Mergent's

HANDBOOK OF
COMMON STOCKS

2016 Summer Common

MERGENT

INTRODUCTION

Mergent's Handbook of Common Stocks provides quick and easy access to basic financial and business information on more than 900 stocks that are included in the Russell 1000, S&P 500, S&P 400 and Mergent's Dividend Achievers. The Tab Section provides one-line information on New York Stock Exchange companies.

The price charts, statistics, and analyses are presented in a format that provides the investor with the necessary perspective for acting on investment advice or suggestions. It also affords investors the opportunity to make investment decisions on their own.

Statistics and analyses are revised quarterly. Every effort is made to secure the most current operating results and dividend information available. In the case of year-end results, preliminary results are shown and analyzed as they are received. Full statistical presentations of annual report information are shown in the following edition. The schedule below describes the publication dates and company reporting periods usually covered in each edition.

The Winter Edition (published in January) covers quarterly reports and preliminary annual reports through September 30.

The Spring Edition (published in April) covers quarterly reports and preliminary annual reports through December 31.

The Summer Edition (published in July) covers quarterly reports and preliminary annual reports through March 31.

The Fall Edition (published in October) covers quarterly reports and preliminary annual reports through June 30.

Note: For various reasons, some companies may not report in time to meet our publication deadlines. Company reports received close to press time are shown in the Addenda. The remainder of late reports are published and analyzed in the next edition of the Handbook.

The special section on these opening pages contains a number of features, including a guide on how to use this book, a classification of companies by their major line of business based on their NAIC code, outstanding stock price movements by company, plus long-term charts on popular stock market averages. The Addenda provide the latest developments available just prior to publication but after the company reports have been completed.

TABLE OF CONTENTS

Page

HOW TO USE THIS BOOK... 4a

SPECIAL FEATURES

Analysis of Stock Price Movements by Company 10a

Short-term Price Scores: Company Rankings... 11a

Rankings by Selected Investment Criteria 12a

Classification of Companies by Industry... 16a

CHARTS

Dow Jones Industrial Average 25a

New York Stock Exchange Composite Index 27a

ADDENDA

Companies Added and Dropped 28a

Recent and Pending Stock Dividends and Splits 29a

Recent Dividend Changes 29a

Recent and Pending Name Changes.. 30a

Latest Developments.. 30a

Common Dividend Achiever Rankings 31a

COMPANY REPORTS

Arranged Alphabetically.. White Section

Tab Section - NYSE Companies T1

HOW TO USE THIS BOOK

The presentation of historical data and analytical comments provides the answers to four basic questions for each company:

1. What does the company do?
   (See G.)
2. How has it done in the past?
   (See B, J.)
3. How is it doing now?
   (See C, D, H.)
4. How will it fare in the future?
   (See I.)

A. CAPSULE STOCK INFORMATION

shows where the stock is traded and its symbol, a recent price and price/earnings ratio, plus the yield afforded by the indicated dividend based on a recent price. The indicated dividend is the current annualized dividend based on the most recent price. Some companies are designated as Dividend Achievers. Dividend Achievers have, by *Mergent's* criteria, increased their cash dividend payments for at least ten consecutive years, adjusting for splits. The number of years of consecutive increases is given for each Dividend Achiever.

B. LONG-TERM PRICE CHART

illustrates the pattern of monthly stock price movements, fully adjusted for stock dividends and splits. The chart points out the degree of volatility in the price movement of the company's stock and what its long-term trend has been. It also shows how it has performed long-term relative to an initial investment in the S&P 500 Index equal to the price of the company's stock at the beginning of the period shown in the price chart. It indicates areas of price support and resistance, plus other technical points to be considered by the investor. The bars at the base of the long-term price chart indicate the monthly trading volume. Monthly trading volume offers the individual an opportunity to recognize at what periods stock accumulation occurs and what percent of a company's outstanding shares are traded.

PRICE SCORES

– Above each company's price/volume chart are its *Mergent's Price Scores*. These are basic measures of the stock's performance. Each stock is measured against the New York Stock Exchange Composite Index.

A score of 100 indicates that the stock did as well as the New York Stock Exchange Composite Index during the time period. A score of less than 100 means that the stock did not do as well; a score of more than 100 means that the stock outperformed the NYSE Composite Index. All stock prices are adjusted for splits and stock dividends. The time periods measured for each company conclude with the date of the recent price shown in the top line of each company's profile.

The *7 YEAR PRICE SCORE* mirrors the common stock's price growth over the previous seven years. The higher the price score, the better the relative performance. It is based on the ratio of the latest 12-month average price to the current seven-year average. This ratio is then indexed against the same ratio for the market as a whole (the New York Stock Exchange Composite Index), which is taken as 100.

The *12 MONTH PRICE SCORE* is a similar measurement but for a shorter period of time. It is based on the ratio of the latest two-month average price to the current 12-month average. As was done for the Long-Term Price Score, this ratio is also indexed to the same ratio for the market as a whole.

C. INTERIM EARNINGS (Per Share) –

Figures are reported after the effect of extraordinary items, discontinued operations and cumulative effects of accounting changes. Each figure is for the quarterly period indicated. These figures are essentially as reported by the company, although all figures are adjusted for all stock dividends and splits.

ILLUSTRATIVE INC.

Exchange A	**Symbol**	**Price**	**52Wk Range**		**Yield**		**P/E**
NYS	A00	$48.60 (5/30/2016)	49.34-39.75		1.98		17.61

*7 Year Price Score 108.48 *NYSE Composite Index=100 *12 Month Price Score 105.26

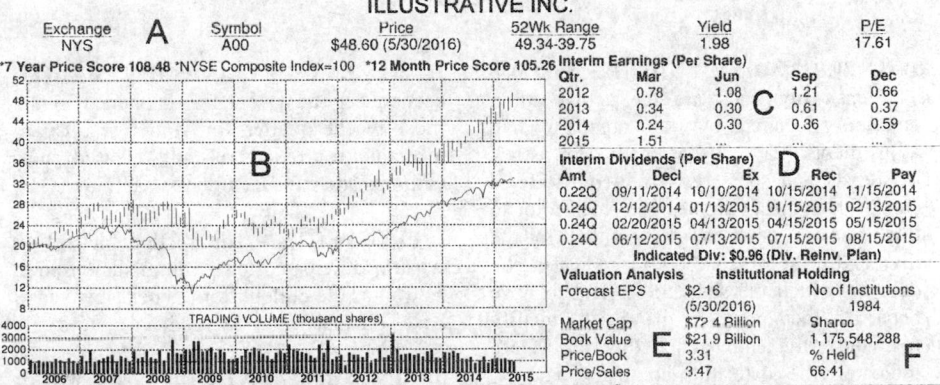

Interim Earnings (Per Share) C

Qtr.	Mar	Jun	Sep	Dec
2012	0.78	1.08	1.21	0.66
2013	0.34	0.30	0.61	0.37
2014	0.24	0.30	0.36	0.59
2015	1.51	...	...	...

Interim Dividends (Per Share) D

Amt	Decl	Ex	Rec	Pay
0.22Q	09/11/2014	10/10/2014	10/15/2014	11/15/2014
0.24Q	12/12/2014	01/13/2015	01/15/2015	02/13/2015
0.24Q	02/20/2015	04/13/2015	04/15/2015	05/15/2015
0.24Q	06/12/2015	07/13/2015	07/15/2015	08/15/2015

Indicated Div: $0.96 (Div. Reinv. Plan)

Valuation Analysis   **Institutional Holding**

Forecast EPS	$2.16 (5/30/2016)	No of Institutions 1984
Market Cap	$72.4 Billion E	Shares
Book Value	$21.9 Billion	1,175,548,288
Price/Book	3.31	% Held F
Price/Sales	3.47	66.41

TRADING VOLUME (thousand shares)

Business Summary: Pharmaceuticals (MIC: 4.1.1 SIC: 2834 NAIC: 325412) G

Illustrative Incorporated is engaged in the discovery, development, manufacture and sale of a line of health care products. Co.'s reportable segments are: Established Pharmaceutical Products, which sells a line of generic pharmaceutical products; Diagnostic Products, which sells diagnostic systems and tests for blood banks, hospitals, commercial laboratories and alternate-care testing sites; Nutritional Products, which sells a line of adult and pediatric nutritional products; and Vascular Products, which includes a line of coronary, endovascular, structural heart, vessel closure and other medical device products. Non-reportable segments include the Diabetes Care and Medical Optics segments.

Recent Developments: For the quarter ended Sept 30, 2015, income from continuing operations increased 136.2% to US$529.0 million from US$224.0 million in the year-earlier quarter. Net income increased 511.2% to US$2.29 billion from US$375.0 million in the year-earlier quarter. Revenues were US$4.90 billion, up 3.0% from US$4.76 billion the year before. Operating income was US$610.0 million versus US$365.0 million in the prior-year quarter, an increase of 67.1%. Direct operating expenses declined 8.5% to US$2.08 billion from US$2.27 billion in the comparable period the year before. Indirect operating expenses increased 4.3% to US$2.21 billion from US$2.12 billion in the equivalent prior-year period. H

Prospects: Our evaluation of Illustrative Incorporated as of June 14, 2015 is the result of our systematic analysis on three basic characteristics: earnings strength, relative valuation, and recent stock price movement. The company has managed to produce a neutral trend in earnings per share over the past 5 quarters and while recent estimates for the company have been mixed, Aoo has posted better than expected results. Based on operating earnings yield, the company is about fairly valued when compared to all of the companies in our coverage universe. Share price changes over the past year indicates that A00 will perform well over the near term. I

Financial Data (US$ in Thousands) J	3 Mos	12/31/2014	12/31/2013	12/31/2012	12/31/2011	12/31/2010	12/31/2009	12/31/2008
Earnings Per Share	2.76	1.49	1.62	3.72	3.01	2.96	3.69	3.12
Cash Flow Per Share	2.22	2.42	2.13	5.90	5.76	5.65	4.70	4.51
Tang Book Value Per Share	4.06	3.49	6.24	1.50	N.M.	N.M.	2.17	1.51
Dividends Per Share	0.900	0.880	0.560	2.010	1.880	1.720	1.560	1.405
Dividend Payout %	32.61	59.06	34.57	54.03	62.46	58.11	42.28	45.03
Income Statement								
Total Revenue	4,897,000	20,247,000	21,848,000	39,873,910	38,851,259	35,166,721	30,764,707	29,527,552
EBITDA	1,040,000	4,139,000	4,330,000	9,674,326	8,855,110	9,243,371	9,515,184	7,861,635
Depn & Amortn	371,000	1,548,000	1,719,000	2,898,534	3,211,523	3,082,855	1,939,533	1,797,101
Income Before Taxes	653,000	2,518,000	2,521,000	6,262,614	5,198,642	5,712,834	7,193,774	5,737,289
Income Taxes	124,000	797,000	138,000	299,694	470,193	1,086,662	1,447,936	1,122,070
Net Income	2,292,000	2,284,000	2,576,000	5,962,920	4,728,449	4,626,172	5,745,838	4,880,719
Average Shares	1,515,537	1,527,000	1,574,000	1,591,838	1,567,389	1,556,022	1,555,126	1,560,753
Balance Sheet								
Current Assets	19,985,000	15,261,000	19,247,000	31,322,583	23,768,774	22,317,529	23,313,891	17,042,559
Total Assets	43,095,000	41,275,000	42,953,000	67,234,944	60,276,893	59,462,266	52,416,623	42,419,204
Current Liabilities	9,206,000	10,532,000	9,507,000	13,280,176	15,480,228	17,262,434	13,049,489	11,591,908
Long-Term Obligations	5,931,000	3,408,000	3,388,000	18,085,302	12,039,822	12,523,517	11,266,294	8,713,327
Total Liabilities	21,221,000	19,749,000	17,782,000	40,513,983	35,837,060	37,074,131	29,560,885	24,939,235
Stockholders' Equity	21,874,000	21,526,000	25,171,000	26,720,961	24,439,833	22,388,135	22,855,627	17,479,551
Shares Outstanding	1,488,757	1,508,035	1,548,098	1,576,667	1,570,378	1,546,983	1,551,167	1,552,432
Statistical Record								
Return on Assets %	9.91	5.42	4.68	9.33	7.90	8.27	12.12	11.85
Return on Equity %	18.56	9.78	9.93	23.25	20.19	20.45	28.49	27.61
EBITDA Margin %	21.24	20.44	19.82	24.26	22.79	26.28	30.93	26.62
Net Margin %	46.80	11.28	11.79	14.95	12.17	13.15	18.68	16.53
Asset Turnover	0.49	0.48	0.40	0.62	0.65	0.63	0.65	0.72
Current Ratio	2.17	1.45	2.02	2.36	1.54	1.29	1.79	1.47
Debt to Equity	0.27	0.16	0.13	0.68	0.49	0.56	0.49	0.50
Price Range	47.83-37.02	46.37-35.85	38.71-31.34	34.51-25.91	26.95-21.61	26.91-21.94	27.39-19.87	28.95-23.66
P/E Ratio	17.33-13.41	31.12-24.06	23.90-19.35	9.28-6.96	8.95-7.18	9.09-7.41	7.42-5.38	9.28-7.58
Average Yield %	2.11	2.15	1.57	6.66	7.70	7.41	7.08	5.32

Address: 000 Illusus Park Road, Abbott Park, IL 60064-6400 **Telephone:** 200-000-0000 K	**Web Site:** www.ill.com **Officers:** Mike Smith - Chairman, Chief Executive Officer Thomas Jones - Executive Vice President, Chief Financial Officer	**Auditors:** Ernst & Young LLP **Investor Contact:** 000-000-0000 **Transfer Agents:** Computershare Trust Co., NA, Providence, RI

HOW TO USE THIS BOOK

D. INTERIM DIVIDENDS (Per Share) – The cash dividends are the actual dollar amounts declared by the company. No adjustments have been made for stock dividends and splits. **Ex-Dividend Date**: a stockholder must purchase the stock prior to this date in order to be entitled to the dividend. The **Record Date** indicates the date on which the shareholder had to have been a holder of record in order to qualify for the dividend. The **Payable Date** indicates the date the company paid or intends to pay the dividend. The cash amount shown in the first column is followed by a letter (example "Q" for quarterly) to indicate the frequency of the dividend. A notation of "Dividend payment suspended" indicates that dividend payments have been suspended within the most recent ten years.

Indicated Dividend This is the annualized amount (fully adjusted for splits) of the latest regular cash dividend. Companies with Dividend Reinvestment Plans are indicated here.

E. VALUATION ANALYSIS is a tool for evaluating a company's stock. Included are: Forecast Earnings Per Share (EPS), Market Capitalization, Book Value, Price/Book and Price/Sales.

F. INSTITUTIONAL HOLDINGS – indicates the number of investment companies, insurance companies, mutual funds, bank trust and college endowment funds holding the stock and the total number of shares held as last reported.

G. BUSINESS SUMMARY explains what a company does in terms of the products or services it sells, its markets, and the position the company occupies in its industry. For a quick reference, included are the Company's Standard Industrial Classification (SIC), North American Industry Classification (NAIC) and Mergent's Industry Classification (MIC).

H. RECENT DEVELOPMENTS – This section captures what has happened in the most recent quarter for which results are available. It provides recently released sales, earnings and expense figures.

I. PROSPECTS – This section focuses on what is anticipated for the immediate future, as well as the outlook for the next few years, based on analysis by Mergent.

J. FINANCIAL DATA (fully adjusted for stock dividends and splits) is provided for at least the past seven fiscal years preceded by the most recent three-, six- and nine-month results if available.

Fiscal Years are the annual financial reporting periods as determined by each company. Annual prices and dividends are displayed based on the Company's fiscal year.

Per Share Data:

The Earnings Per Share figure is based on a trailing 12-month period. Earnings per share, and all per share figures, are adjusted for subsequent stock dividends and splits.

Cash Flow Per Share represents the annualized cash flow from operating activities (or for quarters, TTM cash flow from operating activities) divided by the average shares outstanding.

Tangible Book Value Per Share is calculated as stockholders equity (the value of common shares, paid-in capital and retained earnings) minus preferred stock and intangibles such as goodwill, patents and excess acquisition costs, divided by shares outstanding. It demonstrates the underlying cash value of each common share if the company were to be liquidated as of that date.

Dividends Per Share is the total of cash payments made per share to shareholders for the trailing 12-month period.

HOW TO USE THIS BOOK

Dividend Payout % is the proportion of earnings available for common stock that is paid to common shareholders in the form of cash dividends. It is significant because it indicates what percentage of earnings is being reinvested in the business for internal growth.

EDITOR'S NOTE: TTM net income is net income for the last 365 days (normally four reported quarters) ended on the quarterly balance sheet date. Where that last 365 days does not exactly equate to the last four reported quarters the net income for any included partial quarter is adjusted on a pro-rata basis.

INCOME STATEMENT, BALANCE SHEET AND STATISTICAL RECORD

Includes pertinent earnings and balance sheet information essential to analyzing a corporation's performance. The comparisons provide the necessary historical perspective to intelligently review the various operating and financial trends. Generic definitions follow.

Income Statement:
Total Revenues consists of all revenues from operations.

EBITDA represents earnings before, interest, taxes, depreciation and amortization, and special items.

Depreciation and Amortization includes all non-cash charges such as depletion and amortization as well as depreciation.

Income Before Taxes is the remaining income *after* deducting all costs, expenses, property charges, interest etc. but *before* deducting income taxes.

Income Taxes includes the amount charged against earnings to provide for current and deferred income taxes.

Net Income consists of all revenues less all expenses (operating and non-operating), and is presented before preference and common dividends.

Average Shares Outstanding is the weighted average number of shares including common equivalent shares outstanding during the year, as reported by the corporation and fully adjusted for all stock dividends and splits. The use of *average shares* minimizes the distortion in *earnings per share* which could result from issuance of a large amount of stock or the company's purchase of a large amount of its own stock during the year.

Balance Sheet:
Current Assets includes the short-term assets expected to be realized or consumed within one year. Normally includes cash and cash equivalents, short term investments, receivables, prepayments and inventories.

Total Assets represents all of the assets of the company, including tangible and intangible, and current and non-current.

Current Liabilities are all of the obligations of the company normally expected to be paid within one year. Includes bank overdrafts, short-term debt, payables and accruals.

Long-Term Obligations are the total long-term debts (due beyond one year) reported by the company, including bonds, capital lease obligations, notes, mortgages, debentures, etc.

Total Liabilities represents all liabilities of the company, whether current or non-current.

Stockholders' Equity is the sum of all capital stock accounts – paid in capital (including additional premium), retained earnings, and all other capital balances.

Shares Outstanding is the number of shares outstanding as of the date of the company's quarterly/annual report, exclusive of treasury stock and adjusted for subsequent stock dividends and splits.

Statistical Record:
Return on Assets % represents the ratio of annualized net income (or for Mos, TTM net income) to average total assets. This ratio

HOW TO USE THIS BOOK

represents how effectively assets are being used to produce a profit.

Return on Equity % is the ratio of annualized net income (or for Mos, TTM net income) to average stockholders' equity, expressed as a percentage. This ratio illustrates how effectively the investment of the stockholders is being utilized to earn a profit.

EBITDA Margin % represents earnings before interest, taxes, depreciation and amortization as a percentage of total revenue.

Net Margin % is net income expressed as a percentage of total revenues.

Asset Turnover is annualized total revenue (or for Mos, TTM total revenue) divided by average total assets. A measure of efficiency for the use of assets.

Current Ratio represents current assets divided by current liabilities. The higher the figure the better the company is able to meet its current liabilities out of its current assets. A key measure of liquidity for industrial companies.

Debt to Equity is the ratio of long-term obligations to stockholders' equity.

Price Ranges are based on each Company's fiscal year. Where actual stock sales did not take place, a range of lowest bid and highest asked prices is shown.

Price/Earnings Ratio is shown as a range. The figures are calculated by dividing the stock's highest price for the year and its lowest price by the year's earnings per share. Growth stocks tend to command higher P/Es than cyclical stocks.

Average Yield % is the ratio of annual dividends to the real average of the prices over the fiscal year.

EDITOR'S NOTE: In order to preserve the historical relationships between prices, earnings and dividends, figures are not restated to reflect subsequent events. Figures are presented in U.S. dollars unless otherwise indicated.

K. ADDITIONAL INFORMATION on each stock includes the officers of the company, investor relations contact, address, telephone number, web site and transfer agents.

OTHER DEFINITIONS

Factors Pertaining Especially to Real Estate Investment Trusts
Property Income is income from property rental and other associated activities.

Non-Property Income includes interest income and other income not from property activities.

Factors Pertaining Especially to Utilities
PPE Turnover represents annualized total revenue (or for Mos, TTM total revenue) divided by average net property, plant and equipment.

Factors Pertaining Especially to Banks
Interest Income is all interest income, including income from loans and leases, securities and deposits.

Interest Expense is all interest expense, including from loans and leases, securities and deposits.

Net Interest Income is interest income less interest expense. This figure is presented before provision for losses.

Provision for Losses represents the amount charged against earnings to increase the provision made for losses on loans and leases.

Non-Interest Income is any income that is not interest-related. Such income could include trading revenue and gains on the sale of assets.

Non-Interest Expense is all expenses that are not interest-related, including employment costs, office costs, marketing costs, etc.

Net Loans & Leases includes all loans and leases net of provisions for losses. May include commercial, agricultural, real estate, consumer and foreign loans.

Total Deposits are all time and demand deposits entrusted to a bank.

Net Interest Margin % is net interest income before provisions expressed as a

HOW TO USE THIS BOOK

percentage of total interest income. A key measure of bank profitability.

Efficiency Ratio % is non-interest expense expressed as a percentage of total revenue.

Loans to Deposits are net loans and leases divided by total deposits. A key measure of bank liquidity.

Factors Pertaining Especially to Insurance Companies

Premium Income is the amount of insurance premiums received from policyholders. This is the primary revenue source for insurance companies.

Benefits and Claims represents the payments made to policyholders under the terms of insurance contracts.

Loss Ratio % is benefits and claims expressed as a percentage of premium income. A key ratio of insurance company profitability.

ABBREVIATIONS AND SYMBOLS

A...Annual
ASE...............American Stock Exchange
()...Deficit
(Div. Reinv. Plan)..Dividend Reinvest Plan offered
E..Extra
M......................................…...Monthly
N/A...........................…....Not Applicable
N.M............................…....Not Meaningful
NMS................. National Market Systems
NYS...............New York Stock Exchange
Q....................................…..Quarterly
S..................................…Semi-Annual
Sp...........…...................Special Dividend
U.......................…....Frequency Unknown

ANALYSIS OF STOCK PRICE MOVEMENTS BY COMPANY

For the three-month period beginning Mar. 1, 2016 and ending May 31, 2016, the Dow Jones Industrial Average advanced 7.50%, while the broader New York Stock Exchange Composite rose 8.46%. The Dow and NYSE began the period at 16,545.67 and 9,626.88, respectively. The Dow and NYSE posted their three-month period highs of 18,167.63 and 10,523.79 on Apr. 20, 2016 and Apr. 27, 2016, respectively. The Dow and NYSE's highs were aided by some investors' views that U.S. economic growth, although uninspiring, would continue over the intermediate term. Factors for such optimism included the Labor Department's report of the addition of 215,000 jobs in March as well as signs of factory activity expansion, according to the Institute for Supply Management. Too, the Federal Reserve left interest rates unchanged, citing low U.S. inflation, tepid growth from overseas economies and the potential British exit from the European Union. Conversely, the Dow and NYSE would post their respective three-month period lows of 16,545.67 and 9,613.96 on Mar. 1, 2016. The indices' period lows were influenced by investor concerns of the willingness or ability of central banks to lift their economies. Specifically, despite central banks' ongoing efforts the outlook for inflation seemed uncertain as U.S. inflation remained subdued, growth in China wavered and oil prices showed weakness. The Dow would close the three-month period at 17,787.20, while the NYSE would finish at 10,441.

Over the last twelve months, the best performing stock was **Newmont Mining Corp.** Co.'s gold production has benefited from gains at its Asia Pacific operations.

The second-best price performer was **Manitowoc Company Inc.** Co.'s top line is benefiting from continued strength in tower cranes as a result of improving residential and commercial construction trends, as well as new product introductions.

AK Steel Holding Corp. was the third-best performing stock. Co. remains focused on optimizing its operational footprint and reducing exposure to commodity products.

The fourth-best performing stock was **Cliffs Natural Resources Inc.** Co. is seeing some improved sentiment about steel demand in China and signs of high-cost capacity closures in addition to less aggressive supply expansion expectations from the major iron ore producers.

Tyson Foods, Inc. was the fifth-best performing stock. Co.'s recent operating profit reflects gains across its Chicken, Beef, Pork and Prepared Foods segments.

The sixth-best performing stock was **Tahoe Resources, Inc.** Co. is benefiting from lower unit costs, as well as the recent commissioning of its Shahuindo project in Peru.

Teekay Corp. was the worst performing stock over the last twelve months. Co. is focusing on strengthening its financial position through financing initiatives to help fund its growth capital expenditures.

The second-worst performer was **Cobalt International Energy Inc.** Co. continues to seek funding alternatives to maintain its exploration, appraisal and development activities.

The third-worst price performer was **Restoration Hardware Holdings, Inc.** Co. noted that its results have been affected by recent weakness in consumer spending at the luxury end of the retail market.

The fourth-worst performing stock was **Community Health Systems, Inc.** Co. intends to initiate debt reduction actions and focus on a higher-margin group of hospitals with opportunities for performance gains.

Global Partners LP was the fifth-worst performing stock. Co. remains focused on implementing its strategic divestiture program to streamline its retail portfolio.

Tidewater Inc. was the sixth-worst price performer. Co.'s results have been hurt by lower crude oil prices and reduced exploration and production spending.

HIGHEST-LOWEST

SHORT-TERM PRICE SCORES: COMPANY RANKINGS

25 HIGHEST	SHORT-TERM PRICE SCORE♦	LONG-TERM PRICE SCORE♦	PRICE RANGE (52 Wks.)	RECENT PRICE
Newmont Mining Corp.	143.1	47.1	35.55 - 15.55	32.41
Manitowoc Company Inc.	139.5	92.0	6.05 - 2.64	5.70
AK Steel Holding Corp.	134.4	30.0	5.57-1.83	4.28
Cliffs Natural Resources, Corp.	131.7	7.2	5.52-1.26	4.28
Tyson Foods, Inc.	125.4	159.3	69.27-39.75	63.78
Tahoe Resources Inc.	125.3	...	15.01 - 6.83	11.93
Albemarle Corp.	125.2	85.3	80.09 - 41.78	78.50
United States Steel Corp.	124.6	38.5	25.78 - 6.67	14.47
Valspar Corp.	124.1	128.6	108.32 - 70.82	108.32
Edwards Lifesciences Corp.	123.5	153.8	108.93 - 65.63	98.50
Westar Energy Inc.	122.2	116.4	56.33 - 34.11	56.33
Black Hills Corporation	121.7	102.4	61.74 - 37.29	60.54
Dolby Laboratories Inc.	120.3	76.1	47.92 - 30.50	47.45
Digital Realty Trust, Inc.	119.8	103.4	97.28 - 61.52	95.45
Worthington Industries, Inc.	119.7	102.0	38.26 - 21.88	37.36
3D Systems Corp.	119.0	45.4	21.98 - 6.42	13.39
American Water Works Co,Inc.	118.9	133.1	75.20 - 48.63	74.10
SPX Corp.	117.7	63.9	18.94 - 7.79	16.57
Ingredion Inc.	117.1	133.6	120.31 - 79.31	117.41
Cabot Corp.	117.0	88.9	50.18 - 30.90	45.71
Pioneer Natural Resources Co.	116.5	97.7	168.7 - 107.2	160.32
Realty Income Corp.	116.4	111.9	64.22 - 43.38	60.09
Global Payments, Inc.	116.1	166.0	77.69 - 51.09	77.69
Piedmont Natural Gas Co Inc.	116.0	127.4	60.06 - 35.28	60.06
Boston Scientific Corp.	116.0	150.2	22.71 - 15.78	22.71

25 LOWEST				
Teekay Corp.	42.2	57.5	48.27 - 4.92	10.52
Cobalt International Energy Inc.	47.6	...	10.67 - 2.07	2.24
Restoration Hardware Holdings, Inc.	52.6	...	105.64 - 31.01	33.26
Community Health Systems, Inc.	53.2	81.8	52.71 - 11.98	13.44
Global Partners LP	55.2	71.2	41.59 - 12.31	13.29
Tidewater Inc.	56.1	23.8	24.33 - 3.90	4.33
Williams Cos Inc.	56.5	90.7	60.86 - 11.16	22.16
Tableau Software, Inc.	58.6	...	128.74 - 37.22	51.44
Energy Transfer Equity LP	59.1	103.1	35.24 - 4.05	12.64
Carbo Ceramics Inc.	60.8	23.9	46.00 - 10.63	12.33
Hertz Global Holdings Inc.	62.5	72.5	21.17 - 7.10	9.69
Twitter Inc.	63.7	...	37.00 - 14.01	15.22
Waddell & Reed Financial, Inc.	63.9	71.9	49.85 - 18.87	21.37
Atwood Oceanics, Inc.	64.4	33.3	31.30 - 5.32	10.67
LinkedIn Corp.	65.6	...	255.5 - 100.9	136.50
TravelCenters of America LLC	67.1	121.6	16.70 - 6.47	7.07
American Equity Investment Life Holding	67.2	115.6	29.54 - 12.81	16.21
Platform Specialty Products Corp.	67.3	...	28.35 - 5.55	9.49
Western Refining Inc.	67.5	126.9	50.24 - 20.78	21.24
CF Industries Holdings Inc.	68.4	104.9	68.92 - 27.61	27.66
Block (H&R), Inc.	68.5	116.3	37.40 - 19.46	21.36
Whiting Petroleum Corp.	68.9	29.2	35.97 - 3.53	12.35
Pandora Media Inc.	70.2	...	21.98 - 7.88	11.79
Ensco plc	71.3	28.8	24.67 - 7.88	9.89
Kinder Morgan Inc.	71.4	...	41.29 - 12.01	18.08

♦For definition see page 4a.

Ranking by Total Revenues

Based on most recent fiscal year-end figures.

Rank	Company Name	Revenues ($Mill)	Rank	Company Name	Revenues ($Mill)
1.	Wal-Mart Stores, Inc.	482,130.0	26.	Anthem Inc	79,156.5
2.	Exxon Mobil Corp.	268,882.0	27.	Procter & Gamble Co.	76,279.0
3.	Berkshire Hathaway Inc	210,821.0	28.	Philip Morris International	73,908.0
4.	McKesson Corp.	190,884.0	29.	Target Corp	73,785.0
5.	UnitedHealth Group Inc	157,107.0	30.	Marathon Petroleum Corp.	72,258.0
6.	CVS Health Corporation	153,290.0	31.	Johnson & Johnson	70,074.0
7.	General Motors Co.	152,356.0	32.	MetLife Inc	69,951.0
8.	Ford Motor Co.	149,558.0	33.	Archer Daniels Midland Co.	67,702.0
9.	AT&T Inc	146,801.0	34.	PepsiCo Inc	63,056.0
10.	Chevron Corporation	138,477.0	35.	Aetna Inc.	60,336.5
11.	AmerisourceBergen Corp.	135,961.8	36.	Lowe's Companies Inc	59,074.0
12.	Verizon Communications	131,620.0	37.	United Parcel Service Inc	58,363.0
13.	General Electric Co	117,386.0	38.	American Intl. Group Inc	58,327.0
14.	Kroger Co	109,830.0	39.	Prudential Financial, Inc.	57,119.0
15.	HP Inc	103,355.0	40.	United Technologies Corp	56,098.0
16.	Cardinal Health, Inc.	102,531.0	41.	Humana Inc.	54,289.0
17.	JPMorgan Chase & Co	101,006.0	42.	Disney (Walt) Co.	52,465.0
18.	Phillips 66	100,949.0	43.	Hewlett Packard Enterprise	52,107.0
19.	Boeing Co.	96,114.0	44.	Pfizer Inc	48,851.0
20.	Bank of America Corp.	93,056.0	45.	Dow Chemical Co.	48,778.0
21.	Wells Fargo & Co.	90,033.0	46.	Sysco Corp	48,680.8
22.	Home Depot Inc	88,519.0	47.	FedEx Corp	47,453.0
23.	Citigroup Inc	88,275.0	48.	Caterpillar Inc.	47,011.0
24.	Valero Energy Corp.	87,804.0	49.	Lockheed Martin Corp.	46,132.0
25.	Intl. Bus. Machines Corp.	81,741.0	50.	Coca-Cola Co	44,294.0

Ranking by Net Income

Based on most recent fiscal year-end figures.

Rank	Company Name	Net Income ($Mill)	Rank	Company Name	Net Income ($Mill)
1.	JPMorgan Chase & Co	24,442.0	26.	U.S. Bancorp	5,879.0
2.	Berkshire Hathaway Inc	24,083.0	27.	UnitedHealth Group Inc	5,813.0
3.	Wells Fargo & Co.	22,894.0	28.	Prudential Financial, Inc.	5,642.0
4.	Verizon Communications	17,879.0	29.	PepsiCo Inc	5,452.0
5.	Citigroup Inc	17,242.0	30.	MetLife Inc	5,310.0
6.	Exxon Mobil Corp.	16,150.0	31.	Altria Group Inc	5,241.0
7.	Bank of America Corp.	15,888.0	32.	CVS Health Corporation	5,237.0
8.	Johnson & Johnson	15,409.0	33.	Boeing Co.	5,176.0
9.	Wal-Mart Stores, Inc.	14,694.0	34.	American Express Co.	5,163.0
10.	AT&T Inc	13,345.0	35.	AbbVie Inc.	5,144.0
11.	Intl. Bus. Machines Corp.	13,190.0	36.	United Parcel Service Inc	4,844.0
12.	General Motors Co.	9,687.0	37.	3M Co	4,833.0
13.	Oracle Corp	8,901.0	38.	Union Pacific Corp	4,772.0
14.	Disney (Walt) Co.	8,382.0	39.	Honeywell International Inc	4,768.0
15.	Dow Chemical Co.	7,685.0	40.	Chevron Corporation	4,587.0
16.	United Technologies Corp	7,608.0	41.	HP Inc	4,554.0
17.	Ford Motor Co.	7,373.0	42.	McDonald's Corp	4,529.3
18.	Coca-Cola Co	7,351.0	43.	Delta Air Lines, Inc.	4,526.0
19.	United Continental Holdings	7,340.0	44.	Merck & Co., Inc	4,442.0
20.	Procter & Gamble Co.	7,036.0	45.	Abbott Laboratories	4,423.0
21.	Home Depot Inc	7,009.0	46.	Phillips 66	4,227.0
22.	Pfizer Inc	6,960.0	47.	PNC Financial Services Grp	4,143.0
23.	Philip Morris International	6,873.0	48.	Capital One Financial Corp	4,050.0
24.	Visa Inc	6,328.0	49.	Valero Energy Corp.	3,990.0
25.	Morgan Stanley	6,127.0	50.	Allergan PLC	3,915.2

Ranking by Total Assets

Based on most recent fiscal year-end figures.

Rank	Company Name	Assets ($Mill)	Rank	Company Name	Assets ($Mill)
1.	JPMorgan Chase & Co	2,351,698.0	26.	BB&T Corp.	209,947.0
2.	Bank of America Corp.	2,144,316.0	27.	Wal-Mart Stores, Inc.	199,581.0
3.	Wells Fargo & Co.	1,787,632.0	28.	General Motors Co.	194,520.0
4.	Citigroup Inc	1,731,210.0	29.	SunTrust Banks, Inc.	190,817.0
5.	MetLife Inc	877,933.0	30.	Schwab (Charles) Corp.	183,718.0
6.	Morgan Stanley	787,465.0	31.	Pfizer Inc	167,460.0
7.	Prudential Financial, Inc.	757,388.0	32.	American Express Co.	161,184.0
8.	Berkshire Hathaway Inc	552,257.0	33.	Ally Financial Inc	158,581.0
9.	American Intl. Group Inc	496,943.0	34.	Ameriprise Financial Inc	145,342.0
10.	General Electric Co	492,692.0	35.	Allergan PLC	135,840.7
11.	U.S. Bancorp	421,853.0	36.	Johnson & Johnson	133,411.0
12.	AT&T Inc	402,672.0	37.	Procter & Gamble Co.	129,495.0
13.	Bank of New York Mellon	393,780.0	38.	Regions Financial Corp	126,050.0
14.	PNC Financial Services Grp	358,493.0	39.	M & T Bank Corp	122,787.9
15.	Exxon Mobil Corp.	336,758.0	40.	Duke Energy Corp	121,156.0
16.	Capital One Financial Corp	334,048.0	41.	AFLAC Inc.	118,296.0
17.	Chevron Corporation	266,103.0	42.	Oracle Corp	112,180.0
18.	Lincoln National Corp.	251,937.0	43.	UnitedHealth Group Inc	111,383.0
19.	State Street Corp.	245,192.0	44.	Intl. Bus. Machines Corp.	110,495.0
20.	Verizon Communications	244,640.0	45.	HP Inc	106,882.0
21.	Hartford Financial Services	228,348.0	46.	Genworth Financial, Inc.	106,431.0
22.	BlackRock, Inc.	225,261.0	47.	Allstate Corp.	104,656.0
23.	Ford Motor Co.	224,925.0	48.	Chubb Ltd	102,366.0
24.	Principal Financial Group	218,685.9	49.	Merck & Co., Inc	101,779.0
25.	Voya Financial Inc	218,249.6	50.	Travelers Companies Inc	100,184.0

Ranking by Market Capitalization

Based on most recent fiscal year-end figures and closing prices at 5/31/2016

Rank	Company Name	Market Cap ($Mill)	Rank	Company Name	Market Cap ($Mill)
1.	WABCO Holdings Inc	21,758,709.6	26.	Altria Group Inc	124,506.9
2.	Exxon Mobil Corp.	369,131.3	27.	Bristol-Myers Squibb Co.	119,689.3
3.	Johnson & Johnson	309,970.1	28.	Medtronic PLC	112,248.0
4.	General Electric Co	277,984.7	29.	McDonald's Corp	107,151.3
5.	Wells Fargo & Co.	257,507.9	30.	CVS Health Corporation	103,589.4
6.	AT&T Inc	241,007.4	31.	MasterCard Inc	103,444.1
7.	JPMorgan Chase & Co	238,670.1	32.	3M Co	102,088.5
8.	Wal-Mart Stores, Inc.	220,596.3	33.	AbbVie Inc.	101,780.4
9.	Procter & Gamble Co.	215,716.5	34.	Accenture plc	96,955.6
10.	Pfizer Inc	210,450.2	35.	Schlumberger Ltd.	95,553.1
11.	Verizon Communications	207,483.1	36.	Honeywell International Inc	86,751.6
12.	Coca-Cola Co	192,948.5	37.	United Technologies Corp	84,172.0
13.	Chevron Corporation	190,354.9	38.	Lilly (Eli) & Co.	82,820.9
14.	Berkshire Hathaway Inc	176,461.8	39.	Boeing Co.	80,359.0
15.	Oracle Corp	165,733.7	40.	U.S. Bancorp	73,924.6
16.	Home Depot Inc	164,358.2	41.	NIKE Inc	73,523.8
17.	Disney (Walt) Co.	160,978.6	42.	Lockheed Martin Corp.	71,920.9
18.	Merck & Co., Inc	155,729.1	43.	United Parcel Service Inc	71,178.6
19.	Philip Morris International	153,078.8	44.	Lowe's Companies Inc	71,003.6
20.	Bank of America Corp.	151,921.6	45.	Reynolds American Inc	70,938.9
21.	Visa Inc	150,364.2	46.	Union Pacific Corp	70,806.7
22.	Intl. Bus. Machines Corp.	147,584.5	47.	Danaher Corp	67,740.1
23.	PepsiCo Inc	146,131.7	48.	Colgate-Palmolive Co.	62,877.4
24.	Citigroup Inc	135,313.9	49.	American Express Co.	62,539.9
25.	UnitedHealth Group Inc	127,094.0	50.	Simon Property Group, Inc.	61,151.6

Ranking by Current Yield

Based on closing prices at 5/312016

Rank	Company Name	Yield %	Rank	Company Name	Yield %
1.	Allergan PLC	23.33	26.	Buckeye Partners, L.P.	6.67
2.	Global Partners LP	13.92	27.	TC PipeLines, LP	6.45
3.	Plains All American Pipeline	12.11	28.	Corrections Corp of America	6.43
4.	Williams Cos Inc	11.55	29.	Medical Properties Trust Inc	6.26
5.	Annaly Capital Management	11.34	30.	Las Vegas Sands Corp	6.23
6.	StoneMor Partners L P	11.19	31.	Transocean Ltd.	6.13
7.	MFA Financial, Inc.	11.10	32.	OUTFRONT Media Inc	6.12
8.	CBL & Associates Properties	11.02	33.	W.P. Carey Inc	6.11
9.	WP Glimcher Inc	9.78	34.	Covanta Holding Corp	6.00
10.	SPX Corp.	9.05	35.	Columbia Property Trust Inc	5.82
11.	Energy Transfer Equity LP	9.02	36.	GUESS ?, Inc.	5.71
12.	Care Capital Properties Inc	8.77	37.	Enterprise Products Partners	5.69
13.	Waddell & Reed Financial	8.61	38.	Oneok Inc	5.69
14.	Targa Resources Corp	8.50	39.	Kohl's Corp.	5.55
15.	Senior Housing Properties	8.35	40.	EPR Properties	5.39
16.	Noble Corp plc	8.33	41.	Iron Mountain Inc	5.28
17.	Hospitality Properties Trust	7.97	42.	General Cable Corp.	5.27
18.	CenturyLink, Inc.	7.96	43.	Host Hotels & Resorts Inc	5.19
19.	LaSalle Hotel Properties	7.79	44.	Barnes & Noble Inc	5.16
20.	Vector Group Ltd	7.45	45.	National Health Investors	5.16
21.	Omega Healthcare Investors	7.27	46.	The Gap, Inc.	5.11
22.	Western Refining Inc	7.16	47.	Liberty Property Trust	5.09
23.	Genesis Energy L.P.	7.14	48.	GameStop Corp	5.09
24.	Sunoco Logistics Partners	7.13	49.	Spectra Energy Corp	5.08
25.	HCP, Inc.	7.00	50.	Welltower Inc	4.99

Ranking by Return on Equity

Based on most recent fiscal year-end figures.

Rank	Company Name	Return on Equity %	Rank	Company Name	Return on Equity %
1.	Energy Transfer Equity	3,603.03	26.	Lazard Ltd	97.65
2.	Gartner Inc	1,220.92	27.	Masco Corp.	89.99
3.	Clorox Co	426.47	28.	Home Depot Inc	89.89
4.	Lennox International Inc	340.51	29.	Boeing Co.	69.01
5.	S&P Global Inc	339.00	30.	Taubman Centers, Inc.	62.22
6.	Colgate-Palmolive Co.	327.19	31.	Western Union Co	61.94
7.	Pitney Bowes Inc	318.73	32.	Brown-Forman Corp.	61.38
8.	Crown Holdings Inc	298.86	33.	Delphi Automotive Plc	60.92
9.	Kimberly-Clark Corp.	293.20	34.	MasterCard Inc	59.42
10.	Visteon Corp.	237.67	35.	NewMarket Corp	59.02
11.	United Parcel Service Inc	210.11	36.	Graco Inc	56.30
12.	AbbVie Inc.	180.90	37.	Wyndham Worldwide Corp	55.51
13.	Altria Group Inc	177.84	38.	Mettler-Toledo Intl., Inc.	54.28
14.	Catalent Inc	161.49	39.	TJX Companies, Inc.	53.29
15.	CEB Inc	142.55	40.	Tenneco Inc	53.12
16.	United Continental Hldgs	129.20	41.	Oneok Inc	52.80
17.	Six Flags Entertainment	124.69	42.	Rite Aid Corp.	51.97
18.	Verizon Communications	124.48	43.	Accenture plc	51.47
19.	Sherwin-Williams Co	113.05	44.	Grace (WR) & Co	50.27
20.	Lockheed Martin Corp.	110.97	45.	Polaris Industries Inc.	48.81
21.	USG Corp	107.54	46.	Motorola Solutions Inc.	46.41
22.	Tupperware Brands Corp	107.45	47.	Toro Co.	46.30
23.	Yum! Brands, Inc.	105.50	48.	Campbell Soup Co.	46.27
24.	Intl. Bus. Machines Corp.	100.96	49.	FactSet Research Systems	46.24
25.	Booz Allen Hamilton Hldg	98.59	50.	Delta Air Lines, Inc.	46.04

Ranking by High P/E Ratio

Based on closing prices at 5/31/2016

Rank	Company Name	P/E Ratio	Rank	Company Name	P/E Ratio
1.	Global Partners LP	1,329.00	26.	Tyler Technologies, Inc.	89.12
2.	Chico's FAS Inc	1,085.00	27.	Hill-Rom Holdings, Inc.	87.73
3.	Kinder Morgan Inc.	904.00	28.	Digital Realty Trust, Inc.	87.57
4.	AECOM	802.75	29.	Bristol-Myers Squibb Co.	77.10
5.	Zimmer Biomet Holdings	321.34	30.	Ball Corp	76.91
6.	MSG Network Inc	288.50	31.	PBF Energy Inc	75.34
7.	TC PipeLines, LP	276.15	32.	Valmont Industries Inc	73.97
8.	Sotheby's	230.00	33.	Red Hat Inc	72.39
9.	PNM Resources Inc	218.93	34.	Alexandria Real Estate Eq	72.31
10.	SeaWorld Entertainment	218.25	35.	Rayonier Inc.	72.03
11.	Newmont Mining Corp	202.56	36.	Under Armour Inc	69.87
12.	Ciena Corp	194.00	37.	American Tower Corp	68.25
13.	Bard (CR) Inc	154.25	38.	Babcock & Wilcox Enterprs.	67.97
14.	Chevron Corporation	146.38	39.	Johnson Controls Inc	65.90
15.	Spectra Energy Corp	127.44	40.	West Pharmaceutical Srvcs.	65.29
16.	Calpine Corp	123.33	41.	Lindsay Corp	64.27
17.	MBIA Inc.	120.00	42.	Corning Inc	63.30
18.	TravelCenters of America	117.83	43.	Grace (WR) & Co	63.12
19.	Harris Corp.	110.94	44.	Helmerich & Payne, Inc.	62.40
20.	Healthcare Trust Of America	107.79	45.	American Campus Commun.	61.87
21.	Allied World Assur Co Hldg	103.00	46.	Zoetis Inc	61.58
22.	Brady Corp	99.34	47.	Armstrong World Industries	60.81
23.	Clean Harbors, Inc	97.15	48.	Essex Property Trust Inc	60.43
24.	Carpenter Technology Corp.	97.09	49.	Schlumberger Ltd.	60.08
25.	Douglas Emmett Inc	94.14	50.	Columbia Property Trust Inc	57.28

Ranking by Low P/E Ratio

Based on closing prices at 5/31/2016

Rank	Company Name	P/E Ratio	Rank	Company Name	P/E Ratio
1.	Visteon Corp.	1.46	26.	Waddell & Reed Financial	8.25
2.	Atwood Oceanics, Inc.	1.63	27.	Spirit AeroSystems Hldgs	8.27
3.	Transocean Ltd.	2.35	28.	XL Group Plc	8.54
4.	United Continental Holdings	2.35	29.	TRI Pointe Group Inc	8.57
5.	Trinity Industries, Inc.	3.94	30.	Asbury Automotive Group	8.77
6.	USG Corp	4.10	31.	The Gap, Inc.	9.04
7.	Assured Guaranty Ltd	4.32	32.	MFA Financial, Inc.	9.13
8.	Lazard Ltd	4.70	33.	Highwoods Properties, Inc.	9.22
9.	Noble Corp plc	4.74	34.	GATX Corp	9.25
10.	General Motors Co.	4.75	35.	Dillard's Inc.	9.28
11.	Equity Residential	5.95	36.	Mosaic Co	9.31
12.	Western Refining Inc	6.07	37.	Citigroup Inc	9.35
13.	Ford Motor Co.	6.08	38.	Westlake Chemical Corp	9.37
14.	Baxter International Inc.	6.09	39.	HollyFrontier Corp.	9.39
15.	Tesoro Corporation	6.60	40.	Genesis Energy L.P.	9.46
16.	Diebold, Inc.	6.95	41.	Everest Re Group Ltd	9.50
17.	Supervalu Inc.	7.02	42.	Marathon Petroleum Corp.	9.60
18.	HP Inc	7.08	43.	Alaska Air Group, Inc.	9.62
19.	Delta Air Lines, Inc.	7.30	44.	Michael Kors Holdings	9.62
20.	Prudential Financial, Inc.	7.39	45.	Pitney Bowes Inc	9.65
21.	Valero Energy Corp.	7.61	46.	Avnet Inc	9.75
22.	American Eq. Inv. Life Hldg.	7.79	47.	MetLife Inc	9.75
23.	GameStop Corp	7.80	48.	Jabil Circuit, Inc.	9.99
24.	Cliffs Natural Resources, Inc	8.08	49.	Air Lease Corp	10.02
25.	NeuStar, Inc.	8.12	50.	Dow Chemical Co.	10.03

CLASSIFICATION BY INDUSTRY

Accommodation and Food Services
Accommodation
  Choice Hotels International, Inc.
  Hilton Worldwide Holdings Inc.
  Host Hotels & Resorts Inc.
  Hyatt Hotels Corp.
  Park Place Entertainment Corp.
  Wyndham Worldwide Corp.

Food Services and Drinking Places
  Brinker International, Inc.
  Chipotle Mexican Grill Inc
  *Darden Restaurants, Inc.
  *McDonald's Corporation
  Ruby Tuesday, Inc.
  *Yum! Brands, Inc.

Administrative & Support and Waste Management & Remediation Services
Administrative and Support Services
  *Equifax Inc.
  *ManpowerGroup
  Mid Atlantic Medical Services
  Robert Half International, Inc.
  *Rollins, Inc.

Waste Management and Remediation Services
  Clean Harbors, Inc.
  *Johnson Controls, Inc.
  Republic Services, Inc.
  *Waste Management, Inc.

Arts, Entertainment, and Recreation
  *Carnival Corp.
  *Disney (Walt) Company (The)
  GTECH Holdings Corp.
  Las Vegas Sands Corp.
  Live Nation Entertainment, Inc.
  MGM Resorts International
  Royal Caribbean Cruises Ltd.
  SeaWorld Entertainment Inc
  Six Flags Entertainment Corp
  Vista Outdoor Inc

Construction
  ABM Industries Incorporated
  *Boston Properties, Inc.
  CalAtlantic Group Inc
  Chicago Bridge & Iron Co., N.V.
  Eagle Materials Inc.
  EMCOR Group, Inc.
  Fortune Brands Home & Security, Inc.
  *Granite Construction Inc.
  Horton (D.R.) Inc.
  Jacobs Engineering Group Inc.
  KB Home
  KBR Inc.
  Lennar Corporation
  M.D.C. Holdings, Inc.
  Martin Marietta Materials, Inc.
  *MDU Resources Group, Inc.
  NVR Inc.

Owens Corning
Pulte Homes, Inc.
Quanta Services, Inc.
Taylor Morrison Home Corp
Toll Brothers, Inc.
TRI Pointe Group Inc.a

Educational Services
  DeVry Education Group Inc.
  Graham Holdings Co.

Electric Power Generation
  Calpine Corp.
  Covanta Holding Corp.
  NRG Energy, Inc.
  Ormat Technologies Inc

Finance and Insurance
Commercial Banking
  Ally Financial Inc
  Associated Banc-Corp
  *BancorpSouth, Inc.
  *Bank of America Corporation
  *Bank of Hawaii Corporation
  *Bank of New York Mellon Corp.
  BankUnited Inc.
  *BB&T Corporation
  *Comerica, Inc.
  *Community Bank System, Inc.
  Cullen/Frost Bankers, Inc.
  *First Horizon National Corporation
  First Republic Bank (San Francisco, CA)
  *Hudson United Bancorp
  *J.P. Morgan Chase & Co.
  *KeyCorp
  *M&T Bank Corporation
  *North Fork Bancorporation, Inc.
  *PNC Financial Services Group
  Prosperity Bancshares Inc.
  *Regions Financial Corp.
  *State Street Corporation
  *SunTrust Banks, Inc.
  Synchrony Financial
  *Synovus Financial Corporation
  *TCF Financial Corp.
  *U.S. Bancorp
  *Valley National Bancorp
  *Wells Fargo & Company
  *Wilmington Trust Corporation

Direct Health and Medical Insurance Carriers
  *AFLAC Incorporated
  Cigna Corp.
  Humana Inc.
  Pacificare Health Systems, Inc.
  Reinsurance Group of America
  UnitedHealth Group Inc.
  Universal American Corp.
  *UnumProvident Corporation
  WellCare Health Plans Inc.
Direct Life Insurance Carriers

American Equity Investment Life Holding Co.
Assurant Inc.
*Genworth Financial Inc. (Holding Co)
*Lincoln National Corporation
Primerica Inc.
Principal Financial Group, Inc.
*Protective Life Corporation
Prudential Financial, Inc.
*Torchmark Corporation
Voya Financial Inc.

Direct Property and Casualty Insurance Carriers
Allied World Assurance Company Holdings AG
Allmerica Financial Corporation
*Allstate Corporation (The)
*American Financial Group, Inc.
American International Group
Aspen Insurance Holdings Ltd
Berkley (W.R.) Corporation
Berkshire Hathaway Inc.
CNA Financial Corporation
Endurance Specialty Holdings Ltd
Everest Re Group Ltd
Hanover Insurance Group Inc.
*Kemper Corp.
Leucadia National Corporation
Loews Corporation
Markel Corporation
Mercury General Corporation
ProAssurance Corp.
Progressive Corporation (The)
RenaissanceRe Holdings Ltd
*RLI Corp.
*The St Paul Travelers Companies Inc.
White Mountains Insurance Group, Ltd
XL Capital Plc

Direct Title Insurance Carriers
Alleghany Corporation
*CoreLogic Inc.
Fidelity National Financial Inc.
First American Financial Corp

Insurance Agencies and Brokerages
Aetna, Inc.
Anthem Inc.
Brown & Brown, Inc.
Centene Corp
Gallagher (Arthur J.) & Company
*Hartford Financial Services Group
Metlife, Inc.
Molina Healthcare Inc.

Mortgage and Nonmortgage Loan Brokers
Nationstar Mortgage Holdings Inc.
*New York Community Bancorp, Inc.

Nondepository Credit Intermediation
*American Express Company
Ameriprise Financial Inc.
*Capital One Financial Corp.
Discover Financial Services
Invesco Ltd
Lazard Ltd
*Morgan Stanley

Real Estate Investment Trusts
Alexandria Real Estate Equities, Inc.
American Campus Communities Inc.
American Homes 4 Rent
American Tower Corp
AMB Property Corporation
*Annaly Capital Management Inc.
Apartment Investment & Mngmnt
AvalonBay Communities, Inc.
*Brandywine Realty Trust
*Brixmor Property Group Inc
Camden Property Trust
Care Capital Properties Inc.
CBL & Associates Properties, Inc.
*Chimera Investment Corp.
Columbia Property Trust Inc
Corporate Office Properties Trust
*Crown Castle International Corp.
*DDR Corp
Digital Realty Trust Inc.
Douglas Emmett Inc.
*Duke Realty Corporation
*Equity Commonwealth
Equity Lifestyle Properties Inc
*Equity One, Inc.
*Equity Residential Prop. Trust
*EPR Properties
*Essex Property Trust, Inc.
Extra Space Storage Inc
*Federal Realty Investment Trust
General Growth Properties Inc.
*HCP, Inc.
Healthcare Trust of America Inc
*Highwoods Properties, Inc.
*Hospitality Properties Trust
*Kilroy Realty Corp.
*Kimco Realty Corp.
LaSalle Hotel Properties
*Liberty Property Trust
*Macerich Company (The)
*Mack-Cali Realty Corporation
Medical Properties Trust Inc.
MFA Financial, Inc.
*Mid-America Apartment Communities Inc
National Health Investors, Inc.
*National Retail Properties Inc.
*Omega Healthcare Investors, Inc.
OUTFRONT Media Inc
Piedmont Office Realty Trust Inc
*ProLogis
Public Storage, Inc.
Realty Income Corp.
*Regency Centers Corporation
Retail Properties of America, Inc
*Shurgard Storage Centers, Inc.
*Simon Property Group, Inc.
SL Green Realty Corp.
*Senior Housing Properties Trust
Starwood Hotels & Resorts
*Tanger Factory Outlet Centers, Inc.
*Taubman Centers, Inc.
*UDR Inc.

*Universal Health Realty Inc. Trust
*Urban Edge Properties
*Urstadt Biddle Properties Inc.
*Ventas, Inc.
*Vornado Realty Trust
*Weingarten Realty Investors
*Welltower Inc.
 WP Glimcher Inc.

 Reinsurance Carriers
*Chubb Ltd.
*Marsh & McLennan Cos. Inc.
 MBIA Inc.
*Old Republic International Corp.

Savings Institutions
*Sovereign Bancorp, Inc.
*Webster Financial Corp.

*Securities, Commodity Contracts, and Other
Financial Investments and Related Activities*
 Affiliated Managers Group Inc.
 Assured Guaranty Ltd
 Broadridge Financial Solutions Inc.
*Citigroup Inc.
 CME Group Inc.
 Eaton Vance Corporation
 Federated Investors, Inc.
*Franklin Resources, Inc.
 Goldman Sachs Group, Inc.
 IntercontinentalExchange Inc.
 Janus Capital Group, Inc.
 Legg Mason, Inc.
 Raymond James Financial, Inc.
*Waddell & Reed Financial, Inc.
 Westwood Holdings Group, Inc.

Other Financial Vehicles
 BlackRock, Inc.

Health Care and Social Assistance
 Brookdale Senior Living Inc.
 Community Health Systems, Inc.
 DaVita Inc.
 Envision Healthcare Holdings Inc.
 HCA Holdings Inc.
 Health Management Associates
 Kindred Healthcare, Inc.
 Laboratory Corp. of America
 Mednax, Inc.
*Tenet Healthcare Corporation
 Universal Health Services, Inc.

Information
*Cable Networks, Program Distribution and
Internet Service Providers*
 Cablevision Systems Corp.
 Scripps Networks Interactive Inc.
 Time Warner Inc.

*Information Services and Data Processing
Services*
 Alliance Data Systems Corp.
 Concord EFS, Inc.
 DST Systems, Inc.

 Dun & Bradstreet Corp. (The)
 Fair Isaac Corporation
 FactSet Research Systems Inc.
 FleetCor Technologies Inc.
 Green Dot Corp
*Hewlett Packard Enterprise Co
 IHS Inc.
 IMS Health Holdings Inc.
 Lender Processing Services Inc.
 MasterCard Inc.
 Nielsen Holdings PLC
 NCR Corporation
 Rackspace Hosting Inc
*Thomson Reuters Corp
 Total System Services, Inc.

 Vantiv Inc.
 VeriFone Systems
 Visa Inc.
 Western Union Co.

Motion Picture and Sound Recording Industries
 Cinemark Holdings Inc
 DreamWorks Animation SKG Inc.
 News Corp.
 Regal Entertainment Group

Publishing Industries
 3D Systems Corp.
 Gannett Co. Inc
 Meredith Corporation
 Monster Worldwide Inc.
 MSCI Inc.
*New York Times Company
 Oracle Corp.
*Reader's Digest Association, Inc.
 ServiceNow Inc
 Solera Holdings Inc.
*S&P Global Inc.
 Time Inc.
 Tyler Technologies, Inc.
 VMWARE, Inc.
 Wiley (John) & Sons Inc.

Radio and Television Broadcasting
 Cable One Inc
 Dolby Laboratories Inc.
 MSG Network Inc
 Pandora Media Inc
 Tegna Inc
 Westwood One, Inc.

Telecommunications
*AT&T Inc
*CenturyLink, Inc.
*Citizens Communications Co.
 Fidelity National Information Services Inc.
 Level 3 Communications, Inc.
 Neustar Inc.
 Qwest Communications International
 Sprint Nextel Corporation
*Telephone and Data Systems, Inc.
 United States Cellular Corp.

*Verizon Communications Inc.

Manufacturing
Beverage and Tobacco Product Manufacturing
*Altria Group, Inc.
 Boston Beer Co., Inc.
*Brown-Forman Corporation
*Coca-Cola Company (The)
 Constellation Brands, Inc.
 Dr Pepper Snapple Group Inc
 Molson Coors Brewing Company
*PepsiCo Inc.
*Philip Morris International Inc.
*Reynolds American Inc.
*Vector Group Inc.

Chemical Manufacturing
*3M Company
*Air Products & Chemicals, Inc.
*Albemarle Corporation
 Alberto-Culver Company
*Avon Products, Inc.
*Ashland, Inc.
*Cabot Corporation
 Celanese Corp.
 CF Industries Holdings Inc.
 Charles River Laboratories Int.
 Chemtura Corp.
*Church & Dwight Company, Inc.
*Clorox Company (The)
*Colgate-Palmolive Company
 Compass Minerals International Inc.
 *Dow Chemical Company
*du Pont (E.I.) de Nemours & Co.
*Eastman Chemical Company
*Ecolab, Inc.
*Fuller (H.B.) Company
 Grace (W.R.) Co.
 Huntsman Corp.
 IMC Global, Inc.
*International Flavors & Fragrances
 Monsanto Co.
*Olin Corporation
 Platform Specialty Products Corp
*PPG Industries, Inc.
*Praxair, Inc.
*Procter & Gamble Company
 Rockwood Holdings Inc.
*Rohm & Haas Company
*RPM International Inc.
 Scotts Company (The)
*Sherwin-Williams Company
 Stepan Co.
 Westlake Chemical Corp.
*Valspar Corporation (The)

Computer and Electronic Product Manufacturing
 Advanced Micro Devices, Inc.
 Agilent Technologies, Inc.
*Allegheny Technologies Inc.
*Ametek, Inc.
*AVX Corporation
 Ciena Corp.
*Corning Incorporated

 EMC Corporation
*Emerson Electric Co.
 Esterline Technologies Corp
 Global Payments Inc.
 Harman International Industries
 Juniper Networks Inc.
*Harris Corporation
*HP Inc
 Knowles Corp
*International Business Machines
 Jabil Circuit, Inc.
 L-3 Communications Holdings
 Lexmark International, Inc.
 Mettler-Toledo International Inc.
 Micron Technology, Inc.
*Motorola Solutions Inc.
 Plantronics, Inc.
*Raytheon Company
*Rockwell Collins, Inc.
 Teradyne, Inc.
 Teradata Corp.
 Thermo Fisher Scientific Inc.
 TE Connectivity Ltd
 Vishay Intertechnology, Inc.
 Waters Corporation

Electrical Equipment, Appliance, and Component Manufacturing
 Acuity Brands Inc.
 Amphenol Corp.
 Anixter International Inc.
 Belden Inc.
*Eaton Corporation
 Edgewell Personal Care Co.
 Energizer Holdings Inc
 General Cable Corp.
*General Electric Company
*Hubbell, Inc.
 Regal Beloit Corp.
*Rockwell Automation
*Smith (A.O.) Corporation
 Spectrum Brands Holdings Inc
*Whirlpool Corporation

Fabricated Metal Product Manufacturing
*Badger Meter, Inc.
*Ball Corporation
*Crane Co.
 Crown Holdings, Inc.
 Danaher Corporation
 Greif Inc.
 Orbital ATK Inc
*Parker-Hannifin Corp.
 Shaw Group Inc. (The)
*Snap-On Incorporated
*Stanley Works
*Timken Company (The)
 Valmont Industries, Inc.

Food Manufacturing
*Archer Daniels Midland Co.
 Bunge Ltd
*Campbell Soup Company

*ConAgra Foods, Inc.
Corn Products International Inc.
Dean Foods Company
*Flowers Foods, Inc.
*General Mills, Inc.
*Hershey Foods Corporation
Hillshire Brands Co
*Hormel Foods Corporation
*Kellogg Company
*McCormick & Company, Inc.
Mead Johnson Nutrition Co.
Pinnacle Foods Inc.
Post Holdings Inc
Ralcorp Holdings Inc.
*Sensient Technologies Corp.
*Smucker (J.M.) Company
Tootsie Roll Industries, Inc.
TreeHouse Foods Inc
*Tyson Foods, Inc.
Whitewave Foods Co.

Furniture and Related Product Manufacturing
HNI Corporation
Leggett & Platt, Incorporated
*Masco Corporation
Tempur Sealy International Inc.
Steelcase Inc.

Machinery Manufacturing
AGCO Corporation
Babcock & Wilcox Enterprises Inc.
*Brunswick Corporation
BWX Technologies Inc.
*Caterpillar Inc.
Colfax Corp
*Cummins Inc.
*Curtiss-Wright Corp.
*Deere & Company
*Diebold, Inc.
*Donaldson Company, Inc.
*Dover Corporation
Flowserve Corporation
FMC Corporation
FMC Technologies, Inc.
Gardner Denver, Inc.
*Graco Inc.
*IDEX Corporation
Ingersoll-Rand Plc
Joy Global Inc.
*Kennametal Inc.
Lindsay Corp
*Manitowoc Company, Inc. (The)
Lennox International Inc.
Pentair Ltd
Roper Technologies Inc.
SPX Corporation
Terex Corporation
*Tennant Company
*Toro Co. (The)
Varian Medical Systems, Inc.
Watsco Inc.
*Xerox Corporation
Xylem Inc.
*York International Corporation

Medical Equipment and Supplies Manufacturing
Advanced Medical Optics Inc.
Alere Inc.
*Bard (C.R.), Inc.
*Baxter International Inc.
*Becton, Dickinson and Company
Bio-Rad Laboratories, Inc.
Boston Scientific Corporation
CareFusion Corp
Cooper Companies, Inc.
Covidien Plc
Halyard Health Inc
Hill-Rom Holdings, Inc.
*Medtronic PLC
Mine Safety Appliances Company
ResMed Inc.
St. Jude Medical, Inc.
Steris plc
Stryker Corporation
*Teleflex Inc.
Zimmer Biomet Holdings, Inc.

Nonmetallic Mineral Product Manufacturing
Brink's Company (The)
Carbo Ceramics Inc.
Minerals Technologies Inc.
Oil-Dri Corp. of America
Owens-Illinois, Inc.
USG Corporation

Paper and Wood Product Manufacturing
*Avery Dennison Corporation
*Bemis Company, Inc.
*Boise Cascade Corporation
Domtar Corp.
*International Paper Company
*Kimberly-Clark Corporation
*Louisiana-Pacific Corporation
Packaging Corp. of America
*Rayonier Inc.
*Sonoco Products Company
Tenneco Inc.

Petroleum and Coal Products Manufacturing
*Chevron Corp.
Cobalt International Energy Inc.
*ConocoPhillips
*Exxon Mobil Corporation
*Hess Corp.
HollyFrontier Corp
*Marathon Petroleum Corp
Murphy Oil Corporation
PBF Energy, Inc.
Phillips 66
Tesoro Corporation
Valero Energy Corporation
Western Refining Inc.

Pharmaceutical Preparation Manufacturing
*Abbott Laboratories
AbbVie Inc.
*Allergan, Inc.
AmerisourceBergen Corporation
*Bristol-Myers Squibb Company
Catalent Inc
Edwards Lifesciences Corp.

Genentech, Inc.
*Johnson & Johnson
*Lilly (Eli) & Company
*Merck & Co., Inc.
*Pfizer Inc.
Prestige Brands Holdings Inc.
Zoetis Inc.

Plastics and Rubber Products Manufacturing
AptarGroup Inc.
Armstrong World Industry Inc.
*Carlisle Companies Incorporated
Hexcel Corp
*Illinois Tool Works, Incorporated
*Myers Industries, Inc.
*Newell Brands Inc.
PolyOne Corp.d
Sealed Air Corporation
Tupperware Brands Corporation
*West Pharmaceutical Services

Primary Metal Manufacturing
*AK Steel Holding Corporation
*Alcoa, Inc.
Carpenter Technology Corp.
Commercial Metals Co.
*Nucor Corporation
*United States Steel Corporation
*Worthington Industries, Inc.

Printing and Related Support Activities
Deluxe Corporation

Textiles, Apparel, and Leather Manufacturing
Coach, Inc.
GUESS ?, Inc.
Kate Spade & Co.
Michael Kors Holdings Ltd
Mohawk Industries, Inc.
*NIKE, Inc.
PVH Corp.
Ralph Lauren Corp
Under Armour Inc.
*VF Corporation

Transportation Equipment Manufacturing
Allison Transmission Holdings Inc
Autoliv, Inc.
*Boeing Company (The)
*BorgWarner Inc.
*Clarcor Inc.
Dana Holding Corp
Delphi Automotive Plc
*Ford Motor Company
General Dynamics Corporation
General Motors Co.
*Harley-Davidson, Inc.
*Honeywell International Inc.
Huntington Ingalls Industries Inc
Lear Corp.
*Lockheed Martin Corporation
*Meritor Inc.
*Modine Manufacturing Company
Navistar International Inc.
*Oshkosh Corp.

*Polaris Industries Inc.
Sequa Corporation
Spirit AeroSystems Holdings Inc.
*Textron Inc.
Thor Industries, Inc.
Transdigm Group Inc.
Trinity Industries, Inc.
Triumph Group Inc.
*United Technologies Corp.
Visteon Corp.
WABCO Holdings Inc.
Wabtec Corp.

Other Manufacturing
*Brady Corporation
Coty, Inc.
*Estee Lauder Companies, Inc.

Mining
Activities Support for Mining
*Baker Hughes Inc.
Diamond Offshore Drilling, Inc.
Dril Quip, Inc.
Ensco plc
Frank's International N.V.
EOG Resources, Inc.
Halliburton Company
Helmerich & Payne, Inc.
*Marathon Oil Corporation
MRC Global Inc.
Noble Corp
Now Inc.
Oceaneering International, Inc.
Oil States International, Inc.
Pride International, Inc.
Rowan Companies Plc
RPC, Inc.
Schlumberger Ltd.
Superior Energy Services, Inc.
Transocean Ltd

Mining (except Oil and Gas)
*Arch Coal, Inc.
Cliffs Natural Resources, Inc.
CONSOL Energy Inc.
Freeport-McMoRan Inc.
*Massey Energy Co.
Mosaic Co. (The)
Newmont Mining Corporation
*Southern Copper Corp.
Tahoe Resources Inc.
*Vulcan Materials Company

Oil and Gas Extraction
*Anadarko Petroleum Corp.
*Apache Corporation
Atwood Oceanics, Inc.
Cabot Oil & Gas Corp.
Chesapeake Energy Corp.
Cimarex Energy Co.
Concho Resources Inc
Continental Resources Inc.
Denbury Resources, Inc.
Devon Energy Corporation

*Kerr-McGee Corporation
Kosmos Energy Ltd
Laredo Petroleum, Inc.
Nabors Industries Ltd.
Newfield Exploration Co.
Noble Corp.
Noble Energy, Inc.
*Occidental Petroleum Corp.
Pioneer Natural Resources Co.
QEP Resources Inc
Range Resources Corp.
St. Mary Land & Exploration Co.
Southwestern Energy Company
Ultra Petroleum Corp
Unit Corp.
Whiting Petroleum Corp.
WPX Energy, Inc.

Other Services
Aramark
Clear Channel Outdoor Holdings
Corrections Corporation of America
Genpact Ltd
Hillenbrand Inc.
ITC Holdings Corp.
Leidos Holdings Inc.
Netsuite Inc
Palo Alto Networks, Inc
Red Hat Inc.
*Regis Corporation
Reliance Steel & Aluminum Co.
Salesforce.Com Inc.
Service Corporation International
StoneMor Partners LP
Tableau Software Inc
TravelCenters of America LLC
Twitter Inc
*Universal Corporation
Valassis Communications, Inc.
Workday Inc.
Wex Inc.
Yelp Inc.

Professional, Scientific, and Technical Services
Accenture Ltd
AECOM Technology Corp.
Agere Systems Inc.
*Block (H & R), Inc.
Booz Allen Hamilton Holding Corp.
CEB Inc
Computer Sciences Corporation
Convergys Corporation
Covance Inc.
Fluor Corporation
FTI Consulting Inc.
Gartner Group, Inc.
*Interpublic Group of Companies
Korn/Ferry International
LinkedIn Corp
Moody's Corporation
*Omnicom Group, Inc.
*PerkinElmer, Inc.
Quest Diagnostics, Incorporated
Quintiles Transnational Holdings Inc

Synnex Corp.

Real Estate and Rental and Leasing
Real Estate
Alexander & Baldwin Inc.
CBRE Group Inc.
Howard Hughes Corp
Jones Lang LaSalle Inc.
Realogy Holdings Corp
*W.P. Carey & Co. LLC

Rental and Leasing Services
Air Lease Corp
Hertz Global Holdings Inc.
United Rentals, Inc.

Retail Trade
Building Material and Garden Equipment and Supplies Dealers
*Home Depot (The), Inc.
*Lowe's Companies, Inc.
Wesco International, Inc.

Clothing and Clothing Accessories Stores
Abercrombie & Fitch Co.
American Eagle Outfitters, Inc.
Carter's Inc
Chico's FAS, Inc.
Deckers Outdoor Corp.
DSW Inc.
*Foot Locker, Inc.
Gap, Inc. (The)
Nordstrom, Inc.
Payless ShoeSource Inc.
*Tiffany & Co.
TJX Companies, Inc. (The)

Furniture and Consumer Electronics
Aaron's, Inc.
Best Buy Co., Inc.
GameStop Corp.
*RadioShack Corporation
Williams-Sonoma, Inc.

General Merchandise Stores
Big Lots, Inc.
Dillard's, Inc.
Dollar General Corp.
Kohl's Corporation
Macys Inc.
Penney (J.C.) Company, Inc.
*Target Corporation
*Wal-Mart Stores, Inc.

Grocery Stores
Kroger Company (The)
*Ruddick Corporation
Safeway Inc.

Health and Personal Care Stores
*CVS Health Corp
GNC Holdings Inc
*Rite Aid Corporation
*Walgreen Co.

Motor Vehicle and Parts Dealers
Advance Auto Parts, Inc.

Asbury Automotive Group, Inc.
AutoNation, Inc.
AutoZone, Inc.
Carmax Inc.
Group 1 Automotive, Inc.
KAR Auction Services Inc.
Lithia Motors, Inc
Penske Automotive Group Inc.
Sonic Automotive, Inc.

Sporting Goods, Hobby, Book, and Music Stores and other
Barnes & Noble, Inc.
Cabelas Inc.
CST Brands Inc.
Dick's Sporting Goods, Inc.
Murphy USA Inc.
Sally Beauty Holdings Inc.
Signet Jewelers Ltd.
*Sotheby's Holdings, Inc.

Transportation and Warehousing
AirTran Holdings, Inc.
Alaska Air Group, Inc.
*Atmos Energy Corporation
*Buckeye Partners, L.P.
Delta Air Lines, Inc.
*Energy Transfer Equity L P
*Enterprise Products Partners L.P.
*FedEx Corporation
*GATX Corporation
Genesee & Wyoming Inc.
Genesis Energy L.P.
Global Partners LP
Iron Mountain Incorporated
Kansas City Southern
Kinder Morgan Inc.
Kirby Corp.
Magellan Midstream Partners LP
*Norfolk Southern Corporation
*OGE Energy Corp.
*Oneok Inc.
Plains All American Pipeline, L.P.
*Ryder System, Inc.
Southwest Airlines Co.
*Spectra Energy Corp.
Targa Resources Corp
TC PipeLines, LP
Teekay Corp
*Tidewater Inc.
*Union Pacific Corp.
United Parcel Service, Inc.
Western Gas Resources, Inc.
Williams Companies, Inc. (The)

Utilities
Utilities - Electric
AES Corporation (The)
*Alliant Energy Corporation
*Ameren Corporation
*American Electric Power Co.
*Avista Corp.
*Black Hills Corporation
*CenterPoint Energy, Inc.

*Cleco Corp.
*CMS Energy Corporation
*Consolidated Edison, Inc.
*Dominion Resources, Inc.
*DTE Energy Co.
*Duke Energy Corporation
*Edison International
*Entergy Corporation
*Eversource Energy
*Exelon Corporation
*FirstEnergy Corporation
*Great Plains Energy Incorporated
*Hawaiian Electric Industries, Inc.
*Idacorp, Inc.
*NextEra Energy Inc.
New Jersey Resources Corp.
*NiSource, Inc.
*PG&E Corporation
*Pinnacle West Capital Corp.
*PNM Resources, Inc.
*PPL Corporation
*Puget Energy, Inc.
RRI Energy, Inc.
*SCANA Corporation
*Southern Company (The)
*TECO Energy, Inc.
*WEC Energy Group Inc.
*Westar Energy, Inc.
*Xcel Energy, Inc.

Utilities - Natural Gas
*AGL Resources Inc.
*Chesapeake Utilities Corp.
*Energen Corporation
*Equitable Resources, Inc.
*National Fuel Gas Company
Northwest Natural Gas Co.
One Gas, Inc.
*Piedmont Natural Gas Company
*Questar Corporation
*Sempra Energy
South Jersey Industries, Inc.
*Spire Inc.
*UGI Corporation
*Vectren Corporation
*WGL Holdings, Inc.

Utilities - Water
*American States Water Co.
American Water Works Co., Inc.
*Aqua America, Inc.
*California Water Service Group
SJW Corp.

Wholesale Trade
Wholesale Trade, Durable Goods
Arrow Electronics, Inc.
*Avnet, Inc.
Ceridian Corporation
*Genuine Parts Company
Grainger (W.W.), Inc.
Hughes Supply, Inc.
Ingram Micro Inc.
MSC Industrial Direct Co., Inc.
National-Oilwell, Inc.

*Owens & Minor, Inc.
*Pitney Bowes Inc.
*Weyerhaeuser Company
 World Fuel Services Corp.

Wholesale Trade, Nondurable Goods
 Cardinal Health, Inc.
*Crompton Corporation

*Dominos Pizza Inc.
 Herbalife Ltd.
*McKesson Corporation
 Nu Skin Enterprises, Inc.
*Supervalu Inc.
*Sysco Corporation

* **Designates companies offering dividend reinvestment plans.**

DOW JONES INDUSTRIAL AVERAGE
PRICES - EARNINGS - DIVIDENDS

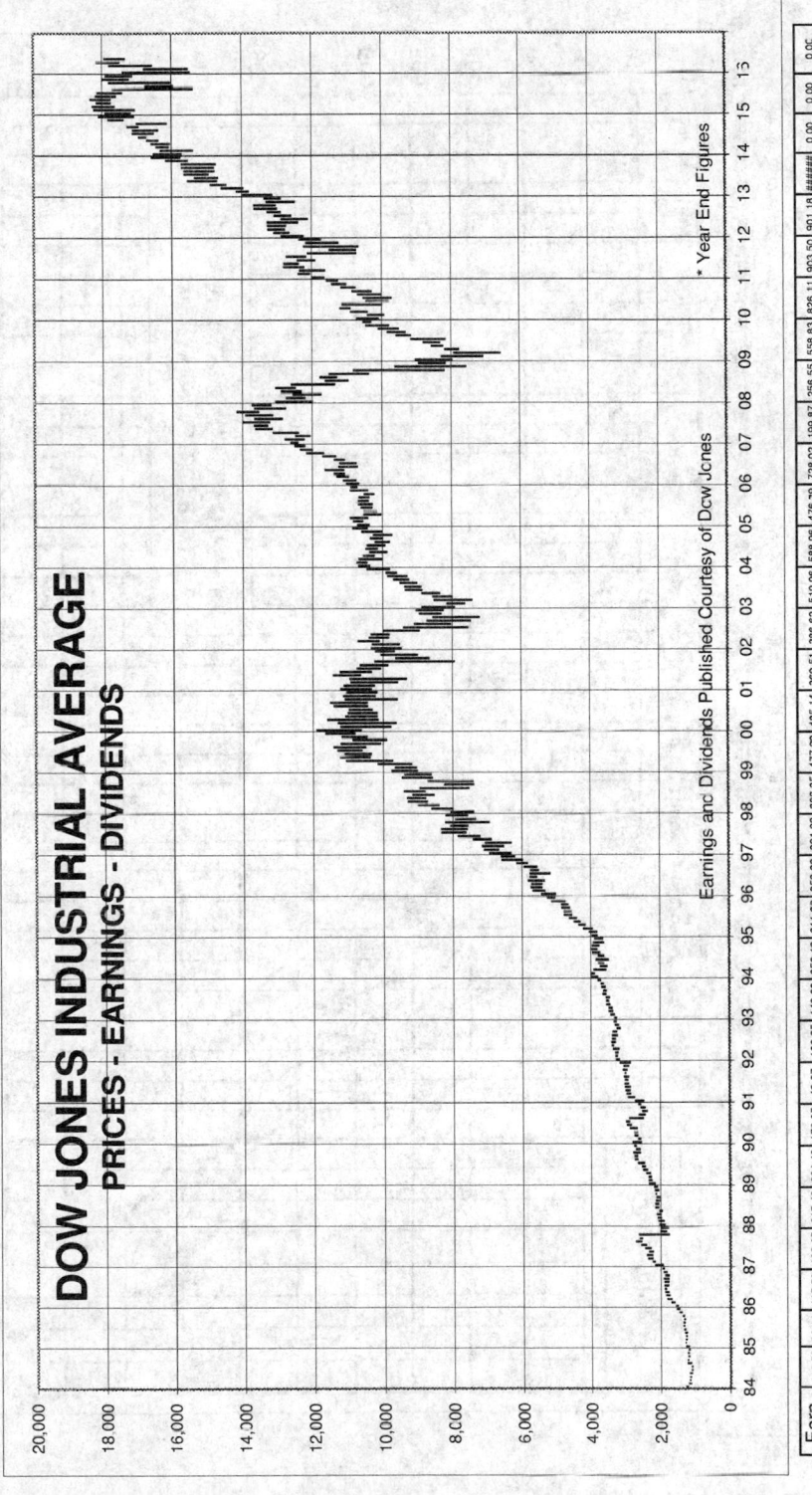

Earnings and Dividends Published Courtesy of Dow Jones

* Year End Figures

	84	85	86	87	88	89	90	91	92	93	94	95	96	97	98	99	00	01	02	03	04	05	06	07	08	09	10	11	12	13	14	15
Earn.	113.58	96.11	115.59	133.05	215.46	221.48	172.05	49.27	108.25	146.82	256.13	311.02	353.88	391.29	363.35	477.22	485.14	369.51	386.62	519.96	588.96	476.39	728.02	199.87	256.55	558.83	826.11	903.50	901.18	####	0.00	0.00
Div.	60.63	62.03	67.04	71.20	79.53	103.00	103.70	95.18	100.72	99.66	105.65	116.56	131.14	136.10	151.13	168.52	172.08	181.07	189.68	209.42	239.27	246.65	287.75	298.99	316.40	277.38	286.86	318.37	353.97	360.10	0.00	0.00
*Price	1,212	1,547	1,896	1,939	2,169	2,753	2,634	3,169	3,301	3,754	3,834	5,117	6,448	7,908	9,181	11,497	10,787	10,022	8,342	10,454	10,783	10,718	12,463	13,265	8,776	10,428	11,578	12,218	13,104	16,577	0	0
P/E Ratio	0	0	0	0	0	0	0	0	0	0	0	0	0	0	0	0	22.20	27.10	21.60	20.10	18.30	22.50	17.0	34.20	18.70	14.00	13.70	14.50	12.80	15.60	0.00	0.00

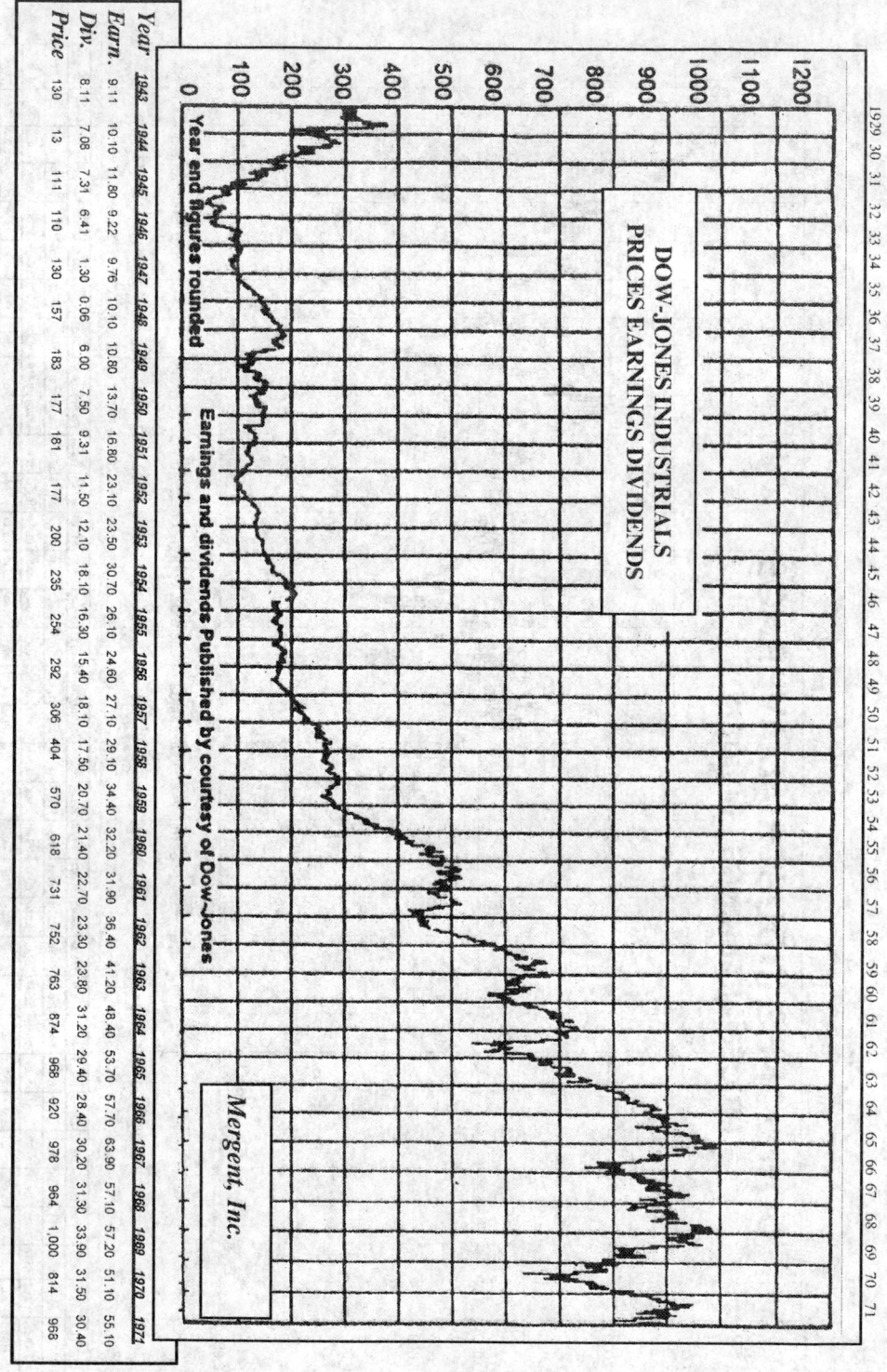

DOW-JONES INDUSTRIALS
PRICES EARNINGS DIVIDENDS

Mergent, Inc.

Earnings and dividends Published by courtesy of Dow-Jones
Year end figures rounded

Year	1943	1944	1945	1946	1947	1948	1949	1950	1951	1952	1953	1954	1955	1956	1957	1958	1959	1960	1961	1962	1963	1964	1965	1966	1967	1968	1969	1970	1971
Earn.	9.11	10.10	11.80	9.22	9.76	10.10	10.80	13.70	16.80	23.10	23.50	30.70	26.10	24.60	27.10	29.10	34.40	32.20	31.90	36.40	41.20	48.40	53.70	57.70	63.90	57.10	57.20	51.10	55.10
Div.	8.11	7.08	7.31	6.41	1.30	0.06	6.00	7.50	9.31	11.50	12.10	18.10	16.30	15.40	18.10	17.50	20.70	21.40	22.70	23.30	23.80	31.20	29.40	28.40	30.20	31.30	33.90	31.50	30.40
Price	130	130	111	110	130	157	183	177	181	177	200	235	254	292	306	404	570	618	731	752	763	874	968	920	978	964	1,000	814	968

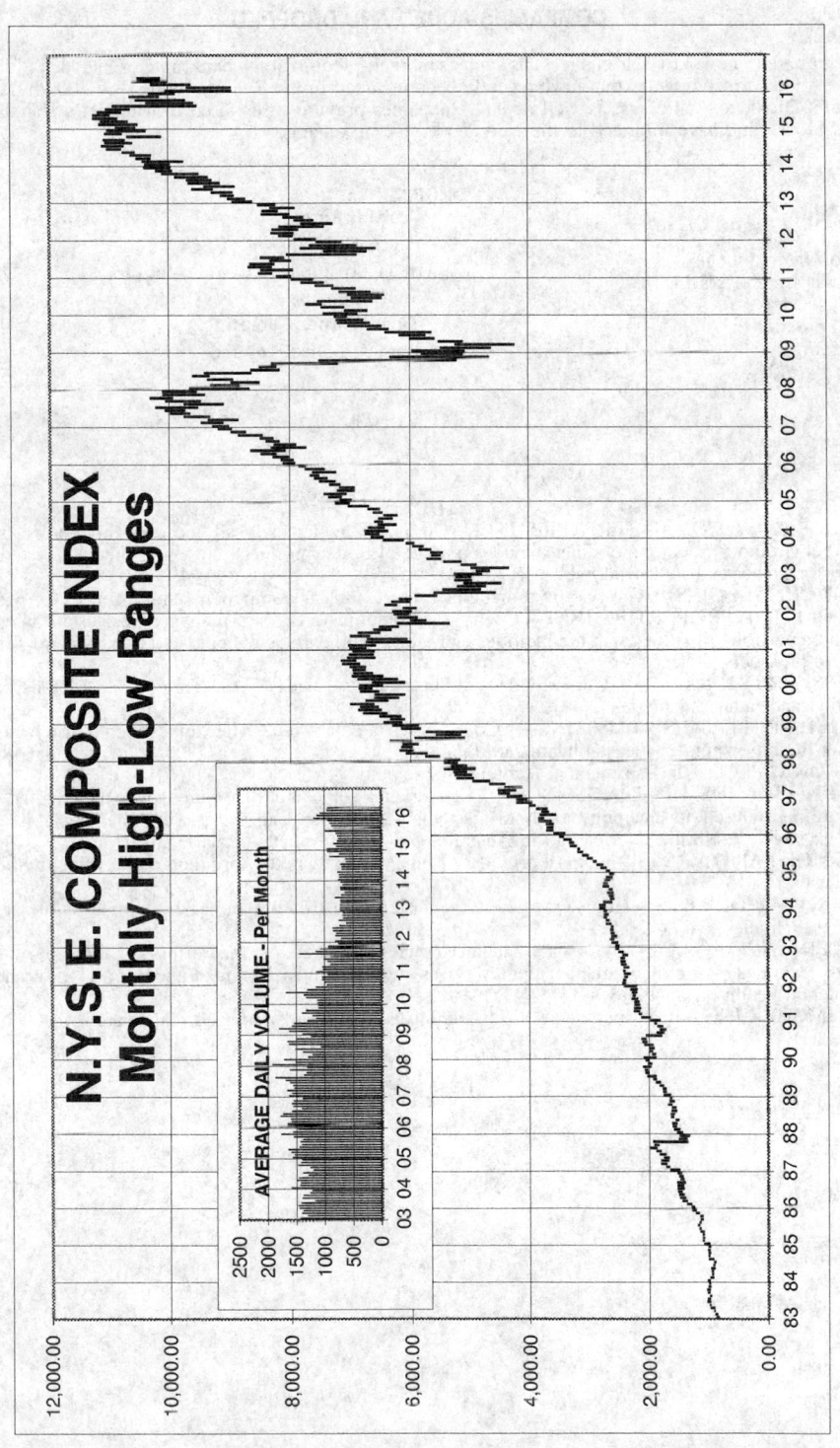

N.Y.S.E. COMPOSITE INDEX
Monthly High-Low Ranges

AVERAGE DAILY VOLUME - Per Month

ADDENDA

COMPANIES ADDED AND DROPPED

Companies are removed for various reasons such as mergers, acquisitions, bankruptcies and lack of investor interest. Added are companies that have recently been included in the Russell 1000, S&P 500, S&P 400 or Mergent's Dividend Achievers, as well as any companies previously covered in Mergent's Handbook of Nasdaq Stocks that have migrated to the New York Stock Exchange.

DROPPED

ADT Corp
Airgas Inc.
Cameron International Corp
Coca-Cola Enterprises Inc
Health Net, Inc.
ITT Corporation
Jarden Corp

Peabody Energy Corp
Pepco Holdings Inc
StanCorp Financial Group Inc.
SunEdison Inc
Time Warner Cable Inc.
Waste Connections Inc.

ADDED

BABCOCK & WILCOX ENTERPRISES INC. – Co. is a provider of fossil and renewable power generation and environmental equipment that includes a range of boiler products and environmental systems, and services for power and industrial uses.

BWX TECHNOLOGIES INC. – Co. is a manufacturer of nuclear components and a service provider.

CARE CAPITAL PROPERTIES INC. – Co. is a self-administered, self-managed real estate investment trust with a portfolio of skilled nursing facilities and other healthcare assets operated by private regional and local care providers.

CURTISS-WRIGHT CORP. – Co. provides products and services to the commercial, defense, power generation and industrial markets.

MEDICAL PROPERTIES TRUST INC. – Co. is a self-advised real estate investment trust focused on investing in and owning net-leased healthcare facilities.

MEDTRONIC PLC – Co. is a medical technology company.

PRESTIGE BRANDS HOLDINGS INC. – Co. markets, sells and distributes over-the-counter (OTC) healthcare and household cleaning brands to mass merchandisers, drug stores, supermarkets, convenience and dollar stores in North America and in Australia and certain other international markets.

STONEMOR PARTNERS LP – Co. is a provider of funeral and cemetery products and services in the death care industry.

TRI POINTE GROUP INC. – Co. is engaged in the design, construction and sale of single-family detached and attached homes.

VOYA FINANCIAL INC. – Co. is a financial services organization that offers a range of retirement services, annuities, investment management services mutual funds, life insurance, group insurance and supplemental health products.

WP GLIMCHER INC. – Co. operates as a self-administered and self-managed real estate investment trust.

ADDENDA (Continued)

RECENT AND PENDING STOCK DIVIDENDS AND SPLITS

Company	Amount	Ex-Div. Date	Date of Record	Payable Date
Alliant Energy Corp.	2-for-1	5/20/2016	5/4/2016	5/19/2016
Brown-Forman Corp.	100%	8/19/2016	8/8/2016	8/18/2016
Hertz Global Holdings Inc.	1-for-15	7/1/2016	. . .	. . .
Tootsie Roll Industries Inc.	3%	3/4/2016	3/8/2016	4/8/2016

RECENT DIVIDEND CHANGES

Company	–Latest Dividend– Amount	Payable	Company	–Latest Dividend– Amount	Payable
Increased			**Increased**		
American Campus Communities	0.42 Q	5/12/16	MetLife Inc.	0.40 Q	5/5/16
American Tower Corp.	0.51 Q	4/8/16	MSA Safety Inc.	0.33 Q	5/19/16
American Water Works Co, Inc.	0.38 Q	5/5/16	Omega Healthcare Investors, Inc.	0.58 Q	4/28/16
Ameriprise Financial Inc.	0.75 Q	5/5/16	Penske Automotive Group Inc.	0.27 Q	5/12/16
Aspen Insurance Holdings Ltd	0.22 Q	5/5/16	Phillips 66	0.63 Q	5/16/16
Autoliv Inc.	0.58 Q	5/16/16	PPG Industries Inc.	0.40 Q	5/6/16
Avery Dennison Corp.	0.41 Q	5/27/16	Procter & Gamble Co.	0.67 Q	4/14/16
Bank of Hawaii Corp.	0.48 Q	5/26/16	Quest Diagnostics, Inc.	0.40 Q	4/4/16
BB&T Corp.	0.28 Q	5/11/16	Raytheon Co	0.73 Q	4/4/16
Buckeye Partners, L.P.	1.20 Q	5/12/16	RLI Corp.	0.20 Q	5/26/16
Cabot Corp.	0.30 Q	5/25/16	Schwab (Charles) Corp.	0.07 Q	5/11/16
Carnival Corp.	0.35 Q	5/25/16	Signet Jewelers Ltd.	0.26 Q	4/27/16
Celanese Corp.	0.36 Q	4/28/16	Sonoco Products Co.	0.37 Q	5/11/16
Colgate-Palmolive Co.	0.39 Q	4/20/16	Southern Company	0.56 Q	5/12//16
Constellation Brands Inc.	0.40 Q	5/6/16	Southern Copper Corp.	0.05 Q	5/6/16
Cullen/Frost Bankers, Inc.	0.54 Q	5/26/16	Sunoco Logistics Partners L.P.	0.49 Q	5/5/16
Enterprise Products Partners L.P.	0.40 Q	4/27/16	Tanger Factory Outlet Centers, Inc.	0.33 Q	4/27/16
Exelon Corp.	0.32 Q	5/11/16	TE Connectivity Ltd.	0.37 Q	5/25/16
Exxon Mobil Corp.	0.75 Q	5/11/16	TJX Companies, Inc.	0.26 Q	5/10/16
FactSet Research Systems Inc.	0.50 Q	5/26/16	UDR Inc.	0.30 Q	4/7/16
First Republic Bank	0.16 Q	4/26/16	United Technologies Corp.	0.66 Q	5/18/16
Foot Locker, Inc.	0.28 Q	4/13/16	Webster Financial Corp.	0.25 Q	5/5/16
Fuller (H.B.) Company	0.14 Q	4/19/16	Wells Fargo & Co.	0.38 Q	5/4/16
General Dynamics Corp.	0.76 Q	4/6//16	WGL Holdings Inc.	0.49 Q	4/6/16
General Mills, Inc.	0.46 Q	4/7/16	Whirlpool Corp.	1.00 Q	5/18/16
Genesis Energy L.P.	0.67 Q	4/27/16	Williams Sonoma Inc.	0.37 Q	4/27/16
Grainger (W.W.) Inc.	1.22 Q	5/5/16			
Group 1 Automotive, Inc.	0.23 Q	5/27/16	**Decreased**		
Hexcel Corp.	0.11 Q	5/2/16	Anadarko Petroleum Corp.	0.05 Q	3/7/16
HNI Corp.	0.28 Q	5/18/16	Best Buy Inc.	0.28 Q	3/15/16
Hospitality Properties Trust	0.51 Q	4/21/16	Cimarex Energy Co.	0.08 Q	5/11/16
IDEX Corporation	0.34 Q	4/14/16	CNA Financial Corp.	0.25 Q	5/12/16
International Business Machines	1.40 Q	5/6//16	Ensco plc	0.01 Q	3/3/16
Invesco Ltd.	0.28 Q	5/11/16	Equity Residential	0.50 Q	3/22/16
Janus Capital Group Inc.	0.11 Q	5/5/16	Lazard Ltd.	0.38 Q	4/29/16
Johnson & Johnson	0.80 Q	5/20/16	NIKE Inc.	0.16 Q	3/3/16
Jones Lang LaSalle Inc.	0.31 Q	5/11/16	Noble Corp. plc	0.02 Q	4/28/16
KeyCorp	0.09 Q	5/26/16	NRG Energy Inc.	0.03 Q	4/28/16
Lithia Motors, Inc.	0.25 Q	5/11/16	ProAssurance Corp.	0.31 Q	3/28/16
Magellan Midstream Partners LP	0.80 Q	4/28/16	Range Resources Corp.	0.02 Q	3/11/16
ManpowerGroup	0.86 Q	5/27/16			

RECENT AND PENDING NAME CHANGES

Old	New
Lacede Group Inc.	Spire Inc.
Newell Rubbermaid Inc.	Newell Brands Inc.
McGraw Hill Financial, Inc.	S&P Global Inc.

LATEST DEVELOPMENTS

GANNETT CO INC. – On June 27, 2016, Co. announced the execution of a definitive merger agreement whereby Co. would acquire the outstanding shares of ReachLocal, Inc. for $4.60 per share in cash. This represents a total enterprise value of approximately $156.0 million.

MEDTRONIC PLC – On June 27, 2016, Co. and HeartWare International, Inc., an innovator of less-invasive, miniaturized circulatory support technologies for the treatment of advanced heart failure, announced that the companies have entered into a definitive merger agreement under which Co. will acquire HeartWare in a transaction valued at approximately $1.10 billion. The acquisition is expected to close during Co.'s second fiscal quarter ending Oct. 28, 2016.

MARATHON OIL CORP – On June 20, 2016, Co. announced the signing of a definitive purchase and sale agreement to acquire PayRock Energy Holdings, LLC, a portfolio company of EnCap Investments, for $888.0 million. PayRock has approximately 61,000 net surface acres and production of 9,000 net barrels of oil equivalent per day in the oil window of the Anadarko Basin STACK play in Oklahoma.

The 2016 Summer Common Dividend Achievers

Companies listed below qualified for the 2016 Summer Edition of Mergent's Dividend Achievers. Also shown are total numbers of consecutive years of dividend growth.

Company	Years	Company	Years
3M Co	57	Dominion Resources Inc	12
Aaron's Inc	12	Donaldson Co. Inc.	20
Abbott Laboratories	42	Dover Corp	60
ABM Industries. Inc.	51	Duke Energy Corp	11
AFLAC Inc.	33	Eaton Vance Corp	34
AGL Resources Inc.	13	Ecolab. Inc.	23
Air Products & Chemicals. Inc.	33	Edison International	11
Albemarle Corp.	21	Emerson Electric Co.	59
Alliant Energy Corp	12	Enterprise Products Partners L.P.	17
Altria Group Inc	49	EOG Resources. Inc.	16
American Equity Investment Life	12	Equity Lifestyle Properties Inc	11
American Financial Group Inc	10	Essex Property Trust Inc	21
American States Water Co	61	Eversource Energy	12
AmeriGas Partners. L.P.	11	Exxon Mobil Corp.	33
Ameriprise Financial Inc	10	FactSet Research Systems Inc.	16
AmerisourceBergen Corp.	11	Federal Realty Investment Trust (MD)	48
AptarGroup Inc.	22	FedEx Corp	12
Aqua America Inc	23	Flowers Foods. Inc.	12
Archer Daniels Midland Co.	41	Franklin Resources. Inc.	26
Assurant Inc	11	Fuller (H.B.) Company	48
AT&T Inc	31	General Dynamics Corp.	24
Atmos Energy Corp.	28	General Mills. Inc.	12
Avista Corp.	13	Genesis Energy L.P.	12
Badger Meter. Inc.	23	Genuine Parts Co.	59
Bard (CR) Inc	44	Graco Inc	16
Becton. Dickinson and Co.	43	Grainger (W.W.) Inc.	44
Bemis Co Inc	32	Hanover Insurance Group Inc	10
Berkley (WR) Corp	14	Harris Corp.	14
Best Buy Inc	11	HCP. Inc.	30
Black Hills Corporation	44	Helmerich & Payne. Inc.	39
Brady Corp	31	Holly Energy Partners LP	11
Brown & Brown. Inc.	22	Hormel Foods Corp.	49
Brown-Forman Corp.	31	Illinois Tool Works. Inc.	53
Buckeye Partners. L.P.	20	International Business Machines Corp.	20
California Water Service Group (DE)	48	International Flavors & Fragrances Inc.	13
Cardinal Health. Inc.	19	Johnson & Johnson	51
Carlisle Companies Inc.	39	Kellogg Co	11
Caterpillar Inc.	22	Kimberly-Clark Corp.	41
CenterPoint Energy. Inc	10	L-3 Communications Holdings. Inc.	11
Chesapeake Utilities Corp.	12	Leggett & Platt. Inc.	44
Chevron Corporation	28	Lindsay Corp	13
Church & Dwight Co.. Inc.	19	Lockheed Martin Corp.	13
Clarcor Inc.	35	Lowe's Companies Inc	54
Clorox Co (The)	39	Magellan Midstream Partners LP	14
Coca-Cola Co (The)	53	McCormick & Co.. Inc.	29
Colgate-Palmolive Co.	53	McDonald's Corp	39
Community Bank System. Inc.	24	MDU Resources Group Inc.	25
Compass Minerals International Inc	11	Mercury General Corp.	29
ConocoPhillips	15	Meredith Corp	22
Consolidated Edison Inc	41	Monsanto Co.	14
Crane Co.	11	MSA Safety Inc	45
Cullen/Frost Bankers. Inc.	22	MSC Industrial Direct Co.. Inc.	12
Cummins. Inc.	10	Murphy Oil Corp	16
CVS Health Corporation	12	National Fuel Gas Co. (NJ)	44
Deere & Co.	12	National Health Investors. Inc.	13
Digital Realty Trust. Inc.	11	National Retail Properties Inc	26

The 2016 Summer Common Dividend Achievers (Cont.)

Company Name	Years of Growth	Company Name	Years of Growth
New Jersey Resources Corp	20	Southern Company (The)	14
NextEra Energy Inc	20	Spire Inc	12
NIKE Inc	14	Stanley Black & Decker Inc	48
Norfolk Southern Corp.	14	Stepan Co.	48
Northrop Grumman Corp	12	StoneMor Partners L P	10
Northwest Natural Gas Co.	60	Stryker Corp.	23
Northwestern Corp.	10	Sunoco Logistics Partners L.P.	13
NU Skin Enterprises. Inc.	14	Sysco Corp.	39
Nucor Corp.	43	Tanger Factory Outlet Centers. Inc.	22
Occidental Petroleum Corp	13	Target Corp	44
Oil-Dri Corp. of America	13	TC PipeLines. LP	16
Old Republic International Corp.	34	Telephone & Data Systems. Inc.	41
Omega Healthcare Investors. Inc.	13	Tennant Co.	43
Oneok Inc	13	The Gap. Inc.	11
ONEOK Partners LP	10	Tiffany & Co.	13
Owens & Minor. Inc.	18	TJX Companies. Inc.	19
Parker Hannifin Corp.	59	Tootsie Roll Industries Inc	52
PepsiCo Inc	44	Torchmark Corp.	10
Piedmont Natural Gas Co Inc	36	Toro Co. (The)	12
Plains All American Pipeline. L.P.	16	TransMontaigne Partners L.P.	10
Polaris Industries Inc.	20	Travelers Companies Inc (The)	10
PPG Industries Inc	44	UGI Corp.	28
PPL Corp	16	United Technologies Corp	22
Praxair. Inc.	23	Universal Corp.	45
Procter & Gamble Co.	62	Universal Health Realty Income Trust	28
Prosperity Bancshares Inc.	16	Urstadt Biddle Properties Inc	17
Questar Corp	36	Valmont Industries Inc	14
Raytheon Co.	11	Valspar Corp	37
Realty Income Corp	21	Vector Group Ltd	17
Regal Beloit Corp	11	Vectren Corp	40
Republic Services Inc	12	Verizon Communications Inc	11
Reynolds American Inc	11	VF Corp.	43
RLI Corp.	39	W.P. Carey Inc	17
Robert Half International Inc.	11	Wal-Mart Stores. Inc.	40
Rollins. Inc.	13	Waste Management. Inc. (DE)	12
Roper Technologies Inc	23	WEC Energy Group Inc	12
RPM International Inc (DE)	42	Welltower Inc	12
Ryder System. Inc.	11	West Pharmaceutical Services. Inc.	23
S&P Global Inc	42	Westar Energy Inc	12
SCANA Corp	15	Westlake Chemical Corp	11
Sensient Technologies Corp.	10	Westwood Holdings Group. Inc.	13
Sherwin-Williams Co (The)	36	WGL Holdings Inc	39
SJW Corp.	48	Wiley (John) & Sons Inc.	22
Smith (A.O.) Corp	23	Williams Cos Inc (The)	12
Smucker (J.M.) Co.	18	Xcel Energy. Inc.	12
Sonoco Products Co.	32	Yum! Brands. Inc.	11
South Jersey Industries. Inc.	16		

AARON'S INC

Exchange	Symbol	Price	52Wk Range	Yield	P/E	Div Achiever
NYS	AAN	$25.10 (5/31/2016)	40.46-20.33	0.40	13.42	12 Years

*7 Year Price Score 96.92 *NYSE Composite Index=100 ***12 Month Price Score 87.86**

Interim Earnings (Per Share)

Qtr	Mar	Jun	Sep	Dec
2013	0.67	0.34	0.28	0.30
2014	0.53	0.12	0.13	0.31
2015	0.68	0.56	0.33	0.30
2016	0.68	...	...	...

Interim Dividends (Per Share)

Amt	Decl	Ex	Rec	Pay
0.023Q	08/07/2015	09/01/2015	09/03/2015	10/01/2015
0.025Q	11/09/2015	11/27/2015	12/01/2015	01/04/2016
0.025Q	02/29/2016	03/11/2016	03/15/2016	04/01/2016
0.025Q	05/09/2016	06/02/2016	06/04/2016	07/01/2016

Indicated Div: $0.10

Valuation Analysis / Institutional Holding

Forecast EPS	$2.23 (05/14/2016)	No of Institutions	300
Market Cap	$1.8 Billion	Shares	72,023,672
Book Value	$1.4 Billion	% Held	N/A
Price/Book	1.29		
Price/Sales	0.57		

TRADING VOLUME (thousand shares)

Business Summary: Retail - Furniture & Home Furnishings (MIC: 2.1.6 SIC: 5712 NAIC: 442110)

Aaron's is a retailer of furniture, consumer electronics, computers, appliances and household accessories. Co. is engaged in the lease ownership and retail sale of products such as televisions, computers, tablets, mobile phones, living room, dining room and bedroom furniture, mattresses, washers, dryers and refrigerators. Co. carries brands such as Samsung®, Frigidaire®, Hewlett-Packard®, LG®, Whirlpool®, Simmons®, Philips®, JVC®, Sharp® and Magnavox®. At Dec 31 2015, Co. had 2,039 stores, comprised of 1,305 Co.-operated stores in 28 states, District of Columbia and Canada and 734 independently-owned franchised stores in 47 states and Canada.

Recent Developments: For the quarter ended Mar 31 2016, net income increased 0.9% to US$49.7 million from US$49.2 million in the year-earlier quarter. Revenues were US$854.4 million, up 4.0% from US$821.8 million the year before. Operating income was US$86.0 million versus US$84.8 million in the prior-year quarter, an increase of 1.4%. Direct operating expenses declined 17.0% to US$78.5 million from US$94.6 million in the comparable period the year before. Indirect operating expenses increased 7.4% to US$690.0 million from US$642.4 million in the equivalent prior-year period.

Prospects: Our evaluation of Aaron's Inc as of June 19, 2016 is the result of our systematic analysis on three basic characteristics: earnings strength, relative valuation, and recent stock price movement. The company has managed to produce a neutral trend in earnings per share over the past 5 quarters and while recent estimates for the company have remained steady, AAN has posted results that fell short of analysts expectations. Based on operating earnings yield, the company is undervalued when compared to all of the companies in our coverage universe. Share price changes over the past year indicates that AAN will perform in line with the market over the near term.

Financial Data

(US$ in Thousands)	3 Mos	12/31/2015	12/31/2014	12/31/2013	12/31/2012	12/31/2011	12/31/2010	12/31/2009
Earnings Per Share	1.87	1.86	1.08	1.58	2.25	1.43	1.44	1.37
Cash Flow Per Share	1.88	2.30	(0.68)	4.07	0.79	...	0.61	2.39
Tang Book Value Per Share	8.59	7.59	5.45	12.30	11.83	9.93	9.65	8.45
Dividends Per Share	0.096	0.094	0.086	0.072	0.062	0.054	0.049	0.046
Dividend Payout %	5.13	5.05	7.96	4.56	2.76	3.78	3.40	3.36
Income Statement								
Total Revenue	854,427	3,179,756	2,725,239	2,234,631	2,222,588	2,024,049	1,876,847	1,752,787
EBITDA	433,921	286,274	191,698	240,875	332,806	233,286	235,282	221,438
Depn & Amortn	348,302	52,000	53,700	53,300	53,100	45,200	41,400	40,700
Income Before Taxes	79,728	213,120	121,704	184,960	276,855	183,377	190,786	176,439
Income Taxes	30,041	77,411	43,471	64,294	103,812	69,610	72,410	63,561
Net Income	49,687	135,709	78,233	120,666	173,043	113,767	118,376	112,601
Average Shares	73,217	73,043	72,723	76,390	76,826	...	82,102	81,951
Balance Sheet								
Current Assets	1,411,647	1,617,652	1,409,286	1,353,167	1,342,110	1,283,122	1,090,949	894,264
Total Assets	2,548,767	2,658,875	2,456,844	1,827,176	1,812,693	1,735,149	1,502,072	1,321,456
Current Liabilities	612,804	374,326	358,690	317,551	271,554	317,844	253,352	215,482
Long-Term Obligations	518,041	610,450	606,082	142,704	141,528	153,789	41,790	55,044
Total Liabilities	1,130,845	1,292,257	1,233,323	687,213	676,803	758,595	522,655	434,196
Stockholders' Equity	1,417,922	1,366,618	1,223,521	1,139,963	1,136,126	976,554	979,417	887,260
Shares Outstanding	72,749	72,600	72,488	72,956	75,720	75,640	80,087	81,357
Statistical Record								
Return on Assets %	5.50	5.31	3.65	6.63	9.73	7.03	8.38	8.82
Return on Equity %	10.11	10.48	6.62	10.60	16.34	11.63	12.68	13.66
EBITDA Margin %	50.79	9.00	7.03	10.78	14.97	11.53	12.54	12.63
Net Margin %	5.82	4.27	2.87	5.40	7.79	5.62	6.31	6.42
Asset Turnover	1.30	1.24	1.27	1.23	1.25	1.25	1.33	1.37
Current Ratio	2.30	4.32	3.93	4.26	4.94	4.04	4.31	4.15
Debt to Equity	0.37	0.45	0.50	0.13	0.12	0.16	0.04	0.06
Price Range	40.46-20.33	40.46-21.74	35.90-23.27	30.60-26.68	31.16-24.83	29.16-19.19	20.79-13.00	20.30-11.47
P/E Ratio	21.64-10.87	21.75-11.69	33.24-21.55	19.37-16.89	13.85-11.04	20.39-13.42	14.44-9.03	14.82-8.37
Average Yield %	0.32	0.30	0.30	0.25	0.22	0.21	0.29	2.90

Address: 309 E. Paces Ferry Road, N.E., Atlanta, GA 30305-2377 **Telephone:** 404-231-0011	**Web Site:** www.aarons.com **Officers:** R. Charles Loudermilk - Chairman Emeritus, Chairman, Chief Executive Officer Steven A. Michaels - President, Chief Financial Officer, Division Officer	**Auditors:** Ernst & Young LLP **Investor Contact:** 678-402-3116 **Transfer Agents:** Computershare Investor Services, Canton, MA

ABBVIE INC.

Exchange	Symbol	Price	52Wk Range	Yield	P/E
NYS	ABBV	$62.93 (5/31/2016)	71.23-48.27	3.62	18.95

*7 Year Price Score N/A   *NYSE Composite Index=100   *12 Month Price Score 99.62

Interim Earnings (Per Share)

Qtr.	Mar	Jun	Sep	Dec
2013	0.60	0.66	0.60	0.70
2014	0.61	0.68	0.31	(0.50)
2015	0.63	0.83	0.74	0.92
2016	0.83			

Interim Dividends (Per Share)

Amt	Decl	Ex	Rec	Pay
0.51Q	09/11/2015	10/13/2015	10/15/2015	11/16/2015
0.57Q	10/30/2015	01/13/2016	01/15/2016	02/16/2016
0.57Q	02/18/2016	04/13/2016	04/15/2016	05/16/2016
0.57Q	06/16/2016	07/13/2016	07/15/2016	08/15/2016

Indicated Div: $2.28

Valuation Analysis

		Institutional Holding	
Forecast EPS	$4.76	No of Institutions	
	(05/20/2016)	1856	
Market Cap	$101.8 Billion	Shares	
Book Value	$4.6 Billion	1,165,989,888	
Price/Book	21.92	% Held	
Price/Sales	4.28	69.34	

TRADING VOLUME (thousand shares)

Business Summary: Biotechnology (MIC: 4.1.2 SIC: 2834 NAIC: 325412)

AbbVie is a research-based biopharmaceutical company that develops and markets therapies that address diseases. Co.'s products are focused on treating conditions such as chronic autoimmune diseases in rheumatology, gastroenterology and dermatology; oncology, including blood cancers; virology, including hepatitis C and human immunodeficiency virus; neurological disorders, such as Parkinson's disease and metabolic diseases; as well as other serious health conditions. Co. also has a pipeline of medicines, including over 50 compounds or indications in clinical development across such medical specialties as immunology, virology/liver disease, oncology, neurological diseases and women's health.

Recent Developments: For the quarter ended Mar 31 2016, net income increased 32.5% to US$1.35 billion from US$1.02 billion in the year-earlier quarter. Revenues were US$5.96 billion, up 18.2% from US$5.04 billion the year before. Operating income was US$2.28 billion versus US$1.69 billion in the prior-year quarter, an increase of 35.0%. Direct operating expenses rose 45.3% to US$1.37 billion from US$942.0 million in the comparable period the year before. Indirect operating expenses decreased 4.1% to US$2.31 billion from US$2.41 billion in the equivalent prior-year period.

Prospects: Our evaluation of AbbVie Inc. as of June 19, 2016 is the result of our systematic analysis on three basic characteristics: earnings strength, relative valuation, and recent stock price movement. The company has managed to produce a neutral trend in earnings per share over the past 5 quarters. However, while recent estimates for the company have been mixed, ABBV has posted better than expected results. Based on operating earnings yield, the company is undervalued when compared to all of the companies in our coverage universe. Share price changes over the past year indicates that ABBV will perform in line with the market over the near term.

Financial Data

(US$ in Thousands)	3 Mos	12/31/2015	12/31/2014	12/31/2013	12/31/2012	12/31/2011	12/31/2010	12/31/2009
Earnings Per Share	3.32	3.13	1.10	2.56	3.35	...	...	...
Cash Flow Per Share	5.00	4.64	2.23	3.94	4.01	...	...	...
Dividends Per Share	2.100	2.020	1.660	1.600		...	...	...
Dividend Payout %	63.25	64.54	150.91	62.50	...	...	...	...
Income Statement								
Total Revenue	5,958,000	22,859,000	19,960,000	18,790,000	18,380,000	17,443,951	15,637,731	14,214,196
EBITDA	2,244,000	8,167,000	3,546,000	6,507,000	6,959,000	4,940,721	6,019,858	6,647,809
Depn & Amortn	268,000	836,000	786,000	897,000	1,150,000	1,272,194	1,184,361	697,492
Income Before Taxes	1,776,000	6,645,000	2,369,000	5,332,000	5,725,000	3,668,527	4,835,497	5,950,317
Income Taxes	422,000	1,501,000	595,000	1,204,000	450,000	235,399	657,631	1,313,802
Net Income	1,354,000	5,144,000	1,774,000	4,128,000	5,275,000	3,433,128	4,177,866	4,636,515
Average Shares	1,625,000	1,637,000	1,610,000	1,604,000	1,577,000	...	...	...
Balance Sheet								
Current Assets	16,622,000	16,314,000	16,088,000	17,848,000	15,354,000	7,354,155	8,218,493	...
Total Assets	53,720,000	53,050,000	27,547,000	29,198,000	27,008,000	19,657,166	21,134,705	...
Current Liabilities	10,662,000	10,894,000	11,400,000	6,879,000	6,776,000	5,896,678	3,761,248	...
Long-Term Obligations	29,490,000	29,240,000	10,565,000	14,292,000	14,630,000			...
Total Liabilities	49,077,000	49,105,000	25,805,000	24,706,000	23,645,000	7,433,453	5,431,706	...
Stockholders' Equity	4,643,000	3,945,000	1,742,000	4,492,000	3,363,000	12,223,713	15,702,999	...
Shares Outstanding	1,617,358	1,609,892	1,591,389	1,587,360	1,577,334	...	...	...
Statistical Record								
Return on Assets %	13.62	12.76	6.25	14.69	22.55	16.83	...	...
Return on Equity %	181.93	180.90	56.91	105.11	67.50	24.59	...	...
EBITDA Margin %	37.66	35.73	17.77	34.63	37.86	28.32	38.50	46.77
Net Margin %	22.73	22.50	8.89	21.97	28.70	19.68	26.72	32.62
Asset Turnover	0.59	0.57	0.70	0.67	0.79	0.86	...	...
Current Ratio	1.56	1.50	1.41	2.59	2.27	1.25	2.19	...
Debt to Equity	6.35	7.41	6.06	3.18	4.35		...	...
Price Range	71.23-48.27	71.23-48.27	69.71-46.46	54.32-33.71	...	...	...	...
P/E Ratio	21.45-14.54	22.76-15.42	63.37-42.24	21.22-13.17	...	...	...	...
Average Yield %	3.44	3.25	2.99	3.66	...	...	...	...

Address: 1 North Waukegan Road, North Chicago, IL 60064-6400 **Telephone:** 847-932-7900	**Web Site:** www.abbvie.com **Officers:** Richard A. Gonzalez - Chairman, Chief Executive Officer Michael E. Severino - Executive Vice President, Chief Scientific Officer	**Auditors:** Ernst & Young LLP **Transfer Agents:** Computershare Trust Company, N.A., Canton, MA

ABBOTT LABORATORIES

Exchange	Symbol	Price	52Wk Range	Yield	P/E	Div Achiever
NYS	ABT	$39.63 (5/31/2016)	51.20-36.34	2.62	24.46	42 Years

*7 Year Price Score 111.61   *NYSE Composite Index=100   *12 Month Price Score 91.42

Interim Earnings (Per Share)

Qtr.	Mar	Jun	Sep	Dec
2013	0.34	0.30	0.61	0.37
2014	0.24	0.30	0.36	0.59
2015	1.51	0.52	0.38	0.51
2016	0.21	...	...	...

Interim Dividends (Per Share)

Amt	Decl	Ex	Rec	Pay
0.24Q	09/17/2015	10/13/2015	10/15/2015	11/15/2015
0.26Q	12/11/2015	01/13/2016	01/15/2016	02/16/2016
0.26Q	02/19/2016	04/13/2016	04/15/2016	05/16/2016
0.26Q	06/10/2016	07/13/2016	07/15/2016	08/15/2016

Indicated Div: $1.04 (Div. Reinv. Plan)

Valuation Analysis | **Institutional Holding**

Forecast EPS	$2.21	No of Institutions	
	(05/20/2016)	2056	
Market Cap	$58.2 Billion	Shares	
Book Value	$20.7 Billion	1,190,967,296	
Price/Book	2.81	% Held	
Price/Sales	2.86	66.41	

TRADING VOLUME (thousand shares)

Business Summary: Pharmaceuticals (MIC: 4.1.1 SIC: 2834 NAIC: 325412)

Abbott Laboratories is engaged in the discovery, development, manufacture and sale of a line of health care products. Co.'s reportable segments are: Established Pharmaceutical Products, which sells a line of generic pharmaceutical products; Diagnostic Products, which sells diagnostic systems and tests for blood banks, hospitals, commercial laboratories and alternate-care testing sites; Nutritional Products, which sells a line of adult and pediatric nutritional products; and Vascular Products, which includes a line of coronary, endovascular, structural heart, vessel closure and other medical device products. Non-reportable segments include the Diabetes Care and Medical Optics segments.

Recent Developments: For the quarter ended Mar 31 2016, income from continuing operations decreased 89.4% to US$56.0 million from US$529.0 million in the year-earlier quarter. Net income decreased 86.2% to US$316.0 million from US$2.29 billion in the year-earlier quarter. Revenues were US$4.89 billion, down 0.2% from US$4.90 billion the year before. Operating income was US$524.0 million versus US$610.0 million in the prior-year quarter, a decrease of 14.1%. Direct operating expenses rose 2.8% to US$2.14 billion from US$2.08 billion in the comparable period the year before. Indirect operating expenses increased 0.7% to US$2.22 billion from US$2.21 billion in the equivalent prior-year period.

Prospects: Our evaluation of Abbott Laboratories as of June 19, 2016 is the result of our systematic analysis on three basic characteristics: earnings strength, relative valuation, and recent stock price movement. The company has managed to produce a neutral trend in earnings per share over the past 5 quarters and while recent estimates for the company have remained steady, ABT has posted better than expected results. Based on operating earnings yield, the company is undervalued when compared to all of the companies in our coverage universe. Share price changes over the past year indicates that ABT will perform in line with the market over the near term.

Financial Data

(US$ in Thousands)	3 Mos	12/31/2015	12/31/2014	12/31/2013	12/31/2012	12/31/2011	12/31/2010	12/31/2009
Earnings Per Share	1.62	2.92	1.49	1.62	3.72	3.01	2.96	3.69
Cash Flow Per Share	1.94	1.98	2.42	2.13	5.90	5.76	5.65	4.70
Tang Book Value Per Share	3.74	4.08	3.49	6.24	1.50	N.M.	N.M.	2.17
Dividends Per Share	0.980	0.960	0.880	0.560	2.010	1.880	1.720	1.560
Dividend Payout %	60.49	32.88	59.06	34.57	54.03	62.46	58.11	42.28
Income Statement								
Total Revenue	4,885,000	20,405,000	20,247,000	21,848,000	39,873,910	38,851,259	35,166,721	30,764,707
EBITDA	374,000	4,713,000	4,139,000	4,330,000	9,674,326	8,855,110	9,243,371	9,515,184
Depn & Amortn	347,000	1,472,000	1,548,000	1,719,000	2,898,534	3,211,523	3,082,855	1,939,533
Income Before Taxes	2,000	3,183,000	2,518,000	2,521,000	6,262,614	5,198,642	5,712,834	7,193,774
Income Taxes	(54,000)	577,000	797,000	138,000	299,694	470,193	1,086,662	1,447,936
Net Income	316,000	4,423,000	2,284,000	2,576,000	5,962,920	4,728,449	4,626,172	5,745,838
Average Shares	1,483,673	1,506,000	1,527,000	1,574,000	1,591,838	1,567,389	1,556,022	1,555,126
Balance Sheet								
Current Assets	12,406,000	14,155,000	15,261,000	19,247,000	31,322,583	23,768,774	22,317,529	23,313,891
Total Assets	39,637,000	41,247,000	41,275,000	42,953,000	67,234,944	60,276,893	59,462,266	52,416,623
Current Liabilities	8,393,000	9,186,000	10,532,000	9,507,000	13,280,176	15,480,228	17,262,434	13,049,489
Long-Term Obligations	5,977,000	5,871,000	3,408,000	3,388,000	18,085,302	12,039,822	12,523,517	11,266,294
Total Liabilities	18,915,000	20,036,000	19,749,000	17,782,000	40,513,983	35,837,060	37,074,131	29,560,885
Stockholders' Equity	20,722,000	21,211,000	21,526,000	25,171,000	26,720,961	24,439,833	22,388,135	22,855,627
Shares Outstanding	1,469,152	1,472,665	1,508,035	1,548,098	1,576,667	1,570,378	1,546,983	1,551,167
Statistical Record								
Return on Assets %	5.92	10.72	5.42	4.68	9.33	7.90	8.27	12.12
Return on Equity %	11.49	20.70	9.78	9.93	23.25	20.19	20.45	28.49
EBITDA Margin %	7.66	23.10	20.44	19.82	24.26	22.79	26.28	30.93
Net Margin %	6.47	21.68	11.28	11.79	14.95	12.17	13.15	18.68
Asset Turnover	0.49	0.49	0.48	0.40	0.62	0.65	0.63	0.65
Current Ratio	1.48	1.54	1.45	2.02	2.36	1.54	1.29	1.79
Debt to Equity	0.29	0.28	0.16	0.13	0.68	0.49	0.56	0.49
Price Range	51.20-36.34	51.20-39.06	46.37-35.85	38.71-31.34	34.51-25.91	26.95-21.61	26.91-21.94	27.39-19.87
P/E Ratio	31.60-22.43	17.53-13.38	31.12-24.06	23.90-19.35	9.28-6.96	8.95-7.18	9.09-7.41	7.42-5.38
Average Yield %	2.19	2.07	2.15	1.57	6.66	7.70	7.08	6.73

Address: 100 Abbott Park Road, Abbott Park, IL 60064-6400
Telephone: 224-667-6100

Web Site: www.abbott.com
Officers: Miles D. White - Chairman, Chief Executive Officer Hubert L. Allen - Executive Vice President, Secretary, General Counsel

Auditors: Ernst & Young LLP
Investor Contact: 847-937-7300
Transfer Agents: Computershare Trust Co., NA, Providence, RI

3

ABERCROMBIE & FITCH CO.

Exchange	Symbol	Price	52Wk Range	Yield	P/E
NYS	ANF	$19.89 (5/31/2016)	32.46-16.45	4.02	23.96

*7 Year Price Score 52.10   ***NYSE Composite Index=100**   ***12 Month Price Score 108.48**

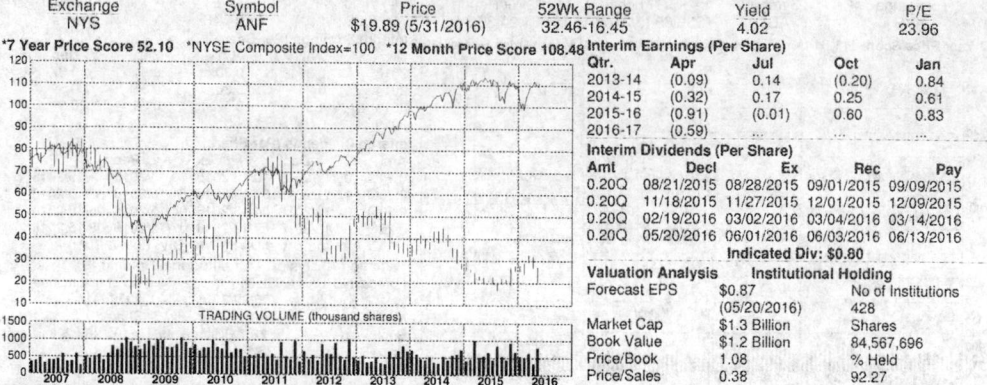

Interim Earnings (Per Share)

Qtr.	Apr	Jul	Oct	Jan
2013-14	(0.09)	0.14	(0.20)	0.84
2014-15	(0.32)	0.17	0.25	0.61
2015-16	(0.91)	(0.01)	0.60	0.83
2016-17	(0.59)	...	...	...

Interim Dividends (Per Share)

Amt	Decl	Ex	Rec	Pay
0.20Q	08/21/2015	08/28/2015	09/01/2015	09/09/2015
0.20Q	11/18/2015	11/27/2015	12/01/2015	12/09/2015
0.20Q	02/19/2016	03/02/2016	03/04/2016	03/14/2016
0.20Q	05/20/2016	06/01/2016	06/03/2016	06/13/2016

Indicated Div: $0.80

Valuation Analysis

		Institutional Holding	
Forecast EPS	$0.87	No of Institutions	
	(05/20/2016)	428	
Market Cap	$1.3 Billion	Shares	
Book Value	$1.2 Billion	84,567,696	
Price/Book	1.08	% Held	
Price/Sales	0.38	92.27	

Business Summary: Retail - Apparel and Accessories (MIC: 2.1.5 SIC: 5651 NAIC: 448140)

Abercrombie & Fitch, through its subsidiaries, is a retailer that primarily operates stores and direct-to-consumer operations. Through these channels, Co. sells a range of products, including: casual sportswear apparel, including knit tops and woven shirts, graphic t-shirts, fleece, jeans and woven pants, shorts, sweaters, and outerwear; personal care products; and accessories for men, women and kids under the Abercrombie & Fitch, abercrombie kids, and Hollister brands. As of Jan 30 2016, Co. operated 754 stores in the U.S. and 178 stores outside of the U.S.

Recent Developments: For the quarter ended Apr 30 2016, net loss amounted to US$38.6 million versus a net loss of US$63.2 million in the year-earlier quarter. Revenues were US$685.5 million, down 3.4% from US$709.4 million the year before. Operating loss was US$54.9 million versus a loss of US$90.2 million in the prior-year quarter. Direct operating expenses declined 12.8% to US$259.8 million from US$297.9 million in the comparable period the year before. Indirect operating expenses decreased 4.2% to US$480.6 million from US$501.7 million in the equivalent prior-year period.

Prospects: Our evaluation of Abercrombie & Fitch Co. as of June 19, 2016 is the result of our systematic analysis on three basic characteristics: earnings strength, relative valuation, and recent stock price movement. The company has suffered a very negative trend in earnings per share over the past 5 quarters. However, while recent estimates for the company have been lowered by analysts, ANF has posted results that fell short of analysts expectations. Based on operating earnings yield, the company is about fairly valued when compared to all of the companies in our coverage universe. Share price changes over the past year indicates that ANF will perform very well over the near term.

Financial Data

(US$ in Thousands)	3 Mos	01/30/2016	01/31/2015	02/01/2014	02/02/2013	01/28/2012	01/29/2011	01/30/2010
Earnings Per Share	0.83	0.51	0.71	0.69	2.85	1.43	1.67	...
Cash Flow Per Share	4.84	4.51	4.36	2.28	8.21	4.22	4.46	4.59
Tang Book Value Per Share	18.48	19.17	20.04	22.64	23.18	21.75	21.67	20.78
Dividends Per Share	0.800	0.800	0.800	0.800	0.700	0.700	0.700	0.700
Dividend Payout %	96.39	156.86	112.68	115.94	24.56	48.95	41.92	...
Income Statement								
Total Revenue	685,483	3,518,680	3,744,030	4,116,897	4,510,805	4,158,058	3,468,777	2,928,626
EBITDA	(61,417)	257,899	301,503	270,168	552,536	374,728	412,712	309,482
Depn & Amortn	(6,506)	185,061	187,984	189,345	178,303	184,698	180,780	191,570
Income Before Taxes	(59,417)	54,590	99,154	73,277	366,945	186,453	228,570	119,510
Income Taxes	(20,787)	16,031	47,333	18,649	129,934	59,591	78,287	40,557
Net Income	(39,587)	35,576	51,821	54,628	237,011	127,658	150,283	254
Average Shares	67,625	69,417	72,937	78,666	83,175	89,537	89,851	88,609
Balance Sheet								
Current Assets	1,094,528	1,178,980	1,164,972	1,320,566	1,307,824	1,488,775	1,433,268	1,235,846
Total Assets	2,344,182	2,433,039	2,505,167	2,850,997	2,987,401	3,048,153	2,947,902	2,821,866
Current Liabilities	477,645	534,703	485,956	568,222	690,801	705,353	558,851	449,372
Long-Term Obligations	336,615	333,675	341,831	180,726	63,942	57,851	68,566	71,213
Total Liabilities	1,094,526	1,141,976	1,115,466	1,121,504	1,169,133	1,185,697	1,057,118	993,949
Stockholders' Equity	1,249,656	1,291,063	1,389,701	1,729,493	1,818,268	1,862,456	1,890,784	1,827,917
Shares Outstanding	67,605	67,348	69,352	76,402	78,445	85,638	87,246	87,985
Statistical Record								
Return on Assets %	2.52	1.44	1.94	1.88	7.73	4.27	5.22	0.01
Return on Equity %	4.63	2.66	3.33	3.09	12.67	6.82	8.10	0.01
EBITDA Margin %	N.M.	7.33	8.05	6.56	12.25	9.01	11.90	10.57
Net Margin %	N.M.	1.01	1.38	1.33	5.25	3.07	4.33	0.01
Asset Turnover	1.48	1.43	1.40	1.41	1.47	1.39	1.21	1.04
Current Ratio	2.29	2.20	2.40	2.32	1.89	2.11	2.56	2.75
Debt to Equity	0.27	0.26	0.25	0.10	0.04	0.03	0.04	0.04
Price Range	32.46-16.45	27.63-16.45	44.83-25.52	54.41-31.72	53.53-29.06	77.14-44.23	58.14-30.39	41.84-17.11
P/E Ratio	39.11-19.82	54.18-32.25	63.14-35.94	78.86-45.97	18.78-10.20	53.94-30.93	34.81-18.20	N.M.
Average Yield %	3.35	3.57	2.22	1.87	1.71	1.13	1.67	2.38

Address: 6301 Fitch Path, New Albany, OH 43054 **Telephone:** 614-283-6500	**Web Site:** www.abercrombie.com **Officers:** Arthur C. Martinez - Executive Chairman Fran Horowitz - President, Officer, Division Officer	**Auditors:** PricewaterhouseCoopers LLP **Investor Contact:** 614-283-6751 **Transfer Agents:** American Stock Transfer & Trust Company, LLC, Brooklyn, NY

ABM INDUSTRIES, INC.

Exchange	Symbol	Price	52Wk Range	Yield	P/E	Div Achiever
NYS	ABM	$34.17 (5/31/2016)	34.17-26.58	1.93	33.17	51 Years

*7 Year Price Score 107.15 *NYSE Composite Index=100 *12 Month Price Score 105.07

Interim Earnings (Per Share)

Qtr.	Jan	Apr	Jul	Oct
2012-13	0.24	0.35	0.29	0.43
2013-14	0.23	0.27	0.34	0.48
2014-15	0.31	0.32	0.03	0.68
2015-16	0.24	0.08	...	...

Interim Dividends (Per Share)

Amt	Decl	Ex	Rec	Pay
0.16Q	09/02/2015	09/29/2015	10/01/2015	11/02/2015
0.165Q	12/08/2015	01/05/2016	01/07/2016	02/01/2016
0.165Q	03/08/2016	04/05/2016	04/07/2016	05/02/2016
0.165Q	06/08/2016	07/05/2016	07/07/2016	08/01/2016

Indicated Div: $0.66

Valuation Analysis **Institutional Holding**

Forecast EPS	$1.60	No of Institutions
(05/16/2016)		274
Market Cap	$1.9 Billion	Shares
Book Value	$992.2 Million	54,062,588
Price/Book	1.93	% Held
Price/Sales	0.39	84.31

Business Summary: Sanitation Services (MIC: 7.5.3 SIC: 7349 NAIC: 561720)

ABM Industries is a provider of end-to-end, integrated facility solutions. Co.'s segments consist of: Janitorial, which provides a range of cleaning services; Facility Services, which provides onsite mechanical engineering and technical services and solutions for facilities and infrastructure systems; Parking, which provides parking and transportation services; Building and Energy Solutions, which provides energy solutions, electrical, HVAC, lighting, and other maintenance and repair services; and Other, which provides facility solutions to aviation service companies related to access control, aircraft cabin cleaning, certain shuttle bus operations, and passenger assistance.

Recent Developments: For the quarter ended Apr 30 2016, income from continuing operations decreased 57.5% to US$6.8 million from US$16.0 million in the year-earlier quarter. Net income decreased 76.0% to US$4.4 million from US$18.3 million in the year-earlier quarter. Revenues were US$1.26 billion, up 6.9% from US$1.18 billion the year before. Operating income was US$11.8 million versus US$27.2 million in the prior-year quarter, a decrease of 56.6%. Direct operating expenses rose 7.6% to US$1.13 billion from US$1.05 billion in the comparable period the year before. Indirect operating expenses increased 16.9% to US$112.9 million from US$96.6 million in the equivalent prior-year period.

Prospects: Our evaluation of ABM Industries Inc. as of June 19, 2016 is the result of our systematic analysis on three basic characteristics: earnings strength, relative valuation, and recent stock price movement. The company has suffered a very negative trend in earnings per share over the past 5 quarters. However, while recent estimates for the company have been mixed, ABM has posted better than expected results. Based on operating earnings yield, the company is about fairly valued when compared to all of the companies in our coverage universe. Share price changes over the past year indicates that ABM will perform poorly over the near term.

Financial Data

(US$ in Thousands)	6 Mos	3 Mos	10/31/2015	10/31/2014	10/31/2013	10/31/2012	10/31/2011	10/31/2010
Earnings Per Share	1.03	1.27	1.33	1.32	1.30	1.14	1.27	1.23
Cash Flow Per Share	2.88	2.58	2.56	2.15	2.47	2.78	3.01	2.88
Tang Book Value Per Share	N.M.	N.M.	0.51	N.M.	N.M.	N.M.	N.M.	1.51
Dividends Per Share	0.650	0.645	0.640	0.620	0.600	0.580	0.560	0.540
Dividend Payout %	63.11	50.79	48.12	46.97	46.15	50.88	44.09	43.90
Income Statement								
Total Revenue	2,525,500	1,268,400	4,897,800	5,032,800	4,809,281	4,300,265	4,246,842	3,495,747
EBITDA	38,400	20,000	130,600	185,900	179,378	147,117	170,216	144,976
Depn & Amortn	13,000	6,400	57,000	57,300	60,353	50,864	52,648	36,264
Income Before Taxes	20,300	10,900	63,400	117,900	106,133	86,254	101,763	104,073
Income Taxes	3,200	(300)	18,300	48,800	39,552	29,931	36,980	40,203
Net Income	18,400	14,000	76,300	75,600	72,900	62,582	68,504	64,121
Average Shares	56,900	57,100	57,400	57,100	56,067	54,914	54,103	52,908
Balance Sheet								
Current Assets	903,400	953,000	947,200	927,200	864,632	767,427	733,757	608,756
Total Assets	2,184,500	2,255,200	2,149,800	2,192,900	2,119,236	1,869,251	1,879,598	1,548,670
Current Liabilities	568,200	565,200	568,200	526,400	508,524	473,910	443,196	333,851
Long-Term Obligations	208,900	286,700	158,000	319,800	314,870	215,000	300,000	140,500
Total Liabilities	1,192,300	1,259,500	1,142,300	1,224,100	1,201,729	1,018,853	1,083,712	809,645
Stockholders' Equity	992,200	995,700	1,007,500	968,800	917,507	850,398	795,886	739,025
Shares Outstanding	55,938	56,045	56,105	55,691	55,477	54,393	53,333	52,635
Statistical Record								
Return on Assets %	2.67	3.24	3.51	3.51	3.66	3.33	4.00	4.18
Return on Equity %	5.89	7.34	7.72	8.02	8.25	7.58	8.93	8.99
EBITDA Margin %	1.52	1.58	2.67	3.69	3.73	3.42	4.01	4.15
Net Margin %	0.73	1.10	1.56	1.50	1.52	1.46	1.61	1.83
Asset Turnover	2.22	2.17	2.26	2.33	2.41	2.29	2.48	2.28
Current Ratio	1.59	1.69	1.67	1.76	1.70	1.62	1.66	1.82
Debt to Equity	0.21	0.29	0.16	0.33	0.34	0.25	0.38	0.19
Price Range	33.80-26.58	33.80-26.58	33.80-26.70	29.43-24.57	28.99-18.27	24.50-17.95	27.00-17.29	22.77-18.35
P/E Ratio	32.82-25.81	26.61-20.93	25.41-20.08	22.30-18.61	22.30-14.05	21.49-15.75	21.26-13.61	18.51-14.92
Average Yield %	2.11	2.10	2.10	2.29	2.59	2.79	2.41	2.59

Address: 551 Fifth Avenue, Suite 300, New York, NY 10176 Telephone: 212-297-0200	Web Site: www.abm.com Officers: Maryellen C. Herringer - Chairman Scott B. Salmirs - President, Chief Executive Officer, Executive Vice President	Auditors: KPMG LLP Investor Contact: 212-297-0200 Transfer Agents: Computershare, Providence, RI

ACCENTURE PLC

Exchange	Symbol	Price	52Wk Range	Yield	P/E
NYS	ACN	$118.97 (5/31/2016)	119.12-92.14	1.85	20.69

*7 Year Price Score 129.70 ***NYSE Composite Index=100** ***12 Month Price Score 109.45**

Interim Earnings (Per Share)

Qtr.	Nov	Feb	May	Aug
2012-13	1.06	1.65	1.21	1.01
2013-14	1.15	1.03	1.26	1.08
2014-15	1.29	1.08	1.24	1.15
2015-16	1.28	2.08	...	...

Interim Dividends (Per Share)

Amt	Decl	Ex	Rec	Pay
1.02S	09/23/2014	10/15/2014	10/17/2014	11/17/2014
1.02S	03/25/2015	04/08/2015	04/10/2015	05/15/2015
1.10S	09/24/2015	10/14/2015	10/16/2015	11/13/2015
1.10S	03/24/2016	04/13/2016	04/15/2016	05/13/2016

Indicated Div: $2.20

Valuation Analysis   **Institutional Holding**

Forecast EPS	N/A	No of Institutions
		N/A
Market Cap	$76.9 Billion	Shares
Book Value	$6.8 Billion	N/A
Price/Book	11.29	% Held
Price/Sales	2.30	N/A

Business Summary: IT Services (MIC: 6.3.1 SIC: 7389 NAIC: 561499)

Accenture is a services company providing management consulting, technology and outsourcing services. Co.'s segments are: Communications, Media & Technology, which serves communications, electronics, technology, media and entertainment industries; Financial Services, which serves banking, capital markets and insurance industries; Health & Public Service, which serves healthcare payers and providers, public service organizations, educational institutions and non-profit organizations; Products, which serves a set of interconnected consumer-relevant industries; and Resources, which serves chemicals, energy, forest products, metals and mining, utilities and related industries.

Recent Developments: For the quarter ended Feb 29 2016, net income increased 88.4% to US$1.40 billion from US$743.2 million in the year-earlier quarter. Revenues were US$8.40 billion, up 5.9% from US$7.93 billion the year before. Operating income was US$1.09 billion versus US$1.02 billion in the prior-year quarter, an increase of 6.6%. Direct operating expenses rose 5.9% to US$6.03 billion from US$5.69 billion in the comparable period the year before. Indirect operating expenses increased 5.1% to US$1.28 billion from US$1.22 billion in the equivalent prior-year period.

Prospects: Our evaluation of Accenture PLC as of July 19, 2015 is the result of our systematic analysis on three basic characteristics: earnings strength, relative valuation, and recent stock price movement. The company has managed to produce a neutral trend in earnings per share over the past 5 quarters and while recent estimates for the company have been raised by analysts, ACN has posted better than expected results. Based on operating earnings yield, the company is about fairly valued when compared to all of the companies in our coverage universe. Share price changes over the past year indicates that ACN will perform in line with the market over the near term.

Financial Data

(US$ in Thousands)	6 Mos	3 Mos	08/31/2015	08/31/2014	08/31/2013	08/31/2012	08/31/2011	08/31/2010
Earnings Per Share	5.75	4.75	4.76	4.52	4.93	3.84	3.40	2.66
Cash Flow Per Share	6.14	6.11	6.53	5.50	5.12	6.60	5.33	4.85
Tang Book Value Per Share	5.12	3.67	4.93	5.08	4.71	4.33	3.98	2.89
Dividends Per Share	2.120	2.120	2.040	1.860	1.620	1.350	0.900	1.125
Dividend Payout %	36.87	44.63	42.86	41.15	32.86	35.16	26.47	42.29
Income Statement								
Total Revenue	16,863,037	8,465,984	32,914,424	31,874,678	30,394,285	29,777,985	27,352,914	23,094,078
EBITDA	3,200,324	1,407,171	5,037,040	4,611,862	4,645,433	4,194,677	3,783,488	3,168,187
Depn & Amortn	354,627	181,882	645,923	326,910	324,997	317,992	297,549	269,072
Income Before Taxes	2,850,955	1,228,363	4,410,530	4,297,701	4,339,294	3,904,174	3,512,022	2,914,369
Income Taxes	582,416	359,682	1,136,741	1,121,743	784,775	1,079,241	958,782	853,910
Net Income	2,145,419	818,899	3,053,581	2,941,498	3,281,878	2,553,510	2,277,677	1,780,656
Average Shares	668,125	671,300	678,757	692,389	712,763	726,416	742,184	766,047
Balance Sheet								
Current Assets	10,678,800	10,623,048	11,579,394	11,904,442	11,844,178	12,587,931	11,471,183	9,563,625
Total Assets	18,147,778	17,993,875	18,266,058	17,930,452	16,867,049	16,665,415	15,731,510	12,835,253
Current Liabilities	7,573,179	8,472,398	8,532,199	8,158,079	8,160,990	8,109,205	7,906,589	6,567,604
Long-Term Obligations	26,866	25,807	25,587	26,403	25,600	22	...	1,445
Total Liabilities	11,336,117	12,093,450	12,132,333	12,198,417	11,906,863	12,519,582	11,852,559	9,999,507
Stockholders' Equity	6,811,661	5,900,425	6,133,725	5,732,035	4,960,186	4,145,833	3,878,951	2,835,746
Shares Outstanding	646,678	648,550	650,036	656,556	666,355	676,750	690,799	690,063
Statistical Record								
Return on Assets %	20.93	17.07	16.87	16.91	19.57	15.72	15.95	14.19
Return on Equity %	57.44	53.43	51.47	55.02	72.08	63.47	67.84	62.24
EBITDA Margin %	18.98	16.62	15.30	14.47	15.28	14.09	13.83	13.72
Net Margin %	12.72	9.67	9.28	9.23	10.80	8.58	8.33	7.71
Asset Turnover	1.91	1.85	1.82	1.83	1.81	1.83	1.92	1.84
Current Ratio	1.41	1.25	1.36	1.46	1.45	1.55	1.45	1.46
Debt to Equity	N.M.	N.M.	N.M.	N.M.	N.M.	0.01	N.M.	N.M.
Price Range	109.73-86.86	109.73-81.88	105.20-75.85	85.40-70.28	83.09-61.06	65.89-49.82	63.44-36.60	44.67-33.00
P/E Ratio	19.08-15.11	23.10-17.24	22.10-15.93	18.89-15.55	16.85-12.39	17.16-12.97	18.66-10.76	16.79-12.41
Average Yield %	2.14	2.21	2.26	2.35	2.22	2.32	1.76	2.82

Address: 1 Grand Canal Square, Grand Canal Harbour, Dublin, 2 Telephone: 164-620-00	Web Site: www.accenture.com Officers: Pierre Nanterme - Chairman, Chief Executive Officer David P. Rowland - Chief Financial Officer, Senior Vice President	Auditors: KPMG LLP Investor Contact: 353-140-78203 Transfer Agents: Computershare, Canton, MA

ACUITY BRANDS INC (HOLDING COMPANY)

Exchange	Symbol	Price	52Wk Range	Yield	P/E
NYS	AYI	$259.04 (5/31/2016)	259.54-169.87	0.20	43.83

*7 Year Price Score 189.83 *NYSE Composite Index=100 ***12 Month Price Score 115.13**

TRADING VOLUME (thousand shares)

Interim Earnings (Per Share)

Qtr.	Nov	Feb	May	Aug
2012-13	0.61	0.57	0.73	1.04
2013-14	1.03	0.75	1.01	1.20
2014-15	1.17	1.07	1.48	1.37
2015-16	1.57	1.49	...	...

Interim Dividends (Per Share)

Amt	Decl	Ex	Rec	Pay
0.13Q	06/26/2015	07/16/2015	07/20/2015	08/03/2015
0.13Q	10/02/2015	10/15/2015	10/19/2015	11/02/2015
0.13Q	01/06/2016	01/15/2016	01/20/2016	02/01/2016
0.13Q	04/01/2016	04/14/2016	04/18/2016	05/02/2016

Indicated Div: $0.52

Valuation Analysis / Institutional Holding

Forecast EPS	$7.95	No of Institutions	572
	(05/20/2016)		
Market Cap	$11.3 Billion	Shares	48,169,968
Book Value	$1.5 Billion	% Held	93.41
Price/Book	7.55		
Price/Sales	3.81		

Business Summary: Electrical Equipment (MIC: 7.3.1 SIC: 3648 NAIC: 335129)

Acuity Brands is a provider of lighting solutions for commercial, institutional, industrial, infrastructure, and residential applications throughout North America and certain international markets. Co.'s lighting solutions include devices such as luminaires, lighting controls, lighting components, power supplies, prismatic skylights, light-emitting diode lamps, and integrated lighting systems for indoor and outdoor applications utilizing a combination of light sources, including daylight, and other devices controlled by software that monitors and manages light levels.

Recent Developments: For the quarter ended Feb 29 2016, net income increased 41.2% to US$65.5 million from US$46.4 million in the year-earlier quarter. Revenues were US$777.8 million, up 26.2% from US$616.1 million the year before. Operating income was US$106.7 million versus US$78.6 million in the prior-year quarter, an increase of 35.8%. Direct operating expenses rose 22.3% to US$440.9 million from US$360.4 million in the comparable period the year before. Indirect operating expenses increased 30.0% to US$230.2 million from US$177.1 million in the equivalent prior-year period.

Prospects: Our evaluation of Acuity Brands Inc. as of June 19, 2016 is the result of our systematic analysis on three basic characteristics: earnings strength, relative valuation, and recent stock price movement. The company has enjoyed a very positive trend in earnings per share over the past 5 quarters and while recent estimates for the company have been raised by analysts, AYI has posted better than expected results. Based on operating earnings yield, the company is about fairly valued when compared to all of the companies in our coverage universe. Share price changes over the past year indicates that AYI will perform very well over the near term.

Financial Data

(US$ in Thousands)	6 Mos	3 Mos	08/31/2015	08/31/2014	08/31/2013	08/31/2012	08/31/2011	08/31/2010
Earnings Per Share	5.91	5.49	5.09	4.05	2.95	2.72	2.42	1.80
Cash Flow Per Share	7.65	6.77	6.70	5.45	3.14	4.15	3.82	3.78
Tang Book Value Per Share	3.61	9.28	13.16	8.40	4.18	1.06	N.M.	N.M.
Dividends Per Share	0.520	0.520	0.520	0.520	0.520	0.520	0.520	0.520
Dividend Payout %	8.80	9.47	10.22	12.84	17.63	19.12	21.49	28.89
Income Statement								
Total Revenue	1,514,400	736,600	2,706,700	2,393,500	2,089,100	1,933,700	1,795,700	1,626,900
EBITDA	251,600	127,400	409,500	329,600	253,300	237,200	216,300	176,700
Depn & Amortn	30,700	14,300	34,400	31,800	29,000	27,500	28,800	28,500
Income Before Taxes	204,800	105,200	343,600	265,700	193,100	179,000	157,600	118,800
Income Taxes	70,900	36,800	121,500	89,900	65,700	62,700	52,100	39,800
Net Income	133,900	68,400	222,100	175,800	127,400	116,300	105,500	79,600
Average Shares	43,800	43,600	43,400	43,000	42,500	41,900	42,800	43,300
Balance Sheet								
Current Assets	997,700	1,255,200	1,436,500	1,186,700	913,500	779,000	630,500	626,300
Total Assets	2,619,800	2,506,300	2,429,600	2,168,100	1,903,800	1,736,900	1,597,400	1,503,600
Current Liabilities	513,400	512,700	520,900	470,500	386,200	364,800	331,400	321,300
Long-Term Obligations	353,500	352,400	352,400	353,600	353,600	353,500	353,400	353,300
Total Liabilities	1,126,400	1,071,400	1,069,600	1,004,600	910,300	902,900	840,400	809,200
Stockholders' Equity	1,493,400	1,434,900	1,360,000	1,163,500	993,500	834,000	757,000	694,400
Shares Outstanding	43,516	43,510	43,305	42,862	42,486	41,789	41,488	42,116
Statistical Record								
Return on Assets %	10.69	10.16	9.66	8.63	7.00	6.96	6.80	5.70
Return on Equity %	18.83	18.10	17.60	16.30	13.94	14.58	14.54	11.65
EBITDA Margin %	16.61	17.30	15.13	13.77	12.12	12.27	12.05	10.86
Net Margin %	8.84	9.29	8.21	7.34	6.10	6.01	5.88	4.89
Asset Turnover	1.22	1.19	1.18	1.18	1.15	1.16	1.16	1.16
Current Ratio	1.94	2.45	2.76	2.52	2.37	2.14	1.90	1.95
Debt to Equity	0.24	0.25	0.26	0.30	0.36	0.42	0.47	0.51
Price Range	240.14-158.57	231.59-128.36	211.15-117.71	143.65-84.43	88.34-59.86	64.98-33.97	60.96-38.74	47.56-30.98
P/E Ratio	40.63-26.83	42.18-23.38	41.48-23.13	35.47-20.85	29.95-20.29	23.89-12.49	25.19-16.01	26.42-17.21
Average Yield %	0.27	0.29	0.32	0.44	0.72	0.97	0.98	1.36

Address: 1170 Peachtree Street, N.E., Suite 2300, Atlanta, GA 30309-7676 **Telephone:** 404-853-1400 **Fax:** 404-853-1300	**Web Site:** www.acuitybrands.com **Officers:** Vernon J. Nagel - Chairman, President, Chief Executive Officer Richard K Reece - Executive Vice President, Chief Financial Officer	**Auditors:** Ernst & Young LLP **Investor Contact:** 404-853-1400 **Transfer Agents:** Computershare Shareowner Services, Pittsburgh, PA

ADVANCE AUTO PARTS INC

Exchange	Symbol	Price	52Wk Range	Yield	P/E
NYS	AAP	$153.84 (5/31/2016)	200.38-138.41	0.16	23.52

*7 Year Price Score 149.29 *NYSE Composite Index=100 ***12 Month Price Score 92.57**

TRADING VOLUME (thousand shares)

Interim Earnings (Per Share)

Qtr.	Apr	Jul	Sep	Dec
2014	2.01	1.89	1.66	1.15
Qtr.	Apr	Jul	Oct	Dec
2015-16	2.00	2.03	1.63	0.74
2016	2.14	...	...	...

Interim Dividends (Per Share)

Amt	Decl	Ex	Rec	Pay
0.06Q	08/12/2015	09/16/2015	09/18/2015	10/02/2015
0.06Q	11/09/2015	12/22/2015	12/24/2015	01/08/2016
0.06Q	02/09/2016	03/16/2016	03/18/2016	04/01/2016
0.06Q	05/17/2016	06/15/2016	06/17/2016	07/01/2016

Indicated Div: $0.24

Valuation Analysis / **Institutional Holding**

Forecast EPS	$7.82 (05/20/2016)	No of Institutions	678
Market Cap	$11.3 Billion	Shares	83,836,192
Book Value	$2.6 Billion	% Held	
Price/Book	4.30		93.15
Price/Sales	1.17		

Business Summary: Retail - Automotive (MIC: 2.1.4 SIC: 5531 NAIC: 441310)

Advance Auto Parts is a retailer of automotive aftermarket part provider in North America, serving both do-it-for-me (Commercial), and do-it-yourself (DIY), customers. Co. operated primarily within the U.S., with additional locations in Canada, Puerto Rico and the U.S. Virgin Islands. Co.'s stores operate primarily under trade names Advance Auto Parts, Autopart International and Carquest and Co.'s distribution branches operate under the Worldpac trade name. In addition, Co. served approximately 1,300 independently-owned Carquest stores and operated a total of 5,171 stores and 122 distribution branches as of Jan. 2, 2016.

Recent Developments: For the quarter ended Apr 23 2016, net income increased 7.2% to US$158.8 million from US$148.1 million in the year-earlier quarter. Revenues were US$2.98 billion, down 1.9% from US$3.04 billion the year before. Operating income was US$271.0 million versus US$262.5 million in the prior-year quarter, an increase of 3.2%. Direct operating expenses declined 0.9% to US$1.63 billion from US$1.64 billion in the comparable period the year before. Indirect operating expenses decreased 4.6% to US$1.08 billion from US$1.13 billion in the equivalent prior-year period.

Prospects: Our evaluation of Advance Auto Parts Inc. as of June 19, 2016 is the result of our systematic analysis on three basic characteristics: earnings strength, relative valuation, and recent stock price movement. The company has managed to produce a neutral trend in earnings per share over the past 5 quarters. However, while recent estimates for the company have been lowered by analysts, AAP has posted results that fell short of analysts expectations. Based on operating earnings yield, the company is about fairly valued when compared to all of the companies in our coverage universe. Share price changes over the past year indicates that AAP will perform in line with the market over the near term.

Financial Data

(US$ in Thousands)	3 Mos	01/02/2016	01/03/2015	12/28/2013	12/29/2012	12/31/2011	01/01/2011	01/02/2010
Earnings Per Share	6.54	6.40	6.71	5.32	5.22	5.11	3.95	2.83
Cash Flow Per Share	...	9.45	9.56	7.50	9.40	10.99	7.76	7.43
Tang Book Value Per Share	13.04	10.69	3.55	17.39	15.06	10.17	11.95	13.05
Dividends Per Share	0.240	0.240	0.240	0.240	0.240	0.240	0.240	0.240
Dividend Payout %	3.67	3.75	3.58	4.51	4.60	4.70	6.08	8.48
Income Statement								
Total Revenue	2,979,778	9,737,018	9,843,861	6,493,814	6,205,003	6,170,462	5,925,203	5,412,623
EBITDA	353,442	1,042,024	1,089,842	862,837	843,824	838,404	747,294	604,761
Depn & Amortn	79,320	223,728	235,040	199,821	185,909	174,219	163,378	149,769
Income Before Taxes	255,179	752,888	781,394	626,398	624,074	633,236	557,055	431,655
Income Taxes	96,366	279,490	287,569	234,640	236,404	238,554	211,002	161,282
Net Income	158,813	473,398	493,825	391,758	387,670	394,682	346,053	270,373
Average Shares	73,847	73,733	73,414	73,414	74,062	77,071	87,155	95,113
Balance Sheet								
Current Assets	5,266,227	4,940,746	4,741,040	3,989,384	3,184,200	2,293,820	2,124,271	1,887,618
Total Assets	8,438,963	8,134,565	7,962,358	5,564,774	4,613,814	3,655,754	3,354,217	3,072,963
Current Liabilities	3,908,563	3,797,477	3,743,066	2,764,785	2,559,638	2,187,875	1,848,049	1,466,027
Long-Term Obligations	1,229,888	1,213,161	1,636,311	1,052,668	604,461	415,136	300,851	202,927
Total Liabilities	5,809,824	5,673,917	5,959,446	4,048,569	3,403,120	2,807,840	2,314,843	1,790,598
Stockholders' Equity	2,629,139	2,460,648	2,002,912	1,516,205	1,210,694	847,914	1,039,374	1,282,365
Shares Outstanding	73,556	73,314	73,074	72,840	73,383	72,799	81,956	93,623
Statistical Record								
Return on Assets %	...	5.90	7.18	7.72	9.40	11.29	10.80	8.98
Return on Equity %	...	21.27	27.61	28.81	37.77	41.94	29.89	23.00
EBITDA Margin %	11.86	10.70	11.07	13.29	13.60	13.59	12.61	11.17
Net Margin %	5.33	4.86	5.02	6.03	6.25	6.40	5.84	5.00
Asset Turnover	...	1.21	1.43	1.28	1.50	1.77	1.85	1.80
Current Ratio	1.35	1.30	1.27	1.44	1.24	1.05	1.15	1.29
Debt to Equity	0.47	0.49	0.82	0.69	0.50	0.49	0.29	0.16
Price Range	200.38-138.41	200.38-143.00	161.22-109.63	110.28-71.76	92.37-65.59	72.16-50.04	68.54-39.16	47.06-30.13
P/E Ratio	30.64-21.16	31.31-22.34	24.03-16.34	20.73-13.49	17.70-12.57	14.12-9.79	17.35-9.91	16.63-10.65
Average Yield %	0.15	0.15	0.18	0.28	0.32	0.38	0.44	0.60

Address: 5008 Airport Road, Roanoke, VA 24012 **Telephone:** 540-362-4911	**Web Site:** www.AdvanceAutoParts.com **Officers:** George E. Sherman - President, Interim Chief Executive Officer Michael A. Norona - Chief Financial Officer, Executive Vice President, Secretary	**Auditors:** Deloitte & Touche LLP **Investor Contact:** 540-561-6444 **Transfer Agents:** BNY Mellon Shareowner Services, Pittsburgh, PA

AECOM

*7 Year Price Score 92.32 ***NYSE Composite Index=100** ***12 Month Price Score 104.97**

Interim Earnings (Per Share)

Qtr.	Dec	Mar	Jun	Sep
2012-13	0.36	0.53	0.70	0.77
2013-14	0.58	0.41	0.70	0.64
2014-15	(0.98)	0.00	(0.11)	0.01
2015-16	(0.13)	0.27	...	...

Interim Dividends (Per Share)

No Dividends Paid

Valuation Analysis | Institutional Holding

Forecast EPS	$3.24	No of Institutions
	(05/20/2016)	359
Market Cap	$4.9 Billion	Shares
Book Value	$3.5 Billion	133,203,400
Price/Book	1.42	% Held
Price/Sales	0.27	87.20

Business Summary: Construction Services (MIC: 7.5.4 SIC: 8711 NAIC: 541330)

AECOM designs, builds, finances and operates infrastructure assets for governments, businesses and organizations in more than 150 countries. Co.'s business segments are: Design and Consulting Services, which include planning, consulting, architectural and engineering design, program management and construction management for industrial, commercial, institutional and government clients; Construction Services, which provides construction, program and construction management services; and Management Services, which include program and facilities management, training, logistics, consulting, systems engineering and technical assistance, and systems integration and information technology.

Recent Developments: For the quarter ended Mar 31 2016, net income increased 223.2% to US$66.6 million from US$20.6 million in the year-earlier quarter. Revenues were US$4.38 billion, down 2.8% from US$4.51 billion the year before. Operating income was US$140.8 million versus US$6.5 million in the prior-year quarter, an increase of. Direct operating expenses declined 4.7% to US$4.20 billion from US$4.40 billion in the comparable period the year before. Indirect operating expenses decreased 55.9% to US$42.7 million from US$96.8 million in the equivalent prior-year period.

Prospects: Our evaluation of AECOM as of June 19, 2016 is the result of our systematic analysis on three basic characteristics: earnings strength, relative valuation, and recent stock price movement. The company has generated a negative trend in earnings per share over the past 5 quarters and while recent estimates for the company have been raised by analysts, ACM has posted better than expected results. Based on operating earnings yield, the company is undervalued when compared to all of the companies in our coverage universe. Share price changes over the past year indicates that ACM will perform well over the near term.

Financial Data

(US$ in Thousands)	6 Mos	3 Mos	09/30/2015	09/30/2014	09/30/2013	09/30/2012	09/30/2011	09/30/2010
Earnings Per Share	0.04	...	(1.04)	2.33	2.35	(0.52)	2.33	2.05
Cash Flow Per Share	4.04	3.64	5.11	3.71	4.06	3.86	1.12	1.39
Tang Book Value Per Share	N.M.	N.M.	N.M.	1.64	1.32	2.78	1.19	2.52
Income Statement								
Total Revenue	8,678,947	4,297,651	17,989,880	8,356,783	8,153,495	8,218,180	8,037,374	6,545,791
EBITDA	353,857	144,188	233,182	366,806	426,892	91,029	452,972	389,358
Depn & Amortn	218,199	111,018	191,300	69,100	70,700	77,100	73,200	59,300
Income Before Taxes	13,417	(26,348)	(257,745)	256,864	311,455	(31,167)	339,361	320,130
Income Taxes	11,505	(682)	(80,237)	82,024	92,578	74,416	100,090	91,696
Net Income	21,461	(20,367)	(154,845)	229,854	239,243	(58,567)	275,800	236,887
Average Shares	155,448	153,619	149,605	98,657	101,942	111,875	118,345	115,463
Balance Sheet								
Current Assets	6,285,936	5,896,574	6,246,085	3,434,113	3,131,602	3,147,293	2,990,066	2,946,499
Total Assets	13,989,215	13,529,403	14,014,298	6,123,377	5,665,623	5,664,568	5,789,328	5,242,909
Current Liabilities	5,260,488	4,755,094	4,836,052	2,455,769	2,053,549	2,078,402	1,814,446	1,852,260
Long-Term Obligations	4,130,087	4,366,424	4,446,527	939,565	1,089,060	907,141	1,144,723	914,686
Total Liabilities	10,530,775	10,214,822	10,606,550	3,936,860	3,644,180	3,495,104	3,449,617	3,152,897
Stockholders' Equity	3,458,440	3,314,581	3,407,748	2,186,517	2,021,443	2,169,464	2,339,711	2,090,012
Shares Outstanding	152,913	152,452	151,263	96,715	96,016	107,041	113,248	115,316
Statistical Record								
Return on Assets %	0.04	N.M.	N.M.	3.90	4.22	N.M.	5.00	5.25
Return on Equity %	0.15	N.M.	N.M.	10.92	11.42	N.M.	12.45	12.40
EBITDA Margin %	4.08	3.36	1.30	4.39	5.24	1.11	5.64	5.95
Net Margin %	0.25	N.M.	N.M.	2.75	2.93	N.M.	3.43	3.62
Asset Turnover	1.28	1.30	1.79	1.42	1.44	1.43	1.46	1.45
Current Ratio	1.19	1.24	1.29	1.40	1.52	1.51	1.65	1.59
Debt to Equity	1.19	1.32	1.30	0.43	0.54	0.42	0.49	0.44
Price Range	35.36-23.15	35.36-24.92	35.36-24.92	38.13-27.47	35.20-18.87	24.06-14.91	29.93-17.67	30.73-22.02
P/E Ratio	884.00-578.75	...	...	16.36-11.79	14.98-8.03	...	12.85-7.58	14.99-10.74

Address: 1999 Avenue of the Stars, Suite 2600, Los Angeles, CA 90067 **Telephone:** 213-593-8000	**Web Site:** www.aecom.com **Officers:** Michael S. Burke - Chairman, President, Chief Executive Officer Daniel R. Tishman - Vice-Chairman	**Auditors:** Ernst & Young LLP **Investor Contact:** 212-973-2982 **Transfer Agents:** Computershare Investor Services, LLC, Canton, MA

AES CORP.

Exchange	Symbol	Price	52Wk Range	Yield	P/E
NYS	AES	$11.09 (5/31/2016)	13.94-8.54	3.97	25.79

*7 Year Price Score 75.74 *NYSE Composite Index=100 *12 Month Price Score 100.78

TRADING VOLUME (thousand shares)

Interim Earnings (Per Share)

Qtr.	Mar	Jun	Sep	Dec
2013	0.11	0.22	0.09	(0.28)
2014	(0.08)	0.18	0.67	0.28
2015	0.20	0.10	0.26	(0.12)
2016	0.19	...	...	...

Interim Dividends (Per Share)

Amt	Decl	Ex	Rec	Pay
0.10Q	07/17/2015	07/30/2015	08/03/2015	08/17/2015
0.10Q	10/16/2015	10/29/2015	11/02/2015	11/16/2015
0.11Q	12/14/2015	01/29/2016	02/02/2016	02/16/2016
0.11Q	04/15/2016	04/28/2016	05/02/2016	05/16/2016

Indicated Div: $0.44

Valuation Analysis

		Institutional Holding	
Forecast EPS	$1.00 (05/20/2016)	No of Institutions	611
Market Cap	$7.3 Billion	Shares	700,441,984
Book Value	$3.9 Billion	% Held	83.52
Price/Book	1.89		
Price/Sales	0.51		

Business Summary: Electric Utilities (MIC: 3.1.1 SIC: 4911 NAIC: 221121)

AES is a holding company. Through its subsidiaries and affiliates, Co. operates a portfolio of electricity generation and distribution businesses. Co. owns and/or operates power plants to generate and sell power to customers, such as utilities, industrial users, and other intermediaries. Additionally, Co. owns and/or operates utilities to generate or purchase, distribute, transmit and sell electricity to end-user customers in the residential, commercial, industrial and governmental sectors within a defined service area. In certain circumstances, Co.'s utilities also generate and sell electricity on the wholesale market. As of Dec 31 2015, Co. served 10.5 million utility customers.

Recent Developments: For the quarter ended Mar 31 2016, net income decreased 70.9% to US$74.0 million from US$254.0 million in the year-earlier quarter. Revenues were US$3.47 billion, down 12.9% from US$3.98 billion the year before. Direct operating expenses declined 9.1% to US$2.97 billion from US$3.26 billion in the comparable period the year before. Indirect operating expenses decreased 12.7% to US$48.0 million from US$55.0 million in the equivalent prior-year period.

Prospects: Our evaluation of AES Corp. as of June 19, 2016 is the result of our systematic analysis on three basic characteristics: earnings strength, relative valuation, and recent stock price movement. The company has generated a negative trend in earnings per share over the past 5 quarters. However, while recent estimates for the company have been mixed, AES has posted results that fell short of analysts expectations. Based on operating earnings yield, the company is undervalued when compared to all of the companies in our coverage universe. Share price changes over the past year indicates that AES will perform poorly over the near term.

Financial Data

(US$ in Millions)	3 Mos	12/31/2015	12/31/2014	12/31/2013	12/31/2012	12/31/2011	12/31/2010	12/31/2009
Earnings Per Share	0.43	0.44	1.06	0.15	(1.21)	0.07	0.01	0.98
Cash Flow Per Share	3.54	3.11	2.49	3.65	3.83	3.71	4.56	3.32
Tang Book Value Per Share	3.80	3.47	3.71	3.44	2.98	2.25	6.03	4.38
Dividends Per Share	0.410	0.400	0.200	0.160	0.040	...	...	...
Dividend Payout %	95.35	90.91	18.87	106.67	...	...	...	...
Income Statement								
Total Revenue	3,471	14,963	17,146	15,891	18,141	17,274	16,647	14,119
EBITDA	684	3,138	3,886	3,448	2,788	4,536	3,259	4,515
Depn & Amortn	290	1,104	1,204	1,193	1,251	1,154	1,100	1,005
Income Before Taxes	160	1,122	1,576	1,048	314	2,179	1,044	2,343
Income Taxes	92	465	419	343	708	636	307	599
Net Income	126	306	769	114	(912)	58	9	658
Average Shares	663	689	724	748	755	783	769	670
Balance Sheet								
Current Assets	6,947	6,866	7,826	7,739	8,465	9,228	9,446	8,787
Total Assets	36,900	36,850	38,966	40,411	41,830	45,333	40,511	39,535
Current Liabilities	6,572	6,950	6,997	7,653	8,319	8,446	8,065	6,621
Long-Term Obligations	18,337	18,278	18,725	18,869	18,519	20,116	16,693	17,943
Total Liabilities	33,027	33,163	34,616	36,003	37,183	39,309	33,978	34,800
Stockholders' Equity	3,873	3,687	4,350	4,408	4,647	6,024	6,533	4,735
Shares Outstanding	658	666	703	722	744	765	787	667
Statistical Record								
Return on Assets %	0.77	0.81	1.94	0.28	N.M.	0.14	0.02	1.77
Return on Equity %	7.06	7.61	17.56	2.52	N.M.	0.92	0.16	15.66
EBITDA Margin %	19.71	20.97	22.66	21.70	15.37	26.26	19.58	31.98
Net Margin %	3.63	2.05	4.49	0.72	N.M.	0.34	0.05	4.66
Asset Turnover	0.39	0.39	0.43	0.39	0.42	0.40	0.42	0.38
Current Ratio	1.06	0.99	1.12	1.01	1.02	1.09	1.17	1.33
Debt to Equity	4.73	4.96	4.30	4.28	3.99	3.34	2.56	3.79
Price Range	13.94-8.54	13.94-8.83	15.57-12.79	15.31-10.70	13.80-9.72	13.38-9.44	14.13-8.90	15.24-4.91
P/E Ratio	32.42-19.86	31.68-20.07	14.69-12.07	102.07-71.33	...	191.14-134.86	N.M.	15.55-5.01
Average Yield %	3.60	3.33	1.40	1.25	0.34	...	...	...

Address: 4300 Wilson Boulevard, Arlington, VA 22203	Web Site: www.aes.com	Auditors: Ernst & Young LLP
Telephone: 703-522-1315	Officers: Andres R. Gluski - President, Chief Executive Officer, Executive Vice President, Chief Operating Officer Brian A. Miller - Executive Vice President, Secretary, General Counsel	Investor Contact: 703-682-6451
Fax: 703-528-4510		Transfer Agents: Computershare Investor Services, Canton, MA

AETNA INC.

Exchange	Symbol	Price	52Wk Range	Yield	P/E
NYS	AET	$113.23 (5/31/2016)	132.60-94.31	0.88	17.05

*7 Year Price Score 158.73 *NYSE Composite Index=100   *12 Month Price Score 98.98

Interim Earnings (Per Share)

Qtr.	Mar	Jun	Sep	Dec
2013	1.48	1.49	1.38	0.98
2014	1.82	1.52	1.67	0.65
2015	2.20	2.08	1.59	0.91
2016	2.06	...	...	...

Interim Dividends (Per Share)

Amt	Decl	Ex	Rec	Pay
0.25Q	09/25/2015	10/13/2015	10/15/2015	10/30/2015
0.25Q	12/04/2015	01/12/2016	01/14/2016	01/29/2016
0.25Q	02/19/2016	04/12/2016	04/14/2016	04/29/2016
0.25Q	05/20/2016	07/12/2016	07/14/2016	07/29/2016

Indicated Div: $1.00

Valuation Analysis

		Institutional Holding	
Forecast EPS	$8.04	No of Institutions	
	(05/20/2016)	1122	
Market Cap	$39.7 Billion	Shares	
Book Value	$16.8 Billion	384,480,864	
Price/Book	2.36	% Held	
Price/Sales	0.65	82.39	

Business Summary: Life & Health (MIC: 5.2.2 SIC: 6324 NAIC: 524114)

Aetna is a health care benefits company. Co. has three segments: Health Care, which provides medical, pharmacy benefit management services, dental, behavioral health and vision plans provided on both an insured basis and an employer-funded, or administrative services contract, basis and emerging businesses products and services such as Accountable Care Solutions; Group Insurance, which consists primarily of life insurance products, disability insurance products and long-term care insurance products; and Large Case Pensions, which manages a variety of retirement products including pension and annuity products primarily for tax-qualified pension plans.

Recent Developments: For the quarter ended Mar 31 2016, net income decreased 6.2% to US$727.9 million from US$776.3 million in the year-earlier quarter. Revenues were US$15.69 billion, up 4.0% from US$15.09 billion the year before. Net premiums earned were US$14.01 billion versus US$13.48 billion in the prior-year quarter, an increase of 3.9%. Net investment income fell 6.5% to US$217.7 million from US$232.9 million a year ago.

Prospects: Our evaluation of Aetna Inc. as of June 19, 2016 is the result of our systematic analysis on three basic characteristics: earnings strength, relative valuation, and recent stock price movement. The company has managed to produce a neutral trend in earnings per share over the past 5 quarters. However, while recent estimates for the company have been mixed, AET has posted better than expected results. Based on operating earnings yield, the company is undervalued when compared to all of the companies in our coverage universe. Share price changes over the past year indicates that AET will perform poorly over the near term.

Financial Data
(US$ in Thousands)

	3 Mos	12/31/2015	12/31/2014	12/31/2013	12/31/2012	12/31/2011	12/31/2010	12/31/2009
Earnings Per Share	6.64	6.78	5.68	5.33	4.81	5.22	4.18	2.84
Cash Flow Per Share	11.90	11.07	...	6.41	5.34	6.73	3.40	5.64
Tang Book Value Per Share	12.98	10.84	5.49	4.70	10.30	8.46	11.05	8.74
Dividends Per Share	1.000	1.000	0.900	0.800	0.700	0.450	0.040	0.040
Dividend Payout %	15.06	14.75	15.85	15.01	14.55	8.62	0.96	1.41
Income Statement								
Premium Income	14,009,100	53,788,800	51,748,500	41,836,600	31,715,400	28,965,000	29,432,700	30,136,200
Total Revenue	15,693,400	60,336,500	58,003,200	47,294,600	36,595,900	33,779,800	34,246,000	34,764,100
Benefits & Claims	528,900	2,120,600	2,165,000	2,350,400	2,949,500	1,876,500	2,013,400	2,078,100
Income Before Taxes	1,288,600	4,235,600	3,499,900	2,940,500	2,545,400	3,077,800	2,644,200	1,901,200
Income Taxes	560,700	1,841,000	1,454,700	1,028,600	887,500	1,092,100	877,400	624,700
Net Income	726,600	2,390,200	2,040,800	1,913,600	1,657,900	1,985,700	1,766,800	1,276,500
Average Shares	353,100	352,600	359,100	359,200	345,000	380,200	422,900	449,500
Balance Sheet								
Total Assets	56,423,700	53,424,100	53,402,100	49,871,800	41,494,500	38,593,100	37,739,400	38,550,400
Total Liabilities	39,610,200	37,309,800	38,850,300	35,846,300	31,088,700	28,472,900	27,848,600	29,046,600
Stockholders' Equity	16,813,500	16,114,300	14,482,600	14,025,500	10,405,800	10,120,200	9,890,800	9,503,800
Shares Outstanding	350,600	349,500	349,800	362,200	327,600	349,700	384,400	430,800
Statistical Record								
Return on Assets %	4.18	4.47	3.95	4.19	4.13	5.20	4.63	3.43
Return on Equity %	14.68	15.62	14.32	15.67	16.11	19.85	18.22	14.43
Loss Ratio %	3.78	3.94	4.18	5.62	9.30	6.48	6.84	6.90
Net Margin %	4.63	3.96	3.52	4.05	4.53	5.88	5.16	3.67
Price Range	132.60-94.31	132.60-87.60	90.84-65.15	68.93-44.38	50.23-35.30	45.90-30.51	35.38-25.99	34.52-18.99
P/E Ratio	19.97-14.20	19.56-12.92	15.99-11.47	12.93-8.33	10.44-7.34	8.79-5.84	8.46-6.22	12.15-6.69
Average Yield %	0.90	0.92	1.15	1.35	1.65	1.15	0.13	0.15

Address: 151 Farmington Avenue, Hartford, CT 06156
Telephone: 860 273-0123

Web Site: www.aetna.com
Officers: Mark T. Bertolini - Chairman, President, Chief Executive Officer Karen S. Rohan - President, Executive Vice President

Auditors: KPMG LLP
Investor Contact: 860 273-2402
Transfer Agents: Computershare Trust Company, N.A, Providence, RI

AFFILIATED MANAGERS GROUP INC.

Exchange	Symbol	Price	52Wk Range	Yield	P/E
NYS	AMG	$173.52 (5/31/2016)	227.92-117.80	N/A	19.45

*7 Year Price Score 108.56 *NYSE Composite Index=100   *12 Month Price Score 95.46

Interim Earnings (Per Share)

Qtr.	Mar	Jun	Sep	Dec
2013	1.15	1.18	1.37	2.85
2014	1.40	1.77	1.84	3.00
2015	2.28	2.31	1.98	2.71
2016	1.92	...	...	...

Interim Dividends (Per Share)

No Dividends Paid

Valuation Analysis

		Institutional Holding	
Forecast EPS	$13.35	No of Institutions	
	(05/20/2016)	661	
Market Cap	$9.7 Billion	Shares	
Book Value	$2.9 Billion	64,229,800	
Price/Book	3.38	% Held	
Price/Sales	4.04	95.84	

Business Summary: Wealth Management (MIC: 5.5.2 SIC: 6282 NAIC: 523920)

Affiliated Managers Group is a global asset management company with equity investments in boutique investment management firms, (Affiliates). Co.'s Affiliates provide investment management services globally to institutional clients, mutual funds and high net worth individuals. In addition, Co. provides centralized assistance to its Affiliates in strategic matters, marketing, distribution, product development and operations. Co. perates in three business segments representing Co.'s three principal distribution channels: Institutional, Mutual Fund and High Net Worth.

Recent Developments: For the quarter ended Mar 31 2016, net income decreased 21.2% to US$174.0 million from US$220.7 million in the year-earlier quarter. Revenues were US$545.4 million, down 14.1% from US$635.0 million the year before. Operating income was US$178.8 million versus US$231.4 million in the prior-year quarter, a decrease of 22.7%. Indirect operating expenses decreased 9.2% to US$366.6 million from US$403.6 million in the equivalent prior-year period.

Prospects: Our evaluation of Affiliated Managers Group Inc. as of June 19, 2016 is the result of our systematic analysis on three basic characteristics: earnings strength, relative valuation, and recent stock price movement. The company has enjoyed a very positive trend in earnings per share over the past 5 quarters. However, while recent estimates for the company have been mixed, AMG has posted better than expected results. Based on operating earnings yield, the company is undervalued when compared to all of the companies in our coverage universe. Share price changes over the past year indicates that AMG will perform well over the near term.

Financial Data
(US$ in Thousands)

	3 Mos	12/31/2015	12/31/2014	12/31/2013	12/31/2012	12/31/2011	12/31/2010	12/31/2009
Earnings Per Share	8.92	9.28	8.01	6.55	3.28	3.11	2.81	1.38
Cash Flow Per Share	20.59	22.19	25.31	18.02	12.21	13.68	10.14	5.88
Income Statement								
Total Revenue	545,400	2,484,500	2,510,900	2,188,800	1,805,500	1,704,800	1,358,242	841,840
EBITDA	210,600	992,600	977,600	817,100	644,700	578,800	457,003	292,930
Depn & Amortn	27,800	142,300	139,100	142,200	222,300	97,700	60,066	32,939
Income Before Taxes	162,500	801,700	731,800	555,900	365,500	380,000	305,800	181,862
Income Taxes	56,500	256,900	227,900	194,100	83,800	93,100	91,523	28,003
Net Income	104,500	516,000	452,100	360,500	174,000	164,900	138,633	59,473
Average Shares	56,500	57,200	58,400	56,700	53,000	53,000	49,398	43,333
Balance Sheet								
Current Assets	1,145,500	1,304,200	1,316,300	1,210,200	912,300	876,400	769,430	585,582
Total Assets	8,091,300	7,784,800	7,698,100	6,318,800	6,187,100	5,218,900	5,291,215	3,390,906
Current Liabilities	571,000	729,400	808,300	514,700	375,800	417,600	407,457	227,115
Long-Term Obligations	2,300,800	1,589,600	1,591,800	865,000	1,630,600	1,198,200	1,391,990	964,334
Total Liabilities	5,223,000	4,947,700	5,071,100	4,184,600	4,102,900	3,352,900	3,491,252	2,281,216
Stockholders' Equity	2,868,300	2,837,100	2,627,000	2,134,200	2,084,200	1,866,000	1,799,963	1,109,690
Shares Outstanding	55,800	55,800	54,600	53,900	53,900	53,900	53,944	45,795
Statistical Record								
Return on Assets %	6.32	6.67	6.45	5.77	3.04	3.14	3.19	1.79
Return on Equity %	18.15	18.89	18.99	17.09	8.79	9.00	9.53	5.40
EBITDA Margin %	38.61	39.95	38.93	37.33	35.71	33.95	33.65	34.80
Net Margin %	19.16	20.77	18.01	16.47	9.64	9.67	10.21	7.06
Asset Turnover	0.31	0.32	0.36	0.35	0.32	0.32	0.31	0.25
Current Ratio	2.01	1.79	1.63	2.35	2.43	2.10	1.89	2.58
Debt to Equity	0.80	0.56	0.61	0.41	0.78	0.64	0.77	0.87
Price Range		228.02-117.80	228.02-144.01	216.88-179.30	216.88-130.15	132.30-96.00	112.20-72.88	101.86-59.70	73.28-29.19
P/E Ratio		25.56-13.21	24.57-15.52	27.08-22.38	33.11-19.87	40.34-29.27	36.08-23.43	36.25-21.25	53.10-21.15

Address: 777 South Flagler Drive, West Palm Beach, FL 33401 **Telephone:** 800-345-1100	**Web Site:** www.amg.com **Officers:** Sean M. Healey - Chairman, Chief Executive Officer John Kingston - Vice-Chairman, Executive Vice President, General Counsel, Secretary	**Auditors:** PricewaterhouseCoopers LLP **Investor Contact:** 617-747-3300 **Transfer Agents:** American Stock Transfer & Trust Company, New York, NY

AFLAC INC.

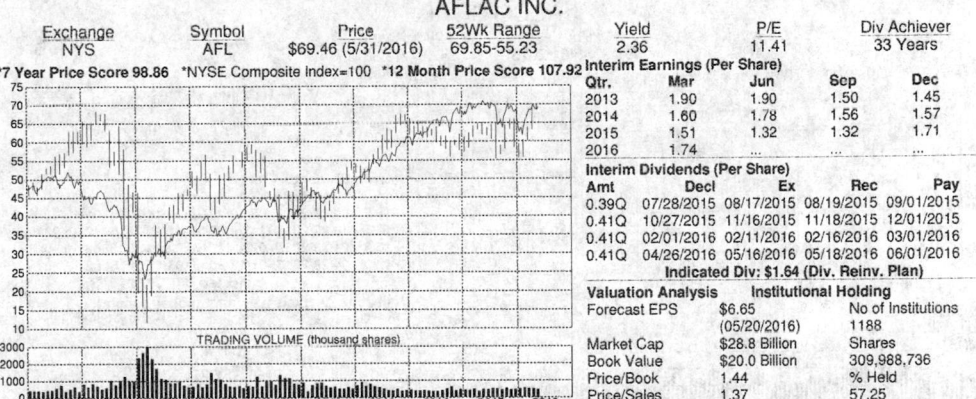

*7 Year Price Score 98.86   *NYSE Composite Index=100   *12 Month Price Score 107.92

Interim Earnings (Per Share)

Qtr.	Mar	Jun	Sep	Dec
2013	1.90	1.90	1.50	1.45
2014	1.60	1.78	1.56	1.57
2015	1.51	1.32	1.32	1.71
2016	1.74	...	...	...

Interim Dividends (Per Share)

Amt	Decl	Ex	Rec	Pay
0.39Q	07/28/2015	08/17/2015	08/19/2015	09/01/2015
0.41Q	10/27/2015	11/16/2015	11/18/2015	12/01/2015
0.41Q	02/01/2016	02/11/2016	02/16/2016	03/01/2016
0.41Q	04/26/2016	05/16/2016	05/18/2016	06/01/2016

Indicated Div: $1.64 (Div. Reinv. Plan)

Valuation Analysis   **Institutional Holding**

Forecast EPS	$6.65	No of Institutions
	(05/20/2016)	1188
Market Cap	$28.8 Billion	Shares
Book Value	$20.0 Billion	309,988,736
Price/Book	1.44	% Held
Price/Sales	1.37	57.25

Business Summary: Life & Health (MIC: 5.2.2 SIC: 6321 NAIC: 524114)

AFLAC is a holding company. Through its subsidiary, American Family Life Assurance Company of Columbus, which operates in the U.S. (Aflac U.S.) and as a branch in Japan (Aflac Japan), Co. provides supplemental health and life insurance. Aflac Japan sells voluntary supplemental insurance products, including cancer plans, general medical indemnity plans, medical/sickness riders, care plans, living benefit life plans, ordinary life insurance plans and annuities. Aflac U.S. sells voluntary supplemental insurance products including products designed to protect individuals from depletion of assets and loss-of-income products.

Recent Developments: For the quarter ended Mar 31 2016, net income increased 10.3% to US$731.0 million from US$663.0 million in the year-earlier quarter. Revenues were US$5.45 billion, up 4.3% from US$5.23 billion the year before. Net premiums earned were US$4.60 billion versus US$4.43 billion in the prior-year quarter, an increase of 3.8%. Net investment income rose 2.4% to US$801.0 million from US$782.0 million a year ago.

Prospects: Our evaluation of AFLAC Inc. as of June 19, 2016 is the result of our systematic analysis on three basic characteristics: earnings strength, relative valuation, and recent stock price movement. The company has managed to produce a neutral trend in earnings per share over the past 5 quarters. However, while recent estimates for the company have been mixed, AFL has posted better than expected results. Based on operating earnings yield, the company is undervalued when compared to all of the companies in our coverage universe. Share price changes over the past year indicates that AFL will perform well over the near term.

Financial Data

(US$ in Thousands)	3 Mos	12/31/2015	12/31/2014	12/31/2013	12/31/2012	12/31/2011	12/31/2010	12/31/2009
Earnings Per Share	6.09	5.85	6.50	6.76	6.11	4.18	4.95	3.19
Cash Flow Per Share	15.87	15.73	14.52	22.71	31.94	23.24	14.90	13.21
Tang Book Value Per Share	48.22	41.73	41.47	31.82	34.16	28.96	23.54	17.96
Dividends Per Share	1.600	1.580	1.500	1.420	1.340	1.230	1.140	1.120
Dividend Payout %	26.27	27.01	23.08	21.01	21.93	29.43	23.03	35.11
Income Statement								
Premium Income	4,602,000	17,570,000	19,072,000	20,135,000	22,148,000	20,362,000	18,073,000	16,621,000
Total Revenue	5,451,000	20,872,000	22,728,000	23,939,000	25,364,000	22,171,000	20,732,000	18,254,000
Benefits & Claims	3,025,000	11,746,000	12,937,000	13,813,000	15,330,000	13,749,000	12,106,000	11,308,000
Income Before Taxes	1,117,000	3,862,000	4,491,000	4,816,000	4,302,000	2,992,000	3,585,000	2,235,000
Income Taxes	386,000	1,329,000	1,540,000	1,658,000	1,436,000	1,028,000	1,241,000	738,000
Net Income	731,000	2,533,000	2,951,000	3,158,000	2,866,000	1,964,000	2,344,000	1,497,000
Average Shares	420,920	433,172	454,000	467,408	469,287	469,370	473,085	469,063
Balance Sheet								
Total Assets	127,766,000	118,296,000	119,767,000	121,307,000	131,094,000	117,102,000	101,039,000	84,106,000
Total Liabilities	107,745,000	100,588,000	101,420,000	106,687,000	115,116,000	103,596,000	89,983,000	75,689,000
Stockholders' Equity	20,021,000	17,708,000	18,347,000	14,620,000	15,978,000	13,506,000	11,056,000	8,417,000
Shares Outstanding	415,203	424,380	442,445	459,413	467,786	466,310	469,661	468,568
Statistical Record								
Return on Assets %	2.09	2.13	2.45	2.50	2.30	1.80	2.53	1.83
Return on Equity %	13.46	14.05	17.90	20.64	19.39	15.99	24.07	19.89
Loss Ratio %	65.73	66.85	67.83	68.60	69.22	67.52	66.98	68.03
Net Margin %	13.41	12.14	12.98	13.19	11.30	8.86	11.31	8.20
Price Range	65.99-55.23	65.99-55.23	66.80-55.80	67.48-48.65	54.70-38.45	59.28-31.46	57.85-40.48	47.14-11.49
P/E Ratio	10.84-9.07	11.28-9.44	10.28-8.58	9.98-7.20	8.95-6.29	14.18-7.53	11.69-8.18	14.78-3.60
Average Yield %	2.61	2.56	2.44	2.45	2.90	2.62	2.25	3.25

Address: 1932 Wynnton Road, Columbus, GA 31999	**Web Site:** www.aflac.com	**Auditors:** KPMG LLP
Telephone: 706-323-3431	**Officers:** Daniel P. Amos - Chairman, Chief Executive Officer Kriss Cloninger - President, Chief Financial Officer, Treasurer	**Investor Contact:** 706-596-3264
Fax: 706-596-3488		**Transfer Agents:** Atlac Incorporated Shareholder Services, Columbus, GA

AGCO CORP.

Exchange	Symbol	Price	52Wk Range	Yield	P/E
NYS	AGCO	$51.93 (5/31/2016)	57.87-43.83	1.00	18.48

*7 Year Price Score 91.84 *NYSE Composite Index=100 *12 Month Price Score 102.21

Interim Earnings (Per Share)

Qtr.	Mar	Jun	Sep	Dec
2013	1.19	2.15	1.27	1.40
2014	1.03	1.77	0.69	0.86
2015	0.34	1.22	0.77	0.73
2016	0.09	...	...	...

Interim Dividends (Per Share)

Amt	Decl	Ex	Rec	Pay
0.12Q	07/23/2015	08/12/2015	08/14/2015	09/15/2015
0.12Q	10/22/2015	11/12/2015	11/16/2015	12/15/2015
0.13Q	01/28/2016	02/11/2016	02/16/2016	03/15/2016
0.13Q	04/28/2016	05/12/2016	05/16/2016	06/15/2016

Indicated Div: $0.52

Valuation Analysis

		Institutional Holding	
Forecast EPS	$2.35	No of Institutions	
	(05/20/2016)	525	
Market Cap	$4.3 Billion	Shares	
Book Value	$2.9 Billion	89,088,744	
Price/Book	1.49	% Held	
Price/Sales	0.58	83.38	

Business Summary: Industrial Machinery & Equipment (MIC: 7.2.1 SIC: 3523 NAIC: 333111)

AGCO is a manufacturer and distributor of agricultural equipment and related replacement parts. Co. sells a range of agricultural equipment, including tractors, combines, self-propelled sprayers, hay tools, forage equipment, seeding and tillage, implements, and grain storage and protein production systems. Co.'s products are marketed under a number of well-known brands, including Challenger®, Fendt®, GSI®, Massey Ferguson® and Valtra®. In addition, Co. also provides retail and wholesale financing through its finance joint ventures with Cooperatieve Centrale Raiffeisen-Boerenleenbank B.A.

Recent Developments: For the quarter ended Mar 31 2016, net income decreased 65.9% to US$10.2 million from US$29.9 million in the year-earlier quarter. Revenues were US$1.56 billion, down 8.4% from US$1.70 billion the year before. Operating income was US$19.4 million versus US$46.8 million in the prior-year quarter, a decrease of 58.5%. Direct operating expenses declined 8.1% to US$1.24 billion from US$1.35 billion in the comparable period the year before. Indirect operating expenses decreased 1.9% to US$295.3 million from US$301.1 million in the equivalent prior-year period.

Prospects: Our evaluation of AGCO Corp. as of June 19, 2016 is the result of our systematic analysis on three basic characteristics: earnings strength, relative valuation, and recent stock price movement. The company has generated a negative trend in earnings per share over the past 5 quarters and while recent estimates for the company have remained steady, AGCO has posted better than expected results. Based on operating earnings yield, the company is undervalued when compared to all of the companies in our coverage universe. Share price changes over the past year indicates that AGCO will perform well over the near term.

Financial Data

(US$ in Thousands)	3 Mos	12/31/2015	12/31/2014	12/31/2013	12/31/2012	12/31/2011	12/31/2010	12/31/2009
Earnings Per Share	2.81	3.06	4.36	6.01	5.30	5.95	2.29	1.44
Cash Flow Per Share	5.57	6.03	4.69	8.19	6.84	7.59	4.73	3.81
Tang Book Value Per Share	14.18	14.51	19.09	23.27	17.20	11.67	19.91	17.31
Dividends Per Share	0.490	0.480	0.440	0.400	...	...	...	...
Dividend Payout %	17.44	15.69	10.09	6.66	...	...	...	...
Income Statement								
Total Revenue	1,559,300	7,467,300	9,723,700	10,786,900	9,962,200	8,773,200	6,896,600	6,630,400
EBITDA	75,000	584,900	877,800	1,120,000	888,300	764,700	462,500	344,700
Depn & Amortn	66,900	260,100	280,400	259,400	229,900	173,500	154,300	147,600
Income Before Taxes	(2,400)	279,400	539,000	802,600	600,800	561,000	274,900	153,800
Income Taxes	(400)	72,500	187,700	258,500	137,900	24,600	104,400	56,500
Net Income	7,800	264,000	404,200	592,300	516,400	585,300	220,200	135,700
Average Shares	83,100	87,100	94,200	99,400	98,600	98,100	96,400	94,100
Balance Sheet								
Current Assets	3,213,100	2,898,300	3,527,900	4,517,100	3,954,700	3,662,800	3,121,000	2,788,900
Total Assets	6,976,200	6,501,300	7,395,900	8,438,800	7,721,800	7,257,200	5,436,900	5,062,200
Current Liabilities	2,263,300	2,185,400	2,216,900	2,812,000	2,464,800	2,205,500	1,912,900	1,718,100
Long-Term Obligations	1,257,500	928,800	997,600	938,500	1,035,600	1,409,700	443,000	454,000
Total Liabilities	4,102,000	3,663,000	3,947,400	4,428,600	4,257,100	4,262,000	2,778,500	2,660,700
Stockholders' Equity	2,874,200	2,838,300	3,448,500	4,010,200	3,464,700	2,995,200	2,658,400	2,401,500
Shares Outstanding	82,458	83,814	89,146	97,362	96,815	97,194	93,143	92,453
Statistical Record								
Return on Assets %	3.42	3.80	5.11	7.33	6.88	9.22	4.19	2.71
Return on Equity %	8.20	8.40	10.84	15.85	15.94	20.71	8.70	6.23
EBITDA Margin %	4.81	7.83	9.03	10.38	8.92	8.72	6.71	5.20
Net Margin %	0.50	3.54	4.16	5.49	5.18	6.67	3.19	2.05
Asset Turnover	1.03	1.07	1.23	1.33	1.33	1.38	1.31	1.32
Current Ratio	1.42	1.33	1.59	1.61	1.60	1.66	1.63	1.62
Debt to Equity	0.44	0.33	0.29	0.23	0.30	0.47	0.17	0.19
Price Range	57.87-43.83	57.87-42.72	59.19-42.08	64.42-48.02	52.94-38.56	58.13-32.39	50.94-25.86	33.50-15.10
P/E Ratio	20.59-15.60	18.91-13.96	13.58-9.65	10.72-7.99	9.99-7.28	9.77-5.44	22.24-11.29	23.26-10.49
Average Yield %	0.99	0.98	0.87	0.72	...	...	...	...

Address: 4205 River Green Parkway, Duluth, GA 30096 Telephone: 770-813-9200	Web Site: www.agcocorp.com Officers: Martin H. Richenhagen - Chairman, President, Chief Executive Officer Andrew H. Beck - Senior Vice President, Chief Financial Officer	Auditors: KPMG LLP Investor Contact: 770-232-8229 Transfer Agents: Computershare Trust Company, N.A., Canton, MA

AGILENT TECHNOLOGIES, INC.

Exchange	Symbol	Price	52Wk Range	Yield	P/E
NYS	A	$45.89 (5/31/2016)	45.89-33.37	1.00	33.01

*7 Year Price Score 104.59 *NYSE Composite index=100 *12 Month Price Score 106.49

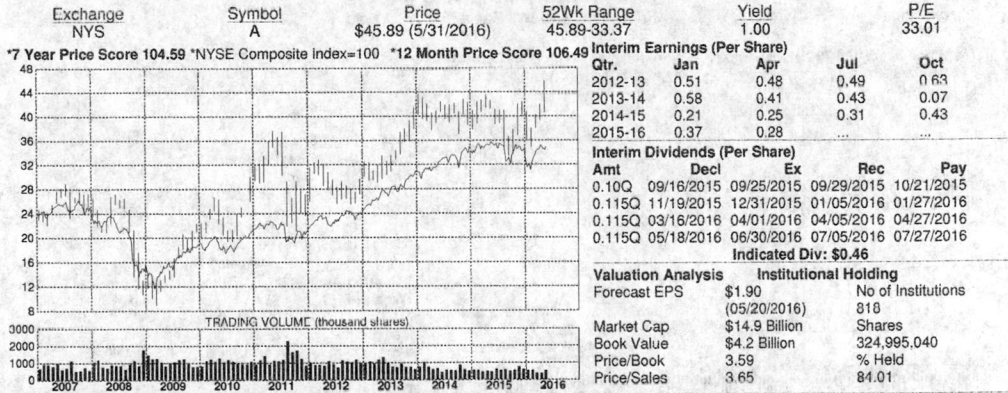

Interim Earnings (Per Share)

Qtr.	Jan	Apr	Jul	Oct
2012-13	0.51	0.48	0.49	0.63
2013-14	0.58	0.41	0.43	0.07
2014-15	0.21	0.25	0.31	0.43
2015-16	0.37	0.28	...	...

Interim Dividends (Per Share)

Amt	Decl	Ex	Rec	Pay
0.10Q	09/16/2015	09/25/2015	09/29/2015	10/21/2015
0.115Q	11/19/2015	12/31/2015	01/05/2016	01/27/2016
0.115Q	03/16/2016	04/01/2016	04/05/2016	04/27/2016
0.115Q	05/18/2016	06/30/2016	07/05/2016	07/27/2016

Indicated Div: $0.46

Valuation Analysis   **Institutional Holding**

Forecast EPS	$1.90	No of Institutions
(05/20/2016)		818
Market Cap	$14.9 Billion	Shares
Book Value	$4.2 Billion	324,995,040
Price/Book	3.59	% Held
Price/Sales	3.65	84.01

Business Summary: Medical Instruments & Equipment (MIC: 4.3.1 SIC: 3825 NAIC: 334515)

Agilent Technologies is engaged in life sciences, diagnostics and applied chemical markets. Co.'s life sciences and applied markets business provides instruments and software that enable customers to identify, quantify and analyze the physical and biological properties of substances and products, as well as enable customers in the clinical and life sciences research areas to interrogate samples at the molecular level. Co.'s diagnostics and genomics business is comprised of three areas of activity providing solutions that include reagents, instruments, software and consumables. The Agilent CrossLab business spans the lab with its consumables and services portfolio

Recent Developments: For the quarter ended Apr 30 2016, income from continuing operations decreased 1.1% to US$91.0 million from US$92.0 million in the year-earlier quarter. Net income increased 4.6% to US$91.0 million from US$87.0 million in the year-earlier quarter. Revenues were US$1.02 billion, up 5.8% from US$963.0 million the year before. Operating income was US$131.0 million versus US$107.0 million in the prior-year quarter, an increase of 22.4%. Direct operating expenses rose 1.2% to US$489.0 million from US$483.0 million in the comparable period the year before. Indirect operating expenses increased 7.0% to US$399.0 million from US$373.0 million in the equivalent prior-year period.

Prospects: Our evaluation of Agilent Technologies Inc. as of June 19, 2016 is the result of our systematic analysis on three basic characteristics: earnings strength, relative valuation, and recent stock price movement. The company has produced a positive trend in earnings per share over the past 5 quarters and while recent estimates for the company have been mixed, A has posted better than expected results. Based on operating earnings yield, the company is about fairly valued when compared to all of the companies in our coverage universe. Share price changes over the past year indicates that A will perform well over the near term.

Financial Data

(US$ in Millions)	6 Mos	3 Mos	10/31/2015	10/31/2014	10/31/2013	10/31/2012	10/31/2011	10/31/2010
Earnings Per Share	1.39	1.36	1.20	1.49	2.10	3.27	2.85	1.94
Cash Flow Per Share	2.11	1.87	1.47	2.14	3.38	3.52	3.63	2.07
Tang Book Value Per Share	3.43	3.21	4.09	5.17	3.98	3.09	6.67	3.69
Dividends Per Share	0.430	0.415	0.400	0.528	0.460	0.300	...	...
Dividend Payout %	30.94	30.51	33.33	35.44	21.90	9.17	...	...
Income Statement								
Total Revenue	2,047	1,028	4,038	6,981	6,782	6,858	6,615	5,444
EBITDA	420	224	637	944	1,140	1,306	1,246	892
Depn & Amortn	130	66	98	194	181	171	142	124
Income Before Taxes	259	142	480	646	859	1,043	1,032	692
Income Taxes	45	19	42	142	135	(110)	20	8
Net Income	214	123	401	504	724	1,153	1,012	684
Average Shares	328	332	335	338	345	353	355	353
Balance Sheet								
Current Assets	3,488	3,399	3,686	5,500	4,983	4,629	5,569	6,169
Total Assets	7,640	7,302	7,479	10,831	10,686	10,536	9,057	9,696
Current Liabilities	1,133	947	976	1,702	1,602	1,893	1,837	3,083
Long-Term Obligations	1,654	1,653	1,655	2,762	2,699	2,112	1,932	2,190
Total Liabilities	3,478	3,257	3,312	5,533	5,400	5,354	4,749	6,468
Stockholders' Equity	4,162	4,045	4,167	5,298	5,286	5,182	4,308	3,228
Shares Outstanding	325	328	331	334	332	346	346	346
Statistical Record								
Return on Assets %	6.11	6.10	4.38	4.68	6.82	11.74	10.79	7.90
Return on Equity %	11.06	10.92	8.47	9.52	13.83	24.23	26.86	23.86
EBITDA Margin %	20.52	21.79	15.78	13.52	16.81	19.04	18.84	16.39
Net Margin %	10.45	11.96	9.93	7.22	10.68	16.81	15.30	12.56
Asset Turnover	0.54	0.55	0.44	0.65	0.64	0.70	0.71	0.63
Current Ratio	3.08	3.59	3.78	3.23	3.11	2.45	3.03	2.00
Debt to Equity	0.40	0.41	0.40	0.52	0.51	0.41	0.45	0.68
Price Range	42.63-33.37	43.55-33.37	43.55-33.37	43.57-35.79	37.89-25.56	32.79-23.55	37.60-21.02	26.62-17.90
P/E Ratio	30.67-24.01	32.02-24.54	36.29-27.81	29.24-24.02	18.04-12.17	10.03-7.20	13.19-7.38	13.72-9.23
Average Yield %	1.11	1.05	1.01	1.31	1.46	1.06	...	...

Address: 5301 Stevens Creek Blvd., Santa Clara, CA 95051 Telephone: 408-345-8886	Web Site: www.investor.agilent.com Officers: Michael R. McMullen - Chief Executive Officer, Senior Vice President, Division Officer Henrik Ancher-Jensen - Senior Vice President, Region Officer	Auditors: PricewaterhouseCoopers LLP Investor Contact: 408-345-8948 Transfer Agents: ComputerShare Investor Services, Chicago, IL

AGL RESOURCES INC.

Exchange	Symbol	Price	52Wk Range	Yield	P/E	Div Achiever
NYS	GAS	$65.80 (5/31/2016)	66.39-46.56	3.22	23.17	13 Years

*7 Year Price Score 114.79 *NYSE Composite Index=100 *12 Month Price Score 107.63

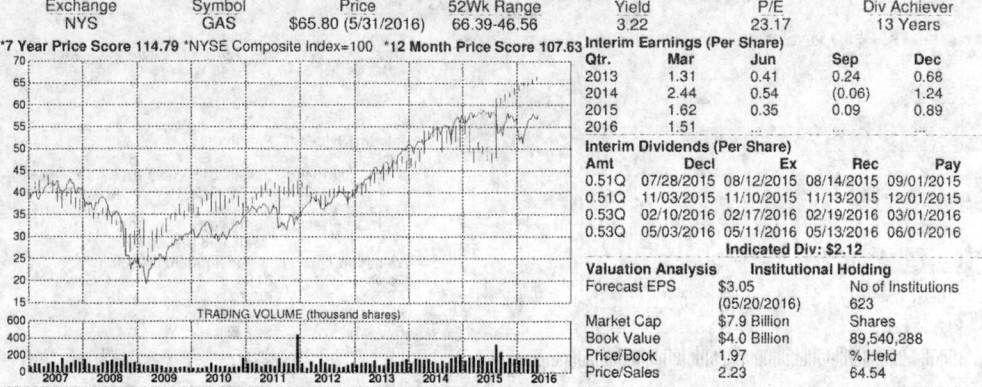

Interim Earnings (Per Share)

Qtr.	Mar	Jun	Sep	Dec
2013	1.31	0.41	0.24	0.68
2014	2.44	0.54	(0.06)	1.24
2015	1.62	0.35	0.09	0.89
2016	1.51	...	...	...

Interim Dividends (Per Share)

Amt	Decl	Ex	Rec	Pay
0.51Q	07/28/2015	08/12/2015	08/14/2015	09/01/2015
0.51Q	11/03/2015	11/10/2015	11/13/2015	12/01/2015
0.53Q	02/10/2016	02/17/2016	02/19/2016	03/01/2016
0.53Q	05/03/2016	05/11/2016	05/13/2016	06/01/2016

Indicated Div: $2.12

Valuation Analysis | **Institutional Holding**

Forecast EPS	$3.05	No of Institutions
(05/20/2016)		623
Market Cap	$7.9 Billion	Shares
Book Value	$4.0 Billion	89,540,288
Price/Book	1.97	% Held
Price/Sales	2.23	64.54

Business Summary: Gas Utilities (MIC: 3.3.1 SIC: 4924 NAIC: 221210)

AGL Resources is an energy services holding company. Co.'s operating segments includes: distribution operations engaged in the operation, construction and maintenance of natural gas pipeline and storage facilities to provide natural gas to customers; retail operations, which provides natural gas commodity and related services to customers; wholesale services, which involve natural gas storage, gas pipeline arbitrage and provides natural gas asset management and related logistics services; midstream operations consists primarily of natural gas storage facilities and select pipelines, enabling the provision of various sources of natural gas supplies to its customers.

Recent Developments: For the quarter ended Mar 31 2016, net income decreased 5.9% to US$193.0 million from US$205.0 million in the year-earlier quarter. Revenues were US$1.33 billion, down 22.5% from US$1.72 billion the year before. Operating income was US$348.0 million versus US$364.0 million in the prior-year quarter, a decrease of 4.4%. Direct operating expenses declined 38.2% to US$578.0 million from US$935.0 million in the comparable period the year before. Indirect operating expenses decreased 3.3% to US$408.0 million from US$422.0 million in the equivalent prior-year period.

Prospects: Our evaluation of AGL Resources Inc. as of June 19, 2016 is the result of our systematic analysis on three basic characteristics: earnings strength, relative valuation, and recent stock price movement. The company has managed to produce a neutral trend in earnings per share over the past 5 quarters. Because the company lacks sufficient analyst estimate data, we place greater weight on the historical EPS trend as the measure of earnings strength. Based on operating earnings yield, the company is about fairly valued when compared to all of the companies in our coverage universe. Share price changes over the past year indicates that GAS will perform very well over the near term.

Financial Data
(US$ in Thousands)

	3 Mos	12/31/2015	12/31/2014	12/31/2013	12/31/2012	12/31/2011	12/31/2010	12/31/2009
Earnings Per Share	2.84	2.94	4.04	2.64	2.31	2.12	3.00	2.88
Cash Flow Per Share	9.18	11.55	5.51	8.24	8.55	5.61	6.80	7.71
Tang Book Value Per Share	17.52	16.67	15.31	13.21	12.56	11.97	17.88	17.57
Dividends Per Share	2.060	2.040	1.960	1.880	1.741	1.899	1.760	1.720
Dividend Payout %	72.54	69.39	48.51	71.21	75.37	89.57	58.67	59.72
Income Statement								
Total Revenue	1,334,000	3,941,000	5,385,000	4,617,000	3,922,000	2,338,000	2,373,000	2,317,000
EBITDA	453,000	1,156,000	1,489,000	1,121,000	1,049,000	633,000	659,000	643,000
Depn & Amortn	102,000	397,000	380,000	418,000	415,000	186,000	160,000	158,000
Income Before Taxes	304,000	586,000	930,000	522,000	450,000	311,000	390,000	384,000
Income Taxes	111,000	213,000	350,000	191,000	164,000	125,000	140,000	135,000
Net Income	182,000	353,000	482,000	313,000	271,000	172,000	234,000	222,000
Average Shares	120,400	119,900	119,200	118,300	117,500	80,900	77,800	77,100
Balance Sheet								
Current Assets	1,537,000	2,115,000	2,890,000	2,733,000	2,668,000	2,746,000	2,162,000	2,000,000
Total Assets	14,336,000	14,754,000	14,909,000	14,656,000	14,141,000	13,913,000	7,518,000	7,074,000
Current Liabilities	2,489,000	3,000,000	3,219,000	3,122,000	3,338,000	3,084,000	2,428,000	1,772,000
Long-Term Obligations	3,273,000	3,275,000	3,602,000	3,813,000	3,327,000	3,561,000	1,673,000	1,974,000
Total Liabilities	10,304,000	10,825,000	11,125,000	11,025,000	10,728,000	10,595,000	5,705,000	5,294,000
Stockholders' Equity	4,032,000	3,929,000	3,784,000	3,631,000	3,413,000	3,318,000	1,813,000	1,780,000
Shares Outstanding	120,679	120,376	119,647	118,888	117,855	117,000	78,000	77,500
Statistical Record								
Return on Assets %	2.40	2.38	3.26	2.17	1.93	1.61	3.21	3.22
Return on Equity %	8.60	9.15	13.00	8.89	8.03	6.70	13.03	12.94
EBITDA Margin %	33.96	29.33	27.65	24.28	26.75	27.07	27.77	27.75
Net Margin %	13.64	8.96	8.95	6.78	6.91	7.36	9.86	9.58
Asset Turnover	0.25	0.27	0.36	0.32	0.28	0.22	0.33	0.34
Current Ratio	0.62	0.70	0.90	0.88	0.80	0.89	0.89	1.13
Debt to Equity	0.81	0.83	0.95	1.05	0.97	1.07	0.92	1.11
Price Range	65.20-46.56	63.82-46.56	56.54-45.47	48.25-39.61	42.28-36.85	43.50-34.98	39.98-34.62	37.48-24.18
P/E Ratio	22.96-16.39	21.71-15.84	14.00-11.25	18.28-14.93	18.30-15.95	20.52-16.50	13.33-11.54	13.01-8.40
Average Yield %	3.59	3.75	3.82	4.29	4.40	4.77	4.70	5.36

Address: Ten Peachtree Place N.E., Atlanta, GA 30309 **Telephone:** 404-584-4000	**Web Site:** www.aglresources.com **Officers:** James A. Rubright - Chairman Andrew W. Evans - President, Chief Operating Officer, Chief Executive Officer, Executive Vice President, Chief Financial Officer	**Auditors:** PricewaterhouseCoopers LLP **Investor Contact:** 404-584-4577 **Transfer Agents:** Wells Fargo Shareowner Services, St. Paul, MN

AIR LEASE CORP

Exchange	Symbol	Price	52Wk Range	Yield	P/E
NYS	AL	$30.05 (5/31/2016)	38.45-22.73	0.67	10.02

*7 Year Price Score N/A *NYSE Composite Index=100 *12 Month Price Score 95.80

Interim Earnings (Per Share)

Qtr.	Mar	Jun	Sep	Dec
2013	0.38	0.41	0.46	0.55
2014	0.57	0.58	0.58	0.65
2015	0.19	0.70	0.71	0.74
2016	0.85	...	...	...

Interim Dividends (Per Share)

Amt	Decl	Ex	Rec	Pay
0.04Q	08/05/2015	09/08/2015	09/10/2015	10/06/2015
0.05Q	11/05/2015	12/10/2015	12/14/2015	01/06/2016
0.05Q	02/25/2016	03/17/2016	03/21/2016	04/05/2016
0.05Q	05/02/2016	06/09/2016	06/13/2016	07/07/2016

Indicated Div: $0.20

Valuation Analysis

		Institutional Holding	
Forecast EPS	$3.42	No of Institutions	
	(05/20/2016)	282	
Market Cap	$3.1 Billion	Shares	
Book Value	$3.1 Billion	95,814,800	
Price/Book	1.00	% Held	
Price/Sales	2.40	86.86	

Business Summary: Miscellaneous Transportation Services (MIC: 7.4.5 SIC: 7359 NAIC: 532411)

Air Lease is an aircraft leasing company. Co. is principally engaged in purchasing new commercial jet transport aircraft directly from aircraft manufacturers, such as The Boeing Company and Airbus S.A.S., and leasing those aircraft to airlines. In addition to its leasing activities, Co. sells aircraft from its operating lease portfolio to third parties, including other leasing companies, financial services companies and airlines. Co. also provides fleet management services to investors and owners of aircraft portfolios. As of Dec 31 2014, Co. owned 213 aircraft, comprised of 163 single-aisle narrowbody jet aircraft, 32 twin-aisle widebody jet aircraft and 18 turboprop aircraft.

Recent Developments: For the quarter ended Mar 31 2016, net income increased 380.3% to US$92.9 million from US$19.3 million in the year-earlier quarter. Revenues were US$343.3 million, up 23.4% from US$278.3 million the year before. Indirect operating expenses decreased 19.7% to US$199.3 million from US$248.3 million in the equivalent prior-year period.

Prospects: Our evaluation of Air Lease Corp as of June 19, 2016 is the result of our systematic analysis on three basic characteristics: earnings strength, relative valuation, and recent stock price movement. The company has produced a positive trend in earnings per share over the past 5 quarters. However, while recent estimates for the company have been mixed, AL has posted better than expected results. Based on operating earnings yield, the company is undervalued when compared to all of the companies in our coverage universe. Share price changes over the past year indicates that AL will perform very well over the near term.

Financial Data

(US$ in Thousands)	3 Mos	12/31/2015	12/31/2014	12/31/2013	12/31/2012	12/31/2011	12/31/2010
Earnings Per Share	3.00	2.34	2.38	1.80	1.28	0.59	(1.32)
Cash Flow Per Share	8.36	8.19	7.53	6.44	4.85	2.98	1.14
Tang Book Value Per Share	30.19	29.44	27.07	24.78	23.04	21.61	18.73
Dividends Per Share	0.180	0.170	0.130	0.105	...	...	...
Dividend Payout %	6.00	7.26	5.46	5.83	...	...	...
Income Statement							
Total Revenue	343,328	1,222,840	1,050,493	858,675	655,746	336,741	58,366
EBITDA	327,848	1,056,857	952,023	765,849	567,605	252,840	10,090
Depn & Amortn	115,736	397,760	336,657	280,037	216,219	112,307	19,262
Income Before Taxes	143,991	392,953	394,776	293,442	203,973	82,841	(60,915)
Income Taxes	51,133	139,562	138,778	103,031	72,054	29,609	(8,875)
Net Income	92,858	253,391	255,998	190,411	131,919	53,232	(52,040)
Average Shares	110,563	110,628	110,192	108,963	107,656	90,416	39,511
Balance Sheet							
Current Assets	179,304	1,244,238	1,434,891	1,432,504	901,114	783,511	569,739
Total Assets	12,783,410	12,355,098	10,774,784	9,332,604	7,353,624	5,164,593	2,276,282
Current Liabilities	192,389	1,069,313	889,124	701,070	502,392	338,802	131,328
Long-Term Obligations	8,017,501	7,712,421	6,714,362	5,853,317	4,384,732	2,602,799	911,981
Total Liabilities	9,679,007	9,335,186	8,002,722	6,809,170	5,021,003	2,988,310	1,051,347
Stockholders' Equity	3,104,403	3,019,912	2,772,062	2,523,434	2,332,621	2,176,283	1,224,935
Shares Outstanding	102,829	102,582	102,392	101,822	101,247	100,714	65,393
Statistical Record							
Return on Assets %	2.73	2.19	2.55	2.28	2.10	1.43	...
Return on Equity %	11.10	8.75	9.67	7.84	5.84	3.13	...
EBITDA Margin %	95.49	86.43	90.63	89.19	86.56	75.08	17.29
Net Margin %	27.05	20.72	24.37	22.17	20.12	15.81	N.M.
Asset Turnover	0.11	0.11	0.10	0.10	0.10	0.09	...
Current Ratio	0.93	1.16	1.61	2.04	1.79	2.31	4.34
Debt to Equity	2.58	2.55	2.42	2.32	1.88	1.20	0.74
Price Range	40.21-22.73	40.21-29.83	42.44-30.27	33.29-21.50	25.58-18.62	29.70-17.83	...
P/E Ratio	13.40-7.58	17.18-12.75	17.83-12.72	18.49-11.94	19.98-14.55	50.34-30.22	...
Average Yield %	0.54	0.48	0.36	0.38	...	...	...

Address: 2000 Avenue of the Stars, Suite 1000N, Los Angeles, CA 90067 Telephone: 310-553-0555	Web Site: www.airleasecorp.com Officers: Steven F. Udvar-Házy - Chairman, Chief Executive Officer John L. Plueger - President, Chief Operating Officer, Chief Executive Officer	Auditors: KPMG LLP Investor Contact: 310-553-0555 Transfer Agents: American Stock Transfer & Trust Company, LLC, Seattle, WA

AIR PRODUCTS & CHEMICALS, INC.

Exchange	Symbol	Price	52Wk Range	Yield	P/E	Div Achiever
NYS	APD	$142.64 (5/31/2016)	149.20-116.31	2.41	55.94	33 Years

*7 Year Price Score 114.35 *NYSE Composite Index=100 *12 Month Price Score 104.44

Interim Earnings (Per Share)

Qtr.	Dec	Mar	Jun	Sep
2012-13	1.31	1.38	1.36	0.64
2013-14	1.35	1.32	1.46	0.48
2014-15	1.50	1.33	1.47	1.58
2015-16	1.67	(2.17)	...	...

Interim Dividends (Per Share)

Amt	Decl	Ex	Rec	Pay
0.81Q	09/16/2015	09/29/2015	10/01/2015	11/09/2015
0.81Q	11/19/2015	12/30/2015	01/04/2016	02/08/2016
0.86Q	03/17/2016	03/30/2016	04/01/2016	05/09/2016
0.86Q	05/19/2016	06/29/2016	07/01/2016	08/08/2016

Indicated Div: $3.44 (Div. Reinv. Plan)

Valuation Analysis / **Institutional Holding**

Forecast EPS	$7.49	No of Institutions
	(05/20/2016)	1139
Market Cap	$30.8 Billion	Shares
Book Value	$6.9 Billion	231,194,832
Price/Book	4.46	% Held
Price/Sales	3.23	88.94

Business Summary: Specialty Chemicals (MIC: 8.3.2 SIC: 2813 NAIC: 325120)

Air Products and Chemicals manufactures and distributes products in two lines of business: Industrial Gases and Materials Technologies. Industrial Gases' primary products are atmospheric gases, process gases, and equipment for air separation. Materials Technologies' primary products are performance materials and chemicals, such as epoxy amine curing agents, polyurethane catalysts, additives, and specialty surfactants, and electronics materials such as specialty gases, chemical mechanical planarization slurries, and specialty chemicals. Co. also designs and manufactures equipment for natural gas liquefaction and helium distribution.

Recent Developments: For the quarter ended Mar 31 2016, income from continuing operations increased 29.7% to US$387.6 million from US$298.8 million in the year-earlier quarter. Net loss amounted to US$465.5 million versus net income of US$296.9 million in the year-earlier quarter. Revenues were US$2.27 billion, down 5.9% from US$2.41 billion the year before. Operating income was US$513.3 million versus US$376.9 million in the prior-year quarter, an increase of 36.2%. Direct operating expenses declined 10.6% to US$1.52 billion from US$1.70 billion in the comparable period the year before. Indirect operating expenses decreased 29.6% to US$238.9 million from US$339.4 million in the equivalent prior-year period.

Prospects: Our evaluation of Air Products & Chemicals Inc. as of June 19, 2016 is the result of our systematic analysis on three basic characteristics: earnings strength, relative valuation, and recent stock price movement. The company has produced a positive trend in earnings per share over the past 5 quarters and while recent estimates for the company have remained steady, APD has posted better than expected results. Based on operating earnings yield, the company is undervalued when compared to all of the companies in our coverage universe. Share price changes over the past year indicates that APD will perform well over the near term.

Financial Data

(US$ in Thousands)	6 Mos	3 Mos	09/30/2015	09/30/2014	09/30/2013	09/30/2012	09/30/2011	09/30/2010
Earnings Per Share	2.55	6.05	5.88	4.61	4.68	5.44	5.63	4.74
Cash Flow Per Share	11.84	11.70	11.34	10.28	7.41	8.33	8.23	7.17
Tang Book Value Per Share	24.37	26.71	26.05	25.82	22.12	19.38	22.09	20.33
Dividends Per Share	3.290	3.240	3.200	3.020	2.770	2.500	2.230	1.920
Dividend Payout %	129.02	53.55	54.42	65.51	59.19	45.96	39.61	40.51
Income Statement								
Total Revenue	4,627,000	2,355,800	9,894,900	10,439,000	10,180,400	9,611,700	10,082,000	9,026,000
EBITDA	1,488,700	725,700	2,560,400	2,233,600	2,182,700	2,094,200	2,473,000	2,231,700
Depn & Amortn	464,800	232,700	900,400	914,800	864,700	817,200	856,500	846,100
Income Before Taxes	976,000	470,800	1,561,100	1,203,100	1,182,600	1,158,700	1,506,700	1,267,100
Income Taxes	268,400	132,500	415,900	366,000	307,900	287,300	408,400	339,500
Net Income	(109,700)	363,600	1,277,900	991,700	994,200	1,167,300	1,224,200	1,029,100
Average Shares	217,900	217,600	217,300	215,220	212,300	214,700	217,600	217,100
Balance Sheet								
Current Assets	3,031,200	2,779,000	2,910,800	3,294,800	3,439,100	3,415,800	3,189,800	3,033,800
Total Assets	16,810,800	17,260,300	17,438,100	17,779,100	17,850,100	16,941,800	14,290,700	13,505,900
Current Liabilities	3,839,100	3,572,400	3,648,100	2,963,000	3,227,600	2,689,900	2,342,000	2,244,100
Long-Term Obligations	3,573,200	3,870,500	3,949,100	4,824,500	5,056,300	4,584,200	3,927,500	3,659,800
Total Liabilities	9,894,200	9,893,200	10,189,100	10,413,300	10,808,000	10,464,600	8,494,900	7,959,000
Stockholders' Equity	6,916,600	7,367,100	7,249,000	7,365,800	7,042,100	6,477,200	5,795,800	5,546,900
Shares Outstanding	216,081	215,650	215,359	213,538	211,179	212,475	210,185	213,802
Statistical Record								
Return on Assets %	3.23	7.55	7.26	5.57	5.72	7.45	8.81	7.76
Return on Equity %	7.77	17.89	17.49	13.77	14.71	18.97	21.59	19.91
EBITDA Margin %	32.17	30.80	25.88	21.40	21.44	21.79	24.53	24.73
Net Margin %	N.M.	15.43	12.91	9.50	9.77	12.14	12.14	11.40
Asset Turnover	0.56	0.56	0.56	0.59	0.59	0.61	0.73	0.68
Current Ratio	0.79	0.78	0.80	1.11	1.07	1.27	1.36	1.35
Debt to Equity	0.52	0.53	0.54	0.65	0.72	0.71	0.68	0.66
Price Range	152.96-116.31	158.13-125.25	158.13-119.03	136.32-102.58	110.02-77.09	92.68-73.87	97.79-74.80	84.71-64.81
P/E Ratio	59.98-45.61	26.14-20.70	26.89-20.24	29.57-22.25	23.51-16.47	17.04-13.58	17.37-13.29	17.87-13.67
Average Yield %	2.38	2.27	2.24	2.54	3.05	2.96	2.54	2.53

Address: 7201 Hamilton Boulevard, Allentown, PA 18195-1501	**Web Site:** www.airproducts.com	**Auditors:** KPMG
Telephone: 610-481-4911	**Officers:** Seifollah (Seifi) Ghasemi - Chairman, President, Chief Executive Officer M. Scott Crocco - Senior Vice President, Chief Financial Officer, Vice President, Controller, Principal Accounting Officer	**Investor Contact:** 610-481-7461
Fax: 610-481-5900		**Transfer Agents:** Broadridge Corporate Issuer Solutions, Inc., Brentwood, NY

AK STEEL HOLDING CORP.

Exchange	Symbol	Price	52Wk Range	Yield	P/E
NYS	AKS	$4.28 (5/31/2016)	5.57-1.83	N/A	N/A

*7 Year Price Score 29.96 ***NYSE Composite Index=100** ***12 Month Price Score 134.38**

TRADING VOLUME (thousand shares)

Interim Earnings (Per Share)

Qtr.	Mar	Jun	Sep	Dec
2013	(0.07)	(0.30)	(0.23)	0.26
2014	(0.63)	(0.13)	(0.05)	0.14
2015	(1.72)	(0.36)	0.04	(0.81)
2016	(0.08)	...	...	...

Interim Dividends (Per Share)

No Dividends Paid

Valuation Analysis   Institutional Holding

Forecast EPS	$0.04	No of Institutions
	(05/20/2016)	303
Market Cap	$763.5 Million	Shares
Book Value	N/A	104,700,448
Price/Book	N/A	% Held
Price/Sales	0.12	94.62

Business Summary: Non-Precious Metals (MIC: 8.2.2 SIC: 3312 NAIC: 331111)

AK Steel Holding is a producer of flat-rolled carbon, stainless and electrical steels and tubular products through its subsidiary, AK Steel Corporation. Co. operates steelmaking and finishing plants, coke plants and tube manufacturing plants across six states. These operations produce flat-rolled carbon, specialty stainless and electrical steels that Co. sells in sheet and strip form, and carbon and stainless steel that Co. finishes into welded steel tubing. Co. also produces metallurgical coal through its AK Coal Resources, Inc. subsidiary. In addition, Co. operates trading companies in Mexico and Europe that buy and sell steel products and other materials.

Recent Developments: For the quarter ended Mar 31 2016, net income amounted to US$4.4 million versus a net loss of US$290.8 million in the year-earlier quarter. Revenues were US$1.52 billion, down 13.3% from US$1.75 billion the year before. Operating income was US$48.0 million versus US$33.8 million in the prior-year quarter, an increase of 42.0%. Direct operating expenses declined 15.1% to US$1.37 billion from US$1.61 billion in the comparable period the year before. Indirect operating expenses decreased 2.9% to US$105.3 million from US$108.5 million in the equivalent prior-year period.

Prospects: Our evaluation of AK Steel Holding Corp. as of June 19, 2016 is the result of our systematic analysis on three basic characteristics: earnings strength, relative valuation, and recent stock price movement. The company has enjoyed a very positive trend in earnings per share over the past 5 quarters. Because the company lacks sufficient analyst estimate data, we place greater weight on the historical EPS trend as the measure of earnings strength. Based on operating earnings yield, the company is about fairly valued when compared to all of the companies in our coverage universe. Share price changes over the past year indicates that AKS will perform very poorly over the near term.

Financial Data
(US$ in Thousands)

	3 Mos	12/31/2015	12/31/2014	12/31/2013	12/31/2012	12/31/2011	12/31/2010	12/31/2009
Earnings Per Share	(1.21)	(2.86)	(0.65)	(0.34)	(9.06)	(1.41)	(1.17)	(0.68)
Cash Flow Per Share	1.91	1.13	(2.18)	(0.81)	(2.39)	(1.64)	(1.21)	0.54
Tang Book Value Per Share	...	...	...	...	...	3.19	5.52	7.71
Dividends Per Share	...	...	...	...	0.100	0.200	0.200	0.200
Income Statement								
Total Revenue	1,518,800	6,692,900	6,505,700	5,570,400	5,933,700	6,468,000	5,968,300	4,076,800
EBITDA	106,300	6,200	320,200	324,500	70,100	(21,600)	54,000	140,900
Depn & Amortn	59,000	216,000	201,900	190,100	192,000	185,000	197,100	204,600
Income Before Taxes	4,500	(382,800)	(26,400)	7,000	(208,600)	(254,100)	(174,500)	(98,000)
Income Taxes	100	63,400	7,700	(10,400)	790,000	(94,000)	(43,800)	(20,000)
Net Income	(13,600)	(509,000)	(96,900)	(46,800)	(1,027,300)	(155,600)	(128,900)	(74,600)
Average Shares	177,500	177,200	148,100	135,800	113,000	109,800	109,600	109,000
Balance Sheet								
Current Assets	1,742,400	1,806,200	2,025,700	1,273,200	1,442,700	1,274,400	1,404,100	1,630,100
Total Assets	3,987,300	4,084,400	4,858,500	3,605,700	3,903,100	4,449,900	4,188,600	4,274,700
Current Liabilities	991,700	1,042,600	1,125,200	831,400	812,400	1,137,100	844,500	740,700
Long-Term Obligations	2,336,400	2,354,100	2,452,500	1,506,200	1,411,200	650,000	650,600	605,800
Total Liabilities	4,977,800	5,062,000	5,351,000	3,826,700	4,408,400	4,061,400	3,543,900	3,393,900
Stockholders' Equity	(990,500)	(977,600)	(492,500)	(221,000)	(505,300)	388,500	644,700	880,800
Shares Outstanding	178,377	177,893	177,215	136,380	135,944	110,284	109,986	109,394
Statistical Record								
EBITDA Margin %	7.00	0.09	4.92	5.83	1.18	N.M.	0.90	3.46
Asset Turnover	1.51	1.50	1.54	1.48	1.42	1.50	1.41	0.91
Current Ratio	1.76	1.73	1.80	1.53	1.78	1.12	1.66	2.20
Debt to Equity	...	...	...	...	...	1.67	1.01	0.69
Price Range	5.77-1.83	5.97-2.04	11.19-5.20	8.20-2.82	10.04-3.57	17.61-5.77	25.77-11.52	23.39-5.45
Average Yield %	...	...	...	...	1.60	...	1.20	1.29

Address: 9227 Centre Pointe Drive, West Chester, OH 45069	Web Site: www.aksteel.com	Auditors: Ernst & Young LLP
Telephone: 513-425-5000	Officers: Roger K. Newport - Executive Vice President, Senior Vice President, Vice President, Vice President, Chief Financial Officer, Chief Executive Officer Jaime Vasquez - Vice President, Chief Financial Officer	Investor Contact: 513-425-5270
Fax: 513-425-5220		Transfer Agents: Computershare Investor Services, LLC, Canton, MA

ALASKA AIR GROUP, INC.

Exchange	Symbol	Price	52Wk Range	Yield	P/E
NYS	ALK	$66.40 (5/31/2016)	86.33-60.65	1.66	9.62

*7 Year Price Score 195.33 *NYSE Composite Index=100 *12 Month Price Score 95.65

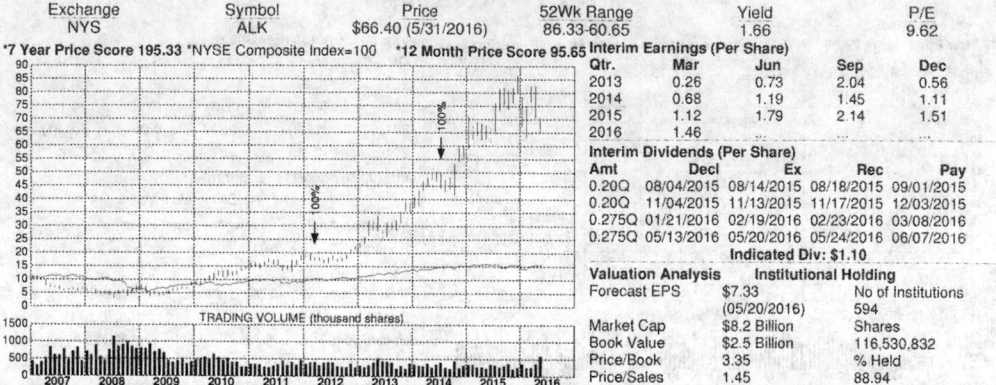

Interim Earnings (Per Share)

Qtr.	Mar	Jun	Sep	Dec
2013	0.26	0.73	2.04	0.56
2014	0.68	1.19	1.45	1.11
2015	1.12	1.79	2.14	1.51
2016	1.46			

Interim Dividends (Per Share)

Amt	Decl	Ex	Rec	Pay
0.20Q	08/04/2015	08/14/2015	08/18/2015	09/01/2015
0.20Q	11/04/2015	11/13/2015	11/17/2015	12/03/2015
0.275Q	01/21/2016	02/19/2016	02/23/2016	03/08/2016
0.275Q	05/13/2016	05/20/2016	05/24/2016	06/07/2016

Indicated Div: $1.10

Valuation Analysis

		Institutional Holding	
Forecast EPS	$7.33 (05/20/2016)	No of Institutions	594
Market Cap	$8.2 Billion	Shares	116,530,832
Book Value	$2.5 Billion	% Held	88.94
Price/Book	3.35		
Price/Sales	1.45		

Business Summary: Airlines/Air Freight (MIC: 7.4.4 SIC: 4512 NAIC: 481111)

Alaska Air Group is a holding company. Co. operates through Alaska Airlines, Inc. (Alaska), which operates a fleet of passenger jets (mainline) and contracts with Horizon Air Industries, Inc (Horizon), SkyWest Airlines, Inc. and Peninsula Airways, Inc. for regional capacity; and Horizon, which operates a fleet of turboprop aircraft and sells all of its capacity to Alaska pursuant to a capacity purchase arrangement. Co.'s mainline operations provides north/south service within the western U.S., Canada, Mexico, and Costa Rica, and passenger and cargo services within Alaska. Co.'s regional operations carried passengers, primarily in Washington, Oregon, Idaho and California.

Recent Developments: For the quarter ended Mar 31 2016, net income increased 23.5% to US$184.0 million from US$149.0 million in the year-earlier quarter. Revenues were US$1.35 billion, up 6.1% from US$1.27 billion the year before. Operating income was US$290.0 million versus US$238.0 million in the prior-year quarter, an increase of 21.8%. Direct operating expenses declined 9.1% to US$378.0 million from US$416.0 million in the comparable period the year before. Indirect operating expenses increased 10.4% to US$679.0 million from US$615.0 million in the equivalent prior-year period.

Prospects: Our evaluation of Alaska Air Group Inc. as of June 19, 2016 is the result of our systematic analysis on three basic characteristics: earnings strength, relative valuation, and recent stock price movement. The company has generated a negative trend in earnings per share over the past 5 quarters. However, while recent estimates for the company have been lowered by analysts, ALK has posted better than expected results. Based on operating earnings yield, the company is undervalued when compared to all of the companies in our coverage universe. Share price changes over the past year indicates that ALK will perform very well over the near term.

Financial Data

(US$ in Thousands)	3 Mos	12/31/2015	12/31/2014	12/31/2013	12/31/2012	12/31/2011	12/31/2010	12/31/2009
Earnings Per Share	6.90	6.56	4.42	3.58	2.20	1.67	1.71	0.84
Cash Flow Per Share	12.81	12.34	7.60	7.01	5.31	4.85	3.86	2.13
Tang Book Value Per Share	19.81	19.26	16.18	14.76	10.10	8.27	7.69	6.13
Dividends Per Share	0.875	0.800	0.500	0.200	...	...	...	...
Dividend Payout %	12.68	12.20	11.31	5.59	...	...	...	...
Income Statement								
Total Revenue	1,347,000	5,598,000	5,368,000	5,156,000	4,657,000	4,317,800	3,832,300	3,399,800
EBITDA	379,000	1,619,000	1,276,000	1,103,000	805,000	693,500	709,100	482,400
Depn & Amortn	88,000	320,000	294,000	270,000	264,000	246,900	230,500	219,200
Income Before Taxes	292,000	1,312,000	975,000	816,000	514,000	393,700	405,900	202,900
Income Taxes	108,000	464,000	370,000	308,000	198,000	149,200	154,800	81,300
Net Income	184,000	848,000	605,000	508,000	316,000	244,500	251,100	121,600
Average Shares	125,328	129,372	136,801	141,878	143,568	146,840	147,144	144,616
Balance Sheet								
Current Assets	1,923,000	1,663,000	1,756,000	1,762,000	1,737,000	1,595,500	1,662,000	1,634,300
Total Assets	6,829,000	6,533,000	6,181,000	5,838,000	5,505,000	5,195,000	5,016,600	4,985,000
Current Liabilities	2,069,000	1,806,000	1,671,000	1,580,000	1,501,000	1,509,600	1,424,700	1,258,300
Long-Term Obligations	531,000	571,000	686,000	754,000	871,000	1,099,000	1,313,000	1,699,200
Total Liabilities	4,374,000	4,122,000	4,054,000	3,809,000	4,084,000	4,021,800	3,911,200	4,112,900
Stockholders' Equity	2,455,000	2,411,000	2,127,000	2,029,000	1,421,000	1,173,200	1,105,400	872,100
Shares Outstanding	123,913	125,175	131,481	137,491	140,753	141,899	143,695	142,364
Statistical Record								
Return on Assets %	13.34	13.34	10.07	8.96	5.89	4.79	5.02	2.48
Return on Equity %	38.22	37.37	29.11	29.45	24.30	21.46	25.40	15.85
EBITDA Margin %	28.14	28.92	23.77	21.39	17.29	16.06	18.50	14.19
Net Margin %	13.66	15.15	11.27	9.85	6.79	5.66	6.55	3.58
Asset Turnover	0.86	0.88	0.89	0.91	0.87	0.85	0.77	0.69
Current Ratio	0.93	0.92	1.05	1.12	1.16	1.06	1.17	1.30
Debt to Equity	0.22	0.24	0.32	0.37	0.61	0.94	1.19	1.95
Price Range	86.33-60.65	86.33-58.77	59.77-36.59	39.09-21.55	22.46-16.10	19.13-12.83	14.77-7.84	9.04-3.48
P/E Ratio	12.51-8.79	13.16-8.96	13.52-8.28	10.92-6.02	10.21-7.32	11.45-7.68	8.63-4.58	10.76-4.15
Average Yield %	1.19	1.12	1.06	0.66	...	...	...	...

Address: 19300 International Boulevard, Seattle, WA 98188 **Telephone:** 206-392-5040	**Web Site:** www.alaskaair.com **Officers:** Bradley D. Tilden - Chairman, Chief Executive Officer Kyle B. Levine - Vice President, General Counsel	**Auditors:** KPMG LLP **Investor Contact:** 206-392-5260 **Transfer Agents:** Computershare Trust Company N.A., Providence, RI

ALBEMARLE CORP.

Exchange	Symbol	Price	52Wk Range	Yield	P/E	Div Achiever
NYS	ALB	$78.50 (5/31/2016)	80.09-41.78	1.55	16.99	21 Years

*7 Year Price Score 85.26 *NYSE Composite Index=100 *12 Month Price Score 125.19

Interim Earnings (Per Share)

Qtr.	Mar	Jun	Sep	Dec
2013	0.94	0.98	1.11	1.88
2014	0.71	0.28	0.93	(0.22)
2015	0.40	0.46	0.58	1.56
2016	2.02	...	...	...

Interim Dividends (Per Share)

Amt	Decl	Ex	Rec	Pay
0.29Q	07/09/2015	09/14/2015	09/16/2015	10/01/2015
0.29Q	10/05/2015	12/11/2015	12/15/2015	01/04/2016
0.305Q	02/26/2016	03/14/2016	03/16/2016	04/01/2016
0.305Q	05/10/2016	06/13/2016	06/15/2016	07/01/2016

Indicated Div: $1.22 (Div. Reinv. Plan)

Valuation Analysis

Forecast EPS $4.11 (05/20/2016)

Institutional Holding

No of Institutions 479

Market Cap	$8.8 Billion	Shares	114,505,152
Book Value	$3.5 Billion	% Held	
Price/Book	2.49		102.55
Price/Sales	2.43		

Business Summary: Specialty Chemicals (MIC: 8.3.2 SIC: 2821 NAIC: 325211)

Albemarle is a developer, manufacturer and marketer of chemicals across a range of end markets including the petroleum refining, consumer electronics, energy storage, construction, automotive, steel and aerospace, lubricants, pharmaceuticals, crop protection, household appliances, heating, ventilation, aluminum finishing, food safety and custom chemistry services. Co. has three segments: Performance Chemicals, which consist of lithium, performance catalyst solutions, and bromine; Refining Solutions, which consist of clean fuels technologies and heavy oil upgrading; and Chemetall® Surface Treatment, which is a supplier of applied surface treatments and services.

Recent Developments: For the quarter ended Mar 31 2016, net income increased 399.6% to US$235.5 million from US$47.1 million in the year-earlier quarter. Revenues were US$865.4 million, down 2.1% from US$884.4 million the year before. Operating income was US$274.8 million versus US$36.7 million in the prior-year quarter, an increase of 649.1%. Direct operating expenses declined 15.6% to US$528.0 million from US$625.9 million in the comparable period the year before. Indirect operating expenses decreased 71.8% to US$62.6 million from US$221.8 million in the equivalent prior-year period.

Prospects: Our evaluation of Albemarle Corp. as of June 19, 2016 is the result of our systematic analysis on three basic characteristics: earnings strength, relative valuation, and recent stock price movement. The company has enjoyed a very positive trend in earnings per share over the past 5 quarters and while recent estimates for the company have been raised by analysts, ALB has posted better than expected results. Based on operating earnings yield, the company is about fairly valued when compared to all of the companies in our coverage universe. Share price changes over the past year indicates that ALB will perform in line with the market over the near term.

Financial Data

(US$ in Thousands)	3 Mos	12/31/2015	12/31/2014	12/31/2013	12/31/2012	12/31/2011	12/31/2010	12/31/2009
Earnings Per Share	4.62	3.00	1.69	4.90	3.47	4.77	3.51	1.94
Cash Flow Per Share	4.34	3.24	6.26	5.16	5.47	5.38	3.63	3.92
Tang Book Value Per Share	N.M.	N.M.	13.74	15.68	16.45	13.37	11.02	8.33
Dividends Per Share	1.175	1.160	1.100	0.960	0.800	0.670	0.560	0.500
Dividend Payout %	25.43	38.67	65.09	19.59	23.05	14.05	15.95	25.77
Income Statement								
Total Revenue	865,398	3,651,335	2,445,548	2,616,416	2,745,420	2,869,005	2,362,764	2,005,394
EBITDA	335,770	671,609	352,437	675,286	495,693	671,797	500,136	272,157
Depn & Amortn	60,552	180,700	97,900	99,300	88,300	83,600	82,500	87,300
Income Before Taxes	249,967	358,187	213,179	544,427	374,593	550,623	392,103	160,273
Income Taxes	30,985	29,122	18,484	136,322	82,533	130,014	92,719	(7,028)
Net Income	228,186	334,906	133,316	413,171	311,536	436,280	323,720	178,368
Average Shares	112,770	111,556	79,102	84,322	89,884	91,522	92,184	92,046
Balance Sheet								
Current Assets	1,615,391	1,831,003	3,348,850	1,482,915	1,407,313	1,355,620	1,348,198	1,032,087
Total Assets	9,438,968	9,615,014	5,223,103	3,584,797	3,437,291	3,203,824	3,068,081	2,771,557
Current Liabilities	1,225,098	1,616,685	1,139,886	436,363	385,009	401,178	364,177	353,264
Long-Term Obligations	3,105,351	3,174,674	2,223,035	1,054,310	686,588	749,257	851,927	776,403
Total Liabilities	5,898,663	6,360,622	3,863,638	1,957,436	1,603,693	1,612,547	1,652,007	1,565,861
Stockholders' Equity	3,540,305	3,254,392	1,359,465	1,627,361	1,833,598	1,591,277	1,416,074	1,205,696
Shares Outstanding	112,296	112,219	78,030	80,052	88,899	88,841	91,593	91,509
Statistical Record								
Return on Assets %	5.41	4.51	3.03	11.77	9.36	13.91	11.09	6.32
Return on Equity %	15.64	14.52	8.93	23.88	18.14	29.01	24.69	15.71
EBITDA Margin %	38.80	18.39	14.41	25.81	18.06	23.42	21.17	13.57
Net Margin %	26.37	9.17	5.45	15.79	11.35	15.21	13.70	8.89
Asset Turnover	0.38	0.49	0.56	0.75	0.82	0.91	0.81	0.71
Current Ratio	1.32	1.13	2.94	3.40	3.66	3.38	3.70	2.92
Debt to Equity	0.88	0.98	1.64	0.65	0.37	0.47	0.60	0.64
Price Range	64.38-41.78	64.38-41.78	72.62-53.16	69.55-57.75	67.70-51.56	71.11-39.00	56.73-34.86	37.27-15.81
P/E Ratio	13.94-9.04	21.46-13.93	42.97-31.46	14.19-11.79	19.51-14.86	14.91-8.18	16.16-9.93	19.21-8.15
Average Yield %	2.19	2.16	1.71	1.50	1.34	1.17	1.27	1.77

Address: 451 Florida Street, Baton Rouge, LA 70801
Telephone: 225-388-8011

Web Site: www.albemarle.com
Officers: Jim W. Nokes - Chairman William M Gottwald - Vice-Chairman

Auditors: PricewaterhouseCoopers LLP
Investor Contact: 225-388-8011
Transfer Agents: Wells Fargo Bank, N.A. Shareowner Services, St. Paul, MN

ALCOA, INC.

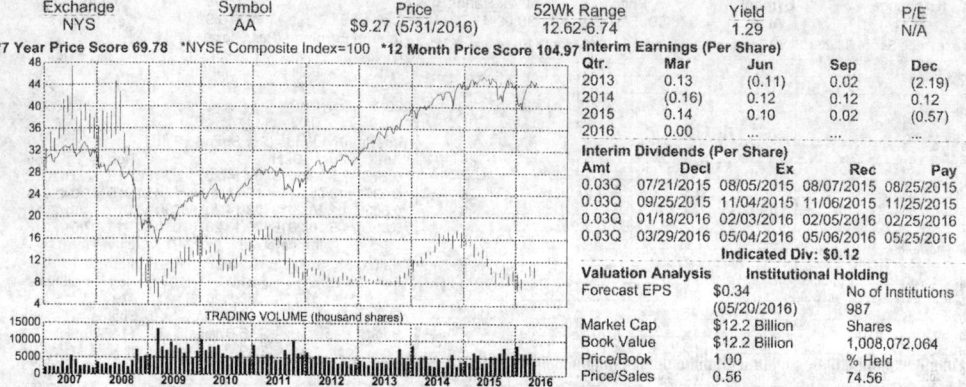

Exchange	Symbol	Price	52Wk Range	Yield	P/E
NYS	AA	$9.27 (5/31/2016)	12.62-6.74	1.29	N/A

*7 Year Price Score 69.78 *NYSE Composite Index=100 *12 Month Price Score 104.97

Interim Earnings (Per Share)

Qtr.	Mar	Jun	Sep	Dec
2013	0.13	(0.11)	0.02	(2.19)
2014	(0.16)	0.12	0.12	0.12
2015	0.14	0.10	0.02	(0.57)
2016	0.00	...	...	...

Interim Dividends (Per Share)

Amt	Decl	Ex	Rec	Pay
0.03Q	07/21/2015	08/05/2015	08/07/2015	08/25/2015
0.03Q	09/25/2015	11/04/2015	11/06/2015	11/25/2015
0.03Q	01/18/2016	02/03/2016	02/05/2016	02/25/2016
0.03Q	03/29/2016	05/04/2016	05/06/2016	05/25/2016

Indicated Div: $0.12

Valuation Analysis / **Institutional Holding**

Forecast EPS	$0.34 (05/20/2016)	No of Institutions 987
Market Cap	$12.2 Billion	Shares
Book Value	$12.2 Billion	1,008,072,064
Price/Book	1.00	% Held
Price/Sales	0.56	74.56

TRADING VOLUME (thousand shares)

Business Summary: Non-Precious Metals (MIC: 8.2.2 SIC: 3334 NAIC: 331312)

Alcoa is primarily a producer of aluminum products. Co.'s operations consist of five reportable segments: Alumina, which consists of its refinery system; Primary Metals, which consists of its smelter system; Global Rolled Products, which represents Co.'s midstream operations and produces aluminum sheet and plate for a variety of end markets; and Engineered Products and Solutions, which produces products that are used mostly in the aerospace, commercial transportation, and power generation end markets; as well as Transportation and Construction Solutions, which produces products that are used mostly in the nonresidential building and construction and commercial transportation end markets.

Recent Developments: For the quarter ended Mar 31 2016, net income decreased 95.7% to US$11.0 million from US$255.0 million in the year-earlier quarter. Revenues were US$4.95 billion, down 15.0% from US$5.82 billion the year before. Direct operating expenses declined 9.0% to US$4.04 billion from US$4.44 billion in the comparable period the year before. Indirect operating expenses decreased 8.4% to US$831.0 million from US$907.0 million in the equivalent prior-year period.

Prospects: Our evaluation of Alcoa Inc. as of June 19, 2016 is the result of our systematic analysis on three basic characteristics: earnings strength, relative valuation, and recent stock price movement. The company has enjoyed a very positive trend in earnings per share over the past 5 quarters. However, while recent estimates for the company have been mixed, AA has posted better than expected results. Based on operating earnings yield, the company is overvalued when compared to all of the companies in our coverage universe. Share price changes over the past year indicates that AA will perform poorly over the near term.

Financial Data

(US$ in Thousands)	3 Mos	12/31/2015	12/31/2014	12/31/2013	12/31/2012	12/31/2011	12/31/2010	12/31/2009
Earnings Per Share	(0.45)	(0.31)	0.21	(2.14)	0.18	0.55	0.24	(1.23)
Cash Flow Per Share	1.01	1.26	1.44	1.47	1.40	2.07	2.22	1.46
Tang Book Value Per Share	5.14	4.14	5.15	6.28	7.09	7.56	7.75	6.94
Dividends Per Share	0.120	0.120	0.120	0.120	0.120	0.120	0.120	0.260
Dividend Payout %	...	...	57.14	...	66.67	21.82	50.00	...
Income Statement								
Total Revenue	4,947,000	22,534,000	23,906,000	23,032,000	23,700,000	24,951,000	21,013,000	18,439,000
EBITDA	495,000	2,099,000	2,415,000	114,000	2,273,000	3,033,000	2,460,000	279,000
Depn & Amortn	309,000	1,280,000	1,372,000	1,422,000	1,462,000	1,481,000	1,451,000	1,311,000
Income Before Taxes	63,000	337,000	589,000	(1,748,000)	352,000	1,048,000	534,000	(1,484,000)
Income Taxes	30,000	445,000	320,000	428,000	162,000	255,000	148,000	(574,000)
Net Income	16,000	(322,000)	268,000	(2,285,000)	191,000	611,000	254,000	(1,151,000)
Average Shares	1,314,000	1,259,000	1,180,000	1,070,000	1,076,000	1,161,000	1,025,000	935,000
Balance Sheet								
Current Assets	7,665,000	7,953,000	8,269,000	6,969,000	7,700,000	7,713,000	6,869,000	7,022,000
Total Assets	36,140,000	36,528,000	37,399,000	35,742,000	40,179,000	40,120,000	39,293,000	38,472,000
Current Liabilities	5,555,000	5,211,000	5,541,000	6,105,000	5,942,000	6,013,000	5,236,000	5,414,000
Long-Term Obligations	8,257,000	9,044,000	8,769,000	7,607,000	8,311,000	8,640,000	8,842,000	8,974,000
Total Liabilities	23,914,000	24,482,000	25,093,000	25,149,000	26,980,000	26,276,000	25,682,000	26,012,000
Stockholders' Equity	12,226,000	12,046,000	12,306,000	10,593,000	13,199,000	13,844,000	13,611,000	12,460,000
Shares Outstanding	1,315,107	1,310,160	1,216,663	1,071,011	1,067,211	1,064,412	1,022,025	974,378
Statistical Record								
Return on Assets %	N.M.	N.M.	0.73	N.M.	0.47	1.54	0.65	N.M.
Return on Equity %	N.M.	N.M.	2.34	N.M.	1.41	4.45	1.95	N.M.
EBITDA Margin %	10.01	9.31	10.10	0.49	9.59	12.16	11.71	1.51
Net Margin %	0.32	N.M.	1.12	N.M.	0.81	2.45	1.21	N.M.
Asset Turnover	0.60	0.61	0.65	0.61	0.59	0.63	0.54	0.48
Current Ratio	1.38	1.53	1.49	1.14	1.30	1.28	1.31	1.30
Debt to Equity	0.68	0.75	0.71	0.72	0.63	0.62	0.65	0.72
Price Range	14.15-6.74	17.07-7.82	17.60-10.10	10.69-7.70	10.76-8.02	18.13-8.52	17.45-10.00	16.34-5.22
P/E Ratio	...	...	83.81-48.10	...	59.78-44.56	32.96-15.49	72.71-41.67	...
Average Yield %	1.19	1.03	0.83	1.40	1.31	0.86	0.94	2.40

Address: 390 Park Avenue, New York, NY 10022-4608
Telephone: 212-836-2732

Web Site: www.alcoa.com
Officers: Klaus Kleinfeld - Chairman, President, Chief Executive Officer, Chief Operating Officer
Olivier M. Jarrault - Executive Vice President, Division Officer

Auditors: PricewaterhouseCoopers LLP
Investor Contact: 212-836-2674
Transfer Agents: Computershares

ALERE INC.

Exchange	Symbol	Price	52Wk Range	Yield	P/E
NYS	ALR	$42.95 (5/31/2016)	55.39-35.47	N/A	12.22

*7 Year Price Score 117.12 *NYSE Composite Index=100 ***12 Month Price Score 90.33**

Interim Earnings (Per Share)

Qtr.	Mar	Jun	Sep	Dec
2012	(0.05)	(0.23)	(0.11)	(0.84)
2013	0.09	(0.81)	(0.30)	(0.10)
2014	(0.14)	(0.67)	(1.10)	1.77
2015	2.42	0.17	0.00	...

Interim Dividends (Per Share)

No Dividends Paid

Valuation Analysis | Institutional Holding

Forecast EPS	$2.19	No of Institutions
	(05/20/2016)	359
Market Cap	$3.7 Billion	Shares
Book Value	$2.1 Billion	89,056,912
Price/Book	1.76	% Held
Price/Sales	1.66	N/A

TRADING VOLUME (thousand shares)

Business Summary: Medical Instruments & Equipment (MIC: 4.3.1 SIC: 2835 NAIC: 325413)

Alere is a provider of point-of-care diagnostics and services. Co. operates in three segments: professional diagnostics, which includes a range of diagnostic test products and other in vitro diagnostic tests marketed to medical professionals and laboratories for detection of diseases and conditions; health information solutions, which provides services designed to provide physicians with actionable data that allow them to make decisions and deliver care; and consumer diagnostics, which consists primarily of manufacturing operations related to Co.'s role as a manufacturer of products for SPD Swiss Precision Diagnostics GmbH, its 50/50 joint venture with The Procter & Gamble Company.

Recent Developments: For the quarter ended Sep 30 2015, income from continuing operations was US$5.5 million compared with a loss of US$84.3 million in the year-earlier quarter. Net income amounted to US$5.5 million versus a net loss of US$98.7 million in the year-earlier quarter. Revenues were US$602.0 million, down 7.3% from US$649.2 million the year before. Operating income was US$29.2 million versus US$35.3 million in the prior-year quarter, a decrease of 17.5%. Direct operating expenses declined 5.9% to US$327.0 million from US$347.6 million in the comparable period the year before. Indirect operating expenses decreased 7.7% to US$245.9 million from US$266.3 million in the equivalent prior-year period.

Prospects: Our evaluation of Alere Inc. as of June 19, 2016 is the result of our systematic analysis on three basic characteristics: earnings strength, relative valuation, and recent stock price movement. The company has produced a positive trend in earnings per share over the past 5 quarters and while recent estimates for the company have remained steady, ALR has posted results that fell short of analysts expectations. Based on operating earnings yield, the company is about fairly valued when compared to all of the companies in our coverage universe. Share price changes over the past year indicates that ALR will perform in line with the market over the near term.

Financial Data

(US$ in Thousands)	9 Mos	6 Mos	3 Mos	12/31/2014	12/31/2013	12/31/2012	12/31/2011	12/31/2010
Earnings Per Share	4.36	3.26	2.42	(0.14)	(1.13)	(1.23)	(1.58)	(12.33)
Cash Flow Per Share	1.80	1.66	1.85	2.82	3.00	3.96	3.26	3.26
Income Statement								
Total Revenue	1,839,353	1,237,309	608,153	2,586,690	3,029,442	2,818,825	2,386,527	2,155,347
EBITDA	163,109	128,691	29,484	186,600	242,524	228,789	121,624	(860,651)
Depn & Amortn	10,627	7,784	3,946	98,300	120,900	109,700	83,700	67,700
Income Before Taxes	(2,114)	16,309	(20,294)	(118,500)	(134,032)	(121,471)	(166,047)	(1,067,786)
Income Taxes	(10,009)	8,915	(8,786)	66,722	(46,311)	(30,319)	(24,214)	(29,931)
Net Income	234,606	229,044	209,140	9,918	(71,254)	(78,182)	(133,542)	(1,017,310)
Average Shares	87,169	86,635	84,338	82,938	81,542	80,587	83,128	84,445
Balance Sheet								
Current Assets	1,886,710	1,938,283	1,439,248	1,832,793	1,472,414	1,406,737	1,293,727	1,194,257
Total Assets	6,574,165	6,651,394	6,148,371	6,718,041	7,060,814	7,067,928	6,672,701	6,330,374
Current Liabilities	1,126,015	1,138,012	661,243	743,784	673,186	648,809	624,452	782,858
Long-Term Obligations	2,993,928	2,964,949	3,031,594	3,631,945	3,787,195	3,641,592	3,280,080	2,379,968
Total Liabilities	4,476,729	4,492,812	4,081,024	4,760,074	4,982,848	4,887,506	4,443,467	3,755,336
Stockholders' Equity	2,097,436	2,158,582	2,067,347	1,957,967	2,077,966	2,180,422	2,229,234	2,575,038
Shares Outstanding	86,189	85,545	84,882	83,853	81,987	80,897	79,968	84,928
Statistical Record								
Return on Assets %	5.78	4.32	3.42	0.14	N.M.	N.M.	N.M.	N.M.
Return on Equity %	19.40	13.97	10.88	0.49	N.M.	N.M.	N.M.	N.M.
EBITDA Margin %	8.87	10.40	4.85	7.21	8.01	8.12	5.10	N.M.
Net Margin %	12.75	18.51	34.39	0.38	N.M.	N.M.	N.M.	N.M.
Asset Turnover	0.33	0.35	0.38	0.38	0.43	0.41	0.37	0.32
Current Ratio	1.68	1.70	2.18	2.46	2.19	2.17	2.07	1.53
Debt to Equity	1.43	1.37	1.47	1.85	1.82	1.67	1.47	0.92
Price Range	55.39-36.31	52.75-34.26	49.06-32.86	41.14-32.86	36.58-18.50	26.01-17.40	41.00-18.51	44.85-25.80
P/E Ratio	12.70-8.33	16.18-10.51	20.27-13.58	...	...	...	...	...

Address: 51 Sawyer Road, Suite 200, Waltham, MA 02453	**Web Site:** www.alere.com	**Auditors:** PricewaterhouseCoopers, LLP
Telephone: 781-647-3900	**Officers:** Namal Nawana - President, Chief Operating Officer, Interim Chief Executive Officer, Chief Executive Officer James F. Hinrichs - Executive Vice President, Chief Financial Officer	**Transfer Agents:** Computershare, Providence, RI
Fax: 781-647-3939		

23

ALEXANDER & BALDWIN INC.

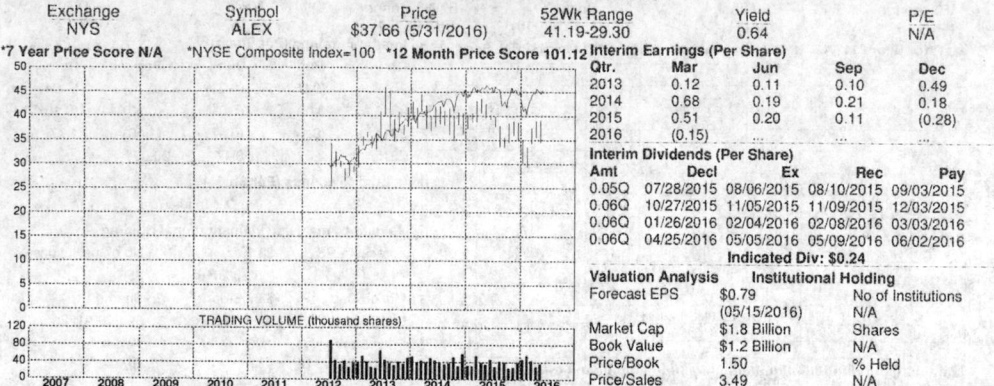

Exchange	Symbol	Price	52Wk Range	Yield	P/E
NYS	ALEX	$37.66 (5/31/2016)	41.19-29.30	0.64	N/A

*7 Year Price Score N/A *NYSE Composite Index=100 *12 Month Price Score 101.12

Interim Earnings (Per Share)

Qtr.	Mar	Jun	Sep	Dec
2013	0.12	0.11	0.10	0.49
2014	0.68	0.19	0.21	0.18
2015	0.51	0.20	0.11	(0.28)
2016	(0.15)	...	...	...

Interim Dividends (Per Share)

Amt	Decl	Ex	Rec	Pay
0.05Q	07/28/2015	08/06/2015	08/10/2015	09/03/2015
0.06Q	10/27/2015	11/05/2015	11/09/2015	12/03/2015
0.06Q	01/26/2016	02/04/2016	02/08/2016	03/03/2016
0.06Q	04/25/2016	05/05/2016	05/09/2016	06/02/2016

Indicated Div: $0.24

Valuation Analysis | **Institutional Holding**

Forecast EPS	$0.79 (05/15/2016)	No of Institutions	N/A
Market Cap	$1.8 Billion	Shares	N/A
Book Value	$1.2 Billion	% Held	N/A
Price/Book	1.50		
Price/Sales	3.49		

Business Summary: Property, Real Estate & Development (MIC: 5.3.2 SIC: 6531 NAIC: 531390)

Alexander & Baldwin is a Hawaii company with interests in real estate development, real estate leasing, materials and construction, and agribusiness. Co. operates in four segments: Real Estate Development and Sales, which engages in land stewardship, planning, entitlement, development, real estate investment and sale of land and commercial and residential properties; Real Estate Leasing, which owns, operates, and manages a portfolio of retail, office and industrial properties in Hawaii and on the Mainland; Materials and Construction, which performs asphalt paving as prime contractor and subcontractor; and Agribusiness, which produces bulk raw sugar, food grade sugars, and molasses.

Recent Developments: For the quarter ended Mar 31 2016, net loss amounted to US$7.0 million versus net income of US$25.9 million in the year-earlier quarter. Revenues were US$108.8 million, down 27.8% from US$150.7 million the year before. Revenues from property income fell 45.9% to US$35.1 million from US$64.9 million in the corresponding quarter a year earlier.

Prospects: Our evaluation of Alexander & Baldwin Inc. as of June 19, 2016 is the result of our systematic analysis on three basic characteristics: earnings strength, relative valuation, and recent stock price movement. The company has suffered a very negative trend in earnings per share over the past 5 quarters. However, while recent estimates for the company have been mixed, ALEX has posted results that fell short of analysts expectations. Based on operating earnings yield, the company is overvalued when compared to all of the companies in our coverage universe. Share price changes over the past year indicates that ALEX will perform in line with the market over the near term.

Financial Data

(US$ in Thousands)	3 Mos	12/31/2015	12/31/2014	12/31/2013	12/31/2012	12/31/2011	12/31/2010	12/31/2009
Earnings Per Share	(0.12)	0.54	1.25	0.82	0.48	0.56	...	...
Cash Flow Per Share	2.19	2.63	0.80	(0.86)	0.26	0.25	...	...
Tang Book Value Per Share	21.75	22.06	21.26	20.42	21.31	...	...	...
Dividends Per Share	0.220	0.210	0.170	0.040	...	...	...	...
Dividend Payout %	...	38.89	13.60	4.88	...	...	...	...
Income Statement								
Total Revenue	108,800	570,500	560,000	365,200	296,700	268,700	263,000	190,800
EBITDA	(3,100)	117,000	106,700	81,700	66,400	67,200	46,200	8,300
Depn & Amortn	...	43,800	55,000	41,700	35,100	34,800	35,200	34,800
Income Before Taxes	(9,700)	47,600	28,800	23,600	16,500	15,600	(3,600)	(42,900)
Income Taxes	(2,700)	16,500	(1,400)	8,500	(1,200)	6,800	(2,200)	(18,100)
Net Income	(7,500)	29,600	61,400	36,900	20,500	23,500	33,100	10,900
Average Shares	48,900	49,300	49,300	45,100	42,900	42,100	...	...
Balance Sheet								
Current Assets	157,900	152,500	175,900	171,400	63,400	68,800	70,300	...
Total Assets	2,319,000	2,243,500	2,329,900	2,285,200	1,437,300	1,386,600	1,341,500	...
Current Liabilities	186,200	184,700	183,000	218,200	69,600	90,000	175,600	...
Long-Term Obligations	591,800	497,800	631,500	605,500	220,000	327,200	249,600	...
Total Liabilities	1,091,100	1,008,300	1,126,000	1,119,300	522,900	660,800	652,900	...
Stockholders' Equity	1,227,900	1,235,200	1,203,900	1,165,900	914,400	725,800	688,600	...
Shares Outstanding	48,982	48,900	48,800	48,600	42,900	...	...	...
Statistical Record								
Return on Assets %	N.M.	1.29	2.66	1.98	...	1.72	...	...
Return on Equity %	N.M.	2.43	5.18	3.55	...	3.32	...	...
EBITDA Margin %	N.M.	20.51	19.05	22.37	22.38	25.01	17.57	4.35
Net Margin %	N.M.	5.19	10.96	10.10	6.91	8.75	12.59	5.71
Asset Turnover	0.23	0.25	0.24	0.20	...	0.20	...	...
Current Ratio	0.85	0.83	0.96	0.79	0.91	0.76	0.40	...
Debt to Equity	0.48	0.40	0.52	0.52	0.24	0.45	0.36	...
Price Range	43.52-29.30	43.52-33.34	44.56-34.74	45.92-29.21	34.25-25.30	...	...	...
P/E Ratio	...	80.59-61.74	35.65-27.79	56.00-35.62	71.35-52.71	...	...	...
Average Yield %	0.60	0.55	0.43	0.11	...	...	...	...

Address: 822 Bishop Street, Honolulu, HI 96813 **Telephone:** 808-525-6611	**Web Site:** www.alexanderbaldwin.com **Officers:** Stanley M. Kuriyama - Chairman, President, Chief Executive Officer Christopher J. Benjamin - President, Chief Executive Officer, Chief Operating Officer	**Auditors:** Deloitte & Touche LLP **Transfer Agents:** Computershare Shareowner Services LLC

ALEXANDRIA REAL ESTATE EQUITIES, INC.

Exchange	Symbol	Price	52Wk Range	Yield	P/E
NYS	ARE	$96.90 (5/31/2016)	98.26-71.65	3.30	72.31

*7 Year Price Score 102.63 *NYSE Composite Index=100 *12 Month Price Score 104.81

TRADING VOLUME (thousand shares)

Interim Earnings (Per Share)

Qtr.	Mar	Jun	Sep	Dec
2013	0.36	0.38	0.35	0.52
2014	0.46	0.39	0.39	(0.23)
2015	0.25	0.44	0.46	0.49
2016	(0.05)	...	...	...

Interim Dividends (Per Share)

Amt	Decl	Ex	Rec	Pay
0.77Q	09/14/2015	09/28/2015	09/30/2015	10/15/2015
0.77Q	12/08/2015	12/29/2015	12/31/2015	01/15/2016
0.80Q	03/07/2016	03/29/2016	03/31/2016	04/15/2016
0.80Q	06/06/2016	06/28/2016	06/30/2016	07/15/2016

Indicated Div: $3.20

Valuation Analysis / Institutional Holding

Forecast EPS	$1.37	No of Institutions
	(05/20/2016)	410
Market Cap	$7.1 Billion	Shares
Book Value	$3.9 Billion	78,383,064
Price/Book	1.83	% Held
Price/Sales	8.18	96.52

Business Summary: REITs (MIC: 5.3.1 SIC: 6798 NAIC: 525930)

Alexandria Real Estate Equities is a self-administered, and self-managed urban office real estate investment trust focused on collaborative science and technology campuses. Co.'s tenants include multinational pharmaceutical companies, public and private biotechnology, life science product and service, medical device, digital health, and technology companies; academic and medical research institutions; U.S. government research agencies; non-profits; and venture capital firms. Co.'s properties are primarily located in the following markets: Greater Boston, San Francisco, New York City, San Diego, Seattle, Maryland, and Research Triangle Park.

Recent Developments: For the quarter ended Mar 31 2016, income from continuing operations decreased 60.2% to US$10.0 million from US$25.1 million in the year-earlier quarter. Net income decreased 60.1% to US$10.0 million from US$25.0 million in the year-earlier quarter. Revenues were US$216.1 million, up 9.8% from US$196.8 million the year before. Revenues from property income rose 9.8% to US$210.9 million from US$192.0 million in the corresponding quarter a year earlier.

Prospects: Our evaluation of Alexandria Real Estate Equities Inc. as of June 19, 2016 is the result of our systematic analysis on three basic characteristics: earnings strength, relative valuation, and recent stock price movement. The company has generated a negative trend in earnings per share over the past 5 quarters. Because the company lacks sufficient analyst estimate data, we place greater weight on the historical EPS trend as the measure of earnings strength. Based on operating earnings yield, the company is overvalued when compared to all of the companies in our coverage universe. Share price changes over the past year indicates that ARE will perform in line with the market over the near term.

Financial Data

(US$ in Thousands)	3 Mos	12/31/2015	12/31/2014	12/31/2013	12/31/2012	12/31/2011	12/31/2010	12/31/2009
Earnings Per Share	1.34	1.63	1.01	1.60	1.09	1.73	2.19	2.72
Cash Flow Per Share	4.65	4.79	4.70	4.60	4.90	4.18	4.53	5.34
Tang Book Value Per Share	48.33	49.73	48.43	49.69	48.41	48.65	46.38	44.33
Dividends Per Share	3.110	3.050	2.880	2.610	2.090	1.860	1.500	1.850
Dividend Payout %	232.09	187.12	285.15	163.13	191.74	107.51	68.49	68.01
Income Statement								
Total Revenue	216,089	843,474	726,877	631,151	586,073	573,443	487,303	480,140
EBITDA	36,918	516,121	410,164	400,404	369,778	361,455	285,591	345,507
Depn & Amortn	1,700	265,802	232,277	197,927	199,148	161,813	136,663	127,806
Income Before Taxes	10,363	144,506	98,588	134,525	101,446	136,235	79,286	136,430
Net Income	5,936	144,217	106,778	140,249	105,528	135,393	139,022	141,648
Average Shares	72,584	71,528	71,169	68,038	62,160	59,077	48,405	38,600
Balance Sheet								
Current Assets	171,061	164,455	123,443	95,323	189,367	109,351	125,078	121,821
Total Assets	8,971,532	8,911,120	8,136,036	7,529,764	7,150,116	6,574,129	5,905,861	5,457,227
Current Liabilities	692,742	651,361	547,899	489,762	465,109	361,972	335,371	304,202
Long-Term Obligations	4,091,499	3,965,795	3,678,579	3,061,061	3,181,949	2,779,264	2,584,162	2,746,946
Total Liabilities	5,105,812	4,936,033	4,307,597	3,612,975	3,708,265	3,199,828	2,977,036	3,133,819
Stockholders' Equity	3,865,720	3,975,087	3,828,439	3,916,789	3,441,851	3,374,301	2,928,825	2,323,408
Shares Outstanding	72,873	72,548	71,463	71,172	63,244	61,560	54,966	43,846
Statistical Record								
Return on Assets %	1.46	1.69	1.36	1.91	1.53	2.17	2.45	2.68
Return on Equity %	3.32	3.70	2.76	3.81	3.09	4.30	5.29	7.09
EBITDA Margin %	17.08	61.19	56.43	63.44	63.09	63.03	58.61	71.96
Net Margin %	2.75	17.10	14.69	22.22	18.01	23.61	28.53	29.50
Asset Turnover	0.10	0.10	0.09	0.09	0.09	0.09	0.09	0.09
Current Ratio	0.25	0.25	0.23	0.19	0.41	0.30	0.37	0.40
Debt to Equity	1.06	1.00	0.96	0.78	0.92	0.82	0.88	1.18
Price Range	98.04-71.65	102.42-83.40	90.19-63.62	78.09-61.02	76.65-64.75	84.93-57.19	75.07-56.89	66.98-30.71
P/E Ratio	73.16-53.47	62.83-51.17	89.30-62.99	48.81-38.14	70.32-59.40	49.09-33.06	34.28-25.98	24.63-11.29
Average Yield %	3.50	3.30	3.75	3.83	2.91	2.53	2.20	3.90

Address: 385 East Colorado Boulevard, Suite 299, Pasadena, CA 91101 Telephone: 626-578-0777	Web Site: www.are.com Officers: Joel S. Marcus - Chairman, President, Chief Executive Officer Dean A. Shigenaga - Senior Vice President, Chief Financial Officer, Treasurer	Auditors: Ernst & Young LLP Investor Contact: 626-396-4828 Transfer Agents: American Stock Transfer & Trust Company, LLC, Brooklyn, NY

ALLEGHANY CORP.

Exchange	Symbol	Price	52Wk Range	Yield	P/E
NYS	Y	$544.83 (5/31/2016)	544.83-450.94	N/A	14.62

*7 Year Price Score 113.40 *NYSE Composite Index=100 *12 Month Price Score 104.75

TRADING VOLUME (thousand shares)

Interim Earnings (Per Share)

Qtr.	Mar	Jun	Sep	Dec
2013	11.67	6.78	6.75	12.24
2014	12.28	9.06	11.40	8.66
2015	7.82	11.40	6.07	9.83
2016	9.96			

Interim Dividends (Per Share)

Amt	Decl	Ex	Rec	Pay
2%	02/26/2010	03/30/2010	04/01/2010	04/23/2010
2%	02/25/2011	03/30/2011	04/01/2011	04/29/2011

Valuation Analysis

	Institutional Holding	
Forecast EPS $29.60 (05/15/2016)	No of Institutions	428
Market Cap $8.4 Billion	Shares	
Book Value $7.8 Billion		16,865,138
Price/Book 1.08	% Held	
Price/Sales 1.58		79.00

Business Summary: General Insurance (MIC: 5.2.1 SIC: 6331 NAIC: 524127)

Alleghany is an insurance holding company. Co. is engaged in the property and casualty reinsurance and insurance operations. Co. manages, sources, executes and monitors its private capital investments through its subsidiary, Alleghany Capital Corporation. Co.'s private capital investments include: Stranded Oil Resources Corporation; Bourn & Koch, Inc.; R.C. Tway Company, LLC; IPS-Integrated Project Services, LLC; an approximately 40% equity interest in ORX Exploration, Inc.; and a 30% equity interest in Jazwares, LLC. Co. has two segments: reinsurance, which consists of property and casualty reinsurance operations; and insurance, which consists of property and casualty insurance operations.

Recent Developments: For the quarter ended Mar 31 2016, net income increased 23.3% to US$154.7 million from US$125.4 million in the year-earlier quarter. Revenues were US$1.48 billion, up 27.8% from US$1.16 billion the year before. Net premiums earned were US$1.22 billion versus US$1.02 billion in the prior-year quarter, an increase of 20.1%. Net investment income fell 7.5% to US$104.9 million from US$113.4 million a year ago.

Prospects: Our evaluation of Alleghany Corp. as of June 19, 2016 is the result of our systematic analysis on three basic characteristics: earnings strength, relative valuation, and recent stock price movement. The company has managed to produce a neutral trend in earnings per share over the past 5 quarters and while recent estimates for the company have remained steady, Y has posted better than expected results. Based on operating earnings yield, the company is undervalued when compared to all of the companies in our coverage universe. Share price changes over the past year indicates that Y will perform well over the near term.

Financial Data

(US$ in Thousands)	3 Mos	12/31/2015	12/31/2014	12/31/2013	12/31/2012	12/31/2011	12/31/2010	12/31/2009
Earnings Per Share	37.26	35.13	41.40	37.44	45.48	16.20	21.85	28.51
Cash Flow Per Share	9.59	20.54	22.72	34.78	32.02	10.63	6.70	15.84
Tang Book Value Per Share	480.71	463.26	450.23	399.42	366.57	325.87	309.39	278.99
Income Statement								
Premium Income	1,221,565	4,230,286	4,410,647	4,239,216	3,733,005	747,639	768,134	845,015
Total Revenue	1,478,950	4,999,478	5,231,809	4,971,654	4,753,212	981,837	985,352	1,184,392
Benefits & Claims	664,644	2,339,790	2,494,565	2,479,353	2,630,170	429,986	377,937	442,104
Income Before Taxes	212,321	757,368	931,909	855,236	719,276	190,837	277,371	395,380
Income Taxes	57,668	195,173	251,777	225,882	17,032	47,586	78,869	124,381
Net Income	154,505	560,315	679,239	628,421	702,244	143,251	198,502	270,999
Average Shares	15,464	15,879	16,405	16,786	15,441	8,811	9,081	9,518
Balance Sheet								
Total Assets	23,055,343	22,846,333	23,489,436	23,361,088	22,807,967	6,478,089	6,431,699	6,192,770
Total Liabilities	15,283,607	15,291,626	16,016,008	16,437,331	16,404,180	3,552,412	3,522,831	3,475,249
Stockholders' Equity	7,771,736	7,554,707	7,473,428	6,923,757	6,403,787	2,925,677	2,908,868	2,717,521
Shares Outstanding	15,437	15,544	16,054	16,766	16,890	8,551	8,941	9,218
Statistical Record								
Return on Assets %	2.53	2.42	2.90	2.72	4.78	2.22	3.14	4.38
Return on Equity %	7.66	7.46	9.44	9.43	15.01	4.91	7.06	10.10
Loss Ratio %	54.41	55.31	56.56	58.49	70.46	57.51	49.20	52.32
Net Margin %	10.45	11.21	12.98	12.64	14.77	14.59	20.15	22.88
Price Range	515.25-450.94	515.25-440.61	482.00-363.60	417.39-335.42	355.46-284.25	338.90-277.26	304.90-248.75	287.82-214.73
P/E Ratio	13.83-12.10	14.67-12.54	11.64-8.78	11.15-8.96	7.82-6.25	20.92-17.11	13.95-11.38	10.10-7.53

Address: 7 Times Square Tower, 17th Floor, New York, NY 10036 **Telephone:** 212-752 1356	**Web Site:** www.alleghany.com **Officers:** John J. Burns - Chairman Weston M. Hicks - President, Chief Executive Officer	**Auditors:** Ernst & Young LLP **Transfer Agents:** Computershare Trust Company, N.A., Providence, RI

ALLEGHENY TECHNOLOGIES, INC

Exchange	Symbol	Price	52Wk Range	Yield	P/E
NYS	ATI	$12.38 (5/31/2016)	33.29-7.62	2.58	N/A

*7 Year Price Score 38.76   *NYSE Composite Index=100   *12 Month Price Score 87.97

Interim Earnings (Per Share)

Qtr.	Mar	Jun	Sep	Dec
2013	0.09	0.04	(0.32)	1.62
2014	(0.19)	(0.03)	(0.01)	0.20
2015	0.09	(0.15)	(1.35)	(2.12)
2016	(0.94)	...	...	...

Interim Dividends (Per Share)

Amt	Decl	Ex	Rec	Pay
0.18Q	07/30/2015	08/17/2015	08/19/2015	09/16/2015
0.08Q	12/10/2015	12/17/2015	12/21/2015	12/30/2015
0.08Q	02/26/2016	03/09/2016	03/11/2016	03/24/2016
0.08Q	05/06/2016	05/25/2016	05/27/2016	06/09/2016

Indicated Div: $0.32

Valuation Analysis

		Institutional Holding	
Forecast EPS	$-0.95 (05/15/2016)	No of Institutions	403
Market Cap	$1.3 Billion	Shares	106,710,288
Book Value	$2.0 Billion	% Held	79.34
Price/Book	0.68		
Price/Sales	0.40		

Business Summary: Non-Precious Metals (MIC: 8.2.2 SIC: 3317 NAIC: 331210)

Allegheny Technologies is a materials and components producer. Co. operates two segments: High Performance Materials and Components, which produces, converts and distributes materials, including titanium and titanium-based alloys, nickel- and cobalt-based alloys and superalloys, zirconium and related alloys such as hafnium and niobium, powder alloys and other specialty materials; and Flat Rolled Products, which produces, converts and distributes stainless steel, nickel-based alloys, specialty alloys, and titanium and titanium-based alloys, in a range of product forms including plate, sheet, engineered strip, and Precision Rolled Strip® products, as well as grain-oriented electrical steel.

Recent Developments: For the quarter ended Mar 31 2016, net loss amounted to US$98.1 million versus net income of US$12.6 million in the year-earlier quarter. Revenues were US$757.5 million, down 32.7% from US$1.13 billion the year before. Operating loss was US$104.8 million versus an income of US$46.4 million in the prior-year quarter. Direct operating expenses declined 22.2% to US$790.7 million from US$1.02 billion in the comparable period the year before. Indirect operating expenses increased 13.5% to US$71.6 million from US$63.1 million in the equivalent prior-year period.

Prospects: Our evaluation of Allegheny Technologies Inc. as of June 19, 2016 is the result of our systematic analysis on three basic characteristics: earnings strength, relative valuation, and recent stock price movement. The company has generated a negative trend in earnings per share over the past 5 quarters. Because the company lacks sufficient analyst estimate data, we place greater weight on the historical EPS trend as the measure of earnings strength. Based on operating earnings yield, the company is overvalued when compared to all of the companies in our coverage universe. Share price changes over the past year indicates that ATI will perform in line with the market over the near term.

Financial Data

(US$ in Thousands)	3 Mos	12/31/2015	12/31/2014	12/31/2013	12/31/2012	12/31/2011	12/31/2010	12/31/2009
Earnings Per Share	(4.56)	(3.53)	(0.03)	1.44	1.43	1.97	0.72	0.32
Cash Flow Per Share	0.54	1.22	0.52	3.45	4.02	2.90	0.28	2.25
Tang Book Value Per Share	12.36	13.11	16.72	20.06	16.20	16.34	18.61	18.40
Dividends Per Share	0.520	0.620	0.720	0.720	0.720	0.720	0.720	0.720
Dividend Payout %	...	...	...	50.00	50.35	36.55	100.00	225.00
Income Statement								
Total Revenue	757,500	3,719,600	4,223,400	4,043,500	5,031,500	5,183,000	4,047,800	3,054,900
EBITDA	(59,900)	(177,900)	286,800	91,000	509,600	606,100	329,900	216,800
Depn & Amortn	44,100	189,900	176,600	180,600	194,000	174,400	141,500	132,600
Income Before Taxes	(132,300)	(478,000)	1,500	(154,800)	244,000	339,400	125,700	64,900
Income Taxes	(34,200)	(112,100)	(8,700)	(63,600)	76,200	116,300	47,000	26,900
Net Income	(101,200)	(377,900)	(2,600)	154,000	158,400	214,300	70,700	31,700
Average Shares	107,300	107,300	107,100	106,800	116,600	113,900	98,720	98,130
Balance Sheet								
Current Assets	1,800,700	1,867,600	2,482,100	2,950,800	2,510,600	2,569,500	2,115,100	1,997,600
Total Assets	5,719,100	5,751,700	6,582,600	6,898,500	6,247,800	6,046,900	4,493,600	4,346,000
Current Liabilities	828,700	686,500	959,900	1,211,000	871,500	861,800	791,000	624,600
Long-Term Obligations	1,492,700	1,491,800	1,509,100	1,527,400	1,463,000	1,482,000	921,900	1,037,600
Total Liabilities	3,723,900	3,668,900	3,984,200	4,004,300	3,768,200	3,571,600	2,452,800	2,333,800
Stockholders' Equity	1,995,200	2,082,800	2,598,400	2,894,200	2,479,600	2,475,300	2,040,800	2,012,200
Shares Outstanding	108,916	109,174	108,710	107,983	107,398	106,354	98,542	98,070
Statistical Record								
Return on Assets %	N.M.	N.M.	N.M.	2.34	2.57	4.07	1.60	0.74
Return on Equity %	N.M.	N.M.	N.M.	5.73	6.38	9.49	3.49	1.60
EBITDA Margin %	N.M.	N.M.	6.79	2.25	10.13	11.69	8.15	7.10
Net Margin %	N.M.	N.M.	N.M.	3.81	3.15	4.13	1.75	1.04
Asset Turnover	0.55	0.60	0.63	0.62	0.82	0.98	0.92	0.72
Current Ratio	2.17	2.72	2.59	2.44	2.88	2.98	2.67	3.20
Debt to Equity	0.75	0.72	0.58	0.53	0.59	0.60	0.45	0.52
Price Range	37.45-7.62	37.45-10.46	46.23-29.86	35.64-26.00	51.62-25.61	72.74-32.78	58.97-39.73	45.73-17.49
P/E Ratio	...	...	...	24.75-18.06	36.10-17.91	36.92-16.64	81.90-55.18	142.91-54.66
Average Yield %	2.60	2.52	1.92	2.39	2.06	1.28	1.46	2.32

Address: 1000 Six PPG Place, Pittsburgh, PA 15222-5479 **Telephone:** 412-394 2800	**Web Site:** www.atimetals.com **Officers:** Richard J. Harshman - Chairman, President, Chief Executive Officer I. Patrick Hassey - Chairman, Outgoing Chief Executive Officer	**Auditors:** Ernst & Young LLP **Investor Contact:** 412-394-3004 **Transfer Agents:** Computershare

ALLERGAN PLC

Exchange	Symbol	Price	52Wk Range	Yield	P/E
NYS	AGN PRA	$235.75 (5/31/2016)	339.50-201.65	N/A	21.91

*7 Year Price Score 180.28 *NYSE Composite Index=100   *12 Month Price Score 80.15

Interim Earnings (Per Share)

Qtr.	Mar	Jun	Sep	Dec
2013	(0.79)	(4.27)	0.49	(0.70)
2014	0.55	0.28	(3.95)	(3.03)
2015	(1.85)	(0.80)	13.29	(2.20)
2016	0.47	...	...	...

Interim Dividends (Per Share)

No Dividends Paid

Valuation Analysis   **Institutional Holding**

Forecast EPS	N/A	No of Institutions
		1259
Market Cap	$93.2 Billion	Shares
Book Value	$77.5 Billion	346,698,080
Price/Book	1.20	% Held
Price/Sales	5.23	N/A

Business Summary: Pharmaceuticals (MIC: 4.1.1 SIC: 2834 NAIC: 325412)

Allergan is a pharmaceutical company engaged in the development, manufacturing, marketing, sale and distribution of brand name pharmaceutical products, medical aesthetics, biosimilar and over-the-counter pharmaceutical products. Co. has four segments: U.S. Brands, which provides branded products within the U.S., including Botox® therapies; U.S. Medical Aesthetics, which includes provides aesthetics and dermatology products within the U.S., including Botox® therapies; International Brands, which includes provides products sold outside of the U.S.; and Anda Distribution, which includes distribution of generic and branded pharmaceutical products manufactured by third parties, as well as by Co.

Recent Developments: For the quarter ended Mar 31 2016, loss from continuing operations was US$81.0 million compared with a loss of US$786.7 million in the year-earlier quarter. Net income amounted to US$256.4 million versus a net loss of US$512.3 million in the year-earlier quarter. Revenues were US$3.80 billion, up 48.1% from US$2.56 billion the year before. Operating loss was US$153.8 million versus a loss of US$677.7 million in the prior-year quarter. Direct operating expenses declined 20.4% to US$811.8 million from US$1.02 billion in the comparable period the year before. Indirect operating expenses increased 41.3% to US$3.14 billion from US$2.22 billion in the equivalent prior-year period.

Prospects: Our evaluation of Allergan PLC as of Aug. 2, 2015 is the result of our systematic analysis on three basic characteristics: earnings strength, relative valuation, and recent stock price movement. The company has managed to produce a neutral trend in earnings per share over the past 5 quarters. However, while recent estimates for the company have been lowered by analysts, AGN has posted better than expected results. Based on operating earnings yield, the company is about fairly valued when compared to all of the companies in our coverage universe. Share price changes over the past year indicates that AGN will perform in line with the market over the near term.

Financial Data

(US$ in Thousands)	3 Mos	12/31/2015	12/31/2014	12/31/2013	12/31/2012	12/31/2011	12/31/2010	12/31/2009
Earnings Per Share	10.76	10.01	(7.42)	(5.27)	0.76	2.06	1.48	1.96
Cash Flow Per Share	13.23	12.32	10.21	8.53	5.28	5.08	4.67	3.59
Tang Book Value Per Share	N.M.	N.M.	N.M.	N.M.	N.M.	1.90	0.97	N.M.
Income Statement								
Total Revenue	3,795,900	15,071,000	13,062,300	8,677,600	5,914,900	4,584,400	3,566,900	2,793,000
EBITDA	1,533,300	(3,119,700)	(1,078,300)	(207,400)	455,500	633,800	433,400	477,400
Depn & Amortn	1,686,600	128,600	230,900	202,000	97,500	93,600	101,900	96,400
Income Before Taxes	(483,000)	(4,430,200)	(1,712,100)	(644,400)	243,800	460,500	249,000	351,800
Income Taxes	(402,000)	(1,561,900)	(81,900)	112,700	146,800	196,900	67,300	140,600
Net Income	255,700	3,915,200	(1,630,500)	(750,400)	97,300	260,900	184,400	222,000
Average Shares	394,800	367,800	219,700	142,300	128,400	126,500	124,200	116,400
Balance Sheet								
Current Assets	10,091,500	8,615,400	6,881,700	4,434,700	3,879,700	2,569,700	1,799,400	1,771,000
Total Assets	136,073,700	135,840,700	52,529,100	22,725,900	14,103,500	6,698,300	5,827,300	5,992,200
Current Liabilities	10,195,500	8,328,300	5,018,600	3,294,900	2,710,600	1,839,500	820,700	1,052,400
Long-Term Obligations	38,551,800	40,293,400	14,846,300	8,517,400	6,257,100	665,300	849,700	999,000
Total Liabilities	58,623,700	59,249,300	24,198,000	13,193,800	10,269,700	3,134,700	2,545,600	2,969,100
Stockholders' Equity	77,450,000	76,591,400	28,331,100	9,532,100	3,833,800	3,563,600	3,281,700	3,023,100
Shares Outstanding	395,400	394,500	247,600	174,200	127,700	127,200	125,800	123,400
Statistical Record								
Return on Assets %	3.40	4.16	N.M.	N.M.	0.93	4.17	3.12	4.59
Return on Equity %	6.29	7.46	N.M.	N.M.	2.62	7.62	5.85	8.65
EBITDA Margin %	40.39	N.M.	N.M.	N.M.	7.70	13.83	12.15	17.09
Net Margin %	6.74	25.98	N.M.	N.M.	1.64	5.69	5.17	7.95
Asset Turnover	0.13	0.16	0.35	0.47	0.57	0.73	0.60	0.58
Current Ratio	0.99	1.03	1.37	1.35	1.43	1.40	2.19	1.68
Debt to Equity	0.50	0.53	0.52	0.89	1.63	0.19	0.26	0.33
Price Range	339.50-252.10	339.50-252.10	270.61-167.93	168.00-83.10	90.85-55.89	72.10-50.59	51.95-37.69	40.12-23.74
P/E Ratio	31.55-23.43	33.92-25.18	...	...	119.54-73.54	35.00-24.56	35.10-25.47	20.47-12.11

Address: Clonshaugh Business and Technology Park, Coolock, 07054 **Telephone:** 862-261-7000	**Web Site:** www.allergan.com **Officers:** Paul M. Bisaro - Chairman, President, Chief Executive Officer Brenton L. Saunders - President, Chief Executive Officer	**Auditors:** PricewaterhouseCoopers LLP **Investor Contact:** 862-261-7488 **Transfer Agents:** American Stock Transfer and Trust Company, New York, NY

ALLIANCE DATA SYSTEMS CORP.

Exchange	Symbol	Price	52Wk Range	Yield	P/E
NYS	ADS	$222.19 (5/31/2016)	305.50-177.12	N/A	25.02

*7 Year Price Score 131.13 *NYSE Composite Index=100 *12 Month Price Score 82.93

Interim Earnings (Per Share)

Qtr.	Mar	Jun	Sep	Dec
2013	1.92	1.71	2.01	1.79
2014	2.08	2.19	2.74	0.89
2015	2.32	2.11	2.08	2.34
2016	2.35	...	...	...

Interim Dividends (Per Share)

No Dividends Paid

Valuation Analysis   Institutional Holding

Forecast EPS	$16.75	No of Institutions
	(05/20/2016)	713
Market Cap	$13.1 Billion	Shares
Book Value	$1.7 Billion	66,266,912
Price/Book	7.53	% Held
Price/Sales	2.01	105.83

TRADING VOLUME (thousand shares)

Business Summary: Business Services (MIC: 7.5.2 SIC: 7389 NAIC: 522320)

Alliance Data Systems is a provider of data-driven marketing and loyalty solutions. Co. provides a portfolio of integrated outsourced marketing solutions, including customer loyalty programs, database marketing services, end-to-end marketing services, analytics and creative services, direct marketing services and private label and co-brand retail credit card programs. Co. focuses on facilitating and managing interactions between its clients and their customers through all consumer marketing channels, including in-store, online, email, social media, mobile, direct mail and telephone. Co.'s products and services are reported under three segments: LoyaltyOne®, Epsilon and Card Services.

Recent Developments: For the quarter ended Mar 31 2016, net income decreased 3.6% to US$158.9 million from US$164.8 million in the year-earlier quarter. Revenues were US$1.68 billion, up 4.7% from US$1.60 billion the year before. Operating income was US$344.3 million versus US$324.5 million in the prior-year quarter, an increase of 6.1%. Direct operating expenses rose 1.4% to US$1.00 billion from US$989.9 million in the comparable period the year before. Indirect operating expenses increased 14.4% to US$327.9 million from US$286.8 million in the equivalent prior-year period.

Prospects: Our evaluation of Alliance Data Systems Corp. as of June 19, 2016 is the result of our systematic analysis on three basic characteristics: earnings strength, relative valuation, and recent stock price movement. The company has produced a positive trend in earnings per share over the past 5 quarters and while recent estimates for the company have been raised by analysts, ADS has posted better than expected results. Based on operating earnings yield, the company is undervalued when compared to all of the companies in our coverage universe. Share price changes over the past year indicates that ADS will perform poorly over the near term.

Financial Data

(US$ in Thousands)	3 Mos	12/31/2015	12/31/2014	12/31/2013	12/31/2012	12/31/2011	12/31/2010	12/31/2009
Earnings Per Share	8.88	8.85	7.87	7.42	6.58	5.45	3.48	2.49
Cash Flow Per Share	29.91	27.57	23.84	20.40	22.62	19.95	17.18	6.43
Income Statement								
Total Revenue	1,676,100	6,439,746	5,302,940	4,319,063	3,641,390	3,173,287	2,791,421	1,964,341
EBITDA	352,700	1,698,049	1,368,994	1,284,440	1,114,038	940,206	747,140	512,747
Depn & Amortn	8,400	436,189	270,527	185,528	139,674	127,526	117,920	104,990
Income Before Taxes	245,500	931,676	837,941	793,412	682,904	514,095	310,890	262,946
Income Taxes	86,600	326,248	321,801	297,242	260,648	198,809	115,252	86,227
Net Income	157,100	605,428	516,140	496,170	422,256	315,286	193,737	143,734
Average Shares	60,200	62,301	62,445	66,866	64,143	57,804	55,710	57,706
Balance Sheet								
Current Assets	16,230,200	16,250,417	13,814,776	10,400,842	9,132,143	6,606,967	6,129,535	2,359,505
Total Assets	22,399,100	22,421,830	20,263,977	13,244,257	12,000,139	8,980,249	8,272,152	5,225,667
Current Liabilities	6,643,100	6,405,559	6,305,483	4,512,498	5,032,777	3,855,171	3,862,188	2,130,012
Long-Term Obligations	5,151,000	10,136,018	8,134,248	2,435,792	2,051,570	2,874,848	2,030,593	2,422,889
Total Liabilities	20,657,900	20,411,800	17,867,597	12,388,496	11,471,652	8,804,283	8,249,058	4,952,891
Stockholders' Equity	1,741,200	2,010,030	2,396,380	855,761	528,487	175,966	23,094	272,776
Shares Outstanding	59,000	60,877	63,812	51,550	49,603	49,830	51,371	52,199
Statistical Record								
Return on Assets %	2.88	2.84	3.08	3.93	4.01	3.65	2.87	3.00
Return on Equity %	32.69	27.48	31.74	71.69	119.55	316.77	130.96	43.11
EBITDA Margin %	21.04	26.37	25.82	29.74	30.59	29.63	26.77	26.10
Net Margin %	9.37	9.40	9.73	11.49	11.60	9.94	6.94	7.32
Asset Turnover	0.31	0.30	0.32	0.34	0.35	0.37	0.41	0.41
Current Ratio	2.44	2.54	2.19	2.30	1.81	1.71	1.59	1.11
Debt to Equity	2.96	5.04	3.39	2.85	3.88	16.34	87.93	8.88
Price Range		309.91-177.12	309.91-247.05	294.27-233.67	262.93-144.76	148.02-100.94	105.74-70.68	77.98-53.05	68.52-23.78
P/E Ratio		34.90-19.95	35.02-27.92	37.39-29.69	35.44-19.51	22.50-15.34	19.40-12.97	22.41-15.24	27.52-9.55

Address: 7500 Dallas Parkway, Suite 700, Plano, TX 75024
Telephone: 214-494-3000

Web Site: www.alliancedata.com
Officers: Edward J. Heffernan - President, Chief Executive Officer Bryan J. Kennedy - Executive Vice President, Division Officer

Auditors: Deloitte & Touche LLP
Investor Contact: 212-850-5721
Transfer Agents: ComputerShare Investor Services, Providence, RI

ALLIANT ENERGY CORP

Exchange	Symbol	Price	52Wk Range	Yield	P/E	Div Achiever
NYS	LNT	$37.05 (5/31/2016)	37.52-27.27	3.17	22.19	12 Years

*7 Year Price Score 114.35 *NYSE Composite Index=100 *12 Month Price Score 112.27

Interim Earnings (Per Share)

Qtr.	Mar	Jun	Sep	Dec
2013	0.32	0.29	0.71	0.29
2014	0.48	0.28	0.69	0.27
2015	0.44	0.30	0.80	0.15
2016	0.42	...	...	...

Interim Dividends (Per Share)

Amt	Decl	Ex	Rec	Pay
0.275Q	10/09/2015	10/28/2015	10/30/2015	11/13/2015
0.294Q	01/15/2016	01/27/2016	01/29/2016	02/12/2016
0.294Q	04/08/2016	04/27/2016	04/29/2016	05/13/2016
2-for-1	04/20/2016	05/20/2016	05/04/2016	05/19/2016

Indicated Div: $1.18 (Div. Reinv. Plan)

Valuation Analysis | **Institutional Holding**

Forecast EPS	$1.89 (05/10/2016)	No of Institutions 550
Market Cap	$8.4 Billion	Shares
Book Value	$3.8 Billion	82,752,744
Price/Book	2.24	% Held
Price/Sales	2.63	60.53

Business Summary: Electric Utilities (MIC: 3.1.1 SIC: 4931 NAIC: 221122)

Alliant Energy is a public utility holding company. Through its subsidiaries, Co. principally generates and distributes electricity and distributes and transports natural gas to retail customers in select markets in Iowa and Wisconsin, and sells electricity to wholesale customers in Wisconsin. As of Dec 31 2015, Co. provided regulated electric and natural gas service to approximately 950,000 electric and about 410,000 natural gas customers in the Midwest. Co.'s non-utility operations consist of its non-regulated generation, transportation, and other non-regulated investments including an interest in American Transmission Company LLC, a transmission-only utility operating in the Midwest.

Recent Developments: For the quarter ended Mar 31 2016, income from continuing operations increased 1.0% to US$100.2 million from US$99.2 million in the year-earlier quarter. Net income decreased 0.1% to US$99.1 million from US$99.2 million in the year-earlier quarter. Revenues were US$843.8 million, down 6.0% from US$897.4 million the year before. Operating income was US$145.9 million versus US$152.9 million in the prior-year quarter, a decrease of 4.6%. Direct operating expenses declined 7.9% to US$569.1 million from US$617.8 million in the comparable period the year before. Indirect operating expenses increased 1.7% to US$128.8 million from US$126.7 million in the equivalent prior-year period.

Prospects: Our evaluation of Alliant Energy Corp. as of June 19, 2016 is the result of our systematic analysis on three basic characteristics: earnings strength, relative valuation, and recent stock price movement. The company has generated a negative trend in earnings per share over the past 5 quarters and while recent estimates for the company have been mixed, LNT has posted better than expected results. Based on operating earnings yield, the company is about fairly valued when compared to all of the companies in our coverage universe. Share price changes over the past year indicates that LNT will perform well over the near term.

Financial Data

(US$ in Thousands)	3 Mos	12/31/2015	12/31/2014	12/31/2013	12/31/2012	12/31/2011	12/31/2010	12/31/2009
Earnings Per Share	1.67	1.68	1.73	1.62	1.45	1.37	1.30	0.51
Cash Flow Per Share	3.46	3.87	4.02	3.30	3.79	3.18	4.46	2.98
Tang Book Value Per Share	16.57	16.41	15.50	14.79	14.39	13.84	13.32	12.80
Dividends Per Share	2.237	2.200	2.040	1.880	1.800	1.700	1.580	1.500
Dividend Payout %	133.98	130.95	117.92	116.41	124.57	124.09	121.54	297.03
Income Statement								
Total Revenue	843,800	3,253,600	3,350,300	3,276,800	3,094,500	3,665,300	3,416,100	3,432,800
EBITDA	261,600	1,027,600	1,020,700	975,800	929,500	870,500	918,900	552,000
Depn & Amortn	102,500	413,700	442,300	411,100	387,900	380,100	344,100	317,700
Income Before Taxes	111,300	427,500	399,600	392,300	388,900	336,400	415,100	83,600
Income Taxes	21,600	70,400	44,300	53,900	89,400	55,100	145,200	(9,200)
Net Income	99,100	388,400	393,300	376,200	335,700	321,900	306,300	129,700
Average Shares	226,800	225,400	221,600	221,600	221,536	221,356	221,042	220,704
Balance Sheet								
Current Assets	768,500	826,800	1,043,100	1,011,200	994,300	866,500	1,092,700	1,377,300
Total Assets	12,535,000	12,495,200	12,085,900	11,112,400	10,785,500	9,687,900	9,282,900	9,036,000
Current Liabilities	1,348,500	1,359,300	1,214,700	1,433,300	1,020,000	855,000	866,700	1,074,100
Long-Term Obligations	3,522,700	3,522,200	3,606,700	2,977,800	3,136,600	2,703,100	2,703,400	2,404,500
Total Liabilities	8,770,400	8,771,100	8,647,200	7,831,000	7,590,600	6,614,900	6,329,300	6,203,400
Stockholders' Equity	3,764,600	3,724,100	3,438,700	3,281,400	3,194,900	3,073,000	2,953,600	2,832,600
Shares Outstanding	227,125	226,918	221,871	221,887	221,974	222,037	221,787	221,312
Statistical Record								
Return on Assets %	3.16	3.16	3.39	3.44	3.27	3.39	3.34	1.50
Return on Equity %	10.55	10.84	11.71	11.62	10.68	10.68	10.59	4.40
EBITDA Margin %	31.00	31.58	30.47	29.78	30.04	23.75	26.90	16.08
Net Margin %	11.74	11.94	11.74	11.48	10.85	8.78	8.97	3.78
Asset Turnover	0.26	0.26	0.29	0.30	0.30	0.39	0.37	0.40
Current Ratio	0.57	0.61	0.86	0.71	0.97	1.01	1.26	1.28
Debt to Equity	0.94	0.95	1.05	0.91	0.98	0.88	0.92	0.85
Price Range	37.14-27.27	35.16-27.27	34.66-25.25	26.97-21.95	23.75-21.05	22.16-17.15	18.82-15.13	15.60-10.23
P/E Ratio	22.24-16.33	20.93-16.24	20.03-14.59	16.65-13.55	16.38-14.52	16.18-12.52	14.47-11.64	30.58-20.06
Average Yield %	7.25	7.19	7.08	7.49	8.13	8.56	9.22	11.44

Address: 4902 N. Biltmore Lane, Madison, WI 53718 **Telephone:** 608-458-3311 **Fax:** 608-458-4824	**Web Site:** www.alliantenergy.com **Officers:** Patricia L. Kampling - President, Chief Executive Officer, Chief Operating Officer John O. Larsen - Senior Vice President	**Auditors:** Deloitte & Touche LLP **Investor Contact:** 608-458-3956 **Transfer Agents:** Wells Fargo Shareowner Services, Mendota Heights, MN

ALLIED WORLD ASSURANCE COMPANY HOLDINGS AG

Exchange	Symbol	Price	52Wk Range	Yield	P/E
NYS	AWH	$37.08 (5/31/2016)	44.84-30.75	2.80	103.00

*7 Year Price Score 117.34 *NYSE Composite Index=100 *12 Month Price Score 94.15

TRADING VOLUME (thousand shares)

Interim Earnings (Per Share)

Qtr.	Mar	Jun	Sep	Dec
2013	1.50	(0.02)	1.18	1.33
2014	1.74	1.52	0.31	1.32
2015	1.27	0.10	(0.57)	0.02
2016	0.81	...	...	...

Interim Dividends (Per Share)

Amt	Decl	Ex	Rec	Pay
0.26Q	09/08/2015	09/18/2015	09/22/2015	10/01/2015
0.26Q	11/30/2015	12/18/2015	12/22/2015	12/31/2015
0.26Q	03/03/2016	03/18/2016	03/22/2016	03/31/2016
0.26Q	06/08/2016	06/17/2016	06/21/2016	06/30/2016

Indicated Div: $1.04

Valuation Analysis

		Institutional Holding	
Forecast EPS	N/A	No of Institutions	306
Market Cap	$3.3 Billion	Shares	82,650,096
Book Value	$3.5 Billion	% Held	N/A
Price/Book	0.94		
Price/Sales	1.31		

Business Summary: General Insurance (MIC: 5.2.1 SIC: 6331 NAIC: 524126)

Allied World Assurance Company Holdings is a holding company. Co. is engaged in providing property and casualty insurance and reinsurance via operations in Australia, Bermuda, the U. S., Canada, Europe, Hong Kong, Labuan, and Singapore. Co. has three segments: North American Insurance, which provides specialty liability products, with a focus on coverages for healthcare and professional liability risks; Global Markets Insurance, which includes its direct insurance operations outside of North America; and Reinsurance, which includes the reinsurance of property, general casualty, professional liability, specialty lines and property catastrophe coverages written by other insurance companies.

Recent Developments: For the quarter ended Mar 31 2016, net income decreased 40.4% to US$74.1 million from US$124.4 million in the year-earlier quarter. Revenues were US$652.9 million, down 0.9% from US$659.0 million the year before. Net premiums earned were US$580.1 million versus US$568.5 million in the prior-year quarter, an increase of 2.0%. Net investment income rose 19.6% to US$53.3 million from US$44.6 million a year ago.

Prospects: Our evaluation of Allied World Assurance Company Holdings AG as of Mar. 20, 2016 is the result of our systematic analysis on three basic characteristics: earnings strength, relative valuation, and recent stock price movement. The company has suffered a very negative trend in earnings per share over the past 5 quarters and while recent estimates for the company have remained steady, AWH has posted results that fell short of analysts expectations. Based on operating earnings yield, the company is about fairly valued when compared to all of the companies in our coverage universe. Share price changes over the past year indicates that AWH will perform in line with the market over the near term.

Financial Data
(US$ in Thousands)

	3 Mos	12/31/2015	12/31/2014	12/31/2013	12/31/2012	12/31/2011	12/31/2010	12/31/2009
Earnings Per Share	0.36	0.89	4.92	3.98	4.43	2.31	4.44	3.89
Cash Flow Per Share	6.01	5.54	4.27	1.12	5.80	4.80	3.24	4.50
Tang Book Value Per Share	33.73	33.29	35.90	31.95	28.80	24.97	24.07	19.33
Dividends Per Share	1.040	1.005	0.842	0.625	0.500	0.375	0.350	0.247
Dividend Payout %	288.89	112.92	17.11	15.69	11.28	16.26	7.88	6.34
Income Statement								
Premium Income	580,100	2,488,400	2,182,758	2,005,833	1,748,898	1,456,992	1,359,548	1,316,892
Total Revenue	652,900	2,546,400	2,450,653	2,222,922	2,222,475	1,764,761	1,890,048	1,695,848
Benefits & Claims	372,400	1,586,300	1,199,190	1,123,242	1,139,264	959,156	707,883	604,060
Income Before Taxes	75,200	89,700	520,782	427,660	511,447	305,528	691,950	643,531
Income Taxes	1,100	5,800	30,523	9,780	18,440	30,980	26,945	36,644
Net Income	74,100	83,900	490,259	417,880	493,007	274,548	665,005	606,887
Average Shares	91,559	94,174	99,591	104,865	111,209	119,003	149,739	155,978
Balance Sheet								
Total Assets	13,728,000	13,511,900	12,421,563	11,945,830	12,029,946	11,122,158	10,427,631	9,653,153
Total Liabilities	10,192,600	9,979,400	8,643,272	8,426,004	8,703,611	7,973,136	7,351,811	6,439,858
Stockholders' Equity	3,535,400	3,532,500	3,778,291	3,519,826	3,326,335	3,149,022	3,075,820	3,213,295
Shares Outstanding	89,840	90,959	96,195	100,253	104,393	113,226	114,267	149,203
Statistical Record								
Return on Assets %	0.26	0.65	4.02	3.49	4.25	2.55	6.62	6.48
Return on Equity %	0.91	2.30	13.44	12.21	15.19	8.82	21.15	21.56
Loss Ratio %	64.20	63.75	54.94	56.00	65.14	65.83	52.07	45.87
Net Margin %	11.35	3.29	20.01	18.80	22.18	15.56	35.18	35.79
Price Range	44.84-30.75	44.84-35.10	39.47-32.31	37.63-26.27	27.54-20.33	21.67-16.51	20.39-13.84	16.25-11.00
P/E Ratio	124.56-85.42	50.38-39.44	8.02-6.57	9.46-6.60	6.22-4.59	9.38-7.15	4.59-3.12	4.18-2.83
Average Yield %	2.68	2.51	2.31	1.97	2.01	1.92	2.10	1.77

Address: Gubelstrasse 24, Park Tower, 15th Floor, Zug, 6300
Telephone: 417-681-080

Web Site: www.awac.com
Officers: Scott A. Carmilani - Chairman, President, Chief Executive Officer Bart Friedman Vice-Chairman

Auditors: Deloitte & Touche LLP
Transfer Agents: Continental Stock Transfer & Trust Company

ALLISON TRANSMISSION HOLDINGS INC

Exchange	Symbol	Price	52Wk Range	Yield	P/E
NYS	ALSN	$28.09 (5/31/2016)	30.71-21.58	2.14	30.20

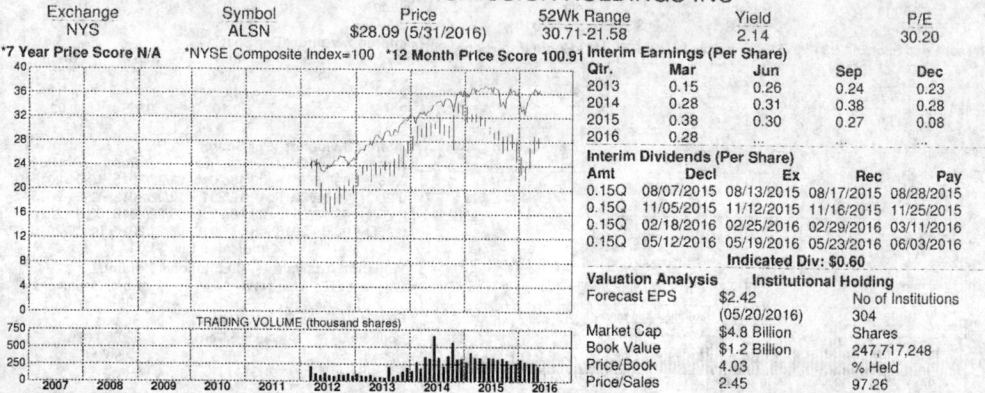

*7 Year Price Score N/A   *NYSE Composite Index=100   *12 Month Price Score 100.91

Interim Earnings (Per Share)

Qtr.	Mar	Jun	Sep	Dec
2013	0.15	0.26	0.24	0.23
2014	0.28	0.31	0.38	0.28
2015	0.38	0.30	0.27	0.08
2016	0.28	...	...	...

Interim Dividends (Per Share)

Amt	Decl	Ex	Rec	Pay
0.15Q	08/07/2015	08/13/2015	08/17/2015	08/28/2015
0.15Q	11/05/2015	11/12/2015	11/16/2015	11/25/2015
0.15Q	02/18/2016	02/25/2016	02/29/2016	03/11/2016
0.15Q	05/12/2016	05/19/2016	05/23/2016	06/03/2016

Indicated Div: $0.60

Valuation Analysis

		Institutional Holding	
Forecast EPS	$2.42 (05/20/2016)	No of Institutions	304
Market Cap	$4.8 Billion	Shares	247,717,248
Book Value	$1.2 Billion	% Held	97.26
Price/Book	4.03		
Price/Sales	2.45		

Business Summary: Construction Services (MIC: 7.5.4 SIC: 3714 NAIC: 336350)

Allison Transmission is a manufacturer of fully-automatic transmissions for medium- and heavy-duty commercial vehicles and medium- and heavy-tactical U.S. defense vehicles. Co.'s transmissions are used in a variety of applications, including on-highway trucks (distribution, refuse, construction, fire and emergency), buses, motorhomes, off-highway vehicles and equipment (primarily energy, mining and construction) and defense vehicles (wheeled and tracked). Co. has 13 transmission product lines. Co. has developed over 100 different models that are used in more than 2,500 different vehicle configurations and are compatible with more than 500 combinations of engine brands, models and ratings.

Recent Developments: For the quarter ended Mar 31 2016, net income decreased 29.4% to US$48.3 million from US$68.4 million in the year-earlier quarter. Revenues were US$462.1 million, down 8.2% from US$503.6 million the year before. Operating income was US$110.7 million versus US$142.3 million in the prior-year quarter, a decrease of 22.2%. Direct operating expenses declined 6.6% to US$247.0 million from US$264.4 million in the comparable period the year before. Indirect operating expenses increased 7.7% to US$104.4 million from US$96.9 million in the equivalent prior-year period.

Prospects: Our evaluation of Allison Transmission Holding as of June 19, 2016 is the result of our systematic analysis on three basic characteristics: earnings strength, relative valuation, and recent stock price movement. The company has produced a positive trend in earnings per share over the past 5 quarters and while recent estimates for the company have remained steady, ALSN has posted better than expected results. Based on operating earnings yield, the company is undervalued when compared to all of the companies in our coverage universe. Share price changes over the past year indicates that ALSN will perform in line with the market over the near term.

Financial Data

(US$ in Thousands)	3 Mos	12/31/2015	12/31/2014	12/31/2013	12/31/2012	12/31/2011	12/31/2010	12/31/2009
Earnings Per Share	0.93	1.03	1.25	0.88	2.76	0.56	0.16	(1.79)
Cash Flow Per Share	3.62	3.30	3.10	2.46	2.73	2.59	2.14	0.93
Dividends Per Share	0.600	0.600	0.510	0.420	0.180	...	...	...
Dividend Payout %	64.52	58.25	40.80	47.73	6.52	...	...	...
Income Statement								
Total Revenue	462,100	1,985,800	2,127,400	1,926,800	2,141,800	2,162,800	1,926,300	1,766,700
EBITDA	156,700	588,700	699,100	603,000	619,900	623,600	614,600	213,500
Depn & Amortn	46,100	185,400	192,600	204,000	252,500	255,700	253,800	261,800
Income Before Taxes	76,500	288,800	368,100	266,100	216,200	150,600	83,300	(282,500)
Income Taxes	28,200	106,500	139,500	100,700	(298,000)	47,600	53,700	41,400
Net Income	48,300	182,300	228,600	165,400	514,200	103,000	29,600	(323,900)
Average Shares	171,500	177,200	182,300	187,900	186,200	183,275	181,367	181,322
Balance Sheet								
Current Assets	690,300	616,800	758,000	606,900	490,300	702,700	645,500	...
Total Assets	4,441,200	4,408,400	4,804,200	4,812,600	4,866,000	5,192,600	5,310,400	...
Current Liabilities	319,500	304,600	345,900	387,200	377,800	449,900	417,500	...
Long-Term Obligations	2,348,300	2,352,700	2,502,600	2,660,400	2,801,300	3,345,000	3,637,700	...
Total Liabilities	3,258,400	3,219,800	3,406,400	3,373,800	3,509,100	4,370,900	4,568,700	...
Stockholders' Equity	1,182,800	1,188,600	1,397,800	1,438,800	1,356,900	821,700	741,700	...
Shares Outstanding	169,774	171,157	179,488	183,376	184,084	181,375	181,375	...
Statistical Record								
Return on Assets %	3.51	3.96	4.75	3.42	10.20	1.96	...	...
Return on Equity %	12.47	14.10	16.12	11.83	47.08	13.18	...	...
EBITDA Margin %	33.91	29.65	32.86	31.30	28.94	28.83	31.91	12.08
Net Margin %	10.45	9.18	10.75	8.58	24.01	4.76	1.54	N.M.
Asset Turnover	0.42	0.43	0.44	0.40	0.42	0.41	...	...
Current Ratio	2.16	2.02	2.19	1.57	1.30	1.56	1.55	...
Debt to Equity	1.99	1.98	1.79	1.85	2.06	4.07	4.90	...
Price Range	32.31-21.58	33.90-24.64	34.38-26.46	28.04-20.42	25.02-16.21	...	...	...
P/E Ratio	34.74-23.20	32.91-23.92	27.50-21.17	31.86-23.20	9.07-5.87	...	...	...
Average Yield %	2.15	2.02	1.68	1.76	0.91	...	...	...

Address: One Allison Way, Indianapolis, IN 46222 Telephone: 317-242-5000	Web Site: www.allisontransmission.com Officers: Lawrence E. Dewey - Chairman, President, Chief Executive Officer David S. Graziosi - President, Executive Vice President, Chief Financial Officer, Treasurer, Assistant Secretary	Auditors: PricewaterhouseCoopers LLP Transfer Agents: American Stock Transfer & Trust Company, LLC, Brooklyn, NY

ALLSTATE CORP.

Exchange	Symbol	Price	52Wk Range	Yield	P/E
NYS	ALL	$67.51 (5/31/2016)	69.38-56.99	1.96	16.55

*7 Year Price Score 121.37 *NYSE Composite Index=100 *12 Month Price Score 103.65

Interim Earnings (Per Share)

Qtr.	Mar	Jun	Sep	Dec
2013	1.47	0.92	0.66	1.74
2014	1.30	1.39	1.74	1.85
2015	1.53	0.79	1.54	1.18
2016	0.57	...	...	...

Interim Dividends (Per Share)

Amt	Decl	Ex	Rec	Pay
0.30Q	07/14/2015	08/27/2015	08/31/2015	10/01/2015
0.30Q	11/19/2015	11/25/2015	11/30/2015	01/04/2016
0.33Q	02/12/2016	02/25/2016	02/29/2016	04/01/2016
0.33Q	05/24/2016	06/01/2016	06/03/2016	07/01/2016

Indicated Div: $1.32 (Div. Reinv. Plan)

Valuation Analysis

		Institutional Holding	
Forecast EPS	$4.29	No of Institutions	
	(05/20/2016)	1160	
Market Cap	$25.3 Billion	Shares	
Book Value	$20.3 Billion	350,592,128	
Price/Book	1.24	% Held	
Price/Sales	0.71	71.10	

Business Summary: General Insurance (MIC: 5.2.1 SIC: 6331 NAIC: 524126)

Allstate is a holding company. Through its subsidiaries, Co. is engaged in the property-liability insurance and life insurance business. Co. has four business segments which include: Allstate Protection, which sells private passenger auto and homeowners insurance; Allstate Financial, which provides life insurance, voluntary accident and health insurance products; Discontinued Lines and Coverages, which includes results from insurance coverage that Co. no longer writes and results for certain commercial and other businesses in run-off; and Corporate and Other, which is comprised of holding company activities and certain non-insurance operations.

Recent Developments: For the quarter ended Mar 31 2016, net income decreased 63.7% to US$246.0 million from US$677.0 million in the year-earlier quarter. Revenues were US$8.87 billion, down 0.9% from US$8.95 billion the year before. Net premiums earned were US$8.29 billion versus US$7.96 billion in the prior-year quarter, an increase of 4.1%. Net investment income fell 14.0% to US$731.0 million from US$850.0 million a year ago.

Prospects: Our evaluation of Allstate Corp. as of June 19, 2016 is the result of our systematic analysis on three basic characteristics: earnings strength, relative valuation, and recent stock price movement. The company has generated a negative trend in earnings per share over the past 5 quarters. However, while recent estimates for the company have been lowered by analysts, ALL has posted better than expected results. Based on operating earnings yield, the company is undervalued when compared to all of the companies in our coverage universe. Share price changes over the past year indicates that ALL will perform well over the near term.

Financial Data
(US$ in Millions)

	3 Mos	12/31/2015	12/31/2014	12/31/2013	12/31/2012	12/31/2011	12/31/2010	12/31/2009
Earnings Per Share	4.08	5.05	6.27	4.81	4.68	1.51	1.71	1.58
Cash Flow Per Share	9.96	9.02	7.50	9.13	6.22	3.70	6.83	7.97
Tang Book Value Per Share	46.33	44.78	46.27	43.33	40.38	34.79	34.04	29.45
Dividends Per Share	1.230	1.200	1.120	1.000	0.880	0.840	0.800	0.800
Dividend Payout %	30.15	23.76	17.86	20.79	18.80	55.63	46.78	50.63
Income Statement								
Premium Income	8,289	32,467	31,086	29,970	28,978	28,180	28,125	28,152
Total Revenue	8,871	35,653	35,239	34,507	33,315	32,654	31,400	32,013
Benefits & Claims	455	22,837	21,193	19,828	20,302	21,922	20,766	20,363
Income Before Taxes	355	3,282	4,236	3,396	3,306	960	1,126	1,248
Income Taxes	109	1,111	1,386	1,116	1,000	172	198	394
Net Income	246	2,171	2,850	2,280	2,306	788	928	854
Average Shares	382	406	438	470	493	523	542	540
Balance Sheet								
Total Assets	105,947	104,656	108,533	123,520	126,947	125,563	130,874	132,652
Total Liabilities	85,607	84,631	86,229	102,040	106,367	106,889	111,858	115,960
Stockholders' Equity	20,340	20,025	22,304	21,480	20,580	18,674	19,016	16,692
Shares Outstanding	375	381	418	449	479	501	533	537
Statistical Record								
Return on Assets %	1.63	2.04	2.46	1.82	1.82	0.61	0.70	0.64
Return on Equity %	8.18	10.26	13.02	10.84	11.72	4.18	5.20	5.82
Loss Ratio %	5.49	70.34	68.18	66.16	70.06	77.79	73.83	72.33
Net Margin %	2.77	6.09	8.09	6.61	6.92	2.41	2.96	2.67
Price Range	72.12-56.99	72.58-56.99	71.00-49.55	54.71-40.17	42.62-27.56	34.31-22.68	35.43-27.26	33.26-14.12
P/E Ratio	17.68-13.97	14.37-11.29	11.32-7.90	11.37-8.35	9.11-5.89	22.72-15.02	20.72-15.94	21.05-8.94
Average Yield %	1.92	1.82	1.89	2.02	2.47	2.91	2.61	3.09

Address: 2775 Sanders Road, Northbrook, IL 60062
Telephone: 847-402-5000

Web Site: www.allstate.com
Officers: Thomas J. Wilson - Chairman, President, Chief Executive Officer, Division Officer Matthew E. Winter - President, Division Officer

Auditors: Deloitte & Touche LLP
Investor Contact: 800-416-8803
Transfer Agents: Wells Fargo Bank, N.A. Shareowner Services, St. Paul, MN

33

Exchange	Symbol	Price	52Wk Range	Yield	P/E
NYS	ALLY	$17.94 (5/31/2016)	23.66-15.33	N/A	N/A

*7 Year Price Score N/A *NYSE Composite Index=100 *12 Month Price Score 88.67

Interim Earnings (Per Share)

Qtr.	Mar	Jun	Sep	Dec
2013	2.16	(2.73)	(0.26)	(0.81)
2014	0.33	0.54	0.74	0.23
2015	1.06	(2.22)	0.47	(1.98)
2016	0.49			

Interim Dividends (Per Share)

No Dividends Paid

Valuation Analysis / **Institutional Holding**

Valuation Analysis		Institutional Holding	
Forecast EPS	$2.27	No of Institutions	3
	(05/20/2016)		
Market Cap	$8.7 Billion	Shares	
Book Value	$13.8 Billion		107,200
Price/Book	0.63	% Held	
Price/Sales	0.90		N/A

TRADING VOLUME (thousand shares)

2007 2008 2009 2010 2011 2012 2013 2014 2015 2016

Business Summary: Credit & Lending (MIC: 5.4.1 SIC: 6141 NAIC: 522291)

Ally Financial is a holding company and a financial services firm. Co.'s Dealer Financial Services includes its Automotive Finance operations and Insurance operations, providing a range of financial services and insurance products to automotive dealerships and their retail customers. Co.'s banking subsidiary, Ally Bank, acquires deposits directly from customers through direct banking via the internet, telephone, mobile, and mail channels. Ally Bank's products include savings and money market accounts, certificates of deposit, interest-bearing checking accounts, and individual retirement accounts. At Dec 31 2014, Co. had total assets of $151.83 billion and total deposits of $58.22 billion.

Recent Developments: For the quarter ended Mar 31 2016, income from continuing operations increased 38.0% to US$247.0 million from US$179.0 million in the year-earlier quarter. Net income decreased 56.6% to US$250.0 million from US$576.0 million in the year-earlier quarter. Net interest income decreased 0.7% to US$1.46 billion from US$1.47 billion in the year-earlier quarter. Provision for loan losses was US$220.0 million versus US$116.0 million in the prior-year quarter, an increase of 89.7%. Non-interest income rose 54.7% to US$376.0 million from US$243.0 million, while non-interest expense declined 7.4% to US$1.22 billion.

Prospects: Our evaluation of Ally Financial Inc as of June 19, 2016 is the result of our systematic analysis on three basic characteristics: earnings strength, relative valuation, and recent stock price movement. The company has managed to produce a neutral trend in earnings per share over the past 5 quarters. However, while recent estimates for the company have been mixed, ALLY has posted results that fell short of analysts expectations. Based on operating earnings yield, the company is undervalued when compared to all of the companies in our coverage universe. Share price changes over the past year indicates that ALLY will perform in line with the market over the near term.

Financial Data
(US$ in Millions)

	3 Mos	12/31/2015	12/31/2014	12/31/2013	12/31/2012	12/31/2011	12/31/2010	12/31/2009
Earnings Per Share	(3.24)	(2.66)	1.83	(1.64)	0.95	(2.23)	...	...
Cash Flow Per Share	12.47	10.55	7.07	5.95	12.20	13.31	...	...
Tang Book Value Per Share	27.15	26.44	29.46	27.00	29.03	22.77	22.43	18.48
Income Statement								
Total Revenue	2,485	9,487	9,667	9,577	10,497	13,246	16,712	17,500
Income Before Taxes	397	1,341	1,246	357	(755)	(19)	1,123	(6,976)
Income Taxes	150	496	321	(59)	(1,284)	179	153	74
Net Income	250	1,289	1,150	361	1,196	(157)	1,075	(10,298)
Average Shares	484	482	481	420	412	412	...	...
Balance Sheet								
Total Assets	156,505	158,581	151,828	151,167	182,347	184,059	172,008	172,306
Total Liabilities	142,682	145,142	136,429	136,959	162,449	164,688	151,519	151,467
Stockholders' Equity	13,823	13,439	15,399	14,208	19,898	19,371	20,489	20,839
Shares Outstanding	483	481	480	479	412	412	412	247
Statistical Record								
Return on Assets %	0.62	0.83	0.76	0.22	0.65	N.M.	0.62	...
Return on Equity %	6.47	8.94	7.77	2.12	6.07	N.M.	5.20	...
Net Margin %	10.06	13.59	11.90	3.77	11.39	N.M.	6.43	N.M.
Asset Turnover	0.06	0.06	0.06	0.06	0.06	0.07	0.10	...
Price Range	23.66-15.33	23.88-18.33	27.90-20.12	...	...	...	...	...
P/E Ratio	...	...	15.25-10.99	...	...	...	...	...

Address: 200 Renaissance Center, P.O. Box 200, Detroit, MI 48265-2000
Telephone: 866-710-4623

Web Site: www.ally.com
Officers: Franklin W. Hobbs - Chairman William F. Muir - President

Auditors: Deloitte & Touche LLP
Investor Contact: 866-710-4623
Transfer Agents: Computershare Limited

ALTRIA GROUP INC

Exchange	Symbol	Price	52Wk Range	Yield	P/E	Div Achiever
NYS	MO	$63.64 (5/31/2016)	65.02-47.54	3.55	22.89	50 Years

*7 Year Price Score 138.60 *NYSE Composite Index=100 *12 Month Price Score 108.02

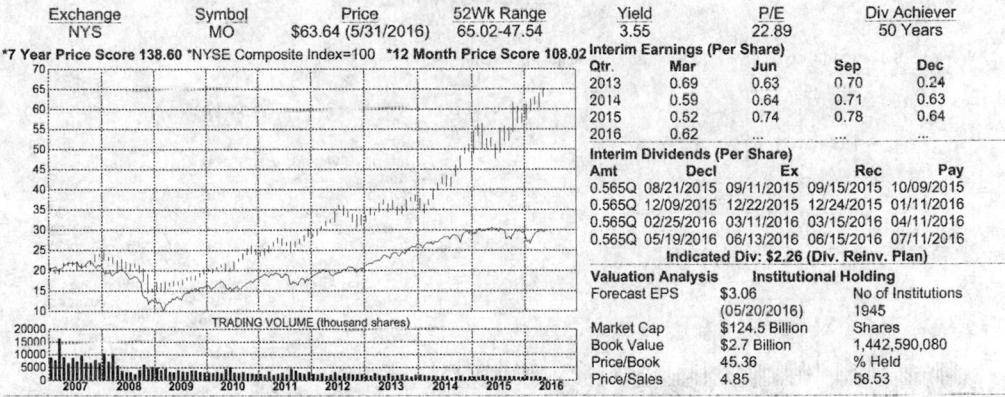

Interim Earnings (Per Share)

Qtr.	Mar	Jun	Sep	Dec
2013	0.69	0.63	0.70	0.24
2014	0.59	0.64	0.71	0.63
2015	0.52	0.74	0.78	0.64
2016	0.62	...	...	...

Interim Dividends (Per Share)

Amt	Decl	Ex	Rec	Pay
0.565Q	08/21/2015	09/11/2015	09/15/2015	10/09/2015
0.565Q	12/09/2015	12/22/2015	12/24/2015	01/11/2016
0.565Q	02/25/2016	03/11/2016	03/15/2016	04/11/2016
0.565Q	05/19/2016	06/13/2016	06/15/2016	07/11/2016

Indicated Div: $2.26 (Div. Reinv. Plan)

Valuation Analysis   **Institutional Holding**

Forecast EPS	$3.06	No of Institutions
	(05/20/2016)	1945
Market Cap	$124.5 Billion	Shares
Book Value	$2.7 Billion	1,442,590,080
Price/Book	45.36	% Held
Price/Sales	4.85	58.53

Business Summary: Tobacco Products (MIC: 1.3.1 SIC: 2111 NAIC: 312221)

Altria Group is a holding company. Co.'s subsidiaries include: Philip Morris USA Inc., which is engaged in the manufacture and sale of cigarettes; John Middleton Co., which is engaged in the manufacture and sale of machine-made cigars and pipe tobacco; UST LLC, which through its direct and indirect subsidiaries, including U.S. Smokeless Tobacco Company LLC and Ste. Michelle Wine Estates Ltd., is engaged in the manufacture and sale of smokeless tobacco products and wine; Nu Mark LLC, which is engaged in the manufacture and sale of innovative tobacco products; and Philip Morris Capital Corporation, which maintains a portfolio of finance assets.

Recent Developments: For the quarter ended Mar 31 2016, net income increased 19.6% to US$1.22 billion from US$1.02 billion in the year-earlier quarter. Revenues were US$6.07 billion, up 4.5% from US$5.80 billion the year before. Operating income was US$1.98 billion versus US$1.87 billion in the prior-year quarter, an increase of 6.0%. Direct operating expenses rose 2.4% to US$3.41 billion from US$3.33 billion in the comparable period the year before. Indirect operating expenses increased 11.3% to US$679.0 million from US$610.0 million in the equivalent prior-year period.

Prospects: Our evaluation of Altria Group Inc. as of June 19, 2016 is the result of our systematic analysis on three basic characteristics: earnings strength, relative valuation, and recent stock price movement. The company has produced a positive trend in earnings per share over the past 5 quarters and while recent estimates for the company have been mixed, MO has posted better than expected results. Based on operating earnings yield, the company is about fairly valued when compared to all of the companies in our coverage universe. Share price changes over the past year indicates that MO will perform very well over the near term.

Financial Data

(US$ in Thousands)	3 Mos	12/31/2015	12/31/2014	12/31/2013	12/31/2012	12/31/2011	12/31/2010	12/31/2009
Earnings Per Share	2.78	2.67	2.56	2.26	2.06	1.64	1.87	1.54
Cash Flow Per Share	3.07	2.96	2.36	2.19	1.92	1.75	1.33	1.67
Dividends Per Share	2.215	2.170	2.000	1.840	1.700	1.580	1.460	1.320
Dividend Payout %	79.68	81.27	78.13	81.42	82.52	96.34	78.07	85.71
Income Statement								
Total Revenue	6,066,000	25,434,000	24,522,000	24,466,000	24,618,000	23,800,000	24,363,000	23,556,000
EBITDA	2,066,000	8,342,000	7,764,000	7,212,000	6,604,000	6,321,000	6,504,000	5,753,000
Depn & Amortn	49,000	204,000	188,000	212,000	225,000	253,000	276,000	291,000
Income Before Taxes	1,817,000	7,321,000	6,768,000	5,951,000	5,253,000	4,852,000	5,095,000	4,277,000
Income Taxes	665,000	2,835,000	2,704,000	2,407,000	2,294,000	2,189,000	1,816,000	1,669,000
Net Income	1,217,000	5,241,000	5,070,000	4,535,000	4,180,000	3,390,000	3,905,000	3,206,000
Average Shares	1,956,000	1,961,000	1,978,000	1,999,000	2,024,000	2,064,000	2,079,000	2,071,000
Balance Sheet								
Current Assets	7,498,000	6,086,000	6,878,000	6,590,000	6,315,000	7,131,000	5,981,000	5,773,000
Total Assets	34,063,000	32,535,000	34,475,000	34,859,000	35,329,000	36,962,000	37,402,000	36,677,000
Current Liabilities	8,616,000	7,078,000	7,673,000	7,058,000	8,251,000	7,643,000	6,840,000	7,992,000
Long-Term Obligations	12,846,000	12,915,000	13,693,000	13,992,000	12,419,000	13,089,000	12,194,000	11,185,000
Total Liabilities	31,318,000	29,655,000	31,461,000	30,740,000	32,161,000	33,282,000	32,210,000	32,608,000
Stockholders' Equity	2,745,000	2,880,000	3,014,000	4,119,000	3,168,000	3,680,000	5,192,000	4,069,000
Shares Outstanding	1,956,710	1,960,059	1,971,474	1,993,479	2,009,740	2,044,419	2,088,739	2,076,028
Statistical Record								
Return on Assets %	15.94	15.64	14.62	12.92	11.53	9.12	10.54	10.04
Return on Equity %	206.14	177.84	142.16	124.47	121.75	76.42	84.33	92.97
EBITDA Margin %	34.06	32.80	31.66	29.48	26.83	26.56	26.70	24.42
Net Margin %	20.06	20.61	20.68	18.54	16.98	14.24	16.03	13.61
Asset Turnover	0.75	0.76	0.71	0.70	0.68	0.64	0.66	0.74
Current Ratio	0.87	0.86	0.90	0.93	0.77	0.93	0.87	0.72
Debt to Equity	4.68	4.48	4.54	3.40	3.92	3.56	2.35	2.75
Price Range	63.00-47.54	61.53-47.54	51.27-34.00	38.57-31.44	36.16-28.14	30.31-23.51	26.15-19.37	20.37-14.62
P/E Ratio	22.66-17.10	23.04-17.81	20.03-13.28	17.07-13.91	17.55-13.66	18.48-14.34	13.98-10.36	13.23-9.49
Average Yield %	3.98	4.03	4.75	5.19	5.26	5.96	6.62	7.60

Address: 6601 West Broad Street, Richmond, VA 23230 Telephone: 804-274-2200	Web Site: www.altria.com Officers: Martin J. Barrington - Chairman, President, Chief Executive Officer, Vice-Chairman Howard A. Willard - Executive Vice President, Chief Financial Officer, Chief Operating Officer	Auditors: PricewaterhouseCoopers LLP Investor Contact: 804-484-8222 Transfer Agents: Computershare Trust Company, N.A., Providence, RI

AMEREN CORP

Exchange	Symbol	Price	52Wk Range	Yield	P/E
NYS	AEE	$49.55 (5/31/2016)	50.83-37.51	3.43	19.28

*7 Year Price Score 109.14 *NYSE Composite Index=100 *12 Month Price Score 109.17

Interim Earnings (Per Share)

Qtr.	Mar	Jun	Sep	Dec
2013	(0.60)	0.39	1.24	0.15
2014	0.40	0.61	1.20	0.20
2015	0.45	0.61	1.41	0.12
2016	0.43	...	...	...

Interim Dividends (Per Share)

Amt	Decl	Ex	Rec	Pay
0.41Q	08/14/2015	09/08/2015	09/10/2015	09/30/2015
0.425Q	10/09/2015	12/07/2015	12/09/2015	12/31/2015
0.425Q	02/12/2016	03/07/2016	03/09/2016	03/31/2016
0.425Q	04/29/2016	06/06/2016	06/08/2016	06/30/2016

Indicated Div: $1.70

Valuation Analysis

		Institutional Holding	
Forecast EPS	$2.50 (05/20/2016)	No of Institutions	666
Market Cap	$12.0 Billion	Shares	
Book Value	$6.9 Billion		191,316,736
Price/Book	1.75	% Held	
Price/Sales	2.01		64.53

Business Summary: Electric Utilities (MIC: 3.1.1 SIC: 4931 NAIC: 221111)

Ameren is a public utility holding company. Through its subsidiary, Union Electric Company, doing business as Ameren Missouri, Co. operates a rate-regulated electric generation, transmission, and distribution business and a rate-regulated natural gas transmission and distribution business in Missouri. Through its subsidiary, Ameren Illinois Company, doing business as Ameren Illinois, Co. operates rate-regulated electric and natural gas transmission and distribution businesses in Illinois. Co. also has a subsidiary, Ameren Transmission Company of Illinois, that operates a Federal Energy Regulatory Commission rate-regulated electric transmission business.

Recent Developments: For the quarter ended Mar 31 2016, income from continuing operations decreased 2.7% to US$107.0 million from US$110.0 million in the year-earlier quarter. Net income decreased 2.7% to US$107.0 million from US$110.0 million in the year-earlier quarter. Revenues were US$1.43 billion, down 7.8% from US$1.56 billion the year before. Operating income was US$220.0 million versus US$256.0 million in the prior-year quarter, a decrease of 14.1%. Direct operating expenses declined 9.1% to US$893.0 million from US$982.0 million in the comparable period the year before. Indirect operating expenses increased 0.9% to US$321.0 million from US$318.0 million in the equivalent prior-year period.

Prospects: Our evaluation of Ameren Corp. as of June 19, 2016 is the result of our systematic analysis on three basic characteristics: earnings strength, relative valuation, and recent stock price movement. The company has generated a negative trend in earnings per share over the past 5 quarters and while recent estimates for the company have been mixed, AEE has posted better than expected results. Based on operating earnings yield, the company is about fairly valued when compared to all of the companies in our coverage universe. Share price changes over the past year indicates that AEE will perform well over the near term.

Financial Data

(US$ in Thousands)	3 Mos	12/31/2015	12/31/2014	12/31/2013	12/31/2012	12/31/2011	12/31/2010	12/31/2009
Earnings Per Share	2.57	2.59	2.40	1.18	(4.01)	2.15	0.58	2.78
Cash Flow Per Share	8.52	8.31	6.39	6.98	6.95	7.78	7.71	8.97
Tang Book Value Per Share	26.62	26.94	25.98	25.19	25.51	30.92	30.42	29.04
Dividends Per Share	1.670	1.655	1.610	1.600	1.600	1.555	1.540	1.540
Dividend Payout %	64.98	63.90	67.08	135.59	...	72.33	265.52	55.40
Income Statement								
Total Revenue	1,434,000	6,098,000	6,053,000	5,838,000	6,828,000	7,531,000	7,638,000	7,090,000
EBITDA	252,000	2,158,000	2,087,000	1,958,000	(397,000)	2,084,000	1,800,000	2,260,000
Depn & Amortn	30,000	896,000	813,000	761,000	842,000	829,000	860,000	826,000
Income Before Taxes	138,000	948,000	970,000	829,000	(1,654,000)	836,000	476,000	956,000
Income Taxes	31,000	363,000	377,000	311,000	(680,000)	310,000	325,000	332,000
Net Income	105,000	630,000	586,000	289,000	(974,000)	519,000	139,000	612,000
Average Shares	242,600	243,600	244,400	244,500	242,600	241,500	238,800	220,400
Balance Sheet								
Current Assets	1,458,000	1,917,000	2,046,000	1,972,000	2,369,000	2,295,000	2,894,000	2,842,000
Total Assets	23,385,000	23,640,000	22,676,000	21,042,000	21,835,000	23,645,000	23,515,000	23,790,000
Current Liabilities	1,839,000	2,093,000	2,249,000	2,461,000	1,698,000	1,785,000	1,888,000	1,711,000
Long-Term Obligations	6,881,000	6,880,000	6,120,000	5,504,000	6,626,000	6,677,000	7,313,000	7,943,000
Total Liabilities	16,516,000	16,694,000	15,963,000	14,498,000	15,219,000	15,726,000	15,785,000	15,937,000
Stockholders' Equity	6,869,000	6,946,000	6,713,000	6,544,000	6,616,000	7,919,000	7,730,000	7,853,000
Shares Outstanding	242,600	242,600	242,600	242,600	242,600	242,600	240,400	237,400
Statistical Record								
Return on Assets %	2.71	2.72	2.68	1.35	N.M.	2.20	0.59	2.64
Return on Equity %	9.24	9.22	8.84	4.39	N.M.	6.63	1.78	8.15
EBITDA Margin %	17.57	35.39	34.48	33.54	N.M.	27.67	23.57	31.88
Net Margin %	7.32	10.33	9.68	4.95	N.M.	6.89	1.82	8.63
Asset Turnover	0.26	0.26	0.28	0.27	0.30	0.32	0.32	0.31
Current Ratio	0.79	0.92	0.91	0.80	1.40	1.29	1.53	1.66
Debt to Equity	1.00	0.99	0.91	0.84	1.00	0.84	0.95	1.01
Price Range	50.10-37.51	46.54-37.51	47.92-35.40	37.03-30.72	34.71-28.55	33.81-25.97	29.83-23.59	34.92-19.76
P/E Ratio	19.49-14.60	17.97-14.48	19.97-14.75	31.38-26.03	...	15.73-12.08	51.43-40.67	12.56-7.11
Average Yield %	3.93	3.96	4.02	4.62	4.96	5.28	5.77	5.97

Address: 1901 Chouteau Avenue, St. Louis, MO 63103 **Telephone:** 314-621-3222	**Web Site:** www.ameren.com **Officers:** Warner L. Baxter - Chairman, President, Chief Executive Officer Martin J. Lyons - Executive Vice President, Senior Vice President, Chief Financial Officer	**Auditors:** PricewaterhouseCoopers LLP **Transfer Agents:** Ameren Services Company, St. Louis, MO

AMERICAN CAMPUS COMMUNITIES INC

Exchange	Symbol	Price	52Wk Range	Yield	P/E
NYS	ACC	$47.02 (5/31/2016)	48.05-32.26	3.57	61.87

*7 Year Price Score 93.47   *NYSE Composite Index=100   *12 Month Price Score 112.08

Interim Earnings (Per Share)

Qtr.	Mar	Jun	Sep	Dec
2013	0.20	0.07	0.45	0.26
2014	0.27	0.12	(0.06)	0.25
2015	0.62	0.14	0.01	0.25
2016	0.36	...	...	...

Interim Dividends (Per Share)

Amt	Decl	Ex	Rec	Pay
0.40Q	08/05/2015	08/13/2015	08/17/2015	08/27/2015
0.40Q	11/05/2015	11/12/2015	11/16/2015	11/30/2015
0.40Q	01/26/2016	02/04/2016	02/08/2016	02/19/2016
0.42Q	05/04/2016	05/12/2016	05/16/2016	05/27/2016

Indicated Div: $1.68

Valuation Analysis | **Institutional Holding**

Forecast EPS	$0.80
	(05/20/2016)
Market Cap	$6.1 Billion
Book Value	$3.5 Billion
Price/Book	1.77
Price/Sales	8.06

No of Institutions	403
Shares	142,444,544
% Held	102.50

Business Summary: REITs (MIC: 5.3.1 SIC: 6798 NAIC: 525930)

American Campus Communities is a real estate investment trust. Through American Campus Communities Operating Partnership L.P., Co. owns, manages and develops student housing properties. Co. focuses on the acquisition, design, financing, development, construction management, leasing and management of student housing properties. Co. has four reportable segments: Wholly-Owned Properties, On-Campus Participating Properties, Development Services, and Property Management Services. As of Dec 31 2015, Co.'s property portfolio contained 162 properties, with 134 owned off-campus student housing properties, 23 American Campus Equity properties, and five on-campus participating properties.

Recent Developments: For the quarter ended Mar 31 2016, net income decreased 35.2% to US$46.2 million from US$71.3 million in the year-earlier quarter. Revenues were US$200.0 million, up 3.9% from US$192.5 million the year before. Revenues from property income rose 3.5% to US$195.7 million from US$189.1 million in the corresponding quarter a year earlier.

Prospects: Our evaluation of American Campus Communities Inc. as of June 19, 2016 is the result of our systematic analysis on three basic characteristics: earnings strength, relative valuation, and recent stock price movement. The company has managed to produce a neutral trend in earnings per share over the past 5 quarters and while recent estimates for the company have remained steady, ACC has posted better than expected results. Based on operating earnings yield, the company is overvalued when compared to all of the companies in our coverage universe. Share price changes over the past year indicates that ACC will perform very well over the near term.

Financial Data
(US$ in Thousands)

	3 Mos	12/31/2015	12/31/2014	12/31/2013	12/31/2012	12/31/2011	12/31/2010	12/31/2009
Earnings Per Share	0.76	1.02	0.58	0.98	0.65	0.80	0.26	(0.28)
Cash Flow Per Share	2.03	2.33	2.47	2.35	2.39	1.89	2.05	1.63
Tang Book Value Per Share	26.54	24.66	24.35	25.05	25.30	18.90	18.15	17.22
Dividends Per Share	1.600	1.580	1.500	1.418	1.350	1.350	1.350	1.350
Dividend Payout %	210.53	154.90	258.62	144.64	207.69	168.75	519.23	...
Income Statement								
Total Revenue	199,995	753,381	733,915	657,462	491,290	390,317	344,991	309,590
EBITDA	67,390	206,371	151,286	137,179	118,644	98,873	89,951	73,048
Depn & Amortn	(512)	3,700	2,400	13,700	6,800	4,100	1,800	10,200
Income Before Taxes	46,554	119,303	62,692	48,456	57,027	43,143	27,684	221
Income Taxes	345	1,242	1,308	1,020	725	433	570	540
Net Income	45,587	115,991	62,839	104,644	56,636	56,629	16,210	(12,840)
Average Shares	124,266	114,032	105,711	105,382	85,309	69,807	59,338	48,706
Balance Sheet								
Current Assets	434,609	68,809	67,144	83,440	72,366	50,679	146,007	101,373
Total Assets	6,367,537	6,025,947	5,834,748	5,598,040	5,118,962	3,008,582	2,693,484	2,234,981
Current Liabilities	49,306	71,988	70,629	65,088	56,046	36,884	34,771	26,543
Long-Term Obligations	2,623,267	2,967,980	2,972,719	2,744,387	2,221,105	1,447,530	1,345,103	1,223,455
Total Liabilities	2,905,260	3,255,751	3,225,194	2,973,139	2,470,581	1,633,366	1,479,522	1,335,951
Stockholders' Equity	3,462,277	2,770,196	2,609,554	2,624,901	2,648,381	1,375,216	1,213,962	899,030
Shares Outstanding	130,433	112,350	107,175	104,782	104,665	72,759	66,875	52,203
Statistical Record								
Return on Assets %	1.50	1.96	1.10	1.95	1.39	1.99	0.66	N.M.
Return on Equity %	2.90	4.31	2.40	3.97	2.81	4.37	1.53	N.M.
EBITDA Margin %	33.70	27.39	20.61	20.86	24.15	25.33	26.07	23.60
Net Margin %	22.79	15.40	8.56	15.92	11.53	14.51	4.70	N.M.
Asset Turnover	0.12	0.13	0.13	0.12	0.12	0.14	0.14	0.14
Current Ratio	8.81	0.96	0.95	1.28	1.29	1.37	4.20	3.82
Debt to Equity	0.76	1.07	1.14	1.05	0.84	1.05	1.11	1.36
Price Range	47.09-32.26	44.84-32.26	41.88-32.21	47.88-31.80	47.69-40.86	42.39-30.78	33.39-24.62	28.68-15.61
P/E Ratio	61.96-42.45	43.96-31.63	72.21-55.53	48.86-32.45	73.37-62.86	52.99-38.48	128.42-94.69	...
Average Yield %	4.02	3.98	3.95	3.55	3.04	3.79	4.68	5.84

Address: 12700 Hill Country Blvd., Suite T-200, Austin, TX 78738
Telephone: 512-732-1000

Web Site: www.americancampus.com
Officers: William C. Bayless - President, Chief Executive Officer Brian B. Nickel - Senior Executive Vice President, Chief Investment Officer, Secretary

Auditors: Ernst & Young LLP
Investor Contact: 512-732-1041
Transfer Agents: Wells Fargo Bank N.A., Mendota Heights, MN

AMERICAN EAGLE OUTFITTERS, INC.

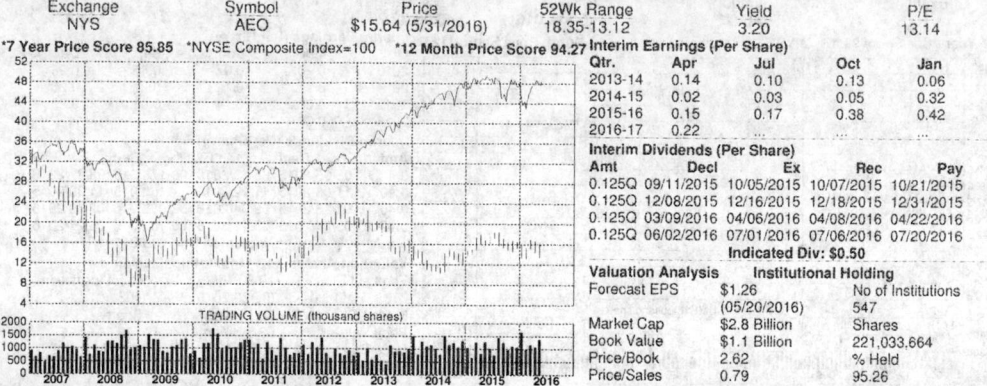

Exchange	Symbol	Price	52Wk Range	Yield	P/E
NYS	AEO	$15.64 (5/31/2016)	18.35-13.12	3.20	13.14

*7 Year Price Score 85.85 *NYSE Composite Index=100 *12 Month Price Score 94.27

Interim Earnings (Per Share)

Qtr.	Apr	Jul	Oct	Jan
2013-14	0.14	0.10	0.13	0.06
2014-15	0.02	0.03	0.05	0.32
2015-16	0.15	0.17	0.38	0.42
2016-17	0.22			

Interim Dividends (Per Share)

Amt	Decl	Ex	Rec	Pay
0.125Q	09/11/2015	10/05/2015	10/07/2015	10/21/2015
0.125Q	12/08/2015	12/16/2015	12/18/2015	12/31/2015
0.125Q	03/09/2016	04/06/2016	04/08/2016	04/22/2016
0.125Q	06/02/2016	07/01/2016	07/06/2016	07/20/2016
		Indicated Div: $0.50		

Valuation Analysis

		Institutional Holding	
Forecast EPS	$1.26	No of Institutions	
	(05/20/2016)	547	
Market Cap	$2.8 Billion	Shares	
Book Value	$1.1 Billion	221,033,664	
Price/Book	2.62	% Held	
Price/Sales	0.79	95.26	

Business Summary: Retail - Apparel and Accessories (MIC: 2.1.5 SIC: 5651 NAIC: 448140)

American Eagle Outfitters is a specialty retailer operating retail stores and online at ae.com and aerie.com in the U.S. and internationally. Co. provides an assortment of apparel and accessories for men and women under the American Eagle Outfitters brand, and intimates, apparel and personal care products for women under the Aerie brand. Co. operates stores in the U.S., Canada, Mexico, Hong Kong, China and the U.K. Co. also has license agreements with third parties to operate American Eagle Outfitters and Aerie stores throughout Asia, Europe, Latin America and the Middle East. As of Jan 30 2016, Co. operated 949 American Eagle Outfitters stores and 97 Aerie stand-alone stores.

Recent Developments: For the quarter ended Apr 30 2016, net income increased 39.3% to US$40.5 million from US$29.1 million in the year-earlier quarter. Revenues were US$749.4 million, up 7.1% from US$699.5 million the year before. Operating income was US$58.7 million versus US$42.0 million in the prior-year quarter, an increase of 39.7%. Direct operating expenses rose 4.3% to US$456.0 million from US$437.3 million in the comparable period the year before. Indirect operating expenses increased 6.6% to US$234.8 million from US$220.2 million in the equivalent prior-year period.

Prospects: Our evaluation of American Eagle Outfitters Inc. as of June 19, 2016 is the result of our systematic analysis on three basic characteristics: earnings strength, relative valuation, and recent stock price movement. The company has generated a negative trend in earnings per share over the past 5 quarters and while recent estimates for the company have been raised by analysts, AEO has posted better than expected results. Based on operating earnings yield, the company is undervalued when compared to all of the companies in our coverage universe. Share price changes over the past year indicates that AEO will perform poorly over the near term.

Financial Data (US$ in Thousands)	3 Mos	01/30/2016	01/31/2015	02/01/2014	02/02/2013	01/28/2012	01/29/2011	01/30/2010
Earnings Per Share	1.19	1.11	0.42	0.43	1.16	0.77	0.70	0.81
Cash Flow Per Share	2.13	1.76	1.75	1.20	2.51	1.23	2.02	1.88
Tang Book Value Per Share	5.58	5.45	5.55	5.71	6.08	7.04	6.89	7.58
Dividends Per Share	0.500	0.500	0.500	0.375	2.050	0.440	0.930	0.400
Dividend Payout %	42.02	45.05	119.05	87.21	176.72	57.14	132.86	49.38
Income Statement								
Total Revenue	749,416	3,521,848	3,282,867	3,305,802	3,475,802	3,159,818	2,967,559	2,990,520
EBITDA	102,691	462,487	292,031	258,838	524,794	374,944	434,253	377,274
Depn & Amortn	39,080	140,616	132,529	116,761	122,756	137,934	139,169	144,883
Income Before Taxes	63,611	321,871	159,502	142,077	402,038	237,010	295,084	232,391
Income Taxes	23,135	108,580	70,715	59,094	137,940	85,305	113,150	63,369
Net Income	40,476	218,138	80,322	82,983	232,108	151,705	140,647	169,022
Average Shares	182,927	196,237	195,135	194,475	200,665	196,314	201,818	209,512
Balance Sheet								
Current Assets	729,327	723,375	890,513	923,560	1,141,800	1,287,488	1,174,410	1,167,030
Total Assets	1,596,296	1,612,246	1,696,908	1,694,164	1,756,053	1,950,802	1,879,998	2,138,148
Current Liabilities	418,486	463,682	459,093	415,478	435,902	405,401	387,837	408,955
Total Liabilities	518,988	560,870	557,162	527,986	534,866	533,951	528,927	559,631
Stockholders' Equity	1,077,308	1,051,376	1,139,746	1,166,178	1,221,187	1,416,851	1,351,071	1,578,517
Shares Outstanding	180,804	180,135	194,516	193,149	192,604	193,848	194,366	206,832
Statistical Record								
Return on Assets %	14.04	13.22	4.75	4.82	12.32	7.94	7.02	8.26
Return on Equity %	20.66	19.97	6.99	6.97	17.31	10.99	9.63	11.35
EBITDA Margin %	13.70	13.13	8.90	7.83	15.10	11.87	14.63	12.62
Net Margin %	5.40	6.19	2.45	2.51	6.68	4.80	4.74	5.65
Asset Turnover	2.19	2.13	1.94	1.92	1.85	1.65	1.48	1.46
Current Ratio	1.74	1.56	1.94	2.22	2.62	3.18	3.03	2.85
Price Range	18.35-13.12	18.35-13.24	14.85-10.28	22.55-12.77	23.80-13.58	16.18-10.17	19.34-11.60	19.62-8.44
P/E Ratio	15.42-11.03	16.53-11.93	35.36-24.48	52.44-29.70	20.52-11.71	21.01-13.21	27.63-16.57	24.22-10.42
Average Yield %	3.12	3.08	3.93	2.18	10.55	3.21	6.13	2.75

Address: 77 Hot Metal Street, Pittsburgh, PA 15203-2329
Telephone: 412-432-3300

Web Site: www.ae.com
Officers: Jay L. Schottenstein - Executive Chairman, Chairman, Chief Executive Officer, Interim Chief Executive Officer Fredrick W. Grover - Executive Vice President

Auditors: Ernst & Young LLP
Investor Contact: 412-432-3300
Transfer Agents: Computershare Trust Company, N.A., Providence, RI

AMERICAN ELECTRIC POWER COMPANY, INC.

Exchange	Symbol	Price	52Wk Range	Yield	P/E
NYS	AEP	$64.73 (5/31/2016)	67.01-52.54	3.46	16.55

*7 Year Price Score 111.98 *NYSE Composite Index=100 *12 Month Price Score 108.62

Interim Earnings (Per Share)

Qtr.	Mar	Jun	Sep	Dec
2013	0.75	0.69	0.89	0.71
2014	1.15	0.80	1.01	0.39
2015	1.29	0.88	1.06	0.95
2016	1.02	...	...	...

Interim Dividends (Per Share)

Amt	Decl	Ex	Rec	Pay
0.53Q	07/21/2015	08/06/2015	08/10/2015	09/10/2015
0.56Q	10/20/2015	11/06/2015	11/10/2015	12/10/2015
0.56Q	01/25/2016	02/08/2016	02/10/2016	03/10/2016
0.56Q	04/26/2016	05/06/2016	05/10/2016	06/10/2016

Indicated Div: $2.24

Valuation Analysis

Forecast EPS	$3.69	**Institutional Holding**	
	(05/20/2016)	No of Institutions	1109
Market Cap	$31.8 Billion	Shares	384,335,200
Book Value	$18.1 Billion	% Held	66.29
Price/Book	1.75		
Price/Sales	1.98		

Business Summary. Electric Utilities (MIC: 3.1.1 SIC: 4911 NAIC: 221122)

American Electric Power Company is a public utility holding company. The public utility subsidiaries of Co. provide electric service, consisting of generation, transmission and distribution, on an integrated basis to their retail customers. The service areas of Co.'s public utility subsidiaries cover portions of the states of Arkansas, Indiana, Kentucky, Louisiana, Michigan, Ohio, Oklahoma, Tennessee, Texas, Virginia and West Virginia. Transmission networks are interconnected with distribution facilities in the territories served.

Recent Developments: For the quarter ended Mar 31 2016, income from continuing operations decreased 18.9% to US$503.1 million from US$620.2 million in the year-earlier quarter. Net income decreased 20.2% to US$503.1 million from US$630.7 million in the year-earlier quarter. Revenues were US$4.04 billion, down 11.7% from US$4.58 billion the year before. Operating income was US$892.9 million versus US$1.10 billion in the prior-year quarter, a decrease of 19.0%. Direct operating expenses declined 12.3% to US$2.40 billion from US$2.74 billion in the comparable period the year before. Indirect operating expenses increased 1.4% to US$751.2 million from US$741.1 million in the equivalent prior-year period.

Prospects: Our evaluation of American Electric Power Company Inc. as of June 19, 2016 is the result of our systematic analysis on three basic characteristics: earnings strength, relative valuation, and recent stock price movement. The company has generated a negative trend in earnings per share over the past 5 quarters. However, while recent estimates for the company have been mixed, AEP has posted results that fell short of analysts expectations. Based on operating earnings yield, the company is undervalued when compared to all of the companies in our coverage universe. Share price changes over the past year indicates that AEP will perform very well over the near term.

Financial Data

(US$ in Thousands)	3 Mos	12/31/2015	12/31/2014	12/31/2013	12/31/2012	12/31/2011	12/31/2010	12/31/2009
Earnings Per Share	3.91	4.17	3.34	3.04	2.60	4.02	2.53	2.96
Cash Flow Per Share	8.74	9.68	9.44	8.44	7.83	7.86	5.55	5.40
Tang Book Value Per Share	36.79	36.33	34.18	32.79	31.19	30.18	28.30	27.46
Dividends Per Share	2.180	2.150	2.030	1.950	1.880	1.850	1.710	1.640
Dividend Payout %	55.75	51.56	60.78	64.14	72.31	46.02	67.59	55.41
Income Statement								
Total Revenue	4,044,900	16,453,200	17,020,000	15,357,000	14,945,000	15,116,000	14,427,000	13,489,000
EBITDA	969,000	5,639,900	5,448,000	4,890,000	4,728,000	5,092,000	4,628,000	4,571,000
Depn & Amortn	40,500	2,154,700	2,073,000	1,874,000	1,918,000	1,792,000	1,780,000	1,660,000
Income Before Taxes	713,600	2,611,300	2,490,000	2,110,000	1,822,000	2,367,000	1,849,000	1,938,000
Income Taxes	235,500	908,000	942,000	684,000	604,000	818,000	643,000	575,000
Net Income	501,200	2,047,100	1,634,000	1,480,000	1,259,000	1,946,000	1,214,000	1,360,000
Average Shares	491,332	490,574	488,899	487,040	485,084	482,460	479,601	458,982
Balance Sheet								
Current Assets	4,146,300	4,072,400	4,478,000	4,310,000	4,589,000	4,182,000	5,016,000	4,756,000
Total Assets	62,486,500	61,683,100	59,633,000	56,414,000	54,367,000	52,223,000	50,455,000	48,348,000
Current Liabilities	7,221,900	7,108,500	7,967,000	6,112,000	6,823,000	6,611,000	6,518,000	5,327,000
Long-Term Obligations	17,749,300	17,740,900	16,181,000	16,828,000	15,586,000	15,083,000	15,502,000	15,757,000
Total Liabilities	44,360,000	43,791,400	42,813,000	40,329,000	39,130,000	37,559,000	36,773,000	35,147,000
Stockholders' Equity	18,126,500	17,891,700	16,820,000	16,085,000	15,237,000	14,664,000	13,682,000	13,201,000
Shares Outstanding	491,243	491,052	489,402	487,777	485,668	483,422	480,807	478,054
Statistical Record								
Return on Assets %	3.13	3.37	2.82	2.67	2.36	3.79	2.46	2.91
Return on Equity %	10.85	11.79	9.93	9.45	8.40	13.73	9.03	11.35
EBITDA Margin %	23.96	34.28	32.01	31.84	31.64	33.69	32.08	33.89
Net Margin %	12.39	12.44	9.60	9.64	8.42	12.87	8.41	10.08
Asset Turnover	0.26	0.27	0.29	0.28	0.28	0.29	0.29	0.29
Current Ratio	0.57	0.57	0.56	0.71	0.67	0.63	0.77	0.89
Debt to Equity	0.98	0.99	0.96	1.05	1.02	1.03	1.13	1.19
Price Range	66.40-52.54	64.57-52.54	62.91-46.08	51.43-41.92	45.27-37.22	41.65-33.60	37.70-30.97	35.58-24.28
P/E Ratio	16.98-13.44	15.48-12.60	18.84-13.80	16.92-13.79	17.41-14.32	10.36-8.36	14.90-12.24	12.02-8.20
Average Yield %	3.81	3.79	3.84	4.24	4.59	4.96	4.90	5.49

Address: 1 Riverside Plaza, Columbus, OH 43215-2373	**Web Site:** www.aep.com	**Auditors:** Deloitte & Touche LLP
Telephone: 614-716-1000	**Officers:** Nicholas K. Akins - Chairman, President, Chief Executive Officer David M. Feinberg - Executive Vice President, Senior Vice President, Secretary, General Counsel	**Investor Contact:** 614-716-2819
Fax: 614-223-1823		**Transfer Agents:** Computershare Trust Company, N.A., Providence, RI

AMERICAN EQUITY INVESTMENT LIFE HOLDING CO

Exchange	Symbol	Price	52Wk Range	Yield	P/E	Div Achiever
NYS	AEL	$16.21 (5/31/2016)	29.54-12.81	1.36	7.79	12 Years

*7 Year Price Score 115.63 *NYSE Composite Index=100   *12 Month Price Score 67.21

TRADING VOLUME (thousand shares)

Interim Earnings (Per Share)

Qtr.	Mar	Jun	Sep	Dec
2013	0.38	1.71	0.75	0.59
2014	(0.13)	0.46	0.85	0.39
2015	0.07	1.05	1.19	0.39
2016	(0.55)	...	...	...

Interim Dividends (Per Share)

Amt	Decl	Ex	Rec	Pay
0.15A	11/15/2012	11/29/2012	12/03/2012	12/17/2012
0.18A	11/20/2013	11/27/2013	12/02/2013	12/16/2013
0.20A	11/21/2014	11/26/2014	12/01/2014	12/15/2014
0.22A	11/19/2015	11/25/2015	11/30/2015	12/14/2015

Indicated Div: $0.22

Valuation Analysis

		Institutional Holding	
Forecast EPS	$2.12 (05/20/2016)	No of Institutions	318
Market Cap	$1.3 Billion	Shares	89,180,264
Book Value	$2.2 Billion	% Held	98.34
Price/Book	0.60		
Price/Sales	0.87		

Business Summary: Life & Health (MIC: 5.2.2 SIC: 6311 NAIC: 524113)

American Equity Investment Life Holding is a holding company. Co. is engaged in the development and sale of fixed index and fixed rate annuity products. Co. is an underwriter of fixed annuity and life insurance products through its wholly-owned life insurance subsidiaries, American Equity Investment Life Insurance Company, American Equity Investment Life Insurance Company of New York, and Eagle Life Insurance Company. Co.'s life insurance products include ordinary and term, universal life and other interest-sensitive life insurance products. As of Dec 31 2014, Co. was licensed to sell its products in 50 states in the U.S. and the District of Columbia.

Recent Developments: For the quarter ended Mar 31 2016, net loss amounted to US$44.8 million versus net income of US$5.9 million in the year-earlier quarter. Revenues were US$417.6 million, up 2.1% from US$409.0 million the year before. Net premiums earned were US$43.9 million versus US$35.7 million in the prior-year quarter, an increase of 22.9%. Net investment income rose 12.8% to US$450.8 million from US$399.7 million a year ago.

Prospects: Our evaluation of American Equity Investment Life Holding Co as of June 19, 2016 is the result of our systematic analysis on three basic characteristics: earnings strength, relative valuation, and recent stock price movement. The company has managed to produce a neutral trend in earnings per share over the past 5 quarters. However, while recent estimates for the company have been mixed, AEL has posted results that fell short of analysts expectations. Based on operating earnings yield, the company is undervalued when compared to all of the companies in our coverage universe. Share price changes over the past year indicates that AEL will perform very poorly over the near term.

Financial Data
(US$ in Thousands)

	3 Mos	12/31/2015	12/31/2014	12/31/2013	12/31/2012	12/31/2011	12/31/2010	12/31/2009
Earnings Per Share	2.08	2.72	1.58	3.38	0.89	1.37	0.68	1.18
Cash Flow Per Share	9.58	6.40	9.51	13.16	12.77	4.67	7.19	9.20
Tang Book Value Per Share	27.20	23.90	28.13	19.63	27.86	24.36	16.47	13.43
Dividends Per Share	0.220	0.220	0.200	0.180	0.150	0.120	0.100	0.080
Dividend Payout %	10.58	8.09	12.66	5.33	16.85	8.76	14.71	6.78
Income Statement								
Total Revenue	417,604	1,518,937	2,168,973	2,610,692	1,588,558	1,139,775	1,285,592	1,188,913
Income Before Taxes	(69,103)	337,314	196,064	389,332	85,989	132,914	65,266	86,164
Income Taxes	(24,262)	117,484	70,041	136,049	28,191	46,666	22,333	17,634
Net Income	(44,841)	219,830	126,023	253,283	57,798	86,248	42,933	68,530
Average Shares	82,961	80,961	79,893	75,040	65,675	63,619	64,580	58,915
Balance Sheet								
Total Assets	51,262,936	49,041,163	43,989,734	39,621,499	35,133,478	30,874,719	26,426,763	21,312,004
Total Liabilities	49,028,620	47,096,628	41,849,858	38,236,812	33,413,241	29,466,040	25,488,716	20,557,381
Stockholders' Equity	2,234,316	1,944,535	2,139,876	1,384,687	1,720,237	1,408,679	938,047	754,623
Shares Outstanding	82,155	81,354	76,062	70,535	61,750	57,836	56,968	56,203
Statistical Record								
Return on Assets %	0.35	0.47	0.30	0.68	0.17	0.30	0.18	0.36
Return on Equity %	7.41	10.76	7.15	16.31	3.68	7.35	5.07	10.99
Net Margin %	N.M.	14.47	5.81	9.70	3.64	7.57	3.34	5.76
Asset Turnover	0.03	0.03	0.05	0.07	0.05	0.04	0.05	0.06
Price Range	29.67-12.81	29.67-22.76	29.46-20.43	26.38-12.21	12.95-10.05	13.85-8.17	12.95-6.90	8.46-3.09
P/E Ratio	14.26-6.16	10.91-8.37	18.65-12.93	7.80-3.61	14.55-11.29	10.11-5.96	19.04-10.15	7.17-2.62
Average Yield %	0.92	0.82	0.83	1.01	1.30	1.03	0.99	1.26

Address: 6000 Westown Parkway, West Des Moines, IA 50266
Telephone: 515-221-0002

Web Site: www.american-equity.com
Officers: David J. Noble - Chairman John M. Matovina - Vice-Chairman, President, Chief Executive Officer, Chief Financial Officer, Treasurer

Auditors: KPMG LLP
Investor Contact: 515-273-3602
Transfer Agents: Computershare Trust Company, N.A., Providence, RI

AMERICAN EXPRESS CO.

Exchange	Symbol	Price	52Wk Range	Yield	P/E
NYS	AXP	$65.76 (5/31/2016)	81.36-51.11	1.76	13.13

*7 Year Price Score 95.84   *NYSE Composite Index=100   *12 Month Price Score 90.93

TRADING VOLUME (thousand shares)

Interim Earnings (Per Share)

Qtr.	Mar	Jun	Sep	Dec
2013	1.15	1.27	1.25	1.21
2014	1.33	1.43	1.40	1.39
2015	1.48	1.42	1.24	0.90
2016	1.45	...	...	...

Interim Dividends (Per Share)

Amt	Decl	Ex	Rec	Pay
0.29Q	09/28/2015	10/07/2015	10/09/2015	11/10/2015
0.29Q	12/01/2015	01/06/2016	01/08/2016	02/10/2016
0.29Q	03/28/2016	04/06/2016	04/08/2016	05/10/2016
0.29Q	05/03/2016	06/29/2016	07/01/2016	08/10/2016

Indicated Div: $1.16

Valuation Analysis

		Institutional Holding	
Forecast EPS	$5.59 (05/20/2016)	No of Institutions	1800
Market Cap	$62.5 Billion	Shares	892,601,216
Book Value	$20.7 Billion	% Held	77.64
Price/Book	3.02		
Price/Sales	1.81		

Business Summary: Credit & Lending (MIC: 5.4.1 SIC: 6141 NAIC: 522210)

American Express is a bank holding company. Through its subsidiaries, Co. is a global services company. Co. engages in businesses comprising four reportable operating segments: U.S. Card Services, International Card Services, Global Commercial Services and Global Network and Merchant Services. Co.'s range of products and services includes: charge and credit card products; network services; merchant acquisition and processing, servicing and settlement, and point-of-sale, marketing and information products and services for merchants; fee services, including fraud prevention services; expense management products and services; travel-related services; and stored value/prepaid products.

Recent Developments: For the quarter ended Mar 31 2016, net income decreased 6.5% to US$1.43 billion from US$1.53 billion in the year-earlier quarter. Net interest income increased 9.2% to US$1.58 billion from US$1.45 billion in the year-earlier quarter. Provision for loan losses was US$434.0 million versus US$420.0 million in the prior-year quarter, an increase of 3.3%. Non-interest income rose 0.1% to US$6.51 billion from US$6.50 billion, while non-interest expense advanced 4.9% to US$5.47 billion.

Prospects: Our evaluation of American Express Co. as of June 19, 2016 is the result of our systematic analysis on three basic characteristics: earnings strength, relative valuation, and recent stock price movement. The company has enjoyed a very positive trend in earnings per share over the past 5 quarters and while recent estimates for the company have remained steady, AXP has posted better than expected results. Based on operating earnings yield, the company is undervalued when compared to all of the companies in our coverage universe. Share price changes over the past year indicates that AXP will perform in line with the market over the near term.

Financial Data
(US$ in Thousands)

	3 Mos	12/31/2015	12/31/2014	12/31/2013	12/31/2012	12/31/2011	12/31/2010	12/31/2009
Earnings Per Share	5.01	5.05	5.56	4.88	3.89	4.12	3.35	1.54
Cash Flow Per Share	11.77	10.98	10.52	7.90	6.22	8.89	7.82	5.47
Tang Book Value Per Share	21.79	17.68	16.42	14.55	13.31	12.43	10.54	9.53
Dividends Per Share	0.870	1.100	0.980	0.860	0.780	0.720	0.720	0.720
Dividend Payout %	17.37	21.78	17.63	17.62	20.05	17.48	21.49	46.75
Income Statement								
Total Revenue	8,513,000	34,441,000	35,999,000	34,932,000	33,808,000	32,282,000	30,242,000	26,730,000
Income Before Taxes	2,184,000	7,938,000	8,991,000	7,888,000	6,451,000	6,956,000	5,964,000	2,841,000
Income Taxes	758,000	2,775,000	3,106,000	2,529,000	1,969,000	2,057,000	1,907,000	704,000
Net Income	1,426,000	5,163,000	5,885,000	5,359,000	4,482,000	4,935,000	4,057,000	2,130,000
Average Shares	963,000	1,003,000	1,051,000	1,089,000	1,141,000	1,184,000	1,195,000	1,171,000
Balance Sheet								
Total Assets	158,816,000	161,184,000	159,103,000	153,375,000	153,140,000	153,337,000	147,042,000	124,088,000
Total Liabilities	138,089,000	140,511,000	138,430,000	133,879,000	134,254,000	134,543,000	130,812,000	109,682,000
Stockholders' Equity	20,727,000	20,673,000	20,673,000	19,496,000	18,886,000	18,794,000	16,230,000	14,406,000
Shares Outstanding	951,000	969,000	1,023,000	1,064,000	1,105,000	1,164,000	1,197,000	1,192,000
Statistical Record								
Return on Assets %	3.23	3.22	3.77	3.50	2.92	3.29	2.99	1.70
Return on Equity %	23.80	24.97	29.30	27.92	23.72	28.18	26.49	16.23
Net Margin %	16.75	14.99	16.35	15.34	13.26	15.29	13.42	7.97
Asset Turnover	0.22	0.22	0.23	0.23	0.22	0.21	0.22	0.21
Price Range	81.36-51.11	93.04-67.87	95.84-80.24	90.73-57.48	61.05-48.24	53.59-42.36	48.05-36.79	41.83-10.26
P/E Ratio	16.24-10.20	18.42-13.44	17.24-14.43	18.59-11.78	15.69-12.40	13.01-10.28	14.34-10.98	27.16-6.66
Average Yield %	1.21	1.41	1.09	1.18	1.39	1.52	1.73	2.67

Address: 200 Vesey Street, New York, NY 10285	Web Site: www.americanexpress.com	Auditors: PricewaterhouseCoopers LLP
Telephone: 212-640-2000	Officers: Kenneth I. Chenault - Chairman, Chief Executive Officer Stephen J. Squeri - Vice Chairman, Division Officer	Transfer Agents: Computershare Shareowner Services LLC, Canton, MA
Fax: 212-640-0404		

AMERICAN FINANCIAL GROUP INC

Exchange	Symbol	Price	52Wk Range	Yield	P/E	Div Achiever
NYS	AFG	$73.28 (5/31/2016)	75.17-63.53	1.53	15.05	10 Years

*7 Year Price Score 130.34 *NYSE Composite Index=100 *12 Month Price Score 99.94

Interim Earnings (Per Share)

Qtr.	Mar	Jun	Sep	Dec
2013	1.32	1.20	0.92	1.72
2014	1.13	1.15	1.28	1.41
2015	0.21	1.57	0.71	1.45
2016	1.14	...	...	...

Interim Dividends (Per Share)

Amt	Decl	Ex	Rec	Pay
0.28Q	10/01/2015	10/13/2015	10/15/2015	10/26/2015
1.00Sp	11/04/2015	12/11/2015	12/15/2015	12/24/2015
0.28Q	01/04/2016	01/13/2016	01/15/2016	01/25/2016
0.28Q	04/01/2016	04/13/2016	04/15/2016	04/25/2016

Indicated Div: $1.12 (Div. Reinv. Plan)

Valuation Analysis / Institutional Holding

Forecast EPS	$5.65 (05/13/2016)	No of Institutions	422
Market Cap	$6.4 Billion	Shares	64,209,584
Book Value	$4.8 Billion	% Held	
Price/Book	1.34	Price/Sales	1.01	57.65

Business Summary: General Insurance (MIC: 5.2.1 SIC: 6331 NAIC: 524126)

American Financial Group is a holding company. Co.'s segments include: Property and Casualty Insurance, which includes Property and Transportation(inland and ocean marine, agricultural-related, and commercial automobile), Specialty Casualty (executive and professional liability, umbrella and excess liability, excess and surplus, general liability, targeted programs, and workers' compensation), and Specialty Financial (fidelity and surety and lease and loan services); Annuity, which sells fixed and fixed-indexed annuities in the retail, financial institutions and education markets; and Other, which includes commercial real estate operations.

Recent Developments: For the quarter ended Mar 31 2016, net income increased 316.0% to US$104.0 million from US$25.0 million in the year-earlier quarter. Revenues were US$1.48 billion, up 13.7% from US$1.30 billion the year before. Net premiums earned were US$1.00 billion versus US$971.0 million in the prior-year quarter, an increase of 3.4%.

Prospects: Our evaluation of American Financial Group Inc. as of June 19, 2016 is the result of our systematic analysis on three basic characteristics: earnings strength, relative valuation, and recent stock price movement. The company has managed to produce a neutral trend in earnings per share over the past 5 quarters and while recent estimates for the company have remained steady, AFG has posted better than expected results. Based on operating earnings yield, the company is undervalued when compared to all of the companies in our coverage universe. Share price changes over the past year indicates that AFG will perform well over the near term.

Financial Data
(US$ in Thousands)

	3 Mos	12/31/2015	12/31/2014	12/31/2013	12/31/2012	12/31/2011	12/31/2010	12/31/2009
Earnings Per Share	4.87	3.94	4.97	5.16	5.09	3.33	4.33	4.45
Cash Flow Per Share	14.90	15.49	...	8.51	8.65	6.58	7.91	7.90
Tang Book Value Per Share	52.39	50.22	53.34	49.31	49.37	44.55	40.73	31.52
Dividends Per Share	2.060	2.030	1.91	1.805	0.970	0.662	0.575	0.520
Dividend Payout %	42.30	51.52	38.43	34.98	19.06	19.89	13.28	11.69
Income Statement								
Premium Income	1,004,000	4,328,000	3,986,000	3,318,000	3,165,000	3,189,000	3,001,000	2,855,900
Total Revenue	1,475,000	6,145,000	5,713,000	5,092,000	5,062,000	4,750,000	4,497,000	4,320,600
Benefits & Claims	818,000	3,558,000	3,306,000	2,731,000	2,779,000	2,623,000	2,269,000	1,982,800
Income Before Taxes	156,000	565,000	626,000	689,000	537,000	560,000	689,000	812,900
Income Taxes	52,000	195,000	220,000	236,000	135,000	240,000	266,000	282,200
Net Income	101,000	352,000	452,000	471,000	488,000	343,000	479,000	519,300
Average Shares	88,500	89,400	91,000	91,200	95,900	102,900	110,500	116,800
Balance Sheet								
Total Assets	51,038,000	49,859,000	47,535,000	42,087,000	39,171,000	36,042,000	32,454,000	27,683,300
Total Liabilities	46,283,000	45,267,000	42,306,000	37,488,000	34,593,000	31,497,000	27,984,000	23,902,200
Stockholders' Equity	4,755,000	4,592,000	4,879,000	4,599,000	4,578,000	4,545,000	4,470,000	3,781,100
Shares Outstanding	86,966	87,474	91,000	89,513	88,979	97,846	105,168	113,386
Statistical Record								
Return on Assets %	0.87	0.72	1.01	1.16	1.29	1.00	1.59	1.92
Return on Equity %	8.97	7.43	9.54	10.26	10.67	7.61	11.61	16.56
Loss Ratio %	81.47	82.21	82.94	82.31	87.80	82.25	75.61	69.43
Net Margin %	6.85	5.73	7.91	9.25	9.64	7.22	10.65	12.02
Price Range	75.17-63.13	75.17-58.04	62.36-52.93	58.16-39.52	40.25-36.58	37.30-30.09	32.61-24.30	26.42-13.04
P/E Ratio	15.44-12.96	19.08-14.73	12.55-10.65	11.27-7.66	7.91-7.19	11.20-9.04	7.53-5.61	5.94-2.93
Average Yield %	3.00	3.03	3.31	3.60	2.54	1.94	1.99	2.38

Address: 301 East Fourth Street, Cincinnati, OH 45202 **Telephone:** 513-579-2121	**Web Site:** www.afginc.com **Officers:** Carl H. Lindner - Chairman Carl H. Lindner - Co-President, Co-Chief Executive Officer	**Auditors:** Ernst & Young LLP **Investor Contact:** 513-579-6739 **Transfer Agents:** American Stock Transfer & Trust Company, New York, NY

AMERICAN HOMES 4 RENT

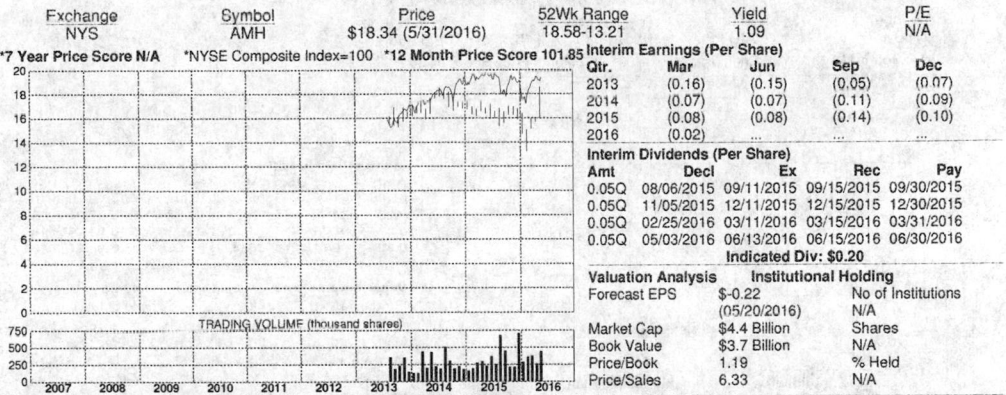

Exchange	Symbol	Price	52Wk Range	Yield	P/E
NYS	AMH	$18.34 (5/31/2016)	18.58-13.21	1.09	N/A

*7 Year Price Score N/A   *NYSE Composite Index=100   *12 Month Price Score 101.85

Interim Earnings (Per Share)

Qtr.	Mar	Jun	Sep	Dec
2013	(0.16)	(0.15)	(0.05)	(0.07)
2014	(0.07)	(0.07)	(0.11)	(0.09)
2015	(0.08)	(0.08)	(0.14)	(0.10)
2016	(0.02)	...	...	...

Interim Dividends (Per Share)

Amt	Decl	Ex	Rec	Pay
0.05Q	08/06/2015	09/11/2015	09/15/2015	09/30/2015
0.05Q	11/05/2015	12/11/2015	12/15/2015	12/30/2015
0.05Q	02/25/2016	03/11/2016	03/15/2016	03/31/2016
0.05Q	05/03/2016	06/13/2016	06/15/2016	06/30/2016

Indicated Div: $0.20

Valuation Analysis		Institutional Holding	
Forecast EPS	$-0.22	No of Institutions	
	(05/20/2016)	N/A	
Market Cap	$4.4 Billion	Shares	
Book Value	$3.7 Billion	N/A	
Price/Book	1.19	% Held	
Price/Sales	6.33	N/A	

TRADING VOLUME (thousand shares)

Business Summary: REITs (MIC: 5.3.1 SIC: 6798 NAIC: 525930)

American Homes 4 Rent is an internally managed Maryland real estate investment trust engaged in acquiring, renovating, leasing and operating single-family homes as rental properties. As of Dec 31 2014, Co. owned 34,599 single-family properties in 22 states. As of the same date, Co.'s entire portfolio of single-family properties was internally managed through its proprietary property management platform.

Recent Developments: For the quarter ended Mar 31 2016, net income amounted to US$5.0 million versus a net loss of US$8.3 million in the year-earlier quarter. Revenues were US$195.2 million, up 48.2% from US$131.7 million the year before. Revenues from property income rose 46.7% to US$191.2 million from US$130.4 million in the corresponding quarter a year earlier.

Prospects: Our evaluation of American Homes 4 Rent as of June 19, 2016 is the result of our systematic analysis on three basic characteristics: earnings strength, relative valuation, and recent stock price movement. The company has enjoyed a very positive trend in earnings per share over the past 5 quarters. Because the company lacks sufficient analyst estimate data, we place greater weight on the historical EPS trend as the measure of earnings strength. Based on operating earnings yield, the company is overvalued when compared to all of the companies in our coverage universe. Share price changes over the past year indicates that AMH will perform in line with the market over the near term.

Financial Data
(US$ in Thousands)

	3 Mos	12/31/2015	12/31/2014	12/31/2013	12/31/2012	12/31/2011
Earnings Per Share	(0.34)	(0.40)	(0.34)	(0.36)	(1.42)	(0.01)
Cash Flow Per Share	1.04	0.96	0.82	0.13	(0.90)	(0.01)
Tang Book Value Per Share	14.89	15.10	15.74	15.17	23.40	0.09
Dividends Per Share	0.200	0.200	0.200	0.050	...	...
Income Statement						
Total Revenue	195,193	630,576	398,874	139,032	4,540	65
EBITDA	100,219	265,196	152,305	51,283	(8,125)	(21)
Depn & Amortn	64,214	223,731	165,516	70,987	2,111	21
Income Before Taxes	5,028	(47,948)	(33,092)	(20,074)	(10,236)	(42)
Net Income	5,028	(47,948)	(33,092)	(19,066)	(10,236)	...
Average Shares	219,157	210,600	196,348	123,592	7,225	3,301
Balance Sheet						
Current Assets	220,518	168,968	185,985	175,419	397,198	...
Total Assets	8,097,710	6,807,786	6,227,351	4,224,144	921,458	3,523
Current Liabilities	638,946	291,591	486,723	573,485	16,294	49
Long-Term Obligations	2,955,407	2,580,962	1,571,034	...	...	...
Total Liabilities	4,410,823	3,548,441	2,777,250	1,289,200	16,784	49
Stockholders' Equity	3,686,887	3,259,345	3,450,101	2,934,944	904,674	3,474
Shares Outstanding	239,554	207,870	211,473	185,504	38,664	38,664
Statistical Record						
EBITDA Margin %	51.34	42.06	38.18	36.89	N.M.	N.M.
Net Margin %	2.58	N.M.	N.M.	N.M.	N.M.	...
Asset Turnover	0.09	0.10	0.08	0.05	0.01	...
Current Ratio	0.35	0.58	0.38	0.31	24.38	...
Debt to Equity	0.80	0.79	0.46	...	...	...
Price Range	17.33-13.21	17.48-15.30	18.51-15.87	16.90-15.22	...	...
Average Yield %	1.24	1.21	1.16	0.31	...	...

Address: 30601 Agoura Road, Suite 200, Agoura Hills, CA 91301
Telephone: 805-413-5300

Web Site: www.americanhomes4rent.com
Officers: David P. Singelyn - Chief Executive Officer, Interim Chief Financial Officer David Goldberg - Executive Vice President

Auditors: BDO USA, LLP
Transfer Agents: American Stock Transfer & Trust Company, LLC

AMERICAN INTERNATIONAL GROUP INC

Exchange	Symbol	Price	52Wk Range	Yield	P/E
NYS	AIG	$57.88 (5/31/2016)	64.54-50.20	2.21	N/A

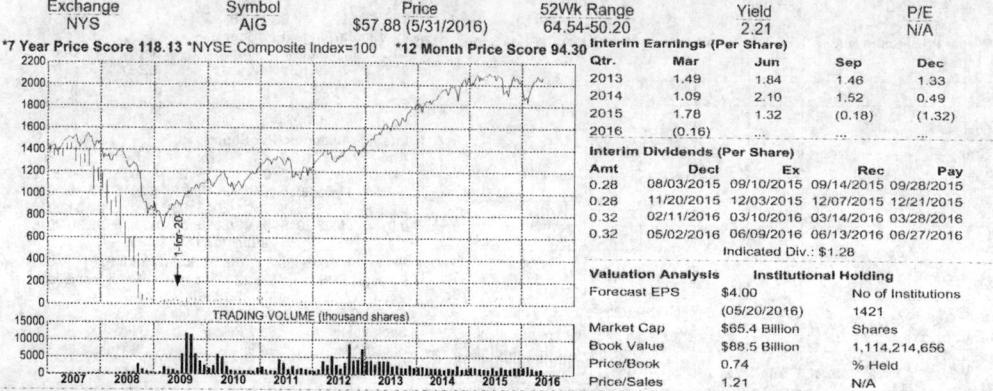

*7 Year Price Score 118.13 *NYSE Composite Index=100 *12 Month Price Score 94.30

Interim Earnings (Per Share)

Qtr.	Mar	Jun	Sep	Dec
2013	1.49	1.84	1.46	1.33
2014	1.09	2.10	1.52	0.49
2015	1.78	1.32	(0.18)	(1.32)
2016	(0.16)			

Interim Dividends (Per Share)

Amt	Decl	Ex	Rec	Pay
0.28	08/03/2015	09/10/2015	09/14/2015	09/28/2015
0.28	11/20/2015	12/03/2015	12/07/2015	12/21/2015
0.32	02/11/2016	03/10/2016	03/14/2016	03/28/2016
0.32	05/02/2016	06/09/2016	06/13/2016	06/27/2016

Indicated Div.: $1.28

Valuation Analysis / **Institutional Holding**

Forecast EPS	$4.00	No of Institutions
	(05/20/2016)	1421
Market Cap	$65.4 Billion	Shares
Book Value	$88.5 Billion	1,114,214,656
Price/Book	0.74	% Held
Price/Sales	1.21	N/A

Business Summary: General Insurance (MIC: 5.2.1 SIC: 6331 NAIC: 524126)

American International Group is a holding company. Co. provides a range of property casualty insurance, life insurance, retirement products, mortgage insurance and other financial services to customers in more than 100 countries and jurisdictions. Co. has two reportable segments: Commercial Insurance, which provides insurance products and services for commercial and institutional customers, and its operating segments consist of Property Casualty, Mortgage Guaranty and Institutional Markets; and Consumer Insurance, which provides a portfolio of retirement, life insurance and personal insurance products, and its operating segments consist of Retirement, Life, and Personal Insurance.

Recent Developments: For the quarter ended Mar 31 2016, loss from continuing operations was US$156.0 million compared with income of US$2.48 billion in the year-earlier quarter. Net loss amounted to US$203.0 million versus net income of US$2.48 billion in the year-earlier quarter. Revenues were US$11.78 billion, down 26.3% from US$15.98 billion the year before. Net premiums earned were US$8.81 billion versus US$8.82 billion in the prior-year quarter, a decrease of 0.2%. Net investment income fell 25.0% to US$2.62 billion from US$3.50 billion a year ago.

Prospects: Our evaluation of American International Group Inc. as of June 19, 2016 is the result of our systematic analysis on three basic characteristics: earnings strength, relative valuation, and recent stock price movement. The company has produced a positive trend in earnings per share over the past 5 quarters. However, while recent estimates for the company have been lowered by analysts, AIG has posted results that fell short of analysts expectations. Based on operating earnings yield, the company is overvalued when compared to all of the companies in our coverage universe. Share price changes over the past year indicates that AIG will perform well over the near term.

Financial Data
(US$ in Thousands)

	3 Mos	12/31/2015	12/31/2014	12/31/2013	12/31/2012	12/31/2011	12/31/2010	12/31/2009
Earnings Per Share	(0.34)	1.65	5.20	6.13	2.04	9.44	11.60	(90.48)
Cash Flow Per Share	1.32	2.21	3.51	3.98	2.17	0.02	123.80	137.33
Tang Book Value Per Share	78.28	75.10	77.69	68.62	66.38	55.33	85.45	N.M.
Dividends Per Share	1.005	0.810	0.500	0.200	...	...	...	...
Dividend Payout %	...	49.09	9.62	3.26	...	...	...	...
Income Statement								
Premium Income	8,806,000	36,655,000	37,254,000	37,350,000	38,011,000	38,990,000	48,029,000	64,702,000
Total Revenue	11,779,000	58,327,000	64,406,000	68,678,000	65,656,000	64,237,000	77,301,000	96,004,000
Benefits & Claims	6,387,000	...	...	...	...	...	...	...
Income Before Taxes	(214,000)	3,281,000	10,501,000	9,368,000	9,322,000	(1,065,000)	17,936,000	(13,648,000)
Income Taxes	(58,000)	1,059,000	2,927,000	360,000	1,570,000	(18,036,000)	5,859,000	(1,878,000)
Net Income	(183,000)	2,196,000	7,529,000	9,085,000	3,438,000	17,798,000	7,786,000	(10,949,000)
Average Shares	1,156,548	1,334,464	1,447,553	1,481,206	1,687,226	1,799,458	136,649	135,324
Balance Sheet								
Total Assets	502,777,000	496,943,000	515,581,000	541,329,000	548,633,000	555,773,000	683,443,000	847,585,000
Total Liabilities	414,259,000	407,285,000	408,683,000	440,859,000	450,631,000	450,822,000	598,124,000	777,761,000
Stockholders' Equity	88,518,000	89,658,000	106,898,000	100,470,000	98,002,000	104,951,000	85,319,000	69,824,000
Shares Outstanding	1,130,738	1,193,916	1,375,926	1,464,063	1,476,321	1,896,821	140,463	135,070
Statistical Record								
Return on Assets %	N.M.	0.43	1.42	1.67	0.62	2.87	1.02	N.M.
Return on Equity %	N.M.	2.23	7.26	9.15	3.38	18.71	10.04	N.M.
Loss Ratio %	72.53	...	...	...	...	...	...	...
Net Margin %	(1.55)	3.76	11.69	13.23	5.24	27.71	10.07	(11.40)
Price Range	64.54-50.20	64.54-48.87	56.51-46.88	52.30-34.84	37.21-23.54	61.18-20.10	59.38-22.16	50.23-7.00
P/E Ratio	...	39.12-29.62	10.87-9.02	8.53-5.68	18.24-11.54	6.48-2.13	5.12-1.91	...
Average Yield %	1.71	1.38	0.95	0.45	...	...	...	...

Address: 175 Water Street, New York, NY 10038 Telephone: 212-770-7000	Web Site: www.aig.com Officers: Robert Steven Miller - Chairman Peter D. Hancock - President, Chief Executive Officer	Auditors: PricewaterhouseCoopers LLP Transfer Agents: Wells Fargo Bank, N.A. Shareowner Services, St. Paul, MN

AMERICAN STATES WATER CO

Exchange	Symbol	Price	52Wk Range	Yield	P/E	Div Achiever
NYS	AWR	$39.06 (5/31/2016)	47.18-36.00	2.29	25.04	62 Years

*7 Year Price Score 133.80 *NYSE Composite Index=100 *12 Month Price Score 98.51

Interim Earnings (Per Share)

Qtr.	Mar	Jun	Sep	Dec
2013	0.34	0.42	0.63	0.30
2014	0.28	0.39	0.54	0.35
2015	0.32	0.41	0.56	0.31
2016	0.28	...	...	...

Interim Dividends (Per Share)

Amt	Decl	Ex	Rec	Pay
0.224Q	07/29/2015	08/12/2015	08/14/2015	09/01/2015
0.224Q	10/29/2015	11/12/2015	11/16/2015	12/01/2015
0.224Q	01/27/2016	02/11/2016	02/16/2016	03/01/2016
0.224Q	05/02/2016	05/16/2016	05/18/2016	06/01/2016

Indicated Div: $0.90 (Div. Reinv. Plan)

Valuation Analysis | **Institutional Holding**

Forecast EPS	$1.68	No of Institutions
	(05/20/2016)	286
Market Cap	$1.4 Billion	Shares
Book Value	$467.4 Million	24,632,712
Price/Book	3.05	% Held
Price/Sales	3.16	59.46

TRADING VOLUME (thousand shares)

Business Summary: Water Utilities (MIC: 3.2.1 SIC: 4941 NAIC: 221310)

American States Water is a holding company. Co. is the parent company of Golden State Water Company (GSWC) and American States Utility Services, Inc. (ASUS) and its subsidiaries. Co. has three reportable segments: water, electric and contracted services. Within the segments, Co. has two principal business units, water and electric service utility operations, conducted through GSWC, and contracted services conducted through ASUS and its subsidiaries. GSWC is a California public utility company engaged principally in the purchase, production and distribution of water in 10 counties in the State of California. At Dec 31 2015, GSWC served 260,151 water customers and 23,846 electric customers.

Recent Developments: For the quarter ended Mar 31 2016, net income decreased 16.5% to US$10.2 million from US$12.1 million in the year-earlier quarter. Revenues were US$93.5 million, down 7.3% from US$100.9 million the year before. Operating income was US$21.2 million versus US$24.9 million in the prior-year quarter, a decrease of 14.7%. Indirect operating expenses decreased 4.9% to US$72.3 million from US$76.0 million in the equivalent prior-year period.

Prospects: Our evaluation of American States Water Co. as of June 19, 2016 is the result of our systematic analysis on three basic characteristics: earnings strength, relative valuation, and recent stock price movement. The company has managed to produce a neutral trend in earnings per share over the past 5 quarters and while recent estimates for the company have remained steady, AWR has posted results that fell short of analysts expectations. Based on operating earnings yield, the company is about fairly valued when compared to all of the companies in our coverage universe. Share price changes over the past year indicates that AWR will perform in line with the market over the near term.

Financial Data

(US$ in Thousands)	3 Mos	12/31/2015	12/31/2014	12/31/2013	12/31/2012	12/31/2011	12/31/2010	12/31/2009
Earnings Per Share	1.56	1.60	1.57	1.61	1.41	1.22	0.89	0.81
Cash Flow Per Share	2.31	2.54	4.22	3.51	2.66	2.14	1.45	2.01
Tang Book Value Per Share	12.76	12.73	13.21	12.69	11.79	10.85	10.10	9.58
Dividends Per Share	0.885	0.874	0.831	0.760	0.635	0.550	0.520	0.505
Dividend Payout %	56.73	54.63	52.93	47.20	45.04	45.27	58.76	62.35
Income Statement								
Total Revenue	93,527	458,641	465,791	472,077	466,908	419,274	398,942	360,973
EBITDA	31,379	161,519	161,547	161,144	154,759	133,257	111,523	103,272
Depn & Amortn	9,965	42,674	41,751	40,967	43,234	38,349	38,167	33,557
Income Before Taxes	15,963	98,215	99,106	98,469	90,093	72,086	54,126	48,356
Income Taxes	5,813	37,731	38,048	35,783	35,945	30,076	23,035	18,825
Net Income	10,150	60,484	61,058	62,686	54,148	45,859	33,197	29,531
Average Shares	36,697	37,614	38,880	38,869	38,262	37,674	37,472	36,376
Balance Sheet								
Current Assets	131,125	132,697	209,451	191,617	184,033	165,601	204,984	96,015
Total Assets	1,368,891	1,348,600	1,378,298	1,310,183	1,280,943	1,238,362	1,192,035	1,113,293
Current Liabilities	139,051	123,507	99,290	100,906	93,697	104,370	178,842	99,706
Long-Term Obligations	320,910	325,541	325,798	326,079	332,463	340,395	299,839	305,866
Total Liabilities	901,490	882,655	871,497	817,779	826,364	829,696	814,494	753,863
Stockholders' Equity	467,401	465,945	506,801	492,404	454,579	408,666	377,541	359,430
Shares Outstanding	36,554	36,501	38,286	38,720	38,474	37,577	37,261	37,064
Statistical Record								
Return on Assets %	4.27	4.44	4.54	4.84	4.29	3.77	2.88	2.72
Return on Equity %	12.12	12.44	12.22	13.24	12.51	11.67	9.01	8.82
EBITDA Margin %	33.55	35.22	34.68	34.14	33.15	31.78	27.95	28.61
Net Margin %	10.85	13.19	13.11	13.28	11.60	10.94	8.32	8.18
Asset Turnover	0.33	0.34	0.35	0.36	0.37	0.35	0.35	0.33
Current Ratio	0.94	1.07	2.11	1.90	1.96	1.59	1.15	0.96
Debt to Equity	0.69	0.70	0.64	0.66	0.73	0.83	0.79	0.85
Price Range	47.18-36.00	43.57-36.00	38.71-27.15	32.86-23.99	23.99-17.15	18.16-15.64	19.53-15.80	19.27-14.89
P/E Ratio	30.24-23.08	27.23-22.50	24.66-17.29	20.41-14.90	17.01-12.16	14.89-12.82	21.94-17.75	23.79-18.38
Average Yield %	2.20	2.21	2.21	2.64	2.76	3.16	3.20	2.94

Address: 630 E. Foothill Boulevard, San Dimas, CA 91773-1212 Telephone: 909-394-3600	Web Site: www.aswater.com Officers: Lloyd E. Ross - Chairman Robert J. Sprowls - President, Chief Executive Officer	Auditors: PricewaterhouseCoopers LLP Investor Contact: 909-394-3600 Transfer Agents: Computershare Shareowner Services, Jersey City, NJ

AMERICAN TOWER CORP

Exchange	Symbol	Price	52Wk Range	Yield	P/E
NYS	AMT	$105.78 (5/31/2016)	107.18-83.66	2.00	68.25

*7 Year Price Score 117.28 *NYSE Composite Index=100 *12 Month Price Score 107.40

TRADING VOLUME (thousand shares)

Interim Earnings (Per Share)

Qtr.	Mar	Jun	Sep	Dec
2013	0.43	0.25	0.45	0.25
2014	0.51	0.58	0.50	0.42
2015	0.45	0.30	0.18	0.49
2016	0.58	...	...	...

Interim Dividends (Per Share)

Amt	Decl	Ex	Rec	Pay
0.46Q	09/10/2015	09/21/2015	09/23/2015	10/07/2015
0.49Q	12/03/2015	12/14/2015	12/16/2015	01/13/2016
0.51Q	03/09/2016	04/08/2016	04/12/2016	04/28/2016
0.53Q	06/02/2016	06/15/2016	06/17/2016	07/15/2016

Indicated Div: $2.12

Valuation Analysis

Forecast EPS	$2.31
	(05/20/2016)
Market Cap	$44.9 Billion
Book Value	$6.9 Billion
Price/Book	6.48
Price/Sales	9.02

Institutional Holding

No of Institutions	1048
Shares	456,415,648
% Held	N/A

Business Summary: REITs (MIC: 5.3.1 SIC: 6798 NAIC: 525930)

American Tower is a holding company. Through its subsidiaries, Co. is a real estate investment trusts and independent owner, operator and developer of communications real estate. Co.'s property operations leases space on communications sites to wireless service providers, radio and television broadcast companies, wireless data providers, government agencies and municipalities and tenants in a number of other industries. Co. services operations provides tower-related services in the U.S., including site acquisition, zoning and permitting and structural analysis, which primarily support its site leasing business, including the addition of new tenants and equipment on its sites.

Recent Developments: For the quarter ended Mar 31 2016, net income increased 43.9% to US$281.3 million from US$195.5 million in the year-earlier quarter. Revenues were US$1.29 billion, up 19.4% from US$1.08 billion the year before.

Prospects: Our evaluation of Americann Tower REIT, Inc. as of June 19, 2016 is the result of our systematic analysis on three basic characteristics: earnings strength, relative valuation, and recent stock price movement. The company has enjoyed a very positive trend in earnings per share over the past 5 quarters. However, while recent estimates for the company have been mixed, AMT has posted better than expected results. Based on operating earnings yield, the company is overvalued when compared to all of the companies in our coverage universe. Share price changes over the past year indicates that AMT will perform well over the near term.

Financial Data

(US$ in Thousands)	3 Mos	12/31/2015	12/31/2014	12/31/2013	12/31/2012	12/31/2011	12/31/2010	12/31/2009
Earnings Per Share	1.55	1.41	2.00	1.38	1.60	0.99	0.92	0.61
Cash Flow Per Share	5.27	5.21	5.39	4.05	3.57	2.95	2.55	2.11
Dividends Per Share	1.810	1.810	1.400	1.100	0.900	0.350	...	...
Dividend Payout %	116.77	128.37	70.00	79.71	56.25	35.35	...	...
Income Statement								
Total Revenue	1,289,047	4,771,516	4,100,048	3,361,407	2,875,960	2,443,532	1,985,335	1,724,114
EBITDA	805,695	2,059,623	1,973,189	1,451,704	1,492,921	1,150,557	1,068,807	1,079,815
Depn & Amortn	341,634	661,400	551,800	483,600	411,900	353,400	286,000	424,457
Income Before Taxes	310,431	829,962	865,704	541,749	701,294	506,695	556,025	421,487
Income Taxes	29,124	157,955	62,505	59,541	107,304	125,080	182,489	182,565
Net Income	275,159	685,074	824,910	551,333	637,283	396,462	372,936	246,595
Average Shares	427,888	423,015	400,086	399,146	399,287	400,195	404,072	406,948
Balance Sheet								
Current Assets	1,036,516	996,468	947,968	952,656	829,528	842,771	1,404,174	651,356
Total Assets	27,064,315	26,904,272	21,331,545	20,272,571	14,089,129	12,232,430	10,368,014	8,512,668
Current Liabilities	1,198,156	1,200,029	1,929,692	924,758	632,178	779,591	542,195	391,244
Long-Term Obligations	16,884,242	17,068,807	13,711,084	14,408,146	8,693,345	7,134,492	5,512,492	4,141,060
Total Liabilities	20,131,066	20,252,593	17,377,985	16,738,406	10,516,028	8,945,210	6,866,570	5,197,586
Stockholders' Equity	6,933,249	6,651,679	3,953,560	3,534,165	3,573,101	3,287,220	3,501,444	3,315,082
Shares Outstanding	424,563	423,885	396,698	394,864	395,091	393,642	398,677	401,596
Statistical Record								
Return on Assets %	2.89	2.84	3.97	3.21	4.83	3.51	3.95	2.95
Return on Equity %	10.74	12.92	22.03	15.51	18.53	11.68	10.94	7.82
EBITDA Margin %	62.50	43.16	48.13	43.19	51.91	47.09	53.84	62.63
Net Margin %	21.35	14.36	20.12	16.40	22.16	16.22	18.78	14.30
Asset Turnover	0.19	0.20	0.20	0.20	0.22	0.22	0.21	0.21
Current Ratio	0.87	0.83	0.49	1.03	1.31	1.08	2.59	1.66
Debt to Equity	2.44	2.57	3.47	4.08	2.43	2.17	1.57	1.25
Price Range	104.06-83.66	104.06-87.01	105.01-78.83	84.64-68.36	77.27-58.81	60.70-46.35	53.14-38.86	43.47-25.69
P/E Ratio	67.14-53.97	73.80-61.71	52.51-39.41	61.33-49.54	48.29-36.76	61.31-46.82	57.76-42.24	71.26-42.11
Average Yield %	1.91	1.89	1.55	1.44	1.31	0.66	...	...

Address: 116 Huntington Avenue, Boston, MA 02116 **Telephone:** 617-375-7500	**Web Site:** www.americantower.com **Officers:** James D. Taiclet - Chairman, President, Chief Executive Officer Thomas A. Bartlett - Executive Vice President, Chief Financial Officer, Treasurer	**Auditors:** Deloitte & Touche LLP **Investor Contact:** 617-375-7500 **Transfer Agents:** Computershare

46

AMERICAN WATER WORKS CO, INC.

Exchange	Symbol	Price	52Wk Range	Yield	P/E
NYS	AWK	$74.10 (5/31/2016)	75.20-48.63	2.02	27.96

*7 Year Price Score 133.06 *NYSE Composite Index=100 *12 Month Price Score 118.87

TRADING VOLUME (thousand shares)

Interim Earnings (Per Share)

Qtr.	Mar	Jun	Sep	Dec
2013	0.32	0.57	0.84	0.30
2014	0.38	0.61	0.85	0.52
2015	0.44	0.68	0.96	0.55
2016	0.46	...	...	...

Interim Dividends (Per Share)

Amt	Decl	Ex	Rec	Pay
0.34Q	07/24/2015	08/06/2015	08/10/2015	09/01/2015
0.34Q	10/30/2015	11/05/2015	11/09/2015	12/01/2015
0.34Q	12/11/2015	02/04/2016	02/08/2016	03/01/2016
0.375Q	04/22/2016	05/05/2016	05/09/2016	06/01/2016

Indicated Div: $1.50

Valuation Analysis / **Institutional Holding**

Forecast EPS	$2.83 (05/20/2016)	No of Institutions 703
Market Cap	$13.2 Billion	Shares 172,625,952
Book Value	$5.1 Billion	% Held 79.40
Price/Book	2.59	
Price/Sales	1.11	

Business Summary: Water Utilities (MIC: 3.2.1 SIC: 4941 NAIC: 221310)

American Water Works Company is a holding company. Through its subsidiaries, Co. provides drinking water, wastewater and other water related services in 47 states and one Canadian province. Co. has two operating segments: the Regulated Businesses, which provides water and wastewater services to customers; and the Market-Based Operations, which provides a range of market-based water and wastewater services and products including homeowner water and sewer line maintenance services, water and wastewater facility operations and maintenance services and wastewater residuals management services.

Recent Developments: For the quarter ended Mar 31 2016, net income increased 2.5% to US$82.0 million from US$80.0 million in the year-earlier quarter. Revenues were US$743.0 million, up 6.4% from US$698.0 million the year before. Operating income was US$214.0 million versus US$204.0 million in the prior-year quarter, an increase of 4.9%. Indirect operating expenses increased 7.1% to US$529.0 million from US$494.0 million in the equivalent prior-year period.

Prospects: Our evaluation of American Water Works Co. Inc. as of June 19, 2016 is the result of our systematic analysis on three basic characteristics: earnings strength, relative valuation, and recent stock price movement. The company has managed to produce a neutral trend in earnings per share over the past 5 quarters and while recent estimates for the company have remained steady, AWK has posted results that fell short of analysts expectations. Based on operating earnings yield, the company is about fairly valued when compared to all of the companies in our coverage universe. Share price changes over the past year indicates that AWK will perform very well over the near term.

Financial Data
(US$ in Thousands)

	3 Mos	12/31/2015	12/31/2014	12/31/2013	12/31/2012	12/31/2011	12/31/2010	12/31/2009
Earnings Per Share	2.65	2.64	2.35	2.06	2.01	1.75	1.53	(1.39)
Cash Flow Per Share	6.90	6.59	6.13	5.04	5.40	4.61	4.43	3.55
Tang Book Value Per Share	21.21	21.02	20.66	19.73	18.28	17.31	16.44	15.75
Dividends Per Share	1.360	1.330	1.210	0.840	1.210	0.900	0.860	0.820
Dividend Payout %	51.32	50.38	51.49	40.78	60.20	51.43	56.21	...
Income Statement								
Total Revenue	743,000	3,159,000	3,011,328	2,901,858	2,876,889	2,666,236	2,710,677	2,440,703
EBITDA	268,000	1,495,000	1,349,306	1,232,271	1,233,328	1,066,028	1,024,036	428,995
Depn & Amortn	52,000	405,000	356,952	337,653	314,639	268,987	275,844	262,825
Income Before Taxes	136,000	782,000	709,814	605,470	631,258	503,680	449,436	(111,665)
Income Taxes	54,000	306,000	279,973	236,206	257,008	198,751	181,609	121,418
Net Income	82,000	476,000	423,108	369,264	358,070	309,613	267,827	(233,083)
Average Shares	179,000	180,000	179,806	179,056	177,671	176,531	175,124	168,164
Balance Sheet								
Current Assets	638,000	657,000	661,369	550,390	499,447	1,397,659	534,307	499,127
Total Assets	17,417,000	17,241,000	16,130,956	15,069,533	14,718,976	14,776,391	14,079,773	13,452,651
Current Liabilities	1,614,000	1,533,000	1,240,998	1,235,533	994,832	1,489,105	774,506	607,392
Long-Term Obligations	5,850,000	5,862,000	5,432,744	5,212,881	5,190,509	5,339,947	5,410,271	5,288,180
Total Liabilities	12,335,000	12,192,000	11,215,365	10,341,729	10,273,988	10,536,007	9,947,501	9,447,235
Stockholders' Equity	5,082,000	5,049,000	4,915,591	4,727,804	4,444,988	4,240,384	4,132,272	4,005,416
Shares Outstanding	177,735	178,282	179,462	178,379	176,988	175,664	174,996	174,630
Statistical Record								
Return on Assets %	2.84	2.85	2.71	2.48	2.42	2.15	1.95	N.M.
Return on Equity %	9.49	9.55	8.78	8.05	8.22	7.40	6.58	N.M.
EBITDA Margin %	36.07	47.33	44.81	42.46	42.87	39.98	37.78	17.58
Net Margin %	11.04	15.07	14.05	12.73	12.45	11.61	9.88	N.M.
Asset Turnover	0.19	0.19	0.19	0.19	0.19	0.18	0.20	0.18
Current Ratio	0.40	0.43	0.53	0.45	0.50	0.94	0.69	0.82
Debt to Equity	1.15	1.16	1.11	1.10	1.17	1.26	1.31	1.32
Price Range	69.97-48.63	60.61-48.63	55.86-41.16	43.50-37.13	38.35-31.38	32.55-25.23	25.73-19.92	22.68-16.53
P/E Ratio	26.40-18.35	22.96-18.42	23.77-17.51	21.12-18.02	19.08-15.61	18.60-14.42	16.82-13.02	...
Average Yield %	2.39	2.45	2.53	2.05	3.43	3.12	3.84	4.20

Address: 1025 Laurel Oak Road, Voorhees, NJ 08043
Telephone: 856-346-8200
Web Site: www.amwater.com
Officers: George MacKenzie - Chairman Susan N. Story - President, Chief Executive Officer, Senior Vice President, Chief Financial Officer
Auditors: PricewaterhouseCoopers LLP
Investor Contact: 856-566-4005
Transfer Agents: American Stock Transfer & Trust Company, Brooklyn, N

AMERIPRISE FINANCIAL INC

Exchange	Symbol	Price	52Wk Range	Yield	P/E	Div Achiever
NYS	AMP	$101.67 (5/31/2016)	129.86-76.27	2.95	11.98	10 Years

*7 Year Price Score 118.98 *NYSE Composite Index=100 *12 Month Price Score 89.86

TRADING VOLUME (thousand shares)

Interim Earnings (Per Share)

Qtr.	Mar	Jun	Sep	Dec
2013	1.58	1.54	1.86	1.47
2014	2.01	1.91	2.17	2.22
2015	2.08	2.23	2.17	2.00
2016	2.09	...	...	...

Interim Dividends (Per Share)

Amt	Decl	Ex	Rec	Pay
0.67Q	07/22/2015	07/30/2015	08/03/2015	08/14/2015
0.67Q	10/21/2015	10/29/2015	11/02/2015	11/13/2015
0.67Q	01/27/2016	02/10/2016	02/12/2016	02/26/2016
0.75Q	04/27/2016	05/05/2016	05/09/2016	05/20/2016

Indicated Div: $3.00 (Div. Reinv. Plan)

Valuation Analysis / Institutional Holding

Forecast EPS	$9.57	No of Institutions	897
	(05/20/2016)		
Market Cap	$17.0 Billion	Shares	166,305,264
Book Value	$7.1 Billion	% Held	83.93
Price/Book	2.39		
Price/Sales	1.43		

Business Summary: Wealth Management (MIC: 5.5.2 SIC: 6282 NAIC: 523930)

Ameriprise Financial is a holding company. Co. provides a range of products and services to individual and institutional clients. Co.'s segments include Advice & Wealth Management, which provides financial planning and advice, as well as brokerage services, primarily to retail clients through Co.'s advisors; Asset Management, which provides investment advice and investment products to institutional clients; Annuities, which provides variable and fixed annuity products; Protection, which provides a range of products to address the protection and risk management needs of Co.'s retail clients including life, disability income and property-casualty insurance; and Corporate & Other.

Recent Developments: For the quarter ended Mar 31 2016, net income decreased 24.0% to US$364.0 million from US$479.0 million in the year-earlier quarter. Revenues were US$2.77 billion, down 9.4% from US$3.05 billion the year before. Direct operating expenses declined 5.7% to US$1.51 billion from US$1.60 billion in the comparable period the year before. Indirect operating expenses decreased 6.5% to US$782.0 million from US$836.0 million in the equivalent prior-year period.

Prospects: Our evaluation of Ameriprise Financial Inc. as of June 19, 2016 is the result of our systematic analysis on three basic characteristics: earnings strength, relative valuation, and recent stock price movement. The company has managed to produce a neutral trend in earnings per share over the past 5 quarters. However, while recent estimates for the company have been mixed, AMP has posted results that fell short of analysts expectations. Based on operating earnings yield, the company is undervalued when compared to all of the companies in our coverage universe. Share price changes over the past year indicates that AMP will perform poorly over the near term.

Financial Data
(US$ in Millions)

	3 Mos	12/31/2015	12/31/2014	12/31/2013	12/31/2012	12/31/2011	12/31/2010	12/31/2009
Earnings Per Share	8.49	8.48	8.30	6.44	4.62	4.37	4.18	2.95
Cash Flow Per Share	13.21	14.16	12.52	6.71	6.86	9.02	7.91	(5.19)
Tang Book Value Per Share	42.52	42.20	44.37	42.64	44.58	46.21	43.47	36.35
Dividends Per Share	2.680	2.590	2.260	2.010	1.430	0.870	0.710	0.680
Dividend Payout %	31.57	30.54	27.23	31.21	30.95	19.91	16.99	23.05
Income Statement								
Total Revenue	2,765	12,170	12,268	11,199	10,217	10,192	9,976	7,805
EBITDA	595	2,679	3,019	2,395	1,666	1,845	2,051	1,229
Depn & Amortn	65	150	144	144	152	143	167	182
Income Before Taxes	475	2,142	2,547	1,970	1,238	1,385	1,594	920
Income Taxes	111	455	545	492	335	355	334	183
Net Income	364	1,562	1,619	1,334	1,029	1,076	1,097	722
Average Shares	174	184	195	207	222	246	262	244
Balance Sheet								
Current Assets	2,795	8,133	8,055	7,661	7,265	8,869	9,946	9,165
Total Assets	140,250	145,342	148,810	144,576	134,729	133,986	131,192	113,774
Current Liabilities	10,330	10,440	9,387	8,991	8,351	11,419	10,335	9,472
Long-Term Obligations	5,356	10,246	9,929	8,456	7,384	7,571	7,852	2,249
Total Liabilities	133,157	138,125	140,686	136,384	125,637	123,731	120,467	104,501
Stockholders' Equity	7,093	7,217	8,124	8,192	9,092	10,255	10,725	9,273
Shares Outstanding	166	171	183	192	203	221	246	255
Statistical Record								
Return on Assets %	1.05	1.06	1.10	0.96	0.76	0.81	0.90	0.69
Return on Equity %	20.05	20.36	19.85	15.44	10.61	10.26	10.97	9.35
EBITDA Margin %	21.52	22.01	24.61	21.39	16.31	18.10	20.56	15.75
Net Margin %	13.16	12.83	13.20	11.91	10.07	10.56	11.00	9.25
Asset Turnover	0.08	0.08	0.08	0.08	0.08	0.08	0.08	0.07
Current Ratio	0.27	0.78	0.86	0.85	0.87	0.78	0.96	0.97
Debt to Equity	0.76	1.42	1.22	1.03	0.81	0.74	0.73	0.24
Price Range	131.62-76.27	137.81-103.08	136.76-101.47	115.05-62.63	63.52-45.46	64.73-37.34	57.97-35.83	39.52-13.80
P/E Ratio	15.50-8.98	16.25-12.16	16.48-12.23	17.86-9.73	13.75-9.84	14.81-8.54	13.87-8.57	13.40-4.68
Average Yield %	2.39	2.12	1.92	2.38	2.61	1.63	1.58	2.44

Address: 1099 Ameriprise Financial Center, Minneapolis, MN 55474 **Telephone:** 612-671-3131	**Web Site:** www.ameriprise.com **Officers:** James M. Cracchiolo - Chairman, Chief Executive Officer Kelli A. Hunter - Executive Vice President	**Auditors:** PricewaterhouseCoopers LLP **Investor Contact:** 612-671-2080 **Transfer Agents:** Computershare Trust Company, N.A, Providence, RI

AMERISOURCEBERGEN CORP.

Exchange	Symbol	Price	52Wk Range	Yield	P/E	Div Achiever
NYS	ABC	$74.98 (5/31/2016)	114.95-73.66	1.81	11.22	11 Years

*7 Year Price Score 146.69 *NYSE Composite Index=100 ***12 Month Price Score 86.06**

Interim Earnings (Per Share)

Qtr.	Dec	Mar	Jun	Sep
2012-13	0.71	0.19	0.71	0.21
2013-14	0.17	0.76	(0.06)	0.30
2014-15	(0.91)	(2.33)	0.89	1.65
2015-16	1.46	2.68		

Interim Dividends (Per Share)

Amt	Decl	Ex	Rec	Pay
0.29Q	08/06/2015	08/13/2015	08/17/2015	09/01/2015
0.34Q	11/06/2015	11/12/2015	11/16/2015	12/01/2015
0.34Q	02/09/2016	02/18/2016	02/22/2016	03/07/2016
0.34Q	05/10/2016	05/19/2016	05/23/2016	06/06/2016

Indicated Div: $1.36

Valuation Analysis

Forecast EPS	$5.50
	(05/20/2016)
Market Cap	$16.8 Billion
Book Value	$2.2 Billion
Price/Book	7.67
Price/Sales	0.12

Institutional Holding

No of Institutions	957
Shares	210,632,880
% Held	80.88

TRADING VOLUME (thousand shares)

Business Summary: Pharmaceuticals (MIC: 4.1.1 SIC: 5122 NAIC: 424210)

AmerisourceBergen is a pharmaceutical sourcing and distribution services company. Co. distributes brand-name and generic pharmaceuticals, over-the-counter healthcare products, home healthcare supplies and equipment, and related services to a range of healthcare providers. Co. also provides pharmacy services to certain drug patients. Additionally, Co. furnishes healthcare providers and pharmaceutical manufacturers with a range of related services, including reimbursement and pharmaceutical consulting services, logistics services, inventory management, pharmacy automation, and pharmacy management. Co.'s operations are comprised of the Pharmaceutical Distribution reportable segment and Other.

Recent Developments: For the quarter ended Mar 31 2016, net income amounted to US$604.1 million versus a net loss of US$513.4 million in the year-earlier quarter. Revenues were US$35.70 billion, up 9.3% from US$32.67 billion the year before. Operating income was US$948.7 million versus a loss of US$364.2 million in the prior-year quarter. Direct operating expenses rose 9.0% to US$34.62 billion from US$31.76 billion in the comparable period the year before. Indirect operating expenses decreased 90.1% to US$126.6 million from US$1.28 billion in the equivalent prior-year period.

Prospects: Our evaluation of AmerisourceBergen Corp. as of June 19, 2016 is the result of our systematic analysis on three basic characteristics: earnings strength, relative valuation, and recent stock price movement. The company has managed to produce a neutral trend in earnings per share over the past 5 quarters and while recent estimates for the company have been mixed, ABC has posted better than expected results. Based on operating earnings yield, the company is undervalued when compared to all of the companies in our coverage universe. Share price changes over the past year indicates that ABC will perform poorly over the near term.

Financial Data
(US$ in Thousands)

	6 Mos	3 Mos	09/30/2015	09/30/2014	09/30/2013	09/30/2012	09/30/2011	09/30/2010
Earnings Per Share	6.68	1.67	(0.62)	1.17	1.84	2.80	2.54	2.22
Cash Flow Per Share	18.82	18.31	18.00	6.44	3.41	5.15	4.29	3.93
Tang Book Value Per Share	N.M.	N.M.	N.M.	N.M.	N.M.	N.M.	0.01	0.39
Dividends Per Share	1.260	1.210	1.160	0.940	0.840	0.520	0.430	0.320
Dividend Payout %	18.86	72.46	...	80.34	45.65	18.57	16.93	14.41
Income Statement								
Total Revenue	72,407,403	36,709,046	135,961,803	119,569,127	87,959,167	79,489,596	80,217,558	77,953,979
EBITDA	954,887	(92,052)	561,085	912,379	1,037,045	1,377,084	1,312,105	1,183,016
Depn & Amortn	184,940	87,469	187,935	162,089	138,690	118,529	104,743	82,753
Income Before Taxes	705,955	(210,400)	274,149	673,428	824,458	1,163,131	1,130,641	1,027,769
Income Taxes	(228,557)	(540,777)	409,036	389,398	331,023	454,945	424,017	391,021
Net Income	934,512	330,377	(134,887)	276,484	433,707	718,986	706,624	636,748
Average Shares	225,450	226,718	217,786	235,405	235,345	256,903	277,417	287,246
Balance Sheet								
Current Assets	22,070,068	20,361,675	20,334,488	16,800,205	14,393,651	10,987,151	11,217,623	10,748,350
Total Assets	32,495,355	30,755,802	27,736,157	21,532,183	18,918,638	15,444,126	14,982,671	14,434,843
Current Liabilities	23,770,910	24,024,341	22,700,765	17,250,160	14,870,635	11,214,482	10,855,120	9,906,344
Long-Term Obligations	4,368,586	4,393,317	3,493,048	1,995,632	1,396,606	1,446,770	972,863	1,343,158
Total Liabilities	30,304,193	29,455,783	27,102,637	19,575,284	16,598,893	12,987,414	12,115,813	11,480,546
Stockholders' Equity	2,191,162	1,300,019	633,520	1,956,899	2,319,745	2,456,712	2,866,858	2,954,297
Shares Outstanding	224,001	206,315	206,891	221,908	229,994	235,394	260,991	277,521
Statistical Record								
Return on Assets %	5.09	1.42	N.M.	1.37	2.52	4.71	4.80	4.55
Return on Equity %	73.67	25.78	N.M.	12.93	18.16	26.94	24.28	22.46
EBITDA Margin %	1.32	N.M.	0.41	0.76	1.18	1.73	1.64	1.52
Net Margin %	1.29	0.90	N.M.	0.23	0.49	0.90	0.88	0.82
Asset Turnover	4.78	5.00	5.52	5.91	5.12	5.21	5.45	5.57
Current Ratio	0.93	0.85	0.90	0.97	0.97	0.98	1.03	1.08
Debt to Equity	1.99	3.38	5.51	1.02	0.60	0.59	0.34	0.45
Price Range	115.48-83.62	115.48-89.69	115.48-75.02	78.33-61.10	62.23-38.99	42.08-35.57	43.09-30.66	32.88-21.62
P/E Ratio	17.29-12.52	69.15-53.71	...	66.95-52.22	33.82-21.19	15.03-12.70	16.96-12.07	14.81-9.74
Average Yield %	1.24	1.16	1.15	1.34	1.67	1.37	1.15	1.14

Address: 1300 Morris Drive, Chesterbrook, PA 19087-5594	**Web Site:** www.amerisourcebergen.com	**Auditors:** Ernst & Young LLP
Telephone: 610-727-7000	**Officers:** Steven H. Collis - President, Chief Executive Officer John G. Chou - Executive Vice President, Senior Vice President, Secretary, General Counsel	**Investor Contact:** 610-727-7199
Fax: 610-647-0141		**Transfer Agents:** ComputerShare, College Station, TX

AMETEK, INC.

Exchange	Symbol	Price	52Wk Range	Yield	P/E
NYS	AME	$47.82 (5/31/2016)	57.50-44.75	0.75	19.60

*7 Year Price Score 119.40 *NYSE Composite Index=100   *12 Month Price Score 93.21

Interim Earnings (Per Share)

Qtr.	Mar	Jun	Sep	Dec
2013	0.51	0.52	0.52	0.55
2014	0.57	0.61	0.57	0.62
2015	0.59	0.64	0.65	0.58
2016	0.57	...	...	...

Interim Dividends (Per Share)

Amt	Decl	Ex	Rec	Pay
0.09Q	07/30/2015	09/14/2015	09/16/2015	09/30/2015
0.09Q	11/04/2015	12/02/2015	12/04/2015	12/18/2015
0.09Q	02/04/2016	03/15/2016	03/17/2016	03/31/2016
0.09Q	05/04/2016	06/14/2016	06/16/2016	06/30/2016

Indicated Div: $0.36

Valuation Analysis   **Institutional Holding**

Forecast EPS	$2.45 (05/20/2016)	No of Institutions	615
Market Cap	$11.2 Billion	Shares	229,519,248
Book Value	$3.3 Billion	% Held	87.34
Price/Book	3.39		
Price/Sales	2.84		

TRADING VOLUME (thousand shares)

Business Summary: Electrical Equipment (MIC: 7.3.1 SIC: 3621 NAIC: 335312)

AMETEK is a manufacturer of electronic instruments and electromechanical devices with operations in North America, Europe, Asia and South America. Co.'s products are marketed and sold through two operating groups: the Electronic Instruments Group, which is engaged in the design and manufacture of instruments for the process, aerospace, power and industrial markets; and the Electromechanical Group, which supplies electrical interconnects, precision motion control solutions, specialty metals, thermal management systems, and floor care and technical motors. Co.'s end markets include aerospace and defense, medical, factory automation, mass transit, petrochemical and other industrial markets.

Recent Developments: For the quarter ended Mar 31 2016, net income decreased 5.6% to US$134.2 million from US$142.1 million in the year-earlier quarter. Revenues were US$944.4 million, down 4.0% from US$984.1 million the year before. Operating income was US$208.5 million versus US$221.0 million in the prior-year quarter, a decrease of 5.6%. Direct operating expenses declined 4.8% to US$605.4 million from US$636.0 million in the comparable period the year before. Indirect operating expenses increased 2.7% to US$130.5 million from US$127.1 million in the equivalent prior-year period.

Prospects: Our evaluation of Ametek Inc. as of June 19, 2016 is the result of our systematic analysis on three basic characteristics: earnings strength, relative valuation, and recent stock price movement. The company has managed to produce a neutral trend in earnings per share over the past 5 quarters. However, while recent estimates for the company have been mixed, AME has posted results that fell short of analysts expectations. Based on operating earnings yield, the company is undervalued when compared to all of the companies in our coverage universe. Share price changes over the past year indicates that AME will perform well over the near term.

Financial Data

(US$ in Thousands)	3 Mos	12/31/2015	12/31/2014	12/31/2013	12/31/2012	12/31/2011	12/31/2010	12/31/2009
Earnings Per Share	2.44	2.45	2.37	2.10	1.88	1.58	1.17	0.85
Cash Flow Per Share	2.99	2.80	2.96	2.71	2.53	2.12	1.77	1.52
Dividends Per Share	0.360	0.360	0.330	0.240	0.220	0.160	0.120	0.107
Dividend Payout %	14.75	14.69	13.92	11.43	11.70	10.13	10.23	12.57
Income Statement								
Total Revenue	944,398	3,974,295	4,021,964	3,594,136	3,334,213	2,989,914	2,470,952	2,098,355
EBITDA	224,768	966,882	948,484	855,605	791,624	675,244	519,192	405,592
Depn & Amortn	18,325	68,707	63,724	57,238	53,677	48,873	45,420	42,209
Income Before Taxes	183,042	806,380	804,832	724,795	662,475	556,642	406,250	294,633
Income Taxes	48,872	215,521	220,372	207,796	203,343	172,178	122,318	88,863
Net Income	134,170	590,859	584,460	516,999	459,132	384,464	283,932	205,770
Average Shares	236,216	241,586	247,102	246,065	243,986	243,162	241,326	242,662
Balance Sheet								
Current Assets	1,662,590	1,619,613	1,578,604	1,369,129	1,164,743	1,059,119	974,492	969,430
Total Assets	6,994,702	6,664,530	6,420,963	5,877,902	5,190,056	4,319,490	3,818,915	3,246,032
Current Liabilities	1,290,554	1,025,172	936,144	874,545	879,969	628,875	550,859	424,282
Long-Term Obligations	1,552,674	1,556,045	1,427,825	1,141,750	1,133,121	1,123,416	1,071,360	955,880
Total Liabilities	3,698,016	3,409,904	3,181,402	2,741,781	2,654,905	2,266,685	2,043,711	1,679,008
Stockholders' Equity	3,296,686	3,254,626	3,239,561	3,136,121	2,535,151	2,052,805	1,775,204	1,567,024
Shares Outstanding	233,410	235,515	241,335	245,006	243,395	240,557	241,064	242,738
Statistical Record								
Return on Assets %	8.75	9.03	9.50	9.34	9.63	9.45	8.04	6.53
Return on Equity %	17.77	18.20	18.33	18.23	19.96	20.09	16.99	14.42
EBITDA Margin %	23.80	24.33	23.58	23.81	23.74	22.58	21.01	19.33
Net Margin %	14.21	14.87	14.53	14.38	13.77	12.86	11.49	9.81
Asset Turnover	0.59	0.61	0.65	0.65	0.70	0.73	0.70	0.67
Current Ratio	1.29	1.58	1.69	1.57	1.32	1.68	1.77	2.28
Debt to Equity	0.47	0.48	0.44	0.36	0.45	0.55	0.60	0.61
Price Range	57.50-44.75	57.50-47.90	54.20-46.12	52.67-37.57	38.02-28.17	31.18-20.95	27.47-16.07	17.49-10.96
P/E Ratio	23.57-18.34	23.47-19.55	22.87-19.46	25.08-17.89	20.22-14.98	19.73-13.26	23.48-13.74	20.58-12.89
Average Yield %	0.68	0.67	0.64	0.54	0.65	0.59	0.60	0.72

Address: 1100 Cassatt Road, Berwyn, PA 19312-1177
Telephone: 610-647-2121
Fax: 610-647-0211

Web Site: www.ametek.com
Officers: Frank S. Hermance - Chairman, Chief Executive Officer David A. Zapico - Chief Executive Officer, Chief Operating Officer, Executive Vice President, Division Officer

Auditors: Ernst & Young LLP
Transfer Agents: American Stock Transfer & Trust Co., New York, NY

AMPHENOL CORP.

Exchange NYS	Symbol APH	Price $58.72 (5/31/2016)	52Wk Range 59.05-45.42	Yield 0.95	P/E 25.09

*7 Year Price Score 128.00 *NYSE Composite Index=100 *12 Month Price Score 104.81

Interim Earnings (Per Share)

Qtr.	Mar	Jun	Sep	Dec
2013	0.47	0.47	0.50	0.52
2014	0.49	0.56	0.57	0.61
2015	0.57	0.56	0.65	0.63
2016	0.50	...	...	...

Interim Dividends (Per Share)

Amt	Decl	Ex	Rec	Pay
0.14Q	07/22/2015	09/04/2015	09/09/2015	10/02/2015
0.14Q	10/29/2015	12/11/2015	12/15/2015	01/06/2016
0.14Q	01/28/2016	03/11/2016	03/15/2016	04/06/2016
0.14Q	04/29/2016	06/10/2016	06/14/2016	07/07/2016

Indicated Div: $0.56

Valuation Analysis

		Institutional Holding	
Forecast EPS	$2.60 (05/20/2016)	No of Institutions	689
Market Cap	$18.1 Billion	Shares	329,710,016
Book Value	$3.4 Billion	% Held	97.63
Price/Book	5.34		
Price/Sales	3.17		

Business Summary: Electrical Equipment (MIC: 7.3.1 SIC: 3678 NAIC: 334417)

Amphenol is engaged in designing, manufacturing and marketing electrical, electronic and fiber optic connectors, interconnect systems, antennas, sensors and sensor-based products and coaxial and high-speed specialty cable. Co. has two reportable business segments: Interconnect Products and Assemblies, which designs, manufacturers and markets a range of connector and connector systems, antennas and sensors used in a range of applications; and Cable Products and Solutions, which primarily designs, manufacturers and markets cable, other products and components for use primarily in the broadband communications and information technology markets as well as certain applications in other markets.

Recent Developments: For the quarter ended Mar 31 2016, net income decreased 12.9% to US$158.4 million from US$181.8 million in the year-earlier quarter. Revenues were US$1.45 billion, up 9.4% from US$1.33 billion the year before. Operating income was US$239.4 million versus US$260.2 million in the prior-year quarter, a decrease of 8.0%. Direct operating expenses rose 9.9% to US$992.0 million from US$902.5 million in the comparable period the year before. Indirect operating expenses increased 33.7% to US$219.8 million from US$164.4 million in the equivalent prior-year period.

Prospects: Our evaluation of Amphenol Corp. as of June 19, 2016 is the result of our systematic analysis on three basic characteristics: earnings strength, relative valuation, and recent stock price movement. The company has managed to produce a neutral trend in earnings per share over the past 5 quarters and while recent estimates for the company have remained steady, APH has posted better than expected results. Based on operating earnings yield, the company is about fairly valued when compared to all of the companies in our coverage universe. Share price changes over the past year indicates that APH will perform in line with the market over the near term.

Financial Data
(US$ in Thousands)

	3 Mos	12/31/2015	12/31/2014	12/31/2013	12/31/2012	12/31/2011	12/31/2010	12/31/2009
Earnings Per Share	2.34	2.41	2.21	1.96	1.70	1.52	1.41	0.92
Cash Flow Per Share	3.37	3.33	2.81	2.42	2.08	1.67	1.22	1.70
Tang Book Value Per Share	N.M.	1.77	0.94	9.04	1.56	1.30	2.24	1.09
Dividends Per Share	0.545	0.530	0.450	0.305	0.210	0.030	0.030	0.030
Dividend Payout %	23.29	21.99	20.36	15.56	12.39	1.97	2.13	3.28
Income Statement								
Total Revenue	1,451,200	5,568,700	5,345,500	4,614,669	4,292,065	3,939,786	3,554,101	2,820,065
EBITDA	302,300	1,274,300	1,200,800	1,031,708	948,721	868,975	802,229	579,483
Depn & Amortn	61,900	171,600	168,100	136,482	121,779	119,439	102,846	98,524
Income Before Taxes	222,300	1,052,800	972,500	846,645	778,841	716,752	663,688	446,527
Income Taxes	63,900	280,500	257,300	207,896	219,333	187,910	161,275	119,311
Net Income	156,600	763,500	709,100	635,672	555,317	524,191	496,405	317,834
Average Shares	314,200	316,500	320,430	324,548	327,894	343,651	352,651	347,883
Balance Sheet								
Current Assets	2,989,600	3,850,000	3,504,100	3,157,567	2,706,915	2,181,237	1,992,130	1,420,395
Total Assets	7,890,000	7,458,400	7,027,000	6,168,028	5,215,463	4,445,225	4,015,857	3,219,184
Current Liabilities	1,069,600	1,008,400	1,045,600	1,609,878	888,514	642,415	654,990	503,159
Long-Term Obligations	2,866,200	2,813,200	2,672,300	1,431,437	1,606,204	1,376,831	799,640	753,050
Total Liabilities	4,503,800	4,219,900	4,119,600	3,308,519	2,785,504	2,273,456	1,695,002	1,473,107
Stockholders' Equity	3,386,200	3,238,500	2,907,400	2,859,509	2,429,959	2,171,769	2,320,855	1,746,077
Shares Outstanding	307,700	308,000	309,884	316,412	319,715	326,244	351,101	346,419
Statistical Record								
Return on Assets %	9.93	10.54	10.75	11.17	11.47	12.39	13.72	10.23
Return on Equity %	23.37	24.85	24.59	24.04	24.07	23.34	24.41	20.54
EBITDA Margin %	20.83	22.88	22.46	22.36	22.10	22.06	22.57	20.55
Net Margin %	10.79	13.71	13.27	13.78	12.94	13.31	13.97	11.27
Asset Turnover	0.76	0.77	0.81	0.81	0.89	0.93	0.98	0.91
Current Ratio	2.80	3.82	3.35	1.96	3.05	3.40	3.04	2.82
Debt to Equity	0.85	0.87	0.92	0.50	0.66	0.63	0.34	0.43
Price Range	59.54-45.42	60.20-49.06	55.45-42.34	44.59-32.35	32.51-22.91	29.30-19.90	26.65-19.26	23.48-10.95
P/E Ratio	25.44-19.41	24.98-20.36	25.09-19.16	22.75-16.51	19.12-13.48	19.28-13.09	18.90-13.66	25.53-11.90
Average Yield %	1.01	0.96	0.93	0.79	0.73	0.12	0.13	0.18

Address: 358 Hall Avenue, Wallingford, CT 06492 Telephone: 203-265-8900 Fax: 203-265-8746	Web Site: www.amphenol.com Officers: Richard Adam Norwitt - President, Chief Executive Officer Gary A. Anderson - Senior Vice President, Division Officer	Auditors: Deloitte & Touche LLP Transfer Agents: Computershare Trust Company, N.A., Providence, RI

ANADARKO PETROLEUM CORP

Exchange	Symbol	Price	52Wk Range	Yield	P/E
NYS	APC	$51.86 (5/31/2016)	84.79-30.54	0.39	N/A

*7 Year Price Score 67.27   *NYSE Composite Index=100   *12 Month Price Score 83.37

Interim Earnings (Per Share)

Qtr.	Mar	Jun	Sep	Dec
2013	0.91	1.83	0.36	(1.52)
2014	(5.30)	0.45	2.12	(0.78)
2015	(6.45)	0.12	(4.41)	(2.45)
2016	(2.03)	...	...	...

Interim Dividends (Per Share)

Amt	Decl	Ex	Rec	Pay
0.27Q	08/04/2015	09/04/2015	09/09/2015	09/23/2015
0.27Q	11/03/2015	12/07/2015	12/09/2015	12/23/2015
0.05Q	02/09/2016	03/07/2016	03/09/2016	03/23/2016
0.05Q	05/10/2016	06/06/2016	06/08/2016	06/22/2016

Indicated Div: $0.20

Valuation Analysis

		Institutional Holding	
Forecast EPS	$-3.44 (05/20/2016)	No of Institutions	1225
Market Cap	$26.5 Billion	Shares	552,077,376
Book Value	$11.7 Billion	% Held	
Price/Book	2.27		85.18
Price/Sales	3.29		

Business Summary: Production & Extraction (MIC: 9.1.1 SIC: 1311 NAIC: 211111)

Anadarko Petroleum is an independent exploration and production company. Co. has three segments: oil and gas exploration and production, which explores for and produces natural gas, crude oil, condensate, and natural gas liquids (NGLs); midstream, which is engaged in gathering, processing, treating, and transporting Co. and third-party oil, natural-gas, and NGLs production; and marketing, which sells much of its production, as well as third-party purchased volumes. At Dec 31 2015, Co.'s proved reserves consisted of 2.06 billion barrels of oil equivalent, of which 6.02 trillion cubic feet were natural gas, 713.00 billion barrels were oil and condensate and 340.0 million barrels were NGLs.

Recent Developments: For the quarter ended Mar 31 2016, net loss amounted to US$998.0 million versus a net loss of US$3.24 billion in the year-earlier quarter. Revenues were US$1.67 billion, down 27.9% from US$2.32 billion the year before. Operating loss was US$864.0 million versus a loss of US$4.21 billion in the prior-year quarter. Direct operating expenses declined 59.2% to US$791.0 million from US$1.94 billion in the comparable period the year before. Indirect operating expenses decreased 61.9% to US$1.75 billion from US$4.59 billion in the equivalent prior-year period.

Prospects: Our evaluation of Anadarko Petroleum Corp. as of June 19, 2016 is the result of our systematic analysis on three basic characteristics: earnings strength, relative valuation, and recent stock price movement. The company has produced a positive trend in earnings per share over the past 5 quarters. Because the company lacks sufficient analyst estimate data, we place greater weight on the historical EPS trend as the measure of earnings strength. Based on operating earnings yield, the company is overvalued when compared to all of the companies in our coverage universe. Share price changes over the past year indicates that APC will perform very poorly over the near term.

Financial Data

(US$ in Thousands)	3 Mos	12/31/2015	12/31/2014	12/31/2013	12/31/2012	12/31/2011	12/31/2010	12/31/2009
Earnings Per Share	(8.77)	(13.18)	(3.47)	1.58	4.74	(5.32)	1.52	(0.28)
Cash Flow Per Share	4.89	(3.69)	16.73	17.71	16.63	5.03	10.60	8.18
Tang Book Value Per Share	10.50	12.76	25.97	32.15	29.87	24.63	30.98	29.65
Dividends Per Share	0.860	1.080	0.990	0.540	0.360	0.360	0.360	0.360
Dividend Payout %	...	...	...	34.18	7.59	...	23.68	...
Income Statement								
Total Revenue	1,674,000	8,698,000	18,470,000	14,581,000	13,411,000	13,967,000	10,984,000	9,000,000
EBITDA	(15,000)	(4,261,000)	5,376,000	6,719,000	8,271,000	1,245,000	6,210,000	4,126,000
Depn & Amortn	1,149,000	4,603,000	4,550,000	3,927,000	3,964,000	3,830,000	3,714,000	3,532,000
Income Before Taxes	(1,381,000)	(9,689,000)	54,000	2,106,000	3,565,000	(3,424,000)	1,641,000	(108,000)
Income Taxes	(383,000)	(2,877,000)	1,617,000	1,165,000	1,120,000	(856,000)	820,000	(5,000)
Net Income	(1,034,000)	(6,692,000)	(1,750,000)	801,000	2,391,000	(2,649,000)	761,000	(135,000)
Average Shares	509,000	508,000	506,000	505,000	502,000	498,000	497,000	480,000
Balance Sheet								
Current Assets	5,767,000	3,982,000	11,221,000	7,108,000	6,795,000	6,931,000	6,675,000	6,083,000
Total Assets	47,922,000	46,414,000	61,689,000	55,781,000	52,589,000	51,779,000	51,559,000	50,123,000
Current Liabilities	6,657,000	4,181,000	10,234,000	5,703,000	3,994,000	4,899,000	4,114,000	3,824,000
Long-Term Obligations	15,726,000	15,718,000	15,092,000	13,065,000	13,269,000	15,060,000	12,722,000	11,149,000
Total Liabilities	36,236,000	33,595,000	41,964,000	33,924,000	31,960,000	33,674,000	30,875,000	30,195,000
Stockholders' Equity	11,686,000	12,819,000	19,725,000	21,857,000	20,629,000	18,105,000	20,684,000	19,928,000
Shares Outstanding	510,400	508,300	506,600	503,700	500,500	498,400	496,200	492,600
Statistical Record								
Return on Assets %	N.M.	N.M.	N.M.	1.48	4.57	N.M.	1.50	N.M.
Return on Equity %	N.M.	N.M.	N.M.	3.77	12.31	N.M.	3.75	N.M.
EBITDA Margin %	N.M.	N.M.	29.11	46.08	61.67	8.91	56.54	45.84
Net Margin %	N.M.	N.M.	N.M.	5.49	17.83	N.M.	6.93	N.M.
Asset Turnover	0.16	0.16	0.31	0.27	0.26	0.27	0.22	0.18
Current Ratio	0.87	0.95	1.10	1.25	1.70	1.41	1.62	1.59
Debt to Equity	1.35	1.23	0.77	0.60	0.64	0.83	0.62	0.56
Price Range	94.54-30.54	94.54-45.67	112.69-72.01	97.76-74.31	88.05-57.12	84.71-60.53	76.16-34.83	69.36-31.15
P/E Ratio	...	...	...	61.87-47.03	18.58-12.05	...	50.11-22.91	...
Average Yield %	1.32	1.44	1.04	0.62	0.49	0.47	0.60	0.72

Address: 1201 Lake Robbins Drive, The Woodlands, TX 77380-1046 **Telephone:** 832-636-1000	**Web Site:** www.anadarko.com **Officers:** James T. Hackett - Executive Chairman, Chairman, Chief Executive Officer James J. Kleckner - Executive Vice President	**Auditors:** KPMG LLP **Investor Contact:** 855-820-6605 **Transfer Agents:** BNYMellon Shareowner Services, Jersey City, NJ

ANIXTER INTERNATIONAL INC

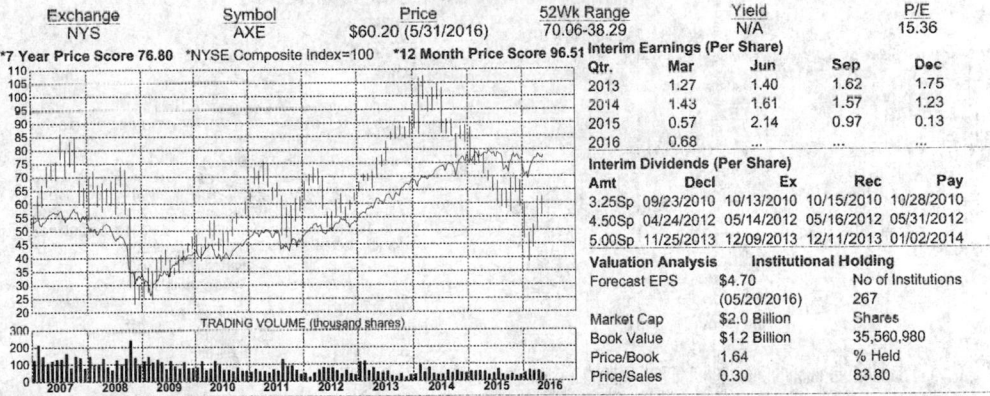

Exchange	Symbol	Price	52Wk Range	Yield	P/E
NYS	AXE	$60.20 (5/31/2016)	70.06-38.29	N/A	15.36

*7 Year Price Score 76.80   ***NYSE Composite Index=100**   ***12 Month Price Score 96.51**

Interim Earnings (Per Share)

Qtr.	Mar	Jun	Sep	Dec
2013	1.27	1.40	1.62	1.75
2014	1.43	1.61	1.57	1.23
2015	0.57	2.14	0.97	0.13
2016	0.68	...	...	...

Interim Dividends (Per Share)

Amt	Decl	Ex	Rec	Pay
3.25Sp	09/23/2010	10/13/2010	10/15/2010	10/28/2010
4.50Sp	04/24/2012	05/14/2012	05/16/2012	05/31/2012
5.00Sp	11/25/2013	12/09/2013	12/11/2013	01/02/2014

Valuation Analysis   **Institutional Holding**

Forecast EPS	$4.70	No of Institutions
	(05/20/2016)	267
Market Cap	$2.0 Billion	Shares
Book Value	$1.2 Billion	35,560,980
Price/Book	1.64	% Held
Price/Sales	0.30	83.80

Business Summary: Electrical Equipment (MIC: 7.3.1 SIC: 5063 NAIC: 423610)

Anixter International is engaged in the distribution of network and security solutions, electrical and electronic solutions, and utility power solutions through Anixter Inc. and its subsidiaries. The Network and Security Solutions segment supplies products and customized supply chain solutions. The Electrical and Electronic Solutions segment supplies wire and cable products and customized supply chain solutions. The Utility Power Solutions segment supplies electrical transmission and distribution products, power plant maintenance, repair and operations supplies and smart-grid products, and arranges materials management and procurement outsourcing.

Recent Developments: For the quarter ended Apr 1 2016, income from continuing operations decreased 12.5% to US$23.2 million from US$26.5 million in the year-earlier quarter. Net income increased 19.4% to US$22.8 million from US$19.1 million in the year-earlier quarter. Revenues were US$1.82 billion, up 31.1% from US$1.39 billion the year before. Operating income was US$60.3 million versus US$59.3 million in the prior-year quarter, an increase of 1.7%. Direct operating expenses rose 34.4% to US$1.45 billion from US$1.08 billion in the comparable period the year before. Indirect operating expenses increased 24.2% to US$310.5 million from US$250.0 million in the equivalent prior-year period.

Prospects: Our evaluation of Anixter International Inc. as of June 19, 2016 is the result of our systematic analysis on three basic characteristics: earnings strength, relative valuation, and recent stock price movement. The company has enjoyed a very positive trend in earnings per share over the past 5 quarters and while recent estimates for the company have been raised by analysts, AXE has posted better than expected results. Based on operating earnings yield, the company is undervalued when compared to all of the companies in our coverage universe. Share price changes over the past year indicates that AXE will perform poorly over the near term.

Financial Data

(US$ in Thousands)	3 Mos	01/01/2016	01/02/2015	01/03/2014	12/28/2012	12/31/2011	12/31/2010	01/01/2010
Earnings Per Share	3.92	3.81	5.84	6.04	3.69	5.36	3.05	(0.83)
Cash Flow Per Share	4.17	2.78	3.17	10.03	4.30	4.22	5.74	12.60
Tang Book Value Per Share	0.38	N.M.	16.62	20.86	19.30	19.55	18.54	19.20
Dividends Per Share	...	...	...	5.000	4.500	...	3.250	...
Dividend Payout %	...	...	...	82.78	121.95	...	106.56	...
Income Statement								
Total Revenue	1,816,200	6,190,500	6,445,500	6,226,500	6,253,100	6,146,900	5,472,100	4,982,400
EBITDA	74,700	294,300	378,600	373,500	301,400	387,100	339,900	120,400
Depn & Amortn	17,200	47,600	35,700	30,100	32,500	33,500	107,000	37,100
Income Before Taxes	37,400	182,900	294,800	296,000	209,200	303,500	179,300	17,200
Income Taxes	14,200	86,000	100,000	95,600	84,600	102,800	70,800	46,500
Net Income	22,800	127,600	194,800	200,500	124,800	188,200	108,500	(29,300)
Average Shares	33,400	33,400	33,300	33,200	33,800	35,100	35,500	35,100
Balance Sheet								
Current Assets	2,647,200	2,727,800	2,589,800	2,275,700	2,450,100	2,402,900	2,281,200	2,051,000
Total Assets	4,070,500	4,142,000	3,586,500	2,860,800	3,089,600	3,034,000	2,933,300	2,671,700
Current Liabilities	1,123,800	1,156,200	1,030,500	902,400	967,300	1,026,900	1,071,200	670,000
Long-Term Obligations	1,563,600	1,642,900	1,207,700	836,000	982,200	806,800	688,800	821,400
Total Liabilities	2,846,600	2,962,600	2,453,500	1,833,400	2,119,700	2,032,800	1,922,500	1,647,600
Stockholders' Equity	1,223,900	1,179,400	1,133,000	1,027,400	969,900	1,001,200	1,010,800	1,024,100
Shares Outstanding	33,368	33,278	33,141	32,853	32,537	33,228	34,323	34,700
Statistical Record								
Return on Assets %	3.46	3.31	6.06	6.63	4.10	6.31	3.88	N.M.
Return on Equity %	11.23	11.07	18.08	19.75	12.73	18.71	10.69	N.M.
EBITDA Margin %	4.11	4.75	5.87	6.00	4.82	6.30	6.21	2.42
Net Margin %	1.26	2.06	3.02	3.22	2.00	3.06	1.98	N.M.
Asset Turnover	1.75	1.61	2.00	2.06	2.05	2.06	1.96	1.73
Current Ratio	2.36	2.36	2.51	2.52	2.53	2.34	2.13	3.06
Debt to Equity	1.28	1.39	1.07	0.81	1.01	0.81	0.68	0.80
Price Range	78.07-38.29	88.18-56.66	107.51-76.57	92.36-62.64	73.37-49.76	75.58-45.10	60.80-38.74	47.95-24.60
P/E Ratio	19.92-9.77	23.14-14.87	18.41-13.11	15.29-10.37	19.88-13.49	14.10-8.41	19.93-12.70	...
Average Yield %	...	...	...	6.40	7.30	...	6.58	...

Address: 2301 Patriot Blvd., Glenview, IL 60026	Web Site: www.anixter.com	Auditors: Ernst & Young LLP
Telephone: 224-521-8000	**Officers:** Samuel Zell - Chairman Robert J. Eck - President, Chief Executive Officer	**Investor Contact:** 224-521-8895
		Transfer Agents: Wells Fargo Shareowner Services, Mendota Heights, MN

ANNALY CAPITAL MANAGEMENT INC

Exchange	Symbol	Price	52Wk Range	Yield	P/E
NYS	NLY	$10.58 (5/31/2016)	11.12-8.69	11.34	N/A

*7 Year Price Score 59.57 *NYSE Composite Index=100 *12 Month Price Score 104.51

Interim Earnings (Per Share)

Qtr.	Mar	Jun	Sep	Dec
2013	0.87	1.64	0.18	1.05
2014	(0.23)	(0.37)	0.35	(0.71)
2015	(0.52)	0.93	(0.68)	0.69
2016	(0.96)	...	...	...

Interim Dividends (Per Share)

Amt	Decl	Ex	Rec	Pay
0.30Q	09/17/2015	09/28/2015	09/30/2015	10/30/2015
0.30Q	12/17/2015	12/29/2015	12/31/2015	01/29/2016
0.30Q	03/14/2016	03/29/2016	03/31/2016	04/29/2016
0.30Q	06/16/2016	06/28/2016	06/30/2016	07/29/2016

Indicated Div: $1.20

Valuation Analysis   **Institutional Holding**

Forecast EPS	$1.19
	(05/20/2016)
Market Cap	$9.8 Billion
Book Value	$11.6 Billion
Price/Book	0.84
Price/Sales	12.90

No of Institutions 728
Shares 587,398,912
% Held 50.37

Business Summary: REITs (MIC: 5.3.1 SIC: 6798 NAIC: 525930)

Annaly Capital Management is a mortgage real estate investment trust that is externally managed by Annaly Management Company LLC. Co. owns a portfolio of real estate related investments, including mortgage pass-through certificates, collateralized mortgage obligations, agency callable debentures, other securities representing interests in or obligations backed by pools of mortgage loans, commercial real estate assets and corporate debt. In addition, Co. may directly or indirectly invests part of its assets in other types of securities, including, unrated debt and equity securities and derivative instruments.

Recent Developments: For the quarter ended Mar 31 2016, net loss amounted to US$868.1 million versus a net loss of US$476.5 million in the year-earlier quarter. Revenues were a negative US$673.5 million, compared with a negative US$296.1 million the year before.

Prospects: Our evaluation of Annaly Capital Management Inc. as of June 19, 2016 is the result of our systematic analysis on three basic characteristics: earnings strength, relative valuation, and recent stock price movement. The company has managed to produce a neutral trend in earnings per share over the past 5 quarters and while recent estimates for the company have remained steady, NLY has posted results that were in line with analysts expectations. Based on operating earnings yield, the company is undervalued when compared to all of the companies in our coverage universe. Share price changes over the past year indicates that NLY will perform very well over the near term.

Financial Data
(US$ in Thousands)

	3 Mos	12/31/2015	12/31/2014	12/31/2013	12/31/2012	12/31/2011	12/31/2010	12/31/2009
Earnings Per Share	(0.02)	0.42	(0.96)	3.74	1.71	0.37	2.04	3.52
Cash Flow Per Share	1.88	(3.34)	6.47	(13.61)	7.83	2.77	18.47	19.78
Tang Book Value Per Share	11.49	11.62	13.00	12.03	15.78	16.04	15.32	17.00
Dividends Per Share	1.200	1.200	1.200	1.500	2.050	2.440	2.650	2.540
Dividend Payout %	...	285.71	...	40.11	119.88	659.45	129.80	92.15
Income Statement								
Interest Income	388,143	2,170,697	2,632,647	2,918,562	3,259,145	3,579,618	2,683,134	2,922,602
Interest Expense	147,447	471,596	512,659	624,714	667,172	480,326	1,163,332	1,295,762
Net Interest Income	240,696	1,699,101	2,119,988	2,293,848	2,591,973	3,099,292	1,519,802	1,626,840
Non-Interest Income	(1,061,668)	(1,035,068)	(2,747,604)	1,676,144	(584,602)	(2,459,576)	(79,224)	483,988
Non-Interest Expense	47,945	200,240	209,338	232,081	235,559	237,344	171,847	131,908
Income Before Taxes	(868,917)	463,793	(836,954)	3,737,911	1,771,812	402,372	1,299,769	1,996,104
Income Taxes	(837)	(1,954)	5,325	8,213	35,912	59,051	35,434	34,381
Net Income	(867,918)	466,556	(842,083)	3,729,698	1,735,900	344,461	1,267,280	1,961,471
Average Shares	926,813	947,276	947,539	995,557	1,005,755	874,518	625,307	553,130
Balance Sheet								
Net Loans & Leases	278,600	278,600	...	...	...	...	...	...
Total Assets	77,443,965	75,190,893	88,355,367	81,922,460	133,452,295	109,630,002	83,026,590	69,376,190
Total Liabilities	65,795,513	63,294,919	75,026,876	69,517,405	117,527,851	93,837,088	73,121,658	59,758,650
Stockholders' Equity	11,648,452	11,895,974	13,328,491	12,405,055	15,924,444	15,792,914	9,904,932	9,617,540
Shares Outstanding	924,853	935,929	947,643	947,432	947,213	970,161	631,594	553,134
Statistical Record								
Return on Assets %	0.10	0.57	N.M.	3.46	1.42	0.36	1.66	3.09
Return on Equity %	0.61	3.70	N.M.	26.33	10.92	2.68	12.98	23.22
Net Interest Margin %	62.01	78.27	80.53	78.60	79.53	86.58	56.64	55.66
Efficiency Ratio %	...	17.63	...	5.05	8.81	21.19	6.60	3.87
Price Range	10.55-8.69	11.04-9.06	11.92-9.97	16.13-9.74	17.75-14.01	18.72-15.48	18.70-15.34	19.67-12.50
P/E Ratio	...	26.29-21.57	...	4.31-2.60	10.38-8.19	50.59-41.84	9.17-7.52	5.59-3.55
Average Yield %	12.47	11.94	10.96	11.60	12.91	14.27	15.57	12.92

Address: 1211 Avenue of the Americas, New York, NY 10036 **Telephone:** 212-696-0100 **Fax:** 212-696-9809	**Web Site:** www.annaly.com **Officers:** Wellington J. Denahan-Norris - Chairman, Vice-Chairman, Chief Executive Officer, Co-Chief Executive Officer, Chief Operating Officer Kevin G. Keyes - President, Chief Executive Officer, Chief Strategy Officer, Managing Director	**Auditors:** Ernst & Young LLP **Investor Contact:** 888-826-6259 **Transfer Agents:** Computershare Shareowner Services LLC, Jersey City, NJ

54

ANTHEM INC

Exchange	Symbol	Price	52Wk Range	Yield	P/E
NYS	ANTM	$132.16 (5/31/2016)	171.04-117.22	1.97	14.83

*7 Year Price Score 139.40 ***NYSE Composite Index=100** ***12 Month Price Score 97.15**

TRADING VOLUME (thousand shares)

Interim Earnings (Per Share)

Qtr.	Mar	Jun	Sep	Dec
2013	2.89	2.64	2.16	0.51
2014	2.40	2.56	2.22	1.81
2015	3.09	3.13	2.43	0.72
2016	2.63	...	...	...

Interim Dividends (Per Share)

Amt	Decl	Ex	Rec	Pay
0.625Q	07/28/2015	09/08/2015	09/10/2015	09/25/2015
0.625Q	10/27/2015	12/02/2015	12/04/2015	12/21/2015
0.65Q	02/18/2016	03/08/2016	03/10/2016	03/25/2016
0.65Q	04/26/2016	06/08/2016	06/10/2016	06/24/2016

Indicated Div: $2.60

Valuation Analysis

		Institutional Holding	
Forecast EPS	$10.93	No of Institutions	
	(05/20/2016)	837	
Market Cap	$34.7 Billion	Shares	
Book Value	$23.5 Billion	223,709,584	
Price/Book	1.48	% Held	
Price/Sales	0.43	0.17	

Business Summary: Hospitals & Health Care Facilities (MIC: 4.2.1 SIC: 6324 NAIC: 524114)

Anthem is an insurance holding company. Through its subsidiaries, Co. provides a range of network-based managed care health benefit plans to large and small employer, individual, Medicaid and Medicare markets. Co.'s managed care plans include: preferred provider organizations; health maintenance organizations; point-of-service plans; indemnity plans and other hybrid plans, including consumer-driven health plans; and hospital only and limited benefit products. Co. has three reportable segments: Commercial and Specialty Business; Government Business; and Other. Co. served 38.6 million medical members through its affiliated health plans as of Dec 31 2015.

Recent Developments: For the quarter ended Mar 31 2016, net income decreased 18.7% to US$703.0 million from US$865.2 million in the year-earlier quarter. Revenues were US$20.29 billion, up 6.5% from US$19.05 billion the year before. Net premiums earned were US$18.99 billion versus US$17.61 billion in the prior-year quarter, an increase of 7.8%. Net investment income rose 2.1% to US$171.1 million from US$167.6 million a year ago.

Prospects: Our evaluation of Anthem Inc. as of June 19, 2016 is the result of our systematic analysis on three basic characteristics: earnings strength, relative valuation, and recent stock price movement. The company has managed to produce a neutral trend in earnings per share over the past 5 quarters and while recent estimates for the company have been raised by analysts, ANTM has posted better than expected results. Based on operating earnings yield, the company is undervalued when compared to all of the companies in our coverage universe. Share price changes over the past year indicates that ANTM will perform well over the near term.

Financial Data
(US$ in Thousands)

	3 Mos	12/31/2015	12/31/2014	12/31/2013	12/31/2012	12/31/2011	12/31/2010	12/31/2009
Earnings Per Share	8.91	9.38	8.99	8.20	8.18	7.25	6.94	9.88
Cash Flow Per Share	14.40	15.65	12.21	10.23	8.51	9.37	3.45	6.38
Tang Book Value Per Share	N.M.	N.M.	N.M.	N.M.	N.M.	4.41	6.75	7.42
Dividends Per Share	2.525	2.500	1.750	1.500	1.150	1.000	...	...
Dividend Payout %	28.34	26.65	19.47	18.29	14.06	13.79	...	...
Income Statement								
Total Revenue	20,288,500	79,156,500	73,874,100	71,023,500	61,711,700	60,710,700	58,801,800	65,028,100
Income Before Taxes	1,312,000	4,631,000	4,368,100	3,840,200	3,865,500	3,957,900	4,353,800	7,403,000
Income Taxes	609,000	2,071,000	1,808,000	1,205,900	1,210,000	1,311,200	1,466,700	2,657,100
Net Income	703,000	2,560,000	2,569,700	2,489,700	2,655,500	2,646,700	2,887,100	4,745,900
Average Shares	267,500	272,900	285,900	303,800	324,800	365,100	415,800	480,500
Balance Sheet								
Total Assets	63,858,700	61,717,800	62,065,000	59,574,500	58,955,400	52,018,800	50,166,900	52,125,400
Total Liabilities	40,311,600	38,673,700	37,813,700	34,809,300	35,152,700	28,730,600	26,354,300	27,262,100
Stockholders' Equity	23,547,100	23,044,100	24,251,300	24,765,200	23,802,700	23,288,200	23,812,600	24,863,300
Shares Outstanding	262,840	261,238	268,109	293,273	304,715	339,372	377,736	449,789
Statistical Record								
Return on Assets %	3.71	4.14	4.23	4.20	4.77	5.18	5.64	9.44
Return on Equity %	10.02	10.83	10.49	10.25	11.25	11.24	11.86	20.50
Net Margin %	3.47	3.23	3.48	3.51	4.30	4.36	4.91	7.30
Price Range	171.04-117.22	171.04-123.26	129.16-84.25	93.92-58.93	73.80-52.93	81.78-56.86	68.06-47.43	60.36-30.10
P/E Ratio	19.20-13.16	18.23-13.14	14.37-9.37	11.45-7.19	9.02-6.47	11.28-7.84	9.81-6.83	6.11-3.05
Average Yield %	1.74	1.70	1.62	1.91	1.82	1.46	...	...

Address: 120 Monument Circle, Indianapolis, IN 46204-4903 **Telephone:** 317-488-6000	**Web Site:** www.antheminc.com **Officers:** Joseph R. Swedish - President, Chief Executive Officer Randal L. Brown - Executive Vice President, Chief Human Resources Officer	**Auditors:** Ernst & Young LLP **Investor Contact:** 212-476-1473 **Transfer Agents:** EquiServe Trust Company, N.A., Providence, RI

APACHE CORP.

Exchange	Symbol	Price	52Wk Range	Yield	P/E
NYS	APA	$57.14 (5/31/2016)	59.60-34.38	1.75	N/A

*7 Year Price Score 46.96 *NYSE Composite Index=100 *12 Month Price Score 112.64

Interim Earnings (Per Share)

Qtr.	Mar	Jun	Sep	Dec
2013	1.76	2.54	0.75	0.44
2014	0.60	1.31	(3.50)	(12.54)
2015	(12.34)	(14.83)	(14.95)	(19.08)
2016	(1.29)	...	...	...

Interim Dividends (Per Share)

Amt	Decl	Ex	Rec	Pay
0.25Q	09/17/2015	10/20/2015	10/22/2015	11/23/2015
0.25Q	12/17/2015	01/20/2016	01/22/2016	02/22/2016
0.25Q	02/04/2016	04/20/2016	04/22/2016	05/23/2016
0.25Q	05/12/2016	07/20/2016	07/22/2016	08/22/2016

Indicated Div: $1.00

Valuation Analysis

		Institutional Holding	
Forecast EPS	$-0.72 (05/20/2016)	No of Institutions	1139
Market Cap	$21.6 Billion	Shares	423,797,824
Book Value	$2.0 Billion	% Held	81.21
Price/Book	10.72		
Price/Sales	3.74		

Business Summary: Production & Extraction (MIC: 9.1.1 SIC: 1311 NAIC: 211111)

Apache is an independent energy company that explores for, develops, and produces natural gas, crude oil, and natural gas liquids. As of Dec 31 2015 Co. had exploration and production interests in four countries: the U.S., Canada, Egypt, and the U.K. (North Sea). Co. also pursues exploration interests in other countries. As of Dec 31 2015, Co. had total estimated proved reserves of 0.79 billion barrels of oil of crude oil, 198.0 million barrels of natural gas liquids and 3.40 trillion cubic feet of natural gas.

Recent Developments: For the quarter ended Mar 31 2016, net loss amounted to US$561.0 million versus a net loss of US$4.64 billion in the year-earlier quarter. Revenues were US$1.05 billion, down 35.5% from US$1.63 billion the year before. Direct operating expenses declined 19.9% to US$430.0 million from US$537.0 million in the comparable period the year before. Indirect operating expenses decreased 84.6% to US$1.33 billion from US$8.62 billion in the equivalent prior-year period.

Prospects: Our evaluation of Apache Corp. as of June 19, 2016 is the result of our systematic analysis on three basic characteristics: earnings strength, relative valuation, and recent stock price movement. The company has produced a positive trend in earnings per share over the past 5 quarters. Because the company lacks sufficient analyst estimate data, we place greater weight on the historical EPS trend as the measure of earnings strength. Based on operating earnings yield, the company is overvalued when compared to all of the companies in our coverage universe. Share price changes over the past year indicates that APA will perform well over the near term.

Financial Data

(US$ in Thousands)	3 Mos	12/31/2015	12/31/2014	12/31/2013	12/31/2012	12/31/2011	12/31/2010	12/31/2009
Earnings Per Share	(50.15)	(61.20)	(14.06)	5.50	4.92	11.47	8.46	(0.87)
Cash Flow Per Share	6.90	7.89	22.03	24.90	21.80	25.92	19.11	12.58
Tang Book Value Per Share	5.33	6.79	68.66	80.92	73.58	69.38	57.84	46.34
Dividends Per Share	1.000	1.000	0.950	0.770	0.660	0.600	0.600	0.600
Dividend Payout %	...	...	...	14.00	13.41	5.23	7.09	...
Income Statement								
Total Revenue	1,052,000	6,366,000	13,851,000	16,054,000	17,078,000	16,888,000	12,092,000	8,614,826
EBITDA	465,000	1,406,000	7,382,000	11,106,000	12,151,000	12,455,000	8,518,000	5,781,853
Depn & Amortn	1,082,000	29,372,000	10,158,000	6,700,000	7,109,000	4,204,000	3,083,000	5,213,224
Income Before Taxes	(707,000)	(28,226,000)	(2,906,000)	4,216,000	4,877,000	8,093,000	5,206,000	326,391
Income Taxes	(146,000)	(5,469,000)	1,637,000	1,928,000	2,876,000	3,509,000	2,174,000	610,789
Net Income	(561,000)	(23,528,000)	(5,060,000)	2,288,000	2,001,000	4,584,000	3,032,000	(284,398)
Average Shares	378,000	378,000	384,000	406,000	391,000	400,000	359,000	335,852
Balance Sheet								
Current Assets	3,222,000	3,752,000	6,415,000	6,366,000	4,962,000	4,803,000	3,480,000	4,585,849
Total Assets	17,679,000	18,842,000	55,952,000	61,637,000	60,737,000	52,051,000	43,425,000	28,185,743
Current Liabilities	1,598,000	1,841,000	3,664,000	4,700,000	5,536,000	4,963,000	3,524,000	2,392,558
Long-Term Obligations	8,718,000	8,777,000	11,245,000	9,672,000	11,355,000	6,785,000	8,095,000	4,950,390
Total Liabilities	15,661,000	16,276,000	30,015,000	28,241,000	29,406,000	23,058,000	19,048,000	12,407,122
Stockholders' Equity	2,018,000	2,566,000	25,937,000	33,396,000	31,331,000	28,993,000	24,377,000	15,778,621
Shares Outstanding	378,532	378,034	376,504	395,772	391,640	384,117	382,391	336,436
Statistical Record								
Return on Assets %	N.M.	N.M.	N.M.	3.74	3.54	9.60	8.47	N.M.
Return on Equity %	N.M.	N.M.	N.M.	7.07	6.62	17.18	15.10	N.M.
EBITDA Margin %	44.20	22.09	53.30	69.18	71.15	73.75	70.44	67.12
Net Margin %	N.M.	N.M.	N.M.	14.25	11.72	27.14	25.07	N.M.
Asset Turnover	0.17	0.17	0.24	0.26	0.30	0.35	0.34	0.30
Current Ratio	2.02	2.04	1.75	1.35	0.90	0.97	0.99	1.92
Debt to Equity	4.32	3.42	0.43	0.29	0.36	0.23	0.33	0.31
Price Range	71.40-34.38	71.40-36.20	103.48-55.20	94.42-68.84	111.57-75.07	133.37-76.50	119.92-82.75	105.13-51.38
P/E Ratio	...	...	...	17.17-12.52	22.68-15.26	11.63-6.67	14.17-9.78	...
Average Yield %	2.03	1.84	1.11	0.93	0.74	0.54	0.60	0.73

Address: One Post Oak Central, 2000 Post Oak Boulevard, Suite 100, Houston, TX 77056-4400
Telephone: 713-296-6000

Web Site: www.apachecorp.com
Officers: John J. Christmann - President, Chief Executive Officer, Vice President, Region Officer Margery M. Harris - Executive Vice President, Vice President

Auditors: Ernst & Young LLP
Investor Contact: 281-302-2286
Transfer Agents: Wells Fargo Bank, N.A., South St. Paul, MN

APARTMENT INVESTMENT & MANAGEMENT CO

Exchange	Symbol	Price	52Wk Range	Yield	P/E
NYS	AIV	$42.65 (5/31/2016)	43.10-34.85	3.09	39.13

*7 Year Price Score 119.12 *NYSE Composite Index=100 *12 Month Price Score 105.60

TRADING VOLUME (thousand shares)

Interim Earnings (Per Share)

Qtr.	Mar	Jun	Sep	Dec
2013	0.03	0.07	0.46	0.84
2014	0.44	0.51	0.85	0.25
2015	0.58	0.39	0.12	0.43
2016	0.15	...	...	...

Interim Dividends (Per Share)

Amt	Decl	Ex	Rec	Pay
0.30Q	07/28/2015	08/12/2015	08/14/2015	08/31/2015
0.30Q	10/27/2015	11/16/2015	11/18/2015	11/30/2015
0.33Q	01/26/2016	02/17/2016	02/19/2016	02/29/2016
0.33Q	04/28/2016	05/18/2016	05/20/2016	05/31/2016

Indicated Div: $1.32

Valuation Analysis Institutional Holding

Forecast EPS	$0.71 (05/20/2016)	No of Institutions 437
Market Cap	$6.7 Billion	Shares 190,615,376
Book Value	$1.6 Billion	% Held 98.96
Price/Book	4.17	
Price/Sales	6.79	

Business Summary: REITs (MIC: 5.3.1 SIC: 6798 NAIC: 525930)

Apartment Investment and Management is a self-administered and self-managed real estate investment trust. AIMCO Properties, L.P. (Aimco Operating Partnership) conducts Co.'s business, which is focused on the ownership, management, redevelopment and limited development of apartment communities. Co., through its wholly-owned subsidiaries, AIMCO-GP, Inc. and AIMCO-LP Trust, owns a majority of the ownership interests in the Aimco Operating Partnership. As of Dec. 31, 2015, Co.'s real estate portfolio consisted of 196 apartment communities with 49,149 apartment homes.

Recent Developments: For the quarter ended Mar 31 2016, income from continuing operations increased 28.4% to US$23.7 million from US$18.5 million in the year-earlier quarter. Net income decreased 71.3% to US$29.9 million from US$104.2 million in the year-earlier quarter. Revenues were US$246.2 million, up 0.8% from US$244.3 million the year before.

Prospects: Our evaluation of Apartment Investment & Management Co. as of June 19, 2016 is the result of our systematic analysis on three basic characteristics: earnings strength, relative valuation, and recent stock price movement. The company has produced a positive trend in earnings per share over the past 5 quarters. Because the company lacks sufficient analyst estimate data, we place greater weight on the historical EPS trend as the measure of earnings strength. Based on operating earnings yield, the company is overvalued when compared to all of the companies in our coverage universe. Share price changes over the past year indicates that AIV will perform very well over the near term.

Financial Data

(US$ in Thousands)	3 Mos	12/31/2015	12/31/2014	12/31/2013	12/31/2012	12/31/2011	12/31/2010	12/31/2009
Earnings Per Share	1.09	1.52	2.06	1.40	0.61	(0.86)	(1.08)	(1.00)
Cash Flow Per Share	2.37	2.32	2.21	2.24	2.35	2.17	2.21	2.05
Tang Book Value Per Share	9.22	9.36	7.11	6.16	5.82	2.08	3.47	5.23
Dividends Per Share	1.230	1.180	1.040	0.960	0.760	0.480	0.300	0.400
Dividend Payout %	112.84	77.63	50.49	68.57	124.59	...	...	...
Income Statement								
Total Revenue	246,239	981,310	984,363	974,053	1,033,197	1,079,584	1,144,934	1,195,763
EBITDA	143,439	568,089	547,943	549,525	576,113	554,385	576,037	566,394
Depn & Amortn	79,828	311,487	286,422	296,825	350,692	385,191	435,802	455,258
Income Before Taxes	17,812	63,866	47,428	31,711	(11,427)	(131,545)	(161,210)	(203,683)
Income Taxes	(5,886)	(27,524)	(20,047)	(1,959)	(929)	(7,166)	(18,433)	(18,671)
Net Income	26,057	248,710	309,249	207,290	132,456	(57,087)	(71,728)	(64,274)
Average Shares	156,117	155,570	146,002	145,532	134,479	119,312	116,369	114,301
Balance Sheet								
Current Assets	154,612	137,745	120,416	185,933	368,189	430,784	508,600	524,427
Total Assets	6,142,213	6,144,194	6,097,028	6,079,413	6,401,380	6,871,862	7,378,566	7,906,468
Current Liabilities	97,753	36,123	41,919	43,161	30,747	66,091	109,662	118,640
Long-Term Obligations	3,917,590	3,873,160	4,135,139	4,388,185	4,688,447	5,172,320	5,457,783	5,637,253
Total Liabilities	4,539,051	4,521,803	4,869,293	5,111,956	5,485,955	5,963,533	6,312,524	6,636,750
Stockholders' Equity	1,603,162	1,622,391	1,227,735	967,457	915,425	908,329	1,066,042	1,269,718
Shares Outstanding	156,605	156,326	146,403	145,917	145,563	120,916	117,642	116,479
Statistical Record								
Return on Assets %	2.94	4.06	5.08	3.32	1.99	N.M.	N.M.	N.M.
Return on Equity %	11.28	17.45	28.18	22.02	14.49	N.M.	N.M.	N.M.
EBITDA Margin %	58.25	57.89	55.66	56.42	55.76	51.35	50.31	47.37
Net Margin %	10.58	25.34	31.42	21.28	12.82	N.M.	N.M.	N.M.
Asset Turnover	0.16	0.16	0.16	0.16	0.16	0.15	0.15	0.14
Current Ratio	1.58	3.81	2.87	4.31	11.97	6.52	4.64	4.42
Debt to Equity	2.44	2.39	3.37	4.54	5.12	5.69	5.12	4.44
Price Range	41.82-34.85	41.19-34.85	38.32-25.72	33.20-25.00	28.27-22.40	27.97-20.29	25.93-15.21	16.73-4.94
P/E Ratio	38.37-31.97	27.10-22.93	18.60-12.49	23.71-17.86	46.34-36.72	...	...	...
Average Yield %	3.22	3.07	3.22	3.32	2.92	1.94	1.44	3.87

Address: 4582 South Ulster Street, Suite 1100, Denver, CO 80237	**Web Site:** www.aimco.com	**Auditors:** Ernst & Young LLP
Telephone: 303-757-8101	**Officers:** Terry Considine - Chairman, Chief Executive Officer Charles A. Higdon - Senior Vice President, Chief Accounting Officer, Associate/Affiliate Company Officer	**Investor Contact:** 303-691-4350
Fax: 303-759-3226		**Transfer Agents:** Computershare Trust Company, N.A., Providence, RI

APTARGROUP INC.

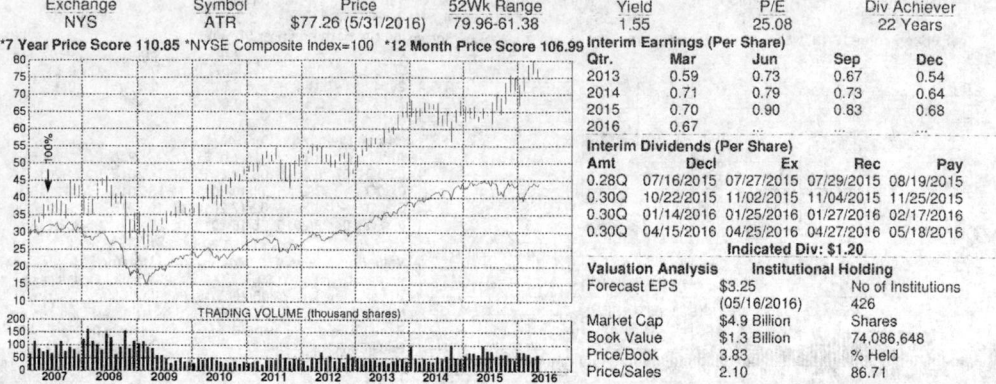

Exchange	Symbol	Price	52Wk Range	Yield	P/E	Div Achiever
NYS	ATR	$77.26 (5/31/2016)	79.96-61.38	1.55	25.08	22 Years

*7 Year Price Score 110.85 *NYSE Composite Index=100 *12 Month Price Score 106.99

Interim Earnings (Per Share)

Qtr.	Mar	Jun	Sep	Dec
2013	0.59	0.73	0.67	0.54
2014	0.71	0.79	0.73	0.64
2015	0.70	0.90	0.83	0.68
2016	0.67	...	...	...

Interim Dividends (Per Share)

Amt	Decl	Ex	Rec	Pay
0.28Q	07/16/2015	07/27/2015	07/29/2015	08/19/2015
0.30Q	10/22/2015	11/02/2015	11/04/2015	11/25/2015
0.30Q	01/14/2016	01/25/2016	01/27/2016	02/17/2016
0.30Q	04/15/2016	04/25/2016	04/27/2016	05/18/2016

Indicated Div: $1.20

Valuation Analysis

		Institutional Holding	
Forecast EPS	$3.25	No of Institutions	426
	(05/16/2016)		
Market Cap	$4.9 Billion	Shares	
Book Value	$1.3 Billion		74,086,648
Price/Book	3.83	% Held	
Price/Sales	2.10		86.71

Business Summary: Plastics (MIC: 8.4.2 SIC: 3089 NAIC: 326199)

AptarGroup is a provider of a range of packaging, dispensing and sealing solutions, primarily for the beauty, personal care, home care, prescription drug, consumer health care, injectables, food and beverage markets. While Co. provides a range of dispensing and sealing solutions, its primary products are: dispensing pumps, which dispense a spray or lotion from non-pressurized containers; closures, which are plastic caps which allow a product to be dispensed without removing the cap; aerosol valves, which dispense product from pressurized containers; and elastomeric primary packaging components, which include stoppers for infusion, antibiotic, lyophilization and diagnostic vials.

Recent Developments: For the quarter ended Mar 31 2016, net income decreased 2.7% to US$43.9 million from US$45.1 million in the year-earlier quarter. Revenues were US$582.3 million, down 1.3% from US$589.8 million the year before. Operating income was US$69.2 million versus US$73.6 million in the prior-year quarter, a decrease of 5.9%. Direct operating expenses declined 3.1% to US$374.2 million from US$386.0 million in the comparable period the year before. Indirect operating expenses increased 6.6% to US$138.9 million from US$130.2 million in the equivalent prior-year period.

Prospects: Our evaluation of AptarGroup Inc. as of June 19, 2016 is the result of our systematic analysis on three basic characteristics: earnings strength, relative valuation, and recent stock price movement. The company has managed to produce a neutral trend in earnings per share over the past 5 quarters. However, while recent estimates for the company have been mixed, ATR has posted results that fell short of analysts expectations. Based on operating earnings yield, the company is about fairly valued when compared to all of the companies in our coverage universe. Share price changes over the past year indicates that ATR will perform very well over the near term.

Financial Data

(US$ in Thousands)	3 Mos	12/31/2015	12/31/2014	12/31/2013	12/31/2012	12/31/2011	12/31/2010	12/31/2009
Earnings Per Share	3.08	3.09	2.85	2.52	2.38	2.65	2.48	1.79
Cash Flow Per Share	4.74	5.19	4.84	4.32	4.71	3.92	3.89	4.34
Tang Book Value Per Share	11.61	12.89	11.85	16.38	14.81	15.96	15.67	15.05
Dividends Per Share	1.160	1.140	1.090	1.000	0.880	0.800	0.660	0.600
Dividend Payout %	37.66	36.89	38.25	39.68	36.97	30.19	26.61	33.52
Income Statement								
Total Revenue	582,338	2,317,149	2,597,809	2,520,013	2,331,036	2,337,183	2,076,719	1,841,616
EBITDA	103,860	458,955	451,343	427,470	391,629	418,585	394,832	324,755
Depn & Amortn	35,887	134,647	146,893	144,923	133,845	132,048	129,339	127,709
Income Before Taxes	59,966	295,289	288,218	265,266	241,830	274,959	254,370	183,894
Income Taxes	15,979	95,276	94,677	92,457	78,953	91,312	80,796	59,461
Net Income	43,863	199,348	191,658	171,994	162,612	183,683	173,481	124,623
Average Shares	65,063	64,492	67,292	68,208	68,395	69,274	69,815	69,785
Balance Sheet								
Current Assets	1,271,095	1,294,994	1,213,938	1,198,411	1,038,933	1,143,950	1,063,983	943,491
Total Assets	2,679,033	2,438,726	2,437,190	2,497,762	2,324,412	2,159,295	2,032,718	1,956,193
Current Liabilities	522,766	411,900	604,738	542,821	455,323	518,849	423,322	417,315
Long-Term Obligations	773,182	762,524	588,892	354,814	352,860	254,910	258,773	209,616
Total Liabilities	1,411,678	1,289,315	1,333,783	1,018,005	944,522	869,519	753,795	703,348
Stockholders' Equity	1,267,355	1,149,411	1,103,407	1,479,757	1,379,890	1,289,776	1,278,923	1,252,845
Shares Outstanding	62,900	62,516	61,931	65,384	65,928	65,900	66,800	67,300
Statistical Record								
Return on Assets %	7.90	8.18	7.77	7.13	7.23	8.76	8.70	6.58
Return on Equity %	17.27	17.70	14.84	12.03	12.15	14.30	13.70	10.46
EBITDA Margin %	17.84	19.81	17.37	16.96	16.80	17.91	19.01	17.63
Net Margin %	7.53	8.60	7.38	6.83	6.98	7.86	8.35	6.77
Asset Turnover	0.92	0.95	1.05	1.05	1.04	1.12	1.04	0.97
Current Ratio	2.43	3.14	2.01	2.21	2.28	2.20	2.51	2.26
Debt to Equity	0.61	0.66	0.53	0.24	0.26	0.20	0.20	0.17
Price Range	78.73-61.38	75.72-61.38	68.38-56.18	67.81-47.72	55.26-45.80	54.34-42.79	48.22-35.03	38.89-25.30
P/E Ratio	25.56-19.93	24.50-19.86	23.99-19.71	26.91-18.94	23.22-19.24	20.51-16.15	19.44-14.13	21.73-14.13
Average Yield %	1.68	1.71	1.69	1.72	1.71	1.61	1.58	1.80

Address: 475 West Terra Cotta Avenue, Suite E, Crystal Lake, IL 60014	**Web Site:** www.aptar.com	**Auditors:** PricewaterhouseCoopers LLP
Telephone: 815-477-0424	**Officers:** King W. Harris - Chairman Peter H. Pfeiffer - President, Chief Executive Officer	**Investor Contact:** 815-477-0424
Fax: 815-477-0481		**Transfer Agents:** Wells Fargo Shareowner Services, South St. Paul, MN

AQUA AMERICA INC

Exchange	Symbol	Price	52Wk Range	Yield	P/E	Div Achiever
NYS	WTR	$32.31 (5/31/2016)	32.89-24.49	2.20	28.10	24 Years

*7 Year Price Score 115.24 *NYSE Composite Index=100 *12 Month Price Score 108.91

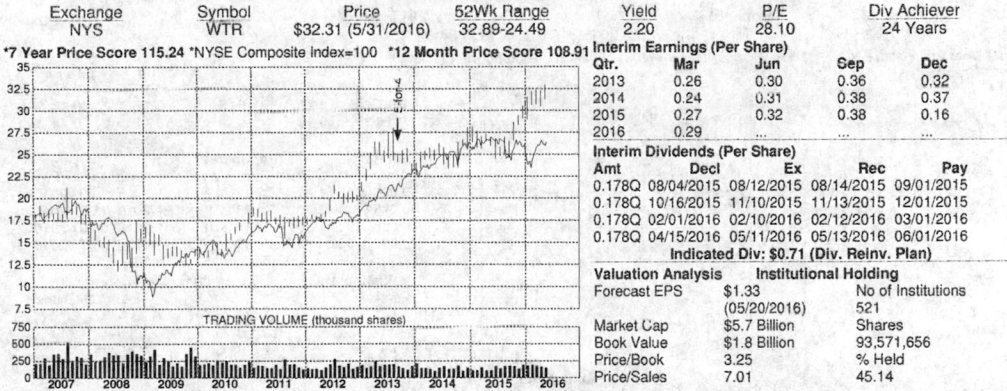

Interim Earnings (Per Share)

Qtr.	Mar	Jun	Sep	Dec
2013	0.26	0.30	0.36	0.32
2014	0.24	0.31	0.38	0.37
2015	0.27	0.32	0.38	0.16
2016	0.29	...	...	...

Interim Dividends (Per Share)

Amt	Decl	Ex	Rec	Pay
0.178Q	08/04/2015	08/12/2015	08/14/2015	09/01/2015
0.178Q	10/16/2015	11/10/2015	11/13/2015	12/01/2015
0.178Q	02/01/2016	02/10/2016	02/12/2016	03/01/2016
0.178Q	04/15/2016	05/11/2016	05/13/2016	06/01/2016

Indicated Div: $0.71 (Div. Reinv. Plan)

Valuation Analysis		Institutional Holding	
Forecast EPS	$1.33	No of Institutions	
	(05/20/2016)	521	
Market Cap	$5.7 Billion	Shares	
Book Value	$1.8 Billion	93,571,656	
Price/Book	3.25	% Held	
Price/Sales	7.01	45.14	

Business Summary: Water Utilities (MIC: 3.2.1 SIC: 4941 NAIC: 221310)

Aqua America is the holding company for regulated utilities providing water or wastewater services in Pennsylvania, Ohio, Texas, Illinois, North Carolina, New Jersey, Indiana, and Virginia. Co.'s Aqua Pennsylvania, Inc. subsidiary provides water or wastewater services in counties north and west of the City of Philadelphia and in 27 other counties in Pennsylvania. Co.'s Aqua Resources, Inc. subsidiary provides water and wastewater service through operating and maintenance contracts with municipal authorities and other parties. Co.'s Aqua Infrastructure, LLC subsidiary provides non-utility raw water supply services for firms in the natural gas drilling industry.

Recent Developments: For the quarter ended Mar 31 2016, net income increased 6.6% to US$51.7 million from US$48.5 million in the year-earlier quarter. Revenues were US$192.6 million, up 1.2% from US$190.3 million the year before. Operating income was US$72.3 million versus US$71.2 million in the prior-year quarter, an increase of 1.6%. Direct operating expenses rose 0.5% to US$73.5 million from US$73.2 million in the comparable period the year before. Indirect operating expenses increased 1.7% to US$46.7 million from US$46.0 million in the equivalent prior-year period.

Prospects: Our evaluation of Aqua America Inc. as of June 19, 2016 is the result of our systematic analysis on three basic characteristics: earnings strength, relative valuation, and recent stock price movement. The company has produced a positive trend in earnings per share over the past 5 quarters and while recent estimates for the company have remained steady, WTR has posted better than expected results. Based on operating earnings yield, the company is about fairly valued when compared to all of the companies in our coverage universe. Share price changes over the past year indicates that WTR will perform very well over the near term.

Financial Data

(US$ in Thousands)	3 Mos	12/31/2015	12/31/2014	12/31/2013	12/31/2012	12/31/2011	12/31/2010	12/31/2009
Earnings Per Share	1.15	1.14	1.31	1.25	1.12	0.82	0.72	0.62
Cash Flow Per Share	2.12	2.10	2.06	2.09	2.11	2.12	1.54	1.52
Tang Book Value Per Share	9.69	9.58	9.19	8.52	7.75	7.06	6.58	6.25
Dividends Per Share	0.699	0.686	0.634	0.622	0.536	0.504	0.472	0.440
Dividend Payout %	60.78	60.18	48.40	49.76	47.86	61.17	65.56	71.43
Income Statement								
Total Revenue	192,607	814,204	779,903	768,643	757,760	711,956	726,072	670,539
EBITDA	106,991	453,755	442,543	426,922	438,516	405,597	400,788	355,741
Depn & Amortn	32,145	125,290	123,054	119,258	111,767	111,942	121,067	114,939
Income Before Taxes	54,993	251,929	243,092	230,348	248,992	215,853	204,069	172,195
Income Taxes	3,007	14,962	25,219	22,690	66,881	71,091	80,094	67,842
Net Income	51,737	201,790	233,239	221,300	196,563	143,069	123,975	104,353
Average Shares	177,819	177,517	177,763	176,814	174,917	173,361	171,620	170,161
Balance Sheet								
Current Assets	122,733	128,370	152,522	171,669	260,894	320,453	145,419	121,571
Total Assets	5,815,443	5,741,038	5,406,752	5,051,817	4,858,517	4,348,420	4,072,466	3,762,597
Current Liabilities	174,343	193,199	225,335	266,910	274,164	425,673	223,715	201,007
Long-Term Obligations	1,744,108	1,743,612	1,560,655	1,468,583	1,543,954	1,395,457	1,531,976	1,386,557
Total Liabilities	4,054,736	4,015,108	3,751,409	3,516,982	3,472,813	3,097,107	2,898,212	2,653,693
Stockholders' Equity	1,760,707	1,725,930	1,655,343	1,534,835	1,385,704	1,251,313	1,174,254	1,108,904
Shares Outstanding	177,265	176,544	176,753	176,750	175,209	173,518	172,219	170,607
Statistical Record								
Return on Assets %	3.63	3.62	4.46	4.47	4.26	3.40	3.16	2.88
Return on Equity %	11.93	11.94	14.62	15.15	14.87	11.80	10.86	9.63
EBITDA Margin %	55.55	55.73	56.74	55.54	57.87	56.97	55.20	53.05
Net Margin %	26.86	24.78	29.91	28.79	25.94	20.10	17.07	15.56
Asset Turnover	0.14	0.15	0.15	0.16	0.16	0.17	0.19	0.19
Current Ratio	0.70	0.66	0.68	0.64	0.95	0.75	0.65	0.60
Debt to Equity	0.99	1.01	0.94	0.96	1.11	1.12	1.30	1.25
Price Range	32.33-24.49	30.51-24.49	28.05-22.59	27.99-20.34	21.48-16.94	18.92-15.42	18.31-13.27	16.95-12.36
P/E Ratio	28.11-21.30	26.76-21.48	21.41-17.24	22.39-16.27	19.18-15.13	23.07-18.81	25.43-18.43	27.34-19.94
Average Yield %	2.51	2.56	2.55	2.54	2.80	2.85	3.10	3.10

Address: 762 W. Lancaster Avenue, Bryn Mawr, PA 19010-3489 **Telephone:** 610-527-8000	**Web Site:** www.aquaamerica.com **Officers:** Nicholas DeBenedictis - Chairman, Senior Advisor, President, Chief Executive Officer Christopher H. Franklin - Chief Executive Officer, Executive Vice President, Senior Vice President, Region Officer, Division Officer	**Auditors:** PricewaterhouseCoopers LLP **Investor Contact:** 610-645-1191 **Transfer Agents:** Computershare Trust Company, N.A., Providence, RI

ARAMARK

Exchange	Symbol	Price	52Wk Range	Yield	P/E
NYS	ARMK	$33.29 (5/31/2016)	34.34-28.81	1.14	32.64

*7 Year Price Score N/A   *NYSE Composite Index=100   *12 Month Price Score 103.53

Interim Earnings (Per Share)

Qtr.	Dec	Mar	Jun	Sep
2012-13	0.20	(0.20)	0.13	0.18
2013-14	0.21	0.05	0.19	0.18
2014-15	0.35	0.24	0.14	0.23
2015-16	0.38	0.27		

Interim Dividends (Per Share)

Amt	Decl	Ex	Rec	Pay
0.086Q	08/04/2015	08/14/2015	08/18/2015	09/08/2015
0.095Q	11/18/2015	11/25/2015	11/30/2015	12/09/2015
0.095Q	02/02/2016	02/11/2016	02/16/2016	03/07/2016
0.095Q	05/04/2016	05/16/2016	05/18/2016	06/07/2016

Indicated Div: $0.38

Valuation Analysis   **Institutional Holding**

Forecast EPS	$1.70 (05/20/2016)	No of Institutions	351
Market Cap	$8.1 Billion	Shares	229,725,376
Book Value	$2.0 Billion	% Held	89.92
Price/Book	3.94		
Price/Sales	0.56		

Business Summary: Hotels, Restaurants & Travel (MIC: 2.2.1 SIC: 5812 NAIC: 722110)

Aramark provides food, facilities and uniform services to education, healthcare, business and industry, and sports, leisure and corrections clients. Co. has three segments: Food and Support Services (FSS) North America, FSS International and Uniform and Career Apparel (Uniform). The FSS segments manage interrelated services-including food, hospitality and facility services-for school districts, colleges and universities, healthcare facilities, businesses, sports, entertainment and recreational venues, conference and convention centers, national and state parks and correctional institutions. The Uniform segment provides uniforms and other garments and work clothes and ancillary items.

Recent Developments: For the quarter ended Apr 1 2016, net income increased 10.6% to US$66.5 million from US$60.1 million in the year-earlier quarter. Revenues were US$3.57 billion, down 0.6% from US$3.59 billion the year before. Operating income was US$172.1 million versus US$154.9 million in the prior-year quarter, an increase of 11.1%. Direct operating expenses declined 0.9% to US$3.21 billion from US$3.24 billion in the comparable period the year before. Indirect operating expenses decreased 3.8% to US$193.0 million from US$200.6 million in the equivalent prior-year period.

Prospects: Our evaluation of Aramark as of June 19, 2016 is the result of our systematic analysis on three basic characteristics: earnings strength, relative valuation, and recent stock price movement. The company has enjoyed a very positive trend in earnings per share over the past 5 quarters and while recent estimates for the company have been mixed, ARMK has posted better than expected results. Based on operating earnings yield, the company is about fairly valued when compared to all of the companies in our coverage universe. Share price changes over the past year indicates that ARMK will perform well over the near term.

Financial Data

(US$ in Thousands)	6 Mos	3 Mos	10/02/2015	10/03/2014	09/27/2013	09/28/2012	09/30/2011
Earnings Per Share	1.02	0.99	0.96	0.63	0.33	0.49	0.40
Cash Flow Per Share	3.37	3.04	2.88	1.73	3.46	3.41	1.49
Dividends Per Share	0.362	0.354	0.345	0.225	...	...	...
Dividend Payout %	35.54	35.73	35.94	35.71			
Income Statement							
Total Revenue	7,285,097	3,710,275	14,329,135	14,832,913	13,945,657	13,505,426	13,082,377
EBITDA	634,016	341,611	849,925	799,681	748,924	815,174	777,956
Depn & Amortn	247,809	127,518	226,600	239,900	239,100	236,600	234,500
Income Before Taxes	243,136	142,773	341,996	229,677	90,629	124,968	95,969
Income Taxes	83,203	49,337	105,020	80,218	19,233	18,066	(734)
Net Income	159,697	93,343	235,946	148,956	69,356	103,551	83,846
Average Shares	248,270	247,613	246,616	237,451	209,370	209,707	209,999
Balance Sheet							
Current Assets	2,421,271	2,386,667	2,379,123	2,464,976	2,287,165	2,185,501	...
Total Assets	10,328,420	10,149,894	10,224,050	10,455,693	10,267,106	10,487,354	...
Current Liabilities	1,899,412	1,728,319	2,180,988	2,378,873	2,389,253	2,163,674	...
Long-Term Obligations	5,366,112	5,485,964	5,212,290	5,355,789	5,758,229	5,971,305	...
Total Liabilities	8,279,077	8,180,118	8,340,691	8,737,657	9,363,399	9,554,337	...
Stockholders' Equity	2,049,343	1,969,776	1,883,359	1,718,036	903,707	933,017	...
Shares Outstanding	242,354	241,789	239,917	233,910	201,798	202,573	...
Statistical Record							
Return on Assets %	2.43	2.38	2.29	1.41	0.67	...	...
Return on Equity %	12.96	13.09	13.14	11.18	7.57	...	...
EBITDA Margin %	8.70	9.21	5.93	5.39	5.37	6.04	5.95
Net Margin %	2.19	2.52	1.65	1.00	0.50	0.77	0.64
Asset Turnover	1.39	1.40	1.39	1.41	1.35	...	...
Current Ratio	1.27	1.38	1.09	1.04	0.96	1.01	...
Debt to Equity	2.62	2.79	2.77	3.12	6.37	6.40	...
Price Range	34.03-28.81	34.03-28.81	33.49-25.35	29.89-22.70	...	...	...
P/E Ratio	33.36-28.25	34.37-29.10	34.89-26.41	47.44-36.03	...	...	...
Average Yield %	1.15	1.12	1.12	0.84	...	...	...

Address: Aramark Tower, 1101 Market Street, Philadelphia, PA 19107
Telephone: 215-238-3000

Web Site: www.aramark.com
Officers: Joseph Neubauer - Chairman Eric J. Foss - President, Chief Executive Officer

Auditors: KPMG LLP
Transfer Agents: Computershare Trust Company, N.A.

ARCHER DANIELS MIDLAND CO.

Exchange	Symbol	Price	52Wk Range	Yield	P/E	Div Achiever
NYS	ADM	$42.77 (5/31/2016)	53.03-30.51	2.81	16.45	41 Years

*7 Year Price Score 97.90 *NYSE Composite Index=100 *12 Month Price Score 94.39

Interim Earnings (Per Share)

Qtr.	Mar	Jun	Sep	Dec
2013	0.41	0.34	0.72	0.56
2014	0.40	0.81	1.14	1.08
2015	0.77	0.62	0.41	1.18
2016	0.39	...	...	...

Interim Dividends (Per Share)

Amt	Decl	Ex	Rec	Pay
0.28Q	08/06/2015	08/17/2015	08/19/2015	09/09/2015
0.28Q	11/04/2015	11/16/2015	11/18/2015	12/09/2015
0.30Q	02/02/2016	02/11/2016	02/16/2016	03/08/2016
0.30Q	05/05/2016	05/16/2016	05/18/2016	06/08/2016

Indicated Div: $1.20 (Div. Reinv. Plan)

Valuation Analysis — **Institutional Holding**

Forecast EPS	$2.43	No of Institutions
	(05/20/2016)	992
Market Cap	$25.1 Billion	Shares
Book Value	$17.9 Billion	557,304,704
Price/Book	1.40	% Held
Price/Sales	0.39	72.56

Business Summary: Food (MIC: 1.2.1 SIC: 2041 NAIC: 311211)

Archer-Daniels-Midland is a processor of oilseeds, corn, wheat, cocoa, and other agricultural commodities and is a manufacturer of protein meal, vegetable oil, corn sweeteners, flour, biodiesel, ethanol, and other food and feed ingredients. Co. has four segments: Agricultural Services, which buys, stores, cleans, and transports agricultural commodities; Corn Processing, which is engaged in corn wet milling and dry milling activities; Oilseeds Processing, which is engaged in the origination, merchandising, crushing, and further processing of oilseeds; and Wild Flavors and Specialty Ingredients, which consists of WILD Flavors businesses, Specialty Commodities Inc. subsidiary and Eatern Foods.

Recent Developments: For the quarter ended Mar 31 2016, net income decreased 53.3% to US$230.0 million from US$493.0 million in the year-earlier quarter. Revenues were US$14.38 billion, down 17.8% from US$17.51 billion the year before. Direct operating expenses declined 17.2% to US$13.59 billion from US$16.40 billion in the comparable period the year before. Indirect operating expenses decreased 2.0% to US$488.0 million from US$498.0 million in the equivalent prior-year period.

Prospects: Our evaluation of Archer Daniels Midland Co. as of June 19, 2016 is the result of our systematic analysis on three basic characteristics: earnings strength, relative valuation, and recent stock price movement. The company has managed to produce a neutral trend in earnings per share over the past 5 quarters and while recent estimates for the company have been raised by analysts, ADM has posted results that fell short of analysts expectations. Based on operating earnings yield, the company is about fairly valued when compared to all of the companies in our coverage universe. Share price changes over the past year indicates that ADM will perform very poorly over the near term.

Financial Data
(US$ in Thousands)

	3 Mos	12/31/2015	12/31/2014	12/31/2013	12/31/2012	06/30/2012	06/30/2011	06/30/2010
Earnings Per Share	2.60	2.98	3.43	2.02	1.05	1.84	3.13	3.00
Cash Flow Per Share	4.13	4.01	7.60	7.91	2.49	4.34	(3.64)	4.17
Tang Book Value Per Share	23.87	23.88	25.58	29.43	27.87	26.35	26.93	22.04
Dividends Per Share	1.140	1.120	0.960	0.760	0.700	0.685	0.620	0.580
Dividend Payout %	43.85	37.58	27.99	37.62	66.67	37.23	19.81	19.33
Income Statement								
Total Revenue	14,384,000	67,702,000	81,201,000	89,804,000	46,729,000	89,038,000	80,676,000	61,682,000
EBITDA	520,000	2,930,000	3,853,000	2,751,000	1,331,000	2,470,000	3,696,000	3,358,000
Depn & Amortn	231,000	799,000	850,000	827,000	435,000	848,000	877,000	912,000
Income Before Taxes	241,000	1,894,000	2,758,000	1,613,000	742,000	1,293,000	2,473,000	2,024,000
Income Taxes	76,000	438,000	877,000	670,000	303,000	523,000	997,000	666,000
Net Income	230,000	1,849,000	2,248,000	1,342,000	692,000	1,223,000	2,036,000	1,930,000
Average Shares	597,000	621,000	656,000	663,000	661,000	666,000	654,000	644,000
Balance Sheet								
Current Assets	20,970,000	21,829,000	26,028,000	28,530,000	29,762,000	26,954,000	27,504,000	18,134,000
Total Assets	39,681,000	40,157,000	44,027,000	43,752,000	45,136,000	41,553,000	42,193,000	31,548,000
Current Liabilities	12,867,000	13,505,000	15,602,000	15,658,000	16,993,000	14,626,000	13,218,000	8,573,000
Long-Term Obligations	5,851,000	5,779,000	5,558,000	5,347,000	6,456,000	6,535,000	8,266,000	6,830,000
Total Liabilities	21,782,000	22,258,000	24,452,000	23,596,000	26,216,000	23,584,000	23,385,000	16,939,000
Stockholders' Equity	17,899,000	17,899,000	19,575,000	20,156,000	18,920,000	17,969,000	18,808,000	14,609,000
Shares Outstanding	587,000	595,000	637,000	659,000	659,000	659,000	676,000	639,000
Statistical Record								
Return on Assets %	3.90	4.39	5.12	3.02	1.05	2.91	5.52	6.11
Return on Equity %	8.66	9.87	11.32	6.87	2.43	6.63	12.19	13.73
EBITDA Margin %	3.62	4.33	4.75	3.06	2.85	2.77	4.58	5.44
Net Margin %	1.60	2.73	2.77	1.49	1.48	1.37	2.52	3.13
Asset Turnover	1.59	1.61	1.85	2.02	0.71	2.12	2.19	1.95
Current Ratio	1.63	1.62	1.67	1.82	1.75	1.84	2.08	2.12
Debt to Equity	0.33	0.32	0.28	0.27	0.34	0.36	0.44	0.47
Price Range	53.17-30.51	53.17-34.18	53.71-38.23	43.79-27.39	29.10-24.48	33.50-24.16	37.65-25.50	32.61-24.51
P/E Ratio	20.45-11.73	17.84-11.47	15.66-11.15	21.68-13.56	27.71-23.31	18.21-13.13	12.03-8.15	10.87-8.17
Average Yield %	2.66	2.44	2.08	2.15	2.59	2.31	1.93	2.00

Address: 77 West Wacker Drive, Suite 4600, Chicago, IL 60601 Telephone: 312-634-8100	Web Site: www.adm.com Officers: Juan R. Luciano - Chairman, President, Chief Executive Officer, Executive Vice President, Chief Operating Officer Ray G. Young - Executive Vice President, Senior Vice President, Chief Financial Officer	Auditors: Ernst & Young LLP Investor Contact: 217-424-5656 Transfer Agents: Hickory Point Bank & Trust, fsb, Decatur, IL

ARMSTRONG WORLD INDUSTRIES INC

Exchange	Symbol	Price	52Wk Range	Yield	P/E
NYS	AWI	$41.35 (5/31/2016)	51.99-31.45	N/A	60.81

*7 Year Price Score 89.84   *NYSE Composite Index=100   ***12 Month Price Score 96.89**

Interim Earnings (Per Share)

Qtr.	Mar	Jun	Sep	Dec
2013	0.05	0.50	0.85	0.21
2014	0.30	0.34	0.57	(0.07)
2015	0.83	0.53	0.57	(0.24)
2016	(0.18)	...	...	...

Interim Dividends (Per Share)

Amt	Decl	Ex	Rec	Pay
13.74U	11/23/2010	12/13/2010	12/03/2010	12/10/2010
8.55U	03/23/2012	03/30/2012	04/03/2012	04/10/2012
0.00U	03/11/2016	04/04/2016	03/21/2016	04/01/2016

Valuation Analysis   **Institutional Holding**

Forecast EPS	$2.25
	(05/20/2016)
Market Cap	$2.3 Billion
Book Value	$770.3 Million
Price/Book	2.98
Price/Sales	0.94

No of Institutions 246
Shares 62,010,248
% Held 93.85

Business Summary: Metal Products (MIC: 8.2.3 SIC: 3448 NAIC: 332311)

Armstrong World Industries produces flooring products and ceiling systems for use in the construction and renovation of residential, commercial and institutional buildings. Co.'s segments include: Building Products, which produces suspended mineral fiber, soft fiber and metal ceiling systems; Resilient Flooring, which produces and sources floor coverings, sources and sells laminate flooring and vinyl tile products, vinyl sheet products, adhesives, linoleum products, installation and maintenance materials and accessories; and Wood Flooring, which produces and sources wood flooring products such as pre-finished solid and engineered wood floors in various wood species, and related accessories.

Recent Developments: For the quarter ended Mar 31 2016, loss from continuing operations was US$11.6 million compared with income of US$3.8 million in the year-earlier quarter. Net loss amounted to US$9.9 million versus net income of US$46.6 million in the year-earlier quarter. Revenues were US$571.8 million, up 3.7% from US$551.4 million the year before. Operating income was US$18.3 million versus US$35.8 million in the prior-year quarter, a decrease of 48.9%. Direct operating expenses rose 4.4% to US$440.3 million from US$421.9 million in the comparable period the year before. Indirect operating expenses increased 20.8% to US$113.2 million from US$93.7 million in the equivalent prior-year period.

Prospects: Our evaluation of Armstrong World Industries Inc. as of June 19, 2016 is the result of our systematic analysis on three basic characteristics: earnings strength, relative valuation, and recent stock price movement. The company has produced a positive trend in earnings per share over the past 5 quarters and while recent estimates for the company have been mixed, AWI has posted better than expected results. Based on operating earnings yield, the company is about fairly valued when compared to all of the companies in our coverage universe. Share price changes over the past year indicates that AWI will perform in line with the market over the near term.

Financial Data

(US$ in Thousands)	3 Mos	12/31/2015	12/31/2014	12/31/2013	12/31/2012	12/31/2011	12/31/2010	12/31/2009
Earnings Per Share	0.68	1.68	1.14	1.60	2.19	1.90	0.19	1.36
Cash Flow Per Share	3.11	3.67	3.80	3.70	3.72	3.64	3.30	4.58
Tang Book Value Per Share	5.11	5.04	2.68	2.76	3.25	10.01	9.21	22.75
Dividends Per Share	...	...	...	...	8.550	...	13.740	...
Dividend Payout %	...	...	...	...	390.41	...	7,231.58	...
Income Statement								
Total Revenue	571,800	2,420,000	2,515,300	2,719,900	2,618,900	2,859,500	2,766,400	2,780,000
EBITDA	34,500	219,200	293,000	287,100	327,900	297,700	185,500	199,600
Depn & Amortn	30,200	118,300	129,400	109,000	112,700	113,800	143,300	146,800
Income Before Taxes	(17,600)	57,800	120,100	112,500	164,600	138,200	21,700	35,200
Income Taxes	12,100	71,300	83,200	71,400	76,100	80,700	55,700	(2,500)
Net Income	(9,900)	94,200	63,800	94,100	131,300	112,400	11,000	77,700
Average Shares	55,600	55,900	55,400	58,400	59,500	58,800	58,200	57,000
Balance Sheet								
Current Assets	816,000	880,800	811,500	884,000	1,019,900	1,209,300	1,020,700	1,331,600
Total Assets	2,625,900	2,691,900	2,606,200	2,916,600	2,854,300	2,994,700	2,922,400	3,302,600
Current Liabilities	405,800	436,300	388,100	410,900	384,700	386,100	382,900	357,300
Long-Term Obligations	925,700	950,900	1,003,000	1,042,600	1,038,000	822,900	839,600	432,500
Total Liabilities	1,855,600	1,923,100	1,957,100	2,243,400	2,135,200	1,864,500	1,831,600	1,403,300
Stockholders' Equity	770,300	768,800	649,100	673,200	719,100	1,130,200	1,090,800	1,899,300
Shares Outstanding	55,477	55,359	55,126	54,406	58,934	58,424	58,070	57,433
Statistical Record								
Return on Assets %	1.45	3.56	2.31	3.26	4.48	3.80	0.35	2.34
Return on Equity %	5.14	13.29	9.65	13.52	14.16	10.12	0.74	4.27
EBITDA Margin %	6.03	9.06	11.65	10.56	12.52	10.41	6.71	7.18
Net Margin %	N.M.	3.89	2.54	3.46	5.01	3.93	0.40	2.79
Asset Turnover	0.94	0.91	0.91	0.94	0.89	0.97	0.89	0.84
Current Ratio	2.01	2.02	2.09	2.15	2.65	3.13	2.67	3.73
Debt to Equity	1.20	1.24	1.55	1.55	1.44	0.73	0.77	0.23
Price Range	51.99-31.45	51.99-31.45	53.19-39.27	49.93-40.06	50.38-33.50	41.61-28.43	46.41-24.78	38.73-8.19
P/E Ratio	76.45-46.25	30.95-23.06	46.65-34.44	31.20-25.04	23.00-15.29	21.90-14.96	244.25-130.41	28.48-6.02
Average Yield %	...	...	...	...	20.81	...	40.60	...

Address: 2500 Columbia Avenue, Lancaster, PA 17603
Telephone: 717-397-0611

Web Site: www.armstrong.com
Officers: James J. O'Connor - Chairman Victor D. Grizzle - President, Chief Executive Officer, Executive Vice President, Division Officer

Auditors: KPMG LLP
Investor Contact: 717-396-6354
Transfer Agents: American Stock Transfer & Trust Company, New York, NY

ARROW ELECTRONICS, INC.

Exchange	Symbol	Price	52Wk Range	Yield	P/E
NYS	ARW	$64.62 (5/31/2016)	65.32-46.66	N/A	12.31

*7 Year Price Score 113.78 *NYSE Composite Index=100 ***12 Month Price Score 108.45**

TRADING VOLUME (thousand shares)

Interim Earnings (Per Share)

Qtr.	Mar	Jun	Sep	Dec
2013	0.72	0.86	0.95	1.32
2014	1.06	1.27	1.47	1.18
2015	1.09	1.28	1.15	1.68
2016	1.14	...	...	...

Interim Dividends (Per Share)

No Dividends Paid

Valuation Analysis   **Institutional Holding**

Forecast EPS	$6.78	No of Institutions
	(05/20/2016)	505
Market Cap	$5.9 Billion	Shares
Book Value	$4.3 Billion	108,102,272
Price/Book	1.37	% Held
Price/Sales	0.25	89.56

Business Summary: Electrical Equipment (MIC: 7.3.1 SIC: 5045 NAIC: 334419)

Arrow Electronics is a provider of products, services, and solutions to industrial and commercial users of electronic components and enterprise computing solutions. Co.'s customer base consists of original equipment manufacturers, contract manufacturers, and other commercial customers. Co. has two segments: Global Components, which markets and distributes electronic components and provides a range of value-added capabilities throughout the entire life cycle of technology products and services; and Global Enterprise Computing Solutions, which provides computing solutions and services.

Recent Developments: For the quarter ended Apr 2 2016, net income increased 0.5% to US$106.6 million from US$106.1 million in the year-earlier quarter. Revenues were US$5.47 billion, up 9.4% from US$5.00 billion the year before. Operating income was US$181.4 million versus US$177.4 million in the prior-year quarter, an increase of 2.2%. Direct operating expenses rose 9.5% to US$4.73 billion from US$4.32 billion in the comparable period the year before. Indirect operating expenses increased 11.7% to US$567.5 million from US$507.9 million in the equivalent prior-year period.

Prospects: Our evaluation of Arrow Electronics Inc. as of June 19, 2016 is the result of our systematic analysis on three basic characteristics: earnings strength, relative valuation, and recent stock price movement. The company has enjoyed a very positive trend in earnings per share over the past 5 quarters and while recent estimates for the company have remained steady, ARW has posted better than expected results. Based on operating earnings yield, the company is undervalued when compared to all of the companies in our coverage universe. Share price changes over the past year indicates that ARW will perform in line with the market over the near term.

Financial Data

(US$ in Thousands)	3 Mos	12/31/2015	12/31/2014	12/31/2013	12/31/2012	12/31/2011	12/31/2010	12/31/2009
Earnings Per Share	5.25	5.20	4.98	3.85	4.56	5.17	4.01	1.03
Cash Flow Per Share	9.40	6.92	6.82	4.39	6.16	1.06	1.87	7.09
Tang Book Value Per Share	16.36	15.22	18.24	17.16	17.52	16.12	16.70	16.61
Income Statement								
Total Revenue	5,474,177	23,282,020	22,768,674	21,357,285	20,405,128	21,390,264	18,744,676	14,684,101
EBITDA	190,241	1,023,575	989,978	857,287	954,019	1,051,743	863,508	369,832
Depn & Amortn	8,877	203,028	197,978	168,064	149,896	142,707	114,303	102,357
Income Before Taxes	145,789	685,146	676,015	574,790	702,247	803,065	672,634	184,190
Income Taxes	41,053	191,697	184,943	182,343	203,642	210,485	199,378	65,416
Net Income	106,592	497,726	498,045	399,420	506,332	598,810	479,630	123,512
Average Shares	92,787	95,686	99,947	103,699	111,077	115,932	119,577	120,489
Balance Sheet								
Current Assets	8,427,570	9,186,471	9,032,607	8,585,770	7,715,301	7,024,591	7,085,834	5,839,628
Total Assets	12,352,787	13,021,930	12,442,856	12,060,883	10,785,687	9,829,079	9,600,538	7,762,366
Current Liabilities	4,920,803	6,056,152	5,838,021	5,301,946	4,910,211	3,958,927	4,343,243	3,332,246
Long-Term Obligations	2,649,042	2,380,575	2,075,453	2,226,132	1,587,478	1,927,823	1,761,203	1,276,138
Total Liabilities	8,033,407	8,879,487	8,288,886	7,880,651	6,802,465	6,160,267	6,349,343	4,845,406
Stockholders' Equity	4,319,380	4,142,443	4,153,970	4,180,232	3,983,222	3,668,812	3,251,195	2,916,960
Shares Outstanding	91,623	90,923	95,895	99,936	106,001	111,814	114,647	119,828
Statistical Record								
Return on Assets %	4.26	3.91	4.07	3.50	4.90	6.16	5.52	1.66
Return on Equity %	12.02	12.00	11.95	9.79	13.20	17.31	15.55	4.42
EBITDA Margin %	3.48	4.40	4.35	4.01	4.68	4.92	4.61	2.52
Net Margin %	1.95	2.14	2.19	1.87	2.48	2.80	2.56	0.84
Asset Turnover	2.02	1.83	1.86	1.87	1.97	2.20	2.16	1.97
Current Ratio	1.71	1.52	1.55	1.62	1.57	1.77	1.63	1.75
Debt to Equity	0.61	0.57	0.50	0.53	0.40	0.53	0.54	0.44
Price Range	65.32-46.66	64.67-50.79	62.71-46.42	54.25-36.47	42.63-31.02	46.53-25.98	34.39-22.01	29.98-15.17
P/E Ratio	12.44-8.89	12.44-9.77	12.59-9.32	14.09-9.47	9.35-6.80	9.00-5.03	8.58-5.49	29.11-14.73

Address: 9201 East Dry Creek Road, Centennial, CO 80112 **Telephone:** 303-824-4000	**Web Site:** www.arrow.com **Officers:** Michael J. Long - Chairman, President, Chief Executive Officer, Chief Operating Officer Paul J. Reilly - Executive Vice President, Chief Financial Officer, Interim Chief Accounting Officer	**Auditors:** Ernst & Young LLP **Investor Contact:** 303-824-4000 **Transfer Agents:** Wells Fargo Shareowner Services, South St. Paul, MN

ASBURY AUTOMOTIVE GROUP, INC

Exchange	Symbol	Price	52Wk Range	Yield	P/E
NYS	ABG	$56.10 (5/31/2016)	95.54-45.07	N/A	8.77

*7 Year Price Score 153.13 *NYSE Composite Index=100 *12 Month Price Score 79.44

Interim Earnings (Per Share)

Qtr.	Mar	Jun	Sep	Dec
2013	1.04	0.87	0.73	0.87
2014	1.02	1.18	1.08	0.43
2015	1.30	1.52	1.96	1.65
2016	1.27			

Interim Dividends (Per Share)

No Dividends Paid

Valuation Analysis

		Institutional Holding	
Forecast EPS	$6.10	No of Institutions	
	(05/20/2016)	286	
Market Cap	$1.3 Billion	Shares	
Book Value	$241.8 Million	27,025,310	
Price/Book	5.38	% Held	
Price/Sales	0.20	92.94	

Business Summary: Retail - Automotive (MIC: 2.1.4 SIC: 5599 NAIC: 441229)

Asbury Automotive Group is an automotive retailer with its store operations conducted by its subsidiaries. As of Dec 31 2015, Co. owned and operated 99 new vehicle franchises (81 dealership locations), representing 28 brands of automobiles and 25 collision centers in 17 metropolitan markets within nine states. Co.'s stores provide a range of automotive products and services, including new and used vehicles, repair and maintenance services, collision repair services, and finance and insurance products. In addition, as of Dec 31 2015, Co. owned and operated three stand-alone used vehicle stores under the Q auto brand name in Florida.

Recent Developments: For the quarter ended Mar 31 2016, income from continuing operations decreased 13.4% to US$31.1 million from US$35.9 million in the year-earlier quarter. Net income decreased 13.6% to US$31.0 million from US$35.9 million in the year-earlier quarter. Revenues were US$1.55 billion, up 0.6% from US$1.54 billion the year before. Operating income was US$68.9 million versus US$73.1 million in the prior-year quarter, a decrease of 5.7%. Direct operating expenses was unchanged at US$1.29 billion versus the comparable period the year before. Indirect operating expenses increased 4.7% to US$191.9 million from US$183.3 million in the equivalent prior-year period.

Prospects: Our evaluation of Asbury Automotive Group Inc. as of June 19, 2016 is the result of our systematic analysis on three basic characteristics: earnings strength, relative valuation, and recent stock price movement. The company has generated a negative trend in earnings per share over the past 5 quarters and while recent estimates for the company have remained steady, ABG has posted better than expected results. Based on operating earnings yield, the company is undervalued when compared to all of the companies in our coverage universe. Share price changes over the past year indicates that ABG will perform poorly over the near term.

Financial Data

(US$ in Thousands)	3 Mos	12/31/2015	12/31/2014	12/31/2013	12/31/2012	12/31/2011	12/31/2010	12/31/2009
Earnings Per Share	6.40	6.41	3.71	3.51	2.61	2.08	1.14	0.41
Cash Flow Per Share	4.95	5.91	2.82	1.65	(0.66)	(5.69)	0.31	3.47
Tang Book Value Per Share	2.72	5.47	10.25	12.92	10.84	8.76	7.07	6.94
Income Statement								
Total Revenue	1,550,800	6,588,300	5,867,700	5,334,900	4,640,300	4,276,700	3,936,000	3,650,600
EBITDA	74,000	366,000	262,700	243,600	208,100	155,000	133,800	118,100
Depn & Amortn	5,100	29,500	26,400	24,300	22,600	22,700	21,100	23,500
Income Before Taxes	50,300	273,400	183,000	165,300	133,300	77,600	60,500	38,600
Income Taxes	19,200	104,000	71,000	64,200	50,000	29,600	23,200	14,400
Net Income	31,000	169,200	111,600	109,100	82,200	67,900	38,100	13,400
Average Shares	24,400	26,400	30,100	31,100	31,500	32,600	33,300	32,900
Balance Sheet								
Current Assets	1,369,300	1,343,000	1,276,700	1,108,600	986,400	792,500	877,300	815,600
Total Assets	2,335,500	2,305,900	2,192,000	1,888,600	1,661,400	1,419,400	1,486,300	1,400,900
Current Liabilities	1,114,400	1,007,800	1,041,100	834,200	779,800	636,300	635,800	598,800
Long-Term Obligations	931,700	940,400	678,700	543,300	461,400	439,100	534,900	528,800
Total Liabilities	2,093,700	1,991,400	1,747,100	1,398,000	1,258,600	1,092,800	1,199,200	1,157,300
Stockholders' Equity	241,800	314,500	444,900	490,600	402,800	326,600	287,100	243,600
Shares Outstanding	23,201	24,810	28,523	30,765	31,316	31,320	32,798	32,430
Statistical Record								
Return on Assets %	7.28	7.52	5.47	6.15	5.32	4.67	2.64	0.88
Return on Equity %	52.97	44.56	23.86	24.42	22.48	22.13	14.36	5.75
EBITDA Margin %	4.77	5.56	4.48	4.57	4.48	3.62	3.40	3.24
Net Margin %	2.00	2.57	1.90	2.05	1.77	1.59	0.97	0.37
Asset Turnover	2.92	2.93	2.88	3.01	3.00	2.94	2.73	2.39
Current Ratio	1.23	1.33	1.23	1.33	1.26	1.25	1.38	1.36
Debt to Equity	3.85	2.99	1.53	1.11	1.15	1.34	1.86	2.17
Price Range	95.54-45.07	95.54-66.76	77.56-45.42	55.61-32.03	32.03-21.50	21.66-15.04	18.80-9.82	14.86-2.01
P/E Ratio	14.93-7.04	14.90-10.41	20.91-12.24	15.84-9.13	12.27-8.24	10.41-7.23	16.49-8.61	36.24-4.90

Address: 2905 Premiere Parkway N.W., Suite 300, Duluth, GA 30097	Web Site: www.asburyauto.com	Auditors: Ernst & Young LLP
Telephone: 770-418-8200	Officers: Charles R. Oglesby - Executive Chairman Craig T. Monaghan - President, Chief Executive Officer	Investor Contact: 770-418-8210 Transfer Agents: Computershare Trust Company, N.A.

ASHLAND INC

Exchange	Symbol	Price	52Wk Range	Yield	P/E
NYS	ASH	$113.36 (5/31/2016)	128.35-89.25	1.38	32.11

*7 Year Price Score 118.76 *NYSE Composite Index=100 *12 Month Price Score 102.71

Interim Earnings (Per Share)

Qtr.	Dec	Mar	Jun	Sep
2012-13	1.26	0.66	1.55	5.10
2013-14	1.40	(0.57)	1.25	0.91
2014-15	0.46	3.26	1.56	(0.76)
2015-16	1.35	1.38	...	...

Interim Dividends (Per Share)

Amt	Decl	Ex	Rec	Pay
0.39Q	07/16/2015	08/19/2015	08/21/2015	09/15/2015
0.39Q	11/19/2015	11/27/2015	12/01/2015	12/15/2015
0.39Q	01/28/2016	02/17/2016	02/19/2016	03/15/2016
0.39Q	05/18/2016	06/01/2016	06/03/2016	06/15/2016

Indicated Div: $1.56

Valuation Analysis

Forecast EPS	$7.10
	(05/20/2016)
Market Cap	$7.0 Billion
Book Value	$2.7 Billion
Price/Book	2.58
Price/Sales	1.39

Institutional Holding

No of Institutions	520
Shares	59,996,544
% Held	82.19

Business Summary: Specialty Chemicals (MIC: 8.3.2 SIC: 5169 NAIC: 325199)

Ashland provides specialty chemicals. Co.'s chemistry is used in a variety of markets and applications, including architectural coatings, adhesives, automotive, construction, energy, food and beverage, personal care, and pharmaceutical. Co. has three reportable segments: Specialty Ingredients, which provides cellulose ethers, vinyl pyrrolidones and biofunctionals; Performance Materials, which provides gelcoats, maleic anhydride, butanediol, tetrahydrofuran, N-Methylpyrrolidone and other intermediates and solvents; and Valvoline, which is a producer and distributor of automotive, commercial and industrial lubricants and automotive chemicals.

Recent Developments: For the quarter ended Mar 31 2016, income from continuing operations decreased 8.4% to US$87.0 million from US$95.0 million in the year-earlier quarter. Net income decreased 61.2% to US$87.0 million from US$224.0 million in the year-earlier quarter. Revenues were US$1.25 billion, down 7.6% from US$1.35 billion the year before. Operating income was US$147.0 million versus US$193.0 million in the prior-year quarter, a decrease of 23.8%. Direct operating expenses declined 11.0% to US$823.0 million from US$925.0 million in the comparable period the year before. Indirect operating expenses increased 19.4% to US$277.0 million from US$232.0 million in the equivalent prior-year period.

Prospects: Our evaluation of Ashland Inc. as of June 19, 2016 is the result of our systematic analysis on three basic characteristics: earnings strength, relative valuation, and recent stock price movement. The company has managed to produce a neutral trend in earnings per share over the past 5 quarters. However, while recent estimates for the company have been mixed, ASH has posted better than expected results. Based on operating earnings yield, the company is undervalued when compared to all of the companies in our coverage universe. Share price changes over the past year indicates that ASH will perform in line with the market over the near term.

Financial Data

(US$ in Thousands)	6 Mos	3 Mos	09/30/2015	09/30/2014	09/30/2013	09/30/2012	09/30/2011	09/30/2010
Earnings Per Share	3.53	5.41	4.48	3.00	8.57	0.33	5.17	4.18
Cash Flow Per Share	3.92	1.62	1.31	7.53	10.14	4.92	3.12	6.63
Tang Book Value Per Share	N.M.	N.M.	N.M.	N.M.	N.M.	N.M.	N.M.	5.85
Dividends Per Share	1.560	1.510	1.460	1.360	1.130	0.800	0.650	0.450
Dividend Payout %	44.19	27.91	32.59	45.33	13.19	242.42	12.57	10.77
Income Statement								
Total Revenue	2,410,000	1,163,000	5,387,000	6,121,000	7,813,000	8,206,000	6,502,000	9,012,000
EBITDA	304,000	156,000	592,000	345,000	1,529,000	713,000	443,000	963,000
Depn & Amortn	6,000	3,000	263,000	304,000	309,000	484,000	325,000	385,000
Income Before Taxes	213,000	111,000	169,000	(116,000)	951,000	(14,000)	3,000	392,000
Income Taxes	35,000	20,000	(22,000)	(188,000)	274,000	(52,000)	(53,000)	91,000
Net Income	176,000	89,000	309,000	233,000	683,000	26,000	414,000	332,000
Average Shares	63,000	66,000	69,000	78,000	80,000	80,000	80,000	79,000
Balance Sheet								
Current Assets	2,912,000	2,932,000	3,248,000	3,561,000	2,873,000	3,209,000	3,387,000	2,833,000
Total Assets	9,901,000	9,673,000	10,064,000	10,951,000	12,088,000	12,524,000	12,966,000	9,531,000
Current Liabilities	1,702,000	1,594,000	1,448,000	1,687,000	1,727,000	1,913,000	1,739,000	1,687,000
Long-Term Obligations	3,328,000	3,337,000	3,348,000	2,942,000	2,947,000	3,131,000	3,648,000	1,108,000
Total Liabilities	7,178,000	7,126,000	7,027,000	7,368,000	7,535,000	8,495,000	8,831,000	5,728,000
Stockholders' Equity	2,723,000	2,547,000	3,037,000	3,583,000	4,553,000	4,029,000	4,135,000	3,803,000
Shares Outstanding	62,060	63,225	67,000	70,000	77,000	79,000	78,000	79,000
Statistical Record								
Return on Assets %	2.33	3.66	2.94	2.02	5.55	0.20	3.68	3.50
Return on Equity %	7.98	12.47	9.34	5.73	15.92	0.64	10.43	8.99
EBITDA Margin %	12.61	13.41	10.99	5.64	19.57	8.69	6.81	10.69
Net Margin %	7.30	7.65	5.74	3.81	8.74	0.32	6.37	3.68
Asset Turnover	0.51	0.52	0.51	0.53	0.63	0.64	0.58	0.95
Current Ratio	1.71	1.84	2.24	2.11	1.66	1.68	1.95	1.68
Debt to Equity	1.22	1.31	1.10	0.82	0.65	0.78	0.88	0.29
Price Range	131.52-89.25	131.52-98.93	131.52-96.38	109.37-85.09	93.42-68.27	76.73-42.79	68.34-44.14	63.28-34.14
P/E Ratio	37.26-25.28	24.31-18.29	29.36-21.51	36.46-28.36	10.90-7.97	232.52-129.67	13.22-8.54	15.14-8.17
Average Yield %	1.40	1.29	1.24	1.37	1.38	1.28	1.16	0.95

Address: 50 E. RiverCenter Boulevard, P.O. Box 391, Covington, KY 41012-0391
Telephone: 859-815-3333

Web Site: www.ashland.com
Officers: William A. Wulfsohn - Chairman, Chief Executive Officer J. Kevin Willis - Senior Vice President, Chief Financial Officer

Auditors: PricewaterhouseCoopers LLP
Investor Contact: 859-815-3527
Transfer Agents: Wells Fargo Shareowner Services, South St. Paul, MN

ASPEN INSURANCE HOLDINGS LTD

Exchange	Symbol	Price	52Wk Range	Yield	P/E
NYS	AHL	$47.85 (5/31/2016)	51.19-41.07	1.84	11.03

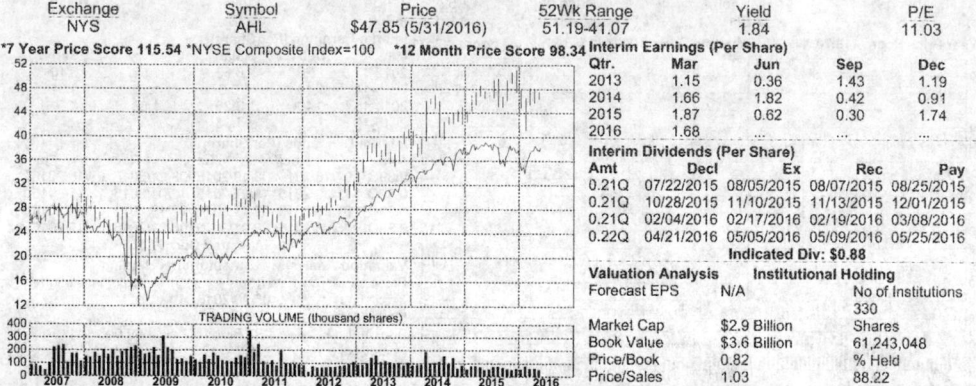

*7 Year Price Score 115.54 *NYSE Composite Index=100 *12 Month Price Score 98.34

Interim Earnings (Per Share)

Qtr.	Mar	Jun	Sep	Dec
2013	1.15	0.36	1.43	1.19
2014	1.66	1.82	0.42	0.91
2015	1.87	0.62	0.30	1.74
2016	1.68	...	...	...

Interim Dividends (Per Share)

Amt	Decl	Ex	Rec	Pay
0.21Q	07/22/2015	08/05/2015	08/07/2015	08/25/2015
0.21Q	10/28/2015	11/10/2015	11/13/2015	12/01/2015
0.21Q	02/04/2016	02/17/2016	02/19/2016	03/08/2016
0.22Q	04/21/2016	05/05/2016	05/09/2016	05/25/2016

Indicated Div: $0.88

Valuation Analysis

		Institutional Holding	
Forecast EPS	N/A	No of Institutions	330
Market Cap	$2.9 Billion	Shares	61,243,048
Book Value	$3.6 Billion	% Held	88.22
Price/Book	0.82		
Price/Sales	1.03		

Business Summary: General Insurance (MIC: 5.2.1 SIC: 6331 NAIC: 524126)

Aspen Insurance Holdings is a holding company. Through its principal operating subsidiaries, Co. operates in the global markets for property and casualty insurance and reinsurance. Co. is organized into two business segments: reinsurance, which consists of property catastrophe reinsurance, other property reinsurance (risk excess, pro rata and facultative), casualty reinsurance (U.S. treaty, international treaty and global facultative) and specialty reinsurance (credit and surety, agriculture, marine, aviation and other specialty lines); and insurance, which consists of property and casualty insurance, marine, aviation and energy insurance and financial and professional lines insurance.

Recent Developments: For the quarter ended Mar 31 2016, net income decreased 10.6% to US$114.4 million from US$128.0 million in the year-earlier quarter. Revenues were US$779.6 million, up 11.0% from US$702.3 million the year before. Net premiums earned were US$663.1 million versus US$593.6 million in the prior-year quarter, an increase of 11.7%. Net investment income rose 4.4% to US$49.5 million from US$47.4 million a year ago.

Prospects: Our evaluation of Aspen Insurance Holdings Ltd. as of July 19, 2015 is the result of our systematic analysis on three basic characteristics: earnings strength, relative valuation, and recent stock price movement. The company has managed to produce a neutral trend in earnings per share over the past 5 quarters. However, while recent estimates for the company have been lowered by analysts, AHL has posted better than expected results. Based on operating earnings yield, the company is undervalued when compared to all of the companies in our coverage universe. Share price changes over the past year indicates that AHL will perform in line with the market over the near term.

Financial Data
(US$ in Thousands)

	3 Mos	12/31/2015	12/31/2014	12/31/2013	12/31/2012	12/31/2011	12/31/2010	12/31/2009
Earnings Per Share	4.34	4.54	4.82	4.14	3.38	(1.82)	3.62	5.64
Cash Flow Per Share	9.24	9.37	9.41	8.47	6.96	4.86	8.18	7.82
Tang Book Value Per Share	57.38	55.82	54.83	50.06	49.03	44.61	42.18	39.57
Dividends Per Share	0.840	0.830	0.780	0.710	0.660	0.600	0.600	0.600
Dividend Payout %	19.35	18.28	16.18	17.15	19.53	...	16.57	10.64
Income Statement								
Premium Income	663,100	2,473,300	2,405,300	2,171,800	2,083,500	1,888,500	1,898,900	1,823,000
Total Revenue	779,600	2,753,400	2,646,400	2,423,300	2,329,400	2,077,700	2,190,400	2,074,900
Benefits & Claims	357,400	...	...	...	...	...	...	...
Income Before Taxes	116,900	337,500	367,900	342,700	295,400	(143,000)	340,300	534,700
Income Taxes	2,500	14,400	12,100	13,400	15,000	(37,200)	27,600	60,800
Net Income	114,600	323,100	355,800	329,300	280,400	(105,800)	312,700	473,900
Average Shares	62,483	62,687	65,872	69,417	73,689	70,665	80,014	85,327
Balance Sheet								
Total Assets	11,505,400	11,048,800	10,716,300	10,230,500	10,310,600	9,476,500	8,832,100	8,257,200
Total Liabilities	7,949,400	7,630,200	7,297,500	6,930,600	6,822,400	6,304,900	5,590,700	4,951,800
Stockholders' Equity	3,556,000	3,418,600	3,418,800	3,299,900	3,488,200	3,171,600	3,241,400	3,305,400
Shares Outstanding	60,675	60,918	62,017	65,546	70,753	70,655	76,342	83,327
Statistical Record								
Return on Assets %	2.75	2.97	3.40	3.21	2.83	N.M.	3.66	6.10
Return on Equity %	8.80	9.45	10.59	9.70	8.40	N.M.	9.55	15.58
Loss Ratio %	53.90	...	...	...	...	...	...	...
Net Margin %	14.70	11.73	13.44	13.59	12.04	(5.09)	14.28	22.84
Price Range	51.19-41.07	51.19-42.32	46.94-36.63	41.31-32.08	33.58-26.17	30.74-22.16	31.50-24.31	28.25-18.60
P/E Ratio	11.79-9.46	11.28-9.32	9.74-7.60	9.98-7.75	9.93-7.74	...	8.70-6.72	5.01-3.30
Average Yield %	1.77	1.75	1.84	1.90	2.27	2.26	2.15	2.47

Address: 141 Front Street, Hamilton, HM 19 **Telephone:** 441-295-8201	**Web Site:** www.aspen.bm **Officers:** Glyn Jones - Chairman Christopher O'Kane - Chief Executive Officer
Auditors: KPMG LLP **Investor Contact:** 646-502-1076 **Transfer Agents:** Computershare Investor Services, Jersey City, NJ	

ASSOCIATED BANC-CORP

Exchange	Symbol	Price	52Wk Range	Yield	P/E
NYS	ASB	$18.69 (5/31/2016)	20.84-15.48	2.35	16.11

*7 Year Price Score 105.40 *NYSE Composite Index=100 ***12 Month Price Score 94.76**

TRADING VOLUME (thousand shares)

Interim Earnings (Per Share)

Qtr.	Mar	Jun	Sep	Dec
2013	0.27	0.28	0.27	0.28
2014	0.27	0.28	0.31	0.31
2015	0.30	0.31	0.31	0.27
2016	0.27	...	...	...

Interim Dividends (Per Share)

Amt	Decl	Ex	Rec	Pay
0.10Q	07/21/2015	08/28/2015	09/01/2015	09/15/2015
0.11Q	10/20/2015	11/27/2015	12/01/2015	12/15/2015
0.11Q	02/02/2016	02/26/2016	03/01/2016	03/15/2016
0.11Q	04/26/2016	05/27/2016	06/01/2016	06/15/2016

Indicated Div: $0.44

Valuation Analysis / Institutional Holding

Forecast EPS	$1.21	No of Institutions
(05/15/2016)		301
Market Cap	$2.8 Billion	Shares
Book Value	$3.0 Billion	120,909,592
Price/Book	0.95	% Held
Price/Sales	2.58	70.05

Business Summary: Banking (MIC: 5.1.1 SIC: 6022 NAIC: 522110)

Associated Banc is a bank holding company. Through banking and various nonbanking subsidiaries, Co. provides banking and nonbanking products and services. Co. has three segments: Corporate and Commercial Specialty, which provides lending solutions such as commercial loans, deposit and cash management solutions; Community, Consumer, and Business, which includes lending solutions such as residential mortgages, deposit and transactional solutions; and Risk Management and Shared Services, which includes corporate risk management, credit administration, treasury, finance, operations and technology functions. As of Dec 2015, Co. had total assets of $27.72 billion and deposits of $21.01 billion.

Recent Developments: For the quarter ended Mar 31 2016, net income decreased 8.9% to US$42.5 million from US$46.7 million in the year-earlier quarter. Net interest income increased 2.5% to US$172.0 million from US$167.8 million in the year-earlier quarter. Provision for loan losses was US$20.0 million versus US$4.5 million in the prior-year quarter, an increase of 344.4%. Non-interest income rose 4.2% to US$83.2 million from US$79.8 million, while non-interest expense was unchanged at US$174.0 million.

Prospects: Our evaluation of Associated Banc-Corp. as of June 19, 2016 is the result of our systematic analysis on three basic characteristics: earnings strength, relative valuation, and recent stock price movement. The company has managed to produce a neutral trend in earnings per share over the past 5 quarters and while recent estimates for the company have remained steady, ASB has posted results that fell short of analysts expectations. Based on operating earnings yield, the company is undervalued when compared to all of the companies in our coverage universe. Share price changes over the past year indicates that ASB will perform well over the near term.

Financial Data

(US$ in Thousands)	3 Mos	12/31/2015	12/31/2014	12/31/2013	12/31/2012	12/31/2011	12/31/2010	12/31/2009
Earnings Per Share	1.16	1.19	1.16	1.10	1.00	0.66	(0.18)	(1.26)
Cash Flow Per Share	2.06	2.02	1.35	2.94	2.03	1.79	2.95	0.95
Tang Book Value Per Share	12.01	11.70	11.51	11.12	11.06	10.34	9.36	9.39
Dividends Per Share	0.420	0.410	0.370	0.330	0.230	0.040	0.040	0.470
Dividend Payout %	36.21	34.45	31.90	30.00	23.00	6.06	...	...
Income Statement								
Interest Income	194,069	753,662	736,745	708,983	718,284	741,622	806,126	981,256
Interest Expense	22,082	77,384	55,778	63,440	92,292	128,791	172,347	255,251
Net Interest Income	171,987	676,278	680,967	645,543	625,992	612,831	633,779	726,005
Provision for Losses	20,000	37,500	16,000	10,000	3,000	52,000	390,010	750,645
Non-Interest Income	83,192	328,409	290,319	313,099	313,290	282,469	345,523	350,961
Non-Interest Expense	173,971	697,399	679,241	680,749	681,823	659,873	630,320	611,420
Income Before Taxes	61,208	269,788	276,045	267,893	254,459	183,427	(41,028)	(285,099)
Income Taxes	18,674	81,487	85,536	79,201	75,486	43,728	(40,172)	(153,240)
Net Income	42,534	188,301	190,509	188,692	178,973	139,699	(856)	(131,859)
Average Shares	149,454	150,603	158,254	165,802	172,357	173,372	171,230	127,858
Balance Sheet								
Net Loans & Leases	19,078,209	18,564,994	17,482,479	15,692,684	15,375,023	13,902,115	12,284,730	13,636,330
Total Assets	28,178,867	27,715,021	26,821,774	24,226,920	23,487,735	21,924,217	21,785,596	22,874,142
Total Deposits	20,685,460	21,007,665	18,763,504	17,267,167	16,939,865	15,090,655	15,225,393	16,728,613
Total Liabilities	25,196,369	24,777,775	24,021,523	21,335,630	20,551,336	19,058,423	18,626,805	20,135,534
Stockholders' Equity	2,982,498	2,937,246	2,800,251	2,891,290	2,936,399	2,865,794	3,158,791	2,738,608
Shares Outstanding	150,993	151,239	151,541	164,138	170,239	174,591	173,887	128,403
Statistical Record								
Return on Assets %	0.67	0.69	0.75	0.79	0.79	0.64	N.M.	N.M.
Return on Equity %	6.28	6.56	6.69	6.48	6.15	4.64	N.M.	N.M.
Net Interest Margin %	88.62	89.73	92.43	91.05	87.15	82.63	78.62	73.99
Efficiency Ratio %	62.75	64.45	66.13	66.60	66.10	64.43	54.73	45.89
Loans to Deposits	0.92	0.88	0.93	0.91	0.91	0.92	0.81	0.82
Price Range	20.84-15.48	20.84-16.62	19.36-15.58	17.60-13.12	14.63-11.43	15.36-8.95	16.10-11.01	21.39-9.21
P/E Ratio	17.97-13.34	17.51-13.97	16.69-13.43	16.00-11.93	14.63-11.43	23.27-13.56	...	...
Average Yield %	2.23	2.16	2.08	2.11	1.77	0.31	0.30	3.59

Address: 433 Main Street, Green Bay, WI 54301
Telephone: 920-491-7500

Web Site: www.associatedbank.com
Officers: William R. Hutchinson - Chairman Philip B. Flynn - President, Chief Executive Officer

Auditors: KPMG LLP
Investor Contact: 920-491-7059
Transfer Agents: Wells Fargo Shareowner Services, Saint Paul, MN

ASSURANT INC

Exchange	Symbol	Price	52Wk Range	Yield	P/E	Div Achiever
NYS	AIZ	$87.39 (5/31/2016)	88.67-65.55	2.29	18.71	11 Years

*7 Year Price Score 133.58 *NYSE Composite Index=100 *12 Month Price Score 106.92

Interim Earnings (Per Share)

Qtr.	Mar	Jun	Sep	Dec
2013	1.46	1.70	1.68	1.46
2014	1.86	1.95	1.92	0.70
2015	0.71	0.47	(0.10)	0.96
2016	3.34	...	...	...

Interim Dividends (Per Share)

Amt	Decl	Ex	Rec	Pay
0.30Q	07/08/2015	08/27/2015	08/31/2015	09/15/2015
0.50Q	09/09/2015	11/25/2015	11/30/2015	12/14/2015
0.50Q	01/15/2016	02/25/2016	02/29/2016	03/14/2016
0.50Q	05/13/2016	05/26/2016	05/31/2016	06/14/2016

Indicated Div: $2.00

Valuation Analysis

Forecast EPS	$6.05 (05/20/2016)
Market Cap	$5.5 Billion
Book Value	$4.6 Billion
Price/Book	1.20
Price/Sales	0.55

Institutional Holding

No of Institutions	511
Shares	71,834,544
% Held	89.36

TRADING VOLUME (thousand shares)

Business Summary: Life & Health (MIC: 5.2.2 SIC: 6321 NAIC: 524114)

Assurant is a holding company. Co. provides insurance products and related services in North America, Latin America, Europe and other select markets. Co.'s segments include Assurant Solutions, which focuses on domestic and international extended service contracts and warranties including mobile device protection; preneed life insurance and international credit insurance; Assurant Specialty Property, which focuses on lender-placed homeowners insurance, and adjacent niches such as multi-family housing insurance; and Assurant Employee Benefits, which provides group disability, dental, life, vision and supplemental products as well as individual dental products.

Recent Developments: For the quarter ended Mar 31 2016, net income increased 340.2% to US$220.3 million from US$50.0 million in the year-earlier quarter. Revenues were US$2.15 billion, down 17.4% from US$2.60 billion the year before. Net premiums earned were US$1.42 billion versus US$2.16 billion in the prior-year quarter, a decrease of 34.5%. Net investment income fell 10.9% to US$135.7 million from US$152.3 million a year ago.

Prospects: Our evaluation of Assurant Inc. as of June 19, 2016 is the result of our systematic analysis on three basic characteristics: earnings strength, relative valuation, and recent stock price movement. The company has generated a negative trend in earnings per share over the past 5 quarters and while recent estimates for the company have been mixed, AIZ has posted better than expected results. Based on operating earnings yield, the company is undervalued when compared to all of the companies in our coverage universe. Share price changes over the past year indicates that AIZ will perform very well over the near term.

Financial Data
(US$ in Thousands)

	3 Mos	12/31/2015	12/31/2014	12/31/2013	12/31/2012	12/31/2011	12/31/2010	12/31/2009
Earnings Per Share	4.67	2.05	6.44	6.30	5.67	5.58	2.50	3.63
Cash Flow Per Share	1.43	3.73	5.46	13.41	8.04	8.85	4.89	2.29
Tang Book Value Per Share	54.46	51.83	57.12	51.43	54.43	46.13	40.79	33.66
Dividends Per Share	1.600	1.370	1.060	0.960	0.810	0.700	0.630	0.590
Dividend Payout %	34.26	66.83	16.46	15.24	14.29	12.54	25.20	16.25
Income Statement								
Total Revenue	2,147,527	10,325,494	10,381,653	9,047,657	8,508,270	8,272,804	8,527,722	8,700,501
Income Before Taxes	337,507	201,181	744,137	789,699	757,751	714,955	606,444	709,606
Income Taxes	117,189	59,626	273,230	300,792	274,046	169,116	327,267	279,032
Net Income	220,318	141,555	470,907	488,907	483,705	545,839	279,177	430,574
Average Shares	65,920	69,017	73,152	77,654	85,307	97,795	111,473	118,495
Balance Sheet								
Total Assets	30,287,195	30,043,128	31,562,466	29,714,689	28,946,607	27,115,445	26,397,018	25,841,796
Total Liabilities	25,722,550	25,519,161	26,381,159	24,881,210	23,761,241	22,088,509	21,616,481	20,988,547
Stockholders' Equity	4,564,645	4,523,967	5,181,307	4,833,479	5,185,366	5,026,936	4,780,537	4,853,249
Shares Outstanding	62,643	65,850	69,299	71,828	78,664	88,524	102,000	116,648
Statistical Record								
Return on Assets %	1.02	0.46	1.54	1.67	1.72	2.04	1.07	1.71
Return on Equity %	6.43	2.92	9.40	9.76	9.45	11.13	5.80	10.06
Net Margin %	10.26	1.37	4.54	5.40	5.69	6.60	3.27	4.95
Asset Turnover	0.32	0.34	0.34	0.31	0.30	0.31	0.33	0.35
Price Range	86.81-59.86	86.81-59.86	69.52-60.81	66.37-34.70	43.35-32.57	41.71-31.23	41.68-29.48	33.04-16.95
P/E Ratio	18.59-12.82	42.35-29.20	10.80-9.44	10.53-5.51	7.65-5.74	7.47-5.60	16.67-11.79	9.10-4.67
Average Yield %	2.15	1.92	1.60	1.88	2.18	1.88	1.76	2.20

Address: 28 Liberty Street, 41st Floor, New York, NY 10005 **Telephone:** 212-859-7000	**Web Site:** www.assurant.com **Officers:** Alan B. Colberg - President, Chief Executive Officer, Executive Vice President Christopher J. Pagano - Executive Vice President, Chief Risk Officer, Chief Financial Officer, Chief Investment Officer, Treasurer, Division Officer	**Auditors:** PricewaterhouseCoopers LLP **Investor Contact:** 212-859-7197 **Transfer Agents:** Computershare, Providence, RI

ASSURED GUARANTY LTD

Exchange	Symbol	Price	52Wk Range	Yield	P/E
NYS	AGO	$26.89 (5/31/2016)	29.52-22.04	1.93	4.32

*7 Year Price Score 110.27 *NYSE Composite Index=100 *12 Month Price Score 98.82

TRADING VOLUME (thousand shares)

Interim Earnings (Per Share)

Qtr.	Mar	Jun	Sep	Dec
2013	(0.74)	1.16	2.09	1.87
2014	0.23	0.89	2.09	3.13
2015	1.28	1.96	0.88	2.95
2016	0.43	...	...	...

Interim Dividends (Per Share)

Amt	Decl	Ex	Rec	Pay
0.12Q	08/05/2015	08/17/2015	08/19/2015	09/02/2015
0.12Q	11/04/2015	11/16/2015	11/18/2015	12/02/2015
0.13Q	02/24/2016	03/07/2016	03/09/2016	03/23/2016
0.13Q	05/04/2016	05/16/2016	05/18/2016	06/01/2016

Indicated Div: $0.52

Valuation Analysis

		Institutional Holding	
Forecast EPS	$2.80	No of Institutions	
	(05/20/2016)	361	
Market Cap	$3.6 Billion	Shares	
Book Value	$6.1 Billion	150,219,056	
Price/Book	0.59	% Held	
Price/Sales	1.74	83.38	

Business Summary: General Insurance (MIC: 5.2.1 SIC: 6351 NAIC: 524298)

Assured Guaranty is a Bermuda based holding company that provides, through its subsidiaries, credit protection products to the U.S. and international public finance (including infrastructure) and structured finance markets. Co. markets its financial guaranty insurance directly to issuers and underwriters of public finance and structured finance securities as well as to investors in such obligations. Co. guarantees obligations issued principally in the U.S. and the U.K., including Australia and Western Europe. Co.'s financial guaranty direct and assumed businesses provide credit enhancement, on public finance, infrastructure and structured finance obligations.

Recent Developments: For the quarter ended Mar 31 2016, net income decreased 70.6% to US$59.0 million from US$201.0 million in the year-earlier quarter. Revenues were US$245.0 million, down 33.6% from US$369.0 million the year before. Net premiums earned were US$183.0 million versus US$142.0 million in the prior-year quarter, an increase of 28.9%. Net investment income fell 2.0% to US$99.0 million from US$101.0 million a year ago.

Prospects: Our evaluation of Assured Guaranty Ltd. as of June 19, 2016 is the result of our systematic analysis on three basic characteristics: earnings strength, relative valuation, and recent stock price movement. The company has managed to produce a neutral trend in earnings per share over the past 5 quarters and while recent estimates for the company have remained steady, AGO has posted better than expected results. Based on operating earnings yield, the company is undervalued when compared to all of the companies in our coverage universe. Share price changes over the past year indicates that AGO will perform in line with the market over the near term.

Financial Data
(US$ in Thousands)

	3 Mos	12/31/2015	12/31/2014	12/31/2013	12/31/2012	12/31/2011	12/31/2010	12/31/2009
Earnings Per Share	6.22	7.08	6.26	4.30	0.57	4.18	2.90	0.75
Cash Flow Per Share	(1.21)	(0.35)	3.34	1.31	(0.87)	3.68	0.57	2.21
Tang Book Value Per Share	45.25	43.96	36.37	28.08	25.74	25.89	20.67	19.12
Dividends Per Share	0.490	0.480	0.440	0.400	0.360	0.180	0.180	0.180
Dividend Payout %	7.88	6.78	7.03	9.30	63.16	4.31	6.21	24.00
Income Statement								
Total Revenue	245,000	2,207,000	1,994,000	1,608,000	973,000	1,819,313	1,401,301	929,587
Income Before Taxes	65,000	1,431,000	1,531,000	1,142,000	132,000	1,034,462	635,522	142,668
Income Taxes	6,000	375,000	443,000	334,000	22,000	258,842	86,609	36,862
Net Income	59,000	1,056,000	1,088,000	808,000	110,000	775,620	548,913	97,186
Average Shares	137,000	149,000	173,600	187,600	190,700	185,500	188,900	129,128
Balance Sheet								
Total Assets	14,452,000	14,544,000	14,925,000	16,287,000	17,242,000	18,091,531	20,471,512	16,593,436
Total Liabilities	8,339,000	8,481,000	9,167,000	11,172,000	12,248,000	13,373,095	16,672,748	13,072,928
Stockholders' Equity	6,113,000	6,063,000	5,758,000	5,115,000	4,994,000	4,718,436	3,798,764	3,520,508
Shares Outstanding	135,083	137,928	158,306	182,177	194,003	182,235	183,744	184,162
Statistical Record								
Return on Assets %	6.28	7.17	6.97	4.82	0.62	4.02	2.96	0.92
Return on Equity %	15.36	17.87	20.01	15.99	2.26	18.21	15.00	3.57
Net Margin %	24.08	47.85	54.56	50.25	11.31	42.63	39.17	10.45
Asset Turnover	0.14	0.15	0.13	0.10	0.05	0.09	0.08	0.09
Price Range	29.52-22.04	29.52-23.62	26.65-20.73	24.65-14.23	18.98-11.26	19.75-9.19	24.62-13.13	25.91-2.95
P/E Ratio	4.75-3.54	4.17-3.34	4.26-3.31	5.73-3.31	33.30-19.75	4.72-2.20	8.49-4.53	34.55-3.93
Average Yield %	1.88	1.82	1.84	1.93	2.53	1.27	0.96	1.28

Address: 30 Woodbourne Avenue, Hamilton, HM 08 Telephone: 441-279-5700	Web Site: www.assuredguaranty.com Officers: Robin Monro-Davies - Chairman Dominic J. Frederico - President, Chief Executive Officer	Auditors: PricewaterhouseCoopers LLP Investor Contact: 441-279-5700 Transfer Agents: Mellon Investor Services LLC

AT&T INC

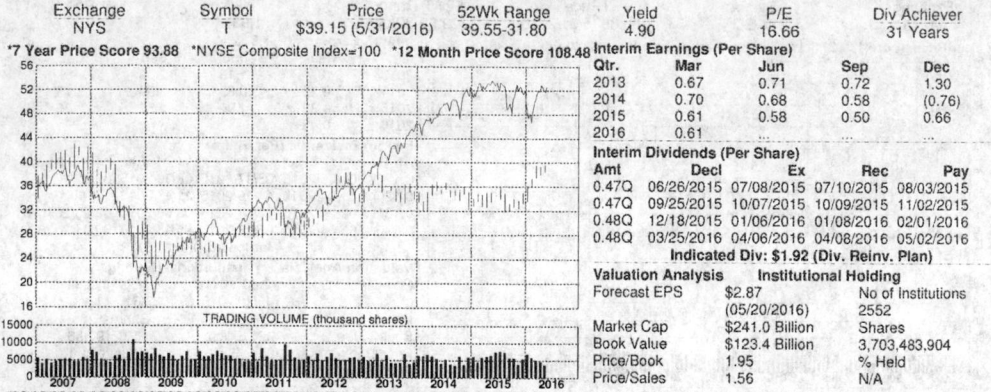

Exchange	Symbol	Price	52Wk Range	Yield	P/E	Div Achiever
NYS	T	$39.15 (5/31/2016)	39.55-31.80	4.90	16.66	31 Years

*7 Year Price Score 93.88   *NYSE Composite Index=100   *12 Month Price Score 108.48

Interim Earnings (Per Share)

Qtr.	Mar	Jun	Sep	Dec
2013	0.67	0.71	0.72	1.30
2014	0.70	0.68	0.58	(0.76)
2015	0.61	0.58	0.50	0.66
2016	0.61	...	...	...

Interim Dividends (Per Share)

Amt	Decl	Ex	Rec	Pay
0.47Q	06/26/2015	07/08/2015	07/10/2015	08/03/2015
0.47Q	09/25/2015	10/07/2015	10/09/2015	11/02/2015
0.48Q	12/18/2015	01/06/2016	01/08/2016	02/01/2016
0.48Q	03/25/2016	04/06/2016	04/08/2016	05/02/2016

Indicated Div: $1.92 (Div. Reinv. Plan)

Valuation Analysis

Forecast EPS	$2.87	Institutional Holding	
	(05/20/2016)	No of Institutions	2552
Market Cap	$241.0 Billion	Shares	3,703,483,904
Book Value	$123.4 Billion	% Held	N/A
Price/Book	1.95		
Price/Sales	1.56		

TRADING VOLUME (thousand shares)

Business Summary: Services (MIC: 6.1.2 SIC: 4813 NAIC: 517110)

AT&T is a holding company. Co. is a provider of communications and digital entertainment services in the U.S. and the world. Co. provides its services and products to consumers in the U.S., Mexico and Latin America and to businesses and other providers of telecommunications services worldwide. The services and products that Co. provides vary by market, and include: wireless communications, data/broadband and Internet services, digital video services, local and long-distance telephone services, telecommunications equipment, managed networking, and wholesale services. Co. has four reportable segments: Business Solutions, Entertainment Group, Consumer Mobility and International.

Recent Developments: For the quarter ended Mar 31 2016, net income increased 16.4% to US$3.89 billion from US$3.34 billion in the year-earlier quarter. Revenues were US$40.54 billion, up 24.4% from US$32.58 billion the year before. Operating income was US$7.13 billion versus US$5.56 billion in the prior-year quarter, an increase of 28.3%. Direct operating expenses rose 27.1% to US$18.40 billion from US$14.48 billion in the comparable period the year before. Indirect operating expenses increased 19.7% to US$15.00 billion from US$12.54 billion in the equivalent prior-year period.

Prospects: Our evaluation of AT&T Inc. as of June 19, 2016 is the result of our systematic analysis on three basic characteristics: earnings strength, relative valuation, and recent stock price movement. The company has managed to produce a neutral trend in earnings per share over the past 5 quarters. However, while recent estimates for the company have been mixed, T has posted better than expected results. Based on operating earnings yield, the company is undervalued when compared to all of the companies in our coverage universe. Share price changes over the past year indicates that T will perform well over the near term.

Financial Data
(US$ in Thousands)

	3 Mos	12/31/2015	12/31/2014	12/31/2013	12/31/2012	12/31/2011	12/31/2010	12/31/2009
Earnings Per Share	2.35	2.37	1.19	3.39	1.25	0.66	3.35	2.12
Cash Flow Per Share	6.00	6.38	6.02	6.48	6.73	5.84	5.92	5.84
Dividends Per Share	1.890	1.880	1.840	1.800	1.760	1.720	1.680	1.640
Dividend Payout %	80.43	79.32	154.62	53.10	140.80	260.61	50.15	77.36
Income Statement								
Total Revenue	40,535,000	146,801,000	132,447,000	128,752,000	127,434,000	126,723,000	124,280,000	123,018,000
EBITDA	13,764,000	44,022,000	31,171,000	48,797,000	30,064,000	25,835,000	36,872,000	37,603,000
Depn & Amortn	6,563,000	19,289,000	17,773,000	17,722,000	16,933,000	16,368,000	16,402,000	15,959,000
Income Before Taxes	5,994,000	20,613,000	9,785,000	27,135,000	9,687,000	5,932,000	17,476,000	18,265,000
Income Taxes	2,122,000	7,005,000	3,442,000	9,224,000	2,900,000	2,532,000	(1,162,000)	6,156,000
Net Income	3,803,000	13,345,000	6,224,000	18,249,000	7,264,000	3,944,000	19,864,000	12,535,000
Average Shares	6,189,999	5,645,999	5,220,999	5,384,999	5,820,999	5,949,999	5,937,999	5,923,999
Balance Sheet								
Current Assets	38,001,000	35,992,000	32,028,000	23,196,000	22,706,000	23,027,000	19,951,000	24,334,000
Total Assets	403,638,000	402,672,000	292,829,000	277,787,000	272,315,000	270,344,000	268,488,000	268,752,000
Current Liabilities	44,528,000	47,816,000	37,282,000	34,995,000	31,787,000	30,794,000	33,951,000	36,705,000
Long-Term Obligations	122,104,000	118,515,000	76,011,000	69,290,000	66,358,000	61,300,000	58,971,000	64,720,000
Total Liabilities	280,206,000	280,001,000	206,459,000	186,799,000	179,953,000	164,810,000	156,841,000	166,852,000
Stockholders' Equity	123,432,000	122,671,000	86,370,000	90,988,000	92,362,000	105,534,000	111,647,000	101,900,000
Shares Outstanding	6,156,223	6,144,939	5,186,912	5,226,315	5,581,394	5,926,511	5,911,086	5,901,930
Statistical Record								
Return on Assets %	3.89	3.84	2.18	6.63	2.67	1.46	7.39	4.69
Return on Equity %	13.19	12.77	7.02	19.91	7.32	3.63	18.60	12.65
EBITDA Margin %	33.96	29.99	23.53	37.90	23.59	20.39	29.67	30.57
Net Margin %	9.38	9.09	4.70	14.17	5.70	3.11	15.98	10.19
Asset Turnover	0.43	0.42	0.46	0.47	0.47	0.47	0.46	0.46
Current Ratio	0.85	0.75	0.86	0.66	0.71	0.75	0.59	0.66
Debt to Equity	0.99	0.97	0.88	0.76	0.72	0.58	0.53	0.64
Price Range	39.45-31.80	36.18-31.80	36.74-31.86	39.00-33.11	38.34-29.16	31.86-27.33	29.44-24.13	29.42-21.72
P/E Ratio	16.79-13.53	15.27-13.42	30.87-26.77	11.50-9.77	30.67-23.33	48.27-41.41	8.79-7.20	13.88-10.25
Average Yield %	5.47	5.56	5.32	5.08	5.20	5.86	6.30	6.40

Address: 208 S. Akard St., Dallas, TX 75202 **Telephone:** 210-821-4105	**Web Site:** www.att.com **Officers:** Randall L. Stephenson - Chairman, President, Chief Executive Officer, Senior Executive Vice President, Chief Financial Officer, Chief Operating Officer William A. Blase - Senior Executive Vice President	**Auditors:** Ernst & Young LLP **Investor Contact:** 210-351-2058 **Transfer Agents:** Computershare Trust Company, N.A, Providence, RI

70

ATMOS ENERGY CORP.

Exchange NYS	Symbol ATO	Price $72.90 (5/31/2016)	52Wk Range 74.99-51.28	Yield 2.30	P/E 23.07	Div Achiever 28 Years

*7 Year Price Score 129.88 *NYSE Composite Index=100 *12 Month Price Score 114.44

TRADING VOLUME (thousand shares)

Interim Earnings (Per Share)

Qtr.	Dec	Mar	Jun	Sep
2012-13	0.88	1.27	0.42	0.07
2013-14	0.95	1.38	0.45	0.18
2014-15	0.96	1.35	0.55	0.23
2015-16	1.00	1.38	...	...

Interim Dividends (Per Share)

Amt	Decl	Ex	Rec	Pay
0.39Q	08/05/2015	08/20/2015	08/24/2015	09/08/2015
0.42Q	11/04/2015	11/19/2015	11/23/2015	12/07/2015
0.42Q	02/02/2016	02/18/2016	02/22/2016	03/07/2016
0.42Q	05/04/2016	05/19/2016	05/23/2016	06/06/2016

Indicated Div: $1.68 (Div. Reinv. Plan)

Valuation Analysis

		Institutional Holding	
Forecast EPS	$3.29	No of Institutions	503
	(05/20/2016)		
Market Cap	$7.5 Billion	Shares	83,546,392
Book Value	$3.3 Billion	% Held	74.56
Price/Book	2.23		
Price/Sales	2.20		

Business Summary: Gas Utilities (MIC: 3.3.1 SIC: 4924 NAIC: 221210)

Atmos Energy is engaged primarily in the regulated natural gas distribution and pipeline businesses as well as other nonregulated natural gas businesses. Co. operates in three segments: regulated distribution, which includes its regulated distribution and related sales operations; regulated pipeline, which includes the regulated pipeline and storage operations of its Atmos Pipeline - Texas Division; and nonregulated, which includes its nonregulated natural gas management, nonregulated natural gas transmission, storage and other services. As of Sep 30 2015, Co. delivered natural gas to over 3.0 million residential, commercial, public authority and industrial customers in eight states.

Recent Developments: For the quarter ended Mar 31 2016, net income increased 3.0% to US$141.8 million from US$137.7 million in the year-earlier quarter. Revenues were US$1.13 billion, down 26.5% from US$1.54 billion the year before. Operating income was US$250.0 million versus US$250.2 million in the prior-year quarter, a decrease of 0.1%. Direct operating expenses declined 39.7% to US$614.5 million from US$1.02 billion in the comparable period the year before. Indirect operating expenses decreased 1.0% to US$267.8 million from US$270.5 million in the equivalent prior-year period.

Prospects: Our evaluation of Atmos Energy Corp. as of June 19, 2016 is the result of our systematic analysis on three basic characteristics: earnings strength, relative valuation, and recent stock price movement. The company has produced a positive trend in earnings per share over the past 5 quarters and while recent estimates for the company have remained steady, ATO has posted results that were in line with analysts expectations. Based on operating earnings yield, the company is about fairly valued when compared to all of the companies in our coverage universe. Share price changes over the past year indicates that ATO will perform very well over the near term.

Financial Data

(US$ in Thousands)	6 Mos	3 Mos	09/30/2015	09/30/2014	09/30/2013	09/30/2012	09/30/2011	09/30/2010
Earnings Per Share	3.16	3.13	3.09	2.96	2.64	2.37	2.27	2.20
Cash Flow Per Share	7.30	8.56	8.21	7.58	6.77	6.49	6.46	7.91
Tang Book Value Per Share	25.46	24.78	24.16	23.35	20.29	17.93	16.78	15.95
Dividends Per Share	1.620	1.590	1.560	1.480	1.400	1.380	1.360	1.340
Dividend Payout %	51.27	50.80	50.49	50.00	53.03	58.23	59.91	60.91
Income Statement								
Total Revenue	2,038,514	906,221	4,142,136	4,940,916	3,886,257	3,438,483	4,347,634	4,789,690
EBITDA	588,183	266,561	903,017	861,070	739,289	678,173	696,781	706,230
Depn & Amortn	143,856	71,565	276,005	254,956	237,607	246,577	233,383	217,133
Income Before Taxes	386,284	164,513	510,771	476,819	373,297	290,422	312,573	334,626
Income Taxes	141,613	61,652	195,696	187,002	142,599	98,226	113,689	128,787
Net Income	244,671	102,861	315,075	289,817	243,194	216,717	207,601	205,839
Average Shares	102,946	102,713	101,892	97,608	91,711	91,172	90,652	92,422
Balance Sheet								
Current Assets	652,912	863,270	630,985	775,840	683,266	827,962	1,010,953	875,192
Total Assets	9,543,926	9,554,653	9,092,945	8,594,704	7,940,401	7,495,675	7,282,871	6,763,791
Current Liabilities	1,227,353	1,515,056	1,154,823	910,650	978,486	1,275,954	867,598	1,166,079
Long-Term Obligations	2,455,559	2,455,474	2,455,388	2,455,986	2,455,671	1,956,305	2,206,117	1,809,551
Total Liabilities	6,199,361	6,282,544	5,898,148	5,508,472	5,359,992	5,136,432	5,027,450	4,585,443
Stockholders' Equity	3,344,565	3,272,109	3,194,797	3,086,232	2,580,409	2,359,243	2,255,421	2,178,348
Shares Outstanding	102,209	102,079	101,478	100,388	90,640	90,239	90,296	90,164
Statistical Record								
Return on Assets %	3.51	3.43	3.56	3.51	3.15	2.92	2.96	3.14
Return on Equity %	10.01	10.11	10.03	10.23	9.85	9.37	9.36	9.45
EBITDA Margin %	28.85	29.41	21.80	17.43	19.02	19.72	16.03	14.74
Net Margin %	12.00	11.35	7.61	5.87	6.26	6.30	4.78	4.30
Asset Turnover	0.37	0.41	0.47	0.60	0.50	0.46	0.62	0.73
Current Ratio	0.53	0.57	0.55	0.85	0.70	0.65	1.17	0.75
Debt to Equity	0.73	0.75	0.77	0.80	0.95	0.83	0.98	0.83
Price Range	74.33-51.28	64.25-51.28	58.81-47.35	53.40-41.08	45.19-33.20	36.94-30.60	34.98-28.87	30.06-26.41
P/E Ratio	23.52-16.23	20.53-16.38	19.03-15.32	18.04-13.88	17.12-12.58	15.59-12.91	15.41-12.72	13.66-12.00
Average Yield %	2.72	2.83	2.89	3.11	3.52	4.11	4.20	4.70

Address: Three Lincoln Centre, Suite 1800, 5430 LBJ Freeway, Dallas, TX 75240 Telephone: 972-934-9227 Fax: 972-855-3075	Web Site: www.atmosenergy.com Officers: Robert W. Best - Chairman, Executive Chairman, Chief Executive Officer Michael E. Haefner - President, Chief Operating Officer, Executive Vice President, Senior Vice President	Auditors: Ernest & Young LLP Investor Contact: 972-855-3729 Transfer Agents: American Stock Transfer & Trust Company, New York, NY

ATWOOD OCEANICS, INC.

Exchange	Symbol	Price	52Wk Range	Yield	P/E
NYS	ATW	$10.67 (5/31/2016)	31.30-5.32	N/A	1.63

*7 Year Price Score 33.26 *NYSE Composite Index=100 *12 Month Price Score 64.43

TRADING VOLUME (thousand shares)

Interim Earnings (Per Share)

Qtr.	Dec	Mar	Jun	Sep
2012-13	1.10	1.28	1.37	1.57
2013-14	1.28	1.13	1.11	1.72
2014-15	0.71	1.89	1.73	2.32
2015-16	0.60	1.89	...	...

Interim Dividends (Per Share)

Dividend Payment Suspended

Valuation Analysis

		Institutional Holding	
Forecast EPS	$4.52	No of Institutions	
	(05/20/2016)	376	
Market Cap	$691.4 Million	Shares	
Book Value	$3.1 Billion	78,507,528	
Price/Book	0.22	% Held	
Price/Sales	0.53	98.92	

Business Summary: Equipment & Services (MIC: 9.1.3 SIC: 1381 NAIC: 213111)

Atwood Oceanics is a global offshore drilling contractor engaged in the drilling and completion of exploratory and developmental oil and gas wells. As of Sep 30 2015, Co. owned a fleet of 11 mobile offshore drilling units, which consisted of ultra-deepwater drillships, semisubmersible rigs, and jackup drilling rigs, located in the U.S. Gulf of Mexico, the Mediterranean Sea, offshore West Africa, offshore Southeast Asia and offshore Australia. In addition, Co. is constructing two ultra-deepwater drillships. Co.'s customers consist primarily of integrated oil and natural gas companies and independent oil and natural gas companies.

Recent Developments: For the quarter ended Mar 31 2016, net income decreased 0.2% to US$122.4 million from US$122.7 million in the year-earlier quarter. Revenues were US$296.4 million, down 15.4% from US$350.4 million the year before. Operating income was US$145.1 million versus US$147.8 million in the prior-year quarter, a decrease of 1.8%. Direct operating expenses declined 31.4% to US$89.9 million from US$131.1 million in the comparable period the year before. Indirect operating expenses decreased 14.2% to US$61.3 million from US$71.5 million in the equivalent prior-year period.

Prospects: Our evaluation of Atwood Oceanics Inc. as of June 19, 2016 is the result of our systematic analysis on three basic characteristics: earnings strength, relative valuation, and recent stock price movement. The company has suffered a very negative trend in earnings per share over the past 5 quarters. Because the company lacks sufficient analyst estimate data, we place greater weight on the historical EPS trend as the measure of earnings strength. Based on operating earnings yield, the company is undervalued when compared to all of the companies in our coverage universe. Share price changes over the past year indicates that ATW will perform very poorly over the near term.

Financial Data

(US$ in Thousands)	6 Mos	3 Mos	09/30/2015	09/30/2014	09/30/2013	09/30/2012	09/30/2011	09/30/2010
Earnings Per Share	6.54	6.54	6.65	5.24	5.32	4.14	4.15	3.95
Cash Flow Per Share	9.80	9.72	9.36	6.89	6.64	3.91	5.25	4.76
Tang Book Value Per Share	47.92	46.07	45.58	39.71	34.46	29.63	25.44	21.26
Dividends Per Share	0.575	1.000	1.000	...	...	...	...	...
Dividend Payout %	8.79	15.29	15.04	...	...	...	...	...
Income Statement								
Total Revenue	604,170	307,819	1,395,851	1,173,953	1,063,663	787,421	645,076	650,562
EBITDA	303,057	108,129	703,377	586,142	546,981	390,009	372,257	359,370
Depn & Amortn	85,487	44,077	171,947	147,358	117,510	70,599	43,597	37,030
Income Before Taxes	186,721	50,295	478,970	397,293	404,801	313,304	324,847	319,979
Income Taxes	25,203	11,214	46,397	56,471	54,577	41,133	53,173	62,983
Net Income	161,518	39,081	432,573	340,822	350,224	272,171	271,674	256,996
Average Shares	64,825	64,921	65,030	65,074	65,845	65,781	65,403	65,028
Balance Sheet								
Current Assets	604,569	517,241	607,675	497,807	453,760	370,534	460,931	359,994
Total Assets	4,834,992	4,748,446	4,809,011	4,507,228	3,657,266	2,943,762	2,375,391	1,724,440
Current Liabilities	95,668	116,289	135,448	167,377	156,872	136,667	159,323	93,460
Long-Term Obligations	1,595,018	1,608,399	1,685,946	1,742,122	1,263,232	830,000	520,000	230,000
Total Liabilities	1,729,885	1,764,907	1,861,841	1,951,704	1,449,895	1,004,340	722,604	354,306
Stockholders' Equity	3,105,107	2,983,539	2,947,170	2,555,524	2,207,371	1,939,422	1,652,787	1,370,134
Shares Outstanding	64,794	64,768	64,654	64,362	64,057	65,452	64,960	64,443
Statistical Record								
Return on Assets %	9.07	9.15	9.29	8.35	10.61	10.21	13.25	15.89
Return on Equity %	14.60	15.22	15.72	14.31	16.89	15.11	17.97	20.79
EBITDA Margin %	50.16	35.13	50.39	49.93	51.42	49.53	57.71	55.24
Net Margin %	26.73	12.70	30.99	29.03	32.93	34.56	42.12	39.50
Asset Turnover	0.28	0.29	0.30	0.29	0.32	0.30	0.31	0.40
Current Ratio	6.32	4.45	4.49	2.97	2.89	2.71	2.89	3.85
Debt to Equity	0.51	0.54	0.57	0.68	0.57	0.43	0.31	0.17
Price Range	35.35-5.32	35.35-10.12	43.69-14.56	58.04-42.98	59.13-43.75	49.34-31.98	48.33-29.73	40.09-24.21
P/E Ratio	5.41-0.81	5.41-1.55	6.57-2.19	11.08-8.20	11.11-8.22	11.92-7.72	11.65-7.16	10.15-6.13
Average Yield %	3.13	4.21	3.46	...	...	...	...	...

Address: 15011 Katy Freeway, Suite 800, Houston, TX 77094
Telephone: 281-749-7800
Fax: 281-492-7871

Web Site: www.atwd.com
Officers: George S. Dotson - Chairman Robert J. Saltiel - President, Chief Executive Officer

Auditors: PricewaterhouseCoopers LLP
Investor Contact: 281-749-7902
Transfer Agents: Continental Stock Transfer & Trust Company, New York, NY

AUTOLIV INC.

Exchange	Symbol	Price	52Wk Range	Yield	P/E
NYS	ALV	$122.61 (5/31/2016)	128.95-96.57	1.89	19.52

*7 Year Price Score 125.55 *NYSE Composite Index=100 *12 Month Price Score 103.28

Interim Earnings (Per Share)

Qtr.	Mar	Jun	Sep	Dec
2013	1.29	1.44	1.29	1.05
2014	1.38	0.89	1.16	1.63
2015	0.40	1.55	1.12	2.10
2016	1.51	...	...	...

Interim Dividends (Per Share)

Amt	Decl	Ex	Rec	Pay
0.56Q	08/03/2015	11/16/2015	11/18/2015	12/03/2015
0.56Q	12/18/2015	02/16/2016	02/18/2016	03/03/2016
0.58Q	02/16/2016	05/16/2016	05/18/2016	06/02/2016
0.58Q	05/10/2016	08/16/2016	08/18/2016	09/01/2016

Indicated Div: $2.32

Valuation Analysis

	Institutional Holding	
Forecast EPS	$7.07	No of Institutions
	(05/20/2016)	369
Market Cap	$10.8 Billion	Shares
Book Value	$3.6 Billion	38,416,148
Price/Book	3.00	% Held
Price/Sales	1.15	34.18

Business Summary: Auto Parts (MIC: 1.8.2 SIC: 3714 NAIC: 336399)

Autoliv is a holding company. Through its subsidiaries, Autoliv AB and Autoliv ASP, Inc., Co. is a developer, manufacturer and supplier to the automotive industry of automotive safety systems with a range of products, including modules and components for passenger and driver-side airbags, side-impact airbag protection systems, seatbelts, steering wheels, safety electronics, whiplash protection systems and child seats, including components for such systems, and vision and night vision systems, radar and other safety systems. Co.'s geographical regions are in Europe, the Americas, China, Japan and the Rest of Asia. Co. has two segments; passive safety products and active safety products.

Recent Developments: For the quarter ended Mar 31 2016, net income increased 273.9% to US$133.5 million from US$35.7 million in the year-earlier quarter. Revenues were US$2.43 billion, up 11.8% from US$2.17 billion the year before. Operating income was US$205.2 million versus US$80.0 million in the prior-year quarter, an increase of 156.5%. Direct operating expenses rose 10.2% to US$1.93 billion from US$1.75 billion in the comparable period the year before. Indirect operating expenses decreased 13.8% to US$295.8 million from US$343.3 million in the equivalent prior-year period.

Prospects: Our evaluation of Autoliv Inc. as of June 19, 2016 is the result of our systematic analysis on three basic characteristics: earnings strength, relative valuation, and recent stock price movement. The company has generated a negative trend in earnings per share over the past 5 quarters. However, while recent estimates for the company have been mixed, ALV has posted better than expected results. Based on operating earnings yield, the company is undervalued when compared to all of the companies in our coverage universe. Share price changes over the past year indicates that ALV will perform well over the near term.

Financial Data

(US$ in Thousands)	3 Mos	12/31/2015	12/31/2014	12/31/2013	12/31/2012	12/31/2011	12/31/2010	12/31/2009
Earnings Per Share	6.28	5.17	5.06	5.07	5.08	6.65	6.39	0.12
Cash Flow Per Share	9.84	8.51	7.74	8.77	7.34	8.50	10.59	6.04
Tang Book Value Per Share	17.06	18.86	19.90	24.30	21.48	18.11	13.55	7.75
Dividends Per Share	2.240	2.220	2.120	2.000	1.890	1.730	0.650	0.210
Dividend Payout %	35.67	42.94	41.90	39.45	37.20	26.02	10.17	175.00
Income Statement								
Total Revenue	2,430,000	9,169,600	9,240,500	8,803,400	8,266,700	8,232,400	7,170,600	5,120,700
EBITDA	211,900	1,052,400	1,024,100	1,041,700	972,000	1,146,900	1,132,600	378,300
Depn & Amortn	7,900	319,000	305,400	286,000	273,200	268,300	281,700	314,300
Income Before Taxes	189,700	671,000	660,100	726,700	660,500	821,500	800,000	1,700
Income Taxes	56,800	218,200	198,000	244,100	183,000	201,300	210,000	(7,100)
Net Income	133,200	456,800	467,800	485,800	483,100	623,400	590,600	10,000
Average Shares	88,300	88,400	92,400	95,900	95,100	93,700	92,400	84,500
Balance Sheet								
Current Assets	4,060,100	4,038,300	4,136,200	3,700,400	3,289,200	3,000,300	2,688,600	2,179,600
Total Assets	8,144,300	7,525,500	7,442,900	6,983,000	6,570,300	6,117,300	5,664,500	5,185,600
Current Liabilities	2,416,500	2,226,400	2,138,600	2,428,500	1,849,800	2,085,900	1,834,500	1,693,500
Long-Term Obligations	1,499,400	1,499,400	1,521,200	279,100	562,900	363,500	637,700	820,700
Total Liabilities	4,544,100	4,069,900	4,015,800	3,001,700	2,811,700	2,783,900	2,737,200	2,797,400
Stockholders' Equity	3,600,200	3,455,600	3,427,100	3,981,300	3,758,600	3,333,400	2,927,300	2,388,200
Shares Outstanding	88,200	88,107	88,726	94,396	95,500	89,293	88,963	85,100
Statistical Record								
Return on Assets %	7.17	6.10	6.49	7.17	7.59	10.58	10.89	0.19
Return on Equity %	16.28	13.27	12.63	12.55	13.59	19.91	22.22	0.44
EBITDA Margin %	8.72	11.48	11.08	11.83	11.76	13.93	15.80	7.39
Net Margin %	5.48	4.98	5.06	5.52	5.84	7.57	8.24	0.20
Asset Turnover	1.22	1.23	1.28	1.30	1.30	1.40	1.32	0.99
Current Ratio	1.68	1.81	1.93	1.52	1.78	1.44	1.47	1.29
Debt to Equity	0.42	0.43	0.44	0.07	0.15	0.11	0.22	0.34
Price Range	130.81-96.57	130.81-96.57	108.03-86.27	94.41-64.13	69.05-51.89	83.53-46.14	81.49-40.91	44.35-12.33
P/E Ratio	20.83-15.38	25.30-18.68	21.35-17.05	18.62-12.65	13.59-10.21	12.56-6.94	12.75-6.40	369.58-102.75
Average Yield %	1.95	1.94	2.14	2.53	3.10	2.63	1.14	0.73

Address: Vasagatan 11, 7th Floor, SE-111 20, Box 70381, Stockholm, SE-107 24	**Web Site:** www.autoliv.com	**Auditors:** Ernst & Young AB
Telephone: 858-720-600	**Officers:** Jan Carlson - Interim Chairman, President, Chief Executive Officer Mats Backman - Chief Financial Officer, Division Officer	**Investor Contact:** 248-223-8107 **Transfer Agents:** Computershare Trust Company, N.A., Providence, RI

AUTONATION, INC.

Exchange	Symbol	Price	52Wk Range	Yield	P/E
NYS	AN	$50.44 (5/31/2016)	66.20-41.53	N/A	13.24

*7 Year Price Score 116.51 *NYSE Composite Index=100   *12 Month Price Score 84.51

TRADING VOLUME (thousand shares)

Interim Earnings (Per Share)

Qtr.	Mar	Jun	Sep	Dec
2013	0.67	0.73	0.75	0.89
2014	0.78	0.83	0.90	1.01
2015	0.97	1.00	1.04	0.88
2016	0.89			

Interim Dividends (Per Share)

No Dividends Paid

Valuation Analysis   Institutional Holding

Forecast EPS	$4.20	No of Institutions
	(05/20/2016)	525
Market Cap	$5.2 Billion	Shares
Book Value	$2.1 Billion	88,980,048
Price/Book	2.49	% Held
Price/Sales	0.25	58.63

Business Summary: Retail - Automotive (MIC: 2.1.4 SIC: 5511 NAIC: 441110)

AutoNation, through its subsidiaries, is an automotive retailer. Co. provides a range of automotive products and services, including new vehicles, used vehicles, parts and service, which includes automotive repair and maintenance services as well as wholesale parts and collision businesses, and automotive finance and insurance products, which include vehicle service and other protection products, as well as the arranging of financing for vehicle purchases through third-party finance sources. At Dec 31 2015, Co. owned and operated 342 new vehicle franchises from 254 stores located in the U.S. At Dec 31 2015, Co. had three operating segments: Domestic, Import, and Premium Luxury.

Recent Developments: For the quarter ended Mar 31 2016, income from continuing operations decreased 13.9% to US$96.2 million from US$111.7 million in the year-earlier quarter. Net income decreased 14.0% to US$95.9 million from US$111.5 million in the year-earlier quarter. Revenues were US$5.12 billion, up 3.5% from US$4.94 billion the year before. Operating income was US$207.4 million versus US$214.9 million in the prior-year quarter, a decrease of 3.5%. Direct operating expenses rose 3.6% to US$4.29 billion from US$4.14 billion in the comparable period the year before. Indirect operating expenses increased 5.7% to US$618.5 million from US$585.0 million in the equivalent prior-year period.

Prospects: Our evaluation of AutoNation Inc. as of June 19, 2016 is the result of our systematic analysis on three basic characteristics: earnings strength, relative valuation, and recent stock price movement. The company has generated a negative trend in earnings per share over the past 5 quarters. However, while recent estimates for the company have been lowered by analysts, AN has posted results that fell short of analysts expectations. Based on operating earnings yield, the company is undervalued when compared to all of the companies in our coverage universe. Share price changes over the past year indicates that AN will perform poorly over the near term.

Financial Data

(US$ in Thousands)	3 Mos	12/31/2015	12/31/2014	12/31/2013	12/31/2012	12/31/2011	12/31/2010	12/31/2009
Earnings Per Share	3.81	3.89	3.52	3.04	2.52	1.91	1.43	1.12
Cash Flow Per Share	4.74	4.50	4.14	3.99	2.55	2.60	1.60	2.09
Tang Book Value Per Share	0.96	4.65	3.55	3.86	1.32	3.72	4.95	5.84
Income Statement								
Total Revenue	5,119,600	20,862,000	19,108,800	17,517,600	15,668,800	13,832,300	12,461,000	10,757,800
EBITDA	205,300	1,003,900	934,700	846,900	741,800	657,300	558,800	509,300
Depn & Amortn	1,300	132,100	112,600	101,000	92,900	88,000	80,300	80,700
Income Before Taxes	156,900	722,700	682,300	604,400	516,800	461,300	381,300	351,000
Income Taxes	60,700	279,000	262,500	228,600	199,500	177,100	146,000	116,800
Net Income	95,900	442,600	418,700	374,900	316,400	281,400	226,600	198,000
Average Shares	107,400	113,900	118,900	123,300	125,800	147,300	158,600	177,300
Balance Sheet								
Current Assets	4,872,700	4,711,400	3,999,200	3,830,000	3,361,100	2,676,200	2,629,100	2,250,600
Total Assets	9,997,600	9,558,300	8,399,700	7,914,100	7,203,000	6,198,800	5,974,200	5,407,300
Current Liabilities	5,860,500	5,169,100	3,882,000	3,751,800	3,201,700	2,462,600	2,399,400	1,863,400
Long-Term Obligations	1,742,600	1,753,700	2,103,400	1,809,800	2,066,300	1,634,400	1,340,600	1,105,000
Total Liabilities	7,907,000	7,209,000	6,327,600	5,852,400	5,514,500	4,304,200	3,895,300	3,104,100
Stockholders' Equity	2,090,600	2,349,300	2,072,100	2,061,700	1,688,500	1,894,600	2,078,900	2,303,200
Shares Outstanding	103,100	110,804	113,313	120,915	120,856	135,784	148,364	171,731
Statistical Record								
Return on Assets %	4.63	4.93	5.13	4.96	4.71	4.62	3.98	3.47
Return on Equity %	19.88	20.02	20.26	19.99	17.61	14.16	10.34	8.80
EBITDA Margin %	4.01	4.81	4.89	4.83	4.73	4.75	4.48	4.73
Net Margin %	1.87	2.12	2.19	2.14	2.02	2.03	1.82	1.84
Asset Turnover	2.28	2.32	2.34	2.32	2.33	2.27	2.19	1.88
Current Ratio	0.83	0.91	1.03	1.02	1.05	1.09	1.10	1.21
Debt to Equity	0.83	0.75	1.02	0.88	1.22	0.86	0.64	0.48
Price Range	66.20-41.53	66.20-56.12	61.23-46.84	54.10-39.59	48.45-32.54	40.93-27.53	28.46-17.59	21.17-7.91
P/E Ratio	17.38-10.90	17.02-14.43	17.39-13.31	17.80-13.02	19.23-12.91	21.43-14.41	19.90-12.30	18.90-7.06

Address: 200 S.W. 1st Avenue, Fort Lauderdale, FL 33301 **Telephone:** 954-769-6000	**Web Site:** www.autonation.com **Officers:** Cheryl Miller - Executive Vice President, Chief Financial Officer Michael J. Jackson - Chairman, President, Chief Executive Officer	**Auditors:** KPMG LLP **Investor Contact:** 954-769-7342 **Transfer Agents:** Computershare Trust Company, N.A.

AUTOZONE, INC.

Exchange	Symbol	Price	52Wk Range	Yield	P/E
NYS	AZO	$762.20 (5/31/2016)	805.40-663.16	N/A	19.45

*7 Year Price Score 152.48 ***NYSE Composite Index=100** ***12 Month Price Score 102.99**

Interim Earnings (Per Share)

Qtr.	Nov	Feb	May	Aug
2013 14	6.29	5.63	8.46	11.23

Qtr.	Nov	Feb	Apr	Aug
2014-15	7.27	6.51	9.57	12.70
2015-16	8.29	7.43	10.77	...

Interim Dividends (Per Share)

No Dividends Paid

Valuation Analysis **Institutional Holding**

Forecast EPS	$40.80	No of Institutions
	(05/20/2016)	807
Market Cap	$22.5 Billion	Shares
Book Value	N/A	37,224,000
Price/Book	N/A	% Held
Price/Sales	2.14	87.47

TRADING VOLUME (thousand shares)

2007 2008 2009 2010 2011 2012 2013 2014 2015 2016

Business Summary: Retail - Automotive (MIC: 2.1.4 SIC: 5531 NAIC: 441310)

AutoZone is a retailer and a distributor of automotive replacement parts and accessories. At Aug. 30, 2014, Co. operated 5,141 stores in the U.S., including Puerto Rico; 441 stores in Mexico; seven stores in Brazil; and 20 Interamerican Motor Corporation (IMC) branches. Each of Co.'s stores carries a product line for cars, sport utility vehicles, vans and light trucks, including new and remanufactured automotive hard parts, maintenance items, accessories and non-automotive products. Co. also has commercial programs in select stores in Mexico, as well as in its stores in Brazil. Co. also sells the ALLDATA brand automotive diagnostic and repair software through www.alldata.com.

Recent Developments: For the quarter ended May 7 2016, net income increased 6.0% to US$327.5 million from US$309.1 million in the year-earlier quarter. Revenues were US$2.59 billion, up 4.0% from US$2.49 billion the year before. Operating income was US$536.4 million versus US$513.9 million in the prior-year quarter, an increase of 4.4%. Direct operating expenses rose 2.8% to US$1.22 billion from US$1.19 billion in the comparable period the year before. Indirect operating expenses increased 5.7% to US$834.1 million from US$788.8 million in the equivalent prior-year period.

Prospects: Our evaluation of AutoZone Inc. as of June 19, 2016 is the result of our systematic analysis on three basic characteristics: earnings strength, relative valuation, and recent stock price movement. The company has enjoyed a very positive trend in earnings per share over the past 5 quarters. However, while recent estimates for the company have been lowered by analysts, AZO has posted results that fell short of analysts expectations. Based on operating earnings yield, the company is undervalued when compared to all of the companies in our coverage universe. Share price changes over the past year indicates that AZO will perform very well over the near term.

Financial Data

(US$ in Thousands)	9 Mos	6 Mos	3 Mos	08/29/2015	08/30/2014	08/31/2013	08/25/2012	08/27/2011
Earnings Per Share	39.19	37.99	37.07	36.03	31.57	27.79	23.48	19.47
Cash Flow Per Share	52.77	52.34	48.31	48.46	40.43	38.73	31.72	30.38
Income Statement								
Total Revenue	7,236,907	4,643,235	2,386,043	10,187,340	9,475,313	9,147,530	8,603,863	8,072,973
EBITDA	1,362,436	824,193	439,721	2,229,200	2,088,346	2,008,588	1,848,788	1,699,974
Depn & Amortn	5,407	3,538	1,726	276,149	258,123	235,490	219,897	205,171
Income Before Taxes	1,255,136	752,813	402,985	1,802,612	1,662,714	1,587,683	1,452,986	1,324,246
Income Taxes	440,897	266,088	144,873	642,371	592,970	571,203	522,613	475,272
Net Income	814,239	486,725	258,112	1,160,241	1,069,744	1,016,480	930,373	848,974
Average Shares	30,405	30,778	31,138	32,206	33,882	36,581	39,625	43,603
Balance Sheet								
Current Assets	4,225,486	4,209,813	4,053,871	3,970,294	3,580,612	3,278,013	2,978,946	2,792,425
Total Assets	8,464,105	8,366,414	8,217,528	8,102,349	7,517,858	6,892,089	6,265,639	5,869,602
Current Liabilities	4,647,589	4,994,661	4,775,241	4,712,873	4,541,094	4,169,150	3,655,592	3,430,896
Long-Term Obligations	4,953,697	4,387,811	4,754,101	4,624,876	4,162,890	4,013,267	3,718,302	3,317,600
Total Liabilities	10,327,387	10,107,727	9,995,649	9,803,739	9,139,715	8,579,408	7,813,664	7,123,834
Stockholders' Equity	(1,863,282)	(1,741,313)	(1,778,121)	(1,701,390)	(1,621,857)	(1,687,319)	(1,548,025)	(1,254,232)
Shares Outstanding	29,501	30,101	30,271	30,659	32,304	34,293	37,028	40,109
Statistical Record								
Return on Assets %	14.73	14.67	14.81	14.90	14.89	15.20	15.38	14.88
EBITDA Margin %	18.83	17.75	18.43	21.88	22.04	21.96	21.49	21.06
Net Margin %	11.25	10.48	10.82	11.39	11.29	11.11	10.81	10.52
Asset Turnover	1.28	1.28	1.29	1.31	1.32	1.37	1.42	1.42
Current Ratio	0.91	0.84	0.85	0.84	0.79	0.79	0.81	0.81
Price Range	805.40-663.16	797.29-615.15	797.29-568.55	750.13-501.78	543.84-411.89	448.58-344.99	397.13-307.00	304.10-209.78
P/E Ratio	20.55-16.92	20.99-16.19	21.51-15.34	20.82-13.93	17.23-13.05	16.14-12.41	16.91-13.07	15.62-10.77

Address: 123 South Front Street, Memphis, TN 38103
Telephone: 901-495-6500

Web Site: www.autozone.com
Officers: William C. Rhodes - Chairman, President, Chief Executive Officer, Customer Satisfaction William T, Giles - Executive Vice President, Chief Financial Officer, Treasurer, Customer Satisfaction

Auditors: Ernst & Young LLP
Transfer Agents: ComputerShare Investor Services, Providence, RI

AVALONBAY COMMUNITIES, INC.

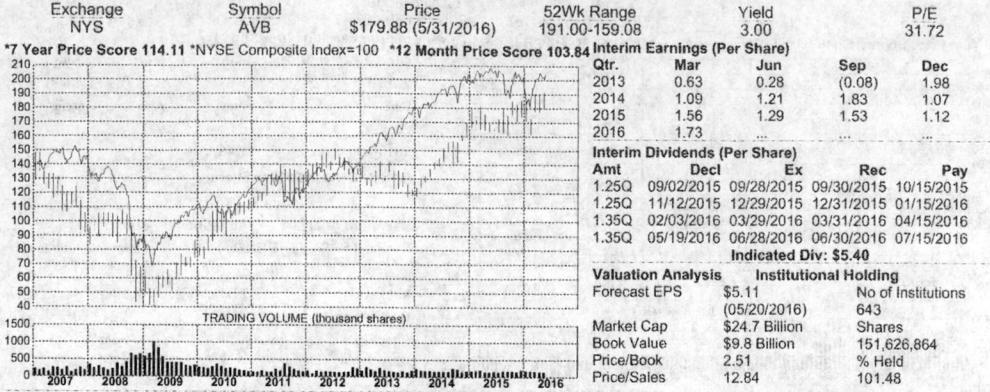

Exchange	Symbol	Price	52Wk Range	Yield	P/E
NYS	AVB	$179.88 (5/31/2016)	191.00-159.08	3.00	31.72

*7 Year Price Score 114.11 *NYSE Composite Index=100 *12 Month Price Score 103.84

Interim Earnings (Per Share)

Qtr.	Mar	Jun	Sep	Dec
2013	0.63	0.28	(0.08)	1.98
2014	1.09	1.21	1.83	1.07
2015	1.56	1.29	1.53	1.12
2016	1.73	...	...	...

Interim Dividends (Per Share)

Amt	Decl	Ex	Rec	Pay
1.25Q	09/02/2015	09/28/2015	09/30/2015	10/15/2015
1.25Q	11/12/2015	12/29/2015	12/31/2015	01/15/2016
1.35Q	02/03/2016	03/29/2016	03/31/2016	04/15/2016
1.35Q	05/19/2016	06/28/2016	06/30/2016	07/15/2016

Indicated Div: $5.40

Valuation Analysis

		Institutional Holding	
Forecast EPS	$5.11 (05/20/2016)	No of Institutions	643
Market Cap	$24.7 Billion	Shares	151,626,864
Book Value	$9.8 Billion	% Held	101.48
Price/Book	2.51		
Price/Sales	12.84		

Business Summary: REITs (MIC: 5.3.1 SIC: 6798 NAIC: 525930)

AvalonBay Communities is a real estate investment trust. Co. focuses on the development, redevelopment, acquisition, ownership and operation of multifamily communities primarily in New England, the New York/New Jersey metro area, the Mid-Atlantic, the Pacific Northwest, and Northern and Southern California. Co.'s reportable segments are: Established Communities, Other Stabilized Communities and Development/Redevelopment Communities. At Dec 31 2015, Co. owned or held a direct or indirect ownership interest in 259 operating apartment communities containing 75,584 apartment homes in 11 states and the District of Columbia.

Recent Developments: For the quarter ended Mar 31 2016, net income increased 14.3% to US$237.9 million from US$208.1 million in the year-earlier quarter. Revenues were US$508.5 million, up 14.9% from US$442.4 million the year before.

Prospects: Our evaluation of AvalonBay Communities Inc. as of June 19, 2016 is the result of our systematic analysis on three basic characteristics: earnings strength, relative valuation, and recent stock price movement. The company has enjoyed a very positive trend in earnings per share over the past 5 quarters. Because the company lacks sufficient analyst estimate data, we place greater weight on the historical EPS trend as the measure of earnings strength. Based on operating earnings yield, the company is about fairly valued when compared to all of the companies in our coverage universe. Share price changes over the past year indicates that AVB will perform very well over the near term.

Financial Data

(US$ in Thousands)	3 Mos	12/31/2015	12/31/2014	12/31/2013	12/31/2012	12/31/2011	12/31/2010	12/31/2009
Earnings Per Share	5.67	5.51	5.21	2.78	4.32	4.87	2.07	1.93
Cash Flow Per Share	8.03	7.91	6.79	5.71	5.54	4.78	3.96	4.74
Tang Book Value Per Share	71.79	71.83	68.51	66.42	59.76	46.18	38.54	37.41
Dividends Per Share	5.100	5.000	4.640	4.280	3.880	3.570	3.570	3.570
Dividend Payout %	89.95	90.74	89.06	153.96	89.81	73.31	172.46	184.97
Income Statement								
Total Revenue	508,498	1,856,028	1,685,061	1,462,921	1,038,660	968,711	895,266	851,582
EBITDA	381,563	1,327,114	1,143,050	815,098	640,856	579,266	505,457	443,581
Depn & Amortn	128,208	477,923	442,682	573,715	260,094	250,269	232,942	218,286
Income Before Taxes	209,945	673,576	519,750	68,981	243,842	160,818	97,306	74,972
Income Taxes	37	1,861	9,368	...	...	...	...	...
Net Income	237,931	741,733	683,567	353,141	423,869	441,622	175,331	155,647
Average Shares	137,383	134,593	131,237	127,265	98,025	90,777	84,632	80,599
Balance Sheet								
Current Assets	267,902	535,405	634,702	406,694	2,808,399	713,926	502,058	340,013
Total Assets	17,043,390	16,931,305	16,176,723	15,328,143	11,160,078	8,482,390	7,821,488	7,457,605
Current Liabilities	379,539	264,474	244,027	227,314	182,648	156,473	142,954	141,488
Long-Term Obligations	6,502,580	6,456,948	6,525,852	6,145,391	3,851,033	3,632,296	4,067,657	3,974,872
Total Liabilities	7,196,858	7,090,779	7,130,318	6,732,011	4,322,863	4,087,649	4,510,870	4,407,478
Stockholders' Equity	9,846,532	9,840,526	9,046,405	8,596,132	6,837,215	4,394,741	3,310,618	3,050,127
Shares Outstanding	137,162	137,002	132,050	129,416	114,403	95,175	85,899	81,528
Statistical Record								
Return on Assets %	4.63	4.48	4.34	2.67	4.30	5.42	2.30	2.13
Return on Equity %	8.15	7.85	7.75	4.58	7.53	11.46	5.51	5.22
EBITDA Margin %	75.04	71.50	67.83	55.72	61.70	59.80	56.46	52.09
Net Margin %	46.79	39.96	40.57	24.14	40.81	45.59	19.58	18.28
Asset Turnover	0.12	0.11	0.11	0.11	0.11	0.12	0.12	0.12
Current Ratio	0.71	2.02	2.60	1.79	15.38	4.56	3.51	2.40
Debt to Equity	0.66	0.66	0.72	0.71	0.56	0.83	1.23	1.30
Price Range	190.20-159.08	185.54-159.08	169.20-117.53	141.46-116.86	151.00-124.26	139.51-109.16	114.80-73.21	86.59-40.11
P/E Ratio	33.54-28.06	33.67-28.87	32.48-22.56	50.88-42.04	34.95-28.76	28.65-22.41	55.46-35.37	44.87-20.78
Average Yield %	2.95	2.91	3.26	3.30	2.81	2.88	3.63	5.84

Address: Ballston Tower, 671 N. Glebe Road, Suite 800, Arlington, VA 22203 **Telephone:** 703-329-6300 **Fax:** 703-329-9130	**Web Site:** www.avalonbay.com **Officers:** Timothy J. Naughton - Chairman, President, Chief Executive Officer Leo S. Horey - Executive Vice President, Chief Administrative Officer
Auditors: Ernst & Young LLP **Investor Contact:** 703-317-4681 **Transfer Agents:** Computershare, Pittsburgh, PA	

AVERY DENNISON CORP.

Exchange	Symbol	Price	52Wk Range	Yield	P/E
NYS	AVY	$74.38 (5/31/2016)	76.74-55.59	2.20	23.61

*7 Year Price Score 128.49 *NYSE Composite Index=100 *12 Month Price Score 113.55

Interim Earnings (Per Share)

Qtr.	Mar	Jun	Sep	Dec
2013	0.57	0.68	0.47	0.44
2014	0.73	0.44	0.68	0.76
2015	0.77	0.68	0.88	0.61
2016	0.98	...	...	...

Interim Dividends (Per Share)

Amt	Decl	Ex	Rec	Pay
0.37Q	07/23/2015	08/31/2015	09/02/2015	09/16/2015
0.37Q	10/22/2015	11/30/2015	12/02/2015	12/16/2015
0.37Q	02/03/2016	02/29/2016	03/02/2016	03/16/2016
0.41Q	04/28/2016	05/27/2016	06/01/2016	06/15/2016

Indicated Div: $1.64 (Div. Reinv. Plan)

Valuation Analysis — **Institutional Holding**

Forecast EPS	$3.84	No of Institutions
	(05/20/2016)	671
Market Cap	$6.6 Billion	Shares
Book Value	$968.3 Million	101,634,448
Price/Book	6.86	% Held
Price/Sales	1.12	84.13

TRADING VOLUME (thousand shares)

Business Summary: Containers & Packaging (MIC: 8.1.3 SIC: 2672 NAIC: 322222)

Avery Dennison operates in three segments: Pressure-sensitive Materials, which manufactures and sells Fasson®-, JAC®-, and Avery Dennison®-brand pressure-sensitive label and packaging materials, Avery Dennison®-brand graphics, Avery Dennison®-brand reflective products, Avery Dennison®-brand tapes, and performance polymers (used to manufacture pressure-sensitive materials); Retail Branding and Information Solutions, which designs, manufactures and sells a range of branding and information solutions to retailers, brand owners, apparel manufacturers, distributors and industrial customers; and Vancive Medical Technologies, which manufactures a range of pressure-sensitive adhesive products.

Recent Developments: For the quarter ended Apr 2 2016, net income increased 24.6% to US$89.6 million from US$71.9 million in the year-earlier quarter. Revenues were US$1.49 billion, down 2.8% from US$1.53 billion the year before. Direct operating expenses declined 3.2% to US$1.06 billion from US$1.10 billion in the comparable period the year before. Indirect operating expenses decreased 9.4% to US$299.1 million from US$330.0 million in the equivalent prior-year period.

Prospects: Our evaluation of Avery Dennison Corp. as of June 19, 2016 is the result of our systematic analysis on three basic characteristics: earnings strength, relative valuation, and recent stock price movement. The company has produced a positive trend in earnings per share over the past 5 quarters. However, while recent estimates for the company have been mixed, AVY has posted better than expected results. Based on operating earnings yield, the company is about fairly valued when compared to all of the companies in our coverage universe. Share price changes over the past year indicates that AVY will perform very well over the near term.

Financial Data

(US$ in Thousands)	3 Mos	01/02/2016	01/03/2015	12/28/2013	12/29/2012	12/31/2011	01/01/2011	01/02/2010
Earnings Per Share	3.15	2.95	2.60	2.16	2.08	1.78	2.97	(7.21)
Cash Flow Per Share	5.14	5.22	3.92	3.26	5.02	4.01	4.61	5.40
Tang Book Value Per Share	2.60	2.60	3.07	6.71	6.92	6.94	4.52	1.42
Dividends Per Share	1.480	1.460	1.340	1.140	1.080	1.000	0.800	1.220
Dividend Payout %	46.98	49.49	51.54	52.78	51.92	56.18	26.94	...
Income Statement								
Total Revenue	1,485,500	5,966,900	6,330,300	6,140,000	6,035,600	6,026,300	6,512,700	5,952,700
EBITDA	183,100	594,600	563,200	557,700	478,400	471,900	600,800	(518,000)
Depn & Amortn	44,300	125,200	135,500	135,600	150,100	168,000	172,900	187,600
Income Before Taxes	123,500	408,900	364,400	363,100	255,500	232,900	351,300	(790,900)
Income Taxes	33,900	134,500	113,300	118,800	86,400	78,500	34,400	(44,200)
Net Income	89,600	274,300	248,900	215,800	215,400	190,100	316,900	(746,700)
Average Shares	91,100	92,900	95,700	100,100	103,500	106,800	106,800	103,600
Balance Sheet								
Current Assets	1,887,400	1,775,400	1,921,300	2,091,800	2,411,700	2,218,800	1,951,900	1,733,200
Total Assets	4,249,400	4,133,700	4,360,200	4,610,600	5,105,300	4,972,700	5,099,400	5,002,800
Current Liabilities	1,594,200	1,459,100	1,597,800	1,554,100	2,074,500	1,647,100	1,831,800	1,867,700
Long-Term Obligations	963,300	963,600	945,300	950,600	702,200	954,200	956,200	1,088,700
Total Liabilities	3,281,100	3,168,000	3,293,700	3,118,400	3,524,400	3,314,200	3,453,700	3,640,200
Stockholders' Equity	968,300	965,700	1,066,500	1,492,200	1,580,900	1,658,500	1,645,700	1,362,600
Shares Outstanding	89,276	89,967	90,458	96,178	99,915	106,269	105,391	105,298
Statistical Record								
Return on Assets %	6.81	6.48	5.46	4.45	4.29	3.79	6.29	N.M.
Return on Equity %	29.24	27.07	19.14	14.08	13.34	11.54	21.13	N.M.
EBITDA Margin %	12.33	9.96	8.90	9.08	7.93	7.83	9.23	N.M.
Net Margin %	6.03	4.60	3.93	3.51	3.57	3.15	4.87	N.M.
Asset Turnover	1.38	1.41	1.39	1.27	1.20	1.20	1.29	1.06
Current Ratio	1.18	1.22	1.20	1.35	1.16	1.35	1.07	0.93
Debt to Equity	0.99	1.00	0.89	0.64	0.44	0.58	0.58	0.80
Price Range	72.86-51.07	66.18-51.07	52.67-41.28	50.65-34.92	34.97-26.38	43.11-23.97	42.49-30.79	40.02-17.26
P/E Ratio	23.13-16.21	22.43-17.31	20.26-15.88	23.45-16.17	16.81-12.68	24.22-13.47	14.31-10.37	...
Average Yield %	2.40	2.49	2.74	2.63	3.54	2.89	2.22	4.12

Address: 207 Goode Avenue, Glendale, CA 91203
Telephone: 626-304-2000

Web Site: www.averydennison.com
Officers: Dean A. Scarborough - Executive Chairman, Chairman, President, Chairman, President, Chief Executive Officer, Chief Executive Officer Mitchell R. Butler - President, Senior Vice President, Chief Executive Officer, Senior Vice President, Chief Financial Officer, Chief Operating Officer, Chief Financial Officer, Chief Operating Officer

Auditors: PricewaterhouseCoopers LLP
Investor Contact: 626-304-2000
Transfer Agents: Broadridge Corporate Issuer Solutions, Inc., Brentwood, NY

AVISTA CORP.

Exchange	Symbol	Price	52Wk Range	Yield	P/E	Div Achiever
NYS	AVA	$40.22 (5/31/2016)	41.64-29.93	3.41	18.97	13 Years

*7 Year Price Score 110.86 *NYSE Composite Index=100 *12 Month Price Score 112.60

Interim Earnings (Per Share)

Qtr.	Mar	Jun	Sep	Dec
2013	0.71	0.43	0.19	0.53
2014	0.81	1.67	0.16	0.51
2015	0.74	0.40	0.21	0.62
2016	0.89	...	...	...

Interim Dividends (Per Share)

Amt	Decl	Ex	Rec	Pay
0.33Q	08/21/2015	09/01/2015	09/03/2015	09/15/2015
0.33Q	11/06/2015	11/17/2015	11/19/2015	12/15/2015
0.343Q	02/05/2016	02/17/2016	02/19/2016	03/15/2016
0.343Q	05/12/2016	05/24/2016	05/26/2016	06/15/2016

Indicated Div: $1.37

Valuation Analysis / Institutional Holding

Forecast EPS	$2.03	No of Institutions
	(05/16/2016)	321
Market Cap	$2.5 Billion	Shares
Book Value	$1.6 Billion	46,763,176
Price/Book	1.60	% Held
Price/Sales	1.75	67.46

Business Summary: Electric Utilities (MIC: 3.1.1 SIC: 4931 NAIC: 221121)

Avista is a holding company. Through its subsidiaries, Co. is primarily engaged as an electric and natural gas utility with certain other business ventures. Co. has two reportable business segments: Avista Utilities, which generates, transmits and distributes electricity and distributes natural gas, serving electric and gas customers in eastern Washington and northern Idaho and natural gas customers in parts of Oregon; and Alaska Electric Light and Power Company, which provides electric services in Juneau, AK. Co. has other businesses, including sheet metal fabrication, venture fund investments and real estate investments.

Recent Developments: For the quarter ended Mar 31 2016, net income increased 20.7% to US$56.1 million from US$46.5 million in the year-earlier quarter. Revenues were US$418.2 million, down 6.3% from US$446.5 million the year before. Operating income was US$106.1 million versus US$89.6 million in the prior-year quarter, an increase of 18.4%. Direct operating expenses declined 12.7% to US$276.7 million from US$317.0 million in the comparable period the year before. Indirect operating expenses decreased 11.2% to US$35.4 million from US$39.9 million in the equivalent prior-year period.

Prospects: Our evaluation of Avista Corp. as of June 19, 2016 is the result of our systematic analysis on three basic characteristics: earnings strength, relative valuation, and recent stock price movement. The company has produced a positive trend in earnings per share over the past 5 quarters and while recent estimates for the company have remained steady, AVA has posted better than expected results. Based on operating earnings yield, the company is about fairly valued when compared to all of the companies in our coverage universe. Share price changes over the past year indicates that AVA will perform very well over the near term.

Financial Data
(US$ in Thousands)

	3 Mos	12/31/2015	12/31/2014	12/31/2013	12/31/2012	12/31/2011	12/31/2010	12/31/2009
Earnings Per Share	2.12	1.97	3.10	1.85	1.32	1.72	1.65	1.58
Cash Flow Per Share	5.34	6.03	4.34	4.05	5.35	4.66	4.11	4.73
Tang Book Value Per Share	24.24	23.61	22.91	19.68	19.01	19.63	19.26	18.72
Dividends Per Share	1.333	1.320	1.270	1.220	1.160	1.100	1.000	0.810
Dividend Payout %	62.85	67.01	40.97	65.95	87.88	63.95	60.61	51.27
Income Statement								
Total Revenue	418,173	1,484,776	1,472,562	1,618,505	1,547,002	1,619,780	1,558,740	1,512,565
EBITDA	118,393	450,490	404,802	391,648	343,932	372,558	325,519	353,718
Depn & Amortn	10,426	188,677	142,075	141,458	149,849	142,537	104,695	156,807
Income Before Taxes	88,010	185,619	192,106	175,524	120,061	160,171	146,105	134,971
Income Taxes	31,942	67,449	72,240	63,230	41,261	56,632	51,157	46,323
Net Income	56,052	123,227	192,041	111,077	78,210	100,224	92,425	87,071
Average Shares	62,907	62,708	61,887	59,997	59,201	58,092	55,824	54,942
Balance Sheet								
Current Assets	279,224	306,046	395,347	549,679	505,794	614,556	579,565	418,923
Total Assets	4,956,013	4,906,649	4,712,331	4,361,923	4,313,179	4,214,531	3,940,095	3,606,959
Current Liabilities	431,841	474,680	385,269	625,340	576,149	627,174	579,175	503,417
Long-Term Obligations	1,531,338	1,531,658	1,543,609	1,371,403	1,301,752	1,254,176	1,199,517	1,087,696
Total Liabilities	3,366,422	3,378,023	3,228,660	3,063,657	3,053,702	3,028,830	2,814,311	2,555,672
Stockholders' Equity	1,589,591	1,528,626	1,483,671	1,298,266	1,259,477	1,185,701	1,125,784	1,051,287
Shares Outstanding	63,208	62,312	62,243	60,076	59,812	58,422	57,119	54,836
Statistical Record								
Return on Assets %	2.75	2.56	4.23	2.56	1.83	2.46	2.45	2.41
Return on Equity %	8.58	8.18	13.81	8.69	6.38	8.67	8.49	8.50
EBITDA Margin %	28.31	30.34	27.49	24.20	22.23	23.00	20.88	23.39
Net Margin %	13.40	8.30	13.04	6.86	5.06	6.19	5.93	5.76
Asset Turnover	0.30	0.31	0.32	0.37	0.36	0.40	0.41	0.42
Current Ratio	0.65	0.64	1.03	0.88	0.88	0.98	1.00	0.83
Debt to Equity	0.96	1.00	1.04	1.06	1.03	1.06	1.07	1.03
Price Range	41.12-29.93	38.30-29.93	37.27-27.73	29.15-24.11	27.86-23.07	26.41-21.39	22.72-18.79	22.28-12.77
P/E Ratio	19.40-14.12	19.44-15.19	12.02-8.95	15.76-13.03	21.11-17.48	15.35-12.44	13.77-11.39	14.10-8.08
Average Yield %	3.92	3.96	4.01	4.51	4.55	4.55	4.76	4.49

Address: 1411 East Mission Avenue, Spokane, WA 99202-2600	Web Site: www.avistacorp.com	Auditors: Doloitte & Touche LLP
Telephone: 509-489-0500	Officers: Scott L. Morris - Chairman, President, Chief Executive Officer Mark T. Thies - Senior Vice President, Chief Financial Officer, Treasurer	Investor Contact: 509-489-0500
Fax: 509-482-4361		Transfer Agents: Computershare, Pittsburgh, PA

AVNET INC

Exchange	Symbol	Price	52Wk Range	Yield	P/E
NYS	AVT	$41.03 (5/31/2016)	46.95-37.78	1.66	9.75

*7 Year Price Score 102.16 *NYSE Composite Index=100 *12 Month Price Score 96.86

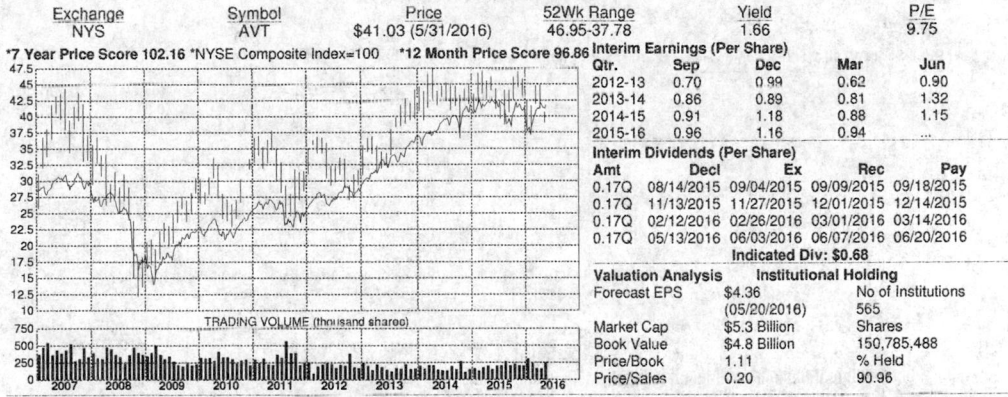

Interim Earnings (Per Share)

Qtr.	Sep	Dec	Mar	Jun
2012-13	0.70	0.99	0.62	0.90
2013-14	0.86	0.89	0.81	1.32
2014-15	0.91	1.18	0.88	1.15
2015-16	0.96	1.16	0.94	

Interim Dividends (Per Share)

Amt	Decl	Ex	Rec	Pay
0.17Q	08/14/2015	09/04/2015	09/09/2015	09/18/2015
0.17Q	11/13/2015	11/27/2015	12/01/2015	12/14/2015
0.17Q	02/12/2016	02/26/2016	03/01/2016	03/14/2016
0.17Q	05/13/2016	06/03/2016	06/07/2016	06/20/2016

Indicated Div: $0.68

Valuation Analysis

		Institutional Holding	
Forecast EPS	$4.36	No of Institutions	
	(05/20/2016)	565	
Market Cap	$5.3 Billion	Shares	
Book Value	$4.8 Billion	150,785,488	
Price/Book	1.11	% Held	
Price/Sales	0.20	90.96	

Business Summary: Electrical Equipment (MIC: 7.3.1 SIC: 5065 NAIC: 423690)

Avnet is a distributor of electronic components, enterprise computer and storage products, information technology solutions and services and embedded subsystems. In addition, Co. provides engineering design, materials management and logistics services, system integration and configuration, and supply chain services to meet specific requirements of both customers and suppliers. Co. has two primary operating groups: Electronics Marketing, which markets and sells semiconductors, interconnect, passive and electromechanical devices and embedded products; and Technology Solutions, which focuses on creating and delivering datacenter and IT lifecycle solutions to end-users.

Recent Developments: For the quarter ended Apr 2 2016, net income increased 1.6% to US$123.5 million from US$121.5 million in the year-earlier quarter. Revenues were US$6.17 billion, down 8.3% from US$6.74 billion the year before. Operating income was US$181.6 million versus US$203.7 million in the prior-year quarter, a decrease of 10.8%. Direct operating expenses declined 8.8% to US$5.44 billion from US$5.96 billion in the comparable period the year before. Indirect operating expenses decreased 2.7% to US$555.2 million from US$570.6 million in the equivalent prior-year period.

Prospects: Our evaluation of Avnet Inc. as of June 19, 2016 is the result of our systematic analysis on three basic characteristics: earnings strength, relative valuation, and recent stock price movement. The company has managed to produce a neutral trend in earnings per share over the past 5 quarters and while recent estimates for the company have been mixed, AVT has posted better than expected results. Based on operating earnings yield, the company is undervalued when compared to all of the companies in our coverage universe. Share price changes over the past year indicates that AVT will perform in line with the market over the near term.

Financial Data

(US$ in Thousands)	9 Mos	6 Mos	3 Mos	06/27/2015	06/28/2014	06/29/2013	06/30/2012	07/02/2011
Earnings Per Share	4.21	4.15	4.17	4.12	3.89	3.21	3.79	4.34
Cash Flow Per Share	4.59	3.36	4.42	4.28	1.73	5.06	3.60	1.83
Tang Book Value Per Share	26.28	25.13	24.77	24.41	24.29	22.09	19.68	20.75
Dividends Per Share	0.670	0.660	0.650	0.640	0.600	...	...	...
Dividend Payout %	15.91	15.90	15.59	15.53	15.42	...	...	...
Income Statement								
Total Revenue	19,992,467	13,817,751	6,969,694	27,924,657	27,499,654	25,458,924	25,707,522	26,534,413
EBITDA	696,852	482,658	231,720	904,230	898,450	745,221	952,286	1,020,934
Depn & Amortn	92,295	61,919	30,612	95,600	92,500	88,303	70,645	57,516
Income Before Taxes	535,251	374,714	177,506	712,965	701,127	549,265	790,782	870,966
Income Taxes	125,526	88,448	47,252	141,052	155,523	99,192	223,763	201,897
Net Income	409,725	286,266	130,254	571,913	545,604	450,073	567,019	669,069
Average Shares	131,650	134,918	136,326	138,791	140,119	140,003	149,553	154,337
Balance Sheet								
Current Assets	8,938,101	9,142,387	8,714,523	8,642,073	8,954,199	8,356,878	8,254,439	8,227,207
Total Assets	11,125,460	11,302,352	10,864,456	10,799,953	11,255,517	10,474,680	10,167,866	9,905,569
Current Liabilities	4,564,420	5,363,298	4,960,255	4,272,296	4,978,826	4,821,444	4,798,652	4,477,728
Long-Term Obligations	1,610,539	1,072,188	1,075,752	1,646,501	1,213,814	1,206,993	1,271,985	1,273,509
Total Liabilities	6,365,259	6,628,350	6,233,185	6,114,932	6,365,324	6,185,555	6,262,134	5,849,499
Stockholders' Equity	4,760,201	4,674,002	4,631,271	4,685,021	4,890,193	4,289,125	3,905,732	4,056,070
Shares Outstanding	128,514	131,297	132,174	135,464	138,248	137,088	142,548	152,797
Statistical Record								
Return on Assets %	5.23	4.97	5.26	5.20	5.04	4.37	5.66	7.59
Return on Equity %	12.28	12.08	12.18	11.98	11.92	11.01	14.28	18.99
EBITDA Margin %	3.49	3.49	3.32	3.24	3.27	2.93	3.70	3.85
Net Margin %	2.05	2.07	1.87	2.05	1.98	1.77	2.21	2.52
Asset Turnover	2.46	2.40	2.57	2.54	2.54	2.47	2.57	3.01
Current Ratio	1.96	1.70	1.76	2.02	1.80	1.73	1.72	1.84
Debt to Equity	0.34	0.23	0.23	0.35	0.25	0.28	0.33	0.31
Price Range	46.95-37.78	47.12-38.63	47.12-36.54	47.12-36.54	47.50-33.97	36.86-27.01	36.83-24.19	37.81-22.86
P/E Ratio	11.15-8.97	11.35-9.31	11.30-8.76	11.44-8.87	12.21-8.73	11.48-8.41	9.72-6.38	8.71-5.27
Average Yield %	1.56	1.51	1.51	1.47	1.44	...	...	...

Address: 2211 South 47th Street, Phoenix, AZ 85034 **Telephone:** 480-643-2000	**Web Site:** www.avnet.com **Officers:** Richard P. Hamada - President, Chief Executive Officer, Chief Operating Officer Gerard W. Fay - Senior Vice President, Chief Logistics and Global Operations Officer, Division Officer	**Auditors:** KPMG LLP **Investor Contact:** 480-643-7053 **Transfer Agents:** American Stock Transfer & Trust Company, Brooklyn, NY

AVON PRODUCTS, INC.

Exchange	Symbol	Price	52Wk Range	Yield	P/E
NYS	AVP	$3.90 (5/31/2016)	7.00-2.38	N/A	N/A

*7 Year Price Score 19.93   *NYSE Composite Index=100   *12 Month Price Score 100.81

Interim Earnings (Per Share)

Qtr.	Mar	Jun	Sep	Dec
2013	(0.03)	0.07	(0.01)	(0.16)
2014	(0.38)	0.04	0.21	(0.75)
2015	(0.33)	0.07	(1.58)	(0.76)
2016	(0.38)	...	...	...

Interim Dividends (Per Share)

Amt	Decl	Ex	Rec	Pay
0.06Q	02/12/2015	02/19/2015	02/23/2015	03/02/2015
0.06Q	04/30/2015	05/12/2015	05/14/2015	06/01/2015
0.06Q	07/30/2015	08/11/2015	08/13/2015	09/01/2015
0.06Q	11/04/2015	11/12/2015	11/16/2015	12/01/2015

Valuation Analysis

		Institutional Holding	
Forecast EPS	$0.13	No of Institutions	503
	(05/20/2016)		
Market Cap	$1.7 Billion	Shares	423,354,976
Book Value	N/A	% Held	99.42
Price/Book	N/A		
Price/Sales	0.30		

Business Summary: Household & Personal Products (MIC: 1.7.1 SIC: 2844 NAIC: 446120)

Avon Products is a manufacturer and marketer of beauty and related products. Co.'s product categories are Beauty and Fashion & Home. Beauty consists of skincare (which includes personal care), fragrance and color (cosmetics). Fashion & Home consists of fashion jewelry, watches, apparel, footwear, accessories, gift and decorative products, housewares, entertainment and leisure products, children's products and nutritional products. Co.'s business is conducted primarily in one channel, direct selling. Co.'s reportable segments are based on geographic operations and include commercial business units in Latin America; Europe, Middle East and Africa; and Asia Pacific.

Recent Developments: For the quarter ended Mar 31 2016, loss from continuing operations was US$155.8 million compared with a loss of US$142.6 million in the year-earlier quarter. Net loss amounted to US$165.4 million versus a net loss of US$146.4 million in the year-earlier quarter. Revenues were US$1.31 billion, down 15.8% from US$1.55 billion the year before. Operating income was US$7.8 million versus a loss of US$32.9 million in the prior-year quarter. Direct operating expenses declined 15.2% to US$518.8 million from US$611.7 million in the comparable period the year before. Indirect operating expenses decreased 19.9% to US$779.9 million from US$973.3 million in the equivalent prior-year period.

Prospects: Our evaluation of Avon Products Inc. as of June 19, 2016 is the result of our systematic analysis on three basic characteristics: earnings strength, relative valuation, and recent stock price movement. The company has enjoyed a very positive trend in earnings per share over the past 5 quarters and while recent estimates for the company have been mixed, AVP has posted results that fell short of analysts expectations. Based on operating earnings yield, the company is overvalued when compared to all of the companies in our coverage universe. Share price changes over the past year indicates that AVP will perform poorly over the near term.

Financial Data

(US$ in Thousands)	3 Mos	12/31/2015	12/31/2014	12/31/2013	12/31/2012	12/31/2011	12/31/2010	12/31/2009
Earnings Per Share	(2.65)	(2.60)	(0.88)	(0.13)	(0.10)	1.18	1.39	1.45
Cash Flow Per Share	0.23	0.21	0.83	1.25	1.28	1.52	1.61	1.83
Tang Book Value Per Share	...	...	N.M.	1.55	1.13	1.49	1.10	2.16
Dividends Per Share	0.180	0.240	0.240	0.240	0.750	0.920	0.880	0.840
Dividend Payout %	...	...	...	...	...	77.97	63.31	57.93
Income Statement								
Total Revenue	1,306,500	6,160,500	8,851,400	9,955,000	10,717,100	11,291,600	10,862,800	10,382,800
EBITDA	(101,800)	224,700	401,800	422,100	470,200	993,000	1,163,700	1,144,100
Depn & Amortn	27,600	94,000	141,300	164,800	162,400	174,000	145,200	133,000
Income Before Taxes	(158,100)	22,700	164,200	162,600	218,600	742,600	945,400	926,500
Income Taxes	(2,300)	819,200	549,100	163,600	256,800	216,200	350,200	298,300
Net Income	(165,900)	(1,148,900)	(388,600)	(56,400)	(42,500)	513,600	606,300	625,800
Average Shares	435,900	435,200	434,500	433,400	431,900	432,100	431,350	428,540
Balance Sheet								
Current Assets	2,209,700	2,341,100	2,964,500	3,479,100	3,928,900	4,098,800	4,184,300	4,189,300
Total Assets	3,629,100	3,879,500	5,496,800	6,492,300	7,382,500	7,735,000	7,873,700	6,832,700
Current Liabilities	1,605,100	2,195,100	2,047,200	2,240,500	2,704,600	2,891,000	2,956,300	2,274,800
Long-Term Obligations	2,145,000	2,159,600	2,463,900	2,532,700	2,623,900	2,459,100	2,408,600	2,307,800
Total Liabilities	4,079,800	4,949,800	5,207,000	5,382,200	6,165,400	6,164,600	6,217,200	5,560,100
Stockholders' Equity	(450,700)	(1,070,300)	289,800	1,110,100	1,217,100	1,570,400	1,656,500	1,272,600
Shares Outstanding	436,789	435,500	434,700	433,900	432,200	430,800	429,500	427,480
Statistical Record								
Return on Assets %	N.M.	N.M.	N.M.	N.M.	N.M.	6.58	8.25	9.70
Return on Equity %	...	...	N.M.	N.M.	N.M.	31.83	41.40	64.27
EBITDA Margin %	N.M.	3.65	4.54	4.24	4.39	8.79	10.71	11.02
Net Margin %	N.M.	N.M.	N.M.	N.M.	N.M.	4.55	5.58	6.03
Asset Turnover	1.33	1.31	1.48	1.43	1.41	1.45	1.48	1.61
Current Ratio	1.38	1.07	1.45	1.55	1.45	1.42	1.42	1.84
Debt to Equity	...	...	8.50	2.28	2.16	1.57	1.45	1.81
Price Range	9.15-2.38	9.39-2.50	17.22-9.11	24.20-14.36	23.52-13.80	30.91-16.09	35.49-25.73	36.12-15.20
P/E Ratio	...	...	...	...	...	26.19-13.64	25.53-18.51	24.91-10.48
Average Yield %	3.64	3.94	1.78	1.19	4.42	3.70	3.24	3.09

Address: 777 Third Avenue, New York, NY 10017-1307	**Web Site:** www.avon.com	**Auditors:** PricewaterhouseCoopers LLP
Telephone: 212-282-5000	**Officers:** Sherilyn S. McCoy - Chief Executive Officer James S. Scully - Executive Vice President, Chief Financial Officer	**Investor Contact:** 212-282-5320
		Transfer Agents: Computershare Investor Services, Canton, MA

80

AVX CORP.

Exchange	Symbol	Price	52Wk Range	Yield	P/E
NYS	AVX	$13.81 (5/31/2016)	14.27-10.70	3.04	23.02

*7 Year Price Score 84.45 ***NYSE Composite Index=100** ***12 Month Price Score 99.98**

Interim Earnings (Per Share)

Qtr.	Jun	Sep	Dec	Mar
2011-12	0.40	0.36	0.22	(0.08)
2012-13	(0.81)	0.17	0.12	0.15
2013-14	0.16	0.17	0.19	0.23
2014-15	0.24	0.27	0.23	0.60
2015-16	0.21	0.17	0.03	0.19

Interim Dividends (Per Share)

Amt	Decl	Ex	Rec	Pay
0.105Q	07/23/2015	08/05/2015	08/07/2015	08/21/2015
0.105Q	10/21/2015	11/04/2015	11/06/2015	11/20/2015
0.105Q	02/03/2016	02/17/2016	02/19/2016	03/04/2016
0.105Q	05/13/2016	06/01/2016	06/03/2016	06/17/2016

Indicated Div: $0.42

Valuation Analysis		Institutional Holding	
Forecast EPS	$0.75	No of Institutions	
	(05/20/2016)	194	
Market Cap	$2.3 Billion	Shares	
Book Value	$2.2 Billion	47,999,100	
Price/Book	1.06	% Held	
Price/Sales	1.93	24.12	

Business Summary: Electrical Equipment (MIC: 7.3.1 SIC: 3675 NAIC: 334414)

AVX is a manufacturer and supplier of passive electronic components and related products. Co. has three segments: Passive Components, which manufactures a line of multi-layered ceramic and solid tantalum capacitors, ceramic and film power capacitors, film packages of multiple passive integrated components, varistors, thermistors, inductors and resistive products; Kyocera Electronic Devices Resale, which distributes and sells certain Kyocera Corporation of Japan manufactured electronic component and connector products to certain customers and in certain territories outside of Japan; and Interconnect, which manufactures and sells electronic connectors and interconnect systems.

Recent Developments: For the year ended Mar 31 2016, net income decreased 55.0% to US$101.5 million from US$225.9 million in the prior year. Revenues were US$1.20 billion, down 11.7% from US$1.35 billion the year before. Operating income was US$124.0 million versus US$212.7 million in the prior year, a decrease of 41.7%. Direct operating expenses declined 11.5% to US$906.5 million from US$1.02 billion in the comparable period the year before. Indirect operating expenses increased 42.5% to US$165.1 million from US$115.8 million in the equivalent prior-year period.

Prospects: Our evaluation of AVX Corp. as of June 19, 2016 is the result of our systematic analysis on three basic characteristics: earnings strength, relative valuation, and recent stock price movement. The company has produced a positive trend in earnings per share over the past 5 quarters and while recent estimates for the company have remained steady, AVX has posted better than expected results. Based on operating earnings yield, the company is about fairly valued when compared to all of the companies in our coverage universe. Share price changes over the past year indicates that AVX will perform poorly over the near term.

Financial Data

(US$ in Thousands)	03/31/2016	03/31/2015	03/31/2014	03/31/2013	03/31/2012	03/31/2011	03/31/2010	03/31/2009
Earnings Per Share	0.60	1.34	0.75	(0.38)	0.90	1.43	0.84	0.47
Cash Flow Per Share	0.99	1.18	(0.42)	1.15	0.87	0.89	1.18	0.38
Tang Book Value Per Share	11.38	11.04	10.50	10.08	11.08	10.55	9.12	8.32
Dividends Per Share	0.420	0.400	0.357	0.300	0.260	0.190	0.160	0.160
Dividend Payout %	70.00	29.85	47.67	...	28.89	13.29	19.05	34.04
Income Statement								
Total Revenue	1,195,529	1,353,228	1,442,604	1,414,400	1,545,254	1,653,176	1,304,966	1,389,613
EBITDA	161,580	252,096	204,621	(75,601)	216,313	370,910	223,146	137,904
Depn & Amortn	33,918	37,073	43,731	42,480	42,499	43,220	53,798	61,738
Income Before Taxes	132,152	218,599	163,357	(113,322)	179,905	334,259	176,357	97,139
Income Taxes	30,617	(7,272)	36,320	(49,010)	27,100	90,256	33,499	16,293
Net Income	101,535	225,871	127,037	(64,312)	152,805	244,003	142,858	80,846
Average Shares	167,961	168,402	168,658	169,124	170,134	170,390	170,274	170,689
Balance Sheet								
Current Assets	1,686,891	1,744,552	1,768,723	1,945,533	1,727,145	1,602,115	1,316,358	1,132,504
Total Assets	2,409,819	2,459,015	2,384,988	2,601,995	2,468,012	2,319,482	2,051,492	1,872,529
Current Liabilities	180,302	266,309	161,934	330,877	297,073	235,665	193,273	149,402
Total Liabilities	232,713	327,052	337,303	629,065	347,259	280,065	250,485	202,776
Stockholders' Equity	2,177,106	2,131,963	2,047,685	1,972,930	2,120,753	2,039,417	1,801,007	1,669,753
Shares Outstanding	167,492	168,191	168,221	168,633	169,601	170,142	170,074	170,384
Statistical Record								
Return on Assets %	4.16	9.33	5.09	N.M.	6.37	11.16	7.28	4.06
Return on Equity %	4.70	10.81	6.32	N.M.	7.33	12.71	8.23	4.62
EBITDA Margin %	13.52	18.63	14.18	N.M.	14.00	22.44	17.10	9.92
Net Margin %	8.49	16.69	8.81	N.M.	9.89	14.76	10.95	5.82
Asset Turnover	0.49	0.56	0.58	0.56	0.64	0.76	0.67	0.70
Current Ratio	9.36	6.55	10.92	5.88	5.81	6.80	6.81	7.58
Price Range	14.91-10.70	15.04-11.88	14.09-11.16	13.36-9.20	16.48-11.10	16.24-12.16	14.34-9.08	13.72-7.38
P/E Ratio	24.85-17.83	11.22-8.87	18.79-14.88	...	18.31-12.33	11.36-8.50	17.07-10.81	29.19-15.70
Average Yield %	3.23	2.95	2.79	2.76	1.91	1.32	1.40	1.57

Address: 1 AVX Boulevard, Fountain Inn, SC 29644	Web Site: www.avx.com	Auditors: PricewaterhouseCoopers LLP
Telephone: 864-967-2150	Officers: Tetsuo Kuba - Chairman John Sarvis - President, Chief Executive Officer, Division Officer	Investor Contact: 843-448-9411
		Transfer Agents: The American Stock Transfer and Trust Company, Brooklyn, NY

81

BABCOCK & WILCOX ENTERPRISES INC

Exchange	Symbol	Price	52Wk Range	Yield	P/E
NYS	BW	$21.75 (5/31/2016)	23.66-16.08	N/A	67.97

*7 Year Price Score N/A   *NYSE Composite Index=100   *12 Month Price Score 111.71

Interim Earnings (Per Share)

Qtr.	Mar	Jun	Sep	Dec
2015	0.24	0.10	0.11	(0.09)
2016	0.20	...	...	...

Interim Dividends (Per Share)

No Dividends Paid

Valuation Analysis   **Institutional Holding**

Forecast EPS	$1.39	No of Institutions
	(05/20/2016)	185
Market Cap	$1.0 Billion	Shares
Book Value	$730.2 Million	50,060,660
Price/Book	1.42	% Held
Price/Sales	0.59	N/A

Business Summary: Miscellaneous (MIC: 0.0.0 SIC: 3433 NAIC: 333414)

Babcock & Wilcox Enterprises is engaged in the power generation business. Co. is a technology-based provider of fossil and renewable power generation equipment that includes a suite of boiler products and environmental systems, and services for power and industrial uses. Co. specializes in engineering, manufacturing, procurement, and erection of equipment and technology used in the power generation industry and various other industries. Co. operates in three segments: Global Power, Global Services and Industrial Environmental.

Recent Developments: For the quarter ended Mar 31 2016, income from continuing operations decreased 6.7% to US$10.6 million from US$11.4 million in the year-earlier quarter. Net income decreased 16.9% to US$10.6 million from US$12.7 million in the year-earlier quarter. Revenues were US$404.1 million, up 1.8% from US$397.2 million the year before. Operating income was unchanged at US$17.3 million versus the prior-year quarter. Direct operating expenses rose 3.3% to US$324.0 million from US$313.8 million in the comparable period the year before. Indirect operating expenses decreased 4.8% to US$62.9 million from US$66.1 million in the equivalent prior-year period.

Prospects: Our evaluation of Babcock & Wilcox Enterprises Inc. as of June 19, 2016 is the result of our systematic analysis on three basic characteristics: earnings strength, relative valuation, and recent stock price movement. The company has suffered a very negative trend in earnings per share over the past 5 quarters. However, while recent estimates for the company have been mixed, BW has posted better than expected results. Based on operating earnings yield, the company is undervalued when compared to all of the companies in our coverage universe. Share price changes over the past year indicates that BW will perform very well over the near term.

Financial Data
(US$ in Thousands)

	3 Mos	12/31/2015	12/31/2014	12/31/2013	12/31/2012
Earnings Per Share	0.32	0.36	...	...	...
Cash Flow Per Share	1.64	3.19	...	...	...
Tang Book Value Per Share	10.30	9.96	...	...	...
Income Statement					
Total Revenue	404,116	1,757,295	1,589,719	1,921,163	2,039,100
EBITDA	20,945	44,388	(38,740)	262,778	205,731
Depn & Amortn	6,293	23,500	26,300	25,200	18,800
Income Before Taxes	14,543	20,447	(64,373)	238,634	187,815
Income Taxes	6,626	3,671	(29,528)	82,206	64,323
Net Income	10,507	19,141	(26,529)	174,526	140,753
Average Shares	52,221	53,708	...	...	...
Balance Sheet					
Current Assets	924,311	978,184	854,694	749,752	...
Total Assets	1,610,097	1,663,045	1,522,806	1,296,469	...
Current Liabilities	525,963	561,352	488,090	518,477	...
Long-Term Obligations	...	...	...	225	...
Total Liabilities	879,909	915,337	830,145	765,508	...
Stockholders' Equity	730,188	747,708	692,661	530,961	...
Shares Outstanding	47,732	51,104	...	...	...
Statistical Record					
Return on Assets %	1.09	1.20	N.M.	...	...
Return on Equity %	2.42	2.66	N.M.	...	...
EBITDA Margin %	5.18	2.53	N.M.	13.68	10.09
Net Margin %	2.60	1.09	N.M.	9.08	6.90
Asset Turnover	1.14	1.10	1.13	...	...
Current Ratio	1.76	1.74	1.75	1.45	...
Price Range	22.01-16.08	21.35-16.08	...	...	...
P/E Ratio	68.78-50.25	59.31-44.67	...	...	...

Address: The Harris Building, 13024 Ballantyne Corporate Place, Suite 700, Charlotte, NC 28277 **Telephone:** 704-625-4900	**Web Site:** www.babcock.com **Officers:** E. James Ferland - Chairman Jenny L. Apker - Senior Vice President, Chief Financial Officer	**Auditors:** Deloitte & Touche LLP **Transfer Agents:** Computershare Trust Company, N.A., Canton, MA

BADGER METER, INC.

Exchange	Symbol	Price	52Wk Range	Yield	P/E	Div Achiever
NYS	BMI	$75.00 (5/31/2016)	75.00-53.21	1.07	36.41	23 Years

*7 Year Price Score 114.53 *NYSE Composite Index=100 *12 Month Price Score 113.06

TRADING VOLUME (thousand shares)

Interim Earnings (Per Share)

Qtr.	Mar	Jun	Sep	Dec
2013	0.20	0.44	0.63	0.44
2014	0.32	0.61	0.71	0.40
2015	0.29	0.55	0.58	0.38
2016	0.55	...	...	...

Interim Dividends (Per Share)

Amt	Decl	Ex	Rec	Pay
0.20Q	08/14/2015	08/27/2015	08/31/2015	09/15/2015
0.20Q	11/13/2015	11/25/2015	11/30/2015	12/15/2015
0.20Q	02/12/2016	02/25/2016	02/29/2016	03/15/2016
0.20Q	04/29/2016	05/26/2016	05/31/2016	06/15/2016

Indicated Div: $0.80 (Div. Reinv. Plan)

Valuation Analysis		Institutional Holding	
Forecast EPS	$2.37	No of Institutions	
	(05/16/2016)	188	
Market Cap	$1.1 Billion	Shares	
Book Value	$238.6 Million	13,533,366	
Price/Book	4.57	% Held	
Price/Sales	2.76	76.62	

Business Summary: Electronic Instruments & Related Products (MIC: 6.2.3 SIC: 3824 NAIC: 334514)

Badger Meter is a manufacturer and marketer of products incorporating flow measurement, control and communication solutions. Co.'s product lines fall into two categories: sales of water meters and related technologies to municipal water utilities (municipal water), which includes mechanical and ultrasonic (electronic) water meters and related technologies and services used by municipal water utilities; and sales of meters to various industries for water and other fluids (flow instrumentation), which includes meters and valves sold worldwide to measure and control materials flowing through a pipe or pipeline including water, air, steam, oil, and other liquids and gases.

Recent Developments: For the quarter ended Mar 31 2016, net income increased 89.0% to US$8.0 million from US$4.2 million in the year-earlier quarter. Revenues were US$100.6 million, up 20.2% from US$83.6 million the year before. Operating income was US$12.8 million versus US$7.1 million in the prior-year quarter, an increase of 81.6%. Direct operating expenses rose 14.9% to US$61.6 million from US$53.6 million in the comparable period the year before. Indirect operating expenses increased 13.8% to US$26.2 million from US$23.0 million in the equivalent prior-year period.

Prospects: Our evaluation of Badger Meter Inc. as of June 19, 2016 is the result of our systematic analysis on three basic characteristics: earnings strength, relative valuation, and recent stock price movement. The company has enjoyed a very positive trend in earnings per share over the past 5 quarters. However, while recent estimates for the company have been mixed, BMI has posted better than expected results. Based on operating earnings yield, the company is about fairly valued when compared to all of the companies in our coverage universe. Share price changes over the past year indicates that BMI will perform very well over the near term.

Financial Data
(US$ in Thousands)

	3 Mos	12/31/2015	12/31/2014	12/31/2013	12/31/2012	12/31/2011	12/31/2010	12/31/2009
Earnings Per Share	2.06	1.80	2.06	1.70	1.95	1.27	1.91	2.28
Cash Flow Per Share	3.27	2.49	2.50	2.42	2.42	2.09	1.23	2.47
Tang Book Value Per Share	9.27	8.74	7.26	6.56	5.38	9.01	8.31	7.61
Dividends Per Share	0.790	0.780	0.740	0.700	0.660	0.600	0.520	0.460
Dividend Payout %	38.35	43.33	35.92	41.18	33.85	47.24	27.23	20.18
Income Statement								
Total Revenue	100,570	377,698	364,768	334,122	319,660	262,915	276,634	250,337
EBITDA	18,305	52,362	54,938	47,619	52,056	34,678	51,527	48,974
Depn & Amortn	5,499	9,993	8,891	8,512	7,587	7,144	6,704	6,731
Income Before Taxes	12,536	41,152	44,912	38,009	43,471	27,349	44,438	42,333
Income Taxes	4,546	15,214	15,234	13,392	15,439	8,188	15,776	15,553
Net Income	7,990	25,938	29,678	24,617	28,032	19,161	28,662	34,170
Average Shares	14,498	14,447	14,378	14,440	14,399	15,049	15,006	14,948
Balance Sheet								
Current Assets	150,758	149,328	141,105	127,163	121,374	101,195	97,337	86,680
Total Assets	356,434	355,480	341,158	316,058	290,453	218,910	215,864	191,016
Current Liabilities	98,841	104,544	107,075	98,041	94,080	22,413	32,679	26,261
Total Liabilities	117,853	123,205	126,827	119,495	119,206	39,629	47,481	46,555
Stockholders' Equity	238,581	232,275	214,331	196,563	171,247	179,281	168,383	144,461
Shares Outstanding	14,538	14,524	14,461	14,411	14,314	15,122	15,048	14,972
Statistical Record								
Return on Assets %	8.50	7.45	9.03	8.12	10.98	8.81	14.09	17.69
Return on Equity %	13.07	11.62	14.45	13.39	15.95	11.02	18.32	26.75
EBITDA Margin %	18.20	13.86	15.06	14.25	16.28	13.19	18.63	19.56
Net Margin %	7.94	6.87	8.14	7.37	8.77	7.29	10.36	13.65
Asset Turnover	1.13	1.08	1.11	1.10	1.25	1.21	1.36	1.30
Current Ratio	1.53	1.43	1.32	1.30	1.29	4.52	2.98	3.30
Price Range	69.19-53.21	65.58-55.31	60.04-47.58	55.35-42.54	48.27-29.68	45.19-27.06	45.05-35.22	43.84-23.10
P/E Ratio	33.59-25.83	36.43-30.73	29.15-23.10	32.56-25.02	24.75-15.22	35.58-21.31	23.59-18.44	19.23-10.13
Average Yield %	1.30	1.30	1.41	1.43	1.78	1.68	1.30	1.30

Address: 4545 W. Brown Deer Road, Milwaukee, WI 53223
Telephone: 414-355-0400

Web Site: www.badgermeter.com
Officers: Richard A. Meeusen - Chairman, President, Chief Executive Officer Kimberly K. Stoll - Vice President

Auditors: Ernst & Young LLP
Investor Contact: 414-371-5702
Transfer Agents: American Stock Transfer & Trust Company, LLC, New York, NY

BAKER HUGHES INC.

Exchange	Symbol	Price	52Wk Range	Yield	P/E
NYS	BHI	$46.38 (5/31/2016)	65.22-38.88	1.47	N/A

*7 Year Price Score 81.76   *NYSE Composite Index=100   *12 Month Price Score 88.12

Interim Earnings (Per Share)

Qtr.	Mar	Jun	Sep	Dec
2013	0.60	0.54	0.77	0.56
2014	0.74	0.80	0.86	1.52
2015	(1.35)	(0.43)	(0.36)	(2.36)
2016	(2.22)	...	...	...

Interim Dividends (Per Share)

Amt	Decl	Ex	Rec	Pay
0.17Q	07/23/2015	08/31/2015	09/02/2015	09/23/2015
0.17Q	10/21/2015	12/01/2015	12/03/2015	12/24/2015
0.17Q	01/28/2016	02/29/2016	03/02/2016	03/23/2016
0.17Q	04/18/2016	05/27/2016	06/01/2016	06/22/2016

Indicated Div: $0.68

Valuation Analysis

		Institutional Holding	
Forecast EPS	$-1.86	No of Institutions	
	(05/20/2016)	948	
Market Cap	$20.3 Billion	Shares	
Book Value	$15.3 Billion	402,970,368	
Price/Book	1.33	% Held	
Price/Sales	1.47	85.56	

TRADING VOLUME (thousand shares)

Business Summary: Equipment & Services (MIC: 9.1.3 SIC: 3533 NAIC: 333132)

Baker Hughes is a supplier of oilfield services, products, technology and systems used in the oil and natural gas industry. Co.'s oilfield products and services fall into one of two categories, Drilling and Evaluation or Completion and Production. Co.'s Drilling and Evaluation products and services include drilling services. Co.'s Completion and Production products and services include artificial lift. Co.'s oilfield operations are organized into four geographical operating segments: North America, Latin America, Europe/Africa/Russia Caspian, and Middle East/Asia Pacific. Co.'s Industrial Services consists of its downstream chemicals, and process and pipeline services businesses.

Recent Developments: For the quarter ended Mar 31 2016, net loss amounted to US$981.0 million versus a net loss of US$593.0 million in the year-earlier quarter. Revenues were US$2.67 billion, down 41.9% from US$4.59 billion the year before. Operating loss was US$559.0 million versus a loss of US$774.0 million in the prior-year quarter. Direct operating expenses declined 38.8% to US$2.66 billion from US$4.34 billion in the comparable period the year before. Indirect operating expenses decreased 44.3% to US$571.0 million from US$1.03 billion in the equivalent prior-year period.

Prospects: Our evaluation of Baker Hughes Inc. as of June 19, 2016 is the result of our systematic analysis on three basic characteristics: earnings strength, relative valuation, and recent stock price movement. The company has produced a positive trend in earnings per share over the past 5 quarters. Because the company lacks sufficient analyst estimate data, we place greater weight on the historical EPS trend as the measure of earnings strength. Based on operating earnings yield, the company is overvalued when compared to all of the companies in our coverage universe. Share price changes over the past year indicates that BHI will perform poorly over the near term.

Financial Data

(US$ in Thousands)	3 Mos	12/31/2015	12/31/2014	12/31/2013	12/31/2012	12/31/2011	12/31/2010	12/31/2009
Earnings Per Share	(5.37)	(4.49)	3.92	2.47	2.97	3.97	2.06	1.36
Cash Flow Per Share	3.26	4.10	6.76	7.14	4.16	3.46	2.17	4.00
Tang Book Value Per Share	19.86	22.07	27.03	24.80	22.94	19.79	15.42	18.18
Dividends Per Share	0.680	0.680	0.640	0.600	0.600	0.600	0.600	0.600
Dividend Payout %	...	...	16.33	24.29	20.20	15.11	29.13	44.12
Income Statement								
Total Revenue	2,670,000	15,742,000	24,551,000	22,364,000	21,361,000	19,831,000	14,414,000	9,664,000
EBITDA	(205,000)	(759,000)	4,565,000	3,528,000	3,619,000	3,781,000	2,492,000	1,447,000
Depn & Amortn	354,000	1,637,000	1,706,000	1,579,000	1,427,000	1,221,000	1,069,000	711,000
Income Before Taxes	(614,000)	(2,613,000)	2,627,000	1,715,000	1,982,000	2,339,000	1,282,000	611,000
Income Taxes	367,000	(639,000)	896,000	612,000	665,000	596,000	463,000	190,000
Net Income	(981,000)	(1,967,000)	1,719,000	1,096,000	1,311,000	1,739,000	812,000	421,000
Average Shares	442,000	438,000	439,000	444,000	441,000	438,000	395,000	311,000
Balance Sheet								
Current Assets	8,771,000	9,268,000	12,045,000	11,295,000	10,417,000	9,797,000	8,707,000	6,225,000
Total Assets	22,936,000	24,080,000	28,827,000	27,934,000	26,689,000	24,847,000	22,986,000	11,439,000
Current Liabilities	2,462,000	2,775,000	4,637,000	4,578,000	4,124,000	3,502,000	3,139,000	1,613,000
Long-Term Obligations	3,885,000	3,890,000	3,913,000	3,882,000	3,837,000	3,845,000	3,554,000	1,785,000
Total Liabilities	7,617,000	7,782,000	10,202,000	10,221,000	9,620,000	9,101,000	8,886,000	4,155,000
Stockholders' Equity	15,319,000	16,298,000	18,625,000	17,713,000	17,069,000	15,746,000	14,100,000	7,284,000
Shares Outstanding	437,913	437,000	434,000	438,000	441,000	437,000	432,000	312,000
Statistical Record								
Return on Assets %	N.M.	N.M.	6.06	4.01	5.07	7.27	4.72	3.61
Return on Equity %	N.M.	N.M.	9.46	6.30	7.97	11.65	7.59	5.98
EBITDA Margin %	N.M.	N.M.	18.59	15.78	16.94	19.07	17.29	14.97
Net Margin %	N.M.	N.M.	7.00	4.90	6.14	8.77	5.63	4.36
Asset Turnover	0.55	0.60	0.87	0.82	0.83	0.83	0.84	0.83
Current Ratio	3.56	3.34	2.60	2.47	2.53	2.80	2.77	3.86
Debt to Equity	0.25	0.24	0.21	0.22	0.22	0.24	0.25	0.25
Price Range	69.13-38.88	69.13-43.36	75.35-50.02	58.66-40.85	52.40-38.13	79.94-44.47	57.17-35.87	47.67-26.58
P/E Ratio	...	...	19.22-12.76	23.75-16.54	17.64-12.84	20.14-11.20	27.75-17.41	35.05-19.54
Average Yield %	1.26	...	1.17	1.00	1.24	1.36	0.94	1.30	1.61

Address: 2929 Allen Parkway, Suite 2100, Houston, TX 77019-2118 **Telephone:** 713-439-8600 **Fax:** 713-439-8699	**Web Site:** www.bakerhughes.com **Officers:** Martin S. Craighead - Chairman, President, Chief Executive Officer Kimberly A. Ross - Senior Vice President, Chief Financial Officer	**Auditors:** Deloitte & Touche LLP **Investor Contact:** 713-439-8039 **Transfer Agents:** Computershare Shareowner Services, LLC, Jersey City, NJ

BALL CORP

Exchange	Symbol	Price	52Wk Range	Yield	P/E
NYS	BLL	$72.30 (5/31/2016)	75.84-60.50	0.72	76.91

*7 Year Price Score 126.97 *NYSE Composite Index=100 *12 Month Price Score 104.06

Interim Earnings (Per Share)

Qtr.	Mar	Jun	Sep	Dec
2013	0.47	0.63	0.70	0.85
2014	0.65	1.07	1.04	0.54
2015	0.15	1.13	0.32	0.39
2016	(0.90)	...	...	...

Interim Dividends (Per Share)

Amt	Decl	Ex	Rec	Pay
0.13Q	07/29/2015	08/28/2015	09/01/2015	09/15/2015
0.13Q	10/28/2015	11/27/2015	12/01/2015	12/15/2015
0.13Q	01/27/2016	02/26/2016	03/01/2016	03/15/2016
0.13Q	04/27/2016	05/27/2016	06/01/2016	06/15/2016

Indicated Div: $0.52

Valuation Analysis

Forecast EPS	$3.61	No of Institutions
	(05/17/2016)	614
Market Cap	$10.2 Billion	Shares
Book Value	$1.1 Billion	134,862,880
Price/Book	9.58	% Held
Price/Sales	1.31	72.59

Institutional Holding

Business Summary: Metal Products (MIC: 8.2.3 SIC: 3411 NAIC: 332431)

Ball is a supplier of metal packaging to the beverage, food, personal care and household products industries. Co. also provides aerospace and other technologies and services to governmental and commercial customers. Co.'s main product lines are aluminum and steel beverage containers. Co. also produces steel food, aerosol, paint, general line and decorative containers, and extruded aluminum aerosol and beverage containers and aluminum slugs. Co. has four reportable segments: metal beverage packaging, Americas and Asia; metal beverage packaging, Europe; metal food and household products packaging; and aerospace and technologies.

Recent Developments: For the quarter ended Mar 31 2016, net loss amounted to US$127.0 million versus net income of US$27.5 million in the year-earlier quarter. Revenues were US$1.76 billion, down 8.7% from US$1.92 billion the year before. Operating loss was US$110.0 million versus an income of US$125.9 million in the prior-year quarter. Direct operating expenses declined 9.3% to US$1.42 billion from US$1.56 billion in the comparable period the year before. Indirect operating expenses increased 90.4% to US$450.0 million from US$236.3 million in the equivalent prior-year period.

Prospects: Our evaluation of Ball Corp. as of June 19, 2016 is the result of our systematic analysis on three basic characteristics: earnings strength, relative valuation, and recent stock price movement. The company has produced a positive trend in earnings per share over the past 5 quarters and while recent estimates for the company have remained steady, BLL has posted results that fell short of analysts expectations. Based on operating earnings yield, the company is about fairly valued when compared to all of the companies in our coverage universe. Share price changes over the past year indicates that BLL will perform well over the near term.

Financial Data

(US$ in Thousands)	3 Mos	12/31/2015	12/31/2014	12/31/2013	12/31/2012	12/31/2011	12/31/2010	12/31/2009
Earnings Per Share	0.94	1.99	3.30	2.73	2.55	2.63	2.55	2.04
Cash Flow Per Share	5.65	7.33	7.31	5.75	5.50	5.74	2.85	2.98
Dividends Per Share	0.520	0.520	0.520	0.520	0.400	0.280	0.200	0.200
Dividend Payout %	55.32	26.13	15.76	19.05	15.69	10.65	7.84	9.80
Income Statement								
Total Revenue	1,756,000	7,997,000	8,570,000	8,468,100	8,735,700	8,630,900	7,630,000	7,345,300
EBITDA	(45,000)	852,500	1,078,100	1,056,700	1,038,800	1,116,500	1,016,800	922,400
Depn & Amortn	65,000	247,300	239,500	261,300	248,300	279,600	252,200	267,800
Income Before Taxes	(209,000)	345,500	645,600	583,600	595,600	659,800	606,400	537,400
Income Taxes	(83,000)	47,000	149,900	149,600	165,000	201,300	175,800	162,800
Net Income	(127,000)	280,900	470,000	406,800	403,500	444,000	468,000	387,900
Average Shares	141,793	140,984	142,430	149,223	158,084	168,590	183,538	189,978
Balance Sheet								
Current Assets	2,323,000	2,184,000	2,313,500	2,465,700	2,339,400	2,321,900	2,305,700	1,923,300
Total Assets	10,059,000	9,777,000	7,571,000	7,819,800	7,507,100	7,284,600	6,927,700	6,488,300
Current Liabilities	2,232,000	2,141,600	2,006,800	1,927,400	1,685,800	1,856,100	1,383,300	1,428,600
Long-Term Obligations	5,408,000	5,054,200	2,993,800	3,182,500	3,085,300	2,696,700	2,701,600	2,283,900
Total Liabilities	8,991,000	8,525,700	6,537,900	6,619,900	6,392,500	6,065,500	5,409,700	4,907,000
Stockholders' Equity	1,068,000	1,251,300	1,033,100	1,199,900	1,114,600	1,219,100	1,518,000	1,581,300
Shares Outstanding	141,580	142,289	136,966	142,118	149,729	160,315	172,158	188,041
Statistical Record								
Return on Assets %	1.50	3.24	6.11	5.31	5.44	6.25	6.98	6.03
Return on Equity %	13.26	24.59	42.10	35.15	34.49	32.44	30.20	29.09
EBITDA Margin %	N.M.	10.66	12.58	12.48	11.89	12.94	13.33	12.56
Net Margin %	N.M.	3.51	5.48	4.80	4.62	5.14	6.13	5.28
Asset Turnover	0.88	0.92	1.11	1.10	1.18	1.21	1.14	1.14
Current Ratio	1.04	1.02	1.15	1.28	1.39	1.25	1.67	1.35
Debt to Equity	5.06	4.04	2.90	2.65	2.77	2.21	1.78	1.44
Price Range	74.91-60.50	77.16-60.50	70.15-48.27	51.79-41.54	45.46-36.25	40.36-30.22	34.83-24.13	26.13-18.45
P/E Ratio	79.69-64.36	38.77-30.40	21.26-14.63	18.97-15.22	17.83-14.22	15.35-11.49	13.66-9.46	12.81-9.04
Average Yield %	0.75	0.75	0.84	0.86	1.13	0.96	0.78	0.90

Address: 10 Longs Peak Drive, P.O. Box 5000, Broomfield, CO 80021-2510 **Telephone:** 303-469-3131	**Web Site:** www.ball.com **Officers:** John A. Hayes - Chairman, President, Chief Executive Officer Charles E. Baker - Vice President, General Counsel, Assistant Secretary, Corporate Secretary	**Auditors:** PricewaterhouseCoopers LLP **Investor Contact:** 303-460-3537 **Transfer Agents:** Computershare, Providence, RI

BANCORPSOUTH INC.

Exchange	Symbol	Price	52Wk Range	Yield	P/E
NYS	BXS	$23.89 (5/31/2016)	26.93-18.96	1.67	19.27

*7 Year Price Score 106.83 *NYSE Composite Index=100 *12 Month Price Score 94.62

Interim Earnings (Per Share)

Qtr.	Mar	Jun	Sep	Dec
2013	0.22	0.22	0.26	0.29
2014	0.30	0.32	0.30	0.29
2015	0.33	0.41	0.36	0.23
2016	0.24	...	...	...

Interim Dividends (Per Share)

Amt	Decl	Ex	Rec	Pay
0.10Q	07/22/2015	09/11/2015	09/15/2015	10/01/2015
0.10Q	10/28/2015	12/11/2015	12/15/2015	01/04/2016
0.10Q	01/27/2016	03/11/2016	03/15/2016	04/01/2016
0.10Q	04/27/2016	06/13/2016	06/15/2016	07/01/2016

Indicated Div: $0.40 (Div. Reinv. Plan)

Valuation Analysis

		Institutional Holding	
Forecast EPS	$1.54	No of Institutions	
	(05/14/2016)	233	
Market Cap	$2.3 Billion	Shares	
Book Value	$1.7 Billion	66,104,336	
Price/Book	1.34	% Held	
Price/Sales	3.05	65.90	

Business Summary: Banking (MIC: 5.1.1 SIC: 6022 NAIC: 522110)

BancorpSouth is a financial holding company. Through its subsidiary, BancorpSouth Bank, Co. provides financial services to individuals and small-to-medium size businesses. Co. has three segments: Community Banking, which provides deposit products, commercial loans and consumer loans; Insurance Agencies, which serves as agents in the sale of commercial lines of insurance and lines of property and casualty, life, health and employee benefits products and services; and General Corporate and Other, which includes mortgage lending, trust services, credit card activities, investment services and others. At Dec 31 2015, Co. had total assets of $13.80 billion and total deposits of $11.33 billion.

Recent Developments: For the quarter ended Mar 31 2016, net income decreased 30.1% to US$22.5 million from US$32.3 million in the year-earlier quarter. Net interest income increased 4.8% to US$111.2 million from US$106.1 million in the year-earlier quarter. Provision for loan losses was US$1.0 million versus a credit for loan losses of US$5.0 million in the prior-year quarter. Non-interest income fell 10.6% to US$65.5 million from US$73.3 million, while non-interest expense advanced 3.9% to US$142.3 million.

Prospects: Our evaluation of BancorpSouth Inc. as of June 19, 2016 is the result of our systematic analysis on three basic characteristics: earnings strength, relative valuation, and recent stock price movement. The company has managed to produce a neutral trend in earnings per share over the past 5 quarters and while recent estimates for the company have remained steady, BXS has posted better than expected results. Based on operating earnings yield, the company is undervalued when compared to all of the companies in our coverage universe. Share price changes over the past year indicates that BXS will perform in line with the market over the near term.

Financial Data

(US$ in Thousands)	3 Mos	12/31/2015	12/31/2014	12/31/2013	12/31/2012	12/31/2011	12/31/2010	12/31/2009
Earnings Per Share	1.24	1.33	1.21	0.99	0.90	0.45	0.27	0.99
Cash Flow Per Share	1.89	1.39	1.48	2.14	1.42	3.07	2.69	3.36
Tang Book Value Per Share	14.49	14.27	13.40	12.60	12.43	11.88	11.41	12.06
Dividends Per Share	0.375	0.350	0.250	0.120	0.040	0.140	0.880	0.880
Dividend Payout %	30.24	26.32	20.66	12.12	4.44	31.11	325.93	88.89
Income Statement								
Interest Income	117,972	464,378	450,257	449,507	486,424	537,853	582,762	615,414
Interest Expense	6,813	28,696	33,595	50,558	71,833	102,940	141,620	170,515
Net Interest Income	111,159	435,682	416,662	398,949	414,591	434,913	441,142	444,899
Provision for Losses	1,000	(13,000)	...	7,500	28,000	130,081	204,016	117,324
Non-Interest Income	65,515	277,968	269,146	275,066	280,149	270,845	264,144	275,276
Non-Interest Expense	142,300	539,911	518,406	534,849	549,193	533,633	487,033	490,017
Income Before Taxes	33,374	186,739	167,402	131,666	117,547	42,044	14,237	112,834
Income Taxes	10,825	59,248	50,652	37,551	33,252	4,475	(8,705)	30,105
Net Income	22,549	127,491	116,750	94,115	84,295	37,569	22,942	82,729
Average Shares	94,594	96,124	96,302	95,332	93,864	83,509	83,515	83,430
Balance Sheet								
Net Loans & Leases	10,468,237	10,404,227	9,711,508	8,874,372	8,601,661	8,758,651	9,229,891	9,679,436
Total Assets	13,926,398	13,798,662	13,326,369	13,029,733	13,397,198	12,995,851	13,615,010	13,167,867
Total Deposits	11,486,697	11,331,161	10,972,339	10,773,836	11,088,146	10,955,189	11,490,021	10,677,702
Total Liabilities	12,246,605	12,143,218	11,720,310	11,516,603	11,948,146	11,732,939	12,392,766	11,891,571
Stockholders' Equity	1,679,793	1,655,444	1,606,059	1,513,130	1,449,052	1,262,912	1,222,244	1,276,296
Shares Outstanding	94,438	94,162	96,254	95,231	94,437	83,483	83,481	83,450
Statistical Record								
Return on Assets %	0.85	0.94	0.89	0.71	0.64	0.28	0.17	0.62
Return on Equity %	7.08	7.82	7.49	6.35	6.20	3.02	1.84	6.57
Net Interest Margin %	94.22	93.82	92.54	88.75	85.23	80.86	75.70	72.29
Efficiency Ratio %	77.55	72.73	72.06	73.82	71.64	65.99	57.51	55.02
Loans to Deposits	0.91	0.92	0.89	0.82	0.78	0.80	0.80	0.91
Price Range	26.93-18.96	26.93-19.76	25.90-19.62	25.45-14.28	15.57-10.89	16.67-8.34	24.49-12.56	25.13-16.55
P/E Ratio	21.72-15.29	20.25-14.86	21.40-16.21	25.71-14.42	17.30-12.10	37.04-18.53	90.70-46.52	25.38-16.72
Average Yield %	1.57	1.45	1.09	0.65	0.29	1.12	4.97	4.01

Address: One Mississippi Plaza, 201 South Spring Street, Tupelo, MS 38804
Telephone: 662-680-2000

Web Site: www.bancorpsouth.com
Officers: James D. Rollins - Chairman, Chief Executive Officer Chris A. Bagley - President, Chief Operating Officer

Auditors: KPMG LLP
Investor Contact: 662-680-2000
Transfer Agents: Computershare, Canton, MA

BANK OF AMERICA CORP.

Exchange	Symbol	Price	52Wk Range	Yield	P/E
NYS	BAC	$14.79 (5/31/2016)	18.45-11.16	1.35	11.83

*7 Year Price Score 98.91   *NYSE Composite Index=100   *12 Month Price Score 89.89

Interim Earnings (Per Share)

Qtr.	Mar	Jun	Sep	Dec
2013	0.10	0.32	0.20	0.28
2014	(0.05)	0.19	(0.04)	0.26
2015	0.27	0.45	0.37	0.22
2016	0.21			

Interim Dividends (Per Share)

Amt	Decl	Ex	Rec	Pay
0.05Q	07/23/2015	09/02/2015	09/04/2015	09/25/2015
0.05Q	10/22/2015	12/02/2015	12/04/2015	12/24/2015
0.05Q	01/21/2016	03/02/2016	03/04/2016	03/25/2016
0.05Q	04/27/2016	06/01/2016	06/03/2016	06/24/2016

Indicated Div: $0.20 (Div. Reinv. Plan)

Valuation Analysis

Forecast EPS	$1.31
	(05/20/2016)
Market Cap	$152.5 Billion
Book Value	$262.8 Billion
Price/Book	0.58
Price/Sales	1.67

Institutional Holding

No of Institutions	2201
Shares	6,728,424,960
% Held	60.51

Business Summary: Banking (MIC: 5.1.1 SIC: 6021 NAIC: 522110)

Bank of America is a bank and financial holding company. Through its banking and various nonbanking subsidiaries throughout the U.S. and in international markets, Co. serves individual consumers, small- and middle-market businesses, institutional investors, corporations and governments with a range of banking, investing, asset management and other financial and risk management products and services. Co. provides its services and products through five segments: Consumer Banking, Global Wealth & Investment Management, Global Banking, Global Markets and Legacy Assets & Servicing. As of Dec 31 2015, Co. had total assets of $2.14 trillion and total deposits of $1.20 trillion.

Recent Developments: For the quarter ended Mar 31 2016, net income decreased 13.5% to US$2.68 billion from US$3.10 billion in the year-earlier quarter. Net interest income decreased 2.6% to US$9.17 billion from US$9.41 billion in the year-earlier quarter. Provision for loan losses was US$997.0 million versus US$765.0 million in the prior-year quarter, an increase of 30.3%. Non-interest income fell 10.1% to US$10.34 billion from US$11.50 billion, while non-interest expense declined 6.4% to US$14.82 billion.

Prospects: Our evaluation of Bank of America Corp. as of June 19, 2016 is the result of our systematic analysis on three basic characteristics: earnings strength, relative valuation, and recent stock price movement. The company has generated a negative trend in earnings per share over the past 5 quarters. However, while recent estimates for the company have been mixed, BAC has posted better than expected results. Based on operating earnings yield, the company is undervalued when compared to all of the companies in our coverage universe. Share price changes over the past year indicates that BAC will perform in line with the market over the near term.

Financial Data
(US$ in Millions)

	3 Mos	12/31/2015	12/31/2014	12/31/2013	12/31/2012	12/31/2011	12/31/2010	12/31/2009
Earnings Per Share	1.25	1.31	0.36	0.90	0.25	0.01	(0.37)	(0.29)
Cash Flow Per Share	4.18	2.65	2.54	8.65	(1.29)	6.36	8.44	16.79
Tang Book Value Per Share	15.75	15.16	13.91	13.11	12.59	11.98	11.18	8.80
Dividends Per Share	0.200	0.200	0.120	0.040	0.040	0.040	0.040	0.040
Dividend Payout %	16.00	15.27	33.33	4.44	16.00	400.00	...	...
Income Statement								
Interest Income	11,695	49,800	50,886	55,020	57,400	66,236	75,497	77,916
Interest Expense	2,524	10,549	10,934	12,755	16,744	21,620	23,974	30,807
Net Interest Income	9,171	39,251	39,952	42,265	40,656	44,616	51,523	47,109
Provision for Losses	997	3,161	2,275	3,556	8,169	13,410	28,435	48,570
Non-Interest Income	10,341	43,256	44,295	46,677	42,678	48,838	58,697	72,534
Non-Interest Expense	14,816	57,192	75,117	69,214	72,093	80,274	83,108	66,713
Income Before Taxes	3,699	22,154	6,855	16,172	3,072	(230)	(1,323)	4,360
Income Taxes	1,019	6,266	2,022	4,741	(1,116)	(1,676)	915	(1,916)
Net Income	2,680	15,888	4,833	11,431	4,188	1,446	(2,238)	6,276
Average Shares	11,101	11,215	10,584	11,492	10,841	10,254	9,790	7,729
Balance Sheet								
Net Loans & Leases	895,236	898,220	879,808	922,167	903,053	906,179	933,613	906,802
Total Assets	2,185,498	2,144,316	2,104,534	2,102,273	2,209,974	2,129,046	2,264,909	2,223,299
Total Deposits	1,217,261	1,197,259	1,118,936	1,119,271	1,105,261	1,033,041	1,010,430	991,611
Total Liabilities	1,922,722	1,888,111	1,861,063	1,869,588	1,973,018	1,898,945	2,036,661	1,991,855
Stockholders' Equity	262,776	256,205	243,471	232,685	236,956	230,101	228,248	231,444
Shares Outstanding	10,312	10,380	10,516	10,591	10,779	10,536	10,085	8,650
Statistical Record								
Return on Assets %	0.70	0.75	0.23	0.53	0.19	0.07	N.M.	0.31
Return on Equity %	5.93	6.36	2.03	4.87	1.79	0.63	N.M.	3.07
Net Interest Margin %	78.42	78.82	78.51	76.82	70.83	67.36	68.25	60.46
Efficiency Ratio %	67.24	61.46	78.92	68.06	72.04	69.76	61.93	44.34
Loans to Deposits	0.74	0.75	0.79	0.82	0.82	0.88	0.92	0.91
Price Range	18.45-11.16	18.45-15.15	18.13-14.51	15.88-11.03	11.61-5.80	15.25-4.99	19.48-10.95	18.59-3.14
P/E Ratio	14.76-8.93	14.08-11.56	50.36-40.31	17.64-12.26	46.44-23.20	N.M.	...	...
Average Yield %	1.25	1.21	0.73	0.30	0.47	0.40	0.27	0.32

Address: Bank of America Corporate Center, 100 N. Tryon Street, Charlotte, NC 28255 Telephone: 704-386-5681	Web Site: www.bankofamerica.com Officers: Brian T. Moynihan - Chairman, President, Chief Executive Officer, Division Officer Gary G. Lynch - Vice-Chairman, Global General Counsel, Head	Auditors: PricewaterhouseCoopers LLP Investor Contact: 800-521-3984 Transfer Agents: Computershare Trust Company, N.A., Providence, RI

BANK OF HAWAII CORP

Exchange	Symbol	Price	52Wk Range	Yield	P/E
NYS	BOH	$71.85 (5/31/2016)	71.85-55.26	2.67	18.47

*7 Year Price Score 107.55 *NYSE Composite Index=100 *12 Month Price Score 104.18

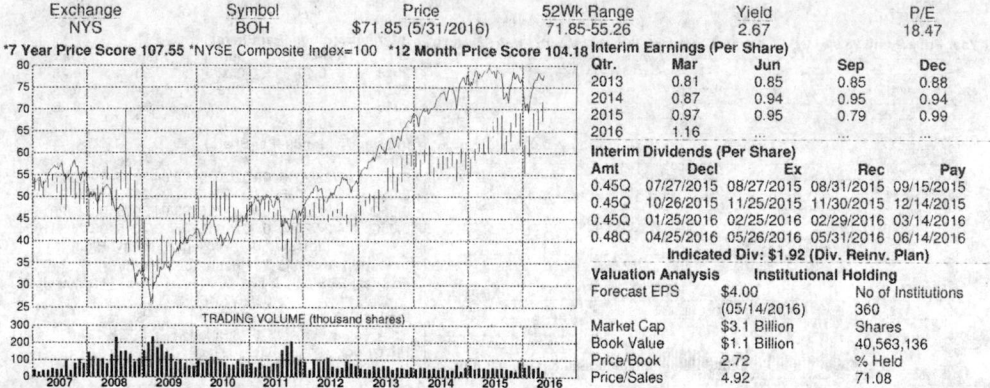

Interim Earnings (Per Share)

Qtr.	Mar	Jun	Sep	Dec
2013	0.81	0.85	0.85	0.88
2014	0.87	0.94	0.95	0.94
2015	0.97	0.95	0.79	0.99
2016	1.16			

Interim Dividends (Per Share)

Amt	Decl	Ex	Rec	Pay
0.45Q	07/27/2015	08/27/2015	08/31/2015	09/15/2015
0.45Q	10/26/2015	11/25/2015	11/30/2015	12/14/2015
0.45Q	01/25/2016	02/29/2016	02/29/2016	03/14/2016
0.48Q	04/25/2016	05/26/2016	05/31/2016	06/14/2016

Indicated Div: $1.92 (Div. Reinv. Plan)

Valuation Analysis

		Institutional Holding	
Forecast EPS	$4.00 (05/14/2016)	No of Institutions	360
Market Cap	$3.1 Billion	Shares	40,563,136
Book Value	$1.1 Billion	% Held	71.08
Price/Book	2.72		
Price/Sales	4.92		

Business Summary: Banking (MIC: 5.1.1 SIC: 6022 NAIC: 522110)

Bank of Hawaii is a bank holding company. Through its subsidiary, Bank of Hawaii, Co. provides a range of financial products and services primarily to customers in Hawaii, Guam, and other Pacific Islands. Co.'s segments include: Retail Banking, which provides loan and lease, deposit, and retail insurance products; Commercial Banking, which provides corporate banking and commercial real estate loans, among others; Investment Services, which includes trust services and investment management, among others; and Treasury and Other, which consists of corporate asset and liability management activities. As of Dec 31 2015, Co. had total assets of $15.46 billion and total deposits of $13.25 billion.

Recent Developments: For the quarter ended Mar 31 2016, net income increased 18.3% to US$50.2 million from US$42.4 million in the year-earlier quarter. Net interest income increased 6.5% to US$103.0 million from US$96.8 million in the year-earlier quarter. Credit for loan losses was US$2.0 million versus a provision for loan losses of nil in the prior-year quarter. Non-interest income rose 7.5% to US$56.2 million from US$52.3 million, while non-interest expense advanced 0.5% to US$87.4 million.

Prospects: Our evaluation of Bank of Hawaii Corp. as of June 19, 2016 is the result of our systematic analysis on three basic characteristics: earnings strength, relative valuation, and recent stock price movement. The company has managed to produce a neutral trend in earnings per share over the past 5 quarters and while recent estimates for the company have remained steady, BOH has posted better than expected results. Based on operating earnings yield, the company is undervalued when compared to all of the companies in our coverage universe. Share price changes over the past year indicates that BOH will perform well over the near term.

Financial Data

(US$ in Thousands)	3 Mos	12/31/2015	12/31/2014	12/31/2013	12/31/2012	12/31/2011	12/31/2010	12/31/2009
Earnings Per Share	3.89	3.70	3.69	3.38	3.67	3.39	3.80	3.00
Cash Flow Per Share	5.53	5.41	4.77	5.45	4.92	4.88	4.17	6.29
Tang Book Value Per Share	25.18	24.53	22.84	21.41	21.56	20.61	19.84	17.46
Dividends Per Share	1.800	1.800	1.800	1.800	1.800	1.800	1.800	1.800
Dividend Payout %	46.27	48.65	48.78	53.25	49.05	53.10	47.37	60.00
Income Statement								
Interest Income	113,069	432,110	417,633	398,505	420,489	439,693	465,251	497,794
Interest Expense	10,045	38,023	37,977	39,598	43,218	49,485	58,771	85,460
Net Interest Income	103,024	394,087	379,656	358,907	377,271	390,208	406,480	412,334
Provision for Losses	(2,000)	1,000	(4,864)	...	979	12,690	55,287	107,878
Non-Interest Income	56,207	186,219	180,017	186,223	200,286	197,655	255,258	267,808
Non-Interest Expense	87,386	348,104	326,899	330,969	334,288	348,193	347,579	350,024
Income Before Taxes	73,845	231,202	237,638	214,161	242,290	226,980	260,215	222,240
Income Taxes	23,635	70,498	74,596	63,659	76,214	66,937	76,273	78,207
Net Income	50,210	160,704	163,042	150,502	166,076	160,043	183,942	144,033
Average Shares	43,126	43,454	44,125	44,572	45,249	47,224	48,355	48,009
Balance Sheet								
Net Loans & Leases	7,977,787	7,780,913	6,794,037	5,986,368	5,747,038	5,418,655	5,205,998	5,632,671
Total Assets	15,654,695	15,455,016	14,787,208	14,084,280	13,728,372	13,846,391	13,126,787	12,414,827
Total Deposits	13,488,892	13,251,103	12,633,089	11,914,656	11,529,482	10,592,623	9,888,995	9,409,676
Total Liabilities	14,515,942	14,338,756	13,732,122	13,072,304	12,706,707	12,843,724	12,115,654	11,518,854
Stockholders' Equity	1,138,753	1,116,260	1,055,086	1,011,976	1,021,665	1,002,667	1,011,133	895,973
Shares Outstanding	43,080	43,282	43,724	44,490	44,754	45,947	48,097	48,018
Statistical Record								
Return on Assets %	1.09	1.06	1.13	1.08	1.20	1.19	1.44	1.24
Return on Equity %	15.22	14.80	15.78	14.80	16.36	15.89	19.29	17.08
Net Interest Margin %	91.12	91.20	90.91	90.06	89.72	88.75	87.37	82.83
Efficiency Ratio %	51.62	56.30	54.70	56.60	53.85	54.63	48.24	45.72
Loans to Deposits	0.59	0.59	0.54	0.50	0.50	0.51	0.53	0.60
Price Range	69.22-55.26	69.22-54.53	61.52-53.53	59.67-44.05	49.60-42.04	49.11-35.03	53.53-42.21	47.92-25.70
P/E Ratio	17.79-14.21	18.71-14.74	16.67-14.51	17.65-13.03	13.51-11.46	14.49-10.33	14.09-11.11	15.97-8.57
Average Yield %	2.81	2.85	3.12	3.44	3.90	4.07	3.84	4.65

Address: 130 Merchant Street, Honolulu, HI 96813 **Telephone:** 888-643-3888	**Web Site:** www.boh.com **Officers:** Peter S. Ho - Chairman, President, Chief Executive Officer, Chief Banking Officer Wayne Y. Hamano - Vice-Chairman, Chief Commercial Officer	**Auditors:** Ernst & Young LLP **Investor Contact:** 808-694-8430 **Transfer Agents:** Computershare Investor Services, LLC, Canton, MA

BANK OF NEW YORK MELLON CORP

Exchange	Symbol	Price	52Wk Range	Yield	P/E
NYS	BK	$42.06 (5/31/2016)	45.26-32.74	1.62	15.13

*7 Year Price Score 111.33 *NYSE Composite Index=100 *12 Month Price Score 97.56

Interim Earnings (Per Share)

Qtr.	Mar	Jun	Sep	Dec
2013	(0.23)	0.71	0.82	0.44
2014	0.57	0.48	0.93	0.18
2015	0.67	0.73	0.74	0.58
2016	0.73	...	...	...

Interim Dividends (Per Share)

Amt	Decl	Ex	Rec	Pay
0.17Q	07/21/2015	07/30/2015	08/03/2015	08/13/2015
0.17Q	10/20/2015	11/02/2015	11/04/2015	11/13/2015
0.17Q	01/21/2016	01/29/2016	02/02/2016	02/12/2016
0.17Q	04/21/2016	04/29/2016	05/03/2016	05/13/2016

Indicated Div: $0.68

Valuation Analysis

		Institutional Holding	
Forecast EPS	$3.09 (05/20/2016)	No of Institutions	1208
Market Cap	$45.3 Billion	Shares	953,949,376
Book Value	$38.5 Billion	% Held	79.82
Price/Book	1.18		
Price/Sales	2.93		

Business Summary: Banking (MIC: 5.1.1 SIC: 6022 NAIC: 522110)

Bank of New York Mellon is a bank holding company. Through its subsidiaries, Co. provides financial products and services in domestic and international markets. Co.'s principal segments are: Investment Management, comprised of its affiliated investment management boutiques that deliver a portfolio of investment strategies; and Investment Services, which provides global custody and related services, government clearing, global collateral services, corporate trust and depositary receipt and clearing services, as well as global payment/working capital solutions to global financial institutional clients. As of Dec 31 2015, Co. had total assets of $393.78 billion and deposits of $279.61 billion.

Recent Developments: For the quarter ended Mar 31 2016, net income decreased 0.2% to US$808.0 million from US$810.0 million in the year-earlier quarter. Net interest income increased 5.2% to US$766.0 million from US$728.0 million in the year-earlier quarter. Provision for loan losses was US$10.0 million versus US$2.0 million in the prior-year quarter, an increase of 400.0%. Non-interest income fell 3.3% to US$2.96 billion from US$3.06 billion, while non-interest expense declined 2.6% to US$2.63 billion.

Prospects: Our evaluation of Bank of New York Mellon Corp. as of June 19, 2016 is the result of our systematic analysis on three basic characteristics: earnings strength, relative valuation, and recent stock price movement. The company has managed to produce a neutral trend in earnings per share over the past 5 quarters and while recent estimates for the company have remained steady, BK has posted better than expected results. Based on operating earnings yield, the company is undervalued when compared to all of the companies in our coverage universe. Share price changes over the past year indicates that BK will perform in line with the market over the near term.

Financial Data
(US$ in Thousands)

	3 Mos	12/31/2015	12/31/2014	12/31/2013	12/31/2012	12/31/2011	12/31/2010	12/31/2009
Earnings Per Share	2.78	2.71	2.15	1.74	2.03	2.03	2.05	(1.16)
Cash Flow Per Share	5.54	3.74	3.97	(0.56)	1.38	1.81	3.34	3.21
Tang Book Value Per Share	12.22	11.67	11.22	10.67	9.77	7.75	6.22	5.42
Dividends Per Share	0.680	0.680	0.660	0.580	0.520	0.480	0.360	0.510
Dividend Payout %	24.46	25.09	30.70	33.33	25.62	23.65	17.56	...
Income Statement								
Total Revenue	3,847,000	15,494,000	16,046,000	15,326,000	15,249,000	15,334,000	14,483,000	8,279,000
Income Before Taxes	1,091,000	4,235,000	3,563,000	3,712,000	3,302,000	3,617,000	3,694,000	(2,208,000)
Income Taxes	283,000	1,013,000	912,000	1,520,000	779,000	1,048,000	1,047,000	(1,395,000)
Net Income	817,000	3,158,000	2,567,000	2,111,000	2,445,000	2,569,000	2,581,000	(1,083,000)
Average Shares	1,085,284	1,112,511	1,137,480	1,154,441	1,178,430	1,223,026	1,216,214	1,178,907
Balance Sheet								
Total Assets	372,870,000	393,780,000	385,303,000	374,310,000	358,990,000	325,266,000	247,259,000	212,224,000
Total Liabilities	334,411,000	355,743,000	347,862,000	336,789,000	322,559,000	291,849,000	214,905,000	183,247,000
Stockholders' Equity	38,459,000	38,037,000	37,441,000	37,521,000	36,431,000	33,417,000	32,354,000	28,977,000
Shares Outstanding	1,077,082	1,085,342	1,118,227	1,142,249	1,163,490	1,209,674	1,241,530	1,207,834
Statistical Record								
Return on Assets %	0.83	0.81	0.68	0.58	0.71	0.90	1.12	N.M.
Return on Equity %	8.43	8.37	6.85	5.71	6.98	7.81	8.42	N.M.
Net Margin %	21.24	20.38	16.00	13.77	16.03	16.75	17.82	N.M.
Asset Turnover	0.04	0.04	0.04	0.04	0.04	0.05	0.06	0.04
Price Range	45.26-32.74	45.26-35.66	41.53-30.91	34.94-25.70	26.20-19.51	32.37-17.71	32.54-24.16	32.56-18.02
P/E Ratio	16.28-11.78	16.70-13.16	19.32-14.38	20.08-14.77	12.91-9.61	15.95-8.72	15.87-11.79	...
Average Yield %	1.67	1.65	1.81	1.94	2.30	1.92	1.30	1.87

Address: 225 Liberty Street, New York, NY 10286
Telephone: 212-495-1784

Web Site: www.bnymellon.com
Officers: Gerald L. Hassell - Chairman, President, Chief Executive Officer Steven G. Elliott - Senior Vice Chairman

Auditors: KPMG LLP
Investor Contact: 412-234-4633
Transfer Agents: Computershare Sharcowner Services LLC, Jersey City, NJ

BANKUNITED INC.

Exchange	Symbol	Price	52Wk Range	Yield	P/E
NYS	BKU	$33.10 (5/31/2016)	39.34-29.85	2.54	13.73

*7 Year Price Score N/A   *NYSE Composite Index=100   *12 Month Price Score 95.88

Interim Earnings (Per Share)

Qtr.	Mar	Jun	Sep	Dec
2013	0.47	0.52	0.52	0.50
2014	0.53	0.46	0.51	0.45
2015	0.44	0.43	0.95	0.52
2016	0.51	...	...	...

Interim Dividends (Per Share)

Amt	Decl	Ex	Rec	Pay
0.21Q	06/15/2015	06/29/2015	07/01/2015	07/15/2015
0.21Q	09/16/2015	09/29/2015	10/01/2015	10/15/2015
0.21Q	12/29/2015	01/13/2016	01/15/2016	01/29/2016
0.21Q	03/24/2016	04/13/2016	04/15/2016	04/29/2016

Indicated Div: $0.84

Valuation Analysis

Forecast EPS	$2.16 (05/20/2016)
Market Cap	$3.4 Billion
Book Value	$2.3 Billion
Price/Book	1.52
Price/Sales	3.33

Institutional Holding

No of Institutions	297
Shares	119,596,000
% Held	96.53

Business Summary: Banking (MIC: 5.1.1 SIC: 6035 NAIC: 522190)

BankUnited is a bank holding company. Co.'s primary banking markets are Florida, in particular the Miami metropolitan statistical area, and the Tri-State market of New York, New Jersey and Connecticut. Co.'s primary lending focus is to serve commercial and middle-market businesses. Co. provides a range of lending products including small business loans, commercial real estate loans, equipment loans and leases, term loans, formula-based loans, municipal loans and leases, commercial lines of credit, letters of credit, residential mortgages and consumer loans. As of Dec 31 2014, Co. had total assets of $19.21 billion and total deposits of $13.51 billion.

Recent Developments: For the quarter ended Mar 31 2016, net income increased 18.1% to US$54.9 million from US$46.5 million in the year-earlier quarter. Net interest income increased 19.7% to US$206.8 million from US$172.7 million in the year-earlier quarter. Provision for loan losses was US$3.7 million versus US$8.1 million in the prior-year quarter, a decrease of 54.5%. Non-interest income rose 11.8% to US$23.2 million from US$20.7 million, while non-interest expense advanced 24.5% to US$142.1 million.

Prospects: Our evaluation of BankUnited Inc as of June 19, 2016 is the result of our systematic analysis on three basic characteristics: earnings strength, relative valuation, and recent stock price movement. The company has generated a negative trend in earnings per share over the past 5 quarters. However, while recent estimates for the company have been lowered by analysts, BKU has posted results that fell short of analysts expectations. Based on operating earnings yield, the company is undervalued when compared to all of the companies in our coverage universe. Share price changes over the past year indicates that BKU will perform well over the near term.

Financial Data (US$ in Thousands)	3 Mos	12/31/2015	12/31/2014	12/31/2013	12/31/2012	12/31/2011	12/31/2010	12/31/2009
Earnings Per Share	2.41	2.35	1.95	2.01	2.05	0.62	1.99	1.29
Cash Flow Per Share	2.41	2.13	(0.50)	(0.68)	(3.74)	(2.60)	(4.82)	(3.81)
Tang Book Value Per Share	20.99	20.90	19.52	18.41	18.28	15.01	12.74	11.14
Dividends Per Share	0.630	0.630	1.050	0.630	0.720	0.560	...	...
Dividend Payout %	26.14	26.81	53.85	31.34	35.12	90.32	...	...
Income Statement								
Total Revenue	274,005	983,040	867,909	769,927	810,103	801,314	855,467	588,352
Income Before Taxes	84,223	296,893	293,250	318,002	344,865	192,744	312,540	199,421
Income Taxes	29,349	45,233	89,035	109,066	133,605	129,576	127,805	80,375
Net Income	54,874	251,660	204,215	208,936	211,260	63,168	184,735	119,046
Average Shares	103,553	102,972	100,595	99,751	93,828	95,605	92,950	92,664
Balance Sheet								
Total Assets	24,819,488	23,883,467	19,210,529	15,046,649	12,375,953	11,322,038	10,869,560	11,129,961
Total Liabilities	22,555,236	21,639,569	17,157,995	13,117,951	10,569,273	9,786,758	9,616,052	10,035,701
Stockholders' Equity	2,264,252	2,243,898	2,052,534	1,928,698	1,806,680	1,535,280	1,253,508	1,094,260
Shares Outstanding	104,149	103,626	101,656	101,013	95,006	97,700	92,971	92,767
Statistical Record								
Return on Assets %	1.16	1.17	1.19	1.52	1.78	0.57	1.68	...
Return on Equity %	11.88	11.71	10.26	11.19	12.61	4.53	15.74	...
Net Margin %	20.03	25.60	23.53	27.14	26.08	7.88	21.59	20.23
Asset Turnover	0.05	0.05	0.05	0.06	0.07	0.07	0.08	...
Price Range	39.34-29.85	39.34-26.74	35.38-27.66	33.22-24.44	26.15-22.04	29.72-19.39	...	...
P/E Ratio	16.32-12.39	16.74-11.38	18.14-14.18	16.53-12.16	12.76-10.75	47.94-31.27	...	...
Average Yield %	1.79	1.82	3.30	2.23	3.00	2.23	...	...

Address: 14817 Oak Lane, Miami Lakes, FL 33016
Telephone: 305-569-2000

Web Site: www.bankunited.com
Officers: John Adam Kanas - Chairman, President, Chief Executive Officer Randy R. Melby - Senior Executive Vice President, Chief Risk Officer

Auditors: KPMG LLP
Investor Contact: 305-231-6400
Transfer Agents: Registrar and Transfer Company

BARD (CR) INC

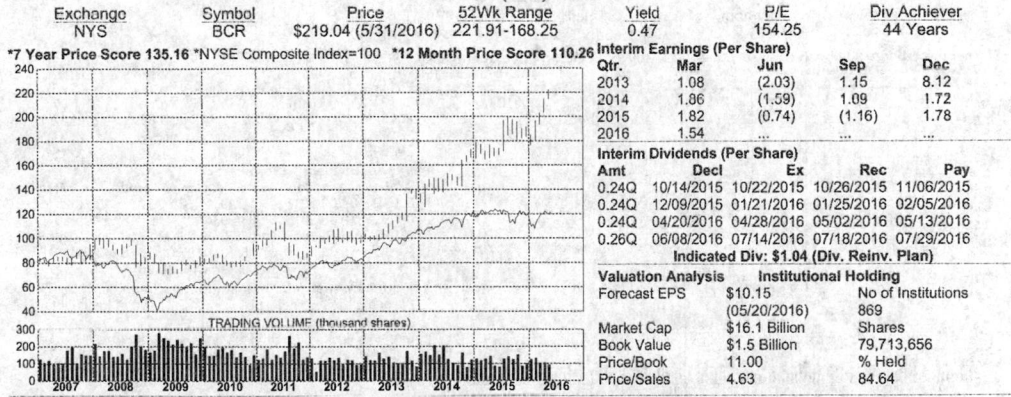

Exchange	Symbol	Price	52Wk Range	Yield	P/E	Div Achiever
NYS	BCR	$219.04 (5/31/2016)	221.91-168.25	0.47	154.25	44 Years

*7 Year Price Score 135.16   *NYSE Composite Index=100   *12 Month Price Score 110.26

Interim Earnings (Per Share)

Qtr.	Mar	Jun	Sep	Dec
2013	1.08	(2.03)	1.15	8.12
2014	1.86	(1.59)	1.09	1.72
2015	1.82	(0.74)	(1.16)	1.78
2016	1.54	...	...	...

Interim Dividends (Per Share)

Amt	Decl	Ex	Rec	Pay
0.24Q	10/14/2015	10/22/2015	10/26/2015	11/06/2015
0.24Q	12/09/2015	01/21/2016	01/25/2016	02/05/2016
0.24Q	04/20/2016	04/28/2016	05/02/2016	05/13/2016
0.26Q	06/08/2016	07/14/2016	07/18/2016	07/29/2016

Indicated Div: $1.04 (Div. Reinv. Plan)

Valuation Analysis

		Institutional Holding	
Forecast EPS	$10.15	No of Institutions	
	(05/20/2016)	869	
Market Cap	$16.1 Billion	Shares	
Book Value	$1.5 Billion	79,713,656	
Price/Book	11.00	% Held	
Price/Sales	4.63	84.64	

Business Summary: Medical Instruments & Equipment (MIC: 4.3.1 SIC: 3841 NAIC: 339112)

Bard (C.R.) designs, develops, manufactures, packages, distributes and sells medical, surgical, diagnostic and patient care devices. Co. has four product groups: vascular, urology, oncology and surgical products. Co.'s vascular products cover a range of minimally invasive devices for the treatment of peripheral vascular disease and heart arrhythmias. Co.'s urology products include drainage, continence, urological and Targeted Temperature Management™ products. Co.'s oncology products cover devices used in the treatment and management of various cancers and other diseases and disorders. Co.'s surgical products include implanted grafts and fixation devices for hernia and soft tissue repairs.

Recent Developments: For the quarter ended Mar 31 2016, net income decreased 16.9% to US$116.2 million from US$139.8 million in the year-earlier quarter. Revenues were US$873.5 million, up 6.6% from US$819.7 million the year before. Direct operating expenses rose 3.0% to US$320.4 million from US$311.2 million in the comparable period the year before. Indirect operating expenses increased 13.8% to US$350.2 million from US$307.6 million in the equivalent prior-year period.

Prospects: Our evaluation of Bard (C.R.) Inc. as of June 19, 2016 is the result of our systematic analysis on three basic characteristics: earnings strength, relative valuation, and recent stock price movement. The company has produced a positive trend in earnings per share over the past 5 quarters and while recent estimates for the company have been mixed, BCR has posted better than expected results. Based on operating earnings yield, the company is about fairly valued when compared to all of the companies in our coverage universe. Share price changes over the past year indicates that BCR will perform well over the near term.

Financial Data

(US$ in Thousands)	3 Mos	12/31/2015	12/31/2014	12/31/2013	12/31/2012	12/31/2011	12/31/2010	12/31/2009
Earnings Per Share	1.42	1.77	3.76	8.39	6.16	3.69	5.32	4.60
Cash Flow Per Share	10.15	10.77	8.73	14.17	7.92	8.41	6.83	6.34
Tang Book Value Per Share	N.M.	N.M.	N.M.	N.M.	1.10	0.17	5.69	13.34
Dividends Per Share	0.940	0.920	0.860	0.820	0.780	0.740	0.700	0.660
Dividend Payout %	66.20	51.98	22.87	9.77	12.66	20.05	13.16	14.35
Income Statement								
Total Revenue	873,500	3,416,000	3,323,600	3,049,500	2,958,100	2,896,400	2,720,200	2,534,900
EBITDA	206,900	455,700	545,400	1,308,200	813,500	586,900	778,500	730,700
Depn & Amortn	53,000	62,300	56,800	51,100	47,000	43,200	51,800	51,000
Income Before Taxes	142,900	349,400	445,800	1,213,400	732,400	510,800	717,700	671,500
Income Taxes	26,700	214,000	151,300	523,600	202,300	182,800	208,100	210,100
Net Income	116,200	135,400	294,500	689,800	530,100	328,000	509,200	460,100
Average Shares	75,200	75,400	77,100	80,700	84,400	87,300	94,600	99,000
Balance Sheet								
Current Assets	2,074,900	2,093,200	2,047,100	2,090,400	1,847,200	1,685,900	1,529,300	1,491,800
Total Assets	5,176,900	4,942,900	5,092,600	5,041,100	4,151,300	3,931,100	3,171,500	2,906,900
Current Liabilities	1,393,600	1,261,800	614,600	586,500	447,600	904,100	397,700	281,700
Long-Term Obligations	1,144,500	1,147,800	1,401,900	1,405,700	1,409,600	908,700	896,900	149,880
Total Liabilities	3,717,000	3,487,600	3,287,700	2,952,900	2,225,600	2,148,900	1,540,000	713,300
Stockholders' Equity	1,459,900	1,455,300	1,804,900	2,088,200	1,925,700	1,782,200	1,631,500	2,193,600
Shares Outstanding	73,318	73,697	74,893	77,436	81,697	84,543	84,973	95,917
Statistical Record								
Return on Assets %	2.18	2.70	5.81	15.01	13.08	9.24	16.75	16.51
Return on Equity %	6.97	8.31	15.13	34.37	28.51	19.22	26.62	22.06
EBITDA Margin %	23.69	13.34	16.41	42.90	27.50	20.26	28.62	28.83
Net Margin %	13.30	3.96	8.86	22.62	17.92	11.32	18.72	18.15
Asset Turnover	0.68	0.68	0.66	0.66	0.73	0.82	0.90	0.91
Current Ratio	1.49	1.66	3.33	3.56	4.13	1.86	3.85	5.30
Debt to Equity	0.78	0.79	0.78	0.67	0.73	0.51	0.55	0.07
Price Range	202.88-165.24	200.53-164.52	172.68-125.42	139.85-97.74	107.83-85.45	113.32-82.39	95.72-76.18	88.41-70.39
P/E Ratio	142.87-116.37	113.29-92.95	45.93-33.36	16.67-11.65	17.50-13.87	30.71-22.33	17.99-14.32	19.22-15.30
Average Yield %	0.51	0.51	0.58	0.73	0.79	0.77	0.85	0.85

Address: 730 Central Avenue, Murray Hill, NJ 07974 Telephone: 908-277-8000	Web Site: www.crbard.com Officers: Timothy M. Ring - Chairman, Chief Executive Officer John H. Weiland - President, Chief Operating Officer	Auditors: KPMG LLP Transfer Agents: Computershare Trust Company, N.A., Canton, MA

BARNES & NOBLE INC

Exchange	Symbol	Price	52Wk Range	Yield	P/E
NYS	BKS	$11.63 (5/31/2016)	18.77-7.33	5.16	N/A

*7 Year Price Score 93.68   *NYSE Composite Index=100   *12 Month Price Score 90.40

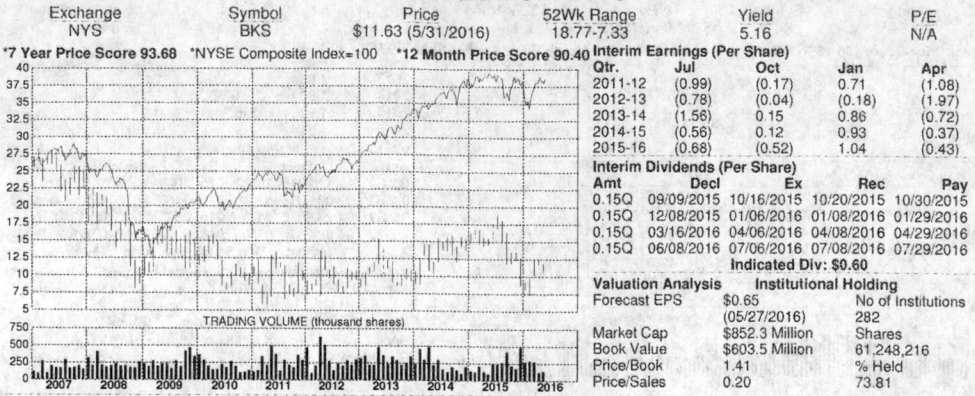

Interim Earnings (Per Share)

Qtr.	Jul	Oct	Jan	Apr
2011-12	(0.99)	(0.17)	0.71	(1.08)
2012-13	(0.78)	(0.04)	(0.18)	(1.97)
2013-14	(1.56)	0.15	0.86	(0.72)
2014-15	(0.56)	0.12	0.93	(0.37)
2015-16	(0.68)	(0.52)	1.04	(0.43)

Interim Dividends (Per Share)

Amt	Decl	Ex	Rec	Pay
0.15Q	09/09/2015	10/16/2015	10/20/2015	10/30/2015
0.15Q	12/08/2015	01/06/2016	01/08/2016	01/29/2016
0.15Q	03/16/2016	04/06/2016	04/08/2016	04/29/2016
0.15Q	06/08/2016	07/06/2016	07/08/2016	07/29/2016
		Indicated Div: $0.60		

Valuation Analysis

		Institutional Holding	
Forecast EPS	$0.65 (05/27/2016)	No of Institutions	282
Market Cap	$852.3 Million	Shares	61,248,216
Book Value	$603.5 Million	% Held	73.81
Price/Book	1.41		
Price/Sales	0.20		

Business Summary: Retail - Specialty (MIC: 2.1.3 SIC: 5942 NAIC: 451211)

Barnes & Noble is a content and commerce company providing customers access to trade books and other content across its multi-channel distribution platform. Co. has two operating segments: B&N Retail, which operates retail bookstores and includes Co.'s eCommerce site and Sterling Publishing Co., Inc., a provider in trade book publishing; and NOOK, which includes Co.'s digital business, providing digital books and magazines for sale online, NOOK®2 reading devices, Co.-branded NOOK® tablets and reading software. As of Apr 30, 2016, Co. operated 640 bookstores in 50 states, maintained an eCommerce site, developed digital reading products and operated a digital bookstore.

Recent Developments: For the year ended Apr 30 2016, income from continuing operations decreased 55.3% to US$14.7 million from US$32.9 million a year earlier. Net loss amounted to US$24.4 million versus net income of US$36.6 million in the prior year. Revenues were US$4.16 billion, down 3.1% from US$4.30 billion the year before. Operating income was US$14.7 million versus US$90.2 million in the prior year, a decrease of 83.8%. Direct operating expenses declined 1.2% to US$2.84 billion from US$2.87 billion in the comparable period the year before. Indirect operating expenses decreased 1.7% to US$1.31 billion from US$1.34 billion in the equivalent prior-year period.

Prospects: Our evaluation of Barnes & Noble Inc. as of June 26, 2016 is the result of our systematic analysis on three basic characteristics: earnings strength, relative valuation, and recent stock price movement. The company has managed to produce a neutral trend in earnings per share over the past 5 quarters. However, while recent estimates for the company have been mixed, BKS has posted results that were in line with analysts expectations. Based on operating earnings yield, the company is overvalued when compared to all of the companies in our coverage universe. Share price changes over the past year indicates that BKS will perform poorly over the near term.

Financial Data

(US$ in Thousands)	04/30/2016	05/02/2015	05/03/2014	04/27/2013	04/28/2012	04/30/2011	05/01/2010	05/02/2009
Earnings Per Share	(0.49)	0.21	(1.12)	(3.02)	(1.41)	(1.31)	0.63	(0.05)
Cash Flow Per Share	2.71	0.92	5.34	2.02	(0.42)	3.53	2.32	(2.15)
Tang Book Value Per Share	1.11	2.94	N.M.	N.M.	N.M.	N.M.	N.M.	10.40
Dividends Per Share	0.600	...	...	...	...	0.750	1.000	1.000
Dividend Payout %	...	...	...	...	...	...	158.73	...
Income Statement								
Total Revenue	4,163,844	6,069,497	6,381,357	6,839,005	7,129,199	6,998,565	5,810,564	1,105,152
EBITDA	149,506	312,635	256,956	12,600	176,745	179,475	287,710	43,182
Depn & Amortn	134,850	179,462	222,764	232,604	238,048	244,734	214,464	46,426
Income Before Taxes	5,886	115,283	4,685	(255,349)	(96,607)	(122,609)	45,009	(3,443)
Income Taxes	(8,814)	78,687	51,953	(97,543)	(27,740)	(48,652)	8,365	(1,374)
Net Income	(24,446)	36,596	(47,268)	(157,806)	(68,867)	(73,920)	36,676	(2,693)
Average Shares	72,542	60,928	58,971	58,247	57,337	56,588	56,153	54,759
Balance Sheet								
Current Assets	1,178,390	1,729,315	1,980,438	2,047,135	1,997,793	1,747,021	1,719,477	1,518,561
Total Assets	2,012,782	3,229,505	3,537,449	3,732,536	3,765,249	3,596,466	3,705,686	2,780,105
Current Liabilities	1,193,871	1,447,259	1,721,645	1,715,470	1,827,280	1,734,677	1,724,408	1,291,696
Long-Term Obligations	47,200	...	...	77,000	324,200	313,100	260,400	...
Total Liabilities	1,409,272	2,040,147	2,878,753	3,018,793	3,017,592	2,776,556	2,803,868	1,869,864
Stockholders' Equity	603,510	1,189,358	658,696	713,743	747,657	819,910	901,818	910,241
Shares Outstanding	73,287	63,274	59,176	58,706	57,654	57,055	55,708	55,077
Statistical Record								
Return on Assets %	N.M.	1.08	N.M.	N.M.	N.M.	N.M.	1.13	N.M.
Return on Equity %	N.M.	3.97	N.M.	N.M.	N.M.	N.M.	4.06	N.M.
EBITDA Margin %	3.59	5.15	4.03	0.18	2.48	2.56	4.95	3.91
Net Margin %	N.M.	0.60	N.M.	N.M.	N.M.	N.M.	0.63	N.M.
Asset Turnover	1.59	1.80	1.73	1.83	1.94	1.92	1.80	0.29
Current Ratio	0.99	1.19	1.15	1.19	1.09	1.01	1.00	1.18
Debt to Equity	0.08	...	...	0.11	0.43	0.38	0.29	...
Price Range	18.77-7.33	16.98-10.26	15.27-8.40	13.59-7.40	13.37-6.54	14.80-5.74	17.54-10.81	21.00-8.02
P/E Ratio	...	80.85-48.88	...	...	...	...	27.84-17.17	...
Average Yield %	4.59	...	...	...	...	...	7.69	7.18	6.93

Address: 122 Fifth Avenue, New York, NY 10011 **Telephone:** 212-633-3300	**Web Site:** www.barnesandnoble.com **Officers:** Leonard Riggio - Chairman Ronald D. Boire - Chief Executive Officer, Division Officer	**Auditors:** Ernst & Young LLP **Investor Contact:** 212-633-3489 **Transfer Agents:** Computershare, Jersey City, NJ	

BAXTER INTERNATIONAL INC.

*7 Year Price Score 97.18   *NYSE Composite Index=100   *12 Month Price Score 112.07

Interim Earnings (Per Share)

Qtr.	Mar	Jun	Sep	Dec
2013	1.00	1.07	0.99	0.60
2014	1.01	0.95	0.86	1.74
2015	0.78	0.60	0.00	0.37
2016	6.12	...	...	...

Interim Dividends (Per Share)

Amt	Decl	Ex	Rec	Pay
0.115Q	07/29/2015	09/02/2015	09/04/2015	10/01/2015
0.115Q	11/10/2015	12/02/2015	12/04/2015	01/04/2016
0.115Q	02/16/2016	03/02/2016	03/04/2016	04/01/2016
0.13Q	05/03/2016	06/01/2016	06/03/2016	07/01/2016

Indicated Div: $0.52

Valuation Analysis · **Institutional Holding**

Forecast EPS	$1.63	No of Institutions	
	(05/20/2016)	1346	
Market Cap	$23.8 Billion	Shares	
Book Value	$9.0 Billion	550,421,952	
Price/Book	2.64	% Held	
Price/Sales	2.09	78.71	

Business Summary: Medical Instruments & Equipment (MIC: 4.3.1 SIC: 3841 NAIC: 339112)

Baxter International, through its subsidiaries, provides a portfolio of renal and hospital products, including home, acute and in-center dialysis; sterile intravenous (IV) solutions; infusion systems and devices; parenteral nutrition; biosurgery products and anesthetics; and pharmacy automation, software and services. These products are used by hospitals, kidney dialysis centers, nursing homes, rehabilitation centers, doctors' offices and by patients at home under physician supervision. As of Dec 31 2015, Co. manufactures products in approximately 25 countries and sells them in approximately 120 countries. Co. operates in two segments: Hospital Products and Renal.

Recent Developments: For the quarter ended Mar 31 2016, income from continuing operations increased to US$3.39 billion from US$134.0 million in the year-earlier quarter. Net income increased 686.0% to US$3.38 billion from US$430.0 million in the year-earlier quarter. Revenues were US$2.38 billion, down 1.2% from US$2.40 billion the year before. Operating income was US$188.0 million versus US$92.0 million in the prior-year quarter, an increase of 104.3%. Direct operating expenses rose 1.9% to US$1.41 billion from US$1.38 billion in the comparable period the year before. Indirect operating expenses decreased 16.2% to US$777.0 million from US$927.0 million in the equivalent prior-year period.

Prospects: Our evaluation of Baxter International Inc. as of June 19, 2016 is the result of our systematic analysis on three basic characteristics: earnings strength, relative valuation, and recent stock price movement. The company has enjoyed a very positive trend in earnings per share over the past 5 quarters and while recent estimates for the company have been mixed, BAX has posted better than expected results. Based on operating earnings yield, the company is about fairly valued when compared to all of the companies in our coverage universe. Share price changes over the past year indicates that BAX will perform very well over the near term.

Financial Data

(US$ in Millions)	3 Mos	12/31/2015	12/31/2014	12/31/2013	12/31/2012	12/31/2011	12/31/2010	12/31/2009
Earnings Per Share	7.09	1.76	4.56	3.66	4.18	3.88	2.39	3.59
Cash Flow Per Share	2.22	3.02	5.93	5.89	5.62	4.95	5.09	4.79
Tang Book Value Per Share	8.95	8.78	4.00	3.62	6.63	6.14	6.98	8.08
Dividends Per Share	0.865	1.270	2.050	1.920	1.570	1.265	1.180	1.070
Dividend Payout %	12.20	72.16	44.96	52.46	37.56	32.60	49.37	29.81
Income Statement								
Total Revenue	2,375	9,968	16,671	15,259	14,190	13,893	12,843	12,562
EBITDA	3,546	1,313	3,589	3,445	3,661	3,537	2,674	3,482
Depn & Amortn	189	759	1,005	823	712	670	685	638
Income Before Taxes	3,329	428	2,439	2,494	2,862	2,813	1,902	2,746
Income Taxes	(58)	35	493	537	563	553	463	519
Net Income	3,380	968	2,497	2,012	2,326	2,224	1,420	2,205
Average Shares	552	549	547	549	556	573	594	614
Balance Sheet								
Current Assets	8,017	11,796	10,351	10,004	9,260	8,650	7,989	8,271
Total Assets	17,350	20,975	25,917	25,869	20,390	19,073	17,489	17,354
Current Liabilities	3,823	5,750	6,042	5,906	4,759	4,857	4,041	4,464
Long-Term Obligations	2,068	3,935	7,606	8,126	5,580	4,749	4,363	3,440
Total Liabilities	8,331	12,129	17,797	17,406	13,452	12,488	10,922	10,163
Stockholders' Equity	9,019	8,846	8,120	8,463	6,938	6,585	6,567	7,191
Shares Outstanding	551	547	542	543	546	560	580	600
Statistical Record								
Return on Assets %	18.56	4.13	9.64	8.70	11.76	12.17	8.15	13.46
Return on Equity %	48.14	11.41	30.12	26.13	34.31	33.82	20.64	32.86
EBITDA Margin %	149.31	13.17	21.53	22.58	25.80	25.46	20.82	27.72
Net Margin %	142.32	9.71	14.98	13.19	16.39	16.01	11.06	17.55
Asset Turnover	0.54	0.43	0.64	0.66	0.72	0.76	0.74	0.77
Current Ratio	2.10	2.05	1.71	1.69	1.95	1.78	1.98	1.85
Debt to Equity	0.23	0.44	0.94	0.96	0.80	0.72	0.66	0.48
Price Range	42.13-32.27	42.13-32.27	41.83-36.12	40.43-34.71	37.38-26.64	33.90-25.89	33.52-21.99	32.87-25.21
P/E Ratio	5.94-4.55	23.94-18.34	9.17-7.92	11.05-9.48	8.94-6.37	8.74-6.67	14.03-9.20	9.16-7.02
Average Yield %	2.31	3.39	5.22	5.10	4.98	4.29	4.35	3.65

Address: One Baxter Parkway, Deerfield, IL 60015
Telephone: 224-948-2000
Fax: 847-948-2964

Web Site: www.baxter.com
Officers: Jose E. Almeida - Chairman, President, Chief Executive Officer Brik V. Eyre - Corporate Vice-President, Division Officer

Auditors: PricewaterhouseCoopers LLP
Transfer Agents: Computershare Trust Company, N.A., Providence, RI

BB&T CORP.

Exchange	Symbol	Price	52Wk Range	Yield	P/E
NYS	BBT	$36.37 (5/31/2016)	41.60-30.28	3.08	14.15

*7 Year Price Score 98.70   ***NYSE Composite Index=100**   ***12 Month Price Score 93.74**

Interim Earnings (Per Share)

Qtr.	Mar	Jun	Sep	Dec
2013	0.29	0.77	0.37	0.75
2014	0.69	0.58	0.71	0.76
2015	0.67	0.62	0.64	0.64
2016	0.67			

Interim Dividends (Per Share)

Amt	Decl	Ex	Rec	Pay
0.27Q	07/21/2015	08/12/2015	08/14/2015	09/01/2015
0.27Q	10/19/2015	11/10/2015	11/13/2015	12/01/2015
0.27Q	01/26/2016	02/10/2016	02/12/2016	03/01/2016
0.28Q	04/26/2016	05/11/2016	05/13/2016	06/01/2016

Indicated Div: $1.12 (Div. Reinv. Plan)

Valuation Analysis   Institutional Holding

Forecast EPS	$2.77 (05/20/2016)	No of Institutions	1039
Market Cap	$28.5 Billion	Shares	526,730,944
Book Value	$28.2 Billion	% Held	63.09
Price/Book	1.01		
Price/Sales	2.69		

Business Summary: Banking (MIC: 5.1.1 SIC: 6021 NAIC: 522110)

BB&T is a financial holding company. Through its subsidiary, Branch Banking and Trust Company, Co. provides insurance premium financing, commercial real estate financing arrangements, loan servicing for third-party investors; direct consumer finance loans to individuals; credit card lending; automobile financing; factoring and equipment financing. Co. also markets a range of other services, including deposits; discount and full service brokerage, annuities and mutual funds; life insurance, property and casualty insurance, health insurance and commercial general liability insurance. At Dec 31 2015, Co. had total assets of $209.95 billion and total deposits of $149.12 billion.

Recent Developments: For the quarter ended Mar 31 2016, net income increased 4.2% to US$570.0 million from US$547.0 million in the year-earlier quarter. Net interest income increased 16.5% to US$1.53 billion from US$1.31 billion in the year-earlier quarter. Provision for loan losses was US$184.0 million versus US$99.0 million in the prior-year quarter, an increase of 85.9%. Non-interest income rose 1.9% to US$1.02 billion from US$997.0 million, while non-interest expense advanced 8.6% to US$1.55 billion.

Prospects: Our evaluation of BB&T Corp. as of June 19, 2016 is the result of our systematic analysis on three basic characteristics: earnings strength, relative valuation, and recent stock price movement. The company has managed to produce a neutral trend in earnings per share over the past 5 quarters and while recent estimates for the company have remained steady, BBT has posted better than expected results. Based on operating earnings yield, the company is undervalued when compared to all of the companies in our coverage universe. Share price changes over the past year indicates that BBT will perform poorly over the near term.

Financial Data

(US$ in Thousands)	3 Mos	12/31/2015	12/31/2014	12/31/2013	12/31/2012	12/31/2011	12/31/2010	12/31/2009
Earnings Per Share	2.57	2.56	2.75	2.19	2.70	1.83	1.16	1.15
Cash Flow Per Share	4.31	3.90	4.54	7.59	5.28	6.55	4.18	(0.78)
Tang Book Value Per Share	19.26	18.70	18.76	16.59	15.63	14.82	13.09	12.56
Dividends Per Share	1.080	1.050	0.950	1.120	0.760	0.640	0.600	1.240
Dividend Payout %	42.02	41.02	34.55	51.14	28.15	34.97	51.72	107.83
Income Statement								
Interest Income	1,721,000	6,327,000	6,142,000	6,507,000	6,917,000	6,885,000	7,115,000	6,884,000
Interest Expense	192,000	735,000	768,000	891,000	1,060,000	1,378,000	1,795,000	2,040,000
Net Interest Income	1,529,000	5,592,000	5,374,000	5,616,000	5,857,000	5,507,000	5,320,000	4,844,000
Provision for Losses	184,000	428,000	251,000	592,000	1,057,000	1,190,000	2,638,000	2,811,000
Non-Interest Income	1,016,000	4,019,000	3,784,000	3,937,000	3,820,000	3,113,000	3,957,000	3,934,000
Non-Interest Expense	1,546,000	6,266,000	5,921,000	5,837,000	5,828,000	5,802,000	5,670,000	4,931,000
Income Before Taxes	816,000	2,917,000	2,986,000	3,124,000	2,792,000	1,628,000	969,000	1,036,000
Income Taxes	246,000	794,000	760,000	1,395,000	764,000	296,000	115,000	159,000
Net Income	570,000	2,123,000	2,226,000	1,729,000	2,028,000	1,332,000	854,000	877,000
Average Shares	790,176	757,765	728,372	714,363	708,877	705,168	701,039	635,619
Balance Sheet								
Net Loans & Leases	135,183,000	135,526,000	119,833,000	115,407,000	116,346,000	108,949,000	104,556,000	103,607,000
Total Assets	212,405,000	209,947,000	186,814,000	183,010,000	183,872,000	174,579,000	157,081,000	165,764,000
Total Deposits	150,500,000	149,124,000	129,040,000	127,475,000	133,075,000	124,939,000	107,213,000	114,965,000
Total Liabilities	184,205,000	182,641,000	162,476,000	160,251,000	162,714,000	157,161,000	140,645,000	149,573,000
Stockholders' Equity	28,200,000	27,306,000	24,338,000	22,759,000	21,158,000	17,418,000	16,436,000	16,191,000
Shares Outstanding	782,379	780,337	720,698	706,620	699,728	697,143	694,381	689,750
Statistical Record								
Return on Assets %	1.07	1.07	1.20	0.94	1.13	0.80	0.53	0.55
Return on Equity %	8.12	8.22	9.45	7.87	10.49	7.87	5.23	5.44
Net Interest Margin %	88.84	88.38	87.50	86.31	84.68	79.99	74.77	70.37
Efficiency Ratio %	56.49	60.56	59.65	55.89	54.28	58.03	51.21	45.58
Loans to Deposits	0.90	0.91	0.93	0.91	0.87	0.87	0.98	0.90
Price Range	41.60-30.28	41.60-34.78	40.77-35.20	37.32-29.11	33.99-25.79	29.17-19.17	35.61-21.87	29.53-13.32
P/E Ratio	16.19-11.78	16.25-13.59	14.83-12.80	17.04-13.29	12.59-9.55	15.94-10.48	30.70-18.85	25.68-11.58
Average Yield %	2.90	2.74	2.50	3.39	2.51	2.56	2.19	5.42

Address: 200 West Second Street, Winston-Salem, NC 27101 **Telephone:** 336-733-2000 **Fax:** 336-671-2399	**Web Site:** www.bbt.com **Officers:** Kelly S. King - Chairman, President, Chief Executive Officer, Chief Operating Officer, President (frmr) Christopher L. Henson - Senior Executive Vice President, Chief Operating Officer	**Auditors:** PricewaterhouseCoopers LLP **Investor Contact:** 336-733-3021 **Transfer Agents:** Computershare Trust Company, N.A., Providence, RI

BECTON, DICKINSON AND CO.

Exchange	Symbol	Price	52Wk Range	Yield	P/E	Div Achiever
NYS	BDX	$166.45 (5/31/2016)	168.57-130.40	1.59	44.39	43 Years

*7 Year Price Score 126.28 *NYSE Composite Index=100 *12 Month Price Score 108.07

TRADING VOLUME (thousand shares)

Interim Earnings (Per Share)

Qtr.	Dec	Mar	Jun	Sep
2012-13	3.13	1.39	1.52	0.45
2013-14	1.37	1.45	1.65	1.52
2014-15	1.20	1.08	0.30	0.83
2015-16	1.06	1.56	...	...

Interim Dividends (Per Share)

Amt	Decl	Ex	Rec	Pay
0.60Q	07/28/2015	09/04/2015	09/09/2015	09/30/2015
0.66Q	11/23/2015	12/08/2015	12/10/2015	12/31/2015
0.66Q	01/25/2016	03/08/2016	03/10/2016	03/31/2016
0.66Q	05/24/2016	06/07/2016	06/09/2016	06/30/2016

Indicated Div: $2.64 (Div. Reinv. Plan)

Valuation Analysis		Institutional Holding	
Forecast EPS	$8.55	No of Institutions	
	(05/20/2016)	1305	
Market Cap	$35.3 Billion	Shares	
Book Value	$7.7 Billion	209,204,896	
Price/Book	4.61	% Held	
Price/Sales	2.89	84.12	

Business Summary: Medical Instruments & Equipment (MIC: 4.3.1 SIC: 3841 NAIC: 339112)

Becton, Dickinson and Company is a medical technology company engaged mainly in the development, manufacture and sale of medical devices, instrument systems and reagents. Co.'s operations consist of two business segments: BD Medical, which produces an array of medical devices that are used in a range of healthcare settings; BD Life Sciences, which provides products for the safe collection and transport of diagnostics specimens, and instruments and reagent systems to detect a range of infectious diseases, healthcare-associated infections and cancers. In addition, BD Life Sciences segment produces research and clinical tools that facilitate the study of cells, and the components of cells.

Recent Developments: For the quarter ended Mar 31 2016, net income increased 56.5% to US$338.0 million from US$216.0 million in the year-earlier quarter. Revenues were US$3.07 billion, up 49.5% from US$2.05 billion the year before. Operating income was US$466.0 million versus US$293.0 million in the prior-year quarter, an increase of 59.0%. Direct operating expenses rose 57.6% to US$1.58 billion from US$1.01 billion in the comparable period the year before. Indirect operating expenses increased 35.2% to US$1.02 billion from US$753.0 million in the equivalent prior-year period.

Prospects: Our evaluation of Becton, Dickinson and Co. as of June 19, 2016 is the result of our systematic analysis on three basic characteristics: earnings strength, relative valuation, and recent stock price movement. The company has managed to produce a neutral trend in earnings per share over the past 5 quarters. However, while recent estimates for the company have been lowered by analysts, BDX has posted better than expected results. Based on operating earnings yield, the company is about fairly valued when compared to all of the companies in our coverage universe. Share price changes over the past year indicates that BDX will perform well over the near term.

Financial Data

(US$ in Thousands)	6 Mos	3 Mos	09/30/2015	09/30/2014	09/30/2013	09/30/2012	09/30/2011	09/30/2010
Earnings Per Share	3.75	3.27	3.35	5.99	6.49	5.59	5.62	5.49
Cash Flow Per Share	10.52	9.01	8.54	9.03	8.80	8.22	7.74	7.08
Tang Book Value Per Share	N.M.	N.M.	N.M.	14.79	14.07	9.65	12.67	16.87
Dividends Per Share	2.520	2.460	2.400	2.180	1.980	1.800	1.640	1.480
Dividend Payout %	67.20	75.23	71.64	36.39	30.51	32.20	29.18	26.96
Income Statement								
Total Revenue	6,054,000	2,986,000	10,282,000	8,446,000	8,054,000	7,708,382	7,828,904	7,372,333
EBITDA	1,398,000	646,000	1,986,000	2,173,000	1,809,000	2,067,671	2,261,162	2,179,407
Depn & Amortn	569,000	289,000	891,000	562,000	546,000	510,938	504,089	502,113
Income Before Taxes	642,000	266,000	739,000	1,522,000	1,165,000	1,472,408	1,716,263	1,661,160
Income Taxes	75,000	37,000	44,000	337,000	236,000	362,880	451,411	484,820
Net Income	567,000	229,000	695,000	1,185,000	1,293,000	1,169,927	1,270,994	1,317,610
Average Shares	216,538	216,294	207,509	197,709	199,193	209,181	226,280	240,136
Balance Sheet								
Current Assets	6,612,000	5,641,000	6,045,000	6,131,000	5,873,000	5,322,071	4,668,331	4,505,250
Total Assets	26,236,000	26,046,000	26,820,000	12,447,000	12,149,000	11,360,909	10,430,428	9,650,694
Current Liabilities	4,380,000	4,529,000	4,386,000	2,235,000	2,130,000	1,978,055	1,823,228	1,671,673
Long-Term Obligations	10,864,000	10,858,000	11,370,000	3,769,000	3,763,000	3,761,112	2,484,665	1,495,357
Total Liabilities	18,571,000	18,823,000	19,656,000	7,396,000	7,106,000	7,225,020	5,602,253	4,216,114
Stockholders' Equity	7,666,000	7,223,000	7,164,000	5,053,000	5,043,000	4,135,889	4,828,175	5,434,580
Shares Outstanding	212,202	211,816	210,695	191,892	193,999	196,911	214,818	229,816
Statistical Record								
Return on Assets %	2.97	3.09	3.54	9.64	11.00	10.71	12.66	13.90
Return on Equity %	10.93	11.20	11.38	23.47	28.17	26.03	24.77	24.91
EBITDA Margin %	23.09	21.63	19.32	25.73	22.46	26.82	28.88	29.56
Net Margin %	9.37	7.67	6.76	14.03	16.05	15.18	16.23	17.87
Asset Turnover	0.45	0.50	0.52	0.69	0.69	0.71	0.78	0.78
Current Ratio	1.51	1.25	1.38	2.74	2.76	2.69	2.56	2.70
Debt to Equity	1.42	1.50	1.59	0.75	0.75	0.91	0.51	0.28
Price Range	156.53-130.40	156.53-130.40	153.86-113.60	120.33-98.33	104.50-74.63	79.91-70.65	89.74-73.25	80.14-66.60
P/E Ratio	41.74-34.77	47.87-39.88	45.93-33.91	20.09-16.42	16.10-11.50	14.30-12.64	15.97-13.03	14.60-12.13
Average Yield %	1.75	1.71	1.72	1.93	2.18	2.39	2.01	2.01

Address: 1 Becton Drive, Franklin Lakes, NJ 07417-1880
Telephone: 201-847-6800

Web Site: www.bd.com
Officers: Vincent A. Forlenza - Chairman, President, Chief Executive Officer, Chief Operating Officer Gary M. Cohen - Executive Vice President

Auditors: Ernst & Young LLP
Investor Contact: 180-028-46845
Transfer Agents: Computershare Trust Company, N.A., Canton, MA

BELDEN INC

Exchange	Symbol	Price	52Wk Range	Yield	P/E
NYS	BDC	$64.67 (5/31/2016)	86.35-37.15	0.31	27.06

*7 Year Price Score 105.15 *NYSE Composite Index=100 ***12 Month Price Score 106.04**

Interim Earnings (Per Share)

Qtr.	Mar	Jun	Sep	Dec
2013	0.49	0.66	0.65	0.51
2014	0.56	0.00	0.77	0.37
2015	(0.46)	0.50	0.34	1.16
2016	0.39	...	...	...

Interim Dividends (Per Share)

Amt	Decl	Ex	Rec	Pay
0.05Q	08/24/2015	09/14/2015	09/16/2015	10/02/2015
0.05Q	12/03/2015	12/14/2015	12/16/2015	01/05/2016
0.05Q	02/25/2016	03/14/2016	03/16/2016	04/05/2016
0.05Q	05/26/2016	06/14/2016	06/16/2016	07/06/2016

Indicated Div: $0.20

Valuation Analysis — **Institutional Holding**

Forecast EPS	$5.32	No of Institutions
	(05/07/2016)	286
Market Cap	$2.7 Billion	Shares
Book Value	$838.0 Million	52,929,320
Price/Book	3.25	% Held
Price/Sales	1.18	91.89

TRADING VOLUME (thousand shares)

Business Summary: Electrical Equipment (MIC: 7.3.1 SIC: 3357 NAIC: 335921)

Belden is a signal transmission solutions company. Co. has five segments: Broadcast Solutions, which provides production, distribution, and connectivity systems for television broadcast, cable, satellite, and IPTV industries; Enterprise Connectivity Solutions, which provides network infrastructure solutions for enterprise customers; Industrial Connectivity Solutions, which provides networking components and connectivity products; Industrial IT Solutions, which provides networking systems for markets such as discrete automation, process automation, energy, and transportation systems; and Network Security Solutions, which provides threat protection, security, and compliance solutions.

Recent Developments: For the quarter ended Apr 3 2016, net income amounted to US$16.4 million versus a net loss of US$19.6 million in the year-earlier quarter. Revenues were US$541.5 million, down 1.0% from US$547.0 million the year before. Operating income was US$41.0 million versus US$4.9 million in the prior-year quarter, an increase of 736.3%. Direct operating expenses declined 6.7% to US$316.5 million from US$339.3 million in the comparable period the year before. Indirect operating expenses decreased 9.2% to US$184.1 million from US$202.8 million in the equivalent prior-year period.

Prospects: Our evaluation of Belden Inc. as of June 19, 2016 is the result of our systematic analysis on three basic characteristics: earnings strength, relative valuation, and recent stock price movement. The company has managed to produce a neutral trend in earnings per share over the past 5 quarters and while recent estimates for the company have remained steady, BDC has posted better than expected results. Based on operating earnings yield, the company is undervalued when compared to all of the companies in our coverage universe. Share price changes over the past year indicates that BDC will perform poorly over the near term.

Financial Data

(US$ in Thousands)	3 Mos	12/31/2015	12/31/2014	12/31/2013	12/31/2012	12/31/2011	12/31/2010	12/31/2009
Earnings Per Share	2.39	1.54	1.69	2.31	4.23	2.38	2.27	(0.53)
Cash Flow Per Share	7.08	5.58	4.48	3.75	3.08	3.92	2.38	3.26
Tang Book Value Per Share	N.M.	N.M.	N.M.	N.M.	N.M.	4.25	3.66	2.04
Dividends Per Share	0.200	0.200	0.200	0.200	0.200	0.200	0.200	0.200
Dividend Payout %	8.37	12.99	11.83	8.66	4.73	8.40	8.81	...
Income Statement								
Total Revenue	541,497	2,309,222	2,308,265	2,069,193	1,840,739	1,981,953	1,617,090	1,415,262
EBITDA	78,196	289,174	261,290	285,131	104,225	224,009	167,503	62,277
Depn & Amortn	37,232	150,391	102,126	94,403	57,892	50,172	48,789	55,880
Income Before Taxes	16,568	38,170	77,591	118,127	(4,662)	126,722	70,072	(34,414)
Income Taxes	143	(26,568)	7,114	22,315	(38,194)	24,638	12,714	(10,909)
Net Income	16,524	66,204	74,449	103,313	194,490	114,345	108,459	(24,901)
Average Shares	42,440	42,953	43,997	44,737	45,942	48,104	47,783	46,594
Balance Sheet								
Current Assets	752,910	843,164	1,414,150	1,195,498	959,582	925,421	860,855	764,318
Total Assets	3,223,595	3,315,841	3,262,827	2,751,753	2,584,583	1,788,120	1,696,484	1,620,578
Current Liabilities	492,813	549,263	525,359	401,566	452,482	381,566	357,924	357,953
Long-Term Obligations	1,689,664	1,750,521	1,765,422	1,364,536	1,135,527	550,926	551,155	543,942
Total Liabilities	2,385,611	2,491,742	2,455,641	1,915,212	1,772,723	1,093,571	1,057,969	1,069,530
Stockholders' Equity	837,984	824,099	807,186	836,541	811,860	694,549	638,515	551,048
Shares Outstanding	42,071	41,981	42,464	43,455	44,168	45,825	47,045	46,660
Statistical Record								
Return on Assets %	3.06	2.01	2.48	3.87	8.87	6.56	6.54	N.M.
Return on Equity %	12.52	8.12	9.06	12.53	25.75	17.16	18.24	N.M.
EBITDA Margin %	14.44	12.52	11.32	13.78	5.66	11.30	10.36	4.40
Net Margin %	3.05	2.87	3.23	4.99	10.57	5.77	6.71	N.M.
Asset Turnover	0.69	0.70	0.77	0.78	0.84	1.14	0.98	0.87
Current Ratio	1.53	1.54	2.69	2.98	2.12	2.43	2.41	2.14
Debt to Equity	2.02	2.12	2.19	1.63	1.40	0.79	0.86	0.99
Price Range	95.14-37.15	95.14-45.10	80.96-58.56	71.30-44.99	44.99-30.24	40.32-23.93	38.69-20.55	26.66-8.40
P/E Ratio	39.81-15.54	61.78-29.29	47.91-34.65	30.87-19.48	10.64-7.15	16.94-10.05	17.04-9.05	...
Average Yield %	0.32	0.28	0.28	0.35	0.55	0.59	0.75	1.07

Address: 1 North Brentwood Boulevard, 15th Floor, St. Louis, MO 63105
Telephone: 314-854-8000
Fax: 314-854-8001

Web Site: www.belden.com
Officers: Bryan C. Cressey - Chairman John S. Stroup - President, Chief Executive Officer

Auditors: Ernst & Young LLP
Investor Contact: 314-854-8054
Transfer Agents: American Stock Transfer & Trust Company, Brooklyn, NY

BEMIS CO INC

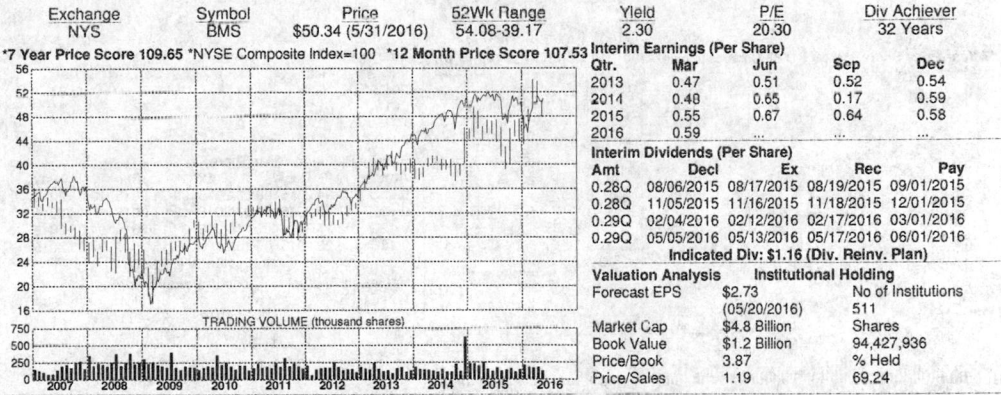

Exchange	Symbol	Price	52Wk Range	Yield	P/E	Div Achiever
NYS	BMS	$50.34 (5/31/2016)	54.08-39.17	2.30	20.30	32 Years

*7 Year Price Score 109.65 *NYSE Composite Index=100 *12 Month Price Score 107.53

Interim Earnings (Per Share)

Qtr.	Mar	Jun	Sep	Dec
2013	0.47	0.51	0.52	0.54
2014	0.48	0.65	0.17	0.59
2015	0.55	0.67	0.64	0.58
2016	0.59	...	...	...

Interim Dividends (Per Share)

Amt	Decl	Ex	Rec	Pay
0.28Q	08/06/2015	08/17/2015	08/19/2015	09/01/2015
0.28Q	11/05/2015	11/16/2015	11/18/2015	12/01/2015
0.29Q	02/04/2016	02/12/2016	02/17/2016	03/01/2016
0.29Q	05/05/2016	05/13/2016	05/17/2016	06/01/2016

Indicated Div: $1.16 (Div. Reinv. Plan)

Valuation Analysis

Valuation Analysis	**Institutional Holding**	
Forecast EPS	$2.73	No of Institutions
	(05/20/2016)	511
Market Cap	$4.8 Billion	Shares
Book Value	$1.2 Billion	94,427,936
Price/Book	3.87	% Held
Price/Sales	1.19	69.24

TRADING VOLUME (thousand shares)

Business Summary: Containers & Packaging (MIC: 8.1.3 SIC: 2671 NAIC: 322221)

Bemis Co is a manufacturer of packaging products with two segments. The U.S. Packaging segment includes food, consumer, and industrial products packaging-related manufacturing operations located in the U.S. that manufactures multilayer polymer, blown and cast film structures to produce packaging sold for food, personal care and non-food applications. The Global Packaging segment includes packaging-related manufacturing operations located outside of the U.S., medical device and pharmaceutical packaging manufacturing operations that manufactures multilayer polymer, blown and cast film structures to produce packaging for a range of food, medical, electronics and pharmaceutical, among others.

Recent Developments: For the quarter ended Mar 31 2016, income from continuing operations decreased 1.4% to US$56.2 million from US$57.0 million in the year-earlier quarter. Net income increased 3.3% to US$56.2 million from US$54.4 million in the year-earlier quarter. Revenues were US$967.9 million, down 6.9% from US$1.04 billion the year before. Operating income was US$99.4 million versus US$97.4 million in the prior-year quarter, an increase of 2.1%. Direct operating expenses declined 7.7% to US$759.1 million from US$822.6 million in the comparable period the year before. Indirect operating expenses decreased 8.9% to US$109.4 million from US$120.1 million in the equivalent prior-year period.

Prospects: Our evaluation of Bemis Co Inc. as of June 19, 2016 is the result of our systematic analysis on three basic characteristics: earnings strength, relative valuation, and recent stock price movement. The company has managed to produce a neutral trend in earnings per share over the past 5 quarters and while recent estimates for the company have remained steady, BMS has posted results that fell short of analysts expectations. Based on operating earnings yield, the company is undervalued when compared to all of the companies in our coverage universe. Share price changes over the past year indicates that BMS will perform well over the near term.

Financial Data

(US$ in Thousands)	3 Mos	12/31/2015	12/31/2014	12/31/2013	12/31/2012	12/31/2011	12/31/2010	12/31/2009
Earnings Per Share	2.48	2.44	1.89	2.04	1.66	1.73	1.85	1.38
Cash Flow Per Share	5.48	5.71	2.48	3.63	4.07	4.02	3.39	4.60
Tang Book Value Per Share	1.30	1.14	3.07	4.34	3.93	3.02	6.18	9.90
Dividends Per Share	1.130	1.120	1.080	1.040	1.000	0.960	0.920	0.900
Dividend Payout %	45.56	45.90	57.14	50.98	60.24	55.49	49.73	65.22
Income Statement								
Total Revenue	967,900	4,071,400	4,343,500	5,029,800	5,139,200	5,322,670	4,835,042	3,514,586
EBITDA	140,100	559,800	594,500	578,800	555,200	590,232	611,272	442,470
Depn & Amortn	40,800	144,200	170,000	190,300	205,700	221,200	210,500	160,108
Income Before Taxes	83,900	363,900	363,700	320,300	278,600	292,223	327,284	240,310
Income Taxes	27,700	122,000	124,600	107,700	104,800	104,900	117,600	87,800
Net Income	56,200	239,300	191,100	212,600	173,800	184,081	205,111	147,221
Average Shares	95,900	97,900	101,200	103,900	103,900	105,072	108,750	103,601
Balance Sheet								
Current Assets	1,164,600	1,119,000	1,287,800	1,504,500	1,525,000	1,549,011	1,466,919	2,005,348
Total Assets	3,573,100	3,489,800	3,615,100	4,110,200	4,185,700	4,320,444	4,285,831	3,928,705
Current Liabilities	564,800	589,100	481,400	601,900	643,000	681,965	675,259	524,855
Long-Term Obligations	1,437,200	1,353,900	1,315,900	1,421,400	1,417,600	1,554,750	1,283,525	1,227,514
Total Liabilities	2,340,700	2,282,400	2,182,100	2,425,400	2,544,800	2,738,341	2,406,208	2,124,973
Stockholders' Equity	1,232,400	1,207,400	1,433,000	1,684,800	1,640,900	1,582,103	1,879,623	1,803,732
Shares Outstanding	94,700	95,100	98,200	101,900	103,200	102,983	107,673	108,223
Statistical Record								
Return on Assets %	6.75	6.74	4.95	5.13	4.08	4.28	4.99	4.36
Return on Equity %	18.83	18.13	12.26	12.79	10.76	10.64	11.14	9.35
EBITDA Margin %	14.47	13.75	13.69	11.51	10.80	11.09	12.64	12.59
Net Margin %	5.81	5.88	4.40	4.23	3.38	3.46	4.24	4.19
Asset Turnover	1.12	1.15	1.12	1.21	1.21	1.24	1.18	1.04
Current Ratio	2.06	1.90	2.68	2.50	2.37	2.27	2.17	3.82
Debt to Equity	1.17	1.12	0.92	0.84	0.86	0.98	0.68	0.68
Price Range	54.08-39.17	49.33-39.17	46.08-37.17	42.23-33.46	33.79-29.78	34.25-27.53	33.90-26.72	30.90-17.09
P/E Ratio	21.81-15.79	20.22-16.05	24.38-19.67	20.70-16.40	20.36-17.94	19.80-15.91	18.32-14.44	22.39-12.38
Average Yield %	2.48	2.48	2.70	2.66	3.17	3.07	3.06	3.60

Address: One Neenah Center, 4th Floor, P.O. Box 669, Neenah, WI 54957-0669
Telephone: 920 527 5000

Web Site: www.bemis.com
Officers: Henry J. Theisen - Executive Chairman, President, Chief Executive Officer Jeffrey H. Curler Chairman Emeritus, Chairman

Auditors: PricewaterhouseCoopers LLP
Investor Contact: 920-727-4100
Transfer Agents: Wells Fargo Bank, N.A., South St. Paul, MN

BERKLEY (WR) CORP

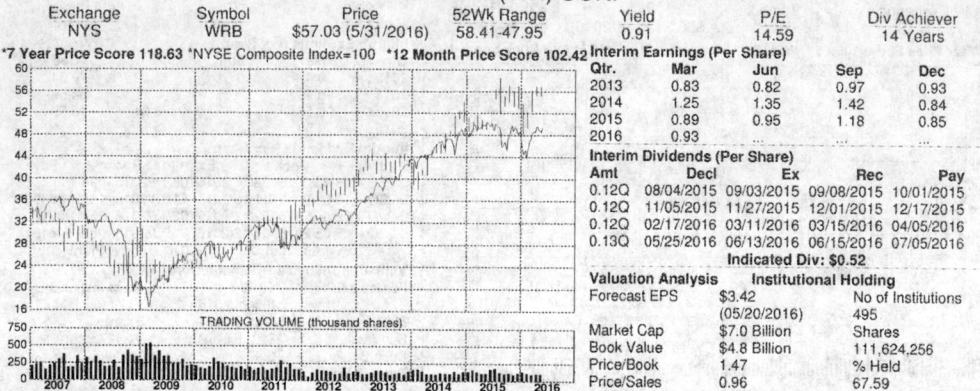

Exchange	Symbol	Price	52Wk Range	Yield	P/E	Div Achiever
NYS	WRB	$57.03 (5/31/2016)	58.41-47.95	0.91	14.59	14 Years

*7 Year Price Score 118.63 *NYSE Composite Index=100 *12 Month Price Score 102.42

Interim Earnings (Per Share)

Qtr.	Mar	Jun	Sep	Dec
2013	0.83	0.82	0.97	0.93
2014	1.25	1.35	1.42	0.84
2015	0.89	0.95	1.18	0.85
2016	0.93	...	...	...

Interim Dividends (Per Share)

Amt	Decl	Ex	Rec	Pay
0.12Q	08/04/2015	09/03/2015	09/08/2015	10/01/2015
0.12Q	11/05/2015	11/27/2015	12/01/2015	12/17/2015
0.12Q	02/17/2016	03/11/2016	03/15/2016	04/05/2016
0.13Q	05/25/2016	06/13/2016	06/15/2016	07/05/2016

Indicated Div: $0.52

Valuation Analysis

Forecast EPS	$3.42 (05/20/2016)
Market Cap	$7.0 Billion
Book Value	$4.8 Billion
Price/Book	1.47
Price/Sales	0.96

Institutional Holding

No of Institutions	495
Shares	111,624,256
% Held	67.59

TRADING VOLUME (thousand shares)

Business Summary: General Insurance (MIC: 5.2.1 SIC: 6331 NAIC: 524126)

W. R. Berkley is an insurance holding company. Co. operates in three business segments: Insurance-Domestic, which underwrites commercial insurance business primarily throughout the U.S.; Insurance-International, which writes business in almost 60 countries worldwide, with branches or offices in 19 locations outside the U.S., including the U.K., Continental Europe, South America, Canada, Scandinavia, Asia, and Australia; and Reinsurance-Global, which provides other insurance companies and self-insureds with assistance in managing their net risk through reinsurance on either a portfolio basis, through treaty reinsurance, or on an individual basis, through facultative reinsurance.

Recent Developments: For the quarter ended Mar 31 2016, net income increased 1.5% to US$120.2 million from US$118.4 million in the year-earlier quarter. Revenues were US$1.81 billion, up 3.6% from US$1.74 billion the year before. Net premiums earned were US$1.53 billion versus US$1.47 billion in the prior-year quarter, an increase of 3.8%. Net investment income rose 4.7% to US$130.1 million from US$124.2 million a year ago.

Prospects: Our evaluation of Berkley (W. R.) Corp. as of June 19, 2016 is the result of our systematic analysis on three basic characteristics: earnings strength, relative valuation, and recent stock price movement. The company has managed to produce a neutral trend in earnings per share over the past 5 quarters. However, while recent estimates for the company have been lowered by analysts, WRB has posted better than expected results. Based on operating earnings yield, the company is undervalued when compared to all of the companies in our coverage universe. Share price changes over the past year indicates that WRB will perform well over the near term.

Financial Data
(US$ in Thousands)

	3 Mos	12/31/2015	12/31/2014	12/31/2013	12/31/2012	12/31/2011	12/31/2010	12/31/2009
Earnings Per Share	3.91	3.87	4.86	3.55	3.56	2.71	2.90	1.86
Cash Flow Per Share	7.83	7.10	5.75	6.06	4.91	4.80	3.03	1.97
Tang Book Value Per Share	37.50	36.06	35.02	31.96	31.01	28.49	25.62	22.29
Dividends Per Share	0.480	0.470	1.430	0.390	1.350	0.310	0.270	0.240
Dividend Payout %	12.28	12.14	29.42	10.99	37.92	11.44	9.31	12.90
Income Statement								
Premium Income	1,527,335	6,040,609	5,744,418	5,226,537	4,673,516	4,160,867	3,835,582	3,805,849
Total Revenue	1,807,211	7,206,457	7,128,928	6,408,534	5,823,554	5,155,984	4,724,069	4,431,178
Benefits & Claims	922,321	3,656,270	3,490,567	3,197,024	2,948,479	2,658,365	2,309,867	2,336,707
Income Before Taxes	174,676	732,030	952,196	698,888	701,928	518,283	603,305	382,230
Income Taxes	54,428	227,923	302,593	193,587	191,285	123,550	153,739	73,150
Net Income	120,248	504,107	649,603	505,301	510,643	394,733	449,566	309,080
Average Shares	128,529	130,188	133,652	140,742	143,314	145,672	155,081	166,574
Balance Sheet								
Total Assets	22,230,934	21,730,967	21,716,691	20,551,796	20,155,896	18,487,731	17,528,547	17,328,596
Total Liabilities	17,479,721	17,130,721	17,126,746	16,215,761	15,849,679	14,479,305	13,825,671	13,732,529
Stockholders' Equity	4,751,213	4,600,246	4,589,945	4,336,035	4,306,217	4,008,426	3,702,876	3,596,067
Shares Outstanding	122,599	123,307	126,748	132,233	136,017	137,520	141,009	156,552
Statistical Record								
Return on Assets %	2.30	2.32	3.07	2.48	2.64	2.19	2.58	1.85
Return on Equity %	10.85	10.97	14.56	11.69	12.25	10.24	12.32	9.31
Loss Ratio %	60.39	60.53	60.76	61.17	63.09	63.89	60.22	61.40
Net Margin %	6.65	7.00	9.11	7.88	8.77	7.66	9.52	6.98
Price Range	58.41-47.95	58.41-48.40	53.96-37.93	45.39-37.74	40.21-33.85	35.68-26.71	28.55-24.11	31.00-18.86
P/E Ratio	14.94-12.26	15.09-12.51	11.10-7.80	12.79-10.63	11.29-9.51	13.17-9.86	9.84-8.31	16.67-10.14
Average Yield %	0.90	0.89	3.13	0.92	3.60	1.00	1.01	1.00

Address: 475 Steamboat Road, Greenwich, CT 06830 **Telephone:** 203-629-3000	**Web Site:** www.wrberkley.com **Officers:** William R. Berkley - Executive Chairman, Chairman, Chief Executive Officer W. Robert Berkley - President, Chief Executive Officer, Chief Operating Officer	**Auditors:** KPMG LLP **Investor Contact:** 203-629-3040 **Transfer Agents:** Wells Fargo Bank, N.A., Mendota Heights, MN

BERKSHIRE HATHAWAY INC

Exchange	Symbol	Price	52Wk Range	Yield	P/E
NYS	BRK B	$140.54 (5/31/2016)	147.60-124.13	N/A	N/A

*7 Year Price Score 114.05 ***NYSE Composite Index=100** ***12 Month Price Score 104.41**

TRADING VOLUME (thousand shares)

Interim Earnings (Per Share)

Qtr.	Mar	Jun	Sep	Dec
2013	2977.00	2763.00	3074.00	3036.00
2014	2862.00	3889.00	2811.00	2530.00
2015	3143.00	2442.00	5737.00	3333.00
2016	3401.00	...	...	...

Interim Dividends (Per Share)

No Dividends Paid

Valuation Analysis / Institutional Holding

Forecast EPS	$7.20	No of Institutions	
	(05/20/2016)	2223	
Market Cap	$176.5 Million	Shares	
Book Value	$258.7 Billion		886,035,264
Price/Book	0.00	% Held	
Price/Sales	0.00		13.59

Business Summary: General Insurance (MIC: 5.2.1 SIC: 6331 NAIC: 524126)

Berkshire Hathaway is a holding company. Co.'s subsidiaries are engaged in a number of business activities which include: property and casualty insurance and reinsurance; railroad, which operates railroad systems in North America through BNSF Railway Company; investing, manufactured housing business and related consumer financing, transportation equipment, manufacturing and leasing, and furniture leasing; manufacturing and service businesses; wholesale distribution of groceries and non-food items; regulated electric and gas utility, including power generation and distribution activities; and domestic real estate brokerage and brokerage franchisor.

Recent Developments: For the quarter ended Mar 31 2016, net income increased 8.1% to US$5.66 billion from US$5.23 billion in the year-earlier quarter. Revenues were US$52.40 billion, up 7.7% from US$48.64 billion the year before. Net premiums earned were US$11.12 billion versus US$9.54 billion in the prior-year quarter, an increase of 16.6%.

Prospects: Our evaluation of Berkshire Hathaway Inc. as of June 19, 2016 is the result of our systematic analysis on three basic characteristics: earnings strength, relative valuation, and recent stock price movement. The company has enjoyed a very positive trend in earnings per share over the past 5 quarters and while recent estimates for the company have remained steady, BRK.B has posted results that fell short of analysts expectations. Based on operating earnings yield, the company is undervalued when compared to all of the companies in our coverage universe. Share price changes over the past year indicates that BRK.B will perform well over the near term.

Financial Data
(US$ in Thousands)

	3 Mos	12/31/2015	12/31/2014	12/31/2013	12/31/2012	12/31/2011	12/31/2010	12/31/2009
Earnings Per Share	14,913.00	14,656.00	12,092.00	11,850.00	8,977.00	6,215.00	7,928.00	5,193.00
Cash Flow Per Share	20,084.73	19,164.63	19,477.25	16,855.55	12,652.36	12,410.52	10,940.53	10,215.49
Tang Book Value Per Share	114,865.69	146,452.91	109,230.64	100,294.17	81,027.67	67,625.75	65,718.52	62,593.93
Income Statement								
Premium Income	11,124,000	41,294,000	41,253,000	36,684,000	34,545,000	32,075,000	30,749,000	27,884,000
Total Revenue	52,403,000	210,821,000	194,673,000	182,150,000	162,463,000	143,688,000	136,185,000	112,493,000
Benefits & Claims	8,699,000	31,940,000	31,587,000	26,347,000	25,227,000	25,708,000	22,540,000	20,089,000
Income Before Taxes	6,456,000	34,946,000	28,105,000	28,796,000	22,236,000	15,314,000	19,051,000	11,552,000
Income Taxes	799,000	10,532,000	7,935,000	8,951,000	6,924,000	4,568,000	5,607,000	3,538,000
Net Income	5,589,000	24,083,000	19,872,000	19,476,000	14,824,000	10,254,000	12,967,000	8,055,000
Average Shares	1,643	1,643	1,643	1,643	1,651	1,649	1,635	1,551
Balance Sheet								
Total Assets	586,315,000	552,257,000	526,186,000	484,931,000	427,452,000	392,647,000	372,229,000	297,119,000
Total Liabilities	327,654,000	296,707,000	286,016,000	263,041,000	239,805,000	227,797,000	214,911,000	166,017,000
Stockholders' Equity	258,661,000	255,550,000	240,170,000	221,890,000	187,647,000	164,850,000	157,318,000	131,102,000
Shares Outstanding	1,256	1,254	1,642	1,643	1,642	1,650	1,648	1,551
Statistical Record								
Return on Assets %	4.39	4.47	3.93	4.27	3.61	2.68	3.87	2.85
Return on Equity %	9.80	9.72	8.60	9.51	8.39	6.37	8.99	6.70
Loss Ratio %	78.20	77.35	76.57	71.82	73.03	80.15	73.30	72.04
Net Margin %	10.67	11.42	10.21	10.69	9.12	7.14	9.52	7.16
Price Range	148.31-124.13	151.37-127.74	152.67-108.78	118.94-89.70	90.69-76.29	87.28-66.00	83.72-64.94	70.80-46.00

Address: 3555 Farnam Street, Omaha, NE 68131	Web Site: www.berkshirehathaway.com	Auditors: Deloitte & Touche LLP
	Officers: Warren Edward Buffett - Chairman, Chief	Transfer Agents: Wells Fargo Bank,
Telephone: 402-346-1400	Executive Officer Charles T. Munger - Vice-Chairman	N.A., St. Paul, MN

BEST BUY INC

Exchange	Symbol	Price	52Wk Range	Yield	P/E	Div Achiever
NYS	BBY	$32.17 (5/31/2016)	38.96-25.87	3.48	11.09	11 Years

*7 Year Price Score 89.41 *NYSE Composite Index=100 *12 Month Price Score 96.22

Interim Earnings (Per Share)

Qtr.	Apr	Jul	Oct	Jan
2013-14	(0.24)	0.77	0.16	0.84
2014-15	1.31	0.42	0.30	1.47
2015-16	0.36	0.46	0.36	1.38
2016-17	0.70	...	...	...

Interim Dividends (Per Share)

Amt	Decl	Ex	Rec	Pay
0.23Q	11/20/2015	12/08/2015	12/10/2015	12/31/2015
0.45Sp	02/25/2016	03/15/2016	03/17/2016	04/07/2016
0.28Q	02/25/2016	03/15/2016	03/17/2016	04/07/2016
0.28Q	05/25/2016	06/10/2016	06/14/2016	07/05/2016

Indicated Div: $1.12 (Div. Reinv. Plan)

Valuation Analysis

Forecast EPS	$2.92 (05/20/2016)
Market Cap	$10.4 Billion
Book Value	$4.4 Billion
Price/Book	2.35
Price/Sales	0.26

Institutional Holding

No of Institutions	750
Shares	299,658,112
% Held	80.89

TRADING VOLUME (thousand shares)

Business Summary: Retail - Appliances and Electronics (MIC: 2.1.7 SIC: 5731 NAIC: 443112)

Best Buy is a provider of technology products, services and solutions. Co. provides these products and services to the customers who visit its stores, engage with Geek Squad agents or use its websites or mobile applications. Co. has operations in the U.S., Canada and Mexico. Co. operates in two segments: Domestic and International. Co.'s Domestic and International segments have offerings in six categories: Consumer Electronics, Computing and Mobile Phones, Entertainment, Appliances, Services and Other. As of Jan 31 2016, Co. had approximately 1,200 large-format and 400 small-format stores.

Recent Developments: For the quarter ended Apr 30 2016, income from continuing operations increased 510.8% to US$226.0 million from US$37.0 million in the year-earlier quarter. Net income increased 77.5% to US$229.0 million from US$129.0 million in the year-earlier quarter. Revenues were US$8.44 billion, down 1.3% from US$8.56 billion the year before. Operating income was US$372.0 million versus US$86.0 million in the prior-year quarter, an increase of 332.6%. Direct operating expenses declined 3.5% to US$6.30 billion from US$6.53 billion in the comparable period the year before. Indirect operating expenses decreased 8.8% to US$1.77 billion from US$1.94 billion in the equivalent prior-year period.

Prospects: Our evaluation of Best Buy Inc. as of June 19, 2016 is the result of our systematic analysis on three basic characteristics: earnings strength, relative valuation, and recent stock price movement. The company has generated a negative trend in earnings per share over the past 5 quarters and while recent estimates for the company have been mixed, BBY has posted better than expected results. Based on operating earnings yield, the company is undervalued when compared to all of the companies in our coverage universe. Share price changes over the past year indicates that BBY will perform very well over the near term.

Financial Data

(US$ in Thousands)	3 Mos	01/30/2016	01/31/2015	02/01/2014	02/02/2013	03/03/2012	02/26/2011	02/27/2010
Earnings Per Share	2.90	2.56	3.49	1.53	(1.30)	(3.36)	3.08	3.10
Cash Flow Per Share	5.61	3.83	5.55	3.21	4.66	8.84	2.94	5.31
Tang Book Value Per Share	12.29	12.15	12.84	9.98	6.50	6.01	9.71	8.19
Dividends Per Share	1.420	1.430	0.720	0.680	0.660	0.620	0.580	0.560
Dividend Payout %	48.97	55.86	20.63	44.44	...	...	18.83	18.06
Income Statement								
Total Revenue	8,443,000	39,528,000	40,339,000	42,410,000	45,085,000	50,705,000	50,272,000	49,694,000
EBITDA	542,000	2,047,000	2,133,000	1,903,000	758,000	2,122,000	3,143,000	3,215,000
Depn & Amortn	162,000	657,000	656,000	716,000	832,000	945,000	978,000	926,000
Income Before Taxes	360,000	1,310,000	1,387,000	1,087,000	(186,000)	1,043,000	2,078,000	2,195,000
Income Taxes	134,000	503,000	141,000	398,000	231,000	709,000	714,000	802,000
Net Income	229,000	897,000	1,233,000	532,000	(441,000)	(1,231,000)	1,277,000	1,317,000
Average Shares	326,700	350,700	353,600	347,600	338,600	366,300	416,500	427,500
Balance Sheet								
Current Assets	9,282,000	9,886,000	11,729,000	10,485,000	12,047,000	10,297,000	10,473,000	10,566,000
Total Assets	12,901,000	13,519,000	15,256,000	14,013,000	16,787,000	16,005,000	17,849,000	18,302,000
Current Liabilities	6,334,000	6,925,000	7,777,000	7,436,000	10,810,000	8,855,000	8,663,000	8,978,000
Long-Term Obligations	1,334,000	1,339,000	1,580,000	1,612,000	1,153,000	1,685,000	711,000	1,104,000
Total Liabilities	8,475,000	9,141,000	10,261,000	10,027,000	13,726,000	12,260,000	11,247,000	11,982,000
Stockholders' Equity	4,426,000	4,378,000	4,995,000	3,986,000	3,061,000	3,745,000	6,602,000	6,320,000
Shares Outstanding	324,000	323,779	351,468	346,751	338,276	341,400	392,590	418,815
Statistical Record								
Return on Assets %	7.49	6.25	8.45	3.46	N.M.	N.M.	7.08	7.74
Return on Equity %	21.45	19.19	27.53	15.14	N.M.	N.M.	19.82	24.09
EBITDA Margin %	6.42	5.18	5.29	4.49	1.68	4.18	6.25	6.47
Net Margin %	2.71	2.27	3.06	1.25	N.M.	N.M.	2.54	2.65
Asset Turnover	2.96	2.75	2.76	2.76	2.99	2.95	2.79	2.92
Current Ratio	1.47	1.43	1.51	1.41	1.11	1.16	1.21	1.18
Debt to Equity	0.30	0.31	0.32	0.40	0.38	0.45	0.11	0.17
Price Range	38.96-25.87	41.77-25.87	39.91-22.78	44.33-15.12	27.51-11.29	33.03-22.12	48.58-31.39	45.37-24.71
P/E Ratio	13.43-8.92	16.32-10.11	11.44-6.53	28.97-9.88	...	...	15.77-10.19	14.64-7.97
Average Yield %	4.32	4.13	2.35	2.20	3.62	2.25	1.50	1.49

Address: 7601 Penn Avenue South, Richfield, MN 55423 **Telephone:** 612-291-1000	**Web Site:** www.bestbuy.com **Officers:** Hubert Joly - Chairman, President, Chief Executive Officer Richard M. Schulze - Chairman Emeritus, Chairman	**Auditors:** Deloitte & Touche LLP **Transfer Agents:** Computershare, Providence, RI

BIG LOTS, INC.

Exchange	Symbol	Price	52Wk Range	Yield	P/E
NYS	BIG	$52.30 (5/31/2016)	52.30-35.88	1.61	17.67

*7 Year Price Score 101.73 ***NYSE Composite Index=100** ***12 Month Price Score 104.47**

TRADING VOLUME (thousand shares)

Interim Earnings (Per Share)

Qtr.	Apr	Jul	Oct	Jan
2013-14	0.31	0.31	(0.17)	1.45
2014-15	0.06	0.36	(0.00)	1.71
2015-16	0.60	0.34	(0.03)	1.86
2016-17	0.79	...	...	...

Interim Dividends (Per Share)

Amt	Decl	Ex	Rec	Pay
0.19Q	08/28/2015	09/09/2015	09/11/2015	09/25/2015
0.19Q	12/04/2015	12/15/2015	12/17/2015	12/31/2015
0.21Q	03/04/2016	03/16/2016	03/18/2016	04/01/2016
0.21Q	05/26/2016	06/08/2016	06/10/2016	06/24/2016

Indicated Div: $0.84

Valuation Analysis / Institutional Holding

Forecast EPS	$3.46	No of Institutions
(05/20/2016)		413
Market Cap	$2.4 Billion	Shares
Book Value	$620.1 Million	64,444,248
Price/Book	3.90	% Held
Price/Sales	0.46	88.67

Business Summary: Retail - General Merchandise/Department Stores (MIC: 2.1.1 SIC: 5331 NAIC: 452990)

Big Lots is a retailer. Co.'s merchandising categories are food, such as beverage and grocery; Consumables, such as health and beauty, plastics, paper, chemical, and pet departments; Soft Home, such as home decor, frames, fashion bedding, utility bedding, bath, window, decorative textile, and area rugs departments; Hard Home, such as appliances, table top, food preparation, stationery and home maintenance departments; Furniture, such as upholstery, mattress, ready-to-assemble, and case goods departments; Seasonal, such as lawn and garden, summer, and other holiday departments; Electronics and Accessories, such as electronics, jewelry, hosiery, and infant accessories departments.

Recent Developments: For the quarter ended Apr 30 2016, income from continuing operations increased 19.5% to US$38.6 million from US$32.3 million in the year-earlier quarter. Net income increased 20.0% to US$38.7 million from US$32.2 million in the year-earlier quarter. Revenues were US$1.31 billion, up 2.5% from US$1.28 billion the year before. Operating income was US$62.6 million versus US$52.6 million in the prior-year quarter, an increase of 18.9%. Direct operating expenses rose 2.4% to US$794.9 million from US$776.3 million in the comparable period the year before. Indirect operating expenses increased 0.8% to US$455.1 million from US$451.5 million in the equivalent prior-year period.

Prospects: Our evaluation of Big Lots Inc. as of June 19, 2016 is the result of our systematic analysis on three basic characteristics: earnings strength, relative valuation, and recent stock price movement. The company has managed to produce a neutral trend in earnings per share over the past 5 quarters and while recent estimates for the company have been raised by analysts, BIG has posted better than expected results. Based on operating earnings yield, the company is undervalued when compared to all of the companies in our coverage universe. Share price changes over the past year indicates that BIG will perform poorly over the near term.

Financial Data

(US$ in Thousands)	3 Mos	01/30/2016	01/31/2015	02/01/2014	02/02/2013	01/28/2012	01/29/2011	01/30/2010
Earnings Per Share	2.96	2.80	2.06	2.16	2.93	2.99	2.83	2.42
Cash Flow Per Share	6.88	6.80	5.81	3.46	4.62	4.67	4.07	4.82
Tang Book Value Per Share	13.40	14.67	14.92	15.66	13.00	12.75	12.81	12.22
Dividends Per Share	0.780	0.760	0.510	...	...	...	...	...
Dividend Payout %	26.35	27.14	24.76	...	...	...	...	...
Income Statement								
Total Revenue	1,312,575	5,190,582	5,177,078	5,301,912	5,400,119	5,202,269	4,952,244	4,726,772
EBITDA	92,948	353,233	344,188	304,326	404,805	435,702	435,951	399,914
Depn & Amortn	29,699	122,700	119,700	115,100	106,300	90,280	78,606	74,904
Income Before Taxes	62,615	226,850	221,900	185,887	294,313	341,892	355,384	323,345
Income Taxes	24,002	83,842	85,239	61,118	117,148	134,657	132,837	121,975
Net Income	38,659	142,873	114,276	125,295	177,121	207,064	222,524	200,369
Average Shares	48,888	50,964	55,552	57,958	60,476	69,419	78,581	82,681
Balance Sheet								
Current Assets	956,165	994,432	1,038,429	1,121,061	1,090,630	1,006,656	1,051,719	1,122,966
Total Assets	1,606,621	1,640,370	1,635,891	1,739,599	1,753,626	1,641,310	1,619,599	1,669,493
Current Liabilities	654,801	678,448	587,829	577,447	629,634	584,820	541,931	542,520
Long-Term Obligations	153,800	62,300	62,100	77,000	171,200	65,900	...	...
Total Liabilities	986,547	919,900	846,341	838,172	995,484	818,077	672,806	668,081
Stockholders' Equity	620,074	720,470	789,550	901,427	758,142	823,233	946,793	1,001,412
Shares Outstanding	46,270	49,101	52,912	57,548	57,269	63,609	73,894	81,922
Statistical Record								
Return on Assets %	9.17	8.75	6.79	7.19	10.27	12.73	13.57	12.95
Return on Equity %	21.12	18.98	13.55	15.14	22.04	23.46	22.91	22.62
EBITDA Margin %	7.08	6.81	6.65	5.74	7.50	8.38	8.80	8.46
Net Margin %	2.95	2.75	2.21	2.36	3.28	3.98	4.49	4.24
Asset Turnover	3.21	3.18	3.08	3.04	3.13	3.20	3.02	3.06
Current Ratio	1.46	1.47	1.77	1.94	1.73	1.72	1.94	2.07
Debt to Equity	0.25	0.09	0.08	0.09	0.23	0.08	...	...
Price Range	50.01-35.88	50.96-35.88	50.80-25.71	38.96-26.79	46.81-26.86	44.04-29.02	41.14-27.91	31.17-12.99
P/E Ratio	16.90-12.12	18.20-12.81	24.66-12.48	18.04-12.40	15.98-9.17	14.73-9.71	14.54-9.86	12.88-5.37
Average Yield %	1.78	1.68	1.22	...	...	...	...	...

Address: 300 Phillipi Road, P.O. Box 28512, Columbus, OH 43228-5311
Telephone: 614-278-6800
Fax: 614-278-6666

Web Site: www.biglots.com
Officers: David J. Campisi - President, Chief Executive Officer Lisa M. Bachmann - Executive Vice President, Senior Vice President, Chief Operating Officer, Chief Information Officer, Chief Merchandising Officer

Auditors: Deloitte & Touche LLP
Investor Contact: 614-278-6622
Transfer Agents: Computershare Investor Services, Canton, MA

BIO-RAD LABORATORIES, INC.

Exchange	Symbol	Price	52Wk Range	Yield	P/E
NYS	BIO	$148.85 (5/31/2016)	151.93-123.93	N/A	40.67

*7 Year Price Score 105.47 *NYSE Composite Index=100 *12 Month Price Score 100.79

Interim Earnings (Per Share)

Qtr.	Mar	Jun	Sep	Dec
2013	0.68	1.20	(0.25)	1.04
2014	0.23	1.09	0.39	1.34
2015	0.61	0.97	0.59	1.68
2016	0.42	...	...	...

Interim Dividends (Per Share)

No Dividends Paid

Valuation Analysis

		Institutional Holding	
Forecast EPS	$3.31	No of Institutions	
	(05/09/2016)	320	
Market Cap	$4.4 Billion	Shares	
Book Value	$2.5 Billion	19,664,596	
Price/Book	1.72	% Held	
Price/Sales	2.17	65.21	

Business Summary: Biotechnology (MIC: 4.1.2 SIC: 3826 NAIC: 334516)

Bio-Rad Laboratories is a manufacturer and distributor of its own life science research and clinical diagnostics products. Co. has two primary segments: Life Science, which is engaged in developing, manufacturing and marketing a range of reagents, apparatus and laboratory instruments used for biological research; and Clinical Diagnostics, which designs, manufactures, sells and supports test systems, informatics systems, test kits and quality controls that serve clinical laboratories in the diagnostics market. Co. sells its products and services to a diverse client base comprised of scientific research, healthcare, education and government customers.

Recent Developments: For the quarter ended Mar 31 2016, net income decreased 31.1% to US$12.3 million from US$17.8 million in the year-earlier quarter. Revenues were US$471.2 million, down 0.3% from US$472.8 million the year before. Operating income was US$25.7 million versus US$34.3 million in the prior-year quarter, a decrease of 25.1%. Direct operating expenses rose 2.2% to US$207.2 million from US$202.7 million in the comparable period the year before. Indirect operating expenses increased 1.1% to US$238.3 million from US$235.8 million in the equivalent prior-year period.

Prospects: Our evaluation of Bio-Rad Laboratories Inc. as of June 19, 2016 is the result of our systematic analysis on three basic characteristics: earnings strength, relative valuation, and recent stock price movement. The company has enjoyed a very positive trend in earnings per share over the past 5 quarters and while recent estimates for the company have been raised by analysts, BIO has posted results that fell short of analysts expectations. Based on operating earnings yield, the company is overvalued when compared to all of the companies in our coverage universe. Share price changes over the past year indicates that BIO will perform in line with the market over the near term.

Financial Data

(US$ in Thousands)	3 Mos	12/31/2015	12/31/2014	12/31/2013	12/31/2012	12/31/2011	12/31/2010	12/31/2009
Earnings Per Share	3.66	3.85	3.05	2.69	5.72	6.26	6.59	5.20
Cash Flow Per Share	5.08	6.38	9.46	6.14	9.83	9.27	8.17	11.86
Tang Book Value Per Share	60.98	60.64	49.21	48.75	44.04	36.03	34.78	26.42
Income Statement								
Total Revenue	471,197	2,019,441	2,175,044	2,132,694	2,069,235	2,073,529	1,927,118	1,784,244
EBITDA	58,665	289,239	290,088	307,456	393,043	401,697	353,300	296,656
Depn & Amortn	34,090	131,800	149,900	147,200	130,400	121,000	74,500	69,500
Income Before Taxes	20,195	145,847	131,557	112,385	222,931	235,762	220,283	185,832
Income Taxes	7,919	32,754	42,712	34,574	59,084	57,739	33,348	36,667
Net Income	12,276	113,093	88,845	77,790	163,778	178,223	185,490	144,620
Average Shares	29,506	29,409	29,133	28,906	28,642	28,468	28,151	27,828
Balance Sheet								
Current Assets	1,775,264	1,777,596	1,716,367	1,747,856	1,929,932	1,798,155	1,975,346	1,562,674
Total Assets	3,753,413	3,711,542	3,341,278	3,388,790	3,436,753	3,096,803	3,062,764	2,535,853
Current Liabilities	400,888	441,351	446,761	487,472	469,920	459,115	666,627	419,972
Long-Term Obligations	434,000	435,707	435,710	435,615	732,414	731,698	731,100	737,919
Total Liabilities	1,208,964	1,221,039	1,156,123	1,202,068	1,426,018	1,352,866	1,526,068	1,276,127
Stockholders' Equity	2,544,449	2,490,503	2,185,155	2,186,722	2,010,735	1,743,937	1,536,696	1,259,726
Shares Outstanding	29,396	29,359	29,069	28,776	28,481	28,184	27,852	27,526
Statistical Record								
Return on Assets %	3.04	3.21	2.64	2.28	5.00	5.79	6.63	6.32
Return on Equity %	4.54	4.84	4.06	3.71	8.70	10.87	13.27	12.57
EBITDA Margin %	12.45	14.32	13.34	14.42	18.99	19.37	18.33	16.63
Net Margin %	2.61	5.60	4.08	3.65	7.91	8.60	9.63	8.11
Asset Turnover	0.57	0.57	0.65	0.62	0.63	0.67	0.69	0.78
Current Ratio	4.43	4.03	3.84	3.59	4.11	3.92	2.96	3.72
Debt to Equity	0.17	0.17	0.20	0.20	0.36	0.42	0.48	0.59
Price Range	151.93-123.93	151.93-113.77	133.73-106.48	126.00-105.05	114.25-92.30	126.34-87.54	113.63-81.50	100.46-53.10
P/E Ratio	41.51-33.86	39.46-29.55	43.85-34.91	46.84-39.05	19.97-16.14	20.18-13.98	17.24-12.37	19.32-10.21

Address: 1000 Alfred Nobel Drive, Hercules, CA 94547 Telephone: 510-724-7000	Web Site: www.bio-rad.com Officers: David Schwartz - Chairman Norman D. Schwartz - President, Chief Executive Officer	Auditors: KPMG LLP Investor Contact: 510-741-6104 Transfer Agents: Computershare, Canton, MA

BLACK HILLS CORPORATION

Exchange	Symbol	Price	52Wk Range	Yield	P/E	Div Achiever
NYS	BKH	$60.54 (5/31/2016)	61.74-37.29	2.78	N/A	44 Years

*7 Year Price Score 102.44 *NYSE Composite Index=100 *12 Month Price Score 121.67

Interim Earnings (Per Share)

Qtr.	Mar	Jun	Sep	Dec
2013	0.97	0.69	0.52	0.41
2014	1.08	0.44	0.60	0.78
2015	1.07	(0.94)	(0.22)	(0.31)
2016	0.77	...	...	...

Interim Dividends (Per Share)

Amt	Decl	Ex	Rec	Pay
0.405Q	07/28/2015	08/14/2015	08/18/2015	09/01/2015
0.405Q	10/27/2015	11/13/2015	11/17/2015	12/01/2015
0.42Q	01/27/2016	02/11/2016	02/16/2016	03/01/2016
0.42Q	04/25/2016	05/16/2016	05/18/2016	06/01/2016

Indicated Div: $1.68 (Div. Reinv. Plan)

Valuation Analysis

		Institutional Holding	
Forecast EPS	$3.00	No of Institutions	
	(05/14/2016)	324	
Market Cap	$3.1 Billion	Shares	
Book Value	$1.5 Billion	50,382,992	
Price/Book	2.10	% Held	
Price/Sales	2.37	73.32	

Business Summary: Electric Utilities (MIC: 3.1.1 SIC: 4911 NAIC: 221121)

Black Hills is a holding company. Through its subsidiaries, Co. operates in the U.S. with two primary business groups: Utilities, which comprised of its regulated Electric Utilities and regulated Gas Utilities segments; and Non-regulated Energy, which comprised of its Power Generation, Coal Mining and Oil and Gas segments. As of Dec 31 2015, Co.'s Electric Utilities segment generated, transmitted and distributed electricity to approximately 207,200 electric customers in South Dakota, Wyoming, Colorado and Montana and also distributed natural gas to approximately 44,200 gas utility customers of Cheyenne Light, Fuel and Power Company in and around Cheyenne, WY.

Recent Developments: For the quarter ended Mar 31 2016, net income increased 18.3% to US$40.1 million from US$33.9 million in the year-earlier quarter. Revenues were US$450.0 million, up 1.8% from US$442.0 million the year before. Operating income was US$73.6 million versus US$70.5 million in the prior-year quarter, an increase of 4.4%. Direct operating expenses declined 6.5% to US$278.9 million from US$298.5 million in the comparable period the year before. Indirect operating expenses increased 33.4% to US$97.5 million from US$73.0 million in the equivalent prior-year period.

Prospects: Our evaluation of Black Hills Corp. as of June 19, 2016 is the result of our systematic analysis on three basic characteristics: earnings strength, relative valuation, and recent stock price movement. The company has produced a positive trend in earnings per share over the past 5 quarters and while recent estimates for the company have been mixed, BKH has posted better than expected results. Based on operating earnings yield, the company is about fairly valued when compared to all of the companies in our coverage universe. Share price changes over the past year indicates that BKH will perform very well over the near term.

Financial Data

(US$ in Thousands)	3 Mos	12/31/2015	12/31/2014	12/31/2013	12/31/2012	12/31/2011	12/31/2010	12/31/2009
Earnings Per Share	(0.70)	(0.71)	2.89	2.59	1.85	1.24	1.76	2.11
Cash Flow Per Share	8.13	9.45	7.29	7.35	7.21	5.61	3.80	7.01
Tang Book Value Per Share	3.18	21.54	22.82	21.37	19.80	19.40	18.88	18.65
Dividends Per Share	1.635	1.620	1.560	1.520	1.480	1.460	1.440	1.420
Dividend Payout %	...	...	53.98	58.69	80.00	117.74	81.82	67.30
Income Statement								
Total Revenue	449,959	1,304,605	1,393,570	1,275,852	1,173,884	1,272,188	1,307,251	1,269,578
EBITDA	76,651	193,413	412,428	434,978	408,195	281,493	308,348	309,212
Depn & Amortn	1,666	161,734	150,210	147,980	160,187	135,591	126,894	121,297
Income Before Taxes	44,302	(49,522)	194,177	177,540	136,895	57,468	92,424	110,728
Income Taxes	4,252	(22,160)	65,395	61,608	48,400	18,224	25,298	33,315
Net Income	40,050	(32,111)	128,781	114,962	81,528	49,730	68,685	81,555
Average Shares	51,858	45,288	44,598	44,419	44,073	40,081	39,091	38,684
Balance Sheet								
Current Assets	423,146	822,151	454,036	345,288	405,106	758,921	670,871	624,870
Total Assets	6,324,653	4,655,501	4,279,806	3,875,178	3,729,471	4,127,083	3,711,509	3,317,698
Current Liabilities	660,262	422,029	651,281	378,394	734,889	878,067	787,440	644,859
Long-Term Obligations	3,159,055	1,866,866	1,267,589	1,396,948	938,877	1,280,409	1,186,050	1,015,912
Total Liabilities	4,843,970	3,189,634	2,903,782	2,567,430	2,496,962	2,917,747	2,611,239	2,232,861
Stockholders' Equity	1,480,683	1,465,867	1,376,024	1,307,748	1,232,509	1,209,336	1,100,270	1,084,837
Shares Outstanding	51,446	51,192	44,671	44,499	44,206	43,924	39,269	38,968
Statistical Record								
Return on Assets %	N.M.	N.M.	3.16	3.02	2.07	1.27	1.95	2.44
Return on Equity %	N.M.	N.M.	9.60	9.05	6.66	4.31	6.29	7.64
EBITDA Margin %	17.04	14.83	29.60	34.09	34.77	22.13	23.59	24.36
Net Margin %	8.90	N.M.	9.24	9.01	6.95	3.91	5.25	6.42
Asset Turnover	0.25	0.29	0.34	0.34	0.30	0.32	0.37	0.38
Current Ratio	0.64	1.95	0.70	0.91	0.55	0.86	0.85	0.97
Debt to Equity	2.13	1.27	0.92	1.07	0.76	1.06	1.08	0.94
Price Range	60.76-37.29	53.12-37.29	61.39-47.48	54.82-36.34	36.95-30.67	34.80-26.61	34.11-25.86	27.82-14.59
P/E Ratio	...	...	21.24-16.43	21.17-14.03	19.97-16.58	28.06-21.46	19.38-14.69	13.18-6.91
Average Yield %	3.52	3.54	2.84	3.21	4.40	4.65	4.79	6.15

Address: 625 Ninth Street, Rapid City, SD 57701 **Telephone:** 605-721-1700	**Web Site:** www.blackhillscorp.com **Officers:** David R. Emery - Chairman, President, Chief Executive Officer Linden R. Evans - Division Officer, President, Chief Operating Officer	**Auditors:** Deloitte & Touche LLP **Investor Contact:** 605-721-1171 **Transfer Agents:** Wells Fargo Shareowner Services, St. Paul, MN

103

BLACKROCK, INC.

Exchange	Symbol	Price	52Wk Range	Yield	P/E
NYS	BLK	$363.85 (5/31/2016)	367.47-289.72	2.52	19.28

*7 Year Price Score 114.42 *NYSE Composite Index=100 *12 Month Price Score 104.59

Interim Earnings (Per Share)

Qtr.	Mar	Jun	Sep	Dec
2013	3.62	4.19	4.21	4.85
2014	4.40	4.72	5.37	4.77
2015	4.84	4.84	5.00	5.11
2016	3.92	...	...	...

Interim Dividends (Per Share)

Amt	Decl	Ex	Rec	Pay
2.18Q	07/30/2015	08/31/2015	09/02/2015	09/22/2015
2.18Q	11/17/2015	12/01/2015	12/03/2015	12/23/2015
2.29Q	01/14/2016	03/03/2016	03/07/2016	03/23/2016
2.29Q	05/25/2016	06/02/2016	06/06/2016	06/23/2016

Indicated Div: $9.16

Valuation Analysis — **Institutional Holding**

Forecast EPS	$19.66	No of Institutions
	(05/20/2016)	1119
Market Cap	$59.5 Billion	Shares
Book Value	$28.4 Billion	157,735,584
Price/Book	2.10	% Held
Price/Sales	5.27	79.83

Business Summary: Finance Intermediaries & Services (MIC: 5.5.1 SIC: 6211 NAIC: 523999)

BlackRock is an investment management firm. Co. provides investment and risk management services to institutional and retail clients. Co.'s products include single- and multi-asset class portfolios investing in equities, fixed income, alternatives and money market instruments. The products are provided in a variety of vehicles, including open-end and closed-end mutual funds, iShares® exchange-traded funds, separate accounts and collective investment funds. Co. also provides its BlackRock Solutions® investment and risk management technology platform, Aladdin®, risk analytics and advisory services to institutional investors. At Dec 31 2015, Co. had $4.65 trillion of assets under management.

Recent Developments: For the quarter ended Mar 31 2016, net income decreased 21.6% to US$647.0 million from US$825.0 million in the year-earlier quarter. Revenues were US$2.62 billion, down 3.6% from US$2.72 billion the year before. Operating income was US$963.0 million versus US$1.07 billion in the prior-year quarter, a decrease of 9.7%. Indirect operating expenses were unchanged at US$1.66 billion versus the equivalent prior-year period.

Prospects: Our evaluation of BlackRock Inc. as of June 19, 2016 is the result of our systematic analysis on three basic characteristics: earnings strength, relative valuation, and recent stock price movement. The company has managed to produce a neutral trend in earnings per share over the past 5 quarters. However, while recent estimates for the company have been lowered by analysts, BLK has posted results that fell short of analysts expectations. Based on operating earnings yield, the company is undervalued when compared to all of the companies in our coverage universe. Share price changes over the past year indicates that BLK will perform well over the near term.

Financial Data

(US$ in Thousands)	3 Mos	12/31/2015	12/31/2014	12/31/2013	12/31/2012	12/31/2011	12/31/2010	12/31/2009
Earnings Per Share	18.87	19.79	19.25	16.87	13.79	12.37	10.55	6.11
Cash Flow Per Share	17.71	18.05	18.31	21.40	12.77	15.34	13.06	10.24
Dividends Per Share	8.830	8.720	7.720	6.720	6.000	5.500	4.000	3.120
Dividend Payout %	46.79	44.06	40.10	39.83	43.51	44.46	37.91	51.06
Income Statement								
Total Revenue	2,624,000	11,401,000	11,081,000	10,180,000	9,337,000	9,081,000	8,612,000	4,700,000
EBITDA	971,000	5,049,000	4,901,000	4,473,000	3,971,000	3,605,000	3,476,000	1,572,000
Depn & Amortn	10,000	243,000	274,000	289,000	286,000	294,000	305,000	232,000
Income Before Taxes	915,000	4,602,000	4,395,000	3,973,000	3,470,000	3,135,000	3,021,000	1,272,000
Income Taxes	268,000	1,250,000	1,131,000	1,022,000	1,030,000	796,000	971,000	375,000
Net Income	657,000	3,345,000	3,294,000	2,932,000	2,458,000	2,337,000	2,063,000	875,000
Average Shares	167,398	169,038	171,112	173,828	178,017	187,116	192,692	139,481
Balance Sheet								
Current Assets	7,507,000	8,320,000	7,843,000	6,637,000	6,856,000	5,466,000	5,462,000	6,438,000
Total Assets	222,958,000	225,261,000	239,808,000	219,873,000	200,451,000	179,896,000	178,459,000	177,994,000
Current Liabilities	2,057,000	3,039,000	2,900,000	2,831,000	2,716,000	2,428,000	2,745,000	5,000,000
Long-Term Obligations	4,968,000	4,930,000	4,938,000	4,939,000	5,687,000	4,690,000	3,259,000	3,434,000
Total Liabilities	194,564,000	196,758,000	212,442,000	193,413,000	175,048,000	154,848,000	152,365,000	153,665,000
Stockholders' Equity	28,394,000	28,503,000	27,366,000	26,460,000	25,403,000	25,048,000	26,094,000	24,329,000
Shares Outstanding	163,587	163,461	164,786	166,589	168,875	138,463	131,216	61,896
Statistical Record								
Return on Assets %	1.37	1.44	1.43	1.40	1.29	1.30	1.16	0.88
Return on Equity %	11.40	11.97	12.24	11.31	9.72	9.14	8.18	4.81
EBITDA Margin %	37.00	44.29	44.23	43.94	42.53	39.70	40.36	33.45
Net Margin %	25.04	29.34	29.73	28.80	26.33	25.74	23.95	18.62
Asset Turnover	0.05	0.05	0.05	0.05	0.05	0.05	0.05	0.05
Current Ratio	3.65	2.74	2.70	2.34	2.52	2.25	1.99	1.29
Debt to Equity	0.17	0.17	0.18	0.19	0.22	0.19	0.12	0.14
Price Range	377.85-289.72	380.33-293.52	364.40-286.39	316.47-206.71	209.29-163.37	207.06-141.77	242.81-139.44	240.80-90.57
P/E Ratio	20.02-15.35	19.22-14.83	18.93-14.88	18.76-12.25	15.18-11.85	16.74-11.46	23.02-13.22	39.41-14.82
Average Yield %	2.63	2.51	2.42	2.49	3.24	3.07	2.21	1.81

Address: 55 East 52nd Street, New York, NY 10055 Telephone: 212-810-5300	Web Site: www.blackrock.com Officers: Laurence D. Fink - Chairman, Chief Executive Officer Robert W. Fairbairn - Vice-Chairman, Senior Managing Director, Division Officer	Auditors: Deloitte & Touche LLP Transfer Agents: Computershare, Jersey City, NJ

BLOCK (H & R), INC.

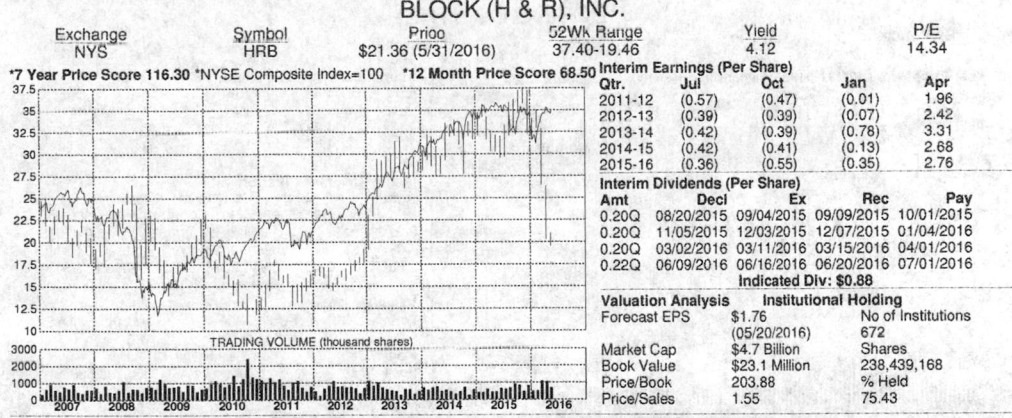

Exchange	Symbol	Price	52Wk Range	Yield	P/E
NYS	HRB	$21.36 (5/31/2016)	37.40-19.46	4.12	14.34

*7 Year Price Score 116.30 *NYSE Composite Index=100 *12 Month Price Score 68.50

Interim Earnings (Per Share)

Qtr.	Jul	Oct	Jan	Apr
2011-12	(0.57)	(0.47)	(0.01)	1.96
2012-13	(0.39)	(0.39)	(0.07)	2.42
2013-14	(0.42)	(0.39)	(0.78)	3.31
2014-15	(0.42)	(0.41)	(0.13)	2.68
2015-16	(0.36)	(0.55)	(0.35)	2.76

Interim Dividends (Per Share)

Amt	Decl	Ex	Rec	Pay
0.20Q	08/20/2015	09/04/2015	09/09/2015	10/01/2015
0.20Q	11/05/2015	12/03/2015	12/07/2015	01/04/2016
0.20Q	03/02/2016	03/11/2016	03/15/2016	04/01/2016
0.22Q	06/09/2016	06/16/2016	06/20/2016	07/01/2016

Indicated Div: $0.88

Valuation Analysis

		Institutional Holding	
Forecast EPS	$1.76	No of Institutions	
	(05/20/2016)	672	
Market Cap	$4.7 Billion	Shares	
Book Value	$23.1 Million	238,439,168	
Price/Book	203.88	% Held	
Price/Sales	1.55	75.43	

Business Summary: Miscellaneous Consumer Services (MIC: 2.2.3 SIC: 7291 NAIC: 541213)

Block (H&R) and its subsidiaries are engaged in providing tax preparation and other services. Co. provides assisted income tax return preparation, digital do-it-yourself (DIY) tax solutions and other services and products related to income tax return preparation to the general public primarily in the U.S., Canada, Australia, and their respective territories. Co. provides a number of DIY tax solutions, including online tax services and desktop spftware. In addition to its tax services and products, Co. provides clients additional services, including refund transfers that include a fee deduction feature, H&R Block Emerald Advance® lines of credit, and H&R Block Emerald Prepaid MasterCard®.

Recent Developments: For the year ended Apr 30 2016, income from continuing operations decreased 21.2% to US$383.6 million from US$486.7 million a year earlier. Net income decreased 21.0% to US$374.3 million from US$473.7 million in the prior year. Revenues were US$3.04 billion, down 1.3% from US$3.08 billion the year before. Direct operating expenses rose 3.4% to US$1.69 billion from US$1.63 billion in the comparable period the year before. Indirect operating expenses increased 10.6% to US$731.9 million from US$661.4 million in the equivalent prior-year period.

Prospects: Our evaluation of Block (H & R) Inc. as of June 19, 2016 is the result of our systematic analysis on three basic characteristics: earnings strength, relative valuation, and recent stock price movement. The company has managed to produce a neutral trend in earnings per share over the past 5 quarters. However, while recent estimates for the company have been lowered by analysts, HRB has posted better than expected results. Based on operating earnings yield, the company is undervalued when compared to all of the companies in our coverage universe. Share price changes over the past year indicates that HRB will perform poorly over the near term.

Financial Data

(US$ in Thousands)	04/30/2016	04/30/2015	04/30/2014	04/30/2013	04/30/2012	04/30/2011	04/30/2010	04/30/2009
Earnings Per Share	1.49	1.71	1.72	1.58	0.89	1.31	1.43	1.45
Cash Flow Per Share	2.13	2.28	2.96	1.82	1.21	1.66	1.77	3.08
Tang Book Value Per Share	N.M.	3.48	2.79	2.00	2.17	0.77	0.72	0.51
Dividends Per Share	0.800	0.800	0.800	0.800	0.700	0.600	0.600	0.593
Dividend Payout %	53.69	46.78	46.51	50.63	78.65	45.80	41.96	40.86
Income Statement								
Total Revenue	3,038,153	3,078,658	3,024,295	2,905,943	2,893,771	3,774,296	3,874,332	4,083,577
EBITDA	730,693	889,351	851,816	770,211	645,370	769,225	881,035	935,970
Depn & Amortn	100,800	101,300	84,700	68,200	69,300	92,200	96,900	96,600
Income Before Taxes	569,479	742,805	767,116	702,011	576,070	677,025	784,135	839,370
Income Taxes	185,926	256,061	267,019	236,853	230,102	257,620	295,189	326,315
Net Income	374,267	473,663	475,157	433,948	265,932	406,110	479,242	485,673
Average Shares	250,818	277,136	276,027	274,359	298,601	309,777	333,236	334,539
Balance Sheet								
Current Assets	1,222,298	2,951,301	3,114,006	2,462,343	2,500,994	2,477,731	2,649,036	2,571,080
Total Assets	2,857,775	4,515,420	4,693,529	4,537,779	4,649,567	5,207,961	5,234,318	5,359,722
Current Liabilities	1,039,605	1,878,289	2,313,116	2,012,205	2,526,428	2,214,675	2,321,491	2,398,280
Long-Term Obligations	1,501,925	505,298	505,837	905,958	409,115	1,049,754	1,060,144	1,107,122
Total Liabilities	2,834,672	2,682,471	3,136,980	3,274,232	3,323,675	3,758,387	3,793,688	3,953,863
Stockholders' Equity	23,103	1,832,949	1,556,549	1,263,547	1,325,892	1,449,574	1,440,630	1,405,859
Shares Outstanding	220,517	275,275	274,228	272,635	292,119	305,366	323,306	334,101
Statistical Record								
Return on Assets %	10.12	10.29	10.29	9.45	5.38	7.78	9.05	8.84
Return on Equity %	40.22	27.95	33.70	33.52	19.11	28.10	33.67	40.58
EBITDA Margin %	24.05	28.89	28.17	26.50	22.30	20.38	22.74	22.92
Net Margin %	12.32	15.39	15.71	14.93	9.19	10.76	12.37	11.89
Asset Turnover	0.82	0.67	0.66	0.63	0.59	0.72	0.73	0.74
Current Ratio	1.18	1.57	1.35	1.22	0.99	1.12	1.14	1.07
Debt to Equity	65.01	0.28	0.32	0.72	0.31	0.72	0.74	0.79
Price Range	37.40-20.24	35.64-27.64	32.19-26.05	29.42-14.47	17.48-12.73	18.92-10.62	23.07-13.94	26.50-14.78
P/E Ratio	25.10-13.58	20.84-16.16	18.72-15.15	18.62-9.16	19.64-14.30	14.44-8.11	16.13-9.75	18.28-10.19
Average Yield %	2.47	2.48	2.76	4.11	4.51	4.18	3.29	2.81

Address: One H&R Block Way, Kansas City, MO 64105
Telephone: 816-854-3000

Web Site: www.hrblock.com
Officers: Robert A. Gerard - Chairman William C. Cobb - President, Chief Executive Officer

Auditors: Deloitte & Touche LLP
Transfer Agents: Wells Fargo Shareowner Services, St. Paul, MN

BOEING CO. (THE)

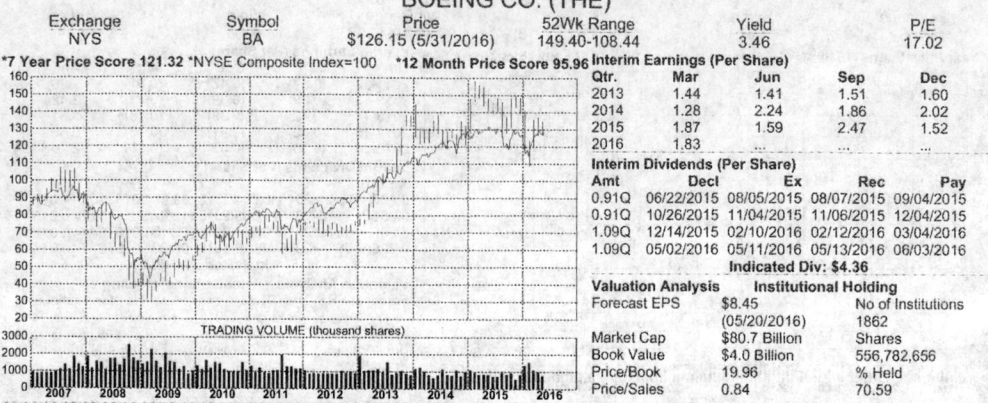

Exchange	Symbol	Price	52Wk Range	Yield	P/E
NYS	BA	$126.15 (5/31/2016)	149.40-108.44	3.46	17.02

*7 Year Price Score 121.32 *NYSE Composite Index=100 *12 Month Price Score 95.96

Interim Earnings (Per Share)

Qtr.	Mar	Jun	Sep	Dec
2013	1.44	1.41	1.51	1.60
2014	1.28	2.24	1.86	2.02
2015	1.87	1.59	2.47	1.52
2016	1.83	...	...	...

Interim Dividends (Per Share)

Amt	Decl	Ex	Rec	Pay
0.91Q	06/22/2015	08/05/2015	08/07/2015	09/04/2015
0.91Q	10/26/2015	11/04/2015	11/06/2015	12/04/2015
1.09Q	12/14/2015	02/10/2016	02/12/2016	03/04/2016
1.09Q	05/02/2016	05/11/2016	05/13/2016	06/03/2016

Indicated Div: $4.36

Valuation Analysis

		Institutional Holding	
Forecast EPS	$8.45	No of Institutions	1862
	(05/20/2016)		
Market Cap	$80.7 Billion	Shares	556,782,656
Book Value	$4.0 Billion		
Price/Book	19.96	% Held	70.59
Price/Sales	0.84		

TRADING VOLUME (thousand shares)

Business Summary: Aerospace (MIC: 7.1.1 SIC: 3721 NAIC: 336411)

Boeing is an aerospace firm. Co. engages in the design, development, manufacture, sale, service and support of commercial jetliners, military aircraft, satellites, missile defense, human space flight and launch systems and services. While its principal operations are in the U.S., Co. conducts operations in various countries and has a network of international partners, suppliers and subcontractors. As of Dec 31 2015, Co. operated five principal segments: Commercial Airplanes; Defense, Space and Security, which is comprised of the Boeing Military Aircraft, Network and Space Systems and Global Services and Support segments; and Boeing Capital.

Recent Developments: For the quarter ended Mar 31 2016, net income decreased 8.8% to US$1.22 billion from US$1.34 billion in the year-earlier quarter. Revenues were US$22.63 billion, up 2.2% from US$22.15 billion the year before. Operating income was US$1.79 billion versus US$2.02 billion in the prior-year quarter, a decrease of 11.4%. Direct operating expenses rose 3.2% to US$19.10 billion from US$18.50 billion in the comparable period the year before. Indirect operating expenses increased 6.9% to US$1.75 billion from US$1.63 billion in the equivalent prior-year period.

Prospects: Our evaluation of Boeing Co. as of June 19, 2016 is the result of our systematic analysis on three basic characteristics: earnings strength, relative valuation, and recent stock price movement. The company has managed to produce a neutral trend in earnings per share over the past 5 quarters and while recent estimates for the company have been raised by analysts, BA has posted results that fell short of analysts expectations. Based on operating earnings yield, the company is undervalued when compared to all of the companies in our coverage universe. Share price changes over the past year indicates that BA will perform well over the near term.

Financial Data

(US$ in Millions)	3 Mos	12/31/2015	12/31/2014	12/31/2013	12/31/2012	12/31/2011	12/31/2010	12/31/2009
Earnings Per Share	7.41	7.44	7.38	5.96	5.11	5.34	4.45	1.84
Cash Flow Per Share	15.93	13.61	12.15	10.75	9.88	5.39	4.00	7.90
Tang Book Value Per Share	N.M.	N.M.	0.96	9.07	N.M.	N.M.	N.M.	N.M.
Dividends Per Share	3.820	3.640	2.920	1.940	1.760	1.680	1.680	1.680
Dividend Payout %	51.55	48.92	39.57	32.55	34.44	31.46	37.75	91.30
Income Statement								
Total Revenue	22,632	96,114	90,762	86,623	81,698	68,735	64,306	68,281
EBITDA	2,203	8,513	8,597	7,742	7,353	6,935	6,069	3,094
Depn & Amortn	443	1,357	1,414	1,338	1,248	1,322	1,313	1,273
Income Before Taxes	1,687	6,881	6,850	6,018	5,642	5,115	4,240	1,482
Income Taxes	522	1,979	1,691	1,646	2,007	1,382	1,196	396
Net Income	1,219	5,176	5,446	4,585	3,900	4,018	3,307	1,312
Average Shares	665	696	738	769	763	753	744	713
Balance Sheet								
Current Assets	65,587	68,234	67,785	65,074	57,309	49,810	40,572	35,275
Total Assets	91,547	94,408	99,198	92,663	88,896	79,986	68,565	62,053
Current Liabilities	49,517	50,412	56,717	51,486	44,982	41,274	35,395	32,883
Long-Term Obligations	8,721	8,730	8,141	8,072	8,973	10,018	11,473	12,217
Total Liabilities	87,504	88,073	90,533	77,788	83,029	76,471	65,799	59,925
Stockholders' Equity	4,043	6,335	8,665	14,875	5,867	3,515	2,766	2,128
Shares Outstanding	639	666	706	747	755	744	735	755
Statistical Record								
Return on Assets %	5.34	5.35	5.68	5.05	4.61	5.41	5.06	2.27
Return on Equity %	84.68	69.01	46.27	44.21	82.91	127.94	135.15	314.63
EBITDA Margin %	9.73	8.86	9.47	8.94	9.00	10.09	9.44	4.53
Net Margin %	5.39	5.39	6.00	5.29	4.77	5.85	5.14	1.92
Asset Turnover	1.02	0.99	0.95	0.95	0.96	0.93	0.98	1.18
Current Ratio	1.32	1.35	1.20	1.26	1.27	1.21	1.15	1.07
Debt to Equity	2.16	1.38	0.94	0.54	1.53	2.85	4.15	5.74
Price Range	154.38-108.44	158.31-125.49	144.37-118.34	138.36-73.65	77.27-67.24	79.95-57.41	75.59-54.13	56.05-29.36
P/E Ratio	20.83-14.63	21.28-16.87	19.56-16.04	23.21-12.36	15.12-13.16	14.97-10.75	16.99-12.16	30.46-15.96
Average Yield %	2.76	2.54	2.27	1.88	2.40	2.41	2.54	3.72

| **Address:** 100 North Riverside Plaza, Chicago, IL 60606-1596
Telephone: 312-544-2000 | **Web Site:** www.boeing.com
Officers: Dennis A. Muilenburg - Chairman, Vice-Chairman, President, Chief Executive Officer, Chief Operating Officer, Executive Vice President, Division Officer Bertrand-Marc Allen - Senior Vice President, Division Officer | **Auditors:** Deloitte & Touche LLP
Transfer Agents: Computershare Trust Company, N.A., Providence, RI |

BOOZ ALLEN HAMILTON HOLDING CORP.

Exchange	Symbol	Price	52Wk Range	Yield	P/E
NYS	BAH	$29.27 (5/31/2016)	31.13-24.77	2.05	15.09

*7 Year Price Score N/A *NYSE Composite Index=100 *12 Month Price Score 101.28

Interim Earnings (Per Share)

Qtr.	Jun	Sep	Dec	Mar
2011-12	0.37	0.53	0.44	0.36
2012-13	0.43	0.27	0.68	0.37
2013-14	0.48	0.45	0.31	0.30
2014-15	0.47	0.42	0.35	0.28
2015-16	0.43	0.37	0.71	0.43

Interim Dividends (Per Share)

Amt	Decl	Ex	Rec	Pay
0.13Q	07/28/2015	08/06/2015	08/10/2015	08/31/2015
0.13Q	10/28/2015	11/06/2015	11/10/2015	11/30/2015
0.15Q	01/27/2016	02/08/2016	02/10/2016	02/29/2016
0.15Q	05/17/2016	06/08/2016	06/10/2016	06/30/2016

Indicated Div: $0.60

Valuation Analysis

		Institutional Holding	
Forecast EPS	$1.71 (05/15/2016)	No of Institutions	269
Market Cap	$4.3 Billion	Shares	226,380,528
Book Value	$408.5 Million	% Held	88.04
Price/Book	10.60		
Price/Sales	0.80		

Business Summary: Business Services (MIC: 7.5.2 SIC: 8742 NAIC: 541611)

Booz Allen Hamilton Holding is a holding company. Through its subsidiaries, Co. is a provider of management and technology, consulting, and engineering services to the U.S. and international governments, corporations, and non-profit organizations. Co.'s functional service offerings are: Systems Delivery, which include cloud experts and Software Developers and Systems Architects; Engineering and Science, which include engineers that provide prototyping and reverse engineering, among others and Networks and Information Technology Infrastructure; Cyber, which focuses on prevention; Analytics, which include decision analysts' capabilities, and data scientists; and Consulting.

Recent Developments: For the year ended Mar 31 2016, net income increased 26.5% to US$294.1 million from US$232.6 million in the prior year. Revenues were US$5.41 billion, up 2.5% from US$5.27 billion the year before. Operating income was US$444.6 million versus US$458.8 million in the prior year, a decrease of 3.1%. Direct operating expenses declined 0.5% to US$2.58 billion from US$2.59 billion in the comparable period the year before. Indirect operating expenses increased 7.2% to US$2.38 billion from US$2.22 billion in the equivalent prior-year period.

Prospects: Our evaluation of Booz Allen Hamilton Holding as of June 19, 2016 is the result of our systematic analysis on three basic characteristics: earnings strength, relative valuation, and recent stock price movement. The company has produced a positive trend in earnings per share over the past 5 quarters and while recent estimates for the company have been mixed, BAH has posted results that were in line with analysts expectations. Based on operating earnings yield, the company is undervalued when compared to all of the companies in our coverage universe. Share price changes over the past year indicates that BAH will perform well over the near term.

Financial Data

(US$ in Thousands)	03/31/2016	03/31/2015	03/31/2014	03/31/2013	03/31/2012	03/31/2011	03/31/2010	03/31/2009
Earnings Per Share	1.94	1.52	1.54	1.45	1.70	0.66	0.22	(0.37)
Cash Flow Per Share	1.70	2.13	2.35	3.46	2.76	2.59	2.54	2.57
Dividends Per Share	0.540	1.460	2.400	8.360	0.090	...	...	...
Dividend Payout %	27.84	96.05	155.84	576.55	5.29	...	...	...
Income Statement								
Total Revenue	5,405,738	5,274,770	5,478,693	5,758,059	5,859,218	5,591,296	5,122,633	2,941,275
EBITDA	500,377	510,450	516,417	497,895	450,752	311,956	253,462	67,860
Depn & Amortn	50,100	52,700	57,600	59,300	58,800	52,000	55,200	35,300
Income Before Taxes	379,462	385,918	380,787	368,311	343,874	128,064	48,994	(60,930)
Income Taxes	85,368	153,349	148,599	149,253	103,919	43,370	23,575	(22,147)
Net Income	294,094	232,569	232,188	219,058	239,955	84,694	25,419	(38,783)
Average Shares	149,719	150,375	148,681	144,854	140,812	127,448	116,228	105,695
Balance Sheet								
Current Assets	1,189,771	1,163,208	1,255,977	1,424,352	1,657,663	1,365,649	1,370,168	1,432,893
Total Assets	3,010,171	2,877,493	2,940,818	3,177,528	3,314,791	3,024,023	3,062,223	3,182,249
Current Liabilities	939,913	848,994	917,104	964,646	914,446	866,135	785,920	643,585
Long-Term Obligations	1,484,448	1,569,272	1,585,231	1,659,611	922,925	964,328	1,546,782	1,220,502
Total Liabilities	2,601,683	2,690,995	2,769,182	2,950,735	2,129,606	2,116,773	2,552,640	2,121,906
Stockholders' Equity	408,488	186,498	171,636	226,793	1,185,185	907,250	509,583	1,060,343
Shares Outstanding	147,992	149,089	149,295	146,206	142,552	140,215	120,647	120,498
Statistical Record								
Return on Assets %	9.96	7.99	7.59	6.75	7.55	2.78	0.81	...
Return on Equity %	98.59	129.88	116.55	31.03	22.87	11.96	3.24	...
EBITDA Margin %	9.26	9.68	9.43	8.65	7.69	5.58	4.95	2.31
Net Margin %	5.44	4.41	4.24	3.80	4.10	1.51	0.50	N.M.
Asset Turnover	1.83	1.81	1.79	1.77	1.84	1.84	1.64	...
Current Ratio	1.27	1.37	1.37	1.48	1.81	1.58	1.74	2.23
Debt to Equity	3.63	8.41	9.24	7.32	0.78	1.06	3.04	1.15
Price Range	31.13-24.45	30.46-20.82	22.16-12.90	19.06-11.90	19.87-13.52	20.00-18.00	...	...
P/E Ratio	16.05-12.60	20.04-13.70	14.39-8.38	13.14-8.21	11.69-7.95	30.30-27.27	...	...
Average Yield %	1.94	5.87	13.04	56.23	0.52	...	...	...

Address: 8283 Greensboro Drive, McLean, VA 22102	**Web Site:** www.boozallen.com	**Auditors:** Ernst & Young LLP
Telephone: 703-902-5000	**Officers:** Ralph W. Shrader - Chairman, President, Chief Executive Officer Horacio D. Rozanski - President, Executive Vice President, Chief Operating Officer, Chief Executive Officer	**Investor Contact:** 703-377-5332 **Transfer Agents:** Computershare, Jersey City, NJ

BORGWARNER INC

Exchange	Symbol	Price	52Wk Range	Yield	P/E
NYS	BWA	$34.03 (5/31/2016)	61.62-28.23	1.53	16.68

*7 Year Price Score 91.24   *NYSE Composite Index=100   *12 Month Price Score 83.99

Interim Earnings (Per Share)

Qtr.	Mar	Jun	Sep	Dec
2013	0.61	0.75	0.72	0.62
2014	0.69	0.83	0.73	0.61
2015	0.79	0.65	0.70	0.56
2016	0.13	...	...	...

Interim Dividends (Per Share)

Amt	Decl	Ex	Rec	Pay
0.13Q	07/29/2015	08/28/2015	09/01/2015	09/15/2015
0.13Q	11/11/2015	11/27/2015	12/01/2015	12/15/2015
0.13Q	02/10/2016	02/26/2016	03/01/2016	03/15/2016
0.13Q	04/27/2016	05/27/2016	06/01/2016	06/15/2016

Indicated Div: $0.52

Valuation Analysis | **Institutional Holding**

Forecast EPS	$3.25 (05/20/2016)	No of Institutions 656
Market Cap	$7.4 Billion	Shares
Book Value	$3.7 Billion	220,899,520
Price/Book	2.01	% Held
Price/Sales	0.89	90.53

Business Summary: Auto Parts (MIC: 1.8.2 SIC: 3714 NAIC: 336350)

Borg Warner is a supplier of engineered automotive systems and components primarily for powertrain applications. These products are manufactured and sold primarily to original equipment manufacturers (OEMs) of light vehicles. Co.'s products are also sold to other OEMs of commercial vehicles and off-highway vehicles. Co.'s products fall into two reporting segments: Engine and Drivetrain. The Engine segment's products include turbochargers, timing devices and chain products, emissions systems, thermal systems, diesel coldstart and gasoline ignition technology. The Drivetrain segment's products include transmission components and systems and all-wheel drive torque management systems.

Recent Developments: For the quarter ended Mar 31 2016, net income decreased 7.7% to US$173.2 million from US$187.7 million in the year-earlier quarter. Revenues were US$2.27 billion, up 14.3% from US$1.98 billion the year before. Operating income was US$264.2 million versus US$259.6 million in the prior-year quarter, an increase of 1.8%. Direct operating expenses rose 16.0% to US$1.80 billion from US$1.56 billion in the comparable period the year before. Indirect operating expenses increased 18.1% to US$200.1 million from US$169.4 million in the equivalent prior-year period.

Prospects: Our evaluation of Borg Warner Inc. as of June 19, 2016 is the result of our systematic analysis on three basic characteristics: earnings strength, relative valuation, and recent stock price movement. The company has enjoyed a very positive trend in earnings per share over the past 5 quarters and while recent estimates for the company have remained steady, BWA has posted better than expected results. Based on operating earnings yield, the company is undervalued when compared to all of the companies in our coverage universe. Share price changes over the past year indicates that BWA will perform poorly over the near term.

Financial Data

(US$ in Thousands)	3 Mos	12/31/2015	12/31/2014	12/31/2013	12/31/2012	12/31/2011	12/31/2010	12/31/2009
Earnings Per Share	2.04	2.70	2.86	2.70	2.09	2.23	1.53	0.12
Cash Flow Per Share	4.00	3.87	3.53	3.14	3.89	3.24	2.36	1.51
Tang Book Value Per Share	6.34	5.71	9.98	9.63	7.33	4.42	4.35	4.17
Dividends Per Share	0.520	0.520	0.510	0.250	...	...	...	0.060
Dividend Payout %	25.49	19.26	17.83	9.26	...	...	...	52.17
Income Statement								
Total Revenue	2,268,600	8,023,200	8,305,100	7,436,600	7,183,200	7,114,700	5,652,800	3,961,800
EBITDA	358,600	1,259,900	1,294,100	1,154,600	1,046,800	1,100,800	775,500	324,400
Depn & Amortn	94,400	320,200	330,400	299,400	293,900	303,300	271,200	273,600
Income Before Taxes	244,500	886,800	932,800	825,800	718,200	727,700	438,300	(3,900)
Income Taxes	80,400	280,400	292,600	218,230	238,600	195,300	81,700	(18,500)
Net Income	164,100	609,700	655,800	624,300	500,900	550,100	377,400	27,000
Average Shares	218,137	225,648	228,924	231,337	242,754	256,936	259,150	233,878
Balance Sheet								
Current Assets	3,182,400	3,135,300	2,970,800	2,798,500	2,472,800	2,137,800	2,059,900	1,551,800
Total Assets	8,940,700	8,841,500	7,228,000	6,917,000	6,400,800	5,958,600	5,555,000	4,811,400
Current Liabilities	2,310,400	2,357,300	2,168,200	1,623,900	1,603,100	1,905,400	1,392,300	1,046,200
Long-Term Obligations	2,131,900	2,124,600	716,300	1,021,000	823,800	751,300	1,051,900	773,200
Total Liabilities	5,247,500	5,287,800	3,611,800	3,356,400	3,318,200	3,570,700	3,296,400	2,626,100
Stockholders' Equity	3,693,200	3,553,700	3,616,200	3,560,600	3,082,600	2,387,900	2,258,600	2,185,300
Shares Outstanding	217,619	219,324	226,430	227,932	231,145	217,028	224,632	233,675
Statistical Record								
Return on Assets %	7.23	7.59	9.27	9.38	8.08	9.56	7.28	0.57
Return on Equity %	16.53	17.01	18.28	18.80	18.26	23.68	16.99	1.29
EBITDA Margin %	15.81	15.70	15.58	15.53	14.57	15.47	13.72	8.19
Net Margin %	7.23	7.60	7.90	8.39	6.97	7.73	6.68	0.68
Asset Turnover	1.01	1.00	1.17	1.12	1.16	1.24	1.09	0.84
Current Ratio	1.38	1.33	1.37	1.72	1.54	1.12	1.48	1.48
Debt to Equity	0.58	0.60	0.20	0.29	0.27	0.31	0.47	0.35
Price Range	62.08-28.23	63.01-38.89	67.38-50.24	55.96-35.42	43.52-30.27	40.83-28.07	36.57-16.61	17.93-7.59
P/E Ratio	30.43-13.84	23.34-14.40	23.56-17.57	20.73-13.12	20.83-14.48	18.31-12.59	23.90-10.86	149.38-63.25
Average Yield %	1.13	1.00	0.86	0.56	...	...	...	0.43

Address: 3850 Hamlin Road, Auburn Hills, MI 48326 **Telephone:** 248-754-9200	**Web Site:** www.borgwarner.com **Officers:** Timothy M. Manganello - Chairman, Chief Executive Officer James R. Verrier - President, Chief Executive Officer, Vice President, Chief Operating Officer	**Auditors:** PricewaterhouseCoopers LLP **Investor Contact:** 248-754-0881 **Transfer Agents:** BNY Mellon Shareowner Services, Jersey City, NJ

BOSTON BEER CO INC (THE)

Exchange	Symbol	Price	52Wk Range	Yield	P/E
NYS	SAM	$155.40 (5/31/2016)	261.32-146.42	N/A	22.89

*7 Year Price Score 118.43 *NYSE Composite Index=100 ***12 Month Price Score 78.48**

TRADING VOLUME (thousand shares)

Interim Earnings (Per Share)

Qtr.	Mar	Jun	Sep	Dec
2013	0.51	1 45	1.89	1.33
2014	0.62	1.88	2.79	1.40
2015	1.00	2.18	2.85	1.23
2016	0.53	...	...	...

Interim Dividends (Per Share)

No Dividends Paid

Valuation Analysis

		Institutional Holding	
Forecast EPS	$6.71	No of Institutions	
	(05/20/2016)	289	
Market Cap	$2.0 Billion	Shares	
Book Value	$435.3 Million	10,886,599	
Price/Book	4.52	% Held	
Price/Sales	2.07	65.06	

Business Summary: Beverages (MIC: 1.2.2 SIC: 2082 NAIC: 312120)

Boston Beer Company is engaged in the business of selling alcohol beverages throughout the U.S. and in selected international markets. Co. consists of two operating segments that each produce and sell alcohol beverages. The first is the Boston Beer Company operating segment comprised of Co.'s Samuel Adams®, Twisted Tea® and Angry Orchard® brands. The second is the A&S Brewing Collaborative operating segment which is comprised of The Traveler Beer Company, Coney Island Brewing Company, Angel City Brewing Company and Concrete Beach Brewing Company. Co. produces malt beverages and hard cider at Co.-owned breweries and under contract arrangements at other brewery locations.

Recent Developments: For the quarter ended Mar 26 2016, net income decreased 48.8% to US$7.0 million from US$13.7 million in the year-earlier quarter. Revenues were US$188.8 million, down 5.4% from US$199.5 million the year before. Operating income was US$11.2 million versus US$22.1 million in the prior-year quarter, a decrease of 49.2%. Direct operating expenses declined 2.6% to US$97.3 million from US$99.9 million in the comparable period the year before. Indirect operating expenses increased 3.6% to US$80.3 million from US$77.5 million in the equivalent prior-year period.

Prospects: Our evaluation of Boston Beer Co. Inc. as of June 19, 2016 is the result of our systematic analysis on three basic characteristics: earnings strength, relative valuation, and recent stock price movement. The company has generated a negative trend in earnings per share over the past 5 quarters. However, while recent estimates for the company have been mixed, SAM has posted results that fell short of analysts expectations. Based on operating earnings yield, the company is about fairly valued when compared to all of the companies in our coverage universe. Share price changes over the past year indicates that SAM will perform poorly over the near term.

Financial Data

(US$ in Thousands)	3 Mos	12/26/2015	12/27/2014	12/28/2013	12/29/2012	12/31/2011	12/25/2010	12/26/2009
Earnings Per Share	6.79	7.25	6.69	5.18	4.39	4.81	3.52	2.17
Cash Flow Per Share	12.06	12.89	10.92	7.85	7.47	5.50	4.98	4.68
Tang Book Value Per Share	34.09	35.87	33.09	23.41	18.93	14.30	12.26	12.05
Income Statement								
Total Revenue	188,827	959,934	903,007	739,053	580,222	513,000	463,798	415,053
EBITDA	23,047	198,354	180,373	138,210	115,686	121,946	98,329	71,055
Depn & Amortn	12,029	43,400	34,800	25,700	20,200	18,500	17,300	16,800
Income Before Taxes	11,041	155,010	145,594	112,541	95,517	103,500	81,108	54,367
Income Taxes	4,009	56,596	54,851	42,149	36,050	37,441	30,966	23,249
Net Income	7,032	98,414	90,743	70,392	59,467	66,059	50,142	31,118
Average Shares	13,088	13,520	13,484	13,504	13,435	13,741	14,228	14,356
Balance Sheet								
Current Assets	182,495	223,603	207,462	164,278	162,342	125,723	112,004	113,030
Total Assets	607,831	645,400	605,161	444,075	359,484	272,488	258,530	262,936
Current Liabilities	101,521	111,160	110,170	104,377	88,894	67,049	72,199	73,786
Long-Term Obligations	411	471	528	584	566	...	...	...
Total Liabilities	172,484	184,179	169,021	141,990	114,393	87,743	92,942	89,781
Stockholders' Equity	435,347	461,221	436,140	302,085	245,091	184,745	165,588	173,155
Shares Outstanding	12,660	12,756	13,069	12,747	12,811	12,822	13,395	14,249
Statistical Record								
Return on Assets %	14.52	15.78	17.34	17.57	18.87	24.48	19.28	12.93
Return on Equity %	19.71	21.99	24.65	25.80	27.75	37.10	29.69	19.93
EBITDA Margin %	12.21	20.66	19.97	18.70	19.94	23.77	21.20	17.12
Net Margin %	3.72	10.25	10.05	9.52	10.25	12.88	10.81	7.50
Asset Turnover	1.50	1.54	1.73	1.84	1.84	1.90	1.78	1.72
Current Ratio	1.80	2.01	1.88	1.57	1.83	1.88	1.55	1.53
Price Range	272.83-163.55	323.99-197.05	297.78-203.81	259.25-134.45	139.24-94.52	112.88-72.13	99.53-44.25	46.81-18.33
P/E Ratio	40.18-24.09	44.69-27.18	44.51-30.46	50.05-25.96	31.72-21.53	23.47-15.00	28.28-12.57	21.57-8.45

Address: One Design Center Place, Suite 850, Boston, MA 02210	Web Site: www.bostonbeer.com	Auditors: Deloitte Touche Tohmatsu Limited
Telephone: 617-368-5000	Officers: C. James Koch - Chairman Martin F. Roper - President, Chief Executive Officer	Investor Contact: 617-368-5060
Fax: 617-368-5500		Transfer Agents: Computershare Shareownor Services LLC, Jersey Clty, NJ

BOSTON PROPERTIES, INC.

Exchange	Symbol	Price	52Wk Range	Yield	P/E
NYS	BXP	$125.63 (5/31/2016)	133.13-108.18	2.07	32.97

*7 Year Price Score 101.62 *NYSE Composite Index=100 *12 Month Price Score 103.68

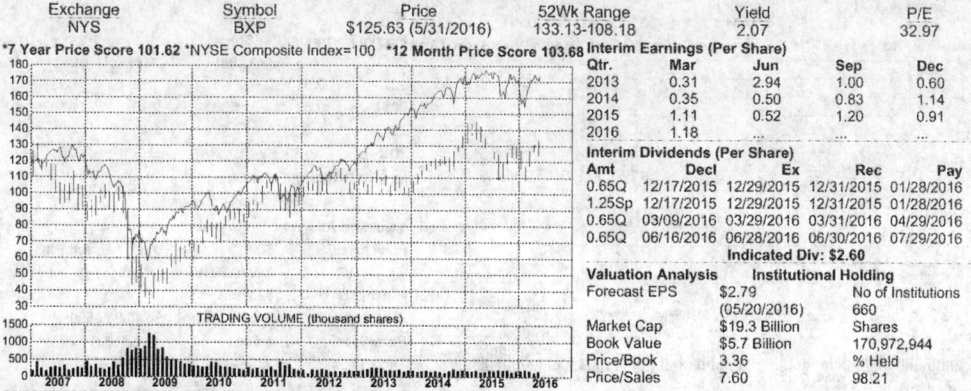

Interim Earnings (Per Share)

Qtr.	Mar	Jun	Sep	Dec
2013	0.31	2.94	1.00	0.60
2014	0.35	0.50	0.83	1.14
2015	1.11	0.52	1.20	0.91
2016	1.18	...	...	...

Interim Dividends (Per Share)

Amt	Decl	Ex	Rec	Pay
0.65Q	12/17/2015	12/29/2015	12/31/2015	01/28/2016
1.25Sp	12/17/2015	12/29/2015	12/31/2015	01/28/2016
0.65Q	03/09/2016	03/29/2016	03/31/2016	04/29/2016
0.65Q	06/16/2016	06/28/2016	06/30/2016	07/29/2016

Indicated Div: $2.60

Valuation Analysis

		Institutional Holding	
Forecast EPS	$2.79	No of Institutions	660
	(05/20/2016)		
Market Cap	$19.3 Billion	Shares	170,972,944
Book Value	$5.7 Billion	% Held	98.21
Price/Book	3.36		
Price/Sales	7.60		

Business Summary: REITs (MIC: 5.3.1 SIC: 6798 NAIC: 525930)

Boston Properties is a self-administered and self-managed real estate investment trust. Co. is also an owner and developer of office properties in the U.S. Co.'s properties are focused in four markets: Boston, New York, San Francisco and Washington, DC. At Dec 31 2015, Co. owned or had interests in 168 commercial real estate properties, which consisted of: 158 office properties, including 127 Class A office properties (includingincluding nine properties under construction/redevelopment) and 31 Office/Technical properties; one hotel; five retail properties; and four residential properties (including two under construction). Co. also owns or controls undeveloped land parcels.

Recent Developments: For the quarter ended Mar 31 2016, income from continuing operations increased 30.3% to US$148.6 million from US$114.1 million in the year-earlier quarter. Net income increased 3.4% to US$216.2 million from US$209.2 million in the year-earlier quarter. Revenues were US$666.0 million, up 7.7% from US$618.5 million the year before. Revenues from property income rose 7.7% to US$650.5 million from US$604.1 million in the corresponding quarter a year earlier.

Prospects: Our evaluation of Boston Properties Inc. as of June 19, 2016 is the result of our systematic analysis on three basic characteristics: earnings strength, relative valuation, and recent stock price movement. The company has enjoyed a very positive trend in earnings per share over the past 5 quarters. Because the company lacks sufficient analyst estimate data, we place greater weight on the historical EPS trend as the measure of earnings strength. Based on operating earnings yield, the company is overvalued when compared to all of the companies in our coverage universe. Share price changes over the past year indicates that BXP will perform well over the near term.

Financial Data

(US$ in Thousands)	3 Mos	12/31/2015	12/31/2014	12/31/2013	12/31/2012	12/31/2011	12/31/2010	12/31/2009
Earnings Per Share	3.81	3.73	2.83	4.86	1.92	1.86	1.14	1.76
Cash Flow Per Share	6.16	5.21	4.54	5.11	4.27	4.16	2.70	4.71
Tang Book Value Per Share	36.13	35.87	35.90	36.56	34.35	33.23	31.59	32.41
Dividends Per Share	3.850	3.850	7.100	4.850	2.300	2.050	2.000	2.180
Dividend Payout %	101.05	103.22	250.88	99.79	119.79	110.22	175.44	123.86
Income Statement								
Total Revenue	665,985	2,490,821	2,396,998	2,135,539	1,876,267	1,759,526	1,550,804	1,522,249
EBITDA	410,060	1,472,991	1,429,565	1,254,860	1,112,752	1,061,245	867,269	895,195
Depn & Amortn	159,448	639,542	628,573	565,397	454,044	439,184	338,371	321,681
Income Before Taxes	146,808	401,253	345,249	242,583	245,144	227,930	150,819	250,681
Net Income	184,365	583,106	443,611	749,811	289,650	272,679	159,072	231,014
Average Shares	153,917	153,844	153,308	152,521	150,711	146,218	140,057	131,512
Balance Sheet								
Current Assets	2,518,650	1,650,256	2,988,994	3,133,405	2,152,220	2,836,349	1,629,480	2,197,161
Total Assets	19,175,830	18,379,456	19,886,767	20,162,251	15,462,321	14,782,966	13,348,263	12,348,703
Current Liabilities	587,384	792,415	1,289,267	867,235	382,051	316,145	329,417	376,683
Long-Term Obligations	10,160,366	9,216,513	10,086,984	11,521,508	8,912,369	8,704,138	7,786,001	6,719,771
Total Liabilities	13,426,047	12,670,021	14,189,469	14,369,786	10,254,380	9,861,316	8,919,968	7,847,049
Stockholders' Equity	5,749,783	5,709,435	5,697,298	5,792,465	5,207,941	4,921,650	4,428,295	4,501,654
Shares Outstanding	153,604	153,579	153,113	152,983	151,601	148,107	140,199	138,880
Statistical Record								
Return on Assets %	3.10	3.05	2.22	4.21	1.91	1.94	1.24	1.99
Return on Equity %	10.30	10.22	7.72	13.63	5.70	5.83	3.56	5.75
EBITDA Margin %	61.57	59.14	59.64	58.76	59.31	60.31	55.92	58.81
Net Margin %	27.68	23.41	18.51	35.11	15.44	15.50	10.26	15.18
Asset Turnover	0.13	0.13	0.12	0.12	0.12	0.13	0.12	0.13
Current Ratio	4.29	2.08	2.32	3.61	5.63	8.97	4.95	5.83
Debt to Equity	1.77	1.61	1.77	1.99	1.71	1.77	1.76	1.49
Price Range	142.17-108.18	144.74-108.65	136.28-100.37	114.59-98.27	116.07-97.49	112.36-84.66	90.73-62.49	70.80-31.49
P/E Ratio	37.31-28.39	38.80-29.13	48.16-35.47	23.58-20.22	60.45-50.78	60.41-45.52	79.59-54.82	40.23-17.89
Average Yield %	3.11	2.99	6.00	4.58	2.16	2.10	2.54	4.13

Address: Prudential Center, 800 Boylston Street, Suite 1900, Boston, MA 02199-8103 **Telephone:** 617-236-3300	**Web Site:** www.bostonproperties.com **Officers:** Douglas T. Linde - President, Chief Merchandising Officer, Principal Operating Officer Owen D. Thomas - Chief Executive Officer	**Auditors:** PricewaterhouseCoopers LLP **Investor Contact:** 617-236-3322 **Transfer Agents:** Computershare Trust Company, N.A., Providence, RI

BOSTON SCIENTIFIC CORP.

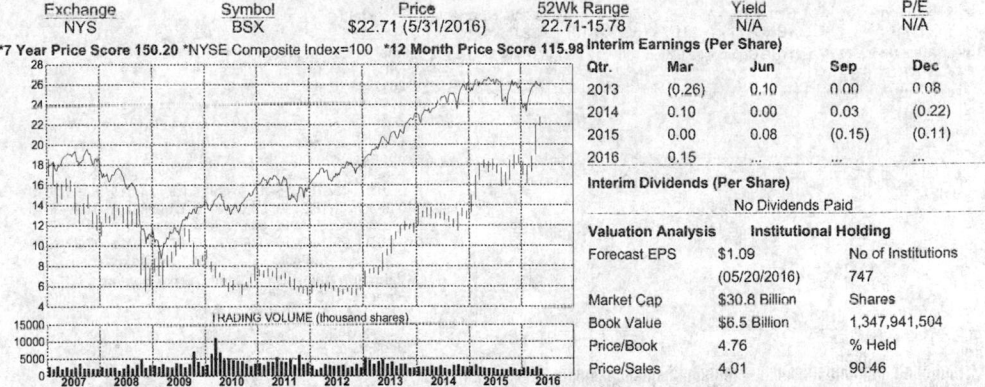

Exchange	Symbol	Price	52Wk Range	Yield	P/E
NYS	BSX	$22.71 (5/31/2016)	22.71-15.78	N/A	N/A

*7 Year Price Score 150.20 ***NYSE Composite Index=100** ***12 Month Price Score 115.98**

Interim Earnings (Per Share)

Qtr.	Mar	Jun	Sep	Dec
2013	(0.26)	0.10	0.00	0.08
2014	0.10	0.00	0.03	(0.22)
2015	0.00	0.08	(0.15)	(0.11)
2016	0.15	...	...	...

Interim Dividends (Per Share)

No Dividends Paid

Valuation Analysis / Institutional Holding

Valuation Analysis		Institutional Holding	
Forecast EPS	$1.09	No of Institutions	
	(05/20/2016)	747	
Market Cap	$30.8 Billion	Shares	
Book Value	$6.5 Billion	1,347,941,504	
Price/Book	4.76	% Held	
Price/Sales	4.01	90.46	

Business Summary: Medical Instruments & Equipment (MIC: 4.3.1 SIC: 3841 NAIC: 339112)

Boston Scientific is a developer, manufacturer and marketer of medical devices. Co.'s products include: drug-eluting coronary stent systems, core coronary technology, and structural heart therapy for Interventional Cardiology; stents, balloon catheters, wires, peripheral embolization devices and vena cava filters for Peripheral Interventions; a range of implantable devices that monitor the heart for Cardiac Rhythm Management; radio frequency generators for Electrophysiology; devices for gastroenterology and interventional bronchoscopy for Endoscopy; devices to treat urological and pelvic conditions for Urology/Women's Health; and pain management products for Neuromodulation.

Recent Developments: For the quarter ended Mar 31 2016, net income amounted to US$202.0 million versus a net loss of US$1.0 million in the year-earlier quarter. Revenues were US$1.96 billion, up 11.1% from US$1.77 billion the year before. Operating income was US$293.0 million versus US$24.0 million in the prior-year quarter, an increase of. Direct operating expenses rose 10.2% to US$573.0 million from US$520.0 million in the comparable period the year before. Indirect operating expenses decreased 10.3% to US$1.10 billion from US$1.22 billion in the equivalent prior-year period.

Prospects: Our evaluation of Boston Scientific Corp. as of June 19, 2016 is the result of our systematic analysis on three basic characteristics: earnings strength, relative valuation, and recent stock price movement. The company has produced a positive trend in earnings per share over the past 5 quarters and while recent estimates for the company have remained steady, BSX has posted better than expected results. Based on operating earnings yield, the company is about fairly valued when compared to all of the companies in our coverage universe. Share price changes over the past year indicates that BSX will perform well over the near term.

Financial Data

(US$ in Thousands)	3 Mos	12/31/2015	12/31/2014	12/31/2013	12/31/2012	12/31/2011	12/31/2010	12/31/2009
Earnings Per Share	(0.03)	(0.18)	(0.09)	(0.09)	(2.89)	0.29	(0.70)	(0.68)
Cash Flow Per Share	0.68	0.45	0.96	0.81	0.89	0.67	0.21	0.55
Income Statement								
Total Revenue	1,964,000	7,477,000	7,380,000	7,143,000	7,249,000	7,622,000	7,806,000	8,188,000
EBITDA	348,000	(97,000)	(11,000)	374,000	(3,563,000)	1,219,000	(367,000)	(578,000)
Depn & Amortn	64,000	274,000	287,000	279,000	288,000	296,000	303,000	323,000
Income Before Taxes	228,000	(650,000)	(509,000)	(223,000)	(4,107,000)	642,000	(1,063,000)	(1,308,000)
Income Taxes	26,000	(411,000)	(390,000)	(102,000)	(39,000)	201,000	2,000	(283,000)
Net Income	202,000	(239,000)	(119,000)	(121,000)	(4,068,000)	441,000	(1,065,000)	(1,025,000)
Average Shares	1,369,900	1,341,200	1,324,300	1,341,200	1,406,700	1,519,000	1,517,800	1,507,900
Balance Sheet								
Current Assets	3,164,000	3,471,000	3,606,000	3,011,000	3,022,000	3,105,000	3,615,000	4,061,000
Total Assets	17,718,000	18,133,000	17,042,000	16,571,000	17,154,000	21,290,000	22,128,000	25,177,000
Current Liabilities	2,608,000	2,430,000	2,846,000	1,824,000	1,772,000	1,807,000	2,609,000	3,022,000
Long-Term Obligations	5,424,000	5,674,000	3,859,000	4,237,000	4,252,000	4,257,000	4,934,000	5,915,000
Total Liabilities	11,261,000	11,813,000	10,585,000	10,032,000	10,284,000	9,937,000	10,832,000	12,876,000
Stockholders' Equity	6,457,000	6,320,000	6,457,000	6,539,000	6,870,000	11,353,000	11,296,000	12,301,000
Shares Outstanding	1,354,567	1,346,647	1,327,451	1,322,296	1,355,711	1,449,055	1,520,780	1,510,753
Statistical Record								
Return on Assets %	N.M.	N.M.	N.M.	N.M.	N.M.	2.03	N.M.	N.M.
Return on Equity %	N.M.	N.M.	N.M.	N.M.	N.M.	3.89	N.M.	N.M.
EBITDA Margin %	17.72	N.M.	N.M.	5.24	N.M.	15.99	N.M.	N.M.
Net Margin %	10.29	N.M.	N.M.	N.M.	N.M.	5.79	N.M.	N.M.
Asset Turnover	0.45	0.43	0.44	0.42	0.38	0.35	0.33	0.31
Current Ratio	1.21	1.43	1.27	1.65	1.71	1.72	1.39	1.34
Debt to Equity	0.84	0.90	0.60	0.65	0.62	0.37	0.44	0.48
Price Range	18.94-15.78	18.94-13.22	13.98-11.37	12.38-5.73	6.36-4.97	7.79-5.09	9.62-5.13	11.75-6.14
P/E Ratio	...	...	...	...	...	26.86-17.55	...	...

Address: 300 Boston Scientific Way, Marlborough, MA 01752-1234	Web Site: www.bostonscientific.com	Auditors: Ernst & Young LLP
Telephone: 508-683-4000	Officers: Michael F. Mahoney - Chairman, President, Chief Executive Officer Supratim Bose - Executive Vice President, Region Officer	Investor Contact: 508-650-8023
		Transfer Agents: Computershare Shareowner Services, Providence, RI

BRADY CORP

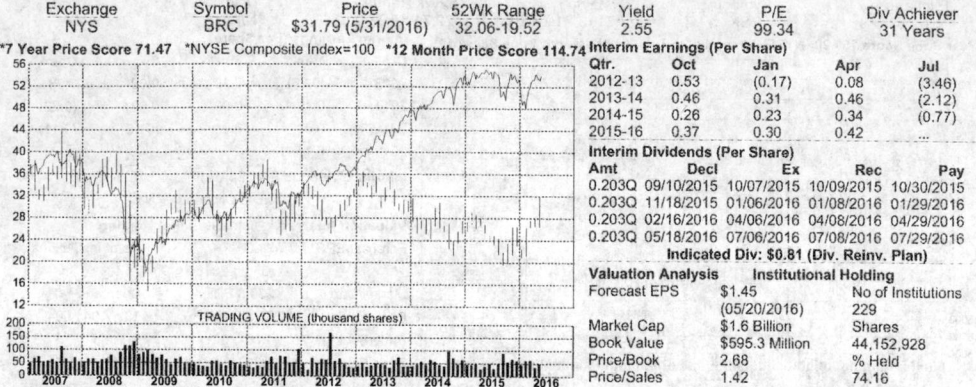

Exchange	Symbol	Price	52Wk Range	Yield	P/E	Div Achiever
NYS	BRC	$31.79 (5/31/2016)	32.06-19.52	2.55	99.34	31 Years

*7 Year Price Score 71.47   *NYSE Composite Index=100   *12 Month Price Score 114.74

Interim Earnings (Per Share)

Qtr.	Oct	Jan	Apr	Jul
2012-13	0.53	(0.17)	0.08	(3.46)
2013-14	0.46	0.31	0.46	(2.12)
2014-15	0.26	0.23	0.34	(0.77)
2015-16	0.37	0.30	0.42	...

Interim Dividends (Per Share)

Amt	Decl	Ex	Rec	Pay
0.203Q	09/10/2015	10/07/2015	10/09/2015	10/30/2015
0.203Q	11/18/2015	01/06/2016	01/08/2016	01/29/2016
0.203Q	02/16/2016	04/06/2016	04/08/2016	04/29/2016
0.203Q	05/18/2016	07/06/2016	07/08/2016	07/29/2016

Indicated Div: $0.81 (Div. Reinv. Plan)

Valuation Analysis

Forecast EPS	$1.45	Institutional Holding	
	(05/20/2016)	No of Institutions	229
Market Cap	$1.6 Billion	Shares	44,152,928
Book Value	$595.3 Million	% Held	74.16
Price/Book	2.68		
Price/Sales	1.42		

TRADING VOLUME (thousand shares)

Business Summary: Printing (MIC: 7.5.5 SIC: 3993 NAIC: 339950)

Brady is a manufacturer of identification solutions and specialty materials, and workplace safety products that identify and protect premises, products and people. Co. provides customers with a range of customized and diverse products for use in various applications. Co. operates in two business segments: Identification Solutions (ID Solutions), which includes identification and healthcare products that are sold to a range of maintenance, repair, and operations (MRO) and original equipment manufacturing customers; and Workplace Safety, which includes workplace safety and compliance products, sold to a range of MRO customers.

Recent Developments: For the quarter ended Apr 30 2016, income from continuing operations increased 21.9% to US$21.0 million from US$17.2 million in the year-earlier quarter. Net income increased 21.9% to US$21.0 million from US$17.2 million in the year-earlier quarter. Revenues were US$286.8 million, down 1.2% from US$290.2 million the year before. Operating income was US$30.8 million versus US$24.3 million in the prior-year quarter, an increase of 26.8%. Direct operating expenses declined 5.3% to US$141.4 million from US$149.2 million in the comparable period the year before. Indirect operating expenses decreased 1.8% to US$114.7 million from US$116.7 million in the equivalent prior-year period.

Prospects: Our evaluation of Brady Corp. as of June 19, 2016 is the result of our systematic analysis on three basic characteristics: earnings strength, relative valuation, and recent stock price movement. The company has enjoyed a very positive trend in earnings per share over the past 5 quarters and while recent estimates for the company have been raised by analysts, BRC has posted better than expected results. Based on operating earnings yield, the company is about fairly valued when compared to all of the companies in our coverage universe. Share price changes over the past year indicates that BRC will perform poorly over the near term.

Financial Data

(US$ in Thousands)	9 Mos	6 Mos	3 Mos	07/31/2015	07/31/2014	07/31/2013	07/31/2012	07/31/2011
Earnings Per Share	0.32	0.24	0.17	0.06	(0.89)	(3.02)	(0.35)	2.04
Cash Flow Per Share	2.77	2.53	2.06	1.82	1.80	2.80	2.75	3.18
Tang Book Value Per Share	1.93	1.42	1.49	1.67	2.48	1.09	4.82	5.00
Dividends Per Share	0.808	0.805	0.802	0.800	0.780	0.760	0.740	0.720
Dividend Payout %	252.34	335.42	472.06	1,333.33	...	...	...	35.29
Income Statement								
Total Revenue	838,519	551,703	283,073	1,171,731	1,225,034	1,152,109	1,324,269	1,339,597
EBITDA	108,341	69,442	38,232	63,506	(12,082)	(33,380)	85,827	215,009
Depn & Amortn	24,896	17,502	8,889	27,355	26,727	48,725	43,987	48,827
Income Before Taxes	77,326	47,659	27,192	24,995	(53,109)	(98,746)	22,750	144,058
Income Taxes	22,352	13,666	8,489	20,093	(4,963)	42,070	40,661	35,406
Net Income	54,974	33,993	18,703	2,987	(45,968)	(154,535)	(17,911)	108,652
Average Shares	50,505	50,647	51,089	51,383	51,866	51,330	52,453	53,133
Balance Sheet								
Current Assets	429,433	405,909	407,208	408,582	463,842	512,490	650,854	758,287
Total Assets	1,061,275	1,031,285	1,048,849	1,062,897	1,253,665	1,438,683	1,607,719	1,861,505
Current Liabilities	163,782	157,132	169,960	209,247	291,945	323,497	267,018	301,881
Long-Term Obligations	236,310	247,689	241,434	200,774	159,296	201,150	254,944	331,914
Total Liabilities	465,935	468,797	476,091	475,209	520,589	607,886	598,366	705,313
Stockholders' Equity	595,340	562,488	572,758	587,688	733,076	830,797	1,009,353	1,156,192
Shares Outstanding	50,262	50,244	50,578	51,319	51,322	52,173	51,554	53,132
Statistical Record								
Return on Assets %	1.41	1.09	0.71	0.26	N.M.	N.M.	N.M.	6.02
Return on Equity %	2.49	1.96	1.29	0.45	N.M.	N.M.	N.M.	10.05
EBITDA Margin %	12.92	12.59	13.51	5.42	N.M.	N.M.	6.48	16.05
Net Margin %	6.56	6.16	6.61	0.25	N.M.	N.M.	N.M.	8.11
Asset Turnover	1.02	1.04	1.01	1.01	0.91	0.76	0.76	0.74
Current Ratio	2.62	2.58	2.40	1.95	1.59	1.58	2.44	2.51
Debt to Equity	0.40	0.44	0.42	0.34	0.22	0.24	0.25	0.29
Price Range	27.82-19.52	28.91-19.52	28.91-19.52	28.91-21.19	35.54-24.26	36.33-26.34	34.40-24.73	38.49-25.35
P/E Ratio	86.94-61.00	120.46-81.33	170.06-114.82	481.83-353.17	...	...	...	18.87-12.43
Average Yield %	3.36	3.30	3.21	3.12	2.69	2.38	2.51	2.23

Address: 6555 West Good Hope Road, Milwaukee, WI 53223
Telephone: 414-358-6600

Web Site: www.bradycorp.com
Officers: J. Michael Nauman - President, Chief Executive Officer Aaron James Pearce - Chief Financial Officer, Senior Vice President, Vice President, Chief Accounting Officer, Treasurer, Director

Auditors: Deloitte & Touche LLP
Investor Contact: 414-438-6940
Transfer Agents: Wells Fargo Bank Minnesota, N.A., St. Paul, MN

BRANDYWINE REALTY TRUST

Exchange	Symbol	Price	52Wk Range	Yield	P/E
NYS	BDN	$15.79 (5/31/2016)	15.79-11.29	4.05	N/A

*7 Year Price Score 90.64 *NYSE Composite Index=100 *12 Month Price Score 109.68

Interim Earnings (Per Share)

Qtr.	Mar	Jun	Sep	Dec
2013	0.01	0.03	0.06	0.12
2014	(0.03)	0.00	0.04	(0.02)
2015	0.04	0.01	0.10	(0.36)
2016	0.25	...	...	...

Interim Dividends (Per Share)

Amt	Decl	Ex	Rec	Pay
0.15Q	09/15/2015	10/01/2015	10/05/2015	10/19/2015
0.15Q	12/08/2015	01/04/2016	01/06/2016	01/20/2016
0.15Q	03/09/2016	03/31/2016	04/04/2016	04/18/2016
0.16Q	05/24/2016	07/01/2016	07/06/2016	07/20/2016

Indicated Div: $0.64

Valuation Analysis   **Institutional Holding**

Forecast EPS	$0.18	No of Institutions
	(05/20/2016)	322
Market Cap	$2.8 Billion	Shares
Book Value	$1.9 Billion	217,113,600
Price/Book	1.42	% Held
Price/Sales	4.69	97.05

Business Summary: REITs (MIC: 5.3.1 SIC: 6798 NAIC: 525930)

Brandywine Realty Trust is a real estate investment trust. Co. provides leasing, property management, development, redevelopment, acquisition and other tenant-related services for a portfolio of properties. Co.'s segments are Pennsylvania Suburbs; Philadelphia Central Business District; Metropolitan Washington D.C.; New Jersey/Delaware; Richmond, VA; Austin, TX; and California. At Dec 31 2014, Co. owned 200 properties, consisting of 167 office properties, 20 industrial facilities, five mixed-use properties, one retail property, two properties classified as held for sale, three development properties, one redevelopment property and one re-entitlement property.

Recent Developments: For the quarter ended Mar 31 2016, net income increased 438.9% to US$46.3 million from US$8.6 million in the year-earlier quarter. Revenues were US$136.5 million, down 9.2% from US$150.4 million the year before. Revenues from property income fell 8.0% to US$135.7 million from US$147.6 million in the corresponding quarter a year earlier.

Prospects: Our evaluation of Brandywine Realty Trust as of June 19, 2016 is the result of our systematic analysis on three basic characteristics: earnings strength, relative valuation, and recent stock price movement. The company has managed to produce a neutral trend in earnings per share over the past 5 quarters. Because the company lacks sufficient analyst estimate data, we place greater weight on the historical EPS trend as the measure of earnings strength. Based on operating earnings yield, the company is overvalued when compared to all of the companies in our coverage universe. Share price changes over the past year indicates that BDN will perform in line with the market over the near term.

Financial Data

(US$ in Thousands)	3 Mos	12/31/2015	12/31/2014	12/31/2013	12/31/2012	12/31/2011	12/31/2010	12/31/2009
Earnings Per Share	...	(0.21)	...	0.23	(0.06)	(0.10)	(0.19)	...
Cash Flow Per Share	0.77	1.10	1.14	1.20	1.09	1.32	1.41	1.97
Tang Book Value Per Share	10.55	10.43	11.39	11.28	11.72	12.52	13.03	13.83
Dividends Per Share	0.750	0.600	0.600	0.600	0.600	0.600	0.600	0.600
Dividend Payout %	...	...	...	260.87	...	...	...	...
Income Statement								
Total Revenue	136,502	602,631	596,982	562,210	559,833	581,805	566,897	582,219
EBITDA	72,359	284,798	339,506	367,574	310,238	337,860	291,505	333,109
Depn & Amortn	1,220	219,936	210,946	205,715	206,148	220,284	193,260	192,426
Income Before Taxes	46,713	(50,425)	1,913	35,318	(32,895)	(17,007)	(34,943)	1,579
Net Income	45,921	(30,401)	6,975	42,777	6,595	(4,499)	(17,074)	8,026
Average Shares	175,471	178,162	166,202	154,414	143,257	135,444	131,743	113,251
Balance Sheet								
Current Assets	571,264	218,912	410,310	406,891	139,213	125,595	130,729	102,472
Total Assets	4,378,064	4,554,511	4,859,173	4,765,095	4,506,709	4,557,718	4,690,378	4,663,750
Current Liabilities	140,498	158,518	184,369	180,912	178,178	193,393	216,410	110,398
Long-Term Obligations	2,184,948	2,384,717	2,451,308	2,595,381	2,465,330	2,393,995	2,430,446	2,454,577
Total Liabilities	2,432,047	2,620,586	2,718,346	2,864,875	2,754,431	2,701,127	2,840,876	2,780,318
Stockholders' Equity	1,946,017	1,933,925	2,140,827	1,900,220	1,752,278	1,856,591	1,849,502	1,883,432
Shares Outstanding	174,890	174,688	179,293	156,731	143,538	142,690	134,485	128,582
Statistical Record								
Return on Assets %	0.15	N.M.	0.14	0.92	0.15	N.M.	N.M.	0.17
Return on Equity %	0.34	N.M.	0.35	2.34	0.36	N.M.	N.M.	0.45
EBITDA Margin %	53.01	47.26	56.87	65.38	55.42	58.07	51.42	57.21
Net Margin %	33.64	N.M.	1.17	7.61	1.18	N.M.	N.M.	1.38
Asset Turnover	0.13	0.13	0.12	0.12	0.12	0.13	0.12	0.12
Current Ratio	4.07	1.38	2.23	2.25	0.78	0.65	0.60	0.93
Debt to Equity	1.12	1.23	1.15	1.37	1.41	1.29	1.31	1.30
Price Range	16.10-11.29	17.00-11.72	16.29-13.77	15.94-12.18	12.88-9.40	12.76-7.09	13.36-10.00	11.85-2.52
P/E Ratio	N.M.	...	N.M.	69.30-52.96	...	...	...	...
Average Yield %	5.60	4.23	4.00	4.36	5.17	5.65	5.17	7.68

Address: 555 East Lancaster Avenue, Radnor, PA 19087
Telephone: 610-325-5600

Web Site: www.brandywinerealty.com
Officers: Gerard H. Sweeney - President, Chief Executive Officer Thomas E. Wirth - Executive Vice President, Chief Financial Officer, Principal Accounting Officer

Auditors: PricewaterhouseCoopers LLP
Investor Contact: 610-832-7702
Transfer Agents: Computershare, Providence, RI

BRINKER INTERNATIONAL, INC.

Exchange	Symbol	Price	52Wk Range	Yield	P/E
NYS	EAT	$44.97 (5/31/2016)	59.90-43.42	2.85	13.84

*7 Year Price Score 121.65 *NYSE Composite Index=100 *12 Month Price Score 90.24

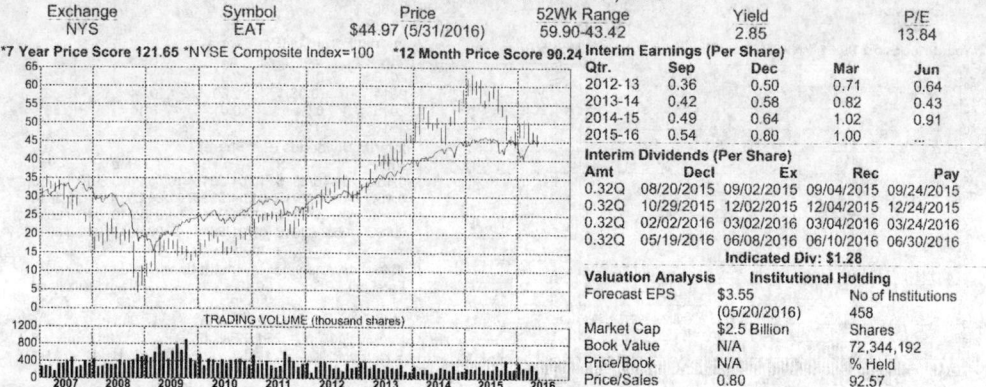

Interim Earnings (Per Share)

Qtr.	Sep	Dec	Mar	Jun
2012-13	0.36	0.50	0.71	0.64
2013-14	0.42	0.58	0.82	0.43
2014-15	0.49	0.64	1.02	0.91
2015-16	0.54	0.80	1.00	...

Interim Dividends (Per Share)

Amt	Decl	Ex	Rec	Pay
0.32Q	08/20/2015	09/02/2015	09/04/2015	09/24/2015
0.32Q	10/29/2015	12/02/2015	12/04/2015	12/24/2015
0.32Q	02/02/2016	03/02/2016	03/04/2016	03/24/2016
0.32Q	05/19/2016	06/08/2016	06/10/2016	06/30/2016

Indicated Div: $1.28

Valuation Analysis

	Institutional Holding
Forecast EPS $3.55	No of Institutions
(05/20/2016)	458
Market Cap $2.5 Billion	Shares
Book Value N/A	72,344,192
Price/Book N/A	% Held
Price/Sales 0.80	92.57

Business Summary: Hotels, Restaurants & Travel (MIC: 2.2.1 SIC: 5812 NAIC: 722110)

Brinker International owns, develops, operates and franchises the Chili's Grill & Bar (Chili's) and Maggiano's Little Italy (Maggiano's) restaurant brands. Co.'s Chili's restaurants menu includes Baby Back Ribs, burgers, Mix and Match Fajitas, Tableside Guacamole and Chips and Salsa, as well as a range of appetizers, entrees and desserts. Co.'s Maggiano's Italian-American restaurants serve appetizers, entrees with pasta, chicken, seafood, veal and steaks, and desserts, as well as alcoholic beverages. At June 24 2015, Co.'s system of company-owned and franchised restaurants included 1,629 restaurants located in 49 states and Washington, D.C. Co. also has restaurants in other countries.

Recent Developments: For the quarter ended Mar 23 2016, net income decreased 12.1% to US$57.5 million from US$65.4 million in the year-earlier quarter. Revenues were US$824.6 million, up 5.2% from US$784.2 million the year before. Operating income was US$86.3 million versus US$103.2 million in the prior-year quarter, a decrease of 16.4%. Direct operating expenses rose 7.7% to US$665.3 million from US$617.7 million in the comparable period the year before. Indirect operating expenses increased 15.4% to US$73.1 million from US$63.3 million in the equivalent prior-year period.

Prospects: Our evaluation of Brinker International Inc. as of June 19, 2016 is the result of our systematic analysis on three basic characteristics: earnings strength, relative valuation, and recent stock price movement. The company has enjoyed a very positive trend in earnings per share over the past 5 quarters. However, while recent estimates for the company have been mixed, EAT has posted better than expected results. Based on operating earnings yield, the company is undervalued when compared to all of the companies in our coverage universe. Share price changes over the past year indicates that EAT will perform in line with the market over the near term.

Financial Data

(US$ in Thousands)	9 Mos	6 Mos	3 Mos	06/24/2015	06/25/2014	06/26/2013	06/27/2012	06/29/2011
Earnings Per Share	3.25	3.27	3.11	3.05	2.26	2.20	1.87	1.53
Cash Flow Per Share	6.94	6.11	5.70	5.86	5.45	4.06	3.87	2.87
Tang Book Value Per Share	...	...	...	...	N.M.	0.11	2.48	3.80
Dividends Per Share	1.240	1.200	1.160	1.120	0.960	0.800	0.640	0.560
Dividend Payout %	38.15	36.70	37.30	36.72	42.48	36.36	34.22	36.60
Income Statement								
Total Revenue	2,375,808	1,551,169	762,559	3,002,278	2,905,452	2,846,098	2,820,722	2,761,386
EBITDA	336,587	210,984	95,691	458,525	380,460	390,914	360,663	340,087
Depn & Amortn	117,335	78,285	39,171	145,242	136,081	131,481	125,054	128,447
Income Before Taxes	195,175	117,025	48,753	284,277	216,288	230,315	208,809	183,329
Income Taxes	56,772	36,124	15,546	87,583	62,249	66,956	57,577	42,269
Net Income	138,403	80,901	33,207	196,694	154,039	163,359	151,232	141,060
Average Shares	57,407	59,899	61,208	64,404	68,152	74,158	80,664	92,320
Balance Sheet								
Current Assets	196,724	253,938	192,197	189,717	210,854	198,591	194,846	221,360
Total Assets	1,489,188	1,579,884	1,549,331	1,435,873	1,490,604	1,452,603	1,436,072	1,484,568
Current Liabilities	422,291	449,010	393,153	418,475	466,110	390,211	401,749	405,601
Long-Term Obligations	1,174,660	1,156,493	1,125,410	970,825	832,302	780,121	587,890	502,572
Total Liabilities	1,732,850	1,744,816	1,657,471	1,514,333	1,427,510	1,303,246	1,126,199	1,045,658
Stockholders' Equity	(243,662)	(164,932)	(108,140)	(78,460)	63,094	149,357	309,873	438,910
Shares Outstanding	55,761	58,255	60,131	60,585	64,558	67,444	74,342	82,938
Statistical Record								
Return on Assets %	13.37	13.01	13.03	13.48	10.50	11.34	10.38	8.48
Return on Equity %	...	...	...	...	145.41	71.34	40.51	24.23
EBITDA Margin %	14.17	13.60	12.55	15.27	13.09	13.74	12.79	12.32
Net Margin %	5.83	5.22	4.35	6.55	5.30	5.74	5.36	5.11
Asset Turnover	2.15	1.98	2.02	2.06	1.98	1.98	1.94	1.66
Current Ratio	0.47	0.57	0.49	0.45	0.45	0.51	0.48	0.55
Debt to Equity	...	...	...	...	13.19	5.22	1.90	1.15
Price Range	61.82-43.42	63.12-43.42	63.12-49.55	63.12-44.16	55.00-38.19	41.60-28.71	32.69-20.01	26.03-14.12
P/E Ratio	19.02-13.36	19.30-13.28	20.30-15.93	20.70-14.48	24.34-16.90	18.91-13.05	17.48-10.70	17.01-9.23
Average Yield %	2.37	2.17	2.04	2.04	2.08	2.08	2.32	2.67

Address: 6820 LBJ Freeway, Dallas, TX 75240	Web Site: www.brinker.com	Auditors: KPMG LLP
Telephone: 972-980-9917	Officers: Douglas H. Brooks - Chairman, President, Chief Executive Officer Wyman T. Roberts - President, Chief Executive Officer, Division Officer	Investor Contact: 972-980-9917
		Transfer Agents: Computershare, Canton, MA

BRISTOL-MYERS SQUIBB CO.

Exchange	Symbol	Price	52Wk Range	Yield	P/E
NYS	BMY	$71.70 (5/31/2016)	72.83-57.30	2.12	77.10

*7 Year Price Score 135.06 NYSE Composite Index=100   *12 Month Price Score 105.90

TRADING VOLUME (thousand shares)

Interim Earnings (Per Share)

Qtr.	Mar	Jun	Sep	Dec
2013	0.37	0.32	0.42	0.43
2014	0.56	0.20	0.43	0.01
2015	0.71	(0.08)	0.42	(0.12)
2016	0.71	...	...	...

Interim Dividends (Per Share)

Amt	Decl	Ex	Rec	Pay
0.37Q	09/17/2015	09/30/2015	10/02/2015	11/02/2015
0.38Q	12/08/2015	12/30/2015	01/04/2016	02/01/2016
0.38Q	03/03/2016	03/30/2016	04/01/2016	05/02/2016
0.38Q	06/07/2016	06/29/2016	07/01/2016	08/01/2016

Indicated Div: $1.52

Valuation Analysis

Forecast EPS	$2.57
	(05/20/2016)
Market Cap	$119.1 Billion
Book Value	$14.4 Billion
Price/Book	8.28
Price/Sales	7.04

Institutional Holding

No of Institutions	2036
Shares	1,396,721,152
% Held	71.85

Business Summary: Pharmaceuticals (MIC: 4.1.1 SIC: 2834 NAIC: 325412)

Bristol-Myers Squibb is engaged in the discovery, development, licensing, manufacturing, marketing, distribution and sale of biopharmaceutical products. Co. has products in the following therapeutic classes, among others: virology, including human immunodeficiency virus infection; oncology; neuroscience; immunoscience; and cardiovascular. Co.'s products include: Abilify, an atypical antipsychotic agent for adult patients with schizophrenia, bipolar mania disorder and depressive disorder; and Baraclude (entecavir) is a selective inhibitor of hepatitis B virus that was approved by the U.S. Food and Drug Administration for the treatment of chronic hepatitis B virus infection.

Recent Developments:
For the quarter ended Mar 31 2016, net income increased 0.6% to US$1.21 billion from US$1.20 billion in the year-earlier quarter. Revenues were US$4.39 billion, up 8.7% from US$4.04 billion the year before. Direct operating expenses rose 24.2% to US$1.05 billion from US$847.0 million in the comparable period the year before. Indirect operating expenses increased 7.8% to US$2.20 billion from US$2.05 billion in the equivalent prior-year period.

Prospects:
Our evaluation of Bristol-Myers Squibb Co. as of June 19, 2016 is the result of our systematic analysis on three basic characteristics: earnings strength, relative valuation, and recent stock price movement. The company has produced a positive trend in earnings per share over the past 5 quarters and while recent estimates for the company have been mixed, BMY has posted better than expected results. Based on operating earnings yield, the company is about fairly valued when compared to all of the companies in our coverage universe. Share price changes over the past year indicates that BMY will perform well over the near term.

Financial Data
(US$ in Millions)

	3 Mos	12/31/2015	12/31/2014	12/31/2013	12/31/2012	12/31/2011	12/31/2010	12/31/2009
Earnings Per Share	0.93	0.93	1.20	1.54	1.16	2.16	1.79	5.34
Cash Flow Per Share	0.49	1.10	1.90	2.16	4.14	2.85	2.62	2.06
Tang Book Value Per Share	3.69	3.57	3.66	3.48	N.M.	4.29	4.17	3.94
Dividends Per Share	1.870	1.490	1.450	1.760	1.360	1.320	0.960	1.250
Dividend Payout %	201.08	160.22	120.83	114.29	117.24	61.11	53.63	23.41
Income Statement								
Total Revenue	4,391	16,560	15,879	16,385	17,621	21,244	19,484	18,808
EBITDA	1,814	2,761	3,127	3,543	2,798	7,202	6,301	5,651
Depn & Amortn	142	500	543	453	382	448	473	469
Income Before Taxes	1,629	2,077	2,381	2,891	2,340	6,700	5,758	5,052
Income Taxes	449	446	352	311	(161)	1,721	1,558	1,182
Net Income	1,195	1,565	2,004	2,563	1,960	3,709	3,102	10,612
Average Shares	1,680	1,679	1,670	1,662	1,688	1,717	1,727	1,978
Balance Sheet								
Current Assets	11,215	10,415	14,608	18,916	9,521	15,318	13,273	13,958
Total Assets	31,892	31,748	33,749	38,592	35,897	32,970	31,076	31,008
Current Liabilities	7,597	8,017	8,461	12,440	8,279	7,780	6,739	6,313
Long-Term Obligations	6,593	6,550	7,242	7,981	6,568	5,376	5,328	6,130
Total Liabilities	17,506	17,482	18,897	23,438	22,274	17,014	15,363	16,165
Stockholders' Equity	14,386	14,266	14,852	15,154	13,623	15,956	15,713	14,843
Shares Outstanding	1,661	1,669	1,661	1,649	1,630	1,690	1,704	1,714
Statistical Record								
Return on Assets %	4.81	4.78	5.54	6.88	5.68	11.58	9.99	35.05
Return on Equity %	10.52	10.75	13.36	17.81	13.22	23.42	20.30	78.36
EBITDA Margin %	41.31	16.67	19.69	21.62	15.88	33.90	32.34	30.05
Net Margin %	27.21	9.45	12.62	15.64	11.12	17.46	15.92	56.42
Asset Turnover	0.52	0.51	0.44	0.44	0.51	0.66	0.63	0.62
Current Ratio	1.48	1.30	1.73	1.52	1.15	1.97	1.97	2.21
Debt to Equity	0.46	0.46	0.49	0.53	0.48	0.34	0.34	0.41
Price Range	70.71-57.30	70.71-57.30	61.30-46.59	53.84-32.59	36.15-30.81	35.29-24.97	27.93-22.44	25.96-17.51
P/E Ratio	76.03-61.61	76.03-61.61	51.08-38.83	34.96-21.16	31.16-26.56	16.34-11.56	15.60-12.54	4.86-3.28
Average Yield %	2.89	2.31	2.78	4.02	4.08	4.56	3.74	5.75

Address: 345 Park Avenue, New York, NY 10154	Web Site: www.bms.com	Auditors: Deloitte & Touche LLP
Telephone: 212-546-4000	Officers: Lamberto Andreotti - President, Chief Executive Officer Charles A. Bancroft - Executive Vice President, Chief Financial Officer, Acting Chief Financial Officer	Investor Contact: 609-252-4611
Fax: 212-546-4020		Transfer Agents: Wells Fargo Shareowner Services, Mendota Heights, MN

BRIXMOR PROPERTY GROUP INC

Exchange	Symbol	Price	52Wk Range	Yield	P/E
NYS	BRX	$25.25 (5/31/2016)	26.76-21.10	3.88	33.67

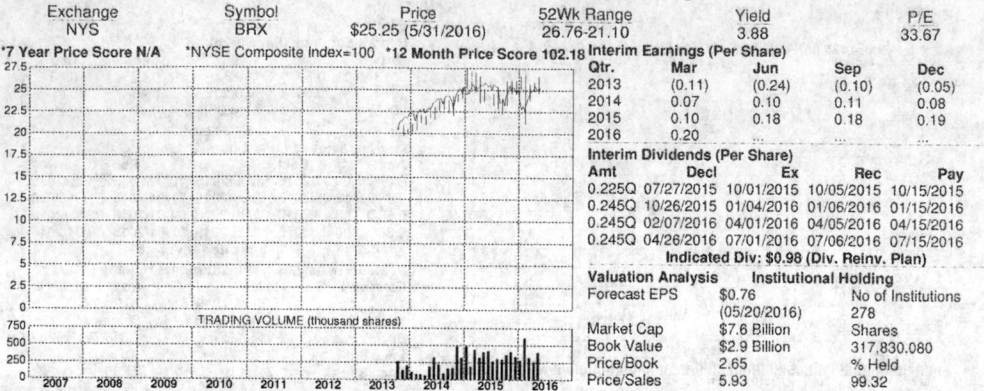

*7 Year Price Score N/A   *NYSE Composite Index=100   *12 Month Price Score 102.18

Interim Earnings (Per Share)

Qtr.	Mar	Jun	Sep	Dec
2013	(0.11)	(0.24)	(0.10)	(0.05)
2014	0.07	0.10	0.11	0.08
2015	0.10	0.18	0.18	0.19
2016	0.20	...	...	...

Interim Dividends (Per Share)

Amt	Decl	Ex	Rec	Pay
0.225Q	07/27/2015	10/01/2015	10/05/2015	10/15/2015
0.245Q	10/26/2015	01/04/2016	01/06/2016	01/15/2016
0.245Q	02/07/2016	04/01/2016	04/05/2016	04/15/2016
0.245Q	04/26/2016	07/01/2016	07/06/2016	07/15/2016

Indicated Div: $0.98 (Div. Reinv. Plan)

Valuation Analysis | **Institutional Holding**

Forecast EPS	$0.76 (05/20/2016)	No of Institutions 278
Market Cap	$7.6 Billion	Shares
Book Value	$2.9 Billion	317,830.080
Price/Book	2.65	% Held
Price/Sales	5.93	99.32

Business Summary: REITs (MIC: 5.3.1 SIC: 6798 NAIC: 525930)

Brixmor Property Group is an internally-managed real estate investment trust. Co. conducts all of its operations through Brixmor Operating Partnership LP and subsidiaries (Operating Partnership). Through the Operating Partnership, Co. is engaged in the ownership, management, leasing, acquisition and development of retail shopping centers, comprising a portfolio of grocery-anchored community and neighborhood shopping centers. As of Dec 31 2014, Co.'s portfolio was comprised of 521 shopping centers.

Recent Developments: For the quarter ended Mar 31 2016, net income increased 97.7% to US$61.5 million from US$31.1 million in the year-earlier quarter. Revenues were US$323.1 million, up 2.5% from US$315.3 million the year before. Revenues from property income rose 3.1% to US$251.1 million from US$243.6 million in the corresponding quarter a year earlier.

Prospects: Our evaluation of Brixmor Property Group Inc as of June 19, 2016 is the result of our systematic analysis on three basic characteristics: earnings strength, relative valuation, and recent stock price movement. The company has managed to produce a neutral trend in earnings per share over the past 5 quarters. However, while recent estimates for the company have been mixed, BRX has posted better than expected results. Based on operating earnings yield, the company is about fairly valued when compared to all of the companies in our coverage universe. Share price changes over the past year indicates that BRX will perform well over the near term.

Financial Data

(US$ in Thousands)	3 Mos	12/31/2015	12/31/2014	12/31/2013	12/31/2012	12/31/2011	06/27/2011	12/31/2010
Earnings Per Share	0.75	0.65	0.36	(0.50)	...	...	...	...
Cash Flow Per Share	1.79	1.79	1.97	1.76	...	...	...	...
Tang Book Value Per Share	9.53	9.59	9.79	10.29	23.04	24.85	...	...
Dividends Per Share	0.920	0.900	0.727	...	...	...	...	...
Dividend Payout %	122.67	138.46	201.94	...	...	...	...	...
Income Statement								
Total Revenue	323,104	1,265,980	1,236,599	1,174,697	1,125,797	565,619	553,934	1,125,104
EBITDA	105,665	482,117	402,055	287,090	323,882	443,976	139,023	66,259
Depn & Amortn	(13,147)	40,343	29,264	41,921	91,519	85,142	(14,989)	(16,581)
Income Before Taxes	61,442	197,077	110,581	(101,995)	(152,879)	154,761	(37,095)	(289,345)
Income Taxes	...	...	...	...	...	...	...	(16,494)
Net Income	61,549	193,720	89,002	(93,534)	(122,567)	115,351	(47,843)	(321,387)
Average Shares	299,379	305,017	244,588	188,993	...	...	...	...
Balance Sheet								
Current Assets	429,744	400,625	410,941	473,399	445,320	480,713	...	...
Total Assets	9,465,258	9,498,007	9,702,402	10,171,916	9,603,729	10,032,266	...	...
Current Liabilities	552,785	603,439	679,102	709,529	632,112	691,154	...	...
Long-Term Obligations	6,007,397	5,974,266	6,042,997	5,981,289	6,499,356	6,694,549	...	...
Total Liabilities	6,612,040	6,628,224	6,798,692	7,807,981	7,860,767	8,152,213	...	...
Stockholders' Equity	2,853,218	2,869,783	2,903,710	2,363,935	1,742,962	1,880,053	...	...
Shares Outstanding	299,347	299,138	296,552	229,689	75,649	75,649	...	...
Statistical Record								
Return on Assets %	2.39	2.02	0.90	N.M.	N.M.	...	...	...
Return on Equity %	7.93	6.71	3.38	N.M.	N.M.	...	...	...
EBITDA Margin %	32.70	38.08	32.51	24.44	28.77	78.49	25.10	5.89
Net Margin %	19.05	15.30	7.20	N.M.	N.M.	20.39	N.M.	N.M.
Asset Turnover	0.13	0.13	0.12	0.12	0.11	...	...	...
Current Ratio	0.78	0.66	0.61	0.67	0.70	0.70	...	...
Debt to Equity	2.11	2.08	2.08	2.53	3.73	3.56	...	...
Price Range	26.76-21.10	27.39-22.23	25.24-20.13	20.94-19.66	...	...	...	...
P/E Ratio	35.68-28.13	42.14-34.20	70.11-55.92	...	...	...	...	...
Average Yield %	3.76	3.62	3.23	...	...	...	...	...

Address: 450 Lexington Avenue, New York, NY 10017 Telephone: 212-869-3000	Web Site: www.brixmor.com Officers: John G. Schreiber - Chairman James M. Taylor - President, Chief Executive Officer	Auditors: Deloitte & Touche LLP Transfer Agents: Computershare Trust Company, N.A., Canton, MA

BROADRIDGE FINANCIAL SOLUTIONS INC

Exchange	Symbol	Price	52Wk Range	Yield	P/E
NYS	BR	$64.19 (5/31/2016)	65.36-49.64	1.87	25.88

*7 Year Price Score 147.80 *NYSE Composite Index=100 *12 Month Price Score 108.61

Interim Earnings (Per Share)

Qtr.	Sep	Dec	Mar	Jun
2012-13	0.14	0.13	0.35	1.07
2013-14	0.30	0.22	0.41	1.13
2014-15	0.26	0.28	0.43	1.35
2015-16	0.28	0.33	0.52	...

Interim Dividends (Per Share)

Amt	Decl	Ex	Rec	Pay
0.30Q	08/06/2015	09/11/2015	09/15/2015	10/01/2015
0.30Q	11/12/2015	12/10/2015	12/14/2015	01/04/2016
0.30Q	02/02/2016	03/10/2016	03/14/2016	04/01/2016
0.30Q	05/03/2016	06/15/2016	06/17/2016	07/01/2016

Indicated Div: $1.20

Valuation Analysis / Institutional Holding

Valuation Analysis		Institutional Holding	
Forecast EPS	$2.73 (05/17/2016)	No of Institutions	626
Market Cap	$7.5 Billion	Shares	122,023,392
Book Value	$902.6 Million	% Held	85.49
Price/Book	8.36		
Price/Sales	2.64		

Business Summary: Finance Intermediaries & Services (MIC: 5.5.1 SIC: 7389 NAIC: 523999)

Broadridge Financial Solutions provides investor communications and technology solutions to banks, broker-dealers, mutual funds and corporate issuers. Co.'s businesses operate in two business segments: Investor Communication Solutions, which involves the processing and distribution of proxy materials to investors in equity securities and mutual funds, as well as the facilitation of related vote processing; and Global Technology and Operations, which provides a suite of computerized real-time transaction processing services that automate the securities transaction lifecycle, from desktop productivity tools, data aggregation, performance reporting, and portfolio management.

Recent Developments: For the quarter ended Mar 31 2016, net income increased 18.0% to US$63.7 million from US$54.0 million in the year-earlier quarter. Revenues were US$688.8 million, up 8.6% from US$634.2 million the year before. Operating income was US$100.6 million versus US$89.0 million in the prior-year quarter, an increase of 13.0%. Direct operating expenses rose 7.5% to US$486.5 million from US$452.6 million in the comparable period the year before. Indirect operating expenses increased 9.8% to US$101.7 million from US$92.6 million in the equivalent prior-year period.

Prospects: Our evaluation of Broadridge Financial Solutions Inc. as of June 19, 2016 is the result of our systematic analysis on three basic characteristics: earnings strength, relative valuation, and recent stock price movement. The company has produced a positive trend in earnings per share over the past 5 quarters and while recent estimates for the company have been mixed, BR has posted better than expected results. Based on operating earnings yield, the company is about fairly valued when compared to all of the companies in our coverage universe. Share price changes over the past year indicates that BR will perform well over the near term.

Financial Data
(US$ in Thousands)

	9 Mos	6 Mos	3 Mos	06/30/2015	06/30/2014	06/30/2013	06/30/2012	06/30/2011
Earnings Per Share	2.48	2.39	2.34	2.32	2.12	1.69	0.97	1.32
Cash Flow Per Share	3.69	3.40	3.29	3.60	3.24	2.22	2.34	1.53
Dividends Per Share	1.170	1.140	1.110	1.080	0.840	0.720	0.640	0.600
Dividend Payout %	47.18	47.70	47.44	46.55	39.62	42.60	65.98	45.45
Income Statement								
Total Revenue	1,922,500	1,233,700	594,700	2,694,200	2,558,000	2,430,800	2,303,500	2,166,900
EBITDA	269,100	141,700	66,300	530,300	475,500	392,400	270,900	313,500
Depn & Amortn	43,500	28,700	14,600	63,300	58,100	57,000	58,500	36,100
Income Before Taxes	206,400	113,000	51,700	444,400	395,500	323,200	200,900	269,700
Income Taxes	68,900	39,200	18,100	151,800	132,500	111,100	75,900	97,900
Net Income	137,400	73,800	33,500	287,100	263,000	212,100	123,600	169,600
Average Shares	121,700	122,000	121,700	124,000	124,100	125,400	127,500	128,300
Balance Sheet								
Current Assets	1,003,800	828,200	795,500	861,400	880,600	807,000	777,400	751,400
Total Assets	2,524,000	2,353,600	2,299,500	2,368,100	2,192,100	2,018,200	1,987,600	1,904,000
Current Liabilities	581,300	428,400	413,000	508,900	484,400	469,500	410,300	782,700
Long-Term Obligations	819,500	754,500	734,400	689,400	524,100	524,500	524,400	124,300
Total Liabilities	1,621,500	1,412,000	1,375,300	1,440,300	1,230,400	1,202,200	1,137,100	1,106,700
Stockholders' Equity	902,600	941,500	924,200	927,800	961,700	816,000	850,500	797,300
Shares Outstanding	117,500	118,500	118,300	118,200	119,500	119,000	124,800	123,700
Statistical Record								
Return on Assets %	12.62	13.19	13.16	12.59	12.49	10.59	6.33	9.17
Return on Equity %	33.68	30.52	30.40	30.39	29.59	25.45	14.96	21.14
EBITDA Margin %	14.00	11.49	11.15	19.68	18.59	16.14	11.76	14.47
Net Margin %	7.15	5.98	5.63	10.66	10.28	8.73	5.37	7.83
Asset Turnover	1.19	1.26	1.25	1.18	1.22	1.21	1.18	1.17
Current Ratio	1.73	1.93	1.93	1.69	1.82	1.72	1.89	0.96
Debt to Equity	0.91	0.80	0.79	0.74	0.54	0.64	0.62	0.16
Price Range	59.90-49.64	59.90-44.92	57.13-39.11	55.53-39.11	42.13-26.93	27.97-20.41	24.85-19.18	24.07-18.96
P/E Ratio	24.15-20.02	25.06-18.79	24.41-16.71	23.94-16.86	19.87-12.70	16.55-12.08	25.62-19.77	18.23-14.36
Average Yield %	2.15	2.13	2.21	2.29	2.36	3.04	2.88	2.72

Address: 5 Dakota Drive, Lake Success, NY 11042 **Telephone:** 516-472-5400	**Web Site:** www.broadridge.com **Officers:** Richard J. Daly - President, Chief Executive Officer Michael Liberatore - Executive Officer, Acting Principal Financial Officer	**Auditors:** Deloitte & Touche LLP **Investor Contact:** 516-472-5400 **Transfer Agents:** Broadridge Corporate Issuer Solutions, Inc.

BROOKDALE SENIOR LIVING INC

Exchange	Symbol	Price	52Wk Range	Yield	P/E
NYS	BKD	$17.94 (5/31/2016)	37.82-11.80	N/A	N/A

*7 Year Price Score 81.94   *NYSE Composite Index=100   *12 Month Price Score 77.02

TRADING VOLUME (thousand shares)

Interim Earnings (Per Share)

Qtr.	Mar	Jun	Sep	Dec
2013	0.03	(0.04)	(0.01)	(0.01)
2014	(0.02)	(0.03)	(0.23)	(0.70)
2015	(0.71)	(0.46)	(0.37)	(0.94)
2016	(0.26)			

Interim Dividends (Per Share)

No Dividends Paid

Valuation Analysis   **Institutional Holding**

Forecast EPS	$2.48	No of Institutions
	(05/20/2016)	341
Market Cap	$3.4 Billion	Shares
Book Value	$2.4 Billion	199,099,472
Price/Book	1.41	% Held
Price/Sales	0.69	103.59

Business Summary: Hospitals & Health Care Facilities (MIC: 4.2.1 SIC: 8052 NAIC: 623311)

Brookdale Senior Living is a holding company. Through its subsidiaries, Co. operates independent living, assisted living and dementia-care communities and continuing care retirement centers (CCRCs). Co. manages certain of its communities for third parties or unconsolidated ventures in which Co. has an ownership interest pursuant to management agreements. Through its ancillary program, Co. provides outpatient therapy, home health and hospice services to residents of its communities and to seniors living outside of its communities. At Dec 31 2015, Co. operated 130 retirement center communities, 915 assisted living communities and 78 CCRCs; and provided management services to 164 communities.

Recent Developments: For the quarter ended Mar 31 2016, net loss amounted to US$48.8 million versus a net loss of US$130.7 million in the year-earlier quarter. Revenues were US$1.26 billion, up 1.2% from US$1.25 billion the year before. Operating income was US$41.4 million versus a loss of US$116.9 million in the prior-year quarter. Indirect operating expenses decreased 10.5% to US$1.22 billion from US$1.36 billion in the equivalent prior-year period.

Prospects: Our evaluation of Brookdale Senior Living Inc. as of June 19, 2016 is the result of our systematic analysis on three basic characteristics: earnings strength, relative valuation, and recent stock price movement. The company has enjoyed a very positive trend in earnings per share over the past 5 quarters. However, while recent estimates for the company have been mixed, BKD has posted results that were in line with analysts expectations. Based on operating earnings yield, the company is overvalued when compared to all of the companies in our coverage universe. Share price changes over the past year indicates that BKD will perform poorly over the near term.

Financial Data
(US$ in Thousands)

	3 Mos	12/31/2015	12/31/2014	12/31/2013	12/31/2012	12/31/2011	12/31/2010	12/31/2009
Earnings Per Share	(2.03)	(2.48)	(1.01)	(0.03)	(0.54)	(0.56)	(0.41)	(0.60)
Cash Flow Per Share	1.90	1.59	1.64	2.96	2.38	2.22	1.90	2.13
Tang Book Value Per Share	8.25	8.52	10.64	5.89	5.79	6.19	6.27	6.32
Income Statement								
Total Revenue	1,263,156	4,960,608	3,831,706	2,891,966	2,770,085	2,457,918	2,213,264	2,023,068
EBITDA	44,279	558,601	445,043	396,848	331,158	318,473	320,983	266,534
Depn & Amortn	(3,752)	721,000	529,100	264,100	248,500	247,100	258,000	233,900
Income Before Taxes	(48,170)	(549,560)	(330,902)	(3,312)	(60,113)	(67,267)	(80,501)	(99,621)
Income Taxes	1,665	(92,209)	(181,305)	1,756	2,044	2,340	(31,432)	(32,926)
Net Income	(48,775)	(458,155)	(149,426)	(3,584)	(65,645)	(68,175)	(48,901)	(66,255)
Average Shares	185,153	184,333	148,185	123,671	121,991	121,161	120,010	111,288
Balance Sheet								
Current Assets	467,499	497,943	614,789	294,862	309,038	280,875	328,109	317,421
Total Assets	9,988,672	10,048,564	10,521,363	4,737,757	4,665,978	4,466,061	4,530,470	4,645,943
Current Liabilities	855,915	840,148	877,762	870,844	1,121,503	620,950	606,358	689,309
Long-Term Obligations	6,156,259	6,196,809	5,993,691	2,434,624	2,169,826	2,415,971	2,498,620	2,459,341
Total Liabilities	7,569,036	7,589,676	7,639,639	3,716,820	3,663,261	3,425,853	3,470,473	3,559,361
Stockholders' Equity	2,419,636	2,458,888	2,881,724	1,020,937	1,002,717	1,040,208	1,059,997	1,086,582
Shares Outstanding	190,829	188,338	187,037	127,726	126,689	125,354	124,316	123,206
Statistical Record								
EBITDA Margin %	3.51	11.26	11.61	13.72	11.95	12.96	14.50	13.17
Asset Turnover	0.49	0.48	0.50	0.62	0.61	0.55	0.48	0.44
Current Ratio	0.55	0.59	0.70	0.34	0.28	0.45	0.54	0.46
Debt to Equity	2.54	2.52	2.08	2.38	2.16	2.32	2.36	2.26
Price Range	38.74-11.80	38.74-17.69	36.86-26.37	29.97-24.96	25.72-15.19	28.05-11.54	22.07-12.77	20.54-2.55

Address: 111 Westwood Place, Suite 400, Brentwood, TN 37027 **Telephone:** 615-221-2250	**Web Site:** www.brookdale.com **Officers:** William B. Doniger - Vice-Chairman T. Andrew Smith - President, Chief Executive Officer, Executive Vice President, Secretary, General Counsel	**Auditors:** Ernst & Young LLP **Investor Contact:** 615-564-8104 **Transfer Agents:** American Stock Transfer & Trust Company, New York, NY

BROWN & BROWN, INC.

Exchange	Symbol	Price	52Wk Range	Yield	P/E	Div Achiever
NYS	BRO	$36.06 (5/31/2016)	36.06-28.87	1.36	20.61	22 Years

*7 Year Price Score 104.29 *NYSE Composite Index=100 *12 Month Price Score 106.32

Interim Earnings (Per Share)

Qtr.	Mar	Jun	Sep	Dec
2013	0.41	0.36	0.39	0.32
2014	0.30	0.42	0.47	0.17
2015	0.39	0.43	0.47	0.41
2016	0.44	...	...	...

Interim Dividends (Per Share)

Amt	Decl	Ex	Rec	Pay
0.11Q	07/20/2015	08/05/2015	08/07/2015	08/12/2015
0.123Q	10/19/2015	11/02/2015	11/04/2015	11/12/2015
0.123Q	01/20/2016	02/01/2016	02/03/2016	02/17/2016
0.123Q	04/18/2016	05/05/2016	05/09/2016	05/18/2016

Indicated Div: $0.49

Valuation Analysis		Institutional Holding	
Forecast EPS	$1.77	No of Institutions	
	(05/20/2016)	340	
Market Cap	$5.1 Billion	Shares	
Book Value	$2.2 Billion	122,393,072	
Price/Book	2.30	% Held	
Price/Sales	3.01	69.39	

Business Summary: Brokers & Intermediaries (MIC: 5.2.3 SIC: 6411 NAIC: 524210)

Brown & Brown is an insurance agency, wholesale brokerage, insurance programs and service organization. Co. markets and sells insurance products and services, primarily in the property, casualty and employee benefits areas. Co. has four segments: Retail, which provides a range of insurance products and services; National Programs, which has five categories: Professional Programs, Arrowhead Insurance Programs, Commercial Programs, Public Entity-Related Programs, and National Flood Program; Wholesale Brokerage, which markets and sells excess and surplus commercial insurance products and services to retail insurance agencies; and Services, which provide a range of insurance-related services.

Recent Developments: For the quarter ended Mar 31 2016, net income increased 9.0% to US$62.1 million from US$57.0 million in the year-earlier quarter. Revenues were US$424.2 million, up 4.9% from US$404.3 million the year before.

Prospects: Our evaluation of Brown & Brown Inc. as of June 19, 2016 is the result of our systematic analysis on three basic characteristics: earnings strength, relative valuation, and recent stock price movement. The company has produced a positive trend in earnings per share over the past 5 quarters. However, while recent estimates for the company have been mixed, BRO has posted better than expected results. Based on operating earnings yield, the company is about fairly valued when compared to all of the companies in our coverage universe. Share price changes over the past year indicates that BRO will perform well over the near term.

Financial Data
(US$ in Thousands)

	3 Mos	12/31/2015	12/31/2014	12/31/2013	12/31/2012	12/31/2011	12/31/2010	12/31/2009
Earnings Per Share	1.75	1.70	1.41	1.48	1.26	1.13	1.12	1.08
Cash Flow Per Share	2.90	2.99	2.73	2.76	1.58	1.71	2.15	1.62
Dividends Per Share	0.465	0.453	0.410	0.370	0.345	0.325	0.313	0.302
Dividend Payout %	26.57	26.62	29.08	25.00	27.38	28.76	27.90	28.01
Income Statement								
Total Revenue	424,173	1,660,509	1,575,796	1,363,279	1,200,032	1,013,542	973,492	967,877
EBITDA	139,851	462,707	389,052	391,534	336,281	297,045	293,208	282,593
Depn & Amortn	27,405	20,900	20,895	17,485	15,373	12,392	12,639	13,240
Income Before Taxes	102,549	402,559	339,749	357,609	304,811	270,521	266,098	254,754
Income Taxes	40,479	159,241	132,853	140,497	120,766	106,526	104,346	101,460
Net Income	62,070	243,318	206,896	217,112	184,045	163,995	161,752	153,294
Average Shares	136,940	140,112	142,891	142,624	142,010	140,264	139,318	137,507
Balance Sheet								
Current Assets	1,496,621	1,537,389	1,570,108	928,036	759,512	708,127	652,809	613,699
Total Assets	4,992,960	5,012,739	4,956,458	3,649,508	3,128,058	2,607,011	2,400,814	2,224,226
Current Liabilities	1,283,356	1,328,547	1,269,153	906,877	567,781	481,620	470,157	478,953
Long-Term Obligations	1,058,327	1,079,878	1,152,846	380,000	450,000	250,033	250,067	250,209
Total Liabilities	2,794,427	2,862,963	2,842,713	1,642,367	1,320,725	963,048	894,470	854,352
Stockholders' Equity	2,198,533	2,149,776	2,113,745	2,007,141	1,807,333	1,643,963	1,506,344	1,369,874
Shares Outstanding	140,173	138,985	143,486	145,419	143,878	143,352	142,795	142,076
Statistical Record								
Return on Assets %	5.05	4.88	4.81	6.41	6.40	6.55	6.99	7.06
Return on Equity %	11.66	11.41	10.04	11.38	10.64	10.41	11.25	11.74
EBITDA Margin %	32.97	27.87	24.69	28.72	28.02	29.31	30.12	29.20
Net Margin %	14.63	14.65	13.13	15.93	15.34	16.18	16.62	15.84
Asset Turnover	0.34	0.33	0.37	0.40	0.42	0.40	0.42	0.45
Current Ratio	1.17	1.16	1.24	1.02	1.34	1.47	1.39	1.28
Debt to Equity	0.48	0.50	0.55	0.19	0.25	0.15	0.17	0.18
Price Range	35.80-28.87	34.47-30.74	33.26-28.28	34.12-25.46	27.64-22.29	26.91-17.00	24.20-16.50	21.39-15.65
P/E Ratio	20.46-16.50	20.28-18.08	23.59-20.06	23.05-17.20	21.94-17.69	23.81-15.04	21.61-14.73	19.81-14.49
Average Yield %	1.43	1.39	1.32	1.18	1.36	1.41	1.58	1.61

Address: 220 South Ridgewood Avenue, Daytona Beach, FL 32114
Telephone: 386-252-9601

Web Site: www.bbinsurance.com
Officers: J. Hyatt Brown - Chairman Jim W. Henderson - Vice-Chairman, Chief Operating Officer

Auditors: Deloitte & Touche LLP
Investor Contact: 386-252-9601
Transfer Agents: American Stock Transfer & Trust Co., Brooklyn, NY

BROWN-FORMAN CORP.

Exchange	Symbol	Price	52Wk Range	Yield	P/E	Div Achiever
NYS	BF B	$98.07 (5/31/2016)	110.81-90.60	1.39	18.79	31 Years

*7 Year Price Score 128.97 *NYSE Composite Index=100 *12 Month Price Score 95.71

Interim Earnings (Per Share)

Qtr.	Jul	Oct	Jan	Apr
2011-12	0.54	0.73	0.62	0.49
2012-13	0.69	0.80	0.73	0.53
2013-14	0.66	0.96	0.82	0.61
2014-15	0.70	0.97	0.87	0.67
2015-16	0.75	0.97	0.94	2.57

Interim Dividends (Per Share)

Amt	Decl	Ex	Rec	Pay
0.34Q	11/19/2015	12/01/2015	12/03/2015	12/30/2015
0.34Q	01/28/2016	03/07/2016	03/09/2016	04/01/2016
0.34Q	05/26/2016	06/02/2016	06/06/2016	07/01/2016
100%	05/26/2016	08/19/2016	08/08/2016	08/18/2016

Indicated Div: $1.36

Valuation Analysis

		Institutional Holding	
Forecast EPS	$3.55	No of Institutions	
	(05/20/2016)	156	
Market Cap	$19.4 Billion	Shares	
Book Value	$1.6 Billion	42,442,192	
Price/Book	12.42	% Held	
Price/Sales	6.28	29.49	

Business Summary: Beverages (MIC: 1.2.2 SIC: 2084 NAIC: 312130)

Brown-Forman primarily manufactures, bottles, imports, exports, markets, and sells a range of alcoholic beverage brands. Co.'s principal brands are: Jack Daniel's Tennessee Whiskey, Jack Daniel's ready-to-drink cocktails (RTDs), Jack Daniel's Tennessee Honey, Gentleman Jack Rare Tennessee Whiskey, Jack Daniel's Tennessee Fire, Jack Daniel's Single Barrel, Jack Daniel's Sinatra Select, Jack Daniel's Winter Jack, Jack Daniel's No. 27 Gold Tennessee Whiskey, Finlandia RTDs, Korbel California Champagnes, Korbel California Brandy, Woodford Reserve Kentucky Bourbons, el Jimador Tequilas, el Jimador New Mix RTDs, Canadian Mist Canadian Whisky, Sonoma-Cutrer California Wines, among others.

Recent Developments: For the year ended Apr 30 2016, net income increased 56.0% to US$1.07 billion from US$684.0 million in the prior year. Revenues were US$3.09 billion, down 1.4% from US$3.13 billion the year before. Operating income was US$1.53 billion versus US$1.03 billion in the prior year, an increase of 49.3%. Direct operating expenses declined 0.6% to US$945.0 million from US$951.0 million in the comparable period the year before. Indirect operating expenses decreased 47.1% to US$611.0 million from US$1.16 billion in the equivalent prior-year period.

Prospects: Our evaluation of Brown-Forman Corp. as of June 19, 2016 is the result of our systematic analysis on three basic characteristics: earnings strength, relative valuation, and recent stock price movement. The company has managed to produce a neutral trend in earnings per share over the past 5 quarters. However, while recent estimates for the company have been mixed, BF.B has posted better than expected results. Based on operating earnings yield, the company is about fairly valued when compared to all of the companies in our coverage universe. Share price changes over the past year indicates that BF.B will perform well over the near term.

Financial Data

(US$ in Thousands)	04/30/2016	04/30/2015	04/30/2014	04/30/2013	04/30/2012	04/30/2011	04/30/2010	04/30/2009
Earnings Per Share	5.22	3.21	3.06	2.75	2.37	2.60	2.01	1.91
Cash Flow Per Share	2.57	2.87	3.04	2.52	2.40	2.41	2.46	2.18
Tang Book Value Per Share	1.91	3.29	3.44	1.61	3.68	3.52	2.54	2.02
Dividends Per Share	1.310	1.210	1.090	4.977	0.893	1.493	0.783	0.746
Dividend Payout %	25.10	37.69	35.62	180.97	37.64	57.44	38.91	38.99
Income Statement								
Total Revenue	3,089,000	3,134,000	2,991,000	2,849,000	2,723,000	2,586,000	2,469,000	2,481,000
EBITDA	1,589,000	1,078,000	1,021,000	949,000	837,000	911,000	769,000	716,000
Depn & Amortn	56,000	51,000	50,000	51,000	49,000	56,000	59,000	55,000
Income Before Taxes	1,489,000	1,002,000	947,000	865,000	760,000	829,000	682,000	630,000
Income Taxes	422,000	318,000	288,000	274,000	247,000	257,000	233,000	195,000
Net Income	1,067,000	684,000	659,000	591,000	513,000	572,000	449,000	435,000
Average Shares	204,280	213,083	215,082	214,986	216,150	219,769	222,862	227,283
Balance Sheet								
Current Assets	2,233,000	2,254,000	2,177,000	1,821,000	1,749,000	1,976,000	1,527,000	1,574,000
Total Assets	4,183,000	4,193,000	4,103,000	3,626,000	3,477,000	3,712,000	3,383,000	3,475,000
Current Liabilities	791,000	958,000	561,000	473,000	404,000	707,000	546,000	836,000
Long-Term Obligations	1,230,000	748,000	997,000	997,000	503,000	504,000	508,000	509,000
Total Liabilities	2,621,000	2,288,000	2,071,000	1,998,000	1,408,000	1,652,000	1,488,000	1,659,000
Stockholders' Equity	1,562,000	1,905,000	2,032,000	1,628,000	2,069,000	2,060,000	1,895,000	1,816,000
Shares Outstanding	197,742	208,700	213,455	213,707	213,111	217,485	220,444	225,190
Statistical Record								
Return on Assets %	25.41	16.49	17.05	16.64	14.23	16.12	13.09	12.65
Return on Equity %	61.38	34.75	36.01	31.97	24.78	28.93	24.20	24.57
EBITDA Margin %	51.44	34.40	34.14	33.31	30.74	35.23	31.15	28.86
Net Margin %	34.54	21.83	22.03	20.74	18.84	22.12	18.19	17.53
Asset Turnover	0.74	0.76	0.77	0.80	0.76	0.73	0.72	0.72
Current Ratio	2.82	2.35	3.88	3.85	4.33	2.79	2.80	1.88
Debt to Equity	0.79	0.39	0.49	0.61	0.24	0.24	0.27	0.28
Price Range	110.81-90.23	97.05-83.61	90.44-66.50	71.86-56.00	57.71-41.49	48.68-36.30	40.12-27.83	41.85-24.67
P/E Ratio	21.23-17.29	30.23-26.05	29.57-21.73	26.13-20.36	24.35-17.51	18.72-13.96	19.96-13.85	21.91-12.91
Average Yield %	1.31	1.33	1.45	7.73	1.76	3.51	2.36	2.19

Address: 850 Dixie Highway, Louisville, KY 40210 **Telephone:** 502-585-1100 **Fax:** 502-774-7876	**Web Site:** www.brown-forman.com **Officers:** Paul C. Varga - Chairman, Chief Executive Officer Jane C. Morreau - Senior Vice President, Executive Vice President, Chief Financial Officer, Chief Production Officer, Director	**Auditors:** PricewaterhouseCoopers LLP **Transfer Agents:** Computershare, Providence, RI

BRUNSWICK CORP.

Exchange	Symbol	Price	52Wk Range	Yield	P/E
NYS	BC	$47.87 (5/31/2016)	55.49-37.98	1.25	17.93

*7 Year Price Score 135.10 *NYSE Composite Index=100 *12 Month Price Score 97.23

Interim Earnings (Per Share)

Qtr.	Mar	Jun	Sep	Dec
2013	0.53	0.86	0.61	6.19
2014	0.60	0.93	1.10	(0.05)
2015	0.60	1.25	0.81	(0.09)
2016	0.70	...	...	...

Interim Dividends (Per Share)

Amt	Decl	Ex	Rec	Pay
0.125Q	07/21/2015	08/21/2015	08/25/2015	09/15/2015
0.15Q	10/20/2015	11/20/2015	11/24/2015	12/15/2015
0.15Q	02/11/2016	02/19/2016	02/23/2016	03/15/2016
0.15Q	05/04/2016	05/20/2016	05/24/2016	06/15/2016

Indicated Div: $0.60

Valuation Analysis

		Institutional Holding	
Forecast EPS	$3.46	No of Institutions	
	(05/20/2016)	454	
Market Cap	$4.3 Billion	Shares	
Book Value	$1.3 Billion	98,980,992	
Price/Book	3.33	% Held	
Price/Sales	1.04	98.68	

Business Summary: Leisure Equipment (MIC: 1.6.1 SIC: 3511 NAIC: 333611)

Brunswick is a designer, manufacturer and marketer of recreation products. Co. operates in three reportable segments: marine engine, which manufactures and markets a range of outboard engines, sterndrive engines, inboard engines and marine parts and accessories; boat, which designs, manufactures and markets fiberglass pleasure boats, offshore fishing boats, yachts and sport yachts, aluminum fishing boats, pontoon boats, deck boats and inflatable boats; and fitness, which designs, manufactures and markets fitness equipment, including treadmills, total body cross-trainers, stair climbers, stationary bikes and strength-training equipment as well as billiards tables and accessories.

Recent Developments: For the quarter ended Apr 2 2016, income from continuing operations increased 11.7% to US$63.2 million from US$56.6 million in the year-earlier quarter. Net income increased 13.7% to US$64.8 million from US$57.0 million in the year-earlier quarter. Revenues were US$1.07 billion, up 8.6% from US$985.7 million the year before. Operating income was US$96.0 million versus US$88.7 million in the prior-year quarter, an increase of 8.2%. Direct operating expenses rose 8.4% to US$788.2 million from US$726.9 million in the comparable period the year before. Indirect operating expenses increased 9.4% to US$186.1 million from US$170.1 million in the equivalent prior-year period.

Prospects: Our evaluation of Brunswick Corp. as of June 19, 2016 is the result of our systematic analysis on three basic characteristics: earnings strength, relative valuation, and recent stock price movement. The company has managed to produce a neutral trend in earnings per share over the past 5 quarters and while recent estimates for the company have been raised by analysts, BC has posted better than expected results. Based on operating earnings yield, the company is undervalued when compared to all of the companies in our coverage universe. Share price changes over the past year indicates that BC will perform in line with the market over the near term.

Financial Data
(US$ in Thousands)

	3 Mos	12/31/2015	12/31/2014	12/31/2013	12/31/2012	12/31/2011	12/31/2010	12/31/2009
Earnings Per Share	2.67	2.56	2.58	8.20	0.54	0.78	(1.25)	(6.63)
Cash Flow Per Share	3.95	3.48	2.53	1.87	1.78	1.00	2.32	1.42
Tang Book Value Per Share	8.69	10.21	8.94	7.70	N.M.	N.M.	N.M.	N.M.
Dividends Per Share	0.550	0.525	0.450	0.100	0.050	0.050	0.050	0.050
Dividend Payout %	20.60	20.51	17.44	1.22	9.26	6.41	...	...
Income Statement								
Total Revenue	1,070,300	4,105,700	3,838,700	3,887,500	3,717,600	3,748,000	3,403,300	2,776,100
EBITDA	122,400	423,000	393,000	358,700	335,900	269,100	128,600	(440,000)
Depn & Amortn	25,400	85,900	78,300	84,800	85,900	97,200	119,500	146,100
Income Before Taxes	90,600	311,500	286,100	231,500	184,800	94,000	(81,700)	(669,000)
Income Taxes	28,200	87,800	93,000	(545,600)	33,600	17,400	25,900	(98,500)
Net Income	64,800	241,400	245,700	769,200	50,000	71,900	(110,600)	(586,200)
Average Shares	92,800	94,300	95,100	93,800	92,400	92,200	88,700	88,400
Balance Sheet								
Current Assets	1,609,400	1,984,900	1,967,800	1,508,600	1,360,100	1,356,100	1,535,800	1,458,700
Total Assets	3,122,700	3,152,500	3,134,400	2,915,800	2,424,200	2,494,000	2,678,000	2,709,400
Current Liabilities	896,200	908,100	900,100	883,100	937,200	908,100	951,600	906,600
Long-Term Obligations	446,100	442,500	450,200	453,400	563,600	690,400	828,400	839,400
Total Liabilities	1,817,400	1,871,200	1,962,900	1,877,400	2,346,500	2,463,100	2,607,600	2,499,100
Stockholders' Equity	1,305,300	1,281,300	1,171,500	1,038,400	77,700	30,900	70,400	210,300
Shares Outstanding	90,712	90,813	92,694	92,409	89,631	89,104	88,661	88,263
Statistical Record								
Return on Assets %	8.10	7.68	8.12	28.81	2.03	2.78	N.M.	N.M.
Return on Equity %	19.92	19.68	22.24	137.84	91.83	141.95	N.M.	N.M.
EBITDA Margin %	11.44	10.30	10.24	9.23	9.04	7.18	3.78	N.M.
Net Margin %	6.05	5.88	6.40	19.79	1.34	1.92	N.M.	N.M.
Asset Turnover	1.36	1.31	1.27	1.46	1.51	1.45	1.26	0.94
Current Ratio	1.80	2.19	2.19	1.71	1.45	1.49	1.61	1.61
Debt to Equity	0.34	0.35	0.38	0.44	7.25	22.34	11.77	3.99
Price Range	55.49-37.98	56.39-46.50	51.94-38.95	46.48-29.09	29.09-18.49	27.01-13.50	22.69-10.37	13.11-2.18
P/E Ratio	20.78-14.22	22.03-18.16	20.13-15.10	5.67-3.55	53.87-34.24	34.63-17.31	...	...
Average Yield %	1.11	1.01	1.03	0.27	0.21	0.26	0.32	0.73

Address: 1 N. Field Court, Lake Forest, IL 60045-4811	Web Site: www.brunswick.com	Auditors: Deloitte & Touche LLP
Telephone: 847-735-4700	Officers: Mark D. Schwabero - Chairman, President, Chief Executive Officer, Chief Operating Officer, Vice President, Division Officer William L. Metzger - Senior Vice President, Chief Financial Officer, Vice President, Treasurer	Investor Contact: 847-735-4612 Transfer Agents: ComputerShare Investor Services, Providence, RI

BUCKEYE PARTNERS, L.P.

Exchange	Symbol	Price	52Wk Range	Yield	P/E	Div Achiever
NYS	BPL	$71.92 (5/31/2016)	79.00-50.35	6.67	20.32	20 Years

*7 Year Price Score 89.30   *NYSE Composite Index=100   *12 Month Price Score 102.89

Interim Earnings (Per Share)

Qtr.	Mar	Jun	Sep	Dec
2013	0.86	0.72	0.72	(0.81)
2014	0.78	0.20	0.86	0.43
2015	0.87	0.71	0.78	1.04
2016	1.01	...	...	...

Interim Dividends (Per Share)

Amt	Decl	Ex	Rec	Pay
1.163Q	07/31/2015	08/06/2015	08/10/2015	08/17/2015
1.175Q	10/30/2015	11/05/2015	11/09/2015	11/17/2015
1.188Q	02/12/2016	02/19/2016	02/23/2016	03/01/2016
1.20Q	05/06/2016	05/12/2016	05/16/2016	05/23/2016

Indicated Div: $4.80

Valuation Analysis

		Institutional Holding	
Forecast EPS	$4.13	No of Institutions	
	(05/20/2016)	478	
Market Cap	$9.4 Billion	Shares	
Book Value	N/A	100,822,320	
Price/Book	N/A	% Held	
Price/Sales	2.98	77.76	

Business Summary: Equipment & Services (MIC: 9.1.3 SIC: 4613 NAIC: 486910)

Buckeye Partners is a holding company. Through its subsidiaries, Co. operates in four business segments: Pipelines and Terminals, which operates pipeline located primarily in the northeastern and upper midwestern portions of the U.S.; Global Marine Terminals, which provides bulk storage, marine terminal throughput services, and other related services; Merchant Services, which is a wholesale distributor of refined petroleum products in the continental U.S. and in the Caribbean; as well as Development and Logistics, which provides operations and maintenance, asset development and construction services for third-party pipeline and energy assets across the U.S.

Recent Developments: For the quarter ended Mar 31 2016, income from continuing operations increased 20.5% to US$135.0 million from US$112.0 million in the year-earlier quarter. Net income increased 21.4% to US$135.0 million from US$111.2 million in the year-earlier quarter. Revenues were US$780.6 million, down 28.3% from US$1.09 billion the year before. Operating income was US$180.2 million versus US$151.8 million in the prior-year quarter, an increase of 18.7%. Direct operating expenses declined 48.6% to US$368.6 million from US$717.5 million in the comparable period the year before. Indirect operating expenses increased 5.9% to US$231.7 million from US$218.8 million in the equivalent prior-year period.

Prospects: Our evaluation of Buckeye Partners, L.P. as of June 19, 2016 is the result of our systematic analysis on three basic characteristics: earnings strength, relative valuation, and recent stock price movement. The company has produced a positive trend in earnings per share over the past 5 quarters. However, while recent estimates for the company have been lowered by analysts, BPL has posted results that fell short of analysts expectations. Based on operating earnings yield, the company is undervalued when compared to all of the companies in our coverage universe. Share price changes over the past year indicates that BPL will perform well over the near term.

Financial Data
(US$ in Thousands)

	3 Mos	12/31/2015	12/31/2014	12/31/2013	12/31/2012	12/31/2011	12/31/2010	12/31/2009
Earnings Per Share	3.54	3.40	2.28	1.49	2.32	1.20	1.65	1.84
Cash Flow Per Share	5.23	5.54	5.03	3.60	4.53	4.47	11.24	1.11
Dividends Per Share	4.675	4.625	4.425	4.225	4.150	4.025	3.825	3.625
Dividend Payout %	132.06	136.03	194.08	283.56	178.88	335.42	231.82	197.01
Income Statement								
Total Revenue	780,594	3,453,434	6,620,247	5,054,101	4,357,242	4,759,610	3,151,268	1,770,372
EBITDA	177,519	762,914	643,319	601,036	458,956	329,291	333,514	259,920
Depn & Amortn	(2,768)	158,700	148,400	122,700	120,200	105,500	54,700	50,700
Income Before Taxes	132,504	432,884	323,684	347,416	223,776	104,230	189,645	134,369
Income Taxes	615	874	451	1,060	(675)	...	...	...
Net Income	131,113	437,223	272,954	160,273	226,417	108,501	43,080	140,982
Average Shares	130,129	128,617	119,899	107,677	97,635	90,772	26,086	50,663
Balance Sheet								
Current Assets	521,181	551,550	632,299	901,086	634,322	626,036	626,631	613,723
Total Assets	8,380,184	8,369,281	8,086,088	7,005,563	5,981,009	5,570,376	3,574,216	3,255,649
Current Liabilities	528,476	504,309	621,955	685,043	594,366	554,979	516,520	417,733
Long-Term Obligations	3,701,717	3,732,824	3,388,986	3,092,711	2,735,244	2,393,574	1,519,393	1,498,970
Total Liabilities	4,628,204	4,633,892	4,383,460	3,939,898	3,608,696	3,267,207	2,181,811	2,040,511
Shares Outstanding	130,296	129,523	127,043	115,063	98,345	93,273	71,436	51,682
Statistical Record								
Return on Assets %	5.56	5.31	3.62	2.47	3.91	2.37	1.26	4.48
EBITDA Margin %	22.74	22.09	9.72	11.89	10.53	6.92	10.58	14.68
Net Margin %	16.80	12.66	4.12	3.17	5.20	2.28	1.37	7.96
Asset Turnover	0.38	0.42	0.88	0.78	0.75	1.04	0.92	0.56
Current Ratio	0.99	1.09	1.02	1.32	1.07	1.13	1.21	1.47
Price Range	82.04-50.35	82.04-54.00	83.91-66.87	73.13-45.41	64.17-44.65	68.52-57.61	69.80-52.33	55.59-32.25
P/E Ratio	23.18-14.22	24.13-15.88	36.80-29.33	49.08-30.48	27.66-19.25	57.10-48.01	42.30-31.72	30.21-17.53
Average Yield %	6.81	6.42	5.76	6.59	7.84	6.30	6.26	8.27

Address: One Greenway Plaza, Suite 600, Houston, TX 77046 Telephone: 832-615-8600	Web Site: www.buckeye.com Officers: Clark C. Smith - President, Chief Executive Officer, Chief Operating Officer, Associate/Affiliate Company Officer Mark S. Esselman - Senior Vice President	Auditors: Deloitte & Touche LLP Investor Contact: 800-422-2825 Transfer Agents: First Chicago Trust Company a Division of Equiserv, Jersey City, NJ

BUNGE LTD.

Exchange	Symbol	Price	52Wk Range	Yield	P/E
NYS	BG	$67.07 (5/31/2016)	92.85-47.79	2.50	13.69

*7 Year Price Score 84.06   *NYSE Composite Index=100   *12 Month Price Score 88.11

TRADING VOLUME (thousand shares)

Interim Earnings (Per Share)

Qtr.	Mar	Jun	Sep	Dec
2013	1.15	0.75	(1.13)	0.77
2014	(0.18)	1.81	1.90	(0.41)
2015	1.67	0.50	1.56	1.30
2016	1.54	...	...	...

Interim Dividends (Per Share)

Amt	Decl	Ex	Rec	Pay
0.38Q	08/05/2015	11/12/2015	11/16/2015	12/02/2015
0.38Q	12/09/2015	02/12/2016	02/17/2016	03/02/2016
0.38Q	03/01/2016	05/17/2016	05/19/2016	06/02/2016
0.42Q	05/24/2016	08/17/2016	08/19/2016	09/02/2016

Indicated Div: $1.68

Valuation Analysis   Institutional Holding

Forecast EPS	N/A	No of Institutions 569
		Shares
Market Cap	$9.4 Billion	122,526,048
Book Value	$6.8 Billion	% Held
Price/Book	1.38	79.92
Price/Sales	0.23	

Business Summary: Food (MIC: 1.2.1 SIC: 2079 NAIC: 311225)

Bunge is a holding company. Through its subsidiaries, Co. is an agribusiness and food company operating in the farm-to-consumer food chain. Co. conducts its operations in five segments: agribusiness, involved in the purchase, storage, transport, processing and sale of agricultural commodities and commodity products; edible oil products and milling products ; sugar and bioenergy, where Co. is a producer of sugar and ethanol in Brazil, and a trader and merchandiser of sugar; and fertilizer, where Co. produces, blends and distributes a range of nitrogen, phosphate, and potassium fertilizers, including phosphate-based liquid and solid nitrogen fertilizers.

Recent Developments: For the quarter ended Mar 31 2016, income from continuing operations decreased 2.0% to US$241.0 million from US$246.0 million in the year-earlier quarter. Net income decreased 10.8% to US$232.0 million from US$260.0 million in the year-earlier quarter. Revenues were US$8.92 billion, down 17.5% from US$10.81 billion the year before. Direct operating expenses declined 17.8% to US$8.30 billion from US$10.10 billion in the comparable period the year before. Indirect operating expenses decreased 5.1% to US$314.0 million from US$331.0 million in the equivalent prior-year period.

Prospects: Our evaluation of Bunge Ltd. as of July 19, 2015 is the result of our systematic analysis on three basic characteristics: earnings strength, relative valuation, and recent stock price movement. The company has produced a positive trend in earnings per share over the past 5 quarters. However, while recent estimates for the company have been lowered by analysts, BG has posted better than expected results. Based on operating earnings yield, the company is undervalued when compared to all of the companies in our coverage universe. Share price changes over the past year indicates that BG will perform well over the near term.

Financial Data

(US$ in Millions)	3 Mos	12/31/2015	12/31/2014	12/31/2013	12/31/2012	12/31/2011	12/31/2010	12/31/2009
Earnings Per Share	4.90	5.07	3.17	1.55	0.19	6.07	15.06	2.22
Cash Flow Per Share	2.69	4.25	9.57	15.12	(3.12)	17.83	(17.25)	(2.91)
Tang Book Value Per Share	38.04	35.14	49.08	57.17	65.09	68.93	70.99	54.77
Dividends Per Share	1.480	1.440	1.280	1.140	1.040	0.960	0.880	0.800
Dividend Payout %	30.20	28.40	40.38	73.55	547.37	15.82	5.84	36.04
Income Statement								
Total Revenue	8,916	43,455	57,161	61,347	60,991	58,743	45,707	41,926
EBITDA	435	1,784	1,570	1,825	1,117	1,637	3,699	733
Depn & Amortn	113	518	576	524	504	497	420	427
Income Before Taxes	275	1,051	734	1,014	372	940	3,050	145
Income Taxes	34	296	249	904	(6)	44	689	(110)
Net Income	235	791	515	306	64	942	2,354	361
Average Shares	149	152	147	148	147	155	156	127
Balance Sheet								
Current Assets	11,423	10,916	13,081	17,772	17,264	13,128	15,815	11,783
Total Assets	18,939	17,922	21,432	26,781	27,280	23,275	26,001	21,286
Current Liabilities	7,092	7,340	8,704	12,535	11,561	6,947	10,004	6,207
Long-Term Obligations	3,845	2,934	2,855	3,179	3,532	3,348	2,551	3,618
Total Liabilities	12,167	11,481	12,986	16,924	16,418	11,568	13,781	11,792
Stockholders' Equity	6,772	6,441	8,446	9,857	10,862	11,707	12,220	9,494
Shares Outstanding	139	142	145	147	146	143	146	134
Statistical Record								
Return on Assets %	4.08	4.02	2.14	1.13	0.25	3.82	9.96	1.74
Return on Equity %	10.93	10.63	5.63	2.95	0.57	7.87	21.68	4.26
EBITDA Margin %	4.88	4.11	2.75	2.97	1.83	2.79	8.09	1.75
Net Margin %	2.64	1.82	0.90	0.50	0.10	1.60	5.15	0.86
Asset Turnover	2.22	2.21	2.37	2.27	2.41	2.38	1.93	2.02
Current Ratio	1.61	1.49	1.50	1.42	1.49	1.89	1.58	1.90
Debt to Equity	0.57	0.46	0.34	0.32	0.33	0.29	0.21	0.38
Price Range	92.85-47.79	92.85-61.81	92.91-73.51	83.11-66.40	73.82-57.22	75.44-55.51	71.29-46.29	72.41-41.61
P/E Ratio	18.95-9.75	18.31-12.19	29.31-23.19	53.62-42.84	388.53-301.16	12.43-9.14	4.73-3.07	32.62-18.74
Average Yield %	2.01	1.79	1.58	1.51	1.59	1.45	1.52	1.36

Address: 50 Main Street, White Plains, NY 10606 **Telephone:** 914-684-2800	**Web Site:** www.bunge.com **Officers:** Soren Schroder - Chief Executive Officer, Region Officer D. Benedict Pearcy - Chief Development Officer, Division Officer	**Auditors:** Deloitte & Touche LLP **Transfer Agents:** Computershare Investor Services LLC

BWX TECHNOLOGIES INC

Exchange	Symbol	Price $35.17 (5/31/2016)	52Wk Range 35.17-16.36	Yield 1.02	P/E 28.14

*7 Year Price Score N/A   ***NYSE Composite Index=100**   ***12 Month Price Score 115.35**

TRADING VOLUME (thousand shares)

Interim Earnings (Per Share)

Qtr.	Mar	Jun	Sep	Dec
2013	0.41	0.65	0.54	1.47
2014	0.41	0.24	0.57	(0.94)
2015	0.42	(0.16)	0.96	(0.01)
2016	0.46	...	...	...

Interim Dividends (Per Share)

Amt	Decl	Ex	Rec	Pay
0.06Q	07/31/2015	08/18/2015	08/20/2015	09/10/2015
0.06Q	10/30/2015	11/18/2015	11/20/2015	12/16/2015
0.09Q	02/23/2016	03/03/2016	03/07/2016	03/24/2016
0.09Q	04/29/2016	05/12/2016	05/16/2016	06/06/2016

Indicated Div: $0.36

Valuation Analysis		Institutional Holding	
Forecast EPS	$1.62 (05/15/2016)	No of Institutions	321
Market Cap	$3.7 Billion	Shares	102,227,664
Book Value	$267.6 Million	% Held	91.30
Price/Book	13.69		
Price/Sales	2.54		

Business Summary: Industrial Machinery & Equipment (MIC: 7.2.1 SIC: 3511 NAIC: 333611)

BWX Technologies provides a range of products and services. As of June 30 2015, Co. operated in three segments: Nuclear Operations, which mainly manufactures naval nuclear reactors for the U.S. Department of Energy/National Nuclear Security Administration's Naval Nuclear Propulsion Program, which in turn supplies them to the U.S. Navy for use in submarines and aircraft carriers; Technical Services, which provides various services to the U.S. Government, including uranium processing, environmental site restoration services and management and operating services; and Nuclear Energy, which supplies commercial nuclear steam generators, components and services to nuclear utility customers.

Recent Developments: For the quarter ended Mar 31 2016, income from continuing operations increased 44.0% to US$48.9 million from US$34.0 million in the year-earlier quarter. Net income increased 8.6% to US$48.9 million from US$45.0 million in the year-earlier quarter. Revenues were US$364.8 million, up 8.7% from US$335.5 million the year before. Operating income was US$42.6 million versus US$53.8 million in the prior-year quarter, a decrease of 20.8%. Direct operating expenses rose 9.3% to US$248.8 million from US$227.6 million in the comparable period the year before. Indirect operating expenses increased 35.8% to US$73.4 million from US$54.1 million in the equivalent prior-year period.

Prospects: Our evaluation of BWX Technologies Inc. as of June 19, 2016 is the result of our systematic analysis on three basic characteristics: earnings strength, relative valuation, and recent stock price movement. The company has produced a positive trend in earnings per share over the past 5 quarters and while recent estimates for the company have remained steady, BWXT has posted better than expected results. Based on operating earnings yield, the company is about fairly valued when compared to all of the companies in our coverage universe. Share price changes over the past year indicates that BWXT will perform very well over the near term.

Financial Data

(US$ in Thousands)	3 Mos	12/31/2015	12/31/2014	12/31/2013	12/31/2012	12/31/2011	12/31/2010	12/31/2009
Earnings Per Share	1.25	1.22	0.27	3.07	1.91	1.43	1.30	...
Cash Flow Per Share	2.94	3.09	0.69	1.23	1.56	1.48	1.65	...
Tang Book Value Per Share	0.39	0.37	4.77	7.26	6.12	4.65	3.79	...
Dividends Per Share	0.310	0.320	0.400	0.340	0.080	...	...	...
Dividend Payout %	24.80	26.23	148.15	11.07	4.19	...	...	...
Income Statement								
Total Revenue	364,826	1,415,529	2,923,019	3,269,208	3,291,359	2,952,040	2,688,811	2,854,632
EBITDA	75,052	242,819	63,161	512,987	314,353	221,281	234,590	260,958
Depn & Amortn	11,905	55,300	92,900	62,200	59,400	61,800	61,100	62,600
Income Before Taxes	61,591	207,669	(36,290)	449,115	252,709	156,280	161,738	177,207
Income Taxes	16,230	80,416	(15,991)	184,583	101,861	72,982	82,294	84,381
Net Income	48,791	131,465	29,388	346,078	227,695	169,654	153,262	147,764
Average Shares	105,762	107,583	108,761	112,685	119,021	118,404	117,626	...
Balance Sheet								
Current Assets	634,239	647,294	1,473,802	1,437,424	1,521,086	1,487,076	1,209,116	1,306,715
Total Assets	1,365,712	1,382,139	2,856,936	2,609,153	2,840,355	2,789,111	2,500,510	2,603,859
Current Liabilities	372,792	353,780	819,636	927,228	1,079,288	1,154,807	981,827	1,235,176
Long-Term Obligations	274,884	285,000	285,000	225	430	633	855	324,790
Total Liabilities	1,098,126	1,116,423	1,858,232	1,444,466	1,853,920	1,963,317	1,787,651	2,483,153
Stockholders' Equity	267,586	265,716	998,704	1,164,687	986,435	825,794	712,859	120,706
Shares Outstanding	104,163	105,297	106,688	110,468	115,235	118,107	116,862	...
Statistical Record								
Return on Assets %	6.49	6.20	1.08	12.70	8.07	6.41	6.01	5.78
Return on Equity %	20.78	20.79	2.72	32.18	25.06	22.05	36.77	577.68
EBITDA Margin %	20.57	17.15	2.16	15.69	9.55	7.50	8.72	9.14
Net Margin %	13.37	9.29	1.01	10.59	6.92	5.75	5.70	5.18
Asset Turnover	0.70	0.67	1.07	1.20	1.17	1.12	1.05	1.12
Current Ratio	1.70	1.83	1.80	1.55	1.41	1.29	1.23	1.06
Debt to Equity	1.03	1.07	0.29	N.M.	N.M.	N.M.	N.M.	2.69
Price Range	34.33-16.36	32.23-16.36	25.39-19.81	24.70-18.11	19.84-16.47	25.45-13.27	18.58-15.21	...
P/E Ratio	27.46-13.09	26.42-13.41	94.05-73.38	8.05-5.90	10.38-8.62	17.80-9.28	14.29-11.70	...
Average Yield %	1.15	1.30	1.77	1.59	0.45	...	...	...

Address: 800 Main Street, 4th Floor, Lynchburg, VA 24504 Telephone: 980-365-4300	Web Site: www.babcock.com Officers: John A. Fees - Chairman P. Sandy Baker - President, Chief Executive Officer	Auditors: Deloitte & Touche LLP Investor Contact: 704-625-4944 Transfer Agents: Computershare Trust Company, N.A., Canton, MA

CABELAS INC

Exchange	Symbol	Price	52Wk Range	Yield	P/E
NYS	CAB	$48.56 (5/31/2016)	53.60-33.42	N/A	18.39

*7 Year Price Score 98.16 *NYSE Composite Index=100 *12 Month Price Score 107.41

TRADING VOLUME (thousand shares)

Interim Earnings (Per Share)

Qtr.	Mar	Jun	Sep	Dec
2013	0.70	0.62	0.70	1.12
2014	0.36	0.61	0.75	1.10
2015	0.37	0.56	0.62	1.13
2016	0.33	...	...	...

Interim Dividends (Per Share)

No Dividends Paid

Valuation Analysis | **Institutional Holding**

Forecast EPS	$3.20	No of Institutions
	(05/20/2016)	370
Market Cap	$3.3 Billion	Shares
Book Value	$1.9 Billion	60,454,240
Price/Book	1.77	% Held
Price/Sales	0.82	75.88

Business Summary: Retail - Specialty (MIC: 2.1.3 SIC: 5941 NAIC: 451110)

Cabelas is a retailer, which operated 77 retail stores, 68 stores in 36 states and nine stores in Canada at the end of 2015. Co. sells products through its e-commerce websites and direct mail catalogs. Through its wholly-owned bank subsidiary, World's Foremost Bank, Co. issues and manages the Cabela's CLUB Visa credit card, a reward based credit card program. Co.'s product categories include hunting equipment for hunting and sport shooting; general outdoors equipment and accessories for outdoor activities; clothing and footwear including fieldwear apparel, sportswear apparel, and workwear products; and Cabela's branded products, including casual apparel, footwear and selected hard goods.

Recent Developments: For the quarter ended Apr 2 2016, net income decreased 14.5% to US$22.9 million from US$26.8 million in the year-earlier quarter. Revenues were US$864.7 million, up 4.5% from US$827.1 million the year before. Operating income was US$44.4 million versus US$44.5 million in the prior-year quarter, a decrease of 0.4%. Direct operating expenses rose 4.7% to US$488.1 million from US$466.4 million in the comparable period the year before. Indirect operating expenses increased 5.1% to US$332.2 million from US$316.1 million in the equivalent prior-year period.

Prospects: Our evaluation of Cabelas Inc. as of June 19, 2016 is the result of our systematic analysis on three basic characteristics: earnings strength, relative valuation, and recent stock price movement. The company has managed to produce a neutral trend in earnings per share over the past 5 quarters and while recent estimates for the company have remained steady, CAB has posted better than expected results. Based on operating earnings yield, the company is undervalued when compared to all of the companies in our coverage universe. Share price changes over the past year indicates that CAB will perform in line with the market over the near term.

Financial Data
(US$ in Thousands)

	3 Mos	01/02/2016	12/27/2014	12/28/2013	12/29/2012	12/31/2011	01/01/2011	01/02/2010
Earnings Per Share	2.64	2.67	2.81	3.13	2.42	2.00	1.62	0.74
Cash Flow Per Share	5.18	4.59	3.64	4.91	3.37	5.31	2.48	4.32
Tang Book Value Per Share	27.45	26.92	25.52	22.68	19.58	17.10	14.95	14.54
Income Statement								
Total Revenue	864,662	3,997,702	3,647,650	3,599,577	3,112,682	2,811,166	2,663,242	2,632,240
EBITDA	80,967	450,205	453,416	458,789	361,106	310,237	263,994	170,199
Depn & Amortn	35,710	132,696	113,097	93,407	79,269	71,343	69,872	70,566
Income Before Taxes	36,026	294,627	318,477	343,528	261,714	214,467	166,680	76,524
Income Taxes	13,137	105,297	116,762	119,138	88,201	71,847	54,521	26,907
Net Income	22,889	189,330	201,715	224,390	173,513	142,620	112,159	49,617
Average Shares	68,687	70,968	71,877	71,778	71,709	71,274	69,086	67,453
Balance Sheet								
Current Assets	6,095,720	6,484,945	5,937,672	4,986,512	4,589,028	4,111,281	3,546,061	1,341,092
Total Assets	8,101,209	8,472,503	7,675,317	6,396,864	5,748,163	5,133,771	4,531,179	2,491,885
Current Liabilities	2,479,840	2,475,903	2,121,040	1,112,780	1,429,350	1,619,690	1,798,937	721,738
Long-Term Obligations	2,926,697	3,366,329	3,071,031	2,774,987	2,155,633	1,314,035	1,237,422	345,178
Total Liabilities	6,228,229	6,643,860	5,857,807	4,790,530	4,372,184	3,952,455	3,506,631	1,507,464
Stockholders' Equity	1,872,980	1,828,643	1,817,510	1,606,334	1,375,979	1,181,316	1,024,548	984,421
Shares Outstanding	68,243	67,818	71,093	70,630	70,053	68,840	68,156	67,287
Statistical Record								
Return on Assets %	2.40	2.31	2.87	3.71	3.20	2.96	3.20	2.00
Return on Equity %	10.01	10.22	11.82	15.09	13.61	12.97	11.20	5.14
EBITDA Margin %	9.36	11.26	12.43	12.75	11.60	11.04	9.91	6.47
Net Margin %	2.65	4.74	5.53	6.23	5.57	5.07	4.21	1.88
Asset Turnover	0.52	0.49	0.52	0.59	0.57	0.58	0.76	1.06
Current Ratio	2.46	2.62	2.80	4.48	3.21	2.54	1.97	1.86
Debt to Equity	1.56	1.84	1.69	1.73	1.57	1.11	1.21	0.35
Price Range	57.32-33.42	58.30-33.42	71.54-46.60	71.71-41.75	56.48-24.23	31.19-19.66	23.11-12.97	16.37-5.24
P/E Ratio	21.71-12.66	21.84-12.52	25.46-16.58	22.91-13.34	23.34-10.01	15.60-9.83	14.27-8.01	22.12-7.08

Address: One Cabela Drive, Sidney, NE 69160	**Web Site:** www.cabelas.com	**Auditors:** Deloitte & Touche LLP
Telephone: 308 254 5505	**Officers:** Richard N. Cabela - Chairman James W. Cabela - Vice-Chairman	**Investor Contact:** 308 255-2905
		Transfer Agents: Wells Fargo Shareowner Services, St. Paul, MN

CABLE ONE INC

Exchange	Symbol	Price	52Wk Range	Yield	P/E
NYS	CABO	$489.99 (5/31/2016)	498.51-376.91	1.22	30.51

*7 Year Price Score N/A ***NYSE Composite Index=100** ***12 Month Price Score 106.15**

Interim Earnings (Per Share)

Qtr.	Mar	Jun	Sep	Dec
2014	4.17	4.60	11.84	4.60
2015	3.78	3.67	3.30	4.44
2016	4.65	...	...	...

Interim Dividends (Per Share)

Amt	Decl	Ex	Rec	Pay
1.50Q	11/03/2015	11/13/2015	11/17/2015	12/04/2015
1.50Q	02/02/2016	02/11/2016	02/16/2016	03/04/2016
1.50Q	05/03/2016	05/13/2016	05/17/2016	06/03/2016

Indicated Div: $6.00

Valuation Analysis | **Institutional Holding**

Forecast EPS	$18.23	No of Institutions
	(05/16/2016)	235
Market Cap	$2.8 Billion	Shares
Book Value	$422.2 Million	4,147,375
Price/Book	6.68	% Held
Price/Sales	3.49	N/A

TRADING VOLUME (thousand shares)

Business Summary: Radio & Television (MIC: 2.3.1 SIC: 4841 NAIC: 515210)

Cable One is a provider of data, video and voice services in 19 Western, Midwestern and Southern states. Co. provides these broadband services to residential and business customers in 38 cable systems covering over 400 cities and towns. Co.'s product lines include residential video services, residential data services, residential voice services, data, voice and video services products to its business customers, as well as advertising. As of Dec 31 2015, Co. provided service to 664,604 residential and business customers. Of these customers, 501,241 subscribed to data services, 364,150 to video services and 127,094 to voice services.

Recent Developments: For the quarter ended Mar 31 2016, net income increased 22.3% to US$27.0 million from US$22.1 million in the year-earlier quarter. Revenues were US$202.8 million, down 0.1% from US$202.9 million the year before. Operating income was US$47.4 million versus US$35.9 million in the prior-year quarter, an increase of 31.9%. Indirect operating expenses decreased 6.9% to US$155.4 million from US$167.0 million in the equivalent prior-year period.

Prospects: Our evaluation of Cable ONE Inc. as of June 19, 2016 is the result of our systematic analysis on three basic characteristics: earnings strength, relative valuation, and recent stock price movement. The company has enjoyed a very positive trend in earnings per share over the past 5 quarters. However, while recent estimates for the company have been mixed, CABO has posted better than expected results. Based on operating earnings yield, the company is about fairly valued when compared to all of the companies in our coverage universe. Share price changes over the past year indicates that CABO will perform well over the near term.

Financial Data

(US$ in Thousands)	3 Mos	12/31/2015	12/31/2014	12/31/2013	12/31/2012
Earnings Per Share	16.06	15.19	...	...	...
Cash Flow Per Share	...	42.10	...	...	...
Tang Book Value Per Share	N.M.	N.M.	...	...	...
Dividends Per Share	3.000	1.500	...	...	...
Dividend Payout %	18.68	9.87	...	...	...
Income Statement					
Total Revenue	202,805	807,266	814,812	825,707	804,992
EBITDA	82,997	302,110	372,009	289,811	276,711
Depn & Amortn	35,104	140,600	134,000	125,500	126,500
Income Before Taxes	40,338	145,420	238,009	164,311	150,211
Income Taxes	13,294	56,387	90,700	59,800	56,300
Net Income	27,044	89,033	147,309	104,511	93,911
Average Shares	5,810	5,860	1,000.00	1,000.00	1,000.00
Balance Sheet					
Current Assets	151,727	166,353	50,121	46,768	...
Total Assets	1,377,664	1,408,595	1,262,040	1,248,344	...
Current Liabilities	122,522	126,832	95,623	105,142	...
Long-Term Obligations	534,663	545,301	...	...	...
Total Liabilities	955,486	973,249	408,752	413,085	...
Stockholders' Equity	422,178	435,346	853,288	835,259	...
Shares Outstanding	5,757	5,833	1,000.00	1,000.00	...
Statistical Record					
Return on Assets %	...	...	11.74	...	...
Return on Equity %	...	...	17.45	...	...
EBITDA Margin %	40.92	37.42	45.66	35.10	34.37
Net Margin %	13.33	11.03	18.08	12.66	11.67
Asset Turnover	...	...	0.65	...	...
Current Ratio	1.24	1.31	0.52	0.44	...
Debt to Equity	1.27	1.25	...	...	...
Price Range	490.48-376.91	490.48-376.91	...	...	...
P/E Ratio	30.54-23.47	32.29-24.81	...	...	...
Average Yield %	0.70	0.35	...	...	...

Address: 210 E. Earll Drive, Phoenix, AZ 85012 **Telephone:** 602-364-6000	**Web Site:** www.cableone.net **Officers:** Thomas O. Might - Chairman, Chief Executive Officer Stephen A. Fox - Senior Vice President, Chief Technology Officer	**Auditors:** PricewaterhouseCoopers LLP **Transfer Agents:** Computershare Trust Company, N.A.

CABLEVISION SYSTEMS CORP

Exchange	Symbol	Price	52Wk Range	Yield	P/E
NYS	CVC	$34.68 (5/31/2016)	34.68-22.59	N/A	43.35

*7 Year Price Score 120.57 *NYSE Composite Index=100 *12 Month Price Score 109.58

Interim Earnings (Per Share)

Qtr.	Mar	Jun	Sep	Dec
2013	(0.06)	0.51	1.10	0.19
2014	0.33	0.35	0.26	0.20
2015	0.16	0.27	0.08	0.11
2016	0.34	...	...	...

Interim Dividends (Per Share)

Amt	Decl	Ex	Rec	Pay
0.15Q	11/05/2014	11/19/2014	11/21/2014	12/12/2014
0.15Q	02/24/2015	03/12/2015	03/16/2015	04/03/2015
0.15Q	05/01/2015	05/20/2015	05/22/2015	06/12/2015
0.15Q	08/06/2015	08/19/2015	08/21/2015	09/10/2015

Valuation Analysis — **Institutional Holding**

Valuation Analysis		Institutional Holding	
Forecast EPS	$0.91	No of Institutions	
	(05/20/2016)	542	
Market Cap	$9.6 Billion	Shares	
Book Value	N/A	211,828,416	
Price/Book	N/A	% Held	
Price/Sales	1.47	92.27	

Business Summary: Radio & Television (MIC: 2.3.1 SIC: 4841 NAIC: 515210)

Cablevision Systems is a holding company. Through its CSC Holdings, LLC subsidiary and their subsidiaries, Co. is engaged as a cable operator, serving video customers in and around the New York metropolitan area. Co. also provides data and Voice over Internet Protocol services using its broadband network. Through its Cablevision Lightpath, Inc. subsidiary (Lightpath), Co. provides Ethernet-based data, Internet, voice and video transport and managed services to the business market in the New York metropolitan area. In addition, through its Newsday LLC indirect subsidiary, Co. operates a newspaper publishing business. Co. operates through three reportable segments: Cable, Lightpath and Other.

Recent Developments: For the quarter ended Mar 31 2016, income from continuing operations increased 71.8% to US$94.3 million from US$54.9 million in the year-earlier quarter. Net income increased 112.4% to US$94.3 million from US$44.4 million in the year-earlier quarter. Revenues were US$1.64 billion, up 1.6% from US$1.61 billion the year before. Operating income was US$251.3 million versus US$223.8 million in the prior-year quarter, an increase of 12.3%. Indirect operating expenses were unchanged at US$1.39 billion versus the equivalent prior-year period.

Prospects: Our evaluation of Cablevision Systems Corp. as of June 19, 2016 is the result of our systematic analysis on three basic characteristics: earnings strength, relative valuation, and recent stock price movement. The company has enjoyed a very positive trend in earnings per share over the past 5 quarters and while recent estimates for the company have been raised by analysts, CVC has posted better than expected results. Based on operating earnings yield, the company is overvalued when compared to all of the companies in our coverage universe. Share price changes over the past year indicates that CVC will perform very well over the near term.

Financial Data

(US$ in Thousands)	3 Mos	12/31/2015	12/31/2014	12/31/2013	12/31/2012	12/31/2011	12/31/2010	12/31/2009
Earnings Per Share	0.80	0.63	1.15	1.75	0.87	1.02	1.20	0.96
Cash Flow Per Share	4.41	4.67	5.21	4.35	4.38	5.06	5.78	5.61
Dividends Per Share	0.300	0.450	0.600	0.600	0.600	0.575	0.475	0.400
Dividend Payout %	37.50	71.43	52.17	34.29	68.97	56.37	39.58	41.67
Income Statement								
Total Revenue	1,640,757	6,509,743	6,460,946	6,232,152	6,705,461	6,700,848	7,231,249	7,773,276
EBITDA	312,786	1,792,752	1,861,401	1,665,286	1,842,812	2,172,774	2,361,179	2,349,905
Depn & Amortn	7,207	865,252	860,671	871,689	1,065,957	1,003,974	985,747	1,082,248
Income Before Taxes	157,097	342,661	425,150	192,960	57,184	423,094	591,269	521,019
Income Taxes	62,786	154,872	115,768	65,635	23,821	184,436	225,550	235,702
Net Income	94,377	175,449	311,439	465,661	233,523	291,857	360,948	285,572
Average Shares	279,013	276,339	270,703	265,935	267,330	284,904	301,880	298,444
Balance Sheet								
Current Assets	1,836,861	1,875,586	1,930,666	1,724,434	1,373,487	1,354,952	1,639,875	2,055,365
Total Assets	6,732,386	6,867,293	6,765,171	6,591,076	7,246,224	7,143,325	8,840,685	9,325,725
Current Liabilities	2,094,013	2,188,642	1,750,168	1,441,052	1,692,948	1,595,428	2,162,113	2,070,240
Long-Term Obligations	8,510,557	8,620,404	9,134,654	9,419,783	10,578,202	10,792,752	12,126,732	10,839,677
Total Liabilities	11,564,935	11,778,609	11,806,640	11,875,406	12,885,388	12,719,180	15,137,603	14,481,680
Stockholders' Equity	(4,832,549)	(4,911,316)	(5,041,469)	(5,284,330)	(5,639,164)	(5,575,855)	(6,296,918)	(5,155,955)
Shares Outstanding	276,326	276,709	274,357	267,736	264,698	274,307	295,203	302,022
Statistical Record								
Return on Assets %	3.35	2.57	4.66	6.73	3.24	3.65	3.97	3.05
EBITDA Margin %	19.06	27.54	28.81	26.72	27.48	32.43	32.65	30.23
Net Margin %	5.75	2.70	4.82	7.47	3.48	4.36	4.99	3.67
Asset Turnover	0.97	0.96	0.97	0.90	0.93	0.84	0.80	0.83
Current Ratio	0.88	0.86	1.10	1.20	0.81	0.85	0.76	0.99
Price Range	33.30-17.95	33.19-17.72	21.32-15.85	19.79-13.73	18.52-10.97	37.72-12.75	34.72-20.76	21.60-7.82
P/E Ratio	41.63-22.44	52.68-28.13	18.54-13.78	11.31-7.85	21.29-12.61	36.98-12.50	28.93-17.30	22.50-8.14
Average Yield %	1.07	1.80	3.36	3.73	4.16	2.16	1.83	2.47

Address: 1111 Stewart Avenue, Bethpage, NY 11714
Telephone: 516-803-2300

Web Site: www.cablevision.com
Officers: Dexter Goei - President, Chief Executive Officer Charles Stewart - Chief Financial Officer, Treasurer

Auditors: KPMG LLP
Transfer Agents: Wells Fargo Shareowner Services, St. Paul, MN

CABOT CORP.

Exchange	Symbol	Price	52Wk Range	Yield	P/E
NYS	CBT	$45.71 (5/31/2016)	50.18-30.90	2.63	N/A

*7 Year Price Score 88.87 *NYSE Composite Index=100 *12 Month Price Score 117.05

Interim Earnings (Per Share)

Qtr.	Dec	Mar	Jun	Sep
2012-13	0.31	0.42	0.90	0.73
2013-14	1.23	0.54	0.78	0.48
2014-15	0.69	0.41	(7.04)	0.61
2015-16	(0.11)	0.76		

Interim Dividends (Per Share)

Amt	Decl	Ex	Rec	Pay
0.22Q	07/10/2015	08/26/2015	08/28/2015	09/11/2015
0.22Q	11/13/2015	11/24/2015	11/27/2015	12/11/2015
0.22Q	01/08/2016	02/24/2016	02/26/2016	03/11/2016
0.30Q	05/24/2016	05/25/2016	05/27/2016	06/10/2016

Indicated Div: $1.20

Valuation Analysis

		Institutional Holding	
Forecast EPS	$3.15	No of Institutions	377
	(05/16/2016)		
Market Cap	$2.8 Billion	Shares	60,005,944
Book Value	$1.3 Billion	% Held	87.29
Price/Book	2.26		
Price/Sales	1.12		

Business Summary: Specialty Chemicals (MIC: 8.3.2 SIC: 2895 NAIC: 325182)

Cabot is a chemicals and performance materials company. Co.'s business segments are: Reinforcement Materials, which include rubber blacks products used in tires and industrial products; Performance Chemicals, which manufactures and sells carbon black, compounds and inkjet colorants, and fumed silica, fumed alumina and dispersions thereof and aerogel; Purification Solutions, which include activated carbon products used for the purification of water, air, food and beverages, pharmaceuticals and other liquids and gases; and Specialty Fluids, which produces and markets cesium formate as a drilling and completion fluid for use in high pressure and high temperature oil and gas well construction.

Recent Developments: For the quarter ended Mar 31 2016, net income increased 92.6% to US$52.0 million from US$27.0 million in the year-earlier quarter. Revenues were US$568.0 million, down 18.2% from US$694.0 million the year before. Operating income was US$77.0 million versus US$54.0 million in the prior-year quarter, an increase of 42.6%. Direct operating expenses declined 24.7% to US$418.0 million from US$555.0 million in the comparable period the year before. Indirect operating expenses decreased 14.1% to US$73.0 million from US$85.0 million in the equivalent prior-year period.

Prospects: Our evaluation of Cabot Corp. as of June 19, 2016 is the result of our systematic analysis on three basic characteristics: earnings strength, relative valuation, and recent stock price movement. The company has enjoyed a very positive trend in earnings per share over the past 5 years. However, while recent estimates for the company have been mixed, CBT has posted results that fell short of analysts expectations. Based on operating earnings yield, the company is undervalued when compared to all of the companies in our coverage universe. Share price changes over the past year indicates that CBT will perform very well over the near term.

Financial Data

(US$ in Thousands)	6 Mos	3 Mos	09/30/2015	09/30/2014	09/30/2013	09/30/2012	09/30/2011	09/30/2010
Earnings Per Share	(5.78)	(6.13)	(5.27)	3.03	2.36	5.99	3.57	2.35
Cash Flow Per Share	7.72	8.42	7.87	4.89	6.57	6.53	3.02	3.89
Tang Book Value Per Share	15.32	13.74	14.84	16.45	17.77	15.83	22.66	19.26
Dividends Per Share	0.880	0.880	0.880	0.840	0.800	0.760	0.720	0.720
Dividend Payout %	...	...	...	27.72	33.90	12.69	20.17	30.64
Income Statement								
Total Revenue	1,171,000	603,000	2,871,000	3,647,000	3,463,000	3,300,000	3,102,000	2,893,000
EBITDA	160,000	45,000	(159,000)	544,000	438,000	440,000	378,000	388,000
Depn & Amortn	82,000	41,000	169,000	184,000	176,000	153,000	138,000	142,000
Income Before Taxes	54,000	(8,000)	(377,000)	308,000	205,000	245,000	203,000	208,000
Income Taxes	6,000	(5,000)	(45,000)	92,000	58,000	55,000	6,000	46,000
Net Income	41,000	(7,000)	(334,000)	199,000	153,000	388,000	236,000	154,000
Average Shares	62,800	62,500	63,400	65,100	64,500	64,200	65,400	64,000
Balance Sheet								
Current Assets	1,028,000	999,000	1,048,000	1,364,000	1,495,000	1,443,000	1,555,000	1,438,000
Total Assets	2,998,000	2,955,000	3,075,000	4,084,000	4,233,000	4,399,000	3,141,000	2,886,000
Current Liabilities	655,000	709,000	441,000	630,000	844,000	919,000	656,000	539,000
Long-Term Obligations	669,000	670,000	970,000	1,004,000	1,020,000	1,172,000	556,000	600,000
Total Liabilities	1,739,000	1,796,000	1,841,000	2,142,000	2,282,000	2,586,000	1,654,000	1,584,000
Stockholders' Equity	1,259,000	1,159,000	1,234,000	1,942,000	1,951,000	1,813,000	1,487,000	1,302,000
Shares Outstanding	62,348	62,350	62,458	64,382	63,970	63,347	63,860	65,370
Statistical Record								
Return on Assets %	N.M.	N.M.	N.M.	4.79	3.54	10.26	7.83	5.54
Return on Equity %	N.M.	N.M.	N.M.	10.22	8.13	23.45	16.92	12.64
EBITDA Margin %	13.66	7.46	N.M.	14.92	12.65	13.33	12.19	13.41
Net Margin %	3.50	N.M.	N.M.	5.46	4.42	11.76	7.61	5.32
Asset Turnover	0.75	0.77	0.80	0.88	0.80	0.87	1.03	1.04
Current Ratio	1.57	1.41	2.38	2.17	1.77	1.57	2.37	2.67
Debt to Equity	0.53	0.58	0.79	0.52	0.52	0.65	0.37	0.46
Price Range	49.34-30.90	47.86-30.90	50.77-30.90	60.30-42.48	43.93-32.41	44.66-23.27	47.83-24.78	33.65-21.04
P/E Ratio	...	...	...	19.90-14.02	18.61-13.73	7.46-3.88	13.40-6.94	14.32-8.95
Average Yield %	2.20	2.18	2.11	1.58	2.09	2.08	1.86	2.59

Address: Two Seaport Lane, Boston, MA 02210-2019 **Telephone:** 617-345-0100	**Web Site:** www.cabotcorp.com **Officers:** Sean D. Keohane - President, Chief Executive Officer, Executive Vice President, Division Officer Nicholas S. Cross - Executive Vice President, Division Officer	**Auditors:** Deloitte & Touche LLP **Investor Contact:** 617-342-6090 **Transfer Agents:** Computershare Trust Company, N.A., Providence, RI

CABOT OIL & GAS CORP.

Exchange	Symbol	Price	52Wk Range	Yield	P/E
NYS	COG	$23.97 (5/31/2016)	34.17-15.03	0.33	N/A

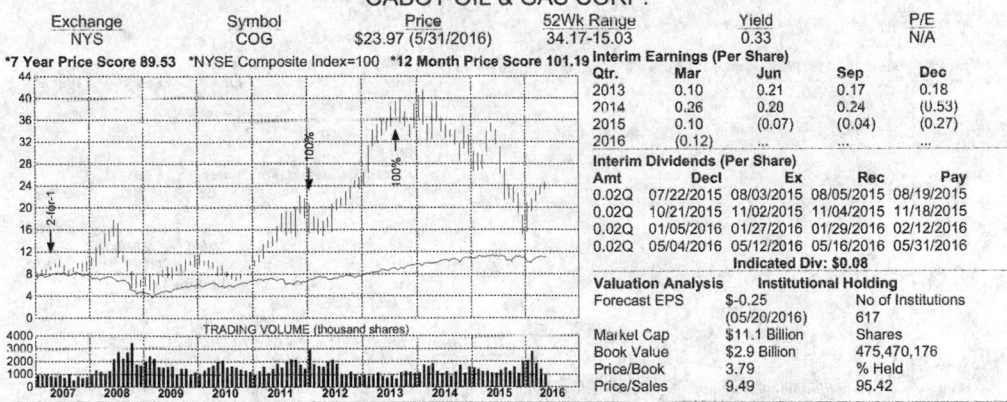

*7 Year Price Score 89.53   *NYSE Composite Index=100   *12 Month Price Score 101.19

Interim Earnings (Per Share)

Qtr.	Mar	Jun	Sep	Dec
2013	0.10	0.21	0.17	0.18
2014	0.26	0.20	0.24	(0.53)
2015	0.10	(0.07)	(0.04)	(0.27)
2016	(0.12)	...	...	...

Interim Dividends (Per Share)

Amt	Decl	Ex	Rec	Pay
0.02Q	07/22/2015	08/03/2015	08/05/2015	08/19/2015
0.02Q	10/21/2015	11/02/2015	11/04/2015	11/18/2015
0.02Q	01/05/2016	01/27/2016	01/29/2016	02/12/2016
0.02Q	05/04/2016	05/12/2016	05/16/2016	05/31/2016

Indicated Div: $0.08

Valuation Analysis

Forecast EPS	$-0.25
	(05/20/2016)
Market Cap	$11.1 Billion
Book Value	$2.9 Billion
Price/Book	3.79
Price/Sales	9.49

Institutional Holding

No of Institutions	617
Shares	475,470,176
% Held	95.42

Business Summary: Production & Extraction (MIC: 9.1.1 SIC: 1311 NAIC: 211111)

Cabot Oil & Gas is engaged in the development, exploitation, exploration, production and marketing of natural gas, oil and, to a lesser extent, natural gas liquids (NGLs). Co. also transports, stores, gathers and purchases natural gas for resale. Co.'s exploration, development and production operations are primarily focused on two unconventional plays: the Marcellus Shale in northeast Pennsylvania and the Eagle Ford Shale in south Texas. Co. also has operations in various other conventional and unconventional plays throughout the continental U.S. As of Dec 31 2015, Co. had proved natural gas reserves of 7.86 trillion cubic feet and proved crude oil and NGLs reserves of 55.7 million barrels.

Recent Developments: For the quarter ended Mar 31 2016, net loss amounted to US$51.2 million versus net income of US$40.3 million in the year-earlier quarter. Revenues were US$281.9 million, down 39.3% from US$464.8 million the year before. Operating loss was US$55.6 million versus an income of US$87.3 million in the prior-year quarter. Direct operating expenses declined 14.1% to US$138.3 million from US$161.0 million in the comparable period the year before. Indirect operating expenses decreased 7.9% to US$199.3 million from US$216.5 million in the equivalent prior-year period.

Prospects: Our evaluation of Cabot Oil & Gas Corp. as of June 19, 2016 is the result of our systematic analysis on three basic characteristics: earnings strength, relative valuation, and recent stock price movement. The company has produced a positive trend in earnings per share over the past 5 quarters. Because the company lacks sufficient analyst estimate data, we place greater weight on the historical EPS trend as the measure of earnings strength. Based on operating earnings yield, the company is overvalued when compared to all of the companies in our coverage universe. Share price changes over the past year indicates that COG will perform poorly over the near term.

Financial Data

(US$ in Thousands)	3 Mos	12/31/2015	12/31/2014	12/31/2013	12/31/2012	12/31/2011	12/31/2010	12/31/2009
Earnings Per Share	(0.50)	(0.28)	0.25	0.66	0.31	0.29	0.25	0.35
Cash Flow Per Share	1.24	1.79	2.97	2.44	1.55	1.20	1.17	1.48
Tang Book Value Per Share	6.33	4.85	5.19	5.29	5.07	5.04	4.50	4.37
Dividends Per Share	0.080	0.080	0.080	0.060	0.040	0.030	0.030	0.030
Dividend Payout %	...	...	32.00	9.09	12.90	10.34	12.24	8.45
Income Statement								
Total Revenue	281,941	1,357,150	2,173,011	1,746,278	1,204,546	979,864	844,035	879,276
EBITDA	(54,398)	529,888	740,620	1,205,225	762,803	654,372	596,903	503,539
Depn & Amortn	1,191	626,665	637,514	654,745	456,670	347,522	330,464	221,270
Income Before Taxes	(79,964)	(193,688)	29,321	485,538	237,840	235,187	198,498	223,290
Income Taxes	(28,770)	(73,382)	(72,067)	205,765	106,110	112,779	95,112	74,947
Net Income	(51,194)	(113,891)	104,468	279,773	131,730	122,408	103,386	148,343
Average Shares	431,841	413,696	417,601	422,375	421,986	421,522	420,780	418,730
Balance Sheet								
Current Assets	720,687	144,786	413,447	378,899	270,310	345,800	203,008	281,502
Total Assets	5,702,708	5,261,899	5,437,716	4,981,080	4,616,313	4,331,493	4,005,031	3,683,401
Current Liabilities	199,382	235,552	499,018	407,905	444,139	343,344	303,835	308,741
Long-Term Obligations	1,583,192	2,005,000	1,752,000	1,147,000	1,012,000	950,000	975,000	805,000
Total Liabilities	2,758,648	3,252,711	3,294,983	2,776,478	2,484,866	2,226,725	2,132,331	1,870,887
Stockholders' Equity	2,944,060	2,009,188	2,142,733	2,204,602	2,131,447	2,104,768	1,872,700	1,812,514
Shares Outstanding	464,999	413,875	413,022	416,396	420,050	417,230	416,031	414,616
Statistical Record								
Return on Assets %	N.M.	N.M.	2.01	5.83	2.94	2.94	2.69	4.02
Return on Equity %	N.M.	N.M.	4.81	12.90	6.20	6.16	5.61	8.23
EBITDA Margin %	N.M.	39.04	34.08	69.02	63.33	66.78	70.72	57.27
Net Margin %	N.M.	N.M.	4.81	16.02	10.94	12.49	12.25	16.87
Asset Turnover	0.21	0.25	0.42	0.36	0.27	0.24	0.22	0.24
Current Ratio	3.61	0.61	0.83	0.93	0.61	1.01	0.67	0.91
Debt to Equity	0.54	1.00	0.82	0.52	0.47	0.45	0.52	0.44
Price Range	35.40-15.03	35.40-15.03	41.61-28.48	39.93-23.77	25.54-14.77	22.15-9.36	11.56-6.75	11.43-4.54
P/E Ratio	...	...	166.44-113.92	60.50-36.01	82.37-47.65	76.37-32.27	46.23-26.99	32.66-12.96
Average Yield %	0.32	0.34	0.23	0.18	0.20	0.20	0.34	0.37

Address: Three Memorial City Plaza, 840 Gessner Road, Suite 1400, Houston, TX 77024	**Web Site:** www.cabotog.com	**Auditors:** PricewaterhouseCoopers LLP
	Officers: Dan O. Dinges - Chairman, President, Chief Executive Officer Scott C. Schroeder - Vice President, Chief Financial Officer	**Investor Contact:** 281-589-4993
Telephone: 281-589-4600		**Transfer Agents:** Wells Fargo Bank N.A., Mendota Heights, MN
Fax: 281-589-4653		

CALATLANTIC GROUP INC

Exchange	Symbol	Price	52Wk Range	Yield	P/E
NYS	CAA	$36.99 (5/31/2016)	46.50-27.88	0.43	15.67

*7 Year Price Score 107.11 *NYSE Composite Index=100 *12 Month Price Score 88.25

Interim Earnings (Per Share)

Qtr.	Mar	Jun	Sep	Dec
2013	0.25	0.55	0.75	0.80
2014	0.45	0.70	0.70	0.85
2015	0.40	0.70	0.59	0.55
2016	0.52	...	...	...

Interim Dividends (Per Share)

Amt	Decl	Ex	Rec	Pay
0.04Q	11/02/2015	12/11/2015	12/15/2015	12/30/2015
0.04Q	02/11/2016	03/11/2016	03/15/2016	03/30/2016
0.04Q	05/03/2016	06/13/2016	06/15/2016	06/30/2016

Indicated Div: $0.16

Valuation Analysis

		Institutional Holding	
Forecast EPS	$3.56	No of Institutions	426
	(05/20/2016)		
Market Cap	$4.4 Billion	Shares	137,050,208
Book Value	$3.9 Billion		
Price/Book	1.11	% Held	N/A
Price/Sales	1.03		

Business Summary: Builders (MIC: 2.2.5 SIC: 1531 NAIC: 236117)

CalAtlantic Group is a builder of single-family attached and detached homes. Co. also provides mortgage, title and escrow services. Co. operates two principal businesses: homebuilding, which acquires and develops land and constructs and sells single-family attached and detached homes, and is divided into four reportable segments: North, Southeast, Southwest and West; and financial services, which consists of mortgage financing operations and title services operations. Mortgage financing operations provides mortgage financing to Co.'s homebuyers in substantially all of the markets in which Co. operates, while title services operations provides title examinations for its homebuyers.

Recent Developments: For the quarter ended Mar 31 2016, net income increased 129.9% to US$72.7 million from US$31.6 million in the year-earlier quarter. Revenues were US$1.20 billion, up 153.0% from US$475.7 million the year before. Direct operating expenses rose 163.4% to US$949.1 million from US$360.4 million in the comparable period the year before. Indirect operating expenses increased 106.9% to US$136.7 million from US$66.1 million in the equivalent prior-year period.

Prospects: Our evaluation of CalAtlantic Group Inc. as of June 19, 2016 is the result of our systematic analysis on three basic characteristics: earnings strength, relative valuation, and recent stock price movement. The company has managed to produce a neutral trend in earnings per share over the past 5 quarters. However, while recent estimates for the company have been lowered by analysts, CAA has posted better than expected results. Based on operating earnings yield, the company is undervalued when compared to all of the companies in our coverage universe. Share price changes over the past year indicates that CAA will perform poorly over the near term.

Financial Data

(US$ in Thousands)	3 Mos	12/31/2015	12/31/2014	12/31/2013	12/31/2012	12/31/2011	12/31/2010	12/31/2009
Earnings Per Share	2.36	2.26	2.70	2.35	7.20	(0.25)	(0.25)	(0.30)
Cash Flow Per Share	(1.70)	(3.78)	(6.50)	(3.05)	(6.99)	(8.32)	(3.85)	21.95
Tang Book Value Per Share	25.04	24.14	30.47	26.46	29.45	15.71	15.81	20.69
Dividends Per Share	0.080	0.040	...	...	...	...	...	...
Dividend Payout %	3.39	1.77	...	...	...	...	...	...
Income Statement								
Total Revenue	1,203,235	3,540,113	2,435,297	1,939,519	1,258,258	893,900	924,874	1,179,542
EBITDA	117,801	397,298	364,029	269,340	96,304	22,982	41,577	(41,046)
Depn & Amortn	3,786	56,775	13,397	12,591	9,631	14,494	14,850	16,380
Income Before Taxes	114,015	340,523	350,632	256,749	80,277	(16,680)	(13,447)	(104,884)
Income Taxes	42,543	128,980	134,099	68,983	(453,234)	(56)	(557)	(96,265)
Net Income	72,661	213,509	215,865	188,715	531,421	(16,417)	(11,724)	(13,786)
Average Shares	138,430	81,512	63,257	58,234	44,103	38,781	21,040	19,124
Balance Sheet								
Current Assets	6,637,513	6,398,703	3,611,272	3,034,920	2,429,312	1,991,793	1,969,342	1,624,592
Total Assets	8,431,737	8,345,505	4,174,420	3,662,105	3,113,074	2,200,383	2,133,123	1,861,011
Current Liabilities	924,013	670,474	268,968	250,037	220,590	203,719	159,843	218,837
Long-Term Obligations	3,565,755	3,791,121	2,225,495	1,940,462	1,634,177	1,371,756	1,350,598	1,197,721
Total Liabilities	4,489,768	4,484,069	2,497,732	2,193,145	1,857,258	1,576,629	1,511,261	1,425,213
Stockholders' Equity	3,941,969	3,861,436	1,676,688	1,468,960	1,255,816	623,754	621,862	435,798
Shares Outstanding	118,731	121,286	55,028	55,523	42,649	39,712	39,328	21,058
Statistical Record								
Return on Assets %	4.03	3.41	5.51	5.57	19.95	N.M.	N.M.	N.M.
Return on Equity %	9.04	7.71	13.72	13.85	56.39	N.M.	N.M.	N.M.
EBITDA Margin %	9.79	11.22	14.95	13.89	7.65	2.57	4.50	N.M.
Net Margin %	6.04	6.03	8.86	9.73	42.23	N.M.	N.M.	N.M.
Asset Turnover	0.68	0.57	0.62	0.57	0.47	0.41	0.46	0.57
Current Ratio	7.18	9.54	13.43	12.14	11.01	9.78	12.32	7.42
Debt to Equity	0.90	0.98	1.33	1.32	1.30	2.20	2.17	2.75
Price Range	46.50-27.88	46.50-33.45	45.75-34.40	49.05-35.45	38.95-15.65	24.75-10.80	34.40-15.15	22.15-3.35
P/E Ratio	19.70-11.81	20.58-14.80	16.94-12.74	20.87-15.09	5.41-2.17	...	...	...
Average Yield %	0.20	0.10	...	...	...	...	...	...

Address: 15360 Barranca Parkway, Irvine, CA 92618 **Telephone:** 949-789-1600	**Web Site:** www.calatlantichomes.com **Officers:** Scott D. Stowell - Executive Chairman, President, Chief Executive Officer, Chief Operating Officer Larry T. Nicholson - President, Chief Executive Officer	**Auditors:** Ernst & Young LLP **Transfer Agents:** Computershare Shareowner Services LLC, Pittsburgh, PA

CALIFORNIA WATER SERVICE GROUP (DE)

Exchange	Symbol	Price	52Wk Range	Yield	P/E	Div Achiever
NYS	CWT	$29.15 (5/31/2016)	29.15-19.68	2.37	32.75	48 Years

*7 Year Price Score 99.47   *NYSE Composite Index=100   *12 Month Price Score 114.86

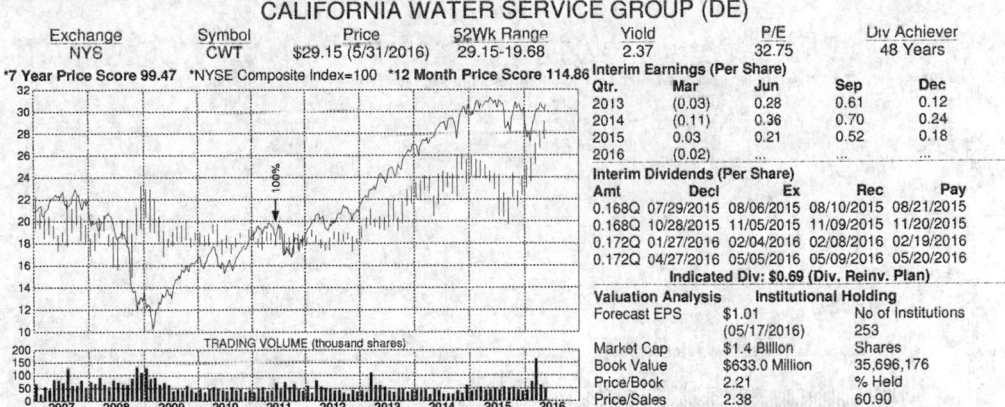

Interim Earnings (Per Share)

Qtr.	Mar	Jun	Sep	Dec
2013	(0.03)	0.28	0.61	0.12
2014	(0.11)	0.36	0.70	0.24
2015	0.03	0.21	0.52	0.18
2016	(0.02)	...	...	...

Interim Dividends (Per Share)

Amt	Decl	Ex	Rec	Pay
0.168Q	07/29/2015	08/06/2015	08/10/2015	08/21/2015
0.168Q	10/28/2015	11/05/2015	11/09/2015	11/20/2015
0.172Q	01/27/2016	02/04/2016	02/08/2016	02/19/2016
0.172Q	04/27/2016	05/05/2016	05/09/2016	05/20/2016

Indicated Div: $0.69 (Div. Reinv. Plan)

Valuation Analysis   Institutional Holding

Forecast EPS	$1.01	No of Institutions	
	(05/17/2016)	253	
Market Cap	$1.4 Billion	Shares	
Book Value	$633.0 Million	35,696,176	
Price/Book	2.21	% Held	
Price/Sales	2.38	60.90	

Business Summary: Water Utilities (MIC: 3.2.1 SIC: 4941 NAIC: 221310)

California Water Service Group is a holding company. Through its subsidiaries, Co. is engaged in the production, purchase, storage, treatment, testing, distribution and sale of water for domestic, industrial, public and irrigation uses, and for fire protection. Co. also provides non-regulated water-related services that include water system operation, billing and meter reading services. As of Dec 31 2014, Co. provided its services to approximately 477,900 customers in 83 California communities; 4,300 customers on the islands of Maui and Hawaii; 16,000 customers in Tacoma and Olympia, WA; and approximately 7,600 customers in the Belen, Los Lunas and Elephant Butte areas in New Mexico.

Recent Developments: For the quarter ended Mar 31 2016, net loss amounted to US$798,000 versus net income of US$1.6 million in the year-earlier quarter. Revenues were US$121.7 million, down 0.2% from US$122.0 million the year before. Operating income was US$6.3 million versus US$7.5 million in the prior-year quarter, a decrease of 16.4%. Direct operating expenses rose 1.4% to US$66.4 million from US$65.5 million in the comparable period the year before. Indirect operating expenses were unchanged at US$49.0 million versus the equivalent prior-year period.

Prospects: Our evaluation of California Water Service Group as of June 19, 2016 is the result of our systematic analysis on three basic characteristics: earnings strength, relative valuation, and recent stock price movement. The company has enjoyed a very positive trend in earnings per share over the past 5 quarters and while recent estimates for the company have remained steady, CWT has posted results that fell short of analysts expectations. Based on operating earnings yield, the company is about fairly valued when compared to all of the companies in our coverage universe. Share price changes over the past year indicates that CWT will perform poorly over the near term.

Financial Data

(US$ in Thousands)	3 Mos	12/31/2015	12/31/2014	12/31/2013	12/31/2012	12/31/2011	12/31/2010	12/31/2009
Earnings Per Share	0.89	0.94	1.19	1.02	1.17	0.90	0.91	0.97
Cash Flow Per Share	3.11	3.02	2.68	2.68	3.14	2.66	1.81	1.75
Tang Book Value Per Share	13.14	13.36	13.05	12.49	11.24	10.69	10.39	10.07
Dividends Per Share	0.675	0.670	0.650	0.640	0.630	0.615	0.595	0.590
Dividend Payout %	75.84	71.28	54.62	62.75	53.85	68.33	65.75	60.51
Income Statement								
Total Revenue	121,727	588,368	597,499	584,103	559,966	501,814	460,399	449,372
EBITDA	22,066	160,783	174,346	156,421	154,252	143,439	133,314	129,186
Depn & Amortn	16,454	64,007	64,119	61,331	57,973	53,063	46,244	42,613
Income Before Taxes	(1,723)	69,545	83,465	66,301	68,184	60,737	60,725	65,366
Income Taxes	(925)	24,528	26,727	19,047	19,356	23,025	23,069	24,812
Net Income	(798)	45,017	56,738	47,254	48,828	37,712	37,656	40,554
Average Shares	47,905	47,880	47,829	46,417	41,892	41,772	41,638	41,532
Balance Sheet								
Current Assets	148,521	127,578	154,124	139,490	146,564	113,888	126,210	92,241
Total Assets	2,299,805	2,246,095	2,187,351	1,959,855	1,995,924	1,854,587	1,692,066	1,525,581
Current Liabilities	158,143	148,455	217,706	166,584	243,067	151,875	107,348	110,358
Long-Term Obligations	557,849	512,287	419,233	426,142	434,467	481,632	479,181	374,269
Total Liabilities	1,666,838	1,603,940	1,560,725	1,361,099	1,522,212	1,404,758	1,256,540	1,104,947
Stockholders' Equity	632,967	642,155	626,626	598,756	473,712	449,829	435,526	420,634
Shares Outstanding	47,974	47,875	47,806	47,740	41,908	41,817	41,666	41,530
Statistical Record								
Return on Assets %	1.89	2.03	2.74	2.39	2.53	2.13	2.34	2.76
Return on Equity %	6.80	7.10	9.26	8.81	10.55	8.52	8.80	9.85
EBITDA Margin %	18.13	27.33	29.18	26.78	27.55	28.58	28.96	28.75
Net Margin %	N.M.	7.65	9.50	8.09	8.72	7.52	8.18	9.02
Asset Turnover	0.26	0.27	0.29	0.30	0.29	0.28	0.29	0.31
Current Ratio	0.94	0.86	0.71	0.84	0.60	0.75	1.18	0.84
Debt to Equity	0.88	0.80	0.67	0.71	0.92	1.07	1.10	0.89
Price Range	27.08-19.68	25.96-19.68	26.09-20.44	23.23-18.35	19.21-17.22	19.21-16.89	19.77-16.98	23.22-16.77
P/E Ratio	30.43-22.11	27.62-20.94	21.92-17.18	22.77-17.99	16.42-14.72	21.34-18.77	21.73-18.66	23.93-17.29
Average Yield %	2.89	2.87	2.87	3.12	3.46	3.37	3.24	3.07

Address: 1720 North First Street, San Jose, CA 95112 **Telephone:** 408-367-8200	**Web Site:** www.calwatergroup.com **Officers:** Peter C. Nelson - Chairman, President, Chief Executive Officer Martin A. Kropelnicki - Vice President, Chief Financial Officer, Treasurer, Acting Principal Accounting Officer, President, Chief Operating Officer, Chief Executive Officer	**Auditors:** Deloitte & Touche LLP **Investor Contact:** 408-367-8200 **Transfer Agents:** American Stock Transfer & Trust Company, Brooklyn, NY

CALPINE CORP

Exchange	Symbol	Price	52Wk Range	Yield	P/E
NYS	CPN	$14.80 (5/31/2016)	20.13-11.80	N/A	123.33

*7 Year Price Score 77.78 *NYSE Composite Index=100 *12 Month Price Score 96.31

Interim Earnings (Per Share)

Qtr.	Mar	Jun	Sep	Dec
2013	(0.28)	(0.16)	0.70	(0.22)
2014	(0.04)	0.33	1.52	0.54
2015	(0.03)	0.05	0.76	(0.13)
2016	(0.56)	...	...	...

Interim Dividends (Per Share)

No Dividends Paid

Valuation Analysis   **Institutional Holding**

Forecast EPS	$0.57	No of Institutions
	(05/20/2016)	450
Market Cap	$5.3 Billion	Shares
Book Value	$2.9 Billion	333,933,504
Price/Book	1.82	% Held
Price/Sales	0.82	N/A

Business Summary: Electric Utilities (MIC: 3.1.1 SIC: 4911 NAIC: 221122)

Calpine is a power generation company engaged in the ownership and operation of natural gas-fired and geothermal power plants in North America. Co. sells wholesale power, steam, capacity, renewable energy credits and ancillary services to its customers, including utilities, independent electric system operators, industrial and agricultural companies, retail power providers, municipalities, power marketers and others. Co. purchases primarily natural gas and some fuel oil as fuel for its power plants and engages in related natural gas transportation and storage transactions. Co. also purchases electric transmission rights to deliver power to its customers.

Recent Developments: For the quarter ended Mar 31 2016, net loss amounted to US$194.0 million versus a net loss of US$7.0 million in the year-earlier quarter. Revenues were US$1.62 billion, down 1.9% from US$1.65 billion the year before. Operating income was US$3.0 million versus US$166.0 million in the prior-year quarter, a decrease of 98.2%. Direct operating expenses rose 8.7% to US$1.38 billion from US$1.27 billion in the comparable period the year before. Indirect operating expenses increased 10.0% to US$231.0 million from US$210.0 million in the equivalent prior-year period.

Prospects: Our evaluation of Calpine Corp. as of June 19, 2016 is the result of our systematic analysis on three basic characteristics: earnings strength, relative valuation, and recent stock price movement. The company has suffered a very negative trend in earnings per share over the past 5 quarters. However, while recent estimates for the company have been lowered by analysts, CPN has posted results that fell short of analysts expectations. Based on operating earnings yield, the company is undervalued when compared to all of the companies in our coverage universe. Share price changes over the past year indicates that CPN will perform in line with the market over the near term.

Financial Data
(US$ in Thousands)

	3 Mos	12/31/2015	12/31/2014	12/31/2013	12/31/2012	12/31/2011	12/31/2010	12/31/2009
Earnings Per Share	0.12	0.64	2.31	0.03	0.42	(0.39)	0.06	0.31
Cash Flow Per Share	2.56	2.38	2.11	1.25	1.39	1.60	1.91	1.57
Tang Book Value Per Share	8.12	8.72	8.84	8.19	8.74	8.93	10.45	9.87
Income Statement								
Total Revenue	1,615,000	6,472,000	8,030,000	6,301,000	5,478,000	6,800,000	6,545,000	6,564,000
EBITDA	223,000	1,368,000	2,188,000	1,334,000	1,472,000	1,079,000	1,100,000	1,392,000
Depn & Amortn	226,000	595,000	591,000	654,000	557,000	560,000	568,000	469,000
Income Before Taxes	(159,000)	149,000	958,000	(10,000)	190,000	(232,000)	(246,000)	110,000
Income Taxes	35,000	(76,000)	22,000	2,000	19,000	(22,000)	(68,000)	15,000
Net Income	(198,000)	235,000	946,000	14,000	199,000	(190,000)	31,000	149,000
Average Shares	353,501	364,886	409,360	444,773	471,743	485,381	487,294	486,319
Balance Sheet								
Current Assets	3,775,000	4,095,000	4,220,000	2,856,000	2,832,000	3,562,000	3,429,000	4,099,000
Total Assets	18,659,000	18,833,000	18,378,000	16,559,000	16,549,000	17,371,000	17,256,000	16,650,000
Current Liabilities	3,085,000	3,048,000	3,199,000	1,531,000	1,318,000	2,162,000	1,789,000	2,749,000
Long-Term Obligations	11,672,000	11,868,000	11,083,000	10,908,000	10,635,000	10,321,000	10,104,000	8,996,000
Total Liabilities	15,744,000	15,724,000	15,000,000	13,045,000	12,555,000	13,067,000	12,613,000	12,202,000
Stockholders' Equity	2,915,000	3,109,000	3,378,000	3,514,000	3,994,000	4,304,000	4,643,000	4,448,000
Shares Outstanding	359,027	356,662	381,921	429,038	457,048	481,743	444,435	442,998
Statistical Record								
Return on Assets %	0.25	1.26	5.42	0.08	1.17	N.M.	0.18	0.80
Return on Equity %	1.55	7.25	27.45	0.37	4.78	N.M.	0.68	3.38
EBITDA Margin %	13.81	21.14	27.25	21.17	26.87	15.87	16.81	21.21
Net Margin %	N.M.	3.63	11.78	0.22	3.63	N.M.	0.47	2.27
Asset Turnover	0.35	0.35	0.46	0.38	0.32	0.39	0.39	0.35
Current Ratio	1.22	1.34	1.32	1.87	2.15	1.65	1.92	1.49
Debt to Equity	4.00	3.82	3.28	3.10	2.66	2.40	2.18	2.02
Price Range	23.26-11.80	23.26-11.80	24.29-18.53	22.01-18.05	18.90-14.51	16.88-12.93	14.02-10.80	14.68-4.78
P/E Ratio	193.83-98.33	36.34-18.44	10.52-8.02	733.67-601.67	45.00-34.55	...	233.67-180.00	47.35-15.42

Address: 717 Texas Avenue, Suite 1000, Houston, TX 77002
Telephone: 713-830-2000

Web Site: www.calpine.com
Officers: Frank Cassidy - Chairman John B. (Thad) Hill - President, Chief Executive Officer, Executive Vice President, Chief Operating Officer, Chief Commercial Officer

Auditors: PricewaterhouseCoooers LLP
Investor Contact: 713-830-8775
Transfer Agents: Computershare, Inc., Providence, RI

CAMDEN PROPERTY TRUST

Exchange	Symbol	Price	52Wk Range	Yield	P/E
NYS	CPT	$85.21 (5/31/2016)	86.80-69.45	3.52	43.92

*7 Year Price Score 105.18 *NYSE Composite Index=100   *12 Month Price Score 106.63

TRADING VOLUME (thousand shares)

Interim Earnings (Per Share)

Qtr.	Mar	Jun	Sep	Dec
2013	0.72	0.81	0.80	1.44
2014	0.45	0.40	0.43	1.99
2015	1.27	0.40	0.41	0.67
2016	0.46	...	...	...

Interim Dividends (Per Share)

Amt	Decl	Ex	Rec	Pay
0.70Q	09/15/2015	09/28/2015	09/30/2015	10/16/2015
0.70Q	12/03/2015	12/15/2015	12/17/2015	01/15/2016
0.75Q	01/28/2016	03/29/2016	03/31/2016	04/18/2016
0.75Q	06/15/2016	06/28/2016	06/30/2016	07/18/2016

Indicated Div: $3.00

Valuation Analysis   **Institutional Holding**

Forecast EPS	$1.93	No of Institutions
	(05/20/2016)	473
Market Cap	$8.3 Billion	Shares
Book Value	$2.8 Billion	94,697,872
Price/Book	2.98	% Held
Price/Sales	9.22	86.52

Business Summary: REITs (MIC: 5.3.1 SIC: 6798 NAIC: 525930)

Camden Property Trust is a real estate investment trust. Co. is primarily engaged in the ownership, management, development, redevelopment, acquisition, and construction of multifamily apartment communities. Co.'s properties typically consist of mid-rise buildings or two and three story buildings in a landscaped setting and provide residents with a variety of amenities common to multifamily rental properties. As of Dec 31 2015, Co. owned interests in, operated, or were developing 180 multifamily properties comprised of 62,649 apartment homes across the U.S. Co. also owns land holdings which it may develop into multifamily communities in the future.

Recent Developments: For the quarter ended Mar 31 2016, income from continuing operations decreased 67.4% to US$37.9 million from US$116.2 million in the year-earlier quarter. Net income decreased 64.5% to US$42.9 million from US$121.1 million in the year-earlier quarter. Revenues were US$219.4 million, up 7.0% from US$205.0 million the year before. Revenues from property income rose 7.9% to US$217.6 million from US$201.6 million in the corresponding quarter a year earlier.

Prospects: Our evaluation of Camden Property Trust as of June 19, 2016 is the result of our systematic analysis on three basic characteristics: earnings strength, relative valuation, and recent stock price movement. The company has enjoyed a very positive trend in earnings per share over the past 5 quarters. Because the company lacks sufficient analyst estimate data, we place greater weight on the historical EPS trend as the measure of earnings strength. Based on operating earnings yield, the company is overvalued when compared to all of the companies in our coverage universe. Share price changes over the past year indicates that CPT will perform very well over the near term.

Financial Data

(US$ in Thousands)	3 Mos	12/31/2015	12/31/2014	12/31/2013	12/31/2012	12/31/2011	12/31/2010	12/31/2009
Earnings Per Share	1.94	2.76	3.27	3.78	3.30	0.66	0.33	(0.80)
Cash Flow Per Share	4.96	4.75	4.75	4.64	3.86	3.37	3.27	3.49
Tang Book Value Per Share	28.61	28.87	28.85	27.85	26.64	21.97	21.66	21.15
Dividends Per Share	2.850	2.800	2.640	2.520	2.240	1.960	1.800	2.050
Dividend Payout %	146.91	101.45	80.73	66.67	67.88	296.97	545.45	...
Income Statement								
Total Revenue	219,423	900,260	858,589	810,048	744,315	677,263	638,741	649,369
EBITDA	122,339	608,360	628,446	453,904	468,132	329,751	324,927	242,477
Depn & Amortn	62,091	257,082	238,989	223,198	213,480	187,668	178,567	176,340
Income Before Taxes	36,682	253,966	296,194	132,577	150,370	29,669	20,467	(62,159)
Income Taxes	315	1,872	1,903	1,826	1,208	2,220	1,581	967
Net Income	42,940	258,262	301,314	346,291	293,900	59,961	31,142	(44,203)
Average Shares	90,509	89,490	88,468	88,494	85,556	73,701	68,957	62,359
Balance Sheet								
Current Assets	36,324	41,688	185,793	52,117	66,285	91,270	211,177	149,773
Total Assets	6,040,455	6,037,612	6,056,907	5,632,141	5,385,172	4,622,075	4,699,737	4,607,999
Current Liabilities	235,510	242,851	256,767	205,742	180,317	154,994	139,189	130,686
Long-Term Obligations	2,765,817	2,724,687	2,743,539	2,530,766	2,510,468	2,432,112	2,563,754	2,625,199
Total Liabilities	3,252,296	3,221,055	3,241,305	2,940,605	2,822,073	2,765,433	2,915,393	2,979,663
Stockholders' Equity	2,788,159	2,816,557	2,815,602	2,691,536	2,563,099	1,856,642	1,784,344	1,628,336
Shares Outstanding	97,455	97,571	97,604	96,660	96,201	84,517	82,386	76,996
Statistical Record								
Return on Assets %	2.97	4.27	5.16	6.29	5.86	1.29	0.67	N.M.
Return on Equity %	6.38	9.17	10.94	13.18	13.26	3.29	1.83	N.M.
EBITDA Margin %	55.75	67.58	73.20	56.03	62.89	48.69	50.87	37.34
Net Margin %	19.57	28.69	35.09	42.75	39.49	8.85	4.88	N.M.
Asset Turnover	0.15	0.15	0.15	0.15	0.15	0.15	0.14	0.14
Current Ratio	0.15	0.17	0.72	0.25	0.37	0.59	1.52	1.15
Debt to Equity	0.99	0.97	0.97	0.94	0.98	1.31	1.44	1.61
Price Range	84.09-69.45	81.28-69.45	77.87-56.88	75.46-56.79	71.59-59.61	69.32-53.09	54.13-36.77	44.01-17.56
P/E Ratio	43.35-35.80	29.45-25.16	23.81-17.39	19.96-15.02	21.69-18.06	105.03-80.44	164.03-111.42	...
Average Yield %	3.75	3.68	3.77	3.76	3.39	3.27	3.93	6.59

Address: 11 Greenway Plaza, Suite 2400, Houston, TX 77046
Telephone: 713-354-2500

Web Site: www.camdenliving.com
Officers: Richard J. Campo - Chairman, Chief Executive Officer D. Keith Oden - President

Auditors: Deloitte & Touche LLP
Investor Contact: 713-354-2549
Transfer Agents: American Stock Transfer and Trust Company, New York, NY

CAMPBELL SOUP CO.

Exchange	Symbol	Price	52Wk Range	Yield	P/E
NYS	CPB	$60.57 (5/31/2016)	66.50-46.15	2.06	26.45

*7 Year Price Score 115.09 *NYSE Composite Index=100 *12 Month Price Score 115.03

Interim Earnings (Per Share)

Qtr.	Oct	Jan	Apr	Jul
2012-13	0.78	0.60	0.57	(0.50)
2013-14	0.54	1.03	0.58	0.43
2014-15	0.74	0.66	0.58	0.23
2015-16	0.62	0.85	0.59	...

Interim Dividends (Per Share)

Amt	Decl	Ex	Rec	Pay
0.312Q	06/25/2015	07/09/2015	07/13/2015	08/03/2015
0.312Q	09/28/2015	10/09/2015	10/14/2015	11/02/2015
0.312Q	11/19/2015	01/07/2016	01/11/2016	02/01/2016
0.312Q	03/23/2016	04/07/2016	04/11/2016	05/02/2016

Indicated Div: $1.25

Valuation Analysis / Institutional Holding

Valuation Analysis		Institutional Holding	
Forecast EPS	$2.97 (05/20/2016)	No of Institutions	835
Market Cap	$18.7 Billion	Shares	168,573,648
Book Value	$1.7 Billion	% Held	40.31
Price/Book	11.17		
Price/Sales	2.35		

Business Summary: Food (MIC: 1.2.1 SIC: 2032 NAIC: 311422)

Campbell Soup is a manufacturer and marketer of convenience food products. Co. operates in five segments: U.S. Simple Meals, which includes Prego pasta sauces, Pace Mexican sauces, and Swanson canned poultry; Global Baking and Snacking, which includes Pepperidge Farm cookies, crackers, bakery and frozen products; International Simple Meals and Beverages, which aggregates the retail business in Canada and the simple meals and beverages business in Asia Pacific, Latin America and China; U.S. Beverages, which consist of the U.S. retail beverages business, including V8 juices and beverages; and Bolthouse and Foodservice, which includes the Bolthouse Farms carrot products operating segment.

Recent Developments: For the quarter ended May 1 2016, net income increased 3.4% to US$185.0 million from US$179.0 million in the year-earlier quarter. Revenues were US$1.87 billion, down 1.6% from US$1.90 billion the year before. Operating income was US$268.0 million versus US$285.0 million in the prior-year quarter, a decrease of 6.0%. Direct operating expenses declined 0.7% to US$1.21 billion from US$1.22 billion in the comparable period the year before. Indirect operating expenses decreased 1.3% to US$392.0 million from US$397.0 million in the equivalent prior-year period.

Prospects: Our evaluation of Campbell Soup Co. as of June 19, 2016 is the result of our systematic analysis on three basic characteristics: earnings strength, relative valuation, and recent stock price movement. The company has generated a negative trend in earnings per share over the past 5 quarters and while recent estimates for the company have been raised by analysts, CPB has posted better than expected results. Based on operating earnings yield, the company is about fairly valued when compared to all of the companies in our coverage universe. Share price changes over the past year indicates that CPB will perform very well over the near term.

Financial Data
(US$ in Thousands)

	9 Mos	6 Mos	3 Mos	08/02/2015	08/03/2014	07/28/2013	07/29/2012	07/31/2011
Earnings Per Share	2.29	2.28	2.09	2.21	2.59	1.44	2.41	2.42
Cash Flow Per Share	4.51	4.27	3.91	3.80	2.82	3.25	3.54	3.51
Dividends Per Share	1.248	1.248	1.248	1.248	1.248	1.160	1.160	1.145
Dividend Payout %	54.50	54.74	59.71	56.47	48.19	80.56	48.13	47.31
Income Statement								
Total Revenue	6,274,000	4,404,000	2,203,000	8,082,000	8,268,000	8,052,000	7,707,000	7,719,000
EBITDA	1,225,000	881,000	389,000	1,381,000	1,479,000	1,473,000	1,470,000	1,544,000
Depn & Amortn	228,000	152,000	74,000	286,000	287,000	393,000	258,000	265,000
Income Before Taxes	914,000	674,000	287,000	990,000	1,073,000	955,000	1,106,000	1,168,000
Income Taxes	270,000	215,000	93,000	299,000	347,000	275,000	342,000	366,000
Net Income	644,000	459,000	194,000	691,000	818,000	458,000	774,000	805,000
Average Shares	311,000	312,000	312,000	313,000	316,000	317,000	319,000	329,000
Balance Sheet								
Current Assets	2,042,000	2,132,000	2,337,000	2,092,000	2,100,000	2,221,000	1,771,000	1,963,000
Total Assets	8,081,000	8,079,000	8,304,000	8,089,000	8,113,000	8,323,000	6,530,000	6,862,000
Current Liabilities	2,377,000	2,566,000	2,904,000	2,806,000	2,989,000	3,282,000	2,070,000	1,989,000
Long-Term Obligations	2,552,000	2,551,000	2,551,000	2,552,000	2,244,000	2,544,000	2,004,000	2,427,000
Total Liabilities	6,405,000	6,553,000	6,890,000	6,709,000	6,498,000	7,106,000	5,632,000	5,774,000
Stockholders' Equity	1,676,000	1,526,000	1,414,000	1,380,000	1,615,000	1,217,000	898,000	1,088,000
Shares Outstanding	309,000	309,000	310,000	310,000	313,000	312,000	312,000	320,000
Statistical Record								
Return on Assets %	8.99	8.87	7.84	8.55	9.79	6.18	11.59	12.29
Return on Equity %	43.51	46.46	42.94	46.27	56.83	43.43	78.16	80.16
EBITDA Margin %	19.53	20.00	17.66	17.09	17.89	18.29	19.07	20.00
Net Margin %	10.26	10.42	8.81	8.55	9.89	5.69	10.04	10.43
Asset Turnover	1.01	1.00	0.97	1.00	0.99	1.09	1.15	1.18
Current Ratio	0.86	0.83	0.80	0.75	0.70	0.68	0.86	0.99
Debt to Equity	1.52	1.67	1.80	1.85	1.39	2.09	2.23	2.23
Price Range	65.47-45.20	56.41-44.70	51.67-42.72	49.31-41.60	47.89-38.60	48.14-32.47	34.44-29.77	37.47-32.77
P/E Ratio	28.59-19.74	24.74-19.61	24.72-20.44	22.31-18.82	18.49-14.90	33.43-22.55	14.29-12.35	15.48-13.54
Average Yield %	2.37	2.55	2.65	2.75	2.87	2.93	3.56	3.30

Address: 1 Campbell Place, Camden, NJ 08103-1799 Telephone: 856-342-4800 Fax: 856-342-3878	Web Site: www.campbellsoupcompany.com Officers: Denise M. Morrison - President, Chief Executive Officer Anthony P. DiSilvestro - Chief Financial Officer, Senior Vice President, Senior Vice President (frmr), Principal Accounting Officer	Auditors: PricewaterhouseCoopers LLP Investor Contact: 856-342-6081 Transfer Agents: Computershare Trust Company, N.A., Providence, RI

CAPITAL ONE FINANCIAL CORP

Exchange	Symbol	Price	52Wk Range	Yield	P/E
NYS	COF	$73.24 (5/31/2016)	91.71-58.66	2.18	10.60

*7 Year Price Score 108.51 *NYSE Composite Index=100 *12 Month Price Score 94.32

Interim Earnings (Per Share)

Qtr.	Mar	Jun	Sep	Dec
2013	1.79	1.87	1.86	1.45
2014	1.96	2.04	1.86	1.73
2015	2.00	1.50	1.98	1.59
2016	1.84	...	...	...

Interim Dividends (Per Share)

Amt	Decl	Ex	Rec	Pay
0.40Q	07/30/2015	08/06/2015	08/10/2015	08/20/2015
0.40Q	10/29/2015	11/05/2015	11/09/2015	11/19/2015
0.40Q	02/03/2016	02/11/2016	02/16/2016	02/26/2016
0.40Q	05/05/2016	05/12/2016	05/16/2016	05/26/2016

Indicated Div: $1.60

Valuation Analysis — **Institutional Holding**

Forecast EPS	$7.55
(05/20/2016)	No of Institutions 1120
Market Cap	$37.7 Billion — Shares
Book Value	$47.7 Billion — 497,403,264
Price/Book	0.79 — % Held
Price/Sales	1.47 — 84.82

Business Summary: Credit & Lending (MIC: 5.4.1 SIC: 6022 NAIC: 522110)

Capital One Financial is a financial services holding company. Through its subsidiaries, Co. provides a range of financial products and services to consumers, small businesses and commercial clients through branches, the internet and other distribution channels. Co.'s Capital One Bank (USA), National Association subsidiary provides credit and debit card products, other lending products and deposit products. Co.'s Capital One, National Association subsidiary provides a range of banking products and financial services to consumers, small businesses and commercial clients. As of Dec 31 2015, Co. had total assets of $334.05 billion and deposits of $217.72 billion.

Recent Developments: For the quarter ended Mar 31 2016, income from continuing operations decreased 10.2% to US$1.02 billion from US$1.13 billion in the year-earlier quarter. Net income decreased 12.1% to US$1.01 billion from US$1.15 billion in the year-earlier quarter. Net interest income increased 10.5% to US$5.06 billion from US$4.58 billion in the year-earlier quarter. Provision for loan losses was US$1.53 billion versus US$935.0 million in the prior-year quarter, an increase of 63.3%. Non-interest income rose 8.7% to US$1.16 billion from US$1.07 billion, while non-interest expense advanced 5.7% to US$3.22 billion.

Prospects: Our evaluation of Capital One Financial Corp. as of June 19, 2016 is the result of our systematic analysis on three basic characteristics: earnings strength, relative valuation, and recent stock price movement. The company has managed to produce a neutral trend in earnings per share over the past 5 quarters. However, while recent estimates for the company have been lowered by analysts, COF has posted results that fell short of analysts expectations. Based on operating earnings yield, the company is undervalued when compared to all of the companies in our coverage universe. Share price changes over the past year indicates that COF will perform well over the near term.

Financial Data

(US$ in Thousands)	3 Mos	12/31/2015	12/31/2014	12/31/2013	12/31/2012	12/31/2011	12/31/2010	12/31/2009
Earnings Per Share	6.91	7.07	7.59	6.96	6.16	6.80	6.01	0.74
Cash Flow Per Share	23.37	18.69	16.52	17.22	16.11	16.35	18.01	6.53
Tang Book Value Per Share	64.56	62.22	56.15	48.48	45.68	34.95	28.34	28.55
Dividends Per Share	1.600	1.500	1.200	0.950	0.200	0.200	0.200	0.525
Dividend Payout %	23.15	21.22	15.81	13.65	3.25	2.94	3.33	70.95
Income Statement								
Interest Income	5,517,000	20,459,000	19,397,000	19,898,000	18,964,000	14,987,000	15,353,000	10,664,585
Interest Expense	461,000	1,625,000	1,579,000	1,792,000	2,375,000	2,246,000	2,896,000	2,967,470
Net Interest Income	5,056,000	18,834,000	17,818,000	18,106,000	16,589,000	12,741,000	12,457,000	7,697,115
Provision for Losses	1,527,000	4,536,000	3,541,000	3,453,000	4,415,000	2,360,000	3,907,000	4,230,111
Non-Interest Income	1,164,000	4,579,000	4,472,000	4,278,000	4,807,000	3,538,000	3,714,000	5,286,152
Non-Interest Expense	3,223,000	12,996,000	12,180,000	12,514,000	11,946,000	9,332,000	7,934,000	7,417,054
Income Before Taxes	1,470,000	5,881,000	6,569,000	6,417,000	5,035,000	4,587,000	4,330,000	1,336,102
Income Taxes	452,000	1,869,000	2,146,000	2,025,000	1,301,000	1,334,000	1,280,000	349,485
Net Income	1,013,000	4,050,000	4,428,000	4,159,000	3,517,000	3,147,000	2,743,000	883,781
Average Shares	528,000	548,000	571,900	587,600	566,000	459,000	456,000	431,415
Balance Sheet								
Net Loans & Leases	223,448,000	225,625,000	204,559,000	193,102,000	200,934,000	131,843,000	120,547,000	86,759,911
Total Assets	330,346,000	334,048,000	308,854,000	297,048,000	312,918,000	206,019,000	197,503,000	169,646,363
Total Deposits	221,779,000	217,721,000	205,548,000	204,523,000	212,485,000	128,226,000	122,210,000	115,809,096
Total Liabilities	282,639,000	286,764,000	263,801,000	255,304,000	272,419,000	176,353,000	170,962,000	143,056,953
Stockholders' Equity	47,707,000	47,284,000	45,053,000	41,744,000	40,499,000	29,666,000	26,541,000	26,589,410
Shares Outstanding	514,479	527,259	553,391	572,675	582,207	459,947	457,013	455,170
Statistical Record								
Return on Assets %	1.23	1.26	1.46	1.36	1.35	1.56	1.49	0.53
Return on Equity %	8.37	8.77	10.20	10.11	10.00	11.20	10.33	3.32
Net Interest Margin %	91.64	92.06	91.86	90.99	87.48	85.01	81.14	72.17
Efficiency Ratio %	48.24	51.91	51.03	51.76	50.25	50.38	41.61	46.50
Loans to Deposits	1.01	1.04	1.00	0.94	0.95	1.03	0.99	0.75
Price Range	91.71-58.66	91.71-71.55	84.95-68.66	76.61-50.80	61.40-43.75	56.21-37.63	46.73-34.63	41.05-8.31
P/E Ratio	13.27-8.49	12.97-10.12	11.19-9.05	11.01-7.30	9.97-7.10	8.27-5.53	7.78-5.76	55.47-11.23
Average Yield %	2.08	1.88	1.53	1.50	0.37	0.42	0.50	1.94

Address: 1680 Capital One Drive, McLean, VA 22102
Telephone: 703-720-1000

Web Site: www.capitalone.com
Officers: Richard D. Fairbank - Chairman, President, Chief Executive Officer Stephen S. Crawford - Chief Financial Officer, Chief Financial Officer designate, Head

Auditors: Ernst & Young LLP
Investor Contact: 703-720-2455
Transfer Agents: ComputerShare Investor Services, Providence, RI

CARBO CERAMICS INC.

Exchange	Symbol	Price	52Wk Range	Yield	P/E
NYS	CRR	$12.33 (5/31/2016)	46.00-10.63	N/A	N/A

*7 Year Price Score 23.91 *NYSE Composite Index=100 *12 Month Price Score 60.82

Interim Earnings (Per Share)

Qtr.	Mar	Jun	Sep	Dec
2013	0.76	0.71	1.31	0.90
2014	0.80	1.00	0.60	0.02
2015	(1.24)	(0.74)	(0.60)	(2.17)
2016	(1.07)	...	...	...

Interim Dividends (Per Share)

Amt	Decl	Ex	Rec	Pay
0.33Q	01/20/2015	01/29/2015	02/02/2015	02/17/2015
0.10Q	03/17/2015	04/29/2015	05/01/2015	05/15/2015
0.10Q	07/21/2015	07/30/2015	08/03/2015	08/17/2015
0.10Q	09/22/2015	10/29/2015	11/02/2015	11/16/2015

Valuation Analysis / Institutional Holding

Forecast EPS	$-3.28 (05/20/2016)	No of Institutions	225
Market Cap	$289.5 Million	Shares	28,007,332
Book Value	$620.2 Million	% Held	98.55
Price/Book	0.47		
Price/Sales	1.21		

TRADING VOLUME (thousand shares)

Business Summary: Equipment & Services (MIC: 9.1.3 SIC: 3299 NAIC: 327999)

CARBO Ceramics is a supplier of ceramic proppant. Co. also sells resin-coated sand. Co. is a provider of fracture simulation software, and a provider of fracture design and consulting services, and a range of technologies for spill prevention, containment and countermeasures. Co. sells the majority of its products and services to operators of oil and natural gas wells and to oilfield service companies. Co.'s products and services are primarily used in the hydraulic fracturing of natural gas and oil wells. Co. primarily manufactures six ceramic proppants: KRYPTOSPHERE-H, CARBOHSP®, CARBOPROP®, CARBOLITE®, CARBOECONOPROP® and CARBOHYDROPROP®.

Recent Developments: For the quarter ended Mar 31 2016, net loss amounted to US$24.7 million versus a net loss of US$28.6 million in the year-earlier quarter. Revenues were US$33.1 million, down 55.1% from US$73.7 million the year before. Operating loss was US$36.1 million versus a loss of US$42.5 million in the prior-year quarter. Direct operating expenses declined 43.1% to US$56.7 million from US$99.7 million in the comparable period the year before. Indirect operating expenses decreased 24.8% to US$12.4 million from US$16.5 million in the equivalent prior-year period.

Prospects: Our evaluation of Carbo Ceramics Inc. as of June 19, 2016 is the result of our systematic analysis on three basic characteristics: earnings strength, relative valuation, and recent stock price movement. The company has enjoyed a very positive trend in earnings per share over the past 5 quarters. Because the company lacks sufficient analyst estimate data, we place greater weight on the historical EPS trend as the measure of earnings strength. Based on operating earnings yield, the company is overvalued when compared to all of the companies in our coverage universe. Share price changes over the past year indicates that CRR will perform very poorly over the near term.

Financial Data

(US$ in Thousands)	3 Mos	12/31/2015	12/31/2014	12/31/2013	12/31/2012	12/31/2011	12/31/2010	12/31/2009
Earnings Per Share	(4.58)	(4.76)	2.41	3.67	4.59	5.62	3.40	2.27
Cash Flow Per Share	0.40	3.07	4.61	5.99	6.79	4.84	4.00	0.95
Tang Book Value Per Share	26.27	27.44	33.08	32.77	30.35	26.75	22.02	19.22
Dividends Per Share	0.300	0.630	1.260	1.140	1.020	0.880	0.760	0.700
Dividend Payout %	...	...	52.28	31.06	22.22	15.66	22.35	30.84
Income Statement								
Total Revenue	33,102	279,574	648,325	667,398	645,536	625,705	473,082	341,872
EBITDA	(23,697)	(108,822)	143,134	171,896	203,419	233,268	146,899	104,248
Depn & Amortn	12,291	54,457	50,860	47,472	44,893	36,015	27,728	24,905
Income Before Taxes	(36,785)	(163,749)	92,871	125,201	158,590	197,450	119,349	79,794
Income Taxes	(12,101)	(54,205)	37,283	40,315	52,657	67,314	40,633	26,984
Net Income	(24,684)	(109,544)	55,588	84,886	105,933	130,136	78,716	52,810
Average Shares	23,062	22,999	22,946	22,957	22,969	23,012	22,977	23,111
Balance Sheet								
Current Assets	216,070	285,277	337,611	371,382	349,917	302,565	237,655	218,870
Total Assets	759,523	836,369	934,226	878,951	808,878	740,865	599,571	513,412
Current Liabilities	42,448	70,290	77,415	56,688	50,830	79,066	51,247	32,458
Long-Term Obligations	52,651	55,000	...	...	...	...	...	...
Total Liabilities	139,327	194,063	158,169	110,364	95,800	110,707	77,592	56,096
Stockholders' Equity	620,196	642,306	776,057	768,587	713,078	630,158	521,979	457,316
Shares Outstanding	23,476	23,280	23,092	23,080	23,092	23,106	23,108	23,077
Statistical Record								
Return on Assets %	N.M.	N.M.	6.13	10.06	13.63	19.42	14.15	9.94
Return on Equity %	N.M.	N.M.	7.20	11.46	15.73	22.59	16.08	11.74
EBITDA Margin %	N.M.	N.M.	22.08	25.76	31.51	37.28	31.05	30.49
Net Margin %	N.M.	N.M.	8.57	12.72	16.41	20.80	16.64	15.45
Asset Turnover	0.28	0.32	0.72	0.79	0.83	0.93	0.85	0.64
Current Ratio	5.09	4.06	4.36	6.55	6.88	3.83	4.64	6.74
Debt to Equity	0.08	0.09	...	...	...	...	...	...
Price Range	46.00-14.20	46.00-15.40	154.12-34.10	126.00-65.63	133.99-61.00	180.25-94.18	103.81-59.27	70.77-27.43
P/E Ratio	...	...	63.95-14.15	34.33-17.88	29.19-13.29	32.07-16.76	30.53-17.43	31.18-12.08
Average Yield %	1.14	2.05	1.21	1.27	1.23	0.65	0.99	1.63

Address: 575 North Dairy Ashford, Suite 300, Houston, TX 77079
Telephone: 281-921-6400

Web Site: www.carboceramics.com
Officers: William C. Morris - Chairman Gary A. Kolstad - President, Chief Executive Officer

Auditors: Ernst & Young
Investor Contact: 281-921-6400
Transfer Agents: Computershare, Canton, MA

CARDINAL HEALTH, INC.

Exchange	Symbol	Price	52Wk Range	Yield	P/E	Div Achiever
NYS	CAH	$78.95 (5/31/2016)	90.85-76.16	2.27	18.89	19 Years

*7 Year Price Score 132.19 *NYSE Composite Index=100   *12 Month Price Score 95.55

Interim Earnings (Per Share)

Qtr.	Sep	Dec	Mar	Jun
2012-13	0.79	0.88	1.00	(1.70)
2013-14	0.90	0.80	0.91	0.68
2014-15	0.78	0.86	1.09	0.88
2015-16	1.15	0.98	1.17	...

Interim Dividends (Per Share)

Amt	Decl	Ex	Rec	Pay
0.387Q	08/05/2015	09/29/2015	10/01/2015	10/15/2015
0.387Q	11/04/2015	12/30/2015	01/04/2016	01/15/2016
0.387Q	02/02/2016	03/30/2016	04/01/2016	04/15/2016
0.449Q	05/04/2016	06/29/2016	07/01/2016	07/15/2016

Indicated Div: $1.80

Valuation Analysis | **Institutional Holding**

Forecast EPS	$5.25	No of Institutions
	(05/20/2016)	1052
Market Cap	$25.7 Billion	Shares
Book Value	$6.7 Billion	311,892,096
Price/Book	3.83	% Held
Price/Sales	0.22	82.85

Business Summary: Pharmaceuticals (MIC: 4.1.1 SIC: 5122 NAIC: 424210)

Cardinal Health is a healthcare services and products company. Co.'s segments are: Pharmaceutical and Medical. The Pharmaceutical segment distributes branded and generic pharmaceutical, over-the-counter healthcare and consumer products; operates nuclear pharmacies and cyclotron facilities; and distributes specialty pharmaceutical products, provides services to pharmaceutical manufacturers, third-party payors and healthcare providers, and provides specialty pharmacies services. The Medical segment distributes a range of medical, surgical and laboratory products to hospitals, ambulatory surgery centers, clinical laboratories and other healthcare providers and to patients in the home.

Recent Developments: For the quarter ended Mar 31 2016, net income increased 5.8% to US$386.0 million from US$365.0 million in the year-earlier quarter. Revenues were US$30.66 billion, up 20.8% from US$25.38 billion the year before. Operating income was US$656.0 million versus US$591.0 million in the prior-year quarter, an increase of 11.0%. Direct operating expenses rose 21.1% to US$28.97 billion from US$23.92 billion in the comparable period the year before. Indirect operating expenses increased 19.0% to US$1.03 billion from US$868.0 million in the equivalent prior-year period.

Prospects: Our evaluation of Cardinal Health Inc. as of June 19, 2016 is the result of our systematic analysis on three basic characteristics: earnings strength, relative valuation, and recent stock price movement. The company has generated a negative trend in earnings per share over the past 5 quarters. However, while recent estimates for the company have been mixed, CAH has posted better than expected results. Based on operating earnings yield, the company is undervalued when compared to all of the companies in our coverage universe. Share price changes over the past year indicates that CAH will perform well over the near term.

Financial Data

(US$ in Thousands)	9 Mos	6 Mos	3 Mos	06/30/2015	06/30/2014	06/30/2013	06/30/2012	06/30/2011
Earnings Per Share	4.18	4.10	3.98	3.62	3.38	0.97	3.06	2.72
Cash Flow Per Share	9.75	8.93	7.40	7.65	7.40	5.06	3.40	4.00
Tang Book Value Per Share	N.M.	N.M.	N.M.	0.73	1.58	1.18	5.40	4.53
Dividends Per Share	1.548	1.504	1.459	1.415	1.250	1.090	0.882	0.800
Dividend Payout %	37.03	36.67	36.66	39.07	36.98	112.37	28.84	29.41
Income Statement								
Total Revenue	90,162,000	59,499,000	28,055,000	102,531,000	91,084,000	101,093,000	107,552,000	102,644,200
EBITDA	2,299,000	1,483,000	749,000	2,362,000	2,196,000	1,270,000	2,034,000	1,854,100
Depn & Amortn	465,000	306,000	137,000	254,000	265,000	259,000	241,000	243,000
Income Before Taxes	1,700,000	1,087,000	568,000	1,967,000	1,798,000	888,000	1,698,000	1,518,300
Income Taxes	604,000	377,000	184,000	755,000	635,000	553,000	628,000	552,100
Net Income	1,095,000	709,000	383,000	1,215,000	1,166,000	334,000	1,069,000	959,000
Average Shares	331,000	332,000	331,000	335,000	345,000	344,000	349,000	352,500
Balance Sheet								
Current Assets	22,291,000	21,829,000	21,218,000	21,752,000	17,939,000	17,770,000	17,510,000	16,315,900
Total Assets	34,055,000	33,507,000	31,222,000	30,142,000	26,033,000	25,819,000	24,260,000	22,845,900
Current Liabilities	19,385,000	18,879,000	17,782,000	17,243,000	15,115,000	14,590,000	14,174,000	13,369,500
Long-Term Obligations	5,195,000	5,171,000	5,231,000	5,211,000	3,171,000	3,686,000	2,418,000	2,175,300
Total Liabilities	27,342,000	26,796,000	24,717,000	23,886,000	19,632,000	19,844,000	18,016,000	16,997,300
Stockholders' Equity	6,713,000	6,711,000	6,505,000	6,256,000	6,401,000	5,975,000	6,244,000	5,848,600
Shares Outstanding	326,000	330,000	329,000	328,000	337,000	339,000	343,000	351,100
Statistical Record								
Return on Assets %	4.49	4.51	4.68	4.33	4.50	1.33	4.53	4.48
Return on Equity %	21.25	21.37	20.88	19.20	18.84	5.47	17.63	17.24
EBITDA Margin %	2.55	2.49	2.67	2.30	2.41	1.26	1.89	1.81
Net Margin %	1.21	1.19	1.37	1.19	1.28	0.33	0.99	0.93
Asset Turnover	3.80	3.70	3.74	3.65	3.51	4.04	4.55	4.79
Current Ratio	1.15	1.16	1.19	1.26	1.19	1.22	1.24	1.22
Debt to Equity	0.77	0.77	0.80	0.83	0.50	0.62	0.39	0.37
Price Range	91.50-76.16	91.50-76.72	91.50-72.13	91.50-68.56	73.54-47.02	48.76-37.75	46.83-37.99	45.54-29.96
P/E Ratio	21.89-18.22	22.32-18.71	22.99-18.12	25.28-18.94	21.76-13.91	50.27-38.92	15.30-12.42	16.74-11.01
Average Yield %	1.83	1.75	1.73	1.74	2.01	2.54	2.10	2.10

Address: 7000 Cardinal Place, Dublin, OH 43017
Telephone: 614-757-5000

Web Site: www.cardinalhealth.com
Officers: George S. Barrett - Chairman, Chief Executive Officer Jeffrey William Henderson - Executive Vice President, Chief Financial Officer, Division Officer

Auditors: Ernst & Young LLP
Investor Contact: 614-757-7115
Transfer Agents: Computershare Trust Company, N.A., Canton, MA

CARE CAPITAL PROPERTIES INC

Exchange	Symbol	Price	52Wk Range	Yield	P/E
NYS	CCP	$25.99 (5/31/2016)	35.61-24.19	8.77	N/A

*7 Year Price Score N/A ***NYSE Composite Index=100** ***12 Month Price Score N/A**

Interim Earnings (Per Share)

Qtr.	Mar	Jun	Sep	Dec
2014	0.49	0.55	0.40	0.45
2015	0.44	0.45	0.43	0.38
2016	0.36	...	...	...

Interim Dividends (Per Share)

Amt	Decl	Ex	Rec	Pay
0.57Q	09/02/2015	09/10/2015	09/14/2015	09/30/2015
0.57Q	12/11/2015	12/17/2015	12/21/2015	12/31/2015
0.57Q	03/10/2016	03/17/2016	03/21/2016	03/31/2016
0.57Q	05/10/2016	06/08/2016	06/10/2016	06/30/2016

Indicated Div: $2.28

Valuation Analysis

Forecast EPS	$1.54
	(05/20/2016)
Market Cap	$2.2 Billion
Book Value	$1.2 Billion
Price/Book	1.83
Price/Sales	6.53

Institutional Holding

No of Institutions	348
Shares	76,667,128
% Held	N/A

TRADING VOLUME (thousand shares)

Business Summary: REITs (MIC: 5.3.1 SIC: 6798 NAIC: 525930)

Care Capital Properties is a self-administered, self-managed real estate investment trust with a portfolio of skilled nursing facilities (SNFs) and other healthcare assets operated by private regional and local care providers. Co. leases its properties to unaffiliated tenants. In addition, Co. originates and manages a portfolio of secured and unsecured loans, made primarily to its SNF operators and other post-acute care providers. At Dec 31 2015, Co.'s portfolio consisted of 358 properties operated by 39 private regional and local care providers, spread across 36 states. Co. conducts all of its operations through its operating partnership, Care Capital Properties, LP and its subsidiaries.

Recent Developments: For the quarter ended Mar 31 2016, net income decreased 20.1% to US$29.8 million from US$37.3 million in the year-earlier quarter. Revenues were US$84.5 million, up 7.6% from US$78.6 million the year before. Revenues from property income rose 7.2% to US$84.2 million from US$78.6 million in the corresponding quarter a year earlier.

Prospects: Our evaluation of Care Capital Properties Inc. as of June 19, 2016 is the result of our systematic analysis on three basic characteristics: earnings strength, relative valuation, and recent stock price movement. The company has generated a negative trend in earnings per share over the past 5 quarters and while recent estimates for the company have remained steady, CCP has posted results that fell short of analysts expectations. Based on operating earnings yield, the company is undervalued when compared to all of the companies in our coverage universe. Share price changes over the past year indicates that CCP will perform very poorly over the near term.

Financial Data
(US$ in Thousands)

	3 Mos	12/31/2015	12/31/2014	12/31/2013	12/31/2012
Earnings Per Share	1.62	1.71	...	...	...
Cash Flow Per Share	...	3.20	...	...	...
Tang Book Value Per Share	12.51	12.76	...	...	...
Dividends Per Share	1.710	1.140	...	...	...
Dividend Payout %	105.56	66.67	...	...	...
Income Statement					
Total Revenue	84,543	327,941	295,364	291,632	290,537
EBITDA	30,593	147,040	146,657	163,547	163,541
Depn & Amortn	269	(8,968)	(11,184)	(10,978)	(9,227)
Income Before Taxes	30,324	143,661	157,841	174,525	172,768
Income Taxes	421	938	...	...	...
Net Income	29,766	143,166	157,595	174,290	172,421
Average Shares	83,620	83,607	...	...	...
Balance Sheet					
Current Assets	12,548	16,995	2,424	2,167	...
Total Assets	2,927,891	2,954,969	2,331,750	2,405,764	...
Current Liabilities	202,236	214,259	208,671	214,464	...
Long-Term Obligations	1,530,112	1,524,863	...	...	...
Total Liabilities	1,733,747	1,740,537	213,534	219,563	...
Stockholders' Equity	1,194,144	1,214,432	2,118,216	2,186,201	...
Shares Outstanding	83,943	83,803	...	...	...
Statistical Record					
Return on Assets %	4.64	5.42	6.65	...	...
Return on Equity %	6.96	8.59	7.32	...	...
EBITDA Margin %	36.19	44.84	49.65	56.08	56.29
Net Margin %	35.21	43.66	53.36	59.76	59.35
Asset Turnover	0.11	0.12	0.12	...	...
Current Ratio	0.06	0.08	0.01	0.01	...
Debt to Equity	1.28	1.26	...	...	...
Price Range	35.61-24.19	35.61-29.91	...	...	...
P/E Ratio	21.98-14.93	20.82-17.49	...	...	...
Average Yield %	5.63	3.56	...	...	...

Address: 191 N. Wacker Dr., Suite 1200, Chicago, IL 60606
Telephone: 312-881-4700

Web Site: www.carecapitalproperties.com
Officers: Raymond J. Lewis - Chief Executive Officer
Lori B. Wittman - Executive Vice President, Chief Financial Officer

Auditors: KPMG LLP
Transfer Agents: Wells Fargo Shareowner Services, St. Paul, MN

CARLISLE COMPANIES INC.

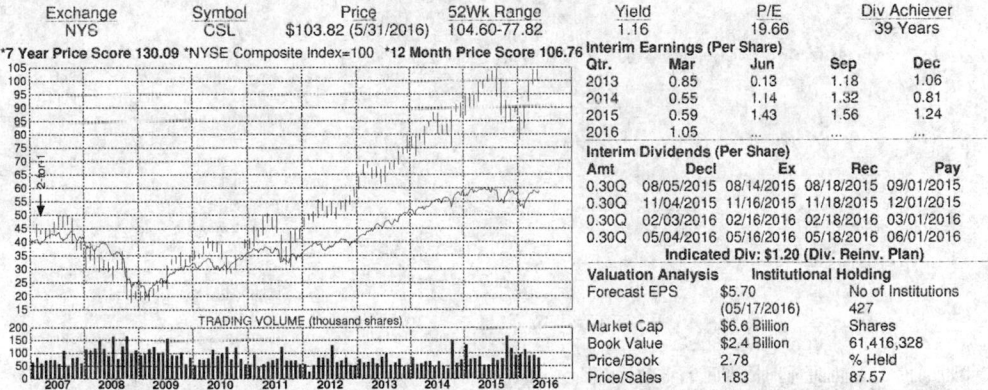

Exchange	Symbol	Price	52Wk Range	Yield	P/E	Div Achiever
NYS	CSL	$103.82 (5/31/2016)	104.60-77.82	1.16	19.66	39 Years

*7 Year Price Score 130.09 *NYSE Composite Index=100 *12 Month Price Score 106.76

Interim Earnings (Per Share)

Qtr.	Mar	Jun	Sep	Dec
2013	0.85	0.13	1.18	1.06
2014	0.55	1.14	1.32	0.81
2015	0.59	1.43	1.56	1.24
2016	1.05	...	...	...

Interim Dividends (Per Share)

Amt	Decl	Ex	Rec	Pay
0.30Q	08/05/2015	08/14/2015	08/18/2015	09/01/2015
0.30Q	11/04/2015	11/16/2015	11/18/2015	12/01/2015
0.30Q	02/03/2016	02/16/2016	02/18/2016	03/01/2016
0.30Q	05/04/2016	05/16/2016	05/18/2016	06/01/2016

Indicated Div: $1.20 (Div. Reinv. Plan)

Valuation Analysis

Valuation Analysis		Institutional Holding	
Forecast EPS	$5.70	No of Institutions	
	(05/17/2016)	427	
Market Cap	$6.6 Billion	Shares	
Book Value	$2.4 Billion	61,416,328	
Price/Book	2.78	% Held	
Price/Sales	1.83	87.57	

Business Summary: Rubber Products (MIC: 8.4.1 SIC: 3069 NAIC: 326299)

Carlisle Companies is a holding company. Through its subsidiaries, Co. is a manufacturing company consisting of five segments: Construction Materials, which provides rubber, thermoplastic polyolefin, and polyvinyl chloride membrane roofing systems; Interconnect Technologies, which provides wire, cable, connectors, contacts, and cable assemblies; Fluid Technologies, which designs, manufactures, and sells liquid finishing equipment; Brake and Friction, which provides braking systems and friction products; and FoodService Products, which manufactures, distributes, and sells commercial foodservice and janitorial products.

Recent Developments: For the quarter ended Mar 31 2016, income from continuing operations increased 73.4% to US$68.5 million from US$39.5 million in the year-earlier quarter. Net income increased 73.9% to US$68.5 million from US$39.4 million in the year-earlier quarter. Revenues were US$794.0 million, up 11.9% from US$709.3 million the year before. Direct operating expenses rose 2.3% to US$548.6 million in the comparable period the year before. Indirect operating expenses increased 26.7% to US$135.4 million from US$106.9 million in the equivalent prior-year period.

Prospects: Our evaluation of Carlisle Companies Inc. as of June 19, 2016 is the result of our systematic analysis on three basic characteristics: earnings strength, relative valuation, and recent stock price movement. The company has generated a negative trend in earnings per share over the past 5 quarters and while recent estimates for the company have been raised by analysts, CSL has posted better than expected results. Based on operating earnings yield, the company is undervalued when compared to all of the companies in our coverage universe. Share price changes over the past year indicates that CSL will perform well over the near term.

Financial Data

(US$ in Thousands)	3 Mos	12/31/2015	12/31/2014	12/31/2013	12/31/2012	12/31/2011	12/31/2010	12/31/2009
Earnings Per Share	5.28	4.82	3.82	3.22	4.22	2.86	2.34	2.34
Cash Flow Per Share	9.20	8.16	4.61	6.53	7.75	3.11	1.76	7.38
Tang Book Value Per Share	5.64	5.08	9.72	8.60	3.36	2.85	6.16	9.79
Dividends Per Share	1.150	1.100	0.940	0.840	0.760	0.700	0.660	0.630
Dividend Payout %	21.78	22.82	24.61	26.09	18.01	24.48	28.21	26.92
Income Statement								
Total Revenue	794,000	3,543,200	3,204,000	2,943,000	3,629,400	3,224,500	2,527,700	2,379,500
EBITDA	144,100	575,400	473,000	442,200	498,900	343,200	254,900	263,500
Depn & Amortn	33,500	73,500	64,700	75,400	74,600	68,100	58,800	56,600
Income Before Taxes	102,200	467,900	376,100	333,000	398,800	253,900	187,800	197,900
Income Taxes	33,700	148,300	124,400	97,800	131,500	72,000	57,200	46,100
Net Income	68,500	319,700	251,300	209,700	270,200	180,300	145,600	144,600
Average Shares	64,876	65,804	65,304	64,806	63,610	62,495	61,592	61,234
Balance Sheet								
Current Assets	1,382,700	1,319,500	1,611,500	1,535,000	1,205,300	1,214,100	1,016,900	799,800
Total Assets	4,025,800	3,954,100	3,758,700	3,493,000	3,457,300	3,137,900	2,529,500	1,914,100
Current Liabilities	628,800	605,900	392,200	376,400	470,600	613,500	456,400	301,100
Long-Term Obligations	595,800	598,700	749,800	751,000	752,500	604,300	405,100	156,100
Total Liabilities	1,638,300	1,606,700	1,553,700	1,506,900	1,669,200	1,637,800	1,188,800	695,500
Stockholders' Equity	2,387,500	2,347,400	2,205,000	1,986,100	1,788,100	1,500,100	1,340,700	1,218,600
Shares Outstanding	63,961	64,051	64,691	63,658	63,127	61,664	61,024	60,645
Statistical Record								
Return on Assets %	8.97	8.29	6.93	6.03	8.17	6.36	6.55	7.25
Return on Equity %	15.16	14.05	11.99	11.11	16.39	12.69	11.38	12.50
EBITDA Margin %	18.15	16.24	14.76	15.03	13.75	10.64	10.08	11.07
Net Margin %	8.63	9.02	7.84	7.13	7.44	5.59	5.76	6.08
Asset Turnover	0.93	0.92	0.88	0.85	1.10	1.14	1.14	1.19
Current Ratio	2.20	2.18	4.11	4.08	2.56	1.98	2.23	2.66
Debt to Equity	0.25	0.26	0.34	0.38	0.42	0.40	0.30	0.13
Price Range	104.60-77.82	104.60-84.11	91.54-71.67	79.62-58.76	59.36-45.56	50.55-30.52	41.63-28.05	36.28-18.11
P/E Ratio	19.81-14.74	21.70-17.45	23.96-18.76	24.73-18.25	14.07-10.80	17.67-10.67	17.79-11.99	15.50-7.74
Average Yield %	1.23	1.16	1.14	1.24	1.45	1.65	1.84	2.34

Address: 11605 North Community House Road, Suite 600, Charlotte, NC 28277	Web Site: www.carlisle.com	Auditors: Ernst & Young LLP
	Officers: David A. Roberts - Chairman, President, Chief Executive Officer D. Christian Koch - President, Chief Operating Officer, Region Officer, Chief Executive Officer	Investor Contact: 800-897-9071
Telephone: 704-501-1100		Transfer Agent: Computershare
Fax: 704-501-1190		Investor Services, LLC, Chicago, IL

CARMAX INC.

Exchange	Symbol	Price	52Wk Range	Yield	P/E
NYS	KMX	$53.66 (5/31/2016)	73.70-42.15	N/A	17.71

*7 Year Price Score 121.11 *NYSE Composite Index=100   *12 Month Price Score 92.02

Interim Earnings (Per Share)

Qtr.	May	Aug	Nov	Feb
2011-12	0.55	0.49	0.36	0.40
2012-13	0.52	0.48	0.41	0.46
2013-14	0.64	0.62	0.47	0.43
2014-15	0.76	0.70	0.60	0.67
2015-16	0.86	0.82	0.63	0.71

Interim Dividends (Per Share)
No Dividends Paid

Valuation Analysis / Institutional Holding

Valuation Analysis		Institutional Holding	
Forecast EPS	$3.31	No of Institutions	
	(05/20/2016)	587	
Market Cap	$10.4 Billion	Shares	
Book Value	$2.9 Billion	253,724,752	
Price/Book	3.60	% Held	
Price/Sales	0.69	96.58	

Business Summary: Retail - Automotive (MIC: 2.1.4 SIC: 5521 NAIC: 441120)

CarMax is a holding company. Through its subsidiaries, Co. is engaged as a retailer of used vehicles. Co. operates in two segments: CarMax Sales Operations, which sells used vehicles, purchases used vehicles from customers and other sources, sells related products and services, and arranges financing options for customers; and CarMax Auto Finance, which consists of finance operation that provides vehicle financing to customer buying vehicles from Co. Co.'s products and services include retail merchandising, wholesale auctions, extended protection plans, reconditioning and service, and customer credit. At Feb 29 2016, Co. operated 158 used car stores in 78 metropolitan markets.

Recent Developments: For the year ended Feb 29 2016, net income increased 4.4% to US$623.4 million from US$597.4 million in the prior year. Revenues were US$15.15 billion, up 6.2% from US$14.27 billion the year before. Direct operating expenses rose 6.1% to US$13.13 billion from US$12.38 billion in the comparable period the year before. Indirect operating expenses increased 9.9% to US$1.01 billion from US$918.2 million in the equivalent prior-year period.

Prospects: Our evaluation of Carmax Inc. as of June 19, 2016 is the result of our systematic analysis on three basic characteristics: earnings strength, relative valuation, and recent stock price movement. The company has managed to produce a neutral trend in earnings per share over the past 5 quarters. However, while recent estimates for the company have been lowered by analysts, KMX has posted better than expected results. Based on operating earnings yield, the company is undervalued when compared to all of the companies in our coverage universe. Share price changes over the past year indicates that KMX will perform poorly over the near term.

Financial Data
(US$ in Thousands)

	02/29/2016	02/28/2015	02/28/2014	02/28/2013	02/29/2012	02/28/2011	02/28/2010	02/28/2009
Earnings Per Share	3.03	2.73	2.16	1.87	1.79	1.67	1.26	0.27
Cash Flow Per Share	(0.73)	(4.49)	(2.74)	(3.41)	(0.27)	(0.08)	0.23	1.22
Tang Book Value Per Share	14.92	15.11	14.96	13.36	11.77	10.15	8.67	7.23
Income Statement								
Total Revenue	15,149,675	14,268,716	12,574,299	10,962,818	10,003,599	8,975,554	7,470,193	6,973,966
EBITDA	1,173,302	1,099,504	918,556	816,008	775,824	675,541	513,724	155,839
Depn & Amortn	127,000	105,700	90,400	82,300	75,200	59,421	58,328	54,741
Income Before Taxes	1,009,944	969,331	797,322	701,351	666,910	613,490	452,496	96,798
Income Taxes	386,516	371,973	304,736	267,067	253,115	232,612	170,828	37,585
Net Income	623,428	597,358	492,586	434,284	413,795	380,878	281,668	59,213
Average Shares	205,540	218,691	227,584	231,823	230,721	227,601	222,234	220,513
Balance Sheet								
Current Assets	2,471,781	2,599,038	2,643,224	2,310,131	1,853,448	1,410,098	1,556,412	1,287,752
Total Assets	14,481,576	13,198,201	11,707,157	9,888,602	8,331,543	6,839,909	2,556,191	2,379,187
Current Liabilities	1,005,193	997,173	875,497	684,173	646,313	508,217	477,351	490,770
Long-Term Obligations	10,342,323	8,818,750	7,340,431	6,009,627	4,863,318	3,909,492	27,371	178,062
Total Liabilities	11,576,790	10,041,416	8,390,160	6,869,435	5,658,431	4,548,279	622,609	786,120
Stockholders' Equity	2,904,786	3,156,785	3,316,997	3,019,167	2,673,112	2,291,630	1,933,582	1,593,067
Shares Outstanding	194,712	208,869	221,685	225,906	227,118	225,885	223,065	220,392
Statistical Record								
Return on Assets %	4.49	4.80	4.56	4.77	5.44	8.11	11.41	2.51
Return on Equity %	20.51	18.45	15.55	15.26	16.62	18.03	15.97	3.84
EBITDA Margin %	7.74	7.71	7.31	7.44	7.76	7.53	6.88	2.23
Net Margin %	4.12	4.19	3.92	3.96	4.14	4.24	3.77	0.85
Asset Turnover	1.09	1.15	1.16	1.20	1.32	1.91	3.03	2.96
Current Ratio	2.46	2.61	3.02	3.38	2.87	2.77	3.26	2.62
Debt to Equity	3.56	2.79	2.21	1.99	1.82	1.71	0.01	0.11
Price Range	74.73-42.15	68.30-42.88	53.05-38.38	40.10-25.22	35.38-23.41	36.83-18.67	24.50-8.68	21.73-6.23
P/E Ratio	24.66-13.91	25.02-15.71	24.56-17.77	21.44-13.49	19.77-13.08	22.05-11.18	19.44-6.89	80.48-23.07

Address: 12800 Tuckahoe Creek Parkway, Richmond, VA 23238
Telephone: 804-747-0422

Web Site: www.carmax.com
Officers: William R. Tiefel - Chairman William D. Nash - President, Executive Vice President, Senior Vice President, Vice President

Auditors: KPMG LLP
Investor Contact: 804-935-4591
Transfer Agents: American Stock Transfer & Trust Company, LLC, Brooklyn, NY

CARNIVAL CORP

Exchange	Symbol	Price	52Wk Range	Yield	P/E
NYS	CCL	$47.74 (5/31/2016)	55.14-41.92	2.93	20.06

*7 Year Price Score 111.10 *NYSE Composite Index=100 *12 Month Price Score 98.70

Interim Earnings (Per Share)

Qtr.	Feb	May	Aug	Nov
2012-13	0.05	0.05	1.20	0.09
2013-14	(0.02)	0.14	1.60	(0.13)
2014-15	0.06	0.29	1.56	0.35
2015-16	0.18	...	...	...

Interim Dividends (Per Share)

Amt	Decl	Ex	Rec	Pay
0.30Q	07/16/2015	08/19/2015	08/21/2015	09/11/2015
0.30Q	10/16/2015	11/18/2015	11/20/2015	12/11/2015
0.30Q	01/14/2016	02/17/2016	02/19/2016	03/11/2016
0.35Q	04/13/2016	05/25/2016	05/27/2016	06/17/2016

Indicated Div: $1.40

Valuation Analysis / Institutional Holding

Forecast EPS	$3.40	No of Institutions
	(05/20/2016)	894
Market Cap	$36.0 Billion	Shares
Book Value	$22.6 Billion	485,970,784
Price/Book	1.59	% Held
Price/Sales	2.28	57.93

Business Summary: Hotels, Restaurants & Travel (MIC: 2.2.1 SIC: 4489 NAIC: 483212)

Carnival is a leisure travel company. As of Nov 30 2015, Co. operated 99 cruise ships within a portfolio of cruise brands that sell cruise products and services. Co. has three cruise segments: North America cruise brands, which includes Carnival Cruise Lines, Princess Cruises, Holland America Line, and Seabourn; Europe, Australia & Asia cruise brands, which includes Costa Cruises, AIDA Cruises, P&O Cruises (U.K.), P&O Cruises (Australia), and Cunard; and Cruise Support, which includes certain of its port and related facilities. Co. also has a Tour and Other segment, which includes the hotel and transportation operations of Holland America Princess Alaska Tours.

Recent Developments: For the quarter ended Feb 29 2016, net income increased 189.8% to US$142.0 million from US$49.0 million in the year-earlier quarter. Revenues were US$3.65 billion, up 3.4% from US$3.53 billion the year before. Operating income was US$434.0 million versus US$266.0 million in the prior-year quarter, an increase of 63.2%. Direct operating expenses declined 3.9% to US$2.24 billion from US$2.34 billion in the comparable period the year before. Indirect operating expenses increased 4.7% to US$974.0 million from US$930.0 million in the equivalent prior-year period.

Prospects: Our evaluation of Carnival Corp. as of June 19, 2016 is the result of our systematic analysis on three basic characteristics: earnings strength, relative valuation, and recent stock price movement. The company has managed to produce a neutral trend in earnings per share over the past 5 quarters. However, while recent estimates for the company have been mixed, CCL has posted better than expected results. Based on operating earnings yield, the company is undervalued when compared to all of the companies in our coverage universe. Share price changes over the past year indicates that CCL will perform very well over the near term.

Financial Data

(US$ in Thousands)	3 Mos	11/30/2015	11/30/2014	11/30/2013	11/30/2012	11/30/2011	11/30/2010	11/30/2009
Earnings Per Share	2.38	2.26	1.59	1.39	1.67	2.42	2.47	2.24
Cash Flow Per Share	5.97	5.85	4.42	3.66	3.84	4.79	4.85	4.25
Tang Book Value Per Share	24.31	25.29	25.60	25.84	25.05	24.68	23.28	21.90
Dividends Per Share	1.150	1.100	1.000	1.500	1.000	1.000	0.400	...
Dividend Payout %	48.32	48.67	62.89	107.91	59.88	41.32	16.19	...
Income Statement								
Total Revenue	3,651,000	15,714,000	15,884,000	15,456,000	15,382,000	15,793,000	14,469,000	13,157,000
EBITDA	616,000	3,634,000	3,160,000	2,968,000	3,155,000	3,788,000	3,761,000	3,481,000
Depn & Amortn	423,000	1,626,000	1,635,000	1,588,000	1,527,000	1,522,000	1,416,000	1,309,000
Income Before Taxes	143,000	1,799,000	1,245,000	1,072,000	1,302,000	1,912,000	1,979,000	1,806,000
Income Taxes	1,000	42,000	9,000	(6,000)	4,000	...	1,000	16,000
Net Income	142,000	1,757,000	1,236,000	1,078,000	1,298,000	1,912,000	1,978,000	1,790,000
Average Shares	769,000	779,000	778,000	777,000	779,000	789,000	805,000	804,000
Balance Sheet								
Current Assets	1,860,000	2,451,000	1,503,000	1,937,000	1,821,000	1,312,000	1,244,000	1,518,000
Total Assets	38,446,000	39,237,000	39,532,000	40,104,000	39,161,000	38,637,000	37,490,000	36,835,000
Current Liabilities	6,664,000	6,956,000	6,921,000	6,720,000	7,340,000	6,105,000	5,755,000	4,967,000
Long-Term Obligations	7,990,000	7,413,000	7,363,000	8,092,000	7,168,000	8,053,000	8,011,000	9,097,000
Total Liabilities	15,821,000	15,466,000	15,244,000	15,548,000	15,232,000	14,805,000	14,459,000	14,800,000
Stockholders' Equity	22,625,000	23,771,000	24,288,000	24,556,000	23,929,000	23,832,000	23,031,000	22,035,000
Shares Outstanding	755,000	772,000	777,000	776,000	776,000	777,000	790,000	787,000
Statistical Record								
Return on Assets %	4.80	4.46	3.10	2.72	3.33	5.02	5.32	5.10
Return on Equity %	8.05	7.31	5.06	4.45	5.42	8.16	8.78	8.70
EBITDA Margin %	16.87	23.13	19.89	19.20	20.51	23.99	25.99	26.46
Net Margin %	3.89	11.18	7.78	6.97	8.44	12.11	13.67	13.60
Asset Turnover	0.41	0.40	0.40	0.39	0.39	0.41	0.39	0.37
Current Ratio	0.28	0.35	0.22	0.29	0.25	0.21	0.22	0.31
Debt to Equity	0.35	0.31	0.30	0.33	0.30	0.34	0.35	0.41
Price Range	55.14-41.92	54.08-42.39	44.16-33.88	39.32-31.60	39.16-29.48	47.85-29.42	44.70-30.14	33.95-16.98
P/E Ratio	23.17-17.61	23.93-18.76	27.77-21.31	28.29-22.73	23.45-17.65	19.77-12.16	18.10-12.20	15.16-7.58
Average Yield %	2.33	2.29	2.59	4.22	2.96	2.64	1.10	...

Address: 3655 N.W. 87th Avenue, Miami, FL 33178-2428 **Telephone:** 305-599-2600	**Web Site:** www.carnivalcorporation.com **Officers:** Micky Meir Arison - Chairman, Chief Executive Officer Arnold W. Donald - President, Chief Executive Officer	**Auditors:** PricewaterhouseCoopers LLP **Investor Contact:** 305-406-5539 **Transfer Agents:** ComputerShare Investor Services, Providence, RI

CARPENTER TECHNOLOGY CORP.

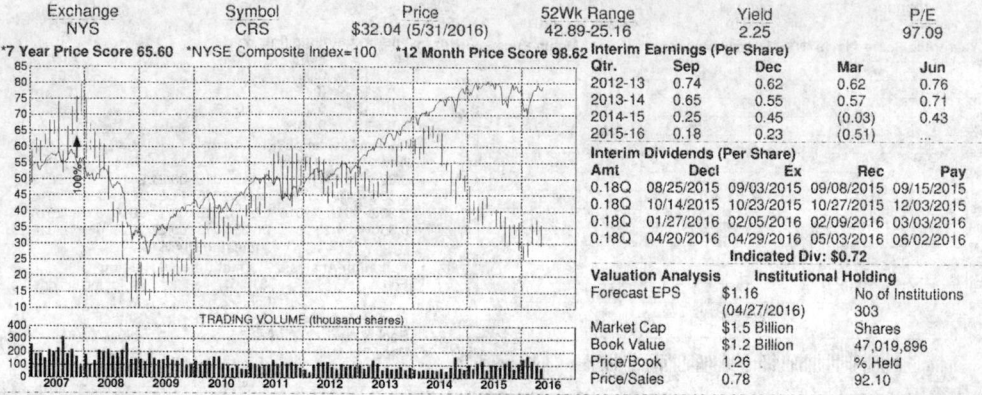

Exchange	Symbol	Price	52Wk Range	Yield	P/E
NYS	CRS	$32.04 (5/31/2016)	42.89-25.16	2.25	97.09

*7 Year Price Score 65.60   *NYSE Composite Index=100   *12 Month Price Score 98.62

Interim Earnings (Per Share)

Qtr.	Sep	Dec	Mar	Jun
2012-13	0.74	0.62	0.62	0.76
2013-14	0.65	0.55	0.57	0.71
2014-15	0.25	0.45	(0.03)	0.43
2015-16	0.18	0.23	(0.51)	

Interim Dividends (Per Share)

Amt	Decl	Ex	Rec	Pay
0.18Q	08/25/2015	09/03/2015	09/08/2015	09/15/2015
0.18Q	10/14/2015	10/23/2015	10/27/2015	12/03/2015
0.18Q	01/27/2016	02/05/2016	02/09/2016	03/03/2016
0.18Q	04/20/2016	04/29/2016	05/03/2016	06/02/2016

Indicated Div: $0.72

Valuation Analysis

		Institutional Holding	
Forecast EPS	$1.16 (04/27/2016)	No of Institutions	303
Market Cap	$1.5 Billion	Shares	
Book Value	$1.2 Billion		47,019,896
Price/Book	1.26	% Held	
Price/Sales	0.78		92.10

TRADING VOLUME (thousand shares)

Business Summary: Non-Precious Metals (MIC: 8.2.2 SIC: 3312 NAIC: 331111)

Carpenter Technology is engaged in the manufacturing, fabrication and distribution of metals. Co. provides material solutions for the aerospace and defense, energy, transportation, medical and industrial and consumer industries. Co.'s segments are Specialty Alloys Operations, which consists of alloy and stainless steel manufacturing operations; and Performance Engineered Products, which includes the Dynamet titanium business, the Carpenter Powder Products business, the Amega West Services business, the Specialty Steel Supply and the Latrobe and Mexico distribution business. Co.'s classes of products are: alloys, stainless steels, titanium products, powder metals, and alloy and tools steels.

Recent Developments: For the quarter ended Mar 31 2016, net loss amounted to US$23.9 million versus a net loss of US$1.4 million in the year-earlier quarter. Revenues were US$456.3 million, down 20.0% from US$570.6 million the year before. Operating loss was US$24.3 million versus an income of US$4.8 million in the prior-year quarter. Direct operating expenses declined 17.4% to US$408.8 million from US$494.8 million in the comparable period the year before. Indirect operating expenses increased 1.1% to US$71.8 million from US$71.0 million in the equivalent prior-year period.

Prospects: Our evaluation of Carpenter Technology Corp. as of June 19, 2016 is the result of our systematic analysis on three basic characteristics: earnings strength, relative valuation, and recent stock price movement. The company has generated a negative trend in earnings per share over the past 5 quarters and while recent estimates for the company have remained steady, CRS has posted results that fell short of analysts expectations. Based on operating earnings yield, the company is about fairly valued when compared to all of the companies in our coverage universe. Share price changes over the past year indicates that CRS will perform very poorly over the near term.

Financial Data

(US$ in Thousands)	9 Mos	6 Mos	3 Mos	06/30/2015	06/30/2014	06/30/2013	06/30/2012	06/30/2011
Earnings Per Share	0.33	0.81	1.03	1.11	2.47	2.73	2.53	1.59
Cash Flow Per Share	5.76	6.69	6.22	5.37	4.50	4.07	3.39	1.46
Tang Book Value Per Share	18.83	18.97	19.35	19.81	21.94	18.01	13.99	15.66
Dividends Per Share	0.720	0.720	0.720	0.720	0.720	0.720	0.720	0.720
Dividend Payout %	218.18	88.89	69.90	64.86	29.15	26.37	28.46	45.28
Income Statement								
Total Revenue	1,355,700	899,400	455,600	2,226,700	2,173,000	2,271,700	2,028,700	1,675,100
EBITDA	108,400	104,500	52,300	223,800	305,900	321,300	282,400	160,400
Depn & Amortn	90,000	60,300	29,900	107,200	93,300	85,100	71,500	59,200
Income Before Taxes	(2,400)	30,600	15,800	89,000	195,800	215,500	188,000	85,200
Income Taxes	1,800	10,800	7,200	30,400	63,600	70,300	67,000	16,100
Net Income	(3,600)	20,400	8,900	58,700	132,800	146,100	121,200	71,000
Average Shares	47,100	48,900	49,900	52,700	53,600	53,400	47,800	44,700
Balance Sheet								
Current Assets	1,016,100	1,036,200	1,047,000	1,070,400	1,194,500	1,281,500	1,249,700	1,157,600
Total Assets	2,786,500	2,840,600	2,871,100	2,905,900	3,057,500	2,882,900	2,627,800	1,991,900
Current Liabilities	315,100	335,300	324,400	322,100	430,600	421,200	554,200	395,400
Long-Term Obligations	612,900	608,400	611,000	607,100	604,300	604,200	305,900	407,800
Total Liabilities	1,599,500	1,612,600	1,593,900	1,580,000	1,553,200	1,579,800	1,524,000	1,226,200
Stockholders' Equity	1,187,000	1,228,000	1,277,200	1,325,900	1,504,300	1,303,100	1,103,800	765,700
Shares Outstanding	46,582	47,605	49,121	50,318	53,137	52,773	52,412	44,107
Statistical Record								
Return on Assets %	0.66	1.41	1.84	1.97	4.47	5.30	5.23	3.97
Return on Equity %	1.47	3.07	3.92	4.15	9.46	12.14	12.93	10.60
EBITDA Margin %	8.00	11.62	11.48	10.05	14.08	14.14	13.92	9.58
Net Margin %	N.M.	2.27	1.95	2.64	6.11	6.43	5.97	4.24
Asset Turnover	0.67	0.69	0.72	0.75	0.73	0.82	0.88	0.94
Current Ratio	3.22	3.09	3.23	3.32	2.77	3.04	2.25	2.93
Debt to Equity	0.52	0.50	0.48	0.46	0.40	0.46	0.28	0.53
Price Range	44.61-25.16	49.25-27.92	52.87-29.34	64.32-35.69	66.64-45.59	55.70-43.77	59.53-41.32	57.68-30.58
P/E Ratio	135.18-76.24	60.80-34.47	51.33-28.49	57.95-32.15	26.98-18.46	20.40-16.03	23.53-16.33	36.28-19.23
Average Yield %	2.04	1.90	1.73	1.55	1.21	1.47	1.41	1.78

Address: P.O. Box 14662, Reading, PA 19610 Telephone: 610-208-2000	Web Site: www.cartech.com Officers: Gregory A. Pratt - Interim Executive Chairman, Chairman, Interim President, Interim Chief Executive Officer Tony R. Thene - President, Chief Executive Officer, Senior Vice President, Chief Financial Officer	Auditors: PricewaterhouseCoopers LLP Investor Contact: 610-208-3476 Transfer Agents: American Stock Transfer & Trust Company

CARTER'S INC

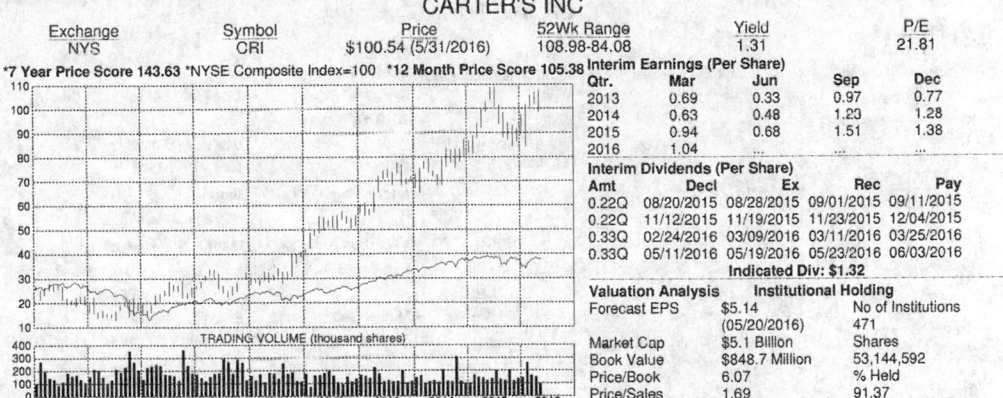

Exchange	Symbol	Price	52Wk Range	Yield	P/E
NYS	CRI	$100.54 (5/31/2016)	108.98-84.08	1.31	21.81

*7 Year Price Score 143.63 *NYSE Composite Index=100 *12 Month Price Score 105.38

Interim Earnings (Per Share)

Qtr.	Mar	Jun	Sep	Dec
2013	0.69	0.33	0.97	0.77
2014	0.63	0.48	1.23	1.28
2015	0.94	0.68	1.51	1.38
2016	1.04	...	...	...

Interim Dividends (Per Share)

Amt	Decl	Ex	Rec	Pay
0.22Q	08/20/2015	08/28/2015	09/01/2015	09/11/2015
0.22Q	11/12/2015	11/19/2015	11/23/2015	12/04/2015
0.33Q	02/24/2016	03/09/2016	03/11/2016	03/25/2016
0.33Q	05/11/2016	05/19/2016	05/23/2016	06/03/2016

Indicated Div: $1.32

Valuation Analysis — **Institutional Holding**

Forecast EPS	$5.14
	(05/20/2016)
Market Cap	$5.1 Billion
Book Value	$848.7 Million
Price/Book	6.07
Price/Sales	1.69

No of Institutions	471
Shares	53,144,592
% Held	91.37

Business Summary: Apparel, Footwear & Accessories (MIC: 1.4.2 SIC: 5641 NAIC: 315291)

Carter's is a marketer of apparel for babies and young children. Under its Carter's brand, Co. designs, sources, and markets a range of products, mainly for sizes newborn to eight. Under its OshKosh B'gosh (OshKosh) brand, Co. designs, sources, and markets a range of young children's apparel, mainly for children in sizes newborn to 12. Co. provides several product categories, including baby, sleepwear, playclothes, and related accessories. As of Jan 2 2016, Co. operated 594 Carter's and 241 OshKosh stores in the U.S., and its products are sold through 147 Co.-operated stores in Canada in addition to its international wholesale, licensing, and online channels.

Recent Developments: For the quarter ended Apr 2 2016, net income increased 8.4% to US$54.0 million from US$49.8 million in the year-earlier quarter. Revenues were US$724.1 million, up 5.7% from US$684.8 million the year before. Operating income was US$93.0 million versus US$84.5 million in the prior-year quarter, an increase of 10.1%. Direct operating expenses rose 3.1% to US$413.2 million from US$400.7 million in the comparable period the year before. Indirect operating expenses increased 9.2% to US$217.9 million from US$199.5 million in the equivalent prior-year period.

Prospects: Our evaluation of Carter Holdings Inc. as of June 19, 2016 is the result of our systematic analysis on three basic characteristics: earnings strength, relative valuation, and recent stock price movement. The company has generated a negative trend in earnings per share over the past 5 quarters and while recent estimates for the company have remained steady, CRI has posted better than expected results. Based on operating earnings yield, the company is about fairly valued when compared to all of the companies in our coverage universe. Share price changes over the past year indicates that CRI will perform in line with the market over the near term.

Financial Data

(US$ in Thousands)	3 Mos	01/02/2016	01/03/2015	12/28/2013	12/29/2012	12/31/2011	01/01/2011	01/02/2010
Earnings Per Share	4.61	4.50	3.62	2.75	2.69	1.94	2.46	1.97
Cash Flow Per Share	6.82	5.96	5.28	3.69	4.80	1.41	1.48	3.33
Tang Book Value Per Share	7.06	7.52	5.45	3.38	8.28	5.30	4.13	1.93
Dividends Per Share	0.990	0.880	0.760	0.480	...	...	...	...
Dividend Payout %	21.48	19.56	20.99	17.45	...	...	...	...
Income Statement								
Total Revenue	724,085	3,013,879	2,893,868	2,638,711	2,381,734	2,109,734	1,749,256	1,589,677
EBITDA	91,171	463,136	405,093	330,521	301,631	220,536	273,206	224,170
Depn & Amortn	1,356	68,417	74,937	68,288	39,500	32,500	29,950	28,557
Income Before Taxes	83,283	368,188	302,906	249,465	255,391	180,888	233,386	183,828
Income Taxes	29,303	130,366	108,236	89,058	94,241	66,872	86,914	68,188
Net Income	53,980	237,822	194,670	160,407	161,150	114,016	146,472	115,640
Average Shares	51,644	52,334	53,093	57,522	59,069	58,214	59,016	58,347
Balance Sheet								
Current Assets	1,032,841	1,131,465	1,041,458	970,381	957,703	782,147	716,263	675,668
Total Assets	1,912,463	2,009,113	1,893,096	1,812,484	1,630,109	1,402,709	1,257,182	1,208,599
Current Liabilities	192,881	262,718	247,971	269,139	244,235	152,753	183,372	170,617
Long-Term Obligations	580,319	584,431	586,000	586,000	186,000	236,000	236,000	331,020
Total Liabilities	1,063,746	1,134,062	1,106,412	1,111,753	644,630	597,000	577,246	652,575
Stockholders' Equity	848,717	875,051	786,684	700,731	985,479	805,709	679,936	556,024
Shares Outstanding	51,206	51,764	52,712	54,541	59,126	58,595	57,493	58,081
Statistical Record								
Return on Assets %	12.85	12.22	10.34	9.34	10.66	8.60	11.91	10.26
Return on Equity %	29.26	28.70	25.75	19.08	18.04	15.39	23.77	23.60
EBITDA Margin %	12.59	15.37	14.00	12.53	12.66	10.45	15.62	14.10
Net Margin %	7.45	7.89	6.73	6.08	6.77	5.40	8.37	7.27
Asset Turnover	1.62	1.55	1.54	1.54	1.57	1.59	1.42	1.41
Current Ratio	5.35	4.31	4.20	3.61	3.92	5.12	3.91	3.96
Debt to Equity	0.68	0.67	0.74	0.84	0.19	0.29	0.35	0.60
Price Range	108.98-84.08	108.98-80.98	87.31-64.84	77.33-55.55	57.44-39.49	40.62-27.04	33.63-22.34	29.13-14.13
P/E Ratio	23.64-18.24	24.22-18.00	24.12-17.91	28.12-20.20	21.35-14.68	20.94-13.94	13.67-9.08	14.79-7.17
Average Yield %	1.03	0.93	1.00	0.71	...	...	...	...

Address: Phipps Tower, 3438 Peachtree Road N.E., Suite 1800, Atlanta, GA 30326
Telephone: 678-791-1000

Web Site: www.carters.com
Officers: Michael Dennis Casey - Chairman, President, Chief Executive Officer Brian J. Lynch - President, Executive Vice President

Auditors: PricewaterhouseCoopers LLP
Investor Contact: 404-745-2889
Transfer Agents: American Stock Transfer & Trust Company, LLC, Brooklyn, NY

CATALENT INC

Exchange	Symbol	Price	52Wk Range	Yield	P/E
NYS	CTLT	$28.12 (5/31/2016)	34.21-20.86	N/A	17.04

*7 Year Price Score N/A   *NYSE Composite Index=100   *12 Month Price Score 99.02

TRADING VOLUME (thousand shares)

Interim Earnings (Per Share)

Qtr.	Sep	Dec	Mar	Jun
2013-14	0.02	(0.26)	0.09	0.36
2014-15	(0.18)	0.37	0.25	1.26
2015-16	0.07	0.24	0.08	...

Interim Dividends (Per Share)

No Dividends Paid

Valuation Analysis   Institutional Holding

Forecast EPS	$1.22	No of Institutions
	(05/20/2016)	208
Market Cap	$3.5 Billion	Shares
Book Value	$602.9 Million	125,967,160
Price/Book	5.81	% Held
Price/Sales	1.92	94.66

Business Summary: Pharmaceuticals (MIC: 4.1.1 SIC: 2834 NAIC: 325412)

Catalent is a provider of delivery technologies and development solutions for drugs, biologics and consumer health products. Co.'s segments include: Oral Technologies, which formulates, develops and manufactures prescription and consumer health products; Medication Delivery Solutions, which formulates, develops and manufactures prefilled syringes and other injectable formats; blow-fill-seal unit dose development and manufacturing as well as biologic cell line development and manufacturing; and Development and Clinical Services, which among others manufactures, packaging, storage, distribution and inventory management for global clinical trials of drugs and biologics.

Recent Developments: For the quarter ended Mar 31 2016, income from continuing operations decreased 68.2% to US$9.8 million from US$30.8 million in the year-earlier quarter. Net income decreased 68.2% to US$9.8 million from US$30.8 million in the year-earlier quarter. Revenues were US$438.0 million, down 1.9% from US$446.6 million the year before. Operating income was US$31.5 million versus US$65.8 million in the prior-year quarter, a decrease of 52.1%. Direct operating expenses rose 5.9% to US$311.8 million from US$294.4 million in the comparable period the year before. Indirect operating expenses increased 9.6% to US$94.7 million from US$86.4 million in the equivalent prior-year period.

Prospects: Our evaluation of Catalent Inc as of June 19, 2016 is the result of our systematic analysis on three basic characteristics: earnings strength, relative valuation, and recent stock price movement. The company has generated a negative trend in earnings per share over the past 5 quarters and while recent estimates for the company have remained steady, CTLT has posted results that fell short of analysts expectations. Based on operating earnings yield, the company is undervalued when compared to all of the companies in our coverage universe. Share price changes over the past year indicates that CTLT will perform very well over the near term.

Financial Data
(US$ in Thousands)

	9 Mos	6 Mos	3 Mos	06/30/2015	06/30/2014	06/30/2013	06/30/2012	06/30/2011
Earnings Per Share	1.65	1.82	1.95	1.75	0.21	(0.62)	(0.54)	(0.72)
Cash Flow Per Share	1.59	1.95	2.06	1.44	2.38	1.84	1.17	1.33
Income Statement								
Total Revenue	1,315,900	877,900	423,000	1,830,800	1,827,700	1,800,300	1,694,800	1,531,800
EBITDA	137,700	100,900	37,600	311,800	331,000	350,500	346,200	285,600
Depn & Amortn	3,400	2,300	1,100	94,300	100,500	171,200	144,400	125,500
Income Before Taxes	67,600	53,600	13,800	112,500	67,400	(23,900)	18,600	(5,400)
Income Taxes	18,300	14,100	4,900	(97,700)	49,500	24,100	16,500	23,700
Net Income	49,600	39,800	9,100	212,200	16,200	(46,700)	(40,400)	(54,000)
Average Shares	125,772	125,826	126,190	121,348	76,123	74,970	75,384	74,693
Balance Sheet								
Current Assets	727,500	679,500	691,200	737,500	687,500	677,900	704,700	205,100
Total Assets	3,057,700	3,035,200	3,056,400	3,145,400	3,090,200	3,056,800	3,139,000	2,729,100
Current Liabilities	371,500	340,200	352,900	399,000	453,000	410,300	439,300	...
Long-Term Obligations	1,844,900	1,848,300	1,859,900	1,864,100	2,685,400	2,656,600	2,640,300	...
Total Liabilities	2,454,800	2,427,800	2,459,200	2,511,400	3,461,400	3,467,500	3,489,700	...
Stockholders' Equity	602,900	607,400	597,200	634,000	(371,200)	(410,700)	(350,700)	...
Shares Outstanding	124,654	124,523	124,521	124,319	74,821	74,796	74,756	74,729
Statistical Record								
Return on Assets %	6.74	7.41	8.02	6.81	0.53	N.M.	N.M.	...
Return on Equity %	37.96	40.88	43.74	161.49	...	...	...	...
EBITDA Margin %	10.46	11.49	8.89	17.03	18.11	19.47	20.43	18.64
Net Margin %	3.77	4.53	2.15	11.59	0.89	N.M.	N.M.	N.M.
Asset Turnover	0.61	0.60	0.61	0.59	0.59	0.59	0.58	...
Current Ratio	1.96	2.00	1.96	1.85	1.52	1.65	1.60	...
Debt to Equity	3.06	3.04	3.11	2.94	...	...	...	...
Price Range	34.21-20.86	34.21-23.98	34.21-23.52	31.96-19.85	...	...	...	...
P/E Ratio	20.73-12.64	18.80-13.18	17.54-12.06	18.26-11.34	...	...	...	...

Address: 14 Schoolhouse Road, Somerset, NJ 08873 **Telephone:** 732-537-6200	**Web Site:** www.catalent.com **Officers:** Chinh E. Chu - Chairman John R. Chiminski - President, Chief Executive Officer	**Auditors:** Ernst & Young LLP **Transfer Agents:** Computershare Trust Company, N.A.

CATERPILLAR INC.

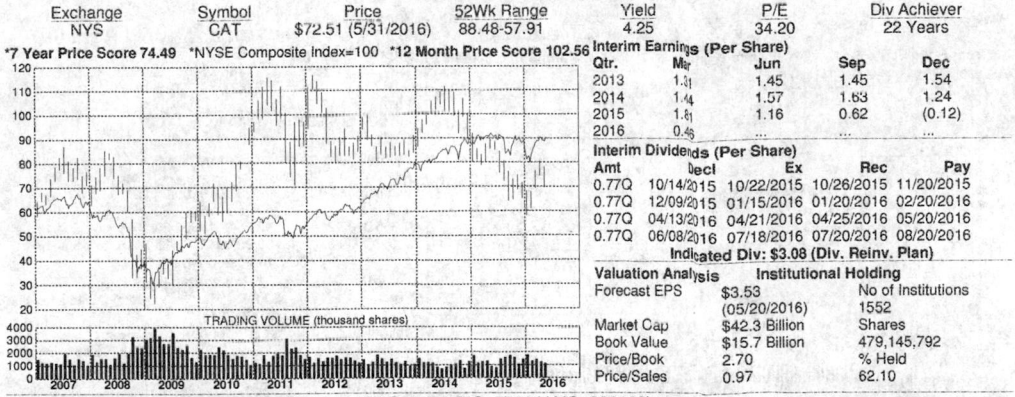

Exchange	Symbol	Price	52Wk Range	Yield	P/E	Div Achiever
NYS	CAT	$72.51 (5/31/2016)	88.48-57.91	4.25	34.20	22 Years

*7 Year Price Score 74.49 *NYSE Composite Index=100 *12 Month Price Score 102.56

Interim Earnings (Per Share)

Qtr.	Mar	Jun	Sep	Dec
2013	1.31	1.45	1.45	1.54
2014	1.44	1.57	1.63	1.24
2015	1.81	1.16	0.62	(0.12)
2016	0.46	...	...	...

Interim Dividends (Per Share)

Amt	Decl	Ex	Rec	Pay
0.77Q	10/14/2015	10/22/2015	10/26/2015	11/20/2015
0.77Q	12/09/2015	01/15/2016	01/20/2016	02/20/2016
0.77Q	04/13/2016	04/21/2016	04/25/2016	05/20/2016
0.77Q	06/08/2016	07/18/2016	07/20/2016	08/20/2016

Indicated Div: $3.08 (Div. Reinv. Plan)

Valuation Analysis

		Institutional Holding	
Forecast EPS	$3.53	No of Institutions	
	(05/20/2016)	1552	
Market Cap	$42.3 Billion	Shares	479,145,792
Book Value	$15.7 Billion	% Held	
Price/Book	2.70		62.10
Price/Sales	0.97		

TRADING VOLUME (thousand shares)

Business Summary: Construction Services (MIC: 7.5.4 SIC: 3531 NAIC: 333120)

Caterpillar is engaged in manufacturing construction and mining equipment, diesel and natural gas engines, industrial gas turbines and diesel-electric locomotives. Co.'s segments include: Construction Industries, which supports customers using machinery in infrastructure and building construction applications; Resource Industries, which supports customers using machinery in mine and quarry applications; Energy and Transportation, which supports customers using reciprocating engines, turbines, diesel-electric locomotives, and related parts across industries such as power generation and industrial; and Financial Products, which provides retail and wholesale financing for Co.'s products.

Recent Developments: For the quarter ended Mar 31 2016, net income decreased 78.2% to US$272.0 million from US$1.25 billion in the year-earlier quarter. Revenues were US$9.46 billion, down 25.5% from US$12.70 billion the year before. Operating income was US$494.0 million versus US$1.70 billion in the prior-year quarter, a decrease of 71.0%. Direct operating expenses declined 22.1% to US$6.82 billion from US$8.76 billion in the comparable period the year before. Indirect operating expenses decreased 4.2% to US$2.15 billion from US$2.24 billion in the equivalent prior-year period.

Prospects: Our evaluation of Caterpillar Inc. as of June 19, 2016 is the result of our systematic analysis on three basic characteristics: earnings strength, relative valuation, and recent stock price movement. The company has managed to produce a neutral trend in earnings per share over the past 5 quarters. However, while recent estimates for the company have been mixed, CAT has posted results that fell short of analysts expectations. Based on operating earnings yield, the company is about fairly valued when compared to all of the companies in our coverage universe. Share price changes over the past year indicates that CAT will perform poorly over the near term.

Financial Data

(US$ in Thousands)	3 Mos	12/31/2015	12/31/2014	12/31/2013	12/31/2012	12/31/2011	12/31/2010	12/31/2009
Earnings Per Share	2.12	3.50	5.88	5.75	8.48	7.40	4.15	1.43
Cash Flow Per Share	10.11	11.23	13.05	15.80	8.01	10.87	7.93	10.31
Tang Book Value Per Share	10.66	9.23	11.51	16.08	10.04	2.22	11.59	9.61
Dividends Per Share	3.010	2.940	2.600	1.720	2.480	1.800	1.720	1.680
Dividend Payout %	141.98	84.00	44.22	29.91	29.25	24.32	41.45	117.48
Income Statement								
Total Revenue	9,461,000	47,011,000	55,184,000	55,656,000	65,875,000	60,138,000	42,588,000	32,396,000
EBITDA	1,386,000	6,654,000	8,986,000	9,030,000	11,921,000	10,158,000	7,209,000	4,257,000
Depn & Amortn	740,000	2,705,000	2,795,000	2,710,000	2,421,000	2,211,000	2,202,000	2,254,000
Income Before Taxes	365,000	2,855,000	5,083,000	5,128,000	8,236,000	6,725,000	3,750,000	569,000
Income Taxes	92,000	742,000	1,380,000	1,319,000	2,528,000	1,720,000	968,000	(270,000)
Net Income	271,000	2,102,000	3,695,000	3,789,000	5,681,000	4,928,000	2,700,000	895,000
Average Shares	587,700	601,300	628,900	658,600	669,600	666,100	650,400	626,000
Balance Sheet								
Current Assets	33,748,000	34,418,000	38,867,000	38,335,000	42,524,000	38,128,000	31,810,000	26,789,000
Total Assets	78,307,000	78,497,000	84,681,000	84,896,000	89,356,000	81,446,000	64,020,000	60,038,000
Current Liabilities	26,215,000	26,303,000	27,877,000	27,297,000	29,755,000	28,561,000	22,020,000	19,292,000
Long-Term Obligations	24,470,000	25,247,000	27,784,000	26,719,000	27,752,000	24,944,000	20,437,000	21,847,000
Total Liabilities	62,631,000	63,688,000	67,935,000	64,085,000	71,824,000	68,563,000	53,196,000	51,298,000
Stockholders' Equity	15,676,000	14,809,000	16,746,000	20,811,000	17,532,000	12,883,000	10,824,000	8,740,000
Shares Outstanding	583,868	582,321	606,166	637,822	655,048	647,533	638,822	624,722
Statistical Record								
Return on Assets %	1.57	2.58	4.36	4.35	6.63	6.78	4.35	1.40
Return on Equity %	7.73	13.32	19.68	19.76	37.25	41.57	27.60	12.07
EBITDA Margin %	14.65	14.15	16.28	16.22	18.10	16.89	16.93	13.14
Net Margin %	2.86	4.47	6.70	6.81	8.62	8.19	6.34	2.76
Asset Turnover	0.54	0.58	0.65	0.64	0.77	0.83	0.69	0.51
Current Ratio	1.29	1.31	1.39	1.40	1.43	1.33	1.44	1.39
Debt to Equity	1.56	1.70	1.66	1.28	1.58	1.94	1.89	2.50
Price Range	89.33-57.91	91.88-63.79	111.40-86.17	99.49-80.43	116.20-79.4	115.41-70.55	94.63-50.78	60.40-22.17
P/E Ratio	42.14-27.32	26.25-18.23	18.95-14.65	17.30-13.99	13.70-9.9	15.60-9.53	22.80-12.24	42.24-15.50
Average Yield %	4.02	3.73	2.58	1.92	2.4	1.86	2.49	4.00

Address: 100 N.E. Adams Street,	Web Site: www.caterpillar.com	Auditors: PricewaterhouseCoopers LLP
Peoria, IL 61629	Officers: Douglas R. Oberhelman - Chairman,	Investor Contact: 309-675-4549
Telephone: 309-675-1000	Vice-Chairman, Chief Executive Officer Bradley M.	Transfer Agents: ComputerShare,
Fax: 309-675-4332	Halverson Vice President, Group President, Chief Financial Officer, Controller	College Station, TX

CBL & ASSOCIATES PROPERTIES INC

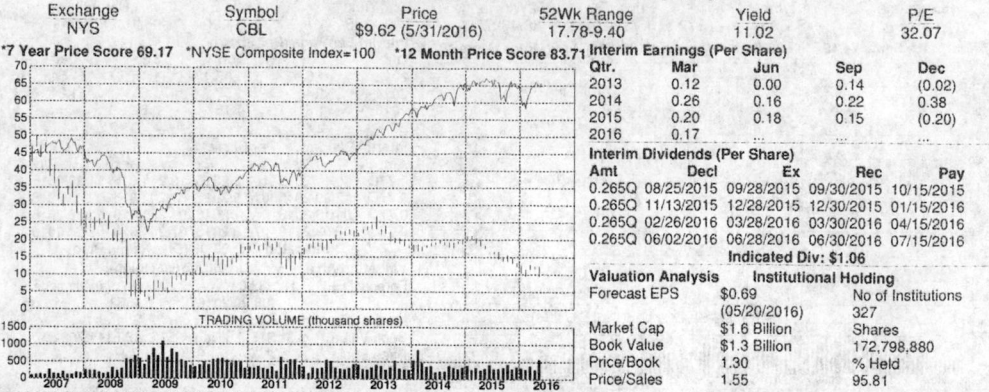

Exchange	Symbol	Price	52Wk Range	Yield	P/E
NYS	CBL	$9.62 (5/31/2016)	17.78-9.40	11.02	32.07

*7 Year Price Score 69.17 *NYSE Composite Index=100 *12 Month Price Score 83.71

Interim Earnings (Per Share)

Qtr.	Mar	Jun	Sep	Dec
2013	0.12	0.00	0.14	(0.02)
2014	0.26	0.16	0.22	0.38
2015	0.20	0.18	0.15	(0.20)
2016	0.17	...	...	...

Interim Dividends (Per Share)

Amt	Decl	Ex	Rec	Pay
0.265Q	08/25/2015	09/28/2015	09/30/2015	10/15/2015
0.265Q	11/13/2015	12/28/2015	12/30/2015	01/15/2016
0.265Q	02/26/2016	03/28/2016	03/30/2016	04/15/2016
0.265Q	06/02/2016	06/28/2016	06/30/2016	07/15/2016

Indicated Div: $1.06

Valuation Analysis

		Institutional Holding	
Forecast EPS	$0.69	No of Institutions	327
	(05/20/2016)		
Market Cap	$1.6 Billion	Shares	172,798,880
Book Value	$1.3 Billion	% Held	95.81
Price/Book	1.30		
Price/Sales	1.55		

Business Summary: REITs (MIC: 5.3.1 SIC: 6798 NAIC: 525930)

CBL & Associates Properties is a real estate investment trust. Co. owns, develops, acquires, leases, manages, and operates regional shopping malls, open-air centers, outlet centers, associated centers, community centers and office properties located in 27 states. As of Dec 31 2014, Co. owned a controlling interest in 72 malls and non-controlling interests in nine malls; a controlling interest in 25 associated centers and a non-controlling interest in four associated centers; a controlling interest in six community centers and a non-controlling interest in five community centers; and a controlling interest in eight offfice buildings and a non-controlling interest in five office buildings.

Recent Developments: For the quarter ended Mar 31 2016, net income decreased 21.3% to US$41.9 million from US$53.2 million in the year-earlier quarter. Revenues were US$263.1 million, up 0.8% from US$260.9 million the year before. Revenues from property income rose 1.2% to US$256.3 million from US$253.3 million in the corresponding quarter a year earlier.

Prospects: Our evaluation of CBL & Associates Properties Inc. as of June 19, 2016 is the result of our systematic analysis on three basic characteristics: earnings strength, relative valuation, and recent stock price movement. The company has produced a positive trend in earnings per share over the past 5 quarters. Because the company lacks sufficient analyst estimate data, we place greater weight on the historical EPS trend as the measure of earnings strength. Based on operating earnings yield, the company is undervalued when compared to all of the companies in our coverage universe. Share price changes over the past year indicates that CBL will perform well over the near term.

Financial Data
(US$ in Thousands)

	3 Mos	12/31/2015	12/31/2014	12/31/2013	12/31/2012	12/31/2011	12/31/2010	12/31/2009
Earnings Per Share	0.30	0.34	1.02	0.24	0.54	0.62	0.21	(0.35)
Cash Flow Per Share	2.78	2.90	2.75	2.78	3.10	2.98	3.11	4.06
Tang Book Value Per Share	7.41	7.54	8.26	8.26	8.24	8.51	8.79	8.11
Dividends Per Share	1.060	1.060	1.000	0.935	0.880	0.840	0.800	0.580
Dividend Payout %	353.33	311.76	98.04	389.58	162.96	135.48	380.95	...
Income Statement								
Total Revenue	263,078	1,055,018	1,060,739	1,053,625	1,034,640	1,067,340	1,071,804	1,089,489
EBITDA	63,931	629,162	764,424	616,432	702,059	703,795	672,079	476,259
Depn & Amortn	95	302,530	296,046	290,395	275,267	285,703	297,802	201,300
Income Before Taxes	8,965	103,756	242,675	105,006	186,315	149,347	91,571	(13,881)
Income Taxes	(537)	2,941	4,499	1,305	1,404	(269)	(6,417)	(1,222)
Net Income	40,074	103,371	219,150	85,204	131,600	133,936	62,151	(14,989)
Average Shares	170,669	170,499	170,247	167,027	154,807	148,334	138,416	106,366
Balance Sheet								
Current Assets	132,629	142,136	141,853	168,742	165,678	141,844	140,881	129,394
Total Assets	6,383,928	6,479,991	6,616,299	6,785,971	7,089,736	6,719,428	7,506,554	7,729,110
Current Liabilities	299,691	344,434	328,352	333,875	358,874	303,577	314,651	248,333
Long-Term Obligations	4,683,487	4,710,628	4,700,460	4,857,523	4,745,683	4,489,355	5,209,747	5,616,139
Total Liabilities	5,117,745	5,195,021	5,209,747	5,381,058	5,761,043	5,456,150	6,206,216	6,611,214
Stockholders' Equity	1,266,183	1,284,970	1,406,552	1,404,913	1,328,693	1,263,278	1,300,338	1,117,896
Shares Outstanding	170,791	170,490	170,260	170,048	161,309	148,364	147,923	137,888
Statistical Record								
Return on Assets %	1.51	1.58	3.27	1.23	1.90	1.88	0.82	N.M.
Return on Equity %	7.34	7.68	15.59	6.23	10.13	10.45	5.14	N.M.
EBITDA Margin %	24.30	59.64	72.07	58.51	67.86	65.94	62.71	43.71
Net Margin %	15.23	9.80	20.66	8.09	12.72	12.55	5.80	N.M.
Asset Turnover	0.16	0.16	0.16	0.15	0.15	0.15	0.14	0.14
Current Ratio	0.44	0.41	0.43	0.51	0.46	0.47	0.45	0.52
Debt to Equity	3.70	3.67	3.34	3.46	3.57	3.55	4.01	5.02
Price Range	19.91-9.40	21.28-12.17	19.91-16.40	26.58-17.57	22.81-15.63	19.24-10.91	18.47-9.58	10.69-2.06
P/E Ratio	66.37-31.33	62.59-35.79	19.52-16.08	110.75-73.21	42.24-28.94	31.03-17.60	87.95-45.62	...
Average Yield %	7.22	6.31	5.43	4.36	4.47	5.15	5.77	8.64

Address: 2030 Hamilton Place Blvd., Suite 500, Chattanooga, TN 37421-6000 **Telephone:** 423-855-0001	**Web Site:** www.cblproperties.com **Officers:** Charles B. Lebovitz - Chairman Stephen D. Lebovitz - President, Chief Executive Officer	**Auditors:** Deloitte & Touche LLP **Transfer Agents:** Computershare, Providence, RI

146

CBRE GROUP INC

Exchange	Symbol	Price	52Wk Range	Yield	P/E
NYS	CBG	$29.85 (5/31/2016)	38.56-23.32	N/A	18.77

*7 Year Price Score 119.78 *NYSE Composite Index=100 *12 Month Price Score 88.20

Interim Earnings (Per Share)

Qtr.	Mar	Jun	Sep	Dec
2013	0.11	0.21	0.28	0.34
2014	0.20	0.32	0.32	0.61
2015	0.28	0.37	0.44	0.54
2016	0.24	...	...	...

Interim Dividends (Per Share)

No Dividends Paid

Valuation Analysis | **Institutional Holding**

Forecast EPS	$2.30	No of Institutions
	(05/20/2016)	665
Market Cap	$10.0 Billion	Shares
Book Value	$2.8 Billion	366,548,960
Price/Book	3.55	% Held
Price/Sales	0.86	N/A

Business Summary: Property, Real Estate & Development (MIC: 5.3.2 SIC: 6531 NAIC: 531210)

CBRE Group is a holding company. Through its subsidiaries, Co. provides services to occupiers, owners, lenders and investors in office, retail, industrial, multifamily and other types of commercial real estate. Co. provides commercial real estate services under the CBRE brand name, investment management services under the CBRE Global Investors brand name and development services under the Trammell Crow brand name. Co.'s business is focused on several competencies, including commercial property, corporate facilities, project and transaction management, tenant/occupier and property/agency leasing, real estate investment management, valuation, development services and proprietary research.

Recent Developments: For the quarter ended Mar 31 2016, net income decreased 9.1% to US$84.6 million from US$93.1 million in the year-earlier quarter. Revenues were US$2.85 billion, up 38.7% from US$2.05 billion the year before.

Prospects: Our evaluation of CBRE Group Inc. as of June 19, 2016 is the result of our systematic analysis on three basic characteristics: earnings strength, relative valuation, and recent stock price movement. The company has managed to produce a neutral trend in earnings per share over the past 5 quarters. However, while recent estimates for the company have been lowered by analysts, CBG has posted better than expected results. Based on operating earnings yield, the company is undervalued when compared to all of the companies in our coverage universe. Share price changes over the past year indicates that CBG will perform in line with the market over the near term.

Financial Data
(US$ in Thousands)

	3 Mos	12/31/2015	12/31/2014	12/31/2013	12/31/2012	12/31/2011	12/31/2010	12/31/2009
Earnings Per Share	1.59	1.63	1.45	0.95	0.97	0.74	0.63	0.12
Cash Flow Per Share	1.51	1.96	2.00	2.27	0.90	1.13	1.96	0.77
Income Statement								
Total Revenue	2,846,734	10,855,810	9,049,918	7,184,794	6,514,099	5,905,411	5,115,316	4,165,820
EBITDA	113,443	966,650	904,150	671,456	672,374	519,768	486,931	275,867
Depn & Amortn	2,648	137,200	122,800	98,100	76,200	54,200	58,700	59,400
Income Before Taxes	77,464	716,881	675,548	444,563	428,749	324,762	245,496	33,450
Income Taxes	50,125	320,853	263,759	187,187	185,322	189,103	130,368	26,993
Net Income	82,167	547,132	484,503	316,538	315,555	239,162	200,345	33,341
Average Shares	337,506	336,414	334,171	331,762	327,044	323,723	319,016	279,995
Balance Sheet								
Current Assets	4,086,896	5,305,223	3,524,504	2,879,812	4,084,550	3,550,047	2,260,870	2,266,725
Total Assets	9,835,135	11,017,943	7,647,105	6,998,414	7,809,542	7,219,143	5,121,568	5,039,406
Current Liabilities	3,696,420	4,994,157	2,875,634	2,605,740	2,972,293	2,680,648	1,956,768	1,629,041
Long-Term Obligations	2,635,045	2,645,111	1,852,416	1,866,890	2,543,707	2,611,187	1,851,901	2,372,302
Total Liabilities	7,017,540	8,305,291	5,387,275	5,102,629	6,270,331	6,067,662	4,213,353	4,410,284
Stockholders' Equity	2,817,595	2,712,652	2,259,830	1,895,785	1,539,211	1,151,481	908,215	629,122
Shares Outstanding	335,292	334,230	332,991	331,927	330,082	327,972	323,594	321,767
Statistical Record								
Return on Assets %	6.14	5.86	6.62	4.28	4.19	3.88	3.94	0.68
Return on Equity %	21.13	22.01	23.32	18.43	23.39	23.22	26.06	8.96
EBITDA Margin %	3.99	8.90	9.99	9.35	10.32	8.80	9.52	6.62
Net Margin %	2.89	5.04	5.35	4.41	4.84	4.05	3.92	0.80
Asset Turnover	1.33	1.16	1.24	0.97	0.86	0.96	1.01	0.85
Current Ratio	1.11	1.06	1.23	1.11	1.37	1.32	1.16	1.39
Debt to Equity	0.94	0.98	0.82	0.98	1.65	2.27	2.04	3.77
Price Range	38.92-23.32	38.92-30.93	35.06-25.47	26.31-19.90	20.86-15.10	29.70-12.78	21.31-12.16	14.04-2.36
P/E Ratio	24.48-14.67	23.88-18.98	24.18-17.57	27.69-20.95	21.51-15.57	40.14-17.27	33.83-19.30	117.00-19.67

Address: 400 South Hope Street, 25th Floor, Los Angeles, CA 90071
Telephone: 213-613-3333

Web Site: www.cbre.com
Officers: Robert E. Sulentic - President, Chief Executive Officer James R. Groch - Chief Financial Officer, Director, Executive Vice President, Chief Investment Officer, Global Chief Investment Officer, Division Officer

Auditors: KPMG LLP
Investor Contact: 213-613-3732
Transfer Agents: Broadridge Corporate Issuer Solutions, Inc., Edgewood, NY

CBS CORP

Exchange	Symbol	Price	52Wk Range	Yield	P/E
NYS	CBS	$55.20 (5/31/2016)	62.22-38.67	1.09	17.64

*7 Year Price Score 113.49 *NYSE Composite Index=100 *12 Month Price Score 108.97

Interim Earnings (Per Share)

Qtr.	Mar	Jun	Sep	Dec
2013	0.69	0.76	0.80	0.76
2014	0.78	0.76	3.03	0.83
2015	0.78	0.67	0.88	0.56
2016	1.02			

Interim Dividends (Per Share)

Amt	Decl	Ex	Rec	Pay
0.15Q	07/28/2015	09/08/2015	09/10/2015	10/01/2015
0.15Q	11/24/2015	12/09/2015	12/11/2015	01/01/2016
0.15Q	01/28/2016	03/09/2016	03/11/2016	04/01/2016
0.15Q	05/26/2016	06/08/2016	06/10/2016	07/01/2016

Indicated Div: $0.60

Valuation Analysis

		Institutional Holding	
Forecast EPS	$4.05 (05/20/2016)	No of Institutions	968
Market Cap	$25.1 Billion	Shares	415,748.032
Book Value	$5.5 Billion	% Held	
Price/Book	4.57		
Price/Sales	1.76	N/A	

Business Summary: Radio & Television (MIC: 2.3.1 SIC: 4833 NAIC: 515120)

CBS is a mass media company. Co. segments include: Entertainment, which is composed of the CBS® Television Network, CBS Television Studios®, CBS Global Distribution Groupâ„¢, CBS Interactiveâ„¢, and CBS Films®; Cable Networks, which is composed of Showtime Networks that operates Co.'s premium subscription program services; CBS Sports Network®, that operates cable network focused on college athletics and other sports; and Smithsonian Networks that operates Smithsonian Channel, a basic cable program service; Publishing, which is composed of Simon & Schuster that publishes and distributes consumer books; and Local Broadcasting, which is composed of CBS Television Stations, and CBS Radio®.

Recent Developments: For the quarter ended Mar 31 2016, net income increased 20.1% to US$473.0 million from US$394.0 million in the year-earlier quarter. Revenues were US$3.85 billion, up 10.0% from US$3.50 billion the year before. Operating income was US$821.0 million versus US$721.0 million in the prior-year quarter, an increase of 13.9%. Direct operating expenses rose 10.0% to US$2.36 billion from US$2.14 billion in the comparable period the year before. Indirect operating expenses increased 5.5% to US$672.0 million from US$637.0 million in the equivalent prior-year period.

Prospects: Our evaluation of CBS Corp. as of June 19, 2016 is the result of our systematic analysis on three basic characteristics: earnings strength, relative valuation, and recent stock price movement. The company has managed to produce a neutral trend in earnings per share over the past 5 quarters. However, while recent estimates for the company have been mixed, CBS has posted better than expected results. Based on operating earnings yield, the company is undervalued when compared to all of the companies in our coverage universe. Share price changes over the past year indicates that CBS will perform in line with the market over the near term.

Financial Data

(US$ in Thousands)	3 Mos	12/31/2015	12/31/2014	12/31/2013	12/31/2012	12/31/2011	12/31/2010	12/31/2009
Earnings Per Share	3.13	2.89	5.27	3.01	2.39	1.92	1.04	0.33
Cash Flow Per Share	4.37	2.88	2.32	3.08	2.82	2.63	2.56	1.39
Dividends Per Share	0.600	0.600	0.540	0.480	0.440	0.350	0.200	0.200
Dividend Payout %	19.17	20.76	10.25	15.95	18.41	18.23	19.23	60.61
Income Statement								
Total Revenue	3,849,000	13,886,000	13,806,000	15,284,000	14,089,000	14,245,000	14,059,800	13,014,600
EBITDA	882,000	2,631,000	2,763,000	3,622,000	3,326,000	2,938,000	2,177,200	1,427,700
Depn & Amortn	64,000	240,000	249,000	357,000	369,000	426,000	432,400	448,700
Income Before Taxes	725,000	2,023,000	2,164,000	2,897,000	2,561,000	2,083,000	1,221,500	443,000
Income Taxes	231,000	587,000	762,000	978,000	892,000	755,000	462,700	182,800
Net Income	473,000	1,413,000	2,959,000	1,879,000	1,574,000	1,305,000	724,200	226,500
Average Shares	464,000	489,000	561,000	624,000	659,000	681,000	694,500	682,900
Balance Sheet								
Current Assets	5,534,000	5,747,000	5,589,000	5,370,000	5,720,000	5,543,000	5,334,700	5,636,900
Total Assets	23,501,000	23,765,000	24,072,000	26,387,000	26,466,000	26,197,000	26,142,600	26,962,000
Current Liabilities	3,384,000	3,560,000	4,033,000	4,207,000	3,941,000	3,933,000	4,025,500	4,746,500
Long-Term Obligations	8,226,000	8,226,000	6,510,000	5,940,000	5,904,000	5,958,000	5,973,500	6,553,300
Total Liabilities	18,018,000	18,202,000	17,102,000	16,421,000	16,253,000	16,289,000	16,322,000	17,942,600
Stockholders' Equity	5,483,000	5,563,000	6,970,000	9,966,000	10,213,000	9,908,000	9,820,600	9,019,400
Shares Outstanding	454,000	463,000	507,000	596,000	630,000	651,000	680,200	674,800
Statistical Record								
Return on Assets %	6.31	5.91	11.73	7.11	5.96	4.99	2.73	0.84
Return on Equity %	25.12	22.55	34.94	18.62	15.60	13.23	7.69	2.57
EBITDA Margin %	22.92	18.95	20.01	23.70	23.61	20.62	15.49	10.97
Net Margin %	12.29	10.18	21.43	12.29	11.17	9.16	5.15	1.74
Asset Turnover	0.60	0.58	0.55	0.58	0.53	0.54	0.53	0.48
Current Ratio	1.64	1.61	1.39	1.28	1.45	1.41	1.33	1.19
Debt to Equity	1.50	1.48	0.93	0.60	0.58	0.60	0.61	0.73
Price Range	62.77-38.67	63.35-38.67	67.55-48.91	63.74-37.52	38.05-27.27	29.54-18.95	19.59-12.67	14.35-3.09
P/E Ratio	20.05-12.35	21.92-13.38	12.82-9.28	21.18-12.47	15.92-11.41	15.39-9.87	18.84-12.18	43.48-9.36
Average Yield %	1.17	1.12	0.92	0.95	1.33	1.43	1.23	2.22

Address: 51 W. 52nd Street, New York, NY 10019 **Telephone:** 212-975-4321	**Web Site:** www.cbscorporation.com **Officers:** Leslie Moonves - Chairman, President, Chief Executive Officer Sumner M. Redstone - Chairman Emeritus, Executive Chairman	**Auditors:** PricewaterhouseCoopers LLP **Investor Contact:** 187-722-70787 **Transfer Agents:** Wells Fargo Shareowner Services, St. Paul, MN

CEB INC

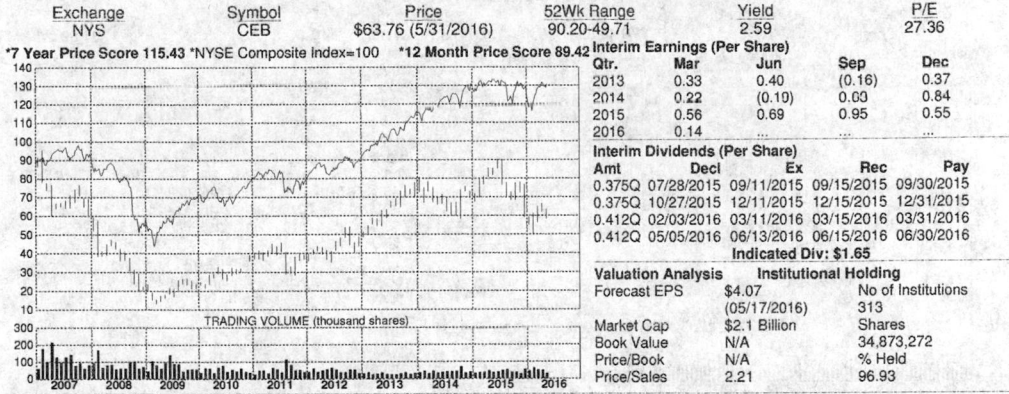

Exchange	Symbol	Price	52Wk Range	Yield	P/E
NYS	CEB	$63.76 (5/31/2016)	90.20-49.71	2.59	27.36

*7 Year Price Score 115.43 *NYSE Composite Index=100 *12 Month Price Score 89.42

Interim Earnings (Per Share)

Qtr.	Mar	Jun	Sep	Dec
2013	0.33	0.40	(0.16)	0.37
2014	0.22	(0.10)	0.60	0.84
2015	0.56	0.69	0.95	0.55
2016	0.14	...	...	...

Interim Dividends (Per Share)

Amt	Decl	Ex	Rec	Pay
0.375Q	07/28/2015	09/11/2015	09/15/2015	09/30/2015
0.375Q	10/27/2015	12/11/2015	12/15/2015	12/31/2015
0.412Q	02/03/2016	03/11/2016	03/15/2016	03/31/2016
0.412Q	05/05/2016	06/13/2016	06/15/2016	06/30/2016

Indicated Div: $1.65

Valuation Analysis

		Institutional Holding	
Forecast EPS	$4.07 (05/17/2016)	No of Institutions	313
Market Cap	$2.1 Billion	Shares	34,873,272
Book Value	N/A	% Held	96.93
Price/Book	N/A		
Price/Sales	2.21		

TRADING VOLUME (thousand shares)

Business Summary: Business Services (MIC: 7.5.2 SIC: 8742 NAIC: 541611)

CEB is an insight and technology company with two reporting segments. The CEB segment provides data analysis, research, and advisory services that align to executive leadership roles and recurring decisions. This includes Co.'s membership programs for senior executives and their teams. The CEB Talent Assessment segment includes cloud-based solutions for talent assessment, development, strategy, analytics, decision support, and services that support those solutions, enabling client access to data, analytics and insights for assessing and managing employees and applicants. This segment assists clients with determining potential candidates for employment and developing existing employees.

Recent Developments: For the quarter ended Mar 31 2016, net income decreased 76.2% to US$4.5 million from US$19.1 million in the year-earlier quarter. Revenues were US$223.2 million, up 0.7% from US$221.6 million the year before. Operating income was US$16.1 million versus US$30.0 million in the prior-year quarter, a decrease of 46.2%. Direct operating expenses rose 1.4% to US$79.7 million from US$78.7 million in the comparable period the year before. Indirect operating expenses increased 12.7% to US$127.3 million from US$113.0 million in the equivalent prior-year period.

Prospects: Our evaluation of CEB Inc as of June 19, 2016 is the result of our systematic analysis on three basic characteristics: earnings strength, relative valuation, and recent stock price movement. The company has managed to produce a neutral trend in earnings per share over the past 5 quarters and while recent estimates for the company have been raised by analysts, CEB has posted better than expected results. Based on operating earnings yield, the company is undervalued when compared to all of the companies in our coverage universe. Share price changes over the past year indicates that CEB will perform poorly over the near term.

Financial Data

(US$ in Thousands)	3 Mos	12/31/2015	12/31/2014	12/31/2013	12/31/2012	12/31/2011	12/31/2010	12/31/2009
Earnings Per Share	2.33	2.75	1.50	0.94	1.10	1.53	1.17	1.33
Cash Flow Per Share	4.46	4.44	5.41	4.43	3.64	2.94	2.48	0.84
Tang Book Value Per Share	...	N.M.	N.M.	N.M.	N.M.	1.10	1.16	0.32
Dividends Per Share	1.538	1.500	1.050	0.900	0.700	0.600	0.440	0.740
Dividend Payout %	65.99	54.55	70.00	95.74	63.64	39.22	37.61	55.64
Income Statement								
Total Revenue	223,198	928,434	908,974	820,053	622,654	484,663	438,907	442,906
EBITDA	16,518	171,248	139,296	107,974	105,019	109,807	83,010	90,918
Depn & Amortn	393	32,100	29,400	25,200	19,600	13,500	14,600	17,300
Income Before Taxes	9,056	118,969	91,850	60,438	74,620	96,307	68,410	73,618
Income Taxes	4,513	25,004	40,678	28,467	37,569	38,860	28,047	27,989
Net Income	4,543	92,528	51,172	31,971	37,051	52,655	40,363	45,629
Average Shares	32,886	33,672	34,039	33,943	33,821	34,419	34,553	34,293
Balance Sheet								
Current Assets	435,535	449,512	464,861	462,169	367,019	348,276	298,759	203,436
Total Assets	1,299,619	1,338,552	1,357,384	1,383,675	1,322,249	533,692	510,149	423,195
Current Liabilities	637,490	602,996	623,565	574,402	520,053	368,886	344,358	298,792
Long-Term Obligations	550,410	556,418	490,287	505,554	528,280	...	...	...
Total Liabilities	1,322,880	1,294,875	1,271,247	1,243,933	1,206,747	454,128	427,333	372,918
Stockholders' Equity	(23,261)	43,677	86,137	139,742	115,502	79,564	82,816	50,277
Shares Outstanding	32,238	32,906	33,445	33,624	33,337	33,302	34,322	34,147
Statistical Record								
Return on Assets %	5.93	6.86	3.73	2.36	3.98	10.09	8.65	10.49
Return on Equity %	479.03	142.55	45.31	25.05	37.88	64.85	60.65	115.69
EBITDA Margin %	7.40	18.44	15.32	13.17	16.87	22.66	18.91	20.53
Net Margin %	2.04	9.97	5.63	3.90	5.95	10.86	9.20	10.30
Asset Turnover	0.71	0.69	0.66	0.61	0.67	0.93	0.94	1.02
Current Ratio	0.68	0.75	0.75	0.80	0.71	0.94	0.87	0.68
Debt to Equity	...	12.74	5.69	3.62	4.57	...	...	...
Price Range	90.20-49.71	90.20-58.98	80.34-58.05	77.59-47.46	53.86-34.86	45.45-28.21	38.92-21.29	26.51-12.93
P/E Ratio	38.71-21.33	32.80-21.45	53.56-38.70	82.54-50.49	48.96-31.69	29.71-18.44	33.26-18.20	19.93-9.72
Average Yield %	2.11	1.95	1.51	1.42	1.62	1.59	1.51	3.67

Address: 1919 North Lynn Street, Arlington, VA 22209
Telephone: 571-303-3000

Web Site: www.cebglobal.com
Officers: Thomas L. Monahan - Chairman, Chief Executive Officer Haniel Lynn - Group President

Auditors: Ernst & Young LLP
Investor Contact: 571-303-3000
Transfer Agents: Computershare, Jersey City, NJ

CELANESE CORP (DE)

Exchange	Symbol	Price	52Wk Range	Yield	P/E
NYS	CE	$70.48 (5/31/2016)	73.72-54.48	2.04	31.89

*7 Year Price Score 118.10 *NYSE Composite Index=100 *12 Month Price Score 104.98

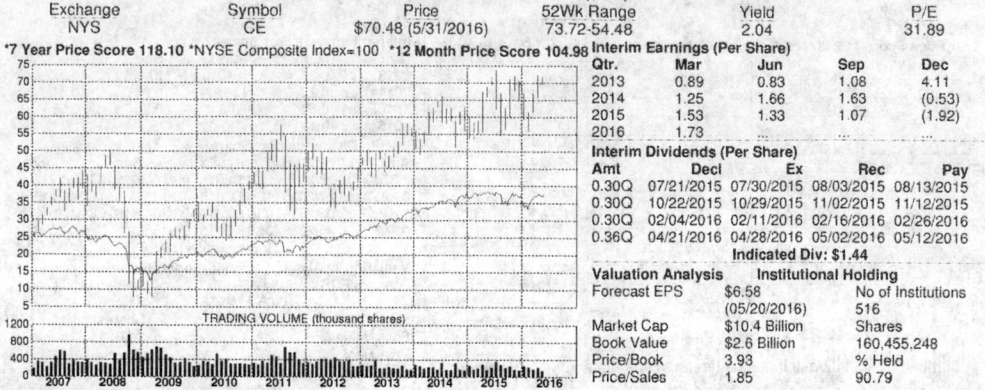

Interim Earnings (Per Share)

Qtr.	Mar	Jun	Sep	Dec
2013	0.89	0.83	1.08	4.11
2014	1.25	1.66	1.63	(0.53)
2015	1.53	1.33	1.07	(1.92)
2016	1.73	...	...	...

Interim Dividends (Per Share)

Amt	Decl	Ex	Rec	Pay
0.30Q	07/21/2015	07/30/2015	08/03/2015	08/13/2015
0.30Q	10/22/2015	10/29/2015	11/02/2015	11/12/2015
0.30Q	02/04/2016	02/11/2016	02/16/2016	02/26/2016
0.36Q	04/21/2016	04/28/2016	05/02/2016	05/12/2016

Indicated Div: $1.44

Valuation Analysis

		Institutional Holding	
Forecast EPS	$6.58 (05/20/2016)	No of Institutions	516
Market Cap	$10.4 Billion	Shares	160,455,248
Book Value	$2.6 Billion	% Held	90.79
Price/Book	3.93		
Price/Sales	1.85		

Business Summary: Specialty Chemicals (MIC: 8.3.2 SIC: 5169 NAIC: 424690)

Celanese is a technology and specialty materials company. Co. operates four business segments: Advanced Engineered Materials, which includes its engineered materials business that uses polymer technology to produce a portfolio of specialty polymers used automotive, medical and electronics products, as well as other consumer and industrial applications; Consumer Specialties, which includes Co.'s cellulose derivatives and food ingredients businesses; Industrial Specialties, which includes Co.'s emulsion polymers and ethylene vinyl acetate polymers businesses; and Acetyl Intermediates, which includes its intermediate chemistry business, which produces and supplies acetyl products.

Recent Developments: For the quarter ended Mar 31 2016, income from continuing operations increased 10.3% to US$258.0 million from US$234.0 million in the year-earlier quarter. Net income increased 10.7% to US$259.0 million from US$234.0 million in the year-earlier quarter. Revenues were US$1.40 billion, down 3.2% from US$1.45 billion the year before. Operating income was US$287.0 million versus US$257.0 million in the prior-year quarter, an increase of 11.7%. Direct operating expenses declined 5.1% to US$1.01 billion from US$1.07 billion in the comparable period the year before. Indirect operating expenses decreased 16.9% to US$103.0 million from US$124.0 million in the equivalent prior-year period.

Prospects: Our evaluation of Celanese Corp. as of June 19, 2016 is the result of our systematic analysis on three basic characteristics: earnings strength, relative valuation, and recent stock price movement. The company has produced a positive trend in earnings per share over the past 5 quarters and while recent estimates for the company have remained steady, CE has posted better than expected results. Based on operating earnings yield, the company is undervalued when compared to all of the companies in our coverage universe. Share price changes over the past year indicates that CE will perform well over the near term.

Financial Data

(US$ in Thousands)	3 Mos	12/31/2015	12/31/2014	12/31/2013	12/31/2012	12/31/2011	12/31/2010	12/31/2009
Earnings Per Share	2.21	2.00	4.00	6.91	3.79	3.82	2.38	3.11
Cash Flow Per Share	5.96	5.71	6.21	4.80	4.55	4.08	2.92	4.15
Tang Book Value Per Share	12.19	10.55	12.67	11.21	4.94	2.45	N.M.	N.M.
Dividends Per Share	1.200	1.150	0.930	0.525	0.270	0.220	0.180	0.160
Dividend Payout %	54.30	57.50	23.25	7.60	7.12	5.76	7.56	5.14
Income Statement								
Total Revenue	1,404,000	5,674,000	6,802,000	6,510,000	6,418,000	6,763,000	5,918,000	5,082,000
EBITDA	314,000	782,000	1,133,000	1,912,000	910,000	1,075,000	823,000	682,000
Depn & Amortn	2,000	357,000	292,000	312,000	312,000	294,000	256,000	290,000
Income Before Taxes	280,000	307,000	695,000	1,429,000	415,000	563,000	370,000	193,000
Income Taxes	60,000	201,000	314,000	508,000	48,000	149,000	112,000	(243,000)
Net Income	257,000	304,000	624,000	1,101,000	605,000	607,000	377,000	488,000
Average Shares	148,131	152,287	156,166	159,334	159,796	158,947	158,372	157,115
Balance Sheet								
Current Assets	2,503,000	2,787,000	2,698,000	3,182,000	2,839,000	2,703,000	2,668,000	2,856,000
Total Assets	8,392,000	8,586,000	8,818,000	9,018,000	9,000,000	8,518,000	8,281,000	8,410,000
Current Liabilities	1,095,000	1,550,000	1,338,000	1,545,000	1,355,000	1,385,000	1,542,000	1,607,000
Long-Term Obligations	2,487,000	2,468,000	2,608,000	2,887,000	2,930,000	2,873,000	2,990,000	3,259,000
Total Liabilities	5,747,000	6,208,000	6,000,000	6,319,000	7,270,000	7,177,000	7,355,000	7,826,000
Stockholders' Equity	2,645,000	2,378,000	2,818,000	2,699,000	1,730,000	1,341,000	926,000	584,000
Shares Outstanding	147,439	146,782	152,902	156,939	159,642	156,463	155,759	144,394
Statistical Record								
Return on Assets %	3.82	3.49	7.00	12.22	6.89	7.23	4.52	6.27
Return on Equity %	11.81	11.70	22.62	49.72	39.29	53.55	49.93	127.42
EBITDA Margin %	22.36	13.78	16.66	29.37	14.18	15.90	13.91	13.42
Net Margin %	18.30	5.36	9.17	16.91	9.43	8.98	6.37	9.60
Asset Turnover	0.66	0.65	0.76	0.72	0.73	0.81	0.71	0.65
Current Ratio	2.29	1.80	2.02	2.06	2.10	1.95	1.73	1.78
Debt to Equity	0.94	1.04	0.93	1.07	1.69	2.14	3.23	5.58
Price Range	73.72-54.48	73.72-53.41	66.05-48.83	58.25-41.97	52.22-33.28	57.66-31.49	41.17-23.84	33.08-7.52
P/E Ratio	33.36-24.65	36.86-26.70	16.51-12.21	8.43-6.07	13.78-8.78	15.09-8.24	17.30-10.02	10.64-2.42
Average Yield %	1.85	1.81	1.59	1.06	0.64	0.49	0.57	0.74

Address: 222 W. Las Colinas Blvd., Suite 900N, Irving, TX 75039-5421
Telephone: 972-443-4000

Web Site: www.celanese.com
Officers: Mark C. Rohr - Chairman, Chief Executive Officer Scott M. Sutton - Executive Vice President, Division Officer

Auditors: KPMG LLP
Investor Contact: 972-443-4965
Transfer Agents: ComputerShare Investor Services, Providence, RI

CENTENE CORP

Exchange	Symbol	Price	52Wk Range	Yield	P/E
NYS	CNC	$62.35 (5/31/2016)	81.48-52.66	N/A	27.96

*7 Year Price Score 182.86 *NYSE Composite Index=100 *12 Month Price Score 95.65

Interim Earnings (Per Share)

Qtr.	Mar	Jun	Sep	Dec
2013	0.21	0.35	0.44	0.47
2014	0.28	0.41	0.68	0.88
2015	0.51	0.72	0.76	0.89
2016	(0.14)	...	...	...

Interim Dividends (Per Share)

No Dividends Paid

Valuation Analysis

		Institutional Holding	
Forecast EPS	$4.20	No of Institutions	
	(05/20/2016)	669	
Market Cap	$10.6 Billion	Shares	
Book Value	$5.3 Billion	169,530,352	
Price/Book	2.01	% Held	
Price/Sales	0.43	103.39	

TRADING VOLUME (thousand shares)

Business Summary: Hospitals & Health Care Facilities (MIC: 4.2.1 SIC: 6324 NAIC: 524114)

Centene is a healthcare enterprise that provides programs and services to government sponsored healthcare programs. Co. operates in two segments: Managed Care, which provides health plan coverage to individuals through government subsidized programs, including Medicaid, the State Children's Health Insurance Program, Long Term Care, Foster Care, dual-eligible individuals and the Supplemental Security Income Program, also known as the Aged, Blind or Disabled Program, and to individuals covered through federally facilitated and state-based Health Insurance Marketplaces; and Specialty Services, which consists of Co.'s companies providing a range of healthcare services and products.

Recent Developments: For the quarter ended Mar 31 2016, loss from continuing operations was US$15.0 million compared with income of US$65.0 million in the year-earlier quarter. Net loss amounted to US$16.0 million versus net income of US$64.0 million in the year-earlier quarter. Revenues were US$6.95 billion, up 35.5% from US$5.13 billion the year before.

Prospects: Our evaluation of Centene Corp. as of June 19, 2016 is the result of our systematic analysis on three basic characteristics: earnings strength, relative valuation, and recent stock price movement. The company has produced a positive trend in earnings per share over the past 5 quarters and while recent estimates for the company have been mixed, CNC has posted better than expected results. Based on operating earnings yield, the company is undervalued when compared to all of the companies in our coverage universe. Share price changes over the past year indicates that CNC will perform very poorly over the near term.

Financial Data

(US$ in Thousands)	3 Mos	12/31/2015	12/31/2014	12/31/2013	12/31/2012	12/31/2011	12/31/2010	12/31/2009
Earnings Per Share	2.23	2.88	2.25	1.47	0.01	1.06	0.94	0.94
Cash Flow Per Share	6.44	5.52	10.51	3.53	2.70	2.61	1.73	2.88
Tang Book Value Per Share	N.M.	9.64	7.35	7.56	6.46	6.16	4.91	4.10
Income Statement								
Total Revenue	6,953,000	22,760,000	16,560,000	10,863,329	8,667,612	5,340,582	4,448,323	4,102,864
EBITDA	44,000	818,000	557,000	348,108	58,948	237,454	209,405	186,929
Depn & Amortn	9,000	78,000	65,000	52,234	50,112	42,249	37,131	33,103
Income Before Taxes	2,000	697,000	457,000	268,917	(11,624)	174,885	154,282	137,508
Income Taxes	17,000	339,000	196,000	107,080	(329)	66,522	59,900	48,841
Net Income	(17,000)	355,000	271,000	165,099	1,859	111,218	94,836	83,671
Average Shares	125,543	123,066	120,360	112,494	107,428	104,948	100,895	88,632
Balance Sheet								
Current Assets	7,551,000	3,605,000	3,034,000	1,800,173	1,373,602	940,010	656,821	616,134
Total Assets	18,652,000	7,339,000	5,838,000	3,529,300	2,741,682	2,190,336	1,943,882	1,702,364
Current Liabilities	7,871,000	3,629,000	2,900,000	1,559,121	1,197,090	837,613	765,246	715,908
Long-Term Obligations	4,276,000	1,216,000	888,000	665,697	535,481	348,344	327,824	307,085
Total Liabilities	13,355,000	5,182,000	4,094,000	2,295,259	1,788,626	1,254,702	1,149,943	1,101,519
Stockholders' Equity	5,297,000	2,157,000	1,744,000	1,234,041	953,056	935,634	793,939	600,845
Shares Outstanding	170,449	120,342	118,433	110,638	104,658	101,729	99,233	86,358
Statistical Record								
Return on Assets %	2.17	5.39	5.79	5.27	0.08	5.38	5.20	5.31
Return on Equity %	7.71	18.20	18.20	15.10	0.20	12.86	13.60	15.18
EBITDA Margin %	0.63	3.59	3.36	3.20	0.68	4.45	4.71	4.56
Net Margin %	N.M.	1.56	1.64	1.52	0.02	2.08	2.13	2.04
Asset Turnover	1.94	3.45	3.54	3.46	3.51	2.58	2.44	2.60
Current Ratio	0.96	0.99	1.05	1.15	1.15	1.12	0.86	0.86
Debt to Equity	0.81	0.56	0.51	0.54	0.56	0.37	0.41	0.51
Price Range	81.48-52.66	81.48-51.92	53.58-27.83	33.19-20.45	25.40-13.42	20.27-12.67	13.15-8.94	11.14-7.52
P/E Ratio	36.54-23.61	28.29-18.03	23.81-12.37	22.58-13.91	N.M.	19.12-11.95	13.99-9.51	11.85-8.00

Address: 7700 Forsyth Boulevard, St. Louis, MO 63105 Telephone: 314-725-4477 Fax: 314-725-5180	Web Site: www.centene.com Officers: Michael F. Neidorff - Chairman, President, Chief Executive Officer Jeffrey A. Schwaneke - Chief Financial Officer, Executive Vice President, Senior Vice President, Vice President, Chief Accounting Officer, Corporate Controller	Auditors: KPMG LLP Transfer Agents: Broadridge Corporate Issuer Solutions, Inc., Philadelphia, PA

151

CENTERPOINT ENERGY, INC

Exchange	Symbol	Price	52Wk Range	Yield	P/E	Div Achiever
NYS	CNP	$22.53 (5/31/2016)	22.53-16.14	4.57	N/A	10 Years

*7 Year Price Score 83.75 *NYSE Composite Index=100 *12 Month Price Score 111.70

Interim Earnings (Per Share)

Qtr.	Mar	Jun	Sep	Dec
2013	0.34	(0.23)	0.35	0.26
2014	0.43	0.25	0.33	0.41
2015	0.30	0.18	(0.91)	(1.18)
2016	0.36	...	...	...

Interim Dividends (Per Share)

Amt	Decl	Ex	Rec	Pay
0.248Q	07/24/2015	08/12/2015	08/14/2015	09/10/2015
0.248Q	10/21/2015	11/10/2015	11/13/2015	12/10/2015
0.258Q	01/20/2016	02/11/2016	02/16/2016	03/10/2016
0.258Q	04/28/2016	05/12/2016	05/16/2016	06/10/2016

Indicated Div: $1.03 (Div. Reinv. Plan)

Valuation Analysis

		Institutional Holding	
Forecast EPS	$1.15 (05/20/2016)	No of Institutions	641
Market Cap	$9.7 Billion	Shares	
Book Value	$3.5 Billion		325,819,648
Price/Book	2.77	% Held	
Price/Sales	1.40		75.72

Business Summary: Electric Utilities (MIC: 3.1.1 SIC: 4911 NAIC: 221111)

CenterPoint Energy is a public utility holding company whose subsidiaries include: CenterPoint Energy Houston Electric, LLC, which engages in the electric transmission and distribution business in the Texas Gulf Coast that includes the city of Houston; and CenterPoint Energy Resources Corp. (CERC Corp), which owns and operates natural gas distribution systems. Co. also provides variable and fixed-price physical natural gas supplies primarily to commercial and industrial customers and electric and gas utilities. Co.'s business segments are electric transmission and distribution, natural gas distribution, energy services, interstate pipelines, midstream investments and other operations.

Recent Developments: For the quarter ended Mar 31 2016, net income increased 17.6% to US$154.0 million from US$131.0 million in the year-earlier quarter. Revenues were US$1.98 billion, down 18.5% from US$2.43 billion the year before. Operating income was US$250.0 million versus US$256.0 million in the prior-year quarter, a decrease of 2.3%. Direct operating expenses declined 37.1% to US$852.0 million from US$1.35 billion in the comparable period the year before. Indirect operating expenses increased 7.2% to US$882.0 million from US$823.0 million in the equivalent prior-year period.

Prospects: Our evaluation of Centerpoint Energy Inc. as of June 19, 2016 is the result of our systematic analysis on three basic characteristics: earnings strength, relative valuation, and recent stock price movement. The company has managed to produce a neutral trend in earnings per share over the past 5 quarters and while recent estimates for the company have remained steady, CNP has posted better than expected results. Based on operating earnings yield, the company is about fairly valued when compared to all of the companies in our coverage universe. Share price changes over the past year indicates that CNP will perform well over the near term.

Financial Data

(US$ in Thousands)	3 Mos	12/31/2015	12/31/2014	12/31/2013	12/31/2012	12/31/2011	12/31/2010	12/31/2009
Earnings Per Share	(1.55)	(1.61)	1.42	0.72	0.97	3.17	1.07	1.01
Cash Flow Per Share	4.26	4.34	3.25	3.76	4.34	4.44	3.38	5.04
Tang Book Value Per Share	6.19	6.10	8.62	8.13	6.62	5.93	3.53	2.41
Dividends Per Share	1.000	0.990	0.950	0.830	0.810	0.790	0.780	0.760
Dividend Payout %	...	...	66.90	115.28	83.51	24.92	72.90	75.25
Income Statement								
Total Revenue	1,984,000	7,386,000	9,226,000	8,106,000	7,452,000	8,450,000	8,785,000	8,281,000
EBITDA	297,000	1,930,000	2,061,000	1,608,000	1,857,000	2,256,000	1,828,000	1,673,000
Depn & Amortn	6,000	970,000	1,013,000	531,000	562,000	529,000	531,000	496,000
Income Before Taxes	180,000	503,000	577,000	593,000	726,000	1,144,000	676,000	533,000
Income Taxes	86,000	(438,000)	274,000	470,000	340,000	404,000	263,000	176,000
Net Income	154,000	(692,000)	611,000	311,000	417,000	1,357,000	442,000	372,000
Average Shares	433,000	430,000	432,000	430,930	429,794	428,724	413,000	367,681
Balance Sheet								
Current Assets	2,335,000	2,689,000	3,268,000	2,658,000	2,874,000	2,337,000	2,582,000	2,904,000
Total Assets	21,004,000	21,334,000	23,200,000	21,870,000	22,871,000	21,703,000	20,111,000	19,773,000
Current Liabilities	2,534,000	2,467,000	3,475,000	3,019,000	3,575,000	2,593,000	2,620,000	3,038,000
Long-Term Obligations	7,354,000	7,901,000	8,009,000	7,817,000	8,357,000	8,641,000	9,001,000	9,119,000
Total Liabilities	17,498,000	17,873,000	18,652,000	17,541,000	18,570,000	17,481,000	16,913,000	17,134,000
Stockholders' Equity	3,506,000	3,461,000	4,548,000	4,329,000	4,301,000	4,222,000	3,198,000	2,639,000
Shares Outstanding	430,614	430,000	430,000	429,000	428,000	426,000	425,000	391,000
Statistical Record								
Return on Assets %	N.M.	N.M.	2.71	1.39	1.87	6.49	2.22	1.89
Return on Equity %	N.M.	N.M.	13.77	7.21	9.76	36.58	15.14	15.91
EBITDA Margin %	14.97	26.13	22.34	19.84	24.92	26.70	20.81	20.20
Net Margin %	7.76	N.M.	6.62	3.84	5.60	16.06	5.03	4.49
Asset Turnover	0.32	0.33	0.41	0.36	0.33	0.40	0.44	0.42
Current Ratio	0.92	1.09	0.94	0.88	0.80	0.90	0.99	0.96
Debt to Equity	2.10	2.28	1.76	1.81	1.94	2.05	2.81	3.46
Price Range	21.31-16.14	23.63-16.14	25.54-21.54	25.16-19.25	21.75-18.23	21.29-15.20	16.92-12.90	14.81-8.88
P/E Ratio	...	...	17.99-15.17	34.94-26.74	22.42-18.79	6.72-4.79	15.81-12.06	14.66-8.79
Average Yield %	5.30	5.05	3.95	3.58	4.03	4.27	5.30	6.38

Address: 1111 Louisiana, Houston, TX 77002	**Web Site:** www.centerpointenergy.com	**Auditors:** Deloitte & Touche LLP
Telephone: 713-207-1111	**Officers:** Milton Carroll - Executive Chairman Scott M. Prochazka - President, Chief Executive Officer, Executive Vice President, Chief Operating Officer	**Investor Contact:** 713-207-6500 **Transfer Agents:** CenterPoint Energy Investor Services

CENTURYLINK, INC.

Exchange	Symbol	Price	52Wk Range	Yield	P/E
NYS	CTL	$27.12 (5/31/2016)	32.99-22.24	7.96	16.14

*7 Year Price Score 67.54   *NYSE Composite Index=100   *12 Month Price Score 106.98

Interim Earnings (Per Share)

Qtr.	Mar	Jun	Sep	Dec
2013	0.48	0.44	(1.76)	0.39
2014	0.35	0.04	0.33	0.34
2015	0.34	0.26	0.37	0.61
2016	0.44	...	...	...

Interim Dividends (Per Share)

Amt	Decl	Ex	Rec	Pay
0.54Q	08/25/2015	09/03/2015	09/08/2015	09/22/2015
0.54Q	11/10/2015	11/20/2015	11/24/2015	12/08/2015
0.54Q	02/23/2016	03/02/2016	03/04/2016	03/18/2016
0.54Q	05/18/2016	05/26/2016	05/31/2016	06/14/2016

Indicated Div: $2.16 (Div. Reinv. Plan)

Valuation Analysis

Forecast EPS	$2.59 (05/20/2016)
Market Cap	$14.8 Billion
Book Value	$14.0 Billion
Price/Book	1.06
Price/Sales	0.83

Institutional Holding

No of Institutions	916
Shares	434,947,584
% Held	73.15

Business Summary: Services (MIC: 6.1.2 SIC: 4813 NAIC: 517110)

CenturyLink is a holding company. Through its subsidiaries, Co. is a communications company engaged primarily in providing a range of communications services. Co.'s communications services include local and long-distance voice, internet, Multi Protocol Label Switching, private line (including special access), data integration, Ethernet, colocation, managed hosting (including cloud hosting), network, public access, wireless, video and other services. Co. has two segments: Business, which provides products and services to enterprise, wholesale and governmental customers, including other communication providers; and Consumer, which provides products and services to residential consumers.

Recent Developments: For the quarter ended Mar 31 2016, net income increased 22.9% to US$236.0 million from US$192.0 million in the year-earlier quarter. Revenues were US$4.40 billion, down 1.1% from US$4.45 billion the year before. Operating income was US$694.0 million versus US$649.0 million in the prior-year quarter, an increase of 6.9%. Direct operating expenses declined 0.6% to US$1.90 billion from US$1.91 billion in the comparable period the year before. Indirect operating expenses decreased 4.4% to US$1.81 billion from US$1.89 billion in the equivalent prior-year period.

Prospects: Our evaluation of CenturyLink, Inc. as of June 19, 2016 is the result of our systematic analysis on three basic characteristics: earnings strength, relative valuation, and recent stock price movement. The company has produced a positive trend in earnings per share over the past 5 quarters. However, while recent estimates for the company have been mixed, CTL has posted better than expected results. Based on operating earnings yield, the company is undervalued when compared to all of the companies in our coverage universe. Share price changes over the past year indicates that CTL will perform well over the near term.

Financial Data
(US$ in Thousands)

	3 Mos	12/31/2015	12/31/2014	12/31/2013	12/31/2012	12/31/2011	12/31/2010	12/31/2009
Earnings Per Share	1.68	1.58	1.36	(0.40)	1.25	1.07	3.13	3.23
Cash Flow Per Share	9.72	9.29	9.13	9.25	9.75	7.89	6.80	7.92
Dividends Per Share	2.160	2.160	2.160	2.160	2.900	2.900	2.900	2.800
Dividend Payout %	128.57	136.71	158.82	...	232.00	271.03	92.65	86.69
Income Statement								
Total Revenue	4,401,000	17,900,000	18,031,000	18,095,000	18,376,000	15,351,000	7,041,534	4,974,239
EBITDA	710,000	5,428,000	5,379,000	4,474,000	5,667,000	4,621,000	3,316,563	2,023,726
Depn & Amortn	(1,000)	2,836,000	2,958,000	2,952,000	3,098,000	2,601,000	1,227,000	838,800
Income Before Taxes	380,000	1,280,000	1,110,000	224,000	1,250,000	948,000	1,532,085	814,512
Income Taxes	144,000	402,000	338,000	463,000	473,000	375,000	582,951	301,881
Net Income	236,000	878,000	772,000	(239,000)	777,000	573,000	947,705	647,211
Average Shares	540,187	555,093	569,739	600,892	622,285	534,121	301,297	199,057
Balance Sheet								
Current Assets	2,926,000	2,650,000	3,576,000	3,907,000	3,613,000	3,523,000	1,143,129	1,123,591
Total Assets	47,517,000	47,604,000	50,147,000	51,787,000	54,020,000	56,139,000	22,038,098	22,562,729
Current Liabilities	3,826,000	4,604,000	3,918,000	4,409,000	4,595,000	4,019,000	1,011,042	1,707,195
Long-Term Obligations	19,508,000	18,722,000	20,121,000	20,181,000	19,400,000	21,356,000	7,316,004	7,253,653
Total Liabilities	33,481,000	33,544,000	35,124,000	34,596,000	34,731,000	35,312,000	12,396,857	13,101,790
Stockholders' Equity	14,036,000	14,060,000	15,023,000	17,191,000	19,289,000	20,827,000	9,641,241	9,460,939
Shares Outstanding	546,164	543,800	568,517	583,637	625,658	618,514	304,947	299,189
Statistical Record								
Return on Assets %	1.90	1.80	1.51	N.M.	1.41	1.47	4.25	4.20
Return on Equity %	6.40	6.04	4.79	N.M.	3.86	3.76	9.92	10.25
EBITDA Margin %	16.13	30.32	29.83	24.73	30.84	30.10	47.10	40.68
Net Margin %	5.36	4.91	4.28	N.M.	4.23	3.73	13.46	13.01
Asset Turnover	0.37	0.37	0.35	0.34	0.33	0.39	0.32	0.32
Current Ratio	0.76	0.58	0.91	0.89	0.79	0.88	1.13	0.66
Debt to Equity	1.39	1.33	1.34	1.17	1.01	1.03	0.76	0.77
Price Range	36.78-22.24	40.52-24.38	41.81-28.09	41.76-30.30	42.95-36.59	46.73-31.82	46.80-32.93	36.82-23.56
P/E Ratio	21.89-13.24	25.65-15.43	30.74-20.65	...	34.36-29.27	43.67-29.74	14.95-10.52	11.40-7.29
Average Yield %	7.41	6.87	5.92	6.18	7.37	7.49	7.82	9.13

Address: 100 CenturyLink Drive, Monroe, LA 71203
Telephone: 318 388-9000
Fax: 318-789-8656

Web Site: www.centurylink.com
Officers: Glen F. Post - President, Chief Executive Officer David D. Cole - Executive Vice President, Senior Vice President, Controller

Auditors: KPMG LLP
Investor Contact: 800-833-1188
Transfer Agents: Computershare Trust Company, Providence, RI

CF INDUSTRIES HOLDINGS INC

Exchange	Symbol	Price	52Wk Range	Yield	P/E
NYS	CF	$27.66 (5/31/2016)	68.92-27.61	4.34	13.11

*7 Year Price Score 104.93 *NYSE Composite Index=100   *12 Month Price Score 68.39

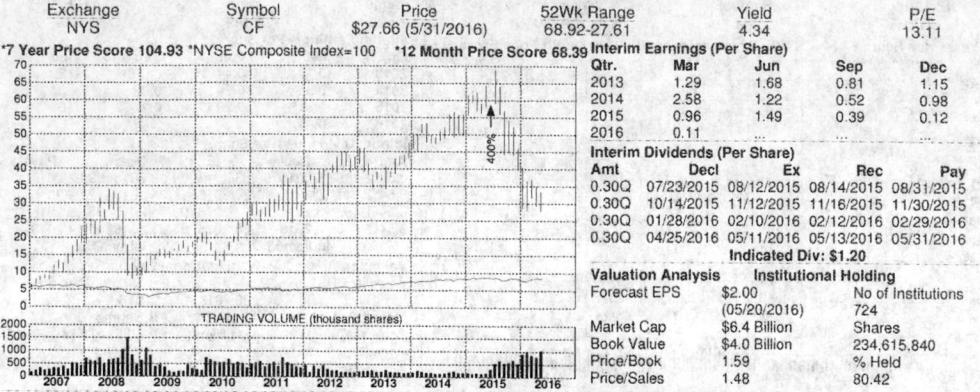

Interim Earnings (Per Share)

Qtr.	Mar	Jun	Sep	Dec
2013	1.29	1.68	0.81	1.15
2014	2.58	1.22	0.52	0.98
2015	0.96	1.49	0.39	0.12
2016	0.11	...	...	...

Interim Dividends (Per Share)

Amt	Decl	Ex	Rec	Pay
0.30Q	07/23/2015	08/12/2015	08/14/2015	08/31/2015
0.30Q	10/14/2015	11/16/2015	11/16/2015	11/30/2015
0.30Q	01/28/2016	02/10/2016	02/12/2016	02/29/2016
0.30Q	04/25/2016	05/11/2016	05/13/2016	05/31/2016

Indicated Div: $1.20

Valuation Analysis

Forecast EPS	$2.00 (05/20/2016)
Market Cap	$6.4 Billion
Book Value	$4.0 Billion
Price/Book	1.59
Price/Sales	1.48

Institutional Holding

No of Institutions	724
Shares	234,615,840
% Held	80.42

Business Summary: Agricultural Chemicals (MIC: 8.3.3 SIC: 2875 NAIC: 325314)

CF Industries Holdings is engaged in manufacturing and distributing nitrogen fertilizer and other nitrogen products. Co.'s principal nitrogen fertilizer products are ammonia, granular urea, urea ammonium nitrate solution (UAN) and ammonium nitrate (AN). Co.'s other nitrogen products include diesel exhaust fluid, urea liquor, nitric acid and aqua ammonia. Co. also exports nitrogen fertilizer products, primarily from its Donaldsonville, LA; Yazoo City, MS; and Billingham, the U.K. manufacturing facilities. Co.'s reportable segments consist of ammonia, granular urea, UAN, AN, Other, and phosphate. Co.'s customers are cooperatives, fertilizer distributors, farmers and industrial users.

Recent Developments: For the quarter ended Mar 31 2016, net income decreased 80.1% to US$47.0 million from US$236.0 million in the year-earlier quarter. Revenues were US$1.00 billion, up 5.2% from US$954.0 million the year before. Operating income was US$97.0 million versus US$367.0 million in the prior-year quarter, a decrease of 73.6%. Direct operating expenses rose 46.3% to US$787.0 million from US$538.0 million in the comparable period the year before. Indirect operating expenses increased 144.9% to US$120.0 million from US$49.0 million in the equivalent prior-year period.

Prospects: Our evaluation of CF Industries Holdings Inc. as of June 19, 2016 is the result of our systematic analysis on three basic characteristics: earnings strength, relative valuation, and recent stock price movement. The company has generated a negative trend in earnings per share over the past 5 quarters. However, while recent estimates for the company have been lowered by analysts, CF has posted results that fell short of analysts expectations. Based on operating earnings yield, the company is undervalued when compared to all of the companies in our coverage universe. Share price changes over the past year indicates that CF will perform poorly over the near term.

Financial Data

(US$ in Thousands)	3 Mos	12/31/2015	12/31/2014	12/31/2013	12/31/2012	12/31/2011	12/31/2010	12/31/2009
Earnings Per Share	2.11	2.96	5.42	4.95	5.72	4.40	1.07	1.48
Cash Flow Per Share	4.37	5.12	5.50	4.98	7.42	5.99	3.69	2.81
Tang Book Value Per Share	7.11	7.06	8.76	10.51	12.04	7.43	5.35	7.12
Dividends Per Share	1.200	1.200	1.000	0.440	0.320	0.200	0.080	0.080
Dividend Payout %	56.87	40.54	18.46	8.89	5.60	4.55	7.49	5.39
Income Statement								
Total Revenue	1,004,000	4,308,300	4,743,200	5,474,700	6,104,000	6,097,900	3,965,000	2,608,400
EBITDA	245,000	1,289,600	2,375,400	2,726,100	3,333,300	3,157,100	1,291,700	793,600
Depn & Amortn	146,000	65,400	53,900	410,600	419,800	416,200	394,800	101,000
Income Before Taxes	62,000	1,092,600	2,144,200	2,168,000	2,782,500	2,595,400	677,100	695,600
Income Taxes	15,000	395,800	773,000	686,500	964,200	926,500	273,700	246,000
Net Income	26,000	699,900	1,390,300	1,464,600	1,848,700	1,539,200	349,200	365,600
Average Shares	233,500	236,100	256,500	296,000	323,500	350,000	327,000	246,000
Balance Sheet								
Current Assets	3,520,000	1,127,100	2,614,500	2,630,100	2,807,600	1,798,600	1,341,400	1,283,100
Total Assets	15,581,000	12,738,900	11,338,200	10,678,100	10,166,900	8,974,500	8,758,500	2,494,900
Current Liabilities	1,273,000	1,215,200	979,700	828,300	950,200	1,031,200	946,600	479,800
Long-Term Obligations	5,539,000	5,592,700	4,592,500	3,098,100	1,600,000	1,617,800	1,954,100	4,700
Total Liabilities	11,539,000	8,703,700	7,128,500	5,602,000	4,264,700	4,427,500	4,708,100	766,000
Stockholders' Equity	4,042,000	4,035,200	4,209,700	5,076,100	5,902,200	4,547,000	4,050,400	1,728,900
Shares Outstanding	233,079	233,081	241,673	279,240	314,753	327,102	356,335	242,849
Statistical Record								
Return on Assets %	3.66	5.81	12.63	14.05	19.26	17.36	6.21	14.98
Return on Equity %	12.22	16.98	29.94	26.68	35.29	35.81	12.08	23.84
EBITDA Margin %	24.40	29.93	50.08	49.79	54.61	51.77	32.58	30.42
Net Margin %	2.59	16.25	29.31	26.75	30.29	25.24	8.81	14.02
Asset Turnover	0.32	0.36	0.43	0.53	0.64	0.69	0.70	1.07
Current Ratio	2.77	0.93	2.67	3.18	2.95	1.74	1.42	2.67
Debt to Equity	1.37	1.39	1.09	0.61	0.27	0.36	0.48	N.M.
Price Range	68.92-27.83	68.92-40.07	56.55-44.98	47.41-34.06	44.90-30.76	37.96-24.20	27.33-11.71	18.99-8.85
P/E Ratio	32.66-13.19	23.28-13.54	10.43-8.30	9.58-6.88	7.85-5.38	8.63-5.50	25.55-10.95	12.83-5.98
Average Yield %	2.41	2.13	1.99	1.09	0.83	0.72	0.42	0.53

Address: 4 Parkway North, Suite 400, Deerfield, IL 60015 Telephone: 847-405-2400	Web Site: www.cfindustries.com Officers: Stephen A. Furbacher - Chairman W. Anthony Will - President, Chief Executive Officer, Senior Vice President, Vice President	Auditors: KPMG LLP Investor Contact: 847-405-2550 Transfer Agents: Computershare, Providence, RI

CHARLES RIVER LABORATORIES INTERNATIONAL INC.

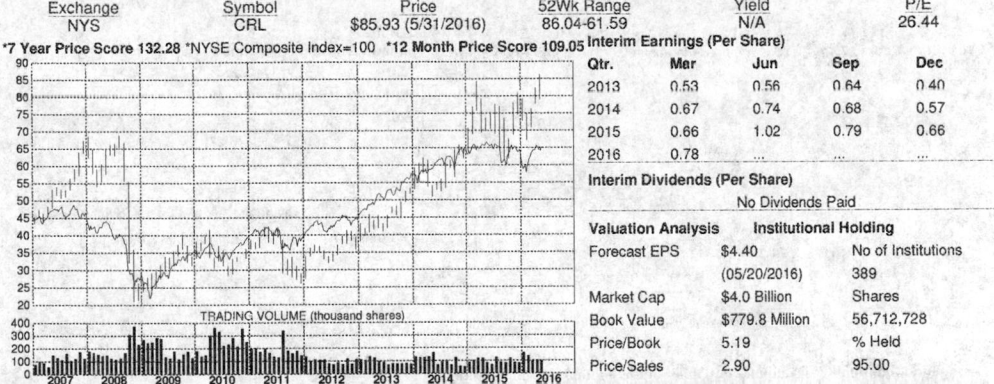

Exchange	Symbol	Price	52Wk Range	Yield	P/E
NYS	CRL	$85.93 (5/31/2016)	86.04-61.59	N/A	26.44

*7 Year Price Score 132.28 *NYSE Composite Index=100 *12 Month Price Score 109.05

Interim Earnings (Per Share)

Qtr.	Mar	Jun	Sep	Dec
2013	0.53	0.56	0.64	0.40
2014	0.67	0.74	0.68	0.57
2015	0.66	1.02	0.79	0.66
2016	0.78	...	...	...

Interim Dividends (Per Share)

No Dividends Paid

Valuation Analysis — **Institutional Holding**

Forecast EPS	$4.40	No of Institutions
	(05/20/2016)	389
Market Cap	$4.0 Billion	Shares
Book Value	$779.8 Million	56,712,728
Price/Book	5.19	% Held
Price/Sales	2.90	95.00

Business Summary: Biotechnology (MIC: 4.1.2 SIC: 8731 NAIC: 541710)

Charles River Laboratories International is a provider of laboratory animal medicine and science to develop a portfolio of discovery and safety assessment services. Co. has three segments: Research Models and Services, which is engaged in supplying research models to the drug development industry; Discovery and Safety Assessment, which provides discovery and safety assessment services in which Co. includes both in vivo and in vitro studies, supporting laboratory services, and preclinical consulting and program management to support product development; and Manufacturing Support, which includes Microbial Solutions, Avian Vaccine Services and Biologics Testing Solutions.

Recent Developments: For the quarter ended Mar 26 2016, income from continuing operations increased 18.8% to US$37.6 million from US$31.6 million in the year-earlier quarter. Net income increased 18.8% to US$37.5 million from US$31.6 million in the year-earlier quarter. Revenues were US$354.9 million, up 10.8% from US$320.4 million the year before. Operating income was US$51.5 million versus US$43.0 million in the prior-year quarter, an increase of 19.7%. Direct operating expenses rose 6.6% to US$214.1 million from US$200.8 million in the comparable period the year before. Indirect operating expenses increased 16.5% to US$89.3 million from US$76.7 million in the equivalent prior-year period.

Prospects: Our evaluation of Charles River Laboratories International Inc. as of June 19, 2016 is the result of our systematic analysis on three basic characteristics: earnings strength, relative valuation, and recent stock price movement. The company has managed to produce a neutral trend in earnings per share over the past 5 quarters and while recent estimates for the company have been mixed, CRL has posted better than expected results. Based on operating earnings yield, the company is about fairly valued when compared to all of the companies in our coverage universe. Share price changes over the past year indicates that CRL will perform well over the near term.

Financial Data
(US$ in Thousands)

	3 Mos	12/26/2015	12/27/2014	12/28/2013	12/29/2012	12/31/2011	12/25/2010	12/26/2009
Earnings Per Share	3.25	3.13	2.66	2.12	2.01	2.14	(5.38)	1.74
Cash Flow Per Share	6.76	6.22	5.42	4.39	4.35	4.00	2.70	3.34
Tang Book Value Per Share	1.71	0.29	3.64	6.85	6.37	4.80	6.52	10.73
Income Statement								
Total Revenue	354,868	1,363,302	1,297,662	1,165,528	1,129,530	1,142,647	1,133,416	1,202,551
EBITDA	55,907	304,386	284,848	255,202	243,774	259,126	(206,340)	262,565
Depn & Amortn	409	94,929	96,457	96,636	81,275	85,231	93,649	93,553
Income Before Taxes	51,550	195,428	177,595	138,327	129,746	132,662	(334,082)	149,107
Income Taxes	13,975	43,391	47,671	32,911	27,628	17,140	23	39,725
Net Income	37,143	149,313	126,698	102,828	97,295	109,566	(336,669)	114,441
Average Shares	47,617	47,634	47,558	48,489	48,406	51,318	62,561	65,635
Balance Sheet								
Current Assets	637,391	559,234	606,898	552,550	485,252	425,843	552,894	595,601
Total Assets	2,103,718	2,068,497	1,885,192	1,644,621	1,586,344	1,558,320	1,733,373	2,204,093
Current Liabilities	309,989	311,761	296,170	247,034	342,247	216,797	259,780	249,773
Long-Term Obligations	840,481	845,997	745,958	641,808	527,075	703,170	670,270	457,419
Total Liabilities	1,323,894	1,335,430	1,212,989	1,003,637	985,539	1,032,737	1,045,950	828,850
Stockholders' Equity	779,824	733,067	672,203	640,984	600,805	525,583	687,423	1,375,243
Shares Outstanding	47,114	46,698	47,327	47,553	48,220	48,875	56,441	65,877
Statistical Record								
Return on Assets %	7.84	7.57	7.20	6.38	6.20	6.55	N.M.	5.26
Return on Equity %	21.46	21.31	19.35	16.61	17.32	17.77	N.M.	8.92
EBITDA Margin %	15.75	22.33	21.95	21.90	21.58	22.68	N.M.	21.83
Net Margin %	10.47	10.95	9.76	8.82	8.61	9.59	N.M.	9.52
Asset Turnover	0.71	0.69	0.74	0.72	0.72	0.68	0.58	0.55
Current Ratio	2.06	1.79	2.05	2.24	1.42	1.96	2.13	2.38
Debt to Equity	1.08	1.15	1.11	1.00	0.88	1.34	0.98	0.33
Price Range	80.54-61.59	84.20-61.59	65.59-50.74	53.33-37.47	41.24-27.39	42.47-25.95	41.56-28.25	40.09-23.15
P/E Ratio	24.78-18.95	26.90-19.68	24.66-19.08	25.16-17.67	20.52-13.63	19.85-12.13	...	23.04-13.30

Address: 251 Ballardvale Street, Wilmington, MA 01887 **Telephone:** 781-222-6000	**Web Site:** www.criver.com **Officers:** James C. Foster - Chairman, President, Chief Executive Officer David R. Smith Executive Vice President, Chief Financial Officer	**Auditors:** PricewaterhouseCoopers LLP **Investor Contact:** 781-222-6000 **Transfer Agent:** ComputerShare Investor Services, Providence, RI

CHESAPEAKE ENERGY CORP.

Exchange	Symbol	Price	52Wk Range	Yield	P/E
NYS	CHK	$4.29 (5/31/2016)	14.05-1.59	N/A	N/A

*7 Year Price Score 27.41   *NYSE Composite Index=100   *12 Month Price Score 80.17

Interim Earnings (Per Share)

Qtr.	Mar	Jun	Sep	Dec
2013	0.02	0.66	0.24	(0.23)
2014	0.54	0.22	0.26	0.83
2015	(5.72)	(6.27)	(7.08)	(3.36)
2016	(1.44)	...	...	...

Interim Dividends (Per Share)

Dividend Payment Suspended

Valuation Analysis   **Institutional Holding**

Forecast EPS	$-0.36	No of Institutions
	(05/20/2016)	779
Market Cap	$2.9 Billion	Shares
Book Value	$1.3 Billion	565,060,032
Price/Book	2.24	% Held
Price/Sales	0.25	84.92

Business Summary: Production & Extraction (MIC: 9.1.1 SIC: 1311 NAIC: 211111)

Chesapeake Energy is an oil and natural gas exploration and production company engaged in the acquisition, exploration and development of properties for the production of oil, natural gas and natural gas liquids (NGL) from underground reservoirs. Co. also owns oil and natural gas marketing and natural gas gathering and compression businesses. Co.'s operations are located onshore in the U.S. Co. has two geographic operating divisions: Southern Division, and Northern Division. As of Dec 31 2015, Co. had estimated total proved reserves of 314.0 million barrels of oil, 6.04 billion cubic feet of natural gas, and 183.0 million barrels of NGL.

Recent Developments: For the quarter ended Mar 31 2016, net loss amounted to US$921.0 million versus a net loss of US$3.72 billion in the year-earlier quarter. Revenues were US$1.95 billion, down 39.3% from US$3.22 billion the year before. Operating loss was US$952.0 million versus a loss of US$5.04 billion in the prior-year quarter. Direct operating expenses declined 33.7% to US$1.65 billion from US$2.49 billion in the comparable period the year before. Indirect operating expenses decreased 78.2% to US$1.26 billion from US$5.77 billion in the equivalent prior-year period.

Prospects: Our evaluation of Chesapeake Energy Corp. as of June 19, 2016 is the result of our systematic analysis on three basic characteristics: earnings strength, relative valuation, and recent stock price movement. The company has enjoyed a very positive trend in earnings per share over the past 5 quarters. Because the company lacks sufficient analyst estimate data, we place greater weight on the historical EPS trend as the measure of earnings strength. Based on operating earnings yield, the company is overvalued when compared to all of the companies in our coverage universe. Share price changes over the past year indicates that CHK will perform very poorly over the near term.

Financial Data

(US$ in Thousands)	3 Mos	12/31/2015	12/31/2014	12/31/2013	12/31/2012	12/31/2011	12/31/2010	12/31/2009
Earnings Per Share	(18.15)	(22.43)	1.87	0.73	(1.46)	2.32	2.51	(9.57)
Cash Flow Per Share	0.58	1.86	7.03	7.07	4.40	9.27	8.11	7.12
Tang Book Value Per Share	...	...	20.87	19.47	18.83	20.57	18.65	16.95
Dividends Per Share	0.087	0.175	0.350	0.350	0.350	0.250	0.300	0.300
Dividend Payout %	...	...	18.72	47.95	...	10.78	11.95	...
Income Statement								
Total Revenue	1,953,000	12,764,000	20,951,000	17,506,000	12,316,000	11,635,000	9,366,000	7,702,000
EBITDA	(559,000)	(16,552,000)	6,204,000	4,572,000	1,914,000	4,847,000	4,368,000	(7,481,000)
Depn & Amortn	300,000	2,229,000	2,915,000	2,903,000	2,811,000	1,923,000	1,692,000	1,694,000
Income Before Taxes	(921,000)	(19,098,000)	3,200,000	1,442,000	(974,000)	2,880,000	2,657,000	(9,288,000)
Income Taxes	...	(4,463,000)	1,144,000	548,000	(380,000)	1,123,000	1,110,000	(3,483,000)
Net Income	(921,000)	(14,685,000)	1,917,000	724,000	(769,000)	1,742,000	1,774,000	(5,830,000)
Average Shares	668,000	662,000	772,000	653,000	643,000	752,000	706,000	612,000
Balance Sheet								
Current Assets	1,492,000	2,480,000	7,468,000	3,656,000	2,948,000	3,177,000	3,266,000	2,446,000
Total Assets	15,357,000	17,357,000	40,751,000	41,782,000	41,611,000	41,835,000	37,179,000	29,914,000
Current Liabilities	2,833,000	3,685,000	5,863,000	5,515,000	6,266,000	7,082,000	4,490,000	2,688,000
Long-Term Obligations	10,062,000	10,383,000	11,184,000	12,917,000	12,356,000	10,824,000	12,640,000	12,295,000
Total Liabilities	14,046,000	15,219,000	23,848,000	25,787,000	26,042,000	25,211,000	21,915,000	18,470,000
Stockholders' Equity	1,311,000	2,138,000	16,903,000	15,995,000	15,569,000	16,624,000	15,264,000	11,444,000
Shares Outstanding	683,176	663,357	663,329	664,190	664,319	659,335	654,029	647,671
Statistical Record								
Return on Assets %	N.M.	N.M.	4.65	1.74	N.M.	4.41	5.29	N.M.
Return on Equity %	N.M.	N.M.	11.65	4.59	N.M.	10.93	13.28	N.M.
EBITDA Margin %	N.M.	N.M.	29.61	26.12	15.54	41.66	46.64	N.M.
Net Margin %	N.M.	N.M.	9.15	4.14	N.M.	14.97	18.94	N.M.
Asset Turnover	0.48	0.44	0.51	0.42	0.29	0.29	0.28	0.23
Current Ratio	0.53	0.67	1.27	0.66	0.47	0.45	0.73	0.91
Debt to Equity	7.68	4.86	0.66	0.81	0.79	0.65	0.83	1.07
Price Range	16.54-1.59	21.26-3.72	29.50-16.71	27.13-15.62	24.07-12.75	33.50-20.75	27.25-18.85	27.72-12.70
P/E Ratio	...	...	15.78-8.94	37.17-21.39	...	14.44-8.95	10.86-7.51	...
Average Yield %	1.07	1.51	1.42	1.63	1.90	0.90	1.37	1.47

Address: 6100 North Western Avenue, Oklahoma City, OK 73118 Telephone: 405-848-8000	Web Site: www.chk.com Officers: Robert Douglas Lawler - President, Chief Executive Officer Domenic J. (Nick) Dell'Osso - Executive Vice President, Chief Financial Officer	Auditors: PricewaterhouseCoopers LLP Investor Contact: 405-935-4763 Transfer Agents: Computershare Trust Company, N.A., Canton, MA

CHESAPEAKE UTILITIES CORP.

Exchange	Symbol	Price	52Wk Range	Yield	P/E	Div Achiever
NYS	CPK	$57.69 (5/31/2016)	66.37-46.62	2.11	21.94	12 Years

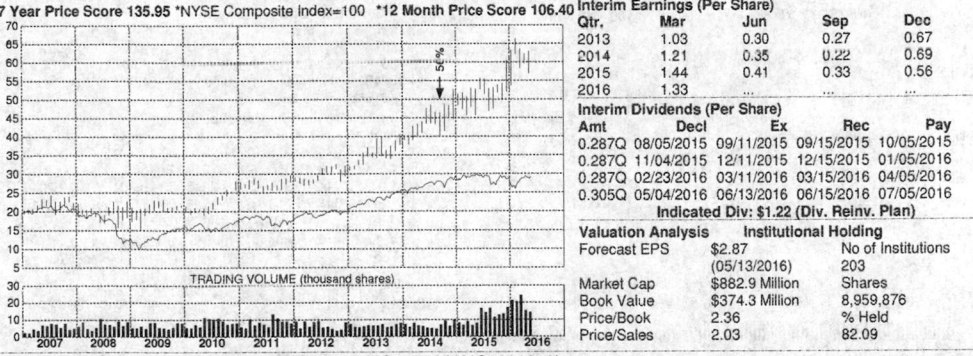

*7 Year Price Score 135.95 *NYSE Composite Index=100 *12 Month Price Score 106.40

Interim Earnings (Per Share)

Qtr.	Mar	Jun	Sep	Dec
2013	1.03	0.30	0.27	0.67
2014	1.21	0.35	0.22	0.69
2015	1.44	0.41	0.33	0.56
2016	1.33	...	...	...

Interim Dividends (Per Share)

Amt	Decl	Ex	Rec	Pay
0.287Q	08/05/2015	09/11/2015	09/15/2015	10/05/2015
0.287Q	11/04/2015	12/11/2015	12/15/2015	01/05/2016
0.287Q	02/23/2016	03/11/2016	03/15/2016	04/05/2016
0.305Q	05/04/2016	06/13/2016	06/15/2016	07/05/2016

Indicated Div: $1.22 (Div. Reinv. Plan)

Valuation Analysis / Institutional Holding

Valuation Analysis		Institutional Holding	
Forecast EPS	$2.87	No of Institutions	
	(05/13/2016)	203	
Market Cap	$882.9 Million	Shares	
Book Value	$374.3 Million	8,959,876	
Price/Book	2.36	% Held	
Price/Sales	2.03	82.09	

Business Summary: Gas Utilities (MIC: 3.3.1 SIC: 4923 NAIC: 221210)

Chesapeake Utilities is a utility company engaged in regulated energy businesses, unregulated energy businesses, and other unregulated businesses, including information services. Co. operates within three segments: Regulated Energy, which includes natural gas distribution, natural gas transmission and electric distribution operations; Unregulated Energy, which includes propane distribution, propane wholesale marketing and natural gas marketing operations, as well as other unregulated energy services, such as energy-related merchandise sales and heating, ventilation and air conditioning, plumbing and electrical services; and Other, which consists primarily of information services operation.

Recent Developments: For the quarter ended Mar 31 2016, net income decreased 3.5% to US$20.4 million from US$21.1 million in the year-earlier quarter. Revenues were US$146.3 million, down 14.0% from US$170.1 million the year before. Operating income was US$36.4 million versus US$37.5 million in the prior-year quarter, a decrease of 3.0%. Direct operating expenses declined 19.2% to US$98.6 million from US$122.0 million in the comparable period the year before. Indirect operating expenses increased 7.5% to US$11.3 million from US$10.6 million in the equivalent prior-year period.

Prospects: Our evaluation of Chesapeake Utilities Corp. as of June 19, 2016 is the result of our systematic analysis on three basic characteristics: earnings strength, relative valuation, and recent stock price movement. The company has managed to produce a neutral trend in earnings per share over the past 5 quarters. However, while recent estimates for the company have been mixed, CPK has posted better than expected results. Based on operating earnings yield, the company is about fairly valued when compared to all of the companies in our coverage universe. Share price changes over the past year indicates that CPK will perform very well over the near term.

Financial Data

(US$ in Thousands)	3 Mos	12/31/2015	12/31/2014	12/31/2013	12/31/2012	12/31/2011	12/31/2010	12/31/2009
Earnings Per Share	2.63	2.72	2.47	2.26	1.99	1.91	1.82	1.43
Cash Flow Per Share	5.46	6.97	5.45	5.05	4.57	4.96	4.29	4.18
Tang Book Value Per Share	23.33	22.35	20.08	18.78	17.35	16.28	13.10	12.19
Dividends Per Share	1.150	1.133	1.067	1.013	0.960	0.910	0.870	0.833
Dividend Payout %	43.73	41.64	43.18	44.84	48.16	47.56	47.80	58.14
Income Statement								
Total Revenue	146,296	459,244	498,834	444,306	392,502	418,027	427,546	268,785
EBITDA	37,992	85,029	76,096	69,229	62,453	59,727	55,258	36,690
Depn & Amortn	1,646	6,978	6,577	6,123	5,547	5,116	3,133	2,789
Income Before Taxes	33,696	68,045	60,037	54,872	48,159	45,611	42,979	26,815
Income Taxes	13,329	26,905	23,945	22,085	19,296	17,989	16,923	10,918
Net Income	20,367	41,140	36,092	32,787	28,863	27,622	26,056	15,897
Average Shares	15,331	15,143	14,604	14,543	14,507	14,476	14,373	11,160
Balance Sheet								
Current Assets	100,375	112,538	122,373	126,409	100,597	127,760	137,229	116,575
Total Assets	1,081,984	1,068,586	904,469	837,522	733,746	709,066	670,993	617,102
Current Liabilities	274,449	279,593	194,235	221,942	162,166	157,499	197,642	170,600
Long-Term Obligations	148,602	149,340	158,486	117,592	101,907	110,285	89,642	98,814
Total Liabilities	707,732	710,448	604,147	558,749	477,148	468,286	444,754	407,321
Stockholders' Equity	374,252	358,138	300,322	278,773	256,598	240,780	226,239	209,781
Shares Outstanding	15,304	15,270	14,588	14,457	14,396	14,350	14,286	14,091
Statistical Record								
Return on Assets %	4.05	4.17	4.14	4.17	3.99	4.00	4.05	3.17
Return on Equity %	11.68	12.50	12.46	12.25	11.57	11.83	11.95	9.55
EBITDA Margin %	25.97	18.51	15.25	15.58	15.91	14.29	12.92	13.65
Net Margin %	13.92	8.96	7.24	7.38	7.35	6.61	6.09	5.91
Asset Turnover	0.44	0.47	0.57	0.57	0.54	0.61	0.66	0.54
Current Ratio	0.37	0.40	0.63	0.57	0.62	0.81	0.69	0.68
Debt to Equity	0.40	0.42	0.53	0.42	0.40	0.46	0.40	0.47
Price Range	66.37-45.54	60.31-45.54	52.60-37.78	40.48-30.27	32.45-26.83	29.55-25.21	27.96-18.80	23.09-14.92
P/E Ratio	25.24-17.32	22.17-16.74	21.30-15.30	17.91-13.39	16.31-13.48	15.47-13.20	15.36-10.33	16.14-10.43
Average Yield %	2.12	2.21	2.44	2.88	3.25	3.37	3.92	4.10

Address: 909 Silver Lake Boulevard, Dover, DE 19904
Telephone: 302-734-6799

Web Site: www.chpk.com
Officers: John R. Schimkaitis - Vice-Chairman, Chief Executive Officer Michael P. McMasters - President, Executive Vice President, Chief Operating Officer

Auditors: Baker Tilly Virchow Krause LLP
Investor Contact: 888-742-5275
Transfer Agents: Computershare Trust Company, N.A., Providence, RI

CHEVRON CORPORATION

Exchange	Symbol	Price	52Wk Range	Yield	P/E	Div Achiever
NYS	CVX	$101.00 (5/31/2016)	103.85-70.02	4.24	146.38	28 Years

*7 Year Price Score 76.33   *NYSE Composite Index=100   ***12 Month Price Score 109.86**

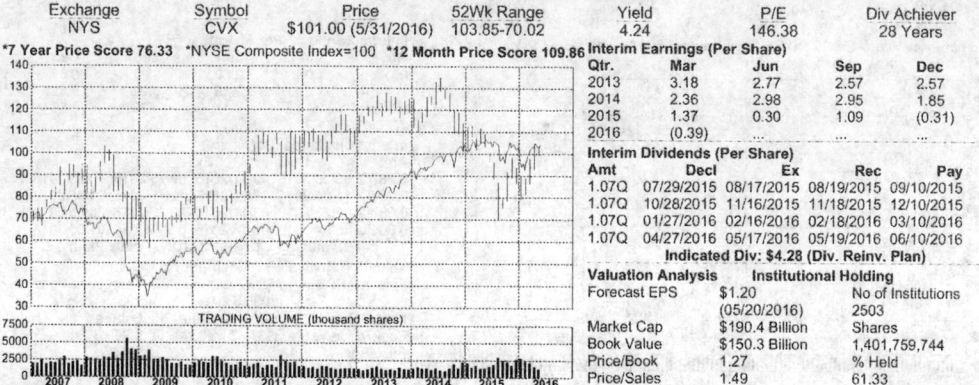

Interim Earnings (Per Share)

Qtr.	Mar	Jun	Sep	Dec
2013	3.18	2.77	2.57	2.57
2014	2.36	2.98	2.95	1.85
2015	1.37	0.30	1.09	(0.31)
2016	(0.39)	...	...	...

Interim Dividends (Per Share)

Amt	Decl	Ex	Rec	Pay
1.07Q	07/29/2015	08/17/2015	08/19/2015	09/10/2015
1.07Q	10/28/2015	11/16/2015	11/18/2015	12/10/2015
1.07Q	01/27/2016	02/16/2016	02/18/2016	03/10/2016
1.07Q	04/27/2016	05/17/2016	05/19/2016	06/10/2016

Indicated Div: $4.28 (Div. Reinv. Plan)

Valuation Analysis		Institutional Holding	
Forecast EPS	$1.20 (05/20/2016)	No of Institutions	2503
Market Cap	$190.4 Billion	Shares	
Book Value	$150.3 Billion		1,401,759,744
Price/Book	1.27	% Held	
Price/Sales	1.49		61.33

Business Summary: Refining & Marketing (MIC: 9.1.2 SIC: 2911 NAIC: 324110)

Chevron is engaged in energy and chemicals operations. Upstream operations consist of, among others, exploring for, developing and producing crude oil and natural gas; transporting, storage and marketing of natural gas; and a gas-to-liquids plant. Downstream operations consist of, among others, refining crude oil into petroleum products; marketing of crude oil and refined products; and manufacturing and marketing of commodity petrochemicals, plastics and fuel and lubricant additives. At Dec 31 2015, Co. had net proved reserves of 6.27 billion barrels of crude oil, condensate, natural gas liquids and synthetic oil, and 29.44 billion cubic feet of natural gas.

Recent Developments: For the quarter ended Mar 31 2016, net loss amounted to US$707.0 million versus net income of US$2.60 billion in the year-earlier quarter. Revenues were US$23.55 billion, down 31.8% from US$34.56 billion the year before. Direct operating expenses declined 34.7% to US$11.23 billion from US$17.19 billion in the comparable period the year before. Indirect operating expenses decreased 2.9% to US$14.04 billion from US$14.46 billion in the equivalent prior-year period.

Prospects: Our evaluation of Chevron Corporation as of June 19, 2016 is the result of our systematic analysis on three basic characteristics: earnings strength, relative valuation, and recent stock price movement. The company has enjoyed a very positive trend in earnings per share over the past 5 quarters and while recent estimates for the company have been raised by analysts, CVX has posted better than expected results. Based on operating earnings yield, the company is overvalued when compared to all of the companies in our coverage universe. Share price changes over the past year indicates that CVX will perform well over the near term.

Financial Data

(US$ in Millions)	3 Mos	12/31/2015	12/31/2014	12/31/2013	12/31/2012	12/31/2011	12/31/2010	12/31/2009
Earnings Per Share	0.69	2.45	10.14	11.09	13.32	13.44	9.48	5.24
Cash Flow Per Share	9.78	10.42	16.72	18.27	19.85	20.69	15.70	9.73
Tang Book Value Per Share	77.32	78.67	80.03	75.50	67.75	58.92	50.04	43.48
Dividends Per Share	4.280	4.280	4.210	3.900	3.510	3.090	2.840	2.660
Dividend Payout %	620.29	174.69	41.52	35.17	26.35	22.99	29.96	50.76
Income Statement								
Total Revenue	23,553	138,477	211,970	228,848	241,909	253,706	204,928	171,636
EBITDA	2,692	25,879	47,995	50,091	59,745	60,545	45,168	30,666
Depn & Amortn	4,403	21,037	16,793	14,186	13,413	12,911	13,063	12,110
Income Before Taxes	(1,711)	4,842	31,202	35,905	46,332	47,634	32,055	18,528
Income Taxes	(1,004)	132	11,892	14,308	19,996	20,626	12,919	7,965
Net Income	(725)	4,587	19,241	21,423	26,179	26,895	19,024	10,483
Average Shares	1,869	1,875	1,898	1,932	1,965	2,001	2,007	2,001
Balance Sheet								
Current Assets	31,713	35,347	42,232	50,250	55,720	53,234	48,841	37,216
Total Assets	263,842	266,103	266,026	253,753	232,982	209,474	184,769	164,621
Current Liabilities	29,162	26,464	31,926	33,018	34,212	33,600	29,012	26,211
Long-Term Obligations	32,709	33,664	24,028	20,057	12,065	9,812	11,289	10,130
Total Liabilities	113,535	113,387	110,998	104,640	96,458	88,092	79,688	72,707
Stockholders' Equity	150,307	152,716	155,028	149,113	136,524	121,382	105,081	91,914
Shares Outstanding	1,884	1,882	1,879	1,913	1,946	1,981	2,007	2,007
Statistical Record								
Return on Assets %	0.49	1.72	7.40	8.80	11.80	13.64	10.89	6.44
Return on Equity %	0.85	2.98	12.65	15.00	20.25	23.75	19.31	11.74
EBITDA Margin %	11.43	18.69	22.64	21.89	24.70	23.86	22.04	17.87
Net Margin %	N.M.	3.31	9.08	9.36	10.82	10.60	9.28	6.11
Asset Turnover	0.48	0.52	0.82	0.94	1.09	1.29	1.17	1.05
Current Ratio	1.09	1.34	1.32	1.52	1.63	1.58	1.68	1.42
Debt to Equity	0.22	0.22	0.15	0.13	0.09	0.08	0.11	0.11
Price Range	111.73-70.02	112.78-70.02	134.85-100.86	127.76-108.14	117.96-96.41	109.66-89.88	91.60-67.31	79.64-56.46
P/E Ratio	161.93-101.48	46.03-28.58	13.30-9.95	11.52-9.75	8.86-7.24	8.16-6.69	9.66-7.10	15.20-10.77
Average Yield %	4.66	4.44	3.49	3.25	3.26	3.07	3.53	3.79

Address: 6001 Bollinger Canyon Road, San Ramon, CA 94583-2324 Telephone: 925-842-1000 Fax: 925-894-6017	Web Site: www.chevron.com Officers: John S. Watson - Chairman, Vice-Chairman, Chief Executive Officer Patricia E. Yarrington - Vice President, Chief Financial Officer	Auditors: PricewaterhouseCoopers LLP Investor Contact: 925-842-5690 Transfer Agents: Computershare, Providence, RI

CHICAGO BRIDGE & IRON CO., N.V. (NETHERLANDS)

Exchange	Symbol	Price	52Wk Range	Yield	P/E
NYS	CBI	$38.24 (5/31/2016)	56.66-31.52	0.73	N/A

*7 Year Price Score 82.50   *NYSE Composite Index=100   *12 Month Price Score 89.73

Interim Earnings (Per Share)

Qtr.	Mar	Jun	Sep	Dec
2013	0.32	0.98	1.08	1.82
2014	0.82	1.31	1.48	1.37
2015	1.21	1.55	(7.02)	(0.64)
2016	1.01	...	...	...

Interim Dividends (Per Share)

Amt	Decl	Ex	Rec	Pay
0.07Q	09/11/2015	09/17/2015	09/21/2015	09/30/2015
0.07Q	12/03/2015	12/16/2015	12/18/2015	12/31/2015
0.07Q	02/17/2016	03/17/2016	03/21/2016	03/31/2016
0.07Q	05/04/2016	06/16/2016	06/20/2016	06/30/2016

Indicated Div: $0.28

Valuation Analysis   **Institutional Holding**

Forecast EPS	$5.00
(05/20/2016)	No of Institutions 622
Market Cap	$4.0 Billion
Book Value	$2.1 Billion
Price/Book	1.88
Price/Sales	0.32

No of Institutions 622
Shares 85,073,832
% Held 71.09

Business Summary: Construction Services (MIC: 7.5.4 SIC: 1799 NAIC: 238990)

Chicago Bridge & Iron Company has four operating groups: engineering, construction and maintenance, which provides engineering, procurement and construction services for energy infrastructure facilities; fabrication services, which consists of fabrication of piping systems, process and nuclear modules, fabrication and erection of steel plate structures and manufacturing and distribution of pipe and fittings; technology, which provides licensed process technologies, catalysts, and engineered products, as well as process planning and project development services; and environmental solutions, which provides services that include remediation and restoration of contaminated sites, among others.

Recent Developments: For the quarter ended Mar 31 2016, net income decreased 23.5% to US$120.0 million from US$156.7 million in the year-earlier quarter. Revenues were US$2.67 billion, down 14.7% from US$3.13 billion the year before. Operating income was US$187.9 million versus US$246.8 million in the prior-year quarter, a decrease of 23.8%. Direct operating expenses declined 13.6% to US$2.38 billion from US$2.76 billion in the comparable period the year before. Indirect operating expenses decreased 19.2% to US$99.7 million from US$123.4 million in the equivalent prior-year period.

Prospects: Our evaluation of Chicago Bridge & Iron Co., N.V. as of June 19, 2016 is the result of our systematic analysis on three basic characteristics: earnings strength, relative valuation, and recent stock price movement. The company has produced a positive trend in earnings per share over the past 5 quarters. However, while recent estimates for the company have been mixed, CBI has posted results that fell short of analysts expectations. Based on operating earnings yield, the company is undervalued when compared to all of the companies in our coverage universe. Share price changes over the past year indicates that CBI will perform in line with the market over the near term.

Financial Data

(US$ in Thousands)	3 Mos	12/31/2015	12/31/2014	12/31/2013	12/31/2012	12/31/2011	12/31/2010	12/31/2009
Earnings Per Share	(5.10)	(4.72)	4.98	4.23	3.07	2.55	2.04	1.79
Cash Flow Per Share	3.58	(0.53)	2.44	(1.07)	2.09	4.21	2.93	2.58
Tang Book Value Per Share	N.M.	N.M.	N.M.	N.M.	2.84	0.65	N.M.	N.M.
Dividends Per Share	0.280	0.280	0.280	0.200	0.200	0.200	...	...
Dividend Payout %	...	...	5.62	4.73	6.51	7.84	...	...
Income Statement								
Total Revenue	2,667,733	12,929,504	12,974,930	11,094,527	5,485,206	4,550,542	3,642,318	4,556,503
EBITDA	195,227	(279,671)	1,138,781	841,060	504,133	408,494	356,681	358,690
Depn & Amortn	11,277	161,135	181,398	180,026	66,421	70,184	72,885	79,531
Income Before Taxes	160,541	(526,881)	882,317	580,386	426,135	335,076	272,065	259,593
Income Taxes	44,569	(81,231)	271,417	91,270	127,003	96,765	79,966	114,917
Net Income	106,925	(504,415)	543,607	454,120	301,655	255,032	204,559	174,289
Average Shares	105,785	106,766	109,122	107,452	98,230	100,204	100,458	97,244
Balance Sheet								
Current Assets	3,688,030	3,369,428	3,530,459	3,389,565	2,721,555	1,661,321	1,202,486	1,195,578
Total Assets	9,480,703	9,202,357	9,381,031	9,389,593	4,329,675	3,291,983	2,909,534	3,016,767
Current Liabilities	5,314,410	4,859,077	4,322,230	4,797,624	1,772,522	1,743,424	1,440,633	1,679,875
Long-Term Obligations	1,492,365	1,800,000	1,564,158	1,625,000	800,000	...	40,000	80,000
Total Liabilities	7,341,262	7,188,367	6,642,939	7,045,014	2,961,922	2,114,249	1,854,072	2,142,947
Stockholders' Equity	2,139,441	2,013,990	2,738,092	2,344,579	1,367,753	1,177,734	1,055,462	873,820
Shares Outstanding	105,124	104,427	107,806	107,478	96,835	97,595	99,342	100,203
Statistical Record								
Return on Assets %	N.M.	N.M.	5.79	6.62	7.89	8.22	6.90	5.79
Return on Equity %	N.M.	N.M.	21.39	24.47	23.64	22.84	21.21	24.38
EBITDA Margin %	7.32	N.M.	8.78	7.58	9.19	8.98	9.79	7.87
Net Margin %	4.01	N.M.	4.19	4.09	5.50	5.60	5.62	3.83
Asset Turnover	1.30	1.39	1.38	1.62	1.44	1.47	1.23	1.51
Current Ratio	0.69	0.69	0.82	0.71	1.54	0.95	0.83	0.71
Debt to Equity	0.70	0.89	0.57	0.69	0.58	...	0.04	0.09
Price Range	58.63-31.52	58.63-34.51	87.65-37.78	83.14-46.35	47.40-33.47	44.51-26.68	33.20-16.94	20.88-4.87
P/E Ratio	...	...	17.60-7.59	19.65-10.96	15.44-10.90	17.45-10.46	16.27-8.30	11.66-2.72
Average Yield %	0.64	0.62	0.41	0.32	0.50	0.55	...	...

Address: Prinses Beatrixlaan 35, The Hague, 2595 AK	Web Site: www.cbi.com	Auditors: Ernst & Young LLP
Telephone: 703-732-010	Officers: Philip K. Asherman - President, Chief Executive Officer, Managing Director Richard E. Chandler - Executive Vice President, Chief Legal Officer, Secretary	Transfer Agents: The Bank of New York

CHICO'S FAS INC

Exchange	Symbol	Price	52Wk Range	Yield	P/E
NYS	CHS	$10.85 (5/31/2016)	17.19-9.69	2.95	1085.00

*7 Year Price Score 78.36 *NYSE Composite Index=100 *12 Month Price Score 89.05

TRADING VOLUME (thousand shares)

Interim Earnings (Per Share)

Qtr.	Apr	Jul	Oct	Jan
2013-14	0.31	0.27	(0.18)	0.00
2014-15	0.26	0.20	0.17	(0.21)
2015-16	0.22	0.02	(0.09)	(0.15)
2016-17	0.23	...	...	...

Interim Dividends (Per Share)

Amt	Decl	Ex	Rec	Pay
0.077Q	11/24/2015	12/03/2015	12/07/2015	12/21/2015
0.08Q	02/25/2016	03/10/2016	03/14/2016	03/28/2016
0.08Q	04/08/2016	06/09/2016	06/13/2016	06/27/2016
0.08Q	06/17/2016	09/08/2016	09/12/2016	09/26/2016

Indicated Div: $0.32

Valuation Analysis   **Institutional Holding**

Forecast EPS	$0.65 (05/20/2016)	No of Institutions	387
Market Cap	$1.4 Billion	Shares	
Book Value	$613.5 Million		139,221,408
Price/Book	2.35	% Held	
Price/Sales	0.56		87.92

Business Summary: Retail - Apparel and Accessories (MIC: 2.1.5 SIC: 5621 NAIC: 448120)

Chico's FAS, Inc. operates as a retailer of private branded, casual-to-dressy clothing, intimates, complementary accessories, and other non-clothing items. Co.'s portfolio consists of three brands: Chico's, White House I Black Market (WHIBM), and Soma Intimates (Soma). Co.'s products include apparel as well as accessories such as shoes, belts, scarves and jewelry, including earrings, necklaces and bracelets. Co. sells its products through retail stores, catalog, and via the Internet. As of Jan 30 2016, Co. operated 1,518 stores across 48 states, Puerto Rico, the U.S. Virgin Islands and Canada and sold merchandise through 37 franchise locations in Mexico.

Recent Developments: For the quarter ended Apr 30 2016, net income decreased 4.4% to US$31.1 million from US$32.5 million in the year-earlier quarter. Revenues were US$643.0 million, down 7.9% from US$697.8 million the year before. Operating income was US$50.5 million versus US$52.7 million in the prior-year quarter, a decrease of 4.1%. Direct operating expenses declined 5.3% to US$380.6 million from US$402.1 million in the comparable period the year before. Indirect operating expenses decreased 12.8% to US$211.8 million from US$242.9 million in the equivalent prior-year period.

Prospects: Our evaluation of Chico's FAS Inc. as of June 19, 2016 is the result of our systematic analysis on three basic characteristics: earnings strength, relative valuation, and recent stock price movement. The company has suffered a very negative trend in earnings per share over the past 5 quarters. However, while recent estimates for the company have been lowered by analysts, CHS has posted results that fell short of analysts expectations. Based on operating earnings yield, the company is undervalued when compared to all of the companies in our coverage universe. Share price changes over the past year indicates that CHS will perform poorly over the near term.

Financial Data

(US$ in Thousands)	3 Mos	01/30/2016	01/31/2015	02/01/2014	02/02/2013	01/28/2012	01/29/2011	01/30/2010
Earnings Per Share	0.01	0.01	0.42	0.41	1.08	0.82	0.64	0.39
Cash Flow Per Share	1.43	1.43	1.91	1.53	2.22	1.51	1.36	1.22
Tang Book Value Per Share	3.60	3.72	4.50	4.07	4.46	3.85	5.22	4.75
Dividends Per Share	0.313	0.310	0.300	0.240	0.210	0.200	0.160	...
Dividend Payout %	3,125.00	3,100.00	71.43	58.54	19.44	24.39	25.00	...
Income Statement								
Total Revenue	642,977	2,642,309	2,675,211	2,586,037	2,581,057	2,196,360	1,904,954	1,713,150
EBITDA	78,500	103,516	234,143	254,983	396,009	321,807	271,195	204,525
Depn & Amortn	27,957	116,600	117,800	113,800	108,471	99,430	94,113	96,372
Income Before Taxes	50,084	(14,954)	116,441	141,683	288,419	223,974	178,794	109,846
Income Taxes	19,000	(16,900)	51,800	75,800	108,200	83,100	63,400	40,200
Net Income	31,084	1,946	64,641	65,883	180,219	140,874	115,394	69,646
Average Shares	131,689	138,741	149,126	155,994	164,119	170,250	178,033	178,857
Balance Sheet								
Current Assets	450,527	465,321	562,959	441,289	597,993	497,426	756,765	599,980
Total Assets	1,136,116	1,166,052	1,438,581	1,371,191	1,580,628	1,425,152	1,416,021	1,318,803
Current Liabilities	296,858	298,131	302,930	273,327	302,411	238,109	221,277	194,706
Long-Term Obligations	79,735	82,219	...	...	...	...	...	...
Total Liabilities	522,639	526,264	494,960	462,088	487,429	415,924	351,114	336,885
Stockholders' Equity	613,477	639,788	943,621	909,103	1,093,199	1,009,228	1,064,907	981,918
Shares Outstanding	132,609	135,531	152,916	152,195	162,774	165,736	177,899	178,126
Statistical Record								
Return on Assets %	0.04	0.15	4.61	4.48	11.80	9.94	8.46	5.49
Return on Equity %	0.08	0.25	7.00	6.60	16.87	13.62	11.31	7.41
EBITDA Margin %	12.21	3.92	8.75	9.86	15.34	14.65	14.24	11.94
Net Margin %	4.83	0.07	2.42	2.55	6.98	6.41	6.06	4.07
Asset Turnover	2.09	2.03	1.91	1.76	1.69	1.55	1.40	1.35
Current Ratio	1.52	1.56	1.86	1.61	1.98	2.09	3.42	3.08
Debt to Equity	0.13	0.13	...	...	...	...	...	...
Price Range	17.29-9.69	18.38-9.69	18.00-14.56	19.73-15.33	19.64-11.41	16.26-9.94	16.42-8.26	14.74-3.42
P/E Ratio	N.M.	N.M.	42.86-34.67	48.12-37.39	18.19-10.56	19.83-12.12	25.66-12.91	37.79-8.77
Average Yield %	2.26	2.04	1.89	1.38	1.27	1.52	1.36	...

Address: 11215 Metro Parkway, Fort Myers, FL 33966
Telephone: 239-277-6200

Web Site: www.chicosfas.com
Officers: David F. Walker - Chairman David F. Dyer - President, Chief Executive Officer, Vice-Chairman

Auditors: Ernst & Young, LLP
Transfer Agents: Registrar and Transfer Company, Cranford, NJ

CHIMERA INVESTMENT CORP

Exchange	Symbol	Price	52Wk Range	Yield	P/E
NYS	CIM	$14.99 (5/31/2016)	15.12-11.39	N/A	10.94

*7 Year Price Score 72.79   *NYSE Composite Index=100   *12 Month Price Score 102.24

Interim Earnings (Per Share)
Qtr.	Mar	Jun	Sep	Dec
2013	0.40	0.70	0.35	0.35
2014	0.50	0.50	1.85	0.00
2015	0.33	0.57	(0.24)	0.60
2016	0.44	...	...	...

Interim Dividends (Per Share)
Amt	Decl	Ex	Rec	Pay
0.09Q	09/17/2014	09/26/2014	09/30/2014	10/29/2014
0.09Q	12/18/2014	12/29/2014	12/31/2014	01/29/2015
0.096Q	03/17/2015	03/27/2015	03/31/2015	04/30/2015
1-for-5	...	04/06/2015	...	...

Valuation Analysis   Institutional Holding
Forecast EPS	$2.20	No of Institutions
	(05/17/2016)	317
Market Cap	$2.8 Billion	Shares
Book Value	$2.9 Billion	193,437,328
Price/Book	0.97	% Held
Price/Sales	4.56	62.19

Business Summary: REITs (MIC: 5.3.1 SIC: 6798 NAIC: 525930)

Chimera Investment is a finance company that invests, either directly or indirectly through its subsidiaries, in residential mortgage-backed securities, residential mortgage loans, commercial mortgage loans, real estate-related securities and various other asset classes. Co. is externally managed by Fixed Income Discount Advisory Company, an investment advisor.

Recent Developments: For the quarter ended Mar 31 2016, net income increased 24.0% to US$83.1 million from US$67.0 million in the year-earlier quarter. Revenues were US$161.4 million, up 9.2% from US$147.9 million the year before.

Prospects: Our evaluation of Chimera Investment Corp. as of June 19, 2016 is the result of our systematic analysis on three basic characteristics: earnings strength, relative valuation, and recent stock price movement. The company has produced a positive trend in earnings per share over the past 5 quarters and while recent estimates for the company have been raised by analysts, CIM has posted better than expected results. Based on operating earnings yield, the company is undervalued when compared to all of the companies in our coverage universe. Share price changes over the past year indicates that CIM will perform in line with the market over the near term.

Financial Data
(US$ in Thousands)	3 Mos	12/31/2015	12/31/2014	12/31/2013	12/31/2012	12/31/2011	12/31/2010	12/31/2009
Earnings Per Share	1.37	1.25	2.85	1.75	1.60	0.65	3.25	3.20
Cash Flow Per Share	2.50	1.99	0.89	1.48	1.63	2.18	1.86	1.66
Tang Book Value Per Share	15.52	15.70	17.55	16.21	17.24	14.83	17.93	15.86
Dividends Per Share	2.420	1.440	1.800	2.800	1.900	2.550	3.450	2.150
Dividend Payout %	176.64	115.20	63.16	160.00	118.75	392.31	106.15	67.19
Income Statement								
Total Revenue	161,410	603,111	768,360	498,786	513,493	337,320	735,471	391,934
EBITDA	93,833	271,308	528,190	299,773	276,037	89,781	286,172	274,735
Depn & Amortn	10,706	20,958	(61,017)	(62,915)	(51,731)	(48,154)	(247,435)	(49,249)
Income Before Taxes	83,127	250,350	589,207	362,688	327,768	137,935	533,607	323,984
Income Taxes	29	1,000.00	2	2	1,000.00	606	756	1,000.00
Net Income	83,098	250,349	589,205	362,686	327,767	137,329	532,851	323,983
Average Shares	187,840	199,650	205,508	205,514	205,499	205,434	164,523	101,408
Balance Sheet								
Current Assets	255,506	180,309	235,719	110,623	660,483	255,624	56,261	57,407
Total Assets	15,306,957	15,344,646	19,155,005	6,936,081	7,742,489	7,747,135	8,073,700	4,618,328
Current Liabilities	8,270,340	8,127,509	10,425,034	1,957,862	1,622,897	2,789,220	2,122,576	2,092,425
Long-Term Obligations	4,109,401	...	...	...	...	...	2,245,315	390,350
Total Liabilities	12,393,322	12,398,458	15,547,315	3,604,571	4,200,010	4,699,516	4,390,694	2,491,766
Stockholders' Equity	2,913,635	2,946,188	3,607,690	3,331,510	3,542,479	3,047,619	3,683,006	2,126,562
Shares Outstanding	187,729	187,711	205,546	205,525	205,519	205,493	205,406	134,074
Statistical Record								
Return on Assets %	1.63	1.45	4.52	4.94	4.22	1.74	8.40	10.63
Return on Equity %	8.28	7.64	16.98	10.55	9.92	4.08	18.34	25.50
EBITDA Margin %	58.13	44.98	68.74	60.10	53.76	26.62	38.91	70.10
Net Margin %	51.48	41.51	76.68	72.71	63.83	40.71	72.45	82.66
Asset Turnover	0.04	0.03	0.06	0.07	0.07	0.04	0.12	0.13
Current Ratio	0.03	0.02	0.02	0.06	0.41	0.09	0.03	0.03
Debt to Equity	1.41	...	...	...	...	...	0.61	0.18
Price Range	15.94-11.39	16.45-12.86	16.95-14.95	16.60-13.05	15.60-10.65	21.55-12.55	21.50-17.55	21.50-12.45
P/E Ratio	11.64-8.31	13.16-10.29	5.95-5.25	9.49-7.46	9.75-6.66	33.15-19.31	6.62-5.40	6.72-3.89
Average Yield %	17.31	9.79	11.36	18.40	14.05	14.75	17.39	12.13

Address: 520 Madison Avenue, 32nd Floor, New York, NY 10022	Web Site: www.chimerareit.com	Auditors: Ernst & Young LLP
Telephone: 212-626-2300	Officers: Matthew Lambiase - President, Chief Executive Officer Choudhary Yarlagadda - Chief Operating Officer	Investor Contact: 866-315-9930
		Transfer Agents: Computershare Shareowner Services LLC, Jersey City, NJ

CHIPOTLE MEXICAN GRILL INC

Exchange	Symbol	Price	52Wk Range	Yield	P/E
NYS	CMG	$441.96 (5/31/2016)	757.77-404.26	N/A	42.74

*7 Year Price Score 126.94 *NYSE Composite Index=100 ***12 Month Price Score 76.96**

TRADING VOLUME (thousand shares)

Interim Earnings (Per Share)

Qtr.	Mar	Jun	Sep	Dec
2013	2.45	2.82	2.66	2.54
2014	2.64	3.50	4.15	3.84
2015	3.88	4.45	4.59	2.18
2016	(0.88)	...	...	...

Interim Dividends (Per Share)

No Dividends Paid

Valuation Analysis

		Institutional Holding	
Forecast EPS	$4.81	No of Institutions	
	(05/20/2016)	748	
Market Cap	$13.0 Billion	Shares	
Book Value	$1.5 Billion	32,776,536	
Price/Book	8.42	% Held	
Price/Sales	3.05	91.52	

Business Summary: Hotels, Restaurants & Travel (MIC: 2.2.1 SIC: 5812 NAIC: 722110)

Chipotle Mexican Grill together with its subsidiaries operates Chipotle Mexican Grill restaurants, which serve a focused menu of burritos, tacos, burrito bowls (a burrito without the tortilla) and salads, made using fresh ingredients. As of Dec 31 2015, Co. operated Chipotle restaurants throughout the U.S., as well as Canada, England, France, and Germany. Additionally, Co.'s restaurants included ShopHouse Southeast Asian Kitchen restaurants, serving Asian-inspired cuisine, and Co. is an investor in a consolidated entity that owned and operated Pizzeria Locale restaurants, a fast casual pizza concept.

Recent Developments: For the quarter ended Mar 31 2016, net loss amounted to US$26.4 million versus net income of US$122.6 million in the year-earlier quarter. Revenues were US$834.5 million, down 23.4% from US$1.09 billion the year before. Operating loss was US$46.6 million versus an income of US$197.8 million in the prior-year quarter. Direct operating expenses declined 1.6% to US$777.6 million from US$789.9 million in the comparable period the year before. Indirect operating expenses increased 2.1% to US$103.4 million from US$101.3 million in the equivalent prior-year period.

Prospects: Our evaluation of Chipotle Mexican Grill Inc. as of June 19, 2016 is the result of our systematic analysis on three basic characteristics: earnings strength, relative valuation, and recent stock price movement. The company has suffered a very negative trend in earnings per share over the past 5 quarters. However, while recent estimates for the company have been lowered by analysts, CMG has posted better than expected results. Based on operating earnings yield, the company is overvalued when compared to all of the companies in our coverage universe. Share price changes over the past year indicates that CMG will perform very well over the near term.

Financial Data
(US$ in Thousands)

	3 Mos	12/31/2015	12/31/2014	12/31/2013	12/31/2012	12/31/2011	12/31/2010	12/31/2009
Earnings Per Share	10.34	15.10	14.13	10.47	8.75	6.76	5.64	3.95
Cash Flow Per Share	16.80	21.98	21.98	17.08	13.29	13.17	9.26	8.21
Tang Book Value Per Share	51.73	68.86	64.15	48.86	39.37	32.71	25.39	21.65
Income Statement								
Total Revenue	834,459	4,501,223	4,108,269	3,214,591	2,731,224	2,269,548	1,835,922	1,518,417
EBITDA	(11,816)	900,235	824,777	630,525	541,815	425,500	356,752	265,013
Depn & Amortn	34,788	130,368	110,474	96,054	84,130	74,938	68,921	61,308
Income Before Taxes	(44,478)	769,867	714,303	534,471	457,685	349,705	289,061	204,225
Income Taxes	(18,046)	294,265	268,929	207,033	179,685	134,760	110,080	77,380
Net Income	(26,432)	475,602	445,374	327,438	278,000	214,945	178,981	126,845
Average Shares	29,893	31,494	31,512	31,281	31,783	31,775	31,735	32,102
Balance Sheet								
Current Assets	374,740	814,647	878,479	666,307	546,607	501,192	406,221	297,454
Total Assets	2,140,820	2,725,066	2,546,285	2,009,280	1,668,667	1,425,308	1,121,605	961,505
Current Liabilities	271,963	279,942	245,710	199,228	186,852	157,453	123,054	102,153
Long-Term Obligations	...	...	...	...	3,386	3,529	3,661	3,782
Total Liabilities	600,566	597,092	533,916	470,992	422,741	381,082	310,732	258,044
Stockholders' Equity	1,540,254	2,127,974	2,012,369	1,538,288	1,245,926	1,044,226	810,873	703,461
Shares Outstanding	29,348	30,584	31,027	31,033	31,093	31,252	31,074	31,483
Statistical Record								
Return on Assets %	13.48	18.04	19.55	17.81	17.92	16.88	17.18	14.20
Return on Equity %	17.77	22.97	25.09	23.52	24.21	23.17	23.64	19.13
EBITDA Margin %	N.M.	20.00	20.08	19.61	19.84	18.75	19.43	17.45
Net Margin %	N.M.	10.57	10.84	10.19	10.18	9.47	9.75	8.35
Asset Turnover	1.75	1.71	1.80	1.75	1.76	1.78	1.76	1.70
Current Ratio	1.38	2.91	3.58	3.34	2.93	3.18	3.30	2.91
Debt to Equity	...	...	...	...	N.M.	N.M.	N.M.	0.01
Price Range	757.77-404.26	757.77-479.85	692.69-476.28	546.97-280.94	440.40-236.24	343.37-212.66	258.82-86.43	97.05-47.42
P/E Ratio	73.23-39.10	50.18-31.78	49.02-33.71	52.24-26.83	50.33-27.00	50.79-31.46	45.89-15.32	24.57-12.01

Address: 1401 Wynkoop Street, Suite 500, Denver, CO 80202 Telephone: 303-595-4000	Web Site: www.chipotle.com Officers: Steve Ells - Chairman, Co-Chief Executive Officer Montgomery F. Moran - Co-Chief Executive Officer, Corporate Secretary	Auditors: Ernst & Young LLP Transfer Agents: Wells Fargo Shareowner Services, Mendota Heights, MN

CHOICE HOTELS INTERNATIONAL, INC.

Exchange	Symbol	Price	52Wk Range	Yield	P/E
NYS	CHH	$45.38 (5/31/2016)	57.14-41.85	1.81	20.63

*7 Year Price Score 104.28 ***NYSE Composite Index=100** ***12 Month Price Score 97.86**

Interim Earnings (Per Share)

Qtr.	Mar	Jun	Sep	Dec
2013	0.26	0.48	0.70	0.46
2014	0.32	0.60	0.67	0.44
2015	0.37	0.62	0.72	0.51
2016	0.35	...	...	...

Interim Dividends (Per Share)

Amt	Decl	Ex	Rec	Pay
0.195Q	09/14/2015	09/30/2015	10/02/2015	10/16/2015
0.205Q	12/14/2015	12/30/2015	01/04/2016	01/18/2016
0.205Q	03/01/2016	03/31/2016	04/04/2016	04/18/2016
0.205Q	04/26/2016	06/29/2016	07/01/2016	07/15/2016

Indicated Div: $0.82

Valuation Analysis

		Institutional Holding	
Forecast EPS	$2.32	No of Institutions	
	(05/20/2016)	181	
Market Cap	$2.6 Billion	Shares	
Book Value	N/A	29,439,948	
Price/Book	N/A	% Held	
Price/Sales	2.87	N/A	

Business Summary: Hotels, Restaurants & Travel (MIC: 2.2.1 SIC: 7011 NAIC: 721110)

Choice Hotels International is a hotel franchisor with franchise agreements representing 6,379 hotels open and 603 hotels under construction, awaiting conversion or approved for development as of Dec 31 2014 with 505,278 rooms and 47,951 rooms, respectively, in 50 states, the District of Columbia and more than 35 countries and territories outside the U.S. Co. franchises lodging properties under the following proprietary brand names: Comfort Inn®, Comfort Suites®, Quality®, Clarion®, Sleep Inn®, Econo Lodge®, Rodeway Inn®, MainStay Suites®, Suburban Extended Stay Hotel®, Cambria® hotels & suites, and Ascend Hotel Collection®.

Recent Developments: For the quarter ended Mar 31 2016, net income decreased 9.2% to US$19.6 million from US$21.6 million in the year-earlier quarter. Revenues were US$207.1 million, up 18.2% from US$175.2 million the year before. Operating income was US$42.9 million versus US$41.4 million in the prior-year quarter, an increase of 3.5%. Direct operating expenses rose 28.0% to US$126.4 million from US$98.7 million in the comparable period the year before. Indirect operating expenses increased 7.8% to US$37.9 million from US$35.1 million in the equivalent prior-year period.

Prospects: Our evaluation of Choice Hotels International Inc. as of June 19, 2016 is the result of our systematic analysis on three basic characteristics: earnings strength, relative valuation, and recent stock price movement. The company has managed to produce a neutral trend in earnings per share over the past 5 quarters. However, while recent estimates for the company have been mixed, CHH has posted results that fell short of analysts expectations. Based on operating earnings yield, the company is about fairly valued when compared to all of the companies in our coverage universe. Share price changes over the past year indicates that CHH will perform in line with the market over the near term.

Financial Data
(US$ in Thousands)

	3 Mos	12/31/2015	12/31/2014	12/31/2013	12/31/2012	12/31/2011	12/31/2010	12/31/2009
Earnings Per Share	2.20	2.22	2.10	1.91	2.07	1.85	1.80	1.63
Cash Flow Per Share	2.73	2.81	3.19	2.62	2.79	2.29	2.46	1.87
Dividends Per Share	0.800	0.790	0.750	0.740	11.150	0.740	0.740	0.740
Dividend Payout %	36.36	35.59	35.71	38.74	538.65	40.00	41.11	45.40
Income Statement								
Total Revenue	207,118	859,878	757,970	724,307	691,509	638,793	596,076	564,178
EBITDA	45,576	230,439	217,241	199,374	197,005	172,021	163,162	150,873
Depn & Amortn	2,765	4,300	3,100	3,100	2,400	2,600	2,400	2,800
Income Before Taxes	32,558	184,886	174,416	156,284	168,956	157,788	156,985	149,521
Income Taxes	10,780	55,956	52,285	44,317	48,481	47,661	50,770	52,384
Net Income	19,598	128,029	123,160	112,601	120,687	110,396	107,441	98,250
Average Shares	56,025	57,273	58,256	58,335	57,653	58,934	59,041	60,224
Balance Sheet								
Current Assets	338,116	310,953	351,414	258,646	233,470	194,796	163,582	127,862
Total Assets	787,263	717,010	647,270	539,899	510,772	447,689	411,722	340,037
Current Liabilities	220,327	208,016	200,098	174,338	176,137	184,565	165,258	131,806
Long-Term Obligations	892,447	812,945	782,082	783,471	847,150	252,032	251,554	277,700
Total Liabilities	1,173,128	1,112,909	1,076,071	1,004,144	1,059,676	473,250	469,793	454,249
Stockholders' Equity	(385,865)	(395,899)	(428,801)	(464,245)	(548,904)	(25,561)	(58,071)	(114,212)
Shares Outstanding	56,487	56,336	57,337	58,638	58,171	58,277	59,583	59,541
Statistical Record								
Return on Assets %	17.40	18.77	20.75	21.43	25.11	25.69	28.58	29.40
EBITDA Margin %	22.00	26.80	28.66	27.53	28.49	26.93	27.37	26.74
Net Margin %	9.46	14.89	16.25	15.55	17.45	17.28	18.02	17.41
Asset Turnover	1.23	1.26	1.28	1.38	1.44	1.49	1.59	1.69
Current Ratio	1.53	1.49	1.76	1.48	1.33	1.06	0.99	0.97
Price Range	64.08-41.85	64.85-46.62	57.34-43.71	49.71-33.62	44.21-30.80	41.25-26.54	39.55-29.57	32.94-23.25
P/E Ratio	29.13-19.02	29.21-21.00	27.30-20.81	26.03-17.60	21.36-14.88	22.30-14.35	21.97-16.43	20.21-14.26
Average Yield %	1.53	1.43	1.52	1.79	31.06	2.11	2.12	2.59

Address: 1 Choice Hotels Circle, Suite 400, Rockville, MD 20850	**Web Site:** www.choicehotels.com	**Auditors:** Ernst & Young LLP
Telephone: 301-592-5000	**Officers:** Stewart Bainum - Chairman Charles A. Ledsinger - Vice-Chairman	**Investor Contact:** 301-592 5026
		Transfer Agents: Computershare, Providence, RI

CHUBB LTD

Exchange	Symbol	Price	52Wk Range	Yield	P/E
NYS	CB	$126.61 (5/31/2016)	127.22-99.72	2.18	16.79

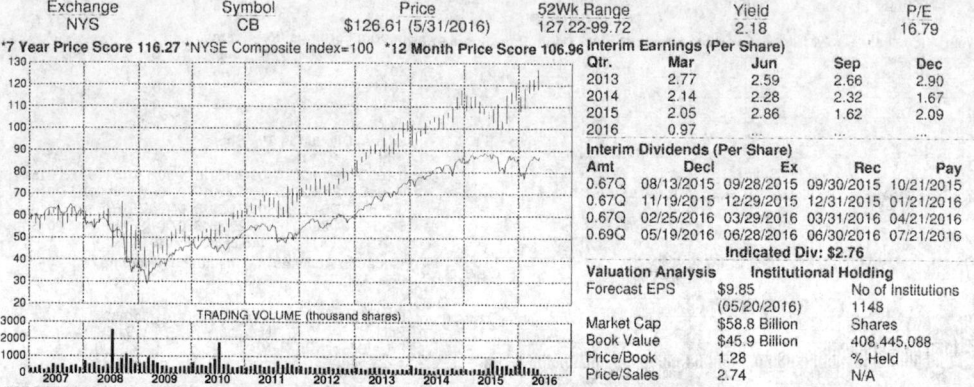

*7 Year Price Score 116.27 *NYSE Composite Index=100 *12 Month Price Score 106.96

Interim Earnings (Per Share)

Qtr.	Mar	Jun	Sep	Dec
2013	2.77	2.59	2.66	2.90
2014	2.14	2.28	2.32	1.67
2015	2.05	2.86	1.62	2.09
2016	0.97			

Interim Dividends (Per Share)

Amt	Decl	Ex	Rec	Pay
0.67Q	08/13/2015	09/28/2015	09/30/2015	10/21/2015
0.67Q	11/19/2015	12/29/2015	12/31/2015	01/21/2016
0.67Q	02/25/2016	03/29/2016	03/31/2016	04/21/2016
0.69Q	05/19/2016	06/28/2016	06/30/2016	07/21/2016

Indicated Div: $2.76

Valuation Analysis

		Institutional Holding	
Forecast EPS	$9.85	No of Institutions	
	(05/20/2016)	1148	
Market Cap	$58.8 Billion	Shares	
Book Value	$45.9 Billion	408,445,088	
Price/Book	1.28	% Held	
Price/Sales	2.74	N/A	

Business Summary: General Insurance (MIC: 5.2.1 SIC: 6331 NAIC: 524130)

Chubb is a holding company. Through its subsidiaries, Co. is an insurance and reinsurance organization. Co. provides commercial insurance products and service offerings such as risk management programs, loss control and engineering and claims management. Co. provides insurance products ranging from Directors & Officers and professional liability to several specialty-casualty and umbrella and excess casualty lines. Co. also provides personal lines insurance coverage including homeowners, umbrella liability and recreational marine products. Co.'s segments are: Insurance - North American P&C, Insurance - North American Agriculture, Insurance - Overseas General, Global Reinsurance, and Life.

Recent Developments: For the quarter ended Mar 31 2016, net income decreased 35.5% to US$439.0 million from US$681.0 million in the year-earlier quarter. Revenues were US$6.88 billion, up 56.7% from US$4.39 billion the year before. Net premiums earned were US$6.60 billion versus US$3.93 billion in the prior-year quarter, an increase of 68.0%. Net investment income rose 22.3% to US$674.0 million from US$551.0 million a year ago.

Prospects: Our evaluation of Chubb Ltd. as of June 19, 2016 is the result of our systematic analysis on three basic characteristics: earnings strength, relative valuation, and recent stock price movement. The company has managed to produce a neutral trend in earnings per share over the past 5 quarters and while recent estimates for the company have been raised by analysts, CB has posted better than expected results. Based on operating earnings yield, the company is undervalued when compared to all of the companies in our coverage universe. Share price changes over the past year indicates that CB will perform very well over the near term.

Financial Data
(US$ in Thousands)

	3 Mos	12/31/2015	12/31/2014	12/31/2013	12/31/2012	12/31/2011	12/31/2010	12/31/2009
Earnings Per Share	7.54	8.62	8.42	10.92	7.89	4.65	9.11	7.55
Cash Flow Per Share	8.53	11.87	13.40	11.80	11.72	10.26	10.44	9.90
Tang Book Value Per Share	48.54	72.26	72.61	68.93	66.28	58.43	54.67	46.76
Dividends Per Share	2.680	2.660	3.210	1.510	2.410	1.030	1.300	1.460
Dividend Payout %	35.54	30.86	38.12	13.83	30.54	22.15	14.27	19.34
Income Statement								
Premium Income	6,597,000	17,213,000	17,426,000	16,613,000	15,677,000	15,387,000	13,504,000	13,240,000
Total Revenue	6,877,000	18,987,000	19,171,000	19,261,000	17,936,000	16,834,000	16,006,000	15,075,000
Benefits & Claims	3,800,000	10,027,000	10,166,000	9,863,000	10,174,000	9,921,000	7,936,000	7,747,000
Income Before Taxes	578,000	3,183,000	3,256,000	4,119,000	2,896,000	2,053,000	3,600,000	3,119,000
Income Taxes	124,000	462,000	634,000	480,000	270,000	506,000	559,000	528,000
Net Income	439,000	2,834,000	2,853,000	3,758,000	2,706,000	1,585,000	3,108,000	2,549,000
Average Shares	450,009	328,835	338,986	344,147	342,746	340,780	341,246	337,539
Balance Sheet								
Total Assets	156,644,000	102,366,000	98,248,000	94,510,000	92,545,000	87,505,000	83,355,000	77,980,000
Total Liabilities	110,747,000	73,231,000	68,661,000	65,685,000	65,014,000	62,989,000	60,381,000	58,313,000
Stockholders' Equity	45,897,000	29,135,000	29,587,000	28,825,000	27,531,000	24,516,000	22,974,000	19,667,000
Shares Outstanding	464,283	324,563	328,659	339,793	340,321	336,927	334,942	336,524
Statistical Record								
Return on Assets %	2.03	2.83	2.96	4.02	3.00	1.86	3.85	3.40
Return on Equity %	6.86	9.65	9.77	13.34	10.37	6.68	14.58	14.94
Loss Ratio %	57.60	58.25	58.34	59.37	64.90	64.48	58.77	58.51
Net Margin %	6.38	14.93	14.88	19.51	15.09	9.42	19.42	16.91
Price Range	122.47-99.72	119.47-99.72	117.58-92.19	103.53-79.80	81.70-68.98	73.33-58.98	62.37-47.50	55.14-31.84
P/E Ratio	16.24-13.23	13.86-11.57	13.96-10.95	9.48-7.31	10.35-8.74	15.77-12.68	6.85-5.21	7.30-4.22
Average Yield %	2.44	2.43	3.10	1.66	3.23	1.59	2.40	3.12

Address: Baerengasse 32, Zurich, CH-8001	**Web Site:** www.acegroup.com	**Auditors:** PricewaterhouseCoopers LLP
Telephone: 434-567-600	**Officers:** Evan G. Greenberg - Chairman, Vice-Chairman, President, Chief Executive Officer, Chief Operating Officer John W. Keogh - Vice-Chairman, Chief Operating Officer	**Transfer Agents:** Mellon Investor Services LLC, Ridgefield Park, NJ

CHURCH & DWIGHT CO., INC.

Exchange	Symbol	Price	52Wk Range	Yield	P/E	Div Achiever
NYS	CHD	$98.48 (5/31/2016)	99.09-78.23	1.44	31.46	19 Years

*7 Year Price Score 131.67 *NYSE Composite Index=100 *12 Month Price Score 107.32

Interim Earnings (Per Share)

Qtr.	Mar	Jun	Sep	Dec
2013	0.76	0.61	0.76	0.65
2014	0.73	0.65	0.85	0.78
2015	0.80	0.55	0.90	0.82
2016	0.86	...	...	...

Interim Dividends (Per Share)

Amt	Decl	Ex	Rec	Pay
0.335Q	07/28/2015	08/07/2015	08/11/2015	09/01/2015
0.335Q	10/28/2015	11/06/2015	11/10/2015	12/01/2015
0.355Q	02/02/2016	02/11/2016	02/16/2016	03/01/2016
0.355Q	05/04/2016	05/12/2016	05/16/2016	06/01/2016

Indicated Div: $1.42 (Div. Reinv. Plan)

Valuation Analysis — **Institutional Holding**

Forecast EPS	$3.53	No of Institutions
	(05/20/2016)	821
Market Cap	$12.6 Billion	Shares
Book Value	$1.9 Billion	124,886,672
Price/Book	6.57	% Held
Price/Sales	3.68	77.18

Business Summary: Household & Personal Products (MIC: 1.7.1 SIC: 2841 NAIC: 325611)

Church & Dwight Co. develops, manufactures and markets a range of household, personal care and specialty products. Co. sells its consumer products under a variety of brands through a distribution platform such as supermarkets, mass merchandisers, wholesale clubs, drugstores, convenience stores, home stores, dollar, pet and other specialty stores and websites. Co. has three segments: consumer domestic, which include household and personal care products; consumer international, which sells a range of personal care products, household and over-the-counter products in international markets; and specialty products, which focuses on animal nutrition, specialty chemicals and specialty cleaners.

Recent Developments: For the quarter ended Mar 31 2016, net income increased 5.4% to US$113.0 million from US$107.2 million in the year-earlier quarter. Revenues were US$849.0 million, up 4.5% from US$812.3 million the year before. Operating income was US$179.5 million versus US$172.1 million in the prior-year quarter, an increase of 4.3%. Direct operating expenses rose 2.9% to US$470.0 million from US$456.8 million in the comparable period the year before. Indirect operating expenses increased 8.8% to US$199.5 million from US$183.4 million in the equivalent prior-year period.

Prospects: Our evaluation of Church & Dwight Co. Inc. as of June 19, 2016 is the result of our systematic analysis on three basic characteristics: earnings strength, relative valuation, and recent stock price movement. The company has enjoyed a very positive trend in earnings per share over the past 5 quarters and while recent estimates for the company have remained steady, CHD has posted better than expected results. Based on operating earnings yield, the company is about fairly valued when compared to all of the companies in our coverage universe. Share price changes over the past year indicates that CHD will perform well over the near term.

Financial Data

(US$ in Thousands)	3 Mos	12/31/2015	12/31/2014	12/31/2013	12/31/2012	12/31/2011	12/31/2010	12/31/2009
Earnings Per Share	3.13	3.07	3.01	2.79	2.45	2.12	1.88	1.71
Cash Flow Per Share	4.94	4.62	4.00	3.60	3.73	3.06	3.02	2.85
Tang Book Value Per Share	N.M.	N.M.	N.M.	N.M.	N.M.	1.88	0.99	N.M.
Dividends Per Share	1.360	1.340	1.240	1.120	0.960	0.680	0.310	0.230
Dividend Payout %	43.45	43.65	41.20	40.14	39.18	32.08	16.53	13.49
Income Statement								
Total Revenue	849,000	3,394,800	3,297,600	3,194,300	2,921,900	2,749,300	2,589,220	2,520,922
EBITDA	206,000	730,000	697,800	682,400	603,600	543,100	485,109	472,675
Depn & Amortn	27,900	58,300	57,100	59,700	56,000	49,800	44,113	56,921
Income Before Taxes	171,300	641,200	613,300	595,000	533,600	484,600	413,219	380,186
Income Taxes	60,000	225,000	211,000	203,400	192,700	185,000	147,562	148,715
Net Income	113,000	410,400	413,900	394,400	349,800	309,600	270,717	243,533
Average Shares	131,800	133,600	137,500	141,200	142,700	145,800	144,402	142,954
Balance Sheet								
Current Assets	785,500	906,000	1,032,500	1,115,800	933,800	755,200	649,481	928,265
Total Assets	4,292,300	4,256,900	4,381,300	4,259,700	4,098,100	3,117,600	2,945,194	3,118,446
Current Liabilities	1,012,800	872,700	905,300	651,200	725,600	383,600	447,092	567,032
Long-Term Obligations	699,800	692,800	698,600	649,500	649,400	249,700	249,673	597,347
Total Liabilities	2,372,000	2,233,700	2,279,400	1,959,800	2,037,200	1,077,000	1,074,505	1,516,863
Stockholders' Equity	1,920,300	2,023,200	2,101,900	2,299,900	2,060,900	2,040,600	1,870,689	1,601,583
Shares Outstanding	128,169	129,954	133,351	138,964	138,781	142,287	142,409	141,098
Statistical Record								
Return on Assets %	9.64	9.50	9.58	9.44	9.67	10.21	8.93	8.23
Return on Equity %	21.74	19.90	18.81	18.09	17.01	15.83	15.59	16.61
EBITDA Margin %	24.26	21.50	21.16	21.36	20.66	19.75	18.74	18.75
Net Margin %	13.31	12.09	12.55	12.35	11.97	11.26	10.46	9.66
Asset Turnover	0.79	0.79	0.76	0.76	0.81	0.91	0.85	0.85
Current Ratio	0.78	1.04	1.14	1.71	1.29	1.97	1.45	1.64
Debt to Equity	0.36	0.34	0.33	0.28	0.32	0.12	0.13	0.37
Price Range	92.29-78.23	90.57-77.56	80.53-62.06	66.91-53.57	58.76-44.80	46.34-34.28	35.33-29.86	30.97-23.14
P/E Ratio	29.49-24.99	29.50-25.26	26.75-20.62	23.98-19.20	23.98-18.29	21.86-16.17	18.79-15.89	18.11-13.53
Average Yield %	1.59	1.58	1.77	1.81	1.84	1.67	0.94	0.84

Address: 500 Charles Ewing Boulevard, Ewing, NJ 08628	Web Site: www.churchdwight.com	Auditors: Deloitte & Touche LLP
Telephone: 609-806-1200	Officers: James R. Craigie - Chairman, Chief Executive Officer Matthew Thomas Farrell - President,	Investor Contact: 609-497-7111
Fax: 609-497-7269	Chief Executive Officer, Executive Vice President, Chief Financial Officer, Chief Operating Officer	Transfer Agents: Computershare Inc., Canton, MA

CIENA CORP

Exchange	Symbol	Price	52Wk Range	Yield	P/E
NYS	CIEN	$17.46 (5/31/2016)	26.03-15.73	N/A	194.00

*7 Year Price Score 101.52 *NYSE Composite Index=100 ***12 Month Price Score 80.06**

Interim Earnings (Per Share)

Qtr.	Jan	Apr	Jul	Oct
2012-13	(0.47)	(0.27)	(0.01)	(0.09)
2013-14	(0.15)	(0.10)	0.15	(0.29)
2014-15	(0.17)	0.17	0.19	(0.12)
2015-16	(0.08)	0.10	...	...

Interim Dividends (Per Share)

No Dividends Paid

Valuation Analysis — **Institutional Holding**

Forecast EPS	$1.38	No of Institutions
	(05/20/2016)	453
Market Cap	$2.4 Billion	Shares
Book Value	$669.0 Million	149,908,752
Price/Book	3.60	% Held
Price/Sales	0.96	N/A

TRADING VOLUME (thousand shares)

Business Summary: IT Services (MIC: 6.3.1 SIC: 7373 NAIC: 541512)

Ciena provides equipment, software and services that support the transport, switching, aggregation, service delivery and management of voice, video and data traffic on communications networks. Co.'s Converged Packet Optical, Packet Networking, and Optical Transport products are used by communications service providers, cable and multiservice operators, Web-scale providers, submarine network operators, governments, enterprises, research and education institutions, and other network operators. To complement its product portfolio, Co. provides a range of consulting and support services that help customers design, optimize, deploy, manage and maintain their communications networks.

Recent Developments: For the quarter ended Apr 30 2016, net income decreased 32.2% to US$14.0 million from US$20.7 million in the year-earlier quarter. Revenues were US$640.7 million, up 3.1% from US$621.6 million the year before. Operating income was US$28.2 million versus US$42.4 million in the prior-year quarter, a decrease of 33.4%. Direct operating expenses rose 2.4% to US$357.6 million from US$349.2 million in the comparable period the year before. Indirect operating expenses increased 10.8% to US$254.9 million from US$230.0 million in the equivalent prior-year period.

Prospects: Our evaluation of CIENA Corp. as of June 19, 2016 is the result of our systematic analysis on three basic characteristics: earnings strength, relative valuation, and recent stock price movement. The company has suffered a very negative trend in earnings per share over the past 5 quarters and while recent estimates for the company have been raised by analysts, CIEN has posted better than expected results. Based on operating earnings yield, the company is about fairly valued when compared to all of the companies in our coverage universe. Share price changes over the past year indicates that CIEN will perform very poorly over the near term.

Financial Data

(US$ in Thousands)	6 Mos	3 Mos	10/31/2015	10/31/2014	10/31/2013	10/31/2012	10/31/2011	10/31/2010
Earnings Per Share	0.09	0.16	0.10	(0.38)	(0.83)	(1.45)	(2.04)	(3.58)
Cash Flow Per Share	2.01	1.87	2.21	0.85	0.44	1.08	(0.94)	(2.46)
Tang Book Value Per Share	1.57	1.37	1.19	...	...	...	N.M.	N.M.
Income Statement								
Total Revenue	1,213,832	573,115	2,445,669	2,288,289	2,082,546	1,833,923	1,741,970	1,236,636
EBITDA	95,677	43,645	202,050	125,295	89,203	45,951	(9,517)	(151,353)
Depn & Amortn	65,288	32,406	125,966	103,751	119,608	125,797	146,427	165,518
Income Before Taxes	6,345	(10,247)	23,764	(26,673)	(80,191)	(134,699)	(187,848)	(331,573)
Income Taxes	3,894	1,299	12,097	13,964	5,240	9,322	7,673	1,941
Net Income	2,451	(11,546)	11,667	(40,637)	(85,431)	(144,021)	(195,521)	(333,514)
Average Shares	138,889	136,675	120,101	105,783	102,350	99,341	95,854	93,103
Balance Sheet								
Current Assets	2,078,049	1,751,020	1,864,210	1,693,190	1,395,802	1,415,690	1,332,838	1,441,568
Total Assets	2,981,583	2,589,315	2,695,051	2,072,632	1,802,770	1,881,143	1,951,418	2,118,093
Current Liabilities	630,132	555,229	667,034	781,136	615,055	684,970	453,493	469,945
Long-Term Obligations	1,505,389	1,258,316	1,285,433	1,279,380	1,212,019	1,225,806	1,442,364	1,442,705
Total Liabilities	2,312,571	1,962,288	2,074,175	2,142,247	1,885,447	1,970,115	1,937,545	1,958,800
Stockholders' Equity	669,012	627,027	620,876	(69,615)	(82,677)	(88,972)	13,873	159,293
Shares Outstanding	138,008	137,436	135,612	106,979	103,705	100,601	97,440	94,060
Statistical Record								
Return on Assets %	0.48	0.81	0.49	N.M.	N.M.	N.M.	N.M.	N.M.
Return on Equity %	3.03	7.02	4.23	...	...	...	N.M.	N.M.
EBITDA Margin %	7.88	7.62	8.26	5.48	4.28	2.51	N.M.	N.M.
Net Margin %	0.20	N.M.	0.48	N.M.	N.M.	N.M.	N.M.	N.M.
Asset Turnover	0.99	1.07	1.03	1.18	1.13	0.95	0.86	0.68
Current Ratio	3.30	3.15	2.79	2.17	2.27	2.07	2.94	3.07
Debt to Equity	2.25	2.01	2.07	...	...	...	103.97	9.06
Price Range	26.03-16.63	26.03-17.28	26.03-14.81	26.20-14.16	27.67-12.42	17.98-10.38	28.81-10.28	19.24-10.67
P/E Ratio	289.22-184.78	162.69-108.00	260.30-148.10	...	...	...	...	...

Address: 7035 Ridge Road, Hanover, MD 21076
Telephone: 410-694-5700
Fax: 410-694-5750

Web Site: www.ciena.com
Officers: Patrick H. Nettles - Executive Chairman
Gary B. Smith - President, Chief Executive Officer

Auditors: PricewaterhouseCoopers LLP
Transfer Agents: Computershare Trust Company, N.A., Providence, RI

CIGNA CORP

Exchange	Symbol	Price	52Wk Range	Yield	P/E
NYS	CI	$128.11 (5/31/2016)	169.77-124.81	0.03	16.01

*7 Year Price Score 168.77 *NYSE Composite Index=100   *12 Month Price Score 94.65

Interim Earnings (Per Share)

Qtr.	Mar	Jun	Sep	Dec
2013	0.20	1.76	1.95	1.29
2014	1.02	2.12	2.01	1.78
2015	2.04	2.26	2.10	1.64
2016	2.00	...	...	...

Interim Dividends (Per Share)

Amt	Decl	Ex	Rec	Pay
0.04A	02/27/2013	03/08/2013	03/12/2013	04/10/2013
0.04A	02/26/2014	03/10/2014	03/12/2014	04/09/2014
0.04A	02/25/2015	03/10/2015	03/12/2015	04/09/2015
0.04A	02/24/2016	03/09/2016	03/11/2016	04/11/2016

Indicated Div: $0.04

Valuation Analysis

Forecast EPS	$9.27
	(05/20/2016)
Market Cap	$32.9 Billion
Book Value	$12.7 Billion
Price/Book	2.59
Price/Sales	0.86

Institutional Holding

No of Institutions	982
Shares	250,656,688
% Held	80.86

TRADING VOLUME (thousand shares)

Business Summary: Life & Health (MIC: 5.2.2 SIC: 6324 NAIC: 524114)

Cigna is a holding company. Co is a health services organization. Through its subsidiaries, Co. provides medical, dental, disability, life and accident insurance and related products and services, the majority of which are provide through employers and other groups such as governmental and non-governmental organizations, unions and associations. Co. also provides commercial health and dental insurance, Medicare and Medicaid products and health, life and accident insurance coverages to individuals in the U.S. and selected international markets. Co.'s segments include: Global Health Care; Global Supplemental Benefits; Group Disability and Life; and Other Operations.

Recent Developments: For the quarter ended Mar 31 2016, net income decreased 3.2% to US$514.0 million from US$531.0 million in the year-earlier quarter. Revenues were US$9.88 billion, up 4.4% from US$9.47 billion the year before. Net premiums earned were US$7.75 billion versus US$7.40 billion in the prior-year quarter, an increase of 4.6%. Net investment income fell 1.4% to US$272.0 million from US$276.0 million a year ago.

Prospects: Our evaluation of Cigna Corp. as of June 19, 2016 is the result of our systematic analysis on three basic characteristics: earnings strength, relative valuation, and recent stock price movement. The company has generated a negative trend in earnings per share over the past 5 quarters and while recent estimates for the company have remained steady, CI has posted better than expected results. Based on operating earnings yield, the company is undervalued when compared to all of the companies in our coverage universe. Share price changes over the past year indicates that CI will perform in line with the market over the near term.

Financial Data
(US$ in Millions)

	3 Mos	12/31/2015	12/31/2014	12/31/2013	12/31/2012	12/31/2011	12/31/2010	12/31/2009
Earnings Per Share	8.00	8.04	7.83	5.18	5.61	4.84	4.89	4.73
Cash Flow Per Share	11.56	10.61	7.56	2.57	8.23	5.51	6.39	2.72
Tang Book Value Per Share	25.91	23.45	18.46	16.47	13.18	18.14	12.97	9.27
Dividends Per Share	0.040	0.040	0.040	0.040	0.040	0.040	0.040	0.040
Dividend Payout %	0.50	0.50	0.51	0.77	0.71	0.83	0.82	0.85
Income Statement								
Premium Income	7,746	29,642	27,214	28,976	26,187	19,089	18,393	16,041
Total Revenue	9,884	37,876	34,914	32,380	29,119	21,998	21,253	18,414
Benefits & Claims	6,129	23,290	21,334	20,865	17,859	12,724	12,288	10,030
Income Before Taxes	819	3,327	3,304	2,176	2,477	1,968	1,870	1,898
Income Taxes	305	1,250	1,210	698	853	640	521	594
Net Income	519	2,094	2,102	1,476	1,623	1,327	1,345	1,302
Average Shares	259	260	268	284	289	274	275	275
Balance Sheet								
Total Assets	58,884	57,088	55,896	54,336	53,734	51,047	45,682	43,013
Total Liabilities	46,209	45,053	45,122	43,769	43,965	42,703	39,037	37,596
Stockholders' Equity	12,675	12,035	10,774	10,567	9,769	8,344	6,645	5,417
Shares Outstanding	256	256	259	275	285	285	271	274
Statistical Record								
Return on Assets %	3.56	3.71	3.81	2.73	3.09	2.74	3.03	3.08
Return on Equity %	17.61	18.36	19.70	14.52	17.87	17.71	22.30	28.90
Loss Ratio %	79.12	78.57	78.39	72.01	68.20	66.66	66.81	62.53
Net Margin %	5.25	5.53	6.02	4.56	5.57	6.03	6.33	7.07
Price Range	169.77-124.64	169.77-101.06	105.20-75.64	88.18-53.46	54.49-39.66	52.62-36.66	38.26-29.77	37.19-12.87
P/E Ratio	21.22-15.58	21.12-12.57	13.44-9.66	17.02-10.32	9.71-7.07	10.87-7.57	7.82-6.09	7.86-2.72
Average Yield %	0.03	0.03	0.04	0.06	0.09	0.09	0.12	0.16

Address: 900 Cottage Grove Road, Bloomfield, CT 06002
Telephone: 860-226-6000
Fax: 860-226-6741

Web Site: www.cigna.com
Officers: Isaiah Harris - Chairman David M. Cordani - President, Chief Executive Officer

Auditors: PricewaterhouseCoopers LLP
Investor Contact: 215-761-1414
Transfer Agents: Computershare Shareowner Services, Providence, RI

CIMAREX ENERGY CO

Exchange	Symbol	Price	52Wk Range	Yield	P/E
NYS	XEC	$116.28 (5/31/2016)	122.96-75.60	0.28	N/A

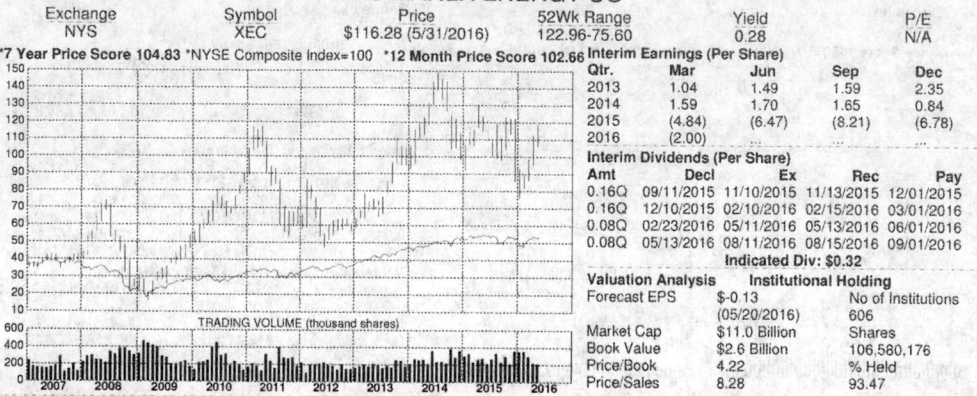

*7 Year Price Score 104.83 *NYSE Composite Index=100 *12 Month Price Score 102.66

Interim Earnings (Per Share)

Qtr.	Mar	Jun	Sep	Dec
2013	1.04	1.49	1.59	2.35
2014	1.59	1.70	1.65	0.84
2015	(4.84)	(6.47)	(8.21)	(6.78)
2016	(2.00)	...	...	...

Interim Dividends (Per Share)

Amt	Decl	Ex	Rec	Pay
0.16Q	09/11/2015	11/10/2015	11/13/2015	12/01/2015
0.16Q	12/10/2015	02/10/2016	02/15/2016	03/01/2016
0.08Q	02/23/2016	05/11/2016	05/13/2016	06/01/2016
0.08Q	05/13/2016	08/11/2016	08/15/2016	09/01/2016

Indicated Div: $0.32

Valuation Analysis / **Institutional Holding**

Forecast EPS	$-0.13	No of Institutions
	(05/20/2016)	606
Market Cap	$11.0 Billion	Shares
Book Value	$2.6 Billion	106,580,176
Price/Book	4.22	% Held
Price/Sales	8.28	93.47

Business Summary: Production & Extraction (MIC: 9.1.1 SIC: 1311 NAIC: 211111)

Cimarex Energy is an independent oil and gas exploration and production company. Co.'s operations are mainly located in Oklahoma, Texas and New Mexico. Co.'s operations are focused in two main areas: the Permian Basin and the Mid-Continent region. Co.'s Permian Basin region encompasses west Texas and southeast New Mexico. Co.'s Mid-Continent region consists of Oklahoma and the Texas Panhandle. As of Dec 31 2015, Co.'s proved oil and gas reserves totaled 2.91 trillion cubic feet of natural gas equivalent, consisted of 1.52 trillion cubic feet of gas, and 107.8 million barrels of oil and 124.3 million barrels of natural gas liquids.

Recent Developments: For the quarter ended Mar 31 2016, net loss amounted to US$186.1 million versus a net loss of US$414.9 million in the year-earlier quarter. Revenues were US$240.6 million, down 33.4% from US$361.0 million the year before. Operating loss was US$278.1 million versus a loss of US$635.4 million in the prior-year quarter. Direct operating expenses declined 14.0% to US$70.7 million from US$82.2 million in the comparable period the year before. Indirect operating expenses decreased 51.0% to US$448.0 million from US$914.2 million in the equivalent prior-year period.

Prospects: Our evaluation of Cimarex Energy Co as of June 19, 2016 is the result of our systematic analysis on three basic characteristics: earnings strength, relative valuation, and recent stock price movement. The company has suffered a very negative trend in earnings per share over the past 5 quarters. Because the company lacks sufficient analyst estimate data, we place greater weight on the historical EPS trend as the measure of earnings strength. Based on operating earnings yield, the company is overvalued when compared to all of the companies in our coverage universe. Share price changes over the past year indicates that XEC will perform in line with the market over the near term.

Financial Data

(US$ in Thousands)	3 Mos	12/31/2015	12/31/2014	12/31/2013	12/31/2012	12/31/2011	12/31/2010	12/31/2009
Earnings Per Share	(23.46)	(25.92)	5.78	6.47	4.07	6.15	6.70	(3.82)
Cash Flow Per Share	7.13	7.44	18.90	15.53	14.03	15.06	13.25	8.02
Tang Book Value Per Share	21.03	22.96	44.30	39.03	32.96	28.44	22.51	16.12
Dividends Per Share	0.640	0.640	0.620	0.540	0.460	0.380	0.300	0.240
Dividend Payout %	...	...	10.73	8.35	11.30	6.18	4.48	...
Income Statement								
Total Revenue	240,600	1,452,619	2,424,176	1,998,051	1,623,938	1,757,889	1,613,683	1,009,794
EBITDA	(148,331)	(2,948,304)	1,648,862	1,533,030	1,088,609	1,238,496	1,225,351	(206,413)
Depn & Amortn	128,099	778,923	806,021	615,874	513,916	390,461	304,222	265,699
Income Before Taxes	(292,331)	(3,782,384)	805,901	893,700	560,550	841,481	913,731	(488,481)
Income Taxes	(106,200)	(1,373,436)	298,697	329,011	206,727	311,549	338,949	(176,538)
Net Income	(186,131)	(2,408,948)	507,204	564,689	353,823	529,932	574,782	(311,943)
Average Shares	93,000	92,992	85,810	85,409	85,034	86,232	85,782	84,192
Balance Sheet								
Current Assets	931,090	1,077,930	931,804	469,139	470,137	457,895	561,767	407,258
Total Assets	4,901,261	5,243,286	8,725,293	7,253,135	6,305,152	5,428,577	4,358,247	3,444,537
Current Liabilities	357,092	410,067	776,327	683,167	645,982	616,339	512,313	388,763
Long-Term Obligations	1,486,211	1,485,620	1,500,000	924,000	750,000	405,000	350,000	392,793
Total Liabilities	2,286,930	2,445,608	4,224,661	3,230,927	2,830,416	2,297,964	1,748,415	1,406,431
Stockholders' Equity	2,614,331	2,797,678	4,500,632	4,022,208	3,474,736	3,130,613	2,609,832	2,038,106
Shares Outstanding	94,815	94,820	87,592	87,152	86,595	85,774	85,234	83,541
Statistical Record								
Return on Assets %	N.M.	N.M.	6.35	8.33	6.01	10.83	14.73	N.M.
Return on Equity %	N.M.	N.M.	11.90	15.06	10.68	18.46	24.73	N.M.
EBITDA Margin %	N.M.	N.M.	68.02	76.73	67.04	70.45	75.94	N.M.
Net Margin %	N.M.	N.M.	20.92	28.26	21.79	30.15	35.62	N.M.
Asset Turnover	0.21	0.21	0.30	0.29	0.28	0.36	0.41	0.27
Current Ratio	2.61	2.63	1.20	0.69	0.73	0.74	1.10	1.05
Debt to Equity	0.57	0.53	0.33	0.23	0.22	0.13	0.13	0.19
Price Range	129.44-75.60	129.44-85.27	148.77-92.73	110.43-57.73	86.41-46.96	117.56-53.37	89.85-49.21	53.95-15.92
P/E Ratio	...	...	25.74-16.04	17.07-8.92	21.23-11.54	19.12-8.68	13.41-7.34	...
Average Yield %	0.60	0.58	0.51	0.67	0.75	0.45	0.43	0.71

Address: 1700 Lincoln Street, Suite 3700, Denver, CO 80203
Telephone: 303-295-3995

Web Site: www.cimarex.com
Officers: Thomas E. Jorden - Executive Vice President, President, Chief Executive Officer Joseph R. Albi - Executive Vice President, Chief Operating Officer

Auditors: KPMG LLP
Investor Contact: 303-295-3995
Transfer Agents: Continental Stock Transfer & Trust Company, New York, NY

CINEMARK HOLDINGS INC

Exchange	Symbol	Price	52Wk Range
NYS	CNK	$36.18 (5/31/2016)	42.06-27.15

Yield	P/E
2.99	18.00

*7 Year Price Score 116.27 *NYSE Composite Index=100 *12 Month Price Score 99.60

Interim Earnings (Per Share)

Qtr.	Mar	Jun	Sep	Dec
2013	0.28	0.18	0.69	0.13
2014	0.31	0.62	0.33	0.41
2015	0.37	0.61	0.40	0.50
2016	0.50	...	...	...

Interim Dividends (Per Share)

Amt	Decl	Ex	Rec	Pay
0.25Q	08/20/2015	08/27/2015	08/31/2015	09/11/2015
0.25Q	11/13/2015	11/30/2015	12/02/2015	12/16/2015
0.27Q	02/24/2016	03/03/2016	03/07/2016	03/18/2016
0.27Q	05/26/2016	06/06/2016	06/08/2016	06/22/2016

Indicated Div: $1.08

Valuation Analysis / Institutional Holding

Valuation Analysis		Institutional Holding	
Forecast EPS	$2.00 (05/20/2016)	No of Institutions	392
Market Cap	$4.2 Billion	Shares	110,218,360
Book Value	$1.1 Billion	% Held	88.88
Price/Book	3.69		
Price/Sales	1.44		

Business Summary: Entertainment (MIC: 2.3.2 SIC: 7832 NAIC: 512131)

Cinemark Holdings is a holding company. Through its subsidiaries, Co. is engaged in the motion picture exhibition industry, with theatres in the U. S., Brazil, Argentina, Chile, Colombia, Peru, Ecuador, Honduras, El Salvador, Nicaragua, Costa Rica, Panama, Guatemala, Bolivia and Curacao. At Dec 31 2015, Co. managed its business under two segments: U.S. markets and international markets. As of the same date, Co. operated 513 theatres and 5,796 screens in the U.S. and Latin America. Co. develops and expands new platforms and markets adaptive concepts for its theatre circuit, such as XD, Movie Bistro, Cinemark Reserve, Luxury Lounger reclining seats, D-BOX seating, CineArts and other concepts.

Recent Developments: For the quarter ended Mar 31 2016, net income increased 37.6% to US$59.0 million from US$42.9 million in the year-earlier quarter. Revenues were US$704.9 million, up 9.2% from US$645.4 million the year before. Operating income was US$114.8 million versus US$90.4 million in the prior-year quarter, an increase of 27.0%. Direct operating expenses rose 12.0% to US$268.8 million from US$240.1 million in the comparable period the year before. Indirect operating expenses increased 2.0% to US$321.2 million from US$314.8 million in the equivalent prior-year period.

Prospects: Our evaluation of Cinemark Holdings Inc. as of June 19, 2016 is the result of our systematic analysis on three basic characteristics: earnings strength, relative valuation, and recent stock price movement. The company has managed to produce a neutral trend in earnings per share over the past 5 quarters. However, while recent estimates for the company have been mixed, CNK has posted better than expected results. Based on operating earnings yield, the company is undervalued when compared to all of the companies in our coverage universe. Share price changes over the past year indicates that CNK will perform well over the near term.

Financial Data
(US$ in Thousands)

	3 Mos	12/31/2015	12/31/2014	12/31/2013	12/31/2012	12/31/2011	12/31/2010	12/31/2009
Earnings Per Share	2.01	1.87	1.66	1.28	1.47	1.14	1.29	0.87
Cash Flow Per Share	4.33	3.96	3.97	2.72	3.48	3.47	2.37	1.63
Dividends Per Share	1.020	1.000	1.000	0.920	0.840	0.840	0.750	0.720
Dividend Payout %	50.75	53.48	60.24	71.88	57.14	73.68	58.14	82.76
Income Statement								
Total Revenue	704,869	2,852,609	2,626,990	2,682,894	2,473,531	2,279,613	2,141,144	1,976,500
EBITDA	157,913	610,472	548,557	522,345	544,395	465,124	455,915	388,159
Depn & Amortn	45,843	186,898	173,138	160,071	143,394	150,149	138,637	144,055
Income Before Taxes	85,363	319,541	267,320	241,182	283,709	199,981	210,939	146,508
Income Taxes	33,459	128,939	96,064	113,316	125,398	73,050	57,838	44,845
Net Income	58,525	216,869	192,610	148,470	168,949	130,557	146,120	97,108
Average Shares	115,527	115,399	114,966	114,396	113,824	113,224	112,151	110,255
Balance Sheet								
Current Assets	685,907	715,151	741,010	729,599	845,161	627,118	577,053	507,297
Total Assets	4,128,715	4,126,497	4,151,980	4,144,163	3,863,226	3,522,408	3,421,478	3,276,448
Current Liabilities	389,894	439,793	414,407	395,712	338,204	305,027	271,940	280,832
Long-Term Obligations	2,000,268	1,981,882	2,016,552	2,025,453	1,893,571	1,691,633	1,654,417	1,664,506
Total Liabilities	2,989,156	3,026,789	3,039,180	3,050,741	2,779,161	2,509,531	2,399,931	2,376,616
Stockholders' Equity	1,139,559	1,099,708	1,112,800	1,093,422	1,084,065	1,012,877	1,021,547	899,832
Shares Outstanding	116,139	115,924	115,700	115,382	114,949	114,201	113,750	110,917
Statistical Record								
Return on Assets %	5.70	5.24	4.64	3.71	4.56	3.76	4.36	3.06
Return on Equity %	20.96	19.60	17.46	13.64	16.07	12.83	15.21	11.35
EBITDA Margin %	22.40	21.40	20.88	19.47	22.01	20.40	21.29	19.64
Net Margin %	8.30	7.60	7.33	5.53	6.83	5.73	6.82	4.91
Asset Turnover	0.71	0.69	0.63	0.67	0.67	0.66	0.64	0.62
Current Ratio	1.76	1.63	1.79	1.84	2.50	2.06	2.12	1.81
Debt to Equity	1.76	1.80	1.81	1.85	1.75	1.67	1.62	1.85
Price Range	45.52-27.15	45.52-31.56	36.37-27.73	34.17-25.98	27.20-18.04	21.75-16.82	19.35-12.95	14.53-6.83
P/E Ratio	22.65-13.51	24.34-16.88	21.91-16.70	26.70-20.30	18.50-12.27	19.08-14.75	15.00-10.04	16.70-7.85
Average Yield %	2.81	2.62	3.07	3.06	3.64	4.31	4.59	6.98

Address: 3900 Dallas Parkway, Suite 500, Plano, TX 75093 **Telephone:** 972-665-1000	**Web Site:** www.cinemark.com **Officers:** Lee Roy Mitchell - Chairman Timothy C. Warner - Vice-Chairman, President, Chief Executive Officer, Chief Operating Officer	**Auditors:** Deloitte & Touche LLP **Investor Contact:** 972-665-1500 **Transfer Agents:** Wells Fargo Shareholder Services

CITIGROUP INC

Exchange	Symbol	Price	52Wk Range	Yield	P/E
NYS	C	$46.57 (5/31/2016)	60.34-34.98	0.42	9.35

*7 Year Price Score 97.87   *NYSE Composite Index=100   *12 Month Price Score 88.81

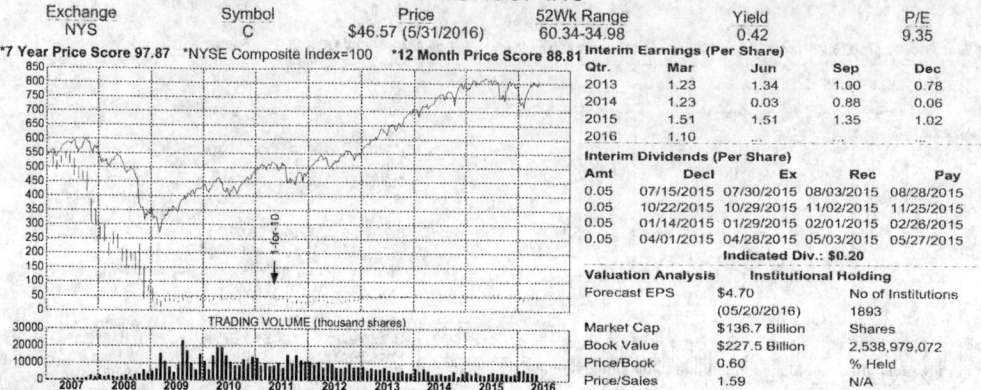

Interim Earnings (Per Share)

Qtr.	Mar	Jun	Sep	Dec
2013	1.23	1.34	1.00	0.78
2014	1.23	0.03	0.88	0.06
2015	1.51	1.51	1.35	1.02
2016	1.10			

Interim Dividends (Per Share)

Amt	Decl	Ex	Rec	Pay
0.05	07/15/2015	07/30/2015	08/03/2015	08/28/2015
0.05	10/22/2015	10/29/2015	11/02/2015	11/25/2015
0.05	01/14/2016	01/29/2015	02/01/2016	02/26/2015
0.05	04/01/2015	04/28/2015	05/03/2015	05/27/2015

Indicated Div.: $0.20

Valuation Analysis

		Institutional Holding	
Forecast EPS	$4.70	No of Institutions	
	(05/20/2016)	1893	
Market Cap	$136.7 Billion	Shares	
Book Value	$227.5 Billion	2,538,979,072	
Price/Book	0.60	% Held	
Price/Sales	1.59	N/A	

Business Summary: Banking (MIC: 5.1.1 SIC: 6021 NAIC: 522110)

Citigroup is a financial services holding company whose businesses provide consumers, corporations, governments and institutions with financial products and services, including consumer banking and credit, corporate and investment banking, securities brokerage, securities services and wealth management. Co. operates in two primary business segments: Citicorp, consisting of Global Consumer Banking businesses and Institutional Clients Group; and Citi Holdings, consisting of businesses and portfolios of assets that Co. has determined are not central to its core Citicorp businesses. As of Dec 31 2015, Co. had total assets of $1.73 trillion and total deposits of $907.88 billion.

Recent Developments: For the quarter ended Mar 31 2016, income from continuing operations decreased 27.2% to US$3.51 billion from US$4.82 billion in the year-earlier quarter. Net income decreased 27.1% to US$3.51 billion from US$4.81 billion in the year-earlier quarter. Net interest income decreased 3.0% to US$11.23 billion from US$11.57 billion in the year-earlier quarter. Provision for loan losses was US$1.96 billion versus US$1.72 billion in the prior-year quarter, an increase of 13.9%. Non-interest income fell 22.5% to US$6.33 billion from US$8.16 billion, while non-interest expense declined 4.2% to US$10.61 billion.

Prospects: Our evaluation of Citigroup Inc. as of June 19, 2016 is the result of our systematic analysis on three basic characteristics: earnings strength, relative valuation, and recent stock price movement. The company has suffered a very negative trend in earnings per share over the past 5 quarters. However, while recent estimates for the company have been lowered by analysts, C has posted better than expected results. Based on operating earnings yield, the company is undervalued when compared to all of the companies in our coverage universe. Share price changes over the past year indicates that C will perform in line with the market over the near term.

Financial Data

(US$ in Thousands)	3 Mos	12/31/2015	12/31/2014	12/31/2013	12/31/2012	12/31/2011	12/31/2010	12/31/2009
Earnings Per Share	4.98	5.40	2.20	4.35	2.44	3.63	3.50	(8.00)
Cash Flow Per Share	12.84	13.23	14.99	18.91	4.86	15.38	12.40	(48.17)
Tang Book Value Per Share	62.07	60.03	56.24	54.41	50.57	48.88	43.00	39.23
Dividends Per Share	0.200	0.160	0.040	0.040	0.040	0.030	...	0.100
Dividend Payout %	4.02	2.96	1.82	0.92	1.64	0.83	...	...
Income Statement								
Interest Income	14,167,000	58,551,000	61,683,000	62,970,000	68,138,000	72,681,000	79,516,000	76,635,000
Interest Expense	2,940,000	11,921,000	13,690,000	16,177,000	20,535,000	24,234,000	24,864,000	27,721,000
Net Interest Income	11,227,000	46,630,000	47,993,000	46,793,000	47,603,000	48,447,000	54,652,000	48,914,000
Provision for Losses	1,957,000	7,108,000	6,828,000	7,604,000	10,848,000	11,773,000	25,194,000	38,760,000
Non-Interest Income	6,328,000	29,724,000	28,889,000	29,573,000	22,570,000	29,906,000	31,949,000	31,371,000
Non-Interest Expense	10,611,000	44,420,000	55,690,000	49,265,000	51,389,000	51,956,000	48,223,000	49,324,000
Income Before Taxes	4,987,000	24,826,000	14,364,000	19,497,000	7,936,000	14,624,000	13,184,000	(7,799,000)
Income Taxes	1,479,000	7,440,000	6,864,000	5,867,000	27,000	3,521,000	2,233,000	(6,733,000)
Net Income	3,501,000	17,242,000	7,313,000	13,673,000	7,541,000	11,067,000	10,602,000	(1,606,000)
Average Shares	2,943,100	3,007,700	3,037,000	3,041,600	3,015,500	2,998,800	2,967,810	1,209,900
Balance Sheet								
Net Loans & Leases	606,112,000	604,991,000	628,641,000	645,824,000	630,009,000	617,127,000	608,139,000	555,471,000
Total Assets	1,800,967,000	1,731,210,000	1,842,530,000	1,880,382,000	1,864,660,000	1,873,878,000	1,913,902,000	1,856,646,000
Total Deposits	934,591,000	907,887,000	899,332,000	968,273,000	930,560,000	865,936,000	844,968,000	835,903,000
Total Liabilities	1,573,445,000	1,509,353,000	1,631,996,000	1,676,043,000	1,675,611,000	1,696,072,000	1,750,434,000	1,703,946,000
Stockholders' Equity	227,522,000	221,857,000	210,534,000	204,339,000	189,049,000	177,806,000	163,468,000	152,700,000
Shares Outstanding	2,934,929	2,953,279	3,023,918	3,029,243	3,028,884	2,923,878	2,905,836	2,848,327
Statistical Record								
Return on Assets %	0.88	0.96	0.39	0.73	0.40	0.58	0.56	N.M.
Return on Equity %	7.23	7.98	3.53	6.95	4.10	6.49	6.71	N.M.
Net Interest Margin %	79.25	79.64	77.81	74.31	69.86	66.66	68.73	63.83
Efficiency Ratio %	51.77	50.32	61.49	53.23	56.65	50.65	43.26	45.67
Loans to Deposits	0.65	0.67	0.70	0.67	0.68	0.71	0.72	0.66
Price Range	60.34-34.98	60.34-46.95	56.37-45.68	53.29-39.56	40.17-24.82	51.30-23.11	49.70-31.50	74.60-10.20
P/E Ratio	12.12-7.02	11.17-8.69	25.62-20.76	12.25-9.09	16.46-10.17	14.13-6.37	14.20-9.00	...
Average Yield %	0.39	0.30	0.08	0.08	0.12	0.08	...	0.27

Address: 388 Greenwich Street, New York, NY 10013
Telephone: 212-559-1000

Web Site: www.citigroup.com
Officers: Michael E. O'Neill - Chairman Michael S. Helfer - Vice-Chairman, General Counsel, Corporate Secretary

Auditors: KPMG LLP
Investor Contact: 212-559-2718
Transfer Agents: Computershare Trust Company, N.A., Providence, RI

CLARCOR INC.

Exchange	Symbol	Price	52Wk Range	Yield	P/E	Div Achiever
NYS	CLC	$59.30 (5/31/2016)	63.53-44.29	1.48	20.38	35 Years

*7 Year Price Score 93.36   *NYSE Composite Index=100   *12 Month Price Score 106.13

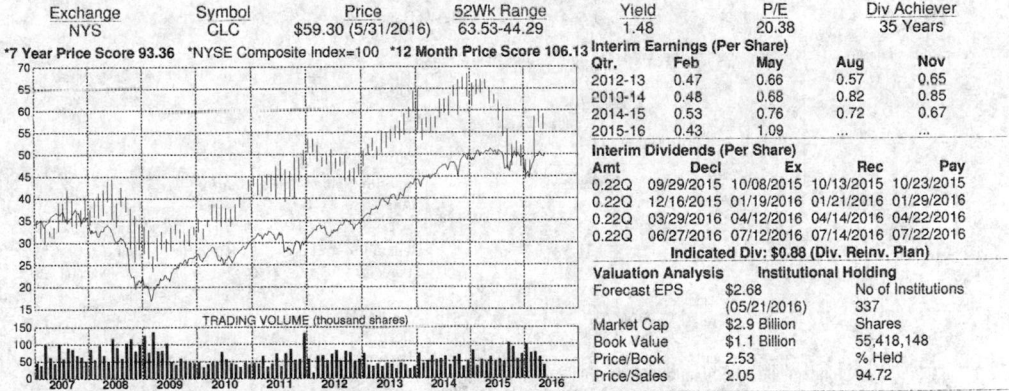

Interim Earnings (Per Share)

Qtr.	Feb	May	Aug	Nov
2012-13	0.47	0.66	0.57	0.65
2013-14	0.48	0.68	0.82	0.85
2014-15	0.53	0.76	0.72	0.67
2015-16	0.43	1.09	...	...

Interim Dividends (Per Share)

Amt	Decl	Ex	Rec	Pay
0.22Q	09/29/2015	10/08/2015	10/13/2015	10/23/2015
0.22Q	12/16/2015	01/19/2016	01/21/2016	01/29/2016
0.22Q	03/29/2016	04/12/2016	04/14/2016	04/22/2016
0.22Q	06/27/2016	07/12/2016	07/14/2016	07/22/2016

Indicated Div: $0.88 (Div. Reinv. Plan)

Valuation Analysis		Institutional Holding	
Forecast EPS	$2.68		
	(05/21/2016)	No of Institutions	337
Market Cap	$2.9 Billion	Shares	
Book Value	$1.1 Billion		55,418,148
Price/Book	2.53	% Held	
Price/Sales	2.05		94.72

Business Summary: Industrial Machinery & Equipment (MIC: 7.2.1 SIC: 3714 NAIC: 336399)

Clarcor is a provider of filtration products, filtration systems and services, and consumer and industrial packaging products. Co. has three reportable segments: Engine/Mobile Filtration, which manufactures and sells filtration products for on-road and off-road mobile and stationary applications; Industrial/Environmental Filtration, which manufactures and sells filtration products used in industrial and commercial processes, and in buildings and infrastructures of various types; and Packaging; which manufactured a range of different types and sizes of containers and packaging capabilities.

Recent Developments: For the quarter ended May 28 2016, net income increased 38.4% to US$53.4 million from US$38.6 million in the year-earlier quarter. Revenues were US$365.0 million, down 8.7% from US$399.8 million the year before. Operating income was US$53.8 million versus US$58.9 million in the prior-year quarter, a decrease of 8.8%. Direct operating expenses declined 8.7% to US$243.1 million from US$266.2 million in the comparable period the year before. Indirect operating expenses decreased 8.8% to US$68.1 million from US$74.7 million in the equivalent prior-year period.

Prospects: Our evaluation of Clarcor Inc. as of June 26, 2016 is the result of our systematic analysis on three basic characteristics: earnings strength, relative valuation, and recent stock price movement. The company has enjoyed a very positive trend in earnings per share over the past 5 quarters. However, while recent estimates for the company have been mixed, CLC has posted better than expected results. Based on operating earnings yield, the company is about fairly valued when compared to all of the companies in our coverage universe. Share price changes over the past year indicates that CLC will perform in line with the market over the near term.

Financial Data
(US$ in Thousands)

	6 Mos	3 Mos	11/28/2015	11/29/2014	11/30/2013	11/30/2012	12/03/2011	11/27/2010
Earnings Per Share	2.91	2.58	2.67	2.83	2.34	2.42	2.42	1.88
Cash Flow Per Share	...	...	3.08	3.11	2.71	2.72	2.33	2.82
Tang Book Value Per Share	6.32	5.26	5.58	4.97	13.91	11.34	9.98	8.69
Dividends Per Share	0.860	0.840	0.820	0.710	0.575	0.495	0.435	0.398
Dividend Payout %	29.55	32.56	30.71	25.09	24.57	20.45	17.98	21.14
Income Statement								
Total Revenue	681,240	316,272	1,481,026	1,512,854	1,130,770	1,121,765	1,126,601	1,011,429
EBITDA	142,385	46,506	234,226	244,908	200,554	208,849	207,954	169,800
Depn & Amortn	29,194	14,033	31,075	30,065	26,329	25,925	26,826	26,119
Income Before Taxes	109,469	30,490	197,965	211,563	174,300	182,997	181,308	143,423
Income Taxes	34,908	9,300	63,052	67,380	55,950	59,657	56,947	47,072
Net Income	74,517	21,163	134,704	144,084	118,076	122,986	124,003	96,081
Average Shares	49,153	49,104	50,429	50,871	50,538	50,882	51,191	51,156
Balance Sheet								
Current Assets	641,492	644,299	664,795	728,907	892,121	654,594	600,899	526,273
Total Assets	1,789,957	1,782,257	1,818,456	1,888,769	1,448,843	1,205,502	1,134,933	1,042,411
Current Liabilities	195,769	192,013	203,700	224,380	207,761	174,891	160,050	163,457
Long-Term Obligations	329,795	395,841	397,368	411,330	116,413	16,391	15,981	17,331
Total Liabilities	646,554	700,704	708,887	784,709	416,995	304,658	300,206	285,941
Stockholders' Equity	1,143,403	1,081,553	1,109,569	1,104,060	1,031,848	900,844	834,727	756,470
Shares Outstanding	48,760	48,500	49,110	50,204	50,370	49,652	50,144	50,334
Statistical Record								
Return on Assets %	7.80	7.02	7.29	8.66	8.90	10.57	11.21	9.56
Return on Equity %	12.70	11.82	12.20	13.53	12.22	14.25	15.33	13.35
EBITDA Margin %	20.90	14.70	15.82	16.19	17.74	18.62	18.46	16.79
Net Margin %	10.94	6.69	9.10	9.52	10.44	10.96	11.01	9.50
Asset Turnover	0.76	0.79	0.80	0.91	0.85	0.96	1.02	1.01
Current Ratio	3.28	3.36	3.26	3.25	4.29	3.74	3.75	3.22
Debt to Equity	0.29	0.37	0.36	0.37	0.11	0.02	0.02	0.02
Price Range	63.53-44.29	67.04-44.29	68.32-46.54	67.45-53.08	60.65-45.13	53.47-43.14	49.23-39.17	42.01-30.72
P/E Ratio	21.83-15.22	25.98-17.17	25.59-17.43	23.83-18.76	25.92-19.29	22.10-17.83	20.34-16.19	22.35-16.34
Average Yield %	1.60	1.50	1.36	1.18	1.08	1.02	0.99	1.11

Address: 840 Crescent Centre Drive, Suite 600, Franklin, TN 37067 Telephone: 615-771-3100 Fax: 615-771-5603	Web Site: www.clarcor.com Officers: Christopher L. Conway - Chairman, President, Chief Executive Officer, Chief Operating Officer David J. Lindsay - Vice President, Chief Administrative Officer	Auditors: PricewaterhouseCoopers LLP Investor Contact: 615-771-3100 Transfer Agents: Computershare Investor Services, Canton, MA

CLEAN HARBORS, INC

Exchange	Symbol	Price	52Wk Range	Yield	P/E
NYS	CLH	$51.49 (5/31/2016)	56.51-39.35	N/A	97.15

*7 Year Price Score 82.20   *NYSE Composite Index=100   *12 Month Price Score 103.34

TRADING VOLUME (thousand shares)

Interim Earnings (Per Share)

Qtr.	Mar	Jun	Sep	Dec
2013	0.17	0.38	0.58	0.44
2014	0.15	0.47	(1.55)	0.45
2015	(0.12)	0.18	0.69	0.02
2016	(0.36)	...	...	...

Interim Dividends (Per Share)

Amt	Decl	Ex	Rec	Pay
100%	06/08/2011	07/27/2011	07/06/2011	07/26/2011

Valuation Analysis   Institutional Holding

Forecast EPS	$0.67 (05/17/2016)	No of Institutions 333
Market Cap	$3.0 Billion	Shares
Book Value	$1.1 Billion	61,891,404
Price/Book	2.65	% Held
Price/Sales	0.93	96.12

Business Summary: Sanitation Services (MIC: 7.5.3 SIC: 4953 NAIC: 562112)

Clean Harbors is a provider of environmental, energy and industrial services throughout North America. Co.'s operations are managed in six reportable segments: Technical Services, which provides a range of hazardous material management services; Industrial and Field Services, which provides industrial and specialty services; Kleen Performance Products, which processes used oil into high quality base and blended lubricating oils; SK Environmental Services, which consists of Safety-Kleen's branches and provides a range of environmental services; Lodging Services, which provides lodges and remote workforce accommodation facilities; and Oil and Gas Field Services, which provides fluid handling.

Recent Developments:
For the quarter ended Mar 31 2016, net loss amounted to US$20.9 million versus a net loss of US$7.1 million in the year-earlier quarter. Revenues were US$636.1 million, down 13.2% from US$732.5 million the year before. Operating loss was US$4.1 million versus an income of US$7.3 million in the prior-year quarter. Direct operating expenses declined 15.0% to US$464.3 million from US$546.5 million in the comparable period the year before. Indirect operating expenses decreased 1.6% to US$175.9 million from US$178.7 million in the equivalent prior-year period.

Prospects:
Our evaluation of Clean Harbors Inc. as of June 19, 2016 is the result of our systematic analysis on three basic characteristics: earnings strength, relative valuation, and recent stock price movement. The company has suffered a very negative trend in earnings per share over the past 5 quarters and while recent estimates for the company have been raised by analysts, CLH has posted results that fell short of analysts expectations. Based on operating earnings yield, the company is overvalued when compared to all of the companies in our coverage universe. Share price changes over the past year indicates that CLH will perform poorly over the near term.

Financial Data

(US$ in Thousands)	3 Mos	12/31/2015	12/31/2014	12/31/2013	12/31/2012	12/31/2011	12/31/2010	12/31/2009
Earnings Per Share	0.53	0.76	(0.47)	1.57	2.40	2.39	2.46	0.73
Cash Flow Per Share	6.09	6.80	4.93	6.86	6.00	3.39	4.26	1.88
Tang Book Value Per Share	2.67	2.37	4.76	5.52	4.40	12.01	11.49	8.45
Income Statement								
Total Revenue	636,083	3,275,137	3,401,636	3,509,656	2,187,908	1,984,136	1,731,244	1,074,220
EBITDA	(3,506)	420,199	355,590	434,761	338,456	348,302	307,807	144,366
Depn & Amortn	931	234,000	239,400	212,500	163,439	124,235	95,394	66,895
Income Before Taxes	(23,417)	109,646	38,522	143,885	127,730	184,678	184,477	61,472
Income Taxes	(2,546)	65,544	66,850	48,319	(1,944)	57,426	56,756	26,225
Net Income	(20,871)	44,102	(28,328)	95,566	129,674	127,252	130,515	36,686
Average Shares	57,617	58,434	60,311	60,728	54,079	53,324	52,934	49,866
Balance Sheet								
Current Assets	1,063,621	921,196	1,126,433	1,171,179	1,086,793	891,868	752,537	620,250
Total Assets	3,641,675	3,431,428	3,704,278	3,953,678	3,825,806	2,085,803	1,602,475	1,401,068
Current Liabilities	465,510	517,120	572,471	639,545	569,052	381,742	306,284	233,320
Long-Term Obligations	1,631,603	1,382,543	1,395,000	1,401,435	1,402,879	530,578	270,846	299,348
Total Liabilities	2,525,102	2,335,146	2,441,407	2,478,039	2,393,734	1,184,816	821,648	787,243
Stockholders' Equity	1,116,573	1,096,282	1,262,871	1,475,639	1,432,072	900,987	780,827	613,825
Shares Outstanding	57,551	57,593	58,903	60,672	60,385	53,182	52,772	52,461
Statistical Record								
Return on Assets %	0.84	1.24	N.M.	2.46	4.38	6.90	8.69	3.19
Return on Equity %	2.66	3.74	N.M.	6.57	11.09	15.13	18.72	7.04
EBITDA Margin %	N.M.	12.83	10.45	12.39	15.47	17.55	17.78	13.44
Net Margin %	N.M.	1.35	N.M.	2.72	5.93	6.41	7.54	3.42
Asset Turnover	0.88	0.92	0.89	0.90	0.74	1.08	1.15	0.93
Current Ratio	2.28	1.78	1.97	1.83	1.91	2.34	2.46	2.66
Debt to Equity	1.46	1.26	1.10	0.95	0.98	0.59	0.35	0.49
Price Range	58.87-39.35	58.87-40.22	64.51-44.98	62.53-50.30	70.30-47.16	64.17-40.58	42.09-26.75	31.84-20.54
P/E Ratio	111.08-74.25	77.46-52.92	...	39.83-32.04	29.29-19.65	26.85-16.98	17.11-10.87	43.61-28.14

Address: 42 Longwater Drive, Norwell, MA 02061-9149 Telephone: 781-792-5000	Web Site: www.cleanharbors.com Officers: Alan S. McKim - Chairman, President, Chief Executive Officer James M. Rutledge - Vice-Chairman, President, Chief Financial Officer, Executive Vice President, Chief Operating Officer, Treasurer	Auditors: Deloitte & Touche LLP Investor Contact: 617-542-5300 Transfer Agents: American Stock Transfer & Trust Company, New York, NY

CLEAR CHANNEL OUTDOOR HOLDINGS INC

Exchange	Symbol	Price	52Wk Range	Yield	P/E
NYS	CCO	$6.43 (5/31/2016)	11.58-3.41	N/A	30.62

*7 Year Price Score 63.22 *NYSE Composite Index=100 *12 Month Price Score 77.17

Interim Earnings (Per Share)

Qtr.	Mar	Jun	Sep	Dec
2013	(0.22)	0.02	0.01	0.04
2014	(0.27)	0.14	(0.02)	0.12
2015	(0.09)	0.00	(0.06)	(0.12)
2016	0.39	...	...	...

Interim Dividends (Per Share)

Amt	Decl	Ex	Rec	Pay
0.558Sp	10/21/2013	11/12/2013	11/05/2013	11/08/2013
0.486Sp	07/23/2014	08/12/2014	08/04/2014	08/11/2014
0.603Sp	12/21/2015	01/08/2016	01/04/2016	01/07/2016
1.494Sp	01/21/2016	02/05/2016	02/01/2016	02/04/2016

Valuation Analysis

	Institutional Holding	
Forecast EPS	$0.44	No of Institutions
	(05/14/2016)	146
Market Cap	$2.3 Billion	Shares
Book Value	N/A	35,238,072
Price/Book	N/A	% Held
Price/Sales	0.84	9.90

Business Summary: Advertising (MIC: 2.3.4 SIC: 7312 NAIC: 541850)

Clear Channel Outdoor Holdings is a holding company. Co. provides clients with advertising opportunities through billboards, street furniture displays, transit displays and other out-of-home advertising displays, such as wallscapes, and spectaculars, which it owns or operates. Co. has two reportable operating segments: Americas outdoor advertising (Americas) and International outdoor advertising (International). The Americas segment primarily includes operations in the U. S. and Canada. The International segment primarily includes operations in Europe, Asia, Latin America and Australia. As of Dec 31 2014, Co. owned or operated more than 640,000 advertising displays worldwide.

Recent Developments: For the quarter ended Mar 31 2016, net income amounted to US$141.1 million versus a net loss of US$33.0 million in the year-earlier quarter. Revenues were US$590.7 million, down 4.0% from US$615.0 million the year before. Operating income was US$291.4 million versus a loss of US$3.3 million in the prior-year quarter. Direct operating expenses declined 5.3% to US$343.7 million from US$363.0 million in the comparable period the year before. Indirect operating income amounted to US$44.3 million compared with an expense of US$255.4 million in the equivalent prior-year period.

Prospects: Our evaluation of Clear Channel Outdoor Holdings Inc. as of June 19, 2016 is the result of our systematic analysis on three basic characteristics: earnings strength, relative valuation, and recent stock price movement. The company has produced a positive trend in earnings per share over the past 5 quarters. Because the company lacks sufficient analyst estimate data, we place greater weight on the historical EPS trend as the measure of earnings strength. Based on operating earnings yield, the company is overvalued when compared to all of the companies in our coverage universe. Share price changes over the past year indicates that CCO will perform very poorly over the near term.

Financial Data

(US$ in Thousands)	3 Mos	12/31/2015	12/31/2014	12/31/2013	12/31/2012	12/31/2011	12/31/2010	12/31/2009
Earnings Per Share	0.21	(0.27)	(0.03)	(0.14)	(0.54)	0.11	(0.26)	(2.46)
Cash Flow Per Share	0.85	0.83	0.97	1.16	0.99	1.45	1.48	1.24
Dividends Per Share	2.096	...	0.486	0.558	6.083	...	...	...
Dividend Payout %	998.24	...	...	...	...	...	...	...
Income Statement								
Total Revenue	590,721	2,806,204	2,961,259	2,946,190	2,946,944	3,003,874	2,797,994	2,698,024
EBITDA	288,176	658,120	712,532	702,880	453,200	729,497	588,699	(497,552)
Depn & Amortn	2,613	384,732	414,903	411,732	410,227	432,035	413,588	338,456
Income Before Taxes	204,403	(20,842)	4,543	(7,425)	(267,142)	100,486	(44,882)	(990,203)
Income Taxes	62,912	50,177	(8,787)	14,809	(107,089)	43,296	21,599	(149,110)
Net Income	140,100	(96,072)	(9,590)	(48,460)	(183,112)	42,946	(87,523)	(868,189)
Average Shares	360,904	359,508	358,565	357,662	356,915	356,528	355,568	355,377
Balance Sheet								
Current Assets	1,358,903	1,577,211	1,079,949	1,238,428	1,515,400	1,453,728	1,569,978	1,640,545
Total Assets	5,739,384	6,357,199	6,362,411	6,759,392	7,105,782	7,088,185	7,096,050	7,192,422
Current Liabilities	666,187	920,613	717,829	773,590	811,405	720,983	785,421	771,093
Long-Term Obligations	5,108,621	5,156,924	4,930,468	4,919,377	4,935,388	2,522,103	2,522,133	2,561,805
Total Liabilities	6,871,410	7,114,641	6,706,686	6,801,330	6,907,627	4,579,488	4,597,789	4,624,775
Stockholders' Equity	(1,132,026)	(757,442)	(344,275)	(41,938)	198,155	2,508,697	2,498,261	2,567,647
Shares Outstanding	362,062	361,427	360,090	359,001	357,247	356,028	355,802	355,798
Statistical Record								
Return on Assets %	1.30	N.M.	N.M.	N.M.	N.M.	0.61	N.M.	N.M.
Return on Equity %	...	...	...	N.M.	N.M.	1.72	N.M.	N.M.
EBITDA Margin %	48.78	23.45	24.06	23.86	15.38	24.29	21.04	N.M.
Net Margin %	23.72	N.M.	N.M.	N.M.	N.M.	1.43	N.M.	N.M.
Asset Turnover	0.47	0.44	0.45	0.42	0.41	0.42	0.39	0.35
Current Ratio	2.04	1.71	1.50	1.60	1.87	2.02	2.00	2.13
Debt to Equity	...	...	...	...	24.91	1.01	1.01	1.00
Price Range	11.61-3.41	11.61-4.78	10.59-6.34	10.20-7.01	14.36-4.69	15.36-8.81	14.25-8.37	11.12-2.43
P/E Ratio	55.29-16.24	...	...	...	...	139.64-80.09	...	...
Average Yield %	27.73	...	5.92	6.95	79.37	...	...	...

Address: 200 East Basse Road, Suite 100, San Antonio, TX 78209	Web Site: www.clearchanneloutdoor.com	Auditors: Ernst & Young LLP
Telephone: 210-832-3700	Officers: Randall T. Mays - President, Holding/Parent Company Officer, Sister Company Officer Richard J. Dressler - Chief Financial Officer, Holding/Parent Company Officer	Transfer Agents: Computershare Shareowner Services LLC, College Station, TX

CLIFFS NATURAL RESOURCES, INC.

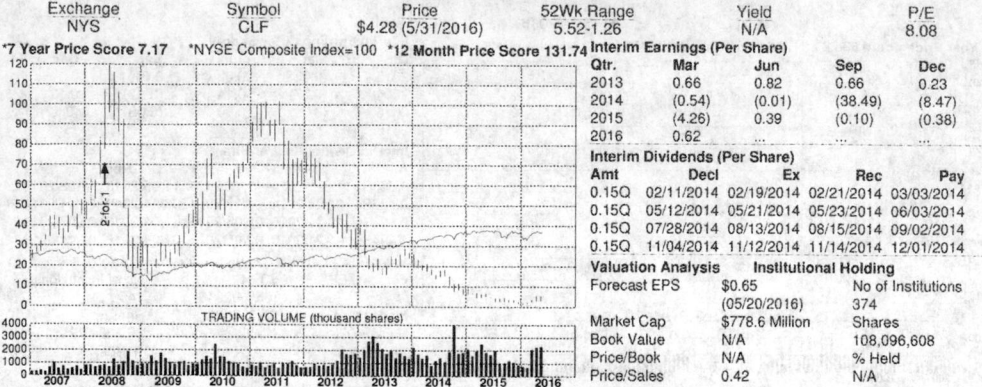

Exchange	Symbol	Price	52Wk Range	Yield	P/E
NYS	CLF	$4.28 (5/31/2016)	5.52-1.26	N/A	8.08

*7 Year Price Score 7.17   *NYSE Composite Index=100   *12 Month Price Score 131.74

Interim Earnings (Per Share)

Qtr.	Mar	Jun	Sep	Dec
2013	0.66	0.82	0.66	0.23
2014	(0.54)	(0.01)	(38.49)	(8.47)
2015	(4.26)	0.39	(0.10)	(0.38)
2016	0.62	...	...	...

Interim Dividends (Per Share)

Amt	Decl	Ex	Rec	Pay
0.15Q	02/11/2014	02/19/2014	02/21/2014	03/03/2014
0.15Q	05/12/2014	05/21/2014	05/23/2014	06/03/2014
0.15Q	07/28/2014	08/13/2014	08/15/2014	09/02/2014
0.15Q	11/04/2014	11/12/2014	11/14/2014	12/01/2014

Valuation Analysis   Institutional Holding

Forecast EPS	$0.65	No of Institutions	
	(05/20/2016)	374	
Market Cap	$778.6 Million	Shares	
Book Value	N/A	108,096,608	
Price/Book	N/A	% Held	
Price/Sales	0.42	N/A	

Business Summary: Non-Precious Metals (MIC: 8.2.2 SIC: 1099 NAIC: 212299)

Cliffs Natural Resources is a mining and natural resources company, and a producer of iron ore and low-volatile metallurgical coal. Co.'s operations are formed according to product category and geographic location: U.S. Iron Ore, which manages and operates iron ore mines located in Michigan and Minnesota; Asia Pacific Iron Ore, which has operations in Western Australia and consists solely of Co.'s wholly owned Koolyanobbing complex; North American Coal, which owns and operates low-volatile metallurgical coal operations located in Alabama and West Virginia; and Eastern Canadian Iron Ore, which owns iron ore mines in Eastern Canada, the Bloom Lake mine and the Wabush Scully mine.

Recent Developments: For the quarter ended Mar 31 2016, income from continuing operations decreased 31.5% to US$114.3 million from US$166.8 million in the year-earlier quarter. Net income amounted to US$116.8 million versus a net loss of US$761.7 million in the year-earlier quarter. Revenues were US$305.5 million, down 31.5% from US$446.0 million the year before. Operating loss was US$300,000 versus an income of US$71.9 million in the prior-year quarter. Direct operating expenses declined 24.8% to US$274.6 million from US$365.2 million in the comparable period the year before. Indirect operating expenses increased 250.6% to US$31.2 million from US$8.9 million in the equivalent prior-year period.

Prospects: Our evaluation of Cliffs Natural Resources, Inc. as of June 19, 2016 is the result of our systematic analysis on three basic characteristics: earnings strength, relative valuation, and recent stock price movement. The company has suffered a very negative trend in earnings per share over the past 5 quarters. Because the company lacks sufficient analyst estimate data, we place greater weight on the historical EPS trend as the measure of earnings strength. Based on operating earnings yield, the company is overvalued when compared to all of the companies in our coverage universe. Share price changes over the past year indicates that CLF will perform very poorly over the near term.

Financial Data

(US$ in Thousands)	3 Mos	12/31/2015	12/31/2014	12/31/2013	12/31/2012	12/31/2011	12/31/2010	12/31/2009
Earnings Per Share	0.53	(5.13)	(47.52)	2.37	(6.32)	11.48	7.49	1.64
Cash Flow Per Share	0.81	0.25	2.34	7.55	3.60	16.32	9.76	1.49
Tang Book Value Per Share	...	...	...	34.86	30.43	31.59	25.64	17.97
Dividends Per Share	...	...	0.600	0.600	2.155	0.840	0.507	0.255
Dividend Payout %	...	...	...	25.32	...	7.32	6.78	15.55
Income Statement								
Total Revenue	305,500	2,013,300	4,623,700	5,691,400	5,872,700	6,794,300	4,682,200	2,342,000
EBITDA	212,400	660,800	(9,385,900)	1,035,300	(12,700)	2,686,300	1,523,400	439,400
Depn & Amortn	33,800	119,200	32,600	366,900	293,500	237,800	165,400	120,600
Income Before Taxes	121,800	313,100	(9,603,700)	489,300	(501,800)	2,241,500	1,298,200	290,600
Income Taxes	7,500	169,300	(1,302,000)	55,100	255,900	420,100	292,000	20,800
Net Income	108,000	(749,300)	(7,224,200)	413,500	(899,400)	1,619,100	1,019,900	205,100
Average Shares	171,962	153,605	153,098	174,323	142,351	141,012	136,138	125,751
Balance Sheet								
Current Assets	792,000	982,700	1,448,900	1,560,000	1,650,000	1,790,700	2,583,700	1,161,200
Total Assets	1,886,300	2,135,500	3,164,000	13,121,900	13,574,900	14,541,700	7,778,200	4,639,300
Current Liabilities	439,800	581,700	958,600	1,085,500	1,381,500	1,493,300	1,028,700	570,400
Long-Term Obligations	2,499,100	2,699,400	2,962,300	3,022,600	3,960,700	3,608,700	1,713,100	525,000
Total Liabilities	3,745,700	4,116,900	4,595,300	7,052,400	8,942,200	8,756,700	3,932,300	2,096,500
Stockholders' Equity	(1,859,400)	(1,981,400)	(1,431,300)	6,069,500	4,632,700	5,785,000	3,845,900	2,542,800
Shares Outstanding	181,909	153,591	153,246	153,126	142,495	142,021	135,456	130,971
Statistical Record								
Return on Assets %	5.16	N.M.	N.M.	3.10	N.M.	14.51	16.43	4.69
Return on Equity %	...	...	N.M.	7.73	N.M.	33.62	31.93	9.55
EBITDA Margin %	69.53	32.82	N.M.	18.19	N.M.	39.54	32.54	18.76
Net Margin %	35.35	N.M.	N.M.	7.27	N.M.	23.83	21.78	8.76
Asset Turnover	0.82	0.76	0.57	0.43	0.42	0.61	0.75	0.54
Current Ratio	1.80	1.69	1.51	1.44	1.19	1.20	2.51	2.04
Debt to Equity	...	...	...	0.50	0.85	0.62	0.45	0.21
Price Range	6.58-1.26	9.07-1.55	26.21-6.06	38.81-15.68	76.63-28.40	101.43-48.30	79.98-39.95	47.41-12.01
P/E Ratio	12.42-2.38	...	...	16.38-6.62	...	8.84-4.21	10.68-5.33	28.91-7.32
Average Yield %	...	...	3.90	2.54	4.23	1.03	0.84	0.90

Address: 200 Public Square, Cleveland, OH 44114-2315 **Telephone:** 216-694-5700	**Web Site:** www.cliffsnaturalresources.com **Officers:** Lourenco Goncalves - Chairman, President, Chief Executive Officer P. Kelly Tompkins - Executive Vice President, Executive Vice President (frmr), Chief Legal Officer, Chief Administrative Officer, Division Officer, Chief Financial Officer	**Auditors:** Deloitte & Touche LLP **Investor Contact:** 216-694-5700 **Transfer Agents:** Wells Fargo Shareowner Services, St. Paul, MN

CLOROX CO (THE)

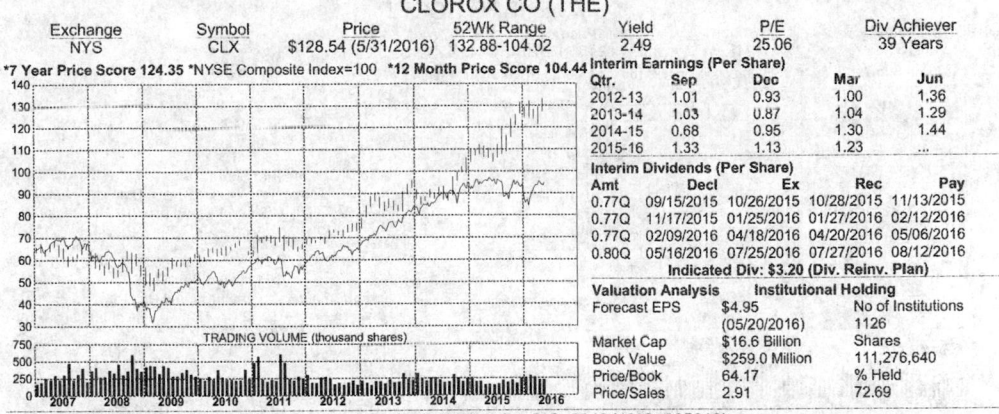

Exchange	Symbol	Price	52Wk Range	Yield	P/E	Div Achiever
NYS	CLX	$128.54 (5/31/2016)	132.88-104.02	2.49	25.06	39 Years

*7 Year Price Score 124.35 *NYSE Composite Index=100 *12 Month Price Score 104.44

Interim Earnings (Per Share)

Qtr.	Sep	Dec	Mar	Jun
2012-13	1.01	0.93	1.00	1.36
2013-14	1.03	0.87	1.04	1.29
2014-15	0.68	0.95	1.30	1.44
2015-16	1.33	1.13	1.23	...

Interim Dividends (Per Share)

Amt	Decl	Ex	Rec	Pay
0.77Q	09/15/2015	10/26/2015	10/28/2015	11/13/2015
0.77Q	11/17/2015	01/25/2016	01/27/2016	02/12/2016
0.77Q	02/09/2016	04/18/2016	04/20/2016	05/06/2016
0.80Q	05/16/2016	07/25/2016	07/27/2016	08/12/2016

Indicated Div: $3.20 (Div. Reinv. Plan)

Valuation Analysis / **Institutional Holding**

Forecast EPS	$4.95	No of Institutions
	(05/20/2016)	1126
Market Cap	$16.6 Billion	Shares
Book Value	$259.0 Million	111,276,640
Price/Book	64.17	% Held
Price/Sales	2.91	72.69

Business Summary: Household & Personal Products (MIC: 1.7.1 SIC: 2842 NAIC: 325612)

Clorox is a manufacturer and marketer of consumer products. Co. sells its products primarily through mass retail outlets, e-commerce channels, wholesale distributors, and medical supply distributors. Co. markets brand names, including its namesake bleach and cleaning products, Pine-Sol® cleaners, Liquid-Plumr® clog removers, Poett® home care products, Fresh Step® cat litter, Glad® bags, wraps and containers, Kingsford® charcoal, Hidden Valley® dressings and sauces, Brita® water-filtration products and Burt's Bees® natural personal care products. Co. has four main segments: Cleaning, Household, Lifestyle and International.

Recent Developments: For the quarter ended Mar 31 2016, income from continuing operations increased 10.4% to US$159.0 million from US$144.0 million in the year-earlier quarter. Net income decreased 6.9% to US$162.0 million from US$174.0 million in the year-earlier quarter. Revenues were US$1.43 billion, up 1.8% from US$1.40 billion the year before. Direct operating expenses declined 2.0% to US$780.0 million from US$796.0 million in the comparable period the year before. Indirect operating expenses increased 5.4% to US$409.0 million from US$388.0 million in the equivalent prior-year period.

Prospects: Our evaluation of Clorox Co. as of June 19, 2016 is the result of our systematic analysis on three basic characteristics: earnings strength, relative valuation, and recent stock price movement. The company has generated a negative trend in earnings per share over the past 5 quarters and while recent estimates for the company have remained steady, CLX has posted better than expected results. Based on operating earnings yield, the company is about fairly valued when compared to all of the companies in our coverage universe. Share price changes over the past year indicates that CLX will perform very well over the near term.

Financial Data

(US$ in Thousands)	9 Mos	6 Mos	3 Mos	06/30/2015	06/30/2014	06/30/2013	06/30/2012	06/30/2011
Earnings Per Share	5.13	5.20	5.02	4.37	4.23	4.30	4.09	4.02
Cash Flow Per Share	6.37	6.04	6.02	6.71	5.92	5.91	4.66	5.11
Dividends Per Share	3.050	3.020	2.990	2.960	2.840	2.560	2.400	2.200
Dividend Payout %	59.45	58.08	59.56	67.73	67.14	59.53	58.68	54.73
Income Statement								
Total Revenue	4,161,000	2,735,000	1,390,000	5,655,000	5,591,000	5,623,000	5,468,000	5,231,000
EBITDA	920,000	621,000	328,000	1,154,000	1,116,000	1,124,000	1,064,000	815,000
Depn & Amortn	122,000	82,000	41,000	165,000	169,000	171,000	167,000	162,000
Income Before Taxes	731,000	494,000	264,000	893,000	847,000	834,000	772,000	533,000
Income Taxes	248,000	170,000	91,000	315,000	299,000	279,000	248,000	276,000
Net Income	483,000	321,000	172,000	580,000	558,000	572,000	541,000	557,000
Average Shares	131,647	131,546	131,220	132,776	131,742	132,969	132,310	138,101
Balance Sheet								
Current Assets	1,590,000	1,490,000	1,410,000	1,429,000	1,395,000	1,420,000	1,376,000	1,279,000
Total Assets	4,284,000	4,175,000	4,095,000	4,164,000	4,258,000	4,311,000	4,355,000	4,163,000
Current Liabilities	1,387,000	1,358,000	1,351,000	1,405,000	1,638,000	1,134,000	2,061,000	1,365,000
Long-Term Obligations	1,796,000	1,796,000	1,796,000	1,796,000	1,595,000	2,170,000	1,571,000	2,125,000
Total Liabilities	4,025,000	3,977,000	3,976,000	4,046,000	4,104,000	4,165,000	4,490,000	4,249,000
Stockholders' Equity	259,000	198,000	119,000	118,000	154,000	146,000	(135,000)	(86,000)
Shares Outstanding	129,296	129,357	128,787	128,614	128,796	130,366	129,562	131,066
Statistical Record								
Return on Assets %	15.84	15.50	16.06	13.77	13.02	13.20	12.67	12.78
Return on Equity %	240.29	286.43	459.72	426.47	372.00	10,400.00	...	...
EBITDA Margin %	22.11	22.71	23.60	20.41	19.96	19.99	19.46	15.58
Net Margin %	11.61	11.74	12.37	10.26	9.98	10.17	9.89	10.65
Asset Turnover	1.34	1.29	1.38	1.34	1.30	1.30	1.28	1.20
Current Ratio	1.15	1.10	1.04	1.02	0.85	1.25	0.67	0.94
Debt to Equity	6.93	9.07	15.09	15.22	10.36	14.86	...	...
Price Range	131.81-104.02	131.34-103.87	119.39-95.46	111.93-86.39	95.83-81.49	89.53-70.10	74.55-63.71	71.26-61.57
P/E Ratio	25.69-20.28	25.26-19.97	23.78-19.02	25.61-19.77	22.65-19.26	20.82-16.30	18.23-15.58	17.73-15.32
Average Yield %	2.59	2.67	2.79	2.91	3.23	3.27	3.52	3.33

Address: 1221 Broadway, Oakland, CA 94612-1888	Web Site: www.thecloroxcompany.com	Auditors: Ernst & Young LLP
Telephone: 510-271-7000	Officers: George J. Harad - Chairman Benno O. Dorer - Chief Executive Officer, Executive Vice President, Senior Vice President, Division Officer	Transfer Agents: Computershare, Providence, RI

CMS ENERGY CORP

Exchange	Symbol	Price	52Wk Range	Yield	P/E
NYS	CMS	$41.82 (5/31/2016)	42.71-31.39	2.77	23.90

*7 Year Price Score 125.05 *NYSE Composite Index=100 *12 Month Price Score 110.54

Interim Earnings (Per Share)

Qtr.	Mar	Jun	Sep	Dec
2013	0.53	0.29	0.46	0.37
2014	0.75	0.30	0.34	0.35
2015	0.73	0.25	0.53	0.38
2016	0.59	...	...	...

Interim Dividends (Per Share)

Amt	Decl	Ex	Rec	Pay
0.29Q	07/13/2015	08/05/2015	08/07/2015	08/31/2015
0.29Q	10/16/2015	11/04/2015	11/06/2015	11/30/2015
0.31Q	01/21/2016	02/03/2016	02/05/2016	02/29/2016
0.31Q	04/21/2016	05/04/2016	05/06/2016	05/31/2016

Indicated Div: $1.16

Valuation Analysis

		Institutional Holding	
Forecast EPS	$2.02	No of Institutions	629
	(05/20/2016)		
Market Cap	$11.7 Billion	Shares	279,913,088
Book Value	$4.1 Billion	% Held	87.26
Price/Book	2.84		
Price/Sales	1.90		

Business Summary: Electric Utilities (MIC: 3.1.1 SIC: 4931 NAIC: 221119)

CMS Energy is a holding company. Co. has several subsidiaries, including Consumers Energy Company (Consumers), an electric and gas utility, and CMS Enterprises Company (CMS Enterprises), primarily a domestic independent power producer. Consumers serves individuals and businesses operating in the alternative energy, automotive, chemical, metal, and food products industries, as well as a group of other industries. CMS Enterprises, through its subsidiaries and equity investments, is engaged primarily in independent power production and owns power generation facilities fueled mostly by natural gas and biomass. Co. has three business segments: electric utility, gas utility, and enterprises.

Recent Developments: For the quarter ended Mar 31 2016, net income decreased 18.8% to US$164.0 million from US$202.0 million in the year-earlier quarter. Revenues were US$1.80 billion, down 14.7% from US$2.11 billion the year before. Operating income was US$336.0 million versus US$397.0 million in the prior-year quarter, a decrease of 15.4%. Direct operating expenses declined 19.2% to US$1.14 billion from US$1.41 billion in the comparable period the year before. Indirect operating expenses increased 7.3% to US$325.0 million from US$303.0 million in the equivalent prior-year period.

Prospects: Our evaluation of CMS Energy Corp. as of June 19, 2016 is the result of our systematic analysis on three basic characteristics: earnings strength, relative valuation, and recent stock price movement. The company has generated a negative trend in earnings per share over the past 5 quarters and while recent estimates for the company have remained steady, CMS has posted better than expected results. Based on operating earnings yield, the company is about fairly valued when compared to all of the companies in our coverage universe. Share price changes over the past year indicates that CMS will perform very well over the near term.

Financial Data

(US$ in Millions)	3 Mos	12/31/2015	12/31/2014	12/31/2013	12/31/2012	12/31/2011	12/31/2010	12/31/2009
Earnings Per Share	1.75	1.89	1.74	1.66	1.42	1.58	1.28	0.91
Cash Flow Per Share	5.46	5.95	5.35	5.37	4.75	4.66	4.14	3.73
Tang Book Value Per Share	14.72	14.21	13.34	12.98	12.09	11.92	11.19	11.42
Dividends Per Share	1.180	1.160	1.080	1.020	0.960	0.840	0.660	0.500
Dividend Payout %	67.43	61.38	62.07	61.45	67.61	53.16	51.56	54.95
Income Statement								
Total Revenue	1,801	6,456	7,179	6,566	6,253	6,503	6,432	6,205
EBITDA	578	1,916	1,801	1,766	1,587	1,549	1,607	1,360
Depn & Amortn	238	750	685	628	598	546	616	612
Income Before Taxes	234	782	714	743	605	597	579	337
Income Taxes	74	271	250	302	245	191	224	115
Net Income	164	525	479	454	382	415	340	229
Average Shares	277	276	274	271	268	263	252	237
Balance Sheet								
Current Assets	1,890	2,320	2,597	2,526	2,422	2,565	2,759	2,742
Total Assets	20,037	20,340	19,185	17,416	17,131	16,452	15,616	15,256
Current Liabilities	2,047	2,302	2,014	1,945	1,797	2,338	2,021	1,954
Long-Term Obligations	8,284	8,559	8,139	7,239	6,863	6,207	6,636	6,092
Total Liabilities	15,928	16,402	15,515	13,962	13,937	13,424	12,823	12,415
Stockholders' Equity	4,109	3,938	3,670	3,454	3,194	3,028	2,793	2,841
Shares Outstanding	279	277	275	266	264	254	249	227
Statistical Record								
Return on Assets %	2.48	2.66	2.62	2.63	2.27	2.59	2.20	1.52
Return on Equity %	12.31	13.80	13.45	13.66	12.25	14.26	12.07	8.19
EBITDA Margin %	32.09	29.68	25.09	26.90	25.38	23.82	24.98	21.92
Net Margin %	9.11	8.13	6.67	6.91	6.11	6.38	5.29	3.69
Asset Turnover	0.31	0.33	0.39	0.38	0.37	0.41	0.42	0.41
Current Ratio	0.92	1.01	1.29	1.30	1.35	1.10	1.37	1.40
Debt to Equity	2.02	2.17	2.22	2.10	2.15	2.05	2.38	2.14
Price Range	42.44-31.39	38.20-31.39	36.42-26.12	29.94-24.38	24.81-21.33	22.35-17.16	19.16-14.26	16.04-10.09
P/E Ratio	24.25-17.94	20.21-16.61	20.93-15.01	18.04-14.69	17.47-15.02	14.15-10.86	14.97-11.14	17.63-11.09
Average Yield %	3.32	3.35	3.60	3.77	4.16	4.26	4.26	3.97

Address: One Energy Plaza, Jackson, MI 49201	Web Site: www.cmsenergy.com	Auditors: PricewaterhouseCoopers LLP
Telephone: 517-788-0550	Officers: David W. Joos - Chairman Patricia K. Poppe - President, Chief Executive Officer, Division Officer	Investor Contact: 517-788-1868
		Transfer Agents: Investor Services Department, Jackson, MI

CNA FINANCIAL CORP.

Exchange	Symbol	Price	52Wk Range	Yield	P/E
NYS	CNA	$32.86 (5/31/2016)	40.43-28.21	3.04	28.33

*7 Year Price Score 94.45 *NYSE Composite Index=100 *12 Month Price Score 91.21

Interim Earnings (Per Share)

Qtr.	Mar	Jun	Sep	Dec
2013	0.93	0.72	1.01	0.82
2014	0.05	0.98	0.79	0.73
2015	0.86	0.51	0.66	(0.26)
2016	0.25	...	...	...

Interim Dividends (Per Share)

Amt	Decl	Ex	Rec	Pay
0.25Q	11/02/2015	11/12/2015	11/16/2015	12/02/2015
0.25Q	02/08/2016	02/18/2016	02/22/2016	03/09/2016
2.00Sp	02/08/2016	02/18/2016	02/22/2016	03/09/2016
0.25Q	05/02/2016	05/12/2016	05/16/2016	06/01/2016

Indicated Div: $1.00

Valuation Analysis

Forecast EPS	$2.77
	(04/16/2016)
Market Cap	$8.9 Billion
Book Value	$11.5 Billion
Price/Book	0.77
Price/Sales	0.99

Institutional Holding

No of Institutions	227
Shares	272,283,488
% Held	99.04

TRADING VOLUME (thousand shares)

Business Summary: General Insurance (MIC: 5.2.1 SIC: 6331 NAIC: 524126)

CNA Financial is an insurance holding company. Co.'s insurance products include commercial property and casualty coverages, including surety. Co.'s services include risk management, information services, warranty and claims administration. Co.'s products and services are marketed through independent agents, brokers and managing general underwriters to a range of customers such as businesses, insurance companies, associations, and other groups. Co.'s core business, commercial property and casualty insurance operations are reported in three segments: Specialty, Commercial and Hardy. Co.'s non-core businesses are managed in two segments: Life & Group Non-Core and Corporate & Other Non-Core.

Recent Developments: For the quarter ended Mar 31 2016, net income decreased 71.7% to US$66.0 million from US$233.0 million in the year-earlier quarter. Revenues were US$2.20 billion, down 6.7% from US$2.35 billion the year before. Net premiums earned were US$1.70 billion versus US$1.69 billion in the prior-year quarter, an increase of 0.7%. Net investment income fell 22.0% to US$435.0 million from US$558.0 million a year ago.

Prospects: Our evaluation of CNA Financial Corp. as of June 19, 2016 is the result of our systematic analysis on three basic characteristics: earnings strength, relative valuation, and recent stock price movement. The company has produced a positive trend in earnings per share over the past 5 quarters and while recent estimates for the company have remained steady, CNA has posted results that fell short of analysts expectations. Based on operating earnings yield, the company is undervalued when compared to all of the companies in our coverage universe. Share price changes over the past year indicates that CNA will perform well over the near term.

Financial Data
(US$ in Thousands)

	3 Mos	12/31/2015	12/31/2014	12/31/2013	12/31/2012	12/31/2011	12/31/2010	12/31/2009
Earnings Per Share	1.16	1.77	2.55	3.47	2.33	2.28	2.28	1.10
Cash Flow Per Share	6.02	5.13	5.34	4.46	4.63	6.32	(0.33)	4.68
Tang Book Value Per Share	41.85	42.94	46.83	46.33	45.14	42.40	40.18	35.38
Dividends Per Share	3.000	3.000	2.000	0.800	0.600	0.400	...	...
Dividend Payout %	258.62	169.49	78.43	23.05	25.75	17.54	...	...
Income Statement								
Premium Income	1,699,000	6,921,000	7,212,000	7,271,000	6,882,000	6,603,000	6,515,000	6,721,000
Total Revenue	2,195,000	9,101,000	9,692,000	10,113,000	9,547,000	8,947,000	9,209,000	8,472,000
Benefits & Claims	...	5,384,000	5,591,000	5,947,000	5,896,000	5,489,000	4,985,000	5,290,000
Income Before Taxes	57,000	549,000	1,207,000	1,313,000	872,000	877,000	1,112,000	540,000
Income Taxes	(9,000)	70,000	319,000	376,000	244,000	246,000	333,000	57,000
Net Income	66,000	479,000	691,000	937,000	628,000	614,000	690,000	419,000
Average Shares	270,900	270,700	270,600	270,200	269,800	269,600	269,500	269,100
Balance Sheet								
Total Assets	55,502,000	55,047,000	55,566,000	57,194,000	58,522,000	55,179,000	55,331,000	55,298,000
Total Liabilities	44,032,000	43,291,000	42,772,000	44,543,000	46,208,000	43,622,000	44,377,000	44,638,000
Stockholders' Equity	11,470,000	11,756,000	12,794,000	12,651,000	12,314,000	11,557,000	10,954,000	10,660,000
Shares Outstanding	270,479	270,274	269,980	269,717	269,399	269,274	269,139	269,026
Statistical Record								
Return on Assets %	0.56	0.87	1.23	1.62	1.10	1.11	1.25	0.78
Return on Equity %	2.61	3.90	5.43	7.51	5.25	5.46	6.38	4.78
Loss Ratio %	...	77.79	77.52	81.79	85.67	83.13	76.52	78.71
Net Margin %	3.01	5.26	7.13	9.27	6.58	6.86	7.49	4.95
Price Range	41.82-28.21	43.40-34.24	43.08-36.29	42.89-28.01	30.67-25.91	31.04-21.58	28.99-22.15	25.99-6.49
P/E Ratio	36.05-24.32	24.52-19.34	16.89-14.23	12.36-8.07	13.16-11.12	13.61-9.46	12.71-9.71	23.63-5.90
Average Yield %	8.28	7.82	5.01	2.27	2.14	1.48	...	...

Address: 333 South Wabash, Chicago, IL 60604
Telephone: 312 822 5000
Fax: 312-822-6419

Web Site: www.cna.com
Officers: Dino E. Robusto - Incoming Chairman, Incoming Chief Executive Officer Thomas F. Motamed - Chairman, Chief Executive Officer

Auditors: Deloitte & Touche LLP
Investor Contact: 312 822-4278
Transfer Agents: Wells Fargo Bank, N.A., St. Paul, MN

COACH, INC.

Exchange	Symbol	Price	52Wk Range	Yield	P/E
NYS	COH	$39.42 (5/31/2016)	42.00-27.44	3.42	28.16

*7 Year Price Score 62.38   *NYSE Composite Index=100   *12 Month Price Score 115.38

Interim Earnings (Per Share)

Qtr.	Sep	Dec	Mar	Jun
2012-13	0.77	1.23	0.84	0.77
2013-14	0.77	1.06	0.68	0.28
2014-15	0.43	0.66	0.32	0.04
2015-16	0.35	0.61	0.40	

Interim Dividends (Per Share)

Amt	Decl	Ex	Rec	Pay
0.338Q	07/31/2015	09/03/2015	09/08/2015	09/28/2015
0.338Q	11/12/2015	12/02/2015	12/04/2015	12/28/2015
0.338Q	02/18/2016	03/02/2016	03/04/2016	03/28/2016
0.338Q	05/18/2016	06/01/2016	06/03/2016	07/05/2016

Indicated Div: $1.35

Valuation Analysis

		Institutional Holding	
Forecast EPS	$1.92	No of Institutions	
	(05/20/2016)	916	
Market Cap	$11.0 Billion	Shares	
Book Value	$2.6 Billion	280,524,864	
Price/Book	4.17	% Held	
Price/Sales	2.52	82.73	

Business Summary: Apparel, Footwear & Accessories (MIC: 1.4.2 SIC: 3171 NAIC: 316992)

Coach is a marketer of accessories and gifts for women and men. Co.'s product offerings include women's and men's bags, accessories, footwear, wearables, jewelry, travel bags, sunwear, watches and fragrance. Co.'s segments include: North America, which includes sales to North American consumers through Co.-operated stores, including the Internet, and sales to wholesale customers and distributors; and International, which includes sales to consumers through Co.-operated stores in Japan and mainland China, Co.-operated stores and concession shop-in-shops in Hong Kong, Macau, Singapore, Taiwan, Malaysia, South Korea, the U.K., France, Ireland, Spain, Portugal, Germany, Italy and Belgium.

Recent Developments: For the quarter ended Mar 26 2016, net income increased 27.7% to US$112.5 million from US$88.1 million in the year-earlier quarter. Revenues were US$1.03 billion, up 11.2% from US$929.3 million the year before. Operating income was US$134.3 million versus US$124.0 million in the prior-year quarter, an increase of 8.3%. Direct operating expenses rose 21.3% to US$320.1 million from US$263.8 million in the comparable period the year before. Indirect operating expenses increased 6.9% to US$578.7 million from US$541.5 million in the equivalent prior-year period.

Prospects: Our evaluation of Coach Inc. as of June 19, 2016 is the result of our systematic analysis on three basic characteristics: earnings strength, relative valuation, and recent stock price movement. The company has enjoyed a very positive trend in earnings per share over the past 5 quarters and while recent estimates for the company have remained steady, COH has posted better than expected results. Based on operating earnings yield, the company is about fairly valued when compared to all of the companies in our coverage universe. Share price changes over the past year indicates that COH will perform well over the near term.

Financial Data

(US$ in Thousands)	9 Mos	6 Mos	3 Mos	06/27/2015	06/28/2014	06/29/2013	06/30/2012	07/02/2011
Earnings Per Share	1.40	1.32	1.37	1.45	2.79	3.61	3.53	2.92
Cash Flow Per Share	2.50	2.39	2.91	3.41	3.56	5.02	4.25	3.51
Tang Book Value Per Share	6.56	6.41	6.07	6.13	7.47	7.29	5.64	4.41
Dividends Per Share	1.350	1.350	1.350	1.350	1.350	1.238	0.975	0.675
Dividend Payout %	96.43	102.27	98.54	93.10	48.39	34.28	27.62	23.12
Income Statement								
Total Revenue	3,337,200	2,304,100	1,030,300	4,191,600	4,806,226	5,075,390	4,763,180	4,158,507
EBITDA	693,300	509,500	195,800	809,800	1,309,434	1,681,144	1,637,852	1,425,294
Depn & Amortn	156,600	107,100	54,400	191,800	189,360	162,987	132,909	125,106
Income Before Taxes	517,200	389,400	134,700	611,600	1,122,255	1,520,526	1,505,663	1,301,219
Income Taxes	138,200	122,900	38,300	209,200	340,919	486,106	466,753	420,419
Net Income	379,000	266,500	96,400	402,400	781,336	1,034,420	1,038,910	880,800
Average Shares	279,500	278,400	278,300	277,200	280,379	286,307	294,129	301,558
Balance Sheet								
Current Assets	2,265,100	2,301,600	2,351,600	2,506,500	1,855,217	2,070,947	1,804,528	1,452,388
Total Assets	4,676,500	4,603,700	4,554,400	4,666,900	3,663,131	3,531,897	3,104,321	2,635,116
Current Liabilities	731,500	704,000	751,000	834,700	813,118	722,510	718,160	593,017
Long-Term Obligations	868,500	872,000	875,600	879,100	...	485	985	23,360
Total Liabilities	2,051,100	2,036,400	2,080,900	2,177,000	1,242,478	1,122,739	1,111,390	1,022,547
Stockholders' Equity	2,625,400	2,567,300	2,473,500	2,489,900	2,420,653	2,409,158	1,992,931	1,612,569
Shares Outstanding	277,900	277,700	277,500	276,600	274,361	281,902	285,118	288,514
Statistical Record								
Return on Assets %	8.50	8.91	9.23	9.69	21.78	31.26	36.30	34.62
Return on Equity %	15.13	14.41	15.46	16.43	32.44	47.13	57.79	56.66
EBITDA Margin %	20.77	22.11	19.00	19.32	27.24	33.12	34.39	34.27
Net Margin %	11.36	11.57	9.36	9.60	16.26	20.38	21.81	21.18
Asset Turnover	0.94	1.03	1.02	1.01	1.34	1.53	1.66	1.63
Current Ratio	3.10	3.27	3.13	3.00	2.28	2.87	2.51	2.45
Debt to Equity	0.33	0.34	0.35	0.35	...	N.M.	N.M.	0.01
Price Range	43.03-27.44	43.56-27.44	43.56-28.40	43.56-33.00	59.55-34.02	62.60-46.50	79.03-45.96	65.99-34.37
P/E Ratio	30.74-19.60	33.00-20.79	31.80-20.73	30.04-22.76	21.34-12.19	17.34-12.88	22.39-13.02	22.60-11.77
Average Yield %	3.96	3.85	3.74	3.62	2.67	2.23	1.50	1.33

Address: 516 West 34th Street, New York, NY 10001
Telephone: 212-594-1850
Fax: 212-594-1682

Web Site: www.coach.com
Officers: Jide J. Zeitlin - Chairman Victor Luis - President, Chief Executive Officer, Chief Commercial Officer

Auditors: Deloitte & Touche LLP
Transfer Agents: Mellon Investor Services, Jersey City, NJ

COBALT INTERNATIONAL ENERGY INC.

Exchange	Symbol	Price	52Wk Range	Yield	P/E
NYS	CIE	$2.24 (5/31/2016)	10.67-2.07	N/A	N/A

*7 Year Price Score N/A   *NYSE Composite Index=100   *12 Month Price Score 47.58

Interim Earnings (Per Share)

Qtr.	Mar	Jun	Sep	Dec
2010	(0.31)	(0.19)	(0.39)	(0.55)
2014	(0.14)	(0.23)	(0.35)	(0.53)
2015	(0.20)	(0.16)	(0.14)	(1.20)
2016	(0.11)	...	...	...

Interim Dividends (Per Share)

No Dividends Paid

Valuation Analysis / Institutional Holding

Valuation Analysis		Institutional Holding	
Forecast EPS	$-0.45	No of Institutions	
	(05/20/2016)	260	
Market Cap	$917.8 Million	Shares	
Book Value	$1.4 Billion	519,851,872	
Price/Book	0.65	% Held	
Price/Sales	561.00	103.26	

Business Summary: Production & Extraction (MIC: 9.1.1 SIC: 1311 NAIC: 211111)

Cobalt International Energy is a holding company. Through its subsidiaries, Co. is an independent exploration and production company with operations focused in the deepwater U.S. Gulf of Mexico. Co.'s exploration activities in the U.S. Gulf of Mexico include the North Platte, Shenandoah, Anchor, and Heidelberg fields, each of which are in various stages of appraisal and development. Co. also has a non-operated interest in the Diaba Block offshore Gabon. As of Dec 31 2015, Co.'s estimated net proved undeveloped reserves totaled 1.80 billion cubic feet of natural gas, 300,000 barrels of natural gas liquids, and 5.6 million barrels of oil and condensate.

Recent Developments: For the quarter ended Mar 31 2016, loss from continuing operations was US$30.8 million compared with a loss of US$70.5 million in the year-earlier quarter. Net loss amounted to US$46.6 million versus a net loss of US$81.6 million in the year-earlier quarter. Operating loss was US$16.5 million versus a loss of US$52.1 million in the prior-year quarter. Indirect operating expenses decreased 65.2% to US$18.1 million from US$52.1 million in the equivalent prior-year period.

Prospects: Our evaluation of Cobalt International Energy Inc. as of June 19, 2016 is the result of our systematic analysis on three basic characteristics: earnings strength, relative valuation, and recent stock price movement. The company has produced a positive trend in earnings per share over the past 5 quarters. Because the company lacks sufficient analyst estimate data, we place greater weight on the historical EPS trend as the measure of earnings strength. Based on operating earnings yield, the company is overvalued when compared to all of the companies in our coverage universe. Share price changes over the past year indicates that CIE will perform very well over the near term.

Financial Data
(US$ in Thousands)

	3 Mos	12/31/2015	12/31/2014	12/31/2013	12/31/2012	12/31/2011	12/31/2010	12/31/2009
Earnings Per Share	(1.61)	(1.70)	(1.25)	(1.45)	(0.70)	(0.35)	(0.39)	...
Cash Flow Per Share	(0.52)	(0.62)	(0.16)	(0.53)	(0.35)	(0.15)	(0.38)	...
Tang Book Value Per Share	3.43	3.54	5.18	5.23	6.61	5.36	4.90	5.11
Income Statement								
Total Revenue	1,636	...	...	...	...	...	...	...
EBITDA	12,508	(439,856)	(437,353)	(527,791)	(283,628)	(137,136)	(137,258)	(81,070)
Depn & Amortn	29,006	1,400	4,600	1,900	1,200	700	800	700
Income Before Taxes	(30,802)	(498,545)	(510,763)	(589,024)	(282,999)	(133,637)	(136,476)	(81,257)
Net Income	(46,615)	(694,426)	(510,763)	(589,024)	(282,999)	(133,637)	(136,476)	(81,257)
Average Shares	409,260	408,535	407,116	406,839	403,356	376,603	349,342	...
Balance Sheet								
Current Assets	3,009,809	3,146,291	2,003,134	1,967,443	2,456,742	1,335,094	889,632	1,154,487
Total Assets	4,066,983	4,094,103	4,450,863	3,633,673	4,011,459	2,527,944	1,746,443	1,812,105
Current Liabilities	647,843	628,018	303,601	340,967	160,956	238,069	24,559	70,523
Long-Term Obligations	2,006,620	2,014,779	1,928,528	1,035,980	991,191	...	...	...
Total Liabilities	2,659,698	2,647,966	2,336,597	1,504,527	1,322,241	449,030	27,409	70,523
Stockholders' Equity	1,407,285	1,446,137	2,114,266	2,129,146	2,689,218	2,078,914	1,719,034	1,741,582
Shares Outstanding	409,731	408,740	408,505	406,949	406,596	387,531	350,733	340,517
Statistical Record								
EBITDA Margin %	764.55	...	...	...	...	...	...	...
Current Ratio	4.65	5.01	6.60	5.77	15.26	5.61	36.22	16.37
Debt to Equity	1.43	1.39	0.91	0.49	0.37	...	...	...
Price Range	11.04-2.10	11.04-5.27	19.46-7.63	30.20-14.84	33.03-15.86	16.81-7.06	15.72-6.52	13.88-13.34

Address: Cobalt Center, 920 Memorial City Way, Suite 100, Houston, TX 77024 Telephone: 713-579-9100	Web Site: www.cobaltintl.com Officers: William P. Utt - Interim Chairman Timothy J. Cutt - Chief Executive Officer	Auditors: Ernst & Young LLP Investor Contact: 713-452-2322 Transfer Agents: Continental Stock Transfer & Trust Company

COCA-COLA CO (THE)

Exchange	Symbol	Price	52Wk Range	Yield	P/E	Div Achiever
NYS	KO	$44.60 (5/31/2016)	46.89-37.99	3.14	26.87	53 Years

*7 Year Price Score 99.52 *NYSE Composite Index=100 *12 Month Price Score 105.31

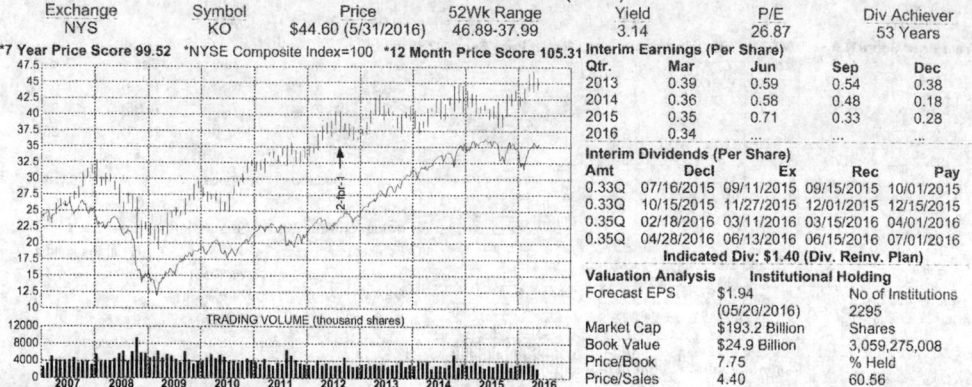

Interim Earnings (Per Share)

Qtr.	Mar	Jun	Sep	Dec
2013	0.39	0.59	0.54	0.38
2014	0.36	0.58	0.48	0.18
2015	0.35	0.71	0.33	0.28
2016	0.34	...	...	...

Interim Dividends (Per Share)

Amt	Decl	Ex	Rec	Pay
0.33Q	07/16/2015	09/11/2015	09/15/2015	10/01/2015
0.33Q	10/15/2015	11/27/2015	12/01/2015	12/15/2015
0.35Q	02/18/2016	03/11/2016	03/15/2016	04/01/2016
0.35Q	04/28/2016	06/13/2016	06/15/2016	07/01/2016

Indicated Div: $1.40 (Div. Reinv. Plan)

Valuation Analysis		Institutional Holding	
Forecast EPS	$1.94	No of Institutions	
	(05/20/2016)		2295
Market Cap	$193.2 Billion	Shares	
Book Value	$24.9 Billion		3,059,275,008
Price/Book	7.75	% Held	
Price/Sales	4.40		60.56

Business Summary: Beverages (MIC: 1.2.2 SIC: 2086 NAIC: 312111)

Coca-Cola is a beverage company. Co. owns or licenses and markets nonalcoholic beverage brands, primarily sparkling beverages but also a range of still beverages such as waters, enhanced waters, juices and juice drinks, ready-to-drink teas and coffees, and energy and sports drinks. Co.'s primary nonalcoholic sparkling beverage brands include Coca-Cola, Diet Coke, Fanta and Sprite. Co. markets, manufactures and sells beverage concentrates and syrups, including fountain syrups; and finished sparkling and still beverages. Co.'s organizational structure consists of the following operating segments: Eurasia and Africa; Europe; Latin America; North America; Asia Pacific; and Bottling Investments.

Recent Developments: For the quarter ended Apr 1 2016, net income decreased 4.7% to US$1.49 billion from US$1.57 billion in the year-earlier quarter. Revenues were US$10.28 billion, down 4.0% from US$10.71 billion the year before. Operating income was US$2.14 billion versus US$2.30 billion in the prior-year quarter, a decrease of 6.8%. Direct operating expenses declined 0.8% to US$4.07 billion from US$4.10 billion in the comparable period the year before. Indirect operating expenses decreased 5.6% to US$4.07 billion from US$4.31 billion in the equivalent prior-year period.

Prospects: Our evaluation of Coca-Cola Co as of June 19, 2016 is the result of our systematic analysis on three basic characteristics: earnings strength, relative valuation, and recent stock price movement. The company has managed to produce a neutral trend in earnings per share over the past 5 quarters and while recent estimates for the company have remained steady, KO has posted better than expected results. Based on operating earnings yield, the company is about fairly valued when compared to all of the companies in our coverage universe. Share price changes over the past year indicates that KO will perform very well over the near term.

Financial Data

(US$ in Thousands)	3 Mos	12/31/2015	12/31/2014	12/31/2013	12/31/2012	12/31/2011	12/31/2010	12/31/2009
Earnings Per Share	1.66	1.67	1.60	1.90	1.97	1.85	2.53	1.47
Cash Flow Per Share	2.21	2.42	2.42	2.38	2.36	2.07	2.06	1.77
Tang Book Value Per Share	0.20	0.33	0.90	1.26	1.22	0.88	0.89	2.60
Dividends Per Share	1.340	1.320	1.220	1.120	1.020	0.940	0.880	0.820
Dividend Payout %	80.72	79.04	76.25	58.95	51.78	50.95	34.78	55.97
Income Statement								
Total Revenue	10,282,000	44,294,000	45,998,000	46,854,000	48,017,000	46,542,000	35,119,000	30,990,000
EBITDA	2,257,000	11,112,000	10,181,000	12,547,000	12,639,000	12,355,000	14,838,000	9,294,000
Depn & Amortn	458,000	1,753,000	1,736,000	1,743,000	1,723,000	1,672,000	1,204,000	1,023,000
Income Before Taxes	1,802,000	9,116,000	8,556,000	10,875,000	10,990,000	10,749,000	13,218,000	8,165,000
Income Taxes	401,000	2,239,000	2,201,000	2,851,000	2,723,000	2,805,000	2,384,000	2,040,000
Net Income	1,483,000	7,351,000	7,098,000	8,584,000	9,019,000	8,572,000	11,809,000	6,824,000
Average Shares	4,381,999	4,404,999	4,449,999	4,508,999	4,583,999	4,645,999	4,665,999	4,657,999
Balance Sheet								
Current Assets	36,510,000	33,395,000	32,986,000	31,304,000	30,328,000	25,497,000	21,579,000	17,551,000
Total Assets	91,263,000	90,093,000	92,023,000	90,055,000	86,174,000	79,974,000	72,921,000	48,671,000
Current Liabilities	30,987,000	26,930,000	32,374,000	27,811,000	27,821,000	24,283,000	18,508,000	13,721,000
Long-Term Obligations	26,990,000	28,407,000	19,063,000	19,154,000	14,736,000	13,656,000	14,041,000	5,059,000
Total Liabilities	66,349,000	64,539,000	61,703,000	56,882,000	53,384,000	48,339,000	41,918,000	23,872,000
Stockholders' Equity	24,914,000	25,554,000	30,320,000	33,173,000	32,790,000	31,635,000	31,003,000	24,799,000
Shares Outstanding	4,331,999	4,323,999	4,365,999	4,401,999	4,468,999	4,525,999	4,583,999	4,605,999
Statistical Record								
Return on Assets %	7.98	8.07	7.80	9.74	10.83	11.21	19.42	15.30
Return on Equity %	27.08	26.31	22.36	26.03	27.92	27.37	42.32	30.15
EBITDA Margin %	21.95	25.09	22.13	26.78	26.32	26.55	42.25	29.99
Net Margin %	14.42	16.60	15.43	18.32	18.78	18.42	33.63	22.02
Asset Turnover	0.48	0.49	0.51	0.53	0.58	0.61	0.58	0.69
Current Ratio	1.18	1.24	1.02	1.13	1.09	1.05	1.17	1.28
Debt to Equity	1.08	1.11	0.63	0.58	0.45	0.43	0.45	0.20
Price Range	46.83-37.99	43.84-37.99	44.83-37.10	43.09-36.25	40.56-33.49	35.62-30.80	32.88-25.02	29.56-18.93
P/E Ratio	28.21-22.89	26.25-22.75	28.02-23.19	22.68-19.08	20.59-17.00	19.25-16.65	13.00-9.89	20.11-12.87
Average Yield %	3.22	3.20	2.99	2.82	2.75	2.82	3.11	3.36

Address: One Coca-Cola Plaza, Atlanta, GA 30313
Telephone: 404-676-2121
Fax: 404-676-6792

Web Site: www.coca-colacompany.com
Officers: Ahmet Muhtar Kent - Chairman, President, Chief Executive Officer Kathy N. Waller - Executive Vice President, Vice President, Chief Financial Officer, Vice President (frmr), Controller

Auditors: Ernst & Young LLP
Investor Contact: 404-676-7563
Transfer Agents: Computershare Trust Company, N.A., Providence, RI

COLGATE-PALMOLIVE CO.

Exchange	Symbol	Price	52Wk Range	Yield	P/E	Div Achiever
NYS	CL	$70.41 (5/31/2016)	72.65-60.37	2.22	46.32	53 Years

*7 Year Price Score 106.20 *NYSE Composite Index=100 ***12 Month Price Score 104.68**

Interim Earnings (Per Share)

Qtr.	Mar	Jun	Sep	Dec
2013	0.48	0.60	0.70	0.60
2014	0.42	0.67	0.59	0.68
2015	0.59	0.63	0.80	(0.50)
2016	0.59	...	...	...

Interim Dividends (Per Share)

Amt	Decl	Ex	Rec	Pay
0.38Q	09/10/2015	10/21/2015	10/23/2015	11/16/2015
0.38Q	01/14/2016	01/21/2016	01/25/2016	02/16/2016
0.39Q	03/10/2016	04/20/2016	04/22/2016	05/16/2016
0.39Q	06/09/2016	07/20/2016	07/22/2016	08/15/2016

Indicated Div: $1.56 (Div. Reinv. Plan)

Valuation Analysis / Institutional Holding

Valuation Analysis		Institutional Holding	
Forecast EPS	$2.81	No of Institutions	
	(05/20/2016)	1715	
Market Cap	$62.9 Billion	Shares	
Book Value	N/A	726,320,768	
Price/Book	N/A	% Held	
Price/Sales	4.00	71.82	

TRADING VOLUME (thousand shares)

Business Summary: Household & Personal Products (MIC: 1.7.1 SIC: 2844 NAIC: 325611)

Colgate-Palmolive is engaged primarily in the manufacture and market a range of consumer products. Co. has two product segments. Oral, Personal and Home Care products include toothpaste, toothbrushes and mouthwash, bar and liquid hand soaps, shower gels, shampoos, conditioners, deodorants and antiperspirants, laundry and dishwashing detergents, fabric conditioners, household cleaners, bleaches and other similar items. These products are sold to retail trade customers and wholesale distributors. Pet Nutrition products include pet nutrition products manufactured and marketed by Hill's Pet Nutrition. The principal customers for Pet Nutrition products are pet supply retailers and veterinarians.

Recent Developments: For the quarter ended Mar 31 2016, net income decreased 1.5% to US$574.0 million from US$583.0 million in the year-earlier quarter. Revenues were US$3.76 billion, down 7.6% from US$4.07 billion the year before. Operating income was US$867.0 million versus US$860.0 million in the prior-year quarter, an increase of 0.8%. Direct operating expenses declined 9.8% to US$1.51 billion from US$1.68 billion in the comparable period the year before. Indirect operating expenses decreased 9.9% to US$1.38 billion from US$1.53 billion in the equivalent prior-year period.

Prospects: Our evaluation of Colgate-Palmolive Co. as of June 19, 2016 is the result of our systematic analysis on three basic characteristics: earnings strength, relative valuation, and recent stock price movement. The company has enjoyed a very positive trend in earnings per share over the past 5 quarters and while recent estimates for the company have been mixed, CL has posted results that fell short of analysts expectations. Based on operating earnings yield, the company is about fairly valued when compared to all of the companies in our coverage universe. Share price changes over the past year indicates that CL will perform well over the near term.

Financial Data

(US$ in Thousands)	3 Mos	12/31/2015	12/31/2014	12/31/2013	12/31/2012	12/31/2011	12/31/2010	12/31/2009
Earnings Per Share	1.52	1.52	2.36	2.38	2.58	2.47	2.15	2.19
Cash Flow Per Share	3.17	3.27	3.60	3.44	3.35	2.97	3.29	3.28
Dividends Per Share	1.520	1.500	1.420	1.330	1.220	1.135	1.015	0.860
Dividend Payout %	100.00	98.68	60.17	55.88	47.38	45.95	47.10	39.36
Income Statement								
Total Revenue	3,762,000	16,034,000	17,277,000	17,420,000	17,085,000	16,734,000	15,564,000	15,327,000
EBITDA	973,000	2,814,000	3,582,000	3,583,000	3,913,000	3,863,000	3,506,000	3,632,000
Depn & Amortn	106,000	33,000	32,000	32,000	31,000	28,000	22,000	22,000
Income Before Taxes	839,000	2,755,000	3,526,000	3,560,000	3,867,000	3,783,000	3,425,000	3,533,000
Income Taxes	265,000	1,215,000	1,194,000	1,155,000	1,243,000	1,235,000	1,117,000	1,141,000
Net Income	533,000	1,384,000	2,180,000	2,241,000	2,472,000	2,431,000	2,203,000	2,291,000
Average Shares	900,200	909,700	924,300	939,900	960,200	984,000	1,021,800	1,049,200
Balance Sheet								
Current Assets	4,490,000	4,384,000	4,863,000	4,822,000	4,556,000	4,402,000	3,730,000	3,810,000
Total Assets	12,448,000	11,958,000	13,459,000	13,876,000	13,394,000	12,724,000	11,172,000	11,134,000
Current Liabilities	4,463,000	3,534,000	3,946,000	4,470,000	3,736,000	3,716,000	3,728,000	3,599,000
Long-Term Obligations	5,877,000	6,269,000	5,644,000	4,749,000	4,926,000	4,430,000	2,815,000	2,821,000
Total Liabilities	12,818,000	12,257,000	12,314,000	11,571,000	11,205,000	10,349,000	8,497,000	8,018,000
Stockholders' Equity	(370,000)	(299,000)	1,145,000	2,305,000	2,189,000	2,375,000	2,675,000	3,116,000
Shares Outstanding	893,017	892,738	906,712	919,946	935,728	960,036	989,700	988,330
Statistical Record								
Return on Assets %	10.74	10.89	15.95	16.44	18.88	20.35	19.75	21.70
Return on Equity %	3,055.56	327.19	126.38	99.73	108.03	96.28	76.08	90.95
EBITDA Margin %	25.86	17.55	20.73	20.57	22.90	23.08	22.53	23.70
Net Margin %	14.17	8.63	12.62	12.86	14.47	14.53	14.15	14.95
Asset Turnover	1.23	1.26	1.26	1.28	1.30	1.40	1.40	1.45
Current Ratio	1.01	1.24	1.23	1.08	1.22	1.18	1.00	1.06
Debt to Equity	...	...	4.93	2.06	2.25	1.87	1.05	0.91
Price Range	70.72-60.37	71.46-60.37	71.00-60.17	66.26-52.27	55.31-44.13	46.98-37.97	42.91-36.88	43.16-27.52
P/E Ratio	46.53-39.72	47.01-39.72	30.08-25.50	27.84-21.96	21.44-17.10	19.02-15.37	19.96-17.15	19.71-12.57
Average Yield %	2.28	2.23	2.15	2.23	2.42	2.66	2.54	2.45

Address: 300 Park Avenue, New York, NY 10022
Telephone: 212-310-2000
Fax: 212-310-3284

Web Site: www.colgatepalmolive.com
Officers: Ian M. Cook - Chairman, President, Chief Executive Officer Dennis J. Hickey - Vice President, Chief Financial Officer, Corporate Controller

Auditors: PricewaterhouseCoopers LLP
Investor Contact: 212-310-2575
Transfer Agents: Computershare, Providence, RI

COLFAX CORP

Exchange	Symbol	Price	52Wk Range	Yield	P/E
NYS	CFX	$27.09 (5/31/2016)	51.22-19.29	N/A	24.63

*7 Year Price Score 77.20 *NYSE Composite Index=100 *12 Month Price Score 93.14

Interim Earnings (Per Share)

Qtr.	Mar	Jun	Sep	Dec
2013	0.21	0.52	0.48	0.33
2014	0.22	1.53	0.59	0.64
2015	0.42	0.42	0.15	0.35
2016	0.18	...	...	...

Interim Dividends (Per Share)

No Dividends Paid

Valuation Analysis   **Institutional Holding**

Forecast EPS	$1.50	No of Institutions
	(05/20/2016)	N/A
Market Cap	$3.3 Billion	Shares
Book Value	$3.0 Billion	N/A
Price/Book	1.09	% Held
Price/Sales	0.84	N/A

Business Summary: Industrial Machinery & Equipment (MIC: 7.2.1 SIC: 3561 NAIC: 333911)

Colfax provides gas- and fluid-handling and fabrication technology products and services to commercial and governmental customers. Co.'s gas- and fluid-handling segment is a supplier of a range of products, including centrifugal and axial fans, rotary heat exchangers, gas compressors, pumps, fluid-handling systems and controls and specialty valves, which serves customers in the power generation, oil, gas and petrochemical, mining, marine and general industrial and other end markets. Co.'s fabrication technology segment formulates, develops, manufactures and supplies consumable products and equipment for use in the cutting and joining of steels, aluminum and other metals and metal alloys.

Recent Developments: For the quarter ended Apr 1 2016, net income decreased 53.4% to US$26.2 million from US$56.3 million in the year-earlier quarter. Revenues were US$876.8 million, down 3.8% from US$911.1 million the year before. Operating income was US$48.5 million versus US$77.5 million in the prior-year quarter, a decrease of 37.4%. Direct operating expenses declined 3.3% to US$596.3 million from US$616.6 million in the comparable period the year before. Indirect operating expenses increased 6.9% to US$232.1 million from US$217.0 million in the equivalent prior-year period.

Prospects: Our evaluation of Colfax Corp. as of June 19, 2016 is the result of our systematic analysis on three basic characteristics: earnings strength, relative valuation, and recent stock price movement. The company has enjoyed a very positive trend in earnings per share over the past 5 quarters and while recent estimates for the company have been mixed, CFX has posted better than expected results. Based on operating earnings yield, the company is undervalued when compared to all of the companies in our coverage universe. Share price changes over the past year indicates that CFX will perform very poorly over the near term.

Financial Data
(US$ in Thousands)

	3 Mos	12/31/2015	12/31/2014	12/31/2013	12/31/2012	12/31/2011	12/31/2010	12/31/2009
Earnings Per Share	1.10	1.34	3.02	1.56	(0.92)	0.10	0.37	0.50
Cash Flow Per Share	2.61	2.45	3.18	3.65	1.80	1.31	1.43	0.89
Tang Book Value Per Share	N.M.	N.M.	N.M.	N.M.	N.M.	N.M.	0.36	0.45
Income Statement								
Total Revenue	876,843	3,967,053	4,624,476	4,207,209	3,913,856	693,392	541,987	525,024
EBITDA	86,183	375,341	504,053	484,492	211,709	39,006	46,472	50,259
Depn & Amortn	37,717	90,700	94,500	78,100	71,700	13,100	12,100	11,800
Income Before Taxes	39,346	236,902	358,248	302,795	48,439	19,987	27,688	31,247
Income Taxes	13,136	49,724	(62,025)	93,652	90,703	15,432	11,473	9,525
Net Income	22,615	167,739	392,098	178,628	(64,402)	4,555	16,215	21,722
Average Shares	123,242	124,869	122,666	100,366	91,069	44,268	43,667	43,325
Balance Sheet								
Current Assets	1,784,746	1,759,765	2,099,463	2,138,346	2,130,782	351,208	321,056	289,561
Total Assets	6,723,748	6,732,919	7,245,098	6,582,853	6,129,727	1,088,543	1,022,077	1,003,131
Current Liabilities	1,097,661	1,116,344	1,285,535	1,375,090	1,175,458	240,042	191,510	144,199
Long-Term Obligations	1,440,309	1,411,755	1,529,389	1,457,642	1,693,512	101,518	72,500	82,516
Total Liabilities	3,678,156	3,662,944	4,098,272	4,068,964	4,217,375	899,268	805,706	804,299
Stockholders' Equity	3,045,592	3,069,975	3,146,826	2,513,889	1,912,352	189,275	216,371	198,832
Shares Outstanding	122,637	123,486	123,730	101,921	94,067	43,697	43,413	43,229
Statistical Record								
Return on Assets %	2.02	2.40	5.67	2.81	N.M.	0.43	1.60	2.27
Return on Equity %	4.54	5.40	13.85	8.07	N.M.	2.25	7.81	11.88
EBITDA Margin %	9.83	9.46	10.90	11.52	5.41	5.63	8.57	9.57
Net Margin %	2.58	4.23	8.48	4.25	N.M.	0.66	2.99	4.14
Asset Turnover	0.58	0.57	0.67	0.66	1.08	0.66	0.54	0.55
Current Ratio	1.63	1.58	1.63	1.56	1.81	1.46	1.68	2.01
Debt to Equity	0.47	0.46	0.49	0.58	0.89	0.54	0.34	0.42
Price Range	52.65-19.29	53.47-22.00	74.92-47.20	63.69-40.35	40.35-24.80	31.80-18.17	18.90-10.26	13.63-5.41
P/E Ratio	47.86-17.54	39.90-16.42	24.81-15.63	40.83-25.87	...	318.00-181.70	51.08-27.73	27.26-10.82

Address: 420 National Business Parkway, 5th Floor, Annapolis Junction, MD 20701
Telephone: 301-323-9000

Web Site: www.colfaxcorp.com
Officers: Mitchell P. Rales - Chairman Matthew L. Trerotola - President, Chief Executive Officer

Auditors: Ernst & Young LLP
Investor Contact: 301-323-9090
Transfer Agents: Registrar and Transfer Company, Cranford, NJ

COLUMBIA PROPERTY TRUST INC

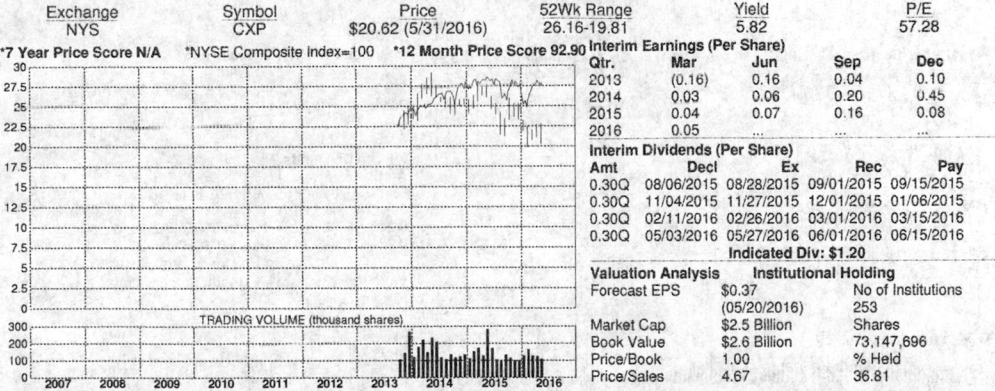

Exchange	Symbol	Price	52Wk Range	Yield	P/E
NYS	CXP	$20.62 (5/31/2016)	26.16-19.81	5.82	57.28

*7 Year Price Score N/A   *NYSE Composite Index=100   *12 Month Price Score 92.90

Interim Earnings (Per Share)

Qtr.	Mar	Jun	Sep	Dec
2013	(0.16)	0.16	0.04	0.10
2014	0.03	0.06	0.20	0.45
2015	0.04	0.07	0.16	0.08
2016	0.05	...	...	...

Interim Dividends (Per Share)

Amt	Decl	Ex	Rec	Pay
0.30Q	08/06/2015	08/28/2015	09/01/2015	09/15/2015
0.30Q	11/04/2015	11/27/2015	12/01/2015	01/06/2016
0.30Q	02/11/2016	02/26/2016	03/01/2016	03/15/2016
0.30Q	05/03/2016	05/27/2016	06/01/2016	06/15/2016

Indicated Div: $1.20

Valuation Analysis   Institutional Holding

Forecast EPS	$0.37	No of Institutions
	(05/20/2016)	253
Market Cap	$2.5 Billion	Shares
Book Value	$2.6 Billion	73,147,696
Price/Book	1.00	% Held
Price/Sales	4.67	36.81

Business Summary: REITs (MIC: 5.3.1 SIC: 6798 NAIC: 525930)

Columbia Property Trust is a real estate investment trust that owns and operates commercial real estate properties. Co. conducts its business primarily through Columbia Property Trust Operating Partnership, L.P., which acquires, develops, owns, leases, and operates real properties directly, through wholly owned subsidiaries, or through joint ventures. Co. typically invests in office properties. As of Dec 31 2014, Co. owned interests in 35 office properties and one hotel located in 12 states and the District of Columbia. All of the properties are wholly owned except for one property, which is owned through a consolidated subsidiary.

Recent Developments: For the quarter ended Mar 31 2016, income from continuing operations increased 25.2% to US$7.0 million from US$5.6 million in the year-earlier quarter. Net income increased 19.6% to US$6.7 million from US$5.6 million in the year-earlier quarter. Revenues were US$126.6 million, down 14.2% from US$147.5 million the year before.

Prospects: Our evaluation of Columbia Property Trust Inc as of June 19, 2016 is the result of our systematic analysis on three basic characteristics: earnings strength, relative valuation, and recent stock price movement. The company has enjoyed a very positive trend in earnings per share over the past 5 quarters. Because the company lacks sufficient analyst estimate data, we place greater weight on the historical EPS trend as the measure of earnings strength. Based on operating earnings yield, the company is overvalued when compared to all of the companies in our coverage universe. Share price changes over the past year indicates that CXP will perform in line with the market over the near term.

Financial Data

(US$ in Thousands)	3 Mos	12/31/2015	12/31/2014	12/31/2013	12/31/2012	12/31/2011	12/31/2010
Earnings Per Share	0.36	0.36	0.74	0.12	0.36	0.40	0.16
Cash Flow Per Share	1.79	1.79	1.90	1.63	1.84	2.06	2.06
Tang Book Value Per Share	20.12	20.40	21.03	21.14	22.33	23.64	...
Dividends Per Share	1.200	1.200	1.200	0.300	1.880	2.000	2.280
Dividend Payout %	333.33	333.33	162.16	250.00	522.22	500.00	1,425.00
Income Statement							
Total Revenue	126,579	566,065	540,797	526,578	576,691	576,389	510,514
EBITDA	68,770	231,811	206,241	214,067	227,930	231,471	161,107
Depn & Amortn	44,042	131,490	117,766	119,835	120,307	119,772	102,558
Income Before Taxes	8,636	22,279	20,039	26,320	41,103	47,789	19,594
Income Taxes	77	378	662	500	586	(276)	(226)
Net Income	6,697	44,619	92,635	15,720	48,043	56,656	23,340
Average Shares	123,412	124,847	124,918	134,085	136,672	135,680	131,212
Balance Sheet							
Current Assets	197,107	153,377	273,224	220,861	187,756	170,017	...
Total Assets	4,634,798	4,678,118	4,738,878	4,592,482	5,730,949	5,776,567	...
Current Liabilities	85,351	136,113	106,276	99,678	104,778	75,678	...
Long-Term Obligations	1,920,187	1,845,830	1,800,066	1,609,179	2,236,296	2,115,486	...
Total Liabilities	2,080,578	2,063,924	2,005,400	1,804,659	2,467,443	2,316,765	...
Stockholders' Equity	2,554,220	2,614,194	2,733,478	2,787,823	3,263,506	3,459,802	...
Shares Outstanding	123,458	124,363	124,973	124,830	136,900	136,549	135,226
Statistical Record							
Return on Assets %	0.93	0.95	1.99	0.30	0.83	...	...
Return on Equity %	1.74	1.67	3.36	0.52	1.43	...	...
EBITDA Margin %	54.33	40.95	38.14	40.65	39.52	40.16	31.56
Net Margin %	5.29	7.88	17.13	2.99	8.33	9.83	4.57
Asset Turnover	0.11	0.12	0.12	0.10	0.10	...	...
Current Ratio	2.31	1.13	2.57	2.22	1.79	2.25	...
Debt to Equity	0.75	0.71	0.66	0.58	0.69	0.61	...
Price Range	27.45-19.81	27.67-21.16	29.13-23.12	25.07-22.16	...	...	...
P/E Ratio	76.25-55.03	76.86-58.78	39.36-31.24	208.92-184.67	...	...	...
Average Yield %	5.01	4.81	4.67	1.29	...	...	...

Address: One Glenlake Parkway, Suite 1200, Atlanta, GA 30328 **Telephone:** 404-465-2200	**Web Site:** www.columbiapropertytrust.com **Officers:** John L. Dixon - Chairman E. Nelson Mills - President, Chief Executive Officer	**Auditors:** Deloitte & Touche LLP **Transfer Agents:** DST Systems Inc

COMERICA, INC.

Exchange	Symbol	Price	52Wk Range	Yield	P/E
NYS	CMA	$47.10 (5/31/2016)	52.65-31.02	1.87	19.22

*7 Year Price Score 96.27 *NYSE Composite Index=100 *12 Month Price Score 99.17

Interim Earnings (Per Share)

Qtr.	Mar	Jun	Sep	Dec
2013	0.70	0.76	0.78	0.62
2014	0.73	0.80	0.82	0.81
2015	0.73	0.73	0.74	0.64
2016	0.34	...	...	...

Interim Dividends (Per Share)

Amt	Decl	Ex	Rec	Pay
0.21Q	07/28/2015	09/11/2015	09/15/2015	10/01/2015
0.21Q	11/10/2015	12/11/2015	12/15/2015	01/01/2016
0.21Q	01/26/2016	03/11/2016	03/15/2016	04/01/2016
0.22Q	04/26/2016	06/13/2016	06/15/2016	07/01/2016

Indicated Div: $0.88 (Div. Reinv. Plan)

Valuation Analysis

		Institutional Holding	
Forecast EPS	$2.50	No of Institutions	
	(05/20/2016)	589	
Market Cap	$8.2 Billion	Shares	
Book Value	$7.6 Billion	173,864,640	
Price/Book	1.08	% Held	
Price/Sales	2.88	83.43	

TRADING VOLUME (thousand shares)

Business Summary: Banking (MIC: 5.1.1 SIC: 6021 NAIC: 522110)

Comerica is a financial holding company. Co.'s principal activity is lending to and accepting deposits from businesses and individuals. Co.'s principal business segments are: Business Bank, which provides products and services to middle market businesses, multinational corporations and governmental entities; Retail Bank, which provides small business banking and personal financial services, as well as consumer products; and Wealth Management, which provides products and services such as fiduciary services and private banking, and sells annuity products, disability and long-term care insurance products. As of Dec 31 2015, Co. had total assets of $71.88 billion and deposits of $59.85 billion.

Recent Developments: For the quarter ended Mar 31 2016, net income decreased 55.2% to US$60.0 million from US$134.0 million in the year-earlier quarter. Net interest income increased 8.2% to US$447.0 million from US$413.0 million in the year-earlier quarter. Provision for loan losses was US$148.0 million versus US$14.0 million in the prior-year quarter, an increase of 957.1%. Non-interest income fell 2.4% to US$246.0 million from US$252.0 million, while non-interest expense advanced 0.9% to US$460.0 million.

Prospects: Our evaluation of Comerica Inc. as of June 19, 2016 is the result of our systematic analysis on three basic characteristics: earnings strength, relative valuation, and recent stock price movement. The company has generated a negative trend in earnings per share over the past 5 quarters and while recent estimates for the company have remained steady, CMA has posted results that fell short of analysts expectations. Based on operating earnings yield, the company is undervalued when compared to all of the companies in our coverage universe. Share price changes over the past year indicates that CMA will perform in line with the market over the near term.

Financial Data

(US$ in Thousands)	3 Mos	12/31/2015	12/31/2014	12/31/2013	12/31/2012	12/31/2011	12/31/2010	12/31/2009
Earnings Per Share	2.45	2.84	3.16	2.85	2.67	2.09	0.88	(0.79)
Cash Flow Per Share	4.45	4.90	3.57	4.57	3.94	4.88	7.56	0.61
Tang Book Value Per Share	43.66	43.03	41.35	39.24	36.87	34.80	32.81	32.27
Dividends Per Share	0.840	0.830	0.790	0.680	0.550	0.400	0.250	0.200
Dividend Payout %	34.29	29.23	25.00	23.86	20.60	19.14	28.41	...
Income Statement								
Interest Income	472,000	1,784,000	1,750,000	1,784,000	1,863,000	1,809,000	1,853,000	2,105,000
Interest Expense	25,000	95,000	95,000	112,000	135,000	156,000	207,000	538,000
Net Interest Income	447,000	1,689,000	1,655,000	1,672,000	1,728,000	1,653,000	1,646,000	1,567,000
Provision for Losses	148,000	147,000	27,000	46,000	79,000	153,000	480,000	1,082,000
Non-Interest Income	246,000	1,050,000	868,000	826,000	818,000	792,000	789,000	1,050,000
Non-Interest Expense	460,000	1,842,000	1,658,000	1,722,000	1,757,000	1,762,000	1,640,000	1,650,000
Income Before Taxes	85,000	750,000	870,000	730,000	710,000	530,000	315,000	(115,000)
Income Taxes	25,000	229,000	277,000	189,000	189,000	137,000	55,000	(131,000)
Net Income	60,000	521,000	593,000	541,000	521,000	393,000	277,000	17,000
Average Shares	176,000	181,000	185,000	187,000	192,000	186,000	173,000	149,000
Balance Sheet								
Net Loans & Leases	48,653,000	48,450,000	47,999,000	44,872,000	45,428,000	41,953,000	39,335,000	41,176,000
Total Assets	69,007,000	71,877,000	69,190,000	65,227,000	65,359,000	61,008,000	53,667,000	59,249,000
Total Deposits	56,351,000	59,853,000	57,486,000	53,292,000	52,202,000	47,755,000	40,471,000	39,665,000
Total Liabilities	61,363,000	64,317,000	61,788,000	58,074,000	58,417,000	54,140,000	47,874,000	52,220,000
Stockholders' Equity	7,644,000	7,560,000	7,402,000	7,153,000	6,942,000	6,868,000	5,793,000	7,029,000
Shares Outstanding	175,078	175,707	179,018	182,304	188,275	197,333	176,535	151,179
Statistical Record								
Return on Assets %	0.65	0.74	0.88	0.83	0.82	0.69	0.49	0.03
Return on Equity %	5.90	6.96	8.15	7.68	7.52	6.21	4.32	0.24
Net Interest Margin %	94.70	94.67	94.57	93.72	92.75	91.38	88.83	74.44
Efficiency Ratio %	64.07	65.00	63.33	65.98	65.54	67.74	62.07	52.30
Loans to Deposits	0.86	0.81	0.83	0.84	0.87	0.88	0.97	1.04
Price Range	52.65-31.02	52.65-40.41	52.37-43.06	47.63-30.34	33.57-26.72	43.36-21.98	44.60-29.57	31.70-12.36
P/E Ratio	21.49-12.66	18.54-14.23	16.57-13.63	16.71-10.65	12.57-10.01	20.75-10.52	50.68-33.60	...
Average Yield %	1.93	1.82	1.63	1.73	1.81	1.25	0.66	0.86

Address: Comerica Bank Tower, 1717 Main Street, MC 6404, Dallas, TX 75201 Telephone: 214-462-6831	Web Site: www.comerica.com Officers: Ralph W. Babb - Chairman, President, Chief Executive Officer Curtis C. Farmer - Vice-Chairman, President, Executive Vice President	Auditors: Ernst & Young LLP Investor Contact: 214-462-6831 Transfer Agents: Wells Fargo Shareowner Services, St. Paul, MN

COMMERCIAL METALS CO.

Exchange NYS	**Symbol** CMC	**Price** $17.17 (5/31/2016)	**52Wk Range** 18.30-12.91	**Yield** 2.80	**P/E** 23.20

*7 Year Price Score 84.52   *NYSE Composite Index=100   *12 Month Price Score 110.91

Interim Earnings (Per Share)

Qtr.	Nov	Feb	May	Aug
2012-13	0.42	0.04	0.16	0.04
2013-14	0.30	0.09	0.20	0.29
2014-15	0.30	0.46	0.49	(0.05)
2015-16	0.21	0.09	...	...

Interim Dividends (Per Share)

Amt	Decl	Ex	Rec	Pay
0.12Q	06/24/2015	07/07/2015	07/09/2015	07/23/2015
0.12Q	10/28/2015	11/06/2015	11/11/2015	11/25/2015
0.12Q	01/04/2016	01/14/2016	01/19/2016	02/02/2016
0.12Q	03/23/2016	04/06/2016	04/06/2016	04/21/2016

Indicated Div: $0.48

Valuation Analysis

		Institutional Holding	
Forecast EPS	$0.92	No of Institutions	
	(05/20/2016)	362	
Market Cap	$2.0 Billion	Shares	
Book Value	$1.3 Billion	112,059,112	
Price/Book	1.46	% Held	
Price/Sales	0.39	84.35	

Business Summary: Non-Precious Metals (MIC: 8.2.2 SIC: 3312 NAIC: 331111)

Commercial Metals manufactures, recycles and markets steel and metal products, related materials and services. Co. has five segments: Americas Recycling , which processes scrap metals; Americas Mills, which include steel mills, scrap metal shredders and scrap metal processing facilities; Americas Fabrication, which bends, welds, cuts and fabricates steel, sells or rents products for the installation of concrete, produces steel fence posts; International Mills, which is comprised of all mill, recycling and fabrication operations; and International Marketing and Distribution, which sells, distributes and processes steel products, ferrous and nonferrous metals and other industrial products.

Recent Developments: For the quarter ended Feb 29 2016, income from continuing operations decreased 19.4% to US$10.8 million from US$13.5 million in the year-earlier quarter. Net income increased 69.5% to US$10.5 million from US$6.2 million in the year-earlier quarter. Revenues were US$1.02 billion, down 26.7% from US$1.39 billion the year before. Direct operating expenses declined 28.9% to US$884.9 million from US$1.24 billion in the comparable period the year before. Indirect operating expenses decreased 5.4% to US$121.9 million from US$128.9 million in the equivalent prior-year period.

Prospects: Our evaluation of Commercial Metals Co. as of June 19, 2016 is the result of our systematic analysis on three basic characteristics: earnings strength, relative valuation, and recent stock price movement. The company has suffered a very negative trend in earnings per share over the past 5 quarters. However, while recent estimates for the company have been mixed, CMC has posted better than expected results. Based on operating earnings yield, the company is about fairly valued when compared to all of the companies in our coverage universe. Share price changes over the past year indicates that CMC will perform well over the near term.

Financial Data

(US$ in Thousands)	6 Mos	3 Mos	08/31/2015	08/31/2014	08/31/2013	08/31/2012	08/31/2011	08/31/2010
Earnings Per Share	0.74	1.11	1.20	0.97	0.66	1.78	(1.13)	(1.81)
Cash Flow Per Share	6.81	5.28	2.69	1.17	1.27	1.69	0.24	0.40
Tang Book Value Per Share	11.20	11.18	10.83	10.81	10.26	10.05	9.37	10.31
Dividends Per Share	0.480	0.480	0.480	0.480	0.480	0.480	0.480	0.480
Dividend Payout %	64.86	43.24	40.00	49.48	72.73	26.97	...	...
Income Statement								
Total Revenue	2,174,556	1,154,859	5,988,605	7,039,959	6,889,575	7,828,440	7,918,430	6,306,102
EBITDA	81,449	53,810	447,470	350,959	326,622	363,784	120,283	39,836
Depn & Amortn	(3,798)	(1,899)	125,182	128,407	124,078	131,495	159,576	168,934
Income Before Taxes	50,318	37,405	244,528	144,811	132,936	162,793	(110,099)	(204,606)
Income Taxes	13,836	11,772	83,206	42,724	57,979	(46,190)	19,328	(38,118)
Net Income	35,565	25,063	141,634	115,551	77,315	207,484	(129,617)	(205,344)
Average Shares	116,507	117,339	117,949	118,607	117,552	116,783	114,995	113,524
Balance Sheet								
Current Assets	1,980,374	2,259,438	2,307,101	2,553,791	2,366,195	2,239,831	2,326,253	2,175,206
Total Assets	3,043,511	3,302,707	3,372,302	3,688,520	3,494,801	3,441,246	3,683,131	3,706,153
Current Liabilities	451,255	515,019	617,348	891,153	781,109	901,134	1,198,854	1,102,959
Long-Term Obligations	1,071,832	1,275,410	1,277,882	1,281,042	1,278,814	1,157,073	1,167,497	1,197,282
Total Liabilities	1,694,872	1,936,678	2,053,101	2,340,040	2,224,802	2,194,878	2,522,706	2,455,417
Stockholders' Equity	1,348,639	1,366,029	1,319,201	1,348,480	1,269,999	1,246,368	1,160,425	1,250,736
Shares Outstanding	114,535	116,232	115,635	117,829	117,010	116,351	115,533	114,325
Statistical Record								
Return on Assets %	2.61	3.77	4.01	3.22	2.23	5.81	N.M.	N.M.
Return on Equity %	6.50	9.64	10.62	8.83	6.14	17.19	N.M.	N.M.
EBITDA Margin %	3.75	4.66	7.47	4.99	4.74	4.65	1.52	0.63
Net Margin %	1.64	2.17	2.37	1.64	1.12	2.65	N.M.	N.M.
Asset Turnover	1.54	1.58	1.70	1.96	1.99	2.19	2.14	1.71
Current Ratio	4.39	4.39	3.74	2.87	3.03	2.49	1.94	1.97
Debt to Equity	0.79	0.93	0.97	0.95	1.01	0.93	1.01	0.96
Price Range	17.29-12.91	17.29-12.99	18.54-12.99	20.58-14.91	17.41-12.74	15.30-8.69	18.09-10.72	21.11-12.39
P/E Ratio	23.36-17.45	15.58-11.70	15.45-10.83	21.22-15.37	26.38-19.30	8.60-4.88	...	...
Average Yield %	3.16	3.11	3.02	3.74	2.61	3.21	3.70	3.06

Address: 6565 North MacArthur Blvd, Irving, TX 75039 **Telephone:** 214-689-4300 **Fax:** 214 689 5886	**Web Site:** www.cmc.com **Officers:** Joseph A. Alvarado - Chairman, President, Chief Executive Officer Terry P. Hatten - Vice President, Chief Human Resources Officer	**Auditors:** Deloitte & Touche LLP **Investor Contact:** 214 689 4300 **Transfer Agents:** StockTrans®, a Broadridge Company

COMMUNITY BANK SYSTEM, INC.

Exchange	Symbol	Price	52Wk Range	Yield	P/E	Div Achiever
NYS	CBU	$41.24 (5/31/2016)	43.13-34.21	3.01	18.75	24 Years

*7 Year Price Score 110.20 *NYSE Composite Index=100 *12 Month Price Score 100.74

Interim Earnings (Per Share)

Qtr.	Mar	Jun	Sep	Dec
2013	0.50	0.52	0.54	0.38
2014	0.54	0.57	0.54	0.57
2015	0.54	0.58	0.60	0.47
2016	0.55			

Interim Dividends (Per Share)

Amt	Decl	Ex	Rec	Pay
0.31Q	08/20/2015	09/11/2015	09/15/2015	10/09/2015
0.31Q	11/20/2015	12/11/2015	12/15/2015	01/11/2016
0.31Q	02/18/2016	03/11/2016	03/15/2016	04/11/2016
0.31Q	05/20/2016	06/13/2016	06/15/2016	07/11/2016

Indicated Div: $1.24 (Div. Reinv. Plan)

Valuation Analysis **Institutional Holding**

Forecast EPS	$2.28	No of Institutions
	(04/24/2016)	204
Market Cap	$1.8 Billion	Shares
Book Value	$1.2 Billion	31,184,908
Price/Book	1.51	% Held
Price/Sales	4.55	62.28

Business Summary: Banking (MIC: 5.1.1 SIC: 6021 NAIC: 522110)

Community Bank System is a holding company. Through its subsidiaries, Community Bank, N.A. (the Bank), Co. operates as a community bank providing a range of banking and financial services to retail, commercial, and municipal customers. Among others, the Bank owns: CBNA Insurance Agency, Inc., which providing personal and commercial property insurance and other risk management products and services; CBNA Treasury Management Corporation, which provides cash management, and investment to the Bank; and Community Investment Services, Inc., which provide broker-dealer and investment advisory services. At Dec 31 2015, Co. had total assets of $8.55 billion and total deposits of $6.87 billion.

Recent Developments: For the quarter ended Mar 31 2016, net income increased 9.4% to US$24.4 million from US$22.3 million in the year-earlier quarter. Net interest income increased 11.8% to US$66.9 million from US$59.8 million in the year-earlier quarter. Provision for loan losses was US$1.3 million versus US$623,000 in the prior-year quarter, an increase of 115.2%. Non-interest income rose 31.8% to US$38.3 million from US$29.0 million, while non-interest expense advanced 20.9% to US$67.7 million.

Prospects: Our evaluation of Community Bank System Inc. as of June 19, 2016 is the result of our systematic analysis on three basic characteristics: earnings strength, relative valuation, and recent stock price movement. The company has managed to produce a neutral trend in earnings per share over the past 5 quarters and while recent estimates for the company have remained steady, CBU has posted better than expected results. Based on operating earnings yield, the company is undervalued when compared to all of the companies in our coverage universe. Share price changes over the past year indicates that CBU will perform well over the near term.

Financial Data

(US$ in Thousands)	3 Mos	12/31/2015	12/31/2014	12/31/2013	12/31/2012	12/31/2011	12/31/2010	12/31/2009
Earnings Per Share	2.20	2.19	2.22	1.94	1.93	2.01	1.89	1.26
Cash Flow Per Share	2.73	2.84	3.04	2.58	2.76	2.73	2.95	1.33
Tang Book Value Per Share	16.24	15.00	14.75	12.00	13.01	11.19	8.87	7.56
Dividends Per Share	1.230	1.220	1.160	1.100	1.060	1.000	0.940	0.880
Dividend Payout %	55.91	55.71	52.25	56.70	54.92	49.75	49.74	69.84
Income Statement								
Interest Income	69,756	259,622	256,220	264,159	281,400	270,969	248,281	248,782
Interest Expense	2,875	11,202	11,792	26,065	50,976	61,556	66,597	83,282
Net Interest Income	66,881	248,420	244,428	238,094	230,424	209,413	181,684	165,500
Provision for Losses	1,341	6,447	7,178	7,992	9,108	4,736	7,205	9,790
Non-Interest Income	38,281	123,299	119,020	102,180	99,246	89,222	88,792	83,535
Non-Interest Expense	67,669	233,055	226,580	221,255	211,757	190,372	176,886	186,178
Income Before Taxes	36,152	132,217	129,690	111,027	108,805	103,527	86,385	53,067
Income Taxes	11,749	40,987	38,337	32,198	31,737	30,385	23,065	11,622
Net Income	24,403	91,230	91,353	78,829	77,068	73,142	63,320	41,445
Average Shares	44,196	41,401	41,029	40,504	39,671	36,182	33,269	32,821
Balance Sheet								
Net Loans & Leases	4,775,915	4,756,906	4,191,907	4,065,492	3,822,688	3,429,344	2,987,805	3,059,354
Total Assets	8,615,901	8,552,669	7,489,440	7,095,864	7,496,800	6,488,275	5,444,506	5,402,813
Total Deposits	7,119,062	6,873,474	5,935,264	5,896,044	5,628,039	4,795,245	3,934,045	3,924,486
Total Liabilities	7,415,236	7,412,022	6,501,536	6,220,052	6,594,022	5,713,692	4,837,248	4,837,116
Stockholders' Equity	1,200,665	1,140,647	987,904	875,812	902,778	774,583	607,258	565,697
Shares Outstanding	44,069	43,774	40,747	40,431	39,625	36,986	33,318	32,800
Statistical Record								
Return on Assets %	1.15	1.14	1.25	1.08	1.10	1.23	1.17	0.78
Return on Equity %	8.43	8.57	9.80	8.86	9.16	10.59	10.80	7.47
Net Interest Margin %	95.88	95.69	95.40	90.13	81.88	77.28	73.18	66.52
Efficiency Ratio %	62.64	60.86	60.38	60.40	55.63	52.85	52.48	56.02
Loans to Deposits	0.67	0.69	0.71	0.69	0.68	0.72	0.76	0.78
Price Range	43.13-34.21	43.13-33.60	39.91-32.84	40.27-27.36	29.38-25.55	28.34-21.81	28.58-17.87	24.39-13.74
P/E Ratio	19.60-15.55	19.69-15.34	17.98-14.79	20.76-14.10	15.22-13.24	14.10-10.85	15.12-9.46	19.36-10.90
Average Yield %	3.26	3.27	3.18	3.42	3.84	4.03	4.03	4.98

Address: 5790 Widewaters Parkway, DeWitt, NY 13214-1883 Telephone: 315-445-2282	Web Site: www.communitybankna.com Officers: Nicholas A. DiCerbo - Chairman Mark E. Tryniski - President, Chief Executive Officer	Auditors: PricewaterhouseCoopersLLP Investor Contact: 315-445-3121 Transfer Agents: American Stock Transfer & Trust Company LLC, Brooklyn, NY

COMMUNITY HEALTH SYSTEMS, INC.

Exchange	Symbol	Price	52Wk Range	Yield	P/E
NYS	CYH	$13.44 (5/31/2016)	52.71-11.98	N/A	17.23

*7 Year Price Score 81.79   ***NYSE Composite Index=100**   ***12 Month Price Score 53.24**

TRADING VOLUME (thousand shares)

Interim Earnings (Per Share)

Qtr.	Mar	Jun	Sep	Dec
2013	0.86	0.32	0.04	0.30
2014	(1.04)	0.37	0.54	0.89
2015	0.68	0.95	0.44	(0.71)
2016	0.10	...	...	...

Interim Dividends (Per Share)

Amt	Decl	Ex	Rec	Pay
0.25U	12/07/2012	12/13/2012	12/17/2012	12/28/2012
0.00U	...	05/02/2016	04/22/2016	04/29/2016

Valuation Analysis   Institutional Holding

Forecast EPS	$2.20 (05/20/2016)	No of Institutions 434
Market Cap	$1.5 Billion	Shares
Book Value	$4.0 Billion	123,012,768
Price/Book	0.38	% Held
Price/Sales	0.08	97.50

Business Summary: Hospitals & Health Care Facilities (MIC: 4.2.1 SIC: 8062 NAIC: 622110)

Community Health Systems is an operator of hospitals. Services provided via Co.'s hospitals and affiliated businesses include general acute care, emergency room, general and specialty surgery, critical care, internal medicine, obstetrics, diagnostic, psychiatric and rehabilitation services. Co. also provides additional outpatient services at urgent care centers, occupational medicine clinics, imaging centers, cancer centers, ambulatory surgery centers and home health and hospice agencies. Through its subsidiary, Quorum Health Resources, LLC, Co. provides management and consulting services to non-affiliated general acute care hospitals. As of Dec 31 2015, Co. owned or leased 194 hospitals.

Recent Developments: For the quarter ended Mar 31 2016, income from continuing operations decreased 67.0% to US$37.0 million from US$112.0 million in the year-earlier quarter. Net income decreased 63.6% to US$36.0 million from US$99.0 million in the year-earlier quarter. Revenues were US$5.00 billion, up 1.8% from US$4.91 billion the year before. Operating income was US$294.0 million versus US$399.0 million in the prior-year quarter, a decrease of 26.3%. Indirect operating expenses increased 4.3% to US$4.71 billion from US$4.51 billion in the equivalent prior-year period.

Prospects: Our evaluation of Community Health Systems Inc. as of June 19, 2016 is the result of our systematic analysis on three basic characteristics: earnings strength, relative valuation, and recent stock price movement. The company has managed to produce a neutral trend in earnings per share over the past 5 quarters. However, while recent estimates for the company have been mixed, CYH has posted results that fell short of analysts expectations. Based on operating earnings yield, the company is undervalued when compared to all of the companies in our coverage universe. Share price changes over the past year indicates that CYH will perform very poorly over the near term.

Financial Data

(US$ in Thousands)	3 Mos	12/31/2015	12/31/2014	12/31/2013	12/31/2012	12/31/2011	12/31/2010	12/31/2009
Earnings Per Share	0.78	1.37	0.82	1.51	2.96	2.23	3.01	2.66
Cash Flow Per Share	11.57	8.05	14.47	11.75	14.31	14.03	12.96	11.88
Dividends Per Share	...	...	...	...	0.250	...	...	...
Dividend Payout %	...	...	...	...	8.45	...	...	...
Income Statement								
Total Revenue	4,999,000	19,437,000	18,639,000	12,997,693	13,028,985	13,626,168	12,986,500	12,107,613
EBITDA	592,000	2,495,000	1,341,000	1,661,043	1,810,229	1,726,131	1,724,767	1,625,116
Depn & Amortn	298,000	1,174,000	75,000	782,675	725,558	657,665	609,839	566,543
Income Before Taxes	43,000	348,000	294,000	263,221	461,738	424,056	463,002	409,609
Income Taxes	26,000	116,000	82,000	88,594	157,502	137,653	159,993	141,325
Net Income	11,000	158,000	92,000	141,203	265,640	201,948	279,983	243,150
Average Shares	110,309	115,272	112,549	93,815	89,806	90,666	92,946	91,517
Balance Sheet								
Current Assets	5,256,000	5,166,000	5,566,000	3,747,963	3,419,142	2,846,089	2,871,193	2,674,995
Total Assets	26,724,000	26,861,000	27,421,000	17,117,295	16,606,335	15,208,840	14,698,123	14,021,472
Current Liabilities	3,054,000	3,072,000	3,589,000	2,457,483	2,143,220	1,911,139	1,642,040	1,457,796
Long-Term Obligations	16,665,000	16,822,000	16,681,000	9,286,495	9,451,394	8,782,798	8,808,382	8,844,638
Total Liabilities	22,721,000	22,842,000	23,418,000	14,049,468	13,875,128	12,811,744	12,508,659	12,070,837
Stockholders' Equity	4,003,000	4,019,000	4,003,000	3,067,827	2,731,207	2,397,096	2,189,464	1,950,635
Shares Outstanding	113,756	112,757	116,725	95,011	91,950	90,571	92,669	93,037
Statistical Record								
Return on Assets %	0.34	0.58	0.41	0.84	1.67	1.35	1.95	1.75
Return on Equity %	2.25	3.94	2.60	4.87	10.33	8.81	13.53	13.42
EBITDA Margin %	11.84	12.84	7.19	12.78	13.89	12.67	13.28	13.42
Net Margin %	0.22	0.81	0.49	1.09	2.04	1.48	2.16	2.01
Asset Turnover	0.73	0.72	0.84	0.77	0.82	0.91	0.90	0.87
Current Ratio	1.72	1.68	1.55	1.53	1.60	1.49	1.75	1.83
Debt to Equity	4.16	4.19	4.17	3.03	3.46	3.66	4.02	4.53
Price Range	52.71-11.98	52.71-20.73	47.29-28.99	42.13-25.30	26.06-13.74	34.65-12.59	34.38-21.46	30.94-10.80
P/E Ratio	67.58-15.36	38.48-15.13	57.67-35.35	27.90-16.76	8.80-4.64	15.54-5.64	11.42-7.13	11.63-4.06
Average Yield %	...	...	...	...	1.21	...	...	...

Address: 4000 Meridian Boulevard, Franklin, TN 37067 **Telephone:** 615-465-7000	**Web Site:** www.chs.net **Officers:** Wayne T. Smith - Chairman, President, Chief Executive Officer David L. Miller - President, Chief Operating Officer, Division Officer	**Auditors:** Deloitte & Touche LLP **Investor Contact:** 615-465-7000 **Transfer Agents:** Registrar and Transfer Company, Cranford, NJ

COMPASS MINERALS INTERNATIONAL INC

Exchange	Symbol	Price	52Wk Range	Yield	P/E	Div Achiever
NYS	CMP	$77.95 (5/31/2016)	88.10-66.62	3.57	17.84	11 Years

*7 Year Price Score 85.35   *NYSE Composite Index=100   *12 Month Price Score 93.46

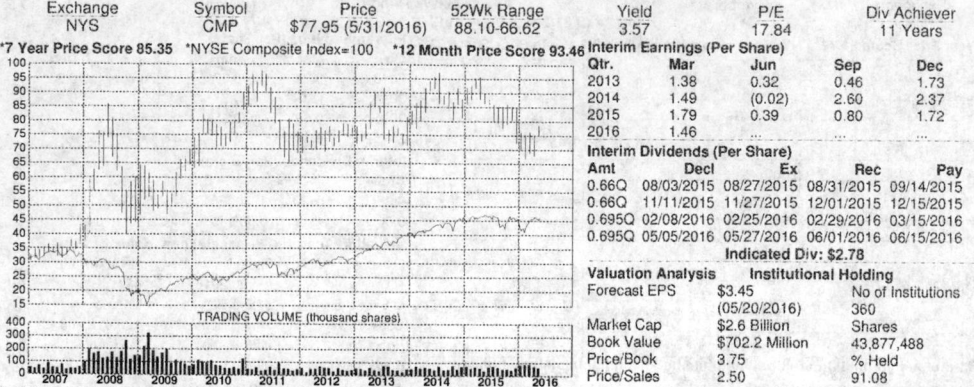

Interim Earnings (Per Share)

Qtr.	Mar	Jun	Sep	Dec
2013	1.38	0.32	0.46	1.73
2014	1.49	(0.02)	2.60	2.37
2015	1.79	0.39	0.80	1.72
2016	1.46	...	...	...

Interim Dividends (Per Share)

Amt	Decl	Ex	Rec	Pay
0.66Q	08/03/2015	08/27/2015	08/31/2015	09/14/2015
0.66Q	11/11/2015	11/27/2015	12/01/2015	12/15/2015
0.695Q	02/08/2016	02/25/2016	02/29/2016	03/15/2016
0.695Q	05/05/2016	05/27/2016	06/01/2016	06/15/2016

Indicated Div: $2.78

Valuation Analysis

		Institutional Holding	
Forecast EPS	$3.45	No of Institutions	360
	(05/20/2016)		
Market Cap	$2.6 Billion	Shares	43,877,488
Book Value	$702.2 Million	% Held	91.08
Price/Book	3.75		
Price/Sales	2.50		

Business Summary: Mining (MIC: 8.2.4 SIC: 1499 NAIC: 212399)

Compass Minerals International is a holding company, which produces and markets minerals, such as salt, sulfate of potash specialty fertilizer magnesium chloride and micronutrients. Co. also sells micronutrient products under its Wolf Trax brand. Additionally, Co. produces and markets consumer deicing and water conditioning products, ingredients used in consumer and commercial food preparation, and other mineral-based products for consumer, agricultural and industrial applications. In the U.K., Co. operates a records management business utilizing excavated areas of its Winsford salt mine with one other locations in London, England. Co. has two segments: salt, and plant nutrition.

Recent Developments: For the quarter ended Mar 31 2016, net income decreased 18.0% to US$49.7 million from US$60.6 million in the year-earlier quarter. Revenues were US$345.7 million, down 12.0% from US$393.0 million the year before. Operating income was US$74.3 million versus US$84.7 million in the prior-year quarter, a decrease of 12.3%. Direct operating expenses declined 13.1% to US$243.1 million from US$279.8 million in the comparable period the year before. Indirect operating expenses decreased 0.7% to US$28.3 million from US$28.5 million in the equivalent prior-year period.

Prospects: Our evaluation of Compass Minerals International Inc. as of June 19, 2016 is the result of our systematic analysis on three basic characteristics: earnings strength, relative valuation, and recent stock price movement. The company has generated a negative trend in earnings per share over the past 5 quarters and while recent estimates for the company have remained steady, CMP has posted better than expected results. Based on operating earnings yield, the company is undervalued when compared to all of the companies in our coverage universe. Share price changes over the past year indicates that CMP will perform in line with the market over the near term.

Financial Data

(US$ in Thousands)	3 Mos	12/31/2015	12/31/2014	12/31/2013	12/31/2012	12/31/2011	12/31/2010	12/31/2009
Earnings Per Share	4.37	4.69	6.44	3.88	2.65	4.45	4.51	4.92
Cash Flow Per Share	3.20	4.09	7.24	7.13	4.57	7.67	7.37	3.65
Tang Book Value Per Share	16.34	14.73	14.25	14.39	12.89	11.78	10.04	6.23
Dividends Per Share	2.675	2.640	2.400	2.180	1.980	1.800	1.560	1.420
Dividend Payout %	61.21	56.29	37.27	56.19	74.72	40.45	34.59	28.86
Income Statement								
Total Revenue	345,700	1,098,700	1,282,500	1,129,600	941,900	1,105,700	1,068,900	963,100
EBITDA	75,800	315,500	391,100	266,200	195,300	284,500	271,200	307,800
Depn & Amortn	300	79,500	79,200	74,200	65,800	66,200	53,300	44,900
Income Before Taxes	69,700	214,500	291,800	174,100	111,300	197,300	195,200	237,100
Income Taxes	20,000	55,300	73,900	43,300	22,400	48,300	44,600	73,200
Net Income	49,700	159,200	217,900	130,800	88,900	149,000	150,600	163,900
Average Shares	33,748	33,692	33,581	33,420	33,135	32,934	32,763	32,596
Balance Sheet								
Current Assets	459,800	512,300	702,700	577,400	506,900	515,800	521,400	483,400
Total Assets	1,651,900	1,628,900	1,637,200	1,404,800	1,300,600	1,205,500	1,114,300	1,003,800
Current Liabilities	136,100	170,800	237,700	257,600	199,300	326,800	182,600	184,600
Long-Term Obligations	712,500	722,100	622,500	474,700	478,400	326,700	482,500	486,600
Total Liabilities	949,700	989,200	983,600	850,600	797,100	758,900	766,500	780,700
Stockholders' Equity	702,200	639,700	653,600	554,200	503,500	446,600	347,800	223,100
Shares Outstanding	33,782	33,701	33,609	33,476	33,272	33,023	32,809	32,643
Statistical Record								
Return on Assets %	9.26	9.75	14.33	9.67	7.08	12.85	14.22	17.95
Return on Equity %	22.00	24.62	36.08	24.73	18.66	37.51	52.76	113.98
EBITDA Margin %	21.93	28.72	30.50	23.57	20.73	25.73	25.37	31.96
Net Margin %	14.38	14.49	16.99	11.58	9.44	13.48	14.09	17.02
Asset Turnover	0.66	0.67	0.84	0.84	0.75	0.95	1.01	1.05
Current Ratio	3.38	3.00	2.96	2.24	2.54	1.58	2.86	2.62
Debt to Equity	1.01	1.13	0.95	0.86	0.95	0.73	1.39	2.18
Price Range	95.60-66.62	95.60-72.12	97.20-77.09	91.64-71.09	78.85-68.38	97.61-64.80	89.66-63.04	69.87-46.51
P/E Ratio	21.88-15.24	20.38-15.38	15.09-11.97	23.62-18.32	29.75-25.80	21.93-14.56	19.88-13.98	14.20-9.45
Average Yield %	3.31	3.08	2.76	2.78	2.68	2.17	2.03	2.47

Address: 9900 West 109th Street, Suite 100, Overland Park, KS 66210 Telephone: 913-344-9200	Web Site: www.compassminerals.com Officers: Francis Joseph Malecha - President, Chief Executive Officer Robert D. Miller - Senior Vice President	Auditors: Ernst & Young LLP Investor Contact: 913-344-9200 Transfer Agents: Computershare Trust Company, N.A., Providence, RI

COMPUTER SCIENCES CORP

Exchange	Symbol	Price	52Wk Range	Yield	P/E
NYS	CSC	$49.20 (5/31/2016)	50.65-27.05	1.14	27.64

*7 Year Price Score 105.89 *NYSE Composite Index=100 *12 Month Price Score 106.19

Interim Earnings (Per Share)

Qtr.	Jun	Sep	Dec	Mar
2011-12	1.17	(18.56)	(8.96)	(1.02)
2012-13	0.26	0.83	3.27	1.82
2013-14	1.02	1.34	0.94	1.16
2014-15	0.98	1.04	(2.23)	0.07
2015-16	1.14	1.19	0.30	(0.84)

Interim Dividends (Per Share)

Amt	Decl	Ex	Rec	Pay
10.50Sp	11/04/2015	11/30/2015	11/18/2015	11/30/2015
0.14Q	11/30/2015	12/31/2015	01/05/2016	01/26/2016
0.14Q	03/16/2016	04/01/2016	04/05/2016	04/29/2016
0.14Q	05/17/2016	06/10/2016	06/14/2016	07/11/2016

Indicated Div: $0.56

Valuation Analysis   **Institutional Holding**

Forecast EPS	$2.88	No of Institutions
	(05/20/2016)	511
Market Cap	$6.8 Billion	Shares
Book Value	$2.0 Billion	148,418,208
Price/Book	3.36	% Held
Price/Sales	0.96	88.95

Business Summary: IT Services (MIC: 6.3.1 SIC: 7373 NAIC: 541512)

Computer Sciences is a provider of information technology services and solutions. Co.'s reportable segments are Global Business Services (GBS) and Global Infrastructure Services (GIS). The GBS segment provides technology solutions including consulting, applications services, and software. The GIS segment provides managed and virtual desktop solutions, unified communications and collaboration services, data center management, cyber security, compute and managed storage solutions to commercial clients. Geographically, Co. has operations throughout North America, Europe, Asia and Australia.

Recent Developments: For the year ended Apr 1 2016, income from continuing operations was US$72.0 million compared with a loss of US$207.0 million a year earlier. Net income increased to US$263.0 million from US$17.0 million in the prior year. Revenues were US$7.11 billion, down 12.5% from US$8.12 billion the year before. Direct operating expenses declined 15.8% to US$5.19 billion from US$6.16 billion in the comparable period the year before. Indirect operating expenses decreased 30.8% to US$1.74 billion from US$2.51 billion in the equivalent prior-year period.

Prospects: Our evaluation of Computer Sciences Corp. as of June 19, 2016 is the result of our systematic analysis on three basic characteristics: earnings strength, relative valuation, and recent stock price movement. The company has managed to produce a neutral trend in earnings per share over the past 5 quarters and while recent estimates for the company have been raised by analysts, CSC has posted better than expected results. Based on operating earnings yield, the company is undervalued when compared to all of the companies in our coverage universe. Share price changes over the past year indicates that CSC will perform very poorly over the near term.

Financial Data

(US$ in Thousands)	04/01/2016	04/03/2015	03/28/2014	03/29/2013	03/30/2012	04/01/2011	04/02/2010	04/03/2009
Earnings Per Share	1.78	(0.05)	4.47	6.18	(27.37)	4.73	5.28	7.31
Cash Flow Per Share	5.82	9.89	10.59	7.26	7.61	10.15	10.81	12.91
Tang Book Value Per Share	N.M.	1.25	8.03	3.35	N.M.	14.61	9.27	3.74
Dividends Per Share	11.240	0.920	0.800	0.800	0.800	0.700	...	...
Dividend Payout %	631.46	...	17.90	12.94	...	14.80	...	...
Income Statement								
Total Revenue	7,106,000	12,173,000	12,998,000	14,993,000	15,877,000	16,042,000	16,128,000	16,739,900
EBITDA	478,000	458,000	1,702,000	1,347,000	(3,456,000)	2,228,000	2,405,000	2,438,600
Depn & Amortn	383,000	606,000	661,000	715,000	763,000	1,140,000	1,156,000	1,270,000
Income Before Taxes	10,000	(276,000)	910,000	471,000	(4,357,000)	957,000	1,024,000	949,100
Income Taxes	(62,000)	(312,000)	289,000	(35,000)	(121,000)	243,000	204,000	(166,100)
Net Income	251,000	(8,000)	674,000	961,000	(4,242,000)	740,000	817,000	1,115,200
Average Shares	141,330	145,780	150,761	155,557	155,012	156,605	154,754	152,614
Balance Sheet								
Current Assets	3,412,000	4,905,000	5,628,000	5,673,000	4,883,000	7,557,000	8,422,000	7,707,200
Total Assets	7,736,000	10,201,000	11,389,000	11,251,000	11,189,000	16,120,000	16,455,000	15,618,700
Current Liabilities	2,608,000	3,601,000	3,462,000	3,349,000	4,536,000	4,178,000	4,122,000	4,016,200
Long-Term Obligations	1,934,000	1,765,000	2,207,000	2,498,000	1,486,000	2,409,000	3,669,000	4,172,600
Total Liabilities	5,711,000	7,280,000	7,476,000	8,116,000	8,410,000	8,616,000	10,009,000	10,108,800
Stockholders' Equity	2,025,000	2,921,000	3,913,000	3,135,000	2,779,000	7,504,000	6,446,000	5,509,900
Shares Outstanding	138,380	138,773	145,571	150,164	155,200	154,480	153,949	151,498
Statistical Record								
Return on Assets %	2.81	N.M.	5.97	8.59	N.M.	4.56	5.11	6.99
Return on Equity %	10.18	N.M.	19.18	32.59	N.M.	10.64	13.70	20.00
EBITDA Margin %	6.73	3.76	13.09	8.98	N.M.	13.89	14.91	14.57
Net Margin %	3.53	N.M.	5.19	6.41	N.M.	4.61	5.07	6.66
Asset Turnover	0.79	1.11	1.15	1.34	1.17	0.99	1.01	1.05
Current Ratio	1.31	1.36	1.63	1.69	1.08	1.81	2.04	1.92
Debt to Equity	0.96	0.60	0.56	0.80	0.53	0.32	0.57	0.76
Price Range	40.51-27.05	41.20-31.80	36.53-24.46	29.00-12.92	29.28-13.17	32.47-22.86	33.39-20.76	28.23-14.02
P/E Ratio	22.76-15.20	...	8.17-5.47	4.69-2.09	...	6.87-4.83	6.32-3.93	3.86-1.92
Average Yield %	31.90	2.57	2.69	4.09	4.21	2.53	...	...

Address: 1775 Tysons Boulevard, Tysons, VA 22102 **Telephone:** 703-876-1000	**Web Site:** www.csc.com **Officers:** John Michael Lawrie - President, Chief Executive Officer Paul N. Saleh - Executive Vice President, Vice President, Chief Financial Officer, Principal Accounting Officer	**Auditors:** Deloitte & Touche LLP **Investor Contact:** 703-245-9700 **Transfer Agents:** Computershare, Providence, RI

CONAGRA FOODS, INC.

Exchange	Symbol	Price	52Wk Range	Yield	P/E
NYS	CAG	$45.70 (5/31/2016)	46.43-37.42	2.19	N/A

*7 Year Price Score 120.49 *NYSE Composite Index=100 *12 Month Price Score 106.03

TRADING VOLUME (thousand shares)

Interim Earnings (Per Share)

Qtr.	Aug	Nov	Feb	May
2012-13	0.61	0.51	0.29	0.45
2013-14	0.34	0.58	0.55	(0.76)
2014-15	1.12	0.02	(2.23)	0.49
2015-16	(2.65)	0.35	0.46	...

Interim Dividends (Per Share)

Amt	Decl	Ex	Rec	Pay
0.25Q	07/14/2015	07/28/2015	07/30/2015	09/01/2015
0.25Q	09/25/2015	10/28/2015	10/30/2015	12/01/2015
0.25Q	12/15/2015	01/27/2016	01/29/2016	03/01/2016
0.25Q	04/07/2016	04/27/2016	04/29/2016	06/01/2016

Indicated Div: $1.00 (Div. Reinv. Plan)

Valuation Analysis | **Institutional Holding**

Forecast EPS	$2.07	No of Institutions
	(05/20/2016)	931
Market Cap	$19.9 Billion	Shares
Book Value	$3.7 Billion	386,446,816
Price/Book	5.46	% Held
Price/Sales	1.54	73.45

Business Summary: Food (MIC: 1.2.1 SIC: 2024 NAIC: 311520)

ConAgra Foods is a packaged food company providing branded and private branded food, as well as a commercial foods business serving restaurants and foodservice operations. As of May 31 2015, Co. had three reportable segments: Consumer Foods, which includes branded food sold in various retail channels primarily in North America; Commercial Foods, which includes commercially branded and private branded food and ingredients, which are sold primarily to commercial, restaurants, foodservice, food manufacturing, and industrial customers; and Private Brands, which includes private brand and customized food products which are sold in various retail channels, primarily in North America.

Recent Developments: For the quarter ended Feb 28 2016, income from continuing operations decreased 11.6% to US$187.6 million from US$212.3 million in the year-earlier quarter. Net income amounted to US$206.3 million versus a net loss of US$952.7 million in the year-earlier quarter. Revenues were US$2.92 billion, up 0.6% from US$2.91 billion the year before. Direct operating expenses declined 2.9% to US$2.12 billion from US$2.19 billion in the comparable period the year before. Indirect operating expenses increased 28.7% to US$566.5 million from US$440.1 million in the equivalent prior-year period.

Prospects: Our evaluation of ConAgra Foods Inc. as of June 19, 2016 is the result of our systematic analysis on three basic characteristics: earnings strength, relative valuation, and recent stock price movement. The company has generated a negative trend in earnings per share over the past 5 quarters and while recent estimates for the company have remained steady, CAG has posted results that fell short of analysts expectations. Based on operating earnings yield, the company is about fairly valued when compared to all of the companies in our coverage universe. Share price changes over the past year indicates that CAG will perform well over the near term.

Financial Data

(US$ in Thousands)	9 Mos	6 Mos	3 Mos	05/31/2015	05/25/2014	05/26/2013	05/27/2012	05/29/2011
Earnings Per Share	(1.35)	(4.04)	(4.37)	(0.60)	0.70	1.85	1.12	1.88
Cash Flow Per Share	3.29	3.18	3.05	3.42	3.69	3.45	2.55	3.16
Tang Book Value Per Share	N.M.	N.M.	N.M.	N.M.	N.M.	N.M.	N.M.	0.38
Dividends Per Share	1.000	1.000	1.000	1.000	1.000	0.990	0.950	0.890
Dividend Payout %	...	...	...	...	142.86	53.51	84.82	47.34
Income Statement								
Total Revenue	8,815,400	5,886,500	2,793,800	15,832,400	17,702,600	15,491,400	13,262,600	12,303,100
EBITDA	1,191,900	787,500	387,000	(55,100)	1,066,800	1,480,600	850,300	1,420,200
Depn & Amortn	281,700	188,800	91,600	108,500	111,400	56,200	21,100	17,800
Income Before Taxes	673,400	438,800	215,100	(495,500)	576,400	1,148,800	625,200	1,224,900
Income Taxes	259,300	168,100	84,900	234,000	298,200	400,200	195,800	421,000
Net Income	(794,600)	(999,200)	(1,154,100)	(252,600)	303,100	773,900	467,900	817,000
Average Shares	439,600	437,900	435,700	426,100	427,500	417,600	418,300	434,300
Balance Sheet								
Current Assets	3,527,500	3,912,500	3,702,000	3,667,700	4,230,800	4,379,800	3,218,800	3,899,300
Total Assets	13,187,200	15,994,600	15,834,300	17,542,200	19,366,400	20,405,300	11,441,900	11,408,700
Current Liabilities	2,615,600	3,953,600	3,846,900	3,310,200	2,642,400	3,401,300	2,225,200	2,125,600
Long-Term Obligations	4,902,700	6,400,400	6,299,600	6,888,900	8,767,600	8,886,900	2,858,600	2,870,300
Total Liabilities	9,533,700	12,560,800	12,471,000	13,016,200	14,107,900	15,140,900	7,002,400	6,707,200
Stockholders' Equity	3,653,500	3,433,800	3,363,300	4,526,000	5,258,500	5,264,400	4,439,500	4,701,500
Shares Outstanding	436,414	434,129	432,911	428,204	421,915	419,465	407,612	410,494
Statistical Record								
Return on Assets %	N.M.	N.M.	N.M.	N.M.	1.53	4.87	4.11	7.08
Return on Equity %	N.M.	N.M.	N.M.	N.M.	5.78	15.99	10.27	17.02
EBITDA Margin %	13.52	13.38	13.85	N.M.	6.03	9.56	6.41	11.54
Net Margin %	N.M.	N.M.	N.M.	N.M.	1.71	5.00	3.53	6.64
Asset Turnover	0.83	0.78	0.85	0.84	0.89	0.98	1.16	1.07
Current Ratio	1.35	0.99	0.96	1.11	1.60	1.29	1.45	1.83
Debt to Equity	1.34	1.86	1.87	1.52	1.67	1.69	0.64	0.61
Price Range	45.49-33.58	45.49-33.57	45.49-32.01	38.90-28.73	37.23-28.26	36.16-23.81	27.18-22.72	25.58-21.14
P/E Ratio	...	...	...	...	53.19-40.37	19.55-12.87	24.27-20.29	13.61-11.24
Average Yield %	2.48	2.55	2.68	2.91	3.08	3.34	3.73	3.86

Address: One ConAgra Drive, Omaha, NE 68102-5001	**Web Site:** www.conagrafoods.com	**Auditors:** KPMG LLP
Telephone: 402-240-4000	**Officers:** Sean M. Connolly - President, Chief Executive Officer Colleen R. Batcheler - Executive Vice President, General Counsel, Corporate Secretary	**Investor Contact:** 402-240-4154 **Transfer Agents:** Wells Fargo Shareowner Services, St. Paul, MN

CONCHO RESOURCES INC

Exchange	Symbol	Price	52Wk Range	Yield	P/E
NYS	CXO	$121.34 (5/31/2016)	125.67-72.52	N/A	N/A

*7 Year Price Score 97.64 *NYSE Composite Index=100 *12 Month Price Score 107.74

TRADING VOLUME (thousand shares)

2007 2008 2009 2010 2011 2012 2013 2014 2015 2016

Interim Earnings (Per Share)

Qtr.	Mar	Jun	Sep	Dec
2013	0.29	0.81	0.29	1.01
2014	0.87	0.11	2.69	1.15
2015	0.06	(1.02)	1.49	(0.02)
2016	(7.95)	...	...	...

Interim Dividends (Per Share)

No Dividends Paid

Valuation Analysis		Institutional Holding	
Forecast EPS	$-0.34	No of Institutions	
	(05/20/2016)	554	
Market Cap	$16.0 Billion	Shares	
Book Value	$6.2 Billion	140,551,632	
Price/Book	2.59	% Held	
Price/Sales	9.54	107.15	

Business Summary: Production & Extraction (MIC: 9.1.1 SIC: 1311 NAIC: 211111)

Concho Resources is an independent oil and natural gas company engaged in the acquisition, development, exploration and production of oil and natural gas properties. Co.'s three core operating areas include: New Mexico Shelf, where it primarily targets the Yeso, San Andres and Grayburg formations; Delaware Basin, where it primarily targets the oil-prone Bone Spring formation that includes three Bone Spring sandstone members and the Avalon shale and the Wolfcamp shale; and Midland Basin, where it primarily targets the Spraberry and Wolfcamp zones. As of Dec 31 2014, Co. had total proved reserves of 367.8 million barrels of oil and 1,534.1 billion cubic feet of natural gas.

Recent Developments: For the quarter ended Mar 31 2016, net loss amounted to US$1.02 billion versus net income of US$7.5 million in the year-earlier quarter. Revenues were US$283.6 million, down 31.4% from US$413.5 million the year before. Operating loss was US$1.55 billion versus an income of US$69.5 million in the prior-year quarter. Direct operating expenses declined 8.4% to US$115.0 million from US$125.5 million in the comparable period the year before. Indirect operating expenses increased 688.4% to US$1.72 billion from US$218.5 million in the equivalent prior-year period.

Prospects: Our evaluation of Concho Resources Inc. as of June 19, 2016 is the result of our systematic analysis on three basic characteristics: earnings strength, relative valuation, and recent stock price movement. The company has suffered a very negative trend in earnings per share over the past 5 quarters. Because the company lacks sufficient analyst estimate data, we place greater weight on the historical EPS trend as the measure of earnings strength. Based on operating earnings yield, the company is overvalued when compared to all of the companies in our coverage universe. Share price changes over the past year indicates that CXO will perform in line with the market over the near term.

Financial Data

(US$ in Thousands)	3 Mos	12/31/2015	12/31/2014	12/31/2013	12/31/2012	12/31/2011	12/31/2010	12/31/2009
Earnings Per Share	(7.50)	0.54	4.88	2.39	4.15	5.28	2.18	(0.12)
Cash Flow Per Share	6.88	7.48	15.38	13.13	11.96	11.69	7.04	4.23
Tang Book Value Per Share	46.62	53.56	46.49	35.49	32.86	28.42	22.85	15.37
Income Statement								
Total Revenue	283,564	1,803,573	2,660,147	2,319,919	1,819,814	1,739,967	972,576	544,447
EBITDA	(1,250,032)	330,955	2,052,361	1,348,348	1,417,104	1,293,188	615,620	203,901
Depn & Amortn	310,082	18,300	979,740	772,608	575,128	428,377	249,850	206,143
Income Before Taxes	(1,614,252)	97,271	855,960	357,159	659,271	746,451	305,683	(30,534)
Income Taxes	(593,772)	31,371	317,785	118,237	251,041	285,848	122,649	(20,732)
Net Income	(1,020,480)	65,900	538,175	251,003	431,689	548,137	204,370	(9,802)
Average Shares	128,396	120,373	109,132	103,913	103,972	103,653	93,837	84,912
Balance Sheet								
Current Assets	1,388,567	1,314,550	1,188,396	520,875	458,882	411,023	330,633	217,258
Total Assets	11,286,521	12,641,876	11,799,963	9,591,164	8,589,437	6,849,576	5,368,494	3,171,085
Current Liabilities	604,948	596,420	1,427,193	756,868	740,086	701,477	506,989	337,014
Long-Term Obligations	3,332,854	3,332,188	3,517,320	3,630,421	3,101,103	2,080,141	1,668,521	845,836
Total Liabilities	5,127,749	5,699,325	6,519,175	5,833,215	5,123,241	3,868,837	2,984,620	1,835,657
Stockholders' Equity	6,158,772	6,942,551	5,280,788	3,757,949	3,466,196	2,980,739	2,383,874	1,335,428
Shares Outstanding	131,564	129,137	113,004	105,095	104,581	103,700	102,810	85,803
Statistical Record								
Return on Assets %	N.M.	0.54	5.03	2.76	5.58	8.97	4.79	N.M.
Return on Equity %	N.M.	1.08	11.91	6.95	13.36	20.44	10.99	N.M.
EBITDA Margin %	N.M.	18.35	77.15	58.12	77.87	74.32	63.30	37.45
Net Margin %	N.M.	3.65	20.23	10.82	23.72	31.50	21.01	N.M.
Asset Turnover	0.14	0.15	0.25	0.26	0.24	0.28	0.23	0.18
Current Ratio	2.30	2.20	0.83	0.69	0.62	0.59	0.65	0.64
Debt to Equity	0.54	0.48	0.67	0.97	0.89	0.70	0.70	0.63
Price Range	128.31-72.52	128.31-86.67	148.00-83.01	120.72-80.14	113.43-77.80	109.79-67.25	88.43-42.86	46.17-17.38
P/E Ratio	...	237.61-160.50	30.33-17.01	50.51-33.53	27.33-18.75	20.79-12.74	40.56-19.66	...

Address: One Concho Center, 600 West Illinois Avenue, Midland, TX 79701 Telephone: 432-683-7443 Fax: 432-683-7441	Web Site: www.conchoresources.com Officers: Timothy A. Leach - Chairman, President, Chief Executive Officer Jack F. Harper - Executive Vice President, Senior Vice President, Chief of Staff, Chief Financial Officer, Treasurer	Auditors: Grant Thornton LLP Investor Contact: 432-685-2533 Transfer Agents: American Stock Transfer & Trust Company, New York, NY

CONOCOPHILLIPS

Exchange	Symbol	Price	52Wk Range	Yield	P/E	Div Achiever
NYS	COP	$43.79 (5/31/2016)	64.07-31.88	2.28	N/A	15 Years

*7 Year Price Score 73.63   *NYSE Composite Index=100   *12 Month Price Score 91.03

Interim Earnings (Per Share)

Qtr.	Mar	Jun	Sep	Dec
2013	1.73	1.65	2.00	2.00
2014	1.71	1.67	2.17	(0.03)
2015	0.22	(0.15)	(0.87)	(2.78)
2016	(1.18)	...	...	...

Interim Dividends (Per Share)

Amt	Decl	Ex	Rec	Pay
0.74Q	07/16/2015	07/23/2015	07/27/2015	09/01/2015
0.74Q	10/09/2015	10/15/2015	10/19/2015	12/01/2015
0.25Q	02/04/2016	02/11/2016	02/16/2016	03/01/2016
0.25Q	05/10/2016	05/18/2016	05/20/2016	06/01/2016

Indicated Div: $1.00 (Div. Reinv. Plan)

Valuation Analysis		Institutional Holding	
Forecast EPS	$-2.33	No of Institutions	
	(05/20/2016)	1981	
Market Cap	$54.2 Billion	Shares	
Book Value	$39.1 Billion	909,579,712	
Price/Book	1.39	% Held	
Price/Sales	1.94	67.11	

Business Summary: Production & Extraction (MIC: 9.1.1 SIC: 2911 NAIC: 324110)

ConocoPhillips is engaged in exploring for, producing, transporting and marketing crude oil, bitumen, natural gas, liquefied natural gas (LNG) and natural gas liquids. Co. manages its operations through six operating segments, which are defined by geographic region: Alaska, Lower 48, Canada, Europe and North Africa, Asia Pacific and Middle East, and Other International. At Dec 31 2015, Co.'s continuing operations were producing in the U.S., Norway, the U.K., Canada, Australia, Timor-Leste, Indonesia, China, Malaysia, and Qatar. As of Dec 31 2015, Co. had total net proved reserves of 8.18 billion barrels of oil equivalent.

Recent Developments: For the quarter ended Mar 31 2016, net loss amounted to US$1.46 billion versus net income of US$286.0 million in the year-earlier quarter. Revenues were US$5.02 billion, down 37.3% from US$8.00 billion the year before. Direct operating expenses declined 29.0% to US$3.58 billion from US$5.04 billion in the comparable period the year before. Indirect operating expenses increased 10.3% to US$3.66 billion from US$3.32 billion in the equivalent prior-year period.

Prospects: Our evaluation of ConocoPhillips as of June 19, 2016 is the result of our systematic analysis on three basic characteristics: earnings strength, relative valuation, and recent stock price movement. The company has enjoyed a very positive trend in earnings per share over the past 5 quarters. Because the company lacks sufficient analyst estimate data, we place greater weight on the historical EPS trend as the measure of earnings strength. Based on operating earnings yield, the company is overvalued when compared to all of the companies in our coverage universe. Share price changes over the past year indicates that COP will perform poorly over the near term.

Financial Data

(US$ in Thousands)	3 Mos	12/31/2015	12/31/2014	12/31/2013	12/31/2012	12/31/2011	12/31/2010	12/31/2009
Earnings Per Share	(4.98)	(3.58)	5.51	7.38	6.72	8.97	7.62	3.24
Cash Flow Per Share	4.92	6.10	13.53	13.07	11.16	14.29	11.52	8.39
Tang Book Value Per Share	31.56	32.17	42.16	42.49	39.33	47.56	43.69	38.04
Dividends Per Share	2.460	2.940	2.840	2.700	2.640	2.640	2.150	1.910
Dividend Payout %	...	...	51.54	36.59	39.29	29.43	28.22	58.95
Income Statement								
Total Revenue	5,015,000	30,935,000	55,517,000	58,248,000	62,004,000	251,226,000	198,655,000	152,840,000
EBITDA	304,000	2,794,000	18,367,000	22,492,000	22,712,000	31,907,000	29,997,000	20,616,000
Depn & Amortn	2,247,000	9,113,000	8,329,000	7,434,000	6,580,000	7,934,000	9,060,000	9,295,000
Income Before Taxes	(2,224,000)	(7,239,000)	9,390,000	14,446,000	15,423,000	23,001,000	19,750,000	10,032,000
Income Taxes	(768,000)	(2,868,000)	3,583,000	6,409,000	7,942,000	10,499,000	8,333,000	5,096,000
Net Income	(1,469,000)	(4,428,000)	6,869,000	9,156,000	8,428,000	12,436,000	11,358,000	4,858,000
Average Shares	1,244,557	1,241,919	1,245,863	1,239,803	1,253,093	1,387,100	1,491,067	1,497,608
Balance Sheet								
Current Assets	10,934,000	8,789,000	15,068,000	19,023,000	23,989,000	30,218,000	34,660,000	21,167,000
Total Assets	99,834,000	97,484,000	116,539,000	118,057,000	117,144,000	153,230,000	156,314,000	152,588,000
Current Liabilities	8,825,000	9,256,000	11,537,000	15,129,000	17,443,000	28,068,000	27,419,000	23,695,000
Long-Term Obligations	27,376,000	23,453,000	22,383,000	21,073,000	20,770,000	21,610,000	22,656,000	26,925,000
Total Liabilities	60,745,000	57,722,000	64,628,000	65,967,000	69,157,000	88,006,000	87,752,000	90,121,000
Stockholders' Equity	39,089,000	39,762,000	51,911,000	52,090,000	47,987,000	65,224,000	68,562,000	62,467,000
Shares Outstanding	1,238,387	1,235,995	1,231,352	1,225,939	1,220,017	1,285,669	1,467,655	1,524,998
Statistical Record								
Return on Assets %	N.M.	N.M.	5.86	7.79	6.22	8.04	7.35	3.29
Return on Equity %	N.M.	N.M.	13.21	18.30	14.85	18.59	17.34	8.26
EBITDA Margin %	6.06	9.03	33.08	38.61	36.63	12.70	15.10	13.49
Net Margin %	N.M.	N.M.	12.37	15.72	13.59	4.95	5.72	3.18
Asset Turnover	0.27	0.29	0.47	0.50	0.46	1.62	1.29	1.03
Current Ratio	1.24	0.95	1.31	1.26	1.38	1.08	1.26	0.89
Debt to Equity	0.70	0.59	0.43	0.40	0.43	0.33	0.33	0.43
Price Range	69.40-31.88	69.88-42.19	86.76-61.69	74.34-56.81	59.63-50.82	61.91-46.49	51.91-36.11	42.45-26.78
P/E Ratio	...	...	15.75-11.20	10.07-7.70	8.87-7.56	6.90-5.18	6.81-4.74	13.10-8.27
Average Yield %	4.76	5.05	3.83	4.18	4.71	4.84	5.08	5.50

Address: 600 North Dairy Ashford, Houston, TX 77079
Telephone: 281-293-1000
Fax: 281-661-7636

Web Site: www.conocophillips.com
Officers: Ryan M. Lance - Chairman, President, Chief Executive Officer, Region Officer, Division Officer
Don E. Wallette - Chief Financial Officer, Executive Vice President, Executive Vice President (frmr)

Auditors: Ernst & Young LLP
Investor Contact: 212-207-1996
Transfer Agents: Computershare, Canton, MA

CONSOL ENERGY INC

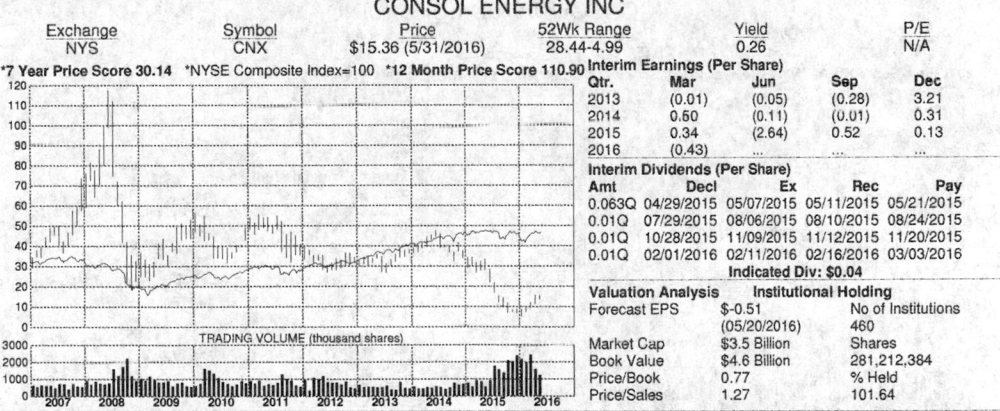

Exchange	Symbol	Price	52Wk Range	Yield	P/E
NYS	CNX	$15.36 (5/31/2016)	28.44-4.99	0.26	N/A

*7 Year Price Score 30.14   *NYSE Composite Index=100   *12 Month Price Score 110.90

Interim Earnings (Per Share)

Qtr.	Mar	Jun	Sep	Dec
2013	(0.01)	(0.05)	(0.28)	3.21
2014	0.50	(0.11)	(0.01)	0.31
2015	0.34	(2.64)	0.52	0.13
2016	(0.43)	...	...	...

Interim Dividends (Per Share)

Amt	Decl	Ex	Rec	Pay
0.063Q	04/29/2015	05/07/2015	05/11/2015	05/21/2015
0.01Q	07/29/2015	08/06/2015	08/10/2015	08/24/2015
0.01Q	10/28/2015	11/09/2015	11/12/2015	11/20/2015
0.01Q	02/01/2016	02/11/2016	02/16/2016	03/03/2016

Indicated Div: $0.04

Valuation Analysis

		Institutional Holding	
Forecast EPS	$-0.51	No of Institutions	
	(05/20/2016)	460	
Market Cap	$3.5 Billion	Shares	
Book Value	$4.6 Billion	281,212,384	
Price/Book	0.77	% Held	
Price/Sales	1.27	101.64	

Business Summary: Mining (MIC: 8.2.4 SIC: 1221 NAIC: 212111)

CONSOL Energy is an energy company. Co. is consists of two principal business divisions: oil and gas exploration and production (E&P) and Coal. The principal activity of the E&P division is to produce pipeline quality natural gas for sale primarily to gas wholesalers. The principal activities of the Coal division are mining, preparation and marketing of thermal coal, sold primarily to power generators, and metallurgical coal, sold to metal and coke producers. The Coal division's reportable segments are Pennsylvania Operations, Virginia Operations, and Other Coal. At Dec 31 2015, Co. had proved reserves of 5.60 trillion cubic feet of natural gas equivalents.

Recent Developments: For the quarter ended Mar 31 2016, loss from continuing operations was US$50.3 million compared with a loss of US$165.3 million in the year-earlier quarter. Net loss amounted to US$96.5 million versus net income of US$79.0 million in the year-earlier quarter. Revenues were US$558.5 million, down 29.5% from US$792.7 million the year before. Direct operating expenses rose 35.2% to US$115.0 million from US$85.0 million in the comparable period the year before. Indirect operating expenses decreased 23.1% to US$520.7 million from US$677.0 million in the equivalent prior-year period.

Prospects: Our evaluation of Consol Energy Inc. as of June 19, 2016 is the result of our systematic analysis on three basic characteristics: earnings strength, relative valuation, and recent stock price movement. The company has enjoyed a very positive trend in earnings per share over the past 5 quarters. Because the company lacks sufficient analyst estimate data, we place greater weight on the historical EPS trend as the measure of earnings strength. Based on operating earnings yield, the company is overvalued when compared to all of the companies in our coverage universe. Share price changes over the past year indicates that CNX will perform very poorly over the near term.

Financial Data
(US$ in Thousands)

	3 Mos	12/31/2015	12/31/2014	12/31/2013	12/31/2012	12/31/2011	12/31/2010	12/31/2009
Earnings Per Share	(2.42)	(1.64)	0.70	2.87	1.70	2.76	1.60	2.95
Cash Flow Per Share	1.77	2.21	4.07	2.88	3.19	6.74	5.26	5.23
Tang Book Value Per Share	20.01	20.53	23.14	21.85	17.33	15.90	13.02	9.86
Dividends Per Share	0.092	0.145	0.250	0.375	0.625	0.425	0.400	0.400
Dividend Payout %	...	...	35.71	13.07	36.76	15.40	25.00	13.56
Income Statement								
Total Revenue	558,514	3,114,401	3,726,804	3,299,685	5,430,307	6,117,242	5,236,021	4,621,875
EBITDA	132,800	349,970	977,879	726,395	1,344,772	1,662,302	1,244,768	1,261,151
Depn & Amortn	160,067	649,601	571,191	461,122	627,438	626,005	571,823	441,387
Income Before Taxes	(77,133)	(498,900)	183,124	46,075	497,274	787,953	467,913	788,345
Income Taxes	(26,847)	(134,425)	14,347	(33,189)	109,201	155,456	109,287	221,203
Net Income	(97,572)	(374,885)	163,090	660,442	388,470	632,497	346,781	539,717
Average Shares	229,259	229,186	231,580	230,077	229,141	229,003	217,037	182,821
Balance Sheet								
Current Assets	1,146,443	804,763	1,166,350	1,445,592	1,539,094	1,897,977	1,115,006	941,036
Total Assets	10,715,870	10,929,902	11,759,530	11,393,667	12,670,909	12,525,700	12,070,610	7,725,401
Current Liabilities	1,584,931	1,680,937	1,147,961	1,119,971	1,387,099	1,388,397	1,664,785	1,428,586
Long-Term Obligations	2,758,961	2,748,205	3,275,878	3,163,559	3,174,586	3,177,423	3,186,138	422,908
Total Liabilities	6,126,540	6,227,875	6,430,072	6,387,378	8,717,117	8,914,815	9,126,133	5,939,853
Stockholders' Equity	4,589,330	4,702,027	5,329,458	5,006,289	3,953,792	3,610,885	2,944,477	1,785,548
Shares Outstanding	229,363	229,054	230,265	229,145	228,094	227,056	226,162	181,086
Statistical Record								
Return on Assets %	N.M.	N.M.	1.41	5.49	3.08	5.14	3.50	7.15
Return on Equity %	N.M.	N.M.	3.16	14.74	10.24	19.30	14.66	33.24
EBITDA Margin %	23.78	11.24	26.24	22.01	24.76	27.17	23.77	27.29
Net Margin %	N.M.	N.M.	4.38	20.02	7.15	10.34	6.62	11.68
Asset Turnover	0.25	0.27	0.32	0.27	0.43	0.50	0.53	0.61
Current Ratio	0.72	0.48	1.02	1.29	1.11	1.37	0.67	0.66
Debt to Equity	0.60	0.58	0.61	0.63	0.80	0.88	1.08	0.24
Price Range	33.34-4.99	34.34-6.50	47.45-32.13	38.42-26.51	39.37-26.80	55.49-31.70	56.34-31.21	52.87-22.58
P/E Ratio	...	...	67.79-45.90	13.39-9.24	23.16-15.76	20.11-11.49	35.21-19.51	17.92-7.65
Average Yield %	0.61	0.70	0.63	1.13	1.93	0.92	0.96	1.08

Address: 1000 Consol Energy Drive, Canonsburg, PA 15317-6506 **Telephone:** 724-485-4000	**Web Site:** www.consolenergy.com **Officers:** William N. Thorndike - Chairman John L. Whitmire Chairman, Vice-Chairman	**Auditors:** PricewaterhouseCoopers LLP **Investor Contact:** 724-485-3157 **Transfer Agents:** ComputerShare, College Station, TX

CONSOLIDATED EDISON INC

Exchange	Symbol	Price	52Wk Range	Yield	P/E	Div Achiever
NYS	ED	$73.26 (5/31/2016)	76.99-57.21	3.66	19.13	41 Years

*7 Year Price Score 101.93 *NYSE Composite Index=100 *12 Month Price Score 109.17

Interim Earnings (Per Share)

Qtr.	Mar	Jun	Sep	Dec
2013	0.65	0.59	1.58	0.80
2014	1.23	0.72	1.48	0.27
2015	1.26	0.74	1.45	0.59
2016	1.05			

Interim Dividends (Per Share)

Amt	Decl	Ex	Rec	Pay
0.65Q	07/16/2015	08/17/2015	08/19/2015	09/15/2015
0.65Q	10/22/2015	11/16/2015	11/18/2015	12/15/2015
0.67Q	01/21/2016	02/12/2016	02/17/2016	03/15/2016
0.67Q	04/21/2016	05/16/2016	05/18/2016	06/15/2016

Indicated Div: $2.68 (Div. Reinv. Plan)

Valuation Analysis

Valuation Analysis		Institutional Holding	
Forecast EPS	$3.99	No of Institutions	
	(05/20/2016)	993	
Market Cap	$21.5 Billion	Shares	
Book Value	$13.2 Billion	178,255,584	
Price/Book	1.63	% Held	
Price/Sales	1.86	51.88	

Business Summary: Electric Utilities (MIC: 3.1.1 SIC: 4931 NAIC: 221121)

Consolidated Edison is a holding company. Co. owns Consolidated Edison Company of New York, Inc., which delivers electricity, natural gas and steam to customers in New York City and Westchester County; Orange and Rockland Utilities, Inc., which delivers electricity and natural gas to customers in southeastern New York, northern New Jersey and northeastern Pennsylvania; competitive energy businesses, which sell to customers electricity purchased in wholesale markets and provide energy-related products and services to customers, and develop, own and operate renewable and energy infrastructure projects; and Consolidated Edison Transmission, LLC, which invests in a transmission company.

Recent Developments: For the quarter ended Mar 31 2016, net income decreased 16.2% to US$310.0 million from US$370.0 million in the year-earlier quarter. Revenues were US$3.16 billion, down 12.7% from US$3.62 billion the year before. Operating income was US$642.0 million versus US$726.0 million in the prior-year quarter, a decrease of 11.6%. Direct operating expenses declined 19.3% to US$1.71 billion from US$2.11 billion in the comparable period the year before. Indirect operating expenses increased 4.0% to US$807.0 million from US$776.0 million in the equivalent prior-year period.

Prospects: Our evaluation of Consolidated Edison Inc. as of June 19, 2016 is the result of our systematic analysis on three basic characteristics: earnings strength, relative valuation, and recent stock price movement. The company has managed to produce a neutral trend in earnings per share over the past 5 quarters. However, while recent estimates for the company have been mixed, ED has posted results that fell short of analysts expectations. Based on operating earnings yield, the company is undervalued when compared to all of the companies in our coverage universe. Share price changes over the past year indicates that ED will perform well over the near term.

Financial Data

(US$ in Thousands)	3 Mos	12/31/2015	12/31/2014	12/31/2013	12/31/2012	12/31/2011	12/31/2010	12/31/2009
Earnings Per Share	3.83	4.05	3.71	3.61	3.86	3.57	3.47	3.14
Cash Flow Per Share	11.04	11.18	9.67	8.71	8.85	10.72	8.37	8.96
Tang Book Value Per Share	43.41	43.08	41.46	40.33	39.05	38.30	37.18	35.72
Dividends Per Share	2.620	2.600	2.520	2.460	2.420	2.400	2.380	2.360
Dividend Payout %	68.41	64.20	67.92	68.14	62.69	67.23	68.59	75.16
Income Statement								
Total Revenue	3,156,000	12,554,000	12,919,000	12,354,000	12,188,000	12,938,000	13,325,000	13,032,000
EBITDA	580,000	3,529,000	3,424,000	3,291,000	3,342,000	3,189,000	3,013,000	2,658,000
Depn & Amortn	(63,000)	1,078,000	1,173,000	1,034,000	997,000	933,000	853,000	728,000
Income Before Taxes	474,000	1,798,000	1,660,000	1,538,000	1,741,000	1,662,000	1,551,000	1,319,000
Income Taxes	164,000	605,000	568,000	476,000	600,000	600,000	548,000	440,000
Net Income	310,000	1,193,000	1,092,000	1,062,000	1,141,000	1,062,000	1,003,000	879,000
Average Shares	294,800	294,400	294,000	294,400	294,500	294,400	285,900	276,300
Balance Sheet								
Current Assets	3,185,000	3,836,000	3,854,000	3,891,000	3,451,000	3,638,000	3,507,000	3,243,000
Total Assets	45,580,000	45,642,000	44,308,000	40,647,000	41,209,000	39,214,000	36,146,000	33,873,000
Current Liabilities	4,436,000	4,720,000	3,781,000	4,730,000	3,945,000	2,987,000	2,366,000	2,952,000
Long-Term Obligations	12,222,000	12,006,000	11,631,000	10,490,000	10,064,000	10,145,000	10,678,000	9,868,000
Total Liabilities	32,387,000	32,590,000	31,732,000	28,402,000	29,340,000	27,565,000	24,872,000	23,411,000
Stockholders' Equity	13,193,000	13,052,000	12,576,000	12,245,000	11,869,000	11,649,000	11,274,000	10,462,000
Shares Outstanding	294,000	293,000	292,876	292,872	292,871	292,888	291,616	281,123
Statistical Record								
Return on Assets %	2.51	2.65	2.57	2.59	2.83	2.82	2.86	2.61
Return on Equity %	8.67	9.31	8.80	8.81	9.68	9.27	9.23	8.63
EBITDA Margin %	18.38	28.11	26.50	26.64	27.42	24.65	22.61	20.40
Net Margin %	9.82	9.50	8.45	8.60	9.36	8.21	7.53	6.74
Asset Turnover	0.26	0.28	0.30	0.30	0.30	0.34	0.38	0.39
Current Ratio	0.72	0.81	1.02	0.82	0.87	1.22	1.48	1.10
Debt to Equity	0.93	0.92	0.92	0.86	0.85	0.87	0.95	0.94
Price Range	76.64-57.21	71.40-57.21	68.50-52.46	63.66-54.33	64.94-54.10	62.59-48.85	51.00-41.66	46.13-32.70
P/E Ratio	20.01-14.94	17.63-14.13	18.46-14.14	17.63-15.05	16.82-14.02	17.53-13.68	14.70-12.01	14.69-10.41
Average Yield %	4.05	4.11	4.39	4.25	4.07	4.46	5.16	5.99

Address: 4 Irving Place, New York, NY 10003	Web Site: www.conedison.com	Auditors: PricewaterhouseCoopers LLP
Telephone: 212-460-4600	Officers: John McAvoy - Chairman, President, Chief Executive Officer Robert N. Hoglund - Chief Financial Officer, Senior Vice President	Investor Contact: 212-460-6611 Transfer Agents: Computershare, Pittsburgh, PA

CONSTELLATION BRANDS INC

Exchange	Symbol	Price	52Wk Range	Yield	P/E
NYS	STZ	$153.15 (5/31/2016)	163.52-115.54	1.04	29.57

*7 Year Price Score 207.24 *NYSE Composite Index=100 ***12 Month Price Score 112.80**

Interim Earnings (Per Share)

Qtr.	May	Aug	Nov	Feb
2011-12	0.35	0.76	0.52	0.51
2012-13	0.38	0.67	0.58	0.42
2013-14	0.27	7.74	1.07	0.76
2014-15	1.03	0.98	1.10	1.06
2015-16	1.18	1.49	1.33	1.19

Interim Dividends (Per Share)

Amt	Decl	Ex	Rec	Pay
0.31Q	06/30/2015	08/07/2015	08/11/2015	08/25/2015
0.31Q	10/06/2015	11/05/2015	11/09/2015	11/24/2015
0.31Q	01/06/2016	02/05/2016	02/09/2016	02/24/2016
0.40Q	04/05/2016	05/06/2016	05/10/2016	05/24/2016

Indicated Div: $1.60

Valuation Analysis / **Institutional Holding**

Forecast EPS	$6.25
	(05/20/2016)
Market Cap	$30.5 Billion
Book Value	$6.6 Billion
Price/Book	4.66
Price/Sales	4.66

No of Institutions	906
Shares	183,602,848
% Held	81.46

Business Summary: Beverages (MIC: 1.2.2 SIC: 2084 NAIC: 312130)

Constellation Brands is an international beverage alcohol company. Co. is a producer and marketer of beer and wine. Co.'s wine portfolio is complemented by select spirits brands and other select beverage alcohol products. Co. is a multi-category supplier (beer, wine and spirits) of beverage alcohol in the U.S. Co. operates in three segments: Beer, Wine and Spirits, and Corporate Operations and Other. Co. sells a number of brands in the import and craft beer categories. Some of Co.'s wine and spirits brands sold in the U.S., which comprise its U.S. Focus Brands, including: Black Box, Clos du Bois, Estancia, Franciscan Estate, Inniskillin, and SVEDKA Vodka.

Recent Developments: For the year ended Feb 29 2016, net income increased 26.8% to US$1.06 billion from US$836.2 million in the prior year. Revenues were US$6.55 billion, up 8.6% from US$6.03 billion the year before. Operating income was US$1.77 billion versus US$1.50 billion in the prior year, an increase of 17.7%. Direct operating expenses rose 4.5% to US$3.61 billion from US$3.45 billion in the comparable period the year before. Indirect operating expenses increased 9.2% to US$1.18 billion from US$1.08 billion in the equivalent prior-year period.

Prospects: Our evaluation of Constellation Brands Inc. as of June 19, 2016 is the result of our systematic analysis on three basic characteristics: earnings strength, relative valuation, and recent stock price movement. The company has generated a negative trend in earnings per share over the past 5 quarters. However, while recent estimates for the company have been lowered by analysts, STZ has posted better than expected results. Based on operating earnings yield, the company is about fairly valued when compared to all of the companies in our coverage universe. Share price changes over the past year indicates that STZ will perform very well over the near term.

Financial Data

(US$ in Thousands)	02/29/2016	02/28/2015	02/28/2014	02/28/2013	02/29/2012	02/28/2011	02/28/2010	02/28/2009
Earnings Per Share	5.18	4.17	9.83	2.04	2.13	2.62	0.45	(1.40)
Cash Flow Per Share	7.17	5.61	4.39	3.05	3.83	2.94	1.83	2.33
Dividends Per Share	1.240	...	...	...	...	...	...	...
Dividend Payout %	23.94	...	...	...	...	...	...	...
Income Statement								
Total Revenue	6,548,400	6,028,000	4,867,700	2,796,100	2,654,300	3,332,000	3,364,800	3,654,600
EBITDA	1,985,000	1,697,800	2,593,000	625,800	584,900	621,700	454,600	166,600
Depn & Amortn	221,000	202,000	155,300	115,400	98,400	119,200	143,800	143,600
Income Before Taxes	1,450,100	1,158,100	2,114,500	283,300	305,500	307,200	45,700	(293,400)
Income Taxes	440,600	343,400	259,200	128,600	89,000	(8,500)	160,000	194,600
Net Income	1,054,900	839,300	1,943,100	387,800	445,000	559,500	99,300	(301,400)
Average Shares	203,821	201,224	197,570	190,307	208,655	213,765	221,210	193,906
Balance Sheet								
Current Assets	2,977,600	2,910,800	2,747,200	2,471,200	2,034,300	2,083,000	2,589,100	2,534,500
Total Assets	16,965,000	15,144,500	14,302,100	7,638,100	7,109,900	7,167,600	8,094,300	8,036,500
Current Liabilities	2,272,300	1,130,700	2,025,700	677,900	1,199,600	662,900	1,372,600	1,326,400
Long-Term Obligations	6,816,200	7,137,500	6,373,300	3,277,800	2,421,400	3,136,700	3,277,100	3,971,100
Total Liabilities	10,405,400	9,373,800	9,320,800	4,777,800	4,433,900	4,615,700	5,518,000	6,128,200
Stockholders' Equity	6,559,600	5,770,700	4,981,300	2,860,300	2,676,000	2,551,900	2,576,300	1,908,300
Shares Outstanding	199,458	194,541	191,470	184,776	214,601	211,162	222,241	219,144
Statistical Record								
Return on Assets %	6.55	5.70	17.71	5.26	6.22	7.33	1.23	N.M.
Return on Equity %	17.06	15.61	49.56	14.01	16.98	21.82	4.43	N.M.
EBITDA Margin %	30.31	28.17	53.27	22.38	22.04	18.66	13.51	4.56
Net Margin %	16.11	13.92	39.92	13.87	16.77	16.79	2.95	N.M.
Asset Turnover	0.41	0.41	0.44	0.38	0.37	0.44	0.42	0.40
Current Ratio	1.31	2.57	1.36	3.65	1.70	3.14	1.89	1.91
Debt to Equity	1.04	1.24	1.28	1.15	0.90	1.23	1.27	2.08
Price Range	154.36-110.91	115.78-77.97	82.07-43.25	44.71-18.69	22.97-16.63	22.40-15.26	17.42-10.95	22.98-10.80
P/E Ratio	29.80-21.41	27.76-18.70	8.35-4.40	21.92-9.16	10.78-7.81	8.55-5.82	38.71-24.33	...
Average Yield %	0.97	...	...	...	...	...	...	...

Address: 207 High Point Drive, Building 100, Victor, NY 14564 **Telephone:** 585-678-7100	**Web Site:** www.cbrands.com **Officers:** Richard Sands - Chairman Robert Sands - President, Chief Executive Officer	**Auditors:** KPMG LLP **Investor Contact:** 585-678-7483 **Transfer Agents:** Computershare Shareowner Services, College Station, TX

CONTINENTAL RESOURCES INC.

Exchange	Symbol	Price	52Wk Range	Yield	P/E
NYS	CLR	$42.06 (5/31/2016)	47.60-16.04	N/A	N/A

*7 Year Price Score 71.65 *NYSE Composite Index=100 *12 Month Price Score 114.05

TRADING VOLUME (thousand shares)

Interim Earnings (Per Share)

Qtr.	Mar	Jun	Sep	Dec
2013	0.38	0.88	0.46	0.35
2014	0.61	0.28	1.44	0.31
2015	(0.36)	0.00	(0.22)	(0.38)
2016	(0.54)	...	...	...

Interim Dividends (Per Share)

No Dividends Paid

Valuation Analysis / Institutional Holding

Valuation Analysis		Institutional Holding	
Forecast EPS	$-0.95	No of Institutions	
	(05/20/2016)	470	
Market Cap	$15.8 Billion	Shares	
Book Value	$4.5 Billion	93,557,440	
Price/Book	3.52	% Held	
Price/Sales	6.28	54.55	

Business Summary: Production & Extraction (MIC: 9.1.1 SIC: 1311 NAIC: 211111)

Continental Resources is a crude oil and natural gas exploration and production company with properties in the North, South and East regions of the U.S. The North region consists of properties north of Kansas and west of the Mississippi River. The South region includes Kansas and all properties south of Kansas and west of the Mississippi River including various plays in the South Central Oklahoma Oil Province, Northwest Cana, and Arkoma areas of Oklahoma. The East region is comprised of undeveloped leasehold acreage east of the Mississippi River. At Dec 31 2014, Co.'s estimated proved reserves were 1,351.1 million barrels of crude oil equivalent.

Recent Developments: For the quarter ended Mar 31 2016, net loss amounted to US$198.3 million versus a net loss of US$132.0 million in the year-earlier quarter. Revenues were US$453.2 million, down 27.6% from US$625.6 million the year before. Operating loss was US$239.1 million versus a loss of US$111.3 million in the prior-year quarter. Indirect operating expenses decreased 6.1% to US$692.3 million from US$736.9 million in the equivalent prior-year period.

Prospects: Our evaluation of Continental Resources Inc. as of June 19, 2016 is the result of our systematic analysis on three basic characteristics: earnings strength, relative valuation, and recent stock price movement. The company has enjoyed a very positive trend in earnings per share over the past 5 quarters. Because the company lacks sufficient analyst estimate data, we place greater weight on the historical EPS trend as the measure of earnings strength. Based on operating earnings yield, the company is overvalued when compared to all of the companies in our coverage universe. Share price changes over the past year indicates that CLR will perform very poorly over the near term.

Financial Data

(US$ in Thousands)	3 Mos	12/31/2015	12/31/2014	12/31/2013	12/31/2012	12/31/2011	12/31/2010	12/31/2009
Earnings Per Share	(1.14)	(0.96)	2.64	2.06	2.04	1.21	0.50	0.21
Cash Flow Per Share	4.36	5.03	9.10	6.96	4.49	3.01	1.93	1.11
Tang Book Value Per Share	11.95	12.52	13.35	10.65	8.52	6.38	3.54	3.03
Income Statement								
Total Revenue	453,174	2,680,167	4,801,618	3,455,150	2,572,520	1,649,789	839,065	626,211
EBITDA	226,732	1,524,448	3,214,277	2,413,761	1,990,602	1,156,011	554,362	342,125
Depn & Amortn	465,451	1,746,454	1,368,311	965,437	694,698	391,844	242,748	208,885
Income Before Taxes	(319,672)	(535,085)	1,562,038	1,213,049	1,155,196	687,445	258,467	110,008
Income Taxes	(121,346)	(181,417)	584,697	448,830	415,811	258,373	90,212	38,670
Net Income	(198,326)	(353,668)	977,341	764,219	739,385	429,072	168,255	71,338
Average Shares	370,062	369,540	370,758	369,698	363,692	356,460	339,558	339,058
Balance Sheet								
Current Assets	760,181	822,339	1,389,601	1,147,266	946,783	936,373	582,326	236,028
Total Assets	14,633,389	14,919,808	15,145,070	11,941,182	9,140,009	5,646,086	3,591,785	2,314,927
Current Liabilities	865,358	923,028	1,952,013	1,473,156	1,125,865	1,111,801	702,222	219,710
Long-Term Obligations	7,203,440	7,115,644	5,995,837	4,713,821	3,537,771	1,254,301	925,991	523,524
Total Liabilities	10,158,269	10,250,908	10,177,226	7,988,064	5,976,310	3,337,960	2,383,630	1,284,648
Stockholders' Equity	4,475,120	4,668,900	4,967,844	3,953,118	3,163,699	2,308,126	1,208,155	1,030,279
Shares Outstanding	374,583	372,959	372,005	371,317	371,209	361,743	340,817	339,936
Statistical Record								
Return on Assets %	N.M.	N.M.	7.22	7.25	9.97	9.29	5.70	3.15
Return on Equity %	N.M.	N.M.	21.91	21.48	26.95	24.40	15.03	7.21
EBITDA Margin %	50.03	56.88	66.94	69.86	77.38	70.07	66.07	54.63
Net Margin %	N.M.	N.M.	20.35	22.12	28.74	26.01	20.05	11.39
Asset Turnover	0.17	0.18	0.35	0.33	0.35	0.36	0.28	0.28
Current Ratio	0.88	0.89	0.71	0.78	0.84	0.84	0.83	1.07
Debt to Equity	1.61	1.52	1.21	1.19	1.12	0.54	0.77	0.51
Price Range	52.63-16.04	52.63-20.00	80.64-30.95	60.50-36.53	47.47-31.29	36.06-22.72	29.56-18.68	22.73-7.14
P/E Ratio	...	...	30.55-11.72	29.37-17.74	23.27-15.34	29.80-18.77	59.11-37.35	108.26-34.00

Address: 20 N. Broadway, Oklahoma City, OK 73102 Telephone: 405-234-9000	Web Site: www.clr.com Officers: Harold G. Hamm - Chairman, Chief Executive Officer Jeffrey B. Hume - Vice-Chairman, President, Chief Operating Officer	Auditors: Grant Thornton LLP Investor Contact: 405-234-9127 Transfer Agents: American Stock Transfer & Trust Company, New York

CONVERGYS CORP

Exchange	Symbol	Price	52Wk Range	Yield	P/E
NYS	CVG	$28.19 (5/31/2016)	28.19-21.17	1.28	16.88

*7 Year Price Score 127.93 *NYSE Composite Index=100 *12 Month Price Score 106.51

Interim Earnings (Per Share)

Qtr.	Mar	Jun	Sep	Dec
2013	0.23	0.22	0.31	(0.20)
2014	0.13	0.23	0.31	0.45
2015	0.37	0.28	0.56	0.40
2016	0.43	...	...	...

Interim Dividends (Per Share)

Amt	Decl	Ex	Rec	Pay
0.08Q	08/04/2015	09/16/2015	09/18/2015	10/02/2015
0.08Q	11/04/2015	12/22/2015	12/24/2015	01/08/2016
0.08Q	02/23/2016	03/22/2016	03/24/2016	04/08/2016
0.09Q	05/09/2016	06/22/2016	06/24/2016	07/08/2016

Indicated Div: $0.36

Valuation Analysis

		Institutional Holding	
Forecast EPS	$1.90	No of Institutions	
	(05/20/2016)	362	
Market Cap	$2.7 Billion	Shares	
Book Value	$1.3 Billion	106,198,080	
Price/Book	2.05	% Held	
Price/Sales	0.93	96.89	

Business Summary: Miscellaneous Consumer Services (MIC: 2.2.3 SIC: 8742 NAIC: 541510)

Convergys is engaged in the design, development and deployment of customer management solutions. Co.'s contact center technology solutions include: Multichannel Interaction Solutions (Intelligent Self-Service, Voice, Chat, Email, and Knowledge Management), Cross-Channel Integration Framework, Real-Time Decisioning Engine, Intelligent Notifications, Campaign Management, Personalized Care, Personalized Selling, Agent Productivity, and Retention. Co. operates a distributed data processing environment that can integrate call center data servers and databases with two primary data centers in Orlando, FL and Cincinnati, OH.

Recent Developments: For the quarter ended Mar 31 2016, income from continuing operations increased 13.2% to US$44.5 million from US$39.3 million in the year-earlier quarter. Net income increased 12.9% to US$44.5 million from US$39.4 million in the year-earlier quarter. Revenues were US$722.2 million, down 2.5% from US$740.5 million the year before. Operating income was US$59.0 million versus US$49.2 million in the prior-year quarter, an increase of 19.9%. Direct operating expenses declined 4.5% to US$451.2 million from US$472.4 million in the comparable period the year before. Indirect operating expenses decreased 3.2% to US$212.0 million from US$218.9 million in the equivalent prior-year period.

Prospects: Our evaluation of Convergys Corp. as of June 19, 2016 is the result of our systematic analysis on three basic characteristics: earnings strength, relative valuation, and recent stock price movement. The company has managed to produce a neutral trend in earnings per share over the past 5 quarters and while recent estimates for the company have remained steady, CVG has posted better than expected results. Based on operating earnings yield, the company is undervalued when compared to all of the companies in our coverage universe. Share price changes over the past year indicates that CVG will perform very well over the near term.

Financial Data

(US$ in Thousands)	3 Mos	12/31/2015	12/31/2014	12/31/2013	12/31/2012	12/31/2011	12/31/2010	12/31/2009
Earnings Per Share	1.67	1.61	1.13	0.56	0.86	2.72	(0.43)	(0.63)
Cash Flow Per Share	2.70	2.54	2.59	2.03	1.00	1.64	1.58	2.16
Tang Book Value Per Share	1.82	1.32	0.21	6.74	7.32	4.88	2.65	0.87
Dividends Per Share	0.320	0.310	0.270	0.240	0.150	...	...	...
Dividend Payout %	19.16	19.25	23.89	42.86	17.44	...	...	...
Income Statement								
Total Revenue	722,200	2,950,600	2,855,500	2,046,100	2,005,000	2,262,000	2,203,400	2,827,200
EBITDA	90,900	336,700	291,500	228,000	125,300	265,000	11,600	(10,800)
Depn & Amortn	31,800	141,500	142,900	85,500	82,400	86,900	97,300	118,900
Income Before Taxes	54,600	177,000	129,300	131,000	29,300	162,000	(105,200)	(158,600)
Income Taxes	10,100	8,600	12,800	72,500	1,100	118,900	16,700	(40,300)
Net Income	44,500	169,000	120,000	60,900	100,600	334,800	(53,200)	(77,300)
Average Shares	103,800	104,700	106,200	109,200	117,100	122,900	123,100	122,800
Balance Sheet								
Current Assets	852,600	823,400	890,900	1,060,400	1,100,600	951,100	705,500	961,100
Total Assets	2,378,700	2,358,100	2,516,500	1,956,700	2,037,900	2,325,900	2,125,300	2,613,600
Current Liabilities	326,900	338,400	368,500	292,600	286,500	382,200	471,200	889,100
Long-Term Obligations	316,000	337,400	368,400	60,200	59,900	121,000	119,300	64,400
Total Liabilities	1,053,600	1,081,900	1,289,300	667,100	666,000	914,400	941,200	1,407,200
Stockholders' Equity	1,325,100	1,276,200	1,227,200	1,289,600	1,371,900	1,411,500	1,184,100	1,206,400
Shares Outstanding	96,482	96,800	99,400	100,800	105,900	115,400	122,100	123,100
Statistical Record								
Return on Assets %	7.11	6.93	5.37	3.05	4.60	15.04	N.M.	N.M.
Return on Equity %	13.68	13.50	9.54	4.58	7.21	25.80	N.M.	N.M.
EBITDA Margin %	12.59	11.41	10.21	11.14	6.25	11.72	0.53	N.M.
Net Margin %	6.16	5.73	4.20	2.98	5.02	14.80	N.M.	N.M.
Asset Turnover	1.20	1.21	1.28	1.02	0.92	1.02	0.93	1.04
Current Ratio	2.61	2.43	2.42	3.62	3.84	2.49	1.50	1.08
Debt to Equity	0.24	0.26	0.30	0.05	0.04	0.09	0.10	0.05
Price Range	27.77-21.17	26.47-19.16	22.60-17.45	21.22-15.88	16.83-12.19	14.72-8.61	13.72-9.52	11.93-5.56
P/E Ratio	16.63-12.68	16.44-11.90	20.00-15.44	37.89-28.36	19.57-14.17	5.41-3.17	...	...
Average Yield %	1.30	1.31	1.32	1.32	1.03	...	...	...

Address: 201 East Fourth Street, Cincinnati, OH 45202 **Telephone:** 513-723-7000	**Web Site:** www.convergys.com **Officers:** Andrea J. Ayers - President, Chief Executive Officer, Division Officer Julia A. Houston - Senior Vice President, General Counsel, Corporate Secretary	**Auditors:** Ernst & Young LLP **Investor Contact:** 513-723-7000 **Transfer Agents:** ComputerShare Investment Services, LLC, Canto

COOPER COMPANIES, INC. (THE)

	Exchange NYS	Symbol COO	Price $162.81 (5/31/2016)	52Wk Range 184.84-121.01	Yield 0.04	P/E 38.49

*7 Year Price Score 130.49 ***NYSE Composite Index=100** ***12 Month Price Score 101.78**

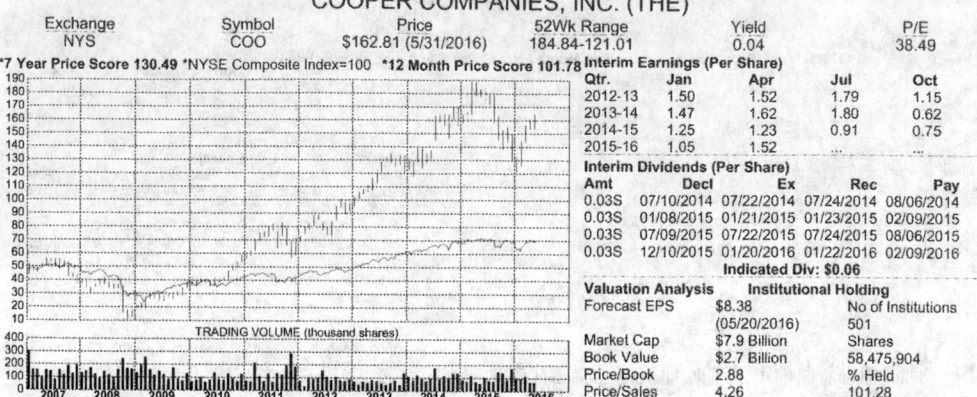

Interim Earnings (Per Share)

Qtr.	Jan	Apr	Jul	Oct
2012-13	1.50	1.52	1.79	1.15
2013-14	1.47	1.62	1.80	0.62
2014-15	1.25	1.23	0.91	0.75
2015-16	1.05	1.52	...	...

Interim Dividends (Per Share)

Amt	Decl	Ex	Rec	Pay
0.03S	07/10/2014	07/22/2014	07/24/2014	08/06/2014
0.03S	01/08/2015	01/21/2015	01/23/2015	02/09/2015
0.03S	07/09/2015	07/22/2015	07/24/2015	08/06/2015
0.03S	12/10/2015	01/20/2016	01/22/2016	02/09/2016

Indicated Div: $0.06

Valuation Analysis

		Institutional Holding	
Forecast EPS	$8.38	No of Institutions	
	(05/20/2016)	501	
Market Cap	$7.9 Billion	Shares	
Book Value	$2.7 Billion	58,475,904	
Price/Book	2.88	% Held	
Price/Sales	4.26	101.28	

Business Summary: Medical Instruments & Equipment (MIC: 4.3.1 SIC: 3851 NAIC: 339115)

Cooper Companies is a medical device company. Co. operates through two business units, CooperVision, Inc. (CooperVision) and CooperSurgical, Inc. (CooperSurgical). CooperVision develops, manufactures and markets a range of soft contact lenses including single-use spherical, toric and multifocal lenses under Co.'s clariti 1day brand and a single-use silicone hydrogel spherical lens under MyDay®. CooperSurgical develops, manufactures and markets medical devices and procedure solutions to improve healthcare delivery to women with products in three categories: hospitals, obstetricians and gynecologists medical offices and fertility clinics.

Recent Developments: For the quarter ended Apr 30 2016, net income increased 21.8% to US$74.5 million from US$61.1 million in the year-earlier quarter. Revenues were US$483.8 million, up 11.3% from US$434.7 million the year before. Operating income was US$89.8 million versus US$71.0 million in the prior-year quarter, an increase of 26.5%. Direct operating expenses rose 11.0% to US$185.3 million from US$167.0 million in the comparable period the year before. Indirect operating expenses increased 6.1% to US$208.7 million from US$196.7 million in the equivalent prior-year period.

Prospects: Our evaluation of Cooper Companies Inc. as of June 19, 2016 is the result of our systematic analysis on three basic characteristics: earnings strength, relative valuation, and recent stock price movement. The company has produced a positive trend in earnings per share over the past 5 quarters and while recent estimates for the company have been raised by analysts, COO has posted better than expected results. Based on operating earnings yield, the company is about fairly valued when compared to all of the companies in our coverage universe. Share price changes over the past year indicates that COO will perform poorly over the near term.

Financial Data

(US$ in Thousands)	6 Mos	3 Mos	10/31/2015	10/31/2014	10/31/2013	10/31/2012	10/31/2011	10/31/2010
Earnings Per Share	4.23	3.94	4.14	5.51	5.96	5.05	3.63	2.43
Cash Flow Per Share	8.01	8.29	8.07	9.46	8.56	6.56	7.17	5.88
Tang Book Value Per Share	1.40	0.74	1.23	N.M.	17.05	12.55	11.13	6.34
Dividends Per Share	0.060	0.060	0.060	0.060	0.060	0.060	0.060	0.060
Dividend Payout %	1.42	1.52	1.45	1.09	1.01	1.19	1.65	2.47
Income Statement								
Total Revenue	933,433	449,641	1,797,060	1,717,776	1,587,725	1,445,136	1,330,835	1,158,517
EBITDA	176,769	72,207	380,147	442,700	446,788	398,437	308,255	255,095
Depn & Amortn	30,515	16,203	146,559	138,201	125,349	111,214	98,149	94,001
Income Before Taxes	133,368	50,730	215,485	296,534	312,271	275,452	192,764	124,426
Income Taxes	7,172	(1,011)	10,341	24,705	15,365	26,808	17,334	11,623
Net Income	125,481	51,356	203,523	269,856	296,151	248,339	175,430	112,803
Average Shares	48,853	48,840	49,179	48,960	49,685	49,152	48,309	46,505
Balance Sheet								
Current Assets	915,115	844,504	841,818	791,617	747,241	657,860	540,347	491,340
Total Assets	4,601,253	4,401,802	4,460,610	4,458,340	3,137,261	2,941,384	2,624,518	2,525,018
Current Liabilities	322,217	347,969	569,172	442,182	321,253	262,552	267,206	199,520
Long-Term Obligations	1,411,182	1,330,627	1,105,764	1,280,833	301,670	348,422	327,453	591,977
Total Liabilities	1,863,177	1,801,845	1,793,101	1,888,462	732,726	748,633	687,030	858,242
Stockholders' Equity	2,738,076	2,599,957	2,667,509	2,569,878	2,404,535	2,192,751	1,937,488	1,666,776
Shares Outstanding	48,448	48,391	48,268	48,143	47,995	48,440	47,846	45,827
Statistical Record								
Return on Assets %	4.61	4.43	4.56	7.11	9.74	8.90	6.81	4.44
Return on Equity %	7.75	7.59	7.77	10.85	12.88	11.99	9.73	7.03
EBITDA Margin %	18.94	16.06	21.15	25.77	28.14	27.57	23.16	22.02
Net Margin %	13.44	11.42	11.33	15.71	18.65	17.18	13.18	9.74
Asset Turnover	0.41	0.41	0.40	0.45	0.52	0.52	0.52	0.46
Current Ratio	2.84	2.43	1.48	1.79	2.33	2.51	2.02	2.46
Debt to Equity	0.52	0.51	0.41	0.50	0.13	0.16	0.17	0.36
Price Range	184.84-121.01	189.09-121.01	189.09-137.62	164.29-117.30	134.97-89.40	100.67-56.64	83.00-48.98	50.82-28.45
P/E Ratio	43.70-28.61	47.99-30.71	45.67-33.24	29.82-21.29	22.65-15.00	19.93-11.22	22.87-13.49	20.91-11.71
Average Yield %	0.04	0.04	0.04	0.04	0.05	0.08	0.09	0.15

Address: 6140 Stoneridge Mall Road, Suite 590, Pleasanton, CA 94588 Telephone: 925-460-3600 Fax: 925-460-3648	Web Site: www.coopercos.com Officers: A. Thomas Bender - Chairman Allan E. Rubenstein - Vice-Chairman	Auditors: KPMG LLP Investor Contact: 925-460-3663 Transfer Agents: American Stock Transfer & Trust Company, New York, NY

CORELOGIC INC.

Exchange	Symbol	Price	52Wk Range	Yield	P/E
NYS	CLGX	$37.27 (5/31/2016)	42.18-32.19	N/A	26.81

*7 Year Price Score 126.31 *NYSE Composite Index=100 *12 Month Price Score 95.86

TRADING VOLUME (thousand shares)

Interim Earnings (Per Share)

Qtr.	Mar	Jun	Sep	Dec
2013	0.34	0.45	0.46	(0.13)
2014	(0.03)	0.17	0.50	0.15
2015	0.32	0.36	0.31	0.41
2016	0.31	...	...	...

Interim Dividends (Per Share)

No Dividends Paid

Valuation Analysis / Institutional Holding

Valuation Analysis		Institutional Holding	
Forecast EPS	$2.15	No of Institutions	
	(05/15/2016)		355
Market Cap	$3.3 Billion	Shares	
Book Value	$1.1 Billion		87,230,760
Price/Book	3.02	% Held	
Price/Sales	2.05	N/A	

Business Summary: Business Services (MIC: 7.5.2 SIC: 7374 NAIC: 519190)

CoreLogic is a property information, analytics and data-enabled services provider operating in North America, Western Europe and Asia Pacific. Co. has two segments: Property Intelligence, which owns or licenses real property, mortgage and consumer information, including loan information, property sales and characteristic information, and property risk and replacement cost; and Risk Management and Work Flow segment, which owns or licenses real property information, mortgage information and consumer information, including loan information, property sales and characteristic information, natural hazard data, parcel maps, employment verification, criminal records and eviction records.

Recent Developments: For the quarter ended Mar 31 2016, income from continuing operations decreased 6.6% to US$27.5 million from US$29.5 million in the year-earlier quarter. Net income decreased 6.5% to US$27.5 million from US$29.4 million in the year-earlier quarter. Revenues were US$453.5 million, up 24.3% from US$364.8 million the year before. Operating income was US$57.3 million versus US$49.3 million in the prior-year quarter, an increase of 16.3%. Direct operating expenses rose 32.2% to US$245.4 million from US$185.5 million in the comparable period the year before. Indirect operating expenses increased 16.1% to US$150.9 million from US$130.0 million in the equivalent prior-year period.

Prospects: Our evaluation of CoreLogic Inc. as of June 19, 2016 is the result of our systematic analysis on three basic characteristics: earnings strength, relative valuation, and recent stock price movement. The company has produced a positive trend in earnings per share over the past 5 quarters and while recent estimates for the company have remained steady, CLGX has posted better than expected results. Based on operating earnings yield, the company is about fairly valued when compared to all of the companies in our coverage universe. Share price changes over the past year indicates that CLGX will perform in line with the market over the near term.

Financial Data

(US$ in Thousands)	3 Mos	12/31/2015	12/31/2014	12/31/2013	12/31/2012	12/31/2011	12/31/2010	12/31/2009
Earnings Per Share	1.39	1.41	0.79	1.11	1.09	(0.68)	(0.60)	2.09
Cash Flow Per Share	4.25	3.69	3.54	3.72	3.52	1.47	1.85	5.16
Tang Book Value Per Share	N.M.	N.M.	N.M.	N.M.	N.M.	N.M.	N.M.	2.70
Dividends Per Share	...	...	...	...	...	...	...	0.880
Dividend Payout %	...	...	...	...	...	...	...	42.11
Income Statement								
Total Revenue	453,543	1,528,110	1,405,040	1,330,630	1,567,633	1,338,547	1,623,272	5,972,777
EBITDA	77,745	308,216	241,940	246,708	297,044	212,390	174,763	700,481
Depn & Amortn	20,685	73,700	68,300	61,800	77,300	63,700	59,300	219,922
Income Before Taxes	43,407	173,226	106,658	137,259	167,276	90,400	85,050	423,797
Income Taxes	15,779	57,394	29,770	34,473	80,396	67,175	35,313	154,621
Net Income	27,480	127,844	73,200	107,728	112,293	(74,609)	(67,330)	199,651
Average Shares	89,919	90,564	92,429	97,109	104,050	109,712	112,363	95,478
Balance Sheet								
Current Assets	476,593	542,266	500,625	641,614	589,924	655,979	855,777	1,696,529
Total Assets	3,606,645	3,701,050	3,516,362	3,003,355	3,029,827	3,110,071	3,219,832	8,723,097
Current Liabilities	585,790	614,476	550,590	538,027	517,091	527,252	729,634	2,238,605
Long-Term Obligations	1,278,941	1,315,511	1,319,211	811,776	792,324	846,027	487,437	791,083
Total Liabilities	2,511,731	2,651,560	2,502,195	1,958,982	1,860,526	1,867,550	1,675,492	5,568,802
Stockholders' Equity	1,094,914	1,049,490	1,014,167	1,044,373	1,169,301	1,242,521	1,544,340	3,154,295
Shares Outstanding	88,843	88,228	89,343	91,254	97,698	106,544	115,499	103,283
Statistical Record								
Return on Assets %	3.56	3.54	2.25	3.57	3.65	N.M.	N.M.	2.29
Return on Equity %	11.88	12.39	7.11	9.73	9.29	N.M.	N.M.	6.83
EBITDA Margin %	17.14	20.17	17.22	18.54	18.95	15.87	10.77	11.73
Net Margin %	6.06	8.37	5.21	8.10	7.16	N.M.	N.M.	3.34
Asset Turnover	0.46	0.42	0.43	0.44	0.51	0.42	0.27	0.68
Current Ratio	0.81	0.88	0.91	1.19	1.14	1.24	1.17	0.76
Debt to Equity	1.17	1.25	1.30	0.78	0.68	0.68	0.32	0.25
Price Range	42.18-32.19	42.18-30.75	35.86-26.00	35.93-21.88	28.00-12.55	20.91-7.80	20.34-16.02	18.35-10.61
P/E Ratio	30.35-23.16	29.91-21.81	45.39-32.91	32.37-19.71	25.69-11.51	...	...	8.78-5.08
Average Yield %	...	...	...	...	...	...	...	5.75

Address: 40 Pacifica, Irvine, CA 92618-7471
Telephone: 949-214-1000

Web Site: www.corelogic.com
Officers: Anand K. Nallathambi - President, Chief Executive Officer Michael Anthony Rasic - Senior Vice President, Chief Financial Officer

Auditors: PwC
Investor Contact: 703-610-5410
Transfer Agents: Wells Fargo Shareowner Services, South Saint Paul, MN

CORNING INC

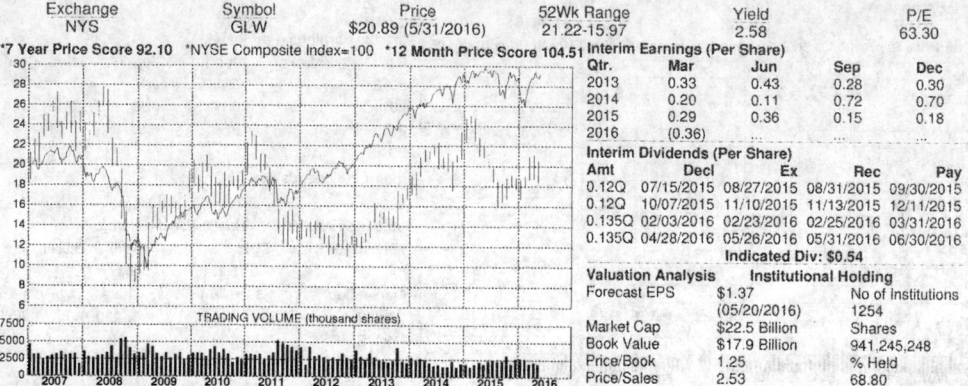

Exchange	Symbol	Price	52Wk Range	Yield	P/E
NYS	GLW	$20.89 (5/31/2016)	21.22-15.97	2.58	63.30

*7 Year Price Score 92.10 *NYSE Composite Index=100 *12 Month Price Score 104.51

Interim Earnings (Per Share)

Qtr.	Mar	Jun	Sep	Dec
2013	0.33	0.43	0.28	0.30
2014	0.20	0.11	0.72	0.70
2015	0.29	0.36	0.15	0.18
2016	(0.36)			

Interim Dividends (Per Share)

Amt	Decl	Ex	Rec	Pay
0.12Q	07/15/2015	08/27/2015	08/31/2015	09/30/2015
0.12Q	10/07/2015	11/10/2015	11/13/2015	12/11/2015
0.135Q	02/03/2016	02/23/2016	02/25/2016	03/31/2016
0.135Q	04/28/2016	05/26/2016	05/31/2016	06/30/2016

Indicated Div: $0.54

Valuation Analysis

		Institutional Holding	
Forecast EPS	$1.37	No of Institutions	1254
	(05/20/2016)		
Market Cap	$22.5 Billion	Shares	941,245,248
Book Value	$17.9 Billion	% Held	
Price/Book	1.25		68.80
Price/Sales	2.53		

Business Summary: Electrical Equipment (MIC: 7.3.1 SIC: 3211 NAIC: 327211)

Corning is a provider of high-performance glass for notebook computers, flat panel desktop monitors, LCD televisions, and other information display applications; carrier network and enterprise network products for the telecommunications industry; ceramic substrates for gasoline and diesel engines in automotive and heavy duty vehicle markets; laboratory products for the scientific community and specialized polymer products for biotechnology applications; optical materials for the semiconductor industry and the scientific community; and other technologies. Co.'s segments include: Display Technologies, Optical Communications, Environmental Technologies, Specialty Materials and Life Sciences.

Recent Developments: For the quarter ended Mar 31 2016, net loss amounted to US$368.0 million versus net income of US$407.0 million in the year-earlier quarter. Revenues were US$2.05 billion, down 9.6% from US$2.27 billion the year before. Operating income was US$177.0 million versus US$412.0 million in the prior-year quarter, a decrease of 57.0%. Direct operating expenses declined 4.0% to US$1.28 billion from US$1.34 billion in the comparable period the year before. Indirect operating expenses increased 13.5% to US$587.0 million from US$517.0 million in the equivalent prior-year period.

Prospects: Our evaluation of Corning Inc. as of June 19, 2016 is the result of our systematic analysis on three basic characteristics: earnings strength, relative valuation, and recent stock price movement. The company has enjoyed a very positive trend in earnings per share over the past 5 quarters. However, while recent estimates for the company have been mixed, GLW has posted results that were in line with analysts expectations. Based on operating earnings yield, the company is undervalued when compared to all of the companies in our coverage universe. Share price changes over the past year indicates that GLW will perform in line with the market over the near term.

Financial Data

(US$ in Thousands)	3 Mos	12/31/2015	12/31/2014	12/31/2013	12/31/2012	12/31/2011	12/31/2010	12/31/2009
Earnings Per Share	0.33	1.00	1.73	1.34	1.15	1.77	2.25	1.28
Cash Flow Per Share	1.93	2.30	3.61	1.92	2.14	2.04	2.46	1.34
Tang Book Value Per Share	12.57	12.75	13.84	14.02	13.60	13.30	11.95	9.57
Dividends Per Share	0.495	0.480	0.400	0.390	0.315	0.225	0.200	0.200
Dividend Payout %	150.00	48.00	23.12	29.10	27.39	12.71	8.89	15.63
Income Statement								
Total Revenue	2,047,000	9,111,000	9,715,000	7,819,000	8,012,000	7,890,000	6,632,000	5,395,000
EBITDA	(404,000)	2,490,000	4,599,000	3,040,000	2,396,000	2,766,000	2,837,000	1,354,000
Depn & Amortn	292,000	1,184,000	1,200,000	1,002,000	997,000	957,000	854,000	792,000
Income Before Taxes	(731,000)	1,187,000	3,302,000	1,926,000	1,302,000	1,739,000	1,885,000	499,000
Income Taxes	(304,000)	147,000	1,096,000	512,000	389,000	408,000	287,000	(74,000)
Net Income	(368,000)	1,339,000	2,472,000	1,961,000	1,728,000	2,805,000	3,558,000	2,008,000
Average Shares	1,103,000	1,343,000	1,427,000	1,462,000	1,506,000	1,583,000	1,581,000	1,568,000
Balance Sheet								
Current Assets	7,178,000	8,269,000	10,238,000	8,891,000	9,695,000	8,677,000	8,859,000	5,521,000
Total Assets	27,945,000	28,547,000	30,063,000	28,478,000	29,375,000	27,848,000	25,833,000	21,295,000
Current Liabilities	2,564,000	2,814,000	2,324,000	1,746,000	1,956,000	2,097,000	1,986,000	1,539,000
Long-Term Obligations	3,910,000	3,910,000	3,227,000	3,272,000	3,382,000	2,364,000	2,262,000	1,930,000
Total Liabilities	10,027,000	9,759,000	8,484,000	7,316,000	7,889,000	6,770,000	6,458,000	5,752,000
Stockholders' Equity	17,918,000	18,788,000	21,579,000	21,162,000	21,486,000	21,078,000	19,375,000	15,543,000
Shares Outstanding	1,075,000	1,130,000	1,274,000	1,399,000	1,470,000	1,515,000	1,561,000	1,553,000
Statistical Record								
Return on Assets %	1.97	4.57	8.45	6.78	6.02	10.45	15.10	9.90
Return on Equity %	2.88	6.63	11.57	9.20	8.10	13.87	20.38	13.85
EBITDA Margin %	N.M.	27.33	47.34	38.88	29.91	35.06	42.78	25.10
Net Margin %	N.M.	14.70	25.45	25.08	21.57	35.55	53.65	37.22
Asset Turnover	0.31	0.31	0.33	0.27	0.28	0.29	0.28	0.27
Current Ratio	2.80	2.94	4.41	5.09	4.96	4.14	4.46	3.59
Debt to Equity	0.22	0.21	0.15	0.15	0.16	0.11	0.12	0.12
Price Range	22.79-15.97	25.00-15.97	23.32-17.05	17.82-11.79	14.62-10.88	23.37-11.88	20.92-15.68	19.34-9.13
P/E Ratio	69.06-48.39	25.00-15.97	13.48-9.86	13.30-8.80	12.71-9.46	13.20-6.71	9.30-6.97	15.11-7.13
Average Yield %	2.60	2.37	1.97	2.67	2.45	1.29	1.14	1.36

Address: One Riverfront Plaza, Corning, NY 14831 **Telephone:** 607-974-9000	**Web Site:** www.corning.com **Officers:** Wendell P. Weeks - Chairman, President, Chief Executive Officer Clark S. Kinlin - Executive Vice President	**Auditors:** PricewaterhouseCoopers LLP **Investor Contact:** 888-267-6464 **Transfer Agents:** ComputerShare Investor Services, Chicago, IL

CORPORATE OFFICE PROPERTIES TRUST

Exchange	Symbol	Price	52Wk Range	Yield	P/E
NYS	OFC	$27.03 (5/31/2016)	27.12-20.04	4.07	16.28

*7 Year Price Score 70.12 *NYSE Composite Index=100 *12 Month Price Score 111.25

Interim Earnings (Per Share)

Qtr.	Mar	Jun	Sep	Dec
2013	0.11	(0.16)	(0.09)	0.97
2014	0.00	0.02	0.22	0.01
2015	0.10	0.13	0.91	0.59
2016	0.03	...	...	...

Interim Dividends (Per Share)

Amt	Decl	Ex	Rec	Pay
0.275Q	09/10/2015	09/28/2015	09/30/2015	10/15/2015
0.275Q	12/10/2015	12/29/2015	12/31/2015	01/15/2016
0.275Q	02/10/2016	03/29/2016	03/31/2016	04/15/2016
0.275Q	05/12/2016	06/28/2016	06/30/2016	07/15/2016

Indicated Div: $1.10

Valuation Analysis		Institutional Holding	
Forecast EPS	$0.53	No of Institutions	
	(05/20/2016)	334	
Market Cap	$2.6 Billion	Shares	
Book Value	$1.5 Billion	101,210,152	
Price/Book	1.69	% Held	
Price/Sales	4.20	103.25	

Business Summary: REITs (MIC: 5.3.1 SIC: 6798 NAIC: 525930)

Corporate Office Properties Trust is a real estate investment trust. Through Corporate Office Properties, L.P. and subsidiaries, Co. is engaged in owning, managing, leasing, developing and acquiring office and data center properties. The majority of Co.'s portfolio is in locations that support U.S. Government agencies and their contractors, most of whom are engaged in national security, defense and information technology related activities. As of Dec 31 2015, Co.'s properties included the following: 177 operating office properties; 13 office properties under, or contractually committed for, construction or redevelopment; 1,439 acres of land that Co. controlled; and a wholesale data center.

Recent Developments: For the quarter ended Mar 31 2016, income from continuing operations decreased 26.3% to US$8.1 million from US$11.0 million in the year-earlier quarter. Net income decreased 45.1% to US$8.1 million from US$14.7 million in the year-earlier quarter. Revenues were US$144.3 million, down 10.4% from US$161.0 million the year before. Revenues from property income rose 8.5% to US$133.1 million from US$122.7 million in the corresponding quarter a year earlier.

Prospects: Our evaluation of Corporate Office Properties Trust as of June 19, 2016 is the result of our systematic analysis on three basic characteristics: earnings strength, relative valuation, and recent stock price movement. The company has enjoyed a very positive trend in earnings per share over the past 5 quarters. However, while recent estimates for the company have been mixed, OFC has posted results that fell short of analysts expectations. Based on operating earnings yield, the company is overvalued when compared to all of the companies in our coverage universe. Share price changes over the past year indicates that OFC will perform in line with the market over the near term.

Financial Data

(US$ in Thousands)	3 Mos	12/31/2015	12/31/2014	12/31/2013	12/31/2012	12/31/2011	12/31/2010	12/31/2009
Earnings Per Share	1.66	1.74	0.25	0.83	(0.03)	(1.94)	0.43	0.70
Cash Flow Per Share	2.22	2.17	2.20	1.87	2.60	2.19	2.62	3.48
Tang Book Value Per Share	12.83	13.19	12.96	12.78	11.81	14.53	16.63	15.88
Dividends Per Share	1.100	1.100	1.100	1.100	1.100	1.650	1.610	1.530
Dividend Payout %	66.27	63.22	440.00	132.53	...	...	374.42	218.57
Income Statement								
Total Revenue	144,307	625,466	586,473	523,360	528,007	556,841	564,475	767,519
EBITDA	31,976	353,188	266,137	241,263	208,502	121,364	266,766	255,449
Depn & Amortn	1,495	147,819	144,077	126,383	113,480	148,730	135,453	117,311
Income Before Taxes	8,078	120,812	34,590	36,704	7,570	(123,044)	39,016	61,094
Income Taxes	(8)	199	310	1,978	381	(10,679)	108	196
Net Income	6,826	178,300	40,255	93,707	20,977	(117,675)	42,760	56,329
Average Shares	94,298	97,667	88,263	85,224	73,454	69,382	59,944	56,407
Balance Sheet								
Current Assets	340,441	100,454	48,703	95,283	51,398	69,917	60,994	74,599
Total Assets	3,937,908	3,909,312	3,670,257	3,629,952	3,653,759	3,867,524	3,844,517	3,380,022
Current Liabilities	142,271	159,081	183,908	159,357	154,252	161,011	164,288	177,072
Long-Term Obligations	2,140,212	2,077,752	1,920,057	1,927,703	2,019,168	2,426,303	2,323,681	2,053,841
Total Liabilities	2,425,152	2,364,787	2,218,834	2,204,368	2,288,335	2,732,099	2,617,880	2,352,502
Stockholders' Equity	1,512,756	1,544,525	1,451,423	1,425,584	1,365,424	1,135,425	1,226,637	1,027,520
Shares Outstanding	94,661	94,531	93,255	87,394	80,952	72,011	66,931	58,342
Statistical Record								
Return on Assets %	4.45	4.70	1.10	2.57	0.56	N.M.	1.18	1.74
Return on Equity %	11.55	11.90	2.80	6.71	1.67	N.M.	3.79	5.75
EBITDA Margin %	22.16	56.47	45.38	46.10	39.49	21.80	47.26	33.28
Net Margin %	4.73	28.51	6.86	17.90	3.97	N.M.	7.58	7.34
Asset Turnover	0.16	0.17	0.16	0.14	0.14	0.14	0.16	0.24
Current Ratio	2.39	0.63	0.26	0.60	0.33	0.43	0.37	0.42
Debt to Equity	1.41	1.35	1.32	1.35	1.48	2.14	1.89	2.00
Price Range	29.86-20.04	30.75-20.34	29.29-23.69	29.75-21.79	26.12-20.96	36.74-19.37	43.19-33.16	39.34-21.36
P/E Ratio	17.99-12.07	17.67-11.69	117.16-94.76	35.84-26.25	...	...	100.44-77.12	56.20-30.51
Average Yield %	4.65	4.36	4.06	4.31	4.69	5.56	4.28	4.88

Address: 6711 Columbia Gateway Drive, Suite 300, Columbia, MD 21046	Web Site: www.copt.com	Auditors: PricewaterhouseCoopers LLP
Telephone: 443-285-5400	Officers: Jay H. Shidler - Chairman Clay W. Hamlin - Vice Chairman	Investor Contact: 443-285-5400
		Transfer Agents: Wells Fargo Shareowner Services, St. Paul, MN

CORRECTIONS CORPORATION OF AMERICA

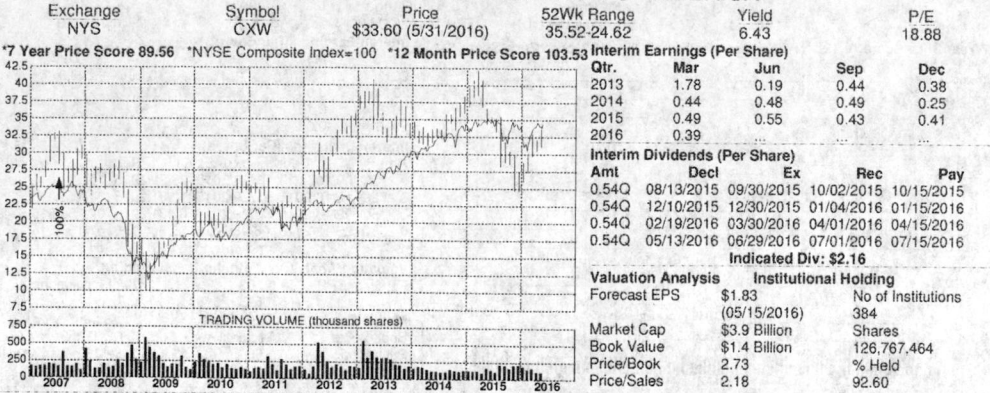

Exchange	Symbol	Price	52Wk Range	Yield	P/E
NYS	CXW	$33.60 (5/31/2016)	35.52-24.62	6.43	18.88

*7 Year Price Score 89.56 *NYSE Composite Index=100 *12 Month Price Score 103.53

Interim Earnings (Per Share)

Qtr.	Mar	Jun	Sep	Dec
2013	1.78	0.19	0.44	0.38
2014	0.44	0.48	0.49	0.25
2015	0.49	0.55	0.43	0.41
2016	0.39	...	...	...

Interim Dividends (Per Share)

Amt	Decl	Ex	Rec	Pay
0.54Q	08/13/2015	09/30/2015	10/02/2015	10/15/2015
0.54Q	12/10/2015	12/30/2015	01/04/2016	01/15/2016
0.54Q	02/19/2016	03/30/2016	04/01/2016	04/15/2016
0.54Q	05/13/2016	06/29/2016	07/01/2016	07/15/2016

Indicated Div: $2.16

Valuation Analysis

		Institutional Holding	
Forecast EPS	$1.83	No of Institutions	384
	(05/15/2016)		
Market Cap	$3.9 Billion	Shares	126,767,464
Book Value	$1.4 Billion	% Held	92.60
Price/Book	2.73		
Price/Sales	2.18		

TRADING VOLUME (thousand shares)

Business Summary: REITs (MIC: 5.3.1 SIC: 6798 NAIC: 525930)

Corrections Corporation of America is an owner of privatized correctional and detention facilities and a prison operator. Co. is engaged in owning, operating, and managing prisons and other correctional facilities and providing residential, community re-entry, and prisoner transportation services for governmental agencies. Co.'s facilities provide a variety of rehabilitation and educational programs, including basic education, faith-based services, life skills and employment training and substance abuse treatment. Co. also provides or makes available to offenders health care (including medical, dental, and mental health services), food services, and work and recreational programs.

Recent Developments: For the quarter ended Mar 31 2016, net income decreased 19.2% to US$46.3 million from US$57.3 million in the year-earlier quarter. Revenues were US$447.4 million, up 5.0% from US$426.0 million the year before.

Prospects: Our evaluation of Corrections Corporation of America as of June 19, 2016 is the result of our systematic analysis on three basic characteristics: earnings strength, relative valuation, and recent stock price movement. The company has managed to produce a neutral trend in earnings per share over the past 5 quarters. However, while recent estimates for the company have been lowered by analysts, CXW has posted better than expected results. Based on operating earnings yield, the company is undervalued when compared to all of the companies in our coverage universe. Share price changes over the past year indicates that CXW will perform in line with the market over the near term.

Financial Data

(US$ in Thousands)	3 Mos	12/31/2015	12/31/2014	12/31/2013	12/31/2012	12/31/2011	12/31/2010	12/31/2009
Earnings Per Share	1.78	1.88	1.66	2.70	1.56	1.54	1.39	1.32
Cash Flow Per Share	3.44	3.42	3.65	3.37	2.84	3.35	2.28	2.71
Tang Book Value Per Share	12.01	11.82	12.34	12.60	15.08	14.02	13.29	12.32
Dividends Per Share	2.160	2.160	2.040	8.600	0.600	...	...	...
Dividend Payout %	121.35	114.89	122.89	318.52	38.46	...	...	...
Income Statement								
Total Revenue	447,385	1,793,087	1,646,867	1,694,297	1,759,885	1,735,613	1,675,031	1,669,963
EBITDA	65,803	431,311	355,500	327,523	417,172	440,851	429,421	414,068
Depn & Amortn	792	151,400	114,000	112,800	114,100	109,100	106,400	103,800
Income Before Taxes	47,467	230,215	201,965	169,597	244,709	258,811	251,894	237,488
Income Taxes	1,160	8,361	6,943	(134,995)	87,586	96,301	94,297	81,745
Net Income	46,307	221,854	195,022	300,835	156,761	162,510	157,193	154,954
Average Shares	117,769	117,785	117,312	111,250	100,623	105,535	112,977	117,290
Balance Sheet								
Current Assets	291,761	342,058	365,985	352,734	350,742	359,429	378,293	325,255
Total Assets	3,273,804	3,356,018	3,127,191	3,007,425	2,974,742	3,019,631	2,983,228	2,905,743
Current Liabilities	317,247	324,595	318,988	254,406	166,458	198,362	205,855	194,583
Long-Term Obligations	1,400,128	1,447,077	1,200,000	1,205,003	1,111,545	1,245,014	1,156,568	1,149,099
Total Liabilities	1,827,348	1,893,270	1,645,691	1,504,918	1,453,122	1,611,609	1,512,357	1,463,197
Stockholders' Equity	1,446,456	1,462,748	1,481,500	1,502,507	1,521,620	1,408,022	1,470,871	1,442,546
Shares Outstanding	117,477	117,232	116,764	115,923	100,105	99,528	109,754	115,962
Statistical Record								
Return on Assets %	6.56	6.84	6.36	10.06	5.22	5.41	5.34	5.36
Return on Equity %	14.44	15.07	13.07	19.90	10.67	11.29	10.79	10.98
EBITDA Margin %	14.71	24.05	21.59	19.33	23.70	25.40	25.64	24.80
Net Margin %	10.35	12.37	11.84	17.76	8.91	9.36	9.38	9.28
Asset Turnover	0.56	0.55	0.54	0.57	0.59	0.58	0.57	0.58
Current Ratio	0.92	1.05	1.15	1.39	2.11	1.81	1.84	1.67
Debt to Equity	0.97	0.99	0.81	0.80	0.73	0.88	0.79	0.80
Price Range	40.61-24.62	42.10-24.62	38.33-31.13	40.78-31.60	35.87-20.96	26.35-18.64	26.71-17.83	26.20-9.82
P/E Ratio	22.81-13.83	22.39-13.10	23.09-18.75	15.10-11.70	22.99-13.44	17.11-12.10	19.22-12.83	19.85-7.44
Average Yield %	6.90	6.40	6.00	24.14	2.02	...	...	...

Address: 10 Burton Hills Blvd., Nashville, TN 37215 **Telephone:** 615-263-3000	**Web Site:** www.cca.com **Officers:** John D. Ferguson - Chairman, Vice-Chairman, President, Chief Executive Officer Damon T. Hininger - President, Chief Executive Officer	**Auditors:** Ernst & Young LLP **Investor Contact:** 615-263-3005 **Transfer Agents:** American Stock Transfer and Trust Company LLC, New York, NY

COTY, INC.

Exchange	Symbol	Price	52Wk Range	Yield	P/E
NYS	COTY	$26.34 (5/31/2016)	32.68-21.79	0.95	47.04

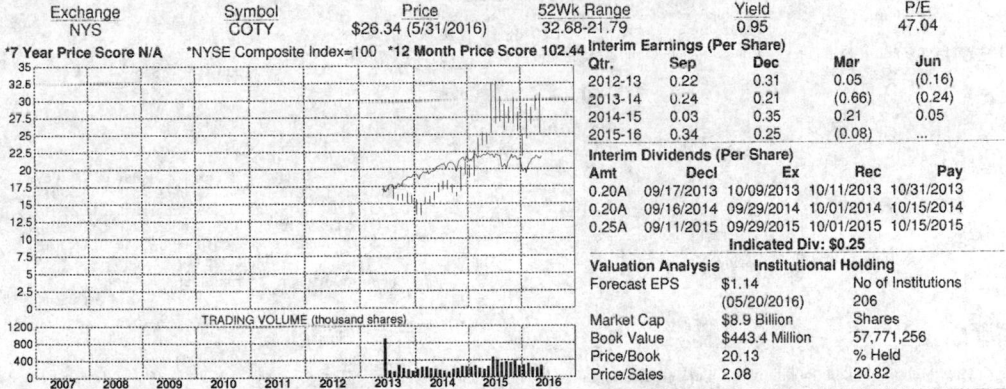

*7 Year Price Score N/A   *NYSE Composite Index=100   *12 Month Price Score 102.44

Interim Earnings (Per Share)

Qtr.	Sep	Dec	Mar	Jun
2012-13	0.22	0.31	0.05	(0.16)
2013-14	0.24	0.21	(0.66)	(0.24)
2014-15	0.03	0.35	0.21	0.05
2015-16	0.34	0.25	(0.08)	...

Interim Dividends (Per Share)

Amt	Decl	Ex	Rec	Pay
0.20A	09/17/2013	10/09/2013	10/11/2013	10/31/2013
0.20A	09/16/2014	09/29/2014	10/01/2014	10/15/2014
0.25A	09/11/2015	09/29/2015	10/01/2015	10/15/2015

Indicated Div: $0.25

Valuation Analysis   **Institutional Holding**

Forecast EPS	$1.14	No of Institutions
	(05/20/2016)	206
Market Cap	$8.9 Billion	Shares
Book Value	$443.4 Million	57,771,256
Price/Book	20.13	% Held
Price/Sales	2.08	20.82

Business Summary: Household & Personal Products (MIC: 1.7.1 SIC: 2844 NAIC: 325620)

Coty is a beauty company with a portfolio of brands that compete in the three segments in which it operates: Fragrances, Color Cosmetics, and Skin and Body Care. Co.'s fragrance products include a variety of men's and women's products. The brands in this segment include brands associated with fashion designers, Lifestyle brands and brands related to entertainment personalities. Co.'s color cosmetics products include lip, eye, nail and facial color products, with brands that include Rimmel, Sally Hansen and OPI. Co.'s skin and body care products include shower gels, deodorants, skin care and sun treatment products. Co.'s skin and body care brands are adidas, Lancaster, philosophy and TJoy.

Recent Developments: For the quarter ended Mar 31 2016, net loss amounted to US$20.3 million versus net income of US$82.2 million in the year-earlier quarter. Revenues were US$950.7 million, up 1.8% from US$933.8 million the year before. Operating income was US$23.0 million versus US$114.7 million in the prior-year quarter, a decrease of 79.9%. Direct operating expenses rose 4.9% to US$369.0 million from US$351.8 million in the comparable period the year before. Indirect operating expenses increased 19.6% to US$558.7 million from US$467.3 million in the equivalent prior-year period.

Prospects: Our evaluation of Coty, Inc. as of June 19, 2016 is the result of our systematic analysis on three basic characteristics: earnings strength, relative valuation, and recent stock price movement. The company has generated a negative trend in earnings per share over the past 5 quarters. However, while recent estimates for the company have been mixed, COTY has posted results that fell short of analysts expectations. Based on operating earnings yield, the company is about fairly valued when compared to all of the companies in our coverage universe. Share price changes over the past year indicates that COTY will perform in line with the market over the near term.

Financial Data

(US$ in Thousands)	9 Mos	6 Mos	3 Mos	06/30/2015	06/30/2014	06/30/2013	06/30/2012	06/30/2011
Earnings Per Share	0.56	0.85	0.95	0.64	(0.26)	0.42	(0.87)	0.18
Cash Flow Per Share	1.73	2.00	1.71	1.49	1.41	1.22	1.58	1.27
Dividends Per Share	0.250	0.250	0.250	0.200	0.200	0.150	...	0.100
Dividend Payout %	44.64	29.41	26.32	31.25	...	35.71	...	55.56
Income Statement								
Total Revenue	3,273,500	2,322,800	1,112,300	4,395,200	4,551,600	4,649,100	4,611,300	4,086,100
EBITDA	409,500	328,800	139,500	462,500	189,400	564,600	(95,600)	410,300
Depn & Amortn	171,000	112,900	57,500	156,200	165,000	169,400	145,900	133,800
Income Before Taxes	167,900	176,600	66,000	233,300	(44,100)	318,700	(331,100)	185,000
Income Taxes	(42,500)	(54,100)	(67,100)	(26,100)	20,100	116,800	(37,800)	95,100
Net Income	187,900	214,700	125,700	232,500	(97,400)	168,000	(324,400)	61,700
Average Shares	337,900	354,300	369,900	362,900	381,700	396,400	373,000	339,100
Balance Sheet								
Current Assets	1,899,100	1,940,600	2,038,000	1,856,400	2,784,800	2,416,900	2,138,500	...
Total Assets	7,024,900	6,511,700	6,157,000	6,018,900	6,592,500	6,470,000	6,183,400	...
Current Liabilities	1,730,200	1,712,900	1,687,200	1,526,200	1,597,300	1,463,200	1,913,000	...
Long-Term Obligations	3,997,100	3,570,900	2,750,600	2,605,900	3,260,100	2,590,100	2,270,200	...
Total Liabilities	6,581,500	6,105,900	5,282,500	5,049,100	5,748,700	4,976,000	5,153,800	...
Stockholders' Equity	443,400	405,800	874,500	969,800	843,800	1,494,000	1,029,600	...
Shares Outstanding	338,800	337,000	356,500	360,800	353,900	383,800	381,900	370,000
Statistical Record								
Return on Assets %	3.18	4.82	5.52	3.69	N.M.	2.66	...	...
Return on Equity %	44.15	59.44	44.59	25.64	N.M.	13.31	...	...
EBITDA Margin %	12.51	14.16	12.54	10.52	4.16	12.14	N.M.	10.04
Net Margin %	5.74	9.24	11.30	5.29	N.M.	3.61	N.M.	1.51
Asset Turnover	0.65	0.66	0.69	0.70	0.70	0.73	...	...
Current Ratio	1.10	1.13	1.21	1.22	1.74	1.65	1.12	...
Debt to Equity	9.01	8.80	3.15	2.69	3.86	1.73	2.20	...
Price Range	32.68-21.79	32.68-18.71	32.68-15.94	32.45-15.94	17.85-13.25	17.52-16.61	...	...
P/E Ratio	58.36-38.91	38.45-22.01	34.40-16.78	50.70-24.91	...	41.71-39.55	...	...
Average Yield %	0.92	0.96	1.06	0.96	1.26	0.88	...	...

Address: 350 Fifth Avenue, New York, NY 10118	**Web Site:** www.coty.com	**Auditors:** Deloitte & Touche LLP
Telephone: 212-389-7300	**Officers:** Lambertus (Bart) J.H. Becht - Chairman, Interim Chief Executive Officer Camillo Pane Executive Vice President	**Investor Contact:** 212 479-4300

COVANTA HOLDING CORP

Exchange	Symbol	Price	52Wk Range	Yield	P/E
NYS	CVA	$16.67 (5/31/2016)	22.58-12.62	6.00	34.02

*7 Year Price Score 82.09   *NYSE Composite Index=100   *12 Month Price Score 95.45

Interim Earnings (Per Share)

Qtr.	Mar	Jun	Sep	Dec
2013	(0.19)	(0.30)	0.22	0.22
2014	(0.07)	0.00	0.05	0.01
2015	(0.28)	(0.05)	0.25	0.58
2016	(0.29)	...	...	...

Interim Dividends (Per Share)

Amt	Decl	Ex	Rec	Pay
0.25Q	09/17/2015	09/28/2015	09/30/2015	10/07/2015
0.25Q	12/03/2015	12/28/2015	12/30/2015	01/07/2016
0.25Q	03/03/2016	03/24/2016	03/29/2016	04/05/2016
0.25Q	05/05/2016	06/23/2016	06/27/2016	07/06/2016

Indicated Div: $1.00

Valuation Analysis / **Institutional Holding**

Forecast EPS	$0.10	No of Institutions
	(05/17/2016)	327
Market Cap	$2.2 Billion	Shares
Book Value	$553.0 Million	116,865,360
Price/Book	3.95	% Held
Price/Sales	1.31	N/A

Business Summary: Electric Utilities (MIC: 3.1.1 SIC: 4911 NAIC: 221111)

Covanta Holding is a holding company. Co. is an owner and operator of infrastructure for the conversion of waste to energy, as well as other waste disposal and renewable energy production businesses. Co. conducts all of its operations through subsidiaries which are engaged predominantly in the businesses of waste and energy services. Co. has one reportable segment, which is North America and is comprised of waste and energy services operations primarily in the U.S. and Canada. Co. holds equity interests in energy-from-waste facilities in China and Italy.

Recent Developments: For the quarter ended Mar 31 2016, net loss was unchanged at US$37.0 million versus US$37.0 million the year-earlier quarter. Revenues were US$403.0 million, up 5.2% from US$383.0 million the year before. Operating loss was US$14.0 million versus an income of US$7.0 million in the prior-year quarter. Direct operating expenses rose 9.0% to US$315.0 million from US$289.0 million in the comparable period the year before. Indirect operating expenses increased 17.2% to US$102.0 million from US$87.0 million in the equivalent prior-year period.

Prospects: Our evaluation of Covanta Holding Corp. as of June 19, 2016 is the result of our systematic analysis on three basic characteristics: earnings strength, relative valuation, and recent stock price movement. The company has managed to produce a neutral trend in earnings per share over the past 5 quarters and while recent estimates for the company have remained steady, CVA has posted results that fell short of analysts expectations. Based on operating earnings yield, the company is overvalued when compared to all of the companies in our coverage universe. Share price changes over the past year indicates that CVA will perform in line with the market over the near term.

Financial Data

(US$ in Thousands)	3 Mos	12/31/2015	12/31/2014	12/31/2013	12/31/2012	12/31/2011	12/31/2010	12/31/2009
Earnings Per Share	0.49	0.51	(0.01)	(0.05)	0.86	1.54	0.40	0.66
Cash Flow Per Share	1.84	1.89	2.62	2.45	2.58	2.56	2.82	2.58
Tang Book Value Per Share	1.63	0.11	1.33	2.11	2.86	2.49	2.31	4.62
Dividends Per Share	1.000	1.000	0.860	0.660	0.600	0.300	1.500	...
Dividend Payout %	204.08	196.08	...	...	69.77	19.48	375.00	...
Income Statement								
Total Revenue	403,000	1,645,000	1,682,000	1,630,000	1,644,000	1,650,000	1,582,301	1,550,467
Income Before Taxes	(50,000)	(28,000)	4,000	78,000	134,000	107,000	56,501	137,436
Income Taxes	(10,000)	(84,000)	15,000	40,000	26,000	28,000	23,355	50,044
Net Income	(37,000)	68,000	(2,000)	(7,000)	114,000	219,000	61,654	101,645
Average Shares	129,000	133,000	130,000	130,000	133,000	142,000	153,928	154,994
Balance Sheet								
Total Assets	4,200,000	4,259,000	4,204,000	4,378,000	4,526,000	4,385,000	4,676,302	4,934,282
Total Liabilities	3,647,000	3,621,000	3,422,000	3,471,000	3,478,000	3,302,000	3,548,616	3,551,276
Stockholders' Equity	553,000	638,000	782,000	907,000	1,048,000	1,083,000	1,127,686	1,383,006
Shares Outstanding	131,000	131,000	133,000	130,000	132,000	136,000	149,891	154,936
Statistical Record								
Return on Assets %	1.63	1.61	N.M.	N.M.	2.55	4.83	1.28	2.21
Return on Equity %	11.31	9.58	N.M.	N.M.	10.67	19.81	4.91	8.02
Net Margin %	(9.18)	4.13	(0.12)	(0.43)	6.93	13.27	3.90	6.56
Price Range	22.75-12.62	22.83-13.79	25.10-16.48	21.79-17.16	18.96-13.49	17.59-13.02	19.54-14.30	22.68-12.92
P/E Ratio	46.43-25.76	44.76-27.04	...	...	22.05-15.69	11.42-8.45	48.85-35.75	34.36-19.58
Average Yield %	5.49	5.04	4.30	3.34	3.59	1.88	9.16	

Address: 445 South Street, Morristown, NJ 07960	**Web Site:** www.covanta.com	**Auditors:** Ernst & Young LLP
Telephone: 862-345-5000	**Officers:** Samuel Zell - Chairman Stephen J. Jones - President, Chief Executive Officer	**Investor Contact:** 862-345-5456
		Transfer Agents: American Stock Transfer and Trust Company, New York, NY

CRANE CO.

Exchange	Symbol	Price	52Wk Range	Yield	P/E	Div Achiever
NYS	CR	$57.40 (5/31/2016)	61.63-43.14	2.30	14.49	11 Years

*7 Year Price Score 90.92   *NYSE Composite Index=100   *12 Month Price Score 104.83

Interim Earnings (Per Share)

Qtr.	Mar	Jun	Sep	Dec
2013	0.99	0.93	0.97	0.84
2014	0.82	1.00	0.47	0.95
2015	0.87	0.95	0.97	1.11
2016	0.93	...	...	...

Interim Dividends (Per Share)

Amt	Decl	Ex	Rec	Pay
0.33Q	07/27/2015	08/27/2015	08/31/2015	09/09/2015
0.33Q	10/26/2015	11/25/2015	11/30/2015	12/09/2015
0.33Q	01/25/2016	02/25/2016	02/29/2016	03/10/2016
0.33Q	04/25/2016	05/26/2016	05/31/2016	06/10/2016

Indicated Div: $1.32

Valuation Analysis

		Institutional Holding	
Forecast EPS	$4.01	No of Institutions	
	(05/20/2016)	350	
Market Cap	$4.2 Billion	Shares	
Book Value	$1.2 Billion	45,758,756	
Price/Book	3.43	% Held	
Price/Sales	1.53	69.56	

Business Summary: Industrial Machinery & Equipment (MIC: 7.2.1 SIC: 3499 NAIC: 332999)

Crane is a manufacturer of industrial products. Co. has four segments: Fluid Handling, which provides fluid handling equipment; Payment and Merchandising Technologies, which provides technology payment acceptance products and vending equipment and related solutions; Aerospace and Electronics, which provides products such as custom designed, engineered products used in landing systems, sensing and utility systems, fluid management, seat actuation, power and microelectronic applications, and microwave systems; and Engineered Materials, which manufactures fiberglass-reinforced plastic panels and coils for use in the manufacturing of recreational vehicles, truck bodies, truck trailers.

Recent Developments: For the quarter ended Mar 31 2016, net income increased 7.6% to US$55.2 million from US$51.3 million in the year-earlier quarter. Revenues were US$660.0 million, down 2.8% from US$678.8 million the year before. Operating income was US$85.5 million versus US$86.0 million in the prior-year quarter, a decrease of 0.6%. Direct operating expenses declined 3.6% to US$426.1 million from US$442.0 million in the comparable period the year before. Indirect operating expenses decreased 1.5% to US$148.4 million from US$150.7 million in the equivalent prior-year period.

Prospects: Our evaluation of Crane Co. as of June 19, 2016 is the result of our systematic analysis on three basic characteristics: earnings strength, relative valuation, and recent stock price movement. The company has produced a positive trend in earnings per share over the past 5 quarters and while recent estimates for the company have remained steady, CR has posted better than expected results. Based on operating earnings yield, the company is undervalued when compared to all of the companies in our coverage universe. Share price changes over the past year indicates that CR will perform poorly over the near term.

Financial Data

(US$ in Thousands)	3 Mos	12/31/2015	12/31/2014	12/31/2013	12/31/2012	12/31/2011	12/31/2010	12/31/2009
Earnings Per Share	3.96	3.89	3.23	3.73	3.72	0.44	2.59	2.28
Cash Flow Per Share	3.83	3.95	4.50	4.14	4.08	2.58	2.28	3.23
Tang Book Value Per Share	N.M.	N.M.	N.M.	N.M.	N.M.	N.M.	0.21	0.09
Dividends Per Share	1.320	1.320	1.260	1.160	1.080	0.980	0.860	0.800
Dividend Payout %	33.33	33.93	39.01	31.10	29.03	222.73	33.20	35.09
Income Statement								
Total Revenue	660,000	2,740,500	2,924,997	2,595,281	2,579,068	2,545,867	2,217,825	2,196,343
EBITDA	101,700	411,300	360,365	389,309	349,957	84,974	277,586	223,312
Depn & Amortn	16,500	39,100	41,700	38,700	40,400	39,900	41,000	14,067
Income Before Taxes	76,600	336,500	281,156	326,016	284,605	20,454	210,929	184,926
Income Taxes	21,400	106,500	87,587	105,065	88,416	(6,062)	56,739	50,846
Net Income	55,200	230,000	193,569	220,951	217,821	26,516	154,190	134,080
Average Shares	58,900	58,800	59,603	58,839	58,293	59,204	59,562	58,812
Balance Sheet								
Current Assets	1,254,700	1,203,500	1,195,184	1,149,092	1,180,521	1,032,232	988,661	1,046,346
Total Assets	3,395,000	3,341,600	3,450,785	3,559,607	2,889,878	2,843,531	2,706,697	2,712,898
Current Liabilities	575,600	572,800	640,025	668,902	511,888	533,095	498,554	466,782
Long-Term Obligations	744,800	749,300	749,213	749,170	399,092	398,914	398,736	398,557
Total Liabilities	2,181,800	2,202,200	2,391,033	2,355,288	1,971,495	2,029,978	1,721,753	1,827,136
Stockholders' Equity	1,213,200	1,139,400	1,059,752	1,204,319	918,383	813,553	984,944	885,762
Shares Outstanding	72,426	58,109	58,121	58,185	57,106	57,614	58,160	58,526
Statistical Record								
Return on Assets %	6.90	6.77	5.52	6.85	7.58	0.96	5.69	4.89
Return on Equity %	21.03	20.92	17.10	20.82	25.08	2.95	16.48	16.51
EBITDA Margin %	15.41	15.01	12.32	15.00	13.57	3.34	12.52	10.17
Net Margin %	8.36	8.39	6.62	8.51	8.45	1.04	6.95	6.10
Asset Turnover	0.80	0.81	0.83	0.80	0.90	0.92	0.82	0.80
Current Ratio	2.18	2.10	1.87	1.72	2.31	1.94	1.98	2.24
Debt to Equity	0.61	0.66	0.71	0.62	0.43	0.49	0.40	0.45
Price Range	64.31-43.14	69.78-45.27	76.33-53.63	67.25-46.28	51.07-35.53	51.06-34.03	41.30-28.97	32.21-12.85
P/E Ratio	16.24-10.89	17.94-11.64	23.63-16.60	18.03-12.41	13.73-9.55	116.05-77.34	15.95-11.19	14.13-5.64
Average Yield %	2.47	2.33	1.87	1.99	2.54	2.18	2.44	3.50

Address: 100 First Stamford Place, Stamford, CT 06902	**Web Site:** www.craneco.com	**Auditors:** Deloitte & Touche LLP
Telephone: 203 363-7300	**Officers:** R. S. Evans - Chairman Max H. Mitchell - President, Chief Executive Officer, Executive Vice President, Chief Operating Officer	**Investor Contact:** 203 363-7352
		Transfer Agents: First Chicago Trust Company of New York, Jersey City, NJ

CROWN CASTLE INTERNATIONAL CORP

Exchange	Symbol	Price	52Wk Range	Yield	P/E
NYS	CCI	$90.81 (5/31/2016)	91.29-76.58	3.90	21.67

*7 Year Price Score 118.17 *NYSE Composite Index=100 *12 Month Price Score 103.06

Interim Earnings (Per Share)

Qtr.	Mar	Jun	Sep	Dec
2013	0.05	0.18	0.16	(0.13)
2014	0.27	0.07	0.29	0.41
2015	0.34	3.42	0.28	0.38
2016	0.11	...		

Interim Dividends (Per Share)

Amt	Decl	Ex	Rec	Pay
0.82Q	08/03/2015	09/16/2015	09/18/2015	09/30/2015
0.885Q	10/22/2015	12/16/2015	12/18/2015	12/31/2015
0.885Q	02/18/2016	03/16/2016	03/18/2016	03/31/2016
0.885Q	05/20/2016	06/15/2016	06/17/2016	06/30/2016

Indicated Div: $3.54

Valuation Analysis

		Institutional Holding	
Forecast EPS	$0.97	No of Institutions	
	(05/20/2016)	758	
Market Cap	$30.7 Billion	Shares	
Book Value	$7.2 Billion	343,534,944	
Price/Book	4.29	% Held	
Price/Sales	8.29	N/A	

Business Summary: REITs (MIC: 5.3.1 SIC: 6798 NAIC: 525930)

Crown Castle International owns, operates and leases shared wireless infrastructure, including: towers and other structures, such as rooftops; small cell networks supported by fiber. Co. conducts its operations through subsidiaries of its subsdiary, Crown Castle Operating Company. Co.'s main business is providing access, including space or capacity, to its shared wireless infrastructure via long-term contracts in various forms, including license, sublease and lease agreements. As part of its activity to provide solutions, Co. provides certain network services relating to its wireless infrastructure, primarily consisting of site development services and installation services.

Recent Developments: For the quarter ended Mar 31 2016, income from continuing operations decreased 57.2% to US$47.8 million from US$111.7 million in the year-earlier quarter. Net income decreased 61.8% to US$47.8 million from US$125.1 million in the year-earlier quarter. Revenues were US$934.4 million, up 3.8% from US$900.5 million the year before. Revenues from property income rose 9.3% to US$799.3 million from US$731.4 million in the corresponding quarter a year earlier.

Prospects: Our evaluation of Crown Castle International Corp. as of June 19, 2016 is the result of our systematic analysis on three basic characteristics: earnings strength, relative valuation, and recent stock price movement. The company has generated a negative trend in earnings per share over the past 5 quarters and while recent estimates for the company have remained steady, CCI has posted results that fell short of analysts expectations. Based on operating earnings yield, the company is overvalued when compared to all of the companies in our coverage universe. Share price changes over the past year indicates that CCI will perform in line with the market over the near term.

Financial Data
(US$ in Thousands)

	3 Mos	12/31/2015	12/31/2014	12/31/2013	12/31/2012	12/31/2011	12/31/2010	12/31/2009
Earnings Per Share	4.19	4.42	1.04	0.26	0.64	0.52	(1.16)	(0.47)
Cash Flow Per Share	5.30	5.39	5.01	4.15	2.66	2.27	2.10	1.99
Dividends Per Share	3.410	3.345	0.820	...	...	...	...	...
Dividend Payout %	81.38	75.68	78.85	...	...	...	...	...
Income Statement								
Total Revenue	934,384	3,663,851	3,689,884	3,022,384	2,432,680	2,032,729	1,878,658	1,685,407
EBITDA	182,127	1,773,951	1,718,209	1,442,904	1,136,215	1,074,528	529,863	629,546
Depn & Amortn	4,211	774,900	757,400	562,100	438,900	387,800	379,300	379,600
Income Before Taxes	51,712	473,829	388,134	292,529	100,827	179,807	(338,105)	(190,523)
Income Taxes	3,872	(51,457)	(10,640)	198,628	(100,061)	8,347	(26,846)	(76,400)
Net Income	47,840	1,520,992	390,513	90,111	188,584	171,077	(310,940)	(114,332)
Average Shares	334,929	334,062	333,265	299,293	291,270	285,947	286,764	286,622
Balance Sheet								
Current Assets	820,882	981,245	931,502	892,683	1,581,324	599,152	545,145	1,196,033
Total Assets	21,718,251	22,036,245	21,143,276	20,594,908	16,088,709	10,545,096	10,469,529	10,956,606
Current Liabilities	811,946	855,369	898,935	756,387	1,237,858	402,106	440,885	754,105
Long-Term Obligations	11,778,176	12,143,019	11,807,526	11,490,914	10,923,186	6,853,182	6,750,207	6,361,954
Total Liabilities	14,565,257	14,947,024	14,427,051	13,668,191	13,149,963	7,853,819	7,707,575	7,704,711
Stockholders' Equity	7,152,994	7,089,221	6,716,225	6,926,717	2,938,746	2,691,277	2,761,954	3,251,895
Shares Outstanding	337,559	333,771	333,856	334,070	293,164	284,449	290,826	292,729
Statistical Record								
Return on Assets %	6.75	7.04	1.87	0.49	1.41	1.63	N.M.	N.M.
Return on Equity %	21.13	22.03	5.72	1.83	6.68	6.27	N.M.	N.M.
EBITDA Margin %	19.49	48.42	46.57	47.74	46.71	52.86	28.20	37.35
Net Margin %	5.12	41.51	10.58	2.98	7.75	8.42	N.M.	N.M.
Asset Turnover	0.17	0.17	0.18	0.16	0.18	0.19	0.18	0.16
Current Ratio	1.01	1.15	1.04	1.18	1.28	1.49	1.24	1.59
Debt to Equity	1.65	1.71	1.76	1.66	3.72	2.55	2.44	1.96
Price Range	88.41-76.58	88.71-76.58	84.75-68.96	79.77-66.66	72.16-44.92	46.17-37.37	44.15-34.82	39.79-15.84
P/E Ratio	21.10-18.28	20.07-17.33	81.49-66.3	1306.81-256.38	112.75-70.19	88.79-71.87	...	...
Average Yield %	4.08	4.00	1.07	...	...	...	...	...

Address: 1220 Augusta Drive, Suite 600, Houston, TX 77057-2261 **Telephone:** 713-570-3000	**Web Site:** www.crowncastle.com **Officers:** J. Landis Martin - Chairman W. Benjamin Moreland - Incoming Executive Vice-Chairman, President, Chief Executive Officer	**Auditors:** PricewaterhouseCoopers LLP **Investor Contact:** 713-570-3050 **Transfer Agents:** Mellon Investor Services LLC, Jersey City, NJ

CROWN HOLDINGS INC

Exchange	Symbol	Price	52Wk Range	Yield	P/E
NYS	CCK	$52.17 (5/31/2016)	56.46-44.21	N/A	16.99

*7 Year Price Score 109.41 *NYSE Composite Index=100 *12 Month Price Score 102.71

Interim Earnings (Per Share)

Qtr.	Mar	Jun	Sep	Dec
2013	0.28	0.93	0.73	0.36
2014	0.17	0.76	1.76	0.09
2015	0.32	1.02	1.01	0.47
2016	0.57	...	...	...

Interim Dividends (Per Share)

No Dividends Paid

Valuation Analysis **Institutional Holding**

Forecast EPS	$3.90	No of Institutions
	(05/20/2016)	506
Market Cap	$7.3 Billion	Shares
Book Value	$249.0 Million	139,374,448
Price/Book	29.22	% Held
Price/Sales	0.84	91.80

Business Summary: Metal Products (MIC: 8.2.3 SIC: 3411 NAIC: 332431)

Crown Holdings is engaged in the design, manufacture and sale of packaging products for consumer goods. Co.'s primary products include steel and aluminum cans for food, beverage, household and other consumer products and metal vacuum closures and caps. These products are sold through Co.'s sales organization to the soft drink, food, citrus, brewing, household products, personal care and various other industries. Co.'s business is organized geographically within three divisions: Americas, which include Americas Beverage segment and North America Food segment; European, which includes European Beverage segment and European Food segment; and Asia-Pacific.

Recent Developments: For the quarter ended Mar 31 2016, net income increased 59.7% to US$99.0 million from US$62.0 million in the year-earlier quarter. Revenues were US$1.89 billion, down 5.2% from US$2.00 billion the year before. Operating income was US$219.0 million versus US$168.0 million in the prior-year quarter, an increase of 30.4%. Direct operating expenses declined 7.6% to US$1.58 billion from US$1.71 billion in the comparable period the year before. Indirect operating expenses decreased 21.2% to US$93.0 million from US$118.0 million in the equivalent prior-year period.

Prospects: Our evaluation of Crown Holdings Inc. as of June 19, 2016 is the result of our systematic analysis on three basic characteristics: earnings strength, relative valuation, and recent stock price movement. The company has managed to produce a neutral trend in earnings per share over the past 5 quarters and while recent estimates for the company have remained steady, CCK has posted better than expected results. Based on operating earnings yield, the company is undervalued when compared to all of the companies in our coverage universe. Share price changes over the past year indicates that CCK will perform in line with the market over the near term.

Financial Data
(US$ in Millions)

	3 Mos	12/31/2015	12/31/2014	12/31/2013	12/31/2012	12/31/2011	12/31/2010	12/31/2009
Earnings Per Share	3.07	2.82	2.79	2.30	3.75	1.83	2.00	2.06
Cash Flow Per Share	6.05	6.93	6.65	6.34	4.22	2.50	3.70	4.75
Income Statement								
Total Revenue	1,893	8,762	9,097	8,656	8,470	8,644	7,941	7,938
EBITDA	258	1,135	952	941	1,035	948	980	894
Depn & Amortn	60	237	190	134	180	140	172	194
Income Before Taxes	137	639	516	576	636	587	614	459
Income Taxes	38	178	41	148	(17)	194	165	7
Net Income	79	393	387	324	557	282	324	334
Average Shares	139	139	138	140	148	154	162	161
Balance Sheet								
Current Assets	2,904	3,049	3,624	3,180	2,750	2,603	2,649	2,242
Total Assets	9,940	10,020	9,708	8,030	7,490	6,868	6,899	6,532
Current Liabilities	2,718	2,908	2,926	2,920	2,518	2,285	2,377	1,925
Long-Term Obligations	5,293	5,255	5,007	3,469	3,289	3,337	2,649	2,739
Total Liabilities	9,691	9,876	9,589	8,026	7,652	7,341	6,995	6,538
Stockholders' Equity	249	144	119	4	(162)	(473)	(96)	(6)
Shares Outstanding	139	139	139	138	143	148	155	161
Statistical Record								
Return on Assets %	4.26	3.98	4.36	4.18	7.74	4.10	4.82	5.02
Return on Equity %	385.59	298.86	629.27	...	...	...	...	...
EBITDA Margin %	13.63	12.95	10.46	10.87	12.22	10.97	12.34	11.26
Net Margin %	4.17	4.49	4.25	3.74	6.58	3.26	4.08	4.21
Asset Turnover	0.86	0.89	1.03	1.12	1.18	1.26	1.18	1.19
Current Ratio	1.07	1.05	1.24	1.09	1.09	1.14	1.11	1.16
Debt to Equity	21.26	36.49	42.08	867.25	...	...	...	...
Price Range	56.63-44.21	56.63-44.31	52.31-40.12	45.22-36.81	38.79-32.69	41.19-29.30	33.85-22.66	29.21-17.87
P/E Ratio	18.45-14.40	20.08-15.71	18.75-14.38	19.66-16.00	10.34-8.72	22.51-16.01	16.93-11.33	14.18-8.67

Address: One Crown Way, Philadelphia, PA 19154-4599
Telephone: 215-698-5100

Web Site: www.crowncork.com
Officers: John W. Conway - Chairman, President, Chief Executive Officer, Chief Operating Officer Timothy J. Donahue - President, Executive Vice President, Chief Financial Officer, Chief Operating Officer, Chief Executive Officer

Auditors: PricewaterhouseCoopers LLP
Investor Contact: 215-698-5341
Transfer Agents: Wells Fargo Shareowner Services, St. Paul, MN

CST BRANDS INC

Exchange	Symbol	Price	52Wk Range	Yield	P/E
NYS	CST	$37.93 (5/31/2016)	41.30-32.00	0.66	18.78

*7 Year Price Score N/A   *NYSE Composite Index=100   *12 Month Price Score 100.95

Interim Earnings (Per Share)

Qtr.	Mar	Jun	Sep	Dec
2013	0.03	0.57	0.55	0.45
2014	0.14	0.43	0.83	1.23
2015	0.18	0.32	1.12	0.34
2016	0.24			

Interim Dividends (Per Share)

Amt	Decl	Ex	Rec	Pay
0.063Q	09/11/2015	09/28/2015	09/30/2015	10/15/2015
0.063Q	12/09/2015	12/29/2015	12/31/2015	01/15/2016
0.063Q	03/03/2016	03/29/2016	03/31/2016	04/15/2016
0.063Q	06/08/2016	06/28/2016	06/30/2016	07/15/2016

Indicated Div: $0.25

Valuation Analysis

		Institutional Holding	
Forecast EPS	$1.82	No of Institutions	353
	(05/20/2016)		
Market Cap	$2.9 Billion	Shares	
Book Value	$937.0 Million		68,512,160
Price/Book	3.06	% Held	
Price/Sales	0.26		89.45

TRADING VOLUME (thousand shares)

Business Summary: Retail - Food & Beverage, Drug & Tobacco (MIC: 2.1.2 SIC: 5541 NAIC: 447110)

CST Brands is a holding company. Through its subsidiaries, Co. is an independent retailer of motor fuel and convenience merchandise in the U.S. and eastern Canada. Co.'s retail operations include the sale of motor fuel at convenience stores, commission agents and cardlocks; the sale of food, convenience merchandise items and services at convenience stores; and the sale of heating oil to residential customers and heating oil and motor fuel to commercial customers. As of Dec 31 2015, Co. had three operating segments, U.S. Retail, Canadian Retail and CrossAmerica.

Recent Developments: For the quarter ended Mar 31 2016, net income increased 100.0% to US$12.0 million from US$6.0 million in the year-earlier quarter. Revenues were US$2.37 billion, down 11.1% from US$2.67 billion the year before. Operating income was US$26.0 million versus US$21.0 million in the prior-year quarter, an increase of 23.8%. Direct operating expenses declined 13.8% to US$2.03 billion from US$2.36 billion in the comparable period the year before. Indirect operating expenses increased 8.7% to US$311.0 million from US$286.0 million in the equivalent prior-year period.

Prospects: Our evaluation of CST Brands Inc. as of June 19, 2016 is the result of our systematic analysis on three basic characteristics: earnings strength, relative valuation, and recent stock price movement. The company has managed to produce a neutral trend in earnings per share over the past 5 quarters and while recent estimates for the company have been mixed, CST has posted better than expected results. Based on operating earnings yield, the company is undervalued when compared to all of the companies in our coverage universe. Share price changes over the past year indicates that CST will perform very poorly over the near term.

Financial Data
(US$ in Millions)

	3 Mos	12/31/2015	12/31/2014	12/31/2013	12/31/2012	12/31/2011	12/31/2010
Earnings Per Share	2.02	1.95	2.63	1.84	...	...	...
Cash Flow Per Share	5.03	4.75	4.68	5.84	...	...	...
Tang Book Value Per Share	N.M.	1.73	1.10	7.67	15.92	...	...
Dividends Per Share	0.250	0.250	0.250	0.125	...	...	...
Dividend Payout %	12.38	12.82	9.51	6.79	...	...	...
Income Statement							
Total Revenue	2,371	11,444	12,758	12,777	13,135	12,863	10,371
EBITDA	97	407	448	348	419	419	385
Depn & Amortn	61	122	114	106	103	101	94
Income Before Taxes	21	227	289	215	315	317	290
Income Taxes	9	88	109	76	105	103	97
Net Income	19	149	200	139	210	214	193
Average Shares	75	76	76	75			
Balance Sheet							
Current Assets	612	720	798	766	384	485	...
Total Assets	4,248	3,840	3,641	2,303	1,709	1,691	...
Current Liabilities	582	621	550	463	228	212	...
Long-Term Obligations	1,735	1,317	1,227	1,006	4	5	...
Total Liabilities	3,311	2,930	2,828	1,676	462	442	...
Stockholders' Equity	937	910	813	627	1,247	1,249	...
Shares Outstanding	75	75	77	75	75		...
Statistical Record							
Return on Assets %	3.88	3.98	6.73	6.93	12.32	...	...
Return on Equity %	18.34	17.30	27.78	14.83	16.78	...	...
EBITDA Margin %	4.09	3.56	3.51	2.72	3.19	3.26	3.71
Net Margin %	0.80	1.30	1.57	1.09	1.60	1.66	1.86
Asset Turnover	2.81	3.06	4.29	6.37	7.71	...	...
Current Ratio	1.05	1.16	1.45	1.65	1.68	2.29	...
Debt to Equity	1.85	1.45	1.51	1.60	N.M.	N.M.	...
Price Range	44.75-32.00	45.07-32.97	44.32-30.00	36.72-29.19	...	...	...
P/E Ratio	22.15-15.84	23.11-16.91	16.85-11.41	19.96-15.86	...	...	...
Average Yield %	0.66	0.63	0.72	0.39	...	...	...

Address: One Valero Way, Building D, Suite 200, San Antonio, TX 78249
Telephone: 210-692-5000

Web Site: www.CSTBrands.com
Officers: Kimberly S. Bowers Lubel - President, Chief Executive Officer Anthony P. Bartys - Senior Vice President, Chief Operating Officer

Auditors: KPMG LLP
Investor Contact: 800-456-3533
Transfer Agents: American Stock Transfer & Trust Company, Brookly, NY

CULLEN/FROST BANKERS, INC.

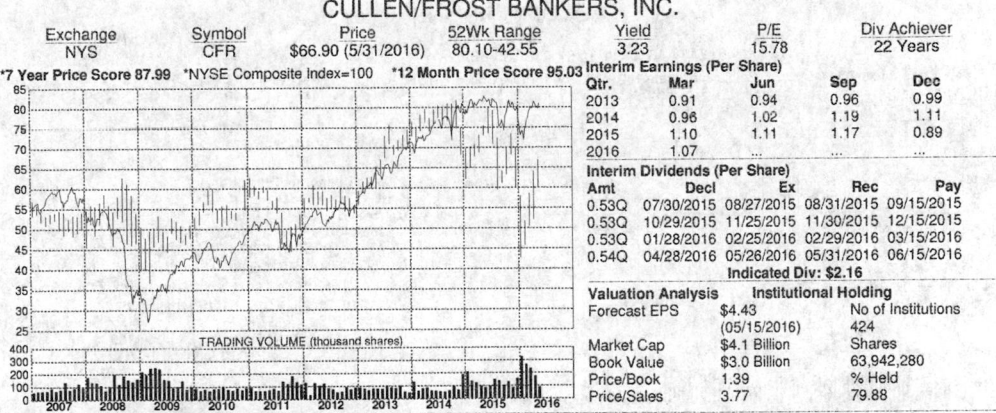

Exchange	Symbol	Price	52Wk Range	Yield	P/E	Div Achiever
NYS	CFR	$66.90 (5/31/2016)	80.10-42.55	3.23	15.78	22 Years

*7 Year Price Score 87.99   *NYSE Composite Index=100   *12 Month Price Score 95.03

Interim Earnings (Per Share)

Qtr.	Mar	Jun	Sep	Dec
2013	0.91	0.94	0.96	0.99
2014	0.96	1.02	1.19	1.11
2015	1.10	1.11	1.17	0.89
2016	1.07	...	...	...

Interim Dividends (Per Share)

Amt	Decl	Ex	Rec	Pay
0.53Q	07/30/2015	08/27/2015	08/31/2015	09/15/2015
0.53Q	10/29/2015	11/25/2015	11/30/2015	12/15/2015
0.53Q	01/28/2016	02/25/2016	02/29/2016	03/15/2016
0.54Q	04/28/2016	05/26/2016	05/31/2016	06/15/2016

Indicated Div: $2.16

Valuation Analysis

		Institutional Holding	
Forecast EPS	$4.43	No of Institutions	
	(05/15/2016)	424	
Market Cap	$4.1 Billion	Shares	
Book Value	$3.0 Billion	63,942,280	
Price/Book	1.39	% Held	
Price/Sales	3.77	79.88	

Business Summary: Banking (MIC: 5.1.1 SIC: 6021 NAIC: 522110)

Cullen/Frost Bankers is a financial holding company and a bank holding company. Through its subsidiaries, Co. provides a range of products and services throughout various Texas markets. In addition to general commercial and consumer banking, other products and services provided include trust and investment management, investment banking, insurance, brokerage, leasing, treasury management and item processing. Co.'s operations are managed along two reportable operating segments consisting of Banking and Frost Wealth Advisors. As of Dec 31 2015, Co. had total assets of $28.57 billion and total deposits of $24.34 billion.

Recent Developments: For the quarter ended Mar 31 2016, net income decreased 4.7% to US$68.8 million from US$72.2 million in the year-earlier quarter. Net interest income increased 5.0% to US$189.7 million from US$180.7 million in the year-earlier quarter. Provision for loan losses was US$28.5 million versus US$8.2 million in the prior-year quarter, an increase of 249.2%. Non-interest income rose 15.5% to US$96.1 million from US$83.2 million, while non-interest expense advanced 4.5% to US$179.2 million.

Prospects: Our evaluation of Cullen/Frost Bankers Inc. as of June 19, 2016 is the result of our systematic analysis on three basic characteristics: earnings strength, relative valuation, and recent stock price movement. The company has managed to produce a neutral trend in earnings per share over the past 5 quarters and while recent estimates for the company have been raised by analysts, CFR has posted better than expected results. Based on operating earnings yield, the company is undervalued when compared to all of the companies in our coverage universe. Share price changes over the past year indicates that CFR will perform poorly over the near term.

Financial Data (US$ in Thousands)	3 Mos	12/31/2015	12/31/2014	12/31/2013	12/31/2012	12/31/2011	12/31/2010	12/31/2009
Earnings Per Share	4.24	4.28	4.29	3.80	3.86	3.54	3.44	3.00
Cash Flow Per Share	7.57	6.27	4.62	2.88	4.88	4.49	7.03	4.61
Tang Book Value Per Share	35.25	33.60	32.32	30.16	30.48	28.48	24.95	22.44
Dividends Per Share	2.120	2.100	2.030	1.980	1.900	1.830	1.780	1.710
Dividend Payout %	50.00	49.07	47.32	52.11	49.22	51.69	51.74	57.00
Income Statement								
Interest Income	192,604	749,496	701,471	642,500	631,612	623,017	617,339	623,036
Interest Expense	2,880	12,864	14,537	21,945	26,751	41,241	53,880	86,357
Net Interest Income	189,724	736,632	686,934	620,555	604,861	581,776	563,459	536,679
Provision for Losses	28,500	51,845	16,314	20,582	10,080	27,445	43,611	65,392
Non-Interest Income	96,143	328,730	320,144	302,818	288,787	290,002	282,033	293,706
Non-Interest Expense	179,159	693,718	654,740	611,910	575,093	558,098	535,541	532,238
Income Before Taxes	78,208	319,799	336,024	290,881	308,475	286,235	266,340	232,755
Income Taxes	9,429	40,471	58,047	53,015	70,523	68,700	57,576	53,721
Net Income	68,779	279,328	277,977	237,866	237,952	217,535	208,764	179,034
Average Shares	62,079	63,473	62,973	61,116	61,643	61,277	60,585	59,513
Balance Sheet								
Net Loans & Leases	11,380,155	11,350,672	10,887,993	9,423,262	9,119,395	7,884,982	7,990,704	8,242,471
Total Assets	28,400,086	28,567,118	28,277,775	24,312,939	23,124,069	20,317,245	17,617,092	16,288,038
Total Deposits	24,156,975	24,343,595	24,135,930	20,688,786	19,497,366	16,756,748	14,479,342	13,313,310
Total Liabilities	25,407,846	25,676,775	25,426,372	21,798,778	20,706,587	18,033,708	15,555,412	14,393,614
Stockholders' Equity	2,992,240	2,890,343	2,851,403	2,514,161	2,417,482	2,283,537	2,061,680	1,894,424
Shares Outstanding	61,984	61,982	63,149	60,566	61,479	61,263	60,909	60,038
Statistical Record								
Return on Assets %	0.98	0.98	1.06	1.00	1.09	1.15	1.23	1.14
Return on Equity %	9.35	9.73	10.36	9.65	10.10	10.01	10.55	9.79
Net Interest Margin %	98.50	98.28	97.93	96.58	95.76	93.38	91.27	86.14
Efficiency Ratio %	62.05	64.34	64.09	64.73	62.48	61.13	59.55	58.06
Loans to Deposits	0.47	0.47	0.45	0.46	0.47	0.47	0.55	0.62
Price Range	80.10-42.55	80.10-59.40	81.67-68.06	75.58-54.27	60.67-53.66	62.57-44.29	62.01-50.00	53.19-36.61
P/E Ratio	18.89-10.04	18.71-13.88	19.04-15.86	19.89-14.28	15.72-13.90	17.68-12.51	18.03-14.53	17.73-12.20
Average Yield %	3.25	3.05	2.66	2.98	3.36	3.36	3.27	3.61

Address: 100 W. Houston Street, San Antonio, TX 78205	**Web Site:** www.frostbank.com	**Auditors:** Ernst & Young LLP
Telephone: 210-220-4011	**Officers:** Richard W. Evans - Chairman, President, Chief Executive Officer Phillip D. Green - Group	**Investor Contact:** 210-220-5632
Fax: 210-220-5578	Executive Vice President, Chief Financial Officer, President	**Transfer Agents:** American Stock Transfer & Trust Company, LLC, Brooklyn, NY

CUMMINS, INC.

Exchange	Symbol	Price	52Wk Range	Yield	P/E	Div Achiever
NYS	CMI	$114.47 (5/31/2016)	137.85-83.52	3.41	15.12	10 Years

*7 Year Price Score 88.89 ***NYSE Composite Index=100** ***12 Month Price Score 101.55**

Interim Earnings (Per Share)

Qtr.	Mar	Jun	Sep	Dec
2013	1.49	2.20	1.90	2.31
2014	1.83	2.43	2.32	2.44
2015	2.14	2.62	2.14	0.94
2016	1.87	...	...	...

Interim Dividends (Per Share)

Amt	Decl	Ex	Rec	Pay
0.975Q	07/14/2015	08/19/2015	08/21/2015	09/01/2015
0.975Q	10/13/2015	11/18/2015	11/20/2015	12/01/2015
0.975Q	02/09/2016	02/17/2016	02/19/2016	03/01/2016
0.975Q	05/10/2016	05/18/2016	05/20/2016	06/01/2016

Indicated Div: $3.90 (Div. Reinv. Plan)

Valuation Analysis / Institutional Holding

Forecast EPS	$7.99 (05/20/2016)	No of Institutions	1100
Market Cap	$19.5 Billion	Shares	169,972,304
Book Value	$6.9 Billion	% Held	76.87
Price/Book	2.82		
Price/Sales	1.04		

Business Summary: Auto Parts (MIC: 1.8.2 SIC: 3519 NAIC: 333618)

Cummins is a diesel engine manufacturer. Co. has four complementary operating segments: Engine, which produces engines and parts for sale to customers in on-highway and various industrial markets; Distribution, which includes wholly-owned and partially-owned distributorships engaged in wholesaling engines, generator sets and service parts, as well as performing service and repair activities on Co.'s products and maintaining relationships with various original equipment manufacturers; Components, which sells filtration products, aftertreatment systems, turbochargers and fuel systems; and Power Generation, which provides power systems and sells engines, generator sets and alternators.

Recent Developments: For the quarter ended Apr 3 2016, net income decreased 17.6% to US$333.0 million from US$404.0 million in the year-earlier quarter. Revenues were US$4.29 billion, down 8.9% from US$4.71 billion the year before. Operating income was US$470.0 million versus US$548.0 million in the prior-year quarter, a decrease of 14.2%. Direct operating expenses declined 7.9% to US$3.24 billion from US$3.51 billion in the comparable period the year before. Indirect operating expenses decreased 9.4% to US$586.0 million from US$647.0 million in the equivalent prior-year period.

Prospects: Our evaluation of Cummins Inc. as of June 19, 2016 is the result of our systematic analysis on three basic characteristics: earnings strength, relative valuation, and recent stock price movement. The company has managed to produce a neutral trend in earnings per share over the past 5 quarters. However, while recent estimates for the company have been mixed, CMI has posted better than expected results. Based on operating earnings yield, the company is undervalued when compared to all of the companies in our coverage universe. Share price changes over the past year indicates that CMI will perform in line with the market over the near term.

Financial Data

(US$ in Thousands)	3 Mos	12/31/2015	12/31/2014	12/31/2013	12/31/2012	12/31/2011	12/31/2010	12/31/2009
Earnings Per Share	7.57	7.84	9.02	7.91	8.67	9.55	5.28	2.16
Cash Flow Per Share	12.51	11.56	12.41	11.17	8.07	10.74	5.11	5.76
Tang Book Value Per Share	35.75	37.65	38.02	35.84	30.50	25.66	20.63	15.80
Dividends Per Share	3.705	3.510	2.810	2.250	1.800	1.325	...	...
Dividend Payout %	48.94	44.77	31.15	28.45	20.76	13.87	...	...
Income Statement								
Total Revenue	4,291,000	19,110,000	19,221,000	17,301,000	17,334,000	18,048,000	13,226,000	10,800,000
EBITDA	481,000	2,485,000	2,826,000	2,451,000	2,565,000	2,945,000	1,884,000	936,000
Depn & Amortn	3,000	419,000	351,000	318,000	287,000	264,000	248,000	269,000
Income Before Taxes	465,000	2,025,000	2,434,000	2,119,000	2,271,000	2,671,000	1,617,000	640,000
Income Taxes	132,000	555,000	698,000	531,000	533,000	725,000	477,000	156,000
Net Income	321,000	1,399,000	1,651,000	1,483,000	1,645,000	1,848,000	1,040,000	428,000
Average Shares	172,000	178,406	183,079	187,417	189,668	193,597	197,148	197,695
Balance Sheet								
Current Assets	7,468,000	7,947,000	9,055,000	8,639,000	7,167,000	7,091,000	6,289,000	5,003,000
Total Assets	14,827,000	15,134,000	15,776,000	14,728,000	12,548,000	11,668,000	10,402,000	8,816,000
Current Liabilities	3,917,000	3,803,000	4,021,000	3,368,000	3,136,000	3,657,000	3,260,000	2,432,000
Long-Term Obligations	1,614,000	1,576,000	1,589,000	1,672,000	698,000	658,000	709,000	637,000
Total Liabilities	7,907,000	7,728,000	8,027,000	7,218,000	5,945,000	6,176,000	5,732,000	5,043,000
Stockholders' Equity	6,920,000	7,406,000	7,749,000	7,510,000	6,603,000	5,492,000	4,670,000	3,773,000
Shares Outstanding	170,400	175,200	182,200	186,700	189,800	192,000	197,800	201,300
Statistical Record								
Return on Assets %	8.72	9.05	10.82	10.87	13.55	16.75	10.82	4.94
Return on Equity %	18.23	18.46	21.64	21.02	27.13	36.37	24.64	12.22
EBITDA Margin %	11.21	13.00	14.70	14.17	14.80	16.32	14.24	8.67
Net Margin %	7.48	7.32	8.59	8.57	9.49	10.24	7.86	3.96
Asset Turnover	1.22	1.24	1.26	1.27	1.43	1.64	1.38	1.25
Current Ratio	1.91	2.09	2.25	2.57	2.29	1.94	1.93	2.06
Debt to Equity	0.23	0.21	0.21	0.22	0.11	0.12	0.15	0.17
Price Range	143.22-83.52	147.85-85.21	160.55-123.70	140.97-103.66	128.00-83.53	120.18-79.91	111.25-45.16	50.55-18.45
P/E Ratio	18.92-11.03	18.86-10.87	17.80-13.71	17.82-13.10	14.76-9.63	12.58-8.37	21.07-8.55	23.40-8.54
Average Yield %	3.24	2.80	1.91	1.95	1.76	1.32	...	...

Address: 500 Jackson Street, P.O. Box 3005, Columbus, IN 47202-3005
Telephone: 812-377-5000
Fax: 812-377-4937

Web Site: www.cummins.com
Officers: Norman Thomas Linebarger - Chairman, President, Chief Executive Officer, Executive Vice President, Vice President, Chief Financial Officer, Chief Operating Officer, Division Officer Richard Joseph Freeland - President, Vice President, Chief Operating Officer, Division Officer

Auditors: PricewaterhouseCoopers LLP
Investor Contact: 812-377-3121
Transfer Agents: Wells Fargo Shareowner Services

CURTISS-WRIGHT CORP.

Exchange	Symbol	Price	52Wk Range	Yield	P/E
NYS	CW	$83.22 (5/31/2016)	83.77-61.97	0.62	24.12

*7 Year Price Score 130.02 *NYSE Composite Index=100 ***12 Month Price Score 109.88**

TRADING VOLUME (thousand shares)

Interim Earnings (Per Share)

Qtr.	Mar	Jun	Sep	Dec
2013	0.44	0.70	0.76	0.98
2014	0.72	0.74	0.51	0.34
2015	0.33	0.53	0.71	1.48
2016	0.73	...	...	...

Interim Dividends (Per Share)

Amt	Decl	Ex	Rec	Pay
0.13Q	09/23/2015	09/30/2015	10/02/2015	10/16/2015
0.13Q	11/12/2015	11/24/2015	11/27/2015	12/11/2015
0.13Q	02/10/2016	03/30/2016	04/01/2016	04/15/2016
0.13Q	05/11/2016	06/21/2016	06/23/2016	07/07/2016

Indicated Div: $0.52

Valuation Analysis / Institutional Holding

Forecast EPS	$4.13
(05/15/2016)	
Market Cap	$3.7 Billion
Book Value	$1.3 Billion
Price/Book	2.88
Price/Sales	1.72

No of Institutions	284
Shares	41,948,568
% Held	79.44

Business Summary: Industrial Machinery & Equipment (MIC: 7.2.1 SIC: 3599 NAIC: 333999)

Curtiss-Wright provides products and services to the commercial, defense, power generation and industrial markets. Co. has three segments: Commercial/Industrial, is primarily engaged with the general industrial and commercial aerospace markets and, the defense and power generation markets; Defense, provides a range of offerings of products including: Commercial Off-the-Shelf embedded computing board level modules, integrated subsystems, flight test equipment, instrumentation and control systems, turret aiming and stabilization products, and weapons handling systems; and Power, is primarily engaged with the nuclear power generation market and, to the naval defense market.

Recent Developments: For the quarter ended Mar 31 2016, income from continuing operations decreased 24.1% to US$32.8 million from US$43.2 million in the year-earlier quarter. Net income increased 105.2% to US$32.8 million from US$16.0 million in the year-earlier quarter. Revenues were US$503.5 million, down 7.8% from US$546.2 million the year before. Operating income was US$57.3 million versus US$72.8 million in the prior-year quarter, a decrease of 21.4%. Direct operating expenses declined 6.6% to US$331.6 million from US$355.1 million in the comparable period the year before. Indirect operating expenses decreased 3.1% to US$114.6 million from US$118.3 million in the equivalent prior-year period.

Prospects: Our evaluation of Curtiss-Wright Corp. as of June 19, 2016 is the result of our systematic analysis on three basic characteristics: earnings strength, relative valuation, and recent stock price movement. The company has generated a negative trend in earnings per share over the past 5 quarters and while recent estimates for the company have been mixed, CW has posted better than expected results. Based on operating earnings yield, the company is about fairly valued when compared to all of the companies in our coverage universe. Share price changes over the past year indicates that CW will perform in line with the market over the near term.

Financial Data

(US$ in Thousands)	3 Mos	12/31/2015	12/31/2014	12/31/2013	12/31/2012	12/31/2011	12/31/2010	12/31/2009
Earnings Per Share	3.45	3.05	2.31	2.88	2.40	2.77	2.30	2.08
Cash Flow Per Share	9.06	3.48	6.91	5.06	3.25	4.36	3.75	4.35
Tang Book Value Per Share	0.05	N.M.	2.73	N.M.	N.M.	4.48	4.91	2.98
Dividends Per Share	0.520	0.520	0.520	0.390	0.350	0.320	0.320	0.320
Dividend Payout %	15.07	17.05	22.51	13.54	14.58	11.55	13.91	15.38
Income Statement								
Total Revenue	503,507	2,205,683	2,243,126	2,510,771	2,097,716	2,054,130	1,893,134	1,809,690
EBITDA	81,984	375,932	349,338	306,573	224,491	265,323	234,302	220,425
Depn & Amortn	24,487	64,700	66,600	71,600	62,800	59,500	53,900	50,100
Income Before Taxes	47,564	275,194	246,944	197,953	135,362	184,989	158,295	145,259
Income Taxes	14,745	82,946	76,995	59,972	43,073	54,566	51,697	50,038
Net Income	32,819	145,461	113,338	137,981	113,844	130,423	106,598	95,221
Average Shares	45,240	47,616	49,075	47,912	47,412	47,013	46,322	45,695
Balance Sheet								
Current Assets	1,260,204	1,316,620	1,571,075	1,337,283	1,175,761	1,167,134	900,027	837,501
Total Assets	2,963,652	3,029,378	3,399,511	3,458,274	3,114,588	2,652,837	2,242,018	2,142,041
Current Liabilities	457,179	525,187	571,993	534,593	639,748	505,384	427,939	524,319
Long-Term Obligations	966,861	953,083	953,279	958,604	751,990	583,928	391,042	384,112
Total Liabilities	1,676,945	1,773,955	1,921,078	1,905,569	1,801,996	1,423,798	1,081,915	1,115,284
Stockholders' Equity	1,286,707	1,255,423	1,478,433	1,552,705	1,312,592	1,229,039	1,160,103	1,026,757
Shares Outstanding	44,599	44,621	47,904	47,638	46,449	46,484	46,133	45,624
Statistical Record								
Return on Assets %	5.33	4.53	3.31	4.20	3.94	5.33	4.86	4.55
Return on Equity %	12.08	10.64	7.48	9.63	8.93	10.92	9.75	10.06
EBITDA Margin %	16.28	17.04	15.57	12.21	10.70	12.92	12.38	12.18
Net Margin %	6.52	6.59	5.05	5.50	5.43	6.35	5.63	5.26
Asset Turnover	0.71	0.69	0.65	0.76	0.73	0.84	0.86	0.87
Current Ratio	2.76	2.51	2.75	2.50	1.84	2.31	2.10	1.60
Debt to Equity	0.75	0.76	0.64	0.62	0.57	0.48	0.34	0.37
Price Range	77.08-61.97	77.08-61.97	73.16-58.77	62.23-31.05	38.82-28.90	38.26-26.16	37.16-26.59	36.38-22.74
P/E Ratio	22.34-17.96	25.27-20.32	31.67-25.44	21.61-10.78	16.18-12.04	13.81-9.44	16.16-11.56	17.49-10.93
Average Yield %	0.75	0.75	0.78	0.95	1.07	0.98	1.01	1.02

Address: 13925 Ballantyne Corporate Place, Suite 400, Charlotte, NC 28277 **Telephone:** 704-869-4600	**Web Site:** www.curtisswright.com **Officers:** Martin R. Benante - Chairman, Chief Executive Officer David C. Adams - President, Chief Executive Officer, Vice President, Co-Chief Operating Officer, Chief Operating Officer	**Auditors:** Deloitte & Touche LLP **Investor Contact:** 973-541-3700 **Transfer Agents:** Broadridge Corporate Issuer Solutions, Inc., Brentwood, NY

CVS HEALTH CORPORATION

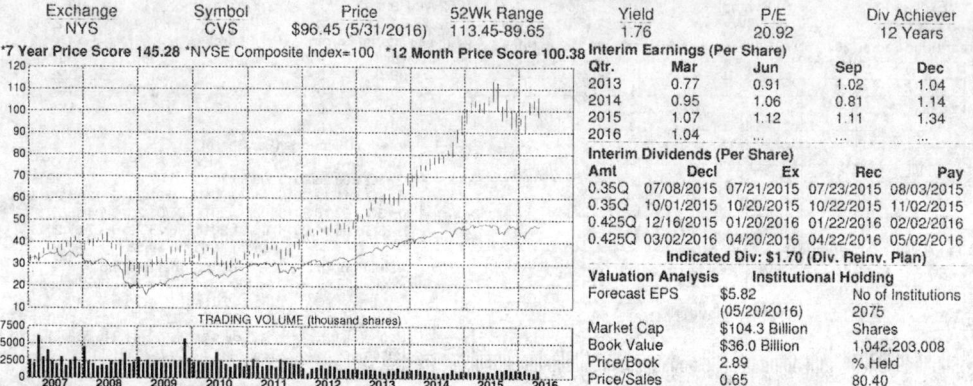

Exchange	Symbol	Price	52Wk Range	Yield	P/E	Div Achiever
NYS	CVS	$96.45 (5/31/2016)	113.45-89.65	1.76	20.92	12 Years

*7 Year Price Score 145.28 *NYSE Composite Index=100 *12 Month Price Score 100.38

Interim Earnings (Per Share)

Qtr.	Mar	Jun	Sep	Dec
2013	0.77	0.91	1.02	1.04
2014	0.95	1.06	0.81	1.14
2015	1.07	1.12	1.11	1.34
2016	1.04	...	...	...

Interim Dividends (Per Share)

Amt	Decl	Ex	Rec	Pay
0.35Q	07/08/2015	07/21/2015	07/23/2015	08/03/2015
0.35Q	10/01/2015	10/20/2015	10/22/2015	11/02/2015
0.425Q	12/16/2015	01/20/2016	01/22/2016	02/02/2016
0.425Q	03/02/2016	04/20/2016	04/22/2016	05/02/2016

Indicated Div: $1.70 (Div. Reinv. Plan)

Valuation Analysis — **Institutional Holding**

Forecast EPS	$5.82 (05/20/2016)	No of Institutions 2075
Market Cap	$104.3 Billion	Shares
Book Value	$36.0 Billion	1,042,203,008
Price/Book	2.89	% Held
Price/Sales	0.65	80.40

Business Summary: Retail - Food & Beverage, Drug & Tobacco (MIC: 2.1.2 SIC: 5912 NAIC: 446110)

CVS Health is a pharmacy health care provider. Co. has three reportable segments: Pharmacy Services, which provides pharmacy benefit management services, and through its SilverScript Insurance Company subsidiary, is a provider of drug benefits to eligible beneficiaries under the federal government's Medicare Part D program; Retail/LTC, which sells prescription drugs and a range of over-the-counter and personal care products, beauty and cosmetic products, and general merchandise (front store products); and Corporate, which provides management and administrative services to support the overall operations of Co.

Recent Developments: For the quarter ended Mar 31 2016, net income decreased 6.1% to US$1.15 billion in the year-earlier quarter. Revenues were US$43.22 billion, up 18.9% from US$36.33 billion the year before. Operating income was US$2.18 billion versus US$2.13 billion in the prior-year quarter, an increase of 2.1%. Direct operating expenses rose 20.9% to US$36.47 billion from US$30.17 billion in the comparable period the year before. Indirect operating expenses increased 13.3% to US$4.57 billion from US$4.03 billion in the equivalent prior-year period.

Prospects: Our evaluation of CVS Health Corp. as of June 19, 2016 is the result of our systematic analysis on three basic characteristics: earnings strength, relative valuation, and recent stock price movement. The company has generated a negative trend in earnings per share over the past 5 quarters and while recent estimates for the company have been raised by analysts, CVS has posted better than expected results. Based on operating earnings yield, the company is undervalued when compared to all of the companies in our coverage universe. Share price changes over the past year indicates that CVS will perform very well over the near term.

Financial Data
(US$ in Thousands)

	3 Mos	12/31/2015	12/31/2014	12/31/2013	12/31/2012	12/31/2011	12/31/2010	12/31/2009
Earnings Per Share	4.61	4.63	3.96	3.74	3.03	2.57	2.49	2.55
Cash Flow Per Share	8.10	7.52	7.01	4.75	5.23	4.38	3.50	2.81
Tang Book Value Per Share	N.M.	N.M.	0.04	1.58	1.26	1.33	1.65	N.M.
Dividends Per Share	1.475	1.400	1.100	0.900	0.650	0.500	0.350	0.305
Dividend Payout %	32.00	30.24	27.78	24.06	21.45	19.46	14.06	11.96
Income Statement								
Total Revenue	43,215,000	153,290,000	139,367,000	126,761,000	123,133,000	107,100,000	96,413,000	98,729,000
EBITDA	2,793,000	10,954,000	9,678,000	9,437,000	8,180,000	7,898,000	7,634,000	7,827,000
Depn & Amortn	617,000	1,500,000	1,400,000	1,400,000	1,300,000	1,568,000	1,469,000	1,389,000
Income Before Taxes	1,893,000	8,616,000	7,678,000	7,528,000	6,323,000	5,746,000	5,629,000	5,913,000
Income Taxes	746,000	3,386,000	3,033,000	2,928,000	2,441,000	2,258,000	2,190,000	2,205,000
Net Income	1,146,000	5,237,000	4,644,000	4,592,000	3,877,000	3,461,000	3,427,000	3,696,000
Average Shares	1,099,000	1,126,000	1,169,000	1,226,000	1,280,000	1,347,000	1,377,000	1,450,000
Balance Sheet								
Current Assets	29,413,000	30,378,000	25,983,000	25,325,000	19,852,000	18,594,000	17,706,000	17,537,000
Total Assets	92,634,000	93,657,000	74,252,000	71,526,000	65,912,000	64,543,000	62,169,000	61,641,000
Current Liabilities	24,537,000	23,169,000	19,027,000	15,425,000	13,790,000	11,956,000	11,070,000	12,300,000
Long-Term Obligations	26,267,000	26,267,000	11,695,000	12,841,000	9,133,000	9,208,000	8,652,000	8,756,000
Total Liabilities	56,609,000	56,461,000	36,294,000	33,588,000	28,208,000	26,492,000	24,469,000	25,873,000
Stockholders' Equity	36,025,000	37,196,000	37,958,000	37,938,000	37,704,000	38,051,000	37,700,000	35,768,000
Shares Outstanding	1,081,000	1,101,000	1,140,000	1,180,000	1,231,000	1,298,000	1,363,000	1,391,000
Statistical Record								
Return on Assets %	6.20	6.24	6.37	6.68	5.93	5.46	5.54	6.03
Return on Equity %	14.14	13.94	12.24	12.14	10.21	9.14	9.33	10.51
EBITDA Margin %	6.46	7.15	6.94	7.44	6.64	7.37	7.92	7.93
Net Margin %	2.65	3.42	3.33	3.62	3.15	3.23	3.55	3.74
Asset Turnover	1.92	1.83	1.91	1.84	1.88	1.69	1.56	1.61
Current Ratio	1.20	1.31	1.37	1.64	1.44	1.56	1.60	1.43
Debt to Equity	0.73	0.71	0.31	0.34	0.24	0.24	0.23	0.24
Price Range	113.45-89.65	113.45-91.56	98.25-65.44	71.58-48.35	49.24-41.46	41.16-32.06	37.37-26.98	38.01-23.98
P/E Ratio	24.61-19.45	24.50-19.78	24.81-16.53	19.14-12.93	16.25-13.68	16.02-12.47	15.01-10.84	14.91-9.40
Average Yield %	1.46	1.38	1.40	1.54	1.43	1.39	1.08	0.97

Address: One CVS Drive, Woonsocket, RI 02895
Telephone: 401-765-1500
Fax: 401-762-2137

Web Site: www.cvshealth.com
Officers: Larry J. Merlo - President, Chief Executive Officer Troyen A. Brennan - Executive Vice President, Chief Medical Officer

Auditors: Ernst & Young LLP
Investor Contact: 800-201-0938
Transfer Agents: Computershare, Providence, RI

DAVITA HEALTHCARE PARTNERS INC

Exchange	Symbol	Price	52Wk Range	Yield	P/E
NYS	DVA	$77.32 (5/31/2016)	83.96-62.24	N/A	34.67

*7 Year Price Score 118.76 *NYSE Composite Index=100 *12 Month Price Score 100.06

Interim Earnings (Per Share)

Qtr.	Mar	Jun	Sep	Dec
2013	0.14	1.19	0.64	0.99
2014	0.85	0.68	0.85	0.95
2015	(0.52)	0.78	1.00	(0.02)
2016	0.47	...	...	...

Interim Dividends (Per Share)

No Dividends Paid

Valuation Analysis		Institutional Holding	
Forecast EPS	$3.98	No of Institutions	
	(05/17/2016)	678	
Market Cap	$16.0 Billion	Shares	
Book Value	$4.7 Billion	186,439,632	
Price/Book	3.39	% Held	
Price/Sales	1.13	84.44	

Business Summary: Diagnostic & Health Related Services (MIC: 4.2.2 SIC: 8092 NAIC: 621492)

DaVita HealthCare Partners operates two primary divisions: Kidney Care, which primarily includes its U.S. dialysis and related lab services providing kidney dialysis services; and HealthCare Partners, which is a patient- and physician-focused health care delivery and management company. As of Dec 31 2015, Co. operated or provided administrative services through a network of 2,251 outpatient dialysis centers in 46 states and the District of Columbia, and acute inpatient dialysis services in approximately 900 hospitals and related laboratory services throughout the U.S.; and operated or provided administrative services to 118 outpatient dialysis centers in 10 countries outside of the U.S.

Recent Developments: For the quarter ended Mar 31 2016, net income amounted to US$138.2 million versus a net loss of US$76.1 million in the year-earlier quarter. Revenues were US$3.58 billion, up 8.9% from US$3.29 billion the year before. Operating income was US$364.9 million versus a loss of US$64.2 million in the prior-year quarter. Direct operating expenses rose 9.3% to US$2.58 billion from US$2.36 billion in the comparable period the year before. Indirect operating expenses decreased 35.9% to US$633.9 million from US$989.5 million in the equivalent prior-year period.

Prospects: Our evaluation of Davita HealthCare Partners Inc. as of June 19, 2016 is the result of our systematic analysis on three basic characteristics: earnings strength, relative valuation, and recent stock price movement. The company has managed to produce a neutral trend in earnings per share over the past 5 quarters. However, while recent estimates for the company have been lowered by analysts, DVA has posted better than expected results. Based on operating earnings yield, the company is undervalued when compared to all of the companies in our coverage universe. Share price changes over the past year indicates that DVA will perform well over the near term.

Financial Data
(US$ in Thousands)

	3 Mos	12/31/2015	12/31/2014	12/31/2013	12/31/2012	12/31/2011	12/31/2010	12/31/2009
Earnings Per Share	2.23	1.25	3.33	2.95	2.73	2.48	1.97	2.03
Cash Flow Per Share	7.71	7.35	6.87	8.45	5.72	6.23	4.14	3.22
Income Statement								
Total Revenue	3,581,136	13,781,837	12,795,106	11,764,050	8,186,280	6,731,806	6,447,391	6,108,800
EBITDA	432,949	1,180,295	1,714,748	1,463,527	1,284,737	1,156,889	954,773	970,297
Depn & Amortn	169,355	475,484	428,309	373,107	299,810	249,060	219,314	214,515
Income Before Taxes	263,594	704,811	1,286,439	1,090,420	984,927	907,829	735,459	755,782
Income Taxes	126,822	295,726	446,343	381,013	359,845	325,292	260,239	278,465
Net Income	97,434	269,732	723,114	633,446	536,017	478,001	405,683	422,684
Average Shares	207,928	216,251	216,927	214,763	195,942	193,064	206,118	208,335
Balance Sheet								
Current Assets	4,199,560	4,503,280	3,876,797	3,472,278	2,878,794	2,281,608	2,622,854	2,302,521
Total Assets	18,514,198	18,514,875	17,942,715	17,098,877	16,018,596	8,892,172	8,114,424	7,558,236
Current Liabilities	2,443,618	2,399,138	2,088,652	2,462,049	2,018,174	1,153,116	924,345	1,046,941
Long-Term Obligations	8,979,855	9,001,308	8,383,280	8,141,231	8,326,534	4,417,624	4,233,850	3,532,217
Total Liabilities	13,810,272	13,644,095	12,772,202	12,666,398	12,255,459	6,751,097	6,136,002	5,423,170
Stockholders' Equity	4,703,926	4,870,780	5,170,513	4,432,479	3,763,137	2,141,075	1,978,422	2,135,066
Shares Outstanding	206,392	209,754	215,640	213,163	210,997	187,282	192,003	206,125
Statistical Record								
Return on Assets %	2.59	1.48	4.13	3.83	4.29	5.62	5.18	5.69
Return on Equity %	9.88	5.37	15.06	15.46	18.11	23.21	19.72	20.68
EBITDA Margin %	12.09	8.56	13.40	12.44	15.69	17.19	14.81	15.88
Net Margin %	2.72	1.96	5.65	5.38	6.55	7.10	6.29	6.92
Asset Turnover	0.76	0.76	0.73	0.71	0.66	0.79	0.82	0.82
Current Ratio	1.72	1.88	1.86	1.41	1.43	1.98	2.84	2.20
Debt to Equity	1.91	1.85	1.62	1.84	2.21	2.06	2.14	1.65
Price Range	84.23-62.24	84.23-67.79	78.07-62.74	65.59-53.76	57.49-38.56	44.68-30.32	37.06-28.41	30.77-21.17
P/E Ratio	37.77-27.91	67.38-54.23	23.44-18.84	22.24-18.22	21.06-14.13	18.02-12.23	18.81-14.42	15.16-10.43

Address: 2000 16th Street, Denver, CO 80202	Web Site: www.davita.com	Auditors: KPMG LLP
Telephone: 303 405-2100	Officers: Kent J. Thiry - Chairman, Co-Chairman, Chief Executive Officer Michael D. Staffieri - Division Officer	Investor Contact: 310-536-2585 Transfer Agents: Computershare

DANA HOLDING CORP

Exchange	Symbol	Price	52Wk Range	Yield	P/E
NYS	DAN	$12.02 (5/31/2016)	22.14-11.03	2.00	13.07

*7 Year Price Score 84.45 *NYSE Composite Index=100 *12 Month Price Score 81.30

Interim Earnings (Per Share)

Qtr.	Mar	Jun	Sep	Dec
2013	0.19	0.44	(1.16)	0.26
2014	0.19	0.49	0.52	0.64
2015	0.38	0.36	0.75	(0.49)
2016	0.30			

Interim Dividends (Per Share)

Amt	Decl	Ex	Rec	Pay
0.06Q	07/29/2015	08/19/2015	08/21/2015	09/11/2015
0.06Q	10/28/2015	11/10/2015	11/13/2015	12/04/2015
0.06Q	02/23/2016	03/09/2016	03/11/2016	04/01/2016
0.06Q	04/28/2016	05/11/2016	05/13/2016	06/03/2016

Indicated Div: $0.24

Valuation Analysis

Forecast EPS	$1.63
	(05/20/2016)
Market Cap	$1.8 Billion
Book Value	$778.0 Million
Price/Book	2.29
Price/Sales	0.30

Institutional Holding

No of Institutions	340
Shares	162,804,256
% Held	N/A

Business Summary: Auto Parts (MIC: 1.8.2 SIC: 3714 NAIC: 336399)

Dana Holding is a holding company that provides driveline, sealing and thermal-management products. Co has four segments: Light Vehicle Driveline Technologies, which provide front and rear axles, drive shafts, differentials, torque couplings and modular assemblies; Commercial Vehicle Driveline Technologies, which provide steer axles, drive axles, drive shafts, and tire inflation systems; Off-Highway Driveline Technologies, which provide front and rear axles, driveshafts, transmissions, torque converters, tire inflation systems, and electronic controls; and Power Technologies, which provide gaskets, cover modules, heat shields, engine sealing systems, cooling, and heat transfer products.

Recent Developments: For the quarter ended Mar 31 2016, net income decreased 35.1% to US$48.0 million from US$74.0 million in the year-earlier quarter. Revenues were US$1.45 billion, down 9.9% from US$1.61 billion the year before. Direct operating expenses declined 9.4% to US$1.25 billion from US$1.38 billion in the comparable period the year before. Indirect operating expenses decreased 6.5% to US$101.0 million from US$108.0 million in the equivalent prior-year period.

Prospects: Our evaluation of Dana Holding Corp. as of June 19, 2016 is the result of our systematic analysis on three basic characteristics: earnings strength, relative valuation, and recent stock price movement. The company has generated a negative trend in earnings per share over the past 5 quarters and while recent estimates for the company have remained steady, DAN has posted results that fell short of analysts expectations. Based on operating earnings yield, the company is undervalued when compared to all of the companies in our coverage universe. Share price changes over the past year indicates that DAN will perform poorly over the near term.

Financial Data

(US$ in Thousands)	3 Mos	12/31/2015	12/31/2014	12/31/2013	12/31/2012	12/31/2011	12/31/2010	12/31/2009
Earnings Per Share	0.92	0.99	1.84	(0.09)	1.40	1.02	(0.16)	(4.19)
Cash Flow Per Share	2.67	2.55	3.23	3.94	2.28	2.52	2.04	1.89
Tang Book Value Per Share	3.88	3.64	4.94	4.16	4.48	3.29	3.24	2.58
Dividends Per Share	0.240	0.230	0.200	0.200	0.200	...	...	...
Dividend Payout %	26.09	23.23	10.87	...	14.29	...	...	...
Income Statement								
Total Revenue	1,449,000	6,060,000	6,617,000	6,769,000	7,224,000	7,592,000	6,109,000	5,228,000
EBITDA	140,000	566,000	576,000	704,000	701,000	655,000	408,000	58,000
Depn & Amortn	44,000	174,000	213,000	262,000	277,000	307,000	314,000	397,000
Income Before Taxes	72,000	292,000	260,000	368,000	364,000	296,000	35,000	(454,000)
Income Taxes	24,000	82,000	(70,000)	119,000	51,000	85,000	31,000	(27,000)
Net Income	45,000	159,000	319,000	244,000	300,000	219,000	10,000	(431,000)
Average Shares	149,900	160,000	173,500	146,400	214,700	215,300	140,800	110,200
Balance Sheet								
Current Assets	2,563,000	2,474,000	2,954,000	3,165,000	2,953,000	3,049,000	2,933,000	2,582,000
Total Assets	4,468,000	4,326,000	4,930,000	5,129,000	5,144,000	5,305,000	5,099,000	5,064,000
Current Liabilities	1,152,000	1,091,000	1,261,000	1,268,000	1,310,000	1,493,000	1,407,000	1,156,000
Long-Term Obligations	1,574,000	1,553,000	1,613,000	1,567,000	803,000	831,000	780,000	969,000
Total Liabilities	3,690,000	3,598,000	3,850,000	3,820,000	3,301,000	3,568,000	3,414,000	3,385,000
Stockholders' Equity	778,000	728,000	1,080,000	1,309,000	1,843,000	1,737,000	1,685,000	1,679,000
Shares Outstanding	148,074	150,068	166,070	145,338	148,264	147,319	144,126	139,414
Statistical Record								
Return on Assets %	3.06	3.44	6.34	4.75	5.73	4.21	0.20	N.M.
Return on Equity %	15.94	17.59	26.71	15.48	16.71	12.80	0.59	N.M.
EBITDA Margin %	9.66	9.34	8.70	10.40	9.70	8.63	6.68	1.11
Net Margin %	3.11	2.62	4.82	3.60	4.15	2.88	0.16	N.M.
Asset Turnover	1.28	1.31	1.32	1.32	1.38	1.46	1.20	0.98
Current Ratio	2.22	2.27	2.34	2.50	2.25	2.04	2.08	2.23
Debt to Equity	2.02	2.13	1.49	1.20	0.44	0.48	0.46	0.58
Price Range	22.14-11.03	23.20-13.11	24.60-17.21	23.32-15.52	16.49-11.31	18.99-9.95	17.65-9.20	10.95-0.20
P/E Ratio	24.07-11.99	23.43-13.24	13.37-9.35	...	11.78-8.08	18.62-9.75	...	...
Average Yield %	1.41	1.20	0.93	1.05	1.44	...	...	...

Address: 3939 Technology Drive, Maumee, OH 43537 **Telephone:** 419-887-3000 **Fax:** 419-887-5200	**Web Site:** www.dana.com **Officers:** James K. Kamsickas - President, Chief Executive Officer Jonathan M. Collins - Senior Vice President, Chief Financial Officer	**Auditors:** PricewaterhouseCoopers LLP **Investor Contact:** 800-537-8823 **Transfer Agents:** Wells Fargo Shareowner Services

DANAHER CORP

Exchange	Symbol	Price	52Wk Range	Yield	P/E
NYS	DHR	$98.36 (5/31/2016)	99.97-82.40	0.65	19.44

*7 Year Price Score 125.81 *NYSE Composite Index=100 *12 Month Price Score 105.21

Interim Earnings (Per Share)

Qtr.	Mar	Jun	Sep	Dec
2013	0.98	0.87	0.84	1.11
2014	0.81	0.95	0.95	0.92
2015	0.79	0.97	2.01	0.99
2016	1.09	...	...	...

Interim Dividends (Per Share)

Amt	Decl	Ex	Rec	Pay
0.135Q	12/08/2015	12/17/2015	12/21/2015	01/29/2016
0.16Q	02/23/2016	03/22/2016	03/24/2016	04/29/2016
0.16Q	05/10/2016	06/01/2016	06/03/2016	07/29/2016

Indicated Div: $0.64

Valuation Analysis — **Institutional Holding**

Forecast EPS	$4.94	No of Institutions
	(05/20/2016)	1415
Market Cap	$67.7 Billion	Shares
Book Value	$24.5 Billion	581,837,184
Price/Book	2.76	% Held
Price/Sales	3.16	77.66

TRADING VOLUME (thousand shares)

Business Summary: Industrial Machinery & Equipment (MIC: 7.2.1 SIC: 3823 NAIC: 334515)

Danaher operates in five segments. The Test & Measurement segment provides products, software and services to measure and monitor physical parameters in industrial applications. The Environmental segment helps protect water supply and facilitate environmental stewardship. The Life Sciences & Diagnostics segment provides research tools that scientists use to study the basic building blocks of life. The Dental segment provides products that are used to diagnose, treat and prevent disease and ailments of the teeth, gums and supporting bone. The Industrial Technologies segment provides solutions that help protect food supply, improve packaging design and verify pharmaceutical dosages.

Recent Developments: For the quarter ended Apr 1 2016, income from continuing operations increased 35.9% to US$758.4 million from US$558.0 million in the year-earlier quarter. Net income increased 33.1% to US$758.4 million from US$569.8 million in the year-earlier quarter. Revenues were US$5.39 billion, up 14.8% from US$4.69 billion the year before. Operating income was US$882.1 million versus US$755.1 million in the prior-year quarter, an increase of 16.8%. Direct operating expenses rose 13.4% to US$2.52 billion from US$2.23 billion in the comparable period the year before. Indirect operating expenses increased 15.6% to US$1.98 billion from US$1.71 billion in the equivalent prior-year period.

Prospects: Our evaluation of Danaher Corp. as of June 19, 2016 is the result of our systematic analysis on three basic characteristics: earnings strength, relative valuation, and recent stock price movement. The company has managed to produce a neutral trend in earnings per share over the past 5 quarters. However, while recent estimates for the company have been lowered by analysts, DHR has posted better than expected results. Based on operating earnings yield, the company is about fairly valued when compared to all of the companies in our coverage universe. Share price changes over the past year indicates that DHR will perform very well over the near term.

Financial Data

(US$ in Thousands)	3 Mos	12/31/2015	12/31/2014	12/31/2013	12/31/2012	12/31/2011	12/31/2010	12/31/2009
Earnings Per Share	5.06	4.74	3.63	3.80	3.36	3.11	2.64	1.73
Cash Flow Per Share	5.88	5.45	5.35	5.15	4.91	3.88	3.19	2.81
Tang Book Value Per Share	N.M.	N.M.	N.M.	0.14	N.M.	N.M.	N.M.	N.M.
Dividends Per Share	0.565	0.540	0.400	0.100	0.100	0.090	0.080	0.065
Dividend Payout %	11.17	11.39	11.02	2.63	2.98	2.89	3.03	3.76
Income Statement								
Total Revenue	5,387,200	20,563,100	19,913,800	19,118,000	18,260,400	16,090,540	13,202,602	11,184,938
EBITDA	1,415,600	4,055,000	4,140,400	4,236,100	3,593,000	2,868,219	2,632,641	1,727,000
Depn & Amortn	310,100	573,500	552,600	529,900	497,800	350,660	197,998	184,524
Income Before Taxes	1,043,800	3,324,000	3,481,800	3,566,000	2,940,900	2,381,069	2,319,937	1,424,854
Income Taxes	285,400	725,300	883,400	871,000	711,500	512,562	549,705	273,150
Net Income	758,400	3,357,400	2,598,400	2,695,000	2,392,200	2,172,264	1,793,000	1,151,704
Average Shares	697,100	708,500	716,100	711,000	713,100	701,191	683,275	671,484
Balance Sheet								
Current Assets	7,747,200	7,836,700	9,431,300	9,113,700	7,587,800	6,272,357	5,729,513	5,220,628
Total Assets	48,385,600	48,222,200	36,991,700	34,672,200	32,941,000	29,949,447	22,217,130	19,595,420
Current Liabilities	5,321,300	6,170,400	5,396,400	4,527,400	4,206,100	4,172,028	3,304,754	2,760,960
Long-Term Obligations	12,194,700	12,025,200	3,401,500	3,436,700	5,287,600	5,206,800	2,783,907	2,889,023
Total Liabilities	23,880,900	24,531,900	13,613,600	12,286,900	13,924,500	13,044,713	8,506,117	7,965,244
Stockholders' Equity	24,504,700	23,690,300	23,378,100	22,385,300	19,016,500	16,904,783	13,711,010	11,630,176
Shares Outstanding	688,600	686,800	704,300	698,100	687,500	687,730	656,360	645,470
Statistical Record								
Return on Assets %	8.40	7.88	7.25	7.97	7.59	8.33	8.58	6.21
Return on Equity %	14.83	14.27	11.36	13.02	13.28	14.19	14.15	10.74
EBITDA Margin %	26.28	19.72	20.79	22.16	19.68	17.83	19.94	15.44
Net Margin %	14.08	16.33	13.05	14.10	13.10	13.50	13.58	10.30
Asset Turnover	0.51	0.48	0.56	0.57	0.58	0.62	0.63	0.60
Current Ratio	1.46	1.27	1.75	2.01	1.80	1.50	1.73	1.89
Debt to Equity	0.50	0.51	0.15	0.15	0.28	0.31	0.20	0.25
Price Range	97.35-81.88	97.35-81.88	87.06-71.70	77.20-55.90	56.83-48.33	55.77-40.42	47.37-35.08	38.05-24.02
P/E Ratio	19.24-16.18	20.54-17.27	23.98-19.75	20.32-14.71	16.91-14.38	17.93-13.00	17.94-13.29	21.99-13.88
Average Yield %	0.64	0.61	0.61	0.52	0.15	0.19	0.18	0.21

Address: 2200 Pennsylvania Avenue, N.W., Suite 800W, Washington, DC 20037-1701	**Web Site:** www.danaher.com	**Auditors:** Ernst & Young LLP
Telephone: 202-828-0850	**Officers:** Steven M. Rales - Chairman Thomas Patrick Joyce - President, Chief Executive Officer, Executive Vice President	**Investor Contact:** 202-828-0850
Fax: 202-828-0860		**Transfer Agents:** Computershare, Providence, RI

DARDEN RESTAURANTS, INC.

Exchange	Symbol	Price	52Wk Range	Yield	P/E
NYS	DRI	$67.83 (5/31/2016)	67.83-53.93	2.95	25.60

*7 Year Price Score 116.11 *NYSE Composite Index=100 *12 Month Price Score 103.53

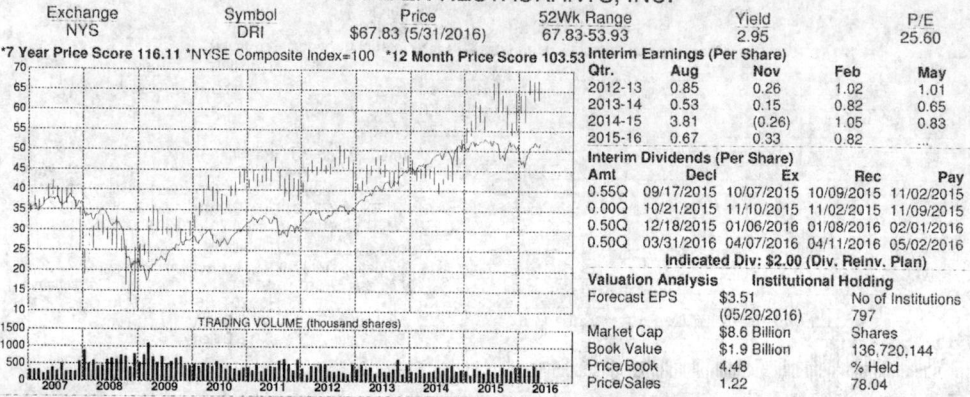

Interim Earnings (Per Share)

Qtr.	Aug	Nov	Feb	May
2012-13	0.85	0.26	1.02	1.01
2013-14	0.53	0.15	0.82	0.65
2014-15	3.81	(0.26)	1.05	0.83
2015-16	0.67	0.33	0.82	

Interim Dividends (Per Share)

Amt	Decl	Ex	Rec	Pay
0.55Q	09/17/2015	10/07/2015	10/09/2015	11/02/2015
0.00Q	10/21/2015	11/02/2015	11/09/2015	
0.50Q	12/18/2015	01/06/2016	01/08/2016	02/01/2016
0.50Q	03/31/2016	04/07/2016	04/11/2016	05/02/2016

Indicated Div: $2.00 (Div. Reinv. Plan)

Valuation Analysis   **Institutional Holding**

Forecast EPS	$3.51	No of Institutions	797
	(05/20/2016)		
Market Cap	$8.6 Billion	Shares	136,720,144
Book Value	$1.9 Billion	% Held	78.04
Price/Book	4.48		
Price/Sales	1.22		

Business Summary: Hotels, Restaurants & Travel (MIC: 2.2.1 SIC: 5812 NAIC: 722110)

Darden Restaurants is a service restaurant company. Co. has four reportable segments: Olive Garden; LongHorn Steakhouse; Fine Dining (which includes The Capital Grille and Eddie V's); and Other Business (which includes Yard House, Seasons 52, Bahama Breeze, consumer-packaged goods and franchise revenues). As of May 31, 2015, Co. owned and operated 1,534 restaurants through subsidiaries in the U.S. and Canada under the Olive Garden®, LongHorn Steakhouse®, The Capital Grille®, Yard House®, Seasons 52®, Bahama Breeze®, and Eddie V's Prime Seafood® and Wildfish Seafood Grille® (collectively Eddie V's) trademarks and Co. also had 34 restaurants operated by independent third parties.

Recent Developments: For the quarter ended Feb 28 2016, income from continuing operations decreased 15.7% to US$108.2 million from US$128.4 million in the year-earlier quarter. Net income decreased 20.9% to US$105.8 million from US$133.8 million in the year-earlier quarter. Revenues were US$1.85 billion, up 6.7% from US$1.73 billion the year before. Operating income was US$221.2 million versus US$170.4 million in the prior-year quarter, an increase of 29.8%. Direct operating expenses rose 5.5% to US$1.42 billion from US$1.34 billion in the comparable period the year before. Indirect operating expenses decreased 3.4% to US$210.8 million from US$218.2 million in the equivalent prior-year period.

Prospects: Our evaluation of Darden Restaurants Inc. as of June 19, 2016 is the result of our systematic analysis on three basic characteristics: earnings strength, relative valuation, and recent stock price movement. The company has generated a negative trend in earnings per share over the past 5 quarters and while recent estimates for the company have been raised by analysts, DRI has posted better than expected results. Based on operating earnings yield, the company is undervalued when compared to all of the companies in our coverage universe. Share price changes over the past year indicates that DRI will perform well over the near term.

Financial Data

(US$ in Thousands)	9 Mos	6 Mos	3 Mos	05/31/2015	05/25/2014	05/26/2013	05/27/2012	05/29/2011
Earnings Per Share	2.65	2.88	2.29	5.47	2.15	3.13	3.57	3.39
Cash Flow Per Share	7.17	6.77	7.34	6.74	4.25	7.38	5.87	6.56
Tang Book Value Per Share	3.72	4.23	7.63	7.00	5.37	3.74	5.97	6.67
Dividends Per Share	2.150	2.200	2.200	2.200	2.200	2.000	1.720	1.280
Dividend Payout %	81.13	76.39	96.07	40.22	102.33	63.90	48.18	37.76
Income Statement								
Total Revenue	5,143,300	3,295,800	1,687,000	6,764,000	6,285,600	8,551,900	7,998,700	7,500,200
EBITDA	440,500	219,000	136,000	695,500	627,100	1,056,100	1,095,400	1,060,800
Depn & Amortn	3,400	3,100	1,800	327,900	318,200	407,800	355,800	319,600
Income Before Taxes	274,300	136,200	111,800	175,300	174,600	522,400	638,000	647,600
Income Taxes	55,000	25,100	30,800	(21,100)	(8,600)	109,800	161,500	168,900
Net Income	235,400	129,600	86,400	709,500	286,200	411,900	475,500	476,300
Average Shares	129,400	129,900	129,300	129,700	133,200	131,600	133,200	140,300
Balance Sheet								
Current Assets	729,900	1,383,500	1,204,600	1,056,400	1,976,400	764,900	757,600	663,800
Total Assets	4,501,900	5,182,300	6,026,500	5,994,700	7,100,700	6,936,900	5,944,200	5,466,600
Current Liabilities	1,201,100	1,815,400	1,142,600	1,196,700	1,618,500	1,416,400	1,774,100	1,286,800
Long-Term Obligations	439,700	439,500	1,437,600	1,452,300	2,533,400	2,548,700	1,508,100	1,463,300
Total Liabilities	2,583,700	3,192,500	3,602,400	3,661,200	4,943,800	4,877,400	4,102,200	3,530,400
Stockholders' Equity	1,918,200	1,989,800	2,424,100	2,333,500	2,156,900	2,059,500	1,842,000	1,936,200
Shares Outstanding	126,725	128,236	128,138	126,700	132,300	130,300	129,000	134,600
Statistical Record								
Return on Assets %	6.49	6.72	4.82	10.66	4.09	6.41	8.36	8.92
Return on Equity %	16.40	18.01	12.86	31.09	13.61	21.17	25.24	24.94
EBITDA Margin %	8.56	6.64	8.06	10.28	9.98	12.35	13.69	14.14
Net Margin %	4.58	3.93	5.12	10.49	4.55	4.82	5.94	6.35
Asset Turnover	1.34	1.26	1.13	1.02	0.90	1.33	1.41	1.40
Current Ratio	0.61	0.76	1.05	0.88	1.22	0.54	0.43	0.52
Debt to Equity	0.23	0.22	0.59	0.62	1.17	1.24	0.82	0.76
Price Range	67.08-53.93	67.08-50.06	67.08-42.16	62.44-39.18	48.94-40.99	51.23-39.79	48.02-37.19	46.59-33.68
P/E Ratio	25.31-20.35	23.29-17.38	29.29-18.41	11.41-7.16	22.76-19.07	16.37-12.71	13.45-10.42	13.74-9.93
Average Yield %	3.56	3.76	3.98	4.41	4.89	4.43	3.99	3.13

Address: 1000 Darden Center Drive, Orlando, FL 32837
Telephone: 407-245-4000

Web Site: www.darden.com
Officers: Charles M. Sonsteby - Chairman Eugene I. Lee - President, Chief Executive Officer, Interim Chief Executive Officer, Division Officer

Auditors: KPMG LLP
Investor Contact: 800-832-7336
Transfer Agents: Wells Fargo Shareowner Services, Mendota Heights, MN

DDR CORP.

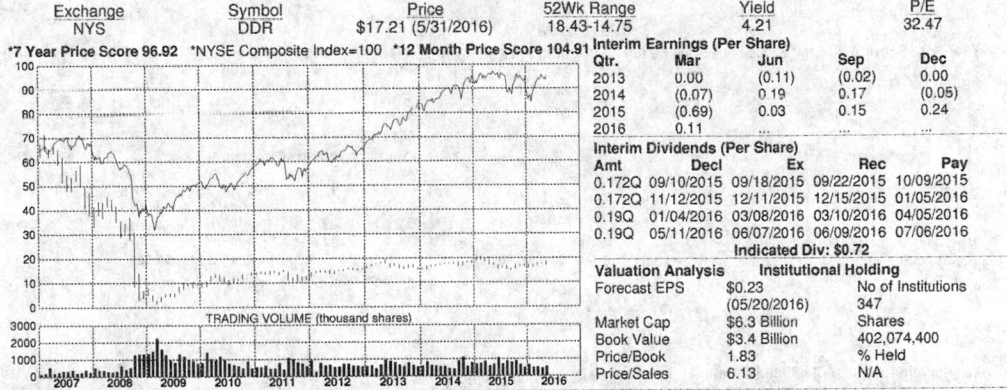

Exchange	Symbol	Price	52Wk Range	Yield	P/E
NYS	DDR	$17.21 (5/31/2016)	18.43-14.75	4.21	32.47

*7 Year Price Score 96.92   *NYSE Composite Index=100   *12 Month Price Score 104.91

Interim Earnings (Per Share)

Qtr.	Mar	Jun	Sep	Dec
2013	0.00	(0.11)	(0.02)	0.00
2014	(0.07)	0.19	0.17	(0.05)
2015	(0.69)	0.03	0.15	0.24
2016	0.11	...	...	...

Interim Dividends (Per Share)

Amt	Decl	Ex	Rec	Pay
0.172Q	09/10/2015	09/18/2015	09/22/2015	10/09/2015
0.172Q	11/12/2015	12/11/2015	12/15/2015	01/05/2016
0.19Q	01/04/2016	03/08/2016	03/10/2016	04/05/2016
0.19Q	05/11/2016	06/07/2016	06/09/2016	07/06/2016

Indicated Div: $0.72

Valuation Analysis		Institutional Holding	
Forecast EPS	$0.23	No of Institutions	
	(05/20/2016)	347	
Market Cap	$6.3 Billion	Shares	
Book Value	$3.4 Billion	402,074,400	
Price/Book	1.83	% Held	
Price/Sales	6.13	N/A	

Business Summary: REITs (MIC: 5.3.1 SIC: 6798 NAIC: 525930)

DDR is a real estate investment trust. Co. owns, develops, redevelops, expands, leases and manages shopping centers. Co. also engages in the origination and acquisition of loans and debt securities, which are collateralized by shopping centers. As of Dec 31 2014, Co.'s portfolio consisted of 415 shopping centers in which it had an economic interest. These properties consist of shopping centers and enclosed malls owned in the U.S. and Puerto Rico. At Dec 31 2014, Co. owned and managed more than 118.0 million total square feet of gross leasable area. Co. also owns more than 1,100 acres of undeveloped land, including interests in land.

Recent Developments: For the quarter ended Mar 31 2016, income from continuing operations was US$33.5 million compared with a loss of US$268.0 million in the year-earlier quarter. Net income amounted to US$45.9 million versus a net loss of US$242.9 million in the year-earlier quarter. Revenues were US$254.4 million, down 1.7% from US$258.8 million the year before. Revenues from property income fell 2.1% to US$240.9 million from US$246.2 million in the corresponding quarter a year earlier.

Prospects: Our evaluation of DDR Corp. as of June 19, 2016 is the result of our systematic analysis on three basic characteristics: earnings strength, relative valuation, and recent stock price movement. The company has generated a negative trend in earnings per share over the past 5 quarters. Because the company lacks sufficient analyst estimate data, we place greater weight on the historical EPS trend as the measure of earnings strength. Based on operating earnings yield, the company is overvalued when compared to all of the companies in our coverage universe. Share price changes over the past year indicates that DDR will perform well over the near term.

Financial Data

(US$ in Thousands)	3 Mos	12/31/2015	12/31/2014	12/31/2013	12/31/2012	12/31/2011	12/31/2010	12/31/2009
Earnings Per Share	0.53	(0.27)	0.25	(0.14)	(0.21)	(0.28)	(1.03)	(2.51)
Cash Flow Per Share	1.24	1.20	1.17	1.15	1.04	1.01	1.14	1.44
Tang Book Value Per Share	7.64	7.67	8.43	8.62	8.93	9.49	9.85	11.34
Dividends Per Share	0.708	0.690	0.620	0.540	0.480	0.220	0.080	0.440
Dividend Payout %	133.49	...	248.00	...	...	...	...	...
Income Statement								
Total Revenue	254,423	1,028,071	985,675	888,788	800,375	771,018	803,069	819,307
EBITDA	69,037	382,693	695,022	542,368	448,625	390,678	348,295	547,011
Depn & Amortn	661	396,730	431,204	338,277	265,195	245,069	240,573	244,861
Income Before Taxes	19,529	(226,551)	42,625	(1,239)	(22,195)	(74,277)	(111,396)	76,316
Income Taxes	458	6,286	1,855	2,713	1,160	1,044	47,992	(691)
Net Income	45,573	(72,168)	117,282	(10,175)	(25,822)	(15,854)	(209,358)	(356,593)
Average Shares	365,042	360,946	358,122	326,426	291,726	271,472	244,712	158,816
Balance Sheet								
Current Assets	202,300	204,143	221,218	327,991	249,778	283,557	267,290	343,651
Total Assets	8,935,627	9,097,088	9,541,895	9,693,073	8,055,837	7,469,425	7,768,090	8,426,606
Current Liabilities	465,033	494,082	509,660	470,520	370,234	286,949	139,807	141,389
Long-Term Obligations	5,031,673	5,139,537	5,234,707	5,294,674	4,319,143	4,104,584	4,302,000	5,178,663
Total Liabilities	5,505,224	5,641,903	5,771,647	5,788,412	4,713,699	4,423,741	4,671,488	5,563,417
Stockholders' Equity	3,430,403	3,455,185	3,770,248	3,904,661	3,342,138	3,045,684	3,096,602	2,863,189
Shares Outstanding	364,448	364,347	359,754	358,348	314,261	276,280	255,555	201,085
Statistical Record								
Return on Assets %	2.39	N.M.	1.22	N.M.	N.M.	N.M.	N.M.	N.M.
Return on Equity %	6.30	N.M.	3.06	N.M.	N.M.	N.M.	N.M.	N.M.
EBITDA Margin %	27.13	37.22	70.51	61.02	56.05	50.67	43.37	66.77
Net Margin %	17.91	N.M.	11.90	N.M.	N.M.	N.M.	N.M.	N.M.
Asset Turnover	0.11	0.11	0.10	0.10	0.10	0.10	0.10	0.09
Current Ratio	0.44	0.41	0.43	0.70	0.67	0.99	1.91	2.43
Debt to Equity	1.47	1.49	1.39	1.36	1.29	1.35	1.39	1.81
Price Range	19.09-14.75	20.36-14.75	18.70-15.06	19.41-14.95	15.86-12.28	15.14-10.17	14.09-8.25	10.45-1.43
P/E Ratio	36.02-27.83	...	74.80-60.24	...	...	...	...	...
Average Yield %	4.26	4.01	3.61	3.21	3.26	1.69	0.69	7.14

Address: 3300 Enterprise Parkway, Beachwood, OH 44122
Telephone: 216-755-5500
Fax: 216-755-1500

Web Site: www.ddr.com
Officers: David J. Oakes - President, Chief Executive Officer, Senior Executive Vice President, Chief Financial Officer, Interim Principal Financial Officer Paul W. Freddo - Senior Executive Vice President

Auditors: PricewaterhouseCoopers LLP
Transfer Agents: Computershare, Providence, RI

DEAN FOODS CO.

Exchange	Symbol	Price	52Wk Range	Yield	P/E
NYS	DF	$18.28 (5/31/2016)	20.96-15.76	1.97	16.18

*7 Year Price Score 102.56 *NYSE Composite Index=100 ***12 Month Price Score 97.11**

Interim Earnings (Per Share)

Qtr.	Mar	Jun	Sep	Dec
2013	5.26	(0.61)	4.35	(0.42)
2014	(0.09)	(0.01)	(0.17)	0.05
2015	(0.78)	0.28	0.22	0.20
2016	0.43			

Interim Dividends (Per Share)

Amt	Decl	Ex	Rec	Pay
0.07Q	08/12/2015	08/20/2015	08/24/2015	09/03/2015
0.07Q	11/11/2015	11/19/2015	11/23/2015	12/03/2015
0.09Q	03/03/2016	03/10/2016	03/14/2016	03/23/2016
0.09Q	05/11/2016	05/19/2016	05/23/2016	06/02/2016

Indicated Div: $0.36

Valuation Analysis

		Institutional Holding	
Forecast EPS	$1.54	No of Institutions	
	(05/20/2016)	405	
Market Cap	$1.7 Billion	Shares	
Book Value	$577.9 Million	132,332,064	
Price/Book	2.90	% Held	
Price/Sales	0.21	N/A	

Business Summary: Food (MIC: 1.2.1 SIC: 2024 NAIC: 311520)

Dean Foods is a food and beverage company and a processor and distributor of fluid milk and other dairy and dairy case products. Co. manufactures, markets and distributes dairy case products, including fluid milk, ice cream, cultured dairy products, creamers, ice cream mix and other dairy products. Co.'s portfolio includes DairyPure®, its white milk brand, and TruMoo®, the flavored milk brand, along with dairy brands such as Alta Dena ®, Berkeley Farms ®, Country Fresh ®, Dean's ®, Garelick Farms ®, LAND O LAKES ® milk and cultured products (licensed brand), Lehigh Valley Dairy Farms ®, Mayfield ®, McArthur ®, Meadow Gold®, Oak Farms ®, PET ® (licensed brand), T.G. Lee ®, Tuscan ® and more.

Recent Developments: For the quarter ended Mar 31 2016, income from continuing operations was US$39.2 million compared with a loss of US$73.7 million in the year-earlier quarter. Net income amounted to US$39.2 million versus a net loss of US$73.7 million in the year-earlier quarter. Revenues were US$1.88 billion, down 8.4% from US$2.05 billion the year before. Operating income was US$78.5 million versus a loss of US$59.2 million in the prior-year quarter. Direct operating expenses declined 12.6% to US$1.37 billion from US$1.57 billion in the comparable period the year before. Indirect operating expenses decreased 20.8% to US$425.5 million from US$537.5 million in the equivalent prior-year period.

Prospects: Our evaluation of Dean Foods Co. as of June 19, 2016 is the result of our systematic analysis on three basic characteristics: earnings strength, relative valuation, and recent stock price movement. The company has generated a negative trend in earnings per share over the past 5 quarters and while recent estimates for the company have been mixed, DF has posted better than expected results. Based on operating earnings yield, the company is undervalued when compared to all of the companies in our coverage universe. Share price changes over the past year indicates that DF will perform very well over the near term.

Financial Data

(US$ in Thousands)	3 Mos	12/31/2015	12/31/2014	12/31/2013	12/31/2012	12/31/2011	12/31/2010	12/31/2009
Earnings Per Share	1.13	(0.09)	(0.22)	8.58	1.70	(17.18)	1.00	2.76
Cash Flow Per Share	3.24	4.37	1.63	(3.38)	4.76	4.90	5.88	7.70
Tang Book Value Per Share	5.35	5.02	5.74	6.62	N.M.	...	N.M.	N.M.
Dividends Per Share	0.300	0.280	0.280	6.62	...	...	...	...
Dividend Payout %	26.55	...	...	...	...	...	...	...
Income Statement								
Total Revenue	1,878,828	8,121,661	9,503,196	9,016,321	11,462,277	13,055,493	12,122,887	11,158,388
EBITDA	85,861	224,856	168,125	649,061	675,077	(1,789,108)	410,818	635,954
Depn & Amortn	6,325	171,353	159,389	165,469	246,583	10,539	11,295	9,637
Income Before Taxes	62,660	(13,310)	(52,283)	283,034	263,922	(2,052,598)	151,222	379,823
Income Taxes	23,459	(5,229)	(32,096)	(42,325)	146,509	(456,811)	73,482	152,065
Net Income	39,201	(8,508)	(20,296)	813,178	158,622	(1,575,621)	91,491	240,308
Average Shares	92,168	93,298	93,916	94,796	93,065	91,694	91,430	86,929
Balance Sheet								
Current Assets	1,046,289	1,077,563	1,180,060	1,150,698	2,202,778	1,716,322	1,816,216	1,628,969
Total Assets	2,452,354	2,528,015	2,769,636	2,802,045	5,687,091	5,754,363	7,956,667	7,843,941
Current Liabilities	668,005	761,895	794,451	781,087	1,340,993	1,495,542	1,440,965	1,478,525
Long-Term Obligations	833,704	840,932	916,481	896,564	3,077,258	3,563,389	3,893,275	3,980,627
Total Liabilities	1,874,406	1,982,511	2,142,318	2,087,730	5,329,904	5,857,761	6,457,142	6,491,995
Stockholders' Equity	577,948	545,504	627,318	714,315	357,187	(103,398)	1,499,525	1,351,946
Shares Outstanding	91,766	91,428	94,080	94,831	92,781	91,872	91,127	90,471
Statistical Record								
Return on Assets %	4.21	N.M.	N.M.	19.16	2.77	N.M.	1.16	3.23
Return on Equity %	18.51	N.M.	N.M.	151.78	124.66	N.M.	6.42	25.16
EBITDA Margin %	4.57	2.77	1.77	7.20	5.89	N.M.	3.39	5.70
Net Margin %	2.09	N.M.	N.M.	9.02	1.38	N.M.	0.75	2.15
Asset Turnover	3.20	3.07	3.41	2.12	2.00	1.90	1.53	1.50
Current Ratio	1.57	1.41	1.49	1.47	1.64	1.15	1.26	1.10
Debt to Equity	1.44	1.54	1.46	1.26	8.62	...	2.60	2.94
Price Range	20.96-15.76	19.56-15.41	19.40-12.70	22.70-14.35	17.48-9.82	12.91-7.41	17.23-6.75	20.39-14.79
P/E Ratio	18.55-13.95	...	...	2.65-1.67	10.28-5.78	...	17.23-6.75	7.39-5.36
Average Yield %	1.68	1.61	1.78	...	...	...	...	...

Address: 2711 North Haskell Avenue, Suite 3400, Dallas, TX 75204 Telephone: 214-303-3400	Web Site: www.deanfoods.com Officers: Tom C. Davis - Chairman Gregg A. Tanner - Chief Executive Officer, Executive Vice President, Chief Supply Chain Officer	Auditors: Deloitte & Touche LLP Investor Contact: 214-303-3400 Transfer Agents: Computershare Shareowner Services LLC, Providence, RI

DECKERS OUTDOOR CORP.

Exchange	Symbol	Price	52Wk Range	Yield	P/E
NYS	DECK	$52.59 (5/31/2016)	76.14-42.27	N/A	14.21

*7 Year Price Score 78.34   *NYSE Composite Index=100   *12 Month Price Score 94.78

TRADING VOLUME (thousand shares)

Interim Earnings (Per Share)

Qtr.	Jun	Sep	Dec	Mar
2014-15	(1.07)	1.17	4.50	0.07
2015-16	(1.43)	1.11	4.78	(0.70)

Interim Dividends (Per Share)

No Dividends Paid

Valuation Analysis   Institutional Holding

Forecast EPS	$4.24	No of Institutions
	(05/20/2016)	386
Market Cap	$1.7 Billion	Shares
Book Value	$967.5 Million	36,767,232
Price/Book	1.74	% Held
Price/Sales	0.90	109.11

Business Summary: Apparel, Footwear & Accessories (MIC: 1.4.2 SIC: 3021 NAIC: 316211)

Deckers Outdoor is engaged in designing, marketing and distributing footwear, apparel, and accessories developed for both everyday casual lifestyle use and for other activities. Co. markets its products under: UGG®, a brand in footwear, handbags, apparel, and cold weather accessories; Teva®, which includes outdoors footwear; and Sanuk®, which is Co.'s casual footwear. Co.'s other brands include: Hoka One One® (Hoka), a line of footwear; Ahnu®, a line of outdoor and yoga footwear; and Koolaburra® by UGG (Koolaburra), a line of fashion casual footwear using sheepskin and other plush materials. At Mar 31 2016, Co. had a total of 153 retail stores worldwide.

Recent Developments: For the year ended Mar 31 2016, net income decreased 24.4% to US$122.3 million from US$161.8 million in the prior year. Revenues were US$1.88 billion, up 3.2% from US$1.82 billion the year before. Operating income was US$162.1 million versus US$224.4 million in the prior year, a decrease of 27.8%. Direct operating expenses rose 9.5% to US$1.03 billion from US$938.9 million in the comparable period the year before. Indirect operating expenses increased 4.7% to US$684.5 million from US$653.7 million in the equivalent prior-year period.

Prospects: Our evaluation of Deckers Outdoor Corp. as of June 19, 2016 is the result of our systematic analysis on three basic characteristics: earnings strength, relative valuation, and recent stock price movement. The company has generated a negative trend in earnings per share over the past 5 quarters. However, while recent estimates for the company have been lowered by analysts, DECK has posted better than expected results. Based on operating earnings yield, the company is undervalued when compared to all of the companies in our coverage universe. Share price changes over the past year indicates that DECK will perform very poorly over the near term.

Financial Data

(US$ in Thousands)	03/31/2016	03/31/2015	03/31/2014	12/31/2013	12/31/2012	12/31/2011	12/31/2010	12/31/2009
Earnings Per Share	3.70	4.66	4.06	4.18	3.45	5.07	4.03	2.96
Cash Flow Per Share	3.85	4.93	...	7.60	4.43	0.78	3.62	4.75
Tang Book Value Per Share	23.63	21.67	...	19.24	14.95	16.06	16.28	12.11
Income Statement								
Total Revenue	1,875,197	1,817,057	294,716	1,556,618	1,414,398	1,377,283	1,000,989	813,177
EBITDA	212,303	274,445	10,278	250,051	221,108	314,308	262,724	191,532
Depn & Amortn	50,024	49,293	10,569	41,439	33,367	28,977	12,283	10,194
Income Before Taxes	156,885	221,139	(742)	205,557	184,118	285,262	250,109	183,223
Income Taxes	34,620	59,359	1,943	59,868	55,104	83,404	89,732	66,304
Net Income	122,265	161,780	(2,685)	145,689	128,866	199,052	158,235	116,786
Average Shares	33,039	34,733	34,621	34,829	37,334	39,265	39,292	39,393
Balance Sheet								
Current Assets	785,765	686,593	623,862	829,304	691,586	817,902	715,732	520,987
Total Assets	1,278,068	1,169,933	1,064,204	1,259,729	1,068,064	1,146,196	808,994	599,043
Current Liabilities	238,498	167,542	122,215	320,518	267,017	232,079	144,863	100,870
Long-Term Obligations	32,631	33,154	...	...	...	...	...	...
Total Liabilities	310,597	232,921	175,355	371,610	329,263	310,260	156,007	107,685
Stockholders' Equity	967,471	937,012	888,849	888,119	738,801	835,936	652,987	491,358
Shares Outstanding	32,020	33,292	34,624	34,618	34,400	38,692	38,581	38,604
Statistical Record								
Return on Assets %	9.96	14.48	N.M.	12.52	11.61	20.36	22.48	21.57
Return on Equity %	12.80	17.72	N.M.	17.91	16.32	26.74	27.66	26.68
EBITDA Margin %	11.32	15.10	3.49	16.06	15.63	22.82	26.25	23.55
Net Margin %	6.52	8.90	N.M.	9.36	9.11	14.45	15.81	14.36
Asset Turnover	1.53	1.63	1.03	1.34	1.27	1.41	1.42	1.50
Current Ratio	3.29	4.10	5.10	2.59	2.59	3.52	4.94	5.16
Debt to Equity	0.03	0.04	...	...	...	...	...	...
Price Range	76.58-42.27	99.38-66.05	88.56-72.86	86.09-36.12	90.21-28.63	117.66-72.38	87.02-31.53	34.62-12.57
P/E Ratio	20.70-11.42	21.33-14.17	21.82-17.95	20.60-8.64	26.15-8.30	23.21-14.28	21.59-7.82	11.70-4.25

Address: 250 Coromar Drive, Goleta, CA 93117	**Web Site:** www.deckers.com	**Auditors:** KPMG LLP
Telephone: 805-967-7611	**Officers:** Angel R. Martinez - Chairman, President, Chief Executive Officer Thomas A. George - Chief Financial Officer, Principal Financial Officer, Principal Accounting Officer	**Investor Contact:** 203-.68-2.8200
		Transfer Agents: Mellon Investor Services LLC, South Hackensack, NJ

DEERE & CO.

Exchange	Symbol	Price	52Wk Range	Yield	P/E	Div Achiever
NYS	DE	$82.29 (5/31/2016)	97.33-71.78	2.92	16.49	12 Years

*7 Year Price Score 89.19   *NYSE Composite Index=100   *12 Month Price Score 97.50

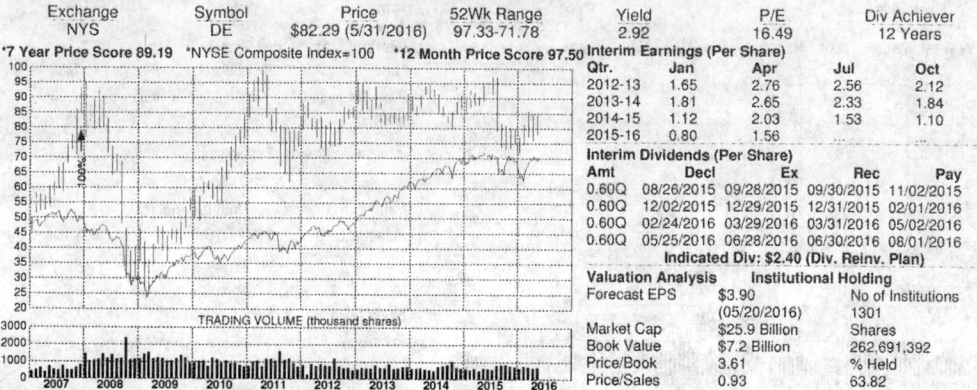

Interim Earnings (Per Share)

Qtr.	Jan	Apr	Jul	Oct
2012-13	1.65	2.76	2.56	2.12
2013-14	1.81	2.65	2.33	1.84
2014-15	1.12	2.03	1.53	1.10
2015-16	0.80	1.56		

Interim Dividends (Per Share)

Amt	Decl	Ex	Rec	Pay
0.60Q	08/26/2015	09/28/2015	09/30/2015	11/02/2015
0.60Q	12/02/2015	12/29/2015	12/31/2015	02/01/2016
0.60Q	02/24/2016	03/29/2016	03/31/2016	05/02/2016
0.60Q	05/25/2016	06/28/2016	06/30/2016	08/01/2016

Indicated Div: $2.40 (Div. Reinv. Plan)

Valuation Analysis		Institutional Holding	
Forecast EPS	$3.90	No of Institutions	1301
	(05/20/2016)		
Market Cap	$25.9 Billion	Shares	262,691,392
Book Value	$7.2 Billion		
Price/Book	3.61	% Held	63.82
Price/Sales	0.93		

Business Summary: Industrial Machinery & Equipment (MIC: 7.2.1 SIC: 3523 NAIC: 332212)

Deere & Company operates in three business segments. The agriculture and turf segment primarily manufactures and distributes a line of agriculture and turf equipment and related service parts, including loaders; combines, and corn pickers among others. The construction and forestry segment primarily manufactures and distributes a range of machines and service parts used in construction, earthmoving, material handling and timber harvesting, including backhoe loaders; crawler dozers and loaders; and excavators among others. The financial services segment primarily finances sales and leases by Co.'s dealers of new and used agriculture and turf equipment and construction and forestry equipment.

Recent Developments:
For the quarter ended Apr 30 2016, net income decreased 28.4% to US$494.7 million from US$690.8 million in the year-earlier quarter. Revenues were US$7.88 billion, down 3.6% from US$8.17 billion the year before. Direct operating expenses declined 2.9% to US$5.53 billion from US$5.69 billion in the comparable period the year before. Indirect operating expenses increased 10.4% to US$1.61 billion from US$1.46 billion in the equivalent prior-year period.

Prospects:
Our evaluation of Deere & Co. as of June 19, 2016 is the result of our systematic analysis on three basic characteristics: earnings strength, relative valuation, and recent stock price movement. The company has managed to produce a neutral trend in earnings per share over the past 5 quarters. However, while recent estimates for the company have been lowered by analysts, DE has posted better than expected results. Based on operating earnings yield, the company is undervalued when compared to all of the companies in our coverage universe. Share price changes over the past year indicates that DE will perform in line with the market over the near term.

Financial Data

(US$ in Thousands)	6 Mos	3 Mos	10/31/2015	10/31/2014	10/31/2013	10/31/2012	10/31/2011	10/31/2010
Earnings Per Share	4.99	5.46	5.77	8.63	9.09	7.63	6.63	4.35
Cash Flow Per Share	11.37	10.98	11.21	9.71	8.45	2.93	5.57	5.38
Tang Book Value Per Share	19.76	18.43	18.80	23.74	25.00	15.00	13.97	12.26
Dividends Per Share	2.400	2.400	2.400	2.220	1.990	1.790	1.520	1.160
Dividend Payout %	48.10	43.96	41.59	25.72	21.89	23.46	22.93	26.67
Income Statement								
Total Revenue	13,399,900	5,524,500	28,862,800	36,066,900	37,795,400	36,157,100	32,012,500	26,004,600
EBITDA	2,210,600	898,600	4,152,100	6,157,400	6,861,700	6,072,200	5,498,200	4,376,600
Depn & Amortn	761,800	374,200	692,000	696,000	637,000	555,000	516,000	540,000
Income Before Taxes	1,084,500	351,200	2,780,100	4,797,400	5,483,400	4,734,400	4,222,800	3,025,200
Income Taxes	333,300	95,500	840,100	1,626,500	1,945,900	1,659,400	1,423,600	1,161,600
Net Income	749,800	254,400	1,940,000	3,161,700	3,537,300	3,064,700	2,799,900	1,865,000
Average Shares	316,500	317,600	336,000	366,100	389,200	401,500	422,400	428,600
Balance Sheet								
Current Assets	14,526,100	12,709,400	12,492,000	14,019,600	15,316,900	16,942,400	13,478,600	11,510,500
Total Assets	59,183,300	56,036,200	57,947,600	61,336,400	59,521,300	56,265,800	48,207,400	43,266,800
Current Liabilities	20,308,100	17,981,000	20,408,600	21,232,500	21,979,000	19,092,000	17,552,100	14,220,500
Long-Term Obligations	24,648,000	24,533,200	23,833,000	24,381,000	21,578,000	22,453,000	16,960,000	16,815,000
Total Liabilities	52,019,000	49,446,000	51,204,200	52,273,800	49,255,500	49,423,700	41,407,100	36,976,500
Stockholders' Equity	7,164,300	6,590,200	6,743,400	9,062,600	10,265,800	6,842,100	6,800,300	6,290,300
Shares Outstanding	314,258	315,325	316,687	345,504	373,802	387,805	406,069	422,180
Statistical Record								
Return on Assets %	2.72	3.16	3.25	5.23	6.11	5.85	6.12	4.42
Return on Equity %	21.03	24.37	24.55	32.72	41.35	44.81	42.78	33.58
EBITDA Margin %	16.50	16.27	14.39	17.07	18.15	16.79	17.18	16.83
Net Margin %	5.60	4.60	6.72	8.77	9.36	8.48	8.75	7.17
Asset Turnover	0.47	0.49	0.48	0.60	0.65	0.69	0.70	0.62
Current Ratio	0.72	0.71	0.61	0.66	0.70	0.89	0.77	0.81
Debt to Equity	3.44	3.72	3.53	2.69	2.10	3.28	2.49	2.67
Price Range	97.33-71.78	97.33-71.78	97.33-72.89	94.53-80.01	95.05-80.90	88.40-70.59	99.24-61.72	77.25-46.30
P/E Ratio	19.51-14.38	17.83-13.15	16.87-12.63	10.95-9.27	10.46-8.90	11.59-9.25	14.97-9.31	17.76-10.64
Average Yield %	2.89	2.81	2.73	2.54	2.31	2.26	1.83	1.93

Address: One John Deere Place,	Web Site: www.johndeere.com	Auditors: Deloitte & Touche LLP
Moline, IL 61265	Officers: Samuel R. Allen - Chairman, President,	Investor Contact: 309-765-4491
Telephone: 309-765-8000	Chief Executive Officer, Chief Operating Officer,	Transfer Agents: ComputerShare,
Fax: 309-765-9929	Division Officer Max A. Guinn - President, Senior	College Station, TX
	Vice President	

DELPHI AUTOMOTIVE PLC

Exchange	Symbol	Price	52Wk Range	Yield	P/E
NYS	DLPH	$67.96 (5/31/2016)	89.16-57.01	1.71	11.56

*7 Year Price Score N/A   *NYSE Composite Index=100   *12 Month Price Score 92.73

Interim Earnings (Per Share)

Qtr.	Mar	Jun	Sep	Dec
2013	0.88	1.17	0.87	0.97
2014	1.04	1.28	1.02	1.16
2015	0.72	2.23	1.42	0.70
2016	1.53	...	...	...

Interim Dividends (Per Share)

Amt	Decl	Ex	Rec	Pay
0.25Q	07/23/2015	08/10/2015	08/12/2015	08/26/2015
0.25Q	10/22/2015	11/09/2015	11/12/2015	11/25/2015
0.29Q	01/12/2016	02/12/2016	02/17/2016	02/29/2016
0.29Q	04/28/2016	05/09/2016	05/11/2016	05/25/2016

Indicated Div: $1.16

Valuation Analysis

		Institutional Holding	
Forecast EPS	N/A	No of Institutions	605
Market Cap	$18.6 Billion	Shares	265,205,152
Book Value	$2.3 Billion	% Held	88.32
Price/Book	8.21		
Price/Sales	1.21		

TRADING VOLUME (thousand shares)

Business Summary: Auto Parts (MIC: 1.8.2 SIC: 3714 NAIC: 336399)

Delphi Automotive is a vehicle components manufacturer. Co.'s business is organized into three segments: Electrical/Electronic Architecture, which provides vehicle's electrical architectures, such as connectors, wiring assemblies and harnesses, electrical centers, and hybrid high voltage and safety distribution systems; Powertrain Systems, which provides products for engine management systems and supplies fuel handling systems for gasoline, diesel, flexfuel and biodiesel configurations; and Electronics and Safety, which provides a range of electronic and safety equipment and software in the areas of controls, security, infotainment, communications, safety systems and power electronics.

Recent Developments: For the quarter ended Mar 31 2016, income from continuing operations increased 10.2% to US$335.0 million from US$304.0 million in the year-earlier quarter. Net income increased 93.4% to US$443.0 million from US$229.0 million in the year-earlier quarter. Revenues were US$4.05 billion, up 6.7% from US$3.80 billion the year before. Operating income was US$441.0 million versus US$446.0 million in the prior-year quarter, a decrease of 1.1%. Direct operating expenses rose 6.8% to US$3.27 billion from US$3.06 billion in the comparable period the year before. Indirect operating expenses increased 16.9% to US$345.0 million in the equivalent prior-year period.

Prospects: Our evaluation of Delphi Automotive PLC as of July 26, 2015 is the result of our systematic analysis on three basic characteristics: earnings strength, relative valuation, and recent stock price movement. The company has managed to produce a neutral trend in earnings per share over the past 5 quarters. However, while recent estimates for the company have been lowered by analysts, DLPH has posted better than expected results. Based on operating earnings yield, the company is undervalued when compared to all of the companies in our coverage universe. Share price changes over the past year indicates that DLPH will perform very well over the near term.

Financial Data

(US$ in Millions)	3 Mos	12/31/2015	12/31/2014	12/31/2013	12/31/2012	12/31/2011	12/31/2010	12/31/2009
Earnings Per Share	5.88	5.06	4.48	3.89	3.33	2.72	...	...
Cash Flow Per Share	6.64	5.97	7.11	5.63	4.56	3.27	...	...
Tang Book Value Per Share	N.M.	N.M.	3.80	5.52	3.39	3.33	...	...
Dividends Per Share	1.040	1.000	1.000	0.680	...	...	...	...
Dividend Payout %	17.69	19.76	22.32	17.48	...	...	...	...
Income Statement								
Total Revenue	4,051	15,165	17,023	16,463	15,519	16,041	13,817	3,421
EBITDA	609	2,077	2,316	2,088	1,866	1,994	1,296	91
Depn & Amortn	165	447	486	436	402	396	351	123
Income Before Taxes	404	1,508	1,705	1,523	1,345	1,506	944	(35)
Income Taxes	75	263	282	256	212	305	258	(27)
Net Income	425	1,450	1,351	1,212	1,077	1,145	631	(18)
Average Shares	277	286	301	311	323	421	...	...
Balance Sheet								
Current Assets	5,082	5,121	5,224	5,752	5,227	5,501	7,666	6,835
Total Assets	12,071	11,973	10,746	11,047	10,176	9,128	11,082	10,307
Current Liabilities	4,061	3,927	3,889	3,894	3,659	3,712	3,719	3,426
Long-Term Obligations	3,985	3,956	2,417	2,351	2,324	1,996	71	94
Total Liabilities	9,806	9,723	8,236	8,136	7,831	7,440	5,441	5,369
Stockholders' Equity	2,265	2,250	2,510	2,911	2,345	1,688	5,641	4,938
Shares Outstanding	273	278	291	306	315	328	...	...
Statistical Record								
Return on Assets %	14.79	12.76	12.40	11.42	11.13	11.33	5.90	...
Return on Equity %	75.38	60.92	49.84	46.12	53.26	31.25	11.93	...
EBITDA Margin %	15.03	13.70	13.61	12.68	12.02	12.43	9.38	2.66
Net Margin %	10.49	9.56	7.94	7.36	6.94	7.14	4.57	N.M.
Asset Turnover	1.37	1.34	1.56	1.55	1.60	1.59	1.29	...
Current Ratio	1.25	1.30	1.34	1.48	1.43	1.48	2.06	2.00
Debt to Equity	1.76	1.76	0.96	0.81	0.99	1.18	0.01	0.02
Price Range	89.16-57.01	89.16-66.59	74.14-58.30	60.13-37.62	38.25-22.14	22.13-19.63	...	...
P/E Ratio	15.16-9.70	17.62-13.16	16.55-13.01	15.46-9.67	11.49-6.65	8.14-7.22	...	...
Average Yield %	1.32	1.24	1.49	1.35	...	...	...	...

Address: Courtney Road, Hoath Way, Gillingham, ME8 0RU	**Web Site:** www.delphi.com	**Auditors:** Ernst & Young LLP
Telephone: 441-634-234422	**Officers:** Rajiv L. Gupta - Chairman Kevin P. Clark - President, Chief Executive Officer, Executive Vice President, Senior Vice President, Chief Operating Officer, Chief Financial Officer	**Investor Contact:** 248-813-2494
		Transfer Agents: Computershare Trust Company, N.A., Providence

DELTA AIR LINES, INC. (DE)

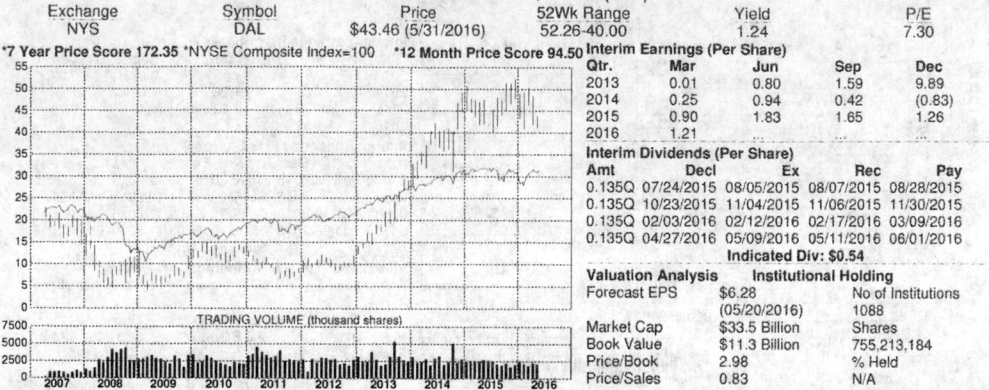

Exchange	Symbol	Price	52Wk Range	Yield	P/E
NYS	DAL	$43.46 (5/31/2016)	52.26-40.00	1.24	7.30

*7 Year Price Score 172.35 *NYSE Composite Index=100   *12 Month Price Score 94.50

Interim Earnings (Per Share)

Qtr.	Mar	Jun	Sep	Dec
2013	0.01	0.80	1.59	9.89
2014	0.25	0.94	0.42	(0.83)
2015	0.90	1.83	1.65	1.26
2016	1.21			

Interim Dividends (Per Share)

Amt	Decl	Ex	Rec	Pay
0.135Q	07/24/2015	08/05/2015	08/07/2015	08/28/2015
0.135Q	10/23/2015	11/04/2015	11/06/2015	11/30/2015
0.135Q	02/03/2016	02/12/2016	02/17/2016	03/09/2016
0.135Q	04/27/2016	05/09/2016	05/11/2016	06/01/2016

Indicated Div: $0.54

Valuation Analysis

Forecast EPS	$6.28	No of Institutions	
	(05/20/2016)	1088	
Market Cap	$33.5 Billion	Shares	
Book Value	$11.3 Billion	755,213,184	
Price/Book	2.98	% Held	
Price/Sales	0.83	N/A	

Institutional Holding

Business Summary: Airlines/Air Freight (MIC: 7.4.4 SIC: 4512 NAIC: 481111)

Delta Air Lines provides scheduled air transportation for passengers and cargo in the U.S. and around the world. Co.'s route network is centered around a system of hub and international gateway airports that it operates in Amsterdam, Atlanta, Boston, Detroit, London-Heathrow, Los Angeles, Minneapolis-St. Paul, New York-LaGuardia, New York-JFK, Paris-Charles de Gaulle, Salt Lake City, Seattle and Tokyo-Narita. Each of these operations includes flights that gather and distribute traffic from markets in the geographic region surrounding the hub or gateway to domestic and international cities and to other hubs or gateways. Co.'s network is supported by a fleet of aircraft varied in size.

Recent Developments: For the quarter ended Mar 31 2016, net income increased 26.8% to US$946.0 million from US$746.0 million in the year-earlier quarter. Revenues were US$9.25 billion, down 1.5% from US$9.39 billion the year before. Operating income was US$1.54 billion versus US$1.40 billion in the prior-year quarter, an increase of 10.2%. Direct operating expenses declined 14.6% to US$3.76 billion from US$4.40 billion in the comparable period the year before. Indirect operating expenses increased 10.2% to US$3.95 billion from US$3.59 billion in the equivalent prior-year period.

Prospects: Our evaluation of Delta Air Lines Inc. as of June 19, 2016 is the result of our systematic analysis on three basic characteristics: earnings strength, relative valuation, and recent stock price movement. The company has produced a positive trend in earnings per share over the past 5 quarters. However, while recent estimates for the company have been lowered by analysts, DAL has posted better than expected results. Based on operating earnings yield, the company is undervalued when compared to all of the companies in our coverage universe. Share price changes over the past year indicates that DAL will perform very well over the near term.

Financial Data

(US$ in Thousands)	3 Mos	12/31/2015	12/31/2014	12/31/2013	12/31/2012	12/31/2011	12/31/2010	12/31/2009
Earnings Per Share	5.95	5.63	0.78	12.29	1.19	1.01	0.70	(1.50)
Cash Flow Per Share	9.43	9.95	5.92	5.31	2.92	3.38	3.40	1.67
Dividends Per Share	0.495	0.450	0.300	0.120	...	...	...	...
Dividend Payout %	8.32	7.99	38.46	0.98	...	...	...	...
Income Statement								
Total Revenue	9,251,000	40,704,000	40,362,000	37,773,000	36,670,000	35,115,000	31,755,000	28,063,000
EBITDA	2,027,000	9,438,000	3,422,000	4,779,000	3,430,000	3,263,000	3,520,000	1,576,000
Depn & Amortn	486,000	1,800,000	1,700,000	1,400,000	1,400,000	1,400,000	1,727,000	1,906,000
Income Before Taxes	1,434,000	7,157,000	1,072,000	2,527,000	1,025,000	769,000	608,000	(1,581,000)
Income Taxes	488,000	2,631,000	413,000	(8,013,000)	16,000	(85,000)	15,000	(344,000)
Net Income	946,000	4,526,000	659,000	10,540,000	1,009,000	854,000	593,000	(1,237,000)
Average Shares	780,000	804,000	845,000	858,000	850,000	844,000	843,000	827,000
Balance Sheet								
Current Assets	9,306,000	9,056,000	12,465,000	9,651,000	8,272,000	7,729,000	7,307,000	7,741,000
Total Assets	53,342,000	53,134,000	54,121,000	52,252,000	44,550,000	43,499,000	43,188,000	43,539,000
Current Liabilities	18,108,000	17,526,000	16,879,000	14,152,000	13,270,000	12,701,000	11,385,000	9,797,000
Long-Term Obligations	6,920,000	6,766,000	8,561,000	9,795,000	11,082,000	11,847,000	13,179,000	15,665,000
Total Liabilities	42,090,000	42,284,000	45,308,000	40,609,000	46,681,000	44,895,000	42,291,000	43,294,000
Stockholders' Equity	11,252,000	10,850,000	8,813,000	11,643,000	(2,131,000)	(1,396,000)	897,000	245,000
Shares Outstanding	771,581	778,783	825,258	851,443	851,402	845,245	834,723	783,954
Statistical Record								
Return on Assets %	8.83	8.44	1.24	21.78	2.29	1.97	1.37	N.M.
Return on Equity %	46.57	46.04	6.44	221.61	...	...	103.85	N.M.
EBITDA Margin %	21.91	23.19	8.48	12.65	9.35	9.29	11.08	5.62
Net Margin %	10.23	11.12	1.63	27.90	2.75	2.43	1.87	N.M.
Asset Turnover	0.76	0.76	0.76	0.78	0.83	0.81	0.73	0.63
Current Ratio	0.51	0.52	0.74	0.68	0.62	0.61	0.64	0.79
Debt to Equity	0.62	0.62	0.97	0.84	...	...	14.69	63.94
Price Range	52.26-40.00	52.26-40.00	49.23-27.47	29.34-11.87	12.10-8.01	13.00-6.62	14.93-9.96	12.38-3.93
P/E Ratio	8.78-6.72	9.28-7.10	63.12-35.22	2.39-0.97	10.17-6.73	12.87-6.55	21.33-14.23	...
Average Yield %	1.07	0.98	0.80	0.60	...	...	...	...

Address: Post Office Box 20706, Atlanta, GA 30320-6001 **Telephone:** 404-715-2600	**Web Site:** ir.delta.com **Officers:** Richard H. Anderson - Executive Chairman, Chief Executive Officer Glen W. Hauenstein - President, Executive Vice President, Chief Revenue Officer, Executive Vice President (frmr)	**Auditors:** Ernst & Young LLP **Investor Contact:** 404-715-2170 **Transfer Agents:** Wells Fargo Shareowner Services, St. Paul, MN

DELUXE CORP.

Exchange	Symbol	Price	52Wk Range	Yield	P/E
NYS	DLX	$65.13 (5/31/2016)	65.36-51.00	1.84	14.10

*7 Year Price Score 134.61 *NYSE Composite Index=100 *12 Month Price Score 104.45

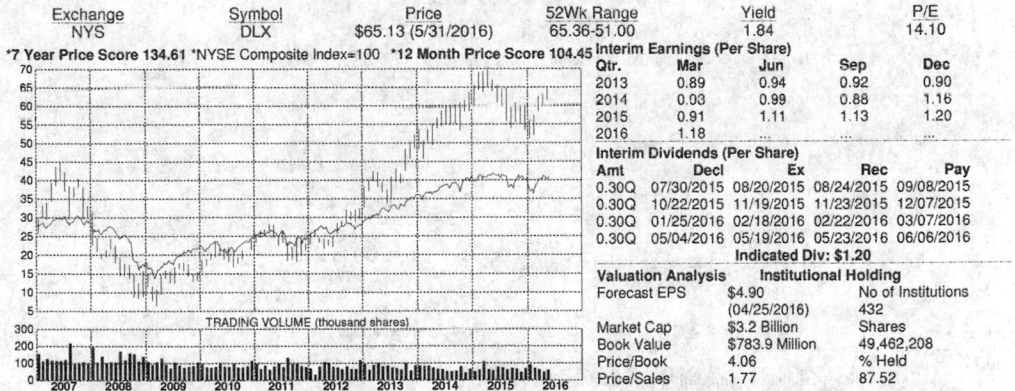

Interim Earnings (Per Share)

Qtr.	Mar	Jun	Sep	Dec
2013	0.89	0.94	0.92	0.90
2014	0.03	0.99	0.88	1.16
2015	0.91	1.11	1.13	1.20
2016	1.18	...	...	...

Interim Dividends (Per Share)

Amt	Decl	Ex	Rec	Pay
0.30Q	07/30/2015	08/20/2015	08/24/2015	09/08/2015
0.30Q	10/22/2015	11/19/2015	11/23/2015	12/07/2015
0.30Q	01/25/2016	02/18/2016	02/22/2016	03/07/2016
0.30Q	05/04/2016	05/19/2016	05/23/2016	06/06/2016

Indicated Div: $1.20

Valuation Analysis / **Institutional Holding**

Forecast EPS	$4.90
	(04/25/2016)
Market Cap	$3.2 Billion
Book Value	$783.9 Million
Price/Book	4.06
Price/Sales	1.77

No of Institutions 432
Shares 49,462,208
% Held 87.52

Business Summary: Printing (MIC: 7.5.5 SIC: 2761 NAIC: 323116)

Deluxe provides payment solutions. To promote and sell a range of products and services, Co. uses printed and electronic marketing; a direct sales force; referrals from financial institutions, telecommunication clients and other partners; purchased search results from online search engines; and independent distributors and dealers. Small Business Services segment provides products and services small business customers and Co.'s Direct Checks segment provides products and services to consumers. Through its Financial Services segment, Co. provides products and services to financial institution clients. Co.'s product and service offerings include checks.

Recent Developments: For the quarter ended Mar 31 2016, net income increased 26.5% to US$58.1 million from US$45.9 million in the year-earlier quarter. Revenues were US$459.3 million, up 5.9% from US$433.6 million the year before. Operating income was US$92.6 million versus US$85.3 million in the prior-year quarter, an increase of 8.6%. Direct operating expenses rose 7.6% to US$164.3 million from US$152.7 million in the comparable period the year before. Indirect operating expenses increased 3.4% to US$202.4 million from US$195.6 million in the equivalent prior-year period.

Prospects: Our evaluation of Deluxe Corp. as of June 19, 2016 is the result of our systematic analysis on three basic characteristics: earnings strength, relative valuation, and recent stock price movement. The company has managed to produce a neutral trend in earnings per share over the past 5 quarters and while recent estimates for the company have remained steady, DLX has posted better than expected results. Based on operating earnings yield, the company is undervalued when compared to all of the companies in our coverage universe. Share price changes over the past year indicates that DLX will perform poorly over the near term.

Financial Data
(US$ in Thousands)

	3 Mos	12/31/2015	12/31/2014	12/31/2013	12/31/2012	12/31/2011	12/31/2010	12/31/2009
Earnings Per Share	4.62	4.36	3.96	3.65	3.32	2.80	2.96	1.94
Cash Flow Per Share	6.21	6.23	5.63	5.17	4.79	4.61	4.16	4.06
Dividends Per Share	1.200	1.200	1.150	1.000	1.000	1.000	1.000	1.000
Dividend Payout %	25.97	27.52	29.04	27.40	30.12	35.71	33.78	51.55
Income Statement								
Total Revenue	459,298	1,772,817	1,674,082	1,584,824	1,514,917	1,417,596	1,402,237	1,344,195
EBITDA	119,279	485,646	448,627	430,484	408,982	389,020	354,029	269,066
Depn & Amortn	26,486	137,400	114,917	111,124	111,382	125,139	73,915	67,765
Income Before Taxes	87,550	327,947	297,181	281,059	250,753	216,084	235,949	155,021
Income Taxes	29,448	109,318	97,387	94,407	80,261	71,489	82,554	55,656
Net Income	58,102	218,629	199,794	186,652	170,492	144,595	152,624	99,365
Average Shares	49,175	49,825	50,262	51,010	51,076	51,415	51,325	50,925
Balance Sheet								
Current Assets	312,573	325,988	318,890	319,313	219,743	192,575	171,237	159,499
Total Assets	1,832,757	1,844,402	1,688,391	1,569,529	1,412,440	1,388,809	1,308,691	1,211,210
Current Liabilities	706,635	751,043	467,248	490,071	220,110	300,367	211,512	243,048
Long-Term Obligations	198,027	196,222	393,401	385,115	652,581	656,131	748,122	742,753
Total Liabilities	1,048,891	1,099,333	1,040,894	1,019,072	979,505	1,086,120	1,082,493	1,094,000
Stockholders' Equity	783,866	745,069	647,497	550,457	432,935	302,689	226,198	117,210
Shares Outstanding	48,910	49,019	49,742	50,344	50,614	50,826	51,338	51,189
Statistical Record								
Return on Assets %	13.19	12.38	12.27	12.52	12.14	10.72	12.11	8.18
Return on Equity %	31.54	31.40	33.36	37.96	46.23	54.68	88.89	116.71
EBITDA Margin %	25.97	27.39	26.80	27.16	27.00	27.44	25.25	20.02
Net Margin %	12.65	12.33	11.93	11.78	11.25	10.20	10.88	7.39
Asset Turnover	1.03	1.00	1.03	1.06	1.08	1.05	1.11	1.11
Current Ratio	0.44	0.43	0.68	0.65	1.00	0.64	0.81	0.66
Debt to Equity	0.25	0.26	0.61	0.70	1.51	2.17	3.31	6.34
Price Range	69.57-51.00	69.57-53.36	63.54-45.52	52.19-32.24	32.24-21.51	28.12-18.05	23.85-14.79	17.93-6.23
P/E Ratio	15.06-11.04	15.96-12.24	16.05-11.49	14.30-8.83	9.71-6.48	10.04-6.45	8.06-5.00	9.24-3.21
Average Yield %	2.00	1.93	2.08	2.44	3.76	4.21	5.06	7.23

Address: 3680 Victoria Street North, Shoreview, MN 55126-2966	**Web Site:** www.deluxe.com	**Auditors:** PricewaterhouseCoopers LLP
Telephone: 651-483-7111	**Officers:** Lee J. Schram - Chief Executive Officer	**Investor Contact:** 651-787-1068
Fax: 651-483-7337	Terry D. Peterson - Senior Vice President, Chief Financial Officer, Principal Financial Officer, Principal Accounting Officer	**Transfer Agents:** Wells Fargo Bank Minnesota, N.A., St. Paul, MN

DENBURY RESOURCES, INC. (DE)

Exchange	Symbol	Price	52Wk Range	Yield	P/E
NYS	DNR	$4.01 (5/31/2016)	7.35-0.95	N/A	N/A

*7 Year Price Score 20.10 *NYSE Composite Index=100 *12 Month Price Score 103.34

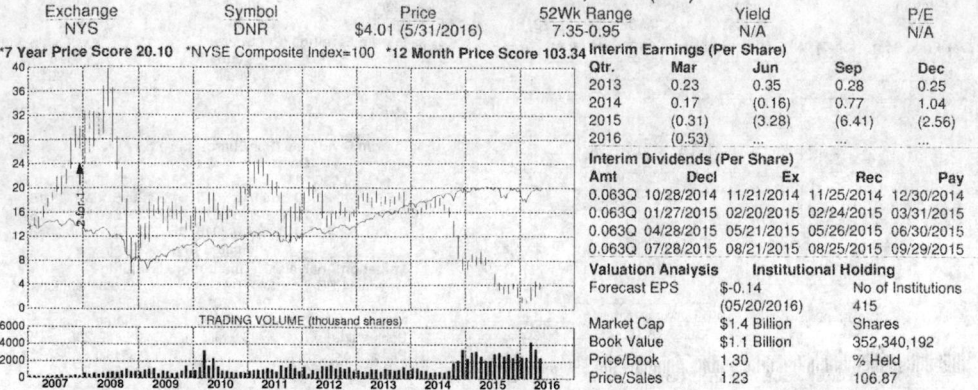

Interim Earnings (Per Share)

Qtr.	Mar	Jun	Sep	Dec
2013	0.23	0.35	0.28	0.25
2014	0.17	(0.16)	0.77	1.04
2015	(0.31)	(3.28)	(6.41)	(2.56)
2016	(0.53)	...	...	...

Interim Dividends (Per Share)

Amt	Decl	Ex	Rec	Pay
0.063Q	10/28/2014	11/21/2014	11/25/2014	12/30/2014
0.063Q	01/27/2015	02/20/2015	02/24/2015	03/31/2015
0.063Q	04/28/2015	05/21/2015	05/26/2015	06/30/2015
0.063Q	07/28/2015	08/21/2015	08/25/2015	09/29/2015

Valuation Analysis   **Institutional Holding**

Forecast EPS	$-0.14	No of Institutions
	(05/20/2016)	415
Market Cap	$1.4 Billion	Shares
Book Value	$1.1 Billion	352,340,192
Price/Book	1.30	% Held
Price/Sales	1.23	106.87

Business Summary: Production & Extraction (MIC: 9.1.1 SIC: 1311 NAIC: 211111)

Denbury Resources is an independent oil and natural gas company. Co. operations are focused in two key operating areas: the Gulf Coast and Rocky Mountain regions. Co.'s properties with proved and producing reserves in the Gulf Coast region are situated in Mississippi, Texas, Louisiana and Alabama, and in the Rocky Mountain region are situated in Montana, North Dakota and Wyoming. Co.'s primary focus is using carbon dioxide in enhanced oil recovery. At Dec 31 2015, Co.'s total estimated proved reserves were 288.6 million barrels of oil equivalent, which consisted of 282.3 million barrels of crude oil and 38.31 billion cubic feet of natural gas.

Recent Developments: For the quarter ended Mar 31 2016, net loss amounted to US$185.2 million versus a net loss of US$107.7 million in the year-earlier quarter. Revenues were US$194.8 million, down 36.7% from US$307.6 million the year before. Direct operating expenses declined 27.4% to US$103.1 million from US$142.0 million in the comparable period the year before. Indirect operating expenses increased 10.1% to US$372.1 million from US$337.8 million in the equivalent prior-year period.

Prospects: Our evaluation of Denbury Resources Inc. as of June 19, 2016 is the result of our systematic analysis on three basic characteristics: earnings strength, relative valuation, and recent stock price movement. The company has managed to produce a neutral trend in earnings per share over the past 5 quarters. Because the company lacks sufficient analyst estimate data, we place greater weight on the historical EPS trend as the measure of earnings strength. Based on operating earnings yield, the company is about fairly valued when compared to all of the companies in our coverage universe. Share price changes over the past year indicates that DNR will perform very poorly over the near term.

Financial Data

(US$ in Thousands)	3 Mos	12/31/2015	12/31/2014	12/31/2013	12/31/2012	12/31/2011	12/31/2010	12/31/2009
Earnings Per Share	(12.78)	(12.57)	1.81	1.11	1.35	1.43	0.72	(0.30)
Cash Flow Per Share	2.10	2.48	3.50	3.71	3.65	3.04	2.31	2.15
Tang Book Value Per Share	3.08	3.55	12.51	11.08	10.20	9.18	7.87	6.89
Dividends Per Share	...	0.188	0.250	...	...	...	...	...
Dividend Payout %	...	...	13.81	...	...	...	...	...
Income Statement								
Total Revenue	194,844	1,257,560	2,435,205	2,517,127	2,456,472	2,309,324	1,921,791	882,493
EBITDA	(234,836)	(5,625,933)	1,812,008	1,307,055	1,532,671	1,514,555	1,107,366	156,907
Depn & Amortn	3,306	540,781	606,448	523,966	522,233	426,150	452,183	238,323
Income Before Taxes	(280,313)	(6,325,982)	1,022,557	642,380	856,857	924,045	479,070	(128,846)
Income Taxes	(95,120)	(1,940,534)	387,066	232,783	331,497	350,712	193,543	(47,033)
Net Income	(185,193)	(4,385,448)	635,491	409,597	525,360	573,333	271,723	(75,156)
Average Shares	347,235	348,802	351,167	369,877	388,938	400,958	376,255	246,917
Balance Sheet								
Current Assets	272,975	344,708	812,680	414,559	1,542,754	684,113	864,318	255,762
Total Assets	5,538,547	5,919,824	12,727,802	11,788,737	11,139,342	10,184,424	9,065,063	4,269,978
Current Liabilities	324,402	373,015	640,125	675,199	616,421	661,267	579,345	393,790
Long-Term Obligations	3,222,497	3,277,866	3,535,900	3,260,625	3,104,462	2,669,729	2,416,208	1,301,068
Total Liabilities	4,457,269	4,670,912	7,023,946	6,487,331	6,024,453	5,377,926	4,684,356	2,297,741
Stockholders' Equity	1,081,278	1,248,912	5,703,856	5,301,406	5,114,889	4,806,498	4,380,707	1,972,237
Shares Outstanding	350,605	351,417	353,364	362,504	375,561	388,980	400,212	261,773
Statistical Record								
Return on Assets %	N.M.	N.M.	5.18	3.57	4.91	5.96	4.08	N.M.
Return on Equity %	N.M.	N.M.	11.55	7.86	10.56	12.48	8.55	N.M.
EBITDA Margin %	N.M.	N.M.	74.41	51.93	62.39	65.58	57.62	17.78
Net Margin %	N.M.	N.M.	26.10	16.27	21.39	24.83	14.14	N.M.
Asset Turnover	0.13	0.13	0.20	0.22	0.23	0.24	0.29	0.22
Current Ratio	0.84	0.92	1.27	0.61	2.50	1.03	1.49	0.65
Debt to Equity	2.98	2.62	0.62	0.62	0.61	0.56	0.55	0.66
Price Range	9.44-0.95	9.44-1.89	18.50-6.34	19.48-15.98	20.91-13.46	24.86-10.86	19.79-13.55	18.48-9.94
P/E Ratio	...	...	10.22-3.50	17.55-14.40	15.49-9.97	17.38-7.59	27.49-18.82	...
Average Yield %	...	3.35	1.65	...	...	...	...	...

Address: 5320 Legacy Drive, Plano, TX 75024	**Web Site:** www.denbury.com	**Auditors:** PricewaterhouseCoopers LLP
Telephone: 972-673-2000	**Officers:** Wieland F. Wettstein - Chairman Phil Rykhoek - President, Chief Executive Officer	**Investor Contact:** 972-673-2028
Fax: 972-673-2150		**Transfer Agents:** American Stock Transfer and Trust Company, New York, NY

DEVON ENERGY CORP.

Exchange	Symbol	Price	52Wk Range	Yield	P/E
NYS	DVN	$36.09 (5/31/2016)	64.83-18.65	0.67	N/A

*7 Year Price Score 52.99 *NYSE Composite Index=100 *12 Month Price Score 83.41

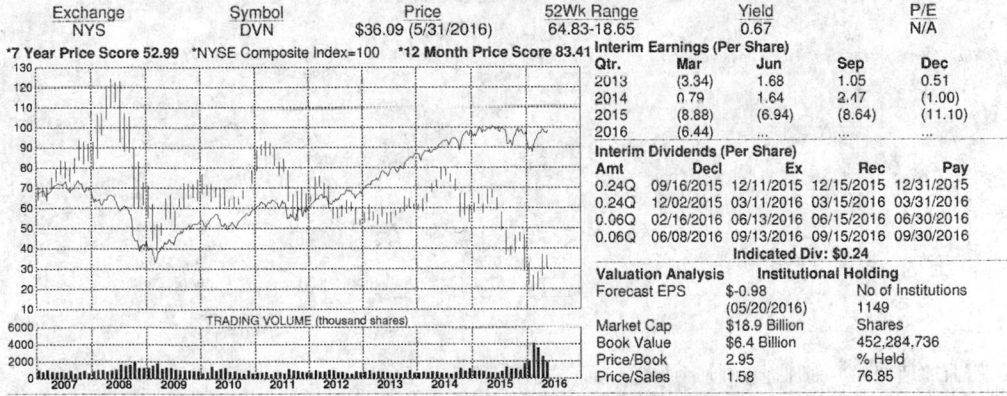

Interim Earnings (Per Share)

Qtr.	Mar	Jun	Sep	Dec
2013	(3.34)	1.68	1.05	0.51
2014	0.79	1.64	2.17	(1.00)
2015	(8.88)	(6.94)	(8.64)	(11.10)
2016	(6.44)	...	...	...

Interim Dividends (Per Share)

Amt	Decl	Ex	Rec	Pay
0.24Q	09/16/2015	12/11/2015	12/15/2015	12/31/2015
0.24Q	12/02/2015	03/11/2016	03/15/2016	03/31/2016
0.06Q	02/16/2016	06/13/2016	06/15/2016	06/30/2016
0.06Q	06/08/2016	09/13/2016	09/15/2016	09/30/2016

Indicated Div: $0.24

Valuation Analysis		Institutional Holding	
Forecast EPS	$-0.98	No of Institutions	
	(05/20/2016)	1149	
Market Cap	$18.9 Billion	Shares	
Book Value	$6.4 Billion	452,284,736	
Price/Book	2.95	% Held	
Price/Sales	1.58	76.85	

Business Summary: Production & Extraction (MIC: 9.1.1 SIC: 1311 NAIC: 211111)

Devon Energy is an independent energy company engaged primarily in the exploration, development and production of oil, natural gas and natural gas liquids. Co.'s operations are concentrated in various North American onshore areas in the U.S. and Canada. Co.'s operating areas consist of Delaware Basin, the STACK development, Eagle Ford, Rockies Oil, Heavy Oi, Barnett Shale, and Other assets located primarily in the Midland Basin, east Texas, Granite Wash and Mississippian-Lime areas. Co. also owns natural gas pipelines, plants and treatment facilities through its ownership in EnLink Midstream Partners, LP. As of Dec 31 2015, Co. had 2.18 billion barrels of oil equivalent proved reserves.

Recent Developments: For the quarter ended Mar 31 2016, net loss amounted to US$3.47 billion versus a net loss of US$3.59 billion in the year-earlier quarter. Revenues were US$2.13 billion, down 34.9% from US$3.27 billion the year before. Operating loss was US$3.50 billion versus a loss of US$5.50 billion in the prior-year quarter. Direct operating expenses declined 24.2% to US$1.51 billion from US$1.99 billion in the comparable period the year before. Indirect operating expenses decreased 39.2% to US$4.12 billion from US$6.77 billion in the equivalent prior-year period.

Prospects: Our evaluation of Devon Energy Corp. as of June 19, 2016 is the result of our systematic analysis on three basic characteristics: earnings strength, relative valuation, and recent stock price movement. The company has produced a positive trend in earnings per share over the past 5 quarters. Because the company lacks sufficient analyst estimate data, we place greater weight on the historical EPS trend as the measure of earnings strength. Based on operating earnings yield, the company is overvalued when compared to all of the companies in our coverage universe. Share price changes over the past year indicates that DVN will perform very poorly over the near term.

Financial Data
(US$ in Thousands)

	3 Mos	12/31/2015	12/31/2014	12/31/2013	12/31/2012	12/31/2011	12/31/2010	12/31/2009
Earnings Per Share	(33.12)	(35.55)	3.91	(0.06)	(0.52)	11.25	10.31	(5.58)
Cash Flow Per Share	8.19	13.23	14.77	13.52	12.36	15.11	12.59	10.79
Tang Book Value Per Share	4.30	4.83	37.25	36.06	37.44	38.19	30.53	21.58
Dividends Per Share	0.960	0.960	0.940	0.860	0.800	0.670	0.640	0.640
Dividend Payout %	...	...	24.04	...	...	5.96	6.21	...
Income Statement								
Total Revenue	2,126,000	13,145,000	19,566,000	10,397,000	9,502,000	11,454,000	9,940,000	8,015,000
EBITDA	(2,979,000)	(17,622,000)	7,904,000	3,346,000	2,900,000	6,890,000	5,861,000	(2,069,000)
Depn & Amortn	542,000	3,129,000	3,319,000	2,780,000	2,811,000	2,248,000	1,930,000	2,108,000
Income Before Taxes	(3,685,000)	(21,268,000)	4,059,000	149,000	(317,000)	4,290,000	3,568,000	(4,526,000)
Income Taxes	(217,000)	(6,065,000)	2,368,000	169,000	(132,000)	2,156,000	1,235,000	(1,773,000)
Net Income	(3,056,000)	(14,454,000)	1,607,000	(20,000)	(206,000)	4,704,000	4,550,000	(2,479,000)
Average Shares	474,000	407,000	407,000	402,000	400,000	414,000	436,000	439,000
Balance Sheet								
Current Assets	2,950,000	4,026,000	6,498,000	8,005,000	8,971,000	9,305,000	5,555,000	2,992,000
Total Assets	28,637,000	29,532,000	50,637,000	42,877,000	43,326,000	41,117,000	32,927,000	29,686,000
Current Liabilities	2,600,000	3,295,000	5,935,000	6,655,000	6,003,000	6,738,000	4,583,000	3,802,000
Long-Term Obligations	12,195,000	12,137,000	9,830,000	7,956,000	8,455,000	5,969,000	3,819,000	5,847,000
Total Liabilities	22,227,000	22,483,000	29,098,000	22,378,000	22,048,000	19,687,000	13,674,000	14,116,000
Stockholders' Equity	6,410,000	7,049,000	21,539,000	20,499,000	21,278,000	21,430,000	19,253,000	15,570,000
Shares Outstanding	524,000	418,000	409,000	406,000	406,000	403,700	431,500	446,700
Statistical Record								
Return on Assets %	N.M.	N.M.	3.44	N.M.	N.M.	12.71	14.53	N.M.
Return on Equity %	N.M.	N.M.	7.65	N.M.	N.M.	23.13	26.13	N.M.
EBITDA Margin %	N.M.	N.M.	40.40	32.18	30.52	60.15	58.96	N.M.
Net Margin %	N.M.	N.M.	8.21	N.M.	N.M.	41.07	45.77	N.M.
Asset Turnover	0.32	0.33	0.42	0.24	0.22	0.31	0.32	0.26
Current Ratio	1.13	1.22	1.09	1.20	1.49	1.38	1.21	0.79
Debt to Equity	1.90	1.72	0.46	0.39	0.40	0.28	0.20	0.38
Price Range	69.03-18.65	69.03-28.67	79.50-52.66	65.52-51.44	75.81-51.15	93.10-53.34	78.51-59.79	74.20-38.84
P/E Ratio	...	...	20.33-13.47	...	...	8.28-4.74	7.61-5.80	...
Average Yield %	2.17	1.81	1.39	1.49	1.30	0.88	0.95	1.06

Address: 333 West Sheridan Avenue, Oklahoma City, OK 73102-5015
Telephone: 405-235-3611

Web Site: www.devonenergy.com
Officers: J. Larry Nichols - Executive Chairman, President, Chief Executive Officer John Richels - Vice Chairman, President, Chief Executive Officer

Auditors: KPMG LLP
Investor Contact: 405-552-4505
Transfer Agents: Computershare Trust Company, N.A., Providence, RI

DEVRY EDUCATION GROUP INC

Exchange	Symbol	Price	52Wk Range	Yield	P/E
NYS	DV	$18.10 (5/31/2016)	33.99-15.99	1.99	32.32

*7 Year Price Score 52.04 *NYSE Composite Index=100 *12 Month Price Score 72.87

Interim Earnings (Per Share)

Qtr.	Sep	Dec	Mar	Jun
2012-13	0.49	0.78	0.88	(0.50)
2013-14	(0.11)	0.74	0.86	0.58
2014-15	0.31	0.65	0.72	0.46
2015-16	0.08	(0.79)	0.81	..

Interim Dividends (Per Share)

Amt	Decl	Ex	Rec	Pay
0.18S	11/06/2014	12/03/2014	12/05/2014	12/26/2014
0.18S	05/14/2015	06/03/2015	06/05/2015	06/26/2015
0.18S	11/05/2015	12/02/2015	12/04/2015	12/23/2015
0.18S	05/16/2016	06/01/2016	06/03/2016	06/24/2016

Indicated Div: $0.36

Valuation Analysis   **Institutional Holding**

Forecast EPS	$2.37	No of Institutions	283
	(05/14/2016)		
Market Cap	$1.1 Billion	Shares	70,144,048
Book Value	$1.6 Billion	% Held	92.17
Price/Book	0.73		
Price/Sales	0.62		

TRADING VOLUME (thousand shares)

Business Summary: Educational Services (MIC: 2.2.2 SIC: 8221 NAIC: 611310)

DeVry Education Group is a provider of educational services. Co.'s institutions provide a range of programs in healthcare, business, technology, accounting, finance and law. Co. conducts its operations through three segments. The Medical and Healthcare segment includes the operations of DeVry Medical International, Chamberlain College of Nursing, and Carrington College. The International and Professional Education segment includes the operations of DeVry Brasil and Becker Professional Education. The Business, Technology and Management segment includes the operations of DeVry University.

Recent Developments: For the quarter ended Mar 31 2016, income from continuing operations increased 24.7% to US$51.9 million from US$41.6 million in the year-earlier quarter. Net income increased 10.0% to US$51.9 million from US$47.2 million in the year-earlier quarter. Revenues were US$474.2 million, down 3.2% from US$489.8 million the year before. Operating income was US$60.8 million versus US$49.5 million in the prior-year quarter, an increase of 23.0%. Direct operating expenses declined 0.1% to US$252.9 million from US$253.2 million in the comparable period the year before. Indirect operating expenses decreased 14.3% to US$160.5 million from US$187.2 million in the equivalent prior-year period.

Prospects: Our evaluation of DeVry Education Group Inc. as of June 19, 2016 is the result of our systematic analysis on three basic characteristics: earnings strength, relative valuation, and recent stock price movement. The company has enjoyed a very positive trend in earnings per share over the past 5 quarters and while recent estimates for the company have remained steady, DV has posted better than expected results. Based on operating earnings yield, the company is undervalued when compared to all of the companies in our coverage universe. Share price changes over the past year indicates that DV will perform in line with the market over the near term.

Financial Data

(US$ in Thousands)	9 Mos	6 Mos	3 Mos	06/30/2015	06/30/2014	06/30/2013	06/30/2012	06/30/2011
Earnings Per Share	0.56	0.47	1.91	2.14	2.07	1.65	2.09	4.68
Cash Flow Per Share	3.34	2.92	2.78	3.15	4.14	4.07	4.12	5.84
Tang Book Value Per Share	9.85	8.94	11.11	11.14	11.29	9.63	8.05	9.77
Dividends Per Share	0.360	0.360	0.360	0.360	0.340	0.340	0.300	0.240
Dividend Payout %	64.29	76.60	18.85	16.82	16.43	20.61	14.35	5.13
Income Statement								
Total Revenue	1,371,836	897,615	441,413	1,909,943	1,923,371	1,964,375	2,089,781	2,182,371
EBITDA	76,554	(5,860)	29,272	241,918	264,007	250,039	285,081	552,208
Depn & Amortn	63,839	42,272	21,025	85,008	82,739	83,111	77,149	58,033
Income Before Taxes	7,528	(51,938)	6,048	153,660	179,367	164,969	206,138	494,432
Income Taxes	683	(6,853)	662	18,537	27,699	39,227	63,757	163,602
Net Income	6,803	(45,122)	5,465	139,899	134,032	106,786	141,565	330,403
Average Shares	64,353	64,654	64,729	65,277	64,853	64,611	67,705	70,620
Balance Sheet								
Current Assets	594,606	400,288	718,114	601,057	577,091	442,164	401,114	624,650
Total Assets	2,115,897	1,908,912	2,136,742	2,074,193	1,997,636	1,857,018	1,838,616	1,850,503
Current Liabilities	401,554	291,809	439,400	321,909	316,812	316,217	315,209	316,431
Total Liabilities	559,962	442,075	593,373	489,383	464,243	459,862	482,223	460,987
Stockholders' Equity	1,555,935	1,466,837	1,543,369	1,584,810	1,533,393	1,397,156	1,356,393	1,389,516
Shares Outstanding	62,909	63,284	63,573	63,623	63,624	62,946	64,722	68,635
Statistical Record								
Return on Assets %	1.72	1.65	5.85	6.87	6.95	5.78	7.65	19.00
Return on Equity %	2.35	2.11	8.10	8.97	9.15	7.76	10.28	25.72
EBITDA Margin %	5.58	N.M.	6.63	12.67	13.73	12.73	13.64	25.30
Net Margin %	0.50	N.M.	1.24	7.32	6.97	5.44	6.77	15.14
Asset Turnover	0.87	0.96	0.88	0.94	1.00	1.06	1.13	1.25
Current Ratio	1.48	1.37	1.63	1.87	1.82	1.40	1.27	1.97
Price Range	37.57-16.74	47.47-22.46	49.18-25.17	49.18-29.98	45.99-28.32	34.03-18.35	66.55-26.58	61.86-37.50
P/E Ratio	67.09-29.89	101.00-47.79	25.75-13.18	22.98-14.01	22.22-13.68	20.62-11.12	31.84-12.72	13.22-8.01
Average Yield %	1.35	1.15	0.98	0.89	0.93		1.29	0.77	0.48

Address: 3005 Highland Parkway, Downers Grove, IL 60515 **Telephone:** 630-515-7700	**Web Site:** www.devryeducationgroup.com **Officers:** Christopher B. Begley - Chairman Lisa W. Wardell - President, Chief Executive Officer	**Auditors:** PricewaterhouseCoopers LLP **Investor Contact:** 630-353-3800 **Transfer Agents:** Computershare Investor Services, L.L.C.

DIAMOND OFFSHORE DRILLING, INC.

Exchange	Symbol	Price	52Wk Range	Yield	P/E
NYS	DO	$25.82 (5/31/2016)	31.35-15.55	N/A	51.64

*7 Year Price Score 32.26 *NYSE Composite Index=100 *12 Month Price Score 105.44

Interim Earnings (Per Share)

Qtr.	Mar	Jun	Sep	Dec
2013	1.27	1.33	0.68	0.67
2014	1.05	0.65	0.38	0.72
2015	(1.86)	0.66	0.99	(1.79)
2016	0.64	...	...	...

Interim Dividends (Per Share)

Amt	Decl	Ex	Rec	Pay
0.125Q	02/09/2015	02/18/2015	02/20/2015	03/02/2015
0.125Q	05/04/2015	05/13/2015	05/15/2015	06/01/2015
0.125Q	08/03/2015	08/12/2015	08/14/2015	09/01/2015
0.125Q	11/02/2015	11/10/2015	11/13/2015	12/01/2015

Valuation Analysis

		Institutional Holding	
Forecast EPS	$1.34	No of Institutions	
	(05/20/2016)	478	
Market Cap	$3.5 Billion	Shares	
Book Value	$4.2 Billion	147,045,200	
Price/Book	0.84	% Held	
Price/Sales	1.56	98.45	

Business Summary: Equipment & Services (MIC: 9.1.3 SIC: 1381 NAIC: 213111)

Diamond Offshore Drilling, Inc. engaged in offshore drilling, providing contract drilling services to the energy industry around the world with a fleet of 32 offshore drilling rigs, which includes four jack-up rigs. Co.'s fleet consists of 23 semisubmersibles, including the Ocean GreatWhite, which is under construction, five jack-ups and four dynamically positioned drillships, including the Ocean BlackLion. Co. provides a range of services worldwide, primarily in the floater market (ultra-deepwater, deepwater and mid-water).

Recent Developments: For the quarter ended Mar 31 2016, net income amounted to US$87.4 million versus a net loss of US$255.7 million in the year-earlier quarter. Revenues were US$470.5 million, down 24.1% from US$620.1 million the year before. Operating income was US$111.6 million versus a loss of US$269.5 million in the prior-year quarter. Direct operating expenses declined 35.4% to US$239.6 million from US$370.8 million in the comparable period the year before. Indirect operating expenses decreased 77.0% to US$119.3 million from US$518.8 million in the equivalent prior-year period.

Prospects: Our evaluation of Diamond Offshore Drilling Inc. as of June 19, 2016 is the result of our systematic analysis on three basic characteristics: earnings strength, relative valuation, and recent stock price movement. The company has suffered a very negative trend in earnings per share over the past 5 quarters and while recent estimates for the company have been raised by analysts, DO has posted better than expected results. Based on operating earnings yield, the company is undervalued when compared to all of the companies in our coverage universe. Share price changes over the past year indicates that DO will perform in line with the market over the near term.

Financial Data

(US$ in Thousands)	3 Mos	12/31/2015	12/31/2014	12/31/2013	12/31/2012	12/31/2011	12/31/2010	12/31/2009
Earnings Per Share	0.50	(2.00)	2.81	3.95	5.18	6.92	6.87	9.89
Cash Flow Per Share	5.96	5.37	7.22	7.67	9.41	10.21	9.22	10.91
Tang Book Value Per Share	30.58	29.99	32.46	33.35	32.92	31.17	27.78	26.11
Dividends Per Share	0.375	0.500	3.500	3.500	3.500	3.500	5.250	8.000
Dividend Payout %	75.00	...	124.56	88.61	67.57	50.58	76.42	80.89
Income Statement								
Total Revenue	470,543	2,419,393	2,814,671	2,920,421	2,986,508	3,322,419	3,322,974	3,631,284
EBITDA	212,779	202,426	1,032,926	1,186,474	1,352,300	1,644,352	1,816,982	2,259,990
Depn & Amortn	104,240	493,162	456,483	388,092	392,913	398,612	393,177	346,446
Income Before Taxes	83,196	(381,348)	515,191	774,240	918,081	1,179,271	1,336,016	1,868,431
Income Taxes	(4,229)	(107,063)	128,180	225,554	197,604	216,729	380,559	492,212
Net Income	87,425	(274,285)	387,011	548,686	720,477	962,542	955,457	1,376,219
Average Shares	137,206	137,157	137,523	139,064	139,048	139,038	139,070	139,097
Balance Sheet								
Current Assets	615,034	669,595	899,059	2,718,110	2,132,943	1,992,683	1,863,498	1,723,370
Total Assets	6,944,599	7,164,889	8,021,289	8,391,434	7,235,286	6,964,157	6,726,984	6,264,261
Current Liabilities	380,987	625,723	856,646	745,582	485,546	427,291	626,288	413,475
Long-Term Obligations	1,980,049	1,994,773	1,994,526	2,244,189	1,496,066	1,495,823	1,495,593	1,495,375
Total Liabilities	2,749,819	3,052,119	3,569,726	3,754,176	2,658,892	2,631,094	2,865,272	2,633,619
Stockholders' Equity	4,194,780	4,112,770	4,451,563	4,637,258	4,576,394	4,333,063	3,861,712	3,630,642
Shares Outstanding	137,169	137,158	137,147	139,035	139,031	139,027	139,026	139,026
Statistical Record								
Return on Assets %	0.95	N.M.	4.72	7.02	10.12	14.06	14.71	24.57
Return on Equity %	1.64	N.M.	8.52	11.91	16.13	23.49	25.50	39.44
EBITDA Margin %	45.22	8.37	36.70	40.63	45.28	49.49	54.68	62.24
Net Margin %	18.58	N.M.	13.75	18.79	24.12	28.97	28.75	37.90
Asset Turnover	0.31	0.32	0.34	0.37	0.42	0.49	0.51	0.65
Current Ratio	1.61	1.07	1.05	3.65	4.39	4.66	2.98	4.17
Debt to Equity	0.47	0.49	0.45	0.48	0.33	0.35	0.39	0.41
Price Range	34.81-15.55	37.23-16.81	56.92-29.37	76.48-55.39	72.43-55.61	80.14-52.90	106.34-56.94	107.01-54.29
P/E Ratio	69.62-31.10	...	20.26-10.45	19.36-14.02	13.98-10.74	11.58-7.64	15.48-8.29	10.82-5.49
Average Yield %	1.60	1.91	7.82	5.24	5.36	5.18	7.12	9.68

Address: 15415 Katy Freeway, Houston, TX 77094	**Web Site:** www.diamondoffshore.com	**Auditors:** Deloitte & Touche LLP
Telephone: 281-492-5300	**Officers:** James S. Tisch - Chairman Ronald Woll - Senior Vice President, Chief Commercial Officer	**Investor Contact:** 281-492-5393
Fax: 281-492-5316		**Transfer Agents:** Computershare, Providence, R.I.

DICK'S SPORTING GOODS, INC

Exchange	Symbol	Price	52Wk Range	Yield	P/E
NYS	DKS	$42.90 (5/31/2016)	54.18-34.24	1.41	15.32

*7 Year Price Score 91.86   *NYSE Composite Index=100   *12 Month Price Score 97.34

Interim Earnings (Per Share)

Qtr.	Apr	Jul	Oct	Jan
2013-14	0.52	0.67	0.40	1.11
2014-15	0.57	0.57	0.41	1.29
2015-16	0.53	0.77	0.41	1.12
2016-17	0.50			

Interim Dividends (Per Share)

Amt	Decl	Ex	Rec	Pay
0.138Q	08/12/2015	09/09/2015	09/11/2015	09/30/2015
0.138Q	11/12/2015	12/09/2015	12/11/2015	12/31/2015
0.151Q	02/23/2016	03/09/2016	03/11/2016	03/31/2016
0.151Q	05/13/2016	06/08/2016	06/10/2016	06/30/2016

Indicated Div: $0.60

Valuation Analysis   **Institutional Holding**

Forecast EPS	$2.80	No of Institutions
	(05/20/2016)	569
Market Cap	$4.8 Billion	Shares
Book Value	$1.8 Billion	91,356,904
Price/Book	2.66	% Held
Price/Sales	0.65	71.90

TRADING VOLUME (thousand shares)

Business Summary: Retail - Specialty (MIC: 2.1.3 SIC: 5941 NAIC: 451110)

Dick's Sporting Goods is a sporting goods retailer providing sports equipment, apparel, footwear and accessories through a blend of associates, in-store services and shop-in-shops. Co. also owns and operates Golf Galaxy, Field & Stream and other specialty concept stores as well as eCommerce websites at www.DICKS.com, www.golfgalaxy.com, www.fieldandstreamshop.com and www.caliastudio.com. At Jan 30 2016, Co. operated 644 Dick's Sporting Goods stores in 47 states, 73 Golf Galaxy stores in 29 states, and 19 Field & Stream stores in nine states. Co.'s Dick's Sporting Goods stores typically contain the following shops: footwear, team sports, outdoor lodge, golf, fitness and athletic apparel.

Recent Developments: For the quarter ended Apr 30 2016, net income decreased 10.2% to US$56.9 million from US$63.3 million in the year-earlier quarter. Revenues were US$1.66 billion, up 6.1% from US$1.57 billion the year before. Operating income was US$90.7 million versus US$101.9 million in the prior-year quarter, a decrease of 11.0%. Direct operating expenses rose 6.2% to US$1.16 billion from US$1.10 billion in the comparable period the year before. Indirect operating expenses increased 10.4% to US$405.1 million from US$367.1 million in the equivalent prior-year period.

Prospects: Our evaluation of Dick's Sporting Goods Inc. as of June 19, 2016 is the result of our systematic analysis on three basic characteristics: earnings strength, relative valuation, and recent stock price movement. The company has managed to produce a neutral trend in earnings per share over the past 5 quarters. However, while recent estimates for the company have been lowered by analysts, DKS has posted better than expected results. Based on operating earnings yield, the company is undervalued when compared to all of the companies in our coverage universe. Share price changes over the past year indicates that DKS will perform in line with the market over the near term.

Financial Data
(US$ in Thousands)

	3 Mos	01/30/2016	01/31/2015	02/01/2014	02/02/2013	01/28/2012	01/29/2011	01/30/2010
Earnings Per Share	2.80	2.83	2.84	2.69	2.31	2.10	1.50	1.15
Cash Flow Per Share	5.42	5.60	5.10	3.30	3.55	3.42	3.36	3.56
Tang Book Value Per Share	13.35	13.24	12.88	11.52	10.47	11.39	9.37	7.27
Dividends Per Share	0.564	0.550	0.500	0.500	2.500	0.500	...	...
Dividend Payout %	20.13	19.43	17.61	18.59	108.23	23.81	...	...
Income Statement								
Total Revenue	1,660,343	7,270,965	6,814,479	6,213,173	5,836,119	5,211,802	4,871,492	4,412,835
EBITDA	140,768	715,387	720,829	702,836	621,159	558,994	418,627	325,971
Depn & Amortn	47,990	180,500	161,600	153,800	125,300	113,100	107,100	100,400
Income Before Taxes	91,647	530,875	556,014	546,107	489,825	432,026	297,511	223,176
Income Taxes	34,770	200,484	211,816	208,509	199,116	168,120	115,434	87,817
Net Income	56,877	330,391	344,198	337,598	290,709	263,906	182,077	135,359
Average Shares	113,276	116,794	121,238	125,628	125,995	125,768	121,724	117,955
Balance Sheet								
Current Assets	2,070,678	1,812,690	1,850,384	1,620,071	1,595,889	1,868,393	1,564,330	1,222,361
Total Assets	3,878,367	3,559,336	3,436,198	3,071,487	2,887,807	2,996,452	2,597,536	2,245,333
Current Liabilities	1,283,310	1,191,675	1,118,833	1,002,587	1,000,768	940,146	848,543	795,675
Long-Term Obligations	162,780	5,324	5,913	6,476	7,762	151,596	139,846	141,265
Total Liabilities	2,074,234	1,770,149	1,603,973	1,379,308	1,300,483	1,363,707	1,233,955	1,162,106
Stockholders' Equity	1,804,133	1,789,187	1,832,225	1,692,179	1,587,324	1,632,745	1,363,581	1,083,227
Shares Outstanding	111,908	111,751	118,106	120,966	123,005	121,333	118,729	114,808
Statistical Record								
Return on Assets %	8.74	9.47	10.61	11.36	9.72	9.46	7.54	6.45
Return on Equity %	18.26	18.30	19.59	20.64	17.76	17.66	14.92	13.72
EBITDA Margin %	8.48	9.84	10.58	11.31	10.64	10.73	8.59	7.39
Net Margin %	3.43	4.54	5.05	5.43	4.98	5.06	3.74	3.07
Asset Turnover	1.99	2.08	2.10	2.09	1.95	1.87	2.02	2.10
Current Ratio	1.61	1.52	1.65	1.62	1.59	1.99	1.84	1.54
Debt to Equity	0.09	N.M.	N.M.	N.M.	N.M.	0.09	0.10	0.13
Price Range	56.29-34.24	58.98-34.24	57.26-41.90	58.58-45.11	53.93-40.80	42.58-29.86	37.81-22.46	26.05-10.77
P/E Ratio	20.10-12.23	20.84-12.10	20.16-14.75	21.78-16.77	23.35-17.66	20.28-14.22	25.21-14.97	22.65-9.37
Average Yield %	1.22	1.12	1.03	0.97	5.12	1.33	...	...

Address: 345 Court Street, Coraopolis, PA 15108 Telephone: 724-273-3400	Web Site: www.DICKS.com Officers: Edward W. Stack - Chairman, Chief Executive Officer William J. Colombo - Vice-Chairman, Chief Marketing Officer	Auditors: Deloitte & Touche LLP ha Transfer Agents: American Stock Transfer & Trust Company, New York, NY

DIEBOLD, INC.

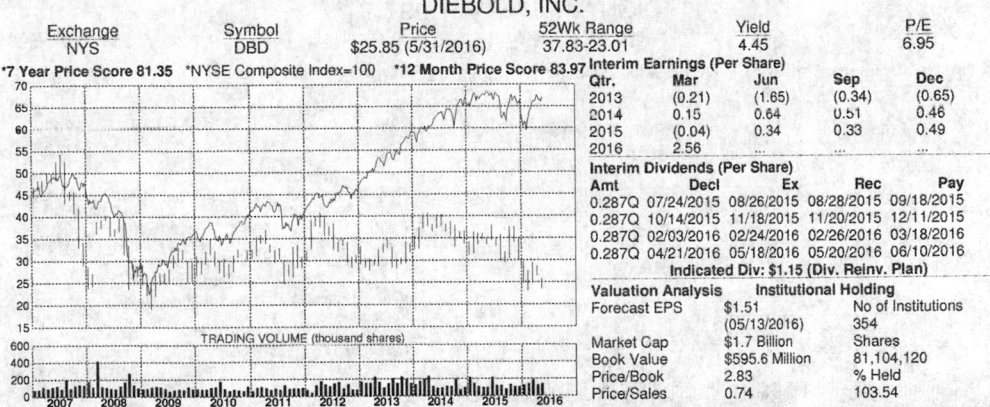

Exchange	Symbol	Price	52Wk Range	Yield	P/E
NYS	DBD	$25.85 (5/31/2016)	37.83-23.01	4.45	6.95

*7 Year Price Score 81.35   *NYSE Composite Index=100   *12 Month Price Score 83.97

Interim Earnings (Per Share)

Qtr.	Mar	Jun	Sep	Dec
2013	(0.21)	(1.65)	(0.34)	(0.65)
2014	0.15	0.64	0.51	0.46
2015	(0.04)	0.34	0.33	0.49
2016	2.56	...	...	...

Interim Dividends (Per Share)

Amt	Decl	Ex	Rec	Pay
0.287Q	07/24/2015	08/26/2015	08/28/2015	09/18/2015
0.287Q	10/14/2015	11/18/2015	11/20/2015	12/11/2015
0.287Q	02/03/2016	02/24/2016	02/26/2016	03/18/2016
0.287Q	04/21/2016	05/18/2016	05/20/2016	06/10/2016

Indicated Div: $1.15 (Div. Reinv. Plan)

Valuation Analysis

		Institutional Holding	
Forecast EPS	$1.51	No of Institutions	
	(05/13/2016)	354	
Market Cap	$1.7 Billion	Shares	
Book Value	$595.6 Million	81,104,120	
Price/Book	2.83	% Held	
Price/Sales	0.74	103.54	

TRADING VOLUME (thousand shares)

Business Summary: Computer Hardware & Equipment (MIC: 6.2.1 SIC: 3578 NAIC: 333313)

Diebold is engaged in providing of exceptional self-service innovation, security and services to financial, retail, commercial and other markets. Co. has two lines of business: Financial Self-Service, which provides a line of self-service solutions and technology, including automated teller machine (ATM) outsourcing, ATM security, deposit automation, recycling and payment terminals and software; and Security Solutions, which provides physical and electronic security systems as well as assisted transactions, providing total security systems solutions to financial, commercial, retail, and other markets.

Recent Developments: For the quarter ended Mar 31 2016, income from continuing operations was US$20.7 million compared with a loss of US$10.1 million in the year-earlier quarter. Net income amounted to US$168.5 million versus a net loss of US$5.6 million in the year-earlier quarter. Revenues were US$509.6 million, down 11.3% from US$574.8 million the year before. Operating loss was US$5.7 million versus a loss of US$3.0 million in the prior-year quarter. Direct operating expenses declined 10.8% to US$370.8 million from US$415.5 million in the comparable period the year before. Indirect operating expenses decreased 11.0% to US$144.5 million from US$162.3 million in the equivalent prior-year period.

Prospects: Our evaluation of Diebold Inc. as of June 19, 2016 is the result of our systematic analysis on three basic characteristics: earnings strength, relative valuation, and recent stock price movement. The company has generated a negative trend in earnings per share over the past 5 quarters and while recent estimates for the company have remained steady, DBD has posted results that fell short of analysts expectations. Based on operating earnings yield, the company is about fairly valued when compared to all of the companies in our coverage universe. Share price changes over the past year indicates that DBD will perform poorly over the near term.

Financial Data

(US$ in Thousands)	3 Mos	12/31/2015	12/31/2014	12/31/2013	12/31/2012	12/31/2011	12/31/2010	12/31/2009
Earnings Per Share	3.72	1.12	1.76	(2.85)	1.23	2.24	(0.31)	0.39
Cash Flow Per Share	(0.25)	0.57	2.90	1.95	2.14	3.35	4.15	4.52
Tang Book Value Per Share	6.58	3.86	5.56	6.51	8.49	9.18	10.53	8.98
Dividends Per Share	1.150	1.150	1.150	1.150	1.140	1.120	1.080	1.040
Dividend Payout %	30.91	102.68	65.34	...	92.68	50.00	...	266.67
Income Statement								
Total Revenue	509,600	2,419,300	3,051,053	2,857,491	2,991,693	2,835,848	2,823,793	2,718,292
EBITDA	34,600	119,000	250,211	(40,422)	199,203	249,397	86,915	209,344
Depn & Amortn	3,200	40,700	48,202	50,151	51,447	50,549	51,425	50,085
Income Before Taxes	19,900	45,800	170,589	(119,807)	117,426	164,392	(2,397)	123,807
Income Taxes	(800)	(13,700)	53,570	56,715	29,905	12,815	14,561	44,477
Net Income	168,200	73,700	114,417	(181,605)	78,454	144,815	(20,252)	26,026
Average Shares	65,700	65,600	65,154	63,659	63,914	64,792	65,907	66,867
Balance Sheet								
Current Assets	1,687,600	1,643,600	1,655,530	1,555,350	1,814,857	1,732,355	1,714,036	1,588,085
Total Assets	2,278,000	2,249,300	2,342,136	2,183,491	2,592,987	2,517,443	2,519,790	2,554,865
Current Liabilities	990,100	955,800	1,027,723	893,736	838,855	824,217	809,765	743,091
Long-Term Obligations	428,900	613,100	479,794	480,242	617,534	606,154	550,368	540,000
Total Liabilities	1,682,400	1,836,900	1,810,532	1,586,727	1,783,024	1,690,457	1,558,635	1,508,486
Stockholders' Equity	595,600	412,400	531,604	596,764	809,963	826,986	961,155	1,046,379
Shares Outstanding	65,144	65,001	64,632	64,068	63,240	62,513	65,717	66,327
Statistical Record								
Return on Assets %	10.66	3.21	5.06	N.M.	3.06	5.75	N.M.	1.02
Return on Equity %	46.83	15.61	20.28	N.M.	9.56	16.20	N.M.	2.61
EBITDA Margin %	6.79	4.92	8.20	N.M.	6.66	8.79	3.08	7.70
Net Margin %	33.01	3.05	3.75	N.M.	2.62	5.11	N.M.	0.96
Asset Turnover	0.99	1.05	1.35	1.20	1.17	1.13	1.11	1.07
Current Ratio	1.70	1.72	1.61	1.74	2.16	2.10	2.12	2.14
Debt to Equity	0.72	1.49	0.90	0.80	0.76	0.73	0.57	0.52
Price Range	37.83-23.01	37.83-29.36	40.61-32.35	35.10-27.61	40.68-28.26	36.94-24.76	34.87-25.94	32.93-19.05
P/E Ratio	10.17-6.19	33.78-26.21	23.07-18.38	...	33.07-22.98	16.49-11.05	...	84.44-48.85
Average Yield %	3.59	3.40	3.12	3.73	3.31	3.58	3.58	3.85

Address: 5995 Mayfair Road, P.O. Box 3077, North Canton, OH 44720-8077	**Web Site:** www.diebold.com	**Auditors:** KPMG LLP
Telephone: 330-490-4000	**Officers:** Andreas W. Mattes - President, Chief Executive Officer Kevin J. Krakora - Executive Vice President	**Investor Contact:** 330-490-6319
		Transfer Agents: Wells Fargo Shareowner Services

DIGITAL REALTY TRUST, INC.

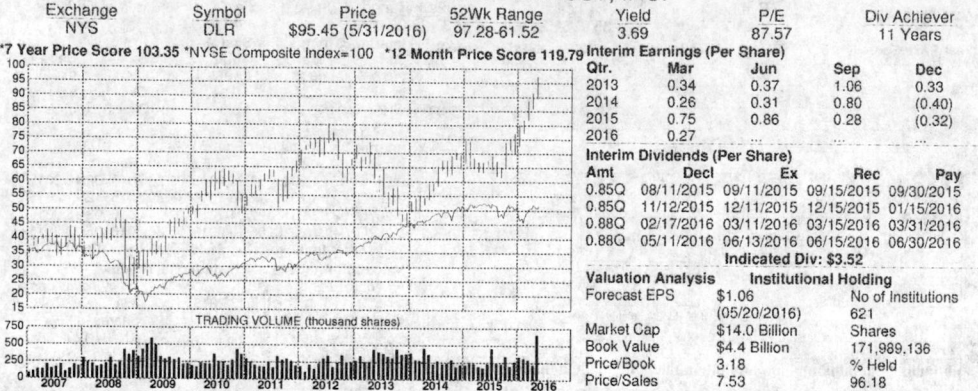

Exchange	Symbol	Price	52Wk Range	Yield	P/E	Div Achiever
NYS	DLR	$95.45 (5/31/2016)	97.28-61.52	3.69	87.57	11 Years

*7 Year Price Score 103.35 *NYSE Composite Index=100 *12 Month Price Score 119.79

Interim Earnings (Per Share)

Qtr.	Mar	Jun	Sep	Dec
2013	0.34	0.37	1.06	0.33
2014	0.26	0.31	0.80	(0.40)
2015	0.75	0.86	0.28	(0.32)
2016	0.27	...	...	...

Interim Dividends (Per Share)

Amt	Decl	Ex	Rec	Pay
0.85Q	08/11/2015	09/11/2015	09/15/2015	09/30/2015
0.85Q	11/12/2015	12/11/2015	12/15/2015	01/15/2016
0.88Q	02/17/2016	03/11/2016	03/15/2016	03/31/2016
0.88Q	05/11/2016	06/13/2016	06/15/2016	06/30/2016

Indicated Div: $3.52

Valuation Analysis

Forecast EPS	$1.06
	(05/20/2016)
Market Cap	$14.0 Billion
Book Value	$4.4 Billion
Price/Book	3.18
Price/Sales	7.53

Institutional Holding

No of Institutions	621
Shares	171,989.136
% Held	96.18

Business Summary: REITs (MIC: 5.3.1 SIC: 6798 NAIC: 525930)

Digital Realty Trust is a real estate investment trust. Co. owns, acquires, develops and manages technology-related real estate. Digital Realty Trust, L.P. is the entity through which Co. conducts its business and owns its assets. At Dec 31 2014, Co.'s portfolio consisted of 131 properties, including 14 properties held as investments in unconsolidated joint ventures and developable land, of which, 105 are located throughout North America, 21 are located in Europe, three are located in Australia and two in Asia. The types of properties within Co.'s focus include: corporate datacenters, Internet gateway datacenters, technology manufacturing properties, and offices of technology companies.

Recent Developments: For the quarter ended Mar 31 2016, net income decreased 49.0% to US$62.3 million from US$122.3 million in the year-earlier quarter. Revenues were US$504.2 million, up 24.0% from US$406.6 million the year before. Revenues from property income rose 12.8% to US$457.1 million from US$405.2 million in the corresponding quarter a year earlier.

Prospects: Our evaluation of Digital Realty Trust Inc. as of June 19, 2016 is the result of our systematic analysis on three basic characteristics: earnings strength, relative valuation, and recent stock price movement. The company has managed to produce a neutral trend in earnings per share over the past 5 quarters and while recent estimates for the company have been raised by analysts, DLR has posted better than expected results. Based on operating earnings yield, the company is overvalued when compared to all of the companies in our coverage universe. Share price changes over the past year indicates that DLR will perform very well over the near term.

Financial Data
(US$ in Thousands)

	3 Mos	12/31/2015	12/31/2014	12/31/2013	12/31/2012	12/31/2011	12/31/2010	12/31/2009
Earnings Per Share	1.09	1.56	0.99	2.12	1.48	1.32	0.68	0.62
Cash Flow Per Share	5.73	5.78	4.92	5.13	4.68	4.07	4.26	3.74
Tang Book Value Per Share	18.77	19.67	20.87	22.70	23.14	18.42	16.02	11.67
Dividends Per Share	3.430	3.400	3.320	3.120	2.920	2.720	2.020	1.470
Dividend Payout %	314.68	217.95	335.35	147.17	197.30	206.06	297.06	237.10
Income Statement								
Total Revenue	504,199	1,763,336	1,616,438	1,482,259	1,279,067	1,062,710	865,401	637,142
EBITDA	164,999	1,067,980	935,904	986,718	757,123	630,664	518,381	388,067
Depn & Amortn	46,750	578,064	557,356	486,805	393,995	327,400	281,455	211,316
Income Before Taxes	60,364	286,100	190,126	310,653	207,912	157,174	100,158	89,062
Income Taxes	2,109	...	...	...	...	...	...	...
Net Income	61,549	296,689	200,183	314,488	210,334	156,265	102,294	87,662
Average Shares	147,433	138,865	133,637	128,127	116,006	99,169	86,013	77,020
Balance Sheet								
Current Assets	231,189	252,460	188,807	278,333	268,617	186,376	142,118	156,216
Total Assets	11,421,975	11,451,267	9,526,784	9,685,745	8,819,214	6,098,566	5,329,483	3,745,059
Current Liabilities	570,652	735,268	720,942	765,196	739,861	390,588	288,841	188,233
Long-Term Obligations	6,156,730	5,934,241	4,673,127	4,961,892	4,278,565	2,940,210	2,806,954	1,784,444
Total Liabilities	7,015,177	6,951,135	5,648,528	6,075,229	5,350,909	3,575,649	3,366,965	2,186,064
Stockholders' Equity	4,406,798	4,500,132	3,878,256	3,610,516	3,468,305	2,522,917	1,962,518	1,558,995
Shares Outstanding	146,797	146,384	135,626	128,455	125,140	106,039	91,159	76,812
Statistical Record								
Return on Assets %	2.29	2.83	2.08	3.40	2.81	2.73	2.25	2.50
Return on Equity %	5.79	7.08	5.35	8.89	7.00	6.97	5.81	5.74
EBITDA Margin %	32.72	60.57	57.90	66.57	59.19	59.34	59.90	60.91
Net Margin %	12.21	16.83	12.38	21.22	16.44	14.70	11.82	13.76
Asset Turnover	0.18	0.17	0.17	0.16	0.17	0.19	0.19	0.18
Current Ratio	0.41	0.34	0.26	0.36	0.36	0.48	0.49	0.83
Debt to Equity	1.40	1.32	1.20	1.37	1.23	1.17	1.43	1.14
Price Range	88.49-61.52	77.01-61.52	70.27-49.12	73.77-44.53	80.31-59.28	67.14-50.63	63.94-46.69	50.28-26.33
P/E Ratio	81.18-56.44	49.37-39.44	70.98-49.62	34.80-21.00	54.26-40.05	50.86-38.36	94.03-68.66	81.10-42.47
Average Yield %	4.84	5.01	5.56	5.21	4.12	4.61	3.58	3.77

Address: Four Embarcadero Center, Suite 3200, San Francisco, CA 94111 **Telephone:** 415-738-6500 **Fax:** 415-738-6501	**Web Site:** www.digitalrealty.com **Officers:** Dennis E. Singleton - Interim Chairman A. William Stein - Interim Chief Executive Officer, Chief Executive Officer, Chief Financial Officer, Chief Investment Officer	**Auditors:** KPMG LLP **Investor Contact:** 415-738-6500 **Transfer Agents:** American Stock Transfer & Trust Company, New York, NY

DILLARD'S INC.

Exchange	Symbol	Price	52Wk Range	Yield	P/E
NYS	DDS	$59.11 (5/31/2016)	117.19-55.45	0.47	9.28

*7 Year Price Score 106.30 *NYSE Composite index=100   ***12 Month Price Score 82.61**

TRADING VOLUME (thousand shares)

Interim Earnings (Per Share)

Qtr.	Apr	Jul	Oct	Jan
2013-14	2.50	0.79	1.13	2.67
2014-15	2.56	0.80	1.30	3.12
2015-16	2.66	0.75	1.19	2.26
2016-17	2.17	...	...	...

Interim Dividends (Per Share)

Amt	Decl	Ex	Rec	Pay
0.07Q	08/20/2015	09/28/2015	09/30/2015	11/02/2015
0.07Q	11/19/2015	12/29/2015	12/31/2015	02/01/2016
0.07Q	02/25/2016	03/29/2016	03/31/2016	05/02/2016
0.07Q	05/23/2016	06/28/2016	06/30/2016	08/01/2016

Indicated Div: $0.28

Valuation Analysis

		Institutional Holding	
Forecast EPS	$5.81	No of Institutions	
	(05/14/2016)	320	
Market Cap	$2.0 Billion	Shares	
Book Value	$1.8 Billion	38,068,464	
Price/Book	1.13	% Held	
Price/Sales	0.31	79.67	

Business Summary: Retail - General Merchandise/Department Stores (MIC: 2.1.1 SIC: 5311 NAIC: 452111)

Dillard's is a fashion apparel, cosmetics and home furnishing retailer. As of Jan 30 2016, Co. operated 297 Dillard's stores, including 24 clearance centers, and an Internet store providing a selection of merchandise including fashion apparel for women, men and children, accessories, cosmetics, home furnishings and other consumer goods. Co. also operates a contracting construction company, CDI Contractors, LLC, a portion of whose business includes constructing and remodeling stores for Co. As of Jan 30 2016, Co. operated retail department stores in 29 states, primarily in the southwest, southeast and midwest regions of the U. S.

Recent Developments: For the quarter ended Apr 30 2016, net income decreased 29.3% to US$77.4 million from US$109.6 million in the year-earlier quarter. Revenues were US$1.54 billion, down 4.6% from US$1.61 billion the year before. Direct operating expenses declined 2.3% to US$938.6 million from US$960.4 million in the comparable period the year before. Indirect operating expenses decreased 1.0% to US$480.6 million from US$485.7 million in the equivalent prior-year period.

Prospects: Our evaluation of Dillard's Inc. as of June 19, 2016 is the result of our systematic analysis on three basic characteristics: earnings strength, relative valuation, and recent stock price movement. The company has managed to produce a neutral trend in earnings per share over the past 5 quarters. However, while recent estimates for the company have been mixed, DDS has posted results that fell short of analysts expectations. Based on operating earnings yield, the company is undervalued when compared to all of the companies in our coverage universe. Share price changes over the past year indicates that DDS will perform in line with the market over the near term.

Financial Data

(US$ in Thousands)	3 Mos	01/30/2016	01/31/2015	02/01/2014	02/02/2013	01/28/2012	01/29/2011	01/30/2010
Earnings Per Share	6.37	6.91	7.79	7.10	6.87	8.52	2.67	0.93
Cash Flow Per Share	10.63	11.57	14.39	11.04	10.69	9.39	7.66	7.53
Tang Book Value Per Share	52.47	49.98	49.02	45.33	41.24	41.50	34.79	31.21
Dividends Per Share	0.270	0.260	0.240	0.220	5.200	0.190	0.160	0.160
Dividend Payout %	4.24	3.76	3.08	3.10	75.69	2.23	5.99	17.20
Income Statement								
Total Revenue	1,538,797	6,754,545	6,780,129	6,691,777	6,751,595	6,399,765	6,253,535	6,226,628
EBITDA	196,522	719,707	823,074	815,729	809,346	726,728	604,508	421,528
Depn & Amortn	61,188	250,000	251,000	255,000	260,000	258,000	262,000	263,000
Income Before Taxes	119,620	408,784	510,768	496,224	479,750	396,669	268,716	84,525
Income Taxes	42,200	140,770	179,480	173,400	145,060	(62,518)	84,450	12,690
Net Income	77,431	269,370	331,853	323,671	335,962	463,909	179,620	68,531
Average Shares	35,652	39,005	42,603	45,586	48,911	54,448	67,174	73,783
Balance Sheet								
Current Assets	1,882,694	1,668,883	1,888,442	1,660,156	1,491,980	1,591,729	1,701,926	1,749,529
Total Assets	4,025,646	3,865,625	4,170,071	4,050,739	4,048,744	4,306,137	4,374,166	4,606,327
Current Liabilities	899,886	751,216	885,323	778,311	767,116	870,364	831,212	769,022
Long-Term Obligations	820,147	822,054	820,704	821,544	822,309	823,938	908,629	970,009
Total Liabilities	2,213,634	2,070,320	2,150,801	2,058,542	2,078,569	2,254,118	2,287,446	2,302,224
Stockholders' Equity	1,812,012	1,795,305	2,019,270	1,992,197	1,970,175	2,052,019	2,086,720	2,304,103
Shares Outstanding	34,535	35,920	41,192	43,948	47,769	49,441	59,977	73,831
Statistical Record								
Return on Assets %	5.58	6.72	8.10	8.01	7.91	10.72	4.01	1.47
Return on Equity %	12.05	14.16	16.59	16.38	16.44	22.48	8.20	3.02
EBITDA Margin %	12.77	10.66	12.14	12.19	11.99	11.36	9.67	6.77
Net Margin %	5.03	3.99	4.89	4.84	4.98	7.25	2.87	1.10
Asset Turnover	1.57	1.69	1.65	1.66	1.59	1.48	1.40	1.34
Current Ratio	2.09	2.22	2.13	2.13	1.94	1.83	2.05	2.28
Debt to Equity	0.45	0.46	0.41	0.41	0.42	0.40	0.44	0.42
Price Range	133.38-61.24	142.22-61.24	125.81-83.60	97.21-75.77	89.05-43.89	60.28-38.56	41.96-15.61	20.02-3.00
P/E Ratio	20.94-9.61	20.58-8.86	16.15-10.73	13.69-10.67	12.96-6.39	7.08-4.53	15.72-5.85	21.53-3.23
Average Yield %	0.30	0.26	0.22	0.26	7.26	0.40	0.60	1.45

Address: 1600 Cantrell Road, Little Rock, AR 72201 **Telephone:** 501-376-5200	**Web Site:** www.dillards.com **Officers:** William T. Dillard - Chairman, Chief Executive Officer Alex Dillard - President	**Auditors:** KPMG LLP **Investor Contact:** 501-376-5965 **Transfer Agents:** Registrar and Transfer Company, Cranford, NJ

DISCOVER FINANCIAL SERVICES

Exchange	Symbol	Price	52Wk Range	Yield	P/E
NYS	DFS	$56.81 (5/31/2016)	59.66-43.25	1.97	10.90

*7 Year Price Score 119.51 *NYSE Composite Index=100 *12 Month Price Score 100.96

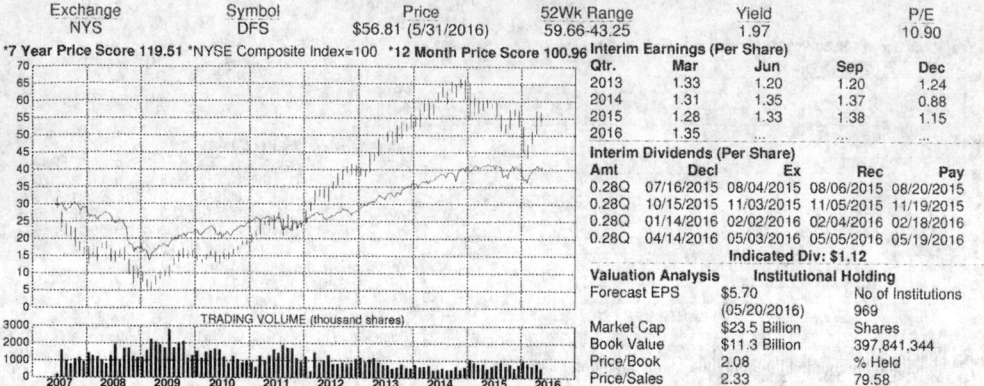

Interim Earnings (Per Share)

Qtr.	Mar	Jun	Sep	Dec
2013	1.33	1.20	1.20	1.24
2014	1.31	1.35	1.37	0.88
2015	1.28	1.33	1.38	1.15
2016	1.35	...	...	...

Interim Dividends (Per Share)

Amt	Decl	Ex	Rec	Pay
0.28Q	07/16/2015	08/04/2015	08/06/2015	08/20/2015
0.28Q	10/15/2015	11/03/2015	11/05/2015	11/19/2015
0.28Q	01/14/2016	02/02/2016	02/04/2016	02/18/2016
0.28Q	04/14/2016	05/03/2016	05/05/2016	05/19/2016

Indicated Div: $1.12

Valuation Analysis — **Institutional Holding**

Forecast EPS	$5.70	No of Institutions
	(05/20/2016)	969
Market Cap	$23.5 Billion	Shares
Book Value	$11.3 Billion	397,841,344
Price/Book	2.08	% Held
Price/Sales	2.33	79.58

Business Summary: Credit & Lending (MIC: 5.4.1 SIC: 6141 NAIC: 522210)

Discover Financial Services is a bank and financial holding company.Co. provides direct banking products and services and payment services through its subsidiaries. Co. provides its customers credit card loans, private student loans, personal loans, home loans, home equity loans and deposit products. Co. also operates the Discover Network, the PULSE network, and Diners Club International. The Discover Network processes transactions for Discover-branded credit cards and provides payment transaction processing and settlement services. At Dec 31 2015, Co. had total assets of $86.94 billion and total deposits of $47.59 billion.

Recent Developments: For the quarter ended Mar 31 2016, net income decreased 1.9% to US$575.0 million from US$586.0 million in the year-earlier quarter. Net interest income increased 7.4% to US$1.75 billion from US$1.63 billion in the year-earlier quarter. Provision for loan losses was US$424.0 million versus US$390.0 million in the prior-year quarter, an increase of 8.7%. Non-interest income fell 12.5% to US$474.0 million from US$542.0 million, while non-interest expense advanced 1.5% to US$886.0 million.

Prospects: Our evaluation of Discover Financial Services as of June 19, 2016 is the result of our systematic analysis on three basic characteristics: earnings strength, relative valuation, and recent stock price movement. The company has enjoyed a very positive trend in earnings per share over the past 5 quarters and while recent estimates for the company have been raised by analysts, DFS has posted better than expected results. Based on operating earnings yield, the company is undervalued when compared to all of the companies in our coverage universe. Share price changes over the past year indicates that DFS will perform in line with the market over the near term.

Financial Data
(US$ in Thousands)

	3 Mos	12/31/2015	12/31/2014	12/31/2013	11/30/2012	11/30/2011	11/30/2010	11/30/2009
Earnings Per Share	5.21	5.13	4.90	4.96	4.46	4.06	1.22	2.39
Cash Flow Per Share	9.47	8.82	8.28	6.68	5.84	6.66	7.12	7.13
Tang Book Value Per Share	24.95	24.41	22.58	20.71	17.56	14.75	11.04	12.57
Dividends Per Share	1.120	1.080	0.920	0.600	0.400	0.200	0.080	0.120
Dividend Payout %	21.50	21.05	18.78	12.10	8.97	4.93	6.56	5.02
Income Statement								
Total Revenue	2,558,000	10,002,000	9,611,000	9,370,000	8,984,000	8,550,313	8,241,217	7,913,039
Income Before Taxes	914,000	3,612,000	3,694,000	3,944,000	3,753,000	3,511,244	1,268,859	2,120,898
Income Taxes	339,000	1,315,000	1,371,000	1,474,000	1,408,000	1,284,536	504,071	844,713
Net Income	575,000	2,297,000	2,323,000	2,470,000	2,345,000	2,226,708	764,788	1,276,185
Average Shares	417,000	437,498	463,412	486,861	520,000	542,626	548,760	511,803
Balance Sheet								
Total Assets	88,093,000	86,936,000	83,126,000	79,340,000	75,283,000	68,783,937	60,784,968	46,020,987
Total Liabilities	76,777,000	75,661,000	71,992,000	68,531,000	65,505,000	60,541,726	54,328,122	37,585,440
Stockholders' Equity	11,316,000	11,275,000	11,134,000	10,809,000	9,778,000	8,242,211	6,456,846	8,435,547
Shares Outstanding	414,226	421,678	449,188	472,244	497,871	528,830	544,681	542,922
Statistical Record								
Return on Assets %	2.65	2.70	2.86	2.94	3.25	3.44	1.43	2.97
Return on Equity %	20.30	20.50	21.17	22.12	25.96	30.30	10.27	17.78
Net Margin %	22.48	22.97	24.17	26.36	26.10	26.04	9.28	16.13
Asset Turnover	0.12	0.12	0.12	0.11	0.12	0.13	0.15	0.18
Price Range	60.34-43.25	65.49-50.60	66.38-52.21	55.95-37.80	41.61-23.07	27.52-18.02	19.09-12.43	17.08-4.89
P/E Ratio	11.58-8.30	12.77-9.86	13.55-10.66	11.28-7.62	9.33-5.17	6.78-4.44	15.65-10.19	7.15-2.05
Average Yield %	2.06	1.89	1.52	1.28	1.19	0.87	0.53	1.13

Address: 2500 Lake Cook Road, Riverwoods, IL 60015 **Telephone:** 224-405-0900	**Web Site:** www.discover.com **Officers:** David W. Nelms - Chairman, Chief Executive Officer Roger C. Hochschild - President, Chief Operating Officer	**Auditors:** Deloitte & Touche LLP **Investor Contact:** 224-405-4555 **Transfer Agents:** Computershare, Jersey City, NJ

DISNEY (WALT) CO. (THE)

Exchange	Symbol	Price	52Wk Range	Yield	P/E
NYS	DIS	$99.22 (5/31/2016)	121.69-88.85	1.43	18.27

*7 Year Price Score 146.79 ***NYSE Composite Index=100** ***12 Month Price Score 95.08**

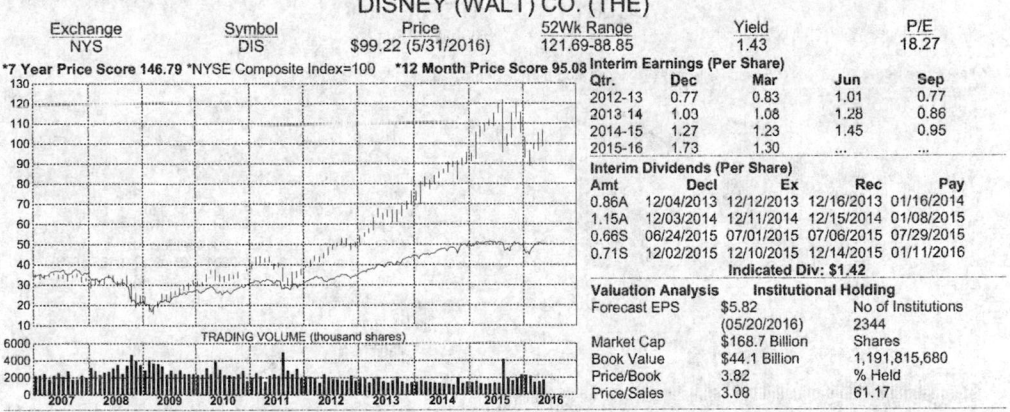

Interim Earnings (Per Share)
Qtr.	Dec	Mar	Jun	Sep
2012-13	0.77	0.83	1.01	0.77
2013 14	1.03	1.08	1.28	0.86
2014-15	1.27	1.23	1.45	0.95
2015-16	1.73	1.30	...	...

Interim Dividends (Per Share)
Amt	Decl	Ex	Rec	Pay
0.86A	12/04/2013	12/12/2013	12/16/2013	01/16/2014
1.15A	12/03/2014	12/11/2014	12/15/2014	01/08/2015
0.66S	06/24/2015	07/01/2015	07/06/2015	07/29/2015
0.71S	12/02/2015	12/10/2015	12/14/2015	01/11/2016

Indicated Div: $1.42

Valuation Analysis
		Institutional Holding	
Forecast EPS	$5.82 (05/20/2016)	No of Institutions	2344
Market Cap	$168.7 Billion	Shares	1,191,815,680
Book Value	$44.1 Billion	% Held	61.17
Price/Book	3.82		
Price/Sales	3.08		

Business Summary: Entertainment (MIC: 2.3.2 SIC: 4841 NAIC: 515210)

Walt Disney is an entertainment company with five segments: Media Networks, which operates cable and broadcast television networks and television production operations; Parks and Resorts, which owns and operates the Walt Disney World Resort in Florida and the Disneyland Resort in California; Studio Entertainment, which produces and acquires live-action and animated motion pictures, direct-to-video content, musical recordings and live stage plays; Consumer Products, which designs, develops, publishes, promotes and sells a variety of products based on its intellectual property; and Interactive, which creates and delivers entertainment and lifestyle content across interactive media platforms.

Recent Developments: For the quarter ended Apr 2 2016, net income increased 2.2% to US$2.28 billion from US$2.23 billion in the year-earlier quarter. Revenues were US$12.97 billion, up 4.1% from US$12.46 billion the year before. Direct operating expenses rose 2.6% to US$6.86 billion from US$6.69 billion in the comparable period the year before. Indirect operating expenses increased 2.9% to US$2.74 billion from US$2.67 billion in the equivalent prior-year period.

Prospects: Our evaluation of Disney (Walt) Co. as of June 19, 2016 is the result of our systematic analysis on three basic characteristics: earnings strength, relative valuation, and recent stock price movement. The company has managed to produce a neutral trend in earnings per share over the past 5 quarters. However, while recent estimates for the company have been mixed, DIS has posted results that fell short of analysts expectations. Based on operating earnings yield, the company is undervalued when compared to all of the companies in our coverage universe. Share price changes over the past year indicates that DIS will perform in line with the market over the near term.

Financial Data
(US$ in Thousands)	6 Mos	3 Mos	10/03/2015	09/27/2014	09/28/2013	09/29/2012	10/01/2011	10/02/2010
Earnings Per Share	5.43	5.36	4.90	4.26	3.38	3.13	2.52	2.03
Cash Flow Per Share	7.29	6.90	6.34	5.64	5.29	4.45	3.73	3.44
Tang Book Value Per Share	5.44	5.32	5.95	5.65	5.96	5.41	4.61	4.40
Dividends Per Share	1.370	1.370	1.810	0.860	0.750	0.600	0.400	0.350
Dividend Payout %	25.23	25.56	36.94	20.19	22.19	19.17	15.87	17.24
Income Statement								
Total Revenue	28,213,000	15,244,000	52,465,000	48,813,000	45,041,000	42,278,000	40,893,000	38,063,000
EBITDA	8,374,000	4,458,000	15,525,000	13,657,000	11,140,000	10,989,000	9,642,000	8,198,000
Depn & Amortn	1,103,000	550,000	2,354,000	2,288,000	2,192,000	1,987,000	1,841,000	1,602,000
Income Before Taxes	7,180,000	3,884,000	13,054,000	11,392,000	8,713,000	8,633,000	7,458,000	6,187,000
Income Taxes	2,618,000	1,448,000	5,016,000	4,242,000	2,984,000	3,087,000	2,785,000	2,314,000
Net Income	5,023,000	2,880,000	8,382,000	7,501,000	6,136,000	5,682,000	4,807,000	3,963,000
Average Shares	1,643,000	1,668,000	1,709,000	1,759,000	1,813,000	1,818,000	1,909,000	1,948,000
Balance Sheet								
Current Assets	16,999,000	17,768,000	16,758,000	15,176,000	14,109,000	13,709,000	13,757,000	12,225,000
Total Assets	90,264,000	90,121,000	88,182,000	84,186,000	81,241,000	74,898,000	72,124,000	69,206,000
Current Liabilities	17,073,000	18,796,000	16,334,000	13,292,000	11,704,000	12,813,000	12,088,000	11,000,000
Long-Term Obligations	15,367,000	12,965,000	12,773,000	12,676,000	13,050,000	10,981,000	11,210,000	10,354,000
Total Liabilities	46,140,000	46,163,000	43,657,000	39,228,000	35,812,000	35,139,000	34,739,000	31,687,000
Stockholders' Equity	44,124,000	43,958,000	44,525,000	44,958,000	45,429,000	39,759,000	37,385,000	37,519,000
Shares Outstanding	1,700,000	1,700,000	1,600,000	1,707,000	1,800,000	1,780,000	1,762,200	1,896,900
Statistical Record								
Return on Assets %	10.36	10.25	9.57	9.09	7.88	7.75	6.82	6.01
Return on Equity %	20.22	20.61	18.43	16.64	14.45	14.77	12.87	11.15
EBITDA Margin %	29.68	29.24	29.59	27.98	24.73	25.99	23.58	21.54
Net Margin %	17.80	18.89	15.98	15.37	13.62	13.44	11.76	10.41
Asset Turnover	0.62	0.61	0.60	0.59	0.58	0.58	0.58	0.58
Current Ratio	1.00	0.95	1.03	1.14	1.21	1.07	1.14	1.11
Debt to Equity	0.35	0.29	0.29	0.28	0.29	0.28	0.30	0.28
Price Range	121.69-88.85	121.69-90.96	121.69-81.74	90.94-63.59	67.67-47.06	52.92-29.00	44.07-29.55	37.56-27.21
P/E Ratio	22.41-16.36	22.70-16.97	24.83-16.68	21.35-14.93	20.02-13.92	16.91-9.27	17.49-11.73	18.50-13.40
Average Yield %	1.30	1.29	1.77	1.09	1.29	1.41	1.04	1.08

Address: 500 South Buena Vista Street, Burbank, CA 91521 **Telephone:** 818-560-1000	**Web Site:** www.disney.com **Officers:** Robert A. Iger - Chairman, President, Chief Executive Officer Alan N. Braverman - Senior Executive Vice President, Secretary, General Counsel	**Auditors:** PricewaterhouseCoopers LLP **Investor Contact:** 818 553-7200 **Transfer Agents:** Broadridge Corporate Issuer Solutions, Brentwood, NY

DOLBY LABORATORIES INC

Exchange	Symbol	Price	52Wk Range	Yield	P/E
NYS	DLB	$47.45 (5/31/2016)	47.92-30.50	1.01	26.96

*7 Year Price Score 76.10 *NYSE Composite Index=100 *12 Month Price Score 120.35

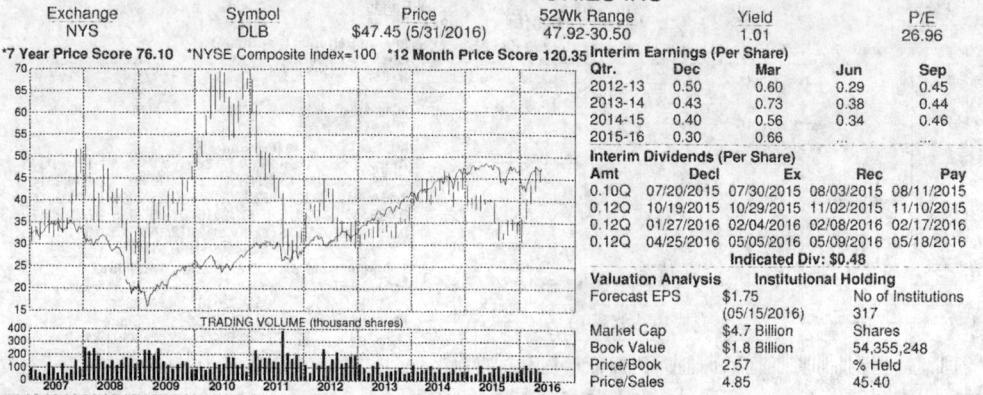

Interim Earnings (Per Share)

Qtr.	Dec	Mar	Jun	Sep
2012-13	0.50	0.60	0.29	0.45
2013-14	0.43	0.73	0.38	0.44
2014-15	0.40	0.56	0.34	0.46
2015-16	0.30	0.66	...	...

Interim Dividends (Per Share)

Amt	Decl	Ex	Rec	Pay
0.10Q	07/20/2015	07/30/2015	08/03/2015	08/11/2015
0.12Q	10/19/2015	10/29/2015	11/02/2015	11/10/2015
0.12Q	01/27/2016	02/04/2016	02/08/2016	02/17/2016
0.12Q	04/25/2016	05/05/2016	05/09/2016	05/18/2016

Indicated Div: $0.48

Valuation Analysis

		Institutional Holding	
Forecast EPS	$1.75	No of Institutions	
	(05/15/2016)	317	
Market Cap	$4.7 Billion	Shares	
Book Value	$1.8 Billion	54,355,248	
Price/Book	2.57	% Held	
Price/Sales	4.85	45.40	

Business Summary: Manufacturing (MIC: 6.1.1 SIC: 3663 NAIC: 334220)

Dolby Laboratories designs and manufactures audio and imaging products for the film production, cinema, and television broadcast industries. Co.'s products include digital cinema server products, which are used to load, store, decrypt, decode, and watermark digital film files for presentation on digital cinema projectors; Dolby Cinema Audio Products including its Cinema Processors that decode and render digital cinema soundtracks including those using Dolby Atmos, an object-oriented audio platform. Co. also provides products that author, encrypt, encode and package Dolby Atmos sound tracks. Co.'s other products include broadcast hardware and software to encode and decode audio for DTV.

Recent Developments: For the quarter ended Apr 1 2016, net income increased 15.4% to US$67.5 million from US$58.5 million in the year-earlier quarter. Revenues were US$274.3 million, up 0.9% from US$272.0 million the year before. Operating income was US$82.3 million versus US$78.6 million in the prior-year quarter, an increase of 4.7%. Direct operating expenses declined 3.1% to US$24.4 million from US$25.1 million in the comparable period the year before. Indirect operating expenses decreased 0.3% to US$167.6 million from US$168.2 million in the equivalent prior-year period.

Prospects: Our evaluation of Dolby Laboratories Inc. as of June 19, 2016 is the result of our systematic analysis on three basic characteristics: earnings strength, relative valuation, and recent stock price movement. The company has enjoyed a very positive trend in earnings per share over the past 5 quarters and while recent estimates for the company have remained steady, DLB has posted better than expected results. Based on operating earnings yield, the company is about fairly valued when compared to all of the companies in our coverage universe. Share price changes over the past year indicates that DLB will perform in line with the market over the near term.

Financial Data

(US$ in Thousands)	6 Mos	3 Mos	09/25/2015	09/26/2014	09/27/2013	09/28/2012	09/30/2011	09/24/2010
Earnings Per Share	1.76	1.66	1.75	1.99	1.84	2.46	2.75	2.46
Cash Flow Per Share	2.87	3.71	3.03	3.55	2.70	3.66	3.56	2.89
Tang Book Value Per Share	13.19	12.61	13.58	13.38	11.40	13.41	12.33	10.19
Dividends Per Share	0.440	0.420	0.400	...	4.000	...	...	...
Dividend Payout %	25.00	25.30	22.86	...	217.39		...	...
Income Statement								
Total Revenue	515,154	240,814	970,638	960,176	909,674	926,264	955,505	922,713
EBITDA	123,483	39,821	289,621	310,672	284,773	393,376	454,740	448,217
Depn & Amortn	2,661	1,605	48,200	38,100	37,400	30,600	24,100	17,800
Income Before Taxes	123,307	39,484	245,782	276,099	250,646	368,991	440,643	437,012
Income Taxes	24,751	8,473	62,542	67,379	60,344	103,857	130,061	154,185
Net Income	98,299	30,901	181,390	206,103	189,271	264,302	309,267	283,447
Average Shares	101,555	101,931	103,862	103,632	102,788	107,541	112,554	115,388
Balance Sheet								
Current Assets	786,287	737,941	918,330	1,005,851	812,722	970,286	1,158,598	1,060,413
Total Assets	2,158,851	2,113,604	2,133,293	1,984,012	1,737,945	1,960,798	1,884,387	1,711,772
Current Liabilities	198,487	196,535	209,681	189,370	172,815	156,840	159,385	165,756
Total Liabilities	313,490	310,108	326,225	273,995	256,835	240,529	220,874	238,035
Stockholders' Equity	1,845,361	1,803,496	1,807,068	1,710,017	1,481,110	1,720,269	1,663,513	1,473,737
Shares Outstanding	100,055	100,770	101,034	102,268	101,739	103,095	109,420	112,084
Statistical Record								
Return on Assets %	8.44	8.27	8.84	11.11	10.26	13.78	16.92	17.26
Return on Equity %	9.94	9.66	10.34	12.95	11.86	15.66	19.40	20.19
EBITDA Margin %	23.97	16.54	29.84	32.36	31.30	42.47	47.59	48.58
Net Margin %	19.08	12.83	18.69	21.47	20.81	28.53	32.37	30.72
Asset Turnover	0.46	0.47	0.47	0.52	0.49	0.48	0.52	0.56
Current Ratio	3.96	3.75	4.38	5.31	4.70	6.19	7.27	6.40
Price Range	43.52-30.50	43.41-30.91	45.99-30.91	46.93-34.39	35.60-28.98	45.11-26.28	69.51-27.44	69.37-37.40
P/E Ratio	24.73-17.33	26.15-18.62	26.28-17.66	23.58-17.28	19.35-15.75	18.34-10.68	25.28-9.98	28.20-15.20
Average Yield %	1.21	1.14	1.02	...	12.23	...	...	...

Address: 1275 Market Street, San Francisco, CA 94103-1410 **Telephone:** 415-558-0200	**Web Site:** www.dolby.com **Officers:** Peter Gotcher - Chairman Kevin J. Yeaman - President, Chief Executive Officer	**Auditors:** KPMG LLP **Transfer Agents:** Computershare Trust Company, N.A., Providence, RI

DOLLAR GENERAL CORP

Exchange	Symbol	Price	52Wk Range	Yield	P/E
NYS	DG	$89.90 (5/31/2016)	89.90-60.02	1.11	21.71

*7 Year Price Score N/A   *NYSE Composite Index=100   *12 Month Price Score 111.34

Interim Earnings (Per Share)

Qtr.	Apr	Jul	Oot	Jan
2013-14	0.67	0.76	0.74	1.01
2014 15	0.72	0.83	0.78	1.17
2015-16	0.84	0.95	0.86	1.30
2016-17	1.03	...	...	...

Interim Dividends (Per Share)

Amt	Decl	Ex	Rec	Pay
0.22Q	08/27/2015	09/14/2015	09/16/2015	09/30/2015
0.22Q	12/03/2015	12/21/2015	12/23/2015	01/06/2016
0.25Q	03/08/2016	03/24/2016	03/29/2016	04/12/2016
0.25Q	05/24/2016	06/13/2016	06/15/2016	06/29/2016

Indicated Div: $1.00

Valuation Analysis

		Institutional Holding	
Forecast EPS	$4.64	No of Institutions	
	(05/20/2016)	773	
Market Cap	$25.5 Billion	Shares	
Book Value	$5.4 Billion	272,303,712	
Price/Book	4.73	% Held	
Price/Sales	1.23	N/A	

TRADING VOLUME (thousand shares)

Business Summary: Retail - General Merchandise/Department Stores (MIC: 2.1.1 SIC: 5331 NAIC: 452990)

Dollar General is a discount retailer offering a wide selection of merchandise. At Feb 26, 2016, Co. operated 12,575 stores located in 43 states, primarily in the southern, southwestern, midwestern and eastern U.S. Co.'s consumables category includes paper and cleaning products, packaged food, perishables, snacks, health and beauty; seasonal products include decorations, toys, batteries, small electronics, automotive and home office supplies; home products include kitchen supplies, cookware, frames, craft supplies and kitchen, and bed and bath soft goods; and apparel category includes casual everyday apparel, as well as socks, underwear, disposable diapers, shoes and accessories.

Recent Developments: For the quarter ended Apr 29 2016, net income increased 16.5% to US$295.1 million from US$253.2 million in the year-earlier quarter. Revenues were US$5.27 billion, up 7.0% from US$4.92 billion the year before. Operating income was US$480.7 million versus US$428.2 million in the prior-year quarter, an increase of 12.3%. Direct operating expenses rose 6.8% to US$3.65 billion from US$3.42 billion in the comparable period the year before. Indirect operating expenses increased 5.7% to US$1.13 billion from US$1.07 billion in the equivalent prior-year period.

Prospects: Our evaluation of Dollar General Inc. as of June 19, 2016 is the result of our systematic analysis on three basic characteristics: earnings strength, relative valuation, and recent stock price movement. The company has produced a positive trend in earnings per share over the past 5 quarters and while recent estimates for the company have been raised by analysts, DG has posted better than expected results. Based on operating earnings yield, the company is about fairly valued when compared to all of the companies in our coverage universe. Share price changes over the past year indicates that DG will perform in line with the market over the near term.

Financial Data

(US$ in Thousands)	3 Mos	01/29/2016	01/30/2015	01/31/2014	02/01/2013	02/03/2012	01/28/2011	01/29/2010
Earnings Per Share	4.14	3.95	3.49	3.17	2.85	2.22	1.82	1.04
Cash Flow Per Share	5.03	4.69	4.33	3.77	3.41	3.03	2.42	2.08
Tang Book Value Per Share	N.M.	N.M.	0.56	N.M.	N.M.	N.M.	N.M.	N.M.
Dividends Per Share	0.910	0.880	...	...	...	...	...	0.752
Dividend Payout %	21.98	22.28	...	...	...	...	...	72.36
Income Statement								
Total Revenue	5,265,432	20,368,562	18,909,588	17,504,167	16,022,128	14,807,188	13,035,000	11,796,380
EBITDA	573,067	2,290,568	2,104,993	2,032,614	1,902,520	1,673,889	1,474,664	1,098,816
Depn & Amortn	92,324	350,600	335,900	315,300	277,200	243,700	215,700	201,100
Income Before Taxes	456,662	1,853,024	1,680,861	1,628,330	1,497,394	1,225,289	984,972	552,116
Income Taxes	161,538	687,944	615,516	603,214	544,732	458,604	357,115	212,674
Net Income	295,124	1,165,080	1,065,345	1,025,116	952,662	766,685	627,857	339,442
Average Shares	286,978	295,211	305,681	323,854	334,469	345,117	344,800	324,836
Balance Sheet								
Current Assets	3,477,346	3,432,410	3,532,609	3,205,607	2,677,113	2,275,074	2,367,825	1,845,449
Total Assets	11,316,384	11,257,885	11,224,104	10,867,524	10,367,682	9,688,520	9,546,222	8,863,519
Current Liabilities	2,011,594	1,995,596	1,987,740	1,811,971	1,738,547	1,509,902	1,365,373	1,206,500
Long-Term Obligations	2,989,663	2,969,175	2,639,427	2,742,788	2,771,336	2,617,891	3,287,070	3,399,715
Total Liabilities	5,928,001	5,880,009	5,514,066	5,465,331	5,382,352	5,013,938	5,482,590	5,454,735
Stockholders' Equity	5,388,383	5,377,876	5,710,038	5,402,193	4,985,330	4,674,582	4,063,632	3,408,784
Shares Outstanding	283,778	286,694	303,447	317,058	327,069	338,089	341,507	340,586
Statistical Record								
Return on Assets %	10.84	10.39	9.67	9.68	9.53	7.84	6.84	3.83
Return on Equity %	22.40	21.07	19.23	19.79	19.78	17.26	16.85	10.88
EBITDA Margin %	10.88	11.25	11.13	11.61	11.87	11.30	11.31	9.31
Net Margin %	5.60	5.72	5.63	5.86	5.95	5.18	4.82	2.88
Asset Turnover	1.86	1.82	1.72	1.65	1.60	1.51	1.42	1.33
Current Ratio	1.73	1.72	1.78	1.77	1.54	1.51	1.73	1.53
Debt to Equity	0.55	0.55	0.46	0.51	0.56	0.56	0.81	1.00
Price Range	87.31-60.02	81.18-60.02	71.29-53.50	62.87-43.80	55.06-41.64	42.70-26.85	33.28-21.71	24.55-22.15
P/E Ratio	21.09-14.50	20.55-15.19	20.43-15.33	19.83-13.82	19.32-14.61	19.23-12.09	18.29-11.93	23.61-21.30
Average Yield %	1.22	1.21	...	...	...	...	...	3.23

Address: 100 Mission Ridge, Goodlettsville, TN 37072
Telephone: 615-855-4000
Fax: 615-855-5527

Web Site: www.dollargeneral.com
Officers: Todd J. Vasos - Chief Executive Officer, Executive Vice President, Chief Merchandising Officer, Chief Operating Officer, Division Officer John W. Garratt - Senior Vice President, Interim Chief Financial Officer, Executive Vice President, Chief Financial Officer

Auditors: Ernst & Young LLP
Investor Contact: 615-855-4000
Transfer Agents: Wells Fargo Bank, N.A., St. Paul, MN

DOMINION RESOURCES INC

Exchange	Symbol	Price	52Wk Range	Yield	P/E	Div Achiever
NYS	D	$72.25 (5/31/2016)	76.22-64.89	3.88	22.72	12 Years

*7 Year Price Score 107.31 *NYSE Composite Index=100 *12 Month Price Score 100.96

Interim Earnings (Per Share)

Qtr.	Mar	Jun	Sep	Dec
2013	0.86	0.35	0.98	0.74
2014	0.65	0.27	0.90	0.41
2015	0.91	0.70	1.00	0.60
2016	0.88	...	...	...

Interim Dividends (Per Share)

Amt	Decl	Ex	Rec	Pay
0.647Q	08/04/2015	08/26/2015	08/28/2015	09/20/2015
0.647Q	10/22/2015	11/23/2015	11/25/2015	12/20/2015
0.70Q	01/21/2016	03/02/2016	03/04/2016	03/20/2016
0.70Q	05/11/2016	06/01/2016	06/03/2016	06/20/2016

Indicated Div: $2.80 (Div. Reinv. Plan)

Valuation Analysis — **Institutional Holding**

Forecast EPS	$3.80 (05/20/2016)	No of Institutions	1303
Market Cap	$43.1 Billion	Shares	436,348,448
Book Value	$12.9 Billion	% Held	63.75
Price/Book	3.35		
Price/Sales	3.85		

Business Summary: Electric Utilities (MIC: 3.1.1 SIC: 4911 NAIC: 221121)

Dominion Resources is a producer and transporter of energy. Co.'s subsidiary, Dominion Gas Holdings, LLC conducts business activities through a regulated interstate natural gas transmission pipeline and underground storage system in the Northeast, mid-Atlantic and Midwest states, regulated gas transportation and distribution operations in Ohio, and gas gathering and processing activities primarily in West Virginia, Ohio and Pennsylvania. Co.'s nonregulated operations include merchant generation, energy marketing and price risk management activities, and retail energy marketing operations. As of Dec 31 2015, Co. served over 5.0 million utility and retail energy customers in 14 states .

Recent Developments: For the quarter ended Mar 31 2016, net income decreased 1.7% to US$531.0 million from US$540.0 million in the year-earlier quarter. Revenues were US$2.92 billion, down 14.3% from US$3.41 billion the year before. Operating income was US$882.0 million versus US$1.00 billion in the prior-year quarter, a decrease of 12.0%. Direct operating expenses declined 19.7% to US$1.52 billion from US$1.90 billion in the comparable period the year before. Indirect operating expenses increased 1.4% to US$515.0 million from US$508.0 million in the equivalent prior-year period.

Prospects: Our evaluation of Dominion Resources Inc. as of June 19, 2016 is the result of our systematic analysis on three basic characteristics: earnings strength, relative valuation, and recent stock price movement. The company has managed to produce a neutral trend in earnings per share over the past 5 quarters. However, while recent estimates for the company have been mixed, D has posted better than expected results. Based on operating earnings yield, the company is about fairly valued when compared to all of the companies in our coverage universe. Share price changes over the past year indicates that D will perform well over the near term.

Financial Data
(US$ in Thousands)

	3 Mos	12/31/2015	12/31/2014	12/31/2013	12/31/2012	12/31/2011	12/31/2010	12/31/2009
Earnings Per Share	3.18	3.20	2.24	2.93	0.53	2.45	4.76	2.17
Cash Flow Per Share	7.60	7.55	5.90	5.93	7.20	5.21	3.10	6.38
Tang Book Value Per Share	16.06	14.77	13.57	14.20	12.43	13.90	14.58	12.35
Dividends Per Share	2.643	2.590	2.400	2.250	2.110	1.970	1.830	1.750
Dividend Payout %	83.10	80.94	107.14	76.79	398.11	80.41	38.45	80.65
Income Statement								
Total Revenue	2,921,000	11,683,000	12,436,000	13,120,000	13,093,000	14,379,000	15,197,000	15,131,000
EBITDA	1,360,000	5,401,000	4,079,000	4,971,000	2,822,000	4,328,000	7,127,000	4,129,000
Depn & Amortn	424,000	1,669,000	1,560,000	1,390,000	1,443,000	1,288,000	1,258,000	1,319,000
Income Before Taxes	710,000	2,828,000	1,326,000	2,704,000	497,000	2,171,000	5,037,000	1,916,000
Income Taxes	179,000	905,000	452,000	892,000	146,000	745,000	2,057,000	612,000
Net Income	524,000	1,899,000	1,310,000	1,697,000	302,000	1,408,000	2,808,000	1,287,000
Average Shares	598,200	593,700	584,500	579,500	573,900	574,600	590,100	593,700
Balance Sheet								
Current Assets	3,711,000	4,191,000	5,615,000	5,940,000	5,140,000	5,430,000	5,400,000	6,817,000
Total Assets	59,505,000	58,797,000	54,327,000	50,096,000	46,838,000	45,614,000	42,817,000	42,554,000
Current Liabilities	7,518,000	8,120,000	7,198,000	6,994,000	7,763,000	6,962,000	5,773,000	6,833,000
Long-Term Obligations	24,186,000	23,616,000	21,805,000	19,330,000	16,851,000	17,394,000	15,758,000	15,481,000
Total Liabilities	46,625,000	46,133,000	42,772,000	38,197,000	36,013,000	33,911,000	30,563,000	31,112,000
Stockholders' Equity	12,880,000	12,664,000	11,555,000	11,899,000	10,825,000	11,703,000	12,254,000	11,442,000
Shares Outstanding	597,000	596,000	585,000	581,000	576,000	570,000	581,000	599,000
Statistical Record								
Return on Assets %	3.29	3.36	2.51	3.50	0.65	3.18	6.58	3.04
Return on Equity %	15.16	15.68	11.17	14.94	2.67	11.75	23.70	11.82
EBITDA Margin %	46.56	46.23	32.80	37.89	21.55	30.10	46.90	27.29
Net Margin %	17.94	16.25	10.53	12.93	2.31	9.79	18.48	8.51
Asset Turnover	0.20	0.21	0.24	0.27	0.28	0.33	0.36	0.36
Current Ratio	0.49	0.52	0.78	0.85	0.66	0.78	0.94	1.00
Debt to Equity	1.88	1.86	1.89	1.62	1.56	1.49	1.29	1.35
Price Range	76.22-64.89	79.27-64.89	80.23-63.51	67.80-51.80	54.97-49.19	53.53-42.26	44.92-36.27	39.61-27.29
P/E Ratio	23.97-20.41	24.77-20.28	35.82-28.35	23.14-17.68	103.72-92.81	21.85-17.25	9.44-7.62	18.25-12.58
Average Yield %	3.77	3.65	3.43	3.79	4.05	4.14	4.42	5.20

Address: 120 Tredegar Street, Richmond, VA 23219 Telephone: 804-819-2000 Fax: 804-775-5819	Web Site: www.dom.com Officers: Thomas F. Farrell - Chairman, President, Chief Executive Officer, Division Officer Mark F. McGettrick - Executive Vice President, Chief Financial Officer	Auditors: Deloitte & Touche LLP Investor Contact: 804-819-2205 Transfer Agents: Dominion Resources Services, Inc. Richmond, VA

DOMINOS PIZZA INC.

Exchange	Symbol	Price	52Wk Range	Yield	P/E
NYS	DPZ	$120.88 (5/31/2016)	140.01-101.62	1.26	34.15

*7 Year Price Score 184.08 *NYSE Composite Index=100 *12 Month Price Score 108.12

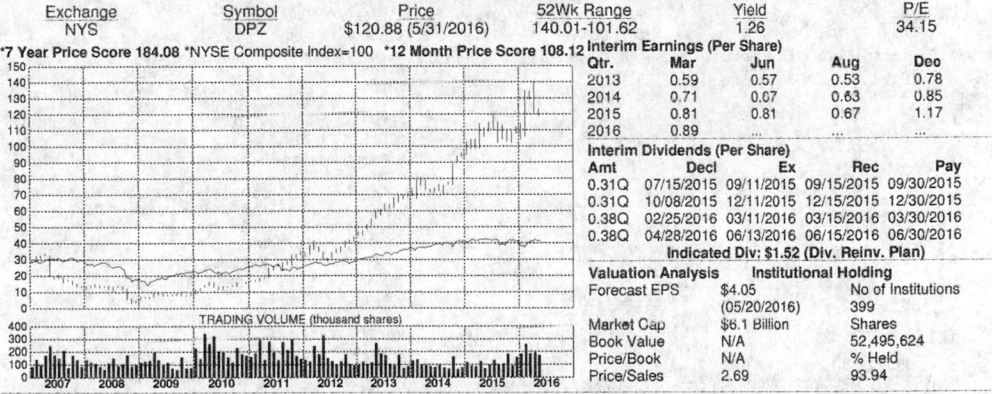

Interim Earnings (Per Share)

Qtr.	Mar	Jun	Aug	Deo
2013	0.59	0.57	0.53	0.78
2014	0.71	0.67	0.63	0.85
2015	0.81	0.81	0.67	1.17
2016	0.89	...	...	...

Interim Dividends (Per Share)

Amt	Decl	Ex	Rec	Pay
0.31Q	07/15/2015	09/11/2015	09/15/2015	09/30/2015
0.31Q	10/08/2015	12/11/2015	12/15/2015	12/30/2015
0.38Q	02/25/2016	03/11/2016	03/15/2016	03/30/2016
0.38Q	04/28/2016	06/13/2016	06/15/2016	06/30/2016

Indicated Div: $1.52 (Div. Reinv. Plan)

Valuation Analysis

		Institutional Holding	
Forecast EPS	$4.05	No of Institutions	
	(05/20/2016)	399	
Market Cap	$6.1 Billion	Shares	
Book Value	N/A	52,495,624	
Price/Book	N/A	% Held	
Price/Sales	2.69	93.94	

Business Summary: Hotels, Restaurants & Travel (MIC: 2.2.1 SIC: 5812 NAIC: 722211)

Domino's Pizza is engaged in the delivery and carryout segments of the pizza industry. Co.'s activities include the retail sales of food via Co.-owned Domino's Pizza stores; sales of food, equipment and supplies to Co.-owned and franchised Domino's Pizza stores via Co.-owned supply chain centers; and receipt of royalties and fees from domestic and international Domino's Pizza franchisees. As of Jan 3 2016, Co. had three segments: domestic stores, which consisted of 4,816 franchised stores and 384 domestic Co.-owned stores; international franchise, which included a network of franchised stores in 80 international markets and operates 7,330 international franchise stores; and supply chain.

Recent Developments: For the quarter ended Mar 27 2016, net income decreased 1.8% to US$45.5 million from US$46.3 million in the year earlier quarter. Revenues were US$539.2 million, up 7.4% from US$502.0 million the year before. Operating income was US$98.7 million versus US$94.3 million in the prior-year quarter, an increase of 4.7%. Direct operating expenses rose 7.8% to US$372.0 million from US$345.0 million in the comparable period the year before. Indirect operating expenses increased 9.1% to US$68.5 million from US$62.8 million in the equivalent prior-year period.

Prospects: Our evaluation of Dominos Pizza Inc. as of June 19, 2016 is the result of our systematic analysis on three basic characteristics: earnings strength, relative valuation, and recent stock price movement. The company has generated a negative trend in earnings per share over the past 5 quarters and while recent estimates for the company have remained steady, DPZ has posted results that fell short of analysts expectations. Based on operating earnings yield, the company is about fairly valued when compared to all of the companies in our coverage universe. Share price changes over the past year indicates that DPZ will perform well over the near term.

Financial Data

(US$ in Thousands)	3 Mos	01/03/2016	12/28/2014	12/29/2013	12/30/2012	01/01/2012	01/02/2011	01/03/2010
Earnings Per Share	3.54	3.47	2.86	2.48	1.91	1.71	1.45	1.38
Cash Flow Per Share	4.51	5.33	3.51	3.51	3.13	2.61	2.20	1.74
Dividends Per Share	1.310	1.240	1.000	0.800	3.000	...	...	...
Dividend Payout %	37.01	35.73	34.97	32.26	157.07			
Income Statement								
Total Revenue	539,175	2,216,528	1,993,833	1,802,223	1,678,439	1,652,193	1,570,894	1,404,057
EBITDA	100,372	450,266	386,895	345,688	320,098	289,377	267,400	279,469
Depn & Amortn	1,660	44,827	41,534	31,877	37,767	30,232	31,889	33,685
Income Before Taxes	72,842	306,215	258,623	225,099	181,187	167,806	138,945	135,522
Income Taxes	27,391	113,426	96,036	82,114	68,795	62,445	51,028	55,778
Net Income	45,451	192,789	162,587	142,985	112,392	105,361	87,917	79,744
Average Shares	51,230	55,532	56,931	57,720	58,997	61,653	60,815	57,827
Balance Sheet								
Current Assets	626,486	602,637	428,361	351,540	306,267	326,843	305,038	278,668
Total Assets	820,759	799,845	619,280	525,255	478,197	480,543	460,837	453,761
Current Liabilities	333,726	375,983	265,608	254,611	229,498	197,175	186,126	219,423
Long-Term Obligations	2,173,403	2,181,460	1,523,546	1,512,299	1,536,443	1,450,369	1,451,321	1,522,463
Total Liabilities	2,551,038	2,600,096	1,838,745	1,815,457	1,813,720	1,690,282	1,671,488	1,774,755
Stockholders' Equity	(1,730,279)	(1,800,251)	(1,219,465)	(1,290,202)	(1,335,523)	(1,209,739)	(1,210,651)	(1,320,994)
Shares Outstanding	50,110	49,838	55,553	55,768	56,313	57,741	60,139	58,572
Statistical Record								
Return on Assets %	26.34	26.73	28.49	28.58	23.51	22.45	19.28	17.10
EBITDA Margin %	18.62	20.31	19.40	19.18	19.07	17.51	17.02	19.90
Net Margin %	8.43	8.70	8.15	7.93	6.70	6.38	5.60	5.68
Asset Turnover	3.09	3.07	3.49	3.60	3.51	3.52	3.44	3.01
Current Ratio	1.88	1.60	1.61	1.38	1.33	1.66	1.64	1.27
Price Range	134.39-98.36	119.43-94.17	95.93-67.17	70.68-43.55	43.46-28.75	34.91-16.17	16.16-8.68	9.67-5.17
P/E Ratio	37.96-27.79	34.42-27.14	33.54-23.49	28.50-17.56	22.75-15.05	20.42-9.46	11.14-5.99	7.01-3.75
Average Yield %	1.18	1.16	1.29	1.36	8.41	...	...	...

Address: 30 Frank Lloyd Wright Drive, Ann Arbor, MI 48105 **Telephone:** 734-930-3030	**Web Site:** www.dominos.com **Officers:** David A. Brandon - Chairman, Chief Executive Officer J. Patrick Doyle - President, Chief Executive Officer, Region Officer	**Auditors:** PricewaterhouseCoopers LLP **Investor Contact:** 734-930-3008 **Transfer Agents:** ComputerShare Investor Services, Providence, RI

DOMTAR CORP

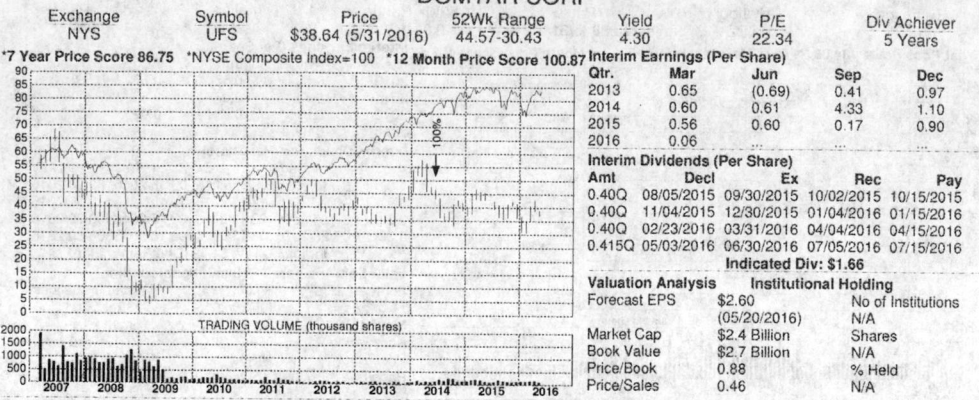

Exchange	Symbol	Price	52Wk Range	Yield	P/E	Div Achiever
NYS	UFS	$38.64 (5/31/2016)	44.57-30.43	4.30	22.34	5 Years

*7 Year Price Score 86.75   *NYSE Composite Index=100   *12 Month Price Score 100.87

Interim Earnings (Per Share)

Qtr.	Mar	Jun	Sep	Dec
2013	0.65	(0.69)	0.41	0.97
2014	0.60	0.61	4.33	1.10
2015	0.56	0.60	0.17	0.90
2016	0.06	...	...	...

Interim Dividends (Per Share)

Amt	Decl	Ex	Rec	Pay
0.40Q	08/05/2015	09/30/2015	10/02/2015	10/15/2015
0.40Q	11/04/2015	12/30/2015	01/04/2016	01/15/2016
0.40Q	02/23/2016	03/31/2016	04/04/2016	04/15/2016
0.415Q	05/03/2016	06/30/2016	07/05/2016	07/15/2016

Indicated Div: $1.66

Valuation Analysis

		Institutional Holding	
Forecast EPS	$2.60 (05/20/2016)	No of Institutions	N/A
Market Cap	$2.4 Billion	Shares	
Book Value	$2.7 Billion		N/A
Price/Book	0.88	% Held	N/A
Price/Sales	0.46		N/A

Business Summary: Paper & Forest Products (MIC: 8.1.2 SIC: 2621 NAIC: 322121)

Domtar is engaged in designing, manufacturing, marketing and distributing a range of fiber-based products including communication papers, specialty and packaging papers and absorbent hygiene products. Co.'s segments includes Pulp and Paper, which consists of the design, manufacturing, marketing and distribution of communication, specialty and packaging papers, as well as softwood, fluff and hardwood market pulp; and Personal Care, which consists of the design, manufacturing, marketing and distribution of absorbent hygiene products, including both adult incontinence and baby diapers. Co. markets and produces incontinence care products under the Attends®, IncoPack® and Indasec® brand names.

Recent Developments: For the quarter ended Mar 31 2016, net income decreased 88.9% to US$4.0 million from US$36.0 million in the year-earlier quarter. Revenues were US$1.29 billion, down 4.5% from US$1.35 billion the year before. Operating income was US$18.0 million versus US$71.0 million in the prior-year quarter, a decrease of 74.6%. Direct operating expenses declined 1.1% to US$1.05 billion from US$1.06 billion in the comparable period the year before. Indirect operating expenses increased 1.9% to US$219.0 million from US$215.0 million in the equivalent prior-year period.

Prospects: Our evaluation of Domtar Corp. as of June 19, 2016 is the result of our systematic analysis on three basic characteristics: earnings strength, relative valuation, and recent stock price movement. The company has generated a negative trend in earnings per share over the past 5 quarters. However, while recent estimates for the company have been mixed, UFS has posted better than expected results. Based on operating earnings yield, the company is undervalued when compared to all of the companies in our coverage universe. Share price changes over the past year indicates that UFS will perform in line with the market over the near term.

Financial Data

(US$ in Thousands)	3 Mos	12/31/2015	12/31/2014	12/31/2013	12/31/2012	12/31/2011	12/31/2010	12/31/2009
Earnings Per Share	1.73	2.24	6.64	1.36	2.38	4.54	7.00	3.59
Cash Flow Per Share	6.75	7.16	9.78	6.17	7.63	11.07	13.62	9.21
Tang Book Value Per Share	25.10	24.06	25.96	30.94	33.07	35.44	37.06	29.93
Dividends Per Share	1.600	1.600	1.400	1.050	0.850	0.650	0.375	...
Dividend Payout %	92.49	71.43	21.08	77.21	35.71	14.32	5.36	...
Income Statement								
Total Revenue	1,287,000	5,264,000	5,563,000	5,391,000	5,482,000	5,612,000	5,850,000	5,465,000
EBITDA	107,000	628,000	727,000	527,000	752,000	968,000	998,000	1,020,000
Depn & Amortn	89,000	340,000	363,000	366,000	385,000	376,000	395,000	405,000
Income Before Taxes	1,000	156,000	261,000	72,000	236,000	505,000	448,000	490,000
Income Taxes	(3,000)	14,000	(170,000)	(20,000)	58,000	133,000	(157,000)	180,000
Net Income	4,000	142,000	431,000	91,000	172,000	365,000	605,000	310,000
Average Shares	62,800	63,400	64,900	66,800	72,200	80,400	86,400	86,400
Balance Sheet								
Current Assets	1,572,000	1,554,000	1,670,000	2,077,000	2,015,000	1,934,000	2,000,000	2,202,000
Total Assets	5,759,000	5,663,000	6,185,000	6,278,000	6,123,000	5,869,000	6,026,000	6,519,000
Current Liabilities	778,000	788,000	926,000	709,000	758,000	716,000	725,000	771,000
Long-Term Obligations	1,211,000	1,219,000	1,181,000	1,510,000	1,128,000	837,000	825,000	1,701,000
Total Liabilities	3,023,000	3,011,000	3,295,000	3,496,000	3,246,000	2,897,000	2,824,000	3,857,000
Stockholders' Equity	2,736,000	2,652,000	2,890,000	2,782,000	2,877,000	2,972,000	3,202,000	2,662,000
Shares Outstanding	62,585	62,849	64,010	64,837	69,692	73,500	84,895	86,089
Statistical Record								
Return on Assets %	1.88	2.40	6.92	1.47	2.86	6.14	9.65	4.91
Return on Equity %	4.04	5.12	15.20	3.22	5.87	11.82	20.63	12.90
EBITDA Margin %	8.31	11.93	13.07	9.78	13.72	17.25	17.06	18.66
Net Margin %	0.31	2.70	7.75	1.69	3.14	6.50	10.34	5.67
Asset Turnover	0.89	0.89	0.89	0.87	0.91	0.94	0.93	0.87
Current Ratio	2.02	1.97	1.80	2.93	2.66	2.70	2.76	2.86
Debt to Equity	0.44	0.46	0.41	0.54	0.39	0.28	0.26	0.64
Price Range	46.22-30.43	46.86-35.49	57.56-33.06	47.99-32.69	50.30-34.87	52.50-32.51	41.97-23.48	29.25-3.60
P/E Ratio	26.72-17.59	20.92-15.84	8.67-4.98	35.29-24.03	21.13-14.65	11.56-7.16	6.00-3.35	8.15-1.00
Average Yield %	4.07	3.88	3.19	2.72	2.07	1.53	1.17	...

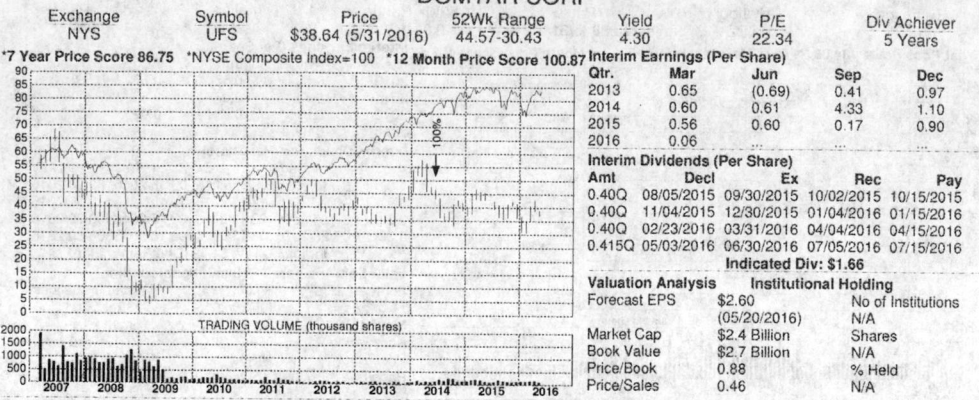

Address: 234 Kingsley Park Drive, Fort Mill, SC 29715 **Telephone:** 803-802-7500	**Web Site:** www.domtar.com **Officers:** Harold H. MacKay - Chairman John D. Williams - President, Chief Executive Officer	**Auditors:** PricewaterhouseCoopers LLP **Investor Contact:** 514-848-5555 **Transfer Agents:** ComputerShare Investor Services, Providence, RI

DR PEPPER SNAPPLE GROUP INC

Exchange	Symbol	Price	52Wk Range	Yield	P/E
NYS	DPS	$91.40 (5/31/2016)	95.56-72.75	2.32	22.18

*7 Year Price Score 144.99 *NYSE Composite Index=100 ***12 Month Price Score 104.85**

Interim Earnings (Per Share)

Qtr.	Mar	Jun	Sep	Dec
2013	0.51	0.76	1.01	0.77
2014	0.78	1.06	0.96	0.77
2015	0.81	1.14	1.05	0.97
2016	0.96	...	...	...

Interim Dividends (Per Share)

Amt	Decl	Ex	Rec	Pay
0.48Q	08/06/2015	09/10/2015	09/14/2015	10/02/2015
0.48Q	11/18/2015	12/10/2015	12/14/2015	01/06/2016
0.53Q	02/11/2016	03/11/2016	03/15/2016	04/05/2016
0.53Q	05/18/2016	06/13/2016	06/14/2016	07/07/2016

Indicated Div: $2.12

Valuation Analysis   **Institutional Holding**

Forecast EPS	$4.34	No of Institutions
	(05/20/2016)	789
Market Cap	$17.1 Billion	Shares
Book Value	$2.1 Billion	192,417,824
Price/Book	8.12	% Held
Price/Sales	2.70	88.76

Business Summary: Beverages (MIC: 1.2.2 SIC: 2086 NAIC: 312111)

Dr Pepper Snapple Group is a brand owner, manufacturer and distributor of non-alcoholic beverages in the U.S., Canada and Mexico with a portfolio of flavored carbonated soft drinks (CSDs) and non-carbonated beverages (NCBs), including ready-to-drink teas, juice drinks, water and mixers. In the CSD market, Co.'s brands are Dr Pepper, Canada Dry, 7UP, Squirt, Crush, A&W, Sunkist soda, Schweppes, Sun Drop. In the NCB market segment in the U.S., Co. participates primarily in the ready-to-drink tea, juice, juice drinks and mixer categories. Co.'s NCB brands are Hawaiian Punch, Snapple, Mott's, and Clamato. Co.'s segments are: Beverage Concentrates, Packaged Beverages and Latin America Beverages.

Recent Developments: For the quarter ended Mar 31 2016, net income increased 15.9% to US$182.0 million from US$157.0 million in the year-earlier quarter. Revenues were US$1.49 billion, up 2.5% from US$1.45 billion the year before. Operating income was US$313.0 million versus US$270.0 million in the prior-year quarter, an increase of 15.9%. Direct operating expenses was unchanged at US$602.0 million versus the comparable period the year before. Indirect operating expenses decreased 1.2% to US$572.0 million from US$579.0 million in the equivalent prior-year period.

Prospects: Our evaluation of Dr Pepper Snapple Group Inc. as of June 19, 2016 is the result of our systematic analysis on three basic characteristics: earnings strength, relative valuation, and recent stock price movement. The company has managed to produce a neutral trend in earnings per share over the past 5 quarters and while recent estimates for the company have remained steady, DPS has posted better than expected results. Based on operating earnings yield, the company is about fairly valued when compared to all of the companies in our coverage universe. Share price changes over the past year indicates that DPS will perform very well over the near term.

Financial Data

(US$ in Thousands)	3 Mos	12/31/2015	12/31/2014	12/31/2013	12/31/2012	12/31/2011	12/31/2010	12/31/2009
Earnings Per Share	4.12	3.97	3.56	3.05	2.96	2.74	2.17	2.17
Cash Flow Per Share	5.69	5.19	5.22	4.27	2.17	3.48	10.54	3.40
Dividends Per Share	1.970	1.920	1.640	1.520	1.360	1.210	0.900	0.150
Dividend Payout %	47.82	48.36	46.07	49.84	45.95	44.16	41.47	6.91
Income Statement								
Total Revenue	1,487,000	6,282,000	6,121,000	5,997,000	5,995,000	5,903,000	5,636,000	5,531,000
EBITDA	354,000	1,491,000	1,379,000	859,000	1,304,000	1,234,000	1,131,000	1,274,000
Depn & Amortn	40,000	192,000	199,000	196,000	203,000	198,000	185,000	167,000
Income Before Taxes	281,000	1,184,000	1,073,000	542,000	978,000	925,000	821,000	868,000
Income Taxes	99,000	420,000	371,000	(81,000)	349,000	320,000	294,000	315,000
Net Income	182,000	764,000	703,000	624,000	629,000	606,000	528,000	555,000
Average Shares	189,000	192,400	197,400	204,500	212,300	221,200	242,600	255,200
Balance Sheet								
Current Assets	1,283,000	1,817,000	1,211,000	1,119,000	1,335,000	1,757,000	1,309,000	1,279,000
Total Assets	8,364,000	8,869,000	8,273,000	8,201,000	8,928,000	9,283,000	8,859,000	8,776,000
Current Liabilities	1,176,000	1,583,000	1,038,000	1,030,000	1,232,000	1,915,000	1,338,000	854,000
Long-Term Obligations	2,907,000	2,875,000	2,588,000	2,588,000	2,508,000	2,554,000	1,687,000	2,960,000
Total Liabilities	6,262,000	6,686,000	5,979,000	5,924,000	6,648,000	7,020,000	6,400,000	5,589,000
Stockholders' Equity	2,102,000	2,183,000	2,294,000	2,277,000	2,280,000	2,263,000	2,459,000	3,187,000
Shares Outstanding	186,694	187,841	192,957	197,979	205,292	212,130	223,936	254,109
Statistical Record								
Return on Assets %	9.50	8.91	8.53	7.29	6.89	6.68	5.99	6.37
Return on Equity %	36.50	34.13	30.76	27.39	27.62	25.67	18.70	19.16
EBITDA Margin %	23.81	23.73	22.53	14.32	21.75	20.90	20.07	23.03
Net Margin %	12.24	12.16	11.49	10.41	10.49	10.27	9.37	10.03
Asset Turnover	0.76	0.73	0.74	0.70	0.66	0.65	0.64	0.64
Current Ratio	1.09	1.15	1.17	1.09	1.08	0.92	0.98	1.50
Debt to Equity	1.38	1.32	1.13	1.10	1.12	1.00	0.69	0.93
Price Range	95.53-72.75	94.99-71.38	74.00-47.22	50.36-42.47	45.91-37.33	42.81-33.73	40.10-26.84	30.09-11.90
P/E Ratio	23.19-17.66	23.93-17.98	20.79-13.26	16.51-13.92	15.51-12.61	15.62-12.31	18.48-12.37	13.87-5.48
Average Yield %	2.36	2.39	2.77	3.28	3.22	3.18	2.57	0.67

Address: 5301 Legacy Drive, Plano, TX 75024
Telephone: 972-673-7000

Web Site: www.drpeppersnapplegroup.com
Officers: Wayne R. Sanders - Chairman Larry D. Young - President, Chief Executive Officer

Auditors: Deloitte & Touche LLP
Investor Contact: 972-673-7935
Transfer Agents: Computershare Investor Services, Canton, MA

DONALDSON CO. INC.

Exchange	Symbol	Price	52Wk Range	Yield	P/E	Div Achiever
NYS	DCI	$33.51 (5/31/2016)	36.35-26.17	2.09	24.11	20 Years

*7 Year Price Score 82.96   ***NYSE Composite Index=100**   ***12 Month Price Score 102.87**

Interim Earnings (Per Share)

Qtr.	Oct	Jan	Apr	Jul
2012-13	0.36	0.34	0.46	0.48
2013-14	0.41	0.39	0.46	0.50
2014-15	0.40	0.35	0.33	0.41
2015-16	0.29	0.28	0.41	

Interim Dividends (Per Share)

Amt	Decl	Ex	Rec	Pay
0.17Q	07/31/2015	08/17/2015	08/19/2015	09/03/2015
0.17Q	11/20/2015	12/04/2015	12/08/2015	12/23/2015
0.17Q	01/28/2016	02/11/2016	02/16/2016	03/02/2016
0.175Q	05/25/2016	06/08/2016	06/10/2016	06/29/2016

Indicated Div: $0.70 (Div. Reinv. Plan)

Valuation Analysis

		Institutional Holding	
Forecast EPS	$1.54 (05/10/2016)	No of Institutions	417
Market Cap	$4.5 Billion	Shares	
Book Value	$799.6 Million		128,120,032
Price/Book	5.58	% Held	
Price/Sales	1.99		68.96

Business Summary: Industrial Machinery & Equipment (MIC: 7.2.1 SIC: 3564 NAIC: 333411)

Donaldson is a manufacturer of filtration systems and replacement parts. Co. has two segments: Engine Products, which provides air filtration systems, exhaust and emissions systems, liquid filtration systems including hydraulics, fuel, and lube systems, and replacement filters; and Industrial Products, which provides dust, fume, and mist collectors, compressed air purification systems, air filtration systems for gas turbines, PTFE membrane-based products, and air and gas filtration systems for applications including computer hard disk drives and semi-conductor manufacturing. Products are sold to original equipment manufacturers, distributors, dealers, and directly to end-users.

Recent Developments: For the quarter ended Apr 30 2016, net income increased 14.6% to US$54.8 million from US$47.8 million in the year-earlier quarter. Revenues were US$571.3 million, down 0.7% from US$575.6 million the year before. Operating income was US$74.9 million versus US$67.1 million in the prior-year quarter, an increase of 11.6%. Direct operating expenses declined 1.8% to US$374.7 million from US$381.5 million in the comparable period the year before. Indirect operating expenses decreased 4.2% to US$121.7 million from US$127.0 million in the equivalent prior-year period.

Prospects: Our evaluation of Donaldson Co. Inc. as of June 19, 2016 is the result of our systematic analysis on three basic characteristics: earnings strength, relative valuation, and recent stock price movement. The company has enjoyed a very positive trend in earnings per share over the past 5 quarters. However, while recent estimates for the company have been mixed, DCI has posted better than expected results. Based on operating earnings yield, the company is about fairly valued when compared to all of the companies in our coverage universe. Share price changes over the past year indicates that DCI will perform poorly over the near term.

Financial Data

(US$ in Thousands)	9 Mos	6 Mos	3 Mos	07/31/2015	07/31/2014	07/31/2013	07/31/2012	07/31/2011
Earnings Per Share	1.39	1.31	1.38	1.49	1.76	1.64	1.73	1.44
Cash Flow Per Share	1.89	1.77	1.65	1.55	2.18	2.13	1.72	1.59
Tang Book Value Per Share	3.97	3.25	3.50	3.81	5.70	6.01	4.75	4.70
Dividends Per Share	0.680	0.675	0.670	0.665	0.575	0.410	0.320	0.268
Dividend Payout %	48.92	51.53	48.55	44.63	32.67	25.00	18.50	18.64
Income Statement								
Total Revenue	1,626,500	1,055,200	538,000	2,371,213	2,473,466	2,436,948	2,493,248	2,294,029
EBITDA	246,600	149,900	77,000	370,660	432,903	417,891	437,569	379,288
Depn & Amortn	55,900	36,600	18,600	66,900	62,000	58,800	55,300	54,500
Income Before Taxes	174,900	102,800	53,400	288,603	360,703	348,181	370,780	312,263
Income Taxes	43,600	26,300	14,900	80,492	100,479	100,804	106,479	86,972
Net Income	131,300	76,500	38,500	208,111	260,224	247,377	264,301	225,291
Average Shares	134,700	134,400	134,856	139,381	147,641	150,455	152,940	157,196
Balance Sheet								
Current Assets	1,028,900	1,006,700	1,013,400	1,030,716	1,225,277	1,055,662	1,085,662	1,066,582
Total Assets	1,824,700	1,788,900	1,800,100	1,809,534	1,942,411	1,743,556	1,730,082	1,726,093
Current Liabilities	523,700	587,500	584,900	560,647	609,580	476,435	498,523	496,244
Long-Term Obligations	391,800	389,000	389,300	389,218	243,726	102,774	203,483	205,748
Total Liabilities	1,025,100	1,087,100	1,064,500	1,034,765	939,928	658,369	820,068	791,382
Stockholders' Equity	799,600	701,800	735,600	774,769	1,002,483	1,085,187	910,014	934,711
Shares Outstanding	133,108	132,930	132,637	134,598	140,405	146,152	147,662	150,794
Statistical Record								
Return on Assets %	10.22	9.84	10.39	11.09	14.12	14.24	15.25	13.97
Return on Equity %	22.77	23.47	23.42	23.42	24.93	24.80	28.58	26.80
EBITDA Margin %	15.16	14.21	14.31	15.63	17.50	17.15	17.55	16.53
Net Margin %	8.07	7.25	7.16	8.78	10.52	10.15	10.60	9.82
Asset Turnover	1.22	1.23	1.26	1.26	1.34	1.40	1.44	1.42
Current Ratio	1.96	1.71	1.73	1.84	2.01	2.22	2.18	2.15
Debt to Equity	0.49	0.55	0.53	0.50	0.24	0.09	0.22	0.22
Price Range	37.70-26.17	38.41-26.17	42.91-27.38	42.91-31.93	43.58-35.15	39.26-32.02	38.20-23.31	31.29-20.95
P/E Ratio	27.12-18.83	29.32-19.98	31.09-19.84	28.80-21.43	24.76-19.97	23.94-19.52	22.08-13.47	21.73-14.55
Average Yield %	2.16	2.04	1.88	1.75	1.41	1.15	0.97	0.98

Address: 1400 West 94th Street, Minneapolis, MN 55431 **Telephone:** 952-887-3131	**Web Site:** www.donaldson.com **Officers:** Tod E. Carpenter - President, Chief Executive Officer, Chief Operating Officer, Division Officer Scott J. Robinson - Chief Financial Officer, Vice President	**Auditors:** PwC **Investor Contact:** 952-887-3753 **Transfer Agents:** Wells Fargo Shareowner Services, St. Paul, MN

DOUGLAS EMMETT INC

Exchange	Symbol	Price	52Wk Range	Yield	P/E
NYS	DEI	$33.89 (5/31/2016)	34.03-24.95	2.60	94.14

*7 Year Price Score 112.38 *NYSE Composite Index=100 ***12 Month Price Score 107.75**

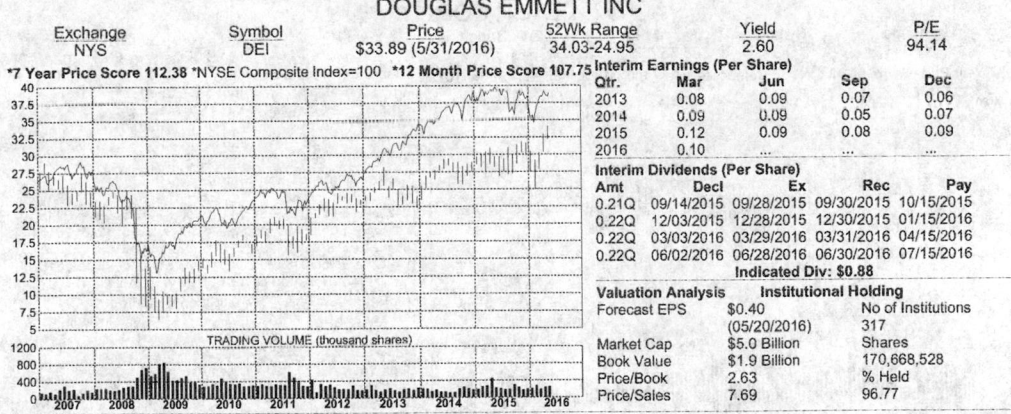

Interim Earnings (Per Share)

Qtr.	Mar	Jun	Sep	Dec
2013	0.08	0.09	0.07	0.06
2014	0.09	0.09	0.05	0.07
2015	0.12	0.09	0.08	0.09
2016	0.10	...	...	...

Interim Dividends (Per Share)

Amt	Decl	Ex	Rec	Pay
0.21Q	09/14/2015	09/28/2015	09/30/2015	10/15/2015
0.22Q	12/03/2015	12/28/2015	12/30/2015	01/15/2016
0.22Q	03/03/2016	03/29/2016	03/31/2016	04/15/2016
0.22Q	06/02/2016	06/28/2016	06/30/2016	07/15/2016

Indicated Div: $0.88

Valuation Analysis

		Institutional Holding	
Forecast EPS	$0.40	No of Institutions	
	(05/20/2016)	317	
Market Cap	$5.0 Billion	Shares	
Book Value	$1.9 Billion	170,668,528	
Price/Book	2.63	% Held	
Price/Sales	7.69	96.77	

Business Summary: REITs (MIC: 5.3.1 SIC: 6798 NAIC: 525930)

Douglas Emmett is a real estate investment trust. Through its interest in Douglas Emmett Properties, LP and its subsidiaries, including its investments in its unconsolidated institutional real estate funds (Funds), Co. owns or partially owns, acquires, develops and manages real estate, consisting primarily of office and multifamily properties. At Dec 31 2015, Co.'s total portfolio of 72 properties consisted of 54 office properties that Co. directly owned and operated, eight office properties that Co. operated and indirectly owned via its equity interest in its Funds, and 10 wholly-owned multifamily properties. Co. also owned the fee interests in two parcels of land subject to ground leases.

Recent Developments: For the quarter ended Mar 31 2016, net income decreased 27.4% to US$16.0 million from US$22.1 million in the year-earlier quarter. Revenues were US$168.6 million, up 8.9% from US$154.8 million the year before.

Prospects: Our evaluation of Douglas Emmett Inc. as of June 19, 2016 is the result of our systematic analysis on three basic characteristics: earnings strength, relative valuation, and recent stock price movement. The company has managed to produce a neutral trend in earnings per share over the past 5 quarters and while recent estimates for the company have been mixed, DEI has posted better than expected results. Based on operating earnings yield, the company is overvalued when compared to all of the companies in our coverage universe. Share price changes over the past year indicates that DEI will perform in line with the market over the near term.

Financial Data
(US$ in Thousands)

	3 Mos	12/31/2015	12/31/2014	12/31/2013	12/31/2012	12/31/2011	12/31/2010	12/31/2009
Earnings Per Share	0.36	0.39	0.30	0.31	0.16	0.01	(0.22)	(0.22)
Cash Flow Per Share	1.96	1.86	1.71	1.71	1.50	1.65	1.54	1.48
Tang Book Value Per Share	12.82	13.07	13.38	13.78	13.97	14.17	14.63	14.64
Dividends Per Share	0.860	0.850	0.810	0.740	0.630	0.490	0.400	0.400
Dividend Payout %	236.91	220.21	270.00	238.71	393.75	4,900.00	...	...
Income Statement								
Total Revenue	168,572	635,774	599,539	591,536	578,999	575,337	570,844	571,060
EBITDA	53,818	424,050	397,979	385,857	375,329	362,710	373,177	382,632
Depn & Amortn	2,112	227,536	220,331	205,570	198,581	209,130	232,255	228,713
Income Before Taxes	16,046	61,061	49,141	49,739	30,055	5,125	(25,985)	(30,878)
Net Income	15,366	58,384	44,621	45,311	22,942	1,451	(26,423)	(27,064)
Average Shares	151,451	150,604	176,221	174,802	173,120	159,966	122,714	121,552
Balance Sheet								
Current Assets	165,466	190,262	102,071	121,375	441,788	471,484	330,213	129,277
Total Assets	7,291,424	6,066,161	5,954,596	5,847,789	6,103,807	6,231,602	6,279,289	6,059,932
Current Liabilities	151,025	157,027	168,196	176,297	171,914	193,074	212,300	256,894
Long-Term Obligations	4,469,957	3,611,276	3,435,290	3,241,140	3,441,140	3,624,156	3,668,133	3,273,459
Total Liabilities	5,394,897	4,139,950	4,011,138	3,877,392	4,124,151	4,366,496	4,452,228	4,266,569
Stockholders' Equity	1,896,527	1,926,211	1,943,458	1,970,397	1,979,656	1,865,106	1,827,061	1,793,363
Shares Outstanding	147,383	146,919	144,869	142,605	141,245	131,070	124,131	121,596
Statistical Record								
Return on Assets %	0.83	0.97	0.76	0.76	0.37	0.02	N.M.	N.M.
Return on Equity %	2.87	3.02	2.28	2.29	1.19	0.08	N.M.	N.M.
EBITDA Margin %	31.93	66.70	66.38	65.23	64.82	63.04	65.37	67.00
Net Margin %	9.12	9.18	7.44	7.66	3.96	0.25	N.M.	N.M.
Asset Turnover	0.10	0.11	0.10	0.10	0.09	0.09	0.09	0.09
Current Ratio	1.10	1.21	0.61	0.69	2.57	2.44	1.56	0.50
Debt to Equity	2.36	1.87	1.77	1.64	1.74	1.94	2.01	1.83
Price Range	31.79-24.95	31.79-26.85	29.38-23.29	28.18-22.27	24.48-18.46	21.05-15.54	18.56-13.00	14.85-6.36
P/E Ratio	88.31-69.31	81.51-68.85	97.93-77.63	90.90-71.84	153.00-115.38	N.M.	...	...
Average Yield %	2.94	2.89	2.96	3.02	2.78	2.63	2.51	3.73

Address: 808 Wilshire Boulevard, Suite 200, Santa Monica, CA 90401 **Telephone:** 310-255-7700	**Web Site:** www.douglasemmett.com **Officers:** Dan A. Emmett - Chairman Jordan L. Kaplan - President, Chief Executive Officer	**Auditors:** Ernst & Young LLP **Investor Contact:** 310-255-7751 **Transfer Agents:** Computershare Investor Services

DOVER CORP

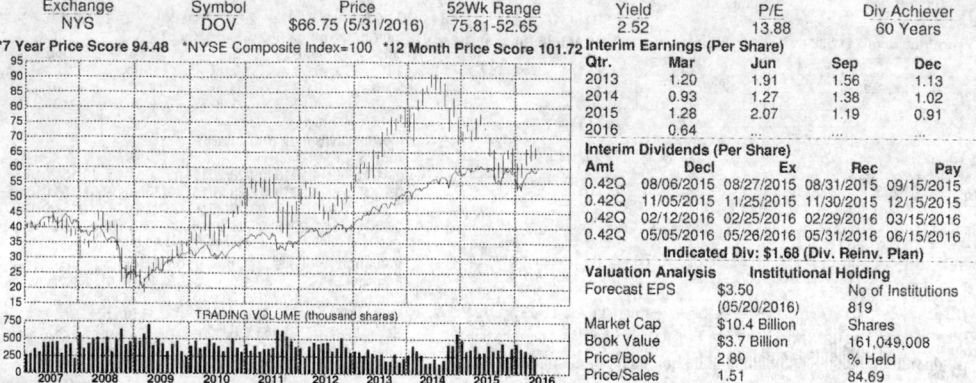

Exchange	Symbol	Price	52Wk Range	Yield	P/E	Div Achiever
NYS	DOV	$66.75 (5/31/2016)	75.81-52.65	2.52	13.88	60 Years

*7 Year Price Score 94.48   *NYSE Composite Index=100   *12 Month Price Score 101.72

Interim Earnings (Per Share)

Qtr.	Mar	Jun	Sep	Dec
2013	1.20	1.91	1.56	1.13
2014	0.93	1.27	1.38	1.02
2015	1.28	2.07	1.19	0.91
2016	0.64			

Interim Dividends (Per Share)

Amt	Decl	Ex	Rec	Pay
0.42Q	08/06/2015	08/27/2015	08/31/2015	09/15/2015
0.42Q	11/05/2015	11/25/2015	11/30/2015	12/15/2015
0.42Q	02/12/2016	02/25/2016	02/29/2016	03/15/2016
0.42Q	05/05/2016	05/26/2016	05/31/2016	06/15/2016

Indicated Div: $1.68 (Div. Reinv. Plan)

Valuation Analysis   **Institutional Holding**

Forecast EPS	$3.50 (05/20/2016)	No of Institutions	819
Market Cap	$10.4 Billion	Shares	161,049,008
Book Value	$3.7 Billion	% Held	84.69
Price/Book	2.80		
Price/Sales	1.51		

Business Summary: Industrial Machinery & Equipment (MIC: 7.2.1 SIC: 3559 NAIC: 333220)

Dover is a diversified global manufacturer operating via four main segments: Energy, which is a provider of solutions and services for production and processing of oil, natural gas liquids, and gas worldwide; Engineered Systems, which is focused on the design, manufacture and service of critical equipment and components serving the printing and identification, vehicle service, environmental solutions and industrial end markets; Fluids, is focused on the handling of critical fluids across the retail fueling, chemical, hygienic, and industrial end markets; and Refrigeration & Food Equipment, which provides equipment and systems serving the commercial refrigeration and food service industries.

Recent Developments: For the quarter ended Mar 31 2016, income from continuing operations decreased 15.2% to US$99.4 million from US$117.2 million in the year-earlier quarter. Net income decreased 52.6% to US$99.4 million from US$209.5 million in the year-earlier quarter. Revenues were US$1.62 billion, down 5.4% from US$1.72 billion the year before. Operating income was US$145.8 million versus US$192.5 million in the prior-year quarter, a decrease of 24.3%. Direct operating expenses declined 5.1% to US$1.03 billion from US$1.09 billion in the comparable period the year before. Indirect operating expenses increased 2.0% to US$443.4 million from US$434.6 million in the equivalent prior-year period.

Prospects: Our evaluation of Dover Corp. as of June 19, 2016 is the result of our systematic analysis on three basic characteristics: earnings strength, relative valuation, and recent stock price movement. The company has managed to produce a neutral trend in earnings per share over the past 5 quarters and while recent estimates for the company have been mixed, DOV has posted better than expected results. Based on operating earnings yield, the company is about fairly valued when compared to all of the companies in our coverage universe. Share price changes over the past year indicates that DOV will perform poorly over the near term.

Financial Data

(US$ in Thousands)	3 Mos	12/31/2015	12/31/2014	12/31/2013	12/31/2012	12/31/2011	12/31/2010	12/31/2009
Earnings Per Share	4.81	5.46	4.59	5.78	4.41	4.74	3.70	1.91
Cash Flow Per Share	6.13	6.02	5.70	6.88	6.93	5.69	5.09	4.31
Tang Book Value Per Share	N.M.	N.M.	N.M.	N.M.	N.M.	N.M.	1.35	N.M.
Dividends Per Share	1.660	1.640	1.550	1.450	1.330	1.180	1.070	1.020
Dividend Payout %	34.51	30.04	33.77	25.09	30.16	24.89	28.92	53.40
Income Statement								
Total Revenue	1,622,273	6,956,311	7,752,728	8,729,813	8,104,339	7,950,140	7,132,648	5,775,689
EBITDA	204,367	1,095,383	1,373,465	1,593,512	1,460,528	1,386,757	1,195,340	751,593
Depn & Amortn	45,029	167,516	152,079	235,358	201,816	175,997	163,915	159,600
Income Before Taxes	127,624	800,610	1,094,207	1,237,412	1,137,571	1,095,164	925,084	491,618
Income Taxes	28,268	204,729	316,067	271,607	304,452	248,799	217,176	119,724
Net Income	99,356	869,829	775,235	1,003,129	811,070	895,243	700,104	356,438
Average Shares	156,161	159,172	168,842	173,547	183,993	188,887	189,170	186,736
Balance Sheet								
Current Assets	2,345,756	2,420,779	2,896,822	3,240,162	3,027,844	3,397,130	3,261,871	2,522,707
Total Assets	8,980,895	8,619,763	9,090,385	10,838,172	10,443,943	9,501,450	8,562,894	7,882,403
Current Liabilities	1,648,809	1,367,182	2,039,354	1,615,580	1,986,628	1,202,981	1,194,386	969,176
Long-Term Obligations	2,610,642	2,617,342	2,253,041	2,599,201	2,189,350	2,186,230	1,790,886	1,825,260
Total Liabilities	5,282,762	4,975,188	5,389,660	5,460,776	5,524,713	4,570,895	4,036,332	3,798,795
Stockholders' Equity	3,698,133	3,644,575	3,700,725	5,377,396	4,919,230	4,930,555	4,526,562	4,083,608
Shares Outstanding	155,148	155,003	163,011	169,906	174,717	183,591	186,488	186,876
Statistical Record								
Return on Assets %	8.62	9.82	7.78	9.43	8.11	9.91	8.51	4.53
Return on Equity %	20.88	23.68	17.08	19.48	16.42	18.93	16.26	9.05
EBITDA Margin %	12.60	15.75	17.72	18.25	18.02	17.44	16.76	13.01
Net Margin %	6.12	12.50	10.00	11.49	10.01	11.26	9.82	6.17
Asset Turnover	0.78	0.79	0.78	0.82	0.81	0.88	0.87	0.73
Current Ratio	1.42	1.77	1.42	2.01	1.52	2.82	2.73	2.60
Debt to Equity	0.71	0.72	0.61	0.48	0.45	0.44	0.40	0.45
Price Range	77.77-52.65	77.77-55.99	91.07-67.76	80.08-54.51	55.26-42.26	57.93-37.03	48.91-34.05	35.56-18.30
P/E Ratio	16.17-10.95	14.24-10.25	19.84-14.76	13.86-9.43	12.53-9.58	12.22-7.81	13.22-9.20	18.62-9.58
Average Yield %	2.56	2.43	1.89	2.16	2.69	2.38	2.26	3.61

Address: 3005 Highland Parkway, Downers Grove, IL 60515 **Telephone:** 630-541-1540	**Web Site:** www.dovercorporation.com **Officers:** Michael F. Johnston - Chairman Robert A. Livingston - President, Chief Executive Officer	**Auditors:** PricewaterhouseCoopers LLP **Investor Contact:** 212-922-1640 **Transfer Agents:** ComputerShare Investor Services, Providence, RI

DOW CHEMICAL CO.

Exchange	Symbol	Price	52Wk Range	Yield	P/E
NYS	DOW	$51.36 (5/31/2016)	56.97-39.39	3.58	10.03

*7 Year Price Score 111.99 *NYSE Composite Index=100 *12 Month Price Score 105.10

Interim Earnings (Per Share)

Qtr.	Mar	Jun	Sep	Dec
2013	0.46	1.87	0.49	0.80
2014	0.79	0.73	0.71	0.63
2015	1.18	0.97	1.09	2.91
2016	0.15	...	...	...

Interim Dividends (Per Share)

Amt	Decl	Ex	Rec	Pay
0.42Q	09/04/2015	09/28/2015	09/30/2015	10/30/2015
0.46Q	10/22/2015	12/29/2015	12/31/2015	01/29/2016
0.46Q	02/11/2016	03/29/2016	03/31/2016	04/29/2016
0.46Q	05/12/2016	06/28/2016	06/30/2016	07/29/2016

Indicated Div: $1.84

Valuation Analysis / Institutional Holding

Valuation Analysis		Institutional Holding	
Forecast EPS	$3.50	No of Institutions	
	(05/20/2016)	1543	
Market Cap	$57.7 Billion	Shares	
Book Value	$25.6 Billion	855,534,848	
Price/Book	2.25	% Held	
Price/Sales	1.22	65.65	

Business Summary: Plastics (MIC: 8.4.2 SIC: 2821 NAIC: 325211)

Dow Chemical is a manufacturer and supplier of products used primarily as raw materials in the manufacture of customer products and services. Co. serves the following industries: appliance; automotive; agricultural; building and construction; chemical processing; electronics; furniture; housewares; oil and gas; packaging; paints, coatings and adhesives; personal care; pharmaceutical; processed foods; pulp and paper; textile and carpet; utilities; and water treatment. Co. conducts its operations through five segments: Agricultural Sciences, Consumer Solutions, Infrastructure Solutions, Performance Materials & Chemicals and Performance Plastics.

Recent Developments: For the quarter ended Mar 31 2016, net income decreased 81.9% to US$275.0 million from US$1.52 billion in the year-earlier quarter. Revenues were US$10.70 billion, down 13.5% from US$12.37 billion the year before. Direct operating expenses declined 16.6% to US$7.95 billion from US$9.54 billion in the comparable period the year before. Indirect operating expenses decreased 2.7% to US$1.20 billion from US$1.24 billion in the equivalent prior-year period.

Prospects: Our evaluation of Dow Chemical Co. as of June 19, 2016 is the result of our systematic analysis on three basic characteristics: earnings strength, relative valuation, and recent stock price movement. The company has managed to produce a neutral trend in earnings per share over the past 5 quarters and while recent estimates for the company have been mixed, DOW has posted better than expected results. Based on operating earnings yield, the company is undervalued when compared to all of the companies in our coverage universe. Share price changes over the past year indicates that DOW will perform in line with the market over the near term.

Financial Data
(US$ in Millions)

	3 Mos	12/31/2015	12/31/2014	12/31/2013	12/31/2012	12/31/2011	12/31/2010	12/31/2009
Earnings Per Share	5.12	6.15	2.87	3.68	0.70	2.05	1.72	0.32
Cash Flow Per Share	5.72	6.65	5.55	6.60	3.47	3.38	3.64	1.99
Tang Book Value Per Share	5.16	5.02	1.75	4.80	N.M.	0.24	N.M.	N.M.
Dividends Per Share	1.760	1.720	1.530	1.280	1.210	0.900	0.600	0.600
Dividend Payout %	34.38	27.97	53.31	34.78	172.86	43.90	34.88	187.50
Income Statement								
Total Revenue	10,703	48,778	58,167	57,080	56,786	59,985	53,674	44,875
EBITDA	410	12,458	7,934	9,342	4,892	6,352	5,924	4,061
Depn & Amortn	103	2,327	2,572	2,512	2,535	2,673	2,798	2,690
Income Before Taxes	126	9,256	4,430	5,770	1,129	2,378	1,690	(161)
Income Taxes	(110)	2,147	1,426	1,988	565	817	481	(97)
Net Income	254	7,685	3,772	4,787	1,182	2,742	2,310	648
Average Shares	1,117	1,241	1,187	1,290	1,176	1,158	1,143	1,053
Balance Sheet								
Current Assets	23,334	24,475	24,267	24,977	23,684	23,422	23,781	19,560
Total Assets	68,440	68,026	68,796	69,501	69,605	69,224	69,588	65,937
Current Liabilities	11,682	11,215	11,593	11,971	11,493	13,634	13,896	13,106
Long-Term Obligations	16,229	16,215	18,838	16,820	19,919	18,310	20,605	19,152
Total Liabilities	42,841	42,652	46,373	42,603	48,728	46,943	47,749	45,382
Stockholders' Equity	25,599	25,374	22,423	26,898	20,877	22,281	21,839	20,555
Shares Outstanding	1,122	1,116	1,157	1,205	1,203	1,184	1,167	1,150
Statistical Record								
Return on Assets %	9.49	11.23	5.45	6.88	1.70	3.95	3.41	1.16
Return on Equity %	27.01	32.16	15.30	20.04	5.46	12.43	10.90	3.75
EBITDA Margin %	3.83	25.54	13.64	16.37	8.61	10.59	11.04	9.05
Net Margin %	2.37	15.76	6.48	8.39	2.08	4.57	4.30	1.44
Asset Turnover	0.69	0.71	0.84	0.82	0.82	0.86	0.79	0.81
Current Ratio	2.00	2.18	2.09	2.09	2.06	1.72	1.71	1.49
Debt to Equity	0.63	0.64	0.84	0.95	0.95	0.82	0.94	0.93
Price Range	56.97-39.39	56.97-39.39	54.80-41.89	44.86-30.18	36.08-27.74	41.34-21.51	34.41-22.97	29.42-6.33
P/E Ratio	11.13-7.69	9.26-6.40	19.09-14.60	12.19-8.20	51.54-39.63	20.17-10.49	20.01-13.35	91.94-19.78
Average Yield %	3.61	3.54	3.10	3.57	3.84	2.76	2.09	3.25

Address: 2030 Dow Center, Midland, MI 48674
Telephone: 989-636-1000
Fax: 989-638-1740

Web Site: www.dow.com
Officers: Andrew N. Liveris - Chairman, President, Chief Executive Officer James R. Fitterling - Vice-Chairman, President, Chief Operating Officer

Auditors: Deloitte & Touche LLP
Investor Contact: 800 422-8193
Transfer Agents: Computershare, Providence, RI

DRIL-QUIP INC

Exchange	Symbol	Price	52Wk Range	Yield	P/E
NYS	DRQ	$61.03 (5/31/2016)	79.06-49.90	N/A	13.33

*7 Year Price Score 72.50 *NYSE Composite Index=100 *12 Month Price Score 97.57

Interim Earnings (Per Share)

Qtr.	Mar	Jun	Sep	Dec
2013	0.98	1.05	0.98	1.15
2014	1.04	1.27	1.40	1.49
2015	1.38	1.01	1.32	1.28
2016	0.97	...	...	...

Interim Dividends (Per Share)

No Dividends Paid

Valuation Analysis

Institutional Holding	
Forecast EPS	$2.59
(05/20/2016)	No of Institutions: 362
Market Cap	$2.3 Billion
Book Value	$1.4 Billion
	Shares: 45,127,188
Price/Book	1.70
Price/Sales	2.95
	% Held: 93.70

TRADING VOLUME (thousand shares)

Business Summary: Equipment & Services (MIC: 9.1.3 SIC: 3533 NAIC: 333132)

Dril-Quip designs, manufactures, sells and services offshore drilling and production equipment. Co.'s primary products consist of subsea and surface wellheads, subsea and surface production trees, subsea control systems and manifolds, mudline hanger systems, specialty connectors and associated pipe, drilling and production riser systems, liner hangers, wellhead connectors and diverters. Co. also provides technical advisory assistance on an as-requested basis during installation of its products, as well as rework and reconditioning services for Co.'s customer-owned products. Co.'s customers may rent or purchase running tools from Co. for use in the installation and retrieval of its products.

Recent Developments: For the quarter ended Mar 31 2016, net income decreased 31.5% to US$36.8 million from US$53.7 million in the year-earlier quarter. Revenues were US$166.6 million, down 26.3% from US$226.0 million the year before. Operating income was US$49.3 million versus US$71.7 million in the prior-year quarter, a decrease of 31.2%. Direct operating expenses declined 25.6% to US$93.1 million from US$125.1 million in the comparable period the year before. Indirect operating expenses decreased 17.3% to US$24.1 million from US$29.2 million in the equivalent prior-year period.

Prospects: Our evaluation of Dril-Quip Inc. as of June 19, 2016 is the result of our systematic analysis on three basic characteristics: earnings strength, relative valuation, and recent stock price movement. The company has generated a negative trend in earnings per share over the past 5 quarters and while recent estimates for the company have been mixed, DRQ has posted better than expected results. Based on operating earnings yield, the company is undervalued when compared to all of the companies in our coverage universe. Share price changes over the past year indicates that DRQ will perform poorly over the near term.

Financial Data

(US$ in Thousands)	3 Mos	12/31/2015	12/31/2014	12/31/2013	12/31/2012	12/31/2011	12/31/2010	12/31/2009
Earnings Per Share	4.58	4.98	5.19	4.16	2.94	2.36	2.55	2.66
Cash Flow Per Share	4.12	4.96	3.74	3.99	(0.20)	2.54	2.69	3.48
Tang Book Value Per Share	35.92	34.90	31.98	30.54	26.35	23.03	20.68	17.78
Income Statement								
Total Revenue	166,561	844,310	930,957	872,372	733,031	601,342	566,251	540,204
EBITDA	57,118	279,335	309,948	252,845	187,916	152,652	159,588	160,037
Depn & Amortn	7,775	30,500	31,200	29,300	26,224	23,013	20,875	17,997
Income Before Taxes	49,821	249,771	279,380	224,097	162,122	130,004	138,903	142,391
Income Taxes	13,052	57,763	70,668	54,270	42,913	34,737	36,677	37,250
Net Income	36,769	192,008	208,712	169,827	119,209	95,267	102,226	105,141
Average Shares	37,847	38,531	40,190	40,865	40,523	40,322	40,060	39,538
Balance Sheet								
Current Assets	1,164,616	1,124,298	1,127,140	1,078,813	924,388	799,302	688,249	617,356
Total Assets	1,470,458	1,428,250	1,449,251	1,394,612	1,231,447	1,085,858	948,551	817,246
Current Liabilities	104,899	100,815	198,642	142,790	155,089	151,000	111,329	104,625
Long-Term Obligations	...	...	...	...	...	...	58	316
Total Liabilities	107,163	103,792	204,059	152,594	165,015	160,614	120,537	112,161
Stockholders' Equity	1,363,295	1,324,458	1,245,192	1,242,018	1,066,432	925,244	828,014	705,085
Shares Outstanding	37,957	37,951	38,932	40,673	40,475	40,175	40,041	39,658
Statistical Record								
Return on Assets %	12.05	13.35	14.68	12.93	10.26	9.37	11.58	14.04
Return on Equity %	13.30	14.94	16.78	14.71	11.94	10.87	13.34	16.63
EBITDA Margin %	34.29	33.08	33.29	28.98	25.64	25.39	28.18	29.63
Net Margin %	22.08	22.74	22.42	19.47	16.26	15.84	18.05	19.46
Asset Turnover	0.54	0.59	0.65	0.66	0.63	0.59	0.64	0.72
Current Ratio	11.10	11.15	5.67	7.56	5.96	5.29	6.18	5.90
Price Range	80.20-49.90	80.20-55.11	115.81-70.00	119.38-73.05	76.61-58.72	81.36-49.38	82.28-40.95	58.79-18.38
P/E Ratio	17.51-10.90	16.10-11.07	22.31-13.49	28.70-17.56	26.06-19.97	34.47-20.92	32.27-16.06	22.10-6.91

Address: 6401 N. Eldridge Parkway, Houston, TX 77041	Web Site: www.dril-quip.com	Auditors: PricewaterhouseCoopers LLP
Telephone: 713-939-7711	Officers: John V. Lovoi - Chairman Larry E. Reimert - Co-Chairman	Investor Contact: 713-939-7711
Fax: 713-939-8063		Transfer Agents: Computershare, Jersey City, NJ

DST SYSTEMS INC. (DE)

Exchange	Symbol	Price	52Wk Range	Yield	P/E
NYS	DST	$120.92 (5/31/2016)	134.17-95.56	1.09	13.98

*7 Year Price Score 136.99 *NYSE Composite Index=100 *12 Month Price Score 103.05

Interim Earnings (Per Share)

Qtr.	Mar	Jun	Sep	Dec
2013	2.04	1.77	2.23	1.97
2014	2.37	3.34	2.51	6.44
2015	2.87	2.91	2.08	1.96
2016	1.70	...	...	...

Interim Dividends (Per Share)

Amt	Decl	Ex	Rec	Pay
0.30Q	07/29/2015	08/26/2015	08/28/2015	09/11/2015
0.30Q	10/30/2015	11/23/2015	11/25/2015	12/11/2015
0.33Q	01/27/2016	02/29/2016	03/02/2016	03/15/2016
0.33Q	05/10/2016	05/25/2016	05/27/2016	06/15/2016

Indicated Div: $1.32

Valuation Analysis

Forecast EPS	$6.87
	(05/20/2016)
Market Cap	$4.1 Billion
Book Value	$997.8 Million
Price/Book	4.10
Price/Sales	1.42

Institutional Holding

No of Institutions	450
Shares	33,352,516
% Held	70.46

Business Summary: IT Services (MIC: 6.3.1 SIC: 7374 NAIC: 518210)

DST Systems is a provider of technology-based information processing and servicing solutions. Co. has three segments: Financial Services, which provides investor, investment, advisor/intermediary and asset distribution services to companies within the Financial Services industry; Healthcare Services, which provide healthcare organizations with pharmacy, healthcare administration, and health outcomes optimization solutions; and Customer Communications, which provides a range of integrated print, mail, and electronic solutions. Co.'s Investments and Other Segment is comprised of its investments in equity securities, private equity investments, real estate and other financial interests.

Recent Developments: For the quarter ended Mar 31 2016, net income decreased 47.1% to US$57.0 million from US$107.8 million in the year-earlier quarter. Revenues were US$745.8 million, up 6.2% from US$702.3 million the year before. Operating income was US$75.4 million versus US$79.1 million in the prior-year quarter, a decrease of 4.7%. Indirect operating expenses increased 7.6% to US$670.4 million from US$623.2 million in the equivalent prior-year period.

Prospects: Our evaluation of DST Systems Inc. as of June 19, 2016 is the result of our systematic analysis on three basic characteristics: earnings strength, relative valuation, and recent stock price movement. The company has enjoyed a very positive trend in earnings per share over the past 5 quarters. However, while recent estimates for the company have been lowered by analysts, DST has posted better than expected results. Based on operating earnings yield, the company is undervalued when compared to all of the companies in our coverage universe. Share price changes over the past year indicates that DST will perform well over the near term.

Financial Data

(US$ in Thousands)	3 Mos	12/31/2015	12/31/2014	12/31/2013	12/31/2012	12/31/2011	12/31/2010	12/31/2009
Earnings Per Share	8.65	9.83	14.66	8.00	7.08	3.95	6.73	4.84
Cash Flow Per Share	5.72	6.12	7.81	9.15	4.80	8.85	7.56	7.31
Tang Book Value Per Share	8.26	11.85	18.60	14.90	11.40	3.72	11.79	8.31
Dividends Per Share	1.230	1.200	1.200	1.200	0.800	0.700	0.600	...
Dividend Payout %	14.22	12.21	8.19	15.00	11.30	17.72	8.92	...
Income Statement								
Total Revenue	745,800	2,825,100	2,749,300	2,658,600	2,576,600	2,388,700	2,328,500	2,217,900
EBITDA	89,400	615,600	897,800	683,700	669,900	419,900	613,800	483,100
Depn & Amortn	7,700	105,500	114,900	127,300	139,100	121,100	127,500	123,700
Income Before Taxes	75,600	486,000	756,300	521,900	487,300	252,300	440,200	317,200
Income Taxes	25,300	173,700	198,400	192,300	195,500	95,800	159,100	112,900
Net Income	58,100	358,200	593,300	352,600	324,000	183,100	318,500	241,600
Average Shares	34,300	36,400	40,500	44,100	45,800	46,300	47,300	50,000
Balance Sheet								
Current Assets	837,700	1,055,500	971,900	842,400	954,300	766,900	997,200	678,900
Total Assets	2,604,500	2,813,200	2,942,900	3,090,500	3,392,500	3,428,600	3,339,400	2,912,800
Current Liabilities	783,200	948,700	1,021,900	1,072,800	1,378,500	1,073,700	1,104,900	1,281,200
Long-Term Obligations	566,900	556,500	385,600	399,400	492,200	1,059,500	923,300	563,800
Total Liabilities	1,606,700	1,767,200	1,706,500	1,906,700	2,312,800	2,608,600	2,515,000	2,278,400
Stockholders' Equity	997,800	1,046,000	1,236,400	1,183,800	1,079,700	820,000	824,400	634,400
Shares Outstanding	33,800	34,300	37,600	41,800	44,300	44,100	46,200	49,100
Statistical Record								
Return on Assets %	11.61	12.45	19.67	10.88	9.47	5.41	10.19	8.91
Return on Equity %	28.06	31.39	49.03	31.16	34.02	22.27	43.67	55.37
EBITDA Margin %	11.99	21.79	32.66	25.72	26.00	17.58	26.36	21.78
Net Margin %	7.79	12.68	21.58	13.26	12.57	7.67	13.68	10.89
Asset Turnover	1.08	0.98	0.91	0.82	0.75	0.71	0.74	0.82
Current Ratio	1.07	1.11	0.95	0.79	0.69	0.71	0.90	0.53
Debt to Equity	0.57	0.53	0.31	0.34	0.46	1.29	1.12	0.89
Price Range	134.17-95.56	134.17-92.96	99.67-82.51	91.04-60.60	62.33-46.33	56.10-41.23	46.61-35.68	47.31-25.89
P/E Ratio	15.51-11.05	13.65-9.46	6.80-5.63	11.38-7.58	8.80-6.54	14.20-10.44	6.93-5.30	9.77-5.35
Average Yield %	1.08	1.07	1.30	1.64	1.48	1.44	1.44	...

Address: 333 West 11th Street, Kansas City, MO 64105 Telephone: 816-435-1000	Web Site: www.dstsystems.com Officers: Stephen C. Hooley - Chairman, President, Chief Executive Officer, Chief Operating Officer Jonathan J. Boehm - Executive Vice President	Auditors: PricewaterhouseCoopers LLP Transfer Agents: Computershare Trust Company, N.A., Providence, RI

DSW INC

Exchange	Symbol	Price	52Wk Range	Yield	P/E
NYS	DSW	$21.16 (5/31/2016)	35.78-19.20	3.78	15.45

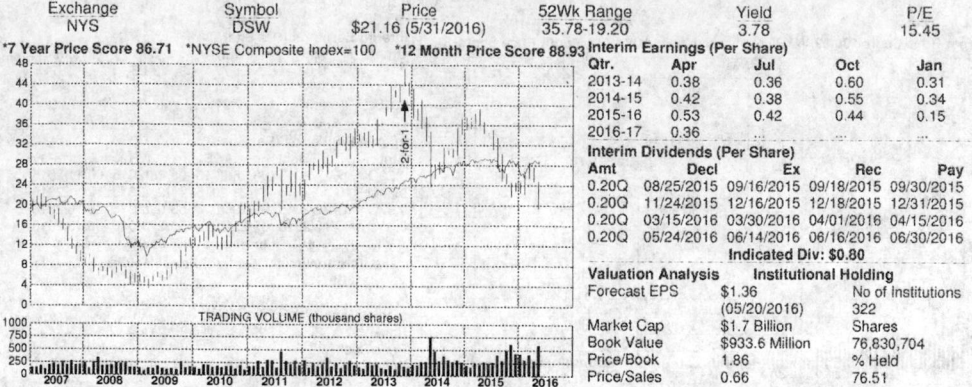

*7 Year Price Score 86.71   *NYSE Composite Index=100   *12 Month Price Score 88.93

Interim Earnings (Per Share)

Qtr.	Apr	Jul	Oct	Jan
2013-14	0.38	0.36	0.60	0.31
2014-15	0.42	0.38	0.55	0.34
2015-16	0.53	0.42	0.44	0.15
2016-17	0.36			

Interim Dividends (Per Share)

Amt	Decl	Ex	Rec	Pay
0.20Q	08/25/2015	09/16/2015	09/18/2015	09/30/2015
0.20Q	11/24/2015	12/16/2015	12/18/2015	12/31/2015
0.20Q	03/15/2016	03/30/2016	04/01/2016	04/15/2016
0.20Q	05/24/2016	06/14/2016	06/16/2016	06/30/2016

Indicated Div: $0.80

Valuation Analysis | **Institutional Holding**

Forecast EPS	$1.36	No of Institutions
	(05/20/2016)	322
Market Cap	$1.7 Billion	Shares
Book Value	$933.6 Million	76,830,704
Price/Book	1.86	% Held
Price/Sales	0.66	76.51

Business Summary: Retail - Apparel and Accessories (MIC: 2.1.5 SIC: 5661 NAIC: 448210)

DSW is a footwear and accessories retailer. Co. has two reportable segments: the DSW segment, which includes DSW stores and dsw.com, and the Affiliated Business Group (ABG) segment. Co. provides an assortment of brand name dress, casual and athletic footwear and accessories for women, men and children. Co. separates its merchandise into four primary categories: women's footwear; men's footwear; athletic footwear; and accessories and other. Through its ABG segment, Co. also partners with four other retailers. As of Jan 31 2015, Co. operated a total of 431 stores located in 42 states, the District of Columbia and Puerto Rico, and dsw.com.

Recent Developments: For the quarter ended Apr 30 2016, net income decreased 36.6% to US$30.0 million from US$47.4 million in the year-earlier quarter. Revenues were US$681.3 million, up 3.9% from US$655.5 million the year before. Operating income was US$48.7 million versus US$73.6 million in the prior-year quarter, a decrease of 33.8%. Direct operating expenses rose 7.8% to US$476.9 million from US$442.4 million in the comparable period the year before. Indirect operating expenses increased 11.6% to US$155.6 million from US$139.5 million in the equivalent prior-year period.

Prospects: Our evaluation of DSW Inc. as of June 19, 2016 is the result of our systematic analysis on three basic characteristics: earnings strength, relative valuation, and recent stock price movement. The company has managed to produce a neutral trend in earnings per share over the past 5 quarters. However, while recent estimates for the company have been lowered by analysts, DSW has posted results that fell short of analysts expectations. Based on operating earnings yield, the company is undervalued when compared to all of the companies in our coverage universe. Share price changes over the past year indicates that DSW will perform well over the near term.

Financial Data

(US$ in Thousands)	3 Mos	01/30/2016	01/31/2015	02/01/2014	02/02/2013	01/28/2012	01/29/2011	01/30/2010
Earnings Per Share	1.37	1.54	1.69	1.65	1.62	2.27	1.20	0.61
Cash Flow Per Share	2.48	2.78	2.21	3.34	2.86	3.05	1.61	1.87
Tang Book Value Per Share	9.90	10.73	11.15	10.72	9.25	8.79	6.96	5.68
Dividends Per Share	0.800	0.800	0.750	0.375	1.435	1.150	...	...
Dividend Payout %	58.39	51.95	44.38	22.73	88.58	50.66	...	...
Income Statement								
Total Revenue	681,267	2,620,248	2,496,092	2,368,668	2,257,778	2,024,329	1,822,376	1,602,605
EBITDA	49,416	295,762	319,900	315,982	301,638	207,773	223,067	137,466
Depn & Amortn	536	79,033	77,768	74,594	64,836	56,323	47,984	46,378
Income Before Taxes	49,401	220,191	244,927	244,007	240,613	142,269	177,279	91,891
Income Taxes	19,078	83,806	95,713	92,705	95,427	(58,069)	69,655	37,150
Net Income	30,014	136,034	153,299	151,302	146,439	174,788	107,624	54,741
Average Shares	82,705	88,501	90,612	91,901	90,606	74,276	89,836	89,034
Balance Sheet								
Current Assets	767,854	795,668	768,470	812,764	821,790	868,007	717,181	606,990
Total Assets	1,456,990	1,369,109	1,438,243	1,421,244	1,262,103	1,207,900	1,008,897	850,756
Current Liabilities	323,285	323,426	283,790	284,402	275,311	307,549	253,716	224,719
Total Liabilities	523,423	464,185	427,123	422,700	403,524	421,313	368,133	325,875
Stockholders' Equity	933,567	904,924	1,011,120	998,544	858,579	786,587	640,764	524,881
Shares Outstanding	82,015	81,918	88,399	90,728	90,024	86,583	88,375	87,782
Statistical Record								
Return on Assets %	7.97	9.72	10.75	11.31	11.67	15.81	11.61	6.98
Return on Equity %	11.97	14.24	15.30	16.34	17.51	24.56	18.52	11.08
EBITDA Margin %	7.25	11.29	12.82	13.34	13.36	10.26	12.24	8.58
Net Margin %	4.41	5.19	6.14	6.39	6.49	8.63	5.91	3.42
Asset Turnover	1.78	1.87	1.75	1.77	1.80	1.83	1.97	2.04
Current Ratio	2.38	2.46	2.71	2.86	2.98	2.82	2.83	2.70
Price Range	36.65-21.62	39.14-21.62	40.98-23.62	47.22-31.45	35.26-24.70	27.66-16.65	20.11-10.96	13.46-3.34
P/E Ratio	26.75-15.78	25.42-14.04	24.25-13.98	28.62-19.06	21.77-15.25	12.18-7.33	16.75-9.13	22.06-5.47
Average Yield %	2.85	2.60	2.31	0.97	4.79	5.00	...	...

Address: 810 DSW Drive, Columbus, OH 43219
Telephone: 614-237-7100

Web Site: www.dswinc.com
Officers: Jay L. Schottenstein - Chairman, Chief Executive Officer Jared A. Poff - Senior Vice President, Interim Chief Financial Officer, Principal Accounting Officer, Principal Financial Officer

Auditors: Deloitte & Touche LLP
Investor Contact: 855-893-5691
Transfer Agents: Computershare

DTE ENERGY CO

Exchange	Symbol	Price	52Wk Range	Yield	P/E
NYS	DTE	$90.68 (5/31/2016)	91.33-73.78	3.22	23.31

*7 Year Price Score 113.24 *NYSE Composite Index=100 *12 Month Price Score 106.55

Interim Earnings (Per Share)

Qtr.	Mar	Jun	Sep	Dec
2013	1.34	0.60	1.13	0.69
2014	1.84	0.70	0.88	1.68
2015	1.53	0.61	1.47	0.44
2016	1.37	...	...	...

Interim Dividends (Per Share)

Amt	Decl	Ex	Rec	Pay
0.73Q	06/25/2015	09/17/2015	09/21/2015	10/15/2015
0.73Q	12/02/2015	12/17/2015	12/21/2015	01/15/2016
0.73Q	02/04/2016	03/17/2016	03/21/2016	04/15/2016
0.73Q	05/05/2016	06/16/2016	06/20/2016	07/15/2016

Indicated Div: $2.92

Valuation Analysis

		Institutional Holding	
Forecast EPS	$4.95	No of Institutions	
	(05/20/2016)	687	
Market Cap	$16.3 Billion	Shares	
Book Value	$8.9 Billion	134,036,152	
Price/Book	1.83	% Held	
Price/Sales	1.64	62.87	

Business Summary: Electric Utilities (MIC: 3.1.1 SIC: 4911 NAIC: 221111)

DTE Energy is a holding company. Co. is engaged in the generation, purchase, distribution and sale of electricity in southeastern Michigan through its DTE Electric Company subsidiary, as well as in the purchase, storage, transportation, distribution and sale of natural gas throughout Michigan and the sale of storage and transportation capacity through its DTE Gas Company subsidiary. Co.'s non-utility operations are: natural gas pipelines, gathering and storage businesses; power and industrial projects; and energy marketing and trading operations. As of Dec 31 2015, DTE Electric and DTE Gas Company served approximately 2.2 million and 1.2 million, respectively, customers throughout Michigan.

Recent Developments: For the quarter ended Mar 31 2016, net income decreased 12.4% to US$240.0 million from US$274.0 million in the year-earlier quarter. Revenues were US$2.57 billion, down 14.0% from US$2.98 billion the year before. Operating income was US$381.0 million versus US$461.0 million in the prior-year quarter, a decrease of 17.4%. Direct operating expenses declined 16.5% to US$1.86 billion from US$2.22 billion in the comparable period the year before. Indirect operating expenses increased 9.7% to US$328.0 million from US$299.0 million in the equivalent prior-year period.

Prospects: Our evaluation of DTE Energy Co. as of June 19, 2016 is the result of our systematic analysis on three basic characteristics: earnings strength, relative valuation, and recent stock price movement. The company has generated a negative trend in earnings per share over the past 5 quarters and while recent estimates for the company have been mixed, DTE has posted better than expected results. Based on operating earnings yield, the company is undervalued when compared to all of the companies in our coverage universe. Share price changes over the past year indicates that DTE will perform well over the near term.

Financial Data

(US$ in Thousands)	3 Mos	12/31/2015	12/31/2014	12/31/2013	12/31/2012	12/31/2011	12/31/2010	12/31/2009
Earnings Per Share	3.89	4.05	5.10	3.76	3.55	4.18	3.74	3.24
Cash Flow Per Share	10.64	10.68	10.39	12.31	12.88	11.88	10.86	11.09
Tang Book Value Per Share	37.78	37.14	35.07	32.64	30.29	29.05	27.36	25.39
Dividends Per Share	2.880	2.840	2.690	2.585	2.415	2.322	2.180	2.120
Dividend Payout %	74.04	70.12	52.75	68.75	68.03	55.56	58.29	65.43
Income Statement								
Total Revenue	2,566,000	10,337,000	12,301,000	9,661,000	8,791,000	8,897,000	8,557,000	8,014,000
EBITDA	440,000	1,492,000	1,771,000	1,420,000	1,465,000	1,536,000	1,552,000	1,374,000
Depn & Amortn	15,000	98,000	77,000	71,000	75,000	65,000	65,000	66,000
Income Before Taxes	323,000	957,000	1,275,000	922,000	960,000	987,000	950,000	782,000
Income Taxes	83,000	237,000	364,000	254,000	286,000	267,000	311,000	247,000
Net Income	247,000	727,000	905,000	661,000	610,000	711,000	630,000	532,000
Average Shares	180,000	179,000	177,000	175,000	172,000	170,000	169,000	164,000
Balance Sheet								
Current Assets	2,362,000	2,575,000	3,087,000	2,806,000	2,915,000	3,196,000	3,167,000	2,877,000
Total Assets	28,564,000	28,737,000	27,974,000	25,935,000	26,339,000	26,009,000	24,896,000	24,195,000
Current Liabilities	2,209,000	2,528,000	2,577,000	3,189,000	2,768,000	2,628,000	2,749,000	2,645,000
Long-Term Obligations	8,758,000	8,835,000	8,343,000	7,214,000	7,014,000	7,187,000	7,089,000	7,370,000
Total Liabilities	19,677,000	19,965,000	19,647,000	18,014,000	18,966,000	19,000,000	18,174,000	17,917,000
Stockholders' Equity	8,887,000	8,772,000	8,327,000	7,921,000	7,373,000	7,009,000	6,722,000	6,278,000
Shares Outstanding	179,435	179,470	176,991	177,087	172,351	169,247	169,428	165,400
Statistical Record								
Return on Assets %	2.48	2.56	3.36	2.53	2.32	2.79	2.57	2.18
Return on Equity %	7.99	8.50	11.14	8.64	8.46	10.36	9.69	8.67
EBITDA Margin %	17.15	14.43	14.40	14.70	16.66	17.26	18.14	17.14
Net Margin %	9.63	7.03	7.36	6.84	6.94	7.99	7.36	6.64
Asset Turnover	0.35	0.36	0.46	0.37	0.33	0.35	0.35	0.33
Current Ratio	1.07	1.02	1.20	0.88	1.05	1.22	1.15	1.09
Debt to Equity	0.99	1.01	1.00	0.91	0.95	1.03	1.05	1.17
Price Range	90.87-73.78	91.54-73.78	90.18-65.10	72.90-60.05	62.10-52.96	55.05-44.03	48.97-41.50	44.64-23.61
P/E Ratio	23.36-18.97	22.60-18.22	17.68-12.76	19.39-15.97	17.49-14.92	13.17-10.53	13.09-11.10	13.78-7.29
Average Yield %	3.57	3.52	3.55	3.84	4.17	4.69	4.76	6.28

Address: One Energy Plaza, Detroit, MI 48226-1279	**Web Site:** www.dteenergy.com	**Auditors:** PricewaterhouseCoopers LLP
Telephone: 313-235-4000	**Officers:** Gerard M. Anderson - Chairman, President, Chief Executive Officer Steven E. Kurmas - Vice-Chairman, President, Chief Operating Officer, Group President	**Transfer Agents:** Wells Fargo Bank, N.A.

DU PONT (E.I.) DE NEMOURS & CO

Exchange	Symbol	Price	52Wk Range	Yield	P/E
NYS	DD	$65.41 (5/31/2016)	74.55-47.32	2.32	27.14

*7 Year Price Score 101.63 *NYSE Composite Index=100 *12 Month Price Score 107.06

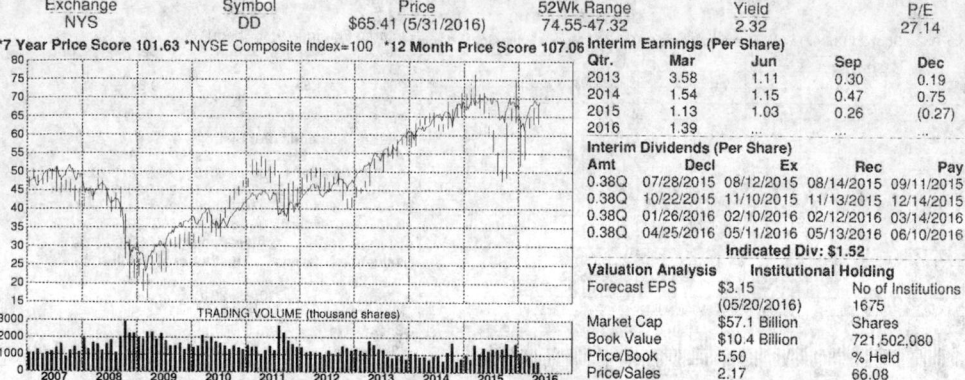

Interim Earnings (Per Share)

Qtr.	Mar	Jun	Sep	Dec
2013	3.58	1.11	0.30	0.19
2014	1.54	1.15	0.47	0.75
2015	1.13	1.03	0.26	(0.27)
2016	1.39			

Interim Dividends (Per Share)

Amt	Decl	Ex	Rec	Pay
0.38Q	07/28/2015	08/12/2015	08/14/2015	09/11/2015
0.38Q	10/22/2015	11/10/2015	11/13/2015	12/14/2015
0.38Q	01/26/2016	02/10/2016	02/12/2016	03/14/2016
0.38Q	04/25/2016	05/11/2016	05/13/2016	06/10/2016

Indicated Div: $1.52

Valuation Analysis

		Institutional Holding	
Forecast EPS	$3.15	No of Institutions	
	(05/20/2016)	1675	
Market Cap	$57.1 Billion	Shares	
Book Value	$10.4 Billion	721,502,080	
Price/Book	5.50	% Held	
Price/Sales	2.17	66.08	

Business Summary: Diversified Chemicals (MIC: 8.3.1 SIC: 2821 NAIC: 325211)

Du Pont (E.I.) de Nemours & Co is engaged in agriculture and nutrition. Co.'s subsidiaries and affiliates conduct manufacturing, seed production or selling activities and some are distributors of products manufactured by it. Co. consists of 10 businesses which are aggregated into six reportable segments. Co.'s reportable segments are Agriculture, Electronics & Communications, Industrial Biosciences, Nutrition & Health, Performance Materials and Safety & Protection. Co. also includes certain businesses not included in the reportable segments, such as pre-commercial programs, nonaligned businesses and pharmaceuticals in Other.

Recent Developments: For the quarter ended Mar 31 2016, net income increased 19.0% to US$1.23 billion from US$1.04 billion in the year-earlier quarter. Revenues were US$7.78 billion, down 3.2% from US$8.04 billion the year before. Direct operating expenses declined 5.1% to US$4.43 billion from US$4.66 billion in the comparable period the year before. Indirect operating expenses decreased 5.8% to US$1.72 billion from US$1.82 billion in the equivalent prior-year period.

Prospects: Our evaluation of Du Pont (E.I.) de Nemours & Co as of June 19, 2016 is the result of our systematic analysis on three basic characteristics: earnings strength, relative valuation, and recent stock price movement. The company has enjoyed a very positive trend in earnings per share over the past 5 quarters and while recent estimates for the company have been mixed, DD has posted better than expected results. Based on operating earnings yield, the company is about fairly valued when compared to all of the companies in our coverage universe. Share price changes over the past year indicates that DD will perform in line with the market over the near term.

Financial Data

(US$ in Thousands)	3 Mos	12/31/2015	12/31/2014	12/31/2013	12/31/2012	12/31/2011	12/31/2010	12/31/2009
Earnings Per Share	2.41	2.16	3.92	5.18	2.95	3.68	3.28	1.92
Cash Flow Per Share	2.97	2.59	4.06	3.43	5.18	5.55	5.02	5.24
Tang Book Value Per Share	2.09	1.57	4.39	6.67	0.12	N.M.	4.06	2.53
Dividends Per Share	1.630	1.720	1.840	1.780	1.700	1.640	1.640	1.640
Dividend Payout %	67.63	79.63	46.94	34.36	57.63	44.57	50.00	85.42
Income Statement								
Total Revenue	7,777,000	25,130,000	36,046,000	36,144,000	35,310,000	38,719,000	32,733,000	27,328,000
EBITDA	2,087,000	4,294,000	7,186,000	5,689,000	5,358,000	6,383,000	5,676,000	4,347,000
Depn & Amortn	360,000	1,539,000	1,818,000	1,752,000	1,779,000	1,654,000	1,375,000	1,755,000
Income Before Taxes	1,635,000	2,542,000	4,991,000	3,489,000	3,115,000	4,282,000	3,711,000	2,184,000
Income Taxes	406,000	696,000	1,370,000	626,000	622,000	772,000	659,000	415,000
Net Income	1,226,000	1,953,000	3,625,000	4,848,000	2,788,000	3,474,000	3,031,000	1,755,000
Average Shares	877,251	899,527	921,873	933,147	942,197	941,029	921,655	908,712
Balance Sheet								
Current Assets	17,865,000	17,755,000	21,748,000	24,384,000	21,191,000	18,058,000	19,059,000	17,288,000
Total Assets	41,801,000	41,166,000	49,876,000	51,499,000	49,736,000	48,492,000	40,410,000	38,185,000
Current Liabilities	8,955,000	10,353,000	12,640,000	13,367,000	13,549,000	11,185,000	9,389,000	9,390,000
Long-Term Obligations	8,126,000	7,642,000	9,271,000	10,741,000	10,465,000	11,736,000	10,137,000	9,528,000
Total Liabilities	31,414,000	31,173,000	36,556,000	35,270,000	39,648,000	39,899,000	31,132,000	30,970,000
Stockholders' Equity	10,387,000	9,993,000	13,320,000	16,229,000	10,088,000	8,593,000	9,278,000	7,215,000
Shares Outstanding	873,409	871,347	904,979	926,986	933,016	926,123	917,310	903,814
Statistical Record								
Return on Assets %	4.88	4.29	7.15	9.58	5.66	7.82	7.71	4.72
Return on Equity %	18.53	16.75	24.54	36.84	29.77	38.88	36.75	24.48
EBITDA Margin %	26.84	17.09	19.94	15.74	15.17	16.49	17.34	15.91
Net Margin %	15.76	7.77	10.06	13.41	7.90	8.97	9.26	6.42
Asset Turnover	0.60	0.55	0.71	0.71	0.72	0.87	0.83	0.73
Current Ratio	1.99	1.71	1.72	1.82	1.56	1.61	2.03	1.84
Debt to Equity	0.78	0.76	0.70	0.66	1.04	1.37	1.09	1.32
Price Range	74.55-47.32	76.47-47.32	71.43-56.59	61.72-42.73	51.11-39.85	53.95-36.56	47.52-30.58	33.61-15.33
P/E Ratio	30.93-19.63	35.40-21.91	18.22-14.44	11.91-8.25	17.32-13.51	14.66-9.94	14.49-9.32	17.51-7.99
Average Yield %	2.67	2.69	2.88	3.41	3.64	3.46	4.30	6.09

Address: 974 Centre Road, Wilmington, DE 19805
Telephone: 302-774-1000

Web Site: www.dupont.com
Officers: Edward D. Breen - Chairman, Interim Chairman, Chief Executive Officer, Interim Chief Executive Officer Nicholas C. Fanandakis - Chief Financial Officer, Executive Vice President, Senior Vice President

Auditors: PricewaterhouseCoopers LLP
Investor Contact: 302-774-4994
Transfer Agents: Computershare Trust Company, N.A., College Station, TX

DUKE ENERGY CORP

Exchange	Symbol	Price	52Wk Range	Yield	P/E	Div Achiever
NYS	DUK	$78.23 (5/31/2016)	81.13-65.83	4.22	20.43	11 Years

*7 Year Price Score 97.85   *NYSE Composite Index=100   *12 Month Price Score 105.33

Interim Earnings (Per Share)

Qtr.	Mar	Jun	Sep	Dec
2013	0.89	0.48	1.42	0.97
2014	(0.14)	0.00	1.80	0.14
2015	1.22	0.78	1.35	0.69
2016	1.01	...	...	...

Interim Dividends (Per Share)

Amt	Decl	Ex	Rec	Pay
0.825Q	07/07/2015	08/12/2015	08/14/2015	09/16/2015
0.825Q	10/29/2015	11/10/2015	11/13/2015	12/16/2015
0.825Q	01/04/2016	02/10/2016	02/12/2016	03/16/2016
0.825Q	05/05/2016	05/18/2016	05/20/2016	06/16/2016

Indicated Div: $3.30 (Div. Reinv. Plan)

Valuation Analysis   **Institutional Holding**

Forecast EPS	$4.60	No of Institutions
	(05/20/2016)	1504
Market Cap	$53.9 Billion	Shares
Book Value	$39.9 Billion	489,476,000
Price/Book	1.35	% Held
Price/Sales	2.34	N/A

Business Summary: Electric Utilities (MIC: 3.1.1 SIC: 4931 NAIC: 221122)

Duke Energy is an energy company. Co. operates three segments: Regulated Utilities, which conducts operations primarily through its utility subsidiaries that served 7.4 million retail electric customers in the Southeast and Midwest regions and 525,000 retail natural gas customers in southwestern Ohio and northern Kentucky at Dec 31 2015; International Energy, which operates and manages power generation facilities and engages in sales and marketing of electric power, natural gas, and natural gas liquids outside the U.S.; and Commercial Portfolio, which acquires, builds, develops, and operates wind and solar renewable generation and energy transmission projects throughout the continental U.S.

Recent Developments: For the quarter ended Mar 31 2016, income from continuing operations decreased 10.3% to US$696.0 million from US$776.0 million in the year-earlier quarter. Net income decreased 19.4% to US$699.0 million from US$867.0 million in the year-earlier quarter. Revenues were US$5.62 billion, down 7.3% from US$6.07 billion the year before. Operating income was US$1.33 billion versus US$1.46 billion in the prior-year quarter, a decrease of 8.4%. Direct operating expenses declined 11.1% to US$3.18 billion from US$3.58 billion in the comparable period the year before. Indirect operating expenses increased 7.6% to US$1.11 billion from US$1.03 billion in the equivalent prior-year period.

Prospects: Our evaluation of Duke Energy Corp. Holding Co as of June 19, 2016 is the result of our systematic analysis on three basic characteristics: earnings strength, relative valuation, and recent stock price movement. The company has managed to produce a neutral trend in earnings per share over the past 5 quarters. However, while recent estimates for the company have been mixed, DUK has posted results that fell short of analysts expectations. Based on operating earnings yield, the company is undervalued when compared to all of the companies in our coverage universe. Share price changes over the past year indicates that DUK will perform well over the near term.

Financial Data

(US$ in Thousands)	3 Mos	12/31/2015	12/31/2014	12/31/2013	12/31/2012	12/31/2011	12/31/2010	12/31/2009
Earnings Per Share	3.83	4.05	2.66	3.76	3.07	3.84	3.00	2.49
Cash Flow Per Share	10.01	9.62	9.32	9.04	9.11	8.27	10.27	8.03
Tang Book Value Per Share	34.17	33.99	34.73	35.40	34.40	41.68	41.08	38.52
Dividends Per Share	3.270	3.240	3.150	3.090	1.530	2.970	2.910	2.820
Dividend Payout %	85.38	80.00	118.42	82.18	49.84	77.34	97.00	113.25
Income Statement								
Total Revenue	5,622,000	23,459,000	23,925,000	24,598,000	19,624,000	14,529,000	14,272,000	12,731,000
EBITDA	2,343,000	9,256,000	9,076,000	8,547,000	6,147,000	5,137,000	4,861,000	4,281,000
Depn & Amortn	931,000	3,613,000	3,507,000	3,229,000	2,652,000	2,026,000	1,994,000	1,846,000
Income Before Taxes	901,000	4,068,000	4,004,000	3,798,000	2,303,000	2,305,000	2,094,000	1,761,000
Income Taxes	213,000	1,326,000	1,669,000	1,261,000	705,000	752,000	890,000	758,000
Net Income	694,000	2,816,000	1,883,000	2,665,000	1,768,000	1,706,000	1,320,000	1,075,000
Average Shares	689,000	694,000	707,000	706,000	575,000	444,333	439,666	431,333
Balance Sheet								
Current Assets	7,943,000	8,322,000	11,575,000	10,516,000	10,122,000	6,880,000	6,223,000	5,766,000
Total Assets	121,709,000	121,156,000	120,709,000	114,779,000	113,856,000	62,526,000	59,090,000	57,040,000
Current Liabilities	10,891,000	11,400,000	11,233,000	8,644,000	10,029,000	5,528,000	3,897,000	4,088,000
Long-Term Obligations	38,232,000	37,495,000	37,213,000	38,152,000	36,351,000	18,679,000	17,935,000	16,113,000
Total Liabilities	81,817,000	81,429,000	79,834,000	73,449,000	72,900,000	39,754,000	36,568,000	35,290,000
Stockholders' Equity	39,892,000	39,727,000	40,875,000	41,330,000	40,956,000	22,772,000	22,522,000	21,750,000
Shares Outstanding	689,000	688,000	707,000	706,000	704,000	445,333	443,000	436,333
Statistical Record								
Return on Assets %	2.17	2.33	1.60	2.33	2.00	2.81	2.27	1.95
Return on Equity %	6.54	6.99	4.58	6.48	5.53	7.53	5.96	5.03
EBITDA Margin %	41.68	39.46	37.94	34.75	31.32	35.36	34.06	33.63
Net Margin %	12.34	12.00	7.87	10.83	9.01	11.74	9.25	8.44
Asset Turnover	0.19	0.19	0.20	0.22	0.22	0.24	0.25	0.23
Current Ratio	0.73	0.73	1.03	1.22	1.01	1.24	1.60	1.41
Debt to Equity	0.96	0.94	0.91	0.92	0.89	0.82	0.80	0.74
Price Range	80.68-65.83	89.36-65.83	86.83-67.13	75.20-63.80	69.84-59.87	66.18-51.75	55.59-46.83	53.43-35.43
P/E Ratio	21.07-17.19	22.06-16.25	32.64-25.24	20.00-16.97	22.75-19.50	17.23-13.48	18.53-15.61	21.46-14.23
Average Yield %	4.45	4.33	4.27	4.46	2.36	5.22	5.71	6.24

Address: 550 South Tryon Street, Charlotte, NC 28202-1803 **Telephone:** 704-382-3853	**Web Site:** www.duke-energy.com **Officers:** Lynn J. Good - Chairman, Vice-Chairman, President, Chief Executive Officer, Group Executive, Chief Financial Officer Dhiaa M. Jamil - Chief Operating Officer, Executive Vice President, Chief Officer	**Auditors:** Deloitte & Touche LLP **Investor Contact:** 704-382-4070 **Transfer Agents:** Duke Energy, Charlotte, NC

DUKE REALTY CORP

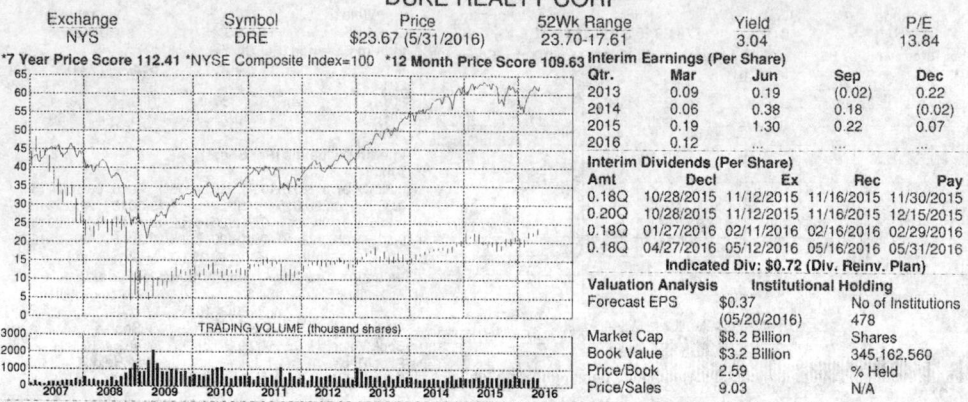

Exchange	Symbol	Price	52Wk Range	Yield	P/E
NYS	DRE	$23.67 (5/31/2016)	23.70-17.61	3.04	13.84

*7 Year Price Score 112.41 *NYSE Composite Index=100 *12 Month Price Score 109.63

Interim Earnings (Per Share)

Qtr.	Mar	Jun	Sep	Dec
2013	0.09	0.19	(0.02)	0.22
2014	0.06	0.38	0.18	(0.02)
2015	0.19	1.30	0.22	0.07
2016	0.12	...	...	...

Interim Dividends (Per Share)

Amt	Decl	Ex	Rec	Pay
0.18Q	10/28/2015	11/12/2015	11/16/2015	11/30/2015
0.20Q	10/28/2015	11/12/2015	11/16/2015	12/15/2015
0.18Q	01/27/2016	02/11/2016	02/16/2016	02/29/2016
0.18Q	04/27/2016	05/12/2016	05/16/2016	05/31/2016

Indicated Div: $0.72 (Div. Reinv. Plan)

Valuation Analysis

		Institutional Holding	
Forecast EPS	$0.37	No of Institutions	478
	(05/20/2016)		
Market Cap	$8.2 Billion	Shares	345,162,560
Book Value	$3.2 Billion	% Held	N/A
Price/Book	2.59		
Price/Sales	9.03		

Business Summary: REITs (MIC: 5.3.1 SIC: 6798 NAIC: 525930)

Duke Realty is a self-administered and self-managed real estate investment trust and is the sole general partner of Duke Realty Limited Partnership. As of Dec 31 2015, Co. owned or jointly controlled 587 industrial, medical office and other properties; and owned, including through ownership interests in unconsolidated joint ventures, approximately 3,200 acres of land and controlled an additional 1,600 acres through purchase options. Co. had four segments at Dec 31 2015, the first three of which consisted of the ownership and rental of industrial, medical office and office real estate investments and its service operations segment. The fourth segment consists of various real estate services.

Recent Developments: For the quarter ended Mar 31 2016, income from continuing operations increased 16.5% to US$43.6 million from US$37.4 million in the year-earlier quarter. Net income decreased 33.7% to US$43.8 million from US$66.0 million in the year-earlier quarter. Revenues were US$225.0 million, down 15.9% from US$267.4 million the year before. Revenues from property income fell 6.0% to US$201.8 million from US$214.6 million in the corresponding quarter a year earlier.

Prospects: Our evaluation of Duke Realty Corp. as of June 19, 2016 is the result of our systematic analysis on three basic characteristics: earnings strength, relative valuation, and recent stock price movement. The company has generated a negative trend in earnings per share over the past 5 quarters. Because the company lacks sufficient analyst estimate data, we place greater weight on the historical EPS trend as the measure of earnings strength. Based on operating earnings yield, the company is about fairly valued when compared to all of the companies in our coverage universe. Share price changes over the past year indicates that DRE will perform in line with the market over the near term.

Financial Data

(US$ in Thousands)	3 Mos	12/31/2015	12/31/2014	12/31/2013	12/31/2012	12/31/2011	12/31/2010	12/31/2009
Earnings Per Share	1.71	1.77	0.60	0.47	(0.48)	0.11	(0.07)	(1.67)
Cash Flow Per Share	1.17	1.10	1.32	1.35	1.11	1.34	1.64	1.99
Tang Book Value Per Share	9.15	9.22	8.31	7.86	7.04	7.59	8.09	8.52
Dividends Per Share	...	0.690	0.680	0.680	0.680	0.680	0.680	0.760
Dividend Payout %	...	38.98	113.33	144.68	...	618.18	...	...
Income Statement								
Total Revenue	224,954	949,432	1,164,704	1,081,790	1,109,440	1,274,274	1,393,603	1,344,089
EBITDA	136,411	611,171	639,454	517,941	414,918	480,821	530,277	192,782
Depn & Amortn	79,116	253,683	290,279	288,583	262,825	267,222	271,058	266,803
Income Before Taxes	22,088	188,581	130,808	2,350	(92,563)	(8,796)	20,370	(293,031)
Income Taxes	343	(3,928)	(844)	(5,080)	(103)	(194)	(1,126)	(6,070)
Net Income	43,756	621,861	246,455	196,549	(75,868)	96,309	65,262	(271,490)
Average Shares	349,674	352,197	340,446	326,712	267,900	259,598	238,920	201,206
Balance Sheet								
Current Assets	170,934	174,619	211,786	182,908	216,229	382,211	173,565	318,615
Total Assets	6,896,960	6,917,113	7,754,839	7,752,614	7,560,101	7,004,437	7,644,276	7,304,279
Current Liabilities	226,480	263,318	323,687	308,945	319,071	282,480	302,702	283,481
Long-Term Obligations	3,381,060	3,341,739	4,453,403	4,254,376	4,446,170	3,809,589	4,207,079	3,854,032
Total Liabilities	3,731,529	3,735,181	4,894,514	4,739,371	4,968,687	4,289,751	4,698,666	4,378,934
Stockholders' Equity	3,165,431	3,181,932	2,860,325	3,013,243	2,591,414	2,714,686	2,945,610	2,925,345
Shares Outstanding	345,935	345,285	344,112	326,399	279,423	252,927	252,195	224,029
Statistical Record								
Return on Assets %	8.20	8.48	3.18	2.57	N.M.	1.31	0.87	N.M.
Return on Equity %	19.86	20.58	8.39	7.01	N.M.	3.40	2.22	N.M.
EBITDA Margin %	60.64	64.37	54.90	47.88	37.40	37.73	38.05	14.34
Net Margin %	19.45	65.50	21.16	18.17	N.M.	7.56	4.68	N.M.
Asset Turnover	0.12	0.13	0.15	0.14	0.15	0.17	0.19	0.18
Current Ratio	0.75	0.66	0.65	0.59	0.68	1.35	0.57	1.12
Debt to Equity	1.07	1.05	1.56	1.41	1.72	1.40	1.43	1.32
Price Range	22.63-17.61	22.58-17.61	20.63-14.53	18.71-13.87	15.77-12.02	15.51-9.70	14.32-10.37	13.16-4.39
P/E Ratio	13.23-10.30	12.76-9.95	34.38-24.22	39.81-29.51	...	141.00-88.18	...	...
Average Yield %	...	3.41	3.86	4.24	4.82	5.31	5.68	7.80

Address: 600 East 96th Street, Suite 100, Indianapolis, IN 46240 **Telephone:** 317-808-6000	**Web Site:** www.dukerealty.com **Officers:** Dennis D. Oklak - Chairman, President, Chief Executive Officer James B. Connor - Senior Executive Vice President, Chief Operating Officer, Region Officer, President, Chief Executive Officer	**Auditors:** KPMG LLP **Investor Contact:** 317-808-6060 **Transfer Agents:** American Stock Transfer & Trust Company, New York, NY

DUN & BRADSTREET CORP (DE)

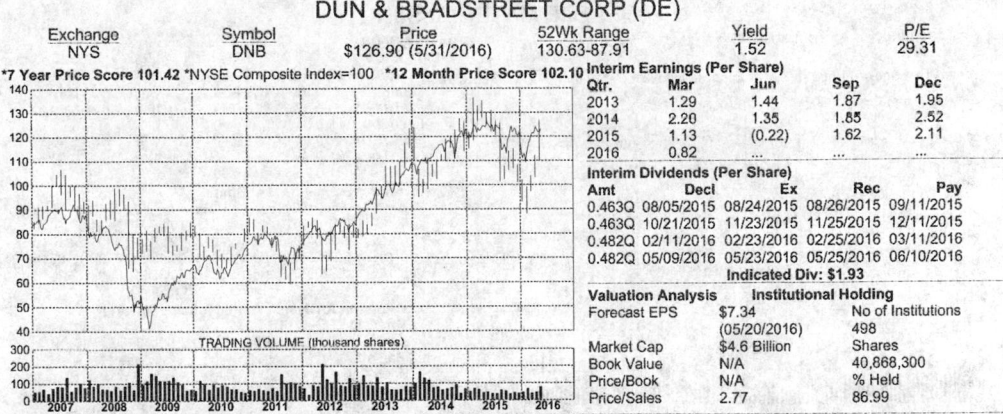

Exchange	Symbol	Price	52Wk Range	Yield	P/E
NYS	DNB	$126.90 (5/31/2016)	130.63-87.91	1.52	29.31

*7 Year Price Score 101.42 *NYSE Composite Index=100 *12 Month Price Score 102.10

Interim Earnings (Per Share)

Qtr.	Mar	Jun	Sep	Dec
2013	1.29	1.44	1.87	1.95
2014	2.20	1.35	1.85	2.52
2015	1.13	(0.22)	1.62	2.11
2016	0.82	...	...	...

Interim Dividends (Per Share)

Amt	Decl	Ex	Rec	Pay
0.463Q	08/05/2015	08/24/2015	08/26/2015	09/11/2015
0.463Q	10/21/2015	11/23/2015	11/25/2015	12/11/2015
0.482Q	02/11/2016	02/23/2016	02/25/2016	03/11/2016
0.482Q	05/09/2016	05/23/2016	05/25/2016	06/10/2016

Indicated Div: $1.93

Valuation Analysis

		Institutional Holding	
Forecast EPS	$7.34	No of Institutions	
	(05/20/2016)	498	
Market Cap	$4.6 Billion	Shares	
Book Value	N/A	40,868,300	
Price/Book	N/A	% Held	
Price/Sales	2.77	86.99	

Business Summary: Business Services (MIC: 7.5.2 SIC: 7323 NAIC: 561450)

Dun & Bradstreet is a provider of commercial data, analytics and insight on businesses. Customers use Risk Management Solutions‚„¢ to mitigate credit, compliance and supplier risk, increase cash flow and drive profitability, and Sales & Marketing Solutions‚„¢ to use data to grow sales and improve marketing effectiveness. Co. manages and reports its business through two segments: Americas, which consists of its operations in the U.S., Canada and Latin America; and.Non-Americas, which primarily consists of its operations in the U.K., the Netherlands, Belgium, Greater China, India and its Worldwide Network.

Recent Developments: For the quarter ended Mar 31 2016, net income decreased 26.8% to US$30.0 million from US$41.0 million in the year-earlier quarter. Revenues were US$375.0 million, up 5.3% from US$356.2 million the year before. Operating income was US$53.2 million versus US$65.1 million in the prior-year quarter, a decrease of 18.3%. Direct operating expenses rose 1.1% to US$132.4 million from US$131.0 million in the comparable period the year before. Indirect operating expenses increased 18.3% to US$189.4 million from US$160.1 million in the equivalent prior-year period.

Prospects: Our evaluation of Dun & Bradstreet Corp. as of June 19, 2016 is the result of our systematic analysis on three basic characteristics: earnings strength, relative valuation, and recent stock price movement. The company has generated a negative trend in earnings per share over the past 5 quarters and while recent estimates for the company have remained steady, DNB has posted better than expected results. Based on operating earnings yield, the company is undervalued when compared to all of the companies in our coverage universe. Share price changes over the past year indicates that DNB will perform poorly over the near term.

Financial Data

(US$ in Thousands)	3 Mos	12/31/2015	12/31/2014	12/31/2013	12/31/2012	12/31/2011	12/31/2010	12/31/2009
Earnings Per Share	4.33	4.64	7.99	6.54	6.43	5.28	4.98	5.99
Cash Flow Per Share	8.70	9.51	8.64	8.52	7.83	6.40	6.40	7.07
Dividends Per Share	1.870	1.850	1.760	1.600	1.520	1.440	1.400	1.360
Dividend Payout %	43.19	39.87	22.03	24.46	23.64	27.27	28.11	22.70
Income Statement								
Total Revenue	375,000	1,637,100	1,681,800	1,655,200	1,663,000	1,758,500	1,676,600	1,687,000
EBITDA	63,000	335,600	398,500	443,500	428,200	415,900	444,200	485,900
Depn & Amortn	9,000	6,200	8,300	8,100	11,200	12,300	12,400	10,700
Income Before Taxes	41,000	280,000	348,600	396,000	378,300	368,100	387,900	432,500
Income Taxes	11,000	74,200	52,600	135,500	83,100	109,200	137,900	112,100
Net Income	30,000	168,800	294,400	258,500	295,500	260,300	252,100	319,400
Average Shares	36,400	36,400	36,900	39,500	46,000	49,300	50,400	52,900
Balance Sheet								
Current Assets	865,800	959,600	935,900	822,400	747,400	726,900	668,300	759,600
Total Assets	2,176,000	2,273,600	1,986,200	1,890,300	1,991,800	1,977,100	1,905,500	1,749,400
Current Liabilities	960,200	959,200	1,158,900	852,300	876,700	953,500	927,700	859,100
Long-Term Obligations	1,725,400	1,804,100	1,352,200	1,516,000	1,290,700	963,900	972,000	961,800
Total Liabilities	3,294,200	3,390,400	3,189,500	2,938,700	3,009,200	2,721,000	2,559,900	2,495,100
Stockholders' Equity	(1,118,200)	(1,116,800)	(1,203,300)	(1,048,400)	(1,017,400)	(743,900)	(654,400)	(745,700)
Shares Outstanding	36,200	36,100	35,900	37,800	41,300	47,700	49,600	51,200
Statistical Record								
Return on Assets %	7.51	7.93	15.19	13.32	14.85	13.41	13.80	19.15
EBITDA Margin %	16.80	20.50	23.69	26.79	25.75	23.65	26.49	28.80
Net Margin %	8.00	10.31	17.51	15.62	17.77	14.80	15.04	18.93
Asset Turnover	0.79	0.77	0.87	0.85	0.84	0.91	0.92	1.01
Current Ratio	0.90	1.00	0.81	0.96	0.85	0.76	0.72	0.88
Price Range	134.74-87.91	135.92-100.97	127.37-94.87	123.42-78.17	86.50-63.34	86.45-59.25	84.37-65.90	84.64-69.80
P/E Ratio	31.12-20.30	29.29-21.76	15.94-11.87	18.87-11.95	13.45-9.85	16.37-11.22	16.94-13.23	14.13-11.65
Average Yield %	1.66	1.55	1.58	1.64	1.95	1.94	1.90	1.75

Address: 103 JFK Parkway, Short Hills, NJ 07078	**Web Site:** www.dnb.com	**Auditors:** PricewaterhouseCoopers LLP
Telephone: 973-921-5500	**Officers:** Robert P. Carrigan - President, Chief Executive Officer Joshua L. Peirez - President, Chief Operating Officer, Division Officer	**Investor Contact:** 973-921-5914
		Transfer Agents: Computershare Shareowner Services LLC, Providence, RI

EAGLE MATERIALS INC

Exchange	Symbol	Price	52Wk Range	Yield	P/E
NYS	EXP	$78.32 (5/31/2016)	84.48-46.85	0.51	25.68

*7 Year Price Score 113.82 *NYSE Composite Index=100 *12 Month Price Score 105.15

Interim Earnings (Per Share)

Qtr.	Jun	Sep	Dec	Mar
2011-12	0.07	0.14	0.07	0.20
2012-13	0.31	0.40	0.37	0.15
2013-14	0.60	0.80	0.63	0.46
2014-15	0.75	1.00	1.03	0.93
2015-16	0.75	0.59	0.92	0.79

Interim Dividends (Per Share)

Amt	Decl	Ex	Rec	Pay
0.10Q	08/12/2015	10/01/2015	10/05/2015	11/06/2015
0.10Q	11/16/2015	12/16/2015	12/18/2015	01/22/2016
0.10Q	02/02/2016	04/13/2016	04/15/2016	05/13/2016
0.10Q	05/20/2016	06/16/2016	06/20/2016	07/22/2016

Indicated Div: $0.40

Valuation Analysis   **Institutional Holding**

Forecast EPS	$4.25	No of Institutions	
	(05/20/2016)	360	
Market Cap	$3.8 Billion	Shares	
Book Value	$1.0 Billion	50,770,616	
Price/Book	3.65	% Held	
Price/Sales	3.32	91.32	

Business Summary: Construction Materials (MIC: 8.5.1 SIC: 3241 NAIC: 327310)

Eagle Materials is a holding company. Co. operates in five business segments: CCement, Gypsum Wallboard, Recycled Paperboard, Oil and Gas Proppants and Concrete and Aggregates. These operations are conducted in the U.S. and include the mining of limestone and the manufacture, production, distribution and sale of Portland cement and specialty oil well cement, the grinding of slag, the mining of gypsum and the manufacture and sale of gypsum wallboard; the manufacture and sale of recycled paperboard to the gypsum wallboard industry and other paperboard converters; the sale of readymix concrete, the mining and sale of aggregates and the mining and sale of sand used in hydraulic fracturing.

Recent Developments: For the year ended Mar 31 2016, net income decreased 18.3% to US$152.6 million from US$186.9 million in the prior year. Revenues were US$1.14 billion, up 7.2% from US$1.07 billion the year before. Direct operating expenses rose 12.3% to US$911.9 million from US$812.2 million in the comparable period the year before. Indirect operating income amounted to US$4.2 million compared with an income of US$10.5 million in the equivalent prior-year period.

Prospects: Our evaluation of Eagle Materials Inc. as of June 19, 2016 is the result of our systematic analysis on three basic characteristics: earnings strength, relative valuation, and recent stock price movement. The company has produced a positive trend in earnings per share over the past 5 quarters and while recent estimates for the company have been raised by analysts, EXP has posted better than expected results. Based on operating earnings yield, the company is about fairly valued when compared to all of the companies in our coverage universe. Share price changes over the past year indicates that EXP will perform in line with the market over the near term.

Financial Data

(US$ in Thousands)	03/31/2016	03/31/2015	03/31/2014	03/31/2013	03/31/2012	03/31/2011	03/31/2010	03/31/2009
Earnings Per Share	3.05	3.71	2.49	1.22	0.42	0.34	0.66	0.95
Cash Flow Per Share	5.36	4.72	3.48	2.67	1.37	1.00	1.48	1.83
Tang Book Value Per Share	18.03	15.91	13.40	10.78	7.10	6.93	6.69	6.31
Dividends Per Share	0.400	0.400	0.400	0.400	0.300	0.400	0.400	0.600
Dividend Payout %	13.11	10.78	16.06	32.79	71.43	117.65	60.61	63.16
Income Statement								
Total Revenue	1,143,492	1,066,368	898,396	642,562	495,023	462,180	467,905	602,182
EBITDA	280,952	289,403	229,575	122,512	58,905	73,916	86,300	108,677
Depn & Amortn	84,200	69,700	67,300	55,100	48,900	48,200	49,700	50,000
Income Before Taxes	180,169	207,964	143,993	51,589	(6,616)	9,196	15,140	29,757
Income Taxes	66,660	66,074	57,561	26,352	3,180	1,913	10,347	20,419
Net Income	152,592	186,853	124,243	57,744	18,732	14,849	28,950	41,764
Average Shares	50,070	50,372	49,939	47,340	44,515	44,251	44,038	43,897
Balance Sheet								
Current Assets	380,003	366,635	306,960	261,271	191,841	174,626	161,274	175,283
Total Assets	1,883,635	1,882,591	1,511,529	1,476,233	985,145	982,810	1,013,776	1,066,668
Current Liabilities	120,589	184,576	108,820	100,229	77,043	70,350	71,884	64,249
Long-Term Obligations	499,714	455,714	371,759	489,259	262,259	287,000	303,000	355,000
Total Liabilities	843,104	871,998	680,030	780,063	512,634	523,246	568,414	638,841
Stockholders' Equity	1,040,531	1,010,593	831,499	696,170	472,511	459,564	445,362	427,827
Shares Outstanding	48,526	50,245	50,053	49,503	45,269	44,447	43,830	43,589
Statistical Record								
Return on Assets %	8.08	11.01	8.32	4.69	1.90	1.49	2.78	3.83
Return on Equity %	14.84	20.29	16.27	9.88	4.01	3.28	6.63	10.02
EBITDA Margin %	24.57	27.14	25.55	19.07	11.90	15.99	18.44	18.05
Net Margin %	13.34	17.52	13.83	8.99	3.78	3.21	6.19	6.94
Asset Turnover	0.61	0.63	0.60	0.52	0.50	0.46	0.45	0.55
Current Ratio	3.15	1.99	2.82	2.61	2.49	2.48	2.24	2.73
Debt to Equity	0.48	0.45	0.45	0.70	0.56	0.62	0.68	0.83
Price Range	87.68-46.85	104.73-69.80	90.88-61.72	71.57-29.84	35.81-15.68	32.79-21.79	29.75-22.18	37.86-14.41
P/E Ratio	28.75-15.36	28.23-18.81	36.50-24.79	58.66-24.46	85.26-37.33	96.44-64.09	45.08-33.61	39.85-15.17
Average Yield %	0.56	0.46	0.54	0.83	1.18	1.47	1.54	2.44

Address: 3811 Turtle Creek Blvd., Suite 1100, Dallas, TX 75219 **Telephone:** 214-432-2000 **Fax:** 214-432-2100	**Web Site:** www.eaglematerials.com **Officers:** Laurence E. Hirsch - Chairman David B. Powers - President, Chief Executive Officer, Executive Vice President, Division Officer	**Auditors:** Ernst & Young LLP **Investor Contact:** 214-432-2000 **Transfer Agents:** Computershare, Inc., Providence , RI

EASTMAN CHEMICAL CO.

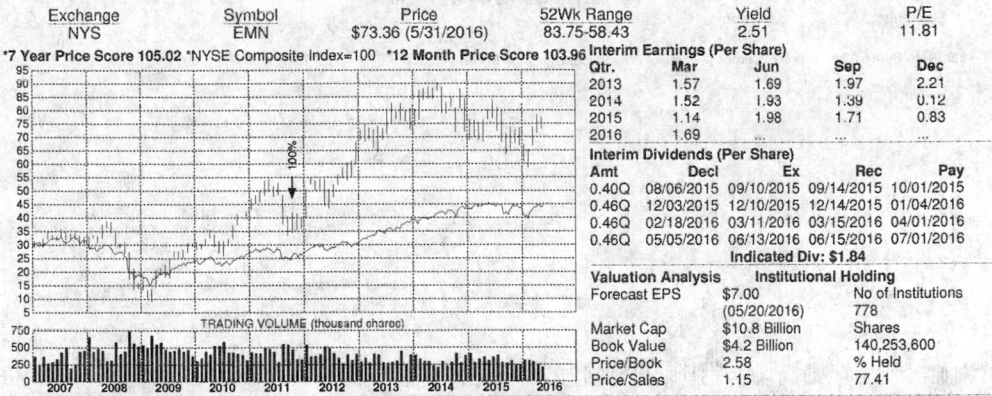

Exchange	Symbol	Price	52Wk Range	Yield	P/E
NYS	EMN	$73.36 (5/31/2016)	83.75-58.43	2.51	11.81

*7 Year Price Score 105.02 *NYSE Composite Index=100 *12 Month Price Score 103.96

Interim Earnings (Per Share)

Qtr.	Mar	Jun	Sep	Dec
2013	1.57	1.69	1.97	2.21
2014	1.52	1.93	1.39	0.12
2015	1.14	1.98	1.71	0.83
2016	1.69	...	...	...

Interim Dividends (Per Share)

Amt	Decl	Ex	Rec	Pay
0.40Q	08/06/2015	09/10/2015	09/14/2015	10/01/2015
0.46Q	12/03/2015	12/10/2015	12/14/2015	01/04/2016
0.46Q	02/18/2016	03/11/2016	03/15/2016	04/01/2016
0.46Q	05/05/2016	06/13/2016	06/15/2016	07/01/2016

Indicated Div: $1.84

Valuation Analysis / **Institutional Holding**

Forecast EPS	$7.00	No of Institutions
	(05/20/2016)	778
Market Cap	$10.8 Billion	Shares
Book Value	$4.2 Billion	140,253,600
Price/Book	2.58	% Held
Price/Sales	1.15	77.41

TRADING VOLUME (thousand shares)

Business Summary: Plastics (MIC: 8.4.2 SIC: 2821 NAIC: 325211)

Eastman Chemical is a chemical company. Co.'s segments are: Additives & Functional Products, which manufactures chemicals for products in the coatings and tires industries; Adhesives & Plasticizers, which manufactures adhesives resins and plasticizers; Advanced Materials, which produces and markets copolyesters, cellulose esters, interlayers, and aftermarket window film products; Fibers, which manufactures and sells Estron™ acetate tow, Estrobond™ triacetin plasticizers, and Estron™ natural and Chromspun™ solution-dyed acetate yarns; and Specialty Fluids & Intermediates, which uses acetyl and olefins streams and manufacturing technology for specialty fluids to manufacture certain products.

Recent Developments: For the quarter ended Mar 31 2016, net income increased 45.9% to US$251.0 million from US$172.0 million in the year-earlier quarter. Revenues were US$2.24 billion, down 8.5% from US$2.44 billion the year before. Operating income was US$399.0 million versus US$311.0 million in the prior-year quarter, an increase of 28.3%. Direct operating expenses declined 10.4% to US$1.60 billion from US$1.79 billion in the comparable period the year before. Indirect operating expenses decreased 31.9% to US$235.0 million from US$345.0 million in the equivalent prior-year period.

Prospects: Our evaluation of Eastman Chemical Co. as of June 19, 2016 is the result of our systematic analysis on three basic characteristics: earnings strength, relative valuation, and recent stock price movement. The company has managed to produce a neutral trend in earnings per share over the past 5 quarters. However, while recent estimates for the company have been lowered by analysts, EMN has posted better than expected results. Based on operating earnings yield, the company is undervalued when compared to all of the companies in our coverage universe. Share price changes over the past year indicates that EMN will perform well over the near term.

Financial Data

(US$ in Thousands)	3 Mos	12/31/2015	12/31/2014	12/31/2013	12/31/2012	12/31/2011	12/31/2010	12/31/2009
Earnings Per Share	6.21	5.66	4.97	7.44	2.93	4.86	2.96	0.93
Cash Flow Per Share	10.61	10.85	9.42	8.42	7.73	4.47	3.99	5.23
Tang Book Value Per Share	N.M.	N.M.	N.M.	N.M.	N.M.	10.69	8.86	8.28
Dividends Per Share	1.720	1.660	1.450	1.250	1.080	0.990	0.895	0.880
Dividend Payout %	27.70	29.33	29.18	16.80	36.86	20.37	30.24	95.14
Income Statement								
Total Revenue	2,236,000	9,648,000	9,527,000	9,350,000	8,102,000	7,178,000	5,842,000	5,047,000
EBITDA	534,000	1,794,000	1,532,000	2,204,000	1,101,000	1,301,000	973,000	566,000
Depn & Amortn	147,000	402,000	355,000	345,000	309,000	261,000	238,000	262,000
Income Before Taxes	323,000	1,129,000	990,000	1,679,000	649,000	964,000	636,000	226,000
Income Taxes	72,000	275,000	235,000	507,000	206,000	307,000	211,000	90,000
Net Income	251,000	848,000	751,000	1,165,000	437,000	696,000	438,000	136,000
Average Shares	148,800	149,800	151,100	156,500	149,100	143,100	147,800	146,800
Balance Sheet								
Current Assets	2,863,000	2,878,000	3,173,000	2,840,000	2,594,000	2,302,000	2,047,000	1,735,000
Total Assets	15,616,000	15,611,000	16,072,000	11,845,000	11,619,000	6,184,000	5,986,000	5,515,000
Current Liabilities	1,847,000	2,056,000	2,022,000	1,470,000	1,364,000	1,114,000	1,070,000	800,000
Long-Term Obligations	6,565,000	6,608,000	7,248,000	4,254,000	4,779,000	1,445,000	1,598,000	1,604,000
Total Liabilities	11,412,000	11,670,000	12,562,000	8,049,000	8,676,000	4,314,000	4,359,000	4,002,000
Stockholders' Equity	4,204,000	3,941,000	3,510,000	3,796,000	2,943,000	1,870,000	1,627,000	1,513,000
Shares Outstanding	147,785	147,761	148,596	152,416	153,894	136,915	141,343	144,770
Statistical Record								
Return on Assets %	5.90	5.35	5.38	9.93	4.90	11.44	7.62	2.52
Return on Equity %	24.27	22.76	20.56	34.57	18.11	39.81	27.90	8.87
EBITDA Margin %	23.88	18.59	16.08	23.57	13.59	18.12	16.66	11.21
Net Margin %	11.23	8.79	7.88	12.46	5.39	9.70	7.50	2.69
Asset Turnover	0.60	0.61	0.68	0.80	0.91	1.18	1.02	0.93
Current Ratio	1.55	1.40	1.57	1.93	1.90	2.07	1.91	2.17
Debt to Equity	1.56	1.68	2.06	1.12	1.62	0.77	0.98	1.06
Price Range	83.75-58.43	83.75-63.30	90.20-71.49	82.60-64.06	68.05-40.09	54.08-33.31	42.04-25.82	30.70-9.00
P/E Ratio	13.49-9.41	14.80-11.18	18.15-14.38	11.10-8.61	23.23-13.68	11.13-6.85	14.20-8.72	33.01-9.68
Average Yield %	2.40	2.27	1.75	1.69	2.03	2.23	2.70	4.13

Address: 200 South Wilcox Drive, Kingsport, TN 37662
Telephone: 423-229-2000

Web Site: www.eastman.com
Officers: Mark J. Costa - Chairman, President, Executive Vice President, Chief Marketing Officer, Chief Executive Officer Brad A. Lich Executive Vice President

Auditors: PricewaterhouseCoopers LLP
Investor Contact: 212-835-1620
Transfer Agents: American Stock Transfer & Trust Company, New York, NY

EATON CORP PLC

Exchange	Symbol	Price	52Wk Range	Yield	P/E
NYS	ETN	$61.63 (5/31/2016)	72.87-47.27	3.70	14.96

*7 Year Price Score 93.01   *NYSE Composite Index=100   *12 Month Price Score 105.04

Interim Earnings (Per Share)
Qtr.	Mar	Jun	Sep	Dec
2013	0.79	1.04	1.07	1.00
2014	0.92	0.36	1.26	1.23
2015	0.99	1.14	0.96	1.14
2016	0.88	...	...	...

Interim Dividends (Per Share)
Amt	Decl	Ex	Rec	Pay
0.55Q	07/21/2015	07/30/2015	08/03/2015	08/21/2015
0.55Q	10/27/2015	11/05/2015	11/09/2015	11/20/2015
0.57Q	02/24/2016	03/03/2016	03/07/2016	03/18/2016
0.57Q	04/26/2016	05/04/2016	05/06/2016	05/20/2016

Indicated Div: $2.28

Valuation Analysis
Forecast EPS	$4.30
	(05/20/2016)
Market Cap	$28.2 Billion
Book Value	$15.5 Billion
Price/Book	1.82
Price/Sales	1.38

Institutional Holding
No of Institutions	954
Shares	338,290,464
% Held	69.95

Business Summary: Electrical Equipment (MIC: 7.3.1 SIC: 3599 NAIC: 336399)

Eaton is a power management company providing energy-efficient solutions. Co.'s segments are: Electrical Products, which includes electrical components, industrial components, residential products, and single phase power quality; Electrical Systems and Services, which includes power distribution and assemblies, three phase power quality, and hazardous duty electrical equipment; Hydraulics, which provides power products, fluid conveyance products, filtration systems solutions, industrial drum and disc brakes, and golf grips; Aerospace, which supplies aerospace fuel, hydraulics and pneumatic systems; and Vehicle, which provides drivetrain and powertrain systems and critical components.

Recent Developments: For the quarter ended Mar 31 2016, net income decreased 13.7% to US$403.0 million from US$467.0 million in the year-earlier quarter. Revenues were US$4.81 billion, down 7.8% from US$5.22 billion the year before. Direct operating expenses declined 8.4% to US$3.29 billion from US$3.59 billion in the comparable period the year before. Indirect operating expenses decreased 3.0% to US$1.04 billion from US$1.07 billion in the equivalent prior-year period.

Prospects: Our evaluation of Eaton Corp PLC as of June 19, 2016 is the result of our systematic analysis on three basic characteristics: earnings strength, relative valuation, and recent stock price movement. The company has enjoyed a very positive trend in earnings per share over the past 5 quarters and while recent estimates for the company have been mixed, ETN has posted better than expected results. Based on operating earnings yield, the company is undervalued when compared to all of the companies in our coverage universe. Share price changes over the past year indicates that ETN will perform in line with the market over the near term.

Financial Data
(US$ in Millions)

	3 Mos	12/31/2015	12/31/2014	12/31/2013	12/31/2012	12/31/2011	12/31/2010	12/31/2009
Earnings Per Share	4.12	4.23	3.76	3.90	3.46	3.93	2.73	1.14
Cash Flow Per Share	5.81	5.09	3.96	4.83	4.77	3.69	3.82	4.23
Dividends Per Share	2.220	2.200	1.960	1.680	1.520	1.360	0.540	1.000
Dividend Payout %	53.88	52.01	52.13	43.08	43.93	34.61	19.78	88.11
Income Statement								
Total Revenue	4,813	20,855	22,552	22,046	16,311	16,049	13,715	11,873
EBITDA	732	2,856	2,502	2,671	2,057	2,227	1,723	1,026
Depn & Amortn	233	479	514	516	598	556	551	573
Income Before Taxes	442	2,145	1,761	1,884	1,251	1,553	1,036	303
Income Taxes	39	164	(42)	11	31	201	99	(82)
Net Income	404	1,979	1,793	1,861	1,217	1,350	929	383
Average Shares	459	467	476	476	350	342	339	335
Balance Sheet								
Current Assets	7,013	6,616	8,100	8,731	7,844	5,826	5,506	4,524
Total Assets	31,583	31,031	33,529	35,491	35,848	17,873	17,252	16,282
Current Liabilities	5,022	4,625	5,355	4,914	5,431	3,637	3,233	2,689
Long-Term Obligations	7,572	7,781	8,024	8,969	9,762	3,366	3,382	3,349
Total Liabilities	16,064	15,845	17,743	18,700	20,762	10,404	9,890	9,505
Stockholders' Equity	15,519	15,186	15,786	16,791	15,086	7,469	7,362	6,777
Shares Outstanding	458	458	467	475	470	334	339	332
Statistical Record								
Return on Assets %	5.96	6.13	5.20	5.22	4.52	7.69	5.54	2.33
Return on Equity %	12.48	12.78	11.01	11.68	10.76	18.21	13.14	5.85
EBITDA Margin %	15.21	13.69	11.09	12.12	12.61	13.88	12.56	8.64
Net Margin %	8.39	9.49	7.95	8.44	7.46	8.41	6.77	3.23
Asset Turnover	0.64	0.65	0.65	0.62	0.61	0.91	0.82	0.72
Current Ratio	1.40	1.43	1.51	1.78	1.44	1.60	1.70	1.68
Debt to Equity	0.49	0.51	0.51	0.53	0.65	0.45	0.46	0.49
Price Range	73.50-47.27	73.50-49.74	79.44-58.27	76.75-54.18	54.66-37.04	56.22-34.16	51.09-30.62	33.10-15.14
P/E Ratio	17.84-11.47	17.38-11.76	21.13-15.50	19.68-13.89	15.80-10.71	14.31-8.69	18.71-11.22	29.04-13.28
Average Yield %	3.71	3.50	2.75	2.57	3.25	2.85	1.39	3.97

Address: Eaton House, 30 Pembroke Road, Dublin 4, 44114-2584 Telephone: 353-163-72900	Web Site: www.eaton.com Officers: Craig Arnold - Chairman, Chief Executive Officer, Division Officer Richard H. Fearon - Vice-Chairman, Chief Financial Officer, Chief Planning Officer	Auditors: Ernst & Young LLP Investor Contact: 216-523-4205 Transfer Agents: Computershare Shareowner Services, Jersey City, NJ

EATON VANCE CORP

Exchange	Symbol	Price	52Wk Range	Yield	P/E	Div Achiever
NYS	EV	$36.36 (5/31/2016)	41.35-27.18	2.92	17.48	34 Years

*7 Year Price Score 88.94   *NYSE Composite Index=100   *12 Month Price Score 98.87

Interim Earnings (Per Share)

Qtr.	Jan	Apr	Jul	Oct
2012-13	0.38	0.50	0.18	0.46
2013-14	0.56	0.59	0.63	0.66
2014-15	0.21	0.58	0.57	0.53
2015-16	0.50	0.48	...	...

Interim Dividends (Per Share)

Amt	Decl	Ex	Rec	Pay
0.25Q	07/08/2015	07/29/2015	07/31/2015	08/12/2015
0.265Q	10/15/2015	10/28/2015	10/30/2015	11/13/2015
0.265Q	01/13/2016	01/27/2016	01/29/2016	02/12/2016
0.265Q	04/13/2016	04/27/2016	04/29/2016	05/13/2016

Indicated Div: $1.06

Valuation Analysis

		Institutional Holding	
Forecast EPS	$2.10	No of Institutions	
	(05/20/2016)	444	
Market Cap	$4.1 Billion	Shares	
Book Value	$613.9 Million	96,012,128	
Price/Book	6.74	% Held	
Price/Sales	3.06	70.05	

Business Summary: Wealth Management (MIC: 5.5.2 SIC: 6282 NAIC: 523930)

Eaton Vance, through its subsidiaries, manages active equity, income and alternative strategies across a range of investment styles and asset classes, including U.S. and global equities, floating-rate bank loans, municipal bonds, global income, high-yield and investment grade bonds. Through its subsidiary, Parametric Portfolio Associates LLC, Co. provides portfolio implementation and overlay services, including tax-managed core and index strategies, centralized portfolio management of multi-manager portfolios and customized exposure management services. As of Oct 31 2015, Co. had $311.35 billion in assets under management.

Recent Developments: For the quarter ended Apr 30 2016, net income decreased 8.5% to US$69.5 million from US$75.9 million in the year-earlier quarter. Revenues were US$323.3 million, down 8.1% from US$351.7 million the year before. Operating income was US$95.8 million versus US$122.2 million in the prior-year quarter, a decrease of 21.6%. Indirect operating expenses decreased 0.8% to US$227.5 million from US$229.4 million in the equivalent prior-year period.

Prospects: Our evaluation of Eaton Vance Corp. as of June 19, 2016 is the result of our systematic analysis on three basic characteristics: earnings strength, relative valuation, and recent stock price movement. The company has enjoyed a very positive trend in earnings per share over the past 5 quarters and while recent estimates for the company have been raised by analysts, EV has posted results that fell short of analysts expectations. Based on operating earnings yield, the company is undervalued when compared to all of the companies in our coverage universe. Share price changes over the past year indicates that EV will perform poorly over the near term.

Financial Data

(US$ in Thousands)	6 Mos	3 Mos	10/31/2015	10/31/2014	10/31/2013	10/31/2012	10/31/2011	10/31/2010
Earnings Per Share	2.08	2.18	1.92	2.44	1.53	1.72	1.75	1.40
Cash Flow Per Share	3.39	3.35	1.94	0.85	1.00	1.59	1.49	0.82
Tang Book Value Per Share	2.76	2.60	2.82	3.05	3.01	3.42	2.17	1.70
Dividends Per Share	1.045	1.030	1.015	0.910	1.820	0.770	0.730	0.660
Dividend Payout %	50.24	47.25	52.86	37.30	118.95	44.77	41.71	47.14
Income Statement								
Total Revenue	654,846	331,556	1,403,563	1,450,294	1,357,503	1,209,036	1,260,031	1,121,661
EBITDA	227,946	110,803	411,816	531,896	410,498	428,309	420,380	373,163
Depn & Amortn	7,737	4,059	11,400	10,900	13,000	16,900	15,800	15,400
Income Before Taxes	200,813	97,566	369,384	491,149	359,453	403,738	381,376	326,961
Income Taxes	73,012	36,843	143,214	186,710	143,896	142,385	156,844	126,263
Net Income	113,353	58,386	230,299	304,316	193,841	203,465	214,902	174,298
Average Shares	113,667	114,603	118,155	121,595	122,444	115,126	119,975	122,632
Balance Sheet								
Current Assets	536,522	560,909	816,015	580,522	668,767	632,423	657,959	499,274
Total Assets	1,920,755	1,893,120	2,116,471	1,860,086	2,407,249	1,979,491	1,831,300	1,280,607
Current Liabilities	184,068	160,843	277,047	275,719	255,222	227,985	210,723	258,001
Long-Term Obligations	958,113	964,504	970,850	725,637	1,100,415	946,605	977,699	500,000
Total Liabilities	1,306,808	1,302,563	1,496,240	1,204,910	1,737,465	1,367,419	1,370,885	870,322
Stockholders' Equity	613,947	590,557	620,231	655,176	669,784	612,072	460,415	410,285
Shares Outstanding	113,867	115,165	115,885	118,261	121,631	116,291	115,623	118,326
Statistical Record								
Return on Assets %	13.23	14.49	11.58	14.26	8.84	10.65	13.81	14.80
Return on Equity %	39.13	43.42	36.11	45.94	30.24	37.84	49.36	46.03
EBITDA Margin %	34.81	33.42	29.34	36.68	30.24	35.43	33.36	33.27
Net Margin %	17.31	17.61	16.41	20.98	14.28	16.83	17.06	15.54
Asset Turnover	0.73	0.77	0.71	0.68	0.62	0.63	0.81	0.95
Current Ratio	2.91	3.49	2.95	2.11	2.62	2.77	3.12	1.94
Debt to Equity	1.56	1.63	1.57	1.11	1.64	1.55	2.12	1.22
Price Range	41.55-27.18	44.00-27.39	44.00-33.06	43.63-34.29	44.18-28.14	29.70-21.78	33.92-20.84	35.72-25.90
P/E Ratio	19.98-13.07	20.18-12.56	22.92-17.22	17.88-14.05	28.88-18.39	17.27-12.66	19.38-11.91	25.51-18.50
Average Yield %	2.97	2.73	2.56	2.38	4.80	2.92	2.51	2.17

Address: Two International Place, Boston, MA 02110 **Telephone:** 617-482-8260 **Fax:** 617-482-2396	**Web Site:** www.eatonvance.com **Officers:** Thomas E. Faust - Chairman, President, Chief Executive Officer Jeffrey P. Beale - Vice President, Chief Administrative Officer	**Auditors:** Deloitte & Touche LLP **Investor Contact:** 617-482-8260 **Transfer Agents:** ComputerShare Investor Services, Providence, RI

ECOLAB, INC.

Exchange	Symbol	Price	52Wk Range	Yield	P/E	Div Achiever
NYS	ECL	$117.24 (5/31/2016)	122.10-100.14	1.19	35.31	23 Years

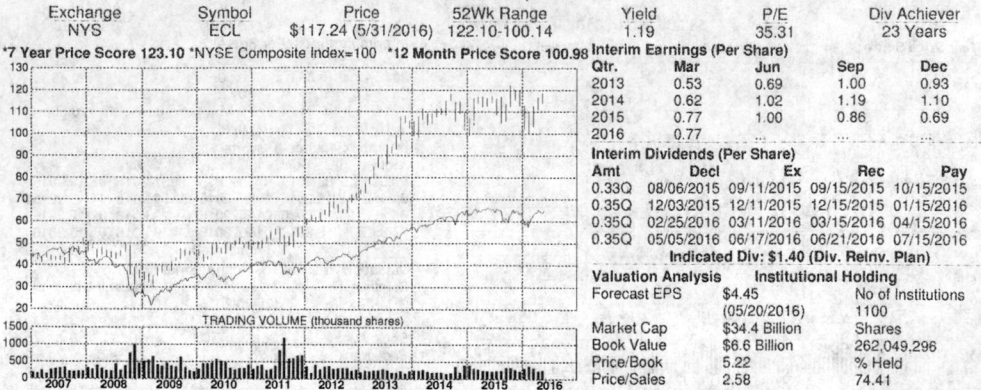

*7 Year Price Score 123.10 *NYSE Composite Index=100 *12 Month Price Score 100.98

Interim Earnings (Per Share)

Qtr.	Mar	Jun	Sep	Dec
2013	0.53	0.69	1.00	0.93
2014	0.62	1.02	1.19	1.10
2015	0.77	1.00	0.86	0.69
2016	0.77	...	...	...

Interim Dividends (Per Share)

Amt	Decl	Ex	Rec	Pay
0.33Q	08/06/2015	09/11/2015	09/15/2015	10/15/2015
0.35Q	12/03/2015	12/11/2015	12/15/2015	01/15/2016
0.35Q	02/25/2016	03/11/2016	03/15/2016	04/15/2016
0.35Q	05/05/2016	06/17/2016	06/21/2016	07/15/2016

Indicated Div: $1.40 (Div. Reinv. Plan)

Valuation Analysis — **Institutional Holding**

Forecast EPS	$4.45	No of Institutions
	(05/20/2016)	1100
Market Cap	$34.4 Billion	Shares
Book Value	$6.6 Billion	262,049,296
Price/Book	5.22	% Held
Price/Sales	2.58	74.41

Business Summary: Specialty Chemicals (MIC: 8.3.2 SIC: 2842 NAIC: 325612)

Ecolab is a provider of water, hygiene and energy technologies and services that protect people and resources. Co.'s products and technologies are used in water treatment, pollution control, energy conservation, oil production and refining, steelmaking, and other industrial processes. Co. has four reportable segments: Global Industrial, which consists of the Water, Food and Beverage, Paper and Textile Care operating units; Global Institutional, which consists of the consists of the Institutional, Specialty and Healthcare operating units; Global Energy, which consists of the Energy operating unit; as well as Other, which consists of the Pest Elimination and Equipment Care operating units.

Recent Developments: For the quarter ended Mar 31 2016, net income decreased 1.4% to US$232.0 million from US$235.4 million in the year-earlier quarter. Revenues were US$3.10 billion, down 6.1% from US$3.30 billion the year before. Operating income was US$371.5 million versus US$387.7 million in the prior-year quarter, a decrease of 4.2%. Direct operating expenses declined 7.6% to US$1.63 billion from US$1.77 billion in the comparable period the year before. Indirect operating expenses decreased 4.4% to US$1.09 billion from US$1.14 billion in the equivalent prior-year period.

Prospects: Our evaluation of Ecolab Inc. as of June 19, 2016 is the result of our systematic analysis on three basic characteristics: earnings strength, relative valuation, and recent stock price movement. The company has managed to produce a neutral trend in earnings per share over the past 5 quarters. However, while recent estimates for the company have been mixed, ECL has posted better than expected results. Based on operating earnings yield, the company is about fairly valued when compared to all of the companies in our coverage universe. Share price changes over the past year indicates that ECL will perform in line with the market over the near term.

Financial Data

(US$ in Thousands)	3 Mos	12/31/2015	12/31/2014	12/31/2013	12/31/2012	12/31/2011	12/31/2010	12/31/2009
Earnings Per Share	3.32	3.32	3.93	3.16	2.35	1.91	2.23	1.74
Cash Flow Per Share	8.02	6.75	6.05	5.20	4.10	2.89	4.07	2.94
Tang Book Value Per Share	N.M.	N.M.	N.M.	N.M.	N.M.	N.M.	2.23	1.16
Dividends Per Share	1.360	1.340	1.155	0.965	0.830	0.725	0.640	0.575
Dividend Payout %	40.96	40.36	29.39	30.54	35.32	37.96	28.70	33.05
Income Statement								
Total Revenue	3,097,400	13,545,100	14,280,500	13,253,400	11,838,700	6,798,500	6,089,700	5,900,600
EBITDA	583,700	2,121,300	2,513,000	2,074,600	1,757,300	1,084,800	1,112,800	971,300
Depn & Amortn	212,200	560,000	558,000	514,000	468,000	331,000	306,000	290,000
Income Before Taxes	305,400	1,317,700	1,698,400	1,298,300	1,012,600	679,600	747,700	620,100
Income Taxes	73,400	300,500	476,200	324,700	311,300	216,300	216,600	201,400
Net Income	230,800	1,002,100	1,202,800	967,800	703,600	462,500	530,300	417,300
Average Shares	298,300	301,400	305,900	305,900	298,900	242,100	237,600	239,900
Balance Sheet								
Current Assets	4,194,900	4,447,500	4,871,100	4,698,400	4,892,000	5,396,000	1,869,900	1,814,200
Total Assets	18,341,800	18,641,700	19,466,700	19,636,500	17,572,300	18,240,800	4,872,200	5,020,900
Current Liabilities	4,159,500	4,764,400	4,386,600	3,488,700	3,052,700	3,166,300	1,324,800	1,250,200
Long-Term Obligations	5,082,800	4,260,200	4,864,000	6,043,500	5,736,100	6,613,200	656,400	868,800
Total Liabilities	11,760,400	11,731,800	12,150,800	12,292,200	11,495,300	12,574,100	2,743,000	3,020,000
Stockholders' Equity	6,581,400	6,909,900	7,315,900	7,344,300	6,077,000	5,666,700	2,129,200	2,000,900
Shares Outstanding	293,300	295,967	299,852	301,135	294,722	291,974	232,512	236,594
Statistical Record								
Return on Assets %	5.32	5.26	6.15	5.20	3.92	4.00	10.72	8.54
Return on Equity %	14.86	14.09	16.41	14.42	11.95	11.87	25.68	23.36
EBITDA Margin %	18.84	15.66	17.60	15.65	14.84	15.96	18.27	16.46
Net Margin %	7.45	7.40	8.42	7.30	5.94	6.80	8.71	7.07
Asset Turnover	0.71	0.71	0.73	0.71	0.66	0.59	1.23	1.21
Current Ratio	1.01	0.93	1.11	1.35	1.60	1.70	1.41	1.45
Debt to Equity	0.77	0.62	0.66	0.82	0.94	1.17	0.31	0.43
Price Range	122.10-100.14	122.10-98.93	118.07-98.03	107.99-71.90	72.72-58.02	57.81-44.53	52.30-41.33	47.48-29.85
P/E Ratio	36.78-30.16	36.78-29.80	30.04-24.94	34.17-22.75	30.94-24.69	30.27-23.31	23.45-18.53	27.29-17.16
Average Yield %	1.21	1.18	1.06	1.08	1.27	1.40	1.36	1.45

Address: 370 Wabasha Street North, St. Paul, MN 55102 Telephone: 800-232-6522	Web Site: www.ecolab.com Officers: Douglas M. Baker - Chairman, President, Chief Executive Officer, Chief Operating Officer Thomas W. Handley - President, Chief Operating Officer, Senior Executive Vice President, Division Officer	Auditors: PricewaterhouseCoopers LLP Investor Contact: 651-293-2545 Transfer Agents: Computershare Trust Company, N.A., Providence, RI

EDGEWELL PERSONAL CARE CO

Exchange	Symbol	Price	52Wk Range	Yield	P/E
NYS	EPC	$79.43 (5/31/2016)	105.69-69.84	N/A	N/A

*7 Year Price Score 107.73 *NYSE Composite Index=100 *12 Month Price Score 95.69

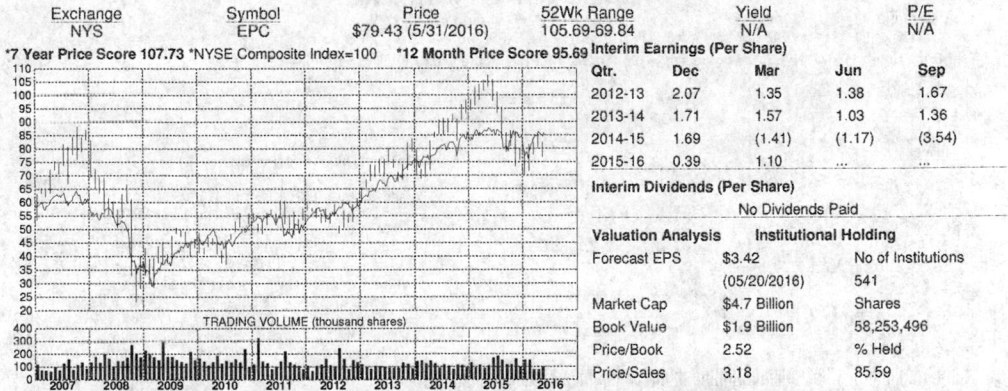

Interim Earnings (Per Share)

Qtr.	Dec	Mar	Jun	Sep
2012-13	2.07	1.35	1.38	1.67
2013-14	1.71	1.57	1.03	1.36
2014-15	1.69	(1.41)	(1.17)	(3.54)
2015-16	0.39	1.10	...	...

Interim Dividends (Per Share)

No Dividends Paid

Valuation Analysis		Institutional Holding	
Forecast EPS	$3.42	No of Institutions	
	(05/20/2016)	541	
Market Cap	$4.7 Billion	Shares	
Book Value	$1.9 Billion	58,253,496	
Price/Book	2.52	% Held	
Price/Sales	3.18	85.59	

Business Summary: Household & Personal Products (MIC: 1.7.1 SIC: 3699 NAIC: 335912)

Edgewell Personal Care is a manufacturer and marketer of personal care products in the wet shave, sun and skin care, feminine care and infant care categories. Co. manages its business in four segments: Wet Shave, which manufactures and distributes Schick and Wilkinson Sword razor systems, composed of razor handles and refillable blades, and disposable shave products for men and women; Sun and Skin Care, in which Co. sells its products under the Banana Boat, Hawaiian Tropic, Wet Ones and Playtex brand names; Feminine Care, in which Co. markets products under the Playtex, Stayfree, Carefree and o.b. brands; and All Other, which includes infant care, pet care and miscellaneous other products.

Recent Developments: For the quarter ended Mar 31 2016, income from continuing operations was US$66.1 million compared with a loss of US$54.6 million in the year-earlier quarter. Net income versus a net loss of US$88.4 million in the year-earlier quarter. Revenues were US$611.2 million, down 6.1% from US$651.1 million the year before. Direct operating expenses declined 5.3% to US$300.1 million from US$316.8 million in the comparable period the year before. Indirect operating expenses decreased 42.0% to US$219.8 million from US$379.1 million in the equivalent prior-year period.

Prospects: Our evaluation of Edgewell Personal Care Co. as of June 19, 2016 is the result of our systematic analysis on three basic characteristics: earnings strength, relative valuation, and recent stock price movement. The company has produced a positive trend in earnings per share over the past 5 quarters and while recent estimates for the company have been mixed, EPC has posted results that were in line with analysts expectations. Based on operating earnings yield, the company is about fairly valued when compared to all of the companies in our coverage universe. Share price changes over the past year indicates that EPC will perform poorly over the near term.

Financial Data
(US$ in Thousands)

	6 Mos	3 Mos	09/30/2015	09/30/2014	09/30/2013	09/30/2012	09/30/2011	09/30/2010
Earnings Per Share	(3.22)	(5.73)	(4.44)	5.69	6.47	6.22	3.72	5.72
Cash Flow Per Share	(0.06)	2.05	2.40	9.23	12.08	9.71	5.93	9.32
Income Statement								
Total Revenue	1,106,300	495,100	2,421,200	4,447,700	4,466,000	4,567,200	4,645,700	4,248,300
EBITDA	202,100	68,600	(285,200)	716,400	863,100	829,400	681,900	788,100
Depn & Amortn	44,600	20,200	73,700	120,300	164,700	136,700	154,500	119,300
Income Before Taxes	122,000	30,700	(458,700)	473,500	567,900	565,400	406,000	543,400
Income Taxes	32,200	7,000	(162,600)	117,400	160,900	156,500	144,800	140,400
Net Income	89,800	23,700	(275,300)	356,100	407,000	408,900	261,200	403,000
Average Shares	59,900	59,900	62,000	62,600	62,900	65,700	70,300	70,500
Balance Sheet								
Current Assets	1,515,500	1,464,000	1,636,600	2,729,600	2,568,400	2,522,600	2,392,600	2,429,500
Total Assets	4,949,400	4,886,500	4,991,700	6,928,700	6,717,400	6,731,200	6,663,400	6,387,900
Current Liabilities	601,400	511,200	666,800	1,573,700	1,153,400	1,307,500	1,159,300	1,253,500
Long-Term Obligations	1,843,400	1,841,300	1,704,000	1,768,900	1,998,800	2,138,600	2,206,500	2,022,500
Total Liabilities	3,076,600	3,090,000	3,127,600	4,406,400	4,263,800	4,661,700	4,562,100	4,288,300
Stockholders' Equity	1,872,800	1,796,500	1,864,100	2,522,300	2,453,600	2,069,500	2,101,300	2,099,600
Shares Outstanding	59,358	59,312	60,176	61,824	62,324	61,522	67,075	70,355
Statistical Record								
Return on Assets %	N.M.	N.M.	N.M.	5.22	6.05	6.09	4.00	6.43
Return on Equity %	N.M.	N.M.	N.M.	14.31	18.00	19.55	12.44	20.87
EBITDA Margin %	18.27	13.86	N.M.	16.11	19.33	18.16	14.68	18.55
Net Margin %	8.12	4.79	N.M.	8.01	9.11	8.95	5.62	9.49
Asset Turnover	0.25	0.32	0.41	0.65	0.66	0.68	0.71	0.68
Current Ratio	2.52	2.86	2.45	1.73	2.23	1.93	2.06	1.94
Debt to Equity	0.98	1.02	0.91	0.70	0.81	1.03	1.05	0.96
Price Range	107.28-69.84	107.28-73.07	107.28-78.40	92.73-67.59	80.20-52.29	59.13-47.72	60.55-48.19	52.84-36.90
P/E Ratio	...	...	...	16.30-11.88	12.40-8.08	9.51-7.67	16.28-12.95	9.24-6.45

Address: 1350 Timberlake Manor Parkway, Chesterfield, MO 63017 **Telephone:** 314-594-1900	**Web Site:** www.energizer.com **Officers:** David P. Hatfield - Chairman, President, Chief Executive Officer Sandra J. Sheldon - Chief Financial Officer	**Auditors:** PricewaterhouseCoopers LLP **Investor Contact:** 314-982-2013 **Transfer Agents:** Continental Stock Transfer & Trust Company, New York, NY

EDISON INTERNATIONAL

Exchange	Symbol	Price	52Wk Range	Yield	P/E	Div Achiever
NYS	EIX	$71.63 (5/31/2016)	72.76-55.58	2.68	23.80	11 Years

*7 Year Price Score 114.03 *NYSE Composite Index=100 *12 Month Price Score 110.57

Interim Earnings (Per Share)

Qtr.	Mar	Jun	Sep	Dec
2013	0.82	(0.29)	1.34	0.91
2014	0.54	1.63	1.46	1.27
2015	0.91	1.15	1.28	(0.24)
2016	0.82			

Interim Dividends (Per Share)

Amt	Decl	Ex	Rec	Pay
0.417Q	08/27/2015	09/28/2015	09/30/2015	10/31/2015
0.48Q	12/10/2015	12/29/2015	12/31/2015	01/31/2016
0.48Q	02/25/2016	03/29/2016	03/31/2016	04/30/2016
0.48Q	04/28/2016	06/28/2016	06/30/2016	07/31/2016

Indicated Div: $1.92 (Div. Reinv. Plan)

Valuation Analysis

		Institutional Holding	
Forecast EPS	$3.90	No of Institutions	
	(05/20/2016)	767	
Market Cap	$23.3 Billion	Shares	
Book Value	$11.4 Billion	286,858,048	
Price/Book	2.04	% Held	
Price/Sales	2.04	79.00	

Business Summary: Electric Utilities (MIC: 3.1.1 SIC: 4911 NAIC: 221111)

Edison International is a holding company. Through its principal subsidiary, Southern California Edison Company (SCE), Co. is primarily engaged in the business of supplying and delivering electricity. Co. is also the parent company of Edison Energy Group, a company that engaged in businesses focused on providing energy services to commercial and industrial customers, engaging in transmission opportunities, and exploring distributed water treatment and recycling. SCE supplies electricity to its customers through transmission and distribution networks. Its transmission facilities include sub-transmission facilities and are located primarily in California as well as in Nevada and Arizona.

Recent Developments: For the quarter ended Mar 31 2016, income from continuing operations decreased 7.2% to US$295.0 million from US$318.0 million in the year-earlier quarter. Net income decreased 6.9% to US$296.0 million from US$318.0 million in the year-earlier quarter. Revenues were US$2.44 billion, down 2.9% from US$2.51 billion the year before. Operating income was US$448.0 million versus US$538.0 million in the prior-year quarter, a decrease of 16.7%. Direct operating expenses was unchanged at US$1.42 billion versus the comparable period the year before. Indirect operating expenses increased 3.1% to US$569.0 million from US$552.0 million in the equivalent prior-year period.

Prospects: Our evaluation of Edison International as of June 19, 2016 is the result of our systematic analysis on three basic characteristics: earnings strength, relative valuation, and recent stock price movement. The company has produced a positive trend in earnings per share over the past 5 quarters and while recent estimates for the company have been mixed, EIX has posted results that fell short of analysts expectations. Based on operating earnings yield, the company is undervalued when compared to all of the companies in our coverage universe. Share price changes over the past year indicates that EIX will perform well over the near term.

Financial Data

(US$ in Thousands)	3 Mos	12/31/2015	12/31/2014	12/31/2013	12/31/2012	12/31/2011	12/31/2010	12/31/2009
Earnings Per Share	3.01	3.10	4.89	2.78	(0.56)	(0.11)	3.82	2.58
Cash Flow Per Share	13.49	13.83	9.96	9.83	10.20	11.98	10.67	9.34
Tang Book Value Per Share	35.11	34.89	33.64	30.50	28.95	30.86	32.48	30.20
Dividends Per Share	1.795	1.732	1.482	1.367	1.313	1.285	1.265	1.245
Dividend Payout %	59.63	55.89	30.32	49.19	...	...	33.12	48.26
Income Statement								
Total Revenue	2,440,000	11,524,000	13,413,000	12,581,000	11,862,000	12,760,000	12,409,000	12,361,000
EBITDA	970,000	3,539,000	4,349,000	3,377,000	4,005,000	2,310,000	3,863,000	3,050,000
Depn & Amortn	499,000	1,420,000	1,815,000	1,622,000	1,634,000	1,889,000	1,640,000	1,538,000
Income Before Taxes	333,000	1,568,000	1,979,000	1,221,000	1,860,000	(350,000)	1,551,000	812,000
Income Taxes	38,000	486,000	443,000	242,000	267,000	(288,000)	354,000	(98,000)
Net Income	271,000	1,020,000	1,612,000	915,000	(183,000)	(37,000)	1,256,000	849,000
Average Shares	328,000	329,000	329,000	329,000	330,000	326,000	329,000	327,000
Balance Sheet								
Current Assets	2,427,000	2,654,000	4,019,000	3,312,000	2,672,000	4,484,000	4,422,000	4,430,000
Total Assets	50,459,000	50,310,000	50,186,000	46,646,000	44,394,000	48,039,000	45,530,000	41,444,000
Current Liabilities	4,233,000	4,927,000	5,479,000	4,881,000	3,744,000	4,348,000	3,952,000	3,787,000
Long-Term Obligations	11,243,000	10,964,000	10,234,000	9,825,000	9,231,000	13,689,000	12,371,000	10,437,000
Total Liabilities	39,020,000	38,942,000	39,226,000	36,708,000	34,962,000	37,984,000	34,947,000	30,696,000
Stockholders' Equity	11,439,000	11,368,000	10,960,000	9,938,000	9,432,000	10,055,000	10,583,000	9,841,000
Shares Outstanding	325,811	325,811	325,811	325,811	325,811	325,811	325,811	325,811
Statistical Record								
Return on Assets %	1.96	2.03	3.33	2.01	N.M.	N.M.	2.89	1.97
Return on Equity %	8.81	9.14	15.43	9.45	N.M.	N.M.	12.30	8.38
EBITDA Margin %	39.75	30.71	32.42	26.84	33.76	18.10	31.13	24.67
Net Margin %	11.11	8.85	12.02	7.27	N.M.	N.M.	10.12	6.87
Asset Turnover	0.23	0.23	0.28	0.28	0.26	0.27	0.29	0.29
Current Ratio	0.57	0.54	0.73	0.68	0.71	1.03	1.12	1.17
Debt to Equity	0.98	0.96	0.93	0.99	0.98	1.36	1.17	1.06
Price Range	72.11-55.58	69.05-55.58	68.27-45.07	53.98-44.36	47.96-39.98	41.52-33.29	39.19-31.13	36.39-23.73
P/E Ratio	23.96-18.47	22.27-17.93	13.96-9.22	19.42-15.96	...	...	10.26-8.15	14.10-9.20
Average Yield %	2.93	2.82	2.63	2.85	2.96	3.37	3.66	3.95

Address: 2244 Walnut Grove Avenue, P.O. Box 976, Rosemead, CA 91770 Telephone: 626-302-2222	Web Site: www.edisoninvestor.com Officers: Theodore F. Craver - Chairman, President, Chief Executive Officer Pedro J. Pizarro - President, Chief Executive Officer	Auditors: PricewaterhouseCoopers LLP Transfer Agents: Wells Fargo Shareowner Services, St. Paul, MN

EDWARDS LIFESCIENCES CORP

Exchange	**Symbol**	**Price**	**52Wk Range**	**Yield**	**P/E**
NYS	EW	$98.50 (5/31/2016)	108.93-65.63	N/A	41.91

*7 Year Price Score 153.84 *NYSE Composite Index=100 *12 Month Price Score 123.45

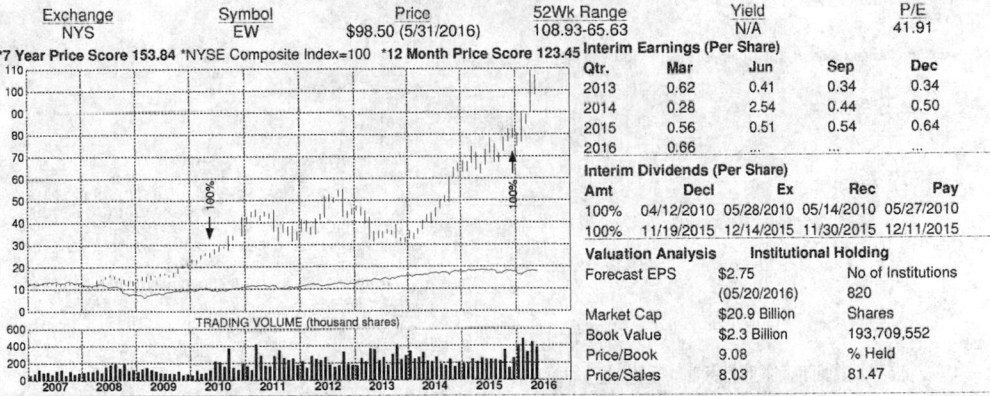

Interim Earnings (Per Share)

Qtr.	Mar	Jun	Sep	Dec
2013	0.62	0.41	0.34	0.34
2014	0.28	2.54	0.44	0.50
2015	0.56	0.51	0.54	0.64
2016	0.66	...	...	...

Interim Dividends (Per Share)

Amt	Decl	Ex	Rec	Pay
100%	04/12/2010	05/28/2010	05/14/2010	05/27/2010
100%	11/19/2015	12/14/2015	11/30/2015	12/11/2015

Valuation Analysis   **Institutional Holding**

Forecast EPS	$2.75	No of Institutions
	(05/20/2016)	820
Market Cap	$20.9 Billion	Shares
Book Value	$2.3 Billion	193,709,552
Price/Book	9.08	% Held
Price/Sales	8.03	81.47

Business Summary: Medical Instruments & Equipment (MIC: 4.3.1 SIC: 3842 NAIC: 339113)

Edwards Lifesciences is focused on technologies that treat structural heart disease and critically ill patients. Co.'s products and technologies are categorized into three areas: Transcatheter Heart Valve Therapy, which includes technologies designed to treat heart valve disease using catheter-based approaches for certain patients deemed at high risk for traditional open-heart surgery; Surgical Heart Valve Therapy, which provides heart valve therapy and a manufacturer of heart valves and repair products; and Critical Care, which provides hemodynamic monitoring systems used to measure a patient's heart function in surgical and intensive care settings.

Recent Developments: For the quarter ended Mar 31 2016, net income increased 15.9% to US$143.0 million from US$123.4 million in the year-earlier quarter. Revenues were US$697.3 million, up 18.1% from US$590.3 million the year before. Direct operating expenses rose 32.6% to US$180.3 million from US$136.0 million in the comparable period the year before. Indirect operating expenses increased 13.2% to US$327.3 million from US$289.2 million in the equivalent prior-year period.

Prospects: Our evaluation of Edwards Lifesciences Corp. as of June 19, 2016 is the result of our systematic analysis on three basic characteristics: earnings strength, relative valuation, and recent stock price movement. The company has produced a positive trend in earnings per share over the past 5 quarters and while recent estimates for the company have remained steady, EW has posted better than expected results. Based on operating earnings yield, the company is overvalued when compared to all of the companies in our coverage universe. Share price changes over the past year indicates that EW will perform very well over the near term.

Financial Data

(US$ in Thousands)	3 Mos	12/31/2015	12/31/2014	12/31/2013	12/31/2012	12/31/2011	12/31/2010	12/31/2009
Earnings Per Share	2.35	2.25	3.74	1.72	1.24	0.99	0.92	0.97
Cash Flow Per Share	2.74	2.55	4.80	2.12	1.62	1.37	1.11	0.73
Tang Book Value Per Share	6.91	7.75	8.31	5.11	4.50	4.04	4.03	3.33
Income Statement								
Total Revenue	697,300	2,493,700	2,322,900	2,045,500	1,899,600	1,678,600	1,447,000	1,321,400
EBITDA	201,600	690,400	1,212,300	574,000	435,400	321,900	308,900	342,300
Depn & Amortn	15,900	58,700	57,500	53,100	44,000	44,000	40,000	38,000
Income Before Taxes	183,300	622,400	1,144,000	515,700	391,800	278,200	267,400	303,200
Income Taxes	40,300	127,500	332,900	123,600	97,900	46,900	50,200	75,300
Net Income	143,000	494,900	811,100	391,700	293,200	236,700	218,000	229,100
Average Shares	217,800	220,300	217,000	227,600	236,600	238,800	238,400	234,800
Balance Sheet								
Current Assets	1,819,300	2,047,900	2,294,600	1,725,800	1,291,900	1,168,500	1,032,600	889,200
Total Assets	3,853,800	4,059,300	3,524,300	2,724,700	2,221,500	1,980,500	1,767,200	1,615,500
Current Liabilities	458,300	476,200	434,400	345,600	347,400	335,200	337,800	290,500
Long-Term Obligations	602,200	599,900	598,100	593,100	189,300	150,400	...	90,300
Total Liabilities	1,554,500	1,556,200	1,332,900	1,165,500	742,200	642,600	459,000	457,600
Stockholders' Equity	2,299,300	2,503,100	2,191,400	1,559,200	1,479,300	1,337,900	1,308,200	1,157,900
Shares Outstanding	211,900	215,400	215,600	218,600	228,600	228,200	230,000	227,200
Statistical Record								
Return on Assets %	14.01	13.05	25.96	15.84	13.92	12.63	12.89	15.19
Return on Equity %	22.80	21.08	43.25	25.78	20.76	17.89	17.68	22.50
EBITDA Margin %	28.91	27.69	52.19	28.06	22.92	19.18	21.35	25.90
Net Margin %	20.51	19.85	34.92	19.15	15.43	14.10	15.07	17.34
Asset Turnover	0.71	0.66	0.74	0.83	0.90	0.90	0.86	0.88
Current Ratio	3.97	4.30	5.28	4.99	3.72	3.49	3.06	3.06
Debt to Equity	0.26	0.24	0.27	0.38	0.13	0.11	...	0.08
Price Range	89.56-61.93	82.56-61.93	66.74-32.09	47.28-30.72	54.88-34.22	45.68-31.25	42.38-21.45	21.95-13.28
P/E Ratio	38.11-26.35	36.69-27.52	17.84-8.58	27.49-17.86	44.25-27.59	46.14-31.57	46.06-23.32	22.62-13.69

Address: One Edwards Way, Irvine, CA 92614	**Web Site:** www.edwards.com	**Auditors:** PricewaterhouseCoopers LLP
Telephone: 949-250-2500	**Officers:** Michael A. Mussallem - Chairman, Chief Executive Officer Denise E. Botticelli - Vice President, Associate General Counsel, Secretary	**Transfer Agents:** ComputerShare Investor Services, Providence, RI

EMC CORP. (MA)

Exchange	Symbol	Price	52Wk Range	Yield	P/E
NYS	EMC	$27.95 (5/31/2016)	28.35-22.67	1.65	27.14

*7 Year Price Score 91.22 *NYSE Composite Index=100 *12 Month Price Score 102.15

Interim Earnings (Per Share)

Qtr.	Mar	Jun	Sep	Dec
2013	0.26	0.32	0.27	0.47
2014	0.19	0.28	0.28	0.56
2015	0.13	0.25	0.25	0.39
2016	0.14	...	...	...

Interim Dividends (Per Share)

Amt	Decl	Ex	Rec	Pay
0.115Q	07/30/2015	09/29/2015	10/01/2015	10/23/2015
0.115Q	12/18/2015	12/30/2015	01/04/2016	01/22/2016
0.115Q	02/12/2016	03/30/2016	04/01/2016	04/22/2016
0.115Q	05/12/2016	06/29/2016	07/01/2016	07/22/2016

Indicated Div: $0.46

Valuation Analysis

		Institutional Holding	
Forecast EPS	$1.80	No of Institutions	
	(05/20/2016)	1676	
Market Cap	$54.6 Billion	Shares	
Book Value	$21.6 Billion	1,803,362,048	
Price/Book	2.53	% Held	
Price/Sales	2.22	80.71	

Business Summary: Computer Hardware & Equipment (MIC: 6.2.1 SIC: 3572 NAIC: 334112)

EMC develops, delivers and supports the Information Technology industry's range of information infrastructure and virtual infrastructure technologies, applications and services. Co. has three businesses: EMC Information Infrastructure, which comprises the Information Storage, Enterprise Content Division and RSA Information Security segments; VMware Virtual Infrastructure, which develops and markets its product and service within three product groups: Software-Defined Data Center, Hybrid Cloud Computing and End-User Computing; as well as Pivotal, which unites strategic technology, people and programs from Co. and VMware, Inc.

Recent Developments: For the quarter ended Mar 31 2016, net income increased 2.1% to US$297.0 million from US$291.0 million in the year-earlier quarter. Revenues were US$5.48 billion, down 2.5% from US$5.61 billion the year before. Operating income was US$410.0 million versus US$379.0 million in the prior-year quarter, an increase of 8.2%. Direct operating expenses declined 2.6% to US$2.22 billion from US$2.27 billion in the comparable period the year before. Indirect operating expenses decreased 3.7% to US$2.85 billion from US$2.96 billion in the equivalent prior-year period.

Prospects: Our evaluation of EMC Corp. as of June 19, 2016 is the result of our systematic analysis on three basic characteristics: earnings strength, relative valuation, and recent stock price movement. The company has produced a positive trend in earnings per share over the past 5 quarters. However, while recent estimates for the company have been mixed, EMC has posted results that fell short of analysts expectations. Based on operating earnings yield, the company is undervalued when compared to all of the companies in our coverage universe. Share price changes over the past year indicates that EMC will perform well over the near term.

Financial Data

(US$ in Thousands)	3 Mos	12/31/2015	12/31/2014	12/31/2013	12/31/2012	12/31/2011	12/31/2010	12/31/2009
Earnings Per Share	1.03	1.01	1.32	1.33	1.23	1.10	0.88	0.53
Cash Flow Per Share	2.69	2.77	3.22	3.34	2.98	2.76	2.21	1.65
Tang Book Value Per Share	1.24	0.98	1.83	3.02	3.08	2.46	1.94	2.51
Dividends Per Share	0.460	0.460	0.545	0.200	...	...	...	...
Dividend Payout %	44.66	45.54	41.29	15.04	...	...	...	...
Income Statement								
Total Revenue	5,475,000	24,704,000	24,440,000	23,222,000	21,713,902	20,007,588	17,015,126	14,025,910
EBITDA	910,000	4,065,000	4,907,000	4,888,000	4,662,818	4,147,636	3,381,628	2,122,575
Depn & Amortn	483,000	1,019,000	998,000	867,000	780,300	727,900	595,300	565,500
Income Before Taxes	386,000	2,882,000	3,762,000	3,865,000	3,803,615	3,249,270	2,607,983	1,374,576
Income Taxes	89,000	710,000	868,000	772,000	917,598	640,385	638,297	252,775
Net Income	268,000	1,990,000	2,714,000	2,889,000	2,732,613	2,461,337	1,899,995	1,088,077
Average Shares	1,965,000	1,962,000	2,059,000	2,160,000	2,205,639	2,229,113	2,147,931	2,055,146
Balance Sheet								
Current Assets	14,600,000	15,063,000	15,733,000	17,278,000	12,208,609	11,582,683	9,783,322	10,538,302
Total Assets	45,703,000	46,612,000	45,885,000	45,849,000	38,068,685	34,268,179	30,833,284	26,812,003
Current Liabilities	11,286,000	12,885,000	11,710,000	11,799,000	10,303,996	10,376,210	9,378,014	5,148,167
Long-Term Obligations	5,477,000	5,475,000	5,495,000	5,494,000	...	...	...	3,100,290
Total Liabilities	24,130,000	25,472,000	23,989,000	23,548,000	15,711,542	15,309,146	13,429,244	11,262,121
Stockholders' Equity	21,573,000	21,140,000	21,896,000	22,301,000	22,357,143	18,959,033	17,404,040	15,549,882
Shares Outstanding	1,953,000	1,943,000	1,985,000	2,020,000	2,106,959	2,048,890	2,069,246	2,052,441
Statistical Record								
Return on Assets %	4.51	4.30	5.92	6.89	7.53	7.56	6.59	4.29
Return on Equity %	9.55	9.25	12.28	12.94	13.19	13.54	11.53	7.61
EBITDA Margin %	16.62	16.45	20.08	21.05	21.47	20.73	19.87	15.13
Net Margin %	4.89	8.06	11.10	12.44	12.58	12.30	11.17	7.76
Asset Turnover	0.55	0.53	0.53	0.55	0.60	0.61	0.59	0.55
Current Ratio	1.29	1.17	1.34	1.46	1.18	1.12	1.04	2.05
Debt to Equity	0.25	0.26	0.25	0.25	...	...	...	0.20
Price Range	28.35-22.67	29.83-22.67	30.89-23.66	27.04-21.50	29.88-21.72	28.47-20.28	23.09-16.63	18.44-9.85
P/E Ratio	27.52-22.01	29.53-22.45	23.40-17.92	20.33-16.17	24.29-17.66	25.88-18.44	26.24-18.90	34.79-18.58
Average Yield %	1.78	1.74	1.97	0.82	...	...	...	...

Address: 176 South Street, Hopkinton, MA 01748	Web Site: www.emc.com	Auditors: PricewaterhouseCoopers LLP
Telephone: 508-435-1000	Officers: Joseph M. Tucci - Chairman, President, President (frmr), Chief Executive Officer William J. Teuber - Vice-Chairman	Transfer Agents: Computershare, College Station, TX
Fax: 508-435-5222		

EMCOR GROUP, INC.

Exchange	Symbol	Price	52Wk Range	Yield	P/E
NYS	EME	$47.55 (5/31/2016)	51.68-42.47	0.67	17.17

*7 Year Price Score 114.59 *NYSE Composite Index=100   ***12 Month Price Score 99.79**

Interim Earnings (Per Share)

Qtr.	Mar	Jun	Sep	Dec
2013	0.44	0.31	0.39	0.68
2014	0.61	0.60	0.67	0.66
2015	0.52	0.74	0.66	0.81
2016	0.56	...	...	...

Interim Dividends (Per Share)

Amt	Decl	Ex	Rec	Pay
0.08Q	07/07/2015	07/15/2015	07/17/2015	07/27/2015
0.08Q	10/08/2015	10/15/2015	10/19/2015	10/30/2015
0.08Q	01/07/2016	01/14/2016	01/19/2016	01/29/2016
0.08Q	04/05/2016	04/14/2016	04/18/2016	04/29/2016

Indicated Div: $0.32

Valuation Analysis   Institutional Holding

Forecast EPS	$2.91	No of Institutions	
	(05/14/2016)	359	
Market Cap	$2.9 Billion	Shares	
Book Value	$1.5 Billion	71,020,032	
Price/Book	1.97	% Held	
Price/Sales	0.42	89.87	

TRADING VOLUME (thousand shares)

Business Summary: Construction Services (MIC: 7.5.4 SIC: 1731 NAIC: 238210)

EMCOR Group is an electrical and mechanical construction and facilities services firm. In addition, Co. provides a number of building services and industrial services. Co.'s services are provided through its operating subsidiaries and joint venture entities. Co. focuses on providing construction services relating to electrical and mechanical systems and in providing various services relating to the operation, maintenance and management of facilities, including refineries and petrochemical plants. Co. also provides its construction services indirectly by acting as a subcontractor to contractors, systems suppliers, property managers and other subcontractors.

Recent Developments: For the quarter ended Mar 31 2016, income from continuing operations increased 4.1% to US$34.4 million from US$33.1 million in the year-earlier quarter. Net income increased 5.0% to US$34.4 million from US$32.7 million in the year-earlier quarter. Revenues were US$1.74 billion, up 9.8% from US$1.59 billion the year before. Operating income was US$55.6 million versus US$55.3 million in the prior-year quarter, an increase of 0.5%. Direct operating expenses rose 10.9% to US$1.52 billion from US$1.37 billion in the comparable period the year before. Indirect operating expenses increased 3.6% to US$167.5 million from US$161.6 million in the equivalent prior-year period.

Prospects: Our evaluation of EMCOR Group Inc. as of June 19, 2016 is the result of our systematic analysis on three basic characteristics: earnings strength, relative valuation, and recent stock price movement. The company has generated a negative trend in earnings per share over the past 5 quarters. However, while recent estimates for the company have been mixed, EME has posted results that fell short of analysts expectations. Based on operating earnings yield, the company is undervalued when compared to all of the companies in our coverage universe. Share price changes over the past year indicates that EME will perform well over the near term.

Financial Data
(US$ in Thousands)

	3 Mos	12/31/2015	12/31/2014	12/31/2013	12/31/2012	12/31/2011	12/31/2010	12/31/2009
Earnings Per Share	2.77	2.72	2.52	1.82	2.16	1.91	(1.31)	2.38
Cash Flow Per Share	4.06	4.25	3.72	2.24	2.76	2.24	1.03	5.45
Tang Book Value Per Share	2.86	2.63	1.27	1.34	6.51	4.48	7.52	5.44
Dividends Per Share	0.320	0.320	0.320	0.180	0.510	0.050	...	...
Dividend Payout %	11.55	11.76	12.70	9.89	23.61	2.62	...	...
Income Statement								
Total Revenue	1,744,970	6,718,726	6,424,965	6,417,158	6,346,679	5,613,459	5,121,285	5,547,942
EBITDA	65,085	361,277	364,344	277,620	310,929	264,543	(12,269)	281,402
Depn & Amortn	9,470	74,195	74,466	67,328	60,962	53,750	16,417	18,977
Income Before Taxes	53,404	278,823	281,645	202,651	244,248	201,352	(38,189)	259,270
Income Taxes	18,969	106,256	103,528	75,297	95,362	76,764	52,395	96,193
Net Income	34,348	172,286	168,664	123,792	146,584	130,826	(86,691)	160,756
Average Shares	61,350	63,307	67,062	68,076	67,738	68,375	66,393	67,445
Balance Sheet								
Current Assets	1,980,927	2,067,419	1,886,603	1,930,105	2,044,453	1,936,653	1,980,167	1,977,365
Total Assets	3,449,659	3,546,470	3,388,967	3,465,915	3,107,070	3,014,076	2,755,542	2,981,894
Current Liabilities	1,319,752	1,413,728	1,283,417	1,298,743	1,294,519	1,330,913	1,232,699	1,334,605
Long-Term Obligations	293,958	300,065	316,399	335,331	154,112	153,335	151,184	150,251
Total Liabilities	1,967,960	2,069,759	1,972,954	1,999,650	1,760,990	1,779,342	1,602,599	1,763,823
Stockholders' Equity	1,481,699	1,476,711	1,416,013	1,466,265	1,346,080	1,234,734	1,152,943	1,218,071
Shares Outstanding	61,340	61,067	62,981	66,896	66,964	66,444	66,660	66,187
Statistical Record								
Return on Assets %	5.14	4.97	4.92	3.77	4.78	4.53	N.M.	5.37
Return on Equity %	11.95	11.91	11.70	8.80	11.33	10.96	N.M.	14.22
EBITDA Margin %	3.73	5.38	5.67	4.33	4.90	4.71	N.M.	5.07
Net Margin %	1.97	2.56	2.63	1.93	2.31	2.33	N.M.	2.90
Asset Turnover	2.03	1.94	1.87	1.95	2.07	1.95	1.79	1.85
Current Ratio	1.50	1.46	1.47	1.49	1.58	1.46	1.61	1.48
Debt to Equity	0.20	0.20	0.22	0.23	0.11	0.12	0.13	0.12
Price Range	51.68-42.47	51.68-39.96	47.79-39.07	43.78-34.61	34.70-25.76	32.65-18.58	29.89-22.33	27.69-13.56
P/E Ratio	18.66-15.33	19.00-14.69	18.96-15.50	24.05-19.02	16.06-11.93	17.09-9.73	...	11.63-5.70
Average Yield %	0.68	0.69	0.73	0.46	1.76	0.18	...	...

Address: 301 Merritt Seven, Norwalk, CT 06851-1092	**Web Site:** www.emcorgroup.com
Telephone: 203-849-7800	**Officers:** Stephen W. Bershad - Chairman Sheldon I. Cammaker - Vice-Chairman, Executive Vice President, Secretary, General Counsel

Auditors: Ernst & Young LLP
Investor Contact: 203-849-7938
Transfer Agents: Computershare Shareowner Services, Pittsburgh, PA

EMERSON ELECTRIC CO.

Exchange	Symbol	Price	52Wk Range	Yield	P/E	Div Achiever
NYS	EMR	$52.02 (5/31/2016)	60.34-42.29	3.65	17.82	59 Years

*7 Year Price Score 79.84   *NYSE Composite Index=100   *12 Month Price Score 106.33

Interim Earnings (Per Share)

Qtr.	Dec	Mar	Jun	Sep
2012-13	0.62	0.77	0.27	1.10
2013-14	0.65	0.77	1.03	0.58
2014-15	0.75	1.42	0.84	0.98
2015-16	0.53	0.57	...	...

Interim Dividends (Per Share)

Amt	Decl	Ex	Rec	Pay
0.47Q	08/04/2015	08/12/2015	08/14/2015	09/10/2015
0.475Q	11/03/2015	11/10/2015	11/13/2015	12/10/2015
0.475Q	02/02/2016	02/10/2016	02/12/2016	03/10/2016
0.475Q	05/03/2016	05/11/2016	05/13/2016	06/10/2016

Indicated Div: $1.90 (Div. Reinv. Plan)

Valuation Analysis / Institutional Holding

Forecast EPS	$3.09 (05/20/2016)	No of Institutions	1731
Market Cap	$33.5 Billion	Shares	543,647,872
Book Value	$7.7 Billion	% Held	69.26
Price/Book	4.35		
Price/Sales	1.60		

Business Summary: Electrical Equipment (MIC: 7.3.1 SIC: 3679 NAIC: 334419)

Emerson Electric is organized into five business segments: process management, which provides measurement, control and diagnostic capabilities for automated industrial processes producing items; industrial automation, which brings integrated manufacturing solutions to various industries; network power, which designs, manufactures, installs and maintains power systems for telecommunications networks, data centers and other critical applications; commercial and residential solutions, which provides tools for professionals and homeowners, residential storage systems and appliance solutions; and climate technologies, which includes heating, air conditioning and refrigeration technology.

Recent Developments: For the quarter ended Mar 31 2016, net income decreased 61.5% to US$377.0 million from US$979.0 million in the year-earlier quarter. Revenues were US$4.93 billion, down 8.7% from US$5.40 billion the year before. Direct operating expenses declined 9.3% to US$2.93 billion from US$3.23 billion in the comparable period the year before. Indirect operating expenses decreased 7.6% to US$1.22 billion from US$1.32 billion in the equivalent prior-year period.

Prospects: Our evaluation of Emerson Electric Co. as of June 19, 2016 is the result of our systematic analysis on three basic characteristics: earnings strength, relative valuation, and recent stock price movement. The company has enjoyed a very positive trend in earnings per share over the past 5 quarters. However, while recent estimates for the company have been mixed, EMR has posted better than expected results. Based on operating earnings yield, the company is undervalued when compared to all of the companies in our coverage universe. Share price changes over the past year indicates that EMR will perform well over the near term.

Financial Data

(US$ in Thousands)	6 Mos	3 Mos	09/30/2015	09/30/2014	09/30/2013	09/30/2012	09/30/2011	09/30/2010
Earnings Per Share	2.92	3.77	3.99	3.03	2.76	2.67	3.27	2.84
Cash Flow Per Share	4.37	3.76	3.76	5.27	5.08	4.17	4.32	4.39
Tang Book Value Per Share	N.M.	N.M.	N.M.	1.79	1.99	0.60	N.M.	N.M.
Dividends Per Share	1.890	1.885	1.880	1.720	1.640	1.600	1.380	1.340
Dividend Payout %	64.73	50.00	47.12	56.77	59.42	59.93	42.20	47.18
Income Statement								
Total Revenue	9,641,000	4,713,000	22,304,000	24,537,000	24,669,000	24,412,000	24,222,000	21,039,000
EBITDA	1,106,000	498,000	5,053,000	4,285,000	4,155,000	4,085,000	4,637,000	3,878,000
Depn & Amortn	(97,000)	(51,000)	721,000	743,000	741,000	746,000	783,000	738,000
Income Before Taxes	1,111,000	503,000	4,161,000	3,348,000	3,196,000	3,115,000	3,631,000	2,879,000
Income Taxes	382,000	151,000	1,428,000	1,164,000	1,130,000	1,091,000	1,127,000	848,000
Net Income	729,000	352,000	2,710,000	2,147,000	2,004,000	1,968,000	2,480,000	2,164,000
Average Shares	644,700	652,500	676,500	704,100	722,900	734,600	753,500	757,000
Balance Sheet								
Current Assets	9,913,000	9,694,000	10,049,000	10,867,000	10,999,000	10,126,000	9,345,000	8,363,000
Total Assets	21,764,000	21,552,000	22,088,000	24,177,000	24,711,000	23,818,000	23,861,000	22,843,000
Current Liabilities	8,182,000	8,202,000	7,800,000	8,454,000	7,625,000	7,133,000	6,465,000	5,849,000
Long-Term Obligations	4,062,000	4,043,000	4,289,000	3,559,000	4,055,000	3,787,000	4,324,000	4,586,000
Total Liabilities	14,072,000	14,096,000	14,007,000	14,058,000	14,126,000	13,523,000	13,462,000	13,051,000
Stockholders' Equity	7,692,000	7,456,000	8,081,000	10,119,000	10,585,000	10,295,000	10,399,000	9,792,000
Shares Outstanding	643,261	643,099	654,608	696,605	706,660	724,113	738,877	752,690
Statistical Record								
Return on Assets %	8.74	11.29	11.72	8.78	8.26	8.23	10.62	10.16
Return on Equity %	23.53	30.13	29.78	20.74	19.20	18.97	24.57	23.59
EBITDA Margin %	11.47	10.57	22.66	17.46	16.84	16.73	19.14	18.43
Net Margin %	7.56	7.47	12.15	8.75	8.12	8.06	10.24	10.29
Asset Turnover	0.94	0.95	0.96	1.00	1.02	1.02	1.04	0.99
Current Ratio	1.21	1.18	1.29	1.29	1.44	1.42	1.45	1.43
Debt to Equity	0.53	0.54	0.53	0.35	0.38	0.37	0.42	0.47
Price Range	61.78-42.29	61.87-42.78	65.77-43.04	70.26-61.79	66.50-47.32	53.37-40.69	61.85-41.31	53.62-37.75
P/E Ratio	21.16-14.48	16.41-11.35	16.48-10.79	23.19-20.39	24.09-17.14	19.99-15.24	18.91-12.63	18.88-13.29
Average Yield %	3.71	3.53	3.29	2.60	2.93	2.93	2.54	2.91

Address: 8000 W. Florissant Avenue, P.O. Box 4100, St. Louis, MO 63136 Telephone: 314-553-2000	Web Site: www.emerson.com Officers: David N. Farr - Chairman, President, Chief Executive Officer Edward L. Monser - President, Chief Operating Officer	Auditors: KPMG LLP Investor Contact: 314-553-2197 Transfer Agents: Computershare, Inc., Providence, RI

ENDURANCE SPECIALTY HOLDINGS LTD

Exchange	Symbol	Price	52Wk Range	Yield	P/E
NYS	ENH	$67.92 (5/31/2016)	69.49-59.35	2.24	12.74

*7 Year Price Score 114.74 *NYSE Composite Index=100 *12 Month Price Score 100.63

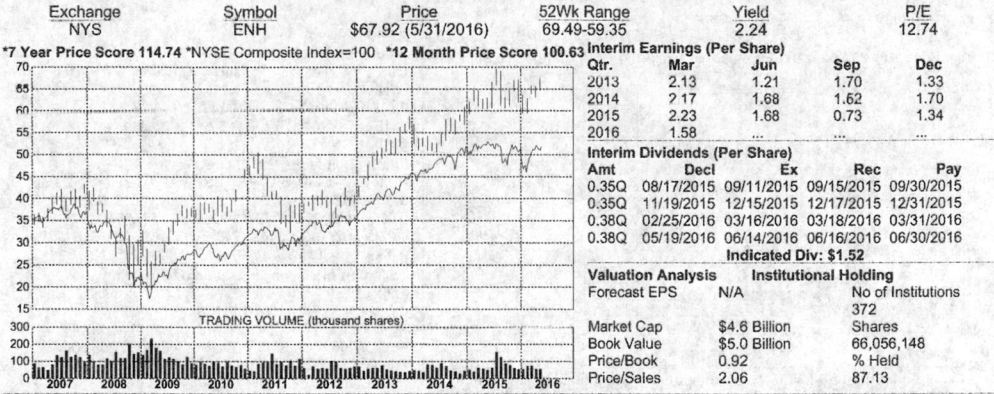

Interim Earnings (Per Share)

Qtr.	Mar	Jun	Sep	Dec
2013	2.13	1.21	1.70	1.33
2014	2.17	1.68	1.62	1.70
2015	2.23	1.68	0.73	1.34
2016	1.58	...	...	...

Interim Dividends (Per Share)

Amt	Decl	Ex	Rec	Pay
0.35Q	08/17/2015	09/11/2015	09/15/2015	09/30/2015
0.35Q	11/19/2015	12/15/2015	12/17/2015	12/31/2015
0.38Q	02/25/2016	03/16/2016	03/18/2016	03/31/2016
0.38Q	05/19/2016	06/14/2016	06/16/2016	06/30/2016

Indicated Div: $1.52

Valuation Analysis | **Institutional Holding**

Forecast EPS	N/A	No of Institutions
		372
Market Cap	$4.6 Billion	Shares
Book Value	$5.0 Billion	66,056,148
Price/Book	0.92	% Held
Price/Sales	2.06	87.13

Business Summary: General Insurance (MIC: 5.2.1 SIC: 6331 NAIC: 524126)

Endurance Specialty Holdings is a holding company. Through its operating subsidiaries based in Bermuda, the U.S. and the U.K., Co. underwrites property and casualty insurance and reinsurance. Co. focuses on the underwriting of specialty lines of insurance and reinsurance. Co.'s operations are organized into two business segments: Insurance, which is comprised of four lines of business: agriculture, casualty and other specialty, professional lines, and property, marine/energy and aviation; and Reinsurance, which is comprised of five lines of business: catastrophe, property, casualty, professional lines, and specialty

Recent Developments: For the quarter ended Mar 31 2016, net income increased 14.9% to US$124.6 million from US$108.5 million in the year-earlier quarter. Revenues were US$575.1 million, up 27.3% from US$451.7 million the year before. Net premiums earned were US$553.2 million versus US$389.9 million in the prior-year quarter, an increase of 41.9%. Net investment income fell 73.3% to US$11.2 million from US$41.9 million a year ago.

Prospects: Our evaluation of Endurance Specialty Holdings Ltd. as of July 26, 2015 is the result of our systematic analysis on three basic characteristics: earnings strength, relative valuation, and recent stock price movement. The company has produced a positive trend in earnings per share over the past 5 quarters. However, while recent estimates for the company have been mixed, ENH has posted better than expected results. Based on operating earnings yield, the company is undervalued when compared to all of the companies in our coverage universe. Share price changes over the past year indicates that ENH will perform poorly over the near term.

Financial Data

(US$ in Thousands)	3 Mos	12/31/2015	12/31/2014	12/31/2013	12/31/2012	12/31/2011	12/31/2010	12/31/2009
Earnings Per Share	5.33	5.73	7.06	6.37	3.00	(2.95)	6.38	8.69
Cash Flow Per Share	4.69	4.66	6.14	3.69	6.39	6.99	8.00	8.44
Tang Book Value Per Share	65.95	64.27	67.34	60.94	58.48	55.98	56.30	46.95
Dividends Per Share	1.430	1.400	1.360	1.280	1.240	1.200	1.000	1.000
Dividend Payout %	26.83	24.43	19.26	20.09	41.33	...	15.67	11.51
Income Statement								
Premium Income	553,191	1,978,453	1,863,978	2,016,484	2,013,900	1,931,393	1,741,113	1,633,192
Total Revenue	575,092	2,097,530	2,003,393	2,194,202	2,256,335	2,103,034	1,958,379	1,907,358
Benefits & Claims	243,328	917,108	970,162	1,219,684	1,520,995	1,632,666	1,038,100	866,640
Income Before Taxes	123,411	359,473	348,840	317,768	165,862	(116,740)	371,898	524,696
Income Taxes	(1,233)	4,362	390	5,853	3,346	(23,006)	7,160	(11,408)
Net Income	115,581	344,095	348,450	311,915	162,516	(93,734)	364,738	536,104
Average Shares	65,696	52,828	43,415	42,818	42,601	40,214	53,728	58,874
Balance Sheet								
Total Assets	14,282,186	13,241,525	9,644,782	8,978,122	8,794,972	8,292,615	7,979,405	7,666,694
Total Liabilities	9,298,829	8,385,263	6,459,600	6,091,573	6,084,375	5,681,450	5,131,252	4,879,411
Stockholders' Equity	4,983,357	4,856,262	3,185,182	2,886,549	2,710,597	2,611,165	2,848,153	2,787,283
Shares Outstanding	67,349	66,797	44,765	44,368	43,116	43,086	47,218	55,115
Statistical Record								
Return on Assets %	2.85	3.01	3.74	3.51	1.90	N.M.	4.66	7.18
Return on Equity %	8.51	8.56	11.48	11.15	6.09	N.M.	12.94	21.47
Loss Ratio %	43.99	46.35	52.05	60.49	75.52	84.53	59.62	53.06
Net Margin %	20.10	16.40	17.39	14.22	7.20	(4.46)	18.62	28.11
Price Range	69.49-59.35	69.49-59.17	60.67-50.45	58.67-39.69	42.36-34.09	50.43-32.19	46.64-34.86	38.44-19.71
P/E Ratio	13.04-11.14	12.13-10.33	8.59-7.15	9.21-6.23	14.12-11.36	...	7.31-5.46	4.42-2.27
Average Yield %	2.25	2.20	2.49	2.54	3.20	2.93	2.56	3.23

Address: Waterloo House, 100 Pitts Bay Road, Pembroke, HM 08
Telephone: 441-278-0400

Web Site: www.endurance.bm
Officers: John R. Charman - Chairman, Chief Executive Officer Michael J. McGuire - Chief Financial Officer

Auditors: Ernst & Young Ltd.
Investor Contact: 441-278-0988
Transfer Agents: EquiServe Trust Company, N A , Providence, Rhode Island

ENERGEN CORP.

Exchange	Symbol	Price	52Wk Range	Yield	P/E
NYS	EGN	$47.62 (5/31/2016)	75.46-22.90	N/A	N/A

*7 Year Price Score 74.52   *NYSE Composite Index=100   *12 Month Price Score 85.64

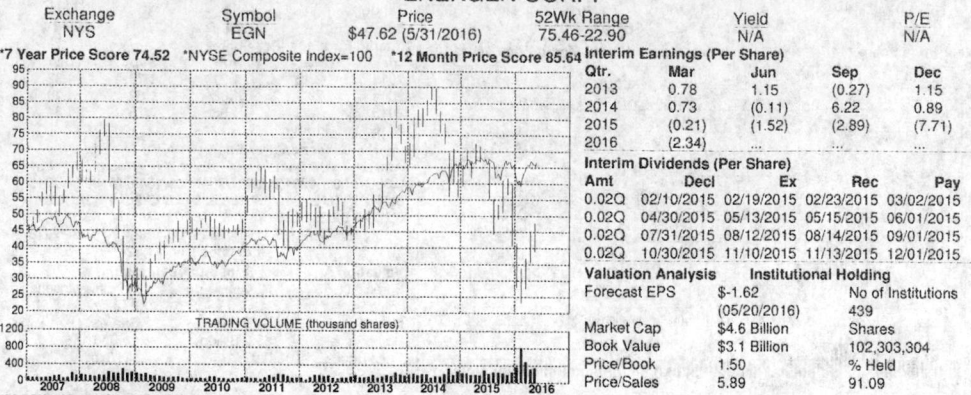

Interim Earnings (Per Share)
Qtr.	Mar	Jun	Sep	Dec
2013	0.78	1.15	(0.27)	1.15
2014	0.73	(0.11)	6.22	0.89
2015	(0.21)	(1.52)	(2.89)	(7.71)
2016	(2.34)	...	...	...

Interim Dividends (Per Share)
Amt	Decl	Ex	Rec	Pay
0.02Q	02/10/2015	02/19/2015	02/23/2015	03/02/2015
0.02Q	04/30/2015	05/13/2015	05/15/2015	06/01/2015
0.02Q	07/31/2015	08/12/2015	08/14/2015	09/01/2015
0.02Q	10/30/2015	11/10/2015	11/13/2015	12/01/2015

Valuation Analysis
		Institutional Holding	
Forecast EPS	$-1.62	No of Institutions	
	(05/20/2016)	439	
Market Cap	$4.6 Billion	Shares	
Book Value	$3.1 Billion	102,303,304	
Price/Book	1.50	% Held	
Price/Sales	5.89	91.09	

Business Summary: Production & Extraction (MIC: 9.1.1 SIC: 1311 NAIC: 211111)

Energen is an oil and natural gas exploration and production company that explores, develops and produces oil, natural gas liquids and natural gas in the Permian Basin in west Texas and the San Juan Basin in New Mexico. Co.'s operations focus on increasing production and adding proved reserves via the development of oil, natural gas liquids and natural gas properties. Co. also explores for and develops new reservoirs, mainly in areas in which it has an operating presence. At Dec 31 2015, Co. had 354.7 million barrels of oil equivalents proved reserves, which consisted of 433.90 billion cubic feet of natural gas, 71.7 million barrels of natural gas liquids, and 210.7 million barrels of oil.

Recent Developments: For the quarter ended Mar 31 2016, net loss amounted to US$203.1 million versus a net loss of US$15.4 million in the year-earlier quarter. Revenues were US$128.2 million, down 42.2% from US$221.9 million the year before. Operating loss was US$301.8 million versus a loss of US$12.4 million in the prior-year quarter. Direct operating expenses declined 29.6% to US$47.7 million from US$67.8 million in the comparable period the year before. Indirect operating expenses increased 129.6% to US$382.3 million from US$166.5 million in the equivalent prior-year period.

Prospects: Our evaluation of Energen Corp. as of June 19, 2016 is the result of our systematic analysis on three basic characteristics: earnings strength, relative valuation, and recent stock price movement. The company has generated a negative trend in earnings per share over the past 5 quarters. Because the company lacks sufficient analyst estimate data, we place greater weight on the historical EPS trend as the measure of earnings strength. Based on operating earnings yield, the company is overvalued when compared to all of the companies in our coverage universe. Share price changes over the past year indicates that EGN will perform very poorly over the near term.

Financial Data
(US$ in Thousands)	3 Mos	12/31/2015	12/31/2014	12/31/2013	12/31/2012	12/31/2011	12/31/2010	12/31/2009
Earnings Per Share	(14.46)	(12.43)	7.75	2.82	3.51	3.59	4.04	3.57
Cash Flow Per Share	6.84	9.39	9.68	12.82	10.17	10.57	9.34	9.48
Tang Book Value Per Share	31.71	36.78	46.84	39.36	37.14	33.79	30.02	27.77
Dividends Per Share	0.060	0.080	0.470	0.580	0.560	0.540	0.520	0.500
Dividend Payout %	...	...	6.06	20.57	15.95	15.04	12.87	14.01
Income Statement								
Total Revenue	128,219	878,554	1,679,213	1,738,650	1,617,169	1,483,479	1,578,534	1,440,420
EBITDA	(182,354)	(843,839)	726,706	895,474	882,535	734,144	744,884	674,759
Depn & Amortn	119,362	593,789	548,564	527,845	419,598	283,997	247,865	235,084
Income Before Taxes	(311,549)	(1,480,736)	140,371	298,429	397,381	405,325	457,797	400,296
Income Taxes	(108,433)	(535,005)	40,728	105,282	143,819	145,701	166,990	143,971
Net Income	(203,116)	(945,731)	568,032	204,554	253,562	259,624	290,807	256,325
Average Shares	86,632	76,078	73,274	72,470	72,316	72,332	72,050	71,885
Balance Sheet								
Current Assets	333,241	246,340	919,360	427,231	425,120	444,168	486,283	515,606
Total Assets	4,393,018	4,613,693	6,138,258	6,622,212	6,175,890	5,237,416	4,363,560	3,803,118
Current Liabilities	217,862	287,521	560,323	1,109,893	1,159,782	543,879	818,611	520,761
Long-Term Obligations	551,147	776,087	1,038,563	1,343,464	1,103,528	1,153,700	405,254	410,786
Total Liabilities	1,316,558	1,717,833	2,723,654	3,764,193	3,499,200	2,805,253	2,209,517	1,814,875
Stockholders' Equity	3,076,460	2,895,860	3,414,604	2,858,019	2,676,690	2,432,163	2,154,043	1,988,243
Shares Outstanding	97,004	78,743	72,895	72,606	72,069	71,970	71,761	71,602
Statistical Record								
Return on Assets %	N.M.	N.M.	8.90	3.20	4.43	5.41	7.12	6.76
Return on Equity %	N.M.	N.M.	18.11	7.39	9.90	11.32	14.04	13.14
EBITDA Margin %	N.M.	N.M.	43.28	51.50	54.57	49.49	47.19	46.84
Net Margin %	N.M.	N.M.	33.83	11.77	15.68	17.50	18.42	17.80
Asset Turnover	0.15	0.16	0.26	0.27	0.28	0.31	0.39	0.38
Current Ratio	1.53	0.86	1.64	0.38	0.37	0.82	0.59	0.99
Debt to Equity	0.18	0.27	0.30	0.47	0.41	0.47	0.19	0.21
Price Range	75.46-22.90	75.46-40.45	90.10-55.49	85.31-44.87	55.50-40.85	65.01-38.80	49.76-42.08	48.26-23.57
P/E Ratio	...	...	11.63-7.16	30.25-15.91	15.81-11.64	18.11-10.81	12.32-10.42	13.52-6.60
Average Yield %	0.11	0.13	0.62	0.97	1.15	1.00	1.13	1.32

Address: 605 Richard Arrington Jr. Boulevard North, Birmingham, AL 35203-2707 Telephone: 205-326-2700	Web Site: www.energen.com Officers: James T. McManus - Chairman, President, Chief Executive Officer, Chief Operating Officer Charles W. Porter - Vice President, Chief Financial Officer, Treasurer	Auditors: PricewaterhouseCoopers LLP Investor Contact: 205-326-8421 Transfer Agents: Computershare Shareowner Services LLC, Providence, RI

ENERGIZER HOLDINGS INC

Exchange	Symbol	Price	52Wk Range	Yield	P/E
NYS	ENR	$47.33 (5/31/2016)	47.33-30.23	2.11	34.55

*7 Year Price Score N/A   *NYSE Composite Index=100   *12 Month Price Score 112.03

Interim Earnings (Per Share)

Qtr.	Dec	Mar	Jun	Sep
2014-15	0.99	(1.11)	(0.32)	0.38
2015-16	1.05	0.20	...	...

Interim Dividends (Per Share)

Amt	Decl	Ex	Rec	Pay
0.25Q	07/02/2015	08/17/2015	08/19/2015	09/09/2015
0.25Q	11/16/2015	11/25/2015	11/30/2015	12/16/2015
0.25Q	02/01/2016	02/17/2016	02/19/2016	03/16/2016
0.25Q	05/10/2016	05/26/2016	05/31/2016	06/20/2016

Indicated Div: $1.00

Valuation Analysis

		Institutional Holding	
Forecast EPS	$2.25 (05/20/2016)	No of Institutions	329
Market Cap	$2.9 Billion	Shares	56,471,384
Book Value	N/A	% Held	N/A
Price/Book	N/A		
Price/Sales	1.81		

Business Summary: Household & Personal Products (MIC: 1.7.1 SIC: 3699 NAIC: 335999)

Energizer Holdings is a manufacturer, marketer and distributor of household batteries, specialty batteries and portable lights under the Energizer and Eveready brand names. Co. provides batteries using lithium, alkaline, carbon zinc, nickel metal hydride, zinc air and silver oxide technologies. Co. also distributes, markets, and licenses lighting products including headlights, lanterns, kid's lights and area lights. Co. markets its flashlights under the Hard Case®, Dolphin®, and WeatherReady® sub-brands. Co. also licenses its brands to companies developing solutions in gaming, automotive batteries, portable power for devices, light-emitting diode light bulbs and other lighting products.

Recent Developments: For the quarter ended Mar 31 2016, net income amounted to US$16.4 million versus a net loss of US$69.2 million in the year-earlier quarter. Revenues were US$334.0 million, down 6.4% from US$356.9 million the year before. Direct operating expenses rose 2.1% to US$192.4 million in the comparable period the year before. Indirect operating expenses decreased 53.0% to US$107.4 million from US$228.3 million in the equivalent prior-year period.

Prospects: Our evaluation of Energizer Holdings Co. as of June 19, 2016 is the result of our systematic analysis on three basic characteristics: earnings strength, relative valuation, and recent stock price movement. The company has managed to produce a neutral trend in earnings per share over the past 5 quarters and while recent estimates for the company have been raised by analysts, ENR has posted better than expected results. Based on operating earnings yield, the company is about fairly valued when compared to all of the companies in our coverage universe. Share price changes over the past year indicates that ENR will perform poorly over the near term.

Financial Data
(US$ in Thousands)

	6 Mos	3 Mos	09/30/2015	09/30/2014	09/30/2013	09/30/2012
Earnings Per Share	1.37	...	(0.06)	...	...	...
Cash Flow Per Share	2.64	3.12	2.60	...	...	...
Dividends Per Share	0.750	0.500	0.250	...	...	...
Dividend Payout %	54.74	...	...	...	...	...
Income Statement						
Total Revenue	840,800	506,800	1,631,600	1,840,400	2,012,200	2,087,700
EBITDA	157,100	115,200	114,300	308,200	284,900	381,800
Depn & Amortn	15,600	7,800	37,100	40,300	54,800	55,300
Income Before Taxes	115,500	94,500	(700)	215,200	162,000	257,600
Income Taxes	33,600	29,000	3,300	57,900	47,100	70,600
Net Income	81,900	65,500	(4,000)	157,300	114,900	187,000
Average Shares	62,300	62,300	62,200	...	...	...
Balance Sheet						
Current Assets	1,043,400	1,086,100	1,126,500	747,100	753,000	...
Total Assets	1,584,400	1,617,500	1,629,600	1,194,700	1,238,800	...
Current Liabilities	400,200	446,800	467,800	380,400	395,100	...
Long-Term Obligations	983,000	983,700	995,000	...	...	...
Total Liabilities	1,594,600	1,650,000	1,689,700	470,200	501,100	...
Stockholders' Equity	(10,200)	(32,500)	(60,100)	724,500	737,700	...
Shares Outstanding	61,830	61,829	62,195	...	...	...
Statistical Record						
EBITDA Margin %	18.68	22.73	7.01	16.75	14.16	18.29
Net Margin %	9.74	12.92	N.M.	8.55	5.71	8.96
Asset Turnover	...	...	1.16	...	...	...
Current Ratio	2.61	2.43	2.41	1.96	1.91	...
Price Range	43.25-30.23	43.25-33.00	42.31-33.00	...	...	...
P/E Ratio	31.57-22.07	N.M.	N.M.	...	...	...
Average Yield %	1.97	1.29	0.64	...	...	...

Address: 533 Maryville University Drive, St. Louis, MO 63141 **Telephone:** 314-985-2000	**Web Site:** www.energizerholdings.com **Officers:** J. Patrick Mulcahy - Chairman Alan R. Hoskins - President, Chief Executive Officer	**Auditors:** PRICEWATERHOUSECOOPERS LLP **Transfer Agents:** Continental Stock Transfer and Trust Company

ENERGY TRANSFER EQUITY L P

Exchange	Symbol	Price	52Wk Range	Yield	P/E
NYS	ETE	$12.64 (5/31/2016)	35.24-4.05	9.02	10.90

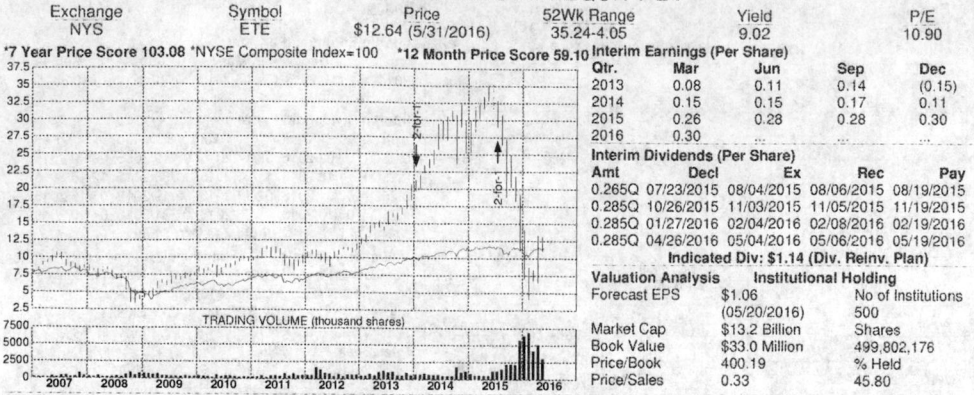

*7 Year Price Score 103.08 *NYSE Composite Index=100   *12 Month Price Score 59.10

Interim Earnings (Per Share)

Qtr.	Mar	Jun	Sep	Dec
2013	0.08	0.11	0.14	(0.15)
2014	0.15	0.15	0.17	0.11
2015	0.26	0.28	0.28	0.30
2016	0.30	...	...	...

Interim Dividends (Per Share)

Amt	Decl	Ex	Rec	Pay
0.265Q	07/23/2015	08/04/2015	08/06/2015	08/19/2015
0.285Q	10/26/2015	11/03/2015	11/05/2015	11/19/2015
0.285Q	01/27/2016	02/04/2016	02/08/2016	02/19/2016
0.285Q	04/26/2016	05/04/2016	05/06/2016	05/19/2016

Indicated Div: $1.14 (Div. Reinv. Plan)

Valuation Analysis   **Institutional Holding**

Forecast EPS	$1.06	No of Institutions
	(05/20/2016)	500
Market Cap	$13.2 Billion	Shares
Book Value	$33.0 Million	499,802,176
Price/Book	400.19	% Held
Price/Sales	0.33	45.80

TRADING VOLUME (thousand shares)

Business Summary: Equipment & Services (MIC: 9.1.3 SIC: 4922 NAIC: 486210)

Energy Transfer Equity is a holding company that owns equity interests in Energy Transfer Partners, L.P. and Regency Energy Partners LP, which are engaged in energy-related services. Co.'s principal reportable segments include: Gathering and Processing, which provides wellhead-to-market services to producers of natural gas; Natural Gas Transportation, which owns intrastate and interstate natural gas pipelines that deliver natural gas; NGL Services, which owns midstream energy assets through Lone Star NGL LLC; Contract Services, which provides natural gas compression services and treating services; and Natural Resources, which includes the management of coal and natural resources properties.

Recent Developments: For the quarter ended Mar 31 2016, net income increased 52.0% to US$336.0 million from US$221.0 million in the year-earlier quarter. Revenues were US$7.68 billion, down 26.0% from US$10.38 billion the year before. Operating income was US$701.0 million versus US$617.0 million in the prior-year quarter, an increase of 13.6%. Direct operating expenses declined 33.8% to US$5.62 billion from US$8.49 billion in the comparable period the year before. Indirect operating expenses increased 6.5% to US$1.36 billion from US$1.28 billion in the equivalent prior-year period.

Prospects: Our evaluation of Energy Transfer Equity L.P. as of June 19, 2016 is the result of our systematic analysis on three basic characteristics: earnings strength, relative valuation, and recent stock price movement. The company has generated a negative trend in earnings per share over the past 5 quarters and while recent estimates for the company have been raised by analysts, ETE has posted better than expected results. Based on earnings yield, the company is undervalued when compared to all of the companies in our coverage universe. Share price changes over the past year indicates that ETE will perform very poorly over the near term.

Financial Data

(US$ in Thousands)	3 Mos	12/31/2015	12/31/2014	12/31/2013	12/31/2012	12/31/2011	12/31/2010	12/31/2009
Earnings Per Share	1.16	1.11	0.57	0.17	0.28	0.34	0.22	0.50
Cash Flow Per Share	3.33	2.89	2.92	2.16	1.01	1.54	1.22	0.81
Dividends Per Share	1.080	1.020	0.750	0.652	0.625	0.588	0.540	0.526
Dividend Payout %	93.10	91.89	130.43	372.50	221.24	170.29	251.16	106.31
Income Statement								
Total Revenue	7,682,000	42,126,000	55,691,000	48,335,000	16,964,000	8,240,703	6,598,132	5,417,295
EBITDA	644,000	4,136,000	3,677,000	2,488,000	3,044,000	1,724,322	1,305,927	1,459,052
Depn & Amortn	(3,000)	1,776,000	1,223,000	1,128,000	801,000	556,569	394,698	304,129
Income Before Taxes	220,000	717,000	1,085,000	139,000	1,225,000	427,942	286,342	686,503
Income Taxes	(55,000)	(100,000)	357,000	93,000	54,000	16,883	13,738	9,229
Net Income	312,000	1,189,000	633,000	196,000	304,000	309,811	192,758	442,473
Average Shares	1,044,800	1,064,400	1,090,800	1,121,800	1,066,888	891,873	891,764	891,592
Balance Sheet								
Current Assets	5,584,000	5,410,000	6,153,000	6,536,000	5,597,000	1,455,444	1,291,010	1,267,959
Total Assets	72,765,000	71,189,000	64,469,000	50,330,000	48,904,000	20,896,793	17,378,730	12,160,509
Current Liabilities	5,691,000	4,910,000	6,782,000	6,500,000	5,845,000	1,841,313	1,081,075	889,745
Long-Term Obligations	37,401,000	36,837,000	29,653,000	22,562,000	21,440,000	10,946,864	9,346,067	7,750,998
Total Liabilities	74,418,000	72,088,000	63,772,000	49,220,000	46,718,000	20,772,165	17,187,119	12,160,357
Stockholders' Equity	33,000	33,000	33,000	32,000	73,000	71,144	70,943	...
Shares Outstanding	1,044,800	1,046,923	1,080,613	1,122,926	1,119,822	891,890	891,764	891,592
Statistical Record								
Return on Assets %	1.74	1.75	1.10	0.40	0.87	1.62	1.31	3.81
Return on Equity %	3,687.88	3,603.03	1,947.69	373.33	420.65	436.09	...	...
EBITDA Margin %	8.38	9.82	6.60	5.15	17.94	20.92	19.79	26.93
Net Margin %	4.06	2.82	1.14	0.41	1.79	3.76	2.92	8.17
Asset Turnover	0.56	0.62	0.97	0.97	0.48	0.43	0.45	0.47
Current Ratio	0.98	1.10	0.91	1.01	0.96	0.79	1.19	1.43
Debt to Equity	1,133.36	1,116.27	898.58	705.06	293.70	153.87	131.74	...
Price Range	35.24-4.05	35.24-11.09	32.24-19.62	20.62-11.37	11.95-8.60	11.56-8.02	10.12-7.04	7.72-4.04
P/E Ratio	30.38-3.49	31.75-9.99	56.56-34.43	121.31-66.88	42.67-30.71	33.99-23.58	45.98-31.99	15.44-8.09
Average Yield %	4.86	3.71	2.85	4.23	5.89	5.87	6.18	8.34

Address: 8111 Westchester Drive, Suite 600, Dallas, TX 75225 **Telephone:** 214-981-0700	**Web Site:** www.energytransfer.com **Officers:** Kelcy L. Warren - Chairman John W. McReynolds - President, Chief Financial Officer	**Auditors:** Grant Thornton LLP **Investor Contact:** 214-981-0795 **Transfer Agents:** American Stock Transfer & Trust, Brooklyn, NY

ENSCO PLC

Exchange	Symbol	Price	52Wk Range	Yield	P/E
NYS	ESV	$9.89 (5/31/2016)	24.67-7.88	0.40	N/A

*7 Year Price Score 28.75 *NYSE Composite Index=100 *12 Month Price Score 71.35

Interim Earnings (Per Share)

Qtr.	Mar	Jun	Sep	Dec
2013	1.36	1.55	1.62	1.54
2014	1.25	(5.07)	1.83	(14.91)
2015	1.38	1.11	1.34	(10.61)
2016	0.74	...	...	...

Interim Dividends (Per Share)

Amt	Decl	Ex	Rec	Pay
0.15Q	08/18/2015	09/02/2015	09/04/2015	09/18/2015
0.15Q	11/10/2015	12/03/2015	12/07/2015	12/18/2015
0.01Q	02/24/2016	03/03/2016	03/07/2016	03/18/2016
0.01Q	05/23/2016	06/02/2016	06/06/2016	06/17/2016

Indicated Div: $0.04

Valuation Analysis / **Institutional Holding**

Forecast EPS	N/A
	No of Institutions 607
Market Cap	$2.3 Billion
	Shares
Book Value	$6.7 Billion
	241,399,056
Price/Book	0.35
	% Held
Price/Sales	0.63
	N/A

TRADING VOLUME (thousand shares)

Business Summary: Equipment & Services (MIC: 9.1.3 SIC: 1381 NAIC: 213111)

Ensco is offshore contract drilling company. As of Dec 31 2015, Co. owned and operated an offshore drilling rig fleet of 64 rigs. Co.'s rig fleet includes ten drillships, 13 dynamically positioned semisubmersible rigs, three moored semisubmersible rigs and 42 jackup rigs, including four rigs under construction. Co.'s business consists of three operating segments: floaters, which include its drillships and semisubmersible rigs, jackups and other, which consists of management services on rigs owned by third-parties. Co.'s two reportable segments, Floaters and Jackups, provide one service, contract drilling.

Recent Developments: For the quarter ended Mar 31 2016, income from continuing operations decreased 45.9% to US$177.6 million from US$328.1 million in the year-earlier quarter. Net income decreased 46.1% to US$176.7 million from US$327.9 million in the year-earlier quarter. Revenues were US$814.0 million, down 30.1% from US$1.16 billion the year before. Operating income was US$313.6 million versus US$478.4 million in the prior-year quarter, a decrease of 34.4%. Direct operating expenses declined 29.8% to US$363.7 million from US$518.3 million in the comparable period the year before. Indirect operating expenses decreased 18.2% to US$136.7 million from US$167.2 million in the equivalent prior-year period.

Prospects: Our evaluation of Ensco PLC as of July 26, 2015 is the result of our systematic analysis on three basic characteristics: earnings strength, relative valuation, and recent stock price movement. The company has suffered a very negative trend in earnings per share over the past 5 quarters. However, while recent estimates for the company have been mixed, ESV has posted better than expected results. Based on operating earnings yield, the company is undervalued when compared to all of the companies in our coverage universe. Share price changes over the past year indicates that ESV will perform well over the near term.

Financial Data
(US$ in Thousands)

	3 Mos	12/31/2015	12/31/2014	12/31/2013	12/31/2012	12/31/2011	12/31/2010	12/31/2009
Earnings Per Share	(7.42)	(6.88)	(16.88)	6.07	5.04	3.08	4.06	5.48
Cash Flow Per Share	6.29	7.31	8.89	8.58	9.56	3.81	5.79	8.70
Tang Book Value Per Share	28.41	27.65	33.68	40.39	36.26	32.01	39.34	36.22
Dividends Per Share	0.460	0.600	3.000	2.250	1.500	1.400	1.075	0.100
Dividend Payout %	...	...	...	37.07	29.76	45.45	26.48	1.82
Income Statement								
Total Revenue	814,000	4,063,400	4,564,500	4,919,800	4,300,700	2,842,700	1,696,800	1,945,900
EBITDA	420,100	(692,300)	(1,862,500)	2,412,600	2,126,000	1,234,200	860,800	1,165,200
Depn & Amortn	108,300	572,500	537,900	611,900	558,600	418,900	216,300	205,900
Income Before Taxes	249,000	(1,471,200)	(2,548,800)	1,658,500	1,466,600	736,600	644,500	959,300
Income Taxes	71,400	(13,900)	140,500	225,600	244,400	131,000	96,000	178,400
Net Income	175,300	(1,594,800)	(3,902,600)	1,418,200	1,169,700	600,400	579,500	779,400
Average Shares	232,500	232,200	231,600	231,100	229,700	192,600	141,000	140,500
Balance Sheet								
Current Assets	2,322,800	2,285,100	2,934,800	1,535,200	1,723,900	1,644,700	1,436,700	1,652,800
Total Assets	13,610,000	13,637,000	16,059,900	19,472,900	18,565,300	17,871,200	7,051,500	6,747,200
Current Liabilities	1,507,400	775,500	1,104,600	1,047,300	989,700	1,323,400	349,000	484,900
Long-Term Obligations	4,991,000	5,895,100	5,885,600	4,718,900	4,798,400	4,877,600	240,100	257,200
Total Liabilities	6,909,300	7,124,100	7,844,900	6,681,300	6,718,900	6,991,900	1,092,000	1,248,000
Stockholders' Equity	6,700,700	6,512,900	8,215,000	12,791,600	11,846,400	10,879,300	5,959,500	5,499,200
Shares Outstanding	235,850	235,350	234,250	233,550	232,450	230,950	142,950	142,550
Statistical Record								
Return on Assets %	N.M.	N.M.	N.M.	7.46	6.40	4.82	8.40	12.39
Return on Equity %	N.M.	N.M.	N.M.	11.51	10.27	7.13	10.11	15.32
EBITDA Margin %	51.61	N.M.	N.M.	49.04	49.43	43.42	50.73	59.88
Net Margin %	21.54	N.M.	N.M.	28.83	27.20	21.12	34.15	40.05
Asset Turnover	0.25	0.27	0.26	0.26	0.24	0.23	0.25	0.31
Current Ratio	1.54	2.95	2.66	1.47	1.74	1.24	4.12	3.41
Debt to Equity	0.74	0.91	0.72	0.37	0.41	0.45	0.04	0.05
Price Range	27.51-7.88	31.93-13.53	57.33-26.41	65.45-51.73	60.33-42.21	59.57-39.51	53.40-34.45	50.32-22.11
P/E Ratio	...	...	...	10.78-8.52	11.97-8.38	19.34-12.83	13.15-8.49	9.18-4.03
Average Yield %	2.69	2.86	6.34	3.83	2.80	2.72	2.43	0.28

Address: 6 Chesterfield Gardens, London, W1J5BQ	**Web Site:** www.enscoplc.com	**Auditors:** KPMG LLP
	Officers: Carl G. Trowell - President, Chief Executive Officer Maria Clara Silva - Vice President	**Investor Contact:** 713-430-4607
Telephone: 207-659-4660		**Transfer Agents:** Computershare Trust Company, N.A.

ENTERGY CORP

Exchange	Symbol	Price	52Wk Range	Yield	P/E
NYS	ETR	$75.92 (5/31/2016)	79.97-61.53	4.48	N/A

*7 Year Price Score 83.64 *NYSE Composite Index=100 *12 Month Price Score 106.58

Interim Earnings (Per Share)

Qtr.	Mar	Jun	Sep	Dec
2013	0.90	0.92	1.34	0.83
2014	2.24	1.05	1.27	0.66
2015	1.65	0.83	(4.04)	0.55
2016	1.28			

Interim Dividends (Per Share)

Amt	Decl	Ex	Rec	Pay
0.83Q	07/31/2015	08/11/2015	08/13/2015	09/01/2015
0.85Q	10/30/2015	11/09/2015	11/12/2015	12/01/2015
0.85Q	01/29/2016	02/09/2016	02/11/2016	03/01/2016
0.85Q	04/06/2016	05/10/2016	05/12/2016	06/01/2016

Indicated Div: $3.40

Valuation Analysis | Institutional Holding
Forecast EPS	$5.07	No of Institutions
	(05/20/2016)	756
Market Cap	$13.5 Billion	Shares
Book Value	$9.7 Billion	157,901,104
Price/Book	1.40	% Held
Price/Sales	1.21	88.50

Business Summary: Electric Utilities (MIC: 3.1.1 SIC: 4911 NAIC: 221122)

Entergy is an integrated energy company engaged primarily in electric power production and retail electric distribution operations. Co. owns and operates power plants. Co. operates through two business segments: Utility, which generates, transmits, distributes and sells electric power to retail and wholesale customers in Arkansas, Louisiana, Mississippi, and Texas, as well as provides natural gas utility services to customers in and around Baton Rouge, LA, and New Orleans, LA; and Entergy Wholesale Commodities, which includes the ownership, operation, and decommissioning of nuclear power plants, and the sale of the electric power produced by its operating plants to wholesale customers.

Recent Developments: For the quarter ended Mar 31 2016, net income decreased 22.3% to US$235.2 million from US$302.9 million in the year-earlier quarter. Revenues were US$2.61 billion, down 10.6% from US$2.92 billion the year before. Operating income was US$498.2 million versus US$542.8 million in the prior-year quarter, a decrease of 8.2%. Direct operating expenses declined 14.2% to US$1.55 billion from US$1.81 billion in the comparable period the year before. Indirect operating expenses decreased 1.5% to US$561.2 million from US$569.9 million in the equivalent prior-year period.

Prospects: Our evaluation of Entergy Corp. as of June 19, 2016 is the result of our systematic analysis on three basic characteristics: earnings strength, relative valuation, and recent stock price movement. The company has generated a negative trend in earnings per share over the past 5 quarters. However, while recent estimates for the company have been mixed, ETR has posted better than expected results. Based on operating earnings yield, the company is undervalued when compared to all of the companies in our coverage universe. Share price changes over the past year indicates that ETR will perform well over the near term.

Financial Data
(US$ in Thousands)

	3 Mos	12/31/2015	12/31/2014	12/31/2013	12/31/2012	12/31/2011	12/31/2010	12/31/2009
Earnings Per Share	(1.38)	(0.99)	5.22	3.99	4.76	7.55	6.66	6.30
Cash Flow Per Share	17.99	18.37	21.67	17.90	16.54	17.63	21.11	15.22
Tang Book Value Per Share	52.14	51.56	54.91	53.07	50.65	49.73	46.64	44.70
Dividends Per Share	3.360	3.340	3.320	3.320	3.320	3.320	3.240	3.000
Dividend Payout %	...	...	63.60	83.21	69.75	43.97	48.65	47.62
Income Statement								
Total Revenue	2,609,852	11,513,251	12,494,921	11,390,947	10,302,079	11,229,073	11,487,577	10,745,650
EBITDA	1,006,811	1,773,982	4,157,567	3,373,366	3,112,375	3,783,583	3,982,587	3,507,237
Depn & Amortn	500,248	2,117,236	2,127,892	2,012,076	1,771,649	1,745,455	1,705,331	1,281,838
Income Before Taxes	375,187	(799,661)	1,549,854	956,553	899,218	1,653,635	1,887,544	1,891,583
Income Taxes	139,945	(642,927)	589,597	225,981	30,855	286,263	617,239	632,740
Net Income	229,966	(156,734)	960,257	730,572	868,363	1,367,372	1,270,305	1,251,050
Average Shares	178,976	179,176	180,296	178,570	177,737	178,370	187,814	195,838
Balance Sheet								
Current Assets	4,001,195	4,067,412	4,389,633	3,929,691	3,683,126	3,622,703	4,339,083	4,534,161
Total Assets	45,933,882	44,647,681	46,527,854	43,406,446	43,202,502	40,701,699	38,685,276	37,364,597
Current Liabilities	3,839,348	3,089,958	3,848,891	4,060,572	4,106,321	4,950,699	2,776,249	3,193,997
Long-Term Obligations	13,526,430	13,138,557	12,529,819	12,171,767	11,954,859	10,082,134	11,359,235	11,059,971
Total Liabilities	36,254,750	35,072,705	36,215,369	33,469,220	33,724,902	31,459,918	29,878,138	28,439,894
Stockholders' Equity	9,679,132	9,574,976	10,312,485	9,937,226	9,477,600	9,241,781	8,807,138	8,924,703
Shares Outstanding	178,389	178,389	179,240	178,370	177,807	176,355	178,745	189,118
Statistical Record								
Return on Assets %	N.M.	N.M.	2.14	1.69	2.06	3.44	3.34	3.38
Return on Equity %	N.M.	N.M.	9.48	7.53	9.25	15.15	14.33	14.55
EBITDA Margin %	38.58	15.41	33.27	29.61	30.21	33.69	34.67	32.64
Net Margin %	8.81	N.M.	7.69	6.41	8.43	12.18	11.06	11.64
Asset Turnover	0.24	0.25	0.28	0.26	0.24	0.28	0.30	0.29
Current Ratio	1.04	1.32	1.14	0.97	0.90	0.73	1.56	1.42
Debt to Equity	1.40	1.37	1.22	1.22	1.26	1.09	1.29	1.24
Price Range	79.61-61.53	89.90-61.53	91.16-60.52	72.35-60.85	73.06-62.04	74.18-59.57	84.07-69.43	85.44-60.53
P/E Ratio	...	...	17.46-11.59	18.13-15.25	15.35-13.03	9.83-7.89	12.62-10.42	13.56-9.61
Average Yield %	4.75	4.58	4.47	5.06	4.91	4.86	4.21	3.97

Address: 639 Loyola Avenue, New Orleans, LA 70113 **Telephone:** 504-576-4000	**Web Site:** www.entergy.com **Officers:** Leo P. Denault - Chairman, Chief Executive Officer, Executive Vice President, Chief Financial Officer Roderick K. West - Executive Vice President, Chief Administrative Officer	**Auditors:** Deloitte & Touche LLP **Investor Contact:** 504-576-4879 **Transfer Agents:** Wells Fargo Shareowner Services, St. Paul, MN

ENTERPRISE PRODUCTS PARTNERS L.P.

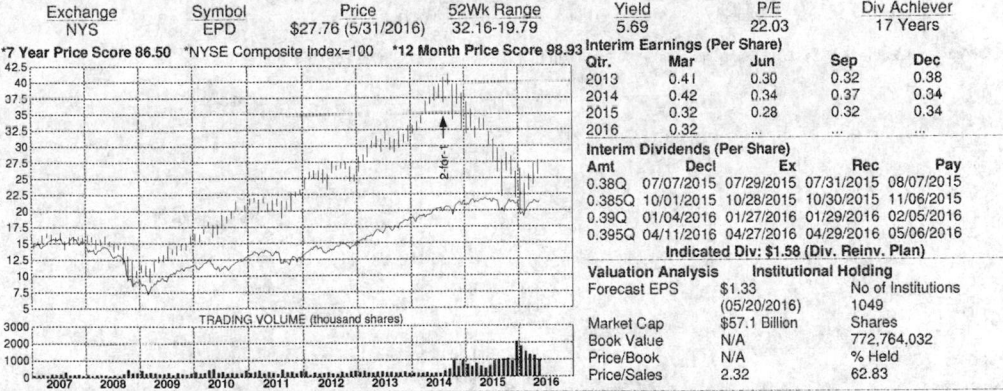

Exchange	Symbol	Price	52Wk Range	Yield	P/E	Div Achiever
NYS	EPD	$27.76 (5/31/2016)	32.16-19.79	5.69	22.03	17 Years

*7 Year Price Score 86.50   *NYSE Composite Index=100   *12 Month Price Score 98.93

Interim Earnings (Per Share)

Qtr.	Mar	Jun	Sep	Dec
2013	0.41	0.30	0.32	0.38
2014	0.42	0.34	0.37	0.34
2015	0.32	0.28	0.32	0.34
2016	0.32	...	...	...

Interim Dividends (Per Share)

Amt	Decl	Ex	Rec	Pay
0.38Q	07/07/2015	07/29/2015	07/31/2015	08/07/2015
0.385Q	10/01/2015	10/28/2015	10/30/2015	11/06/2015
0.39Q	01/04/2016	01/27/2016	01/29/2016	02/05/2016
0.395Q	04/11/2016	04/27/2016	04/29/2016	05/06/2016

Indicated Div: $1.58 (Div. Reinv. Plan)

Valuation Analysis

Forecast EPS	$1.33
	(05/20/2016)
Market Cap	$57.1 Billion
Book Value	N/A
Price/Book	N/A
Price/Sales	2.32

Institutional Holding

No of Institutions	1049
Shares	772,764,032
% Held	62.83

TRADING VOLUME (thousand shares)

Business Summary: Equipment & Services (MIC: 9.1.3 SIC: 4922 NAIC: 486210)

Enterprise Products Partners provides midstream energy services to producers and consumers of natural gas, natural gas liquids (NGLs), crude oil, petrochemicals and refined products. Co.'s midstream energy operations include: natural gas gathering, treating, processing, transportation and storage; NGL transportation, fractionation, storage, and import and export terminals (including liquefied petroleum gas); crude oil gathering, transportation, storage and terminals; offshore production platforms; petrochemical and refined products transportation and services; and a marine transportation business that operates on the U.S. inland and Intracoastal Waterway systems and in the Gulf of Mexico.

Recent Developments: For the quarter ended Mar 31 2016, net income increased 3.0% to US$670.2 million from US$650.6 million in the year-earlier quarter. Revenues were US$5.01 billion, down 33.0% from US$7.47 billion the year before. Operating income was US$915.6 million versus US$896.0 million in the prior-year quarter, an increase of 2.2%. Direct operating expenses declined 37.3% to US$4.15 billion from US$6.62 billion in the comparable period the year before. Indirect operating income amounted to US$57.2 million compared with an income of US$39.9 million in the equivalent prior-year period.

Prospects: Our evaluation of Enterprise Products Partners L.P. as of June 19, 2016 is the result of our systematic analysis on three basic characteristics: earnings strength, relative valuation, and recent stock price movement. The company has enjoyed a very positive trend in earnings per share over the past 5 quarters and while recent estimates for the company have remained steady, EPD has posted results that fell short of analysts expectations. Based on operating earnings yield, the company is about fairly valued when compared to all of the companies in our coverage universe. Share price changes over the past year indicates that EPD will perform poorly over the near term.

Financial Data

(US$ in Thousands)	3 Mos	12/31/2015	12/31/2014	12/31/2013	12/31/2012	12/31/2011	12/31/2010	12/31/2009
Earnings Per Share	1.26	1.26	1.47	1.41	1.36	1.19	0.57	0.86
Cash Flow Per Share	1.94	2.04	2.25	2.16	1.67	2.02	4.19	2.44
Dividends Per Share	1.530	1.510	1.430	1.350	1.266	1.202	1.143	1.083
Dividend Payout %	121.43	119.84	97.28	95.74	93.45	101.05	198.70	125.14
Income Statement								
Total Revenue	5,005,300	27,027,900	47,951,200	47,727,000	42,583,100	44,313,000	33,739,300	25,510,900
EBITDA	1,114,000	4,305,700	4,630,900	4,311,300	4,018,000	3,588,700	2,833,600	2,446,800
Depn & Amortn	295,900	1,161,600	1,114,100	1,012,400	900,500	776,600	745,700	678,100
Income Before Taxes	577,500	2,182,300	2,597,100	2,497,300	2,346,500	2,069,100	1,347,800	1,129,200
Income Taxes	8,400	(2,500)	23,100	57,500	(17,200)	27,200	26,100	25,300
Net Income	670,200	2,558,400	2,833,500	2,607,100	2,428,000	2,088,300	320,800	1,030,900
Average Shares	2,040,500	1,998,600	1,895,200	1,842,600	1,786,400	1,719,800	557,000	975,600
Balance Sheet								
Current Assets	4,592,600	4,313,000	5,490,700	7,023,400	5,843,100	6,068,700	5,507,100	4,246,900
Total Assets	49,737,400	48,952,000	47,100,700	40,138,700	35,934,400	34,125,100	31,360,800	26,151,600
Current Liabilities	6,013,400	7,166,600	7,873,700	8,238,700	7,755,700	7,432,400	5,880,200	4,536,000
Long-Term Obligations	21,919,800	20,826,700	19,157,400	16,226,500	14,655,200	14,029,400	13,281,200	11,346,400
Total Liabilities	28,608,500	28,656,900	29,037,500	24,923,900	22,746,700	22,011,700	19,986,600	16,639,500
Shares Outstanding	2,055,907	2,012,553	1,937,324	1,871,370	1,806,667	1,772,281	1,696,404	1,220,888
Statistical Record								
Return on Assets %	5.36	5.33	6.50	6.85	6.91	6.38	1.12	4.67
EBITDA Margin %	22.26	15.93	9.66	9.03	9.44	8.10	8.40	9.59
Net Margin %	13.39	9.47	5.91	5.46	5.70	4.71	0.95	4.04
Asset Turnover	0.51	0.56	1.10	1.25	1.21	1.35	1.17	1.16
Current Ratio	0.76	0.60	0.70	0.85	0.75	0.82	0.94	0.94
Price Range	34.30-19.79	36.83-21.86	41.11-31.84	33.15-25.04	27.44-23.11	23.20-18.75	22.15-15.17	16.07-8.97
P/E Ratio	27.22-15.71	29.23-17.35	27.97-21.66	23.51-17.76	20.18-17.00	19.50-15.76	38.86-26.61	18.69-10.44
Average Yield %	5.57	5.04	3.91	4.50	4.94	5.64	6.23	8.37

Address: 1100 Louisiana Street, 10th Floor, Houston, TX 77002 **Telephone:** 713-381-6500	**Web Site:** www.enterpriseproducts.com **Officers:** Randa Duncan Williams - Chairman W. Randall Fowler - Executive Vice President, Chief Financial Officer, Chief Administrative Officer	**Auditors:** Deloitte & Touche LLP **Investor Contact:** 866 230-0745 **Transfer Agents:** Wells Fargo Shareowner Services, South St. Paul, MN

ENVISION HEALTHCARE HOLDINGS INC

Exchange	Symbol	Price	52Wk Range	Yield	P/E
NYS	EVHC	$24.81 (5/31/2016)	45.27-18.97	N/A	34.46

*7 Year Price Score N/A   *NYSE Composite Index=100   *12 Month Price Score 73.42

Interim Earnings (Per Share)

Qtr.	Mar	Jun	Sep	Dec
2013	(0.03)	0.07	(0.05)	0.05
2014	0.13	(0.01)	0.28	0.26
2015	0.17	0.27	0.09	0.22
2016	0.14	...	...	...

Interim Dividends (Per Share)

No Dividends Paid

Valuation Analysis

		Institutional Holding	
Forecast EPS	$1.49	No of Institutions	291
	(05/20/2016)		
Market Cap	$4.6 Billion	Shares	
Book Value	$2.0 Billion		204,636,416
Price/Book	2.33	% Held	
Price/Sales	0.80		102.08

Business Summary: Hospitals & Health Care Facilities (MIC: 4.2.1 SIC: 8062 NAIC: 622110)

Envision Healthcare Holdings is a holding company. Through its subsidiaries, Co. is engaged as a provider of physician-led and outsourced medical services under EmCare and AMR brands. Co.'s business is conducted primarily through two operating subsidiaries, EmCare Holdings, Inc. (EmCare) and American Medical Response, Inc. (AMR). EmCare is a provider of integrated facility-based physician services, including emergency, anesthesiology, hospitalist/inpatient care, radiology, tele-radiology and surgery. AMR is a provider and manager of community-based healthcare transportation services, including emergency, non-emergency, managed transportation, fixed-wing air ambulance and disaster response.

Recent Developments: For the quarter ended Mar 31 2016, net income decreased 10.2% to US$30.5 million from US$33.9 million in the year-earlier quarter. Revenues were US$1.60 billion, up 28.4% from US$1.24 billion the year before. Operating income was US$87.5 million versus US$83.3 million in the prior-year quarter, an increase of 5.1%. Indirect operating expenses increased 30.0% to US$1.51 billion from US$1.16 billion in the equivalent prior-year period.

Prospects: Our evaluation of Envision Healthcare Holdings as of June 19, 2016 is the result of our systematic analysis on three basic characteristics: earnings strength, relative valuation, and recent stock price movement. The company has enjoyed a very positive trend in earnings per share over the past 5 quarters and while recent estimates for the company have been mixed, EVHC has posted better than expected results. Based on operating earnings yield, the company is about fairly valued when compared to all of the companies in our coverage universe. Share price changes over the past year indicates that EVHC will perform very poorly over the near term.

Financial Data
(US$ in Thousands)

	3 Mos	12/31/2015	12/31/2014	12/31/2013	12/31/2012	12/31/2011	05/24/2011	12/31/2010
Earnings Per Share	0.72	0.76	0.66	0.04	0.31	0.10	0.05	0.32
Cash Flow Per Share	1.57	1.34	1.51	0.36	1.66	0.89	0.42	0.45
Income Statement								
Total Revenue	1,597,546	5,447,916	4,397,644	3,728,312	3,300,121	1,885,811	1,221,790	2,859,322
EBITDA	148,823	441,769	388,060	272,747	305,329	158,873	92,502	272,342
Depn & Amortn	60,577	76,500	65,600	63,900	56,500	30,900	17,100	43,000
Income Before Taxes	49,726	247,771	209,110	10,178	68,269	22,071	39,767	210,503
Income Taxes	19,392	97,374	89,498	(994)	27,463	9,328	19,242	79,126
Net Income	26,850	144,892	125,508	5,995	41,185	13,019	20,668	131,724
Average Shares	191,930	191,538	189,921	156,962	132,945	130,833	417,085	415,648
Balance Sheet								
Current Assets	1,702,512	1,598,427	1,363,239	1,082,283	753,259	773,676	...	...
Total Assets	6,468,738	6,388,191	4,703,753	4,300,017	4,036,833	4,013,108	...	...
Current Liabilities	783,993	791,745	576,868	451,329	478,694	388,353	...	...
Long-Term Obligations	2,954,829	2,993,100	2,025,877	1,895,381	2,647,098	2,357,699	...	...
Total Liabilities	4,472,710	4,421,652	2,943,176	2,705,294	3,498,676	3,099,618	...	...
Stockholders' Equity	1,996,028	1,966,539	1,760,577	1,594,723	538,157	913,490	...	...
Shares Outstanding	187,121	186,924	183,679	180,382	130,661	130,204	...	...
Statistical Record								
Return on Assets %	2.38	2.61	2.79	0.14	1.02	...	...	...
Return on Equity %	7.27	7.78	7.48	0.56	5.66	...	...	...
EBITDA Margin %	9.32	8.11	8.82	7.32	9.25	8.42	7.57	9.52
Net Margin %	1.68	2.66	2.85	0.16	1.25	0.69	1.69	4.61
Asset Turnover	1.00	0.98	0.98	0.89	0.82	...	...	...
Current Ratio	2.17	2.02	2.36	2.40	1.57	1.99	...	...
Debt to Equity	1.48	1.52	1.15	1.19	4.92	2.58	...	...
Price Range	45.27-18.97	45.27-23.44	37.69-30.41	35.52-25.10	...	...	...	...
P/E Ratio	62.88-26.35	59.57-30.84	57.11-46.08	888.00-627.50	...	...	...	...

Address: 6200 S. Syracuse Way, Suite 200, Greenwood Village, CO 80111 **Telephone:** 303-495-1200	**Web Site:** www.evhc.net **Officers:** William A. Sanger - Executive Chairman, President, Chief Executive Officer Randel G. Owen - Executive Vice President, Chief Financial Officer, Chief Accounting Officer, Chief Operating Officer	**Auditors:** Ernst & Young LLP **Transfer Agents:** American Stock Transfer & Trust Company

EOG RESOURCES, INC.

Exchange	Symbol	Price	52Wk Range	Yield	P/E	Div Achiever
NYS	EOG	$81.36 (5/31/2016)	90.65-60.24	0.82	N/A	16 Years

*7 Year Price Score 99.49 *NYSE Composite Index=100 *12 Month Price Score 101.61

Interim Earnings (Per Share)

Qtr.	Mar	Jun	Sep	Dec
2013	0.91	1.21	0.84	1.05
2014	1.21	1.29	2.01	0.81
2015	(0.31)	0.01	(7.47)	(0.52)
2016	(0.86)	...	...	...

Interim Dividends (Per Share)

Amt	Decl	Ex	Rec	Pay
0.168Q	09/22/2015	10/14/2015	10/16/2015	10/30/2015
0.168Q	12/02/2015	01/13/2016	01/15/2016	01/29/2016
0.168Q	02/25/2016	04/13/2016	04/15/2016	04/29/2016
0.168Q	04/27/2016	07/13/2016	07/15/2016	07/29/2016

Indicated Div: $0.67

Valuation Analysis

	Institutional Holding	
Forecast EPS	$-2.15	No of Institutions
	(05/20/2016)	1210
Market Cap	$44.8 Billion	Shares
Book Value	$12.4 Billion	534,612,480
Price/Book	3.61	% Held
Price/Sales	5.74	90.44

Business Summary: Production & Extraction (MIC: 9.1.1 SIC: 1311 NAIC: 211111)

EOG Resources, together with its subsidiaries, explores for, develops, produces and markets crude oil and natural gas primarily in producing basins in the U.S., The Republic of Trinidad and Tobago, the U.K., The People's Republic of China, Canada and, from time to time, select other international areas. As of Dec 31 2015, Co.'s total estimated net proved reserves were 2.12 billion barrels of oil equivalent, of which 1,098.0 million barrels (MMBbl) were crude oil and condensate reserves, 383.0 MMBbl were natural gas liquids reserves and 5,825.00 billion cubic feet, or 637.0 million barrels of oil equivalent were natural gas reserves.

Recent Developments: For the quarter ended Mar 31 2016, net loss amounted to US$471.8 million versus a net loss of US$169.7 million in the year-earlier quarter. Revenues were US$1.35 billion, down 41.6% from US$2.32 billion the year before. Operating loss was US$638.1 million versus a loss of US$173.0 million in the prior-year quarter. Direct operating expenses declined 26.5% to US$459.8 million from US$625.8 million in the comparable period the year before. Indirect operating expenses decreased 17.9% to US$1.53 billion from US$1.87 billion in the equivalent prior-year period.

Prospects: Our evaluation of EOG Resources Inc. as of June 19, 2016 is the result of our systematic analysis on three basic characteristics: earnings strength, relative valuation, and recent stock price movement. The company has enjoyed a very positive trend in earnings per share over the past 5 quarters. Because the company lacks sufficient analyst estimate data, we place greater weight on the historical EPS trend as the measure of earnings strength. Based on operating earnings yield, the company is overvalued when compared to all of the companies in our coverage universe. Share price changes over the past year indicates that EOG will perform in line with the market over the near term.

Financial Data

(US$ in Thousands)	3 Mos	12/31/2015	12/31/2014	12/31/2013	12/31/2012	12/31/2011	12/31/2010	12/31/2009
Earnings Per Share	(8.84)	(8.29)	5.32	4.02	1.05	2.05	0.32	1.09
Cash Flow Per Share	5.35	6.59	15.92	13.56	9.76	8.71	5.40	5.87
Tang Book Value Per Share	22.55	23.54	32.30	28.23	24.45	23.49	20.13	19.80
Dividends Per Share	0.670	0.670	0.511	0.366	0.335	0.318	0.305	0.285
Dividend Payout %	...	...	9.61	9.11	31.75	15.49	96.83	26.27
Income Statement								
Total Revenue	1,354,349	8,757,428	18,035,340	14,487,118	11,682,636	10,126,115	6,099,896	4,786,959
EBITDA	286,313	(3,370,519)	9,193,814	7,273,322	4,663,995	4,636,543	2,479,488	2,522,100
Depn & Amortn	928,891	3,313,644	3,997,041	3,600,976	3,169,703	2,516,381	1,941,926	1,549,188
Income Before Taxes	(710,968)	(6,921,556)	4,995,315	3,436,886	1,280,740	1,909,799	407,976	872,011
Income Taxes	(239,192)	(2,397,041)	2,079,828	1,239,777	710,461	818,676	247,322	325,384
Net Income	(471,776)	(4,524,515)	2,915,481	2,197,109	570,279	1,091,123	160,654	546,627
Average Shares	546,715	545,697	548,539	546,228	541,524	532,536	509,000	503,768
Balance Sheet								
Current Assets	2,365,812	2,592,244	5,416,021	4,072,015	3,589,884	3,253,938	2,527,446	1,839,541
Total Assets	26,338,423	26,975,244	34,762,687	30,574,238	27,336,578	24,838,797	21,624,233	18,118,667
Current Liabilities	1,547,972	1,819,287	3,384,308	2,861,716	2,924,058	2,522,319	2,220,099	1,345,560
Long-Term Obligations	6,979,029	6,653,685	5,903,354	5,906,642	5,905,602	5,009,166	5,003,341	2,760,000
Total Liabilities	13,932,935	14,032,209	17,050,105	15,155,779	14,051,814	12,197,893	11,392,601	8,120,625
Stockholders' Equity	12,405,488	12,943,035	17,712,582	15,418,459	13,284,764	12,640,904	10,231,632	9,998,042
Shares Outstanding	550,192	549,858	548,294	546,171	543,264	538,038	508,154	505,017
Statistical Record								
Return on Assets %	N.M.	N.M.	8.92	7.59	2.18	4.70	0.81	3.21
Return on Equity %	N.M.	N.M.	17.60	15.31	4.39	9.54	1.59	5.75
EBITDA Margin %	21.14	N.M.	50.98	50.21	39.92	45.79	40.65	52.69
Net Margin %	N.M.	N.M.	16.17	15.17	4.88	10.78	2.63	11.42
Asset Turnover	0.26	0.28	0.55	0.50	0.45	0.44	0.31	0.28
Current Ratio	1.53	1.42	1.60	1.42	1.23	1.29	1.14	1.37
Debt to Equity	0.56	0.51	0.33	0.38	0.44	0.40	0.49	0.28
Price Range	99.74-60.24	99.74-68.36	117.98-80.87	92.58-56.72	62.19-41.98	59.84-34.20	56.86-43.31	50.29-22.80
P/E Ratio	...	...	22.18-15.20	23.03-14.11	59.22-39.98	29.19-16.69	177.69-135.34	46.14-20.91
Average Yield %	0.84	0.79	0.52	0.50	0.62	0.64	0.63	0.78

Address: 1111 Bagby, Sky Lobby 2,	Web Site: www.eogresources.com	Auditors: Deloitte & Touche LLP
Houston, TX 77002	Officers: William R. Thomas - Chairman, President,	Investor Contact: 713-651-7000
Telephone: 713-651-7000	Chief Executive Officer, Senior Executive Vice	Transfer Agents: Computershare Trust
	President Gary L. Thomas - President, Senior	Company, N.A., Providence, RI
	Executive Vice President, Chief Operating Officer	

EPR PROPERTIES

Exchange	Symbol	Price	52Wk Range	Yield	P/E
NYS	EPR	$71.28 (5/31/2016)	71.78-49.57	5.39	23.29

*7 Year Price Score 103.70 *NYSE Composite Index=100 *12 Month Price Score 113.91

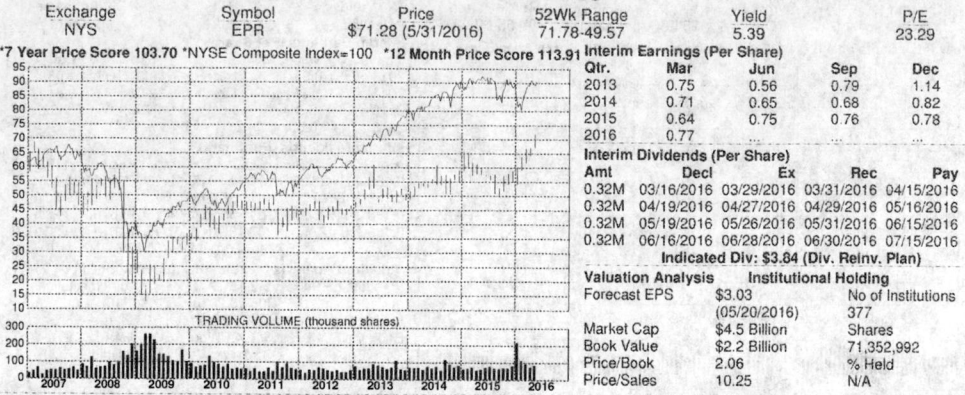

Interim Earnings (Per Share)

Qtr.	Mar	Jun	Sep	Dec
2013	0.75	0.56	0.79	1.14
2014	0.71	0.65	0.68	0.82
2015	0.64	0.75	0.76	0.78
2016	0.77	...	...	...

Interim Dividends (Per Share)

Amt	Decl	Ex	Rec	Pay
0.32M	03/16/2016	03/29/2016	03/31/2016	04/15/2016
0.32M	04/19/2016	04/27/2016	04/29/2016	05/16/2016
0.32M	05/19/2016	05/26/2016	05/31/2016	06/15/2016
0.32M	06/16/2016	06/28/2016	06/30/2016	07/15/2016

Indicated Div: $3.84 (Div. Reinv. Plan)

Valuation Analysis **Institutional Holding**

Forecast EPS	$3.03	No of Institutions
	(05/20/2016)	377
Market Cap	$4.5 Billion	Shares
Book Value	$2.2 Billion	71,352,992
Price/Book	2.06	% Held
Price/Sales	10.25	N/A

Business Summary: REITs (MIC: 5.3.1 SIC: 6798 NAIC: 525930)

EPR Properties is a real estate investment trust. Co.'s operating segments: Entertainment, which consisted of investments in megaplex theatres, entertainment retail centers, family entertainment centers and other retail parcels; Education, which consisted of investments in public charter schools, early education centers and K-12 private schools; Recreation, which consisted of investments in metro ski parks, resorts, waterparks and golf entertainment complexes; and Other, which consisted of investments for development of the casino, golf course, entertainment village, infrastructure and mortgage financing related to one sold winery property.

Recent Developments: For the quarter ended Mar 31 2016, income from continuing operations increased 26.5% to US$54.2 million from US$42.8 million in the year-earlier quarter. Net income increased 26.5% to US$54.2 million from US$42.8 million in the year-earlier quarter. Revenues were US$118.8 million, up 19.4% from US$99.4 million the year before. Revenues from property income rose 20.5% to US$97.6 million from US$81.0 million in the corresponding quarter a year earlier.

Prospects: Our evaluation of EPR Properties as of June 19, 2016 is the result of our systematic analysis on three basic characteristics: earnings strength, relative valuation, and recent stock price movement. The company has produced a positive trend in earnings per share over the past 5 quarters. Because the company lacks sufficient analyst estimate data, we place greater weight on the historical EPS trend as the measure of earnings strength. Based on operating earnings yield, the company is about fairly valued when compared to all of the companies in our coverage universe. Share price changes over the past year indicates that EPR will perform well over the near term.

Financial Data (US$ in Thousands)	3 Mos	12/31/2015	12/31/2014	12/31/2013	12/31/2012	12/31/2011	12/31/2010	12/31/2009
Earnings Per Share	3.06	2.93	2.86	3.24	1.98	1.80	1.86	(0.61)
Cash Flow Per Share	4.63	4.79	4.61	4.87	4.42	4.20	3.99	4.12
Tang Book Value Per Share	34.53	33.95	33.57	32.54	31.13	31.36	33.68	34.19
Dividends Per Share	3.683	3.630	3.420	3.160	3.000	2.800	2.600	2.600
Dividend Payout %	120.34	123.89	119.58	97.52	151.52	155.56	139.78	...
Income Statement								
Total Revenue	118,768	421,017	385,051	343,064	321,786	301,659	313,064	270,811
EBITDA	103,333	359,661	322,977	291,819	256,797	216,395	237,637	103,114
Depn & Amortn	26,220	85,900	63,000	50,700	47,300	45,000	47,200	43,200
Income Before Taxes	53,824	193,846	178,707	160,063	132,841	99,716	115,635	(12,801)
Income Taxes	(144)	482	4,228	(14,176)	...	...	...	...
Net Income	54,180	194,532	179,633	180,226	121,556	115,228	114,874	8,007
Average Shares	62,744	58,328	54,444	48,214	47,049	46,901	45,555	36,122
Balance Sheet								
Current Assets	96,811	73,962	63,690	60,210	73,393	68,942	67,869	69,284
Total Assets	4,343,540	4,217,270	3,702,048	3,272,276	2,946,730	2,733,995	2,923,420	2,680,732
Current Liabilities	160,371	161,482	130,036	108,926	118,000	81,597	100,983	71,352
Long-Term Obligations	1,996,131	1,981,920	1,645,523	1,475,336	1,368,832	1,154,295	1,191,179	1,141,423
Total Liabilities	2,156,502	2,143,402	1,775,936	1,584,639	1,487,209	1,263,946	1,320,181	1,207,870
Stockholders' Equity	2,187,038	2,073,868	1,926,112	1,687,637	1,459,521	1,470,049	1,603,239	1,472,862
Shares Outstanding	63,341	60,823	57,125	51,655	46,887	46,726	46,542	42,872
Statistical Record								
Return on Assets %	4.99	4.91	5.15	5.80	4.27	4.07	4.10	0.30
Return on Equity %	10.05	9.73	9.94	11.45	8.28	7.50	7.47	0.58
EBITDA Margin %	87.00	85.43	83.88	85.06	79.80	71.73	75.91	38.08
Net Margin %	45.62	46.21	46.65	52.53	37.78	38.20	36.69	2.96
Asset Turnover	0.11	0.11	0.11	0.11	0.11	0.11	0.11	0.10
Current Ratio	0.60	0.46	0.49	0.55	0.62	0.84	0.67	0.97
Debt to Equity	0.91	0.96	0.85	0.87	0.94	0.79	0.74	0.77
Price Range	66.62-49.57	65.58-49.57	60.80-48.60	60.70-45.93	48.11-40.40	49.88-35.91	49.61-33.79	36.61-12.70
P/E Ratio	21.77-16.20	22.38-16.92	21.26-16.99	18.73-14.18	24.30-20.40	27.71-19.95	26.67-18.17	...
Average Yield %	6.44	6.33	6.32	6.23	6.71	6.28	6.17	10.01

Address: 909 Walnut Street, Suite 200, Kansas City, MO 64106 **Telephone:** 816-472-1700 **Fax:** 816-472-5794	**Web Site:** www.eprkc.com **Officers:** Robert J. Druten - Chairman Gregory K. Silvers - President, Chief Executive Officer, Executive Vice President, Vice President, Chief Operating Officer, Chief Development Officer, Secretary, General Counsel	**Auditors:** KPMG LLP **Transfer Agents:** Computershare Trust Company, N. A., Providence, RI

272

EQT CORP.

Exchange	Symbol	Price	52Wk Range	Yield	P/E
NYS	EQT	$73.25 (5/31/2016)	86.07-47.75	0.16	N/A

*7 Year Price Score 89.90 *NYSE Composite Index=100 *12 Month Price Score 102.33

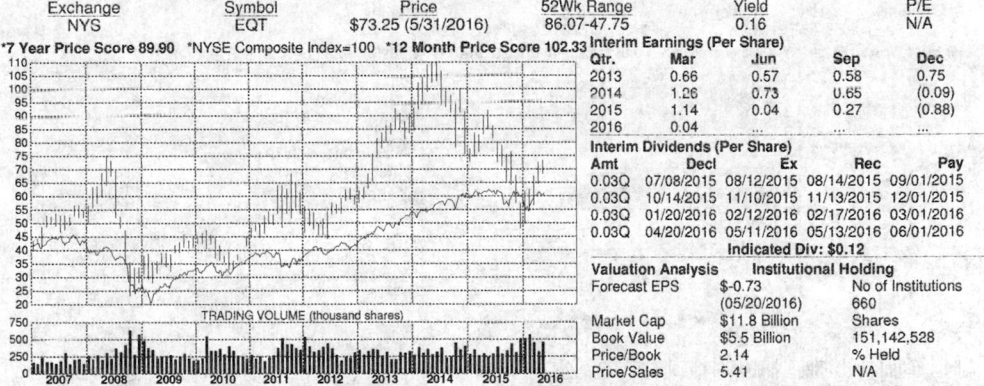

Interim Earnings (Per Share)

Qtr.	Mar	Jun	Sep	Dec
2013	0.66	0.57	0.58	0.75
2014	1.26	0.73	0.65	(0.09)
2015	1.14	0.04	0.27	(0.88)
2016	0.04	...	...	...

Interim Dividends (Per Share)

Amt	Decl	Ex	Rec	Pay
0.03Q	07/08/2015	08/12/2015	08/14/2015	09/01/2015
0.03Q	10/14/2015	11/10/2015	11/13/2015	12/01/2015
0.03Q	01/20/2016	02/12/2016	02/17/2016	03/01/2016
0.03Q	04/20/2016	05/11/2016	05/13/2016	06/01/2016

Indicated Div: $0.12

Valuation Analysis — **Institutional Holding**

Forecast EPS	$-0.73	No of Institutions
	(05/20/2016)	660
Market Cap	$11.8 Billion	Shares
Book Value	$5.5 Billion	151,142,528
Price/Book	2.14	% Held
Price/Sales	5.41	N/A

Business Summary: Production & Extraction (MIC: 9.1.1 SIC: 1311 NAIC: 211111)

EQT conducts its business through two business segments. The EQT Production segment includes Co.'s exploration for, and development and production of, natural gas, natural gas liquids (NGLs) and a limited amount of crude oil, primarily in the Appalachian Basin. The EQT Midstream segment's operations include the natural gas gathering, transmission, storage and marketing activities of Co. Co.'s produced natural gas is sold to marketers, utilities and industrial customers located mainly in the Appalachian Basin and the Northeastern U.S. As of Dec 31 2015, Co. had total proved reserves of 9.98 trillion cubic feet of natural gas, NGLs and crude oil.

Recent Developments: For the quarter ended Mar 31 2016, net income decreased 60.0% to US$88.4 million from US$221.2 million in the year-earlier quarter. Revenues were US$545.1 million, down 23.7% from US$714.8 million the year before. Operating income was US$127.2 million versus US$314.8 million in the prior-year quarter, a decrease of 59.6%. Indirect operating expenses increased 4.5% to US$417.9 million from US$400.1 million in the equivalent prior-year period.

Prospects: Our evaluation of EQT Corp. as of June 19, 2016 is the result of our systematic analysis on three basic characteristics: earnings strength, relative valuation, and recent stock price movement. The company has produced a positive trend in earnings per share over the past 5 quarters. Because the company lacks sufficient analyst estimate data, we place greater weight on the historical EPS trend as the measure of earnings strength. Based on operating earnings yield, the company is overvalued when compared to all of the companies in our coverage universe. Share price changes over the past year indicates that EQT will perform poorly over the near term.

Financial Data

(US$ in Thousands)	3 Mos	12/31/2015	12/31/2014	12/31/2013	12/31/2012	12/31/2011	12/31/2010	12/31/2009
Earnings Per Share	(0.53)	0.56	2.54	2.57	1.22	3.19	1.57	1.19
Cash Flow Per Share	6.69	7.99	9.33	7.97	5.47	6.13	5.47	5.55
Tang Book Value Per Share	34.19	33.29	30.23	26.74	24.01	24.04	20.64	16.43
Dividends Per Share	0.120	0.120	0.120	0.120	0.880	0.880	0.880	0.880
Dividend Payout %	...	21.43	4.72	4.67	72.13	27.59	56.05	73.95
Income Statement								
Total Revenue	545,069	2,339,762	2,469,710	1,862,011	1,641,608	1,639,934	1,322,708	1,269,827
EBITDA	353,272	1,392,308	1,539,546	1,340,416	985,611	1,234,754	743,990	554,945
Depn & Amortn	221,231	819,216	679,298	676,570	499,118	339,297	270,285	196,078
Income Before Taxes	95,861	426,561	723,711	521,158	301,707	759,129	345,548	247,088
Income Taxes	7,436	104,675	214,092	175,186	105,296	279,360	127,520	96,668
Net Income	5,636	85,171	386,965	390,572	183,395	479,769	227,700	156,929
Average Shares	157,195	152,939	152,513	151,787	150,506	150,209	145,232	131,482
Balance Sheet								
Current Assets	2,156,358	2,251,019	1,904,323	1,255,425	852,845	1,690,134	827,940	695,166
Total Assets	14,049,625	13,976,172	12,064,900	9,792,053	8,849,862	8,772,719	7,098,438	5,957,257
Current Liabilities	421,348	795,819	833,479	523,410	570,465	804,910	596,984	612,674
Long-Term Obligations	2,794,481	2,793,343	2,822,889	2,490,354	2,502,969	2,527,627	1,943,200	1,949,200
Total Liabilities	8,558,470	8,898,381	7,482,085	5,757,265	5,246,042	5,178,889	4,019,742	3,806,227
Stockholders' Equity	5,491,155	5,077,791	4,582,815	4,034,788	3,603,820	3,593,830	3,078,696	2,151,030
Shares Outstanding	160,594	152,554	151,596	150,884	150,109	149,477	149,153	130,931
Statistical Record								
Return on Assets %	N.M.	0.65	3.54	4.19	2.08	6.05	3.49	2.78
Return on Equity %	N.M.	1.76	8.98	10.23	5.08	14.38	8.71	7.47
EBITDA Margin %	64.81	59.51	62.34	71.99	60.04	75.29	56.25	43.70
Net Margin %	1.03	3.64	15.67	20.98	11.17	29.26	17.21	12.36
Asset Turnover	0.16	0.18	0.23	0.20	0.19	0.21	0.20	0.23
Current Ratio	5.12	2.83	2.28	2.40	1.50	2.10	1.39	1.13
Debt to Equity	0.51	0.55	0.62	0.62	0.69	0.70	0.63	0.91
Price Range	91.95-47.75	91.95-47.75	109.84-75.38	92.56-57.19	62.74-44.00	68.35-44.42	47.37-32.54	45.74-27.77
P/E Ratio	...	164.20-85.27	43.24-29.68	36.02-22.25	51.43-36.07	21.43-13.92	30.17-20.73	38.44-23.34
Average Yield %	0.17	0.16	0.12	0.15	1.64	1.64	...	2.34

Address: 625 Liberty Avenue, Suite 1700, Pittsburgh, PA 15222
Telephone: 412-553-5700

Web Site: www.eqt.com
Officers: David L. Porges - Chairman, President, Chief Executive Officer, Associate/Affiliate Company Officer Steven T. Schlotterbeck - President, Executive Vice President, Senior Vice President, Vice President, Division Officer

Auditors: Ernst & Young LLP
Investor Contact: 412-553-7833
Transfer Agents: Computershare, College Station, TX

EQUIFAX INC

Exchange	Symbol	Price	52Wk Range	Yield	P/E
NYS	EFX	$125.73 (5/31/2016)	126.29-92.70	1.05	34.17

*7 Year Price Score 155.11 *NYSE Composite Index=100 *12 Month Price Score 111.66

Interim Earnings (Per Share)

Qtr.	Mar	Jun	Sep	Dec
2013	0.82	0.73	0.67	0.61
2014	0.69	0.75	0.75	0.80
2015	0.73	0.92	0.98	0.93
2016	0.85	...	...	...

Interim Dividends (Per Share)

Amt	Decl	Ex	Rec	Pay
0.29Q	08/07/2015	08/19/2015	08/21/2015	09/15/2015
0.29Q	11/05/2015	11/19/2015	11/23/2015	12/15/2015
0.33Q	02/10/2016	03/01/2016	03/03/2016	03/15/2016
0.33Q	05/05/2016	05/23/2016	05/25/2016	06/15/2016

Indicated Div: $1.32

Valuation Analysis

Forecast EPS	$5.21 (05/20/2016)
Market Cap	$15.0 Billion
Book Value	$2.5 Billion
Price/Book	6.02
Price/Sales	5.46

Institutional Holding

No of Institutions	731
Shares	142,055,728
% Held	85.90

TRADING VOLUME (thousand shares)

Business Summary: Business Services (MIC: 7.5.2 SIC: 7323 NAIC: 561450)

Equifax Inc. is a provider of information solutions and human resources business process outsourcing services for businesses, governments and consumers. Co.'s products and services are based on databases of consumer and business information. Co. uses statistical techniques and software tools to analyze all available data, creating insights, decision-making solutions and processing services for its clients. Co. also provides information, technology and services to support debt collections and recovery management. Additionally, Co. provides payroll-related and human resource management business process outsourcing services in the U.S.

Recent Developments: For the quarter ended Mar 31 2016, net income increased 14.3% to US$102.4 million from US$89.6 million in the year-earlier quarter. Revenues were US$728.3 million, up 11.7% from US$651.8 million the year before. Operating income was US$176.2 million versus US$154.2 million in the prior-year quarter, an increase of 14.3%. Direct operating expenses rose 17.8% to US$253.3 million from US$215.1 million in the comparable period the year before. Indirect operating expenses increased 5.8% to US$298.8 million from US$282.5 million in the equivalent prior-year period.

Prospects: Our evaluation of Equifax Inc. as of June 19, 2016 is the result of our systematic analysis on three basic characteristics: earnings strength, relative valuation, and recent stock price movement. The company has enjoyed a very positive trend in earnings per share over the past 5 quarters and while recent estimates for the company have remained steady, EFX has posted better than expected results. Based on operating earnings yield, the company is about fairly valued when compared to all of the companies in our coverage universe. Share price changes over the past year indicates that EFX will perform very well over the near term.

Financial Data

(US$ in Thousands)	3 Mos	12/31/2015	12/31/2014	12/31/2013	12/31/2012	12/31/2011	12/31/2010	12/31/2009
Earnings Per Share	3.68	3.55	2.97	2.84	2.22	1.88	2.11	1.83
Cash Flow Per Share	6.14	6.25	5.08	4.67	4.13	3.35	2.83	3.31
Dividends Per Share	1.200	1.160	1.000	0.880	0.720	0.640	0.280	0.160
Dividend Payout %	32.61	32.68	33.67	30.99	32.43	34.04	13.27	8.74
Income Statement								
Total Revenue	728,300	2,663,600	2,436,400	2,303,900	2,160,500	1,959,800	1,859,500	1,824,500
EBITDA	230,900	900,400	847,000	790,900	659,000	628,200	599,100	572,400
Depn & Amortn	56,800	200,000	204,200	190,300	163,400	164,900	167,800	158,800
Income Before Taxes	154,000	636,600	574,200	530,400	440,200	408,200	375,200	356,600
Income Taxes	51,600	201,800	200,200	188,900	159,400	168,000	131,900	116,100
Net Income	102,100	429,100	367,400	351,800	272,100	232,900	266,700	233,900
Average Shares	120,800	120,900	123,500	123,700	122,500	123,700	126,500	127,900
Balance Sheet								
Current Assets	630,100	561,600	605,100	648,400	529,700	452,300	429,200	416,800
Total Assets	6,732,900	4,509,000	4,674,200	4,539,900	4,511,100	3,508,600	3,433,600	3,550,500
Current Liabilities	1,729,400	603,800	823,100	662,500	646,500	362,800	319,500	492,200
Long-Term Obligations	1,883,800	1,145,900	1,145,700	1,145,500	1,447,400	966,000	978,900	990,900
Total Liabilities	4,245,600	2,198,100	2,474,100	2,239,200	2,577,900	1,806,200	1,742,200	1,949,300
Stockholders' Equity	2,487,300	2,310,900	2,200,100	2,300,700	1,933,200	1,702,400	1,691,400	1,601,200
Shares Outstanding	119,000	118,700	119,400	121,900	120,400	119,600	122,600	126,200
Statistical Record								
Return on Assets %	7.82	9.35	7.97	7.77	6.77	6.71	7.64	6.87
Return on Equity %	19.11	19.02	16.33	16.62	14.93	13.73	16.20	16.06
EBITDA Margin %	31.70	33.80	34.76	34.33	30.50	32.05	32.22	31.37
Net Margin %	14.02	16.11	15.08	15.27	12.59	11.88	14.34	12.82
Asset Turnover	0.48	0.58	0.53	0.51	0.54	0.56	0.53	0.54
Current Ratio	0.36	0.93	0.74	0.98	0.82	1.25	1.34	0.85
Debt to Equity	0.76	0.50	0.52	0.50	0.75	0.57	0.58	0.62
Price Range	114.29-91.84	113.61-80.00	82.15-65.04	69.35-53.13	54.93-38.42	39.81-28.79	36.40-27.78	31.50-19.79
P/E Ratio	31.06-24.96	32.00-22.54	27.66-21.90	24.42-18.71	24.74-17.31	21.18-15.31	17.25-13.17	17.21-10.81
Average Yield %	1.17	1.18	1.36	1.45	1.56	1.82	0.87	0.60

Address: 1550 Peachtree Street, N.W., Atlanta, GA 30309 **Telephone:** 404-885-8000	**Web Site:** www.equifax.com **Officers:** Richard F. Smith - Chairman, Chief Executive Officer John W. Gamble - Chief Financial Officer, Corporate Vice-President	**Auditors:** Ernst & Young LLP **Investor Contact:** 404-885-8804 **Transfer Agents:** American Stock Transfer & Trust Company, Brookly, NY

EQUITY COMMONWEALTH

Exchange	Symbol	Price	52Wk Range	Yield	P/E
NYS	EQC	$28.89 (5/31/2016)	29.67-25.27	N/A	35.23

*7 Year Price Score 110.99 *NYSE Composite Index=100 *12 Month Price Score 101.58

Interim Earnings (Per Share)

Qtr.	Mar	Jun	Sep	Dec
2013	0.15	0.07	(1.92)	(0.11)
2014	0.08	(0.14)	1.16	(1.33)
2015	0.05	0.04	0.18	0.29
2016	0.31	...	...	...

Interim Dividends (Per Share)

Dividend Payment Suspended

Valuation Analysis — **Institutional Holding**

Forecast EPS	$0.00	No of Institutions
	(05/20/2016)	337
Market Cap	$3.6 Billion	Shares
Book Value	$3.4 Billion	131,934,976
Price/Book	1.07	% Held
Price/Sales	5.67	N/A

TRADING VOLUME (thousand shares)

Business Summary: REITs (MIC: 5.3.1 SIC: 6798 NAIC: 525930)

CommonWealth is an internally managed and self-advised real estate investment trust engaged in the ownership and operation primarily of office buildings in central business district (CBD) and suburban locations throughout the U.S. As of Dec 31 2014, Co.'s portfolio included 156 properties (262 buildings) with a combined 42.9 million square feet. Co.'s portfolio consisted of 40 properties (53 buildings) with a combined 21.9 million square feet located in CBD locations, and 116 properties (209 buildings) with a combined 21.0 million square feet located in suburban locations. 11 of Co.'s properties (11 buildings) with a combined 1.8 million square feet are located in Australia.

Recent Developments: For the quarter ended Mar 31 2016, net income increased 240.4% to US$46.4 million from US$13.6 million in the year-earlier quarter. Revenues were US$137.1 million, down 35.6% from US$213.1 million the year before. Revenues from property income fell 34.6% to US$109.9 million from US$168.0 million in the corresponding quarter a year earlier.

Prospects: Our evaluation of Equity Commonwealth as of June 19, 2016 is the result of our systematic analysis on three basic characteristics: earnings strength, relative valuation, and recent stock price movement. The company has managed to produce a neutral trend in earnings per share over the past 5 quarters. Because the company lacks sufficient analyst estimate data, we place greater weight on the historical EPS trend as the measure of earnings strength. Based on operating earnings yield, the company is overvalued when compared to all of the companies in our coverage universe. Share price changes over the past year indicates that EQC will perform well over the near term.

Financial Data
(US$ in Thousands)

	3 Mos	12/31/2015	12/31/2014	12/31/2013	12/31/2012	12/31/2011	12/31/2010	12/31/2009
Earnings Per Share	0.82	0.56	(0.19)	(1.97)	(1.81)	0.81	1.26	2.04
Cash Flow Per Share	1.30	1.41	1.60	2.09	3.30	3.40	3.90	5.30
Tang Book Value Per Share	23.93	23.62	22.64	23.06	29.49	33.32	36.30	39.43
Dividends Per Share	...	...	0.250	1.000	1.750	2.000	1.480	2.040
Dividend Payout %	...	...	...	...	...	246.91	117.46	100.00
Income Statement								
Total Revenue	137,135	714,891	861,857	885,536	1,013,092	911,948	793,370	849,722
EBITDA	105,212	349,436	119,101	336,587	476,565	400,352	394,131	398,460
Depn & Amortn	38,355	145,888	166,076	178,353	188,123	166,444	180,619	155,341
Income Before Taxes	46,477	102,221	(188,644)	(13,548)	85,626	40,602	37,029	70,855
Income Taxes	75	2,364	3,191	2,634	3,207	1,347	550	735
Net Income	46,402	99,857	24,012	(156,967)	(79,845)	109,984	135,409	164,674
Average Shares	127,522	129,437	125,163	112,378	83,750	84,726	72,001	63,353
Balance Sheet								
Current Assets	1,955,058	2,009,650	644,874	468,319	372,239	418,224	390,359	224,224
Total Assets	5,103,149	5,244,372	5,761,639	6,646,434	8,189,634	7,447,026	6,588,520	6,121,321
Current Liabilities	154,146	133,925	176,248	187,216	231,002	193,346	155,344	161,877
Long-Term Obligations	1,557,839	1,710,324	2,207,665	3,005,410	4,349,821	3,577,331	3,206,066	2,992,650
Total Liabilities	1,715,778	1,875,885	2,442,056	3,282,848	5,084,206	3,878,509	3,456,830	3,232,255
Stockholders' Equity	3,387,371	3,368,487	3,319,583	3,363,586	3,105,428	3,568,517	3,131,690	2,889,066
Shares Outstanding	125,502	126,349	129,607	118,386	83,804	83,721	72,138	55,965
Statistical Record								
Return on Assets %	2.45	1.81	0.39	N.M.	N.M.	1.57	2.13	2.71
Return on Equity %	3.96	2.99	0.72	N.M.	N.M.	3.28	4.50	5.67
EBITDA Margin %	76.72	48.88	13.82	38.01	47.04	43.90	49.68	46.89
Net Margin %	33.84	13.97	2.79	N.M.	N.M.	12.06	17.07	19.38
Asset Turnover	0.12	0.13	0.14	0.12	0.13	0.13	0.12	0.14
Current Ratio	12.68	15.01	3.66	2.50	1.61	2.16	2.51	1.39
Debt to Equity	0.46	0.51	0.67	0.89	1.40	1.00	1.02	1.04
Price Range	29.67-25.21	29.67-25.21	28.06-22.40	26.26-15.71	20.61-13.58	28.71-15.95	28.00-6.21	8.07-2.68
P/E Ratio	36.18-30.74	52.98-45.02	...	...	...	35.44-19.69	22.22-4.93	3.96-1.31
Average Yield %	...	...	0.96	4.53	10.25	8.77	9.06	40.28

Address: Two North Riverside Plaza, Suite 2100, Chicago, IL 60606
Telephone: 312-646-2800
Fax: 617-332-2261

Web Site: www.eqcre.com
Officers: Samuel Zell - Chairman David A. Helfand - President, Chief Executive Officer, Interim Chief Financial Officer

Auditors: Ernst & Young LLP
Investor Contact: 617-796-8222
Transfer Agents: Wells Fargo Bank, National Association, Mendota Heights, MN

Exchange	Symbol	Price	52Wk Range	Yield	P/E	Div Achiever
NYS	ELS	$73.30 (5/31/2016)	75.46-52.19	2.32	40.27	11 Years

*7 Year Price Score 139.41 *NYSE Composite Index=100   *12 Month Price Score 112.28

Interim Earnings (Per Share)

Qtr.	Mar	Jun	Sep	Dec
2013	0.42	0.21	0.36	0.29
2014	0.46	0.30	0.31	0.35
2015	0.32	0.38	0.43	0.41
2016	0.60			

Interim Dividends (Per Share)

Amt	Decl	Ex	Rec	Pay
0.375Q	08/04/2015	09/23/2015	09/25/2015	10/09/2015
0.375Q	11/03/2015	12/23/2015	12/28/2015	01/08/2016
0.425Q	03/08/2016	03/22/2016	03/25/2016	04/08/2016
0.425Q	05/10/2016	06/22/2016	06/24/2016	07/08/2016

Indicated Div: $1.70

Valuation Analysis

		Institutional Holding	
Forecast EPS	$1.85 (05/20/2016)	No of Institutions	322
Market Cap	$6.2 Billion	Shares	81,807,984
Book Value	$946.0 Million	% Held	89.27
Price/Book	6.55		
Price/Sales	7.44		

Business Summary: REITs (MIC: 5.3.1 SIC: 6798 NAIC: 525930)

Equity Lifestyle Properties is an owner and operator of lifestyle-oriented properties (Properties). Co. leases individual developed areas with access to utilities for placement of factory built homes, cottages, cabins or recreational vehicles. Co.'s operations are conducted primarily through MHC Operating Limited Partnership. Co.'s Realty Systems, Inc. subsidiary is engaged in the business of purchasing and selling or leasing Site Set homes that are located in Properties owned and managed by Co. As of Dec 31 2014, Co. owned or had an ownership interest in a portfolio of 384 Properties located throughout the U.S. and Canada, consisting of 143,113 residential sites.

Recent Developments: For the quarter ended Mar 31 2016, net income increased 79.8% to US$57.2 million from US$31.8 million in the year-earlier quarter. Revenues were US$220.1 million, up 5.6% from US$208.4 million the year before. Revenues from property income rose 5.8% to US$215.3 million from US$203.5 million in the corresponding quarter a year earlier.

Prospects: Our evaluation of Equity Lifestyle Properties Inc. as of June 19, 2016 is the result of our systematic analysis on three basic characteristics: earnings strength, relative valuation, and recent stock price movement. The company has managed to produce a neutral trend in earnings per share over the past 5 quarters. Because the company lacks sufficient analyst estimate data, we place greater weight on the historical EPS trend as the measure of earnings strength. Based on operating earnings yield, the company is overvalued when compared to all of the companies in our coverage universe. Share price changes over the past year indicates that ELS will perform very well over the near term.

Financial Data

(US$ in Thousands)	3 Mos	12/31/2015	12/31/2014	12/31/2013	12/31/2012	12/31/2011	12/31/2010	12/31/2009
Earnings Per Share	1.82	1.54	1.41	1.28	0.66	0.32	0.63	0.61
Cash Flow Per Share	4.10	4.20	3.43	3.08	2.86	2.47	2.68	2.73
Tang Book Value Per Share	9.57	9.36	9.25	9.09	8.69	11.28	3.67	3.60
Dividends Per Share	1.550	1.500	1.300	1.000	0.875	0.750	0.600	0.550
Dividend Payout %	85.16	97.40	92.20	78.13	132.58	234.38	96.00	90.16
Income Statement								
Total Revenue	220,147	821,654	776,809	728,375	709,877	580,073	511,361	489,934
EBITDA	113,221	366,852	358,057	304,235	302,661	226,687	223,099	215,361
Depn & Amortn	31,278	114,698	111,872	110,505	105,578	86,463	73,347	73,670
Income Before Taxes	56,309	146,423	133,890	75,208	72,559	40,556	58,601	48,499
Net Income	57,190	150,512	138,468	125,905	74,458	42,504	60,397	56,261
Average Shares	92,041	91,907	91,511	91,196	90,862	80,660	71,036	65,888
Balance Sheet								
Current Assets	131,251	146,586	139,440	126,668	115,929	158,489	109,145	187,838
Total Assets	3,415,125	3,420,061	3,446,339	3,391,639	3,398,226	3,496,101	2,048,395	2,166,319
Current Liabilities	293,670	281,657	255,066	236,066	204,058	212,138	175,318	163,991
Long-Term Obligations	2,106,298	2,145,713	2,212,246	2,192,368	2,269,866	2,284,683	1,412,919	1,547,901
Total Liabilities	2,469,139	2,494,993	2,534,346	2,498,306	2,538,978	2,569,774	1,821,365	1,947,789
Stockholders' Equity	945,986	925,068	911,993	893,333	859,248	926,327	227,030	218,530
Shares Outstanding	84,594	84,253	83,879	83,313	83,193	82,156	61,944	60,701
Statistical Record								
Return on Assets %	5.11	4.38	4.05	3.71	2.15	1.53	2.87	2.64
Return on Equity %	18.93	16.39	15.34	14.37	8.32	7.37	27.11	37.86
EBITDA Margin %	51.43	44.65	46.09	41.77	42.64	39.08	43.63	43.96
Net Margin %	25.98	18.32	17.83	17.29	10.49	7.33	11.81	11.48
Asset Turnover	0.24	0.24	0.23	0.21	0.21	0.21	0.24	0.23
Current Ratio	0.45	0.52	0.55	0.54	0.57	0.75	0.62	1.15
Debt to Equity	2.23	2.32	2.43	2.45	2.64	2.47	6.22	7.08
Price Range	73.30-52.19	66.81-51.55	52.42-36.13	42.77-33.48	36.49-31.91	36.05-27.29	29.71-23.40	25.43-14.92
P/E Ratio	40.27-28.68	43.38-33.47	37.18-25.62	33.41-26.16	55.30-48.35	112.66-85.27	47.16-37.14	41.70-24.46
Average Yield %	2.58	2.64	2.98	2.67	2.57	2.44	2.27	2.68

Address: Two North Riverside Plaza, Suite 800, Chicago, IL 60606 **Telephone:** 312-279-1400	**Web Site:** www.equitylifestyle.com **Officers:** Samuel Zell - Chairman Howard Walker - Vice-Chairman	**Auditors:** Ernst & Young LLP **Investor Contact:** 180-024-75279 **Transfer Agents:** American Stock Transfer and Trust Company, LLC, New York, NY

EQUITY ONE, INC.

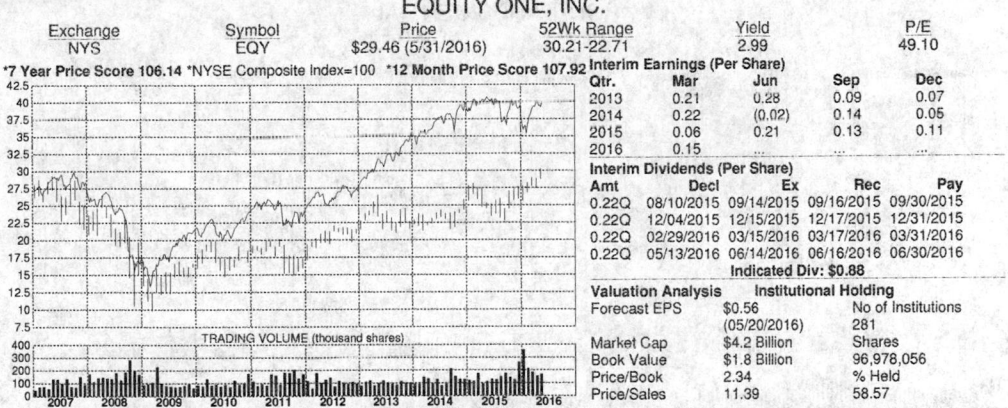

Exchange	Symbol	Price	52Wk Range	Yield	P/E
NYS	EQY	$29.46 (5/31/2016)	30.21-22.71	2.99	49.10

*7 Year Price Score 106.14 *NYSE Composite Index=100 *12 Month Price Score 107.92

Interim Earnings (Per Share)

Qtr.	Mar	Jun	Sep	Dec
2013	0.21	0.28	0.09	0.07
2014	0.22	(0.02)	0.14	0.05
2015	0.06	0.21	0.13	0.11
2016	0.15	...	...	...

Interim Dividends (Per Share)

Amt	Decl	Ex	Rec	Pay
0.22Q	08/10/2015	09/14/2015	09/16/2015	09/30/2015
0.22Q	12/04/2015	12/15/2015	12/17/2015	12/31/2015
0.22Q	02/29/2016	03/15/2016	03/17/2016	03/31/2016
0.22Q	05/13/2016	06/14/2016	06/16/2016	06/30/2016

Indicated Div: $0.88

Valuation Analysis   **Institutional Holding**

Forecast EPS	$0.56	No of Institutions	
	(05/20/2016)	281	
Market Cap	$4.2 Billion	Shares	
Book Value	$1.8 Billion	96,978,056	
Price/Book	2.34	% Held	
Price/Sales	11.39	58.57	

TRADING VOLUME (thousand shares)

Business Summary: REITs (MIC: 5.3.1 SIC: 6798 NAIC: 525930)

Equity One is a real estate investment trust. Co. owns, manages, acquires, develops and redevelops shopping centers and retail properties located primarily in supply constrained suburban and urban communities. As of Dec 31 2015, Co.'s portfolio comprised 126 properties, including 102 retail properties and five non-retail properties. As of Dec 31 2015, Co.'s retail occupancy excluding developments and redevelopments was 96.0% and included national, regional and local tenants. Additionally, Co. had joint venture interests in six retail properties and two office buildings.

Recent Developments: For the quarter ended Mar 31 2016, net income increased 100.5% to US$21.1 million from US$10.5 million in the year-earlier quarter. Revenues were US$94.5 million, up 6.8% from US$88.5 million the year before.

Prospects: Our evaluation of Equity One Inc. as of June 19, 2016 is the result of our systematic analysis on three basic characteristics: earnings strength, relative valuation, and recent stock price movement. The company has generated a negative trend in earnings per share over the past 5 quarters and while recent estimates for the company have been mixed, EQY has posted better than expected results. Based on operating earnings yield, the company is overvalued when compared to all of the companies in our coverage universe. Share price changes over the past year indicates that EQY will perform very well over the near term.

Financial Data

(US$ in Thousands)	3 Mos	12/31/2015	12/31/2014	12/31/2013	12/31/2012	12/31/2011	12/31/2010	12/31/2009
Earnings Per Share	0.60	0.51	0.39	0.65	(0.04)	0.29	0.27	0.99
Cash Flow Per Share	1.23	1.29	1.21	1.13	1.34	0.93	0.78	1.16
Tang Book Value Per Share	11.86	11.29	11.03	10.81	10.76	11.69	11.87	11.60
Dividends Per Share	0.880	0.880	0.880	0.880	0.880	0.880	0.880	1.120
Dividend Payout %	146.67	172.55	225.64	135.38	...	303.45	325.93	113.13
Income Statement								
Total Revenue	94,477	360,153	353,185	332,511	325,611	291,925	285,224	271,390
EBITDA	34,271	111,282	93,756	102,673	49,906	77,946	88,796	135,186
Depn & Amortn	690	(12,158)	(18,269)	(12,303)	(12,469)	(10,584)	(7,487)	(6,775)
Income Before Taxes	20,733	68,118	47,994	46,831	(9,800)	18,378	18,361	68,511
Income Taxes	440	(856)	850	(484)	(2,503)	(5,064)	(3,765)	(5,017)
Net Income	21,066	65,453	48,897	77,954	(3,477)	33,621	25,112	83,817
Average Shares	141,253	128,160	119,725	117,771	114,233	110,241	91,710	83,857
Balance Sheet								
Current Assets	39,924	33,411	39,578	49,367	42,178	121,314	53,514	57,776
Total Assets	3,371,461	3,375,903	3,262,225	3,354,659	3,502,668	3,219,342	2,681,864	2,452,320
Current Liabilities	52,797	56,051	58,608	53,155	64,289	59,010	41,792	42,431
Long-Term Obligations	1,356,086	1,366,722	1,333,041	1,508,409	1,599,350	1,309,071	1,202,873	1,216,891
Total Liabilities	1,589,081	1,811,897	1,778,805	1,959,476	2,105,942	1,802,026	1,395,957	1,387,785
Stockholders' Equity	1,782,380	1,564,006	1,483,420	1,395,183	1,396,726	1,417,316	1,285,907	1,064,535
Shares Outstanding	141,544	129,106	124,281	117,647	116,938	112,599	102,327	86,131
Statistical Record								
Return on Assets %	2.35	1.97	1.48	2.27	N.M.	1.14	0.98	3.73
Return on Equity %	4.66	4.30	3.40	5.58	N.M.	2.49	2.14	8.49
EBITDA Margin %	36.27	30.90	26.55	30.88	15.33	26.70	31.13	49.81
Net Margin %	22.30	18.17	13.84	23.44	N.M.	11.52	8.80	30.88
Asset Turnover	0.11	0.11	0.11	0.10	0.10	0.10	0.11	0.12
Current Ratio	0.76	0.60	0.68	0.93	0.66	2.06	1.28	1.36
Debt to Equity	0.76	0.87	0.90	1.08	1.15	0.92	0.94	1.14
Price Range	28.93-22.71	28.11-22.71	25.76-21.27	26.45-20.90	21.96-17.02	20.05-14.89	19.88-14.72	17.70-9.74
P/E Ratio	48.22-37.85	55.12-44.53	66.05-54.54	40.69-32.15	...	69.14-51.34	73.63-54.52	17.88-9.84
Average Yield %	3.41	3.43	3.80	3.80	4.30	4.91	5.03	7.73

Address: 410 Park Avenue, Suite 1220, New York, NY 10022 **Telephone:** 212-796-1760	**Web Site:** www.equityone.com **Officers:** Chaim Katzman - Chairman Dori Segal - Vice-Chairman	**Auditors:** Ernst & Young LLP **Investor Contact:** 212-796-1760 **Transfer Agents:** American Stock Transfer & Trust Company, New York, NY

EQUITY RESIDENTIAL

Exchange	Symbol	Price	52Wk Range	Yield	P/E
NYS	EQR	$69.21 (5/31/2016)	81.97-66.82	2.91	5.95

*7 Year Price Score 111.04 *NYSE Composite Index=100   *12 Month Price Score 93.70

Interim Earnings (Per Share)

Qtr.	Mar	Jun	Sep	Dec
2013	3.01	0.90	1.04	0.29
2014	0.22	0.31	0.61	0.60
2015	0.49	0.78	0.53	0.56
2016	9.76			

Interim Dividends (Per Share)

Amt	Decl	Ex	Rec	Pay
0.552Q	12/17/2015	12/23/2015	12/28/2015	01/08/2016
8.00Q	02/22/2016	03/01/2016	03/03/2016	03/10/2016
0.504Q	03/11/2016	03/22/2016	03/24/2016	04/08/2016
0.504Q	06/16/2016	06/23/2016	06/27/2016	07/08/2016

Indicated Div: $2.02

Valuation Analysis

		Institutional Holding	
Forecast EPS	$10.72	No of Institutions	719
	(05/20/2016)		
Market Cap	$25.3 Billion	Shares	424,239,648
Book Value	$11.1 Billion	% Held	97.20
Price/Book	2.29		
Price/Sales	9.38		

Business Summary: REITs (MIC: 5.3.1 SIC: 6798 NAIC: 525930)

Equity Residential is a real estate investment trust focused on the acquisition, development and management of apartment properties. Co. is the general partner of, and at Dec 31 2015 owned an approximate 96.2% ownership interest in ERP Operating Limited Partnership (ERPOP), an Illinois limited partnership. All of Co.'s property ownership, development and related business operations are conducted through ERPOP and those entities/subsidiaries owned or controlled by ERPOP. As of Dec 31 2015, Co., directly or indirectly through investments in title holding entities, owned all or a portion of 394 properties located in 12 states and the District of Columbia consisting of 109,652 apartment units.

Recent Developments:
For the quarter ended Mar 31 2016, income from continuing operations increased to US$3.73 billion from US$190.1 million in the year-earlier quarter. Net income increased to US$3.73 billion from US$190.2 million in the year-earlier quarter. Revenues were US$619.1 million, down 7.1% from US$666.4 million the year before.

Prospects:
Our evaluation of Equity Residential Properties Trust as of June 19, 2016 is the result of our systematic analysis on three basic characteristics: earnings strength, relative valuation, and recent stock price movement. The company has produced a positive trend in earnings per share over the past 5 quarters. However, while recent estimates for the company have been lowered by analysts, EQR has posted better than expected results. Based on operating earnings yield, the company is overvalued when compared to all of the companies in our coverage universe. Share price changes over the past year indicates that EQR will perform very well over the near term.

Financial Data

(US$ in Thousands)	3 Mos	12/31/2015	12/31/2014	12/31/2013	12/31/2012	12/31/2011	12/31/2010	12/31/2009
Earnings Per Share	11.63	2.36	1.73	5.16	2.70	2.95	0.95	1.27
Cash Flow Per Share	3.32	3.73	3.67	2.45	3.45	2.71	2.59	2.46
Tang Book Value Per Share	30.17	28.60	28.44	29.01	22.27	18.38	16.85	17.28
Dividends Per Share	10.161	2.210	2.000	1.850	1.780	1.580	1.470	1.640
Dividend Payout %	87.37	93.64	115.61	35.85	65.93	53.56	154.74	129.13
Income Statement								
Total Revenue	619,083	2,744,965	2,614,748	2,387,702	2,123,715	1,989,463	1,995,519	1,943,711
EBITDA	402,221	1,779,145	1,675,625	1,501,328	1,476,136	1,230,368	1,108,945	1,139,962
Depn & Amortn	188,152	765,895	758,861	1,013,353	684,992	663,616	673,403	600,375
Income Before Taxes	(1,759)	558,380	448,485	(121,076)	312,108	80,509	(45,481)	22,965
Income Taxes	350	917	1,394	1,169	539	728	334	2,808
Net Income	3,587,758	908,018	658,683	1,905,353	881,204	935,197	295,983	382,029
Average Shares	382,243	380,620	377,735	354,305	319,766	312,065	282,888	290,105
Balance Sheet								
Current Assets	669,145	155,115	160,468	199,737	872,161	546,850	624,988	562,588
Total Assets	21,301,292	23,157,328	22,950,614	22,834,545	17,201,000	16,659,303	16,184,194	15,417,515
Current Liabilities	540,126	559,305	507,329	512,203	441,759	367,692	339,800	319,916
Long-Term Obligations	8,583,818	10,968,498	10,844,861	10,766,254	8,529,244	9,721,061	9,948,076	9,392,570
Total Liabilities	10,237,520	12,686,960	12,582,158	12,327,344	9,911,187	10,990,288	11,094,008	10,370,176
Stockholders' Equity	11,063,772	10,470,368	10,368,456	10,507,201	7,289,813	5,669,015	5,090,186	5,047,339
Shares Outstanding	365,496	364,755	362,855	360,479	325,054	297,508	290,197	279,959
Statistical Record								
Return on Assets %	19.33	3.94	2.88	9.52	5.19	5.69	1.87	2.39
Return on Equity %	40.05	8.71	6.31	21.41	13.56	17.38	5.84	7.61
EBITDA Margin %	64.97	64.81	64.08	62.88	69.51	61.84	55.57	58.65
Net Margin %	579.53	33.08	25.19	79.80	41.49	47.01	14.83	19.65
Asset Turnover	0.12	0.12	0.11	0.12	0.13	0.12	0.13	0.12
Current Ratio	1.24	0.28	0.32	0.39	1.97	1.49	1.84	1.76
Debt to Equity	0.78	1.05	1.05	1.02	1.17	1.71	1.95	1.86
Price Range	81.97-68.62	81.97-68.95	74.55-51.87	60.75-50.45	65.47-54.06	63.68-49.66	52.29-31.86	36.00-16.71
P/E Ratio	7.05-5.90	34.73-29.22	43.09-29.98	11.77-9.78	24.25-20.02	21.59-16.83	55.04-33.54	28.35-13.16
Average Yield %	13.48	2.90	3.19	3.34	3.00	2.79	3.33	6.45

Address: Two North Riverside Plaza, Chicago, IL 60606	Web Site: www.equityresidential.com	Auditors: Ernst & Young LLP
Telephone: 312-474-1300	Officers: Samuel Zell - Chairman David J. Neithercut - President, Chief Executive Officer	Investor Contact: 888-879-6356
		Transfer Agents: Computershare Trust Company, N.A, Providence, RI

ESSEX PROPERTY TRUST INC

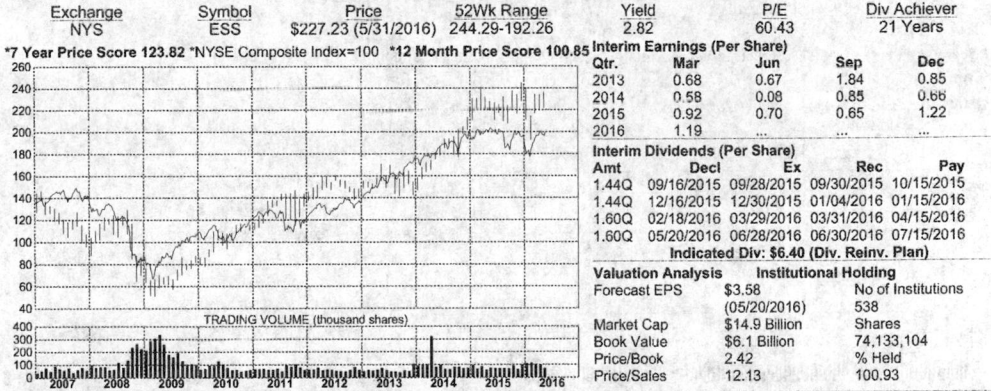

Exchange	Symbol	Price	52Wk Range	Yield	P/E	Div Achiever
NYS	ESS	$227.23 (5/31/2016)	244.29-192.26	2.82	60.43	21 Years

*7 Year Price Score 123.82 *NYSE Composite Index=100 *12 Month Price Score 100.85

Interim Earnings (Per Share)

Qtr.	Mar	Jun	Sep	Dec
2013	0.68	0.67	1.84	0.85
2014	0.58	0.08	0.85	0.66
2015	0.92	0.70	0.65	1.22
2016	1.19	...	...	...

Interim Dividends (Per Share)

Amt	Decl	Ex	Rec	Pay
1.44Q	09/16/2015	09/28/2015	09/30/2015	10/15/2015
1.44Q	12/16/2015	12/30/2015	01/04/2016	01/15/2016
1.60Q	02/18/2016	03/29/2016	03/31/2016	04/15/2016
1.60Q	05/20/2016	06/28/2016	06/30/2016	07/15/2016

Indicated Div: $6.40 (Div. Reinv. Plan)

Valuation Analysis		Institutional Holding	
Forecast EPS	$3.58	No of Institutions	
	(05/20/2016)	538	
Market Cap	$14.9 Billion	Shares	
Book Value	$6.1 Billion	74,133,104	
Price/Book	2.42	% Held	
Price/Sales	12.13	100.93	

TRADING VOLUME (thousand shares)

Business Summary: REITs (MIC: 5.3.1 SIC: 6798 NAIC: 525930)

Essex Property Trust is a self-administered and self-managed real estate investment trust. Co. owns all of its interest in its real estate investments directly or indirectly through Essex Portfolio, L.P. (the Operating Partnership). Co. is engaged primarily in the ownership, operation, management, acquisition, development and redevelopment of predominantly apartment communities. As of Dec 31 2015, Co. owned or held an interest in 246 communities, aggregating 59,160 apartment homes, located along the West Coast, as well as four commercial buildings (totaling approximately 319,079 sq. ft.), and eight active development projects with 2,447 apartment.

Recent Developments: For the quarter ended Mar 31 2016, net income increased 34.2% to US$86.9 million from US$64.8 million in the year earlier quarter. Revenues were US$314.2 million, up 11.1% from US$282.9 million the year before. Revenues from property income rose 11.4% to US$312.2 million from US$280.2 million in the corresponding quarter a year earlier.

Prospects: Our evaluation of Essex Property Trust Inc. as of June 19, 2016 is the result of our systematic analysis on three basic characteristics: earnings strength, relative valuation, and recent stock price movement. The company has enjoyed a very positive trend in earnings per share over the past 5 quarters. Because the company lacks sufficient analyst estimate data, we place greater weight on the historical EPS trend as the measure of earnings strength. Based on operating earnings yield, the company is overvalued when compared to all of the companies in our coverage universe. Share price changes over the past year indicates that ESS will perform very well over the near term.

Financial Data

(US$ in Thousands)	3 Mos	12/31/2015	12/31/2014	12/31/2013	12/31/2012	12/31/2011	12/31/2010	12/31/2009
Earnings Per Share	3.76	3.49	2.06	4.04	3.41	1.24	1.14	2.91
Cash Flow Per Share	10.02	9.52	8.72	8.19	7.61	6.66	5.92	6.37
Tang Book Value Per Share	93.88	94.28	93.42	48.51	46.52	40.37	36.05	35.79
Dividends Per Share	5.920	5.760	5.110	4.840	4.400	4.160	4.130	4.120
Dividend Payout %	157.45	165.04	248.06	119.80	129.03	335.48	362.28	141.58
Income Statement								
Total Revenue	314,202	1,194,407	969,305	613,703	543,425	475,558	415,732	411,389
EBITDA	108,423	833,735	583,880	383,426	356,549	288,820	238,145	237,224
Depn & Amortn	(7,551)	421,673	336,595	193,518	170,686	152,542	125,904	119,866
Income Before Taxes	71,839	226,378	94,545	96,941	99,452	61,723	52,497	44,382
Net Income	81,836	232,120	122,150	156,283	125,284	47,070	35,934	37,108
Average Shares	65,557	65,061	56,696	37,335	35,124	32,628	29,734	29,746
Balance Sheet								
Current Assets	237,278	279,825	237,583	212,105	201,002	176,107	177,448	209,083
Total Assets	12,067,484	12,005,091	11,562,874	5,186,839	4,847,223	4,036,964	3,732,887	3,254,637
Current Liabilities	318,675	272,634	261,248	125,857	115,302	94,440	90,178	82,591
Long-Term Obligations	5,352,802	5,315,464	5,109,817	3,033,524	2,818,683	2,360,858	2,258,745	1,847,442
Total Liabilities	5,925,492	5,767,358	5,540,202	3,297,871	3,078,070	2,595,088	2,578,592	2,197,192
Stockholders' Equity	6,141,992	6,237,733	6,022,672	1,888,968	1,769,153	1,441,876	1,154,295	1,057,445
Shares Outstanding	65,426	65,379	63,682	37,421	36,442	33,888	31,324	28,849
Statistical Record								
Return on Assets %	2.10	1.97	1.46	3.12	2.81	1.21	1.03	1.16
Return on Equity %	4.11	3.79	3.09	8.54	7.78	3.63	3.25	3.62
EBITDA Margin %	34.51	69.80	60.24	62.48	65.61	60.73	57.28	57.66
Net Margin %	26.05	19.43	12.60	25.47	23.05	9.90	8.64	9.02
Asset Turnover	0.10	0.10	0.12	0.12	0.12	0.12	0.12	0.13
Current Ratio	0.74	1.03	0.91	1.69	1.74	1.86	1.97	2.53
Debt to Equity	0.87	0.85	0.85	1.61	1.59	1.64	1.96	1.75
Price Range	244.29-192.26	244.29-206.60	212.86-143.51	170.47-141.49	160.33-136.94	146.45-110.77	116.94-77.66	87.34-50.76
P/E Ratio	64.97-51.13	70.00-59.20	103.33-69.67	42.20-35.02	47.02-40.16	118.10-89.33	102.58-68.12	30.01-17.44
Average Yield %	2.66	2.57	2.82	3.13	2.96	3.20	4.06	5.93

Address: 1100 Park Place Suite 200, San Mateo, CA 94403
Telephone: 650-655-7800

Web Site: www.essex.com
Officers: George M. Marcus - Chairman Michael J. Schall - President, Chief Executive Officer, Senior Executive Vice President, Chief Operating Officer

Auditors: KPMG LLLP
Investor Contact: 650-494-3700
Transfer Agents: Computershare Investor Services, LLC, Chicago, IL

ESTERLINE TECHNOLOGIES CORP

Exchange	Symbol	Price	52Wk Range	Yield	P/E
NYS	ESL	$67.41 (5/31/2016)	108.67-51.76	N/A	N/A

*7 Year Price Score 91.14 ***NYSE Composite Index=100** ***12 Month Price Score 84.55**

Interim Earnings (Per Share)

Qtr.	Jan	Apr	Jul	Oct
2013-14	0.93	1.14	1.19	(0.11)
2014-15	(0.26)	0.63	0.92	0.11
2015-16	0.17	0.50	...	...

Interim Dividends (Per Share)

No Dividends Paid

Valuation Analysis **Institutional Holding**

Forecast EPS	$4.45	No of Institutions
	(05/20/2016)	299
Market Cap	$2.0 Billion	Shares
Book Value	$1.6 Billion	30,732,232
Price/Book	1.27	% Held
Price/Sales	N/A	99.04

Business Summary: Electronic Instruments & Related Products (MIC: 6.2.3 SIC: 3823 NAIC: 334513)

Esterline Technologies designs, manufactures and markets products for the aerospace and defense industry. Co. has three segments: Avionics and Controls, which focuses on cockpit systems, technology interface systems for commercial and military aircraft, and similar devices for land- and sea-based military vehicles, communication systems, military audio and data products, and medical equipment; Sensors and Systems, which includes operations that produce temperature and pressure sensors, electrical power switching, and other systems; and Advanced Materials, which focuses on thermally engineered components, elastomer products, and combustible ordnance and warfare countermeasure devices.

Recent Developments: For the quarter ended Apr 1 2016, income from continuing operations decreased 21.4% to US$17.0 million from US$21.6 million in the year-earlier quarter. Net income decreased 24.4% to US$15.0 million from US$19.8 million in the year-earlier quarter. Revenues were US$490.3 million, down 2.0% from US$500.1 million the year before. Operating income was US$27.8 million versus US$35.0 million in the prior-year quarter, a decrease of 20.4%. Direct operating expenses declined 0.7% to US$334.1 million from US$336.4 million in the comparable period the year before. Indirect operating expenses decreased 0.3% to US$128.3 million from US$128.7 million in the equivalent prior-year period.

Prospects: Our evaluation of Esterline Technologies Corp. as of June 19, 2016 is the result of our systematic analysis on three basic characteristics: earnings strength, relative valuation, and recent stock price movement. The company has produced a positive trend in earnings per share over the past 5 quarters. However, while recent estimates for the company have been mixed, ESL has posted results that fell short of analysts expectations. Based on operating earnings yield, the company is undervalued when compared to all of the companies in our coverage universe. Share price changes over the past year indicates that ESL will perform in line with the market over the near term.

Financial Data
(US$ in Thousands)

	6 Mos	3 Mos	10/02/2015	10/31/2014	10/25/2013	10/26/2012	10/28/2011	10/29/2010
Earnings Per Share	...	...	1.91	3.16	5.19	3.60	4.27	4.66
Cash Flow Per Share	...	...	5.10	6.69	8.07	6.33	6.32	6.02
Tang Book Value Per Share	3.19	1.97	1.47	10.82	5.21	N.M.	N.M.	9.38
Income Statement								
Total Revenue	931,787	441,477	1,774,449	2,051,169	1,969,754	1,992,318	1,717,985	1,526,601
EBITDA	93,694	41,293	190,534	299,489	292,377	241,706	239,583	226,470
Depn & Amortn	48,736	24,171	45,000	56,200	55,400	52,400	42,500	39,500
Income Before Taxes	30,629	9,993	116,022	210,834	197,849	143,533	158,482	154,749
Income Taxes	3,383	(33)	18,956	44,274	30,085	29,958	24,938	24,504
Net Income	20,057	5,084	59,612	102,418	164,734	112,535	133,040	141,920
Average Shares	29,825	29,939	31,215	32,448	31,738	31,282	31,154	30,477
Balance Sheet								
Current Assets	1,113,860	1,098,528	1,128,814	1,169,504	1,091,715	1,035,693	1,039,313	1,076,585
Total Assets	3,012,040	2,919,322	3,007,030	3,193,467	3,262,112	3,227,117	3,378,586	2,587,738
Current Liabilities	413,879	398,737	410,809	408,129	408,092	396,346	418,361	324,377
Long-Term Obligations	863,583	831,358	867,786	609,720	667,859	838,060	1,020,028	598,972
Total Liabilities	1,450,289	1,412,317	1,469,563	1,305,650	1,388,507	1,616,636	1,815,751	1,174,942
Stockholders' Equity	1,561,751	1,507,005	1,537,467	1,887,817	1,873,605	1,610,481	1,562,835	1,412,796
Shares Outstanding	29,448	29,619	29,546	31,854	31,441	30,869	30,613	30,279
Statistical Record								
Return on Assets %	...	...	2.09	3.12	5.09	3.42	4.47	5.81
Return on Equity %	...	...	3.78	5.36	9.48	7.11	8.97	10.68
EBITDA Margin %	10.06	9.35	10.74	14.60	14.84	12.13	13.95	14.83
Net Margin %	2.15	1.15	3.36	4.99	8.36	5.65	7.74	9.30
Asset Turnover	...	...	0.62	0.63	0.61	0.60	0.58	0.62
Current Ratio	2.69	2.76	2.75	2.87	2.68	2.61	2.48	3.32
Debt to Equity	0.55	0.55	0.56	0.32	0.36	0.52	0.65	0.42
Price Range	116.69-51.76	119.45-71.14	120.06-71.14	121.48-78.27	84.80-55.42	75.20-48.71	81.96-48.54	60.44-37.71
P/E Ratio	...	...	62.86-37.25	38.44-24.77	16.34-10.68	20.89-13.53	19.19-11.37	12.97-8.09

Address: 500 108th Avenue N.E., Bellevue, WA 98004 **Telephone:** 425-453-9400	**Web Site:** www.esterline.com **Officers:** Curtis C. Reusser - Chairman, President, Chief Executive Officer Robert D. George - Vice President, Chief Financial Officer, Treasurer, Secretary	**Auditors:** Ernst & Young LLP **Investor Contact:** 425-453-9400 **Transfer Agents:** Mellon Investor Services LLC, Ridgefield, NJ

EVEREST RE GROUP LTD

Exchange	Symbol	Price	52Wk Range	Yield	P/E
NYS	RE	$179.11 (5/31/2016)	199.27-167.74	2.57	9.50

*7 Year Price Score 126.22 *NYSE Composite Index=100 *12 Month Price Score 101.19

Interim Earnings (Per Share)

Qtr.	Mar	Jun	Sep	Dec
2013	7.50	5.56	4.81	7.50
2014	6.21	0.20	6.00	7.44
2015	7.19	4.68	2.00	8.18
2016	4.00	...	...	...

Interim Dividends (Per Share)

Amt	Decl	Ex	Rec	Pay
0.95Q	08/12/2015	08/24/2015	08/26/2015	09/09/2015
1.15Q	11/19/2015	11/30/2015	12/02/2015	12/16/2015
1.15Q	02/24/2016	03/07/2016	03/09/2016	03/23/2016
1.15Q	05/18/2016	05/27/2016	06/01/2016	06/15/2016

Indicated Div: $4.60

Valuation Analysis / **Institutional Holding**

Forecast EPS	$17.65	No of Institutions	
	(05/20/2016)	530	
Market Cap	$7.6 Billion	Shares	
Book Value	$7.8 Billion	44,054,616	
Price/Book	0.97	% Held	
Price/Sales	1.35	88.77	

Business Summary: General Insurance (MIC: 5.2.1 SIC: 6331 NAIC: 524126)

Everest Re Group is a holding company. Through its subsidiaries, Co. provides reinsurance and insurance in the U.S., Bermuda and international markets. Co. operates following segments: U.S. Reinsurance, which writes property and casualty reinsurance and specialty lines of business, including Marine, Aviation, Surety and Accident and Health business; International, which focuses on the international reinsurance markets; Bermuda, which writes property and casualty reinsurance; Insurance, which writes property and casualty insurance, including medical stop loss insurance; and Mt. Logan Re, represents business written for the segregated accounts of Co.'s subsidiary, Mt. Logan Re Ltd.

Recent Developments: For the quarter ended Mar 31 2016, net income decreased 46.8% to US$171.7 million from US$323.0 million in the year-earlier quarter. Revenues were US$1.24 billion, down 13.5% from US$1.44 billion the year before. Net premiums earned were US$1.22 billion versus US$1.27 billion in the prior-year quarter, a decrease of 4.2%. Net investment income fell 16.4% to US$102.5 million from US$122.6 million a year ago.

Prospects: Our evaluation of Everest Re Group Ltd. as of June 19, 2016 is the result of our systematic analysis on three basic characteristics: earnings strength, relative valuation, and recent stock price movement. The company has generated a negative trend in earnings per share over the past 5 quarters. However, while recent estimates for the company have been mixed, RE has posted results that fell short of analysts expectations. Based on operating earnings yield, the company is undervalued when compared to all of the companies in our coverage universe. Share price changes over the past year indicates that RE will perform very well over the near term.

Financial Data
(US$ in Thousands)

	3 Mos	12/31/2015	12/31/2014	12/31/2013	12/31/2012	12/31/2011	12/31/2010	12/31/2009
Earnings Per Share	18.86	22.10	25.91	25.44	15.79	(1.49)	10.70	13.22
Cash Flow Per Share	28.97	30.14	28.95	22.59	12.76	12.26	16.22	12.94
Tang Book Value Per Share	184.91	178.21	166.75	146.57	130.96	112.99	115.45	102.90
Dividends Per Share	4.200	4.000	3.200	2.190	1.920	1.920	1.920	1.920
Dividend Payout %	22.27	18.10	12.35	8.61	12.16	...	17.94	14.52
Income Statement								
Premium Income	1,218,867	5,481,459	5,169,135	4,753,543	4,164,628	4,101,347	3,934,625	3,894,098
Total Revenue	1,242,046	5,837,889	5,790,589	5,640,836	4,922,810	4,693,961	4,705,807	4,498,578
Benefits & Claims	700,749	3,101,915	2,906,534	2,800,251	2,745,265	3,726,204	2,945,712	2,374,058
Income Before Taxes	177,067	1,208,509	1,446,115	1,554,966	939,526	(233,947)	591,238	939,321
Income Taxes	5,381	134,021	187,652	289,706	110,572	(153,461)	(19,516)	132,332
Net Income	171,686	977,869	1,199,156	1,259,382	828,954	(80,486)	610,754	806,989
Average Shares	42,463	43,877	45,802	49,056	52,067	53,916	56,786	60,847
Balance Sheet								
Total Assets	20,855,854	21,426,175	20,817,824	19,808,036	19,777,907	18,893,555	18,407,971	18,001,312
Total Liabilities	13,015,555	13,817,590	13,366,704	12,839,760	13,044,440	12,822,180	12,124,454	11,899,590
Stockholders' Equity	7,840,299	7,608,585	7,451,120	6,968,276	6,733,467	6,071,375	6,283,517	6,101,722
Shares Outstanding	42,399	42,694	44,685	47,543	51,417	53,736	54,428	59,300
Statistical Record								
Return on Assets %	3.92	4.63	5.90	6.36	4.28	N.M.	3.35	4.63
Return on Equity %	10.66	12.99	16.63	18.38	12.91	N.M.	9.86	14.59
Loss Ratio %	57.49	56.59	56.23	58.91	65.92	90.85	74.87	60.97
Net Margin %	13.82	16.75	20.71	22.33	16.84	(1.71)	12.98	17.94
Price Range	197.43-167.74	191.54-166.99	176.27-137.48	159.13-109.95	114.60-83.35	93.76-73.50	88.82-69.24	92.49-58.69
P/E Ratio	10.47-8.89	8.67-7.56	6.80-5.31	6.26-4.32	7.26-5.28	...	8.30-6.47	7.00-4.44
Average Yield %	2.30	2.22	2.01	1.63	1.90	2.28	2.37	2.49

Address: Seon Place - 4th Floor, 141 Front Street, P.O. Box HM 845, Hamilton, HM 19 **Telephone:** 441-295-0006	**Web Site:** www.everestregroup.com **Officers:** Joseph V. Taranto - Chairman, Chief Executive Officer Dominic James Addesso - President, Chief Executive Officer, Executive Vice President, Chief Financial Officer	**Auditors:** PricewaterhouseCoopers, LLP **Investor Contact:** 908-604-3169 **Transfer Agents:** Computershare Trust Company, N.A., Providence, RI

EVERSOURCE ENERGY

Exchange	Symbol	Price	52Wk Range	Yield	P/E	Div Achiever
NYS	ES	$55.24 (5/31/2016)	58.80-45.41	3.22	22.92	16 Years

*7 Year Price Score 112.52 *NYSE Composite Index=100 *12 Month Price Score 107.67

Interim Earnings (Per Share)

Qtr.	Mar	Jun	Sep	Dec
2013	0.72	0.54	0.66	0.56
2014	0.74	0.40	0.74	0.69
2015	0.80	0.65	0.74	0.57
2016	0.45	...	...	...

Interim Dividends (Per Share)

Amt	Decl	Ex	Rec	Pay
0.417Q	09/01/2015	09/10/2015	09/14/2015	09/30/2015
0.417Q	12/02/2015	12/10/2015	12/14/2015	12/31/2015
0.445Q	02/03/2016	02/29/2016	03/02/2016	03/31/2016
0.445Q	05/04/2016	05/26/2016	05/31/2016	06/30/2016

Indicated Div: $1.78 (Div. Reinv. Plan)

Valuation Analysis   **Institutional Holding**

Forecast EPS	$2.98	No of Institutions
	(05/20/2016)	131
Market Cap	$17.5 Billion	Shares
Book Value	$10.4 Billion	24,724,104
Price/Book	1.68	% Held
Price/Sales	2.34	71.53

TRADING VOLUME (thousand shares)

Business Summary: Electric Utilities (MIC: 3.1.1 SIC: 4911 NAIC: 221122)

Eversource Energy is a public utility holding company, which is engaged in the energy delivery business via its wholly owned utility subsidiaries. At Dec 31 2015: The Connecticut Light and Power Company served about 1.2 million customers in Connecticut; NSTAR Electric Company served about 1.2 million customers in Massachusetts; Western Massachusetts Electric Company served about 1.2 million customers in Boston; and Public Service Company of New Hampshire served about 503,000 retail customers in New Hampshire. Co.'s regulated natural gas utilities, NSTAR Gas Company and Yankee Gas Services Company, served about 286,000 and 226,000 customers in Massachusetts and Connecticut, respectively.

Recent Developments: For the quarter ended Mar 31 2016, net income decreased 3.6% to US$246.0 million from US$255.1 million in the year-earlier quarter. Revenues were US$2.06 billion, down 18.2% from US$2.51 billion the year before. Operating income was US$488.5 million versus US$497.5 million in the prior-year quarter, a decrease of 1.8%. Direct operating expenses declined 28.1% to US$1.07 billion from US$1.50 billion in the comparable period the year before. Indirect operating expenses decreased 5.5% to US$492.1 million from US$520.5 million in the equivalent prior-year period.

Prospects: Our evaluation of Eversource Energy as of June 19, 2016 is the result of our systematic analysis on three basic characteristics: earnings strength, relative valuation, and recent stock price movement. The company has managed to produce a neutral trend in earnings per share over the past 5 quarters. However, while recent estimates for the company have been lowered by analysts, ES has posted results that fell short of analysts expectations. Based on operating earnings yield, the company is about fairly valued when compared to all of the companies in our coverage universe. Share price changes over the past year indicates that ES will perform very well over the near term.

Financial Data
(US$ in Thousands)

	3 Mos	12/31/2015	12/31/2014	12/31/2013	12/31/2012	12/31/2011	12/31/2010	12/31/2009
Earnings Per Share	2.41	2.76	2.58	2.49	1.89	2.22	2.19	1.91
Cash Flow Per Share	4.54	4.49	5.17	5.28	4.18	5.47	6.19	5.73
Tang Book Value Per Share	21.81	21.54	20.37	19.32	18.21	21.03	20.63	19.40
Dividends Per Share	1.698	1.670	1.570	1.470	1.323	1.100	1.025	0.950
Dividend Payout %	70.44	60.51	60.85	59.04	69.99	49.55	46.80	49.74
Income Statement								
Total Revenue	2,055,635	7,954,827	7,741,856	7,301,204	6,273,787	4,465,657	4,898,167	5,439,430
EBITDA	685,530	2,460,647	2,272,125	2,170,106	1,656,958	1,124,083	1,142,544	1,096,994
Depn & Amortn	194,983	665,856	614,657	610,777	519,010	302,192	300,737	309,618
Income Before Taxes	392,335	1,422,371	1,295,362	1,220,630	808,003	571,466	604,516	513,739
Income Taxes	146,302	536,367	468,297	426,941	274,926	170,953	210,409	179,947
Net Income	244,153	886,004	819,546	786,007	525,945	394,693	387,949	330,033
Average Shares	318,481	318,432	317,417	316,211	277,993	177,804	176,885	172,717
Balance Sheet								
Current Assets	2,590,547	2,618,786	2,692,465	2,087,049	2,227,295	1,357,472	1,317,742	1,267,854
Total Assets	30,712,475	30,580,309	29,777,975	27,795,537	28,302,824	15,647,066	14,522,042	14,057,679
Current Liabilities	2,593,914	2,989,790	3,134,381	3,275,651	3,643,690	1,947,682	1,238,075	979,412
Long-Term Obligations	9,144,687	8,805,574	8,606,017	7,776,833	7,200,156	4,614,913	4,632,866	4,492,935
Total Liabilities	20,273,976	20,228,094	19,801,160	18,184,009	19,065,774	11,634,396	10,594,666	10,363,577
Stockholders' Equity	10,438,499	10,352,215	9,976,815	9,611,528	9,237,050	4,012,670	3,927,376	3,694,102
Shares Outstanding	317,207	317,191	316,983	315,273	314,053	177,158	176,448	175,620
Statistical Record								
Return on Assets %	2.87	2.94	2.85	2.80	2.39	2.62	2.71	2.35
Return on Equity %	8.48	8.72	8.37	8.34	7.92	9.94	10.18	9.66
EBITDA Margin %	33.35	30.93	29.35	29.72	26.41	25.17	23.33	20.17
Net Margin %	11.88	11.14	10.59	10.77	8.38	8.84	7.92	6.07
Asset Turnover	0.25	0.26	0.27	0.26	0.28	0.30	0.34	0.39
Current Ratio	1.00	0.88	0.86	0.64	0.61	0.70	1.06	1.29
Debt to Equity	0.88	0.85	0.86	0.81	0.78	1.15	1.18	1.22
Price Range	58.53-45.41	56.40-45.41	56.15-41.52	45.33-38.67	40.57-33.53	36.31-30.46	32.05-24.78	26.33-19.45
P/E Ratio	24.29-18.84	20.43-16.45	21.76-16.09	18.20-15.53	21.47-17.74	16.36-13.72	14.63-11.32	13.79-10.18
Average Yield %	3.36	3.34	3.41	3.49	3.53	3.23	3.64	4.16

Address: 300 Cadwell Drive, Springfield, MA 01104 Telephone: 413-785-5871	Web Site: www.eversource.com Officers: James J. Judge - President, Chief Executive Officer, Executive Vice President, Chief Financial Officer David R. McHale - Executive Vice President, Chief Financial Officer, Chief Administrative Officer	Auditors: Deloitte & Touche LLP Investor Contact: 860-728-4650 Transfer Agents: ComputerShare Investor Services, Providence, RI

EXELON CORP

Exchange	Symbol	Price	52Wk Range	Yield	P/E
NYS	EXC	$34.27 (5/31/2016)	35.86-25.46	3.71	17.66

*7 Year Price Score 71.46 *NYSE Composite Index=100 *12 Month Price Score 109.60

Interim Earnings (Per Share)

Qtr.	Mar	Jun	Sep	Dec
2013	(0.01)	0.57	0.86	0.58
2014	0.10	0.60	1.15	0.02
2015	0.80	0.74	0.69	0.32
2016	0.19	...	...	...

Interim Dividends (Per Share)

Amt	Decl	Ex	Rec	Pay
0.31Q	07/28/2015	08/12/2015	08/14/2015	09/10/2015
0.31Q	10/27/2015	11/10/2015	11/13/2015	12/10/2015
0.31Q	01/26/2016	02/10/2016	02/12/2016	03/10/2016
0.318Q	04/26/2016	05/11/2016	05/13/2016	06/10/2016

Indicated Div: $1.27

Valuation Analysis

Forecast EPS	$2.52
	(05/20/2016)
Market Cap	$31.6 Billion
Book Value	$25.9 Billion
Price/Book	1.22
Price/Sales	1.12

Institutional Holding

No of Institutions	1112
Shares	753,670,592
% Held	84.47

Business Summary: Electric Utilities (MIC: 3.1.1 SIC: 4931 NAIC: 221122)

Exelon is a utility services holding company engaged, through its subsidiary, Exelon Generation Company, LLC (Generation), in the energy generation business, and through its other subsidiaries, Commonwealth Edison Company (ComEd), PECO Energy Company (PECO) and Baltimore Gas and Electric Company (BGE), in the energy delivery businesses. Generation also sells renewable energy and other energy-related products and services, and engages in natural gas and oil exploration and production activities. Co. has nine segments consisting of Generation's six segments (Mid-Atlantic, Midwest, New England, New York, Electric Reliability Council of Texas, and Other Regions), ComEd, PECO and BGE.

Recent Developments: For the quarter ended Mar 31 2016, net income decreased 83.3% to US$123.0 million from US$738.0 million in the year-earlier quarter. Revenues were US$7.57 billion, down 14.2% from US$8.83 billion the year before. Operating income was US$483.0 million versus US$1.37 billion in the prior-year quarter, a decrease of 64.6%. Direct operating expenses declined 7.1% to US$6.09 billion from US$6.55 billion in the comparable period the year before. Indirect operating expenses increased 9.6% to US$1.00 billion from US$913.0 million in the equivalent prior-year period.

Prospects: Our evaluation of Exelon Corp. as of June 19, 2016 is the result of our systematic analysis on three basic characteristics: earnings strength, relative valuation, and recent stock price movement. The company has generated a negative trend in earnings per share over the past 5 quarters. However, while recent estimates for the company have been mixed, EXC has posted results that were in line with analysts expectations. Based on operating earnings yield, the company is undervalued when compared to all of the companies in our coverage universe. Share price changes over the past year indicates that EXC will perform well over the near term.

Financial Data

(US$ in Thousands)	3 Mos	12/31/2015	12/31/2014	12/31/2013	12/31/2012	12/31/2011	12/31/2010	12/31/2009
Earnings Per Share	1.94	2.54	1.88	2.00	1.42	3.75	3.87	4.09
Cash Flow Per Share	8.23	8.56	5.18	7.41	7.49	7.32	7.93	9.25
Tang Book Value Per Share	20.87	25.34	23.41	23.68	22.33	17.86	16.65	15.31
Dividends Per Share	1.240	1.240	1.240	1.455	2.100	2.100	2.100	2.100
Dividend Payout %	63.92	48.82	65.96	72.75	147.89	56.00	54.26	51.34
Income Statement								
Total Revenue	7,573,000	29,447,000	27,429,000	24,888,000	23,489,000	18,924,000	18,644,000	17,318,000
EBITDA	750,000	9,222,000	8,007,000	8,055,000	7,556,000	8,408,000	8,986,000	8,506,000
Depn & Amortn	153,000	4,860,000	4,476,000	3,960,000	4,754,000	3,782,000	3,948,000	3,380,000
Income Before Taxes	310,000	3,330,000	2,506,000	2,763,000	1,889,000	3,953,000	4,221,000	4,445,000
Income Taxes	184,000	1,073,000	666,000	1,044,000	627,000	1,457,000	1,658,000	1,712,000
Net Income	173,000	2,250,000	1,820,000	1,729,000	1,171,000	2,495,000	2,563,000	2,707,000
Average Shares	925,000	893,000	864,000	860,000	819,000	665,000	663,000	662,000
Balance Sheet								
Current Assets	11,364,000	15,334,000	12,097,000	10,137,000	10,133,000	5,489,000	6,398,000	5,441,000
Total Assets	111,742,000	95,384,000	86,814,000	79,924,000	78,554,000	55,092,000	52,240,000	49,180,000
Current Liabilities	13,770,000	9,118,000	8,762,000	7,728,000	7,784,000	4,989,000	4,240,000	4,238,000
Long-Term Obligations	29,955,000	24,286,000	20,010,000	18,271,000	18,854,000	12,189,000	12,004,000	11,385,000
Total Liabilities	85,813,000	69,398,000	64,013,000	56,999,000	56,843,000	40,620,000	38,593,000	36,453,000
Stockholders' Equity	25,929,000	25,986,000	22,801,000	22,925,000	21,711,000	14,472,000	13,647,000	12,727,000
Shares Outstanding	922,000	919,924	859,833	857,290	854,781	663,368	661,845	659,798
Statistical Record								
Return on Assets %	1.74	2.47	2.18	2.18	1.75	4.65	5.05	5.58
Return on Equity %	7.04	9.22	7.96	7.75	6.45	17.75	19.44	22.69
EBITDA Margin %	9.90	31.32	29.19	32.36	32.17	44.43	48.20	49.12
Net Margin %	2.28	7.64	6.64	6.95	4.99	13.18	13.75	15.63
Asset Turnover	0.28	0.32	0.33	0.31	0.35	0.35	0.37	0.36
Current Ratio	0.83	1.68	1.38	1.31	1.30	1.10	1.51	1.28
Debt to Equity	1.16	0.93	0.88	0.80	0.87	0.84	0.88	0.89
Price Range	35.86-25.46	37.99-25.46	38.63-26.62	37.78-26.90	42.07-28.57	45.34-39.77	49.66-37.63	57.81-40.15
P/E Ratio	18.48-13.12	14.96-10.02	20.55-14.16	18.89-13.45	29.63-20.12	12.09-10.61	12.83-9.72	14.13-9.82
Average Yield %	3.97	3.87	3.70	4.69	5.72	4.95	4.95	4.25

Address: 10 South Dearborn Street,	Web Site: www.exeloncorp.com	Auditors: PricewaterhouseCoopers LLP
P.O. Box 805379, Chicago, IL	Officers: Mayo A. Shattuck - Executive Chairman	Investor Contact: 312-394-2345
60680-5379	Christopher M. Crane - President, Chief Executive	Transfer Agents: Wells Fargo
Telephone: 800-483-3220	Officer, Chief Operating Officer	

EXTRA SPACE STORAGE INC

Exchange	Symbol	Price	52Wk Range	Yield	P/E
NYS	EXR	$92.97 (5/31/2016)	94.04-65.04	3.36	52.82

*7 Year Price Score 176.50 *NYSE Composite Index=100 *12 Month Price Score 109.41

Interim Earnings (Per Share)

Qtr.	Mar	Jun	Sep	Dec
2013	0.28	0.31	0.26	0.69
2014	0.32	0.36	0.47	0.38
2015	0.46	0.47	0.58	0.05
2016	0.66	...	...	...

Interim Dividends (Per Share)

Amt	Decl	Ex	Rec	Pay
0.59Q	08/28/2015	09/11/2015	09/15/2015	09/30/2015
0.59Q	11/13/2015	12/11/2015	12/15/2015	12/31/2015
0.59Q	02/24/2016	03/11/2016	03/15/2016	03/31/2016
0.78Q	05/25/2016	06/13/2016	06/15/2016	06/30/2016

Indicated Div: $3.12

Valuation Analysis

		Institutional Holding	
Forecast EPS	$2.35	No of Institutions	494
	(05/20/2016)		
Market Cap	$11.6 Billion	Shares	144,640,288
Book Value	$2.1 Billion	% Held	96.50
Price/Book	5.43		
Price/Sales	13.87		

Business Summary: REITs (MIC: 5.3.1 SIC: 6798 NAIC: 525930)

Extra Space Storage is a real estate investment trust (REIT) which is engaged in owning, operating, managing, acquiring, developing and redeveloping self-storage properties. Substantially all of Co.'s business is conducted through Extra Space Storage LP (the Operating Partnership). Co. operate in three segments: rental operations, which include rental operations of stores in which Co. has an ownership interest; tenant reinsurance, which include the reinsurance of risks relating to the loss of goods stored by tenants in Co.'s stores; and property management, acquisition and development, which include managing, acquiring, developing and selling stores.

Recent Developments: For the quarter ended Mar 31 2016, net income increased 52.5% to US$89.4 million from US$58.6 million in the year-earlier quarter. Revenues were US$229.4 million, up 32.5% from US$173.2 million the year before. Revenues from property income rose 34.0% to US$199.5 million from US$148.9 million in the corresponding quarter a year earlier.

Prospects: Our evaluation of Extra Space Storage Inc. as of June 19, 2016 is the result of our systematic analysis on three basic characteristics: earnings strength, relative valuation, and recent stock price movement. The company has managed to produce a neutral trend in earnings per share over the past 5 quarters. However, while recent estimates for the company have been mixed, EXR has posted better than expected results. Based on operating earnings yield, the company is overvalued when compared to all of the companies in our coverage universe. Share price changes over the past year indicates that EXR will perform very well over the near term.

Financial Data
(US$ in Thousands)

	3 Mos	12/31/2015	12/31/2014	12/31/2013	12/31/2012	12/31/2011	12/31/2010	12/31/2009
Earnings Per Share	1.76	1.56	1.53	1.53	1.14	0.54	0.30	0.37
Cash Flow Per Share	3.01	3.07	2.92	2.44	2.10	1.57	1.20	0.94
Tang Book Value Per Share	17.13	16.81	14.87	15.14	13.44	10.71	10.02	10.16
Dividends Per Share	2.360	2.240	1.810	1.450	0.850	0.560	0.400	0.380
Dividend Payout %	134.09	143.59	118.30	94.77	74.56	103.70	133.33	102.70
Income Statement								
Total Revenue	229,403	782,270	647,155	520,613	409,396	329,830	281,497	280,476
EBITDA	95,786	419,908	375,990	310,253	236,757	180,834	147,182	158,334
Depn & Amortn	3,702	123,751	109,531	104,963	79,516	65,358	56,367	58,519
Income Before Taxes	62,419	205,476	188,903	137,855	91,613	52,291	30,783	36,429
Income Taxes	2,765	11,148	7,570	9,984	5,413	1,155	4,162	4,300
Net Income	89,407	209,536	195,896	185,556	127,689	58,423	33,374	39,093
Average Shares	131,956	126,918	121,435	113,105	106,523	96,683	92,050	91,082
Balance Sheet								
Current Assets	97,495	244,197	126,293	187,741	78,720	85,031	99,829	191,358
Total Assets	6,291,419	6,071,407	4,402,107	3,977,140	3,223,477	2,516,250	2,248,468	2,407,556
Current Liabilities	194,333	120,916	204,193	61,272	137,299	260,079	203,324	135,531
Long-Term Obligations	3,564,963	3,499,621	2,232,597	1,948,723	1,496,425	1,154,484	1,083,467	1,309,237
Total Liabilities	4,148,357	3,982,330	2,664,682	2,218,670	1,731,670	1,497,303	1,367,067	1,523,377
Stockholders' Equity	2,143,062	2,089,077	1,737,425	1,758,470	1,491,807	1,018,947	881,401	884,179
Shares Outstanding	125,129	124,119	116,360	115,755	110,737	94,783	87,587	86,721
Statistical Record								
Return on Assets %	4.47	4.00	4.68	5.15	4.44	2.45	1.43	1.66
Return on Equity %	12.40	10.95	11.21	11.42	10.14	6.15	3.78	4.45
EBITDA Margin %	41.75	53.68	58.10	59.59	57.83	54.83	52.29	56.45
Net Margin %	38.97	26.79	30.27	35.64	31.19	17.71	11.86	13.94
Asset Turnover	0.16	0.15	0.15	0.14	0.14	0.14	0.12	0.12
Current Ratio	0.50	2.02	0.62	3.06	0.57	0.33	0.49	1.41
Debt to Equity	1.66	1.68	1.29	1.11	1.00	1.13	1.23	1.48
Price Range	93.46-65.04	90.22-58.64	60.12-41.79	48.65-36.39	36.39-24.00	24.48-17.40	17.57-11.08	12.09-5.10
P/E Ratio	53.10-36.95	57.83-37.59	39.29-27.31	31.80-23.78	31.92-21.05	45.33-32.22	58.57-36.93	32.68-13.78
Average Yield %	3.05	3.10	3.48	3.44	2.74	2.70	2.74	4.36

Address: 2795 East Cottonwood Parkway, Suite 400, Salt Lake City, UT 84121 **Telephone:** 801-365-4600	**Web Site:** www.extraspace.com **Officers:** Kenneth M. Woolley - Executive Chairman, Chairman, Chief Executive Officer Spencer F. Kirk - Chairman, President, Chief Executive Officer	**Auditors:** Ernst & Young LLP **Investor Contact:** 801-365-4600 **Transfer Agents:** American Stock Transfer & Trust Company

EXXON MOBIL CORP.

Exchange	Symbol	Price	52Wk Range	Yield	P/E	Div Achiever
NYS	XOM	$89.02 (5/31/2016)	90.26-68.71	3.37	28.62	33 Years

*7 Year Price Score 83.19   ***NYSE Composite Index=100**   ***12 Month Price Score 107.30**

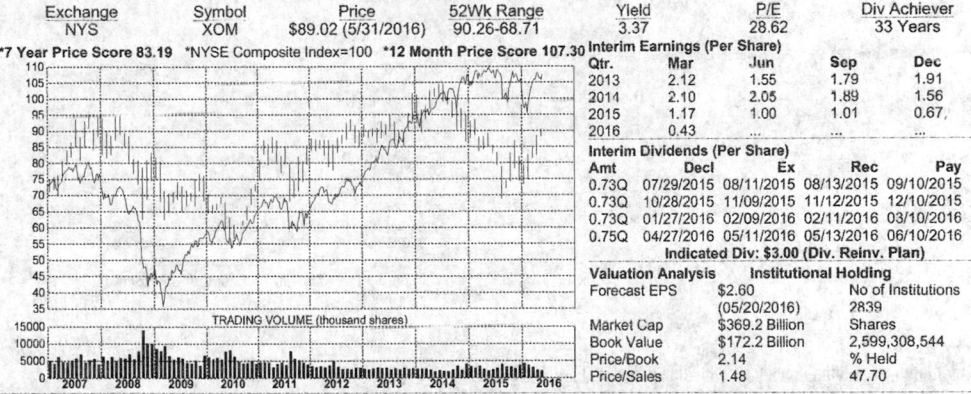

Interim Earnings (Per Share)

Qtr.	Mar	Jun	Sep	Dec
2013	2.12	1.55	1.79	1.91
2014	2.10	2.05	1.89	1.56
2015	1.17	1.00	1.01	0.67,
2016	0.43	...	...	...

Interim Dividends (Per Share)

Amt	Decl	Ex	Rec	Pay
0.73Q	07/29/2015	08/11/2015	08/13/2015	09/10/2015
0.73Q	10/28/2015	11/09/2015	11/12/2015	12/10/2015
0.73Q	01/27/2016	02/09/2016	02/11/2016	03/10/2016
0.75Q	04/27/2016	05/11/2016	05/13/2016	06/10/2016

Indicated Div: $3.00 (Div. Reinv. Plan)

Valuation Analysis		Institutional Holding	
Forecast EPS	$2.60	No of Institutions	
	(05/20/2016)	2839	
Market Cap	$369.2 Billion	Shares	
Book Value	$172.2 Billion	2,599,308,544	
Price/Book	2.14	% Held	
Price/Sales	1.48	47.70	

Business Summary: Production & Extraction (MIC: 9.1.1 SIC: 1311 NAIC: 211111)

Exxon Mobil is engaged in the energy business. Co.'s principal business involves exploration for, and production of, crude oil and natural gas, manufacture of petroleum products and transportation and sale of crude oil, natural gas and petroleum products. Co. is a manufacturer and marketer of commodity petrochemicals, including olefins, aromatics, polyethylene and polypropylene plastics and a range of products. As of Dec 31 2015, Co. had 24.76 billion barrels of oil-equivalent proved reserves.

Recent Developments: For the quarter ended Mar 31 2016, net income decreased 64.9% to US$1.78 billion from US$5.08 billion in the year-earlier quarter. Revenues were US$48.71 billion, down 28.0% from US$67.62 billion the year before. Direct operating expenses declined 29.5% to US$33.08 billion from US$46.96 billion in the comparable period the year before. Indirect operating expenses decreased 0.9% to US$13.89 billion from US$14.03 billion in the equivalent prior-year period.

Prospects: Our evaluation of Exxon Mobil Corp. as of June 19, 2016 is the result of our systematic analysis on three basic characteristics: earnings strength, relative valuation, and recent stock price movement. The company has enjoyed a very positive trend in earnings per share over the past 5 quarters and while recent estimates for the company have been raised by analysts, XOM has posted better than expected results. Based on operating earnings yield, the company is about fairly valued when compared to all of the companies in our coverage universe. Share price changes over the past year indicates that XOM will perform well over the near term.

Financial Data
(US$ in Thousands)

	3 Mos	12/31/2015	12/31/2014	12/31/2013	12/31/2012	12/31/2011	12/31/2010	12/31/2009
Earnings Per Share	3.11	3.85	7.60	7.37	9.70	8.42	6.22	3.98
Cash Flow Per Share	6.50	7.23	10.54	10.16	12.10	11.36	9.91	5.89
Tang Book Value Per Share	41.52	41.10	41.51	40.14	36.84	32.61	29.49	23.39
Dividends Per Share	2.920	2.880	2.700	2.460	2.180	1.850	1.740	1.660
Dividend Payout %	93.89	74.81	35.53	33.38	22.47	21.97	27.97	41.71
Income Statement								
Total Revenue	48,707,000	268,882,000	411,939,000	438,255,000	482,295,000	486,429,000	383,221,000	310,586,000
EBITDA	6,572,000	40,325,000	69,213,000	74,902,000	94,941,000	89,087,000	67,978,000	47,242,000
Depn & Amortn	4,765,000	18,048,000	17,297,000	17,182,000	15,888,000	15,583,000	14,760,000	11,917,000
Income Before Taxes	1,730,000	21,966,000	51,630,000	57,711,000	78,726,000	73,257,000	52,959,000	34,777,000
Income Taxes	(51,000)	5,415,000	18,015,000	24,263,000	31,045,000	31,051,000	21,561,000	15,119,000
Net Income	1,810,000	16,150,000	32,520,000	32,580,000	44,880,000	41,060,000	30,460,000	19,280,000
Average Shares	4,178,000	4,196,000	4,282,000	4,418,999	4,627,999	4,874,999	4,896,999	4,847,999
Balance Sheet								
Current Assets	44,251,000	42,623,000	52,910,000	59,308,000	64,460,000	72,963,000	58,984,000	55,235,000
Total Assets	342,789,000	336,758,000	349,493,000	346,808,000	333,795,000	331,052,000	302,510,000	233,323,000
Current Liabilities	48,726,000	53,976,000	64,633,000	71,724,000	64,139,000	77,505,000	62,633,000	52,061,000
Long-Term Obligations	29,568,000	19,925,000	11,653,000	6,891,000	7,928,000	9,322,000	12,227,000	7,129,000
Total Liabilities	170,602,000	165,947,000	175,094,000	172,805,000	167,932,000	176,656,000	155,671,000	122,754,000
Stockholders' Equity	172,187,000	170,811,000	174,399,000	174,003,000	165,863,000	154,396,000	146,839,000	110,569,000
Shares Outstanding	4,147,000	4,156,000	4,201,000	4,334,999	4,501,999	4,733,999	4,978,999	4,726,999
Statistical Record								
Return on Assets %	3.80	4.71	9.34	9.57	13.46	12.96	11.37	8.36
Return on Equity %	7.58	9.36	18.67	19.17	27.95	27.26	23.67	17.25
EBITDA Margin %	13.49	15.00	16.80	17.09	19.69	18.31	17.74	15.21
Net Margin %	3.72	6.01	7.89	7.43	9.31	8.44	7.95	6.21
Asset Turnover	0.73	0.78	1.18	1.29	1.45	1.54	1.43	1.35
Current Ratio	0.91	0.79	0.82	0.83	1.01	0.94	0.94	1.06
Debt to Equity	0.17	0.12	0.07	0.04	0.05	0.06	0.08	0.06
Price Range	89.11-68.71	93.37-68.71	104.38-86.41	101.51-85.16	93.48-77.60	87.98-68.03	73.42-56.57	81.64-62.22
P/E Ratio	28.65-22.09	24.25-17.85	13.73-11.37	13.77-11.55	9.64-8.00	10.45-8.08	11.80-9.09	20.51-15.63
Average Yield %	3.62	3.48	2.78	2.72	2.52	2.32	2.68	2.34

Address: 5959 Las Colinas Boulevard, Irving, TX 75039-2298 Telephone: 972-444-1000 Fax: 972-444-1505	Web Site: www.exxonmobil.com Officers: Rex W. Tillerson - Chairman, President, Chief Executive Officer, Chief Executive Officer Darren W. Woods - President, Senior Vice President, Vice President, Division Officer	Auditors: PricewaterhouseCoopers LLP Investor Contact: 180-025-21800 Transfer Agents: ComputerShare, College Station, TX

FACTSET RESEARCH SYSTEMS INC.

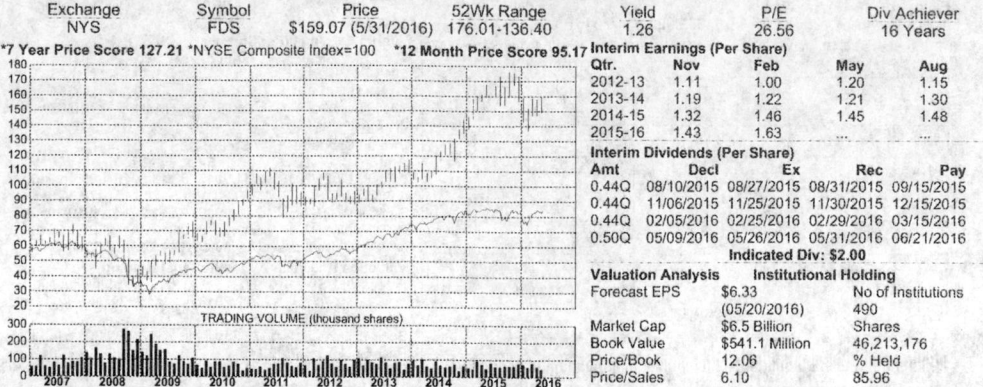

Exchange	Symbol	Price	52Wk Range	Yield	P/E	Div Achiever
NYS	FDS	$159.07 (5/31/2016)	176.01-136.40	1.26	26.56	16 Years

*7 Year Price Score 127.21 *NYSE Composite Index=100 *12 Month Price Score 95.17

Interim Earnings (Per Share)

Qtr.	Nov	Feb	May	Aug
2012-13	1.11	1.00	1.20	1.15
2013-14	1.19	1.22	1.21	1.30
2014-15	1.32	1.46	1.45	1.48
2015-16	1.43	1.63	...	...

Interim Dividends (Per Share)

Amt	Decl	Ex	Rec	Pay
0.44Q	08/10/2015	08/27/2015	08/31/2015	09/15/2015
0.44Q	11/06/2015	11/25/2015	11/30/2015	12/15/2015
0.44Q	02/05/2016	02/25/2016	02/29/2016	03/15/2016
0.50Q	05/09/2016	05/26/2016	05/31/2016	06/21/2016

Indicated Div: $2.00

Valuation Analysis / Institutional Holding

Forecast EPS	$6.33	No of Institutions
	(05/20/2016)	490
Market Cap	$6.5 Billion	Shares
Book Value	$541.1 Million	46,213,176
Price/Book	12.06	% Held
Price/Sales	6.10	85.96

Business Summary: Business Services (MIC: 7.5.2 SIC: 7374 NAIC: 541519)

FactSet Research Systems is a provider of integrated financial information and analytical applications to the investment community. Co. combines content regarding companies and securities from main markets all over the globe into a single online platform of information and analytics. Co. provides smart, streamlined workspaces designed for investment managers, investment bankers, hedge funds managers, quantitative researchers and other professionals. Each personalized solution provides standard features such as wireless connectivity, seamless integration of real-time market data, content choices from hundreds of data sets, Microsoft® Office integration and financial screening capabilities.

Recent Developments: For the quarter ended Feb 29 2016, net income increased 10.0% to US$67.8 million from US$61.6 million in the year-earlier quarter. Revenues were US$281.8 million, up 13.7% from US$247.8 million the year before. Operating income was US$85.3 million versus US$80.6 million in the prior-year quarter, an increase of 5.8%. Direct operating expenses rose 24.5% to US$123.9 million from US$99.5 million in the comparable period the year before. Indirect operating expenses increased 7.3% to US$72.5 million from US$67.6 million in the equivalent prior-year period.

Prospects: Our evaluation of FactSet Research Systems Inc. as of June 19, 2016 is the result of our systematic analysis on three basic characteristics: earnings strength, relative valuation, and recent stock price movement. The company has produced a positive trend in earnings per share over the past 5 quarters. However, while recent estimates for the company have been mixed, FDS has posted better than expected results. Based on operating earnings yield, the company is about fairly valued when compared to all of the companies in our coverage universe. Share price changes over the past year indicates that FDS will perform in line with the market over the near term.

Financial Data
(US$ in Thousands)

	6 Mos	3 Mos	08/31/2015	08/31/2014	08/31/2013	08/31/2012	08/31/2011	08/31/2010
Earnings Per Share	5.99	5.82	5.71	4.92	4.45	4.12	3.61	3.13
Cash Flow Per Share	8.51	7.40	7.37	6.25	6.15	5.17	4.51	4.52
Tang Book Value Per Share	N.M.	N.M.	4.44	4.39	6.02	5.94	5.34	4.96
Dividends Per Share	1.760	1.710	1.660	1.480	1.320	1.160	1.000	0.860
Dividend Payout %	29.38	29.38	29.07	30.08	29.66	28.16	27.70	27.48
Income Statement								
Total Revenue	552,300	270,504	1,006,768	920,335	858,112	805,793	726,510	641,059
EBITDA	190,581	95,838	356,854	329,364	299,310	300,805	266,858	250,981
Depn & Amortn	18,260	8,437	23,100	25,900	28,400	26,100	27,900	28,800
Income Before Taxes	172,321	87,401	333,754	303,464	270,910	274,705	238,958	222,181
Income Taxes	44,594	27,436	92,703	91,921	72,273	85,896	67,912	71,970
Net Income	127,727	59,965	241,051	211,543	198,637	188,809	171,046	150,211
Average Shares	41,536	42,063	42,235	42,970	44,624	45,810	47,355	48,004
Balance Sheet								
Current Assets	327,341	320,848	304,174	249,775	318,034	299,125	273,170	265,145
Total Assets	1,021,705	1,017,687	736,671	663,212	690,197	694,143	657,440	644,608
Current Liabilities	140,037	128,731	139,780	127,291	118,253	113,176	109,423	109,276
Long-Term Obligations	300,000	300,000	35,000	...	...	...	...	...
Total Liabilities	480,647	459,918	205,087	152,130	148,418	141,879	142,252	142,202
Stockholders' Equity	541,058	557,769	531,584	511,082	541,779	552,264	515,188	502,406
Shares Outstanding	41,007	41,382	41,316	41,792	43,324	44,279	45,055	46,024
Statistical Record								
Return on Assets %	29.03	29.46	34.44	31.26	28.70	27.86	26.27	23.51
Return on Equity %	46.97	46.28	46.24	40.18	36.31	35.28	33.62	29.95
EBITDA Margin %	34.51	35.43	35.45	35.79	34.88	37.33	36.73	39.15
Net Margin %	23.13	22.17	23.94	22.99	23.15	23.43	23.54	23.43
Asset Turnover	1.23	1.24	1.44	1.36	1.24	1.19	1.12	1.00
Current Ratio	2.34	2.49	2.18	1.96	2.69	2.64	2.50	2.43
Debt to Equity	0.55	0.54	0.07	...	...	...	...	...
Price Range	176.01-136.40	176.01-134.64	173.20-116.34	127.86-101.94	111.60-87.45	108.52-82.24	111.76-73.55	78.69-54.95
P/E Ratio	29.38-22.77	30.24-23.13	30.33-20.37	25.99-20.72	25.08-19.65	26.34-19.96	30.96-20.37	25.14-17.56
Average Yield %	1.09	1.08	1.11	1.33	1.36	1.23	1.05	1.24

Address: 601 Merritt 7, Norwalk, CT 06851	**Web Site:** www.factset.com	**Auditors:** Ernst & Young LLP
Telephone: 203-810-1000	**Officers:** Philip A. Hadley - Chairman, Chief Executive Officer Philip Snow - President, Chief Executive Officer	**Transfer Agents:** Computershare
Fax: 203-810-1001		

FAIR ISAAC CORP

Exchange	Symbol	Price	52Wk Range	Yield	P/E
NYS	FICO	$111.43 (5/31/2016)	111.57-80.69	0.07	37.77

*7 Year Price Score 163.34 *NYSE Composite Index=100 *12 Month Price Score 112.66

Interim Earnings (Per Share)

Qtr.	Dec	Mar	Jun	Sep
2012-13	0.65	0.51	0.54	0.79
2013-14	0.47	0.59	0.58	1.07
2014-15	0.43	0.58	0.62	1.02
2015-16	0.59	0.72	...	...

Interim Dividends (Per Share)

Amt	Decl	Ex	Rec	Pay
0.02Q	08/27/2015	09/14/2015	09/16/2015	09/30/2015
0.02Q	10/28/2015	11/30/2015	12/02/2015	12/16/2015
0.02Q	02/25/2016	03/07/2016	03/09/2016	03/18/2016
0.02Q	05/12/2016	05/23/2016	05/25/2016	06/08/2016

Indicated Div: $0.08

Valuation Analysis

		Institutional Holding	
Forecast EPS	$3.01	No of Institutions	
	(05/06/2016)	313	
Market Cap	$3.5 Billion	Shares	
Book Value	$425.4 Million	36,369,228	
Price/Book	8.16	% Held	
Price/Sales	4.09	78.64	

Business Summary: Internet & Software (MIC: 6.3.2 SIC: 7389 NAIC: 541512)

Fair Isaac provides analytical solutions, credit scoring and credit account management products and services. Co.'s segments are: Applications, which includes pre-configured decision management applications designed for business problem or process such as marketing, account origination, customer management, fraud, collections and insurance claims management; Scores, which includes business-to-business scoring solutions and services, myFICO® solutions for consumers, and associated services; and tools, which is composed of analytic and decision management software tools that clients can use to create their own custom decision management applications, and its FICO® Decision Management Suit.

Recent Developments: For the quarter ended Mar 31 2016, net income increased 22.5% to US$23.1 million from US$18.9 million in the year-earlier quarter. Revenues were US$206.7 million, down 0.2% from US$207.1 million the year before. Operating income was US$38.5 million versus US$34.4 million in the prior-year quarter, an increase of 12.0%. Direct operating expenses declined 12.2% to US$62.3 million from US$71.0 million in the comparable period the year before. Indirect operating expenses increased 4.1% to US$105.9 million from US$101.7 million in the equivalent prior-year period.

Prospects: Our evaluation of Fair, Isaac & Co. Inc. as of June 19, 2016 is the result of our systematic analysis on three basic characteristics: earnings strength, relative valuation, and recent stock price movement. The company has generated a negative trend in earnings per share over the past 5 quarters and while recent estimates for the company have remained steady, FICO has posted better than expected results. Based on operating earnings yield, the company is about fairly valued when compared to all of the companies in our coverage universe. Share price changes over the past year indicates that FICO will perform very well over the near term.

Financial Data

(US$ in Thousands)	6 Mos	3 Mos	09/30/2015	09/30/2014	09/30/2013	09/30/2012	09/30/2011	09/30/2010
Earnings Per Share	2.95	2.81	2.65	2.72	2.48	2.64	1.79	1.42
Cash Flow Per Share	5.37	5.52	4.23	5.17	3.85	3.71	3.46	2.36
Dividends Per Share	0.080	0.080	0.080	0.080	0.080	0.080	0.080	0.080
Dividend Payout %	2.71	2.85	3.02	2.94	3.23	3.03	4.47	5.63
Income Statement								
Total Revenue	406,754	200,076	838,781	788,985	743,444	676,423	619,683	605,643
EBITDA	76,546	34,080	152,061	173,598	175,746	189,204	151,868	145,641
Depn & Amortn	7,087	3,580	13,673	11,917	13,535	21,544	24,241	30,901
Income Before Taxes	55,920	23,776	109,238	133,131	131,984	136,243	97,455	92,304
Income Taxes	13,563	4,535	22,736	38,252	41,889	44,239	25,893	27,847
Net Income	42,357	19,241	86,502	94,879	90,095	92,004	71,562	64,457
Average Shares	32,262	32,436	32,609	34,864	36,292	36,063	39,988	45,308
Balance Sheet								
Current Assets	276,586	287,545	286,602	288,527	249,188	259,325	364,481	347,175
Total Assets	1,214,941	1,215,250	1,230,163	1,192,298	1,161,547	1,158,611	1,129,468	1,123,716
Current Liabilities	241,331	243,090	243,875	341,404	165,880	209,605	146,498	122,147
Long-Term Obligations	516,000	516,000	516,000	376,000	447,000	455,000	504,000	512,000
Total Liabilities	789,561	793,082	793,165	737,684	630,870	684,205	663,974	648,802
Stockholders' Equity	425,380	422,168	436,998	454,614	530,677	474,406	465,494	474,914
Shares Outstanding	31,159	31,372	31,290	32,047	34,786	34,839	37,084	39,882
Statistical Record								
Return on Assets %	7.80	7.67	7.14	8.06	7.77	8.02	6.35	5.31
Return on Equity %	23.70	22.13	19.40	19.26	17.93	19.52	15.22	11.99
EBITDA Margin %	18.82	17.03	18.13	22.00	23.64	27.97	24.51	24.05
Net Margin %	10.41	9.62	10.31	12.03	12.12	13.60	11.55	10.64
Asset Turnover	0.69	0.71	0.69	0.67	0.64	0.59	0.55	0.50
Current Ratio	1.15	1.18	1.18	0.85	1.50	1.24	2.49	2.84
Debt to Equity	1.21	1.22	1.18	0.83	0.84	0.96	1.08	1.08
Price Range	106.09-80.69	97.25-70.05	97.25-53.89	64.88-51.00	55.29-40.62	45.95-20.26	31.61-21.19	26.57-18.07
P/E Ratio	35.96-27.35	34.61-24.93	36.70-20.34	23.85-18.75	22.29-16.38	17.41-7.67	17.66-11.84	18.71-12.73
Average Yield %	0.09	0.09	0.10	0.14	0.17	0.20	0.30	0.35

Address: 181 Metro Drive, Suite 700, San Jose, CA 95110-1346	**Web Site:** www.fico.com	**Auditors:** Deloitte & Touche LLP
Telephone: 408-535-1500	**Officers:** A. George Battle - Chairman William J. Lansing - Chief Executive Officer	**Investor Contact:** 800-213-5542
		Transfer Agents: Computershare, College Station, TX

FEDERAL REALTY INVESTMENT TRUST (MD)

Exchange	Symbol	Price	52Wk Range	Yield	P/E	Div Achiever
NYS	FRT	$153.19 (5/31/2016)	159.46-124.96	2.45	44.27	48 Years

*7 Year Price Score 118.33 *NYSE Composite Index=100 *12 Month Price Score 106.33

Interim Earnings (Per Share)

Qtr.	Mar	Jun	Sep	Dec
2013	0.53	0.57	0.94	0.42
2014	0.57	0.64	0.69	0.50
2015	0.67	0.63	0.75	0.98
2016	1.10	...	...	...

Interim Dividends (Per Share)

Amt	Decl	Ex	Rec	Pay
0.94Q	08/05/2015	09/18/2015	09/22/2015	10/15/2015
0.94Q	11/04/2015	12/30/2015	01/04/2016	01/15/2016
0.94Q	02/09/2016	03/16/2016	03/18/2016	04/15/2016
0.94Q	05/04/2016	06/20/2016	06/22/2016	07/15/2016

Indicated Div: $3.76 (Div. Reinv. Plan)

Valuation Analysis   Institutional Holding

Forecast EPS	$3.38 (05/20/2016)	No of Institutions	493
Market Cap	$10.9 Billion	Shares	75,912,152
Book Value	$1.9 Billion	% Held	96.88
Price/Book	5.85		
Price/Sales	14.33		

Business Summary: REITs (MIC: 5.3.1 SIC: 6798 NAIC: 525930)

Federal Realty Investment Trust is an equity real estate investment trust. Co. is engaged in the ownership, management, and redevelopment of retail and mixed-use properties. Co.'s properties are located primarily in certain metropolitan markets in the Northeast and Mid-Atlantic regions of the U.S., as well as in California and South Florida. As of Dec 31 2015, Co. owned or had a majority interest in community and neighborhood shopping centers and mixed-use properties which are operated as 90 primarily retail real estate projects. A joint venture in which Co. owns a 30% interest owned six retail real estate projects.

Recent Developments: For the quarter ended Mar 31 2016, income from continuing operations increased 10.7% to US$53.3 million from US$48.2 million in the year-earlier quarter. Net income increased 64.0% to US$79.1 million from US$48.2 million in the year-earlier quarter. Revenues were US$198.3 million, up 7.3% from US$184.8 million the year before. Revenues from property income rose 7.8% to US$195.3 million from US$181.2 million in the corresponding quarter a year earlier.

Prospects: Our evaluation of Federal Realty Investment Trust as of June 19, 2016 is the result of our systematic analysis on three basic characteristics: earnings strength, relative valuation, and recent stock price movement. The company has managed to produce a neutral trend in earnings per share over the past 5 quarters. Because the company lacks sufficient analyst estimate data, we place greater weight on the historical EPS trend as the measure of earnings strength. Based on operating earnings yield, the company is overvalued when compared to all of the companies in our coverage universe. Share price changes over the past year indicates that FRT will perform very well over the near term.

Financial Data

(US$ in Thousands)	3 Mos	12/31/2015	12/31/2014	12/31/2013	12/31/2012	12/31/2011	12/31/2010	12/31/2009
Earnings Per Share	3.46	3.03	2.41	2.46	2.35	2.28	1.98	1.63
Cash Flow Per Share	5.42	5.23	5.14	4.81	4.63	3.92	4.20	4.30
Tang Book Value Per Share	26.04	23.80	23.24	21.56	19.70	18.98	18.53	19.06
Dividends Per Share	3.690	3.620	3.300	3.020	2.840	2.720	2.660	2.620
Dividend Payout %	106.65	119.47	136.93	122.76	120.85	119.30	134.34	160.74
Income Statement								
Total Revenue	198,344	744,012	686,090	637,413	608,018	553,059	544,674	531,019
EBITDA	124,721	457,294	432,549	403,454	399,058	356,369	348,550	324,336
Depn & Amortn	47,799	174,796	170,814	161,099	142,039	126,568	119,817	115,093
Income Before Taxes	53,296	190,094	167,888	137,811	144,372	131,554	127,107	102,356
Net Income	76,955	210,219	164,535	162,681	151,925	143,917	122,790	98,304
Average Shares	69,957	68,981	67,492	65,483	64,056	62,603	61,324	59,830
Balance Sheet								
Current Assets	133,465	173,066	192,230	228,920	166,497	199,925	129,607	255,916
Total Assets	5,125,457	4,911,709	4,546,870	4,219,294	3,898,565	3,659,908	3,159,553	3,222,309
Current Liabilities	248,845	228,309	220,420	221,427	181,571	160,948	155,926	161,571
Long-Term Obligations	2,659,322	2,642,366	2,409,677	2,321,862	2,208,602	2,110,410	1,767,149	1,793,848
Total Liabilities	3,270,506	3,247,960	2,942,469	2,771,134	2,611,753	2,443,816	2,009,720	2,044,972
Stockholders' Equity	1,854,951	1,663,749	1,604,401	1,448,160	1,286,812	1,216,092	1,149,833	1,177,337
Shares Outstanding	70,861	69,493	68,605	66,701	64,815	63,544	61,526	61,242
Statistical Record								
Return on Assets %	4.87	4.45	3.75	4.01	4.01	4.22	3.85	3.11
Return on Equity %	13.98	12.86	10.78	11.90	12.11	12.17	10.55	8.58
EBITDA Margin %	62.88	61.46	63.05	63.30	65.63	64.44	63.99	61.08
Net Margin %	38.80	28.25	23.98	25.52	24.99	26.02	22.54	18.51
Asset Turnover	0.15	0.16	0.16	0.16	0.16	0.16	0.17	0.17
Current Ratio	0.54	0.76	0.87	1.03	0.92	1.24	0.83	1.58
Debt to Equity	1.43	1.59	1.50	1.60	1.72	1.74	1.54	1.52
Price Range	158.96-124.96	150.27-124.96	137.18-100.90	117.96-96.21	110.03-89.23	92.45-75.31	84.32-63.07	70.49-38.82
P/E Ratio	45.94-36.12	49.59-41.24	56.92-41.87	47.95-39.11	46.82-37.97	40.55-33.03	42.59-31.85	43.25-23.82
Average Yield %	2.62	2.60	2.75	2.85	2.79	3.22	3.53	4.70

Address: 1626 East Jefferson Street, Rockville, MD 20852 **Telephone:** 301-998-8100	**Web Site:** www.federalrealty.com **Officers:** Donald C. Wood - President, Chief Executive Officer, Principal Financial Officer Dawn M. Becker - Executive Vice President, Chief Operating Officer, Secretary, General Counsel	**Auditors:** Grant Thornton LLP **Investor Contact:** 800-658-8980 **Transfer Agents:** American Stock Transfer & Trust Company, New York, NY

FEDERATED INVESTORS INC (PA)

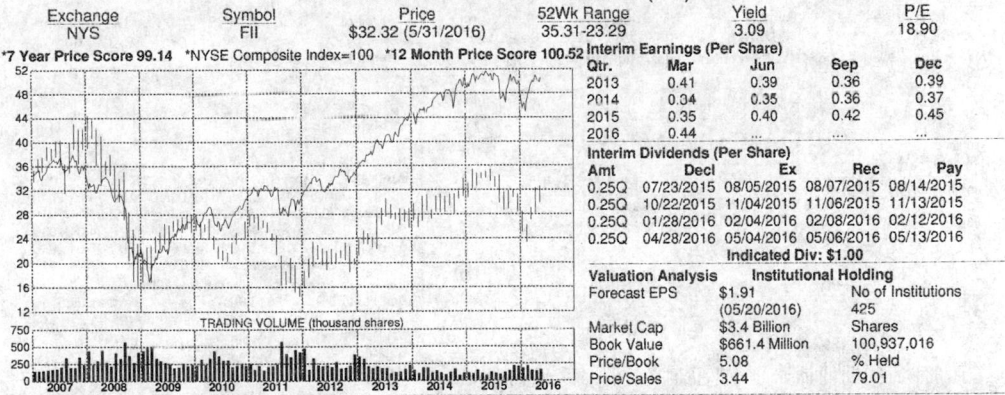

Exchange	Symbol	Price	52Wk Range	Yield	P/E
NYS	FII	$32.32 (5/31/2016)	35.31-23.29	3.09	18.90

*7 Year Price Score 99.14 *NYSE Composite Index=100 *12 Month Price Score 100.52

Interim Earnings (Per Share)

Qtr.	Mar	Jun	Sep	Dec
2013	0.41	0.39	0.36	0.39
2014	0.34	0.35	0.36	0.37
2015	0.35	0.40	0.42	0.45
2016	0.44	...	...	...

Interim Dividends (Per Share)

Amt	Decl	Ex	Rec	Pay
0.25Q	07/23/2015	08/05/2015	08/07/2015	08/14/2015
0.25Q	10/22/2015	11/04/2015	11/06/2015	11/13/2015
0.25Q	01/28/2016	02/04/2016	02/08/2016	02/12/2016
0.25Q	04/28/2016	05/04/2016	05/06/2016	05/13/2016

Indicated Div: $1.00

Valuation Analysis

Forecast EPS	$1.91	
	(05/20/2016)	

Institutional Holding

No of Institutions	425
Shares	100,937,016
% Held	79.01

Market Cap	$3.4 Billion
Book Value	$661.4 Million
Price/Book	5.08
Price/Sales	3.44

Business Summary: Wealth Management (MIC: 5.5.2 SIC: 6282 NAIC: 523930)

Federated Investors, together with its subsidiaries, is a provider of investment management products and related financial services. Co. sponsors, markets and provides investment-related services to various investment products, including mutual funds and Separate Accounts (which include separately managed accounts, institutional accounts, sub-advised funds and other managed products) in both domestic and international markets. Co. markets these funds to banks, broker/dealers and other financial intermediaries who use them to meet the needs of their customers, including retail investors, corporations and retirement plans. As of Dec 31 2015, Co. had $361.11 billion in assets under management.

Recent Developments: For the quarter ended Mar 31 2016, net income increased 33.9% to US$48.8 million from US$36.4 million in the year-earlier quarter. Revenues were US$272.1 million, up 23.4% from US$220.5 million the year before. Operating income was US$74.6 million versus US$59.0 million in the prior-year quarter, an increase of 26.3%. Indirect operating expenses increased 22.3% to US$197.6 million from US$161.5 million in the equivalent prior-year period.

Prospects: Our evaluation of Federated Investors Inc. as of June 19, 2016 is the result of our systematic analysis on three basic characteristics: earnings strength, relative valuation, and recent stock price movement. The company has produced a positive trend in earnings per share over the past 5 quarters and while recent estimates for the company have been raised by analysts, FII has posted better than expected results. Based on operating earnings yield, the company is undervalued when compared to all of the companies in our coverage universe. Share price changes over the past year indicates that FII will perform in line with the market over the near term.

Financial Data

(US$ in Thousands)	3 Mos	12/31/2015	12/31/2014	12/31/2013	12/31/2012	12/31/2011	12/31/2010	12/31/2009
Earnings Per Share	1.71	1.62	1.42	1.55	1.79	1.45	1.73	1.92
Cash Flow Per Share	2.45	2.32	1.91	2.59	3.14	1.13	2.16	2.75
Dividends Per Share	1.000	1.000	1.000	0.980	2.470	0.960	2.220	0.960
Dividend Payout %	58.48	61.73	70.42	63.23	137.99	66.21	128.32	50.00
Income Statement								
Total Revenue	272,109	926,609	859,250	878,365	945,706	895,114	951,943	1,175,950
EBITDA	79,059	284,106	249,352	268,115	316,611	254,671	308,620	334,318
Depn & Amortn	2,904	9,200	10,000	9,100	8,100	8,300	7,500	7,500
Income Before Taxes	76,155	274,906	239,352	259,015	308,511	246,371	301,120	326,818
Income Taxes	27,381	102,920	89,530	92,660	110,883	91,288	111,957	118,278
Net Income	45,258	169,807	149,236	162,177	188,088	150,906	179,114	197,292
Average Shares	99,803	100,477	100,723	100,669	100,313	100,632	99,993	100,056
Balance Sheet								
Current Assets	398,590	395,828	342,055	339,318	300,062	366,511	373,170	184,787
Total Assets	1,190,614	1,187,203	1,140,519	1,135,797	1,090,061	1,150,856	1,153,504	912,433
Current Liabilities	131,626	159,208	149,321	214,205	181,134	187,356	214,352	196,998
Long-Term Obligations	184,875	191,250	216,750	198,333	276,250	318,750	365,686	118,556
Total Liabilities	529,232	539,387	531,025	569,678	594,629	608,897	661,705	384,226
Stockholders' Equity	661,382	647,816	609,494	566,119	495,432	541,959	491,799	528,207
Shares Outstanding	104,044	104,103	104,927	104,798	104,450	103,752	103,673	102,943
Statistical Record								
Return on Assets %	15.48	14.59	13.11	14.57	16.74	13.10	17.34	22.43
Return on Equity %	27.90	27.01	25.39	30.55	36.16	29.20	35.12	41.47
EBITDA Margin %	29.05	30.66	29.02	30.52	33.48	28.45	32.42	28.43
Net Margin %	16.63	18.33	17.37	18.46	19.89	16.86	18.82	16.78
Asset Turnover	0.85	0.80	0.75	0.79	0.84	0.78	0.92	1.34
Current Ratio	3.03	2.49	2.29	1.58	1.66	1.96	1.74	0.94
Debt to Equity	0.28	0.30	0.36	0.35	0.56	0.59	0.74	0.22
Price Range	35.31-23.29	35.34-28.29	33.86-25.73	30.52-20.23	23.45-15.83	28.00-14.38	28.01-20.17	28.02-16.80
P/E Ratio	20.65-13.62	21.81-17.46	23.85-18.12	19.69-13.05	13.10-8.84	19.31-9.92	16.19-11.66	14.59-8.75
Average Yield %	3.25	3.08	3.39	3.74	12.01	4.35	9.26	4.00

Address: Federated Investors Tower,	Web Site: www.federatedinvestors.com	Auditors: Ernst & Young LLP
Pittsburgh, PA 15222-3779	Officers: John F. Donahue - Chairman Paul A	Transfer Agents: ComputerShare
Telephone: 412-288-1900	Uhlman - Vice President	Investor Services, Providence, RI

FEDEX CORP

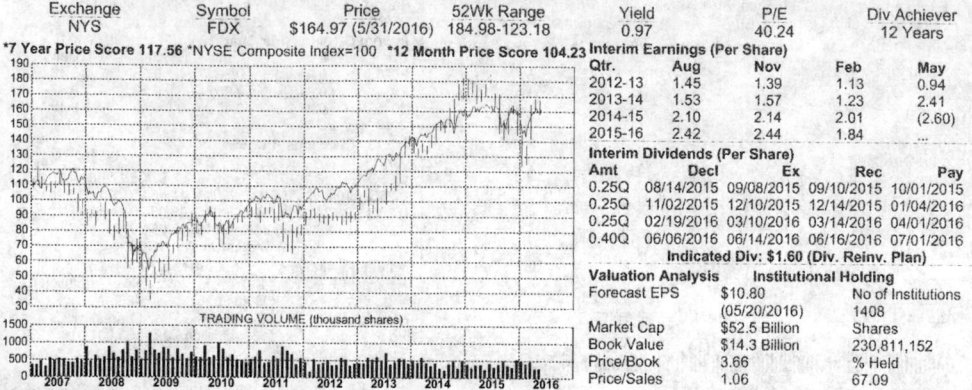

Exchange	Symbol	Price	52Wk Range	Yield	P/E	Div Achiever
NYS	FDX	$164.97 (5/31/2016)	184.98-123.18	0.97	40.24	12 Years

*7 Year Price Score 117.56 *NYSE Composite Index=100 *12 Month Price Score 104.23

Interim Earnings (Per Share)

Qtr.	Aug	Nov	Feb	May
2012-13	1.45	1.39	1.13	0.94
2013-14	1.53	1.57	1.23	2.41
2014-15	2.10	2.14	2.01	(2.60)
2015-16	2.42	2.44	1.84	...

Interim Dividends (Per Share)

Amt	Decl	Ex	Rec	Pay
0.25Q	08/14/2015	09/08/2015	09/10/2015	10/01/2015
0.25Q	11/02/2015	12/10/2015	12/14/2015	01/04/2016
0.25Q	02/19/2016	03/10/2016	03/14/2016	04/01/2016
0.40Q	06/06/2016	06/14/2016	06/16/2016	07/01/2016

Indicated Div: $1.60 (Div. Reinv. Plan)

Valuation Analysis

Forecast EPS	$10.80 (05/20/2016)
Market Cap	$52.5 Billion
Book Value	$14.3 Billion
Price/Book	3.66
Price/Sales	1.06

Institutional Holding

No of Institutions	1408
Shares	230,811,152
% Held	67.09

Business Summary: Airlines/Air Freight (MIC: 7.4.4 SIC: 4513 NAIC: 492110)

FedEx is engaged in the provision of a portfolio of transportation, e-commerce and business services under the FedEx brand. Co.'s primary operating companies are included in four business segments: Federal Express Corporation, a transportation company; FedEx Ground Package System, Inc., a North American provider of small-package ground delivery services; FedEx Freight, Inc., a provider of less-than-truckload freight services; and FedEx Corporate Services, Inc., which provides Co.'s other companies with sales, marketing, information technology, communications and back-office support.

Recent Developments: For the quarter ended Feb 29 2016, net income decreased 19.3% to US$507.0 million from US$628.0 million in the year-earlier quarter. Revenues were US$12.65 billion, up 8.0% from US$11.72 billion the year before. Operating income was US$864.0 million versus US$1.04 billion in the prior-year quarter, a decrease of 16.8%. Direct operating expenses rose 5.3% to US$5.07 billion from US$4.82 billion in the comparable period the year before. Indirect operating expenses increased 14.7% to US$6.72 billion from US$5.86 billion in the equivalent prior-year period.

Prospects: Our evaluation of FedEx Corp. as of June 19, 2016 is the result of our systematic analysis on three basic characteristics: earnings strength, relative valuation, and recent stock price movement. The company has enjoyed a very positive trend in earnings per share over the past 5 quarters. However, while recent estimates for the company have been lowered by analysts, FDX has posted better than expected results. Based on operating earnings yield, the company is undervalued when compared to all of the companies in our coverage universe. Share price changes over the past year indicates that FDX will perform in line with the market over the near term.

Financial Data

(US$ in Thousands)	9 Mos	6 Mos	3 Mos	05/31/2015	05/31/2014	05/31/2013	05/31/2012	05/31/2011
Earnings Per Share	4.10	4.27	3.97	3.65	6.75	4.91	6.41	4.57
Cash Flow Per Share	20.92	20.32	19.95	18.96	13.89	14.88	15.31	12.83
Tang Book Value Per Share	33.22	35.17	40.69	39.60	39.27	46.05	38.93	40.68
Dividends Per Share	0.950	0.900	0.850	0.800	0.600	0.560	0.520	0.480
Dividend Payout %	23.17	21.08	21.41	21.92	8.89	11.41	8.11	10.50
Income Statement								
Total Revenue	37,386,000	24,732,000	12,279,000	47,453,000	45,567,000	44,287,000	42,680,000	39,304,000
EBITDA	5,103,000	3,577,000	1,795,000	4,448,000	6,031,000	4,816,000	5,280,000	4,242,000
Depn & Amortn	1,964,000	1,301,000	648,000	2,600,000	2,600,000	2,300,000	2,100,000	1,900,000
Income Before Taxes	2,921,000	2,139,000	1,084,000	1,627,000	3,289,000	2,455,000	3,141,000	2,265,000
Income Taxes	1,031,000	756,000	392,000	577,000	1,192,000	894,000	1,109,000	813,000
Net Income	1,890,000	1,383,000	692,000	1,050,000	2,097,000	1,561,000	2,032,000	1,452,000
Average Shares	275,000	283,000	286,000	287,000	310,000	317,000	317,000	317,000
Balance Sheet								
Current Assets	10,237,000	11,152,000	10,703,000	10,941,000	9,683,000	11,274,000	9,056,000	8,285,000
Total Assets	37,819,000	38,371,000	37,245,000	37,069,000	33,070,000	33,567,000	29,903,000	27,385,000
Current Liabilities	5,939,000	5,951,000	5,844,000	5,957,000	5,312,000	5,750,000	5,374,000	4,882,000
Long-Term Obligations	8,477,000	8,481,000	7,244,000	7,249,000	4,736,000	2,739,000	1,250,000	1,667,000
Total Liabilities	23,492,000	23,381,000	21,962,000	22,076,000	17,793,000	16,169,000	15,176,000	12,165,000
Stockholders' Equity	14,327,000	14,990,000	15,283,000	14,993,000	15,277,000	17,398,000	14,727,000	15,220,000
Shares Outstanding	318,000	318,000	282,379	282,430	318,000	318,000	317,000	317,000
Statistical Record								
Return on Assets %	3.08	3.39	3.25	2.99	6.29	4.92	7.07	5.55
Return on Equity %	7.50	7.93	7.47	6.94	12.84	9.72	13.53	10.00
EBITDA Margin %	13.65	14.46	14.62	9.37	13.24	10.87	12.37	10.79
Net Margin %	5.06	5.59	5.64	2.21	4.60	3.52	4.76	3.69
Asset Turnover	1.34	1.36	1.38	1.35	1.37	1.40	1.49	1.50
Current Ratio	1.72	1.87	1.83	1.84	1.82	1.96	1.69	1.70
Debt to Equity	0.59	0.57	0.47	0.48	0.31	0.16	0.08	0.11
Price Range	184.98-123.18	184.98-140.74	184.98-145.06	182.03-139.21	144.53-95.71	109.07-84.34	98.50-65.15	98.32-70.11
P/E Ratio	45.12-30.04	43.32-32.96	46.59-36.54	49.87-38.14	21.41-14.18	22.21-17.18	15.37-10.16	21.51-15.34
Average Yield %	0.60	0.54	0.50	0.49	0.48	0.60	0.61	0.55

Address: 942 South Shady Grove Road, Memphis, TN 38120 **Telephone:** 901-818-7500	**Web Site:** www.fedex.com **Officers:** Frederick W. Smith - Chairman, President, Chief Executive Officer Robert B. Carter - Executive Vice President, Chief Information Officer	**Auditors:** Ernst & Young LLP **Investor Contact:** 901-818-7200 **Transfer Agents:** ComputerShare Investor Services, Providence, RI

FIDELITY NATIONAL FINANCIAL INC

Exchange	Symbol	Price	52Wk Range	Yield	P/E
NYS	FNF	$34.95 (5/31/2016)	39.99-29.58	N/A	18.79

*7 Year Price Score N/A   *NYSE Composite Index=100   *12 Month Price Score 94.40

Interim Earnings (Per Share)

Qtr.	Mar	Jun	Sep	Dec
2013	0.39	0.61	0.43	0.29
2014	(0.08)	0.41	0.40	0.35
2015	0.30	0.56	0.53	0.51
2016	0.26	...		

Interim Dividends (Per Share)

Amt	Decl	Ex	Rec	Pay
0.16Q	07/22/2013	09/12/2013	09/16/2013	09/30/2013
0.18Q	10/23/2013	12/12/2013	12/16/2013	12/30/2013
0.18Q	01/28/2014	03/13/2014	03/17/2014	03/31/2014
0.18Q	04/29/2014	06/12/2014	06/16/2014	06/30/2014

Valuation Analysis

		Institutional Holding	
Forecast EPS	$2.30	No of Institutions	
	(05/17/2016)	520	
Market Cap	$12.0 Billion	Shares	
Book Value	$5.7 Billion	262,570,816	
Price/Book	2.10	% Held	
Price/Sales	1.32	N/A	

Business Summary: General Insurance (MIC: 5.2.1 SIC: 6361 NAIC: 524127)

Fidelity National Financial is a title insurance holding company. Co. has organized its business into two groups, FNF Core Operations and FNF Ventures (FNFV). Through its Core Operations, Co. provides title insurance, escrow and other title related services, including collection and trust activities, trustee sales guarantees, recordings and reconveyances and home warranty insurance and technology and transaction services to the real estate and mortgage industries. Through its FNFV group, Co. owns majority and minority equity investment stakes in a number of entities, including American Blue Ribbon Holdings, LLC, Ceridian HCM, Inc. and Fleetcor Technologies, Inc. and Digital Insurance, Inc.

Recent Developments: For the quarter ended Mar 31 2016, income from continuing operations decreased 16.0% to US$84.0 million from US$100.0 million in the year-earlier quarter. Net income decreased 16.0% to US$84.0 million from US$100.0 million in the year-earlier quarter. Revenues were US$2.05 billion, down 0.6% from US$2.06 billion the year before. Net premiums earned were US$952.0 million versus US$858.0 million in the prior-year quarter, an increase of 11.0%.

Prospects: Our evaluation of Fidelity National Financial Inc. as of June 19, 2016 is the result of our systematic analysis on three basic characteristics: earnings strength, relative valuation, and recent stock price movement. The company has generated a negative trend in earnings per share over the past 5 quarters and while recent estimates for the company have remained steady, FNF has posted results that fell short of analysts expectations. Based on operating earnings yield, the company is undervalued when compared to all of the companies in our coverage universe. Share price changes over the past year indicates that FNF will perform in line with the market over the near term.

Financial Data
(US$ in Thousands)

	3 Mos	12/31/2015	12/31/2014	12/31/2013	12/31/2012	12/31/2011	12/31/2010	12/31/2009
Earnings Per Share	1.86	1.89	0.75	1.71	2.68	1.66	1.61	0.97
Cash Flow Per Share	3.56	3.31	4.11	2.10	2.80	0.57	0.81	1.69
Tang Book Value Per Share	N.M.	N.M.	N.M.	10.18	7.48	9.16	7.85	7.16
Dividends Per Share	0.820	0.800	0.370	0.660	0.580	...	...	...
Dividend Payout %	44.09	42.33	49.33	38.60	21.64			
Income Statement								
Premium Income	952,000	4,286,000	3,671,000	4,152,000	3,836,500	3,261,100	3,641,200	3,927,600
Total Revenue	2,048,000	9,132,000	8,024,000	8,565,000	7,201,700	4,839,600	5,740,300	5,828,400
Benefits & Claims	52,000	246,000	228,000	291,000	279,300	222,300	402,900	392,600
Income Before Taxes	131,000	867,000	392,000	651,000	843,400	414,800	562,400	344,900
Income Taxes	49,000	290,000	312,000	205,000	246,700	134,400	185,600	106,800
Net Income	74,000	527,000	583,000	402,000	606,500	369,500	370,100	222,300
Average Shares	281,000	286,000	142,000	235,000	226,000	222,700	229,300	228,500
Balance Sheet								
Total Assets	13,943,000	13,931,000	13,868,000	10,524,000	9,902,600	7,862,100	7,887,500	7,934,400
Total Liabilities	8,216,000	8,177,000	7,874,000	5,456,000	5,634,600	4,229,400	4,460,400	4,608,500
Stockholders' Equity	5,727,000	5,754,000	5,994,000	5,068,000	4,268,000	3,632,700	3,427,100	3,325,900
Shares Outstanding	343,354	347,999	371,777	250,340	228,545	220,677	223,748	230,217
Statistical Record								
Return on Assets %	3.72	3.79	4.78	3.94	6.81	4.69	4.68	2.73
Return on Equity %	8.90	8.97	10.54	8.61	15.31	10.47	10.96	7.25
Loss Ratio %	5.46	5.74	6.21	7.01	7.28	6.82	11.07	10.00
Net Margin %	3.61	5.77	7.27	4.69	8.42	7.63	6.45	3.81
Price Range	39.99-29.58	39.99-32.49	36.02-26.21	...	...	...	...	...
P/E Ratio	21.50-15.90	21.16-17.19	48.03-34.95	...	...	...	...	...
Average Yield %	2.30	2.19	1.27	...	...	...	...	...

Address: 601 Riverside Avenue, Jacksonville, FL 32204
Telephone: 904-854-8100

Web Site: www.fnf.com
Officers: Frank P. Willey - Vice-Chairman Mike Nolan - Co-Chief Operating Officer, President

Auditors: KPMG LLP
Investor Contact: 904-854-8120
Transfer Agents: Continental Stock Transfer & Trust Company, New York, NY

FIDELITY NATIONAL INFORMATION SERVICES INC

Exchange	Symbol	Price	52Wk Range	Yield	P/E
NYS	FIS	$74.27 (5/31/2016)	74.41-56.04	1.40	37.70

*7 Year Price Score 132.64 *NYSE Composite Index=100 *12 Month Price Score 103.39

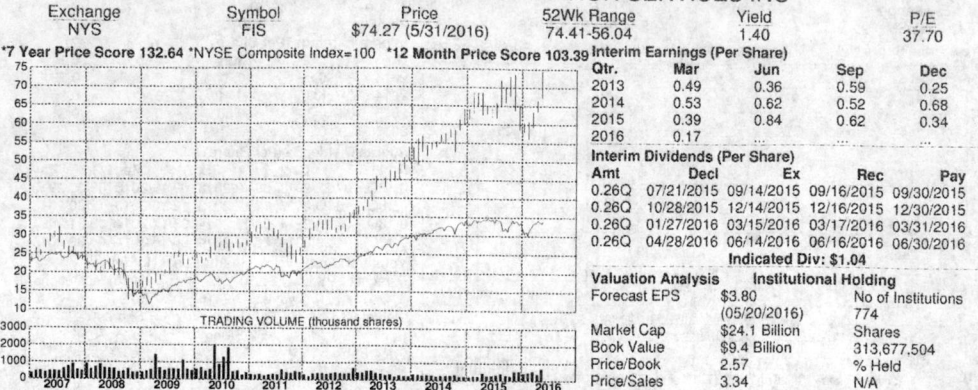

Interim Earnings (Per Share)

Qtr.	Mar	Jun	Sep	Dec
2013	0.49	0.36	0.59	0.25
2014	0.53	0.62	0.52	0.68
2015	0.39	0.84	0.62	0.34
2016	0.17	...	...	...

Interim Dividends (Per Share)

Amt	Decl	Ex	Rec	Pay
0.26Q	07/21/2015	09/14/2015	09/16/2015	09/30/2015
0.26Q	10/28/2015	12/14/2015	12/16/2015	12/30/2015
0.26Q	01/27/2016	03/15/2016	03/17/2016	03/31/2016
0.26Q	04/28/2016	06/14/2016	06/16/2016	06/30/2016

Indicated Div: $1.04

Valuation Analysis / **Institutional Holding**

Forecast EPS	$3.80	No of Institutions
	(05/20/2016)	774
Market Cap	$24.1 Billion	Shares
Book Value	$9.4 Billion	313,677,504
Price/Book	2.57	% Held
Price/Sales	3.34	N/A

Business Summary: Business Services (MIC: 7.5.2 SIC: 6159 NAIC: 522320)

Fidelity National Information Services is engaged in financial services technology. Co. provides a range of solutions in retail and enterprise banking, payments, capital markets, asset and wealth management, risk and compliance, treasury and insurance, as well as providing financial consulting and outsourcing services. Through its Capco brand, Co. provides a range of information technology consulting, advisory and transformational services to financial institutions globally. Co.'s segments include: Integrated Financial Solutions (IFS), Global Financial Solutions (GFS) and Corporate and Other.

Recent Developments: For the quarter ended Mar 31 2016, income from continuing operations decreased 50.2% to US$59.0 million from US$118.5 million in the year-earlier quarter. Net income decreased 48.9% to US$59.0 million from US$115.4 million in the year-earlier quarter. Non-interest income rose 40.3% to US$2.18 billion from US$1.55 billion, while non-interest expense advanced 49.1% to US$2.00 billion.

Prospects: Our evaluation of Fidelity National Information Services Inc. as of June 19, 2016 is the result of our systematic analysis on three basic characteristics: earnings strength, relative valuation, and recent stock price movement. The company has produced a positive trend in earnings per share over the past 5 quarters and while recent estimates for the company have remained steady, FIS has posted better than expected results. Based on operating earnings yield, the company is about fairly valued when compared to all of the companies in our coverage universe. Share price changes over the past year indicates that FIS will perform well over the near term.

Financial Data

(US$ in Thousands)	3 Mos	12/31/2015	12/31/2014	12/31/2013	12/31/2012	12/31/2011	12/31/2010	12/31/2009
Earnings Per Share	1.97	2.19	2.35	1.68	1.55	1.53	1.15	0.44
Cash Flow Per Share	3.98	3.99	4.09	3.66	3.58	3.90	3.10	3.02
Dividends Per Share	1.040	1.040	0.960	0.880	0.800	0.200	0.200	0.200
Dividend Payout %	52.79	47.49	40.85	52.38	51.61	13.07	17.39	45.45
Income Statement								
Total Revenue	2,181,000	6,595,200	6,413,800	6,070,700	5,807,600	5,745,700	5,269,500	3,769,500
EBITDA	188,000	1,359,400	1,341,000	1,132,200	1,171,700	1,113,800	912,600	367,900
Depn & Amortn	5,000	139,100	130,100	119,000	117,800	110,700	123,000	81,300
Income Before Taxes	90,000	1,036,900	1,053,400	825,200	831,200	744,300	616,300	156,000
Income Taxes	31,000	378,800	335,100	309,200	270,900	239,000	215,300	52,100
Net Income	55,000	631,500	679,100	493,100	461,200	469,600	404,500	105,900
Average Shares	327,000	288,700	288,700	294,200	297,500	307,000	352,000	239,400
Balance Sheet								
Current Assets	3,629,000	3,511,400	2,473,100	2,351,900	1,844,200	1,682,700	1,673,000	1,666,100
Total Assets	26,430,000	26,268,800	14,520,500	13,960,100	13,549,700	13,848,300	14,161,800	13,997,600
Current Liabilities	3,322,000	2,363,900	1,598,900	1,672,700	1,256,800	1,354,900	1,285,900	1,234,700
Long-Term Obligations	10,533,000	11,497,800	5,054,600	4,339,800	4,231,600	4,550,600	4,935,200	3,016,600
Total Liabilities	17,037,000	16,947,800	7,963,800	7,379,600	6,908,800	7,345,300	7,758,600	5,688,700
Stockholders' Equity	9,393,000	9,321,000	6,556,700	6,580,500	6,640,900	6,503,000	6,403,200	8,308,900
Shares Outstanding	325,000	324,500	284,900	290,600	294,100	292,900	301,900	374,500
Statistical Record								
Return on Assets %	2.81	3.10	4.77	3.58	3.36	3.35	2.87	0.98
Return on Equity %	7.31	7.95	10.34	7.46	7.00	7.28	5.50	1.79
EBITDA Margin %	8.62	20.61	20.91	18.65	20.18	19.38	17.32	9.76
Net Margin %	2.52	9.58	10.59	8.12	7.94	8.17	7.68	2.81
Asset Turnover	0.35	0.32	0.45	0.44	0.42	0.41	0.37	0.35
Current Ratio	1.09	1.49	1.55	1.41	1.47	1.24	1.30	1.35
Debt to Equity	1.12	1.23	0.77	0.66	0.64	0.70	0.77	0.36
Price Range	73.50-56.04	73.50-58.52	64.04-48.87	53.68-34.81	36.97-26.43	33.54-22.55	29.90-22.28	25.70-15.52
P/E Ratio	37.31-28.45	33.56-26.72	27.25-20.80	31.95-20.72	23.85-17.05	21.92-14.74	26.00-19.37	58.41-35.27
Average Yield %	1.62	1.59	1.73	2.01	2.47	0.69	0.76	0.96

Address: 601 Riverside Avenue, Jacksonville, FL 32204 **Telephone:** 904-438-6000	**Web Site:** www.fisglobal.com **Officers:** Frank R. Martire - Chairman, President, Chief Executive Officer Anthony M. Jabbour - Corporate Executive Vice President, Chief Operating Officer	**Auditors:** KPMG LLP **Transfer Agents:** Computershare Investor Services, LLC, Chicago, IL

FIRST AMERICAN FINANCIAL CORP

Exchange	Symbol	Price	52Wk Range	Yield	P/E
NYS	FAF	$38.24 (5/31/2016)	42.36-32.44	2.72	13.91

*7 Year Price Score N/A   *NYSE Composite Index=100   *12 Month Price Score 97.64

Interim Earnings (Per Share)

Qtr.	Mar	Jun	Sep	Dec
2013	0.33	0.31	0.59	0.48
2014	0.20	0.47	0.74	0.74
2015	0.34	0.85	0.69	0.74
2016	0.47	...	...	...

Interim Dividends (Per Share)

Amt	Decl	Ex	Rec	Pay
0.25Q	08/18/2015	09/03/2015	09/08/2015	09/15/2015
0.25Q	11/04/2015	12/08/2015	12/08/2015	12/15/2015
0.26Q	01/20/2016	03/04/2016	03/08/2016	03/15/2016
0.26Q	05/10/2016	06/06/2016	06/08/2016	06/15/2016

Indicated Div: $1.04

Valuation Analysis   Institutional Holding

Forecast EPS	$2.84	No of Institutions
	(05/20/2016)	304
Market Cap	$4.2 Billion	Shares
Book Value	$2.8 Billion	100,395,800
Price/Book	1.47	% Held
Price/Sales	0.80	96.19

Business Summary: General Insurance (MIC: 5.2.1 SIC: 6361 NAIC: 524127)

First American Financial is a holding company. Through its subsidiaries, Co. is engaged in the business of providing financial services through its title insurance and services segment and its specialty insurance segment. The title insurance and services segment provides title insurance, closing and/or escrow services and similar or related services in connection with residential and commercial real estate transactions. This segment also maintains, manages and provides access to title plant records and images and provides banking, trust and investment advisory services. The specialty insurance segment issues property and casualty insurance policies and sells home warranty products.

Recent Developments: For the quarter ended Mar 31 2016, net income increased 39.4% to US$52.7 million from US$37.8 million in the year-earlier quarter. Revenues were US$1.20 billion, up 8.2% from US$1.11 billion the year before. Net premiums earned were US$1.01 billion versus US$934.3 million in the prior-year quarter, an increase of 8.5%. Net investment income rose 65.7% to US$32.5 million from US$19.6 million a year ago.

Prospects: Our evaluation of First American Financial Corp. as of June 19, 2016 is the result of our systematic analysis on three basic characteristics: earnings strength, relative valuation, and recent stock price movement. The company has produced a positive trend in earnings per share over the past 5 quarters and while recent estimates for the company have remained steady, FAF has posted better than expected results. Based on operating earnings yield, the company is undervalued when compared to all of the companies in our coverage universe. Share price changes over the past year indicates that FAF will perform in line with the market over the near term.

Financial Data
(US$ in Thousands)

	3 Mos	12/31/2015	12/31/2014	12/31/2013	12/31/2012	12/31/2011	12/31/2010	12/31/2009
Earnings Per Share	2.75	2.62	2.15	1.71	2.77	0.73	1.20	...
Cash Flow Per Share	5.10	5.08	3.37	3.54	4.03	1.27	1.49	...
Tang Book Value Per Share	16.67	16.00	14.48	14.74	13.48	10.91	10.51	...
Dividends Per Share	1.010	1.000	0.840	0.480	0.360	0.240	0.400	0.880
Dividend Payout %	36.73	38.17	39.07	28.07	13.00	32.88	33.33	...
Income Statement								
Total Revenue	1,201,712	5,175,456	4,677,949	4,956,077	4,541,821	3,820,574	3,906,612	4,046,834
Income Before Taxes	75,592	432,765	350,560	310,708	467,406	130,293	212,106	204,345
Income Taxes	22,920	143,895	116,345	123,644	165,678	51,714	83,150	70,068
Net Income	52,501	288,086	233,534	186,367	301,041	78,276	127,829	122,389
Average Shares	110,670	109,826	108,688	109,102	108,542	106,914	106,177	...
Balance Sheet								
Total Assets	8,279,255	8,254,351	7,666,100	6,520,600	6,050,847	5,370,337	5,821,826	5,530,281
Total Liabilities	5,435,947	5,495,849	5,093,183	4,067,551	3,702,782	3,341,737	3,841,809	3,510,481
Stockholders' Equity	2,843,308	2,758,502	2,572,917	2,453,049	2,348,065	2,028,600	1,980,017	2,019,800
Shares Outstanding	109,564	109,098	107,541	105,900	107,239	105,410	104,457	...
Statistical Record								
Return on Assets %	3.76	3.62	3.29	2.96	5.26	1.40	...	2.19
Return on Equity %	11.12	10.81	9.29	7.76	13.72	3.91	...	6.26
Net Margin %	4.37	5.57	4.99	3.76	6.63	2.05	3.27	3.02
Asset Turnover	0.65	0.65	0.66	0.79	0.79	0.68	...	0.72
Price Range	42.36-32.44	42.36-32.65	34.30-24.92	28.26-20.53	24.69-12.75	17.06-10.51	15.66-12.31	...
P/E Ratio	15.40-11.80	16.17-12.46	15.95-11.59	16.53-12.01	8.91-4.60	23.37-14.40	13.05-10.26	...
Average Yield %	2.71	2.70	2.99	1.97	1.94	1.65	2.80	...

Address: 1 First American Way, Santa Ana, CA 92707-5913 **Telephone:** 714-250-3000 **Fax:** 714-250-3151	**Web Site:** www.firstam.com **Officers:** Parker S. Kennedy - Executive Chairman George L. Argyros - Chairman, Chief Executive Officer	**Auditors:** PricewaterhouseCoopers LLP **Investor Contact:** 714-250-5214 **Transfer Agents:** Wells Fargo Shareowner Services

293

FIRST HORIZON NATIONAL CORP

Exchange	Symbol	Price	52Wk Range	Yield	P/E
NYS	FHN	$14.56 (5/31/2016)	16.20-11.62	1.92	16.74

*7 Year Price Score 105.40 *NYSE Composite Index=100 *12 Month Price Score 96.83

Interim Earnings (Per Share)

Qtr.	Mar	Jun	Sep	Dec
2013	0.17	0.17	(0.45)	0.21
2014	0.19	0.32	0.19	0.21
2015	(0.33)	0.22	0.25	0.20
2016	0.20	...	...	...

Interim Dividends (Per Share)

Amt	Decl	Ex	Rec	Pay
0.06Q	07/21/2015	09/09/2015	09/11/2015	10/01/2015
0.06Q	10/20/2015	12/09/2015	12/11/2015	01/04/2016
0.07Q	01/26/2016	03/09/2016	03/11/2016	04/01/2016
0.07Q	04/26/2016	06/08/2016	06/10/2016	07/01/2016

Indicated Div: $0.28

Valuation Analysis   **Institutional Holding**

Forecast EPS	$0.92 (05/16/2016)	No of Institutions 370
Market Cap	$3.4 Billion	Shares 201,920,128
Book Value	$2.3 Billion	% Held
Price/Book	1.44	82.19
Price/Sales	2.66	

TRADING VOLUME (thousand shares)

Business Summary: Banking (MIC: 5.1.1 SIC: 6021 NAIC: 522110)

First Horizon National is a bank holding company. Co. provides financial services primarily through its subsidiary, First Tennessee Bank National Association. Co. has four business segments: regional banking, which provides financial products and services; fixed income, which consists of fixed income securities sales, trading, and strategies for institutional clients; corporate, which consists of unallocated corporate expenses, expense on subordinated debt issuances, and unallocated interest income; and non-strategic, which consists of the wind-down national consumer lending activities. As of Dec 31 2015, Co. had total assets of $26.0 billion and total deposits of $20.1 billion.

Recent Developments: For the quarter ended Mar 31 2016, net income amounted to US$52.2 million versus a net loss of US$72.4 million in the year-earlier quarter. Net interest income increased 9.7% to US$172.1 million from US$156.9 million in the year-earlier quarter. Provision for loan losses was US$3.0 million versus US$5.0 million in the prior-year quarter, a decrease of 40.0%. Non-interest income rose 3.6% to US$134.3 million from US$129.7 million, while non-interest expense declined 39.7% to US$226.9 million.

Prospects: Our evaluation of First Horizon National Corp. as of June 19, 2016 is the result of our systematic analysis on three basic characteristics: earnings strength, relative valuation, and recent stock price movement. The company has managed to produce a neutral trend in earnings per share over the past 5 quarters and while recent estimates for the company have remained steady, FHN has posted better than expected results. Based on operating earnings yield, the company is undervalued when compared to all of the companies in our coverage universe. Share price changes over the past year indicates that FHN will perform in line with the market over the near term.

Financial Data
(US$ in Thousands)

	3 Mos	12/31/2015	12/31/2014	12/31/2013	12/31/2012	12/31/2011	12/31/2010	12/31/2009
Earnings Per Share	0.87	0.34	0.91	0.10	(0.11)	0.50	(0.25)	(1.49)
Cash Flow Per Share	1.69	1.57	3.00	1.81	1.49	0.17	3.26	3.56
Tang Book Value Per Share	8.75	8.51	8.63	7.92	7.98	8.10	7.52	7.67
Dividends Per Share	0.250	0.240	0.200	0.200	0.040	0.040	...	...
Dividend Payout %	28.74	70.59	21.98	200.00	...	8.00	...	...
Income Statement								
Interest Income	193,664	736,405	709,249	732,053	798,953	832,437	880,286	992,939
Interest Expense	21,590	82,685	81,531	94,679	110,286	131,605	149,448	216,471
Net Interest Income	172,074	653,720	627,718	637,374	688,667	700,832	730,838	776,468
Provision for Losses	3,000	9,000	27,000	55,000	78,000	44,000	270,000	880,000
Non-Interest Income	134,305	517,325	550,044	584,577	671,329	786,011	955,692	1,233,531
Non-Interest Expense	226,927	1,053,791	841,211	1,158,601	1,383,701	1,292,995	1,367,133	1,550,533
Income Before Taxes	76,452	108,254	309,551	8,350	(101,705)	149,848	49,397	(420,534)
Income Taxes	24,239	10,941	78,501	(32,169)	(85,262)	15,836	(19,083)	(174,945)
Net Income	49,362	85,879	219,523	29,602	(27,759)	131,196	50,201	(269,837)
Average Shares	236,666	236,266	236,735	239,794	248,349	262,861	235,699	220,412
Balance Sheet								
Net Loans & Leases	17,487,230	17,602,602	16,139,003	15,505,417	16,833,556	16,426,673	16,493,062	17,679,471
Total Assets	26,963,682	26,195,136	25,672,887	23,789,833	25,520,140	24,789,384	24,698,952	26,068,678
Total Deposits	20,327,834	19,967,478	18,068,939	16,734,956	16,629,709	16,213,009	15,208,231	14,867,215
Total Liabilities	24,616,165	23,850,981	23,377,350	21,584,513	23,306,099	22,399,912	22,316,112	23,061,375
Stockholders' Equity	2,347,517	2,344,155	2,295,537	2,205,320	2,214,041	2,389,472	2,382,840	3,007,303
Shares Outstanding	232,547	238,586	234,219	236,369	243,597	257,468	263,366	221,980
Statistical Record								
Return on Assets %	0.80	0.33	0.89	0.12	N.M.	0.53	0.20	N.M.
Return on Equity %	9.25	3.70	9.75	1.34	N.M.	5.50	1.86	N.M.
Net Interest Margin %	88.85	88.77	88.50	87.07	86.20	84.19	83.02	78.20
Efficiency Ratio %	69.19	84.05	66.80	88.00	94.11	79.89	74.46	69.64
Loans to Deposits	0.86	0.88	0.89	0.93	1.01	1.01	1.08	1.19
Price Range	16.20-11.62	16.20-12.31	13.91-11.18	12.55-9.72	10.89-7.55	12.53-5.63	14.83-9.24	13.68-6.52
P/E Ratio	18.62-13.36	47.65-36.21	15.29-12.29	125.50-97.20	...	25.06-11.26	...	...
Average Yield %	1.75	1.65	1.66	1.80	0.44	0.43	...	...

Address: 165 Madison Avenue, Memphis, TN 38103 **Telephone:** 901-523-4444	**Web Site:** www.firsthorizon.com **Officers:** D. Bryan Jordan - Chairman, President, Chief Executive Officer David T. Popwell - Chief Operating Officer, Division Officer	**Auditors:** KPMG LLP **Investor Contact:** 800-410-4577 **Transfer Agents:** Wells Fargo

FIRST REPUBLIC BANK (SAN FRANCISCO, CA)

Exchange	Symbol	Price	52Wk Range	Yield	P/E
NYS	FRC	$72.41 (5/31/2016)	72.49-56.59	0.88	21.68

*7 Year Price Score N/A   *NYSE Composite Index=100   *12 Month Price Score 105.29

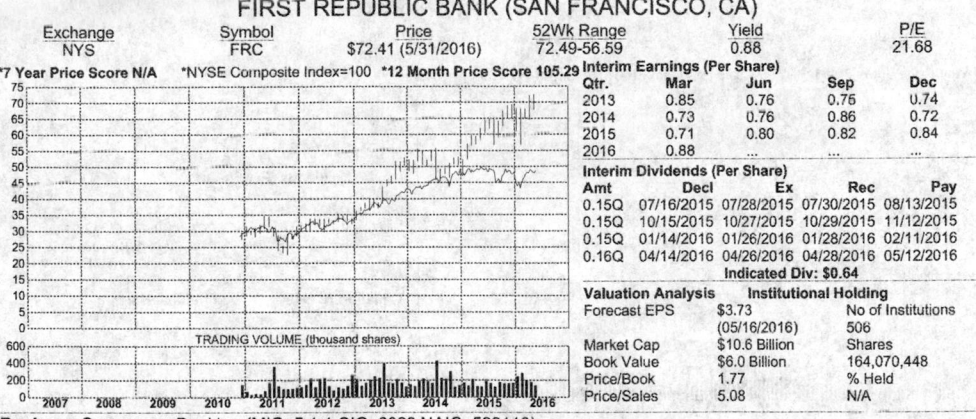

Interim Earnings (Per Share)

Qtr.	Mar	Jun	Sep	Dec
2013	0.85	0.76	0.75	0.74
2014	0.73	0.76	0.86	0.72
2015	0.71	0.80	0.82	0.84
2016	0.88	...	...	...

Interim Dividends (Per Share)

Amt	Decl	Ex	Rec	Pay
0.15Q	07/16/2015	07/28/2015	07/30/2015	08/13/2015
0.15Q	10/15/2015	10/27/2015	10/29/2015	11/12/2015
0.15Q	01/14/2016	01/26/2016	01/28/2016	02/11/2016
0.16Q	04/14/2016	04/26/2016	04/28/2016	05/12/2016

Indicated Div: $0.64

Valuation Analysis / Institutional Holding

Forecast EPS	$3.73	No of Institutions
	(05/16/2016)	506
Market Cap	$10.6 Billion	Shares
Book Value	$6.0 Billion	164,070,448
Price/Book	1.77	% Held
Price/Sales	5.08	N/A

Business Summary: Banking (MIC: 5.1.1 SIC: 6029 NAIC: 522110)

First Republic Bank is commercial bank and trust company. Co. is engaged in providing personalized, relationship-based services, including private banking, private business banking, real estate lending and wealth management services, including trust and custody services, to clients in selected metropolitan areas in the U.S. Co. operates its business through two segments: Commercial Banking and Wealth Management. Co. provides its services in the following areas: San Francisco, Palo Alto, Los Angeles, Santa Barbara, Newport Beach, San Diego, Portland, Boston, Palm Beach, Greenwich and New York City. At Dec 31 2014, Co. had total assets of $48.35 billion and total deposits of $37.13 billion.

Recent Developments: For the quarter ended Mar 31 2016, net income increased 28.4% to US$148.9 million from US$115.9 million in the year-earlier quarter. Net interest income increased 21.9% to US$424.3 million from US$348.0 million in the year-earlier quarter. Provision for loan losses was US$4.5 million versus US$11.9 million in the prior-year quarter, a decrease of 62.2%. Non-interest income rose 27.1% to US$95.3 million from US$74.9 million, while non-interest expense advanced 24.8% to US$319.2 million.

Prospects: Our evaluation of First Republic Bank as of June 19, 2016 is the result of our systematic analysis on three basic characteristics: earnings strength, relative valuation, and recent stock price movement. The company has produced a positive trend in earnings per share over the past 5 quarters. However, while recent estimates for the company have been lowered by analysts, FRC has posted better than expected results. Based on operating earnings yield, the company is undervalued when compared to all of the companies in our coverage universe. Share price changes over the past year indicates that FRC will perform well over the near term.

Financial Data
(US$ in Thousands)

	3 Mos	12/31/2015	12/31/2014	12/31/2013	12/31/2012	12/31/2011	12/31/2010
Earnings Per Share	3.34	3.18	3.07	3.10	2.76	2.65	1.12
Cash Flow Per Share	...	...	3.64	4.28	3.37	0.50	0.17
Tang Book Value Per Share	30.68	29.80	26.21	22.61	19.93	18.10	15.01
Dividends Per Share	0.600	0.590	0.540	0.360	0.300	...	...
Dividend Payout %	17.96	18.55	17.59	11.61	10.87	...	...
Income Statement							
Total Revenue	554,803	1,989,145	1,801,364	1,600,368	1,455,940	1,300,887	593,247
Income Before Taxes	195,879	690,668	669,883	663,559	601,347	554,732	241,265
Income Taxes	47,013	168,523	182,877	201,489	197,337	198,039	96,507
Net Income	148,866	522,145	487,006	462,070	402,472	352,088	142,362
Average Shares	149,719	145,510	140,497	135,949	134,189	132,724	126,776
Balance Sheet							
Total Assets	62,102,510	58,981,285	48,353,330	42,112,763	34,387,677	27,791,801	22,377,633
Total Liabilities	56,117,785	53,275,602	43,574,863	37,952,716	30,989,133	25,274,039	20,239,447
Stockholders' Equity	5,984,725	5,705,683	4,778,467	4,160,047	3,398,544	2,517,762	2,138,186
Shares Outstanding	146,313	146,109	138,268	132,768	131,273	129,371	128,858
Statistical Record							
Return on Assets %	0.98	0.97	1.08	1.21	1.29	1.40	0.67
Return on Equity %	10.04	9.96	10.90	12.23	13.57	15.12	8.29
Net Margin %	26.83	26.25	27.04	28.87	27.64	27.07	24.00
Asset Turnover	0.04	0.04	0.04	0.04	0.05	0.05	0.03
Price Range	69.28-56.59	69.28-47.62	55.62-45.77	52.72-32.78	34.95-29.53	34.60-22.48	29.45-27.31
P/E Ratio	20.74-16.94	21.79-14.97	18.12-14.91	17.01-10.57	12.66-10.70	13.06-8.48	26.29-24.38
Average Yield %	0.95	0.97	1.06	0.85	0.92	...	...

Address: 111 Pine Street, 2nd Floor, San Francisco, CA 94111 **Telephone:** 800-392-1400	**Web Site:** www.firstrepublic.com **Officers:** James H. Herbert - Chairman, Chief Executive Officer Katherine August-deWilde - Vice-Chairman, President, Chief Operating Officer	**Auditors:** KPMG LLP **Investor Contact:** 415-392-1400 **Transfer Agents:** Common and Preferred Stock At** Computershare Shareowner Services, LLC

FIRSTENERGY CORP

Exchange	Symbol	Price	52Wk Range	Yield	P/E
NYS	FE	$32.81 (5/31/2016)	36.34-29.12	4.39	20.38

*7 Year Price Score 72.23 *NYSE Composite Index=100 *12 Month Price Score 101.42

TRADING VOLUME (thousand shares)

Interim Earnings (Per Share)

Qtr.	Mar	Jun	Sep	Dec
2013	0.47	(0.39)	0.52	0.34
2014	0.49	0.15	0.79	(0.73)
2015	0.53	0.44	0.93	(0.53)
2016	0.77			

Interim Dividends (Per Share)

Amt	Decl	Ex	Rec	Pay
0.36Q	07/21/2015	08/05/2015	08/07/2015	09/01/2015
0.36Q	09/15/2015	11/04/2015	11/06/2015	12/01/2015
0.36Q	01/19/2016	02/03/2016	02/05/2016	03/01/2016
0.36Q	03/15/2016	05/04/2016	05/06/2016	06/01/2016

Indicated Div: $1.44

Valuation Analysis **Institutional Holding**

Forecast EPS	$2.68	No of Institutions	745
	(05/20/2016)		
Market Cap	$13.9 Billion	Shares	343,587,808
Book Value	$12.5 Billion	% Held	74.79
Price/Book	1.12		
Price/Sales	0.93		

Business Summary: Electric Utilities (MIC: 3.1.1 SIC: 4911 NAIC: 221121)

FirstEnergy is a public utility holding company. Through its utility operating subsidiaries, Ohio Edison Company, The Cleveland Electric Illuminating Company, The Toledo Edison Company, Pennsylvania Power Company, Jersey Central Power & Light Company, Metropolitan Edison Company, Pennsylvania Electric Company, Monongahela Power Company, The Potomac Edison Company, West Penn Power Company, American Transmission Systems, Inc. and also Trans-Allegheny Interstate Line Company (the Utilities), Co. is engaged in providing electric service. The Utilities' combined service areas encompass approximately 65,000 square miles in Ohio, Pennsylvania, West Virginia, Maryland, New Jersey and New York.

Recent Developments: For the quarter ended Mar 31 2016, net income increased 47.7% to US$328.0 million from US$222.0 million in the year-earlier quarter. Revenues were US$3.87 billion, down 0.7% from US$3.90 billion the year before. Operating income was US$776.0 million versus US$594.0 million in the prior-year quarter, an increase of 30.6%. Direct operating expenses declined 9.7% to US$2.42 billion from US$2.68 billion in the comparable period the year before. Indirect operating expenses increased 8.1% to US$670.0 million from US$620.0 million in the equivalent prior-year period.

Prospects: Our evaluation of FirstEnergy Corp. as of June 19, 2016 is the result of our systematic analysis on three basic characteristics: earnings strength, relative valuation, and recent stock price movement. The company has managed to produce a neutral trend in earnings per share over the past 5 quarters. However, while recent estimates for the company have been lowered by analysts, FE has posted better than expected results. Based on operating earnings yield, the company is undervalued when compared to all of the companies in our coverage universe. Share price changes over the past year indicates that FE will perform well over the near term.

Financial Data

(US$ in Thousands)	3 Mos	12/31/2015	12/31/2014	12/31/2013	12/31/2012	12/31/2011	12/31/2010	12/31/2009
Earnings Per Share	1.61	1.37	0.71	0.94	1.84	2.21	2.57	3.29
Cash Flow Per Share	9.18	8.17	6.46	6.37	5.54	7.68	10.12	8.11
Tang Book Value Per Share	14.23	14.17	14.25	14.99	15.87	16.35	9.74	9.79
Dividends Per Share	1.440	1.440	1.440	2.200	2.200	2.200	2.200	2.200
Dividend Payout %	89.44	105.11	202.82	234.04	119.57	99.55	85.60	66.87
Income Statement								
Total Revenue	3,869,000	15,026,000	15,049,000	14,917,000	15,303,000	16,258,000	13,339,000	12,967,000
EBITDA	1,259,000	3,190,000	2,346,000	2,713,000	3,377,000	3,502,000	2,668,000	2,819,000
Depn & Amortn	455,000	1,282,000	1,220,000	1,202,000	1,124,000	1,121,000	746,000	736,000
Income Before Taxes	541,000	893,000	171,000	570,000	1,324,000	1,443,000	1,242,000	1,235,000
Income Taxes	213,000	315,000	(42,000)	195,000	553,000	574,000	482,000	245,000
Net Income	328,000	578,000	299,000	392,000	770,000	885,000	784,000	1,006,000
Average Shares	426,000	424,000	421,000	419,000	419,000	401,000	305,000	306,000
Balance Sheet								
Current Assets	3,230,000	3,040,000	3,876,000	3,887,000	3,768,000	3,355,000	3,698,000	3,320,000
Total Assets	52,695,000	52,187,000	52,166,000	50,424,000	50,406,000	47,326,000	34,805,000	34,304,000
Current Liabilities	6,389,000	5,602,000	5,561,000	7,637,000	7,605,000	4,855,000	4,698,000	5,288,000
Long-Term Obligations	18,878,000	19,192,000	19,176,000	15,831,000	15,179,000	15,716,000	12,579,000	11,908,000
Total Liabilities	40,232,000	39,766,000	39,746,000	37,732,000	37,322,000	34,046,000	26,260,000	25,745,000
Stockholders' Equity	12,463,000	12,421,000	12,420,000	12,692,000	13,084,000	13,280,000	8,545,000	8,559,000
Shares Outstanding	424,712	423,560	421,102	418,628	418,216	418,216	304,835	304,835
Statistical Record								
Return on Assets %	1.30	1.11	0.58	0.78	1.57	2.16	2.27	2.97
Return on Equity %	5.51	4.65	2.38	3.04	5.83	8.11	9.17	11.95
EBITDA Margin %	32.54	21.23	15.59	18.19	22.07	21.54	20.00	21.74
Net Margin %	8.48	3.85	1.99	2.63	5.03	5.44	5.88	7.76
Asset Turnover	0.29	0.29	0.29	0.30	0.31	0.40	0.39	0.38
Current Ratio	0.51	0.54	0.70	0.51	0.50	0.69	0.79	0.63
Debt to Equity	1.51	1.55	1.54	1.25	1.16	1.18	1.47	1.39
Price Range	36.65-29.12	41.37-29.12	40.77-30.22	46.60-31.60	50.87-40.72	46.02-36.25	47.03-34.03	52.96-35.79
P/E Ratio	22.76-18.09	30.20-21.26	57.42-42.56	49.57-33.62	27.65-22.13	20.82-16.40	18.30-13.24	16.10-10.88
Average Yield %	4.34	4.22	4.26	5.67	4.88	5.24	5.77	5.08

Address: 76 South Main Street, Akron, OH 44308	Web Site: www.firstenergycorp.com	Auditors: PricewaterhouseCoopers LLP
Telephone: 800-736-3402	Officers: Anthony J. Alexander - Chairman, President, Chief Executive Officer Charles E. Jones - President, Chief Executive Officer, Division Officer	Investor Contact: 330-384-3859 Transfer Agents: American Stock Transfer & Trust Company, LLC, New York, NY

FLEETCOR TECHNOLOGIES INC

Exchange	Symbol	Price	52Wk Range	Yield	P/E
NYS	FLT	$148.89 (5/31/2016)	163.86-113.39	N/A	37.04

*7 Year Price Score N/A ***NYSE Composite Index=100** ***12 Month Price Score 102.26**

Interim Earnings (Per Share)

Qtr.	Mar	Jun	Sep	Dec
2013	0.77	0.87	0.93	0.80
2014	0.88	1.03	1.11	1.22
2015	1.00	1.05	1.24	0.56
2016	1.17	...	...	...

Interim Dividends (Per Share)

No Dividends Paid

Valuation Analysis

		Institutional Holding	
Forecast EPS	$6.63	No of Institutions	416
	(05/17/2016)		
Market Cap	$13.8 Billion	Shares	88,797,528
Book Value	$3.0 Billion		
Price/Book	4.61	% Held	91.60
Price/Sales	8.10		

TRADING VOLUME (thousand shares)

Business Summary: Business Services (MIC: 7.5.2 SIC: 7389 NAIC: 522320)

FleetCor Technologies is a provider of fuel cards and workforce payment products and services to businesses, retailers, commercial fleets, oil companies, petroleum marketers and government entities in countries throughout North America, Latin America, Europe, Australia and New Zealand. Co. sells a range of customized fleet and lodging payment programs. Co. provide its customers with various card products that typically function like a charge card to purchase fuel, lodging, food, toll, transportation and related products and services at participating locations. Co. operates in two segments, which it refers to as its North America and International segments.

Recent Developments: For the quarter ended Mar 31 2016, net income increased 16.8% to US$110.0 million from US$94.2 million in the year-earlier quarter. Revenues were US$414.3 million, down 0.5% from US$416.2 million the year before. Operating income was US$176.0 million versus US$163.8 million in the prior-year quarter, an increase of 7.4%. Indirect operating expenses decreased 5.6% to US$238.3 million from US$252.4 million in the equivalent prior-year period.

Prospects: Our evaluation of FleetCor Technologies Inc. as of June 19, 2016 is the result of our systematic analysis on three basic characteristics: earnings strength, relative valuation, and recent stock price movement. The company has generated a negative trend in earnings per share over the past 5 quarters and while recent estimates for the company have remained steady, FLT has posted better than expected results. Based on operating earnings yield, the company is about fairly valued when compared to all of the companies in our coverage universe. Share price changes over the past year indicates that FLT will perform in line with the market over the near term.

Financial Data
(US$ in Thousands)

	3 Mos	12/31/2015	12/31/2014	12/31/2013	12/31/2012	12/31/2011	12/31/2010	12/31/2009
Earnings Per Share	4.02	3.85	4.24	3.36	2.52	1.76	1.34	1.13
Cash Flow Per Share	8.74	8.20	7.21	4.59	1.62	3.47	3.94	5.29
Income Statement								
Total Revenue	414,262	1,702,865	1,199,390	895,171	707,534	519,591	433,841	354,073
EBITDA	213,446	855,251	657,634	486,243	370,283	255,344	200,317	170,478
Depn & Amortn	38,150	190,240	107,249	66,213	46,476	31,090	28,505	23,500
Income Before Taxes	159,105	593,672	521,529	403,569	310,790	210,877	151,280	129,615
Income Taxes	46,940	173,573	144,236	119,068	94,591	63,542	43,384	40,563
Net Income	109,972	362,431	368,707	284,501	216,199	147,335	107,896	89,052
Average Shares	94,329	94,139	86,982	84,655	85,736	83,654	80,751	78,854
Balance Sheet								
Current Assets	2,054,581	1,945,172	2,137,350	1,353,512	1,195,354	1,122,925	618,983	347,242
Total Assets	8,011,830	7,891,868	8,674,506	3,932,235	2,721,870	2,324,492	1,484,118	1,209,545
Current Liabilities	2,238,014	2,248,021	2,896,618	1,908,898	1,142,222	1,121,747	461,122	320,741
Long-Term Obligations	2,032,905	2,061,415	2,168,953	474,939	485,217	278,429	313,796	328,930
Total Liabilities	5,024,061	5,061,821	5,921,369	2,688,342	1,808,048	1,513,056	858,173	735,496
Stockholders' Equity	2,987,769	2,830,047	2,753,137	1,243,893	913,822	811,436	625,945	474,049
Shares Outstanding	92,551	92,376	91,662	82,471	81,037	81,860	79,655	34,025
Statistical Record								
Return on Assets %	4.58	4.38	5.85	8.55	8.55	7.74	8.01	8.33
Return on Equity %	13.12	12.98	18.45	26.37	24.99	20.50	19.62	23.83
EBITDA Margin %	51.52	50.22	54.83	54.32	52.33	49.14	46.17	48.15
Net Margin %	26.55	21.28	30.74	31.78	30.56	28.36	24.87	25.15
Asset Turnover	0.21	0.21	0.19	0.27	0.28	0.27	0.32	0.33
Current Ratio	0.92	0.87	0.74	0.71	1.05	1.00	1.34	1.08
Debt to Equity	0.68	0.73	0.79	0.38	0.53	0.34	0.50	0.69
Price Range	163.86-113.39	163.86-137.02	156.05-101.69	122.70-53.65	53.65-30.55	37.51-25.25	31.06-27.25	...
P/E Ratio	40.76-28.21	42.56-35.59	36.80-23.98	36.52-15.97	21.29-12.12	21.31-14.35	23.18-20.34	...

Address: 5445 Triangle Parkway, Suite 400, Norcross, GA 30092-2575 **Telephone:** 770-449-0479	**Web Site:** www.fleetcor.com **Officers:** Ronald F. Clarke - Chairman, President, Chief Executive Officer John A. Reed - Global Chief Information Officer	**Auditors:** Ernst & Young LLP **Investor Contact:** 770-729-2017 **Transfer Agents:** American Stock Transfer & Trust Company, LLC, Brooklyn, NY

FLOWERS FOODS, INC.

Exchange	Symbol	Price	52Wk Range	Yield	P/E	Div Achiever
NYS	FLO	$18.75 (5/31/2016)	27.09-15.71	3.17	21.31	12 Years

*7 Year Price Score 110.62 *NYSE Composite Index=100   ***12 Month Price Score 85.86**

TRADING VOLUME (thousand shares)

Interim Earnings (Per Share)

Qtr.	Apr	Jul	Oct	Jan
2014-17	0.29	0.20	0.21	0.13
2015-16	0.29	0.24	0.21	0.15
2016-17	0.28	...	...	...

Interim Dividends (Per Share)

Amt	Decl	Ex	Rec	Pay
0.145Q	08/18/2015	08/28/2015	09/01/2015	09/15/2015
0.145Q	11/20/2015	12/02/2015	12/04/2015	12/18/2015
0.145Q	02/19/2016	03/02/2016	03/04/2016	03/18/2016
0.16Q	05/26/2016	06/07/2016	06/09/2016	06/23/2016

Indicated Div: $0.59 (Div. Reinv. Plan)

Valuation Analysis   **Institutional Holding**

Forecast EPS	$1.01	No of Institutions
	(05/20/2016)	398
Market Cap	$3.9 Billion	Shares
Book Value	$1.2 Billion	139,583,920
Price/Book	3.36	% Held
Price/Sales	1.01	61.08

Business Summary: Food (MIC: 1.2.1 SIC: 2053 NAIC: 311813)

Flowers Foods is a producer and marketer of bakery products. Co. has two business segments: a direct-store-delivery (DSD) and a warehouse delivery (warehouse). The DSD Segment operates bakeries that market a range of bakery foods, including breads, buns, rolls, tortillas, and snack cakes. These products are sold through a DSD model to retail and foodservice customers in the Southeast, Mid-Atlantic, New England, Southwest, California and select markets in Nevada. The Warehouse Segment operates bakeries that produce snack cakes, breads and rolls for national retail, foodservice, vending, and co-pack customers, which are delivered through customers' warehouse channels and one bakery mix plant.

Recent Developments: For the quarter ended Apr 23 2016, net income decreased 3.3% to US$59.4 million from US$61.4 million in the year-earlier quarter. Revenues were US$1.20 billion, up 5.1% from US$1.15 billion the year before. Operating income was US$95.2 million versus US$96.5 million in the prior-year quarter, a decrease of 1.4%. Direct operating expenses rose 6.0% to US$621.2 million from US$585.9 million in the comparable period the year before. Indirect operating expenses increased 5.3% to US$488.0 million from US$463.6 million in the equivalent prior-year period.

Prospects: Our evaluation of Flowers Foods Inc. as of June 19, 2016 is the result of our systematic analysis on three basic characteristics: earnings strength, relative valuation, and recent stock price movement. The company has managed to produce a neutral trend in earnings per share over the past 5 quarters. However, while recent estimates for the company have been mixed, FLO has posted results that fell short of analysts expectations. Based on operating earnings yield, the company is undervalued when compared to all of the companies in our coverage universe. Share price changes over the past year indicates that FLO will perform well over the near term.

Financial Data

(US$ in Thousands)	3 Mos	01/02/2016	01/03/2015	12/28/2013	12/29/2012	12/31/2011	01/01/2011	01/02/2010
Earnings Per Share	0.88	0.89	0.82	1.09	0.65	0.60	0.66	0.63
Cash Flow Per Share	...	1.54	1.47	1.30	1.06	0.66	1.49	1.14
Tang Book Value Per Share	N.M.	N.M.	0.93	0.66	0.97	1.95	2.44	2.00
Dividends Per Share	0.580	0.568	0.485	0.444	0.420	0.389	0.344	0.300
Dividend Payout %	65.91	63.76	59.15	40.75	64.29	64.81	52.02	47.87
Income Statement								
Total Revenue	1,204,352	3,778,505	3,748,973	3,751,005	3,046,491	2,773,356	2,573,769	2,600,849
EBITDA	138,623	414,679	392,595	441,933	311,911	276,526	284,962	281,433
Depn & Amortn	43,467	116,800	117,200	106,700	93,400	87,500	79,100	75,100
Income Before Taxes	92,378	293,031	268,054	322,373	208,772	191,966	210,380	207,759
Income Taxes	33,015	103,840	92,315	91,479	72,651	68,538	73,333	74,047
Net Income	59,363	189,191	175,739	230,894	136,121	123,428	137,047	130,297
Average Shares	212,836	213,356	213,092	211,927	207,673	205,321	207,243	208,649
Balance Sheet								
Current Assets	495,129	537,515	460,563	487,405	464,451	378,570	313,714	338,955
Total Assets	2,815,672	2,885,168	2,408,974	2,504,014	1,995,849	1,553,998	1,325,489	1,351,442
Current Liabilities	440,538	403,738	315,553	327,782	354,958	268,419	242,772	221,772
Long-Term Obligations	953,821	933,932	728,940	892,478	535,016	283,406	98,870	225,905
Total Liabilities	1,659,790	1,642,086	1,285,930	1,427,825	1,137,229	795,030	529,699	635,497
Stockholders' Equity	1,155,882	1,243,082	1,123,044	1,076,189	858,620	758,968	795,790	715,945
Shares Outstanding	206,834	212,266	209,347	208,562	207,409	203,971	203,958	205,783
Statistical Record								
Return on Assets %	...	7.17	7.04	10.29	7.69	8.60	10.27	9.66
Return on Equity %	...	16.04	15.72	23.93	16.88	15.92	18.18	19.35
EBITDA Margin %	11.51	10.97	10.47	11.78	10.24	9.97	11.07	10.82
Net Margin %	4.93	5.01	4.69	6.16	4.47	4.45	5.32	5.01
Asset Turnover	...	1.43	1.50	1.67	1.72	1.93	1.93	1.93
Current Ratio	1.12	1.33	1.46	1.49	1.31	1.41	1.29	1.53
Debt to Equity	0.83	0.75	0.65	0.83	0.62	0.37	0.12	0.32
Price Range	27.09-15.71	27.09-18.85	22.19-17.67	25.39-15.51	16.09-12.30	15.31-10.81	12.01-10.41	11.68-9.10
P/E Ratio	30.78-17.85	30.44-21.18	27.06-21.55	23.29-14.23	24.75-18.92	25.52-18.02	18.20-15.77	18.55-14.45
Average Yield %	2.65	2.51	2.43	2.08	3.01	2.99	3.07	2.91

Address: 1919 Flowers Circle, Thomasville, GA 31757	Web Site: www.flowersfoods.com	Auditors: PricewaterhouseCoopers LLP
Telephone: 229-226-9110	Officers: Allen L. Shiver - President, Chief Executive Officer R. Steve Kinsey - Chief Financial Officer, Executive Vice President	Investor Contact: 229-227-2348
		Transfer Agents: Computershare, Providence, RI

FLOWSERVE CORP

Exchange	Symbol	Price	52Wk Range	Yield	P/E
NYS	FLS	$48.13 (5/31/2016)	55.60-35.40	1.58	23.03

*7 Year Price Score 82.19   *NYSE Composite Index=100   *12 Month Price Score 101.28

Interim Earnings (Per Share)

Qtr.	Mar	Jun	Sep	Dec
2013	0.67	0.84	0.90	1.00
2014	0.78	0.90	0.93	1.16
2015	0.20	0.56	0.70	0.54
2016	0.29	...	...	...

Interim Dividends (Per Share)

Amt	Decl	Ex	Rec	Pay
0.18Q	09/14/2015	09/23/2015	09/25/2015	10/09/2015
0.18Q	12/09/2015	12/21/2015	12/23/2015	01/06/2016
0.19Q	02/18/2016	03/22/2016	03/25/2016	04/08/2016
0.19Q	05/19/2016	06/22/2016	06/24/2016	07/08/2016

Indicated Div: $0.76

Valuation Analysis / **Institutional Holding**

Forecast EPS	$2.50	No of Institutions
	(05/20/2016)	606
Market Cap	$6.2 Billion	Shares
Book Value	$1.7 Billion	141,151,280
Price/Book	3.62	% Held
Price/Sales	1.39	90.85

TRADING VOLUME (thousand shares)

Business Summary: Industrial Machinery & Equipment (MIC: 7.2.1 SIC: 3561 NAIC: 333911)

Flowserve develops and manufactures flow control equipment for the movement, control and protection of the flow of materials in its customers' processes. Co.'s product portfolio of pumps, valves, seals, automation and aftermarket services supports infrastructure industries, including oil and gas, chemical, power generation and water management, as well as certain general industrial markets. Through its manufacturing platform and global network of Quick Response Centers, Co. provides a range of aftermarket equipment services, such as installation, diagnostics, repair and retrofitting. Co.'s segments are: Engineered Product Division; Industrial Product Division; and Flow Control Division.

Recent Developments: For the quarter ended Mar 31 2016, net income increased 29.1% to US$38.3 million from US$29.6 million in the year earlier quarter. Revenues were US$947.2 million, down 6.6% from US$1.01 billion the year before. Operating income was US$74.4 million versus US$93.4 million in the prior-year quarter, a decrease of 20.3%. Direct operating expenses declined 6.4% to US$639.2 million from US$682.9 million in the comparable period the year before. Indirect operating expenses decreased 2.0% to US$233.6 million from US$238.4 million in the equivalent prior-year period.

Prospects: Our evaluation of Flowserve Corp. as of June 19, 2016 is the result of our systematic analysis on three basic characteristics: earnings strength, relative valuation, and recent stock price movement. The company has produced a positive trend in earnings per share over the past 5 quarters and while recent estimates for the company have remained steady, FLS has posted results that fell short of analysts expectations. Based on operating earnings yield, the company is undervalued when compared to all of the companies in our coverage universe. Share price changes over the past year indicates that FLS will perform poorly over the near term.

Financial Data

(US$ in Thousands)	3 Mos	12/31/2015	12/31/2014	12/31/2013	12/31/2012	12/31/2011	12/31/2010	12/31/2009
Earnings Per Share	2.09	2.00	3.76	3.41	2.84	2.55	2.29	2.53
Cash Flow Per Share	3.86	3.13	4.17	3.44	3.29	1.31	2.13	2.57
Tang Book Value Per Share	1.96	1.66	5.34	4.39	4.75	6.56	5.71	4.89
Dividends Per Share	0.730	0.720	0.640	0.560	0.480	0.427	0.387	0.360
Dividend Payout %	34.93	36.00	17.02	16.42	16.92	16.75	16.86	14.23
Income Statement								
Total Revenue	947,248	4,561,030	4,877,885	4,954,619	4,751,339	4,510,201	4,032,036	4,365,262
EBITDA	95,176	575,041	873,024	797,681	725,751	693,897	606,654	662,913
Depn & Amortn	28,628	99,501	93,307	90,695	88,572	90,653	60,300	57,200
Income Before Taxes	52,656	412,335	721,075	654,004	594,613	568,644	513,628	568,955
Income Taxes	17,691	148,922	208,305	204,701	160,766	158,524	141,596	156,460
Net Income	37,859	267,669	518,824	485,530	448,339	428,582	388,290	427,887
Average Shares	130,812	133,811	137,843	142,429	157,968	168,306	169,245	169,086
Balance Sheet								
Current Assets	2,429,189	2,631,792	2,794,163	2,847,382	2,740,216	2,628,354	2,523,744	2,499,322
Total Assets	4,981,050	5,103,850	4,968,020	5,036,733	4,810,958	4,622,614	4,459,910	4,248,894
Current Liabilities	1,279,802	1,359,962	1,471,875	1,558,099	1,590,625	1,470,321	1,456,375	1,458,083
Long-Term Obligations	1,573,450	1,570,836	1,101,791	1,127,619	869,116	451,593	476,230	539,373
Total Liabilities	3,258,385	3,437,373	3,036,458	3,166,354	2,920,739	2,352,801	2,356,888	2,452,781
Stockholders' Equity	1,722,665	1,666,477	1,931,562	1,870,379	1,890,219	2,269,813	2,103,022	1,796,113
Shares Outstanding	129,632	129,090	134,349	137,163	144,405	161,718	165,177	164,868
Statistical Record								
Return on Assets %	5.43	5.32	10.37	9.86	9.48	9.44	8.92	10.34
Return on Equity %	15.99	14.88	27.29	25.82	21.50	19.60	19.92	27.05
EBITDA Margin %	10.05	12.61	17.90	16.10	15.27	15.39	15.05	15.19
Net Margin %	4.00	5.87	10.64	9.80	9.44	9.50	9.63	9.80
Asset Turnover	0.88	0.91	0.98	1.01	1.00	0.99	0.93	1.06
Current Ratio	1.90	1.94	1.90	1.83	1.72	1.79	1.73	1.71
Debt to Equity	0.91	0.94	0.57	0.60	0.46	0.20	0.23	0.30
Price Range	58.88-35.40	62.86-39.85	81.55-54.80	78.83-48.93	48.93-33.39	45.00-23.33	39.77-27.67	35.68-14.84
P/E Ratio	28.17-16.94	31.43-19.93	21.69-14.57	23.12-14.35	17.23-11.76	17.65-9.15	17.37-12.08	14.10-5.86
Average Yield %	1.56	1.42	0.88	0.96	1.19	1.19	1.12	1.40

Address: 5215 N. O'Connor Boulevard, Suite 2300, Irving, TX 75039 Telephone: 972-443-6500 Fax: 972-443-6800	Web Site: www.flowserve.com Officers: William C. Rusnack - Chairman Mark A. Blinn - President, Chief Executive Officer	Auditors: PricewaterhouseCoopers LLP Investor Contact: 972-443-6500 Transfer Agents: Wells Fargo Bank, N.A., Mendota Heights, MN

FLUOR CORP.

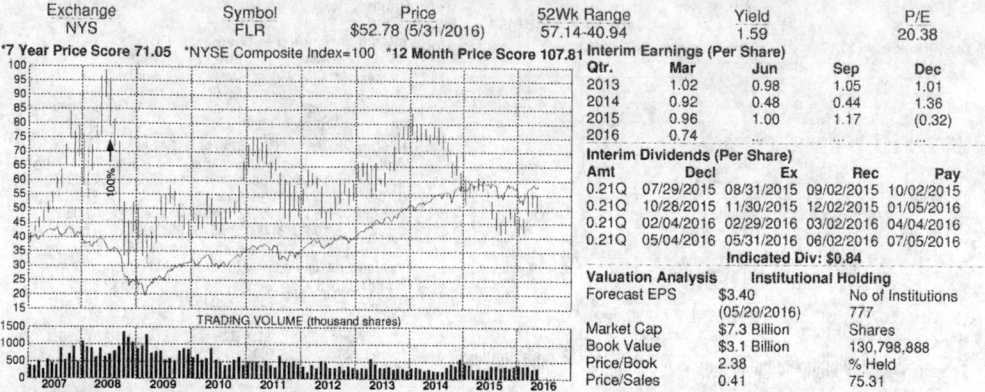

Exchange	Symbol	Price	52Wk Range	Yield	P/E
NYS	FLR	$52.78 (5/31/2016)	57.14-40.94	1.59	20.38

*7 Year Price Score 71.05 *NYSE Composite Index=100 *12 Month Price Score 107.81

Interim Earnings (Per Share)

Qtr.	Mar	Jun	Sep	Dec
2013	1.02	0.98	1.05	1.01
2014	0.92	0.48	0.44	1.36
2015	0.96	1.00	1.17	(0.32)
2016	0.74	...	...	...

Interim Dividends (Per Share)

Amt	Decl	Ex	Rec	Pay
0.21Q	07/29/2015	08/31/2015	09/02/2015	10/02/2015
0.21Q	10/28/2015	11/30/2015	12/02/2015	01/05/2016
0.21Q	02/04/2016	02/29/2016	03/02/2016	04/04/2016
0.21Q	05/04/2016	05/31/2016	06/02/2016	07/05/2016

Indicated Div: $0.84

Valuation Analysis

	Institutional Holding	
Forecast EPS $3.40 (05/20/2016)	No of Institutions 777	
Market Cap $7.3 Billion	Shares 130,798,888	
Book Value $3.1 Billion	% Held 75.31	
Price/Book 2.38		
Price/Sales 0.41		

Business Summary: Construction Services (MIC: 7.5.4 SIC: 1629 NAIC: 237990)

Fluor is a holding company. Through its subsidiaries, Co. is engaged in providing engineering, procurement, construction, fabrication and modularization, commissioning and maintenance as well as project management services. Co. serves a set of industries including oil and gas, chemicals and petrochemicals, transportation, mining and metals, power, life sciences and manufacturing. Co. is also a service provider to the U.S. federal government; and it performs operations and maintenance activities for main industrial clients. Co.'s business is organized into five principal segments: Oil and Gas, Industrial and Infrastructure, Government, Global Services and Power.

Recent Developments: For the quarter ended Mar 31 2016, net income decreased 28.1% to US$119.0 million from US$165.6 million in the year-earlier quarter. Revenues were US$4.42 billion, down 2.7% from US$4.55 billion the year before. Direct operating expenses declined 2.0% to US$4.17 billion from US$4.25 billion in the comparable period the year before. Indirect operating expenses increased 37.1% to US$66.6 million from US$48.6 million in the equivalent prior-year period.

Prospects: Our evaluation of Fluor Corp. as of June 19, 2016 is the result of our systematic analysis on three basic characteristics: earnings strength, relative valuation, and recent stock price movement. The company has managed to produce a neutral trend in earnings per share over the past 5 quarters and while recent estimates for the company have been mixed, FLR has posted results that fell short of analysts expectations. Based on operating earnings yield, the company is undervalued when compared to all of the companies in our coverage universe. Share price changes over the past year indicates that FLR will perform well over the near term.

Financial Data

(US$ in Thousands)	3 Mos	12/31/2015	12/31/2014	12/31/2013	12/31/2012	12/31/2011	12/31/2010	12/31/2009
Earnings Per Share	2.59	2.81	3.20	4.06	2.71	3.40	1.98	3.75
Cash Flow Per Share	6.65	5.86	4.08	4.85	3.75	5.16	3.09	5.02
Tang Book Value Per Share	22.18	20.76	20.17	22.59	19.96	19.53	19.32	17.99
Dividends Per Share	0.840	0.840	0.840	0.640	0.640	0.500	0.500	0.500
Dividend Payout %	32.43	29.89	26.25	15.76	23.62	14.71	25.25	13.33
Income Statement								
Total Revenue	4,423,889	18,114,048	21,531,577	27,351,573	27,577,135	23,381,399	20,849,349	21,990,297
EBITDA	261,999	944,371	1,408,916	1,397,141	946,368	1,187,395	739,566	1,304,627
Depn & Amortn	61,290	189,738	192,594	207,098	212,381	201,939	190,584	182,011
Income Before Taxes	189,220	726,552	1,204,909	1,177,599	733,505	1,001,816	559,596	1,136,788
Income Taxes	70,209	245,888	352,815	354,573	162,438	303,729	118,514	403,913
Net Income	104,323	412,512	510,909	667,711	456,330	593,728	357,496	684,889
Average Shares	140,865	146,722	159,616	164,354	168,491	174,564	180,988	180,862
Balance Sheet								
Current Assets	5,402,869	5,278,287	5,758,047	6,003,683	6,094,137	5,880,623	5,562,825	5,122,088
Total Assets	9,001,727	7,631,506	8,194,429	8,323,850	8,276,043	8,270,276	7,614,923	7,178,483
Current Liabilities	3,589,930	2,935,352	3,330,853	3,407,160	3,887,114	3,840,111	3,523,383	3,301,398
Long-Term Obligations	1,572,001	992,664	991,685	496,604	520,205	513,500	17,759	17,740
Total Liabilities	5,913,116	4,634,159	5,083,558	4,566,863	4,934,748	4,874,751	4,117,924	3,872,950
Stockholders' Equity	3,088,611	2,997,347	3,110,871	3,756,987	3,341,295	3,395,525	3,496,999	3,305,533
Shares Outstanding	139,222	139,018	148,633	161,287	162,359	168,979	176,425	178,824
Statistical Record								
Return on Assets %	4.49	5.21	6.19	8.04	5.50	7.48	4.83	10.07
Return on Equity %	12.11	13.51	14.88	18.81	13.51	17.23	10.51	22.92
EBITDA Margin %	5.92	5.21	6.54	5.11	3.43	5.08	3.55	5.93
Net Margin %	2.36	2.28	2.37	2.44	1.65	2.54	1.71	3.11
Asset Turnover	2.16	2.29	2.61	3.30	3.32	2.94	2.82	3.23
Current Ratio	1.51	1.80	1.73	1.76	1.57	1.53	1.58	1.55
Debt to Equity	0.51	0.33	0.32	0.13	0.16	0.15	0.01	0.01
Price Range	61.20-40.94	61.20-40.94	83.65-56.29	80.29-54.16	63.99-45.12	75.63-45.49	66.63-41.76	58.21-30.46
P/E Ratio	23.63-15.81	21.78-14.57	26.14-17.59	19.78-13.34	23.61-16.65	22.24-13.38	33.65-21.09	15.52-8.12
Average Yield %	1.69	1.61	1.60	0.96	1.17	0.80	1.01	1.10

Address: 6700 Las Colinas Boulevard, Irving, TX 75039 Telephone: 469-398-7000	Web Site: www.fluor.com Officers: David T. Seaton - Chairman, Chief Executive Officer, Chief Operating Officer Glenn Gilkey - Senior Vice President	Auditors: Ernst & Young LLP Investor Contact: 469-398-7189 Transfer Agents: Computershare, Pittsburgh, PA

FMC CORP.

Exchange	Symbol	Price	52Wk Range	Yield	P/E
NYS	FMC	$47.49 (5/31/2016)	57.54-32.93	1.39	10.94

*7 Year Price Score 73.80   *NYSE Composite index=100   *12 Month Price Score 101.93

Interim Earnings (Per Share)

Qtr.	Mar	Jun	Sep	Dec
2013	0.94	0.86	0.13	0.21
2014	0.49	0.81	0.42	0.57
2015	(0.35)	5.52	(0.02)	(1.52)
2016	0.36	...	...	...

Interim Dividends (Per Share)

Amt	Decl	Ex	Rec	Pay
0.165Q	07/21/2015	09/28/2015	09/30/2015	10/15/2015
0.165Q	12/10/2015	12/29/2015	12/31/2015	01/21/2016
0.165Q	02/26/2016	03/29/2016	03/31/2016	04/21/2016
0.165Q	04/26/2016	06/28/2016	06/30/2016	07/21/2016

Indicated Div: $0.66

Valuation Analysis

		Institutional Holding	
Forecast EPS	$2.69	No of Institutions	
	(05/20/2016)	533	
Market Cap	$6.4 Billion	Shares	
Book Value	$2.0 Billion	131,550,512	
Price/Book	3.24	% Held	
Price/Sales	1.86	89.90	

Business Summary: Agricultural Chemicals (MIC: 8.3.3 SIC: 2812 NAIC: 325181)

FMC is chemical company serving agricultural, consumer and industrial markets globally. Co. operates in three business segments: FMC Agricultural Solutions, FMC Health and Nutrition and FMC Lithium. Co.'s FMC Agricultural Solutions segment develops, markets and sells crop protection chemicals - insecticides, herbicides and fungicides. The FMC Health and Nutrition segment focuses on nutritional ingredients, health excipients, and functional health ingredients. Co.'s FMC Lithium segment manufactures lithium for use in a range of lithium products, which are used primarily in energy storage, specialty polymers and chemical synthesis application.

Recent Developments: For the quarter ended Mar 31 2016, income from continuing operations was US$54.8 million compared with a loss of US$61.1 million in the year-earlier quarter. Net income amounted to US$48.7 million versus a net loss of US$45.5 million in the year-earlier quarter. Revenues were US$798.8 million, up 21.1% from US$659.4 million the year before. Direct operating expenses rose 26.6% to US$517.4 million from US$408.7 million in the comparable period the year before. Indirect operating expenses decreased 49.6% to US$174.9 million from US$346.8 million in the equivalent prior-year period.

Prospects: Our evaluation of FMC Corp. as of June 19, 2016 is the result of our systematic analysis on three basic characteristics: earnings strength, relative valuation, and recent stock price movement. The company has enjoyed a very positive trend in earnings per share over the past 5 quarters and while recent estimates for the company have been mixed, FMC has posted better than expected results. Based on operating earnings yield, the company is about fairly valued when compared to all of the companies in our coverage universe. Share price changes over the past year indicates that FMC will perform poorly over the near term.

Financial Data

(US$ in Thousands)	3 Mos	12/31/2015	12/31/2014	12/31/2013	12/31/2012	12/31/2011	12/31/2010	12/31/2009
Earnings Per Share	4.34	3.66	2.29	2.16	3.00	2.55	1.18	1.56
Cash Flow Per Share	0.30	(2.68)	2.80	2.43	2.61	2.68	2.45	2.09
Tang Book Value Per Share	2.17	1.62	6.73	6.21	7.05	5.92	6.55	5.98
Dividends Per Share	0.660	0.660	0.600	0.540	0.405	0.300	0.250	0.250
Dividend Payout %	15.21	18.03	26.20	25.00	13.50	11.76	21.19	16.03
Income Statement								
Total Revenue	798,800	3,276,500	4,037,700	3,874,800	3,748,300	3,377,900	3,116,300	2,826,200
EBITDA	140,100	23,900	649,300	753,600	757,300	688,400	496,500	443,100
Depn & Amortn	33,600	74,100	103,900	94,600	99,100	101,100	109,400	108,400
Income Before Taxes	85,700	(130,300)	485,900	616,800	612,900	547,900	347,800	307,700
Income Taxes	30,900	47,400	73,500	148,600	146,700	136,500	132,000	53,000
Net Income	48,300	489,000	307,500	293,900	416,200	365,900	172,500	228,500
Average Shares	134,304	133,696	134,282	136,137	138,813	143,308	146,160	146,602
Balance Sheet								
Current Assets	2,955,200	2,971,900	2,934,400	2,945,000	2,181,800	1,869,400	1,646,200	1,487,700
Total Assets	6,390,400	6,325,900	5,340,500	5,235,200	4,373,900	3,743,500	3,319,900	3,136,200
Current Liabilities	1,451,300	1,453,300	1,910,400	1,986,700	1,135,400	919,500	963,400	709,200
Long-Term Obligations	1,986,200	2,036,300	1,153,400	1,154,100	908,800	779,100	503,000	588,000
Total Liabilities	4,430,200	4,460,200	3,810,000	3,715,400	2,893,600	2,502,900	2,188,400	2,059,800
Stockholders' Equity	1,960,200	1,865,700	1,530,500	1,519,800	1,480,300	1,240,600	1,131,500	1,076,400
Shares Outstanding	133,751	133,655	133,317	132,885	137,670	139,674	142,971	145,037
Statistical Record								
Return on Assets %	9.98	8.38	5.82	6.12	10.23	10.36	5.34	7.46
Return on Equity %	34.41	28.80	20.16	19.59	30.51	30.85	15.63	23.09
EBITDA Margin %	17.54	0.73	16.08	19.45	20.20	20.38	15.93	15.68
Net Margin %	6.05	14.92	7.62	7.58	11.10	10.83	5.54	8.09
Asset Turnover	0.58	0.56	0.76	0.81	0.92	0.96	0.97	0.92
Current Ratio	2.04	2.04	1.54	1.48	1.92	2.03	1.71	2.10
Debt to Equity	1.01	1.09	0.75	0.76	0.61	0.63	0.44	0.55
Price Range	60.95-32.93	64.59-32.93	83.10-51.60	75.46-55.45	58.59-43.48	46.43-32.91	40.70-25.40	29.00-17.64
P/E Ratio	14.04-7.59	17.65-9.00	36.29-22.53	34.94-25.67	19.53-14.49	18.21-12.91	34.49-21.53	18.59-11.30
Average Yield %	1.47	1.31	0.88	0.83	0.77	0.75	0.78	1.01

Address: 1735 Market Street, Philadelphia, PA 19103	**Web Site:** www.fmc.com	**Auditors:** KPMG LLP
Telephone: 215-299-6000	**Officers:** Pierre R. Brondeau - Chairman, President, Chief Executive Officer Paul W. Graves - Executive Vice President, Chief Financial Officer	**Investor Contact:** 215-299-6119
Fax: 215-299-5998		**Transfer Agents:** Wells Fargo Bank, N.A., Mendota Heights, MN

FMC TECHNOLOGIES INC

Exchange	Symbol	Price	52Wk Range	Yield	P/E
NYS	FTI	$27.23 (5/31/2016)	43.25-22.77	N/A	23.68

*7 Year Price Score 63.54   *NYSE Composite Index=100   *12 Month Price Score 90.41

TRADING VOLUME (thousand shares)

Interim Earnings (Per Share)

Qtr.	Mar	Jun	Sep	Dec
2013	0.43	0.44	0.49	0.75
2014	0.57	0.95	0.72	0.71
2015	0.63	0.46	0.35	0.25
2016	0.09	...	...	...

Interim Dividends (Per Share)

Amt	Decl	Ex	Rec	Pay
2-for-1	02/25/2011	04/01/2011	03/14/2011	03/31/2011

Valuation Analysis / Institutional Holding

Forecast EPS	$1.09	No of Institutions
	(05/20/2016)	599
Market Cap	$6.2 Billion	Shares
Book Value	$2.6 Billion	214,202,400
Price/Book	2.37	% Held
Price/Sales	1.05	92.89

Business Summary: Equipment & Services (MIC: 9.1.3 SIC: 3533 NAIC: 333132)

FMC Technologies designs, manufactures and services systems and products, including subsea production and processing systems, surface wellhead production systems, high pressure fluid control equipment, measurement solutions and marine loading systems for the energy industry. Co. operates in three business segments: Subsea Technologies, which provides subsea systems, schilling robotics, and multiphase and wetgas meters; Surface Technologies, which provides drilling, completion and production wellhead systems, and fluid control; and Energy Infrastructure, which provides measurement solutions, loading systems, and separation systems.

Recent Developments: For the quarter ended Mar 31 2016, net income decreased 86.6% to US$19.8 million from US$148.1 million in the year-earlier quarter. Revenues were US$1.21 billion, down 28.7% from US$1.70 billion the year before. Direct operating expenses declined 26.2% to US$946.8 million from US$1.28 billion in the comparable period the year before. Indirect operating expenses increased 1.5% to US$217.3 million from US$214.0 million in the equivalent prior-year period.

Prospects: Our evaluation of FMC Technologies Inc. as of June 19, 2016 is the result of our systematic analysis on three basic characteristics: earnings strength, relative valuation, and recent stock price movement. The company has generated a negative trend in earnings per share over the past 5 quarters and while recent estimates for the company have been mixed, FTI has posted results that fell short of analysts expectations. Based on operating earnings yield, the company is undervalued when compared to all of the companies in our coverage universe. Share price changes over the past year indicates that FTI will perform in line with the market over the near term.

Financial Data

(US$ in Thousands)	3 Mos	12/31/2015	12/31/2014	12/31/2013	12/31/2012	12/31/2011	12/31/2010	12/31/2009
Earnings Per Share	1.15	1.70	2.95	2.10	1.78	1.64	1.53	1.44
Cash Flow Per Share	3.80	4.04	3.78	3.34	0.58	0.68	0.80	2.39
Tang Book Value Per Share	8.16	7.72	7.00	6.03	3.76	4.33	3.74	2.77
Income Statement								
Total Revenue	1,208,700	6,362,700	7,942,600	7,126,200	6,151,400	5,099,000	4,125,600	4,405,400
EBITDA	96,600	714,400	1,269,600	908,900	740,900	647,100	627,400	605,700
Depn & Amortn	63,300	179,500	170,800	156,000	113,100	86,100	80,700	78,300
Income Before Taxes	25,800	502,600	1,066,300	719,200	601,200	552,800	537,900	517,900
Income Taxes	6,000	107,800	361,000	212,600	166,400	149,300	159,600	155,100
Net Income	19,800	393,100	699,900	501,400	430,000	399,800	375,500	361,800
Average Shares	228,600	231,700	236,900	239,100	240,900	243,200	245,400	251,400
Balance Sheet								
Current Assets	3,837,900	3,948,700	4,436,400	4,023,000	3,488,300	2,787,900	2,345,300	2,225,600
Total Assets	6,313,200	6,437,900	7,175,600	6,605,600	5,902,900	4,271,000	3,644,200	3,509,500
Current Liabilities	2,046,900	2,343,200	2,783,600	2,614,700	1,970,400	2,232,900	1,495,400	1,678,500
Long-Term Obligations	1,218,400	1,134,100	1,297,200	1,329,800	1,580,400	36,000	351,100	391,600
Total Liabilities	3,709,100	3,926,100	4,719,300	4,288,400	4,066,000	2,846,600	2,332,500	2,406,700
Stockholders' Equity	2,604,100	2,511,800	2,456,300	2,317,200	1,836,900	1,424,600	1,311,700	1,102,800
Shares Outstanding	226,200	226,805	231,525	235,800	237,100	237,800	239,600	243,600
Statistical Record								
Return on Assets %	3.99	5.78	10.16	8.02	8.43	10.10	10.50	10.20
Return on Equity %	10.48	15.82	29.32	24.14	26.30	29.22	31.10	40.22
EBITDA Margin %	7.99	11.23	15.98	12.75	12.04	12.69	15.21	13.75
Net Margin %	1.64	6.18	8.81	7.04	6.99	7.84	9.10	8.21
Asset Turnover	0.88	0.93	1.15	1.14	1.21	1.29	1.15	1.24
Current Ratio	1.87	1.69	1.59	1.54	1.77	1.25	1.57	1.33
Debt to Equity	0.47	0.45	0.53	0.57	0.86	0.03	0.27	0.36
Price Range	44.10-22.77	46.84-28.35	63.52-42.75	59.34-42.83	54.36-37.68	53.77-35.96	44.56-23.80	29.42-11.90
P/E Ratio	38.35-19.80	27.55-16.68	21.53-14.49	28.26-20.40	30.54-21.17	32.79-21.93	29.12-15.56	20.43-8.26

Address: 5875 N. Sam Houston Parkway West, Houston, TX 77086 **Telephone:** 281-591-4000	**Web Site:** www.fmctechnologies.com **Officers:** John T. Gremp - Chairman, President, Chief Executive Officer Douglas J. Pferdehirt - President, Executive Vice President, Chief Operating Officer, Chief Executive Officer	**Auditors:** KPMG LLP **Investor Contact:** 281-591-4080 **Transfer Agents:** National City Bank, Cleveland, OH

FOOT LOCKER, INC.

Exchange	Symbol	Price	52Wk Range	Yield	P/E
NYS	FL	$55.92 (5/31/2016)	75.76-54.08	1.97	14.23

*7 Year Price Score 158.46 *NYSE Composite Index=100   *12 Month Price Score 89.95

TRADING VOLUME (thousand shares)

Interim Earnings (Per Share)

Qtr.	Apr	Jul	Oct	Jan
2013-14	0.90	0.44	0.70	0.81
2014-15	1.10	0.63	0.82	1.01
2015-16	1.29	0.84	0.57	1.13
2016-17	1.39	...	...	...

Interim Dividends (Per Share)

Amt	Decl	Ex	Rec	Pay
0.25Q	08/19/2015	10/14/2015	10/16/2015	10/30/2015
0.25Q	11/18/2015	01/13/2016	01/15/2016	01/29/2016
0.275Q	02/17/2016	04/13/2016	04/15/2016	04/29/2016
0.275Q	05/18/2016	07/13/2016	07/15/2016	07/29/2016

Indicated Div: $1.10

Valuation Analysis

		Institutional Holding	
Forecast EPS	$4.73	No of Institutions	
	(05/20/2016)	753	
Market Cap	$7.6 Billion	Shares	
Book Value	$2.7 Billion	164,352,768	
Price/Book	2.84	% Held	
Price/Sales	1.02	91.35	

Business Summary: Retail - Apparel and Accessories (MIC: 2.1.5 SIC: 5661 NAIC: 448210)

Foot Locker is a retailer of athletically inspired shoes and apparel. Co. operates in two segments: Athletic Stores and Direct-to-Customers. The Athletic Stores segment is an athletic footwear and apparel retailer, with formats that include Foot Locker, Lady Foot Locker, SIX:02, Kids Foot Locker, Champs Sports, Footaction, Runners Point and Sidestep. The Direct-to-Customers segment includes Footlocker.com, Inc. and other affiliates, including Eastbay, Inc., and Co.'s international ecommerce businesses, which sell to customers through their Internet and mobile sites and catalogs. As of Jan 30 2016, Co. operated 3,383 mall-based stores in the U. S., Canada, Europe, Australia, and New Zealand.

Recent Developments: For the quarter ended Apr 30 2016, net income increased 3.8% to US$191.0 million from US$184.0 million in the year-earlier quarter. Revenues were US$1.99 billion, up 3.7% from US$1.92 billion the year before. Direct operating expenses rose 3.6% to US$1.29 billion from US$1.25 billion in the comparable period the year before. Indirect operating expenses increased 4.7% to US$398.0 million from US$380.0 million in the equivalent prior-year period.

Prospects: Our evaluation of Foot Locker Inc. as of June 19, 2016 is the result of our systematic analysis on three basic characteristics: earnings strength, relative valuation, and recent stock price movement. The company has managed to produce a neutral trend in earnings per share over the past 5 quarters. However, while recent estimates for the company have been lowered by analysts, FL has posted results that were in line with analysts expectations. Based on operating earnings yield, the company is undervalued when compared to all of the companies in our coverage universe. Share price changes over the past year indicates that FL will perform very well over the near term.

Financial Data

(US$ in Thousands)	3 Mos	01/30/2016	01/31/2015	02/01/2014	02/02/2013	01/28/2012	01/29/2011	01/30/2010
Earnings Per Share	3.93	3.84	3.56	2.85	2.58	1.80	1.07	0.30
Cash Flow Per Share	5.45	5.37	4.96	3.58	2.71	3.26	2.10	2.22
Tang Book Value Per Share	18.18	17.17	16.26	15.58	14.61	12.61	11.69	10.89
Dividends Per Share	1.025	1.000	0.880	0.800	0.720	0.660	0.600	0.600
Dividend Payout %	26.08	26.04	24.72	28.07	27.91	36.67	56.07	200.00
Income Statement								
Total Revenue	1,987,000	7,412,000	7,151,000	6,505,000	6,182,000	5,623,000	5,049,000	4,854,000
EBITDA	337,000	989,000	953,000	801,000	730,000	551,000	372,000	195,000
Depn & Amortn	39,000	148,000	139,000	133,000	118,000	110,000	106,000	112,000
Income Before Taxes	298,000	837,000	809,000	663,000	607,000	435,000	257,000	73,000
Income Taxes	107,000	296,000	289,000	234,000	210,000	157,000	88,000	26,000
Net Income	191,000	541,000	520,000	429,000	397,000	278,000	169,000	48,000
Average Shares	137,800	140,800	146,000	150,500	154,000	154,400	156,700	156,300
Balance Sheet								
Current Assets	2,592,000	2,606,000	2,456,000	2,350,000	2,363,000	2,079,000	1,934,000	1,772,000
Total Assets	3,758,000	3,775,000	3,577,000	3,487,000	3,367,000	3,050,000	2,896,000	2,816,000
Current Liabilities	578,000	700,000	696,000	626,000	636,000	548,000	489,000	433,000
Long-Term Obligations	128,000	129,000	132,000	136,000	133,000	135,000	137,000	138,000
Total Liabilities	1,083,000	1,222,000	1,081,000	991,000	990,000	940,000	871,000	868,000
Stockholders' Equity	2,675,000	2,553,000	2,496,000	2,496,000	2,377,000	2,110,000	2,025,000	1,948,000
Shares Outstanding	135,989	136,977	140,864	145,427	150,070	151,619	154,620	156,541
Statistical Record								
Return on Assets %	14.83	14.76	14.76	12.55	12.17	9.38	5.93	1.69
Return on Equity %	20.96	21.49	20.89	17.66	17.41	13.48	8.53	2.49
EBITDA Margin %	16.96	13.34	13.33	12.31	11.81	9.80	7.37	4.02
Net Margin %	9.61	7.30	7.27	6.59	6.42	4.94	3.35	0.99
Asset Turnover	2.03	2.02	2.03	1.90	1.90	1.90	1.77	1.71
Current Ratio	4.48	3.72	3.53	3.75	3.72	3.79	3.96	4.09
Debt to Equity	0.05	0.05	0.05	0.05	0.06	0.06	0.07	0.07
Price Range	75.76-58.04	75.76-52.43	57.98-36.73	41.44-31.79	37.27-26.24	26.67-16.77	19.81-11.61	12.57-7.28
P/E Ratio	19.28-14.77	19.73-13.65	16.29-10.32	14.54-11.15	14.45-10.17	14.82-9.32	18.51-10.85	41.90-24.27
Average Yield %	1.55	1.54	1.74	2.26	2.21	3.04	3.97	5.65

Address: 330 West 34th Street, New York, NY 10001	**Web Site:** www.footlocker-inc.com	**Auditors:** KPMG
Telephone: 212-720-3700	**Officers:** Ken C. Hicks - Chairman, President, Chief Executive Officer Richard A. Johnson - President, Chief Executive Officer, Executive Vice President, Chief Operating Officer, Division Officer	**Investor Contact:** 212-720-3700
		Transfer Agents: Computershare, Providence, R.I.

FORD MOTOR CO. (DE)

Exchange	Symbol	Price	52Wk Range	Yield	P/E
NYS	F	$13.49 (5/31/2016)	15.68-11.17	4.45	6.08

*7 Year Price Score 88.94 *NYSE Composite Index=100 *12 Month Price Score 95.42

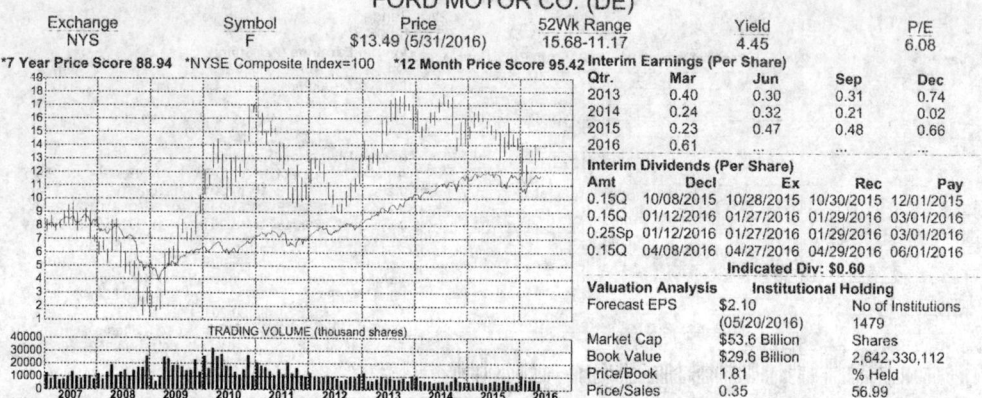

Interim Earnings (Per Share)

Qtr.	Mar	Jun	Sep	Dec
2013	0.40	0.30	0.31	0.74
2014	0.24	0.32	0.21	0.02
2015	0.23	0.47	0.48	0.66
2016	0.61			

Interim Dividends (Per Share)

Amt	Decl	Ex	Rec	Pay
0.15Q	10/08/2015	10/28/2015	10/30/2015	12/01/2015
0.15Q	01/12/2016	01/27/2016	01/29/2016	03/01/2016
0.25Sp	01/12/2016	01/27/2016	01/29/2016	03/01/2016
0.15Q	04/08/2016	04/27/2016	04/29/2016	06/01/2016

Indicated Div: $0.60

Valuation Analysis

Forecast EPS	$2.10 (05/20/2016)
Market Cap	$53.6 Billion
Book Value	$29.6 Billion
Price/Book	1.81
Price/Sales	0.35

Institutional Holding

No of Institutions	1479
Shares	2,642,330,112
% Held	56.99

TRADING VOLUME (thousand shares)

Business Summary: Autos- Manufacturing (MIC: 1.8.1 SIC: 3711 NAIC: 336111)

Ford Motor produces and sells automobiles. Co.'s vehicle brands are Ford and Lincoln. Co. also sells parts and accessories, primarily to its dealerships and to authorized parts distributors. Also, through its wholly-owned subsidiary, Ford Motor Credit Company LLC, Co. provides automotive financing products to and through automotive dealers. Co.'s business is divided in two sectors: Automotive and Financial Services. Reportable segments in the Automotive sector include: North America; South America; Europe; Middle East and Africa; as well as Asia Pacific. Reportable segments in the Financial Services sector include: Ford Motor Credit Company and Other Financial Services.

Recent Developments: For the quarter ended Mar 31 2016, net income increased 112.7% to US$2.46 billion from US$1.15 billion in the year-earlier quarter. Revenues were US$37.72 billion, up 11.3% from US$33.90 billion the year before. Direct operating expenses rose 6.3% to US$30.94 billion from US$29.12 billion in the comparable period the year before. Indirect operating expenses increased 12.0% to US$3.96 billion from US$3.54 billion in the equivalent prior-year period.

Prospects: Our evaluation of Ford Motor Co. as of June 19, 2016 is the result of our systematic analysis on three basic characteristics: earnings strength, relative valuation, and recent stock price movement. The company has generated a negative trend in earnings per share over the past 5 quarters and while recent estimates for the company have been raised by analysts, F has posted better than expected results. Based on operating earnings yield, the company is undervalued when compared to all of the companies in our coverage universe. Share price changes over the past year indicates that F will perform in line with the market over the near term.

Financial Data
(US$ in Millions)

	3 Mos	12/31/2015	12/31/2014	12/31/2013	12/31/2012	12/31/2011	12/31/2010	12/31/2009
Earnings Per Share	2.22	1.84	0.80	1.76	1.42	4.94	1.90	0.86
Cash Flow Per Share	4.50	4.07	3.71	2.65	2.36	2.58	3.33	5.36
Tang Book Value Per Share	7.45	7.22	6.27	6.69	4.04	3.81	...	...
Dividends Per Share	0.850	0.600	0.500	0.400	0.200	0.050	...	...
Dividend Payout %	38.29	32.61	62.50	22.73	14.08	1.01	...	...
Income Statement								
Total Revenue	37,718	149,558	144,077	146,917	134,252	136,264	128,954	118,308
EBITDA	3,310	15,681	10,475	13,522	14,343	15,758	17,001	8,650
Depn & Amortn	...	4,332	4,252	4,064	3,655	3,533	3,876	4,094
Income Before Taxes	3,110	8,434	3,067	5,932	7,132	8,181	6,611	3,016
Income Taxes	1,196	2,881	1,156	(147)	2,056	(11,541)	592	69
Net Income	2,452	7,373	3,187	7,155	5,665	20,213	6,561	2,717
Average Shares	3,997	4,003	4,046	4,088	4,016	4,112	3,450	3,313
Balance Sheet								
Current Assets	154,775	43,495	39,016	44,276	43,305	41,667	41,487	48,278
Total Assets	237,288	224,925	208,527	202,026	190,554	178,348	164,687	194,850
Current Liabilities	69,813	78,336	73,963	74,131	73,428	73,038	75,091	77,073
Long-Term Obligations	93,254	89,856	79,999	76,625	66,296	59,177	62,324	88,427
Total Liabilities	207,683	196,283	183,722	175,643	174,607	163,320	165,360	202,670
Stockholders' Equity	29,605	28,642	24,805	26,383	15,947	15,028	(673)	(7,820)
Shares Outstanding	3,973	3,970	3,956	3,944	3,923	3,923	3,783	3,999
Statistical Record								
Return on Assets %	3.96	3.40	1.55	3.65	3.06	11.78	3.65	1.32
Return on Equity %	32.63	27.59	12.45	33.81	36.48	281.62	...	...
EBITDA Margin %	8.78	10.48	7.27	9.20	10.68	11.56	13.18	7.31
Net Margin %	6.50	4.93	2.21	4.87	4.22	14.83	5.09	2.30
Asset Turnover	0.68	0.69	0.70	0.75	0.73	0.79	0.72	0.57
Current Ratio	2.22	0.56	0.53	0.60	0.59	0.57	0.55	0.63
Debt to Equity	3.15	3.14	3.23	2.90	4.16	3.94	...	...
Price Range	16.14-11.17	16.57-12.90	17.84-13.54	17.76-12.13	12.96-8.92	18.79-9.37	17.00-9.88	10.20-1.58
P/E Ratio	7.27-5.03	9.01-7.01	22.30-16.92	10.09-6.89	9.13-6.28	3.80-1.90	8.95-5.20	11.86-1.84
Average Yield %	5.97	4.00	3.15	2.61	1.83	0.38	...	...

Address: One American Road, Dearborn, MI 48126 **Telephone:** 313-322-3000	**Web Site:** www.corporate.ford.com **Officers:** William Clay Ford - Chairman Mark Fields - President, Chief Executive Officer, Incoming Chief Executive Officer, Executive Vice President, Chief Operating Officer, Region Officer	**Auditors:** PricewaterhouseCoopers LLP **Investor Contact:** 313-845-8540 **Transfer Agents:** Computershare Trust Company, N.A., Providence, RI

FORTUNE BRANDS HOME & SECURITY, INC.

Exchange	Symbol	Price	52Wk Range	Yield	P/E
NYS	FBHS	$58.67 (5/31/2016)	59.19-44.12	1.09	25.62

*7 Year Price Score N/A   *NYSE Composite Index=100   *12 Month Price Score 109.95

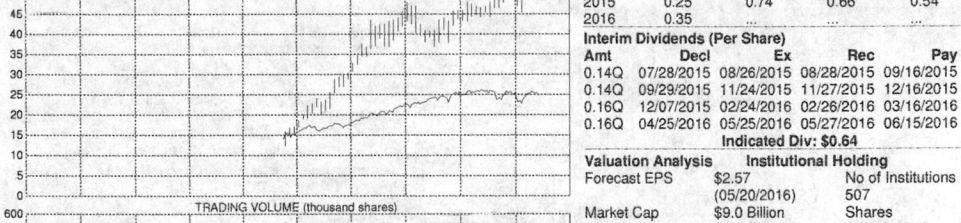

Interim Earnings (Per Share)

Qtr.	Mar	Jun	Sep	Dec
2013	0.22	0.37	0.37	0.37
2014	0.24	0.55	(0.13)	0.28
2015	0.25	0.74	0.66	0.54
2016	0.35	...	...	...

Interim Dividends (Per Share)

Amt	Decl	Ex	Rec	Pay
0.14Q	07/28/2015	08/26/2015	08/28/2015	09/16/2015
0.14Q	09/29/2015	11/24/2015	11/27/2015	12/16/2015
0.16Q	12/07/2015	02/24/2016	02/26/2016	03/16/2016
0.16Q	04/25/2016	05/25/2016	05/27/2016	06/15/2016

Indicated Div: $0.64

Valuation Analysis

	Institutional Holding	
Forecast EPS	$2.57	No of Institutions
	(05/20/2016)	507
Market Cap	$9.0 Billion	Shares
Book Value	$2.2 Billion	148,596,368
Price/Book	4.15	% Held
Price/Sales	1.58	85.07

TRADING VOLUME (thousand shares)

Business Summary: Household Appliances, Electronics & Goods (MIC: 1.5.1 SIC: 1522 NAIC: 236115)

Fortune Brands Home & Security is a holding company, which provides home and security products. Co. has four business segments: Cabinets, which manufactures custom, semi-custom and stock cabinetry, and vanities; Plumbing, which manufactures or assembles and sells faucets, accessories, kitchen sinks and waste disposals; Doors, which manufactures and sells fiberglass, steel entry door systems and urethane millwork product lines; and Security, which manufactures and sells key-controlled and combination padlocks, bicycle and cable locks, built-in locker locks, door hardware, automotive, trailer and towing locks, electronic access control solutions, and other safety and security devices.

Recent Developments: For the quarter ended Mar 31 2016, income from continuing operations increased 36.2% to US$55.7 million from US$40.9 million in the year-earlier quarter. Net income increased 38.2% to US$55.7 million from US$40.3 million in the year-earlier quarter. Revenues were US$1.11 billion, up 16.4% from US$950.8 million the year before. Operating income was US$95.5 million versus US$67.3 million in the prior-year quarter, an increase of 41.9%. Direct operating expenses rose 15.0% to US$728.7 million from US$633.9 million in the comparable period the year before. Indirect operating expenses increased 13.1% to US$282.3 million from US$249.6 million in the equivalent prior-year period.

Prospects: Our evaluation of Fortune Brands Home & Security Inc. as of June 19, 2016 is the result of our systematic analysis on three basic characteristics: earnings strength, relative valuation, and recent stock price movement. The company has managed to produce a neutral trend in earnings per share over the past 5 quarters. However, while recent estimates for the company have been lowered by analysts, FBHS has posted better than expected results. Based on operating earnings yield, the company is about fairly valued when compared to all of the companies in our coverage universe. Share price changes over the past year indicates that FBHS will perform very well over the near term.

Financial Data
(US$ in Thousands)	3 Mos	12/31/2015	12/31/2014	12/31/2013	12/31/2012	12/31/2011	12/31/2010	12/31/2009
Earnings Per Share	2.29	1.93	0.95	1.34	0.71	(0.23)	57,223.00	(41,877.00)
Cash Flow Per Share	2.94	2.58	1.57	1.80	1.76	1.13	138,900.00	269,300.00
Tang Book Value Per Share	N.M.	N.M.	0.85	2.26	1.93	0.36	...	...
Dividends Per Share	0.580	0.560	0.480	0.300	...	3.540	...	...
Dividend Payout %	25.33	29.02	50.53	22.39	...	...	...	...
Income Statement								
Total Revenue	1,106,500	4,579,400	4,013,600	4,157,400	3,591,100	3,328,600	3,233,500	3,006,800
EBITDA	127,000	606,900	498,300	442,500	264,000	94,300	300,400	181,500
Depn & Amortn	31,200	115,100	96,000	90,840	101,300	111,500	111,600	131,100
Income Before Taxes	84,000	459,900	391,900	344,900	154,000	(43,600)	72,500	(34,800)
Income Taxes	28,300	153,400	118,300	114,000	34,300	(9,000)	14,100	6,300
Net Income	55,700	315,000	158,100	229,700	118,700	(35,600)	57,200	(41,900)
Average Shares	158,500	163,000	166,300	171,300	166,100	155,200	1,000.00	1,000.00
Balance Sheet								
Current Assets	1,481,300	1,418,700	1,299,100	1,327,400	1,228,000	953,500	1,467,800	1,369,400
Total Assets	4,942,800	4,878,600	4,052,900	4,178,100	3,873,700	3,637,900	4,259,400	4,191,200
Current Liabilities	684,900	757,900	699,600	738,700	632,600	597,800	576,500	553,000
Long-Term Obligations	1,619,200	1,171,600	643,700	350,000	297,500	389,300	3,230,800	3,248,800
Total Liabilities	2,774,700	2,427,700	1,793,400	1,528,700	1,492,600	1,517,100	4,317,800	4,353,400
Stockholders' Equity	2,168,100	2,450,900	2,259,500	2,649,400	2,381,100	2,120,800	(58,400)	(162,200)
Shares Outstanding	153,376	159,906	158,140	166,667	163,855	156,008	1,000.00	1,000.00
Statistical Record								
Return on Assets %	8.21	7.05	3.84	5.71	3.15	N.M.	1.35	...
Return on Equity %	16.61	13.37	6.44	9.13	5.26	N.M.	...	...
EBITDA Margin %	11.48	13.25	12.42	10.64	7.35	2.83	9.29	6.04
Net Margin %	5.03	6.88	3.94	5.53	3.31	N.M.	1.77	N.M.
Asset Turnover	1.26	1.03	0.98	1.03	0.95	0.84	0.77	...
Current Ratio	2.16	1.87	1.86	1.80	1.94	1.60	2.55	2.48
Debt to Equity	0.75	0.48	0.28	0.13	0.12	0.18	...	...
Price Range	56.47-44.07	56.47-43.04	47.83-36.77	45.70-29.22	30.33-16.82	17.03-12.20	...	...
P/E Ratio	24.66-19.24	29.26-22.30	50.35-38.71	34.10-21.81	42.72-23.69	...	...	...
Average Yield %	1.18	1.16	1.14	0.77	...	23.37	...	...

Address: 520 Lake Cook Road, Deerfield, IL 60015-5611 Telephone: 847-484-4400	Web Site: www.fbhs.com Officers: Christopher J. Klein - President, Chief Executive Officer E. Lee Wyatt - Senior Vice President, Chief Financial Officer	Auditors: PricewaterhouseCoopers LLP Transfer Agents: Wells Fargo Shareowner Services, Mendota Heights, MN

FRANKLIN RESOURCES, INC.

Exchange	Symbol	Price	52Wk Range	Yield	P/E	Div Achiever
NYS	BEN	$37.35 (5/31/2016)	51.44-31.45	1.93	13.53	26 Years

*7 Year Price Score 79.77 *NYSE Composite Index=100 *12 Month Price Score 93.62

Interim Earnings (Per Share)

Qtr.	Dec	Mar	Jun	Sep
2012-13	0.81	0.90	0.86	0.80
2013-14	0.96	0.89	0.92	1.02
2014-15	0.91	0.98	0.82	0.59
2015-16	0.74	0.61	...	...

Interim Dividends (Per Share)

Amt	Decl	Ex	Rec	Pay
0.15Q	09/16/2015	09/28/2015	09/30/2015	10/15/2015
0.18Q	12/15/2015	12/24/2015	12/29/2015	01/13/2016
0.18Q	02/17/2016	03/29/2016	03/31/2016	04/15/2016
0.18Q	06/14/2016	06/28/2016	06/30/2016	07/15/2016

Indicated Div: $0.72 (Div. Reinv. Plan)

Valuation Analysis

	Institutional Holding	
Forecast EPS	$2.72	No of Institutions
	(05/20/2016)	816
Market Cap	$21.9 Billion	Shares
Book Value	$11.8 Billion	318,657,920
Price/Book	1.86	% Held
Price/Sales	3.02	49.69

Business Summary: Wealth Management (MIC: 5.5.2 SIC: 6282 NAIC: 523930)

Franklin Resources is a holding company that, together with its subsidiaries, operates as Franklin Templeton Investments®. Co. is a global investment management organization. Co. provides investment choices under its Franklin®, Templeton®, Mutual Series®, Bissett®, Fiduciary Trustâ„¢, Darby®, Balanced Equity Management® and K2® brand names. In addition to investment management, Co.'s services include fund administration, sales, distribution, shareholder services, transfer agency, trustee, custodial and other fiduciary services, as well as select private banking services. At Sep 30 2015, Co.'s total assets under management were $770.90 billion.

Recent Developments: For the quarter ended Mar 31 2016, net income decreased 42.1% to US$360.8 million from US$622.9 million in the year-earlier quarter. Revenues were US$1.61 billion, down 19.7% from US$2.01 billion the year before. Operating income was US$537.3 million versus US$757.7 million in the prior-year quarter, a decrease of 29.1%. Direct operating expenses declined 25.2% to US$531.7 million from US$710.5 million in the comparable period the year before. Indirect operating expenses increased 0.6% to US$544.9 million from US$541.6 million in the equivalent prior-year period.

Prospects: Our evaluation of Franklin Resources Inc. as of June 19, 2016 is the result of our systematic analysis on three basic characteristics: earnings strength, relative valuation, and recent stock price movement. The company has produced a positive trend in earnings per share over the past 5 quarters. However, while recent estimates for the company have been lowered by analysts, BEN has posted results that fell short of analysts expectations. Based on operating earnings yield, the company is undervalued when compared to all of the companies in our coverage universe. Share price changes over the past year indicates that BEN will perform well over the near term.

Financial Data

(US$ in Thousands)	6 Mos	3 Mos	09/30/2015	09/30/2014	09/30/2013	09/30/2012	09/30/2011	09/30/2010
Earnings Per Share	2.76	3.13	3.29	3.79	3.37	2.98	2.87	2.11
Cash Flow Per Share	2.66	3.30	3.66	3.42	3.22	1.66	2.45	2.43
Tang Book Value Per Share	16.29	16.02	15.88	14.86	12.23	11.09	9.76	8.51
Dividends Per Share	0.660	0.630	1.100	0.480	1.390	1.027	0.333	1.293
Dividend Payout %	23.91	20.13	33.43	12.66	41.25	34.41	11.60	61.29
Income Statement								
Total Revenue	3,371,900	1,758,000	7,948,700	8,491,400	7,985,000	7,101,000	7,140,039	5,852,999
EBITDA	1,256,800	678,500	3,202,000	3,462,400	3,068,900	2,701,700	2,723,200	2,121,149
Depn & Amortn	36,900	22,800	81,600	82,600	76,900	67,900	71,500	67,700
Income Before Taxes	1,206,400	647,300	3,091,600	3,341,500	2,952,600	2,609,600	2,625,277	2,049,860
Income Taxes	391,400	209,700	923,700	997,900	855,900	762,700	803,424	618,312
Net Income	808,200	447,800	2,035,300	2,384,300	2,150,200	1,931,400	1,923,580	1,445,689
Average Shares	587,100	597,700	614,900	625,200	634,100	643,200	666,252	682,059
Balance Sheet								
Current Assets	8,839,000	9,233,100	9,306,800	8,644,100	7,474,400	6,996,500	8,372,635	6,932,798
Total Assets	15,890,900	16,155,500	16,335,700	16,357,100	15,390,300	14,751,500	13,775,843	10,708,088
Current Liabilities	896,000	1,077,300	1,117,800	1,220,200	1,731,800	1,709,100	2,202,253	1,662,390
Long-Term Obligations	2,166,400	2,120,300	2,155,300	2,149,000	2,306,000	2,839,100	2,083,926	949,903
Total Liabilities	4,120,500	4,374,300	4,494,700	4,773,000	5,317,200	5,550,200	5,251,112	2,981,094
Stockholders' Equity	11,770,400	11,781,200	11,841,000	11,584,100	10,073,100	9,201,300	8,524,731	7,726,994
Shares Outstanding	586,134	595,228	603,517	622,893	630,917	636,626	653,080	672,023
Statistical Record								
Return on Assets %	10.32	11.81	12.45	15.02	14.27	13.50	15.71	14.33
Return on Equity %	14.16	16.43	17.38	22.02	22.31	21.73	23.67	18.83
EBITDA Margin %	37.27	38.59	40.28	40.78	38.43	38.05	38.14	36.24
Net Margin %	23.97	25.47	25.61	28.08	26.93	27.20	26.94	24.70
Asset Turnover	0.45	0.47	0.49	0.53	0.53	0.50	0.58	0.58
Current Ratio	9.86	8.57	8.33	7.08	4.32	4.09	3.80	4.17
Debt to Equity	0.18	0.18	0.18	0.19	0.23	0.31	0.24	0.12
Price Range	52.63-31.45	55.49-35.00	58.84-36.36	58.51-49.52	56.11-41.55	42.67-30.13	45.75-31.88	40.44-28.32
P/E Ratio	19.07-11.39	17.73-11.18	17.88-11.05	15.44-13.07	16.65-12.33	14.32-10.11	15.94-11.11	19.16-13.42
Average Yield %	1.56	1.35	2.17	0.88	2.94	2.78	0.83	3.76

Address: One Franklin Parkway, San Mateo, CA 94403 Telephone: 650-312-2000 Fax: 650-312-3655	Web Site: www.franklinresources.com Officers: Gregory E. Johnson - Chairman, President, Chief Executive Officer Rupert H. Johnson - Vice-Chairman	Auditors: PricewaterhouseCoopers LLP Investor Contact: 650-312-4091 Transfer Agents: Computershare, Pittsburgh, PA

FRANK'S INTERNATIONAL NV

Exchange	Symbol	Price	52Wk Range	Yield	P/E
NYS	FI	$16.01 (5/31/2016)	20.60-12.48	3.75	55.21

*7 Year Price Score N/A   *NYSE Composite Index=100   *12 Month Price Score 98.09

TRADING VOLUME (thousand shares)

Interim Earnings (Per Share)

Qtr.	Mar	Jun	Sep	Dec
2013	0.42	0.89	0.29	0.39
2014	0.27	0.23	0.31	0.23
2015	0.21	0.14	0.11	0.04
2016	0.00	...	...	...

Interim Dividends (Per Share)

Amt	Decl	Ex	Rec	Pay
0.15Q	08/03/2015	08/27/2015	08/31/2015	09/18/2015
0.15Q	11/02/2015	11/24/2015	11/27/2015	12/15/2015
0.15Q	02/23/2016	03/03/2016	03/07/2016	03/18/2016
0.15Q	04/27/2016	06/01/2016	06/03/2016	06/17/2016

Indicated Div: $0.60

Valuation Analysis / Institutional Holding

Valuation Analysis		Institutional Holding	
Forecast EPS	$-0.04	No of Institutions	
	(05/20/2016)	171	
Market Cap	$2.5 Billion	Shares	
Book Value	$1.2 Billion	38,433,616	
Price/Book	2.08	% Held	
Price/Sales	2.92	20.45	

Business Summary: Equipment & Services (MIC: 9.1.3 SIC: 1389 NAIC: 213112)

Frank's International is a provider of tubular services to the oil and gas industry. Co. provides its services to exploration and production companies in both offshore and onshore environments, with a focus on wells. Co. provides its tubular services and tubular sales through its three operating segments: International Services, which provides tubular services in international offshore markets and in several onshore international regions; U.S. Services, which provides tubular services in almost all of the active onshore oil and gas drilling regions in the U.S.; and Tubular Sales, which designs and manufactures certain products that it sells directly to external customers.

Recent Developments: For the quarter ended Mar 31 2016, net loss amounted to US$2.4 million versus net income of US$46.4 million in the year-earlier quarter. Revenues were US$153.5 million, down 44.7% from US$277.4 million the year before. Operating loss was US$2.9 million versus an income of US$55.0 million in the prior-year quarter. Direct operating expenses declined 41.5% to US$68.1 million from US$116.4 million in the comparable period the year before. Indirect operating expenses decreased 16.7% to US$88.2 million from US$106.0 million in the equivalent prior-year period.

Prospects: Our evaluation of Frank's International N.V. as of June 19, 2016 is the result of our systematic analysis on three basic characteristics: earnings strength, relative valuation, and recent stock price movement. The company has generated a negative trend in earnings per share over the past 5 quarters. Because the company lacks sufficient analyst estimate data, we place greater weight on the historical EPS trend as the measure of earnings strength. Based on operating earnings yield, the company is overvalued when compared to all of the companies in our coverage universe. Share price changes over the past year indicates that FI will perform in line with the market over the near term.

Financial Data

(US$ in Thousands)	3 Mos	12/31/2015	12/31/2014	12/31/2013	12/31/2012	12/31/2011	12/31/2010
Earnings Per Share	0.29	0.50	1.03	1.85	...	0.99	...
Cash Flow Per Share	2.41	2.77	2.40	2.10	...	1.52	...
Tang Book Value Per Share	7.53	7.65	7.77	7.06	8.56	...	...
Dividends Per Share	0.600	0.600	0.450	0.075	...	...	...
Dividend Payout %	206.90	120.00	43.69	4.05	...	...	...
Income Statement							
Total Revenue	153,486	974,600	1,152,632	1,077,722	1,055,925	719,412	608,208
EBITDA	(3,379)	250,288	394,037	424,875	447,347	236,246	181,060
Depn & Amortn	41	107,200	89,400	77,300	64,800	52,500	46,400
Income Before Taxes	(3,214)	143,429	304,724	346,922	382,811	183,085	133,002
Income Taxes	(806)	37,319	75,412	38,727	31,877	20,287	14,601
Net Income	(772)	79,110	159,037	255,462	350,934	126,980	118,401
Average Shares	155,244	209,152	207,828	185,506	...	172,000	...
Balance Sheet							
Current Assets	993,255	1,023,736	1,107,419	971,196	591,777	...	...
Total Assets	1,677,834	1,726,838	1,758,681	1,561,195	1,107,961	...	...
Current Liabilities	169,759	189,626	207,139	175,724	476,969	...	...
Long-Term Obligations	...	...	...	...	146,843	...	...
Total Liabilities	483,760	514,834	545,986	463,058	660,973	...	...
Stockholders' Equity	1,194,074	1,212,004	1,212,695	1,098,137	446,988	...	...
Shares Outstanding	155,357	155,146	154,327	153,524	50,206	...	...
Statistical Record							
Return on Assets %	2.56	4.54	9.58	...	...	...	...
Return on Equity %	3.65	6.53	13.76	...	...	...	...
EBITDA Margin %	N.M.	25.68	34.19	39.42	42.37	32.84	29.77
Net Margin %	N.M.	8.12	13.80	23.70	33.23	17.65	19.47
Asset Turnover	0.49	0.56	0.69	...	...	...	...
Current Ratio	5.85	5.40	5.35	5.53	1.24	...	...
Debt to Equity	...	...	...	...	0.33	...	...
Price Range	21.21-12.48	21.21-14.09	27.43-14.97	32.22-23.63	...	...	...
P/E Ratio	73.14-43.04	42.42-28.18	26.63-14.53	17.42-12.77	...	...	...
Average Yield %	3.56	3.45	2.06	0.27	...	...	...

Address: Mastenmakersweg 1, Den Helder, 1786 PB	Web Site: www.franksinternational.com	Auditors: PricewaterhouseCoopers LLP
Telephone: 203-670-000	Officers: Gary P. Luquette - President, Chief Executive Officer Jeffrey J. Bird - Executive Vice President, Chief Financial Officer, Interim Principal Accounting Officer	Investor Contact: 713-358-7343
Fax: 281-558-7883		Transfer Agents: American Stock Transfer & Trust Company, Brooklyn, NY

307

FREEPORT-MCMORAN INC

Exchange	Symbol	Price	52Wk Range	Yield	P/E
NYS	FCX	$11.08 (5/31/2016)	20.56-3.74	N/A	N/A

*7 Year Price Score 27.71 *NYSE Composite Index=100 *12 Month Price Score 108.39

TRADING VOLUME (thousand shares)

Interim Earnings (Per Share)

Qtr.	Mar	Jun	Sep	Dec
2013	0.68	0.49	0.79	0.68
2014	0.49	0.46	0.53	(2.73)
2015	(2.38)	(1.78)	(3.58)	(3.54)
2016	(3.35)	...	...	...

Interim Dividends (Per Share)

Dividend Payment Suspended

Valuation Analysis   Institutional Holding

Forecast EPS	$0.48	No of Institutions
	(05/24/2016)	1134
Market Cap	$13.9 Billion	Shares
Book Value	$3.7 Billion	952,140,800
Price/Book	3.76	% Held
Price/Sales	0.91	71.48

Business Summary: Non-Precious Metals (MIC: 8.2.2 SIC: 1021 NAIC: 212234)

Freeport-McMoRan is a natural resources company with a portfolio of mineral assets and oil and natural gas resources. Co.'s portfolio of assets includes the Grasberg minerals district in Indonesia, copper and gold deposit; mining operations in North and South America; the Tenke Fungurume minerals district in the Democratic Republic of Congo in Africa; and the U.S. oil and natural gas assets. Co.'s primary natural resources are copper, gold, molybdenum and oil. At Dec 31 2015, Co.'s estimated proved oil and natural gas reserves totaled 252.0 million barrels of oil equivalents, of which 82.0% was comprised of oil (including natural gas liquids).

Recent Developments: For the quarter ended Mar 31 2016, net loss amounted to US$4.10 billion versus a net loss of US$2.41 billion in the year-earlier quarter. Revenues were US$3.53 billion, down 15.1% from US$4.15 billion the year before. Operating loss was US$3.88 billion versus a loss of US$2.96 billion in the prior-year quarter. Direct operating expenses rose 4.0% to US$7.23 billion from US$6.96 billion in the comparable period the year before. Indirect operating expenses increased 5.0% to US$169.0 million from US$161.0 million in the equivalent prior-year period.

Prospects: Our evaluation of Freeport-McMoRan Inc. as of June 26, 2016 is the result of our systematic analysis on three basic characteristics: earnings strength, relative valuation, and recent stock price movement. The company has enjoyed a very positive trend in earnings per share over the past 5 quarters. However, while recent estimates for the company have been lowered by analysts, FCX has posted better than expected results. Based on operating earnings yield, the company is overvalued when compared to all of the companies in our coverage universe. Share price changes over the past year indicates that FCX will perform poorly over the near term.

Financial Data

(US$ in Thousands)	3 Mos	12/31/2015	12/31/2014	12/31/2013	12/31/2012	12/31/2011	12/31/2010	12/31/2009
Earnings Per Share	(12.25)	(11.31)	(1.26)	2.64	3.19	4.78	4.57	2.93
Cash Flow Per Share	2.59	2.98	5.42	6.13	3.97	6.99	6.86	5.31
Tang Book Value Per Share	2.95	6.03	17.28	17.96	18.13	16.16	12.88	6.86
Dividends Per Share	...	0.261	1.250	2.250	1.250	1.500	1.125	0.075
Dividend Payout %	...	...	...	85.23	39.18	31.38	24.62	2.56
Income Statement								
Total Revenue	3,527,000	15,877,000	21,438,000	20,921,000	18,010,000	20,880,000	18,982,000	15,040,000
EBITDA	(3,116,000)	(9,879,000)	4,069,000	8,228,000	6,852,000	10,056,000	10,102,000	7,539,000
Depn & Amortn	722,000	3,497,000	3,863,000	2,797,000	1,179,000	926,000	1,128,000	1,137,000
Income Before Taxes	(4,038,000)	(14,021,000)	(424,000)	4,913,000	5,487,000	8,818,000	8,512,000	5,816,000
Income Taxes	70,000	(1,935,000)	324,000	1,475,000	1,510,000	3,087,000	2,983,000	2,307,000
Net Income	(4,101,000)	(12,089,000)	(745,000)	3,441,000	3,980,000	5,747,000	5,544,000	3,534,000
Average Shares	1,251,000	1,082,000	1,039,000	1,006,000	954,000	955,000	949,000	938,000
Balance Sheet								
Current Assets	7,233,000	7,462,000	9,045,000	9,972,000	10,297,000	10,047,000	9,851,000	7,433,000
Total Assets	42,664,000	46,577,000	58,795,000	63,473,000	35,440,000	32,070,000	29,386,000	25,996,000
Current Liabilities	4,426,000	4,307,000	5,172,000	4,773,000	3,343,000	2,940,000	3,763,000	3,002,000
Long-Term Obligations	19,638,000	19,779,000	18,492,000	20,394,000	3,525,000	3,533,000	4,660,000	6,330,000
Total Liabilities	38,972,000	38,749,000	40,508,000	42,539,000	17,897,000	16,428,000	16,882,000	16,877,000
Stockholders' Equity	3,692,000	7,828,000	18,287,000	20,934,000	17,543,000	15,642,000	12,504,000	9,119,000
Shares Outstanding	1,252,000	1,246,000	1,039,000	1,038,000	949,000	948,000	945,000	860,000
Statistical Record								
Return on Assets %	N.M.	N.M.	N.M.	6.96	11.76	18.70	20.02	14.32
Return on Equity %	N.M.	N.M.	N.M.	17.89	23.92	40.84	51.28	47.46
EBITDA Margin %	N.M.	N.M.	18.98	39.33	38.05	48.16	53.22	50.13
Net Margin %	N.M.	N.M.	N.M.	16.45	22.10	27.52	29.21	23.50
Asset Turnover	0.31	0.30	0.35	0.42	0.53	0.68	0.69	0.61
Current Ratio	1.63	1.73	1.75	2.09	3.08	3.42	2.62	2.48
Debt to Equity	5.32	2.53	1.01	0.97	0.20	0.23	0.37	0.69
Price Range	23.66-3.74	23.66-6.12	39.04-21.03	37.74-26.82	46.50-30.81	60.92-29.87	60.05-29.09	43.66-11.07
P/E Ratio	...	...	...	14.30-10.16	14.58-9.66	12.74-6.25	13.14-6.37	14.90-3.78
Average Yield %	...	1.69	3.80	6.90	3.35	3.16	2.76	0.27

Address: 333 North Central Avenue, Phoenix, AZ 85004-2189 **Telephone:** 602-366-8100	**Web Site:** www.fcx.com **Officers:** James R. Moffett - Chairman Emeritus, Executive Chairman, Chief Executive Officer Richard C. Adkerson - Vice-Chairman, President, Chief Executive Officer	**Auditors:** Ernst & Young, LLP **Investor Contact:** 602-366-8400 **Transfer Agents:** Computershare, Canton, MA

FTI CONSULTING INC.

Exchange	Symbol	Price	52Wk Range	Yield	P/E
NYS	FCN	$41.85 (5/31/2016)	45.66-30.41	N/A	24.05

*7 Year Price Score 86.34 *NYSE Composite Index=100 *12 Month Price Score 101.90

Interim Earnings (Per Share)

Qtr.	Mar	Jun	Sep	Dec
2013	0.58	0.50	(1.29)	(0.18)
2014	0.45	0.42	0.55	0.01
2015	0.57	0.52	0.25	0.24
2016	0.73	...	...	...

Interim Dividends (Per Share)

No Dividends Paid

Valuation Analysis / Institutional Holding

Valuation Analysis		Institutional Holding	
Forecast EPS	$2.35	No of Institutions	
	(05/06/2016)	264	
Market Cap	$1.7 Billion	Shares	
Book Value	$1.2 Billion	48,817,184	
Price/Book	1.47	% Held	
Price/Sales	0.95	93.00	

TRADING VOLUME (thousand shares)

Business Summary: Business Services (MIC: 7.5.2 SIC: 8742 NAIC: 541618)

FTI Consulting is a business advisory firm. Co. business segments are: Corporate Finance and Restructuring, which advise on a restructuring; Forensic and Litigation Consulting, which provides law firms, companies, and government clients; Economic Consulting, which provides law firms, companies, government entities and other interested parties with analysis of complex economic issues for use in legal, regulatory and arbitration proceedings, strategic decision making and public policy debates; Technology, which provide a suite of software and services; and Strategic Communications, which provide advice and consulting services relating to financial and corporate communications.

Recent Developments: For the quarter ended Mar 31 2016, net income increased 27.4% to US$30.2 million from US$23.7 million in the year-earlier quarter. Revenues were US$470.3 million, up 8.8% from US$432.3 million the year before. Operating income was US$52.2 million versus US$47.8 million in the prior-year quarter, an increase of 9.2%. Direct operating expenses rose 9.5% to US$305.6 million from US$279.0 million in the comparable period the year before. Indirect operating expenses increased 6.6% to US$112.4 million from US$105.5 million in the equivalent prior-year period.

Prospects: Our evaluation of FTI Consulting Inc. as of June 19, 2016 is the result of our systematic analysis on three basic characteristics: earnings strength, relative valuation, and recent stock price movement. The company has managed to produce a neutral trend in earnings per share over the past 5 quarters and while recent estimates for the company have been raised by analysts, FCN has posted better than expected results. Based on operating earnings yield, the company is undervalued when compared to all of the companies in our coverage universe. Share price changes over the past year indicates that FCN will perform poorly over the near term.

Financial Data

(US$ in Thousands)	3 Mos	12/31/2015	12/31/2014	12/31/2013	12/31/2012	12/31/2011	12/31/2010	12/31/2009
Earnings Per Share	1.74	1.58	1.44	(0.27)	(0.92)	2.39	1.51	2.70
Cash Flow Per Share	3.90	3.43	3.41	4.93	2.97	4.23	4.28	5.02
Income Statement								
Total Revenue	470,285	1,779,149	1,756,212	1,652,432	1,576,871	1,566,768	1,401,461	1,399,946
EBITDA	62,816	180,608	188,617	128,867	107,222	253,258	240,004	319,156
Depn & Amortn	10,577	36,626	44,021	49,754	52,786	48,371	77,266	52,502
Income Before Taxes	48,567	105,386	101,411	31,811	3,114	153,127	117,440	227,025
Income Taxes	18,386	39,333	42,604	42,405	40,100	49,224	45,550	83,999
Net Income	30,181	66,053	58,807	(10,594)	(36,986)	103,903	71,890	143,026
Average Shares	41,148	41,729	40,729	39,188	40,316	43,473	47,471	53,044
Balance Sheet								
Current Assets	744,351	741,625	884,173	803,861	674,375	770,954	788,715	499,915
Total Assets	2,225,044	2,229,018	2,430,527	2,364,947	2,275,452	2,411,084	2,414,359	2,077,338
Current Liabilities	287,519	347,077	367,092	384,330	304,197	497,837	289,282	406,202
Long-Term Obligations	501,961	494,772	700,000	711,000	717,024	643,579	785,563	417,397
Total Liabilities	1,043,798	1,081,415	1,327,781	1,322,688	1,207,220	1,304,882	1,247,040	973,124
Stockholders' Equity	1,181,246	1,147,603	1,102,746	1,042,259	1,068,232	1,106,202	1,167,319	1,104,214
Shares Outstanding	41,385	41,234	41,181	40,526	40,755	41,484	46,144	46,985
Statistical Record								
Return on Assets %	3.16	2.84	2.45	N.M.	N.M.	4.31	3.20	6.87
Return on Equity %	6.31	5.87	5.48	N.M.	N.M.	9.14	6.33	12.84
EBITDA Margin %	13.36	10.15	10.74	7.80	6.80	16.16	17.13	22.80
Net Margin %	6.42	3.71	3.35	N.M.	N.M.	6.63	5.13	10.22
Asset Turnover	0.79	0.76	0.73	0.71	0.67	0.65	0.62	0.67
Current Ratio	2.59	2.14	2.41	2.09	2.22	1.55	2.73	1.23
Debt to Equity	0.42	0.43	0.64	0.68	0.67	0.58	0.67	0.38
Price Range	45.66-30.41	45.66-33.62	41.76-28.51	46.11-31.20	44.22-23.11	43.77-32.99	48.06-31.94	56.13-36.54
P/E Ratio	26.24-17.48	28.90-21.28	29.00-19.80	...	...	18.31-13.80	31.83-21.15	20.79-13.53

Address: 1101 K Street N.W., Washington, DC 20005 Telephone: 202-312-9100	Web Site: www.fticonsulting.com Officers: Curtis Lu - General Counsel Dominic DiNapoli - Vice-Chairman	Auditors: KPMG LLP Investor Contact: 617-747-1791 Transfer Agents: American Stock Transfer & Trust Company, New York, NY

FULLER (H.B.) COMPANY

Exchange	Symbol	Price	52Wk Range	Yield	P/E	Div Achiever
NYS	FUL	$45.66 (5/31/2016)	45.66-32.71	1.23	24.42	48 Years

*7 Year Price Score 101.37 *NYSE Composite Index=100 *12 Month Price Score 112.27

Interim Earnings (Per Share)

Qtr.	Feb	May	Aug	Nov
2012-13	0.41	0.51	0.55	0.42
2013-14	0.28	0.40	0.08	0.21
2014-15	0.19	0.49	0.52	0.49
2015-16	0.37			

Interim Dividends (Per Share)

Amt	Decl	Ex	Rec	Pay
0.13Q	07/09/2015	07/21/2015	07/23/2015	08/06/2015
0.13Q	10/01/2015	10/13/2015	10/15/2015	10/29/2015
0.13Q	01/21/2016	02/02/2016	02/04/2016	02/18/2016
0.14Q	04/07/2016	04/19/2016	04/21/2016	05/05/2016

Indicated Div: $0.56 (Div. Reinv. Plan)

Valuation Analysis / Institutional Holding

Forecast EPS	$2.55 (05/20/2016)	No of Institutions	265
Market Cap	$2.3 Billion	Shares	57,160,220
Book Value	$889.4 Million	% Held	95.71
Price/Book	2.57		
Price/Sales	1.09		

Business Summary: Specialty Chemicals (MIC: 8.3.2 SIC: 2891 NAIC: 325520)

H.B. Fuller is a formulator, manufacturer and marketer of adhesives, sealants and other chemical products. Co.'s business is reported in four operating segments: Americas Adhesives; Europe, India, Middle East and Africa (EIMEA); Asia Pacific and Construction Products. Co.'s Americas Adhesives, EIMEA and Asia Pacific operating segments produce and supply industrial adhesives products for applications in various markets including durable assembly, packaging, converting and nonwoven and hygiene. Co.'s Construction Products operating segment includes products used for tile setting, flooring, and heating, ventilation and air conditioning and insulation applications.

Recent Developments: For the quarter ended Feb 27 2016, net income increased 93.6% to US$19.0 million from US$9.8 million in the year-earlier quarter. Revenues were US$474.3 million, up 0.8% from US$470.7 million the year before. Direct operating expenses declined 5.0% to US$336.7 million from US$354.5 million in the comparable period the year before. Indirect operating expenses increased 3.1% to US$100.2 million from US$97.2 million in the equivalent prior-year period.

Prospects: Our evaluation of Fuller (H.B.) Company as of June 19, 2016 is the result of our systematic analysis on three basic characteristics: earnings strength, relative valuation, and recent stock price movement. The company has generated a negative trend in earnings per share over the past 5 quarters. However, while recent estimates for the company have been mixed, FUL has posted better than expected results. Based on operating earnings yield, the company is about fairly valued when compared to all of the companies in our coverage universe. Share price changes over the past year indicates that FUL will perform poorly over the near term.

Financial Data
(US$ in Thousands)

	3 Mos	11/28/2015	11/29/2014	11/30/2013	12/01/2012	12/03/2011	11/27/2010	11/28/2009
Earnings Per Share	1.87	1.69	0.97	1.89	2.48	1.79	1.43	1.70
Cash Flow Per Share	3.74	4.20	0.60	2.67	2.20	2.06	1.53	1.48
Tang Book Value Per Share	6.56	6.11	8.71	8.91	5.82	9.38	7.96	7.12
Dividends Per Share	0.520	0.510	0.460	0.385	0.330	0.295	0.278	0.270
Dividend Payout %	27.81	30.18	47.42	20.37	13.31	16.48	19.44	15.88
Income Statement								
Total Revenue	474,326	2,083,660	2,104,454	2,046,968	1,886,239	1,557,552	1,356,161	1,234,659
EBITDA	52,299	237,746	164,236	204,722	162,100	154,763	127,847	155,964
Depn & Amortn	19,956	74,890	65,524	58,795	54,490	31,054	30,361	34,709
Income Before Taxes	26,035	138,345	79,312	127,544	89,548	114,992	87,718	114,620
Income Taxes	8,760	55,855	34,348	39,949	30,479	34,951	25,307	36,728
Net Income	18,918	86,680	49,773	96,761	125,622	89,105	70,877	83,654
Average Shares	50,995	51,393	51,255	51,136	50,618	49,866	49,608	49,117
Balance Sheet								
Current Assets	791,060	801,051	765,136	794,694	799,344	596,590	533,617	473,656
Total Assets	2,023,336	2,042,252	1,869,006	1,873,028	1,786,320	1,227,709	1,153,457	1,100,445
Current Liabilities	379,086	349,525	317,199	360,778	350,119	254,985	231,333	236,008
Long-Term Obligations	610,969	669,606	547,735	472,315	475,112	179,611	200,978	162,713
Total Liabilities	1,133,956	1,169,332	978,959	942,963	1,008,047	522,505	521,523	509,091
Stockholders' Equity	889,380	872,920	890,047	930,065	778,273	705,204	631,934	591,354
Shares Outstanding	49,989	50,074	50,310	50,228	49,903	49,449	49,194	48,657
Statistical Record								
Return on Assets %	4.65	4.44	2.67	5.30	8.36	7.36	6.31	7.69
Return on Equity %	10.90	9.86	5.48	11.36	16.98	13.11	11.62	14.89
EBITDA Margin %	11.03	11.41	7.80	10.00	8.59	9.94	9.43	12.63
Net Margin %	3.99	4.16	2.37	4.73	6.66	5.72	5.23	6.78
Asset Turnover	1.01	1.07	1.13	1.12	1.26	1.29	1.21	1.13
Current Ratio	2.09	2.29	2.41	2.20	2.28	2.34	2.31	2.01
Debt to Equity	0.69	0.77	0.62	0.51	0.61	0.25	0.32	0.28
Price Range	45.22-32.71	45.74-32.73	52.74-37.46	51.32-32.55	34.00-21.34	25.19-17.06	24.56-18.69	22.88-9.76
P/E Ratio	24.18-17.49	27.07-19.37	54.37-38.62	27.15-17.22	13.71-8.60	14.07-9.53	17.17-13.07	13.46-5.74
Average Yield %	1.33	1.25	0.99	0.95	1.11	1.37	1.30	1.55

Address: 1200 Willow Lake Boulevard, St. Paul, MN 55110-5101 Telephone: 651-236-5900 Fax: 651-236-5161	Web Site: www.hbfuller.com Officers: Lee R. Mitau - Chairman James J. Owens - President, Chief Executive Officer	Auditors: KPMG LLP Investor Contact: 651-236-5062 Transfer Agents: Wells Fargo Shareholder Services, St. Paul, MN

GALLAGHER (ARTHUR J.) & CO.

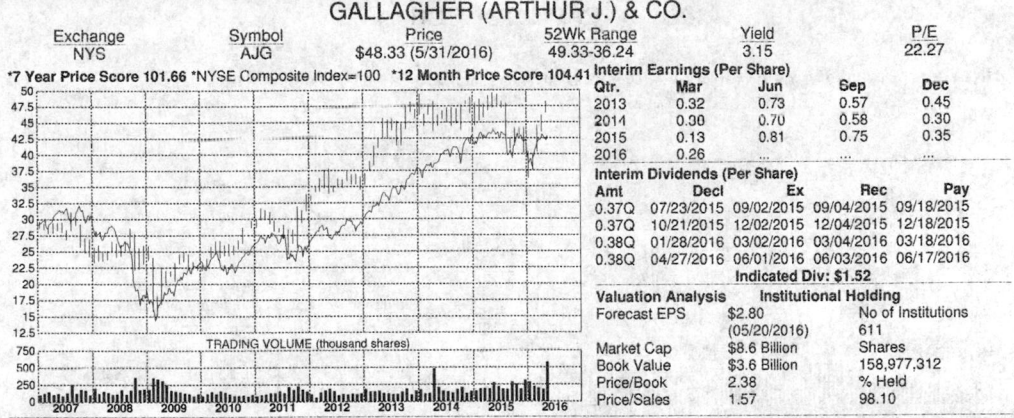

Exchange	Symbol	Price	52Wk Range	Yield	P/E
NYS	AJG	$48.33 (5/31/2016)	49.33-36.24	3.15	22.27

*7 Year Price Score 101.66 *NYSE Composite Index=100 *12 Month Price Score 104.41

Interim Earnings (Per Share)

Qtr.	Mar	Jun	Sep	Dec
2013	0.32	0.73	0.57	0.45
2014	0.30	0.70	0.58	0.30
2015	0.13	0.81	0.75	0.35
2016	0.26	...	...	...

Interim Dividends (Per Share)

Amt	Decl	Ex	Rec	Pay
0.37Q	07/23/2015	09/02/2015	09/04/2015	09/18/2015
0.37Q	10/21/2015	12/02/2015	12/04/2015	12/18/2015
0.38Q	01/28/2016	03/02/2016	03/04/2016	03/18/2016
0.38Q	04/27/2016	06/01/2016	06/03/2016	06/17/2016

Indicated Div: $1.52

Valuation Analysis		Institutional Holding	
Forecast EPS	$2.80	No of Institutions	
	(05/20/2016)	611	
Market Cap	$8.6 Billion	Shares	
Book Value	$3.6 Billion	158,977,312	
Price/Book	2.38	% Held	
Price/Sales	1.57	98.10	

TRADING VOLUME (thousand shares)

Business Summary: Brokers & Intermediaries (MIC: 5.2.3 SIC: 6411 NAIC: 524210)

Arthur J. Gallagher & Co. is engaged in providing insurance brokerage and third-party claims settlement and administration services to entities in the U.S. and abroad. Co. operates three segments: Brokerage, which is comprised of retail and wholesale brokerage operations; Risk Management, which provides contract claim settlement and administration services for enterprises that choose to self-insure some or all of their property/casualty coverages and for insurance companies that choose to outsource some or all of their property/casualty claims departments; and Corporate, which manages Co.'s clean energy and other investments.

Recent Developments: For the quarter ended Mar 31 2016, net income increased 78.7% to US$57.9 million from US$32.4 million in the year-earlier quarter. Revenues were US$1.30 billion, up 5.6% from US$1.23 billion the year before.

Prospects: Our evaluation of Gallagher (Arthur J.) & Co. as of June 19, 2016 is the result of our systematic analysis on three basic characteristics: earnings strength, relative valuation, and recent stock price movement. The company has generated a negative trend in earnings per share over the past 5 quarters. However, while recent estimates for the company have been lowered by analysts, AJG has posted better than expected results. Based on operating earnings yield, the company is undervalued when compared to all of the companies in our coverage universe. Share price changes over the past year indicates that AJG will perform in line with the market over the near term.

Financial Data
(US$ in Thousands)

	3 Mos	12/31/2015	12/31/2014	12/31/2013	12/31/2012	12/31/2011	12/31/2010	12/31/2009
Earnings Per Share	2.17	2.06	1.97	2.06	1.59	1.28	1.66	1.28
Cash Flow Per Share	3.66	3.79	2.63	2.71	2.83	2.53	2.21	2.10
Dividends Per Share	1.490	1.480	1.440	1.400	1.360	1.320	1.280	1.280
Dividend Payout %	68.66	71.84	73.10	67.96	85.53	103.13	77.11	100.00
Income Statement								
Total Revenue	1,300,400	5,392,400	4,626,500	3,179,600	2,520,300	2,134,700	1,864,200	1,729,300
EBITDA	86,100	387,400	336,800	327,900	286,700	243,700	235,300	241,700
Depn & Amortn	30,400	93,900	69,400	53,400	41,400	35,900	32,300	30,600
Income Before Taxes	55,700	293,500	267,400	274,500	245,300	207,800	203,000	211,100
Income Taxes	(2,200)	(95,600)	(36,000)	5,900	50,300	63,700	39,700	78,000
Net Income	46,500	356,800	303,400	268,600	195,000	144,100	174,100	128,600
Average Shares	177,600	173,200	154,300	130,500	122,500	112,500	105,100	100,600
Balance Sheet								
Current Assets	3,939,500	4,335,800	3,811,200	2,875,600	2,429,500	2,199,400	1,726,000	1,540,000
Total Assets	10,712,600	10,913,800	10,010,000	6,860,500	5,352,300	4,483,500	3,596,000	3,250,300
Current Liabilities	4,022,400	4,191,700	3,642,700	3,284,800	2,362,900	2,073,600	1,577,300	1,474,400
Long-Term Obligations	2,071,800	2,075,000	2,125,000	825,000	725,000	675,000	550,000	550,000
Total Liabilities	7,115,500	7,275,500	6,780,600	4,775,000	3,693,700	3,239,900	2,489,300	2,357,400
Stockholders' Equity	3,597,100	3,638,300	3,229,400	2,085,500	1,658,600	1,243,600	1,106,700	892,900
Shares Outstanding	177,100	176,900	164,600	133,600	125,600	114,700	108,400	102,500
Statistical Record								
Return on Assets %	3.73	3.41	3.60	4.40	3.95	3.57	5.09	3.94
Return on Equity %	11.31	10.39	11.42	14.35	13.40	12.26	17.41	15.77
EBITDA Margin %	6.62	7.18	7.28	10.31	11.38	11.42	12.62	13.98
Net Margin %	3.58	6.62	6.56	8.45	7.74	6.75	9.34	7.44
Asset Turnover	0.53	0.52	0.55	0.52	0.51	0.53	0.54	0.53
Current Ratio	0.98	1.03	1.05	0.88	1.03	1.06	1.09	1.04
Debt to Equity	0.58	0.57	0.66	0.40	0.44	0.54	0.50	0.62
Price Range	49.50-36.24	49.50-40.08	49.39-43.59	48.11-34.65	37.73-32.76	33.82-24.51	29.65-22.00	25.91-15.04
P/E Ratio	22.81-16.70	24.03-19.46	25.07-22.13	23.35-16.82	23.73-20.60	26.42-19.15	17.86-13.25	20.24-11.75
Average Yield %	3.38	3.23	3.11	3.26	3.84	4.51	5.00	5.93

Address: Two Pierce Place, Itasca, IL 60143-3141
Telephone: 630-773-3800

Web Site: www.ajg.com
Officers: J. Patrick Gallagher - Chairman, President, Chief Executive Officer Douglas K. Howell - Corporate Vice-President, Chief Financial Officer

Auditors: Ernst & Young LLP
Investor Contact: 630-285-3501
Transfer Agents: Computershare Investor Services, Canton, MA

GAMESTOP CORP

Exchange	Symbol	Price	52Wk Range	Yield	P/E
NYS	GME	$29.10 (5/31/2016)	47.44-25.06	5.09	7.80

*7 Year Price Score 103.01 *NYSE Composite Index=100   ***12 Month Price Score 82.65**

Interim Earnings (Per Share)

Qtr.	Apr	Jul	Oct	Jan
2013-14	0.46	0.09	0.58	1.87
2014-15	0.59	0.22	0.50	2.17
2015-16	0.68	0.24	0.53	2.33
2016-17	0.63			

Interim Dividends (Per Share)

Amt	Decl	Ex	Rec	Pay
0.36Q	08/27/2015	09/04/2015	09/09/2015	09/22/2015
0.36Q	11/23/2015	12/01/2015	12/03/2015	12/15/2015
0.37Q	02/23/2016	03/04/2016	03/08/2016	03/22/2016
0.37Q	05/24/2016	06/06/2016	06/08/2016	06/21/2016

Indicated Div: $1.48

Valuation Analysis   **Institutional Holding**

Forecast EPS	$4.02	No of Institutions
	(05/20/2016)	664
Market Cap	$3.0 Billion	Shares
Book Value	$2.2 Billion	140,582,960
Price/Book	1.40	% Held
Price/Sales	0.33	64.23

Business Summary: Retail - Appliances and Electronics (MIC: 2.1.7 SIC: 5734 NAIC: 443120)

GameStop is a multichannel video game retailer. Co. sells new and pre-owned video game hardware, physical and digital video game software, video game accessories, as well as new and pre-owned mobile and consumer electronics products and other merchandise. As of Jan 30, 2016, Co.'s retail network and family of brands included 7,117 company-operated stores in the U.S., Australia, Canada and Europe, primarily under the names GameStop, EB Games and Micromania. Co. also operates electronic commerce websites under the names www.gamestop.com, www.ebgames.com.au, www.ebgames.co.nz, www.gamestop.ca, www.gamestop.it, www.gamestop.ie, www.gamestop.de, www.gamestop.co.uk and www.micromania.fr.

Recent Developments: For the quarter ended Apr 30 2016, net income decreased 10.8% to US$65.8 million from US$73.8 million in the year-earlier quarter. Revenues were US$1.97 billion, down 4.3% from US$2.06 billion the year before. Operating income was US$114.0 million versus US$123.9 million in the prior-year quarter, a decrease of 8.0%. Direct operating expenses declined 8.8% to US$1.30 billion from US$1.42 billion in the comparable period the year before. Indirect operating expenses increased 9.0% to US$561.5 million from US$515.1 million in the equivalent prior-year period.

Prospects: Our evaluation of GameStop Corp. as of June 19, 2016 is the result of our systematic analysis on three basic characteristics: earnings strength, relative valuation, and recent stock price movement. The company has generated a negative trend in earnings per share over the past 5 quarters. However, while recent estimates for the company have been mixed, GME has posted better than expected results. Based on operating earnings yield, the company is undervalued when compared to all of the companies in our coverage universe. Share price changes over the past year indicates that GME will perform well over the near term.

Financial Data

(US$ in Thousands)	3 Mos	01/30/2016	01/31/2015	02/01/2014	02/02/2013	01/28/2012	01/29/2011	01/30/2010
Earnings Per Share	3.73	3.78	3.47	2.99	(2.13)	2.41	2.65	2.25
Cash Flow Per Share	3.94	6.21	4.29	6.53	4.92	4.48	3.91	3.93
Tang Book Value Per Share	3.18	2.65	4.08	5.57	6.34	5.95	4.43	3.26
Dividends Per Share	1.450	1.440	1.320	1.100	0.800	...	...	...
Dividend Payout %	38.87	38.10	38.04	36.79	...	...	...	...
Income Statement								
Total Revenue	1,971,500	9,363,800	9,296,000	9,039,500	8,886,700	9,550,500	9,473,700	9,077,997
EBITDA	155,000	793,100	762,800	726,400	138,500	760,600	838,400	800,839
Depn & Amortn	41,000	144,900	144,500	152,900	180,100	191,700	181,800	169,129
Income Before Taxes	103,200	625,200	608,300	568,800	(44,900)	549,100	621,400	588,533
Income Taxes	37,400	222,400	215,200	214,600	224,900	210,600	214,600	212,804
Net Income	65,800	402,800	393,100	354,200	(269,700)	339,900	408,000	377,265
Average Shares	104,200	106,700	113,200	118,400	126,400	141,000	154,000	167,875
Balance Sheet								
Current Assets	2,037,100	1,938,800	2,062,500	1,949,600	2,010,900	1,997,300	2,154,800	2,127,304
Total Assets	4,446,000	4,334,900	4,246,300	4,091,400	4,133,600	4,847,400	5,063,800	4,955,327
Current Liabilities	1,366,000	1,794,400	1,639,700	1,726,000	1,715,300	1,633,900	1,747,800	1,655,676
Long-Term Obligations	812,400	350,000	350,600	1,600	...	...	249,000	447,343
Total Liabilities	2,289,900	2,253,900	2,178,600	1,840,000	1,847,300	1,805,300	2,166,500	2,232,170
Stockholders' Equity	2,156,100	2,081,000	2,067,700	2,251,400	2,286,300	3,042,100	2,897,300	2,723,157
Shares Outstanding	104,000	103,300	107,700	115,300	118,200	136,800	146,000	158,662
Statistical Record								
Return on Assets %	9.41	9.41	9.46	8.64	N.M.	6.88	8.17	7.99
Return on Equity %	18.67	19.47	18.25	15.65	N.M.	11.48	14.56	15.06
EBITDA Margin %	7.86	8.47	8.21	8.04	1.56	7.96	8.85	8.82
Net Margin %	3.34	4.30	4.23	3.92	N.M.	3.56	4.31	4.16
Asset Turnover	2.21	2.19	2.24	2.20	1.95	1.93	1.90	1.92
Current Ratio	1.49	1.08	1.26	1.13	1.17	1.22	1.23	1.28
Debt to Equity	0.38	0.17	0.17	N.M.	...	...	0.09	0.16
Price Range	47.44-25.06	47.44-25.06	46.10-31.92	57.59-23.54	27.83-15.73	28.21-19.50	25.46-17.20	32.42-19.64
P/E Ratio	12.72-6.72	12.55-6.63	13.29-9.20	19.26-7.87	...	11.71-8.09	9.61-6.49	14.41-8.73
Average Yield %	3.85	3.61	3.36	2.65	3.68			

Address: 625 Westport Parkway, Grapevine, TX 76051 **Telephone:** 817-424-2000	**Web Site:** www.gamestop.com **Officers:** Daniel A. DeMatteo - Executive Chairman Tony D. Bartel - President, Chief Operating Officer	**Auditors:** Deloitte & Touche LLP **Transfer Agents:** Computershare, Providence, RI

GANNETT CO INC

Exchange	Symbol	Price	52Wk Range	Yield	P/E
NYS	GCI	$15.62 (5/31/2016)	17.75-11.30	4.10	N/A

*7 Year Price Score N/A ***NYSE Composite Index=100** ***12 Month Price Score 106.99**

Interim Earnings (Per Share)

Qtr.	Mar	Jun	Sep	Dec
2014	0.36	0.45	0.44	0.58
2015	0.29	0.46	0.33	0.17
2016	0.26	...	...	...

Interim Dividends (Per Share)

Amt	Decl	Ex	Rec	Pay
0.16Q	07/28/2015	09/02/2015	09/04/2015	10/01/2015
0.16Q	10/28/2015	12/02/2015	12/04/2015	01/04/2016
0.16Q	02/23/2016	03/09/2016	03/11/2016	04/01/2016
0.16Q	05/10/2016	06/02/2016	06/06/2016	06/20/2016

Indicated Div: $0.64

Valuation Analysis

		Institutional Holding	
Forecast EPS	$1.53	No of Institutions	
	(05/03/2016)	302	
Market Cap	$1.8 Billion	Shares	
Book Value	$1.1 Billion	107,564,800	
Price/Book	1.68	% Held	
Price/Sales	N/A	N/A	

TRADING VOLUME (thousand shares)

Business Summary: Publishing (MIC: 2.3.3 SIC: 2721 NAIC: 511120)

Gannett is an international, multi-platform news and information company that delivers content where and when consumers want to engage with it on virtually any device. Co.'s operations comprise USA TODAY, 92 daily local publications in the U.S. and Guam, more than 400 non-daily publications in the U.S., and, through its Newsquest Media Group Limited subsidiary, more than 150 local news brands online, mobile and in print in the U.K. Co.'s operations also include commercial printing, marketing and data services. Certain of Co.'s businesses have strategic relationships with online businesses, including CareerBuilder, Cars.com, and G/O Digital, a digital marketing services business.

Recent Developments: For the quarter ended Mar 27 2016, net income decreased 5.9% to US$31.3 million from US$33.2 million in the year-earlier quarter. Revenues were US$659.4 million, down 8.1% from US$717.4 million the year before. Operating income was US$47.5 million versus US$29.8 million in the prior-year quarter, an increase of 59.2%. Direct operating expenses declined 12.5% to US$419.8 million from US$479.8 million in the comparable period the year before. Indirect operating expenses decreased 7.5% to US$192.1 million from US$207.7 million in the equivalent prior-year period.

Prospects: Our evaluation of Gannett Co Inc. as of June 19, 2016 is the result of our systematic analysis on three basic characteristics: earnings strength, relative valuation, and recent stock price movement. The company has generated a negative trend in earnings per share over the past 5 quarters and while recent estimates for the company have been raised by analysts, GCI has posted better than expected results. Based on operating earnings yield, the company is undervalued when compared to all of the companies in our coverage universe. Share price changes over the past year indicates that GCI will perform very poorly over the near term.

Financial Data

(US$ in Thousands)	3 Mos	12/27/2015	12/28/2014	12/29/2013	12/30/2012
Earnings Per Share	...	1.25	...	...	...
Cash Flow Per Share	...	2.01	...	...	...
Tang Book Value Per Share	3.93	3.66	...	...	...
Dividends Per Share	0.480	0.320	...	...	...
Dividend Payout %	...	25.60	...	...	...
Income Statement					
Total Revenue	659,368	2,885,012	3,171,878	3,324,939	3,470,007
EBITDA	67,195	277,910	373,471	433,093	451,193
Depn & Amortn	23,959	95,916	111,063	110,098	117,789
Income Before Taxes	43,236	181,994	262,408	322,995	333,404
Income Taxes	13,085	47,884	67,560	71,302	67,560
Net Income	31,292	146,091	210,705	274,461	277,230
Average Shares	118,656	116,695	...	...	...
Balance Sheet					
Current Assets	576,941	629,536	531,070	602,281	...
Total Assets	2,332,658	2,427,799	2,384,460	2,494,736	...
Current Liabilities	435,666	490,494	409,583	436,233	...
Total Liabilities	1,250,364	1,369,223	1,446,988	1,229,515	...
Stockholders' Equity	1,082,294	1,058,576	937,472	1,265,221	...
Shares Outstanding	116,492	115,668	...	...	...
Statistical Record					
Return on Assets %	...	...	8.66	...	...
Return on Equity %	...	...	19.18	...	...
EBITDA Margin %	10.19	9.63	11.77	13.03	13.00
Net Margin %	4.75	5.06	6.64	8.25	7.99
Asset Turnover	...	...	1.30	...	...
Current Ratio	1.32	1.28	1.30	1.38	...
Price Range	17.75-11.30	17.75-11.30	...	...	...
P/E Ratio	...	14.20-9.04	...	...	...
Average Yield %	3.25	2.19	...	...	...

Address: 7950 Jones Branch Drive, McLean, VA 22107-0910
Telephone: 703-854-6000

Web Site: www.gannett.com
Officers: John Jeffry Louis - Chairman Robert J Dickey - President, Chief Executive Officer

Auditors: Ernst & Young LLP
Transfer Agents: Wells Fargo Shareowner Services, Mendota Heights, MN

GARTNER INC

Exchange	Symbol	Price	52Wk Range	Yield	P/E
NYS	IT	$101.62 (5/31/2016)	102.35-79.86	N/A	45.77

*7 Year Price Score 141.53 *NYSE Composite Index=100 *12 Month Price Score 103.22

Interim Earnings (Per Share)

Qtr.	Mar	Jun	Sep	Dec
2013	0.38	0.49	0.40	0.65
2014	0.40	0.58	0.38	0.66
2015	0.32	0.61	0.36	0.77
2016	0.48	...	...	...

Interim Dividends (Per Share)

No Dividends Paid

Valuation Analysis — **Institutional Holding**

Forecast EPS	$2.79	No of Institutions
	(05/20/2016)	435
Market Cap	$8.4 Billion	Shares
Book Value	N/A	126,459,024
Price/Book	N/A	% Held
Price/Sales	3.73	88.12

Business Summary: IT Services (MIC: 6.3.1 SIC: 8741 NAIC: 561110)

Gartner is an information technology research and advisory company. Co. provides independent and objective research and analysis on the information technology, computer hardware, software, communications and related technology industries. Co. manages its business through three reportable segments: Research, Consulting and Events. The Research segment consists primarily of subscription-based research products, access to research inquiry, peer networking services, and membership programs. The Consulting segment consists primarily of consulting, measurement engagements, and advisory services. The Events segment consists of various symposia, conferences and exhibitions.

Recent Developments: For the quarter ended Mar 31 2016, net income increased 41.7% to US$40.2 million from US$28.4 million in the year-earlier quarter. Revenues were US$557.3 million, up 18.3% from US$471.2 million the year before. Operating income was US$64.4 million versus US$48.7 million in the prior-year quarter, an increase of 32.3%. Direct operating expenses rose 19.3% to US$212.0 million from US$177.8 million in the comparable period the year before. Indirect operating expenses increased 14.7% to US$280.8 million from US$244.7 million in the equivalent prior-year period.

Prospects: Our evaluation of Gartner Inc. as of June 19, 2016 is the result of our systematic analysis on three basic characteristics: earnings strength, relative valuation, and recent stock price movement. The company has managed to produce a neutral trend in earnings per share over the past 5 quarters and while recent estimates for the company have been raised by analysts, IT has posted better than expected results. Based on operating earnings yield, the company is overvalued when compared to all of the companies in our coverage universe. Share price changes over the past year indicates that IT will perform in line with the market over the near term.

Financial Data

(US$ in Thousands)	3 Mos	12/31/2015	12/31/2014	12/31/2013	12/31/2012	12/31/2011	12/31/2010	12/31/2009
Earnings Per Share	2.22	2.06	2.03	1.93	1.73	1.39	0.96	0.85
Cash Flow Per Share	4.23	4.12	3.88	3.39	2.99	2.66	2.15	1.71
Income Statement								
Total Revenue	557,266	2,163,056	2,021,441	1,784,213	1,615,808	1,468,588	1,288,454	1,139,800
EBITDA	75,558	340,135	324,996	309,722	274,257	244,176	185,526	158,594
Depn & Amortn	9,245	47,142	39,426	34,446	29,802	32,025	35,825	27,036
Income Before Taxes	60,307	272,211	274,683	266,439	235,596	202,184	134,085	115,526
Income Taxes	20,140	96,576	90,917	83,638	69,693	65,282	37,800	32,562
Net Income	40,167	175,635	183,766	182,801	165,903	136,902	96,285	82,964
Average Shares	83,464	85,056	90,719	94,830	95,842	98,846	99,834	97,549
Balance Sheet								
Current Assets	1,179,277	1,140,997	1,096,658	1,084,882	927,466	705,785	621,102	557,825
Total Assets	2,211,509	2,174,686	1,904,351	1,783,582	1,621,277	1,379,872	1,285,658	1,215,279
Current Liabilities	1,291,224	1,323,492	1,215,218	1,159,923	1,070,000	921,137	811,152	898,173
Long-Term Obligations	832,500	790,000	385,000	136,250	115,000	150,000	180,000	124,000
Total Liabilities	2,324,179	2,307,086	1,743,180	1,422,266	1,314,604	1,198,088	1,098,602	1,102,744
Stockholders' Equity	(112,670)	(132,400)	161,171	361,316	306,673	181,784	187,056	112,535
Shares Outstanding	82,499	82,338	87,520	91,965	93,361	93,343	95,988	95,877
Statistical Record								
Return on Assets %	9.37	8.61	9.97	10.74	11.03	10.27	7.70	7.19
Return on Equity %	...	1,220.92	70.34	54.73	67.74	74.23	64.28	181.90
EBITDA Margin %	13.56	15.72	16.08	17.36	16.97	16.63	14.40	13.91
Net Margin %	7.21	8.12	9.09	10.25	10.27	9.32	7.47	7.28
Asset Turnover	1.12	1.06	1.10	1.05	1.07	1.10	1.03	0.99
Current Ratio	0.91	0.86	0.90	0.94	0.87	0.77	0.77	0.62
Debt to Equity	...	...	2.39	0.38	0.37	0.83	0.96	1.10
Price Range	93.87-79.86	93.87-77.92	87.40-62.51	71.22-46.02	51.01-34.67	43.01-32.19	33.75-18.04	20.16-8.38
P/E Ratio	42.28-35.97	45.57-37.83	43.05-30.79	36.90-23.84	29.49-20.04	30.94-23.16	35.16-18.79	23.72-9.86

Address: 56 Top Gallant Road, Stamford, CT 06902-7700
Telephone: 203-316-1111

Web Site: www.gartner.com
Officers: James C. Smith - Chairman Eugene A. Hall - Chief Executive Officer

Auditors: KPMG LLP
Investor Contact: 203-316-6537
Transfer Agents: American Stock Transfer & Trust Company, LLC, New York, NY

314

GATX CORP

Exchange	Symbol	Price	52Wk Range	Yield	P/E
NYS	GMT	$45.87 (5/31/2016)	57.54-35.12	3.49	9.25

*7 Year Price Score 90.86   *NYSE Composite Index=100   *12 Month Price Score 98.16

Interim Earnings (Per Share)

Qtr.	Mar	Jun	Sep	Dec
2013	0.57	0.74	1.15	1.14
2014	0.90	1.15	1.14	1.30
2015	1.39	1.03	0.91	1.36
2016	1.66	...	...	...

Interim Dividends (Per Share)

Amt	Decl	Ex	Rec	Pay
0.38Q	07/31/2015	09/11/2015	09/15/2015	09/30/2015
0.38Q	10/30/2015	12/11/2015	12/15/2015	12/31/2015
0.40Q	01/29/2016	02/24/2016	02/26/2016	03/31/2016
0.40Q	04/22/2016	06/13/2016	06/15/2016	06/30/2016

Indicated Div: $1.60

Valuation Analysis

Forecast EPS	$5.34
	(05/20/2016)
Market Cap	$1.9 Billion
Book Value	$1.3 Billion
Price/Book	1.44
Price/Sales	1.28

Institutional Holding

No of Institutions	335
Shares	55,223,972
% Held	95.42

Business Summary: Services (MIC: 6.1.2 SIC: 4741 NAIC: 488210)

GATX is a railcar lessor, owning fleets in North America, Europe, and Asia. In addition, Co. operates a fleet of US-flagged vessels on the Great Lakes and owns and manages marine assets and other assets. Co. also invests in joint ventures that complement its existing business activities. Co. has four primary business segments: Rail North America, Rail International, American Steamship Company, and Portfolio Management. As of Dec 31 2015, Co. had a wholly owned fleet of 148,425 railcars. As of the same date, Co. also had an ownership interest in 2,375 railcars through investments in affiliated companies, and Co. managed 597 railcars for other third-party owners.

Recent Developments: For the quarter ended Mar 31 2016, net income increased 11.4% to US$69.3 million from US$62.2 million in the year-earlier quarter. Revenues were US$334.4 million, up 4.6% from US$319.7 million the year before. Indirect operating expenses decreased 6.2% to US$224.5 million from US$239.4 million in the equivalent prior-year period.

Prospects: Our evaluation of GATX Corp. as of June 19, 2016 is the result of our systematic analysis on three basic characteristics: earnings strength, relative valuation, and recent stock price movement. The company has generated a negative trend in earnings per share over the past 5 quarters. However, while recent estimates for the company have been mixed, GMT has posted better than expected results. Based on operating earnings yield, the company is undervalued when compared to all of the companies in our coverage universe. Share price changes over the past year indicates that GMT will perform in line with the market over the near term.

Financial Data
(US$ in Thousands)

	3 Mos	12/31/2015	12/31/2014	12/31/2013	12/31/2012	12/31/2011	12/31/2010	12/31/2009
Earnings Per Share	4.96	4.69	4.48	3.59	2.88	2.35	1.72	1.70
Cash Flow Per Share	13.43	12.40	9.98	8.64	7.89	6.61	5.25	5.70
Tang Book Value Per Share	29.91	28.60	27.78	28.39	24.57	22.22	22.02	21.80
Dividends Per Share	1.540	1.520	1.320	1.240	1.200	1.160	1.120	1.120
Dividend Payout %	31.05	32.41	29.46	34.54	41.67	49.36	65.12	65.88
Income Statement								
Total Revenue	334,400	1,449,900	1,451,000	1,321,000	1,243,200	1,308,500	1,204,900	1,153,900
EBITDA	202,300	728,700	676,600	593,400	559,800	386,700	325,500	335,200
Depn & Amortn	72,500	303,300	287,000	267,800	249,400	238,500	228,100	227,300
Income Before Taxes	92,600	270,300	231,200	159,000	143,800	148,200	97,400	107,900
Income Taxes	30,800	110,900	75,700	65,500	26,100	37,400	16,600	26,500
Net Income	69,300	205,300	205,000	169,300	137,300	110,800	80,800	81,400
Average Shares	41,800	43,800	45,800	47,100	47,600	47,200	47,000	48,800
Balance Sheet								
Current Assets	468,100	455,200	576,700	804,900	620,600	713,800	542,300	439,900
Total Assets	7,062,000	6,894,200	6,937,500	6,549,600	6,055,400	5,857,500	5,442,400	5,206,400
Current Liabilities	162,200	178,300	238,000	183,200	451,000	164,200	230,200	193,800
Long-Term Obligations	4,325,900	4,196,800	4,202,100	3,847,400	3,294,300	3,518,500	3,060,900	2,842,000
Total Liabilities	5,756,700	5,614,000	5,623,500	5,152,600	4,811,200	4,730,200	4,328,700	4,103,800
Stockholders' Equity	1,305,300	1,280,200	1,314,000	1,397,000	1,244,200	1,127,300	1,113,700	1,102,600
Shares Outstanding	40,881	41,970	44,198	45,868	46,898	46,653	46,360	46,101
Statistical Record								
Return on Assets %	3.01	2.97	3.04	2.69	2.30	1.96	1.52	1.57
Return on Equity %	16.42	15.83	15.12	12.82	11.55	9.89	7.29	7.31
EBITDA Margin %	60.50	50.26	46.63	44.92	45.03	29.55	27.01	29.05
Net Margin %	20.72	14.16	14.13	12.82	11.04	8.47	6.71	7.05
Asset Turnover	0.21	0.21	0.22	0.21	0.21	0.23	0.23	0.22
Current Ratio	2.89	2.55	2.42	4.39	1.38	4.35	2.36	2.27
Debt to Equity	3.31	3.28	3.20	2.75	2.65	3.12	2.75	2.58
Price Range	60.76-35.12	62.95-39.87	69.10-51.00	53.85-43.30	44.90-35.93	44.33-29.70	36.77-25.94	32.90-13.87
P/E Ratio	12.25-7.08	13.42-8.50	15.42-11.38	15.00-12.06	15.59-12.48	18.86-12.64	21.38-15.08	19.35-8.16
Average Yield %	3.17	2.90	2.12	2.54	2.88	3.14	3.76	4.32

Address: 222 West Adams Street, Chicago, IL 60606-5314 **Telephone:** 312-621-6200	**Web Site:** www.gatx.com **Officers:** Brian A. Kenney - Chairman, President, Chief Executive Officer Thomas A. Ellman - Executive Vice President, Region Officer	**Auditors:** Ernst & Young LLP **Investor Contact:** 312-621-6262 **Transfer Agents:** Computershare, Canton, MA

GENERAL CABLE CORP. (DE)

Exchange	Symbol	Price	52Wk Range	Yield	P/E
NYS	BGC	$13.66 (5/31/2016)	21.10-6.60	5.27	N/A

*7 Year Price Score 44.36   *NYSE Composite Index=100   *12 Month Price Score 100.21

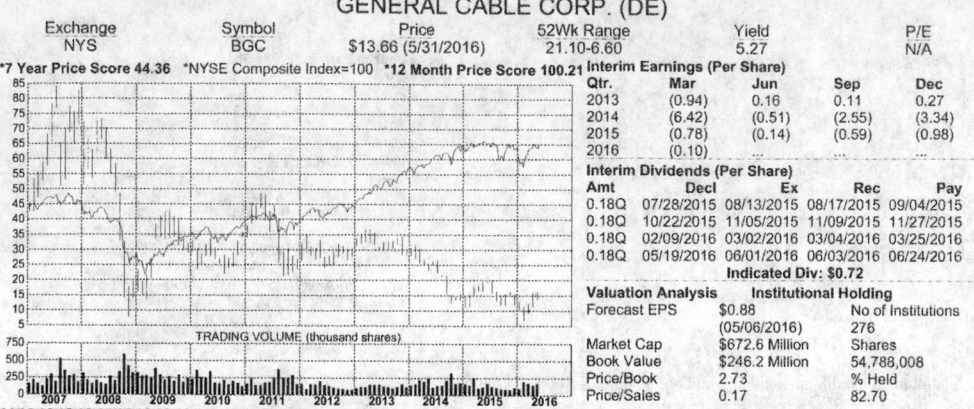

Interim Earnings (Per Share)

Qtr.	Mar	Jun	Sep	Dec
2013	(0.94)	0.16	0.11	0.27
2014	(6.42)	(0.51)	(2.55)	(3.34)
2015	(0.78)	(0.14)	(0.59)	(0.98)
2016	(0.10)	...	...	...

Interim Dividends (Per Share)

Amt	Decl	Ex	Rec	Pay
0.18Q	07/28/2015	08/13/2015	08/17/2015	09/04/2015
0.18Q	10/22/2015	11/05/2015	11/09/2015	11/27/2015
0.18Q	02/09/2016	03/02/2016	03/04/2016	03/25/2016
0.18Q	05/19/2016	06/01/2016	06/03/2016	06/24/2016

Indicated Div: $0.72

Valuation Analysis

		Institutional Holding	
Forecast EPS	$0.88 (05/06/2016)	No of Institutions	276
Market Cap	$672.6 Million	Shares	54,788,008
Book Value	$246.2 Million	% Held	82.70
Price/Book	2.73		
Price/Sales	0.17		

Business Summary: Electrical Equipment (MIC: 7.3.1 SIC: 3357 NAIC: 335929)

General Cable is engaged in the development, design, manufacture, marketing and distribution of copper, aluminum and fiber optic wire and cable products for use in the energy, industrial, construction, specialty and communications markets. Co. additionally engages in the design, integration, and installation on a turn-key basis for products such as high and extra-high voltage terrestrial and submarine systems. Co. four geographic operating and reportable segments are North America, Europe, Latin America, and Africa/Asia Pacific. The majority of products sold by Co.'s four segments include electric utility, electrical infrastructure, communications, construction, and rod mill.

Recent Developments: For the quarter ended Apr 1 2016, loss from continuing operations was US$8.0 million compared with a loss of US$34.7 million in the year-earlier quarter. Net loss amounted to US$4.4 million versus a net loss of US$40.9 million in the year-earlier quarter. Revenues were US$974.0 million, down 16.8% from US$1.17 billion the year before. Operating income was US$15.3 million versus US$16.2 million in the prior-year quarter, a decrease of 5.6%. Direct operating expenses declined 17.9% to US$867.9 million from US$1.06 billion in the comparable period the year before. Indirect operating expenses decreased 6.9% to US$90.8 million from US$97.5 million in the equivalent prior-year period.

Prospects: Our evaluation of General Cable Corp. as of June 19, 2016 is the result of our systematic analysis on three basic characteristics: earnings strength, relative valuation, and recent stock price movement. The company has suffered a very negative trend in earnings per share over the past 5 quarters and while recent estimates for the company have remained steady, BGC has posted better than expected results. Based on operating earnings yield, the company is about fairly valued when compared to all of the companies in our coverage universe. Share price changes over the past year indicates that BGC will perform poorly over the near term.

Financial Data

(US$ in Thousands)	3 Mos	12/31/2015	12/31/2014	12/31/2013	12/31/2012	12/31/2011	12/31/2010	12/31/2009
Earnings Per Share	(1.81)	(2.49)	(12.86)	(0.37)	0.08	1.57	1.31	2.06
Cash Flow Per Share	1.23	4.07	2.73	0.77	5.79	1.87	1.90	10.51
Tang Book Value Per Share	3.87	3.46	7.41	18.40	19.36	21.09	21.18	17.52
Dividends Per Share	0.720	0.540	0.720	0.720	...	...	...	...
Income Statement								
Total Revenue	974,000	4,225,100	5,979,800	6,421,200	6,014,300	5,866,700	4,864,900	4,385,200
EBITDA	32,600	33,600	(414,200)	263,600	284,800	313,700	279,100	341,900
Depn & Amortn	18,700	80,000	110,100	118,600	102,200	97,400	84,800	84,800
Income Before Taxes	(7,300)	(139,300)	(636,100)	27,000	82,300	124,800	122,700	174,100
Income Taxes	800	(14,700)	8,300	38,800	74,200	42,500	47,200	58,400
Net Income	(4,400)	(135,800)	(643,000)	(10,100)	9,800	85,200	76,900	116,600
Average Shares	49,100	48,900	48,800	49,400	51,100	53,700	53,100	52,800
Balance Sheet								
Current Assets	1,884,100	1,741,900	2,396,100	3,006,500	3,234,600	2,887,100	2,805,700	2,462,700
Total Assets	2,587,400	2,466,700	3,366,700	4,578,900	4,919,900	4,370,400	4,327,700	3,924,100
Current Liabilities	1,001,100	949,300	1,482,800	1,555,800	1,977,600	1,522,800	1,420,200	1,182,100
Long-Term Obligations	973,800	923,700	933,900	1,136,600	938,900	892,600	864,500	869,300
Total Liabilities	2,341,200	2,238,700	2,914,600	3,298,700	3,566,600	2,971,800	2,845,700	2,653,900
Stockholders' Equity	246,200	228,000	452,100	1,280,200	1,353,300	1,398,600	1,482,000	1,270,200
Shares Outstanding	49,236	48,908	48,683	49,598	49,693	49,697	52,116	52,008
Statistical Record								
Return on Assets %	N.M.	N.M.	N.M.	N.M.	0.21	1.96	1.86	3.00
Return on Equity %	N.M.	N.M.	N.M.	N.M.	0.71	5.92	5.59	11.79
EBITDA Margin %	3.35	0.80	N.M.	4.11	4.74	5.35	5.74	7.80
Net Margin %	N.M.	N.M.	N.M.	N.M.	0.16	1.45	1.58	2.66
Asset Turnover	1.41	1.45	1.51	1.35	1.29	1.35	1.18	1.13
Current Ratio	1.88	1.83	1.62	1.93	1.64	1.90	1.98	2.08
Debt to Equity	3.96	4.05	2.07	0.89	0.69	0.64	0.58	0.68
Price Range	21.10-6.60	21.10-11.03	31.40-12.51	36.71-28.07	34.54-23.92	48.54-20.89	35.64-21.80	42.50-13.65
P/E Ratio	...	...	...	...	431.75-299.00	30.92-13.31	27.21-16.64	20.63-6.63
Average Yield %	4.90	3.45	3.21	2.24	...	...	...	...

Address: 4 Tesseneer Drive, Highland Heights, KY 41076-9753 **Telephone:** 859-572-8000 **Fax:** 859-572-8458	**Web Site:** www.generalcable.com **Officers:** Michael T. McDonnell - President, Chief Executive Officer Emmanuel Sabonnadiere - Executive Vice President, Region Officer	**Auditors:** Deloitte & Touche LLP **Investor Contact:** 859-572-8373 **Transfer Agents:** Computershare Investor Services, Canton, MA

GENERAL DYNAMICS CORP.

Exchange	Symbol	Price	52Wk Range	Yield	P/E	Div Achiever
NYS	GD	$141.87 (5/31/2016)	153.28-124.18	2.14	15.34	24 Years

*7 Year Price Score 131.91 *NYSE Composite Index=100   *12 Month Price Score 98.86

TRADING VOLUME (thousand shares)

Interim Earnings (Per Share)

Qtr.	Mar	Jun	Sep	Dec
2013	1.62	1.81	1.84	1.40
2014	1.71	1.58	2.06	2.08
2015	2.14	2.27	2.28	2.40
2016	2.30	...	...	...

Interim Dividends (Per Share)

Amt	Decl	Ex	Rec	Pay
0.69Q	08/05/2015	10/07/2015	10/09/2015	11/13/2015
0.69Q	12/02/2015	01/13/2016	01/15/2016	02/05/2016
0.76Q	03/02/2016	04/06/2016	04/08/2016	05/06/2016
0.76Q	06/01/2016	06/29/2016	07/01/2016	08/05/2016

Indicated Div: $3.04

Valuation Analysis

		Institutional Holding	
Forecast EPS	$9.50	No of Institutions	
	(05/20/2016)	1237	
Market Cap	$43.4 Billion	Shares	
Book Value	$10.6 Billion	293,849,280	
Price/Book	4.10	% Held	
Price/Sales	1.38	82.48	

Business Summary: Aerospace (MIC: 7.1.1 SIC: 3721 NAIC: 336411)

General Dynamics is an aerospace and defense company. Co. has four business groups: Aerospace, which produces Gulfstream aircraft, provides aircraft services and performs aircraft completions for other original equipment manufacturers; Combat Systems, which designs and manufactures combat vehicles, weapons systems and munitions; Information Systems and Technology, which provides communications and information technology systems and solutions; and Marine Systems, which designs, constructs and repairs surface ships and submarines. Co.'s primary customer is the U.S. government. Co. also does business with non-U.S. governments and corporate and individual buyers of business aircraft.

Recent Developments: For the quarter ended Apr 3 2016, income from continuing operations increased 2.0% to US$730.0 million from US$716.0 million in the year-earlier quarter. Net income increased 0.1% to US$717.0 million from US$716.0 million in the year-earlier quarter. Revenues were US$7.72 billion, down 0.8% from US$7.78 billion the year before. Operating income was US$1.05 billion versus US$1.03 billion in the prior-year quarter, an increase of 2.5%. Direct operating expenses declined 0.7% to US$6.21 billion from US$6.25 billion in the comparable period the year before. Indirect operating expenses decreased 8.5% to US$460.0 million from US$503.0 million in the equivalent prior-year period.

Prospects: Our evaluation of General Dynamics Corp. as of June 19, 2016 is the result of our systematic analysis on three basic characteristics: earnings strength, relative valuation, and recent stock price movement. The company has managed to produce a neutral trend in earnings per share over the past 5 quarters. However, while recent estimates for the company have been lowered by analysts, GD has posted better than expected results. Based on operating earnings yield, the company is undervalued when compared to all of the companies in our coverage universe. Share price changes over the past year indicates that GD will perform well over the near term.

Financial Data

(US$ in Millions)	3 Mos	12/31/2015	12/31/2014	12/31/2013	12/31/2012	12/31/2011	12/31/2010	12/31/2009
Earnings Per Share	9.25	9.08	7.42	6.67	(0.94)	6.87	6.81	6.17
Cash Flow Per Share	7.12	7.78	11.12	8.86	7.58	8.89	7.83	7.41
Tang Book Value Per Share	N.M.	N.M.	N.M.	3.70	N.M.	N.M.	N.M.	N.M.
Dividends Per Share	2.760	2.690	2.420	1.680	2.510	1.830	1.640	1.490
Dividend Payout %	29.84	29.63	32.61	25.19	...	26.64	24.08	24.15
Income Statement								
Total Revenue	7,724	31,469	30,852	31,218	31,513	32,677	32,466	31,981
EBITDA	1,180	4,667	4,384	4,249	1,317	4,451	4,516	4,235
Depn & Amortn	117	482	496	556	620	592	569	562
Income Before Taxes	1,041	4,102	3,802	3,607	541	3,718	3,790	3,513
Income Taxes	311	1,137	1,129	1,121	873	1,166	1,162	1,106
Net Income	717	2,965	2,533	2,357	(332)	2,526	2,624	2,394
Average Shares	312	326	341	353	353	367	385	387
Balance Sheet								
Current Assets	14,188	14,571	17,407	17,886	15,744	15,368	14,186	13,249
Total Assets	31,702	31,997	35,355	35,448	34,309	34,883	32,545	31,077
Current Liabilities	12,423	12,445	13,751	12,194	11,620	11,145	11,177	10,371
Long-Term Obligations	2,899	2,898	3,410	3,908	3,908	3,907	2,430	3,159
Total Liabilities	21,120	21,259	23,526	20,947	22,919	21,651	19,229	18,654
Stockholders' Equity	10,582	10,738	11,829	14,501	11,390	13,232	13,316	12,423
Shares Outstanding	305	312	332	353	353	356	372	385
Statistical Record								
Return on Assets %	8.98	8.80	7.16	6.76	N.M.	7.49	8.25	8.05
Return on Equity %	26.84	26.28	19.24	18.21	N.M.	19.03	20.39	21.30
EBITDA Margin %	15.28	14.83	14.21	13.61	4.18	13.62	13.91	13.24
Net Margin %	9.28	9.42	8.21	7.55	N.M.	7.73	8.08	7.49
Asset Turnover	0.95	0.93	0.87	0.90	0.91	0.97	1.02	1.08
Current Ratio	1.14	1.17	1.27	1.47	1.35	1.38	1.27	1.28
Debt to Equity	0.27	0.27	0.29	0.27	0.34	0.30	0.18	0.25
Price Range	153.28-124.18	153.28-131.27	145.36-94.46	95.55-64.57	74.09-61.96	78.11-55.67	78.67-55.87	70.66-36.31
P/E Ratio	16.57-13.42	16.88-14.46	19.59-12.73	14.33-9.68	...	11.37-8.10	11.55-8.20	11.45-5.88
Average Yield %	1.97	1.91	2.04	2.11	3.73	2.66	2.43	2.62

Address: 2941 Fairview Park Drive, Suite 100, Falls Church, VA 22042-4513 **Telephone:** 703-876-3000	**Web Site:** www.generaldynamics.com **Officers:** Phebe N. Novakovic - Chairman, President, Chief Executive Officer, Chief Operating Officer, Executive Vice President, Senior Vice President John P. Casey - Executive Vice President, Vice President	**Auditors:** KPMG LLP **Investor Contact:** 703-876-3583 **Transfer Agents:** Computershare, Providence, RI

GENERAL ELECTRIC CO

Exchange	Symbol	Price	52Wk Range	Yield	P/E
NYS	GE	$30.23 (5/31/2016)	31.93-23.27	3.04	41.41

*7 Year Price Score 111.59 *NYSE Composite Index=100 ***12 Month Price Score 106.61**

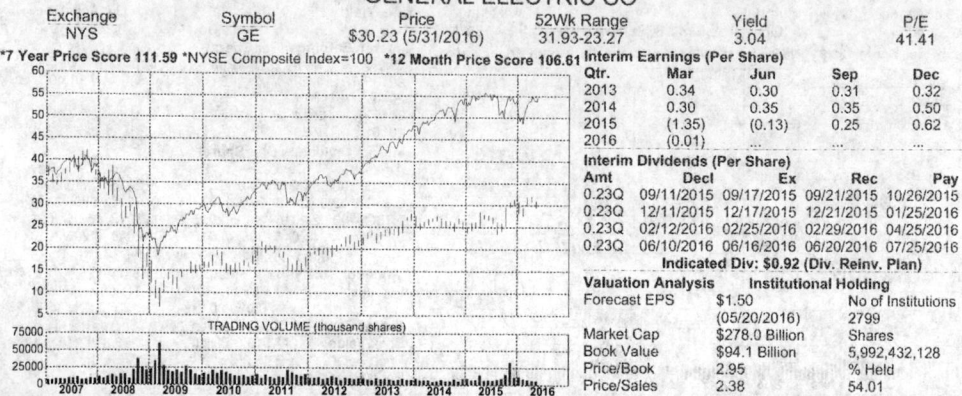

Interim Earnings (Per Share)

Qtr.	Mar	Jun	Sep	Dec
2013	0.34	0.30	0.31	0.32
2014	0.30	0.35	0.35	0.50
2015	(1.35)	(0.13)	0.25	0.62
2016	(0.01)	...	...	...

Interim Dividends (Per Share)

Amt	Decl	Ex	Rec	Pay
0.23Q	09/11/2015	09/17/2015	09/21/2015	10/26/2015
0.23Q	12/11/2015	12/17/2015	12/21/2015	01/25/2016
0.23Q	02/12/2016	02/25/2016	02/29/2016	04/25/2016
0.23Q	06/10/2016	06/16/2016	06/20/2016	07/25/2016

Indicated Div: $0.92 (Div. Reinv. Plan)

Valuation Analysis | **Institutional Holding**

Forecast EPS	$1.50	No of Institutions
	(05/20/2016)	2799
Market Cap	$278.0 Billion	Shares
Book Value	$94.1 Billion	5,992,432,128
Price/Book	2.95	% Held
Price/Sales	2.38	54.01

Business Summary: Electrical Equipment (MIC: 7.3.1 SIC: 3699 NAIC: 335999)

General Electric is a digital industrial company. Co.'s segments include: Power & Water, which is engaged in the field of development, implementation and improvement of products and technologies that harness resources; Oil & Gas, which helps oil and gas companies make use of energy resources; Energy Management, which provides integrated electrical products and systems used to distribute, protect and control energy and equipment; Aviation, which is a provider of jet engines and related services; Appliances & Lighting, which sells and services home appliances; and GE Capital, which provides a range of financial services and products, among others.

Recent Developments: For the quarter ended Mar 31 2016, income from continuing operations was US$378.0 million compared with a loss of US$4.67 billion in the year-earlier quarter. Net income amounted to US$69.0 million versus a net loss of US$13.61 billion in the year-earlier quarter. Revenues were US$27.85 billion, up 6.1% from US$26.24 billion the year before. Direct operating expenses rose 8.9% to US$21.00 billion from US$19.30 billion in the comparable period the year before. Indirect operating expenses increased 24.0% to US$6.60 billion from US$5.32 billion in the equivalent prior-year period.

Prospects: Our evaluation of General Electric Co as of June 19, 2016 is the result of our systematic analysis on three basic characteristics: earnings strength, relative valuation, and recent stock price movement. The company has generated a negative trend in earnings per share over the past 5 quarters. However, while recent estimates for the company have been mixed, GE has posted better than expected results. Based on operating earnings yield, the company is about fairly valued when compared to all of the companies in our coverage universe. Share price changes over the past year indicates that GE will perform well over the near term.

Financial Data
(US$ in Millions)

	3 Mos	12/31/2015	12/31/2014	12/31/2013	12/31/2012	12/31/2011	12/31/2010	12/31/2009
Earnings Per Share	0.73	(0.61)	1.50	1.27	1.29	1.23	1.06	1.01
Cash Flow Per Share	1.55	2.00	2.76	2.80	2.97	3.15	3.39	2.32
Tang Book Value Per Share	1.20	1.71	3.72	3.84	3.61	3.00	4.19	3.73
Dividends Per Share	0.920	0.920	0.890	0.790	0.700	0.610	0.460	0.610
Dividend Payout %	126.03	...	59.33	62.20	54.26	49.59	43.40	60.40
Income Statement								
Total Revenue	27,845	117,386	148,589	146,045	147,359	147,300	150,211	156,783
EBITDA	3,184	13,302	28,500	27,978	31,529	36,375	31,940	31,213
Depn & Amortn	1,210	1,653	1,789	1,711	1,615	1,732	1,749	2,100
Income Before Taxes	238	8,186	17,229	16,151	17,406	20,098	14,208	10,344
Income Taxes	(139)	6,485	1,772	676	2,504	5,732	1,050	(1,090)
Net Income	191	(6,126)	15,233	13,057	13,641	14,151	11,644	11,025
Average Shares	9,372	10,016	10,123	10,289	10,564	10,620	10,678	10,615
Balance Sheet								
Current Assets	157,874	151,993	179,041	171,249	162,740	165,198	153,043	152,646
Total Assets	462,193	492,692	648,349	656,560	685,328	717,242	751,216	781,818
Current Liabilities	104,279	108,197	208,440	206,572	221,403	253,379	224,075	218,399
Long-Term Obligations	134,967	145,301	200,414	221,665	236,084	243,459	293,323	338,215
Total Liabilities	368,069	394,418	520,190	525,994	562,302	600,804	632,280	664,527
Stockholders' Equity	94,124	98,274	128,159	130,566	123,026	116,438	118,936	117,291
Shares Outstanding	9,195	9,379	10,057	10,060	10,405	10,573	10,615	10,663
Statistical Record								
Return on Assets %	1.41	N.M.	2.33	1.95	1.94	1.93	1.52	1.40
Return on Equity %	7.54	N.M.	11.78	10.30	11.36	12.02	9.86	9.93
EBITDA Margin %	11.43	11.33	19.18	19.16	21.40	24.69	21.26	19.91
Net Margin %	0.69	N.M.	10.25	8.94	9.26	9.61	7.75	7.03
Asset Turnover	0.22	0.21	0.23	0.22	0.21	0.20	0.20	0.20
Current Ratio	1.51	1.40	0.86	0.83	0.74	0.65	0.68	0.70
Debt to Equity	1.43	1.48	1.56	1.70	1.92	2.09	2.47	2.88
Price Range	31.83-23.27	31.28-23.27	28.03-23.95	28.03-20.90	23.12-18.15	21.52-14.69	19.50-13.88	17.07-6.66
P/E Ratio	43.60-31.88	...	18.69-15.97	22.07-16.46	17.92-14.07	17.50-11.94	18.40-13.09	16.90-6.59
Average Yield %	3.30	3.43	3.42	3.29	3.46	3.36	2.78	4.56

Address: 3135 Easton Turnpike, Fairfield, CT 06828-0001 **Telephone:** 203-373-2211 **Fax:** 203-373-3131	**Web Site:** www.ge.com **Officers:** Jeffrey R. Immelt - Chairman, President, Chief Executive Officer Daniel C. Heintzelman - Vice-Chairman	**Auditors:** KPMG LLP **Investor Contact:** 203-373-2460 **Transfer Agents:** Computershare, Pittsburgh, PA

GENERAL GROWTH PROPERTIES INC

Exchange	Symbol	Price	52Wk Range	Yield	P/E
NYS	GGP	$26.87 (5/31/2016)	30.17-24.37	2.83	27.70

*7 Year Price Score 122.94 *NYSE Composite Index=100 *12 Month Price Score 103.00

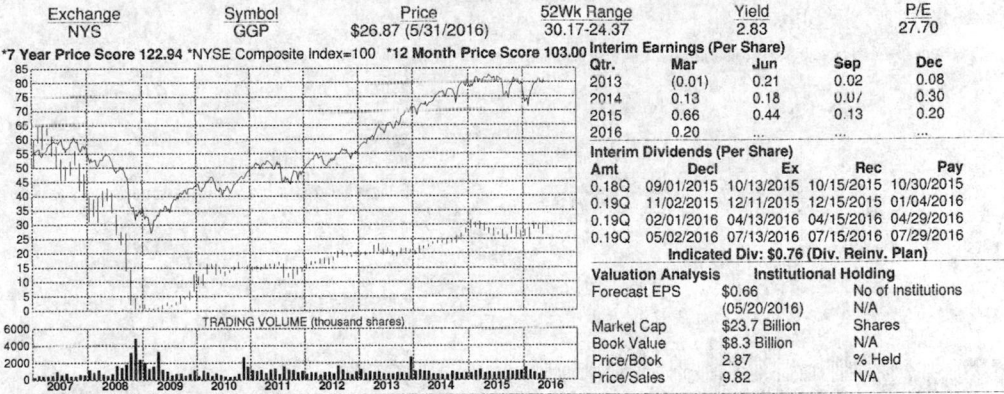

Interim Earnings (Per Share)

Qtr.	Mar	Jun	Sep	Dec
2013	(0.01)	0.21	0.02	0.08
2014	0.13	0.18	0.07	0.30
2015	0.66	0.44	0.13	0.20
2016	0.20	...	...	...

Interim Dividends (Per Share)

Amt	Decl	Ex	Rec	Pay
0.18Q	09/01/2015	10/13/2015	10/15/2015	10/30/2015
0.19Q	11/02/2015	12/11/2015	12/15/2015	01/04/2016
0.19Q	02/01/2016	04/13/2016	04/15/2016	04/29/2016
0.19Q	05/02/2016	07/13/2016	07/15/2016	07/29/2016

Indicated Div: $0.76 (Div. Reinv. Plan)

Valuation Analysis

		Institutional Holding	
Forecast EPS	$0.66	No of Institutions	
	(05/20/2016)	N/A	
Market Cap	$23.7 Billion	Shares	
Book Value	$8.3 Billion	N/A	
Price/Book	2.87	% Held	
Price/Sales	9.82	N/A	

Business Summary: REITs (MIC: 5.3.1 SIC: 6798 NAIC: 525930)

General Growth Properties is a self-administered and self-managed real estate investment trust. Co., through its subsidiaries and affiliates, is an owner and operator of retail properties. As of Dec 31 2015, Co. owned, either entirely or with joint venture partners, 131 retail properties located throughout the U.S. Co. provides management and other services to substantially all of its properties, including properties which it owns through joint venture arrangements. Substantially all of Co.'s business is conducted through its subsidiaries consisting of GGP Operating Partnership, LP, GGP Nimbus, LP and GGP Limited Partnership.

Recent Developments: For the quarter ended Mar 31 2016, net income decreased 69.6% to US$195.3 million from US$641.8 million in the year-earlier quarter. Revenues were US$607.0 million, up 2.2% from US$594.1 million the year before. Revenues from property income fell 1.5% to US$551.7 million from US$560.4 million in the corresponding quarter a year earlier.

Prospects: Our evaluation of General Growth Properties Inc. as of June 19, 2016 is the result of our systematic analysis on three basic characteristics: earnings strength, relative valuation, and recent stock price movement. The company has enjoyed a very positive trend in earnings per share over the past 5 quarters. Because the company lacks sufficient analyst estimate data, we place greater weight on the historical EPS trend as the measure of earnings strength. Based on operating earnings yield, the company is about fairly valued when compared to all of the companies in our coverage universe. Share price changes over the past year indicates that GGP will perform well over the near term.

Financial Data

(US$ in Thousands)	3 Mos	12/31/2015	12/31/2014	12/31/2013	12/31/2012	12/31/2011	12/31/2010	11/09/2010
Earnings Per Share	0.97	1.43	0.69	0.31	(0.52)	(0.37)	(0.27)	(3.74)
Cash Flow Per Share	1.22	1.20	1.07	0.96	0.86	0.53	(0.38)	0.15
Tang Book Value Per Share	8.63	8.63	7.68	7.77	6.99	7.50	8.70	...
Dividends Per Share	0.710	0.710	0.630	0.510	0.420	0.400	0.380	...
Dividend Payout %	73.20	49.65	91.30	164.52	...	...	...	...
Income Statement								
Total Revenue	607,032	2,403,906	2,535,559	2,527,387	2,511,850	2,742,942	416,542	2,406,944
EBITDA	266,057	1,575,382	1,091,273	1,051,835	350,236	1,734,610	34,644	1,478,671
Depn & Amortn	8,586	62,106	76,615	84,229	105,871	1,086,639	153,797	569,307
Income Before Taxes	125,852	954,855	343,986	238,745	(563,805)	(308,177)	(257,560)	(338,556)
Income Taxes	2,920	(38,334)	7,253	345	9,091	9,256	(8,929)	(60,573)
Net Income	191,780	1,374,561	665,850	302,528	(481,233)	(313,172)	(254,216)	(1,185,758)
Average Shares	950,154	951,062	944,721	934,068	938,049	981,136	945,248	316,918
Balance Sheet								
Current Assets	1,195,960	1,306,451	1,036,239	1,056,170	885,675	791,327	1,135,410	...
Total Assets	23,566,314	24,073,555	25,335,734	25,762,303	27,282,405	29,518,151	32,367,379	...
Current Liabilities	831,532	797,770	929,250	963,183	1,170,509	1,882,067	1,846,169	...
Long-Term Obligations	14,085,620	14,433,745	16,216,555	15,891,340	16,186,358	17,335,706	18,047,957	...
Total Liabilities	15,309,437	15,803,512	17,729,815	17,659,182	19,660,707	21,034,822	22,288,277	...
Stockholders' Equity	8,256,877	8,270,043	7,605,919	8,103,121	7,621,698	8,483,329	10,079,102	...
Shares Outstanding	883,123	882,397	884,912	911,194	939,049	935,307	941,880	...
Statistical Record								
Return on Assets %	3.96	5.56	2.61	1.14	N.M.	N.M.	N.M.	...
Return on Equity %	11.40	17.32	8.48	3.85	N.M.	N.M.	N.M.	...
EBITDA Margin %	43.83	65.53	43.04	41.62	13.94	63.24	8.32	61.43
Net Margin %	31.59	57.18	26.26	11.97	N.M.	N.M.	N.M.	N.M.
Asset Turnover	0.10	0.10	0.10	0.10	0.09	0.09	0.01	...
Current Ratio	1.44	1.64	1.12	1.10	0.76	0.42	0.62	...
Debt to Equity	1.71	1.75	2.13	1.96	2.12	2.04	1.79	...
Price Range	30.40-24.37	31.46-24.37	28.66-19.54	23.33-18.69	20.99-14.36	16.90-11.01	16.91-13.91	17.30-3.89
P/E Ratio	31.34-25.12	22.00-17.04	41.54-28.32	75.26-60.29	...	...	...	...
Average Yield %	2.62	2.56	2.67	2.50	2.34	2.78	2.52	...

Address: 110 N. Wacker Dr., Chicago, IL 60606 **Telephone:** 312-960-5000	**Web Site:** www.ggp.com **Officers:** John Bucksbaum - Chairman Sandeep Mathrani - Chief Executive Officer	**Auditors:** Deloitte & Touche LLP **Investor Contact:** 312-960-5529 **Transfer Agents:** American Stock Transfer & Trust Company, LLC, Brooklyn, NY

GENERAL MILLS, INC.

Exchange	Symbol	Price	52Wk Range	Yield	P/E	Div Achiever
NYS	GIS	$62.78 (5/31/2016)	65.36-54.12	2.93	25.62	12 Years

*7 Year Price Score 111.65 *NYSE Composite Index=100 *12 Month Price Score 106.62

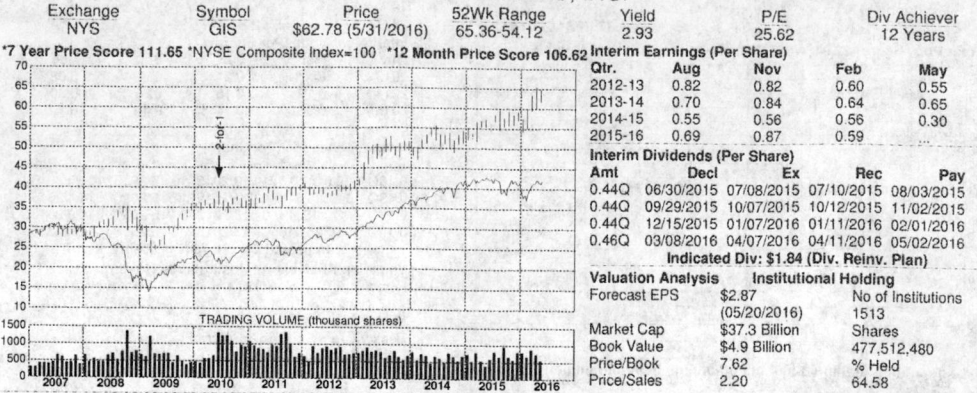

Interim Earnings (Per Share)

Qtr.	Aug	Nov	Feb	May
2012-13	0.82	0.82	0.60	0.55
2013-14	0.70	0.84	0.64	0.65
2014-15	0.55	0.56	0.56	0.30
2015-16	0.69	0.87	0.59	...

Interim Dividends (Per Share)

Amt	Decl	Ex	Rec	Pay
0.44Q	06/30/2015	07/08/2015	07/10/2015	08/03/2015
0.44Q	09/29/2015	10/07/2015	10/12/2015	11/02/2015
0.44Q	12/15/2015	01/07/2016	01/11/2016	02/01/2016
0.46Q	03/08/2016	04/07/2016	04/11/2016	05/02/2016

Indicated Div: $1.84 (Div. Reinv. Plan)

Valuation Analysis		Institutional Holding	
Forecast EPS	$2.87	No of Institutions	
	(05/20/2016)	1513	
Market Cap	$37.3 Billion	Shares	
Book Value	$4.9 Billion	477,512,480	
Price/Book	7.62	% Held	
Price/Sales	2.20	64.58	

Business Summary: Food (MIC: 1.2.1 SIC: 2043 NAIC: 311230)

General Mills is a manufacturer and marketer of branded consumer foods sold through retail stores. Co. is also a supplier of branded and unbranded food products to the North American foodservice and commercial baking industries. Co.'s main product categories in the U.S. are ready-to-eat cereals, refrigerated yogurt, soup, meal kits, shelf stable and frozen vegetables, refrigerated and frozen dough products, dessert and baking mixes, frozen pizza and pizza snacks, grain, fruit and savory snacks, and a range of organic products including meal kits, granola bars, and cereal. Co. has three operating segments: U.S. Retail; International; and Convenience Stores and Foodservice.

Recent Developments: For the quarter ended Feb 28 2016, net income increased 3.9% to US$367.7 million from US$353.8 million in the year-earlier quarter. Revenues were US$4.00 billion, down 8.0% from US$4.35 billion the year before. Operating income was US$586.3 million versus US$537.2 million in the prior-year quarter, an increase of 9.1%. Direct operating expenses declined 11.1% to US$2.64 billion from US$2.98 billion in the comparable period the year before. Indirect operating expenses decreased 8.0% to US$771.2 million from US$838.7 million in the equivalent prior-year period.

Prospects: Our evaluation of General Mills Inc. as of June 19, 2016 is the result of our systematic analysis on three basic characteristics: earnings strength, relative valuation, and recent stock price movement. The company has generated a negative trend in earnings per share over the past 5 quarters and while recent estimates for the company have remained steady, GIS has posted better than expected results. Based on operating earnings yield, the company is about fairly valued when compared to all of the companies in our coverage universe. Share price changes over the past year indicates that GIS will perform well over the near term.

Financial Data

(US$ in Thousands)	9 Mos	6 Mos	3 Mos	05/31/2015	05/25/2014	05/26/2013	05/27/2012	05/29/2011
Earnings Per Share	2.45	2.42	2.11	1.97	2.83	2.79	2.35	2.70
Cash Flow Per Share	4.77	4.73	4.39	4.15	4.05	4.52	3.72	2.38
Dividends Per Share	1.760	1.730	1.700	1.670	1.550	1.320	1.220	1.120
Dividend Payout %	71.84	71.49	80.57	84.77	54.77	47.31	51.91	41.48
Income Statement								
Total Revenue	12,635,200	8,632,800	4,207,900	17,630,300	17,909,600	17,774,100	16,657,900	14,880,200
EBITDA	2,616,500	1,881,500	827,200	2,665,600	3,542,800	3,439,800	3,103,900	3,247,100
Depn & Amortn	441,200	292,500	143,900	588,300	585,400	588,000	541,500	472,600
Income Before Taxes	1,949,000	1,439,900	608,000	1,761,900	2,655,000	2,534,900	2,210,500	2,428,200
Income Taxes	667,700	510,100	198,600	586,800	883,300	741,200	709,600	721,100
Net Income	1,317,800	956,100	426,600	1,221,300	1,824,400	1,855,200	1,567,300	1,798,300
Average Shares	608,500	612,400	615,500	618,800	645,700	665,600	666,700	664,800
Balance Sheet								
Current Assets	4,011,300	4,047,600	4,305,100	3,785,700	4,393,500	4,298,900	3,691,400	3,902,000
Total Assets	21,631,600	21,588,700	22,322,900	21,964,500	23,145,700	22,658,000	21,096,800	18,674,500
Current Liabilities	5,253,700	4,969,400	5,299,900	4,890,100	5,423,500	5,293,900	3,843,200	3,659,200
Long-Term Obligations	7,024,400	7,416,600	7,609,700	7,607,700	6,423,500	5,926,100	6,161,900	5,542,500
Total Liabilities	16,742,800	16,791,700	17,373,800	16,967,800	16,610,900	15,985,800	14,675,100	12,309,000
Stockholders' Equity	4,888,800	4,797,000	4,949,100	4,996,700	6,534,800	6,672,200	6,421,700	6,365,500
Shares Outstanding	593,600	593,300	599,200	598,700	612,300	640,800	648,500	644,800
Statistical Record								
Return on Assets %	6.68	6.49	5.70	5.33	7.99	8.50	7.90	9.92
Return on Equity %	29.13	28.39	23.36	20.84	27.70	28.41	24.58	30.65
EBITDA Margin %	20.71	21.79	19.66	15.12	19.78	19.35	18.63	21.82
Net Margin %	10.43	11.08	10.14	6.93	10.19	10.44	9.41	12.09
Asset Turnover	0.75	0.75	0.77	0.77	0.78	0.81	0.84	0.82
Current Ratio	0.76	0.81	0.81	0.77	0.81	0.81	0.96	1.07
Debt to Equity	1.44	1.55	1.54	1.52	0.98	0.89	0.96	0.87
Price Range	60.14-51.70	59.55-51.13	59.55-48.86	57.14-48.86	54.40-46.86	50.93-37.55	41.05-34.95	39.95-33.57
P/E Ratio	24.55-21.10	24.61-21.13	28.22-23.16	29.01-24.80	19.22-16.56	18.25-13.46	17.47-14.87	14.80-12.43
Average Yield %	3.11	3.11	3.14	3.14	3.09	3.21	3.16	3.07

Address: Number One General Mills Boulevard, Minneapolis, MN 55426 Telephone: 763-764-7600 Fax: 763-764-8330	Web Site: www.generalmills.com Officers: Kendall J. Powell - Chairman, Chief Executive Officer Donal L. Mulligan - Executive Vice President, Chief Financial Officer	Auditors: KPMG LLP Investor Contact: 180-024-55703 Transfer Agents: Wells Fargo Bank, N.A., St. Paul, MN

GENERAL MOTORS CO.

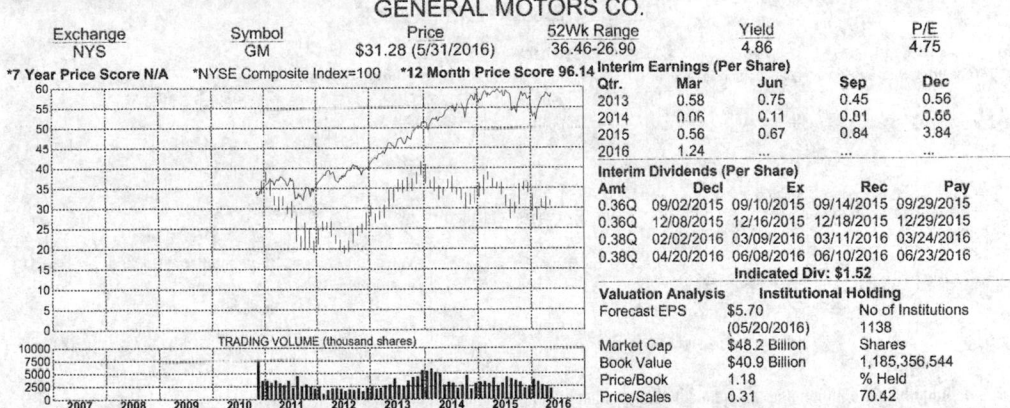

Exchange	Symbol	Price	52Wk Range	Yield	P/E
NYS	GM	$31.28 (5/31/2016)	36.46-26.90	4.86	4.75

*7 Year Price Score N/A   *NYSE Composite Index=100   *12 Month Price Score 96.14

Interim Earnings (Per Share)

Qtr.	Mar	Jun	Sep	Dec
2013	0.58	0.75	0.45	0.56
2014	0.06	0.11	0.01	0.66
2015	0.56	0.67	0.84	3.84
2016	1.24	...	...	...

Interim Dividends (Per Share)

Amt	Decl	Ex	Rec	Pay
0.36Q	09/02/2015	09/10/2015	09/14/2015	09/29/2015
0.36Q	12/08/2015	12/16/2015	12/18/2015	12/29/2015
0.38Q	02/02/2016	03/09/2016	03/11/2016	03/24/2016
0.38Q	04/20/2016	06/08/2016	06/10/2016	06/23/2016

Indicated Div: $1.52

Valuation Analysis   **Institutional Holding**

Forecast EPS	$5.70	No of Institutions
	(05/20/2016)	1138
Market Cap	$48.2 Billion	Shares
Book Value	$40.9 Billion	1,185,356,544
Price/Book	1.18	% Held
Price/Sales	0.31	70.42

Business Summary: Autos- Manufacturing (MIC: 1.8.1 SIC: 3711 NAIC: 336111)

General Motors designs, builds and sells cars, trucks and automobile parts. Co. also provides financing services through General Motors Financial Company, Inc. Co.'s automotive operations are conducted through four segments: GM North America (GMNA), GM Europe, GM International Operations and GM South America. GMNA serves customers in North America with vehicles developed, manufactured and/or marketed under the Buick, Cadillac, Chevrolet and GMC brands. Outside North America Co.'s vehicles are developed, manufactured and/or marketed under the Buick, Cadillac, Chevrolet, GMC, Holden, Opel, and Vauxhall brands. Co. sells its products to dealers for retail sales, and to fleet customers.

Recent Developments: For the quarter ended Mar 31 2016, net income increased 112.7% to US$1.93 billion from US$908.0 million in the year-earlier quarter. Revenues were US$37.27 billion, up 4.3% from US$35.71 billion the year before. Operating income was US$1.97 billion versus US$753.0 million in the prior-year quarter, an increase of 161.9%. Direct operating expenses rose 2.0% to US$32.48 billion from US$31.84 billion in the comparable period the year before. Indirect operating expenses decreased 9.6% to US$2.82 billion from US$3.12 billion in the equivalent prior-year period.

Prospects: Our evaluation of General Motors Co. as of June 19, 2016 is the result of our systematic analysis on three basic characteristics: earnings strength, relative valuation, and recent stock price movement. The company has generated a negative trend in earnings per share over the past 5 quarters and while recent estimates for the company have remained steady, GM has posted better than expected results. Based on operating earnings yield, the company is undervalued when compared to all of the companies in our coverage universe. Share price changes over the past year indicates that GM will perform well over the near term.

Financial Data

(US$ in Millions)	3 Mos	12/31/2015	12/31/2014	12/31/2013	12/31/2012	12/31/2011	12/31/2010	12/31/2009
Earnings Per Share	6.59	5.91	1.65	2.38	2.92	4.58	2.89	(3.58)
Cash Flow Per Share	7.40	7.55	6.27	9.07	6.75	5.32	4.52	1.63
Tang Book Value Per Share	22.76	21.96	18.04	20.30	12.49	N.M.	N.M.	N.M.
Dividends Per Share	1.460	1.380	1.200	...	...	...	...	...
Dividend Payout %	22.15	23.35	72.73	...	...	...	...	...
Income Statement								
Total Revenue	37,265	152,356	155,929	155,427	152,256	150,276	135,592	57,474
EBITDA	2,017	10,566	7,135	9,997	(22,705)	9,782	9,643	(2,359)
Depn & Amortn	45	5,220	5,403	5,078	7,908	4,108	4,363	2,657
Income Before Taxes	1,930	5,524	2,152	5,648	(30,257)	5,985	5,737	(5,283)
Income Taxes	559	(1,897)	228	2,127	(34,831)	(110)	672	(1,000)
Net Income	1,953	9,687	3,949	5,346	6,188	9,190	6,172	(4,297)
Average Shares	1,580	1,640	1,687	1,676	1,675	1,668	1,624	1,239
Balance Sheet								
Current Assets	71,034	78,007	83,670	81,501	69,996	60,247	53,053	59,247
Total Assets	203,618	194,520	177,677	166,344	149,422	144,603	138,898	136,295
Current Liabilities	74,987	71,466	65,701	62,412	53,992	48,932	47,157	52,435
Long-Term Obligations	49,561	43,549	31,853	22,025	10,532	11,650	9,974	5,562
Total Liabilities	162,686	154,649	142,220	123,737	113,178	106,483	102,718	108,048
Stockholders' Equity	40,932	39,871	35,457	42,607	36,244	38,120	36,180	28,247
Shares Outstanding	1,539	1,544	1,610	1,589	1,366	1,564	1,500	1,500
Statistical Record								
Return on Assets %	5.58	5.21	2.30	3.39	4.20	6.48	4.49	N.M.
Return on Equity %	27.69	25.72	10.12	13.56	16.60	24.74	19.16	...
EBITDA Margin %	5.41	6.94	4.58	6.43	N.M.	6.51	7.11	N.M.
Net Margin %	5.24	6.36	2.53	3.44	4.06	6.12	4.55	N.M.
Asset Turnover	0.80	0.82	0.91	0.98	1.03	1.06	0.99	1.05
Current Ratio	0.95	1.09	1.27	1.31	1.30	1.23	1.13	1.13
Debt to Equity	1.21	1.09	0.90	0.52	0.29	0.31	0.28	0.20
Price Range	37.50-26.90	38.87-27.28	40.95-29.69	41.53-26.33	28.83-18.80	38.98-19.05	36.86-33.25	...
P/E Ratio	5.69-4.08	6.58-4.62	24.82-17.99	17.45-11.06	9.87-6.44	8.51-4.16	12.75-11.51	...
Average Yield %	4.45	4.02	3.47	...	...	...	...	...

Address: 300 Renaissance Center, Detroit, MI 48265-3000 **Telephone:** 313-556-5000	**Web Site:** www.gm.com **Officers:** Mary T. Barra - Chairman, Chief Executive Officer, Senior Vice President Daniel Ammann - President, Senior Vice President, Chief Financial Officer	**Auditors:** Deloitte & Touche LLP **Transfer Agents:** Computershare Trust Company, N.A., Providence, RI

GENESEE & WYOMING INC.

Exchange	Symbol	Price	52Wk Range	Yield	P/E
NYS	GWR	$60.07 (5/31/2016)	84.84-44.55	N/A	15.17

*7 Year Price Score 82.51 ***NYSE Composite Index=100** ***12 Month Price Score 95.37**

Interim Earnings (Per Share)

Qtr.	Mar	Jun	Sep	Dec
2013	1.46	1.19	1.16	1.03
2014	0.70	1.07	1.27	1.53
2015	0.42	0.92	1.10	1.47
2016	0.47			

Interim Dividends (Per Share)

No Dividends Paid

Valuation Analysis   Institutional Holding

Forecast EPS	$3.57	No of Institutions
	(05/20/2016)	379
Market Cap	$3.5 Billion	Shares
Book Value	$2.6 Billion	62,094,712
Price/Book	1.35	% Held
Price/Sales	1.67	93.32

TRADING VOLUME (thousand shares)

Business Summary: Rail (MIC: 7.4.3 SIC: 4011 NAIC: 482111)

Genesee & Wyoming owns and operates freight railroads worldwide that are organized in 11 operating regions. As of Dec 31 2015, through its subsidiaries, Co. owned or leased 120 freight railroads. Co.'s subsidiaries provide rail service at more than 40 main ports in North America, Australia and Europe and perform contract coal loading and railcar switching for industrial customers. Co.'s railroads operate over approx. 15,600 miles of track that is owned, jointly owned or leased by Co., which includes the Tarcoola to Darwin rail line. Also, through various track access arrangements, Co. operates over approximately 5,700 additional miles of track that is owned or leased by others.

Recent Developments: For the quarter ended Mar 31 2016, net income increased 13.0% to US$27.0 million from US$23.9 million in the year-earlier quarter. Revenues were US$482.6 million, up 21.6% from US$397.0 million the year before. Operating income was US$57.0 million versus US$72.6 million in the prior-year quarter, a decrease of 21.5%. Direct operating expenses rose 43.7% to US$155.9 million from US$108.5 million in the comparable period the year before. Indirect operating expenses increased 24.9% to US$269.7 million from US$215.9 million in the equivalent prior-year period.

Prospects: Our evaluation of Genesee & Wyoming Inc. as of June 19, 2016 is the result of our systematic analysis on three basic characteristics: earnings strength, relative valuation, and recent stock price movement. The company has managed to produce a neutral trend in earnings per share over the past 5 quarters. However, while recent estimates for the company have been mixed, GWR has posted better than expected results. Based on operating earnings yield, the company is undervalued when compared to all of the companies in our coverage universe. Share price changes over the past year indicates that GWR will perform very poorly over the near term.

Financial Data

(US$ in Thousands)	3 Mos	12/31/2015	12/31/2014	12/31/2013	12/31/2012	12/31/2011	12/31/2010	12/31/2009
Earnings Per Share	3.96	3.89	4.58	4.79	1.02	2.79	1.94	1.57
Cash Flow Per Share	8.23	8.37	8.89	7.69	3.99	4.35	4.44	3.49
Tang Book Value Per Share	10.86	9.77	21.13	16.87	12.51	13.42	10.02	6.90
Income Statement								
Total Revenue	482,616	2,000,401	1,639,012	1,569,011	874,916	829,096	630,195	544,866
EBITDA	107,057	526,623	557,830	501,510	209,116	253,098	174,183	143,128
Depn & Amortn	49,330	159,100	135,000	119,200	66,600	59,700	44,600	41,300
Income Before Taxes	39,827	300,931	368,113	318,387	83,396	158,024	108,833	75,991
Income Taxes	12,808	75,894	107,107	46,296	46,402	38,531	30,164	15,916
Net Income	27,019	225,037	261,006	272,091	52,433	119,484	81,260	61,327
Average Shares	57,964	57,848	56,972	56,679	51,316	42,772	41,889	38,974
Balance Sheet								
Current Assets	501,787	576,560	548,426	548,330	465,252	240,199	208,948	253,243
Total Assets	6,706,052	6,795,604	5,595,753	5,319,821	5,226,115	2,294,157	2,067,560	1,697,032
Current Liabilities	546,789	533,814	464,238	456,508	416,744	261,271	304,886	171,794
Long-Term Obligations	2,142,306	2,223,306	1,548,051	1,540,346	1,770,566	569,026	475,174	421,616
Total Liabilities	4,130,752	4,276,143	3,238,894	3,172,026	3,331,654	1,333,523	1,250,320	1,008,155
Stockholders' Equity	2,575,300	2,519,461	2,356,859	2,147,795	1,894,461	960,634	817,240	688,877
Shares Outstanding	57,948	57,738	53,958	53,543	47,088	42,450	41,835	41,025
Statistical Record								
Return on Assets %	3.39	3.63	4.78	5.16	1.39	5.48	4.32	3.73
Return on Equity %	9.30	9.23	11.59	13.46	3.66	13.44	10.79	10.51
EBITDA Margin %	22.18	26.33	34.03	31.96	23.90	30.53	27.64	26.27
Net Margin %	5.60	11.25	15.92	17.34	5.99	14.41	12.89	11.26
Asset Turnover	0.31	0.32	0.30	0.30	0.23	0.38	0.33	0.33
Current Ratio	0.92	1.08	1.18	1.20	1.12	0.92	0.69	1.47
Debt to Equity	0.83	0.88	0.66	0.72	0.93	0.59	0.58	0.61
Price Range	97.34-44.55	105.15-50.28	105.51-83.33	101.77-76.08	76.28-48.08	61.98-45.19	53.05-28.93	34.04-16.74
P/E Ratio	24.58-11.25	27.03-12.93	23.04-18.19	21.25-15.88	74.78-47.14	22.22-16.20	27.35-14.91	21.68-10.66

Address: 20 West Avenue, Darien, CT 06820
Telephone: 203-202-8900

Web Site: www.gwrr.com
Officers: Mortimer B. Fuller - Chairman John C. Hellmann - President, Chief Executive Officer

Auditors: PricewaterhouseCoopers, LLP
Transfer Agents: Computershare, Providence, RI

GENESIS ENERGY L.P.

Exchange	Symbol	Price	52Wk Range	Yield	P/E	Div Achiever
NYS	GEL	$37.67 (5/31/2016)	49.79-20.43	7.14	9.46	12 Years

*7 Year Price Score 90.25   *NYSE Composite Index=100   *12 Month Price Score 89.02

Interim Earnings (Per Share)

Qtr.	Mar	Jun	Sep	Dec
2013	0.28	0.33	0.22	0.20
2014	0.04	0.24	0.33	0.28
2015	0.21	0.12	3.38	0.16
2016	0.32	...	...	...

Interim Dividends (Per Share)

Amt	Decl	Ex	Rec	Pay
0.625Q	07/07/2015	07/29/2015	07/31/2015	08/14/2015
0.64Q	10/07/2015	10/28/2015	10/30/2015	11/13/2015
0.655Q	01/07/2016	01/27/2016	01/29/2016	02/12/2016
0.672Q	04/13/2016	04/27/2016	04/29/2016	05/13/2016

Indicated Div: $2.69

Valuation Analysis

		Institutional Holding	
Forecast EPS	$1.54	No of Institutions	
	(05/20/2016)	223	
Market Cap	$4.1 Billion	Shares	
Book Value	N/A	88,816,352	
Price/Book	N/A	% Held	
Price/Sales	1.97	66.73	

TRADING VOLUME (thousand shares)

Business Summary: Equipment & Services (MIC: 9.1.3 SIC: 5171 NAIC: 424710)

Genesis Energy is focused on the midstream segment of the oil and gas industry in the Gulf Coast region of the U.S., primarily Texas, Louisiana, Arkansas, Mississippi, Alabama, Florida, Wyoming and in the Gulf of Mexico. Co. manages its businesses through five divisions: onshore pipeline transportation of crude oil and carbon dioxide; offshore pipeline transportation of crude oil; refinery services involving processing of high sulfur gas streams; marine transportation to provide waterborne transportation of petroleum products and crude oil; and supply and logistics services, which include terminaling, blending, storing, marketing, and transporting crude oil and petroleum products.

Recent Developments: For the quarter ended Mar 31 2016, net income increased 74.0% to US$35.2 million from US$20.2 million in the year-earlier quarter. Revenues were US$378.4 million, down 28.2% from US$526.9 million the year before. Operating income was US$59.8 million versus US$24.8 million in the prior-year quarter, an increase of 141.1%. Direct operating expenses declined 43.7% to US$259.7 million from US$461.7 million in the comparable period the year before. Indirect operating expenses increased 45.9% to US$58.9 million from US$40.3 million in the equivalent prior-year period.

Prospects: Our evaluation of Genesis Energy L.P. as of June 19, 2016 is the result of our systematic analysis on three basic characteristics: earnings strength, relative valuation, and recent stock price movement. The company has enjoyed a very positive trend in earnings per share over the past 5 quarters and while recent estimates for the company have been mixed, GEL has posted results that fell short of analysts expectations. Based on operating earnings yield, the company is about fairly valued when compared to all of the companies in our coverage universe. Share price changes over the past year indicates that GEL will perform poorly over the near term.

Financial Data

(US$ in Thousands)	3 Mos	12/31/2015	12/31/2014	12/31/2013	12/31/2012	12/31/2011	12/31/2010	12/31/2009
Earnings Per Share	3.98	4.09	1.18	1.03	1.23	0.75	0.49	0.51
Cash Flow Per Share	2.44	2.81	3.23	1.65	2.41	0.86	2.23	2.28
Dividends Per Share	2.530	2.470	2.230	2.015	1.823	1.650	1.490	1.365
Dividend Payout %	63.57	60.39	188.98	195.63	148.17	220.00	304.08	267.65
Income Statement								
Total Revenue	378,414	2,246,529	3,846,164	4,134,830	4,070,057	3,089,669	2,101,324	1,435,360
EBITDA	98,345	595,918	205,751	157,057	151,000	109,752	(4,884)	46,571
Depn & Amortn	38,497	124,200	73,200	46,300	37,400	27,300	22,500	25,200
Income Before Taxes	25,461	371,122	65,912	62,174	72,769	46,685	(50,308)	7,711
Income Taxes	1,001	3,987	2,845	845	(9,205)	(1,217)	2,588	3,080
Net Income	35,303	422,528	106,202	86,109	96,319	51,249	(48,459)	8,063
Average Shares	109,979	103,004	90,060	83,957	78,363	67,938	40,560	39,603
Balance Sheet								
Current Assets	326,371	306,316	355,366	535,223	404,034	376,104	252,538	189,244
Total Assets	5,569,374	5,459,599	3,230,374	2,862,202	2,109,664	1,730,844	1,506,735	1,148,127
Current Liabilities	257,374	302,136	363,145	446,553	312,651	249,428	206,714	141,428
Long-Term Obligations	3,088,575	2,922,054	1,601,039	1,283,572	850,895	659,300	610,000	366,900
Total Liabilities	3,577,057	3,430,498	2,001,171	1,764,465	1,193,169	938,206	837,471	552,250
Shares Outstanding	109,979	109,979	95,029	88,690	81,202	71,965	64,615	39,488
Statistical Record								
Return on Assets %	9.90	9.72	3.49	3.46	5.00	3.17	N.M.	0.69
EBITDA Margin %	25.99	26.53	5.35	3.80	3.71	3.55	N.M.	3.24
Net Margin %	9.33	18.81	2.76	2.08	2.37	1.66	N.M.	0.56
Asset Turnover	0.47	0.52	1.26	1.66	2.11	1.91	1.58	1.23
Current Ratio	1.27	1.01	0.98	1.20	1.29	1.51	1.22	1.34
Price Range	49.93-20.43	49.93-32.02	57.30-36.23	55.54-35.72	35.87-27.33	29.31-20.94	26.71-16.99	19.51-8.37
P/E Ratio	12.55-5.13	12.21-7.83	48.56-30.70	53.92-34.68	29.16-22.22	39.08-27.92	54.51-34.67	38.25-16.41
Average Yield %	6.43	5.70	4.26	4.17	5.81	6.23	7.01	9.93

Address: 919 Milam, Suite 2100, Houston, TX 77002 **Telephone:** 713-860-2500	**Web Site:** www.genesisenergy.com **Officers:** Grant E. Sims - Chairman, Chief Executive Officer Paul A. Davis - Senior Vice President	**Auditors:** Deloitte & Touche LLP **Transfer Agents:** American Stock Transfer & Trust Company, New York, NY

GENPACT LTD

Exchange	Symbol	Price	52Wk Range	Yield	P/E
NYS	G	$28.19 (5/31/2016)	28.39-21.22	N/A	24.51

*7 Year Price Score 117.93 *NYSE Composite Index=100 *12 Month Price Score 111.08

Interim Earnings (Per Share)

Qtr.	Mar	Jun	Sep	Dec
2013	0.20	0.27	0.30	0.20
2014	0.21	0.22	0.21	0.20
2015	0.20	0.28	0.31	0.29
2016	0.27	...	...	...

Interim Dividends (Per Share)

Amt	Decl	Ex	Rec	Pay
2.24U	08/30/2012	09/06/2012	09/10/2012	09/24/2012

Valuation Analysis   **Institutional Holding**

Forecast EPS	$1.42	No of Institutions
	(05/20/2016)	280
Market Cap	$5.9 Billion	Shares
Book Value	$1.3 Billion	189,366,784
Price/Book	4.40	% Held
Price/Sales	2.39	81.21

Business Summary: Business Services (MIC: 7.5.2 SIC: 7389 NAIC: 541618)

Genpact is engaged in business process outsourcing and information technology (IT) services. Co.'s business focuses on industry verticals in banking and financial services, insurance, capital markets, consumer product goods, life sciences, infrastructure, manufacturing and services, healthcare and high tech. Co.'s offerings in these core vertical activities are driven by its end-to-end process capabilities, which includes: finance and accounting services; analytics and research; business consulting and enterprise risk consulting; re-engineering; supply chain and procurement services; enterprise application services; IT management services; and collections and customer services.

Recent Developments: For the quarter ended Mar 31 2016, net income increased 30.5% to US$58.3 million from US$44.7 million in the year-earlier quarter. Revenues were US$609.7 million, up 3.8% from US$587.2 million the year before. Operating income was US$75.6 million versus US$74.1 million in the prior-year quarter, an increase of 2.1%. Direct operating expenses rose 4.3% to US$372.8 million from US$357.5 million in the comparable period the year before. Indirect operating expenses increased 3.6% to US$161.2 million from US$155.6 million in the equivalent prior-year period.

Prospects: Our evaluation of Genpact Ltd. as of June 19, 2016 is the result of our systematic analysis on three basic characteristics: earnings strength, relative valuation, and recent stock price movement. The company has generated a negative trend in earnings per share over the past 5 quarters and while recent estimates for the company have remained steady, G has posted better than expected results. Based on operating earnings yield, the company is about fairly valued when compared to all of the companies in our coverage universe. Share price changes over the past year indicates that G will perform very well over the near term.

Financial Data

(US$ in Thousands)	3 Mos	12/31/2015	12/31/2014	12/31/2013	12/31/2012	12/31/2011	12/31/2010	12/31/2009
Earnings Per Share	1.15	1.09	0.85	0.97	0.78	0.81	0.63	0.58
Cash Flow Per Share	1.38	1.51	1.23	1.36	1.38	1.20	0.74	0.73
Tang Book Value Per Share	0.97	0.79	0.52	1.17	0.44	1.77	3.96	2.82
Dividends Per Share	...	...	...	...	2.240	...	...	...
Dividend Payout %	...	...	...	...	287.18	...	...	...
Income Statement								
Total Revenue	609,703	2,461,044	2,279,438	2,131,997	1,901,971	1,600,436	1,258,963	1,120,071
EBITDA	93,136	409,892	356,352	399,175	348,457	323,415	247,060	229,151
Depn & Amortn	17,634	76,186	72,572	70,053	69,351	67,279	65,672	71,141
Income Before Taxes	72,664	312,554	254,385	305,982	262,992	262,059	184,247	161,124
Income Taxes	12,243	61,937	57,419	71,100	78,419	70,656	34,203	25,466
Net Income	58,565	239,817	192,002	229,717	178,216	184,294	142,181	127,301
Average Shares	213,892	219,145	225,168	235,754	229,532	226,354	224,838	220,066
Balance Sheet								
Current Assets	1,233,928	1,195,069	1,188,508	1,276,144	1,128,767	985,119	935,780	847,140
Total Assets	2,843,564	2,793,489	2,742,537	2,689,367	2,605,927	2,403,387	1,893,461	1,747,565
Current Liabilities	590,369	594,480	622,114	461,693	517,818	661,828	322,548	395,583
Long-Term Obligations	727,538	739,536	651,974	656,258	659,412	75,631	2,489	28,329
Total Liabilities	1,493,960	1,489,133	1,457,401	1,366,628	1,437,516	970,329	414,789	550,169
Stockholders' Equity	1,349,604	1,304,356	1,285,136	1,322,739	1,168,411	1,433,058	1,478,672	1,197,396
Shares Outstanding	210,490	211,472	218,684	231,262	225,480	222,347	220,916	217,433
Statistical Record								
Return on Assets %	9.09	8.66	7.07	8.68	7.10	8.58	7.81	7.39
Return on Equity %	18.88	18.52	14.72	18.44	13.66	12.66	10.63	12.49
EBITDA Margin %	15.28	16.66	15.63	18.72	18.32	20.21	19.62	20.46
Net Margin %	9.61	9.74	8.42	10.77	9.37	11.52	11.29	11.37
Asset Turnover	0.89	0.89	0.84	0.81	0.76	0.74	0.69	0.65
Current Ratio	2.09	2.01	1.91	2.76	2.18	1.49	2.90	2.14
Debt to Equity	0.54	0.57	0.51	0.50	0.56	0.05	N.M.	0.02
Price Range	27.19-21.22	25.85-18.87	19.30-14.28	21.19-15.46	18.66-14.45	17.83-13.09	18.50-13.50	15.21-7.25
P/E Ratio	23.64-18.45	23.72-17.31	22.71-16.80	21.85-15.94	23.92-18.53	22.01-16.16	29.37-21.43	26.22-12.50
Average Yield %	...	...	...	...	13.70	...	...	...

Address: Canon's Court, 22 Victoria Street, Hamilton, HM12 **Telephone:** 441-295-2244	**Web Site:** www.genpact.com **Officers:** N. V. Tyagarajan - President, Chief Executive Officer Edward J. Fitzpatrick - Senior Vice President, Chief Financial Officer	**Auditors:** KPMG LLP **Transfer Agents:** Computershare, Providence, RI

GENUINE PARTS CO.

Exchange	Symbol	Price	52Wk Range	Yield	P/E	Div Achiever
NYS	GPC	$96.92 (5/31/2016)	99.83-77.40	2.71	20.89	59 Years

*7 Year Price Score 111.94 ***NYSE Composite Index=100** ***12 Month Price Score 107.39**

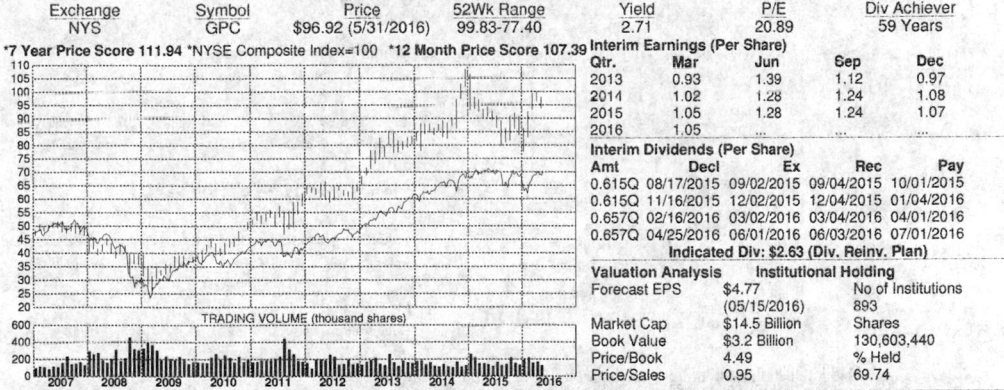

Interim Earnings (Per Share)

Qtr.	Mar	Jun	Sep	Dec
2013	0.93	1.39	1.12	0.97
2014	1.02	1.28	1.24	1.08
2015	1.05	1.28	1.24	1.07
2016	1.05	...	...	...

Interim Dividends (Per Share)

Amt	Decl	Ex	Rec	Pay
0.615Q	08/17/2015	09/02/2015	09/04/2015	10/01/2015
0.615Q	11/16/2015	12/02/2015	12/04/2015	01/04/2016
0.657Q	02/16/2016	03/02/2016	03/04/2016	04/01/2016
0.657Q	04/25/2016	06/01/2016	06/03/2016	07/01/2016

Indicated Div: $2.63 (Div. Reinv. Plan)

Valuation Analysis — **Institutional Holding**

Forecast EPS	$4.77	No of Institutions
	(05/15/2016)	893
Market Cap	$14.5 Billion	Shares
Book Value	$3.2 Billion	130,603,440
Price/Book	4.49	% Held
Price/Sales	0.95	69.74

Business Summary: Auto Parts (MIC: 1.8.2 SIC: 5013 NAIC: 423120)

Genuine Parts is a service organization engaged in the distribution of automotive replacement parts, industrial replacement parts, office products and electrical/electronic materials. Co.'s Automotive Parts Group distributes automotive parts and accessory items. Co.'s Industrial Parts Group distributes industrial replacement parts and related supplies such as bearings and material handling products. Co.'s Office Products Group engages in the wholesale distribution a line of office and other business related products. Co.'s Electrical/Electronic Materials Group distributes materials to electrical and electronic manufacturers, and industrial assembly and specialty wire and cable markets.

Recent Developments: For the quarter ended Mar 31 2016, net income decreased 1.9% to US$158.0 million from US$161.0 million in the year-earlier quarter. Revenues were US$3.72 billion, down 0.5% from US$3.74 billion the year before. Direct operating expenses declined 0.4% to US$2.61 billion from US$2.62 billion in the comparable period the year before. Indirect operating expenses decreased 0.4% to US$857.8 million from US$861.4 million in the equivalent prior-year period.

Prospects: Our evaluation of Genuine Parts Co. as of June 19, 2016 is the result of our systematic analysis on three basic characteristics: earnings strength, relative valuation, and recent stock price movement. The company has produced a positive trend in earnings per share over the past 5 quarters and while recent estimates for the company have been mixed, GPC has posted better than expected results. Based on operating earnings yield, the company is about fairly valued when compared to all of the companies in our coverage universe. Share price changes over the past year indicates that GPC will perform well over the near term.

Financial Data

(US$ in Thousands)	3 Mos	12/31/2015	12/31/2014	12/31/2013	12/31/2012	12/31/2011	12/31/2010	12/31/2009
Earnings Per Share	4.64	4.63	4.61	4.40	4.14	3.58	3.00	2.50
Cash Flow Per Share	7.83	7.64	5.15	6.83	5.82	3.99	4.29	5.30
Tang Book Value Per Share	12.16	11.89	12.50	13.39	16.15	16.08	16.39	15.42
Dividends Per Share	2.502	2.460	2.300	2.150	1.980	1.800	1.640	1.600
Dividend Payout %	53.93	53.13	49.89	48.86	47.83	50.28	54.67	64.00
Income Statement								
Total Revenue	3,718,267	15,280,044	15,341,647	14,077,843	13,013,868	12,458,877	11,207,589	10,057,512
EBITDA	281,299	1,287,018	1,291,140	1,205,232	1,137,797	1,006,778	879,176	762,461
Depn & Amortn	34,654	141,675	148,313	133,957	98,383	88,936	89,332	90,411
Income Before Taxes	246,645	1,123,681	1,117,739	1,044,304	1,018,932	890,806	761,783	644,165
Income Taxes	88,620	418,009	406,453	359,345	370,891	325,690	286,272	244,590
Net Income	158,025	705,672	711,286	684,959	648,041	565,116	475,511	399,575
Average Shares	150,342	152,496	154,375	155,714	156,420	157,660	158,461	159,707
Balance Sheet								
Current Assets	5,770,268	5,555,316	5,592,525	5,221,491	4,820,131	4,576,596	4,414,887	4,032,828
Total Assets	8,450,527	8,144,771	8,246,238	7,680,297	6,807,061	5,879,591	5,465,044	5,004,689
Current Liabilities	4,211,926	3,940,654	3,584,115	3,183,044	2,487,638	1,812,073	1,971,814	1,408,284
Long-Term Obligations	250,000	287,642	540,040	527,815	283,748	534,186	262,622	513,504
Total Liabilities	5,218,797	4,998,204	4,944,990	4,331,223	3,809,174	3,096,356	2,671,225	2,383,359
Stockholders' Equity	3,231,730	3,146,567	3,301,248	3,349,074	2,997,887	2,783,235	2,793,819	2,621,330
Shares Outstanding	149,623	150,081	153,113	153,773	154,841	155,651	157,636	158,917
Statistical Record								
Return on Assets %	8.42	8.61	8.93	9.46	10.19	9.96	9.08	8.16
Return on Equity %	21.92	21.89	21.39	21.58	22.36	20.27	17.56	16.16
EBITDA Margin %	7.57	8.42	8.42	8.56	8.74	8.08	7.84	7.58
Net Margin %	4.25	4.62	4.64	4.87	4.98	4.54	4.24	3.97
Asset Turnover	1.83	1.86	1.93	1.94	2.05	2.20	2.14	2.05
Current Ratio	1.37	1.41	1.56	1.64	1.94	2.53	2.24	2.86
Debt to Equity	0.08	0.09	0.16	0.16	0.09	0.19	0.09	0.20
Price Range	99.36-77.40	106.57-79.53	108.31-77.75	85.03-63.58	66.38-58.53	61.96-46.73	51.50-36.96	39.38-25.06
P/E Ratio	21.41-16.68	23.02-17.18	23.49-16.87	19.32-14.45	16.03-14.14	17.31-13.05	17.17-12.32	15.75-10.02
Average Yield %	2.83	2.72	2.59	2.77	3.16	3.34	3.80	4.63

Address: 2999 Circle 75 Parkway, Atlanta, GA 30339 **Telephone:** 770-953 1700 **Fax:** 770-956-2211	**Web Site:** www.genpt.com **Officers:** Thomas C. Gallagher - Chairman, President, Chief Executive Officer, Chief Operating Officer Paul D. Donahue - President, Chief Executive Officer, Executive Vice President, Division Officer	**Auditors:** Ernst & Young LLP **Investor Contact:** 770-953-1700 **Transfer Agents:** Computershare, Providence, RI

GENWORTH FINANCIAL, INC. (HOLDING CO)

Exchange	Symbol	Price	52Wk Range	Yield	P/E
NYS	GNW	$3.70 (5/31/2016)	8.07-1.61	N/A	N/A

*7 Year Price Score 39.18   *NYSE Composite Index=100   *12 Month Price Score 72.93

TRADING VOLUME (thousand shares)

Interim Earnings (Per Share)

Qtr.	Mar	Jun	Sep	Dec
2013	0.21	0.28	0.22	0.41
2014	0.37	0.35	(1.70)	(1.53)
2015	0.31	(0.39)	(0.57)	(0.59)
2016	0.11			

Interim Dividends (Per Share)

No Dividends Paid

Valuation Analysis   **Institutional Holding**

Forecast EPS	$0.85	No of Institutions	
	(05/20/2016)	499	
Market Cap	$1.8 Billion	Shares	
Book Value	$14.1 Billion	413,711,648	
Price/Book	0.13	% Held	
Price/Sales	0.22	80.32	

Business Summary: Life & Health (MIC: 5.2.2 SIC: 6311 NAIC: 524113)

Genworth Financial is a holding company. Co. operates its business in five operating segments: U.S. Mortgage Insurance, which provides mortgage insurance products predominantly insuring prime-based, individually underwritten residential mortgage loans; Canada Mortgage Insurance, which provides flow mortgage insurance and bulk mortgage insurance in Canada; Australia Mortgage Insurance, which provides flow mortgage insurance and bulk mortgage insurance in Australia; U.S. Life Insurance, which provides long-term care insurance products, and service life insurance and fixed annuity products; and Runoff, which includes the results of non-strategic products which are no longer actively sold.

Recent Developments: For the quarter ended Mar 31 2016, income from continuing operations decreased 37.4% to US$127.0 million from US$203.0 million in the year-earlier quarter. Net income decreased 47.1% to US$108.0 million from US$204.0 million in the year-earlier quarter. Revenues were US$1.79 billion, down 16.4% from US$2.14 billion the year before. Net premiums earned were US$794.0 million versus US$1.14 billion in the prior-year quarter, a decrease of 30.5%. Net investment income rose 1.0% to US$789.0 million from US$781.0 million a year ago.

Prospects: Our evaluation of Genworth Financial Inc. as of June 19, 2016 is the result of our systematic analysis on three basic characteristics: earnings strength, relative valuation, and recent stock price movement. The company has suffered a very negative trend in earnings per share over the past 5 quarters and while recent estimates for the company have remained steady, GNW has posted better than expected results. Based on operating earnings yield, the company is undervalued when compared to all of the companies in our coverage universe. Share price changes over the past year indicates that GNW will perform poorly over the near term.

Financial Data
(US$ in Millions)

	3 Mos	12/31/2015	12/31/2014	12/31/2013	12/31/2012	12/31/2011	12/31/2010	12/31/2009
Earnings Per Share	(1.44)	(1.24)	(2.51)	1.12	0.65	0.25	0.29	(1.02)
Cash Flow Per Share	2.46	3.20	4.91	2.83	1.95	6.37	2.73	4.28
Tang Book Value Per Share	27.64	25.03	29.45	26.52	30.34	29.96	24.06	20.49
Income Statement								
Premium Income	794	4,579	5,431	5,148	5,038	5,705	5,854	6,019
Total Revenue	1,785	8,548	9,565	9,403	10,023	10,344	10,089	9,069
Income Before Taxes	150	(15)	(1,276)	1,050	712	314	76	(792)
Income Taxes	23	(9)	(228)	324	189	53	(209)	(393)
Net Income	53	(615)	(1,244)	560	323	122	142	(460)
Average Shares	499	497	496	498	494	493	493	451
Balance Sheet								
Total Assets	107,173	106,431	111,358	108,045	113,312	114,302	112,395	108,187
Total Liabilities	93,118	93,607	96,435	93,652	96,775	97,761	98,534	95,911
Stockholders' Equity	14,055	12,824	14,923	14,393	16,537	16,541	13,861	12,276
Shares Outstanding	498	498	497	495	492	491	490	489
Statistical Record								
Return on Assets %	N.M.	N.M.	N.M.	0.51	0.28	0.11	0.13	N.M.
Return on Equity %	N.M.	N.M.	N.M.	3.62	1.95	0.80	1.09	N.M.
Net Margin %	2.97	(7.19)	(13.01)	5.96	3.22	1.18	1.41	(5.07)
Price Range	9.15-1.61	9.15-3.47	18.60-7.64	15.63-7.51	9.34-4.12	14.31-4.92	18.96-10.59	13.34-0.84
P/E Ratio	...	...	...	13.96-6.71	14.37-6.34	57.24-19.68	65.38-36.52	...

Address: 6620 West Broad Street, Richmond, VA 23230 **Telephone:** 804-281-6000	**Web Site:** www.genworth.com **Officers:** Thomas J. McInerney - President, Chief Executive Officer, Division Officer Lori M. Evangel - Executive Vice President, Chief Risk Officer	**Auditors:** KPMG LLP **Transfer Agents:** Computershare Shareowner Services LLC, College Station, TX

GLOBAL PARTNERS LP

Exchange	Symbol	Price	52Wk Range	Yield	P/E
NYS	GLP	$13.29 (5/31/2016)	41.59-12.31	13.92	1329.00

*7 Year Price Score 71.16   *NYSE Composite Index=100   *12 Month Price Score 55.22

Interim Earnings (Per Share)

Qtr.	Mar	Jun	Sep	Dec
2013	0.51	0.29	0.09	0.53
2014	2.03	(0.50)	1.50	0.92
2015	0.92	0.15	0.16	(0.09)
2016	(0.21)	...	...	...

Interim Dividends (Per Share)

Amt	Decl	Ex	Rec	Pay
0.693Q	07/22/2015	08/03/2015	08/05/2015	08/14/2015
0.698Q	10/21/2015	11/02/2015	11/04/2015	11/13/2015
0.463Q	01/28/2016	02/08/2016	02/10/2016	02/16/2016
0.463Q	04/26/2016	05/04/2016	05/06/2016	05/16/2016

Indicated Div: $1.85

Valuation Analysis

		Institutional Holding	
Forecast EPS	$-0.41 (05/15/2016)	No of Institutions	95
Market Cap	$445.4 Million	Shares	15,950,623
Book Value	N/A	% Held	37.09
Price/Book	N/A		
Price/Sales	0.05		

Business Summary: Equipment & Services (MIC: 9.1.3 SIC: 5171 NAIC: 424710)

Global Partners is a midstream logistics and marketing company engaged in the purchasing, selling and logistics of transporting petroleum and related products. Co. has three segments: Wholesale, which sells unbranded gasoline and diesel and sells home heating oil, diesel, kerosene, residual oil and propane; Gasoline Distribution and Station Operations, which sells branded and unbranded gasoline to gasoline stations and other sub-jobbers, and operates gasoline stations; and Commercial, which sells and delivers unbranded gasoline, home heating oil, diesel, kerosene, residual oil, renewable fuels and natural gas to customers in the public sector and to commercial and industrial end users.

Recent Developments: For the quarter ended Mar 31 2016, net loss amounted to US$7.8 million versus net income of US$30.4 million in the year-earlier quarter. Revenues were US$1.75 billion, down 41.2% from US$2.98 billion the year before. Operating income was US$14.2 million versus US$45.3 million in the prior-year quarter, a decrease of 68.6%. Direct operating expenses declined 42.3% to US$1.62 billion from US$2.81 billion in the comparable period the year before. Indirect operating expenses decreased 6.0% to US$115.8 million from US$123.2 million in the equivalent prior-year period.

Prospects: On Apr. 29, 2013, Co. began receiving and distributing propane from its new rail-fed propane storage facility in Albany, NY. The 540,000-gallon facility can receive deliveries from Canadian Pacific Railway on a single line haul directly from Midwest and Canadian sources. Separately, Co. has executed a pipeline connection agreement with Tesoro Logistics whereby Tesoro Logistics' High Plains Pipeline System will build, own and operate a new seven-mile pipeline lateral from its Lignite, ND crude oil station to Co.'s crude oil storage tanks at the Basin Transload facility in Columbus, ND. Crude oil is expected to begin flowing on the new Columbus-bound lateral in the third quarter of 2013.

Financial Data
(US$ in Thousands)

	3 Mos	12/31/2015	12/31/2014	12/31/2013	12/31/2012	12/31/2011	12/31/2010	12/31/2009
Earnings Per Share	0.01	1.11	3.95	1.42	1.71	0.87	1.59	2.51
Cash Flow Per Share	3.67	1.94	12.58	9.34	8.78	(0.82)	(5.33)	(4.70)
Dividends Per Share	2.533	2.735	2.527	2.340	2.058	2.000	1.958	1.950
Dividend Payout %	25,325.00	246.40	63.99	164.79	120.32	229.89	123.11	77.69
Income Statement								
Total Revenue	1,750,812	10,314,852	17,269,954	19,589,608	17,625,997	14,835,729	7,801,559	5,818,411
EBITDA	16,310	217,023	233,207	143,309	123,088	75,029	64,948	61,551
Depn & Amortn	2,085	102,300	67,500	57,900	38,500	24,400	15,600	10,800
Income Before Taxes	(8,755)	41,391	117,943	41,872	48,320	19,420	27,038	35,563
Income Taxes	(920)	(1,873)	963	819	1,577	68	...	1,429
Net Income	(7,024)	43,563	114,709	42,615	46,743	19,352	27,038	34,134
Average Shares	33,517	32,323	27,502	27,560	26,567	21,474	16,597	13,279
Balance Sheet								
Current Assets	887,501	867,035	961,223	1,374,311	1,506,933	1,412,864	1,197,645	862,858
Total Assets	2,655,438	2,663,675	2,039,977	2,427,922	2,329,752	1,868,851	1,672,316	1,052,703
Current Liabilities	604,855	594,734	707,491	972,572	1,045,195	771,054	751,681	567,635
Long-Term Obligations	1,172,158	1,075,564	601,936	909,968	762,754	731,095	593,502	312,089
Total Liabilities	2,028,899	2,015,886	1,453,035	2,012,685	1,893,291	1,553,562	1,395,500	895,283
Shares Outstanding	33,517	33,737	30,835	27,491	27,540	21,792	19,105	13,253
Statistical Record								
Return on Assets %	0.23	1.85	5.13	1.79	2.22	1.09	1.98	3.52
EBITDA Margin %	0.93	2.10	1.35	0.73	0.70	0.51	0.83	1.06
Net Margin %	N.M.	0.42	0.66	0.22	0.27	0.13	0.35	0.59
Asset Turnover	3.48	4.39	7.73	8.23	8.37	8.38	5.73	5.99
Current Ratio	1.47	1.46	1.36	1.41	1.44	1.83	1.59	1.52
Price Range	41.82-12.71	41.82-15.26	45.32-31.68	40.65-25.35	27.81-20.19	29.83-14.86	27.60-19.58	26.99-9.21
P/E Ratio	N.M.	37.68-13.75	11.47-8.02	28.63-17.85	16.26-11.81	34.29-17.08	17.36-12.31	10.75-3.67
Average Yield %	9.06	8.21	6.37	6.74	8.67	8.53	8.13	10.64

Address: P.O. Box 9161, 800 South Street, Waltham, MA 02454-9161
Telephone: 781 894-8800

Web Site: www.globalp.com
Officers: Richard Slifka - Chairman, Vice-Chairman
Eric S. Slifka - President, Chief Executive Officer

Auditors: Ernst & Young LLP
Investor Contact: 617-542-5300
Transfer Agents: American Stock Transfer and Trust Company, New York, NY

GLOBAL PAYMENTS, INC.

Exchange	Symbol	Price	52Wk Range	Yield	P/E
NYS	GPN	$77.69 (5/31/2016)	77.69-51.09	0.05	33.93

*7 Year Price Score 165.97 *NYSE Composite Index=100 *12 Month Price Score 116.11

TRADING VOLUME (thousand shares)

Interim Earnings (Per Share)

Qtr.	Aug	Nov	Feb	May
2012-13	0.29	0.45	0.38	0.27
2013-14	0.44	0.51	0.38	0.36
2014-15	0.55	0.55	0.47	0.50
2015-16	0.66	0.60	0.53	...

Interim Dividends (Per Share)

Amt	Decl	Ex	Rec	Pay
100%	10/07/2015	11/03/2015	10/21/2015	11/02/2015
0.01Q	10/07/2015	11/10/2015	11/13/2015	11/27/2015
0.01Q	12/15/2015	02/10/2016	02/12/2016	02/26/2016
0.01Q	03/30/2016	05/11/2016	05/13/2016	05/27/2016

Indicated Div: $0.04

Valuation Analysis / Institutional Holding

Forecast EPS	$2.98	No of Institutions
	(05/20/2016)	556
Market Cap	$10.0 Billion	Shares
Book Value	$840.1 Million	135,462,352
Price/Book	11.95	% Held
Price/Sales	3.51	86.17

Business Summary: Business Services (MIC: 7.5.2 SIC: 7389 NAIC: 561499)

Global Payments is a provider of payment technology services. Co.'s partnerships, technologies and employees enable it to provide a range of services that allow its customers to accept various payment types. Co. provides payment and digital commerce solutions and operates in two reportable segments: North America merchant services and International merchant services. Co.'s business in Europe is primarily located in the U.K, the Republic of Ireland, Spain, the Republic of Malta, the Czech Republic and the Russian Federation. Co.'s Asia-Pacific region includes Australia, Brunei, China, Hong Kong, India, Macau, Malaysia, Maldives, New Zealand, the Philippines, Singapore, Sri Lanka and Taiwan.

Recent Developments:
For the quarter ended Feb 29 2016, net income increased 5.2% to US$72.9 million from US$69.3 million in the year-earlier quarter. Revenues were US$679.9 million, up 2.2% from US$665.0 million the year before. Operating income was US$107.8 million versus US$104.6 million in the prior-year quarter, an increase of 3.0%. Direct operating expenses rose 3.4% to US$258.7 million from US$250.3 million in the comparable period the year before. Indirect operating expenses increased 1.1% to US$313.4 million from US$310.1 million in the equivalent prior-year period.

Prospects:
Our evaluation of Global Payments Inc. as of June 19, 2016 is the result of our systematic analysis on three basic characteristics: earnings strength, relative valuation, and recent stock price movement. The company has managed to produce a neutral trend in earnings per share over the past 5 quarters and while recent estimates for the company have been mixed, GPN has posted better than expected results. Based on operating earnings yield, the company is about fairly valued when compared to all of the companies in our coverage universe. Share price changes over the past year indicates that GPN will perform very well over the near term.

Financial Data
(US$ in Thousands)

	9 Mos	6 Mos	3 Mos	05/31/2015	05/31/2014	05/31/2013	05/31/2012	05/31/2011
Earnings Per Share	2.29	2.22	2.17	2.06	1.69	1.38	1.19	1.30
Cash Flow Per Share	7.39	5.03	7.68	3.17	1.35	1.55	(1.10)	4.45
Tang Book Value Per Share	N.M.	N.M.	N.M.	N.M.	N.M.	N.M.	1.00	0.39
Dividends Per Share	0.040	0.040	0.040	0.040	0.040	0.040	0.040	0.040
Dividend Payout %	1.75	1.80	1.84	1.94	2.37	2.90	3.38	3.08
Income Statement								
Total Revenue	2,151,086	1,471,146	748,796	2,773,718	2,554,236	2,375,923	2,203,847	1,859,802
EBITDA	431,073	302,746	158,620	594,084	527,544	468,978	406,445	413,786
Depn & Amortn	62,331	41,809	20,848	137,487	122,045	111,765	99,096	82,192
Income Before Taxes	331,599	236,002	125,671	417,110	377,350	334,284	300,447	324,207
Income Taxes	82,561	59,876	32,623	107,995	107,398	95,571	82,881	95,076
Net Income	234,479	165,418	86,646	278,040	245,286	216,125	188,161	209,238
Average Shares	130,160	130,353	131,146	134,922	145,376	156,454	158,862	160,956
Balance Sheet								
Current Assets	2,065,103	2,655,821	2,747,038	3,302,295	1,643,444	1,214,492	1,248,739	1,847,975
Total Assets	4,699,101	5,328,101	5,472,918	5,793,548	4,018,650	3,125,056	2,688,143	3,350,531
Current Liabilities	1,748,132	2,267,645	2,390,236	3,015,904	1,211,618	704,114	837,285	1,444,364
Long-Term Obligations	1,787,675	1,915,803	1,932,028	1,680,000	1,376,002	891,134	236,565	268,217
Total Liabilities	3,858,984	4,522,945	4,686,221	5,035,572	3,021,423	1,978,971	1,515,959	2,165,996
Stockholders' Equity	840,117	805,156	786,697	757,976	997,227	1,146,085	1,172,184	1,184,535
Shares Outstanding	129,258	129,362	129,882	130,557	137,691	150,852	157,102	160,669
Statistical Record								
Return on Assets %	6.88	5.94	5.90	5.67	6.87	7.44	6.21	7.76
Return on Equity %	36.01	34.51	33.47	31.68	22.89	18.65	15.92	20.46
EBITDA Margin %	20.04	20.58	21.18	21.42	20.65	19.74	18.44	22.25
Net Margin %	10.90	11.24	11.57	10.02	9.60	9.10	8.54	11.25
Asset Turnover	0.66	0.58	0.57	0.57	0.72	0.82	0.73	0.69
Current Ratio	1.18	1.17	1.15	1.09	1.36	1.72	1.49	1.28
Debt to Equity	2.13	2.38	2.46	2.22	1.38	0.78	0.20	0.23
Price Range	72.66-44.13	72.66-38.63	58.95-34.40	52.70-33.98	36.50-22.91	25.50-19.94	26.74-19.66	26.70-18.05
P/E Ratio	31.73-19.27	32.73-17.40	27.17-15.85	25.58-16.50	21.60-13.55	18.48-14.45	22.47-16.53	20.53-13.88
Average Yield %	0.07	0.08	0.09	0.10	0.13	0.18	0.17	0.18

Address: 10 Glenlake Parkway, North Tower, Atlanta, GA 30328 **Telephone:** 770-829-8000	**Web Site:** www.globalpaymentsinc.com **Officers:** William I. Jacobs - Chairman Jeffrey Steven Sloan - President, Chief Executive Officer	**Auditors:** Deloitte & Touche LLP **Investor Contact:** 770-829-8234 **Transfer Agents:** Computershare Trust Company, N.A, Canton, MA

GNC HOLDINGS INC

Exchange	Symbol	Price	52Wk Range	Yield	P/E
NYS	GNC	$26.05 (5/31/2016)	50.93-23.56	3.07	10.14

*7 Year Price Score N/A   *NYSE Composite Index=100   *12 Month Price Score 78.26

Interim Earnings (Per Share)

Qtr.	Mar	Jun	Sep	Dec
2013	0.73	0.73	0.76	0.50
2014	0.76	0.77	0.71	0.58
2015	0.72	0.79	0.54	0.55
2016	0.69	...	...	...

Interim Dividends (Per Share)

Amt	Decl	Ex	Rec	Pay
0.18Q	07/24/2015	09/09/2015	09/11/2015	09/25/2015
0.18Q	10/23/2015	12/09/2015	12/11/2015	12/28/2015
0.20Q	02/01/2016	03/09/2016	03/11/2016	03/25/2016
0.20Q	04/27/2016	06/08/2016	06/10/2016	06/24/2016

Indicated Div: $0.80

Valuation Analysis | **Institutional Holding**

Forecast EPS	$2.88	No of Institutions	
	(05/20/2016)	299	
Market Cap	$1.8 Billion	Shares	
Book Value	$289.8 Million	71,505,448	
Price/Book	6.17	% Held	
Price/Sales	0.68	84.77	

Business Summary: Retail - Food & Beverage, Drug & Tobacco (MIC: 2.1.2 SIC: 5499 NAIC: 446191)

GNC Holdings, through its subsidiaries, is a retailer of health and wellness products, including vitamins, minerals and herbal supplements (VMHS), sports nutrition products, diet products and other wellness products. Co. has four product categories: VMHS, which sells vitamins and minerals in single vitamin and multi vitamin form and in various potency levels; sports nutrition, which provides a range selection of sports nutrition products; diet products, which provides a variety of diet products; and other wellness, which including cosmetics, food items, health management products, books, DVDs and equipment. As of Dec 31 2015, there were 9,090 GNC store locations globally.

Recent Developments: For the quarter ended Mar 31 2016, net income decreased 19.7% to US$50.8 million from US$63.3 million in the year-earlier quarter. Revenues were US$668.9 million, down 1.8% from US$681.3 million the year before. Operating income was US$94.1 million versus US$109.6 million in the prior-year quarter, a decrease of 14.2%. Direct operating expenses rose 0.3% to US$433.1 million from US$431.8 million in the comparable period the year before. Indirect operating expenses increased 1.4% to US$141.8 million from US$139.8 million in the equivalent prior-year period.

Prospects: Our evaluation of GNC Holdings Inc as of June 19, 2016 is the result of our systematic analysis on three basic characteristics: earnings strength, relative valuation, and recent stock price movement. The company has managed to produce a neutral trend in earnings per share over the past 5 quarters and while recent estimates for the company has remained steady, GNC has posted results that fell short of analysts expectations. Based on operating earnings yield, the company is undervalued when compared to all of the companies in our coverage universe. Share price changes over the past year indicates that GNC will perform poorly over the near term.

Financial Data

(US$ in Thousands)	3 Mos	12/31/2015	12/31/2014	12/31/2013	12/31/2012	12/31/2011	12/31/2010	12/31/2009
Earnings Per Share	2.57	2.60	2.81	2.72	2.29	1.24	0.85	0.58
Cash Flow Per Share	5.20	4.22	3.36	2.47	2.13	1.74	1.62	1.30
Dividends Per Share	0.740	0.720	0.640	0.600	0.440	...	...	...
Dividend Payout %	28.79	27.69	22.78	22.06	19.21	...	...	...
Income Statement								
Total Revenue	668,905	2,639,212	2,613,154	2,630,308	2,429,983	2,072,179	1,822,168	1,707,007
EBITDA	97,164	440,107	485,012	503,298	468,540	321,307	259,393	227,685
Depn & Amortn	3,099	47,000	45,500	42,800	40,700	38,800	46,987	46,659
Income Before Taxes	79,622	342,171	392,804	407,469	380,284	207,604	147,030	111,086
Income Taxes	28,807	122,872	136,932	142,448	140,088	75,271	50,463	41,562
Net Income	50,815	219,299	255,872	265,021	240,196	132,333	96,567	69,524
Average Shares	73,373	84,186	90,918	97,383	104,911	103,010	88,917	87,859
Balance Sheet								
Current Assets	811,392	792,863	876,343	966,047	818,797	705,015	719,294	596,647
Total Assets	2,557,545	2,552,019	2,677,800	2,740,347	2,552,040	2,429,587	2,425,083	2,318,094
Current Liabilities	367,802	277,711	240,343	247,066	245,319	230,533	234,825	199,619
Long-Term Obligations	1,536,390	1,447,904	1,337,638	1,341,656	1,094,745	899,950	1,030,429	1,058,085
Total Liabilities	2,267,721	2,083,458	1,921,757	1,924,768	1,670,001	1,451,125	1,587,219	1,586,118
Stockholders' Equity	289,824	468,561	756,043	815,579	882,039	978,462	837,864	731,976
Shares Outstanding	68,694	76,276	88,335	93,989	99,244	105,044	87,368	87,339
Statistical Record								
Return on Assets %	7.87	8.39	9.45	10.02	9.62	5.45	4.07	...
Return on Equity %	40.24	35.82	32.56	31.22	25.75	14.57	12.30	...
EBITDA Margin %	14.53	16.68	18.56	19.13	19.28	15.51	14.24	13.34
Net Margin %	7.60	8.31	9.79	10.08	9.88	6.39	5.30	4.07
Asset Turnover	1.00	1.01	0.96	0.99	0.97	0.85	0.77	...
Current Ratio	2.21	2.85	3.65	3.91	3.34	3.06	3.06	2.99
Debt to Equity	5.30	3.09	1.77	1.65	1.24	0.92	1.23	1.45
Price Range	50.93-23.56	50.93-28.24	58.45-32.38	60.56-32.20	42.43-26.35	29.24-16.75	...	...
P/E Ratio	19.82-9.17	19.59-10.86	20.80-11.52	22.26-11.84	18.53-11.51	23.58-13.51	...	...
Average Yield %	1.92	1.69	1.53	1.25	1.22	...	...	...

Address: 300 Sixth Avenue, Pittsburgh, PA 15222
Telephone: 412-288-4600

Web Site: www.gnc.com
Officers: Michael G. Archbold - Chief Executive Officer Tricia K. Tolivar - Executive Vice President, Chief Financial Officer

Auditors: PricewaterhouseCoopers LLP
Investor Contact: 412-288-4632
Transfer Agents: American Stock Transfer and Trust Company, LLC, Brooklyn, NY

GRACE (WR) & CO

Exchange	Symbol	Price	52Wk Range	Yield	P/E
NYS	GRA	$77.64 (5/31/2016)	83.89-63.12	N/A	63.12

*7 Year Price Score 126.53 *NYSE Composite Index=100 *12 Month Price Score 99.38

Interim Earnings (Per Share)

Qtr.	Mar	Jun	Sep	Dec
2013	0.69	1.07	0.89	0.66
2014	0.64	1.77	0.99	0.23
2015	0.72	0.78	0.19	0.30
2016	(0.04)	...	...	...

Interim Dividends (Per Share)

No Dividends Paid

Valuation Analysis / **Institutional Holding**

Forecast EPS	$3.10	No of Institutions
	(05/20/2016)	377
Market Cap	$5.5 Billion	Shares
Book Value	$391.4 Million	64,234,200
Price/Book	13.99	% Held
Price/Sales	2.03	80.48

Business Summary: Specialty Chemicals (MIC: 8.3.2 SIC: 2819 NAIC: 331311)

Grace (W.R.) is engaged in the production and sale of chemicals and specialty materials through its three operating segments: Grace Catalysts Technologies, which includes catalysts and related products and technologies used in refining, petrochemical and other chemical manufacturing applications; Grace Materials Technologies, which includes packaging technologies and engineered materials used in consumer, industrial, and pharmaceutical applications; and Grace Construction Products, which includes specialty construction chemicals and specialty building materials used in commercial, infrastructure and residential construction.

Recent Developments: For the quarter ended Mar 31 2016, income from continuing operations decreased 76.8% to US$7.0 million from US$30.2 million in the year-earlier quarter. Net loss amounted to US$2.9 million versus net income of US$52.7 million in the year-earlier quarter. Revenues were US$362.8 million, down 8.6% from US$397.0 million the year before. Direct operating expenses declined 16.0% to US$210.1 million from US$250.0 million in the comparable period the year before. Indirect operating expenses increased 22.2% to US$121.3 million from US$99.3 million in the equivalent prior-year period.

Prospects: Our evaluation of Grace (W.R.) Co. as of June 19, 2016 is the result of our systematic analysis on three basic characteristics: earnings strength, relative valuation, and recent stock price movement. The company has generated a negative trend in earnings per share over the past 5 quarters and while recent estimates for the company have remained steady, GRA has posted better than expected results. Based on operating earnings yield, the company is about fairly valued when compared to all of the companies in our coverage universe. Share price changes over the past year indicates that GRA will perform well over the near term.

Financial Data

(US$ in Thousands)	3 Mos	12/31/2015	12/31/2014	12/31/2013	12/31/2012	12/31/2011	12/31/2010	12/31/2009
Earnings Per Share	1.23	1.99	3.63	3.30	1.23	3.57	2.78	0.98
Cash Flow Per Share	6.47	0.19	(19.55)	6.75	6.04	2.95	4.51	6.00
Tang Book Value Per Share	N.M.	N.M.	N.M.	N.M.	0.38	N.M.	...	...
Income Statement								
Total Revenue	362,800	3,051,500	3,243,000	3,060,700	3,155,500	3,211,900	2,675,000	2,825,000
EBITDA	69,500	521,600	577,500	504,600	204,800	530,400	378,000	240,900
Depn & Amortn	23,200	131,500	137,100	123,100	119,000	120,000	115,600	113,000
Income Before Taxes	24,500	289,200	314,600	337,700	39,300	368,300	222,100	91,000
Income Taxes	24,400	164,700	57,000	102,900	(37,300)	114,700	32,500	11,500
Net Income	(2,700)	144,200	276,300	256,100	94,100	269,400	207,100	71,200
Average Shares	70,600	72,600	76,200	77,700	76,300	75,500	74,400	72,600
Balance Sheet								
Current Assets	893,900	1,184,500	1,690,900	2,294,400	2,440,200	2,149,100	1,904,200	1,628,700
Total Assets	2,888,400	3,676,000	4,095,200	5,396,100	5,090,200	4,496,700	4,271,700	3,968,200
Current Liabilities	464,800	707,400	1,182,100	635,600	646,300	635,600	532,900	494,700
Long-Term Obligations	1,507,700	2,144,300	1,919,000	29,600	35,800	21,600	15,500	10,900
Total Liabilities	2,497,000	3,468,200	3,729,300	4,835,500	4,781,800	4,337,300	4,347,400	4,267,400
Stockholders' Equity	391,400	207,800	365,900	560,600	308,400	159,400	(75,700)	(299,200)
Shares Outstanding	70,533	70,533	72,922	77,046	75,565	73,886	73,120	72,283
Statistical Record								
Return on Assets %	2.67	3.71	5.82	4.88	1.96	6.14	5.03	1.82
Return on Equity %	23.48	50.27	59.64	58.94	40.12	643.73	...	...
EBITDA Margin %	19.16	17.09	17.81	16.49	6.49	16.51	14.13	8.53
Net Margin %	N.M.	4.73	8.52	8.37	2.98	8.39	7.74	2.52
Asset Turnover	0.81	0.79	0.68	0.58	0.66	0.73	0.65	0.72
Current Ratio	1.92	1.67	1.43	3.61	3.78	3.38	3.57	3.29
Debt to Equity	3.85	10.32	5.24	0.05	0.12	0.14	...	...
Price Range	83.89-63.12	83.89-68.23	83.47-65.35	79.35-53.96	54.98-37.05	41.78-25.19	29.07-15.83	21.00-3.27
P/E Ratio	68.20-51.32	42.15-34.29	22.99-18.00	24.05-16.35	44.70-30.12	11.70-7.06	10.46-5.70	21.43-3.33

Address: 7500 Grace Drive, Columbia, MD 21044-4098 **Telephone:** 410-531-4000	**Web Site:** www.grace.com **Officers:** Alfred E. Festa - Chairman, President, Chief Executive Officer Hudson La Force - President, Senior Vice President, Chief Financial Officer, Chief Operating Officer	**Auditors:** PricewaterhouseCoopers LLP **Investor Contact:** 410-531-4167 **Transfer Agents:** Computershare Shareowner Services LLC, Providence, RI

GRACO INC

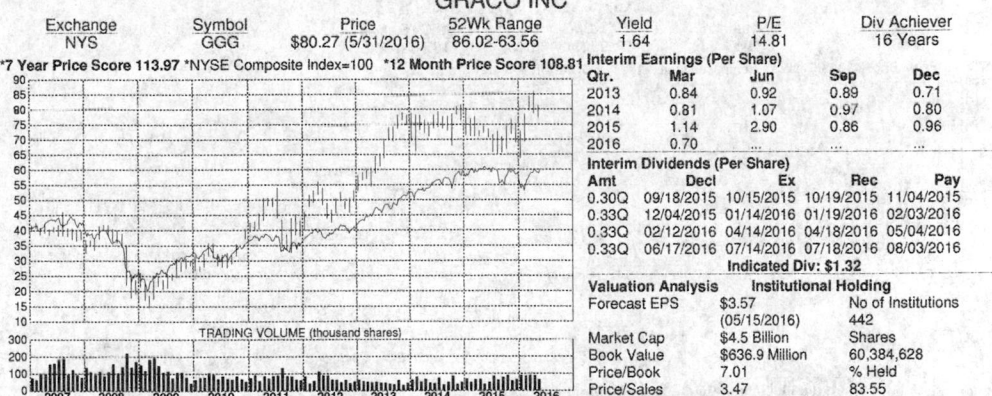

Exchange	Symbol	Price	52Wk Range	Yield	P/E	Div Achiever
NYS	GGG	$80.27 (5/31/2016)	86.02-63.56	1.64	14.81	16 Years

*7 Year Price Score 113.97 *NYSE Composite Index=100 *12 Month Price Score 108.81

Interim Earnings (Per Share)

Qtr.	Mar	Jun	Sep	Dec
2013	0.84	0.92	0.89	0.71
2014	0.81	1.07	0.97	0.80
2015	1.14	2.90	0.86	0.96
2016	0.70	...	...	...

Interim Dividends (Per Share)

Amt	Decl	Ex	Rec	Pay
0.30Q	09/18/2015	10/15/2015	10/19/2015	11/04/2015
0.33Q	12/04/2015	01/14/2016	01/19/2016	02/03/2016
0.33Q	02/12/2016	04/14/2016	04/18/2016	05/04/2016
0.33Q	06/17/2016	07/14/2016	07/18/2016	08/03/2016

Indicated Div: $1.32

Valuation Analysis / **Institutional Holding**

Forecast EPS	$3.57	No of Institutions
	(05/15/2016)	442
Market Cap	$4.5 Billion	Shares
Book Value	$636.9 Million	60,384,628
Price/Book	7.01	% Held
Price/Sales	3.47	83.55

TRADING VOLUME (thousand shares)

Business Summary: Industrial Machinery & Equipment (MIC: 7.2.1 SIC: 3561 NAIC: 333911)

Graco. together with its subsidiaries, design, manufacture and market equipment used to pump, meter, mix and dispense fluid and powder materials. Co. has three segments: Industrial, which includes Co.'s Industrial Products and Applied Fluid Technologies divisions and markets equipment and pre-engineered packages for moving and applying paints, coatings, sealants, adhesives and other fluids; Process, which includes Co.'s Process, Oil and Natural Gas, and Lubrication divisions and markets pumps, valves, meters and accessories to move and dispense fluids; as well as Contractor, which markets sprayers for architectural coatings, corrosion control, texture and line striping.

Recent Developments: For the quarter ended Mar 25 2016, net income decreased 42.5% to US$39.6 million from US$68.8 million in the year earlier quarter. Revenues were US$304.9 million, down 0.5% from US$306.5 million the year before. Operating income was US$60.9 million versus US$65.2 million in the prior-year quarter, a decrease of 6.6%. Direct operating expenses declined 0.8% to US$143.1 million from US$144.3 million in the comparable period the year before. Indirect operating expenses increased 4.1% to US$100.8 million from US$96.9 million in the equivalent prior-year period.

Prospects: Our evaluation of Graco Inc. as of June 19, 2016 is the result of our systematic analysis on three basic characteristics: earnings strength, relative valuation, and recent stock price movement. The company has produced a positive trend in earnings per share over the past 5 quarters and while recent estimates for the company have remained steady, GGG has posted results that fell short of analysts expectations. Based on operating earnings yield, the company is about fairly valued when compared to all of the companies in our coverage universe. Share price changes over the past year indicates that GGG will perform very well over the near term.

Financial Data

(US$ in Thousands)	3 Mos	12/25/2015	12/26/2014	12/27/2013	12/28/2012	12/30/2011	12/31/2010	12/25/2009
Earnings Per Share	5.42	5.86	3.65	3.36	2.42	2.32	1.69	0.81
Cash Flow Per Share	3.03	3.30	4.02	3.98	3.15	2.70	1.65	2.45
Tang Book Value Per Share	N.M.	0.19	2.09	4.80	1.94	3.50	2.38	1.28
Dividends Per Share	1.230	1.200	1.100	1.000	0.900	0.840	0.800	0.760
Dividend Payout %	22.69	20.48	30.14	29.76	37.19	36.21	47.34	93.83
Income Statement								
Total Revenue	304,912	1,286,485	1,221,130	1,104,024	1,012,456	895,283	744,065	579,212
EBITDA	74,105	518,056	357,906	330,369	258,799	239,459	173,924	95,221
Depn & Amortn	12,010	25,700	24,100	23,400	22,200	20,600	21,200	21,700
Income Before Taxes	57,602	474,713	315,073	288,822	217,326	209,728	148,540	68,667
Income Taxes	18,050	129,000	89,500	78,000	68,200	67,400	45,700	19,700
Net Income	39,552	345,713	225,573	210,822	149,126	142,328	102,840	48,967
Average Shares	56,709	59,007	61,745	62,790	61,711	61,370	60,803	60,229
Balance Sheet								
Current Assets	495,844	509,017	859,507	792,593	776,996	582,970	252,408	188,993
Total Assets	1,430,998	1,391,352	1,544,778	1,327,228	1,321,734	874,309	530,474	476,434
Current Liabilities	161,757	194,616	174,480	168,853	151,671	131,282	119,754	103,815
Long-Term Obligations	457,670	392,695	615,000	408,370	556,480	300,000	70,255	86,260
Total Liabilities	794,090	755,801	948,746	692,863	867,620	551,569	266,360	266,780
Stockholders' Equity	636,908	635,551	596,032	634,365	454,114	322,740	264,114	209,654
Shares Outstanding	55,614	55,765	59,198	61,003	60,766	59,747	60,047	59,999
Statistical Record								
Return on Assets %	19.78	23.61	15.75	15.96	13.62	20.32	20.10	9.30
Return on Equity %	50.47	56.30	36.77	38.84	38.50	48.64	42.71	26.03
EBITDA Margin %	24.30	40.27	29.31	29.92	25.56	26.75	23.37	16.44
Net Margin %	12.97	26.87	18.47	19.10	14.73	15.90	13.82	8.45
Asset Turnover	0.80	0.88	0.85	0.84	0.92	1.28	1.45	1.10
Current Ratio	3.07	2.62	4.93	4.69	5.12	4.44	2.11	1.82
Debt to Equity	0.72	0.62	1.03	0.64	1.22	0.93	0.27	0.41
Price Range	84.36-63.56	81.43-64.79	81.43-66.01	78.87-50.85	56.01-39.96	53.84-32.47	40.29-26.38	30.70-14.48
P/E Ratio	15.56-11.73	13.90-11.06	22.31-18.08	23.47-15.13	23.14-16.51	23.21-14.00	23.84-15.61	37.90-17.88
Average Yield %	1.71	1.66	1.46	1.51	1.84	1.96	2.51	3.18

Address: 88 - 11th Avenue N.E, Minneapolis, MN 55413
Telephone: 612-623-6000
Fax: 612-623-6777

Web Site: www.graco.com
Officers: Lee R. Mitau - Chairman Patrick J. McHale - President, Chief Executive Officer

Auditors: Deloitte & Touche LLP
Transfer Agents: Wells Fargo Bank, N.A., St. Paul, MN

GRAHAM HOLDINGS CO.

Exchange	Symbol	Price	52Wk Range	Yield	P/E
NYS	GHC	$497.95 (5/31/2016)	718.70-428.09	0.97	N/A

*7 Year Price Score 136.60 *NYSE Composite Index=100   *12 Month Price Score 86.32

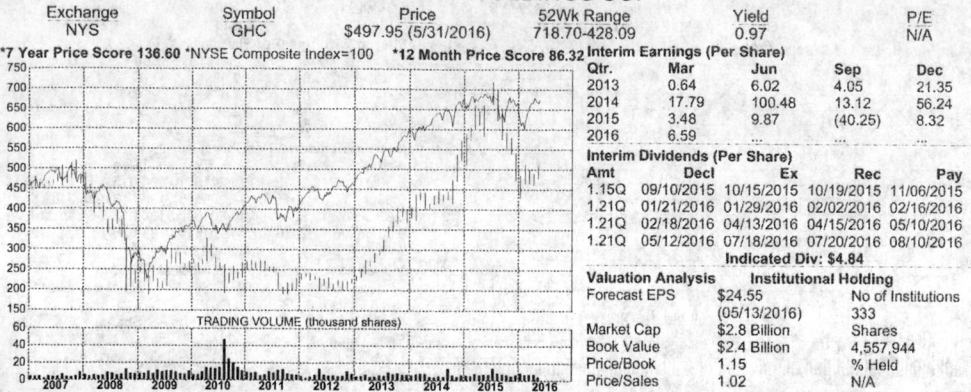

Interim Earnings (Per Share)

Qtr.	Mar	Jun	Sep	Dec
2013	0.64	6.02	4.05	21.35
2014	17.79	100.48	13.12	56.24
2015	3.48	9.87	(40.25)	8.32
2016	6.59	...		

Interim Dividends (Per Share)

Amt	Decl	Ex	Rec	Pay
1.15Q	09/10/2015	10/15/2015	10/19/2015	11/06/2015
1.21Q	01/21/2016	01/29/2016	02/02/2016	02/16/2016
1.21Q	02/18/2016	04/13/2016	04/15/2016	05/10/2016
1.21Q	05/12/2016	07/18/2016	07/20/2016	08/10/2016

Indicated Div: $4.84

Valuation Analysis

		Institutional Holding	
Forecast EPS	$24.55	No of Institutions	
	(05/13/2016)	333	
Market Cap	$2.8 Billion	Shares	
Book Value	$2.4 Billion	4,557,944	
Price/Book	1.15	% Held	
Price/Sales	1.02	N/A	

Business Summary: Educational Services (MIC: 2.2.2 SIC: 8299 NAIC: 611699)

Graham Holdings is a diversified education and media company. Through its Kaplan, Inc. subsidiary, Co. provides educational services for students and personnel, both domestically and outside the U.S. Kaplan conducts its education services through three segments: Kaplan Higher Education, Kaplan Test Preparation and Kaplan International. Co. is also engaged in media operations, which consist of the ownership and operation of five television broadcasting stations, several websites and print publications, as well as a marketing solutions provider. In addition, Co.'s other business operations include home health and hospice services and manufacturing.

Recent Developments: For the quarter ended Mar 31 2016, income from continuing operations was US$38.2 million compared with a loss of US$1.5 million in the year-earlier quarter. Net income increased 75.3% to US$38.2 million from US$21.8 million in the year-earlier quarter. Revenues were US$601.7 million, down 7.1% from US$647.4 million the year before. Operating income was US$51.9 million versus US$8.9 million in the prior-year quarter, an increase of 485.3%. Direct operating expenses declined 5.7% to US$291.6 million from US$309.2 million in the comparable period the year before. Indirect operating expenses decreased 21.6% to US$258.2 million from US$329.3 million in the equivalent prior-year period.

Prospects: Our evaluation of Graham Holdings Co. as of June 19, 2016 is the result of our systematic analysis on three basic characteristics: earnings strength, relative valuation, and recent stock price movement. The company has enjoyed a very positive trend in earnings per share over the past 5 quarters. Because the company lacks sufficient analyst estimate data, we place greater weight on the historical EPS trend as the measure of earnings strength. Based on operating earnings yield, the company is about fairly valued when compared to all of the companies in our coverage universe. Share price changes over the past year indicates that GHC will perform poorly over the near term.

Financial Data

(US$ in Thousands)	3 Mos	12/31/2015	12/31/2014	12/31/2013	12/31/2012	12/31/2011	01/02/2011	01/03/2010
Earnings Per Share	(15.47)	(17.87)	195.03	32.05	17.39	14.70	31.04	9.78
Cash Flow Per Share	29.82	13.06	57.55	45.30	64.66	50.53	78.43	68.84
Tang Book Value Per Share	191.97	231.59	204.94	195.10	93.42	80.74	104.65	98.88
Dividends Per Share	7.660	9.100	10.200	...	19.600	9.400	9.000	8.600
Dividend Payout %	...	...	5.23	...	112.71	63.95	28.99	87.93
Income Statement								
Total Revenue	601,740	2,586,114	3,535,166	3,487,864	4,017,653	4,214,833	4,723,573	4,569,731
EBITDA	89,991	7,530	1,483,888	568,612	429,119	524,491	830,475	529,731
Depn & Amortn	23,023	96,978	222,697	246,798	290,044	283,733	274,991	322,542
Income Before Taxes	59,611	(120,193)	1,226,741	288,011	106,524	211,679	527,557	178,221
Income Taxes	22,400	20,500	406,100	110,000	71,600	96,300	216,600	57,600
Net Income	37,780	(100,655)	1,293,843	236,865	132,113	117,150	278,114	92,774
Average Shares	5,652	5,727	6,559	7,333	7,404	7,905	8,931	9,392
Balance Sheet								
Current Assets	1,605,489	1,860,722	1,690,703	1,702,387	1,453,762	1,245,625	1,361,898	1,388,064
Total Assets	4,312,525	4,352,951	5,752,319	5,811,046	5,105,069	5,016,986	5,158,367	5,186,206
Current Liabilities	735,832	725,149	1,050,792	934,109	1,126,286	995,556	1,008,277	989,583
Long-Term Obligations	399,914	399,926	399,545	447,608	453,384	452,229	396,650	396,236
Total Liabilities	1,872,392	1,862,253	2,601,510	2,500,314	2,507,945	2,403,795	2,332,477	2,235,130
Stockholders' Equity	2,440,133	2,490,698	3,150,809	3,310,732	2,597,124	2,613,191	2,825,890	2,951,076
Shares Outstanding	5,618	5,803	5,798	7,387	7,427	7,591	8,193	9,266
Statistical Record								
Return on Assets %	N.M.	N.M.	22.38	4.34	2.60	2.32	5.39	1.76
Return on Equity %	N.M.	N.M.	40.05	8.02	5.06	4.33	9.65	3.14
EBITDA Margin %	14.96	0.29	41.98	16.30	10.68	12.44	17.58	11.59
Net Margin %	6.28	N.M.	36.60	6.79	3.29	2.78	5.89	2.03
Asset Turnover	0.56	0.51	0.61	0.64	0.79	0.83	0.92	0.87
Current Ratio	2.18	2.57	1.61	1.82	1.29	1.25	1.35	1.40
Debt to Equity	0.16	0.16	0.13	0.14	0.17	0.17	0.14	0.13
Price Range	718.70-428.09	718.70-471.59	571.19-370.98	406.93-220.66	241.68-198.03	272.60-189.12	327.10-190.72	297.49-185.79
P/E Ratio	...	...	2.93-1.90	12.70-6.88	13.90-11.39	18.54-12.87	10.54-6.14	30.42-19.00
Average Yield %	1.32	1.50	2.33	...	8.91	3.96	3.49	3.50

Address: 1300 North 17th Street,	Web Site: www.ghco.com	Auditors: PricewaterhouseCoopers LLP
Arlington, VA 22209	Officers: Donald E. Graham - Chairman, Chief	Transfer Agents: ComputerShare
Telephone: 703-345-6300	Executive Officer Timothy J. O'Shaughnessy - President, Chief Executive Officer	Investor Services, Providence, RI

GRAINGER (W.W.) INC.

Exchange	Symbol	Price	52Wk Range	Yield	P/E	Div Achiever
NYS	GWW	$228.35 (5/31/2016)	245.41-182.78	2.14	19.87	44 Years

*7 Year Price Score 97.90   *NYSE Composite Index=100   *12 Month Price Score 104.54

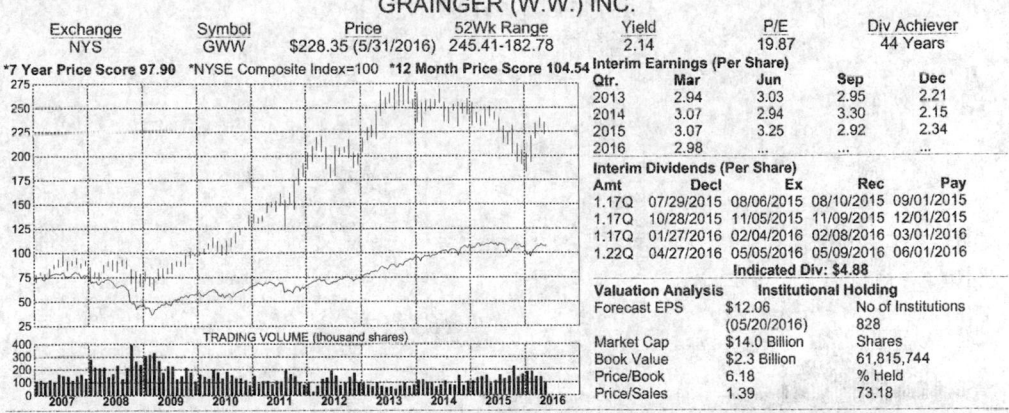

Interim Earnings (Per Share)

Qtr.	Mar	Jun	Sep	Dec
2013	2.94	3.03	2.95	2.21
2014	3.07	2.94	3.30	2.15
2015	3.07	3.25	2.92	2.34
2016	2.98	...	...	...

Interim Dividends (Per Share)

Amt	Decl	Ex	Rec	Pay
1.17Q	07/29/2015	08/06/2015	08/10/2015	09/01/2015
1.17Q	10/28/2015	11/05/2015	11/09/2015	12/01/2015
1.17Q	01/27/2016	02/04/2016	02/08/2016	03/01/2016
1.22Q	04/27/2016	05/05/2016	05/09/2016	06/01/2016

Indicated Div: $4.88

Valuation Analysis

		Institutional Holding	
Forecast EPS	$12.06	No of Institutions	
	(05/20/2016)	828	
Market Cap	$14.0 Billion	Shares	
Book Value	$2.3 Billion	61,815,744	
Price/Book	6.18	% Held	
Price/Sales	1.39	73.18	

Business Summary: Electrical Equipment (MIC: 7.3.1 SIC: 5099 NAIC: 423990)

W.W. Grainger is a distributor of maintenance, repair and operating (MRO) supplies and other related products and services used by businesses and institutions mainly in the U.S. and Canada, and also in Europe, Asia and Latin America. Co.'s U.S. segment provides MRO supplies and other related products and services through sales representatives, catalogs, eCommerce and local branches. Co.'s Canadian segment, through its Acklands – Grainger Inc. subsidiary, distributes tools, fasteners, safety supplies, welding and shop equipment and other items. Co.'s Other businesses include Zoro Tools, Inc., the single channel online business in the U.S., and operations in Europe, Asia and Latin America.

Recent Developments: For the quarter ended Mar 31 2016, net income decreased 10.5% to US$191.6 million from US$214.1 million in the year-earlier quarter. Revenues were US$2.51 billion, up 2.7% from US$2.44 billion the year before. Operating income was US$317.1 million versus US$351.2 million in the prior-year quarter, a decrease of 9.7%. Direct operating expenses rose 8.6% to US$1.46 billion from US$1.35 billion in the comparable period the year before. Indirect operating expenses decreased 2.0% to US$728.0 million from US$742.5 million in the equivalent prior-year period.

Prospects: Our evaluation of Grainger (W.W.) Inc. as of June 19, 2016 is the result of our systematic analysis on three basic characteristics: earnings strength, relative valuation, and recent stock price movement. The company has enjoyed a very positive trend in earnings per share over the past 5 quarters. However, while recent estimates for the company have been lowered by analysts, GWW has posted better than expected results. Based on operating earnings yield, the company is undervalued when compared to all of the companies in our coverage universe. Share price changes over the past year indicates that GWW will perform well over the near term.

Financial Data

(US$ in Thousands)	3 Mos	12/31/2015	12/31/2014	12/31/2013	12/31/2012	12/31/2011	12/31/2010	12/31/2009
Earnings Per Share	11.49	11.58	11.45	11.13	9.52	9.07	6.93	5.62
Cash Flow Per Share	16.01	15.19	14.05	14.20	11.66	10.71	8.42	9.93
Tang Book Value Per Share	19.79	19.68	40.08	39.58	35.70	30.30	26.20	25.08
Dividends Per Share	4.680	4.590	4.170	3.590	3.060	2.520	2.080	1.780
Dividend Payout %	40.73	39.64	36.42	32.26	32.14	27.78	30.01	31.67
Income Statement								
Total Revenue	2,506,538	9,973,384	9,964,953	9,437,758	8,950,045	8,078,185	7,182,158	6,221,991
EBITDA	373,826	1,456,850	1,550,737	1,478,203	1,290,256	1,207,436	1,010,610	860,779
Depn & Amortn	56,294	162,000	208,326	180,613	159,049	149,200	149,678	147,531
Income Before Taxes	303,972	1,262,445	1,334,386	1,287,599	1,117,789	1,051,213	853,960	705,840
Income Taxes	105,940	465,531	522,090	479,850	418,940	385,115	340,196	276,565
Net Income	186,713	768,996	801,729	797,036	689,881	658,423	510,865	430,466
Average Shares	62,099	65,765	69,205	70,576	71,181	71,176	72,138	74,891
Balance Sheet								
Current Assets	3,138,961	3,048,642	2,967,549	3,044,285	2,900,640	2,694,900	2,238,071	2,131,515
Total Assets	5,964,839	5,857,755	5,284,252	5,266,328	5,014,598	4,716,062	3,904,377	3,726,332
Current Liabilities	1,880,440	1,788,534	1,261,716	1,195,790	1,080,003	1,387,925	869,303	776,799
Long-Term Obligations	1,387,124	1,388,414	404,536	445,513	467,048	175,055	420,446	437,500
Total Liabilities	3,697,540	3,591,121	2,074,380	2,015,890	1,990,686	2,087,277	1,699,161	1,562,612
Stockholders' Equity	2,267,299	2,266,634	3,209,872	3,250,438	3,023,912	2,628,785	2,205,216	2,163,720
Shares Outstanding	61,322	62,028	67,432	68,853	69,478	69,962	69,377	72,276
Statistical Record								
Return on Assets %	13.33	13.80	15.20	15.51	14.14	15.28	13.39	11.89
Return on Equity %	27.58	28.08	24.82	25.41	24.34	27.24	23.39	20.51
EBITDA Margin %	14.91	14.61	15.56	15.66	14.42	14.95	14.07	13.83
Net Margin %	7.45	7.71	8.05	8.45	7.71	8.15	7.11	6.92
Asset Turnover	1.80	1.79	1.89	1.84	1.83	1.87	1.88	1.72
Current Ratio	1.67	1.70	2.35	2.55	2.69	1.94	2.57	2.74
Debt to Equity	0.61	0.61	0.13	0.14	0.15	0.07	0.19	0.20
Price Range	251.24-182.78	255.22-190.83	269.22-229.29	274.01-202.37	219.90-177.10	192.31-126.11	138.65-96.83	101.43-61.37
P/E Ratio	21.87-15.91	22.04-16.48	23.51-20.03	24.62-18.18	23.10-18.60	21.20-13.90	20.01-13.97	18.05-10.92
Average Yield %	2.12	2.02	1.67	1.45	1.52	1.67	1.86	2.13

Address: 100 Grainger Parkway, Lake Forest, IL 60045-5201
Telephone: 847-535-1000
Fax: 847-535-0878

Web Site: www.grainger.com
Officers: James T. Ryan - Chairman, President, Chief Executive Officer, Chief Operating Officer Laura D. Brown - Senior Vice President

Auditors: Ernst & Young LLP
Investor Contact: 847-535-0409
Transfer Agents: Computershare Trust Company, N.A., Providence, RI

GRANITE CONSTRUCTION INC.

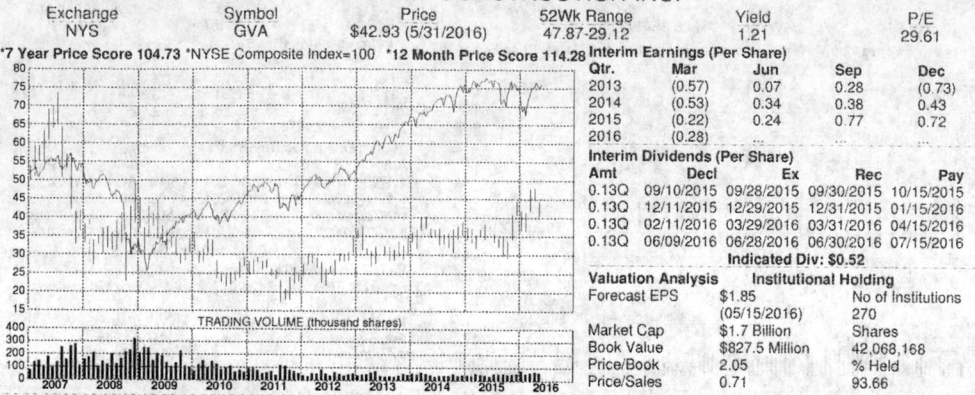

Exchange	Symbol	Price	52Wk Range	Yield	P/E
NYS	GVA	$42.93 (5/31/2016)	47.87-29.12	1.21	29.61

*7 Year Price Score 104.73 *NYSE Composite Index=100 *12 Month Price Score 114.28

Interim Earnings (Per Share)

Qtr.	Mar	Jun	Sep	Dec
2013	(0.57)	0.07	0.28	(0.73)
2014	(0.53)	0.34	0.38	0.43
2015	(0.22)	0.24	0.77	0.72
2016	(0.28)			

Interim Dividends (Per Share)

Amt	Decl	Ex	Rec	Pay
0.13Q	09/10/2015	09/28/2015	09/30/2015	10/15/2015
0.13Q	12/11/2015	12/29/2015	12/31/2015	01/15/2016
0.13Q	02/11/2016	03/29/2016	03/31/2016	04/15/2016
0.13Q	06/09/2016	06/28/2016	06/30/2016	07/15/2016

Indicated Div: $0.52

Valuation Analysis — **Institutional Holding**

Forecast EPS	$1.85	No of Institutions
	(05/15/2016)	270
Market Cap	$1.7 Billion	Shares
Book Value	$827.5 Million	42,068,168
Price/Book	2.05	% Held
Price/Sales	0.71	93.66

Business Summary: Construction Services (MIC: 7.5.4 SIC: 1629 NAIC: 237990)

Granite Construction is a holding company. Through its subsidiaries, Co. is a heavy civil contractor and a construction materials producer. Co.'s segments are: Construction, which performs construction management and civil construction projects focused on new construction and improvement of streets, roads, highways, bridges, site work and other infrastructure projects; Large Project Construction, which focuses on infrastructure projects such as highways, mass transit facilities, bridges, tunnels, waterway locks and dams, pipelines and airport infrastructure; and Construction Materials, which mines and processes aggregates and operates plants that produce construction materials.

Recent Developments: For the quarter ended Mar 31 2016, net loss amounted to US$10.5 million versus a net loss of US$8.6 million in the year-earlier quarter. Revenues were US$439.5 million, up 4.6% from US$420.2 million the year before. Operating loss was US$16.3 million versus a loss of US$11.3 million in the prior-year quarter. Direct operating expenses rose 5.0% to US$400.2 million from US$381.3 million in the comparable period the year before. Indirect operating expenses increased 10.6% to US$55.5 million from US$50.2 million in the equivalent prior-year period.

Prospects: Our evaluation of Granite Construction Inc. as of June 19, 2016 is the result of our systematic analysis on three basic characteristics: earnings strength, relative valuation, and recent stock price movement. The company has suffered a very negative trend in earnings per share over the past 5 quarters. However, while recent estimates for the company have been mixed, GVA has posted results that fell short of analysts expectations. Based on operating earnings yield, the company is about fairly valued when compared to all of the companies in our coverage universe. Share price changes over the past year indicates that GVA will perform very well over the near term.

Financial Data

(US$ in Thousands)	3 Mos	12/31/2015	12/31/2014	12/31/2013	12/31/2012	12/31/2011	12/31/2010	12/31/2009
Earnings Per Share	1.45	1.52	0.64	(0.94)	1.15	1.31	(1.56)	1.90
Cash Flow Per Share	1.61	1.70	1.10	0.14	2.38	2.42	0.78	1.71
Tang Book Value Per Share	19.56	19.93	18.90	18.71	20.00	20.66	19.64	21.50
Dividends Per Share	0.520	0.520	0.520	0.520	0.520	0.520	0.520	0.520
Dividend Payout %	35.86	34.21	81.25	...	45.22	39.69	...	27.37
Income Statement								
Total Revenue	439,452	2,371,029	2,275,270	2,266,901	2,083,037	2,009,531	1,762,965	1,963,479
EBITDA	(1,180)	173,339	131,883	9,968	138,818	150,724	(37,472)	216,562
Depn & Amortn	13,736	61,000	64,900	62,700	51,800	56,000	64,900	74,700
Income Before Taxes	(17,129)	100,217	54,696	(65,333)	79,041	87,240	(107,132)	131,155
Income Taxes	(5,177)	35,179	19,721	(19,263)	21,109	23,348	(43,928)	38,650
Net Income	(11,188)	60,485	25,346	(36,423)	45,283	51,161	(58,983)	73,500
Average Shares	39,433	39,868	39,795	38,803	39,076	38,473	37,820	37,683
Balance Sheet								
Current Assets	962,778	985,222	970,178	950,203	1,022,057	909,722	913,856	1,006,718
Total Assets	1,612,230	1,627,860	1,620,494	1,617,155	1,729,487	1,547,799	1,535,533	1,709,575
Current Liabilities	469,474	466,045	462,826	497,570	531,272	448,468	438,777	506,113
Long-Term Obligations	243,099	245,081	275,621	276,868	271,070	218,413	242,351	489,376
Total Liabilities	784,703	788,623	826,109	835,215	899,534	748,602	774,502	1,123,612
Stockholders' Equity	827,527	839,237	794,385	781,940	829,953	799,197	761,031	830,651
Shares Outstanding	39,563	39,412	39,186	38,917	38,730	38,682	38,745	38,635
Statistical Record								
Return on Assets %	3.62	3.72	1.57	N.M.	2.76	3.32	N.M.	4.26
Return on Equity %	7.20	7.41	3.22	N.M.	5.54	6.56	N.M.	9.20
EBITDA Margin %	N.M.	7.31	5.80	0.44	6.66	7.50	N.M.	11.03
Net Margin %	N.M.	2.55	1.11	N.M.	2.17	2.55	N.M.	3.74
Asset Turnover	1.50	1.46	1.41	1.35	1.27	1.30	1.09	1.14
Current Ratio	2.05	2.11	2.10	1.91	1.92	2.03	2.08	1.99
Debt to Equity	0.29	0.29	0.35	0.35	0.33	0.27	0.32	0.59
Price Range	47.80-29.12	44.25-29.12	40.29-30.52	37.54-26.83	34.43-21.66	29.26-17.15	35.82-21.44	44.78-27.36
P/E Ratio	32.97-20.08	29.11-19.16	62.95-47.69	...	29.94-18.83	22.34-13.09	...	23.57-14.40
Average Yield %	1.40	1.46	1.46	1.66	1.89	2.13	1.89	1.51

Address: 585 West Beach Street, Watsonville, CA 95076 **Telephone:** 831-724-1011	**Web Site:** www.graniteconstruction.com **Officers:** David H. Watts - Chairman James H. Roberts - Executive Vice President, Chief Operating Officer, Division Officer	**Auditors:** PricewaterhouseCoopers LLP **Investor Contact:** 831-724-1011 **Transfer Agents:** Computershare, Canton, MA

334

GREAT PLAINS ENERGY INC

Exchange	Symbol	Price	52Wk Range	Yield	P/E
NYS	GXP	$29.18 (5/31/2016)	32.68-24.16	3.60	20.55

*7 Year Price Score 104.95 *NYSE Composite Index=100 *12 Month Price Score 110.76

Interim Earnings (Per Share)

Qtr.	Mar	Jun	Sep	Dec
2013	0.17	0.41	0.93	0.11
2014	0.15	0.34	0.95	0.13
2015	0.12	0.28	0.82	0.15
2016	0.17	...	...	...

Interim Dividends (Per Share)

Amt	Decl	Ex	Rec	Pay
0.245Q	08/04/2015	08/26/2015	08/28/2015	09/21/2015
0.263Q	11/03/2015	11/25/2015	11/30/2015	12/21/2015
0.263Q	02/10/2016	02/25/2016	02/29/2016	03/21/2016
0.263Q	05/03/2016	05/25/2016	05/27/2016	06/20/2016

Indicated Div: $1.05

Valuation Analysis

		Institutional Holding	
Forecast EPS	$1.73	No of Institutions	
	(05/20/2016)	421	
Market Cap	$4.5 Billion	Shares	
Book Value	$3.7 Billion	135,127,360	
Price/Book	1.24	% Held	
Price/Sales	1.79	76.59	

Business Summary: Electric Utilities (MIC: 3.1.1 SIC: 4911 NAIC: 221122)

Great Plains Energy is a public utility holding company. Co.'s business segment is electric utility, which consists of: Kansas City Power & Light Co., a regulated electric utility that provides electricity to customers primarily in Missouri and Kansas; KCP&L Greater Missouri Operations Co., a regulated electric utility that provides electricity to customers in Missouri and regulated steam service to certain customers in St. Joseph, MO; and GPE Transmission Holding Company, LLC, which owns 13.5% of Transource Energy, LLC, which focuses on developing electric transmission projects. At Dec 31 2015, electric utility served approximately 846,100 customers in western Missouri and eastern Kansas.

Recent Developments: For the quarter ended Mar 31 2016, net income increased 39.7% to US$26.4 million from US$18.9 million in the year-earlier quarter. Revenues were US$572.1 million, up 4.2% from US$549.1 million the year before. Operating income was US$89.9 million versus US$70.1 million in the prior-year quarter, an increase of 28.2%. Direct operating expenses declined 2.0% to US$338.5 million from US$345.4 million in the comparable period the year before. Indirect operating expenses increased 7.6% to US$143.7 million from US$133.6 million in the equivalent prior-year period.

Prospects: Our evaluation of Great Plains Energy Inc. as of June 19, 2016 is the result of our systematic analysis on three basic characteristics: earnings strength, relative valuation, and recent stock price movement. The company has enjoyed a very positive trend in earnings per share over the past 5 quarters. However, while recent estimates for the company have been mixed, GXP has posted better than expected results. Based on operating earnings yield, the company is undervalued when compared to all of the companies in our coverage universe. Share price changes over the past year indicates that GXP will perform very well over the near term.

Financial Data

(US$ in Thousands)	3 Mos	12/31/2015	12/31/2014	12/31/2013	12/31/2012	12/31/2011	12/31/2010	12/31/2009
Earnings Per Share	1.42	1.37	1.57	1.62	1.35	1.25	1.53	1.14
Cash Flow Per Share	5.06	4.88	4.54	5.06	4.55	3.27	4.09	2.59
Tang Book Value Per Share	22.51	22.59	22.17	21.48	20.65	20.50	20.02	19.37
Dividends Per Share	1.015	0.998	0.935	0.882	0.855	0.835	0.830	0.830
Dividend Payout %	71.48	72.81	59.55	54.48	63.33	66.80	54.25	72.81
Income Statement								
Total Revenue	572,100	2,502,200	2,568,200	2,446,300	2,309,900	2,318,000	2,255,500	1,965,000
EBITDA	109,300	833,200	923,800	946,300	856,300	782,500	845,800	668,700
Depn & Amortn	20,700	299,400	376,800	368,300	330,600	305,000	349,100	306,000
Income Before Taxes	37,400	334,500	358,500	379,600	304,900	259,100	311,900	181,800
Income Taxes	11,700	122,700	115,700	129,200	104,600	84,800	99,000	29,500
Net Income	26,400	213,000	242,800	250,200	199,900	174,400	211,700	150,100
Average Shares	155,000	154,800	154,100	153,700	147,200	138,700	136,900	129,800
Balance Sheet								
Current Assets	611,100	664,200	718,900	767,000	723,700	619,100	611,600	612,500
Total Assets	10,743,100	10,738,600	10,475,700	9,795,400	9,647,300	9,118,000	8,818,200	8,482,800
Current Liabilities	899,300	915,700	1,070,800	769,800	1,449,500	1,634,900	1,339,300	958,300
Long-Term Obligations	3,744,400	3,745,100	3,488,000	3,515,700	2,756,800	2,742,300	2,942,700	3,213,000
Total Liabilities	7,092,200	7,043,100	6,850,600	6,282,000	6,268,300	6,119,100	5,893,300	5,651,300
Stockholders' Equity	3,650,900	3,695,500	3,625,100	3,513,400	3,379,000	2,998,900	2,924,900	2,831,500
Shares Outstanding	154,710	154,403	154,162	153,866	153,529	136,141	135,713	135,423
Statistical Record								
Return on Assets %	2.07	2.01	2.40	2.57	2.12	1.94	2.45	1.84
Return on Equity %	6.11	5.82	6.80	7.26	6.25	5.89	7.36	5.54
EBITDA Margin %	19.11	33.30	35.97	38.68	37.07	33.76	37.50	34.03
Net Margin %	4.61	8.51	9.45	10.23	8.65	7.52	9.39	7.64
Asset Turnover	0.24	0.24	0.25	0.25	0.25	0.26	0.26	0.24
Current Ratio	0.68	0.73	0.67	1.00	0.50	0.38	0.46	0.64
Debt to Equity	1.03	1.01	0.96	1.00	0.82	0.91	1.01	1.13
Price Range	32.26-24.16	30.06-24.16	29.38-23.85	24.76-20.31	22.81-19.54	21.97-16.53	19.63-16.85	20.34-11.17
P/E Ratio	22.72-17.01	21.94-17.64	18.71-15.19	15.28-12.54	16.90-14.47	17.58-13.22	12.83-11.01	17.84-9.80
Average Yield %	3.78	3.76	3.62	3.85	4.08	4.15	4.49	5.02

Address: 1200 Main Street, Kansas City, MO 64105	Web Site: www.greatplainsenergy.com	Auditors: Mayer Hoffman McCann P.C.
Telephone: 816-556-2200	Officers: William H. Downey - Executive Vice-Chairman, President, Chief Operating Officer Terry Bassham - Chief Executive Officer, Executive Vice President	Investor Contact: 816-654-1763 Transfer Agents: Computershare Trust Company, N. A., Providence, RI

GREIF INC

Exchange	Symbol	Price	52Wk Range	Yield	P/E
NYS	GEF	$35.86 (5/31/2016)	39.18-24.00	4.68	51.23

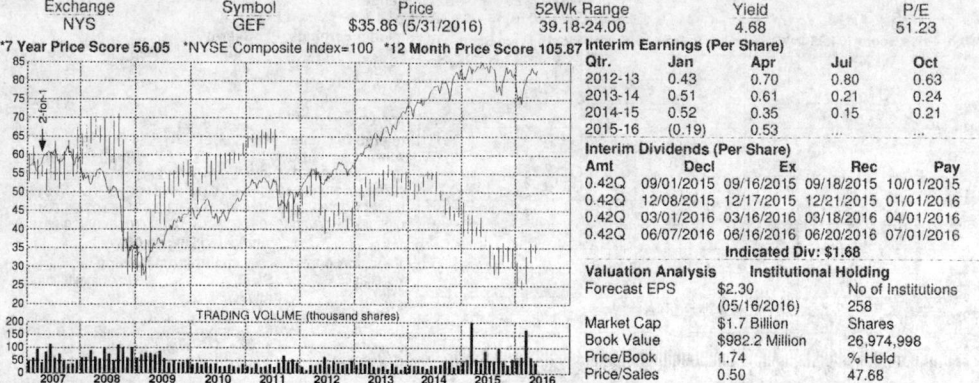

*7 Year Price Score 56.05   *NYSE Composite Index=100   *12 Month Price Score 105.87

Interim Earnings (Per Share)

Qtr.	Jan	Apr	Jul	Oct
2012-13	0.43	0.70	0.80	0.63
2013-14	0.51	0.61	0.21	0.24
2014-15	0.52	0.35	0.15	0.21
2015-16	(0.19)	0.53	...	...

Interim Dividends (Per Share)

Amt	Decl	Ex	Rec	Pay
0.42Q	09/01/2015	09/16/2015	09/18/2015	10/01/2015
0.42Q	12/08/2015	12/17/2015	12/21/2015	01/01/2016
0.42Q	03/01/2016	03/16/2016	03/18/2016	04/01/2016
0.42Q	06/07/2016	06/16/2016	06/20/2016	07/01/2016

Indicated Div: $1.68

Valuation Analysis   **Institutional Holding**

Forecast EPS	$2.30	No of Institutions	258
	(05/16/2016)		
Market Cap	$1.7 Billion	Shares	26,974,998
Book Value	$982.2 Million	% Held	47.68
Price/Book	1.74		
Price/Sales	0.50		

Business Summary: Containers & Packaging (MIC: 8.1.3 SIC: 2655 NAIC: 322214)

Greif is a producer of industrial packaging products and services. Co. has four segments: Rigid Industrial Packaging and Services, which provides steel, fibre and plastic drums, rigid intermediate bulk containers, closure systems for industrial packaging products, transit protection products, water bottles and reconditioned containers, and services; Paper Packaging, which sells containerboard, corrugated sheets, corrugated containers and other corrugated products; Flexible Products and Services, which produces flexible intermediate bulk containers and related services; and Land Management, which focuses on the harvesting and regeneration of its U.S. timber properties.

Recent Developments: For the quarter ended Apr 30 2016, net income increased 58.5% to US$32.5 million from US$20.5 million in the year-earlier quarter. Revenues were US$839.6 million, down 8.3% from US$915.9 million the year before. Operating income was US$82.8 million versus US$51.1 million in the prior-year quarter, an increase of 62.0%. Direct operating expenses declined 9.4% to US$665.9 million from US$734.8 million in the comparable period the year before. Indirect operating expenses decreased 30.1% to US$90.9 million from US$130.0 million in the equivalent prior-year period.

Prospects: Our evaluation of Greif Bros. Corp. as of June 19, 2016 is the result of our systematic analysis on three basic characteristics: earnings strength, relative valuation, and recent stock price movement. The company has enjoyed a very positive trend in earnings per share over the past 5 quarters and while recent estimates for the company have been raised by analysts, GEF has posted results that fell short of analysts expectations. Based on operating earnings yield, the company is undervalued when compared to all of the companies in our coverage universe. Share price changes over the past year indicates that GEF will perform very poorly over the near term.

Financial Data
(US$ in Thousands)

	6 Mos	3 Mos	10/31/2015	10/31/2014	10/31/2013	10/31/2012	10/31/2011	10/31/2010
Earnings Per Share	0.70	0.52	1.23	1.56	2.52	2.17	3.01	3.58
Cash Flow Per Share	6.07	5.02	4.32	5.49	5.27	9.98	3.65	3.78
Tang Book Value Per Share	1.21	0.65	1.59	2.00	2.08	0.55	0.01	8.39
Dividends Per Share	1.680	1.680	1.680	1.680	1.680	1.680	1.680	1.600
Dividend Payout %	240.00	323.08	136.59	107.69	66.67	77.42	55.81	44.69
Income Statement								
Total Revenue	1,611,000	771,400	3,616,700	4,239,100	4,353,400	4,269,500	4,247,954	3,461,537
EBITDA	160,000	46,900	303,000	369,600	459,400	408,400	445,665	416,776
Depn & Amortn	64,300	32,300	113,400	129,800	131,900	131,400	122,700	98,500
Income Before Taxes	57,300	(3,900)	114,800	158,000	243,700	187,100	243,413	252,489
Income Taxes	34,700	6,000	48,400	115,000	97,600	56,800	71,077	40,571
Net Income	20,300	(11,100)	71,900	91,500	147,300	126,100	176,040	209,985
Average Shares	25,766	25,700	25,674	25,552	25,400	25,200	25,044	24,959
Balance Sheet								
Current Assets	928,100	922,300	1,008,500	1,154,700	1,094,000	1,064,000	1,305,337	1,165,889
Total Assets	3,207,200	3,162,800	3,315,700	3,667,400	3,882,200	3,856,900	4,207,282	3,498,445
Current Liabilities	908,700	570,000	647,000	851,700	801,700	862,000	929,768	761,811
Long-Term Obligations	777,000	1,112,100	1,116,200	1,087,400	1,207,200	1,175,300	1,345,138	953,066
Total Liabilities	2,225,000	2,223,000	2,300,100	2,525,300	2,599,000	2,656,100	2,971,931	2,219,724
Stockholders' Equity	982,200	939,800	1,015,600	1,142,100	1,283,200	1,200,800	1,235,351	1,278,721
Shares Outstanding	47,786	47,854	47,813	47,723	47,576	47,403	47,092	47,169
Statistical Record								
Return on Assets %	1.25	0.92	2.06	2.42	3.81	3.12	4.57	6.65
Return on Equity %	4.04	3.02	6.66	7.55	11.86	10.32	14.00	17.71
EBITDA Margin %	9.93	6.08	8.38	8.72	10.55	9.57	10.49	12.04
Net Margin %	1.26	N.M.	1.99	2.16	3.38	2.95	4.14	6.07
Asset Turnover	1.03	1.05	1.04	1.12	1.13	1.06	1.10	1.10
Current Ratio	1.02	1.62	1.56	1.36	1.36	1.23	1.40	1.53
Debt to Equity	0.79	1.18	1.10	0.95	0.94	0.98	1.09	0.75
Price Range	43.21-24.00	44.01-24.92	48.17-27.84	55.74-42.68	57.43-40.00	56.50-38.90	67.04-41.65	60.83-46.52
P/E Ratio	61.73-34.29	84.63-47.92	39.16-22.63	35.73-27.36	22.79-15.87	26.04-17.93	22.27-13.84	16.99-12.99
Average Yield %	5.11	4.75	4.35	3.28	3.36	3.63	2.22	2.86

Address: 425 Winter Road, Delaware, OH 43015 Telephone: 740-549-6000	Web Site: www.greif.com Officers: Michael J. Gasser - Chairman Peter G. Watson - President, Chief Executive Officer, Chief Operating Officer, Division Officer	Auditors: Deloitte & Touche LLP Investor Contact: 740-549-6000 Transfer Agents: The Bank of New York Mellon (Luxembourg) S.A.

GROUP 1 AUTOMOTIVE, INC.

Exchange	Symbol	Price	52Wk Range	Yield	P/E
NYS	GPI	$62.18 (5/31/2016)	96.97-49.80	1.48	15.94

*7 Year Price Score 113.20 *NYSE Composite Index=100   *12 Month Price Score 79.65

Interim Earnings (Per Share)

Qtr.	Mar	Jun	Sep	Dec
2013	0.88	1.43	1.19	0.80
2014	1.19	0.02	1.03	0.78
2015	1.47	1.91	1.88	(1.36)
2016	1.47	...	...	...

Interim Dividends (Per Share)

Amt	Decl	Ex	Rec	Pay
0.21Q	08/13/2015	08/28/2015	09/01/2015	09/15/2015
0.22Q	11/12/2015	11/27/2015	12/01/2015	12/15/2015
0.22Q	02/11/2016	02/26/2016	03/01/2016	03/15/2016
0.23Q	05/18/2016	05/27/2016	06/01/2016	06/15/2016

Indicated Div: $0.92

Valuation Analysis

	Institutional Holding	
Forecast EPS	$7.47	No of Institutions
	(05/20/2016)	294
Market Cap	$1.4 Billion	Shares
Book Value	$912.8 Million	29,077,142
Price/Book	1.57	% Held
Price/Sales	0.13	86.41

Business Summary: Retail - Automotive (MIC: 2.1.4 SIC: 5511 NAIC: 441110)

Group 1 Automotive is an operator in the automotive retail industry. As of Dec 31 2015, Co. owned and operated 199 franchises, representing 32 brands of automobiles, at 152 dealership locations and 35 collision centers worldwide. Through its dealerships, Co. sells new and used cars and light trucks; arranges related vehicle financing; sells service and insurance contracts; provides automotive maintenance and repair services; and sells vehicle parts. Co.'s operations are located in Alabama, California, Florida, Georgia, Kansas, Louisiana, Maryland, Massachusetts, Mississippi, New Hampshire, New Jersey, Oklahoma, South Carolina, Texas, U.K., and Brazil.

Recent Developments: For the quarter ended Mar 31 2016, net income decreased 4.3% to US$34.3 million from US$35.8 million in the year-earlier quarter. Revenues were US$2.61 billion, up 7.2% from US$2.43 billion the year before. Operating income was US$82.0 million versus US$80.7 million in the prior-year quarter, an increase of 1.6%. Direct operating expenses rose 7.3% to US$2.22 billion from US$2.07 billion in the comparable period the year before. Indirect operating expenses increased 7.5% to US$304.4 million from US$283.2 million in the equivalent prior-year period.

Prospects: Our evaluation of Group 1 Automotive Inc. as of June 19, 2016 is the result of our systematic analysis on three basic characteristics: earnings strength, relative valuation, and recent stock price movement. The company has produced a positive trend in earnings per share over the past 5 quarters. However, while recent estimates for the company have been mixed, GPI has posted better than expected results. Based on operating earnings yield, the company is undervalued when compared to all of the companies in our coverage universe. Share price changes over the past year indicates that GPI will perform in line with the market over the near term.

Financial Data

(US$ in Thousands)	3 Mos	12/31/2015	12/31/2014	12/31/2013	12/31/2012	12/31/2011	12/31/2010	12/31/2009
Earnings Per Share	3.90	3.90	3.60	4.32	4.19	3.47	2.16	1.49
Cash Flow Per Share	8.86	6.09	8.48	2.27	(3.47)	9.00	(3.01)	15.50
Tang Book Value Per Share	N.M.	N.M.	N.M.	1.05	5.03	4.62	4.95	2.53
Dividends Per Share	0.850	0.830	0.700	0.650	0.590	0.480	0.100	...
Dividend Payout %	21.79	21.28	19.44	15.05	14.08	13.83	4.63	...
Income Statement								
Total Revenue	2,608,355	10,632,505	9,937,889	8,918,581	7,476,100	6,079,765	5,509,169	4,525,707
EBITDA	82,525	325,538	298,007	308,333	261,496	220,603	168,731	142,071
Depn & Amortn	484	47,200	42,300	35,800	31,500	27,100	26,500	25,800
Income Before Taxes	54,102	182,171	164,400	191,895	160,735	132,094	80,904	54,851
Income Taxes	19,811	88,172	71,396	77,903	60,526	49,700	30,600	20,006
Net Income	34,291	93,999	93,004	113,992	100,209	82,394	50,304	34,845
Average Shares	22,453	23,152	24,885	25,314	22,688	22,409	23,317	23,325
Balance Sheet								
Current Assets	2,254,079	2,202,955	2,035,219	1,967,938	1,566,181	1,175,584	1,019,234	822,038
Total Assets	4,533,846	4,414,929	4,141,492	3,819,478	3,023,015	2,476,343	2,201,964	1,969,414
Current Liabilities	2,103,353	2,039,470	1,922,199	1,865,176	1,395,578	1,044,947	894,934	718,813
Long-Term Obligations	1,256,679	1,203,436	1,008,837	663,689	555,016	482,601	412,950	444,141
Total Liabilities	3,621,053	3,496,677	3,163,482	2,755,209	2,130,226	1,669,243	1,417,596	1,249,258
Stockholders' Equity	912,793	918,252	978,010	1,064,269	892,789	807,100	784,368	720,156
Shares Outstanding	23,008	23,415	24,339	24,314	22,726	22,707	23,793	24,479
Statistical Record								
Return on Assets %	2.14	2.20	2.34	3.33	3.63	3.52	2.41	1.63
Return on Equity %	9.88	9.91	9.11	11.65	11.76	10.35	6.69	5.19
EBITDA Margin %	3.16	3.06	3.00	3.46	3.50	3.63	3.06	3.14
Net Margin %	1.31	0.88	0.94	1.28	1.34	1.36	0.91	0.77
Asset Turnover	2.50	2.49	2.50	2.61	2.71	2.60	2.64	2.12
Current Ratio	1.07	1.08	1.06	1.06	1.12	1.13	1.14	1.14
Debt to Equity	1.38	1.31	1.03	0.62	0.62	0.60	0.53	0.62
Price Range	96.97-49.80	96.97-74.61	92.94-60.32	81.74-55.45	65.51-44.29	51.80-33.93	42.29-22.49	34.47-7.42
P/E Ratio	24.86-12.77	24.86-19.13	25.82-16.76	18.92-12.84	15.63-10.57	14.93-9.78	19.58-10.41	23.13-4.98
Average Yield %	1.07	0.97	0.93	0.97	1.06	1.15	0.32	...

Address: 800 Gessner, Suite 500, Houston, TX 77024
Telephone: 713-647-5700
Fax: 713-647-5858

Web Site: www.group1auto.com
Officers: Earl J. Hesterberg - President, Chief Executive Officer John C. Rickel - Senior Vice President, Chief Financial Officer

Auditors: Ernst & Young LLP
Transfer Agents: American Stock Transfer & Trust Company LLC, Brooklyn, NY

GUESS ?, INC.

Exchange	Symbol	Price	52Wk Range	Yield	P/E
NYS	GES	$15.77 (5/31/2016)	23.29-15.63	5.71	25.44

*7 Year Price Score 56.24   *NYSE Composite Index=100   *12 Month Price Score 86.75

TRADING VOLUME (thousand shares)

Interim Earnings (Per Share)

Qtr.	Apr	Jul	Oct	Jan
2013-14	0.12	0.47	0.40	0.82
2014-15	(0.03)	0.26	0.24	0.64
2015-16	0.04	0.21	0.15	0.56
2016-17	(0.30)			

Interim Dividends (Per Share)

Amt	Decl	Ex	Rec	Pay
0.225Q	08/26/2015	09/04/2015	09/09/2015	09/25/2015
0.225Q	11/24/2015	12/07/2015	12/09/2015	12/24/2015
0.225Q	03/16/2016	03/28/2016	03/30/2016	04/15/2016
0.225Q	05/25/2016	06/06/2016	06/08/2016	06/24/2016

Indicated Div: $0.90

Valuation Analysis

Forecast EPS	$0.60 (05/17/2016)
Market Cap	$1.3 Billion
Book Value	$1.0 Billion
Price/Book	1.32
Price/Sales	0.61

Institutional Holding

No of Institutions	306
Shares	73,233,168
% Held	73.38

Business Summary: Retail - Apparel and Accessories (MIC: 2.1.5 SIC: 2331 NAIC: 315212)

GUESS® designs, markets, distributes and licenses collections of apparel and accessories for men, women and children. The lines include collections of clothing, including among others, jeans, pants, skirts, dresses, shorts, knitwear and intimate apparel. Co. also selectively grants licenses to manufacture and distribute a range of products that complement its apparel lines, including eyewear, watches, handbags, footwear, kids' and infants' apparel, outerwear, swimwear, fragrance, jewelry and other fashion accessories. As of Jan 30 2016, Co. had 1,639 stores globally, of which 1,258 were GUESS® stores, 230 were GUESS® Accessories stores, 77 were G by GUESS stores and 74 were MARCIANO stores.

Recent Developments: For the quarter ended Apr 30 2016, net loss amounted to US$25.2 million versus net income of US$4.0 million in the year-earlier quarter. Revenues were US$448.8 million, down 6.3% from US$478.8 million the year before. Operating loss was US$29.0 million versus an income of US$4.4 million in the prior-year quarter. Direct operating expenses declined 2.3% to US$306.1 million from US$313.3 million in the comparable period the year before. Indirect operating expenses increased 6.6% to US$171.7 million from US$161.1 million in the equivalent prior-year period.

Prospects: Our evaluation of GUESS ® Inc. as of June 19, 2016 is the result of our systematic analysis on three basic characteristics: earnings strength, relative valuation, and recent stock price movement. The company has generated a negative trend in earnings per share over the past 5 quarters. However, while recent estimates for the company have been lowered by analysts, GES has posted results that fell short of analysts expectations. Based on operating earnings yield, the company is about fairly valued when compared to all of the companies in our coverage universe. Share price changes over the past year indicates that GES will perform well over the near term.

Financial Data
(US$ in Thousands)

	3 Mos	01/30/2016	01/31/2015	02/01/2014	02/02/2013	01/28/2012	01/29/2011	01/30/2010
Earnings Per Share	0.62	0.96	1.11	1.80	2.05	2.86	3.11	2.61
Cash Flow Per Share	1.67	2.14	1.82	3.90	3.07	3.99	3.80	3.95
Tang Book Value Per Share	11.46	11.66	12.07	12.97	12.09	12.67	11.01	10.51
Dividends Per Share	0.900	0.900	0.900	0.800	2.000	0.800	2.680	0.450
Dividend Payout %	145.16	93.75	81.08	44.44	97.56	27.97	86.17	17.24
Income Statement								
Total Revenue	448,815	2,204,311	2,417,673	2,569,786	2,658,605	2,688,048	2,487,294	2,128,466
EBITDA	(29,611)	130,283	146,934	235,419	282,739	400,438	424,780	370,261
Depn & Amortn	465	2,096	2,994	2,552	2,501	2,242	3,739	7,853
Income Before Taxes	(29,945)	127,279	143,008	232,959	280,614	399,341	421,377	361,929
Income Taxes	(4,791)	42,464	45,824	75,248	99,128	128,691	126,874	115,599
Net Income	(25,178)	81,851	94,570	153,434	178,744	265,500	289,508	242,761
Average Shares	83,514	84,525	84,837	84,522	86,540	91,948	92,115	91,592
Balance Sheet								
Current Assets	1,025,650	1,036,252	1,111,359	1,216,086	1,107,225	1,261,482	1,163,580	1,123,089
Total Assets	1,552,776	1,538,748	1,601,405	1,764,431	1,713,506	1,844,475	1,685,804	1,530,175
Current Liabilities	319,422	327,059	301,966	370,025	384,966	420,036	431,016	341,679
Long-Term Obligations	23,539	2,318	6,165	7,580	8,314	10,206	12,218	14,137
Total Liabilities	544,026	520,273	527,549	609,917	626,514	668,845	630,928	509,964
Stockholders' Equity	1,008,750	1,018,475	1,073,856	1,154,514	1,086,992	1,175,630	1,054,876	1,020,211
Shares Outstanding	84,326	83,833	85,323	84,962	85,367	89,631	92,290	92,736
Statistical Record								
Return on Assets %	3.43	5.23	5.63	8.85	9.89	15.08	18.05	17.53
Return on Equity %	5.16	7.85	8.51	13.73	15.54	23.87	27.98	27.10
EBITDA Margin %	N.M.	5.91	6.08	9.16	10.63	14.90	17.08	17.40
Net Margin %	N.M.	3.71	3.91	5.97	6.72	9.88	11.64	11.41
Asset Turnover	1.40	1.41	1.44	1.48	1.47	1.53	1.55	1.54
Current Ratio	3.21	3.17	3.68	3.29	2.88	3.00	2.70	3.29
Debt to Equity	0.02	N.M.	0.01	0.01	0.01	0.01	0.01	0.01
Price Range	23.29-16.70	23.29-16.74	30.90-18.78	34.64-24.71	36.72-22.66	47.52-26.30	50.97-31.24	45.28-13.16
P/E Ratio	37.56-26.94	24.26-17.44	27.84-16.92	19.24-13.73	17.91-11.05	16.62-9.20	16.39-10.05	17.35-5.04
Average Yield %	4.50	4.54	3.61	2.67	7.17	2.20	6.56	1.49

Address: 1444 South Alameda Street, Los Angeles, CA 90021 Telephone: 213-765-3100	Web Site: www.guess.com Officers: Paul Marciano - Executive Chairman, Vice-Chairman, Chief Executive Officer, Chief Creative Officer Victor Herrero Amigo - Chief Executive Officer	Auditors: Ernst & Young LLP Investor Contact: 213-765-5578 Transfer Agents: ComputerShare Investor Services, Providence, RI

HALLIBURTON COMPANY

Exchange	Symbol	Price	52Wk Range	Yield	P/E
NYS	HAL	$42.18 (5/31/2016)	46.24-28.48	1.71	N/A

*7 Year Price Score 79.25 *NYSE Composite index=100 *12 Month Price Score 103.26

TRADING VOLUME (thousand shares)

Interim Earnings (Per Share)

Qtr.	Mar	Jun	Sep	Dec
2013	(0.02)	0.69	0.79	0.91
2014	0.73	0.01	1.41	1.06
2015	(0.76)	0.06	(0.06)	(0.03)
2016	(2.81)	...	...	...

Interim Dividends (Per Share)

Amt	Decl	Ex	Rec	Pay
0.18Q	07/16/2015	08/31/2015	09/02/2015	09/23/2015
0.18Q	11/03/2015	12/01/2015	12/03/2015	12/24/2015
0.18Q	02/10/2016	02/29/2016	03/02/2016	03/23/2016
0.18Q	05/19/2016	05/27/2016	06/01/2016	06/22/2016

Indicated Div: $0.72

Valuation Analysis

Forecast EPS	$-0.22
	(05/20/2016)
Market Cap	$36.2 Billion
Book Value	$13.0 Billion
Price/Book	2.78
Price/Sales	1.74

Institutional Holding

No of Institutions	1338
Shares	782,868,096
% Held	75.70

Business Summary: Equipment & Services (MIC: 9.1.3 SIC: 1389 NAIC: 213112)

Halliburton is an oilfield services companies. Co. provides a range of services and products for the exploration, development, and production of oil and natural gas throughout the world. As of Dec. 31, 2015, Co. operated two business segments: Completion and Production which delivers cementing, stimulation, intervention, pressure control, chemicals, artificial lift, and completion products and services; and Drilling and Evaluation segment, which provides field and reservoir modeling, drilling, evaluation, and wellbore placement solutions that enable customers to model, measure, drill, and optimize their well construction activities.

Recent Developments: For the quarter ended Mar 31 2016, loss from continuing operations was US$2.42 billion compared with a loss of US$637.0 million in the year-earlier quarter. Net loss amounted to US$2.42 billion versus a net loss of US$641.0 million in the year-earlier quarter. Revenues were US$4.20 billion, down 40.5% from US$7.05 billion the year before. Operating loss was US$3.08 billion versus a loss of US$548.0 million in the prior-year quarter. Direct operating expenses declined 37.5% to US$3.93 billion from US$6.29 billion in the comparable period the year before. Indirect operating expenses increased 155.3% to US$3.35 billion from US$1.31 billion in the equivalent prior-year period.

Prospects: Our evaluation of Halliburton Co. as of June 19, 2016 is the result of our systematic analysis on three basic characteristics: earnings strength, relative valuation, and recent stock price movement. The company has enjoyed a very positive trend in earnings per share over the past 5 quarters. Because the company lacks sufficient analyst estimate data, we place greater weight on the historical EPS trend as the measure of earnings strength. Based on operating earnings yield, the company is overvalued when compared to all of the companies in our coverage universe. Share price changes over the past year indicates that HAL will perform poorly over the near term.

Financial Data

(US$ in Thousands)	3 Mos	12/31/2015	12/31/2014	12/31/2013	12/31/2012	12/31/2011	12/31/2010	12/31/2009
Earnings Per Share	(2.84)	(0.79)	4.11	2.36	2.84	3.08	2.01	1.27
Cash Flow Per Share	2.24	3.41	4.79	4.95	3.94	4.01	2.44	2.67
Tang Book Value Per Share	12.39	15.60	16.44	13.44	14.67	12.40	9.95	8.46
Dividends Per Share	0.720	0.720	0.630	0.525	0.360	0.360	0.360	0.360
Dividend Payout %	...	...	15.33	22.25	12.68	11.69	17.91	28.35
Income Statement								
Total Revenue	4,198,000	23,633,000	32,870,000	29,402,000	28,503,000	24,829,000	17,973,000	14,675,000
EBITDA	(2,780,000)	1,346,000	7,221,000	4,995,000	5,748,000	6,071,000	4,071,000	2,898,000
Depn & Amortn	346,000	1,835,000	2,126,000	1,900,000	1,628,000	1,359,000	1,119,000	931,000
Income Before Taxes	(3,291,000)	(936,000)	4,712,000	2,764,000	3,822,000	4,449,000	2,655,000	1,682,000
Income Taxes	(875,000)	(274,000)	1,275,000	648,000	1,235,000	1,439,000	853,000	518,000
Net Income	(2,412,000)	(671,000)	3,500,000	2,125,000	2,635,000	2,839,000	1,835,000	1,145,000
Average Shares	858,000	853,000	852,000	902,000	928,000	922,000	911,000	902,000
Balance Sheet								
Current Assets	19,105,000	21,609,000	15,068,000	13,704,000	13,086,000	11,577,000	8,886,000	8,638,000
Total Assets	33,932,000	36,942,000	32,240,000	29,223,000	27,410,000	23,677,000	18,297,000	16,538,000
Current Liabilities	7,412,000	5,359,000	5,883,000	5,026,000	4,752,000	4,121,000	2,757,000	2,889,000
Long-Term Obligations	12,207,000	14,687,000	7,840,000	7,816,000	4,820,000	4,820,000	3,824,000	3,824,000
Total Liabilities	20,917,000	21,480,000	15,973,000	15,642,000	11,645,000	10,479,000	7,924,000	7,810,000
Stockholders' Equity	13,015,000	15,462,000	16,267,000	13,581,000	15,765,000	13,198,000	10,373,000	8,728,000
Shares Outstanding	858,000	856,000	848,000	849,000	929,000	921,000	910,000	902,000
Statistical Record								
Return on Assets %	N.M.	N.M.	11.39	7.50	10.29	13.53	10.54	7.41
Return on Equity %	N.M.	N.M.	23.45	14.48	18.15	24.09	19.21	13.92
EBITDA Margin %	N.M.	5.70	21.97	16.99	20.17	24.45	22.65	19.75
Net Margin %	N.M.	N.M.	10.65	7.23	9.24	11.43	10.21	7.80
Asset Turnover	0.64	0.68	1.07	1.04	1.11	1.18	1.03	0.95
Current Ratio	2.58	4.03	2.56	2.73	2.75	2.81	3.22	2.99
Debt to Equity	0.94	0.95	0.48	0.58	0.31	0.37	0.37	0.44
Price Range	49.21-28.48	49.21-33.40	74.02-37.82	56.26-34.69	38.51-26.70	57.27-28.68	41.15-21.15	31.75-14.78
P/E Ratio	...	...	18.01-9.20	23.84-14.70	13.56-9.40	18.59-9.31	20.47-10.52	25.00-11.64
Average Yield %	1.85	1.75	1.07	1.16	1.09	0.83	1.15	1.57

Address: 3000 North Sam Houston Parkway East, Houston, TX 77032
Telephone: 281-871-2699

Web Site: www.halliburton.com
Officers: David J. Lesar - Chairman, President, Chief Executive Officer Jeffrey Allen Miller - President, Executive Vice President, Chief Operating Officer

Auditors: KPMG LLP
Investor Contact: 888-669 3920
Transfer Agents: Computershare Shareowner Services, Jersey City, NJ

HALYARD HEALTH INC

Exchange	Symbol	Price	52Wk Range	Yield	P/E
NYS	HYH	$31.09 (5/31/2016)	43.12-23.29	N/A	N/A

*7 Year Price Score N/A   *NYSE Composite Index=100   *12 Month Price Score 91.76

TRADING VOLUME (thousand shares)

Interim Earnings (Per Share)

Qtr.	Mar	Jun	Sep	Dec
2014	0.89	(0.10)	(0.16)	(0.05)
2015	0.46	0.17	(10.10)	0.31
2016	0.30	...	...	...

Interim Dividends (Per Share)

No Dividends Paid

Valuation Analysis   Institutional Holding

Forecast EPS	$1.65	No of Institutions
	(05/20/2016)	389
Market Cap	$1.4 Billion	Shares
Book Value	$1.1 Billion	38,443,568
Price/Book	1.34	% Held
Price/Sales	0.93	N/A

Business Summary: Medical Instruments & Equipment (MIC: 4.3.1 SIC: 3842 NAIC: 339113)

Halyard Health is a global company focused on preventing infection, eliminating pain and speeding patient recovery. Co.'s Surgical and Infection Prevention segment provides healthcare supplies and solutions that target the prevention of healthcare related infections. Products include sterilization wraps, surgical drapes and gowns, facial protection, protective apparel and medical exam gloves. Co.'s Medical Devices segment provides products focused on pain management and respiratory and digestive health. These products include post-operative pain management solutions, minimally invasive interventional (or chronic) pain therapies, closed airway suction systems and enteral feeding tubes.

Recent Developments: For the quarter ended Mar 31 2016, net income decreased 34.6% to US$14.2 million from US$21.7 million in the year-earlier quarter. Revenues were US$384.8 million, down 2.4% from US$394.2 million the year before. Operating income was US$33.1 million versus US$40.9 million in the prior-year quarter, a decrease of 19.1%. Direct operating expenses declined 5.3% to US$248.3 million from US$262.1 million in the comparable period the year before. Indirect operating expenses increased 13.4% to US$103.4 million from US$91.2 million in the equivalent prior-year period.

Prospects: Our evaluation of Halyard Health Inc. as of June 19, 2016 is the result of our systematic analysis on three basic characteristics: earnings strength, relative valuation, and recent stock price movement. The company has suffered a very negative trend in earnings per share over the past 5 quarters and while recent estimates for the company have remained steady, HYH has posted better than expected results. Based on operating earnings yield, the company is undervalued when compared to all of the companies in our coverage universe. Share price changes over the past year indicates that HYH will perform very poorly over the near term.

Financial Data

(US$ in Thousands)	3 Mos	12/31/2015	12/31/2014	12/31/2013	12/31/2012	12/31/2011
Earnings Per Share	(9.32)	(9.15)	0.58	...	...	...
Cash Flow Per Share	2.15	2.09	3.18	...	...	...
Tang Book Value Per Share	1.19	0.59	N.M.	...	...	...
Income Statement						
Total Revenue	384,800	1,574,400	1,672,100	1,677,500	1,684,000	1,659,900
EBITDA	43,100	(337,700)	147,300	265,200	266,300	249,000
Depn & Amortn	10,000	40,000	53,000	39,900	38,300	38,300
Income Before Taxes	25,300	(410,500)	91,200	227,800	229,800	214,600
Income Taxes	11,100	15,800	64,100	73,200	77,200	72,200
Net Income	14,200	(426,300)	27,100	154,600	152,600	142,400
Average Shares	46,800	46,600	46,538	...	...	...
Balance Sheet						
Current Assets	706,600	676,000	684,900	585,100	593,700	...
Total Assets	2,019,700	2,000,200	2,527,600	2,484,000	2,534,200	...
Current Liabilities	309,300	315,200	356,000	310,400	359,100	...
Long-Term Obligations	578,500	578,100	632,300	...	...	...
Total Liabilities	939,900	944,900	1,036,400	404,900	478,500	...
Stockholders' Equity	1,079,800	1,055,300	1,491,200	2,079,100	2,055,700	...
Shares Outstanding	46,614	46,614	46,535	...	...	...
Statistical Record						
Return on Assets %	N.M.	N.M.	1.07	6.16	...	...
Return on Equity %	N.M.	N.M.	1.82	7.48	...	...
EBITDA Margin %	11.20	N.M.	8.81	15.81	15.81	15.00
Net Margin %	3.69	N.M.	1.62	9.22	9.06	8.58
Asset Turnover	0.69	0.70	0.66	0.67	...	...
Current Ratio	2.28	2.14	1.92	1.88	1.65	...
Debt to Equity	0.54	0.55	0.42	...	...	...
Price Range	50.41-23.29	50.41-27.00	45.47-35.82	...	...	...
P/E Ratio	...	...	78.40-61.76	...	...	...

Address: 5405 Windward Parkway, Suite 100 South, Alpharetta, GA 30004 **Telephone:** 678-425-9273	**Web Site:** www.halyardhealth.com **Officers:** Robert E. Abernathy - Chairman, Chief Executive Officer S. Ross Mansbach - Vice President, Deputy General Counsel, Corporate Secretary	**Auditors:** Deloitte & Touche LLP **Transfer Agents:** Computershare

HANESBRANDS INC

	Exchange	Symbol	Price	52Wk Range	Yield	P/E
	NYS	HBI	$27.07 (5/31/2016)	34.47-23.82	1.63	23.75

*7 Year Price Score 172.86 *NYSE Composite Index=100 *12 Month Price Score 93.14

Interim Earnings (Per Share)

Qtr.	Mar	Jun	Sep	Dec
2013	0.13	0.30	0.31	0.35
2014	0.10	0.38	0.29	0.55
2015	0.13	0.23	0.40	0.30
2016	0.21	...	...	...

Interim Dividends (Per Share)

Amt	Decl	Ex	Rec	Pay
0.10Q	07/28/2015	08/14/2015	08/18/2015	09/09/2015
0.10Q	10/27/2015	11/13/2015	11/17/2015	12/08/2015
0.11Q	01/26/2016	02/11/2016	02/16/2016	03/08/2016
0.11Q	04/26/2016	05/13/2016	05/17/2016	06/07/2016

Indicated Div: $0.44

Valuation Analysis / **Institutional Holding**

Forecast EPS	$1.93	No of Institutions
	(05/20/2016)	706
Market Cap	$10.2 Billion	Shares
Book Value	$952.0 Million	338,245,696
Price/Book	10.73	% Held
Price/Sales	1.78	87.69

TRADING VOLUME (thousand shares)

Business Summary: Apparel, Footwear & Accessories (MIC: 1.4.2 SIC: 2389 NAIC: 313312)

Hanesbrands is a manufacturer and marketer of apparel under several apparel brands. Co. has four segments: Innerwear, Activewear, Direct to Consumer and International. The Innerwear segment focuses on apparel products, such as intimate apparel, men's underwear, children's underwear and socks. Under its Activewear segment, Co. sells products such as T-shirts and fleece to both retailers and wholesalers as well as provides uniforms for athletic programs. Co.'s Direct to Consumer operations include its domestic Co. operated outlet stores, catalogs and website operations. Co.'s International segment includes products marketed primarily in Europe, Japan, Canada, Mexico, Brazil and Australia.

Recent Developments: For the quarter ended Apr 2 2016, net income increased 52.5% to US$80.3 million from US$52.6 million in the year-earlier quarter. Revenues were US$1.22 billion, up 0.8% from US$1.21 billion the year before. Operating income was US$122.4 million versus US$89.9 million in the prior-year quarter, an increase of 36.1%. Direct operating expenses declined 0.1% to US$761.9 million from US$762.7 million in the comparable period the year before. Indirect operating expenses decreased 6.0% to US$334.9 million from US$356.3 million in the equivalent prior-year period.

Prospects: Our evaluation of Hanesbrands Inc. as of June 19, 2016 is the result of our systematic analysis on three basic characteristics: earnings strength, relative valuation, and recent stock price movement. The company has managed to produce a neutral trend in earnings per share over the past 5 quarters and while recent estimates for the company have been raised by analysts, HBI has posted better than expected results. Based on operating earnings yield, the company is undervalued when compared to all of the companies in our coverage universe. Share price changes over the past year indicates that HBI will perform well over the near term.

Financial Data
(US$ in Thousands)

	3 Mos	01/02/2016	01/03/2015	12/28/2013	12/29/2012	12/31/2011	01/01/2011	01/02/2010
Earnings Per Share	1.14	1.06	1.32	1.08	0.55	0.90	0.72	0.18
Cash Flow Per Share	0.52	0.57	1.66	1.98	1.86	0.57	0.46	1.46
Tang Book Value Per Share	N.M.	N.M.	N.M.	0.76	1.13	0.27	N.M.	N.M.
Dividends Per Share	0.410	0.400	0.300	0.150	...	...	...	...
Dividend Payout %	35.96	37.74	22.67	13.85	...	...	...	...
Income Statement								
Total Revenue	1,219,140	5,731,549	5,324,746	4,627,802	4,525,721	4,637,143	4,326,713	3,891,275
EBITDA	125,515	695,811	659,557	588,575	492,836	562,629	470,579	318,310
Depn & Amortn	3,759	103,903	98,202	90,890	93,036	90,725	86,612	96,755
Income Before Taxes	90,190	473,873	464,968	395,801	262,945	315,607	233,731	58,276
Income Taxes	9,921	45,018	60,449	65,307	30,502	48,919	22,438	6,993
Net Income	80,269	428,855	404,519	330,494	164,681	266,688	211,293	51,283
Average Shares	389,043	403,659	306,033	305,469	300,807	297,753	293,322	287,004
Balance Sheet								
Current Assets	3,117,680	2,917,867	2,765,232	2,243,666	2,027,525	2,330,791	2,147,671	1,822,557
Total Assets	5,822,061	5,619,040	5,221,781	4,090,048	3,631,700	4,034,669	3,790,002	3,326,564
Current Liabilities	1,368,512	1,503,909	1,486,602	999,278	875,668	933,719	829,350	878,975
Long-Term Obligations	2,963,424	2,254,162	1,613,997	1,467,000	1,317,500	1,807,717	1,990,735	1,727,547
Total Liabilities	4,870,020	4,343,149	3,835,009	2,859,425	2,744,834	3,353,608	3,227,328	2,991,845
Stockholders' Equity	952,041	1,275,891	1,386,772	1,230,623	886,866	681,061	562,674	334,719
Shares Outstanding	377,513	391,670	300,591	298,366	294,809	292,551	288,621	286,190
Statistical Record								
Return on Assets %	8.13	7.93	8.55	8.58	4.31	6.84	5.95	1.50
Return on Equity %	38.76	32.30	30.41	31.30	21.06	43.00	47.22	19.78
EBITDA Margin %	10.30	12.14	12.39	12.72	10.89	12.13	10.88	8.18
Net Margin %	6.58	7.48	7.60	7.14	3.64	5.75	4.88	1.32
Asset Turnover	1.02	1.06	1.13	1.20	1.18	1.19	1.22	1.14
Current Ratio	2.28	1.94	1.86	2.25	2.32	2.50	2.59	2.07
Debt to Equity	3.11	1.77	1.16	1.19	1.49	2.65	3.54	5.16
Price Range	34.58-23.82	34.58-26.54	28.93-16.04	17.74-8.90	9.13-5.55	8.31-5.46	7.70-5.42	6.49-1.45
P/E Ratio	30.33-20.89	32.62-25.03	21.92-12.15	16.42-8.24	16.59-10.09	9.24-6.07	10.70-7.52	36.07-8.03
Average Yield %	1.34	1.29	1.31	1.12	...	...	...	...

Address: 1000 East Hanes Mill Road, Winston-Salem, NC 27105 **Telephone:** 336-519-8080	**Web Site:** www.Hanes.com **Officers:** Richard A. Noll - Chairman, Chief Executive Officer Michael E. Faircloth - President, Chief Global Operations	**Auditors:** PricewaterhouseCoopers **Investor Contact:** 336-519-8080 **Transfer Agents:** ComputerShare Investor Services, Providence, RI

HANOVER INSURANCE GROUP INC

Exchange	Symbol	Price	52Wk Range	Yield	P/E	Div Achiever
NYS	THG	$86.68 (5/31/2016)	91.15-71.35	2.12	10.86	10 Years

*7 Year Price Score 132.12 *NYSE Composite Index=100 *12 Month Price Score 105.24

TRADING VOLUME (thousand shares)

Interim Earnings (Per Share)

Qtr.	Mar	Jun	Sep	Dec
2013	1.46	1.19	1.37	1.56
2014	1.22	1.84	1.22	2.00
2015	1.22	2.68	1.74	1.76
2016	1.80	...	...	...

Interim Dividends (Per Share)

Amt	Decl	Ex	Rec	Pay
0.41Q	08/25/2015	09/09/2015	09/11/2015	09/25/2015
0.46Q	12/07/2015	12/16/2015	12/18/2015	12/31/2015
0.46Q	02/23/2016	03/09/2016	03/11/2016	03/25/2016
0.46Q	05/24/2016	06/08/2016	06/10/2016	06/24/2016

Indicated Div: $1.84

Valuation Analysis

Valuation Analysis		Institutional Holding	
Forecast EPS	$6.40	No of Institutions	
	(04/30/2016)	381	
Market Cap	$3.7 Billion	Shares	
Book Value	$3.0 Billion	44,929,216	
Price/Book	1.25	% Held	
Price/Sales	0.75	N/A	

Business Summary: General Insurance (MIC: 5.2.1 SIC: 6331 NAIC: 524126)

The Hanover Insurance Group is a holding company. Co.'s business operations are property and casualty insurance products and services. Co. has four segments: Commercial Lines, which includecommercial multiple peril, commercial automobile, workers' compensation, and other commercial coverages; Personal Lines, which include personal automobile, personal automobile, and other personal coverages; Chaucer Holdings Limited, which includes marine and aviation, property, energy, and casualty and other coverages; and Other, which provides investment advisory services to affiliates and also manages assets for unaffiliated institutions such as insurance companies, retirement plans and foundations.

Recent Developments: For the quarter ended Mar 31 2016, income from continuing operations increased 42.3% to US$78.1 million from US$54.9 million in the year-earlier quarter. Net income increased 42.4% to US$78.2 million from US$54.9 million in the year-earlier quarter. Revenues were US$1.23 billion, down 5.5% from US$1.30 billion the year before. Net premiums earned were US$1.15 billion versus US$1.21 billion in the prior-year quarter, a decrease of 4.9%. Net investment income fell 2.6% to US$68.3 million from US$70.1 million a year ago.

Prospects: Our evaluation of Hanover Insurance Group Inc. as of June 19, 2016 is the result of our systematic analysis on three basic characteristics: earnings strength, relative valuation, and recent stock price movement. The company has generated a negative trend in earnings per share over the past 5 quarters. However, while recent estimates for the company have been lowered by analysts, THG has posted better than expected results. Based on operating earnings yield, the company is undervalued when compared to all of the companies in our coverage universe. Share price changes over the past year indicates that THG will perform very well over the near term.

Financial Data
(US$ in Thousands)

	3 Mos	12/31/2015	12/31/2014	12/31/2013	12/31/2012	12/31/2011	12/31/2010	12/31/2009
Earnings Per Share	7.98	7.40	6.28	5.59	1.23	0.81	3.34	3.86
Cash Flow Per Share	10.05	9.99	12.83	8.71	9.11	4.90	1.83	1.81
Tang Book Value Per Share	64.90	61.82	60.58	55.14	54.41	52.11	50.81	46.05
Dividends Per Share	1.740	1.690	1.520	1.360	1.230	1.125	1.000	0.750
Dividend Payout %	21.80	22.84	24.20	24.33	100.00	138.89	29.94	19.43
Income Statement								
Premium Income	1,151,300	4,704,800	4,710,300	4,450,500	4,239,100	3,598,600	2,841,000	2,546,400
Total Revenue	1,227,600	5,034,000	5,067,600	4,793,700	4,590,700	3,931,600	3,152,200	2,834,100
Benefits & Claims	699,600	2,884,100	2,927,500	2,761,100	2,974,400	2,550,800	1,856,300	1,639,200
Income Before Taxes	108,100	439,400	378,000	329,100	28,700	22,300	211,100	270,900
Income Taxes	30,000	108,600	95,700	83,400	(17,400)	(9,600)	57,900	83,100
Net Income	78,200	331,500	282,000	251,000	55,900	37,100	154,800	197,200
Average Shares	43,500	44,800	44,900	44,900	45,300	45,800	46,300	51,100
Balance Sheet								
Total Assets	14,027,700	13,790,900	13,759,700	13,378,700	13,484,900	12,624,400	8,569,900	8,042,700
Total Liabilities	11,070,700	10,946,500	10,915,700	10,784,200	10,889,500	10,114,600	6,109,400	5,684,100
Stockholders' Equity	2,957,000	2,844,400	2,844,000	2,594,500	2,595,400	2,509,800	2,460,500	2,358,600
Shares Outstanding	42,700	43,000	43,900	43,700	44,300	44,600	44,900	47,500
Statistical Record								
Return on Assets %	2.54	2.41	2.08	1.87	0.43	0.35	1.86	2.28
Return on Equity %	12.12	11.66	10.37	9.67	2.18	1.49	6.42	9.29
Loss Ratio %	60.77	61.30	62.15	62.04	70.17	70.88	65.34	64.37
Net Margin %	6.37	6.59	5.56	5.24	1.22	0.94	4.91	6.96
Price Range	90.68-68.57	86.58-68.18	73.30-53.14	60.99-38.74	41.39-33.99	48.82-31.22	47.73-40.51	45.23-28.49
P/E Ratio	11.36-8.59	11.70-9.21	11.67-8.46	10.91-6.93	33.65-27.63	60.27-38.54	14.29-12.13	11.72-7.38
Average Yield %	2.20	2.22	2.44	2.67	3.25	2.83	2.25	1.96

Address: 440 Lincoln Street, Worcester, MA 01653
Telephone: 508-855-1000
Fax: 508-855-6332

Web Site: www.hanover.com
Officers: Micheal P. Angelini - Chairman Joseph M. Zubretsky - President, Chief Executive Officer

Auditors: PricewaterhouseCoopers LLP
Investor Contact: 508-855-2063
Transfer Agents: ComputerShare Investor Services, Providence, RI

HARLEY-DAVIDSON INC

Exchange	Symbol	Price	52Wk Range	Yield	P/E
NYS	HOG	$46.39 (5/31/2016)	60.41-37.49	3.02	12.31

*7 Year Price Score 91.18   *NYSE Composite Index=100   *12 Month Price Score 93.68

Interim Earnings (Per Share)

Qtr.	Mar	Jun	Sep	Dec
2013	0.99	1.21	0.73	0.35
2014	1.21	1.82	0.69	0.36
2015	1.27	1.44	0.69	0.28
2016	1.36	...	...	...

Interim Dividends (Per Share)

Amt	Decl	Ex	Rec	Pay
0.31Q	09/01/2015	09/11/2015	09/15/2015	09/25/2015
0.31Q	12/01/2015	12/09/2015	12/11/2015	12/28/2015
0.35Q	02/03/2016	02/12/2016	02/17/2016	03/04/2016
0.35Q	04/30/2016	05/24/2016	05/26/2016	06/10/2016

Indicated Div: $1.40 (Div. Reinv. Plan)

Valuation Analysis — **Institutional Holding**

Forecast EPS	$3.99
	(05/20/2016)
Market Cap	$8.4 Billion
Book Value	$1.9 Billion
Price/Book	4.44
Price/Sales	1.38

No of Institutions 785
Shares 191,154,960
% Held 77.34

Business Summary: Autos- Manufacturing (MIC: 1.8.1 SIC: 3751 NAIC: 336991)

Harley-Davidson is the parent company for the groups of companies doing business as Harley-Davidson Motor Company and Harley-Davidson Financial Services (HDFS). Co. operates in two business segments: Motorcycles & Related Products (Motorcycles) and Financial Services. The primary business of the Motorcycles segment is to design, manufacture and sell at wholesale on-road Harley-Davidson motorcycles as well as a line of motorcycle parts, accessories, general merchandise and related services. HDFS is engaged in the business of financing and servicing wholesale inventory receivables and retail consumer loans, primarily for the purchase of Harley-Davidson motorcycles.

Recent Developments: For the quarter ended Mar 27 2016, net income decreased 7.2% to US$250.5 million from US$269.9 million in the year-earlier quarter. Revenues were US$1.75 billion, up 4.6% from US$1.67 billion the year before. Operating income was US$388.8 million versus US$410.1 million in the prior-year quarter, a decrease of 5.2%. Direct operating expenses rose 8.6% to US$1.07 billion from US$985.1 million in the comparable period the year before. Indirect operating expenses increased 5.0% to US$291.8 million from US$277.7 million in the equivalent prior-year period.

Prospects: Our evaluation of Harley-Davidson Inc. as of June 19, 2016 is the result of our systematic analysis on three basic characteristics: earnings strength, relative valuation, and recent stock price movement. The company has produced a positive trend in earnings per share over the past 5 quarters. However, while recent estimates for the company have been lowered by analysts, HOG has posted better than expected results. Based on operating earnings yield, the company is undervalued when compared to all of the companies in our coverage universe. Share price changes over the past year indicates that HOG will perform in line with the market over the near term.

Financial Data
(US$ in Thousands)

	3 Mos	12/31/2015	12/31/2014	12/31/2013	12/31/2012	12/31/2011	12/31/2010	12/31/2009
Earnings Per Share	3.77	3.69	3.88	3.28	2.72	2.55	0.62	(0.24)
Cash Flow Per Share	5.27	5.43	5.30	4.39	3.52	3.80	4.99	2.62
Tang Book Value Per Share	10.15	9.67	13.60	13.54	11.18	10.37	9.24	8.86
Dividends Per Share	1.280	1.240	1.100	0.840	0.620	0.475	0.400	0.400
Dividend Payout %	33.95	33.60	28.35	25.61	22.79	18.63	64.52	...
Income Statement								
Total Revenue	1,749,968	5,995,402	6,228,508	5,899,872	5,580,506	5,311,713	4,859,336	4,781,909
EBITDA	463,969	1,463,875	1,466,782	1,326,633	1,176,523	1,018,338	735,997	446,684
Depn & Amortn	74,375	301,595	179,300	167,072	168,978	180,408	255,171	246,344
Income Before Taxes	382,426	1,150,163	1,283,320	1,114,305	961,512	792,664	390,469	178,660
Income Taxes	131,937	397,956	438,709	380,312	337,587	244,586	130,800	108,019
Net Income	250,489	752,207	844,611	733,993	623,925	599,114	146,545	(55,116)
Average Shares	184,204	203,686	217,706	224,071	229,229	234,918	234,787	233,573
Balance Sheet								
Current Assets	4,491,750	3,983,154	3,948,095	3,988,803	4,050,936	4,542,206	4,066,626	4,341,949
Total Assets	10,467,671	9,991,167	9,528,097	9,405,040	9,170,773	9,674,164	9,430,740	9,155,518
Current Liabilities	2,588,006	2,752,578	2,389,286	2,509,586	1,503,082	2,698,618	2,013,782	2,268,224
Long-Term Obligations	5,460,553	4,845,388	3,761,528	3,416,713	4,370,544	3,843,886	4,520,591	4,114,039
Total Liabilities	8,574,851	8,151,513	6,618,811	6,395,554	6,613,149	7,253,908	7,223,874	7,047,400
Stockholders' Equity	1,892,820	1,839,654	2,909,286	3,009,486	2,557,624	2,420,256	2,206,866	2,108,118
Shares Outstanding	181,090	184,733	211,876	219,959	226,100	230,540	235,520	234,313
Statistical Record								
Return on Assets %	7.07	7.71	8.92	7.90	6.60	6.27	1.58	N.M.
Return on Equity %	30.35	31.68	28.54	26.37	25.00	25.90	6.79	N.M.
EBITDA Margin %	26.51	24.42	23.55	22.49	21.08	19.17	15.15	9.34
Net Margin %	14.31	12.55	13.56	12.44	11.18	11.28	3.02	N.M.
Asset Turnover	0.59	0.61	0.66	0.64	0.59	0.56	0.52	0.56
Current Ratio	1.74	1.45	1.65	1.59	2.70	1.68	2.02	1.91
Debt to Equity	2.88	2.63	1.29	1.14	1.71	1.59	2.05	1.95
Price Range	62.59-37.49	66.13-45.12	73.94-55.48	69.36-48.69	53.49-39.33	45.91-32.10	35.49-21.51	29.58-8.20
P/E Ratio	16.60-9.94	17.92-12.23	19.06-14.30	21.15-14.84	19.67-14.46	18.00-12.59	57.24-34.69	...
Average Yield %	2.47	2.20	1.66	1.45	1.35	1.24	1.40	2.03

Address: 3700 West Juneau Avenue, Milwaukee, WI 53208 **Telephone:** 414-342-4680	**Web Site:** www.harley-davidson.com **Officers:** Matthew S. Levatich - President, Chief Executive Officer William B. Dannehl - Executive Vice President, Chief Organizational Transformation Officer	**Auditors:** Ernst & Young LLP **Investor Contact:** 187-743-78625 **Transfer Agents:** Computershare, Inc., Providence, RI

HARMAN INTERNATIONAL INDUSTRIES, INC.

Exchange	Symbol	Price	52Wk Range	Yield	P/E
NYS	HAR	$78.24 (5/31/2016)	126.92-67.46	1.79	15.71

*7 Year Price Score 125.01 *NYSE Composite Index=100 *12 Month Price Score 82.17

Interim Earnings (Per Share)

Qtr.	Sep	Dec	Mar	Jun
2012-13	0.79	0.68	0.50	0.07
2013-14	0.66	1.03	1.05	0.62
2014-15	1.18	1.65	0.99	1.01
2015-16	1.20	1.55	1.22	...

Interim Dividends (Per Share)

Amt	Decl	Ex	Rec	Pay
0.35Q	08/04/2015	08/12/2015	08/14/2015	08/28/2015
0.35Q	10/29/2015	11/05/2015	11/09/2015	11/24/2015
0.35Q	01/28/2016	02/04/2016	02/08/2016	02/23/2016
0.35Q	04/28/2016	05/05/2016	05/09/2016	05/23/2016

Indicated Div: $1.40

Valuation Analysis

		Institutional Holding	
Forecast EPS	$6.20	No of Institutions	
	(05/20/2016)	616	
Market Cap	$5.5 Billion	Shares	
Book Value	$2.5 Billion	77,362,888	
Price/Book	2.23	% Held	
Price/Sales	0.82	97.18	

Business Summary: Household Appliances, Electronics & Goods (MIC: 1.5.1 SIC: 3651 NAIC: 334310)

Harman International is engaged in the development, manufacture and marketing of audio, visual and infotainment systems, enterprise automation solutions and software services. Co.'s segments include: Infotainment, which designs, manufactures and markets infotainment systems; Lifestyle, which designs, manufactures and markets car audio systems for vehicle applications; Professional, which designs, manufactures and markets a range of audio, lighting, video and control and automation solutions for commercial, enterprise and public space applications; and Services, which creates software solutions that integrate design, mobility, cloud and analytics.

Recent Developments: For the quarter ended Mar 31 2016, net income increased 26.4% to US$88.8 million from US$70.2 million in the year-earlier quarter. Revenues were US$1.63 billion, up 11.2% from US$1.46 billion the year before. Operating income was US$135.4 million versus US$91.5 million in the prior-year quarter, an increase of 47.9%. Direct operating expenses rose 8.5% to US$1.14 billion from US$1.05 billion in the comparable period the year before. Indirect operating expenses increased 9.5% to US$357.5 million from US$326.6 million in the equivalent prior-year period.

Prospects: Our evaluation of Harman International Industries Inc. as of June 19, 2016 is the result of our systematic analysis on three basic characteristics: earnings strength, relative valuation, and recent stock price movement. The company has managed to produce a neutral trend in earnings per share over the past 5 quarters and while recent estimates for the company have remained steady, HAR has posted results that fell short of analysts expectations. Based on operating earnings yield, the company is undervalued when compared to all of the companies in our coverage universe. Share price changes over the past year indicates that HAR will perform poorly over the near term.

Financial Data

(US$ in Thousands)	9 Mos	6 Mos	3 Mos	06/30/2015	06/30/2014	06/30/2013	06/30/2012	06/30/2011
Earnings Per Share	4.98	4.75	4.85	4.84	3.36	2.04	4.57	1.90
Cash Flow Per Share	4.56	4.83	5.37	7.88	8.57	0.61	3.76	4.67
Tang Book Value Per Share	7.82	8.21	6.56	5.87	18.38	20.73	20.05	18.65
Dividends Per Share	1.380	1.360	1.340	1.320	1.200	0.600	0.300	0.050
Dividend Payout %	27.71	28.63	27.63	27.27	35.71	29.41	6.56	2.63
Income Statement								
Total Revenue	5,031,127	3,403,045	1,630,888	6,155,297	5,348,483	4,297,842	4,364,078	3,772,345
EBITDA	521,799	354,028	165,025	592,210	434,521	302,738	391,379	298,296
Depn & Amortn	109,700	70,800	35,700	132,000	119,100	115,600	110,100	115,500
Income Before Taxes	387,541	267,303	121,066	446,281	307,395	174,270	261,153	160,220
Income Taxes	98,019	66,600	33,549	103,269	72,610	31,729	(68,388)	24,304
Net Income	288,820	199,996	87,099	342,680	234,692	142,407	329,541	135,916
Average Shares	72,642	72,830	72,556	70,870	69,889	69,736	72,083	71,635
Balance Sheet								
Current Assets	2,790,906	2,878,442	2,870,154	2,948,770	2,458,871	2,089,052	2,116,245	2,108,155
Total Assets	5,788,397	5,822,778	5,811,081	5,929,752	4,125,590	3,235,685	3,169,464	3,058,495
Current Liabilities	1,662,873	2,000,421	2,078,862	2,120,368	1,485,652	1,077,514	1,381,900	1,047,581
Long-Term Obligations	1,286,809	1,044,531	1,055,767	1,080,667	519,407	255,043	...	378,401
Total Liabilities	3,313,824	3,377,236	3,454,204	3,555,139	2,333,012	1,590,814	1,639,853	1,634,837
Stockholders' Equity	2,474,573	2,445,542	2,356,877	2,374,613	1,792,578	1,644,871	1,529,611	1,423,658
Shares Outstanding	70,554	71,137	71,080	71,219	68,088	68,052	67,286	69,920
Statistical Record								
Return on Assets %	6.89	6.87	7.03	6.82	6.38	4.45	10.55	4.84
Return on Equity %	15.61	15.63	16.48	16.45	13.66	8.97	22.26	10.62
EBITDA Margin %	10.37	10.40	10.12	9.62	8.12	7.04	8.97	7.91
Net Margin %	5.74	5.88	5.34	5.57	4.39	3.31	7.55	3.60
Asset Turnover	1.28	1.31	1.29	1.22	1.45	1.34	1.40	1.34
Current Ratio	1.68	1.44	1.38	1.39	1.66	1.94	1.53	2.01
Debt to Equity	0.52	0.43	0.45	0.46	0.29	0.16	...	0.27
Price Range	146.49-67.46	146.49-88.83	146.49-85.36	146.49-85.36	112.01-53.37	54.20-36.99	50.70-26.20	51.58-29.12
P/E Ratio	29.42-13.55	30.84-18.70	30.20-17.60	30.27-17.64	33.34-15.88	26.57-18.13	11.09-5.73	27.15-15.33
Average Yield %	1.33	1.19	1.16	1.13	1.39		0.74	0.12

Address: 400 Atlantic Street, Suite 1500, Stamford, CT 06901 **Telephone:** 203-328-3500	**Web Site:** www.harman.com **Officers:** Dinesh C. Paliwal - Chairman, President, Chief Executive Officer Sandra E. Rowland - Executive Vice President, Chief Financial Officer	**Auditors:** KPMG LLP **Investor Contact:** 203-328-3500 **Transfer Agents:** Mellon Investor Services LLC

HARRIS CORP.

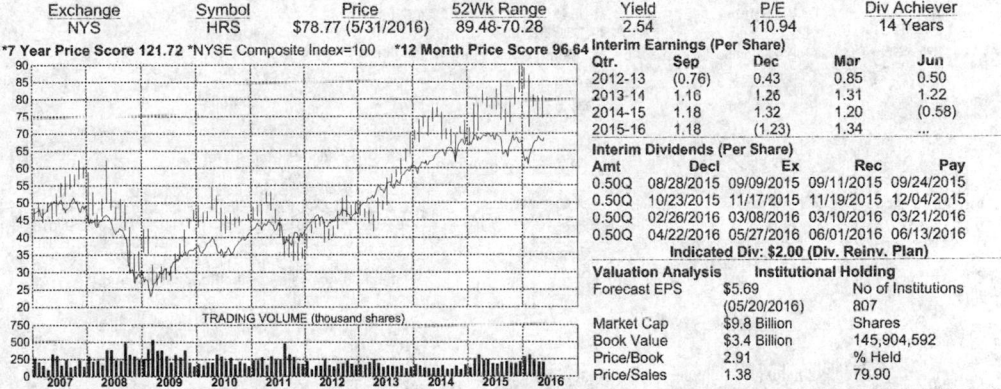

Exchange	Symbol	Price	52Wk Range	Yield	P/E	Div Achiever
NYS	HRS	$78.77 (5/31/2016)	89.48-70.28	2.54	110.94	14 Years

*7 Year Price Score 121.72 *NYSE Composite Index=100   *12 Month Price Score 96.64

Interim Earnings (Per Share)

Qtr.	Sep	Dec	Mar	Jun
2012-13	(0.76)	0.43	0.85	0.50
2013-14	1.16	1.26	1.31	1.22
2014-15	1.18	1.32	1.20	(0.58)
2015-16	1.18	(1.23)	1.34	...

Interim Dividends (Per Share)

Amt	Decl	Ex	Rec	Pay
0.50Q	08/28/2015	09/09/2015	09/11/2015	09/24/2015
0.50Q	10/23/2015	11/17/2015	11/19/2015	12/04/2015
0.50Q	02/26/2016	03/08/2016	03/10/2016	03/21/2016
0.50Q	04/22/2016	05/27/2016	06/01/2016	06/13/2016

Indicated Div: $2.00 (Div. Reinv. Plan)

Valuation Analysis

Forecast EPS $5.69 (05/20/2016)
Market Cap $9.8 Billion
Book Value $3.4 Billion
Price/Book 2.91
Price/Sales 1.38

Institutional Holding

No of Institutions 807
Shares 145,904,592
% Held 79.90

TRADING VOLUME (thousand shares)

Business Summary: Defense (MIC: 7.1.2 SIC: 3812 NAIC: 339111)

Harris has four segments: RF communications, which supplies tactical radio communications and encryption solutions and also of communications systems and equipment for public safety, utility and transportation customers; government communications systems, which conducts research studies, develops prototypes, and produces spaceborne, airborne and terrestrial communications and information processing systems; integrated network solutions, which provides integrated communications and information technology and services; and Exelis, which provides positioning and navigation, sensors, air traffic management solutions, image processing and distribution, communications and information systems.

Recent Developments: For the quarter ended Apr 1 2016, income from continuing operations increased 34.9% to US$170.0 million from US$126.0 million in the year-earlier quarter. Net income increased 33.3% to US$168.0 million from US$126.0 million in the year-earlier quarter. Revenues were US$1.91 billion, up 60.8% from US$1.19 billion the year before. Direct operating expenses rose 74.0% to US$1.31 billion from US$754.0 million in the comparable period the year before. Indirect operating expenses increased 40.9% to US$310.0 million from US$220.0 million in the equivalent prior-year period.

Prospects: Our evaluation of Harris Corp. as of June 19, 2016 is the result of our systematic analysis on three basic characteristics: earnings strength, relative valuation, and recent stock price movement. The company has managed to produce a neutral trend in earnings per share over the past 5 quarters and while recent estimates for the company have been mixed, HRS has posted better than expected results. Based on operating earnings yield, the company is undervalued when compared to all of the companies in our coverage universe. Share price changes over the past year indicates that HRS will perform in line with the market over the near term.

Financial Data

(US$ in Thousands)	9 Mos	6 Mos	3 Mos	07/03/2015	06/27/2014	06/28/2013	06/29/2012	07/01/2011
Earnings Per Share	0.71	0.57	3.12	3.11	4.95	1.01	0.26	4.60
Cash Flow Per Share	7.79	8.23	6.78	7.95	8.03	7.56	7.49	6.67
Dividends Per Share	1.970	1.940	1.910	1.880	1.680	1.480	1.220	1.000
Dividend Payout %	277.46	340.35	61.22	60.45	33.94	146.53	469.23	21.74
Income Statement								
Total Revenue	5,563,000	3,654,000	1,811,000	5,083,000	5,012,000	5,111,700	5,451,300	5,924,600
EBITDA	746,000	384,000	346,000	760,000	1,028,300	917,800	1,095,200	1,103,700
Depn & Amortn	240,000	165,000	83,000	155,000	142,100	146,400	143,000	135,400
Income Before Taxes	368,000	127,000	216,000	477,000	795,400	664,500	841,500	880,700
Income Taxes	185,000	114,000	68,000	143,000	256,200	202,700	286,000	293,600
Net Income	164,000	(4,000)	148,000	334,000	534,800	113,000	30,600	588,000
Average Shares	125,100	123,800	124,700	106,800	107,300	111,200	114,800	126,300
Balance Sheet								
Current Assets	2,866,000	2,835,000	3,053,000	3,524,000	1,991,300	1,948,100	2,600,400	2,216,800
Total Assets	11,900,000	12,097,000	12,564,000	13,129,000	4,931,200	4,858,400	5,592,800	6,172,800
Current Liabilities	2,012,000	2,139,000	1,871,000	2,281,000	1,114,600	1,297,400	1,414,400	1,430,500
Long-Term Obligations	4,319,000	4,443,000	4,901,000	5,053,000	1,575,800	1,577,100	1,883,000	1,887,200
Total Liabilities	8,534,000	8,846,000	9,102,000	9,732,000	3,105,200	3,297,100	3,653,900	3,670,800
Stockholders' Equity	3,366,000	3,251,000	3,462,000	3,397,000	1,826,000	1,561,300	1,938,900	2,502,000
Shares Outstanding	124,481	124,411	124,168	123,675	105,509	106,933	112,147	123,118
Statistical Record								
Return on Assets %	1.29	0.77	4.10	3.64	10.96	2.17	0.52	10.81
Return on Equity %	4.14	2.58	13.58	12.58	31.66	6.47	1.38	25.13
EBITDA Margin %	13.41	10.51	19.11	14.95	20.52	17.95	20.09	18.63
Net Margin %	2.95	N.M.	8.17	6.57	10.67	2.21	0.56	9.92
Asset Turnover	0.85	0.75	0.66	0.55	1.03	0.98	0.93	1.09
Current Ratio	1.42	1.33	1.63	1.54	1.79	1.50	1.84	1.55
Debt to Equity	1.28	1.37	1.42	1.49	0.86	1.01	0.97	0.75
Price Range	89.48-70.28	89.48-67.13	84.59-61.52	82.46-61.52	77.55-49.08	51.97-39.95	45.70-33.23	53.13-41.09
P/E Ratio	126.03-98.99	156.98-117.77	27.11-19.72	26.51-19.78	15.67-9.92	51.46-39.55	175.77-127.81	11.55-8.93
Average Yield %	2.48	2.49	2.55	2.57	2.54	3.14	3.08	2.16

Address: 1025 West NASA Boulevard, Melbourne, FL 32919 **Telephone:** 321-727-9100	**Web Site:** www.harris.com **Officers:** William M. Brown - Chairman, President, Chief Executive Officer Robert L. Duffy - Senior Vice President	**Auditors:** Ernst & Young LLP **Investor Contact:** 321-727-9383 **Transfer Agents:** Computershare, Canton, MA

Exchange	Symbol	Price	52Wk Range	Yield	P/E
NYS	HIG	$45.17 (5/31/2016)	49.53-37.63	1.86	12.31

*7 Year Price Score 128.36 ***NYSE Composite Index=100** ***12 Month Price Score 99.83**

Interim Earnings (Per Share)

Qtr.	Mar	Jun	Sep	Dec
2013	(0.58)	(0.42)	0.60	0.67
2014	1.03	(1.00)	0.86	0.84
2015	1.08	0.96	0.90	1.02
2016	0.79			

Interim Dividends (Per Share)

Amt	Decl	Ex	Rec	Pay
0.21Q	07/27/2015	08/28/2015	09/01/2015	10/01/2015
0.21Q	10/22/2015	11/27/2015	12/01/2015	01/04/2016
0.21Q	02/25/2016	03/03/2016	03/07/2016	04/01/2016
0.21Q	05/19/2016	05/27/2016	06/01/2016	07/01/2016

Indicated Div: $0.84

Valuation Analysis / Institutional Holding

Forecast EPS	$3.90 (05/20/2016)	No of Institutions 938
Market Cap	$17.9 Billion	Shares 432,511,296
Book Value	$18.1 Billion	% Held 84.97
Price/Book	0.99	
Price/Sales	0.98	

Business Summary: General Insurance (MIC: 5.2.1 SIC: 6331 NAIC: 524210)

Hartford Financial Services Group is a holding company. Through its subsidiaries, Co. is a provider of property and casualty insurance, group life and disability products and mutual funds. Co. has six segments: Commercial Lines, which provides workers' compensation, property, automobile, liability, umbrella, marine and livestock insurance products; Personal Lines, which provides automobile, homeowners and personal umbrella coverages; Property & Casualty Other Operations; Group Benefits, which provides group life, accident and disability coverage and group retiree health benefits to members of employer groups, associations, and affinity groups; Mutual Funds; and Talcott Resolution.

Recent Developments: For the quarter ended Mar 31 2016, net income decreased 30.8% to US$323.0 million from US$467.0 million in the year-earlier quarter. Revenues were US$4.39 billion, down 4.9% from US$4.62 billion the year before. Net premiums earned were US$3.40 billion versus US$3.32 billion in the prior-year quarter, an increase of 2.5%. Net investment income fell 14.0% to US$696.0 million from US$809.0 million a year ago.

Prospects: Our evaluation of Hartford Financial Services Group Inc. as of June 19, 2016 is the result of our systematic analysis on three basic characteristics: earnings strength, relative valuation, and recent stock price movement. The company has generated a negative trend in earnings per share over the past 5 quarters. However, while recent estimates for the company have been lowered by analysts, HIG has posted results that fell short of analysts expectations. Based on operating earnings yield, the company is undervalued when compared to all of the companies in our coverage universe. Share price changes over the past year indicates that HIG will perform well over the near term.

Financial Data
(US$ in Thousands)

	3 Mos	12/31/2015	12/31/2014	12/31/2013	12/31/2012	12/31/2011	12/31/2010	12/31/2009
Earnings Per Share	3.67	3.96	1.73	0.34	(0.18)	1.30	2.49	(2.93)
Cash Flow Per Share	6.79	6.63	4.27	2.76	6.11	5.11	7.67	8.59
Tang Book Value Per Share	44.52	42.67	42.93	40.61	48.67	48.24	42.07	35.77
Dividends Per Share	0.810	0.780	0.660	0.500	0.400	0.400	0.200	0.200
Dividend Payout %	22.07	19.70	38.15	147.06	...	30.77	8.03	...
Income Statement								
Premium Income	3,404,000	13,577,000	13,336,000	13,226,000	13,631,000	14,088,000	14,055,000	14,424,000
Total Revenue	4,391,000	18,377,000	18,614,000	26,236,000	26,412,000	21,859,000	22,383,000	24,701,000
Income Before Taxes	381,000	1,978,000	1,699,000	63,000	(527,000)	230,000	2,264,000	(1,728,000)
Income Taxes	58,000	305,000	350,000	(247,000)	(494,000)	(346,000)	584,000	(841,000)
Net Income	323,000	1,682,000	798,000	176,000	(38,000)	662,000	1,680,000	(887,000)
Average Shares	406,300	425,200	460,200	484,400	437,700	478,000	481,500	346,300
Balance Sheet								
Total Assets	227,493,000	228,348,000	245,013,000	277,884,000	298,513,000	304,064,000	318,346,000	307,717,000
Total Liabilities	209,381,000	210,706,000	226,293,000	258,979,000	276,066,000	281,154,000	298,035,000	289,852,000
Stockholders' Equity	18,112,000	17,642,000	18,720,000	18,905,000	22,447,000	22,910,000	20,311,000	17,865,000
Shares Outstanding	395,603	401,821	424,415	453,290	436,305	442,539	444,549	383,007
Statistical Record								
Return on Assets %	0.65	0.71	0.31	0.06	N.M.	0.21	0.54	N.M.
Return on Equity %	8.27	9.25	4.24	0.85	N.M.	3.06	8.80	N.M.
Net Margin %	7.36	9.15	4.29	0.67	(0.14)	3.03	7.51	(3.59)
Price Range	49.53-37.63	49.53-38.90	42.27-32.18	36.62-22.44	22.88-15.93	30.80-14.92	29.64-19.09	29.20-3.62
P/E Ratio	13.50-10.25	12.51-9.82	24.43-18.60	107.71-66.00	...	23.69-11.48	11.90-7.67	...
Average Yield %	1.84	1.78	1.81	1.68	2.07	1.73	0.81	1.17

Address: One Hartford Plaza, Hartford, CT 06155
Telephone: 860-547-5000

Web Site: www.thehartford.com
Officers: Christopher J. Swift - Chairman, Chief Executive Officer, Executive Vice President, Chief Financial Officer, Principal Accounting Officer Douglas G. Elliot - President, Executive Vice President, Division Officer

Auditors: Deloitte & Touche LLP
Investor Contact: 860-547-8691
Transfer Agents: BNY Mellon Shareowner Services, Jersey City, NY

HAWAIIAN ELECTRIC INDUSTRIES INC

Exchange	Symbol	Price	52Wk Range	Yield	P/E
NYS	HE	$32.83 (5/31/2016)	33.98-27.23	3.78	22.03

*7 Year Price Score 99.44   *NYSE Composite Index=100   *12 Month Price Score 107.91

Interim Earnings (Per Share)

Qtr.	Mar	Jun	Sep	Dec
2013	0.34	0.41	0.48	0.39
2014	0.45	0.41	0.46	0.32
2015	0.31	0.33	0.47	0.39
2016	0.30	...	...	...

Interim Dividends (Per Share)

Amt	Decl	Ex	Rec	Pay
0.31Q	08/07/2015	08/20/2015	08/24/2015	09/10/2015
0.31Q	11/04/2015	11/19/2015	11/23/2015	12/10/2015
0.31Q	02/10/2016	02/18/2016	02/22/2016	03/10/2016
0.31Q	05/03/2016	05/26/2016	05/31/2016	06/15/2016

Indicated Div: $1.24

Valuation Analysis / **Institutional Holding**

Forecast EPS	$1.70	No of Institutions	
	(05/20/2016)	314	
Market Cap	$3.5 Billion	Shares	
Book Value	$2.0 Billion	50,635,304	
Price/Book	1.79	% Held	
Price/Sales	1.41	42.13	

Business Summary: Electric Utilities (MIC: 3.1.1 SIC: 4911 NAIC: 221122)

Hawaiian Electric Industries is a holding company. Through its subsidiaries, Co. is engaged in electric utility and banking businesses. Co.'s subsidiary, Hawaiian Electric Company, Inc., and its subsidiaries, Hawaii Electric Light Company, Inc. and Maui Electric Company, Limited, are regulated electric public utilities engaged in the production, purchase, transmission, distribution and sale of electricity. In addition, Co.'s subsidiary, American Savings Bank, F.S.B. is engaged in the origination, purchase and sale of loans, residential mortgage lending, construction and development lending, multifamily residential and commercial real estate lending, consumer lending and commercial lending.

Recent Developments: For the quarter ended Mar 31 2016, net income increased 1.5% to US$32.8 million from US$32.3 million in the year-earlier quarter. Revenues were US$551.0 million, down 13.6% from US$637.9 million the year before. Operating income was US$68.9 million versus US$69.5 million in the prior-year quarter, a decrease of 0.9%. Direct operating expenses declined 15.2% to US$482.1 million from US$568.4 million in the comparable period the year before.

Prospects: Our evaluation of Hawaiian Electric Industries Inc. as of June 19, 2016 is the result of our systematic analysis on three basic characteristics: earnings strength, relative valuation, and recent stock price movement. The company has managed to produce a neutral trend in earnings per share over the past 5 quarters and while recent estimates for the company have been mixed, HE has posted results that fell short of analysts expectations. Based on operating earnings yield, the company is about fairly valued when compared to all of the companies in our coverage universe. Share price changes over the past year indicates that HE will perform well over the near term.

Financial Data

(US$ in Thousands)	3 Mos	12/31/2015	12/31/2014	12/31/2013	12/31/2012	12/31/2011	12/31/2010	12/31/2009
Earnings Per Share	1.49	1.50	1.64	1.62	1.42	1.44	1.21	0.91
Cash Flow Per Share	4.18	3.34	2.96	3.31	2.41	2.62	3.65	3.11
Tang Book Value Per Share	17.56	17.49	17.00	16.58	15.79	15.45	15.16	14.69
Dividends Per Share	1.240	1.240	1.240	1.240	1.240	1.240	1.240	1.240
Dividend Payout %	83.22	82.67	75.61	76.54	87.32	86.11	102.48	136.26
Income Statement								
Total Revenue	550,960	2,602,982	3,239,542	3,238,470	3,374,995	3,242,335	2,664,982	2,309,590
EBITDA	121,112	513,447	508,457	481,041	441,592	443,812	416,750	351,168
Depn & Amortn	50,522	183,966	172,762	160,061	150,389	148,152	154,523	151,282
Income Before Taxes	51,126	254,788	261,922	247,747	217,407	216,052	183,247	128,824
Income Taxes	18,301	93,021	91,712	84,341	76,859	75,932	67,822	43,923
Net Income	32,825	161,767	170,210	163,406	140,548	140,120	115,425	83,011
Average Shares	107,781	106,721	102,937	99,623	97,338	95,820	93,693	91,516
Balance Sheet								
Current Assets	556,241	553,922	558,540	659,367	678,507	712,351	695,411	842,802
Total Assets	11,870,506	11,790,196	11,184,161	10,340,044	10,149,132	9,592,731	9,085,344	8,925,002
Current Liabilities	5,382,595	5,292,882	4,954,148	4,717,006	4,552,246	4,380,070	4,230,555	4,287,743
Long-Term Obligations	1,907,699	1,915,128	1,797,202	1,737,459	1,618,798	1,573,299	1,602,261	1,662,443
Total Liabilities	9,894,034	9,828,263	9,358,440	8,578,681	8,520,974	8,026,489	7,567,414	7,483,354
Stockholders' Equity	1,976,472	1,961,933	1,825,721	1,761,363	1,628,158	1,566,242	1,517,930	1,441,648
Shares Outstanding	107,875	107,460	102,565	101,259	97,928	96,038	94,690	92,520
Statistical Record								
Return on Assets %	1.40	1.41	1.58	1.60	1.42	1.50	1.28	0.91
Return on Equity %	8.30	8.54	9.49	9.64	8.78	9.09	7.80	5.79
EBITDA Margin %	21.98	19.73	15.70	14.85	13.08	13.69	15.64	15.20
Net Margin %	5.96	6.21	5.25	5.05	4.16	4.32	4.33	3.59
Asset Turnover	0.22	0.23	0.30	0.32	0.34	0.35	0.30	0.25
Current Ratio	0.10	0.10	0.11	0.14	0.15	0.16	0.16	0.20
Debt to Equity	0.97	0.98	0.98	0.99	0.99	1.00	1.06	1.15
Price Range	32.64-27.23	34.83-27.23	34.62-23.22	28.30-23.97	29.24-24.00	26.75-21.06	24.75-18.78	22.46-12.24
P/E Ratio	21.91-18.28	23.22-18.15	21.11-14.16	17.47-14.80	20.59-16.90	18.58-14.62	20.45-15.52	24.68-13.45
Average Yield %	4.16	4.05	4.77	4.72	4.69	5.04	5.52	6.88

Address: 1001 Bishop Streetm Suite 2900, Honolulu, HI 96813
Telephone: 808-543-5662
Fax: 808-543-7966

Web Site: www.hei.com
Officers: Jeffrey N. Watanabe - Chairman Constance H. Lau - President, Chief Executive Officer

Auditors: PricewaterhouseCoopers LLP
Investor Contact: 808-543-7384
Transfer Agents: Continental Stock Transfer & Trust Company, New York, NY

HCA HOLDINGS INC

Exchange	Symbol	Price	52Wk Range	Yield	P/E
NYS	HCA	$78.02 (5/31/2016)	94.81-62.83	N/A	14.69

*7 Year Price Score N/A   *NYSE Composite Index=100   *12 Month Price Score 101.92

TRADING VOLUME (thousand shares)

Interim Earnings (Per Share)

Qtr.	Mar	Jun	Sep	Dec
2013	0.74	0.91	0.79	0.93
2014	0.76	1.07	1.16	1.18
2015	1.36	1.18	1.05	1.39
2016	1.69	...	...	...

Interim Dividends (Per Share)

Amt	Decl	Ex	Rec	Pay
2.00U	02/06/2012	02/14/2012	02/16/2012	02/29/2012
2.50U	10/23/2012	10/31/2012	11/02/2012	11/16/2012
2.00U	12/06/2012	12/13/2012	12/17/2012	12/21/2012

Valuation Analysis   Institutional Holding

Forecast EPS	$6.53	No of Institutions	
	(05/20/2016)	753	
Market Cap	$30.7 Billion	Shares	
Book Value	N/A	313,804,352	
Price/Book	N/A	% Held	
Price/Sales	0.76	N/A	

Business Summary: Hospitals & Health Care Facilities (MIC: 4.2.1 SIC: 8062 NAIC: 622110)

HCA Holdings is a holding company. Through its subsidiaries, partnerships and joint ventures, Co. owns, manages or operates hospitals, freestanding surgery centers, freestanding emergency care facilities, urgent care facilities, walk-in clinics, diagnostic and imaging centers, radiation and oncology therapy centers, rehabilitation and physical therapy centers, physician practices and various other facilities. At Dec 31 2015, Co. operated three psychiatric hospitals with 396 licensed beds. Co.'s psychiatric hospitals provide therapeutic programs including child, adolescent and adult psychiatric care, adult and adolescent alcohol and drug abuse treatment and counseling.

Recent Developments: For the quarter ended Mar 31 2016, net income increased 12.6% to US$811.0 million from US$720.0 million in the year-earlier quarter. Revenues were US$10.26 billion, up 6.0% from US$9.68 billion the year before. Indirect operating expenses increased 6.6% to US$9.17 billion from US$8.60 billion in the equivalent prior-year period.

Prospects: Our evaluation of HCA Holdings, Inc. as of June 19, 2016 is the result of our systematic analysis on three basic characteristics: earnings strength, relative valuation, and recent stock price movement. The company has produced a positive trend in earnings per share over the past 5 quarters and while recent estimates for the company have been mixed, HCA has posted better than expected results. Based on operating earnings yield, the company is undervalued when compared to all of the companies in our coverage universe. Share price changes over the past year indicates that HCA will perform in line with the market over the near term.

Financial Data
(US$ in Millions)

	3 Mos	12/31/2015	12/31/2014	12/31/2013	12/31/2012	12/31/2011	12/31/2010	12/31/2009
Earnings Per Share	5.31	4.99	4.16	3.37	3.49	4.97	2.76	2.44
Cash Flow Per Share	12.90	11.43	10.21	8.27	9.46	8.25	7.23	6.45
Dividends Per Share	...	...	...	...	6.500	...	9.430	...
Dividend Payout %	...	...	...	...	186.25	...	341.67	...
Income Statement								
Total Revenue	10,260	39,678	36,918	34,182	33,013	29,682	30,683	30,052
EBITDA	1,988	7,456	6,979	6,498	6,329	6,801	5,462	5,162
Depn & Amortn	489	1,880	1,798	1,733	1,673	1,461	1,416	1,419
Income Before Taxes	1,083	3,911	3,438	2,917	2,858	3,303	1,949	1,756
Income Taxes	284	1,261	1,108	950	888	719	658	627
Net Income	694	2,129	1,875	1,556	1,605	2,465	1,207	1,054
Average Shares	410	426	450	461	459	495	437	432
Balance Sheet								
Current Assets	9,201	9,232	8,930	8,037	7,763	7,233	6,919	6,577
Total Assets	32,776	32,744	31,199	28,831	28,075	26,898	23,852	24,131
Current Liabilities	5,398	5,516	5,480	5,695	6,172	5,554	4,269	4,313
Long-Term Obligations	30,328	30,255	29,307	27,590	27,495	25,645	27,633	24,824
Total Liabilities	40,332	40,343	39,093	37,101	37,735	35,156	35,778	33,117
Stockholders' Equity	(7,556)	(7,599)	(7,894)	(8,270)	(9,660)	(8,258)	(11,926)	(8,986)
Shares Outstanding	393	398	420	439	443	437	427	426
Statistical Record								
Return on Assets %	6.97	6.66	6.25	5.47	5.82	9.71	5.03	...
EBITDA Margin %	19.38	18.79	18.90	19.01	19.17	22.91	17.80	17.18
Net Margin %	6.76	5.37	5.08	4.55	4.86	8.30	3.93	3.51
Asset Turnover	1.26	1.24	1.23	1.20	1.20	1.17	1.28	...
Current Ratio	1.70	1.67	1.63	1.41	1.26	1.30	1.62	1.52
Price Range	94.81-62.83	94.81-64.47	75.00-47.65	48.54-30.17	33.87-20.80	35.24-17.66	...	...
P/E Ratio	17.85-11.83	19.00-12.92	18.03-11.45	14.40-8.95	9.70-5.96	7.09-3.55	...	...
Average Yield %	...	...	...	...	23.25	...	...	...

Address: One Park Plaza, Nashville, TN 37203	**Web Site:** www.hcahealthcare.com	**Auditors:** Ernst & Young LLP
Telephone: 615-344-9551	**Officers:** R. Milton Johnson - Chairman, President, Chief Executive Officer - Designate, Chief Financial Officer Richard M. Bracken - Chairman, Chief Executive Officer	**Investor Contact:** 615-344-2688
		Transfer Agents: Wells Fargo Shareowner Services, St. Paul, MN

HCP, INC.

Exchange	Symbol	Price	52Wk Range	Yield	P/E	Div Achiever
NYS	HCP	$32.87 (5/31/2016)	40.72-26.13	7.00	N/A	30 Years

*7 Year Price Score 79.74 *NYSE Composite Index=100 *12 Month Price Score 93.69

Interim Earnings (Per Share)

Qtr.	Mar	Jun	Sep	Dec
2013	0.51	0.47	0.51	0.64
2014	0.56	0.40	0.54	0.42
2015	(0.52)	0.36	0.25	(1.29)
2016	0.25	...	...	...

Interim Dividends (Per Share)

Amt	Decl	Ex	Rec	Pay
0.565Q	07/30/2015	08/06/2015	08/10/2015	08/25/2015
0.565Q	10/29/2015	11/05/2015	11/09/2015	11/24/2015
0.575Q	01/28/2016	02/04/2016	02/08/2016	02/23/2016
0.575Q	04/27/2016	05/05/2016	05/09/2016	05/24/2016

Indicated Div: $2.30 (Div. Reinv. Plan)

Valuation Analysis

		Institutional Holding	
Forecast EPS	$1.40	No of Institutions	
	(05/20/2016)	890	
Market Cap	$15.3 Billion	Shares	
Book Value	$9.2 Billion	465,498,368	
Price/Book	1.66	% Held	
Price/Sales	5.96	N/A	

Business Summary: REITs (MIC: 5.3.1 SIC: 6798 NAIC: 525930)

HCP is a real estate investment trust, which, together with its consolidated entities, invests primarily in real estate serving the healthcare industry in the U.S. Co. acquires, develops, leases, manages and disposes of healthcare real estate and provides financing to healthcare providers. Co.'s portfolio is comprised of investments in the following healthcare segments: senior housing; post-acute/skilled nursing; life science; medical office; and hospital. At Dec 31 2015, Co. had interests in 528 senior housing facilities, including 22 properties owned by Co.'s unconsolidated joint ventures, 311 post-acute/skilled nursing, 118 life science, 272 medical office, and 16 hospital.

Recent Developments: For the quarter ended Mar 31 2016, net income amounted to US$119.7 million versus a net loss of US$237.5 million in the year-earlier quarter. Revenues were US$640.8 million, up 4.9% from US$610.8 million the year before. Revenues from property income rose 20.7% to US$494.7 million from US$410.0 million in the corresponding quarter a year earlier.

Prospects: Our evaluation of HCP Inc. as of June 19, 2016 is the result of our systematic analysis on three basic characteristics: earnings strength, relative valuation, and recent stock price movement. The company has generated a negative trend in earnings per share over the past 5 quarters. Because the company lacks sufficient analyst estimate data, we place greater weight on the historical EPS trend as the measure of earnings strength. Based on operating earnings yield, the company is about fairly valued when compared to all of the companies in our coverage universe. Share price changes over the past year indicates that HCP will perform poorly over the near term.

Financial Data

(US$ in Thousands)	3 Mos	12/31/2015	12/31/2014	12/31/2013	12/31/2012	12/31/2011	12/31/2010	12/31/2009
Earnings Per Share	(0.43)	(1.21)	2.00	2.13	1.90	1.29	1.00	0.40
Cash Flow Per Share	2.70	2.64	2.72	2.53	2.42	1.82	1.90	1.88
Tang Book Value Per Share	18.41	18.65	22.19	22.28	21.95	20.37	19.70	17.22
Dividends Per Share	2.270	2.260	2.180	2.100	2.000	1.920	1.860	1.840
Dividend Payout %	...	...	109.00	98.59	105.26	148.84	186.00	460.00
Income Statement								
Total Revenue	640,782	2,544,312	2,266,279	2,099,878	1,900,722	1,725,386	1,255,134	1,157,030
EBITDA	305,910	(88,546)	1,332,231	1,280,621	1,171,691	919,658	671,199	388,871
Depn & Amortn	10,157	(1,295)	(949)	(6,646)	(2,232)	(4,510)	(6,378)	(14,780)
Income Before Taxes	173,691	(566,847)	893,438	852,015	756,793	504,831	388,927	104,754
Income Taxes	53,038	(9,011)	250	5,815	(1,636)	1,249	412	1,924
Net Income	116,119	(559,235)	922,233	970,837	832,540	538,891	330,709	146,151
Average Shares	466,262	462,795	458,796	455,702	428,316	400,218	306,900	274,631
Balance Sheet								
Current Assets	186,169	456,045	269,125	365,279	319,671	101,740	1,107,524	188,985
Total Assets	21,199,927	21,449,849	21,369,940	20,075,870	19,915,555	17,408,475	13,331,923	12,209,735
Current Liabilities	433,144	511,512	517,657	417,237	399,903	399,620	461,878	509,856
Long-Term Obligations	10,935,944	11,069,003	9,759,773	8,661,627	8,693,820	7,722,619	4,646,345	5,656,143
Total Liabilities	11,969,180	12,106,206	10,634,643	9,352,570	9,364,318	8,374,993	5,374,556	6,429,198
Stockholders' Equity	9,230,747	9,343,643	10,735,297	10,723,300	10,551,237	9,033,482	7,957,367	5,780,537
Shares Outstanding	466,924	465,488	459,746	456,960	453,191	408,629	370,924	293,548
Statistical Record								
Return on Assets %	N.M.	N.M.	4.45	4.86	4.45	3.51	2.59	1.21
Return on Equity %	N.M.	N.M.	8.60	9.13	8.48	6.34	4.81	2.66
EBITDA Margin %	47.74	N.M.	58.78	60.99	61.64	53.30	53.48	33.61
Net Margin %	18.12	N.M.	40.69	46.23	43.80	31.23	26.35	12.63
Asset Turnover	0.12	0.12	0.11	0.11	0.10	0.11	0.10	0.10
Current Ratio	0.43	0.89	0.52	0.88	0.80	0.25	2.40	0.37
Debt to Equity	1.18	1.18	0.91	0.81	0.82	0.85	0.58	0.98
Price Range	44.59-26.13	48.21-32.75	45.58-36.18	55.28-35.66	47.21-37.87	41.76-28.77	37.97-27.06	32.84-16.08
P/E Ratio	...	...	22.79-18.09	25.95-16.74	24.85-19.93	32.37-22.30	37.97-27.06	82.10-40.20
Average Yield %	6.14	5.70	5.30	4.68	4.65	5.19	5.60	7.43

Address: 1920 Main Street, Suite 1200, Irvine, CA 92614
Telephone: 949-407-0700
Fax: 562-733-5200

Web Site: www.hcpi.com
Officers: Lauralee E. Martin - President, Chief Executive Officer J. Justin Hutchens - Executive Vice President, Chief Investment Officer

Auditors: Deloitte & Touche LLP
Investor Contact: 562-733-5309
Transfer Agents: Wells Fargo Shareowner Services, Saint Paul, MN

HEALTHCARE TRUST OF AMERICA INC

Exchange	Symbol	Price	52Wk Range	Yield	P/E
NYS	HTA	$30.18 (5/31/2016)	30.76-22.69	3.91	107.79

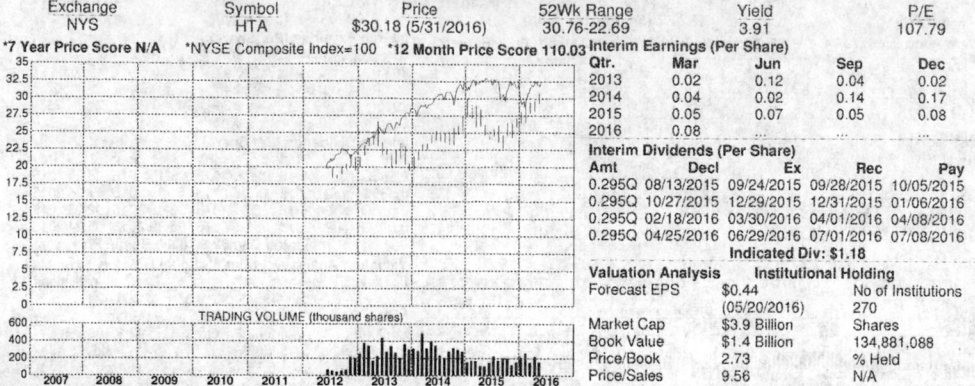

*7 Year Price Score N/A   *NYSE Composite Index=100   *12 Month Price Score 110.03

Interim Earnings (Per Share)

Qtr.	Mar	Jun	Sep	Dec
2013	0.02	0.12	0.04	0.02
2014	0.04	0.02	0.14	0.17
2015	0.05	0.07	0.05	0.08
2016	0.08			

Interim Dividends (Per Share)

Amt	Decl	Ex	Rec	Pay
0.295Q	08/13/2015	09/24/2015	09/28/2015	10/05/2015
0.295Q	10/27/2015	12/29/2015	12/31/2015	01/06/2016
0.295Q	02/18/2016	03/30/2016	04/01/2016	04/08/2016
0.295Q	04/25/2016	06/29/2016	07/01/2016	07/08/2016

Indicated Div: $1.18

Valuation Analysis

Valuation Analysis		Institutional Holding	
Forecast EPS	$0.44	No of Institutions	
	(05/20/2016)	270	
Market Cap	$3.9 Billion	Shares	
Book Value	$1.4 Billion	134,881,088	
Price/Book	2.73	% Held	
Price/Sales	9.56	N/A	

Business Summary: REITs (MIC: 5.3.1 SIC: 6798 NAIC: 525930)

Healthcare Trust of America is a real estate investment trust. Co. is an owner and operator of medical office buildings (MOBs) in the U.S. As of Dec 31 2014, Co.'s portfolio consisted of 74 single-tenant MOBs, 206 multi-tenant MOBs, 10 hospitals and nine senior care facilities. Co.'s properties are primarily located on the campuses of, or aligned with healthcare systems in the U.S. As of Dec 31 2014, Co.'s portfolio was concentrated in following key markets: Boston, MA; Dallas, TX; Phoenix, AZ; Albany, NY; Greenville, SC; Miami, FL; Houston, TX; Pittsburgh, PA; Atlanta, GA; Tampa, FL; Indianapolis, IN; Denver, CO; White Plains, NY; Orlando, FL; Raleigh, NC and Charleston, SC.

Recent Developments: For the quarter ended Mar 31 2016, net income increased 44.6% to US$10.0 million from US$6.9 million in the year-earlier quarter. Revenues were US$107.3 million, up 8.9% from US$98.5 million the year before. Revenues from property income rose 8.9% to US$107.3 million from US$98.5 million in the corresponding quarter a year earlier.

Prospects: Our evaluation of Healthcare Trust Of America as of June 19, 2016 is the result of our systematic analysis on three basic characteristics: earnings strength, relative valuation, and recent stock price movement. The company has produced a positive trend in earnings per share over the past 5 quarters and while recent estimates for the company have been mixed, HTA has posted results that fell short of analysts expectations. Based on operating earnings yield, the company is overvalued when compared to all of the companies in our coverage universe. Share price changes over the past year indicates that HTA will perform well over the near term.

Financial Data

(US$ in Thousands)	3 Mos	12/31/2015	12/31/2014	12/31/2013	12/31/2012	12/31/2011	12/31/2010	12/31/2009
Earnings Per Share	0.28	0.26	0.37	0.20	(0.22)	0.04	(0.10)	(0.44)
Cash Flow Per Share	1.50	1.52	1.41	1.30	1.05	1.00	0.71	0.38
Tang Book Value Per Share	10.72	10.53	11.22	11.29	9.05	11.33	11.67	...
Dividends Per Share	1.175	1.170	0.290	...	...	...	...	...
Dividend Payout %	419.64	450.00	78.38	...	...	...	...	...
Income Statement								
Total Revenue	107,315	403,822	371,505	319,899	299,644	274,438	203,081	129,486
EBITDA	61,900	244,047	246,753	820,036	100,625	112,877	70,332	31,289
Depn & Amortn	37,091	151,614	140,400	755,000	72,000	65,566	48,829	32,487
Income Before Taxes	10,036	33,557	45,994	23,577	(24,368)	5,593	(7,919)	(24,773)
Net Income	9,860	32,931	45,371	24,261	(24,424)	5,541	(7,903)	(25,077)
Average Shares	131,240	128,004	121,168	114,969	111,356	112,195	82,976	56,409
Balance Sheet								
Current Assets	30,514	170,665	175,318	145,532	46,896	98,867	72,334	...
Total Assets	3,310,519	3,172,300	3,041,650	2,752,334	2,414,090	2,291,629	2,271,795	...
Current Liabilities	85,453	94,933	101,042	82,893	63,443	47,801	43,033	...
Long-Term Obligations	1,667,320	1,590,696	1,412,461	1,214,241	1,037,359	639,149	706,526	...
Total Liabilities	1,866,406	1,792,876	1,594,511	1,365,128	1,159,824	724,289	784,549	...
Stockholders' Equity	1,444,113	1,379,424	1,447,139	1,387,206	1,254,266	1,567,340	1,487,246	...
Shares Outstanding	130,662	127,026	125,087	118,440	107,326	114,245	101,321	70,295
Statistical Record								
Return on Assets %	1.13	1.06	1.57	0.94	N.M.	0.24	...	...
Return on Equity %	2.51	2.33	3.20	1.84	N.M.	0.36	...	...
EBITDA Margin %	57.68	60.43	66.42	256.34	33.58	41.13	34.63	24.16
Net Margin %	9.19	8.15	12.21	7.58	N.M.	2.02	N.M.	N.M.
Asset Turnover	0.13	0.13	0.13	0.12	0.13	0.12	...	...
Current Ratio	0.36	1.80	1.74	1.76	0.74	2.07	1.68	...
Debt to Equity	1.15	1.15	0.98	0.88	0.83	0.41	0.48	...
Price Range	29.42-22.69	29.94-22.69	27.40-19.66	26.56-19.46	21.78-18.28	...	...	...
P/E Ratio	105.07-81.04	115.15-87.27	74.05-53.14	132.80-97.30	...	...	...	...
Average Yield %	4.53	4.50	1.22	...	...	...	...	...

Address: 16435 North Scottsdale Road, Suite 320, Scottsdale, AZ 85254	Web Site: www.htareit.com	Auditors: Deloitte & Touche LLP
Telephone: 480-998-3478	**Officers:** Scott D. Peters - Chairman, President, Chief Executive Officer Robert A. Milligan - Executive Vice	**Investor Contact:** 480-998-3478
Fax: 480-991-0755	President, Chief Financial Officer, Secretary, Treasurer	**Transfer Agents:** DST Systems, Inc., Kansas City, MO

HELMERICH & PAYNE, INC.

Exchange	Symbol	Price	52Wk Range	Yield	P/E	Div Achiever
NYS	HP	$61.15 (5/31/2016)	75.12-42.85	4.58	62.40	39 Years

*7 Year Price Score 80.98   *NYSE Composite Index=100   *12 Month Price Score 104.87

Interim Earnings (Per Share)

Qtr.	Dec	Mar	Jun	Sep
2012-13	1.48	1.39	2.46	1.46
2013-14	1.59	1.59	1.75	1.54
2014-15	1.85	1.37	0.83	(0.19)
2015-16	0.15	0.19	...	...

Interim Dividends (Per Share)

Amt	Decl	Ex	Rec	Pay
0.688Q	09/02/2015	11/10/2015	11/13/2015	12/01/2015
0.688Q	12/01/2015	02/10/2016	02/15/2016	03/01/2016
0.688Q	03/02/2016	05/11/2016	05/13/2016	06/01/2016
0.70Q	06/01/2016	08/11/2016	08/15/2016	09/01/2016

Indicated Div: $2.80

Valuation Analysis   **Institutional Holding**

Forecast EPS	$-1.15	No of Institutions
	(05/20/2016)	730
Market Cap	$6.6 Billion	Shares
Book Value	$4.8 Billion	136,276,704
Price/Book	1.38	% Held
Price/Sales	3.07	86.76

Business Summary: Production & Extraction (MIC: 9.1.1 SIC: 1381 NAIC: 213111)

Helmerich & Payne is primarily engaged in contract drilling of oil and gas wells for others. Co.'s contract drilling business is composed of three reportable business segments: U.S. Land, Offshore and International Land. Co. is also engaged in the ownership, development and operation of commercial real estate, and through its subsidiary, TerraVici Drilling Solutions, Inc., in the research and development of rotary steerable technology. Each of the businesses operates independently of the others through wholly-owned subsidiaries. Co.'s real estate investments located within Tulsa, OK, include a shopping center, multi-tenant industrial warehouse properties and undeveloped real estate.

Recent Developments: For the quarter ended Mar 31 2016, income from continuing operations decreased 83.6% to US$25.2 million from US$153.5 million in the year-earlier quarter. Net income decreased 86.2% to US$21.2 million from US$153.5 million in the year-earlier quarter. Revenues were US$438.2 million, down 50.5% from US$885.7 million the year before. Operating income was US$41.6 million versus US$231.3 million in the prior-year quarter, a decrease of 82.0%. Direct operating expenses declined 52.6% to US$221.6 million from US$467.1 million in the comparable period the year before. Indirect operating expenses decreased 6.6% to US$175.0 million from US$187.2 million in the equivalent prior-year period.

Prospects: Our evaluation of Helmerich & Payne Inc. as of June 19, 2016 is the result of our systematic analysis on three basic characteristics: earnings strength, relative valuation, and recent stock price movement. The company has enjoyed a very positive trend in earnings per share over the past 5 quarters. Because the company lacks sufficient analyst estimate data, we place greater weight on the historical EPS trend as the measure of earnings strength. Based on operating earnings yield, the company is overvalued when compared to all of the companies in our coverage universe. Share price changes over the past year indicates that HP will perform poorly over the near term.

Financial Data
(US$ in Thousands)

	6 Mos	3 Mos	09/30/2015	09/30/2014	09/30/2013	09/30/2012	09/30/2011	09/30/2010
Earnings Per Share	0.98	2.16	3.87	6.46	6.79	5.34	3.99	1.45
Cash Flow Per Share	10.17	12.40	13.17	10.38	9.38	9.34	9.17	4.37
Tang Book Value Per Share	44.26	44.63	45.44	45.19	41.64	36.28	30.54	26.53
Dividends Per Share	2.750	2.750	2.750	2.438	0.870	0.280	0.250	0.210
Dividend Payout %	280.61	127.31	71.06	37.73	12.81	5.24	6.27	14.48
Income Statement								
Total Revenue	926,038	487,847	3,165,441	3,719,707	3,387,614	3,151,802	2,543,894	1,875,162
EBITDA	364,887	180,793	1,281,841	1,622,934	1,574,396	1,297,402	1,017,939	716,241
Depn & Amortn	284,204	142,384	606,992	523,549	455,623	387,549	315,468	262,658
Income Before Taxes	71,970	34,618	665,647	1,096,314	1,114,297	902,580	687,067	438,236
Income Taxes	30,898	18,720	243,375	387,548	392,844	328,971	252,399	152,155
Net Income	37,207	16,002	422,225	708,719	736,639	581,045	434,186	156,312
Average Shares	108,466	108,409	108,570	109,141	107,879	108,377	108,632	107,404
Balance Sheet								
Current Assets	1,460,377	1,476,676	1,439,007	1,277,366	1,258,211	895,228	956,313	652,804
Total Assets	7,025,105	7,130,274	7,152,012	6,721,861	6,264,827	5,721,085	5,003,891	4,265,370
Current Liabilities	371,328	408,790	351,228	507,526	452,273	381,164	416,729	232,638
Long-Term Obligations	492,919	492,668	492,443	40,000	80,000	195,000	235,000	360,000
Total Liabilities	2,243,005	2,299,981	2,254,560	1,830,884	1,821,100	1,886,087	1,733,844	1,457,905
Stockholders' Equity	4,782,100	4,830,293	4,897,452	4,890,977	4,443,727	3,834,998	3,270,047	2,807,465
Shares Outstanding	108,039	108,232	107,767	108,232	106,716	105,697	107,086	105,819
Statistical Record								
Return on Assets %	1.49	3.38	6.09	10.91	12.29	10.81	9.37	3.71
Return on Equity %	2.18	4.82	8.63	15.18	17.80	16.31	14.29	5.69
EBITDA Margin %	39.40	37.06	40.49	43.63	46.48	41.16	40.01	38.20
Net Margin %	4.02	3.28	13.34	19.05	21.75	18.44	17.07	8.34
Asset Turnover	0.30	0.37	0.46	0.57	0.57	0.59	0.55	0.45
Current Ratio	3.93	3.61	4.10	2.52	2.78	2.35	2.29	2.81
Debt to Equity	0.10	0.10	0.10	0.01	0.02	0.05	0.07	0.13
Price Range	78.47-42.85	78.47-46.50	97.87-46.50	118.29-68.95	70.82-45.22	65.13-37.39	72.60-40.26	48.58-33.42
P/E Ratio	80.07-43.72	36.33-21.53	25.29-12.02	18.31-10.67	10.43-6.66	12.20-7.00	18.20-10.09	33.50-23.05
Average Yield %	4.60	4.38	4.01	2.52	1.44	0.54	0.44	0.52

Address: 1437 South Boulder Avenue, Tulsa, OK 74119	**Web Site:** www.hpinc.com	**Auditors:** Ernst & Young LLP
Telephone: 918-742-5531	**Officers:** Hans Helmerich - Chairman, President, Chief Executive Officer John W. Lindsay - President, Chief Executive Officer, Executive Vice President, Chief Operating Officer	**Investor Contact:** 918-588-5207
Fax: 918-742-0237		**Transfer Agents:** Computershare Investor Services LLC, Providence, RI

HERBALIFE LTD.

Exchange	Symbol	Price	52Wk Range	Yield	P/E
NYS	HLF	$57.89 (5/31/2016)	63.62-43.42	N/A	13.88

*7 Year Price Score 103.07 *NYSE Composite Index=100 *12 Month Price Score 108.01

Interim Earnings (Per Share)

Qtr.	Mar	Jun	Sep	Dec
2013	1.10	1.34	1.32	4.54
2014	0.74	1.31	0.13	1.18
2015	0.92	0.97	1.09	0.98
2016	1.13	...	...	...

Interim Dividends (Per Share)

Dividend Payment Suspended

Valuation Analysis **Institutional Holding**

Forecast EPS	N/A	No of Institutions
		343
Market Cap	$5.4 Billion	Shares
Book Value	$64.9 Million	104,108,720
Price/Book	82.78	% Held
Price/Sales	1.20	81.24

Business Summary: Household & Personal Products (MIC: 1.7.1 SIC: 5122 NAIC: 424210)

Herbalife is a nutrition company. Co. sells its products through a network of independent members. Co. categorizes its products into five groups: weight management, which provides meal replacement, protein shakes, drink mixes, weight loss solutions and healthy snacks; targeted nutrition, which provides dietary and nutritional supplements containing herbs, vitamins, minerals and other natural ingredients; energy, sports and fitness, which provides products for a healthy active lifestyle; outer nutrition, which provides facial skin care, body care, and hair care products; and literature, promotional and other, which provides start-up kits, sales tools, and educational materials.

Recent Developments: For the quarter ended Mar 31 2016, net income increased 22.5% to US$95.8 million from US$78.2 million in the year-earlier quarter. Revenues were US$1.12 billion, up 1.3% from US$1.11 billion the year before. Operating income was US$168.3 million versus US$135.6 million in the prior-year quarter, an increase of 24.1%. Direct operating expenses declined 1.1% to US$213.1 million from US$215.4 million in the comparable period the year before. Indirect operating expenses decreased 2.1% to US$738.2 million from US$754.4 million in the equivalent prior-year period.

Prospects: Our evaluation of Herbalife Ltd. as of Aug. 2, 2015 is the result of our systematic analysis on three basic characteristics: earnings strength, relative valuation, and recent stock price movement. The company has managed to produce a neutral trend in earnings per share over the past 5 quarters. However, while recent estimates for the company have been mixed, HLF has posted better than expected results. Based on operating earnings yield, the company is undervalued when compared to all of the companies in our coverage universe. Share price changes over the past year indicates that HLF will perform poorly over the near term.

Financial Data

(US$ in Thousands)	3 Mos	12/31/2015	12/31/2014	12/31/2013	12/31/2012	12/31/2011	12/31/2010	12/31/2009
Earnings Per Share	4.17	3.97	3.40	4.91	4.05	3.30	2.34	1.61
Cash Flow Per Share	7.35	7.61	5.93	7.53	5.04	4.33	3.20	2.33
Tang Book Value Per Share	N.M.	...	...	1.34	0.04	1.23	0.62	N.M.
Dividends Per Share	...	...	0.300	1.200	1.200	0.725	0.450	0.400
Dividend Payout %	...	...	8.82	24.44	29.63	21.97	19.27	24.84
Income Statement								
Total Revenue	1,119,600	4,469,000	4,958,600	4,825,308	4,072,330	3,454,537	2,734,226	2,324,577
EBITDA	192,200	663,800	582,000	816,377	732,347	631,170	455,212	358,231
Depn & Amortn	23,900	82,500	81,500	81,100	70,900	68,900	67,700	62,200
Income Before Taxes	143,400	486,400	421,300	716,717	650,906	559,779	380,095	290,928
Income Taxes	47,600	147,300	112,600	189,192	173,716	147,201	89,562	87,582
Net Income	95,800	339,100	308,700	527,525	477,190	412,578	290,533	203,346
Average Shares	85,600	85,300	90,800	107,445	117,856	124,846	124,512	126,194
Balance Sheet								
Current Assets	1,474,100	1,566,300	1,393,400	1,643,120	963,848	768,819	595,586	513,502
Total Assets	2,386,300	2,477,900	2,374,900	2,473,701	1,703,944	1,446,209	1,232,220	1,146,050
Current Liabilities	1,207,900	1,024,400	874,800	922,178	716,891	548,689	470,816	429,966
Long-Term Obligations	992,800	1,392,500	1,711,700	850,019	431,305	202,079	175,046	237,931
Total Liabilities	2,321,400	2,531,400	2,709,300	1,922,255	1,283,189	886,021	745,008	786,739
Stockholders' Equity	64,900	(53,500)	(334,400)	551,446	420,755	560,188	487,212	359,311
Shares Outstanding	92,800	92,700	92,200	101,100	106,900	115,800	117,800	120,400
Statistical Record								
Return on Assets %	14.94	13.98	12.73	25.25	30.21	30.81	24.43	17.94
Return on Equity %	...	...	284.46	108.52	97.03	78.78	68.64	67.66
EBITDA Margin %	17.17	14.85	11.74	16.92	17.98	18.27	16.65	15.41
Net Margin %	8.56	7.59	6.23	10.93	11.72	11.94	10.63	8.75
Asset Turnover	1.88	1.84	2.05	2.31	2.58	2.58	2.30	2.05
Current Ratio	1.22	1.53	1.59	1.78	1.34	1.40	1.27	1.19
Debt to Equity	15.30	...	...	1.54	1.03	0.36	0.36	0.66
Price Range	62.97-40.09	60.77-29.70	81.81-37.16	80.81-32.20	72.69-26.06	62.36-31.88	35.45-18.61	21.99-6.14
P/E Ratio	15.10-9.61	15.31-7.48	24.06-10.93	16.46-6.56	17.95-6.43	18.90-9.66	15.15-7.96	13.66-3.81
Average Yield %	...	...	0.54	2.25	2.27	1.47	1.72	2.79

Address: P.O. Box 309GT, Ugland House, South Church Street, George Town, KY1-1104
Telephone: 213-745-0500

Web Site: www.herbalife.com
Officers: Michael O. Johnson - Chairman, Chief Executive Officer Desmond Walsh - President

Auditors: PricewaterhouseCoopers LLP
Transfer Agents: Mellon Investor Services LLC, South Hackensack, NJ

HERSHEY COMPANY (THE)

Exchange	Symbol	Price	52Wk Range	Yield	P/E
NYS	HSY	$92.85 (5/31/2016)	97.07-83.32	2.51	41.08

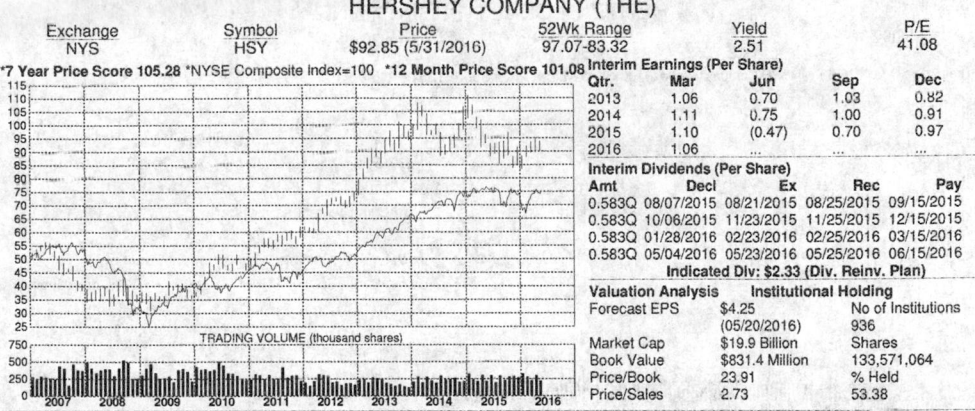

*7 Year Price Score 105.28 *NYSE Composite Index=100 *12 Month Price Score 101.08

Interim Earnings (Per Share)

Qtr.	Mar	Jun	Sep	Dec
2013	1.06	0.70	1.03	0.82
2014	1.11	0.75	1.00	0.91
2015	1.10	(0.47)	0.70	0.97
2016	1.06	...	...	...

Interim Dividends (Per Share)

Amt	Decl	Ex	Rec	Pay
0.583Q	08/07/2015	08/21/2015	08/25/2015	09/15/2015
0.583Q	10/06/2015	11/23/2015	11/25/2015	12/15/2015
0.583Q	01/28/2016	02/23/2016	02/25/2016	03/15/2016
0.583Q	05/04/2016	05/23/2016	05/25/2016	06/15/2016

Indicated Div: $2.33 (Div. Reinv. Plan)

Valuation Analysis

	Institutional Holding	
Forecast EPS	$4.25	No of Institutions
(05/20/2016)		936
Market Cap	$19.9 Billion	Shares
Book Value	$831.4 Million	133,571,064
Price/Book	23.91	% Held
Price/Sales	2.73	53.38

Business Summary: Food (MIC: 1.2.1 SIC: 2064 NAIC: 311320)

Hershey is engaged in the production of chocolate and non-chocolate confectionery. Co. has two reportable segments: North America, which is responsible for Co.'s chocolate and sugar confectionery market position, as well as Co.'s grocery and growing snacks market positions, in the U.S. and Canada; and International and Other, which includes all other countries where Co. manufactures, imports, markets, sells or distributes chocolate and non-chocolate confectionery and other products. Co.'s confectionery offerings include chocolate and non-chocolate confectionery products; gum and mint refreshment products; pantry items; and snack items such as spreads, meat snacks, bars and snack bites.

Recent Developments: For the quarter ended Apr 3 2016, net income decreased 6.1% to US$229.8 million from US$244.7 million in the year-earlier quarter. Revenues were US$1.83 billion, down 5.6% from US$1.94 billion the year before. Operating income was US$339.5 million versus US$384.2 million in the prior-year quarter, a decrease of 11.6%. Direct operating expenses declined 2.5% to US$1.01 billion from US$1.04 billion in the comparable period the year before. Indirect operating expenses decreased 7.5% to US$477.9 million from US$516.7 million in the equivalent prior-year period.

Prospects: Our evaluation of Hershey Foods Corp. as of June 19, 2016 is the result of our systematic analysis on three basic characteristics: earnings strength, relative valuation, and recent stock price movement. The company has managed to produce a neutral trend in earnings per share over the past 5 quarters and while recent estimates for the company have remained steady, HSY has posted better than expected results. Based on operating earnings yield, the company is about fairly valued when compared to all of the companies in our coverage universe. Share price changes over the past year indicates that HSY will perform in line with the market over the near term.

Financial Data

(US$ in Thousands)	3 Mos	12/31/2015	12/31/2014	12/31/2013	12/31/2012	12/31/2011	12/31/2010	12/31/2009
Earnings Per Share	2.26	2.32	3.77	3.61	2.89	2.74	2.21	1.90
Cash Flow Per Share	5.62	5.54	3.77	5.30	4.85	2.56	3.96	4.68
Tang Book Value Per Share	N.M.	N.M.	1.66	3.72	1.05	0.98	1.12	0.10
Dividends Per Share	2.284	2.236	2.040	1.810	1.560	1.380	1.280	1.190
Dividend Payout %	101.06	96.38	54.11	50.14	53.98	50.36	57.92	62.63
Income Statement								
Total Revenue	1,828,812	7,386,626	7,421,768	7,146,079	6,644,252	6,080,788	5,671,009	5,298,668
EBITDA	420,647	1,209,111	1,601,107	1,540,708	1,321,185	1,270,791	1,102,414	944,001
Depn & Amortn	59,913	244,928	211,532	201,033	210,037	215,763	197,116	182,411
Income Before Taxes	339,729	858,410	1,306,043	1,251,319	1,015,579	962,845	808,864	671,131
Income Taxes	109,897	345,459	459,131	430,849	354,648	333,883	299,065	235,137
Net Income	229,832	512,951	846,912	820,470	660,931	628,962	509,799	435,994
Average Shares	217,487	220,651	224,837	227,203	228,337	229,919	230,313	228,995
Balance Sheet								
Current Assets	1,772,918	1,848,598	2,247,047	2,487,334	2,113,485	2,046,558	2,005,217	1,385,434
Total Assets	5,305,840	5,344,371	5,629,516	5,357,488	4,754,839	4,412,199	4,272,732	3,675,031
Current Liabilities	2,336,972	2,217,912	1,935,647	1,408,022	1,471,110	1,173,775	1,298,845	910,628
Long-Term Obligations	1,571,388	1,557,091	1,548,963	1,795,142	1,530,967	1,748,500	1,541,825	1,502,730
Total Liabilities	4,474,401	4,346,374	4,174,454	3,752,654	3,718,090	3,563,177	3,370,416	2,954,572
Stockholders' Equity	831,439	997,997	1,455,062	1,604,834	1,036,749	849,022	902,316	720,459
Shares Outstanding	214,129	216,777	221,044	223,894	223,786	225,205	227,030	227,998
Statistical Record								
Return on Assets %	9.00	9.35	15.42	16.23	14.38	14.48	12.83	11.93
Return on Equity %	47.49	41.82	55.36	62.12	69.91	71.83	62.83	83.95
EBITDA Margin %	23.00	16.37	21.57	21.56	19.88	20.90	19.44	17.82
Net Margin %	12.57	6.94	11.41	11.48	9.95	10.34	8.99	8.23
Asset Turnover	1.32	1.35	1.35	1.41	1.45	1.40	1.43	1.45
Current Ratio	0.76	0.83	1.16	1.77	1.44	1.74	1.54	1.52
Debt to Equity	1.89	1.56	1.06	1.12	1.48	2.06	1.71	2.09
Price Range	101.74-83.32	110.78-83.58	108.07-88.15	100.90-72.22	74.64-59.49	62.00-46.37	51.76-35.79	41.80-30.75
P/E Ratio	45.02-36.87	47.75-36.03	28.67-23.38	27.95-20.01	25.83-20.58	22.63-16.92	23.42-16.19	22.00-16.18
Average Yield %	2.51	2.36	2.09	2.02	2.29	2.48	2.81	3.24

Address: 100 Crystal A Drive, Hershey, PA 17033	**Web Site:** www.hersheys.com	**Auditors:** Ernst & Young LLP
Telephone: 717-534-4200	**Officers:** John P. Bilbrey - Chairman, President, Chief Executive Officer Michele G. Buck - Senior Vice President, Global Chief Marketing Officer, Region Officer, President, Chief Operating Officer	**Investor Contact:** 800-539-0261
Fax: 717-531-6161		**Transfer Agents:** Computershare, Providence, RI

HERTZ GLOBAL HOLDINGS INC

Exchange	Symbol	Price	52Wk Range	Yield	P/E
NYS	HTZ	$9.69 (5/31/2016)	21.17-7.10	N/A	15.89

*7 Year Price Score 72.55 ***NYSE Composite Index=100** ***12 Month Price Score 62.47**

Interim Earnings (Per Share)

Qtr.	Mar	Jun	Sep	Dec
2013	0.04	0.27	0.47	(0.02)
2014	(0.15)	0.15	0.32	(0.51)
2015	(0.15)	0.05	0.52	0.16
2016	(0.12)			

Interim Dividends (Per Share)

No Dividends Paid

Valuation Analysis   **Institutional Holding**

Forecast EPS	$0.94	No of Institutions	
	(05/20/2016)	509	
Market Cap	$4.1 Billion	Shares	
Book Value	$2.0 Billion	555,236,544	
Price/Book	2.02	% Held	
Price/Sales	0.40	103.65	

Business Summary: Miscellaneous Transportation Services (MIC: 7.4.5 SIC: 7514 NAIC: 532111)

Hertz Global Holdings is a holding company. Through its subsidiaries, Co. operates its car rental business through the Hertz, Dollar, Thrifty and Firefly brands. Co. has four segments: U.S. Car Rental, which includes the rental of cars, crossovers and light trucks, as well as ancillary products and services, in the U.S.; International Car Rental, which includes the rental of cars, crossovers and light trucks, as well as ancillary products and services, internationally; Worldwide Equipment Rental, which includes the rental of industrial, construction, material handling and other equipment; and All Other Operations, which is comprised of Co.'s Donlen Corporation subsidiary's business.

Recent Developments: For the quarter ended Mar 31 2016, net loss amounted to US$51.0 million versus a net loss of US$70.0 million in the year-earlier quarter. Revenues were US$2.31 billion, down 5.8% from US$2.45 billion the year before. Direct operating expenses declined 4.8% to US$1.34 billion from US$1.41 billion in the comparable period the year before. Indirect operating expenses decreased 8.2% to US$1.04 billion from US$1.13 billion in the equivalent prior-year period.

Prospects: Our evaluation of Hertz Global Holdings Inc. as of June 19, 2016 is the result of our systematic analysis on three basic characteristics: earnings strength, relative valuation, and recent stock price movement. The company has suffered a very negative trend in earnings per share over the past 5 quarters and while recent estimates for the company have been mixed, HTZ has posted results that fell short of analysts expectations. Based on operating earnings yield, the company is undervalued when compared to all of the companies in our coverage universe. Share price changes over the past year indicates that HTZ will perform very poorly over the near term.

Financial Data
(US$ in Thousands)

	3 Mos	12/31/2015	12/31/2014	12/31/2013	12/31/2012	12/31/2011	12/31/2010	12/31/2009
Earnings Per Share	0.61	0.60	(0.18)	0.76	0.54	0.40	(0.12)	(0.34)
Cash Flow Per Share	7.38	7.37	7.60	8.50	6.45	5.37	5.36	4.78
Income Statement								
Total Revenue	2,311,000	10,535,000	11,046,000	10,771,900	9,020,807	8,298,380	7,562,534	7,101,507
EBITDA	794,000	3,653,000	3,579,000	4,139,300	3,420,591	3,056,094	2,756,171	2,601,935
Depn & Amortn	706,000	2,690,000	2,954,000	2,771,800	2,325,056	2,037,657	2,008,647	2,157,110
Income Before Taxes	(69,000)	341,000	(23,000)	663,100	450,545	324,270	(13,593)	(171,009)
Income Taxes	(18,000)	68,000	59,000	316,900	207,466	128,540	17,068	(59,666)
Net Income	(51,000)	273,000	(82,000)	346,200	243,079	176,170	(48,044)	(126,022)
Average Shares	424,000	456,000	454,000	463,900	448,209	444,778	411,941	371,456
Balance Sheet								
Current Assets	3,432,000	2,960,000	2,725,000	2,888,000	3,097,213	2,940,178	4,025,728	2,769,548
Total Assets	24,028,000	23,358,000	23,985,000	24,588,400	23,286,038	17,673,527	17,332,221	16,002,419
Current Liabilities	2,638,000	2,153,000	2,290,000	2,213,000	2,298,209	2,151,750	2,123,995	1,791,849
Long-Term Obligations	16,072,000	15,907,000	15,993,000	16,309,400	15,448,624	11,317,090	11,306,429	10,364,367
Total Liabilities	21,990,000	21,339,000	21,521,000	21,817,200	20,778,752	15,438,871	15,217,400	13,922,271
Stockholders' Equity	2,038,000	2,019,000	2,464,000	2,771,200	2,507,286	2,234,656	2,114,821	2,080,148
Shares Outstanding	424,000	423,000	459,000	445,800	421,485	417,022	413,462	410,245
Statistical Record								
Return on Assets %	1.15	1.15	N.M.	1.45	1.18	1.01	N.M.	N.M.
Return on Equity %	12.72	12.18	N.M.	13.12	10.22	8.10	N.M.	N.M.
EBITDA Margin %	34.36	34.67	32.40	38.43	37.92	36.83	36.45	36.64
Net Margin %	N.M.	2.59	N.M.	3.21	2.69	2.12	N.M.	N.M.
Asset Turnover	0.43	0.45	0.45	0.45	0.44	0.47	0.45	0.44
Current Ratio	1.30	1.37	1.19	1.31	1.35	1.37	1.90	1.55
Debt to Equity	7.89	7.88	6.49	5.89	6.16	5.06	5.35	4.98
Price Range	22.37-7.10	25.02-13.70	31.56-19.38	28.62-16.27	16.65-10.62	17.25-8.11	14.75-8.51	12.38-2.00
P/E Ratio	36.67-11.64	41.70-22.83	...	37.66-21.41	30.83-19.67	43.13-20.27	...	...

Address: 8501 Williams Road, Estero, FL 33928 **Telephone:** 239-301-7000	**Web Site:** www.hertz.com **Officers:** John P. Tague - Chief Executive Officer Jeffrey T. Foland - Senior Executive Vice President, Chief Revenue Officer	**Auditors:** PricewaterhouseCoopers LLP **Investor Contact:** 201-307-2100 **Transfer Agents:** Computershare Trust Company, N.A., Providence, RI

HESS CORP

Exchange	Symbol	Price	52Wk Range	Yield	P/E
NYS	HES	$59.93 (5/31/2016)	70.23-34.38	1.67	N/A

*7 Year Price Score 70.84 *NYSE Composite Index=100 *12 Month Price Score 103.87

Interim Earnings (Per Share)

Qtr.	Mar	Jun	Sep	Dec
2013	3.72	4.16	1.23	5.71
2014	1.20	2.96	3.31	0.09
2015	(1.37)	(1.99)	(0.98)	(6.43)
2016	(1.72)	...	...	...

Interim Dividends (Per Share)

Amt	Decl	Ex	Rec	Pay
0.25Q	09/09/2015	09/17/2015	09/21/2015	09/30/2015
0.25Q	12/02/2015	12/15/2015	12/17/2015	12/31/2015
0.25Q	03/02/2016	03/15/2016	03/17/2016	03/31/2016
0.25Q	06/01/2016	06/14/2016	06/16/2016	06/30/2016

Indicated Div: $1.00

Valuation Analysis

Forecast EPS	$-5.40 (05/20/2016)
Market Cap	$19.0 Billion
Book Value	$20.6 Billion
Price/Book	0.92
Price/Sales	3.16

Institutional Holding

No of Institutions	838
Shares	286,106,400
% Held	N/A

TRADING VOLUME (thousand shares)

Business Summary: Production & Extraction (MIC: 9.1.1 SIC: 1311 NAIC: 211111)

Hess is an exploration and production company engaged in exploration, development, production, transportation, purchase and sale of crude oil, natural gas liquids, and natural gas with production operations located primarily in the U.S., Denmark, Equatorial Guinea, the Joint Development Area of Malaysia/Thailand, Malaysia, and Norway. The Bakken Midstream operating segment provides services, including crude oil and natural gas gathering. As of Dec 31 2015, Co. had total proved developed and undeveloped reserves of 1.09 billion barrels of oil equivalent, consisted of 827.0 million barrels of crude oil, condensate and natural gas liquids, as well as 1.55 trillion cubic feet of natural gas.

Recent Developments: For the quarter ended Mar 31 2016, loss from continuing operations was US$488.0 million compared with a loss of US$376.0 million in the year-earlier quarter. Net loss amounted to US$488.0 million versus a net loss of US$389.0 million in the year-earlier quarter. Revenues were US$993.0 million, down 35.9% from US$1.55 billion the year before. Direct operating expenses declined 32.0% to US$189.0 million from US$278.0 million in the comparable period the year before. Indirect operating expenses decreased 18.1% to US$1.64 billion from US$2.00 billion in the equivalent prior-year period.

Prospects: Our evaluation of Hess Corp. as of June 19, 2016 is the result of our systematic analysis on three basic characteristics: earnings strength, relative valuation, and recent stock price movement. The company has enjoyed a very positive trend in earnings per share over the past 5 quarters. Because the company lacks sufficient analyst estimate data, we place greater weight on the historical EPS trend as the measure of earnings strength. Based on operating earnings yield, the company is overvalued when compared to all of the companies in our coverage universe. Share price changes over the past year indicates that HES will perform in line with the market over the near term.

Financial Data

(US$ in Thousands)	3 Mos	12/31/2015	12/31/2014	12/31/2013	12/31/2012	12/31/2011	12/31/2010	12/31/2009
Earnings Per Share	(11.12)	(10.78)	7.53	14.82	5.95	5.01	6.47	2.27
Cash Flow Per Share	...	6.99	14.70	14.47	16.68	14.79	13.90	9.40
Tang Book Value Per Share	63.85	66.46	71.18	70.24	55.29	47.68	42.29	37.16
Dividends Per Share	1.000	1.000	1.000	0.700	0.400	0.400	0.400	0.400
Dividend Payout %	...	...	13.28	4.72	6.72	7.98	6.18	17.62
Income Statement								
Total Revenue	993,000	6,561,000	11,439,000	24,421,000	38,373,000	37,871,000	34,613,000	29,569,000
EBITDA	119,000	38,000	5,983,000	7,669,000	7,106,000	5,250,000	5,989,000	4,136,000
Depn & Amortn	868,000	3,955,000	3,224,000	2,770,000	2,949,000	2,406,000	2,317,000	2,254,000
Income Before Taxes	(834,000)	(4,258,000)	2,436,000	4,493,000	3,738,000	2,461,000	3,311,000	1,522,000
Income Taxes	(346,000)	(1,299,000)	744,000	525,000	1,675,000	785,000	1,173,000	715,000
Net Income	(509,000)	(3,056,000)	2,317,000	5,052,000	2,025,000	1,703,000	2,125,000	740,000
Average Shares	299,800	283,600	307,700	340,900	340,300	339,898	328,277	325,965
Balance Sheet								
Current Assets	4,945,000	4,404,000	6,687,000	8,599,000	8,387,000	8,339,000	8,780,000	7,987,000
Total Assets	34,808,000	34,195,000	38,578,000	42,754,000	43,441,000	39,136,000	35,396,000	29,465,000
Current Liabilities	2,193,000	2,628,000	4,851,000	6,558,000	8,382,000	8,100,000	7,613,000	6,850,000
Long-Term Obligations	6,498,000	6,544,000	5,919,000	5,420,000	7,324,000	6,005,000	5,537,000	4,319,000
Total Liabilities	14,210,000	14,809,000	16,373,000	18,034,000	22,351,000	20,620,000	18,707,000	16,081,000
Stockholders' Equity	20,598,000	19,386,000	22,205,000	24,720,000	21,090,000	18,516,000	16,689,000	13,384,000
Shares Outstanding	316,719	286,045	285,834	325,314	341,527	339,976	337,681	327,229
Statistical Record								
Return on Assets %	N.M.	N.M.	5.70	11.72	4.89	4.57	6.55	2.55
Return on Equity %	N.M.	N.M.	9.88	22.06	10.20	9.67	14.13	5.76
EBITDA Margin %	11.98	0.58	52.30	31.40	18.52	13.86	17.30	13.99
Net Margin %	N.M.	N.M.	20.26	20.69	5.28	4.50	6.14	2.50
Asset Turnover	0.17	0.18	0.28	0.57	0.93	1.02	1.07	1.02
Current Ratio	2.25	1.68	1.38	1.31	1.00	1.03	1.15	1.17
Debt to Equity	0.32	0.34	0.27	0.22	0.35	0.32	0.33	0.32
Price Range	78.09-34.38	78.09-47.44	101.10-65.45	84.06-52.96	67.00-39.95	87.03-49.46	76.54-49.69	68.04-47.50
P/E Ratio	...	...	13.43-8.69	5.67-3.57	11.26-6.71	17.37-9.87	11.83-7.68	29.97-20.93
Average Yield %	1.74	1.56	1.15	0.97	0.77	0.57	0.66	0.71

Address: 1185 Avenue of the Americas, New York, NY 10036 Telephone: 212-997-8500	Web Site: www.hess.com Officers: James H. Quigley - Chairman Gregory P. Hill - President, Chief Operating Officer, Executive Vice President, Division Officer	Auditors: Ernst & Young LLP Investor Contact: 212-536-8940 Transfer Agents: Computershare, Providence, RI

HEWLETT PACKARD ENTERPRISE CO

Exchange	Symbol	Price	52Wk Range	Yield	P/E
NYS	HPE	$18.47 (5/31/2016)	18.47-12.06	1.19	N/A

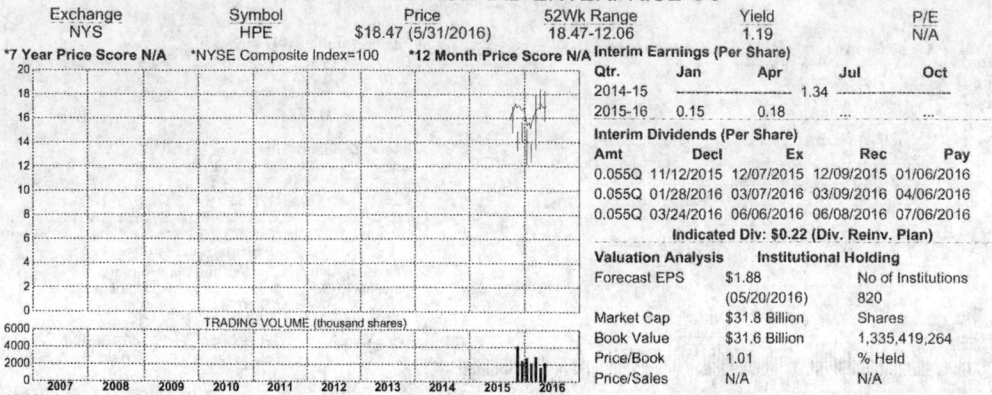

*7 Year Price Score N/A   *NYSE Composite Index=100   *12 Month Price Score N/A

Interim Earnings (Per Share)

Qtr.	Jan	Apr	Jul	Oct
2014-15	---	1.34	---	---
2015-16	0.15	0.18	...	...

Interim Dividends (Per Share)

Amt	Decl	Ex	Rec	Pay
0.055Q	11/12/2015	12/07/2015	12/09/2015	01/06/2016
0.055Q	01/28/2016	03/07/2016	03/09/2016	04/06/2016
0.055Q	03/24/2016	06/06/2016	06/08/2016	07/06/2016

Indicated Div: $0.22 (Div. Reinv. Plan)

Valuation Analysis		Institutional Holding	
Forecast EPS	$1.88	No of Institutions	
	(05/20/2016)	820	
Market Cap	$31.8 Billion	Shares	
Book Value	$31.6 Billion	1,335,419,264	
Price/Book	1.01	% Held	
Price/Sales	N/A	N/A	

Business Summary: IT Services (MIC: 6.3.1 SIC: 7379 NAIC: 541519)

Hewlett Packard Enterprise is a provider of technology solutions. Co. organizes its business into the following five segments: Enterprise Group, which provides customers with technology infrastructure they need to optimize IT; Software, which allows customers to automate IT operations to accelerate and secure business processes; Enterprise Services, which brings Co.'s solutions together through its consulting and support personnel; Financial Services, which enables IT consumption models, financial architectures and customized investment solutions for customers; and Corporate Investments, which includes Hewlett Packard Labs and certain business incubation projects, among others.

Recent Developments: For the quarter ended Apr 30 2016, net income increased 4.9% to US$320.0 million from US$305.0 million in the year-earlier quarter. Revenues were US$12.71 billion, up 1.3% from US$12.55 billion the year before. Operating income was US$492.0 million versus US$428.0 million in the prior-year quarter, an increase of 15.0%. Direct operating expenses rose 1.2% to US$9.01 billion from US$8.90 billion in the comparable period the year before. Indirect operating expenses decreased 0.2% to US$3.21 billion from US$3.22 billion in the equivalent prior-year period.

Prospects: Our evaluation of Hewlett Packard Enterprise Co. as of June 19, 2016 is the result of our systematic analysis on three basic characteristics: earnings strength, relative valuation, and recent stock price movement. The company has suffered a very negative trend in earnings per share over the past 5 quarters. However, while recent estimates for the company have been mixed, HPE has posted better than expected results. Based on operating earnings yield, the company is undervalued when compared to all of the companies in our coverage universe. Share price changes over the past year indicates that HPE will perform very poorly over the near term.

Financial Data

(US$ in Millions)	6 Mos	3 Mos	10/31/2015	10/31/2014	10/31/2013	10/31/2012
Earnings Per Share	...	...	1.34	...	...	...
Cash Flow Per Share	...	...	2.03	...	...	...
Tang Book Value Per Share	3.45	1.20	2.49	...	...	...
Dividends Per Share	0.110	0.055	...	...	...	...
Income Statement						
Total Revenue	25,435	12,724	52,107	55,123	57,371	61,042
EBITDA	1,413	660	5,715	6,718	7,692	(8,981)
Depn & Amortn	419	218	3,952	4,106	4,428	4,841
Income Before Taxes	682	319	1,470	2,244	2,871	(14,314)
Income Taxes	95	52	(991)	596	820	447
Net Income	587	267	2,461	1,648	2,051	(14,761)
Average Shares	1,751	1,778	1,834	...	...	...
Balance Sheet						
Current Assets	31,147	27,756	31,173	22,031	24,379	...
Total Assets	78,064	77,352	81,270	65,071	68,775	...
Current Liabilities	20,597	20,351	22,151	19,760	20,912	...
Long-Term Obligations	15,247	15,229	15,103	485	617	...
Total Liabilities	46,430	46,103	47,735	28,295	30,787	...
Stockholders' Equity	31,634	31,249	33,535	36,776	37,988	...
Shares Outstanding	1,724	1,733	1,742	...	...	...
Statistical Record						
Return on Assets %	...	...	...	2.46	...	...
Return on Equity %	...	...	...	4.41	...	...
EBITDA Margin %	5.56	5.19	10.97	12.19	13.41	N.M.
Net Margin %	2.31	2.10	4.72	2.99	3.57	N.M.
Asset Turnover	...	...	...	0.82	...	...
Current Ratio	1.51	1.36	1.41	1.11	1.17	...
Debt to Equity	0.48	0.49	0.45	0.01	0.02	...
Price Range	18.40-12.06	17.00-12.06	17.00-14.72	...	...	...
P/E Ratio	...	...	12.69-10.99	...	...	...
Average Yield %	0.73	0.38	...	...	...	...

Address: 3000 Hanover Street, Palo Alto, CA 94304 **Telephone:** 650-687-5817	**Web Site:** www.hpe.com **Officers:** Margaret C. Whitman - President, Chief Executive Officer Henry Gomez - Executive Vice President, Chief Marketing Officer, Chief Communications Officer	**Auditors:** Ernst & Young LLP **Transfer Agents:** Wells Fargo Shareowner Services

HEXCEL CORP.

Exchange	Symbol	Price	52Wk Range	Yield	P/E
NYS	HXL	$43.67 (5/31/2016)	54.48-38.38	1.01	18.74

*7 Year Price Score 130.00 *NYSE Composite Index=100 *12 Month Price Score 95.46

Interim Earnings (Per Share)

Qtr.	Mar	Jun	Sep	Dec
2013	0.43	0.48	0.48	0.46
2014	0.50	0.51	0.57	0.54
2015	0.70	0.63	0.55	0.56
2016	0.59	...	...	...

Interim Dividends (Per Share)

Amt	Decl	Ex	Rec	Pay
0.10Q	07/20/2015	07/30/2015	08/03/2015	08/17/2015
0.10Q	10/19/2015	10/29/2015	11/02/2015	11/16/2015
0.10Q	01/21/2016	02/03/2016	02/05/2016	02/12/2016
0.11Q	04/20/2016	05/02/2016	05/04/2016	05/11/2016

Indicated Div: $0.44

Valuation Analysis | **Institutional Holding**

Forecast EPS	$2.50	No of Institutions
	(05/20/2016)	416
Market Cap	$4.1 Billion	Shares
Book Value	$1.2 Billion	109,117,384
Price/Book	3.33	% Held
Price/Sales	2.15	92.32

Business Summary: Plastics (MIC: 8.4.2 SIC: 2821 NAIC: 335991)

Hexcel is a composites company. Co. develops, manufactures, and markets lightweight structural materials, including carbon fibers, specialty reinforcements, prepregs and other fiber-reinforced matrix materials, honeycomb, adhesives, engineered honeycomb and composite structures, for use in Commercial Aerospace, Space and Defense and Industrial markets. Co.'s products are used in a variety of end applications, such as commercial and military aircraft, space launch vehicles and satellites, wind turbine blades, automotive, a variety of recreational products and other industrial applications. Co. has two reportable segments, Composite Materials and Engineered Products.

Recent Developments: For the quarter ended Mar 31 2016, net income decreased 17.8% to US$56.0 million from US$68.1 million in the year-earlier quarter. Revenues were US$497.7 million, up 5.5% from US$471.8 million the year before. Operating income was US$83.9 million versus US$82.6 million in the prior-year quarter, an increase of 1.6%. Direct operating expenses rose 7.5% to US$354.7 million from US$330.0 million in the comparable period the year before. Indirect operating expenses decreased 0.2% to US$59.1 million from US$59.2 million in the equivalent prior-year period.

Prospects: Our evaluation of Hexcel Corp. as of June 19, 2016 is the result of our systematic analysis on three basic characteristics: earnings strength, relative valuation, and recent stock price movement. The company has produced a positive trend in earnings per share over the past 5 quarters and while recent estimates for the company have remained steady, HXL has posted better than expected results. Based on operating earnings yield, the company is undervalued when compared to all of the companies in our coverage universe. Share price changes over the past year indicates that HXL will perform well over the near term.

Financial Data

(US$ in Thousands)	3 Mos	12/31/2015	12/31/2014	12/31/2013	12/31/2012	12/31/2011	12/31/2010	12/31/2009
Earnings Per Share	2.33	2.44	2.12	1.84	1.61	1.35	0.77	0.57
Cash Flow Per Share	3.49	3.14	3.29	2.73	2.31	1.73	1.30	1.78
Tang Book Value Per Share	12.28	11.99	11.41	11.12	9.37	7.54	6.20	5.37
Dividends Per Share	0.400	0.400	...	...	...	...	...	...
Dividend Payout %	17.17	16.39	...	...	...	...	...	...
Income Statement								
Total Revenue	497,700	1,861,200	1,855,500	1,678,200	1,578,200	1,392,400	1,173,600	1,108,300
EBITDA	84,200	408,800	376,500	329,200	304,900	242,400	176,200	150,300
Depn & Amortn	300	76,400	71,200	59,300	57,200	55,300	53,200	46,600
Income Before Taxes	78,300	318,200	297,300	262,600	237,700	175,500	99,800	77,600
Income Taxes	22,700	83,000	89,300	76,000	74,100	41,600	22,900	22,000
Net Income	56,000	237,200	209,400	187,900	164,300	135,500	77,400	56,300
Average Shares	94,800	97,200	98,700	102,100	102,000	100,700	99,900	98,200
Balance Sheet								
Current Assets	691,900	633,800	681,700	656,400	575,700	524,300	497,700	461,100
Total Assets	2,321,600	2,187,400	2,036,400	1,836,100	1,603,100	1,376,100	1,258,100	1,246,600
Current Liabilities	264,200	292,600	310,600	268,700	235,300	247,500	205,900	201,700
Long-Term Obligations	688,000	576,500	415,000	292,000	240,000	238,300	304,600	358,800
Total Liabilities	1,104,100	1,007,800	886,500	675,700	609,000	573,900	598,700	671,000
Stockholders' Equity	1,217,500	1,179,600	1,149,900	1,160,400	994,100	802,200	659,400	575,600
Shares Outstanding	92,900	93,500	95,500	98,900	99,900	98,800	97,300	96,600
Statistical Record								
Return on Assets %	10.21	11.23	10.81	10.93	11.00	10.29	6.18	4.58
Return on Equity %	18.89	20.36	18.13	17.44	18.24	18.54	12.53	10.38
EBITDA Margin %	16.92	21.96	20.29	19.62	19.32	17.41	15.01	13.56
Net Margin %	11.25	12.74	11.29	11.20	10.41	9.73	6.60	5.08
Asset Turnover	0.86	0.88	0.96	0.98	1.06	1.06	0.94	0.90
Current Ratio	2.62	2.17	2.19	2.44	2.45	2.12	2.42	2.29
Debt to Equity	0.57	0.49	0.36	0.25	0.24	0.30	0.46	0.62
Price Range	54.48-38.38	54.48-40.38	46.40-36.92	44.69-26.50	27.80-22.53	25.84-17.58	19.21-10.13	13.56-4.59
P/E Ratio	23.38-16.47	22.33-16.55	21.89-17.42	24.29-14.40	17.27-13.99	19.14-13.02	24.95-13.16	23.79-8.05
Average Yield %	0.85	0.83	...	...	...	...	...	...

Address: Two Stamford Plaza, 281 Tresser Boulevard, Stamford, CT 06901
Telephone: 203-969-0666

Web Site: www.hexcel.com
Officers: Nick L. Stanage - Chairman, President, Chief Operating Officer, Chief Executive Officer
Wayne C. Pensky - Senior Vice President, Chief Financial Officer

Auditors: Ernst & Young LLP
Investor Contact: 203-969-0666
Transfer Agents: American Stock Transfer & Trust Company, New York, NY

HIGHWOODS PROPERTIES, INC.

Exchange	Symbol	Price	52Wk Range	Yield	P/E
NYS	HIW	$48.66 (5/31/2016)	48.85-36.82	3.49	9.22

*7 Year Price Score 101.85 *NYSE Composite Index=100 *12 Month Price Score 108.83

Interim Earnings (Per Share)

Qtr.	Mar	Jun	Sep	Dec
2013	0.15	0.33	0.61	0.33
2014	0.13	0.25	0.57	0.23
2015	0.21	0.27	0.31	0.21
2016	4.49	...	...	...

Interim Dividends (Per Share)

Amt	Decl	Ex	Rec	Pay
0.425Q	07/29/2015	08/13/2015	08/17/2015	09/09/2015
0.425Q	10/15/2015	11/12/2015	11/16/2015	12/08/2015
0.425Q	01/27/2016	02/12/2016	02/17/2016	03/08/2016
0.425Q	04/21/2016	05/16/2016	05/18/2016	06/07/2016

Indicated Div: $1.70

Valuation Analysis **Institutional Holding**

Forecast EPS	$5.36	No of Institutions
	(05/20/2016)	330
Market Cap	$4.7 Billion	Shares
Book Value	$2.0 Billion	110,080,432
Price/Book	2.32	% Held
Price/Sales	7.74	103.08

Business Summary: REITs (MIC: 5.3.1 SIC: 6798 NAIC: 525930)

Highwoods Properties is a real estate investment trust that provides leasing, management, development, construction and other customer-related services for its properties and for third parties. Co. conducts its activities through Highwoods Realty Limited Partnership and is its sole general partner. Co.'s key portfolio consists of office properties in Raleigh, Atlanta, Tampa, Nashville, Memphis, Pittsburgh, Richmond and Orlando, office and industrial properties in Greensboro and retail and office properties in Kansas City. Co. also provides a line of real estate services to its customers, such as build-to-suit construction and space modification, including tenant improvements and expansions.

Recent Developments: For the quarter ended Mar 31 2016, income from continuing operations increased 66.3% to US$28.1 million from US$16.9 million in the year-earlier quarter. Net income increased to US$446.7 million from US$20.8 million in the year-earlier quarter. Revenues were US$164.9 million, up 13.5% from US$145.2 million the year before.

Prospects: Our evaluation of Highwoods Properties Inc. as of June 19, 2016 is the result of our systematic analysis on three basic characteristics: earnings strength, relative valuation, and recent stock price movement. The company has managed to produce a neutral trend in earnings per share over the past 5 quarters. Because the company lacks sufficient analyst estimate data, we place greater weight on the historical EPS trend as the measure of earnings strength. Based on operating earnings yield, the company is overvalued when compared to all of the companies in our coverage universe. Share price changes over the past year indicates that HIW will perform well over the near term.

Financial Data

(US$ in Thousands)	3 Mos	12/31/2015	12/31/2014	12/31/2013	12/31/2012	12/31/2011	12/31/2010	12/31/2009
Earnings Per Share	5.28	1.00	1.19	1.44	1.02	0.54	0.86	0.76
Cash Flow Per Share	3.15	3.06	2.94	3.01	2.54	2.70	2.66	2.78
Tang Book Value Per Share	20.69	16.36	16.09	16.11	14.08	13.12	13.98	14.68
Dividends Per Share	1.700	1.700	1.700	1.700	1.700	1.700	1.700	1.700
Dividend Payout %	32.20	170.00	142.86	118.06	166.67	314.81	197.67	223.68
Income Statement								
Total Revenue	164,859	604,671	608,468	556,810	516,102	482,852	463,321	454,026
EBITDA	48,879	387,910	397,498	336,792	299,864	276,021	296,186	227,817
Depn & Amortn	1,834	223,384	203,324	190,227	165,420	147,786	141,019	116,819
Income Before Taxes	26,857	80,443	113,761	60,459	45,683	39,623	68,157	32,389
Net Income	446,735	101,260	115,972	131,097	84,235	47,971	72,303	61,694
Average Shares	99,357	97,406	93,800	88,836	79,678	76,189	75,578	72,079
Balance Sheet								
Current Assets	453,685	201,274	214,021	176,797	173,550	173,957	132,756	134,209
Total Assets	4,514,024	4,493,432	4,004,909	3,807,101	3,350,428	3,180,992	2,871,835	2,887,101
Current Liabilities	212,106	248,107	237,633	218,962	172,146	148,821	106,716	117,328
Long-Term Obligations	2,100,937	2,499,614	2,094,908	1,982,963	1,888,520	1,934,657	1,556,059	1,506,861
Total Liabilities	2,469,643	2,892,125	2,480,698	2,329,801	2,190,288	2,198,779	1,788,073	1,759,141
Stockholders' Equity	2,044,381	1,601,307	1,524,211	1,477,300	1,160,140	982,213	1,083,762	1,127,960
Shares Outstanding	97,392	96,091	92,907	89,920	80,311	72,647	71,690	71,285
Statistical Record								
Return on Assets %	12.37	2.38	2.97	3.66	2.57	1.59	2.51	2.12
Return on Equity %	29.39	6.48	7.73	9.94	7.84	4.64	6.54	5.54
EBITDA Margin %	29.65	64.15	65.33	60.49	58.10	57.16	63.93	50.18
Net Margin %	270.98	16.75	19.06	23.54	16.32	9.93	15.61	13.59
Asset Turnover	0.14	0.14	0.16	0.16	0.16	0.16	0.16	0.16
Current Ratio	2.14	0.81	0.90	0.81	1.01	1.17	1.24	1.14
Debt to Equity	1.03	1.56	1.37	1.34	1.63	1.97	1.44	1.34
Price Range	47.88-36.82	48.14-36.82	45.13-35.82	41.07-33.00	35.48-29.71	36.92-26.51	35.16-26.54	34.84-16.57
P/E Ratio	9.07-6.97	48.14-36.82	37.92-30.10	28.52-22.92	34.78-29.13	68.37-49.09	40.88-30.86	45.84-21.80
Average Yield %	4.01	3.96	4.21	4.64	5.17	5.30	5.46	6.64

Address: 3100 Smoketree Court, Suite 600, Raleigh, NC 27604 **Telephone:** 919-872-4924 **Fax:** 919-431-1439	**Web Site:** www.highwoods.com **Officers:** O. Temple Sloan - Chairman Edward J. Fritsch - President, Chief Executive Officer	**Auditors:** Deloitte & Touche LLP **Investor Contact:** 919-431-1529 **Transfer Agents:** Wells Fargo Shareholder Services, Mendota Heights, MN

HILL-ROM HOLDINGS, INC.

Exchange	Symbol	Price	52Wk Range	Yield	P/E
NYS	HRC	$49.13 (5/31/2016)	57.79-43.29	1.38	87.73

*7 Year Price Score 117.47 *NYSE Composite Index=100   *12 Month Price Score 96.45

Interim Earnings (Per Share)

Qtr.	Dec	Mar	Jun	Sep
2012-13	0.39	0.37	0.39	0.59
2013-14	0.22	(0.06)	0.45	0.43
2014-15	0.21	0.45	0.33	(0.17)
2015-16	0.07	0.33	...	...

Interim Dividends (Per Share)

Amt	Decl	Ex	Rec	Pay
0.16Q	07/22/2015	09/14/2015	09/16/2015	09/30/2015
0.16Q	11/17/2015	12/11/2015	12/15/2015	12/31/2015
0.17Q	02/26/2016	03/10/2016	03/14/2016	03/28/2016
0.17Q	05/06/2016	06/08/2016	06/10/2016	06/24/2016

Indicated Div: $0.68

Valuation Analysis

Forecast EPS	$3.28
	(05/20/2016)
Market Cap	$3.2 Billion
Book Value	$1.2 Billion
Price/Book	2.75
Price/Sales	1.37

Institutional Holding

No of Institutions	27
Shares	4,651,596
% Held	N/A

Business Summary: Medical Instruments & Equipment (MIC: 4.3.1 SIC: 3841 NAIC: 339112)

Hill-Rom is a medical technology company focusing on Advancing Mobility, Wound Care and Prevention, Clinical Workflow, Surgical Safety and Efficiency, and Respiratory Health. Co.'s segments include: North America, which sells and rents its patient support and near-patient technologies and services, as well as its clinical workflow solutions, in the U.S. and Canada; Surgical and Respiratory Care, which sells and rents its surgical and respiratory care products globally; and International, which sells and rents its patient support and near-patient technologies and services, as well as its clinical workflow solutions, in regions outside of the U.S. and Canada.

Recent Developments: For the quarter ended Mar 31 2016, net income decreased 15.3% to US$22.1 million from US$26.1 million in the year-earlier quarter. Revenues were US$632.6 million, up 33.2% from US$474.8 million the year before. Operating income was US$49.8 million versus US$38.3 million in the prior-year quarter, an increase of 30.0%. Direct operating expenses rose 26.0% to US$328.4 million from US$260.6 million in the comparable period the year before. Indirect operating expenses increased 44.6% to US$254.4 million from US$175.9 million in the equivalent prior-year period.

Prospects: Our evaluation of Hil-Rom Holdings, Inc. as of June 19, 2016 is the result of our systematic analysis on three basic characteristics: earnings strength, relative valuation, and recent stock price movement. The company has managed to produce a neutral trend in earnings per share over the past 5 quarters and while recent estimates for the company have been raised by analysts, HRC has posted better than expected results. Based on operating earnings yield, the company is undervalued when compared to all of the companies in our coverage universe. Share price changes over the past year indicates that HRC will perform poorly over the near term.

Financial Data
(US$ in Thousands)

	6 Mos	3 Mos	09/30/2015	09/30/2014	09/30/2013	09/30/2012	09/30/2011	09/30/2010
Earnings Per Share	0.56	0.68	0.82	1.04	1.74	1.94	2.09	1.97
Cash Flow Per Share	3.28	3.51	3.73	3.65	4.39	4.20	3.52	2.22
Tang Book Value Per Share	N.M.	N.M.	N.M.	2.53	4.50	3.07	8.57	7.80
Dividends Per Share	0.650	0.640	0.632	0.595	0.525	0.487	0.430	0.410
Dividend Payout %	116.07	94.12	77.13	57.21	30.17	25.13	20.57	20.81
Income Statement								
Total Revenue	1,293,800	661,200	1,988,200	1,686,100	1,716,200	1,634,300	1,591,700	1,469,600
EBITDA	182,500	80,400	201,700	231,400	224,700	243,900	242,500	264,400
Depn & Amortn	103,400	52,100	118,200	106,400	71,200	73,900	74,300	72,800
Income Before Taxes	33,900	5,800	65,100	115,200	144,000	163,500	159,700	182,900
Income Taxes	7,500	1,500	18,300	54,600	39,000	42,700	26,200	56,900
Net Income	27,100	4,800	47,700	60,600	105,000	120,800	133,300	125,300
Average Shares	66,382	66,274	58,536	58,523	60,250	62,120	63,899	63,739
Balance Sheet								
Current Assets	983,800	989,300	1,141,000	779,300	688,000	681,800	791,700	739,200
Total Assets	4,242,600	4,271,600	4,457,600	1,752,100	1,586,800	1,627,600	1,299,100	1,245,600
Current Liabilities	491,600	493,400	578,800	442,300	345,400	378,100	334,000	288,700
Long-Term Obligations	2,087,300	2,136,200	2,175,200	364,900	225,800	237,500	50,800	98,500
Total Liabilities	3,074,400	3,134,900	3,310,700	945,600	728,100	815,000	557,400	538,100
Stockholders' Equity	1,168,200	1,136,700	1,146,900	806,500	858,700	812,600	741,700	707,500
Shares Outstanding	65,379	65,299	65,165	57,439	58,523	60,796	61,686	62,786
Statistical Record								
Return on Assets %	1.23	1.34	1.54	3.63	6.53	8.23	10.48	10.11
Return on Equity %	3.87	4.30	4.88	7.28	12.57	15.50	18.40	19.03
EBITDA Margin %	14.11	12.16	10.14	13.72	13.09	14.92	15.24	17.99
Net Margin %	2.09	0.73	2.40	3.59	6.12	7.39	8.37	8.53
Asset Turnover	0.79	0.73	0.64	1.01	1.07	1.11	1.25	1.19
Current Ratio	2.00	2.01	1.97	1.76	1.99	1.80	2.37	2.56
Debt to Equity	1.79	1.88	1.90	0.45	0.26	0.29	0.07	0.14
Price Range	57.79-43.29	57.79-45.13	57.79-40.58	44.39-35.13	37.62-26.40	35.96-25.30	47.48-27.37	35.89-19.59
P/E Ratio	103.20-77.30	84.99-66.37	70.48-49.49	42.68-33.78	21.62-15.17	18.54-13.04	22.72-13.10	18.22-9.94
Average Yield %	1.27	1.25	1.28	1.49	1.59	1.56	1.10	1.48

Address: Two Prudential Plaza, Suite 4100, Chicago, IL 60601 Telephone: 312-819-7200 Fax: 812-934-8189	Web Site: www.Hill-Rom.com Officers: Rolf A. Classon - Chairman John J. Greisch President, Chief Executive Officer	Auditors: PricewaterhouseCoopers LLP Investor Contact: 812-931-2199 Transfer Agents: Computershare Trust Company, N.A., Providence, RI

HILTON WORLDWIDE HOLDINGS INC

Exchange	Symbol	Price	52Wk Range	Yield	P/E
NYS	HLT	$20.78 (5/31/2016)	29.39-17.18	1.35	13.24

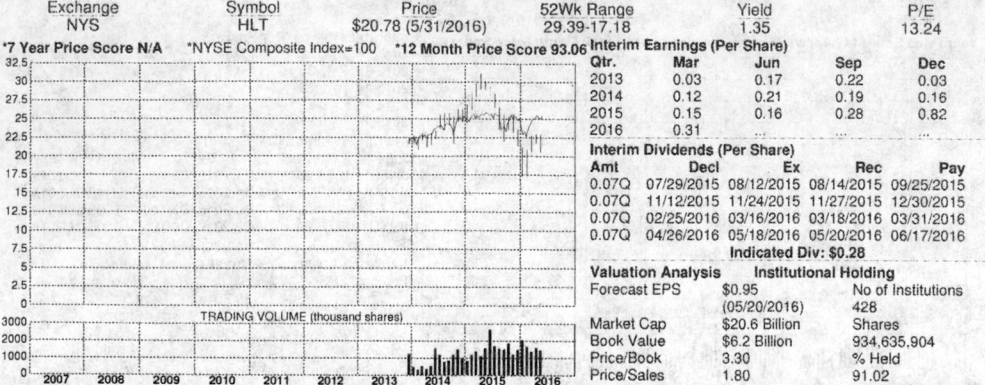

*7 Year Price Score N/A ***NYSE Composite Index=100** ***12 Month Price Score 93.06**

Interim Earnings (Per Share)

Qtr.	Mar	Jun	Sep	Dec
2013	0.03	0.17	0.22	0.03
2014	0.12	0.21	0.19	0.16
2015	0.15	0.16	0.28	0.82
2016	0.31	...	...	...

Interim Dividends (Per Share)

Amt	Decl	Ex	Rec	Pay
0.07Q	07/29/2015	08/12/2015	08/14/2015	09/25/2015
0.07Q	11/12/2015	11/24/2015	11/27/2015	12/30/2015
0.07Q	02/25/2016	03/16/2016	03/18/2016	03/31/2016
0.07Q	04/26/2016	05/18/2016	05/20/2016	06/17/2016
		Indicated Div: $0.28		

Valuation Analysis		Institutional Holding	
Forecast EPS	$0.95	No of Institutions	
	(05/20/2016)	428	
Market Cap	$20.6 Billion	Shares	
Book Value	$6.2 Billion	934,635,904	
Price/Book	3.30	% Held	
Price/Sales	1.80	91.02	

Business Summary: Hotels, Restaurants & Travel (MIC: 2.2.1 SIC: 7011 NAIC: 721110)

Hilton Worldwide Holdings is a holding company. Through its subsidiaries, Co. is engaged in owning, leasing, managing, developing and franchising hotels, resorts and timeshare properties. Co. is a hospitality company with 12 brands that include Hilton Hotels & Resorts, Waldorf Astoria Hotels & Resorts, Conrad Hotels & Resorts, Canopy by Hilton, and Hilton Garden Inn. As of Dec 31 2014, Co. owned, leased, managed or franchised 4,278 hotel and resort properties, totaling 708,268 rooms in 94 countries and territories, as well as 44 timeshare properties comprising 6,794 units. Co. operates its business through three segments: management and franchise, ownership, and timeshare.

Recent Developments: For the quarter ended Mar 31 2016, net income increased 106.7% to US$310.0 million from US$150.0 million in the year-earlier quarter. Revenues were US$2.75 billion, up 5.8% from US$2.60 billion the year before. Operating income was US$409.0 million versus US$490.0 million in the prior-year quarter, a decrease of 16.5%. Indirect operating expenses increased 11.0% to US$2.34 billion from US$2.11 billion in the equivalent prior-year period.

Prospects: Our evaluation of Hilton Worldwide Holdings Inc as of June 19, 2016 is the result of our systematic analysis on three basic characteristics: earnings strength, relative valuation, and recent stock price movement. The company has produced a positive trend in earnings per share over the past 5 quarters and while recent estimates for the company have remained steady, HLT has posted better than expected results. Based on operating earnings yield, the company is about fairly valued when compared to all of the companies in our coverage universe. Share price changes over the past year indicates that HLT will perform poorly over the near term.

Financial Data
(US$ in Millions)

	3 Mos	12/31/2015	12/31/2014	12/31/2013	12/31/2012	12/31/2011	12/31/2010
Earnings Per Share	1.57	1.42	0.68	0.45	...	...	...
Cash Flow Per Share	1.44	1.41	1.39	2.28	...	...	...
Dividends Per Share	0.210	0.140	...	...	...	...	...
Dividend Payout %	13.38	9.86	...	...	...	...	...
Income Statement							
Total Revenue	2,750	11,272	10,502	9,735	9,276	8,783	8,068
EBITDA	484	2,380	2,049	1,611	1,428	1,296	1,709
Depn & Amortn	87	351	313	318	290	323	341
Income Before Taxes	261	1,473	1,128	682	584	341	431
Income Taxes	(46)	80	465	238	214	(59)	308
Net Income	309	1,404	673	415	352	253	128
Average Shares	989	989	985	923	...	...	...
Balance Sheet							
Current Assets	2,738	2,585	2,499	2,383	2,827	3,033	...
Total Assets	25,721	25,716	26,125	26,562	27,066	27,312	...
Current Liabilities	2,545	2,467	2,257	2,142	2,349	2,207	...
Long-Term Obligations	10,255	10,319	11,555	12,671	15,588	16,408	...
Total Liabilities	19,484	19,731	21,373	22,199	24,765	25,444	...
Stockholders' Equity	6,237	5,985	4,752	4,363	2,301	1,868	...
Shares Outstanding	989	987	984	984	920	920	...
Statistical Record							
Return on Assets %	6.06	5.42	2.55	1.55	1.29	...	...
Return on Equity %	28.68	26.15	14.77	12.45	16.84	...	...
EBITDA Margin %	17.60	21.11	19.51	16.55	15.39	14.76	21.18
Net Margin %	11.24	12.46	6.41	4.26	3.79	2.88	1.59
Asset Turnover	0.44	0.43	0.40	0.36	0.34	...	...
Current Ratio	1.08	1.05	1.11	1.11	1.20	1.37	...
Debt to Equity	1.64	1.72	2.43	2.90	6.77	8.78	...
Price Range	31.10-17.18	31.10-21.28	26.42-20.80	22.28-21.50	...	...	...
P/E Ratio	19.81-10.94	21.90-14.99	38.85-30.59	49.51-47.78	...	...	...
Average Yield %	0.85	0.53	...	...	...	...	...

Address: 7930 Jones Branch Drive, Suite 1100, McLean, VA 22102 **Telephone:** 703-883-1000	**Web Site:** www.hiltonworldwide.com **Officers:** Jonathan D. Gray - Chairman Christopher J. Nassetta - President, Chief Executive Officer	**Auditors:** Ernst & Young LLP **Transfer Agents:** Wells Fargo Bank, N.A.

HNI CORP

Exchange	Symbol	Price	52Wk Range	Yield	P/E
NYS	HNI	$46.07 (5/31/2016)	53.20-30.91	2.39	19.28

*7 Year Price Score 110.04 *NYSE Composite Index=100 *12 Month Price Score 99.95

Interim Earnings (Per Share)

Qtr.	Mar	Jun	Sep	Dec
2013	0.03	0.25	0.61	0.50
2014	0.24	0.21	0.74	0.16
2015	0.19	0.52	0.90	0.71
2016	0.26	...	...	...

Interim Dividends (Per Share)

Amt	Decl	Ex	Rec	Pay
0.265Q	08/04/2015	08/12/2015	08/14/2015	09/01/2015
0.265Q	11/12/2015	11/19/2015	11/23/2015	12/01/2015
0.265Q	02/17/2016	02/25/2016	02/29/2016	03/07/2016
0.275Q	05/10/2016	05/18/2016	05/20/2016	06/01/2016

Indicated Div: $1.10

Valuation Analysis

		Institutional Holding	
Forecast EPS	$2.69	No of Institutions	
	(05/20/2016)	228	
Market Cap	$2.0 Billion	Shares	
Book Value	$488.2 Million	41,908,640	
Price/Book	4.19	% Held	
Price/Sales	0.90	67.00	

Business Summary: Office Equipment & Furniture (MIC: 7.5.1 SIC: 2522 NAIC: 337214)

HNI is a provider of office furniture and hearth products. Products are sold primarily through a system of dealers, wholesalers, and office product distributors and also directly to end-user customers and federal, state and local governments. Co. Products and Solutions includes: Office Furniture, where Co. designs, manufactures and markets a range of office furniture systems and seating across a range of price points including panel-based and freestanding furniture systems; and Hearth Products, where Co. is North America's manufacturer and marketer of prefabricated fireplaces, hearth stoves and related products, primarily for the home, including gas, wood and pellet burning fireplaces.

Recent Developments: For the quarter ended Apr 2 2016, net income increased 40.1% to US$11.8 million from US$8.5 million in the year-earlier quarter. Revenues were US$501.0 million, down 4.3% from US$523.5 million the year before. Operating income was US$19.5 million versus US$15.4 million in the prior-year quarter, an increase of 26.6%. Direct operating expenses declined 7.0% to US$315.3 million from US$339.0 million in the comparable period the year before. Indirect operating expenses decreased 1.7% to US$166.2 million from US$169.1 million in the equivalent prior-year period.

Prospects: Our evaluation of HNI Corp. as of June 19, 2016 is the result of our systematic analysis on three basic characteristics: earnings strength, relative valuation, and recent stock price movement. The company has generated a negative trend in earnings per share over the past 5 quarters and while recent estimates for the company have been raised by analysts, HNI has posted better than expected results. Based on operating earnings yield, the company is undervalued when compared to all of the companies in our coverage universe. Share price changes over the past year indicates that HNI will perform very poorly over the near term.

Financial Data

(US$ in Thousands)	3 Mos	01/02/2016	01/03/2015	12/28/2013	12/29/2012	12/31/2011	01/01/2011	01/02/2010
Earnings Per Share	2.39	2.32	1.35	1.39	1.07	1.01	0.59	(0.14)
Cash Flow Per Share	4.57	3.93	3.69	3.66	3.21	3.01	2.10	4.32
Tang Book Value Per Share	4.37	4.51	3.06	3.33	2.94	3.31	3.29	3.51
Dividends Per Share	1.060	1.045	0.990	0.960	0.950	0.920	0.860	0.860
Dividend Payout %	44.35	45.04	73.33	69.06	88.79	91.09	145.76	...
Income Statement								
Total Revenue	501,037	2,304,419	2,222,695	2,059,964	2,004,003	1,833,450	1,686,728	1,656,289
EBITDA	34,770	210,176	158,949	142,287	130,987	127,774	116,540	78,859
Depn & Amortn	15,251	46,500	46,100	36,300	43,360	46,287	58,630	74,867
Income Before Taxes	17,723	157,170	104,931	96,707	77,604	70,159	46,478	(7,673)
Income Taxes	5,881	51,764	43,776	33,338	29,278	24,411	16,797	(1,414)
Net Income	11,843	105,436	61,471	63,683	48,967	45,986	26,941	(6,442)
Average Shares	45,039	45,440	45,578	45,956	45,819	45,694	45,808	44,888
Balance Sheet								
Current Assets	443,495	438,370	455,559	433,228	404,940	434,040	408,161	360,271
Total Assets	1,311,452	1,263,925	1,239,334	1,134,705	1,079,631	1,054,258	997,880	994,326
Current Liabilities	459,207	435,900	457,333	411,584	395,885	388,910	361,351	300,142
Long-Term Obligations	195,000	185,000	197,736	150,197	150,372	150,540	150,111	200,000
Total Liabilities	823,231	786,971	824,747	698,377	659,272	635,201	589,895	575,042
Stockholders' Equity	488,221	476,954	414,587	436,328	420,359	419,057	407,985	419,284
Shares Outstanding	44,375	44,158	44,165	44,981	44,950	44,855	44,840	45,093
Statistical Record								
Return on Assets %	8.50	8.45	5.09	5.77	4.60	4.49	2.71	N.M.
Return on Equity %	23.77	23.72	14.21	14.91	11.70	11.15	6.53	N.M.
EBITDA Margin %	6.94	9.12	7.15	6.91	6.54	6.97	6.91	4.76
Net Margin %	2.36	4.58	2.77	3.09	2.44	2.51	1.60	N.M.
Asset Turnover	1.78	1.85	1.84	1.84	1.88	1.79	1.70	1.54
Current Ratio	0.97	1.01	1.00	1.05	1.02	1.12	1.13	1.20
Debt to Equity	0.40	0.39	0.48	0.34	0.36	0.36	0.37	0.48
Price Range	57.58-30.91	57.58-36.06	52.53-31.50	40.34-30.02	31.68-21.95	33.75-16.23	34.38-23.17	28.95-7.80
P/E Ratio	24.09-12.93	24.82-15.54	38.91-23.33	29.02-21.60	29.61-20.51	33.42-16.07	58.27-39.27	...
Average Yield %	2.41	2.17	2.55	2.70	3.59	3.63	3.14	4.53

Address: P.O. Box 1109, 408 East Second Street, Muscatine, IA 52761-0071
Telephone: 563-272-7400
Fax: 563-272-7114

Web Site: www.hnicorp.com
Officers: Stanley A. Askren - Chairman, President, Chief Executive Officer Kurt A. Tjaden - Chief Financial Officer, Vice President

Auditors: KPMG LLP
Investor Contact: 563-272-7400
Transfer Agents: Wells Fargo Shareowner Services, Mendota Heights, MN

HOLLYFRONTIER CORP.

Exchange	Symbol	Price	52Wk Range	Yield	P/E
NYS	HFC	$26.76 (5/31/2016)	53.80-26.61	4.93	9.39

*7 Year Price Score 104.70 *NYSE Composite Index=100 *12 Month Price Score 79.09

TRADING VOLUME (thousand shares)

Interim Earnings (Per Share)

Qtr.	Mar	Jun	Sep	Dec
2013	1.63	1.27	0.41	0.31
2014	0.76	0.89	0.88	(1.11)
2015	1.16	1.88	1.04	(0.19)
2016	0.12	...	...	...

Interim Dividends (Per Share)

Amt	Decl	Ex	Rec	Pay
0.33Q	08/05/2015	08/31/2015	09/02/2015	09/25/2015
0.33Q	11/11/2015	12/02/2015	12/04/2015	12/30/2015
0.33Q	02/17/2016	03/02/2016	03/04/2016	03/24/2016
0.33Q	05/11/2016	05/25/2016	05/27/2016	06/24/2016

Indicated Div: $1.32

Valuation Analysis

		Institutional Holding	
Forecast EPS	$1.88	No of Institutions	592
	(05/20/2016)		
Market Cap	$4.7 Billion	Shares	
Book Value	$5.1 Billion		159,212,320
Price/Book	0.93	% Held	
Price/Sales	0.39	N/A	

Business Summary: Refining & Marketing (MIC: 9.1.2 SIC: 2911 NAIC: 324110)

HollyFrontier is a petroleum refiner that produces refined products such as gasoline, diesel fuel, jet fuel, lubricant products, and asphalt. Co. has two reportable segments, Refining and its subsidiary, Holly Energy Partners, L.P. (HEP). The Refining segment represents the operations of the El Dorado, Tulsa, Navajo, Cheyenne and Woods Cross Refineries and HollyFrontier Asphalt Company. The HEP segment includes all of the operations of HEP, which owns and operates logistics and refinery assets consisting of petroleum product and crude oil pipelines, terminal, tankage, loading rack facilities and processing units in the Mid-Continent, Southwest and Rocky Mountain regions of the U.S.

Recent Developments: For the quarter ended Mar 31 2016, net income decreased 82.1% to US$43.4 million from US$242.7 million in the year-earlier quarter. Revenues were US$2.02 billion, down 32.9% from US$3.01 billion the year before. Operating income was US$83.6 million versus US$388.6 million in the prior-year quarter, a decrease of 78.5%. Direct operating expenses declined 30.1% to US$1.57 billion from US$2.24 billion in the comparable period the year before. Indirect operating expenses decreased 1.9% to US$366.1 million from US$373.2 million in the equivalent prior-year period.

Prospects: Our evaluation of HollyFrontier Corp. as of June 19, 2016 is the result of our systematic analysis on three basic characteristics: earnings strength, relative valuation, and recent stock price movement. The company has suffered a very negative trend in earnings per share over the past 5 quarters. However, while recent estimates for the company have been lowered by analysts, HFC has posted results that fell short of analysts expectations. Based on operating earnings yield, the company is undervalued when compared to all of the companies in our coverage universe. Share price changes over the past year indicates that HFC will perform very well over the near term.

Financial Data

(US$ in Thousands)	3 Mos	12/31/2015	12/31/2014	12/31/2013	12/31/2012	12/31/2011	12/31/2010	12/31/2009
Earnings Per Share	2.85	3.90	1.42	3.64	8.38	6.42	0.97	0.20
Cash Flow Per Share	4.18	5.19	3.85	4.34	8.08	8.44	2.66	2.10
Tang Book Value Per Share	15.61	16.21	16.28	18.45	18.25	13.70	5.78	5.06
Dividends Per Share	1.320	1.310	3.260	3.200	3.100	1.337	0.300	0.300
Dividend Payout %	46.32	33.59	229.58	87.91	36.99	20.83	30.93	153.85
Income Statement								
Total Revenue	2,018,724	13,237,920	19,764,327	20,160,560	20,090,724	15,439,528	8,322,929	4,834,268
EBITDA	106,704	1,485,685	770,523	1,437,565	3,067,372	1,841,434	356,998	155,585
Depn & Amortn	31,759	233,300	261,800	213,600	182,900	125,000	94,000	78,400
Income Before Taxes	62,933	1,212,306	469,507	1,161,471	2,785,072	1,639,395	189,970	41,884
Income Taxes	22,308	406,060	141,172	391,576	1,027,962	581,991	59,312	7,460
Net Income	21,253	740,101	281,292	735,842	1,727,172	1,023,397	103,964	19,533
Average Shares	176,784	188,940	197,428	201,234	206,184	159,294	107,218	101,206
Balance Sheet								
Current Assets	1,499,270	1,448,065	2,782,998	3,896,444	4,470,265	4,659,124	1,703,435	1,283,011
Total Assets	8,594,287	8,388,299	9,230,640	10,056,739	10,328,997	10,314,621	3,701,475	3,145,939
Current Liabilities	885,608	860,615	1,251,403	1,674,490	1,654,444	2,629,061	1,389,855	1,025,112
Long-Term Obligations	1,308,168	1,040,040	1,054,890	997,519	1,336,238	1,214,742	810,561	707,458
Total Liabilities	3,507,463	3,134,884	3,707,056	4,057,119	4,276,043	5,110,611	3,004,056	2,526,900
Stockholders' Equity	5,086,824	5,253,415	5,523,584	5,999,620	6,052,954	5,204,010	697,419	619,039
Shares Outstanding	176,520	180,234	196,086	198,830	203,551	209,332	106,529	106,132
Statistical Record								
Return on Assets %	5.99	8.40	2.92	7.22	16.69	14.60	3.04	0.78
Return on Equity %	9.98	13.73	4.88	12.21	30.60	34.68	15.79	3.37
EBITDA Margin %	5.29	11.22	3.90	7.13	15.27	11.93	4.29	3.22
Net Margin %	1.05	5.59	1.42	3.65	8.60	6.63	1.25	0.40
Asset Turnover	1.37	1.50	2.05	1.98	1.94	2.20	2.43	1.93
Current Ratio	1.69	1.68	2.22	2.33	2.70	1.77	1.23	1.25
Debt to Equity	0.26	0.20	0.19	0.17	0.22	0.23	1.16	1.14
Price Range	53.80-29.94	53.80-30.19	52.63-36.11	58.43-39.73	47.38-25.24	38.20-20.39	20.49-11.93	16.43-8.54
P/E Ratio	18.88-10.51	13.79-7.74	37.06-25.43	16.05-10.91	5.65-3.01	5.95-3.18	21.12-12.29	82.15-42.67
Average Yield %	3.10	3.01	7.06	6.81	8.65	4.56	2.08	2.57

Address: 2828 N. Harwood, Suite 1300, Dallas, TX 75201-1507 Telephone: 214-871-3555	Web Site: www.hollyfrontier.com Officers: Michael C. Jennings - Chairman, President, Chief Executive Officer, Associate/Affiliate Company Officer Douglas S. Aron - Executive Vice President, Chief Financial Officer	Auditors: Ernst & Young LLP Investor Contact: 214-871-3555 Transfer Agents: Wells Fargo Shareowner Services, Mendota Heights, MN

HOME DEPOT INC

Exchange	Symbol	Price	52Wk Range	Yield	P/E
NYS	HD	$132.12 (5/31/2016)	137.51-109.53	2.09	23.22

*7 Year Price Score 158.57 *NYSE Composite Index=100 *12 Month Price Score 107.79

Interim Earnings (Per Share)

Qtr.	Apr	Jul	Oct	Jan
2013-14	0.83	1.24	0.95	0.74
2014-15	1.00	1.52	1.15	1.05
2015-16	1.21	1.73	1.35	1.17
2016-17	1.44	...	...	...

Interim Dividends (Per Share)

Amt	Decl	Ex	Rec	Pay
0.59Q	08/20/2015	09/01/2015	09/03/2015	09/17/2015
0.59Q	11/19/2015	12/01/2015	12/03/2015	12/17/2015
0.69Q	02/23/2016	03/08/2016	03/10/2016	03/24/2016
0.69Q	05/19/2016	05/31/2016	06/02/2016	06/16/2016

Indicated Div: $2.76 (Div. Reinv. Plan)

Valuation Analysis

		Institutional Holding	
Forecast EPS	$6.30	No of Institutions	
	(05/20/2016)	2227	
Market Cap	$164.5 Billion	Shares	
Book Value	$6.3 Billion	1,080,127,104	
Price/Book	25.97	% Held	
Price/Sales	1.82	66.66	

Business Summary: Retail - Hardware & Home Improvement (MIC: 2.1.8 SIC: 5211 NAIC: 444110)

The Home Depot is a home improvement retailer. Co.'s stores sell a range of building materials, home improvement products and lawn and garden products and provide a number of services. As of Jan 31 2016, Co. had 2,274 The Home Depot stores located throughout the U.S., including the Commonwealth of Puerto Rico and the territories of the U.S. Virgin Islands and Guam, Canada and Mexico. Co. serves three primary customer groups: Do-It-Yourself customers, Do-It-For-Me customers, and professional customers. Co.'s products include EGOâ„¢ 58-volt cordless outdoor power tools; the Husky® 100 platform of mechanics tools; LifeProof Carpet®; and Milwaukee® Cobalt Red Helixâ„¢ drill bits.

Recent Developments: For the quarter ended May 1 2016, net income increased 14.2% to US$1.80 billion from US$1.58 billion in the year-earlier quarter. Revenues were US$22.76 billion, up 9.0% from US$20.89 billion the year before. Operating income was US$3.08 billion versus US$2.60 billion in the prior-year quarter, an increase of 18.5%. Direct operating expenses rose 9.2% to US$14.97 billion from US$13.71 billion in the comparable period the year before. Indirect operating expenses increased 2.9% to US$4.71 billion from US$4.58 billion in the equivalent prior-year period.

Prospects: Our evaluation of Home Depot Inc. as of June 19, 2016 is the result of our systematic analysis on three basic characteristics: earnings strength, relative valuation, and recent stock price movement. The company has produced a positive trend in earnings per share over the past 5 quarters and while recent estimates for the company have been raised by analysts, HD has posted better than expected results. Based on operating earnings yield, the company is about fairly valued when compared to all of the companies in our coverage universe. Share price changes over the past year indicates that HD will perform very well over the near term.

Financial Data

(US$ in Thousands)	3 Mos	01/31/2016	02/01/2015	02/02/2014	02/03/2013	01/29/2012	01/30/2011	01/31/2010
Earnings Per Share	5.69	5.46	4.71	3.76	3.00	2.47	2.01	1.57
Cash Flow Per Share	7.70	7.36	6.18	5.37	4.58	4.27	2.79	3.05
Tang Book Value Per Share	3.38	3.37	6.10	8.14	11.19	10.92	10.91	10.73
Dividends Per Share	2.460	2.360	1.880	1.560	1.160	1.040	0.945	0.900
Dividend Payout %	43.23	43.22	39.92	41.49	38.67	42.11	47.01	57.32
Income Statement								
Total Revenue	22,762,000	88,519,000	83,176,000	78,812,000	74,754,000	70,395,000	67,997,000	66,176,000
EBITDA	3,563,000	13,637,000	12,255,000	10,923,000	9,450,000	8,343,000	7,557,000	6,609,000
Depn & Amortn	486,000	1,863,000	1,786,000	1,757,000	1,684,000	1,682,000	1,718,000	1,806,000
Income Before Taxes	2,840,000	11,021,000	9,976,000	8,467,000	7,221,000	6,068,000	5,273,000	3,982,000
Income Taxes	1,037,000	4,012,000	3,631,000	3,082,000	2,686,000	2,185,000	1,935,000	1,362,000
Net Income	1,803,000	7,009,000	6,345,000	5,385,000	4,535,000	3,883,000	3,338,000	2,661,000
Average Shares	1,252,000	1,283,000	1,346,000	1,434,000	1,511,000	1,570,000	1,658,000	1,692,000
Balance Sheet								
Current Assets	19,010,000	16,993,000	15,302,000	15,279,000	15,372,000	14,520,000	13,479,000	13,900,000
Total Assets	44,576,000	42,549,000	39,946,000	40,518,000	41,084,000	40,518,000	40,125,000	40,877,000
Current Liabilities	15,149,000	12,526,000	11,269,000	10,749,000	11,462,000	9,376,000	10,122,000	10,363,000
Long-Term Obligations	20,904,000	20,888,000	16,869,000	14,691,000	9,475,000	10,758,000	8,707,000	8,662,000
Total Liabilities	38,241,000	36,233,000	30,624,000	27,996,000	23,307,000	22,620,000	21,236,000	21,484,000
Stockholders' Equity	6,335,000	6,316,000	9,322,000	12,522,000	17,777,000	17,898,000	18,889,000	19,393,000
Shares Outstanding	1,245,000	1,252,000	1,307,000	1,380,000	1,484,000	1,537,000	1,623,000	1,698,000
Statistical Record								
Return on Assets %	16.61	17.04	15.81	13.23	10.94	9.66	8.26	6.50
Return on Equity %	93.09	89.89	58.25	35.64	25.01	21.17	17.49	14.36
EBITDA Margin %	15.65	15.41	14.73	13.86	12.64	11.85	11.11	9.99
Net Margin %	7.92	7.92	7.63	6.83	6.07	5.52	4.91	4.02
Asset Turnover	2.08	2.15	2.07	1.94	1.80	1.75	1.68	1.62
Current Ratio	1.25	1.36	1.36	1.42	1.34	1.55	1.33	1.34
Debt to Equity	3.30	3.31	1.81	1.17	0.53	0.60	0.46	0.45
Price Range	136.80-108.06	134.74-104.43	107.62-74.97	82.34-63.92	67.82-44.39	45.41-28.51	37.98-27.07	29.29-18.00
P/E Ratio	24.04-18.99	24.68-19.13	22.85-15.92	21.90-17.00	22.61-14.80	18.38-11.54	18.90-13.47	18.66-11.46
Average Yield %	2.02	2.00	2.15	2.06	2.08	2.83	2.97	3.54

Address: 2455 Paces Ferry Road N.W., Atlanta, GA 30339	**Web Site:** www.homedepot.com	**Auditors:** KPMG LLP
Telephone: 770-433-8211	**Officers:** Craig A. Menear - Chairman, President, Chief Executive Officer, Executive Vice President, Region Officer Matthew A. Carey - Executive Vice President, Chief Information Officer	**Investor Contact:** 770-384-4388
Fax: 770-431-2707		**Transfer Agents:** Computershare Trust Company, N.A., Providence, RI

HONEYWELL INTERNATIONAL INC

Exchange	Symbol	Price	52Wk Range	Yield	P/E
NYS	HON	$113.83 (5/31/2016)	115.80-91.59	2.09	18.45

*7 Year Price Score 125.08 *NYSE Composite Index=100 ***12 Month Price Score 107.88**

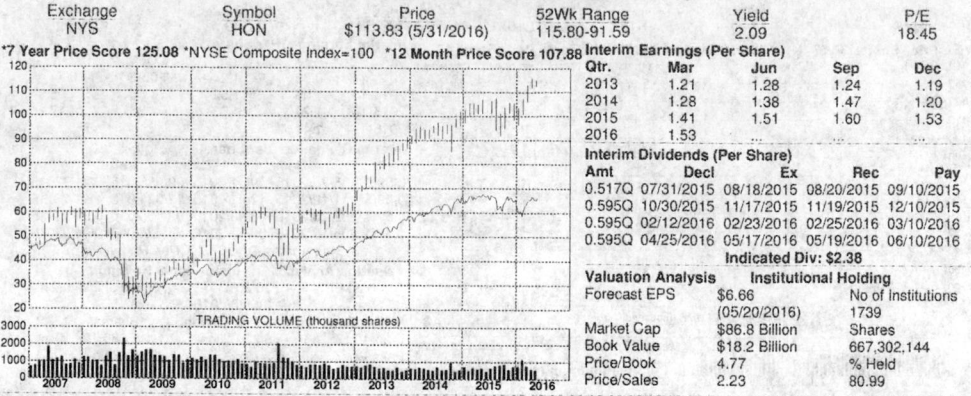

Interim Earnings (Per Share)

Qtr.	Mar	Jun	Sep	Dec
2013	1.21	1.28	1.24	1.19
2014	1.28	1.38	1.47	1.20
2015	1.41	1.51	1.60	1.53
2016	1.53			

Interim Dividends (Per Share)

Amt	Decl	Ex	Rec	Pay
0.517Q	07/31/2015	08/18/2015	08/20/2015	09/10/2015
0.595Q	10/30/2015	11/17/2015	11/19/2015	12/10/2015
0.595Q	02/12/2016	02/23/2016	02/25/2016	03/10/2016
0.595Q	04/25/2016	05/17/2016	05/19/2016	06/10/2016

Indicated Div: $2.38

Valuation Analysis

		Institutional Holding	
Forecast EPS	$6.66	No of Institutions	
	(05/20/2016)	1739	
Market Cap	$86.8 Billion	Shares	
Book Value	$18.2 Billion	667,302,144	
Price/Book	4.77	% Held	
Price/Sales	2.23	80.99	

Business Summary: Auto Parts (MIC: 1.8.2 SIC: 3714 NAIC: 336312)

Honeywell International is a technology and manufacturing company. Co. manages its business operations through three businesses that are reported as operating segments: Aerospace, which is a supplier of aircraft engines, integrated avionics, systems and service solutions, and related products and services; Automation and Control Solutions, which is a provider of environmental and combustion controls, sensing controls, security and life safety products and services, scanning and mobility devices and building solutions and services; and Performance Materials and Technologies, which develops and manufactures materials, process technologies and automation solutions.

Recent Developments: For the quarter ended Mar 31 2016, net income increased 4.4% to US$1.20 billion from US$1.15 billion in the year-earlier quarter. Revenues were US$9.52 billion, up 3.4% from US$9.21 billion the year before. Direct operating expenses rose 2.9% to US$6.55 billion from US$6.36 billion in the comparable period the year before. Indirect operating expenses increased 4.1% to US$1.28 billion from US$1.23 billion in the equivalent prior-year period.

Prospects: Our evaluation of Honeywell International Inc. as of June 19, 2016 is the result of our systematic analysis on three basic characteristics: earnings strength, relative valuation, and recent stock price movement. The company has managed to produce a neutral trend in earnings per share over the past 5 quarters and while recent estimates for the company have remained steady, HON has posted better than expected results. Based on operating earnings yield, the company is undervalued when compared to all of the companies in our coverage universe. Share price changes over the past year indicates that HON will perform well over the near term.

Financial Data

(US$ in Thousands)	3 Mos	12/31/2015	12/31/2014	12/31/2013	12/31/2012	12/31/2011	12/31/2010	12/31/2009
Earnings Per Share	6.17	6.04	5.33	4.92	3.69	2.61	2.59	2.85
Cash Flow Per Share	6.89	6.99	6.40	5.51	4.48	3.63	5.43	5.24
Tang Book Value Per Share	N.M.	N.M.	3.68	2.65	N.M.	N.M.	N.M.	N.M.
Dividends Per Share	2.225	2.148	1.867	1.680	1.528	1.370	1.210	1.210
Dividend Payout %	36.06	35.55	35.04	34.15	41.40	52.49	46.72	42.46
Income Statement								
Total Revenue	9,522,000	38,581,000	40,306,000	39,055,000	37,665,000	36,529,000	33,370,000	30,908,000
EBITDA	1,966,000	7,434,000	6,665,000	6,304,000	4,783,000	3,248,000	3,884,000	4,085,000
Depn & Amortn	253,000	672,000	667,000	670,000	660,000	699,000	724,000	707,000
Income Before Taxes	1,628,000	6,556,000	5,782,000	5,376,000	3,830,000	2,231,000	2,814,000	2,952,000
Income Taxes	432,000	1,739,000	1,489,000	1,450,000	944,000	417,000	808,000	789,000
Net Income	1,186,000	4,768,000	4,239,000	3,924,000	2,926,000	2,067,000	2,022,000	2,153,000
Average Shares	776,900	789,300	795,200	797,300	791,900	791,600	780,900	755,720
Balance Sheet								
Current Assets	19,532,000	20,053,000	22,191,000	21,164,000	17,598,000	16,134,000	15,011,000	13,936,000
Total Assets	50,365,000	49,316,000	45,451,000	45,435,000	41,853,000	39,808,000	37,834,000	36,004,000
Current Liabilities	15,659,000	18,371,000	14,773,000	14,181,000	13,045,000	12,275,000	11,717,000	11,147,000
Long-Term Obligations	9,700,000	5,554,000	6,046,000	6,801,000	6,395,000	6,881,000	5,755,000	6,246,000
Total Liabilities	32,165,000	30,743,000	27,575,000	27,801,000	28,728,000	29,002,000	27,168,000	27,160,000
Stockholders' Equity	18,200,000	18,573,000	17,876,000	17,634,000	13,125,000	10,806,000	10,666,000	8,844,000
Shares Outstanding	762,115	770,400	782,200	783,800	782,800	774,700	783,000	764,209
Statistical Record								
Return on Assets %	10.11	10.06	9.33	8.99	7.15	5.32	5.48	6.02
Return on Equity %	26.89	26.16	23.87	25.51	24.39	19.25	20.73	26.86
EBITDA Margin %	20.65	19.27	16.54	16.14	12.70	8.89	11.64	13.22
Net Margin %	12.46	12.36	10.52	10.05	7.77	5.66	6.06	6.97
Asset Turnover	0.81	0.81	0.89	0.89	0.92	0.94	0.90	0.86
Current Ratio	1.25	1.09	1.50	1.49	1.35	1.31	1.28	1.25
Debt to Equity	0.53	0.30	0.34	0.39	0.49	0.64	0.54	0.71
Price Range	112.98-91.59	107.30-91.59	101.98-85.11	91.37-63.47	64.29-52.92	62.00-41.94	53.72-36.87	41.31-23.23
P/E Ratio	18.31-14.84	17.76-15.16	19.13-15.97	18.57-12.90	17.42-14.34	23.75-16.07	20.74-14.24	14.49-8.15
Average Yield %	2.16	2.10	1.99	2.12	2.59	2.54	2.74	3.54

Address: 115 Tabor Road, Morris Plains, NJ 07950	Web Site: www.honeywell.com	Auditors: Deloitte & Touche LLP
Telephone: 973-455-2000	Officers: David M. Cote - Chairman, Chief Executive Officer Roger Fradin - Co-Vice Chairman, Division Officer	Investor Contact: 973-455-2222
Fax: 973-455-4807		Transfer Agents: American Stock Transfer & Trust Company, LLC, Brookly, NY

HORMEL FOODS CORP.

Exchange	Symbol	Price	52Wk Range	Yield	P/E	Div Achiever
NYS	HRL	$34.41 (5/31/2016)	44.47-28.07	1.69	23.73	49 Years

*7 Year Price Score 155.91 *NYSE Composite Index=100 *12 Month Price Score 108.06

Interim Earnings (Per Share)

Qtr.	Jan	Apr	Jul	Oct
2012-13	0.24	0.23	0.21	0.29
2013-14	0.28	0.26	0.26	0.32
2014-15	0.32	0.34	0.27	0.34
2015-16	0.43	0.40	...	...

Interim Dividends (Per Share)

Amt	Decl	Ex	Rec	Pay
0.145Q	11/23/2015	01/14/2016	01/19/2016	02/16/2016
2-for-1	11/25/2015	02/10/2016	01/26/2016	02/09/2016
0.145Q	03/29/2016	04/14/2016	04/18/2016	05/16/2016
0.145Q	05/23/2016	07/14/2016	07/18/2016	08/15/2016

Indicated Div: $0.58 (Div. Reinv. Plan)

Valuation Analysis — **Institutional Holding**

Forecast EPS	$1.60 (05/17/2016)	No of Institutions	660
Market Cap	$18.2 Billion	Shares	187,118,624
Book Value	$4.3 Billion	% Held	30.40
Price/Book	4.24		
Price/Sales	1.99		

TRADING VOLUME (thousand shares)

Business Summary: Food (MIC: 1.2.1 SIC: 2011 NAIC: 311611)

Hormel Foods is engaged in the production of a variety of meat and food products and the marketing of those products throughout the U.S. and internationally. Co.'s business is reported in five segments: Grocery Products, which processes, markets, and sells shelf-stable food products; Refrigerated Foods, which processes markets, and sells pork and beef products; Jennie-O Turkey Store, which processes, markets, and sells turkey products; Specialty Foods, which packages and sells shelf stable products, nutritional products, sugar, and condiments to industrial, retail, and foodservice customers; and International and Other, which manufactures, markets, and sells Co.'s products internationally

Recent Developments: For the quarter ended Apr 24 2016, net income increased 19.4% to US$215.4 million from US$180.4 million in the year-earlier quarter. Revenues were US$2.30 billion, up 0.9% from US$2.28 billion the year before. Operating income was US$323.8 million versus US$277.7 million in the prior-year quarter, an increase of 16.6%. Direct operating expenses declined 2.5% to US$1.77 billion from US$1.82 billion in the comparable period the year before. Indirect operating expenses increased 11.4% to US$202.5 million from US$181.9 million in the equivalent prior-year period.

Prospects: Our evaluation of Hormel Foods Corp. as of June 19, 2016 is the result of our systematic analysis on three basic characteristics: earnings strength, relative valuation, and recent stock price movement. The company has managed to produce a neutral trend in earnings per share over the past 5 quarters. However, while recent estimates for the company have been mixed, HRL has posted better than expected results. Based on operating earnings yield, the company is about fairly valued when compared to all of the companies in our coverage universe. Share price changes over the past year indicates that HRL will perform very well over the near term.

Financial Data

(US$ in Thousands)	6 Mos	3 Mos	10/25/2015	10/26/2014	10/27/2013	10/28/2012	10/30/2011	10/31/2010
Earnings Per Share	1.45	1.38	1.27	1.12	0.97	0.93	0.87	0.73
Cash Flow Per Share	1.80	1.94	1.88	1.42	1.21	0.99	0.92	0.90
Tang Book Value Per Share	3.37	3.09	2.78	3.46	3.79	3.93	3.59	3.06
Dividends Per Share	0.540	0.520	0.500	0.400	0.340	0.300	0.255	0.210
Dividend Payout %	37.37	37.68	39.37	35.87	34.87	32.26	29.31	28.77
Income Statement								
Total Revenue	4,592,907	2,292,672	9,263,863	9,316,256	8,751,654	8,230,670	7,895,089	7,220,719
EBITDA	726,195	379,867	1,185,009	1,053,431	919,805	854,452	849,168	769,572
Depn & Amortn	63,908	31,804	141,576	139,396	134,329	128,469	133,641	136,123
Income Before Taxes	657,297	342,693	1,033,256	904,567	777,994	719,644	692,079	611,425
Income Taxes	227,814	119,001	369,879	316,126	268,431	253,374	239,640	224,775
Net Income	450,458	235,061	686,088	602,677	526,211	500,050	474,195	395,587
Average Shares	543,769	542,737	541,002	540,432	540,448	537,782	543,830	541,396
Balance Sheet								
Current Assets	1,975,082	1,946,083	2,063,032	2,132,771	2,047,413	2,320,684	1,998,231	1,858,166
Total Assets	6,110,345	6,040,889	6,139,831	5,455,619	4,915,880	4,563,966	4,244,391	4,053,918
Current Liabilities	937,384	1,020,098	1,214,025	954,692	784,009	786,300	778,186	1,101,213
Long-Term Obligations	250,000	250,000	250,000	250,000	250,000	250,000	250,000	...
Total Liabilities	1,803,862	1,880,601	2,141,633	1,849,941	1,604,840	1,744,511	1,587,809	1,653,261
Stockholders' Equity	4,306,483	4,160,288	3,998,198	3,605,678	3,311,040	2,819,455	2,656,582	2,400,657
Shares Outstanding	530,044	529,366	528,411	527,226	527,316	526,088	527,926	531,926
Statistical Record								
Return on Assets %	13.37	12.92	11.87	11.65	11.13	11.39	11.46	10.05
Return on Equity %	19.26	19.00	18.10	17.47	17.21	18.31	18.80	17.21
EBITDA Margin %	15.81	16.57	12.79	11.31	10.51	10.38	10.76	10.66
Net Margin %	9.81	10.25	7.41	6.47	6.01	6.08	6.01	5.48
Asset Turnover	1.57	1.58	1.60	1.80	1.85	1.87	1.91	1.83
Current Ratio	2.11	1.91	1.70	2.23	2.61	2.95	2.57	1.69
Debt to Equity	0.06	0.06	0.06	0.07	0.08	0.09	0.09	...
Price Range	44.47-27.18	40.26-25.61	34.24-25.07	26.27-21.11	22.06-14.77	15.34-13.74	15.19-11.40	11.48-9.21
P/E Ratio	30.67-18.74	29.17-18.56	26.96-19.74	23.46-18.85	22.74-15.22	16.49-14.77	17.45-13.10	15.73-12.62
Average Yield %	1.56	1.67	1.67	1.75	1.69	1.77	2.07	1.87	2.03

Address: 1 Hormel Place, Austin, MN 55912-3680
Telephone: 507-437-5611
Fax: 507-437-5489

Web Site: www.hormel.com
Officers: Jeffrey M. Ettinger - Chairman, President, Chief Executive Officer James P. Snee - President, Chief Operating Officer, Vice President, Group Vice President, Division Officer

Auditors: Ernst & Young LLP
Investor Contact: 507-437-5248
Transfer Agents: Wells Fargo Shareowner Services, Mendota Heights, MN

HORTON (D.R.) INC.

Exchange	Symbol	Price	52Wk Range	Yield	P/E
NYS	DHI	$30.56 (5/31/2016)	33.03-23.23	1.05	14.02

*7 Year Price Score 133.12 *NYSE Composite Index=100 ***12 Month Price Score 101.99**

TRADING VOLUME (thousand shares)

Interim Earnings (Per Share)

Qtr.	Dec	Mar	Jun	Sep
2012-13	0.20	0.32	0.42	0.40
2013-14	0.36	0.38	0.32	0.45
2014-15	0.39	0.40	0.60	0.64
2015-16	0.42	0.52		

Interim Dividends (Per Share)

Amt	Decl	Ex	Rec	Pay
0.063Q	07/28/2015	08/05/2015	08/07/2015	08/18/2015
0.08Q	11/10/2015	11/25/2015	11/30/2015	12/14/2015
0.08Q	01/25/2016	02/03/2016	02/05/2016	02/17/2016
0.08Q	04/21/2016	05/11/2016	05/13/2016	05/27/2016

Indicated Div: $0.32

Valuation Analysis | Institutional Holding

Forecast EPS	$2.38 (05/20/2016)	No of Institutions	723
Market Cap	$11.3 Billion	Shares	341,810,368
Book Value	$6.2 Billion	% Held	91.83
Price/Book	1.81		
Price/Sales	1.00		

Business Summary: Builders (MIC: 2.2.5 SIC: 1531 NAIC: 236117)

D.R. Horton is a homebuilding company. As of Sep 30 2015, Co.'s homebuilding segments were primarily engaged in the acquisition and development of land and construction and sale of residential homes in 27 states and 79 markets. Co. builds single-family detached homes, as well as attached homes such as town homes, duplexes, triplexes and condominiums. Through its financial services operations, Co. provides mortgage financing and title agency services to homebuyers in its homebuilding markets. Co.'s DHI Mortgage subsidiary provides mortgage financing services mainly to its homebuilding customers and sells the mortgages it originates and the related servicing rights to third-party purchasers.

Recent Developments: For the quarter ended Mar 31 2016, net income increased 31.9% to US$195.1 million from US$147.9 million in the year-earlier quarter. Revenues were US$2.77 billion, up 15.4% from US$2.40 billion the year before. Direct operating expenses rose 14.7% to US$2.17 billion from US$1.89 billion in the comparable period the year before. Indirect operating expenses increased 8.0% to US$298.1 million from US$275.9 million in the equivalent prior-year period.

Prospects: Our evaluation of Horton (D.R.) Inc. as of June 19, 2016 is the result of our systematic analysis on three basic characteristics: earnings strength, relative valuation, and recent stock price movement. The company has generated a negative trend in earnings per share over the past 5 quarters. However, while recent estimates for the company have been mixed, DHI has posted better than expected results. Based on operating earnings yield, the company is undervalued when compared to all of the companies in our coverage universe. Share price changes over the past year indicates that DHI will perform well over the near term.

Financial Data

(US$ in Thousands)	6 Mos	3 Mos	09/30/2015	09/30/2014	09/30/2013	09/30/2012	09/30/2011	09/30/2010
Earnings Per Share	2.18	2.06	2.03	1.50	1.33	2.77	0.23	0.77
Cash Flow Per Share	2.42	2.24	1.91	(1.94)	(3.82)	(0.93)	0.05	2.23
Tang Book Value Per Share	16.62	16.15	15.75	13.77	12.45	11.07	8.24	8.15
Dividends Per Share	0.285	0.268	0.250	0.138	0.188	0.150	0.150	0.150
Dividend Payout %	13.07	12.99	12.32	9.17	14.10	5.42	65.22	19.48
Income Statement								
Total Revenue	5,184,300	2,416,400	10,824,000	8,024,900	6,259,300	4,354,000	3,636,800	4,400,200
EBITDA	540,000	239,600	1,161,200	840,600	676,700	278,400	74,300	194,900
Depn & Amortn	2,800	1,400	50,300	36,600	22,300	18,800	19,900	17,200
Income Before Taxes	541,800	241,300	1,123,400	814,200	657,800	242,900	12,100	99,500
Income Taxes	189,000	83,600	372,700	280,700	195,100	(713,400)	(59,700)	(145,600)
Net Income	352,800	157,700	750,700	533,500	462,700	956,300	71,800	245,100
Average Shares	373,700	373,500	369,800	366,600	364,900	359,000	318,500	318,600
Balance Sheet								
Current Assets	9,577,100	9,524,300	9,376,200	8,549,300	7,397,900	5,821,500	4,778,800	5,125,700
Total Assets	11,300,200	11,179,500	11,151,000	10,202,500	8,856,400	7,248,200	5,358,400	5,938,600
Current Liabilities	779,500	753,900	784,600	747,300	636,400	377,600	294,500	186,700
Long-Term Obligations	3,662,800	3,734,300	3,811,500	3,682,800	3,509,000	2,493,100	1,704,600	2,171,800
Total Liabilities	5,051,800	5,120,100	5,256,700	5,086,700	4,797,900	3,656,100	2,737,800	3,325,400
Stockholders' Equity	6,248,400	6,059,400	5,894,300	5,115,800	4,058,500	3,592,100	2,620,600	2,613,200
Shares Outstanding	370,731	369,727	368,647	364,586	322,943	320,891	316,043	318,823
Statistical Record								
Return on Assets %	7.39	7.12	7.03	5.60	5.75	15.13	1.27	3.86
Return on Equity %	13.94	13.53	13.64	11.63	12.10	30.70	2.74	10.06
EBITDA Margin %	10.42	9.92	10.73	10.47	10.81	6.39	2.04	4.43
Net Margin %	6.81	6.53	6.94	6.65	7.39	21.96	1.97	5.57
Asset Turnover	1.03	1.02	1.01	0.84	0.78	0.69	0.64	0.69
Current Ratio	12.29	12.63	11.95	11.44	11.62	15.42	16.23	27.45
Debt to Equity	0.59	0.62	0.65	0.72	0.86	0.69	0.65	0.83
Price Range	33.03-23.23	33.03-22.95	32.21-19.49	25.10-17.69	27.60-17.77	22.37-8.45	13.50-8.94	14.97-9.71
P/E Ratio	15.15-10.66	16.03-11.14	15.87-9.60	16.73-11.79	20.75-13.36	8.08-3.05	58.70-38.87	19.44-12.61
Average Yield %	0.99	0.94	0.95	0.63	0.86	0.98	1.33	1.29

Address: 301 Commerce Street, Suite 500, Fort Worth, TX 76102
Telephone: 817-390-8200

Web Site: www.drhorton.com
Officers: Donald R. Horton - Chairman David V. Auld - President, Chief Executive Officer, Executive Vice President, Chief Operating Officer, Division Officer

Auditors: PricewaterhouseCoopers LLP
Investor Contact: 817-390-8200
Transfer Agents: American Stock Transfer & Trust Co., New York, NY

HOSPITALITY PROPERTIES TRUST

Exchange	Symbol	Price	52Wk Range	Yield	P/E
NYS	HPT	$25.60 (5/31/2016)	30.36-21.77	7.97	24.62

*7 Year Price Score 89.72   *NYSE Composite Index=100   *12 Month Price Score 98.25

Interim Earnings (Per Share)

Qtr.	Mar	Jun	Sep	Dec
2013	0.15	0.27	0.12	0.19
2014	0.22	0.33	0.29	0.35
2015	0.24	0.52	0.37	(0.16)
2016	0.31	...	...	...

Interim Dividends (Per Share)

Amt	Decl	Ex	Rec	Pay
0.50Q	10/13/2015	10/21/2015	10/23/2015	11/19/2015
0.00Q	11/16/2015	12/15/2015	11/27/2015	12/14/2015
0.50Q	01/11/2016	01/20/2016	01/22/2016	02/23/2016
0.51Q	04/13/2016	04/21/2016	04/25/2016	05/19/2016

Indicated Div: $2.04

Valuation Analysis | **Institutional Holding**

Forecast EPS	$1.62	No of Institutions
	(05/16/2016)	485
Market Cap	$3.9 Billion	Shares
Book Value	$2.8 Billion	129,611,424
Price/Book	1.39	% Held
Price/Sales	1.98	81.51

Business Summary: REITs (MIC: 5.3.1 SIC: 6798 NAIC: 525930)

Hospitality Properties Trust is a real estate investment trust. Co. invests in hotels and travel related real estate. As of Dec 31 2015, Co., directly and through subsidiaries, owned 302 hotels and 193 travel centers. Co.'s properties are located in 45 states in the U.S., Canada and Puerto Rico. At Dec 31 2015, Co.'s properties were leased or managed by subsidiaries of the following companies: Marriott International, Inc., InterContinental Hotels Group, plc, Sonesta International Hotels Corporation, Wyndham Hotel Group, Hyatt Hotels Corporation, Carlson Hotels Worldwide, Morgans Hotel Group, and TravelCenters of America LLC.

Recent Developments: For the quarter ended Mar 31 2016, net income increased 25.2% to US$52.1 million from US$41.6 million in the year-earlier quarter. Revenues were US$474.1 million, up 8.9% from US$435.5 million the year before. Revenues from property income rose 17.7% to US$77.6 million from US$65.9 million in the corresponding quarter a year earlier.

Prospects: Our evaluation of Hospitality Properties Trust as of June 19, 2016 is the result of our systematic analysis on three basic characteristics: earnings strength, relative valuation, and recent stock price movement. The company has produced a positive trend in earnings per share over the past 5 quarters. Because the company lacks sufficient analyst estimate data, we place greater weight on the historical EPS trend as the measure of earnings strength. Based on operating earnings yield, the company is about fairly valued when compared to all of the companies in our coverage universe. Share price changes over the past year indicates that HPT will perform poorly over the near term.

Financial Data

(US$ in Thousands)	3 Mos	12/31/2015	12/31/2014	12/31/2013	12/31/2012	12/31/2011	12/31/2010	12/31/2009
Earnings Per Share	1.04	0.97	1.18	0.73	0.84	1.30	(0.07)	1.51
Cash Flow Per Share	3.13	3.52	3.09	2.84	2.94	2.88	2.77	2.96
Tang Book Value Per Share	16.63	16.71	18.08	18.76	18.54	19.50	20.01	21.90
Dividends Per Share	2.000	1.990	1.950	1.890	1.820	1.800	1.800	0.770
Dividend Payout %	192.31	205.15	165.25	258.90	216.67	138.46	...	50.99
Income Statement								
Total Revenue	474,118	1,921,904	1,736,322	1,563,855	1,296,982	1,210,333	1,085,488	1,037,247
EBITDA	95,702	637,427	659,684	579,110	556,072	560,490	405,654	598,861
Depn & Amortn	1,865	335,625	321,369	305,527	267,010	234,647	245,212	256,914
Income Before Taxes	52,349	156,948	198,906	127,750	153,219	191,803	21,990	198,537
Income Taxes	375	1,566	1,945	(5,094)	1,612	1,502	638	5,196
Net Income	52,051	166,418	197,185	133,178	151,923	190,440	21,351	193,341
Average Shares	151,415	151,002	149,817	137,553	123,574	123,470	123,403	107,984
Balance Sheet								
Current Assets	127,224	64,893	45,816	53,373	60,793	181,524	85,503	155,482
Total Assets	6,532,140	6,407,597	5,982,562	5,967,544	5,635,125	5,133,573	5,192,286	5,548,370
Current Liabilities	233,585	308,042	153,796	176,684	178,969	218,557	220,822	262,878
Long-Term Obligations	3,497,694	3,287,473	2,838,613	2,704,005	2,722,358	2,115,714	2,111,223	2,193,561
Total Liabilities	3,731,279	3,595,515	2,992,409	2,880,689	2,901,327	2,334,271	2,332,045	2,456,439
Stockholders' Equity	2,800,861	2,812,082	2,990,153	3,086,855	2,733,798	2,799,302	2,860,241	3,091,931
Shares Outstanding	151,547	151,547	149,920	149,606	123,637	123,521	123,444	123,380
Statistical Record								
Return on Assets %	2.82	2.69	3.30	2.30	2.81	3.69	0.40	3.48
Return on Equity %	6.13	5.74	6.49	4.58	5.48	6.73	0.72	6.79
EBITDA Margin %	20.19	33.17	37.99	37.03	42.87	46.31	37.37	57.74
Net Margin %	10.98	8.66	11.36	8.52	11.71	15.73	1.97	18.64
Asset Turnover	0.31	0.31	0.29	0.27	0.24	0.23	0.20	0.19
Current Ratio	0.54	0.21	0.30	0.30	0.34	0.83	0.39	0.59
Debt to Equity	1.25	1.17	0.95	0.88	1.00	0.76	0.74	0.71
Price Range	33.80-21.77	33.80-24.65	31.74-24.52	32.01-23.24	27.42-21.31	25.51-18.91	27.77-19.00	23.84-9.02
P/E Ratio	32.50-20.93	34.85-25.41	26.90-20.78	43.86-31.84	32.64-25.37	19.63-14.54	...	15.79-5.97
Average Yield %	7.36	6.86	6.83	6.91	7.53	7.80	8.02	4.94

Address: Two Newton Place, 255 Washington Street, Suite 300, Newton, MA 02458-1634	Web Site: www.hptreit.com	Auditors: Ernst & Young LLP
	Officers: John G. Murray - President, Chief Operating Officer, Assistant Secretary Ethan S. Bornstein - Senior Vice President	Investor Contact: 617-796-8232
Telephone: 617-964-8389		Transfer Agents: Wells Fargo Shareowner Services, Mendota Heights, MN

HP INC

	Exchange	Symbol	Price	52Wk Range	Yield	P/E
	NYS	HPQ	$13.38 (5/31/2016)	15.42-9.02	3.71	7.08

*7 Year Price Score 72.02   *NYSE Composite Index=100   *12 Month Price Score 99.08

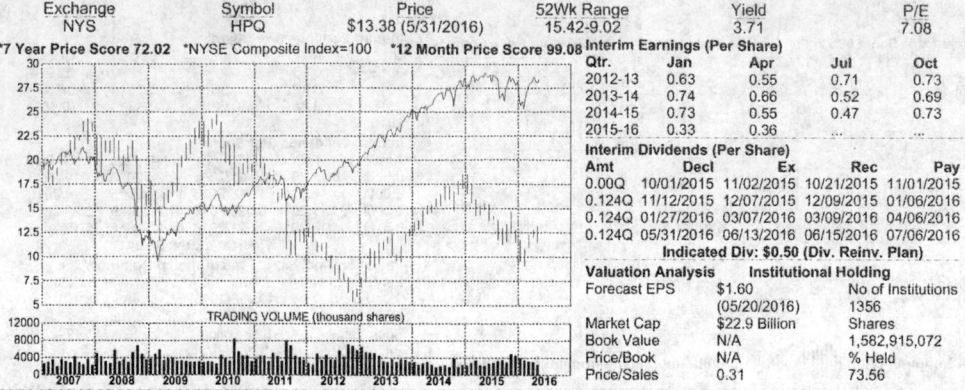

Interim Earnings (Per Share)

Qtr.	Jan	Apr	Jul	Oct
2012-13	0.63	0.55	0.71	0.73
2013-14	0.74	0.66	0.52	0.69
2014-15	0.73	0.55	0.47	0.73
2015-16	0.33	0.36		

Interim Dividends (Per Share)

Amt	Decl	Ex	Rec	Pay
0.00Q	10/01/2015	11/02/2015	10/21/2015	11/01/2015
0.124Q	11/12/2015	12/07/2015	12/09/2015	01/06/2016
0.124Q	01/27/2016	03/07/2016	03/09/2016	04/06/2016
0.124Q	05/31/2016	06/13/2016	06/15/2016	07/06/2016

Indicated Div: $0.50 (Div. Reinv. Plan)

Valuation Analysis / Institutional Holding

Forecast EPS	$1.60	No of Institutions
	(05/20/2016)	1356
Market Cap	$22.9 Billion	Shares
Book Value	N/A	1,582,915,072
Price/Book	N/A	% Held
Price/Sales	0.31	73.56

Business Summary: Computer Hardware & Equipment (MIC: 6.2.1 SIC: 3571 NAIC: 334111)

HP is a provider of products, technologies, software, solutions and services to individual consumers, businesses enterprises, including customers in the government, health and education sectors. Co.'s portolio include personal computing and other access devices, imaging and printing-related products and services, enterprise IT infrastructure products and solutions, multi-vendor customer services and IT management software and solutions. As of Oct 31 2015, Co.'s operations were organized into seven business segments: Personal Systems; Printing; the Enterprise Group; Enterprise Services; Software; HP Financial Services; and Corporate Investments.

Recent Developments: For the quarter ended Apr 30 2016, income from continuing operations decreased 10.0% to US$660.0 million from US$733.0 million in the year-earlier quarter. Net income decreased 37.8% to US$629.0 million from US$1.01 billion in the year-earlier quarter. Revenues were US$11.59 billion, down 10.7% from US$12.98 billion the year before. Operating income was US$841.0 million versus US$997.0 million in the prior-year quarter, a decrease of 15.6%. Direct operating expenses declined 10.3% to US$9.34 billion from US$10.42 billion in the comparable period the year before. Indirect operating expenses decreased 10.0% to US$1.41 billion from US$1.57 billion in the equivalent prior-year period.

Prospects: Our evaluation of HP Inc as of June 19, 2016 is the result of our systematic analysis on three basic characteristics: earnings strength, relative valuation, and recent stock price movement. The company has generated a negative trend in earnings per share over the past 5 quarters. However, while recent estimates for the company have been mixed, HPQ has posted better than expected results. Based on operating earnings yield, the company is undervalued when compared to all of the companies in our coverage universe. Share price changes over the past year indicates that HPQ will perform very poorly over the near term.

Financial Data

(US$ in Millions)	6 Mos	3 Mos	10/31/2015	10/31/2014	10/31/2013	10/31/2012	10/31/2011	10/31/2010
Earnings Per Share	1.89	2.08	2.48	2.62	2.62	(6.41)	3.32	3.69
Cash Flow Per Share	3.34	3.17	3.58	6.55	6.00	5.34	6.04	5.14
Dividends Per Share	0.600	0.636	0.672	0.610	0.554	0.504	0.400	0.320
Dividend Payout %	31.75	30.58	27.10	23.30	21.16	...	12.05	8.67
Income Statement								
Total Revenue	23,834	12,246	103,355	111,454	112,298	120,357	127,245	126,033
EBITDA	1,783	936	9,502	11,485	11,704	(5,973)	14,684	15,758
Depn & Amortn	14	8	4,031	4,300	4,573	5,084	5,007	4,784
Income Before Taxes	1,670	834	4,732	6,557	6,510	(11,933)	8,982	10,974
Income Taxes	360	184	178	1,544	1,397	717	1,908	2,213
Net Income	1,221	592	4,554	5,013	5,113	(12,650)	7,074	8,761
Average Shares	1,731	1,785	1,836	1,912	1,950	1,974	2,128	2,373
Balance Sheet								
Current Assets	15,385	15,155	51,787	50,145	50,364	50,637	51,021	54,184
Total Assets	25,523	25,517	106,882	103,206	105,676	108,768	129,517	124,503
Current Liabilities	16,862	16,761	42,191	43,735	45,521	46,666	50,442	49,403
Long-Term Obligations	6,708	6,683	21,780	16,039	16,608	21,789	22,551	15,258
Total Liabilities	30,309	30,426	79,114	76,475	78,407	86,332	90,892	84,054
Stockholders' Equity	(4,786)	(4,909)	27,768	26,731	27,269	22,436	38,625	40,449
Shares Outstanding	1,711	1,737	1,803	1,839	1,907	1,962	1,990	2,204
Statistical Record								
Return on Assets %	5.35	5.98	4.34	4.80	4.77	N.M.	5.57	7.32
Return on Equity %	30.92	35.00	16.71	18.57	20.57	N.M.	17.89	21.64
EBITDA Margin %	7.48	7.64	9.19	10.30	10.42	N.M.	11.54	12.50
Net Margin %	5.12	4.83	4.41	4.50	4.55	N.M.	5.56	6.95
Asset Turnover	1.18	1.40	0.98	1.07	1.05	1.01	1.00	1.05
Current Ratio	0.91	0.90	1.23	1.15	1.11	1.09	1.01	1.10
Debt to Equity	...	...	0.78	0.60	0.61	0.97	0.58	0.38
Price Range	15.78-9.02	17.51-9.48	18.49-11.15	17.32-11.06	12.39-5.32	13.20-6.29	22.24-10.08	24.75-17.25
P/E Ratio	8.35-4.77	8.42-4.56	7.45-4.50	6.61-4.22	4.73-2.03	...	6.70-3.04	6.71-4.68
Average Yield %	4.74	4.65	4.48	4.20	5.92	4.99	2.37	1.48

Address: 1501 Page Mill Road, Palo Alto, CA 94304
Telephone: 650-857-1501

Web Site: www.hp.com
Officers: Margaret C. Whitman - Chairwoman, President, Chief Executive Officer Jon Flaxman - Chief Operating Officer

Auditors: Ernst & Young LLP
Investor Contact: 800-286-5977
Transfer Agents: Wells Fargo Shareowner Services, St. Paul, MN

HOST HOTELS & RESORTS INC

Exchange	Symbol	Price	52Wk Range	Yield	P/E
NYS	HST	$15.40 (5/31/2016)	21.29-12.82	5.19	18.33

*7 Year Price Score 86.44   *NYSE Composite Index=100   *12 Month Price Score 92.25

TRADING VOLUME (thousand shares)

Interim Earnings (Per Share)

Qtr.	Mar	Jun	Sep	Dec
2013	0.08	0.16	0.03	0.16
2014	0.24	0.21	0.19	0.33
2015	0.13	0.28	0.11	0.21
2016	0.24	...	...	...

Interim Dividends (Per Share)

Amt	Decl	Ex	Rec	Pay
0.20Q	09/14/2015	09/28/2015	09/30/2015	10/15/2015
0.20Q	12/15/2015	12/29/2015	12/31/2015	01/15/2016
0.20Q	02/16/2016	03/29/2016	03/31/2016	04/15/2016
0.20Q	06/15/2016	06/28/2016	06/30/2016	07/15/2016

Indicated Div: $0.80

Valuation Analysis | **Institutional Holding**

Forecast EPS	$0.98	No of Institutions	
	(05/20/2016)	636	
Market Cap	$11.5 Billion	Shares	
Book Value	$7.0 Billion	896,551,104	
Price/Book	1.64	% Held	
Price/Sales	2.12	99.30	

Business Summary: REITs (MIC: 5.3.1 SIC: 6798 NAIC: 525930)

Host Hotels & Resorts is a real estate investment trust. Co. owns properties and conducts operations through Host Hotels & Resorts, L.P., of which it is the sole general partner and in which, as of Dec 31 2015, it held approximately 99% of the partnership interests. As of Feb 19 2016, Co.'s consolidated lodging portfolio consisted 105 hotels, with the majority located in the U.S., and with 12 of the properties located in Australia, Brazil, Canada, Chile, Mexico and New Zealand. The majority of Co.'s hotels operate under brand names among others, Fairmont®, Grand Hyatt®, JW Marriott®, Ritz-Carlton®, St. Regis®, Autograph Collection®, Curio, The Luxury Collection® and W®, and Embassy Suites®.

Recent Developments: For the quarter ended Mar 31 2016, net income increased 85.9% to US$184.0 million from US$99.0 million in the year-earlier quarter. Revenues were US$1.34 billion, up 2.8% from US$1.30 billion the year before.

Prospects: Our evaluation of Host Marriott Corp. as of June 19, 2016 is the result of our systematic analysis on three basic characteristics: earnings strength, relative valuation, and recent stock price movement. The company has enjoyed a very positive trend in earnings per share over the past 5 quarters and while recent estimates for the company have remained steady, HST has posted better than expected results. Based on operating earnings yield, the company is undervalued when compared to all of the companies in our coverage universe. Share price changes over the past year indicates that HST will perform poorly over the near term.

Financial Data

(US$ in Millions)	3 Mos	12/31/2015	12/31/2014	12/31/2013	12/31/2012	12/31/2011	12/31/2010	12/31/2009
Earnings Per Share	0.84	0.74	0.96	0.42	0.08	(0.02)	(0.21)	(0.45)
Cash Flow Per Share	1.62	1.56	1.52	1.37	1.09	0.95	0.79	0.94
Tang Book Value Per Share	9.41	9.41	9.71	9.58	9.42	9.47	9.33	9.43
Dividends Per Share	0.800	0.800	0.750	0.460	0.300	0.140	0.040	0.250
Dividend Payout %	95.24	108.11	78.13	109.52	375.00	...	...	...
Income Statement								
Total Revenue	1,339	5,387	5,354	5,166	5,286	4,998	4,437	4,158
EBITDA	213	1,477	1,670	558	395	337	219	158
Depn & Amortn	2	737	725	10	3	3	1	41
Income Before Taxes	173	510	735	248	42	(17)	(158)	(255)
Income Taxes	(9)	9	14	21	31	(1)	(31)	(39)
Net Income	182	558	732	317	61	(15)	(130)	(252)
Average Shares	749	752	786	747	719	693	656	587
Balance Sheet								
Current Assets	384	254	684	893	453	862	1,154	1,695
Total Assets	11,690	11,784	12,207	12,814	12,994	13,068	12,411	12,555
Current Liabilities	215	243	298	214	194	175	208	174
Long-Term Obligations	3,961	4,017	3,992	4,759	5,411	5,753	5,477	5,837
Total Liabilities	4,670	4,720	4,871	5,586	6,169	6,391	6,108	6,366
Stockholders' Equity	7,020	7,064	7,336	7,228	6,825	6,677	6,303	6,189
Shares Outstanding	746	750	755	754	724	705	675	646
Statistical Record								
Return on Assets %	5.42	4.65	5.85	2.46	0.47	N.M.	N.M.	N.M.
Return on Equity %	8.97	7.75	10.05	4.51	0.90	N.M.	N.M.	N.M.
EBITDA Margin %	15.91	27.42	31.19	10.80	7.47	6.74	4.94	3.80
Net Margin %	13.59	10.36	13.67	6.14	1.15	N.M.	N.M.	N.M.
Asset Turnover	0.46	0.45	0.43	0.40	0.40	0.39	0.36	0.34
Current Ratio	1.79	1.05	2.30	4.17	2.34	4.93	5.55	9.74
Debt to Equity	0.56	0.57	0.54	0.66	0.79	0.86	0.87	0.94
Price Range	21.29-12.82	24.14-15.20	24.33-18.00	19.44-15.67	17.25-13.78	19.77-10.17	17.87-10.60	12.13-3.40
P/E Ratio	25.35-15.26	32.62-20.54	25.34-18.75	46.29-37.31	215.63-172.25	...	...	...
Average Yield %	4.53	4.12	3.41	2.60	1.93	0.90	0.28	2.99

Address: 6903 Rockledge Drive, Suite 1500, Bethesda, MD 20817	Web Site: www.hosthotels.com	Auditors: KPMG LLP
Telephone: 240-744-1000	Officers: Richard E. Marriott - Chairman W. Edward Walter - President, Chief Executive Officer	Transfer Agents: Computershare Trust Company, N.A., Providence, RI

HOWARD HUGHES CORP

Exchange	Symbol	Price	52Wk Range	Yield	P/E
NYS	HHC	$109.26 (5/31/2016)	147.98-81.34	N/A	25.89

*7 Year Price Score N/A   *NYSE Composite Index=100   *12 Month Price Score 89.43

Interim Earnings (Per Share)

Qtr.	Mar	Jun	Sep	Dec
2013	(0.59)	(1.94)	0.17	0.47
2014	(2.19)	(0.37)	0.48	0.81
2015	(2.68)	0.18	0.76	0.59
2016	2.69	...	...	...

Interim Dividends (Per Share)

No Dividends Paid

Valuation Analysis · **Institutional Holding**

Forecast EPS	$6.91	No of Institutions
	(05/20/2016)	278
Market Cap	$4.4 Billion	Shares
Book Value	$2.5 Billion	35,855,732
Price/Book	1.74	% Held
Price/Sales	4.94	82.85

TRADING VOLUME (thousand shares)

Business Summary: Property, Real Estate & Development (MIC: 5.3.2 SIC: 6552 NAIC: 531312)

Howard Hughes is engaged in the development of master planned communities and the ownership, management and the redevelopment or repositioning of real estate assets, as well as other strategic real estate opportunities. Co.'s segments are: Master Planned Communities, which develops and sells land, in large-scale, long-term community development projects in and around Las Vegas, NV, Houston, TX, and Columbia, MD; Operating Assets, which includes retail, office, and multi-family properties, The Woodlands Resort and Conference Center, The Club at Carlton Woods and other real estate investments; Strategic Developments, which includes its condominium projects and properties held for development.

Recent Developments: For the quarter ended Mar 31 2016, net income amounted to US$143.8 million versus a net loss of US$106.0 million in the year-earlier quarter. Revenues were US$239.7 million, up 54.5% from US$155.1 million the year before.

Prospects: Our evaluation of Howard Hughes Corp as of June 19, 2016 is the result of our systematic analysis on three basic characteristics: earnings strength, relative valuation, and recent stock price movement. The company has enjoyed a very positive trend in earnings per share over the past 5 quarters and while recent estimates for the company have been mixed, HHC has posted better than expected results. Based on operating earnings yield, the company is overvalued when compared to all of the companies in our coverage universe. Share price changes over the past year indicates that HHC will perform poorly over the near term.

Financial Data

(US$ in Thousands)	3 Mos	12/31/2015	12/31/2014	12/31/2013	12/31/2012	12/31/2011	12/31/2010	12/31/2009
Earnings Per Share	4.22	1.60	(0.60)	(1.87)	(3.36)	1.17	(1.84)	...
Cash Flow Per Share	0.09	0.61	(1.48)	3.28	4.00	2.28	(1.80)	...
Tang Book Value Per Share	61.52	59.43	56.10	56.56	58.36	61.26	57.47	...
Income Statement								
Total Revenue	239,666	797,088	634,565	474,610	376,886	275,691	142,719	136,348
EBITDA	247,191	286,603	53,409	(68,211)	(113,357)	125,703	(638,185)	(675,530)
Depn & Amortn	24,401	82,275	50,683	29,637	19,455	14,012	14,582	17,145
Income Before Taxes	207,066	146,999	16,104	(78,553)	(124,339)	121,567	(654,820)	(691,963)
Income Taxes	65,233	24,001	62,960	9,570	6,887	(18,325)	(633,459)	(23,969)
Net Income	143,765	126,719	(23,520)	(73,695)	(127,543)	148,470	(69,230)	(703,816)
Average Shares	42,400	42,754	39,464	39,449	38,127	38,982	37,726	...
Balance Sheet								
Current Assets	1,359,374	619,114	721,665	1,383,235	680,397	696,934	655,315	20,563
Total Assets	6,031,974	5,721,582	5,119,931	4,567,868	3,503,042	3,395,149	3,022,707	2,905,227
Current Liabilities	850,128	913,731	898,955	808,099	503,733	459,073	524,940	917,008
Long-Term Obligations	2,543,638	2,443,962	1,993,470	1,514,623	688,312	606,477	318,660	208,860
Total Liabilities	3,535,283	3,361,465	2,896,168	2,329,284	1,197,804	1,070,564	844,424	1,402,607
Stockholders' Equity	2,496,691	2,360,117	2,223,763	2,238,584	2,305,238	2,324,585	2,178,283	1,502,620
Shares Outstanding	39,823	39,714	39,638	39,576	39,498	37,945	37,904	...
Statistical Record								
Return on Assets %	6.67	2.34	N.M.	N.M.	N.M.	4.63	...	N.M.
Return on Equity %	16.31	5.53	N.M.	N.M.	N.M.	6.59	...	N.M.
EBITDA Margin %	103.14	35.96	8.42	N.M.	N.M.	45.60	N.M.	N.M.
Net Margin %	59.99	15.90	N.M.	N.M.	N.M.	53.85	N.M.	N.M.
Asset Turnover	0.16	0.15	0.13	0.12	0.11	0.09	...	0.04
Current Ratio	1.60	0.68	0.80	1.71	1.35	1.52	1.25	0.02
Debt to Equity	1.02	1.04	0.90	0.68	0.30	0.26	0.15	0.14
Price Range	159.12-81.34	159.12-108.49	160.00-118.04	121.13-71.25	75.12-44.27	76.48-37.31	56.00-36.90	...
P/E Ratio	37.71-19.27	99.45-67.81	...	...	...	65.37-31.89	...	...

Address: 13355 Noel Road, 22nd Floor, Dallas, TX 75240 Telephone: 214-741-7744 Fax: 214-741-3021	Web Site: www.howardhughes.com Officers: William A. Ackman - Chairman Grant Herlitz - President	Auditors: Ernst & Young LLP Transfer Agents: Computershare, Jersey City, NJ

370

HUBBELL INC.

Exchange	Symbol	Price	52Wk Range	Yield	P/E
NYS	HUB A	$106.27 (5/31/2016)	109.20-86.29	N/A	22.23

*7 Year Price Score N/A   *NYSE Composite Index=100   *12 Month Price Score N/A

TRADING VOLUME (thousand shares)

Interim Earnings (Per Share)

Qtr.	Mar	Jun	Sep	Dec
2013	1.10	1.37	1.62	1.38
2014	1.08	1.51	1.51	1.38
2015	1.07	1.37	1.27	1.06
2016	1.08	...	...	...

Interim Dividends (Per Share)

Amt	Decl	Ex	Rec	Pay
0.56Q	01/27/2015	02/25/2015	02/27/2015	03/13/2015
0.56Q	04/21/2015	05/27/2015	05/29/2015	06/15/2015
0.56Q	07/21/2015	08/27/2015	08/31/2015	09/15/2015
0.63Q	10/20/2015	11/25/2015	11/30/2015	12/15/2015

Valuation Analysis   **Institutional Holding**

Forecast EPS	$5.30	No of Institutions	
	(05/20/2016)	324	
Market Cap	$5.9 Billion	Shares	
Book Value	$1.6 Billion	49,352,320	
Price/Book	3.75	% Held	
Price/Sales	1.72	9.67	

Business Summary: Electrical Equipment (MIC: 7.3.1 SIC: 3613 NAIC: 334417)

Hubbell is primarily engaged in the design, manufacture and sale of electrical and electronic products a range of non-residential and residential construction, industrial and utility applications. Co. has two segments: electrical, which comprised of businesses that sell stock and custom products including standard and application wiring device products, rough-in electrical products, connector and grounding products, lighting fixtures and controls, as well as other electrical equipment; and power, which consists of operations that design and manufacture a range of distribution, transmission, substation and telecommunications products primarily used by the electrical utility industry.

Recent Developments: For the quarter ended Mar 31 2016, net income decreased 2.2% to US$62.0 million from US$63.4 million in the year-earlier quarter. Revenues were US$834.8 million, up 3.1% from US$809.7 million the year before. Operating income was US$101.9 million versus US$105.0 million in the prior year quarter, a decrease of 3.0%. Direct operating expenses rose 3.0% to US$574.9 million from US$557.9 million in the comparable period the year before. Indirect operating expenses increased 7.6% to US$158.0 million from US$146.8 million in the equivalent prior-year period.

Prospects: Our evaluation of Hubbell Inc. as of Dec. 20, 2015 is the result of our systematic analysis on three basic characteristics: earnings strength, relative valuation, and recent stock price movement. The company has generated a negative trend in earnings per share over the past 5 quarters. However, while recent estimates for the company have been mixed, HUB.B has posted results that fell short of analysts expectations. Based on operating earnings yield, the company is undervalued when compared to all of the companies in our coverage universe. Share price changes over the past year indicates that HUB.B will perform poorly over the near term.

Financial Data
(US$ in Thousands)

	3 Mos	12/31/2015	12/31/2014	12/31/2013	12/31/2012	12/31/2011	12/31/2010	12/31/2009
Earnings Per Share	4.78	4.77	5.48	5.47	5.00	4.42	3.59	3.15
Cash Flow Per Share	6.46	5.74	6.66	6.46	5.89	5.61	4.44	7.00
Tang Book Value Per Share	2.24	7.61	12.47	13.85	10.43	7.96	12.11	9.29
Dividends Per Share	0.630	...	...	1.850	1.680	1.520	1.440	1.400
Dividend Payout %	13.18	...	...	33.82	33.60	34.39	40.11	44.44
Income Statement								
Total Revenue	834,800	3,390,400	3,359,400	3,183,900	3,044,400	2,871,600	2,541,200	2,355,600
EBITDA	123,300	500,800	566,600	549,900	516,700	466,500	398,600	292,546
Depn & Amortn	22,700	51,200	49,900	45,300	44,100	45,800	47,100	46
Income Before Taxes	91,600	418,600	485,500	473,800	441,800	389,800	320,400	261,600
Income Taxes	29,600	136,500	158,300	144,000	139,700	119,600	101,600	80,300
Net Income	60,900	277,300	325,300	326,500	299,700	267,900	217,200	180,100
Average Shares	56,500	58,000	59,200	59,600	59,800	60,400	60,300	57,000
Balance Sheet								
Current Assets	1,425,400	1,387,800	1,629,400	1,632,400	1,456,200	1,353,500	1,226,100	917,900
Total Assets	3,400,900	3,208,700	3,322,800	3,187,200	2,947,000	2,846,500	2,705,800	2,464,500
Current Liabilities	565,500	603,100	499,200	467,000	447,400	492,100	445,000	418,500
Long-Term Obligations	989,500	595,900	597,600	597,200	596,700	596,300	595,900	497,200
Total Liabilities	1,834,000	1,468,100	1,395,700	1,280,800	1,285,800	1,378,700	1,246,600	1,166,300
Stockholders' Equity	1,566,900	1,740,600	1,927,100	1,906,400	1,661,200	1,467,800	1,459,200	1,298,200
Shares Outstanding	55,326	57,836	58,496	59,172	59,236	59,179	60,696	59,660
Statistical Record								
Return on Assets %	8.29	8.49	9.99	10.65	10.32	9.65	8.40	7.86
Return on Equity %	16.09	15.12	16.97	18.30	19.10	18.31	15.75	15.62
EBITDA Margin %	14.77	14.77	16.87	17.27	16.97	16.25	15.69	12.42
Net Margin %	7.30	8.18	9.68	10.25	9.84	9.33	8.55	7.65
Asset Turnover	1.03	1.04	1.03	1.04	1.05	1.03	0.98	1.03
Current Ratio	2.52	2.30	3.26	3.50	3.25	2.75	2.76	2.19
Debt to Equity	0.63	0.34	0.31	0.31	0.36	0.41	0.41	0.38
Price Range	105.93-86.29	103.30-101.04	...	...	...	...	...	...
P/E Ratio	22.16-18.05	21.66-21.18	...	...	...	...	...	...
Average Yield %	0.66	...	...	...	...	...	...	...

Address: 40 Waterview Drive, Shelton, CT 06484 **Telephone:** 475-882-4000	**Web Site:** www.hubbell.com **Officers:** Timothy H. Powers - Chairman, President, Chief Executive Officer David G. Nord - President, Chief Executive Officer, Senior Vice President, Chief Operating Officer, Chief Financial Officer	**Auditors:** PicewaterhouseCoopers LLP **Transfer Agents:** Computershare Inc.

HUMANA INC.

Exchange	Symbol	Price	52Wk Range	Yield	P/E
NYS	HUM	$172.51 (5/31/2016)	214.92-156.96	0.67	24.06

*7 Year Price Score 157.41 *NYSE Composite Index=100   ***12 Month Price Score 96.20**

Interim Earnings (Per Share)

Qtr.	Mar	Jun	Sep	Dec
2013	2.95	2.63	2.31	(0.17)
2014	2.35	2.19	1.85	0.97
2015	2.82	2.85	2.09	0.67
2016	1.56	...	...	...

Interim Dividends (Per Share)

Amt	Decl	Ex	Rec	Pay
0.29Q	08/27/2015	09/28/2015	09/30/2015	10/30/2015
0.29Q	10/29/2015	12/28/2015	12/30/2015	01/29/2016
0.29Q	02/18/2016	03/29/2016	03/31/2016	04/29/2016
0.29Q	04/21/2016	06/28/2016	06/30/2016	07/29/2016

Indicated Div: $1.16

Valuation Analysis

		Institutional Holding	
Forecast EPS	$8.85	No of Institutions	
	(05/20/2016)	791	
Market Cap	$25.7 Billion	Shares	
Book Value	$10.5 Billion	160,487,104	
Price/Book	2.44	% Held	
Price/Sales	0.47	90.88	

Business Summary: Life & Health (MIC: 5.2.2 SIC: 6324 NAIC: 524114)

Humana is a holding company. Through its subsidiaries, Co. is a health and well-being company. Co. manages its business with three reportable segments: Retail consists of Medicare and commercial fully-insured medical and specialty health insurance benefits, including dental, vision, and other supplemental health and financial protection products; Group, consists of employer group commercial fully-insured medical and specialty health insurance benefits, including dental, vision, and other supplemental health and voluntary benefit products; and Healthcare Services includes pharmacy solutions, provider services, home based services, clinical programs, and predictive modeling.

Recent Developments: For the quarter ended Mar 31 2016, net income decreased 45.6% to US$234.0 million from US$430.0 million in the year-earlier quarter. Revenues were US$13.80 billion, down 0.2% from US$13.83 billion the year before. Net premiums earned were US$13.44 billion versus US$13.25 billion in the prior-year quarter, an increase of 1.4%.

Prospects: Our evaluation of Humana Inc. as of June 19, 2016 is the result of our systematic analysis on three basic characteristics: earnings strength, relative valuation, and recent stock price movement. The company has generated a negative trend in earnings per share over the past 5 quarters and while recent estimates for the company have remained steady, HUM has posted better than expected results. Based on operating earnings yield, the company is about fairly valued when compared to all of the companies in our coverage universe. Share price changes over the past year indicates that HUM will perform poorly over the near term.

Financial Data
(US$ in Thousands)

	3 Mos	12/31/2015	12/31/2014	12/31/2013	12/31/2012	12/31/2011	12/31/2010	12/31/2009
Earnings Per Share	7.17	8.44	7.36	7.73	7.47	8.46	6.47	6.15
Cash Flow Per Share	8.33	5.81	10.49	10.90	11.88	12.57	13.36	8.49
Tang Book Value Per Share	48.71	47.75	39.67	36.25	32.89	32.46	25.86	22.23
Dividends Per Share	1.160	1.150	1.110	1.070	1.030	0.750	...	...
Dividend Payout %	16.18	13.63	15.08	13.84	13.79	8.87	...	...
Income Statement								
Premium Income	13,440,000	52,409,000	45,959,000	38,829,000	37,009,000	35,106,000	32,712,323	29,926,751
Total Revenue	13,800,000	54,289,000	48,500,000	41,313,000	39,126,000	36,832,000	33,868,208	30,960,414
Benefits & Claims	11,397,000	44,269,000	38,166,000	32,564,000	30,985,000	28,823,000	27,087,874	24,775,002
Income Before Taxes	500,000	2,431,000	2,170,000	1,921,000	1,911,000	2,235,000	1,749,562	1,601,760
Income Taxes	266,000	1,155,000	1,023,000	690,000	689,000	816,000	650,172	562,085
Net Income	234,000	1,276,000	1,147,000	1,231,000	1,222,000	1,419,000	1,099,390	1,039,675
Average Shares	150,554	151,142	155,874	159,151	163,457	167,827	169,798	169,071
Balance Sheet								
Total Assets	26,934,000	24,705,000	23,466,000	20,735,000	19,979,000	17,708,000	16,103,253	14,153,494
Total Liabilities	16,409,000	14,359,000	13,820,000	11,419,000	11,132,000	9,645,000	9,179,197	8,377,491
Stockholders' Equity	10,525,000	10,346,000	9,646,000	9,316,000	8,847,000	8,063,000	6,924,056	5,776,003
Shares Outstanding	149,036	148,288	149,604	154,030	158,331	164,004	168,449	170,180
Statistical Record								
Return on Assets %	4.11	5.30	5.19	6.05	6.47	8.39	7.27	7.65
Return on Equity %	10.50	12.77	12.10	13.56	14.41	18.94	17.31	20.32
Loss Ratio %	84.80	84.47	83.04	83.87	83.72	82.10	82.81	82.79
Net Margin %	1.70	2.35	2.36	2.98	3.12	3.85	3.25	3.36
Price Range	214.92-156.96	214.92-139.09	149.07-95.59	105.25-66.01	95.50-61.60	89.83-54.74	60.64-43.56	45.80-18.77
P/E Ratio	29.97-21.89	25.46-16.48	20.25-12.99	13.62-8.54	12.78-8.25	10.62-6.47	9.37-6.73	7.45-3.05
Average Yield %	0.64	0.65	0.91	1.26	1.33	1.01	...	...

Address: 500 West Main Street, Louisville, KY 40202 **Telephone:** 502-580-1000	**Web Site:** www.humana.com **Officers:** Kurt J. Hilzinger - Chairman Bruce D. Broussard - President, Chief Executive Officer	**Auditors:** PricewaterhouseCoopers LLP **Investor Contact:** 502-580-3644 **Transfer Agents:** American Stock Transfer & Trust Company, LLC, Brooklyn, NY

372

HUNTINGTON INGALLS INDUSTRIES, INC.

Exchange	Symbol	Price	52Wk Range	Yield	P/E
NYS	HII	$153.41 (5/31/2016)	156.17-103.98	1.30	16.25

*7 Year Price Score N/A   ***NYSE Composite Index=100**   ***12 Month Price Score 115.06**

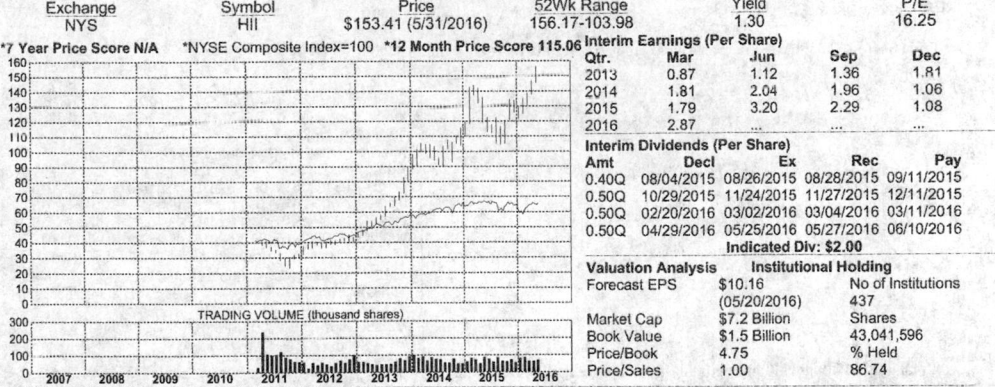

Interim Earnings (Per Share)

Qtr.	Mar	Jun	Sep	Dec
2013	0.87	1.12	1.36	1.81
2014	1.81	2.04	1.96	1.06
2015	1.79	3.20	2.29	1.08
2016	2.87	...	...	...

Interim Dividends (Per Share)

Amt	Decl	Ex	Rec	Pay
0.40Q	08/04/2015	08/26/2015	08/28/2015	09/11/2015
0.50Q	10/29/2015	11/24/2015	11/27/2015	12/11/2015
0.50Q	02/20/2016	03/02/2016	03/04/2016	03/11/2016
0.50Q	04/29/2016	05/25/2016	05/27/2016	06/10/2016

Indicated Div: $2.00

Valuation Analysis

		Institutional Holding	
Forecast EPS	$10.16	No of Institutions	437
	(05/20/2016)		
Market Cap	$7.2 Billion	Shares	43,041,596
Book Value	$1.5 Billion	% Held	86.74
Price/Book	4.75		
Price/Sales	1.00		

Business Summary: Defense (MIC: 7.1.2 SIC: 3731 NAIC: 336611)

Huntington Ingalls Industries is engaged in designing, building, overhauling, and repairing ships primarily for the U.S. Navy and the U.S. Coast Guard. Co. operates its shipbuilding business through its Huntington Ingalls Incorporated subsidiary, which is organized into two segments: Ingalls Shipbuilding, which includes Co.'s non-nuclear ship design, construction, repair, and maintenance businesses; and Newport News Shipbuilding, which includes all of Co.'s nuclear ship design, construction, overhaul, refueling, and repair and maintenance businesses. Co. also provides a range of services to the energy and oil and gas industries, as well as government customers.

Recent Developments: For the quarter ended Mar 31 2016, net income increased 56.3% to US$136.0 million from US$87.0 million in the year-earlier quarter. Revenues were US$1.76 billion, up 12.3% from US$1.57 billion the year before. Operating income was US$198.0 million versus US$156.0 million in the prior-year quarter, an increase of 26.9%. Direct operating expenses rose 12.9% to US$1.43 billion from US$1.27 billion in the comparable period the year before. Indirect operating expenses decreased 8.1% to US$137.0 million from US$149.0 million in the equivalent prior-year period.

Prospects: Our evaluation of Huntington Ingalls Industries Inc. as of June 19, 2016 is the result of our systematic analysis on three basic characteristics: earnings strength, relative valuation, and recent stock price movement. The company has produced a positive trend in earnings per share over the past 5 quarters. However, while recent estimates for the company have been lowered by analysts, HII has posted better than expected results. Based on operating earnings yield, the company is undervalued when compared to all of the companies in our coverage universe. Share price changes over the past year indicates that HII will perform well over the near term.

Financial Data

(US$ in Thousands)	3 Mos	12/31/2015	12/31/2014	12/31/2013	12/31/2012	12/31/2011
Earnings Per Share	9.44	8.36	6.86	5.18	2.91	(1.93)
Cash Flow Per Share	18.83	17.29	14.67	4.75	6.70	10.82
Tang Book Value Per Share	1.59	0.83	N.M.	2.30	N.M.	N.M.
Dividends Per Share	1.800	1.700	1.000	0.500	0.100	...
Dividend Payout %	19.07	20.33	14.58	9.65	3.44	...
Income Statement						
Total Revenue	1,763,000	7,020,000	6,957,000	6,820,000	6,708,000	6,575,000
EBITDA	244,000	949,000	850,000	738,000	542,000	294,000
Depn & Amortn	48,000	180,000	194,000	226,000	184,000	184,000
Income Before Taxes	177,000	632,000	507,000	394,000	241,000	6,000
Income Taxes	41,000	228,000	169,000	133,000	95,000	100,000
Net Income	136,000	404,000	338,000	261,000	146,000	(94,000)
Average Shares	47,400	48,300	49,300	50,400	50,100	48,800
Balance Sheet						
Current Assets	2,203,000	2,284,000	2,546,000	2,676,000	2,484,000	2,268,000
Total Assets	5,896,000	6,024,000	6,269,000	6,225,000	6,392,000	6,001,000
Current Liabilities	1,155,000	1,274,000	1,312,000	1,392,000	1,384,000	1,372,000
Long-Term Obligations	1,275,000	1,273,000	1,592,000	1,700,000	1,779,000	1,830,000
Total Liabilities	4,375,000	4,534,000	4,904,000	4,704,000	5,725,000	5,129,000
Stockholders' Equity	1,521,000	1,490,000	1,365,000	1,521,000	667,000	872,000
Shares Outstanding	47,100	46,900	48,300	48,700	49,600	48,821
Statistical Record						
Return on Assets %	7.42	6.57	5.41	4.14	2.35	N.M.
Return on Equity %	31.23	28.30	23.42	23.86	18.92	N.M.
EBITDA Margin %	13.84	13.52	12.22	10.82	8.08	4.47
Net Margin %	7.71	5.75	4.86	3.83	2.18	N.M.
Asset Turnover	1.18	1.14	1.11	1.08	1.08	2.19
Current Ratio	1.91	1.79	1.94	1.92	1.79	1.65
Debt to Equity	0.84	0.85	1.17	1.12	2.67	2.10
Price Range	142.00-103.98	143.55-103.98	115.48-87.91	90.01-43.17	44.96-31.80	41.50-22.85
P/E Ratio	15.04-11.01	17.17-12.44	16.83-12.81	17.38-8.33	15.45-10.93	...
Average Yield %	1.46	1.38	1.00	0.82	0.26	...

Address: 4101 Washington Avenue, Newport News, VA 23607 **Telephone:** 757-380-2000	**Web Site:** www.huntingtoningalls.com **Officers:** Thomas B. Fargo - Chairman C. Michael Petters - President, Chief Executive Officer	**Auditors:** Deloitte & Touche LLP **Investor Contact:** 757-688-5572 **Transfer Agents:** Computershare Trust Company, N.A., Providence, RI

HUNTSMAN CORP

Exchange	Symbol	Price	52Wk Range	Yield	P/E
NYS	HUN	$14.93 (5/31/2016)	23.50-7.91	3.35	24.88

*7 Year Price Score 73.50 ***NYSE Composite Index=100** ***12 Month Price Score 102.39**

TRADING VOLUME (thousand shares)

Interim Earnings (Per Share)

Qtr.	Mar	Jun	Sep	Dec
2013	(0.10)	0.19	0.26	0.17
2014	0.22	0.48	0.76	(0.16)
2015	0.02	0.12	0.22	0.02
2016	0.24	...	...	...

Interim Dividends (Per Share)

Amt	Decl	Ex	Rec	Pay
0.125Q	08/07/2015	09/11/2015	09/15/2015	09/30/2015
0.125Q	11/09/2015	12/11/2015	12/15/2015	12/31/2015
0.125Q	02/04/2016	03/11/2016	03/15/2016	03/31/2016
0.125Q	05/09/2016	06/13/2016	06/15/2016	06/30/2016

Indicated Div: $0.50

Valuation Analysis

		Institutional Holding	
Forecast EPS	$1.80	No of Institutions	419
	(05/20/2016)		
Market Cap	$3.5 Billion	Shares	189,424,240
Book Value	$1.5 Billion	% Held	80.65
Price/Book	2.35		
Price/Sales	0.35		

Business Summary: Specialty Chemicals (MIC: 8.3.2 SIC: 2899 NAIC: 424690)

Huntsman is a manufacturer of organic chemical products and of inorganic chemical products. Co. operates in five segments: Polyurethanes, Performance Products, Advanced Materials, Textile Effects and Pigments and Additives. Co.'s products comprise a range of chemicals and formulations which it markets to a group of consumer and industrial customers. These products are used in a range of applications, including those in the adhesives, aerospace, automotive, construction products, personal care and hygiene, durable and non-durable consumer products, electronics, medical, packaging, paints and coatings, power generation, refining, synthetic fiber, textile chemicals and dye industries.

Recent Developments: For the quarter ended Mar 31 2016, income from continuing operations increased 270.6% to US$63.0 million from US$17.0 million in the year-earlier quarter. Net income increased 313.3% to US$62.0 million from US$15.0 million in the year-earlier quarter. Revenues were US$2.36 billion, down 9.0% from US$2.59 billion the year before. Operating income was US$138.0 million versus US$77.0 million in the prior-year quarter, an increase of 79.2%. Direct operating expenses declined 9.4% to US$1.94 billion from US$2.14 billion in the comparable period the year before. Indirect operating expenses decreased 25.5% to US$278.0 million from US$373.0 million in the equivalent prior-year period.

Prospects: Our evaluation of Huntsman Corp. as of June 19, 2016 is the result of our systematic analysis on three basic characteristics: earnings strength, relative valuation, and recent stock price movement. The company has produced a positive trend in earnings per share over the past 5 quarters and while recent estimates for the company have been mixed, HUN has posted better than expected results. Based on operating earnings yield, the company is undervalued when compared to all of the companies in our coverage universe. Share price changes over the past year indicates that HUN will perform very poorly over the near term.

Financial Data
(US$ in Thousands)

	3 Mos	12/31/2015	12/31/2014	12/31/2013	12/31/2012	12/31/2011	12/31/2010	12/31/2009
Earnings Per Share	0.60	0.38	1.31	0.53	1.51	1.02	0.11	0.48
Cash Flow Per Share	2.66	2.37	3.14	2.95	3.25	1.54	(0.25)	4.72
Tang Book Value Per Share	5.38	5.23	6.41	7.33	6.66	6.18	6.72	6.94
Dividends Per Share	0.500	0.500	0.500	0.500	0.400	0.400	0.400	0.400
Dividend Payout %	83.33	131.58	38.17	94.34	26.49	39.22	363.64	83.33
Income Statement								
Total Revenue	2,355,000	10,299,000	11,578,000	11,079,000	11,187,000	11,221,000	9,250,000	7,763,000
EBITDA	239,000	752,000	1,016,000	876,000	1,165,000	999,000	588,000	1,114,000
Depn & Amortn	100,000	377,000	413,000	415,000	399,000	398,000	363,000	394,000
Income Before Taxes	89,000	170,000	398,000	271,000	540,000	352,000	(4,000)	482,000
Income Taxes	27,000	46,000	51,000	125,000	169,000	109,000	29,000	370,000
Net Income	56,000	93,000	323,000	128,000	363,000	247,000	27,000	114,000
Average Shares	237,900	245,400	246,000	242,400	240,600	241,700	236,000	238,300
Balance Sheet								
Current Assets	3,830,000	3,834,000	5,039,000	4,159,000	4,119,000	3,946,000	4,008,000	4,140,000
Total Assets	9,840,000	9,820,000	11,002,000	9,188,000	8,884,000	8,657,000	8,714,000	8,626,000
Current Liabilities	1,782,000	1,917,000	2,332,000	2,159,000	2,181,000	1,826,000	2,053,000	1,811,000
Long-Term Obligations	4,725,000	4,626,000	4,939,000	3,639,000	3,418,000	3,734,000	3,631,000	3,786,000
Total Liabilities	8,341,000	8,378,000	9,224,000	7,208,000	7,111,000	6,995,000	6,924,000	6,782,000
Stockholders' Equity	1,499,000	1,442,000	1,778,000	1,980,000	1,773,000	1,662,000	1,790,000	1,844,000
Shares Outstanding	236,271	237,080	243,416	240,401	238,273	235,746	236,799	234,081
Statistical Record								
Return on Assets %	1.40	0.89	3.20	1.42	4.13	2.84	0.31	1.37
Return on Equity %	9.30	5.78	17.19	6.82	21.08	14.31	1.49	6.60
EBITDA Margin %	10.15	7.30	8.78	7.91	10.41	8.90	6.36	14.35
Net Margin %	2.38	0.90	2.79	1.16	3.24	2.20	0.29	1.47
Asset Turnover	0.98	0.99	1.15	1.23	1.27	1.29	1.07	0.93
Current Ratio	2.15	2.00	2.16	1.93	1.89	2.16	1.95	2.29
Debt to Equity	3.15	3.21	2.78	1.84	1.93	2.25	2.03	2.05
Price Range	23.50-7.91	24.40-9.33	28.88-21.22	24.60-15.90	17.07-9.82	20.95-8.78	16.66-8.30	11.51-2.11
P/E Ratio	39.17-13.18	64.21-24.55	22.05-16.20	46.42-30.00	11.30-6.50	20.54-8.61	151.45-75.45	23.98-4.40
Average Yield %	3.21	2.71	1.98	2.61	2.84	2.61	3.40	6.34

Address: 10003 Woodloch Forest Drive, The Woodlands, TX 77380	**Web Site:** www.huntsman.com	**Auditors:** Deloitte & Touche LLP
Telephone: 281-719-6000	**Officers:** Jon M. Huntsman - Chairman Peter R Huntsman - President, Chief Executive Officer	**Investor Contact:** 801-584-5959
		Transfer Agents: Computershare, Providence, RI

HYATT HOTELS CORP

Exchange	Symbol	Price	52Wk Range	Yield	P/E
NYS	H	$45.91 (5/31/2016)	59.79-35.77	N/A	47.82

*7 Year Price Score N/A   *NYSE Composite Index=100   *12 Month Price Score 95.61

TRADING VOLUME (thousand shares)

Interim Earnings (Per Share)

Qtr.	Mar	Jun	Sep	Dec
2013	0.05	0.70	0.35	0.20
2014	0.36	0.49	0.21	1.18
2015	0.15	0.27	0.18	0.26
2016	0.25	...	...	...

Interim Dividends (Per Share)

No Dividends Paid

Valuation Analysis   **Institutional Holding**

Forecast EPS	$1.35	No of Institutions
	(05/20/2016)	203
Market Cap	$6.2 Billion	Shares
Book Value	$4.0 Billion	25,995,458
Price/Book	1.55	% Held
Price/Sales	1.42	22.40

Business Summary: Hotels, Restaurants & Travel (MIC: 2.2.1 SIC: 7011 NAIC: 721110)

Hyatt Hotels is a hospitality company engaged in developing, managing, franchising, licensing and owning a portfolio of properties, including hotels, resorts and residential and vacation ownership properties. Co.'s hotels and resorts operate under Park Hyatt, Andaz, Hyatt, Grand Hyatt and Hyatt Regency brands. Co.'s two select service brands are Hyatt Place and Hyatt House, an extended stay brand. Co. also manages, provides services to or licenses its trademarks with respect to residential ownership units that are often adjacent to a Hyatt-branded hotel. As of Dec 31 2014, Co.'s portfolio of properties consisted of 587 properties (155,265 rooms and units).

Recent Developments: For the quarter ended Mar 31 2016, net income increased 54.5% to US$34.0 million from US$22.0 million in the year-earlier quarter. Revenues were US$1.09 billion, up 3.3% from US$1.05 billion the year before. Direct operating expenses rose 3.6% to US$852.0 million from US$822.0 million in the comparable period the year before. Indirect operating expenses decreased 2.3% to US$169.0 million from US$173.0 million in the equivalent prior-year period.

Prospects: Our evaluation of Hyatt Hotels Corp. as of June 19, 2016 is the result of our systematic analysis on three basic characteristics: earnings strength, relative valuation, and recent stock price movement. The company has enjoyed a very positive trend in earnings per share over the past 5 quarters. However, while recent estimates for the company have been lowered by analysts, H has posted results that were in line with analysts expectations. Based on operating earnings yield, the company is overvalued when compared to all of the companies in our coverage universe. Share price changes over the past year indicates that H will perform poorly over the near term.

Financial Data

(US$ in Thousands)	3 Mos	12/31/2015	12/31/2014	12/31/2013	12/31/2012	12/31/2011	12/31/2010	12/31/2009
Earnings Per Share	0.96	0.86	2.23	1.30	0.53	0.67	0.32	(0.30)
Cash Flow Per Share	4.25	3.77	3.09	2.88	3.02	2.33	2.58	1.82
Tang Book Value Per Share	24.64	24.33	26.44	25.82	26.53	26.38	27.23	26.57
Income Statement								
Total Revenue	1,089,000	4,328,000	4,415,000	4,184,000	3,949,000	3,698,000	3,527,000	3,332,000
EBITDA	144,000	603,000	869,000	673,000	470,000	399,000	405,000	219,000
Depn & Amortn	81,000	289,000	324,000	320,000	327,000	288,000	265,000	255,000
Income Before Taxes	48,000	258,000	500,000	322,000	117,000	79,000	128,000	(42,000)
Income Taxes	16,000	70,000	179,000	116,000	8,000	(28,000)	37,000	(10,000)
Net Income	34,000	124,000	344,000	207,000	88,000	113,000	66,000	(43,000)
Average Shares	135,924	143,999	154,350	159,189	165,377	169,240	174,354	151,486
Balance Sheet								
Current Assets	1,462,000	1,124,000	1,709,000	1,163,000	1,758,000	1,591,000	2,165,000	1,989,000
Total Assets	7,899,000	7,596,000	8,143,000	8,177,000	7,640,000	7,507,000	7,243,000	7,155,000
Current Liabilities	1,012,000	1,107,000	730,000	871,000	618,000	568,000	596,000	495,000
Long-Term Obligations	1,441,000	1,047,000	1,381,000	1,289,000	1,229,000	1,221,000	714,000	840,000
Total Liabilities	3,903,000	3,605,000	3,516,000	3,408,000	2,819,000	2,689,000	2,125,000	2,139,000
Stockholders' Equity	3,996,000	3,991,000	4,627,000	4,769,000	4,821,000	4,818,000	5,118,000	5,016,000
Shares Outstanding	134,786	136,233	149,081	156,111	162,066	165,162	173,953	173,875
Statistical Record								
Return on Assets %	1.72	1.58	4.22	2.62	1.16	1.53	0.92	N.M.
Return on Equity %	3.23	2.88	7.32	4.32	1.82	2.27	1.30	N.M.
EBITDA Margin %	13.22	13.93	19.68	16.09	11.90	10.79	11.48	6.57
Net Margin %	3.12	2.87	7.79	4.95	2.23	3.06	1.87	N.M.
Asset Turnover	0.55	0.55	0.54	0.53	0.52	0.50	0.49	0.50
Current Ratio	1.44	1.02	2.34	1.34	2.84	2.80	3.63	4.02
Debt to Equity	0.36	0.26	0.30	0.27	0.25	0.25	0.14	0.17
Price Range	60.24-35.77	61.76-45.86	63.74-45.88	49.85-38.57	44.10-33.74	49.57-29.79	46.19-28.63	30.31-27.90
P/E Ratio	62.75-37.26	71.81-53.33	28.58-20.57	38.35-29.67	83.21-63.66	73.99-44.46	144.34-89.47	...

Address: 71 South Wacker Drive, 12th Floor, Chicago, IL 60606 **Telephone:** 312-750-1234	**Web Site:** www.hyatt.com **Officers:** Thomas J. Pritzker - Executive Chairman Mark S. Hoplamazian - President, Chief Executive Officer	**Auditors:** Deloitte & Touche LLP **Investor Contact:** 312-750-1234 **Transfer Agents:** Wells Fargo Shareowner Services, South St. Paul, MN

IDACORP INC

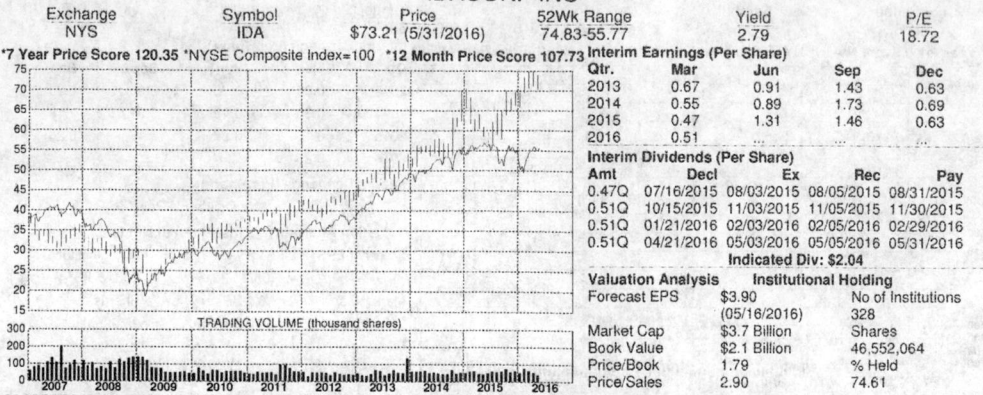

Exchange	Symbol	Price	52Wk Range	Yield	P/E
NYS	IDA	$73.21 (5/31/2016)	74.83-55.77	2.79	18.72

*7 Year Price Score 120.35 *NYSE Composite Index=100 *12 Month Price Score 107.73

Interim Earnings (Per Share)

Qtr.	Mar	Jun	Sep	Dec
2013	0.67	0.91	1.43	0.63
2014	0.55	0.89	1.73	0.69
2015	0.47	1.31	1.46	0.63
2016	0.51	...	...	...

Interim Dividends (Per Share)

Amt	Decl	Ex	Rec	Pay
0.47Q	07/16/2015	08/03/2015	08/05/2015	08/31/2015
0.51Q	10/15/2015	11/03/2015	11/05/2015	11/30/2015
0.51Q	01/21/2016	02/03/2016	02/05/2016	02/29/2016
0.51Q	04/21/2016	05/03/2016	05/05/2016	05/31/2016

Indicated Div: $2.04

Valuation Analysis

		Institutional Holding	
Forecast EPS	$3.90 (05/16/2016)	No of Institutions	328
Market Cap	$3.7 Billion	Shares	46,552,064
Book Value	$2.1 Billion	% Held	74.61
Price/Book	1.79		
Price/Sales	2.90		

TRADING VOLUME (thousand shares)

Business Summary: Electric Utilities (MIC: 3.1.1 SIC: 4911 NAIC: 221122)

Idacorp is a holding company. Co.'s principal operating subsidiary, Idaho Power Company (Idaho Power) is an electric utility engaged in the generation, transmission, distribution, sale, and purchase of electric energy and capacity and is regulated by the state regulatory commissions of Idaho and Oregon and by the Federal Energy Regulatory Commission. Idaho Power is the parent of Idaho Energy Resources Co., a joint venturer in Bridger Coal Company, which mines and supplies coal to the Jim Bridger generating plant owned in part by Idaho Power. Idaho Power holds franchises in the form of right-of-way arrangements and holds certificates from the respective public utility regulatory authorities.

Recent Developments: For the quarter ended Mar 31 2016, net income increased 9.4% to US$25.5 million from US$23.3 million in the year-earlier quarter. Revenues were US$281.0 million, up 0.6% from US$279.4 million the year before. Operating income was US$43.8 million versus US$42.9 million in the prior-year quarter, an increase of 2.1%. Direct operating expenses declined 0.5% to US$189.1 million from US$190.1 million in the comparable period the year before. Indirect operating expenses increased 3.5% to US$48.1 million from US$46.4 million in the equivalent prior-year period.

Prospects: Our evaluation of Idacorp Inc. as of June 19, 2016 is the result of our systematic analysis on three basic characteristics: earnings strength, relative valuation, and recent stock price movement. The company has produced a positive trend in earnings per share over the past 5 quarters and while recent estimates for the company have remained steady, IDA has posted results that fell short of analysts expectations. Based on operating earnings yield, the company is about fairly valued when compared to all of the companies in our coverage universe. Share price changes over the past year indicates that IDA will perform very well over the near term.

Financial Data
(US$ in Thousands)

	3 Mos	12/31/2015	12/31/2014	12/31/2013	12/31/2012	12/31/2011	12/31/2010	12/31/2009
Earnings Per Share	3.91	3.87	3.85	3.64	3.37	3.36	2.95	2.64
Cash Flow Per Share	6.24	7.03	7.27	6.10	4.98	6.27	6.34	6.04
Tang Book Value Per Share	40.61	40.65	38.58	36.53	34.71	32.78	30.56	28.67
Dividends Per Share	1.960	1.920	1.760	1.570	1.370	1.200	1.200	1.200
Dividend Payout %	50.13	49.61	45.71	43.13	40.65	35.71	40.68	45.45
Income Statement								
Total Revenue	280,956	1,270,289	1,282,524	1,246,214	1,080,662	1,026,756	1,036,029	1,049,800
EBITDA	86,624	448,659	410,942	453,348	393,185	305,246	329,756	331,206
Depn & Amortn	35,617	138,110	132,987	129,735	123,941	119,789	115,921	110,626
Income Before Taxes	29,939	228,615	198,154	242,581	195,375	113,931	138,721	147,770
Income Taxes	4,367	45,268	16,772	72,226	26,113	(52,133)	(731)	22,362
Net Income	25,729	194,679	193,480	182,417	168,761	166,693	142,798	124,350
Average Shares	50,337	50,292	50,199	50,126	50,010	49,558	48,340	47,182
Balance Sheet								
Current Assets	587,286	462,036	442,101	476,611	367,253	310,972	460,635	310,406
Total Assets	6,130,450	6,023,314	5,716,853	5,364,563	5,319,516	4,960,609	4,676,055	4,238,727
Current Liabilities	311,819	242,306	241,781	250,372	351,303	368,247	449,059	218,229
Long-Term Obligations	1,744,433	1,725,410	1,614,438	1,615,258	1,466,632	1,387,550	1,488,287	1,409,730
Total Liabilities	4,072,943	3,965,430	3,763,652	3,513,913	3,560,763	3,302,955	3,143,942	2,841,392
Stockholders' Equity	2,057,507	2,057,884	1,953,201	1,850,650	1,758,753	1,657,654	1,532,113	1,397,335
Shares Outstanding	50,415	50,340	50,269	50,232	50,156	49,951	49,405	47,896
Statistical Record								
Return on Assets %	3.26	3.32	3.49	3.41	3.27	3.46	3.20	3.01
Return on Equity %	9.82	9.71	10.17	10.11	9.85	10.45	9.75	9.21
EBITDA Margin %	30.83	35.32	32.04	36.38	36.38	29.73	31.83	31.55
Net Margin %	9.16	15.33	15.09	14.64	15.62	16.23	13.78	11.85
Asset Turnover	0.21	0.22	0.23	0.23	0.21	0.21	0.23	0.25
Current Ratio	1.88	1.91	1.83	1.90	1.05	0.84	1.03	1.42
Debt to Equity	0.85	0.84	0.83	0.87	0.83	0.84	0.97	1.01
Price Range	74.83-55.77	70.34-55.77	69.99-50.77	53.88-43.31	44.80-38.28	42.55-34.31	37.62-30.44	32.63-21.02
P/E Ratio	19.14-14.26	18.18-14.41	18.18-13.19	14.80-11.90	13.29-11.36	12.66-10.21	12.75-10.32	12.36-7.96
Average Yield %	3.04	3.05	3.13	3.22	3.28	3.10	3.44	4.46

Address: 1221 W. Idaho Street, Boise, ID 83702-5627 **Telephone:** 208-388-2200	**Web Site:** www.idacorpinc.com **Officers:** Darrel T. Anderson - President, Chief Executive Officer, Executive Vice President, Chief Financial Officer Steven R. Keen - Senior Vice President, Chief Financial Officer, Treasurer, Vice President, Vice President (frmr)	**Auditors:** Deloitte & Touche LLP **Investor Contact:** 208-388-2664 **Transfer Agents:** Wells Fargo Shareowner Services, Mendota Heights, MN

IDEX CORPORATION

Exchange	Symbol	Price	52Wk Range	Yield	P/E
NYS	IEX	$83.34 (5/31/2016)	84.25-68.33	1.63	22.71

*7 Year Price Score 123.21 *NYSE Composite Index=100   *12 Month Price Score 106.48

Interim Earnings (Per Share)

Qtr.	Mar	Jun	Sep	Dec
2013	0.74	0.76	0.78	0.02
2014	0.91	0.88	0.88	0.77
2015	0.84	0.89	1.02	0.87
2016	0.89	...	...	...

Interim Dividends (Per Share)

Amt	Decl	Ex	Rec	Pay
0.32Q	06/23/2015	07/14/2015	07/16/2015	07/31/2015
0.32Q	09/11/2015	10/14/2015	10/16/2015	10/30/2015
0.32Q	12/01/2015	01/13/2016	01/15/2016	01/29/2016
0.34Q	04/06/2016	04/14/2016	04/15/2016	04/29/2016

Indicated Div: $1.36

Valuation Analysis

		Institutional Holding	
Forecast EPS	$3.73	No of Institutions	398
	(05/20/2016)		
Market Cap	$6.3 Billion	Shares	81,631,288
Book Value	$1.5 Billion	% Held	94.16
Price/Book	4.25		
Price/Sales	3.14		

TRADING VOLUME (thousand shares)

Business Summary: Industrial Machinery & Equipment (MIC: 7.2.1 SIC: 3561 NAIC: 333911)

IDEX is an applied solutions business that sells of pumps, flow meters and other fluidics systems and components and engineered products. Co. has three segments: Fluid and Metering Technologies, which designs, produces and distributes displacement pumps, flow meters, injectors, and other fluid-handling pump modules and systems; Health and Science Technologies, which distribute fluidics, rotary lobe pumps, roll compaction and drying systems used in beverage, food processing, pharmaceutical and cosmetics; and Fire and Safety/Diversified Products, which produces firefighting pumps and controls, rescue tools, lifting bags and other components for the fire and rescue industry.

Recent Developments: For the quarter ended Mar 31 2016, net income increased 3.3% to US$68.1 million from US$66.0 million in the year-earlier quarter. Revenues were US$502.6 million, up 0.1% from US$502.2 million the year before. Operating income was US$102.6 million versus US$101.8 million in the prior-year quarter, an increase of 0.8%. Direct operating expenses rose 1.1% to US$279.2 million from US$276.2 million in the comparable period the year before. Indirect operating expenses decreased 2.8% to US$120.8 million from US$124.3 million in the equivalent prior-year period.

Prospects: Our evaluation of IDEX Corp. as of June 19, 2016 is the result of our systematic analysis on three basic characteristics: earnings strength, relative valuation, and recent stock price movement. The company has produced a positive trend in earnings per share over the past 5 quarters and while recent estimates for the company have been raised by analysts, IEX has posted better than expected results. Based on operating earnings yield, the company is about fairly valued when compared to all of the companies in our coverage universe. Share price changes over the past year indicates that IEX will perform in line with the market over the near term.

Financial Data

(US$ in Thousands)	3 Mos	12/31/2015	12/31/2014	12/31/2013	12/31/2012	12/31/2011	12/31/2010	12/31/2009
Earnings Per Share	3.67	3.62	3.45	3.09	0.45	2.32	1.90	1.40
Cash Flow Per Share	5.03	4.67	4.62	4.93	3.93	2.64	2.29	2.67
Dividends Per Share	1.280	1.240	1.070	0.890	0.770	0.660	0.570	0.480
Dividend Payout %	34.88	34.25	31.01	28.80	171.11	28.45	30.00	34.29
Income Statement								
Total Revenue	502,572	2,020,668	2,147,767	2,024,130	1,954,258	1,838,451	1,513,073	1,329,661
EBITDA	114,569	476,407	477,522	439,662	169,939	338,717	273,765	210,501
Depn & Amortn	11,268	42,426	43,187	44,327	41,485	35,504	25,741	24,496
Income Before Taxes	92,812	392,345	392,440	353,129	86,204	273,881	231,874	168,827
Income Taxes	24,682	109,538	113,054	97,914	48,574	80,024	74,774	55,436
Net Income	68,130	282,807	279,386	255,215	37,630	193,857	157,100	113,391
Average Shares	76,699	77,972	80,728	82,489	83,641	83,543	81,983	80,727
Balance Sheet								
Current Assets	976,508	862,684	1,075,791	990,953	881,865	789,161	692,758	451,712
Total Assets	3,142,298	2,805,443	2,908,070	2,887,577	2,785,390	2,836,107	2,381,695	2,098,157
Current Liabilities	292,282	309,597	411,968	304,609	291,427	258,278	353,668	189,682
Long-Term Obligations	1,094,232	839,707	765,006	772,005	779,241	806,366	408,450	391,754
Total Liabilities	1,649,388	1,362,152	1,421,619	1,314,588	1,320,392	1,322,972	1,006,035	830,053
Stockholders' Equity	1,492,910	1,443,291	1,486,451	1,572,989	1,464,998	1,513,135	1,375,660	1,268,104
Shares Outstanding	76,125	76,534	78,765	81,195	82,726	83,233	82,069	80,970
Statistical Record								
Return on Assets %	9.48	9.90	9.64	9.00	1.34	7.43	7.01	5.31
Return on Equity %	19.36	19.31	18.26	16.80	2.52	13.42	11.88	9.31
EBITDA Margin %	22.80	23.58	22.23	21.72	8.70	18.42	18.09	15.83
Net Margin %	13.56	14.00	13.01	12.61	1.93	10.54	10.38	8.53
Asset Turnover	0.67	0.71	0.74	0.71	0.69	0.70	0.68	0.62
Current Ratio	3.34	2.79	2.61	3.25	3.03	3.06	1.96	2.38
Debt to Equity	0.73	0.58	0.51	0.49	0.53	0.53	0.30	0.31
Price Range	83.63-68.33	80.00-68.86	81.58-66.43	73.85-46.53	46.53-36.00	47.08-29.80	40.04-27.85	32.42-16.74
P/E Ratio	22.79-18.62	22.10-19.02	23.65-19.26	23.90-15.06	103.40-80.00	20.29-12.84	21.07-14.66	23.16-11.96
Average Yield %	1.69	1.64	1.43	1.52	1.88	1.67	1.71	1.87

Address: 1925 West Field Court, Lake Forest, IL 60045	**Web Site:** www.idexcorp.com	**Auditors:** Deloitte & Touche LLP
	Officers: Andrew K. Silvernail - Chief Executive Officer Harold Morgan - Vice President	**Investor Contact:** 847-498-7070
Telephone: 847-498-7070		**Transfer Agents:** Computershare, Providence, RI

IHS INC

Exchange	Symbol	Price	52Wk Range	Yield	P/E
NYS	IHS	$122.93 (5/31/2016)	133.81-93.99	N/A	34.43

*7 Year Price Score 104.55 *NYSE Composite Index=100 *12 Month Price Score 102.65

Interim Earnings (Per Share)

Qtr.	Feb	May	Aug	Nov
2012-13	0.37	0.65	0.35	0.59
2013-14	0.47	0.81	0.68	0.86
2014-15	0.57	0.74	0.86	1.31
2015-16	0.66	...	...	...

Interim Dividends (Per Share)

No Dividends Paid

Valuation Analysis   **Institutional Holding**

Forecast EPS	$6.16	No of Institutions
	(05/20/2016)	394
Market Cap	$8.3 Billion	Shares
Book Value	$2.1 Billion	77,737,616
Price/Book	3.87	% Held
Price/Sales	3.79	97.80

Business Summary: Business Services (MIC: 7.5.2 SIC: 7389 NAIC: 561499)

IHS provides information, insight, and analytics in areas that influence business. Co. is focused on embedding its content and solutions within its customers' organizations, enabling executive level capital deployment strategies and supporting decision-making activities of front-line employees managing daily operations. Co. operates in three segments: Resources, which includes its Energy and Chemicals product offerings; Transportation, which includes its Automotive; Maritime & Trade; and Aerospace, Defense & Security product offerings; and Consolidated Markets & Solutions, which includes its Product Design; Technology, Media & Telecom; and Economics & Country Risk product offerings.

Recent Developments: For the quarter ended Feb 29 2016, net income increased 14.0% to US$45.0 million from US$39.5 million in the year-earlier quarter. Revenues were US$548.4 million, up 6.7% from US$513.9 million the year before. Operating income was US$79.5 million versus US$62.9 million in the prior-year quarter, an increase of 26.3%. Direct operating expenses rose 5.2% to US$210.8 million from US$200.3 million in the comparable period the year before. Indirect operating expenses increased 3.0% to US$258.1 million from US$250.6 million in the equivalent prior-year period.

Prospects: Our evaluation of IHS Inc. as of June 19, 2016 is the result of our systematic analysis on three basic characteristics: earnings strength, relative valuation, and recent stock price movement. The company has generated a negative trend in earnings per share over the past 5 quarters and while recent estimates for the company have been raised by analysts, IHS has posted better than expected results. Based on operating earnings yield, the company is about fairly valued when compared to all of the companies in our coverage universe. Share price changes over the past year indicates that IHS will perform well over the near term.

Financial Data

(US$ in Thousands)	3 Mos	11/30/2015	11/30/2014	11/30/2013	11/30/2012
Earnings Per Share	3.57	3.47	2.81	1.95	2.37
Cash Flow Per Share	8.55	8.95	9.21	7.47	4.76
Income Statement					
Total Revenue	548,446	2,184,335	2,230,794	1,840,631	1,529,869
EBITDA	140,027	392,843	371,892	247,004	243,387
Depn & Amortn	60,515	85,000	68,300	48,800	36,100
Income Before Taxes	51,636	237,791	249,197	154,893	187,713
Income Taxes	10,409	48,853	54,648	23,059	29,564
Net Income	45,044	240,193	194,549	131,733	158,168
Average Shares	68,084	69,289	69,120	67,442	66,735
Balance Sheet					
Current Assets	805,778	955,342	770,587	880,840	863,883
Total Assets	6,562,438	5,601,081	5,348,430	5,359,613	3,549,211
Current Liabilities	1,595,412	960,133	955,057	1,246,435	876,937
Long-Term Obligations	2,410,043	2,095,183	1,806,098	1,779,065	890,922
Total Liabilities	4,423,281	3,400,204	3,188,884	3,452,650	1,964,853
Stockholders' Equity	2,139,157	2,200,877	2,159,546	1,906,963	1,584,358
Shares Outstanding	67,425	67,523	68,372	67,382	65,577
Statistical Record					
Return on Assets %	4.05	4.39	3.63	2.96	4.76
Return on Equity %	11.48	11.02	9.57	7.55	10.63
EBITDA Margin %	25.53	17.98	16.67	13.42	15.91
Net Margin %	8.21	11.00	8.72	7.16	10.34
Asset Turnover	0.36	0.40	0.42	0.41	0.46
Current Ratio	0.51	1.00	0.81	0.71	0.99
Debt to Equity	1.13	0.95	0.84	0.93	0.56
Price Range	133.81-93.99	133.81-105.34	142.47-110.98	115.93-89.83	118.63-82.39
P/E Ratio	37.48-26.33	38.56-30.36	50.70-39.49	59.45-46.07	50.05-34.76

Address: 15 Inverness Way East, Englewood, CO 80112
Telephone: 303-790-0600

Web Site: www.ihs.com
Officers: Jerre L. Stead - Executive Chairman, Chairman, Chief Executive Officer Daniel Yergin - Executive Vice President, Strategic Advisor

Auditors: Ernst & Young LLP
Investor Contact: 303-397-2969
Transfer Agents: American Stock Transfer

378

ILLINOIS TOOL WORKS, INC.

Exchange	Symbol	Price	52Wk Range	Yield	P/E	Div Achiever
NYS	ITW	$106.03 (5/31/2016)	106.03-80.09	2.07	20.35	53 Years

*7 Year Price Score 118.18 *NYSE Composite Index=100 *12 Month Price Score 111.10

Interim Earnings (Per Share)

Qtr.	Mar	Jun	Sep	Dec
2013	0.78	1.03	1.01	0.93
2014	1.11	3.65	1.34	1.19
2015	1.21	1.30	1.39	1.23
2016	1.29	...	...	...

Interim Dividends (Per Share)

Amt	Decl	Ex	Rec	Pay
0.55Q	08/07/2015	09/28/2015	09/30/2015	10/06/2015
0.55Q	10/30/2015	12/29/2015	12/31/2015	01/07/2016
0.55Q	02/12/2016	03/29/2016	03/31/2016	04/07/2016
0.55Q	05/06/2016	06/28/2016	06/30/2016	07/08/2016

Indicated Div: $2.20 (Div. Reinv. Plan)

Valuation Analysis — **Institutional Holding**

Forecast EPS	$5.53	No of Institutions	
	(05/20/2016)	1311	
Market Cap	$38.1 Billion	Shares	
Book Value	$5.2 Billion	356,302,912	
Price/Book	7.30	% Held	
Price/Sales	2.86	52.75	

Business Summary: Industrial Machinery & Equipment (MIC: 7.2.1 SIC: 3569 NAIC: 333999)

Illinois Tool Works operates in the following segments: Automotive OEM, which produces components and fasteners; Test & Measurement and Electronics, which produces equipment, consumables, and related software; Food Equipment, which produces commercial food equipment; Polymers & Fluids, which produces adhesives, sealants, lubrication and cutting fluids, janitorial and hygiene products, and fluids and polymers; Welding, which produces arc welding equipment; Construction Products, which produce construction fastening systems and truss products; and Specialty Products, which produces beverage packaging equipment, product coding and marking equipment, and appliance components and fasteners.

Recent Developments: For the quarter ended Mar 31 2016, net income increased 2.2% to US$468.0 million from US$458.0 million in the year-earlier quarter. Revenues were US$3.27 billion, down 2.0% from US$3.34 billion the year before. Operating income was US$722.0 million versus US$697.0 million in the prior-year quarter, an increase of 3.6%. Direct operating expenses declined 3.8% to US$1.90 billion from US$1.97 billion in the comparable period the year before. Indirect operating expenses decreased 2.8% to US$656.0 million from US$675.0 million in the equivalent prior-year period.

Prospects: Our evaluation of Illinois Tool Works Inc. as of June 19, 2016 is the result of our systematic analysis on three basic characteristics: earnings strength, relative valuation, and recent stock price movement. The company has managed to produce a neutral trend in earnings per share over the past 5 quarters and while recent estimates for the company have been mixed, ITW has posted better than expected results. Based on operating earnings yield, the company is undervalued when compared to all of the companies in our coverage universe. Share price changes over the past year indicates that ITW will perform well over the near term.

Financial Data

(US$ in Thousands)	3 Mos	12/31/2015	12/31/2014	12/31/2013	12/31/2012	12/31/2011	12/31/2010	12/31/2009
Earnings Per Share	5.21	5.13	7.28	3.74	6.06	4.19	3.03	1.89
Cash Flow Per Share	6.45	6.25	4.02	5.67	4.40	3.98	3.12	4.29
Tang Book Value Per Share	N.M.	N.M.	0.92	6.55	6.09	5.35	5.62	4.43
Dividends Per Share	2.135	2.070	1.810	1.600	1.480	1.400	1.300	1.240
Dividend Payout %	40.98	40.35	24.86	42.78	24.42	33.41	42.90	65.61
Income Statement								
Total Revenue	3,274,000	13,405,000	14,484,000	14,135,000	17,924,000	17,786,583	15,870,376	13,877,068
EBITDA	843,000	3,372,000	265,135,000	3,099,000	3,485,000	3,334,240	2,913,307	2,035,248
Depn & Amortn	117,000	475,000	262,242,000	549,000	611,000	589,669	548,278	674,170
Income Before Taxes	668,000	2,723,000	2,708,000	2,361,000	3,633,000	2,592,714	2,211,993	1,213,790
Income Taxes	200,000	820,000	809,000	717,000	1,108,000	575,700	684,800	244,300
Net Income	468,000	1,899,000	2,946,000	1,679,000	2,870,000	2,071,384	1,527,193	947,009
Average Shares	363,900	370,100	404,600	449,300	473,200	494,646	503,350	501,921
Balance Sheet								
Current Assets	6,241,000	6,720,000	8,076,000	9,816,000	7,960,000	6,849,346	5,968,401	5,674,595
Total Assets	15,437,000	15,729,000	17,678,000	19,966,000	19,309,000	17,983,514	16,250,273	16,081,984
Current Liabilities	2,716,000	2,368,000	3,533,000	6,034,000	2,651,000	2,976,727	3,093,592	2,835,638
Long-Term Obligations	6,353,000	6,896,000	5,981,000	2,793,000	4,589,000	3,488,198	2,511,959	2,914,874
Total Liabilities	10,219,000	10,505,000	10,859,000	10,263,000	8,748,000	7,965,723	6,879,997	7,273,777
Stockholders' Equity	5,218,000	5,224,000	6,819,000	9,703,000	10,561,000	10,017,791	9,370,276	8,808,207
Shares Outstanding	359,370	363,710	382,900	430,200	455,100	483,608	497,744	502,336
Statistical Record								
Return on Assets %	12.17	11.37	15.65	8.55	15.35	12.10	9.45	6.05
Return on Equity %	37.45	31.54	35.66	16.57	27.82	21.37	16.80	11.50
EBITDA Margin %	25.75	25.15	1,830.54	21.92	19.44	18.75	18.36	14.67
Net Margin %	14.29	14.17	20.34	11.88	16.01	11.65	9.62	6.82
Asset Turnover	0.85	0.80	0.77	0.72	0.96	1.04	0.98	0.89
Current Ratio	2.30	2.84	2.29	1.63	3.00	2.30	1.93	2.00
Debt to Equity	1.22	1.32	0.88	0.29	0.43	0.35	0.27	0.33
Price Range	102.63-80.09	99.81-80.09	97.21-76.78	84.08-59.77	62.95-47.79	59.02-40.15	53.73-40.77	51.02-26.19
P/E Ratio	19.70-15.37	19.46-15.61	13.35-10.55	22.48-15.98	10.39-7.89	14.09-9.58	17.73-13.46	26.99-13.86
Average Yield %	2.33	2.24	2.12	2.10	2.27	2.61	2.74	3.20

Address: 155 Harlem Avenue, Glenview, IL 60025	**Web Site:** www.itw.com	**Auditors:** Deloitte & Touche LLP
Telephone: 847-724-7500	**Officers:** E. Scott Santi - Chairman, Vice-Chairman, President, Chief Executive Officer, Acting Chief Executive Officer, Chief Operating Officer Christopher A. O'Herlihy - Vice-Chairman, Executive Vice President	**Investor Contact:** 847-657-4104 **Transfer Agents:** Computershare Trust Company, N.A., Providence, RI

IMS HEALTH HOLDINGS INC

Exchange	Symbol	Price	52Wk Range	Yield	P/E
NYS	IMS	$26.11 (5/31/2016)	33.15-22.46	N/A	53.29

*7 Year Price Score N/A   *NYSE Composite Index=100   *12 Month Price Score 92.48

Interim Earnings (Per Share)

Qtr.	Mar	Jun	Sep	Dec
2013	0.04	0.03	(0.07)	0.29
2014	(0.09)	(0.67)	0.14	0.04
2015	0.86	0.14	0.13	0.09
2016	0.13	...	...	...

Interim Dividends (Per Share)

No Dividends Paid

Valuation Analysis

		Institutional Holding	
Forecast EPS	$1.60		No of Institutions
	(05/20/2016)		273
Market Cap	$8.6 Billion		Shares
Book Value	$1.7 Billion		300,506,784
Price/Book	5.13		% Held
Price/Sales	2.81		94.22

TRADING VOLUME (thousand shares)

Business Summary: Internet & Software (MIC: 6.3.2 SIC: 7374 NAIC: 518210)

IMS Health Holdings is a holding company. Co. is a global information and technology services company providing clients in the healthcare industry with solutions to measure and improve their performances. Co. standardizes, organizes, structures and integrates data by applying its analytics and leveraging its global technology infrastructure to assist its clients run their organizations. Co. serves healthcare organizations and decision makers around the world, including pharmaceutical, biotechnology, consumer health and medical device manufacturers, as well as distributors, providers, payers, government agencies, policymakers, researchers and the financial community.

Recent Developments: For the quarter ended Mar 31 2016, net income decreased 85.6% to US$43.0 million from US$298.0 million in the year-earlier quarter. Revenues were US$774.0 million, up 22.5% from US$632.0 million the year before. Operating income was US$113.0 million versus US$91.0 million in the prior-year quarter, an increase of 24.2%. Direct operating expenses rose 29.5% to US$382.0 million from US$295.0 million in the comparable period the year before. Indirect operating expenses increased 13.4% to US$279.0 million from US$246.0 million in the equivalent prior-year period.

Prospects: Our evaluation of IMS Health Holdings Inc as of June 19, 2016 is the result of our systematic analysis on three basic characteristics: earnings strength, relative valuation, and recent stock price movement. The company has suffered a very negative trend in earnings per share over the past 5 quarters. However, while recent estimates for the company have been mixed, IMS has posted better than expected results. Based on operating earnings yield, the company is undervalued when compared to all of the companies in our coverage universe. Share price changes over the past year indicates that IMS will perform in line with the market over the near term.

Financial Data

(US$ in Millions)	3 Mos	12/31/2015	12/31/2014	12/31/2013	12/31/2012	12/31/2011
Earnings Per Share	0.49	1.23	(0.59)	0.29	(0.15)	0.40
Cash Flow Per Share	1.35	1.48	0.34	1.43	1.42	1.20
Income Statement						
Total Revenue	774	2,921	2,641	2,544	2,443	2,364
EBITDA	111	427	(20)	317	252	248
Depn & Amortn	3	44	48	37	42	36
Income Before Taxes	63	217	(285)	(48)	(61)	(62)
Income Taxes	20	(200)	(96)	(130)	(19)	(173)
Net Income	43	417	(189)	82	(42)	111
Average Shares	335	339	319	287	279	279
Balance Sheet						
Current Assets	1,150	1,092	1,014	1,327	1,237	...
Total Assets	7,895	7,459	7,150	7,999	8,215	...
Current Liabilities	1,008	1,033	785	932	843	...
Long-Term Obligations	4,468	4,136	3,743	4,894	4,149	...
Total Liabilities	6,217	5,887	5,608	7,116	6,532	...
Stockholders' Equity	1,678	1,572	1,542	883	1,683	...
Shares Outstanding	329	328	334	280	280	278
Statistical Record						
Return on Assets %	2.14	5.71	N.M.	1.01	...	...
Return on Equity %	9.35	26.78	N.M.	6.39	...	...
EBITDA Margin %	14.34	14.62	N.M.	12.46	10.32	10.49
Net Margin %	5.56	14.28	N.M.	3.22	N.M.	4.70
Asset Turnover	0.40	0.40	0.35	0.31	...	...
Current Ratio	1.14	1.06	1.29	1.42	1.47	...
Debt to Equity	2.66	2.63	2.43	5.54	2.47	...
Price Range	33.15-22.46	33.15-24.60	28.26-22.83	...	...	...
P/E Ratio	67.65-45.84	26.95-20.00	...	...	...	...

Address: 83 Wooster Heights Road, Danbury, CT 06810
Telephone: 203-448-4600

Web Site: www.imshealth.com
Officers: Ari Bousbib - Chairman, President, Chief Executive Officer Stefan C. Linn - Senior Advisor, Senior Vice President

Auditors: PricewaterhouseCoopers LLP
Investor Contact: 203-448-4600
Transfer Agents: American Stock Transfer & Trust Company, Brooklyn, NY

INTERCONTINENTAL EXCHANGE INC.

Exchange	Symbol	Price	52Wk Range	Yield	P/E
NYS	ICE	$271.12 (5/31/2016)	271.12-221.86	1.25	23.23

*7 Year Price Score 127.84 *NYSE Composite Index=100 *12 Month Price Score 100.50

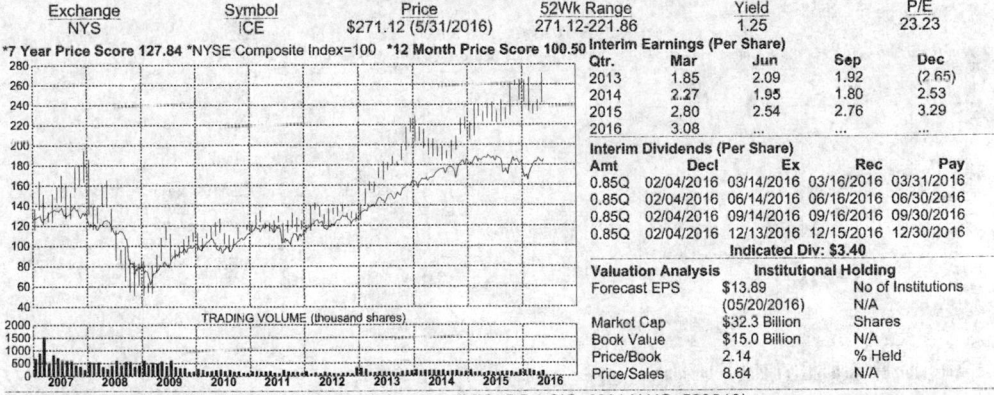

Interim Earnings (Per Share)

Qtr.	Mar	Jun	Sep	Dec
2013	1.85	2.09	1.92	(2.65)
2014	2.27	1.95	1.80	2.53
2015	2.80	2.54	2.76	3.29
2016	3.08	...	...	...

Interim Dividends (Per Share)

Amt	Decl	Ex	Rec	Pay
0.85Q	02/04/2016	03/14/2016	03/16/2016	03/31/2016
0.85Q	02/04/2016	06/14/2016	06/16/2016	06/30/2016
0.85Q	02/04/2016	09/14/2016	09/16/2016	09/30/2016
0.85Q	02/04/2016	12/13/2016	12/15/2016	12/30/2016

Indicated Div: $3.40

Valuation Analysis   **Institutional Holding**

Forecast EPS	$13.89	No of Institutions
	(05/20/2016)	N/A
Market Cap	$32.3 Billion	Shares
Book Value	$15.0 Billion	N/A
Price/Book	2.14	% Held
Price/Sales	8.64	N/A

Business Summary: Finance Intermediaries & Services (MIC: 5.5.1 SIC: 6231 NAIC: 523210)

IntercontinentalExchange is a network of regulated exchanges, clearing houses and data services for financial and commodity markets. Co. operates global marketplaces for trading and clearing a range of securities and derivatives contracts across main asset classes, including energy and agricultural commodities, interest rates, equities, equity derivatives, credit derivatives, bonds and currencies. Co.'s regulated exchanges include: futures exchanges in the U.S., the U.K., Canada, Singapore and Europe, securities exchanges and equity options exchanges. Co. also operates over-the-counter markets for physical energy and credit default swaps and operates central counterparty clearing houses.

Recent Developments: For the quarter ended Mar 31 2016, income from continuing operations decreased 100.0% to nil from US$323.0 million in the year-earlier quarter. Net income increased 16.7% to US$377.0 million from US$323.0 million in the year-earlier quarter. Revenues were US$1.55 billion, up 34.4% from US$1.16 billion the year before. Operating income was US$584.0 million versus US$462.0 million in the prior-year quarter, an increase of 26.4%. Direct operating expenses rose 30.7% to US$400.0 million from US$306.0 million in the comparable period the year before. Indirect operating expenses increased 46.9% to US$570.0 million from US$388.0 million in the equivalent prior-year period.

Prospects: Our evaluation of IntercontinentalExchange Inc. as of June 19, 2016 is the result of our systematic analysis on three basic characteristics: earnings strength, relative valuation, and recent stock price movement. The company has managed to produce a neutral trend in earnings per share over the past 5 quarters. However, while recent estimates for the company have been lowered by analysts, ICE has posted better than expected results. Based on operating earnings yield, the company is undervalued when compared to all of the companies in our coverage universe. Share price changes over the past year indicates that ICE will perform well over the near term.

Financial Data

(US$ in Thousands)	3 Mos	12/31/2015	12/31/2014	12/31/2013	12/31/2012	12/31/2011	12/31/2010	12/31/2009
Earnings Per Share	11.67	11.39	8.55	3.21	7.52	6.90	5.35	4.27
Cash Flow Per Share	12.13	11.81	12.83	9.42	10.05	9.74	7.25	6.67
Tang Book Value Per Share	N.M.	N.M.	N.M.	N.M.	12.51	5.03	N.M.	3.15
Dividends Per Share	3.100	2.900	2.600	0.650	...	...	...	...
Dividend Payout %	26.56	25.46	30.41	20.25	...	...	...	...
Income Statement								
Total Revenue	1,554,000	3,338,000	3,092,000	1,674,000	1,362,965	1,327,491	1,149,944	994,788
EBITDA	729,000	1,963,000	1,685,000	638,000	888,368	848,824	687,694	560,366
Depn & Amortn	143,000	213,000	182,000	85,000	61,400	56,500	50,100	45,700
Income Before Taxes	540,000	1,653,000	1,407,000	500,000	789,692	759,239	610,142	493,705
Income Taxes	163,000	358,000	402,000	230,000	227,955	237,498	202,375	179,551
Net Income	369,000	1,274,000	981,000	254,000	551,576	509,673	398,298	315,988
Average Shares	120,000	112,000	115,000	79,000	73,366	73,895	74,476	74,090
Balance Sheet								
Current Assets	54,554,000	53,313,000	50,245,000	44,259,000	33,750,087	32,605,391	23,575,778	19,459,851
Total Assets	79,160,000	77,987,000	68,279,000	64,818,000	37,214,842	36,147,864	26,642,259	21,884,875
Current Liabilities	55,636,000	54,743,000	50,539,000	44,342,000	32,245,697	31,800,314	23,127,384	18,967,832
Long-Term Obligations	4,718,000	4,717,000	2,247,000	3,923,000	969,500	837,500	325,750	208,500
Total Liabilities	64,112,000	63,179,000	55,919,000	52,235,000	33,571,465	33,026,339	23,864,709	19,485,143
Stockholders' Equity	15,048,000	14,808,000	12,360,000	12,583,000	3,643,377	3,121,525	2,777,550	2,399,732
Shares Outstanding	119,000	119,000	113,000	115,000	72,474	72,425	73,303	73,489
Statistical Record								
Return on Assets %	1.82	1.74	1.47	0.50	1.50	1.62	1.64	1.72
Return on Equity %	9.71	9.38	7.87	3.13	16.26	17.28	15.39	14.34
EBITDA Margin %	46.91	58.81	54.50	38.11	65.18	63.94	59.80	56.33
Net Margin %	23.75	38.17	31.73	15.17	40.47	38.39	34.64	31.76
Asset Turnover	0.05	0.05	0.05	0.03	0.04	0.04	0.05	0.05
Current Ratio	0.98	0.97	0.99	1.00	1.05	1.03	1.02	1.03
Debt to Equity	0.31	0.32	0.18	0.31	0.27	0.27	0.12	0.09
Price Range	266.94-221.86	264.14-204.87	227.82-183.45	226.06-123.81	142.37-112.15	134.72-103.91	126.94-93.92	119.74-50.92
P/E Ratio	22.87-19.01	23.19-17.99	26.65-21.46	70.42-38.57	18.93-14.91	19.52-15.06	23.73-17.56	28.04-11.93
Average Yield %	1.29	1.23	1.28	0.37	...	...	...	...

Address: 5660 New Northside Drive, Atlanta, GA 30328 **Telephone:** 770-857-4700 **Fax:** 770-937-0020	**Web Site:** www.theice.com **Officers:** Jeffrey C. Sprecher - Chairman, Chief Executive Officer Charles A. Vice - President, Chief Operating Officer	**Auditors:** Ernst & Young LLP **Investor Contact:** 770-857-4726 **Transfer Agents:** Computershare Trust Company, N.A., Providence, RI

INGERSOLL-RAND PLC

Exchange	Symbol	Price	52Wk Range	Yield	P/E
NYS	IR	$66.81 (5/31/2016)	69.86-48.80	1.92	23.28

*7 Year Price Score 102.94 *NYSE Composite Index=100 ***12 Month Price Score 107.46**

Interim Earnings (Per Share)

Qtr.	Mar	Jun	Sep	Dec
2013	0.29	1.05	0.56	0.16
2014	0.28	1.12	1.07	0.95
2015	0.19	0.29	1.12	0.88
2016	0.58			

Interim Dividends (Per Share)

Amt	Decl	Ex	Rec	Pay
0.29Q	08/07/2015	09/09/2015	09/11/2015	09/30/2015
0.29Q	10/07/2015	12/09/2015	12/11/2015	12/31/2015
0.32Q	02/03/2016	03/09/2016	03/11/2016	03/31/2016
0.32Q	04/06/2016	06/08/2016	06/10/2016	06/30/2016

Indicated Div: $1.28

Valuation Analysis   **Institutional Holding**

Forecast EPS	N/A	No of Institutions
		N/A
Market Cap	$17.2 Billion	Shares
Book Value	$5.8 Billion	N/A
Price/Book	2.97	% Held
Price/Sales	1.29	N/A

Business Summary: Industrial Machinery & Equipment (MIC: 7.2.1 SIC: 3585 NAIC: 333415)

Ingersoll-Rand is engaged in the design, manufacture, sale and service of industrial and commercial products. Co.'s business segments consist of: Climate, which includes Trane® and American Standard® Heating & Air Conditioning, and commercial and residential building services, parts, support and controls; energy services and building automation through Trane Building Advantage and Nexia; and Thermo King® transport temperature control solutions; and Industrial, which includes compressed air and gas systems and services, power tools, material handling systems, ARO® fluid management equipment, as well as Club Car ® golf, utility and rough terrain vehicles.

Recent Developments: For the quarter ended Mar 31 2016, income from continuing operations increased 105.3% to US$128.7 million from US$62.7 million in the year-earlier quarter. Net income increased 180.9% to US$155.6 million from US$55.4 million in the year-earlier quarter. Revenues were US$2.89 billion, unchanged from the year before. Operating income was US$217.3 million versus US$171.1 million in the prior-year quarter, an increase of 27.0%. Direct operating expenses declined 1.9% to US$2.05 billion from US$2.09 billion in the comparable period the year before. Indirect operating expenses decreased 0.0% to US$629.8 million from US$630.0 million in the equivalent prior-year period.

Prospects: Our evaluation of Ingersoll-Rand Plc. as of July 26, 2015 is the result of our systematic analysis on three basic characteristics: earnings strength, relative valuation, and recent stock price movement. The company has produced a positive trend in earnings per share over the past 5 quarters and while recent estimates for the company have remained steady, IR has posted better than expected results. Based on operating earnings yield, the company is undervalued when compared to all of the companies in our coverage universe. Share price changes over the past year indicates that IR will perform in line with the market over the near term.

Financial Data

(US$ in Thousands)	3 Mos	12/31/2015	12/31/2014	12/31/2013	12/31/2012	12/31/2011	12/31/2010	12/31/2009
Earnings Per Share	2.87	2.48	3.40	2.07	3.28	1.01	1.89	1.37
Cash Flow Per Share	3.72	3.21	3.60	3.98	3.88	3.65	2.14	5.40
Dividends Per Share	1.190	1.160	1.000	0.840	0.640	0.430	0.280	0.500
Dividend Payout %	41.46	46.77	29.41	40.58	19.51	42.57	14.81	36.50
Income Statement								
Total Revenue	2,894,100	13,300,700	12,891,400	12,350,500	14,034,900	14,782,000	14,079,100	13,195,300
EBITDA	314,100	1,657,200	1,613,600	1,297,700	1,758,600	1,107,100	1,524,900	1,102,000
Depn & Amortn	88,000	209,500	199,900	199,500	238,800	236,200	261,800	262,100
Income Before Taxes	171,400	1,235,300	1,201,600	832,200	1,282,600	616,800	995,100	551,000
Income Taxes	41,900	540,800	293,700	189,000	227,000	187,200	224,800	71,300
Net Income	152,400	664,600	931,700	618,800	1,018,600	343,200	642,200	451,300
Average Shares	261,300	267,800	274,300	298,300	310,600	339,300	339,800	329,100
Balance Sheet								
Current Assets	4,812,900	4,609,400	5,707,900	5,716,700	4,942,700	5,182,600	5,370,700	4,827,300
Total Assets	16,952,500	16,738,800	17,298,500	17,658,100	18,492,900	18,754,200	19,990,900	19,991,000
Current Liabilities	3,930,100	3,648,400	3,666,100	3,408,600	4,161,300	4,124,500	4,224,900	3,978,200
Long-Term Obligations	3,714,600	3,734,800	3,741,800	3,153,500	2,269,300	2,879,300	2,922,300	3,219,900
Total Liabilities	11,159,700	10,922,100	11,311,100	10,589,200	11,345,100	11,826,600	12,009,900	12,889,200
Stockholders' Equity	5,792,800	5,816,700	5,987,400	7,068,900	7,147,800	6,927,600	7,981,000	7,101,800
Shares Outstanding	257,300	261,251	262,899	282,700	295,605	297,116	328,164	320,589
Statistical Record								
Return on Assets %	4.46	3.91	5.33	3.42	5.45	1.77	3.21	2.21
Return on Equity %	13.30	11.26	14.27	8.71	14.43	4.60	8.52	6.56
EBITDA Margin %	10.85	12.46	12.52	10.51	12.53	7.49	10.83	8.35
Net Margin %	5.27	5.00	7.23	5.01	7.26	2.32	4.56	3.42
Asset Turnover	0.77	0.78	0.74	0.68	0.75	0.76	0.70	0.65
Current Ratio	1.22	1.26	1.56	1.68	1.19	1.26	1.27	1.21
Debt to Equity	0.64	0.64	0.62	0.45	0.32	0.42	0.37	0.45
Price Range	70.91-48.80	70.91-50.61	64.59-53.57	71.42-47.96	48.87-31.86	52.08-26.48	47.36-31.26	37.23-11.84
P/E Ratio	24.71-17.00	28.59-20.41	19.00-15.76	34.50-23.17	14.90-9.71	51.56-26.22	25.06-16.54	27.18-8.64
Average Yield %	1.99	1.85	1.66	1.44	1.50	1.07	0.75	2.02

Address: 170/175 Lakeview Dr., Airside Business Park, Swords **Telephone:** 018-707-400	**Web Site:** www.ingersollrand.com **Officers:** Michael W. Lamach - Chairman, President, Chief Executive Officer, Chief Operating Officer Susan K. Carter - Senior Vice President, Chief Financial Officer	**Auditors:** PricewaterhouseCoopers LLP **Transfer Agents:** The Bank of New York Mellon, New York, NY

INGRAM MICRO INC.

Exchange	Symbol	Price	52Wk Range	Yield	P/E
NYS	IM	$34.63 (5/31/2016)	36.53-24.07	N/A	31.20

*7 Year Price Score 118.30 *NYSE Composite Index=100 *12 Month Price Score 114.14

Interim Earnings (Per Share)

Qtr.	Mar	Jun	Sep	Dec
2013	0.32	0.45	0.50	0.72
2014	0.16	0.32	0.45	0.74
2015	0.27	(0.22)	0.42	0.90
2016	0.01	...	...	...

Interim Dividends (Per Share)

Amt	Decl	Ex	Rec	Pay
0.10Q	07/30/2015	08/28/2015	09/01/2015	09/15/2015
0.10Q	10/29/2015	11/06/2015	11/10/2015	11/24/2015

Valuation Analysis

		Institutional Holding	
Forecast EPS	$2.48	No of Institutions	489
	(05/20/2016)		
Market Cap	$5.1 Billion	Shares	
Book Value	$4.0 Billion		165,511,136
Price/Book	1.28	% Held	
Price/Sales	0.12		95.29

Business Summary: Computer Hardware & Equipment (MIC: 6.2.1 SIC: 5045 NAIC: 423430)

Ingram Micro is engaged in the distribution of information technology (IT) products, supply chain services and mobile device lifecycle services. Co. operates in North America, Europe, Asia-Pacific, and Latin America. Co. focuses on technology services, mobility lifecycle services, commerce and fulfillment services and cloud services. These services include forward and reverse logistics, subscriber identity module kitting, customization services, eBusiness, airtime activation, managed financial services, advanced planning and trade-in programs, and repair, refurbishment and asset recovery. Co.'s product categories include IT peripherals, systems, software, networking and mobility.

Recent Developments: For the quarter ended Apr 2 2016, net income decreased 95.6% to US$1.9 million from US$43.3 million in the year-earlier quarter. Revenues were US$9.34 billion, down 12.3% from US$10.64 billion the year before. Operating income was US$38.4 million versus US$97.7 million in the prior-year quarter, a decrease of 60.7%. Direct operating expenses declined 13.2% to US$8.70 billion from US$10.03 billion in the comparable period the year before. Indirect operating expenses increased 14.2% to US$593.3 million from US$519.7 million in the equivalent prior-year period.

Prospects: Our evaluation of Ingram Micro Inc. as of June 19, 2016 is the result of our systematic analysis on three basic characteristics: earnings strength, relative valuation, and recent stock price movement. The company has generated a negative trend in earnings per share over the past 5 quarters. However, while recent estimates for the company have been mixed, IM has posted results that fell short of analysts expectations. Based on operating earnings yield, the company is undervalued when compared to all of the companies in our coverage universe. Share price changes over the past year indicates that IM will perform very well over the near term.

Financial Data
(US$ in Thousands)

	3 Mos	12/31/2015	12/31/2014	12/28/2013	12/29/2012	12/31/2011	01/01/2011	01/02/2010
Earnings Per Share	1.11	1.37	1.67	1.99	1.99	1.53	1.94	1.22
Cash Flow Per Share	11.26	9.49	(3.13)	3.06	0.30	1.90	1.12	1.48
Tang Book Value Per Share	18.36	18.54	21.22	19.74	18.70	21.40	19.90	18.32
Dividends Per Share	0.200	0.200	...	...	...	...	...	...
Dividend Payout %	18.02	14.60	...	...	...	...	...	...
Income Statement								
Total Revenue	9,336,601	43,025,852	46,487,426	42,553,918	37,827,299	36,328,701	34,588,984	29,515,446
EBITDA	27,499	437,301	526,559	536,092	462,369	491,989	534,011	356,927
Depn & Amortn	705	62,138	58,962	48,480	20,711	57,282	61,549	68,590
Income Before Taxes	7,463	296,426	394,751	436,099	396,184	387,871	438,061	269,248
Income Taxes	5,564	81,321	128,060	125,516	90,275	143,631	120,001	67,110
Net Income	1,899	215,105	266,691	310,583	305,909	244,240	318,060	202,138
Average Shares	151,821	156,596	159,452	156,272	153,717	159,588	163,861	165,565
Balance Sheet								
Current Assets	9,845,036	10,531,850	11,485,523	10,375,571	10,166,379	8,618,402	8,590,088	7,746,905
Total Assets	11,702,835	12,307,260	12,831,443	11,791,195	11,480,448	9,146,516	9,084,032	8,179,350
Current Liabilities	6,398,602	7,108,115	7,436,433	6,934,416	6,761,831	5,509,875	5,235,186	4,796,660
Long-Term Obligations	1,091,060	1,097,273	1,096,889	797,454	943,275	300,000	531,127	302,424
Total Liabilities	7,679,901	8,339,474	8,665,617	7,841,570	7,869,195	5,873,739	5,842,850	5,167,537
Stockholders' Equity	4,022,934	3,967,786	4,165,826	3,949,625	3,611,253	3,272,777	3,241,182	3,011,813
Shares Outstanding	148,522	148,362	156,214	154,356	150,320	149,484	158,745	164,383
Statistical Record								
Return on Assets %	1.48	1.71	2.15	2.68	2.97	2.69	3.69	2.66
Return on Equity %	4.24	5.29	6.52	8.24	8.91	7.52	10.20	7.15
EBITDA Margin %	0.29	1.02	1.13	1.26	1.22	1.35	1.54	1.21
Net Margin %	0.02	0.50	0.57	0.73	0.81	0.67	0.92	0.68
Asset Turnover	3.55	3.42	3.75	3.67	3.68	4.00	4.02	3.88
Current Ratio	1.54	1.48	1.54	1.50	1.50	1.56	1.64	1.62
Debt to Equity	0.27	0.28	0.26	0.20	0.26	0.09	0.16	0.10
Price Range	36.53-24.07	31.92-23.04	30.78-22.84	24.21-16.92	19.72-14.46	21.50-15.75	19.25-14.87	18.80-9.82
P/E Ratio	32.91-21.68	23.30-16.82	18.43-13.68	12.17-8.50	9.91-7.27	14.05-10.29	9.92-7.66	15.41-8.05
Average Yield %	0.70	0.74	...	...	...	...	...	...

Address: 3351 Michelson Drive, Suite 100, Irvine, CA 92612-0697	**Web Site:** www.ingrammicro.com	**Auditors:** PricewaterhouseCoopers LLP
Telephone: 714-566-1000	**Officers:** Dale R. Laurance - Chairman Alain MoniÃ© - President, Chief Executive Officer	**Investor Contact:** 714-382-5013
Fax: 714-566-7604		**Transfer Agents:** Computershare Trust Company, N.A., Providence, RI

INGREDION INC

Exchange	Symbol	Price	52Wk Range	Yield	P/E
NYS	INGR	$117.41 (5/31/2016)	120.31-79.31	1.53	19.25

*7 Year Price Score 133.63 *NYSE Composite Index=100 ***12 Month Price Score 117.05**

TRADING VOLUME (thousand shares)

Interim Earnings (Per Share)

Qtr.	Mar	Jun	Sep	Dec
2013	1.41	1.20	1.10	1.34
2014	0.96	1.35	1.60	0.85
2015	1.15	1.47	1.48	1.42
2016	1.73	...	...	...

Interim Dividends (Per Share)

Amt	Decl	Ex	Rec	Pay
0.45Q	09/17/2015	09/28/2015	09/30/2015	10/26/2015
0.45Q	12/11/2015	12/29/2015	12/31/2015	01/25/2016
0.45Q	03/16/2016	03/29/2016	03/31/2016	04/25/2016
0.45Q	05/18/2016	06/28/2016	06/30/2016	07/25/2016

Indicated Div: $1.80

Valuation Analysis

		Institutional Holding	
Forecast EPS	$6.67	No of Institutions	572
	(05/20/2016)		
Market Cap	$8.4 Billion	Shares	76,946,288
Book Value	$2.3 Billion	% Held	N/A
Price/Book	3.69		
Price/Sales	1.50		

Business Summary: Food (MIC: 1.2.1 SIC: 2046 NAIC: 311221)

Ingredion is an ingredients solutions provider. Co. turns corn, tapioca, potatoes and other vegetables and fruits into ingredients and biomaterials for the food, beverage, paper and corrugating, brewing and other industries. Co.'s product line includes starches and sweeteners, animal feed products and edible corn oil. Co.'s starch-based products include both food-grade and industrial starches, and biomaterials. Co.'s sweetener products include glucose syrups, high maltose syrups, high fructose corn syrup, caramel color, dextrose, polyols, maltodextrins and glucose and syrup solids. Co. operates four segments: North America, South America, Asia Pacific and Europe, Middle East and Africa.

Recent Developments: For the quarter ended Mar 31 2016, net income increased 51.7% to US$130.0 million from US$85.7 million in the year-earlier quarter. Revenues were US$1.36 billion, up 2.2% from US$1.33 billion the year before. Operating income was US$200.0 million versus US$139.5 million in the prior-year quarter, an increase of 43.4%. Direct operating expenses declined 2.7% to US$1.02 billion from US$1.05 billion in the comparable period the year before. Indirect operating expenses decreased 1.6% to US$139.0 million from US$141.2 million in the equivalent prior-year period.

Prospects: Our evaluation of Ingredion Inc as of June 19, 2016 is the result of our systematic analysis on three basic characteristics: earnings strength, relative valuation, and recent stock price movement. The company has produced a positive trend in earnings per share over the past 5 quarters and while recent estimates for the company have remained steady, INGR has posted better than expected results. Based on operating earnings yield, the company is undervalued when compared to all of the companies in our coverage universe. Share price changes over the past year indicates that INGR will perform very well over the near term.

Financial Data

(US$ in Thousands)	3 Mos	12/31/2015	12/31/2014	12/31/2013	12/31/2012	12/31/2011	12/31/2010	12/31/2009
Earnings Per Share	6.10	5.51	4.74	5.05	5.47	5.32	2.20	0.54
Cash Flow Per Share	9.90	9.58	9.93	8.04	9.54	3.93	5.21	7.82
Tang Book Value Per Share	17.80	15.82	19.76	20.97	20.13	15.75	12.85	19.49
Dividends Per Share	1.770	1.740	1.680	1.560	0.920	0.660	0.560	0.560
Dividend Payout %	29.02	31.58	35.44	30.89	16.82	12.41	25.45	130.70
Income Statement								
Total Revenue	1,360,000	5,621,000	5,668,000	6,328,000	6,532,000	6,219,000	4,367,000	3,672,000
EBITDA	233,000	848,000	775,000	804,000	874,000	880,000	492,000	277,000
Depn & Amortn	47,000	194,000	195,000	194,000	211,000	211,000	155,000	130,000
Income Before Taxes	186,000	599,000	520,000	547,000	596,000	593,000	275,000	115,000
Income Taxes	56,000	187,000	157,000	144,000	167,000	170,000	99,000	68,000
Net Income	127,000	402,000	355,000	396,000	428,000	416,000	169,000	41,000
Average Shares	73,300	73,000	74,900	78,300	78,200	78,200	76,800	75,500
Balance Sheet								
Current Assets	2,068,000	1,950,000	2,144,000	2,214,000	2,360,000	2,102,000	1,753,000	1,045,000
Total Assets	5,228,000	5,074,000	5,091,000	5,360,000	5,592,000	5,317,000	5,071,000	2,952,000
Current Liabilities	693,000	742,000	721,000	820,000	933,000	926,000	891,000	565,000
Long-Term Obligations	1,872,000	1,819,000	1,804,000	1,717,000	1,724,000	1,801,000	1,681,000	408,000
Total Liabilities	2,937,000	2,930,000	2,914,000	2,956,000	3,155,000	3,213,000	3,095,000	1,257,000
Stockholders' Equity	2,291,000	2,144,000	2,177,000	2,404,000	2,437,000	2,104,000	1,976,000	1,695,000
Shares Outstanding	71,966	71,616	71,322	74,311	77,031	75,882	76,023	74,386
Statistical Record								
Return on Assets %	8.37	7.91	6.79	7.23	7.83	8.01	4.21	1.33
Return on Equity %	20.37	18.61	15.50	16.36	18.80	20.39	9.21	2.65
EBITDA Margin %	17.13	15.09	13.67	12.71	13.38	14.15	11.27	7.54
Net Margin %	9.34	7.15	6.26	6.26	6.55	6.69	3.87	1.12
Asset Turnover	1.06	1.11	1.08	1.16	1.19	1.20	1.09	1.19
Current Ratio	2.98	2.63	2.97	2.70	2.53	2.27	1.97	1.85
Debt to Equity	0.82	0.85	0.83	0.71	0.71	0.86	0.85	0.24
Price Range	107.80-76.79	99.34-76.49	86.85-58.88	74.01-61.70	66.59-45.59	59.36-37.74	47.27-26.61	32.26-17.95
P/E Ratio	17.67-12.59	18.03-13.88	18.32-12.42	14.66-12.22	12.17-8.33	11.16-7.09	21.49-12.10	59.74-33.24
Average Yield %	1.97	2.03	2.27	2.31	1.65	1.33	1.56	2.23

Address: 5 Westbrook Corporate Center, Westchester, IL 60154	**Web Site:** www.ingredion.com	**Auditors:** KPMG LLP
Telephone: 708-551-2600	**Officers:** Ilene S. Gordon - Chairman, President, Chief Executive Officer Jack C. Fortnum - Executive Vice President, Vice President, Chief Financial Officer, Division Officer	**Investor Contact:** 708-551-2592
Fax: 708-551-2700		**Transfer Agents:** Computershare, Providence, RI

INTERNATIONAL BUSINESS MACHINES CORP.

Exchange	Symbol	Price	52Wk Range	Yield	P/E	Div Achiever
NYS	IBM	$153.74 (5/31/2016)	173.22-117.85	3.64	11.66	20 Years

*7 Year Price Score 74.97   ***NYSE Composite Index=100**   ***12 Month Price Score 101.09**

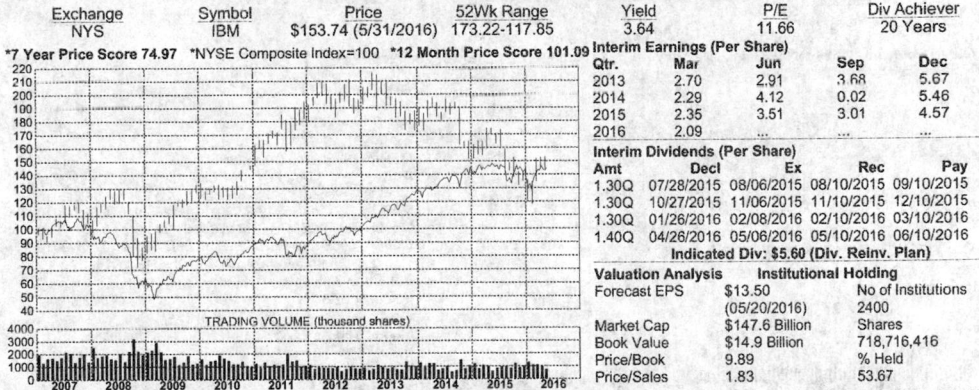

Interim Earnings (Per Share)

Qtr.	Mar	Jun	Sep	Dec
2013	2.70	2.91	3.68	5.67
2014	2.29	4.12	0.02	5.46
2015	2.35	3.51	3.01	4.57
2016	2.09	...	...	...

Interim Dividends (Per Share)

Amt	Decl	Ex	Rec	Pay
1.30Q	07/28/2015	08/06/2015	08/10/2015	09/10/2015
1.30Q	10/27/2015	11/06/2015	11/10/2015	12/10/2015
1.30Q	01/26/2016	02/08/2016	02/10/2016	03/10/2016
1.40Q	04/26/2016	05/06/2016	05/10/2016	06/10/2016

Indicated Div: $5.60 (Div. Reinv. Plan)

Valuation Analysis

		Institutional Holding	
Forecast EPS	$13.50	No of Institutions	
	(05/20/2016)	2400	
Market Cap	$147.6 Billion	Shares	718,716,416
Book Value	$14.9 Billion	% Held	
Price/Book	9.89	53.67	
Price/Sales	1.83		

Business Summary: IT Services (MIC: 6.3.1 SIC: 7379 NAIC: 541519)

International Business Machines operates in five segments: global technology services, which provides information technology infrastructure and business process services; global business services, which provides business outcomes to Co.'s clients across two primary business areas, Consulting and Systems Integration and Application Management Services; software, which consists of middleware and operating systems software; systems hardware, which provides clients with infrastructure technologies to help meet the new requirements of hybrid cloud and cognitive workloads; and global financing, which facilitates clients' acquisition of information technology systems, software and services.

Recent Developments: For the quarter ended Mar 31 2016, income from continuing operations decreased 16.5% to US$2.02 billion from US$2.42 billion in the year-earlier quarter. Net income decreased 13.5% to US$2.01 billion from US$2.33 billion in the year-earlier quarter. Revenues were US$18.68 billion, down 4.6% from US$19.59 billion the year before. Direct operating expenses declined 1.4% to US$10.00 billion from US$10.14 billion in the comparable period the year before. Indirect operating expenses increased 11.8% to US$7.25 billion from US$6.49 billion in the equivalent prior-year period.

Prospects: Our evaluation of International Business Machines Corp. as of June 19, 2016 is the result of our systematic analysis on three basic characteristics: earnings strength, relative valuation, and recent stock price movement. The company has managed to produce a neutral trend in earnings per share over the past 5 quarters. However, while recent estimates for the company have been lowered by analysts, IBM has posted better than expected results. Based on operating earnings yield, the company is undervalued when compared to all of the companies in our coverage universe. Share price changes over the past year indicates that IBM will perform in line with the market over the near term.

Financial Data

(US$ in Thousands)	3 Mos	12/31/2015	12/31/2014	12/31/2013	12/31/2012	12/31/2011	12/31/2010	12/31/2009
Earnings Per Share	13.18	13.42	11.90	14.94	14.37	13.06	11.52	10.01
Cash Flow Per Share	19.80	17.38	16.80	15.85	17.10	16.58	15.41	15.65
Dividends Per Share	5.200	5.000	4.250	3.700	3.300	2.900	2.500	2.150
Dividend Payout %	39.45	37.26	35.71	24.77	22.96	22.21	21.70	21.48
Income Statement								
Total Revenue	18,684,000	81,741,000	92,793,000	99,751,000	104,507,000	106,916,000	99,870,000	95,758,000
EBITDA	2,181,000	20,196,000	24,872,000	24,530,000	26,928,000	26,093,000	24,830,000	23,440,000
Depn & Amortn	1,024,000	3,855,000	4,492,000	4,678,000	4,676,000	4,815,000	4,831,000	4,994,000
Income Before Taxes	1,034,000	15,945,000	19,986,000	19,524,000	21,902,000	21,003,000	19,723,000	18,138,000
Income Taxes	(983,000)	2,581,000	4,234,000	3,041,000	5,298,000	5,148,000	4,890,000	4,713,000
Net Income	2,014,000	13,190,000	12,022,000	16,483,000	16,604,000	15,855,000	14,833,000	13,425,000
Average Shares	964,400	982,700	1,010,000	1,094,486	1,155,449	1,213,767	1,287,355	1,341,352
Balance Sheet								
Current Assets	47,623,000	42,504,000	49,422,000	51,350,000	49,433,000	50,928,000	48,116,000	48,935,000
Total Assets	118,856,000	110,495,000	117,532,000	126,223,000	119,213,000	116,433,000	113,452,000	109,022,000
Current Liabilities	34,664,000	34,269,000	39,600,000	40,154,000	43,625,000	42,123,000	40,562,000	36,002,000
Long-Term Obligations	40,254,000	33,428,000	35,073,000	32,856,000	24,088,000	22,857,000	21,846,000	21,932,000
Total Liabilities	103,931,000	96,233,000	105,664,000	103,431,000	100,353,000	96,294,000	90,405,000	86,385,000
Stockholders' Equity	14,925,000	14,262,000	11,868,000	22,792,000	18,860,000	20,138,000	23,046,000	22,637,000
Shares Outstanding	959,961	965,728	990,523	1,054,390	1,117,367	1,163,182	1,227,993	1,305,337
Statistical Record								
Return on Assets %	11.15	11.57	9.86	13.43	14.05	13.79	13.33	12.29
Return on Equity %	95.15	100.96	69.37	79.15	84.92	73.43	64.94	74.37
EBITDA Margin %	11.67	24.71	26.80	24.59	25.77	24.41	24.86	24.48
Net Margin %	10.78	16.14	12.96	16.52	15.89	14.83	14.85	14.02
Asset Turnover	0.70	0.72	0.76	0.81	0.88	0.93	0.90	0.88
Current Ratio	1.37	1.24	1.25	1.28	1.13	1.21	1.19	1.36
Debt to Equity	2.70	2.34	2.96	1.44	1.28	1.14	0.95	0.97
Price Range	174.40-117.85	174.40-131.75	197.77-151.41	215.80-172.80	211.00-179.16	194.56-146.76	146.92-121.86	132.57-81.98
P/E Ratio	13.23-8.94	13.00-9.82	16.62-12.72	14.44-11.57	14.68-12.47	14.90-11.24	12.75-10.58	13.24-8.19
Average Yield %	3.48	3.22	2.33	1.91	1.68	1.70	1.90	1.97

Address: One New Orchard Road, Armonk, NY 10504	**Web Site:** www.ibm.com	**Auditors:** PricewaterhouseCoopers LLP
Telephone: 914-499-1900	**Officers:** Virginia M. Rometty - Chairman, President, Chief Executive Officer, Senior Vice President Martin I Schroeter - Senior Vice President, Chief Financial Officer, General Manager	**Investor Contact:** 914-499-7777
Fax: 914-765-4190		**Transfer Agents:** Computershare Trust Company, N.A., Providence, RI

INTERNATIONAL FLAVORS & FRAGRANCES INC.

Exchange	Symbol	Price	52Wk Range	Yield	P/E	Div Achiever
NYS	IFF	$129.00 (5/31/2016)	129.34-100.49	1.74	25.54	13 Years

*7 Year Price Score 129.94 *NYSE Composite Index=100 *12 Month Price Score 105.28

TRADING VOLUME (thousand shares)

Interim Earnings (Per Share)

Qtr.	Mar	Jun	Sep	Dec
2013	1.10	1.24	1.20	0.75
2014	1.30	1.35	1.31	1.11
2015	1.57	1.29	1.31	0.98
2016	1.47			

Interim Dividends (Per Share)

Amt	Decl	Ex	Rec	Pay
0.56Q	08/06/2015	09/23/2015	09/25/2015	10/06/2015
0.56Q	12/15/2015	12/23/2015	12/28/2015	01/07/2016
0.56Q	03/10/2016	03/23/2016	03/28/2016	04/07/2016
0.56Q	05/04/2016	06/23/2016	06/27/2016	07/07/2016

Indicated Div: $2.24 (Div. Reinv. Plan)

Valuation Analysis		Institutional Holding	
Forecast EPS	$5.50	No of Institutions	606
	(05/20/2016)		
Market Cap	$10.3 Billion	Shares	85,444,848
Book Value	$1.6 Billion	% Held	77.49
Price/Book	6.31		
Price/Sales	3.39		

Business Summary: Specialty Chemicals (MIC: 8.3.2 SIC: 2869 NAIC: 325199)

International Flavors & Fragrances creates, manufacture and supplies flavors and fragrances for the food, beverage, personal care and household products industries. Co.'s product offerings are Flavors and Fragrances. Flavor compounds are sold to the food and beverage industries for use in consumer products. Fragrances is comprised of Fragrance Compounds, which are used by Co.'s customers in two categories: Fine Fragrances, including perfumes and colognes and Consumer Fragrances, including fragrance compounds for personal care; household products and beauty care; and Fragrance Ingredients, for use in preparation of compounds, and cosmetic, which consist of active and functional ingredients.

Recent Developments: For the quarter ended Mar 31 2016, net income decreased 7.5% to US$118.6 million from US$128.3 million in the year-earlier quarter. Revenues were US$783.3 million, up 1.1% from US$774.9 million the year before. Operating income was US$167.2 million versus US$161.8 million in the prior-year quarter, an increase of 3.4%. Direct operating expenses declined 1.3% to US$423.1 million from US$428.6 million in the comparable period the year before. Indirect operating expenses increased 4.6% to US$193.0 million from US$184.5 million in the equivalent prior-year period.

Prospects: Our evaluation of International Flavors & Fragrances Inc. as of June 19, 2016 is the result of our systematic analysis on three basic characteristics: earnings strength, relative valuation, and recent stock price movement. The company has enjoyed a very positive trend in earnings per share over the past 5 quarters and while recent estimates for the company have remained steady, IFF has posted better than expected results. Based on operating earnings yield, the company is about fairly valued when compared to all of the companies in our coverage universe. Share price changes over the past year indicates that IFF will perform well over the near term.

Financial Data

(US$ in Thousands)	3 Mos	12/31/2015	12/31/2014	12/31/2013	12/31/2012	12/31/2011	12/31/2010	12/31/2009
Earnings Per Share	5.05	5.16	5.06	4.29	3.09	3.26	3.26	2.46
Cash Flow Per Share	5.44	5.39	6.40	5.01	3.98	2.35	3.96	3.72
Tang Book Value Per Share	4.73	4.29	9.49	9.42	6.70	4.89	3.55	0.61
Dividends Per Share	2.150	2.060	1.720	1.460	1.300	1.160	1.040	1.000
Dividend Payout %	42.57	39.92	33.99	34.03	42.07	35.58	31.90	40.65
Income Statement								
Total Revenue	783,312	3,023,189	3,088,533	2,952,896	2,821,446	2,788,018	2,622,862	2,326,158
EBITDA	173,435	659,963	684,482	615,204	561,835	493,512	487,544	344,520
Depn & Amortn	6,061	74,800	89,354	83,227	76,667	75,327	79,242	6,153
Income Before Taxes	154,896	539,101	549,061	485,210	443,415	373,546	359,593	276,549
Income Taxes	36,293	119,854	134,518	131,666	189,281	106,680	96,036	81,023
Net Income	118,603	419,247	414,543	353,544	254,134	266,866	263,557	195,526
Average Shares	80,055	80,891	81,494	81,930	81,833	81,467	80,440	79,094
Balance Sheet								
Current Assets	1,891,529	1,455,884	1,710,027	1,652,903	1,572,559	1,317,220	1,325,195	1,128,066
Total Assets	4,162,460	3,721,454	3,494,621	3,331,731	3,249,600	2,965,581	2,872,455	2,644,774
Current Liabilities	712,748	742,128	518,808	560,366	622,732	564,566	660,951	484,454
Long-Term Obligations	1,369,955	937,844	934,232	932,665	881,104	778,248	787,668	934,749
Total Liabilities	2,532,096	2,131,136	1,976,060	1,868,659	2,000,792	1,861,169	1,873,033	1,875,771
Stockholders' Equity	1,630,364	1,590,318	1,518,561	1,463,072	1,248,808	1,104,412	999,422	769,003
Shares Outstanding	79,777	80,022	80,777	81,384	81,626	80,921	80,210	79,157
Statistical Record								
Return on Assets %	10.68	11.62	12.15	10.74	8.16	9.14	9.55	7.25
Return on Equity %	25.62	26.97	27.81	26.07	21.54	25.37	29.81	29.14
EBITDA Margin %	22.14	21.83	22.16	20.83	19.91	17.70	18.59	14.81
Net Margin %	15.14	13.87	13.42	11.97	9.01	9.57	10.05	8.41
Asset Turnover	0.79	0.84	0.90	0.90	0.91	0.96	0.95	0.86
Current Ratio	2.65	1.96	3.30	2.95	2.53	2.33	2.00	2.33
Debt to Equity	0.84	0.59	0.62	0.64	0.71	0.70	0.79	1.22
Price Range	122.00-100.49	122.77-98.15	105.43-83.84	89.89-66.54	67.41-52.88	65.24-51.31	55.77-39.77	41.85-25.30
P/E Ratio	24.16-19.90	23.79-19.02	20.84-16.57	20.95-15.51	21.82-17.11	20.01-15.74	17.11-12.20	17.01-10.28
Average Yield %	1.90	1.81	1.77	1.85	2.21	1.97	2.21	2.94

Address: 521 West 57th Street, New York, NY 10019-2960 Telephone: 212-765-5500	Web Site: www.iff.com Officers: Andreas Fibig - Chairman, Chief Executive Officer Alison A. Cornell - Executive President, Chief Financial Officer	Auditors: PricewaterhouseCoopers LLP Transfer Agents: American Stock Transfer & Trust Company, New York, NY

INTERNATIONAL PAPER CO

Exchange	Symbol	Price	52Wk Range	Yield	P/E
NYS	IP	$42.16 (5/31/2016)	51.82-32.58	4.17	18.25

*7 Year Price Score 97.14   *NYSE Composite Index=100   *12 Month Price Score 100.01

Interim Earnings (Per Share)

Qtr.	Mar	Jun	Sep	Dec
2013	0.71	0.57	0.85	0.97
2014	(0.21)	0.37	0.83	0.32
2015	0.74	0.54	0.53	0.43
2016	0.81	...	...	...

Interim Dividends (Per Share)

Amt	Decl	Ex	Rec	Pay
0.40Q	07/14/2015	08/12/2015	08/14/2015	09/15/2015
0.44Q	10/13/2015	11/12/2015	11/16/2015	12/15/2015
0.44Q	01/12/2016	02/11/2016	02/16/2016	03/15/2016
0.44Q	05/10/2016	05/25/2016	05/27/2016	06/15/2016

Indicated Div: $1.76

Valuation Analysis

		Institutional Holding	
Forecast EPS	$3.45	No of Institutions	
	(05/20/2016)	983	
Market Cap	$17.3 Billion	Shares	
Book Value	$4.2 Billion	406,224,320	
Price/Book	4.09	% Held	
Price/Sales	0.79	79.59	

Business Summary: Containers & Packaging (MIC: 8.1.3 SIC: 2621 NAIC: 322121)

International Paper is a paper and packaging company with primary markets and manufacturing operations in North America, Europe, Latin America, Russia, Asia, Africa and the Middle East. Co.'s businesses are separated into three segments: Industrial Packaging, which manufactures containerboard in the U.S. and its products include linerboard, medium, whitetop, recycled linerboard, recycled medium and saturating kraft; Printing Papers, which produces printing and writing papers and its products include uncoated papers and pulp; and Consumer Packaging, which produces solid bleached sulfate board and its brands include Everest®, Fortress®, and Starcote®.

Recent Developments: For the quarter ended Mar 31 2016, income from continuing operations increased 9.0% to US$339.0 million from US$311.0 million in the year-earlier quarter. Net income increased 7.4% to US$334.0 million from US$311.0 million in the year-earlier quarter. Revenues were US$5.11 billion, down 7.4% from US$5.52 billion the year before. Direct operating expenses declined 6.1% to US$3.61 billion from US$3.84 billion in the comparable period the year before. Indirect operating expenses decreased 6.3% to US$1.06 billion from US$1.13 billion in the equivalent prior-year period.

Prospects: Our evaluation of International Paper Co. as of June 19, 2016 is the result of our systematic analysis on three basic characteristics: earnings strength, relative valuation, and recent stock price movement. The company has managed to produce a neutral trend in earnings per share over the past 5 quarters. However, while recent estimates for the company have been mixed, IP has posted better than expected results. Based on operating earnings yield, the company is undervalued when compared to all of the companies in our coverage universe. Share price changes over the past year indicates that IP will perform poorly over the near term.

Financial Data
(US$ in Millions)

	3 Mos	12/31/2015	12/31/2014	12/31/2013	12/31/2012	12/31/2011	12/31/2010	12/31/2009
Earnings Per Share	2.31	2.23	1.29	3.11	1.80	3.07	1.48	1.55
Cash Flow Per Share	6.24	6.18	7.19	6.83	6.80	6.19	3.79	10.95
Tang Book Value Per Share	2.14	1.33	3.19	9.44	4.52	9.78	10.34	8.62
Dividends Per Share	1.680	1.640	1.450	1.250	1.087	0.975	0.400	0.325
Dividend Payout %	72.73	73.54	112.40	40.19	60.42	31.76	27.03	20.97
Income Statement								
Total Revenue	5,110	22,365	23,617	29,080	27,833	26,034	25,179	23,366
EBITDA	707	3,034	2,787	2,884	3,095	3,262	2,830	3,340
Depn & Amortn	267	1,213	1,308	1,423	1,399	1,263	1,400	1,472
Income Before Taxes	317	1,266	872	849	1,024	1,458	822	1,199
Income Taxes	41	466	123	(523)	331	311	221	469
Net Income	334	938	555	1,395	794	1,341	644	663
Average Shares	414	420	432	448	440	437	434	428
Balance Sheet								
Current Assets	6,792	6,477	7,959	9,025	8,905	10,456	8,028	7,551
Total Assets	31,043	30,587	28,684	31,528	32,153	26,993	25,368	25,548
Current Liabilities	4,098	3,924	4,909	5,127	4,998	4,738	4,503	4,012
Long-Term Obligations	8,824	8,900	8,631	8,827	9,696	9,189	8,358	8,729
Total Liabilities	26,809	26,703	23,569	23,423	25,849	20,373	18,534	19,525
Stockholders' Equity	4,234	3,884	5,115	8,105	6,304	6,620	6,834	6,023
Shares Outstanding	411	412	420	436	439	436	437	433
Statistical Record								
Return on Assets %	3.25	3.17	1.84	4.38	2.68	5.12	2.53	2.53
Return on Equity %	21.10	20.85	8.40	19.36	12.25	19.93	10.02	13.01
EBITDA Margin %	13.84	13.57	11.80	9.92	11.12	12.53	11.24	14.29
Net Margin %	6.54	4.19	2.35	4.80	2.85	5.15	2.56	2.84
Asset Turnover	0.74	0.75	0.78	0.91	0.94	0.99	0.99	0.89
Current Ratio	1.66	1.65	1.62	1.76	1.78	2.21	1.78	1.88
Debt to Equity	2.08	2.29	1.69	1.09	1.54	1.39	1.22	1.45
Price Range	56.28-32.58	57.59-36.80	55.25-44.25	49.48-39.28	39.28-27.42	32.40-22.33	28.22-19.60	27.27-4.03
P/E Ratio	24.36-14.10	25.83-16.50	42.83-34.30	15.91-12.63	21.82-15.23	10.55-7.27	19.07-13.24	17.59-2.60
Average Yield %	3.84	3.41	3.00	2.77	3.29	3.51	1.66	2.01

Address: 6400 Poplar Avenue, Memphis, TN 38197 **Telephone:** 901-419-9000	**Web Site:** www.internationalpaper.com **Officers:** Mark S. Sutton - Chairman, President, Chief Executive Officer, Chief Operating Officer John N. Balboni - Senior Vice President, Chief Information Officer	**Auditors:** Deloitte & Touche LLP **Investor Contact:** 901-419-1731 **Transfer Agents:** Computershare Trust Company, N.A., Canton, MA

INTERPUBLIC GROUP OF COMPANIES INC.

Exchange	Symbol	Price	52Wk Range	Yield	P/E
NYS	IPG	$23.90 (5/31/2016)	23.90-18.27	2.51	21.73

*7 Year Price Score 132.17 *NYSE Composite Index=100 *12 Month Price Score 107.34

Interim Earnings (Per Share)

Qtr.	Mar	Jun	Sep	Dec
2013	(0.14)	0.18	0.11	0.45
2014	(0.05)	0.23	0.21	0.73
2015	0.00	0.29	0.18	0.62
2016	0.01	...	...	...

Interim Dividends (Per Share)

Amt	Decl	Ex	Rec	Pay
0.12Q	08/11/2015	08/28/2015	09/01/2015	09/15/2015
0.12Q	11/11/2015	11/27/2015	12/01/2015	12/15/2015
0.15Q	02/12/2016	02/26/2016	03/01/2016	03/15/2016
0.15Q	05/19/2016	05/27/2016	06/01/2016	06/15/2016

Indicated Div: $0.60

Valuation Analysis

		Institutional Holding	
Forecast EPS	$1.32	No of Institutions	
	(05/20/2016)	631	
Market Cap	$9.6 Billion	Shares	
Book Value	$1.9 Billion	436,238,464	
Price/Book	4.95	% Held	
Price/Sales	1.25	92.50	

Business Summary: Advertising (MIC: 2.3.4 SIC: 7311 NAIC: 541810)

Interpublic Group of Companies is engaged in providing advertising and marketing services. Co. provides consumer advertising, digital marketing, communications planning and media buying, public relations and other communications disciplines. Co. has two reportable segments: Integrated Agency Networks providing a range of communications and marketing services which includes a range of advertising, marketing communications services and/or marketing services and partner and ; Constituency Management Group providing public relations, meeting and event production, sports and entertainment marketing, corporate and brand identity and marketing consulting.

Recent Developments: For the quarter ended Mar 31 2016, net income amounted to US$2.7 million versus a net loss of US$4.2 million in the year-earlier quarter. Revenues were US$1.74 billion, up 3.9% from US$1.68 billion the year before. Operating income was US$20.9 million versus US$7.8 million in the prior-year quarter, an increase of 167.9%. Indirect operating expenses increased 3.2% to US$1.72 billion from US$1.67 billion in the equivalent prior-year period.

Prospects: Our evaluation of Interpublic Group of Cos. Inc. as of June 19, 2016 is the result of our systematic analysis on three basic characteristics: earnings strength, relative valuation, and recent stock price movement. The company has generated a negative trend in earnings per share over the past 5 quarters and while recent estimates for the company have remained steady, IPG has posted results that fell short of analysts expectations. Based on operating earnings yield, the company is undervalued when compared to all of the companies in our coverage universe. Share price changes over the past year indicates that IPG will perform very well over the near term.

Financial Data
(US$ in Thousands)

	3 Mos	12/31/2015	12/31/2014	12/31/2013	12/31/2012	12/31/2011	12/31/2010	12/31/2009
Earnings Per Share	1.10	1.09	1.12	0.61	0.94	0.99	0.47	0.19
Cash Flow Per Share	2.05	1.65	1.60	1.41	0.82	0.59	1.73	1.16
Dividends Per Share	0.510	0.480	0.380	0.300	0.240	0.240	...	...
Dividend Payout %	46.36	44.04	33.93	49.18	25.53	24.24	...	...
Income Statement								
Total Revenue	1,742,000	7,613,800	7,537,100	7,122,300	6,956,200	7,014,600	6,531,900	6,027,600
EBITDA	28,300	956,100	910,500	696,600	903,100	968,100	690,600	503,600
Depn & Amortn	24,500	130,900	132,300	130,600	124,300	130,700	129,000	150,600
Income Before Taxes	(13,000)	762,200	720,700	468,000	674,800	738,400	450,600	232,400
Income Taxes	(15,600)	282,800	216,500	181,200	213,300	190,200	171,300	90,100
Net Income	2,700	454,600	477,100	267,900	446,700	532,300	261,100	121,300
Average Shares	409,300	415,700	425,400	429,600	481,400	540,600	542,100	508,100
Balance Sheet								
Current Assets	6,486,000	7,693,100	7,810,200	8,084,000	8,738,300	8,286,800	8,453,500	7,637,700
Total Assets	11,516,800	12,585,100	12,747,200	12,905,000	13,493,900	12,876,600	13,070,800	12,263,100
Current Liabilities	6,539,400	7,584,300	7,463,300	8,165,300	7,701,700	8,032,600	7,740,900	6,905,600
Long-Term Obligations	1,609,900	1,610,300	1,623,500	1,129,800	2,060,800	1,210,900	1,583,300	1,638,000
Total Liabilities	9,575,300	10,619,600	10,630,900	10,689,800	11,073,300	10,414,900	10,541,800	9,765,400
Stockholders' Equity	1,941,500	1,965,500	2,116,300	2,215,200	2,420,600	2,461,700	2,529,000	2,497,700
Shares Outstanding	402,405	403,200	413,800	424,500	417,500	449,500	489,100	486,100
Statistical Record								
Return on Assets %	4.04	3.59	3.72	2.03	3.38	4.10	2.06	0.99
Return on Equity %	23.82	22.27	22.03	11.56	18.25	21.33	10.39	4.88
EBITDA Margin %	1.62	12.56	12.08	9.78	12.98	13.80	10.57	8.35
Net Margin %	0.15	5.97	6.33	3.76	6.42	7.59	4.00	2.01
Asset Turnover	0.68	0.60	0.59	0.54	0.53	0.54	0.52	0.49
Current Ratio	0.99	1.01	1.05	0.99	1.13	1.03	1.09	1.11
Debt to Equity	0.83	0.82	0.77	0.51	0.85	0.49	0.63	0.66
Price Range	23.65-18.27	23.65-18.27	20.83-16.05	17.70-11.02	11.97-9.45	13.20-6.95	11.11-6.35	7.59-3.20
P/E Ratio	21.50-16.61	21.70-16.76	18.60-14.33	29.02-18.07	12.73-10.05	13.33-7.02	23.64-13.51	39.95-16.84
Average Yield %	2.41	2.27	2.24	2.06	2.01	2.20	2.29	...

Address: 909 Third Avenue, New York, NY 10022 Telephone: 212-704-1200	Web Site: www.interpublic.com Officers: Michael I. Roth - Chairman, Chief Executive Officer Philippe Krakowsky - Executive Vice President, Chief Strategy Officer, Chief Talent Officer	Auditors: PricewaterhouseCoopers LLP Transfer Agents: Computershare Shareowner Services LLC, Jersey City, NJ

INVESCO LTD

Exchange	Symbol	Price	52Wk Range	Yield	P/E
NYS	IVZ	$31.40 (5/31/2016)	39.87-25.38	3.47	15.39

*7 Year Price Score 99.07 *NYSE Composite Index=100 *12 Month Price Score 92.74

Interim Earnings (Per Share)

Qtr.	Mar	Jun	Sep	Dec
2013	0.49	0.45	0.51	0.65
2014	0.43	0.63	0.59	0.62
2015	0.60	0.60	0.58	0.48
2016	0.38	...	...	...

Interim Dividends (Per Share)

Amt	Decl	Ex	Rec	Pay
0.27Q	07/30/2015	08/18/2015	08/20/2015	09/04/2015
0.27Q	10/29/2015	11/13/2015	11/17/2015	12/07/2015
0.27Q	01/27/2016	02/16/2016	02/18/2016	03/04/2016
0.28Q	04/28/2016	05/11/2016	05/13/2016	06/03/2016

Indicated Div: $1.09

Valuation Analysis

		Institutional Holding	
Forecast EPS	$2.32	No of Institutions	
	(05/20/2016)	697	
Market Cap	$15.4 Billion	Shares	
Book Value	$7.9 Billion	377,521,088	
Price/Book	1.95	% Held	
Price/Sales	3.09	N/A	

Business Summary: Wealth Management (MIC: 5.5.2 SIC: 6282 NAIC: 523930)

Invesco is an investment manager. Co. provides a range of investment capabilities and outcomes, delivered through a range set of investment vehicles. Co. sole business is investment management. Co. operates in North America, U.K., Europe, Middle East and Asia-Pacific. Co.'s asset classes include money market, balanced, equity, fixed income, and alternatives. Co.'s distribution channels consist of: Retail, which is a provider of retail investment solutions to clients in primary markets; and Institutional, which provides investment solutions to institutional investors. As of Dec 31 2015, Co. had US$775.6 billion of assets under management.

Recent Developments: For the quarter ended Mar 31 2016, net income decreased 44.4% to US$157.8 million from US$284.0 million in the year-earlier quarter. Revenues were US$1.15 billion, down 11.1% from US$1.29 billion the year before. Operating income was US$274.4 million versus US$338.1 million in the prior-year quarter, a decrease of 18.8%. Indirect operating expenses decreased 8.3% to US$874.3 million from US$953.5 million in the equivalent prior-year period.

Prospects: Our evaluation of Invesco Ltd as of June 19, 2016 is the result of our systematic analysis on three basic characteristics: earnings strength, relative valuation, and recent stock price movement. The company has managed to produce a neutral trend in earnings per share over the past 5 quarters. However, while recent estimates for the company have been lowered by analysts, IVZ has posted results that fell short of analysts expectations. Based on operating earnings yield, the company is undervalued when compared to all of the companies in our coverage universe. Share price changes over the past year indicates that IVZ will perform in line with the market over the near term.

Financial Data

(US$ in Thousands)	3 Mos	12/31/2015	12/31/2014	12/31/2013	12/31/2012	12/31/2011	12/31/2010	12/31/2009
Earnings Per Share	2.04	2.26	2.27	2.10	1.49	1.57	1.01	0.76
Cash Flow Per Share	2.49	2.46	2.76	1.74	1.81	2.08	0.82	0.87
Tang Book Value Per Share	0.51	0.85	1.16	0.60	N.M.	N.M.	N.M.	0.71
Dividends Per Share	1.080	1.060	0.975	0.848	0.640	0.477	0.433	0.407
Dividend Payout %	52.94	46.90	42.95	40.36	42.95	30.41	42.82	53.62
Income Statement								
Total Revenue	1,148,700	5,122,900	5,147,100	4,644,600	4,177,000	4,092,200	3,487,700	2,627,300
EBITDA	286,900	1,414,600	1,426,500	1,258,900	847,500	925,600	816,200	462,800
Depn & Amortn	24,700	83,000	76,800	71,300	65,400	117,400	96,700	77,600
Income Before Taxes	241,900	1,327,000	1,362,300	1,219,700	829,800	877,600	793,600	330,500
Income Taxes	71,900	398,000	390,600	336,900	272,200	286,100	197,000	148,200
Net Income	161,000	968,100	988,100	940,300	677,100	729,700	465,700	322,500
Average Shares	418,900	429,300	435,600	448,500	453,800	464,700	463,200	423,600
Balance Sheet								
Current Assets	14,497,700	16,888,400	12,009,700	10,505,200	3,907,600	3,834,100	4,274,500	3,121,000
Total Assets	22,658,200	25,073,200	20,462,500	19,270,500	17,492,400	19,347,000	20,444,100	10,909,600
Current Liabilities	11,840,800	1,524,400	3,852,600	3,737,500	2,713,000	2,974,400	3,264,500	2,298,400
Long-Term Obligations	2,073,200	2,072,800	1,589,300	1,588,600	1,186,000	1,069,600	1,315,700	745,700
Total Liabilities	14,754,200	17,187,900	12,136,500	10,877,900	9,175,600	11,227,900	12,179,500	3,996,700
Stockholders' Equity	7,904,000	7,885,300	8,326,000	8,392,600	8,316,800	8,119,100	8,264,600	6,912,900
Shares Outstanding	490,400	417,500	429,900	433,100	441,400	464,000	460,100	431,677
Statistical Record								
Return on Assets %	3.90	4.25	4.97	5.12	3.67	3.67	2.97	3.12
Return on Equity %	10.88	11.94	11.82	11.25	8.22	8.91	6.14	5.12
EBITDA Margin %	24.98	27.61	27.71	27.10	20.29	22.62	23.40	17.62
Net Margin %	14.02	18.90	19.20	20.25	16.21	17.83	13.35	12.27
Asset Turnover	0.22	0.23	0.26	0.25	0.23	0.21	0.22	0.25
Current Ratio	1.22	11.08	3.12	2.81	1.44	1.29	1.31	1.36
Debt to Equity	0.26	0.26	0.19	0.19	0.14	0.13	0.16	0.11
Price Range	41.73-25.38	41.85-30.39	41.28-31.77	36.55-25.64	26.84-20.35	27.42-14.85	24.24-16.63	23.97-9.51
P/E Ratio	20.46-12.44	18.52-13.45	18.19-14.00	17.40-12.21	18.01-13.66	17.46-9.46	24.00-16.47	31.54-12.51
Average Yield %	3.14	2.88	2.61	2.70	2.69	2.18	2.08	2.28

Address: 1555 Peachtree Street N.E., Suite 1800, Atlanta, GA 30309 **Telephone:** 404-892-0896	**Web Site:** www.invesco.com **Officers:** Martin L. Flanagan - President, Chief Executive Officer Gregory Mark Armour - Senior Managing Director, Division Officer, Head	**Auditors:** PricewaterhouseCoopers LLP **Investor Contact:** 404 439-4605 **Transfer Agents.** BNY Mellon Shareowner Services, Pittsburg, PA

IRON MOUNTAIN INC

Exchange	Symbol	Price	52Wk Range	Yield	P/E
NYS	IRM	$36.74 (5/31/2016)	38.15-24.56	5.28	53.25

*7 Year Price Score 86.86 ***NYSE Composite Index=100** ***12 Month Price Score 114.93**

TRADING VOLUME (thousand shares)

Interim Earnings (Per Share)
Qtr.	Mar	Jun	Sep	Dec
2013	0.10	0.14	0.02	0.25
2014	0.22	1.40	0.00	0.04
2015	0.19	0.25	0.11	0.03
2016	0.30	...	...	...

Interim Dividends (Per Share)
Amt	Decl	Ex	Rec	Pay
0.475Q	08/27/2015	09/09/2015	09/11/2015	09/30/2015
0.485Q	10/29/2015	11/27/2015	12/01/2015	12/15/2015
0.485Q	02/18/2016	03/03/2016	03/07/2016	03/21/2016
0.485Q	05/25/2016	06/02/2016	06/06/2016	06/24/2016

Indicated Div: $1.94

Valuation Analysis
	Institutional Holding	
Forecast EPS	$1.19	No of Institutions
	(05/20/2016)	478
Market Cap	$7.8 Billion	Shares
Book Value	$496.4 Million	211,644,208
Price/Book	15.68	% Held
Price/Sales	2.59	N/A

Business Summary: Business Services (MIC: 7.5.2 SIC: 4225 NAIC: 493110)

Iron Mountain stores records, primarily physical records and data backup media, and provides information management services that help organizations protect their information, comply with regulations, and enable corporate disaster recovery. Co. provides storage and information management services to legal, financial, healthcare, insurance, life sciences, energy, businesses services and government organizations. Co. operates in the following business segments: North American Records and Information Management Business, North American Data Management Business, Western European Business, Other International Business, and Corporate and Other Business.

Recent Developments: For the quarter ended Mar 31 2016, net income increased 51.0% to US$63.0 million from US$41.7 million in the year-earlier quarter. Revenues were US$750.7 million, up 0.2% from US$749.3 million the year before. Operating income was US$130.1 million versus US$144.9 million in the prior-year quarter, a decrease of 10.3%. Direct operating expenses rose 1.4% to US$326.1 million from US$321.7 million in the comparable period the year before. Indirect operating expenses increased 4.2% to US$294.5 million from US$282.7 million in the equivalent prior-year period.

Prospects: Our evaluation of Iron Mountain Inc. as of June 19, 2016 is the result of our systematic analysis on three basic characteristics: earnings strength, relative valuation, and recent stock price movement. The company has managed to produce a neutral trend in earnings per share over the past 5 quarters. However, while recent estimates for the company have been lowered by analysts, IRM has posted better than expected results. Based on operating earnings yield, the company is about fairly valued when compared to all of the companies in our coverage universe. Share price changes over the past year indicates that IRM will perform well over the near term.

Financial Data
(US$ in Thousands)	3 Mos	12/31/2015	12/31/2014	12/31/2013	12/31/2012	12/31/2011	12/31/2010	12/31/2009
Earnings Per Share	0.69	0.58	1.66	0.51	0.98	2.02	(0.27)	1.08
Cash Flow Per Share	2.92	2.57	2.42	2.66	2.49	3.16	3.09	3.04
Dividends Per Share	1.920	1.910	5.371	1.080	5.120	0.938	...	...
Dividend Payout %	278.26	329.31	323.57	211.76	522.45	46.41	...	...
Income Statement								
Total Revenue	750,690	3,007,976	3,117,693	3,025,923	3,005,255	3,014,703	3,127,549	3,013,595
EBITDA	231,956	727,156	788,647	700,048	821,563	848,794	628,451	844,194
Depn & Amortn	89,953	301,219	304,557	282,856	280,598	290,638	306,670	283,571
Income Before Taxes	74,941	162,066	223,373	163,018	298,366	352,900	100,795	332,833
Income Taxes	11,900	37,713	(97,275)	63,057	114,873	106,488	149,787	110,527
Net Income	62,774	123,241	326,119	97,262	171,708	395,538	(53,900)	220,877
Average Shares	212,471	212,118	196,749	192,412	174,867	195,938	201,991	204,271
Balance Sheet								
Current Assets	831,896	857,912	917,719	933,607	1,024,092	914,450	1,055,178	1,211,425
Total Assets	6,422,309	6,350,587	6,570,342	6,653,005	6,358,339	6,041,258	6,395,799	6,846,834
Current Liabilities	748,493	841,831	856,736	959,101	904,953	849,030	854,934	814,714
Long-Term Obligations	4,931,296	4,757,610	4,611,436	4,119,139	3,732,116	3,280,268	2,912,465	3,211,223
Total Liabilities	5,925,911	5,841,746	5,713,987	5,605,667	5,208,368	4,795,570	4,439,954	4,705,692
Stockholders' Equity	496,398	508,841	856,355	1,047,338	1,149,971	1,245,688	1,955,845	2,141,142
Shares Outstanding	211,892	211,340	209,818	191,426	190,005	172,140	200,064	203,546
Statistical Record								
Return on Assets %	2.27	1.91	4.93	1.50	2.76	6.36	N.M.	3.35
Return on Equity %	23.39	18.05	34.26	8.85	14.30	24.71	N.M.	11.20
EBITDA Margin %	30.90	24.17	25.30	23.14	27.34	28.16	20.09	28.01
Net Margin %	8.36	4.10	10.46	3.21	5.71	13.12	N.M.	7.33
Asset Turnover	0.47	0.47	0.47	0.47	0.48	0.48	0.47	0.46
Current Ratio	1.11	1.02	1.07	0.97	1.13	1.08	1.23	1.49
Debt to Equity	9.93	9.35	5.38	3.93	3.25	2.63	1.49	1.50
Price Range	37.75-24.56	41.09-26.13	40.27-25.90	39.54-25.30	37.69-27.41	35.40-24.39	28.39-20.25	31.95-17.07
P/E Ratio	54.71-35.59	70.84-45.05	24.26-15.60	77.53-49.61	38.46-27.97	17.52-12.07	...	29.58-15.81
Average Yield %	6.24	5.76	16.71	3.47	16.15	3.07	...	...

Address: One Federal Street, Boston, MA 02110 Telephone: 617-535-4766	Web Site: www.ironmountain.com Officers: William L. Meaney - President, Chief Executive Officer John Tomovcsik - Executive Vice President, General Manager, Chief Operating Officer	Auditors: Deloitte & Touche LLP Investor Contact: 617-535-4766 Transfer Agents: Computershare, Providence, RI

ITC HOLDINGS CORP

Exchange	Symbol	Price	52Wk Range	Yield	P/E
NYS	ITC	$44.52 (5/31/2016)	44.63-31.28	1.68	28.72

*7 Year Price Score 113.74 *NYSE Composite Index=100 *12 Month Price Score 115.91

Interim Earnings (Per Share)

Qtr.	Mar	Jun	Sep	Dec
2013	0.32	0.30	0.37	0.49
2014	0.43	0.34	0.47	0.29
2015	0.43	0.46	0.42	0.25
2016	0.42	...	...	...

Interim Dividends (Per Share)

Amt	Decl	Ex	Rec	Pay
0.188Q	08/19/2015	08/28/2015	09/01/2015	09/15/2015
0.188Q	11/18/2015	11/27/2015	12/01/2015	12/15/2015
0.188Q	02/04/2016	02/26/2016	03/01/2016	03/15/2016
0.188Q	05/19/2016	05/27/2016	06/01/2016	06/15/2016

Indicated Div: $0.75

Valuation Analysis | **Institutional Holding**
Valuation Analysis		Institutional Holding	
Forecast EPS	$2.10	No of Institutions	
	(05/20/2016)	508	
Market Cap	$6.8 Billion	Shares	
Book Value	$1.7 Billion	139,268,976	
Price/Book	3.89	% Held	
Price/Sales	6.46	98.16	

Business Summary: Electric Utilities (MIC: 3.1.1 SIC: 4911 NAIC: 221121)

ITC Holdings is a holding company. Co. is engaged in the transmission of electricity. Through International Transmission Company, Michigan Electric Transmission Company, LLC, ITC Midwest LLC and ITC Great Plains, LLC (together, Regulated Operating Subsidiaries), Co. operates high-voltage systems in Michigan's Lower Peninsula and portions of Iowa, Minnesota, Illinois, Missouri, Kansas and Oklahoma that transmit electricity from generating stations to local distribution facilities connected to its systems. The operations performed by Co.'s Regulated Operating Subsidiaries include: asset planning; engineering, design and construction; maintenance; and real time operations.

Recent Developments: For the quarter ended Mar 31 2016, net income decreased 4.3% to US$64.2 million from US$67.1 million in the year-earlier quarter. Revenues were US$280.1 million, up 2.8% from US$272.5 million the year before. Operating income was US$147.8 million versus US$149.5 million in the prior-year quarter, a decrease of 1.1%. Indirect operating expenses increased 7.6% to US$132.4 million from US$123.0 million in the equivalent prior-year period.

Prospects: Our evaluation of ITC Holdings Corp. as of June 19, 2016 is the result of our systematic analysis on three basic characteristics: earnings strength, relative valuation, and recent stock price movement. The company has managed to produce a neutral trend in earnings per share over the past 5 quarters and while recent estimates for the company have been mixed, ITC has posted better than expected results. Based on operating earnings yield, the company is about fairly valued when compared to all of the companies in our coverage universe. Share price changes over the past year indicates that ITC will perform very well over the near term.

Financial Data
(US$ in Thousands)

	3 Mos	12/31/2015	12/31/2014	12/31/2013	12/31/2012	12/31/2011	12/31/2010	12/31/2009
Earnings Per Share	1.55	1.56	1.54	1.47	1.20	1.10	0.95	0.86
Cash Flow Per Share	3.81	3.62	3.23	2.88	2.14	2.52	2.85	1.82
Tang Book Value Per Share	4.93	4.67	4.32	3.90	2.66	1.70	0.77	0.06
Dividends Per Share	0.725	0.700	0.610	0.535	0.487	0.458	0.437	0.417
Dividend Payout %	46.77	44.87	39.61	36.31	40.56	41.54	46.13	48.45
Income Statement								
Total Revenue	280,133	1,044,768	1,023,048	941,272	830,535	757,397	696,843	621,015
EBITDA	185,750	704,253	679,116	599,928	526,542	482,471	434,873	402,278
Depn & Amortn	38,872	144,672	118,900	109,400	97,300	85,800	77,800	76,800
Income Before Taxes	103,980	383,877	394,405	352,368	296,508	266,434	227,932	208,472
Income Taxes	39,743	141,471	150,322	118,862	108,632	94,749	82,254	77,572
Net Income	64,237	242,406	244,083	233,506	187,876	171,685	145,678	130,900
Average Shares	152,472	154,701	156,817	157,025	154,690	153,236	151,194	150,232
Balance Sheet								
Current Assets	325,511	169,242	186,816	191,538	198,226	201,528	251,742	294,013
Total Assets	7,863,242	7,582,122	6,974,089	6,282,243	5,564,809	4,823,366	4,307,873	4,029,716
Current Liabilities	892,775	719,153	463,014	499,379	1,003,311	315,467	182,404	146,678
Long-Term Obligations	3,947,954	4,060,923	3,928,586	3,412,112	2,495,298	2,645,022	2,496,896	2,434,398
Total Liabilities	6,114,428	5,873,051	5,304,532	4,668,511	4,149,954	3,564,474	3,190,440	3,018,193
Stockholders' Equity	1,748,814	1,709,071	1,669,557	1,613,732	1,414,855	1,258,892	1,117,433	1,011,523
Shares Outstanding	152,766	152,699	155,140	157,500	156,745	153,970	152,147	150,252
Statistical Record								
Return on Assets %	3.20	3.33	3.68	3.94	3.61	3.76	3.49	3.38
Return on Equity %	13.83	14.35	14.87	15.42	14.01	14.45	13.69	13.49
EBITDA Margin %	66.31	67.41	66.38	63.74	63.40	63.70	62.41	64.78
Net Margin %	22.93	23.20	23.86	24.81	22.62	22.67	20.91	21.08
Asset Turnover	0.14	0.14	0.15	0.16	0.16	0.17	0.17	0.16
Current Ratio	0.36	0.24	0.40	0.38	0.20	0.64	1.38	2.00
Debt to Equity	2.26	2.38	2.35	2.11	1.76	2.10	2.23	2.41
Price Range	43.57-31.28	43.91-31.28	41.97-31.27	34.98-25.57	26.54-22.33	25.89-20.66	20.97-16.35	17.46-10.87
P/E Ratio	28.11-20.18	28.15-20.05	27.25-20.31	23.80-17.40	22.12-18.61	23.53-18.78	22.07-17.21	20.31-12.64
Average Yield %	2.02	1.96	1.67	1.79	1.96	1.94	2.31	2.84

Address: 27175 Energy Way, Novi, MI 48377	**Web Site:** www.itc-holdings.com	**Auditors:** Deloitte & Touche LLP
Telephone: 248-946-3000	**Officers:** Joseph L. Welch - Chairman, President, Chief Executive Officer, Treasurer Jon E. Jipping - Executive Vice President, Chief Operating Officer	**Investor Contact:** 248 946-3595 **Transfer Agents:** Computershare Trust Company, N.A., Providence, RI

JABIL CIRCUIT, INC.

Exchange	Symbol	Price	52Wk Range	Yield	P/E
NYS	JBL	$19.08 (5/31/2016)	25.93-16.88	1.68	9.99

*7 Year Price Score 94.67 ***NYSE Composite Index=100** ***12 Month Price Score 85.45**

Interim Earnings (Per Share)

Qtr.	Nov	Feb	May	Aug
2012-13	0.51	0.43	0.24	0.61
2013-14	0.57	(0.19)	0.93	(0.11)
2014-15	0.37	0.27	0.37	0.45
2015-16	0.68	0.41		

Interim Dividends (Per Share)

Amt	Decl	Ex	Rec	Pay
0.08Q	07/16/2015	08/12/2015	08/14/2015	09/01/2015
0.08Q	10/14/2015	11/12/2015	11/16/2015	12/01/2015
0.08Q	01/21/2016	02/11/2016	02/16/2016	03/01/2016
0.08Q	04/21/2016	05/12/2016	05/16/2016	06/01/2016

Indicated Div: $0.32

Valuation Analysis / **Institutional Holding**

Forecast EPS	$1.83	No of Institutions
	(05/20/2016)	501
Market Cap	$3.6 Billion	Shares
Book Value	$2.5 Billion	201,291,184
Price/Book	1.48	% Held
Price/Sales	0.20	84.44

Business Summary: Electrical Equipment (MIC: 7.3.1 SIC: 3672 NAIC: 334412)

Jabil Circuit provides electronic manufacturing services and solutions to companies in the aerospace, automotive, computing, defense, digital home, energy, healthcare, industrial, instrumentation, lifestyles, mobility, mold, networking, packaging, peripherals, storage, telecommunications and wearable technology industries. Co.'s segments consist of: Electronics Manufacturing Services, which is focused around IT, supply chain design and engineering, technologies centered on core electronics; and Diversified Manufacturing Services, which provides engineering solutions, heavy participation in consumer markets, access to higher growth markets and a focus on material sciences and technologies.

Recent Developments: For the quarter ended Feb 29 2016, income from continuing operations increased 35.7% to US$78.4 million from US$57.8 million in the year-earlier quarter. Net income increased 50.0% to US$78.4 million from US$52.3 million in the year-earlier quarter. Revenues were US$4.40 billion, up 2.2% from US$4.31 billion the year before. Operating income was US$154.9 million versus US$124.9 million in the prior-year quarter, an increase of 24.1%. Direct operating expenses rose 1.6% to US$4.00 billion from US$3.94 billion in the comparable period the year before. Indirect operating expenses increased 0.6% to US$244.5 million from US$243.0 million in the equivalent prior-year period.

Prospects: Our evaluation of Jabil Circuit Inc. as of June 19, 2016 is the result of our systematic analysis on three basic characteristics: earnings strength, relative valuation, and recent stock price movement. The company has suffered a very negative trend in earnings per share over the past 5 quarters. However, while recent estimates for the company have been lowered by analysts, JBL has posted results that were in line with analysts expectations. Based on operating earnings yield, the company is undervalued when compared to all of the companies in our coverage universe. Share price changes over the past year indicates that JBL will perform poorly over the near term.

Financial Data

(US$ in Thousands)	6 Mos	3 Mos	08/31/2015	08/31/2014	08/31/2013	08/31/2012	08/31/2011	08/31/2010
Earnings Per Share	1.91	1.77	1.45	1.19	1.79	1.87	1.73	0.78
Cash Flow Per Share	4.12	6.29	6.40	2.46	5.98	3.07	3.86	1.99
Tang Book Value Per Share	8.21	8.39	8.17	8.32	7.85	9.18	8.56	6.87
Dividends Per Share	0.320	0.320	0.320	0.320	0.320	0.320	0.280	0.280
Dividend Payout %	16.75	18.08	22.07	26.89	17.88	17.11	16.18	35.90
Income Statement								
Total Revenue	9,611,571	5,207,977	17,899,196	15,762,146	18,336,894	17,151,941	16,518,827	13,409,411
EBITDA	381,939	220,578	1,069,333	681,594	923,379	966,513	894,899	606,813
Depn & Amortn	16,439	7,840	529,149	485,157	418,154	353,525	319,151	283,334
Income Before Taxes	302,554	181,767	422,046	72,123	386,064	508,900	481,187	247,267
Income Taxes	92,206	49,852	127,861	73,711	15,973	112,811	98,229	76,501
Net Income	210,815	131,885	284,019	241,313	371,482	394,687	381,063	168,840
Average Shares	193,294	193,243	196,005	202,497	207,815	211,181	220,719	217,597
Balance Sheet								
Current Assets	5,565,223	6,317,174	5,866,309	5,359,017	5,820,245	5,639,328	5,135,360	4,654,018
Total Assets	9,898,202	10,221,152	9,603,207	8,479,746	9,153,781	7,803,141	7,057,940	6,367,747
Current Liabilities	5,372,934	5,775,331	5,675,141	4,321,097	4,864,434	3,858,996	3,889,888	3,605,174
Long-Term Obligations	1,811,220	1,818,447	1,346,558	1,669,585	1,690,426	1,658,326	1,112,594	1,018,930
Total Liabilities	7,431,211	7,838,547	7,288,351	6,237,918	6,818,494	5,698,084	5,190,820	4,789,701
Stockholders' Equity	2,466,991	2,382,605	2,314,856	2,241,828	2,335,287	2,105,057	1,867,120	1,578,046
Shares Outstanding	191,187	190,548	192,068	194,113	203,164	206,028	203,416	210,496
Statistical Record								
Return on Assets %	4.01	3.60	3.14	2.74	4.38	5.30	5.68	2.89
Return on Equity %	15.74	14.89	12.47	10.54	16.73	19.82	22.12	11.21
EBITDA Margin %	3.97	4.24	5.97	4.32	5.04	5.64	5.42	4.53
Net Margin %	2.19	2.53	1.59	1.53	2.03	2.30	2.31	1.26
Asset Turnover	2.02	1.94	1.98	1.79	2.16	2.30	2.46	2.30
Current Ratio	1.04	1.09	1.03	1.24	1.20	1.46	1.32	1.29
Debt to Equity	0.73	0.76	0.58	0.74	0.72	0.79	0.60	0.65
Price Range	25.93-17.66	25.59-17.66	24.83-17.66	24.04-15.67	23.90-16.57	27.13-15.76	22.98-10.25	18.36-10.25
P/E Ratio	13.58-9.25	14.46-9.98	17.12-12.18	20.20-13.17	13.35-9.26	14.51-8.43	13.28-5.92	23.54-13.14
Average Yield %	1.45	1.46	1.49	1.63	1.63	1.52	1.34	1.93

Address: 10560 Dr. Martin Luther King, Jr. Street North, St. Petersburg, FL 33716 **Telephone:** 727-577-9749	**Web Site:** www.jabil.com **Officers:** Timothy L. Main - Chairman, President, Chief Executive Officer Thomas A. Sansone - Vice-Chairman	**Auditors:** Ernst & Young LLP **Investor Contact:** 727-803-3349 **Transfer Agents:** Computershare, Providence, RI

JACOBS ENGINEERING GROUP, INC.

Exchange	Symbol	Price	52Wk Range	Yield	P/E
NYS	JEC	$50.69 (5/31/2016)	50.69-35.06	N/A	26.68

*7 Year Price Score 77.56 *NYSE Composite Index=100 *12 Month Price Score 108.15

Interim Earnings (Per Share)

Qtr.	Dec	Mar	Jun	Sep
2012-13	0.76	0.80	0.83	0.84
2013-14	0.71	0.63	0.49	0.65
2014-15	0.77	0.64	0.73	0.25
2015-16	0.38	0.54	...	...

Interim Dividends (Per Share)

No Dividends Paid

Valuation Analysis **Institutional Holding**

Forecast EPS	$3.06	No of Institutions
	(05/20/2016)	669
Market Cap	$6.2 Billion	Shares
Book Value	$4.4 Billion	127,802,576
Price/Book	1.41	% Held
Price/Sales	0.53	86.12

Business Summary: Construction Services (MIC: 7.5.4 SIC: 1629 NAIC: 236210)

Jacobs Engineering Group provides technical and construction services to industrial, commercial, and governmental clients. Co.'s categories of services are: Project Services, including engineering, design, architecture, interiors, planning, environmental, and services; Process, Scientific, and Systems Consulting Services, including services related to scientific testing, analysis, and consulting activities, as well as information technology and systems engineering activities; Construction Services, encompassing field construction services as well as modular construction activities; and Operations and Maintenance services, including services performed in connection with operating facilities.

Recent Developments: For the quarter ended Apr 1 2016, net income decreased 28.1% to US$63.4 million from US$88.1 million in the year-earlier quarter. Revenues were US$2.78 billion, down 4.2% from US$2.90 billion the year before. Operating income was US$86.8 million versus US$133.0 million in the prior-year quarter, a decrease of 34.8%. Direct operating expenses declined 3.1% to US$2.34 billion from US$2.41 billion in the comparable period the year before. Indirect operating expenses decreased 0.1% to US$357.4 million from US$357.9 million in the equivalent prior-year period.

Prospects: Our evaluation of Jacobs Engineering Group Inc. as of June 19, 2016 is the result of our systematic analysis on three basic characteristics: earnings strength, relative valuation, and recent stock price movement. The company has generated a negative trend in earnings per share over the past 5 quarters and while recent estimates for the company have been raised by analysts, JEC has posted better than expected results. Based on operating earnings yield, the company is undervalued when compared to all of the companies in our coverage universe. Share price changes over the past year indicates that JEC will perform in line with the market over the near term.

Financial Data

(US$ in Thousands)	6 Mos	3 Mos	10/02/2015	09/26/2014	09/27/2013	09/28/2012	09/30/2011	10/01/2010
Earnings Per Share	1.90	2.00	2.40	2.48	3.23	2.94	2.60	1.96
Cash Flow Per Share	5.36	3.08	3.81	5.55	3.48	2.36	1.89	1.59
Tang Book Value Per Share	8.01	7.33	7.22	7.61	14.98	11.30	10.24	13.03
Income Statement								
Total Revenue	5,629,697	2,847,934	12,114,832	12,695,157	11,818,376	10,893,778	10,381,664	9,915,517
EBITDA	216,179	93,003	591,670	689,322	767,933	699,797	615,913	485,512
Depn & Amortn	66,677	33,893	149,292	145,412	98,874	100,824	95,370	88,495
Income Before Taxes	148,243	57,787	430,137	542,166	661,548	593,336	516,661	391,934
Income Taxes	34,548	7,481	101,255	190,054	221,366	202,382	181,440	145,647
Net Income	111,764	46,514	302,971	328,108	423,093	378,954	331,029	245,974
Average Shares	121,143	121,959	126,110	132,371	130,945	128,692	127,235	125,790
Balance Sheet								
Current Assets	3,072,828	3,112,296	3,282,976	3,892,071	4,039,558	3,612,077	3,157,353	2,767,042
Total Assets	7,716,805	7,615,851	7,785,926	8,453,659	7,274,144	6,839,433	6,049,428	4,683,917
Current Liabilities	1,918,415	1,784,976	1,981,166	2,349,846	1,887,619	1,747,052	2,058,045	1,239,453
Long-Term Obligations	530,000	621,899	584,434	764,075	415,086	528,260	2,042	509
Total Liabilities	3,340,787	3,310,343	3,494,181	3,984,404	3,061,047	3,116,960	2,736,440	1,824,869
Stockholders' Equity	4,376,018	4,305,508	4,291,745	4,469,255	4,213,097	3,722,473	3,312,988	2,859,048
Shares Outstanding	122,146	122,776	123,152	131,752	131,639	129,935	127,784	125,909
Statistical Record								
Return on Assets %	2.97	3.15	3.67	4.18	6.01	5.90	6.19	5.41
Return on Equity %	5.32	5.70	6.80	7.58	10.69	10.80	10.76	8.99
EBITDA Margin %	3.84	3.27	4.88	5.43	6.50	6.42	5.93	4.90
Net Margin %	1.99	1.63	2.50	2.58	3.58	3.48	3.19	2.48
Asset Turnover	1.49	1.49	1.47	1.62	1.68	1.70	1.94	2.18
Current Ratio	1.60	1.74	1.66	1.66	2.14	2.07	1.53	2.23
Debt to Equity	0.12	0.14	0.14	0.17	0.10	0.14	N.M.	N.M.
Price Range	48.21-35.06	48.21-36.65	49.68-36.65	66.81-49.52	62.33-38.43	47.61-31.55	53.01-31.88	49.97-34.02
P/E Ratio	25.37-18.45	24.11-18.32	20.70-15.27	26.94-19.97	19.30-11.90	16.19-10.73	20.39-12.26	25.49-17.36

Address: 155 North Lake Avenue, Pasadena, CA 91101 **Telephone:** 626-578-3500 **Fax:** 626-568-7144	**Web Site:** www.jacobs.com **Officers:** Steven J. Demetriou - President, Chief Executive Officer Kevin C. Berryman - Executive Vice President, Chief Financial Officer	**Auditors:** Ernst & Young LLP **Transfer Agents:** Wells Fargo Shareowner Services, South St. Paul, MN

JANUS CAPITAL GROUP INC

Exchange	Symbol	Price	52Wk Range	Yield	P/E
NYS	JNS	$15.18 (5/31/2016)	18.75-11.47	2.90	19.97

*7 Year Price Score 109.33 *NYSE Composite Index=100   *12 Month Price Score 98.22

Interim Earnings (Per Share)

Qtr.	Mar	Jun	Sep	Dec
2013	0.15	0.08	0.17	0.21
2014	0.16	0.19	0.22	0.24
2015	0.23	0.23	0.10	0.24
2016	0.19	...	...	...

Interim Dividends (Per Share)

Amt	Decl	Ex	Rec	Pay
0.09Q	07/16/2015	08/05/2015	08/07/2015	08/21/2015
0.09Q	10/15/2015	11/04/2015	11/06/2015	11/20/2015
0.09Q	01/19/2016	02/10/2016	02/12/2016	02/25/2016
0.11Q	04/26/2016	05/05/2016	05/09/2016	05/20/2016

Indicated Div: $0.44

Valuation Analysis

		Institutional Holding	
Forecast EPS	$0.90	No of Institutions	353
	(05/20/2016)		
Market Cap	$2.8 Billion	Shares	194,574,288
Book Value	$1.6 Billion	% Held	103.84
Price/Book	1.76		
Price/Sales	2.64		

TRADING VOLUME (thousand shares)

Business Summary: Wealth Management (MIC: 5.5.2 SIC: 6282 NAIC: 523930)

Janus Capital Group provides investment management, administration, distribution and related services to financial advisors, individuals and institutional clients through mutual funds, separate accounts, other pooled investment vehicles, and subadvised relationships (collectively referred to as investment products) in both domestic and international markets. Through its subsidiaries, Co. provides investment management competencies across a range of disciplines including U.S. and global equities (growth and value), mathematical equities, fixed income and alternatives. Co.'s investment products are distributed through three channels: intermediary, institutional and self-directed.

Recent Developments: For the quarter ended Mar 31 2016, net income decreased 19.9% to US$37.0 million from US$46.2 million in the year-earlier quarter. Revenues were US$248.5 million, down 5.4% from US$262.7 million the year before. Operating income was US$62.6 million versus US$76.0 million in the prior-year quarter, a decrease of 17.6%. Indirect operating expenses decreased 0.4% to US$185.9 million from US$186.7 million in the equivalent prior-year period.

Prospects: Our evaluation of Janus Capital Group Inc. as of June 19, 2016 is the result of our systematic analysis on three basic characteristics: earnings strength, relative valuation, and recent stock price movement. The company has generated a negative trend in earnings per share over the past 5 quarters. However, while recent estimates for the company have been lowered by analysts, JNS has posted results that fell short of analysts expectations. Based on operating earnings yield, the company is undervalued when compared to all of the companies in our coverage universe. Share price changes over the past year indicates that JNS will perform poorly over the near term.

Financial Data

(US$ in Thousands)	3 Mos	12/31/2015	12/31/2014	12/31/2013	12/31/2012	12/31/2011	12/31/2010	12/31/2009
Earnings Per Share	0.76	0.80	0.81	0.62	0.55	0.78	0.88	(4.55)
Cash Flow Per Share	1.61	1.53	1.20	1.21	1.13	1.23	1.37	1.06
Dividends Per Share	0.360	0.350	0.310	0.210	0.290	0.150	0.040	0.040
Dividend Payout %	47.37	43.75	38.27	33.87	52.73	19.23	4.55	...
Income Statement								
Total Revenue	248,500	1,076,200	953,200	873,900	850,000	981,900	1,015,700	848,700
EBITDA	82,200	291,800	343,700	300,700	296,900	362,300	414,700	(598,700)
Depn & Amortn	16,300	11,500	53,500	64,600	75,900	79,200	107,200	78,100
Income Before Taxes	60,900	253,300	257,700	195,500	176,600	232,800	245,000	(750,400)
Income Taxes	23,900	94,000	102,300	73,300	64,700	79,400	76,400	(6,300)
Net Income	35,100	155,800	154,400	114,700	102,300	142,900	159,900	(757,100)
Average Shares	181,300	186,800	184,900	185,900	185,100	184,200	182,000	166,500
Balance Sheet								
Current Assets	796,300	870,700	987,200	990,800	888,400	835,900	893,300	630,600
Total Assets	2,801,100	2,871,500	2,793,200	2,747,300	2,660,400	2,644,000	2,726,800	2,530,300
Current Liabilities	108,300	335,300	229,600	301,700	159,500	148,800	420,800	187,100
Long-Term Obligations	403,300	297,200	450,500	447,700	545,100	595,200	586,700	792,000
Total Liabilities	1,208,600	1,288,800	1,252,400	1,250,500	1,242,500	1,330,800	1,555,300	1,529,200
Stockholders' Equity	1,592,500	1,582,700	1,540,800	1,496,800	1,417,900	1,313,200	1,171,500	1,001,100
Shares Outstanding	184,940	183,660	185,153	188,603	187,522	187,035	184,100	182,024
Statistical Record								
Return on Assets %	5.34	5.50	5.57	4.24	3.85	5.32	6.08	N.M.
Return on Equity %	9.27	9.98	10.17	7.87	7.47	11.50	14.72	N.M.
EBITDA Margin %	33.08	27.11	36.06	34.41	34.93	36.90	40.83	N.M.
Net Margin %	14.12	14.48	16.20	13.13	12.04	14.55	15.74	N.M.
Asset Turnover	0.39	0.38	0.34	0.32	0.32	0.37	0.39	0.29
Current Ratio	7.35	2.60	4.30	3.28	5.57	5.62	2.12	3.37
Debt to Equity	0.25	0.19	0.29	0.30	0.38	0.45	0.50	0.79
Price Range	18.75-11.47	18.75-13.29	16.47-10.32	12.50-8.09	9.55-6.60	14.54-5.63	15.72-8.81	15.82-3.95
P/E Ratio	24.67-15.09	23.44-16.61	20.33-12.74	20.16-13.05	17.36-12.00	18.64-7.22	17.86-10.01	...
Average Yield %	2.34	2.14	2.47	2.24	3.57	1.60	0.34	0.37

Address: 151 Detroit Street, Denver, CO 80206 **Telephone:** 303-333-3863	**Web Site:** www.janus.com **Officers:** Glenn S. Schafer - Chairman Bruce L. Koepfgen - President, Executive Vice President, Chief Financial Officer	**Auditors:** Deloitte & Touche LLP **Transfer Agents:** Wells Fargo Shareowner Services, South St. Paul, MN

JOHNSON CONTROLS INC

Exchange	Symbol	Price	52Wk Range	Yield	P/E
NYS	JCI	$44.15 (5/31/2016)	53.59-34.21	2.63	65.90

*7 Year Price Score 96.73 *NYSE Composite Index=100 *12 Month Price Score 96.79

Interim Earnings (Per Share)

Qtr.	Dec	Mar	Jun	Sep
2012-13	0.52	0.21	0.83	0.15
2013-14	0.69	0.39	0.26	0.46
2014-15	0.76	0.80	0.27	0.53
2015-16	0.69	(0.82)	...	...

Interim Dividends (Per Share)

Amt	Decl	Ex	Rec	Pay
0.26Q	07/22/2015	09/02/2015	09/04/2015	10/02/2015
0.29Q	11/18/2015	12/09/2015	12/11/2015	01/05/2016
0.29Q	01/23/2016	03/09/2016	03/11/2016	04/04/2016
0.29Q	05/17/2016	06/08/2016	06/10/2016	07/05/2016

Indicated Div: $1.16 (Div. Reinv. Plan)

Valuation Analysis

		Institutional Holding	
Forecast EPS	$3.90	No of Institutions	
	(05/20/2016)	1147	
Market Cap	$28.6 Billion	Shares	
Book Value	$10.0 Billion	521,964,672	
Price/Book	2.87	% Held	
Price/Sales	0.79	78.60	

TRADING VOLUME (thousand shares)

Business Summary: Auto Parts (MIC: 1.8.2 SIC: 2531 NAIC: 561790)

Johnson Controls operates in three primary businesses. Building Efficiency, Automotive Experience and Power Solutions. The Building Efficiency business is engaged in providing facility systems and services including comfort and energy management for the residential and non-residential buildings markets. The Automotive Experience business is engaged in designing and manufacturing interior products and systems for passenger cars and light trucks, including vans, pick-up trucks and sport/crossover utility vehicles. The Power Solutions business is engaged in designing and manufacturing automotive batteries for the replacement and original equipment markets.

Recent Developments: For the quarter ended Mar 31 2016, loss from continuing operations was US$469.0 million compared with income of US$479.0 million in the year-earlier quarter. Net loss amounted to US$469.0 million versus net income of US$557.0 million in the year-earlier quarter. Revenues were US$9.03 billion, down 1.8% from US$9.20 billion the year before. Direct operating expenses declined 4.2% to US$7.30 billion from US$7.63 billion in the comparable period the year before. Indirect operating expenses increased 40.8% to US$1.37 billion from US$975.0 million in the equivalent prior-year period.

Prospects: Our evaluation of Johnson Controls Inc. as of June 19, 2016 is the result of our systematic analysis on three basic characteristics: earnings strength, relative valuation, and recent stock price movement. The company has enjoyed a very positive trend in earnings per share over the past 5 quarters and while recent estimates for the company have remained steady, JCI has posted better than expected results. Based on operating earnings yield, the company is undervalued when compared to all of the companies in our coverage universe. Share price changes over the past year indicates that JCI will perform poorly over the near term.

Financial Data

(US$ in Thousands)	6 Mos	3 Mos	09/30/2015	09/30/2014	09/30/2013	09/30/2012	09/30/2011	09/30/2010
Earnings Per Share	0.67	2.29	2.36	1.80	1.71	1.78	2.36	2.19
Cash Flow Per Share	3.12	2.70	2.44	3.59	3.93	2.28	1.59	2.25
Tang Book Value Per Share	2.11	3.09	3.15	3.82	6.90	5.31	4.53	4.20
Dividends Per Share	1.100	1.070	1.040	0.880	0.760	0.720	0.640	0.520
Dividend Payout %	164.18	46.72	44.07	48.89	44.44	40.45	27.12	23.74
Income Statement								
Total Revenue	17,960,000	8,929,000	37,179,000	42,828,000	42,730,000	41,955,000	40,833,000	34,305,000
EBITDA	1,347,000	777,000	2,938,000	2,857,000	3,015,000	2,074,000	2,544,000	2,200,000
Depn & Amortn	445,000	226,000	860,000	955,000	952,000	824,000	731,000	691,000
Income Before Taxes	765,000	483,000	1,776,000	1,640,000	2,063,000	1,250,000	1,813,000	1,509,000
Income Taxes	997,000	129,000	600,000	482,000	1,168,000	237,000	370,000	197,000
Net Income	(80,000)	450,000	1,563,000	1,215,000	1,178,000	1,226,000	1,624,000	1,491,000
Average Shares	648,200	652,800	661,500	674,800	689,200	688,600	689,900	682,500
Balance Sheet								
Current Assets	11,058,000	10,921,000	11,093,000	13,107,000	13,698,000	12,673,000	12,015,000	10,652,000
Total Assets	31,199,000	31,019,000	29,673,000	32,804,000	31,518,000	30,884,000	29,676,000	25,743,000
Current Liabilities	11,792,000	11,301,000	10,495,000	11,694,000	12,117,000	10,855,000	10,782,000	9,910,000
Long-Term Obligations	5,143,000	5,301,000	5,745,000	6,357,000	4,560,000	5,321,000	4,533,000	2,652,000
Total Liabilities	21,215,000	20,513,000	19,297,000	21,493,000	19,204,000	19,329,000	18,634,000	15,672,000
Stockholders' Equity	9,984,000	10,506,000	10,376,000	11,311,000	12,314,000	11,555,000	11,042,000	10,071,000
Shares Outstanding	648,370	648,235	647,367	665,496	684,535	682,307	680,164	673,726
Statistical Record								
Return on Assets %	1.44	4.80	5.00	3.78	3.78	4.04	5.86	5.98
Return on Equity %	4.35	14.12	14.41	10.29	9.87	10.82	15.38	15.52
EBITDA Margin %	7.50	8.70	7.90	6.67	7.06	4.94	6.23	6.41
Net Margin %	N.M.	5.04	4.20	2.84	2.76	2.92	3.98	4.35
Asset Turnover	1.17	1.16	1.19	1.33	1.37	1.38	1.47	1.38
Current Ratio	0.94	0.97	1.06	1.12	1.13	1.17	1.11	1.07
Debt to Equity	0.52	0.50	0.55	0.56	0.37	0.46	0.41	0.26
Price Range	53.59-34.21	53.59-38.75	53.59-38.95	51.92-39.89	43.06-24.94	35.58-23.51	42.71-26.37	35.01-23.77
P/E Ratio	79.99-51.06	23.40-16.92	22.71-16.50	28.84-22.16	25.18-14.58	19.99-13.21	18.10-11.17	15.99-10.85
Average Yield %	2.51	2.29	2.19	1.84	2.24	2.39	1.72	1.79

Address: 5757 North Green Bay Avenue, Milwaukee, WI 53209 Telephone: 414-524-1200	Web Site: www.johnsoncontrols.com Officers: Alex A. Molinaroli - Chairman, President, Chief Executive Officer R. Bruce McDonald - Vice-Chairman, Executive Vice President, Chief Financial Officer	Auditors: PricewaterhouseCoopers LLP Transfer Agents: Wells Fargo Bank, N.A., St. Paul, MN

JOHNSON & JOHNSON

Exchange	Symbol	Price	52Wk Range	Yield	P/E	Div Achiever
NYS	JNJ	$112.69 (5/31/2016)	114.67-90.73	2.84	20.49	51 Years

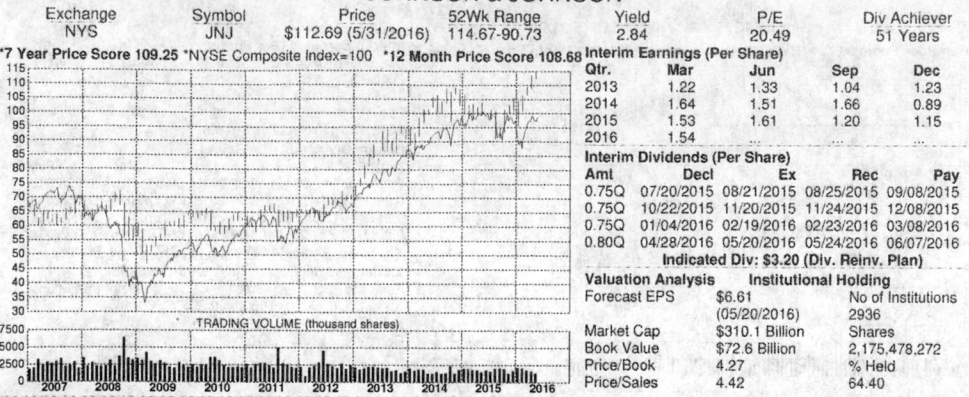

*7 Year Price Score 109.25   *NYSE Composite Index=100   *12 Month Price Score 108.68

Interim Earnings (Per Share)

Qtr.	Mar	Jun	Sep	Dec
2013	1.22	1.33	1.04	1.23
2014	1.64	1.51	1.66	0.89
2015	1.53	1.61	1.20	1.15
2016	1.54			

Interim Dividends (Per Share)

Amt	Decl	Ex	Rec	Pay
0.75Q	07/20/2015	08/21/2015	08/25/2015	09/08/2015
0.75Q	10/22/2015	11/20/2015	11/24/2015	12/08/2015
0.75Q	01/04/2016	02/19/2016	02/23/2016	03/08/2016
0.80Q	04/28/2016	05/20/2016	05/24/2016	06/07/2016

Indicated Div: $3.20 (Div. Reinv. Plan)

Valuation Analysis

		Institutional Holding	
Forecast EPS	$6.61	No of Institutions	
	(05/20/2016)	2936	
Market Cap	$310.1 Billion	Shares	
Book Value	$72.6 Billion	2,175,478,272	
Price/Book	4.27	% Held	
Price/Sales	4.42	64.40	

Business Summary: Pharmaceuticals (MIC: 4.1.1 SIC: 2834 NAIC: 325412)

Johnson & Johnson is a holding company. Through its subsidiaries, Co. is engaged in the research and development, manufacture and sale of a range of products in the health care field. Co. is organized into three business segments: Consumer, which is include a range of products used in the baby care, oral care, skin care, over-the-counter pharmaceutical, women's health and wound care markets. Pharmaceutical, which is focused on five therapeutic areas: immunology, infectious diseases and vaccines, neuroscience, oncology, and cardiovascular and metabolic diseases. Medical Devices, which is include products used in the orthopaedic, surgery, cardiovascular, diabetes care and vision care fields.

Recent Developments: For the quarter ended Apr 3 2016, net income decreased 0.6% to US$4.29 billion from US$4.32 billion in the year-earlier quarter. Revenues were US$17.48 billion, up 0.6% from US$17.37 billion the year before. Direct operating expenses rose 0.9% to US$5.33 billion from US$5.28 billion in the comparable period the year before. Indirect operating expenses increased 5.2% to US$6.86 billion from US$6.52 billion in the equivalent prior-year period.

Prospects: Our evaluation of Johnson & Johnson as of June 19, 2016 is the result of our systematic analysis on three basic characteristics: earnings strength, relative valuation, and recent stock price movement. The company has managed to produce a neutral trend in earnings per share over the past 5 quarters and while recent estimates for the company have remained steady, JNJ has posted better than expected results. Based on operating earnings yield, the company is undervalued when compared to all of the companies in our coverage universe. Share price changes over the past year indicates that JNJ will perform well over the near term.

Financial Data
(US$ in Millions)

	3 Mos	01/03/2016	12/28/2014	12/29/2013	12/30/2012	01/01/2012	01/02/2011	01/03/2010
Earnings Per Share	5.50	5.48	5.70	4.81	3.86	3.49	4.78	4.40
Cash Flow Per Share	6.59	6.84	6.58	6.22	5.61	5.24	5.97	5.91
Tang Book Value Per Share	9.07	8.62	7.44	8.26	4.91	8.37	8.97	7.04
Dividends Per Share	3.000	2.950	2.760	2.590	2.400	2.250	2.110	1.930
Dividend Payout %	54.55	53.83	48.42	53.85	62.18	64.47	44.14	43.86
Income Statement								
Total Revenue	17,482	70,074	74,331	71,312	67,224	65,030	61,587	61,897
EBITDA	6,262	23,320	24,927	19,942	17,889	15,993	20,243	18,891
Depn & Amortn	891	3,700	3,898	4,063	3,646	3,152	2,948	2,775
Income Before Taxes	5,294	19,196	20,563	15,471	13,775	12,361	16,947	15,755
Income Taxes	1,002	3,787	4,240	1,640	3,261	2,689	3,613	3,489
Net Income	4,292	15,409	16,323	13,831	10,853	9,672	13,334	12,266
Average Shares	2,796	2,813	2,864	2,878	2,813	2,776	2,789	2,790
Balance Sheet								
Current Assets	62,738	60,210	59,311	56,407	46,116	54,316	47,307	39,541
Total Assets	136,231	133,411	131,119	132,683	121,347	113,644	102,908	94,682
Current Liabilities	22,134	27,747	25,085	25,675	24,262	22,811	23,072	21,731
Long-Term Obligations	20,233	12,857	15,122	13,328	11,489	12,969	9,156	8,223
Total Liabilities	63,584	62,261	61,367	58,630	56,521	56,564	46,329	44,094
Stockholders' Equity	72,647	71,150	69,752	74,053	64,826	57,080	56,579	50,588
Shares Outstanding	2,752	2,756	2,784	2,821	2,779	2,725	2,739	2,755
Statistical Record								
Return on Assets %	11.62	11.46	12.41	10.92	9.26	8.96	13.53	13.44
Return on Equity %	21.89	21.52	22.76	19.97	17.85	17.07	24.95	25.92
EBITDA Margin %	35.82	33.28	33.54	27.96	26.61	24.59	32.87	30.52
Net Margin %	24.55	21.99	21.96	19.40	16.14	14.87	21.65	19.82
Asset Turnover	0.53	0.52	0.57	0.56	0.57	0.60	0.63	0.68
Current Ratio	2.83	2.17	2.36	2.20	1.90	2.38	2.05	1.82
Debt to Equity	0.28	0.18	0.22	0.18	0.18	0.23	0.16	0.16
Price Range	109.19-90.73	106.39-90.73	109.07-86.62	95.63-70.10	72.52-61.78	67.92-57.66	66.03-57.02	64.96-46.60
P/E Ratio	19.85-16.50	19.41-16.56	19.14-15.20	19.88-14.57	18.79-16.01	19.46-16.52	13.81-11.93	14.76-10.59
Average Yield %	2.99	2.96	2.74	3.02	3.58	3.54	3.33	3.34

Address: One Johnson & Johnson Plaza, New Brunswick, NJ 08933 **Telephone:** 732-524-0400 **Fax:** 732-214-0332	**Web Site:** www.jnj.com **Officers:** Alex Gorsky - Chairman, Chief Executive Officer, Division Officer Dominic J. Caruso - Vice President, Chief Financial Officer	**Auditors:** PricewaterhouseCoopers LLP **Investor Contact:** 800-950-5089 **Transfer Agents:** Computershare Trust Company, N.A., Canton, MA

JONES LANG LASALLE INC

Exchange	Symbol	Price	52Wk Range	Yield	P/E
NYS	JLL	$117.86 (5/31/2016)	179.35-98.58	0.53	12.70

*7 Year Price Score 125.82 *NYSE Composite Index=100 *12 Month Price Score 78.74

TRADING VOLUME (thousand shares)

Interim Earnings (Per Share)

Qtr.	Mar	Jun	Sep	Dec
2013	0.29	1.03	1.39	3.27
2014	0.35	1.58	2.30	4.28
2015	0.92	1.98	2.43	4.31
2016	0.56	...	...	...

Interim Dividends (Per Share)

Amt	Decl	Ex	Rec	Pay
0.25S	10/29/2014	11/12/2014	11/14/2014	12/15/2014
0.27S	04/27/2015	05/13/2015	05/15/2015	06/15/2015
0.29S	10/28/2015	11/10/2015	11/13/2015	12/15/2015
0.31S	04/27/2016	05/11/2016	05/13/2016	06/15/2016

Indicated Div: $0.62

Valuation Analysis / **Institutional Holding**

Forecast EPS	$10.05
(05/16/2016)	
Market Cap	$5.3 Billion
Book Value	$2.7 Billion
Price/Book	1.94
Price/Sales	0.87

No of Institutions	527
Shares	44,288,760
% Held	93.60

Business Summary: Property, Real Estate & Development (MIC: 5.3.2 SIC: 6531 NAIC: 531210)

Jones Lang LaSalle is a financial services firm that provides real estate services on a local, regional and global basis to owner, occupier, investor and developer clients. Services provided include: agency leasing; capital markets; corporate finance; energy and sustainability services; facility management outsourcing (occupiers); investment management; logistics and supply-chain management; mortgage origination and servicing; project and development management/construction; property management (investors); real estate investment banking/merchant banking; research; consulting and advisory services; tenant representation; valuations; and value recovery and receivership services.

Recent Developments: For the quarter ended Mar 31 2016, net income decreased 41.8% to US$25.2 million from US$43.3 million in the year-earlier quarter. Revenues were US$1.34 billion, up 11.1% from US$1.20 billion the year before.

Prospects: Our evaluation of Jones Lang LaSalle Inc. as of June 19, 2016 is the result of our systematic analysis on three basic characteristics: earnings strength, relative valuation, and recent stock price movement. The company has generated a negative trend in earnings per share over the past 5 quarters. However, while recent estimates for the company have been lowered by analysts, JLL has posted better than expected results. Based on operating earnings yield, the company is undervalued when compared to all of the companies in our coverage universe. Share price changes over the past year indicates that JLL will perform poorly over the near term.

Financial Data
(US$ in Thousands)

	3 Mos	12/31/2015	12/31/2014	12/31/2013	12/31/2012	12/31/2011	12/31/2010	12/31/2009
Earnings Per Share	9.28	9.65	8.52	5.98	4.63	3.70	3.48	(0.11)
Cash Flow Per Share	8.31	8.36	11.16	6.62	7.45	4.90	9.09	6.50
Tang Book Value Per Share	5.27	7.11	9.82	5.26	1.17	N.M.	2.23	N.M.
Dividends Per Share	0.560	0.560	0.480	0.440	0.400	0.300	0.200	0.200
Dividend Payout %	6.03	5.80	5.63	7.36	8.64	8.11	5.75	...
Income Statement								
Total Revenue	1,336,800	5,965,671	5,429,603	4,461,591	3,932,830	3,584,544	2,925,613	2,480,736
EBITDA	60,600	626,998	549,864	439,819	355,603	313,805	379,208	250,716
Depn & Amortn	31,200	97,200	84,200	71,000	66,200	62,600	118,550	134,312
Income Before Taxes	20,500	501,671	437,343	334,101	254,230	215,614	214,856	61,386
Income Taxes	8,300	132,805	97,588	92,092	69,244	56,387	49,038	5,677
Net Income	25,700	438,672	386,063	269,865	208,050	164,384	153,902	(3,595)
Average Shares	45,483	45,414	45,260	45,072	44,799	44,367	44,084	38,543
Balance Sheet								
Current Assets	2,463,100	2,650,807	2,118,176	1,724,228	1,515,529	1,300,884	1,194,841	939,918
Total Assets	6,346,800	6,205,159	5,075,336	4,597,353	4,351,499	3,932,636	3,349,861	3,096,933
Current Liabilities	2,026,400	2,505,193	2,047,011	1,658,424	1,661,971	1,348,617	1,296,312	1,095,095
Long-Term Obligations	1,057,900	529,999	275,000	430,000	444,000	463,000	197,500	175,000
Total Liabilities	3,610,200	3,516,396	2,688,539	2,417,684	2,400,316	2,241,507	1,780,930	1,718,004
Stockholders' Equity	2,736,600	2,688,763	2,386,797	2,179,669	1,951,183	1,691,129	1,568,931	1,378,929
Shares Outstanding	45,116	45,049	44,828	44,447	44,054	43,470	42,659	41,843
Statistical Record								
Return on Assets %	7.45	7.78	7.98	6.03	5.01	4.51	4.77	N.M.
Return on Equity %	16.69	17.29	16.91	13.07	11.39	10.08	10.44	N.M.
EBITDA Margin %	4.53	10.51	10.13	9.86	9.04	8.75	12.96	10.11
Net Margin %	1.92	7.35	7.11	6.05	5.29	4.59	5.26	N.M.
Asset Turnover	1.08	1.06	1.12	1.00	0.95	0.98	0.91	0.80
Current Ratio	1.22	1.06	1.03	1.04	0.91	0.96	0.92	0.86
Debt to Equity	0.39	0.20	0.12	0.20	0.23	0.27	0.13	0.13
Price Range	179.35-98.58	179.35-142.69	153.43-101.95	102.80-82.15	87.08-63.21	107.72-47.04	88.51-57.01	61.57-16.94
P/E Ratio	19.33-10.62	18.59-14.79	18.01-11.97	17.19-13.74	18.81-13.65	29.11-12.71	25.43-16.38	...
Average Yield %	0.37	0.35	0.38	0.47	0.53	0.37	0.27	0.53

Address: 200 East Randolph Drive, Chicago, IL 60601 **Telephone:** 312-782-5800 **Fax:** 312-782-4339	**Web Site:** www.jll.com **Officers:** Sheila A. Penrose - Chairman Christian Ulbrich - Region Officer, President	**Auditors:** KPMG LLP **Investor Contact:** 312-782-5800 **Transfer Agents:** Computershare, Pittsburgh, PA

JOY GLOBAL INC

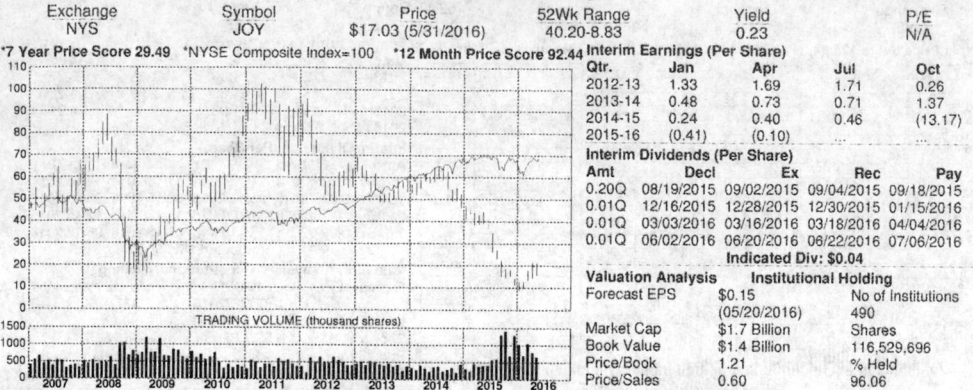

Exchange	Symbol	Price	52Wk Range	Yield	P/E
NYS	JOY	$17.03 (5/31/2016)	40.20-8.83	0.23	N/A

*7 Year Price Score 29.49 *NYSE Composite Index=100 *12 Month Price Score 92.44

Interim Earnings (Per Share)

Qtr.	Jan	Apr	Jul	Oct
2012-13	1.33	1.69	1.71	0.26
2013-14	0.48	0.73	0.71	1.37
2014-15	0.24	0.40	0.46	(13.17)
2015-16	(0.41)	(0.10)	...	...

Interim Dividends (Per Share)

Amt	Decl	Ex	Rec	Pay
0.20Q	08/19/2015	09/02/2015	09/04/2015	09/18/2015
0.01Q	12/16/2015	12/28/2015	12/30/2015	01/15/2016
0.01Q	03/03/2016	03/16/2016	03/18/2016	04/04/2016
0.01Q	06/02/2016	06/20/2016	06/22/2016	07/06/2016

Indicated Div: $0.04

Valuation Analysis | **Institutional Holding**

Forecast EPS	$0.15 (05/20/2016)	No of Institutions 490
Market Cap	$1.7 Billion	Shares 116,529,696
Book Value	$1.4 Billion	% Held
Price/Book	1.21	96.06
Price/Sales	0.60	

TRADING VOLUME (thousand shares)

Business Summary: Industrial Machinery & Equipment (MIC: 7.2.1 SIC: 3532 NAIC: 333131)

Joy Global is a manufacturer and servicer of mining equipment for the extraction of metals and minerals. Co. manufactures and markets original equipment and parts and services for both underground and surface mining and certain industrial applications. Co.'s equipment is used in mining regions to mine coal, copper, iron ore, oil sands, gold, and other minerals and ores. Co. has two business segments: Underground Mining Machinery, a producer of underground mining machinery for the extraction of coal and other bedded materials; and Surface Mining Equipment, a producer of electric mining shovels, blasthole drills, walking draglines and wheel loaders for open-pit mining operations.

Recent Developments: For the quarter ended Apr 29 2016, net loss amounted to US$9.8 million versus net income of US$56.0 million in the year-earlier quarter. Revenues were US$602.0 million, down 25.7% from US$810.5 million the year before. Operating loss was US$4.3 million versus an income of US$92.9 million in the prior-year quarter. Direct operating expenses declined 20.4% to US$458.5 million from US$576.2 million in the comparable period the year before. Indirect operating expenses increased 4.6% to US$147.8 million from US$141.4 million in the equivalent prior-year period.

Prospects: Our evaluation of Joy Global Inc. as of June 19, 2016 is the result of our systematic analysis on three basic characteristics: earnings strength, relative valuation, and recent stock price movement. The company has enjoyed a very positive trend in earnings per share over the past 5 quarters. However, while recent estimates for the company have been mixed, JOY has posted better than expected results. Based on operating earnings yield, the company is overvalued when compared to all of the companies in our coverage universe. Share price changes over the past year indicates that JOY will perform very poorly over the near term.

Financial Data

(US$ in Thousands)	6 Mos	3 Mos	10/30/2015	10/31/2014	10/25/2013	10/26/2012	10/28/2011	10/29/2010
Earnings Per Share	(13.22)	(12.72)	(12.08)	3.28	4.99	7.13	5.72	4.40
Cash Flow Per Share	4.65	4.93	3.65	3.57	6.02	4.19	4.82	5.67
Tang Book Value Per Share	8.08	7.56	8.30	10.24	10.23	5.72	10.83	10.15
Dividends Per Share	0.420	0.610	0.800	0.750	0.700	0.700	0.700	0.700
Dividend Payout %	...	...	...	22.87	14.03	9.82	12.24	15.91
Income Statement								
Total Revenue	1,128,285	526,300	3,172,147	3,778,310	5,012,697	5,660,889	4,403,906	3,524,334
EBITDA	27,981	(5,000)	(1,012,800)	624,540	921,561	1,256,359	979,644	747,293
Depn & Amortn	77,393	40,087	110,900	107,400	99,900	83,800	59,500	51,500
Income Before Taxes	(73,107)	(57,203)	(1,177,129)	461,792	764,157	1,105,131	895,833	679,024
Income Taxes	(17,581)	(16,982)	875	130,755	230,219	337,870	264,831	217,525
Net Income	(50,060)	(40,221)	(1,178,004)	331,037	533,713	762,021	609,656	461,499
Average Shares	97,921	97,851	97,493	100,939	106,996	106,889	106,537	104,905
Balance Sheet								
Current Assets	1,925,175	1,864,406	2,068,442	2,618,359	2,822,444	3,156,077	3,564,007	2,361,927
Total Assets	3,508,100	3,480,734	3,712,446	5,596,986	5,789,582	6,142,503	5,426,354	3,284,041
Current Liabilities	826,928	833,659	910,920	1,174,988	1,360,590	1,780,817	1,724,571	1,023,324
Long-Term Obligations	983,488	992,740	1,060,643	1,269,541	1,256,927	1,306,625	1,356,412	396,326
Total Liabilities	2,128,333	2,136,316	2,292,437	2,755,989	2,931,213	3,565,314	3,474,559	1,928,647
Stockholders' Equity	1,379,767	1,344,418	1,420,009	2,840,997	2,858,369	2,577,189	1,951,795	1,355,394
Shares Outstanding	98,137	97,931	97,597	98,103	102,226	105,926	105,113	103,529
Statistical Record								
Return on Assets %	N.M.	N.M.	N.M.	5.72	8.97	13.21	14.04	14.71
Return on Equity %	N.M.	N.M.	N.M.	11.43	19.69	33.74	36.97	42.67
EBITDA Margin %	2.48	N.M.	N.M.	16.53	18.38	22.19	22.24	21.20
Net Margin %	N.M.	N.M.	N.M.	8.76	10.65	13.46	13.84	13.09
Asset Turnover	0.63	0.68	0.68	0.65	0.84	0.98	1.01	1.12
Current Ratio	2.33	2.24	2.27	2.23	2.07	1.77	2.07	2.31
Debt to Equity	0.71	0.74	0.75	0.45	0.44	0.51	0.69	0.29
Price Range	44.22-8.83	45.07-8.83	54.87-14.32	65.01-48.94	69.01-48.32	95.71-48.77	102.36-60.49	73.12-44.47
P/E Ratio	...	...	...	19.82-14.92	13.83-9.68	13.42-6.84	17.90-10.58	16.62-10.11
Average Yield %	1.96	2.19	2.20	1.30	1.24	1.02	0.81	1.23

Address: 100 East Wisconsin Avenue, Suite 2780, Milwaukee, WI 53202 Telephone: 414-319-8500	Web Site: www.joyglobal.com Officers: John Nils Hanson - Chairman, President, Chief Executive Officer Edward L. Doheny - President, Chief Executive Officer, Executive Vice President	Auditors: Ernst & Young LLP Investor Contact: 414-319-8509 Transfer Agents: The American Stock Transfer & Trust Company, New York, NY

JPMORGAN CHASE & CO

Exchange	Symbol	Price	52Wk Range	Yield	P/E
NYS	JPM	$65.27 (5/31/2016)	70.08-53.07	2.94	11.08

*7 Year Price Score 110.57 ***NYSE Composite Index=100** ***12 Month Price Score 97.20**

Interim Earnings (Per Share)

Qtr.	Mar	Jun	Sep	Dec
2013	1.59	1.60	(0.17)	1.30
2014	1.28	1.46	1.36	1.19
2015	1.45	1.54	1.68	1.32
2016	1.35	...	...	...

Interim Dividends (Per Share)

Amt	Decl	Ex	Rec	Pay
0.44Q	09/15/2015	10/02/2015	10/06/2015	10/31/2015
0.44Q	12/08/2015	01/04/2016	01/06/2016	01/31/2016
0.44Q	03/15/2016	04/04/2016	04/06/2016	04/30/2016
0.48Q	05/17/2016	07/01/2016	07/06/2016	07/31/2016

Indicated Div: $1.92

Valuation Analysis / Institutional Holding

Forecast EPS	$5.65	No of Institutions
(05/20/2016)		2637
Market Cap	$238.7 Billion	Shares
Book Value	$250.2 Billion	3,094,806,016
Price/Book	0.95	% Held
Price/Sales	2.38	73.52

Business Summary: Banking (MIC: 5.1.1 SIC: 6021 NAIC: 522110)

JPMorgan Chase is a financial holding company. Through its subsidiaries, Co., as a financial services firm and banking institution, provides investment banking, financial services for consumers and businesses, commercial banking, financial transaction processing and asset management. Co.'s consumer business is the Consumer and Community Banking segment. The Corporate and Investment Bank, Commercial Banking, and Asset Management segments comprise Co.'s wholesale businesses. Under the J.P. Morgan and Chase brands, Co. serves customers in the corporate, institutional and government clients. As of Dec 31 2015, Co. had total assets of $2.35 trillion and deposits of $1.28 trillion.

Recent Developments: For the quarter ended Mar 31 2016, net income decreased 6.7% to US$5.52 billion from US$5.91 billion in the year-earlier quarter. Net interest income increased 6.6% to US$11.38 billion from US$10.68 billion in the year-earlier quarter. Provision for loan losses was US$1.82 billion versus US$959.0 million in the prior-year quarter, an increase of 90.2%. Non-interest income fell 11.4% to US$11.86 billion from US$13.39 billion, while non-interest expense declined 7.0% to US$13.84 billion.

Prospects: Our evaluation of J.P. Morgan Chase & Co. as of June 19, 2016 is the result of our systematic analysis on three basic characteristics: earnings strength, relative valuation, and recent stock price movement. The company has managed to produce a neutral trend in earnings per share over the past 5 quarters. However, while recent estimates for the company have been mixed, JPM has posted better than expected results. Based on operating earnings yield, the company is undervalued when compared to all of the companies in our coverage universe. Share price changes over the past year indicates that JPM will perform in line with the market over the near term.

Financial Data
(US$ in Millions)

	3 Mos	12/31/2015	12/31/2014	12/31/2013	12/31/2012	12/31/2011	12/31/2010	12/31/2009
Earnings Per Share	5.89	6.00	5.29	4.35	5.20	4.48	3.98	2.26
Cash Flow Per Share	10.14	19.85	9.72	28.54	6.57	24.60	(0.95)	31.56
Tang Book Value Per Share	46.54	45.46	41.92	37.46	36.01	31.05	26.02	22.50
Dividends Per Share	1.720	1.680	1 560	1.360	1.150	0.800	0.200	0.530
Dividend Payout %	29.20	28.00	29.49	31.26	22.12	17.86	5.03	23.45
Income Statement								
Interest Income	13,552	50,973	51,531	52,996	56,063	61,293	63,782	66,350
Interest Expense	2,172	7,463	7,897	9,677	11,153	13,604	12,781	15,198
Net Interest Income	11,380	43,510	43,634	43,319	44,910	47,689	51,001	51,152
Provision for Losses	1,824	3,827	3,139	225	3,385	7,574	16,639	32,015
Non-Interest Income	11,859	50,033	50,571	53,287	52,121	49,545	51,693	49,282
Non-Interest Expense	13,837	59,014	61,274	70,467	64,729	62,911	61,196	52,352
Income Before Taxes	7,578	30,702	29,792	25,914	28,917	26,749	24,859	16,067
Income Taxes	2,058	6,260	8,030	7,991	7,633	7,773	7,489	4,415
Net Income	5,520	24,442	21,762	17,923	21,284	18,976	17,370	11,728
Average Shares	3,970	3,733	3,798	3,815	3,823	3,921	3,977	3,880
Balance Sheet								
Net Loans & Leases	833,319	823,744	743,151	722,154	711,860	696,111	660,661	601,856
Total Assets	2,423,808	2,351,698	2,573,126	2,415,689	2,359,141	2,265,792	2,117,605	2,031,989
Total Deposits	1,321,816	1,279,715	1,363,427	1,287,765	1,193,593	1,127,806	930,369	938,367
Total Liabilities	2,173,651	2,104,125	2,341,061	2,204,511	2,155,072	2,082,219	1,941,499	1,866,624
Stockholders' Equity	250,157	247,573	232,065	211,178	204,069	183,573	176,106	165,365
Shares Outstanding	3,657	3,664	3,715	3,757	3,804	3,773	3,911	3,942
Statistical Record								
Return on Assets %	0.96	0.99	0.87	0.75	0.92	0.87	0.84	0.56
Return on Equity %	9.90	10.19	9.82	8.63	10.95	10.55	10.17	7.06
Net Interest Margin %	83.97	85.36	84.68	81.74	80.11	77.80	79.96	77.09
Efficiency Ratio %	54.45	58.43	60.01	66.30	59.83	56.76	53.00	45.27
Loans to Deposits	0.63	0.64	0.55	0.56	0.60	0.62	0.71	0.64
Price Range	70.08-53.07	70.08-54.38	63.15-53.31	58.48-43.97	46.27-31.00	48.00-28.38	47.81-35.63	47.16-15.90
P/E Ratio	11.90-9.01	11.68-9.06	11.94-10.08	13.44-10.11	8.90-5.96	10.71-6.33	12.01-8.95	20.87-7.04
Average Yield %	2.70	2.63	2.68	2.68	2.62	2.93	2.03	1.49

Address: 270 Park Avenue, New York, NY 10017 Telephone: 212-270-6000	Web Site: www.jpmorganchase.com Officers: James Dimon - Chairman, President, Chief Executive Officer Ashely Bacon - Chief Risk Officer	Auditors: PricewaterhouseCoopers LLP Investor Contact: 212-270-7325 Transfer Agents: Computershare Shareowner Services LLC, Jersey City, NY

JUNIPER NETWORKS INC

Exchange	Symbol	Price	52Wk Range	Yield	P/E
NYS	JNPR	$23.41 (5/31/2016)	32.23-21.62	1.71	14.27

*7 Year Price Score 90.72   *NYSE Composite Index=100   *12 Month Price Score 88.68

Interim Earnings (Per Share)

Qtr.	Mar	Jun	Sep	Dec
2013	0.18	0.19	0.19	0.30
2014	0.22	0.46	0.23	(1.64)
2015	0.19	0.40	0.51	0.50
2016	0.23			

Interim Dividends (Per Share)

Amt	Decl	Ex	Rec	Pay
0.10Q	07/23/2015	08/28/2015	09/01/2015	09/22/2015
0.10Q	10/22/2015	11/27/2015	12/01/2015	12/22/2015
0.10Q	01/27/2016	02/26/2016	03/01/2016	03/22/2016
0.10Q	04/28/2016	05/27/2016	06/01/2016	06/22/2016

Indicated Div: $0.40

Valuation Analysis

		Institutional Holding	
Forecast EPS	$2.01 (05/20/2016)	No of Institutions	695
Market Cap	$9.0 Billion	Shares	392,154,880
Book Value	$4.6 Billion	% Held	72.81
Price/Book	1.95		
Price/Sales	1.85		

Business Summary: Peripherals (MIC: 6.2.2 SIC: 3661 NAIC: 334210)

Juniper Networks designs, develops, and sells products and services for networks. Co. sells its products in more than 100 countries in three geographic regions: Americas; Europe, Middle East, and Africa; and Asia Pacific. Co. sells its network products and service offerings across routing, switching, and security. Co.'s products address network requirements for service providers, cloud environments, enterprises, governments, and research and public sector organizations. Co.'s portfolio addresses domains in the network: the core, the edge, access and aggregation, data centers, Wide Area Networks, and campus and branch.

Recent Developments: For the quarter ended Mar 31 2016, net income increased 14.0% to US$91.4 million from US$80.2 million in the year-earlier quarter. Revenues were US$1.10 billion, up 2.9% from US$1.07 billion the year before. Operating income was US$148.7 million versus US$131.8 million in the prior-year quarter, an increase of 12.8%. Direct operating expenses declined 0.8% to US$407.0 million from US$410.1 million in the comparable period the year before. Indirect operating expenses increased 3.2% to US$542.2 million from US$525.5 million in the equivalent prior-year period.

Prospects: Our evaluation of Juniper Networks Inc. as of June 19, 2016 is the result of our systematic analysis on three basic characteristics: earnings strength, relative valuation, and recent stock price movement. The company has generated a negative trend in earnings per share over the past 5 quarters and while recent estimates for the company have remained steady, JNPR has posted results that fell short of analysts expectations. Based on operating earnings yield, the company is undervalued when compared to all of the companies in our coverage universe. Share price changes over the past year indicates that JNPR will perform in line with the market over the near term.

Financial Data

(US$ in Thousands)	3 Mos	12/31/2015	12/31/2014	12/31/2013	12/31/2012	12/31/2011	12/31/2010	12/31/2009
Earnings Per Share	1.64	1.59	(0.73)	0.86	0.35	0.79	1.15	0.22
Cash Flow Per Share	2.21	2.28	1.67	1.68	1.23	1.86	1.55	1.52
Tang Book Value Per Share	4.19	4.04	4.48	6.34	5.53	5.77	4.87	4.14
Dividends Per Share	0.400	0.400	0.200	...	...	...	...	...
Dividend Payout %	24.39	25.16	...	...	...	...	...	...
Income Statement								
Total Revenue	1,097,900	4,857,800	4,627,100	4,669,100	4,365,400	4,448,709	4,093,266	3,315,912
EBITDA	188,100	1,055,200	112,500	723,400	492,800	759,082	918,731	455,239
Depn & Amortn	47,000	141,500	141,900	148,200	159,400	147,566	151,030	143,416
Income Before Taxes	126,500	852,200	(86,300)	525,500	291,500	571,716	769,501	317,623
Income Taxes	35,100	218,500	248,000	85,700	105,000	146,704	158,781	196,833
Net Income	91,400	633,700	(334,300)	439,800	186,500	425,136	618,402	116,999
Average Shares	389,300	399,400	457,400	510,300	526,200	541,417	538,790	534,015
Balance Sheet								
Current Assets	3,274,200	2,912,400	2,971,900	3,703,900	3,600,700	4,439,661	3,214,370	2,878,959
Total Assets	8,917,700	8,619,200	8,403,100	10,326,000	9,832,100	9,983,820	8,467,851	7,590,263
Current Liabilities	1,515,300	1,801,900	1,527,700	1,441,400	1,422,000	1,466,703	1,471,976	1,375,785
Long-Term Obligations	2,131,800	1,648,800	1,349,000	999,300	999,200	999,034	...	...
Total Liabilities	4,279,600	4,044,800	3,484,000	3,023,800	2,833,100	2,894,638	1,859,651	1,768,127
Stockholders' Equity	4,638,100	4,574,400	4,919,100	7,302,200	6,999,000	7,089,182	6,608,200	5,822,136
Shares Outstanding	386,300	384,000	416,200	495,200	508,400	526,409	525,378	519,341
Statistical Record								
Return on Assets %	7.33	7.45	N.M.	4.36	1.88	4.61	7.70	1.58
Return on Equity %	13.94	13.35	N.M.	6.15	2.64	6.21	9.95	2.00
EBITDA Margin %	17.13	21.72	2.43	15.49	11.29	17.06	22.44	13.73
Net Margin %	8.32	13.05	N.M.	9.42	4.27	9.56	15.11	3.53
Asset Turnover	0.56	0.57	0.49	0.46	0.44	0.48	0.51	0.45
Current Ratio	2.16	1.62	1.95	2.57	2.53	3.03	2.18	2.09
Debt to Equity	0.46	0.36	0.27	0.14	0.14	0.14	...	...
Price Range	32.23-21.62	32.23-21.39	27.95-18.57	22.57-15.69	23.88-14.27	44.46-17.08	37.90-22.82	28.22-12.67
P/E Ratio	19.65-13.18	20.27-13.45	...	26.24-18.24	68.23-40.77	56.28-21.62	32.96-19.84	128.27-57.59
Average Yield %	1.49	1.52	0.84	...	...	...	...	...

Address: 1133 Innovation Way, Sunnyvale, CA 94089	Web Site: www.juniper.net	Auditors: Ernst & Young LLP
Telephone: 408-745-2000	**Officers:** Scott G. Kriens - Chairman, Chief Executive Officer Pradeep S. Sindhu - Vice-Chairman, Chief Technical Officer	**Investor Contact:** 408-936-5396
Fax: 408-745-2100		**Transfer Agents:** Wells Fargo Shareowner Services, Mendota Heights, MN

KANSAS CITY SOUTHERN

Exchange	Symbol	Price	52Wk Range	Yield	P/E
NYS	KSU	$93.10 (5/31/2016)	101.09-64.35	1.42	20.78

*7 Year Price Score 98.00 *NYSE Composite Index=100 *12 Month Price Score 103.47

TRADING VOLUME (thousand shares)

Interim Earnings (Per Share)

Qtr.	Mar	Jun	Sep	Dec
2013	0.94	0.14	1.07	1.03
2014	0.85	1.18	1.25	1.28
2015	0.91	1.01	1.20	1.28
2016	0.99	...	...	...

Interim Dividends (Per Share)

Amt	Decl	Ex	Rec	Pay
0.33Q	08/04/2015	09/10/2015	09/14/2015	10/07/2015
0.33Q	11/12/2015	12/29/2015	12/31/2015	01/20/2016
0.33Q	01/28/2016	03/10/2016	03/14/2016	04/06/2016
0.33Q	05/06/2016	06/09/2016	06/13/2016	07/06/2016

Indicated Div: $1.32

Valuation Analysis

		Institutional Holding	
Forecast EPS	$4.63	No of Institutions	
	(05/20/2016)	668	
Market Cap	$10.1 Billion	Shares	
Book Value	$3.9 Billion	120,625,296	
Price/Book	2.55	% Held	
Price/Sales	4.23	90.30	

Business Summary: Rail (MIC: 7.4.3 SIC: 4011 NAIC: 482111)

Kansas City Southern is a holding company. Co. has domestic and international rail operations in North America that are focused on the north/south freight corridor connecting commercial and industrial markets in the central U.S. with industrial cities in Mexico. As of Dec 31 2015, Co.'s coordinated rail network comprised approximately 6,600 route miles extending from the midwest and southeast portions of the U.S. south into Mexico and connects with all other Class I railroads, providing shippers with an alternative to other railroad routes and giving direct access to Mexico and the southeast and southwest U.S. through alternate interchange hubs.

Recent Developments: For the quarter ended Mar 31 2016, net income increased 6.8% to US$108.1 million from US$101.2 million in the year-earlier quarter. Revenues were US$562.7 million, down 6.7% from US$603.1 million the year before. Operating income was US$187.9 million versus US$178.2 million in the prior-year quarter, an increase of 5.4%. Direct operating expenses declined 29.9% to US$56.8 million from US$81.0 million in the comparable period the year before. Indirect operating expenses decreased 7.5% to US$318.0 million from US$343.9 million in the equivalent prior-year period.

Prospects: Our evaluation of Kansas City Southern Industries Inc. as of June 19, 2016 is the result of our systematic analysis on three basic characteristics: earnings strength, relative valuation, and recent stock price movement. The company has enjoyed a very positive trend in earnings per share over the past 5 quarters. However, while recent estimates for the company have been lowered by analysts, KSU has posted better than expected results. Based on operating earnings yield, the company is undervalued when compared to all of the companies in our coverage universe. Share price changes over the past year indicates that KSU will perform well over the near term.

Financial Data

(US$ in Thousands)	3 Mos	12/31/2015	12/31/2014	12/31/2013	12/31/2012	12/31/2011	12/31/2010	12/31/2009
Earnings Per Share	4.48	4.40	4.55	3.18	3.43	3.00	1.67	0.61
Cash Flow Per Share	8.39	8.29	8.22	7.26	6.12	5.90	4.96	3.14
Tang Book Value Per Share	36.45	36.03	33.96	30.52	28.06	25.10	23.62	21.33
Dividends Per Share	1.320	1.320	1.120	0.860	0.780	...	...	...
Dividend Payout %	29.46	30.00	24.62	27.04	22.74	...	...	...
Income Statement								
Total Revenue	562,700	2,418,800	2,577,100	2,369,300	2,238,600	2,098,300	1,814,800	1,480,200
EBITDA	258,900	1,020,800	1,022,900	836,700	896,300	752,100	612,500	452,100
Depn & Amortn	74,300	284,600	258,100	223,300	198,800	186,200	184,900	182,500
Income Before Taxes	161,000	654,300	692,000	532,800	597,100	436,800	269,500	95,900
Income Taxes	56,800	187,300	208,800	198,300	237,000	123,100	109,200	34,600
Net Income	107,800	483,500	502,600	351,400	377,300	330,300	180,200	68,000
Average Shares	108,275	109,915	110,433	110,340	110,080	109,830	107,534	93,649
Balance Sheet								
Current Assets	451,500	537,000	818,300	942,400	522,300	642,500	598,200	613,800
Total Assets	8,316,000	8,341,000	8,091,000	7,435,400	6,395,900	6,173,000	5,640,900	5,479,100
Current Liabilities	680,700	757,600	898,800	730,600	424,800	437,400	431,200	410,800
Long-Term Obligations	2,038,800	2,045,000	1,841,000	1,856,900	1,547,600	1,602,800	1,621,600	1,911,900
Total Liabilities	4,374,600	4,426,700	4,335,500	4,064,800	3,299,300	3,408,500	3,209,800	3,420,300
Stockholders' Equity	3,941,400	3,914,300	3,755,500	3,370,600	3,096,600	2,764,500	2,431,100	2,058,800
Shares Outstanding	107,973	108,461	110,392	110,229	110,131	109,910	102,648	96,213
Statistical Record								
Return on Assets %	6.03	5.88	6.47	5.08	5.99	5.59	3.24	1.25
Return on Equity %	12.62	12.61	14.11	10.87	12.84	12.71	8.03	3.43
EBITDA Margin %	46.01	42.20	39.69	35.31	40.04	35.84	33.75	30.54
Net Margin %	19.16	19.99	19.50	14.83	16.85	15.74	9.93	4.59
Asset Turnover	0.29	0.29	0.33	0.34	0.36	0.36	0.33	0.27
Current Ratio	0.66	0.71	0.91	1.29	1.23	1.47	1.39	1.49
Debt to Equity	0.52	0.52	0.49	0.55	0.50	0.58	0.67	0.93
Price Range	107.37-64.35	122.03-70.01	125.88-91.12	125.20-83.48	83.82-62.54	69.17-46.00	49.98-29.70	34.13-12.62
P/E Ratio	23.97-14.36	27.73-15.91	27.67-20.03	39.37-26.25	24.44-18.23	23.06-15.33	29.93-17.78	55.95-20.69
Average Yield %	1.48	1.35	1.02	0.79	1.06	...	...	...

Address: 427 West 12th Street, Kansas City, MO 64105 **Telephone:** 816-983-1303 **Fax:** 816 556-0297	**Web Site:** www.kcsouthern.com **Officers:** Patrick J. Ottensmeyer - President, Chief Executive Officer, Executive Vice President Jeffrey M. Songer - Executive Vice President, Chief Operating Officer	**Auditors:** KPMG LLP **Investor Contact:** 816-983-1551 **Transfer Agents:** Computershare Trust Company, N.A., Providence, RI

KAR AUCTION SERVICES INC.

Exchange	Symbol	Price	52Wk Range	Yield	P/E
NYS	KAR	$41.04 (5/31/2016)	41.23-31.98	2.83	26.14

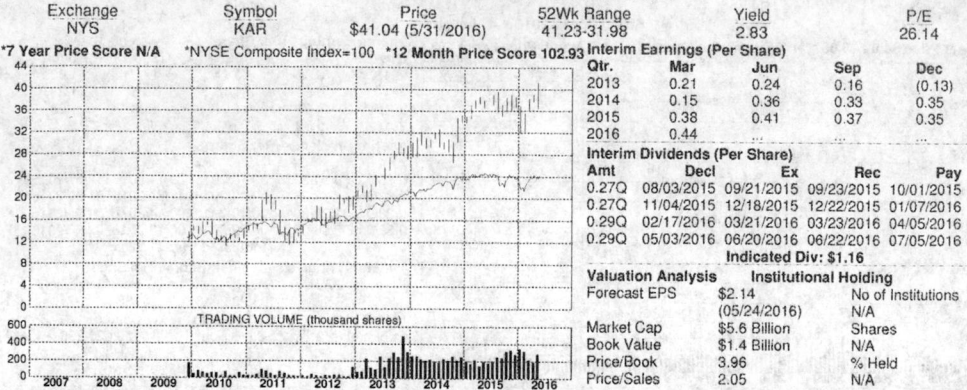

*7 Year Price Score N/A   ***NYSE Composite Index=100**   ***12 Month Price Score 102.93**

Interim Earnings (Per Share)

Qtr.	Mar	Jun	Sep	Dec
2013	0.21	0.24	0.16	(0.13)
2014	0.15	0.36	0.33	0.35
2015	0.38	0.41	0.37	0.35
2016	0.44			

Interim Dividends (Per Share)

Amt	Decl	Ex	Rec	Pay
0.27Q	08/03/2015	09/21/2015	09/23/2015	10/01/2015
0.27Q	11/04/2015	12/18/2015	12/22/2015	01/07/2016
0.29Q	02/17/2016	03/21/2016	03/23/2016	04/05/2016
0.29Q	05/03/2016	06/20/2016	06/23/2016	07/05/2016

Indicated Div: $1.16

Valuation Analysis

		Institutional Holding	
Forecast EPS	$2.14	No of Institutions	
	(05/24/2016)	N/A	
Market Cap	$5.6 Billion	Shares	
Book Value	$1.4 Billion	N/A	
Price/Book	3.96	% Held	
Price/Sales	2.05	N/A	

Business Summary: Retail - Automotive (MIC: 2.1.4 SIC: 5521 NAIC: 441120)

KAR Auction Services is engaged in providing whole car auction services in North America and salvage auction services in North America and the U.K. Co.'s segments are: ADESA Inc. Auctions, which encompasses all physical and online wholesale auctions throughout North America (U.S., Canada and Mexico); Insurance Auto Auctions, Inc., which encompasses all salvage auctions throughout North America (U.S. and Canada); and Automotive Finance Corporation, which provides short-term, inventory-secured financing to independent, used vehicle dealers. As of Dec 31 2015, Co. had a North American network of 66 whole car auction locations and 171 salvage auction locations.

Recent Developments: For the quarter ended Mar 31 2016, net income increased 11.4% to US$60.7 million from US$54.5 million in the year-earlier quarter. Revenues were US$745.0 million, up 17.8% from US$632.4 million the year before. Operating income was US$128.8 million versus US$107.9 million in the prior-year quarter, an increase of 19.4%. Direct operating expenses rose 18.9% to US$418.7 million from US$352.1 million in the comparable period the year before. Indirect operating expenses increased 14.6% to US$197.5 million from US$172.4 million in the equivalent prior-year period.

Prospects: Our evaluation of KAR Aucton Services Inc. as of June 26, 2016 is the result of our systematic analysis on three basic characteristics: earnings strength, relative valuation, and recent stock price movement. The company has enjoyed a very positive trend in earnings per share over the past 5 quarters and while recent estimates for the company have remained steady, KAR has posted better than expected results. Based on operating earnings yield, the company is about fairly valued when compared to all of the companies in our coverage universe. Share price changes over the past year indicates that KAR will perform well over the near term.

Financial Data

(US$ in Thousands)	3 Mos	12/31/2015	12/31/2014	12/31/2013	12/31/2012	12/31/2011	12/31/2010	12/31/2009
Earnings Per Share	1.57	1.51	1.19	0.48	0.66	0.52	0.51	...
Cash Flow Per Share	3.34	3.39	3.08	3.15	2.12	2.25	3.47	2.32
Dividends Per Share	1.100	1.080	1.020	0.820	0.190	...	...	...
Dividend Payout %	70.06	71.52	85.71	170.83	28.79	...	...	...
Income Statement								
Total Revenue	745,000	2,639,600	2,364,500	2,173,300	1,963,400	1,886,300	1,815,000	1,729,600
EBITDA	128,100	506,700	419,000	318,200	343,400	304,800	309,200	289,200
Depn & Amortn	2,000	74,800	67,800	64,300	72,400	71,700	71,000	82,300
Income Before Taxes	97,400	340,500	265,000	149,200	151,600	90,000	96,800	34,300
Income Taxes	36,700	125,900	95,700	81,500	59,600	17,800	27,200	11,100
Net Income	60,700	214,600	169,300	67,700	92,000	72,200	69,600	23,200
Average Shares	139,000	142,300	141,800	140,800	139,000	137,800	135,900	108,100
Balance Sheet								
Current Assets	3,179,900	2,446,100	2,074,900	1,791,500	1,581,400	1,373,200	1,254,700	941,900
Total Assets	6,490,100	5,791,800	5,351,500	5,127,200	4,922,300	4,779,100	4,525,000	4,251,300
Current Liabilities	2,229,900	2,226,100	1,590,600	1,434,600	1,286,900	1,196,200	966,800	642,400
Long-Term Obligations	2,385,500	1,719,300	1,736,600	1,734,700	1,774,600	1,816,900	1,875,700	2,047,300
Total Liabilities	5,066,400	4,405,700	3,804,400	3,645,400	3,478,600	3,435,900	3,280,400	3,109,800
Stockholders' Equity	1,423,700	1,386,100	1,547,100	1,481,800	1,443,700	1,343,200	1,244,600	1,141,500
Shares Outstanding	137,289	137,795	141,316	139,027	136,657	136,271	135,493	134,509
Statistical Record								
Return on Assets %	3.69	3.85	3.23	1.35	1.89	1.55	1.59	0.55
Return on Equity %	14.85	14.63	11.18	4.63	6.58	5.58	5.83	2.45
EBITDA Margin %	17.19	19.20	17.72	14.64	17.49	16.16	17.04	16.72
Net Margin %	8.15	8.13	7.16	3.12	4.69	3.83	3.83	1.34
Asset Turnover	0.46	0.47	0.45	0.43	0.40	0.41	0.41	0.41
Current Ratio	1.43	1.10	1.30	1.25	1.23	1.15	1.30	1.47
Debt to Equity	1.68	1.24	1.12	1.17	1.23	1.35	1.51	1.79
Price Range	39.52-31.98	39.52-33.77	35.18-26.44	30.15-19.30	20.63-13.49	20.91-11.52	15.73-11.19	13.79-11.80
P/E Ratio	25.17-20.37	26.17-22.36	29.56-22.22	62.81-40.21	31.26-20.44	40.21-22.15	30.84-21.94	...
Average Yield %	2.98	2.91	3.33	3.34	1.11	...	...	...

Address: 13085 Hamilton Crossing Boulevard, Carmel, IN 46032 **Telephone:** 800-923-3725	**Web Site:** www.karauctionservices.com **Officers:** James P. Hallett - Chief Executive Officer Eric M. Loughmiller - Executive Vice President, Chief Financial Officer	**Auditors:** KPMG LLP **Investor Contact:** 317-249-4390

KATE SPADE & CO

Exchange	Symbol	Price	52Wk Range	Yield	P/E
NYS	KATE	$21.86 (5/31/2016)	26.23-15.50	N/A	33.12

*7 Year Price Score 106.52 *NYSE Composite Index=100 *12 Month Price Score 115.10

Interim Earnings (Per Share)

Qtr.	Mar	Jun	Sep	Dec
2013	(0.44)	(0.36)	(0.14)	1.52
2014	0.37	(0.03)	(0.07)	0.99
2015	(0.43)	0.07	0.02	0.48
2016	0.09	...	...	...

Interim Dividends (Per Share)

No Dividends Paid

Valuation Analysis / Institutional Holding

Valuation Analysis		Institutional Holding	
Forecast EPS	$0.78	No of Institutions	
	(05/20/2016)	360	
Market Cap	$2.8 Billion	Shares	
Book Value	$267.5 Million	142,194,272	
Price/Book	10.46	% Held	
Price/Sales	2.22	N/A	

Business Summary: Apparel, Footwear & Accessories (MIC: 1.4.2 SIC: 2339 NAIC: 315212)

Kate Spade designs and markets a range of accessories and apparel. Co. operates its kate spade new york and JACK SPADE brands via one operating segment in North America and three operating segments internationally: Japan, Asia (excluding Japan) and Europe. Co.'s kate spade new york brand provides fashion products for women and children, as well as home products, while its JACK SPADE brand provides fashion products for men. The Adelington Design Group reportable segment is also an operating segment. This segment includes supplier arrangements to provide J.C. Penney Corporation, Inc. with LIZ CLAIBORNE and MONET branded jewelry, and a royalty-free license for the LIZ CLAIBORNE NEW YORK brand.

Recent Developments: For the quarter ended Apr 2 2016, income from continuing operations was US$10.9 million compared with a loss of US$53.6 million in the year-earlier quarter. Net income amounted to US$11.6 million versus a net loss of US$55.2 million in the year-earlier quarter. Revenues were US$274.4 million, up 7.5% from US$255.3 million the year before. Operating income was US$17.7 million versus a loss of US$37.1 million in the prior-year quarter. Direct operating expenses rose 4.3% to US$104.9 million from US$100.6 million in the comparable period the year before. Indirect operating expenses decreased 20.9% to US$151.8 million from US$191.9 million in the equivalent prior-year period.

Prospects: Our evaluation of Kate Spade & Co. as of June 19, 2016 is the result of our systematic analysis on three basic characteristics: earnings strength, relative valuation, and recent stock price movement. The company has managed to produce a neutral trend in earnings per share over the past 5 quarters and while recent estimates for the company have remained steady, KATE has posted results that fell short of analysts expectations. Based on operating earnings yield, the company is about fairly valued when compared to all of the companies in our coverage universe. Share price changes over the past year indicates that KATE will perform very well over the near term.

Financial Data
(US$ in Thousands)

	3 Mos	01/02/2016	01/03/2015	12/28/2013	12/29/2012	12/31/2011	01/01/2011	01/02/2010
Earnings Per Share	0.66	0.13	1.25	0.59	(0.68)	(1.35)	(2.67)	(3.26)
Cash Flow Per Share	1.06	0.83	0.11	(0.20)	0.10	(0.18)	1.60	2.21
Tang Book Value Per Share	1.00	0.86	0.35	...	...	...	...	N.M.
Income Statement								
Total Revenue	274,422	1,242,720	1,138,603	1,264,935	1,505,094	1,518,721	2,500,072	3,011,859
EBITDA	29,005	83,188	50,825	165,830	54,392	262,166	(43,149)	(210,291)
Depn & Amortn	11,539	37,800	38,300	47,700	58,700	66,000	109,700	128,300
Income Before Taxes	12,470	26,236	(7,653)	70,889	(55,992)	138,978	(213,042)	(403,675)
Income Taxes	1,554	4,528	(84,379)	(3,035)	3,464	(5,770)	7,941	(109,615)
Net Income	11,636	17,087	159,160	72,995	(74,505)	(171,687)	(251,467)	(305,729)
Average Shares	128,636	128,222	127,019	124,832	109,292	120,692	94,243	93,880
Balance Sheet								
Current Assets	583,732	621,714	474,500	651,713	452,256	551,745	611,923	886,931
Total Assets	951,901	980,361	926,338	977,511	902,523	950,004	1,257,659	1,605,903
Current Liabilities	222,204	267,176	252,795	445,240	415,849	426,973	572,880	642,552
Long-Term Obligations	391,317	397,043	400,284	390,794	383,662	381,569	476,319	516,146
Total Liabilities	684,360	735,140	726,727	1,009,993	1,029,453	1,058,990	1,281,829	1,389,355
Stockholders' Equity	267,541	245,221	199,611	(32,482)	(126,930)	(108,986)	(24,170)	216,548
Shares Outstanding	127,979	127,893	127,371	122,936	116,586	100,844	94,544	94,948
Statistical Record								
Return on Assets %	9.26	1.80	16.45	7.79	N.M.	N.M.	N.M.	N.M.
Return on Equity %	40.11	7.70	187.38	...	...	...	N.M.	N.M.
EBITDA Margin %	10.57	6.69	4.46	13.11	3.61	17.26	N.M.	N.M.
Net Margin %	4.24	1.37	13.98	5.77	N.M.	N.M.	N.M.	N.M.
Asset Turnover	1.39	1.31	1.18	1.35	1.63	1.38	1.75	1.72
Current Ratio	2.63	2.33	1.88	1.46	1.09	1.29	1.07	1.38
Debt to Equity	1.46	1.62	2.01	...	...	...	...	2.38
Price Range	34.38-15.50	35.30-17.04	40.45-24.64	33.59-12.45	13.88-8.61	8.82-4.06	9.33-4.02	7.49-1.65
P/E Ratio	52.09-23.48	271.54-131.08	32.36-19.71	56.93-21.10	...	...	...	...

Address: 2 Park Avenue, New York, NY 10016 **Telephone:** 212-354-4900	**Web Site:** www.katespadeandcompany.com **Officers:** Kay Koplovitz - Chairman George M. Carrara - President, Chief Operating Officer, Executive Vice President, Chief Financial Officer	**Auditors:** Deloitte & Touche LLP **Investor Contact:** 201-295-7861 **Transfer Agents:** Computershare, Jersey City, NJ

403

KB HOME

Exchange	Symbol	Price	52Wk Range	Yield	P/E
NYS	KBH	$13.94 (5/31/2016)	17.32-9.58	0.72	15.49

*7 Year Price Score 82.35 *NYSE Composite Index=100 *12 Month Price Score 98.78

Interim Earnings (Per Share)

Qtr.	Feb	May	Aug	Nov
2012-13	(0.16)	(0.04)	0.30	0.32
2013-14	0.12	0.27	0.28	8.57
2014-15	0.08	0.10	0.23	0.43
2015-16	0.14			

Interim Dividends (Per Share)

Amt	Decl	Ex	Rec	Pay
0.025Q	07/16/2015	08/04/2015	08/06/2015	08/20/2015
0.025Q	10/08/2015	11/03/2015	11/05/2015	11/19/2015
0.025Q	01/21/2016	02/02/2016	02/04/2016	02/18/2016
0.025Q	04/07/2016	05/03/2016	05/05/2016	05/19/2016

Indicated Div: $0.10

Valuation Analysis

Forecast EPS	$1.30	Institutional Holding	
	(05/20/2016)	No of Institutions	342
Market Cap	$1.2 Billion	Shares	87,607,528
Book Value	$1.6 Billion	% Held	88.92
Price/Book	0.73		
Price/Sales	0.37		

Business Summary: Builders (MIC: 2.2.5 SIC: 1531 NAIC: 236115)

KB Home is a homebuilding company. Co.'s homebuilding operations, which is comprised of four segments, provides a range of new homes designed for first-time, move-up and active adult homebuyers, including attached and detached single-family residential homes, townhomes and condominiums. Co. provides homes in development communities, at urban in-fill locations and as part of mixed-use projects. Co.'s financial services segment provides property and casualty insurance and, in certain instances, earthquake, flood and personal property insurance to its homebuyers in the same markets where it builds homes and provides title services in the majority of its markets.

Recent Developments: For the quarter ended Feb 29 2016, net income increased 68.3% to US$13.1 million from US$7.8 million in the year-earlier quarter. Revenues were US$678.4 million, up 16.9% from US$580.1 million the year before. Direct operating expenses rose 15.5% to US$569.7 million from US$493.4 million in the comparable period the year before. Indirect operating expenses increased 23.7% to US$87.9 million from US$71.1 million in the equivalent prior-year period.

Prospects: Our evaluation of KB HOME as of June 19, 2016 is the result of our systematic analysis on three basic characteristics: earnings strength, relative valuation, and recent stock price movement. The company has suffered a very negative trend in earnings per share over the past 5 quarters. However, while recent estimates for the company have been mixed, KBH has posted better than expected results. Based on operating earnings yield, the company is undervalued when compared to all of the companies in our coverage universe. Share price changes over the past year indicates that KBH will perform poorly over the near term.

Financial Data

(US$ in Thousands)	3 Mos	11/30/2015	11/30/2014	11/30/2013	11/30/2012	11/30/2011	11/30/2010	11/30/2009
Earnings Per Share	0.90	0.85	9.25	0.46	(0.76)	(2.32)	(0.90)	(1.33)
Cash Flow Per Share	0.97	1.97	(7.07)	(5.37)	0.45	(4.51)	(1.74)	4.56
Tang Book Value Per Share	19.22	16.51	15.60	5.69	4.29	5.03	7.18	8.03
Dividends Per Share	0.100	0.100	0.100	0.100	0.138	0.250	0.250	0.250
Dividend Payout %	11.11	11.76	1.08	21.74	...	...	...	...
Income Statement								
Total Revenue	678,371	3,032,030	2,400,949	2,097,130	1,560,115	1,315,866	1,589,996	1,824,850
EBITDA	22,643	149,353	126,229	103,094	(9,964)	(94,282)	(7,631)	(226,136)
Depn & Amortn	1,881	3,400	2,400	1,900	1,600	2,000	3,300	5,200
Income Before Taxes	17,217	124,555	93,522	39,296	(80,850)	(144,615)	(77,140)	(275,584)
Income Taxes	2,900	42,400	(823,400)	(1,600)	(20,100)	(2,400)	(7,000)	(209,400)
Net Income	13,127	84,643	918,349	39,963	(58,953)	(178,768)	(69,368)	(101,784)
Average Shares	99,427	102,857	99,314	91,559	77,106	77,043	76,889	76,660
Balance Sheet								
Current Assets	3,960,792	4,038,359	3,731,616	2,946,327	2,338,519	2,277,339	2,824,647	3,128,331
Total Assets	4,922,056	5,015,371	4,757,550	3,193,635	2,561,698	2,512,542	3,109,749	3,435,989
Current Liabilities	411,854	262,795	238,508	193,844	165,936	147,543	276,180	387,279
Long-Term Obligations	2,652,705	2,625,536	2,576,525	2,150,498	1,722,815	1,583,571	1,775,529	1,820,370
Total Liabilities	3,304,998	3,324,537	3,161,640	2,657,549	2,184,892	2,069,885	2,477,871	2,728,765
Stockholders' Equity	1,617,058	1,690,834	1,595,910	536,086	376,806	442,657	631,878	707,224
Shares Outstanding	84,121	102,411	102,289	94,246	87,837	87,956	88,053	88,072
Statistical Record								
Return on Assets %	1.82	1.73	23.10	1.39	N.M.	N.M.	N.M.	N.M.
Return on Equity %	5.59	5.15	86.15	8.76	N.M.	N.M.	N.M.	N.M.
EBITDA Margin %	3.34	4.93	5.26	4.92	N.M.	N.M.	N.M.	N.M.
Net Margin %	1.94	2.79	38.25	1.91	N.M.	N.M.	N.M.	N.M.
Asset Turnover	0.63	0.62	0.60	0.73	0.61	0.47	0.49	0.49
Current Ratio	9.62	15.37	15.65	15.20	14.09	15.44	10.23	8.08
Debt to Equity	1.64	1.55	1.61	4.01	4.57	3.58	2.81	2.57
Price Range	17.32-9.58	17.32-11.87	20.67-13.78	24.82-14.04	16.90-6.34	15.71-5.27	19.33-9.80	20.51-8.11
P/E Ratio	19.24-10.64	20.38-13.96	2.23-1.49	53.96-30.52	...	...	...	...
Average Yield %	0.71	0.68	0.58	0.54	1.32	2.40	1.83	1.71

Address: 10990 Wilshire Boulevard, Los Angeles, CA 90024 Telephone: 310-231-4000 Fax: 310-231-4222	Web Site: www.kbhome.com Officers: Stephen F. Bollenbach - Chairman Jeffrey T. Mezger - President, Chief Executive Officer	Auditors: Ernst & Young LLP Investor Contact: 310-231-4000 Transfer Agents: ComputerShare Investor Services, Providence, RI

KBR INC

Exchange	Symbol	Price	52Wk Range	Yield	P/E
NYS	KBR	$14.55 (5/31/2016)	20.60-11.76	2.20	10.39

*7 Year Price Score 56.42 *NYSE Composite Index=100 *12 Month Price Score 87.17

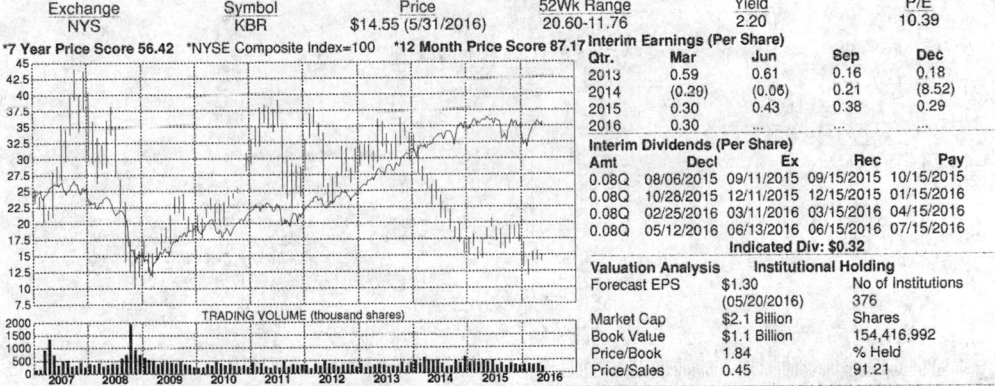

Interim Earnings (Per Share)

Qtr.	Mar	Jun	Sep	Dec
2013	0.59	0.61	0.16	0.18
2014	(0.29)	(0.06)	0.21	(8.52)
2015	0.30	0.43	0.38	0.29
2016	0.30	...	...	...

Interim Dividends (Per Share)

Amt	Decl	Ex	Rec	Pay
0.08Q	08/06/2015	09/11/2015	09/15/2015	10/15/2015
0.08Q	10/28/2015	12/11/2015	12/15/2015	01/15/2016
0.08Q	02/25/2016	03/11/2016	03/15/2016	04/15/2016
0.08Q	05/12/2016	06/13/2016	06/15/2016	07/15/2016

Indicated Div: $0.32

Valuation Analysis | **Institutional Holding**

Forecast EPS	$1.30	No of Institutions	
	(05/20/2016)	376	
Market Cap	$2.1 Billion	Shares	
Book Value	$1.1 Billion	154,416,992	
Price/Book	1.84	% Held	
Price/Sales	0.45	91.21	

Business Summary: Construction Services (MIC: 7.5.4 SIC: 1629 NAIC: 237990)

KBR is an engineering, construction and services company supporting the hydrocarbons and international government services market segments. Co. operates in three business segments: technology and consulting, which provides technologies and consulting services to the oil and gas value chain, from wellhead to crude refining and specialty chemicals production; engineering and construction, which provides engineering, procurement, construction, commissioning and maintenance services for oil and gas, refining, petrochemicals, and chemicals customers; and government services, which focuses on service contracts particularly for the U.K., Australian and the U.S. governments.

Recent Developments: For the quarter ended Mar 31 2016, net income decreased 11.8% to US$45.0 million from US$51.0 million in the year-earlier quarter. Revenues were US$996.0 million, down 30.6% from US$1.44 billion the year before. Operating income was US$65.0 million versus US$64.0 million in the prior-year quarter, an increase of 1.6%. Direct operating expenses declined 32.1% to US$928.0 million from US$1.37 billion in the comparable period the year before. Indirect operating expenses decreased 50.0% to US$3.0 million from US$6.0 million in the equivalent prior-year period.

Prospects: Our evaluation of KBR Inc. as of June 19, 2016 is the result of our systematic analysis on three basic characteristics: earnings strength, relative valuation, and recent stock price movement. The company has suffered a very negative trend in earnings per share over the past 5 quarters and while recent estimates for the company have been mixed, KBR has posted better than expected results. Based on operating earnings yield, the company is undervalued when compared to all of the companies in our coverage universe. Share price changes over the past year indicates that KBR will perform well over the near term.

Financial Data

(US$ in Thousands)	3 Mos	12/31/2015	12/31/2014	12/31/2013	12/31/2012	12/31/2011	12/31/2010	12/31/2009
Earnings Per Share	1.40	1.40	(8.66)	1.54	0.97	3.16	2.07	1.79
Cash Flow Per Share	0.94	0.33	1.16	1.96	0.96	4.33	3.52	(0.23)
Tang Book Value Per Share	5.11	4.97	3.98	11.88	11.27	9.66	7.75	9.60
Dividends Per Share	0.320	0.320	0.320	0.320	0.200	0.200	0.200	0.200
Dividend Payout %	22.86	22.86	...	20.78	20.62	6.33	9.66	11.17
Income Statement								
Total Revenue	996,000	5,096,000	6,366,000	7,283,000	7,921,000	9,261,000	10,099,000	12,105,000
EBITDA	40,000	198,000	(879,000)	385,000	360,000	661,000	665,000	588,000
Depn & Amortn	9,000	35,000	61,000	54,000	65,000	71,000	62,000	55,000
Income Before Taxes	31,000	163,000	(940,000)	326,000	288,000	572,000	586,000	532,000
Income Taxes	15,000	86,000	421,000	136,000	86,000	32,000	191,000	168,000
Net Income	42,000	203,000	(1,262,000)	229,000	144,000	480,000	327,000	290,000
Average Shares	142,000	144,000	146,000	149,000	149,000	151,000	157,000	161,000
Balance Sheet								
Current Assets	1,745,000	1,844,000	2,544,000	3,010,000	3,668,000	3,442,000	3,262,000	3,641,000
Total Assets	3,370,000	3,412,000	4,199,000	5,516,000	5,767,000	5,673,000	5,417,000	5,327,000
Current Liabilities	1,313,000	1,412,000	2,024,000	1,828,000	2,277,000	2,284,000	2,347,000	2,291,000
Long-Term Obligations	50,000	51,000	63,000	...	84,000	88,000	92,000	...
Total Liabilities	2,245,000	2,347,000	3,257,000	2,899,000	3,225,000	3,178,000	3,171,000	3,039,000
Stockholders' Equity	1,125,000	1,065,000	942,000	2,617,000	2,542,000	2,495,000	2,246,000	2,288,000
Shares Outstanding	142,411	142,058	144,837	148,195	147,584	148,143	151,132	160,363
Statistical Record								
Return on Assets %	5.54	5.33	N.M.	4.06	2.51	8.66	6.09	5.17
Return on Equity %	20.06	20.23	N.M.	8.88	5.70	20.25	14.42	13.36
EBITDA Margin %	4.02	3.89	N.M.	5.29	4.54	7.14	6.58	4.86
Net Margin %	4.22	3.98	N.M.	3.14	1.82	5.18	3.24	2.40
Asset Turnover	1.28	1.34	1.31	1.29	1.38	1.67	1.88	2.16
Current Ratio	1.33	1.31	1.26	1.65	1.61	1.51	1.39	1.59
Debt to Equity	0.04	0.05	0.07	...	0.03	0.04	0.04	...
Price Range	20.60-11.76	20.60-14.26	33.62-15.23	36.29-28.01	37.93-22.91	39.12-22.20	30.90-17.60	24.49-11.71
P/E Ratio	14.71-8.40	14.71-10.19	...	23.56-18.19	39.10-23.62	12.38-7.03	14.93-8.50	13.68-6.54
Average Yield %	1.88	1.82	1.35	1.00	0.68	0.62	0.86	1.09

Address: 601 Jefferson Street, Suite 3400, Houston, TX 77002
Telephone: 713-753-3011

Web Site: www.kbr.com
Officers: William P. Utt - Chairman, President, Chief Executive Officer Stuart J.B. Bradie - President, Chief Executive Officer

Auditors: KPMG LLP
Investor Contact: 713-753-5082
Transfer Agents: American Stock Transfer & Trust Company, Brooklyn, NY

KELLOGG CO

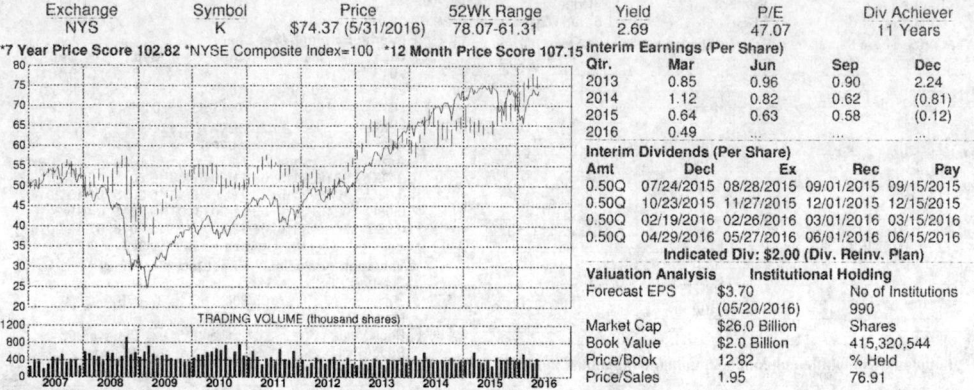

Exchange	Symbol	Price	52Wk Range	Yield	P/E	Div Achiever
NYS	K	$74.37 (5/31/2016)	78.07-61.31	2.69	47.07	11 Years

*7 Year Price Score 102.82 *NYSE Composite Index=100   *12 Month Price Score 107.15

Interim Earnings (Per Share)

Qtr.	Mar	Jun	Sep	Dec
2013	0.85	0.96	0.90	2.24
2014	1.12	0.82	0.62	(0.81)
2015	0.64	0.63	0.58	(0.12)
2016	0.49			

Interim Dividends (Per Share)

Amt	Decl	Ex	Rec	Pay
0.50Q	07/24/2015	08/28/2015	09/01/2015	09/15/2015
0.50Q	10/23/2015	11/27/2015	12/01/2015	12/15/2015
0.50Q	02/19/2016	02/26/2016	03/01/2016	03/15/2016
0.50Q	04/29/2016	05/27/2016	06/01/2016	06/15/2016

Indicated Div: $2.00 (Div. Reinv. Plan)

Valuation Analysis

Forecast EPS	$3.70		No of Institutions
	(05/20/2016)		990
Market Cap	$26.0 Billion		Shares
Book Value	$2.0 Billion		415,320,544
Price/Book	12.82		% Held
Price/Sales	1.95		76.91

Institutional Holding

Business Summary: Food (MIC: 1.2.1 SIC: 2043 NAIC: 311230)

Kellogg manufactures and markets cereal and convenience foods. Co.'s key products are cereals and convenience foods such as cookies, crackers, savory snacks, toaster pastries, cereal bars, fruit-flavored snacks, frozen waffles and veggie foods. Co.'s cereal products are generally marketed under the Kellogg's name and sold to the grocery trade via direct sales forces for resale to consumers. Co. also markets cookies, crackers, crisps, and other convenience foods, under brands such as Kellogg's, Keebler, Cheez-It, Murray, Austin and Famous Amos. Co. operates the following segments: U.S. Morning Foods; U.S. Snacks; U.S. Specialty; North America Other; Europe; Latin America; and Asia Pacific.

Recent Developments: For the quarter ended Apr 2 2016, net income decreased 22.9% to US$175.0 million from US$227.0 million in the year-earlier quarter. Revenues were US$3.40 billion, down 4.5% from US$3.56 billion the year before. Operating income was US$438.0 million versus US$384.0 million in the prior-year quarter, an increase of 14.1%. Direct operating expenses declined 7.0% to US$2.15 billion from US$2.31 billion in the comparable period the year before. Indirect operating expenses decreased 6.3% to US$807.0 million from US$861.0 million in the equivalent prior-year period.

Prospects: Our evaluation of Kellogg Co as of June 19, 2016 is the result of our systematic analysis on three basic characteristics: earnings strength, relative valuation, and recent stock price movement. The company has produced a positive trend in earnings per share over the past 5 quarters and while recent estimates for the company have been mixed, K has posted better than expected results. Based on operating earnings yield, the company is about fairly valued when compared to all of the companies in our coverage universe. Share price changes over the past year indicates that K will perform very well over the near term.

Financial Data

(US$ in Thousands)	3 Mos	01/02/2016	01/03/2015	12/28/2013	12/29/2012	12/31/2011	01/01/2011	01/02/2010
Earnings Per Share	1.58	1.72	1.75	4.94	2.67	3.38	3.30	3.16
Cash Flow Per Share	4.56	4.79	4.93	4.99	4.92	4.42	2.69	4.31
Dividends Per Share	1.990	1.980	1.900	1.800	1.740	1.670	1.560	1.430
Dividend Payout %	125.95	115.12	108.57	36.44	65.17	49.41	47.27	45.25
Income Statement								
Total Revenue	3,395,000	13,525,000	14,580,000	14,792,000	14,197,000	13,198,000	12,397,000	12,575,000
EBITDA	553,000	1,534,000	1,537,000	3,373,000	2,034,000	2,334,000	2,382,000	2,363,000
Depn & Amortn	115,000	534,000	503,000	532,000	448,000	369,000	392,000	384,000
Income Before Taxes	221,000	773,000	825,000	2,606,000	1,325,000	1,732,000	1,742,000	1,684,000
Income Taxes	47,000	159,000	186,000	792,000	363,000	503,000	502,000	476,000
Net Income	175,000	614,000	632,000	1,807,000	961,000	1,231,000	1,247,000	1,212,000
Average Shares	355,000	356,000	360,000	365,000	360,000	364,000	378,000	384,000
Balance Sheet								
Current Assets	3,219,000	3,236,000	3,340,000	3,267,000	3,380,000	3,027,000	2,915,000	2,558,000
Total Assets	15,297,000	15,265,000	15,153,000	15,474,000	15,184,000	11,901,000	11,847,000	11,200,000
Current Liabilities	5,162,000	5,739,000	4,364,000	3,835,000	4,523,000	3,313,000	3,184,000	2,288,000
Long-Term Obligations	6,256,000	5,289,000	5,935,000	6,330,000	6,082,000	5,037,000	4,908,000	4,835,000
Total Liabilities	13,266,000	13,137,000	12,364,000	11,929,000	12,765,000	10,141,000	9,689,000	8,928,000
Stockholders' Equity	2,031,000	2,128,000	2,789,000	3,545,000	2,419,000	1,760,000	2,158,000	2,272,000
Shares Outstanding	350,000	350,024	356,002	362,801	361,266	357,301	365,604	381,379
Statistical Record								
Return on Assets %	3.68	4.05	4.06	11.82	7.12	10.40	10.85	10.98
Return on Equity %	24.56	25.04	19.63	60.76	46.12	63.01	56.45	65.34
EBITDA Margin %	16.29	11.34	10.54	22.80	14.33	17.68	19.21	18.79
Net Margin %	5.15	4.54	4.33	12.22	6.77	9.33	10.06	9.64
Asset Turnover	0.88	0.89	0.94	0.97	1.05	1.11	1.08	1.14
Current Ratio	0.62	0.56	0.77	0.85	0.75	0.91	0.92	1.12
Debt to Equity	3.08	2.49	2.13	1.79	2.51	2.86	2.27	2.13
Price Range	77.86-61.31	73.51-61.31	69.39-56.90	67.46-55.85	56.86-46.51	57.56-48.25	55.58-47.98	54.00-35.84
P/E Ratio	49.28-38.80	42.74-35.65	39.65-32.51	13.66-11.31	21.30-17.42	17.03-14.28	16.84-14.54	17.09-11.34
Average Yield %	2.91	2.94	2.99	2.98	2.89	3.38	3.13	3.12

Address: One Kellogg Square, P.O. Box 3599, Battle Creek, MI 49016-3599	Web Site: www.kelloggcompany.com	Auditors: PricewaterhouseCoopers LLP
Telephone: 269-961-2000	Officers: James M. Jenness - Chairman Gary H. Pilnick - Vice-Chairman, Corporate Development Officer, Chief Legal Officer, Senior Vice President, General Counsel, Secretary	Investor Contact: 269-961-2800
		Transfer Agents: Wells Fargo Bank, N.A., St. Paul, MN

KEMPER CORP. (DE)

Exchange	Symbol	Price	52Wk Range	Yield	P/E
NYS	KMPR	$32.31 (5/31/2016)	41.44-23.80	2.97	23.93

*7 Year Price Score 96.23   *NYSE Composite Index=100   *12 Month Price Score 88.10

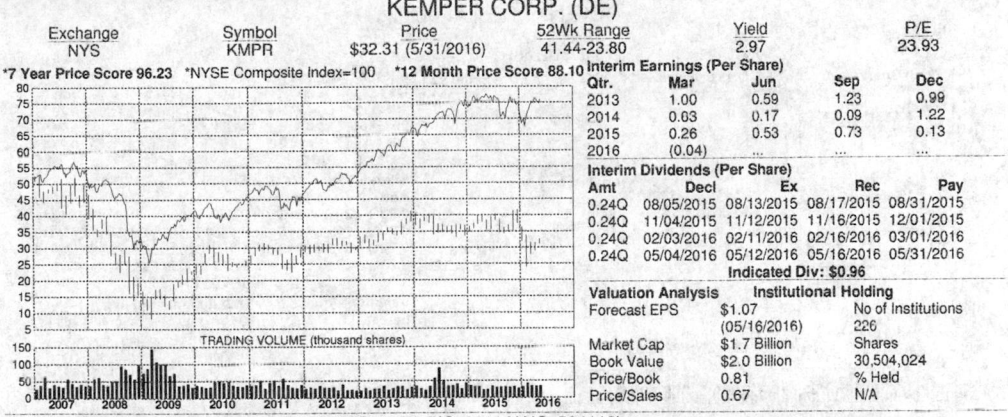

Interim Earnings (Per Share)
Qtr.	Mar	Jun	Sep	Dec
2013	1.00	0.59	1.23	0.99
2014	0.63	0.17	0.09	1.22
2015	0.26	0.53	0.73	0.13
2016	(0.04)	...	...	...

Interim Dividends (Per Share)
Amt	Decl	Ex	Rec	Pay
0.24Q	08/05/2015	08/13/2015	08/17/2015	08/31/2015
0.24Q	11/04/2015	11/12/2015	11/16/2015	12/01/2015
0.24Q	02/03/2016	02/11/2016	02/16/2016	03/01/2016
0.24Q	05/04/2016	05/12/2016	05/16/2016	05/31/2016

Indicated Div: $0.96

Valuation Analysis
		Institutional Holding	
Forecast EPS	$1.07	No of Institutions	
	(05/16/2016)	226	
Market Cap	$1.7 Billion	Shares	
Book Value	$2.0 Billion	30,504,024	
Price/Book	0.81	% Held	
Price/Sales	0.67	N/A	

Business Summary: General Insurance (MIC: 5.2.1 SIC: 6311 NAIC: 524113)

Kemper is an insurance holding company, with subsidiaries that provide automobile, homeowners, life, health, and other insurance products to individuals and businesses. Co. conducts its operations through two operating segments: Property and Casualty Insurance and Life and Health Insurance. The Property and Casualty Insurance segment's principal products are personal automobile insurance, both standard and nonstandard risks, homeowners insurance, other personal insurance and commercial automobile insurance. The Life and Health Insurance segment's principal products are individual life, accident, health and property insurance. Co.'s operations are conducted solely in the U.S.

Recent Developments: For the quarter ended Mar 31 2016, loss from continuing operations was US$2.2 million compared with income of US$13.5 million in the year-earlier quarter. Net loss amounted to US$2.1 million versus net income of US$13.5 million in the year-earlier quarter. Revenues were US$611.3 million, up 22.5% from US$499.2 million the year before. Net premiums earned were US$546.0 million versus US$431.3 million in the prior-year quarter, an increase of 26.6%. Net investment income fell 5.1% to US$67.0 million from US$70.6 million a year ago.

Prospects: Our evaluation of Kemper Corp. as of June 19, 2016 is the result of our systematic analysis on three basic characteristics: earnings strength, relative valuation, and recent stock price movement. The company has suffered a very negative trend in earnings per share over the past 5 quarters and while recent estimates for the company have been mixed, KMPR has posted results that fell short of analysts' expectations. Based on operating earnings yield, the company is overvalued when compared to all of the companies in our coverage universe. Share price changes over the past year indicates that KMPR will perform poorly over the near term.

Financial Data
(US$ in Thousands)	3 Mos	12/31/2015	12/31/2014	12/31/2013	12/31/2012	12/31/2011	12/31/2010	12/31/2009
Earnings Per Share	1.35	1.65	2.12	3.80	1.74	1.38	2.98	2.64
Cash Flow Per Share	5.14	4.17	2.49	2.15	1.11	(0.41)	0.95	2.63
Tang Book Value Per Share	33.60	32.52	33.94	31.26	31.65	31.61	29.50	25.43
Dividends Per Share	0.960	0.960	0.960	0.960	0.960	0.960	0.880	1.070
Dividend Payout %	71.11	58.18	45.28	25.26	55.17	69.57	29.53	40.53
Income Statement								
Premium Income	546,000	2,009,600	1,862,200	2,025,800	2,107,100	2,173,600	2,289,400	2,455,500
Total Revenue	611,300	2,340,800	2,196,600	2,426,500	2,462,300	2,495,000	2,743,400	2,933,400
Income Before Taxes	(6,500)	100,300	160,200	314,400	122,400	82,600	261,300	229,600
Income Taxes	(4,300)	20,100	47,600	99,900	30,600	11,700	77,400	66,400
Net Income	(2,100)	85,700	114,500	217,700	103,400	83,700	184,600	164,700
Average Shares	51,191	51,683	53,867	56,983	58,999	60,366	61,766	62,156
Balance Sheet								
Total Assets	8,169,700	8,036,100	7,833,400	7,656,400	8,009,100	8,085,900	8,358,500	8,573,500
Total Liabilities	6,128,600	6,043,700	5,742,700	5,604,900	5,847,400	5,869,800	6,245,100	6,655,900
Stockholders' Equity	2,041,100	1,992,400	2,090,700	2,051,500	2,161,700	2,216,100	2,113,400	1,917,600
Shares Outstanding	51,133	51,326	52,418	55,653	58,454	60,248	61,066	62,357
Statistical Record								
Return on Assets %	0.87	1.08	1.48	2.78	1.28	1.02	2.18	1.89
Return on Equity %	3.38	4.20	5.53	10.33	4.71	3.87	9.16	9.24
Net Margin %	(0.34)	3.66	5.21	8.97	4.20	3.35	6.73	5.61
Price Range	41.44-23.80	41.44-34.25	40.88-32.97	41.13-29.50	32.93-27.98	31.42-22.29	30.92-21.70	23.77-8.10
P/E Ratio	30.70-17.63	25.12-20.76	19.28-15.55	10.82-7.76	18.93-16.08	22.77-16.15	10.38-7.28	9.00-3.07
Average Yield %	2.67	2.56	2.62	2.79	3.18	3.46	3.45	6.48

Address: One East Wacker Drive, Chicago, IL 60601 **Telephone:** 312-661-4600	**Web Site:** www.kemper.com **Officers:** Robert Joseph Joyce - Chairman Donald G. Southwell - Chairman, President, Chief Executive Officer	**Auditors:** Deloitte & Touche LLP **Investor Contact:** 312-661-4930 **Transfer Agents:** Computershare Trust Company, N.A., Providence, RI

KENNAMETAL INC.

Exchange	Symbol	Price	52Wk Range	Yield	P/E
NYS	KMT	$24.48 (5/31/2016)	36.36-15.91	3.27	N/A

*7 Year Price Score 62.20   *NYSE Composite Index=100   ***12 Month Price Score 90.13**

Interim Earnings (Per Share)
Qtr.	Sep	Dec	Mar	Jun
2012-13	0.57	0.52	0.67	0.76
2013-14	0.48	0.30	0.64	0.57
2014-15	0.49	(4.89)	(0.58)	0.27
2015-16	(0.08)	(2.12)	0.20	...

Interim Dividends (Per Share)
Amt	Decl	Ex	Rec	Pay
0.20Q	07/30/2015	08/07/2015	08/11/2015	08/26/2015
0.20Q	11/03/2015	11/06/2015	11/10/2015	11/24/2015
0.20Q	02/03/2016	02/10/2016	02/12/2016	02/26/2016
0.20Q	05/02/2016	05/11/2016	05/13/2016	05/27/2016

Indicated Div: $0.80

Valuation Analysis
		Institutional Holding	
Forecast EPS	$1.10	No of Institutions	365
	(05/20/2016)		
Market Cap	$2.0 Billion	Shares	81,617,296
Book Value	$1.1 Billion	% Held	96.15
Price/Book	1.70		
Price/Sales	0.88		

Business Summary: Industrial Machinery & Equipment (MIC: 7.2.1 SIC: 3541 NAIC: 333512)

Kennametal provides wear-resistant products, application engineering and services for industrial production, transportation, earthworks, energy, infrastructure and aerospace. Co. has two segments: Industrial and Infrastructure. The Industrial segment focuses on customers in the transportation, general engineering, aerospace and defense market sectors, and the machine tool industry. The Infrastructure segment focuses on customers in the energy and earthworks market sectors that support primary industries such as oil and gas, power generation and chemicals; underground, surface and hard-rock mining; highway construction and road maintenance; process industries such as food and beverage.

Recent Developments: For the quarter ended Mar 31 2016, net income amounted to US$16.7 million versus a net loss of US$45.6 million in the year-earlier quarter. Revenues were US$497.8 million, down 22.1% from US$639.0 million the year before. Operating income was US$27.3 million versus a loss of US$120.4 million in the prior-year quarter. Direct operating expenses declined 22.5% to US$340.5 million from US$439.5 million in the comparable period the year before. Indirect operating expenses decreased 59.4% to US$130.0 million from US$319.9 million in the equivalent prior-year period.

Prospects: Our evaluation of Kennametal Inc. as of June 19, 2016 is the result of our systematic analysis on three basic characteristics: earnings strength, relative valuation, and recent stock price movement. The company has enjoyed a very positive trend in earnings per share over the past 5 quarters. However, while recent estimates for the company have been mixed, KMT has posted better than expected results. Based on operating earnings yield, the company is about fairly valued when compared to all of the companies in our coverage universe. Share price changes over the past year indicates that KMT will perform poorly over the near term.

Financial Data
(US$ in Thousands)	9 Mos	6 Mos	3 Mos	06/30/2015	06/30/2014	06/30/2013	06/30/2012	06/30/2011
Earnings Per Share	(1.73)	(2.51)	(5.28)	(4.71)	1.99	2.52	3.77	2.76
Cash Flow Per Share	3.47	4.02	4.36	4.43	3.46	3.58	3.60	2.81
Tang Book Value Per Share	7.90	7.67	7.74	8.09	7.76	10.76	8.50	12.01
Dividends Per Share	0.780	0.760	0.740	0.720	0.720	0.640	0.540	0.480
Dividend Payout %	...	...	...	...	36.18	25.40	14.32	17.39
Income Statement								
Total Revenue	1,577,212	1,079,376	555,354	2,647,195	2,837,190	2,589,373	2,736,246	2,403,493
EBITDA	(108,812)	(165,381)	37,086	(224,485)	391,482	407,185	521,257	412,364
Depn & Amortn	89,612	62,315	31,559	131,664	130,222	113,104	104,073	93,471
Income Before Taxes	(219,319)	(241,478)	(1,452)	(387,615)	228,809	266,609	389,969	296,133
Income Taxes	(61,499)	(66,964)	4,252	(16,654)	66,611	59,693	79,136	63,856
Net Income	(159,454)	(175,453)	(6,226)	(373,896)	158,366	203,265	307,230	229,727
Average Shares	80,224	79,840	79,728	79,342	79,667	80,612	81,439	83,173
Balance Sheet								
Current Assets	1,099,260	1,062,992	1,168,511	1,258,546	1,525,196	1,499,473	1,282,962	1,287,585
Total Assets	2,491,939	2,440,252	2,752,040	2,849,529	3,868,086	3,301,039	3,034,188	2,754,469
Current Liabilities	421,415	394,983	438,406	482,744	562,756	467,593	578,622	841,521
Long-Term Obligations	699,750	700,711	725,548	735,885	981,666	703,626	490,608	1,919
Total Liabilities	1,347,779	1,315,404	1,442,562	1,503,722	1,938,830	1,519,213	1,390,338	1,116,397
Stockholders' Equity	1,144,160	1,124,848	1,309,478	1,345,807	1,929,256	1,781,826	1,643,850	1,638,072
Shares Outstanding	79,679	79,670	79,607	79,375	78,672	77,842	80,085	81,129
Statistical Record								
Return on Assets %	N.M.	N.M.	N.M.	N.M.	4.42	6.42	10.59	9.15
Return on Equity %	N.M.	N.M.	N.M.	N.M.	8.53	11.87	18.67	15.56
EBITDA Margin %	N.M.	N.M.	6.68	N.M.	13.80	15.73	19.05	17.16
Net Margin %	N.M.	N.M.	N.M.	N.M.	5.58	7.85	11.23	9.56
Asset Turnover	0.81	0.83	0.77	0.79	0.79	0.82	0.94	0.96
Current Ratio	2.61	2.69	2.67	2.61	2.71	3.21	2.22	1.53
Debt to Equity	0.61	0.62	0.55	0.55	0.51	0.39	0.30	N.M.
Price Range	38.95-15.91	38.95-17.94	41.68-24.36	46.35-30.99	52.07-38.16	43.34-32.19	47.51-29.93	44.01-24.34
P/E Ratio	...	...	...	...	26.17-19.18	17.20-12.77	12.60-7.94	15.95-8.82
Average Yield %	2.80	2.43	2.15	1.89	1.58	1.65	1.40	1.35

Address: 600 Grant Street, Suite 5100, Pittsburgh, PA 15219-2706	Web Site: www.kennametal.com	Auditors: PricewaterhouseCoopers LLP
Telephone: 412-248-8000	**Officers:** Lawrence W. Stranghoener - Chairman Ronald M. DeFeo - President, Chief Executive Officer	**Investor Contact:** 724-539-6559 **Transfer Agents:** Computershare, Jersey City, NJ

KEYCORP

Exchange	Symbol	Price	52Wk Range	Yield	P/E
NYS	KEY	$12.82 (5/31/2016)	15.65-10.00	2.65	12.82

*7 Year Price Score 108.70 *NYSE Composite Index=100   *12 Month Price Score 92.08

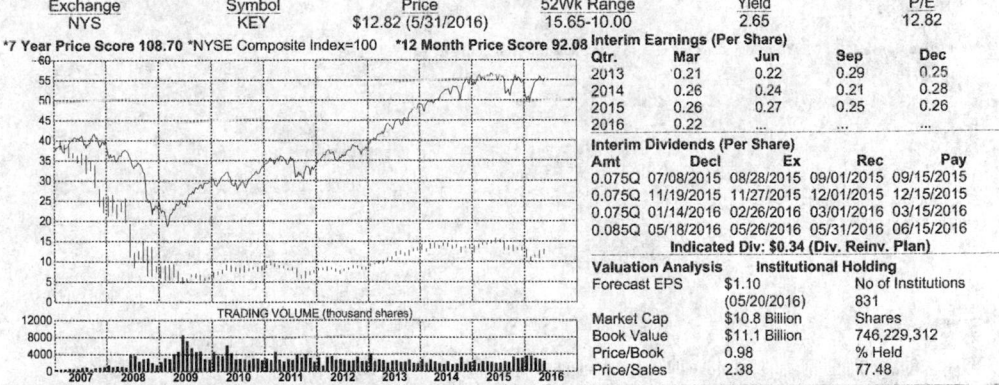

Interim Earnings (Per Share)

Qtr.	Mar	Jun	Sep	Dec
2013	0.21	0.22	0.29	0.25
2014	0.26	0.24	0.21	0.28
2015	0.26	0.27	0.25	0.26
2016	0.22	...	...	...

Interim Dividends (Per Share)

Amt	Decl	Ex	Rec	Pay
0.075Q	07/08/2015	08/28/2015	09/01/2015	09/15/2015
0.075Q	11/19/2015	11/27/2015	12/01/2015	12/15/2015
0.075Q	01/14/2016	02/26/2016	03/01/2016	03/15/2016
0.085Q	05/18/2016	05/26/2016	05/31/2016	06/15/2016

Indicated Div: $0.34 (Div. Reinv. Plan)

Valuation Analysis

		Institutional Holding	
Forecast EPS	$1.10	No of Institutions	
	(05/20/2016)	831	
Market Cap	$10.8 Billion	Shares	
Book Value	$11.1 Billion	746,229,312	
Price/Book	0.98	% Held	
Price/Sales	2.38	77.48	

Business Summary: Banking (MIC: 5.1.1 SIC: 6021 NAIC: 522110)

KeyCorp is a bank holding company. Through its subsidiaries, Co. provides a range of retail and commercial banking, commercial leasing, investment management, consumer finance and investment banking products and services to individual, corporate and institutional clients through two main segments: Key Community Bank and Key Corporate Bank. Co.'s bank and trust company subsidiaries also provide personal, securities lending and custody services, personal financial services, access to mutual funds, treasury services, investment banking and capital markets products, and international banking services. At Dec 31 2015, Co. had total assets of $95.13 billion and total deposits of $71.05 billion.

Recent Developments: For the quarter ended Mar 31 2016, income from continuing operations decreased 18.7% to US$187.0 million from US$230.0 million in the year-earlier quarter. Net income decreased 20.0% to US$188.0 million from US$235.0 million in the year-earlier quarter. Net interest income increased 5.8% to US$604.0 million from US$571.0 million in the year-earlier quarter. Provision for loan losses was US$89.0 million versus US$35.0 million in the prior-year quarter, an increase of 154.3%. Non-interest income fell 1.4% to US$431.0 million from US$437.0 million, while non-interest expense advanced 5.1% to US$703.0 million.

Prospects: Our evaluation of KeyCorp as of June 19, 2016 is the result of our systematic analysis on three basic characteristics: earnings strength, relative valuation, and recent stock price movement. The company has generated a negative trend in earnings per share over the past 5 quarters. However, while recent estimates for the company have been mixed, KEY has posted results that fell short of analysts expectations. Based on operating earnings yield, the company is undervalued when compared to all of the companies in our coverage universe. Share price changes over the past year indicates that KEY will perform in line with the market over the near term.

Financial Data

(US$ in Thousands)	3 Mos	12/31/2015	12/31/2014	12/31/2013	12/31/2012	12/31/2011	12/31/2010	12/31/2009
Earnings Per Share	1.00	1.05	0.99	0.97	0.89	0.87	0.44	(2.34)
Cash Flow Per Share	3.15	1.35	1.51	1.74	1.44	2.03	3.11	3.33
Tang Book Value Per Share	11.47	11.16	10.57	10.00	9.54	9.11	8.45	7.94
Dividends Per Share	0.300	0.290	0.250	0.215	0.180	0.100	0.040	0.092
Dividend Payout %	30.00	27.62	25.25	22.16	20.22	11.49	9.09	...
Income Statement								
Interest Income	683,000	2,622,000	2,554,000	2,620,000	2,705,000	2,889,000	3,408,000	3,795,000
Interest Expense	79,000	274,000	261,000	295,000	441,000	622,000	897,000	1,415,000
Net Interest Income	604,000	2,348,000	2,293,000	2,325,000	2,264,000	2,267,000	2,511,000	2,380,000
Provision for Losses	89,000	166,000	59,000	130,000	229,000	(60,000)	638,000	3,159,000
Non-Interest Income	431,000	1,880,000	1,797,000	1,766,000	1,967,000	1,808,000	1,954,000	2,035,000
Non-Interest Expense	703,000	2,840,000	2,759,000	2,820,000	2,907,000	2,790,000	3,034,000	3,554,000
Income Before Taxes	243,000	1,222,000	1,272,000	1,141,000	1,095,000	1,345,000	793,000	(2,298,000)
Income Taxes	56,000	303,000	326,000	271,000	239,000	369,000	186,000	(1,035,000)
Net Income	188,000	916,000	900,000	910,000	858,000	920,000	554,000	(1,335,000)
Average Shares	835,060	844,489	878,199	912,571	943,259	935,801	878,153	697,155
Balance Sheet								
Net Loans & Leases	60,296,000	59,719,000	57,321,000	54,220,000	52,533,000	49,299,000	48,970,000	56,679,000
Total Assets	98,402,000	95,133,000	93,821,000	92,934,000	89,236,000	88,785,000	91,843,000	93,287,000
Total Deposits	73,382,000	71,046,000	71,998,000	69,262,000	65,993,000	61,956,000	60,610,000	65,571,000
Total Liabilities	87,336,000	84,387,000	83,291,000	82,631,000	78,965,000	78,880,000	80,726,000	82,624,000
Stockholders' Equity	11,066,000	10,746,000	10,530,000	10,303,000	10,271,000	9,905,000	11,117,000	10,663,000
Shares Outstanding	842,289	835,751	859,403	890,724	925,768	953,007	880,607	878,534
Statistical Record								
Return on Assets %	0.90	0.97	0.96	1.00	0.96	1.02	0.60	N.M.
Return on Equity %	8.04	8.61	8.64	8.85	8.48	8.75	5.09	N.M.
Net Interest Margin %	88.43	89.55	89.78	88.74	83.70	78.47	73.68	62.71
Efficiency Ratio %	63.11	63.08	63.41	64.30	62.22	59.40	56.58	60.96
Loans to Deposits	0.82	0.84	0.80	0.78	0.80	0.80	0.81	0.86
Price Range	15.65-10.00	15.65-12.16	14.51-12.14	13.46-8.42	9.04-6.89	9.71-5.71	9.19-5.55	9.23-4.60
P/E Ratio	15.65-10.00	14.90-11.58	14.66-12.26	13.88-8.68	10.16-7.74	11.16-6.56	20.89-12.61	...
Average Yield %	2.25	2.08	1.85	1.94	2.22	1.27	0.51	1.45

Address: 127 Public Square, Cleveland, OH 44114-1306	Web Site: www.key.com	Auditors: Ernst & Young LLP
Telephone: 216-689-3000	Officers: Beth E. Mooney - Chairman, Vice-Chairman, President, Chief Executive Officer, Chief Operating Officer Paul N. Harris - Executive Vice President, Secretary, General Counsel	Investor Contact: 216-689-3000 Transfer Agents: Computershare Investor Services LLC, Providence, RI

KILROY REALTY CORP

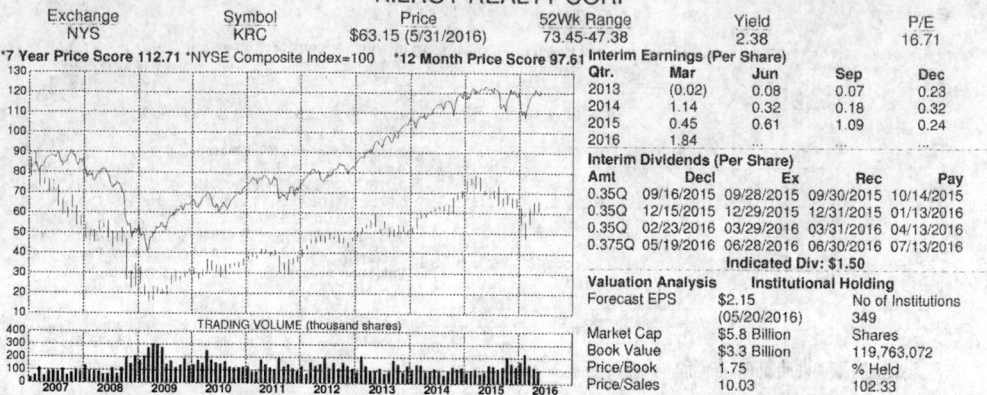

Exchange	Symbol	Price	52Wk Range	Yield	P/E
NYS	KRC	$63.15 (5/31/2016)	73.45-47.38	2.38	16.71

*7 Year Price Score 112.71 *NYSE Composite Index=100 *12 Month Price Score 97.61

Interim Earnings (Per Share)

Qtr.	Mar	Jun	Sep	Dec
2013	(0.02)	0.08	0.07	0.23
2014	1.14	0.32	0.18	0.32
2015	0.45	0.61	1.09	0.24
2016	1.84			

Interim Dividends (Per Share)

Amt	Decl	Ex	Rec	Pay
0.35Q	09/16/2015	09/28/2015	09/30/2015	10/14/2015
0.35Q	12/15/2015	12/29/2015	12/31/2015	01/13/2016
0.35Q	02/23/2016	03/29/2016	03/31/2016	04/13/2016
0.375Q	05/19/2016	06/28/2016	06/30/2016	07/13/2016

Indicated Div: $1.50

Valuation Analysis / **Institutional Holding**

Forecast EPS	$2.15 (05/20/2016)	No of Institutions 349
Market Cap	$5.8 Billion	Shares 119,763,072
Book Value	$3.3 Billion	% Held
Price/Book	1.75	102.33
Price/Sales	10.03	

Business Summary: REITs (MIC: 5.3.1 SIC: 6798 NAIC: 525930)

Kilroy Realty is a real estate investment trust, which owns, develops, acquires and manages real estate assets, consisting primarily of Class A real estate properties in the coastal regions of Los Angeles, Orange County, San Diego County, the San Francisco Bay Area and greater Seattle. Co. owns its interests in all of its properties through Kilroy Realty, L.P. (the Operating Partnership) and Kilroy Realty Finance Partnership, L.P. and generally conducts substantially all of its operations through the Operating Partnership. As of Dec 31 2015, Co. had a stabilized portfolio of 101 office properties.

Recent Developments: For the quarter ended Mar 31 2016, net income increased 304.8% to US$178.1 million from US$44.0 million in the year-earlier quarter. Revenues were US$145.4 million, down 0.4% from US$146.1 million the year before.

Prospects: Our evaluation of Kilroy Realty Corp. as of June 19, 2016 is the result of our systematic analysis on three basic characteristics: earnings strength, relative valuation, and recent stock price movement. The company has generated a negative trend in earnings per share over the past 5 quarters. Because the company lacks sufficient analyst estimate data, we place greater weight on the historical EPS trend as the measure of earnings strength. Based on operating earnings yield, the company is overvalued when compared to all of the companies in our coverage universe. Share price changes over the past year indicates that KRC will perform in line with the market over the near term.

Financial Data

(US$ in Thousands)	3 Mos	12/31/2015	12/31/2014	12/31/2013	12/31/2012	12/31/2011	12/31/2010	12/31/2009
Earnings Per Share	3.78	2.42	1.95	0.36	2.56	0.87	0.07	0.53
Cash Flow Per Share	3.20	3.03	2.95	3.11	2.59	2.44	2.42	3.23
Tang Book Value Per Share	34.00	32.28	28.68	27.62	26.66	21.18	19.84	18.70
Dividends Per Share	1.400	1.400	1.400	1.400	1.400	1.400	1.400	1.630
Dividend Payout %	37.04	57.85	71.79	388.89	54.69	160.92	2,000.00	307.55
Income Statement								
Total Revenue	145,446	581,275	521,725	465,098	404,912	367,131	301,980	279,434
EBITDA	45,278	455,543	280,123	235,372	209,613	199,897	164,214	154,573
Depn & Amortn	1,597	159,500	153,800	145,300	125,900	106,000	86,300	74,000
Income Before Taxes	32,123	238,604	59,313	15,837	5,447	5,059	18,937	35,754
Net Income	174,308	234,081	183,548	43,880	270,914	66,015	19,708	36,990
Average Shares	92,734	90,395	84,967	79,108	69,639	56,717	49,513	38,732
Balance Sheet								
Current Assets	522,435	270,943	274,582	233,031	396,317	120,363	116,513	103,701
Total Assets	6,204,110	5,939,469	5,633,736	5,111,028	4,616,084	3,446,795	2,816,565	2,084,281
Current Liabilities	481,019	281,315	258,729	229,957	183,658	104,405	88,910	69,669
Long-Term Obligations	2,298,393	2,238,508	2,469,413	2,204,938	2,040,935	1,821,286	1,427,776	972,016
Total Liabilities	2,875,802	2,768,503	2,967,526	2,649,716	2,426,454	2,079,440	1,656,576	1,155,695
Stockholders' Equity	3,328,308	3,170,966	2,666,210	2,461,312	2,189,630	1,367,355	1,159,989	928,586
Shares Outstanding	92,229	92,258	86,259	82,153	74,926	58,819	52,349	43,148
Statistical Record								
Return on Assets %	6.12	4.05	3.42	0.90	6.70	2.11	0.80	1.77
Return on Equity %	11.92	8.02	7.16	1.89	15.19	5.22	1.89	4.46
EBITDA Margin %	31.13	78.37	53.69	50.61	51.77	54.45	54.38	55.32
Net Margin %	119.84	40.27	35.18	9.43	66.91	17.98	6.53	13.24
Asset Turnover	0.10	0.10	0.10	0.10	0.10	0.12	0.12	0.13
Current Ratio	1.09	0.96	1.06	1.01	2.16	1.15	1.31	1.49
Debt to Equity	0.69	0.71	0.93	0.90	0.93	1.33	1.23	1.05
Price Range	77.92-47.38	78.86-62.83	71.10-50.18	59.58-47.37	49.88-37.92	41.94-29.25	36.72-26.75	33.46-15.40
P/E Ratio	20.61-12.53	32.59-25.96	36.46-25.73	165.50-131.58	19.48-14.81	48.21-33.62	524.57-382.14	63.13-29.06
Average Yield %	2.14	2.00	2.29	2.69	3.05	3.75	4.34	6.72

Address: 12200 W. Olympic Boulevard, Suite 200, Los Angeles, CA 90064 Telephone: 310-481-8400	Web Site: www.kilroyrealty.com Officers: John B. Kilroy - Chairman, President, Chief Executive Officer Justin William Smart - Executive Vice President	Auditors: Deloitte & Touche LLP Investor Contact: 310-481-8400 Transfer Agents: Computershare Trust Company, N.A., Canton, MA

KIMBERLY-CLARK CORP.

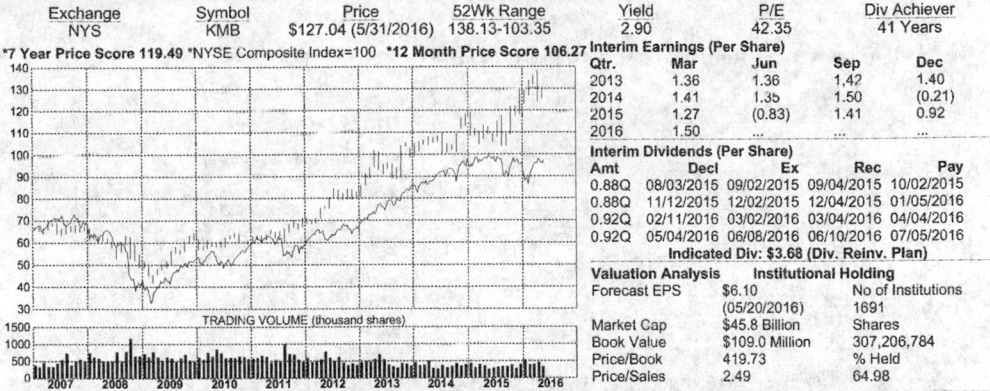

Exchange	Symbol	Price	52Wk Range	Yield	P/E	Div Achiever
NYS	KMB	$127.04 (5/31/2016)	138.13-103.35	2.90	42.35	41 Years

*7 Year Price Score 119.49 *NYSE Composite Index=100 *12 Month Price Score 106.27

Interim Earnings (Per Share)

Qtr.	Mar	Jun	Sep	Dec
2013	1.36	1.36	1.42	1.40
2014	1.41	1.35	1.50	(0.21)
2015	1.27	(0.83)	1.41	0.92
2016	1.50	...	...	...

Interim Dividends (Per Share)

Amt	Decl	Ex	Rec	Pay
0.88Q	08/03/2015	09/02/2015	09/04/2015	10/02/2015
0.88Q	11/12/2015	12/02/2015	12/04/2015	01/05/2016
0.92Q	02/11/2016	03/02/2016	03/04/2016	04/04/2016
0.92Q	05/04/2016	06/08/2016	06/10/2016	07/05/2016

Indicated Div: $3.68 (Div. Reinv. Plan)

Valuation Analysis / **Institutional Holding**

Forecast EPS	$6.10	
	(05/20/2016)	No of Institutions 1691
Market Cap	$45.8 Billion	Shares
Book Value	$109.0 Million	307,206,784
Price/Book	419.73	% Held
Price/Sales	2.49	64.98

Business Summary: Household & Personal Products (MIC: 1.7.1 SIC: 2679 NAIC: 322299)

Kimberly-Clark is principally engaged in the manufacturing and marketing of a range of products primarily made from natural or synthetic fibers using technologies in fibers, nonwovens and absorbency. Co. is organized into three operating segments: personal care brands, which provides disposable diapers, training and youth pants, swimpants, baby wipes, feminine and incontinence care products, and other related products; consumer tissue, which provides facial and bathroom tissue, paper towels, napkins and related products; and K-C professional, which provides wipers, tissue, towels, apparel, soaps and sanitizers.

Recent Developments: For the quarter ended Mar 31 2016, net income increased 15.2% to US$560.0 million from US$486.0 million in the year-earlier quarter. Revenues were US$4.48 billion, down 4.6% from US$4.69 billion the year before. Operating income was US$804.0 million versus US$748.0 million in the prior-year quarter, an increase of 7.5%. Direct operating expenses declined 6.4% to US$2.84 billion from US$3.03 billion in the comparable period the year before. Indirect operating expenses decreased 8.3% to US$835.0 million from US$911.0 million in the equivalent prior-year period.

Prospects: Our evaluation of Kimberly-Clark Corp. as of June 19, 2016 is the result of our systematic analysis on three basic characteristics: earnings strength, relative valuation, and recent stock price movement. The company has enjoyed a very positive trend in earnings per share over the past 5 quarters and while recent estimates for the company have remained steady, KMB has posted better than expected results. Based on operating earnings yield, the company is about fairly valued when compared to all of the companies in our coverage universe. Share price changes over the past year indicates that KMB will perform very well over the near term.

Financial Data
(US$ in Thousands)

	3 Mos	12/31/2015	12/31/2014	12/31/2013	12/31/2012	12/31/2011	12/31/2010	12/31/2009
Earnings Per Share	3.00	2.77	4.04	5.53	4.42	3.99	4.45	4.52
Cash Flow Per Share	7.87	6.34	7.60	7.92	8.34	5.78	6.65	8.37
Tang Book Value Per Share	N.M.	...	N.M.	3.95	5.01	5.54	6.80	7.63
Dividends Per Share	3.560	3.520	3.360	3.240	2.960	2.800	2.640	2.400
Dividend Payout %	118.67	127.08	83.17	58.59	66.97	70.18	59.33	53.10
Income Statement								
Total Revenue	4,476,000	18,591,000	19,724,000	21,152,000	21,063,000	20,846,000	19,746,000	19,115,000
EBITDA	976,000	2,359,000	3,383,000	3,247,000	2,715,000	2,466,000	2,798,000	2,843,000
Depn & Amortn	172,000	746,000	862,000	39,000	29,000	24,000	25,000	18,000
Income Before Taxes	732,000	1,335,000	2,255,000	2,945,000	2,420,000	2,183,000	2,550,000	2,576,000
Income Taxes	207,000	418,000	856,000	929,000	768,000	660,000	788,000	746,000
Net Income	545,000	1,013,000	1,526,000	2,142,000	1,750,000	1,591,000	1,843,000	1,884,000
Average Shares	363,400	366,300	377,400	387,300	396,100	398,600	414,400	416,800
Balance Sheet								
Current Assets	5,151,000	5,426,000	5,559,000	6,550,000	6,589,000	6,283,000	6,328,000	5,864,000
Total Assets	14,820,000	14,842,000	15,526,000	18,919,000	19,873,000	19,373,000	19,864,000	19,209,000
Current Liabilities	5,391,000	6,349,000	6,226,000	5,848,000	6,091,000	5,397,000	5,338,000	4,923,000
Long-Term Obligations	6,904,000	6,106,000	5,630,000	5,386,000	5,070,000	5,426,000	5,120,000	4,792,000
Total Liabilities	14,711,000	14,952,000	14,725,000	13,991,000	14,339,000	13,577,000	13,406,000	12,751,000
Stockholders' Equity	109,000	(110,000)	801,000	4,928,000	5,534,000	5,796,000	6,458,000	6,458,000
Shares Outstanding	360,127	360,900	365,300	380,800	389,300	395,700	406,856	417,000
Statistical Record								
Return on Assets %	7.30	6.67	8.86	11.04	8.89	8.11	9.43	10.10
Return on Equity %	721.85	293.20	53.27	40.95	30.81	25.97	28.54	33.21
EBITDA Margin %	21.81	12.69	17.15	15.35	12.89	11.83	14.17	14.87
Net Margin %	12.18	5.45	7.74	10.13	8.31	7.63	9.33	9.86
Asset Turnover	1.23	1.22	1.15	1.09	1.07	1.06	1.01	1.02
Current Ratio	0.96	0.85	0.89	1.12	1.08	1.16	1.19	1.19
Debt to Equity	63.34	...	7.03	1.09	0.92	0.94	0.79	0.74
Price Range	136.01-103.35	129.54-103.35	118.28-98.99	105.15-80.54	84.28-68.18	70.93-59.97	64.13-56.42	64.04-41.61
P/E Ratio	45.34-34.45	46.77-37.31	29.28-24.50	19.02-14.56	19.07-15.42	17.78-15.03	14.41-12.68	14.17-9.21
Average Yield %	3.04	3.13	3.16	3.45	3.85	4.34	4.39	4.54

Address: P.O. Box 619100, Dallas, TX 75261-9100 **Telephone:** 972-281-1200	**Web Site:** www.kimberly-clark.com **Officers:** Thomas J. Falk - Chairman, President, Chief Executive Officer Mark A. Buthman - Executive Vice President, Senior Vice President, Chief Financial Officer	**Auditors:** Deloitte & Touche LLP **Investor Contact:** 972-281-1440 **Transfer Agents:** ComputerShare Investor Services, Providence, RI

KIMCO REALTY CORP.

Exchange	Symbol	Price	52Wk Range	Yield	P/E
NYS	KIM	$28.18 (5/31/2016)	29.73-22.26	3.62	17.72

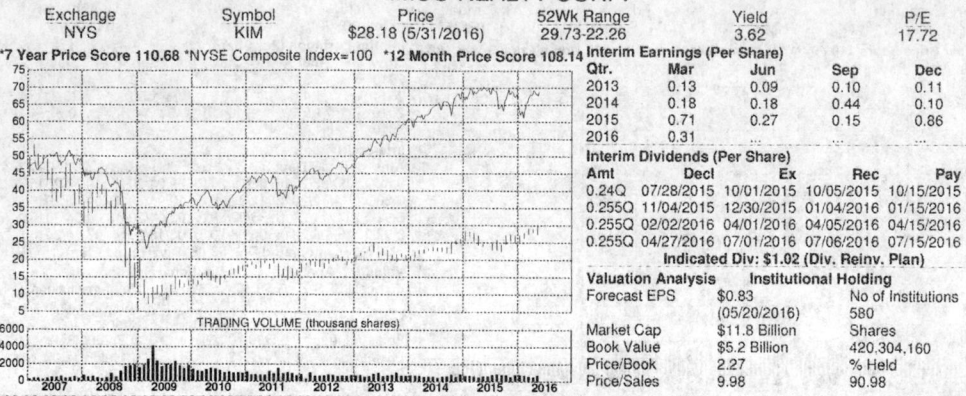

*7 Year Price Score 110.68 *NYSE Composite Index=100 ***12 Month Price Score 108.14**

Interim Earnings (Per Share)

Qtr.	Mar	Jun	Sep	Dec
2013	0.13	0.09	0.10	0.11
2014	0.18	0.18	0.44	0.10
2015	0.71	0.27	0.15	0.86
2016	0.31	...	...	...

Interim Dividends (Per Share)

Amt	Decl	Ex	Rec	Pay
0.24Q	07/28/2015	10/01/2015	10/05/2015	10/15/2015
0.255Q	11/04/2015	12/30/2015	01/04/2016	01/15/2016
0.255Q	02/02/2016	04/01/2016	04/05/2016	04/15/2016
0.255Q	04/27/2016	07/01/2016	07/06/2016	07/15/2016

Indicated Div: $1.02 (Div. Reinv. Plan)

Valuation Analysis		Institutional Holding	
Forecast EPS	$0.83	No of Institutions	580
	(05/20/2016)		
Market Cap	$11.8 Billion	Shares	420,304,160
Book Value	$5.2 Billion	% Held	90.98
Price/Book	2.27		
Price/Sales	9.98		

Business Summary: REITs (MIC: 5.3.1 SIC: 6798 NAIC: 525930)

Kimco Realty is a self-administered real estate investment trust. Co. is the owner and operator of open-air shopping centers. As of Dec 31 2015, Co. had interests in 605 shopping center properties located in 38 states, Puerto Rico and Canada. In addition, Co. had 446 other property interests, primarily through Co.'s preferred equity investments and other real estate investments. Co.'s ownership interests in real estate consist of its consolidated portfolio and portfolios where it owns an economic interest, such as properties in Co.'s investment real estate management programs, where Co. partners with institutional investors and also retains management.

Recent Developments: For the quarter ended Mar 31 2016, income from continuing operations decreased 58.9% to US$115.3 million from US$280.8 million in the year-earlier quarter. Net income decreased 54.5% to US$142.2 million from US$312.7 million in the year-earlier quarter. Revenues were US$297.2 million, up 4.8% from US$283.5 million the year before. Revenues from property income rose 6.4% to US$293.1 million from US$275.5 million in the corresponding quarter a year earlier.

Prospects: Our evaluation of Kimco Realty Corp. as of June 19, 2016 is the result of our systematic analysis on three basic characteristics: earnings strength, relative valuation, and recent stock price movement. The company has suffered a very negative trend in earnings per share over the past 5 quarters. Because the company lacks sufficient analyst estimate data, we place greater weight on the historical EPS trend as the measure of earnings strength. Based on operating earnings yield, the company is about fairly valued when compared to all of the companies in our coverage universe. Share price changes over the past year indicates that KIM will perform well over the near term.

Financial Data

(US$ in Thousands)	3 Mos	12/31/2015	12/31/2014	12/31/2013	12/31/2012	12/31/2011	12/31/2010	12/31/2009
Earnings Per Share	1.59	2.00	0.89	0.43	0.42	0.27	0.22	(0.15)
Cash Flow Per Share	1.00	1.20	1.54	1.40	1.18	1.10	1.18	1.15
Tang Book Value Per Share	12.39	12.21	11.59	11.31	11.69	11.51	12.14	11.96
Dividends Per Share	0.975	0.975	0.915	0.855	0.780	0.730	0.660	0.720
Dividend Payout %	61.32	48.75	102.81	198.84	185.71	270.37	300.00	...
Income Statement								
Total Revenue	297,202	1,166,769	993,897	946,673	922,304	873,694	849,549	786,887
EBITDA	183,945	693,273	577,993	489,434	522,236	540,049	542,367	363,712
Depn & Amortn	84,856	344,527	273,093	257,855	262,742	251,139	247,637	227,776
Income Before Taxes	46,638	168,916	102,107	34,667	34,069	80,441	89,598	(40,845)
Income Taxes	12,112	60,230	22,438	34,520	3,939	19,537	3,415	(36,622)
Net Income	140,713	894,115	424,001	236,281	266,073	169,051	142,868	(3,942)
Average Shares	414,145	412,851	411,038	408,614	406,689	407,669	406,201	350,077
Balance Sheet								
Current Assets	401,721	372,351	449,943	375,860	339,529	296,229	479,681	445,261
Total Assets	11,249,361	11,344,171	10,285,728	9,663,630	9,740,807	9,614,516	9,833,875	10,162,205
Current Liabilities	116,631	4,026,569	3,432,819	3,414,833	3,400,526	3,221,217	3,225,940	3,219,126
Long-Term Obligations	5,162,462	1,614,982	1,428,131	1,035,354	1,003,190	1,130,499	1,076,566	1,434,080
Total Liabilities	6,066,742	6,297,871	5,510,943	5,031,213	4,975,647	4,928,130	4,898,033	5,309,232
Stockholders' Equity	5,182,619	5,046,300	4,774,785	4,632,417	4,765,160	4,686,386	4,935,842	4,852,973
Shares Outstanding	418,281	413,430	411,819	409,731	407,782	406,937	406,423	405,532
Statistical Record								
Return on Assets %	6.30	8.27	4.25	2.44	2.74	1.74	1.43	N.M.
Return on Equity %	14.21	18.21	9.01	5.03	5.61	3.51	2.92	N.M.
EBITDA Margin %	61.89	59.42	58.15	51.70	56.62	61.81	63.84	46.22
Net Margin %	47.35	76.63	42.66	24.96	28.85	19.35	16.82	N.M.
Asset Turnover	0.10	0.11	0.10	0.10	0.10	0.09	0.08	0.08
Current Ratio	3.44	0.09	0.13	0.11	0.10	0.09	0.15	0.14
Debt to Equity	1.00	0.32	0.30	0.22	0.21	0.24	0.22	0.30
Price Range	29.05-22.26	28.33-22.26	25.91-19.75	25.00-19.25	21.03-16.27	20.30-14.11	18.14-12.59	20.45-6.97
P/E Ratio	18.27-14.00	14.16-11.13	29.11-22.19	58.14-44.77	50.07-38.74	75.19-52.26	82.45-57.23	...
Average Yield %	3.84	3.85	4.00	3.97	4.08	4.17	4.32	6.15

Address: 3333 New Hyde Park Road, New Hyde Park, NY 11042 Telephone: 516-869-9000	Web Site: www.kimcorealty.com Officers: Milton Cooper - Chairman Conor C. Flynn - President, Chief Executive Officer, Executive Vice President, Chief Operating Officer, Chief Investment Officer	Auditors: PricewaterhouseCoopers LLP Investor Contact: 866-831-4297 Transfer Agents: Wells Fargo Shareholder Services, St. Paul, MN

KINDRED HEALTHCARE INC

Exchange	Symbol	Price	52Wk Range	Yield	P/E
NYS	KND	$11.87 (5/31/2016)	22.93-8.25	4.04	15.22

*7 Year Price Score 79.55   *NYSE Composite Index=100   *12 Month Price Score 88.65

TRADING VOLUME (thousand shares)

Interim Earnings (Per Share)

Qtr.	Mar	Jun	Sep	Dec
2013	0.06	0.03	(2.04)	(1.27)
2014	0.15	(0.67)	(0.07)	(0.79)
2015	(1.84)	0.25	(0.17)	0.55
2016	0.15	...	...	...

Interim Dividends (Per Share)

Amt	Decl	Ex	Rec	Pay
0.12Q	08/05/2015	08/17/2015	08/19/2015	09/04/2015
0.12Q	11/04/2015	11/16/2015	11/18/2015	12/11/2015
0.12Q	02/25/2016	03/08/2016	03/10/2016	04/01/2016
0.12Q	05/04/2016	05/16/2016	05/18/2016	06/10/2016

Indicated Div: $0.48

Valuation Analysis — **Institutional Holding**

Forecast EPS	$0.91	No of Institutions
	(05/20/2016)	274
Market Cap	$1.0 Billion	Shares
Book Value	$1.5 Billion	86,539,232
Price/Book	0.67	% Held
Price/Sales	0.14	101.13

Business Summary: Hospitals & Health Care Facilities (MIC: 4.2.1 SIC: 8059 NAIC: 623110)

Kindred Healthcare, via its subsidiaries, operates transitional care (TC) hospitals, a home health, hospice and community care business, inpatient rehabilitation hospitals (IRFs), a contract rehabilitation services business, nursing centers and assisted living facilities across the U.S. At Dec 31 2015, Co.'s hospital division operated 95 TC hospitals in 22 states. Co.'s Kindred at Home division primarily provided services from 604 locations in 40 states. Co.'s Kindred Rehabilitation Services division operated 18 IRFs and 100 hospital-based acute rehabilitation units in 46 states. Co.'s nursing center division operated 90 nursing centers and seven assisted living facilities in 18 states.

Recent Developments: For the quarter ended Mar 31 2016, income from continuing operations was US$25.8 million compared with a loss of US$134.6 million in the year-earlier quarter. Net income amounted to US$25.5 million versus a net loss of US$138.0 million in the year-earlier quarter. Revenues were US$1.84 billion, up 9.7% from US$1.68 billion the year before. Indirect operating expenses decreased 2.1% to US$1.80 billion from US$1.84 billion in the equivalent prior-year period.

Prospects: Our evaluation of Kindred Healthcare Inc. as of June 19, 2016 is the result of our systematic analysis on three basic characteristics: earnings strength, relative valuation, and recent stock price movement. The company has suffered a very negative trend in earnings per share over the past 5 quarters and while recent estimates for the company have been mixed, KND has posted better than expected results. Based on operating earnings yield, the company is undervalued when compared to all of the companies in our coverage universe. Share price changes over the past year indicates that KND will perform poorly over the near term.

Financial Data
(US$ in Thousands)

	3 Mos	12/31/2015	12/31/2014	12/31/2013	12/31/2012	12/31/2011	12/31/2010	12/31/2009
Earnings Per Share	0.78	(1.11)	(1.36)	(3.23)	(0.78)	(1.16)	1.43	1.02
Cash Flow Per Share	1.96	1.93	1.80	3.82	5.07	3.32	5.42	6.10
Tang Book Value Per Share	N.M.	N.M.	0.62	N.M.	N.M.	N.M.	17.63	20.99
Dividends Per Share	0.480	0.480	0.480	0.240	...	...	...	...
Dividend Payout %	61.54	...	...	...	...	...	...	...
Income Statement								
Total Revenue	1,837,971	7,054,907	5,027,599	4,900,510	6,181,291	5,521,763	4,359,697	4,270,007
EBITDA	103,143	265,135	308,021	185,233	293,737	169,744	217,244	234,407
Depn & Amortn	7,971	127,400	133,900	135,200	179,100	152,200	120,300	124,800
Income Before Taxes	37,673	(94,660)	5,358	(58,016)	6,741	(63,375)	89,854	101,727
Income Taxes	11,836	(42,797)	462	(13,204)	39,112	(7,104)	33,708	39,115
Net Income	13,001	(93,384)	(79,837)	(168,492)	(40,367)	(53,481)	56,491	40,111
Average Shares	87,249	84,558	58,634	52,249	51,659	46,280	38,954	38,502
Balance Sheet								
Current Assets	1,579,791	1,500,899	1,390,062	1,196,728	1,273,766	1,233,282	836,038	843,651
Total Assets	6,611,304	6,518,936	5,652,964	3,945,869	4,237,946	4,138,493	2,337,415	2,022,224
Current Liabilities	966,466	1,111,212	857,263	792,421	835,331	848,923	621,384	602,619
Long-Term Obligations	3,358,297	3,137,025	2,852,531	1,579,391	1,648,706	1,531,882	365,556	147,647
Total Liabilities	5,109,960	5,019,082	4,211,097	2,863,212	2,981,787	2,849,572	1,305,656	1,055,630
Stockholders' Equity	1,501,344	1,499,854	1,441,867	1,082,657	1,256,159	1,288,921	1,031,759	966,594
Shares Outstanding	85,171	83,792	69,977	54,165	53,280	52,116	39,495	39,104
Statistical Record								
Return on Assets %	1.01	N.M.	N.M.	N.M.	N.M.	N.M.	2.59	1.91
Return on Equity %	4.49	N.M.	N.M.	N.M.	N.M.	N.M.	5.65	4.26
EBITDA Margin %	5.61	3.76	6.13	3.78	4.75	3.07	4.98	5.49
Net Margin %	0.71	N.M.	N.M.	N.M.	N.M.	N.M.	1.30	0.94
Asset Turnover	1.09	1.16	1.05	1.20	1.47	1.71	2.00	2.03
Current Ratio	1.63	1.35	1.62	1.51	1.52	1.45	1.35	1.40
Debt to Equity	2.24	2.09	1.98	1.46	1.31	1.19	0.35	0.15
Price Range	24.42-8.25	24.42-11.44	26.66-17.84	19.87-9.76	13.41-7.79	28.55-7.68	19.59-11.61	19.84-10.91
P/E Ratio	31.31-10.58	...	...	...	...	...	13.70-8.12	19.45-10.70
Average Yield %	2.88	2.52	2.21	1.79	...	...	...	...

Address: 680 South Fourth Street, Louisville, KY 40202-2412 Telephone: 502-596-7300	Web Site: www.kindredhealthcare.com Officers: Edward L. Kuntz - Chairman Steven I. Monaghan - Division Officer	Auditors: PricewaterhouseCoopers LLP Investor Contact: 502-596-7734 Transfer Agents: Computershare

413

KINDER MORGAN INC.

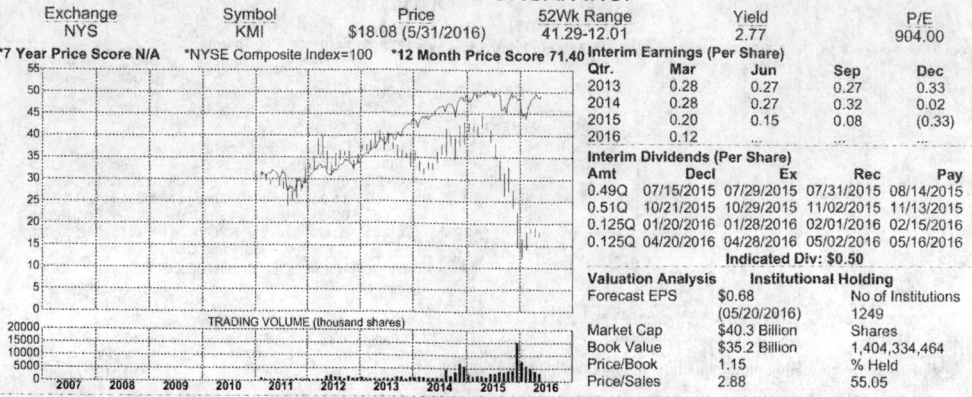

Exchange	Symbol	Price	52Wk Range	Yield	P/E
NYS	KMI	$18.08 (5/31/2016)	41.29-12.01	2.77	904.00

*7 Year Price Score N/A   *NYSE Composite Index=100   *12 Month Price Score 71.40

Interim Earnings (Per Share)

Qtr.	Mar	Jun	Sep	Dec
2013	0.28	0.27	0.27	0.33
2014	0.28	0.27	0.32	0.02
2015	0.20	0.15	0.08	(0.33)
2016	0.12	...	...	...

Interim Dividends (Per Share)

Amt	Decl	Ex	Rec	Pay
0.49Q	07/15/2015	07/29/2015	07/31/2015	08/14/2015
0.51Q	10/21/2015	10/29/2015	11/02/2015	11/13/2015
0.125Q	01/20/2016	01/28/2016	02/01/2016	02/15/2016
0.125Q	04/20/2016	04/28/2016	05/02/2016	05/16/2016

Indicated Div: $0.50

Valuation Analysis

		Institutional Holding	
Forecast EPS	$0.68	No of Institutions	1249
	(05/20/2016)		
Market Cap	$40.3 Billion	Shares	
Book Value	$35.2 Billion		1,404,334,464
Price/Book	1.15	% Held	
Price/Sales	2.88		55.05

Business Summary: Equipment & Services (MIC: 9.1.3 SIC: 4923 NAIC: 221210)

Kinder Morgan is an energy infrastructure company. Co. owns an interest in or operates approximately 84,000 miles of pipelines and approximately 180 terminals. Co.'s pipelines transport natural gas, refined petroleum products, crude oil, condensate, carbon dioxide (CO2) and other products, and its terminals transload and store petroleum products, ethanol and chemicals, and handle such products as coal, petroleum coke and steel. Co. business segments consist of Natural Gas Pipelines, CO2, Terminals, Products Pipelines, Kinder Morgan Canada and Other. As of Dec 31 2015, Co. had total proved reserves of 48.4 million barrels of crude oil and 2.8 million barrels of natural gas liquids.

Recent Developments: For the quarter ended Mar 31 2016, net income decreased 25.1% to US$314.0 million from US$419.0 million in the year-earlier quarter. Revenues were US$3.20 billion, down 11.2% from US$3.60 billion the year before. Operating income was US$816.0 million versus US$1.08 billion in the prior-year quarter, a decrease of 24.3%. Direct operating expenses declined 18.7% to US$1.30 billion from US$1.60 billion in the comparable period the year before. Indirect operating expenses increased 17.2% to US$1.08 billion from US$924.0 million in the equivalent prior-year period.

Prospects: Our evaluation of Kinder Morgan, Inc. as of June 19, 2016 is the result of our systematic analysis on three basic characteristics: earnings strength, relative valuation, and recent stock price movement. The company has enjoyed a very positive trend in earnings per share over the past 5 quarters and while recent estimates for the company have been mixed, KMI has posted better than expected results. Based on operating earnings yield, the company is about fairly valued when compared to all of the companies in our coverage universe. Share price changes over the past year indicates that KMI will perform very poorly over the near term.

Financial Data
(US$ in Thousands)

	3 Mos	12/31/2015	12/31/2014	12/31/2013	12/31/2012	12/31/2011	12/31/2010	12/31/2009
Earnings Per Share	0.02	0.10	0.89	1.15	0.35	0.74	...	...
Cash Flow Per Share	2.29	2.42	3.93	3.92	3.07	3.35	...	...
Tang Book Value Per Share	3.54	3.49	3.35	N.M.	N.M.	N.M.	...	...
Dividends Per Share	1.605	1.930	1.700	1.560	1.340	0.740	...	...
Dividend Payout %	8,025.00	1,930.00	191.01	135.65	382.86	100.00	...	...
Income Statement								
Total Revenue	3,195,000	14,403,000	16,226,000	14,070,000	9,973,000	8,264,900	8,190,600	7,185,200
EBITDA	829,000	4,468,000	6,345,000	5,891,000	3,913,000	2,571,600	2,324,500	2,498,400
Depn & Amortn	14,000	2,059,000	1,862,000	1,663,000	1,324,000	1,022,200	1,025,500	1,047,500
Income Before Taxes	374,000	358,000	2,685,000	2,553,000	1,190,000	869,100	654,100	877,500
Income Taxes	154,000	564,000	648,000	742,000	139,000	362,800	167,600	326,600
Net Income	315,000	253,000	1,026,000	1,193,000	315,000	594,400	(41,300)	495,000
Average Shares	2,229,000	2,193,000	1,137,000	1,036,000	908,000	707,600	...	...
Balance Sheet								
Current Assets	2,481,000	2,824,000	3,752,000	3,868,000	3,674,000	1,663,300	1,786,900	1,380,300
Total Assets	84,229,000	84,104,000	83,198,000	75,185,000	68,185,000	30,717,000	28,908,100	27,581,000
Current Liabilities	4,396,000	4,065,000	6,362,000	6,075,000	5,209,000	4,529,000	3,644,100	2,319,200
Long-Term Obligations	42,105,000	42,406,000	40,246,000	33,887,000	32,000,000	14,356,400	13,812,900	13,240,700
Total Liabilities	49,049,000	48,985,000	49,122,000	62,092,000	54,320,000	27,396,500	25,469,000	23,410,500
Stockholders' Equity	35,180,000	35,119,000	34,076,000	13,093,000	13,865,000	3,320,500	3,439,100	4,170,500
Shares Outstanding	2,229,233	2,229,224	2,125,147	1,030,677	1,035,668	803,344	...	...
Statistical Record								
Return on Assets %	0.16	0.30	1.30	1.66	0.64	1.99	N.M.	1.87
Return on Equity %	0.40	0.73	4.35	8.85	3.66	17.59	N.M.	11.55
EBITDA Margin %	25.95	31.02	39.10	41.87	39.24	31.11	28.38	34.77
Net Margin %	9.86	1.76	6.32	8.48	3.16	7.19	N.M.	6.89
Asset Turnover	0.16	0.17	0.20	0.20	0.20	0.28	0.29	0.27
Current Ratio	0.56	0.69	0.59	0.64	0.71	0.37	0.49	0.60
Debt to Equity	1.20	1.21	1.18	2.59	2.31	4.32	4.02	3.17
Price Range	44.57-12.01	44.57-14.54	43.01-30.96	41.09-32.58	39.85-30.76	32.17-23.66	...	...
P/E Ratio	N.M.	445.70-145.40	48.33-34.79	35.73-28.33	113.86-87.89	43.47-31.97	...	...
Average Yield %	5.55	5.52	4.70	4.20	3.87	2.60	...	...

Address: 1001 Louisiana Street, Suite 1000, Houston, TX 77002 **Telephone:** 713-369-9000	**Web Site:** www.kindermorgan.com **Officers:** Richard D. Kinder - Executive Chairman, Chairman, Chief Executive Officer Steven J. Kean - President, Chief Executive Officer, Chief Operating Officer, Executive Vice President	**Auditors:** PricewaterhouseCoopers LLP **Investor Contact:** 713-369-9449 **Transfer Agents:** Computershare Investor Services, LLC

KIRBY CORP.

Exchange	Symbol	Price	52Wk Range	Yield	P/E
NYS	KEX	$70.08 (5/31/2016)	80.36-45.77	N/A	18.79

*7 Year Price Score 83.24 ***NYSE Composite Index=100** ***12 Month Price Score 99.18**

Interim Earnings (Per Share)

Qtr.	Mar	Jun	Sep	Dec
2013	1.00	1.11	1.21	1.12
2014	1.09	1.31	1.34	1.19
2015	1.09	1.04	1.04	0.94
2016	0.71	...	...	...

Interim Dividends (Per Share)

No Dividends Paid

Valuation Analysis / Institutional Holding

Forecast EPS	$3.00	No of Institutions
	(05/20/2016)	387
Market Cap	$3.8 Billion	Shares
Book Value	$2.3 Billion	63,413,228
Price/Book	1.63	% Held
Price/Sales	1.87	88.05

Business Summary: Shipping (MIC: 7.4.2 SIC: 4449 NAIC: 483211)

Kirby is a domestic tank barge operator. Co. has two segments: marine transportation, which provides marine transportation services, operating tank barges and towing vessels transporting bulk liquid products throughout the Mississippi River System, Gulf Intracoastal Waterway, coastwise along all three U.S. coasts, and in Alaska and Hawaii; and diesel engine services, which provides services for diesel engines, reduction gears and ancillary products for marine and power generation applications, distributes and services diesel engines, transmissions and pumps, and manufactures oilfield service equipment for land-based oilfield service and oil and gas operator and producer markets.

Recent Developments: For the quarter ended Mar 31 2016, net income decreased 37.3% to US$38.5 million from US$61.4 million in the year-earlier quarter. Revenues were US$458.7 million, down 21.9% from US$587.7 million the year before. Operating income was US$65.4 million versus US$103.1 million in the prior-year quarter, a decrease of 36.6%. Direct operating expenses declined 24.9% to US$288.9 million from US$384.8 million in the comparable period the year before. Indirect operating expenses increased 4.6% to US$104.4 million from US$99.8 million in the equivalent prior-year period.

Prospects: Our evaluation of Kirby Corp. as of June 19, 2016 is the result of our systematic analysis on three basic characteristics: earnings strength, relative valuation, and recent stock price movement. The company has managed to produce a neutral trend in earnings per share over the past 5 quarters and while recent estimates for the company have been mixed, KEX has posted results that fell short of analysts expectations. Based on operating earnings yield, the company is about fairly valued when compared to all of the companies in our coverage universe. Share price changes over the past year indicates that KEX will perform poorly over the near term.

Financial Data
(US$ in Thousands)

	3 Mos	12/31/2015	12/31/2014	12/31/2013	12/31/2012	12/31/2011	12/31/2010	12/31/2009
Earnings Per Share	3.73	4.11	4.93	4.44	3.73	3.33	2.15	2.34
Cash Flow Per Share	9.92	9.53	7.74	10.67	5.86	5.76	4.60	6.01
Tang Book Value Per Share	31.96	31.31	29.24	24.97	19.42	17.20	17.31	15.30
Income Statement								
Total Revenue	458,733	2,147,532	2,566,318	2,242,195	2,112,658	1,850,417	1,109,557	1,082,158
EBITDA	72,928	605,469	672,779	612,260	519,578	447,559	306,480	319,587
Depn & Amortn	7,392	225,470	197,312	176,058	154,943	135,257	106,163	103,823
Income Before Taxes	61,343	361,261	454,006	408,330	340,250	294,400	189,357	204,684
Income Taxes	22,859	133,742	169,782	152,379	127,907	109,255	72,258	78,020
Net Income	38,099	226,684	282,006	253,061	209,438	183,026	116,249	125,941
Average Shares	53,483	54,826	56,867	56,552	55,674	54,413	53,466	53,313
Balance Sheet								
Current Assets	598,007	640,776	803,154	544,006	596,256	529,329	425,915	300,097
Total Assets	4,108,986	4,156,266	4,141,909	3,682,517	3,653,128	2,960,411	1,794,937	1,635,963
Current Liabilities	327,582	361,917	594,027	345,989	355,020	358,800	160,259	137,104
Long-Term Obligations	712,163	778,834	600,000	749,150	1,070,110	763,000	200,006	200,204
Total Liabilities	1,802,588	1,887,455	1,887,873	1,671,831	1,958,160	1,517,886	638,838	583,500
Stockholders' Equity	2,306,398	2,268,811	2,254,036	2,010,686	1,694,968	1,442,525	1,156,099	1,052,463
Shares Outstanding	53,804	53,720	56,870	56,846	56,585	55,744	53,557	53,837
Statistical Record								
Return on Assets %	4.93	5.46	7.21	6.90	6.32	7.70	6.78	7.97
Return on Equity %	9.00	10.02	13.23	13.66	13.31	14.09	10.53	12.97
EBITDA Margin %	15.90	28.19	26.22	27.31	24.59	24.19	27.62	29.53
Net Margin %	8.31	10.56	10.99	11.29	9.91	9.89	10.48	11.64
Asset Turnover	0.49	0.52	0.66	0.61	0.64	0.78	0.65	0.68
Current Ratio	1.83	1.77	1.35	1.57	1.68	1.48	2.66	2.19
Debt to Equity	0.31	0.34	0.27	0.37	0.63	0.53	0.17	0.19
Price Range	83.90-45.77	83.90-50.86	123.25-80.32	99.25-61.89	70.00-45.39	65.99-43.75	45.46-31.35	38.81-19.94
P/E Ratio	22.49-12.27	20.41-12.37	25.00-16.29	22.35-13.94	18.77-12.17	19.82-13.14	21.14-14.58	16.59-8.52

Address: 55 Waugh Drive, Suite 1000, Houston, TX 77007 Telephone: 713-435-1000 Fax: 713-435-1010	Web Site: www.kirbycorp.com Officers: Joseph H. Pyne - Chairman, President, Chief Executive Officer David W. Grzebinski - President, Chief Executive Officer, Chief Operating Officer, Executive Vice President, Chief Financial Officer	Auditors: KPMG LLP Transfer Agents: Computershare Trust Company, N.A., Providence, RI

KNOWLES CORP

Exchange	Symbol	Price	52Wk Range	Yield	P/E
NYS	KN	$14.62 (5/31/2016)	21.97-9.98	N/A	N/A

*7 Year Price Score N/A ***NYSE Composite Index=100** ***12 Month Price Score 86.68**

TRADING VOLUME (thousand shares)

Interim Earnings (Per Share)

Qtr.	Mar	Jun	Sep	Dec
2013	0.14	0.20	0.52	0.38
2014	0.09	(0.93)	(0.17)	(0.01)
2015	(0.19)	(0.19)	(0.17)	(2.15)
2016	(0.33)	...	...	...

Interim Dividends (Per Share)

No Dividends Paid

Valuation Analysis		Institutional Holding	
Forecast EPS	$0.86	No of Institutions	
	(05/09/2016)	312	
Market Cap	$1.3 Billion	Shares	
Book Value	$997.5 Million	104,847,368	
Price/Book	1.30	% Held	
Price/Sales	1.26	N/A	

Business Summary: Electronic Instruments & Related Products (MIC: 6.2.3 SIC: 3651 NAIC: 334310)

Knowles is supplier of micro-acoustic, audio processing and specialty component solutions, serving the mobile consumer electronics, communications, medical, military, aerospace and industrial markets. Co.'s Mobile Consumer Electronics segment designs and manufactures acoustic products, including microphones and audio processing technologies used in mobile handsets, tablets and other consumer electronic devices. Co.'s Specialty Components segment specializes in the design and manufacture of specialized electronic components used in medical and life science applications, as well as solutions and components used in communications infrastructure and other markets.

Recent Developments: For the quarter ended Mar 31 2016, loss from continuing operations was US$12.5 million compared with income of US$5.0 million in the year-earlier quarter. Net loss amounted to US$29.4 million versus a net loss of US$15.8 million in the year-earlier quarter. Revenues were US$185.3 million, down 0.7% from US$186.6 million the year before. Operating loss was US$5.9 million versus an income of US$10.3 million in the prior-year quarter. Direct operating expenses declined 4.5% to US$118.5 million from US$124.1 million in the comparable period the year before. Indirect operating expenses increased 39.3% to US$72.7 million from US$52.2 million in the equivalent prior-year period.

Prospects: Our evaluation of Knowles Corp. as of June 19, 2016 is the result of our systematic analysis on three basic characteristics: earnings strength, relative valuation, and recent stock price movement. The company has produced a positive trend in earnings per share over the past 5 quarters and while recent estimates for the company have been mixed, KN has posted better than expected results. Based on operating earnings yield, the company is overvalued when compared to all of the companies in our coverage universe. Share price changes over the past year indicates that KN will perform very poorly over the near term.

Financial Data

(US$ in Thousands)	3 Mos	12/31/2015	12/31/2014	12/31/2013	12/31/2012	12/31/2011
Earnings Per Share	(2.84)	(2.69)	(1.02)	1.24	0.93	1.16
Cash Flow Per Share	1.03	0.90	1.36	2.05	2.05	2.06
Tang Book Value Per Share	N.M.	N.M.	0.60	7.14	...	...
Income Statement						
Total Revenue	185,300	1,084,600	1,141,300	1,214,803	1,117,992	983,318
EBITDA	(6,200)	(100,500)	103,100	274,446	250,264	230,221
Depn & Amortn	200	135,700	151,600	130,912	114,878	84,773
Income Before Taxes	(10,100)	(248,900)	(55,100)	101,510	78,916	105,556
Income Taxes	2,400	(15,100)	31,900	(4,304)	(181)	7,099
Net Income	(29,400)	(233,800)	(87,000)	105,814	79,097	98,457
Average Shares	88,536	86,802	85,046	85,019	85,019	85,019
Balance Sheet						
Current Assets	313,900	419,300	474,000	501,823	377,280	...
Total Assets	1,636,800	1,697,700	1,998,500	2,170,116	2,051,092	...
Current Liabilities	169,900	226,900	288,600	209,975	233,422	...
Long-Term Obligations	371,700	400,000	385,000	...	528,812	...
Total Liabilities	639,300	690,900	762,300	282,989	862,985	...
Stockholders' Equity	997,500	1,006,800	1,236,200	1,887,127	1,188,107	...
Shares Outstanding	88,583	88,451	85,061	85,027	...	...
Statistical Record						
Return on Assets %	N.M.	N.M.	N.M.	5.01	...	...
Return on Equity %	N.M.	N.M.	N.M.	6.88	...	...
EBITDA Margin %	N.M.	N.M.	9.03	22.59	22.39	23.41
Net Margin %	N.M.	N.M.	N.M.	8.71	7.07	10.01
Asset Turnover	0.58	0.59	0.55	0.58	...	...
Current Ratio	1.85	1.85	1.64	2.39	1.62	...
Debt to Equity	0.37	0.40	0.31	...	0.45	...
Price Range	21.97-9.98	24.67-12.88	33.54-18.13	...	...	...

Address: 1151 Maplewood Drive, Itasca, IL 60143
Telephone: 630-250-5100
Fax: 630-250-0575

Web Site: www.knowles.com
Officers: Jean-Pierre M. Ergas - Chairman Jeffrey S. Niew - President, Chief Executive Officer

Auditors: PricewaterhouseCoopers LLP

KOHL'S CORP.

Exchange	Symbol	Price	52Wk Range	Yield	P/E
NYS	KSS	$36.04 (5/31/2016)	65.73-34.56	5.55	12.34

*7 Year Price Score 80.50   *NYSE Composite Index=100   *12 Month Price Score 83.85

Interim Earnings (Per Share)

Qtr.	Apr	Jul	Oct	Jan
2013-14	0.66	1.04	0.81	1.54
2014-15	0.60	1.13	0.70	1.81
2015-16	0.63	0.66	0.63	1.54
2016-17	0.09	...	...	...

Interim Dividends (Per Share)

Amt	Decl	Ex	Rec	Pay
0.45Q	08/11/2015	09/04/2015	09/09/2015	09/23/2015
0.45Q	11/11/2015	12/07/2015	12/09/2015	12/23/2015
0.50Q	02/24/2016	03/07/2016	03/09/2016	03/23/2016
0.50Q	05/11/2016	06/06/2016	06/08/2016	06/22/2016

Indicated Div: $2.00

Valuation Analysis   **Institutional Holding**

Forecast EPS	$3.87	No of Institutions
	(05/20/2016)	889
Market Cap	$6.7 Billion	Shares
Book Value	$5.3 Billion	212,672,832
Price/Book	1.26	% Held
Price/Sales	0.35	96.13

TRADING VOLUME (thousand shares)

Business Summary: Retail - General Merchandise/Department Stores (MIC: 2 1.1 SIC: 5311 NAIC: 452111)

Kohl's sells private label, exclusive and national brand apparel, footwear, accessories, beauty and home products. Co.'s private brands include Apt. 9, Croft & Barrow, Jumping Beans, SO and Sonoma Goods for Life. Co.'s exclusive brands include Food Network, Jennifer Lopez, Marc Anthony, Rock & Republic and Simply Vera Vera Wang. As of Jan. 31, 2016, Co. operated 1,164 department stores in 49 states and an E-Commerce website (www.Kohls.com). Co.'s website includes merchandise which is available in its stores, as well as merchandise which is available only on-line.

Recent Developments: For the quarter ended Apr 30 2016, net income decreased 86.6% to US$17.0 million from US$127.0 million in the year-earlier quarter. Revenues were US$3.97 billion, down 3.7% from US$4.12 billion the year before. Operating income was US$106.0 million versus US$280.0 million in the prior-year quarter, a decrease of 62.1%. Direct operating expenses declined 1.5% to US$2.56 billion from US$2.60 billion in the comparable period the year before. Indirect operating expenses increased 5.1% to US$1.31 billion from US$1.24 billion in the equivalent prior-year period.

Prospects: Our evaluation of Kohl's Corp. as of June 19, 2016 is the result of our systematic analysis on three basic characteristics: earnings strength, relative valuation, and recent stock price movement. The company has generated a negative trend in earnings per share over the past 5 quarters. However, while recent estimates for the company have been lowered by analysts, KSS has posted results that fell short of analysts expectations. Based on operating earnings yield, the company is undervalued when compared to all of the companies in our coverage universe. Share price changes over the past year indicates that KSS will perform poorly over the near term.

Financial Data

(US$ in Thousands)	3 Mos	01/30/2016	01/31/2015	02/01/2014	02/02/2013	01/28/2012	01/29/2011	01/30/2010
Earnings Per Share	2.92	3.46	4.24	4.05	4.17	4.30	3.65	3.23
Cash Flow Per Share	8.26	7.66	10.00	8.67	5.30	7.96	5.53	7.34
Tang Book Value Per Share	28.63	29.52	29.81	28.33	27.24	26.35	27.18	24.92
Dividends Per Share	1.850	1.800	1.560	1.400	1.280	1.000	...	...
Dividend Payout %	63.36	52.02	36.79	34.57	30.70	23.26	...	...
Income Statement								
Total Revenue	3,972,000	19,204,000	19,023,000	19,031,000	19,279,000	18,804,000	18,391,000	17,178,000
EBITDA	340,000	2,318,000	2,575,000	2,631,000	2,723,000	2,936,000	2,570,000	2,303,000
Depn & Amortn	234,000	934,000	886,000	889,000	833,000	778,000	656,000	591,000
Income Before Taxes	27,000	1,057,000	1,349,000	1,404,000	1,561,000	1,859,000	1,782,000	1,588,000
Income Taxes	10,000	384,000	482,000	515,000	575,000	692,000	668,000	597,000
Net Income	17,000	673,000	867,000	889,000	986,000	1,167,000	1,114,000	991,000
Average Shares	184,000	195,000	204,000	220,000	237,000	271,000	306,000	306,000
Balance Sheet								
Current Assets	4,855,000	5,076,000	5,698,000	5,292,000	4,719,000	4,775,000	5,645,000	5,485,000
Total Assets	13,304,000	13,606,000	14,431,000	14,378,000	13,905,000	14,094,000	13,564,000	13,160,000
Current Liabilities	2,647,000	2,714,000	2,859,000	2,736,000	2,535,000	2,590,000	2,710,000	2,390,000
Long-Term Obligations	4,563,000	4,581,000	4,651,000	4,722,000	4,448,000	4,150,000	1,678,000	2,052,000
Total Liabilities	8,007,000	8,115,000	8,440,000	8,400,000	7,857,000	7,586,000	5,462,000	5,307,000
Stockholders' Equity	5,297,000	5,491,000	5,991,000	5,978,000	6,048,000	6,508,000	8,102,000	7,853,000
Shares Outstanding	185,000	186,000	201,000	211,000	222,000	247,000	291,000	307,000
Statistical Record								
Return on Assets %	4.04	4.81	6.04	6.30	6.93	8.46	8.36	8.11
Return on Equity %	9.95	11.75	14.53	14.83	15.45	16.02	14.00	13.62
EBITDA Margin %	8.56	12.07	13.54	13.82	14.12	15.61	13.97	13.41
Net Margin %	0.43	3.50	4.56	4.67	5.11	6.21	6.06	5.77
Asset Turnover	1.37	1.37	1.32	1.35	1.35	1.36	1.38	1.41
Current Ratio	1.83	1.87	1.99	1.93	1.86	1.84	2.08	2.29
Debt to Equity	0.86	0.83	0.78	0.79	0.74	0.64	0.21	0.26
Price Range	74.51-39.69	79.07-42.85	62.50-49.09	58.47-45.21	55.11-41.81	57.00-42.60	58.57-44.27	60.73-33.58
P/E Ratio	25.52-13.59	22.85-12.38	14.74-11.58	14.44-11.16	13.22-10.03	13.26-9.91	16.05-12.13	18.80-10.40
Average Yield %	3.54	3.05	2.78	2.72	2.63	1.95	...	...

Address: N56 W17000 Ridgewood Drive, Menomonee Falls, WI 53051 **Telephone:** 262-703-7000 **Fax:** 262-703-6373	**Web Site:** www.kohls.com **Officers:** Kevin Mansell - Chairman, President, Chief Executive Officer Sona Chawla - Chief Operating Officer	**Auditors:** Ernst & Young LLP **Investor Contact:** 262-703-1440 **Transfer Agents:** Wells Fargo Shareowner Services, St. Paul, MN

KOSMOS ENERGY LTD

Exchange	Symbol	Price	52Wk Range	Yield	P/E
NYS	KOS	$5.74 (5/31/2016)	9.01-3.50	N/A	N/A

*7 Year Price Score N/A   *NYSE Composite Index=100   *12 Month Price Score 91.80

Interim Earnings (Per Share)

Qtr.	Mar	Jun	Sep	Dec
2013	0.05	(0.19)	(0.12)	0.01
2014	0.19	0.15	0.05	0.33
2015	(0.21)	(0.20)	0.15	0.07
2016	(0.15)	...	...	...

Interim Dividends (Per Share)

No Dividends Paid

Valuation Analysis		Institutional Holding	
Forecast EPS	$-0.38	No of Institutions	
	(05/20/2016)	135	
Market Cap	$2.2 Billion	Shares	
Book Value	$1.3 Billion	462,798,336	
Price/Book	1.73	% Held	
Price/Sales	5.51	88.80	

TRADING VOLUME (thousand shares)

Business Summary: Production & Extraction (MIC: 9.1.1 SIC: 1311 NAIC: 211111)

Kosmos Energy is a holding company. Co. is an independent oil and gas exploration and production company focused on areas along the Atlantic Margin. Co.'s assets include existing production and other development projects offshore Ghana, as well as exploration licenses with significant hydrocarbon potential offshore Ireland, Mauritania, Morocco (including Western Sahara), Senegal and Suriname. As of Dec 31 2014, Co. had total net proved reserves of 75.0 million barrels of oil equivalent (MMBoe), comprised of 45.0 MMBoe of proved developed reserves and 31.0 MMBoe of proved undeveloped reserves.

Recent Developments: For the quarter ended Mar 31 2016, net loss amounted to US$59.0 million versus a net loss of US$78.9 million in the year-earlier quarter. Revenues were US$62.1 million, down 53.1% from US$132.6 million the year before. Direct operating expenses declined 8.4% to US$29.4 million from US$32.1 million in the comparable period the year before. Indirect operating expenses decreased 39.0% to US$93.8 million from US$153.7 million in the equivalent prior-year period.

Prospects: Our evaluation of Kosmos Energy Ltd as of June 19, 2016 is the result of our systematic analysis on three basic characteristics: earnings strength, relative valuation, and recent stock price movement. The company has managed to produce a neutral trend in earnings per share over the past 5 quarters. Because the company lacks sufficient analyst estimate data, we place greater weight on the historical EPS trend as the measure of earnings strength. Based on operating earnings yield, the company is overvalued when compared to all of the companies in our coverage universe. Share price changes over the past year indicates that KOS will perform poorly over the near term.

Financial Data

(US$ in Thousands)	3 Mos	12/31/2015	12/31/2014	12/31/2013	12/31/2012	12/31/2011	12/31/2010	12/31/2009
Earnings Per Share	(0.13)	(0.18)	0.72	(0.24)	(0.18)	0.06	...	...
Cash Flow Per Share	1.21	1.15	1.17	1.39	1.00	1.03	...	...
Tang Book Value Per Share	3.31	3.44	3.46	2.56	2.65	2.61	19.09	31.90
Income Statement								
Total Revenue	62,133	471,556	882,738	852,428	672,209	676,780	9,340	10,195
EBITDA	(21,491)	269,245	812,116	326,465	264,963	321,454	(260,998)	(70,100)
Depn & Amortn	29,200	146,600	188,300	213,700	178,600	156,662	2,200	1,900
Income Before Taxes	(61,015)	85,436	578,268	75,954	34,156	99,043	(322,780)	(78,774)
Income Taxes	(2,022)	155,272	298,898	166,998	101,184	76,686	(77,108)	973
Net Income	(58,993)	(69,836)	279,370	(91,044)	(67,028)	22,357	(245,672)	(79,747)
Average Shares	384,435	382,610	386,119	376,819	371,847	354,810	...	...
Balance Sheet								
Current Assets	570,459	734,148	1,010,476	734,961	750,118	1,112,481	559,920	256,728
Total Assets	3,234,819	3,203,050	2,972,766	2,345,826	2,366,123	2,551,934	1,691,535	1,022,057
Current Liabilities	380,765	456,741	448,771	219,324	190,253	339,607	482,057	139,647
Long-Term Obligations	1,013,596	860,878	794,269	900,000	1,000,000	1,110,000	800,000	285,000
Total Liabilities	1,958,697	1,877,537	1,633,807	1,353,491	1,337,217	1,531,208	1,327,440	426,669
Stockholders' Equity	1,276,122	1,325,513	1,338,959	992,335	1,028,906	1,020,726	364,095	595,388
Shares Outstanding	385,157	385,090	386,887	387,574	388,691	390,530	19,069	18,666
Statistical Record								
Return on Assets %	N.M.	N.M.	10.51	N.M.	N.M.	1.05	N.M.	...
Return on Equity %	N.M.	N.M.	23.97	N.M.	N.M.	3.23	N.M.	...
EBITDA Margin %	N.M.	57.10	92.00	38.30	39.42	47.50	N.M.	N.M.
Net Margin %	N.M.	N.M.	31.65	N.M.	N.M.	3.30	N.M.	N.M.
Asset Turnover	0.13	0.15	0.33	0.36	0.27	0.32	0.01	...
Current Ratio	1.50	1.61	2.25	3.35	3.94	3.28	1.16	1.84
Debt to Equity	0.79	0.65	0.59	0.91	0.97	1.09	2.20	0.48
Price Range	9.78-3.50	9.78-4.73	11.23-7.09	13.00-9.75	14.21-9.29	19.24-10.53	...	...
P/E Ratio	...	...	15.60-9.85	...	...	320.67-175.50	...	...

Address: Clarendon House, 2 Church Street, Hamilton, HM 11
Telephone: 441-295-5950

Web Site: www.kosmosenergy.com
Officers: Andrew G. Inglis - Chairman, Chief Executive Officer W. Greg Dunlevy - Executive Vice President, Chief Financial Officer

Auditors: Ernst & Young LLP
Investor Contact: 214-445-9669
Transfer Agents: Computershare Trust Company, N.A., United States

KROGER CO (THE)

Exchange	Symbol	Price	52Wk Range	Yield	P/E
NYS	KR	$35.76 (5/31/2016)	42.64-33.66	1.17	17.36

*7 Year Price Score 165.75 *NYSE Composite Index=100   *12 Month Price Score 95.29

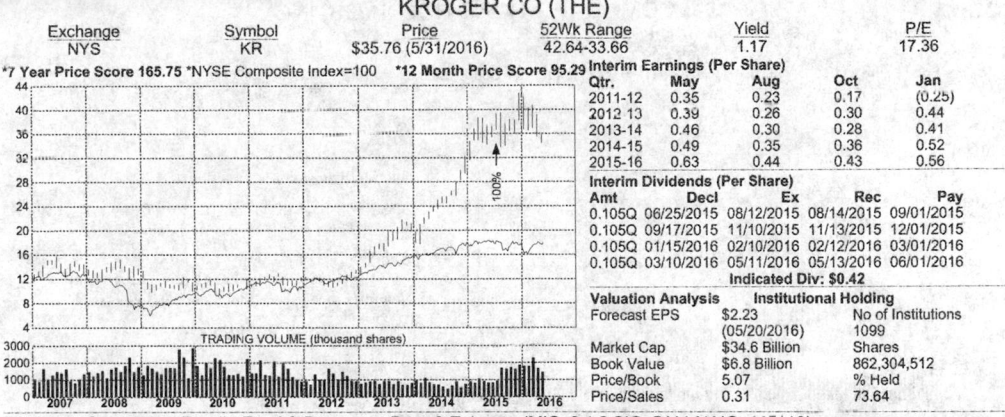

Interim Earnings (Per Share)

Qtr.	May	Aug	Oct	Jan
2011-12	0.35	0.23	0.17	(0.25)
2012-13	0.39	0.26	0.30	0.44
2013-14	0.46	0.30	0.28	0.41
2014-15	0.49	0.35	0.36	0.52
2015-16	0.63	0.44	0.43	0.56

Interim Dividends (Per Share)

Amt	Decl	Ex	Rec	Pay
0.105Q	06/25/2015	08/12/2015	08/14/2015	09/01/2015
0.105Q	09/17/2015	11/10/2015	11/13/2015	12/01/2015
0.105Q	01/15/2016	02/10/2016	02/12/2016	03/01/2016
0.105Q	03/10/2016	05/11/2016	05/13/2016	06/01/2016

Indicated Div: $0.42

Valuation Analysis

		Institutional Holding	
Forecast EPS	$2.23	No of Institutions	
	(05/20/2016)	1099	
Market Cap	$34.6 Billion	Shares	
Book Value	$6.8 Billion	862,304,512	
Price/Book	5.07	% Held	
Price/Sales	0.31	73.64	

Business Summary: Retail - Food & Beverage, Drug & Tobacco (MIC: 2.1.2 SIC: 5411 NAIC: 445110)

Kroger operates retail food and drug stores, multi-department stores, jewelry stores, and convenience stores. As of Jan 30 2016, Co. operated, either directly or through its subsidiaries, 2,778 supermarkets and multi-department stores under a variety of local banner names in 35 states and the District of Columbia. Of these stores, 1,387 have fuel centers. Co. operated through subsidiaries, 784 convenience stores, 323 jewelry stores and an online retailer. The convenience stores provide a limited assortment of staple food items and general merchandise and, in most cases, sell gasoline. Co. also manufactures and processes some of the food for sale in its supermarkets.

Recent Developments: For the year ended Jan 30 2016, net income increased 17.3% to US$2.05 billion from US$1.75 billion in the prior year. Revenues were US$109.83 billion, up 1.3% from US$108.47 billion the year before. Operating income was US$3.58 billion versus US$3.14 billion in the prior year, an increase of 14.0%. Direct operating expenses declined 0.0% to US$85.50 billion from US$85.51 billion in the comparable period the year before. Indirect operating expenses increased 4.8% to US$20.76 billion from US$19.82 billion in the equivalent prior-year period.

Prospects: Our evaluation of Kroger Co. as of June 19, 2016 is the result of our systematic analysis on three basic characteristics: earnings strength, relative valuation, and recent stock price movement. The company has managed to produce a neutral trend in earnings per share over the past 5 quarters and while recent estimates for the company have been mixed, KR has posted better than expected results. Based on operating earnings yield, the company is undervalued when compared to all of the companies in our coverage universe. Share price changes over the past year indicates that KR will perform well over the near term.

Financial Data

(US$ in Thousands)	01/30/2016	01/31/2015	02/01/2014	02/02/2013	01/28/2012	01/29/2011	01/30/2010	01/31/2009
Earnings Per Share	2.06	1.72	1.45	1.39	0.51	0.87	0.06	0.95
Cash Flow Per Share	5.02	4.26	3.30	2.61	2.26	2.66	2.26	2.23
Tang Book Value Per Share	3.15	2.41	2.51	2.89	2.53	3.35	2.86	2.24
Dividends Per Share	0.395	0.340	0.308	0.248	0.215	0.195	0.183	0.172
Dividend Payout %	19.17	19.77	21.21	17.87	42.57	22.41	331.82	18.16
Income Statement								
Total Revenue	109,830,000	108,465,000	98,375,000	96,751,000	90,374,000	82,189,000	76,733,000	76,000,000
EBITDA	5,665,000	5,085,000	4,428,000	4,416,000	2,916,000	3,782,000	2,616,000	3,893,000
Depn & Amortn	2,089,000	1,948,000	1,703,000	1,652,000	1,638,000	1,600,000	1,525,000	1,442,000
Income Before Taxes	3,094,000	2,649,000	2,282,000	2,302,000	843,000	1,734,000	589,000	1,966,000
Income Taxes	1,045,000	902,000	751,000	794,000	247,000	601,000	532,000	717,000
Net Income	2,039,000	1,728,000	1,519,000	1,497,000	602,000	1,116,000	70,000	1,249,000
Average Shares	980,000	994,000	1,040,000	1,074,000	1,186,000	1,276,000	1,300,000	1,318,000
Balance Sheet								
Current Assets	9,892,000	8,911,000	8,830,000	7,959,000	7,325,000	7,621,000	7,450,000	7,206,000
Total Assets	33,897,000	30,556,000	29,281,000	24,652,000	23,476,000	23,505,000	23,093,000	23,211,000
Current Liabilities	12,971,000	11,403,000	10,705,000	11,057,000	9,105,000	8,070,000	7,714,000	7,629,000
Long-Term Obligations	9,709,000	9,771,000	9,653,000	6,145,000	6,850,000	7,304,000	7,477,000	7,505,000
Total Liabilities	27,077,000	25,144,000	23,897,000	20,445,000	19,495,000	18,209,000	18,261,000	18,035,000
Stockholders' Equity	6,820,000	5,412,000	5,384,000	4,207,000	3,981,000	5,296,000	4,832,000	5,176,000
Shares Outstanding	967,000	974,000	1,016,000	1,028,000	1,122,000	1,240,000	1,284,000	1,298,000
Statistical Record								
Return on Assets %	6.34	5.79	5.65	6.12	2.57	4.80	0.30	5.50
Return on Equity %	33.43	32.10	31.76	35.97	13.01	22.10	1.40	24.83
EBITDA Margin %	5.16	4.69	4.50	4.56	3.23	4.60	3.41	5.12
Net Margin %	1.86	1.59	1.54	1.55	0.67	1.36	0.09	1.64
Asset Turnover	3.42	3.64	3.66	3.96	3.86	3.54	3.32	3.35
Current Ratio	0.76	0.78	0.82	0.72	0.80	0.94	0.97	0.94
Debt to Equity	1.42	1.81	1.79	1.46	1.72	1.38	1.55	1.45
Price Range	42.64-33.66	34.67-17.69	21.71-13.84	13.95-10.56	12.91-10.70	11.93-9.58	12.34-9.73	15.18-11.81
P/E Ratio	20.70-16.34	20.16-10.28	14.97-9.54	10.03-7.59	25.32-20.98	13.71-11.01	205.58-162.17	15.97-12.43
Average Yield %	1.05	1.33	1.68	2.07	1.82	1.81	1.69	1.29

Address: 1014 Vine Street, Cincinnati, OH 45202
Telephone: 513-762-4000
Fax: 513-762-1400

Web Site: www.thekrogerco.com
Officers: W. Rodney McMullen - Chairman, Vice-Chairman, President, Chief Executive Officer, Chief Operating Officer J. Michael Schlotman - Executive Vice President, Senior Vice President, Chief Financial Officer, Group Vice President

Auditors: PricewaterhouseCoopers LLP
Investor Contact: 513-762-4366
Transfer Agents: Wells Fargo Shareowner Services, Saint Paul, MN

L-3 COMMUNICATIONS HOLDINGS, INC.

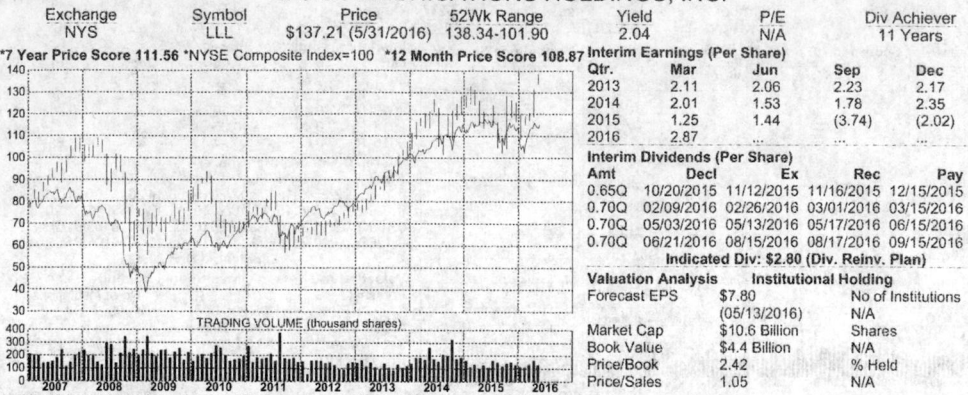

Exchange	Symbol	Price	52Wk Range	Yield	P/E	Div Achiever
NYS	LLL	$137.21 (5/31/2016)	138.34-101.90	2.04	N/A	11 Years

*7 Year Price Score 111.56 *NYSE Composite Index=100 ***12 Month Price Score 108.87**

Interim Earnings (Per Share)

Qtr.	Mar	Jun	Sep	Dec
2013	2.11	2.06	2.23	2.17
2014	2.01	1.53	1.78	2.35
2015	1.25	1.44	(3.74)	(2.02)
2016	2.87	...	...	...

Interim Dividends (Per Share)

Amt	Decl	Ex	Rec	Pay
0.65Q	10/20/2015	11/12/2015	11/16/2015	12/15/2015
0.70Q	02/09/2016	02/26/2016	03/01/2016	03/15/2016
0.70Q	05/03/2016	05/13/2016	05/17/2016	06/15/2016
0.70Q	06/21/2016	08/15/2016	08/17/2016	09/15/2016

Indicated Div: $2.80 (Div. Reinv. Plan)

Valuation Analysis		Institutional Holding	
Forecast EPS	$7.80	No of Institutions	
	(05/13/2016)	N/A	
Market Cap	$10.6 Billion	Shares	
Book Value	$4.4 Billion	N/A	
Price/Book	2.42	% Held	
Price/Sales	1.05	N/A	

Business Summary: Aerospace (MIC: 7.1.1 SIC: 3812 NAIC: 334511)

L-3 Communications Holdings operates through its wholly-owned subsidiary, L-3 Communications Corporation (L-3 Communications). L-3 Communications is a contractor in Intelligence, Surveillance and Reconnaissance systems, aircraft sustainment (including modifications, logistics and maintenance), simulation and training, night vision and image intensification equipment, and security and detection systems. Co. is also a provider of a range of communication and electronic systems and products used on military and commercial platforms. Co. has three reportable segments: Electronic Systems, Aerospace Systems, and Communication Systems.

Recent Developments: For the quarter ended Mar 25 2016, income from continuing operations increased 59.0% to US$167.0 million from US$105.0 million in the year-earlier quarter. Net income increased 111.0% to US$230.0 million from US$109.0 million in the year-earlier quarter. Revenues were US$2.35 billion, down 5.4% from US$2.49 billion the year before. Operating income was US$252.0 million versus US$187.0 million in the prior-year quarter, an increase of 34.8%. Direct operating expenses declined 7.8% to US$2.10 billion from US$2.28 billion in the comparable period the year before. Indirect operating expenses decreased 100.0% to nil from US$22.0 million in the equivalent prior-year period.

Prospects: Our evaluation of L-3 Communications Holdings Inc. as of June 19, 2016 is the result of our systematic analysis on three basic characteristics: earnings strength, relative valuation, and recent stock price movement. The company has managed to produce a neutral trend in earnings per share over the past 5 quarters and while recent estimates for the company have been raised by analysts, LLL has posted better than expected results. Based on operating earnings yield, the company is undervalued when compared to all of the companies in our coverage universe. Share price changes over the past year indicates that LLL will perform in line with the market over the near term.

Financial Data

(US$ in Thousands)	3 Mos	12/31/2015	12/31/2014	12/31/2013	12/31/2012	12/31/2011	12/31/2010	12/31/2009
Earnings Per Share	(1.45)	(2.93)	7.56	8.54	8.30	9.03	8.25	7.61
Cash Flow Per Share	13.71	12.91	13.17	14.13	12.75	14.21	12.78	12.05
Dividends Per Share	2.650	2.600	2.400	2.200	2.000	1.800	1.600	1.400
Dividend Payout %	...	...	31.75	25.76	24.10	19.93	19.39	18.40
Income Statement								
Total Revenue	2,353,000	10,466,000	12,124,000	12,629,000	13,146,000	15,169,000	15,680,000	15,615,000
EBITDA	316,000	640,000	1,257,000	1,424,000	1,508,000	1,736,000	1,896,000	1,804,000
Depn & Amortn	64,000	166,000	172,000	166,000	170,000	173,000	164,000	158,000
Income Before Taxes	215,000	322,000	925,000	1,096,000	1,162,000	1,328,000	1,484,000	1,386,000
Income Taxes	48,000	25,000	248,000	309,000	374,000	360,000	518,000	475,000
Net Income	227,000	(240,000)	664,000	778,000	810,000	956,000	955,000	901,000
Average Shares	79,000	81,900	87,800	91,100	97,600	105,600	115,100	117,400
Balance Sheet								
Current Assets	4,063,000	4,232,000	4,737,000	4,649,000	4,571,000	5,244,000	5,078,000	5,151,000
Total Assets	11,911,000	12,085,000	13,836,000	14,009,000	13,826,000	15,497,000	15,451,000	14,813,000
Current Liabilities	2,679,000	2,879,000	2,525,000	2,523,000	2,597,000	2,690,000	2,733,000	2,482,000
Long-Term Obligations	3,137,000	3,153,000	3,940,000	3,645,000	3,653,000	4,135,000	4,136,000	4,128,000
Total Liabilities	7,533,000	7,730,000	8,551,000	7,986,000	8,363,000	8,862,000	8,687,000	8,246,000
Stockholders' Equity	4,378,000	4,355,000	5,285,000	6,023,000	5,463,000	6,635,000	6,764,000	6,567,000
Shares Outstanding	77,340	78,133	82,040	85,828	90,433	98,979	108,623	115,353
Statistical Record								
Return on Assets %	N.M.	N.M.	4.77	5.59	5.51	6.18	6.31	6.15
Return on Equity %	N.M.	N.M.	11.74	13.55	13.35	14.27	14.33	14.53
EBITDA Margin %	13.43	6.12	10.37	11.28	11.47	11.44	12.09	11.55
Net Margin %	9.65	N.M.	5.48	6.16	6.16	6.30	6.09	5.77
Asset Turnover	0.79	0.81	0.87	0.91	0.89	0.98	1.04	1.07
Current Ratio	1.52	1.47	1.88	1.84	1.76	1.95	1.86	2.08
Debt to Equity	0.72	0.72	0.75	0.61	0.67	0.62	0.61	0.63
Price Range	128.40-101.90	132.87-101.90	128.34-101.39	107.13-74.86	77.91-64.17	84.70-56.53	93.55-63.88	84.88-55.27
P/E Ratio	...	...	16.98-13.41	12.54-8.77	9.39-7.73	9.38-6.26	11.34-7.74	11.15-7.26
Average Yield %	2.27	2.18	2.07	2.48	2.86	2.52	2.24	1.95

Address: 600 Third Avenue, New York, NY 10016 **Telephone:** 212-697-1111	**Web Site:** www.l-3com.com **Officers:** Michael T. Strianese - Chairman, Chief Executive Officer, President Christopher E. Kubasik - President, Chief Operating Officer, Associate/Affiliate Company Officer	**Auditors:** PricewaterhouseCoopers LLP **Investor Contact:** 212-697-1111 **Transfer Agents:** Computershare Trust Company, N.A, Providence, RI

LABORATORY CORPORATION OF AMERICA HOLDINGS

Exchange	Symbol	Price	52Wk Range	Yield	P/E
NYS	LH	$127.95 (5/31/2016)	128.16-100.94	N/A	22.14

*7 Year Price Score 107.37 *NYSE Composite Index=100 *12 Month Price Score 103.45

TRADING VOLUME (thousand shares)

Interim Earnings (Per Share)

Qtr.	Mar	Jun	Sep	Dec
2013	1.50	1.62	1.63	1.44
2014	1.31	1.64	1.59	1.38
2015	0.01	1.64	1.49	1.10
2016	1.55	...	...	...

Interim Dividends (Per Share)

No Dividends Paid

Valuation Analysis **Institutional Holding**

Forecast EPS	$8.80	No of Institutions
	(05/20/2016)	895
Market Cap	$13.1 Billion	Shares
Book Value	$5.2 Billion	113,256,912
Price/Book	2.53	% Held
Price/Sales	1.41	101.76

Business Summary: Diagnostic & Health Related Services (MIC: 4.2.2 SIC: 8071 NAIC: 621511)

Laboratory Corporation of America Holdings is a healthcare diagnostics company, providing clinical laboratory services and end-to-end drug development support. Co. reports its business in two segments: LabCorp Diagnostics (LCD) and Covance Drug Development (CDD). As of Dec 31 2015, Co. had a network of 39 primary laboratories and approximately 1,700 patient service centers, along with a network of branches and STAT laboratories, which performs tests and reports the results to the physician. CDD is engaged in drug development services, and provides a range of drug development solutions, primarily to companies in the pharmaceutical and biotechnology industries.

Recent Developments: For the quarter ended Mar 31 2016, net income increased to US$160.5 million from US$3.4 million in the year-earlier quarter. Revenues were US$2.37 billion, up 32.1% from US$1.79 billion the year before. Operating income was US$301.9 million versus US$132.4 million in the prior-year quarter, an increase of 128.0%. Direct operating expenses rose 36.2% to US$1.59 billion from US$1.17 billion in the comparable period the year before. Indirect operating expenses decreased 3.5% to US$475.4 million from US$492.7 million in the equivalent prior-year period.

Prospects: Our evaluation of Laboratory Corp. of America Holdings as of June 19, 2016 is the result of our systematic analysis on three basic characteristics: earnings strength, relative valuation, and recent stock price movement. The company has managed to produce a neutral trend in earnings per share over the past 5 quarters and while recent estimates for the company have been mixed, LH has posted better than expected results. Based on operating earnings yield, the company is undervalued when compared to all of the companies in our coverage universe. Share price changes over the past year indicates that LH will perform well over the near term.

Financial Data

(US$ in Thousands)	3 Mos	12/31/2015	12/31/2014	12/31/2013	12/31/2012	12/31/2011	12/31/2010	12/31/2009
Earnings Per Share	5.78	4.34	5.91	6.25	5.99	5.11	5.29	4.98
Cash Flow Per Share	11.74	9.94	8.71	9.08	8.77	8.56	8.58	8.03
Income Statement								
Total Revenue	2,368,000	8,680,100	6,011,600	5,808,300	5,671,400	5,542,300	5,003,900	4,694,700
EBITDA	431,500	1,266,900	1,079,500	1,139,900	1,158,400	1,085,600	1,104,100	1,949,000
Depn & Amortn	122,400	269,900	157,600	144,700	141,100	141,500	129,100	130,700
Income Before Taxes	254,600	722,100	812,400	898,700	922,800	856,600	905,000	1,755,400
Income Taxes	95,500	294,100	314,100	340,200	359,400	333,000	344,000	329,000
Net Income	160,200	436,900	511,200	573,800	583,100	519,700	558,200	543,300
Average Shares	103,600	100,600	86,400	91,800	97,400	101,800	105,400	109,100
Balance Sheet								
Current Assets	2,744,900	2,663,000	1,692,700	1,432,100	1,391,800	1,084,800	1,143,800	935,600
Total Assets	14,410,400	14,221,700	7,301,800	6,965,900	6,795,000	6,136,600	6,187,800	4,837,800
Current Liabilities	1,642,700	1,701,500	976,300	735,700	1,028,500	797,400	1,120,500	1,018,400
Long-Term Obligations	5,969,500	5,992,100	2,682,700	2,889,100	2,175,000	2,085,500	1,826,700	977,200
Total Liabilities	9,243,900	9,277,300	4,481,300	4,474,600	4,077,600	3,633,100	3,721,500	2,731,700
Stockholders' Equity	5,166,500	4,944,400	2,820,500	2,491,300	2,717,400	2,503,500	2,466,300	2,106,100
Shares Outstanding	102,100	101,300	84,600	85,700	93,500	97,800	102,400	105,300
Statistical Record								
Return on Assets %	4.17	4.06	7.17	8.34	8.99	8.43	10.13	11.43
Return on Equity %	12.30	11.25	19.25	22.03	22.28	20.91	24.42	28.64
EBITDA Margin %	18.22	14.60	17.96	19.63	20.43	19.59	22.06	41.51
Net Margin %	6.77	5.03	8.50	9.88	10.28	9.38	11.16	11.57
Asset Turnover	0.65	0.81	0.84	0.84	0.87	0.90	0.91	0.99
Current Ratio	1.67	1.57	1.73	1.95	1.35	1.36	1.02	0.92
Debt to Equity	1.16	1.21	0.95	1.16	0.80	0.83	0.74	0.46
Price Range	127.35-100.94	128.18-106.86	109.58-87.86	107.39-86.41	95.25-82.37	100.83-75.99	88.92-70.14	76.45-53.51
P/E Ratio	22.03-17.46	29.53-24.62	18.54-14.87	17.18-13.83	15.90-13.75	19.73-14.87	16.81-13.26	15.35-10.74

Address: 358 South Main Street, Burlington, NC 27215 **Telephone:** 336-229-1127	**Web Site:** www.labcorp.com **Officers:** David P. King - Chairman, President, Chief Executive Officer Glenn A. Eisenberg - Executive Vice President, Chief Financial Officer, Principal Accounting Officer, Treasurer	**Auditors:** PricewaterhouseCoopers LLP **Investor Contact:** 336-436-5076 **Transfer Agents:** American Stock Transfer & Trust Company, Brooklyn, NY

L BRANDS, INC

Exchange	Symbol	Price	52Wk Range	Yield	P/E
NYS	LB	$68.55 (5/31/2016)	100.22-60.62	3.50	17.62

*7 Year Price Score 145.19 *NYSE Composite Index=100 *12 Month Price Score 86.40

Interim Earnings (Per Share)

Qtr.	Apr	Jul	Oct	Jan
2013-14	0.48	0.61	0.31	1.65
2014-15	0.53	0.63	0.44	1.90
2015-16	0.84	0.68	0.55	2.14
2016-17	0.52	...	...	...

Interim Dividends (Per Share)

Amt	Decl	Ex	Rec	Pay
0.50Q	11/06/2015	11/18/2015	11/20/2015	12/04/2015
2.00Q	02/04/2016	02/17/2016	02/19/2016	03/04/2016
0.60Q	02/04/2016	02/17/2016	02/19/2016	03/04/2016
0.60Q	05/20/2016	06/01/2016	06/03/2016	06/17/2016

Indicated Div: $2.40

Valuation Analysis	Institutional Holding	
Forecast EPS	$3.72	No of Institutions
(05/20/2016)		751
Market Cap	$19.7 Billion	Shares
Book Value	N/A	245,569,120
Price/Book	N/A	% Held
Price/Sales	1.61	N/A

Business Summary: Retail - Apparel and Accessories (MIC: 2.1.5 SIC: 5621 NAIC: 448120)

L Brands is a retailer of women's intimate and other apparel, beauty and personal care products and accessories. Co. sells its merchandise through company-owned retail stores in the U.S., Canada and the U.K., which are primarily mall-based, and through its websites and other channels. Co.'s other international operations are primarily through franchise, license and wholesale partners. Co. operates the following retail brands: Victoria's Secret, PINK, Bath & Body Works, La Senza, and Henri Bendel. Co. has three reportable segments: Victoria's Secret, Bath & Body Works and Victoria's Secret and Bath & Body Works International. As of Jan 30 2016, Co. operated a total of 3,005 stores.

Recent Developments: For the quarter ended Apr 30 2016, net income decreased 39.2% to US$152.0 million from US$250.0 million in the year-earlier quarter. Revenues were US$2.61 billion, up 4.1% from US$2.51 billion the year before. Operating income was US$323.0 million versus US$372.0 million in the prior-year quarter, a decrease of 13.2%. Direct operating expenses rose 7.9% to US$1.57 billion from US$1.46 billion in the comparable period the year before. Indirect operating expenses increased 5.3% to US$720.0 million from US$684.0 million in the equivalent prior-year period.

Prospects: Our evaluation of L Brands, Inc. as of June 19, 2016 is the result of our systematic analysis on three basic characteristics: earnings strength, relative valuation, and recent stock price movement. The company has generated a negative trend in earnings per share over the past 5 quarters. However, while recent estimates for the company have been lowered by analysts, LB has posted better than expected results. Based on operating earnings yield, the company is undervalued when compared to all of the companies in our coverage universe. Share price changes over the past year indicates that LB will perform in line with the market over the near term.

Financial Data

(US$ in Thousands)	3 Mos	01/30/2016	01/31/2015	02/01/2014	02/02/2013	01/28/2012	01/29/2011	01/30/2010
Earnings Per Share	3.89	4.22	3.50	3.05	2.54	2.70	2.42	1.37
Cash Flow Per Share	6.64	6.44	6.13	4.32	4.58	4.18	3.99	3.66
Tang Book Value Per Share	...	...	N.M.	...	...	N.M.	N.M.	0.46
Dividends Per Share	4.100	4.000	2.360	1.200	5.000	3.800	4.600	0.600
Dividend Payout %	105.40	94.79	67.43	39.34	196.85	140.74	190.08	43.80
Income Statement								
Total Revenue	2,614,000	12,154,000	11,454,000	10,773,000	10,459,000	10,364,000	9,613,000	8,632,000
EBITDA	440,000	2,725,000	2,398,000	2,166,000	1,983,000	1,860,000	1,846,000	1,263,000
Depn & Amortn	110,000	457,000	438,000	406,000	386,000	387,000	387,000	387,000
Income Before Taxes	233,000	1,934,000	1,636,000	1,446,000	1,281,000	1,227,000	1,251,000	641,000
Income Taxes	81,000	681,000	594,000	543,000	528,000	377,000	446,000	202,000
Net Income	152,000	1,253,000	1,042,000	903,000	753,000	850,000	805,000	448,000
Average Shares	293,000	297,000	298,000	296,000	297,000	314,000	333,000	327,000
Balance Sheet								
Current Assets	2,991,000	4,156,000	3,232,000	3,150,000	2,205,000	2,368,000	2,592,000	3,250,000
Total Assets	7,426,000	8,493,000	7,544,000	7,198,000	6,019,000	6,108,000	6,451,000	7,173,000
Current Liabilities	1,605,000	1,875,000	1,679,000	1,826,000	1,538,000	1,526,000	1,504,000	1,322,000
Long-Term Obligations	5,718,000	5,715,000	4,765,000	4,761,000	4,477,000	3,481,000	2,507,000	2,723,000
Total Liabilities	8,513,000	8,752,000	7,526,000	7,568,000	7,034,000	5,971,000	4,975,000	4,990,000
Stockholders' Equity	(1,087,000)	(259,000)	18,000	(370,000)	(1,015,000)	137,000	1,476,000	2,183,000
Shares Outstanding	288,000	290,000	292,000	291,000	289,000	295,000	321,000	323,000
Statistical Record								
Return on Assets %	16.41	15.67	14.18	13.70	12.22	13.57	11.85	6.35
Return on Equity %	...	...	...	...	...	105.68	44.12	22.15
EBITDA Margin %	16.83	22.42	20.94	20.11	18.96	17.95	19.20	14.63
Net Margin %	5.81	10.31	9.10	8.38	7.20	8.20	8.37	5.19
Asset Turnover	1.74	1.52	1.56	1.63	1.70	1.65	1.42	1.22
Current Ratio	1.86	2.22	1.92	1.73	1.43	1.55	1.72	2.46
Debt to Equity	...	...	264.72	...	...	25.41	1.70	1.25
Price Range	100.22-76.76	100.22-77.87	87.05-50.87	65.60-42.85	52.15-40.83	45.22-29.13	34.90-19.65	20.46-6.26
P/E Ratio	25.76-19.73	23.75-18.45	24.87-14.53	21.51-14.05	20.53-16.07	16.75-10.79	14.42-8.12	14.93-4.57
Average Yield %	4.62	4.41	3.62	2.21	10.58	9.99	17.28	4.31

Address: Three Limited Parkway, Columbus, OH 43230
Telephone: 614-415-7000

Web Site: www.lb.com
Officers: Leslie H. Wexner - Chairman, Chief Executive Officer Stuart B. Burgdoerfer - Executive Vice President, Chief Financial Officer

Auditors: Ernst & Young LLP
Investor Contact: 614-415-6400
Transfer Agents: American Stock Transfer & Trust Company, Brookly, NY

LAREDO PETROLEUM, INC

Exchange	Symbol	Price	52Wk Range	Yield	P/E
NYS	LPI	$12.11 (5/31/2016)	15.05-4.10	N/A	N/A

*7 Year Price Score N/A *NYSE Composite Index=100 *12 Month Price Score 108.51

Interim Earnings (Per Share)

Qtr.	Mar	Jun	Sep	Dec
2013	0.01	0.27	0.09	0.50
2014	0.00	(0.13)	0.58	1.40
2015	0.00	(1.88)	(4.01)	(4.57)
2016	(0.85)	...	...	...

Interim Dividends (Per Share)

No Dividends Paid

Valuation Analysis / Institutional Holding

Forecast EPS	$0.38	No of Institutions
	(05/20/2016)	207
Market Cap	$2.6 Billion	Shares
Book Value	N/A	314,208,544
Price/Book	N/A	% Held
Price/Sales	4.60	N/A

Business Summary: Production & Extraction (MIC: 9.1.1 SIC: 1311 NAIC: 211111)

Laredo Petroleum is a holding company. Through its subsidiaries, Co. is engaged as an independent energy company focused on the acquisition, exploration and development of oil and natural gas properties in the Permian Basin in West Texas. The Permian Basin is comprised of several distinct geological provinces, including: the Midland Basin to the east, the Delaware Basin to the west and the Central Platform in the middle. As of Dec 31 2014, Co.'s net proved reserves were estimated at 247.3 million barrels of oil equivalent, with 140.2 million barrels of oil and condensate and 642.79 billion cubic feet of natural gas.

Recent Developments: For the quarter ended Mar 31 2016, net loss amounted to US$180.4 million versus a net loss of US$472,000 in the year-earlier quarter. Revenues were US$106.6 million, down 29.3% from US$150.7 million the year before. Operating loss was US$176.8 million versus a loss of US$26.5 million in the prior-year quarter. Indirect operating expenses increased 59.9% to US$283.3 million from US$177.2 million in the equivalent prior-year period.

Prospects: Our evaluation of Laredo Petroleum, Inc. as of June 19, 2016 is the result of our systematic analysis on three basic characteristics: earnings strength, relative valuation, and recent stock price movement. The company has produced a positive trend in earnings per share over the past 5 quarters and while recent estimates for the company have been raised by analysts, LPI has posted better than expected results. Based on operating earnings yield, the company is overvalued when compared to all of the companies in our coverage universe. Share price changes over the past year indicates that LPI will perform poorly over the near term.

Financial Data
(US$ in Thousands)

	3 Mos	12/31/2015	12/31/2014	12/31/2013	12/31/2012	12/31/2011	12/31/2010	12/31/2009
Earnings Per Share	(11.46)	(11.10)	1.85	0.88	0.48	0.98	...	...
Cash Flow Per Share	1.63	1.59	3.53	2.75	2.96	3.21	...	...
Tang Book Value Per Share	...	0.61	10.88	8.92	6.48	5.96	...	...
Income Statement								
Total Revenue	106,557	606,640	793,885	665,257	588,080	510,270	242,000	96,574
EBITDA	(116,465)	(2,284,387)	556,030	295,619	183,416	217,800	80,367	(250,164)
Depn & Amortn	42,598	6,500	5,100	4,400	3,300	2,400	1,600	1,100
Income Before Taxes	(182,669)	(2,393,680)	430,051	191,055	94,603	164,928	60,436	(258,501)
Income Taxes	...	(176,945)	164,286	74,507	32,949	59,374	(25,812)	(74,006)
Net Income	(180,371)	(2,209,936)	265,573	118,000	61,654	105,554	86,248	(184,495)
Average Shares	211,560	199,158	143,554	134,378	128,171	108,099	...	...
Balance Sheet								
Current Assets	280,858	332,232	365,253	307,609	137,437	122,938	100,416	...
Total Assets	1,637,164	1,813,287	3,932,549	2,623,760	2,338,304	1,627,652	1,068,160	...
Current Liabilities	156,074	216,815	425,025	253,969	262,068	214,361	150,243	...
Long-Term Obligations	1,476,890	1,416,226	1,801,295	1,051,538	1,216,760	636,961	491,600	...
Total Liabilities	1,682,880	1,681,840	2,369,348	1,351,504	1,506,581	867,639	657,061	...
Stockholders' Equity	(45,716)	131,447	1,563,201	1,272,256	831,723	760,013	411,099	...
Shares Outstanding	213,447	213,808	143,686	142,671	128,298	127,617	...	...
Statistical Record								
Return on Assets %	N.M.	N.M.	8.10	4.76	3.10	7.83	...	...
Return on Equity %	N.M.	N.M.	18.73	11.22	7.73	18.03	...	...
EBITDA Margin %	N.M.	N.M.	70.04	44.44	31.19	42.68	33.21	N.M.
Net Margin %	N.M.	N.M.	33.45	17.74	10.48	20.69	35.64	N.M.
Asset Turnover	0.18	0.21	0.24	0.27	0.30	0.38	...	...
Current Ratio	1.80	1.53	0.86	1.21	0.52	0.57	0.67	...
Debt to Equity	...	10.77	1.15	0.83	1.46	0.84	1.20	...
Price Range	15.80-4.10	15.80-7.05	30.98-7.39	33.52-15.95	26.80-17.41	22.30-18.10	...	...
P/E Ratio	...	...	16.75-3.99	38.09-18.13	55.83-36.27	22.76-18.47	...	...

Address: 15 W. Sixth Street, Suite 900, Tulsa, OK 74119 **Telephone:** 918-513-4570	**Web Site:** www.laredopetro.com **Officers:** Randy A. Foutch - Chairman, Chief Executive Officer Richard C. Buterbaugh - Executive Vice President, Chief Financial Officer	**Auditors:** Grant Thornton LLP **Investor Contact:** 918-858-5504 **Transfer Agents:** American Stock Transfer and Trust Company, Brooklyn, NY

LAS VEGAS SANDS CORP

Exchange	Symbol	Price	52Wk Range	Yield	P/E
NYS	LVS	$46.24 (5/31/2016)	57.23-36.97	6.23	20.74

*7 Year Price Score 85.79 *NYSE Composite Index=100 *12 Month Price Score 98.73

TRADING VOLUME (thousand shares)

Interim Earnings (Per Share)

Qtr.	Mar	Jun	Sep	Dec
2013	0.69	0.64	0.76	0.70
2014	0.95	0.83	0.83	0.90
2015	0.64	0.59	0.65	0.59
2016	0.40			

Interim Dividends (Per Share)

Amt	Decl	Ex	Rec	Pay
0.65Q	07/21/2015	09/18/2015	09/22/2015	09/30/2015
0.65Q	10/21/2015	12/18/2015	12/22/2015	12/31/2015
0.72Q	01/27/2016	03/18/2016	03/22/2016	03/31/2016
0.72Q	04/20/2016	06/20/2016	06/22/2016	06/30/2016

Indicated Div: $2.88

Valuation Analysis

		Institutional Holding	
Forecast EPS	$2.33	No of Institutions	
	(05/20/2016)	688	
Market Cap	$36.7 Billion	Shares	
Book Value	$6.6 Billion	343,321,728	
Price/Book	5.54	% Held	
Price/Sales	3.23	38.47	

Business Summary: Hotels, Restaurants & Travel (MIC: 2.2.1 SIC: 7011 NAIC: 721120)

Las Vegas Sands is a developer of destination properties (integrated resorts) that feature accommodations, gaming, entertainment and retail, convention and exhibition facilities, restaurants and other amenities. Through its 70.1% ownership of Sands China Ltd., Co. owns and operates resort properties, including The Venetian Macao Resort Hotel, Sands Cotai Central, the Four Seasons Hotel Macao, Cotai Strip and the Plaza Casino, and the Sands Macao. In Singapore, Co. owns and operates the Marina Bay Sands, while its properties in the U.S. include The Venetian Resort Hotel Casino and The Palazzo Resort Hotel Casino, the Sands Expo and Convention Center and the Sands Casino Resort Bethlehem.

Recent Developments: For the quarter ended Mar 31 2016, net income decreased 33.1% to US$408.9 million from US$611.0 million in the year-earlier quarter. Revenues were US$2.72 billion, down 9.8% from US$3.01 billion the year before. Operating income was US$585.6 million versus US$711.1 million in the prior-year quarter, a decrease of 17.6%. Direct operating expenses declined 7.8% to US$1.46 billion from US$1.58 billion in the comparable period the year before. Indirect operating expenses decreased 6.4% to US$671.0 million from US$717.2 million in the equivalent prior-year period.

Prospects: Our evaluation of Las Vegas Sands Corp. as of June 19, 2016 is the result of our systematic analysis on three basic characteristics: earnings strength, relative valuation, and recent stock price movement. The company has produced a positive trend in earnings per share over the past 5 quarters. However, while recent estimates for the company have been lowered by analysts, LVS has posted results that fell short of analysts expectations. Based on operating earnings yield, the company is about fairly valued when compared to all of the companies in our coverage universe. Share price changes over the past year indicates that LVS will perform in line with the market over the near term.

Financial Data

(US$ in Thousands)	3 Mos	12/31/2015	12/31/2014	12/31/2013	12/31/2012	12/31/2011	12/31/2010	12/31/2009
Earnings Per Share	2.23	2.47	3.52	2.79	1.85	1.56	0.51	(0.82)
Cash Flow Per Share	4.42	4.33	6.00	5.40	3.78	3.66	2.80	0.97
Tang Book Value Per Share	8.26	8.49	8.93	9.24	8.48	10.60	9.71	10.12
Dividends Per Share	2.670	2.600	2.000	1.400	3.750	...	...	...
Dividend Payout %	119.73	105.26	56.82	50.18	202.70	...	...	...
Income Statement								
Total Revenue	2,716,240	11,688,461	14,583,849	13,769,885	11,131,132	9,410,745	6,853,182	4,563,105
EBITDA	558,103	3,949,486	5,200,486	4,498,054	3,275,631	3,239,918	1,926,478	576,027
Depn & Amortn	19,544	1,077,469	1,119,237	1,099,668	977,743	876,540	772,707	637,906
Income Before Taxes	471,938	2,621,882	3,832,711	3,143,512	2,062,576	2,094,823	855,905	(372,627)
Income Taxes	63,025	236,185	244,640	188,836	180,763	211,704	74,302	(3,884)
Net Income	320,167	1,966,236	2,840,629	2,305,997	1,524,093	1,560,123	599,394	(354,479)
Average Shares	795,032	797,596	808,019	826,316	824,556	811,816	791,760	656,836
Balance Sheet								
Current Assets	2,951,894	3,609,250	5,190,499	5,515,539	4,477,514	5,397,152	4,058,907	5,623,674
Total Assets	20,384,909	20,987,421	22,361,691	22,724,264	22,163,652	22,244,123	21,044,308	20,572,106
Current Liabilities	2,395,700	2,464,135	2,712,494	3,129,665	2,622,823	2,498,706	2,600,413	1,839,305
Long-Term Obligations	9,235,223	9,372,645	9,892,913	9,382,752	10,132,265	9,577,131	9,373,755	10,852,147
Total Liabilities	13,749,921	14,170,680	15,148,105	15,058,770	15,101,810	14,393,434	13,877,938	13,654,838
Stockholders' Equity	6,634,988	6,816,741	7,213,586	7,665,494	7,061,842	7,850,689	7,166,370	6,917,268
Shares Outstanding	794,720	794,645	798,258	818,702	824,297	733,249	707,507	660,322
Statistical Record								
Return on Assets %	8.57	9.07	12.60	10.27	6.85	7.21	2.88	N.M.
Return on Equity %	25.76	28.03	38.18	31.32	20.38	20.78	8.51	N.M.
EBITDA Margin %	20.55	33.79	35.66	32.67	29.43	34.43	28.11	12.62
Net Margin %	11.79	16.82	19.48	16.75	13.69	16.58	8.75	N.M.
Asset Turnover	0.55	0.54	0.65	0.61	0.50	0.43	0.33	0.24
Current Ratio	1.23	1.46	1.91	1.76	1.71	2.16	1.56	3.06
Debt to Equity	1.39	1.37	1.37	1.22	1.43	1.22	1.31	1.57
Price Range	59.56-36.97	60.56-36.98	87.81-52.31	78.87-46.16	61.05-36.41	50.60-36.34	52.80-14.94	19.56-1.42
P/E Ratio	26.71-16.58	24.52-14.97	24.95-14.86	28.27-16.54	33.00-19.68	32.44-23.29	103.53-29.29	...
Average Yield %	5.47	5.08	2.81	2.35	7.91	...	...	...

Address: 3355 Las Vegas Boulevard South, Las Vegas, NV 89109 **Telephone:** 702-414-1000	**Web Site:** www.sands.com **Officers:** Sheldon Gary Adelson - Chairman, Chief Executive Officer, Treasurer Robert G. Goldstein - President, Executive Vice President, Chief Operating Officer, Division Officer	**Auditors:** Deloitte & Touche LLP **Transfer Agents:** American Stock Transfer & Trust Company, New York, NY

LASALLE HOTEL PROPERTIES

Exchange	Symbol	Price	52Wk Range	Yield	P/E
NYS	LHO	$23.11 (5/31/2016)	38.31-20.15	7.79	20.27

*7 Year Price Score 88.25   *NYSE Composite Index=100   *12 Month Price Score 84.06

Interim Earnings (Per Share)

Qtr.	Mar	Jun	Sep	Dec
2013	(0.08)	0.37	0.30	0.14
2014	(0.09)	0.82	0.94	0.21
2015	0.00	0.49	0.39	0.21
2016	0.05	...	...	...

Interim Dividends (Per Share)

Amt	Decl	Ex	Rec	Pay
0.45Q	09/15/2015	09/28/2015	09/30/2015	10/15/2015
0.45Q	12/15/2015	12/29/2015	12/31/2015	01/15/2016
0.45Q	03/10/2016	03/29/2016	03/31/2016	04/15/2016
0.45Q	06/15/2016	06/28/2016	06/30/2016	07/15/2016

Indicated Div: $1.80

Valuation Analysis / Institutional Holding

Valuation Analysis		Institutional Holding	
Forecast EPS	$1.25	No of Institutions	336
	(05/20/2016)		
Market Cap	$2.6 Billion	Shares	
Book Value	$2.3 Billion		131,922,544
Price/Book	1.13	% Held	
Price/Sales	2.13		101.63

Business Summary: REITs (MIC: 5.3.1 SIC: 6798 NAIC: 525930)

LaSalle Hotel Properties is a self-administered and self-managed real estate investment trust. Co. primarily buys, owns, redevelops and leases upscale and luxury full-service hotels located in convention, resort and urban business markets. As of Dec 31 2015, Co. owned interests in 47 hotels with over 12,000 guest rooms located in 10 states and the District of Columbia. Substantially all of Co.'s assets are held directly or indirectly by, and all of its operations are conducted through, the LaSalle Hotel Operating Partnership, L.P. (Operating Partnership). Co. owned, through a combination of direct and indirect interests, 99.9% of the common units of the Operating Partnership at Dec 31 2015.

Recent Developments: For the quarter ended Mar 31 2016, net income increased 231.4% to US$9.1 million from US$2.7 million in the year-earlier quarter. Revenues were US$260.1 million, up 3.7% from US$250.8 million the year before.

Prospects: Our evaluation of LaSalle Hotel Properties as of June 19, 2016 is the result of our systematic analysis on three basic characteristics: earnings strength, relative valuation, and recent stock price movement. The company has enjoyed a very positive trend in earnings per share over the past 5 quarters. Because the company lacks sufficient analyst estimate data, we place greater weight on the historical EPS trend as the measure of earnings strength. Based on operating earnings yield, the company is undervalued when compared to all of the companies in our coverage universe. Share price changes over the past year indicates that LHO will perform poorly over the near term.

Financial Data

(US$ in Thousands)	3 Mos	12/31/2015	12/31/2014	12/31/2013	12/31/2012	12/31/2011	12/31/2010	12/31/2009
Earnings Per Share	1.14	1.09	1.88	0.73	0.52	0.16	(0.36)	(0.34)
Cash Flow Per Share	3.06	3.00	2.72	2.53	2.52	2.04	1.89	2.06
Tang Book Value Per Share	20.50	21.02	21.64	20.23	19.41	21.07	19.76	20.38
Dividends Per Share	1.800	1.725	1.405	0.960	0.710	0.440	0.240	0.040
Dividend Payout %	157.89	158.26	74.73	131.51	136.54	275.00	...	...
Income Statement								
Total Revenue	260,104	1,216,584	1,109,778	977,293	867,075	719,007	600,357	606,999
EBITDA	63,853	377,099	340,212	287,844	254,179	201,699	155,580	160,941
Depn & Amortn	50,186	191,167	162,798	149,282	125,127	112,175	111,510	110,821
Income Before Taxes	3,454	134,537	122,598	90,725	80,639	49,868	7,696	12,227
Income Taxes	(5,620)	(1,292)	2,306	470	9,062	7,048	5,075	4,257
Net Income	9,059	135,552	212,845	89,935	71,296	43,617	1,961	7,618
Average Shares	113,108	113,096	104,545	97,228	85,897	81,326	69,549	54,554
Balance Sheet								
Current Assets	154,663	71,181	166,039	63,773	80,989	60,954	52,341	39,066
Total Assets	4,060,006	4,074,817	3,699,949	3,581,038	3,256,570	2,833,275	2,355,045	2,023,563
Current Liabilities	278,640	267,540	230,473	216,513	145,420	110,635	100,216	80,441
Long-Term Obligations	1,460,488	1,429,794	1,021,090	1,255,062	1,252,220	951,397	808,900	644,148
Total Liabilities	1,742,278	1,700,550	1,258,240	1,477,647	1,403,444	1,067,662	911,578	727,376
Stockholders' Equity	2,317,728	2,374,267	2,441,709	2,103,391	1,853,126	1,765,613	1,443,467	1,296,187
Shares Outstanding	113,059	112,959	112,824	103,963	95,445	83,786	73,059	63,609
Statistical Record								
Return on Assets %	3.51	3.49	5.85	2.63	2.34	1.68	0.09	0.37
Return on Equity %	6.02	5.63	9.37	4.55	3.93	2.72	0.14	0.67
EBITDA Margin %	24.55	31.00	30.66	29.45	29.31	28.05	25.91	26.51
Net Margin %	3.48	11.14	19.18	9.20	8.22	6.07	0.33	1.26
Asset Turnover	0.30	0.31	0.30	0.29	0.28	0.28	0.27	0.29
Current Ratio	0.56	0.27	0.72	0.29	0.56	0.55	0.52	0.49
Debt to Equity	0.63	0.60	0.42	0.60	0.68	0.54	0.56	0.50
Price Range	39.53-20.15	43.47-25.10	41.64-28.89	32.13-23.36	30.12-22.57	29.38-15.72	28.01-19.11	22.27-3.84
P/E Ratio	34.68-17.68	39.88-23.03	22.15-15.37	44.01-32.00	57.92-43.40	183.63-98.25	...	...
Average Yield %	5.89	4.99	4.05	3.50	2.65	1.80	1.05	0.29

Address: 7550 Wisconsin Avenue, 10th Floor, Bethesda, MD 20814 **Telephone:** 301-941-1500 **Fax:** 301-941-1553	**Web Site:** www.lasallehotels.com **Officers:** Stuart L. Scott - Acting Chairman Kenneth G. Fuller - Executive Vice President, Chief Financial Officer, Secretary, Treasurer	**Auditors:** KPMG LLP **Investor Contact:** 301-941-1516 **Transfer Agents:** Wells Fargo Bank, N.A., Saint Paul, MN

LAUDER (ESTEE) COS., INC. (THE)

Exchange	Symbol	Price	52Wk Range	Yield	P/E
NYS	EL	$91.78 (5/31/2016)	97.13-75.73	1.31	29.42

*7 Year Price Score 126.65 *NYSE Composite Index=100 *12 Month Price Score 107.17

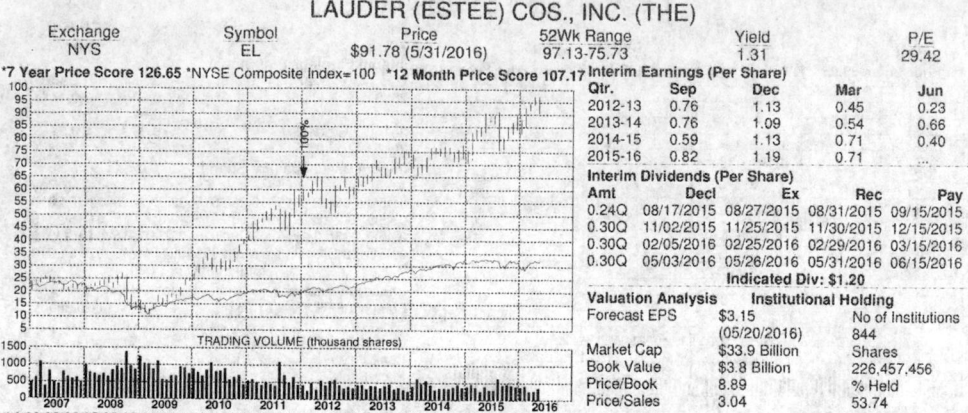

Interim Earnings (Per Share)

Qtr.	Sep	Dec	Mar	Jun
2012-13	0.76	1.13	0.45	0.23
2013-14	0.76	1.09	0.54	0.66
2014-15	0.59	1.13	0.71	0.40
2015-16	0.82	1.19	0.71	

Interim Dividends (Per Share)

Amt	Decl	Ex	Rec	Pay
0.24Q	08/17/2015	08/27/2015	08/31/2015	09/15/2015
0.30Q	11/02/2015	11/25/2015	11/30/2015	12/15/2015
0.30Q	02/05/2016	02/25/2016	02/29/2016	03/15/2016
0.30Q	05/03/2016	05/26/2016	05/31/2016	06/15/2016

Indicated Div: $1.20

Valuation Analysis

Forecast EPS	$3.15
	(05/20/2016)
Market Cap	$33.9 Billion
Book Value	$3.8 Billion
Price/Book	8.89
Price/Sales	3.04

Institutional Holding

No of Institutions	844
Shares	226,457,456
% Held	53.74

Business Summary: Household & Personal Products (MIC: 1.7.1 SIC: 2844 NAIC: 325620)

Estee Lauder Companies manufactures and markets skin care, makeup, fragrance and hair care products. Co.'s products are sold under a number of brand names including: Estee Lauder, Aramis, Clinique, Origins, M.A.C, Bobbi Brown, La Mer and Aveda. Co. is also the licensee for fragrances and/or cosmetics sold under various brand names, including Tommy Hilfiger, Donna Karan New York, DKNY, Michael Kors and Tom Ford. Also, Co. manufactures and sells products under the Prescriptives, GoodSkin Labs, Ojon and Osiao brands. Co. also develops and sells products under a license from Kiton and holds licenses to develop and sell fragrances and other beauty products for the Marni and AERIN brands.

Recent Developments: For the quarter ended Mar 31 2016, net income decreased 2.2% to US$266.6 million from US$272.7 million in the year-earlier quarter. Revenues were US$2.66 billion, up 2.9% from US$2.58 billion the year before. Operating income was US$384.0 million versus US$397.2 million in the prior-year quarter, a decrease of 3.3%. Direct operating expenses rose 0.3% to US$504.2 million from US$502.9 million in the comparable period the year before. Indirect operating expenses increased 5.2% to US$1.77 billion from US$1.68 billion in the equivalent prior-year period.

Prospects: Our evaluation of Lauder (Estee) Cos. Inc. as of June 19, 2016 is the result of our systematic analysis on three basic characteristics: earnings strength, relative valuation, and recent stock price movement. The company has generated a negative trend in earnings per share over the past 5 quarters. However, while recent estimates for the company have been mixed, EL has posted better than expected results. Based on operating earnings yield, the company is about fairly valued when compared to all of the companies in our coverage universe. Share price changes over the past year indicates that EL will perform well over the near term.

Financial Data

(US$ in Thousands)	9 Mos	6 Mos	3 Mos	06/30/2015	06/30/2014	06/30/2013	06/30/2012	06/30/2011
Earnings Per Share	3.12	3.12	3.06	2.82	3.06	2.58	2.16	1.74
Cash Flow Per Share	5.08	5.17	4.90	5.12	3.98	3.16	2.89	2.61
Tang Book Value Per Share	6.05	5.79	5.46	5.79	7.32	5.76	4.27	3.86
Dividends Per Share	1.080	1.020	0.960	0.920	0.780	1.080	0.525	0.375
Dividend Payout %	34.62	32.69	31.37	32.62	25.49	41.86	24.31	21.55
Income Statement								
Total Revenue	8,616,000	5,959,500	2,834,700	10,780,400	10,968,800	10,181,700	9,713,600	8,810,000
EBITDA	1,761,900	1,278,000	548,400	2,006,300	2,205,700	1,878,900	1,609,100	1,372,900
Depn & Amortn	295,300	195,400	95,200	400,000	378,100	329,800	286,900	283,500
Income Before Taxes	1,424,900	1,054,700	439,100	1,560,600	1,776,800	1,475,200	1,261,100	1,025,500
Income Taxes	399,100	295,500	128,300	467,200	567,700	451,400	400,600	321,700
Net Income	1,021,100	755,500	309,300	1,088,900	1,204,100	1,019,800	856,900	700,800
Average Shares	375,600	376,000	379,000	385,700	393,100	394,900	397,000	402,400
Balance Sheet								
Current Assets	4,252,300	4,475,800	4,383,300	4,468,500	4,825,200	4,297,200	3,855,100	3,686,500
Total Assets	8,816,300	8,582,100	8,425,400	8,239,200	7,868,800	7,145,200	6,593,000	6,273,900
Current Liabilities	2,433,700	2,479,400	2,454,300	2,135,600	2,056,700	1,934,600	2,125,800	1,943,300
Long-Term Obligations	1,612,500	1,607,300	1,612,500	1,607,500	1,324,700	1,326,000	1,069,100	1,080,300
Total Liabilities	5,004,500	4,978,300	4,935,000	4,596,000	4,013,900	3,858,300	3,859,800	3,644,500
Stockholders' Equity	3,811,800	3,603,800	3,490,400	3,643,200	3,854,900	3,286,900	2,733,200	2,629,400
Shares Outstanding	369,172	369,394	370,689	374,882	382,884	387,994	388,897	394,562
Statistical Record								
Return on Assets %	13.89	14.36	14.54	13.52	16.04	14.85	13.28	12.07
Return on Equity %	30.63	31.81	32.19	29.04	33.72	33.88	31.87	30.62
EBITDA Margin %	20.45	21.44	19.35	18.61	20.11	18.45	16.57	15.58
Net Margin %	11.85	12.68	10.91	10.10	10.98	10.02	8.82	7.95
Asset Turnover	1.32	1.35	1.37	1.34	1.46	1.48	1.51	1.52
Current Ratio	1.75	1.81	1.79	2.09	2.35	2.22	1.81	1.90
Debt to Equity	0.42	0.45	0.46	0.44	0.34	0.40	0.39	0.41
Price Range	94.42-75.73	91.01-70.40	91.01-70.40	90.22-70.40	76.77-64.71	71.80-50.56	65.35-42.10	52.59-27.86
P/E Ratio	30.26-24.27	29.17-22.56	29.74-23.01	31.99-24.96	25.09-21.15	27.83-19.60	30.25-19.49	30.23-16.01
Average Yield %	1.26	1.22	1.19	1.17	1.10	1.17	0.96	0.94

Address: 767 Fifth Avenue, New York, NY 10153 **Telephone:** 212-572-4200	**Web Site:** www.elcompanies.com **Officers:** William P. Lauder - Executive Chairman Leonard A. Lauder - Chairman Emeritus	**Auditors:** KPMG LLP **Investor Contact:** 800-308-2334 **Transfer Agents:** Computershare, Providence, RI

LAZARD LTD

Exchange	Symbol	Price	52Wk Range	Yield	P/E
NYS	LAZ	$35.18 (5/31/2016)	58.78-30.08	4.32	4.70

*7 Year Price Score 97.52 ***NYSE Composite Index=100** ***12 Month Price Score 80.40**

TRADING VOLUME (thousand shares)

Interim Earnings (Per Share)

Qtr.	Mar	Jun	Sep	Dec
2013	0.12	0.24	0.45	0.40
2014	0.61	0.64	0.67	1.29
2015	0.42	2.82	2.99	1.18
2016	0.50	...	...	...

Interim Dividends (Per Share)

Amt	Decl	Ex	Rec	Pay
0.35Q	10/21/2015	10/29/2015	11/02/2015	11/13/2015
1.20Sp	02/01/2016	02/09/2016	02/11/2016	02/26/2016
0.35Q	02/01/2016	02/09/2016	02/11/2016	02/26/2016
0.38Q	04/20/2016	04/29/2016	05/03/2016	05/13/2016

Indicated Div: $1.52

Valuation Analysis		Institutional Holding	
Forecast EPS	N/A	No of Institutions	390
Market Cap	$4.6 Billion	Shares	110,091,352
Book Value	$1.2 Billion	% Held	76.48
Price/Book	3.92		
Price/Sales	1.97		

Business Summary: Finance Intermediaries & Services (MIC: 5.5.1 SIC: 6282 NAIC: 523930)

Lazard is a financial advisory and asset management firm. Co. focuses primarily on two business segments: Financial Advisory, which provides a range of financial advisory services regarding mergers and acquisitions and other strategic matters, restructurings, capital structure, capital raising and various other financial matters; and Asset Management, which provides a range of global investment solutions and investment management services in equity and fixed income strategies, alternative investments and private equity funds to corporations, public funds, sovereign entities, endowments and foundations, labor funds, financial intermediaries and private clients.

Recent Developments: For the quarter ended Mar 31 2016, net income increased 12.9% to US$70.7 million from US$62.6 million in the year-earlier quarter. Revenues were US$510.1 million, down 14.1% from US$593.9 million the year before. Operating income was US$98.4 million versus US$74.7 million in the prior-year quarter, an increase of 31.8%. Direct operating expenses declined 26.3% to US$11.9 million from US$16.1 million in the comparable period the year before. Indirect operating expenses decreased 20.5% to US$399.8 million from US$503.1 million in the equivalent prior-year period.

Prospects: Our evaluation of Lazard Ltd. as of Apr. 17, 2016 is the result of our systematic analysis on three basic characteristics: earnings strength, relative valuation, and recent stock price movement. The company has generated a negative trend in earnings per share over the past 5 quarters and while recent estimates for the company have been raised by analysts, LAZ has posted better than expected results. Based on operating earnings yield, the company is undervalued when compared to all of the companies in our coverage universe. Share price changes over the past year indicates that LAZ will perform poorly over the near term.

Financial Data

(US$ in Thousands)	3 Mos	12/31/2015	12/31/2014	12/31/2013	12/31/2012	12/31/2011	12/31/2010	12/31/2009
Earnings Per Share	7.49	7.40	3.20	1.21	0.65	1.36	1.36	(1.68)
Cash Flow Per Share	5.97	7.08	6.02	4.36	4.11	3.37	1.62	3.13
Tang Book Value Per Share	6.42	7.86	2.94	1.63	1.53	2.79	2.58	0.44
Dividends Per Share	2.600	2.350	1.200	1.000	1.160	0.605	0.500	0.450
Dividend Payout %	34.71	31.76	37.50	82.64	178.46	44.49	36.76	...
Income Statement								
Total Revenue	510,116	2,404,767	2,363,017	2,064,733	1,994,013	1,919,638	2,003,077	1,638,408
EBITDA	216,161	21,986	560,316	261,671	163,099	271,994	274,229	(154,703)
Depn & Amortn	117,784	38,606	40,851	44,864	39,214	36,495	30,579	27,531
Income Before Taxes	98,377	(16,620)	519,465	216,807	123,885	235,499	243,650	(182,234)
Income Taxes	27,654	(1,009,552)	85,402	51,693	31,100	44,940	49,227	6,011
Net Income	66,823	986,373	427,277	160,212	84,309	174,917	174,979	(130,242)
Average Shares	132,891	133,244	133,813	133,737	129,325	137,629	138,469	78,311
Balance Sheet								
Current Assets	1,637,430	2,054,105	1,875,226	1,661,082	1,685,959	1,869,789	2,227,849	1,607,021
Total Assets	4,011,591	4,486,766	3,332,236	3,011,137	2,986,893	3,081,936	3,422,532	3,147,762
Current Liabilities	760,180	1,186,512	942,468	803,528	740,989	678,015	863,252	854,584
Long-Term Obligations	998,748	1,007,378	1,060,365	1,064,184	1,094,713	1,096,934	1,249,753	1,261,478
Total Liabilities	2,846,263	3,173,311	2,625,492	2,450,928	2,417,237	2,355,793	2,770,134	2,792,371
Stockholders' Equity	1,165,328	1,313,455	706,744	560,209	569,656	726,143	652,398	355,391
Shares Outstanding	129,766	125,512	122,315	120,739	115,413	119,517	112,850	86,315
Statistical Record								
Return on Assets %	29.16	25.23	13.47	5.34	2.77	5.38	5.33	N.M.
Return on Equity %	121.73	97.65	67.45	28.36	12.98	25.38	34.73	N.M.
EBITDA Margin %	42.37	0.91	23.71	12.67	8.18	14.17	13.69	N.M.
Net Margin %	13.10	41.02	18.08	7.76	4.23	9.11	8.74	N.M.
Asset Turnover	0.68	0.62	0.75	0.69	0.66	0.59	0.61	0.55
Current Ratio	2.15	1.73	1.99	2.07	2.28	2.76	2.58	1.88
Debt to Equity	0.86	0.77	1.50	1.90	1.92	1.51	1.92	3.55
Price Range	58.78-30.08	58.78-41.47	54.96-41.37	45.32-29.84	31.49-22.33	45.95-19.65	41.02-26.43	43.55-21.18
P/E Ratio	7.85-4.02	7.94-5.60	17.18-12.93	37.45-24.66	48.45-34.35	33.79-14.45	30.16-19.43	...
Average Yield %	5.49	4.65	2.44	2.77	4.18	1.78	1.42	1.38

Address: Clarendon House, 2 Church Street, Hamilton, HM 11 **Telephone:** 441-295-1422	**Web Site:** www.lazard.com **Officers:** Kenneth M. Jacobs - Chairman, Chief Executive Officer Steven J. Golub - Vice-Chairman, Division Officer	**Auditors:** Deloitte & Touche LLP **Investor Contact:** 212-632-6637 **Transfer Agents:** Computershare, Pittsburgh, PA

LEAR CORP.

Exchange	Symbol	Price	52Wk Range	Yield	P/E
NYS	LEA	$118.76 (5/31/2016)	126.34-94.98	1.01	10.78

*7 Year Price Score N/A ***NYSE Composite Index=100** ***12 Month Price Score 99.58**

Interim Earnings (Per Share)

Qtr.	Mar	Jun	Sep	Dec
2013	1.13	1.60	1.38	0.90
2014	1.47	1.81	1.72	3.22
2015	1.86	2.33	2.34	3.06
2016	3.29	...	...	...

Interim Dividends (Per Share)

Amt	Decl	Ex	Rec	Pay
0.25Q	08/10/2015	08/31/2015	09/02/2015	09/21/2015
0.25Q	11/19/2015	12/09/2015	12/11/2015	12/30/2015
0.30Q	02/12/2016	02/29/2016	03/02/2016	03/23/2016
0.30Q	05/19/2016	06/08/2016	06/10/2016	06/30/2016

Indicated Div: $1.20

Valuation Analysis

Forecast EPS	$12.85 (05/20/2016)
Market Cap	$8.8 Billion
Book Value	$3.0 Billion
Price/Book	2.88
Price/Sales	0.48

Institutional Holding

No of Institutions	631
Shares	92,075,912
% Held	N/A

TRADING VOLUME (thousand shares)

Business Summary: Auto Parts (MIC: 1.8.2 SIC: 3714 NAIC: 336360)

Lear is a designer and manufacturer of automotive seating and electrical distribution systems and related components. Co.'s seating business consists of the design, engineering, assembly and delivery of seat systems, as well as the manufacture of seat components, including seat structures and mechanisms, seat covers, seat foam and headrest. Co.'s electrical business consists of the design, engineering and manufacturing of electrical distribution systems that route electrical signals and manage electrical power within a vehicle. Components of Co.'s electrical business include wiring harnesses, terminals and connectors, junction boxes, electronic control modules and wireless control devices.

Recent Developments: For the quarter ended Apr 2 2016, net income increased 67.5% to US$262.5 million from US$156.7 million in the year-earlier quarter. Revenues were US$4.66 billion, up 3.1% from US$4.52 billion the year before. Direct operating expenses rose 0.8% to US$4.13 billion from US$4.10 billion in the comparable period the year before. Indirect operating expenses decreased 1.7% to US$162.2 million from US$165.0 million in the equivalent prior-year period.

Prospects: Our evaluation of Lear Corp. as of June 19, 2016 is the result of our systematic analysis on three basic characteristics: earnings strength, relative valuation, and recent stock price movement. The company has managed to produce a neutral trend in earnings per share over the past 5 quarters and while recent estimates for the company have remained steady, LEA has posted better than expected results. Based on operating earnings yield, the company is undervalued when compared to all of the companies in our coverage universe. Share price changes over the past year indicates that LEA will perform well over the near term.

Financial Data

(US$ in Thousands)	3 Mos	12/31/2015	12/31/2014	12/31/2013	12/31/2012	12/31/2011	12/31/2010	12/31/2009
Earnings Per Share	11.02	9.59	8.23	4.99	12.85	5.08	4.05	(0.06)
Cash Flow Per Share	21.77	16.56	11.57	9.64	7.40	7.62	6.56	4.69
Tang Book Value Per Share	26.74	25.16	28.62	28.34	28.57	17.95	17.55	14.34
Dividends Per Share	1.050	1.000	0.800	0.680	0.560	0.500	...	...
Dividend Payout %	9.53	10.43	9.72	13.63	4.36	9.84	...	...
Income Statement								
Total Revenue	4,662,900	18,211,400	17,727,300	16,234,000	14,567,000	14,156,500	11,954,600	1,580,900
EBITDA	455,200	1,466,000	1,165,800	964,000	938,400	901,700	740,100	17,000
Depn & Amortn	90,200	347,800	310,900	285,500	239,600	246,300	235,900	39,700
Income Before Taxes	343,900	1,031,500	787,400	610,100	648,900	615,700	448,800	(33,800)
Income Taxes	98,200	285,500	121,400	192,700	(638,000)	68,800	24,600	(24,200)
Net Income	248,400	745,500	672,400	431,400	1,282,800	540,700	438,300	(3,800)
Average Shares	75,474	77,767	81,728	86,415	99,825	106,344	108,122	69,050
Balance Sheet								
Current Assets	5,775,700	5,286,600	5,379,600	4,922,500	4,873,500	4,761,500	4,385,500	3,787,000
Total Assets	9,959,500	9,405,800	9,150,200	8,330,900	8,194,100	7,010,900	6,621,100	6,073,300
Current Liabilities	4,269,500	3,839,600	3,957,800	3,579,100	3,216,900	3,063,500	2,818,500	2,400,800
Long-Term Obligations	1,928,500	1,931,700	1,475,000	1,057,100	626,300	695,400	694,900	927,100
Total Liabilities	6,921,900	6,478,400	6,191,400	5,285,000	4,707,000	4,574,500	4,160,900	3,984,200
Stockholders' Equity	3,037,600	2,927,400	2,958,800	3,045,900	3,487,100	2,436,400	2,460,200	2,089,100
Shares Outstanding	73,767	74,464	78,021	80,751	95,942	100,686	105,176	73,909
Statistical Record								
Return on Assets %	8.65	8.04	7.69	5.22	16.83	7.93	6.91	N.M.
Return on Equity %	28.95	25.33	22.40	13.21	43.19	22.08	19.27	N.M.
EBITDA Margin %	9.76	8.05	6.58	5.94	6.44	6.37	6.19	1.08
Net Margin %	5.33	4.09	3.79	2.66	8.81	3.82	3.67	N.M.
Asset Turnover	1.87	1.96	2.03	1.96	1.91	2.08	1.88	0.24
Current Ratio	1.35	1.38	1.36	1.38	1.51	1.55	1.56	1.58
Debt to Equity	0.63	0.66	0.50	0.35	0.18	0.29	0.28	0.44
Price Range	126.34-94.98	126.34-93.40	103.28-71.97	83.11-46.84	47.01-34.81	55.96-36.03	49.88-31.81	34.29-28.13
P/E Ratio	11.46-8.62	13.17-9.74	12.55-8.74	16.66-9.39	3.66-2.71	11.02-7.09	12.31-7.85	...
Average Yield %	0.94	0.90	0.90	1.06	1.35	1.05	...	...

Address: 21557 Telegraph Road, Southfield, MI 48033 **Telephone:** 248-447-1500 **Fax:** 248-447-5250	**Web Site:** www.lear.com **Officers:** Robert E. Rossiter - Chairman, President, Chief Executive Officer, Advisor Matthew J. Simoncini - President, Chief Executive Officer, Senior Vice President, Chief Financial Officer, Chief Accounting Officer	**Auditors:** Ernst & Young LLP **Investor Contact:** 248-447-1500 **Transfer Agents:** Computershare Trust Company, N.A., Canton, MA

LEGG MASON, INC.

Exchange	Symbol	Price	52Wk Range	Yield	P/E
NYS	LM	$34.50 (5/31/2016)	54.77-25.20	2.55	N/A

*7 Year Price Score 96.52 ***NYSE Composite Index=100** ***12 Month Price Score 81.26**

TRADING VOLUME (thousand shares)

Interim Earnings (Per Share)

Qtr.	Jun	Sep	Dec	Mar
2011-12	0.40	0.39	0.20	0.54
2012-13	(0.07)	0.60	(3.45)	0.19
2013-14	0.38	0.70	0.67	0.58
2014-15	0.61	0.04	0.67	0.72
2015-16	0.84	0.58	(1.31)	(0.42)

Interim Dividends (Per Share)

Amt	Decl	Ex	Rec	Pay
0.20Q	07/31/2015	10/06/2015	10/08/2015	10/26/2015
0.20Q	10/30/2015	12/14/2015	12/16/2015	01/11/2016
0.20Q	01/22/2016	03/08/2016	03/10/2016	04/11/2016
0.22Q	04/29/2016	06/09/2016	06/13/2016	07/05/2016

Indicated Div: $0.88

Valuation Analysis		Institutional Holding	
Forecast EPS	$2.32	No of Institutions	
	(05/20/2016)	579	
Market Cap	$3.7 Billion	Shares	
Book Value	$4.2 Billion	119,797,656	
Price/Book	0.88	% Held	
Price/Sales	1.39	82.72	

Business Summary: Wealth Management (MIC: 5.5.2 SIC: 6282 NAIC: 523930)

Legg Mason is an asset management company. Acting through its subsidiaries, Co. provides investment management and related services to institutional and individual clients, company-sponsored investment funds and retail separately managed account programs. Operating from asset management offices located in the U.S. and the U.K. and a number of other countries worldwide, Co. provides a range of investment management products and services directly and through various financial intermediaries. As of Mar 31 2016, Co. had total assets under management of $7,52 billion.

Recent Developments: For the year ended Mar 31 2016, net loss amounted to US$32.9 million versus net income of US$242.7 million in the prior year. Revenues were US$2.66 billion, down 5.6% from US$2.82 billion the year before. Operating income was US$50.8 million versus US$498.2 million in the prior year, a decrease of 89.8%. Indirect operating expenses increased 12.5% to US$2.61 billion from US$2.32 billion in the equivalent prior-year period.

Prospects: Our evaluation of Legg Mason Inc. as of June 19, 2016 is the result of our systematic analysis on three basic characteristics: earnings strength, relative valuation, and recent stock price movement. The company has suffered a very negative trend in earnings per share over the past 5 quarters. However, while recent estimates for the company have been lowered by analysts, LM has posted better than expected results. Based on operating earnings yield, the company is undervalued when compared to all of the companies in our coverage universe. Share price changes over the past year indicates that LM will perform poorly over the near term.

Financial Data

(US$ in Thousands)	03/31/2016	03/31/2015	03/31/2014	03/31/2013	03/31/2012	03/31/2011	03/31/2010	03/31/2009
Earnings Per Share	(0.25)	2.04	2.33	(2.65)	1.54	1.63	1.32	(13.85)
Cash Flow Per Share	4.22	5.07	3.59	2.28	3.46	2.65	9.29	3.11
Tang Book Value Per Share	N.M.	N.M.	2.67	2.96	3.90	3.87	3.87	N.M.
Dividends Per Share	0.800	0.640	0.520	0.440	0.320	0.200	0.120	0.960
Dividend Payout %	...	31.37	22.32	...	20.78	12.27	9.09	...
Income Statement								
Total Revenue	2,660,844	2,819,106	2,741,757	2,612,650	2,662,574	2,784,317	2,634,879	3,357,367
EBITDA	77,908	473,913	529,030	(367,430)	472,981	550,856	562,684	(2,923,219)
Depn & Amortn	60,297	55,086	62,845	87,848	93,795	102,748	114,078	138,445
Income Before Taxes	(25,218)	367,993	419,641	(510,607)	303,083	365,197	329,656	(3,155,857)
Income Taxes	7,692	125,284	137,805	(150,859)	72,052	119,434	118,676	(1,210,853)
Net Income	(25,032)	237,080	284,784	(353,327)	220,817	253,923	204,357	(1,947,928)
Average Shares	107,406	113,246	122,383	133,226	143,349	155,484	155,362	140,669
Balance Sheet								
Current Assets	2,385,128	1,922,035	2,128,383	1,942,862	2,457,794	2,446,556	2,559,146	2,859,387
Total Assets	7,520,446	7,073,977	7,111,349	7,269,660	8,555,747	8,707,756	8,613,711	9,321,354
Current Liabilities	841,553	815,046	821,245	702,466	975,782	968,972	1,045,355	1,281,193
Long-Term Obligations	1,740,985	1,058,089	1,038,826	1,302,351	1,407,321	1,479,396	1,165,180	2,965,204
Total Liabilities	3,306,883	2,589,076	2,386,625	2,451,309	2,878,456	2,937,372	2,771,987	4,866,877
Stockholders' Equity	4,213,563	4,484,901	4,724,724	4,818,351	5,677,291	5,770,384	5,841,724	4,454,477
Shares Outstanding	107,011	111,469	117,173	125,341	139,874	150,218	161,438	141,853
Statistical Record								
Return on Assets %	N.M.	3.34	3.96	N.M.	2.55	2.93	2.28	N.M.
Return on Equity %	N.M.	5.15	5.97	N.M.	3.85	4.37	3.97	N.M.
EBITDA Margin %	2.93	16.81	19.30	N.M.	17.76	19.78	21.36	N.M.
Net Margin %	N.M.	8.41	10.39	N.M.	8.29	9.12	7.76	N.M.
Asset Turnover	0.36	0.40	0.38	0.33	0.31	0.32	0.29	0.32
Current Ratio	2.83	2.36	2.59	2.77	2.52	2.52	2.45	2.23
Debt to Equity	0.41	0.24	0.22	0.27	0.25	0.26	0.20	0.67
Price Range	55.58-25.20	58.92-43.36	49.04-29.76	32.15-22.38	37.53-22.95	37.58-25.17	33.70-15.90	64.87-10.79
P/E Ratio	...	28.88-21.25	21.05-12.77	...	24.37-14.90	23.06-15.44	25.53-12.05	...
Average Yield %	1.83	1.24	1.24	1.68	1.10	0.62	0.45	2.88

Address: 100 International Drive, Baltimore, MD 21202 **Telephone:** 410-539-0000	**Web Site:** www.leggmason.com **Officers:** Joseph A. Sullivan - President, Chief Executive Officer, Acting Chief Executive Officer, Senior Executive Vice President, Chief Administrative Officer Peter H. Nachtwey - Senior Executive Vice President, Chief Financial Officer	**Auditors:** PricewaterhouseCoopers LLP **Investor Contact:** 410-454-5246 **Transfer Agents:** American Stock Transfer & Trust Company, New York, NY

LEGGETT & PLATT, INC.

Exchange	Symbol	Price	52Wk Range	Yield	P/E	Div Achiever
NYS	LEG	$50.26 (5/31/2016)	51.00-37.79	2.71	20.85	44 Years

*7 Year Price Score 131.31 *NYSE Composite Index=100 *12 Month Price Score 105.66

Interim Earnings (Per Share)

Qtr.	Mar	Jun	Sep	Dec
2013	0.33	0.48	0.49	0.04
2014	0.37	(0.17)	0.34	0.14
2015	0.50	0.54	0.67	0.57
2016	0.63			

Interim Dividends (Per Share)

Amt	Decl	Ex	Rec	Pay
0.32Q	08/12/2015	09/11/2015	09/15/2015	10/15/2015
0.32Q	11/03/2015	12/11/2015	12/15/2015	01/15/2016
0.32Q	02/24/2016	03/11/2016	03/15/2016	04/15/2016
0.34Q	05/17/2016	06/13/2016	06/15/2016	07/15/2016

Indicated Div: $1.36

Valuation Analysis

		Institutional Holding	
Forecast EPS	$2.50 (05/20/2016)	No of Institutions	607
Market Cap	$6.8 Billion	Shares	112,890,160
Book Value	$1.1 Billion	% Held	69.45
Price/Book	6.26		
Price/Sales	1.74		

Business Summary: Furniture (MIC: 1.6.2 SIC: 2519 NAIC: 337121)

Leggett & Platt designs and produces a range of engineered components and products. Co.'s operations are organized into four segments: Residential Furnishings, which supplies a variety of components used by bedding and upholstered furniture manufacturers in the assembly of their finished products; Commercial Products, which designs, manufactures, and distributes a range of components and products primarily for the office seating market; Industrial Materials, which supplies steel wire; and Specialized Products, which designs, manufactures and sells products including automotive seating components, tubing for the aerospace industry, machinery and equipment, and service van interiors.

Recent Developments: For the quarter ended Mar 31 2016, income from continuing operations increased 24.1% to US$91.0 million from US$73.3 million in the year-earlier quarter. Net income increased 25.1% to US$91.1 million from US$72.8 million in the year-earlier quarter. Revenues were US$938.4 million, down 2.9% from US$966.2 million the year before. Operating income was US$127.1 million versus US$111.7 million in the prior-year quarter, an increase of 13.8%. Direct operating expenses declined 5.8% to US$704.8 million from US$748.4 million in the comparable period the year before. Indirect operating expenses increased 0.4% to US$106.5 million from US$106.1 million in the equivalent prior-year period.

Prospects: Our evaluation of Leggett & Platt Inc. as of June 19, 2016 is the result of our systematic analysis on three basic characteristics: earnings strength, relative valuation, and recent stock price movement. The company has managed to produce a neutral trend in earnings per share over the past 5 quarters and while recent estimates for the company have remained steady, LEG has posted better than expected results. Based on operating earnings yield, the company is about fairly valued when compared to all of the companies in our coverage universe. Share price changes over the past year indicates that LEG will perform in line with the market over the near term.

Financial Data
(US$ in Thousands)

	3 Mos	12/31/2015	12/31/2014	12/31/2013	12/31/2012	12/31/2011	12/31/2010	12/31/2009
Earnings Per Share	2.41	2.28	0.68	1.34	1.70	1.04	1.15	0.70
Cash Flow Per Share	3.15	2.55	2.70	2.87	3.11	2.26	2.40	3.55
Tang Book Value Per Share	0.61	0.64	0.89	1.87	1.67	1.82	2.90	3.06
Dividends Per Share	1.270	1.260	1.220	1.180	1.140	1.100	1.060	1.020
Dividend Payout %	52.70	55.26	179.41	88.06	67.06	105.77	92.17	145.71
Income Statement								
Total Revenue	938,400	3,917,200	3,782,300	3,746,000	3,720,800	3,636,000	3,359,100	3,055,100
EBITDA	155,400	590,800	441,100	400,900	457,400	354,700	410,800	360,600
Depn & Amortn	28,300	104,300	109,600	116,100	116,100	116,900	122,800	130,300
Income Before Taxes	118,700	449,800	295,500	247,800	304,400	206,200	255,500	198,400
Income Taxes	27,700	121,800	70,300	55,000	56,300	49,800	71,900	77,300
Net Income	89,500	325,100	98,000	197,300	248,200	153,300	176,600	111,800
Average Shares	141,200	142,900	143,200	147,300	145,963	146,999	153,268	159,964
Balance Sheet								
Current Assets	1,341,900	1,311,200	1,429,600	1,281,700	1,339,100	1,224,000	1,219,100	1,213,600
Total Assets	3,024,400	2,967,600	3,140,600	3,108,100	3,254,900	2,915,100	3,001,000	3,061,200
Current Liabilities	680,000	701,200	992,200	829,500	731,000	586,000	523,100	535,100
Long-Term Obligations	1,032,000	945,400	766,700	688,400	853,900	833,300	762,200	789,300
Total Liabilities	1,945,300	1,882,000	1,994,100	1,716,800	1,820,400	1,617,900	1,493,700	1,507,200
Stockholders' Equity	1,079,100	1,085,600	1,146,500	1,391,300	1,434,500	1,297,200	1,507,300	1,554,000
Shares Outstanding	134,325	135,600	137,800	139,400	142,100	139,400	146,200	148,793
Statistical Record								
Return on Assets %	11.19	10.64	3.14	6.20	8.02	5.18	5.83	3.59
Return on Equity %	31.37	29.13	7.72	13.96	18.12	10.93	11.54	6.97
EBITDA Margin %	16.56	15.08	11.66	10.70	12.29	9.76	12.23	11.80
Net Margin %	9.54	8.30	2.59	5.27	6.67	4.22	5.26	3.66
Asset Turnover	1.27	1.28	1.21	1.18	1.20	1.23	1.11	0.98
Current Ratio	1.97	1.87	1.44	1.55	1.83	2.09	2.33	2.27
Debt to Equity	0.96	0.87	0.67	0.49	0.60	0.64	0.51	0.51
Price Range	51.00-37.79	51.00-40.68	42.95-29.06	34.19-27.22	27.85-19.49	26.37-17.87	25.02-18.26	20.82-10.21
P/E Ratio	21.16-15.68	22.37-17.84	63.16-42.74	25.51-20.31	16.38-11.46	25.36-17.18	21.76-15.88	29.74-14.59
Average Yield %	2.80	2.76	3.53	3.83	4.87	4.83	4.95	6.28

Address: No. 1 Leggett Road, Carthage, MO 64836	Web Site: www.leggett.com	Auditors: PricewaterhouseCoopers LLP
Telephone: 417-358-8131	Officers: Karl G. Glassman - President, Chief Executive Officer, Executive Vice President, Chief Operating Officer Matthew C. Flanigan - Executive Vice President, Senior Vice President, Chief Financial Officer	Investor Contact: 417-358-8131 Transfer Agents: Wells Fargo Shareowner Services, St. Paul, MN

LEIDOS HOLDINGS INC

Exchange	Symbol	Price	52Wk Range	Yield	P/E
NYS	LDOS	$49.40 (5/31/2016)	59.05-38.05	2.59	14.62

*7 Year Price Score 95.91   ***NYSE Composite Index=100**   ***12 Month Price Score 104.68**

Interim Earnings (Per Share)

Qtr.	Apr	Jul	Oct	Jan
2014-15	0.47	(5.92)	0.46	1.55
2015	0.55	0.50	0.67	1.55
2016	0.66	...	...	...

Interim Dividends (Per Share)

Amt	Decl	Ex	Rec	Pay
0.32Q	09/21/2015	10/13/2015	10/15/2015	10/30/2015
0.32Q	12/04/2015	12/11/2015	12/15/2015	12/30/2015
0.32Q	02/22/2016	03/11/2016	03/15/2016	03/30/2016
0.32Q	05/25/2016	06/13/2016	06/15/2016	06/30/2016

Indicated Div: $1.28

Valuation Analysis

		Institutional Holding	
Forecast EPS	$2.92	No of Institutions	
	(05/15/2016)	398	
Market Cap	$3.6 Billion	Shares	
Book Value	$1.1 Billion	71,882,848	
Price/Book	3.23	% Held	
Price/Sales	0.74	N/A	

Business Summary: IT Services (MIC: 6.3.1 SIC: 7373 NAIC: 541330)

Leidos Holdings is a holding company. Through its subsidiaries, Co. is engaged in the following segments: National Security Solutions, which provides solutions and systems for air, land, sea, space and cyberspace for the U.S. intelligence community, the Department of Defense (DoD), the military services, the U.S. Department of Homeland Security and government agencies of U.S. allies abroad; Health and Engineering, which provides products and services to commercial hospitals and the DoD, as well as in energy generation, efficiency and management, environmental services, securing critical infrastructure, and designing and building construction projects; and Corporate and Other.

Recent Developments: For the quarter ended Apr 1 2016, income from continuing operations increased 113.0% to US$49.0 million from US$23.0 million in the year-earlier quarter. Net income increased 19.5% to US$49.0 million from US$41.0 million in the year-earlier quarter. Revenues were US$1.31 billion, up 5.3% from US$1.25 billion the year before. Operating income was US$89.0 million versus US$38.0 million in the prior-year quarter, an increase of 134.2%. Direct operating expenses rose 5.6% to US$1.15 billion from US$1.09 billion in the comparable period the year before. Indirect operating expenses decreased 40.0% to US$69.0 million from US$115.0 million in the equivalent prior-year period.

Prospects: Our evaluation of Leidos Holdings Inc. as of June 19, 2016 is the result of our systematic analysis on three basic characteristics: earnings strength, relative valuation, and recent stock price movement. The company has managed to produce a neutral trend in earnings per share over the past 5 quarters and while recent estimates for the company have remained steady, LDOS has posted better than expected results. Based on operating earnings yield, the company is undervalued when compared to all of the companies in our coverage universe. Share price changes over the past year indicates that LDOS will perform very well over the near term.

Financial Data

(US$ in Millions)	3 Mos	01/01/2016	01/30/2015	01/31/2014	01/31/2013	01/31/2012	01/31/2011	01/31/2010
Earnings Per Share	3.38	3.27	(4.36)	1.94	6.16	0.72	6.52	4.96
Cash Flow Per Share	5.88	2.85	5.37	2.35	4.13	9.19	8.10	6.42
Tang Book Value Per Share	N.M.	N.M.	N.M.	N.M.	2.73	2.10	6.65	7.74
Dividends Per Share	1.600	1.600	1.280	0.640	1.920	...	...	...
Dividend Payout %	47.34	48.93	...	32.99	31.17	...	...	...
Income Statement								
Total Revenue	1,312	4,712	5,063	5,772	11,173	10,587	11,117	10,846
EBITDA	97	437	(162)	237	855	430	1,071	965
Depn & Amortn	8	33	47	81	113	114	111	93
Income Before Taxes	78	355	(283)	88	658	207	883	798
Income Taxes	29	112	47	4	135	215	314	299
Net Income	49	242	(323)	164	525	59	618	497
Average Shares	74	74	74	83	83	84	91	97
Balance Sheet								
Current Assets	1,803	1,793	1,618	1,794	3,079	4,205	3,849	3,193
Total Assets	3,391	3,377	3,281	4,162	5,875	6,667	6,223	5,295
Current Liabilities	1,005	1,040	951	1,009	1,793	3,025	1,748	1,706
Long-Term Obligations	1,089	1,086	1,164	1,331	1,296	1,299	1,849	1,103
Total Liabilities	2,289	2,309	2,283	2,567	3,257	4,486	3,732	3,004
Stockholders' Equity	1,102	1,068	998	1,595	2,618	2,181	2,491	2,291
Shares Outstanding	72	72	74	80	85	85	90	97
Statistical Record								
Return on Assets %	7.46	3.35	N.M.	3.27	8.35	0.92	10.73	9.61
Return on Equity %	23.79	9.48	N.M.	7.79	21.82	2.53	25.85	22.72
EBITDA Margin %	7.39	9.27	N.M.	4.11	7.65	4.06	9.63	8.90
Net Margin %	3.73	5.14	N.M.	2.84	4.70	0.56	5 56	4.58
Asset Turnover	1.43	0.65	1 36	1.15	1.78	1.64	1.93	2.10
Current Ratio	1.79	1.72	1.70	1.78	1.72	1.39	2.20	1.87
Debt to Equity	0.99	1.02	1.17	0.83	0.50	0.60	0.74	0.48
Price Range	59.05-38.05	59.05-38.05	46.07-33.21	49.02-31.06	37.34-28.48	48.17-30.89	54.05-40.82	55.64-46.56
P/E Ratio	17.47-11.26	18.06-11.64	...	25.27-16.01	6.06-4.62	66.91-42.90	8.29-6.26	11.22-9.39
Average Yield %	3.47	3.54	3.26	1.55	5.91	...	...	...

Address: 11951 Freedom Drive, Reston, VA 20190 **Telephone:** 571-526-6000	**Web Site:** www.leidos.com **Officers:** John P. Jumper - Chairman, President, Chief Executive Officer Roger A. Krone - Chief Executive Officer	**Auditors:** Deloitte & Touche LLP **Investor Contact:** 703-676-2283 **Transfer Agents:** BNY Mellon Shareowner Services

431

LENNAR CORP.

Exchange	Symbol	Price	52Wk Range	Yield	P/E
NYS	LEN	$45.57 (5/31/2016)	55.59-37.80	0.35	12.69

*7 Year Price Score 131.93 *NYSE Composite Index=100   ***12 Month Price Score 94.49**

TRADING VOLUME (thousand shares)

Interim Earnings (Per Share)

Qtr.	Feb	May	Aug	Nov
2012-13	0.26	0.61	0.54	0.73
2013-14	0.35	0.61	0.78	1.07
2014-15	0.50	0.79	0.96	1.21
2015-16	0.63			

Interim Dividends (Per Share)

Amt	Decl	Ex	Rec	Pay
0.04Q	06/23/2015	07/06/2015	07/08/2015	07/22/2015
0.04Q	10/07/2015	10/20/2015	10/22/2015	11/05/2015
0.04Q	01/13/2016	01/26/2016	01/28/2016	02/11/2016
0.04Q	04/13/2016	04/25/2016	04/27/2016	05/11/2016

Indicated Div: $0.16

Valuation Analysis

		Institutional Holding	
Forecast EPS	$3.85	No of Institutions	
	(05/20/2016)	677	
Market Cap	$9.8 Billion	Shares	
Book Value	$5.8 Billion	210,539,024	
Price/Book	1.68	% Held	
Price/Sales	1.00	87.77	

Business Summary: Builders (MIC: 2.2.5 SIC: 1521 NAIC: 236115)

Lennar is a homebuilder, a provider of real estate related financial services, and a commercial real estate investment, investment management and finance company. Co.'s homebuilding operations include the construction and sale of single-family attached and detached homes, as well as the purchase, development and sale of residential land. Co.'s Financial Services segment provides mortgage financing, title insurance and closing services for both buyers of its homes and others. Co.'s Rialto segment focuses on real estate investments and asset management. Co.'s Lennar Multifamily segment focuses on developing a portfolio of institutional multifamily rental properties in select U.S. markets.

Recent Developments: For the quarter ended Feb 29 2016, net income increased 24.4% to US$145.5 million from US$116.9 million in the year-earlier quarter. Revenues were US$1.99 billion, up 21.3% from US$1.64 billion the year before. Direct operating expenses rose 21.3% to US$1.77 billion from US$1.46 billion in the comparable period the year before. Indirect operating expenses increased 9.2% to US$47.7 million from US$43.7 million in the equivalent prior-year period.

Prospects: Our evaluation of Lennar Corp. as of June 19, 2016 is the result of our systematic analysis on three basic characteristics: earnings strength, relative valuation, and recent stock price movement. The company has managed to produce a neutral trend in earnings per share over the past 5 quarters. However, while recent estimates for the company have been lowered by analysts, LEN has posted better than expected results. Based on operating earnings yield, the company is undervalued when compared to all of the companies in our coverage universe. Share price changes over the past year indicates that LEN will perform in line with the market over the near term.

Financial Data
(US$ in Thousands)

	3 Mos	11/30/2015	11/30/2014	11/30/2013	11/30/2012	11/30/2011	11/30/2010	11/30/2009
Earnings Per Share	3.59	3.46	2.80	2.15	3.11	0.48	0.51	(2.45)
Cash Flow Per Share	0.45	(2.05)	(3.90)	(4.24)	(2.27)	(1.40)	1.50	2.47
Tang Book Value Per Share	26.92	26.57	23.54	20.39	17.83	14.31	13.98	13.03
Dividends Per Share	0.160	0.160	0.160	0.160	0.160	0.160	0.160	0.160
Dividend Payout %	4.46	4.62	5.71	7.44	5.14	33.33	31.37	...
Income Statement								
Total Revenue	1,993,664	9,474,008	7,779,812	5,935,095	4,104,706	3,095,385	3,074,022	3,119,387
EBITDA	183,444	1,180,426	992,888	783,815	351,191	301,395	180,833	(536,996)
Depn & Amortn	4,777	63,540	59,929	53,846	49,531	42,141	20,080	21,641
Income Before Taxes	177,510	1,104,432	896,408	636,056	207,307	168,604	90,328	(629,487)
Income Taxes	56,241	390,416	341,091	177,015	(435,218)	(14,570)	(25,734)	(314,345)
Net Income	144,080	802,894	638,916	479,674	679,124	92,199	95,261	(417,147)
Average Shares	228,916	230,812	228,240	225,920	218,695	195,185	188,857	170,537
Balance Sheet								
Current Assets	10,111,501	10,171,054	9,230,259	7,700,479	6,609,544	5,750,638	5,644,973	6,036,779
Total Assets	14,195,188	14,419,509	12,958,267	11,273,247	10,362,206	9,154,671	8,787,851	7,314,791
Current Liabilities	442,905	475,909	412,558	271,365	220,690	201,101	168,006	169,596
Long-Term Obligations	6,568,453	5,025,130	4,690,213	4,194,432	4,005,051	3,362,759	3,128,154	2,978,909
Total Liabilities	8,375,074	8,770,565	8,131,247	7,104,346	6,947,442	6,458,203	6,178,902	4,871,312
Stockholders' Equity	5,820,114	5,648,944	4,827,020	4,168,901	3,414,764	2,696,468	2,608,949	2,443,479
Shares Outstanding	214,708	211,145	205,039	204,411	191,547	188,402	186,636	184,896
Statistical Record								
Return on Assets %	6.09	5.87	5.27	4.43	6.94	1.03	1.18	N.M.
Return on Equity %	15.45	15.33	14.20	12.65	22.16	3.48	3.77	N.M.
EBITDA Margin %	9.20	12.46	12.76	13.21	8.56	9.74	5.88	N.M.
Net Margin %	7.23	8.47	8.21	8.08	16.55	2.98	3.10	N.M.
Asset Turnover	0.72	0.69	0.64	0.55	0.42	0.35	0.38	0.42
Current Ratio	22.83	21.37	22.37	28.38	29.95	28.60	33.60	35.60
Debt to Equity	1.13	0.89	0.97	1.01	1.17	1.25	1.20	1.22
Price Range	55.59-37.80	55.59-41.32	47.51-34.22	43.88-31.53	39.05-18.23	21.38-12.71	20.71-11.63	17.38-5.87
P/E Ratio	15.48-10.53	16.07-11.94	16.97-12.22	20.41-14.67	12.56-5.86	44.54-26.48	40.61-22.80	...
Average Yield %	0.33	0.33	0.40	0.43	0.56	0.91	1.03	1.52

Address: 700 Northwest 107th Avenue, Miami, FL 33172	Web Site: www.lennar.com	Auditors: Deloitte & Touche LLP
Telephone: 305-559-4000	Officers: Richard Beckwitt - President Stuart A. Miller - President, Chief Executive Officer	Investor Contact: 305-559-4000
		Transfer Agents: ComputerShare Investor Services, Providence, RI

LENNOX INTERNATIONAL INC

Exchange	Symbol	Price	52Wk Range	Yield	P/E
NYS	LII	$137.35 (5/31/2016)	142.00-107.20	1.25	31.65

*7 Year Price Score 157.98 *NYSE Composite Index=100 *12 Month Price Score 108.38

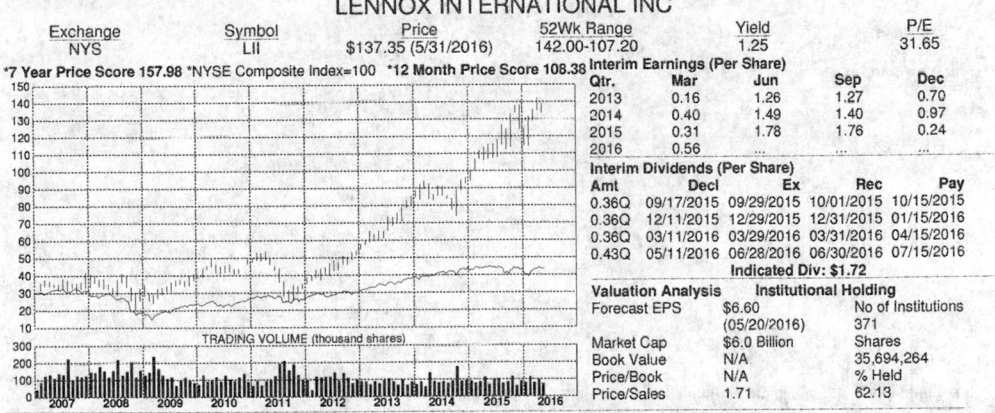

Interim Earnings (Per Share)

Qtr.	Mar	Jun	Sep	Dec
2013	0.16	1.26	1.27	0.70
2014	0.40	1.49	1.40	0.97
2015	0.31	1.78	1.76	0.24
2016	0.56	...	...	...

Interim Dividends (Per Share)

Amt	Decl	Ex	Rec	Pay
0.36Q	09/17/2015	09/29/2015	10/01/2015	10/15/2015
0.36Q	12/11/2015	12/29/2015	12/31/2015	01/15/2016
0.36Q	03/11/2016	03/29/2016	03/31/2016	04/15/2016
0.43Q	05/11/2016	06/28/2016	06/30/2016	07/15/2016

Indicated Div: $1.72

Valuation Analysis / **Institutional Holding**

Forecast EPS	$6.60	No of Institutions
	(05/20/2016)	371
Market Cap	$6.0 Billion	Shares
Book Value	N/A	35,694,264
Price/Book	N/A	% Held
Price/Sales	1.71	62.13

Business Summary: Industrial Machinery & Equipment (MIC: 7.2.1 SIC: 3585 NAIC: 333415)

Lennox International is a provider of climate control solutions and designs, manufactures and markets products for the heating, ventilation, air conditioning and refrigeration markets. Co. has three segments: Residential Heating and Cooling, which provides furnaces, air conditioners, heat pumps, packaged heating and cooling systems, and comfort control products, among others, for the residential replacement and new construction markets; Commercial Heating and Cooling, which manufactures and sells unitary heating and cooling equipment for light commercial applications; and Refrigeration, which provides condensing units, unit coolers, fluid coolers, and air-cooled condensers, among others.

Recent Developments: For the quarter ended Mar 31 2016, income from continuing operations increased 77.9% to US$24.9 million from US$14.0 million in the year-earlier quarter. Net income increased 79.1% to US$24.9 million from US$13.9 million in the year-earlier quarter. Revenues were US$715.2 million, up 4.3% from US$685.8 million the year before. Operating income was US$43.7 million versus US$27.0 million in the prior-year quarter, an increase of 61.9%. Direct operating expenses rose 1.7% to US$531.6 million from US$522.8 million in the comparable period the year before. Indirect operating expenses increased 2.9% to US$139.9 million from US$136.0 million in the equivalent prior-year period.

Prospects: Our evaluation of Lennox International Inc. as of June 19, 2016 is the result of our systematic analysis on three basic characteristics: earnings strength, relative valuation, and recent stock price movement. The company has produced a positive trend in earnings per share over the past 5 quarters and while recent estimates for the company have remained steady, LII has posted better than expected results. Based on operating earnings yield, the company is about fairly valued when compared to all of the companies in our coverage universe. Share price changes over the past year indicates that LII will perform very well over the near term.

Financial Data

(US$ in Thousands)	3 Mos	12/31/2015	12/31/2014	12/31/2013	12/31/2012	12/31/2011	12/31/2010	12/31/2009
Earnings Per Share	4.34	4.09	4.23	3.39	1.75	1.65	2.08	0.90
Cash Flow Per Share	7.73	7.38	3.86	4.22	4.35	1.45	3.40	4.06
Tang Book Value Per Share	...	N.M.	N.M.	5.46	5.43	3.19	5.92	6.17
Dividends Per Share	1.440	1.380	1.140	0.920	0.760	0.720	0.600	0.560
Dividend Payout %	33.18	33.74	26.95	27.14	43.43	43.64	28.85	62.22
Income Statement								
Total Revenue	715,200	3,467,400	3,367,400	3,199,100	2,949,400	3,303,600	3,096,400	2,847,500
EBITDA	53,300	355,600	381,800	335,500	263,700	198,200	232,800	154,700
Depn & Amortn	14,200	62,800	60,800	58,900	55,400	60,400	53,500	52,900
Income Before Taxes	33,300	269,200	303,800	262,100	191,200	121,000	166,500	93,600
Income Taxes	13,000	95,400	109,500	94,400	66,700	42,300	59,500	39,100
Net Income	24,900	186,600	205,800	171,800	90,000	88,300	116,200	51,100
Average Shares	44,700	45,600	48,600	50,600	51,400	53,400	55,800	56,600
Balance Sheet								
Current Assets	1,121,600	938,200	1,014,000	902,400	987,100	903,200	946,900	833,900
Total Assets	1,861,600	1,680,200	1,764,300	1,626,700	1,691,900	1,705,700	1,692,000	1,543,900
Current Liabilities	803,200	824,000	827,300	714,000	639,600	572,900	615,600	593,800
Long-Term Obligations	884,500	508,600	675,000	233,200	351,000	459,600	317,000	193,800
Total Liabilities	1,934,800	1,579,000	1,755,900	1,141,800	1,195,100	1,237,900	1,102,300	939,500
Stockholders' Equity	(73,800)	101,200	8,400	484,900	496,800	467,800	589,700	604,400
Shares Outstanding	43,598	44,678	44,635	49,103	50,232	50,844	53,696	56,274
Statistical Record								
Return on Assets %	10.57	10.83	12.14	10.35	5.28	5.20	7.18	3.19
Return on Equity %	...	340.51	83.44	35.00	18.61	16.70	19.46	9.61
EBITDA Margin %	7.45	10.26	11.34	10.49	8.94	6.00	7.52	5.43
Net Margin %	3.48	5.38	6.11	5.37	3.05	2.67	3.75	1.79
Asset Turnover	1.87	2.01	1.99	1.93	1.73	1.94	1.91	1.78
Current Ratio	1.40	1.14	1.23	1.26	1.54	1.58	1.54	1.40
Debt to Equity	...	5.03	80.36	0.48	0.71	0.98	0.54	0.32
Price Range	137.79-105.61	137.79-93.85	96.04-73.66	85.12-52.52	53.84-34.74	53.63-25.29	49.93-38.22	40.76-23.87
P/E Ratio	31.75-24.33	33.69-22.95	22.70-17.41	25.11-15.49	30.77-19.85	32.50-15.33	24.00-18.37	45.29-26.52
Average Yield %	1.20	1.20	1.31	1.35	1.70	1.77	1.38	1.70

Address: 2140 Lake Park Blvd., Richardson, TX 75080
Telephone: 972-497-5000

Web Site: www.lennoxinternational.com
Officers: Todd M. Bluedorn - Chairman, Chief Executive Officer Michael J. Blatz - Executive Vice President, Division Officer

Auditors: KPMG LLLP
Investor Contact: 972-497-6670
Transfer Agents: Computershare, Providence, RI

LEUCADIA NATIONAL CORP.

Exchange	Symbol	Price	52Wk Range	Yield	P/E
NYS	LUK	$18.10 (5/31/2016)	25.20-14.45	1.38	N/A

*7 Year Price Score 65.47   *NYSE Composite Index=100   *12 Month Price Score 87.15

TRADING VOLUME (thousand shares)

Interim Earnings (Per Share)

Qtr.	Mar	Jun	Sep	Dec
2014	0.25	0.17	0.14	(0.02)
2015	0.99	0.04	(0.47)	0.15
2016	(0.60)	...	...	...

Interim Dividends (Per Share)

Amt	Decl	Ex	Rec	Pay
0.063Q	07/30/2015	09/10/2015	09/14/2015	09/25/2015
0.063Q	10/30/2015	12/10/2015	12/14/2015	12/28/2015
0.063Q	02/19/2016	03/10/2016	03/14/2016	03/28/2016
0.063Q	05/26/2016	06/09/2016	06/13/2016	06/24/2016

Indicated Div: $0.25

Valuation Analysis

		Institutional Holding	
Forecast EPS	$-0.06 (05/06/2016)	No of Institutions	604
Market Cap	$6.6 Billion	Shares	273,569,568
Book Value	$10.2 Billion		
Price/Book	0.64	% Held	68.35
Price/Sales	0.67		

Business Summary: Agricultural Livestock (MIC: 1.1.2 SIC: 0212 NAIC: 112111)

Leucadia National is a diversified holding company engaged through its consolidated subsidiaries in a variety of businesses. Co.'s financial services businesses and investments include investment banking and capital markets, asset management, commercial mortgage banking and servicing, and real estate. Co. also owns and has investments in an array of other businesses, including beef processing, a publicly traded diversified holding company, oil and gas exploration and development, automobile dealerships, fixed wireless broadband services in Italy, manufacturing operations, and a gold and silver mining project.

Recent Developments: For the quarter ended Mar 31 2016, net loss amounted to US$218.6 million versus net income of US$374.4 million in the year-earlier quarter. Revenues were US$2.02 billion, down 36.7% from US$3.18 billion the year before. Direct operating expenses declined 14.3% to US$1.65 billion from US$1.92 billion in the comparable period the year before. Indirect operating expenses decreased 3.7% to US$689.1 million from US$715.8 million in the equivalent prior-year period.

Prospects: Our evaluation of Leucadia National Corp. as of June 19, 2016 is the result of our systematic analysis on three basic characteristics: earnings strength, relative valuation, and recent stock price movement. The company has suffered a very negative trend in earnings per share over the past 5 quarters. Because the company lacks sufficient analyst estimate data, we place greater weight on the historical EPS trend as the measure of earnings strength. Based on operating earnings yield, the company is overvalued when compared to all of the companies in our coverage universe. Share price changes over the past year indicates that LUK will perform poorly over the near term.

Financial Data

(US$ in Thousands)	3 Mos	12/31/2015	12/31/2014	12/31/2013	12/31/2012	12/31/2011	12/31/2010	12/31/2009
Earnings Per Share	(0.88)	0.74	0.54	1.06	3.44	0.10	7.85	2.25
Cash Flow Per Share	0.12	(2.05)	(2.65)	2.07	0.90	0.04	1.77	(0.55)
Tang Book Value Per Share	20.96	21.72	20.97	20.46	24.18	21.66	28.36	17.62
Dividends Per Share	0.250	0.250	0.250	0.250	0.250	0.250	0.250	...
Dividend Payout %	...	33.78	46.30	23.58	7.27	250.00	3.18	...
Income Statement								
Total Revenue	2,015,106	10,886,458	11,486,485	10,429,491	9,193,689	1,570,768	1,320,004	1,119,002
EBITDA	(264,530)	640,021	638,140	695,971	1,229,214	888,098	598,542	(35,793)
Depn & Amortn	35,167	172,073	139,744	138,964	170,113	95,233	104,730	86,377
Income Before Taxes	(322,015)	356,536	381,222	472,043	966,520	680,988	369,003	(250,973)
Income Taxes	(83,361)	109,947	165,971	110,741	376,494	270,253	(1,139,318)	7,143
Net Income	(218,602)	252,111	199,025	362,193	854,466	25,231	1,939,312	550,280
Average Shares	372,367	372,431	373,333	347,734	248,914	244,573	247,672	247,849
Balance Sheet								
Current Assets	10,309,171	12,075,445	15,583,132	14,499,058	2,521,266	1,253,479	985,590	551,474
Total Assets	43,134,365	46,339,812	52,623,908	47,866,781	9,349,118	9,263,189	9,350,298	6,762,364
Current Liabilities	8,564,241	11,187,884	11,389,283	19,336,501	1,280,479	877,132	747,840	624,981
Long-Term Obligations	8,649,030	7,407,594	8,527,929	8,180,865	918,126	1,875,571	1,548,469	1,657,779
Total Liabilities	32,918,060	35,813,601	42,196,750	37,639,319	2,581,850	3,088,793	2,393,540	2,400,717
Stockholders' Equity	10,216,305	10,526,211	10,427,158	10,227,462	6,767,268	6,174,396	6,956,758	4,361,647
Shares Outstanding	362,329	362,617	367,498	364,541	244,582	244,582	243,808	243,288
Statistical Record								
Return on Assets %	N.M.	0.51	0.40	1.27	9.16	0.27	24.07	9.20
Return on Equity %	N.M.	2.41	1.93	4.26	13.17	0.38	34.27	15.64
EBITDA Margin %	N.M.	5.88	5.56	6.67	13.37	56.54	45.34	N.M.
Net Margin %	N.M.	2.32	1.73	3.47	9.29	1.61	146.92	49.18
Asset Turnover	0.20	0.22	0.23	0.36	0.99	0.17	0.16	0.19
Current Ratio	1.20	1.08	1.37	0.75	1.97	1.43	1.32	0.88
Debt to Equity	0.85	0.70	0.82	0.80	0.14	0.30	0.22	0.38
Price Range	25.20-14.45	25.20-16.08	28.65-21.04	32.20-23.79	29.72-19.84	39.02-20.42	29.52-18.89	26.33-10.85
P/E Ratio	...	34.05-21.73	53.06-38.96	30.38-22.44	8.64-5.77	390.20-204.20	3.76-2.41	11.70-4.82
Average Yield %	1.24	1.14	0.98	0.91	1.06	0.82	1.04	...

Address: 520 Madison Avenue, New York, NY 10022 **Telephone:** 212-460-1900 **Fax:** 212-598-4869	**Web Site:** www.leucadia.com **Officers:** Joseph S. Steinberg - Chairman, President Brian P. Friedman - President	**Auditors:** PricewaterhouseCoopers LLP **Investor Contact:** 212-460-1900 **Transfer Agents:** American Stock Transfer & Trust Company, LLC, Brooklyn, NY

LEVEL 3 COMMUNICATIONS, INC.

Exchange	Symbol	Price	52Wk Range	Yield	P/E
NYS	LVLT	$53.95 (5/31/2016)	55.98-41.57	N/A	N/A

*7 Year Price Score 138.86 *NYSE Composite Index=100 *12 Month Price Score 103.87

Interim Earnings (Per Share)

Qtr.	Mar	Jun	Sep	Dec
2013	(0.36)	(0.11)	(0.09)	0.07
2014	0.47	0.21	0.35	0.18
2015	0.35	(0.04)	0.00	9.27
2016	0.34	...	...	...

Interim Dividends (Per Share)

No Dividends Paid

Valuation Analysis		Institutional Holding	
Forecast EPS	$1.72	No of Institutions	
	(05/20/2016)	623	
Market Cap	$19.3 Billion	Shares	
Book Value	$10.3 Billion	495,182,880	
Price/Book	1.86	% Held	
Price/Sales	2.34	N/A	

Business Summary: Services (MIC: 6.1.2 SIC: 4813 NAIC: 517110)

Level 3 Communications is a facilities-based provider of a range of integrated communications services. A facilities-based provider is a provider that owns or leases a substantial portion of the plant, property and equipment necessary to provide its services. Co. provides a range of communications services, which include Internet Protocol and data services, transport and fiber services, voice services, collaboration services, colocation and data center services, and wholesale voice services. Co. provides communications services to a range of wholesale and enterprise customers. Co.'s fiber optic network has reach across North America, Europe and Latin America.

Recent Developments: For the quarter ended Mar 31 2016, net income increased 1.6% to US$124.0 million from US$122.0 million in the year-earlier quarter. Revenues were US$2.05 billion, unchanged from the year before. Operating income was US$362.0 million versus US$316.0 million in the prior-year quarter, an increase of 14.6%. Direct operating expenses declined 4.4% to US$1.03 billion from US$1.08 billion in the comparable period the year before. Indirect operating expenses decreased 0.2% to US$657.0 million from US$658.0 million in the equivalent prior-year period.

Prospects: Our evaluation of Level 3 Communications Inc. as of June 19, 2016 is the result of our systematic analysis on three basic characteristics: earnings strength, relative valuation, and recent stock price movement. The company has generated a negative trend in earnings per share over the past 5 quarters. However, while recent estimates for the company have been mixed, LVLT has posted results that fell short of analysts expectations. Based on operating earnings yield, the company is about fairly valued when compared to all of the companies in our coverage universe. Share price changes over the past year indicates that LVLT will perform well over the near term.

Financial Data

(US$ in Thousands)	3 Mos	12/31/2015	12/31/2014	12/31/2013	12/31/2012	12/31/2011	12/31/2010	12/31/2009
Earnings Per Share	...	9.58	1.21	(0.49)	(1.96)	(5.51)	(5.55)	(5.70)
Cash Flow Per Share	5.77	5.25	4.56	3.21	2.68	2.83	3.06	3.28
Tang Book Value Per Share	4.26	3.51	N.M.	N.M.	N.M.	N.M.	...	N.M.
Income Statement								
Total Revenue	2,051,000	8,229,000	6,777,000	6,313,000	6,376,000	4,333,000	3,651,000	3,762,000
EBITDA	357,000	1,863,000	1,604,000	1,305,000	1,016,000	635,000	653,000	799,000
Depn & Amortn	5,000	939,000	713,000	727,000	659,000	706,000	781,000	823,000
Income Before Taxes	218,000	283,000	238,000	(71,000)	(374,000)	(786,000)	(713,000)	(617,000)
Income Taxes	94,000	(3,150,000)	(76,000)	38,000	48,000	41,000	(91,000)	1,000
Net Income	124,000	3,433,000	314,000	(109,000)	(422,000)	(756,000)	(622,000)	(618,000)
Average Shares	360,339	358,593	258,483	222,368	215,356	137,176	110,679	108,869
Balance Sheet								
Current Assets	2,789,000	1,749,000	1,489,000	1,454,000	1,842,000	1,707,000	972,000	1,259,000
Total Assets	25,039,000	24,145,000	20,947,000	12,874,000	13,307,000	13,188,000	8,355,000	9,062,000
Current Liabilities	2,187,000	1,416,000	1,914,000	1,446,000	1,802,000	1,658,000	956,000	1,519,000
Long-Term Obligations	10,870,000	10,994,000	10,984,000	8,331,000	8,516,000	8,385,000	6,268,000	5,755,000
Total Liabilities	14,697,000	14,019,000	14,584,000	11,463,000	12,136,000	11,995,000	8,512,000	8,571,000
Stockholders' Equity	10,342,000	10,126,000	6,363,000	1,411,000	1,171,000	1,193,000	(157,000)	491,000
Shares Outstanding	357,005	356,374	341,361	234,688	218,380	207,913	111,365	109,607
Statistical Record								
Return on Assets %	14.82	15.23	1.86	N.M.	N.M.	N.M.	N.M.	N.M.
Return on Equity %	40.27	41.64	8.08	N.M.	N.M.	N.M.	N.M.	N.M.
EBITDA Margin %	17.41	22.64	23.67	20.67	15.93	14.65	17.89	21.24
Net Margin %	6.05	41.72	4.63	N.M.	N.M.	N.M.	N.M.	N.M.
Asset Turnover	0.36	0.36	0.40	0.48	0.48	0.40	0.42	0.40
Current Ratio	1.28	1.24	0.78	1.01	1.02	1.03	1.02	0.83
Debt to Equity	1.05	1.09	1.73	5.90	7.27	7.03	...	11.72
Price Range	56.90-41.57	56.90-41.57	50.05-31.01	33.19-19.34	27.53-16.87	39.30-14.70	26.25-12.87	25.65-9.02
P/E Ratio	...	5.94-4.34	41.36-25.63	...	...	...	...	...

Address: 1025 Eldorado Blvd., Broomfield, CO 80021-8869	Web Site: www.level3.com	Auditors: KPMG LLLP
Telephone: 720-888-1000	Officers: James O. Ellis - Chairman Jeff K. Storey - President, Chief Executive Officer, Chief Operating Officer	Investor Contact: 720-888-2518 Transfer Agents: Wells Fargo Shareowner Services, Saint Paul, MN

LEXMARK INTERNATIONAL, INC.

Exchange	Symbol	Price	52Wk Range	Yield	P/E
NYS	LXK	$37.86 (5/31/2016)	47.32-24.45	3.80	N/A

'7 Year Price Score 86.27   *NYSE Composite Index=100   *12 Month Price Score 106.98

Interim Earnings (Per Share)

Qtr.	Mar	Jun	Sep	Dec
2013	0.54	1.39	0.45	1.71
2014	0.46	0.59	0.60	(0.40)
2015	0.32	(0.59)	(0.25)	(0.18)
2016	(0.63)	...	...	...

Interim Dividends (Per Share)

Amt	Decl	Ex	Rec	Pay
0.36Q	07/23/2015	08/26/2015	08/28/2015	09/11/2015
0.36Q	10/22/2015	11/24/2015	11/27/2015	12/11/2015
0.36Q	02/18/2016	02/25/2016	02/29/2016	03/11/2016
0.36Q	04/20/2016	06/01/2016	06/03/2016	06/17/2016

Indicated Div: $1.44

Valuation Analysis

Forecast EPS	$2.73 (05/20/2016)
Market Cap	$2.4 Billion
Book Value	$1.1 Billion
Price/Book	2.22
Price/Sales	0.68

Institutional Holding

No of Institutions	383
Shares	73,700,992
% Held	93.95

TRADING VOLUME (thousand shares)

Business Summary: Peripherals (MIC: 6.2.2 SIC: 3577 NAIC: 334119)

Lexmark International develops, manufactures and supplies printing, imaging, device management, managed print services (MPS), document workflow, and business process and content management solutions. Co.'s products include laser printers and multifunction devices, dot matrix printers and the associated supplies/services. Co. has two segments: Imaging Solutions and Services, which provides color and monochrome laser printers and laser multifunction printers, and supplies, software applications, software solutions and MPS; and Enterprise Software, which provides enterprise content management, business process management and document output management/customer communications management.

Recent Developments: For the quarter ended Mar 31 2016, net loss amounted to US$39.4 million versus net income of US$20.2 million in the year-earlier quarter. Revenues were US$806.2 million, down 5.4% from US$852.0 million the year before. Operating loss was US$38.5 million versus an income of US$42.2 million in the prior-year quarter. Direct operating expenses declined 4.3% to US$499.8 million from US$522.1 million in the comparable period the year before. Indirect operating expenses increased 19.9% to US$344.9 million from US$287.7 million in the equivalent prior-year period.

Prospects: Our evaluation of Lexmark International Inc. as of June 19, 2016 is the result of our systematic analysis on three basic characteristics: earnings strength, relative valuation, and recent stock price movement. The company has generated a negative trend in earnings per share over the past 5 quarters and while recent estimates for the company have remained steady, LXK has posted results that fell short of analysts expectations. Based on operating earnings yield, the company is undervalued when compared to all of the companies in our coverage universe. Share price changes over the past year indicates that LXK will perform poorly over the near term.

Financial Data
(US$ in Thousands)

	3 Mos	12/31/2015	12/31/2014	12/31/2013	12/31/2012	12/31/2011	12/31/2010	12/31/2009
Earnings Per Share	(1.65)	(0.66)	1.25	4.08	1.53	4.12	4.28	1.86
Cash Flow Per Share	3.17	1.75	6.82	7.62	6.01	5.07	6.62	5.14
Tang Book Value Per Share	N.M.	N.M.	6.41	10.55	10.53	14.34	13.41	12.98
Dividends Per Share	1.440	1.440	1.380	1.200	1.150	0.250	...	...
Dividend Payout %	...	...	110.40	29.41	75.16	6.07	...	...
Income Statement								
Total Revenue	806,200	3,551,200	3,710,500	3,667,600	3,797,600	4,173,000	4,199,700	3,879,900
EBITDA	33,200	142,200	339,500	590,700	417,200	639,500	628,800	417,500
Depn & Amortn	72,100	170,500	194,500	189,300	229,600	196,000	181,000	209,100
Income Before Taxes	(50,200)	(67,700)	113,400	368,400	158,000	413,600	421,500	187,000
Income Taxes	(10,800)	(27,300)	34,300	106,600	51,700	92,700	81,500	41,100
Net Income	(39,400)	(40,400)	79,100	261,800	106,300	320,900	340,000	145,900
Average Shares	62,300	61,600	63,200	64,100	69,500	77,900	79,500	78,600
Balance Sheet								
Current Assets	982,800	1,029,300	1,834,300	1,971,700	1,921,600	2,208,800	2,269,600	2,140,700
Total Assets	3,830,800	3,912,400	3,633,100	3,619,500	3,523,400	3,637,000	3,705,200	3,354,200
Current Liabilities	1,188,900	1,171,500	1,211,300	1,146,900	1,443,100	1,123,300	1,246,300	1,191,800
Long-Term Obligations	992,000	1,061,300	699,700	699,600	299,600	649,300	649,100	648,900
Total Liabilities	2,761,800	2,794,400	2,369,800	2,251,200	2,242,200	2,245,300	2,310,900	2,340,600
Stockholders' Equity	1,069,000	1,118,000	1,263,300	1,368,300	1,281,200	1,391,700	1,394,300	1,013,600
Shares Outstanding	62,600	61,900	61,300	62,000	63,900	71,400	78,600	78,100
Statistical Record								
Return on Assets %	N.M.	N.M.	2.18	7.33	2.96	8.74	9.63	4.41
Return on Equity %	N.M.	N.M.	6.01	19.76	7.93	23.04	28.24	15.98
EBITDA Margin %	4.12	4.00	9.15	16.11	10.99	15.32	14.97	10.76
Net Margin %	N.M.	N.M.	2.13	7.14	2.80	7.69	8.10	3.76
Asset Turnover	0.96	0.94	1.02	1.03	1.06	1.14	1.19	1.17
Current Ratio	0.83	0.88	1.51	1.72	1.33	1.97	1.82	1.80
Debt to Equity	0.93	0.95	0.55	0.51	0.23	0.47	0.47	0.64
Price Range	47.32-24.45	47.32-27.92	51.17-34.40	41.11-21.79	37.91-16.77	40.35-26.48	47.72-25.50	28.94-14.48
P/E Ratio	...	...	40.94-27.52	10.08-5.34	24.78-10.96	9.79-6.43	11.15-5.96	15.56-7.78
Average Yield %	4.09	3.79	3.16	3.84	4.26	0.77	...	...

Address: One Lexmark Centre Drive, 740 West New Circle Road, Lexington, KY 40550
Telephone: 859-232-2000

Web Site: www.lexmark.com
Officers: Paul A. Rooke - Chairman, President, Chief Executive Officer, Executive Vice President, Division Officer David Reeder - Chief Financial Officer, Vice President

Auditors: PricewaterhouseCoopers LLP
Investor Contact: 859-232-5568
Transfer Agents: Computershare, Providence, RI

LIBERTY PROPERTY TRUST

Exchange	Symbol	Price	52Wk Range	Yield	P/E
NYS	LPT	$37.32 (5/31/2016)	37.37-27.30	5.09	20.97

*7 Year Price Score 81.47 *NYSE Composite Index=100 *12 Month Price Score 106.82

Interim Earnings (Per Share)

Qtr.	Mar	Jun	Sep	Dec
2013	0.60	0.33	0.21	0.49
2014	0.49	0.20	0.23	0.55
2015	0.21	0.24	0.61	0.54
2016	0.39	...	...	...

Interim Dividends (Per Share)

Amt	Decl	Ex	Rec	Pay
0.475Q	09/11/2015	09/29/2015	10/01/2015	10/15/2015
0.475Q	12/14/2015	12/30/2015	01/04/2016	01/15/2016
0.475Q	03/15/2016	03/29/2016	03/31/2016	04/15/2016
0.475Q	06/15/2016	06/29/2016	07/01/2016	07/15/2016

Indicated Div: $1.90

Valuation Analysis

		Institutional Holding	
Forecast EPS	$1.13	No of Institutions	
	(05/20/2016)	463	
Market Cap	$5.5 Billion	Shares	
Book Value	$2.9 Billion	161,523,664	
Price/Book	1.88	% Held	
Price/Sales	6.91	101.24	

TRADING VOLUME (thousand shares)

Business Summary: REITs (MIC: 5.3.1 SIC: 6798 NAIC: 525930)

Liberty Property Trust is a self-administered and self-managed real estate investment trust. Substantially all of Co.'s operations are conducted directly or indirectly, by its subsidiary, Liberty Property Limited Partnership. Co. provides leasing, property management, development and other tenant-related services for a portfolio of industrial and office properties. As of Dec 31 2015, Co. owned and operated 482 industrial and 128 office properties; and 1,751 acres of developable land; and had an ownership interest, through unconsolidated joint ventures, in 48 industrial and 33 office properties; and 402 acres of developable land.

Recent Developments: For the quarter ended Mar 31 2016, net income increased 85.4% to US$59.1 million from US$31.9 million in the year-earlier quarter. Revenues were US$190.1 million, down 8.1% from US$206.9 million the year before.

Prospects: Our evaluation of Liberty Property Trust as of June 19, 2016 is the result of our systematic analysis on three basic characteristics: earnings strength, relative valuation, and recent stock price movement. The company has managed to produce a neutral trend in earnings per share over the past 5 quarters. Because the company lacks sufficient analyst estimate data, we place greater weight on the historical EPS trend as the measure of earnings strength. Based on operating earnings yield, the company is overvalued when compared to all of the companies in our coverage universe. Share price changes over the past year indicates that LPT will perform in line with the market over the near term.

Financial Data

(US$ in Thousands)	3 Mos	12/31/2015	12/31/2014	12/31/2013	12/31/2012	12/31/2011	12/31/2010	12/31/2009
Earnings Per Share	1.78	1.60	1.47	1.60	1.17	1.59	1.12	0.52
Cash Flow Per Share	2.69	2.60	2.29	2.43	2.71	2.77	2.65	2.78
Tang Book Value Per Share	19.82	20.35	20.70	20.73	17.65	18.96	19.05	19.68
Dividends Per Share	1.900	1.900	1.900	1.900	1.900	1.900	1.900	1.900
Dividend Payout %	106.74	118.75	129.25	118.75	162.39	119.50	169.64	365.38
Income Statement								
Total Revenue	190,140	808,773	792,631	645,930	685,552	667,594	746,830	744,257
EBITDA	62,245	438,132	436,523	365,547	382,305	390,291	427,445	431,646
Depn & Amortn	1,002	181,000	179,100	162,500	140,600	144,300	147,300	144,500
Income Before Taxes	34,429	144,216	123,205	85,811	131,364	132,370	140,864	149,080
Income Taxes	801	3,233	2,967	2,799	976	1,020	1,736	494
Net Income	57,554	238,039	217,910	209,738	137,436	183,999	127,762	56,376
Average Shares	146,531	148,843	147,886	130,909	117,694	115,503	113,606	108,002
Balance Sheet								
Current Assets	189,866	177,501	213,061	328,726	189,119	193,063	273,766	379,796
Total Assets	6,518,298	6,557,629	6,625,536	6,775,560	5,177,971	4,989,673	5,062,833	5,227,421
Current Liabilities	174,775	149,323	148,809	167,506	109,260	104,523	109,622	117,848
Long-Term Obligations	3,145,270	3,147,016	3,163,395	3,253,519	2,657,398	2,222,862	2,359,822	2,456,875
Total Liabilities	3,613,032	3,604,701	3,597,864	3,739,716	3,086,959	2,886,079	2,980,647	3,105,126
Stockholders' Equity	2,905,266	2,952,928	3,027,672	3,035,844	2,091,012	2,103,594	2,082,186	2,122,295
Shares Outstanding	146,603	147,577	148,557	146,596	118,470	116,102	114,280	112,625
Statistical Record								
Return on Assets %	4.11	3.61	3.25	3.51	2.70	3.66	2.48	1.08
Return on Equity %	9.12	7.96	7.19	8.18	6.54	8.79	6.08	2.76
EBITDA Margin %	32.74	54.17	55.07	56.59	55.77	58.46	57.23	58.00
Net Margin %	30.27	29.43	27.49	32.47	20.05	27.56	17.11	7.57
Asset Turnover	0.12	0.12	0.12	0.11	0.13	0.13	0.15	0.14
Current Ratio	1.09	1.19	1.43	1.96	1.73	1.85	2.50	3.22
Debt to Equity	1.08	1.07	1.04	1.07	1.27	1.06	1.13	1.16
Price Range	36.75-27.30	41.42-29.91	40.08-32.77	44.70-32.12	38.57-30.91	36.06-26.16	35.05-27.41	35.11-16.90
P/E Ratio	20.65-15.34	25.89-18.69	27.27-22.29	27.94-20.07	32.97-26.42	22.68-16.45	31.29-24.47	67.52-32.50
Average Yield %	5.82	5.49	5.24	5.03	5.36	5.87	5.99	7.35

Address: 500 Chesterfield Parkway, Malvern, PA 19355
Telephone: 610-648-1700

Web Site: www.libertyproperty.com
Officers: William P. Hankowsky - Chairman, President, Chief Executive Officer Robert E. Fenza - Executive Vice President, Chief Operating Officer

Auditors: Ernst & Young LLP
Investor Contact: 610-648-1704
Transfer Agents: Wells Fargo Shareholder Services, St. Paul, MN

LILLY (ELI) & CO.

Exchange	Symbol	Price	52Wk Range	Yield	P/E
NYS	LLY	$75.03 (5/31/2016)	89.98-69.06	2.72	34.58

*7 Year Price Score 133.23 *NYSE Composite Index=100   ***12 Month Price Score 93.23**

Interim Earnings (Per Share)

Qtr.	Mar	Jun	Sep	Dec
2013	1.42	1.11	1.11	0.68
2014	0.68	0.68	0.47	0.41
2015	0.50	0.56	0.75	0.45
2016	0.41	...	...	...

Interim Dividends (Per Share)

Amt	Decl	Ex	Rec	Pay
0.50Q	10/19/2015	11/10/2015	11/13/2015	12/10/2015
0.51Q	12/08/2015	02/10/2016	02/12/2016	03/10/2016
0.51Q	05/02/2016	05/11/2016	05/13/2016	06/10/2016
0.51Q	06/20/2016	08/11/2016	08/15/2016	09/09/2016

Indicated Div: $2.04 (Div. Reinv. Plan)

Valuation Analysis

		Institutional Holding	
Forecast EPS	$3.57 (05/20/2016)	No of Institutions	1633
Market Cap	$82.8 Billion	Shares	936,653,824
Book Value	$15.0 Billion	% Held	74.52
Price/Book	5.52		
Price/Sales	4.10		

TRADING VOLUME (thousand shares)

Business Summary: Pharmaceuticals (MIC: 4.1.1 SIC: 2834 NAIC: 325412)

Eli Lilly & Company is engaged in discovering, developing, manufacturing, and marketing products in two business segments: human pharmaceutical products and animal health products. Co.'s human pharmaceutical products include: endocrinology products, neurosciences products, oncology products, and cardiovascular products. Co.'s animal health products are comprised of products for food animals, which include Rumensin®, a cattle feed additive, and Tylan®, an antibiotic used to control certain diseases in cattle, swine, and poultry; as well as products for companion animals, which include Trifexis® and Comfortis®, a chewable tablet that kills fleas and prevents flea infestations on dogs.

Recent Developments: For the quarter ended Mar 31 2016, net income decreased 16.9% to US$440.1 million from US$529.5 million in the year-earlier quarter. Revenues were US$4.87 billion, up 4.7% from US$4.64 billion the year before. Direct operating expenses rose 10.9% to US$1.32 billion from US$1.19 billion in the comparable period the year before. Indirect operating expenses decreased 3.4% to US$2.83 billion from US$2.93 billion in the equivalent prior-year period.

Prospects: Our evaluation of Lilly (Eli) & Co. as of June 19, 2016 is the result of our systematic analysis on three basic characteristics: earnings strength, relative valuation, and recent stock price movement. The company has generated a negative trend in earnings per share over the past 5 quarters and while recent estimates for the company have been raised by analysts, LLY has posted results that fell short of analysts expectations. Based on operating earnings yield, the company is about fairly valued when compared to all of the companies in our coverage universe. Share price changes over the past year indicates that LLY will perform in line with the market over the near term.

Financial Data

(US$ in Thousands)	3 Mos	12/31/2015	12/31/2014	12/31/2013	12/31/2012	12/31/2011	12/31/2010	12/31/2009
Earnings Per Share	2.17	2.26	2.23	4.32	3.66	3.90	4.58	3.94
Cash Flow Per Share	2.39	2.61	4.08	5.31	4.75	6.49	6.20	3.95
Tang Book Value Per Share	5.50	4.97	9.66	11.91	8.75	7.27	6.60	5.07
Dividends Per Share	2.010	2.000	1.960	1.960	1.960	1.960	1.960	1.960
Dividend Payout %	92.63	88.50	87.89	45.37	53.55	50.26	42.79	49.75
Income Statement								
Total Revenue	4,865,100	19,958,700	19,615,600	23,113,100	22,603,400	24,286,500	23,076,000	21,836,000
EBITDA	971,500	3,581,800	3,787,200	6,704,500	6,235,000	6,188,000	7,407,900	6,357,400
Depn & Amortn	385,500	717,600	759,100	774,800	754,000	732,400	749,100	813,500
Income Before Taxes	566,800	2,790,000	3,000,300	5,889,300	5,408,200	5,349,500	6,525,200	5,357,800
Income Taxes	126,700	381,600	609,800	1,204,500	1,319,600	1,001,800	1,455,700	1,029,000
Net Income	440,100	2,408,400	2,390,500	4,684,800	4,088,600	4,347,700	5,069,500	4,328,800
Average Shares	1,063,100	1,065,720	1,074,286	1,084,766	1,117,294	1,113,967	1,105,813	1,098,367
Balance Sheet								
Current Assets	11,714,600	12,573,600	12,179,800	13,104,700	13,038,700	14,248,200	14,840,000	12,486,500
Total Assets	34,691,800	35,568,900	37,178,200	35,248,700	34,398,900	33,659,800	31,001,400	27,460,900
Current Liabilities	7,340,900	8,229,600	11,207,500	8,916,600	8,389,500	8,930,900	7,101,400	6,568,100
Long-Term Obligations	7,477,600	7,972,400	5,367,700	4,200,300	5,519,400	5,464,700	6,770,500	6,634,700
Total Liabilities	19,681,900	20,997,600	21,805,000	17,617,300	19,633,700	20,118,100	18,581,100	17,937,200
Stockholders' Equity	15,009,900	14,571,300	15,373,200	17,631,400	14,765,200	13,541,700	12,420,300	9,523,700
Shares Outstanding	1,103,837	1,105,267	1,110,627	1,116,795	1,143,643	1,157,791	1,152,290	1,149,033
Statistical Record								
Return on Assets %	6.59	6.62	6.60	13.45	11.98	13.45	17.34	15.28
Return on Equity %	15.50	16.09	14.49	28.92	28.81	33.49	46.20	53.25
EBITDA Margin %	19.97	17.95	19.31	29.01	27.58	25.48	32.10	29.11
Net Margin %	9.05	12.07	12.19	20.27	18.09	17.90	21.97	19.82
Asset Turnover	0.57	0.55	0.54	0.66	0.66	0.75	0.79	0.77
Current Ratio	1.60	1.53	1.09	1.47	1.55	1.60	2.09	1.90
Debt to Equity	0.50	0.55	0.35	0.24	0.37	0.40	0.55	0.70
Price Range	89.98-69.06	89.98-68.41	72.83-50.73	58.33-47.65	53.81-38.49	41.75-33.63	38.06-32.25	40.57-27.47
P/E Ratio	41.47-31.82	39.81-30.27	32.66-22.75	13.50-11.03	14.70-10.52	10.71-8.62	8.31-7.04	10.30-6.97
Average Yield %	2.52	2.54	3.18	3.72	4.50	5.32	5.58	5.71

Address: Lilly Corporate Center, Indianapolis, IN 46285 **Telephone:** 317-276-2000	**Web Site:** www.lilly.com **Officers:** John C. Lechleiter - Chairman, President, Chief Executive Officer, Chief Operating Officer Derica W. Rice - Acting Chief Executive Officer, Executive Vice President, Chief Financial Officer	**Auditors:** Ernst & Young, LLP **Transfer Agents:** Wells Fargo Shareowner Services, St. Paul, MN

LINCOLN NATIONAL CORP.

Exchange	Symbol	Price	52Wk Range	Yield	P/E
NYS	LNC	$45.85 (5/31/2016)	61.65-30.78	2.18	10.97

*7 Year Price Score 115.52 *NYSE Composite Index=100   *12 Month Price Score 86.44

Interim Earnings (Per Share)

Qtr.	Mar	Jun	Sep	Dec
2013	0.86	1.15	1.23	1.28
2014	1.21	1.48	1.65	1.33
2015	1.15	1.35	0.87	1.14
2016	0.82	...	...	...

Interim Dividends (Per Share)

Amt	Decl	Ex	Rec	Pay
0.20Q	08/13/2015	10/07/2015	10/12/2015	11/01/2015
0.25Q	10/28/2015	01/07/2016	01/11/2016	02/01/2016
0.25Q	02/25/2016	04/07/2016	04/11/2016	05/02/2016
0.25Q	05/27/2016	07/07/2016	07/11/2016	08/01/2016

Indicated Div: $1.00 (Div. Reinv. Plan)

Valuation Analysis

Forecast EPS	$6.15 (05/20/2016)	**Institutional Holding** No of Institutions	850
Market Cap	$11.0 Billion	Shares	
Book Value	$14.7 Billion		227,123,856
Price/Book	0.75	% Held	
Price/Sales	0.81		81.33

Business Summary: Life & Health (MIC: 5.2.2 SIC: 6311 NAIC: 524113)

Lincoln National is a holding company. Co. operates multiple insurance and retirement businesses through its subsidiary companies. Through its business segments, Co. sells a range of wealth protection, accumulation and retirement income products and solutions. These products include fixed and indexed annuities, variable annuities, universal life insurance (UL), variable universal life insurance, linked-benefit UL, term life insurance, indexed universal life insurance, employer-sponsored retirement plans and services, and group life, disability and dental. Co. provides products and services through its Annuities, Retirement Plan Services, Life Insurance and Group Protection segments.

Recent Developments: For the quarter ended Mar 31 2016, net income decreased 30.7% to US$208.0 million from US$300.0 million in the year-earlier quarter. Revenues were US$3.24 billion, down 1.8% from US$3.30 billion the year before. Net premiums earned were US$816.0 million versus US$790.0 million in the prior-year quarter, an increase of 3.3%. Net investment income fell 1.3% to US$1.17 billion from US$1.19 billion a year ago.

Prospects: Our evaluation of Lincoln National Corp. (ID) as of June 19, 2016 is the result of our systematic analysis on three basic characteristics: earnings strength, relative valuation, and recent stock price movement. The company has enjoyed a very positive trend in earnings per share over the past 5 quarters. However, while recent estimates for the company have been mixed, LNC has posted results that fell short of analysts expectations. Based on operating earnings yield, the company is undervalued when compared to all of the companies in our coverage universe. Share price changes over the past year indicates that LNC will perform poorly over the near term.

Financial Data
(US$ in Thousands)

	3 Mos	12/31/2015	12/31/2014	12/31/2013	12/31/2012	12/31/2011	12/31/2010	12/31/2009
Earnings Per Share	4.18	4.51	5.67	4.52	4.56	0.92	2.54	(1.85)
Cash Flow Per Share	9.28	8.95	9.68	3.01	4.51	4.16	5.55	3.35
Tang Book Value Per Share	51.82	46.52	52.49	42.52	46.79	40.82	31.00	26.08
Dividends Per Share	0.850	0.800	0.640	0.480	0.320	0.200	0.040	0.240
Dividend Payout %	20.33	17.74	11.29	10.62	7.02	21.74	1.57	...
Income Statement								
Premium Income	816,000	3,246,000	2,988,000	2,687,000	2,462,000	2,294,000	2,176,000	2,064,000
Total Revenue	3,243,000	13,572,000	13,554,000	11,969,000	11,532,000	10,636,000	10,407,000	8,499,000
Benefits & Claims	1,331,000	5,044,000	4,679,000	3,862,000	3,538,000	3,345,000	3,330,000	2,836,000
Income Before Taxes	235,000	1,430,000	1,997,000	1,631,000	1,568,000	599,000	1,234,000	(521,000)
Income Taxes	27,000	276,000	483,000	387,000	282,000	297,000	283,000	(106,000)
Net Income	208,000	1,154,000	1,515,000	1,244,000	1,313,000	294,000	980,000	(485,000)
Average Shares	245,121	254,938	267,963	275,148	287,590	314,950	319,213	285,635
Balance Sheet								
Total Assets	255,718,000	251,937,000	253,377,000	236,945,000	218,869,000	202,906,000	193,824,000	177,433,000
Total Liabilities	241,060,000	238,320,000	237,637,000	223,493,000	203,896,000	188,742,000	181,018,000	165,733,000
Stockholders' Equity	14,658,000	13,617,000	15,740,000	13,452,000	14,973,000	14,164,000	12,806,000	11,700,000
Shares Outstanding	239,005	243,835	256,551	262,896	271,402	291,319	315,718	302,223
Statistical Record								
Return on Assets %	0.41	0.46	0.62	0.55	0.62	0.15	0.53	N.M.
Return on Equity %	6.88	7.86	10.38	8.75	8.99	2.18	8.00	N.M.
Loss Ratio %	163.11	155.39	156.59	143.73	143.70	145.82	153.03	137.40
Net Margin %	6.41	8.50	11.18	10.39	11.39	2.76	9.42	(5.71)
Price Range	61.65-30.78	61.65-46.07	58.80-45.67	51.95-25.90	27.29-19.29	32.49-14.32	32.90-20.97	27.84-5.01
P/E Ratio	14.75-7.36	13.67-10.22	10.37-8.05	11.49-5.73	5.98-4.23	35.32-15.57	12.95-8.26	...
Average Yield %	1.67	1.45	1.23	1.24	1.37	0.80	0.15	1.30

Address: 150 N. Radnor Chester Road, Suite A305, Radnor, PA 19087 **Telephone:** 484-583-1400	**Web Site:** www.lfg.com **Officers:** Dennis R. Glass - President, Chief Executive Officer Randal Jay Freitag - Executive Vice President, Chief Financial Officer	**Auditors:** Ernst & Young LLP **Transfer Agents:** Computershare, Providence, RI

LINDSAY CORP

Exchange	Symbol	Price	52Wk Range	Yield	P/E	Div Achiever
NYS	LNN	$71.34 (5/31/2016)	89.70-64.06	1.57	64.27	13 Years

*7 Year Price Score 94.55 *NYSE Composite Index=100 *12 Month Price Score 96.04

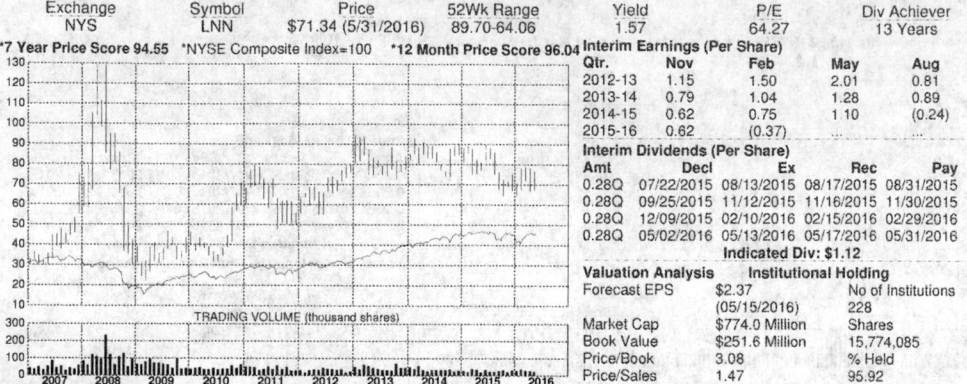

Interim Earnings (Per Share)

Qtr.	Nov	Feb	May	Aug
2012-13	1.15	1.50	2.01	0.81
2013-14	0.79	1.04	1.28	0.89
2014-15	0.62	0.75	1 10	(0.24)
2015-16	0.62	(0.37)		

Interim Dividends (Per Share)

Amt	Decl	Ex	Rec	Pay
0.28Q	07/22/2015	08/13/2015	08/17/2015	08/31/2015
0.28Q	09/25/2015	11/12/2015	11/16/2015	11/30/2015
0.28Q	12/09/2015	02/10/2016	02/15/2016	02/29/2016
0.28Q	05/02/2016	05/13/2016	05/17/2016	05/31/2016

Indicated Div: $1.12

Valuation Analysis

Forecast EPS	$2.37	No of Institutions
	(05/15/2016)	228
Market Cap	$774.0 Million	Shares
Book Value	$251.6 Million	15,774,085
Price/Book	3.08	% Held
Price/Sales	1.47	95.92

Institutional Holding

Business Summary: Industrial Machinery & Equipment (MIC: 7.2.1 SIC: 3523 NAIC: 333111)

Lindsay is a provider of water management and road infrastructure products and services. Co.'s irrigation segment includes the manufacture and marketing of center pivot, lateral move, hose reel irrigation systems, and repair and replacement parts, and the design and manufacture of water pumping stations and controls for the agriculture, golf, landscape and municipal markets. Co.'s infrastructure segment includes the manufacture and marketing of moveable barriers, specialty barriers, crash cushions and end terminals, road marking and road safety equipment, large diameter steel tubing, and railroad signals and structures, and the provision of outsourced manufacturing and production services.

Recent Developments: For the quarter ended Feb 29 2016, net loss amounted to US$4.1 million versus net income of US$9.0 million in the year-earlier quarter. Revenues were US$120.6 million, down 14.5% from US$141.1 million the year before. Operating loss was US$4.7 million versus an income of US$14.5 million in the prior-year quarter. Direct operating expenses declined 13.2% to US$88.1 million from US$101.5 million in the comparable period the year before. Indirect operating expenses increased 48.4% to US$37.1 million from US$25.0 million in the equivalent prior-year period.

Prospects: Our evaluation of Lindsay Corp. as of June 19, 2016 is the result of our systematic analysis on three basic characteristics: earnings strength, relative valuation, and recent stock price movement. The company has produced a positive trend in earnings per share over the past 5 quarters. However, while recent estimates for the company have been lowered by analysts, LNN has posted results that fell short of analysts expectations. Based on operating earnings yield, the company is about fairly valued when compared to all of the companies in our coverage universe. Share price changes over the past year indicates that LNN will perform well over the near term.

Financial Data

(US$ in Thousands)	6 Mos	3 Mos	08/31/2015	08/31/2014	08/31/2013	08/31/2012	08/31/2011	08/31/2010
Earnings Per Share	1.11	2.23	2.22	4.00	5.47	3.38	2.90	1.98
Cash Flow Per Share	2.55	4.57	4.12	7.15	4.48	4.12	3.43	1.91
Tang Book Value Per Share	11.57	13.83	14.16	25.21	23.87	20.11	17.05	13.97
Dividends Per Share	1.110	1.100	1.090	0.920	0.475	0.385	0.345	0.325
Dividend Payout %	100.00	49.33	49.10	23.00	8.68	11.39	11.90	16.41
Income Statement								
Total Revenue	242,195	121,622	560,181	617,933	690,848	551,255	478,890	358,440
EBITDA	14,743	15,723	60,446	88,913	116,915	74,696	65,961	46,087
Depn & Amortn	8,536	4,295	11,700	10,800	9,800	9,600	9,000	8,100
Income Before Taxes	4,203	10,396	46,751	78,655	107,307	65,108	56,514	36,782
Income Taxes	1,388	3,452	20,442	27,143	36,737	21,831	19,712	11,920
Net Income	2,815	6,944	26,309	51,512	70,570	43,277	36,802	24,862
Average Shares	11,024	11,288	11,855	12,882	12,901	12,810	12,692	12,585
Balance Sheet								
Current Assets	284,053	308,708	322,167	374,058	368,791	298,865	257,693	208,011
Total Assets	495,483	521,616	536,468	526,551	512,296	415,531	381,144	325,481
Current Liabilities	84,537	87,555	95,112	116,367	102,092	80,438	79,319	67,082
Long-Term Obligations	117,075	117,124	117,173	...	...	...	4,285	8,571
Total Liabilities	243,864	239,924	247,908	143,904	131,658	104,693	105,479	95,874
Stockholders' Equity	251,619	281,692	288,560	382,647	380,638	310,838	275,665	229,607
Shares Outstanding	10,849	11,182	11,290	12,440	12,873	12,723	12,676	12,486
Statistical Record								
Return on Assets %	2.30	5.08	4.95	9.92	15.21	10.83	10.42	7.85
Return on Equity %	4.28	8.10	7.84	13.50	20.41	14.72	14.57	11.37
EBITDA Margin %	6.09	12.93	10.79	14.39	16.92	13.55	13.77	12.86
Net Margin %	1.16	5.71	4.70	8.34	10.21	7.85	7.68	6.94
Asset Turnover	0.96	1.08	1.05	1.19	1.49	1.38	1.36	1.13
Current Ratio	3.36	3.53	3.39	3.21	3.61	3.72	3.25	3.10
Debt to Equity	0.47	0.42	0.41	...	...	...	0.02	0.04
Price Range	89.70-64.06	89.70-64.06	89.70-73.48	92.93-72.00	94.57-65.36	73.84-49.53	79.19-36.87	45.94-31.44
P/E Ratio	80.81-57.71	40.22-28.73	40.41-33.10	23.23-18.00	17.29-11.95	21.85-14.65	27.31-12.71	23.20-15.88
Average Yield %	1.47	1.39	1.33	1.12	0.60	0.63	0.55	0.86

Address: 2222 North. 111th Street, Omaha, NE 68164 Telephone: 402-829-6800 Fax: 402-829-6834	Web Site: www.lindsay.com Officers: Michael C. Nahl - Chairman Richard W. Parod - President, Chief Executive Officer	Auditors: KPMG LLP Investor Contact: 402-827-6579 Transfer Agents: Wells Fargo Shareowner Services, St. Paul, MN

LINKEDIN CORP

Exchange	Symbol	Price	52Wk Range	Yield	P/E
NYS	LNKD	$136.50 (5/31/2016)	255.54-100.98	N/A	N/A

*7 Year Price Score N/A ***NYSE Composite Index=100** ***12 Month Price Score 65.58**

TRADING VOLUME (thousand shares)

Interim Earnings (Per Share)

Qtr.	Mar	Jun	Sep	Dec
2013	0.20	0.03	(0.03)	0.03
2014	(0.11)	(0.01)	(0.03)	0.02
2015	(0.34)	(0.53)	(0.31)	(0.11)
2016	(0.35)	...	...	...

Interim Dividends (Per Share)

No Dividends Paid

Valuation Analysis   Institutional Holding

Forecast EPS	$3.41	No of Institutions
(05/20/2016)		661
Market Cap	$18.2 Billion	Shares
Book Value	$4.6 Billion	102,190,928
Price/Book	3.95	% Held
Price/Sales	5.67	84.87

Business Summary: Internet & Software (MIC: 6.3.2 SIC: 7371 NAIC: 541511)

LinkedIn operates an online professional network on the Internet through which its members are able to create, manage and share their professional identities, build and engage with their professional networks, access shared knowledge and insights, and find business opportunities.

Recent Developments: For the quarter ended Mar 31 2016, net loss amounted to US$45.3 million versus a net loss of US$42.4 million in the year-earlier quarter. Revenues were US$860.7 million, up 35.0% from US$637.7 million the year before. Operating loss was US$66.2 million versus a loss of US$17.2 million in the prior-year quarter. Direct operating expenses rose 32.9% to US$117.5 million from US$88.4 million in the comparable period the year before. Indirect operating expenses increased 42.9% to US$809.3 million from US$566.5 million in the equivalent prior-year period.

Prospects: Our evaluation of LinkedIn Corp as of June 19, 2016 is the result of our systematic analysis on three basic characteristics: earnings strength, relative valuation, and recent stock price movement. The company has enjoyed a very positive trend in earnings per share over the past 5 quarters. However, while recent estimates for the company have been mixed, LNKD has posted better than expected results. Based on operating earnings yield, the company is overvalued when compared to all of the companies in our coverage universe. Share price changes over the past year indicates that LNKD will perform very poorly over the near term.

Financial Data
(US$ in Thousands)

	3 Mos	12/31/2015	12/31/2014	12/31/2013	12/31/2012	12/31/2011	12/31/2010	12/31/2009
Earnings Per Share	(1.30)	(1.29)	(0.13)	0.23	0.19	0.11	0.07	(0.10)
Cash Flow Per Share	6.73	6.25	4.63	3.84	2.53	1.73	1.28	0.52
Tang Book Value Per Share	20.08	19.60	22.69	20.24	7.00	5.96	2.38	1.95
Income Statement								
Total Revenue	860,650	2,990,911	2,218,767	1,528,545	972,309	522,189	243,099	120,127
EBITDA	40,481	111,381	235,331	164,433	126,089	62,273	37,499	8,170
Depn & Amortn	110,890	285,800	202,300	118,100	70,000	39,500	18,597	11,645
Income Before Taxes	(78,277)	(214,730)	31,205	49,228	57,114	22,942	18,966	(3,125)
Income Taxes	(32,961)	(49,969)	46,525	22,459	35,504	11,030	3,581	848
Net Income	(45,316)	(164,761)	(15,320)	26,769	21,610	11,912	15,385	(3,973)
Average Shares	132,779	129,024	122,800	118,944	112,844	104,118	46,459	41,184
Balance Sheet								
Current Assets	3,968,396	3,935,089	4,122,100	2,755,470	1,018,797	725,927	172,206	121,158
Total Assets	7,209,367	7,011,199	5,427,257	3,352,793	1,382,330	873,697	238,188	148,559
Current Liabilities	1,206,515	1,188,084	882,785	641,991	415,379	226,659	105,472	49,273
Long-Term Obligations	1,138,264	1,126,534	1,081,553	...	...	...	...	...
Total Liabilities	2,597,123	2,542,556	2,101,865	723,399	473,906	248,718	113,958	51,496
Stockholders' Equity	4,612,244	4,468,643	3,325,392	2,629,394	908,424	624,979	124,230	97,063
Shares Outstanding	133,544	132,048	125,041	120,351	108,647	101,480	43,308	41,745
Statistical Record								
Return on Assets %	N.M.	N.M.	N.M.	1.13	1.91	2.14	7.96	...
Return on Equity %	N.M.	N.M.	N.M.	1.51	2.81	3.18	13.90	...
EBITDA Margin %	4.70	3.72	10.61	10.76	12.97	11.93	15.43	6.80
Net Margin %	N.M.	N.M.	N.M.	1.75	2.22	2.28	6.33	N.M.
Asset Turnover	0.50	0.48	0.51	0.65	0.86	0.94	1.26	...
Current Ratio	3.29	3.31	4.67	4.29	2.45	3.20	1.63	2.46
Debt to Equity	0.25	0.25	0.33	...	...	...	...	...
Price Range	265.35-100.98	270.76-169.94	238.43-142.33	256.14-111.17	123.23-61.79	109.97-59.07	...	...
P/E Ratio	...	...	...	N.M.	648.58-325.21	999.73-537.00	...	...

Address: 2029 Stierlin Court, Mountain View, CA 94043	Web Site: www.linkedin.com	Auditors: Deloitte & Touche LLP
Telephone: 650-687 3600	Officers: Reid G. Hoffman - Chairman Jeffrey Weiner - Chief Executive Officer	Transfer Agents: Computershare Trust Company, N.A., Canton, MA

LITHIA MOTORS, INC.

Exchange	Symbol	Price	52Wk Range	Yield	P/E
NYS	LAD	$82.34 (5/31/2016)	126.06-73.79	1.21	11.88

*7 Year Price Score 182.32 *NYSE Composite Index=100   ***12 Month Price Score 80.74**

TRADING VOLUME (thousand shares)

Interim Earnings (Per Share)

Qtr.	Mar	Jun	Sep	Dec
2013	0.86	0.98	1.18	1.04
2014	0.94	1.45	1.31	1.55
2015	1.53	1.93	1.64	1.81
2016	1.55			

Interim Dividends (Per Share)

Amt	Decl	Ex	Rec	Pay
0.20Q	07/22/2015	08/05/2015	08/07/2015	08/21/2015
0.20Q	10/21/2015	11/04/2015	11/06/2015	11/20/2015
0.20Q	02/24/2016	03/09/2016	03/11/2016	03/25/2016
0.25Q	04/21/2016	05/11/2016	05/13/2016	05/27/2016

Indicated Div: $1.00

Valuation Analysis

		Institutional Holding	
Forecast EPS	$7.55	No of Institutions	345
	(05/20/2016)		
Market Cap	$2.1 Billion	Shares	26,441,064
Book Value	$814.7 Million	% Held	89.15
Price/Book	2.60		
Price/Sales	0.26		

Business Summary: Retail - Automotive (MIC: 2.1.4 SIC: 5511 NAIC: 441110)

Lithia Motors is an operator of automotive franchises and a retailer of vehicles and related services. As of Feb 26 2016, Co. provided 31 brands of new vehicles and all brands of used vehicles in 137 stores and online at Lithia.com and DCHauto.com. Co. sells cars and replacement parts; provides vehicle maintenance, warranty, paint and repair services; arranges related financing; and sells service contracts, vehicle protection products and credit insurance. Co. has three segments: Domestic, which sells vehicles manufactured by Chrysler and Ford; Import, which sells vehicles manufactured by Honda, Toyota, and Subaru; and Luxury, which sells vehicles manufactured by Mercedes-Benz and Lexus.

Recent Developments: For the quarter ended Mar 31 2016, net income decreased 0.9% to US$40.3 million from US$40.7 million in the year-earlier quarter. Revenues were US$1.98 billion, up 10.8% from US$1.79 billion the year before. Operating income was US$72.9 million versus US$67.9 million in the prior-year quarter, an increase of 7.4%. Direct operating expenses rose 10.5% to US$1.68 billion from US$1.52 billion in the comparable period the year before. Indirect operating expenses increased 14.0% to US$234.3 million from US$205.5 million in the equivalent prior-year period.

Prospects: Our evaluation of Lithia Motors Inc. as of June 19, 2016 is the result of our systematic analysis on three basic characteristics: earnings strength, relative valuation, and recent stock price movement. The company has generated a negative trend in earnings per share over the past 5 quarters and while recent estimates for the company have remained steady, LAD has posted better than expected results. Based on operating earnings yield, the company is undervalued when compared to all of the companies in our coverage universe. Share price changes over the past year indicates that LAD will perform well over the near term.

Financial Data

(US$ in Thousands)	3 Mos	12/31/2015	12/31/2014	12/31/2013	12/31/2012	12/31/2011	12/31/2010	12/31/2009
Earnings Per Share	6.93	6.91	5.26	4.05	3.07	2.21	0.52	0.41
Cash Flow Per Share	2.73	2.82	1.16	1.24	(8.25)	(0.03)	(0.82)	0.45
Tang Book Value Per Share	23.33	17.44	12.31	15.99	12.99	11.14	10.23	10.25
Dividends Per Share	0.800	0.760	0.610	0.390	0.470	0.260	0.150	...
Dividend Payout %	11.54	11.00	11.60	9.63	15.31	11.76	28.85	...
Income Statement								
Total Revenue	1,982,861	7,864,252	5,390,326	4,005,749	3,316,487	2,699,360	2,131,598	1,749,315
EBITDA	83,052	343,329	261,461	206,546	168,208	129,635	65,948	54,465
Depn & Amortn	11,663	41,600	26,363	20,035	17,314	16,948	17,586	18,821
Income Before Taxes	60,021	262,704	210,495	165,788	128,457	89,175	23,193	10,703
Income Taxes	19,751	79,705	74,955	60,574	49,062	33,408	9,093	4,639
Net Income	40,270	182,999	138,720	106,000	80,362	58,860	13,719	9,151
Average Shares	25,973	26,490	26,382	26,191	26,170	26,664	26,279	22,176
Balance Sheet								
Current Assets	1,899,409	1,878,865	1,615,509	1,081,549	933,209	648,191	508,544	418,063
Total Assets	3,267,618	3,227,299	2,880,932	1,725,121	1,492,702	1,146,133	971,676	895,100
Current Liabilities	1,643,703	1,590,825	1,442,600	872,511	721,304	456,584	345,869	321,177
Long-Term Obligations	595,663	606,463	609,066	245,471	286,876	278,653	268,693	233,065
Total Liabilities	2,452,941	2,399,135	2,207,827	1,190,399	1,064,601	779,012	651,459	588,062
Stockholders' Equity	814,677	828,164	673,105	534,722	428,101	367,121	320,217	307,038
Shares Outstanding	25,755	26,218	26,233	25,891	25,678	25,957	26,285	25,798
Statistical Record								
Return on Assets %	5.90	5.99	6.02	6.59	6.07	5.56	1.47	0.90
Return on Equity %	23.99	24.38	22.97	22.02	20.16	17.13	4.37	3.30
EBITDA Margin %	4.19	4.37	4.85	5.16	5.07	4.80	3.09	3.11
Net Margin %	2.03	2.33	2.57	2.65	2.42	2.18	0.64	0.52
Asset Turnover	2.60	2.57	2.34	2.49	2.51	2.55	2.28	1.72
Current Ratio	1.16	1.18	1.12	1.24	1.29	1.42	1.47	1.30
Debt to Equity	0.73	0.73	0.90	0.46	0.67	0.76	0.84	0.76
Price Range	126.06-73.79	126.06-80.98	96.37-54.17	73.67-37.42	37.42-21.17	24.39-13.50	14.36-5.29	16.19-1.85
P/E Ratio	18.19-10.65	18.24-11.72	18.32-10.30	18.19-9.24	12.19-6.90	11.04-6.11	27.62-10.17	39.49-4.51
Average Yield %	0.76	0.72	0.80	0.69	1.66	1.49	1.70	...

Address: 150 N. Bartlett Street, Medford, OR 97501	**Web Site:** www.lithia.com	**Auditors:** KPMG LLP
Telephone: 541-776-6401	**Officers:** Sidney B. Bartlett - Executive Chairman, Chairman, Chief Executive Officer, Secretary George Liang - Division Officer	**Investor Contact:** 877-331-3084
		Transfer Agents: Broadridge Financial Solutions, Inc., Philadelphia, PA

LIVE NATION ENTERTAINMENT, INC.

Exchange	Symbol	Price	52Wk Range	Yield	P/E
NYS	LYV	$24.15 (5/31/2016)	29.21-19.36	N/A	N/A

*7 Year Price Score 134.89 *NYSE Composite Index=100 *12 Month Price Score 90.50

Interim Earnings (Per Share)

Qtr.	Mar	Jun	Sep	Dec
2013	(0.33)	0.30	0.22	(0.42)
2014	(0.16)	0.11	0.49	(0.94)
2015	(0.31)	0.06	0.38	(0.47)
2016	(0.29)	...	...	...

Interim Dividends (Per Share)

No Dividends Paid

Valuation Analysis		Institutional Holding	
Forecast EPS	$-0.13	No of Institutions	
	(05/20/2016)	352	
Market Cap	$4.9 Billion	Shares	
Book Value	$1.2 Billion	136,028,432	
Price/Book	4.14	% Held	
Price/Sales	0.67	69.80	

Business Summary: Entertainment (MIC: 2.3.2 SIC: 7999 NAIC: 713990)

Live Nation Entertainment is a producer of live music concert, a live entertainment ticketing sales and marketing company, and an artist management company. Co.'s segments are: Concerts, which involves the promotion of live music events, the operation and management of music venues and the production of music festivals; Ticketing, which sells tickets for events on behalf of its clients; Artist Nation, which provides management services to music artists and other clients; and Sponsorship and Advertising, which creates and maintains relationships with sponsors, through opportunities that allow businesses to reach customers through its concert, venue, artist relationship and ticketing assets.

Recent Developments: For the quarter ended Mar 31 2016, net loss amounted to US$56.0 million versus a net loss of US$66.5 million in the year-earlier quarter. Revenues were US$1.21 billion, up 7.8% from US$1.12 billion the year prior. Operating loss was US$33.3 million versus a loss of US$23.9 million in the prior-year quarter. Direct operating expenses rose 8.7% to US$784.2 million from US$721.3 million in the comparable period the year before. Indirect operating expenses increased 8.0% to US$456.8 million from US$423.0 million in the equivalent prior-year period.

Prospects: Our evaluation of Live Nation Entertainment, Inc. as of June 19, 2016 is the result of our systematic analysis on three basic characteristics: earnings strength, relative valuation, and recent stock price movement. The company has produced a positive trend in earnings per share over the past 5 quarters. Because the company lacks sufficient analyst estimate data, we place greater weight on the historical EPS trend as the measure of earnings strength. Based on operating earnings yield, the company is overvalued when compared to all of the companies in our coverage universe. Share price changes over the past year indicates that LYV will perform poorly over the near term.

Financial Data
(US$ in Thousands)

	3 Mos	12/31/2015	12/31/2014	12/31/2013	12/31/2012	12/31/2011	12/31/2010	12/31/2009
Earnings Per Share	(0.32)	(0.33)	(0.49)	(0.22)	(0.87)	(0.46)	(1.39)	(0.73)
Cash Flow Per Share	2.36	1.49	1.35	2.15	1.96	0.74	0.96	0.69
Tang Book Value Per Share	N.M.	N.M.	N.M.	N.M.	N.M.	N.M.	N.M.	0.20
Income Statement								
Total Revenue	1,207,716	7,245,731	6,866,964	6,478,547	5,819,047	5,383,998	5,063,748	4,181,021
EBITDA	72,803	238,352	125,888	222,759	102,081	141,007	54,747	110,337
Depn & Amortn	97,546	134,148	127,168	122,164	124,593	129,177	135,573	162,694
Income Before Taxes	(49,619)	4,851	(103,986)	(5,993)	(142,082)	(104,369)	(193,582)	(116,529)
Income Taxes	6,927	22,122	4,630	30,878	29,736	(26,224)	15,154	11,333
Net Income	(44,518)	(32,508)	(90,807)	(43,378)	(163,227)	(83,016)	(228,390)	(60,179)
Average Shares	201,696	200,973	198,874	193,885	186,955	182,388	164,410	82,652
Balance Sheet								
Current Assets	2,966,254	2,288,315	2,267,691	2,160,104	1,812,812	1,576,790	1,603,497	717,866
Total Assets	6,927,174	6,156,241	5,988,361	5,683,521	5,290,806	5,087,771	5,195,560	2,341,759
Current Liabilities	2,926,237	2,101,206	2,010,781	2,255,518	1,768,172	1,492,553	1,474,221	752,234
Long-Term Obligations	1,992,851	2,002,662	2,015,915	1,530,484	1,677,955	1,663,056	1,677,714	699,037
Total Liabilities	5,742,786	4,919,288	4,691,407	4,274,293	3,935,388	3,626,668	3,831,144	1,649,442
Stockholders' Equity	1,184,388	1,236,953	1,296,954	1,409,228	1,355,418	1,461,103	1,364,416	692,317
Shares Outstanding	202,926	202,483	201,193	199,566	190,853	188,957	174,147	84,448
Statistical Record								
EBITDA Margin %	6.03	3.29	1.83	3.44	1.75	2.62	1.08	2.64
Asset Turnover	1.11	1.19	1.18	1.18	1.12	1.05	1.34	1.73
Current Ratio	1.01	1.09	1.13	0.96	1.03	1.06	1.09	0.95
Debt to Equity	1.68	1.62	1.55	1.09	1.24	1.14	1.23	1.01
Price Range	29.21-19.36	29.21-23.58	27.36-19.76	19.82-9.31	10.88-8.21	12.26-7.33	16.70-8.43	8.90-2.52

Address: 9348 Civic Center Drive,	Web Site: www.livenationentertainment.com	Auditors: Ernst & Young LLP
Beverly Hills, CA 90210	Officers: Irving L. Azoff - Executive Chairman	Investor Contact: 310-867-7000
Telephone: 310-867-7000	Michael Rapino - President, Chief Executive Officer	Transfer Agents: Computershare, Providence, RI

LOCKHEED MARTIN CORP.

Exchange	Symbol	Price	52Wk Range	Yield	P/E	Div Achiever
NYS	LMT	$236.23 (5/31/2016)	244.94-185.52	2.79	20.91	13 Years

*7 Year Price Score 147.60 ***NYSE Composite Index=100** ***12 Month Price Score 108.35**

Interim Earnings (Per Share)

Qtr.	Mar	Jun	Sep	Dec
2013	2.33	2.64	2.66	1.50
2014	2.87	2.76	2.76	2.82
2015	2.74	2.94	2.77	3.01
2016	2.58	...	...	...

Interim Dividends (Per Share)

Amt	Decl	Ex	Rec	Pay
1.50Q	06/24/2015	08/28/2015	09/01/2015	09/25/2015
1.65Q	09/24/2015	11/27/2015	12/01/2015	12/24/2015
1.65Q	01/28/2016	02/26/2016	03/01/2016	03/24/2016
1.65Q	04/27/2016	05/27/2016	06/01/2016	06/24/2016

Indicated Div: $6.60 (Div. Reinv. Plan)

Valuation Analysis

Forecast EPS	$11.85
	(05/20/2016)
Market Cap	$71.9 Billion
Book Value	$3.2 Billion
Price/Book	22.64
Price/Sales	1.51

Institutional Holding

No of Institutions	1445
Shares	304,227,488
% Held	82.83

Business Summary: Defense (MIC: 7.1.2 SIC: 3761 NAIC: 336414)

Lockheed Martin is a security and aerospace company. Co. has five segments: Aeronautics, which researches, designs, develops, manufactures, integrates, sustains, supports, and upgrades military aircraft; Information Systems & Global Solutions, which provides technology systems, information technology applications, and management services across a range of applications; Missiles & Fire Control, which provides air and missile defense systems, tactical missiles and air-to-ground precision strike weapon systems; Mission Systems & Training, which provides ship and submarine combat systems; and Space Systems, which provides satellites, missile systems and space transportation systems.

Recent Developments: For the quarter ended Mar 27 2016, net income decreased 9.6% to US$794.0 million from US$878.0 million in the year-earlier quarter. Revenues were US$11.70 billion, up 15.7% from US$10.11 billion the year before. Operating income was US$1.30 billion versus US$1.36 billion in the prior-year quarter, a decrease of 4.4%. Direct operating expenses rose 18.3% to US$10.47 billion from US$8.85 billion in the comparable period the year before. Indirect operating income amounted to US$62.0 million compared with an income of US$93.0 million in the equivalent prior-year period.

Prospects: Our evaluation of Lockheed Martin Corp. as of June 19, 2016 is the result of our systematic analysis on three basic characteristics: earnings strength, relative valuation, and recent stock price movement. The company has managed to produce a neutral trend in earnings per share over the past 5 quarters. However, while recent estimates for the company have been mixed, LMT has posted results that fell short of analysts expectations. Based on operating earnings yield, the company is about fairly valued when compared to all of the companies in our coverage universe. Share price changes over the past year indicates that LMT will perform very well over the near term.

Financial Data

(US$ in Millions)	3 Mos	12/31/2015	12/31/2014	12/31/2013	12/31/2012	12/31/2011	12/31/2010	12/31/2009
Earnings Per Share	11.30	11.46	11.21	9.13	8.36	7.81	7.94	7.78
Cash Flow Per Share	18.74	16.44	12.20	14.17	4.81	12.66	9.74	8.25
Dividends Per Share	6.300	6.150	5.490	4.780	4.150	3.250	2.640	2.340
Dividend Payout %	55.75	53.66	48.97	52.35	49.64	41.61	33.25	30.08
Income Statement								
Total Revenue	11,702	46,132	45,600	45,358	47,182	46,499	45,803	45,189
EBITDA	1,594	6,492	6,592	5,495	5,443	4,993	4,189	4,288
Depn & Amortn	296	1,026	994	990	988	1,008	92	104
Income Before Taxes	1,134	5,023	5,258	4,155	4,072	3,631	3,826	4,002
Income Taxes	340	1,418	1,644	1,205	1,327	964	1,181	1,260
Net Income	794	3,605	3,614	2,981	2,745	2,655	2,926	3,024
Average Shares	307	314	322	326	328	339	368	388
Balance Sheet								
Current Assets	15,767	16,198	12,329	13,329	13,855	14,094	12,851	12,477
Total Assets	50,158	49,128	37,073	36,188	38,657	37,908	35,067	35,111
Current Liabilities	14,912	14,057	11,112	11,120	12,155	12,130	11,157	10,703
Long-Term Obligations	14,320	14,305	6,169	6,152	6,158	6,460	5,019	5,052
Total Liabilities	46,981	46,031	33,673	31,270	38,618	36,907	31,359	30,982
Stockholders' Equity	3,177	3,097	3,400	4,918	39	1,001	3,708	4,129
Shares Outstanding	304	303	314	319	321	321	346	373
Statistical Record								
Return on Assets %	7.83	8.36	9.87	7.97	7.15	7.28	8.34	8.82
Return on Equity %	105.15	110.97	86.90	120.27	526.44	112.76	74.67	86.47
EBITDA Margin %	13.62	14.07	14.46	12.11	11.54	10.74	9.15	9.49
Net Margin %	6.79	7.81	7.93	6.57	5.82	5.71	6.39	6.69
Asset Turnover	1.06	1.07	1.24	1.21	1.23	1.27	1.31	1.32
Current Ratio	1.06	1.15	1.11	1.20	1.14	1.16	1.15	1.17
Debt to Equity	4.51	4.62	1.81	1.25	157.90	6.45	1.35	1.22
Price Range	226.43-185.52	226.43-185.52	196.84-146.07	148.84-86.70	94.87-79.98	82.27-66.87	86.92-68.04	86.17-58.18
P/E Ratio	20.04-16.42	19.76-16.19	17.56-13.03	16.30-9.50	11.35-9.57	10.53-8.56	10.95-8.57	11.08-7.48
Average Yield %	3.05	3.03	3.25	4.24	4.68	4.21	3.49	3.07

Address: 6801 Rockledge Drive, Bethesda, MD 20817 Telephone: 301-897-6000	Web Site: www.lockheedmartin.com Officers: Robert J. Stevens - Executive Chairman, Chairman, Chief Executive Officer Marillyn A. Hewson - President, Chief Executive Officer, Chief Operating Officer, Executive Vice President	Auditors: Ernst & Young LLP Investor Contact: 301-897-6584 Transfer Agents: Computershare Trust Company, N.A., Providence, RI

LOEWS CORP.

Exchange	Symbol	Price	52Wk Range	Yield	P/E
NYS	L	$40.48 (5/31/2016)	40.73-34.21	0.62	55.45

*7 Year Price Score 80.65 *NYSE Composite Index=100 *12 Month Price Score 103.50

Interim Earnings (Per Share)

Qtr.	Mar	Jun	Sep	Dec
2013	0.62	0.69	0.73	(0.50)
2014	0.15	0.30	0.55	0.55
2015	0.29	0.46	0.50	(0.53)
2016	0.30	...	...	...

Interim Dividends (Per Share)

Amt	Decl	Ex	Rec	Pay
0.063Q	08/11/2015	08/27/2015	08/31/2015	09/14/2015
0.063Q	11/10/2015	11/25/2015	11/30/2015	12/11/2015
0.063Q	02/09/2016	02/26/2016	03/01/2016	03/14/2016
0.063Q	05/10/2016	05/27/2016	06/01/2016	06/14/2016

Indicated Div: $0.25

Valuation Analysis

		Institutional Holding	
Forecast EPS	$2.55	No of Institutions	
	(05/20/2016)	590	
Market Cap	$13.7 Billion	Shares	
Book Value	$17.8 Billion	237,735,872	
Price/Book	0.77	% Held	
Price/Sales	1.05	57.05	

Business Summary: General Insurance (MIC: 5.2.1 SIC: 6331 NAIC: 524126)

Loews is a holding company. Co. is engaged in the following lines of business: commercial property and casualty insurance, including surety through its 90.0% owned subsidiary, CNA Financial Corporation; operation of offshore oil and gas drilling rigs through its 53.0% owned subsidiary, Diamond Offshore Drilling, Inc.; transportation and storage of natural gas and natural gas liquids and gathering and processing of natural gas through its 53% owned subsidiary, Boardwalk Pipeline Partners, LP; and operation a chain of hotels in the U.S. and Canada through its Loews Hotels Holding Corporation subsidiary.

Recent Developments: For the quarter ended Mar 31 2016, income from continuing operations increased 306.1% to US$199.0 million from US$49.0 million in the year-earlier quarter. Net income increased 306.1% to US$199.0 million from US$49.0 million in the year-earlier quarter. Revenues were US$3.17 billion, down 8.8% from US$3.48 billion the year before. Net premiums earned were US$1.70 billion versus US$1.69 billion in the prior-year quarter, an increase of 0.7%. Net investment income fell 28.2% to US$422.0 million from US$588.0 million a year ago.

Prospects: Our evaluation of Loews Corp. as of June 19, 2016 is the result of our systematic analysis on three basic characteristics: earnings strength, relative valuation, and recent stock price movement. The company has produced a positive trend in earnings per share over the past 5 quarters. However, while recent estimates for the company have been mixed, L has posted better than expected results. Based on operating earnings yield, the company is about fairly valued when compared to all of the companies in our coverage universe. Share price changes over the past year indicates that L will perform well over the near term.

Financial Data
(US$ in Thousands)

	3 Mos	12/31/2015	12/31/2014	12/31/2013	12/31/2012	12/31/2011	12/31/2010	12/31/2009
Earnings Per Share	0.73	0.72	1.55	1.53	1.43	2.63	3.07	1.30
Cash Flow Per Share	10.78	9.79	7.83	5.40	7.20	9.80	(0.11)	10.61
Tang Book Value Per Share	51.57	50.63	50.70	49.36	47.12	45.25	42.44	37.74
Dividends Per Share	0.250	0.250	0.250	0.250	0.250	0.250	0.250	0.250
Dividend Payout %	34.25	34.72	16.13	16.34	17.48	9.51	8.14	19.23
Income Statement								
Premium Income	1,699,000	6,921,000	7,212,000	7,271,000	6,882,000	6,603,000	6,515,000	6,721,000
Total Revenue	3,173,000	13,415,000	14,325,000	15,053,000	14,552,000	14,127,000	14,615,000	14,117,000
Benefits & Claims	1,408,000	5,384,000	5,591,000	5,947,000	5,896,000	5,489,000	4,985,000	5,290,000
Income Before Taxes	195,000	244,000	1,810,000	1,429,000	1,399,000	2,232,000	2,902,000	1,730,000
Income Taxes	(4,000)	(43,000)	457,000	360,000	289,000	536,000	895,000	345,000
Net Income	102,000	260,000	591,000	595,000	568,000	1,064,000	1,288,000	564,000
Average Shares	339,250	362,690	382,550	389,510	395,870	405,320	419,520	432,810
Balance Sheet								
Total Assets	77,224,000	76,029,000	78,367,000	79,939,000	80,021,000	75,375,000	76,277,000	74,070,000
Total Liabilities	59,391,000	58,468,000	59,087,000	60,481,000	60,562,000	56,540,000	57,827,000	57,171,000
Stockholders' Equity	17,833,000	17,561,000	19,280,000	19,458,000	19,459,000	18,835,000	18,450,000	16,899,000
Shares Outstanding	339,014	339,897	372,934	386,960	391,805	396,200	414,546	425,070
Statistical Record								
Return on Assets %	0.32	0.34	0.75	0.74	0.73	1.40	1.71	0.78
Return on Equity %	1.36	1.41	3.05	3.06	2.96	5.71	7.29	3.76
Loss Ratio %	82.87	77.79	77.52	81.79	85.67	83.13	76.52	78.71
Net Margin %	3.21	1.94	4.13	3.95	3.90	7.53	8.81	4.00
Price Range	42.40-34.21	42.53-35.36	48.24-39.07	49.20-40.75	43.17-37.31	44.26-33.50	40.08-31.12	36.65-18.02
P/E Ratio	58.08-46.86	59.07-49.11	31.12-25.21	32.16-26.63	30.19-26.09	16.83-12.74	13.06-10.14	28.19-13.86
Average Yield %	0.66	0.64	0.58	0.55	0.62	0.63	0.68	0.86

Address: 667 Madison Avenue, New York, NY 10065-8087 Telephone: 212-521-2000	Web Site: www.loews.com Officers: Jonathan M Tisch - Co Chairman Andrew H. Tisch - Co-Chairman	Auditors: Deloitte & Touche LLP Transfer Agents: Computershare Shareowner Services, Jersey City, NJ

LOUISIANA-PACIFIC CORP.

Exchange	Symbol	Price	52Wk Range	Yield	P/E
NYS	LPX	$18.28 (5/31/2016)	18.70-13.78	N/A	N/A

*7 Year Price Score 112.16 *NYSE Composite Index=100 *12 Month Price Score 105.00

TRADING VOLUME (thousand shares)

Interim Earnings (Per Share)

Qtr.	Mar	Jun	Sep	Dec
2013	0.45	0.65	0.26	(0.14)
2014	(0.10)	0.01	(0.14)	(0.30)
2015	(0.24)	(0.14)	(0.19)	(0.05)
2016	0.07	...	...	...

Interim Dividends (Per Share)

No Dividends Paid

Valuation Analysis | Institutional Holding

Forecast EPS	$0.59	No of Institutions
	(05/15/2016)	295
Market Cap	$2.6 Billion	Shares
Book Value	$1.1 Billion	167,999,664
Price/Book	2.49	% Held
Price/Sales	1.36	104.96

Business Summary: Paper & Forest Products (MIC: 8.1.2 SIC: 2493 NAIC: 321219)

Louisiana-Pacific is a manufacturer of building products. Co.'s products are used primarily in new home construction, repair and remodeling and outdoor structures. Co. operates in four segments: North America oriented strand board (OSB), which manufactures and distributes OSB structural panel products; siding, which includes SmartSide® siding products and related accessories, and CanExel siding and accessories; engineered wood products, which manufactures and distributes laminated veneer lumber, I-Joists, laminated strand lumber and other related products; and South America, which manufactures and distributes OSB and siding products in South America and certain export markets.

Recent Developments: For the quarter ended Mar 31 2016, net income amounted to US$10.3 million versus a net loss of US$34.5 million in the year-earlier quarter. Revenues were US$504.6 million, up 7.0% from US$471.7 million the year before. Operating income was US$18.9 million versus a loss of US$33.2 million in the prior-year quarter. Direct operating expenses declined 2.9% to US$415.5 million from US$427.8 million in the comparable period the year before. Indirect operating expenses decreased 8.9% to US$70.2 million from US$77.1 million in the equivalent prior-year period.

Prospects: Our evaluation of Louisiana-Pacific Corp. as of June 19, 2016 is the result of our systematic analysis on three basic characteristics: earnings strength, relative valuation, and recent stock price movement. The company has enjoyed a very positive trend in earnings per share over the past 5 quarters and while recent estimates for the company have remained steady, LPX has posted better than expected results. Based on operating earnings yield, the company is overvalued when compared to all of the companies in our coverage universe. Share price changes over the past year indicates that LPX will perform well over the near term.

Financial Data

(US$ in Thousands)	3 Mos	12/31/2015	12/31/2014	12/31/2013	12/31/2012	12/31/2011	12/31/2010	12/31/2009
Earnings Per Share	(0.31)	(0.62)	(0.53)	1.23	0.20	(1.36)	(0.30)	(1.12)
Cash Flow Per Share	0.48	0.21	(0.37)	1.74	0.81	(0.30)	0.37	0.56
Tang Book Value Per Share	7.27	7.04	7.78	8.62	7.46	7.29	9.21	9.85
Income Statement								
Total Revenue	504,600	1,892,500	1,934,800	2,085,200	1,715,800	1,356,900	1,383,600	1,054,700
EBITDA	47,300	37,700	25,500	333,900	161,200	(48,300)	98,000	(17,800)
Depn & Amortn	27,900	101,900	100,700	91,300	73,900	78,900	82,000	80,000
Income Before Taxes	13,200	(95,400)	(105,000)	206,600	38,000	(184,100)	(47,900)	(169,400)
Income Taxes	4,400	(2,700)	(27,200)	41,100	7,600	(39,100)	(22,100)	(63,400)
Net Income	10,300	(88,100)	(75,400)	177,100	28,800	(181,300)	(39,000)	(121,400)
Average Shares	145,200	142,400	141,100	144,300	142,600	133,200	129,100	108,500
Balance Sheet								
Current Assets	815,600	769,100	950,300	1,034,200	995,600	656,800	713,600	838,800
Total Assets	2,215,600	2,176,300	2,353,500	2,493,300	2,331,000	2,139,900	2,410,600	2,247,400
Current Liabilities	165,300	143,000	172,700	166,200	239,300	139,500	135,000	306,900
Long-Term Obligations	751,800	751,800	759,500	762,700	782,700	715,900	714,500	337,600
Total Liabilities	1,163,800	1,159,300	1,237,700	1,267,000	1,297,200	1,139,000	1,192,800	997,900
Stockholders' Equity	1,051,800	1,017,000	1,115,800	1,226,300	1,033,800	1,000,900	1,217,800	1,249,500
Shares Outstanding	143,407	142,984	142,226	141,124	138,534	137,139	131,946	126,571
Statistical Record								
Return on Assets %	N.M.	N.M.	N.M.	7.34	1.28	N.M.	N.M.	N.M.
Return on Equity %	N.M.	N.M.	N.M.	15.67	2.82	N.M.	N.M.	N.M.
EBITDA Margin %	9.37	1.99	1.32	16.01	9.40	N.M.	7.08	N.M.
Net Margin %	2.04	N.M.	N.M.	8.49	1.68	N.M.	N.M.	N.M.
Asset Turnover	0.85	0.84	0.80	0.86	0.77	0.60	0.59	0.48
Current Ratio	4.93	5.38	5.50	6.22	4.16	4.71	5.29	2.73
Debt to Equity	0.71	0.74	0.68	0.62	0.76	0.72	0.59	0.27
Price Range	18.70-13.78	18.70-14.19	18.79-12.61	22.18-14.75	19.32-7.68	11.57-4.63	12.86-6.55	7.77-1.19
P/E Ratio	...	...	...	18.03-11.99	96.60-38.40	...	...	...

Address: 414 Union Street, Suite 2000, Nashville, TN 37219 **Telephone:** 615-986-5600 **Fax:** 615-986-5666	**Web Site:** www.lpcorp.com **Officers:** E. Gary Cook - Chairman Curtis M. Stevens - Chief Executive Officer, Executive Vice President, Chief Financial Officer, Chief Operating Officer, Principal Accounting Officer	**Auditors:** Deloitte & Touche LLP **Transfer Agents:** Computershare Trust Company, N.A., Providence, RI

LOWE'S COMPANIES INC

Exchange	Symbol	Price	52Wk Range	Yield	P/E	Div Achiever
NYS	LOW	$80.13 (5/31/2016)	80.35-63.40	1.75	26.62	54 Years

*7 Year Price Score 151.11 *NYSE Composite Index=100 *12 Month Price Score 105.62

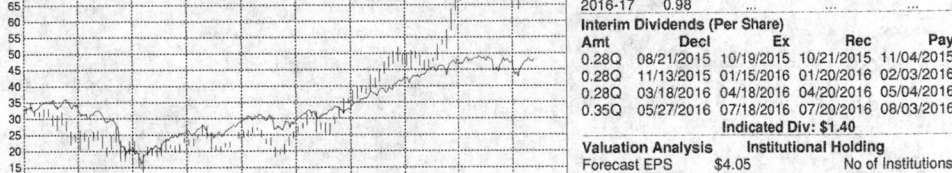

Interim Earnings (Per Share)

Qtr.	Apr	Jul	Oct	Jan
2013-14	0.49	0.88	0.47	0.30
2014-15	0.61	1.04	0.59	0.47
2015-16	0.70	1.20	0.80	0.03
2016-17	0.98	...	...	...

Interim Dividends (Per Share)

Amt	Decl	Ex	Rec	Pay
0.28Q	08/21/2015	10/19/2015	10/21/2015	11/04/2015
0.28Q	11/13/2015	01/15/2016	01/20/2016	02/03/2016
0.28Q	03/18/2016	04/18/2016	04/20/2016	05/04/2016
0.35Q	05/27/2016	07/18/2016	07/20/2016	08/03/2016

Indicated Div: $1.40

Valuation Analysis — **Institutional Holding**

Forecast EPS	$4.05	No of Institutions
(05/20/2016)		1629
Market Cap	$71.6 Billion	Shares
Book Value	$7.2 Billion	807,029,056
Price/Book	9.93	% Held
Price/Sales	1.19	69.67

Business Summary: Retail - Hardware & Home Improvement (MIC: 2.1.8 SIC: 5211 NAIC: 444110)

Lowe's Companies and subsidiaries is a home improvement retailer. As of Jan 29, 2016, Co. operated 1,857 home improvement and hardware stores in the U.S., Canada and Mexico. As of the same date, Co. also had 80 Orchard Supply Hardware stores in California and Oregon. Co. sells home improvement products in the following categories: Lumber and Building Materials; Tools and Hardware; Appliances; Fashion Fixtures; Rough Plumbing and Electrical; Lawn and Garden; Seasonal Living; Paint; Flooring; Millwork; Kitchens; Outdoor Power Equipment, and Home Fashions. Co.'s services includes installation services through independent contractors, and extended protection plans and repair services.

Recent Developments: For the quarter ended Apr 29 2016, net income increased 31.4% to US$884.0 million from US$673.0 million in the year-earlier quarter. Revenues were US$15.23 billion, up 7.8% from US$14.13 billion the year before. Direct operating expenses rose 8.6% to US$9.90 billion from US$9.12 billion in the comparable period the year before. Indirect operating expenses decreased 0.8% to US$3.75 billion from US$3.78 billion in the equivalent prior-year period.

Prospects: Our evaluation of Lowe's Companies Inc. as of June 19, 2016 is the result of our systematic analysis on three basic characteristics: earnings strength, relative valuation, and recent stock price movement. The company has produced a positive trend in earnings per share over the past 5 quarters and while recent estimates for the company have been raised by analysts, LOW has posted better than expected results. Based on operating earnings yield, the company is about fairly valued when compared to all of the companies in our coverage universe. Share price changes over the past year indicates that LOW will perform well over the near term.

Financial Data

(US$ in Thousands)	3 Mos	01/29/2016	01/30/2015	01/31/2014	02/01/2013	02/03/2012	01/28/2011	01/29/2010
Earnings Per Share	3.01	2.73	2.71	2.14	1.69	1.43	1.42	1.21
Cash Flow Per Share	6.16	5.17	5.00	3.89	3.28	3.37	2.76	2.78
Tang Book Value Per Share	8.07	8.41	10.38	11.51	12.48	13.32	13.38	13.07
Dividends Per Share	1.120	1.070	0.870	0.700	0.620	0.530	0.420	0.355
Dividend Payout %	37.21	39.19	32.10	32.71	36.69	37.06	29.58	29.34
Income Statement								
Total Revenue	15,234,000	59,074,000	56,223,000	53,417,000	50,521,000	50,208,000	48,815,000	47,220,000
EBITDA	1,943,000	6,455,000	6,277,000	5,611,000	5,083,000	4,757,000	5,146,000	4,726,000
Depn & Amortn	357,000	1,484,000	1,485,000	1,462,000	1,523,000	1,480,000	1,586,000	1,614,000
Income Before Taxes	1,430,000	4,419,000	4,276,000	3,673,000	3,137,000	2,906,000	3,228,000	2,825,000
Income Taxes	546,000	1,873,000	1,578,000	1,387,000	1,178,000	1,067,000	1,218,000	1,042,000
Net Income	884,000	2,546,000	2,698,000	2,286,000	1,959,000	1,839,000	2,010,000	1,783,000
Average Shares	899,000	929,000	990,000	1,061,000	1,152,000	1,273,000	1,403,000	1,464,000
Balance Sheet								
Current Assets	16,473,000	10,561,000	10,080,000	10,296,000	9,784,000	10,072,000	9,967,000	9,732,000
Total Assets	37,177,000	31,266,000	31,827,000	32,732,000	32,666,000	33,559,000	33,699,000	33,005,000
Current Liabilities	14,121,000	10,492,000	9,348,000	8,876,000	7,708,000	7,891,000	7,119,000	7,355,000
Long-Term Obligations	14,322,000	11,545,000	10,815,000	10,086,000	9,030,000	7,035,000	6,537,000	4,528,000
Total Liabilities	29,965,000	23,612,000	21,859,000	20,879,000	18,809,000	17,026,000	15,587,000	13,936,000
Stockholders' Equity	7,212,000	7,654,000	9,968,000	11,853,000	13,857,000	16,533,000	18,112,000	19,069,000
Shares Outstanding	894,000	910,000	960,000	1,030,000	1,110,000	1,241,000	1,354,000	1,459,000
Statistical Record								
Return on Assets %	7.70	8.09	8.38	7.01	5.93	5.38	6.04	5.44
Return on Equity %	33.04	28.98	24.80	17.83	12.93	10.44	10.84	9.63
EBITDA Margin %	12.75	10.93	11.16	10.50	10.06	9.47	10.54	10.01
Net Margin %	5.80	4.31	4.80	4.28	3.88	3.66	4.12	3.78
Asset Turnover	1.68	1.88	1.75	1.64	1.53	1.47	1.47	1.44
Current Ratio	1.17	1.01	1.08	1.16	1.27	1.28	1.40	1.32
Debt to Equity	1.99	1.51	1.08	0.85	0.65	0.43	0.36	0.24
Price Range	77.61-63.40	77.61-66.25	70.44-44.63	51.95-35.86	38.58-24.85	27.46-18.11	28.22-19.59	24.17-13.39
P/E Ratio	25.78-21.06	28.43-24.27	25.99-16.47	24.28-16.76	22.83-14.70	19.20-12.66	19.87-13.80	19.98-11.07
Average Yield %	1.57	1.49	1.64	1.59	2.03	2.24	1.81	1.74

Address: 1000 Lowe's Blvd., Mooresville, NC 28117 **Telephone:** 704-758-1000	**Web Site:** www.lowes.com **Officers:** Robert A. Niblock - Chairman, President, Chief Executive Officer Ricky D. Damron Executive Vice President, Chief Operating Officer, Division Officer	**Auditors:** Deloitte & Touche LLP **Investor Contact:** 704-758-2033 **Transfer Agents:** Computershare Trust Company N.A., Providence, RI

M & T BANK CORP

Exchange	Symbol	Price	52Wk Range	Yield	P/E
NYS	MTB	$119.50 (5/31/2016)	133.20-100.78	2.34	16.46

*7 Year Price Score 102.76 *NYSE Composite Index=100 *12 Month Price Score 96.71

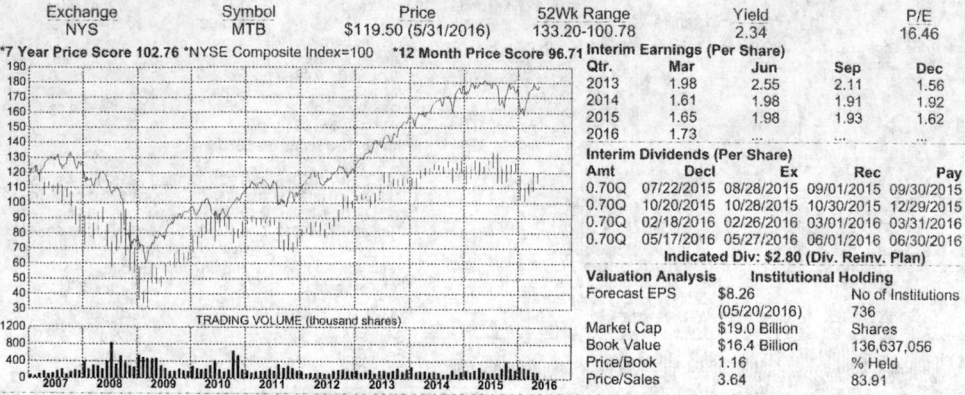

Interim Earnings (Per Share)

Qtr.	Mar	Jun	Sep	Dec
2013	1.98	2.55	2.11	1.56
2014	1.61	1.98	1.91	1.92
2015	1.65	1.98	1.93	1.62
2016	1.73	...	...	...

Interim Dividends (Per Share)

Amt	Decl	Ex	Rec	Pay
0.70Q	07/22/2015	08/28/2015	09/01/2015	09/30/2015
0.70Q	10/20/2015	10/28/2015	10/30/2015	12/29/2015
0.70Q	02/18/2016	02/26/2016	03/01/2016	03/31/2016
0.70Q	05/17/2016	05/27/2016	06/01/2016	06/30/2016

Indicated Div: $2.80 (Div. Reinv. Plan)

Valuation Analysis		Institutional Holding	
Forecast EPS	$8.26	No of Institutions	736
	(05/20/2016)		
Market Cap	$19.0 Billion	Shares	136,637,056
Book Value	$16.4 Billion	% Held	83.91
Price/Book	1.16		
Price/Sales	3.64		

Business Summary: Banking (MIC: 5.1.1 SIC: 6022 NAIC: 522110)

M&T Bank is a bank holding company. Through subsidiaries, Co. provides individuals, corporations and other businesses, and institutions with commercial and retail banking services, including loans and deposits, trust, mortgage banking, asset management, insurance and other financial services. Banking activities are primarily focused on consumers residing in New York State, Maryland, New Jersey, Pennsylvania, Delaware, Connecticut, Virginia, West Virginia and the District of Columbia and on small and medium-size businesses in those areas. Certain subsidiaries also conduct activities in other areas. At Dec 31 2015, Co. had total assets of $122.79 billion and deposits of $91.96 billion.

Recent Developments: For the quarter ended Mar 31 2016, net income increased 23.6% to US$298.5 million from US$241.6 million in the year-earlier quarter. Net interest income increased 32.2% to US$872.0 million from US$659.6 million in the year-earlier quarter. Provision for loan losses was US$49.0 million versus US$38.0 million in the prior-year quarter, an increase of 28.9%. Non-interest income fell 4.4% to US$420.9 million from US$440.2 million, while non-interest expense advanced 13.1% to US$776.1 million.

Prospects: Our evaluation of M & T Bank Corp. as of June 19, 2016 is the result of our systematic analysis on three basic characteristics: earnings strength, relative valuation, and recent stock price movement. The company has produced a positive trend in earnings per share over the past 5 quarters and while recent estimates for the company have been mixed, MTB has posted results that fell short of analysts expectations. Based on operating earnings yield, the company is undervalued when compared to all of the companies in our coverage universe. Share price changes over the past year indicates that MTB will perform in line with the market over the near term.

Financial Data

(US$ in Thousands)	3 Mos	12/31/2015	12/31/2014	12/31/2013	12/31/2012	12/31/2011	12/31/2010	12/31/2009
Earnings Per Share	7.26	7.18	7.42	8.20	7.54	6.35	5.69	2.89
Cash Flow Per Share	10.91	12.74	8.39	7.25	3.96	14.45	14.18	10.37
Tang Book Value Per Share	65.37	63.98	57.02	52.33	44.39	37.44	33.14	28.05
Dividends Per Share	2.800	2.800	2.800	2.800	2.800	2.800	2.800	2.800
Dividend Payout %	38.57	39.00	37.74	34.15	37.14	44.09	49.21	96.89
Income Statement								
Interest Income	972,834	3,170,844	2,956,877	2,957,334	2,941,685	2,792,087	2,729,795	2,725,197
Interest Expense	100,870	328,257	280,431	284,105	343,169	402,331	462,269	669,449
Net Interest Income	871,964	2,842,587	2,676,446	2,673,229	2,598,516	2,389,756	2,267,526	2,055,748
Provision for Losses	49,000	170,000	124,000	185,000	204,000	270,000	368,000	604,000
Non-Interest Income	420,933	1,839,304	1,795,945	1,881,331	1,688,781	1,607,143	1,133,868	1,074,004
Non-Interest Expense	776,095	2,822,932	2,742,857	2,635,885	2,509,260	2,478,068	1,914,837	1,980,563
Income Before Taxes	467,802	1,688,959	1,605,534	1,733,675	1,574,037	1,248,831	1,118,557	545,189
Income Taxes	169,274	595,025	522,616	579,069	523,028	365,121	356,628	139,400
Net Income	298,528	1,079,667	1,066,246	1,138,480	1,029,498	859,479	736,161	379,891
Average Shares	159,181	137,533	131,844	129,603	126,405	123,079	118,843	114,776
Balance Sheet								
Net Loans & Leases	86,909,714	86,533,507	65,749,394	63,156,483	65,645,097	59,187,715	51,087,441	51,058,664
Total Assets	124,625,632	122,787,884	96,685,535	85,162,391	83,008,803	77,924,287	68,021,263	68,880,399
Total Deposits	94,214,576	91,957,841	73,582,053	67,118,612	65,611,253	59,394,649	49,805,284	47,449,838
Total Liabilities	108,270,579	106,614,595	84,349,639	73,856,859	72,806,210	68,653,078	59,663,568	61,127,492
Stockholders' Equity	16,355,053	16,173,289	12,335,896	11,305,532	10,202,593	9,271,209	8,357,695	7,752,907
Shares Outstanding	159,122	159,563	132,312	130,516	128,176	125,683	119,702	118,222
Statistical Record								
Return on Assets %	1.02	0.98	1.17	1.35	1.28	1.18	1.08	0.56
Return on Equity %	7.87	7.57	9.02	10.59	10.54	9.75	9.14	5.23
Net Interest Margin %	89.63	89.65	90.52	90.39	88.33	85.59	83.07	75.43
Efficiency Ratio %	55.68	56.34	57.71	54.48	54.19	56.33	49.56	52.13
Loans to Deposits	0.92	0.94	0.89	0.94	1.00	1.00	1.03	1.08
Price Range	133.20-100.78	133.20-112.28	128.03-109.30	119.30-96.55	104.88-76.98	91.01-67.43	94.45-66.89	68.96-30.50
P/E Ratio	18.35-13.88	18.55-15.64	17.25-14.73	14.55-11.77	13.91-10.21	14.33-10.62	16.60-11.76	23.86-10.55
Average Yield %	2.34	2.28	2.32	2.57	3.18	3.44	3.45	5.22

Address: One M & T Plaza, Buffalo, NY 14203	Web Site: www.mtb.com	Auditors: PricewaterhouseCoopers LLP
Telephone: 716-842-5445	Officers: Robert G. Wilmers - Chairman, Chief Executive Officer Robert T. Brady - Vice Chairman	Investor Contact: 716-842-5138
		Transfer Agents: Registrar and Transfer Company, Cranford, NJ

MACERICH CO. (THE)

Exchange	Symbol	Price	52Wk Range	Yield	P/E
NYS	MAC	$76.32 (5/31/2016)	85.94-72.53	3.56	13.41

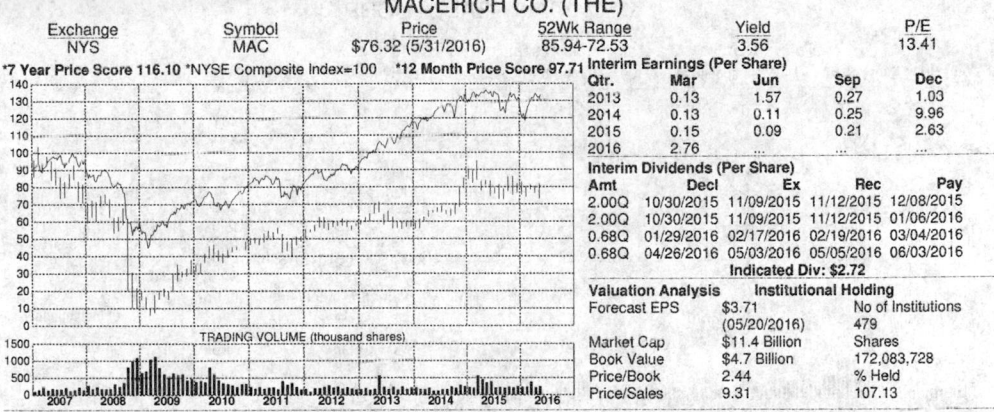

*7 Year Price Score 116.10 *NYSE Composite Index=100 *12 Month Price Score 97.71

Interim Earnings (Per Share)

Qtr.	Mar	Jun	Sep	Dec
2013	0.13	1.57	0.27	1.03
2014	0.13	0.11	0.25	9.96
2015	0.15	0.09	0.21	2.63
2016	2.76	...	...	...

Interim Dividends (Per Share)

Amt	Decl	Ex	Rec	Pay
2.00Q	10/30/2015	11/09/2015	11/12/2015	12/08/2015
2.00Q	10/30/2015	11/09/2015	11/12/2015	01/06/2016
0.68Q	01/29/2016	02/17/2016	02/19/2016	03/04/2016
0.68Q	04/26/2016	05/03/2016	05/05/2016	06/03/2016

Indicated Div: $2.72

Valuation Analysis

		Institutional Holding	
Forecast EPS	$3.71	No of Institutions	
	(05/20/2016)	479	
Market Cap	$11.4 Billion	Shares	
Book Value	$4.7 Billion	172,083,728	
Price/Book	2.44	% Held	
Price/Sales	9.31	107.13	

Business Summary: REITs (MIC: 5.3.1 SIC: 6798 NAIC: 525930)

Macerich is a self-administered and self-managed real estate investment trust. Co. is involved in the acquisition, ownership, development, redevelopment, management and leasing of regional and community/power shopping centers located throughout the U.S. Co. iis the sole general partner of, and owns a majority of the ownership interests in The Macerich Partnership, L.P. (the Operating Partnership). As of Dec 31 2015, the Operating Partnership owned or had an ownership interest in 51 regional shopping centers and seven community/power shopping centers. Co. conducts all of its operations through the Operating Partnership and its management companies.

Recent Developments: For the quarter ended Mar 31 2016, net income increased to US$451.4 million from US$26.7 million in the year-earlier quarter. Revenues were US$256.0 million, down 19.6% from US$318.3 million the year before. Revenues from property income fell 20.5% to US$242.9 million from US$305.3 million in the corresponding quarter a year earlier.

Prospects: Our evaluation of Macerich Co. as of June 19, 2016 is the result of our systematic analysis on three basic characteristics: earnings strength, relative valuation, and recent stock price movement. The company has suffered a very negative trend in earnings per share over the past 5 quarters. Because the company lacks sufficient analyst estimate data, we place greater weight on the historical EPS trend as the measure of earnings strength. Based on operating earnings yield, the company is overvalued when compared to all of the companies in our coverage universe. Share price changes over the past year indicates that MAC will perform in line with the market over the near term.

Financial Data
(US$ in Thousands)

	3 Mos	12/31/2015	12/31/2014	12/31/2013	12/31/2012	12/31/2011	12/31/2010	12/31/2009
Earnings Per Share	5.69	3.08	10.45	3.00	2.51	1.18	0.19	1.45
Cash Flow Per Share	3.20	3.42	2.80	3.02	2.61	1.80	1.67	1.49
Tang Book Value Per Share	30.21	29.59	33.53	22.94	21.46	21.57	22.79	19.25
Dividends Per Share	6.660	6.630	2.510	2.360	2.230	2.050	2.100	2.600
Dividend Payout %	117.05	215.26	24.02	78.67	88.84	173.73	1,105.26	179.31
Income Statement								
Total Revenue	256,000	1,288,149	1,105,247	1,029,475	881,323	791,250	758,559	805,654
EBITDA	564,458	1,041,445	2,021,903	456,788	661,387	339,613	374,516	590,291
Depn & Amortn	83,650	354,977	289,178	269,790	271,025	235,884	221,799	221,276
Income Before Taxes	441,032	474,525	1,542,036	(10,249)	213,584	(91,556)	(60,101)	101,970
Income Taxes	1,317	(3,223)	(4,269)	(1,692)	(4,159)	(6,110)	(9,202)	(4,761)
Net Income	420,915	487,562	1,499,042	420,090	337,426	156,866	25,190	120,742
Average Shares	152,103	158,060	143,291	139,680	134,148	131,628	120,346	81,226
Balance Sheet								
Current Assets	335,013	257,901	230,463	186,055	271,862	269,801	638,097	263,064
Total Assets	10,211,345	11,258,576	13,121,778	9,075,250	9,311,209	7,938,549	7,645,010	7,252,471
Current Liabilities	439,572	815,382	684,122	440,099	388,425	371,968	328,263	336,679
Long-Term Obligations	4,658,968	5,283,742	6,292,400	4,582,727	5,261,370	4,206,074	3,892,070	4,531,634
Total Liabilities	5,544,334	6,543,162	7,481,658	5,716,501	6,233,680	5,125,212	4,754,731	5,394,900
Stockholders' Equity	4,667,011	4,715,414	5,640,120	3,358,749	3,077,529	2,813,337	2,890,279	1,857,571
Shares Outstanding	149,455	154,404	158,201	140,733	137,507	132,153	130,452	96,667
Statistical Record								
Return on Assets %	7.55	4.00	13.51	4.57	3.90	2.01	0.34	1.57
Return on Equity %	17.26	9.42	33.32	13.05	11.42	5.50	1.06	7.50
EBITDA Margin %	220.49	80.85	182.94	44.37	75.04	42.92	49.37	73.27
Net Margin %	164.42	37.85	135.63	40.81	38.29	19.83	3.32	14.99
Asset Turnover	0.10	0.11	0.10	0.11	0.10	0.10	0.10	0.11
Current Ratio	0.76	0.32	0.34	0.42	0.70	0.73	1.94	0.78
Debt to Equity	1.00	1.12	1.12	1.36	1.71	1.50	1.35	2.44
Price Range	85.94-72.53	94.89-72.53	84.87-55.58	70.84-55.25	62.29-50.30	56.20-40.21	49.40-29.97	37.62-5.80
P/E Ratio	15.10-12.75	30.81-23.55	8.12-5.32	23.61-18.42	24.82-20.04	47.63-34.08	260.00-157.74	25.94-4.00
Average Yield %	8.40	8.13	3.80	3.86	3.89	4.18	5.15	12.33

Address: 401 Wilshire Boulevard, Suite 700, Santa Monica, CA 90401 **Telephone:** 310-394-6000	**Web Site:** www.macerich.com **Officers:** Arthur M. Coppola - Chairman, President, Chief Executive Officer Mace Siegel - Chairman Emeritus, Founder	**Auditors:** KPMG LLP **Transfer Agents:** Computershare Trust Company, N.A., Providence, RI

MACK CALI REALTY CORP

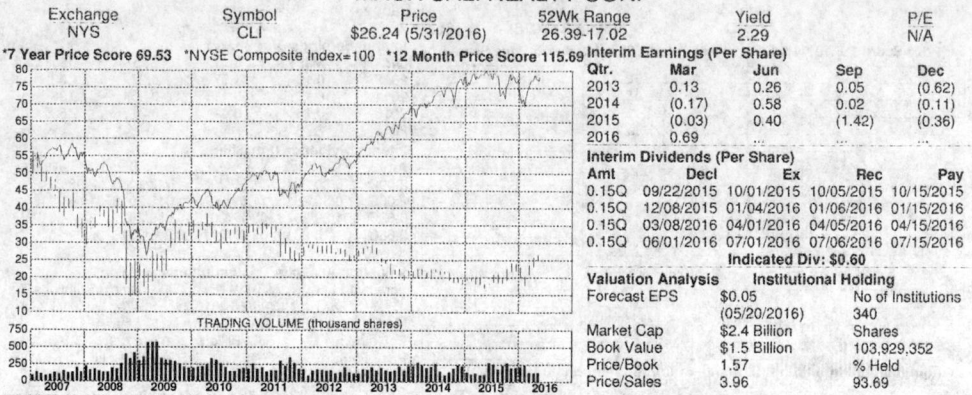

Exchange	Symbol	Price	52Wk Range	Yield	P/E
NYS	CLI	$26.24 (5/31/2016)	26.39-17.02	2.29	N/A

*7 Year Price Score 69.53 *NYSE Composite Index=100 *12 Month Price Score 115.69

Interim Earnings (Per Share)

Qtr.	Mar	Jun	Sep	Dec
2013	0.13	0.26	0.05	(0.62)
2014	(0.17)	0.58	0.02	(0.11)
2015	(0.03)	0.40	(1.42)	(0.36)
2016	0.69			

Interim Dividends (Per Share)

Amt	Decl	Ex	Rec	Pay
0.15Q	09/22/2015	10/01/2015	10/05/2015	10/15/2015
0.15Q	12/08/2015	01/04/2016	01/06/2016	01/15/2016
0.15Q	03/08/2016	04/01/2016	04/05/2016	04/15/2016
0.15Q	06/01/2016	07/01/2016	07/06/2016	07/15/2016

Indicated Div: $0.60

Valuation Analysis

		Institutional Holding	
Forecast EPS	$0.05	No of Institutions	340
	(05/20/2016)		
Market Cap	$2.4 Billion	Shares	103,929,352
Book Value	$1.5 Billion	% Held	93.69
Price/Book	1.57		
Price/Sales	3.96		

Business Summary: REITs (MIC: 5.3.1 SIC: 1542 NAIC: 525930)

Mack-Cali Realty is a self-administered and self-managed real estate investment trust that owns and operates a real estate portfolio comprised of Class A office and office/flex properties located primarily in the Northeast. Co. provides leasing, property management, acquisition, development, construction and tenant-related services for its commercial and other real estate and multi-family real estate portfolio. Co. operates in three industry segments: commercial and other real estate, multi-family real estate, and multi-family services. As of Dec 31 2015, Co. owned or had interests in 275 properties, consisting of 147 office and 109 flex properties.

Recent Developments: For the quarter ended Mar 31 2016, net income amounted to US$68.8 million versus a net loss of US$3.3 million in the year-earlier quarter. Revenues were US$152.9 million, down 0.5% from US$153.7 million the year before. Operating income was US$27.2 million versus US$27.0 million in the prior-year quarter, an increase of 0.8%. Direct operating expenses declined 10.1% to US$47.2 million from US$52.4 million in the comparable period the year before. Indirect operating expenses increased 5.8% to US$78.5 million from US$74.3 million in the equivalent prior-year period.

Prospects: Our evaluation of Mack Cali Realty Corp. as of June 19, 2016 is the result of our systematic analysis on three basic characteristics: earnings strength, relative valuation, and recent stock price movement. The company has enjoyed a very positive trend in earnings per share over the past 5 quarters. Because the company lacks sufficient analyst estimate data, we place greater weight on the historical EPS trend as the measure of earnings strength. Based on operating earnings yield, the company is overvalued when compared to all of the companies in our coverage universe. Share price changes over the past year indicates that CLI will perform well over the near term.

Financial Data

(US$ in Thousands)	3 Mos	12/31/2015	12/31/2014	12/31/2013	12/31/2012	12/31/2011	12/31/2010	12/31/2009
Earnings Per Share	(0.69)	(1.41)	0.32	(0.17)	0.47	0.81	0.67	0.71
Cash Flow Per Share	1.74	1.90	1.79	2.26	2.78	2.93	2.82	3.97
Tang Book Value Per Share	16.70	16.22	18.21	18.58	20.15	21.52	21.77	22.88
Dividends Per Share	0.600	0.600	0.900	1.500	1.800	1.800	1.800	1.990
Dividend Payout %	...	...	281.25	...	382.98	222.22	268.66	280.28
Income Statement								
Total Revenue	152,923	594,883	636,799	667,031	704,743	724,279	787,480	764,525
EBITDA	98,650	145,276	331,703	231,048	363,491	405,233	403,570	411,589
Depn & Amortn	2,665	181,899	188,626	197,609	198,966	199,932	197,853	201,599
Income Before Taxes	70,323	(138,880)	33,814	(87,359)	42,192	79,365	56,474	69,288
Net Income	68,769	(142,052)	31,391	(19,058)	46,269	81,387	63,439	63,728
Average Shares	100,315	100,222	100,041	99,785	99,996	98,962	92,477	88,389
Balance Sheet								
Current Assets	273,533	203,420	196,255	386,735	226,747	182,667	178,473	439,298
Total Assets	4,228,450	4,063,490	4,192,247	4,515,328	4,526,045	4,295,759	4,362,466	4,721,637
Current Liabilities	226,180	224,862	221,582	234,107	253,149	227,544	229,035	241,010
Long-Term Obligations	2,269,287	2,154,920	2,088,654	2,362,766	2,204,389	1,914,215	2,089,494	2,337,437
Total Liabilities	2,728,587	2,607,814	2,567,466	2,872,969	2,759,071	2,406,195	2,604,194	2,890,179
Stockholders' Equity	1,499,863	1,455,676	1,624,781	1,642,359	1,766,974	1,889,564	1,758,272	1,831,458
Shares Outstanding	89,638	89,583	89,076	88,247	87,536	87,799	79,605	78,969
Statistical Record								
Return on Assets %	N.M.	N.M.	0.72	N.M.	1.05	1.88	1.40	1.39
Return on Equity %	N.M.	N.M.	1.92	N.M.	2.52	4.46	3.53	3.78
EBITDA Margin %	64.51	24.42	52.09	34.64	51.58	55.95	51.25	53.84
Net Margin %	44.97	N.M.	4.93	N.M.	6.57	11.24	8.06	8.34
Asset Turnover	0.14	0.14	0.15	0.15	0.16	0.17	0.17	0.17
Current Ratio	1.21	0.90	0.89	1.65	0.90	0.80	0.78	1.82
Debt to Equity	1.51	1.48	1.29	1.44	1.25	1.01	1.19	1.28
Price Range	24.12-16.90	24.12-16.90	22.57-18.02	29.27-19.14	29.33-24.59	35.48-24.37	38.19-27.98	36.44-14.54
P/E Ratio	...	...	70.53-56.31	...	62.40-52.32	43.80-30.09	57.00-41.76	51.32-20.48
Average Yield %	2.96	3.02	4.38	6.12	6.58	5.78	5.47	7.52

Address: 343 Thornall Street, Edison, NJ 08837-2206 Telephone: 732-590-1000 Fax: 732-205-8237	Web Site: www.mack-cali.com Officers: William L. Mack - Chairman Michael J. DeMarco - President, Chief Operating Officer	Auditors: PricewaterhouseCoopers LLP Transfer Agents: Computershare Trust Company, N.A., Providence, RI

MACY'S INC

Exchange	Symbol	Price	52Wk Range	Yield	P/E
NYS	M	$33.21 (5/31/2016)	72.80-30.07	4.55	10.96

*7 Year Price Score 106.17 *NYSE Composite Index=100 *12 Month Price Score 77.05

Interim Earnings (Per Share)

Qtr.	Apr	Jul	Oct	Jan
2013-14	0.55	0.72	0.47	2.12
2014-15	0.60	0.80	0.61	2.21
2015-16	0.56	0.64	0.36	1.66
2016-17	0.37	...	...	...

Interim Dividends (Per Share)

Amt	Decl	Ex	Rec	Pay
0.36Q	08/28/2015	09/11/2015	09/15/2015	10/01/2015
0.36Q	11/09/2015	12/11/2015	12/15/2015	01/04/2016
0.36Q	02/26/2016	03/11/2016	03/15/2016	04/01/2016
0.378Q	05/11/2016	06/13/2016	06/15/2016	07/01/2016

Indicated Div: $1.51

Valuation Analysis / **Institutional Holding**

Forecast EPS	$3.25	No of Institutions
	(05/20/2016)	984
Market Cap	$10.2 Billion	Shares
Book Value	$4.1 Billion	315,898,176
Price/Book	2.47	% Held
Price/Sales	0.38	N/A

Business Summary: Retail - General Merchandise/Department Stores (MIC: 2.1.1 SIC: 5311 NAIC: 452111)

Macy's is an omnichannel retail organization. As of Jan. 31, 2016, the operations of Co. included 870 Macy's, Macy's Backstage, Bloomingdale's, Bloomingdale's Outlet and Bluemercury stores in 45 states, the District of Columbia, Guam and Puerto Rico, as well as macys.com, bloomingdales.com and bluemercury.com. Co. sells a range of merchandise, including apparel and accessories (men's, women's and children's), cosmetics, home furnishings and other consumer goods. The specific assortments vary by size of store, merchandising character and character of customers in the trade areas.

Recent Developments: For the quarter ended Apr 30 2016, net income decreased 40.4% to US$115.0 million from US$193.0 million in the year-earlier quarter. Revenues were US$5.77 billion, down 7.4% from US$6.23 billion the year before. Operating income was US$276.0 million versus US$409.0 million in the prior-year quarter, a decrease of 32.5%. Direct operating expenses declined 7.5% to US$3.52 billion from US$3.80 billion in the comparable period the year before. Indirect operating expenses decreased 2.2% to US$1.98 billion from US$2.02 billion in the equivalent prior-year period.

Prospects: Our evaluation of Macy's Inc. as of June 19, 2016 is the result of our systematic analysis on three basic characteristics: earnings strength, relative valuation, and recent stock price movement. The company has managed to produce a neutral trend in earnings per share over the past 5 quarters. However, while recent estimates for the company have been lowered by analysts, M has posted better than expected results. Based on operating earnings yield, the company is undervalued when compared to all of the companies in our coverage universe. Share price changes over the past year indicates that M will perform very poorly over the near term.

Financial Data

(US$ in Thousands)	3 Mos	01/30/2016	01/31/2015	02/01/2014	02/02/2013	01/28/2012	01/29/2011	01/30/2010
Earnings Per Share	3.03	3.22	4.22	3.86	3.24	2.92	1.98	0.83
Cash Flow Per Share	6.24	6.06	7.65	6.76	5.49	4.94	3.57	4.16
Tang Book Value Per Share	N.M.	N.M.	3.34	5.42	4.51	3.84	2.72	0.67
Dividends Per Share	1.440	1.393	1.188	0.950	0.800	0.350	0.200	0.200
Dividend Payout %	47.52	43.25	28.14	24.61	24.69	11.99	10.10	24.10
Income Statement								
Total Revenue	5,771,000	27,079,000	28,105,000	27,931,000	27,686,000	26,405,000	25,003,000	23,489,000
EBITDA	275,000	3,086,000	3,814,000	3,690,000	3,557,000	3,481,000	3,019,000	2,250,000
Depn & Amortn	(1,000)	1,047,000	1,031,000	1,012,000	1,033,000	1,070,000	1,125,000	1,187,000
Income Before Taxes	178,000	1,678,000	2,390,000	2,290,000	2,102,000	1,968,000	1,320,000	507,000
Income Taxes	63,000	608,000	864,000	804,000	767,000	712,000	473,000	157,000
Net Income	116,000	1,072,000	1,526,000	1,486,000	1,335,000	1,256,000	847,000	350,000
Average Shares	313,500	333,000	361,700	384,800	412,200	430,400	427,300	423,200
Balance Sheet								
Current Assets	7,417,000	7,652,000	8,679,000	8,688,000	7,876,000	8,777,000	6,899,000	6,882,000
Total Assets	20,198,000	20,576,000	21,461,000	21,634,000	20,991,000	22,095,000	20,631,000	21,300,000
Current Liabilities	5,384,000	5,728,000	5,536,000	5,726,000	5,075,000	6,263,000	5,065,000	4,454,000
Long-Term Obligations	6,990,000	6,995,000	7,265,000	6,728,000	6,806,000	6,655,000	6,971,000	8,456,000
Total Liabilities	16,050,000	16,326,000	16,083,000	15,385,000	14,940,000	16,162,000	15,101,000	16,599,000
Stockholders' Equity	4,148,000	4,250,000	5,378,000	6,249,000	6,051,000	5,933,000	5,530,000	4,701,000
Shares Outstanding	308,395	310,256	340,573	364,935	387,701	414,181	423,341	420,843
Statistical Record								
Return on Assets %	4.81	5.11	7.10	6.99	6.10	5.90	4.05	1.62
Return on Equity %	21.27	22.33	26.32	24.23	21.92	21.97	16.60	7.51
EBITDA Margin %	4.77	11.40	13.57	13.21	12.85	13.18	12.07	9.58
Net Margin %	2.01	3.96	5.43	5.32	4.82	4.76	3.39	1.49
Asset Turnover	1.29	1.29	1.31	1.31	1.26	1.24	1.20	1.08
Current Ratio	1.38	1.34	1.57	1.52	1.55	1.40	1.36	1.55
Debt to Equity	1.69	1.65	1.35	1.08	1.12	1.12	1.26	1.80
Price Range	72.80-34.50	72.80-34.50	67.81-50.91	56.23-38.52	41.73-32.83	35.82-22.01	26.00-15.92	20.72-6.58
P/E Ratio	24.03-11.39	22.61-10.71	16.07-12.06	14.57-9.98	12.88-10.13	12.27-7.54	13.13-8.04	24.96-7.93
Average Yield %	2.79	2.43	2.00	2.03	2.09	1.26	0.91	1.43

Address: 151 West 34th Street, New York, NY 10001	**Web Site:** www.macys.com	**Auditors:** KPMG LLP
Telephone: 212-494-1602	**Officers:** Terry J. Lundgren - Chairman, President, Chief Executive Officer Dennis J. Broderick -	**Investor Contact:** 513-579 7028
Fax: 212-494-1838	Executive Vice President, Secretary, General Counsel	**Transfer Agents:** Computershare Shareowner Services, Pittsburgh, PA

MAGELLAN MIDSTREAM PARTNERS LP

Exchange	Symbol	Price	52Wk Range	Yield	P/E	Div Achiever
NYS	MMP	$70.05 (5/31/2016)	79.19-55.08	4.58	18.98	14 Years

*7 Year Price Score 119.39 *NYSE Composite Index=100 *12 Month Price Score 102.09

Interim Earnings (Per Share)

Qtr.	Mar	Jun	Sep	Dec
2013	0.50	0.68	0.55	0.83
2014	1.07	0.64	0.87	1.11
2015	0.81	0.78	1.10	0.90
2016	0.91			

Interim Dividends (Per Share)

Amt	Decl	Ex	Rec	Pay
0.74Q	07/23/2015	08/05/2015	08/07/2015	08/14/2015
0.762Q	10/22/2015	10/29/2015	11/02/2015	11/13/2015
0.785Q	01/26/2016	02/03/2016	02/05/2016	02/12/2016
0.802Q	04/21/2016	04/28/2016	05/02/2016	05/13/2016

Indicated Div: $3.21

Valuation Analysis **Institutional Holding**

Forecast EPS	$3.45	No of Institutions
	(05/20/2016)	692
Market Cap	$16.0 Billion	Shares
Book Value	N/A	158,172,576
Price/Book	N/A	% Held
Price/Sales	7.30	67.74

Business Summary: Equipment & Services (MIC: 9.1.3 SIC: 4613 NAIC: 486910)

Magellan Midstream Partners is principally engaged in the transportation, storage and distribution of refined petroleum products and crude oil. Co. operates in three business segments: refined products segment, which includes the operations of its refined products pipeline system, independent terminals, ammonia pipeline system as well as its blending and fractionation activities; crude oil segment, which is comprised of its crude oil pipelines and storage facilities; and marine storage segment, which is comprised of storage terminals, which provide distribution, storage, blending, inventory management and additive injection services for refiners and other end users of petroleum products.

Recent Developments: For the quarter ended Mar 31 2016, net income increased 12.8% to US$207.1 million from US$183.6 million in the year-earlier quarter. Revenues were US$519.8 million, down 2.0% from US$530.3 million the year before. Operating income was US$216.0 million versus US$219.8 million in the prior-year quarter, a decrease of 1.7%. Direct operating expenses declined 2.5% to US$236.8 million from US$242.9 million in the comparable period the year before. Indirect operating expenses decreased 0.9% to US$67.0 million from US$67.6 million in the equivalent prior-year period.

Prospects: Our evaluation of Magellan Midstream Partners L.P. as of June 19, 2016 is the result of our systematic analysis on three basic characteristics: earnings strength, relative valuation, and recent stock price movement. The company has generated a negative trend in earnings per share over the past 5 quarters and while recent estimates for the company have been mixed, MMP has posted better than expected results. Based on operating earnings yield, the company is about fairly valued when compared to all of the companies in our coverage universe. Share price changes over the past year indicates that MMP will perform poorly over the near term.

Financial Data

(US$ in Thousands)	3 Mos	12/31/2015	12/31/2014	12/31/2013	12/31/2012	12/31/2011	12/31/2010	12/31/2009
Earnings Per Share	3.69	3.59	3.69	2.56	1.92	1.83	1.43	1.11
Cash Flow Per Share	4.78	4.70	4.87	3.41	2.84	2.56	1.94	2.36
Dividends Per Share	3.005	2.915	2.505	2.098	1.784	1.556	1.454	1.420
Dividend Payout %	81.44	81.20	67.89	81.93	92.90	85.04	102.02	127.93
Income Statement								
Total Revenue	519,816	2,188,453	2,303,723	1,897,606	1,772,074	1,748,667	1,557,447	1,014,171
EBITDA	227,968	1,062,252	1,102,931	832,757	673,710	633,203	507,815	389,492
Depn & Amortn	428	164,100	159,000	136,400	126,700	118,900	107,300	95,600
Income Before Taxes	190,313	754,975	824,745	580,575	435,331	408,669	307,219	224,705
Income Taxes	871	2,336	4,620	4,613	2,622	1,866	1,371	1,661
Net Income	207,070	819,122	839,519	582,237	435,670	413,566	311,580	226,475
Average Shares	227,849	227,888	227,626	227,094	226,608	225,974	219,122	114,290
Balance Sheet								
Current Assets	515,531	338,854	402,667	396,733	700,278	612,190	384,583	323,968
Total Assets	6,392,314	6,041,567	5,517,285	4,820,812	4,420,067	4,045,001	3,717,900	3,163,148
Current Liabilities	679,094	713,072	536,155	638,276	392,620	311,055	275,047	229,397
Long-Term Obligations	3,552,032	3,189,287	2,982,895	2,435,316	2,393,408	2,151,775	1,906,148	1,680,004
Total Liabilities	4,354,732	4,019,831	3,649,052	3,173,370	2,904,365	2,581,598	2,262,592	1,966,794
Shares Outstanding	227,781	227,427	227,068	226,679	226,200	225,473	224,962	213,175
Statistical Record								
Return on Assets %	14.05	14.17	16.24	12.60	10.27	10.65	9.06	8.30
EBITDA Margin %	43.86	48.54	47.88	43.88	38.02	36.21	32.61	38.40
Net Margin %	39.84	37.43	36.44	30.68	24.59	23.65	20.01	22.33
Asset Turnover	0.36	0.38	0.45	0.41	0.42	0.45	0.45	0.37
Current Ratio	0.76	0.48	0.75	0.62	1.78	1.97	1.40	1.41
Price Range	85.01-55.08	85.01-55.08	89.12-60.52	63.27-43.19	45.34-32.51	34.48-26.59	28.59-20.52	21.66-12.90
P/E Ratio	23.04-14.93	23.68-15.34	24.15-16.40	24.71-16.87	23.61-16.93	18.84-14.53	20.00-14.35	19.52-11.62
Average Yield %	4.31	3.98	3.23	3.87	4.64	5.19	6.00	8.01

Address: One Williams Center, P.O. Box 22186, Tulsa, OK 74121-2186 **Telephone:** 918-574-7000	**Web Site:** www.magellanlp.com **Officers:** Michael N. Mears - Chairman, President, Chief Executive Officer Richard A. Olson - Senior Vice President	**Auditors:** Ernst & Young LLP **Investor Contact:** 918-574-7650 **Transfer Agents:** Computershare Trust Company, N.A., Providence, RI

MANITOWOC COMPANY INC (THE)

Exchange	Symbol	Price	52Wk Range	Yield	P/E
NYS	MTW	$5.70 (5/31/2016)	6.05-2.64	1.40	N/A

*7 Year Price Score 91.98   *NYSE Composite Index=100   *12 Month Price Score 139.47

Interim Earnings (Per Share)

Qtr.	Mar	Jun	Sep	Dec
2013	0.08	0.43	0.39	0.16
2014	(0.06)	0.34	0.53	0.24
2015	(0.06)	0.17	0.04	0.32
2016	(1.49)	...	...	...

Interim Dividends (Per Share)

Amt	Decl	Ex	Rec	Pay
0.08A	10/30/2013	11/26/2013	11/29/2013	12/10/2013
0.08A	10/21/2014	11/25/2014	11/28/2014	12/10/2014
0.08A	10/28/2015	11/24/2015	11/27/2015	12/10/2015
0.00A	02/11/2016	03/04/2016	02/22/2016	03/04/2016

Indicated Div: $0.08

Valuation Analysis

Institutional Holding	
Forecast EPS	$0.11
	(05/20/2016)
Market Cap	$781.0 Million
Book Value	$767.9 Million
Price/Book	1.02
Price/Sales	0.25

No of Institutions 350

Shares 131,466,608

% Held 75.26

TRADING VOLUME (thousand shares)

Business Summary: Construction Services (MIC: 7.5.4 SIC: 3531 NAIC: 333120)

Manitowoc is a multi-industry, capital goods manufacturer operating in two principal markets: Cranes and Related Products (Crane) and Foodservice Equipment (Foodservice). Crane is a provider of lifting equipment for the construction industry, including mobile telescopic cranes, tower cranes, lattice-boom crawler cranes, and boom trucks. Foodservice is a manufacturer of commercial foodservice equipment serving the ice, beverage, refrigeration, food preparation, and cooking needs of restaurants, convenience stores, hotels, healthcare, and institutional applications.

Recent Developments: For the quarter ended Mar 31 2016, loss from continuing operations was US$200.8 million compared with a loss of US$25.5 million in the year-earlier quarter. Net loss amounted to US$204.0 million versus a net loss of US$8.4 million in the year-earlier quarter. Revenues were US$427.4 million, up 5.1% from US$406.7 million the year before. Operating income was US$3.0 million versus a loss of US$8.3 million in the prior-year quarter. Direct operating expenses rose 4.3% to US$345.5 million from US$331.3 million in the comparable period the year before. Indirect operating expenses decreased 5.7% to US$78.9 million from US$83.7 million in the equivalent prior-year period.

Prospects: Our evaluation of Manitowoc Co. Inc. as of June 19, 2016 is the result of our systematic analysis on three basic characteristics: earnings strength, relative valuation, and recent stock price movement. The company has managed to produce a neutral trend in earnings per share over the past 5 quarters and while recent estimates for the company have remained steady, MTW has posted results that fell short of analysts expectations. Based on operating earnings yield, the company is undervalued when compared to all of the companies in our coverage universe. Share price changes over the past year indicates that MTW will perform very well over the near term.

Financial Data

(US$ in Thousands)	3 Mos	12/31/2015	12/31/2014	12/31/2013	12/31/2012	12/31/2011	12/31/2010	12/31/2009
Earnings Per Share	(0.96)	0.46	1.05	1.05	0.76	(0.08)	(0.56)	(5.41)
Cash Flow Per Share	0.17	0.72	0.73	2.43	1.23	0.12	1.60	2.60
Tang Book Value Per Share	2.44	N.M.	N.M.	N.M.	N.M.	N.M.	N.M.	N.M.
Dividends Per Share	0.080	0.080	0.080	0.080	0.080	0.080	0.080	0.080
Dividend Payout %	...	17.39	7.62	7.62	10.53	...	...	...
Income Statement								
Total Revenue	427,400	3,435,800	3,886,500	4,048,100	3,927,000	3,651,900	3,141,700	3,782,600
EBITDA	(55,000)	262,100	371,300	464,400	382,200	315,400	277,900	(371,500)
Depn & Amortn	13,800	104,300	103,500	103,800	106,600	120,900	125,500	131,100
Income Before Taxes	(78,500)	56,600	169,400	225,200	130,300	37,400	(44,600)	(705,400)
Income Taxes	122,300	(6,700)	8,600	36,100	38,000	15,900	23,900	(58,800)
Net Income	(204,000)	63,500	144,500	141,800	101,700	(10,500)	(73,400)	(704,200)
Average Shares	136,599	137,433	137,351	135,330	133,317	133,377	130,581	130,268
Balance Sheet								
Current Assets	899,000	1,013,600	1,186,100	1,262,900	1,328,000	1,239,800	1,160,600	1,259,900
Total Assets	1,820,400	3,448,900	3,816,600	3,976,600	4,057,300	3,965,200	4,009,300	4,278,700
Current Liabilities	526,600	883,600	1,011,300	1,125,400	1,145,900	1,104,600	1,025,500	1,142,200
Long-Term Obligations	269,300	1,346,600	1,443,200	1,504,100	1,732,000	1,810,900	1,935,600	2,027,500
Total Liabilities	1,052,500	2,629,400	2,992,500	3,201,100	3,457,000	3,481,800	3,527,400	3,670,800
Stockholders' Equity	767,900	819,500	824,100	775,500	600,300	483,400	481,900	607,900
Shares Outstanding	137,016	136,617	135,543	133,717	132,769	131,884	131,388	130,708
Statistical Record								
Return on Assets %	N.M.	1.75	3.71	3.53	2.53	N.M.	N.M.	N.M.
Return on Equity %	N.M.	7.73	18.07	20.61	18.72	N.M.	N.M.	N.M.
EBITDA Margin %	N.M.	7.63	9.55	11.47	9.73	8.64	8.85	N.M.
Net Margin %	N.M.	1.85	3.72	3.50	2.59	N.M.	N.M.	N.M.
Asset Turnover	1.10	0.95	1.00	1.01	0.98	0.92	0.76	0.73
Current Ratio	1.71	1.15	1.17	1.12	1.16	1.12	1.13	1.10
Debt to Equity	0.35	1.64	1.75	1.94	2.89	3.75	4.02	3.34
Price Range	4.74-2.64	4.82-2.99	7.02-3.51	4.95-3.31	3.53-2.05	4.84-1.27	3.37-1.82	2.46-0.51
P/E Ratio	...	10.49-6.50	6.68-3.34	4.72-3.16	4.65-2.70	...	...	...
Average Yield %	2.18	2.06	1.43	1.95	2.85	2.62	3.24	5.38

Address: 2400 South 44th Street, Manitowoc, WI 54221-0066 **Telephone:** 920-684-4410	**Web Site:** www.manitowoc.com **Officers:** Kenneth W. Krueger - Chairman, Interim President, Interim Chief Executive Officer Barry L. Pennypacker - President, Chief Executive Officer, Division Officer	**Auditors:** PricewaterhouseCoopers LLP **Investor Contact:** 920-684-4410 **Transfer Agents:** Computershare Trust Company, N.A, Providence, RI

MANPOWERGROUP

Exchange	Symbol	Price	52Wk Range	Yield	P/E
NYS	MAN	$79.75 (5/31/2016)	96.56-70.33	2.16	14.32

*7 Year Price Score 116.76 *NYSE Composite Index=100   ***12 Month Price Score 93.95**

TRADING VOLUME (thousand shares)

Interim Earnings (Per Share)

Qtr.	Mar	Jun	Sep	Dec
2013	0.31	0.87	1.18	1.26
2014	0.86	1.35	1.61	1.48
2015	0.83	1.33	1.61	1.65
2016	0.98	...	...	...

Interim Dividends (Per Share)

Amt	Decl	Ex	Rec	Pay
0.49S	10/29/2014	11/26/2014	12/01/2014	12/15/2014
0.80S	04/28/2015	05/28/2015	06/01/2015	06/15/2015
0.80S	10/29/2015	11/27/2015	12/01/2015	12/15/2015
0.86S	05/03/2016	05/27/2016	06/01/2016	06/15/2016

Indicated Div: $1.72

Valuation Analysis

		Institutional Holding	
Forecast EPS	$5.95 (05/15/2016)	No of Institutions	537
Market Cap	$6.5 Billion	Shares	83,544,592
Book Value	$2.6 Billion	% Held	91.52
Price/Book	2.51		
Price/Sales	0.34		

Business Summary: Business Services (MIC: 7.5.2 SIC: 7363 NAIC: 561330)

ManpowerGroup provides workforce solutions and services, which include recruitment and assessment, training and development, career management, outsourcing, and workforce consulting. Its brands and offerings include Manpower, Experis, Right Management and ManpowerGroup Solutions. Co.'s portfolio of recruitment services include permanent, temporary and contract recruitment of professionals, as well as administrative and industrial positions, which are provided under its Manpower and Experis brands. Experis focuses on the areas of information technology, engineering, finance and accounting, and healthcare, while Right Management is focused on talent and career management workforce solutions.

Recent Developments: For the quarter ended Mar 31 2016, net income increased 9.1% to US$71.7 million from US$65.7 million in the year-earlier quarter. Revenues were US$4.59 billion, up 1.0% from US$4.54 billion the year before. Operating income was US$131.7 million versus US$122.8 million in the prior-year quarter, an increase of 7.2%. Direct operating expenses rose 0.9% to US$3.81 billion from US$3.78 billion in the comparable period the year before. Indirect operating expenses increased 0.5% to US$642.1 million from US$639.2 million in the equivalent prior-year period.

Prospects: Our evaluation of ManpowerGroup as of June 19, 2016 is the result of our systematic analysis on three basic characteristics: earnings strength, relative valuation, and recent stock price movement. The company has produced a positive trend in earnings per share over the past 5 quarters and while recent estimates for the company have been raised by analysts, MAN has posted better than expected results. Based on operating earnings yield, the company is undervalued when compared to all of the companies in our coverage universe. Share price changes over the past year indicates that MAN will perform well over the near term.

Financial Data

(US$ in Thousands)	3 Mos	12/31/2015	12/31/2014	12/31/2013	12/31/2012	12/31/2011	12/31/2010	12/31/2009
Earnings Per Share	5.57	5.40	5.30	3.62	2.47	3.04	(3.26)	(0.12)
Cash Flow Per Share	8.98	6.66	3.85	5.09	4.16	0.85	2.25	5.29
Tang Book Value Per Share	12.30	14.25	20.24	19.08	14.73	14.31	13.05	15.00
Dividends Per Share	1.600	1.600	0.980	0.920	0.860	0.800	0.740	0.740
Dividend Payout %	28.73	29.63	18.49	25.41	34.82	26.32	...	...
Income Statement								
Total Revenue	4,587,700	19,329,900	20,762,800	20,250,500	20,678,000	22,006,000	18,866,500	16,038,700
EBITDA	149,100	771,900	796,900	603,200	504,100	619,800	(17,600)	124,300
Depn & Amortn	21,300	77,700	83,800	94,300	100,500	104,400	110,100	97,200
Income Before Taxes	119,000	660,700	681,600	475,500	368,400	479,900	(165,200)	(22,900)
Income Taxes	47,300	241,500	254,000	187,500	170,800	228,200	98,400	(13,700)
Net Income	71,700	419,200	427,600	288,000	197,600	251,600	(263,600)	(9,200)
Average Shares	73,500	77,700	80,700	79,600	80,100	82,800	81,000	78,300
Balance Sheet								
Current Assets	5,184,100	5,092,500	5,033,700	5,243,000	5,060,600	4,990,500	4,874,000	4,332,400
Total Assets	7,548,100	7,517,500	7,182,500	7,288,300	7,012,600	6,899,700	6,729,700	6,213,800
Current Liabilities	3,451,000	3,451,000	3,374,400	3,509,600	3,677,200	3,762,200	3,290,100	2,603,000
Long-Term Obligations	850,000	810,900	423,900	481,900	462,100	266,000	669,300	715,600
Total Liabilities	4,943,200	4,892,800	4,239,500	4,374,100	4,511,800	4,416,300	4,332,500	3,677,300
Stockholders' Equity	2,604,900	2,624,700	2,943,000	2,914,200	2,500,800	2,483,400	2,397,200	2,536,500
Shares Outstanding	81,940	73,038	78,114	79,355	76,647	79,903	81,759	78,576
Statistical Record								
Return on Assets %	5.90	5.70	5.91	4.03	2.83	3.69	N.M.	N.M.
Return on Equity %	15.56	15.06	14.60	10.64	7.91	10.31	N.M.	N.M.
EBITDA Margin %	3.25	3.99	3.84	2.98	2.44	2.82	N.M.	0.78
Net Margin %	1.56	2.17	2.06	1.42	0.96	1.14	N.M.	N.M.
Asset Turnover	2.69	2.63	2.87	2.83	2.96	3.23	2.92	2.50
Current Ratio	1.50	1.48	1.49	1.49	1.38	1.33	1.48	1.66
Debt to Equity	0.33	0.31	0.14	0.17	0.18	0.11	0.28	0.28
Price Range	96.56-70.33	96.56-63.79	86.73-59.00	86.66-42.44	47.90-32.41	68.67-32.32	65.14-40.58	61.48-23.75
P/E Ratio	17.34-12.63	17.88-11.81	16.36-11.13	23.94-11.72	19.39-13.12	22.59-10.63	...	...
Average Yield %	1.88	1.89	1.28	1.45	2.19	1.56	1.41	1.70

Address: P.O. Box 2053, 100 Manpower Place, Milwaukee, WI 53212 **Telephone:** 414-961-1000 **Fax:** 414-332-0796	**Web Site:** www.manpower.com **Officers:** Jonas Prising - Chairman, President, Chief Executive Officer, Executive Vice President, Region Officer Darryl Green - President, Chief Operating Officer, Executive Vice President, Region Officer	**Auditors:** Deloitte & Touche LLP **Investor Contact:** 414-906-6807 **Transfer Agents:** ComputerShare, College Station, TX

MARATHON OIL CORP.

Exchange	Symbol	Price	52Wk Range	Yield	P/E
NYS	MRO	$13.07 (5/31/2016)	27.75-6.73	1.53	N/A

*7 Year Price Score 50.15 *NYSE Composite Index=100 *12 Month Price Score 79.46

Interim Earnings (Per Share)

Qtr.	Mar	Jun	Sep	Dec
2013	0.54	0.60	0.80	0.53
2014	1.65	0.80	0.64	1.36
2015	(0.41)	(0.57)	(1.11)	(1.17)
2016	(0.56)	...	...	...

Interim Dividends (Per Share)

Amt	Decl	Ex	Rec	Pay
0.21Q	07/29/2015	08/17/2015	08/19/2015	09/10/2015
0.05Q	10/29/2015	11/16/2015	11/18/2015	12/10/2015
0.05Q	01/27/2016	02/12/2016	02/17/2016	03/10/2016
0.05Q	04/27/2016	05/16/2016	05/18/2016	06/10/2016

Indicated Div: $0.20

Valuation Analysis / **Institutional Holding**

Forecast EPS	$-1.20
	(05/20/2016)
Market Cap	$11.1 Billion
Book Value	$19.4 Billion
Price/Book	0.57
Price/Sales	2.19

No of Institutions	986
Shares	761,694,976
% Held	77.17

Business Summary: Production & Extraction (MIC: 9.1.1 SIC: 1311 NAIC: 211111)

Marathon Oil is an energy company. Co. has three segments: North America Exploration and Production (E&P), which engages in oil and gas exploration, development and/or production activities in the U.S. and Canada; International E&P, which engages in oil and gas exploration, development and/or production activities in Equatorial Guinea, Ethiopia, Gabon, Kenya, the Kurdistan Region of Iraq, Libya and the U.K.; and Oil Sands Mining, which mines, extracts and transports bitumen from oil sands deposits in Alberta, Canada, and upgrades the bitumen to produce and market synthetic crude oil and vacuum gas oil. At Dec 31 2015, Co. had total proved reserves of 2.20 billion barrels of oil equivalents.

Recent Developments: For the quarter ended Mar 31 2016, net loss amounted to US$407.0 million versus a net loss of US$276.0 million in the year-earlier quarter. Revenues were US$730.0 million, down 52.3% from US$1.53 billion the year before. Operating loss was US$598.0 million versus a loss of US$373.0 million in the prior-year quarter. Direct operating expenses declined 34.5% to US$495.0 million from US$756.0 million in the comparable period the year before. Indirect operating expenses decreased 27.5% to US$833.0 million from US$1.15 billion in the equivalent prior-year period.

Prospects: Our evaluation of Marathon Oil Corp. as of June 19, 2016 is the result of our systematic analysis on three basic characteristics: earnings strength, relative valuation, and recent stock price movement. The company has enjoyed a very positive trend in earnings per share over the past 5 quarters. Because the company lacks sufficient analyst estimate data, we place greater weight on the historical EPS trend as the measure of earnings strength. Based on operating earnings yield, the company is overvalued when compared to all of the companies in our coverage universe. Share price changes over the past year indicates that MRO will perform very poorly over the near term.

Financial Data

(US$ in Thousands)	3 Mos	12/31/2015	12/31/2014	12/31/2013	12/31/2012	12/31/2011	12/31/2010	12/31/2009
Earnings Per Share	(3.41)	(3.26)	4.46	2.47	2.23	4.13	3.61	2.06
Cash Flow Per Share	1.82	2.31	8.07	7.48	5.67	9.19	8.27	7.43
Tang Book Value Per Share	22.68	27.23	30.46	27.04	25.12	23.60	31.54	28.94
Dividends Per Share	0.520	0.680	0.800	0.720	0.680	0.800	0.990	0.960
Dividend Payout %	...	...	17.94	29.15	30.49	19.37	27.42	46.60
Income Statement								
Total Revenue	730,000	5,861,000	11,258,000	14,959,000	16,221,000	15,282,000	73,621,000	54,139,000
EBITDA	11,000	300,000	4,493,000	8,015,000	8,821,000	6,827,000	8,174,000	6,124,000
Depn & Amortn	609,000	2,957,000	2,861,000	2,790,000	2,478,000	2,266,000	2,965,000	2,623,000
Income Before Taxes	(683,000)	(2,958,000)	1,361,000	4,930,000	6,113,000	4,427,000	5,122,000	3,441,000
Income Taxes	(276,000)	(754,000)	392,000	3,337,000	4,531,000	2,720,000	2,554,000	2,257,000
Net Income	(407,000)	(2,204,000)	3,046,000	1,753,000	1,582,000	2,946,000	2,568,000	1,463,000
Average Shares	730,000	677,000	683,000	709,000	710,000	714,000	712,000	711,000
Balance Sheet								
Current Assets	3,268,000	2,590,000	4,593,000	2,975,000	3,762,000	3,224,000	13,829,000	10,637,000
Total Assets	32,868,000	32,311,000	36,011,000	35,620,000	35,306,000	31,371,000	50,014,000	47,052,000
Current Liabilities	1,526,000	1,729,000	4,379,000	4,333,000	5,081,000	4,394,000	11,113,000	9,057,000
Long-Term Obligations	7,280,000	7,276,000	5,323,000	6,394,000	6,512,000	4,674,000	7,601,000	8,436,000
Total Liabilities	13,517,000	13,758,000	14,991,000	16,276,000	17,023,000	14,219,000	26,243,000	25,142,000
Stockholders' Equity	19,351,000	18,553,000	21,020,000	19,344,000	18,283,000	17,152,000	23,771,000	21,910,000
Shares Outstanding	848,000	677,000	675,000	697,000	707,000	704,000	710,000	708,000
Statistical Record								
Return on Assets %	N.M.	N.M.	8.50	4.94	4.73	7.24	5.29	3.26
Return on Equity %	N.M.	N.M.	15.09	9.32	8.90	14.40	11.24	6.75
EBITDA Margin %	1.51	5.12	39.91	53.58	54.38	44.67	11.10	11.31
Net Margin %	N.M.	N.M.	27.06	11.72	9.75	19.28	3.49	2.70
Asset Turnover	0.15	0.17	0.31	0.42	0.49	0.38	1.52	1.21
Current Ratio	2.14	1.50	1.05	0.69	0.74	0.73	1.24	1.17
Debt to Equity	0.38	0.39	0.25	0.33	0.36	0.27	0.32	0.39
Price Range	31.19-6.73	31.19-12.38	41.69-24.80	37.93-29.85	35.06-23.32	34.07-20.27	22.55-17.08	21.48-12.74
P/E Ratio	...	...	9.35-5.56	15.36-12.09	15.72-10.46	8.25-4.91	6.25-4.73	10.43-6.18
Average Yield %	2.82	2.99	2.25	2.08	2.32	2.81	5.00	5.24

Address: 5555 San Felipe Street, Houston, TX 77056-2723 **Telephone:** 713-629-6600	**Web Site:** www.marathonoil.com **Officers:** Clarence P. Cazalot - Chairman, President, Chief Executive Officer Lee M. Tillman - President, Chief Executive Officer	**Auditors:** PricewaterhouseCoopers LLP **Investor Contact:** 713-296-4114 **Transfer Agents:** Computershare, Providence, RI

MARATHON PETROLEUM CORP.

Exchange	Symbol	Price	52Wk Range	Yield	P/E
NYS	MPC	$34.83 (5/31/2016)	59.34-30.73	3.67	9.60

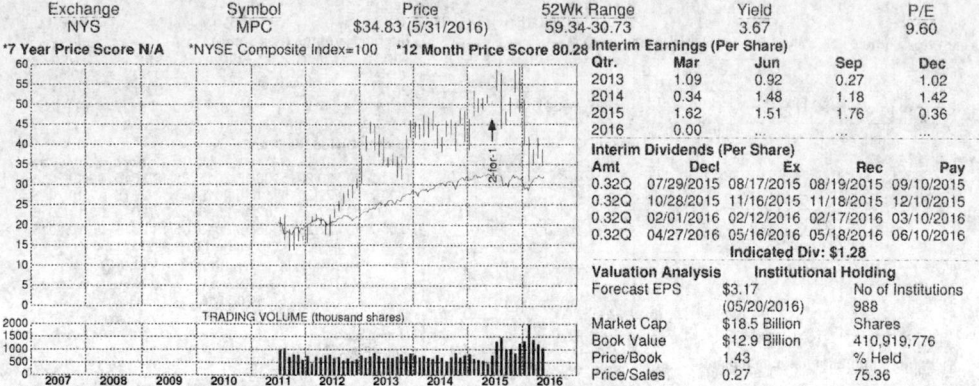

'7 Year Price Score N/A ***NYSE Composite Index=100** ***12 Month Price Score 80.28**

Interim Earnings (Per Share)

Qtr.	Mar	Jun	Sep	Dec
2013	1.09	0.92	0.27	1.02
2014	0.34	1.48	1.18	1.42
2015	1.62	1.51	1.76	0.36
2016	0.00			

Interim Dividends (Per Share)

Amt	Decl	Ex	Rec	Pay
0.32Q	07/29/2015	08/17/2015	08/19/2015	09/10/2015
0.32Q	10/28/2015	11/16/2015	11/18/2015	12/10/2015
0.32Q	02/01/2016	02/12/2016	02/17/2016	03/10/2016
0.32Q	04/27/2016	05/16/2016	05/18/2016	06/10/2016

Indicated Div: $1.28

Valuation Analysis

		Institutional Holding	
Forecast EPS	$3.17	No of Institutions	
	(05/20/2016)	988	
Market Cap	$18.5 Billion	Shares	
Book Value	$12.9 Billion	410,919,776	
Price/Book	1.43	% Held	
Price/Sales	0.27	75.36	

Business Summary: Refining & Marketing (MIC: 9.1.2 SIC: 1311 NAIC: 211111)

Marathon Petroleum is an independent petroleum refining, marketing, retail and transportation company. Co. has three operating segments: Refining and Marketing, which refines crude oil and other feedstocks at Co.'s refineries in the Gulf Coast and Midwest regions of the U.S., purchases refined products and ethanol for resale and distributes refined products; Speedway, which sells transportation fuels and convenience products in the retail market in the Midwest, East Coast and Southeast; and Midstream, which gathers, transports, fractionates, stores and markets natural gas liquids and transports and stores crude oil and refined products.

Recent Developments: For the quarter ended Mar 31 2016, net loss amounted to US$78.0 million versus net income of US$903.0 million in the year-earlier quarter. Revenues were US$12.83 billion, down 25.6% from US$17.24 billion the year before. Operating income was US$75.0 million versus US$1.47 billion in the prior-year quarter, a decrease of 94.9%. Direct operating expenses declined 25.6% to US$9.70 billion from US$13.04 billion in the comparable period the year before. Indirect operating expenses increased 12.0% to US$3.05 billion from US$2.73 billion in the equivalent prior-year period.

Prospects: Our evaluation of Marathon Petroleum Corp. as of June 19, 2016 is the result of our systematic analysis on three basic characteristics: earnings strength, relative valuation, and recent stock price movement. The company has suffered a very negative trend in earnings per share over the past 5 quarters. However, while recent estimates for the company have been lowered by analysts, MPC has posted results that fell short of analysts expectations. Based on operating earnings yield, the company is undervalued when compared to all of the companies in our coverage universe. Share price changes over the past year indicates that MPC will perform well over the near term.

Financial Data

(US$ in Millions)	3 Mos	12/31/2015	12/31/2014	12/31/2013	12/31/2012	12/31/2011	12/31/2010	12/31/2009
Earnings Per Share	3.63	5.26	4.39	3.32	4.95	3.34	...	...
Cash Flow Per Share	6.05	7.55	5.46	5.40	6.59	4.65	...	...
Tang Book Value Per Share	17.46	17.36	16.76	16.80	16.16	12.13	...	...
Dividends Per Share	1.210	1.140	0.920	0.770	0.600	0.225	...	...
Dividend Payout %	33.31	21.67	20.96	23.19	12.13	6.75	...	...
Income Statement								
Total Revenue	12,830	72,258	98,102	100,254	82,492	78,759	62,605	45,639
EBITDA	559	6,302	5,356	4,624	6,317	4,632	1,945	1,315
Depn & Amortn	490	1,646	1,326	1,220	995	891	941	670
Income Before Taxes	(67)	4,374	3,835	3,246	5,238	3,719	1,023	685
Income Taxes	11	1,506	1,280	1,113	1,845	1,330	400	236
Net Income	1	2,852	2,524	2,112	3,389	2,389	623	449
Average Shares	531	542	574	634	684	714	...	...
Balance Sheet								
Current Assets	8,097	9,471	11,339	12,737	13,029	12,001	10,056	7,900
Total Assets	41,758	43,115	30,460	28,385	27,223	25,745	23,232	21,254
Current Liabilities	5,595	6,345	8,579	9,824	8,203	9,591	8,620	6,637
Long-Term Obligations	11,351	11,896	6,610	3,373	3,342	3,292	3,231	2,601
Total Liabilities	28,856	29,878	19,709	17,465	15,529	16,240	14,988	12,082
Stockholders' Equity	12,902	13,237	10,751	10,920	11,694	9,505	8,244	9,172
Shares Outstanding	530	531	548	594	666	714	...	...
Statistical Record								
Return on Assets %	5.45	7.75	8.58	7.60	12.76	9.76	2.80	...
Return on Equity %	16.19	23.78	23.29	18.68	31.89	26.92	7.15	...
EBITDA Margin %	4.36	8.72	5.46	4.61	7.66	5.88	3.11	2.88
Net Margin %	0.01	3.95	2.57	2.11	4.11	3.03	1.00	0.98
Asset Turnover	1.89	1.96	3.33	3.61	3.11	3.22	2.81	...
Current Ratio	1.45	1.49	1.32	1.30	1.59	1.25	1.17	1.19
Debt to Equity	0.88	0.90	0.61	0.31	0.29	0.35	0.39	0.28
Price Range	59.34-30.73	59.34-38.42	48.46-37.90	45.87-30.13	31.50-15.48	22.48-13.53	...	...
P/E Ratio	16.35-8.47	11.28-7.31	11.04-8.63	13.81-9.07	6.36-3.13	6.73-4.05	...	...
Average Yield %	2.51	2.25	2.11	2.02	2.57	1.26	...	...

Address: 539 South Main Street, Findlay, OH 45840-3229 **Telephone:** 419-422-2121	**Web Site:** www.marathonpetroleum.com **Officers:** Gary R. Heminger - President, Chief Executive Officer Randy S. Nickerson - Executive Vice President	**Auditors:** PricewaterhouseCoopers LLP **Investor Contact:** 419-429-5640 **Transfer Agents:** Computershare, Canton, MA

MARKEL CORP (HOLDING CO)

Exchange	Symbol	Price	52Wk Range	Yield	P/E
NYS	MKL	$953.00 (5/31/2016)	982.84-774.24	N/A	24.19

*7 Year Price Score 139.43 *NYSE Composite Index=100 ***12 Month Price Score 105.91**

TRADING VOLUME (thousand shares)

Interim Earnings (Per Share)

Qtr.	Mar	Jun	Sep	Dec
2013	9.50	2.24	4.67	7.15
2014	6.25	2.66	5.30	8.06
2015	13.49	6.72	7.39	14.14
2016	11.15	...	...	...

Interim Dividends (Per Share)

No Dividends Paid

Valuation Analysis		Institutional Holding	
Forecast EPS	$31.27	No of Institutions	
	(05/13/2016)	507	
Market Cap	$13.3 Billion	Shares	
Book Value	$8.2 Billion	15,182,810	
Price/Book	1.62	% Held	
Price/Sales	2.45	75.31	

Business Summary: General Insurance (MIC: 5.2.1 SIC: 6331 NAIC: 524126)

Markel is a financial holding company. Co.'s principal business markets and underwrites specialty insurance products. As of Dec 31 2014, Co. had three reportable segments: U.S. Insurance, which includes all direct business and facultative placements written by Co.'s insurance subsidiaries domiciled in the U.S.; International Insurance, which includes all direct business and facultative placements written by Co.'s insurance subsidiaries domiciled outside of the U.S., including its syndicate at Lloyd's of London; and Reinsurance, which includes property and casualty treaty reinsurance products provided to other insurance and reinsurance companies globally through the broker market.

Recent Developments: For the quarter ended Mar 31 2016, net income decreased 15.6% to US$163.6 million from US$194.0 million in the year-earlier quarter. Revenues were US$1.38 billion, up 5.7% from US$1.30 billion the year before. Net premiums earned were US$957.7 million versus US$943.7 million in the prior-year quarter, an increase of 1.5%. Net investment income fell 1.7% to US$91.3 million from US$92.9 million a year ago.

Prospects: Our evaluation of Markel Corp. as of June 19, 2016 is the result of our systematic analysis on three basic characteristics: earnings strength, relative valuation, and recent stock price movement. The company has generated a negative trend in earnings per share over the past 5 quarters and while recent estimates for the company have remained steady, MKL has posted better than expected results. Based on operating earnings yield, the company is about fairly valued when compared to all of the companies in our coverage universe. Share price changes over the past year indicates that MKL will perform very well over the near term.

Financial Data
(US$ in Thousands)

	3 Mos	12/31/2015	12/31/2014	12/31/2013	12/31/2012	12/31/2011	12/31/2010	12/31/2009
Earnings Per Share	39.40	41.74	22.27	22.48	25.89	14.60	27.27	20.52
Cash Flow Per Share	37.43	46.58	51.26	59.46	40.61	32.14	22.86	28.78
Tang Book Value Per Share	450.46	420.80	418.50	367.58	294.88	261.92	259.89	231.34
Income Statement								
Premium Income	957,686	3,823,532	3,840,912	3,231,616	2,147,128	1,979,340	1,730,921	1,815,835
Total Revenue	1,376,182	5,369,983	5,133,667	4,323,083	3,000,112	2,629,950	2,225,393	2,069,326
Benefits & Claims	473,964	1,938,745	2,202,467	1,816,273	1,154,068	1,209,986	946,229	992,863
Income Before Taxes	214,336	742,105	440,378	361,743	312,050	190,196	295,511	198,637
Income Taxes	50,690	152,963	116,690	77,898	53,802	41,710	27,782	(3,782)
Net Income	163,646	589,142	323,688	283,845	258,248	148,486	267,729	202,419
Average Shares	14,074	14,061	14,057	12,586	9,666	9,726	9,785	9,826
Balance Sheet								
Total Assets	25,685,230	24,941,271	25,200,357	23,955,511	12,556,588	11,532,103	10,825,589	10,241,896
Total Liabilities	17,446,114	17,107,121	17,605,539	17,281,934	8,667,931	8,144,590	7,654,066	7,467,536
Stockholders' Equity	8,239,116	7,834,150	7,594,818	6,673,577	3,888,657	3,387,513	3,171,523	2,774,360
Shares Outstanding	13,968	13,959	13,961	13,985	9,629	9,620	9,717	9,819
Statistical Record								
Return on Assets %	2.19	2.35	1.32	1.55	2.14	1.33	2.54	2.05
Return on Equity %	6.94	7.64	4.54	5.37	7.08	4.53	9.01	8.17
Loss Ratio %	49.49	50.71	57.34	56.20	53.75	61.13	54.67	54.68
Net Margin %	11.89	10.97	6.31	6.57	8.61	5.65	12.03	9.78
Price Range		934.76-740.64	934.76-662.59	703.95-529.00	580.35-433.42	500.68-399.12	425.68-347.36	387.72-321.32	363.00-211.00
P/E Ratio		23.72-18.80	22.39-15.87	31.61-23.75	25.82-19.28	19.34-15.42	29.16-23.79	14.22-11.78	17.69-10.28

Address: 4521 Highwoods Parkway, Glen Allen, VA 23060-6148 **Telephone:** 804-747-0136	**Web Site:** www.markelcorp.com **Officers:** Alan I. Kirshner - Chairman, Chief Executive Officer Steven A. Markel - Vice-Chairman	**Auditors:** KPMG LLP **Investor Contact:** 800-446-6671 **Transfer Agents:** American Stock Transfer & Trust Co., LLC, Brooklyn, NY

MARSH & MCLENNAN COMPANIES INC.

Exchange	Symbol	Price	52Wk Range	Yield	P/E
NYS	MMC	$66.07 (5/31/2016)	66.07-51.29	2.06	22.02

*7 Year Price Score 125.18 *NYSE Composite Index=100 *12 Month Price Score 109.67

Interim Earnings (Per Share)

Qtr.	Mar	Jun	Sep	Dec
2013	0.74	0.69	0.45	0.54
2014	0.80	0.77	0.54	0.54
2015	0.88	0.77	0.61	0.71
2016	0.91			

Interim Dividends (Per Share)

Amt	Decl	Ex	Rec	Pay
0.31Q	09/16/2015	10/07/2015	10/09/2015	11/13/2015
0.31Q	01/13/2016	01/21/2016	01/25/2016	02/12/2016
0.31Q	03/16/2016	04/06/2016	04/08/2016	05/13/2016
0.34Q	05/19/2016	07/07/2016	07/11/2016	08/15/2016

Indicated Div: $1.36

Valuation Analysis | **Institutional Holding**
Forecast EPS $3.40	No of Institutions
(05/20/2016)	829
Market Cap $34.5 Billion	Shares
Book Value $6.7 Billion	513,800,416
Price/Book 5.16	% Held
Price/Sales 2.65	84.80

Business Summary: Brokers & Intermediaries (MIC: 5.2.3 SIC: 6411 NAIC: 524210)

Marsh & McLennan Companies is a holding company. Through its subsidiaries, Co. provides clients advice and solutions in risk, strategy and people. As of Dec 31 2015, Co. provides analysis, advice and transactional capabilities to clients in more than 130 countries. Co. conducts business through two segments: Risk and Insurance Services, which includes risk management activities (risk advice, risk transfer and risk control and mitigation solutions) as well as insurance and reinsurance broking and services; and Consulting, which includes Health, Retirement, Talent and Investments consulting services and products, and specialized management, economic and brand consulting services.

Recent Developments: For the quarter ended Mar 31 2016, income from continuing operations decreased 1.6% to US$490.0 million from US$498.0 million in the year-earlier quarter. Net income decreased 1.0% to US$490.0 million from US$495.0 million in the year-earlier quarter. Revenues were US$3.34 billion, up 3.8% from US$3.22 billion the year before.

Prospects: Our evaluation of Marsh & McLennan Cos. Inc. as of June 19, 2016 is the result of our systematic analysis on three basic characteristics: earnings strength, relative valuation, and recent stock price movement. The company has managed to produce a neutral trend in earnings per share over the past 5 quarters and while recent estimates for the company have remained steady, MMC has posted better than expected results. Based on operating earnings yield, the company is about fairly valued when compared to all of the companies in our coverage universe. Share price changes over the past year indicates that MMC will perform in line with the market over the near term.

Financial Data
(US$ in Thousands)

	3 Mos	12/31/2015	12/31/2014	12/31/2013	12/31/2012	12/31/2011	12/31/2010	12/31/2009
Earnings Per Share	3.00	2.98	2.65	2.43	2.13	1.79	1.55	0.42
Cash Flow Per Share	3.53	3.56	3.88	2.44	2.42	3.15	1.34	1.23
Tang Book Value Per Share	N.M.	N.M.	N.M.	0.99	N.M.	N.M.	N.M.	N.M.
Dividends Per Share	1.210	1.180	1.060	0.960	0.900	0.860	0.810	0.800
Dividend Payout %	40.33	39.60	40.00	39.51	42.25	48.04	52.26	190.48
Income Statement								
Total Revenue	3,336,000	12,893,000	12,951,000	12,261,000	11,924,000	11,526,000	10,550,000	10,493,000
EBITDA	841,000	2,566,000	2,287,000	2,194,000	1,925,000	1,640,000	1,048,000	565,000
Depn & Amortn	111,000	109,000	86,000	72,000	72,000	65,000	66,000	58,000
Income Before Taxes	686,000	2,307,000	2,057,000	1,973,000	1,696,000	1,404,000	769,000	283,000
Income Taxes	196,000	671,000	586,000	594,000	492,000	422,000	204,000	41,000
Net Income	481,000	1,599,000	1,465,000	1,357,000	1,176,000	993,000	855,000	227,000
Average Shares	526,000	536,000	553,000	558,000	552,000	551,000	544,000	524,000
Balance Sheet								
Current Assets	4,798,000	5,044,000	6,055,000	6,300,000	5,963,000	5,648,000	5,276,000	4,931,000
Total Assets	18,128,000	18,216,000	17,840,000	16,980,000	16,288,000	15,454,000	15,310,000	15,337,000
Current Liabilities	3,159,000	3,708,000	3,705,000	3,809,000	3,564,000	3,739,000	3,105,000	3,703,000
Long-Term Obligations	4,748,000	4,402,000	3,376,000	2,621,000	2,658,000	2,668,000	3,026,000	3,034,000
Total Liabilities	11,449,000	11,703,000	10,786,000	9,075,000	9,746,000	9,571,000	8,942,000	9,509,000
Stockholders' Equity	6,679,000	6,513,000	7,054,000	7,905,000	6,542,000	5,883,000	6,368,000	5,828,000
Shares Outstanding	521,521	521,897	540,142	546,759	545,507	539,178	540,509	529,674
Statistical Record								
Return on Assets %	9.14	8.87	8.41	8.16	7.39	6.46	5.58	1.49
Return on Equity %	23.76	23.57	19.59	18.79	18.88	16.21	14.02	3.93
EBITDA Margin %	25.21	19.90	17.66	17.89	16.14	14.23	9.93	5.38
Net Margin %	14.42	12.40	11.31	11.07	9.86	8.62	8.10	2.16
Asset Turnover	0.74	0.72	0.74	0.74	0.75	0.75	0.69	0.69
Current Ratio	1.52	1.36	1.63	1.65	1.67	1.51	1.70	1.33
Debt to Equity	0.71	0.68	0.48	0.33	0.41	0.45	0.48	0.52
Price Range	60.79-51.29	59.84-51.54	58.56-44.40	48.36-34.47	35.78-30.72	32.00-25.71	27.48-20.57	25.39-17.74
P/E Ratio	20.26-17.10	20.08-17.30	22.10-16.75	19.90-14.19	16.80-14.42	17.88-14.36	17.73-13.27	60.45-42.24
Average Yield %	2.15	2.10	2.07	2.34	2.72	2.93	3.41	3.73

Address: 1166 Avenue of the Americas, New York, NY 10036	Web Site: www.mmc.com	Auditors: Deloitte & Touche LLP
Telephone: 212-345-5000	Officers: Daniel S. Glaser - President, Chief Executive Officer, Chief Operating Officer, Division Officer Peter J. Beshar - Executive Vice President, General Counsel	Investor Contact: 212-345-5462
Fax: 212-345-4809		Transfer Agents: Wells Fargo Shareowner Services, St. Paul, MN

MARTIN MARIETTA MATERIALS, INC.

Exchange	Symbol	Price	52Wk Range	Yield	P/E
NYS	MLM	$189.04 (5/31/2016)	193.15-117.00	0.85	38.50

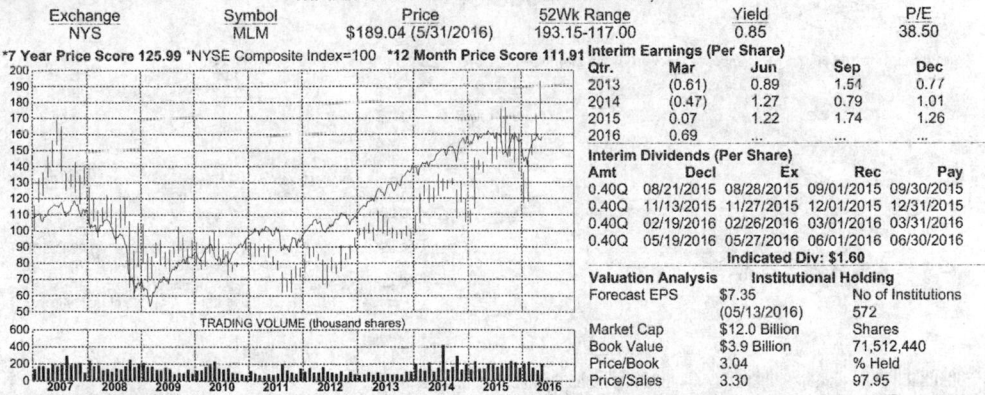

*7 Year Price Score 125.99 *NYSE Composite Index=100 *12 Month Price Score 111.91

Interim Earnings (Per Share)

Qtr.	Mar	Jun	Sep	Dec
2013	(0.61)	0.89	1.54	0.77
2014	(0.47)	1.27	0.79	1.01
2015	0.07	1.22	1.74	1.26
2016	0.69	...	...	...

Interim Dividends (Per Share)

Amt	Decl	Ex	Rec	Pay
0.40Q	08/21/2015	08/28/2015	09/01/2015	09/30/2015
0.40Q	11/13/2015	11/27/2015	12/01/2015	12/31/2015
0.40Q	02/19/2016	02/26/2016	03/01/2016	03/31/2016
0.40Q	05/19/2016	05/27/2016	06/01/2016	06/30/2016

Indicated Div: $1.60

Valuation Analysis

	Institutional Holding	
Forecast EPS	$7.35	No of Institutions
	(05/13/2016)	572
Market Cap	$12.0 Billion	Shares
Book Value	$3.9 Billion	71,512,440
Price/Book	3.04	% Held
Price/Sales	3.30	97.95

Business Summary: Construction Materials (MIC: 8.5.1 SIC: 1411 NAIC: 212311)

Martin Marietta Materials supplies aggregates products for the construction industry, used for the construction of infrastructure, nonresidential, and residential projects. Co.'s Aggregates business mines, processes and sells granite, limestone, sand, gravel, and other aggregate products for the infrastructure, nonresidential and residential construction industries, agriculture, railroad ballast, chemical, and other uses. Co.'s Cement business produces Portland and specialty cements. Co.'s Magnesia Specialties business manufactures and markets magnesia-based chemical products for industrial, agricultural, and environmental applications, and dolomitic lime for use in the steel industry.

Recent Developments: For the quarter ended Mar 31 2016, net income increased 631.5% to US$45.1 million from US$6.2 million in the year-earlier quarter. Revenues were US$788.7 million, up 14.1% from US$691.3 million the year before. Operating income was US$83.8 million versus US$25.6 million in the prior-year quarter, an increase of 227.6%. Direct operating expenses rose 4.4% to US$644.1 million from US$617.1 million in the comparable period the year before. Indirect operating expenses increased 25.0% to US$60.9 million from US$48.7 million in the equivalent prior-year period.

Prospects: Our evaluation of Martin Marietta Materials Inc. as of June 19, 2016 is the result of our systematic analysis on three basic characteristics: earnings strength, relative valuation, and recent stock price movement. The company has produced a positive trend in earnings per share over the past 5 quarters and while recent estimates for the company have been mixed, MLM has posted better than expected results. Based on operating earnings yield, the company is about fairly valued when compared to all of the companies in our coverage universe. Share price changes over the past year indicates that MLM will perform very well over the near term.

Financial Data

(US$ in Thousands)	3 Mos	12/31/2015	12/31/2014	12/31/2013	12/31/2012	12/31/2011	12/31/2010	12/31/2009
Earnings Per Share	4.91	4.29	2.71	2.61	1.83	1.78	2.10	1.91
Cash Flow Per Share	9.43	8.58	6.71	6.69	4.85	5.68	5.93	7.24
Tang Book Value Per Share	27.27	22.93	25.07	18.86	16.17	16.15	17.14	16.05
Dividends Per Share	1.600	1.600	1.600	1.600	1.600	1.600	1.600	1.600
Dividend Payout %	32.59	37.30	59.04	61.30	87.43	89.89	76.19	83.77
Income Statement								
Total Revenue	788,734	3,539,570	2,957,951	2,155,551	2,037,667	1,713,823	1,782,857	1,702,603
EBITDA	153,209	736,962	526,477	386,026	328,192	329,162	374,578	364,772
Depn & Amortn	68,410	246,874	211,242	168,333	171,940	169,974	178,426	176,050
Income Before Taxes	64,765	413,801	249,178	164,226	102,913	100,602	127,696	115,262
Income Taxes	19,710	124,863	94,847	44,045	16,950	20,986	29,217	27,375
Net Income	44,994	288,792	155,601	121,337	84,474	82,379	97,012	85,459
Average Shares	64,350	67,020	57,088	46,285	45,970	45,793	45,659	44,190
Balance Sheet								
Current Assets	998,315	1,082,168	1,288,816	755,366	700,401	657,850	696,211	856,860
Total Assets	7,058,287	6,961,732	7,464,392	3,259,826	3,160,926	3,147,822	3,074,743	3,239,283
Current Liabilities	492,131	367,191	396,648	210,549	173,335	173,712	385,493	373,553
Long-Term Obligations	1,575,327	1,553,649	1,571,059	1,018,518	1,042,183	1,052,902	782,045	1,023,492
Total Liabilities	3,115,636	2,904,448	3,113,226	1,721,949	1,750,381	1,738,501	1,649,303	1,874,043
Stockholders' Equity	3,942,651	4,057,284	4,351,166	1,537,877	1,410,545	1,409,321	1,425,440	1,365,240
Shares Outstanding	63,505	64,479	67,293	46,261	46,002	45,726	45,579	45,399
Statistical Record								
Return on Assets %	4.53	4.00	2.90	3.78	2.67	2.65	3.07	2.73
Return on Equity %	7.91	6.87	5.28	8.23	5.97	5.81	6.95	7.16
EBITDA Margin %	19.42	20.82	17.80	17.91	16.11	19.21	21.01	21.42
Net Margin %	5.70	8.16	5.26	5.63	4.15	4.81	5.44	5.02
Asset Turnover	0.50	0.49	0.55	0.67	0.64	0.55	0.56	0.54
Current Ratio	2.03	2.95	3.25	3.59	4.04	3.79	1.81	2.29
Debt to Equity	0.40	0.38	0.36	0.66	0.74	0.75	0.55	0.75
Price Range	176.51-117.00	176.51-104.58	134.91-98.70	112.09-93.56	95.59-64.56	93.00-61.62	99.81-72.61	104.24-68.37
P/E Ratio	35.95-23.83	41.14-24.38	49.78-36.42	42.95-35.85	52.23-35.28	52.25-34.62	47.53-34.58	54.58-35.80
Average Yield %	1.07	1.09	1.31	1.60	1.96	2.03	1.88	1.88

Address: 2710 Wycliff Road, Raleigh, NC 27607-3033	**Web Site:** www.martinmarietta.com	**Auditors:** PricewaterhouseCoopers LLP
Telephone: 919-781-4550	**Officers:** C. Howard Nye - President, Chief Executive Officer Philip J. Sipling - Executive Vice President, Division Officer	**Transfer Agents:** American Stock Transfer & Trust Company, LLC, Brooklyn, NY

MASCO CORP.

Exchange	Symbol	Price	52Wk Range	Yield	P/E
NYS	MAS	$32.64 (5/31/2016)	32.72-22.63	1.16	28.14

*7 Year Price Score 144.59 *NYSE Composite Index=100 *12 Month Price Score 112.80

Interim Earnings (Per Share)

Qtr.	Mar	Jun	Sep	Dec
2013	0.13	0.21	0.29	0.13
2014	0.21	0.39	1.51	0.28
2015	0.18	0.30	0.32	0.22
2016	0.32			

Interim Dividends (Per Share)

Amt	Decl	Ex	Rec	Pay
0.09Q	06/26/2015	07/09/2015	07/13/2015	08/10/2015
0.095Q	09/25/2015	10/07/2015	10/09/2015	11/09/2015
0.095Q	12/15/2015	01/06/2016	01/08/2016	02/08/2016
0.095Q	03/28/2016	04/06/2016	04/08/2016	05/09/2016

Indicated Div: $0.38 (Div. Reinv. Plan)

Valuation Analysis — **Institutional Holding**

Forecast EPS	$1.51 (05/20/2016)	No of Institutions 748
Market Cap	$10.7 Billion	Shares 358,948,416
Book Value	N/A	% Held 87.05
Price/Book	N/A	
Price/Sales	1.49	

Business Summary: Construction Materials (MIC: 8.5.1 SIC: 2434 NAIC: 337110)

Masco is engaged in the design, manufacture, marketing and distribution of branded home improvement and building products. Co.'s portfolio of brands includes KRAFTMAID® and MERILLAT® cabinets; DELTA®, PEERLESS®, and HANSGROHE® faucets, bath and shower fixtures; HOT SPRING® and CALDERA® spas; BEHR® paint, primer and stain; KILZ® primer; LIBERTY® and BRAINERD® decorative hardware; and MILGARD® windows and doors. Co. has four business segments aggregated by similarity in products and services: Cabinets and Related Products, Plumbing Products, Decorative Architectural Products, and Other Specialty Products.

Recent Developments: For the quarter ended Mar 31 2016, income from continuing operations increased 70.0% to US$119.0 million from US$70.0 million in the year-earlier quarter. Net income increased 63.0% to US$119.0 million from US$73.0 million in the year-earlier quarter. Revenues were US$1.72 billion, up 3.7% from US$1.66 billion the year before. Operating income was US$234.0 million versus US$165.0 million in the prior-year quarter, an increase of 41.8%. Direct operating expenses declined 1.1% to US$1.15 billion from US$1.16 billion in the comparable period the year before. Indirect operating expenses increased 1.5% to US$335.0 million from US$330.0 million in the equivalent prior-year period.

Prospects: Our evaluation of Masco Corp. as of June 19, 2016 is the result of our systematic analysis on three basic characteristics: earnings strength, relative valuation, and recent stock price movement. The company has enjoyed a very positive trend in earnings per share over the past 5 quarters and while recent estimates for the company have been mixed, MAS has posted better than expected results. Based on operating earnings yield, the company is about fairly valued when compared to all of the companies in our coverage universe. Share price changes over the past year indicates that MAS will perform very well over the near term.

Financial Data

(US$ in Thousands)	3 Mos	12/31/2015	12/31/2014	12/31/2013	12/31/2012	12/31/2011	12/31/2010	12/31/2009
Earnings Per Share	1.16	1.02	2.38	0.76	(0.33)	(1.66)	(3.00)	(0.53)
Cash Flow Per Share	2.28	2.07	1.72	1.84	0.80	0.69	1.33	2.01
Dividends Per Share	0.370	0.365	0.330	0.300	0.300	0.300	0.300	0.460
Dividend Payout %	31.90	35.78	13.87	39.47	...	...	...	...
Income Statement								
Total Revenue	1,720,000	7,142,000	8,521,000	8,173,000	7,745,000	7,467,000	7,592,000	7,792,000
EBITDA	233,000	1,030,000	956,000	842,000	497,000	27,000	(266,000)	309,000
Depn & Amortn	...	116,000	157,000	175,000	202,000	246,000	261,000	237,000
Income Before Taxes	177,000	689,000	575,000	434,000	42,000	(472,000)	(777,000)	(151,000)
Income Taxes	58,000	293,000	(333,000)	111,000	83,000	(49,000)	225,000	(49,000)
Net Income	109,000	355,000	856,000	272,000	(114,000)	(575,000)	(1,043,000)	(183,000)
Average Shares	333,000	341,000	352,000	352,000	349,000	348,000	349,000	351,000
Balance Sheet								
Current Assets	4,248,000	3,328,000	3,863,000	3,468,000	3,217,000	3,429,000	3,464,000	3,451,000
Total Assets	6,554,000	5,680,000	7,167,000	6,933,000	6,875,000	7,297,000	8,140,000	9,175,000
Current Liabilities	2,789,000	2,506,000	2,211,000	1,782,000	1,862,000	2,363,000	1,487,000	1,781,000
Long-Term Obligations	2,993,000	2,418,000	2,919,000	3,421,000	3,422,000	3,222,000	4,032,000	3,604,000
Total Liabilities	6,680,000	5,815,000	6,243,000	6,398,000	6,553,000	6,770,000	6,756,000	6,546,000
Stockholders' Equity	(126,000)	(135,000)	924,000	535,000	322,000	527,000	1,384,000	2,629,000
Shares Outstanding	328,700	330,500	345,000	349,500	349,000	347,900	348,600	350,400
Statistical Record								
Return on Assets %	5.71	5.53	12.14	3.94	N.M.	N.M.	N.M.	N.M.
Return on Equity %	124.42	89.99	117.34	63.48	N.M.	N.M.	N.M.	N.M.
EBITDA Margin %	13.55	14.42	11.22	10.30	6.42	0.36	N.M.	3.97
Net Margin %	6.34	4.97	10.05	3.33	N.M.	N.M.	N.M.	N.M.
Asset Turnover	1.03	1.11	1.21	1.18	1.09	0.97	0.88	0.84
Current Ratio	1.52	1.33	1.75	1.95	1.73	1.45	2.33	1.94
Debt to Equity	...	...	3.16	6.39	10.63	6.11	2.91	1.37
Price Range	31.60-22.55	30.50-20.84	22.33-17.18	20.05-14.65	15.02-9.65	12.99-6.08	16.13-8.84	13.30-3.23
P/E Ratio	27.24-19.44	29.90-20.43	9.38-7.22	26.38-19.27	...	...	...	...
Average Yield %	1.41	1.45	1.67	1.69	2.48	3.03	2.66	4.85

Address: 21001 Van Born Road, Taylor, MI 48180 Telephone: 313-274-7400	Web Site: www.masco.com Officers: J. Michael Losh - Chairman Richard A. Manoogian - Chairman Emeritus, Chairman, President, Chief Executive Officer, Vice President	Auditors: PricewaterhouseCoopers LLP Investor Contact: 313-792-5500 Transfer Agents: Computershare, Providence, RI

MASTERCARD INC

Exchange	Symbol	Price	52Wk Range	Yield	P/E
NYS	MA	$95.90 (5/31/2016)	101.50-80.65	0.79	28.89

*7 Year Price Score 148.20 *NYSE Composite Index=100 ***12 Month Price Score 101.53**

TRADING VOLUME (thousand shares)

Interim Earnings (Per Share)

Qtr.	Mar	Jun	Sep	Dec
2013	0.62	0.70	0.73	0.51
2014	0.73	0.80	0.87	0.70
2015	0.89	0.81	0.86	0.79
2016	0.86	...	...	...

Interim Dividends (Per Share)

Amt	Decl	Ex	Rec	Pay
0.16Q	06/10/2015	07/07/2015	07/09/2015	08/10/2015
0.16Q	09/22/2015	10/07/2015	10/09/2015	11/09/2015
0.19Q	12/08/2015	01/06/2016	01/08/2016	02/09/2016
0.19Q	02/02/2016	04/06/2016	04/08/2016	05/09/2016

Indicated Div: $0.76

Valuation Analysis / Institutional Holding

Forecast EPS	$3.55	No of Institutions
	(05/20/2016)	1540
Market Cap	$105.7 Billion	Shares
Book Value	$5.5 Billion	872,115,904
Price/Book	19.29	% Held
Price/Sales	10.69	71.59

Business Summary: Business Services (MIC: 7.5.2 SIC: 7389 NAIC: 561499)

MasterCard is a technology company in the payments industry that connects consumers, financial institutions, merchants, governments and businessess worldwide, enabling them to use electronic forms of payment instead of cash and checks. Co. facilitates the processing of payment transactions, including authorization, clearing and settlement, and delivers related products and services. Co. creates a range of payment solutions and services using its family of brands, including MasterCard®, Maestro® and Cirrus®. Co. also provides offerings such as loyalty and reward programs, information services and consulting.

Recent Developments: For the quarter ended Mar 31 2016, net income decreased 6.0% to US$959.0 million from US$1.02 billion in the year-earlier quarter. Revenues were US$2.45 billion, up 9.7% from US$2.23 billion the year before. Operating income was unchanged at US$1.35 billion versus the prior-year quarter. Indirect operating expenses increased 24.9% to US$1.10 billion from US$879.0 million in the equivalent prior-year period.

Prospects: Our evaluation of MasterCard Inc. as of June 19, 2016 is the result of our systematic analysis on three basic characteristics: earnings strength, relative valuation, and recent stock price movement. The company has managed to produce a neutral trend in earnings per share over the past 5 quarters and while recent estimates for the company have remained steady, MA has posted better than expected results. Based on operating earnings yield, the company is about fairly valued when compared to all of the companies in our coverage universe. Share price changes over the past year indicates that MA will perform well over the near term.

Financial Data
(US$ in Thousands)

	3 Mos	12/31/2015	12/31/2014	12/31/2013	12/31/2012	12/31/2011	12/31/2010	12/31/2009
Earnings Per Share	3.32	3.35	3.10	2.56	2.19	1.49	1.41	1.12
Cash Flow Per Share	3.73	3.57	2.92	3.41	2.35	2.10	1.30	1.06
Tang Book Value Per Share	2.55	2.99	3.95	4.76	4.18	3.30	3.05	2.14
Dividends Per Share	0.670	0.640	0.440	0.210	0.105	0.060	0.060	0.060
Dividend Payout %	20.18	19.10	14.19	8.20	4.79	4.04	4.27	5.38
Income Statement								
Total Revenue	2,446,000	9,667,000	9,473,000	8,346,000	7,391,000	6,714,000	5,539,000	5,098,684
EBITDA	1,561,000	5,150,000	5,208,000	4,573,000	4,000,000	2,804,000	2,831,000	2,353,370
Depn & Amortn	204,000	131,000	107,000	92,000	84,000	77,000	70,000	76,121
Income Before Taxes	1,337,000	4,958,000	5,079,000	4,500,000	3,932,000	2,746,000	2,757,000	2,218,051
Income Taxes	378,000	1,150,000	1,462,000	1,384,000	1,174,000	842,000	910,000	755,427
Net Income	959,000	3,808,000	3,617,000	3,116,000	2,759,000	1,906,000	1,846,000	1,462,532
Average Shares	1,112,000	1,137,000	1,169,000	1,215,000	1,260,000	1,280,000	1,310,000	1,302,320
Balance Sheet								
Current Assets	10,606,000	10,985,000	10,997,000	10,950,000	9,357,000	7,741,000	6,454,000	5,003,147
Total Assets	15,905,000	16,269,000	15,329,000	14,242,000	12,462,000	10,693,000	8,837,000	7,470,279
Current Liabilities	6,440,000	6,269,000	6,222,000	6,032,000	4,906,000	4,217,000	3,143,000	3,167,131
Long-Term Obligations	3,333,000	3,287,000	1,494,000	...	...	...	...	21,598
Total Liabilities	10,426,000	10,241,000	8,539,000	6,758,000	5,545,000	4,825,000	3,632,000	3,966,519
Stockholders' Equity	5,479,000	6,028,000	6,790,000	7,484,000	6,917,000	5,868,000	5,205,000	3,503,760
Shares Outstanding	1,102,000	1,116,000	1,152,561	1,194,188	1,232,439	1,268,637	1,308,986	1,297,729
Statistical Record								
Return on Assets %	24.54	24.10	24.46	23.34	23.77	19.52	22.64	20.97
Return on Equity %	63.62	59.42	50.68	43.27	43.04	34.43	42.39	53.86
EBITDA Margin %	63.82	53.27	54.98	54.79	54.12	41.76	51.11	46.16
Net Margin %	39.21	39.39	38.18	37.34	37.33	28.39	33.33	28.68
Asset Turnover	0.65	0.61	0.64	0.63	0.64	0.69	0.68	0.73
Current Ratio	1.65	1.75	1.77	1.82	1.91	1.84	2.05	1.58
Debt to Equity	0.61	0.55	0.22	...	...	...	...	0.01
Price Range	101.50-80.65	101.50-80.74	89.08-68.68	83.55-49.13	49.85-33.91	38.10-22.09	26.72-19.20	25.84-11.92
P/E Ratio	30.57-24.29	30.30-24.10	28.74-22.15	32.64-19.19	22.76-15.48	25.57-14.82	18.95-13.62	23.07-10.64
Average Yield %	0.72	0.69	0.57	0.34	0.24	0.20	0.26	0.32

Address: 2000 Purchase Street, Purchase, NY 10577 Telephone: 914-249-2000	Web Site: www.mastercard.com Officers: Richard Haythornthwaite - Chairman Walter M Macnee Vice-Chairman	Auditors: PricewaterhouseCoopers LLP Investor Contact: 914-249-4565 Transfer Agents: Computershare, Jersey City, NJ

MBIA INC.

Exchange	Symbol	Price	52Wk Range	Yield	P/E
NYS	MBI	$7.20 (5/31/2016)	9.42-5.41	N/A	120.00

*7 Year Price Score 65.28 *NYSE Composite Index=100 *12 Month Price Score 110.09

Interim Earnings (Per Share)

Qtr.	Mar	Jun	Sep	Dec
2013	0.84	(0.92)	0.67	0.69
2014	1.32	0.45	0.80	0.14
2015	0.37	0.36	(0.23)	0.51
2016	(0.58)	...	...	...

Interim Dividends (Per Share)

No Dividends Paid

Valuation Analysis		Institutional Holding	
Forecast EPS	$0.48	No of Institutions	
	(05/20/2016)	318	
Market Cap	$988.4 Million	Shares	
Book Value	$3.6 Billion	149,762,448	
Price/Book	0.27	% Held	
Price/Sales	1.48	89.31	

Business Summary: General Insurance (MIC: 5.2.1 SIC: 6351 NAIC: 524130)

MBIA provides financial guarantee insurance to the U.S. public finance markets through its indirect, wholly-owned subsidiary, National Public Finance Guarantee Corporation (National). Co. manages four segments: U.S. public finance insurance; international and structured finance insurance; corporate; and advisory services. Co.'s U.S. public finance insurance business is primarily operated through National and its subsidiaries, its international and structured finance insurance business is primarily operated through MBIA Insurance Corporation and its subsidiaries, and its asset management and advisory services business was operated through Cutwater Holdings, LLC and its subsidiaries.

Recent Developments: For the quarter ended Mar 31 2016, net loss amounted to US$78.0 million versus net income of US$69.0 million in the year-earlier quarter. Revenues were US$32.0 million, down 85.4% from US$219.0 million the year before. Net premiums earned were US$75.0 million versus US$101.0 million in the prior-year quarter, a decrease of 25.7%. Net investment income rose 5.4% to US$39.0 million from US$37.0 million a year ago.

Prospects: Our evaluation of MBIA Inc. as of June 19, 2016 is the result of our systematic analysis on three basic characteristics: earnings strength, relative valuation, and recent stock price movement. The company has suffered a very negative trend in earnings per share over the past 5 quarters and while recent estimates for the company have remained steady, MBI has posted results that fell short of analysts expectations. Based on operating earnings yield, the company is overvalued when compared to all of the companies in our coverage universe. Share price changes over the past year indicates that MBI will perform well over the near term.

Financial Data

(US$ in Thousands)	3 Mos	12/31/2015	12/31/2014	12/31/2013	12/31/2012	12/31/2011	12/31/2010	12/31/2009
Earnings Per Share	0.06	1.06	2.76	1.29	6.33	(6.69)	0.26	2.99
Cash Flow Per Share	(0.05)	(0.34)	(1.77)	9.67	(5.28)	(15.11)	(6.21)	(10.53)
Tang Book Value Per Share	26.42	24.61	20.47	17.05	16.22	8.80	14.02	12.50
Income Statement								
Premium Income	75,000	372,000	397,000	457,000	605,000	605,000	594,217	746,336
Total Revenue	32,000	853,000	1,270,000	1,209,000	2,435,000	(1,557,000)	893,798	2,954,021
Benefits & Claims	22,000	123,000	133,000	117,000	50,000	(80,000)	231,944	864,137
Income Before Taxes	(101,000)	289,000	641,000	416,000	1,598,000	(2,239,000)	(95,228)	1,216,881
Income Taxes	(23,000)	109,000	72,000	166,000	364,000	(920,000)	(147,757)	582,821
Net Income	(78,000)	180,000	569,000	250,000	1,234,000	(1,319,000)	52,529	634,060
Average Shares	135,814	164,869	190,898	190,312	194,904	197,019	203,021	208,156
Balance Sheet								
Total Assets	12,751,000	14,855,000	16,284,000	16,953,000	21,724,000	26,873,000	32,279,011	25,684,699
Total Liabilities	9,124,000	11,126,000	12,355,000	13,675,000	18,551,000	25,173,000	29,446,872	23,094,601
Stockholders' Equity	3,627,000	3,729,000	3,929,000	3,278,000	3,173,000	1,700,000	2,832,139	2,590,098
Shares Outstanding	137,277	151,530	191,942	192,249	195,671	193,143	199,745	204,667
Statistical Record								
Return on Assets %	0.23	1.16	3.42	1.29	5.06	N.M.	0.18	2.29
Return on Equity %	0.87	4.70	15.79	7.75	50.51	N.M.	1.94	35.38
Loss Ratio %	29.33	33.06	33.50	25.60	8.26	(13.22)	39.03	115.78
Net Margin %	(243.75)	21.10	44.80	20.68	50.68	...	5.88	21.46
Price Range	9.81-5.41	9.81-5.41	15.08-8.62	15.70-7.85	13.32-6.81	13.61-6.03	13.00-3.98	8.24-2.29
P/E Ratio	163.50-90.17	9.25-5.10	5.46-3.12	12.17-6.09	2.10-1.08	...	50.00-15.31	2.76-0.77

Address: 1 Manhattanville Road, Suite 301, Purchase, NY 10577 Telephone: 914-273-4545	Web Site: www.mbia.com Officers: Joseph W. Brown - Chairman, Chief Executive Officer C. Edward Chaplin - Co-President, Chief Financial Officer, Chief Administrative Officer, Executive Vice President	Auditors: PricewaterhouseCoopers LLP Investor Contact: 914-765-3190 Transfer Agents: Wells Fargo Shareowner Services, St. Paul, MN

MCCORMICK & CO., INC.

Exchange	Symbol	Price	52Wk Range	Yield	P/E	Div Achiever
NYS	MKC	$97.07 (5/31/2016)	100.71-76.02	1.77	29.42	29 Years

*7 Year Price Score 122.07 *NYSE Composite Index=100 *12 Month Price Score 110.09

Interim Earnings (Per Share)

Qtr.	Feb	May	Aug	Nov
2012-13	0.57	0.59	0.78	0.97
2013-14	0.62	0.84	0.94	1.13
2014-15	0.55	0.65	0.76	1.16
2015-16	0.73	...	...	...

Interim Dividends (Per Share)

Amt	Decl	Ex	Rec	Pay
0.40Q	06/30/2015	07/09/2015	07/13/2015	07/27/2015
0.40Q	09/29/2015	10/08/2015	10/13/2015	10/27/2015
0.43Q	11/24/2015	12/29/2015	12/31/2015	01/15/2016
0.43Q	03/30/2016	04/07/2016	04/11/2016	04/25/2016

Indicated Div: $1.72

Valuation Analysis   **Institutional Holding**

Forecast EPS	$3.73	No of Institutions
	(05/20/2016)	828
Market Cap	$12.3 Billion	Shares
Book Value	$1.7 Billion	118,236,096
Price/Book	7.20	% Held
Price/Sales	2.85	73.66

TRADING VOLUME (thousand shares)

Business Summary: Food (MIC: 1.2.1 SIC: 2099 NAIC: 311991)

McCormick & Co. manufactures, markets and distributes spices, seasoning mixes, condiments and other products to the food industry-retail outlets, food manufacturers and foodservice businesses. Co. operates two business segments: consumer and industrial. Co.'s consumer segment sells to retailers, including grocery, mass merchandise, warehouse clubs, discount and drug stores, and e-commerce retailers under the McCormick brand and a variety of brands, including Lawry's, Zatarain's, Simply Asia, Thai Kitchen, Ducros, Schwartz, Club House and Kamis. Co.'s industrial segment sells to food manufacturers and foodservice customers, who are supplied both directly and indirectly through distributors.

Recent Developments: For the quarter ended Feb 29 2016, net income increased 32.5% to US$93.4 million from US$70.5 million in the year-earlier quarter. Revenues were US$1.03 billion, up 2.0% from US$1.01 billion the year before. Operating income was US$129.1 million versus US$93.7 million in the prior-year quarter, an increase of 37.8%. Direct operating expenses rose 0.7% to US$625.2 million from US$620.7 million in the comparable period the year before. Indirect operating expenses decreased 6.8% to US$275.9 million from US$296.0 million in the equivalent prior-year period.

Prospects: Our evaluation of McCormick & Co. Inc. as of June 19, 2016 is the result of our systematic analysis on three basic characteristics: earnings strength, relative valuation, and recent stock price movement. The company has produced a positive trend in earnings per share over the past 5 quarters and while recent estimates for the company have been mixed, MKC has posted better than expected results. Based on operating earnings yield, the company is about fairly valued when compared to all of the companies in our coverage universe. Share price changes over the past year indicates that MKC will perform very well over the near term.

Financial Data
(US$ in Thousands)

	3 Mos	11/30/2015	11/30/2014	11/30/2013	11/30/2012	11/30/2011	11/30/2010	11/30/2009
Earnings Per Share	3.30	3.11	3.34	2.91	3.04	2.79	2.75	2.27
Cash Flow Per Share	4.50	4.61	3.88	3.52	3.42	2.56	2.92	3.18
Dividends Per Share	1.630	1.600	1.480	1.360	1.240	1.120	1.040	0.960
Dividend Payout %	49.39	51.45	44.31	46.74	40.79	40.14	37.82	42.29
Income Statement								
Total Revenue	1,030,200	4,296,300	4,243,200	4,123,400	4,014,200	3,697,600	3,336,800	3,192,100
EBITDA	156,600	655,400	706,800	658,700	683,500	640,900	591,000	550,100
Depn & Amortn	26,400	105,900	102,700	106,000	102,800	98,300	79,000	80,800
Income Before Taxes	116,300	496,200	554,400	499,400	526,100	491,400	462,700	416,500
Income Taxes	31,300	131,300	145,900	133,600	139,800	142,600	118,000	133,000
Net Income	93,400	401,600	437,900	389,000	407,800	374,200	370,200	299,800
Average Shares	128,300	129,200	131,000	133,600	134,300	134,300	134,700	132,300
Balance Sheet								
Current Assets	1,306,200	1,406,500	1,416,200	1,370,200	1,285,400	1,222,900	1,015,900	970,500
Total Assets	4,400,100	4,507,800	4,414,300	4,449,700	4,165,400	4,087,800	3,419,700	3,387,800
Current Liabilities	1,092,200	1,240,600	1,122,000	1,063,100	1,187,600	993,300	834,800	818,200
Long-Term Obligations	1,056,300	1,052,700	1,014,100	1,019,000	779,200	1,029,700	779,900	875,000
Total Liabilities	2,689,900	2,837,600	2,622,100	2,517,200	2,482,500	2,486,100	1,966,000	2,053,200
Stockholders' Equity	1,710,200	1,670,200	1,792,200	1,932,500	1,682,900	1,601,700	1,453,700	1,334,600
Shares Outstanding	126,927	127,300	128,400	131,100	132,500	132,900	133,100	131,800
Statistical Record								
Return on Assets %	9.87	9.00	9.88	9.03	9.86	9.97	10.88	9.07
Return on Equity %	25.01	23.20	23.51	21.52	24.76	24.49	26.55	25.09
EBITDA Margin %	15.20	15.25	16.66	15.97	17.03	17.33	17.71	17.23
Net Margin %	9.07	9.35	10.32	9.43	10.16	10.12	11.09	9.39
Asset Turnover	1.00	0.96	0.96	0.96	0.97	0.99	0.98	0.97
Current Ratio	1.20	1.13	1.26	1.29	1.08	1.23	1.22	1.19
Debt to Equity	0.62	0.63	0.57	0.53	0.46	0.64	0.54	0.66
Price Range	94.10-71.98	86.03-71.39	74.33-63.03	74.76-61.23	66.37-48.54	51.00-43.98	44.81-35.56	36.45-28.53
P/E Ratio	28.52-21.81	27.66-22.95	22.25-18.87	25.69-21.04	21.83-15.97	18.28-15.76	16.29-12.93	16.06-12.57
Average Yield %	2.00	2.04	2.14	1.97	2.17	2.35	2.65	3.00

Address: 18 Loveton Circle, P. O. Box 6000, Sparks, MD 21152-6000
Telephone: 410-771-7301
Fax: 410-771-7462

Web Site: www.mccormickcorporation.com
Officers: Alan D. Wilson - Chairman, President, Chief Executive Officer Gordon M. Stetz - Executive Vice President, Chief Financial Officer

Auditors: Ernst & Young LLP
Investor Contact: 410-771-7244
Transfer Agents: Wells Fargo Bank, N A Shareowner Services, Mendota Heights, MN

MCDONALD'S CORP

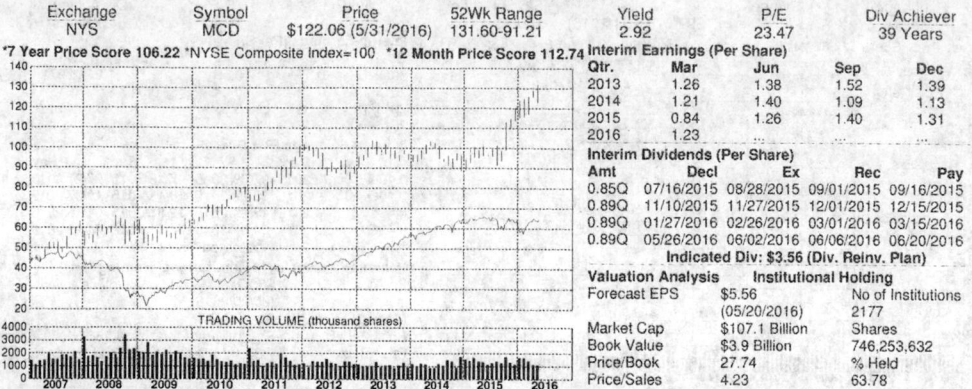

Exchange	Symbol	Price	52Wk Range	Yield	P/E	Div Achiever
NYS	MCD	$122.06 (5/31/2016)	131.60-91.21	2.92	23.47	39 Years

*7 Year Price Score 106.22 *NYSE Composite Index=100 *12 Month Price Score 112.74

Interim Earnings (Per Share)

Qtr.	Mar	Jun	Sep	Dec
2013	1.26	1.38	1.52	1.39
2014	1.21	1.40	1.09	1.13
2015	0.84	1.26	1.40	1.31
2016	1.23	...	...	...

Interim Dividends (Per Share)

Amt	Decl	Ex	Rec	Pay
0.85Q	07/16/2015	08/28/2015	09/01/2015	09/16/2015
0.89Q	11/10/2015	11/27/2015	12/01/2015	12/15/2015
0.89Q	01/27/2016	02/26/2016	03/01/2016	03/15/2016
0.89Q	05/26/2016	06/02/2016	06/06/2016	06/20/2016

Indicated Div: $3.56 (Div. Reinv. Plan)

Valuation Analysis — **Institutional Holding**

Forecast EPS	$5.56	No of Institutions	
	(05/20/2016)	2177	
Market Cap	$107.1 Billion	Shares	
Book Value	$3.9 Billion	746,253,632	
Price/Book	27.74	% Held	
Price/Sales	4.23	63.78	

Business Summary: Hotels, Restaurants & Travel (MIC: 2.2.1 SIC: 5812 NAIC: 722211)

McDonald's franchises and operates McDonald's restaurants. Co.'s menu includes hamburgers and cheeseburgers, Big Mac, Quarter Pounder with Cheese, Filet-O-Fish, several chicken sandwiches, Chicken McNuggets, wraps, french fries, salads, oatmeal, shakes, McFlurry desserts, sundaes, pies, soft drinks, coffee, McCafe beverages and other beverages. Co.'s restaurants also provides breakfast menu that include Egg McMuffin, Sausage McMuffin with Egg, McGriddles, biscuit and bagel sandwiches and hotcakes. At Dec 31 2015, Co. had a total of 36,525 restaurants in 119 countries, including 30,081 that were franchised or licensed, and 6,444 were operated by Co.

Recent Developments: For the quarter ended Mar 31 2016, net income increased 35.4% to US$1.10 billion from US$811.5 million in the year-earlier quarter. Revenues were US$5.90 billion, down 0.9% from US$5.96 billion the year before. Operating income was US$1.78 billion versus US$1.39 billion in the prior-year quarter, an increase of 28.5%. Direct operating expenses declined 5.3% to US$3.18 billion from US$3.35 billion in the comparable period the year before. Indirect operating expenses decreased 22.2% to US$948.3 million from US$1.22 billion in the equivalent prior-year period.

Prospects: Our evaluation of McDonald's Corp. as of June 19, 2016 is the result of our systematic analysis on three basic characteristics: earnings strength, relative valuation, and recent stock price movement. The company has produced a positive trend in earnings per share over the past 5 quarters and while recent estimates for the company have remained steady, MCD has posted better than expected results. Based on operating earnings yield, the company is about fairly valued when compared to all of the companies in our coverage universe. Share price changes over the past year indicates that MCD will perform very well over the near term.

Financial Data

(US$ in Thousands)	3 Mos	12/31/2015	12/31/2014	12/31/2013	12/31/2012	12/31/2011	12/31/2010	12/31/2009
Earnings Per Share	5.20	4.80	4.82	5.55	5.36	5.27	4.58	4.11
Cash Flow Per Share	7.38	6.96	6.86	7.13	6.88	6.93	5.95	5.27
Tang Book Value Per Share	1.47	5.04	10.51	13.26	12.46	11.49	11.44	10.78
Dividends Per Share	3.480	3.440	3.280	3.120	2.870	2.530	2.260	2.050
Dividend Payout %	66.92	71.67	68.05	56.22	53.54	48.01	49.34	49.88
Income Statement								
Total Revenue	5,903,900	25,413,000	27,441,300	28,105,700	27,567,000	27,006,000	24,074,600	22,744,700
EBITDA	2,178,300	8,778,800	9,490,700	10,147,000	9,854,300	9,656,600	8,487,300	7,953,200
Depn & Amortn	383,700	1,438,000	1,539,300	1,498,800	1,402,200	1,329,600	1,200,400	1,160,800
Income Before Taxes	1,580,100	6,702,500	7,380,900	8,126,300	7,935,500	7,834,200	6,836,000	6,319,200
Income Taxes	477,800	2,026,400	2,614,200	2,618,600	2,614,200	2,509,100	2,054,000	1,936,000
Net Income	1,098,600	4,529,300	4,757,800	5,585,900	5,464,800	5,503,100	4,946,300	4,551,000
Average Shares	894,900	944,600	986,300	1,006,100	1,020,200	1,044,900	1,080,300	1,107,400
Balance Sheet								
Current Assets	5,051,600	9,643,000	4,185,500	5,050,100	4,922,100	4,403,000	4,368,500	3,416,300
Total Assets	33,795,400	37,938,700	34,281,400	36,626,300	35,386,500	32,989,900	31,975,200	30,224,900
Current Liabilities	2,858,700	2,950,400	2,747,900	3,170,000	3,403,100	3,509,200	2,924,700	2,988,700
Long-Term Obligations	23,352,600	24,122,100	14,989,700	14,129,800	13,632,500	12,133,800	11,497,000	10,560,300
Total Liabilities	29,932,400	30,850,800	21,428,000	20,616,600	20,092,900	18,599,700	17,341,000	16,191,000
Stockholders' Equity	3,863,000	7,087,900	12,853,400	16,009,700	15,293,600	14,390,200	14,634,200	14,033,900
Shares Outstanding	877,800	906,800	962,900	990,400	1,002,700	1,021,400	1,053,600	1,076,700
Statistical Record								
Return on Assets %	14.61	12.54	13.42	15.51	15.94	16.94	15.90	15.51
Return on Equity %	63.10	45.43	32.97	35.69	36.72	37.92	34.51	33.20
EBITDA Margin %	36.90	34.54	34.59	36.10	35.75	35.76	35.25	34.97
Net Margin %	18.61	17.82	17.34	19.87	19.82	20.38	20.55	20.01
Asset Turnover	0.77	0.70	0.77	0.78	0.80	0.83	0.77	0.78
Current Ratio	1.77	3.27	1.52	1.59	1.45	1.25	1.49	1.14
Debt to Equity	6.05	3.40	1.17	0.88	0.89	0.84	0.79	0.75
Price Range	125.83-91.21	120.07-88.78	103.53-88.46	103.59-88.21	101.74-84.05	100.81-72.67	80.34-61.45	64.53-50.86
P/E Ratio	24.20-17.54	25.01-18.50	21.48-18.35	18.66-15.89	18.98-15.68	19.13-13.79	17.54-13.42	15.70-12.37
Average Yield %	3.28	3.43	3.40	3.21	3.10	3.01	3.19	3.57

Address: One McDonald's Plaza, Oak Brook, IL 60523 **Telephone:** 630-623-3000	**Web Site:** www.mcdonalds.com **Officers:** Stephen J. Easterbrook - President, Chief Executive Officer, Senior Executive Vice President, Region Officer Kevin M. Ozan - Executive Vice President, Chief Financial Officer, Senior Vice President, Corporate Controller	**Auditors:** Ernst & Young LLP **Investor Contact:** 800-228-9623 **Transfer Agents:** Computershare, Providence, RI

MCKESSON CORP.

Exchange	Symbol	Price	52Wk Range	Yield	P/E
NYS	MCK	$183.14 (5/31/2016)	238.27-150.03	0.61	18.88

*7 Year Price Score 131.25 *NYSE Composite Index=100 *12 Month Price Score 89.51

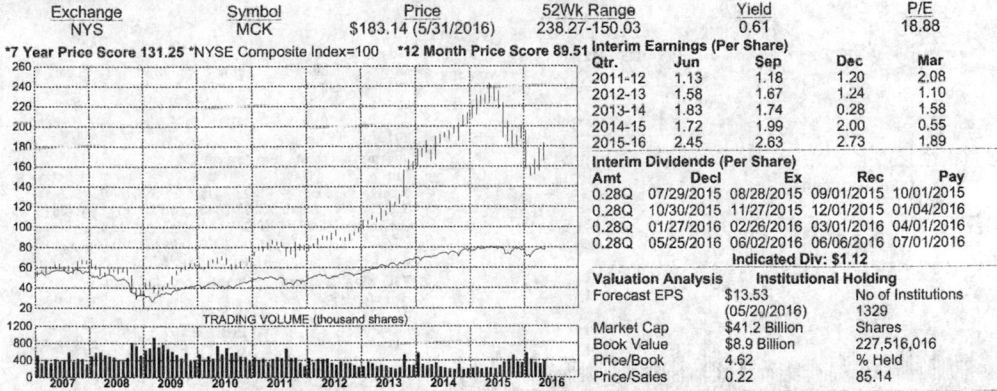

Interim Earnings (Per Share)

Qtr.	Jun	Sep	Dec	Mar
2011-12	1.13	1.18	1.20	2.08
2012-13	1.58	1.67	1.24	1.10
2013-14	1.83	1.74	0.28	1.58
2014-15	1.72	1.99	2.00	0.55
2015-16	2.45	2.63	2.73	1.89

Interim Dividends (Per Share)

Amt	Decl	Ex	Rec	Pay
0.28Q	07/29/2015	08/28/2015	09/01/2015	10/01/2015
0.28Q	10/30/2015	11/27/2015	12/01/2015	01/04/2016
0.28Q	01/27/2016	02/26/2016	03/01/2016	04/01/2016
0.28Q	05/25/2016	06/02/2016	06/06/2016	07/01/2016

Indicated Div: $1.12

Valuation Analysis / Institutional Holding

Valuation Analysis		Institutional Holding	
Forecast EPS	$13.53 (05/20/2016)	No of Institutions	1329
Market Cap	$41.2 Billion	Shares	227,516,016
Book Value	$8.9 Billion	% Held	85.14
Price/Book	4.62		
Price/Sales	0.22		

Business Summary: Pharmaceuticals (MIC: 4.1.1 SIC: 5122 NAIC: 541519)

McKesson is a pharmaceutical distribution services and information technology company. Co. provides offering of pharmaceuticals and medical supplies and provide services to its customers. Co. operates in two segments: the McKesson Distribution Solutions segment, consists of North America pharmaceutical distribution and services, International pharmaceutical distribution and services and Medical-Surgical distribution and services; and the McKesson Technology Solutions segment, provideing a portfolio of information technology and services for healthcare organizations to integrate delivery networks, hospitals, physician practices, home healthcare providers, retail pharmacies and payers.

Recent Developments: For the year ended Mar 31 2016, income from continuing operations increased 27.1% to US$2.34 billion from US$1.84 billion a year earlier. Net income increased 49.7% to US$2.31 billion in the prior year. Revenues were US$190.88 billion, up 6.6% from US$179.05 billion the year before. Operating income was US$3.55 billion versus US$2.97 billion in the prior year, an increase of 19.4%. Direct operating expenses rose 7.1% to US$179.47 billion from US$167.63 billion in the comparable period the year before. Indirect operating expenses decreased 6.8% to US$7.87 billion from US$8.44 billion in the equivalent prior-year period.

Prospects: Our evaluation of McKesson Corp. as of June 19, 2016 is the result of our systematic analysis on three basic characteristics: earnings strength, relative valuation, and recent stock price movement. The company has generated a negative trend in earnings per share over the past 5 quarters and while recent estimates for the company have been mixed, MCK has posted results that fell short of analysts expectations. Based on operating earnings yield, the company is undervalued when compared to all of the companies in our coverage universe. Share price changes over the past year indicates that MCK will perform poorly over the near term.

Financial Data

(US$ in Thousands)	03/31/2016	03/31/2015	03/31/2014	03/31/2013	03/31/2012	03/31/2011	03/31/2010	03/31/2009
Earnings Per Share	9.70	6.27	5.41	5.59	5.59	4.57	4.62	2.95
Cash Flow Per Share	15.92	13.41	13.69	10.57	11.96	9.06	8.61	4.91
Tang Book Value Per Share	N.M.	N.M.	N.M.	N.M	0.21	5.56	12.59	7.39
Dividends Per Share	1.080	0.960	0.920	0.800	0.800	0.720	0.480	0.480
Dividend Payout %	11.13	15.31	17.01	14.31	14.31	15.75	10.39	16.27
Income Statement								
Total Revenue	190,884,000	179,045,000	137,609,000	122,455,000	122,734,000	112,084,000	108,702,000	106,632,000
EBITDA	3,851,000	3,305,000	2,565,000	2,280,000	2,282,000	1,968,000	2,177,000	1,303,000
Depn & Amortn	281,000	306,000	186,000	146,000	140,000	139,000	148,000	133,000
Income Before Taxes	3,235,000	2,645,000	2,099,000	1,916,000	1,910,000	1,641,000	1,858,000	1,057,000
Income Taxes	908,000	815,000	742,000	581,000	516,000	505,000	601,000	241,000
Net Income	2,258,000	1,476,000	1,263,000	1,338,000	1,403,000	1,202,000	1,263,000	823,000
Average Shares	233,000	235,000	233,000	239,000	251,000	263,000	273,000	279,000
Balance Sheet								
Current Assets	38,437,000	36,670,000	32,573,000	23,170,000	23,603,000	22,357,000	21,504,000	18,671,000
Total Assets	56,563,000	53,870,000	51,759,000	34,786,000	33,093,000	30,886,000	28,189,000	25,267,000
Current Liabilities	35,071,000	33,497,000	29,501,000	21,537,000	21,686,000	18,726,000	17,012,000	15,606,000
Long-Term Obligations	6,535,000	8,180,000	8,949,000	4,521,000	3,072,000	3,587,000	2,293,000	2,290,000
Total Liabilities	47,639,000	45,869,000	43,237,000	27,716,000	26,262,000	23,666,000	20,657,000	19,074,000
Stockholders' Equity	8,924,000	8,001,000	8,522,000	7,070,000	6,831,000	7,220,000	7,532,000	6,193,000
Shares Outstanding	225,000	232,000	231,000	227,000	235,000	252,000	271,000	271,000
Statistical Record								
Return on Assets %	4.08	2.79	2.92	3.94	4.37	4.07	4.73	3.30
Return on Equity %	26.61	17.87	16.20	19.25	19.92	16.30	18.40	13.37
EBITDA Margin %	2.02	1.85	1.86	1.86	1.86	1.76	2.00	1.22
Net Margin %	1.18	0.82	0.92	1.09	1.14	1.07	1.16	0.77
Asset Turnover	3.45	3.39	3.18	3.61	3.83	3.79	4.07	4.28
Current Ratio	1.10	1.09	1.10	1.08	1.09	1.19	1.26	1.20
Debt to Equity	0.73	1.02	1.05	0.64	0.45	0.50	0.30	0.37
Price Range	242.75-150.03	230.26-164.68	185.35-104.18	111.23-85.48	88.59-69.35	80.64-58.05	66.72-33.87	58.85-28.60
P/E Ratio	25.03-15.47	36.72-26.26	34.26-19.26	19.90-15.29	15.85-12.41	17.65-12.70	14.44-7.33	19.95-9.69
Average Yield %	0.54	0.48	0.66	0.85	1.00	1.00	0.89	1.01

Address: One Post Street, San Francisco, CA 94104
Telephone: 415-983-8300

Web Site: www.mckesson.com
Officers: John H. Hammergren - Chairman, President, Chief Executive Officer Lori A. Schechter - Executive President, Chief Compliance Officer, General Counsel

Auditors: Deloitte & Touche LLP
Investor Contact: 415-983-8391
Transfer Agents: Wells Fargo Shareowner Services, Mendota Heights, MN

M.D.C. HOLDINGS, INC.

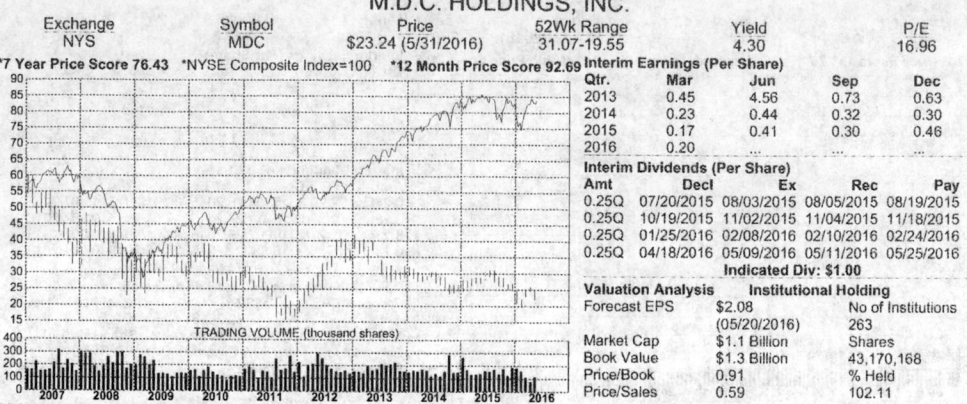

Exchange	Symbol	Price	52Wk Range	Yield	P/E
NYS	MDC	$23.24 (5/31/2016)	31.07-19.55	4.30	16.96

*7 Year Price Score 76.43   *NYSE Composite Index=100   *12 Month Price Score 92.69

Interim Earnings (Per Share)

Qtr.	Mar	Jun	Sep	Dec
2013	0.45	4.56	0.73	0.63
2014	0.23	0.44	0.32	0.30
2015	0.17	0.41	0.30	0.46
2016	0.20	...	...	...

Interim Dividends (Per Share)

Amt	Decl	Ex	Rec	Pay
0.25Q	07/20/2015	08/03/2015	08/05/2015	08/19/2015
0.25Q	10/19/2015	11/02/2015	11/04/2015	11/18/2015
0.25Q	01/25/2016	02/08/2016	02/10/2016	02/24/2016
0.25Q	04/18/2016	05/09/2016	05/11/2016	05/25/2016

Indicated Div: $1.00

Valuation Analysis | **Institutional Holding**

Forecast EPS	$2.08
	(05/20/2016)
Market Cap	$1.1 Billion
Book Value	$1.3 Billion
Price/Book	0.91
Price/Sales	0.59

No of Institutions 263
Shares 43,170,168
% Held 102.11

Business Summary: Builders (MIC: 2.2.5 SIC: 1531 NAIC: 522292)

M.D.C. Holdings is engaged in two primary operations, homebuilding and financial services. Co.'s homebuilding operations consist of wholly-owned subsidiaries that generally purchase finished lots or develop lots to the extent necessary for the construction and sale primarily of single-family detached homes to first-time and first-time move-up homebuyers under the name Richmond American Homes. Co.'s financial services operations include subsidiary companies that provide mortgage financing, place title insurance and homeowner insurance for its homebuyers, and provide general liability insurance for its subsidiaries and most of its subcontractors.

Recent Developments: For the quarter ended Mar 31 2016, net income increased 13.6% to US$9.6 million from US$8.4 million in the year-earlier quarter. Revenues were US$407.8 million, up 5.0% from US$388.5 million the year before. Direct operating expenses rose 3.6% to US$337.9 million from US$326.3 million in the comparable period the year before. Indirect operating expenses increased 11.4% to US$56.3 million from US$50.5 million in the equivalent prior-year period.

Prospects: Our evaluation of M.D.C. Holdings Inc. as of June 19, 2016 is the result of our systematic analysis on three basic characteristics: earnings strength, relative valuation, and recent stock price movement. The company has produced a positive trend in earnings per share over the past 5 quarters. However, while recent estimates for the company have been lowered by analysts, MDC has posted results that fell short of analysts expectations. Based on operating earnings yield, the company is undervalued when compared to all of the companies in our coverage universe. Share price changes over the past year indicates that MDC will perform poorly over the near term.

Financial Data

(US$ in Thousands)	3 Mos	12/31/2015	12/31/2014	12/31/2013	12/31/2012	12/31/2011	12/31/2010	12/31/2009
Earnings Per Share	1.37	1.34	1.29	6.34	1.28	(2.12)	(1.40)	0.52
Cash Flow Per Share	(0.62)	0.00	(3.37)	(5.56)	(2.28)	(1.72)	(4.48)	4.35
Tang Book Value Per Share	25.55	25.57	25.03	24.74	17.97	17.98	20.87	22.82
Dividends Per Share	1.000	1.000	1.000	2.000	2.000	1.000	1.000	1.000
Dividend Payout %	72.99	74.63	77.52	3.55	156.25	...	...	192.31
Income Statement								
Total Revenue	407,761	1,909,036	1,694,584	1,680,434	1,203,023	844,168	958,655	898,303
EBITDA	12,655	95,139	76,292	105,182	40,625	(100,706)	(41,608)	(66,453)
Depn & Amortn	1,073	4,169	4,494	4,083	5,362	16,540	16,943	14,457
Income Before Taxes	14,273	101,424	100,475	129,825	61,115	(107,472)	(70,601)	(107,335)
Income Taxes	4,710	35,633	37,332	(184,560)	(1,584)	(9,082)	(5,831)	(132,014)
Net Income	9,563	65,791	63,143	314,385	62,699	(98,390)	(64,770)	24,679
Average Shares	48,833	48,967	48,817	48,831	48,064	46,796	46,628	46,919
Balance Sheet								
Current Assets	2,080,684	2,081,591	2,012,870	2,229,107	1,747,586	1,692,692	2,349,043	2,248,545
Total Assets	2,385,806	2,415,899	2,358,438	2,595,449	1,945,441	1,858,725	2,547,769	2,429,308
Current Liabilities	271,714	1,159,607	1,130,102	1,382,200	1,062,294	197,279	295,837	329,056
Long-Term Obligations	855,798	...	...	...	...	792,810	1,268,249	1,027,106
Total Liabilities	1,127,512	1,159,607	1,130,102	1,382,200	1,064,544	990,089	1,564,086	1,356,162
Stockholders' Equity	1,258,294	1,256,292	1,228,336	1,213,249	880,897	868,636	983,683	1,073,146
Shares Outstanding	49,006	48,888	48,831	48,788	48,698	47,957	47,142	47,017
Statistical Record								
Return on Assets %	2.85	2.76	2.55	13.85	3.29	N.M.	N.M.	1.01
Return on Equity %	5.39	5.30	5.17	30.03	7.15	N.M.	N.M.	2.29
EBITDA Margin %	3.10	4.98	4.50	6.26	3.38	N.M.	N.M.	N.M.
Net Margin %	2.35	3.45	3.73	18.71	5.21	N.M.	N.M.	2.75
Asset Turnover	0.82	0.80	0.68	0.74	0.63	0.38	0.39	0.37
Current Ratio	7.66	1.80	1.78	1.61	1.65	8.58	7.94	6.83
Debt to Equity	0.68	...	...	...	...	0.91	1.29	0.96
Price Range	31.07-19.55	31.07-24.42	32.24-23.71	41.76-27.12	40.62-17.77	31.80-15.39	38.94-24.63	38.65-23.38
P/E Ratio	22.68-14.27	23.19-18.22	24.99-18.38	6.59-4.28	31.73-13.88	...	...	74.33-44.96
Average Yield %	3.76	3.62	3.58	5.81	6.53	4.30	3.29	3.11

Address: 4350 South Monaco Street, Suite 500, Denver, CO 80237 **Telephone:** 303-773-1100	**Web Site:** www.richmondamerican.com **Officers:** Larry A. Mizel - Chairman, Chief Executive Officer David D. Mandarich - President, Chief Operating Officer	**Auditors:** Ernst & Young LLP **Investor Contact:** 303-773-1100 **Transfer Agents:** Continental Stock Transfer & Trust Company, New York, NY

MDU RESOURCES GROUP INC.

Exchange	Symbol	Price	52Wk Range	Yield	P/E	Div Achiever
NYS	MDU	$22.87 (5/31/2016)	22.87-16.03	3.28	N/A	25 Years

*7 Year Price Score 68.91   *NYSE Composite Index=100   *12 Month Price Score 109.05

Interim Earnings (Per Share)

Qtr.	Mar	Jun	Sep	Dec
2013	0.30	0.24	0.44	0.48
2014	0.30	0.28	0.53	0.44
2015	(1.57)	(1.18)	(0.72)	0.27
2016	0.13	...	...	...

Interim Dividends (Per Share)

Amt	Decl	Ex	Rec	Pay
0.183Q	08/13/2015	09/08/2015	09/10/2015	10/01/2015
0.188Q	11/12/2015	12/08/2015	12/10/2015	01/01/2016
0.188Q	02/11/2016	03/08/2016	03/10/2016	04/01/2016
0.188Q	04/27/2016	06/07/2016	06/09/2016	07/01/2016

Indicated Div: $0.75 (Div. Reinv. Plan)

Valuation Analysis

		Institutional Holding	
Forecast EPS	$1.10	No of Institutions	
	(05/20/2016)	452	
Market Cap	$4.5 Billion	Shares	
Book Value	$2.4 Billion	133,620,552	
Price/Book	1.87	% Held	
Price/Sales	1.05	60.55	

Business Summary: Electric Utilities (MIC: 3.1.1 SIC: 4911 NAIC: 221122)

MDU Resources Group is a diversified natural resource company. Through its subsidiaries, Co. generates, transmits and distributes electricity and distributes natural gas in Montana, North Dakota, South Dakota, Wyoming, Oregon, Washington, Idaho, western Minnesota and southeastern North Dakota. At Dec 31 2015, Co.'s electric operations served over 142,000 residential, commercial, industrial and municipal customers, while its natural gas distribution operations served over 906,000 residential, commercial and industrial customers. Co.'s other businesses include pipeline and midstream, construction materials and contracting, construction services, refining and other, including captive insurer.

Recent Developments: For the quarter ended Mar 31 2016, income from continuing operations decreased 3.3% to US$14.7 million from US$15.2 million in the year-earlier quarter. Net income amounted to US$13.8 million versus a net loss of US$309.4 million in the year-earlier quarter. Revenues were US$905.2 million, up 5.0% from US$862.3 million the year before. Operating income was US$41.8 million versus US$43.7 million in the prior-year quarter, a decrease of 4.4%. Direct operating expenses rose 4.9% to US$759.1 million from US$723.7 million in the comparable period the year before. Indirect operating expenses increased 9.8% to US$104.3 million from US$95.0 million in the equivalent prior-year period.

Prospects: Our evaluation of MDU Resources Group Inc. as of June 19, 2016 is the result of our systematic analysis on three basic characteristics: earnings strength, relative valuation, and recent stock price movement. The company has suffered a very negative trend in earnings per share over the past 5 quarters and while recent estimates for the company have been mixed, MDU has posted results that were in line with analysts expectations. Based on operating earnings yield, the company is overvalued when compared to all of the companies in our coverage universe. Share price changes over the past year indicates that MDU will perform poorly over the near term.

Financial Data
(US$ in Thousands)

	3 Mos	12/31/2015	12/31/2014	12/31/2013	12/31/2012	12/31/2011	12/31/2010	12/31/2009
Earnings Per Share	(1.50)	(3.20)	1.55	1.47	(0.01)	1.12	1.27	(0.67)
Cash Flow Per Share	3.03	3.29	3.20	3.93	3.09	3.32	2.93	4.57
Tang Book Value Per Share	8.80	8.91	12.74	11.40	10.49	11.15	10.71	10.10
Dividends Per Share	0.740	0.735	0.715	0.695	0.675	0.655	0.635	0.623
Dividend Payout %	...	...	46.13	47.28	...	58.48	50.00	...
Income Statement								
Total Revenue	905,153	4,191,549	4,670,558	4,462,404	4,075,431	4,050,492	3,909,695	4,176,501
EBITDA	103,257	500,675	899,555	886,523	385,054	756,282	747,588	186,776
Depn & Amortn	60,259	227,730	401,368	386,856	359,205	343,395	328,843	330,542
Income Before Taxes	19,222	179,877	411,171	415,750	(50,850)	331,533	335,734	(227,865)
Income Taxes	4,558	65,183	119,969	136,736	(31,146)	110,274	122,530	(96,092)
Net Income	13,829	(657,691)	294,338	278,570	(754)	213,026	240,659	(123,274)
Average Shares	195,284	194,986	192,587	189,693	188,826	188,905	188,229	185,175
Balance Sheet								
Current Assets	1,054,936	1,021,042	1,194,973	1,116,688	1,128,081	1,194,638	1,167,168	1,061,658
Total Assets	6,618,400	6,627,608	7,809,978	7,061,332	6,682,491	6,556,125	6,303,549	5,990,952
Current Liabilities	761,467	947,639	968,694	784,900	850,115	898,753	768,076	667,185
Long-Term Obligations	1,822,139	1,627,443	1,825,278	1,842,286	1,610,867	1,285,411	1,433,955	1,486,677
Total Liabilities	4,236,019	4,231,103	4,675,937	4,238,168	4,034,243	3,780,558	3,610,747	3,419,305
Stockholders' Equity	2,382,381	2,396,505	3,134,041	2,823,164	2,648,248	2,775,567	2,692,802	2,571,647
Shares Outstanding	195,304	195,265	194,215	189,329	188,830	188,793	188,362	187,850
Statistical Record								
Return on Assets %	N.M.	N.M.	3.96	4.05	N.M.	3.31	3.91	N.M.
Return on Equity %	N.M.	N.M.	9.88	10.18	N.M.	7.79	9.14	N.M.
EBITDA Margin %	11.41	11.94	19.26	19.87	9.45	18.67	19.12	4.47
Net Margin %	1.53	N.M.	6.30	6.24	N.M.	5.26	6.16	N.M.
Asset Turnover	0.61	0.58	0.63	0.65	0.61	0.63	0.64	0.66
Current Ratio	1.39	1.08	1.23	1.42	1.33	1.33	1.52	1.59
Debt to Equity	0.76	0.68	0.58	0.65	0.61	0.46	0.53	0.58
Price Range	22.90-16.03	24.36-16.36	35.93-21.44	30.87-21.24	23.06-19.76	23.95-18.42	23.91-17.56	24.13-13.04
P/E Ratio	...	...	23.18-13.83	21.00-14.45	...	21.38-16.45	18.83-13.83	...
Average Yield %	3.95	3.70	2.31	2.62	3.09	3.06	3.12	3.22

Address: 1200 West Century Avenue, P.O. Box 5650, Bismarck, ND 58506-5650 **Telephone:** 701-530-1000	**Web Site:** www.mdu.com **Officers:** Harry Jonathan Pearce - Chairman David L. Goodin - President, Chief Executive Officer, Division Officer	**Auditors:** Deloitte & Touche LLP **Investor Contact:** 866-866-8919 **Transfer Agents:** Wells Fargo Bank, N.A., St. Paul, MN

MEAD JOHNSON NUTRITION CO

Exchange	Symbol	Price	52Wk Range	Yield	P/E
NYS	MJN	$82.28 (5/31/2016)	96.96-67.64	2.01	31.17

*7 Year Price Score 94.93 *NYSE Composite Index=100 *12 Month Price Score 104.07

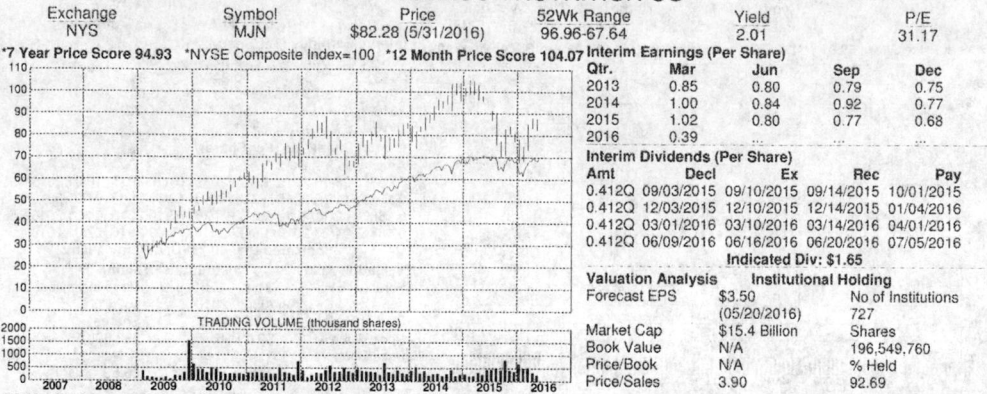

Interim Earnings (Per Share)

Qtr.	Mar	Jun	Sep	Dec
2013	0.85	0.80	0.79	0.75
2014	1.00	0.84	0.92	0.77
2015	1.02	0.80	0.77	0.68
2016	0.39			

Interim Dividends (Per Share)

Amt	Decl	Ex	Rec	Pay
0.412Q	09/03/2015	09/10/2015	09/14/2015	10/01/2015
0.412Q	12/03/2015	12/10/2015	12/14/2015	01/04/2016
0.412Q	03/01/2016	03/10/2016	03/14/2016	04/01/2016
0.412Q	06/09/2016	06/16/2016	06/20/2016	07/05/2016

Indicated Div: $1.65

Valuation Analysis

		Institutional Holding	
Forecast EPS	$3.50	No of Institutions	727
	(05/20/2016)		
Market Cap	$15.4 Billion	Shares	196,549,760
Book Value	N/A	% Held	92.69
Price/Book	N/A		
Price/Sales	3.90		

Business Summary: Food (MIC: 1.2.1 SIC: 2026 NAIC: 311511)

Mead Johnson Nutrition is a nutrition company for infants and children. Co.'s product portfolio consists of two main product categories: infant formula and children's nutrition. Co.'s product categories can be separated into five general product types: routine infant, solutions, specialty, children's nutrition and other. Co.'s routine infant formula is for onsumers while its solutions and specialty products are provided for infants with feeding problems and nutritional needs. Co.'s children's nutrition products are designed to meet the nutritional needs of children at different stages of development. Co.'s other products include vitamins and supplements.

Recent Developments: For the quarter ended Mar 31 2016, net income decreased 63.0% to US$76.7 million from US$207.1 million in the year-earlier quarter. Revenues were US$962.1 million, down 12.1% from US$1.09 billion the year before. Operating income was US$150.1 million versus US$285.2 million in the prior-year quarter, a decrease of 47.4%. Direct operating expenses declined 11.7% to US$347.6 million from US$393.5 million in the comparable period the year before. Indirect operating expenses increased 11.7% to US$464.4 million from US$415.7 million in the equivalent prior-year period.

Prospects: Our evaluation of Mead Johnson Nutrition Company as of June 19, 2016 is the result of our systematic analysis on three basic characteristics: earnings strength, relative valuation, and recent stock price movement. The company has managed to produce a neutral trend in earnings per share over the past 5 quarters and while recent estimates for the company have been mixed, MJN has posted better than expected results. Based on operating earnings yield, the company is about fairly valued when compared to all of the companies in our coverage universe. Share price changes over the past year indicates that MJN will perform in line with the market over the near term.

Financial Data

(US$ in Thousands)	3 Mos	12/31/2015	12/31/2014	12/31/2013	12/31/2012	12/31/2011	12/31/2010	12/31/2009
Earnings Per Share	2.64	3.27	3.54	3.19	2.95	2.47	2.20	1.99
Cash Flow Per Share	4.26	4.57	3.93	3.99	3.39	3.10	2.51	2.87
Tang Book Value Per Share	...	...	1.66	N.M.	N.M.	...	...	...
Dividends Per Share	1.650	1.650	1.500	1.360	1.200	1.040	0.900	0.700
Dividend Payout %	62.50	50.46	42.37	42.63	40.68	42.11	40.91	35.18
Income Statement								
Total Revenue	962,100	4,071,300	4,409,300	4,200,700	3,901,300	3,677,000	3,141,600	2,826,500
EBITDA	175,000	1,019,900	1,064,200	988,300	925,800	831,300	737,500	729,900
Depn & Amortn	24,900	83,700	75,900	63,700	55,800	57,200	54,600	50,300
Income Before Taxes	123,900	871,200	928,000	874,000	805,000	721,900	634,300	587,000
Income Taxes	47,200	215,900	199,200	219,100	192,600	202,900	176,100	176,400
Net Income	72,700	653,500	719,800	649,500	604,500	508,500	452,700	399,600
Average Shares	186,700	199,400	202,700	203,100	204,300	205,000	205,100	200,600
Balance Sheet								
Current Assets	2,634,400	2,602,400	2,418,100	2,118,100	2,015,000	1,889,700	1,449,000	1,336,100
Total Assets	4,016,800	3,998,100	3,776,500	3,474,100	3,258,200	2,766,800	2,293,100	2,070,300
Current Liabilities	1,242,300	1,253,300	1,206,500	1,781,300	1,369,900	1,200,100	976,100	1,100,200
Long-Term Obligations	3,012,600	2,981,000	1,503,900	1,009,100	1,523,200	1,531,900	1,532,500	1,484,900
Total Liabilities	4,652,200	4,630,400	3,202,200	3,182,300	3,239,500	2,945,900	2,660,500	2,745,200
Stockholders' Equity	(635,400)	(632,300)	574,300	291,800	18,700	(179,100)	(367,400)	(674,900)
Shares Outstanding	186,700	186,500	202,300	202,000	202,500	203,700	204,700	204,500
Statistical Record								
Return on Assets %	13.13	16.81	19.85	19.30	20.01	20.10	20.75	23.29
Return on Equity %	998.65	...	166.22	418.36	...	...	...	...
EBITDA Margin %	18.19	25.05	24.14	23.53	23.73	22.61	23.48	25.82
Net Margin %	7.56	16.05	16.32	15.46	15.49	13.83	14.41	14.14
Asset Turnover	1.00	1.05	1.22	1.25	1.29	1.45	1.44	1.65
Current Ratio	2.12	2.08	2.00	1.19	1.47	1.57	1.48	1.21
Debt to Equity	...	...	2.62	3.46	81.45	...	...	...
Price Range	103.11-67.64	105.07-69.64	103.92-73.66	86.19-65.89	88.64-61.66	76.48-55.36	62.55-43.62	47.24-26.22
P/E Ratio	39.06-25.62	32.13-21.30	29.36-20.81	27.02-20.66	30.05-20.90	30.96-22.41	28.43-19.83	23.74-13.18
Average Yield %	1.99	1.84	1.65	1.75	1.59	1.56	1.42	1.97

Address: 2701 Patriot Blvd., Glenview, IL 60026 **Telephone:** 847-832-2420	**Web Site:** www.meadjohnson.com **Officers:** James Milton Cornelius - Chairman Peter Kasper Jakobsen - President, Chief Executive Officer, Executive Vice President, Chief Operating Officer, Region Officer	**Auditors:** Deloitte & Touche LLP **Investor Contact:** 847-832-2182 **Transfer Agents:** Computershare Shareowner Services, Jersey City, NJ

468

MEDICAL PROPERTIES TRUST INC

Exchange	Symbol	Price	52Wk Range	Yield	P/E
NYS	MPW	$14.70 (5/31/2016)	14.70-9.86	6.26	21.00

*7 Year Price Score 90.12 *NYSE Composite Index=100 *12 Month Price Score 110.06

Interim Earnings (Per Share)

Qtr.	Mar	Jun	Sep	Dec
2013	0.18	0.18	0.10	0.10
2014	0.04	0.00	0.16	0.08
2015	0.17	0.11	0.10	0.25
2016	0.24	...	...	...

Interim Dividends (Per Share)

Amt	Decl	Ex	Rec	Pay
0.22Q	08/20/2015	09/15/2015	09/17/2015	10/15/2015
0.22Q	11/12/2015	12/08/2015	12/10/2015	01/14/2016
0.22Q	02/19/2016	03/15/2016	03/17/2016	04/14/2016
0.23Q	05/19/2016	06/14/2016	06/16/2016	07/14/2016

Indicated Div: $0.92

Valuation Analysis

		Institutional Holding	
Forecast EPS	$0.99	No of Institutions	
	(05/15/2016)	375	
Market Cap	$3.5 Billion	Shares	
Book Value	$2.1 Billion	201,630,448	
Price/Book	1.64	% Held	
Price/Sales	7.25	84.30	

TRADING VOLUME (thousand shares)

Business Summary: REITs (MIC: 5.3.1 SIC: 6798 NAIC: 525930)

Medical Properties Trust is a self-advised real estate investment trust focused on investing in and owning net-leased healthcare facilities. Co. acquires and develops healthcare facilities and leases the facilities to healthcare operating companies. At Dec 31 2014, Co.'s portfolio consisted of 132 properties. Co.'s owned facilities consisted of 63 general acute care hospitals, 22 long-term acute care hospitals, 30 inpatient rehabilitation hospitals, three medical office buildings, and six wellness centers. The eight non-owned facilities consisted of four general acute care facilities, one long-term acute care hospital, and three inpatient rehabilitation hospitals.

Recent Developments: For the quarter ended Mar 31 2016, income from continuing operations increased 61.8% to US$58.2 million from US$36.0 million in the year-earlier quarter. Net income increased 61.8% to US$58.2 million from US$36.0 million in the year-earlier quarter. Revenues were US$135.0 million, up 40.7% from US$96.0 million the year before. Revenues from property income rose 43.8% to US$101.2 million from US$70.4 million in the corresponding quarter a year earlier.

Prospects: Our evaluation of Medical Properties Trust Inc. as of June 19, 2016 is the result of our systematic analysis on three basic characteristics: earnings strength, relative valuation, and recent stock price movement. The company has generated a negative trend in earnings per share over the past 5 quarters and while recent estimates for the company have remained steady, MPW has posted results that fell short of analysts expectations. Based on operating earnings yield, the company is undervalued when compared to all of the companies in our coverage universe. Share price changes over the past year indicates that MPW will perform in line with the market over the near term.

Financial Data

(US$ in Thousands)	3 Mos	12/31/2015	12/31/2014	12/31/2013	12/31/2012	12/31/2011	12/31/2010	12/31/2009
Earnings Per Share	0.70	0.63	0.29	0.63	0.67	0.23	0.22	0.45
Cash Flow Per Share	0.99	0.95	0.88	0.93	0.79	0.72	0.60	0.80
Tang Book Value Per Share	8.98	8.88	8.00	8.33	7.70	7.48	8.16	8.53
Dividends Per Share	0.880	0.880	0.840	0.810	0.800	0.800	0.800	0.800
Dividend Payout %	125.71	139.68	289.66	128.57	119.40	347.83	363.64	177.78
Income Statement								
Total Revenue	134,999	441,878	312,532	242,523	201,397	143,319	121,847	129,751
EBITDA	104,435	336,782	201,521	195,915	171,405	107,913	78,125	109,027
Depn & Amortn	1,835	77,912	60,267	42,377	39,050	44,766	32,422	32,133
Income Before Taxes	58,226	141,430	51,138	90,027	75,393	19,431	13,228	39,274
Income Taxes	...	1,503	340	726	...	...	...	...
Net Income	57,927	139,598	50,522	96,991	89,900	26,536	22,913	36,330
Average Shares	237,819	218,304	170,540	152,598	132,333	110,629	100,708	78,117
Balance Sheet								
Current Assets	347,668	324,635	244,806	150,307	118,460	166,581	153,496	62,691
Total Assets	5,710,395	5,609,351	3,747,336	2,904,570	2,178,886	1,621,874	1,348,814	1,309,898
Current Liabilities	161,028	166,714	139,830	118,098	86,570	74,432	59,111	44,597
Long-Term Obligations	3,396,604	3,322,541	2,201,654	1,421,681	1,025,160	689,849	369,970	576,678
Total Liabilities	3,579,285	3,507,083	2,365,289	1,560,362	1,129,072	793,059	449,352	638,453
Stockholders' Equity	2,131,110	2,102,268	1,382,047	1,344,208	1,049,814	828,815	899,462	671,445
Shares Outstanding	237,242	236,744	172,743	161,310	136,335	110,786	110,225	78,725
Statistical Record								
Return on Assets %	3.39	2.98	1.52	3.82	4.72	1.79	1.72	2.77
Return on Equity %	8.23	8.01	3.71	8.10	9.54	3.07	2.92	5.63
EBITDA Margin %	77.36	76.22	64.48	80.78	85.11	75.30	64.12	84.03
Net Margin %	42.91	31.59	16.17	39.99	44.64	18.52	18.80	28.00
Asset Turnover	0.10	0.09	0.09	0.10	0.11	0.10	0.09	0.10
Current Ratio	2.16	1.95	1.75	1.27	1.37	2.24	2.60	1.41
Debt to Equity	1.59	1.58	1.59	1.06	0.98	0.83	0.41	0.86
Price Range	15.32-9.86	15.62-10.73	14.09-12.20	17.46-11.51	11.96-8.69	12.47-8.39	11.51-8.67	10.47-2.91
P/E Ratio	21.89-14.09	24.79-17.03	48.59-42.07	27.71-18.27	17.85-12.97	54.22-36.48	52.32-39.41	23.27-6.47
Average Yield %	7.15	6.70	6.36	5.80	7.91	8.44	7.42	12.13

Address: 1000 Urban Center Drive, Suite 501, Birmingham, AL 35242 **Telephone:** 205-969-3755 **Fax:** 205-969-3756	**Web Site:** www.medicalpropertiestrust.com **Officers:** Edward K. Aldag - Chairman, President, Chief Executive Officer William G. McKenzie - Vice-Chairman	**Auditors:** PricewaterhouseCoopers LLP **Investor Contact:** 205-397-8897 **Transfer Agents:** American Stock Transfer & Trust Company, New York, NY

MEDNAX, INC.

Exchange	Symbol	Price	52Wk Range	Yield	P/E
NYS	MD	$68.45 (5/31/2016)	85.47-61.97	N/A	19.07

*7 Year Price Score 135.36 *NYSE Composite Index=100 *12 Month Price Score 92.43

Interim Earnings (Per Share)

Qtr.	Mar	Jun	Sep	Dec
2013	0.55	0.69	0.76	0.79
2014	0.63	0.79	0.86	0.90
2015	0.72	0.90	0.97	0.99
2016	0.73	...	...	...

Interim Dividends (Per Share)

No Dividends Paid

Valuation Analysis | **Institutional Holding**

Forecast EPS	$4.30	No of Institutions
	(05/20/2016)	503
Market Cap	$6.4 Billion	Shares
Book Value	$2.5 Billion	101,727,328
Price/Book	2.59	% Held
Price/Sales	2.20	N/A

Business Summary: Diagnostic & Health Related Services (MIC: 4.2.2 SIC: 8069 NAIC: 622310)

MEDNAX is a provider of physician services including newborn, anesthesia, maternal-fetal, teleradiology, pediatric cardiology and other pediatric subspecialty care. At Dec 31 2015, Co.'s national network comprised over 3,240 affiliated physicians, including approx. 1,100 physicians who provide neonatal clinical care, in 35 states and Puerto Rico, primarily within hospital-based neonatal intensive care units, to babies born prematurely or with medical complications. Co. also had over 255 affiliated physicians who provide maternal-fetal and obstetrical medical care to expectant mothers experiencing complicated pregnancies, as well as over 1,150 affiliated physicians provide anesthesia care.

Recent Developments: For the quarter ended Mar 31 2016, net income decreased 1.2% to US$67.8 million from US$68.6 million in the year-earlier quarter. Revenues were US$752.6 million, up 17.7% from US$639.4 million the year before. Operating income was US$124.2 million versus US$114.8 million in the prior-year quarter, an increase of 8.2%. Indirect operating expenses increased 19.8% to US$628.4 million from US$524.6 million in the equivalent prior-year period.

Prospects: Our evaluation of Mednax, Inc. as of June 19, 2016 is the result of our systematic analysis on three basic characteristics: earnings strength, relative valuation, and recent stock price movement. The company has managed to produce a neutral trend in earnings per share over the past 5 quarters and while recent estimates for the company have been raised by analysts, MD has posted better than expected results. Based on operating earnings yield, the company is undervalued when compared to all of the companies in our coverage universe. Share price changes over the past year indicates that MD will perform in line with the market over the near term.

Financial Data
(US$ in Thousands)

	3 Mos	12/31/2015	12/31/2014	12/31/2013	12/31/2012	12/31/2011	12/31/2010	12/31/2009
Earnings Per Share	3.59	3.58	3.18	2.78	2.42	2.23	2.13	1.89
Cash Flow Per Share	4.22	3.96	4.29	4.09	3.34	2.84	2.58	2.65
Income Statement								
Total Revenue	752,624	2,779,996	2,438,913	2,154,012	1,816,612	1,588,248	1,401,559	1,288,264
EBITDA	126,147	581,912	531,627	469,327	407,216	371,884	327,845	301,811
Depn & Amortn	1,296	22,200	15,900	15,500	15,800	15,000	13,500	11,200
Income Before Taxes	110,388	536,602	506,836	448,412	388,171	353,245	311,152	287,700
Income Taxes	43,411	204,038	191,413	167,895	147,264	135,248	108,461	111,896
Net Income	67,899	336,320	317,281	280,517	240,907	217,997	202,691	175,804
Average Shares	93,091	93,960	99,887	100,969	99,382	97,592	95,140	92,942
Balance Sheet								
Current Assets	551,439	527,769	467,052	408,839	359,044	337,273	296,009	292,665
Total Assets	4,636,287	4,547,214	3,608,795	3,049,430	2,750,337	2,272,648	2,037,646	1,689,350
Current Liabilities	312,744	428,771	416,273	326,792	268,338	254,301	320,847	346,704
Long-Term Obligations	1,430,837	1,262,820	558,855	27,143	144,233	29,327	146,556	50,209
Total Liabilities	2,175,876	2,109,686	1,344,176	706,442	714,969	541,632	590,192	499,252
Stockholders' Equity	2,460,411	2,437,528	2,264,619	2,342,988	2,035,368	1,731,016	1,447,454	1,190,098
Shares Outstanding	92,922	93,739	96,030	101,207	100,038	97,866	95,874	93,926
Statistical Record								
Return on Assets %	8.10	8.25	9.53	9.67	9.57	10.12	10.88	11.04
Return on Equity %	14.67	14.30	13.77	12.81	12.76	13.72	15.37	16.31
EBITDA Margin %	16.76	20.93	21.80	21.79	22.42	23.41	23.39	23.43
Net Margin %	9.02	12.10	13.01	13.02	13.26	13.73	14.46	13.65
Asset Turnover	0.70	0.68	0.73	0.74	0.72	0.74	0.75	0.81
Current Ratio	1.76	1.23	1.12	1.25	1.34	1.33	0.92	0.84
Debt to Equity	0.58	0.52	0.25	0.01	0.07	0.02	0.10	0.04
Price Range	85.47-62.12	85.47-64.53	67.20-51.25	56.31-39.76	40.67-30.00	37.59-29.31	34.17-23.17	30.61-12.51
P/E Ratio	23.81-17.30	23.87-18.03	21.13-16.12	20.25-14.30	16.81-12.40	16.86-13.14	16.04-10.88	16.19-6.62

Address: 1301 Concord Terrace, Sunrise, FL 33323 Telephone: 954-384-0175	Web Site: www.mednax.com Officers: Cesar L. Alvarez - Chairman Joseph M. Calabro - President, Chief Operating Officer	Auditors: PricewaterhouseCoopers LLP Transfer Agents: ComputerShare Investor Services, Providence, RI

MEDTRONIC PLC

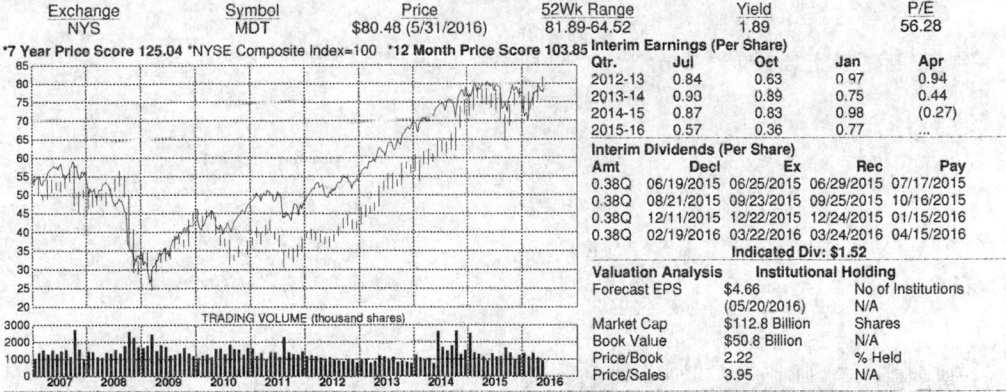

Exchange	Symbol	Price	52Wk Range	Yield	P/E
NYS	MDT	$80.48 (5/31/2016)	81.89-64.52	1.89	56.28

*7 Year Price Score 125.04 *NYSE Composite Index=100 *12 Month Price Score 103.85

Interim Earnings (Per Share)

Qtr.	Jul	Oct	Jan	Apr
2012-13	0.84	0.63	0.97	0.94
2013-14	0.90	0.89	0.75	0.44
2014-15	0.87	0.83	0.98	(0.27)
2015-16	0.57	0.36	0.77	...

Interim Dividends (Per Share)

Amt	Decl	Ex	Rec	Pay
0.38Q	06/19/2015	06/25/2015	06/29/2015	07/17/2015
0.38Q	08/21/2015	09/23/2015	09/25/2015	10/16/2015
0.38Q	12/11/2015	12/22/2015	12/24/2015	01/15/2016
0.38Q	02/19/2016	03/22/2016	03/24/2016	04/15/2016

Indicated Div: $1.52

Valuation Analysis

Forecast EPS	$4.66	Institutional Holding	
	(05/20/2016)	No of Institutions	N/A
Market Cap	$112.8 Billion	Shares	
Book Value	$50.8 Billion	N/A	
Price/Book	2.22	% Held	N/A
Price/Sales	3.95	N/A	

Business Summary: Medical Instruments & Equipment (MIC: 4.3.1 SIC: 3845 NAIC: 334510)

Medtronic is a medical technology company. Co. functions in four segments: cardiac and vascular group, which consists of cardiac rhythm and heart failure disease management, coronary and structural heart disease management, and aortic and peripheral vascular disease management; minimally invasive technologies group; which consists of surgical solutions and patient monitoring and recovery; restorative therapies group; which consists of spine, neuromodulation, surgical technologies, and neurovascular; and diabetes group, which develops, manufactures, and markets diabetes management solutions that include pump therapy, continuous glucose monitoring systems, and therapy management software.

Recent Developments: For the quarter ended Jan 29 2016, net income increased 12.1% to US$1.10 billion from US$977.0 million in the year-earlier quarter. Revenues were US$6.93 billion, up 60.6% from US$4.32 billion the year before. Operating income was US$1.36 billion versus US$1.28 billion in the prior-year quarter, an increase of 6.3%. Direct operating expenses rose 89.8% to US$2.14 billion from US$1.13 billion in the comparable period the year before. Indirect operating expenses increased 79.5% to US$3.44 billion from US$1.92 billion in the equivalent prior-year period.

Prospects: Our evaluation of Medtronic PLC as of June 19, 2016 is the result of our systematic analysis on three basic characteristics: earnings strength, relative valuation, and recent stock price movement. The company has managed to produce a neutral trend in earnings per share over the past 5 quarters. However, while recent estimates for the company have been lowered by analysts, MDT has posted better than expected results. Based on operating earnings yield, the company is undervalued when compared to all of the companies in our coverage universe. Share price changes over the past year indicates that MDT will perform in line with the market over the near term.

Financial Data

(US$ in Thousands)	9 Mos	6 Mos	3 Mos	04/24/2015	04/25/2014	04/26/2013	04/27/2012	04/29/2011
Earnings Per Share	1.43	1.64	2.11	2.41	3.02	3.37	3.41	2.86
Cash Flow Per Share	4.13	4.09	3.81	4.49	4.96	4.80	4.25	3.48
Tang Book Value Per Share	N.M.	N.M.	N.M.	N.M.	6.57	5.58	4.37	3.41
Dividends Per Share	1.445	1.065	0.685	0.305	1.120	1.040	0.970	0.900
Dividend Payout %	101.05	64.94	32.46	12.66	37.09	30.86	28.45	31.47
Income Statement								
Total Revenue	21,266,000	14,332,000	7,274,000	20,261,000	17,005,000	16,590,000	16,184,000	15,933,000
EBITDA	3,808,000	3,395,000	1,612,000	5,072,000	4,663,000	5,221,000	5,127,000	4,465,000
Depn & Amortn	22,000	964,000	481,000	1,306,000	850,000	819,000	833,000	464,000
Income Before Taxes	3,202,000	2,023,000	940,000	3,486,000	3,705,000	4,251,000	4,145,000	3,723,000
Income Taxes	767,000	683,000	120,000	811,000	640,000	784,000	730,000	627,000
Net Income	2,435,000	1,340,000	820,000	2,675,000	3,065,000	3,467,000	3,617,000	3,096,000
Average Shares	1,422,200	1,428,800	1,436,400	1,109,000	1,013,600	1,027,500	1,059,900	1,081,700
Balance Sheet								
Current Assets	27,569,000	28,723,000	29,147,000	30,844,000	21,210,000	17,793,000	9,515,000	9,117,000
Total Assets	102,706,000	104,945,000	104,626,000	106,685,000	37,943,000	34,841,000	33,083,000	30,424,000
Current Liabilities	8,141,000	8,126,000	7,660,000	9,173,000	5,559,000	3,891,000	5,857,000	4,714,000
Long-Term Obligations	33,681,000	33,690,000	33,709,000	33,752,000	10,315,000	9,741,000	7,359,000	8,112,000
Total Liabilities	51,890,000	52,676,000	51,817,000	53,455,000	18,500,000	16,170,000	15,970,000	14,456,000
Stockholders' Equity	50,816,000	52,269,000	52,809,000	53,230,000	19,443,000	18,671,000	17,113,000	15,968,000
Shares Outstanding	1,401,043	1,406,155	1,413,614	1,421,648	998,999	1,016,014	1,037,194	1,070,162
Statistical Record								
Return on Assets %	3.08	3.22	3.69	3.71	8.45	10.24	11.42	10.61
Return on Equity %	6.86	6.46	7.28	7.38	16.13	19.43	21.93	20.29
EBITDA Margin %	17.91	23.69	22.16	25.03	27.42	31.47	31.68	28.02
Net Margin %	11.45	9.35	11.27	13.20	18.02	20.90	22.35	19.43
Asset Turnover	0.36	0.36	0.33	0.28	0.47	0.49	0.51	0.55
Current Ratio	3.39	3.53	3.81	3.36	3.82	4.57	1.62	1.93
Debt to Equity	0.66	0.64	0.64	0.63	0.53	0.52	0.43	0.51
Price Range	79.25-64.52	79.25-64.52	79.25-61.00	79.25-58.21	62.31-46.36	47.72-35.89	43.20-30.41	44.13-31.21
P/E Ratio	55.42-45.12	48.32-39.34	37.56-28.91	32.88-24.15	20.63-15.35	14.16-10.65	12.67-8.92	15.43-10.91
Average Yield %	1.92	1.43	0.95	0.45	2.02	2.47	2.62	2.42

Address: 20 On Hatch, Lower Hatch Street, Dublin, 55432 **Telephone:** 143-817-00	**Web Site:** www.medtronic.com **Officers:** Omar Ishrak - Chairman, Chief Executive Officer Michael J. Coyle - Executive Vice President, Region Officer	**Auditors:** PricewaterhouseCoopers LLP **Transfer Agents:** Wells Fargo Shareowner Services, Mendota Heights, MN

MERCK & CO., INC

Exchange	Symbol	Price	52Wk Range	Yield	P/E
NYS	MRK	$56.26 (5/31/2016)	60.75-48.42	3.27	34.73

*7 Year Price Score 103.20 *NYSE Composite Index=100 *12 Month Price Score 101.12

Interim Earnings (Per Share)

Qtr.	Mar	Jun	Sep	Dec
2013	0.52	0.30	0.38	0.27
2014	0.57	0.68	0.31	2.50
2015	0.33	0.24	0.64	0.34
2016	0.40			

Interim Dividends (Per Share)

Amt	Decl	Ex	Rec	Pay
0.45Q	07/22/2015	09/11/2015	09/15/2015	10/07/2015
0.46Q	11/24/2015	12/11/2015	12/15/2015	01/08/2016
0.46Q	02/23/2016	03/11/2016	03/15/2016	04/07/2016
0.46Q	05/24/2016	06/13/2016	06/15/2016	07/08/2016

Indicated Div: $1.84 (Div. Reinv. Plan)

Valuation Analysis | **Institutional Holding**

Forecast EPS	$3.72	No of Institutions
	(05/20/2016)	2300
Market Cap	$155.8 Billion	Shares
Book Value	$43.8 Billion	2,182,931,200
Price/Book	3.56	% Held
Price/Sales	3.96	N/A

Business Summary: Pharmaceuticals (MIC: 4.1.1 SIC: 2834 NAIC: 325412)

Merck & Co. is a health care company that provides prescription medicines, vaccines, biologic therapies and animal health products. Co.'s operations are comprised of three operating segments: pharmaceutical, which includes human health pharmaceutical and vaccine products marketed either directly by Co. or through joint ventures; animal health, which discovers, develops, manufactures and markets animal health products, including vaccines, which Co. sells to veterinarians, distributors and animal producers; and healthcare services, which provides services and solutions that focus on engagement, health analytics and clinical services to improve the value of care delivered to patients.

Recent Developments: For the quarter ended Mar 31 2016, net income increased 18.0% to US$1.13 billion from US$958.0 million in the year-earlier quarter. Revenues were US$9.31 billion, down 1.2% from US$9.43 billion the year before. Direct operating expenses was unchanged at US$3.57 billion versus the comparable period the year before. Indirect operating expenses decreased 8.0% to US$4.07 billion from US$4.42 billion in the equivalent prior-year period.

Prospects: Our evaluation of Merck & Co. Inc. as of June 19, 2016 is the result of our systematic analysis on three basic characteristics: earnings strength, relative valuation, and recent stock price movement. The company has managed to produce a neutral trend in earnings per share over the past 5 quarters and while recent estimates for the company have been mixed, MRK has posted better than expected results. Based on operating earnings yield, the company is undervalued when compared to all of the companies in our coverage universe. Share price changes over the past year indicates that MRK will perform in line with the market over the near term.

Financial Data

(US$ in Thousands)	3 Mos	12/31/2015	12/31/2014	12/31/2013	12/31/2012	12/31/2011	12/31/2010	12/31/2009
Earnings Per Share	1.62	1.56	4.07	1.47	2.00	2.02	0.28	5.65
Cash Flow Per Share	4.43	4.41	2.72	3.93	3.29	4.03	3.50	1.50
Tang Book Value Per Share	1.68	1.56	5.38	4.67	3.90	2.65	0.82	N.M.
Dividends Per Share	1.820	1.810	1.770	1.730	1.690	1.560	1.520	0.380
Dividend Payout %	112.35	116.03	43.49	117.69	84.50	77.23	542.86	6.73
Income Statement								
Total Revenue	9,312,000	39,498,000	42,237,000	44,033,000	47,267,000	48,047,000	45,987,000	27,428,300
EBITDA	3,244,000	7,179,000	19,992,000	12,666,000	15,557,000	14,701,000	9,079,000	15,880,600
Depn & Amortn	1,561,000	1,600,000	2,500,000	6,988,000	6,978,000	7,427,000	7,381,000	2,576,000
Income Before Taxes	1,590,000	5,196,000	17,026,000	5,141,000	8,097,000	6,724,000	1,066,000	13,056,800
Income Taxes	494,000	942,000	5,349,000	1,028,000	2,440,000	942,000	671,000	2,267,600
Net Income	1,125,000	4,442,000	11,920,000	4,404,000	6,168,000	6,272,000	861,000	12,901,300
Average Shares	2,795,000	2,841,000	2,928,000	2,996,000	3,076,000	3,094,000	3,120,000	2,273,200
Balance Sheet								
Current Assets	28,772,000	29,764,000	33,173,000	35,685,000	34,857,000	33,181,000	29,064,000	28,428,600
Total Assets	98,755,000	101,779,000	98,335,000	105,645,000	106,132,000	105,128,000	105,781,000	112,089,700
Current Liabilities	17,568,000	19,203,000	18,766,000	17,868,000	18,348,000	16,245,000	15,641,000	15,750,700
Long-Term Obligations	23,656,000	23,929,000	18,699,000	20,539,000	16,254,000	15,525,000	15,482,000	16,074,900
Total Liabilities	54,949,000	57,103,000	49,688,000	55,880,000	53,112,000	50,611,000	51,405,000	53,031,700
Stockholders' Equity	43,806,000	44,676,000	48,647,000	49,765,000	53,020,000	54,517,000	54,376,000	59,058,000
Shares Outstanding	2,769,553	2,781,128	2,838,140	2,927,527	3,026,636	3,040,839	3,082,107	3,108,223
Statistical Record								
Return on Assets %	4.46	4.44	11.69	4.16	5.82	5.95	0.79	16.20
Return on Equity %	10.08	9.52	24.22	8.57	11.44	11.52	1.52	33.16
EBITDA Margin %	34.84	18.18	47.33	28.76	32.91	30.60	19.74	57.90
Net Margin %	12.08	11.25	28.22	10.00	13.05	13.05	1.87	47.04
Asset Turnover	0.38	0.39	0.41	0.42	0.45	0.46	0.42	0.34
Current Ratio	1.64	1.55	1.77	2.00	1.90	2.04	1.86	1.80
Debt to Equity	0.54	0.54	0.38	0.41	0.31	0.28	0.28	0.27
Price Range	60.89-48.42	63.03-48.42	61.88-49.49	50.18-40.85	47.96-37.18	37.90-29.81	41.03-31.82	38.00-20.99
P/E Ratio	37.59-29.89	40.40-31.04	15.20-12.16	34.14-27.79	23.98-18.59	18.76-14.76	146.54-113.64	6.73-3.72
Average Yield %	3.33	3.20	3.10	3.73	4.09	4.57	4.22	1.28

Address: 2000 Galloping Hill Road, Keniworth, NJ 07033 Telephone: 908-740-4000 Fax: 908-735-1500	Web Site: www.merck.com Officers: Kenneth C. Frazier - Chairman, President, Chief Executive Officer Robert M. Davis - Executive Vice President, Chief Financial Officer	Auditors: PricewaterhouseCoopers LLP Investor Contact: 908-423-5881 Transfer Agents: Wells Fargo Shareowner Services, South St. Paul, MN

MERCURY GENERAL CORP.

Exchange	Symbol	Price	52Wk Range	Yield	P/E	Div Achiever
NYS	MCY	$52.57 (5/31/2016)	57.53-43.06	4.72	40.75	29 Years

*7 Year Price Score 98.93   *NYSE Composite Index=100   *12 Month Price Score 101.01

Interim Earnings (Per Share)

Qtr.	Mar	Jun	Sep	Dec
2013	1.21	(0.17)	0.72	0.28
2014	1.32	1.73	0.57	(0.39)
2015	0.47	0.17	0.28	0.42
2016	0.42	...	...	...

Interim Dividends (Per Share)

Amt	Decl	Ex	Rec	Pay
0.618Q	08/03/2015	09/08/2015	09/10/2015	09/24/2015
0.62Q	11/02/2015	12/11/2015	12/15/2015	12/29/2015
0.62Q	02/08/2016	03/15/2016	03/17/2016	03/31/2016
0.62Q	05/02/2016	06/14/2016	06/16/2016	06/30/2016

Indicated Div: $2.48

Valuation Analysis   Institutional Holding

Forecast EPS	$2.08	No of Institutions
	(05/15/2016)	281
Market Cap	$2.9 Billion	Shares
Book Value	$1.8 Billion	27,460,732
Price/Book	1.61	% Held
Price/Sales	0.94	38.31

TRADING VOLUME (thousand shares)

Business Summary: General Insurance (MIC: 5.2.1 SIC: 6331 NAIC: 524126)

Mercury General is an insurance holding company. Through its subsidiaries, Co. is primarily engaged in writing personal automobile insurance in 13 states, principally California. Co. also writes homeowners, commercial automobile, commercial property, mechanical breakdown, and umbrella insurance. Co. provides the following types of automobile coverage: collision, property damage, bodily injury, comprehensive, personal injury protection, underinsured and uninsured motorist, and other hazards. Co. provides the following types of homeowner's coverage: dwelling, liability, personal property, fire, and other hazards. Co. sells its policies through independent agents.

Recent Developments: For the quarter ended Mar 31 2016, net income decreased 10.9% to US$23.3 million from US$26.2 million in the year-earlier quarter. Revenues were US$823.9 million, up 10.7% from US$744.5 million the year before. Net premiums earned were US$767.1 million versus US$720.7 million in the prior-year quarter, an increase of 6.4%. Net investment income fell 5.9% to US$29.7 million from US$31.5 million a year ago.

Prospects: Our evaluation of Mercury General Corp. as of June 19, 2016 is the result of our systematic analysis on three basic characteristics: earnings strength, relative valuation, and recent stock price movement. The company has suffered a very negative trend in earnings per share over the past 5 quarters and while recent estimates for the company have remained steady, MCY has posted results that fell short of analysts expectations. Based on operating earnings yield, the company is about fairly valued when compared to all of the companies in our coverage universe. Share price changes over the past year indicates that MCY will perform well over the near term.

Financial Data
(US$ in Thousands)

	3 Mos	12/31/2015	12/31/2014	12/31/2013	12/31/2012	12/31/2011	12/31/2010	12/31/2009
Earnings Per Share	1.29	1.35	3.23	2.04	2.13	3.49	2.78	7.32
Cash Flow Per Share	4.07	3.45	4.48	3.82	2.69	2.89	1.68	3.45
Tang Book Value Per Share	31.39	31.66	32.60	31.62	31.90	32.10	30.87	30.33
Dividends Per Share	2,475	2.473	2.462	2.453	2.442	2.410	2.370	2.330
Dividend Payout %	191.86	183.15	76.24	120.22	114.67	69.05	85.25	31.83
Income Statement								
Premium Income	767,085	2,957,897	2,796,195	2,698,187	2,574,920	2,566,057	2,566,685	2,625,133
Total Revenue	823,920	3,009,300	3,011,773	2,821,041	2,783,370	2,777,285	2,775,885	3,121,493
Benefits & Claims	594,082	2,145,495	1,986,122	1,962,690	1,961,448	1,829,205	1,825,766	1,782,233
Income Before Taxes	26,034	70,567	247,425	132,096	135,310	245,099	182,390	571,541
Income Taxes	2,711	(3,912)	69,476	19,953	18,399	53,935	30,192	168,469
Net Income	23,323	74,479	177,949	112,143	116,911	191,164	152,198	403,072
Average Shares	55,208	55,209	55,020	54,964	54,922	54,845	54,826	55,092
Balance Sheet								
Total Assets	4,692,063	4,628,645	4,600,289	4,315,181	4,189,686	4,070,006	4,203,364	4,232,633
Total Liabilities	2,884,685	2,807,760	2,724,843	2,492,695	2,347,189	2,212,523	2,408,549	2,461,687
Stockholders' Equity	1,807,378	1,820,885	1,875,446	1,822,486	1,842,497	1,857,483	1,794,815	1,770,946
Shares Outstanding	55,254	55,164	55,121	54,975	54,922	54,856	54,803	54,776
Statistical Record								
Return on Assets %	1.54	1.61	3.99	2.64	2.82	4.62	3.61	9.85
Return on Equity %	3.90	4.03	9.62	6.12	6.30	10.47	8.54	24.69
Loss Ratio %	77.45	72.53	71.03	72.74	76.18	71.28	71.13	67.89
Net Margin %	2.83	2.47	5.91	3.98	4.20	6.88	5.48	12.91
Price Range	59.08-43.06	60.20-45.64	58.86-42.97	50.74-36.22	45.63-36.14	46.44-33.86	46.26-37.49	45.99-22.68
P/E Ratio	45.80-33.38	44.59-33.81	18.22-13.30	24.87-17.75	21.42-16.97	13.31-9.70	16.64-13.49	6.28-3.10
Average Yield %	4.70	4.56	5.03	5.60	5.85	5.97	5.64	6.66

Address: 4484 Wilshire Boulevard, Los Angeles, CA 90010 **Telephone:** 323-937-1060 **Fax:** 323-857-7116	**Web Site:** www.mercuryinsurance.com **Officers:** George Joseph - Chairman Gabriel Tirador - President, Chief Executive Officer	**Auditors:** KPMG LLP **Transfer Agents:** Computershare Trust Company, N.A., Canton, MA

473

MEREDITH CORP

*7 Year Price Score 101.17 *NYSE Composite Index=100 *12 Month Price Score 104.84

Interim Earnings (Per Share)

Qtr.	Sep	Dec	Mar	Jun
2012-13	0.55	0.79	0.65	0.74
2013-14	0.53	0.67	0.41	0.89
2014-15	0.65	0.87	0.56	0.94
2015-16	0.24	0.72	1.79	...

Interim Dividends (Per Share)

Amt	Decl	Ex	Rec	Pay
0.458Q	08/12/2015	08/27/2015	08/31/2015	09/15/2015
0.458Q	11/12/2015	11/25/2015	11/30/2015	12/15/2015
0.495Q	02/02/2016	02/25/2016	02/29/2016	03/15/2016
0.495Q	05/11/2016	05/26/2016	05/31/2016	06/15/2016

Indicated Div: $1.98

Valuation Analysis   **Institutional Holding**

Forecast EPS	$3.27	No of Institutions
	(05/20/2016)	311
Market Cap	$2.2 Billion	Shares
Book Value	$1.0 Billion	42,873,232
Price/Book	2.17	% Held
Price/Sales	1.34	81.26

TRADING VOLUME (thousand shares)

Business Summary: Publishing (MIC: 2.3.3 SIC: 2721 NAIC: 511120)

Meredith is a media company focusing primarily on the home and family marketplace. Co. operates two business segments: national media and local media. The national media segment includes magazine publishing, customer relationship marketing, digital and mobile media, brand licensing, database-related activities, and other related operations. The local media segment consists of the operations of network-affiliated television stations and related digital and mobile media assets. As of June 30, 2015, Co.'s local media segment consists of 16 owned television stations and one operated television station located across the U.S.

Recent Developments: For the quarter ended Mar 31 2016, net income increased 220.3% to US$80.9 million from US$25.3 million in the year-earlier quarter. Revenues were US$422.8 million, up 6.2% from US$398.2 million the year before. Operating income was US$128.0 million versus US$47.1 million in the prior-year quarter, an increase of 171.8%. Direct operating expenses rose 1.5% to US$156.7 million from US$154.4 million in the comparable period the year before. Indirect operating expenses decreased 29.8% to US$138.0 million from US$196.6 million in the equivalent prior-year period.

Prospects: Our evaluation of Meredith Corp. as of June 19, 2016 is the result of our systematic analysis on three basic characteristics: earnings strength, relative valuation, and recent stock price movement. The company has enjoyed a very positive trend in earnings per share over the past 5 quarters and while recent estimates for the company have remained steady, MDP has posted better than expected results. Based on operating earnings yield, the company is undervalued when compared to all of the companies in our coverage universe. Share price changes over the past year indicates that MDP will perform in line with the market over the near term.

Financial Data

(US$ in Thousands)	9 Mos	6 Mos	3 Mos	06/30/2015	06/30/2014	06/30/2013	06/30/2012	06/30/2011
Earnings Per Share	3.69	2.46	2.61	3.02	2.50	2.74	2.31	2.78
Cash Flow Per Share	5.44	3.71	4.13	4.32	3.99	4.25	4.05	4.72
Dividends Per Share	1.867	1.830	1.805	1.780	1.680	1.580	1.403	0.970
Dividend Payout %	50.61	74.39	69.16	58.94	67.20	57.66	60.71	34.89
Income Statement								
Total Revenue	1,213,850	791,079	384,666	1,594,176	1,468,708	1,471,340	1,376,687	1,400,480
EBITDA	274,438	127,643	48,301	297,606	230,927	254,101	229,629	272,073
Depn & Amortn	57,275	38,518	19,289	55,494	44,412	43,267	43,858	46,782
Income Before Taxes	201,481	78,547	23,699	222,760	174,339	197,404	172,875	212,353
Income Taxes	77,029	34,999	12,670	85,969	60,798	73,754	68,503	80,743
Net Income	124,452	43,548	11,029	136,791	113,541	123,650	104,372	127,432
Average Shares	45,298	45,358	45,366	45,323	45,410	45,085	45,100	45,832
Balance Sheet								
Current Assets	488,598	531,454	520,052	482,531	470,012	407,692	359,436	333,738
Total Assets	2,823,898	2,878,433	2,878,978	2,843,282	2,543,800	2,140,059	2,016,299	1,712,829
Current Liabilities	509,619	510,093	536,901	531,001	483,103	456,671	482,586	408,992
Long-Term Obligations	631,250	730,000	753,750	732,500	627,500	300,000	275,000	145,000
Total Liabilities	1,806,508	1,914,433	1,932,585	1,891,432	1,652,148	1,285,763	1,218,854	937,844
Stockholders' Equity	1,017,390	964,000	946,393	951,850	891,652	854,296	797,445	774,985
Shares Outstanding	44,554	44,663	44,631	44,620	44,476	44,566	44,507	45,058
Statistical Record								
Return on Assets %	5.91	3.92	4.37	5.08	4.85	5.95	5.58	7.41
Return on Equity %	17.16	11.80	12.82	14.84	13.01	14.97	13.24	17.42
EBITDA Margin %	22.61	16.14	12.56	18.67	15.72	17.27	16.68	19.43
Net Margin %	10.25	5.50	2.87	8.58	7.73	8.40	7.58	9.10
Asset Turnover	0.58	0.57	0.59	0.59	0.63	0.71	0.74	0.81
Current Ratio	0.96	1.04	0.97	0.91	0.97	0.89	0.74	0.82
Debt to Equity	0.62	0.76	0.80	0.77	0.70	0.35	0.34	0.19
Price Range	55.77-36.46	56.96-40.36	56.96-41.36	56.96-42.33	53.34-42.96	48.04-29.68	34.76-21.48	36.81-29.26
P/E Ratio	15.11-9.88	23.15-16.41	21.82-15.85	18.86-14.02	21.34-17.18	17.53-10.83	15.05-9.30	13.24-10.53
Average Yield %	3.97	3.68	3.54	3.51	3.56	4.35	4.84	2.92

Address: 1716 Locust Street, Des Moines, IA 50309-3023
Telephone: 515-284-3000

Web Site: www.meredith.com
Officers: Stephen M. Lacy - Chairman, President, Chief Executive Officer, Principal Accounting Officer, Principal Financial Officer, Acting Vice President D. Mell Meredith Frazier - Vice-Chairman

Auditors: KPMG LLP
Investor Contact: 515-284-3622
Transfer Agents: Wells Fargo Bank, N.A., St. Paul, MN

METLIFE INC

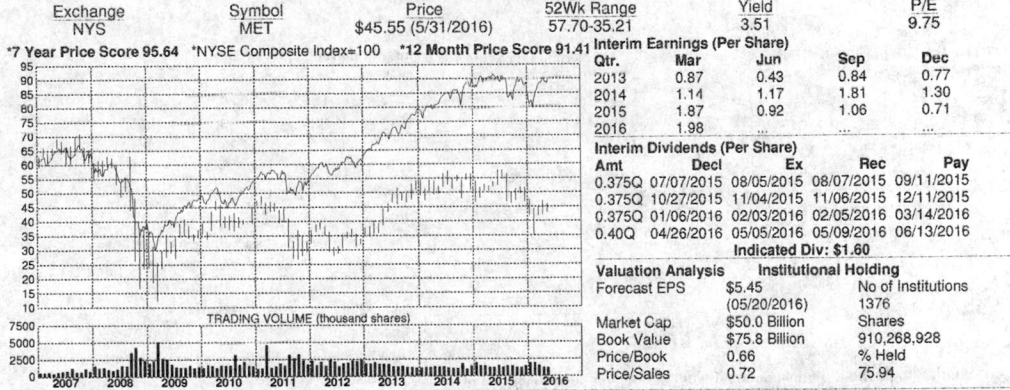

Exchange	Symbol	Price	52Wk Range	Yield	P/E
NYS	MET	$45.55 (5/31/2016)	57.70-35.21	3.51	9.75

*7 Year Price Score 95.64 *NYSE Composite Index=100 *12 Month Price Score 91.41

Interim Earnings (Per Share)

Qtr.	Mar	Jun	Sep	Dec
2013	0.87	0.43	0.84	0.77
2014	1.14	1.17	1.81	1.30
2015	1.87	0.92	1.06	0.71
2016	1.98	...	...	...

Interim Dividends (Per Share)

Amt	Decl	Ex	Rec	Pay
0.375Q	07/07/2015	08/05/2015	08/07/2015	09/11/2015
0.375Q	10/27/2015	11/04/2015	11/06/2015	12/11/2015
0.375Q	01/06/2016	02/03/2016	02/05/2016	03/14/2016
0.40Q	04/26/2016	05/05/2016	05/09/2016	06/13/2016

Indicated Div: $1.60

Valuation Analysis

		Institutional Holding	
Forecast EPS	$5.45	No of Institutions	
	(05/20/2016)	1376	
Market Cap	$50.0 Billion	Shares	
Book Value	$75.8 Billion	910,268,928	
Price/Book	0.66	% Held	
Price/Sales	0.72	75.94	

Business Summary: Life & Health (MIC: 5.2.2 SIC: 6311 NAIC: 524113)

MetLife is a holding company. Through its subsidiaries and affiliates, Co. is a provider of life insurance, annuities, employee benefits and asset management. In the U.S., Co. provides a range of insurance and financial services products, including life, dental, disability, property and casualty, guaranteed interest, stable value and annuities, through both proprietary and independent retail distribution channels, as well as at the workplace. Outside the U.S., Co. provides life, medical, dental, credit and other accident and health insurance, as well as annuities, endowment and retirement and savings products to both individuals and groups.

Recent Developments: For the quarter ended Mar 31 2016, net income increased 1.8% to US$2.20 billion from US$2.16 billion in the year-earlier quarter. Revenues were US$18.43 billion, down 1.5% from US$18.71 billion the year before. Net premiums earned were US$12.04 billion versus US$11.65 billion in the prior-year quarter, an increase of 3.3%. Net investment income fell 16.5% to US$4.56 billion from US$5.46 billion a year ago.

Prospects: Our evaluation of MetLife Inc. as of June 19, 2016 is the result of our systematic analysis on three basic characteristics: earnings strength, relative valuation, and recent stock price movement. The company has enjoyed a very positive trend in earnings per share over the past 5 quarters. However, while recent estimates for the company have been mixed, MET has posted results that fell short of analysts expectations. Based on operating earnings yield, the company is undervalued when compared to all of the companies in our coverage universe. Share price changes over the past year indicates that MET will perform in line with the market over the near term.

Financial Data

(US$ in Millions)	3 Mos	12/31/2015	12/31/2014	12/31/2013	12/31/2012	12/31/2011	12/31/2010	12/31/2009
Earnings Per Share	4.67	4.57	5.42	2.91	1.12	6.29	3.00	(2.89)
Cash Flow Per Share	12.18	12.64	14.51	14.59	15.98	9.71	9.06	4.65
Tang Book Value Per Share	60.12	53.32	55.02	46.25	50.03	45.34	37.49	34.28
Dividends Per Share	1.500	1.475	1.325	1.010	0.740	0.740	0.740	0.740
Dividend Payout %	32.12	32.28	24.45	34.71	66.07	11.76	24.67	...
Income Statement								
Premium Income	12,037	48,052	49,013	47,125	46,531	44,167	33,431	31,663
Total Revenue	18,433	69,951	73,316	68,199	68,150	70,262	52,717	41,058
Benefits & Claims	9,678	38,714	39,102	38,107	37,987	35,457	29,545	28,336
Income Before Taxes	2,922	7,470	8,804	4,052	1,442	10,026	3,958	(4,333)
Income Taxes	719	2,148	2,465	661	128	3,075	1,181	(2,015)
Net Income	2,201	5,310	6,309	3,368	1,324	6,981	2,790	(2,246)
Average Shares	1,108	1,128	1,142	1,116	1,076	1,068	889	818
Balance Sheet								
Total Assets	917,428	877,933	902,337	885,296	836,781	799,625	730,906	539,314
Total Liabilities	841,653	809,907	830,185	822,856	772,207	739,723	682,164	506,193
Stockholders' Equity	75,775	68,026	72,152	62,440	64,574	59,902	48,742	33,121
Shares Outstanding	1,098	1,098	1,131	1,122	1,091	1,057	985	818
Statistical Record								
Return on Assets %	0.58	0.60	0.71	0.39	0.16	0.91	0.44	N.M.
Return on Equity %	7.15	7.58	9.38	5.30	2.12	12.85	6.82	N.M.
Loss Ratio %	80.40	80.57	79.78	80.86	81.64	80.28	88.38	89.49
Net Margin %	11.94	7.59	8.61	4.94	1.94	9.94	5.29	(5.47)
Price Range	57.70-35.21	57.70-46.07	57.22-47.06	54.02-32.94	39.46-27.82	48.63-26.60	47.10-33.64	40.83-12.10
P/E Ratio	12.36-7.54	12.63-10.08	10.56-8.68	18.56-11.32	35.23-24.84	7.73-4.23	15.70-11.21	...
Average Yield %	3.04	2.87	2.50	2.28	2.17	1.90	1.84	2.36

Address: 200 Park Avenue, New York, NY 10166-0188	**Web Site:** www.metlife.com	**Auditors:** Deloitte & Touche LLP
Telephone: 212-578-2211	**Officers:** Steven A. Kandarian - Chairman, President, Chief Executive Officer Ricardo A. Anzaldua - Executive Vice President, General Counsel	**Transfer Agents:** ComputerShare Investor Services, Providence, RI

METTLER-TOLEDO INTERNATIONAL, INC.

Exchange	Symbol	Price	52Wk Range	Yield	P/E
NYS	MTD	$375.32 (5/31/2016)	375.32-277.62	N/A	29.55

*7 Year Price Score 136.09 *NYSE Composite Index=100 ***12 Month Price Score 108.90**

Interim Earnings (Per Share)

Qtr.	Mar	Jun	Sep	Dec
2013	1.69	2.24	2.43	3.44
2014	1.93	2.49	2.89	4.14
2015	2.19	2.73	3.16	4.41
2016	2.40	...	...	...

Interim Dividends (Per Share)

No Dividends Paid

Valuation Analysis		Institutional Holding	
Forecast EPS	$14.31	No of Institutions	
	(05/20/2016)	519	
Market Cap	$10.0 Billion	Shares	
Book Value	$543.3 Million	32,416,952	
Price/Book	18.48	% Held	
Price/Sales	4.19	90.36	

Business Summary: Biotechnology (MIC: 4.1.2 SIC: 3826 NAIC: 334516)

Mettler-Toledo International is a supplier of precision instruments and services. Co. provides weighing instruments for use in laboratory, industrial and food retailing applications. Co. also provides analytical instruments for use in life science, reaction engineering and analytic systems used in drug and chemical compound development and process analytics instruments used for in-line measurement in production processes. In addition, Co. supplies end-of-line inspection systems used in production and packaging for food, pharmaceutical and other industries. Co. has five reportable segments: U.S. Operations, Swiss Operations, Western European Operations, Chinese Operations and Other.

Recent Developments: For the quarter ended Mar 31 2016, net income increased 4.2% to US$65.7 million from US$63.1 million in the year-earlier quarter. Revenues were US$539.7 million, up 0.7% from US$535.7 million the year before. Direct operating expenses rose 1.2% to US$239.8 million from US$236.9 million in the comparable period the year before. Indirect operating expenses decreased 1.3% to US$207.2 million from US$209.9 million in the equivalent prior-year period.

Prospects: Our evaluation of Mettler-Toledo International Inc. as of June 19, 2016 is the result of our systematic analysis on three basic characteristics: earnings strength, relative valuation, and recent stock price movement. The company has managed to produce a neutral trend in earnings per share over the past 5 quarters. However, while recent estimates for the company have been mixed, MTD has posted better than expected results. Based on operating earnings yield, the company is about fairly valued when compared to all of the companies in our coverage universe. Share price changes over the past year indicates that MTD will perform well over the near term.

Financial Data

(US$ in Thousands)	3 Mos	12/31/2015	12/31/2014	12/31/2013	12/31/2012	12/31/2011	12/31/2010	12/31/2009
Earnings Per Share	12.70	12.48	11.44	9.96	9.14	8.21	6.80	5.03
Cash Flow Per Share	15.00	15.42	14.50	11.55	10.53	8.81	8.06	6.90
Tang Book Value Per Share	N.M.	0.70	5.76	12.37	8.46	6.71	7.17	4.87
Income Statement								
Total Revenue	539,674	2,395,447	2,485,983	2,378,972	2,341,528	2,309,328	1,968,178	1,728,853
EBITDA	109,539	523,962	503,158	460,185	438,786	404,092	357,256	279,513
Depn & Amortn	16,546	33,087	33,617	34,765	33,421	31,689	29,686	29,634
Income Before Taxes	86,413	463,424	445,004	402,709	382,601	349,177	307,513	224,762
Income Taxes	20,739	110,604	106,763	96,615	91,754	79,684	75,365	52,169
Net Income	65,674	352,820	338,241	306,094	290,847	269,493	232,148	172,593
Average Shares	27,421	28,269	29,571	30,728	31,824	32,839	34,140	34,290
Balance Sheet								
Current Assets	866,699	862,815	849,430	913,987	864,920	1,018,863	1,144,895	646,107
Total Assets	2,035,273	2,018,485	2,009,110	2,152,819	2,117,400	2,203,474	2,283,063	1,718,787
Current Liabilities	544,792	595,127	678,890	564,188	562,677	609,844	542,186	494,675
Long-Term Obligations	681,872	576,984	335,790	395,960	347,131	476,715	670,301	203,590
Total Liabilities	1,491,940	1,438,028	1,289,515	1,217,767	1,290,181	1,422,337	1,511,479	1,007,649
Stockholders' Equity	543,333	580,457	719,595	935,052	827,219	781,137	771,584	711,138
Shares Outstanding	26,759	27,090	28,243	29,487	30,410	31,590	32,425	33,851
Statistical Record								
Return on Assets %	17.72	17.52	16.25	14.34	13.43	12.01	11.60	10.21
Return on Equity %	58.78	54.28	40.88	34.74	36.07	34.71	31.31	28.42
EBITDA Margin %	20.30	21.87	20.24	19.34	18.74	17.50	18.15	16.17
Net Margin %	12.17	14.73	13.61	12.87	12.42	11.67	11.80	9.98
Asset Turnover	1.20	1.19	1.19	1.11	1.08	1.03	0.98	1.02
Current Ratio	1.59	1.45	1.25	1.62	1.54	1.67	2.11	1.31
Debt to Equity	1.25	0.99	0.47	0.42	0.42	0.61	0.87	0.29
Price Range	347.09-277.62	346.92-277.62	305.89-223.80	253.27-193.30	195.00-148.68	191.95-130.12	157.55-94.10	106.24-45.72
P/E Ratio	27.33-21.86	27.80-22.25	26.74-19.56	25.43-19.41	21.33-16.27	23.38-15.85	23.17-13.84	21.12-9.09

Address: 1900 Polaris Parkway, Columbus, OH 43240 **Telephone:** 614-438-4511 **Fax:** 614-438-4646	**Web Site:** www.mt.com **Officers:** Robert F. Spoerry - Chairman Olivier A. Filliol - President, Chief Executive Officer	**Auditors:** PricewaterhouseCoopers LLP **Investor Contact:** 614-438-4748 **Transfer Agents:** Computershare Shareowner Services LLC, Jersey City, NJ

MFA FINANCIAL, INC.

	Exchange	Symbol	Price	52Wk Range	Yield	P/E
	NYS	MFA	$7.21 (5/31/2016)	7.97-5.78	11.10	9.13

*7 Year Price Score 77.57 *NYSE Composite Index=100 *12 Month Price Score 97.88

Interim Earnings (Per Share)

Qtr.	Mar	Jun	Sep	Dec
2013	0.21	0.19	0.19	0.20
2014	0.20	0.20	0.20	0.21
2015	0.21	0.20	0.20	0.19
2016	0.20	...	...	...

Interim Dividends (Per Share)

Amt	Decl	Ex	Rec	Pay
0.20Q	09/17/2015	09/25/2015	09/29/2015	10/30/2015
0.20Q	12/09/2015	12/23/2015	12/28/2015	01/29/2016
0.20Q	03/11/2016	03/23/2016	03/28/2016	04/29/2016
0.20Q	06/14/2016	06/24/2016	06/28/2016	07/29/2016

Indicated Div: $0.80

Valuation Analysis

		Institutional Holding	
Forecast EPS	$0.76	No of Institutions	
	(05/15/2016)	343	
Market Cap	$2.7 Billion	Shares	
Book Value	$2.9 Billion	340,131,808	
Price/Book	0.93	% Held	
Price/Sales	5.42	83.25	

Business Summary: REITs (MIC: 5.3.1 SIC: 6798 NAIC: 525930)

MFA Financial is a real estate investment trust Co. is principally engaged in the business of investing in residential Agency Mortgage-Backed Securities (MBS) and Non-Agency MBS. Agency MBS refers to MBS that are issued or guaranteed by a federally chartered corporation, such as Fannie Mae or Freddie Mac, or an agency of the U.S. Government, such as Ginnie Mae. Non-Agency MBS are MBS that are not guaranteed by any agency of the U.S. Government or any federally chartered corporation. At Dec 31 2012, Co. had total assets of approximately $12.47 billion.

Recent Developments: For the quarter ended Mar 31 2016, net income decreased 5.0% to US$78.1 million from US$82.2 million in the year-earlier quarter. Revenues were US$140.1 million, up 1.3% from US$138.3 million the year before.

Prospects: Our evaluation of MFA Financial, Inc. as of June 19, 2016 is the result of our systematic analysis on three basic characteristics: earnings strength, relative valuation, and recent stock price movement. The company has managed to produce a neutral trend in earnings per share over the past 5 quarters. However, while recent estimates for the company have been mixed, MFA has posted better than expected results. Based on operating earnings yield, the company is undervalued when compared to all of the companies in our coverage universe. Share price changes over the past year indicates that MFA will perform in line with the market over the near term.

Financial Data

(US$ in Thousands)	3 Mos	12/31/2015	12/31/2014	12/31/2013	12/31/2012	12/31/2011	12/31/2010	12/31/2009
Earnings Per Share	0.79	0.80	0.81	0.78	0.83	0.90	0.93	1.06
Cash Flow Per Share	0.73	0.76	0.69	0.82	0.87	0.98	0.87	1.10
Tang Book Value Per Share	7.71	7.99	8.64	8.59	9.24	6.99	8.00	7.72
Dividends Per Share	0.800	0.800	0.800	1.640	0.880	1.005	0.890	0.990
Dividend Payout %	101.27	100.00	98.77	210.26	106.02	111.67	95.70	93.40
Income Statement								
Interest Income	117,477	492,143	463,817	482,940	499,157	496,747	391,338	505,561
Interest Expense	47,600	176,948	159,808	164,013	171,670	149,411	145,125	229,406
Net Interest Income	69,877	315,195	304,009	318,927	327,487	347,336	246,213	276,155
Non-Interest Income	22,652	(705)	...	...	(1,200)	(10,570)	(12,277)	(17,928)
Non-Interest Expense	14,459	52,429	44,128	35,720	33,569	30,209	24,663	21,254
Net Income	78,070	313,226	313,504	302,709	306,839	316,414	269,762	268,189
Average Shares	370,942	372,114	369,048	362,399	356,762	341,627	281,243	246,424
Balance Sheet								
Net Loans & Leases	1,023,595	895,121	351,395	...	...	...	...	...
Total Assets	12,844,441	13,167,323	12,354,744	12,471,908	13,517,550	11,750,634	8,687,407	9,627,209
Total Liabilities	9,982,795	10,200,062	9,151,472	9,329,657	10,206,544	9,252,874	6,436,960	7,458,947
Stockholders' Equity	2,861,646	2,967,261	3,203,272	3,142,251	3,311,006	2,497,760	2,250,447	2,168,262
Shares Outstanding	370,977	370,584	370,084	365,125	357,546	356,112	280,481	280,078
Statistical Record								
Return on Assets %	2.31	2.45	2.53	2.33	2.42	3.10	2.95	2.65
Return on Equity %	10.19	10.15	9.88	9.38	10.54	13.33	12.21	15.66
Net Interest Margin %	59.48	64.05	65.55	66.04	65.61	69.92	62.92	54.62
Efficiency Ratio %	10.32	10.67	...	...	6.74	6.21	6.51	4.36
Price Range	7.99-5.78	8.19-6.48	8.46-7.06	9.59-7.00	8.70-6.68	8.64-6.25	8.30-6.65	8.32-5.21
P/E Ratio	10.11-7.32	10.24-8.10	10.44-8.72	12.29-8.97	10.48-8.05	9.60-6.94	8.92-7.15	7.85-4.92
Average Yield %	11.16	10.67	9.97	19.93	11.28	13.21	11.87	14.60

Address: 350 Park Avenue, 20th Floor, New York, NY 10022 Telephone: 212-207-6400 Fax: 212-207-6420	Web Site: www.mfafinancial.com Officers: Bryan Wulfsohn - Senior Vice President Craig L. Knutson - President, Executive Vice President, Chief Operating Officer	Auditors: KPMG LLP Transfer Agents: Computershare Shareowner Services LLC, Providence, RI

MGM RESORTS INTERNATIONAL

Exchange	Symbol	Price	52Wk Range	Yield	P/E
NYS	MGM	$22.85 (5/31/2016)	24.14-16.56	N/A	N/A

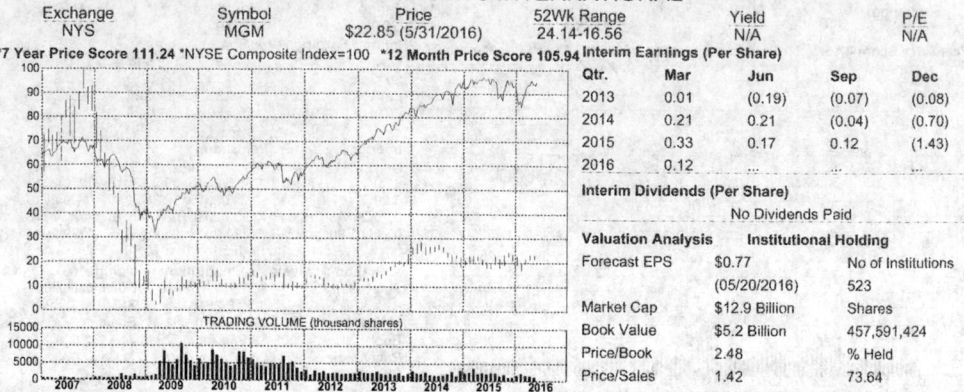

*7 Year Price Score 111.24 *NYSE Composite Index=100 *12 Month Price Score 105.94

Interim Earnings (Per Share)

Qtr.	Mar	Jun	Sep	Dec
2013	0.01	(0.19)	(0.07)	(0.08)
2014	0.21	0.21	(0.04)	(0.70)
2015	0.33	0.17	0.12	(1.43)
2016	0.12	...	...	...

Interim Dividends (Per Share)

No Dividends Paid

Valuation Analysis — **Institutional Holding**

Forecast EPS	$0.77	No of Institutions
	(05/20/2016)	523
Market Cap	$12.9 Billion	Shares
Book Value	$5.2 Billion	457,591,424
Price/Book	2.48	% Held
Price/Sales	1.42	73.64

Business Summary: Hotels, Restaurants & Travel (MIC: 2.2.1 SIC: 7011 NAIC: 721120)

MGM Resorts International is a holding company. Through its subsidiaries, Co. owns and operates casino resorts, which provides gaming, hotel, convention, dining, entertainment, retail and other resort amenities. As of Dec 31 2015, Co. owned and operated casino resorts including Bellagio, MGM Grand Las Vegas, The Mirage in Nevada; two resorts in Mississippi; a golf course located north of its Las Vegas Strip resorts, Primm Valley Golf Club at the California/Nevada state line and Fallen Oak golf course in Saucier, MS; and owned 51.0% in MGM China Holdings Ltd, which through MGM Grand Paradise, S.A, owned the MGM Macau resort and casino and the related gaming subconcession and land concession.

Recent Developments: For the quarter ended Mar 31 2016, net income decreased 57.1% to US$91.2 million from US$212.6 million in the year-earlier quarter. Revenues were US$2.21 billion, down 5.3% from US$2.33 billion the year before. Operating income was US$316.0 million versus US$395.1 million in the prior-year quarter, a decrease of 20.0%. Direct operating expenses declined 10.4% to US$1.30 billion from US$1.45 billion in the comparable period the year before. Indirect operating expenses increased 22.1% to US$592.0 million from US$485.0 million in the equivalent prior-year period.

Prospects: Our evaluation of MGM Resorts International as of June 19, 2016 is the result of our systematic analysis on three basic characteristics: earnings strength, relative valuation, and recent stock price movement. The company has suffered a very negative trend in earnings per share over the past 5 quarters and while recent estimates for the company have been mixed, MGM has posted better than expected results. Based on operating earnings yield, the company is overvalued when compared to all of the companies in our coverage universe. Share price changes over the past year indicates that MGM will perform poorly over the near term.

Financial Data
(US$ in Thousands)

	3 Mos	12/31/2015	12/31/2014	12/31/2013	12/31/2012	12/31/2011	12/31/2010	12/31/2009
Earnings Per Share	(1.02)	(0.82)	(0.31)	(0.32)	(3.62)	5.62	(3.19)	(3.41)
Cash Flow Per Share	1.87	1.85	2.30	2.68	1.85	1.38	1.12	1.55
Tang Book Value Per Share	N.M.	N.M.	N.M.	N.M.	N.M.	N.M.	5.26	7.80
Income Statement								
Total Revenue	2,209,686	9,190,068	10,081,984	9,809,663	9,160,844	7,849,312	6,019,233	5,978,589
EBITDA	313,132	436,078	2,105,320	1,943,896	519,633	4,857,328	(193,874)	(373,987)
Depn & Amortn	12,445	866,163	853,415	884,506	1,001,086	910,946	721,406	740,125
Income Before Taxes	116,018	(1,227,664)	434,844	202,043	(1,597,811)	2,859,550	(2,028,860)	(1,877,239)
Income Taxes	21,310	(6,594)	283,708	31,263	(117,301)	(403,313)	(778,628)	(720,911)
Net Income	66,799	(447,720)	(149,873)	(156,606)	(1,767,691)	3,114,637	(1,437,397)	(1,291,682)
Average Shares	569,455	542,873	490,875	489,661	488,988	560,895	450,449	378,513
Balance Sheet								
Current Assets	2,401,644	2,408,749	3,027,160	2,719,439	2,507,092	2,812,720	1,455,645	3,053,501
Total Assets	25,497,290	25,215,178	26,702,511	26,110,185	26,284,738	27,766,276	18,961,045	22,518,210
Current Liabilities	2,088,311	2,237,951	3,407,925	2,215,328	1,925,671	1,744,764	1,246,221	2,383,601
Long-Term Obligations	12,686,381	12,368,311	12,913,882	13,447,230	13,589,283	13,470,167	12,047,698	12,976,037
Total Liabilities	20,297,391	20,095,251	22,611,594	21,879,006	21,919,190	21,679,698	15,962,500	18,647,778
Stockholders' Equity	5,199,899	5,119,927	4,090,917	4,231,179	4,365,548	6,086,578	2,998,545	3,870,432
Shares Outstanding	565,144	564,838	491,292	490,360	489,234	488,834	488,513	441,222
Statistical Record								
Return on Assets %	N.M.	N.M.	N.M.	N.M.	N.M.	13.33	N.M.	N.M.
Return on Equity %	N.M.	N.M.	N.M.	N.M.	N.M.	68.57	N.M.	N.M.
EBITDA Margin %	14.17	4.75	20.88	19.82	5.67	61.88	N.M.	N.M.
Net Margin %	3.02	N.M.	N.M.	N.M.	N.M.	39.68	N.M.	N.M.
Asset Turnover	0.35	0.35	0.38	0.37	0.34	0.34	0.29	0.26
Current Ratio	1.15	1.08	0.89	1.23	1.30	1.61	1.17	1.28
Debt to Equity	2.44	2.42	3.16	3.18	3.11	2.21	4.02	3.35
Price Range	24.14-16.56	24.14-17.57	28.39-18.01	23.52-11.64	14.71-9.00	16.76-8.23	16.64-9.01	16.10-1.89
P/E Ratio	...	...	...	...	...	2.98-1.46	...	...

Address: 3600 Las Vegas Boulevard South, Las Vegas, NV 89109 Telephone: 702-693-7120	Web Site: www.mgmresorts.com Officers: James J. Murren - Chairman, President, Chief Executive Officer William J. Hornbuckle - President, Chief Marketing Officer, Division Officer	Auditors: Deloitte & Touche LLP Transfer Agents: ComputerShare Investor Services, Providence, RI

MICHAEL KORS HOLDINGS LTD

Exchange	Symbol	Price	52Wk Range	Yield	P/E
NYS	KORS	$42.72 (5/31/2016)	58.54-35.57	N/A	9.62

*7 Year Price Score N/A   *NYSE Composite Index=100   *12 Month Price Score 110.73

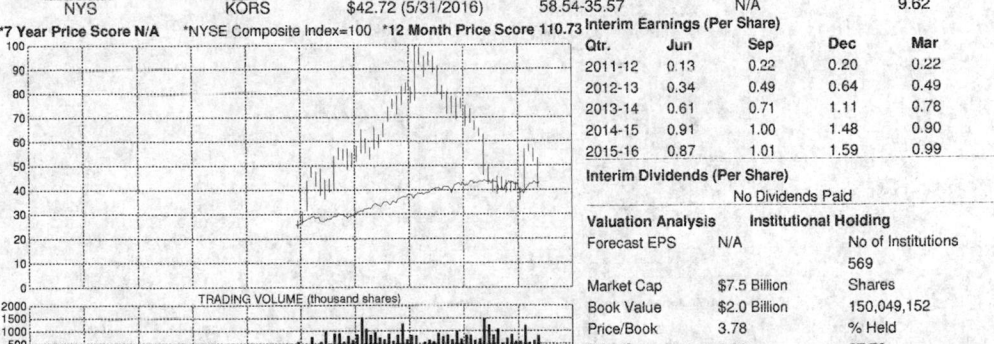

Interim Earnings (Per Share)

Qtr.	Jun	Sep	Dec	Mar
2011-12	0.13	0.22	0.20	0.22
2012-13	0.34	0.49	0.64	0.49
2013-14	0.61	0.71	1.11	0.78
2014-15	0.91	1.00	1.48	0.90
2015-16	0.87	1.01	1.59	0.99

Interim Dividends (Per Share)

No Dividends Paid

Valuation Analysis		Institutional Holding	
Forecast EPS	N/A	No of Institutions	
		569	
Market Cap	$7.5 Billion	Shares	
Book Value	$2.0 Billion	150,049,152	
Price/Book	3.78	% Held	
Price/Sales	1.60	87.73	

Business Summary: Retail - Apparel and Accessories (MIC: 2.1.5 SIC: 3199 NAIC: 316999)

Michael Kors Holdings is a designer, marketer, distributor and retailer of women's apparel and accessories and men's apparel. Co.'s business includes retail, wholesale and licensing segments. Co. has three main collections: the Michael Kors Collection, which provides ready-to-wear and accessories; MICHAEL Michael Kors, which provides women's accessories, mainly handbags, as well as footwear and apparel for women; and Michael Kors Mens, which provides men's ready-to-wear, accessories, and footwear; all of which are provided through its retail and wholesale segments. Co. also provides licensed products primarily through its retail segment. At Apr 2 2016, Co. had 668 retail stores worldwide.

Recent Developments: For the year ended Apr 2 2016, net income decreased 4.9% to US$837.7 million from US$881.0 million in the prior year. Revenues were US$4.71 billion, up 7.8% from US$4.37 billion the year before. Operating income was US$1.18 billion versus US$1.26 billion in the prior year, a decrease of 6.5%. Direct operating expenses rose 11.1% to US$1.91 billion from US$1.72 billion in the comparable period the year before. Indirect operating expenses increased 16.6% to US$1.62 billion from US$1.39 billion in the equivalent prior-year period.

Prospects: Our evaluation of Michael Kors Holdings Ltd. as of Aug. 2, 2015 is the result of our systematic analysis on three basic characteristics: earnings strength, relative valuation, and recent stock price movement. The company has generated a negative trend in earnings per share over the past 5 quarters. However, while recent estimates for the company have been lowered by analysts, KORS has posted results that fell short of analysts expectations. Based on operating earnings yield, the company is undervalued when compared to all of the companies in our coverage universe. Share price changes over the past year indicates that KORS will perform very poorly over the near term.

Financial Data

(US$ in Thousands)	04/02/2016	03/28/2015	03/29/2014	03/30/2013	03/31/2012	04/02/2011	04/03/2010	03/28/2009
Earnings Per Share	4.44	4.28	3.22	1.97	0.78	0.40	0.22	0.08
Cash Flow Per Share	6.49	4.24	3.13	1.82	0.73	0.79	0.20	0.21
Tang Book Value Per Share	10.80	10.85	8.54	5.02	2.22	0.73	0.16	...
Income Statement								
Total Revenue	4,712,100	4,371,469	3,310,843	2,181,732	1,302,254	803,339	508,099	397,074
EBITDA	1,346,200	1,387,438	1,084,640	681,351	286,311	158,680	74,104	36,547
Depn & Amortn	172,200	131,400	76,600	52,700	36,000	23,600	17,100	12,700
Income Before Taxes	1,172,300	1,255,823	1,007,647	627,127	248,816	133,219	54,947	22,247
Income Taxes	334,600	374,800	346,162	229,525	101,452	60,713	15,699	9,208
Net Income	837,700	881,023	661,485	397,602	147,364	72,506	39,248	13,039
Average Shares	189,054	205,865	205,638	201,540	189,299	179,177	179,177	179,177
Balance Sheet								
Current Assets	1,669,800	2,017,431	1,777,169	989,189	464,063	245,398	154,023	...
Total Assets	2,566,800	2,691,893	2,216,973	1,289,565	674,425	399,495	281,852	...
Current Liabilities	435,500	330,081	308,370	164,248	165,006	127,725	102,760	...
Long-Term Obligations	2,300	...	...	...	...	101,650	103,500	...
Total Liabilities	571,100	450,928	410,842	242,319	218,188	267,469	226,135	...
Stockholders' Equity	1,995,700	2,240,965	1,806,131	1,047,246	456,237	132,026	55,717	...
Shares Outstanding	176,441	199,656	204,261	201,454	192,731	140,554	140,554	140,554
Statistical Record								
Return on Assets %	31.34	35.99	37.83	40.60	27.52	21.34	...	...
Return on Equity %	38.91	43.66	46.49	53.04	50.24	77.45	...	...
EBITDA Margin %	28.57	31.74	32.76	31.23	21.99	19.75	14.58	9.20
Net Margin %	17.78	20.15	19.98	18.22	11.32	9.03	7.72	3.28
Asset Turnover	1.76	1.79	1.89	2.23	2.43	2.36	...	...
Current Ratio	3.83	6.11	5.76	6.02	2.81	1.92	1.50	...
Debt to Equity	N.M.	...	...	...	...	0.77	1.86	...
Price Range	66.26-35.57	97.01-64.33	99.84-52.36	64.84-36.04	49.59-24.10	...	...	...
P/E Ratio	14.92-8.01	22.67-15.03	31.01-16.26	32.91-18.29	63.58-30.90	...	...	...

Address: 33 Kingsway, London, WC2B 6UF
Telephone: 207 632-8600

Web Site: www.michaelkors.com
Officers: Michael David Kors - Honorary Chairman, Chief Creative Officer Pascale Meyran - Senior Vice President, Chief Human Resources Officer

Auditors: Ernst & Young LLP
Investor Contact: 203-682-8200
Transfer Agents: American Stock Transfer & Trust Company, LLC, Brooklyn, NY

MID-AMERICA APARTMENT COMMUNITIES INC

Exchange	Symbol	Price	52Wk Range	Yield	P/E
NYS	MAA	$102.99 (5/31/2016)	103.66-72.81	3.18	24.64

*7 Year Price Score 112.73 *NYSE Composite Index=100 *12 Month Price Score 112.63

Interim Earnings (Per Share)

Qtr.	Mar	Jun	Sep	Dec
2013	0.50	1.37	1.04	(0.66)
2014	0.20	0.42	0.89	0.46
2015	0.81	1.81	1.22	0.57
2016	0.58			

Interim Dividends (Per Share)

Amt	Decl	Ex	Rec	Pay
0.77Q	09/24/2015	10/13/2015	10/15/2015	10/30/2015
0.82Q	12/08/2015	01/13/2016	01/15/2016	01/29/2016
0.82Q	03/22/2016	04/13/2016	04/15/2016	04/29/2016
0.82Q	05/17/2016	07/13/2016	07/15/2016	07/29/2016

Indicated Div: $3.28 (Div. Reinv. Plan)

Valuation Analysis | **Institutional Holding**

Forecast EPS	$2.65	No of Institutions
	(05/20/2016)	456
Market Cap	$7.8 Billion	Shares
Book Value	$3.0 Billion	76,426,560
Price/Book	2.61	% Held
Price/Sales	7.38	95.45

TRADING VOLUME (thousand shares)

Business Summary: REITs (MIC: 5.3.1 SIC: 6798 NAIC: 525930)

Mid-America Apartment Communities is a self-administered and self-managed real estate investment trust. Co. owns, operates, acquires and develops apartment communities mainly located in the Southeast and Southwest regions of the U.S. As of Dec 31 2015, Co.'s activities included ownership and operation of 268 multi-family properties and two commercial properties located in Alabama, Arizona, Arkansas, Florida, Georgia, Kansas, Kentucky, Louisiana, Mississippi, Missouri, Nevada, North Carolina, South Carolina, Tennessee, Texas and Virginia. Co.'s business is conducted mainly via Mid-America Apartments, L.P. (Operating Partnership). Co. is the sole general partner of the Operating Partnership.

Recent Developments: For the quarter ended Mar 31 2016, net income decreased 29.2% to US$45.8 million from US$64.7 million in the year-earlier quarter. Revenues were US$269.0 million, up 4.0% from US$258.6 million the year before.

Prospects: Our evaluation of Mid-America Apartment Communities Inc. as of June 19, 2016 is the result of our systematic analysis on three basic characteristics: earnings strength, relative valuation, and recent stock price movement. The company has enjoyed a very positive trend in earnings per share over the past 5 quarters. Because the company lacks sufficient analyst estimate data, we place greater weight on the historical EPS trend as the measure of earnings strength. Based on operating earnings yield, the company is overvalued when compared to all of the companies in our coverage universe. Share price changes over the past year indicates that MAA will perform very well over the near term.

Financial Data

(US$ in Thousands)	3 Mos	12/31/2015	12/31/2014	12/31/2013	12/31/2012	12/31/2011	12/31/2010	12/31/2009
Earnings Per Share	4.18	4.41	1.97	2.25	2.56	1.31	0.56	0.85
Cash Flow Per Share	6.21	6.17	5.12	5.22	5.13	4.66	4.20	4.83
Tang Book Value Per Share	39.45	39.77	38.45	39.39	21.61	18.44	14.86	14.75
Dividends Per Share	3.130	3.080	2.920	2.780	2.640	2.510	2.460	2.460
Dividend Payout %	74.88	69.84	148.22	123.56	103.13	191.60	439.29	289.41
Income Statement								
Total Revenue	269,016	1,042,779	989,296	634,734	497,165	448,992	402,229	378,544
EBITDA	75,491	754,146	545,035	297,550	261,519	218,808	194,713	189,641
Depn & Amortn	(2,656)	279,382	280,462	183,803	131,428	118,969	104,064	96,019
Income Before Taxes	45,968	352,420	145,109	37,832	71,340	41,227	34,653	36,528
Income Taxes	288	1,673	2,050	893	...	...	...	...
Net Income	45,808	332,287	156,277	119,279	105,223	48,821	29,761	37,211
Average Shares	75,489	75,176	74,982	53,116	42,937	39,086	31,977	28,348
Balance Sheet								
Current Assets	49,824	63,641	53,582	133,694	9,883	58,679	47,456	14,380
Total Assets	6,827,921	6,847,781	6,831,028	6,841,925	2,751,068	2,530,468	2,176,048	1,986,826
Current Liabilities	32,531	17,545	18,921	24,337	11,255	8,401	8,508	10,491
Long-Term Obligations	3,443,963	3,427,568	3,524,515	3,472,718	1,673,848	1,649,755	1,500,193	1,399,596
Total Liabilities	3,847,779	3,847,434	3,934,593	3,890,064	1,832,303	1,808,100	1,653,781	1,553,458
Stockholders' Equity	2,980,142	3,000,347	2,896,435	2,951,861	918,765	722,368	522,267	433,368
Shares Outstanding	75,505	75,408	75,267	74,830	42,316	38,959	34,871	29,095
Statistical Record								
Return on Assets %	4.76	4.86	2.29	2.49	3.97	2.07	1.43	1.90
Return on Equity %	11.04	11.27	5.34	6.16	12.79	7.85	6.23	8.78
EBITDA Margin %	28.06	72.32	55.09	46.88	52.60	48.73	48.41	50.10
Net Margin %	17.03	31.87	15.80	18.79	21.16	10.87	7.40	9.83
Asset Turnover	0.15	0.15	0.14	0.13	0.19	0.19	0.19	0.19
Current Ratio	1.53	3.63	2.83	5.49	0.88	6.98	5.58	1.37
Debt to Equity	1.16	1.14	1.22	1.18	1.82	2.28	2.87	3.23
Price Range	102.21-72.81	92.40-71.15	76.24-60.74	74.41-59.70	70.20-58.49	73.25-55.35	64.23-45.58	49.61-22.99
P/E Ratio	24.45-17.42	20.95-16.13	38.70-30.83	33.07-26.53	27.42-22.85	55.92-42.25	114.70-81.39	58.36-27.05
Average Yield %	3.75	3.87	4.19	4.22	4.02	3.93	4.46	6.46

Address: 6584 Poplar Avenue,	Web Site: www.maac.com	Auditors: Ernst & Young LLP
Memphis, TN 38138	Officers: H. Eric Bolton - Chairman, President, Chief	Investor Contact: 901-682-6600
Telephone: 901-682-6600	Executive Officer Thomas L. Grimes - Executive Vice	Transfer Agents: American Stock
Fax: 901-682-6667	President, Chief Operating Officer	Transfer & Trust Company

MINERALS TECHNOLOGIES, INC.

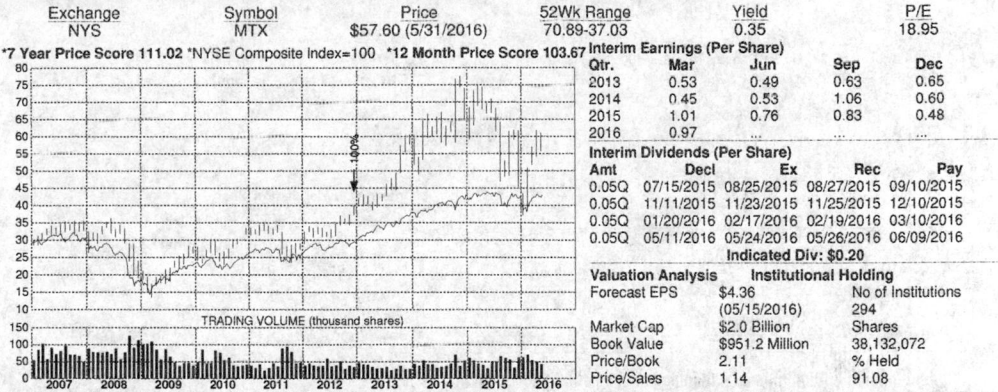

Exchange	Symbol	Price	52Wk Range	Yield	P/E
NYS	MTX	$57.60 (5/31/2016)	70.89-37.03	0.35	18.95

*7 Year Price Score 111.02 *NYSE Composite Index=100 *12 Month Price Score 103.67

Interim Earnings (Per Share)

Qtr.	Mar	Jun	Sep	Dec
2013	0.53	0.49	0.63	0.65
2014	0.45	0.53	1.06	0.60
2015	1.01	0.76	0.83	0.48
2016	0.97	...	...	...

Interim Dividends (Per Share)

Amt	Decl	Ex	Rec	Pay
0.05Q	07/15/2015	08/27/2015	08/27/2015	09/10/2015
0.05Q	11/11/2015	11/23/2015	11/25/2015	12/10/2015
0.05Q	01/20/2016	02/17/2016	02/19/2016	03/10/2016
0.05Q	05/11/2016	05/24/2016	05/26/2016	06/09/2016

Indicated Div: $0.20

Valuation Analysis / **Institutional Holding**

Forecast EPS	$4.36 (05/15/2016)	No of Institutions 294
Market Cap	$2.0 Billion	Shares
Book Value	$951.2 Million	38,132,072
Price/Book	2.11	% Held
Price/Sales	1.14	91.08

Business Summary: Specialty Chemicals (MIC: 8.3.2 SIC: 2819 NAIC: 325188)

Minerals Technologies is a resource- and technology-based company. Co. has five segments: Specialty Minerals, which provides synthetic mineral product precipitated calcium carbonate and processed mineral product quicklime, and mines, processes and sells natural mineral products; Refractories, which provides monolithic and shaped refractory materials and specialty products, and calcium metal and metallurgical wire products; Performance Materials, which supplies bentonite and bentonite-related products; Construction Technologies, which provides products for non-residential construction, environmental and infrastructure projects; and Energy Services, which serves the oil and gas industry.

Recent Developments: For the quarter ended Apr 3 2016, net income decreased 3.3% to US$34.8 million from US$36.0 million in the year-earlier quarter. Revenues were US$410.2 million, down 9.5% from US$453.3 million the year before. Operating income was US$57.6 million versus US$59.9 million in the prior-year quarter, a decrease of 3.8%. Direct operating expenses declined 11.6% to US$297.5 million from US$336.7 million in the comparable period the year before. Indirect operating expenses decreased 2.8% to US$55.1 million from US$56.7 million in the equivalent prior-year period.

Prospects: Our evaluation of Minerals Technologies Inc. as of June 19, 2016 is the result of our systematic analysis on three basic characteristics: earnings strength, relative valuation, and recent stock price movement. The company has produced a positive trend in earnings per share over the past 5 quarters and while recent estimates for the company have remained steady, MTX has posted better than expected results. Based on operating earnings yield, the company is undervalued when compared to all of the companies in our coverage universe. Share price changes over the past year indicates that MTX will perform poorly over the near term.

Financial Data
(US$ in Thousands)

	3 Mos	12/31/2015	12/31/2014	12/31/2013	12/31/2012	12/31/2011	12/31/2010	12/31/2009
Earnings Per Share	3.04	3.08	2.65	2.30	2.09	1.87	1.79	(0.64)
Cash Flow Per Share	8.40	7.78	9.01	3.89	3.95	3.71	3.83	4.29
Tang Book Value Per Share	N.M.	N.M.	N.M.	22.80	20.73	19.17	18.81	17.50
Dividends Per Share	0.200	0.200	0.200	0.200	0.125	0.100	0.100	0.100
Dividend Payout %	6.58	6.49	7.55	8.70	5.98	5.36	5.59	...
Income Statement								
Total Revenue	410,200	1,797,600	1,725,000	1,018,181	1,005,619	1,044,853	1,002,354	907,321
EBITDA	83,800	283,400	246,200	168,657	155,799	152,987	160,620	46,476
Depn & Amortn	24,500	89,900	81,400	44,700	48,700	55,900	61,200	69,000
Income Before Taxes	45,200	132,600	123,000	123,710	107,046	97,740	98,849	(23,140)
Income Taxes	10,700	22,800	30,800	34,515	30,777	27,486	28,963	(5,387)
Net Income	33,900	107,900	92,400	80,330	74,147	67,521	66,869	(23,796)
Average Shares	34,900	35,000	34,800	34,976	35,529	36,236	37,386	37,448
Balance Sheet								
Current Assets	808,000	803,600	924,600	815,117	764,485	720,289	675,572	600,713
Total Assets	2,981,400	2,980,000	3,226,700	1,217,547	1,211,189	1,164,955	1,116,105	1,072,138
Current Liabilities	314,300	318,600	352,900	180,894	250,098	180,902	155,237	152,914
Long-Term Obligations	1,217,700	1,255,300	1,455,500	75,000	8,478	85,449	92,621	92,621
Total Liabilities	2,030,200	2,069,500	2,363,700	370,009	420,778	423,343	360,582	347,977
Stockholders' Equity	951,200	910,500	863,000	847,538	790,411	741,612	755,523	724,161
Shares Outstanding	34,827	34,784	34,649	34,350	34,949	35,309	36,597	37,481
Statistical Record								
Return on Assets %	3.47	3.48	4.16	6.61	6.22	5.92	6.11	N.M.
Return on Equity %	11.69	12.17	10.80	9.81	9.65	9.02	9.04	N.M.
EBITDA Margin %	20.43	15.77	14.27	16.56	15.49	14.64	16.02	5.12
Net Margin %	8.26	6.00	5.36	7.89	7.37	6.46	6.67	N.M.
Asset Turnover	0.57	0.58	0.78	0.84	0.84	0.92	0.92	0.85
Current Ratio	2.57	2.52	2.62	4.51	3.06	3.98	4.35	3.93
Debt to Equity	1.28	1.38	1.69	0.09	0.01	0.12	0.12	0.13
Price Range	74.21-37.03	74.74-45.35	77.40-48.81	60.40-38.43	39.92-28.79	35.05-23.38	33.41-22.86	28.20-13.38
P/E Ratio	24.41-12.18	24.27-14.72	29.21-18.42	26.26-16.71	19.10-13.77	18.74-12.50	18.66-12.77	...
Average Yield %	0.35	0.32	0.32	0.43	0.37	0.33	0.36	0.47

Address: 622 Third Avenue, New York, NY 10017-6707
Telephone: 212-878-1800

Web Site: www.mineralstech.com
Officers: Joseph C. Muscari - Chairman, Chief Executive Officer Douglas T. Dietrich - Senior Vice President, Vice President, Chief Financial Officer

Auditors: KPMG LLP
Investor Contact: 212-878-1831
Transfer Agents: Computershare Trust Company, N. A., Providence, RI

MOHAWK INDUSTRIES, INC.

Exchange	Symbol	Price	52Wk Range	Yield	P/E
NYS	MHK	$196.69 (5/31/2016)	211.33-151.78	N/A	19.10

*7 Year Price Score 155.38 *NYSE Composite Index=100 *12 Month Price Score 102.00

Interim Earnings (Per Share)

Qtr.	Mar	Jun	Sep	Dec
2013	0.72	1.16	1.63	1.29
2014	1.11	2.08	2.06	2.00
2015	0.30	2.53	2.89	2.58
2016	2.30	...	...	...

Interim Dividends (Per Share)

No Dividends Paid

Valuation Analysis

		Institutional Holding	
Forecast EPS	$12.21	No of Institutions	
	(05/20/2016)	662	
Market Cap	$14.6 Billion	Shares	
Book Value	$5.1 Billion	72,619,632	
Price/Book	2.83	% Held	
Price/Sales	1.74	80.64	

Business Summary: Construction Materials (MIC: 8.5.1 SIC: 2273 NAIC: 314110)

Mohawk Industries is a flooring manufacturer for residential and commercial spaces. Co. has three segments: Flooring NA, which designs, manufactures, sources and distributes its floor covering product lines, ceramic tile, laminate, hardwood, resilient floor covering, carpet pad and flooring accessories; Global Ceramic, which designs, manufactures, sources, distributes and markets ceramic tile, porcelain tile and natural stone products; and Flooring ROW, which designs, manufactures, sources, licenses, distributes and markets laminate and hardwood flooring. Co.'s brands include American Olean®, Bigelow®, Daltile®, Durkan®, Karastan®, Lees®, Marazzi®, Mohawk®, Pergo®, Quick-Step® and Unilin®.

Recent Developments: For the quarter ended Apr 2 2016, net income increased 664.8% to US$172.1 million from US$22.5 million in the year-earlier quarter. Revenues were US$2.17 billion, up 15.5% from US$1.88 billion the year before. Operating income was US$245.7 million versus US$43.8 million in the prior-year quarter, an increase of 461.2%. Direct operating expenses rose 11.9% to US$1.53 billion from US$1.37 billion in the comparable period the year before. Indirect operating expenses decreased 15.8% to US$394.0 million from US$468.2 million in the equivalent prior-year period.

Prospects: Our evaluation of Mohawk Industries Inc. as of June 19, 2016 is the result of our systematic analysis on three basic characteristics: earnings strength, relative valuation, and recent stock price movement. The company has enjoyed a very positive trend in earnings per share over the past 5 quarters and while recent estimates for the company have been raised by analysts, MHK has posted better than expected results. Based on operating earnings yield, the company is undervalued when compared to all of the companies in our coverage universe. Share price changes over the past year indicates that MHK will perform well over the near term.

Financial Data

(US$ in Thousands)	3 Mos	12/31/2015	12/31/2014	12/31/2013	12/31/2012	12/31/2011	12/31/2010	12/31/2009
Earnings Per Share	10.30	8.31	7.25	4.82	3.61	2.52	2.65	(0.08)
Cash Flow Per Share	14.86	12.40	9.09	7.32	8.49	4.38	4.66	9.82
Tang Book Value Per Share	25.10	21.97	28.96	26.32	25.74	20.87	17.85	14.67
Income Statement								
Total Revenue	2,172,046	8,071,563	7,803,446	7,348,754	5,787,980	5,642,258	5,319,072	5,344,024
EBITDA	342,437	1,148,433	1,077,938	814,249	596,598	522,071	544,448	272,771
Depn & Amortn	100,194	328,486	315,840	276,432	217,393	220,580	218,649	223,453
Income Before Taxes	229,942	748,861	663,891	445,571	304,492	199,874	192,648	(77,713)
Income Taxes	57,825	131,875	131,637	78,385	53,599	21,649	2,713	(76,694)
Net Income	171,548	615,302	531,965	348,786	250,258	173,922	185,471	(5,499)
Average Shares	74,490	74,043	73,363	72,301	69,306	68,964	68,784	68,452
Balance Sheet								
Current Assets	3,470,551	3,249,972	3,132,270	3,085,718	2,550,046	2,398,164	2,248,613	2,359,000
Total Assets	10,292,315	9,942,364	8,285,544	8,494,177	6,303,684	6,206,228	6,098,926	6,391,446
Current Liabilities	3,323,668	3,259,028	1,955,814	1,320,811	828,649	1,101,346	1,048,914	884,022
Long-Term Obligations	1,173,600	1,196,928	1,402,135	2,132,790	1,327,729	1,200,184	1,302,994	1,801,572
Total Liabilities	5,142,690	5,088,191	3,867,538	4,033,120	2,584,067	2,790,443	2,827,370	3,190,623
Stockholders' Equity	5,149,625	4,854,173	4,418,006	4,461,057	3,719,617	3,415,785	3,271,556	3,200,823
Shares Outstanding	74,082	73,929	72,913	72,686	69,153	68,781	68,629	68,484
Statistical Record								
Return on Assets %	8.23	6.75	6.34	4.71	3.99	2.83	2.97	N.M.
Return on Equity %	16.32	13.27	11.98	8.53	7.00	5.20	5.73	N.M.
EBITDA Margin %	15.77	14.23	13.81	11.08	10.31	9.25	10.24	5.10
Net Margin %	7.90	7.62	6.82	4.75	4.32	3.08	3.49	N.M.
Asset Turnover	0.90	0.89	0.93	0.99	0.92	0.92	0.85	0.83
Current Ratio	1.04	1.00	1.60	2.34	3.08	2.18	2.14	2.67
Debt to Equity	0.23	0.25	0.32	0.48	0.36	0.35	0.40	0.56
Price Range	211.33-151.78	211.33-152.74	157.60-124.77	148.90-90.47	91.29-59.39	68.50-40.75	64.46-41.41	52.97-17.11
P/E Ratio	20.52-14.74	25.43-18.38	21.74-17.21	30.89-18.77	25.29-16.45	27.18-16.17	24.32-15.63	...

Address: 160 S. Industrial Blvd., Calhoun, GA 30701 Telephone: 706-629-7721	Web Site: www.mohawkind.com Officers: Jeffrey S. Lorberbaum - Chairman, Chief Executive Officer Frank H. Boykin - Vice President, Chief Financial Officer	Auditors: KPMG LLP Investor Contact: 706-624-2695 Transfer Agents: American Stock Transfer and Trust Company, Addison, TX

MOLINA HEALTHCARE INC

Exchange	Symbol	Price	52Wk Range	Yield	P/E
NYS	MOH	$48.43 (5/31/2016)	81.50-45.34	N/A	19.93

*7 Year Price Score 158.38 *NYSE Composite Index=100 *12 Month Price Score 83.17

Interim Earnings (Per Share)

Qtr.	Mar	Jun	Sep	Dec
2013	0.64	0.53	0.16	(0.20)
2014	0.09	0.16	0.33	0.70
2015	0.56	0.72	0.77	0.51
2016	0.43	...	...	...

Interim Dividends (Per Share)

No Dividends Paid

Valuation Analysis — **Institutional Holding**

Forecast EPS	$2.72	No of Institutions
(05/20/2016)		371
Market Cap	$2.8 Billion	Shares
Book Value	$1.6 Billion	53,065,984
Price/Book	1.74	% Held
Price/Sales	0.18	84.11

Business Summary: Hospitals & Health Care Facilities (MIC: 4.2.1 SIC: 6324 NAIC: 524114)

Molina Healthcare provides Medicaid-related solutions for low-income families and individuals, and assists state agencies in their administration of the Medicaid program. Co.'s Health Plans segment consists of health plans in 11 states and the Commonwealth of Puerto Rico, and includes Co.'s direct delivery business. The Molina Medicaid Solutions segment provides business processing and information technology development and administrative services to Medicaid agencies in Idaho, Louisiana, Maine, New Jersey, West Virginia, and the U.S. Virgin Islands, and drug rebate administration services in Florida. Co.'s Other segment includes its Pathways behavioral health and social services provider.

Recent Developments: For the quarter ended Mar 31 2016, net income decreased 14.3% to US$24.0 million from US$28.0 million in the year-earlier quarter. Revenues were US$4.34 billion, up 37.0% from US$3.17 billion the year before. Net premiums earned were US$4.10 billion versus US$3.07 billion in the prior-year quarter, an increase of 33.9%.

Prospects: Our evaluation of Molina Healthcare Inc. as of June 19, 2016 is the result of our systematic analysis on three basic characteristics: earnings strength, relative valuation, and recent stock price movement. The company has generated a negative trend in earnings per share over the past 5 quarters. However, while recent estimates for the company have been mixed, MOH has posted results that fell short of analysts expectations. Based on operating earnings yield, the company is about fairly valued when compared to all of the companies in our coverage universe. Share price changes over the past year indicates that MOH will perform poorly over the near term.

Financial Data

(US$ in Thousands)	3 Mos	12/31/2015	12/31/2014	12/31/2013	12/31/2012	12/31/2011	12/31/2010	12/31/2009
Earnings Per Share	2.43	2.58	1.29	1.13	0.21	0.45	1.32	0.79
Cash Flow Per Share	12.92	21.63	22.59	4.16	7.48	4.93	3.93	4.01
Tang Book Value Per Share	14.42	16.36	13.06	12.28	11.84	10.90	8.83	8.55
Income Statement								
Total Revenue	4,343,000	14,178,000	9,666,601	6,588,934	6,028,763	4,769,940	4,085,977	3,669,356
EBITDA	97,000	437,000	226,715	159,817	56,334	97,673	118,901	68,393
Depn & Amortn	8,000	49,000	34,600	26,600	20,500	17,500	13,900	11,000
Income Before Taxes	64,000	322,000	135,304	81,146	19,065	64,654	89,492	43,616
Income Taxes	40,000	179,000	72,726	36,316	9,275	43,836	34,522	12,748
Net Income	24,000	143,000	62,223	52,929	9,790	20,818	54,970	30,868
Average Shares	57,000	56,000	48,340	46,862	46,999	46,425	41,631	38,976
Balance Sheet								
Current Assets	5,764,000	5,306,000	3,245,397	2,039,664	1,349,126	1,048,082	957,939	811,406
Total Assets	7,183,000	6,576,000	4,477,215	3,002,937	1,934,822	1,652,146	1,509,214	1,245,235
Current Liabilities	4,377,000	3,822,000	2,174,773	1,293,976	828,031	601,834	565,548	490,233
Long-Term Obligations	1,163,000	1,160,000	905,048	602,854	261,784	216,929	164,014	158,900
Total Liabilities	5,593,000	5,019,000	3,466,773	2,110,000	1,152,508	897,073	790,157	702,497
Stockholders' Equity	1,590,000	1,557,000	1,010,442	892,937	782,314	755,073	719,057	542,738
Shares Outstanding	57,000	56,000	49,727	45,871	46,762	45,815	45,462	38,410
Statistical Record								
Return on Assets %	2.25	2.59	1.66	2.14	0.54	1.32	3.99	2.58
Return on Equity %	10.55	11.14	6.54	6.32	1.27	2.82	8.71	5.86
EBITDA Margin %	2.23	3.08	2.35	2.43	0.93	2.05	2.91	1.86
Net Margin %	0.55	1.01	0.64	0.80	0.16	0.44	1.35	0.84
Asset Turnover	2.49	2.57	2.58	2.67	3.35	3.02	2.97	3.06
Current Ratio	1.32	1.39	1.49	1.58	1.63	1.74	1.69	1.66
Debt to Equity	0.73	0.75	0.90	0.68	0.33	0.29	0.23	0.29
Price Range	81.50-51.13	81.50-49.87	54.09-32.73	40.69-25.73	35.08-17.77	28.67-14.26	21.14-13.74	16.77-11.21
P/E Ratio	33.54-21.04	31.59-19.33	41.93-25.37	36.01-22.77	167.05-84.62	63.70-31.69	16.02-10.41	21.22-14.19

Address: 200 Oceangate, Suite 100, Long Beach, CA 90802 Telephone: 562-435-3666 Fax: 562-437-1335	Web Site: www.molinahealthcare.com Officers: J. Mario Molina - Chairman, President, Chief Executive Officer John C. Molina - Executive Vice President, Chief Financial Officer, Treasurer	Auditors: Ernst & Young LLP Transfer Agents: American Stock Transfer & Trust Company, New York, NY

MOLSON COORS BREWING CO.

Exchange	Symbol	Price	52Wk Range	Yield	P/E
NYS	TAP	$99.18 (5/31/2016)	100.20-65.19	1.65	43.50

*7 Year Price Score 129.67 *NYSE Composite Index=100 *12 Month Price Score 112.61

Interim Earnings (Per Share)

Qtr.	Mar	Jun	Sep	Dec
2013	0.20	1.51	0.66	0.71
2014	0.88	1.56	(0.19)	0.50
2015	0.43	1.23	0.09	0.18
2016	0.78	...	...	...

Interim Dividends (Per Share)

Amt	Decl	Ex	Rec	Pay
0.41Q	07/16/2015	07/29/2015	07/31/2015	08/17/2015
0.41Q	11/12/2015	11/25/2015	11/30/2015	12/15/2015
0.41Q	02/25/2016	03/03/2016	03/07/2016	03/17/2016
0.41Q	05/26/2016	06/02/2016	06/06/2016	06/16/2016

Indicated Div: $1.64

Valuation Analysis / **Institutional Holding**

Forecast EPS	$3.27	No of Institutions	705
	(05/20/2016)		
Market Cap	$21.3 Billion	Shares	
Book Value	$9.9 Billion		185,391,072
Price/Book	2.15	% Held	
Price/Sales	6.04		70.81

TRADING VOLUME (thousand shares)

Business Summary: Beverages (MIC: 1.2.2 SIC: 2082 NAIC: 312120)

Molson Coors Brewing is a holding company. Co. is a brewer and has a portfolio of owned and partner brands. Co. operates the following segments: Canada, which consists of the production, marketing and sales of its brands, including Coors Light and the Molson brand family, and other owned and licensed brands in Canada; the U.S., which consists of its interest in MillerCoors LLC, its joint venture with SABMiller plc for all U.S. operations; Europe, which consists of the production, marketing and sales of its brands in the U.K., Ireland and Central Europe; and Molson Coors International, which is comprised of its standalone businesses, its export business, and its license business.

Recent Developments: For the quarter ended Mar 31 2016, income from continuing operations increased 98.4% to US$160.1 million from US$80.7 million in the year-earlier quarter. Net income increased 93.2% to US$159.6 million from US$82.6 million in the year-earlier quarter. Revenues were US$657.2 million, down 6.1% from US$700.0 million the year before. Operating income was US$243.3 million versus US$125.3 million in the prior-year quarter, an increase of 94.2%. Direct operating expenses declined 9.0% to US$414.0 million from US$454.8 million in the comparable period the year before. Indirect operating income amounted to US$100,000 compared with an expense of US$119.9 million in the equivalent prior-year period.

Prospects: Our evaluation of Molson Coors Brewing Co. as of June 19, 2016 is the result of our systematic analysis on three basic characteristics: earnings strength, relative valuation, and recent stock price movement. The company has generated a negative trend in earnings per share over the past 5 quarters. However, while recent estimates for the company have been mixed, TAP has posted better than expected results. Based on operating earnings yield, the company is about fairly valued when compared to all of the companies in our coverage universe. Share price changes over the past year indicates that TAP will perform very well over the near term.

Financial Data
(US$ in Thousands)

	3 Mos	12/31/2015	12/31/2014	12/31/2013	12/29/2012	12/31/2011	12/25/2010	12/26/2009
Earnings Per Share	2.28	1.93	2.76	3.08	2.44	3.63	3.78	3.87
Cash Flow Per Share	3.96	3.76	6.88	6.35	5.46	4.62	4.04	4.49
Tang Book Value Per Share	13.44	1.70	N.M.	N.M.	N.M.	8.94	8.86	5.77
Dividends Per Share	1.640	1.640	1.480	1.280	1.280	1.240	1.080	0.920
Dividend Payout %	71.93	84.97	53.62	41.56	52.46	34.16	28.57	23.77
Income Statement								
Total Revenue	657,200	3,567,500	4,146,300	4,206,100	3,916,500	3,515,700	3,254,400	3,032,400
EBITDA	102,300	290,900	426,600	558,100	496,500	601,300	611,900	569,500
Depn & Amortn	16,700	284,500	268,400	272,500	230,300	177,000	159,600	146,900
Income Before Taxes	38,300	(105,600)	24,500	115,500	81,200	316,300	352,900	336,700
Income Taxes	20,600	51,800	69,000	84,000	154,500	99,400	138,700	(14,700)
Net Income	158,800	359,500	514,000	567,300	443,000	676,300	707,700	720,400
Average Shares	204,800	186,400	186,100	184,200	181,800	186,400	187,300	185,900
Balance Sheet								
Current Assets	3,762,800	1,258,800	1,578,900	1,537,700	1,748,000	2,118,000	2,220,900	1,762,800
Total Assets	15,210,300	12,276,300	13,996,300	15,580,100	16,212,200	12,423,800	12,697,600	12,021,100
Current Liabilities	1,221,900	1,217,200	2,325,300	2,142,100	2,598,700	1,277,200	1,333,900	1,580,900
Long-Term Obligations	2,973,400	2,908,700	2,337,100	3,213,000	3,422,500	1,914,900	1,959,600	1,412,700
Total Liabilities	5,311,500	5,233,300	6,133,000	6,941,200	8,245,300	4,775,900	4,898,800	4,941,500
Stockholders' Equity	9,898,800	7,043,000	7,863,300	8,638,900	7,966,900	7,647,900	7,798,800	7,079,600
Shares Outstanding	214,700	184,500	185,500	184,200	181,500	180,000	186,800	185,900
Statistical Record								
Return on Assets %	3.10	2.74	3.48	3.55	3.10	5.30	5.74	6.46
Return on Equity %	5.10	4.82	6.23	6.80	5.69	8.61	9.54	11.09
EBITDA Margin %	15.57	8.15	10.29	13.27	12.68	17.10	18.80	18.78
Net Margin %	24.16	10.08	12.40	13.49	11.31	19.24	21.75	23.76
Asset Turnover	0.25	0.27	0.28	0.26	0.27	0.28	0.26	0.27
Current Ratio	3.08	1.03	0.68	0.72	0.67	1.66	1.66	1.12
Debt to Equity	0.30	0.41	0.30	0.37	0.43	0.25	0.25	0.20
Price Range	96.18-65.19	95.14-65.19	77.75-51.32	56.15-41.83	46.00-38.28	50.51-38.00	50.93-38.90	50.49-31.44
P/E Ratio	42.18-28.59	49.30-33.78	28.17-18.59	18.23-13.58	18.85-15.69	13.91-10.47	13.47-10.29	13.05-8.12
Average Yield %	2.01	2.10	2.21	2.56	3.01	2.80	2.41	2.13

Address: 1555 Notre Dame Street East, Montreal, H2L 2R5 **Telephone:** 514-521-1786	**Web Site:** www.molsoncoors.com **Officers:** Andrew T. Molson - Chairman, Vice-Chairman Geoffrey E. Molson - Chairman	**Auditors:** PricewaterhouseCoopers LLP **Investor Contact:** 303-927-2448 **Transfer Agents:** CST Trust Company, Toronto, Ontario, Canada

MONSANTO CO.

Exchange	Symbol	Price	52Wk Range	Yield	P/E	Div Achiever
NYS	MON	$112.47 (5/31/2016)	116.61-83.11	1.92	34.61	14 Years

*7 Year Price Score 91.33 *NYSE Composite Index=100 *12 Month Price Score 98.79

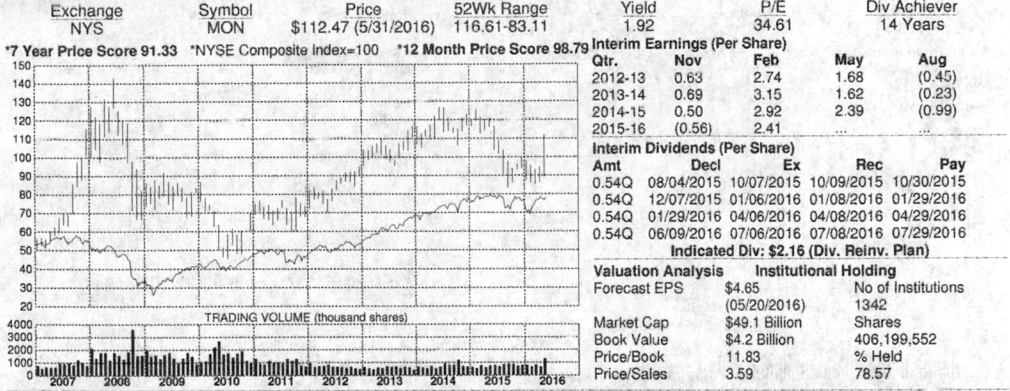

Interim Earnings (Per Share)

Qtr.	Nov	Feb	May	Aug
2012-13	0.63	2.74	1.68	(0.45)
2013-14	0.69	3.15	1.62	(0.23)
2014-15	0.50	2.92	2.39	(0.99)
2015-16	(0.56)	2.41	...	...

Interim Dividends (Per Share)

Amt	Decl	Ex	Rec	Pay
0.54Q	08/04/2015	10/07/2015	10/09/2015	10/30/2015
0.54Q	12/07/2015	01/06/2016	01/08/2016	01/29/2016
0.54Q	01/29/2016	04/06/2016	04/08/2016	04/29/2016
0.54Q	06/09/2016	07/06/2016	07/08/2016	07/29/2016

Indicated Div: $2.16 (Div. Reinv. Plan)

Valuation Analysis   Institutional Holding

Forecast EPS	$4.65	No of Institutions	
	(05/20/2016)	1342	
Market Cap	$49.1 Billion	Shares	
Book Value	$4.2 Billion	406,199,552	
Price/Book	11.83	% Held	
Price/Sales	3.59	78.57	

Business Summary: Agricultural Chemicals (MIC: 8.3.3 SIC: 2879 NAIC: 325320)

Monsanto, along with its subsidiaries, is a provider of agricultural products for farmers. Co. has two business segments: Seeds and Genomics, and Agricultural Productivity. Through its Seeds and Genomics segment, Co. produces seed brands, including DEKALB, Asgrow, Deltapine, Seminis and De Ruiter, and Co. develops biotechnology traits that assist farmers in controlling insects and weeds. Co. also provides other seed companies with genetic material and biotechnology traits for their seed brands. Through its Agricultural Productivity segment, Co. manufactures Roundup and Harness brand herbicides and other herbicides and provides lawn-and-garden herbicide products for the residential market.

Recent Developments: For the quarter ended Feb 29 2016, income from continuing operations decreased 25.1% to US$1.06 billion from US$1.41 billion in the year-earlier quarter. Net income decreased 25.3% to US$1.06 billion from US$1.42 billion in the year-earlier quarter. Revenues were US$4.53 billion, down 12.8% from US$5.20 billion the year before. Operating income was US$1.66 billion versus US$2.02 billion in the prior-year quarter, a decrease of 17.7%. Direct operating expenses declined 10.4% to US$1.93 billion from US$2.16 billion in the comparable period the year before. Indirect operating expenses decreased 8.2% to US$935.0 million from US$1.02 billion in the equivalent prior-year period.

Prospects: Our evaluation of Monsanto Co. as of June 19, 2016 is the result of our systematic analysis on three basic characteristics: earnings strength, relative valuation, and recent stock price movement. The company has managed to produce a neutral trend in earnings per share over the past 5 quarters. However, while recent estimates for the company have been lowered by analysts, MON has posted results that fell short of analysts expectations. Based on operating earnings yield, the company is about fairly valued when compared to all of the companies in our coverage universe. Share price changes over the past year indicates that MON will perform very poorly over the near term.

Financial Data
(US$ in Millions)

	6 Mos	3 Mos	08/31/2015	08/31/2014	08/31/2013	08/31/2012	08/31/2011	08/31/2010
Earnings Per Share	3.25	3.76	4.81	5.22	4.60	3.79	2.96	2.01
Cash Flow Per Share	6.79	6.88	6.52	5.88	5.13	5.70	5.25	2.57
Tang Book Value Per Share	N.M.	N.M.	3.41	4.13	14.77	13.40	12.84	10.42
Dividends Per Share	2.060	2.010	1.960	1.720	1.500	1.200	1.120	1.060
Dividend Payout %	63.38	53.46	40.75	32.95	32.61	31.66	37.84	52.74
Income Statement								
Total Revenue	6,751	2,219	15,001	15,855	14,861	13,504	11,822	10,502
EBITDA	1,560	(116)	4,205	4,664	4,124	3,724	3,075	2,202
Depn & Amortn	364	181	716	691	615	622	613	602
Income Before Taxes	1,001	(406)	3,161	3,827	3,429	2,988	2,374	1,494
Income Taxes	213	(137)	864	1,078	915	901	717	370
Net Income	810	(253)	2,314	2,740	2,482	2,045	1,607	1,109
Average Shares	441	454	481	524	539	540	542	550
Balance Sheet								
Current Assets	8,483	10,467	10,625	9,675	10,077	9,658	8,809	7,122
Total Assets	19,413	21,446	21,920	21,981	20,664	20,224	19,844	17,867
Current Liabilities	5,939	8,501	5,177	5,112	4,336	4,221	4,729	3,541
Long-Term Obligations	7,945	7,939	8,429	7,528	2,061	2,038	1,543	1,862
Total Liabilities	15,261	17,887	14,930	14,106	8,105	8,391	8,299	7,768
Stockholders' Equity	4,152	3,559	6,990	7,875	12,559	11,833	11,545	10,099
Shares Outstanding	436	440	467	485	529	534	535	540
Statistical Record								
Return on Assets %	6.96	8.11	10.54	12.85	12.14	10.18	8.52	6.21
Return on Equity %	24.65	33.15	31.13	26.82	20.35	17.45	14.85	11.00
EBITDA Margin %	23.11	N.M.	28.03	29.42	27.75	27.58	26.01	20.97
Net Margin %	12.00	N.M.	15.43	17.28	16.70	15.14	13.59	10.56
Asset Turnover	0.65	0.64	0.68	0.74	0.73	0.67	0.63	0.59
Current Ratio	1.43	1.23	2.05	1.89	2.32	2.29	1.86	2.01
Debt to Equity	1.91	2.23	1.21	0.96	0.16	0.17	0.13	0.18
Price Range	121.30-83.11	125.46-83.11	125.46-89.42	126.73-99.18	109.22-83.84	88.62-60.04	76.42-47.77	86.65-45.12
P/E Ratio	37.32-25.57	33.37-22.10	26.08-18.59	24.28-19.00	23.74-18.23	23.38-15.84	25.82-16.14	43.11-22.45
Average Yield %	2.02	1.85	1.71	1.52	1.53	1.57	1.69	1.54

Address: 800 North Lindbergh Blvd., St. Louis, MO 63167	**Web Site:** www.monsanto.com	**Auditors:** Deloitte & Touche LLP
Telephone: 314-694-1000	**Officers:** Hugh Grant - Chairman, President, Chief	**Transfer Agents:** ComputerShare, College Station, TX
Fax: 314-694-1057	Executive Officer Brett D. Begemann - President, Executive Vice President, Executive Vice President, Chief Operating Officer, Chief Commercial Officer	

MOODY'S CORP.

Exchange	Symbol	Price	52Wk Range	Yield	P/E
NYS	MCO	$98.64 (5/31/2016)	112.90-78.45	1.50	22.22

*7 Year Price Score 145.70 *NYSE Composite Index=100 *12 Month Price Score 96.29

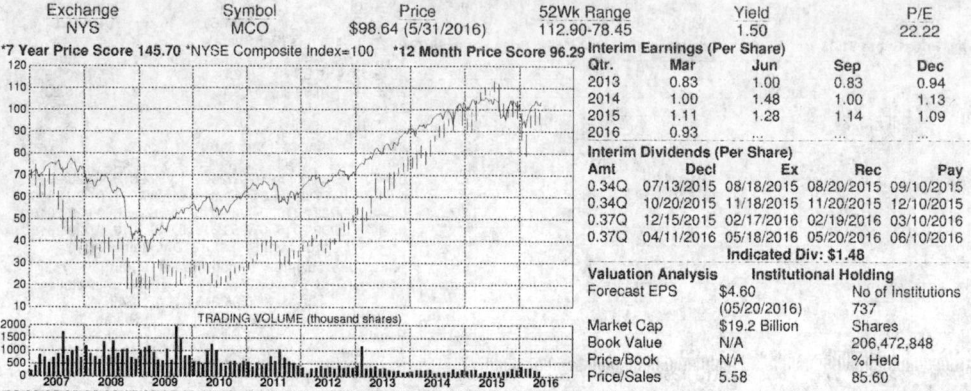

Interim Earnings (Per Share)

Qtr.	Mar	Jun	Sep	Dec
2013	0.83	1.00	0.83	0.94
2014	1.00	1.48	1.00	1.13
2015	1.11	1.28	1.14	1.09
2016	0.93			

Interim Dividends (Per Share)

Amt	Decl	Ex	Rec	Pay
0.34Q	07/13/2015	08/18/2015	08/20/2015	09/10/2015
0.34Q	10/20/2015	11/18/2015	11/20/2015	12/10/2015
0.37Q	12/15/2015	02/17/2016	02/19/2016	03/10/2016
0.37Q	04/11/2016	05/18/2016	05/20/2016	06/10/2016

Indicated Div: $1.48

Valuation Analysis **Institutional Holding**

Forecast EPS	$4.60	No of Institutions	
	(05/20/2016)	737	
Market Cap	$19.2 Billion	Shares	
Book Value	N/A	206,472,848	
Price/Book	N/A	% Held	
Price/Sales	5.58	85.60	

Business Summary: Business Services (MIC: 7.5.2 SIC: 7323 NAIC: 561450)

Moody's provides credit ratings; credit, capital markets and economic related research, data and analytical tools; software and risk management services; quantitative credit risk measures, financial services training and certification services; and outsourced research and analytical services. Co. operates two segments: Moody's Investors Service, which publishes credit ratings on debt obligations, and the entities that issue such obligations, such as corporate and governmental obligations, and commercial paper programs; and Moody's Analytics, which develops products and services that support financial analysis for risk management activities of institutional participants in financial markets.

Recent Developments: For the quarter ended Mar 31 2016, net income decreased 19.3% to US$186.6 million from US$231.3 million in the year-earlier quarter. Revenues were US$816.1 million, down 5.7% from US$865.6 million the year before. Operating income was US$304.1 million versus US$371.3 million in the prior-year quarter, a decrease of 18.1%. Indirect operating expenses increased 3.6% to US$512.0 million from US$494.3 million in the equivalent prior-year period.

Prospects: Our evaluation of Moody's Corp. as of June 19, 2016 is the result of our systematic analysis on three basic characteristics: earnings strength, relative valuation, and recent stock price movement. The company has generated a negative trend in earnings per share over the past 5 quarters and while recent estimates for the company have remained steady, MCO has posted results that fell short of analysts expectations. Based on operating earnings yield, the company is about fairly valued when compared to all of the companies in our coverage universe. Share price changes over the past year indicates that MCO will perform in line with the market over the near term.

Financial Data

(US$ in Thousands)	3 Mos	12/31/2015	12/31/2014	12/31/2013	12/31/2012	12/31/2011	12/31/2010	12/31/2009
Earnings Per Share	4.44	4.63	4.61	3.60	3.05	2.49	2.15	1.69
Cash Flow Per Share	5.79	5.77	4.83	4.22	3.68	3.55	2.78	2.73
Dividends Per Share	1.390	1.360	1.120	0.900	0.640	0.535	0.420	0.400
Dividend Payout %	31.31	29.37	24.30	25.00	20.98	21.49	19.53	23.67
Income Statement								
Total Revenue	816,100	3,484,500	3,334,300	2,972,500	2,730,300	2,280,700	2,032,000	1,797,200
EBITDA	337,700	1,596,400	1,663,800	1,345,700	1,176,500	974,300	830,400	737,600
Depn & Amortn	29,900	113,500	95,600	93,400	93,500	79,200	66,300	64,100
Income Before Taxes	273,700	1,367,800	1,451,400	1,160,500	1,019,200	833,000	711,600	640,100
Income Taxes	89,000	430,000	455,000	353,400	324,300	261,800	201,000	239,100
Net Income	184,400	941,300	988,700	804,500	690,000	571,400	507,800	402,000
Average Shares	197,900	203,400	214,700	223,500	226,600	229,400	236,600	237,800
Balance Sheet								
Current Assets	3,085,300	3,243,100	2,686,400	2,968,800	2,525,700	1,424,400	1,343,000	1,012,900
Total Assets	5,114,900	5,123,400	4,669,000	4,395,100	3,960,900	2,876,100	2,540,300	2,003,300
Current Liabilities	1,151,900	1,218,500	1,199,700	1,141,300	1,164,900	1,134,000	933,800	1,236,000
Long-Term Obligations	3,428,600	3,401,000	2,547,300	2,101,800	1,607,400	1,172,500	1,228,300	746,200
Total Liabilities	5,696,500	5,688,400	4,856,800	4,058,100	3,575,700	3,045,100	2,849,900	2,609,500
Stockholders' Equity	(581,600)	(565,000)	(187,800)	337,000	385,200	(169,000)	(309,600)	(606,200)
Shares Outstanding	194,327	196,075	204,363	213,960	223,252	222,440	230,785	236,857
Statistical Record								
Return on Assets %	17.75	19.23	21.82	19.26	20.13	21.10	22.35	21.29
Return on Equity %	...	...	1,325.34	222.79	636.55	...	...	...
EBITDA Margin %	41.38	45.81	49.90	45.27	43.09	42.72	40.87	41.04
Net Margin %	22.60	27.01	29.65	27.06	25.27	25.05	24.99	22.37
Asset Turnover	0.68	0.71	0.74	0.71	0.80	0.84	0.89	0.95
Current Ratio	2.68	2.66	2.24	2.60	2.17	1.26	1.44	0.82
Debt to Equity	...	...	...	6.24	4.17	...	...	...
Price Range	112.90-78.45	112.90-89.32	101.84-72.65	78.47-43.37	51.54-34.09	41.75-26.54	30.54-18.75	31.23-16.04
P/E Ratio	25.43-17.67	24.38-19.29	22.09-15.76	21.80-12.05	16.90-11.18	16.77-10.66	14.20-8.72	18.48-9.49
Average Yield %	1.37	1.32	1.28	1.44	1.56	1.59	1.67	1.64

Address: 7 World Trade Center, 250 Greenwich Street, New York, NY 10007
Telephone: 212-553-0300

Web Site: www.moodys.com
Officers: Henry A. McKinnell - Chairman Raymond W. McDaniel - Chairman, President, Chief Executive Officer

Auditors: KPMG LLP
Investor Contact: 212-553-4857
Transfer Agents: American Stock Transfer & Trust Company, LLC, Brooklyn, NY

MORGAN STANLEY

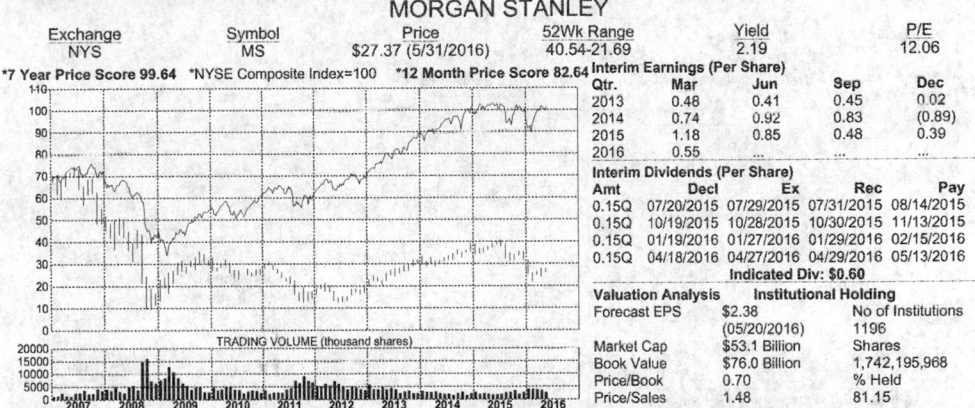

Exchange	Symbol	Price	52Wk Range	Yield	P/E
NYS	MS	$27.37 (5/31/2016)	40.54-21.69	2.19	12.06

*7 Year Price Score 99.64 *NYSE Composite Index=100 *12 Month Price Score 82.64

Interim Earnings (Per Share)

Qtr.	Mar	Jun	Sep	Dec
2013	0.48	0.41	0.45	0.02
2014	0.74	0.92	0.83	(0.89)
2015	1.18	0.85	0.48	0.39
2016	0.55	...	...	...

Interim Dividends (Per Share)

Amt	Decl	Ex	Rec	Pay
0.15Q	07/20/2015	07/29/2015	07/31/2015	08/14/2015
0.15Q	10/19/2015	10/28/2015	10/30/2015	11/13/2015
0.15Q	01/19/2016	01/27/2016	01/29/2016	02/15/2016
0.15Q	04/18/2016	04/27/2016	04/29/2016	05/13/2016

Indicated Div: $0.60

Valuation Analysis — **Institutional Holding**

Forecast EPS	$2.38
	(05/20/2016)
Market Cap	$53.1 Billion
Book Value	$76.0 Billion
Price/Book	0.70
Price/Sales	1.48

No of Institutions	1196
Shares	1,742,195,968
% Held	81.15

Business Summary: Finance Intermediaries & Services (MIC: 5.5.1 SIC: 6211 NAIC: 523110)

Morgan Stanley is a financial holding company. Through its subsidiaries and affiliates, Co. provides its products and services to corporations, governments, financial institutions and individuals. Co. has three segments: Institutional Securities, which provides financial advisory and capital raising services, corporate lending, and sales, trading, financing and market-making activities in equity, fixed income securities and related products; Wealth Management, which provides brokerage and investment advisory services; and Investment Management, which provides a range of investment strategies. As of Dec 31 2015, Co. had total assets of $787.47 billion and total deposits of $156 03 billion.

Recent Developments: For the quarter ended Mar 31 2016, income from continuing operations decreased 53.0% to US$1.16 billion from US$2.47 billion in the year-earlier quarter. Net income decreased 53.0% to US$1.16 billion from US$2.46 billion in the year-earlier quarter. Revenues were US$8.64 billion, down 20.0% from US$10.80 billion the year before. Direct operating expenses declined 4.5% to US$848.0 million from US$888.0 million in the comparable period the year before. Indirect operating expenses decreased 14.2% to US$6.05 billion from US$7.05 billion in the equivalent prior-year period.

Prospects: Our evaluation of Morgan Stanley Dean Witter & Co. as of June 19, 2016 is the result of our systematic analysis on three basic characteristics: earnings strength, relative valuation, and recent stock price movement. The company has suffered a very negative trend in earnings per share over the past 5 quarters. However, while recent estimates for the company have been lowered by analysts, MS has posted better than expected results. Based on operating earnings yield, the company is undervalued when compared to all of the companies in our coverage universe. Share price changes over the past year indicates that MS will perform in line with the market over the near term.

Financial Data
(US$ in Thousands)

	3 Mos	12/31/2015	12/31/2014	12/31/2013	12/31/2012	12/31/2011	12/31/2010	12/31/2009
Earnings Per Share	2.27	2.90	1.60	1.36	(0.02)	1.23	2.63	(0.77)
Cash Flow Per Share	11.08	1.92	0.59	18.65	12.98	4.04	29.58	(38.76)
Tang Book Value Per Share	30.44	30.26	28.26	27.16	25.41	25.72	23.95	18.28
Dividends Per Share	0.600	0.550	0.350	0.200	0.200	0.200	0.200	0.437
Dividend Payout %	26.43	18.97	21.88	14.71	...	16.26	7.60	...
Income Statement								
Interest Income	1,747,000	5,835,000	5,413,000	5,209,000	5,725,000	7,264,000	7,278,000	7,702,000
Interest Expense	848,000	2,742,000	3,678,000	4,431,000	5,924,000	6,907,000	6,414,000	6,712,000
Net Interest Income	899,000	3,093,000	1,735,000	778,000	(199,000)	357,000	864,000	990,000
Non-Interest Income	6,893,000	32,062,000	32,540,000	31,639,000	26,311,000	32,046,000	30,758,000	22,368,000
Non-Interest Expense	6,054,000	26,660,000	30,684,000	27,935,000	25,597,000	26,289,000	25,420,000	22,501,000
Income Before Taxes	1,738,000	8,495,000	3,591,000	4,482,000	515,000	6,114,000	6,202,000	857,000
Income Taxes	578,000	2,200,000	(90,000)	826,000	(239,000)	1,418,000	739,000	(336,000)
Net Income	1,134,000	6,127,000	3,467,000	2,932,000	68,000	4,110,000	4,703,000	1,346,000
Average Shares	1,914,840	1,952,815	1,970,535	1,956,519	1,918,811	1,675,271	1,411,268	1,185,414
Balance Sheet								
Net Loans & Leases	88,802,000	85,759,000	66,577,000	42,874,000	29,046,000	15,369,000	10,576,000	7,259,000
Total Assets	807,497,000	787,465,000	801,510,000	832,702,000	780,960,000	749,898,000	807,698,000	771,462,000
Total Deposits	157,591,000	156,034,000	133,544,000	112,379,000	83,266,000	65,662,000	63,812,000	62,215,000
Total Liabilities	731,487,000	712,283,000	730,610,000	766,781,000	718,851,000	687,849,000	750,487,000	724,774,000
Stockholders' Equity	76,010,000	75,182,000	70,900,000	65,921,000	62,109,000	62,049,000	57,211,000	46,688,000
Shares Outstanding	1,938,294	1,920,024	1,950,980	1,944,868	1,974,042	1,926,986	1,512,022	1,360,595
Statistical Record								
Return on Assets %	0.59	0.77	0.42	0.36	0.01	0.53	0.60	0.19
Return on Equity %	6.48	8.39	5.07	4.58	0.11	6.89	9.05	2.82
Net Interest Margin %	51.46	53.01	32.05	14.94	N.M.	4.91	11.87	12.85
Efficiency Ratio %	70.07	70.35	80.85	75.81	79.90	66.88	66.83	74.83
Loans to Deposits	0.56	0.55	0.50	0.38	0.35	0.23	0.17	0.12
Price Range	40.54-21.69	40.54-31.01	39.00-28.47	31.62-19.12	21.17-12.36	30.99-12.47	32.92-22.83	35.74-13.10
P/E Ratio	17.86-9.56	13.98-10.69	24.38-17.79	23.25-14.06	...	25.20-10.14	12.52-8.68	...
Average Yield %	1.80	1.53	1.07	0.78	1.21	0.92	0.74	1.62

Address: 1585 Broadway, New York, NY 10036	**Web Site:** www.morganstanley.com	**Auditors:** Deloitte & Touche LLP
Telephone: 212-761-4000	**Officers:** James P. Gorman - Chairman, President, Chief Executive Officer Gary G. Lynch - Vice-Chairman, Chief Legal Officer	**Transfer Agents:** Computershare, Providence, RI

MOSAIC CO (THE)

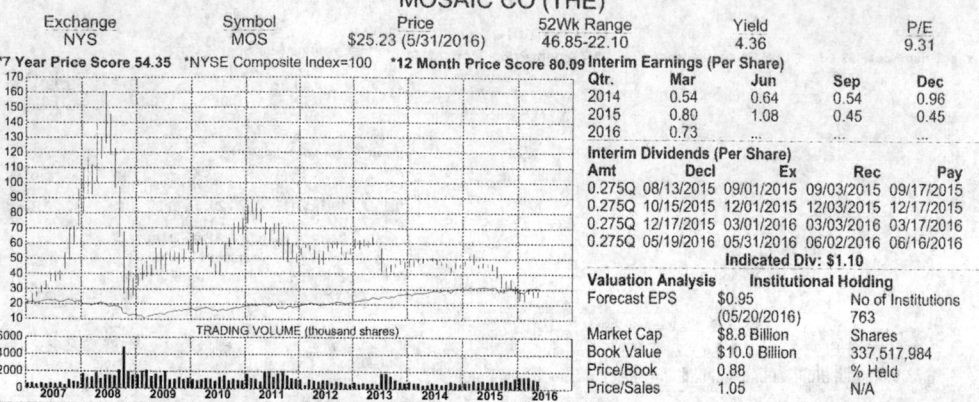

Exchange	Symbol	Price	52Wk Range	Yield	P/E
NYS	MOS	$25.23 (5/31/2016)	46.85-22.10	4.36	9.31

*7 Year Price Score 54.35   ***NYSE Composite Index=100**   ***12 Month Price Score 80.09**

Interim Earnings (Per Share)

Qtr.	Mar	Jun	Sep	Dec
2014	0.54	0.64	0.54	0.96
2015	0.80	1.08	0.45	0.45
2016	0.73	...	...	...

Interim Dividends (Per Share)

Amt	Decl	Ex	Rec	Pay
0.275Q	08/13/2015	09/01/2015	09/03/2015	09/17/2015
0.275Q	10/15/2015	12/01/2015	12/03/2015	12/17/2015
0.275Q	12/17/2015	03/01/2016	03/03/2016	03/17/2016
0.275Q	05/19/2016	05/31/2016	06/02/2016	06/16/2016

Indicated Div: $1.10

Valuation Analysis   **Institutional Holding**

Forecast EPS	$0.95
(05/20/2016)	
Market Cap	$8.8 Billion
Book Value	$10.0 Billion
Price/Book	0.88
Price/Sales	1.05

No of Institutions 763
Shares 337,517,984
% Held N/A

Business Summary: Agricultural Chemicals (MIC: 8.3.3 SIC: 2874 NAIC: 325312)

Mosaic is a producer and marketer of concentrated phosphate and potash crop nutrients. Co. mines phosphate rock in Florida and processes rock into finished phosphate products at facilities in Florida and Louisiana; and mines potash in Saskatchewan and New Mexico. Co. is organized into three reportable business segments: Phosphates, which sells phosphate-based crop nutrients and animal feed ingredients; Potash, which sells potash, primarily as fertilizer, but also for use in industrial applications and, to a lesser degree, as animal feed ingredients; and International Distribution, which serves as a distribution outlet for Co.'s Phosphates and Potash segments.

Recent Developments: For the quarter ended Mar 31 2016, net income decreased 12.8% to US$256.9 million from US$294.6 million in the year-earlier quarter. Revenues were US$1.67 billion, down 21.7% from US$2.14 billion the year before. Operating income was US$163.4 million versus US$318.5 million in the prior-year quarter, a decrease of 48.7%. Direct operating expenses declined 16.4% to US$1.44 billion from US$1.72 billion in the comparable period the year before. Indirect operating expenses decreased 27.2% to US$73.3 million from US$100.7 million in the equivalent prior-year period.

Prospects: Our evaluation of Mosaic Co as of June 19, 2016 is the result of our systematic analysis on three basic characteristics: earnings strength, relative valuation, and recent stock price movement. The company has generated a negative trend in earnings per share over the past 5 quarters. However, while recent estimates for the company have been lowered by analysts, MOS has posted better than expected results. Based on operating earnings yield, the company is undervalued when compared to all of the companies in our coverage universe. Share price changes over the past year indicates that MOS will perform poorly over the near term.

Financial Data

(US$ in Thousands)	3 Mos	12/31/2015	12/31/2014	12/31/2013	05/31/2013	05/31/2012	05/31/2011	05/31/2010
Earnings Per Share	2.71	2.78	2.68	0.80	4.42	4.42	5.62	1.85
Cash Flow Per Share	4.04	5.04	6.13	1.33	4.43	6.20	5.44	3.05
Tang Book Value Per Share	23.83	22.51	24.21	22.32	27.20	23.83	21.97	15.62
Dividends Per Share	1.100	1.075	1.000	1.000	1.000	0.275	0.200	1.500
Dividend Payout %	40.59	38.67	37.31	125.00	22.62	6.22	3.56	81.08
Income Statement								
Total Revenue	1,674,000	8,895,300	9,055,800	4,765,900	9,974,100	11,107,800	9,937,800	6,759,100
EBITDA	435,500	1,933,300	2,075,800	883,700	2,800,500	3,118,300	3,723,800	1,684,300
Depn & Amortn	183,700	732,200	750,900	386,200	604,800	508,100	447,400	445,000
Income Before Taxes	225,700	1,103,300	1,217,300	484,200	2,214,500	2,628,900	3,271,300	1,189,700
Income Taxes	(28,700)	99,100	184,700	152,600	341,000	711,400	752,800	347,300
Net Income	256,800	1,000,400	1,028,600	340,000	1,888,700	1,930,200	2,514,600	827,100
Average Shares	353,200	360,300	375,600	422,000	426,900	436,500	447,500	446,600
Balance Sheet								
Current Assets	3,957,100	4,144,700	5,364,200	8,105,800	6,880,500	6,581,100	6,684,900	4,974,800
Total Assets	17,627,100	17,412,400	18,283,000	19,554,000	18,086,000	16,690,400	15,786,900	12,707,700
Current Liabilities	1,814,300	2,048,300	1,600,400	3,265,900	1,764,900	1,917,700	1,928,500	1,303,900
Long-Term Obligations	3,774,000	3,791,100	3,778,000	3,008,900	1,009,600	1,010,000	761,300	1,245,600
Total Liabilities	7,630,300	7,880,600	7,579,900	8,251,700	4,660,600	4,707,300	4,145,300	3,985,500
Stockholders' Equity	9,996,800	9,531,800	10,703,100	11,302,300	13,425,400	11,983,100	11,641,600	8,722,200
Shares Outstanding	349,797	352,515	367,540	426,005	425,817	425,470	446,572	445,439
Statistical Record								
Return on Assets %	5.46	5.61	5.44	1.18	10.86	11.85	17.65	6.52
Return on Equity %	9.53	9.89	9.35	1.84	14.87	16.30	24.70	9.61
EBITDA Margin %	26.02	21.73	22.92	18.54	28.08	28.07	37.47	24.92
Net Margin %	15.34	11.25	11.36	7.13	18.94	17.38	25.30	12.24
Asset Turnover	0.48	0.50	0.48	0.17	0.57	0.68	0.70	0.53
Current Ratio	2.18	2.02	3.35	2.48	3.90	3.43	3.47	3.82
Debt to Equity	0.38	0.40	0.35	0.27	0.08	0.08	0.07	0.14
Price Range	47.43-22.10	53.56-27.24	50.79-40.76	61.80-40.68	64.30-45.62	73.18-45.68	89.06-38.90	66.70-40.67
P/E Ratio	17.50-8.15	19.27-9.80	18.95-15.21	77.25-50.85	14.55-10.32	16.56-10.33	15.85-6.92	36.05-21.98
Average Yield %	3.03	2.57	2.13	2.08	1.75	0.47	0.30	2.80

Address: 3033 Campus Drive, Suite E490, Plymouth, MN 55441
Telephone: 800-918-8270
Fax: 763-577-2990

Web Site: www.mosaicco.com
Officers: James C. O'Rourke - President, Chief Executive Officer, Executive Vice President, Chief Operating Officer James T. Prokopanko - Senior Advisor, President, Chief Executive Officer

Auditors: KPMG LLP
Investor Contact: 763-577-8213
Transfer Agents: American Stock Transfer & Trust Company, New York, NY

MOTOROLA SOLUTIONS INC.

Exchange	Symbol	Price	52Wk Range	Yield	P/E
NYS	MSI	$69.27 (5/31/2016)	76.32-56.79	2.37	24.83

*7 Year Price Score 111.56 *NYSE Composite Index=100 *12 Month Price Score 108.68

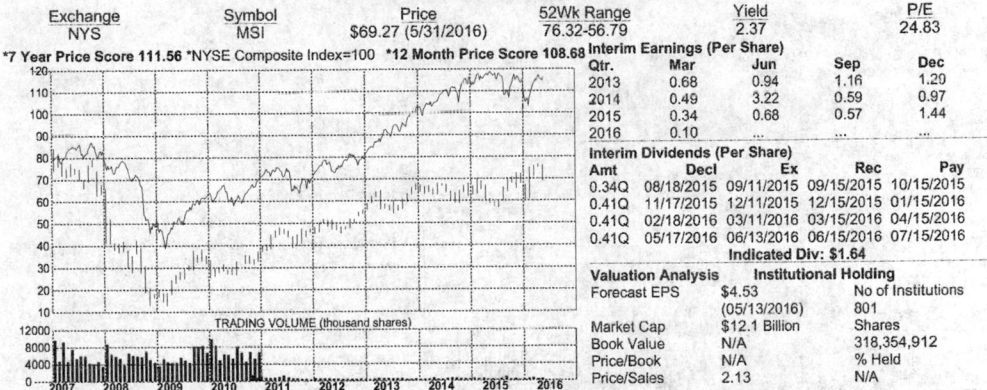

Interim Earnings (Per Share)

Qtr.	Mar	Jun	Sep	Dec
2013	0.68	0.94	1.16	1.29
2014	0.49	3.22	0.59	0.97
2015	0.34	0.68	0.57	1.44
2016	0.10	...	...	...

Interim Dividends (Per Share)

Amt	Decl	Ex	Rec	Pay
0.34Q	08/18/2015	09/11/2015	09/15/2015	10/15/2015
0.41Q	11/17/2015	12/11/2015	12/15/2015	01/15/2016
0.41Q	02/18/2016	03/11/2016	03/15/2016	04/15/2016
0.41Q	05/17/2016	06/13/2016	06/15/2016	07/15/2016

Indicated Div: $1.64

Valuation Analysis / Institutional Holding

Forecast EPS	$4.53	No of Institutions	
	(05/13/2016)	801	
Market Cap	$12.1 Billion	Shares	
Book Value	N/A		318,354,912
Price/Book	N/A	% Held	
Price/Sales	2.13	N/A	

Business Summary: Manufacturing (MIC: 6.1.1 SIC: 3663 NAIC: 334220)

Motorola Solutions is a provider of communication infrastructure, devices, accessories, software and services. The Products segment provides a portfolio of infrastructure, devices, accessories, and software to government, public safety and first-responder agencies, municipalities, and commercial and industrial customers who operate private communications networks and manage a mobile workforce. The Services segment provides a set of service offerings for government, public safety and commercial communication networks including: Integration services, Managed and Support services, and Integrated Digital Enhanced Network services.

Recent Developments: For the quarter ended Apr 2 2016, income from continuing operations decreased 80.7% to US$17.0 million from US$88.0 million in the year-earlier quarter. Net income decreased 77.3% to US$17.0 million from US$75.0 million in the year-earlier quarter. Revenues were US$1.19 billion, down 2.5% from US$1.22 billion the year before. Operating income was US$100.0 million versus US$119.0 million in the prior-year quarter, a decrease of 16.0%. Direct operating expenses rose 2.4% to US$691.0 million from US$675.0 million in the comparable period the year before. Indirect operating expenses decreased 6.3% to US$402.0 million from US$429.0 million in the equivalent prior-year period.

Prospects: Our evaluation of Motorola Solutions Inc. as of June 19, 2016 is the result of our systematic analysis on three basic characteristics: earnings strength, relative valuation, and recent stock price movement. The company has generated a negative trend in earnings per share over the past 5 quarters and while recent estimates for the company have remained steady, MSI has posted better than expected results. Based on operating earnings yield, the company is undervalued when compared to all of the companies in our coverage universe. Share price changes over the past year indicates that MSI will perform very well over the near term.

Financial Data
(US$ in Millions)

	3 Mos	12/31/2015	12/31/2014	12/31/2013	12/31/2012	12/31/2011	12/31/2010	12/31/2009
Earnings Per Share	2.79	3.02	5.29	4.06	2.96	3.41	1.87	(0.14)
Cash Flow Per Share	4.97	5.04	(2.79)	3.55	3.65	2.54	4.60	1.92
Tang Book Value Per Share	...	...	10.60	8.11	5.96	11.73	21.95	18.48
Dividends Per Share	1.500	1.430	1.300	1.140	0.960	0.440	...	0.350
Dividend Payout %	53.76	47.35	24.57	28.08	32.43	12.90	...	...
Income Statement								
Total Revenue	1,193	5,695	5,881	8,696	8,698	8,203	19,282	22,044
EBITDA	119	1,240	(862)	1,486	1,489	1,177	1,378	716
Depn & Amortn	49	150	173	228	208	365	570	749
Income Before Taxes	21	917	(1,161)	1,145	1,215	738	677	(165)
Income Taxes	5	274	(465)	40	337	(3)	406	(77)
Net Income	17	610	1,299	1,099	881	1,158	633	(51)
Average Shares	177	201	245	270	297	339	338	327
Balance Sheet								
Current Assets	4,001	4,582	6,879	7,020	7,401	8,768	17,154	16,032
Total Assets	9,049	8,387	10,423	11,851	12,679	13,929	25,577	25,603
Current Liabilities	2,032	2,193	2,250	3,220	3,335	3,815	8,710	8,261
Long-Term Obligations	5,023	4,386	3,396	2,457	1,859	1,130	2,194	3,365
Total Liabilities	9,196	8,493	7,688	8,192	9,414	8,715	14,692	15,828
Stockholders' Equity	(147)	(106)	2,735	3,659	3,265	5,214	10,885	9,775
Shares Outstanding	174	174	219	254	276	318	336	330
Statistical Record								
Return on Assets %	5.99	6.49	11.66	8.96	6.60	5.86	2.47	N.M.
Return on Equity %	57.04	46.41	40.63	31.74	20.72	14.39	6.13	N.M.
EBITDA Margin %	9.97	21.77	N.M.	17.09	17.12	14.35	7.15	3.25
Net Margin %	1.42	10.71	22.09	12.64	10.13	14.12	3.28	N.M.
Asset Turnover	0.61	0.61	0.53	0.71	0.65	0.42	0.75	0.82
Current Ratio	1.97	2.09	3.06	2.18	2.22	2.30	1.97	1.94
Debt to Equity	...	...	1.24	0.67	0.57	0.22	0.20	0.34
Price Range	76.11-56.79	72.45-56.79	67.87-58.50	67.50-54.01	55.68-44.94	47.87-37.04	37.23-25.19	38.13-12.70
P/E Ratio	27.28-20.35	23.99-18.80	12.83-11.06	16.63-13.30	18.81-15.18	14.04-10.86	19.91-13.47	...
Average Yield %	2.30	2.21	2.02	1.90	1.93	1.02	...	1.33

Address: 1303 East Algonquin Road, Schaumburg, IL 60196 Telephone: 847-576-5000 Fax: 847-576-3477	Web Site: www.motorolasolutions.com Officers: Gregory Q. Brown - Chairman, President, Chief Executive Officer, Division Officer Gino A. Bonanotte - Executive Vice President, Corporate Vice-President, Acting Chief Financial Officer, Chief Financial Officer	Auditors: KPMG LLP Investor Contact: 847-576-6899 Transfer Agents: Computershare, Jersey City, NJ

MRC GLOBAL INC

Exchange	Symbol	Price	52Wk Range	Yield	P/E
NYS	MRC	$14.19 (5/31/2016)	16.01-8.71	N/A	N/A

*7 Year Price Score N/A   *NYSE Composite Index=100   *12 Month Price Score 103.95

Interim Earnings (Per Share)

Qtr.	Mar	Jun	Sep	Dec
2013	0.45	0.43	0.38	0.22
2014	0.23	0.38	0.49	0.30
2015	0.28	0.15	0.10	(3.91)
2016	(0.14)	...	...	...

Interim Dividends (Per Share)

No Dividends Paid

Valuation Analysis

		Institutional Holding	
Forecast EPS	$-0.42	No of Institutions	
	(05/20/2016)	234	
Market Cap	$1.4 Billion	Shares	
Book Value	$1.3 Billion	101,271,512	
Price/Book	1.10	% Held	
Price/Sales	0.35	92.03	

Business Summary: Industrial Machinery & Equipment (MIC: 7.2.1 SIC: 5084 NAIC: 333924)

MRC Global is a holding company. Through its subsidiaries, Co. is a distributor of pipe, valves, fittings and related products to the energy industry across each of the upstream, midstream and downstream sectors. In addition, Co. provides services such as product testing, manufacturer assessments, multiple daily deliveries, volume purchasing, inventory and zone store management and warehousing, technical support, training, just-in-time delivery, truck stocking, order consolidation, product tagging and system interfaces customized to customer and supplier specifications for tracking and replenishing inventory, engineering of control packages, and valve inspection and repair.

Recent Developments: For the quarter ended Mar 31 2016, net loss amounted to US$8.0 million versus net income of US$29.0 million in the year-earlier quarter. Revenues were US$783.0 million, down 39.4% from US$1.29 billion the year before. Operating loss was US$4.0 million versus an income of US$61.0 million in the prior-year quarter. Direct operating expenses declined 39.4% to US$650.0 million from US$1.07 billion in the comparable period the year before. Indirect operating expenses decreased 13.8% to US$137.0 million from US$159.0 million in the equivalent prior-year period.

Prospects: Our evaluation of MRC Global Inc as of June 19, 2016 is the result of our systematic analysis on three basic characteristics: earnings strength, relative valuation, and recent stock price movement. The company has managed to produce a neutral trend in earnings per share over the past 5 quarters. Because the company lacks sufficient analyst estimate data, we place greater weight on the historical EPS trend as the measure of earnings strength. Based on operating earnings yield, the company is overvalued when compared to all of the companies in our coverage universe. Share price changes over the past year indicates that MRC will perform in line with the market over the near term.

Financial Data

(US$ in Thousands)	3 Mos	12/31/2015	12/31/2014	12/31/2013	12/31/2012	12/31/2011	12/31/2010	12/31/2009
Earnings Per Share	(3.80)	(3.38)	1.40	1.48	1.22	0.34	(0.61)	(4.30)
Cash Flow Per Share	6.28	6.76	(1.04)	3.18	2.48	(1.22)	1.34	6.39
Tang Book Value Per Share	3.50	3.61	N.M.	N.M.	N.M.	N.M.	N.M.	...
Dividends Per Share	...	...	...	...	...	...	...	0.040
Income Statement								
Total Revenue	783,000	4,528,613	5,933,212	5,230,792	5,570,858	4,832,423	3,845,536	3,661,922
EBITDA	7,000	(234,808)	355,497	349,668	343,681	243,264	118,316	(191,675)
Depn & Amortn	12,000	60,021	67,799	52,072	49,466	50,652	53,852	46,575
Income Before Taxes	(13,000)	(342,369)	225,946	236,911	181,696	55,768	(75,177)	(354,754)
Income Taxes	(5,000)	(10,790)	81,836	84,816	63,738	26,784	(23,353)	(14,983)
Net Income	(8,000)	(331,579)	144,110	152,095	117,958	28,984	(51,824)	(339,771)
Average Shares	100,700	102,067	102,790	102,522	96,925	84,655	84,384	79,067
Balance Sheet								
Current Assets	1,346,000	1,405,305	2,222,162	1,845,993	1,850,574	1,747,908	1,460,775	...
Total Assets	2,434,000	2,501,546	3,873,821	3,335,682	3,369,727	3,227,687	2,991,194	...
Current Liabilities	417,000	444,366	784,138	762,097	650,104	673,167	618,215	...
Long-Term Obligations	510,000	515,720	1,445,709	978,899	1,250,089	1,526,740	1,360,241	...
Total Liabilities	1,157,000	1,190,234	2,476,606	1,997,414	2,183,805	2,506,825	2,301,436	...
Stockholders' Equity	1,277,000	1,311,312	1,397,215	1,338,268	1,185,922	720,862	689,758	...
Shares Outstanding	98,650	102,203	102,095	101,913	101,563	84,427	84,404	84,368
Statistical Record								
Return on Assets %	N.M.	N.M.	4.00	4.54	3.57	0.93	...	...
Return on Equity %	N.M.	N.M.	10.54	12.05	12.34	4.11	...	...
EBITDA Margin %	0.89	N.M.	5.99	6.68	6.17	5.03	3.08	N.M.
Net Margin %	N.M.	N.M.	2.43	2.91	2.12	0.60	N.M.	N.M.
Asset Turnover	1.31	1.42	1.65	1.56	1.68	1.55	...	...
Current Ratio	3.23	3.16	2.83	2.42	2.85	2.60	2.36	...
Debt to Equity	0.40	0.39	1.03	0.73	1.05	2.12	1.97	...
Price Range	16.87-8.71	16.87-10.37	32.26-13.63	33.70-24.07	28.12-19.60	...	...	...
P/E Ratio	...	...	23.04-9.74	22.77-16.26	23.05-16.07	...	...	...

Address: Fulbright Tower, 1301 Mckinney Street, Suite 2300, Houston, TX 77010
Telephone: 877-294-7574

Web Site: www.mrcglobal.com
Officers: Rhys J. Best - Chairman Andrew R. Lane - Chairman, President, Chief Executive Officer

Auditors: Ernst & Young LLP
Investor Contact: 832-308-2847
Transfer Agents: Computershare, Inc., Providence, RI

MSA SAFETY INC

Exchange	Symbol	Price	52Wk Range	Yield	P/E	Div Achiever
NYS	MSA	$50.37 (5/31/2016)	52.62-38.31	2.62	26.37	45 Years

*7 Year Price Score 96.25   *NYSE Composite Index=100   *12 Month Price Score 105.74

Interim Earnings (Per Share)

Qtr.	Mar	Jun	Sep	Dec
2013	0.51	0.64	0.52	0.60
2014	0.37	0.59	0.51	0.86
2015	0.26	0.63	0.42	0.55
2016	0.31	...	...	...

Interim Dividends (Per Share)

Amt	Decl	Ex	Rec	Pay
0.32Q	08/04/2015	08/17/2015	08/19/2015	09/10/2015
0.32Q	11/10/2015	11/19/2015	11/23/2015	12/10/2015
0.32Q	01/12/2016	02/11/2016	02/16/2016	03/10/2016
0.33Q	05/09/2016	05/19/2016	05/23/2016	06/10/2016

Indicated Div: $1.32

Valuation Analysis — **Institutional Holding**

Forecast EPS	$2.75	No of Institutions
(05/14/2016)		228
Market Cap	$1.9 Billion	Shares
Book Value	$540.0 Million	26,560,404
Price/Book	3.49	% Held
Price/Sales	1.64	N/A

Business Summary: Office Equipment & Furniture (MIC: 7.5.1 SIC: 3842 NAIC: 922160)

Mine Safety Appliances is engaged in the development, manufacture and supply of safety products that protect people and facility insfrastuctures. Co.'s line of safety products is used by workers in a range of markets including the oil and gas, fire service, construction and mining industries. Co.'s primary products include self-contained breathing apparatus, fixed gas and flame detection systems, portable gas detection instruments, industrial head protection, fire and rescue helmets, and fall protection devices. Co. has organized its business into seven geographic operating segments that are aggregated into four geographic segments: North America, Europe, International and Corporate.

Recent Developments: For the quarter ended Mar 31 2016, income from continuing operations increased 44.4% to US$13.2 million from US$9.1 million in the year-earlier quarter. Net income increased 27.8% to US$12.1 million from US$9.5 million in the year-earlier quarter. Revenues were US$280.2 million, up 8.9% from US$257.3 million the year before. Direct operating expenses rose 13.4% to US$158.6 million from US$139.9 million in the comparable period the year before. Indirect operating expenses increased 3.2% to US$95.9 million from US$92.9 million in the equivalent prior-year period.

Prospects: Our evaluation of MSA Safety Inc. as of June 19, 2016 is the result of our systematic analysis on three basic characteristics: earnings strength, relative valuation, and recent stock price movement. The company has produced a positive trend in earnings per share over the past 5 quarters and while recent estimates for the company have been raised by analysts, MSA has posted better than expected results. Based on operating earnings yield, the company is about fairly valued when compared to all of the companies in our coverage universe. Share price changes over the past year indicates that MSA will perform poorly over the near term.

Financial Data

(US$ in Thousands)	3 Mos	12/31/2015	12/31/2014	12/31/2013	12/31/2012	12/31/2011	12/31/2010	12/31/2009
Earnings Per Share	1.91	1.87	2.33	2.34	2.42	1.87	1.05	1.21
Cash Flow Per Share	1.63	1.48	2.88	3.00	4.10	2.35	0.88	3.39
Tang Book Value Per Share	2.93	2.21	6.58	7.20	5.43	4.66	5.06	9.68
Dividends Per Share	1.280	1.270	1.230	1.180	1.380	1.030	0.990	0.960
Dividend Payout %	67.02	67.91	52.79	50.43	57.02	55.08	94.29	79.34
Income Statement								
Total Revenue	280,156	1,129,922	1,136,650	1,111,883	1,179,895	1,178,608	982,668	915,851
EBITDA	38,771	148,780	163,246	157,910	177,332	151,763	95,248	99,782
Depn & Amortn	9,156	26,900	26,200	27,100	31,681	32,828	29,192	27,362
Income Before Taxes	25,713	111,026	127,195	120,133	134,290	104,818	57,349	65,340
Income Taxes	12,511	44,407	41,044	35,145	42,529	34,773	18,290	22,003
Net Income	11,751	70,807	88,506	88,247	90,637	69,852	38,104	43,295
Average Shares	37,759	37,710	37,728	37,450	37,042	36,831	36,422	35,879
Balance Sheet								
Current Assets	521,010	505,027	497,869	500,966	463,548	458,849	477,389	434,025
Total Assets	1,446,230	1,424,818	1,264,792	1,234,270	1,111,746	1,115,052	1,197,188	875,228
Current Liabilities	230,064	251,905	234,057	191,564	188,800	171,770	181,741	168,450
Long-Term Obligations	471,502	459,959	245,000	260,667	272,333	334,046	367,094	82,114
Total Liabilities	906,191	908,322	730,983	667,818	648,791	681,386	745,820	438,612
Stockholders' Equity	540,039	516,496	533,809	566,452	462,955	433,666	451,368	436,616
Shares Outstanding	37,443	37,372	37,448	37,202	37,007	36,692	36,519	35,972
Statistical Record								
Return on Assets %	5.39	5.27	7.08	7.52	8.12	6.04	3.68	4.95
Return on Equity %	13.82	13.48	16.09	17.15	20.16	15.79	8.58	10.43
EBITDA Margin %	13.84	13.17	14.36	14.20	15.03	12.88	9.69	10.90
Net Margin %	4.19	6.27	7.79	7.94	7.68	5.93	3.88	4.73
Asset Turnover	0.85	0.84	0.91	0.95	1.06	1.02	0.95	1.05
Current Ratio	2.26	2.00	2.13	2.62	2.46	2.67	2.63	2.58
Debt to Equity	0.87	0.89	0.46	0.46	0.59	0.77	0.81	0.19
Price Range	52.62-38.31	53.09-38.69	61.02-47.29	54.73-42.71	43.40-32.88	40.22-24.84	32.37-22.73	29.54-15.97
P/E Ratio	27.55-20.06	28.39-20.69	26.19-20.30	23.39-18.25	17.93-13.59	21.51-13.28	30.83-21.65	24.41-13.20
Average Yield %	2.82	2.72	2.28	2.41	3.62	3.11	3.71	4.01

Address: 1000 Cranberry Woods Drive, Cranberry Township, PA 16066-5207
Telephone: 724-776 8600

Web Site: www.msasafety.com
Officers: John T. Ryan - Chairman William M. Lambert - President, Chief Executive Officer

Auditors: Ernst & Young LLP
Investor Contact: 724-741-8534
Transfer Agents: Wells Fargo Shareowner Services, South St.Paul, MN

MSC INDUSTRIAL DIRECT CO., INC.

Exchange	Symbol	Price	52Wk Range	Yield	P/E	Div Achiever
NYS	MSM	$74.95 (5/31/2016)	77.76-55.01	2.29	20.37	12 Years

*7 Year Price Score 83.94   *NYSE Composite Index=100   *12 Month Price Score 110.14

Interim Earnings (Per Share)

Qtr.	Nov	Feb	May	Aug
2012-13	1.00	0.88	0.98	0.89
2013-14	0.93	0.79	1.03	1.00
2014-15	0.91	0.83	1.03	0.96
2015-16	0.89	0.80		

Interim Dividends (Per Share)

Amt	Decl	Ex	Rec	Pay
0.40Q	06/23/2015	07/10/2015	07/14/2015	07/28/2015
0.43Q	10/21/2015	11/06/2015	11/10/2015	11/24/2015
0.43Q	12/16/2015	01/08/2016	01/12/2016	01/26/2016
0.43Q	03/31/2016	04/08/2016	04/12/2016	04/26/2016

Indicated Div: $1.72

Valuation Analysis / Institutional Holding

Valuation Analysis		Institutional Holding	
Forecast EPS	$3.73	No of Institutions	
	(05/20/2016)		384
Market Cap	$4.6 Billion	Shares	
Book Value	$1.4 Billion		54,831,880
Price/Book	3.35	% Held	
Price/Sales	1.61		83.24

TRADING VOLUME (thousand shares)

Business Summary: Industrial Machinery & Equipment (MIC: 7.2.1 SIC: 5084 NAIC: 423830)

MSC Industrial Direct is a direct marketer and distributor of a range of metalworking and maintenance, repair and operations (MRO) products and services. Co. provides approximately 1,000,000 stock-keeping units through its master catalogs, weekly, monthly and quarterly specialty and promotional catalogs, brochures and its websites, mscdirect.com and use-enco.com. Co.'s MRO products include cutting tools; measuring instruments; tooling components; metalworking products; fasteners; flat stock; raw materials; abrasives; machinery hand and power tools; safety and janitorial supplies; plumbing supplies; materials handling products; power transmission components; and electrical supplies.

Recent Developments: For the quarter ended Feb 27 2016, net income decreased 3.9% to US$49.5 million from US$51.5 million in the year-earlier quarter. Revenues were US$684.1 million, down 3.2% from US$706.4 million the year before. Operating income was US$80.5 million versus US$85.9 million in the prior-year quarter, a decrease of 6.2%. Direct operating expenses declined 2.6% to US$375.3 million from US$385.5 million in the comparable period the year before. Indirect operating expenses decreased 2.9% to US$228.2 million from US$235.0 million in the equivalent prior-year period.

Prospects: Our evaluation of MSC Industrial Direct Co. Inc. as of June 19, 2016 is the result of our systematic analysis on three basic characteristics: earnings strength, relative valuation, and recent stock price movement. The company has produced a positive trend in earnings per share over the past 5 quarters. However, while recent estimates for the company have been mixed, MSM has posted better than expected results. Based on operating earnings yield, the company is about fairly valued when compared to all of the companies in our coverage universe. Share price changes over the past year indicates that MSM will perform well over the near term.

Financial Data
(US$ in Thousands)

	6 Mos	3 Mos	08/29/2015	08/30/2014	08/31/2013	09/01/2012	08/27/2011	08/28/2010
Earnings Per Share	3.68	3.71	3.74	3.76	3.75	4.09	3.43	2.37
Cash Flow Per Share	6.29	5.13	4.09	4.40	5.21	3.69	3.35	2.41
Tang Book Value Per Share	10.38	10.07	9.56	10.24	9.53	13.48	10.63	9.23
Dividends Per Share	1.660	1.630	4.600	1.320	1.200	1.000	1.880	0.820
Dividend Payout %	45.11	43.94	122.99	35.11	32.00	24.45	54.81	34.60
Income Statement								
Total Revenue	1,390,936	706,819	2,910,379	2,787,122	2,457,649	2,355,918	2,021,792	1,692,041
EBITDA	207,113	108,376	431,509	430,714	421,645	436,863	371,000	260,512
Depn & Amortn	35,381	17,925	52,799	47,729	36,169	24,676	21,470	18,709
Income Before Taxes	169,208	89,058	373,141	379,525	383,429	412,142	349,330	240,828
Income Taxes	64,654	34,029	141,833	143,458	145,434	153,111	130,544	90,455
Net Income	104,554	55,029	231,308	236,067	237,995	259,031	218,786	150,373
Average Shares	61,313	61,408	61,487	62,339	63,011	62,803	63,324	62,930
Balance Sheet								
Current Assets	971,559	1,004,808	1,032,076	961,415	893,489	920,111	758,434	676,536
Total Assets	2,025,452	2,069,523	2,101,206	2,060,747	1,943,003	1,444,876	1,244,423	1,153,323
Current Liabilities	332,578	376,228	422,337	309,164	213,579	170,515	172,202	190,285
Long-Term Obligations	190,534	203,221	214,789	240,235	241,566	2,189	...	...
Total Liabilities	654,244	710,581	768,336	662,184	552,620	257,765	251,311	253,443
Stockholders' Equity	1,371,208	1,358,942	1,332,870	1,398,563	1,390,383	1,187,111	993,112	899,880
Shares Outstanding	61,373	61,578	61,658	61,618	63,434	62,800	62,800	62,777
Statistical Record								
Return on Assets %	10.97	10.96	11.15	11.82	14.09	18.95	18.30	13.05
Return on Equity %	17.25	17.53	16.98	16.98	18.52	23.38	23.18	17.68
EBITDA Margin %	14.89	15.33	14.83	15.45	17.16	18.54	18.35	15.40
Net Margin %	7.52	7.79	7.95	8.47	9.68	10.99	10.82	8.89
Asset Turnover	1.38	1.38	1.40	1.40	1.45	1.72	1.69	1.47
Current Ratio	2.92	2.67	2.44	3.11	4.18	5.40	4.40	3.56
Debt to Equity	0.14	0.15	0.16	0.17	0.17	N.M.	...	...
Price Range	73.80-55.01	82.60-58.86	91.09-65.04	96.13-75.55	87.79-67.18	84.27-56.13	75.04-44.57	57.47-38.92
P/E Ratio	20.05-14.95	22.26-15.87	24.36-17.39	25.57-20.09	23.41-17.91	20.60-13.72	21.88-12.99	24.25-16.42
Average Yield %	2.49	2.31	6.06	1.55	1.54	1.43	3.02	1.70

Address: 75 Maxess Road, Melville, NY 11747 Telephone: 516-812-2000 Fax: 516-349-7096	Web Site: www.mscdirect.com Officers: Mitchell Jacobson - Chairman David K. Sandler - Executive Vice-Chairman, Vice-Chairman, President, Chief Executive Officer	Auditors: Ernst & Young LLP Investor Contact: 516-812-1216 Transfer Agents: Computershare Trust Company, N.A., Providence, RI

MSCI INC

Exchange	Symbol	Price	52Wk Range	Yield	P/E
NYS	MSCI	$79.79 (5/31/2016)	79.79-57.78	1.10	35.46

*7 Year Price Score 139.08 *NYSE Composite Index=100 ***12 Month Price Score 110.92**

Interim Earnings (Per Share)
Qtr.	Mar	Jun	Sep	Dec
2013	0.48	0.50	0.46	0.39
2014	0.68	0.91	0.44	0.40
2015	0.39	0.50	0.59	0.56
2016	0.60	...	...	...

Interim Dividends (Per Share)
Amt	Decl	Ex	Rec	Pay
0.22Q	07/29/2015	08/17/2015	08/17/2015	08/31/2015
0.22Q	10/28/2015	11/10/2015	11/13/2015	11/30/2015
0.22Q	02/02/2016	02/17/2016	02/19/2016	03/11/2016
0.22Q	04/27/2016	05/11/2016	05/13/2016	05/27/2016

Indicated Div: $0.88

Valuation Analysis
Forecast EPS	$2.90
	(05/20/2016)
Market Cap	$7.7 Billion
Book Value	$615.7 Million
Price/Book	12.51
Price/Sales	7.06

Institutional Holding
No of Institutions	381
Shares	96,854,424
% Held	95.28

Business Summary: Publishing (MIC: 2.3.3 SIC: 7389 NAIC: 523999)

MSCI, together with its wholly-owned subsidiaries, provides content, applications and services to support the needs of institutional investors throughout their investment processes. Co. has four segments: Index, Analytics, ESG and Real Estate. Co.'s products are its equity indexes, custom indexes, factor indexes and environmental, social and governance (ESG) indexes; its analytics products, including multi-factor models, pricing models, methodologies for performance attribution, models for statistical analysis, and tools for portfolio optimization, back testing and stress testing; its ESG research and ratings; and its real estate benchmarks, indexes, business intelligence and analytics.

Recent Developments: For the quarter ended Mar 31 2016, income from continuing operations increased 21.6% to US$60.4 million from US$49.6 million in the year-earlier quarter. Net income increased 37.7% to US$60.4 million from US$43.8 million in the year-earlier quarter. Revenues were US$278.8 million, up 6.1% from US$262.8 million the year before. Operating income was US$113.1 million versus US$88.7 million in the prior-year quarter, an increase of 27.5%. Direct operating expenses declined 9.6% to US$63.2 million from US$69.9 million in the comparable period the year before. Indirect operating expenses decreased 1.5% to US$102.5 million from US$104.1 million in the equivalent prior-year period.

Prospects: Our evaluation of MSCI Inc. as of June 19, 2016 is the result of our systematic analysis on three basic characteristics: earnings strength, relative valuation, and recent stock price movement. The company has managed to produce a neutral trend in earnings per share over the past 5 quarters. However, while recent estimates for the company have been lowered by analysts, MSCI has posted better than expected results. Based on operating earnings yield, the company is about fairly valued when compared to all of the companies in our coverage universe. Share price changes over the past year indicates that MSCI will perform very well over the near term.

Financial Data
(US$ in Thousands)

	3 Mos	12/31/2015	12/31/2014	12/31/2013	12/31/2012	12/31/2011	12/31/2010	11/30/2010
Earnings Per Share	2.25	2.03	2.43	1.83	1.48	1.41	0.11	0.81
Cash Flow Per Share	2.74	2.80	2.64	2.67	2.84	2.11	0.33	1.64
Dividends Per Share	0.840	0.800	0.180	...	...	...	...	...
Dividend Payout %	37.33	39.41	7.41	...	...	...	...	...
Income Statement								
Total Revenue	278,828	1,075,013	996,680	1,035,667	950,141	900,941	72,524	662,901
EBITDA	133,809	488,585	413,624	451,358	426,881	403,589	33,906	262,834
Depn & Amortn	20,749	77,810	74,317	80,503	81,998	85,205	7,364	58,999
Income Before Taxes	90,777	349,554	308,338	345,621	289,409	263,413	20,556	153,491
Income Taxes	30,410	119,516	109,396	123,064	105,171	89,959	6,732	61,321
Net Income	60,367	223,648	284,113	222,557	184,238	173,454	13,824	92,170
Average Shares	99,998	109,926	116,706	121,074	123,204	122,276	121,803	113,357
Balance Sheet								
Current Assets	763,811	1,063,271	770,632	637,035	514,835	677,943	574,962	536,283
Total Assets	2,831,634	3,146,987	2,894,175	3,134,537	3,019,639	3,092,996	3,057,481	3,023,166
Current Liabilities	468,468	498,116	472,912	503,041	509,945	452,805	466,084	466,924
Long-Term Obligations	1,579,960	1,579,404	800,000	788,010	811,623	1,066,548	1,207,966	1,207,881
Total Liabilities	2,215,978	2,245,500	1,461,342	1,558,173	1,594,408	1,787,564	1,955,311	1,943,049
Stockholders' Equity	615,656	901,487	1,432,833	1,576,364	1,425,231	1,305,432	1,102,170	1,080,117
Shares Outstanding	96,535	101,013	112,072	118,083	120,114	121,212	119,594	119,522
Statistical Record								
Return on Assets %	8.39	7.40	9.43	7.23	6.01	5.64	0.60	4.36
Return on Equity %	23.19	19.16	18.88	14.83	13.46	14.41	1.58	11.61
EBITDA Margin %	47.99	45.45	41.50	43.58	44.93	44.80	46.75	39.65
Net Margin %	21.65	20.80	28.51	21.49	19.39	19.25	19.06	13.90
Asset Turnover	0.38	0.36	0.33	0.34	0.31	0.29	0.03	0.31
Current Ratio	1.63	2.13	1.63	1.27	1.01	1.50	1.23	1.15
Debt to Equity	2.57	1.75	0.56	0.50	0.57	0.82	1.10	1.12
Price Range	74.08-57.78	72.85-47.24	48.98-40.28	44.71-30.99	37.81-25.59	39.72-27.94	40.02-34.06	37.96-27.23
P/E Ratio	32.92-25.68	35.89-23.27	20.16-16.58	24.43-16.93	25.55-17.29	28.17-19.82	363.82-309.64	46.86-33.62
Average Yield %	1.29	1.29	0.40	...	...	...	...	...

Address: 7 World Trade Center, 250 Greenwich Street, 49th Floor, New York, NY 10007
Telephone: 212-804-3900

Web Site: www.msci.com
Officers: Henry A. Fernandez - Chairman, President, Chief Executive Officer C.D. Baer Pettit - Chief Operating Officer, Head

Auditors: PricewaterhouseCoopers LLP
Investor Contact: 212 804-3900
Transfer Agents: Broadridge Financial Solutions, Inc.

MSG NETWORK INC

Exchange	Symbol	Price	52Wk Range	Yield	P/E
NYS	MSGN	$17.31 (5/31/2016)	26.12-15.35	N/A	288.50

*7 Year Price Score N/A   *NYSE Composite Index=100   *12 Month Price Score 82.71

Interim Earnings (Per Share)

Qtr.	Sep	Dec	Mar	Jun
2012-13	0.26	0.60	0.49	0.47
2013-14	0.31	0.77	0.24	0.15
2014-15	1.38	0.78	0.51	0.60
2015-16	(1.58)	0.45	0.59	...

Interim Dividends (Per Share)

No Dividends Paid

Valuation Analysis / Institutional Holding

Forecast EPS	$2.08	No of Institutions
	(05/20/2016)	477
Market Cap	$1.3 Billion	Shares
Book Value	N/A	75,258,136
Price/Book	N/A	% Held
Price/Sales	1.46	75.01

Business Summary: Entertainment (MIC: 2.3.2 SIC: 4841 NAIC: 334220)

MSG Network is a holding company. Through its subsidiaries, Co. is engaged in the sports, entertainment and media business. Co. operates in three segments: MSG Media, which is engaged in production and content development for multiple distribution platforms, including content originating from Co.'s venues and is comprised of Co.'s regional sports and entertainment networks; MSG Entertainment, which presents or hosts live entertainment events, including concerts, family shows, performing arts and events in Co.'s collection of venues; and MSG Sports, which owns and operates sports franchises as well as promotes, produces and/or presents a range of other live sporting events.

Recent Developments: For the quarter ended Mar 31 2016, income from continuing operations increased 24.8% to US$44.7 million from US$35.8 million in the year-earlier quarter. Net income increased 12.5% to US$44.7 million from US$39.7 million in the year-earlier quarter. Revenues were US$179.6 million, up 6.3% from US$169.0 million the year before. Operating income was US$84.1 million versus US$72.4 million in the prior-year quarter, an increase of 16.1%. Direct operating expenses rose 21.0% to US$73.3 million from US$60.6 million in the comparable period the year before. Indirect operating expenses decreased 38.3% to US$22.2 million from US$35.9 million in the equivalent prior-year period.

Prospects: Our evaluation of MSG Network Inc. as of June 19, 2016 is the result of our systematic analysis on three basic characteristics: earnings strength, relative valuation, and recent stock price movement. The company has generated a negative trend in earnings per share over the past 5 quarters and while recent estimates for the company have remained steady, MSGN has posted better than expected results. Based on operating earnings yield, the company is undervalued when compared to all of the companies in our coverage universe. Share price changes over the past year indicates that MSGN will perform poorly over the near term.

Financial Data
(US$ in Thousands)

	9 Mos	6 Mos	3 Mos	06/30/2015	06/30/2014	06/30/2013	06/30/2012	06/30/2011
Earnings Per Share	0.06	(0.02)	0.31	3.28	1.47	1.83	1.38	0.36
Cash Flow Per Share	2.41	2.11	2.88	2.00	4.44	3.45	4.44	1.41
Tang Book Value Per Share	...	...	...	10.36	8.53	6.34	4.19	2.42
Income Statement								
Total Revenue	497,674	318,078	148,147	1,621,562	1,555,594	1,340,818	1,284,016	564,287
EBITDA	209,518	122,943	47,043	600,504	279,318	332,609	252,122	86,754
Depn & Amortn	10,260	7,772	4,795	110,723	96,551	78,023	67,523	36,317
Income Before Taxes	178,969	104,686	40,927	487,228	177,869	248,864	179,847	48,221
Income Taxes	58,878	29,305	(404)	191,937	61,478	106,482	73,302	20,607
Net Income	(41,103)	(85,773)	(119,686)	254,701	115,068	142,382	106,545	27,614
Average Shares	75,353	75,373	75,902	77,687	78,167	77,940	77,459	77,193
Balance Sheet								
Current Assets	272,646	381,585	330,774	498,353	399,979	512,173	415,811	509,418
Total Assets	799,542	910,989	863,134	3,019,829	2,925,961	2,732,214	2,524,684	2,280,256
Current Liabilities	137,761	278,202	251,973	574,534	604,201	545,894	516,345	410,607
Long-Term Obligations	1,430,949	1,449,052	1,467,156	...	...	...	...	...
Total Liabilities	1,966,620	2,124,858	2,109,471	1,296,307	1,321,517	1,253,279	1,204,671	1,074,371
Stockholders' Equity	(1,167,078)	(1,213,869)	(1,246,337)	1,723,522	1,604,444	1,478,935	1,320,013	1,205,885
Shares Outstanding	74,882	74,815	74,730	75,796	77,195	76,857	75,605	75,683
Statistical Record								
Return on Assets %	0.24	N.M.	1.37	8.57	4.07	5.42	4.42	2.49
Return on Equity %	1.70	N.M.	11.61	15.31	7.46	10.17	8.41	4.69
EBITDA Margin %	42.10	38.65	31.75	37.03	17.96	24.81	19.64	15.37
Net Margin %	N.M.	N.M.	N.M.	15.71	7.40	10.62	8.30	4.89
Asset Turnover	0.46	0.57	0.78	0.55	0.55	0.51	0.53	0.51
Current Ratio	1.98	1.37	1.31	0.87	0.66	0.94	0.81	1.24
Price Range	26.25-15.35	26.25-18.75	26.25-18.22	26.25-17.90	18.94-14.71	18.90-10.50	11.70-6.62	8.98-5.68
P/E Ratio	437.45-255.83	...	84.67-58.76	8.00-5.46	12.89-10.01	10.33-5.74	8.47-4.80	24.95-15.77

| Address: 11 Pennsylvania Plaza, New York, NY 10001
 Telephone: 212-465-6400 | Web Site: www.thegarden.com
 Officers: James L. Dolan - Executive Chairman, President, Chief Executive Officer, Associate/Affiliate Company Officer Hank J. Ratner - Vice-Chairman, President, Chief Executive Officer | Auditors: KPMG LLP
 Investor Contact: 212-631-5422 |

MURPHY OIL CORP

Exchange	Symbol	Price	52Wk Range	Yield	P/E	Div Achiever
NYS	MUR	$30.91 (5/31/2016)	43.94-15.76	4.53	N/A	16 Years

*7 Year Price Score 49.00 *NYSE Composite Index=100 *12 Month Price Score 107.83

Interim Earnings (Per Share)

Qtr.	Mar	Jun	Sep	Dec
2013	1.88	2.12	1.51	0.43
2014	0.85	0.72	1.37	2.09
2015	(0.08)	(0.42)	(9.26)	(3.41)
2016	(1.16)	...	...	...

Interim Dividends (Per Share)

Amt	Decl	Ex	Rec	Pay
0.35Q	08/05/2015	08/13/2015	08/17/2015	09/01/2015
0.35Q	10/07/2015	11/12/2015	11/16/2015	12/01/2015
0.35Q	02/03/2016	02/11/2016	02/16/2016	03/01/2016
0.35Q	04/06/2016	05/12/2016	05/16/2016	06/01/2016

Indicated Div: $1.40

Valuation Analysis   **Institutional Holding**

Forecast EPS	$-1.70
	(05/20/2016)
Market Cap	$5.3 Billion
Book Value	$5.2 Billion
Price/Book	1.02
Price/Sales	2.09

No of Institutions	588
Shares	176,886,512
% Held	81.30

Business Summary: Production & Extraction (MIC: 9.1.1 SIC: 2911 NAIC: 324110)

Murphy Oil is a holding company. Through its subsidiaries, Co. is an oil and gas exploration and production company. Co. explores for and produces crude oil, natural gas and natural gas liquids worldwide. Co. produces oil and natural gas in the U.S., Canada and Malaysia and conducts oil and natural gas exploration activities worldwide. Co.'s hydrocarbon production is in the U.S., Canada, and Malaysia. MOCL owns a 5% undivided interest in Syncrude Canada Ltd. in northern Alberta, a producer of synthetic crude oil. At Dec 31 2015, Co. had proved reserves of 341.4 million barrels of oil, 114.8 million barrels of synthetic oil, and 1,688.80 billion cubic feet of natural gas.

Recent Developments: For the quarter ended Mar 31 2016, loss from continuing operations was US$199.5 million compared with income of US$3.5 million in the year-earlier quarter. Net loss amounted to US$198.8 million versus a net loss of US$14.4 million in the year-earlier quarter. Revenues were US$430.3 million, down 53.3% from US$921.7 million the year before. Direct operating expenses declined 31.5% to US$159.1 million from US$232.4 million in the comparable period the year before. Indirect operating expenses decreased 33.6% to US$536.2 million from US$807.1 million in the equivalent prior-year period.

Prospects: Our evaluation of Murphy Oil Corp. as of June 19, 2016 is the result of our systematic analysis on three basic characteristics: earnings strength, relative valuation, and recent stock price movement. The company has enjoyed a very positive trend in earnings per share over the past 5 quarters. Because the company lacks sufficient analyst estimate data, we place greater weight on the historical EPS trend as the measure of earnings strength. Based on operating earnings yield, the company is overvalued when compared to all of the companies in our coverage universe. Share price changes over the past year indicates that MUR will perform poorly over the near term.

Financial Data

(US$ in Thousands)	3 Mos	12/31/2015	12/31/2014	12/31/2013	12/31/2012	12/31/2011	12/31/2010	12/31/2009
Earnings Per Share	(14.25)	(13.03)	5.03	5.94	4.99	4.49	4.13	4.35
Cash Flow Per Share	4.03	6.79	17.05	19.36	15.72	11.09	16.31	9.77
Tang Book Value Per Share	30.23	30.85	48.30	46.65	46.68	45.10	42.30	38.22
Dividends Per Share	1.400	1.400	1.325	1.250	3.675	1.100	1.050	1.000
Dividend Payout %	...	...	26.34	21.04	73.65	24.50	25.42	22.99
Income Statement								
Total Revenue	430,295	3,033,080	5,476,084	5,390,089	28,626,046	27,745,549	23,345,071	19,012,392
EBITDA	(222,343)	(1,462,455)	3,357,119	3,173,336	3,166,059	2,826,376	2,760,877	2,329,935
Depn & Amortn	12,471	1,702,432	1,989,030	1,628,749	1,528,145	1,234,693	1,311,918	1,028,371
Income Before Taxes	(265,034)	(3,282,262)	1,252,270	1,472,687	1,622,982	1,550,983	1,414,231	1,277,173
Income Taxes	(65,549)	(1,026,490)	227,297	584,550	658,936	810,051	616,150	536,656
Net Income	(198,802)	(2,270,833)	905,611	1,123,473	970,876	872,702	798,081	837,621
Average Shares	172,114	174,351	180,070	189,271	194,668	194,512	193,157	192,468
Balance Sheet								
Current Assets	1,698,930	1,448,416	3,279,149	3,508,643	4,108,583	3,447,671	3,550,693	3,375,695
Total Assets	11,460,697	11,493,812	16,742,307	17,509,484	17,522,643	14,138,138	14,233,243	12,756,359
Current Liabilities	1,377,755	1,674,629	3,147,887	3,224,031	3,409,081	2,824,928	2,930,910	2,181,608
Long-Term Obligations	3,409,518	3,040,594	2,536,238	2,936,563	2,245,201	249,553	939,350	1,353,183
Total Liabilities	6,255,609	6,187,084	8,168,873	8,913,754	8,580,608	5,359,741	6,033,693	5,410,333
Stockholders' Equity	5,205,088	5,306,728	8,573,434	8,595,730	8,942,035	8,778,397	8,199,550	7,346,026
Shares Outstanding	172,195	172,034	177,499	183,406	190,641	193,723	192,836	191,115
Statistical Record								
Return on Assets %	N.M.	N.M.	5.29	6.41	6.12	6.15	5.91	7.01
Return on Equity %	N.M.	N.M.	10.55	12.81	10.93	10.28	10.27	12.30
EBITDA Margin %	N.M.	N.M.	61.31	58.87	11.06	10.19	11.83	12.25
Net Margin %	N.M.	N.M.	16.54	20.84	3.39	3.15	3.42	4.41
Asset Turnover	0.19	0.21	0.32	0.31	1.80	1.96	1.73	1.59
Current Ratio	1.23	0.86	1.04	1.09	1.21	1.22	1.21	1.55
Debt to Equity	0.66	0.57	0.30	0.34	0.25	0.03	0.11	0.18
Price Range	50.56-15.76	51.77-21.71	67.75-44.39	65.55-51.20	55.89-37.67	66.86-36.33	65.04-41.80	55.80-32.95
P/E Ratio	...	...	13.47-8.83	11.04-8.62	11.20-7.55	14.89-8.09	15.75-10.12	12.83-7.57
Average Yield %	4.48	3.68	2.25	2.19	7.72	2.04	2.09	2.16

Address: 300 Peach Street, P.O. Box 7000, El Dorado, AR 71730-7000	**Web Site:** www.murphyoilcorp.com	**Auditors:** KPMG LLP
Telephone: 870-862-6411	**Officers:** Claiborne P. Deming - Chairman, President, Chief Executive Officer Roger W. Jenkins - President,	**Investor Contact:** 870-864-6501
Fax: 870-864-3673	Chief Executive Officer, Executive Vice President, Chief Operating Officer	**Transfer Agents:** Computershare Trust Company, N A., Chicago, IL

MURPHY USA INC

Exchange	Symbol	Price	52Wk Range	Yield	P/E
NYS	MUSA	$67.99 (5/31/2016)	68.41-48.70	N/A	12.08

*7 Year Price Score N/A   *NYSE Composite Index=100   *12 Month Price Score 103.52

Interim Earnings (Per Share)

Qtr.	Mar	Jun	Sep	Dec
2013	0.47	1.66	0.89	2.00
2014	0.21	1.57	1.36	2.13
2015	0.50	0.59	1.41	1.55
2016	2.08	...	...	...

Interim Dividends (Per Share)

No Dividends Paid

Valuation Analysis

		Institutional Holding	
Forecast EPS	$4.45		No of Institutions
	(05/17/2016)		N/A
Market Cap	$2.7 Billion		Shares
Book Value	$725.6 Million		N/A
Price/Book	3.69		% Held
Price/Sales	0.22		N/A

Business Summary: Retail - General Merchandise/Department Stores (MIC: 2.1.1 SIC: 5541 NAIC: 447110)

Murphy USA's business consists mainly of the marketing of retail motor fuel products and convenience merchandise through a chain of retail stations operated by Co., almost all of which are in close proximity to Walmart stores. Co.'s retail stores are located in 24 states, primarily in the Southwest, Southeast and Midwest U.S. Of these stations, 1,111 were branded Murphy USA and 224 were standalone Murphy Express locations as of Dec 31 2015. Co.'s retail stations under the brand name Murphy USA® participate in the Walmart discount program that Co. provides at most locations. The Walmart discount program provides a cents-off per gallon purchased for fuel when using specific payment methods.

Recent Developments: For the quarter ended Mar 31 2016, income from continuing operations increased 265.2% to US$85.9 million from US$23.5 million in the year-earlier quarter. Net income increased 274.5% to US$85.9 million from US$22.9 million in the year-earlier quarter. Revenues were US$2.49 billion, down 14.7% from US$2.92 billion the year before. Operating income was US$59.2 million versus US$42.0 million in the prior-year quarter, an increase of 40.8%. Direct operating expenses declined 16.7% to US$2.26 billion from US$2.71 billion in the comparable period the year before. Indirect operating expenses increased 3.0% to US$172.2 million from US$167.1 million in the equivalent prior-year period.

Prospects: Our evaluation of Murphy USA Inc. as of June 19, 2016 is the result of our systematic analysis on three basic characteristics: earnings strength, relative valuation, and recent stock price movement. The company has produced a positive trend in earnings per share over the past 5 quarters and while recent estimates for the company have been raised by analysts, MUSA has posted better than expected results. Based on operating earnings yield, the company is undervalued when compared to all of the companies in our coverage universe. Share price changes over the past year indicates that MUSA will perform in line with the market over the near term.

Financial Data

(US$ in Thousands)	3 Mos	12/31/2015	12/31/2014	12/31/2013	12/31/2012	12/31/2011	12/31/2010
Earnings Per Share	5.63	4.02	5.26	5.02	...	...	...
Cash Flow Per Share	6.31	4.97	6.63	7.63	...	...	...
Tang Book Value Per Share	18.42	19.01	18.79	14.04	...	...	...
Income Statement							
Total Revenue	2,490,262	12,699,411	17,209,919	18,083,335	19,655,436	19,273,455	15,592,117
EBITDA	172,139	336,211	485,059	345,217	222,695	407,623	292,189
Depn & Amortn	23,486	86,568	79,234	74,130	76,622	69,550	60,698
Income Before Taxes	139,345	218,289	369,423	257,677	145,740	337,557	227,766
Income Taxes	53,471	80,698	126,341	101,351	62,172	132,284	85,029
Net Income	85,874	176,340	243,863	235,033	83,568	324,020	157,441
Average Shares	41,255	43,794	46,417	46,858	...	...	...
Balance Sheet							
Current Assets	490,591	435,667	665,882	682,416	821,962	588,353	...
Total Assets	2,020,535	1,886,241	1,934,257	1,881,242	1,992,465	1,784,983	...
Current Liabilities	400,053	392,292	413,080	526,517	733,909	492,552	...
Long-Term Obligations	657,766	490,160	492,443	547,578	1,124	1,170	...
Total Liabilities	1,294,921	1,093,951	1,075,552	1,224,906	888,014	666,036	...
Stockholders' Equity	725,614	792,290	858,705	656,336	1,104,451	1,118,947	...
Shares Outstanding	39,396	41,678	45,710	46,743	...	...	...
Statistical Record							
Return on Assets %	12.13	9.23	12.78	...	4.41	...	...
Return on Equity %	30.54	21.36	32.19	...	7.50	...	...
EBITDA Margin %	6.91	2.65	2.82	1.91	1.13	2.11	1.87
Net Margin %	3.45	1.39	1.42	1.30	0.43	1.68	1.01
Asset Turnover	6.25	6.65	9.02	...	10.38	...	...
Current Ratio	1.23	1.11	1.61	1.30	1.12	1.19	...
Debt to Equity	0.91	0.62	0.57	0.83	N.M.	N.M.	...
Price Range	73.47-48.70	73.48-48.70	69.37-37.55	46.31-37.51	...	...	...
P/E Ratio	13.05-8.65	18.28-12.11	13.19-7.14	9.23-7.47	...	...	...

Address: 200 Peach Street, El Dorado, AR 71730-5836
Telephone: 870-875-7600

Web Site: www.murphyusa.com
Officers: R. Madison Murphy - Chairman R. Andrew Clyde - President, Chief Executive Officer

Auditors: KPMG LLP
Transfer Agents: Computershare Trust Company, N.A.

NABORS INDUSTRIES LTD.

Exchange	Symbol	Price	52Wk Range	Yield	P/E
NYS	NBR	$9.40 (5/31/2016)	15.13-5.53	2.55	N/A

*7 Year Price Score 47.37   ***NYSE Composite Index=100**   ***12 Month Price Score 92.65**

TRADING VOLUME (thousand shares)

Interim Earnings (Per Share)

Qtr.	Mar	Jun	Sep	Dec
2013	0.33	(0.01)	(0.35)	0.50
2014	0.16	0.21	0.35	(3.01)
2015	0.42	(0.13)	(1.02)	(0.57)
2016	(1.41)	...	...	...

Interim Dividends (Per Share)

Amt	Decl	Ex	Rec	Pay
0.06Q	07/24/2015	09/04/2015	09/09/2015	09/30/2015
0.06Q	11/03/2015	12/08/2015	12/10/2015	12/31/2015
0.06Q	02/19/2016	03/08/2016	03/10/2016	03/31/2016
0.06Q	04/29/2016	06/08/2016	06/10/2016	07/01/2016

Indicated Div: $0.24

Valuation Analysis | Institutional Holding

Forecast EPS	$-1.65	No of Institutions	
	(05/20/2016)	537	
Market Cap	$2.7 Billion	Shares	
Book Value	$3.9 Billion	293,453,888	
Price/Book	0.68	% Held	
Price/Sales	0.95	89.34	

Business Summary: Production & Extraction (MIC: 9.1.1 SIC: 3533 NAIC: 333132)

Nabors Industries is a holding company, engaged in the land drilling business. Co. also provides drilling technology and equipment and well-site services including engineering, transportation and disposal, construction, maintenance, well logging, directional drilling, rig instrumentation, data collection and other support services in oil and gas markets. Co.'s Drilling & Rig Services business is comprised of land-based and offshore drilling rig operations and other rig services. Through Co.'s investment in C&J Energy Services Ltd. (CJES), Co. is engaged in the completion and production services business. In addition, Co. manufactures and leases or sells top drives and other rig equipment.

Recent Developments: For the quarter ended Mar 31 2016, loss from continuing operations was US$396.6 million compared with income of US$124.4 million in the year-earlier quarter. Net loss amounted to US$397.6 million versus net income of US$123.5 million in the year-earlier quarter. Revenues were US$430.8 million, down 69.7% from US$1.42 billion the year before. Direct operating expenses declined 60.3% to US$365.0 million from US$919.6 million in the comparable period the year before. Indirect operating expenses increased 29.0% to US$514.4 million from US$398.9 million in the equivalent prior-year period.

Prospects: Our evaluation of Nabors Industries Ltd. as of June 19, 2016 is the result of our systematic analysis on three basic characteristics: earnings strength, relative valuation, and recent stock price movement. The company has enjoyed a very positive trend in earnings per share over the past 5 quarters. Because the company lacks sufficient analyst estimate data, we place greater weight on the historical EPS trend as the measure of earnings strength. Based on operating earnings yield, the company is overvalued when compared to all of the companies in our coverage universe. Share price changes over the past year indicates that NBR will perform very poorly over the near term.

Financial Data

(US$ in Thousands)	3 Mos	12/31/2015	12/31/2014	12/31/2013	12/31/2012	12/31/2011	12/31/2010	12/31/2009
Earnings Per Share	(3.13)	(1.29)	(2.28)	0.47	0.56	0.83	0.33	(0.30)
Cash Flow Per Share	2.58	3.03	6.13	4.82	5.37	5.07	3.88	5.71
Tang Book Value Per Share	13.25	14.64	16.36	18.71	19.08	17.93	17.17	17.59
Dividends Per Share	0.240	0.240	0.200	0.160	...	...	...	...
Dividend Payout %	...	...	...	34.04	...	...	...	...
Income Statement								
Total Revenue	430,763	3,791,664	6,809,727	6,248,631	6,751,390	6,136,938	4,215,540	3,503,431
EBITDA	(186,309)	734,970	729,004	1,457,981	1,592,526	1,750,307	1,226,211	803,684
Depn & Amortn	216,669	980,577	1,155,671	1,128,403	1,066,291	1,005,905	871,121	773,852
Income Before Taxes	(448,708)	(427,535)	(604,615)	106,160	274,683	487,769	82,046	(235,116)
Income Taxes	(52,064)	(98,038)	62,666	(55,181)	32,628	142,605	(24,814)	(149,228)
Net Income	(398,294)	(372,675)	(670,659)	139,982	164,034	243,679	94,695	(85,546)
Average Shares	275,851	282,982	290,694	296,592	292,323	292,484	289,996	283,326
Balance Sheet								
Current Assets	1,259,387	1,475,897	2,741,874	2,753,830	3,132,857	3,088,314	2,612,930	2,176,664
Total Assets	8,950,331	9,537,840	11,879,942	12,159,811	12,656,022	12,912,140	11,646,569	10,644,690
Current Liabilities	871,268	1,006,499	1,567,475	1,311,424	1,132,382	1,802,562	2,154,380	608,622
Long-Term Obligations	3,584,402	3,655,200	4,348,859	3,904,117	4,379,336	4,348,490	3,064,126	3,940,605
Total Liabilities	5,046,011	5,255,130	6,971,323	6,121,537	6,641,905	7,255,137	6,249,219	5,477,034
Stockholders' Equity	3,904,320	4,282,710	4,908,619	6,038,274	6,014,117	5,657,003	5,397,350	5,167,656
Shares Outstanding	282,002	281,184	289,408	295,297	290,399	287,628	285,620	284,501
Statistical Record								
Return on Assets %	N.M.	N.M.	N.M.	1.13	1.28	1.98	0.85	N.M.
Return on Equity %	N.M.	N.M.	N.M.	2.32	2.80	4.41	1.79	N.M.
EBITDA Margin %	N.M.	19.38	10.71	23.33	23.59	28.52	29.09	22.94
Net Margin %	N.M.	N.M.	N.M.	2.24	2.43	3.97	2.25	N.M.
Asset Turnover	0.29	0.35	0.57	0.50	0.53	0.50	0.38	0.33
Current Ratio	1.45	1.47	1.75	2.10	2.77	1.71	1.21	3.58
Debt to Equity	0.92	0.85	0.89	0.65	0.73	0.77	0.57	0.76
Price Range	16.70-5.53	16.70-7.73	30.04-10.00	18.14-14.45	22.31-12.65	32.06-11.74	26.87-15.64	23.46-8.50
P/E Ratio				38.60-30.74	39.84-22.59	38.63-14.14	81.42-47.39	...
Average Yield %	2.20	1.99	0.91	0.99	...	...	...	...

Address: Crown House, Second Floor, 4 Par-la-Ville Road, Hamilton, HM08	Web Site: www.nabors.com	Auditors: PricewaterhouseCoopers LLP
Telephone: 441-292-1510	Officers: Anthony G. Petrello - Chairman, Deputy Chairman, President, Chief Executive Officer, Chief Operating Officer William J. Restrepo - Chief Financial Officer	Investor Contact: 441-292-1510 Transfer Agents: Computershare Trust Company, N.A., Providence, RI

NATIONAL FUEL GAS CO. (NJ)

Exchange	Symbol	Price	52Wk Range	Yield	P/E	Div Achiever
NYS	NFG	$55.00 (5/31/2016)	64.29-37.90	2.95	N/A	44 Years

*7 Year Price Score 75.00 *NYSE Composite Index=100 *12 Month Price Score 103.30

TRADING VOLUME (thousand shares)

Interim Earnings (Per Share)

Qtr.	Dec	Mar	Jun	Sep
2012-13	0.81	1.02	0.69	0.56
2013-14	0.97	1.12	0.76	0.67
2014-15	1.00	0.20	(3.44)	(2.25)
2015-16	(2.23)	(1.74)	...	...

Interim Dividends (Per Share)

Amt	Decl	Ex	Rec	Pay
0.395Q	09/18/2015	09/28/2015	09/30/2015	10/15/2015
0.395Q	12/08/2015	12/29/2015	12/31/2015	01/15/2016
0.395Q	03/10/2016	03/29/2016	03/31/2016	04/15/2016
0.405Q	06/09/2016	06/28/2016	06/30/2016	07/15/2016

Indicated Div: $1.62 (Div. Reinv. Plan)

Valuation Analysis / Institutional Holding

Valuation Analysis		Institutional Holding	
Forecast EPS	$2.83	No of Institutions	469
	(05/15/2016)		
Market Cap	$4.7 Billion	Shares	62,957,460
Book Value	$1.6 Billion	% Held	63.01
Price/Book	2.88		
Price/Sales	3.19		

Business Summary: Gas Utilities (MIC: 3.3.1 SIC: 4924 NAIC: 221210)

National Fuel Gas is a holding company. Through its subsidiaries, Co. operates in five segments: Exploration and Production, which is engaged in the exploration for, and the development and production of, natural gas and oil reserves; Pipeline and Storage, which transports and stores natural gas for utilities; Gathering, which builds, owns and operates natural gas processing and pipeline gathering facilities; Utility, which sells natural gas or provides natural gas transportation services; and Energy Marketing, which markets natural gas. At Sep 30 2015, Co. had U.S. proved developed and undeveloped reserves of 33.7 million barrels of oil and 2.14 trillion cubic feet of natural gas.

Recent Developments: For the quarter ended Mar 31 2016, net loss amounted to US$147.7 million versus net income of US$16.7 million in the year-earlier quarter. Revenues were US$449.1 million, down 24.7% from US$596.1 million the year before. Operating loss was US$237.0 million versus an income of US$44.3 million in the prior-year quarter. Direct operating expenses declined 37.2% to US$203.4 million from US$323.8 million in the comparable period the year before. Indirect operating expenses increased 111.8% to US$482.7 million from US$228.0 million in the equivalent prior-year period.

Prospects: Our evaluation of National Fuel Gas Co. as of June 19, 2016 is the result of our systematic analysis on three basic characteristics: earnings strength, relative valuation, and recent stock price movement. The company has enjoyed a very positive trend in earnings per share over the past 5 quarters. However, while recent estimates for the company have been mixed, NFG has posted better than expected results. Based on operating earnings yield, the company is undervalued when compared to all of the companies in our coverage universe. Share price changes over the past year indicates that NFG will perform in line with the market over the near term.

Financial Data

(US$ in Thousands)	6 Mos	3 Mos	09/30/2015	09/30/2014	09/30/2013	09/30/2012	09/30/2011	09/30/2010
Earnings Per Share	(9.66)	(7.72)	(4.50)	3.52	3.08	2.63	3.09	2.73
Cash Flow Per Share	7.77	9.20	10.11	10.84	8.84	7.93	8.21	5.65
Tang Book Value Per Share	19.05	21.33	23.88	28.58	26.17	23.46	22.78	21.19
Dividends Per Share	1.580	1.570	1.560	1.520	1.480	1.440	1.400	1.360
Dividend Payout %	...	...	...	43.18	48.05	54.75	45.31	49.82
Income Statement								
Total Revenue	824,327	375,195	1,760,913	2,113,081	1,829,551	1,626,853	1,778,842	1,760,503
EBITDA	(402,772)	(232,955)	(266,856)	962,915	849,295	724,712	725,274	635,898
Depn & Amortn	134,498	70,551	336,158	383,781	326,760	271,530	226,527	191,809
Income Before Taxes	(597,176)	(333,459)	(698,563)	489,027	432,759	370,631	423,542	353,872
Income Taxes	(260,380)	(144,350)	(319,136)	189,614	172,758	150,554	164,381	137,227
Net Income	(336,796)	(189,109)	(379,427)	299,413	260,001	220,077	258,402	225,913
Average Shares	84,806	84,651	84,387	84,952	84,341	83,739	83,670	82,660
Balance Sheet								
Current Assets	376,509	424,515	513,001	377,332	448,677	355,576	385,312	775,377
Total Assets	5,801,024	6,190,332	6,702,139	6,739,597	6,218,347	5,935,142	5,284,742	5,105,625
Current Liabilities	352,627	411,131	446,140	490,576	302,171	734,479	528,618	524,324
Long-Term Obligations	2,085,123	2,084,562	2,084,009	1,649,000	1,649,000	1,149,000	899,000	1,049,000
Total Liabilities	4,178,545	4,377,651	4,676,699	4,328,914	4,023,618	3,975,047	3,392,857	3,359,654
Stockholders' Equity	1,622,479	1,812,681	2,025,440	2,410,683	2,194,729	1,960,095	1,891,885	1,745,971
Shares Outstanding	84,892	84,739	84,594	84,157	83,661	83,330	82,812	82,075
Statistical Record								
Return on Assets %	N.M.	N.M.	N.M.	4.62	4.28	3.91	4.97	4.58
Return on Equity %	N.M.	N.M.	N.M.	13.00	12.52	11.40	14.21	13.55
EBITDA Margin %	N.M.	N.M.	N.M.	45.57	46.42	44.55	40.77	36.12
Net Margin %	N.M.	N.M.	N.M.	14.17	14.21	13.53	14.53	12.83
Asset Turnover	0.22	0.24	0.26	0.33	0.30	0.29	0.34	0.36
Current Ratio	1.07	1.03	1.15	0.77	1.48	0.48	0.73	1.48
Debt to Equity	1.29	1.15	1.03	0.68	0.75	0.59	0.48	0.60
Price Range	65.92-37.90	70.04-37.90	71.90-48.82	78.30-65.45	68.76-48.69	63.58-42.17	75.40-48.68	54.32-42.98
P/E Ratio	...	...	...	22.24-18.59	22.32-15.81	24.17-16.03	24.40-15.75	19.90-15.74
Average Yield %	3.00	2.75	2.49	2.10	2.52	2.52	2.85	2.13

Address: 6363 Main Street, Williamsville, NY 14221 Telephone: 716-857-7000	Web Site: www.nationalfuelgas.com Officers: David F. Smith - Chairman, Chief Executive Officer Ronald J. Tanski - President, Chief Operating Officer, Chief Executive Officer	Auditors: PricewaterhouseCoopers LLP Investor Contact: 716-857-6987 Transfer Agents: Wells Fargo Shareowner Services, Saint Paul, MN

NATIONAL HEALTH INVESTORS, INC.

Exchange	Symbol	Price	52Wk Range	Yield	P/E	Div Achiever
NYS	NHI	$69.83 (5/31/2016)	71.31-54.10	5.16	17.41	13 Years

'7 Year Price Score 100.28 *NYSE Composite Index=100 *12 Month Price Score 108.08

Interim Earnings (Per Share)

Qtr.	Mar	Jun	Sep	Dec
2013	0.56	0.71	1.53	0.93
2014	0.71	0.77	0.76	0.80
2015	0.79	0.83	0.89	1.44
2016	0.85	...	...	...

Interim Dividends (Per Share)

Amt	Decl	Ex	Rec	Pay
0.85Q	08/05/2015	09/28/2015	09/30/2015	11/10/2015
0.85Q	12/14/2015	12/29/2015	12/31/2015	01/29/2016
0.90Q	02/18/2016	03/29/2016	03/31/2016	05/10/2016
0.90Q	05/06/2016	06/28/2016	06/30/2016	08/10/2016

Indicated Div: $3.60

Valuation Analysis

Forecast EPS	$3.33
	(05/20/2016)
Market Cap	$2.7 Billion
Book Value	$1.1 Billion
Price/Book	2.37
Price/Sales	11.55

Institutional Holding

No of Institutions	264
Shares	27,937,440
% Held	86.51

Business Summary: REITs (MIC: 5.3.1 SIC: 6798 NAIC: 525930)

National Health Investors is a real estate investment trust (REIT) which focuses on sale-leaseback, joint-venture, mortgage and mezzanine financing of senior housing and medical investments. Co.'s portfolio consists of real estate investments in independent, assisted and memory care communities, entrance-fee communities, senior living campuses, skilled nursing facilities, specialty hospitals and medical office buildings. Co.'s other investments include mortgages and notes, the preferred stock and marketable securities of other REITs. At Dec 31 2014, Co.'s operations consisted of investments in real estate and mortgage and other notes receivable involving 183 facilities located in 31 states.

Recent Developments: For the quarter ended Mar 31 2016, net income increased 10.3% to US$33.1 million from US$30.0 million in the year-earlier quarter. Revenues were US$59.0 million, up 5.9% from US$55.8 million the year before. Revenues from property income rose 4.9% to US$55.1 million from US$52.5 million in the corresponding quarter a year earlier.

Prospects: Our evaluation of National Health Investors Inc. as of June 19, 2016 is the result of our systematic analysis on three basic characteristics: earnings strength, relative valuation, and recent stock price movement. The company has managed to produce a neutral trend in earnings per share over the past 5 quarters. Because the company lacks sufficient analyst estimate data, we place greater weight on the historical EPS trend as the measure of earnings strength. Based on operating earnings yield, the company is about fairly valued when compared to all of the companies in our coverage universe. Share price changes over the past year indicates that NHI will perform in line with the market over the

Financial Data

(US$ in Thousands)	3 Mos	12/31/2015	12/31/2014	12/31/2013	12/31/2012	12/31/2011	12/31/2010	12/31/2009
Earnings Per Share	4.01	3.95	3.04	3.74	3.26	2.92	2.50	2.32
Cash Flow Per Share	4.35	4.37	3.78	3.67	3.09	2.77	2.80	2.51
Tang Book Value Per Share	29.44	29.52	27.74	23.19	16.41	15.98	15.98	15.73
Dividends Per Share	3.450	3.400	3.080	3.120	2.640	2.715	2.360	2.300
Dividend Payout %	86.03	86.08	101.32	83.42	80.98	92.98	94.40	99.14
Income Statement								
Total Revenue	59,018	228,988	177,509	117,828	96,953	82,702	78,396	64,221
EBITDA	58,162	204,537	141,201	99,832	91,599	88,445	74,808	65,516
Depn & Amortn	14,550	53,163	38,078	20,658	16,981	11,992	11,203	8,621
Income Before Taxes	33,350	151,374	103,123	79,174	74,618	72,760	62,137	58,136
Income Taxes	...	(707)	...	...	...	...	...	...
Net Income	32,725	150,314	103,052	107,182	90,898	81,132	69,421	64,229
Average Shares	38,414	37,644	33,416	28,397	27,838	27,792	27,732	27,618
Balance Sheet								
Current Assets	93,870	73,063	38,441	30,003	21,542	25,776	8,063	47,907
Total Assets	2,159,234	2,146,349	1,982,960	1,455,820	705,981	579,563	509,341	459,360
Current Liabilities	80,644	52,784	47,582	34,904	33,350	37,105	27,615	23,863
Long-Term Obligations	937,138	926,257	862,726	617,080	203,250	97,300	37,765	...
Total Liabilities	1,028,662	1,013,057	943,035	689,274	248,799	136,078	66,841	24,748
Stockholders' Equity	1,130,572	1,133,292	1,039,925	766,546	457,182	443,485	442,500	434,612
Shares Outstanding	38,403	38,396	37,485	33,051	27,857	27,751	27,689	27,629
Statistical Record								
Return on Assets %	7.29	7.28	5.99	9.92	14.10	14.90	14.33	14.02
Return on Equity %	14.05	13.83	11.41	17.52	20.13	18.31	15.83	14.86
EBITDA Margin %	98.55	89.32	79.55	84.73	94.48	106.94	95.42	102.02
Net Margin %	55.45	65.64	58.05	90.96	93.75	98.10	88.55	100.01
Asset Turnover	0.11	0.11	0.10	0.11	0.15	0.15	0.16	0.14
Current Ratio	1.16	1.38	0.81	0.86	0.65	0.69	0.29	2.01
Debt to Equity	0.83	0.82	0.83	0.81	0.44	0.22	0.09	...
Price Range	72.36-54.10	76.46-54.10	71.19-55.11	72.30-53.28	57.14-43.70	49.19-38.03	48.31-32.03	37.64-21.77
P/E Ratio	18.04-13.49	19.36-13.70	23.42-18.13	19.33-14.25	17.53-13.40	16.85-13.02	19.32-12.81	16.22-9.38
Average Yield %	5.55	5.25	4.94	5.04	5.18	6.04	5.84	7.84

Address: 222 Robert Rose Drive, Murfreesboro, TN 37129 **Telephone:** 615-890-9100	**Web Site:** www.nhireit.com **Officers:** W. Andrew Adams - Chairman, Chief Executive Officer, Acting Chief Financial Officer Kevin Pascoe - Officer	**Auditors:** BDO USA, LLP **Investor Contact:** 615-890-9100 **Transfer Agents:** Computershare Trust Company, N.A. Providence, RI

NATIONAL OILWELL VARCO INC

Exchange	Symbol	Price	52Wk Range	Yield	P/E
NYS	NOV	$32.95 (5/31/2016)	50.20-26.34	0.61	N/A

*7 Year Price Score 56.29 *NYSE Composite Index=100 *12 Month Price Score 86.55

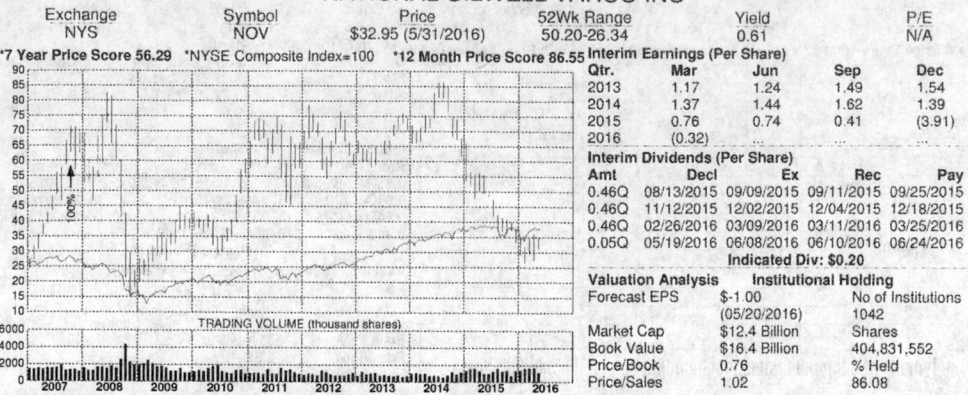

Interim Earnings (Per Share)

Qtr.	Mar	Jun	Sep	Dec
2013	1.17	1.24	1.49	1.54
2014	1.37	1.44	1.62	1.39
2015	0.76	0.74	0.41	(3.91)
2016	(0.32)	...	...	...

Interim Dividends (Per Share)

Amt	Decl	Ex	Rec	Pay
0.46Q	08/13/2015	09/09/2015	09/11/2015	09/25/2015
0.46Q	11/12/2015	12/02/2015	12/04/2015	12/18/2015
0.46Q	02/26/2016	03/09/2016	03/11/2016	03/25/2016
0.05Q	05/19/2016	06/08/2016	06/10/2016	06/24/2016

Indicated Div: $0.20

Valuation Analysis **Institutional Holding**

Forecast EPS	$-1.00	No of Institutions
	(05/20/2016)	1042
Market Cap	$12.4 Billion	Shares
Book Value	$16.4 Billion	404,831,552
Price/Book	0.76	% Held
Price/Sales	1.02	86.08

Business Summary: Equipment & Services (MIC: 9.1.3 SIC: 3533 NAIC: 333132)

National Oilwell Varco provides drilling and well-servicing equipment, products and services to the exploration and production segments of the oil and gas industry. Co. operates in four segments: Rig Systems, which designs, manufactures and sells land rigs, offshore drilling equipment packages, and drilling rig components; Rig Aftermarket, which provides aftermarket products and services to support land and offshore rigs, and drilling rig components; Wellbore Technologies, which designs, manufactures, rents, and sells equipment used to perform drilling operations; and Completion and Production Solutions, which designs, manufactures, and sells equipment for hydraulic fracture stimulation.

Recent Developments: For the quarter ended Mar 31 2016, net loss amounted to US$118.0 million versus net income of US$313.0 million in the year-earlier quarter. Revenues were US$2.19 billion, down 54.6% from US$4.82 billion the year before. Operating loss was US$189.0 million versus an income of US$570.0 million in the prior-year quarter. Direct operating expenses declined 46.6% to US$1.95 billion from US$3.64 billion in the comparable period the year before. Indirect operating expenses decreased 28.7% to US$433.0 million from US$607.0 million in the equivalent prior-year period.

Prospects: Our evaluation of National-Oilwell Inc. as of June 19, 2016 is the result of our systematic analysis on three basic characteristics: earnings strength, relative valuation, and recent stock price movement. The company has generated a negative trend in earnings per share over the past 5 quarters. Because the company lacks sufficient analyst estimate data, we place greater weight on the historical EPS trend as the measure of earnings strength. Based on operating earnings yield, the company is overvalued when compared to all of the companies in our coverage universe. Share price changes over the past year indicates that NOV will perform very poorly over the near term.

Financial Data

(US$ in Thousands)	3 Mos	12/31/2015	12/31/2014	12/31/2013	12/31/2012	12/31/2011	12/31/2010	12/31/2009
Earnings Per Share	(3.08)	(1.99)	5.82	5.44	5.83	4.70	3.98	3.52
Cash Flow Per Share	4.90	3.44	6.11	7.97	1.45	5.08	3.70	5.04
Tang Book Value Per Share	14.72	14.78	18.40	18.97	19.50	17.45	13.90	10.93
Dividends Per Share	1.840	1.840	1.640	0.910	0.490	0.450	0.410	1.100
Dividend Payout %	...	...	28.18	16.73	8.40	9.57	10.30	31.25
Income Statement								
Total Revenue	2,189,000	14,757,000	21,440,000	22,869,000	20,041,000	14,658,000	12,156,000	12,712,000
EBITDA	(35,000)	(122,000)	3,936,000	3,774,000	3,809,000	3,177,000	2,660,000	2,454,000
Depn & Amortn	175,000	391,000	413,000	392,000	323,000	279,000	262,000	249,000
Income Before Taxes	(230,000)	(602,000)	3,436,000	3,283,000	3,447,000	2,876,000	2,361,000	2,161,000
Income Taxes	(118,000)	178,000	1,039,000	1,018,000	1,022,000	937,000	738,000	735,000
Net Income	(119,000)	(769,000)	2,502,000	2,327,000	2,491,000	1,994,000	1,667,000	1,469,000
Average Shares	375,000	387,000	430,000	428,000	427,000	424,000	419,000	417,000
Balance Sheet								
Current Assets	10,048,000	11,801,000	16,162,000	16,423,000	15,678,000	12,110,000	10,535,000	9,598,000
Total Assets	24,754,000	26,725,000	33,562,000	34,812,000	31,484,000	25,515,000	23,050,000	21,532,000
Current Liabilities	3,435,000	4,249,000	7,374,000	6,678,000	5,649,000	5,416,000	4,536,000	4,174,000
Long-Term Obligations	3,372,000	3,928,000	3,014,000	3,149,000	3,148,000	159,000	514,000	876,000
Total Liabilities	8,399,000	10,342,000	12,870,000	12,582,000	11,245,000	7,896,000	7,302,000	7,419,000
Stockholders' Equity	16,355,000	16,383,000	20,692,000	22,230,000	20,239,000	17,619,000	15,748,000	14,113,000
Shares Outstanding	377,066	375,764	418,977	428,433	426,928	423,900	421,141	418,451
Statistical Record								
Return on Assets %	N.M.	N.M.	7.32	7.02	8.72	8.21	7.48	6.83
Return on Equity %	N.M.	N.M.	11.66	10.96	13.12	11.95	11.17	10.99
EBITDA Margin %	N.M.	N.M.	18.36	16.50	19.01	21.67	21.88	19.30
Net Margin %	N.M.	N.M.	11.67	10.18	12.43	13.60	13.71	11.56
Asset Turnover	0.42	0.49	0.63	0.69	0.70	0.60	0.55	0.59
Current Ratio	2.93	2.78	2.19	2.46	2.78	2.24	2.32	2.30
Debt to Equity	0.21	0.24	0.15	0.14	0.16	0.01	0.03	0.06
Price Range	56.00-26.34	65.53-33.27	86.43-61.55	75.97-57.80	78.57-54.07	75.08-45.27	60.61-29.76	44.90-20.14
P/E Ratio	...	...	14.85-10.58	13.97-10.63	13.48-9.27	15.97-9.63	15.23-7.48	12.76-5.72
Average Yield %	4.59	4.01	2.22	1.38	0.73	0.70	1.01	3.40

Address: 7909 Parkwood Circle Drive, Houston, TX 77036-6565 Telephone: 713-346-7500	Web Site: www.natoil.com Officers: Clay C. Williams - Chairman, President, Chief Executive Officer, Executive Vice President, Senior Vice President, Chief Financial Officer, Chief Operating Officer Craig L. Weinstock - Executive Vice President, Secretary, General Counsel	Auditors: Ernst & Young LLP Investor Contact: 713-346-7500 Transfer Agents: American Stock Transfer & Trust Company, New York, NY

NATIONAL RETAIL PROPERTIES INC

Exchange	Symbol	Price	52Wk Range	Yield	P/E	Div Achiever
NYS	NNN	$45.33 (5/31/2016)	47.65-33.99	3.84	34.87	26 Years

*7 Year Price Score 110.44 *NYSE Composite Index=100 *12 Month Price Score 112.43

TRADING VOLUME (thousand shares)

Interim Earnings (Per Share)

Qtr.	Mar	Jun	Sep	Dec
2013	0.25	0.27	0.29	0.29
2014	0.28	0.30	0.31	0.35
2015	0.34	0.28	0.34	0.24
2016	0.44	...	...	...

Interim Dividends (Per Share)

Amt	Decl	Ex	Rec	Pay
0.435Q	07/15/2015	07/29/2015	07/31/2015	08/14/2015
0.435Q	10/15/2015	10/28/2015	10/30/2015	11/16/2015
0.435Q	01/15/2016	01/27/2016	01/29/2016	02/16/2016
0.435Q	04/15/2016	04/27/2016	04/29/2016	05/16/2016

Indicated Div: $1.74 (Div. Reinv. Plan)

Valuation Analysis   **Institutional Holding**

Forecast EPS	$1.44
	(05/20/2016)
Market Cap	$6.5 Billion
Book Value	$3.4 Billion
Price/Book	1.89
Price/Sales	13.15

No of Institutions	
418	
Shares	
153,857,536	
% Held	
N/A	

Business Summary: REITs (MIC: 5.3.1 SIC: 6798 NAIC: 525930)

National Retail Properties is a real estate investment trust. Co. assets include: real estate assets, mortgages and notes receivable, and commercial mortgage residual interests. Co. acquires, owns, invests in and develops properties that are leased primarily to retail tenants under long-term net leases and are primarily held for investment. As of Dec 31 2015, Co. owned 2,257 properties in 47 states.

Recent Developments: For the quarter ended Mar 31 2016, income from continuing operations increased 14.9% to US$53.8 million from US$46.8 million in the year-earlier quarter. Net income increased 30.8% to US$70.7 million from US$54.0 million in the year-earlier quarter. Revenues were US$127.0 million, up 9.3% from US$116.2 million the year before. Revenues from property income rose 9.1% to US$126.1 million from US$115.6 million in the corresponding quarter a year earlier.

Prospects: Our evaluation of National Retail Properties Inc. as of June 19, 2016 is the result of our systematic analysis on three basic characteristics: earnings strength, relative valuation, and recent stock price movement. The company has managed to produce a neutral trend in earnings per share over the past 5 quarters. Because the company lacks sufficient analyst estimate data, we place greater weight on the historical EPS trend as the measure of earnings strength. Based on operating earnings yield, the company is overvalued when compared to all of the companies in our coverage universe. Share price changes over the past year indicates that NNN will perform very well over the near term.

Financial Data

(US$ in Thousands)	3 Mos	12/31/2015	12/31/2014	12/31/2013	12/31/2012	12/31/2011	12/31/2010	12/31/2009
Earnings Per Share	1.30	1.20	1.24	1.10	1.11	0.96	0.80	0.60
Cash Flow Per Share	2.46	2.55	2.39	2.32	2.13	2.08	2.27	1.87
Tang Book Value Per Share	19.96	19.62	18.99	18.05	18.01	18.24	17.17	17.86
Dividends Per Share	1.725	1.710	1.650	1.600	1.560	1.530	1.510	1.500
Dividend Payout %	132.69	142.50	133.06	145.45	140.54	159.38	188.75	250.00
Income Statement								
Total Revenue	126,980	482,914	434,847	392,327	331,752	265,793	229,056	231,799
EBITDA	79,106	428,442	386,076	345,552	280,699	229,444	190,193	175,015
Depn & Amortn	1,738	140,714	121,221	106,304	83,096	65,017	55,278	54,332
Income Before Taxes	53,801	197,829	179,702	155,458	117,333	91,093	71,249	59,907
Income Taxes	...	10,318	(75)	618	(7,086)	779	475	(1,126)
Net Income	70,683	197,836	190,601	160,145	142,015	92,325	72,997	54,810
Average Shares	141,326	134,489	124,710	119,864	109,117	88,837	82,849	79,953
Balance Sheet								
Current Assets	82,150	43,133	39,276	30,389	30,646	29,418	30,986	42,916
Total Assets	5,552,903	5,460,044	4,926,714	4,454,523	3,988,026	3,434,429	2,713,575	2,590,962
Current Liabilities	33,637	20,113	17,396	63,542	191,727	80,708	168,342	7,471
Long-Term Obligations	1,969,789	1,975,944	1,741,054	1,523,659	1,412,764	1,273,509	972,685	987,346
Total Liabilities	2,118,993	2,117,910	1,844,199	1,677,478	1,691,741	1,431,931	1,186,092	1,026,722
Stockholders' Equity	3,433,910	3,342,134	3,082,515	2,777,045	2,296,285	2,002,498	1,527,483	1,564,240
Shares Outstanding	143,235	141,007	132,010	121,991	111,554	104,754	83,613	82,427
Statistical Record								
Return on Assets %	4.06	3.81	4.06	3.79	3.82	3.00	2.75	2.09
Return on Equity %	6.54	6.16	6.51	6.31	6.59	5.23	4.72	3.53
EBITDA Margin %	62.30	88.72	88.78	88.08	84.61	86.32	83.03	75.50
Net Margin %	55.66	40.97	43.83	40.82	42.81	34.74	31.87	23.65
Asset Turnover	0.09	0.09	0.09	0.09	0.09	0.09	0.09	0.09
Current Ratio	2.44	2.14	2.26	0.48	0.16	0.36	0.18	5.74
Debt to Equity	0.57	0.59	0.56	0.55	0.62	0.64	0.64	0.63
Price Range	46.84-33.99	44.24-33.99	40.34-30.33	41.89-30.09	32.25-26.10	27.30-22.92	27.73-19.45	22.29-12.96
P/E Ratio	36.03-26.15	36.87-28.33	32.53-24.46	38.08-27.35	29.05-23.51	28.44-23.88	34.66-24.31	37.15-21.60
Average Yield %	4.43	4.44	4.62	4.68	5.42	5.98	6.38	8.28

Address: 450 South Orange Avenue, Suite 900, Orlando, FL 32801 **Telephone:** 407-265-7348 **Fax:** 407-423-2894	**Web Site:** www.nnnreit.com **Officers:** Craig Macnab - Chairman, Chief Executive Officer Julian E. Whitehurst - President, Chief Operating Officer	**Auditors:** Ernst & Young LLP **Investor Contact:** 407-650-1228 **Transfer Agents:** American Stock Transfer & Trust Company, Brooklyn, NY

NATIONSTAR MORTGAGE HOLDINGS INC

Exchange	Symbol	Price	52Wk Range	Yield	P/E
NYS	NSM	$12.76 (5/31/2016)	19.99-8.61	N/A	N/A

*7 Year Price Score N/A   *NYSE Composite Index=100   *12 Month Price Score 82.26

Interim Earnings (Per Share)

Qtr.	Mar	Jun	Sep	Dec
2013	0.70	1.37	0.91	(0.57)
2014	0.27	0.74	1.22	0.23
2015	(0.53)	0.69	(0.62)	0.76
2016	(1.28)	...	...	...

Interim Dividends (Per Share)

No Dividends Paid

Valuation Analysis   Institutional Holding

		No of Institutions
Forecast EPS	$-0.04	157
	(05/20/2016)	
Market Cap	$1.3 Billion	Shares
Book Value	$1.6 Billion	111,201,440
Price/Book	0.83	% Held
Price/Sales	0.70	104.61

Business Summary: Credit & Lending (MIC: 5.4.1 SIC: 6162 NAIC: 522310)

Nationstar Mortgage Holdings provides servicing, origination and transaction based services to single-family residences. Co. has three operating segments: Servicing, which involves loan administration, payment processing, mortgage escrow account administration, collection of insurance premiums, response to homeowner inquiries, and loss mitigation solutions; Originations, which originates conventional residential mortgage loans through both the Greenlight Financial Services and Nationstar brands; and Solutionstar, which provides data solutions to homebuyers, home sellers, real estate agents and companies engaged in the origination and/or servicing of mortgage loans.

Recent Developments: For the quarter ended Mar 31 2016, net loss amounted to US$133.3 million versus a net loss of US$46.8 million in the year-earlier quarter. Non-interest income fell 31.0% to US$263.8 million from US$382.1 million, while non-interest expense advanced 9.8% to US$421.5 million.

Prospects: Our evaluation of Nationstar Mortgage Holdings as of June 19, 2016 is the result of our systematic analysis on three basic characteristics: earnings strength, relative valuation, and recent stock price movement. The company has enjoyed a very positive trend in earnings per share over the past 5 quarters. However, while recent estimates for the company have been lowered by analysts, NSM has posted results that fell short of analysts expectations. Based on operating earnings yield, the company is undervalued when compared to all of the companies in our coverage universe. Share price changes over the past year indicates that NSM will perform poorly over the near term.

Financial Data
(US$ in Thousands)

	3 Mos	12/31/2015	12/31/2014	12/31/2013	12/31/2012	12/31/2011	12/31/2010	12/31/2009
Earnings Per Share	(0.45)	0.37	2.45	2.40	2.40	...	...	...
Cash Flow Per Share	7.24	4.05	11.83	(20.51)	(22.89)	...	...	...
Tang Book Value Per Share	N.M.	N.M.	N.M.	N.M.	1.23	...	...	...
Income Statement								
Total Revenue	263,769	1,988,635	1,973,068	2,086,985	984,315	377,734	261,428	78,869
EBITDA	138,633	354,743	909,712	707,884	411,756	71,812	23,676	(41,852)
Depn & Amortn	296,256	46,100	287,033	20,045	(5,120)	12,352	16,322	21,660
Income Before Taxes	(215,556)	54,175	285,884	346,254	291,154	20,887	(9,914)	(80,877)
Income Taxes	(82,265)	11,012	64,860	129,200	71,296	...	...	...
Net Income	(132,389)	38,779	220,718	217,054	205,287	20,887	(9,914)	(80,877)
Average Shares	103,098	103,780	90,020	90,268	85,524	...	...	...
Balance Sheet								
Current Assets	932,932	945,346	584,532	6,671,131	3,589,445	696,244	553,623	...
Total Assets	16,551,524	16,654,070	11,112,675	14,026,689	7,126,143	1,787,931	1,947,181	...
Current Liabilities	1,139,400	4,836,036	4,796,483	1,308,450	631,431	183,789	75,054	...
Long-Term Obligations	12,548,706	8,719,292	3,927,542	11,637,294	5,633,766	1,310,463	1,589,173	...
Total Liabilities	14,978,366	14,895,956	9,893,693	13,041,781	6,368,461	1,506,622	1,690,809	...
Stockholders' Equity	1,573,158	1,758,114	1,218,982	984,908	757,682	281,309	256,372	...
Shares Outstanding	102,873	108,837	90,397	90,162	90,460	...	...	...
Statistical Record								
Return on Assets %	N.M.	0.28	1.76	2.05	4.59	1.12	...	...
Return on Equity %	N.M.	2.61	20.03	24.91	39.41	7.77	...	...
EBITDA Margin %	52.56	17.84	46.11	33.92	41.83	19.01	9.06	N.M.
Net Margin %	N.M.	1.95	11.19	10.40	20.86	5.53	N.M.	N.M.
Asset Turnover	0.13	0.14	0.16	0.20	0.22	0.20	...	...
Current Ratio	0.82	0.20	0.12	5.10	5.68	3.79	7.38	...
Debt to Equity	7.98	4.96	3.22	11.82	7.44	4.66	6.20	...
Price Range	26.21-8.61	31.55-11.22	37.70-26.26	57.45-30.98	36.13-13.58	...	...	...
P/E Ratio	...	85.27-30.32	15.39-10.72	23.94-12.91	15.05-5.66	...	...	...

Address: 8950 Cypress Waters Blvd, Coppell, TX 75019 Telephone: 469-549-2000	Web Site: www.nationstarholdings.com Officers: Wesley R. Edens - Chairman Jesse K. Bray - President, President (frmr), Chief Executive Officer, Chief Financial Officer	Auditors: Ernst & Young LLP Transfer Agents: American Stock Transfer & Trust Company, LLC, Brooklyn, NY

NAVISTAR INTERNATIONAL CORP.

Exchange	Symbol	Price	52Wk Range	Yield	P/E
NYS	NAV	$11.25 (5/31/2016)	27.08-6.23	N/A	N/A

*7 Year Price Score 34.00 *NYSE Composite Index=100 *12 Month Price Score 92.33

Interim Earnings (Per Share)

Qtr.	Jan	Apr	Jul	Oct
2012-13	(1.53)	(4.65)	(3.06)	(1.92)
2013-14	(3.05)	(3.65)	(0.02)	(0.87)
2014-15	(0.52)	(0.78)	(0.34)	(0.61)
2015-16	(0.40)	0.05	...	...

Interim Dividends (Per Share)

No Dividends Paid

Valuation Analysis		Institutional Holding	
Forecast EPS	$-0.05	No of Institutions	
	(05/20/2016)	233	
Market Cap	$918.1 Million	Shares	
Book Value	N/A	95,218,992	
Price/Book	N/A	% Held	
Price/Sales	0.10	98.10	

Business Summary: Autos- Manufacturing (MIC: 1.8.1 SIC: 3711 NAIC: 336211)

Navistar International is a holding company. Through its subsidiaries, Co. is an international manufacturer of International® brand commercial and military trucks, proprietary diesel engines, IC Bus™ brand school and commercial buses, as well as a provider of service parts for trucks and diesel engines. Co. also provides retail, wholesale, and lease financing services for its trucks and parts. Co. operates in four industry segments: Truck, Parts, Global Operations, and Financial Services, which consists of its Navistar Financial Corporation subsidiary and its foreign finance operations (collectively referred to as financial services operations).

Recent Developments: For the quarter ended Apr 30 2016, income from continuing operations was US$13.0 million compared with a loss of US$57.0 million in the year-earlier quarter. Net income amounted to US$13.0 million versus a net loss of US$57.0 million in the year-earlier quarter. Revenues were US$2.20 billion, down 18.4% from US$2.69 billion the year before. Direct operating expenses declined 21.8% to US$1.85 billion from US$2.36 billion in the comparable period the year before. Indirect operating expenses decreased 12.9% to US$325.0 million from US$373.0 million in the equivalent prior-year period.

Prospects: Our evaluation of Navistar International Corp. as of June 19, 2016 is the result of our systematic analysis on three basic characteristics: earnings strength, relative valuation, and recent stock price movement. The company has managed to produce a neutral trend in earnings per share over the past 5 quarters. However, while recent estimates for the company have been lowered by analysts, NAV has posted better than expected results. Based on operating earnings yield, the company is undervalued when compared to all of the companies in our coverage universe. Share price changes over the past year indicates that NAV will perform very poorly over the near term.

Financial Data
(US$ in Millions)

	6 Mos	3 Mos	10/31/2015	10/31/2014	10/31/2013	10/31/2012	10/31/2011	10/31/2010
Earnings Per Share	(1.30)	(2.13)	(2.25)	(7.60)	(11.17)	(43.56)	22.64	3.05
Cash Flow Per Share	2.19	1.90	0.56	(4.13)	1.24	8.80	12.09	15.44
Income Statement								
Total Revenue	3,962	1,765	10,140	10,806	10,775	12,948	13,958	12,145
EBITDA	215	81	274	63	(269)	(596)	937	882
Depn & Amortn	54	28	76	314	395	298	299	289
Income Before Taxes	(1)	(28)	(109)	(565)	(985)	(1,153)	391	340
Income Taxes	11	(5)	51	26	(171)	1,780	(1,458)	23
Net Income	(29)	(33)	(184)	(619)	(898)	(3,010)	1,723	223
Average Shares	82	81	81	81	80	69	76	73
Balance Sheet								
Current Assets	4,130	3,939	4,622	5,013	5,459	5,837	7,235	5,835
Total Assets	6,188	5,980	6,692	7,443	8,315	9,102	12,291	9,730
Current Liabilities	3,620	3,800	3,788	4,231	4,261	4,353	4,798	3,589
Long-Term Obligations	3,974	3,607	4,188	3,929	3,922	3,566	3,477	4,238
Total Liabilities	11,316	11,177	11,859	12,095	11,960	12,407	12,313	10,703
Stockholders' Equity	(5,128)	(5,197)	(5,167)	(4,652)	(3,645)	(3,305)	(22)	(973)
Shares Outstanding	81	81	81	81	80	79	70	71
Statistical Record								
Return on Assets %	N.M.	N.M.	N.M.	N.M.	N.M.	N.M.	15.65	2.26
EBITDA Margin %	5.43	4.59	2.70	0.58	N.M.	N.M.	6.71	7.26
Net Margin %	N.M.	N.M.	N.M.	N.M.	N.M.	N.M.	12.34	1.84
Asset Turnover	1.37	1.49	1.43	1.37	1.24	1.21	1.27	1.23
Current Ratio	1.14	1.04	1.22	1.18	1.28	1.34	1.51	1.63
Price Range	29.96-6.23	30.88-6.23	37.76-11.36	40.90-29.49	39.71-18.75	47.20-18.51	70.17-30.68	56.89-32.18
P/E Ratio	...	...	...	...	...	...	3.10-1.36	18.65-10.55

Address: 2701 Navistar Drive, Lisle, IL 60532	**Web Site:** www.navistar.com	**Auditors:** KPMG LLP
Telephone: 331-332-5000	**Officers:** Troy A. Clarke - President, Chief Executive Officer, Chief Operating Officer, Division Officer Persio V. Lisboa - President	**Investor Contact:** 331-332-2143
		Transfer Agents: Computershare Investor Services, Jersey City, NJ

NCR CORP.

Exchange	Symbol	Price	52Wk Range	Yield	P/E
NYS	NCR	$30.88 (5/31/2016)	34.73-19.08	N/A	N/A

*7 Year Price Score 97.21 ***NYSE Composite Index=100** ***12 Month Price Score 110.44**

TRADING VOLUME (thousand shares)

Interim Earnings (Per Share)

Qtr.	Mar	Jun	Sep	Dec
2013	0.36	0.51	0.58	1.17
2014	0.31	0.53	0.09	0.20
2015	0.23	(2.03)	0.57	0.13
2016	0.16	...	...	...

Interim Dividends (Per Share)

No Dividends Paid

Valuation Analysis   Institutional Holding

Forecast EPS	$2.94	No of Institutions
(05/20/2016)		487
Market Cap	$4.1 Billion	Shares
Book Value	$1.3 Billion	127,118,440
Price/Book	3.07	% Held
Price/Sales	0.65	90.38

Business Summary: Computer Hardware & Equipment (MIC: 6.2.1 SIC: 3578 NAIC: 334119)

NCR is a technology company that provides products and services that enable businesses to connect, interact and transact with their customers. Co.'s offerings include software and hardware solutions for automated teller machines and bank branches, retail and hospitality point of sale applications and devices, and self-service kiosks and software applications that can be used by consumers to enable them to interact with businesses from their computer or mobile device. In addition, Co. resells third party networking products and related service offerings to a customers in the telecommunications and technology sectors and servicing third party computer hardware from select manufacturers.

Recent Developments: For the quarter ended Mar 31 2016, income from continuing operations decreased 23.8% to US$32.0 million from US$42.0 million in the year-earlier quarter. Net income decreased 23.8% to US$32.0 million from US$42.0 million in the year-earlier quarter. Revenues were US$1.44 billion, down 2.2% from US$1.48 billion the year before. Operating income was US$101.0 million versus US$95.0 million in the prior-year quarter, an increase of 6.3%. Direct operating expenses declined 2.0% to US$1.06 billion from US$1.09 billion in the comparable period the year before. Indirect operating expenses decreased 5.4% to US$279.0 million from US$295.0 million in the equivalent prior-year period.

Prospects: Our evaluation of NCR Corp. as of June 19, 2016 is the result of our systematic analysis on three basic characteristics: earnings strength, relative valuation, and recent stock price movement. The company has generated a negative trend in earnings per share over the past 5 quarters and while recent estimates for the company have remained steady, NCR has posted better than expected results. Based on operating earnings yield, the company is undervalued when compared to all of the companies in our coverage universe. Share price changes over the past year indicates that NCR will perform poorly over the near term.

Financial Data

(US$ in Thousands)	3 Mos	12/31/2015	12/31/2014	12/31/2013	12/31/2012	12/31/2011	12/31/2010	12/31/2009
Earnings Per Share	(1.17)	(1.09)	1.12	2.62	0.89	0.33	0.83	(0.21)
Cash Flow Per Share	4.79	4.06	3.12	1.70	(1.13)	2.37	1.51	1.40
Tang Book Value Per Share	N.M.	N.M.	N.M.	N.M.	N.M.	N.M.	4.81	2.91
Income Statement								
Total Revenue	1,444,000	6,373,000	6,591,000	6,123,000	5,730,000	5,443,000	4,819,000	4,612,000
EBITDA	180,000	164,000	395,000	719,000	282,000	153,000	160,000	(15,000)
Depn & Amortn	89,000	91,000	83,000	68,000	64,000	96,000	77,000	68,000
Income Before Taxes	45,000	(95,000)	137,000	554,000	182,000	49,000	86,000	(87,000)
Income Taxes	13,000	55,000	(48,000)	98,000	42,000	...	(28,000)	(57,000)
Net Income	32,000	(178,000)	191,000	443,000	146,000	53,000	134,000	(33,000)
Average Shares	132,700	167,600	171,200	169,300	163,800	161,000	161,200	158,900
Balance Sheet								
Current Assets	2,705,000	2,549,000	3,088,000	4,339,000	3,406,000	2,515,000	2,478,000	2,299,000
Total Assets	7,752,000	7,635,000	8,607,000	8,108,000	6,371,000	5,591,000	4,361,000	4,094,000
Current Liabilities	1,984,000	1,781,000	2,070,000	1,881,000	1,742,000	1,565,000	1,416,000	1,382,000
Long-Term Obligations	3,269,000	3,239,000	3,472,000	3,320,000	1,891,000	852,000	10,000	11,000
Total Liabilities	6,413,000	6,117,000	6,736,000	6,339,000	5,124,000	4,792,000	3,478,000	3,530,000
Stockholders' Equity	1,339,000	1,518,000	1,871,000	1,769,000	1,247,000	799,000	883,000	564,000
Shares Outstanding	133,000	133,000	168,600	166,600	162,800	157,600	159,700	159,600
Statistical Record								
Return on Assets %	N.M.	N.M.	2.29	6.12	2.43	1.07	3.17	N.M.
Return on Equity %	N.M.	N.M.	10.49	29.38	14.23	6.30	18.52	N.M.
EBITDA Margin %	12.47	2.57	5.99	11.74	4.92	2.81	3.32	N.M.
Net Margin %	2.22	N.M.	2.90	7.24	2.55	0.97	2.78	N.M.
Asset Turnover	0.78	0.78	0.79	0.85	0.96	1.09	1.14	1.10
Current Ratio	1.36	1.43	1.49	2.31	1.96	1.61	1.75	1.66
Debt to Equity	2.44	2.13	1.86	1.88	1.52	1.07	0.01	0.02
Price Range	34.73-19.08	34.73-22.39	37.50-23.54	41.56-25.48	25.64-16.48	20.83-15.31	15.93-11.13	15.06-6.67
P/E Ratio	...	...	33.48-21.02	15.86-9.73	28.81-18.52	63.12-46.39	19.19-13.41	...

Address: 3097 Satellite Boulevard, Duluth, GA 30096 **Telephone:** 937-445-5000	**Web Site:** www.ncr.com **Officers:** William R. Nuti - Chairman, President, Chief Executive Officer Frederick (Rick) J. Marquardt - Executive Vice President	**Auditors:** PricewaterhouseCoopers LLP **Investor Contact:** 212-589-8569 **Transfer Agents:** Wells Fargo Shareowner Services, St. Paul, MN

504

NETSUITE INC

Exchange	Symbol	Price	52Wk Range	Yield	P/E
NYS	N	$79.31 (5/31/2016)	99.73-53.11	N/A	N/A

*7 Year Price Score 116.78 *NYSE Composite Index=100 *12 Month Price Score 93.05

Interim Earnings (Per Share)

Qtr.	Mar	Jun	Sep	Dec
2013	(0.18)	(0.28)	(0.23)	(0.27)
2014	(0.29)	(0.31)	(0.38)	(0.33)
2015	(0.29)	(0.41)	(0.47)	(0.41)
2016	(0.37)	...	...	...

Interim Dividends (Per Share)

No Dividends Paid

Valuation Analysis

		Institutional Holding	
Forecast EPS	$0.46	No of Institutions	
	(05/20/2016)	253	
Market Cap	$6.4 Billion	Shares	
Book Value	$308.7 Million	47,853,568	
Price/Book	20.66	% Held	
Price/Sales	8.04	50.66	

Business Summary: Internet & Software (MIC: 6.3.2 SIC: 7372 NAIC: 511210)

NetSuite is a provider of cloud-based financials/enterprise resource planning and omnichannel commerce software suites. Co.'s main offering is NetSuite, which is designed to provide the primary business management capabilities. NetSuite, OneWorld and NetSuite CRM+ are designed for use by the majority types of businesses. NetSuite OpenAir is designed for use by services businesses. In addition, Co. provides industry-specific configurations for use by wholesale/distribution, manufacturing and software companies. Co. also sells additional cloud-based application modules. Also, Co. provides customer support and other services related to implementing and supporting its suite of applications.

Recent Developments: For the quarter ended Mar 31 2016, net loss amounted to US$29.7 million versus a net loss of US$22.7 million in the year-earlier quarter. Revenues were US$216.6 million, up 31.4% from US$164.8 million the year before. Operating loss was US$25.1 million versus a loss of US$19.0 million in the prior-year quarter. Direct operating expenses rose 37.2% to US$71.9 million from US$52.4 million in the comparable period the year before. Indirect operating expenses increased 29.2% to US$169.8 million from US$131.4 million in the equivalent prior-year period.

Prospects: Our evaluation of Netsuite Inc. as of June 19, 2016 is the result of our systematic analysis on three basic characteristics: earnings strength, relative valuation, and recent stock price movement. The company has enjoyed a very positive trend in earnings per share over the past 5 quarters and while recent estimates for the company have been mixed, N has posted better than expected results. Based on operating earnings yield, the company is overvalued when compared to all of the companies in our coverage universe. Share price changes over the past year indicates that N will perform poorly over the near term.

Financial Data
(US$ in Thousands)

	3 Mos	12/31/2015	12/31/2014	12/31/2013	12/31/2012	12/31/2011	12/31/2010	12/31/2009
Earnings Per Share	(1.66)	(1.59)	(1.31)	(0.95)	(0.50)	(0.48)	(0.43)	(0.38)
Cash Flow Per Share	1.30	1.28	0.98	0.84	0.77	0.54	0.29	0.08
Tang Book Value Per Share	N.M.	N.M.	1.02	1.40	1.52	1.28	1.02	0.95
Income Statement								
Total Revenue	216,578	741,149	556,284	414,508	308,825	236,326	193,149	166,540
EBITDA	12,113	(67,884)	(53,689)	(38,704)	(17,072)	(17,236)	(13,859)	(13,120)
Depn & Amortn	37,066	48,262	30,093	22,449	15,580	12,986	12,321	10,727
Income Before Taxes	(28,552)	(130,362)	(97,871)	(69,510)	(32,686)	(30,236)	(26,100)	(23,472)
Income Taxes	1,193	(5,619)	2,166	899	2,543	1,771	1,380	640
Net Income	(29,745)	(124,743)	(100,037)	(70,409)	(35,229)	(32,007)	(27,466)	(23,304)
Average Shares	80,086	78,521	76,174	74,085	70,713	66,919	63,772	61,941
Balance Sheet								
Current Assets	670,461	655,100	673,001	599,204	286,728	212,214	154,124	138,779
Total Assets	1,155,463	1,140,976	922,239	772,399	369,775	281,180	217,293	202,224
Current Liabilities	532,635	519,050	392,773	279,564	198,255	141,567	100,107	88,939
Long-Term Obligations	278,031	277,955	265,710	254,038	...	...	...	...
Total Liabilities	846,726	834,775	688,005	562,347	211,006	153,170	111,009	97,391
Stockholders' Equity	308,737	306,201	234,234	210,052	158,769	128,010	106,284	104,833
Shares Outstanding	80,405	79,802	77,031	75,131	72,675	68,785	64,887	62,880
Statistical Record								
EBITDA Margin %	5.59	N.M.	N.M.	N.M.	N.M.	N.M.	N.M.	N.M.
Asset Turnover	0.76	0.72	0.66	0.73	0.95	0.95	0.92	0.81
Current Ratio	1.26	1.26	1.71	2.14	1.45	1.50	1.54	1.56
Debt to Equity	0.90	0.91	1.13	1.21	...	...	...	...
Price Range	99.73-53.11	109.17-79.28	119.63-71.42	111.56-65.94	67.30-38.51	47.30-25.00	26.70-12.13	17.00-6.74

Address: 2955 Campus Drive, Suite 100, San Mateo, CA 94403-2511
Telephone: 650-627-1000

Web Site: www.netsuite.com
Officers: Evan Goldberg - Chairman, Chief Technology Officer Michael Forman - Senior Vice President, Global Controller

Auditors: KPMG LLP
Investor Contact: 415-445-3232
Transfer Agents: Wells Fargo Shareowner Services, Mendota Heights, MN

NEUSTAR, INC.

Exchange	Symbol	Price	52Wk Range	Yield	P/E
NYS	NSR	$23.55 (5/31/2016)	31.91-20.43	N/A	8.12

*7 Year Price Score 72.07   *NYSE Composite Index=100   *12 Month Price Score 90.26

Interim Earnings (Per Share)

Qtr.	Mar	Jun	Sep	Dec
2013	0.50	0.65	0.73	0.59
2014	0.50	0.61	0.84	0.81
2015	0.81	0.80	0.91	0.62
2016	0.57	...	...	...

Interim Dividends (Per Share)

No Dividends Paid

Valuation Analysis

		Institutional Holding	
Forecast EPS	$5.15	No of Institutions	
	(05/20/2016)	359	
Market Cap	$1.3 Billion	Shares	
Book Value	$752.6 Million	76,061,336	
Price/Book	1.70	% Held	
Price/Sales	1.18	101.01	

Business Summary: Services (MIC: 6.1.2 SIC: 4899 NAIC: 517910)

NeuStar is a provider of data sets and proprietary analytics. Co.'s primary services as follows: marketing services, which provide customer intelligence, activation services, and media intelligence; security services, which provide domain name systems services, distributed denial of service protection, and domain name registries; data services, which provide carrier provisioning, caller authentication, common short codes, and user authentication and rights management; as well as number portability administration center services, which include the routing of calls and text messages among all communications service providers in the U.S. and related connection services and system enhancements.

Recent Developments: For the quarter ended Mar 31 2016, net income decreased 32.1% to US$31.4 million from US$46.2 million in the year-earlier quarter. Revenues were US$287.3 million, up 14.3% from US$251.4 million the year before. Operating income was US$64.4 million versus US$79.5 million in the prior-year quarter, a decrease of 18.9%. Direct operating expenses rose 42.4% to US$91.4 million from US$64.2 million in the comparable period the year before. Indirect operating expenses increased 22.1% to US$131.5 million from US$107.8 million in the equivalent prior-year period.

Prospects: Our evaluation of Neustar Inc. as of June 19, 2016 is the result of our systematic analysis on three basic characteristics: earnings strength, relative valuation, and recent stock price movement. The company has managed to produce a neutral trend in earnings per share over the past 5 quarters and while recent estimates for the company have remained steady, NSR has posted results that fell short of analysts expectations. Based on operating earnings yield, the company is undervalued when compared to all of the companies in our coverage universe. Share price changes over the past year indicates that NSR will perform poorly over the near term.

Financial Data

(US$ in Thousands)	3 Mos	12/31/2015	12/31/2014	12/31/2013	12/31/2012	12/31/2011	12/31/2010	12/31/2009
Earnings Per Share	2.90	3.14	2.75	2.46	2.30	2.16	1.40	1.34
Cash Flow Per Share	6.04	6.50	5.55	4.47	4.54	3.10	1.94	2.36
Tang Book Value Per Share	N.M.	N.M.	N.M.	N.M.	N.M.	N.M.	6.15	5.07
Income Statement								
Total Revenue	287,298	1,049,958	963,588	902,041	831,388	620,455	526,812	480,385
EBITDA	68,411	337,287	312,610	328,523	319,404	242,377	209,904	200,561
Depn & Amortn	4,545	56,100	52,700	49,700	42,700	34,100	34,900	30,200
Income Before Taxes	47,474	253,530	235,543	255,124	243,100	204,711	174,935	169,006
Income Taxes	16,099	78,068	71,849	92,372	87,013	81,137	68,726	67,865
Net Income	31,375	175,462	163,694	162,752	156,087	160,823	106,209	101,141
Average Shares	54,940	55,904	59,535	66,108	67,956	74,496	76,065	75,465
Balance Sheet								
Current Assets	322,553	319,540	554,970	436,139	525,756	339,395	460,725	434,768
Total Assets	2,182,295	2,202,247	1,739,108	1,507,081	1,526,724	1,382,638	733,874	647,804
Current Liabilities	362,573	400,968	211,917	171,301	157,430	145,398	115,504	118,505
Long-Term Obligations	934,730	959,340	780,897	610,711	577,505	586,727	4,076	10,766
Total Liabilities	1,429,690	1,478,748	1,120,202	917,507	880,116	880,004	137,762	143,367
Stockholders' Equity	752,605	723,499	618,906	589,574	646,608	502,634	596,112	504,437
Shares Outstanding	54,375	53,518	55,083	61,403	66,174	66,154	73,632	74,460
Statistical Record								
Return on Assets %	8.16	8.90	10.09	10.73	10.70	15.20	15.37	17.33
Return on Equity %	23.11	26.14	27.09	26.33	27.09	29.27	19.30	22.70
EBITDA Margin %	23.81	32.12	32.44	36.42	38.42	39.06	39.84	41.75
Net Margin %	10.92	16.71	16.99	18.04	18.77	25.92	20.16	21.05
Asset Turnover	0.55	0.53	0.59	0.59	0.57	0.59	0.76	0.82
Current Ratio	0.89	0.80	2.62	2.55	3.34	2.33	3.99	3.67
Debt to Equity	1.24	1.33	1.26	1.04	0.89	1.17	0.01	0.02
Price Range	31.91-20.43	31.91-21.66	49.86-24.14	56.51-41.93	43.20-30.40	34.38-22.55	27.00-20.40	24.19-13.75
P/E Ratio	11.00-7.04	10.16-6.90	18.13-8.78	22.97-17.04	18.78-13.22	15.92-10.44	19.29-14.57	18.05-10.26

Address: 21575 Ridgetop Circle, Sterling, VA 20166 **Telephone:** 571-434-5400	**Web Site:** www.neustar.biz **Officers:** Lisa A. Hook - President, Chief Executive Officer Paul S. Lalljie - Senior Vice President, Chief Financial Officer, Treasurer	**Auditors:** Ernst & Young LLP **Investor Contact:** 571-434-3443 **Transfer Agents:** American Stock Transfer & Trust Company, Brooklyn, NY

NEW JERSEY RESOURCES CORP

Exchange	Symbol	Price	52Wk Range	Yield	P/E	Div Achiever
NYS	NJR	$35.15 (5/31/2016)	36.94-27.30	2.73	25.85	20 Years

*7 Year Price Score 114.15 *NYSE Composite Index=100 *12 Month Price Score 110.45

Interim Earnings (Per Share)

Qtr.	Dec	Mar	Jun	Sep
2012-13	0.72	0.54	0.35	(0.23)
2013-14	0.09	2.04	(0.17)	(0.29)
2014-15	1.44	0.71	(0.09)	0.05
2015-16	0.56	0.84	...	...

Interim Dividends (Per Share)

Amt	Decl	Ex	Rec	Pay
0.24Q	07/14/2015	09/11/2015	09/15/2015	10/01/2015
0.24Q	11/11/2015	12/11/2015	12/15/2015	01/04/2016
0.24Q	01/19/2016	03/11/2016	03/15/2016	04/01/2016
0.24Q	05/11/2016	06/13/2016	06/15/2016	07/01/2016

Indicated Div: $0.96 (Div. Reinv. Plan)

Valuation Analysis — **Institutional Holding**

Forecast EPS	$1.60
	(05/20/2016)
Market Cap	$3.0 Billion
Book Value	$1.2 Billion
Price/Book	2.50
Price/Sales	1.58

No of Institutions 344
Shares 56,360,196
% Held 60.16

TRADING VOLUME (thousand shares)

Business Summary: Gas Utilities (MIC: 3.3.1 SIC: 4924 NAIC: 221210)

New Jersey Resources is a holding company that provides regulated gas distribution services and operates certain non-regulated businesses mainly via its subsidiaries: New Jersey Natural Gas Company, which provides natural gas utility service to retail customers in central and northern New Jersey; NJR Energy Services Company, which maintains and transacts around a portfolio of natural gas storage and transportation capacity contracts and provides wholesale energy and energy management services; NJR Clean Energy Ventures Corporation, which is Co.'s distributed power subsidiary; and NJR Midstream Holdings Corporation, which invests in energy-related ventures through its subsidiaries.

Recent Developments: For the quarter ended Mar 31 2016, net income increased 20.4% to US$73.3 million from US$60.9 million in the year-earlier quarter. Revenues were US$574.2 million, down 43.3% from US$1.01 billion the year before. Operating income was US$93.9 million versus US$82.8 million in the prior-year quarter, an increase of 13.4%. Direct operating expenses declined 49.8% to US$446.7 million from US$890.4 million in the comparable period the year before. Indirect operating expenses decreased 15.7% to US$33.6 million from US$39.8 million in the equivalent prior-year period.

Prospects: Our evaluation of New Jersey Resources Corp. as of June 19, 2016 is the result of our systematic analysis on three basic characteristics: earnings strength, relative valuation, and recent stock price movement. The company has suffered a very negative trend in earnings per share over the past 5 quarters and while recent estimates for the company have remained steady, NJR has posted better than expected results. Based on operating earnings yield, the company is about fairly valued when compared to all of the companies in our coverage universe. Share price changes over the past year indicates that NJR will perform very well over the near term.

Financial Data

(US$ in Thousands)	6 Mos	3 Mos	09/30/2015	09/30/2014	09/30/2013	09/30/2012	09/30/2011	09/30/2010
Earnings Per Share	1.36	1.23	2.10	1.67	1.38	1.12	1.22	1.41
Cash Flow Per Share	2.05	3.59	4.55	4.24	1.37	0.61	3.02	1.69
Tang Book Value Per Share	14.05	13.33	12.94	11.45	10.57	9.78	9.37	8.81
Dividends Per Share	0.945	0.930	0.915	0.855	0.810	0.770	0.720	0.680
Dividend Payout %	69.49	75.61	43.57	51.20	58.91	69.06	59.02	48.23
Income Statement								
Total Revenue	1,018,451	444,258	2,733,987	3,738,145	3,198,068	2,248,923	3,009,209	2,639,304
EBITDA	191,736	77,857	316,395	261,483	211,324	152,461	181,948	226,575
Depn & Amortn	34,226	16,482	61,399	52,742	47,310	41,643	35,200	33,192
Income Before Taxes	143,364	54,598	227,275	183,278	140,035	89,974	127,125	172,132
Income Taxes	26,197	8,357	59,724	51,840	35,575	7,729	37,665	64,692
Net Income	121,975	48,647	180,960	141,970	114,809	92,879	101,299	117,457
Average Shares	86,858	86,676	86,265	84,922	83,628	83,264	83,136	83,260
Balance Sheet								
Current Assets	459,861	588,939	544,511	682,731	745,898	647,344	732,367	785,008
Total Assets	3,419,594	3,477,238	3,339,038	3,158,804	3,004,783	2,770,005	2,649,444	2,563,133
Current Liabilities	477,867	574,982	436,100	791,086	851,833	653,139	703,384	705,798
Long-Term Obligations	844,391	848,206	843,595	598,209	512,886	525,169	426,797	428,925
Total Liabilities	2,212,112	2,333,294	2,232,082	2,192,638	2,117,399	1,956,140	1,873,187	1,837,650
Stockholders' Equity	1,207,482	1,143,944	1,106,956	966,166	887,384	813,865	776,257	725,483
Shares Outstanding	85,968	85,809	85,531	84,356	83,923	83,239	82,843	82,347
Statistical Record								
Return on Assets %	3.52	3.07	5.57	4.61	3.98	3.42	3.89	4.81
Return on Equity %	10.07	9.46	17.46	15.32	13.50	11.65	13.49	16.60
EBITDA Margin %	18.83	17.53	11.57	6.99	6.61	6.78	6.05	8.58
Net Margin %	11.98	10.95	6.62	3.80	3.59	4.13	3.37	4.45
Asset Turnover	0.57	0.68	0.84	1.21	1.11	0.83	1.15	1.08
Current Ratio	0.96	1.02	1.25	0.86	0.88	0.99	1.04	1.11
Debt to Equity	0.70	0.74	0.76	0.62	0.58	0.65	0.55	0.59
Price Range	36.81-27.30	33.70-27.30	33.48-24.81	28.66-21.30	23.60-19.50	25.00-20.39	23.57-19.59	19.61-17.02
P/E Ratio	27.07-20.07	27.40-22.20	15.94-11.81	17.16-12.75	17.10-14.13	22.33-18.20	19.32-16.05	13.91-12.07
Average Yield %	3.06	3.09	3.10	3.50	3.72	3.38	3.34	3.70

Address: 1415 Wyckoff Road, Wall, NJ 07719	**Web Site:** www.njresources.com	**Auditors:** Deloitte & Touche LLP
Telephone: 732-938-1480	**Officers:** Laurence M. Downes - Chairman, President, Chief Executive Officer Amanda Mullan - Vice President, Chief Human Resources Officer	**Investor Contact:** 732-378-4967
		Transfer Agents: Wells Fargo Shareowner Services, St. Paul, MN

NEW YORK COMMUNITY BANCORP INC.

Exchange	Symbol	Price	52Wk Range	Yield	P/E
NYS	NYCB	$15.74 (5/31/2016)	19.16-14.44	4.32	N/A

*7 Year Price Score 94.45 ***NYSE Composite Index=100** ***12 Month Price Score 90.84**

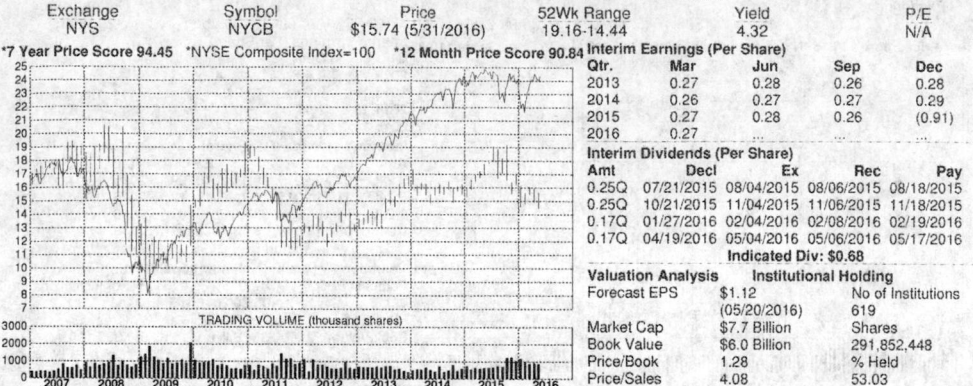

Interim Earnings (Per Share)

Qtr.	Mar	Jun	Sep	Dec
2013	0.27	0.28	0.26	0.28
2014	0.26	0.27	0.27	0.29
2015	0.27	0.28	0.26	(0.91)
2016	0.27			

Interim Dividends (Per Share)

Amt	Decl	Ex	Rec	Pay
0.25Q	07/21/2015	08/04/2015	08/06/2015	08/18/2015
0.25Q	10/21/2015	11/04/2015	11/06/2015	11/18/2015
0.17Q	01/27/2016	02/04/2016	02/08/2016	02/19/2016
0.17Q	04/19/2016	05/04/2016	05/06/2016	05/17/2016

Indicated Div:$0.68

Valuation Analysis | **Institutional Holding**

Forecast EPS	$1.12	No of Institutions
	(05/20/2016)	619
Market Cap	$7.7 Billion	Shares
Book Value	$6.0 Billion	291,852,448
Price/Book	1.28	% Held
Price/Sales	4.08	53.03

TRADING VOLUME (thousand shares)

Business Summary: Credit & Lending (MIC: 5.4.1 SIC: 6036 NAIC: 522120)

New York Community Bancorp is a bank holding company. Co. has two primary subsidiaries: New York Community Bank (Community Bank) and New York Commercial Bank (Commercial Bank). The Community Bank is a producer of multi-family loans, and provides commercial real estate loans, acquisition, development, and construction loans, and commercial and industrial loans. Co. also originates one-to-four family loans originated through its mortgage banking operation. The Commercial Bank provides installment loans, revolving lines of credit, and cash management services, and 24-hour banking online and by phone. At Dec 31 2015, Co. had total assets of $450.32 billion and total deposits of $28.43 billion.

Recent Developments: For the quarter ended Mar 31 2016, net income increased 8.9% to US$129.9 million from US$119.3 million in the year-earlier quarter. Net interest income increased 12.0% to US$327.9 million from US$292.8 million in the year-earlier quarter. Credit for loan losses was US$176,000 versus a provision for loan losses of US$7,000 in the prior-year quarter. Non-interest income fell 32.5% to US$35.2 million from US$52.2 million, while non-interest expense advanced 1.0% to US$158.4 million.

Prospects: Our evaluation of New York Community Bancorp Inc. as of June 19, 2016 is the result of our systematic analysis on three basic characteristics: earnings strength, relative valuation, and recent stock price movement. The company has managed to produce a neutral trend in earnings per share over the past 5 quarters and while recent estimates for the company have remained steady, NYCB has posted results that fell short of analysts expectations. Based on operating earnings yield, the company is undervalued when compared to all of the companies in our coverage universe. Share price changes over the past year indicates that NYCB will perform in line with the market over the near term.

Financial Data

(US$ in Thousands)	3 Mos	12/31/2015	12/31/2014	12/31/2013	12/31/2012	12/31/2011	12/31/2010	12/31/2009
Earnings Per Share	(0.10)	(0.11)	1.09	1.08	1.13	1.09	1.24	1.13
Cash Flow Per Share	(0.38)	(0.94)	1.64	3.13	1.31	1.90	(0.15)	0.60
Tang Book Value Per Share	6.85	6.70	7.03	6.90	6.93	6.77	6.91	6.52
Dividends Per Share	0.920	1.000	1.000	1.000	1.000	1.000	1.000	1.000
Dividend Payout %	...	...	91.74	92.59	88.50	91.74	80.65	88.50
Income Statement								
Interest Income	423,810	1,691,584	1,683,067	1,708,098	1,791,101	1,866,664	1,913,794	1,634,612
Interest Expense	95,944	1,283,509	542,714	541,482	631,080	666,243	733,831	729,287
Net Interest Income	327,866	408,075	1,140,353	1,166,616	1,160,021	1,200,421	1,179,963	905,325
Provision for Losses	(176)	(15,004)	(18,587)	30,758	62,988	100,420	102,903	63,000
Non-Interest Income	35,237	210,763	201,593	218,830	297,353	235,325	337,923	157,639
Non-Interest Expense	158,448	760,511	579,170	591,778	593,833	574,683	546,246	384,003
Income Before Taxes	204,831	(132,013)	773,066	747,126	780,909	734,577	837,471	593,149
Income Taxes	74,922	(84,857)	287,669	271,579	279,803	254,540	296,454	194,503
Net Income	129,909	(47,156)	485,397	475,547	501,106	480,037	541,017	398,646
Average Shares	484,605	448,982	440,988	439,251	437,712	436,143	434,186	351,939
Balance Sheet								
Net Loans & Leases	38,453,936	38,011,995	35,647,639	32,727,507	31,580,636	30,152,154	29,041,595	28,265,208
Total Assets	48,515,572	50,317,796	48,559,217	46,688,287	44,145,100	42,024,302	41,190,689	42,153,869
Total Deposits	28,982,312	28,426,758	28,328,734	25,660,992	24,877,521	22,274,130	21,809,051	22,316,411
Total Liabilities	42,530,772	44,383,100	42,777,402	40,952,625	38,488,836	36,458,598	35,664,469	36,786,967
Stockholders' Equity	5,984,800	5,934,696	5,781,815	5,735,662	5,656,264	5,565,704	5,526,220	5,366,902
Shares Outstanding	486,929	484,943	442,587	440,809	439,050	437,344	435,646	433,197
Statistical Record								
Return on Assets %	N.M.	N.M.	1.02	1.05	1.16	1.15	1.30	1.07
Return on Equity %	N.M.	N.M.	8.43	8.35	8.91	8.66	9.93	8.32
Net Interest Margin %	77.36	24.12	67.75	68.30	64.77	64.31	61.66	55.38
Efficiency Ratio %	34.52	39.98	30.73	30.71	28.43	27.34	24.26	21.43
Loans to Deposits	1.33	1.34	1.26	1.28	1.27	1.35	1.33	1.27
Price Range	19.16-14.51	19.16-15.25	17.34-14.82	16.85-12.96	14.95-11.57	18.97-11.32	19.30-14.42	14.65-7.90
P/E Ratio	...	...	15.91-13.60	15.60-12.00	13.23-10.24	17.40-10.39	15.56-11.63	12.96-6.99
Average Yield %	5.40	5.81	6.30	6.86	7.61	6.69	6.11	8.87

Address: 615 Merrick Avenue, Westbury, NY 11590 **Telephone:** 516-683-4100	**Web Site:** www.mynycb.com **Officers:** Joseph R. Ficalora - Chairman, President, Chief Executive Officer Thomas R. Cangemi - Senior Executive Vice President, Chief Financial Officer	**Auditors:** KPMG LLP **Transfer Agents:** Computershare, Providence, RI

NEW YORK TIMES CO.

Exchange	Symbol	Price	52Wk Range	Yield	P/E
NYS	NYT	$12.09 (5/31/2016)	14.46-11.56	1.32	28.79

*7 Year Price Score 103.38 *NYSE Composite Index=100 *12 Month Price Score 95.83

Interim Earnings (Per Share)

Qtr.	Mar	Jun	Sep	Dec
2013	0.02	0.13	(0.16)	0.42
2014	0.01	0.06	(0.08)	0.21
2015	(0.09)	0.10	0.06	0.31
2016	(0.05)	...	...	...

Interim Dividends (Per Share)

Amt	Decl	Ex	Rec	Pay
0.04Q	06/11/2015	07/13/2015	07/15/2015	07/30/2015
0.04Q	09/17/2015	10/05/2015	10/07/2015	10/22/2015
0.04Q	12/17/2015	01/11/2016	01/13/2016	01/28/2016
0.04Q	02/18/2016	04/04/2016	04/06/2016	04/21/2016

Indicated Div: $0.16

Valuation Analysis

		Institutional Holding	
Forecast EPS	$0.54	No of Institutions	
	(05/15/2016)	304	
Market Cap	$1.9 Billion	Shares	
Book Value	$796.7 Million	133,161,328	
Price/Book	2.44	% Held	
Price/Sales	1.24	75.81	

TRADING VOLUME (thousand shares)

Business Summary: Publishing (MIC: 2.3.3 SIC: 2711 NAIC: 511110)

New York Times principal business consists of distributing content generated by its newsroom through its print, web and mobile platforms. In addition, Co. distributes selected content on third-party platforms. Co. includes newspapers, print and digital products and investments. Co. operates through one segment with businesses that include: The New York Times; the International New York Times; Co.'s websites, NYTimes.com and international.nytimes.com; its mobile applications, including The Times's core news applications, applications such as NYT Cooking, Crossword and others; and related businesses, such as The Times news services division, digital archive distribution, and NYT Live.

Recent Developments: For the quarter ended Mar 27 2016, net loss amounted to US$13.6 million versus a net loss of US$14.4 million in the year-earlier quarter. Revenues were US$379.5 million, down 1.2% from US$384.2 million the year before. Operating income was US$27.9 million versus a loss of US$11.1 million in the prior-year quarter. Direct operating expenses rose 0.8% to US$157.9 million from US$156.6 million in the comparable period the year before. Indirect operating expenses decreased 18.8% to US$193.7 million from US$238.7 million in the equivalent prior-year period.

Prospects: Our evaluation of New York Times Co. as of June 19, 2016 is the result of our systematic analysis on three basic characteristics: earnings strength, relative valuation, and recent stock price movement. The company has generated a negative trend in earnings per share over the past 5 quarters and while recent estimates for the company have remained steady, NYT has posted better than expected results. Based on operating earnings yield, the company is undervalued when compared to all of the companies in our coverage universe. Share price changes over the past year indicates that NYT will perform well over the near term.

Financial Data

(US$ in Thousands)	3 Mos	12/27/2015	12/28/2014	12/29/2013	12/30/2012	12/25/2011	12/26/2010	12/27/2009
Earnings Per Share	0.42	0.38	0.20	0.41	0.87	(0.27)	0.71	0.14
Cash Flow Per Share	0.89	1.07	0.54	0.23	0.53	0.50	1.06	1.79
Tang Book Value Per Share	4.19	4.45	4.06	4.78	3.43	N.M.	N.M.	N.M.
Dividends Per Share	0.160	0.160	0.160	0.040	...	...	...	...
Dividend Payout %	38.10	42.11	80.00	9.76	...	...	...	...
Income Statement								
Total Revenue	379,515	1,579,215	1,588,528	1,577,230	1,990,080	2,323,401	2,393,463	2,440,439
EBITDA	43,407	198,182	171,403	241,564	426,890	197,951	364,198	198,584
Depn & Amortn	15,472	61,597	79,455	85,477	103,775	116,454	120,950	133,775
Income Before Taxes	19,109	97,535	38,218	98,014	260,300	(3,746)	158,186	(16,832)
Income Taxes	(9,201)	33,910	(3,541)	37,892	103,482	36,506	68,516	2,206
Net Income	(8,271)	63,246	33,307	65,105	133,173	(39,669)	107,704	19,891
Average Shares	161,003	166,423	161,323	157,774	152,693	147,190	152,600	146,367
Balance Sheet								
Current Assets	846,128	862,532	1,148,095	1,172,267	1,308,408	748,589	857,232	500,573
Total Assets	2,311,987	2,417,690	2,566,474	2,572,552	2,806,335	2,883,450	3,285,741	3,088,557
Current Liabilities	513,138	563,585	600,508	348,511	422,577	513,308	504,377	500,500
Long-Term Obligations	243,907	242,851	426,458	684,142	696,914	698,220	996,405	769,176
Total Liabilities	1,515,296	1,590,939	1,840,146	1,729,642	2,173,835	2,377,090	2,625,814	2,484,515
Stockholders' Equity	796,691	826,751	726,328	842,910	632,500	506,360	659,927	604,042
Shares Outstanding	160,928	161,389	150,337	149,927	148,605	147,846	146,151	144,513
Statistical Record								
Return on Assets %	2.96	2.54	1.30	2.43	4.61	N.M.	3.39	0.61
Return on Equity %	8.52	8.17	4.26	8.85	23.01	N.M.	17.09	3.60
EBITDA Margin %	11.44	12.55	10.79	15.32	21.45	8.52	15.22	8.14
Net Margin %	N.M.	4.00	2.10	4.13	6.69	N.M.	4.50	0.82
Asset Turnover	0.67	0.64	0.62	0.59	0.69	0.76	0.75	0.75
Current Ratio	1.65	1.53	1.91	3.36	3.10	1.46	1.70	1.00
Debt to Equity	0.31	0.29	0.59	0.81	1.10	1.38	1.51	1.27
Price Range	14.46-11.56	14.46-11.56	17.26-11.22	15.47-8.18	10.88-5.98	10.90-5.65	14.67-7.18	12.16-3.51
P/E Ratio	34.43-27.52	38.05-30.42	86.30-56.10	37.73-19.95	12.51-6.87	...	20.66-10.11	86.86-25.07
Average Yield %	1.22	1.20	1.13	0.36	...	...	...	...

Address: 620 Eighth Avenue, New York, NY 10018	**Web Site:** www.nytco.com	**Auditors:** Ernst & Young LLP
Telephone: 212-556-1234	**Officers:** Arthur Sulzberger - Chairman, Interim Chief Executive Officer Michael Golden - Vice-Chairman	**Investor Contact:** 212-556-4317
		Transfer Agents: Computershare, Providence, RI

NEWELL BRANDS INC

Exchange	Symbol	Price	52Wk Range	Yield	P/E
NYS	NWL	$47.69 (5/31/2016)	49.17-33.76	1.59	38.15

*7 Year Price Score 143.16 *NYSE Composite Index=100 *12 Month Price Score 108.00

TRADING VOLUME (thousand shares)

Interim Earnings (Per Share)

Qtr.	Mar	Jun	Sep	Dec
2013	0.19	0.37	0.66	0.41
2014	0.19	0.54	0.44	0.19
2015	0.20	0.55	0.50	0.05
2016	0.15	...	...	...

Interim Dividends (Per Share)

Amt	Decl	Ex	Rec	Pay
0.19Q	08/13/2015	08/27/2015	08/31/2015	09/15/2015
0.19Q	11/12/2015	11/25/2015	11/30/2015	12/15/2015
0.19Q	02/12/2016	02/25/2016	02/29/2016	03/15/2016
0.19Q	05/12/2016	05/26/2016	05/31/2016	06/15/2016

Indicated Div: $0.76

Valuation Analysis

		Institutional Holding	
Forecast EPS	$2.84	No of Institutions	
	(05/20/2016)	730	
Market Cap	$12.8 Billion	Shares	
Book Value	$1.8 Billion	338,771,168	
Price/Book	7.21	% Held	
Price/Sales	2.14	82.56	

Business Summary: Plastics (MIC: 8.4.2 SIC: 3089 NAIC: 326299)

Newell Brands is a marketer of consumer and commercial products. Co. has five segments: writing, which designs, manufactures and distributes writing and labeling instruments; home solutions, which designs, manufactures and distributes consumer products under multiple brand names; tools, which designs, manufactures and distributes hand and power tool accessories, industrial bandsaw blades, tools and industrial labeling solutions; commercial products, which designs, manufactures and distributes cleaning and refuse products, hygiene systems, material handling solutions and medical and computer carts; and baby & parenting, which designs and distributes infant and juvenile products.

Recent Developments: For the quarter ended Mar 31 2016, income from continuing operations decreased 29.2% to US$40.3 million from US$56.9 million in the year-earlier quarter. Net income decreased 25.1% to US$40.5 million from US$54.1 million in the year-earlier quarter. Revenues were US$1.31 billion, up 4.0% from US$1.26 billion the year before. Operating income was US$125.4 million versus US$98.2 million in the prior-year quarter, an increase of 27.7%. Direct operating expenses rose 4.2% to US$809.3 million from US$776.5 million in the comparable period the year before. Indirect operating expenses decreased 2.3% to US$380.2 million from US$389.3 million in the equivalent prior-year period.

Prospects: Our evaluation of Newell Brands Inc. as of June 19, 2016 is the result of our systematic analysis on three basic characteristics: earnings strength, relative valuation, and recent stock price movement. The company has enjoyed a very positive trend in earnings per share over the past 5 quarters and while recent estimates for the company have remained steady, NWL has posted better than expected results. Based on operating earnings yield, the company is about fairly valued when compared to all of the companies in our coverage universe. Share price changes over the past year indicates that NWL will perform well over the near term.

Financial Data

(US$ in Thousands)	3 Mos	12/31/2015	12/31/2014	12/31/2013	12/31/2012	12/31/2011	12/31/2010	12/31/2009
Earnings Per Share	1.25	1.29	1.35	1.63	1.37	0.42	0.96	0.97
Cash Flow Per Share	1.67	2.10	2.30	2.10	2.12	1.91	2.06	2.15
Dividends Per Share	0.760	0.760	0.660	0.600	0.430	0.290	0.200	0.255
Dividend Payout %	60.80	58.91	48.89	36.81	31.39	69.05	20.83	26.29
Income Statement								
Total Revenue	1,314,900	5,915,700	5,727,000	5,692,500	5,902,700	5,864,600	5,759,200	5,577,600
EBITDA	123,800	503,800	615,700	700,200	750,100	350,800	536,300	689,700
Depn & Amortn	42,800	93,000	93,200	100,400	106,700	110,600	118,000	122,100
Income Before Taxes	51,600	330,900	462,100	539,500	567,300	154,000	299,900	427,600
Income Taxes	11,300	78,200	89,100	122,100	166,300	17,900	7,500	142,700
Net Income	40,500	350,000	377,800	474,600	401,300	125,200	292,800	285,500
Average Shares	270,100	271,500	278,900	291,800	293,600	296,200	305,400	294,400
Balance Sheet								
Current Assets	10,488,900	2,493,500	2,426,600	2,285,600	2,271,100	2,148,000	2,132,000	2,182,100
Total Assets	15,332,800	7,278,000	6,681,100	6,069,700	6,222,000	6,160,900	6,405,300	6,423,900
Current Liabilities	2,194,900	1,988,600	1,890,700	1,604,500	1,570,800	1,660,900	1,665,900	1,759,500
Long-Term Obligations	10,606,600	2,687,600	2,084,500	1,661,600	1,706,500	1,809,300	2,063,900	2,015,300
Total Liabilities	13,557,600	5,455,100	4,829,700	3,998,200	4,225,300	4,311,800	4,503,300	4,645,200
Stockholders' Equity	1,775,200	1,822,900	1,851,400	2,071,500	1,996,700	1,849,100	1,902,000	1,778,700
Shares Outstanding	268,200	267,200	269,200	278,600	286,900	288,300	290,500	277,800
Statistical Record								
Return on Assets %	3.07	5.01	5.93	7.72	6.46	1.99	4.56	4.32
Return on Equity %	19.39	19.05	19.26	23.33	20.81	6.68	15.91	16.83
EBITDA Margin %	9.42	8.52	10.75	12.30	12.71	5.98	9.31	12.37
Net Margin %	3.08	5.92	6.60	8.34	6.80	2.13	5.08	5.12
Asset Turnover	0.54	0.85	0.90	0.93	0.95	0.93	0.90	0.84
Current Ratio	4.78	1.25	1.28	1.42	1.45	1.29	1.28	1.24
Debt to Equity	5.97	1.47	1.13	0.80	0.85	0.98	1.09	1.13
Price Range	48.16-33.76	48.16-36.77	38.41-28.49	32.41-21.80	22.27-16.23	20.21-11.14	18.38-13.36	15.85-4.54
P/E Ratio	38.53-27.01	37.33-28.50	28.45-21.10	19.88-13.37	16.26-11.85	48.12-26.52	19.15-13.92	16.34-4.68
Average Yield %	1.84	1.85	2.04	2.25	2.30	1.79	1.23	2.24

Address: 6655 Peachtree Dunwoody Road, Atlanta, GA 30328	**Web Site:** www.newellrubbermaid.com	**Auditors:** PricewaterhouseCoopers LLP
Telephone: 770-418-7000	**Officers:** Michael B. Polk - President, Chief Executive Officer Paula S. Larson - Executive Vice President	**Investor Contact:** 800-424-1941 **Transfer Agents:** ComputerShare Investor Services, Providence, RI

NEWFIELD EXPLORATION CO

Exchange	Symbol	Price	52Wk Range	Yield	P/E
NYS	NFX	$40.77 (5/31/2016)	41.16-22.31	N/A	N/A

*7 Year Price Score 72.63   *NYSE Composite Index=100   *12 Month Price Score 106.69

Interim Earnings (Per Share)

Qtr.	Mar	Jun	Sep	Dec
2013	(0.06)	0.82	0.05	0.13
2014	2.07	(0.16)	2.02	2.60
2015	(3.30)	(6.09)	(7.52)	(4.01)
2016	(3.52)	...	...	...

Interim Dividends (Per Share)

No Dividends Paid

Valuation Analysis		Institutional Holding	
Forecast EPS	$0.31	No of Institutions	
	(05/20/2016)	576	
Market Cap	$8.1 Billion	Shares	
Book Value	$1.5 Billion	213,766,512	
Price/Book	5.25	% Held	
Price/Sales	5.41	95.22	

Business Summary: Production & Extraction (MIC: 9.1.1 SIC: 1311 NAIC: 211111)

Newfield Exploration is an independent energy company engaged in the exploration, development and production of crude oil, natural gas and natural gas liquids. Co.'s principal areas of operation are the Anadarko and Arkoma basins of Oklahoma, the Williston Basin of North Dakota, the Uinta Basin of Utah and the Maverick and Gulf Coast basins of Texas. In addition, Co. has oil developments offshore China. As of Dec 31 2015, Co. had proved reserves of 509.0 million barrels of oil equivalent, which consisted of 207.0 million barrels of oil and condensate, 1,305.00 billion cubic feet of natural gas, and 84.0 million barrels of natural gas liquids.

Recent Developments: For the quarter ended Mar 31 2016, net loss amounted to US$624.0 million versus a net loss of US$480.0 million in the year earlier quarter. Revenues were US$284.0 million, down 18.6% from US$349.0 million the year before. Operating loss was US$578.0 million versus a loss of US$884.0 million in the prior-year quarter. Direct operating expenses declined 2.2% to US$134.0 million from US$137.0 million in the comparable period the year before. Indirect operating expenses decreased 33.6% to US$728.0 million from US$1.10 billion in the equivalent prior-year period.

Prospects: Our evaluation of Newfield Exploration Co. as of June 19, 2016 is the result of our systematic analysis on three basic characteristics: earnings strength, relative valuation, and recent stock price movement. The company has generated a negative trend in earnings per share over the past 5 quarters and while recent estimates for the company have been raised by analysts, NFX has posted better than expected results. Based on operating earnings yield, the company is overvalued when compared to all of the companies in our coverage universe. Share price changes over the past year indicates that NFX will perform in line with the market over the near term.

Financial Data

(US$ in Thousands)	3 Mos	12/31/2015	12/31/2014	12/31/2013	12/31/2012	12/31/2011	12/31/2010	12/31/2009
Earnings Per Share	(21.14)	(21.18)	6.52	0.94	(8.80)	3.99	3.91	(4.18)
Cash Flow Per Share	6.08	7.60	10.12	10.70	8.47	11.86	12.35	12.14
Tang Book Value Per Share	7.76	8.43	28.35	21.70	20.54	29.11	24.90	20.81
Income Statement								
Total Revenue	284,000	1,557,000	2,288,000	1,789,000	2,567,000	2,471,000	1,883,000	1,338,000
EBITDA	(417,000)	(3,899,000)	2,082,000	1,252,000	104,000	1,700,000	1,571,000	(223,000)
Depn & Amortn	177,000	917,000	903,000	930,000	955,000	767,000	644,000	587,000
Income Before Taxes	(626,000)	(4,947,000)	1,032,000	170,000	(988,000)	840,000	829,000	(885,000)
Income Taxes	(2,000)	(1,585,000)	382,000	62,000	196,000	301,000	306,000	(343,000)
Net Income	(624,000)	(3,362,000)	900,000	147,000	(1,184,000)	539,000	523,000	(542,000)
Average Shares	177,000	159,000	138,000	136,000	135,000	135,000	134,000	130,000
Balance Sheet								
Current Assets	1,088,000	625,000	940,000	901,000	866,000	775,000	731,000	893,000
Total Assets	4,777,000	4,768,000	9,598,000	9,321,000	7,912,000	8,991,000	7,494,000	6,254,000
Current Liabilities	525,000	647,000	1,101,000	1,290,000	959,000	932,000	928,000	873,000
Long-Term Obligations	2,429,000	2,467,000	2,892,000	3,694,000	3,045,000	3,006,000	2,304,000	2,037,000
Total Liabilities	3,239,000	3,389,000	5,705,000	6,365,000	5,132,000	5,071,000	4,151,000	3,486,000
Stockholders' Equity	1,538,000	1,379,000	3,893,000	2,956,000	2,780,000	3,920,000	3,343,000	2,768,000
Shares Outstanding	198,137	163,490	137,328	136,221	135,314	134,684	134,246	133,004
Statistical Record								
Return on Assets %	N.M.	N.M.	9.51	1.71	N.M.	6.54	7.61	N.M.
Return on Equity %	N.M.	N.M.	26.28	5.13	N.M.	14.84	17.12	N.M.
EBITDA Margin %	N.M.	N.M.	91.00	69.98	4.05	68.80	83.43	N.M.
Net Margin %	N.M.	N.M.	39.34	8.22	N.M.	21.81	27.77	N.M.
Asset Turnover	0.21	0.22	0.24	0.21	0.30	0.30	0.27	0.20
Current Ratio	2.07	0.97	0.85	0.70	0.90	0.83	0.79	1.02
Debt to Equity	1.58	1.79	0.74	1.25	1.10	0.77	0.69	0.74
Price Range	41.05-22.31	41.05-22.73	44.98-23.56	31.68-19.84	41.28-23.88	76.45-35.81	73.04-46.60	50.43-17.23
P/E Ratio	...	...	6.90-3.61	33.70-21.11	...	19.16-8.97	18.68-11.92	...

Address: 4 Waterway Square Place, Suite 100, The Woodlands, TX 77380 **Telephone:** 281-210-5100 **Fax:** 281-210-5101	**Web Site:** www.newfield.com **Officers:** Lee K. Boothby - Chairman, President, Chief Executive Officer Brian L. Rickmers - Chief Financial Officer, Controller, Assistant Secretary	**Auditors:** PricewaterhouseCoopers LLP **Investor Contact:** 281-210-5201 **Transfer Agents:** American Stock Transfer & Trust Company, New York, NY

NEWMARKET CORP

Exchange	Symbol	Price	52Wk Range	Yield	P/E
NYS	NEU	$405.00 (5/31/2016)	463.87-324.89	1.58	20.74

*7 Year Price Score 131.32 *NYSE Composite Index=100 *12 Month Price Score 100.91

TRADING VOLUME (thousand shares)

Interim Earnings (Per Share)

Qtr.	Mar	Jun	Sep	Dec
2013	5.07	4.81	5.94	4.09
2014	4.43	5.24	4.53	4.18
2015	5.14	4.72	5.08	4.51
2016	5.22	...	...	...

Interim Dividends (Per Share)

Amt	Decl	Ex	Rec	Pay
1.40Q	08/06/2015	09/11/2015	09/15/2015	10/01/2015
1.60Q	10/21/2015	12/11/2015	12/15/2015	01/01/2016
1.60Q	02/25/2016	03/11/2016	03/15/2016	04/01/2016
1.60Q	04/28/2016	06/13/2016	06/15/2016	07/01/2016

Indicated Div: $6.40

Valuation Analysis

		Institutional Holding	
Forecast EPS	$19.80	No of Institutions	
	(05/10/2016)	323	
Market Cap	$4.8 Billion	Shares	
Book Value	$391.1 Million	8,543,760	
Price/Book	12.27	% Held	
Price/Sales	2.29	N/A	

Business Summary: Specialty Chemicals (MIC: 8.3.2 SIC: 2869 NAIC: 325199)

NewMarket is a holding company and is the parent company of Afton Chemical Corporation (Afton), Ethyl Corporation (Ethyl), NewMarket Services Corporation (NewMarket Services), and NewMarket Development Corporation (NewMarket Development). Afton, a specialty chemicals company, encompasses the petroleum additives business, while Ethyl represents the sale of tetraethyl lead in North America and certain petroleum additives manufacturing operations. NewMarket Development manages the property that Co. owns in Virginia. NewMarket Services provides various administrative services to Co., Afton, Ethyl, and NewMarket Development.

Recent Developments: For the quarter ended Mar 31 2016, net income decreased 3.2% to US$61.9 million from US$63.9 million in the year-earlier quarter. Revenues were US$509.9 million, down 8.9% from US$559.6 million the year before. Operating income was US$95.4 million versus US$99.8 million in the prior-year quarter, a decrease of 4.4%. Direct operating expenses declined 11.6% to US$334.4 million from US$378.3 million in the comparable period the year before. Indirect operating expenses decreased 1.6% to US$80.2 million from US$81.5 million in the equivalent prior-year period.

Prospects: Our evaluation of NewMarket Corp. as of June 19, 2016 is the result of our systematic analysis on three basic characteristics: earnings strength, relative valuation, and recent stock price movement. The company has managed to produce a neutral trend in earnings per share over the past 5 quarters and while recent estimates for the company have been mixed, NEU has posted better than expected results. Based on operating earnings yield, the company is about fairly valued when compared to all of the companies in our coverage universe. Share price changes over the past year indicates that NEU will perform in line with the market over the near term.

Financial Data

(US$ in Thousands)	3 Mos	12/31/2015	12/31/2014	12/31/2013	12/31/2012	12/31/2011	12/31/2010	12/31/2009
Earnings Per Share	19.53	19.45	18.38	19.90	17.85	15.09	12.09	10.65
Cash Flow Per Share	24.14	21.90	18.54	20.92	20.30	13.47	11.30	14.76
Tang Book Value Per Share	32.19	31.52	32.47	41.92	27.70	38.16	31.71	27.16
Dividends Per Share	6.000	5.800	4.700	3.800	28.000	2.390	1.565	1.075
Dividend Payout %	30.72	29.82	25.57	19.10	156.86	15.84	12.94	10.09
Income Statement								
Total Revenue	509,927	2,140,830	2,335,405	2,280,355	2,223,309	2,149,558	1,797,392	1,530,122
EBITDA	103,814	394,327	395,854	401,301	393,639	364,141	315,024	283,098
Depn & Amortn	10,680	40,704	40,188	42,194	41,433	41,604	37,767	32,006
Income Before Taxes	88,946	338,971	339,099	341,311	341,391	303,717	259,996	239,376
Income Taxes	27,015	100,368	105,844	98,964	101,798	96,810	82,871	77,093
Net Income	61,931	238,603	233,255	264,742	239,593	206,907	177,125	162,283
Average Shares	11,839	12,241	12,671	13,286	13,405	13,712	14,650	15,243
Balance Sheet								
Current Assets	773,791	774,767	797,191	897,319	735,495	679,731	602,775	603,139
Total Assets	1,317,440	1,289,915	1,231,925	1,327,274	1,257,510	1,191,662	1,062,741	1,025,192
Current Liabilities	240,105	263,680	259,674	247,614	216,671	216,024	206,387	198,052
Long-Term Obligations	541,124	494,586	363,526	349,467	424,407	232,601	217,544	216,200
Total Liabilities	926,292	902,351	810,884	754,826	855,305	642,069	571,101	567,007
Stockholders' Equity	391,148	387,564	421,041	572,448	402,205	549,593	491,640	458,185
Shares Outstanding	11,848	11,948	12,446	13,099	13,417	13,404	14,034	15,209
Statistical Record								
Return on Assets %	18.37	18.92	18.23	20.48	19.51	18.36	16.97	17.67
Return on Equity %	56.73	59.02	46.96	54.33	50.21	39.74	37.30	43.32
EBITDA Margin %	20.36	18.42	16.95	17.60	17.71	16.94	17.53	18.50
Net Margin %	12.15	11.15	9.99	11.61	10.78	9.63	9.85	10.61
Asset Turnover	1.62	1.70	1.83	1.76	1.81	1.91	1.72	1.67
Current Ratio	3.22	2.94	3.07	3.62	3.39	3.15	2.92	3.05
Debt to Equity	1.38	1.28	0.86	0.61	1.06	0.42	0.44	0.47
Price Range	477.80-324.89	480.33-354.59	413.39-311.61	337.22-241.65	277.43-173.46	203.71-119.76	130.80-81.94	120.33-27.91
P/E Ratio	24.46-16.64	24.70-18.23	22.49-16.95	16.95-12.14	15.54-9.72	13.50-7.94	10.82-6.78	11.30-2.62
Average Yield %	1.48	1.36	1.23	1.35	12.43	1.74	1.45	1.51

Address: 330 South Fourth Street, Richmond, VA 23219-4350
Telephone: 804-788-5000

Web Site: www.newmarket.com
Officers: Bruce C. Gottwald - Chairman Thomas E. Gottwald - President, Chief Executive Officer

Auditors: PricewaterhouseCoopers LLP
Investor Contact: 804-788-5555
Transfer Agents: ComputerShare Investor Services, Providence, RI

NEWMONT MINING CORP (HOLDING CO)

Exchange	Symbol	Price	52Wk Range	Yield	P/E
NYS	NEM	$32.41 (5/31/2016)	35.55-15.55	0.31	202.56

*7 Year Price Score 47.10   *NYSE Composite Index=100   *12 Month Price Score 143.07

Interim Earnings (Per Share)

Qtr.	Mar	Jun	Sep	Dec
2013	0.63	(4.06)	0.82	(2.33)
2014	0.20	0.36	0.43	0.03
2015	0.37	0.14	0.42	(0.50)
2016	0.10	...	...	...

Interim Dividends (Per Share)

Amt	Decl	Ex	Rec	Pay
0.025Q	07/21/2015	09/08/2015	09/10/2015	09/24/2015
0.025Q	10/27/2015	12/09/2015	12/11/2015	12/28/2015
0.025Q	02/11/2016	03/08/2016	03/10/2016	03/24/2016
0.025Q	04/19/2016	06/07/2016	06/09/2016	06/23/2016

Indicated Div: $0.10

Valuation Analysis   Institutional Holding

Forecast EPS	$1.29	No of Institutions
	(05/20/2016)	895
Market Cap	$17.2 Billion	Shares
Book Value	$11.3 Billion	460,794,144
Price/Book	1.52	% Held
Price/Sales	2.21	77.45

Business Summary: Precious Metals (MIC: 8.2.1 SIC: 1041 NAIC: 212221)

Newmont Mining is primarily a gold producer with operations and/or assets in the United States, Australia, Peru, Indonesia, Ghana and Suriname. Co. is also engaged in the production of copper, principally through Batu Hijau in Indonesia, Boddington in Australia and Phoenix in the U.S. Co.'s regions include North America, which consists of Carlin, Phoenix and Twin Creeks in Nevada and Cripple Creek &Victor in Colorado; South America, which consists of Yanacocha in Peru; Asia Pacific, which consists of Boddington, Tanami and Kalgoorlie in Australia and Batu Hijau in Indonesia; and Africa, which consists of Ahafo and Akyem in Ghana.

Recent Developments: For the quarter ended Mar 31 2016, income from continuing operations decreased 27.1% to US$161.0 million from US$221.0 million in the year-earlier quarter. Net income decreased 41.0% to US$135.0 million from US$229.0 million in the year-earlier quarter. Revenues were US$2.03 billion, up 3.0% from US$1.97 billion the year before. Direct operating expenses rose 5.3% to US$1.08 billion from US$1.03 billion in the comparable period the year before. Indirect operating expenses increased 7.1% to US$480.0 million from US$448.0 million in the equivalent prior-year period.

Prospects: Our evaluation of Newmont Mining Corp. as of June 19, 2016 is the result of our systematic analysis on three basic characteristics: earnings strength, relative valuation, and recent stock price movement. The company has enjoyed a very positive trend in earnings per share over the past 5 quarters and while recent estimates for the company have been raised by analysts, NEM has posted better than expected results. Based on operating earnings yield, the company is overvalued when compared to all of the companies in our coverage universe. Share price changes over the past year indicates that NEM will perform very well over the near term.

Financial Data

(US$ in Thousands)	3 Mos	12/31/2015	12/31/2014	12/31/2013	12/31/2012	12/31/2011	12/31/2010	12/31/2009
Earnings Per Share	0.16	0.43	1.02	(4.94)	3.63	0.73	4.55	2.66
Cash Flow Per Share	3.85	4.16	2.88	3.10	4.77	7.26	6.44	6.00
Tang Book Value Per Share	21.39	21.14	20.17	19.91	27.08	25.39	26.52	21.37
Dividends Per Share	0.100	0.100	0.225	1.225	1.400	1.000	0.500	0.400
Dividend Payout %	62.50	23.26	22.06	...	38.57	136.99	10.99	15.04
Income Statement								
Total Revenue	2,032,000	7,729,000	7,292,000	8,322,000	9,868,000	10,358,000	9,540,000	7,705,000
EBITDA	891,000	2,530,000	2,092,000	(1,933,000)	4,383,000	3,079,000	5,210,000	3,823,000
Depn & Amortn	322,000	1,239,000	1,229,000	1,362,000	1,032,000	1,036,000	945,000	806,000
Income Before Taxes	490,000	966,000	506,000	(3,585,000)	3,114,000	1,810,000	3,997,000	2,913,000
Income Taxes	324,000	644,000	133,000	(813,000)	869,000	713,000	856,000	788,000
Net Income	52,000	220,000	508,000	(2,462,000)	1,809,000	366,000	2,277,000	1,297,000
Average Shares	531,000	516,000	499,000	498,000	499,000	504,000	500,000	493,000
Balance Sheet								
Current Assets	4,780,000	4,983,000	5,439,000	4,874,000	5,945,000	5,388,000	7,253,000	5,822,000
Total Assets	24,553,000	25,182,000	24,916,000	24,764,000	29,650,000	27,474,000	25,663,000	22,299,000
Current Liabilities	1,458,000	1,416,000	2,198,000	2,740,000	3,141,000	3,940,000	2,747,000	2,320,000
Long-Term Obligations	5,369,000	6,087,000	6,480,000	6,145,000	6,288,000	3,624,000	4,182,000	4,652,000
Total Liabilities	13,204,000	13,832,000	14,642,000	14,623,000	15,877,000	14,578,000	12,318,000	11,596,000
Stockholders' Equity	11,349,000	11,350,000	10,274,000	10,141,000	13,773,000	12,896,000	13,345,000	10,703,000
Shares Outstanding	530,530	529,650	498,670	497,678	496,723	494,727	492,729	490,730
Statistical Record								
Return on Assets %	0.35	0.88	2.05	N.M.	6.32	1.38	9.50	6.80
Return on Equity %	0.82	2.03	4.98	N.M.	13.53	2.79	18.94	14.57
EBITDA Margin %	43.85	32.73	28.69	N.M.	44.42	29.73	54.61	49.62
Net Margin %	2.56	2.85	6.97	N.M.	18.33	3.53	23.87	16.83
Asset Turnover	0.31	0.31	0.29	0.31	0.34	0.39	0.40	0.40
Current Ratio	3.28	3.52	2.47	1.78	1.89	1.37	2.64	2.51
Debt to Equity	0.47	0.54	0.63	0.61	0.46	0.28	0.31	0.43
Price Range	27.79-15.55	27.69-15.55	27.09-17.78	46.90-22.49	64.04-43.39	72.13-50.39	64.94-42.86	55.83-35.03
P/E Ratio	173.69-97.19	64.40-36.16	26.56-17.43	...	17.64-11.95	98.81-69.03	14.27-9.42	20.99-13.17
Average Yield %	0.47	0.47	0.96	3.74	2.75	1.70	0.89	0.92

Address: 6363 South Fiddler's Green Circle, Greenwood Village, CO 80111	**Web Site:** www.newmont.com	**Auditors:** Ernst & Young LLP
Telephone: 303-863-7414	**Officers:** Gary J. Goldberg - President, Chief Executive Officer, Chief Operating Officer, Executive	**Investor Contact:** 303-837-5362
Fax: 303-837-5837	Vice President Elaine Dorward-King - Executive Vice President	**Transfer Agents:** Computershare, Providence, RI

NEXTERA ENERGY INC

Exchange	Symbol	Price	52Wk Range	Yield	P/E	Div Achiever
NYS	NEE	$120.12 (5/31/2016)	121.48-94.62	2.90	20.09	20 Years

*7 Year Price Score 119.85 *NYSE Composite Index=100 *12 Month Price Score 109.21

Interim Earnings (Per Share)

Qtr.	Mar	Jun	Sep	Dec
2013	0.64	1.44	1.64	0.75
2014	0.98	1.12	1.50	2.00
2015	1.45	1.59	1.93	1.09
2016	1.37	...	...	...

Interim Dividends (Per Share)

Amt	Decl	Ex	Rec	Pay
0.77Q	07/31/2015	08/26/2015	08/28/2015	09/15/2015
0.77Q	10/16/2015	11/24/2015	11/27/2015	12/15/2015
0.87Q	02/12/2016	02/24/2016	02/26/2016	03/15/2016
0.87Q	05/19/2016	05/26/2016	05/31/2016	06/15/2016

Indicated Div: $3.48 (Div. Reinv. Plan)

Valuation Analysis

		Institutional Holding	
Forecast EPS	$6.17	No of Institutions	
	(05/20/2016)	1511	
Market Cap	$55.4 Billion	Shares	
Book Value	$22.9 Billion	388,087,328	
Price/Book	2.42	% Held	
Price/Sales	3.22	N/A	

Business Summary: Electric Utilities (MIC: 3.1.1 SIC: 4911 NAIC: 221121)

NextEra Energy is a holding company. Co. conducts its operations principally through two wholly-owned subsidiaries, Florida Power & Light Company (FPL) and NextEra Energy Resources, LLC (NEER). Co. provides retail and wholesale electric services to customers and owns generation, transmission and distribution facilities to support its services. FPL is engaged primarily in the generation, transmission, distribution and sale of electric energy in Florida. NEER produces its electricity from renewable sources, including wind and solar. NEER also provides energy and capacity requirements services, and engages in power and gas marketing and trading activities.

Recent Developments: For the quarter ended Mar 31 2016, net income decreased 2.0% to US$637.0 million from US$650.0 million in the year-earlier quarter. Revenues were US$3.84 billion, down 6.6% from US$4.10 billion the year before. Operating income was US$1.23 billion versus US$1.13 billion in the prior-year quarter, an increase of 9.3%. Direct operating expenses declined 17.7% to US$1.73 billion from US$2.10 billion in the comparable period the year before. Indirect operating expenses decreased 0.3% to US$874.0 million from US$877.0 million in the equivalent prior-year period.

Prospects: Our evaluation of NextEra Energy Inc. as of June 19, 2016 is the result of our systematic analysis on three basic characteristics: earnings strength, relative valuation, and recent stock price movement. The company has managed to produce a neutral trend in earnings per share over the past 5 quarters. However, while recent estimates for the company have been mixed, NEE has posted better than expected results. Based on operating earnings yield, the company is about fairly valued when compared to all of the companies in our coverage universe. Share price changes over the past year indicates that NEE will perform well over the near term.

Financial Data

(US$ in Thousands)	3 Mos	12/31/2015	12/31/2014	12/31/2013	12/31/2012	12/31/2011	12/31/2010	12/31/2009
Earnings Per Share	5.98	6.06	5.60	4.47	4.56	4.59	4.74	3.97
Cash Flow Per Share	14.07	13.58	12.66	12.03	9.55	9.78	9.34	11.04
Tang Book Value Per Share	49.70	48.97	44.96	41.47	37.90	35.92	34.36	31.35
Dividends Per Share	3.180	3.080	2.900	2.640	2.400	2.200	2.000	1.890
Dividend Payout %	53.18	50.83	51.79	59.06	52.63	47.93	42.19	47.61
Income Statement								
Total Revenue	3,835,000	17,486,000	17,021,000	15,136,000	14,256,000	15,341,000	15,317,000	15,643,000
EBITDA	1,469,000	6,341,000	7,592,000	5,997,000	5,247,000	5,158,000	5,374,000	4,612,000
Depn & Amortn	114,000	3,203,000	2,896,000	2,521,000	1,772,000	1,844,000	2,092,000	2,004,000
Income Before Taxes	864,000	2,083,000	3,552,000	2,496,000	2,590,000	2,397,000	2,431,000	1,890,000
Income Taxes	259,000	(572,000)	1,176,000	801,000	692,000	529,000	532,000	327,000
Net Income	636,000	2,762,000	2,469,000	1,908,000	1,911,000	1,923,000	1,957,000	1,615,000
Average Shares	462,900	454,000	440,100	427,000	419,200	419,000	413,000	407,200
Balance Sheet								
Current Assets	7,096,000	6,795,000	6,944,000	5,842,000	5,237,000	4,872,000	5,258,000	4,337,000
Total Assets	84,637,000	82,479,000	74,929,000	69,306,000	64,439,000	57,188,000	52,994,000	48,458,000
Current Liabilities	10,587,000	10,107,000	9,663,000	9,189,000	8,879,000	6,719,000	6,904,000	6,449,000
Long-Term Obligations	27,791,000	26,681,000	24,367,000	23,969,000	23,177,000	20,810,000	18,013,000	16,300,000
Total Liabilities	61,725,000	59,905,000	55,013,000	51,266,000	48,371,000	42,245,000	38,533,000	35,491,000
Stockholders' Equity	22,912,000	22,574,000	19,916,000	18,040,000	16,068,000	14,943,000	14,461,000	12,967,000
Shares Outstanding	461,000	461,000	443,000	435,000	424,000	416,000	420,861	413,622
Statistical Record								
Return on Assets %	3.44	3.51	3.42	2.85	3.13	3.49	3.86	3.46
Return on Equity %	12.71	13.00	13.01	11.19	12.29	13.08	14.27	13.10
EBITDA Margin %	38.31	36.26	44.60	39.62	36.81	33.62	35.09	29.48
Net Margin %	16.58	15.80	14.51	12.61	13.40	12.54	12.78	10.32
Asset Turnover	0.22	0.22	0.24	0.23	0.23	0.28	0.30	0.34
Current Ratio	0.67	0.67	0.72	0.64	0.59	0.73	0.76	0.67
Debt to Equity	1.21	1.18	1.22	1.33	1.44	1.39	1.25	1.26
Price Range	119.01-94.62	111.66-94.62	110.50-84.25	89.06-69.19	72.05-58.79	61.08-50.17	56.03-45.57	60.05-41.78
P/E Ratio	19.90-15.82	18.43-15.61	19.73-15.04	19.92-15.48	15.80-12.89	13.31-10.93	11.82-9.61	15.13-10.52
Average Yield %	3.05	3.00	3.01	3.31	3.65	3.96	3.90	3.56

Address: 700 Universe Boulevard, Juno Beach, FL 33408
Telephone: 561-694-4000
Fax: 561-694-4620

Web Site: www.nexteraenergy.com
Officers: James L. Robo - Chairman, President, Chief Operating Officer, Chief Executive Officer Shaun J. Francis - Executive Vice President

Auditors: Deloitte & Touche LLP
Investor Contact: 561-694-4697
Transfer Agents: Computershare Trust Company, N.A., Canton, MA

NIELSEN HOLDINGS PLC

Exchange	Symbol	Price	52Wk Range	Yield	P/E
NYS	NLSN	$53.39 (5/31/2016)	53.96-42.80	2.32	32.55

*7 Year Price Score N/A   *NYSE Composite Index=100   *12 Month Price Score 108.63

TRADING VOLUME (thousand shares)

Interim Earnings (Per Share)

Qtr.	Mar	Jun	Sep	Dec
2013	0.09	1.12	0.35	0.37
2014	0.15	0.19	0.24	0.42
2015	0.17	0.31	0.38	0.68
2016	0.27	...	...	...

Interim Dividends (Per Share)

Amt	Decl	Ex	Rec	Pay
0.28Q	10/29/2015	11/20/2015	11/24/2015	12/08/2015
0.28Q	02/18/2016	03/01/2016	03/03/2016	03/17/2016
0.31Q	04/20/2016	05/31/2016	06/02/2016	06/16/2016

Indicated Div: $1.24

Valuation Analysis / Institutional Holding

Forecast EPS	N/A	No of Institutions 482
Market Cap	$19.3 Billion	Shares
Book Value	$4.5 Billion	341,304,672
Price/Book	4.27	% Held
Price/Sales	3.11	75.93

Business Summary: Business Services (MIC: 7.5.2 SIC: 7389 NAIC: 561499)

Nielsen Holdings is an information and measurement company that provides clients with consumer behavior. Co. delivers media and marketing information, analytics and manufacturer and retailer insight about what and where consumers buy and what consumers read, watch and listen to. Co. has two segments: Buy and Watch. Co.'s Buy segment provides retail transactional measurement data, consumer behavior information and analytics primarily to businesses in the consumer packaged goods industry. Co.'s Watch segment provides viewership and listening data and analytics primarily to the media and advertising industries across the television, radio, online and mobile viewing and listening platforms.

Recent Developments: For the quarter ended Mar 31 2016, net income increased 60.3% to US$101.0 million from US$63.0 million in the year-earlier quarter. Revenues were US$1.49 billion, up 2.0% from US$1.46 billion the year before. Operating income was US$224.0 million versus US$199.0 million in the prior-year quarter, an increase of 12.6%. Direct operating expenses rose 3.1% to US$641.0 million from US$622.0 million in the comparable period the year before. Indirect operating expenses decreased 2.4% to US$622.0 million from US$637.0 million in the equivalent prior-year period.

Prospects: Our evaluation of Nielsen N.V. as of July 26, 2015 is the result of our systematic analysis on three basic characteristics: earnings strength, relative valuation, and recent stock price movement. The company has enjoyed a very positive trend in earnings per share over the past 5 quarters. However, while recent estimates for the company have been lowered by analysts, NLSN has posted results that fell short of analysts expectations. Based on operating earnings yield, the company is about fairly valued when compared to all of the companies in our coverage universe. Share price changes over the past year indicates that NLSN will perform very poorly over the near term.

Financial Data
(US$ in Millions)

	3 Mos	12/31/2015	12/31/2014	12/31/2013	12/31/2012	12/31/2011	12/31/2010	12/31/2009
Earnings Per Share	1.64	1.54	1.00	1.94	0.75	0.24	0.46	(1.79)
Cash Flow Per Share	3.29	3.21	2.88	2.40	2.16	1.82	1.96	1.89
Dividends Per Share	0.560	0.280	0.950	0.720	...	...	...	...
Dividend Payout %	34.15	18.18	95.00	37.11	...	...	...	...
Income Statement								
Total Revenue	1,487	6,172	6,288	5,703	5,612	5,532	5,126	4,808
EBITDA	370	1,428	1,080	996	1,000	746	926	195
Depn & Amortn	147	160	162	169	183	171	168	158
Income Before Taxes	145	961	621	520	408	104	103	(603)
Income Taxes	44	383	236	91	140	22	(46)	(197)
Net Income	100	570	384	740	273	84	130	(491)
Average Shares	365	370	384	380	366	357	279	273
Balance Sheet								
Current Assets	2,054	1,908	2,019	2,134	1,676	1,665	1,654	1,646
Total Assets	15,588	15,303	15,376	15,530	14,585	14,504	14,429	14,600
Current Liabilities	1,504	1,687	1,798	1,535	1,751	1,692	1,607	1,624
Long-Term Obligations	7,471	7,028	6,465	6,492	6,229	6,619	8,464	8,548
Total Liabilities	11,072	10,870	10,320	9,801	9,655	9,871	11,542	11,802
Stockholders' Equity	4,516	4,433	5,056	5,729	4,930	4,633	2,887	2,798
Shares Outstanding	361	362	372	378	362	359	276	276
Statistical Record								
Return on Assets %	3.92	3.72	2.48	4.91	1.87	0.58	0.90	N.M.
Return on Equity %	13.08	12.01	7.12	13.88	5.69	2.23	4.57	N.M.
EBITDA Margin %	24.88	23.14	17.18	17.46	17.82	13.49	18.06	4.06
Net Margin %	6.72	9.24	6.11	12.98	4.86	1.52	2.54	N.M.
Asset Turnover	0.40	0.40	0.41	0.38	0.38	0.38	0.35	0.32
Current Ratio	1.37	1.13	1.12	1.39	0.96	0.98	1.03	1.01
Debt to Equity	1.65	1.59	1.28	1.13	1.26	1.43	2.93	3.06
Price Range	52.84-42.80	49.06-42.20	49.51-41.04	45.93-30.59	31.80-25.03	32.06-25.00	...	...
P/E Ratio	32.22-26.10	31.86-27.40	49.51-41.04	23.68-15.77	42.40-33.37	133.58-104.17	...	...
Average Yield %	1.20	0.61	2.10	2.01	...	...	...	...

Address: 85 Broad Street, New York, NY 10004	**Web Site:** www.nielsen.com	**Auditors:** Ernst & Young LLP
Telephone: 646-654-5000	**Officers:** Arvin Kash - Vice-Chairman Dwight Mitch Barns - Chief Executive Officer, Division Officer	**Investor Contact:** 646-654-4602 **Transfer Agents:** Computershare

NIKE INC

Exchange	Symbol	Price	52Wk Range	Yield	P/E	Div Achiever
NYS	NKE	$55.22 (5/31/2016)	67.17-50.67	1.16	25.56	14 Years

*7 Year Price Score 156.43 *NYSE Composite Index=100 ***12 Month Price Score 97.43**

Interim Earnings (Per Share)

Qtr.	Aug	Nov	Feb	May
2012-13	0.31	0.21	0.47	0.36
2013-14	0.43	0.29	0.38	0.39
2014-15	0.55	0.37	0.45	0.49
2015-16	0.67	0.45	0.55	...

Interim Dividends (Per Share)

Amt	Decl	Ex	Rec	Pay
100%	11/19/2015	12/24/2015	12/09/2015	12/23/2015
0.32Q	11/19/2015	12/07/2015	12/09/2015	01/04/2016
0.16Q	02/11/2016	03/03/2016	03/07/2016	04/04/2016
0.16Q	05/13/2016	06/02/2016	06/06/2016	07/05/2016

Indicated Div: $0.64 (Div. Reinv. Plan)

Valuation Analysis | **Institutional Holding**

Forecast EPS	$2.15	No of Institutions
	(05/20/2016)	1695
Market Cap	$93.0 Billion	Shares
Book Value	$12.3 Billion	1,120,565,248
Price/Book	7.56	% Held
Price/Sales	2.92	63.35

TRADING VOLUME (thousand shares)

Business Summary: Apparel, Footwear & Accessories (MIC: 1.4.2 SIC: 3021 NAIC: 316211)

NIKE's principal business activity is the design, development, and worldwide marketing and selling of athletic footwear, apparel, equipment, accessories, and services. Co. sells its products to retail accounts, through Co.-owned retail stores and internet websites (which Co. refers to as its Direct to Consumer operations), and through a mix of independent distributors and licensees throughout the world. Co. focuses its NIKE Brand product offerings in eight primary categories: Running, Basketball, Football (Soccer), Men's Training, Women's Training, Action Sports, Sportswear (its sports lifestyle products), and Golf.

Recent Developments: For the quarter ended Feb 29 2016, net income increased 20.1% to US$950.0 million from US$791.0 million in the year-earlier quarter. Revenues were US$8.03 billion, up 7.7% from US$7.46 billion the year before. Direct operating expenses rose 7.7% to US$4.34 billion from US$4.03 billion in the comparable period the year before. Indirect operating expenses increased 7.3% to US$2.55 billion from US$2.38 billion in the equivalent prior-year period.

Prospects: Our evaluation of NIKE Inc. as of June 19, 2016 is the result of our systematic analysis on three basic characteristics: earnings strength, relative valuation, and recent stock price movement. The company has generated a negative trend in earnings per share over the past 5 quarters and while recent estimates for the company have remained steady, NKE has posted better than expected results. Based on operating earnings yield, the company is about fairly valued when compared to all of the companies in our coverage universe. Share price changes over the past year indicates that NKE will perform very well over the near term.

Financial Data

(US$ in Thousands)	9 Mos	6 Mos	3 Mos	05/31/2015	05/31/2014	05/31/2013	05/31/2012	05/31/2011
Earnings Per Share	2.16	2.06	1.98	1.85	1.49	1.36	1.18	1.10
Cash Flow Per Share	1.92	2.63	2.68	2.72	1.70	1.69	1.03	0.95
Tang Book Value Per Share	7.06	7.61	7.31	7.17	5.98	5.95	5.26	4.89
Dividends Per Share	0.600	0.560	0.420	0.540	0.465	0.405	0.348	0.300
Dividend Payout %	27.78	27.25	21.27	29.19	31.31	29.89	29.45	27.27
Income Statement								
Total Revenue	24,132,000	16,100,000	8,414,000	30,601,000	27,799,000	25,313,000	24,128,000	20,862,000
EBITDA	4,063,000	2,746,000	1,614,000	4,839,000	4,095,000	3,707,000	3,359,000	3,183,000
Depn & Amortn	499,000	322,000	165,000	606,000	518,000	438,000	373,000	335,000
Income Before Taxes	3,550,000	2,415,000	1,445,000	4,205,000	3,544,000	3,272,000	2,983,000	2,844,000
Income Taxes	636,000	451,000	266,000	932,000	851,000	808,000	760,000	711,000
Net Income	2,914,000	1,964,000	1,179,000	3,273,000	2,693,000	2,485,000	2,223,000	2,133,000
Average Shares	1,737,300	1,751,400	1,754,600	1,768,800	1,811,600	1,832,800	1,879,200	1,942,800
Balance Sheet								
Current Assets	15,256,000	16,755,000	15,238,000	15,976,000	13,696,000	13,626,000	11,531,000	11,297,000
Total Assets	20,987,000	22,583,000	20,766,000	21,600,000	18,594,000	17,584,000	15,465,000	14,998,000
Current Liabilities	4,980,000	5,511,000	5,276,000	6,334,000	5,027,000	3,926,000	3,865,000	3,958,000
Long-Term Obligations	2,048,000	2,067,000	1,079,000	1,079,000	1,199,000	1,210,000	228,000	276,000
Total Liabilities	8,687,000	9,178,000	7,872,000	8,893,000	7,770,000	6,428,000	5,084,000	5,155,000
Stockholders' Equity	12,300,000	13,405,000	12,894,000	12,707,000	10,824,000	11,156,000	10,381,000	9,843,000
Shares Outstanding	1,685,000	1,707,000	1,708,000	1,714,000	1,740,000	1,788,000	1,832,000	1,872,000
Statistical Record								
Return on Assets %	18.20	17.34	17.77	16.29	14.89	15.04	14.55	14.50
Return on Equity %	30.64	28.84	29.08	27.82	24.50	23.08	21.92	21.77
EBITDA Margin %	16.84	17.06	19.18	15.81	14.73	14.64	13.92	15.26
Net Margin %	12.08	12.20	14.01	10.70	9.69	9.82	9.21	10.22
Asset Turnover	1.54	1.50	1.58	1.52	1.54	1.53	1.58	1.42
Current Ratio	3.06	3.04	2.89	2.52	2.72	3.47	2.98	2.85
Debt to Equity	0.17	0.15	0.08	0.08	0.11	0.11	0.02	0.03
Price Range	67.17-47.67	67.17-45.59	58.38-39.41	52.49-37.27	39.93-29.98	32.95-21.95	28.60-19.65	23.07-16.80
P/E Ratio	31.09-22.07	32.60-22.13	29.48-19.90	28.37-20.15	26.80-20.12	24.23-16.14	24.24-16.65	20.98-15.27
Average Yield %	1.05	1.04	0.85	1.20	1.30	1.55	1.44	1.50

Address: One Bowerman Drive, Beaverton, OR 97005-6453 **Telephone:** 503-671-6453	**Web Site:** www.nike.com **Officers:** Philip H. Knight - Chairman Mark G. Parker - President, Chief Executive Officer	**Auditors:** PricewaterhouseCoopers LLP **Transfer Agents:** Computershare Trust Company, N.A., Providence, RI

NISOURCE INC. (HOLDING CO.)

Exchange	Symbol	Price	52Wk Range	Yield	P/E
NYS	NI	$23.86 (5/31/2016)	24.30-16.17	2.77	38.48

*7 Year Price Score 147.61 *NYSE Composite Index=100 *12 Month Price Score 115.90

Interim Earnings (Per Share)

Qtr.	Mar	Jun	Sep	Dec
2013	0.83	0.23	0.16	0.48
2014	0.85	0.25	0.10	0.48
2015	0.85	(0.11)	(0.02)	0.19
2016	0.56	...	...	...

Interim Dividends (Per Share)

Amt	Decl	Ex	Rec	Pay
0.155Q	08/04/2015	10/28/2015	10/30/2015	11/20/2015
0.155Q	01/27/2016	02/04/2016	02/08/2016	02/19/2016
0.155Q	03/22/2016	04/27/2016	04/29/2016	05/20/2016
0.165Q	05/11/2016	07/27/2016	07/29/2016	08/19/2016

Indicated Div: $0.66

Valuation Analysis **Institutional Holding**

Forecast EPS	$1.06	No of Institutions
	(05/20/2016)	609
Market Cap	$7.7 Billion	Shares
Book Value	$3.9 Billion	294,714,016
Price/Book	1.98	% Held
Price/Sales	1.70	80.04

Business Summary: Electric Utilities (MIC: 3.1.1 SIC: 4931 NAIC: 221121)

NiSource is an energy holding company. Through its subsidiaries, Co. provides natural gas and electricity to customers. Co.'s business segments are: Gas Distribution Operations, which serve approximately 3,400,000 customers in seven states and operate approximately 59,000 miles of pipeline and also distributes natural gas to approximately 812,000 customers in northern Indiana through its wholly-owned subsidiary Northern Indiana Public Service Company (NIPSCO); and Electric Operations, which generates, transmits and distributes electricity through its subsidiary NIPSCO to approximately 463,000 customers in the northern part of Indiana and engages in wholesale and transmission transactions.

Recent Developments: For the quarter ended Mar 31 2016, income from continuing operations decreased 6.6% to US$179.7 million from US$192.5 million in the year-earlier quarter. Net income decreased 34.7% to US$179.7 million from US$275.3 million in the year-earlier quarter. Revenues were US$1.44 billion, down 22.4% from US$1.85 billion the year before. Operating income was US$381.4 million versus US$386.3 million in the prior-year quarter, a decrease of 1.3%. Direct operating expenses declined 41.5% to US$496.5 million from US$848.2 million in the comparable period the year before. Indirect operating expenses decreased 9.6% to US$558.7 million from US$617.7 million in the equivalent prior-year period.

Prospects: Our evaluation of NiSource Inc. as of June 19, 2016 is the result of our systematic analysis on three basic characteristics: earnings strength, relative valuation, and recent stock price movement. The company has generated a negative trend in earnings per share over the past 5 quarters and while recent estimates for the company have remained steady, NI has posted better than expected results. Based on operating earnings yield, the company is about fairly valued when compared to all of the companies in our coverage universe. Share price changes over the past year indicates that NI will perform well over the near term.

Financial Data

(US$ in Thousands)	3 Mos	12/31/2015	12/31/2014	12/31/2013	12/31/2012	12/31/2011	12/31/2010	12/31/2009
Earnings Per Share	0.62	0.90	1.67	1.70	1.39	1.03	1.04	0.79
Cash Flow Per Share	3.61	4.58	4.19	4.60	4.36	3.10	2.61	6.06
Tang Book Value Per Share	6.01	5.95	7.10	6.20	5.13	3.63	3.36	3.10
Dividends Per Share	0.725	0.830	1.020	0.980	0.940	0.920	0.920	0.920
Dividend Payout %	116.94	92.22	61.08	57.65	67.63	89.32	88.46	116.46
Income Statement								
Total Revenue	1,436,600	4,651,800	6,470,600	5,657,300	5,061,200	6,019,100	6,422,000	6,649,400
EBITDA	384,000	1,252,400	1,849,800	1,714,800	1,578,600	1,372,000	1,413,700	1,375,200
Depn & Amortn	1,900	533,100	615,500	586,700	571,600	547,100	606,600	602,000
Income Before Taxes	291,600	339,900	794,500	716,200	593,900	452,500	421,100	381,000
Income Taxes	111,900	141,300	310,400	261,900	215,500	163,300	141,500	165,800
Net Income	179,700	286,500	530,000	532,100	416,100	299,100	292,000	217,700
Average Shares	322,020	319,836	316,600	313,600	300,400	288,500	280,100	275,800
Balance Sheet								
Current Assets	1,395,400	1,577,200	2,466,500	2,159,200	2,352,400	2,248,200	2,448,900	2,223,600
Total Assets	17,471,400	17,492,500	24,866,300	22,653,900	21,844,700	20,708,300	19,938,800	19,271,700
Current Liabilities	2,495,900	2,657,500	3,954,900	3,178,400	3,301,600	3,646,400	3,649,400	3,149,600
Long-Term Obligations	5,905,500	5,948,500	8,155,900	7,593,200	6,819,100	6,267,100	5,936,100	5,965,100
Total Liabilities	13,599,100	13,649,000	18,691,000	16,767,300	16,290,400	15,710,100	15,015,600	14,417,600
Stockholders' Equity	3,872,300	3,843,500	6,175,300	5,886,600	5,554,300	4,997,300	4,923,200	4,854,100
Shares Outstanding	321,360	319,110	316,037	313,675	310,280	281,853	278,855	276,638
Statistical Record								
Return on Assets %	0.93	1.35	2.23	2.39	1.95	1.47	1.49	1.11
Return on Equity %	3.81	5.72	8.79	9.30	7.87	6.03	5.97	4.54
EBITDA Margin %	26.73	26.92	28.59	30.31	31.19	22.79	22.01	20.68
Net Margin %	12.51	6.16	8.19	9.41	8.22	4.97	4.55	3.27
Asset Turnover	0.21	0.22	0.27	0.25	0.24	0.30	0.33	0.34
Current Ratio	0.56	0.59	0.62	0.68	0.71	0.62	0.67	0.71
Debt to Equity	1.53	1.55	1.32	1.29	1.23	1.25	1.21	1.23
Price Range	23.56-16.17	19.83-16.10	17.41-12.69	12.92-9.78	10.15-8.83	9.38-6.92	7.04-5.60	6.17-3.09
P/E Ratio	38.00-26.08	22.03-17.88	10.43-7.60	7.60-5.75	7.30-6.35	9.11-6.72	6.77-5.38	7.81-3.91
Average Yield %	3.84	4.67	6.85	8.43	9.77	11.53	14.43	19.47

Address: 801 East 86th Avenue, Merrillville, IN 46410 **Telephone:** 877-647-5990	**Web Site:** www.nisource.com **Officers:** Ian M. Rolland - Chairman Joseph Hamrock - President, Chief Executive Officer, Division Officer	**Auditors:** Deloitte & Touche LLP **Investor Contact:** 219 647-5200 **Transfer Agents:** Computershare, Providence, R.I.

NOBLE CORP PLC

Exchange	Symbol	Price	52Wk Range	Yield	P/E
NYS	NE	$8.34 (5/31/2016)	17.30-6.91	8.33	4.74

*7 Year Price Score 32.14 *NYSE Composite Index=100 *12 Month Price Score 86.60

Interim Earnings (Per Share)

Qtr.	Mar	Jun	Sep	Dec
2013	0.59	0.69	1.10	0.68
2014	0.99	0.91	0.49	(2.36)
2015	0.72	0.64	1.32	(0.62)
2016	0.42	...	...	...

Interim Dividends (Per Share)

Amt	Decl	Ex	Rec	Pay
0.375Q	07/24/2015	07/30/2015	08/03/2015	08/10/2015
0.15Q	10/23/2015	10/29/2015	11/02/2015	11/09/2015
0.15Q	01/29/2016	02/04/2016	02/08/2016	02/16/2016
0.02Q	04/22/2016	04/28/2016	05/02/2016	05/09/2016

Indicated Div: $0.69

Valuation Analysis — **Institutional Holding**

Forecast EPS	$0.50	No of Institutions	
	(05/20/2016)	N/A	
Market Cap	$2.0 Billion	Shares	
Book Value	$6.8 Billion	N/A	
Price/Book	0.30	% Held	
Price/Sales	0.64	N/A	

Business Summary: Equipment & Services (MIC: 9.1.3 SIC: 1381 NAIC: 213111)

Noble is an offshore drilling contractor for the oil and gas industry. Co. perform contract drilling services with its fleet of mobile offshore drilling units. Co.'s drilling fleet is composed of the following types of units: drillships, which are self-propelled vessels; semisubmersibles, which are floating platforms which, by means of a water ballasting system, can be submerged to a predetermined depth so that a substantial portion of the hull is below the water surface during drilling operations in order to improve stability; and jackups, which are capable of drilling in water depths up to approximately 500 feet.

Recent Developments: For the quarter ended Mar 31 2016, net income decreased 37.4% to US$124.1 million from US$198.5 million in the year-earlier quarter. Revenues were US$612.0 million, down 23.9% from US$804.3 million the year before. Operating income was US$175.5 million versus US$284.4 million in the prior-year quarter, a decrease of 38.3%. Direct operating expenses declined 21.8% to US$267.3 million from US$341.9 million in the comparable period the year before. Indirect operating expenses decreased 5.0% to US$169.3 million from US$178.1 million in the equivalent prior-year period.

Prospects: Our evaluation of Noble Corp PLC as of June 19, 2016 is the result of our systematic analysis on three basic characteristics: earnings strength, relative valuation, and recent stock price movement. The company has suffered a very negative trend in earnings per share over the past 5 quarters. Because the company lacks sufficient analyst estimate data, we place greater weight on the historical EPS trend as the measure of earnings strength. Based on operating earnings yield, the company is undervalued when compared to all of the companies in our coverage universe. Share price changes over the past year indicates that NE will perform poorly over the near term.

Financial Data

(US$ in Thousands)	3 Mos	12/31/2015	12/31/2014	12/31/2013	12/31/2012	12/31/2011	12/31/2010	12/31/2009
Earnings Per Share	1.76	2.06	0.03	3.05	2.05	1.46	3.02	6.42
Cash Flow Per Share	6.46	7.28	7.03	6.72	5.46	3.02	6.54	8.28
Tang Book Value Per Share	27.84	27.69	26.52	32.84	30.48	29.32	28.39	26.29
Dividends Per Share	1.050	1.275	1.500	0.760	0.542	0.392	0.880	0.180
Dividend Payout %	59.66	61.89	5,000.00	24.92	26.44	40.58	29.14	2.80
Income Statement								
Total Revenue	611,973	3,352,252	3,232,504	4,234,290	3,547,012	2,695,832	2,807,176	3,640,784
EBITDA	186,418	1,593,478	1,095,878	2,044,600	1,542,421	1,149,133	1,455,909	2,419,057
Depn & Amortn	10,958	673,477	909,936	923,042	758,621	658,640	539,829	408,313
Income Before Taxes	117,630	742,433	29,465	1,018,012	703,225	436,250	916,509	2,015,902
Income Taxes	(6,503)	159,232	106,651	167,606	147,088	72,625	143,077	337,260
Net Income	105,485	511,000	8,491	782,697	522,344	370,898	773,429	1,678,642
Average Shares	242,826	242,146	252,909	253,547	252,791	251,989	253,936	258,891
Balance Sheet								
Current Assets	952,019	1,240,618	928,562	1,390,935	1,305,325	1,059,612	830,728	1,483,190
Total Assets	12,454,912	12,891,984	13,286,822	16,217,957	14,607,774	13,495,159	11,221,321	8,396,896
Current Liabilities	728,952	863,657	668,674	1,051,915	911,449	827,180	720,381	433,947
Long-Term Obligations	3,864,060	4,188,904	4,869,020	5,556,251	4,634,375	4,071,964	2,686,484	750,946
Total Liabilities	5,683,635	6,192,755	6,722,092	7,895,374	6,884,608	6,088,638	4,058,318	1,608,464
Stockholders' Equity	6,771,277	6,699,229	6,564,730	8,322,583	7,723,166	7,406,521	7,163,003	6,788,432
Shares Outstanding	243,212	241,977	247,501	253,448	253,348	252,639	252,275	258,224
Statistical Record								
Return on Assets %	3.42	3.90	0.06	5.08	3.71	3.00	7.88	21.66
Return on Equity %	6.58	7.71	0.11	9.76	6.89	5.09	11.09	27.79
EBITDA Margin %	30.46	47.53	33.90	48.29	43.49	42.63	51.86	66.44
Net Margin %	17.24	15.24	0.26	18.48	14.73	13.76	27.55	46.11
Asset Turnover	0.25	0.26	0.22	0.27	0.25	0.22	0.29	0.47
Current Ratio	1.31	1.44	1.39	1.32	1.43	1.28	1.15	3.42
Debt to Equity	0.57	0.63	0.74	0.67	0.60	0.55	0.38	0.11
Price Range	18.16-6.91	19.51-10.46	37.47-14.52	42.26-34.67	41.25-29.13	46.12-27.68	44.87-27.04	44.78-20.81
P/E Ratio	10.32-3.93	9.47-5.08	N.M.	13.86-11.37	20.12-14.21	31.59-18.96	14.86-8.95	6.98-3.24
Average Yield %	8.25	8.82	5.40	1.98	1.54	1.60	2.42	0.55

Address: Devonshire House, 1 Mayfair Place, London, W1J 8AJ Telephone: 203-300-2300	Web Site: www.noblecorp.com Officers: David W. Williams - Chairman, President, Chief Executive Officer, Senior Vice President, Chief Operating Officer (frmr) Julie J. Robertson - Executive Vice President, Senior Vice President, Vice President, Secretary	Auditors: PricewaterhouseCoopers LLP Investor Contact: 281-276-6100 Transfer Agents: Computershare Trust Company, N.A., Canton, MA

NOBLE ENERGY, INC.

Exchange	Symbol	Price	52Wk Range	Yield	P/E
NYS	NBL	$35.75 (5/31/2016)	46.64-25.72	1.12	N/A

*7 Year Price Score 62.57 *NYSE Composite Index=100 *12 Month Price Score 99.31

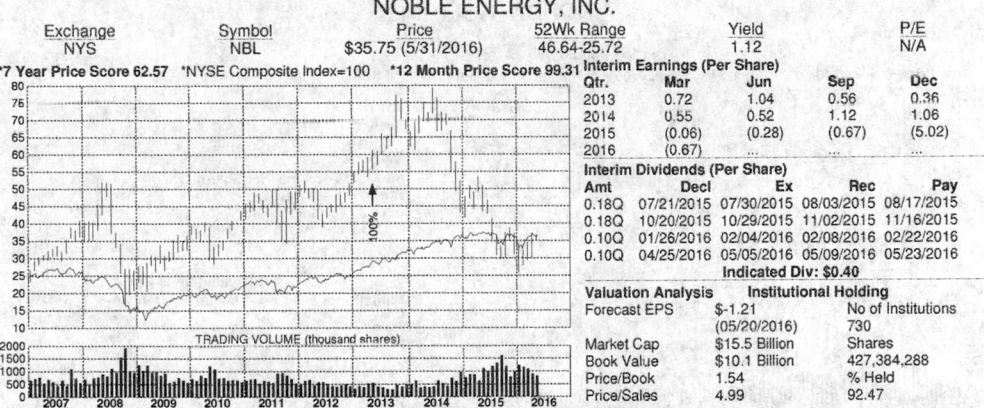

Interim Earnings (Per Share)

Qtr.	Mar	Jun	Sep	Dec
2013	0.72	1.04	0.56	0.36
2014	0.55	0.52	1.12	1.06
2015	(0.06)	(0.28)	(0.67)	(5.02)
2016	(0.67)	...	...	...

Interim Dividends (Per Share)

Amt	Decl	Ex	Rec	Pay
0.18Q	07/21/2015	07/30/2015	08/03/2015	08/17/2015
0.18Q	10/20/2015	10/29/2015	11/02/2015	11/16/2015
0.10Q	01/26/2016	02/04/2016	02/08/2016	02/22/2016
0.10Q	04/25/2016	05/05/2016	05/09/2016	05/23/2016

Indicated Div: $0.40

Valuation Analysis

Valuation Analysis		Institutional Holding	
Forecast EPS	$-1.21	No of Institutions	
	(05/20/2016)	730	
Market Cap	$15.5 Billion	Shares	
Book Value	$10.1 Billion	427,384,288	
Price/Book	1.54	% Held	
Price/Sales	4.99	92.47	

TRADING VOLUME (thousand shares)

Business Summary: Production & Extraction (MIC: 9.1.1 SIC: 1311 NAIC: 211111)

Noble Energy is engaged crude oil, natural gas and natural gas liquids exploration and production. Co.'s properties consist primarily of interests in developed and undeveloped crude oil and natural gas leases and concessions. Co. also owns natural gas processing plants, gathering systems and other pipeline systems. Co. has operations in these areas: the DJ Basin, the Marcellus Shale, Eagle Ford Shale, Permian Basin, the deepwater Gulf of Mexico, offshore West Africa and Eastern Mediterranean. As of Dec 31 2015, Co. had total proved reserves of 1.42 billion barrels of oil equivalent (BoE), of which 485.0 million BoE are proved undeveloped and 936.0 million BoE are proved developed.

Recent Developments: For the quarter ended Mar 31 2016, net loss amounted to US$287.0 million versus a net loss of US$22.0 million in the year-earlier quarter. Revenues were US$724.0 million, down 5.6% from US$767.0 million the year before. Operating loss was US$422.0 million versus a loss of US$134.0 million in the prior-year quarter. Direct operating expenses rose 7.1% to US$272.0 million from US$254.0 million in the comparable period the year before. Indirect operating expenses increased 35.1% to US$874.0 million from US$647.0 million in the equivalent prior-year period.

Prospects: Our evaluation of Noble Energy Inc. as of June 19, 2016 is the result of our systematic analysis on three basic characteristics: earnings strength, relative valuation, and recent stock price movement. The company has produced a positive trend in earnings per share over the past 5 quarters. Because the company lacks sufficient analyst estimate data, we place greater weight on the historical EPS trend as the measure of earnings strength. Based on operating earnings yield, the company is overvalued when compared to all of the companies in our coverage universe. Share price changes over the past year indicates that NBL will perform poorly over the near term.

Financial Data

(US$ in Thousands)	3 Mos	12/31/2015	12/31/2014	12/31/2013	12/31/2012	12/31/2011	12/31/2010	12/31/2009
Earnings Per Share	(6.64)	(6.07)	3.27	2.69	2.86	1.27	2.05	(0.38)
Cash Flow Per Share	4.13	5.13	9.71	8.18	8.22	6.16	5.56	4.36
Tang Book Value Per Share	23.21	24.02	26.61	23.78	21.29	18.45	17.48	15.43
Dividends Per Share	0.640	0.720	0.680	0.545	0.455	0.400	0.360	0.360
Dividend Payout %	...	...	20.80	20.26	15.94	31.50	17.56	...
Income Statement								
Total Revenue	724,000	3,133,000	5,101,000	5,015,000	4,223,000	3,763,000	3,022,000	2,313,000
EBITDA	243,000	288,000	3,679,000	3,072,000	2,883,000	1,737,000	1,979,000	623,000
Depn & Amortn	617,000	2,244,000	1,759,000	1,570,000	1,403,000	965,000	883,000	816,000
Income Before Taxes	(453,000)	(2,219,000)	1,710,000	1,344,000	1,356,000	715,000	1,031,000	(264,000)
Income Taxes	(166,000)	222,000	496,000	437,000	391,000	262,000	306,000	(133,000)
Net Income	(287,000)	(2,441,000)	1,214,000	978,000	1,027,000	453,000	725,000	(131,000)
Average Shares	429,000	402,000	367,000	363,000	360,000	358,000	354,000	346,000
Balance Sheet								
Current Assets	2,092,000	2,276,000	3,075,000	2,611,000	2,771,000	2,418,000	1,838,000	1,678,000
Total Assets	23,413,000	24,196,000	22,553,000	19,642,000	17,554,000	16,444,000	13,282,000	11,807,000
Current Liabilities	1,606,000	1,805,000	2,522,000	2,342,000	2,532,000	2,268,000	1,422,000	990,000
Long-Term Obligations	7,882,000	7,976,000	6,103,000	4,566,000	3,736,000	4,100,000	2,272,000	2,037,000
Total Liabilities	13,361,000	13,826,000	12,228,000	10,458,000	9,296,000	9,179,000	6,434,000	5,650,000
Stockholders' Equity	10,052,000	10,370,000	10,325,000	9,184,000	8,258,000	7,265,000	6,848,000	6,157,000
Shares Outstanding	433,000	431,792	364,693	359,905	358,000	356,000	352,000	350,000
Statistical Record								
Return on Assets %	N.M.	N.M.	5.75	5.26	6.03	3.05	5.78	N.M.
Return on Equity %	N.M.	N.M.	12.45	11.21	13.20	6.42	11.15	N.M.
EBITDA Margin %	33.56	9.19	72.12	61.26	68.27	46.16	65.49	26.93
Net Margin %	N.M.	N.M.	23.80	19.50	24.32	12.04	23.99	N.M.
Asset Turnover	0.13	0.13	0.24	0.27	0.25	0.25	0.24	0.19
Current Ratio	1.30	1.26	1.22	1.11	1.09	1.07	1.29	1.69
Debt to Equity	0.78	0.77	0.59	0.50	0.45	0.56	0.33	0.33
Price Range	53.47-25.72	53.47-29.58	79.23-43.00	77.13-50.87	52.28-38.80	49.84-34.28	43.58-28.11	36.84-20.36
P/E Ratio	...	...	24.23-13.15	28.67-18.91	18.28-13.56	39.24-27.00	21.26-13.71	...
Average Yield %	1.74	1.77	1.03	0.88	0.97	0.90	0.98	1.20

Address: 1001 Noble Energy Way, Houston, TX 77070
Telephone: 281-872-3100
Fax: 281-872-3111

Web Site: www.nobleenergyinc.com
Officers: Charles D. Davidson - Chairman, President, Chief Executive Officer David L. Stover - President, Chief Executive Officer, Chief Operating Officer

Auditors: KPMG LLP
Investor Contact: 281-.87-2.3125
Transfer Agents: Wells Fargo Bank, N. A., South St. Paul, MN

NORDSTROM, INC.

Exchange	Symbol	Price	52Wk Range	Yield	P/E
NYS	JWN	$37.98 (5/31/2016)	79.52-36.37	3.90	13.81

*7 Year Price Score 98.18 ***NYSE Composite Index=100** ***12 Month Price Score 79.07**

TRADING VOLUME (thousand shares)

Interim Earnings (Per Share)

Qtr.	Apr	Jul	Oct	Jan
2013-14	0.73	0.93	0.69	1.36
2014-15	0.72	0.95	0.73	1.32
2015-16	0.66	1.09	0.42	0.98
2016-17	0.26			

Interim Dividends (Per Share)

Amt	Decl	Ex	Rec	Pay
0.37Q	08/19/2015	08/27/2015	08/31/2015	09/15/2015
0.37Q	11/18/2015	11/25/2015	11/30/2015	12/15/2015
0.37Q	02/24/2016	03/03/2016	03/07/2016	03/22/2016
0.37Q	05/19/2016	05/26/2016	05/31/2016	06/15/2016

Indicated Div: $1.48

Valuation Analysis

		Institutional Holding	
Forecast EPS	$2.56	No of Institutions	
	(05/20/2016)	835	
Market Cap	$6.6 Billion	Shares	
Book Value	$875.0 Million	133,360,608	
Price/Book	7.53	% Held	
Price/Sales	0.46	53.51	

Business Summary: Retail - General Merchandise/Department Stores (MIC: 2.1.1 SIC: 5651 NAIC: 448140)

Nordstrom is a retailer that provides a range of fashion brands focused on apparel, shoes, cosmetics and accessories for men, women and children, with operations of 323 U.S. stores located in 39 states as of Mar 14, 2016. Co. has two segments: Retail, which included 118 Nordstrom full-line stores in the U.S. and Nordstrom.com, 197 Nordstrom Rack stores, three Canada full-line stores, Nordstromrack.com/HauteLook, five Trunk Club clubhouses and TrunkClub.com, its two Jeffrey boutiques and one clearance store; and Credit, which customers can access a variety of payment products and services, including a Nordstrom-branded private label card, two Nordstrom VISA credit cards and a debit card.

Recent Developments: For the quarter ended Apr 30 2016, net income decreased 64.1% to US$46.0 million from US$128.0 million in the year-earlier quarter. Revenues were US$3.25 billion, up 1.1% from US$3.22 billion the year before. Operating income was US$106.0 million versus US$245.0 million in the prior-year quarter, a decrease of 56.7%. Direct operating expenses rose 5.1% to US$2.10 billion from US$2.00 billion in the comparable period the year before. Indirect operating expenses increased 7.4% to US$1.04 billion from US$971.0 million in the equivalent prior-year period.

Prospects: Our evaluation of Nordstrom Inc. as of June 19, 2016 is the result of our systematic analysis on three basic characteristics: earnings strength, relative valuation, and recent stock price movement. The company has generated a negative trend in earnings per share over the past 5 quarters. However, while recent estimates for the company have been lowered by analysts, JWN has posted results that fell short of analysts expectations. Based on operating earnings yield, the company is undervalued when compared to all of the companies in our coverage universe. Share price changes over the past year indicates that JWN will perform in line with the market over the near term.

Financial Data
(US$ in Thousands)

	3 Mos	01/30/2016	01/31/2015	02/01/2014	02/02/2013	01/28/2012	01/29/2011	01/30/2010
Earnings Per Share	2.75	3.15	3.72	3.71	3.56	3.14	2.75	2.01
Cash Flow Per Share	13.95	13.19	6.44	6.81	5.38	5.53	5.39	5.79
Tang Book Value Per Share	2.54	2.51	10.55	9.96	8.82	8.58	9.03	6.98
Dividends Per Share	6.330	6.330	1.320	1.200	1.080	0.920	0.760	0.640
Dividend Payout %	230.18	200.95	35.48	32.35	30.34	29.30	27.64	31.84
Income Statement								
Total Revenue	3,249,000	14,437,000	13,506,000	12,540,000	12,148,000	10,877,000	9,700,000	8,627,000
EBITDA	244,000	1,661,000	1,821,000	1,794,000	1,711,000	1,574,000	1,391,000	1,105,000
Depn & Amortn	138,000	560,000	498,000	444,000	366,000	325,000	273,000	271,000
Income Before Taxes	75,000	976,000	1,185,000	1,189,000	1,185,000	1,119,000	991,000	696,000
Income Taxes	29,000	376,000	465,000	455,000	450,000	436,000	378,000	255,000
Net Income	46,000	600,000	720,000	734,000	735,000	683,000	613,000	441,000
Average Shares	175,700	190,100	193,600	197,700	206,700	217,700	222,600	219,700
Balance Sheet								
Current Assets	2,992,000	3,014,000	5,224,000	5,228,000	5,081,000	5,560,000	4,824,000	4,054,000
Total Assets	7,699,000	7,698,000	9,245,000	8,574,000	8,089,000	8,491,000	7,462,000	6,579,000
Current Liabilities	2,936,000	2,911,000	2,800,000	2,541,000	2,226,000	2,575,000	1,879,000	2,014,000
Long-Term Obligations	2,776,000	2,795,000	3,123,000	3,106,000	3,124,000	3,141,000	2,775,000	2,257,000
Total Liabilities	6,824,000	6,827,000	6,805,000	6,494,000	6,176,000	6,535,000	5,441,000	5,007,000
Stockholders' Equity	875,000	871,000	2,440,000	2,080,000	1,913,000	1,956,000	2,021,000	1,572,000
Shares Outstanding	173,400	173,500	190,100	191,200	197,000	207,600	218,000	217,700
Statistical Record								
Return on Assets %	6.00	7.10	8.10	8.83	8.72	8.59	8.76	7.23
Return on Equity %	30.20	36.34	31.95	36.87	37.38	34.44	34.22	31.79
EBITDA Margin %	7.51	11.51	13.48	14.31	14.08	14.47	14.34	12.81
Net Margin %	1.42	4.16	5.33	5.85	6.05	6.28	6.32	5.11
Asset Turnover	1.68	1.71	1.52	1.51	1.44	1.37	1.39	1.41
Current Ratio	1.02	1.04	1.87	2.06	2.28	2.16	2.57	2.01
Debt to Equity	3.17	3.21	1.28	1.49	1.63	1.61	1.37	1.44
Price Range	79.52-45.45	82.32-45.45	79.78-55.38	63.43-52.45	58.20-46.80	52.77-37.45	45.90-28.72	38.93-11.33
P/E Ratio	28.92-16.53	26.13-14.43	21.45-14.89	17.10-14.14	16.35-13.15	16.81-11.93	16.69-10.44	19.37-5.64
Average Yield %	9.90	8.99	1.93	2.05	2.01	1.97	1.98	2.47

Address: 1617 Sixth Avenue, Seattle, WA 98101 Telephone: 206-628-2111	Web Site: www.nordstrom.com Officers: Enrique Hernandez - Chairman Blake W. Nordstrom - Co-President, President, Co-President (fmr), Executive Vice President	Auditors: Deloitte & Touche LLP Investor Contact: 206-303-3200 Transfer Agents: Computershare, Providence, RI

NORFOLK SOUTHERN CORP.

Exchange	Symbol	Price	52Wk Range	Yield	P/E	Div Achiever
NYS	NSC	$84.06 (5/31/2016)	97.56-66.60	2.81	15.60	14 Years

*7 Year Price Score 93.75 *NYSE Composite Index=100 *12 Month Price Score 103.40

Interim Earnings (Per Share)

Qtr.	Mar	Jun	Sep	Dec
2013	1.41	1.46	1.53	1.64
2014	1.17	1.79	1.79	1.64
2015	1.00	1.41	1.49	1.20
2016	1.29	...	...	...

Interim Dividends (Per Share)

Amt	Decl	Ex	Rec	Pay
0.59Q	07/24/2015	08/05/2015	08/07/2015	09/10/2015
0.59Q	10/27/2015	11/04/2015	11/06/2015	12/10/2015
0.59Q	01/26/2016	02/03/2016	02/05/2016	03/10/2016
0.59Q	04/19/2016	05/04/2016	05/06/2016	06/10/2016

Indicated Div: $2.36 (Div. Reinv. Plan)

Valuation Analysis — **Institutional Holding**

Forecast EPS	$5.55
	(05/20/2016)
Market Cap	$24.9 Billion
Book Value	$12.2 Billion
Price/Book	2.03
Price/Sales	2.40

No of Institutions	1323
Shares	232,756,704
% Held	68.43

Business Summary: Rail (MIC: 7.4.3 SIC: 4011 NAIC: 482111)

Norfolk Southern is a holding company engaged principally in the rail transportation business, operating approx. 20,000 miles of road primarily in the East and Midwest. Co.'s Norfolk Southern Railway Company subsidiary and its railroad subsidiaries transport raw materials, intermediate products and finished goods classified in the following commodity groups: coal; intermodal; chemicals; agriculture/consumer products/government; metals/construction; automotive; and, paper/clay/forest products. At Dec 31 2015, Co.'s railroads operated in 22 states and the District of Columbia. Co. also transport overseas freight through several Atlantic and Gulf Coast ports.

Recent Developments: For the quarter ended Mar 31 2016, net income increased 24.8% to US$387.0 million from US$310.0 million in the year-earlier quarter. Revenues were US$2.42 billion, down 5.7% from US$2.57 billion the year before. Operating income was US$723.0 million versus US$606.0 million in the prior-year quarter, an increase of 19.3%. Direct operating expenses declined 22.6% to US$722.0 million from US$933.0 million in the comparable period the year before. Indirect operating expenses decreased 5.2% to US$975.0 million from US$1.03 billion in the equivalent prior-year period.

Prospects: Our evaluation of Norfolk Southern Corp. as of June 19, 2016 is the result of our systematic analysis on three basic characteristics: earnings strength, relative valuation, and recent stock price movement. The company has produced a positive trend in earnings per share over the past 5 quarters. However, while recent estimates for the company have been lowered by analysts, NSC has posted better than expected results. Based on operating earnings yield, the company is undervalued when compared to all of the companies in our coverage universe. Share price changes over the past year indicates that NSC will perform in line with the market over the near term.

Financial Data

(US$ in Thousands)	3 Mos	12/31/2015	12/31/2014	12/31/2013	12/31/2012	12/31/2011	12/31/2010	12/31/2009
Earnings Per Share	5.39	5.10	6.39	6.04	5.37	5.45	4.00	2.76
Cash Flow Per Share	10.60	9.53	9.22	9.87	9.53	9.34	7.41	5.07
Tang Book Value Per Share	41.33	40.93	40.25	36.55	31.08	30.00	29.85	28.06
Dividends Per Share	2.360	2.360	2.220	2.040	1.940	1.660	1.400	1.360
Dividend Payout %	43.78	46.27	34.74	33.77	36.13	30.46	35.00	49.28
Income Statement								
Total Revenue	2,420,000	10,511,000	11,624,000	11,245,000	11,040,000	11,172,000	9,516,000	7,969,000
EBITDA	992,000	4,051,000	4,647,000	4,384,000	4,152,000	4,214,000	3,643,000	2,904,000
Depn & Amortn	253,000	1,059,000	956,000	922,000	922,000	869,000	826,000	845,000
Income Before Taxes	600,000	2,451,000	3,143,000	2,933,000	2,734,000	2,896,000	2,351,000	1,600,000
Income Taxes	213,000	895,000	1,143,000	1,065,000	1,019,000	1,011,000	881,000	598,000
Net Income	387,000	1,556,000	2,000,000	1,910,000	1,749,000	1,916,000	1,496,000	1,034,000
Average Shares	298,900	301,900	312,500	315,500	325,200	351,300	371,800	372,100
Balance Sheet								
Current Assets	1,966,000	2,633,000	2,778,000	3,075,000	2,242,000	1,751,000	2,471,000	2,246,000
Total Assets	33,785,000	34,260,000	33,241,000	32,483,000	30,342,000	28,538,000	28,199,000	27,369,000
Current Liabilities	1,831,000	2,231,000	1,780,000	2,305,000	2,081,000	1,701,000	2,082,000	1,789,000
Long-Term Obligations	9,398,000	9,393,000	8,924,000	8,903,000	8,432,000	7,390,000	6,567,000	6,679,000
Total Liabilities	21,562,000	22,072,000	20,833,000	21,194,000	20,582,000	18,627,000	17,530,000	17,016,000
Stockholders' Equity	12,223,000	12,188,000	12,408,000	11,289,000	9,760,000	9,911,000	10,669,000	10,353,000
Shares Outstanding	295,737	297,795	308,240	308,878	314,034	330,386	357,362	369,019
Statistical Record								
Return on Assets %	4.91	4.61	6.09	6.08	5.92	6.75	5.38	3.85
Return on Equity %	13.40	12.65	16.88	18.15	17.73	18.62	14.23	10.36
EBITDA Margin %	40.99	38.54	39.98	38.99	37.61	37.72	38.28	36.44
Net Margin %	15.99	14.80	17.21	16.99	15.84	17.15	15.72	12.98
Asset Turnover	0.31	0.31	0.35	0.36	0.37	0.39	0.34	0.30
Current Ratio	1.07	1.18	1.56	1.33	1.08	1.03	1.19	1.26
Debt to Equity	0.77	0.77	0.72	0.79	0.86	0.75	0.62	0.65
Price Range	106.35-66.60	111.73-72.44	117.20-87.76	92.87-61.84	78.24-56.34	76.99-60.01	62.99-46.31	54.24-26.95
P/E Ratio	19.73-12.36	21.91-14.20	18.34-13.73	15.38-10.24	14.57-10.49	14.13-11.01	15.75-11.58	19.65-9.76
Average Yield %	2.77	2.55	2.12	2.65	2.83	2.41	2.47	3.23

Address: Three Commercial Place, Norfolk, VA 23510-2191	Web Site: www.nscorp.com	Auditors: KPMG LLP
Telephone: 757-629-2680	Officers: James A. Squires - Chairman, President, Chief Executive Officer, Executive Vice President, Chief Financial Officer, Executive Vice President Marta R. Stewart - Executive Vice President, Chief Financial Officer, Vice President, Treasurer	Investor Contact: 757-629-2861 Transfer Agents: American Stock Transfer & Trust Company, LLC, Brooklyn, NY

NORTHROP GRUMMAN CORP

Exchange	Symbol	Price	52Wk Range	Yield	P/E	Div Achiever
NYS	NOC	$212.67 (5/31/2016)	217.98-156.66	1.69	19.30	12 Years

*7 Year Price Score 163.78 *NYSE Composite Index=100 *12 Month Price Score 112.57

Interim Earnings (Per Share)

Qtr.	Mar	Jun	Sep	Dec
2013	2.03	2.05	2.14	2.13
2014	2.63	2.37	2.26	2.47
2015	2.41	2.74	2.75	2.50
2016	3.03	...	...	...

Interim Dividends (Per Share)

Amt	Decl	Ex	Rec	Pay
0.80Q	08/19/2015	08/27/2015	08/31/2015	09/16/2015
0.80Q	11/18/2015	11/25/2015	11/30/2015	12/16/2015
0.80Q	02/16/2016	02/25/2016	02/29/2016	03/16/2016
0.90Q	05/17/2016	06/02/2016	06/06/2016	06/22/2016

Indicated Div: $3.60 (Div. Reinv. Plan)

Valuation Analysis		Institutional Holding	
Forecast EPS	$10.70	No of Institutions	
	(05/20/2016)	1057	
Market Cap	$38.5 Billion	Shares	
Book Value	$5.6 Billion	200,726,096	
Price/Book	6.84	% Held	
Price/Sales	1.63	76.99	

Business Summary: Defense (MIC: 7.1.2 SIC: 3812 NAIC: 334511)

Northrop Grumman is a global security company. Co. provides products, systems and solutions in unmanned systems; cyber; command, control, communications and computers; intelligence, surveillance, and reconnaissance; strike aircraft; and logistics and modernization to government and commercial customers worldwide through its four sectors: Aerospace Systems, Electronic Systems, Information Systems and Technical Services. Co. conducts most of its business with the U.S. Government, principally the Department of Defense and intelligence community. Co. also conducts business with foreign, state and local governments and commercial customers.

Recent Developments: For the quarter ended Mar 31 2016, net income increased 14.9% to US$556.0 million from US$484.0 million in the year-earlier quarter. Revenues were US$5.96 billion, unchanged from the year before. Operating income was US$739.0 million versus US$780.0 million in the prior-year quarter, a decrease of 5.3%. Direct operating expenses rose 0.4% to US$4.56 billion from US$4.54 billion in the comparable period the year before. Indirect operating expenses increased 3.3% to US$656.0 million from US$635.0 million in the equivalent prior-year period.

Prospects: Our evaluation of Northrop Grumman Corp. as of June 19, 2016 is the result of our systematic analysis on three basic characteristics: earnings strength, relative valuation, and recent stock price movement. The company has produced a positive trend in earnings per share over the past 5 quarters and while recent estimates for the company have been raised by analysts, NOC has posted better than expected results. Based on operating earnings yield, the company is about fairly valued when compared to all of the companies in our coverage universe. Share price changes over the past year indicates that NOC will perform very well over the near term.

Financial Data

(US$ in Thousands)	3 Mos	12/31/2015	12/31/2014	12/31/2013	12/31/2012	12/31/2011	12/31/2010	12/31/2009
Earnings Per Share	11.02	10.39	9.75	8.35	7.81	7.52	6.82	5.21
Cash Flow Per Share	15.20	11.41	12.42	10.81	10.59	7.64	8.26	6.68
Dividends Per Share	3.200	3.100	2.710	2.380	2.150	1.970	1.840	1.690
Dividend Payout %	29.04	29.84	27.79	28.50	27.53	26.20	26.98	32.44
Income Statement								
Total Revenue	5,956,000	23,526,000	23,979,000	24,661,000	25,218,000	26,412,000	34,757,000	33,755,000
EBITDA	855,000	3,558,000	3,681,000	3,615,000	3,625,000	3,766,000	3,482,000	3,132,000
Depn & Amortn	103,000	467,000	462,000	495,000	448,000	462,000	606,000	585,000
Income Before Taxes	676,000	2,790,000	2,937,000	2,863,000	2,965,000	3,083,000	2,595,000	2,266,000
Income Taxes	120,000	800,000	868,000	911,000	987,000	997,000	557,000	693,000
Net Income	556,000	1,990,000	2,069,000	1,952,000	1,978,000	2,118,000	2,053,000	1,686,000
Average Shares	183,400	191,600	212,100	233,900	253,400	281,600	301,100	323,300
Balance Sheet								
Current Assets	5,706,000	6,334,000	8,184,000	9,488,000	8,392,000	7,746,000	9,904,000	8,635,000
Total Assets	23,933,000	24,454,000	26,572,000	26,381,000	26,543,000	25,411,000	31,421,000	30,252,000
Current Liabilities	4,955,000	5,457,000	5,892,000	5,815,000	6,056,000	6,135,000	8,386,000	6,985,000
Long-Term Obligations	6,387,000	6,416,000	5,925,000	5,928,000	3,930,000	3,935,000	4,045,000	4,191,000
Total Liabilities	18,312,000	18,932,000	19,337,000	15,761,000	17,029,000	15,075,000	17,864,000	17,565,000
Stockholders' Equity	5,621,000	5,522,000	7,235,000	10,620,000	9,514,000	10,336,000	13,557,000	12,687,000
Shares Outstanding	180,828	181,303	198,930	217,599	239,209	253,889	290,956	306,865
Statistical Record								
Return on Assets %	8.38	7.80	7.81	7.38	7.59	7.45	6.66	5.58
Return on Equity %	33.34	31.20	23.18	19.39	19.88	17.73	15.65	13.70
EBITDA Margin %	14.36	15.12	15.35	14.66	14.37	14.26	10.02	9.28
Net Margin %	9.34	8.46	8.63	7.92	7.84	8.02	5.91	4.99
Asset Turnover	0.96	0.92	0.91	0.93	0.97	0.93	1.13	1.12
Current Ratio	1.15	1.16	1.39	1.63	1.39	1.26	1.18	1.24
Debt to Equity	1.14	1.16	0.82	0.56	0.41	0.38	0.30	0.33
Price Range	198.73-153.28	191.48-143.37	152.24-110.80	115.32-64.38	71.13-57.11	70.33-49.26	62.94-49.08	51.56-31.16
P/E Ratio	18.03-13.91	18.43-13.80	15.61-11.36	13.81-7.71	9.11-7.31	9.35-6.55	9.23-7.20	9.90-5.98
Average Yield %	1.83	1.85	2.16	2.76	3.37	3.30	3.32	3.87

Address: 2980 Fairview Park Drive, Falls Church, VA 22042 Telephone: 703-280-2900	Web Site: www.northropgrumman.com Officers: Wesley G. Bush - Chairman, President, Chief Executive Officer, Vice President, Chief Financial Officer, Chief Operating Officer Darryl M. Fraser - Vice President	Auditors: Deloitte & Touche LLP Investor Contact: 703-280-2268 Transfer Agents: Computershare, Providence, RI

NORTHWEST NATURAL GAS CO.

Exchange	Symbol	Price	52Wk Range	Yield	P/E	Div Achiever
NYS	NWN	$54.90 (5/31/2016)	57.69-42.18	3.41	24.40	60 Years

*7 Year Price Score 90.31 *NYSE Composite Index=100 *12 Month Price Score 108.97

Interim Earnings (Per Share)

Qtr.	Mar	Jun	Sep	Dec
2013	1.40	0.08	(0.31)	1.07
2014	1.40	0.04	(0.32)	1.05
2015	1.04	0.08	(0.24)	1.08
2016	1.33	...	...	...

Interim Dividends (Per Share)

Amt	Decl	Ex	Rec	Pay
0.465Q	07/02/2015	07/29/2015	07/31/2015	08/14/2015
0.468Q	10/05/2015	10/28/2015	10/30/2015	11/13/2015
0.468Q	01/07/2016	01/27/2016	01/29/2016	02/12/2016
0.468Q	04/07/2016	04/27/2016	04/29/2016	05/13/2016

Indicated Div: $1.87 (Div. Reinv. Plan)

Valuation Analysis — **Institutional Holding**

Forecast EPS	$2.21	No of Institutions	
	(05/15/2016)	255	
Market Cap	$1.5 Billion	Shares	
Book Value	$807.0 Million	18,423,602	
Price/Book	1.87	% Held	
Price/Sales	2.10	59.86	

Business Summary: Gas Utilities (MIC: 3.3.1 SIC: 4924 NAIC: 221210)

Northwest Natural Gas is engaged in the distribution of natural gas. Co. operates in two segments: local gas distribution, which involves building and maintaining a pipeline distribution system, purchasing gas from producers and marketers, contracting for the transportation of gas over interstate pipelines to bring gas from the supply basins into its service territory, and re-selling the gas to customers; and gas storage, which includes natural gas storage services provided to customers primarily from two underground natural gas storage facilities. At Dec 31 2015, Co. had 714,428 utility customers with approximately 89% of its utility customers are located in Oregon and 11% in Washington.

Recent Developments: For the quarter ended Mar 31 2016, net income increased 28.6% to US$36.6 million from US$28.5 million in the year-earlier quarter. Revenues were US$255.5 million, down 2.3% from US$261.7 million the year before. Operating income was US$74.1 million versus US$53.0 million in the prior-year quarter, an increase of 39.8%. Direct operating expenses declined 13.8% to US$108.4 million from US$125.7 million in the comparable period the year before. Indirect operating expenses decreased 11.9% to US$73.0 million from US$83.0 million in the equivalent prior-year period.

Prospects: Our evaluation of Northwest Natural Gas Co. as of June 19, 2016 is the result of our systematic analysis on three basic characteristics: earnings strength, relative valuation, and recent stock price movement. The company has managed to produce a neutral trend in earnings per share over the past 5 quarters and while recent estimates for the company have been raised by analysts, NWN has posted better than expected results. Based on operating earnings yield, the company is about fairly valued when compared to all of the companies in our coverage universe. Share price changes over the past year indicates that NWN will perform well over the near term.

Financial Data
(US$ in Thousands)

	3 Mos	12/31/2015	12/31/2014	12/31/2013	12/31/2012	12/31/2011	12/31/2010	12/31/2009
Earnings Per Share	2.25	1.96	2.16	2.24	2.22	2.39	2.73	2.83
Cash Flow Per Share	7.74	6.75	7.94	6.54	6.28	8.75	4.76	9.07
Tang Book Value Per Share	29.35	28.47	28.12	27.77	27.23	26.70	25.99	24.88
Dividends Per Share	1.865	1.863	1.845	1.825	1.790	1.750	1.680	1.600
Dividend Payout %	82.89	95.03	85.42	81.47	80.63	73.22	61.54	56.54
Income Statement								
Total Revenue	255,529	723,791	754,037	758,518	730,607	848,796	812,106	1,012,711
EBITDA	89,551	234,422	243,426	234,409	220,133	219,322	227,807	225,033
Depn & Amortn	9,104	102,427	98,528	86,994	73,017	70,004	65,124	62,814
Income Before Taxes	70,711	89,456	100,335	102,243	103,959	107,280	122,129	121,793
Income Taxes	34,070	35,753	41,643	41,705	44,104	43,382	49,462	46,671
Net Income	36,641	53,703	58,692	60,538	59,855	63,898	72,667	75,122
Average Shares	27,560	27,417	27,223	27,027	26,907	26,744	26,657	26,576
Balance Sheet								
Current Assets	272,200	332,063	362,560	330,448	283,699	348,689	330,265	328,235
Total Assets	3,002,033	3,076,692	3,064,945	2,970,911	2,818,753	2,746,574	2,616,616	2,399,252
Current Liabilities	362,223	477,714	469,410	432,791	368,436	414,464	468,161	392,569
Long-Term Obligations	569,745	576,700	621,700	681,700	691,700	641,700	591,700	601,700
Total Liabilities	2,195,078	2,295,720	2,297,624	2,219,039	2,085,720	2,032,086	1,923,515	1,739,147
Stockholders' Equity	806,955	780,972	767,321	751,872	733,033	714,488	693,101	660,105
Shares Outstanding	27,493	27,427	27,284	27,075	26,917	26,756	26,668	26,533
Statistical Record								
Return on Assets %	2.07	1.75	1.94	2.09	2.15	2.38	2.90	3.14
Return on Equity %	7.77	6.94	7.73	8.15	8.25	9.08	10.74	11.66
EBITDA Margin %	35.05	32.39	32.28	30.90	30.13	25.84	28.05	22.22
Net Margin %	14.34	7.42	7.78	7.98	8.19	7.53	8.95	7.42
Asset Turnover	0.24	0.24	0.25	0.26	0.26	0.32	0.32	0.42
Current Ratio	0.75	0.70	0.77	0.76	0.77	0.84	0.71	0.84
Debt to Equity	0.71	0.74	0.81	0.91	0.94	0.90	0.85	0.91
Price Range	54.22-42.18	51.98-42.18	52.46-40.36	46.40-40.07	50.47-41.72	48.66-40.09	50.64-41.62	46.19-38.50
P/E Ratio	24.10-18.75	26.52-21.52	24.29-18.69	20.71-17.89	22.73-18.79	20.36-16.77	18.55-15.25	16.32-13.60
Average Yield %	3.95	4.01	4.14	4.21	3.83	3.86	3.63	3.73

Address: 220 N.W. Second Avenue, Portland, OR 97209 Telephone: 503-226-4211	Web Site: www.nwnatural.com Officers: Tod R. Hamachek - Chairman David H. Anderson - President, Executive Vice President, Chief Operating Officer, Executive Vice President (frmr), Senior Vice President, Chief Financial Officer	Auditors: PricewaterhouseCoopers LLP Investor Contact: 503-226-4211ext.24 Transfer Agents: American Stock Transfer & Trust Company, Brooklyn, NY

NOW INC

Exchange	Symbol	Price	52Wk Range	Yield	P/E
NYS	DNOW	$17.34 (5/31/2016)	23.39-12.48	N/A	N/A

*7 Year Price Score N/A   *NYSE Composite Index=100   *12 Month Price Score 98.47

Interim Earnings (Per Share)

Qtr.	Mar	Jun	Sep	Dec
2013	0.37	0.31	0.36	0.32
2014	0.38	0.25	0.30	0.14
2015	(0.09)	(0.18)	(2.09)	(2.32)
2016	(0.59)	...	...	...

Interim Dividends (Per Share)

No Dividends Paid

Valuation Analysis   **Institutional Holding**

Forecast EPS	$-1.46	No of Institutions
	(05/17/2016)	360
Market Cap	$1.9 Billion	Shares
Book Value	$1.4 Billion	107,145,696
Price/Book	1.36	% Held
Price/Sales	0.69	106.22

TRADING VOLUME (thousand shares)

Business Summary: Equipment & Services (MIC: 9.1.3 SIC: 3533 NAIC: 333132)

NOW is a distributor to energy and industrial markets. Co. operates under the DistributionNOW and Wilson Export brands. Co.'s product offering includes consumable maintenance, repair and operating supplies, pipe, valves, fittings, flanges, electrical, artificial lift solutions, mill tools, safety supplies and spare parts. Co. operates three reportable segments: U.S., which serves the upstream, midstream and downstream energy and industrial markets in the U.S.; Canada, which serves the energy exploration, production, drilling and midstream business, providing customers the same products and solutions that it performs in the U.S; and International, which serves international customers.

Recent Developments: For the quarter ended Mar 31 2016, net loss amounted to US$63.0 million versus a net loss of US$10.0 million in the year-earlier quarter. Revenues were US$548.0 million, down 36.5% from US$863.0 million the year before. Operating loss was US$65.0 million versus a loss of US$8.0 million in the prior-year quarter. Direct operating expenses declined 34.9% to US$461.0 million from US$708.0 million in the comparable period the year before. Indirect operating expenses decreased 6.7% to US$152.0 million from US$163.0 million in the equivalent prior-year period.

Prospects: Our evaluation of NOW Inc. as of June 19, 2016 is the result of our systematic analysis on three basic characteristics: earnings strength, relative valuation, and recent stock price movement. The company has managed to produce a neutral trend in earnings per share over the past 5 quarters. Because the company lacks sufficient analyst estimate data, we place greater weight on the historical EPS trend as the measure of earnings strength. Based on operating earnings yield, the company is overvalued when compared to all of the companies in our coverage universe. Share price changes over the past year indicates that DNOW will perform poorly over the near term.

Financial Data

(US$ in Millions)	3 Mos	12/31/2015	12/31/2014	12/31/2013	12/31/2012	12/31/2011
Earnings Per Share	(5.18)	(4.68)	1.06	...	...	...
Cash Flow Per Share	3.98	3.03	1.01	...	...	...
Tang Book Value Per Share	9.33	9.67	14.45	...	...	...
Income Statement						
Total Revenue	548	3,010	4,105	4,296	3,414	1,641
EBITDA	(55)	(493)	194	233	173	132
Depn & Amortn	12	25	16	11	8	4
Income Before Taxes	(67)	(518)	178	222	165	128
Income Taxes	(4)	(16)	62	75	57	43
Net Income	(63)	(502)	116	147	108	85
Average Shares	107	107	108	...	...	...
Balance Sheet						
Current Assets	1,201	1,292	2,047	1,662	1,882	...
Total Assets	1,738	1,832	2,596	2,183	2,373	...
Current Liabilities	302	307	620	363	391	...
Long-Term Obligations	55	108	...	...	...	...
Total Liabilities	370	429	630	381	402	...
Stockholders' Equity	1,368	1,403	1,966	...	...	...
Shares Outstanding	107	107	107	...	...	...
Statistical Record						
Return on Assets %	N.M.	N.M.	4.85	6.45	...	...
EBITDA Margin %	N.M.	N.M.	4.73	5.42	5.07	8.04
Net Margin %	N.M.	N.M.	2.83	3.42	3.16	5.18
Asset Turnover	1.24	1.36	1.72	1.89	...	...
Current Ratio	3.98	4.21	3.30	4.58	4.81	...
Debt to Equity	0.04	0.08	...	...	...	...
Price Range	25.59-12.48	26.79-14.80	37.19-22.50	...	...	...
P/E Ratio	...	...	35.08-21.23	...	...	...

Address: 7402 North Eldridge Parkway, Houston, TX 77041
Telephone: 281-823-4700

Web Site: www.distributionnow.com
Officers: Robert R. Workman - President, Chief Executive Officer Merrill A. Miller - Executive Chairman

Auditors: Ernst & Young LLP
Transfer Agents: American Stock Transfer & Trust Co., LLC , Brooklyn, NY

NRG ENERGY INC

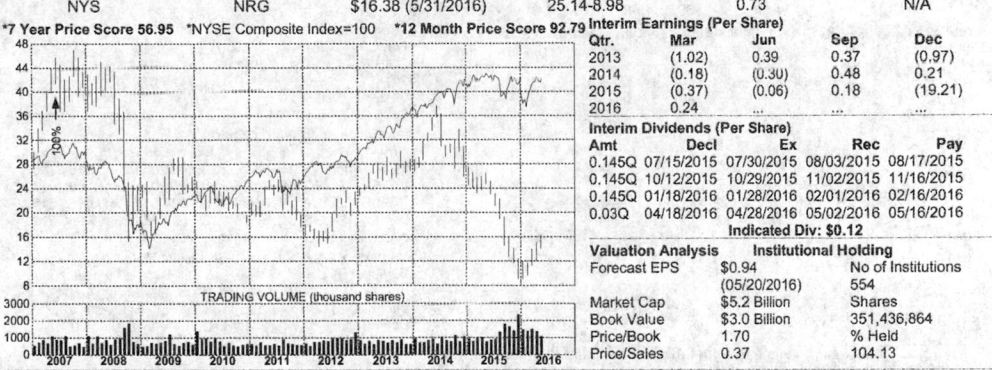

Exchange	Symbol	Price	52Wk Range	Yield	P/E
NYS	NRG	$16.38 (5/31/2016)	25.14-8.98	0.73	N/A

*7 Year Price Score 56.95   *NYSE Composite Index=100   *12 Month Price Score 92.79

Interim Earnings (Per Share)

Qtr.	Mar	Jun	Sep	Dec
2013	(1.02)	0.39	0.37	(0.97)
2014	(0.18)	(0.30)	0.48	0.21
2015	(0.37)	(0.06)	0.18	(19.21)
2016	0.24	...	...	...

Interim Dividends (Per Share)

Amt	Decl	Ex	Rec	Pay
0.145Q	07/15/2015	07/30/2015	08/03/2015	08/17/2015
0.145Q	10/12/2015	10/29/2015	11/02/2015	11/16/2015
0.145Q	01/18/2016	01/28/2016	02/01/2016	02/16/2016
0.03Q	04/18/2016	04/28/2016	05/02/2016	05/16/2016

Indicated Div: $0.12

Valuation Analysis   **Institutional Holding**

Forecast EPS	$0.94
	(05/20/2016)
Market Cap	$5.2 Billion
Book Value	$3.0 Billion
Price/Book	1.70
Price/Sales	0.37

No of Institutions	554
Shares	351,436,864
% Held	104.13

Business Summary: Electric Utilities (MIC: 3.1.1 SIC: 4911 NAIC: 221121)

NRG Energy is a power company, which produces, sells and delivers energy and energy products and services in power markets in the U.S. Co. owns and operates approx. 50,000 megawatt (MW) of generation; engages in the trading of wholesale energy, capacity and related products; transacts in and trades fuel and transportation services; and directly sells energy, services, and products and services to retail customers under the name NRG and various other retail brand names owned by Co. As of Dec 31 2015, Co.'s retail businesses within NRG Home and NRG Business served approximately 2.77 million Recurring customers and approximately 624,000 Discrete customers.

Recent Developments: For the quarter ended Mar 31 2016, net income amounted to US$47.0 million versus a net loss of US$136.0 million in the year-earlier quarter. Revenues were US$3.23 billion, down 15.7% from US$3.83 billion the year before. Operating income was US$476.0 million versus US$76.0 million in the prior-year quarter, an increase of 526.3%. Direct operating expenses declined 28.5% to US$2.19 billion from US$3.06 billion in the comparable period the year before. Indirect operating expenses decreased 18.3% to US$564.0 million from US$690.0 million in the equivalent prior-year period.

Prospects: Our evaluation of NRG Energy Inc. as of June 19, 2016 is the result of our systematic analysis on three basic characteristics: earnings strength, relative valuation, and recent stock price movement. The company has enjoyed a very positive trend in earnings per share over the past 5 quarters. However, while recent estimates for the company have been lowered by analysts, NRG has posted better than expected results. Based on operating earnings yield, the company is about fairly valued when compared to all of the companies in our coverage universe. Share price changes over the past year indicates that NRG will perform in line with the market over the near term.

Financial Data
(US$ in Thousands)

	3 Mos	12/31/2015	12/31/2014	12/31/2013	12/31/2012	12/31/2011	12/31/2010	12/31/2009
Earnings Per Share	(18.85)	(19.46)	0.23	(1.22)	2.35	0.78	1.84	3.44
Cash Flow Per Share	5.09	3.98	4.52	3.93	4.94	4.86	6.44	8.58
Tang Book Value Per Share	N.M.	N.M.	14.59	20.77	22.03	19.47	18.85	16.88
Dividends Per Share	0.580	0.580	0.540	0.450	0.180	...	...	...
Dividend Payout %	...	...	234.78	...	7.66	...	...	...
Income Statement								
Total Revenue	3,229,000	14,674,000	15,868,000	11,295,000	8,422,000	9,079,000	8,849,000	8,952,000
EBITDA	407,000	(3,921,000)	1,280,000	256,000	1,022,000	151,000	1,345,000	2,415,000
Depn & Amortn	48,000	81,000	64,000	49,000	146,000	167,000	4,000	153,000
Income Before Taxes	75,000	(5,130,000)	97,000	(641,000)	215,000	(681,000)	709,000	1,628,000
Income Taxes	21,000	1,342,000	3,000	(282,000)	(327,000)	(843,000)	277,000	728,000
Net Income	82,000	(6,382,000)	134,000	(386,000)	559,000	197,000	477,000	942,000
Average Shares	315,000	329,000	339,000	323,000	234,000	241,000	254,000	271,200
Balance Sheet								
Current Assets	7,346,000	7,391,000	8,582,000	7,596,000	7,956,000	7,597,000	7,137,000	6,208,000
Total Assets	32,680,000	32,882,000	40,665,000	33,902,000	35,128,000	26,715,000	26,896,000	23,378,000
Current Liabilities	4,338,000	4,375,000	4,859,000	4,204,000	4,677,000	5,671,000	4,220,000	3,762,000
Long-Term Obligations	18,677,000	18,983,000	19,900,000	15,767,000	15,733,000	9,745,000	8,748,000	7,847,000
Total Liabilities	29,651,000	29,873,000	30,612,000	24,051,000	24,864,000	18,980,000	18,593,000	15,446,000
Stockholders' Equity	3,029,000	3,009,000	10,053,000	9,851,000	10,264,000	7,735,000	8,303,000	7,932,000
Shares Outstanding	314,906	314,190	336,662	323,779	322,606	227,519	247,197	253,995
Statistical Record								
Return on Assets %	N.M.	N.M.	0.36	N.M.	1.80	0.73	1.90	3.91
Return on Equity %	N.M.	N.M.	1.35	N.M.	6.19	2.46	5.88	12.32
EBITDA Margin %	12.60	N.M.	8.07	2.27	12.13	1.66	15.20	26.98
Net Margin %	2.54	N.M.	0.84	N.M.	6.64	2.17	5.39	10.52
Asset Turnover	0.39	0.40	0.43	0.33	0.27	0.34	0.35	0.37
Current Ratio	1.69	1.69	1.77	1.81	1.70	1.34	1.69	1.65
Debt to Equity	6.17	6.31	1.98	1.60	1.53	1.26	1.05	0.99
Price Range	26.43-8.98	27.50-9.00	37.66-25.83	30.11-22.68	23.65-14.34	25.41-17.57	25.17-18.31	29.13-16.34
P/E Ratio	...	...	163.74-112.30	...	10.06-6.10	32.58-22.53	13.68-9.95	8.47-4.75
Average Yield %	3.35	2.81	1.74	1.69	0.96	...	...	...

Address: 211 Carnegie Center, Princeton, NJ 08540	**Web Site:** www.nrgenergy.com	**Auditors:** KPMG LLP
Telephone: 609-524-4500	**Officers:** Howard E. Cosgrove - Chairman Edward R. Muller - Vice-Chairman	**Investor Contact:** 609-524-4526
		Transfer Agents: Computershare Shareowner Services LLC, College Station, TX

NU SKIN ENTERPRISES, INC.

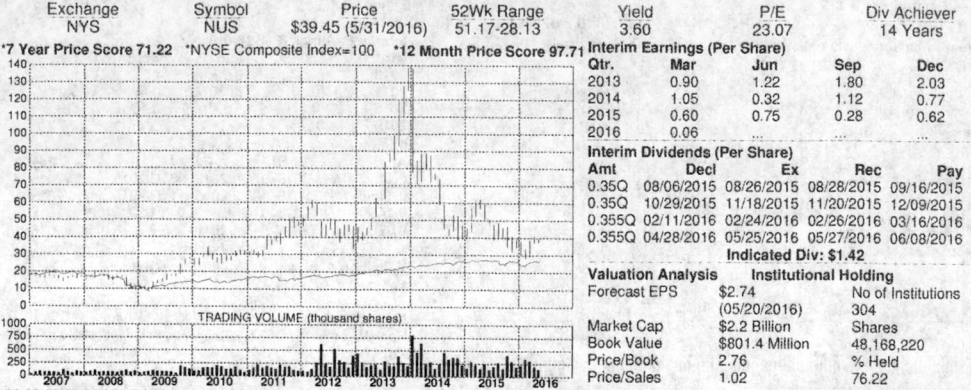

Exchange	Symbol	Price	52Wk Range	Yield	P/E	Div Achiever
NYS	NUS	$39.45 (5/31/2016)	51.17-28.13	3.60	23.07	14 Years

*7 Year Price Score 71.22 *NYSE Composite Index=100 *12 Month Price Score 97.71

Interim Earnings (Per Share)

Qtr.	Mar	Jun	Sep	Dec
2013	0.90	1.22	1.80	2.03
2014	1.05	0.32	1.12	0.77
2015	0.60	0.75	0.28	0.62
2016	0.06			

Interim Dividends (Per Share)

Amt	Decl	Ex	Rec	Pay
0.35Q	08/06/2015	08/26/2015	08/28/2015	09/16/2015
0.35Q	10/29/2015	11/18/2015	11/20/2015	12/09/2015
0.355Q	02/11/2016	02/24/2016	02/26/2016	03/16/2016
0.355Q	04/28/2016	05/25/2016	05/27/2016	06/08/2016

Indicated Div: $1.42

Valuation Analysis

		Institutional Holding	
Forecast EPS	$2.74 (05/20/2016)	No of Institutions	304
Market Cap	$2.2 Billion	Shares	48,168,220
Book Value	$801.4 Million	% Held	76.22
Price/Book	2.76		
Price/Sales	1.02		

Business Summary: Household & Personal Products (MIC: 1.7.1 SIC: 5122 NAIC: 424210)

NU Skin Enterprises is a direct selling company. Co. develops and distributes anti-aging personal care products and nutritional supplements under its Nu Skin and Pharmanex category brands, respectively. Co.'s primary categories in the Nu Skin product line are core skin-care systems and targeted treatment products that address specific skin needs. Products in this category include ageLOC Spa systems, ageLOC Tru Face Essence Ultra anti-aging skin care serum and ageLOC Transformation anti-aging skin care system. Co.'s Pharmanex brand's product line includes its LifePak and ageLOC R2 nutritional supplements and its ageLOC TR90 weight management and body shaping system.

Recent Developments: For the quarter ended Mar 31 2016, net income decreased 90.9% to US$3.3 million from US$36.3 million in the year-earlier quarter. Revenues were US$471.8 million, down 13.2% from US$543.3 million the year before. Operating income was US$8.1 million versus US$68.6 million in the prior-year quarter, a decrease of 88.1%. Direct operating expenses rose 31.2% to US$137.9 million from US$105.1 million in the comparable period the year before. Indirect operating expenses decreased 11.9% to US$325.8 million from US$369.6 million in the equivalent prior-year period.

Prospects: Our evaluation of NU Skin Enterprises Inc. as of June 19, 2016 is the result of our systematic analysis on three basic characteristics: earnings strength, relative valuation, and recent stock price movement. The company has enjoyed a very positive trend in earnings per share over the past 5 quarters and while recent estimates for the company have been raised by analysts, NUS has posted better than expected results. Based on operating earnings yield, the company is undervalued when compared to all of the companies in our coverage universe. Share price changes over the past year indicates that NUS will perform very poorly over the near term.

Financial Data

(US$ in Thousands)	3 Mos	12/31/2015	12/31/2014	12/31/2013	12/31/2012	12/31/2011	12/31/2010	12/31/2009
Earnings Per Share	1.71	2.25	3.11	5.94	3.52	2.38	2.11	1.40
Cash Flow Per Share	4.38	5.55	(0.96)	9.05	5.12	3.61	3.01	2.11
Tang Book Value Per Share	11.02	11.54	12.80	11.24	6.60	6.07	4.52	2.89
Dividends Per Share	1.405	1.400	1.380	1.200	0.800	0.590	0.500	0.460
Dividend Payout %	82.16	62.22	44.37	20.20	22.73	24.79	23.70	32.86
Income Statement								
Total Revenue	471,831	2,247,047	2,569,495	3,176,718	2,169,664	1,743,991	1,537,259	1,331,058
EBITDA	22,231	273,559	345,007	584,040	370,742	252,469	230,313	162,924
Depn & Amortn	16,945	61,600	46,500	27,100	25,500	25,700	22,700	21,800
Income Before Taxes	5,286	211,959	298,507	556,940	345,242	226,769	207,613	141,124
Income Taxes	1,970	78,913	109,331	192,052	123,597	73,439	71,562	51,279
Net Income	3,316	133,046	189,176	364,888	221,645	153,330	136,051	89,845
Average Shares	56,411	59,057	60,887	61,448	63,025	64,546	64,547	64,296
Balance Sheet								
Current Assets	742,158	706,392	834,667	1,118,334	599,403	530,087	422,526	337,943
Total Assets	1,511,473	1,505,843	1,614,434	1,821,062	1,152,907	990,956	892,224	748,449
Current Liabilities	448,063	407,597	418,329	776,792	320,103	241,171	216,448	185,212
Long-Term Obligations	168,377	181,745	164,567	113,852	154,963	107,944	133,013	121,119
Total Liabilities	710,042	680,222	671,996	962,443	562,295	416,720	420,975	372,762
Stockholders' Equity	801,431	825,621	942,438	858,619	590,612	574,236	471,249	375,687
Shares Outstanding	56,000	56,000	59,000	59,000	58,400	62,300	62,100	62,800
Statistical Record								
Return on Assets %	6.41	8.53	11.01	24.54	20.62	16.28	16.58	12.32
Return on Equity %	11.60	15.05	21.01	50.36	37.95	29.33	32.13	25.97
EBITDA Margin %	4.71	12.17	13.43	18.39	17.09	14.48	14.98	12.24
Net Margin %	0.70	5.92	7.36	11.49	10.22	8.79	8.85	6.75
Asset Turnover	1.39	1.44	1.50	2.14	2.02	1.85	1.87	1.83
Current Ratio	1.66	1.73	2.00	1.44	1.87	2.20	1.95	1.82
Debt to Equity	0.21	0.22	0.17	0.13	0.26	0.19	0.28	0.32
Price Range	62.20-28.13	62.20-31.89	138.22-38.28	138.66-37.05	61.50-33.05	51.61-27.81	33.70-23.24	28.04-8.04
P/E Ratio	36.37-16.45	27.64-14.17	44.44-12.31	23.34-6.24	17.47-9.39	21.68-11.68	15.97-11.01	20.03-5.74
Average Yield %	3.36	3.04	2.09	1.59	1.71	1.56	1.75	2.77

Address: 75 West Center Street, Provo, UT 84601 Telephone: 801-345-1000	Web Site: www.nuskinenterprises.com Officers: Blake M. Roney - Chairman Steven J. Lund - Vice-Chairman	Auditors: PricewaterhouseCoopers LLP Investor Contact: 801-345-2657 Transfer Agents: American Stock Transfer & Trust Co. LLC, Brooklyn, NY

NUCOR CORP.

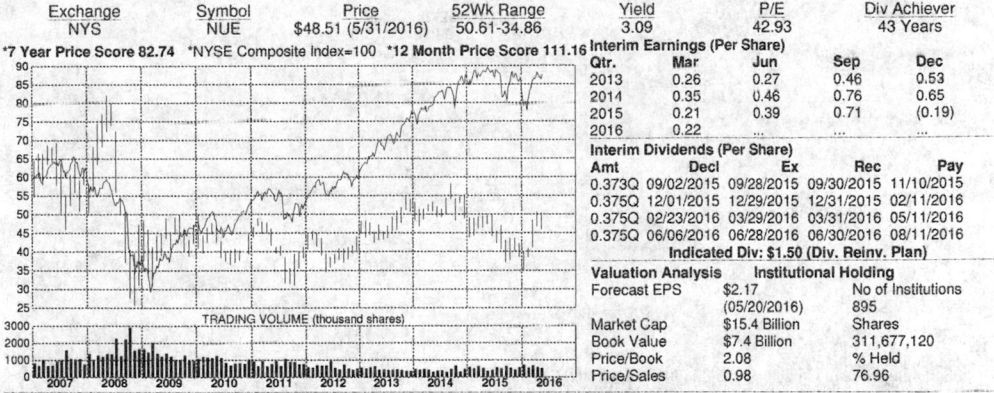

Exchange	Symbol	Price	52Wk Range	Yield	P/E	Div Achiever
NYS	NUE	$48.51 (5/31/2016)	50.61-34.86	3.09	42.93	43 Years

*7 Year Price Score 82.74 *NYSE Composite Index=100 *12 Month Price Score 111.16

Interim Earnings (Per Share)

Qtr.	Mar	Jun	Sep	Dec
2013	0.26	0.27	0.46	0.53
2014	0.35	0.46	0.76	0.65
2015	0.21	0.39	0.71	(0.19)
2016	0.22	...	...	...

Interim Dividends (Per Share)

Amt	Decl	Ex	Rec	Pay
0.373Q	09/02/2015	09/28/2015	09/30/2015	11/10/2015
0.375Q	12/01/2015	12/29/2015	12/31/2015	02/11/2016
0.375Q	02/23/2016	03/29/2016	03/31/2016	05/11/2016
0.375Q	06/06/2016	06/28/2016	06/30/2016	08/11/2016

Indicated Div: $1.50 (Div. Reinv. Plan)

Valuation Analysis

Forecast EPS	$2.17
	(05/20/2016)
Market Cap	$15.4 Billion
Book Value	$7.4 Billion
Price/Book	2.08
Price/Sales	0.98

Institutional Holding

No of Institutions	895
Shares	311,677,120
% Held	76.96

Business Summary: Non-Precious Metals (MIC: 8.2.2 SIC: 3312 NAIC: 331111)

Nucor manufactures steel and steel products. Co. also produces direct reduced iron (DRI) for use in its steel mills. Through its The David J. Joseph Company subsidiary and its affiliates, Co. also processes ferrous and nonferrous metals and brokers ferrous and nonferrous metals, pig iron, hot briquetted iron and DRI. Co.'s primary customers are located in North America, but Co. is doing business outside of North America as well. Co.'s operations include several international trading companies that buy and sell steel and steel products manufactured by it and others. Co. reports its results in three segments: steel mills, steel products and raw materials.

Recent Developments: For the quarter ended Apr 2 2016, net income increased 23.9% to US$104.5 million from US$84.3 million in the year-earlier quarter. Revenues were US$3.72 billion, down 15.5% from US$4.40 billion the year before. Direct operating expenses declined 16.6% to US$3.43 billion from US$4.11 billion in the comparable period the year before. Indirect operating expenses decreased 14.1% to US$145.4 million from US$169.2 million in the equivalent prior-year period.

Prospects: Our evaluation of Nucor Corp. as of June 19, 2016 is the result of our systematic analysis on three basic characteristics: earnings strength, relative valuation, and recent stock price movement. The company has enjoyed a very positive trend in earnings per share over the past 5 quarters and while recent estimates for the company have been raised by analysts, NUE has posted results that fell short of analysts expectations. Based on operating earnings yield, the company is about fairly valued when compared to all of the companies in our coverage universe. Share price changes over the past year indicates that NUE will perform poorly over the near term.

Financial Data

(US$ in Thousands)	3 Mos	12/31/2015	12/31/2014	12/31/2013	12/31/2012	12/31/2011	12/31/2010	12/31/2009
Earnings Per Share	1.13	1.11	2.22	1.52	1.58	2.45	0.42	(0.94)
Cash Flow Per Share	6.72	6.73	4.20	3.38	3.76	3.26	2.76	3.75
Tang Book Value Per Share	14.61	14.58	15.18	15.07	14.73	15.34	14.02	14.88
Dividends Per Share	1.495	1.492	1.482	1.472	1.462	1.452	1.442	1.410
Dividend Payout %	132.30	134.46	66.78	96.88	92.56	59.29	343.45	...
Income Statement								
Total Revenue	3,715,576	16,439,276	21,105,141	19,052,046	19,429,273	20,023,564	15,844,627	11,190,296
EBITDA	347,564	1,503,197	2,012,328	1,464,573	1,562,648	1,950,520	964,437	297,150
Depn & Amortn	170,361	625,757	652,000	535,852	534,010	522,571	512,147	494,035
Income Before Taxes	132,281	703,909	1,191,072	781,826	866,263	1,261,855	299,197	(331,637)
Income Taxes	37,065	213,154	388,787	205,594	259,814	390,828	60,792	(176,800)
Net Income	70,754	357,659	713,946	488,025	504,619	778,188	134,092	(293,613)
Average Shares	319,294	320,693	320,127	319,266	318,240	317,161	316,510	314,873
Balance Sheet								
Current Assets	6,006,149	5,754,380	6,441,888	6,410,046	5,661,364	6,708,081	5,861,175	5,182,248
Total Assets	14,395,104	14,250,399	15,615,927	15,203,283	14,152,059	14,570,350	13,921,910	12,571,904
Current Liabilities	1,550,130	1,385,173	2,097,776	1,960,216	2,029,568	2,396,059	1,504,438	1,227,057
Long-Term Obligations	4,337,875	4,360,600	4,360,600	4,376,900	3,380,200	3,630,200	4,280,200	3,080,200
Total Liabilities	6,968,636	6,833,521	7,843,457	7,557,514	6,510,488	7,095,465	6,801,840	5,181,378
Stockholders' Equity	7,426,468	7,416,878	7,772,470	7,645,769	7,641,571	7,474,885	7,120,070	7,390,526
Shares Outstanding	317,928	317,962	319,033	318,328	317,663	316,749	315,791	314,856
Statistical Record								
Return on Assets %	2.47	2.40	4.63	3.32	3.50	5.46	1.01	N.M.
Return on Equity %	4.80	4.71	9.26	6.38	6.66	10.66	1.85	N.M.
EBITDA Margin %	9.35	9.14	9.53	7.69	8.04	9.74	6.09	2.66
Net Margin %	1.90	2.18	3.38	2.56	2.60	3.89	0.85	N.M.
Asset Turnover	1.08	1.10	1.37	1.30	1.35	1.41	1.20	0.85
Current Ratio	3.87	4.15	3.07	3.27	2.79	2.80	3.90	4.22
Debt to Equity	0.58	0.59	0.56	0.57	0.44	0.49	0.60	0.42
Price Range	49.77-34.86	49.77-37.00	58.09-46.62	54.62-42.23	45.41-34.39	48.88-30.91	49.93-36.38	49.84-30.74
P/E Ratio	44.04-30.85	44.84-33.33	26.17-21.00	35.93-27.78	28.74-21.77	19.95-12.62	118.88-86.62	...
Average Yield %	3.46	3.34	2.87	3.12	3.64	3.57	3.45	3.28

Address: 1915 Rexford Road, Charlotte, NC 28211 **Telephone:** 704-366-7000 **Fax:** 704-362-4208	**Web Site:** www.nucor.com **Officers:** John J. Ferriola - Chairman, President, Chief Executive Officer, Chief Operating Officer James R. Darsey - Executive Vice President	**Auditors:** PricewaterhouseCoopers LLP **Transfer Agents:** American Stock Transfer & Trust Company, New York, NY

NVR INC.

Exchange	Symbol	Price	52Wk Range	Yield	P/E
NYS	NVR	$1733 (5/31/2016)	1799.23-1340.00	N/A	17.96

*7 Year Price Score 139.87 ***NYSE Composite Index=100** ***12 Month Price Score 106.03**

TRADING VOLUME (thousand shares)

Interim Earnings (Per Share)

Qtr.	Mar	Jun	Sep	Dec
2013	6.84	10.11	17.67	20.68
2014	5.16	15.17	20.70	22.91
2015	9.22	21.91	27.11	31.67
2016	15.79	...	...	...

Interim Dividends (Per Share)

No Dividends Paid

Valuation Analysis

		Institutional Holding	
Forecast EPS	$107.89 (05/15/2016)	No of Institutions	407
Market Cap	$6.7 Billion	Shares	
Book Value	$1.3 Billion		5,096,217
Price/Book	5.37	% Held	
Price/Sales	1.26		77.48

Business Summary: Builders (MIC: 2.2.5 SIC: 1531 NAIC: 236117)

NVR is engaged in the construction and sale of single-family detached homes, townhomes and condominium buildings, all of which are primarily constructed on a pre-sold basis. Co.'s homebuilding operations construct and sell single-family detached homes, townhomes and condominium buildings under four trade names: NVHomes and Heartland Homes, which are marketed primarily to move-up and up-scale buyers, and Ryan Homes and Fox Ridge Homes, which are marketed primarily to first-time and first-time move-up buyers. Co. also operates a mortgage banking and title services business. Co.'s mortgage banking operations are operated primarily through a wholly owned subsidiary, NVR Mortgage Finance, Inc.

Recent Developments: For the quarter ended Mar 31 2016, net income increased 67.2% to US$65.3 million from US$39.1 million in the year-earlier quarter. Revenues were US$1.15 billion, up 19.5% from US$959.7 million the year before. Direct operating expenses rose 18.4% to US$925.8 million from US$781.7 million in the comparable period the year before. Indirect operating expenses increased 2.7% to US$112.8 million from US$109.8 million in the equivalent prior-year period.

Prospects: Our evaluation of NVR Inc. as of June 19, 2016 is the result of our systematic analysis on three basic characteristics: earnings strength, relative valuation, and recent stock price movement. The company has generated a negative trend in earnings per share over the past 5 quarters. However, while recent estimates for the company have been mixed, NVR has posted better than expected results. Based on operating earnings yield, the company is undervalued when compared to all of the companies in our coverage universe. Share price changes over the past year indicates that NVR will perform very well over the near term.

Financial Data
(US$ in Thousands)

	3 Mos	12/31/2015	12/31/2014	12/31/2013	12/31/2012	12/31/2011	12/31/2010	12/31/2009
Earnings Per Share	96.48	89.99	63.50	54.81	35.12	23.01	33.42	31.26
Cash Flow Per Share	40.86	50.57	43.14	57.04	52.62	0.27	9.40	41.61
Tang Book Value Per Share	309.10	304.87	264.25	271.93	289.44	266.37	298.65	287.11
Income Statement								
Total Revenue	1,146,725	5,169,562	4,453,139	4,220,908	3,193,204	2,669,608	3,057,369	2,756,153
EBITDA	113,847	648,305	494,300	454,472	290,706	216,140	335,685	319,507
Depn & Amortn	5,447	21,534	17,614	13,391	8,100	6,672	7,263	9,713
Income Before Taxes	103,312	603,212	453,546	418,696	275,077	207,576	322,393	298,414
Income Taxes	38,009	220,285	171,916	152,219	94,489	78,156	116,388	106,234
Net Income	65,303	382,927	281,630	266,477	180,588	129,420	206,005	192,180
Average Shares	4,135	4,255	4,435	4,861	5,141	5,623	6,164	6,148
Balance Sheet								
Current Assets	1,592,951	1,430,852	1,414,424	1,604,150	1,830,732	1,013,482	1,624,721	1,668,868
Total Assets	2,541,651	2,515,131	2,351,335	2,486,148	2,604,842	1,779,485	2,260,061	2,395,770
Current Liabilities	389,914	370,693	337,174	304,483	283,819	213,267	182,454	203,361
Long-Term Obligations	595,999	599,260	599,230	602,440	603,562	6,596	99,681	147,880
Total Liabilities	1,285,188	1,275,966	1,227,080	1,224,796	1,124,365	404,686	519,687	638,508
Stockholders' Equity	1,256,463	1,239,165	1,124,255	1,261,352	1,480,477	1,374,799	1,740,374	1,757,262
Shares Outstanding	3,894	3,890	4,049	4,433	4,914	4,977	5,663	5,950
Statistical Record								
Return on Assets %	16.64	15.74	11.64	10.47	8.22	6.41	8.85	8.54
Return on Equity %	33.79	32.40	23.61	19.44	12.61	8.31	11.78	12.28
EBITDA Margin %	9.93	12.54	11.10	10.77	9.10	8.10	10.98	11.59
Net Margin %	5.69	7.41	6.32	6.31	5.66	4.85	6.74	6.97
Asset Turnover	2.18	2.12	1.84	1.66	1.45	1.32	1.31	1.23
Current Ratio	4.09	3.86	4.19	5.27	6.45	4.75	8.90	8.21
Debt to Equity	0.47	0.48	0.53	0.48	0.41	N.M.	0.06	0.08
Price Range	1799.23-1306.88	1720.00-1224.13	1276.68-997.49	1080.11-835.74	959.25-671.00	804.32-575.28	753.00-604.16	731.00-319.56
P/E Ratio	18.65-13.55	19.11-13.60	20.11-15.71	19.71-15.25	27.31-19.11	34.96-25.00	22.53-18.08	23.38-10.22

Address: 11700 Plaza America Drive, Suite 500, Reston, VA 20190 **Telephone:** 703-956-4000	**Web Site:** www.nvrinc.com **Officers:** Dwight C. Schar - Chairman Paul C. Saville - President, Chief Executive Officer	**Auditors:** KPMG LLP **Transfer Agents:** Computershare Trust Company, N.A., Providence, RI

OCCIDENTAL PETROLEUM CORP

Exchange	Symbol	Price	52Wk Range	Yield	P/E	Div Achiever
NYS	OXY	$75.44 (5/31/2016)	79.41-59.60	3.98	N/A	13 Years

*7 Year Price Score 73.64   *NYSE Composite Index=100   *12 Month Price Score 102.63

Interim Earnings (Per Share)

Qtr.	Mar	Jun	Sep	Dec
2013	1.68	1.64	1.96	2.04
2014	1.75	1.82	1.55	(4.34)
2015	(0.28)	0.23	(3.42)	(6.77)
2016	0.10	...	...	...

Interim Dividends (Per Share)

Amt	Decl	Ex	Rec	Pay
0.75Q	10/08/2015	12/08/2015	12/10/2015	01/15/2016
0.00Q	02/18/2016	02/25/2016	02/29/2016	03/24/2016
0.75Q	02/18/2016	03/08/2016	03/10/2016	04/15/2016
0.75Q	04/28/2016	06/08/2016	06/10/2016	07/15/2016

Indicated Div: $3.00

Valuation Analysis	Institutional Holding
Forecast EPS $-0.68	No of Institutions
(05/20/2016)	1465
Market Cap $57.6 Billion	Shares
Book Value $23.8 Billion	681,238,976
Price/Book 2.42	% Held
Price/Sales 4.85	76.03

Business Summary: Production & Extraction (MIC: 9.1.1 SIC: 1311 NAIC: 211111)

Occidental Petroleum's principal businesses consist of three segments: oil and gas, which explores for, develops and produces oil and condensate, natural gas liquids (NGLs) and natural gas; chemical, which mainly manufactures and markets basic chemicals and vinyls; and midstream, marketing and other, which gathers, processes, transports, stores, purchases and markets oil, condensate, NGLs, natural gas, carbon dioxide and power. As of Dec 31 2015, Co. had 2.20 billion barrels of oil equivalent of proved reserves, which consisted of 1.41 billion barrels of oil, 330.0 million barrels of NGLs and 3.34 trillion cubic feet of natural gas.

Recent Developments: For the quarter ended Mar 31 2016, loss from continuing operations was US$360.0 million compared with a loss of US$215.0 million in the year-earlier quarter. Net income amounted to US$78.0 million versus a net loss of US$218.0 million in the year-earlier quarter. Revenues were US$2.28 billion, down 26.3% from US$3.10 billion the year before. Direct operating expenses declined 17.7% to US$1.28 billion from US$1.56 billion in the comparable period the year before. Indirect operating expenses decreased 11.8% to US$1.60 billion from US$1.81 billion in the equivalent prior-year period.

Prospects: Our evaluation of Occidental Petroleum Corp. as of June 19, 2016 is the result of our systematic analysis on three basic characteristics: earnings strength, relative valuation, and recent stock price movement. The company has enjoyed a very positive trend in earnings per share over the past 5 quarters. Because the company lacks sufficient analyst estimate data, we place greater weight on the historical EPS trend as the measure of earnings strength. Based on operating earnings yield, the company is overvalued when compared to all of the companies in our coverage universe. Share price changes over the past year indicates that OXY will perform well over the near term.

Financial Data

(US$ in Thousands)	3 Mos	12/31/2015	12/31/2014	12/31/2013	12/31/2012	12/31/2011	12/31/2010	12/31/2009
Earnings Per Share	(9.86)	(10.23)	0.79	7.32	5.67	8.32	5.56	3.58
Cash Flow Per Share	4.56	4.38	14.17	16.08	13.94	15.12	11.51	7.17
Tang Book Value Per Share	31.14	31.89	39.26	48.46	49.68	46.39	39.97	35.82
Dividends Per Share	3.000	2.970	2.880	2.560	2.160	1.840	1.470	1.310
Dividend Payout %	...	...	364.56	34.97	38.10	22.12	26.44	36.59
Income Statement								
Total Revenue	2,281,000	12,699,000	21,947,000	25,736,000	24,253,000	24,119,000	19,157,000	15,531,000
EBITDA	566,000	(4,993,000)	5,562,000	14,747,000	12,031,000	14,348,000	10,628,000	7,926,000
Depn & Amortn	1,102,000	4,544,000	4,261,000	5,347,000	4,511,000	3,591,000	3,153,000	3,117,000
Income Before Taxes	(596,000)	(9,684,000)	1,224,000	9,282,000	7,390,000	10,459,000	7,359,000	4,669,000
Income Taxes	(203,000)	(1,330,000)	1,685,000	3,755,000	3,118,000	4,201,000	2,995,000	1,918,000
Net Income	78,000	(7,829,000)	616,000	5,903,000	4,598,000	6,771,000	4,530,000	2,915,000
Average Shares	763,400	765,600	781,100	804,600	810,000	812,900	813,800	813,800
Balance Sheet								
Current Assets	8,237,000	9,402,000	13,873,000	11,323,000	9,492,000	11,542,000	13,059,000	8,086,000
Total Assets	42,018,000	43,437,000	56,259,000	69,443,000	64,210,000	60,044,000	52,432,000	44,229,000
Current Liabilities	6,826,000	6,842,000	8,244,000	8,434,000	7,290,000	7,947,000	7,825,000	6,092,000
Long-Term Obligations	5,608,000	6,883,000	6,838,000	6,939,000	7,023,000	5,871,000	5,111,000	2,557,000
Total Liabilities	18,229,000	19,087,000	21,300,000	26,317,000	24,194,000	22,424,000	19,948,000	15,148,000
Stockholders' Equity	23,789,000	24,350,000	34,959,000	43,126,000	40,016,000	37,620,000	32,484,000	29,081,000
Shares Outstanding	763,839	763,678	890,557	889,919	805,514	811,009	812,794	811,921
Statistical Record								
Return on Assets %	N.M.	N.M.	0.98	8.83	7.38	12.04	9.37	6.80
Return on Equity %	N.M.	N.M.	1.58	14.20	11.81	19.32	14.72	10.34
EBITDA Margin %	24.81	N.M.	25.34	57.30	49.61	59.49	55.48	51.03
Net Margin %	3.42	N.M.	2.81	22.94	18.96	28.07	23.65	18.77
Asset Turnover	0.25	0.25	0.35	0.39	0.39	0.43	0.40	0.36
Current Ratio	1.21	1.37	1.68	1.34	1.30	1.45	1.67	1.33
Debt to Equity	0.24	0.28	0.20	0.16	0.18	0.16	0.16	0.09
Price Range	81.48-59.60	83.08-63.61	100.90-73.13	95.32-73.49	101.16-70.58	111.02-65.78	94.99-69.29	81.04-45.62
P/E Ratio	...	...	127.73-92.57	13.02-10.04	17.84-12.45	13.34-7.91	17.09-12.46	22.64-12.74
Average Yield %	4.18	3.99	3.18	2.99	2.56	2.01	1.86	2.03

Address: 5 Greenway Plaza, Suite 110, Houston, TX 77046
Telephone: 713-215-7000

Web Site: www.oxy.com
Officers: Vicki A. Hollub - President, Chief Executive Officer, Chief Operating Officer, Senior Executive Vice President, Division Officer Christopher G. Stavros - Chief Financial Officer, Executive Vice President

Auditors: KPMG LLP
Transfer Agents: American Stock Transfer and Trust Company, LLC, Brooklyn, NY

OCEANEERING INTERNATIONAL, INC.

Exchange	Symbol	Price	52Wk Range	Yield	P/E
NYS	OII	$33.06 (5/31/2016)	51.16-26.16	3.27	17.40

*7 Year Price Score 67.68   ***NYSE Composite Index=100**   ***12 Month Price Score 86.49**

Interim Earnings (Per Share)

Qtr.	Mar	Jun	Sep	Dec
2013	0.69	0.91	0.96	0.86
2014	0.84	1.02	1.16	0.99
2015	0.70	0.66	0.70	0.28
2016	0.26	...	...	...

Interim Dividends (Per Share)

Amt	Decl	Ex	Rec	Pay
0.27Q	07/22/2015	08/26/2015	08/28/2015	09/18/2015
0.27Q	10/28/2015	11/24/2015	11/27/2015	12/18/2015
0.27Q	02/10/2016	02/24/2016	02/26/2016	03/18/2016
0.27Q	04/25/2016	05/25/2016	05/27/2016	06/17/2016

Indicated Div: $1.08

Valuation Analysis

		Institutional Holding	
Forecast EPS	$1.00	No of Institutions	499
	(05/20/2016)		
Market Cap	$3.2 Billion	Shares	106,734,096
Book Value	$1.6 Billion	% Held	84.62
Price/Book	2.01		
Price/Sales	1.12		

TRADING VOLUME (thousand shares)

Business Summary: Equipment & Services (MIC: 9.1.3 SIC: 1389 NAIC: 213112)

Oceaneering International provides oilfield engineered services and products, primarily to the offshore oil and gas industry, with a focus on deepwater applications. Co. also serves the defense, aerospace and commercial theme park industries. Co.'s services and products include remotely operated vehicles, specialty subsea hardware, engineering and project management, subsea intervention services, including manned diving, survey and positioning services and asset integrity and nondestructive testing services. Co.'s segments are contained within two businesses: Oilfield, which includes Remotely Operated Vehicles, Subsea Products, Subsea Projects and Asset Integrity; and Advanced Technologies.

Recent Developments: For the quarter ended Mar 31 2016, net income decreased 63.9% to US$25.1 million from US$69.5 million in the year-earlier quarter. Revenues were US$608.3 million, down 22.7% from US$786.8 million the year before. Operating income was US$48.1 million versus US$106.7 million in the prior-year quarter, a decrease of 54.9%. Direct operating expenses declined 18.0% to US$510.9 million from US$623.3 million in the comparable period the year before. Indirect operating expenses decreased 13.1% to US$49.4 million from US$56.8 million in the equivalent prior-year period.

Prospects: Our evaluation of Oceaneering International Inc. as of June 19, 2016 is the result of our systematic analysis on three basic characteristics: earnings strength, relative valuation, and recent stock price movement. The company has enjoyed a very positive trend in earnings per share over the past 5 quarters. However, while recent estimates for the company have been lowered by analysts, OII has posted results that fell short of analysts expectations. Based on operating earnings yield, the company is undervalued when compared to all of the companies in our coverage universe. Share price changes over the past year indicates that OII will perform in line with the market over the near term.

Financial Data

(US$ in Thousands)	3 Mos	12/31/2015	12/31/2014	12/31/2013	12/31/2012	12/31/2011	12/31/2010	12/31/2009
Earnings Per Share	1.90	2.34	4.00	3.42	2.66	2.16	1.83	1.70
Cash Flow Per Share	6.19	5.69	6.77	4.89	4.05	2.66	4.05	3.82
Tang Book Value Per Share	11.92	10.81	12.70	15.07	13.46	11.33	11.52	9.96
Dividends Per Share	1,080	1.080	1.030	0.840	0.690	0.450	...	...
Dividend Payout %	56.84	46.15	25.75	24.56	25.94	20.83	...	...
Income Statement								
Total Revenue	608,344	3,062,754	3,659,624	3,287,019	2,782,604	2,192,663	1,917,045	1,822,081
EBITDA	101,892	599,709	857,722	746,071	599,015	485,519	462,225	416,565
Depn & Amortn	59,781	241,235	229,779	202,228	176,483	151,227	153,651	122,945
Income Before Taxes	36,014	334,031	623,528	542,203	420,249	334,084	303,144	286,533
Income Taxes	11,437	105,250	195,148	170,836	132,905	102,227	104,691	101,422
Net Income	25,103	231,011	428,329	371,500	289,017	235,658	200,531	188,353
Average Shares	98,286	98,808	107,091	108,731	108,617	109,001	109,534	110,052
Balance Sheet								
Current Assets	1,426,495	1,517,493	1,713,550	1,433,275	1,202,990	984,122	983,502	874,139
Total Assets	3,364,173	3,429,536	3,511,701	3,128,500	2,768,118	2,400,544	2,030,506	1,880,287
Current Liabilities	523,212	615,956	679,137	727,088	617,185	501,375	439,856	388,547
Long-Term Obligations	800,560	795,836	750,000	...	94,000	120,000	...	120,000
Total Liabilities	1,752,525	1,850,802	1,854,081	1,085,060	952,658	842,582	640,291	655,964
Stockholders' Equity	1,611,648	1,578,734	1,657,620	2,043,440	1,815,460	1,557,962	1,390,215	1,224,323
Shares Outstanding	98,058	97,849	99,613	108,197	107,907	108,034	108,230	109,835
Statistical Record								
Return on Assets %	5.56	6.66	12.90	12.60	11.15	10.64	10.26	10.61
Return on Equity %	11.68	14.28	23.15	19.25	17.09	15.99	15.34	17.19
EBITDA Margin %	16.75	19.58	23.44	22.70	21.53	22.14	24.11	22.86
Net Margin %	4.13	7.54	11.70	11.30	10.39	10.75	10.46	10.34
Asset Turnover	0.86	0.88	1.10	1.11	1.07	0.99	0.98	1.03
Current Ratio	2.73	2.46	2.52	1.97	1.95	1.96	2.24	2.25
Debt to Equity	0.50	0.50	0.45	...	0.05	0.08	...	0.10
Price Range	59.12-26.16	59.12-37.06	78.88-57.49	86.68-53.79	57.42-43.76	48.78-33.16	37.63-20.18	30.03-14.06
P/E Ratio	31.12-13.77	25.26-15.84	19.72-14.37	25.35-15.73	21.59-16.45	22.58-15.35	20.57-11.03	17.66-8.27
Average Yield %	2.56	2.27	1.48	1.14	1.34	1.10	...	...

Address: 11911 FM 529, Houston, TX 77041	Web Site: www.oceaneering.com	Auditors: Ernst & Young LLP
Telephone: 713-329-4500	Officers: John R. Huff - Chairman Roderick A. Larson - President, Senior Vice President, Chief Operating Officer	Investor Contact: 713-329-4500
		Transfer Agents: Computershare Trust Company, N.A., Providence, RI

OGE ENERGY CORP.

Exchange	Symbol	Price	52Wk Range	Yield	P/E
NYS	OGE	$30.19 (5/31/2016)	31.45-23.86	3.64	23.77

*7 Year Price Score 86.06   ***NYSE Composite Index=100**   ***12 Month Price Score 104.33**

Interim Earnings (Per Share)

Qtr.	Mar	Jun	Sep	Dec
2013	0.12	0.46	1.08	0.28
2014	0.25	0.50	0.94	0.29
2015	0.22	0.44	0.55	0.15
2016	0.13	...	...	...

Interim Dividends (Per Share)

Amt	Decl	Ex	Rec	Pay
0.275Q	09/30/2015	10/07/2015	10/12/2015	10/30/2015
0.275Q	12/02/2015	01/06/2016	01/08/2016	01/29/2016
0.275Q	02/25/2016	04/06/2016	04/08/2016	04/29/2016
0.275Q	05/19/2016	07/06/2016	07/08/2016	07/29/2016

Indicated Div: $1.10

Valuation Analysis | **Institutional Holding**
Forecast EPS	$1.78	No of Institutions
	(05/17/2016)	482
Market Cap	$6.0 Billion	Shares
Book Value	$3.3 Billion	141,550,416
Price/Book	1.83	% Held
Price/Sales	2.80	63.47

Business Summary: Electric Utilities (MIC: 3.1.1 SIC: 4911 NAIC: 221121)

OGE Energy is a holding company. Through its subsidiaries, Co. is an energy and energy services provider providing physical delivery and related services for electricity and natural gas. At Dec 31 2015, Co. conducted these activities through two segments: Electric Utility, which generate, transmit, distribute and sell electric energy in 241 communities in Oklahoma and 26 communities in western Arkansas; and Natural Gas Midstream Operations, which consist of Co.'s investment in Enable Midstream Partners, LP (Enable). Enable is engaged in the business of gathering, processing, transporting and storing natural gas. Enable also owns a crude oil gathering business in the Bakken shale formation.

Recent Developments: For the quarter ended Mar 31 2016, net income decreased 41.7% to US$25.2 million from US$43.2 million in the year-earlier quarter. Revenues were US$433.1 million, down 9.8% from US$480.1 million the year before. Operating income was US$37.9 million versus US$56.4 million in the prior-year quarter, a decrease of 32.8%. Direct operating expenses declined 7.2% to US$370.3 million from US$399.2 million in the comparable period the year before. Indirect operating expenses increased 1.6% to US$24.9 million from US$24.5 million in the equivalent prior-year period.

Prospects: Our evaluation of OGE Energy Corp. as of June 19, 2016 is the result of our systematic analysis on three basic characteristics: earnings strength, relative valuation, and recent stock price movement. The company has enjoyed a very positive trend in earnings per share over the past 5 quarters and while recent estimates for the company have been mixed, OGE has posted better than expected results. Based on operating earnings yield, the company is about fairly valued when compared to all of the companies in our coverage universe. Share price changes over the past year indicates that OGE will perform well over the near term.

Financial Data

(US$ in Thousands)	3 Mos	12/31/2015	12/31/2014	12/31/2013	12/31/2012	12/31/2011	12/31/2010	12/31/2009
Earnings Per Share	1.27	1.36	1.98	1.94	1.79	1.73	1.50	1.33
Cash Flow Per Share	4.00	4.34	3.62	3.14	5.29	4.26	4.02	3.40
Tang Book Value Per Share	16.52	16.65	16.27	15.30	13.16	12.17	11.73	10.52
Dividends Per Share	1.050	1.025	0.925	0.835	0.785	0.750	0.725	0.710
Dividend Payout %	82.68	75.37	46.72	43.04	43.85	43.48	48.49	53.38
Income Statement								
Total Revenue	433,100	2,196,900	2,453,100	2,867,700	3,671,200	3,915,900	3,716,900	2,869,700
EBITDA	121,900	810,100	825,800	868,300	1,058,400	971,800	893,500	780,800
Depn & Amortn	78,500	307,900	281,400	298,600	374,800	307,100	292,400	262,600
Income Before Taxes	7,100	353,200	396,000	422,200	520,100	524,300	461,400	382,200
Income Taxes	10,200	97,400	172,800	130,300	135,100	160,700	161,000	121,100
Net Income	25,200	271,300	395,800	387,600	355,000	342,900	295,300	258,300
Average Shares	199,700	199,600	199,900	199,400	198,200	198,400	197,800	194,400
Balance Sheet								
Current Assets	455,900	570,200	705,800	694,600	794,200	652,700	632,100	826,100
Total Assets	9,523,300	9,597,400	9,527,800	9,134,700	9,922,200	8,906,000	7,669,100	7,266,700
Current Liabilities	706,500	752,800	573,300	1,093,800	1,276,400	998,500	814,500	1,275,700
Long-Term Obligations	2,629,300	2,645,600	2,755,300	2,300,100	2,848,600	2,737,100	2,362,900	2,088,900
Total Liabilities	6,225,000	6,271,400	6,283,400	6,097,600	7,155,000	6,342,700	5,379,500	5,225,900
Stockholders' Equity	3,298,300	3,326,000	3,244,400	3,037,100	2,767,200	2,563,300	2,289,600	2,040,800
Shares Outstanding	199,701	199,700	199,400	198,500	197,600	196,200	195,200	194,000
Statistical Record								
Return on Assets %	2.66	2.84	4.24	4.07	3.76	4.14	3.95	3.75
Return on Equity %	7.75	8.26	12.60	13.36	13.28	14.13	13.64	13.12
EBITDA Margin %	28.15	36.87	33.66	30.28	28.83	24.82	24.04	27.21
Net Margin %	5.82	12.35	16.13	13.52	9.67	8.76	7.94	9.00
Asset Turnover	0.23	0.23	0.26	0.30	0.39	0.47	0.50	0.42
Current Ratio	0.65	0.76	1.23	0.64	0.62	0.65	0.78	0.65
Debt to Equity	0.80	0.80	0.85	0.76	1.03	1.07	1.03	1.02
Price Range	32.86-23.86	36.20-24.37	39.08-33.18	38.36-28.16	29.09-25.20	28.41-20.58	22.98-17.39	18.77-9.92
P/E Ratio	25.87-18.79	26.62-17.92	19.74-16.76	19.77-14.51	16.25-14.08	16.42-11.90	15.32-11.59	14.11-7.46
Average Yield %	3.72	3.42	2.56	2.44	2.90	3.03	3.64	4.93

Address: 321 North Harvey, P.O. Box 321, Oklahoma City, OK 73101-0321
Telephone: 405-553-3000

Web Site: www.oge.com
Officers: Sean Trauschke - Chairman, President, Chief Executive Officer, Vice President, Chief Financial Officer Steve E. Merrill Vice President, Chief Financial Officer

Auditors: Ernst & Young LLP
Investor Contact: 405-553-3966
Transfer Agents: Computershare, Providence, RI

OIL-DRI CORP. OF AMERICA

Exchange	Symbol	Price	52Wk Range	Yield	P/E	Div Achiever
NYS	ODC	$32.51 (5/31/2016)	38.30-22.11	2.71	17.48	13 Years

*7 Year Price Score 104.41 *NYSE Composite Index=100 *12 Month Price Score 105.18

TRADING VOLUME (thousand shares)

Interim Earnings (Per Share)

Qtr.	Oct	Jan	Apr	Jul
2012-13	0.64	0.31	0.46	0.67
2013-14	0.41	0.60	0.10	0.06
2014-15	0.30	0.39	0.19	0.71
2015-16	0.75	0.53	(0.13)	...

Interim Dividends (Per Share)

Amt	Decl	Ex	Rec	Pay
0.21Q	10/15/2015	11/18/2015	11/20/2015	12/04/2015
0.21Q	12/08/2015	02/17/2016	02/19/2016	03/04/2016
0.21Q	03/15/2016	05/18/2016	05/20/2016	06/03/2016
0.22Q	06/09/2016	08/17/2016	08/19/2016	09/02/2016

Indicated Div: $0.88

Valuation Analysis

		Institutional Holding	
Forecast EPS	N/A	No of Institutions	87
Market Cap	$235.7 Million	Shares	4,026,452
Book Value	$116.6 Million	% Held	53.44
Price/Book	2.02		
Price/Sales	0.90		

Business Summary: Household & Personal Products (MIC: 1.7.1 SIC: 3999 NAIC: 339999)

Oil-Dri Corp of America develops, manufactures and/or markets sorbent products. Co.'s sorbent products are principally produced from clay minerals, primarily consisting of montmorillonite and attapulgite and other clay-like sorbent materials, such as Antelope shale. Co.'s sorbent technologies include absorbent and adsorbent products. Co.'s absorbent clay products include cat litter, industrial floor absorbents, and agricultural chemical carriers. Co.'s adsorbent products include synthetic sorbents and bleaching clay products. Co. has two reportable operating segments, which are based on its primary customer groups: retail and wholesale products group and business to business products group.

Recent Developments: For the quarter ended Apr 30 2016, net loss amounted to US$892,000 versus net income of US$1.4 million in the year-earlier quarter. Revenues were US$64.2 million, down 1.5% from US$65.2 million the year before. Operating loss was US$1.2 million versus an income of US$1.9 million in the prior-year quarter. Direct operating expenses declined 10.0% to US$45.7 million from US$50.8 million in the comparable period the year before. Indirect operating expenses increased 58.1% to US$19.8 million from US$12.5 million in the equivalent prior-year period.

Prospects: Our evaluation of Oil-Dri Corp. of America as of June 19, 2016 is the result of our systematic analysis on three basic characteristics: earnings strength, relative valuation, and recent stock price movement. The company has suffered a very negative trend in earnings per share over the past 5 quarters. Because the company lacks sufficient analyst estimate data, we place greater weight on the historical EPS trend as the measure of earnings strength. Based on operating earnings yield, the company is about fairly valued when compared to all of the companies in our coverage universe. Share price changes over the past year indicates that ODC will perform in line with the market over the near term

Financial Data

(US$ in Thousands)	9 Mos	6 Mos	3 Mos	07/31/2015	07/31/2014	07/31/2013	07/31/2012	07/31/2011
Earnings Per Share	1.86	2.18	2.04	1.59	1.17	2.07	0.85	1.26
Cash Flow Per Share	4.28	4.75	4.81	3.87	2.33	3.40	3.33	1.87
Tang Book Value Per Share	14.06	14.23	13.81	13.44	12.36	13.79	11.40	12.39
Dividends Per Share	0.830	0.820	0.810	0.800	0.760	0.720	0.680	0.640
Dividend Payout %	44.62	37.61	39.71	50.31	64.96	34.78	80.00	50.79
Income Statement								
Total Revenue	197,397	133,162	67,795	261,402	266,313	250,583	240,681	226,755
EBITDA	12,120	13,109	10,735	25,835	22,172	28,177	19,677	22,636
Depn & Amortn	(6)	(2)	2,939	10,352	9,289	8,939	9,287	8,503
Income Before Taxes	11,376	12,609	7,540	14,169	11,337	17,499	8,361	12,141
Income Taxes	3,024	3,365	2,117	2,801	2,981	2,913	2,263	3,090
Net Income	8,352	9,244	5,423	11,368	8,356	14,586	6,098	9,051
Average Shares	7,041	7,096	7,063	7,037	7,004	6,927	7,062	7,103
Balance Sheet								
Current Assets	89,945	92,720	86,117	82,643	83,516	103,372	95,202	91,816
Total Assets	196,149	199,055	192,086	190,031	186,204	183,559	174,267	173,393
Current Liabilities	30,647	32,154	28,744	28,888	29,500	31,447	29,122	26,480
Long-Term Obligations	12,333	12,333	12,333	15,417	18,900	22,400	25,900	29,700
Total Liabilities	79,598	80,984	76,860	79,503	81,896	80,621	88,959	78,095
Stockholders' Equity	116,551	118,071	115,226	110,528	104,308	102,938	85,308	95,298
Shares Outstanding	7,249	7,249	7,244	7,068	7,071	7,021	6,924	7,156
Statistical Record								
Return on Assets %	7.03	8.19	7.87	6.04	4.52	8.15	3.50	5.53
Return on Equity %	11.98	13.95	13.30	10.58	8.06	15.50	6.73	9.74
EBITDA Margin %	6.14	9.84	15.83	9.88	8.33	11.24	8.18	9.98
Net Margin %	4.23	6.94	8.00	4.35	3.14	5.82	2.53	3.99
Asset Turnover	1.38	1.38	1.41	1.39	1.44	1.40	1.38	1.39
Current Ratio	2.93	2.88	3.00	2.86	2.83	3.29	3.27	3.47
Debt to Equity	0.11	0.10	0.11	0.14	0.18	0.22	0.30	0.31
Price Range	38.30-22.11	38.30-22.11	33.85-22.11	33.85-24.60	40.64-28.97	31.88-21.00	22.35-16.95	22.95-18.91
P/E Ratio	20.59-11.89	17.57-10.14	16.59-10.84	21.29-15.47	34.74-24.76	15.40-10.14	26.29-19.94	18.21-15.01
Average Yield %	2.68	2.71	2.77	2.65	2.26	2.79	3.33	3.06

Address: 410 North Michigan Avenue, Suite 400, Chicago, IL 60611-4213	Web Site: www.oildri.com	Auditors: Grant Thornton LLP
Telephone: 312-321-1515	Officers: Richard M. Jaffee - Chairman Joseph C. Miller - Vice-Chairman	Investor Contact: 312-321-1515
Fax: 312-321-9525		Transfer Agents: ComputerShare Investor Services, Chicago, IL

OIL STATES INTERNATIONAL, INC.

Exchange	Symbol	Price	52Wk Range	Yield	P/E
NYS	OIS	$32.86 (5/31/2016)	42.59-22.36	N/A	N/A

*7 Year Price Score 64.53 ***NYSE Composite Index=100** ***12 Month Price Score 105.29**

Interim Earnings (Per Share)

Qtr.	Mar	Jun	Sep	Dec
2013	1.85	1.38	3.01	1.29
2014	1.32	(0.15)	1.05	1.09
2015	0.38	0.12	0.03	0.03
2016	(0.26)	...	...	...

Interim Dividends (Per Share)

No Dividends Paid

Valuation Analysis / Institutional Holding

Forecast EPS	$-1.05	No of Institutions
	(05/20/2016)	320
Market Cap	$1.7 Billion	Shares
Book Value	$1.2 Billion	61,495,620
Price/Book	1.36	% Held
Price/Sales	1.81	95.41

TRADING VOLUME (thousand shares)

Business Summary: Equipment & Services (MIC: 9.1.3 SIC: 3533 NAIC: 333132)

Oil States International, through its subsidiaries, is a provider of products and services to oil and natural gas companies. Co. operates in two principal business segments: offshore products, which provides products and services for offshore oil and natural gas production systems and facilities, as well as certain products and services to the offshore drilling market; and well site services, which provides completion services and, to a lesser extent, land drilling services. Co. operates in oil and natural gas producing regions, including onshore and offshore U.S., Canada, West Africa, the North Sea, South America and Southeast and Central Asia.

Recent Developments: For the quarter ended Mar 31 2016, net loss amounted to US$13.2 million versus net income of US$19.6 million in the year-earlier quarter. Revenues were US$169.7 million, down 49.7% from US$337.4 million the year before. Operating loss was US$20.1 million versus an income of US$33.8 million in the prior-year quarter. Direct operating expenses declined 45.8% to US$128.8 million from US$237.7 million in the comparable period the year before. Indirect operating expenses decreased 7.5% to US$60.9 million from US$65.9 million in the equivalent prior-year period.

Prospects: Our evaluation of Oil States International Inc. as of June 19, 2016 is the result of our systematic analysis on three basic characteristics: earnings strength, relative valuation, and recent stock price movement. The company has enjoyed a very positive trend in earnings per share over the past 5 quarters. Because the company lacks sufficient analyst estimate data, we place greater weight on the historical EPS trend as the measure of earnings strength. Based on operating earnings yield, the company is overvalued when compared to all of the companies in our coverage universe. Share price changes over the past year indicates that OIS will perform poorly over the near term.

Financial Data
(US$ in Thousands)

	3 Mos	12/31/2015	12/31/2014	12/31/2013	12/31/2012	12/31/2011	12/31/2010	12/31/2009
Earnings Per Share	(0.08)	0.56	3.31	7.53	8.10	5.86	3.19	1.18
Cash Flow Per Share	3.96	5.10	8.29	12.50	12.00	4.22	4.60	9.14
Tang Book Value Per Share	17.93	18.30	19.53	36.47	32.86	26.66	19.93	23.33
Income Statement								
Total Revenue	169,655	1,099,977	1,819,609	2,670,163	4,413,088	3,479,180	2,411,984	2,108,250
EBITDA	(19,704)	179,952	330,279	726,445	910,491	685,938	377,512	233,843
Depn & Amortn	195	123,500	117,700	216,200	216,500	174,900	121,600	114,700
Income Before Taxes	(21,252)	50,568	195,966	436,696	626,652	455,232	240,389	104,257
Income Taxes	(8,016)	22,197	69,117	119,992	177,047	131,647	72,023	46,097
Net Income	(13,239)	28,597	179,003	421,258	448,609	322,453	168,018	59,114
Average Shares	50,042	50,335	53,151	55,327	55,384	55,007	52,700	50,219
Balance Sheet								
Current Assets	549,447	611,473	826,666	1,525,907	1,826,092	1,489,659	1,100,004	925,568
Total Assets	1,516,242	1,599,138	1,809,612	4,131,261	4,439,962	3,703,641	3,015,999	1,932,386
Current Liabilities	131,674	154,200	271,412	373,836	518,532	474,949	554,175	315,223
Long-Term Obligations	89,158	128,554	146,835	972,692	1,279,805	1,142,505	731,732	164,074
Total Liabilities	273,338	343,466	468,955	1,507,844	1,975,557	1,741,485	1,388,093	551,538
Stockholders' Equity	1,242,904	1,255,672	1,340,657	2,623,417	2,464,405	1,962,156	1,627,906	1,380,848
Shares Outstanding	51,362	50,953	53,017	54,181	54,695	51,288	50,838	49,814
Statistical Record								
Return on Assets %	N.M.	1.68	6.03	9.83	10.99	9.60	6.79	2.79
Return on Equity %	N.M.	2.20	9.03	16.56	20.21	17.96	11.17	4.55
EBITDA Margin %	N.M.	16.36	18.15	27.21	20.63	19.72	15.65	11.09
Net Margin %	N.M.	2.60	9.84	15.78	10.17	9.27	6.97	2.80
Asset Turnover	0.57	0.65	0.61	0.62	1.08	1.04	0.97	1.00
Current Ratio	4.17	3.97	3.05	4.08	3.52	3.14	1.98	2.94
Debt to Equity	0.07	0.10	0.11	0.37	0.52	0.58	0.45	0.12
Price Range	47.59-22.36	48.90-23.60	65.37-42.42	62.57-40.87	49.50-35.01	48.85-26.82	37.31-19.54	22.75-6.55
P/E Ratio	...	87.32-42.14	19.75-12.82	8.31-5.43	6.11-4.32	8.34-4.58	11.70-6.12	19.28-5.55

Address: Three Allen Center, 333 Clay Street, Suite 4620, Houston, TX 77002 **Telephone:** 713-652-0582	**Web Site:** www.oilstatesintl.com **Officers:** Stephen A. Wells - Chairman Cynthia B. Taylor President, Chief Executive Officer	**Auditors:** Ernst & Young LLP **Transfer Agents:** Computershare, Pittsburgh, PA

OLD REPUBLIC INTERNATIONAL CORP.

Exchange	Symbol	Price	52Wk Range	Yield	P/E	Div Achiever
NYS	ORI	$19.16 (5/31/2016)	19.26-14.89	3.91	12.36	34 Years

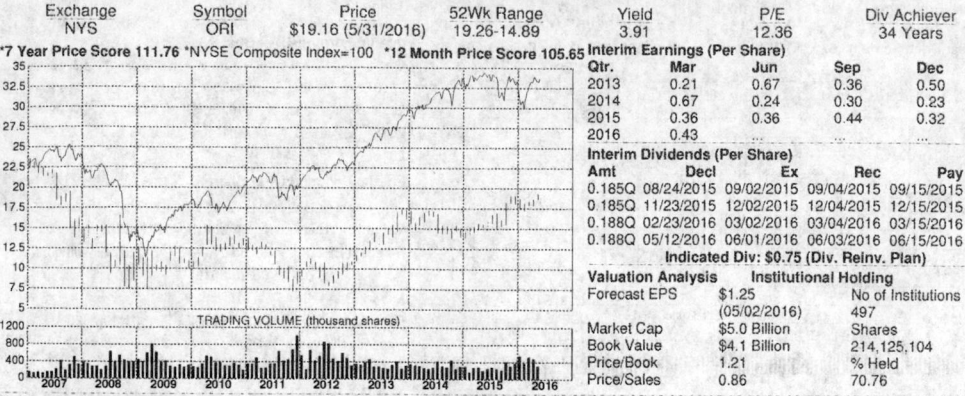

*7 Year Price Score 111.76 *NYSE Composite Index=100 *12 Month Price Score 105.65

Interim Earnings (Per Share)

Qtr.	Mar	Jun	Sep	Dec
2013	0.21	0.67	0.36	0.50
2014	0.67	0.24	0.30	0.23
2015	0.36	0.36	0.44	0.32
2016	0.43	...	...	...

Interim Dividends (Per Share)

Amt	Decl	Ex	Rec	Pay
0.185Q	08/24/2015	09/02/2015	09/04/2015	09/15/2015
0.185Q	11/23/2015	12/02/2015	12/04/2015	12/15/2015
0.188Q	02/23/2016	03/02/2016	03/04/2016	03/15/2016
0.188Q	05/12/2016	06/01/2016	06/03/2016	06/15/2016

Indicated Div: $0.75 (Div. Reinv. Plan)

Valuation Analysis   **Institutional Holding**

Forecast EPS	$1.25 (05/02/2016)	No of Institutions 497
Market Cap	$5.0 Billion	Shares
Book Value	$4.1 Billion	214,125,104
Price/Book	1.21	% Held
Price/Sales	0.86	70.76

Business Summary: General Insurance (MIC: 5.2.1 SIC: 6351 NAIC: 524127)

Old Republic International is a holding company engaged in the single business of insurance underwriting and related services. Co. conducts its operations through three segments, namely, General Insurance Group (property and liability insurance), which is a commercial lines insurance business focused on liability insurance coverages; Title Insurance Group, which consists of the issuance of policies to real estate purchasers and investors based upon searches of the public records, which contain information concerning interests in real property; and the Republic Financial Indemnity Group Run-off Business, which consists of its mortgage guaranty and consumer credit indemnity operations.

Recent Developments: For the quarter ended Mar 31 2016, net income increased 18.9% to US$122.9 million from US$103.4 million in the year-earlier quarter. Revenues were US$1.42 billion, up 6.3% from US$1.33 billion the year before. Net premiums earned were US$1.15 billion versus US$1.10 billion in the prior-year quarter, an increase of 4.3%. Net investment income rose 5.4% to US$98.0 million from US$93.0 million a year ago.

Prospects: Our evaluation of Old Republic International Corp. as of June 19, 2016 is the result of our systematic analysis on three basic characteristics: earnings strength, relative valuation, and recent stock price movement. The company has generated a negative trend in earnings per share over the past 5 quarters and while recent estimates for the company have remained steady, ORI has posted better than expected results. Based on operating earnings yield, the company is undervalued when compared to all of the companies in our coverage universe. Share price changes over the past year indicates that ORI will perform very well over the near term.

Financial Data
(US$ in Thousands)

	3 Mos	12/31/2015	12/31/2014	12/31/2013	12/31/2012	12/31/2011	12/31/2010	12/31/2009
Earnings Per Share	1.55	1.48	1.44	1.74	(0.27)	(0.55)	0.13	(0.42)
Cash Flow Per Share	2.41	2.65	(0.70)	2.67	2.07	(0.37)	(1.17)	2.26
Tang Book Value Per Share	15.80	14.81	15.04	14.49	13.86	14.55	15.90	16.17
Dividends Per Share	0.743	0.740	0.730	0.720	0.710	0.700	0.690	0.680
Dividend Payout %	47.90	50.00	50.69	41.38	...	...	530.77	...
Income Statement								
Premium Income	1,150,800	4,758,800	4,446,300	4,456,600	4,043,800	3,695,500	3,225,500	3,111,500
Total Revenue	1,413,500	5,766,100	5,530,700	5,442,700	4,970,100	4,645,500	4,102,700	3,803,600
Benefits & Claims	...	2,441,300	2,500,000	2,223,000	2,747,400	2,730,600	2,253,200	2,591,000
Income Before Taxes	182,300	631,800	...	...	...	...	27,600	...
Income Taxes	59,300	209,600	199,700	225,000	(59,800)	(96,100)	(2,500)	(174,400)
Net Income	122,900	422,100	409,700	447,800	(68,600)	(140,500)	30,100	(99,100)
Average Shares	295,543	296,088	295,073	293,684	255,812	255,045	241,327	235,657
Balance Sheet								
Total Assets	17,433,300	17,110,500	16,988,100	16,534,400	16,226,800	16,050,400	15,882,700	14,190,000
Total Liabilities	13,290,600	13,229,600	13,064,000	12,759,400	12,630,600	12,277,800	11,761,300	10,298,600
Stockholders' Equity	4,142,600	3,880,800	3,924,000	3,775,000	3,596,200	3,772,500	4,121,400	3,891,400
Shares Outstanding	262,175	261,968	260,946	260,462	259,490	259,328	259,222	240,685
Statistical Record								
Return on Assets %	2.55	2.48	2.44	2.73	N.M.	N.M.	0.20	N.M.
Return on Equity %	10.83	10.82	10.64	12.15	N.M.	N.M.	0.75	N.M.
Loss Ratio %	...	51.30	56.23	49.88	67.94	73.89	69.86	83.27
Net Margin %	8.69	7.32	7.41	8.23	(1.38)	(3.02)	0.73	(2.61)
Price Range	19.02-14.85	19.02-13.87	17.27-13.74	17.36-10.65	11.19-7.83	13.84-7.18	15.29-10.04	12.71-7.40
P/E Ratio	12.27-9.58	12.85-9.37	11.99-9.54	9.98-6.12	...	...	117.62-77.23	...
Average Yield %	4.41	4.61	4.67	5.15	7.29	6.36	5.42	6.36

Address: 307 North Michigan Avenue, Chicago, IL 60601 **Telephone:** 312-346-8100	**Web Site:** www.oldrepublic.com **Officers:** Aldo C. Zucaro - Chairman, Chief Executive Officer James A. Kellogg - Executive Vice-Chairman	**Auditors:** KPMG LLP **Investor Contact:** 800-468-9716 **Transfer Agents:** Wells Fargo Shareholder Services, St. Paul, MN

OLIN CORP.

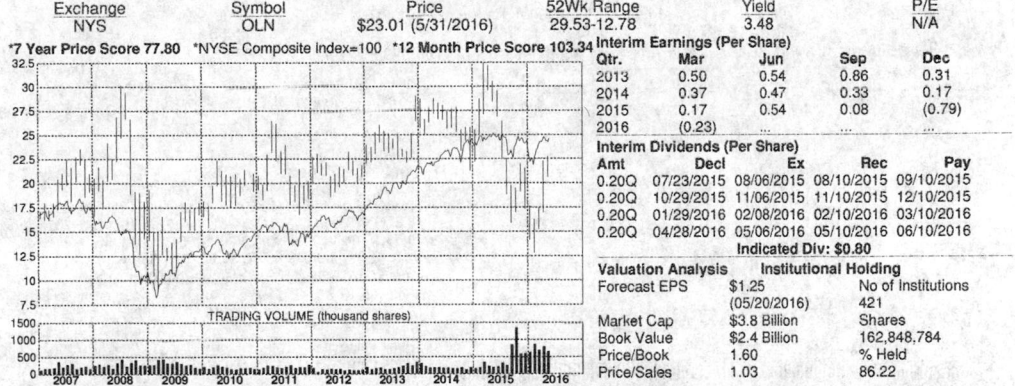

Exchange	Symbol	Price	52Wk Range	Yield	P/E
NYS	OLN	$23.01 (5/31/2016)	29.53-12.78	3.48	N/A

*7 Year Price Score 77.80   *NYSE Composite Index=100   *12 Month Price Score 103.34

Interim Earnings (Per Share)

Qtr.	Mar	Jun	Sep	Dec
2013	0.50	0.54	0.86	0.31
2014	0.37	0.47	0.33	0.17
2015	0.17	0.54	0.08	(0.79)
2016	(0.23)	...	...	...

Interim Dividends (Per Share)

Amt	Decl	Ex	Rec	Pay
0.20Q	07/23/2015	08/06/2015	08/10/2015	09/10/2015
0.20Q	10/29/2015	11/06/2015	11/10/2015	12/10/2015
0.20Q	01/29/2016	02/08/2016	02/10/2016	03/10/2016
0.20Q	04/28/2016	05/06/2016	05/10/2016	06/10/2016

Indicated Div: $0.80

Valuation Analysis

		Institutional Holding	
Forecast EPS	$1.25	No of Institutions	
	(05/20/2016)	421	
Market Cap	$3.8 Billion	Shares	
Book Value	$2.4 Billion	162,848,784	
Price/Book	1.60	% Held	
Price/Sales	1.03	86.22	

Business Summary: Diversified Chemicals (MIC: 8.3.1 SIC: 2812 NAIC: 325181)

Olin is a manufacturer concentrated in three business segments: the Chlor Alkali Products and Vinyls segment manufactures and sells chlorine and caustic soda, ethylene dichloride and vinyl chloride monomer, methyl chloride, methylene chloride, chloroform, carbon tetrachloride, perchloroethylene, bleach products and others; the Epoxy segment produces and sells a range of epoxy materials, including allyl chloride, epichlorohydrin, liquid epoxy resins and downstream products such as converted epoxy resins and additives; and the Winchester segment, which produces and sells sporting ammunition, reloading components, small caliber military ammunition and components, and industrial cartridges.

Recent Developments: For the quarter ended Mar 31 2016, net loss amounted to US$37.9 million versus net income of US$13.1 million in the year-earlier quarter. Revenues were US$1.35 billion, up 160.3% from US$518.0 million the year before. Operating loss was US$7.4 million versus an income of US$26.0 million in the prior-year quarter. Direct operating expenses rose 171.3% to US$1.18 billion from US$433.2 million in the comparable period the year before. Indirect operating expenses increased 206.5% to US$180.2 million from US$58.8 million in the equivalent prior-year period.

Prospects: Our evaluation of Olin Corp. as of June 19, 2016 is the result of our systematic analysis on three basic characteristics: earnings strength, relative valuation, and recent stock price movement. The company has generated a negative trend in earnings per share over the past 5 quarters and while recent estimates for the company have remained steady, OLN has posted better than expected results. Based on operating earnings yield, the company is about fairly valued when compared to all of the companies in our coverage universe. Share price changes over the past year indicates that OLN will perform very poorly over the near term.

Financial Data

(US$ in Thousands)	3 Mos	12/31/2015	12/31/2014	12/31/2013	12/31/2012	12/31/2011	12/31/2010	12/31/2009
Earnings Per Share	(0.40)	(0.01)	1.33	2.21	1.85	2.99	0.81	1.73
Cash Flow Per Share	1.66	2.10	2.03	3.97	3.48	2.70	1.46	2.56
Tang Book Value Per Share	N.M.	N.M.	1.84	2.72	1.23	4.23	6.47	6.42
Dividends Per Share	0.800	0.800	0.800	0.800	0.800	0.800	0.800	0.800
Dividend Payout %	...	...	60.15	36.20	43.24	26.76	98.77	46.24
Income Statement								
Total Revenue	1,348,200	2,854,400	2,241,200	2,515,000	2,184,700	1,961,100	1,585,900	1,531,500
EBITDA	122,300	324,800	342,600	420,500	358,500	498,300	158,300	254,400
Depn & Amortn	129,700	223,900	139,100	135,300	110,900	99,300	86,900	71,700
Income Before Taxes	(55,600)	5,000	161,000	247,200	222,200	369,800	47,000	172,200
Income Taxes	(17,500)	8,100	57,700	71,400	75,600	137,700	12,100	74,200
Net Income	(37,900)	(1,400)	105,700	178,600	149,600	241,700	64,800	135,700
Average Shares	165,100	103,400	79,700	80,900	81,000	80,800	79,900	78,300
Balance Sheet								
Current Assets	1,877,400	1,933,400	816,100	839,900	749,100	780,300	882,800	860,300
Total Assets	9,116,900	9,321,800	2,698,100	2,802,800	2,777,700	2,449,600	2,048,700	1,932,000
Current Liabilities	1,049,600	1,147,700	377,700	407,500	434,000	399,100	391,000	310,900
Long-Term Obligations	3,627,900	3,675,200	658,700	678,400	690,100	524,200	418,200	398,400
Total Liabilities	6,744,100	6,903,000	1,684,800	1,701,700	1,779,300	1,463,800	1,218,400	1,109,700
Stockholders' Equity	2,372,800	2,418,800	1,013,300	1,101,100	998,400	985,800	830,300	822,300
Shares Outstanding	165,200	165,100	77,400	79,400	80,200	80,100	79,579	78,721
Statistical Record								
Return on Assets %	N.M.	N.M.	3.84	6.40	5.71	10.75	3.26	7.39
Return on Equity %	N.M.	N.M.	10.00	17.01	15.04	26.62	7.84	17.77
EBITDA Margin %	9.07	11.38	15.29	16.72	16.41	25.41	9.98	16.61
Net Margin %	N.M.	N.M.	4.72	7.10	6.85	12.32	4.09	8.86
Asset Turnover	0.62	0.47	0.81	0.90	0.83	0.87	0.80	0.83
Current Ratio	1.79	1.68	2.16	2.06	1.73	1.96	2.26	2.77
Debt to Equity	1.53	1.52	0.65	0.62	0.69	0.53	0.50	0.48
Price Range	32.18-12.78	32.41-15.82	28.85-21.22	29.03-21.59	23.19-18.51	26.40-16.71	22.33-15.40	19.30-9.05
P/E Ratio	...	...	21.69-15.95	13.14-9.77	12.54-10.01	8.83-5.59	27.57-19.01	11.16-5.23
Average Yield %	3.73	3.31	3.03	3.32	3.80	3.77	4.16	5.42

Address: 190 Carondelet Plaza, Suite 1530, Clayton, MO 63105 **Telephone:** 314-480-1400	**Web Site:** www.olin.com **Officers:** Joseph D. Rupp - Chairman, President, Chief Executive Officer John E. Fischer - President, Chief Executive Officer, Chief Operating Officer, Senior Vice President, Vice President, Controller, Chief Financial Officer	**Auditors:** KPMG LLP **Investor Contact:** 314-480-1452 **Transfer Agents:** Wells Fargo Shareowner Services, St. Paul, MN

OMEGA HEALTHCARE INVESTORS, INC.

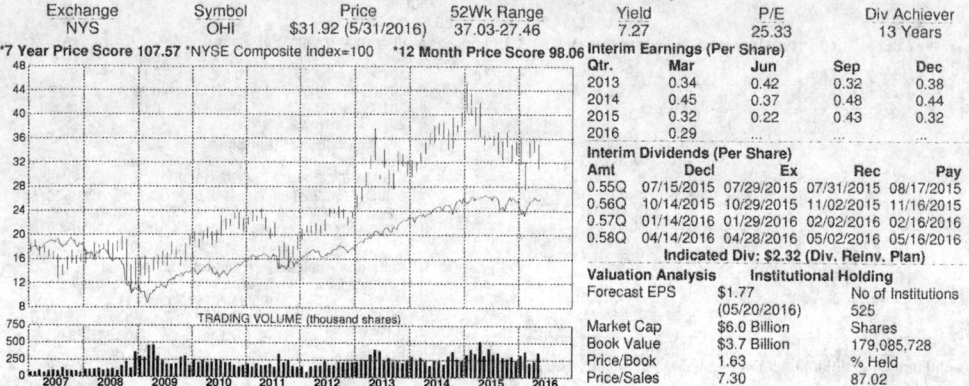

Exchange	Symbol	Price	52Wk Range	Yield	P/E	Div Achiever
NYS	OHI	$31.92 (5/31/2016)	37.03-27.46	7.27	25.33	13 Years

*7 Year Price Score 107.57 *NYSE Composite Index=100 *12 Month Price Score 98.06

Interim Earnings (Per Share)

Qtr.	Mar	Jun	Sep	Dec
2013	0.34	0.42	0.32	0.38
2014	0.45	0.37	0.48	0.44
2015	0.32	0.22	0.43	0.32
2016	0.29			

Interim Dividends (Per Share)

Amt	Decl	Ex	Rec	Pay
0.55Q	07/15/2015	07/29/2015	07/31/2015	08/17/2015
0.56Q	10/14/2015	10/29/2015	11/02/2015	11/16/2015
0.57Q	01/14/2016	01/29/2016	02/02/2016	02/16/2016
0.58Q	04/14/2016	04/28/2016	05/02/2016	05/16/2016

Indicated Div: $2.32 (Div. Reinv. Plan)

Valuation Analysis

		Institutional Holding	
Forecast EPS	$1.77	No of Institutions	
	(05/20/2016)	525	
Market Cap	$6.0 Billion	Shares	
Book Value	$3.7 Billion	179,085,728	
Price/Book	1.63	% Held	
Price/Sales	7.30	87.02	

Business Summary: REITs (MIC: 5.3.1 SIC: 6798 NAIC: 525930)

Omega Healthcare Investors is a real estate investment trust, investing in healthcare facilities, mainly long-term care facilities in the U.S. and the U.K. Co. provides lease or mortgage financing to operators of skilled nursing facilities (SNFs), assisted living facilities (ALFs), independent living facilities and rehabilitation and acute care facilities. As of Dec 31 2015, Co.'s portfolio of investments included 949 healthcare facilities located in 42 states and the U.K. operated by 83 third-party operators, comprising: 782 SNFs, 85 ALFs, 16 specialty facilities and one medical office building; fixed rate mortgages on 56 SNFs and two ALFs; and seven facilities closed or held-for-sale.

Recent Developments: For the quarter ended Mar 31 2016, net income increased 35.2% to US$58.2 million from US$43.1 million in the year-earlier quarter. Revenues were US$212.9 million, up 59.6% from US$133.4 million the year before. Revenues from property income rose 75.0% to US$176.7 million from US$101.0 million in the corresponding quarter a year earlier.

Prospects: Our evaluation of Omega Healthcare Investors Inc. as of June 19, 2016 is the result of our systematic analysis on three basic characteristics: earnings strength, relative valuation, and recent stock price movement. The company has enjoyed a very positive trend in earnings per share over the past 5 quarters. Because the company lacks sufficient analyst estimate data, we place greater weight on the historical EPS trend as the measure of earnings strength. Based on operating earnings yield, the company is undervalued when compared to all of the companies in our coverage universe. Share price changes over the past year indicates that OHI will perform in line with the market over the near term.

Financial Data

(US$ in Thousands)	3 Mos	12/31/2015	12/31/2014	12/31/2013	12/31/2012	12/31/2011	12/31/2010	12/31/2009
Earnings Per Share	1.26	1.29	1.74	1.46	1.12	0.46	0.52	0.87
Cash Flow Per Share	2.59	2.69	2.67	2.39	1.93	1.66	1.68	1.76
Tang Book Value Per Share	16.20	16.50	10.98	10.52	9.00	8.50	9.03	8.57
Dividends Per Share	1.860	2.180	2.020	1.860	1.690	1.550	1.370	1.200
Dividend Payout %	147.62	168.99	116.09	127.40	150.89	336.96	263.46	137.93
Income Statement								
Total Revenue	212,879	743,617	504,787	418,714	350,460	292,204	258,321	197,438
EBITDA	96,217	650,259	472,750	384,930	350,947	245,496	235,579	170,249
Depn & Amortn	(1,870)	232,810	124,576	120,402	124,182	106,031	86,646	49,084
Income Before Taxes	58,443	234,526	221,349	172,521	120,698	52,606	58,436	82,111
Income Taxes	247	1,211	...	...	...	...	...	...
Net Income	58,196	233,315	221,349	172,521	120,698	52,606	58,436	82,111
Average Shares	198,350	180,508	127,294	118,100	108,011	102,177	94,237	83,649
Balance Sheet								
Current Assets	230,003	223,893	201,741	181,879	163,551	135,127	122,139	93,214
Total Assets	8,615,452	8,019,009	3,921,645	3,462,216	2,982,005	2,557,312	2,304,007	1,655,033
Current Liabilities	1,100,000	15,352	...	...	...	...	...	...
Long-Term Obligations	3,119,192	3,569,086	2,378,503	2,024,418	1,824,932	1,551,400	1,176,965	738,149
Total Liabilities	4,922,417	4,281,023	2,520,318	2,162,113	1,970,676	1,678,828	1,299,941	789,806
Stockholders' Equity	3,693,035	3,737,986	1,401,327	1,300,103	1,011,329	878,484	1,004,066	865,227
Shares Outstanding	188,167	187,399	127,606	123,530	112,393	103,410	99,233	88,266
Statistical Record								
Return on Assets %	3.76	3.91	6.00	5.35	4.35	2.16	2.95	5.44
Return on Equity %	9.09	9.08	16.39	14.93	12.74	5.59	6.25	9.93
EBITDA Margin %	45.20	87.45	93.65	91.93	100.14	84.02	91.20	86.23
Net Margin %	27.34	31.38	43.85	41.20	34.44	18.00	22.62	41.59
Asset Turnover	0.12	0.12	0.14	0.13	0.13	0.12	0.13	0.13
Current Ratio	0.21	14.58	...	...	...	...	...	...
Debt to Equity	0.84	0.95	1.70	1.56	1.80	1.77	1.17	0.85
Price Range	41.94-27.46	45.16-32.08	40.29-29.56	37.61-23.85	24.75-19.19	24.27-14.42	23.67-17.67	19.85-11.83
P/E Ratio	33.29-21.79	35.01-24.87	23.16-16.99	25.76-16.34	22.10-17.13	52.76-31.35	45.52-33.98	22.82-13.60
Average Yield %	5.34	5.91	5.68	6.10	7.59	7.73	6.59	7.57

Address: 200 International Circle, Suite 3500, Hunt Valley, MD 21030 Telephone: 410-427-1700 Fax: 410-427-8800	Web Site: www.omegahealthcare.com Officers: Bernard J. Korman - Chairman C. Taylor Pickett - President, Chief Executive Officer	Auditors: Ernst & Young LLP Investor Contact: 410-427-1700 Transfer Agents: Registrar and Transfer Company, Cranford, NJ

OMNICOM GROUP, INC.

Exchange	Symbol	Price	52Wk Range	Yield	P/E
NYS	OMC	$83.33 (5/31/2016)	85.25-64.79	2.64	18.60

*7 Year Price Score 112.58 *NYSE Composite Index=100 *12 Month Price Score 111.11

Interim Earnings (Per Share)

Qtr.	Mar	Jun	Sep	Dec
2013	0.76	1.09	0.74	1.13
2014	0.77	1.23	0.95	1.29
2015	0.83	1.26	0.97	1.35
2016	0.90	...	...	...

Interim Dividends (Per Share)

Amt	Decl	Ex	Rec	Pay
0.50Q	07/16/2015	09/18/2015	09/22/2015	10/08/2015
0.50Q	12/03/2015	12/16/2015	12/18/2015	01/07/2016
0.50Q	02/02/2016	03/07/2016	03/09/2016	04/07/2016
0.55Q	05/24/2016	06/09/2016	06/13/2016	07/11/2016

Indicated Div: $2.20

Valuation Analysis   **Institutional Holding**

Forecast EPS	$4.77	No of Institutions	
	(05/20/2016)	905	
Market Cap	$19.8 Billion	Shares	
Book Value	$2.4 Billion	280,484,000	
Price/Book	8.34	% Held	
Price/Sales	1.31	88.98	

Business Summary: Advertising (MIC: 2.3.4 SIC: 7311 NAIC: 541810)

Omnicom Group is a holding company, engaged in providing advertising, marketing and corporate communications services to clients through its networks and agencies. Co.'s networks and agencies provide a range of services in four fundamental disciplines: advertising, customer relationship management, public relations and specialty communications. Co. develops and delivers the marketing message in a similar way by providing client-specific advertising and marketing services. Co.'s networks and agencies conduct business on a global basis and operate in the following geographic regions: The Americas, EMEA, and, Asia Pacific.

Recent Developments: For the quarter ended Mar 31 2016, net income increased 2.8% to US$236.3 million from US$229.8 million in the year-earlier quarter. Revenues were US$3.50 billion, up 0.9% from US$3.47 billion the year before. Operating income was US$392.1 million versus US$377.7 million in the prior-year quarter, an increase of 3.8%. Direct operating expenses rose 11.6% to US$2.92 billion from US$2.62 billion in the comparable period the year before. Indirect operating expenses decreased 61.3% to US$182.3 million from US$470.7 million in the equivalent prior-year period.

Prospects: Our evaluation of Omnicom Group Inc. as of June 19, 2016 is the result of our systematic analysis on three basic characteristics: earnings strength, relative valuation, and recent stock price movement. The company has enjoyed a very positive trend in earnings per share over the past 5 quarters and while recent estimates for the company have remained steady, OMC has posted better than expected results. Based on operating earnings yield, the company is undervalued when compared to all of the companies in our coverage universe. Share price changes over the past year indicates that OMC will perform very well over the near term.

Financial Data

(US$ in Thousands)	3 Mos	12/31/2015	12/31/2014	12/31/2013	12/31/2012	12/31/2011	12/31/2010	12/31/2009
Earnings Per Share	4.48	4.41	4.24	3.71	3.61	3.33	2.70	2.53
Cash Flow Per Share	8.12	8.90	5.82	6.99	5.39	4.71	4.97	5.62
Dividends Per Share	2.000	2.000	1.900	1.600	1.200	1.000	0.800	0.600
Dividend Payout %	44.64	45.35	44.81	43.13	33.24	30.03	29.63	23.72
Income Statement								
Total Revenue	3,499,100	15,134,400	15,317,800	14,584,500	14,219,400	13,872,500	12,542,500	11,720,700
EBITDA	462,200	2,211,200	2,238,500	2,110,100	2,086,900	1,944,800	1,713,200	1,617,700
Depn & Amortn	70,100	291,100	294,400	284,800	282,700	273,700	253,000	242,800
Income Before Taxes	352,000	1,778,600	1,810,000	1,660,900	1,659,600	1,549,000	1,350,400	1,274,200
Income Taxes	115,500	583,600	593,100	565,200	527,100	505,800	460,200	433,600
Net Income	218,400	1,093,900	1,104,000	991,100	998,300	952,600	827,700	793,000
Average Shares	241,100	245,200	255,300	260,400	270,000	283,300	303,500	310,400
Balance Sheet								
Current Assets	10,545,400	11,980,500	11,190,500	11,652,300	11,661,400	10,421,500	10,194,100	8,788,500
Total Assets	21,067,700	22,110,700	21,559,700	22,098,700	22,151,900	20,505,400	19,566,100	17,920,700
Current Liabilities	12,939,400	14,219,600	12,061,100	12,277,700	11,875,800	11,671,000	11,023,100	10,082,500
Long-Term Obligations	3,612,700	3,564,200	4,562,600	4,033,400	4,448,500	3,182,900	3,124,600	2,220,600
Total Liabilities	18,692,200	19,658,300	18,709,700	18,516,300	18,691,100	17,001,100	15,985,600	13,725,900
Stockholders' Equity	2,375,500	2,452,400	2,850,000	3,582,400	3,460,800	3,504,300	3,580,500	4,194,800
Shares Outstanding	237,749	239,700	246,700	257,600	262,000	273,400	285,500	308,400
Statistical Record								
Return on Assets %	5.36	5.01	5.06	4.48	4.67	4.75	4.42	4.50
Return on Equity %	46.30	41.26	34.33	28.14	28.59	26.89	21.29	20.55
EBITDA Margin %	13.21	14.61	14.61	14.47	14.68	14.02	13.66	13.80
Net Margin %	6.24	7.23	7.21	6.80	7.02	6.87	6.60	6.77
Asset Turnover	0.74	0.69	0.70	0.66	0.66	0.69	0.67	0.67
Current Ratio	0.81	0.84	0.93	0.95	0.98	0.89	0.92	0.87
Debt to Equity	1.52	1.45	1.60	1.13	1.29	0.91	0.87	0.53
Price Range	83.32-64.79	80.52-64.79	78.41-64.93	74.37-49.96	54.23-44.04	50.90-35.95	47.51-33.77	39.84-22.06
P/E Ratio	18.60-14.46	18.26-14.69	18.49-15.31	20.05-13.47	15.02-12.20	15.29-10.80	17.60-12.51	15.75-8.72
Average Yield %	2.72	2.71	2.64	2.56	2.43	2.23	2.01	1.87

Address: 437 Madison Avenue, New York, NY 10022	**Web Site:** www.omnicomgroup.com	**Auditors:** KPMG LLP
Telephone: 212-415-3600	**Officers:** Bruce Crawford - Chairman John D. Wren - President, Chief Executive Officer	**Investor Contact:** 212 415-3393
Fax: 212-415-3393		**Transfer Agents:** Wells Fargo Bank, NA, South St. Paul, MN

ONE GAS, INC.

Exchange NYS	Symbol OGS	Price $58.65 (5/31/2016)	52Wk Range 61.78-41.43	Yield 2.39	P/E 25.17

*7 Year Price Score N/A   ***NYSE Composite Index=100**   ***12 Month Price Score 115.38**

Interim Earnings (Per Share)

Qtr.	Mar	Jun	Sep	Dec
2014	1.13	0.18	0.09	0.69
2015	1.13	0.23	0.14	0.74
2016	1.22	...	...	...

Interim Dividends (Per Share)

Amt	Decl	Ex	Rec	Pay
0.30Q	07/20/2015	08/12/2015	08/14/2015	09/01/2015
0.30Q	10/28/2015	11/10/2015	11/13/2015	12/01/2015
0.35Q	01/19/2016	02/24/2016	02/26/2016	03/11/2016
0.35Q	05/02/2016	05/12/2016	05/16/2016	06/01/2016

Indicated Div: $1.40

Valuation Analysis / Institutional Holding

Forecast EPS	$2.52	No of Institutions
	(05/20/2016)	319
Market Cap	$3.1 Billion	Shares
Book Value	$1.9 Billion	38,013,092
Price/Book	1.64	% Held
Price/Sales	2.22	70.39

Business Summary: Electric Utilities (MIC: 3.1.1 SIC: 4924 NAIC: 221210)

ONE Gas is a regulated natural gas distribution utility. Co. provides natural gas distribution services to customers through its divisions in Oklahoma, Kansas and Texas through Oklahoma Natural Gas, Kansas Gas Service and Texas Gas Service, respectively. Co. serves residential, commercial, industrial and transportation customers in all three states. In addition, Co. provides natural gas distribution services to wholesale and public authority customers. As of Dec 31 2015, Co. served a total of 2.1 million customers in Oklahoma, Kansas and Texas.

Recent Developments: For the quarter ended Mar 31 2016, net income increased 7.2% to US$64.7 million from US$60.4 million in the year-earlier quarter. Revenues were US$508.4 million, down 24.9% from US$676.5 million the year before. Operating income was US$116.1 million versus US$109.0 million in the prior-year quarter, an increase of 6.5%. Direct operating expenses declined 43.0% to US$235.7 million from US$413.6 million in the comparable period the year before. Indirect operating expenses increased 1.7% to US$156.6 million from US$154.0 million in the equivalent prior-year period.

Prospects: Our evaluation of One Gas Inc. as of June 19, 2016 is the result of our systematic analysis on three basic characteristics: earnings strength, relative valuation, and recent stock price movement. The company has enjoyed a very positive trend in earnings per share over the past 5 quarters and while recent estimates for the company have remained steady, OGS has posted better than expected results. Based on operating earnings yield, the company is about fairly valued when compared to all of the companies in our coverage universe. Share price changes over the past year indicates that OGS will perform very well over the near term.

Financial Data

(US$ in Thousands)	3 Mos	12/31/2015	12/31/2014	12/31/2013	12/31/2012	12/31/2011
Earnings Per Share	2.33	2.24	2.07	...	...	...
Cash Flow Per Share	6.34	7.50	4.71	...	...	...
Tang Book Value Per Share	32.77	32.22	31.41	...	...	...
Dividends Per Share	1.250	1.200	0.840	...	...	...
Dividend Payout %	53.65	53.57	40.58	...	...	...
Income Statement						
Total Revenue	508,364	1,547,692	1,818,906	1,689,952	1,376,649	1,621,334
EBITDA	150,320	369,602	349,692	367,591	347,303	329,093
Depn & Amortn	34,684	133,023	125,722	144,758	130,150	132,212
Income Before Taxes	104,789	192,009	178,128	161,467	156,360	142,762
Income Taxes	40,046	72,979	68,338	62,272	59,851	56,004
Net Income	64,743	119,030	109,790	99,195	96,509	86,758
Average Shares	53,107	53,254	52,946	...	...	...
Balance Sheet						
Current Assets	417,611	482,845	667,501	602,184	457,094	...
Total Assets	4,598,104	4,644,410	4,649,210	3,846,475	3,491,332	...
Current Liabilities	228,593	304,221	392,433	769,077	578,702	...
Long-Term Obligations	1,191,854	1,201,305	1,201,311	1,028,949	1,028,954	...
Total Liabilities	2,730,917	2,802,855	2,855,173	2,607,452	2,336,535	...
Stockholders' Equity	1,867,187	1,841,555	1,794,037	1,239,023	1,154,797	...
Shares Outstanding	52,161	52,259	52,083	...	...	...
Statistical Record						
Return on Assets %	2.68	2.56	2.58	2.70	...	...
Return on Equity %	6.66	6.55	7.24	8.29	...	...
EBITDA Margin %	29.57	23.88	19.23	21.75	25.23	20.30
Net Margin %	12.74	7.69	6.04	5.87	7.01	5.35
Asset Turnover	0.30	0.33	0.43	0.46	...	...
Current Ratio	1.83	1.59	1.70	0.78	0.79	...
Debt to Equity	0.64	0.65	0.67	0.83	0.89	...
Price Range	61.78-41.41	51.34-39.38	44.19-32.25	...	...	...
P/E Ratio	26.52-17.77	22.92-17.58	21.35-15.58	...	...	...
Average Yield %	2.62	2.70	2.28	...	...	...

Address: 15 East Fifth Street, Tulsa, OK 74103 Telephone: 918-947-7000	Web Site: www.onegas.com Officers: John W. Gibson - Chairman Mark A. Bender - Senior Vice President, Chief Information Officer	Auditors: PricewaterhouseCoopers LLP

ONEOK INC

Exchange	Symbol	Price	52Wk Range	Yield	P/E	Div Achiever
NYS	OKE	$43.25 (5/31/2016)	43.25-18.93	5.69	34.06	13 Years

*7 Year Price Score 69.67   *NYSE Composite Index=100   *12 Month Price Score 111.26

Interim Earnings (Per Share)

Qtr.	Mar	Jun	Sep	Dec
2013	0.54	0.00	0.30	0.43
2014	0.45	0.29	0.31	0.45
2015	0.29	0.36	0.39	0.12
2016	0.40	...	...	...

Interim Dividends (Per Share)

Amt	Decl	Ex	Rec	Pay
0.605Q	07/23/2015	07/30/2015	08/03/2015	08/14/2015
0.615Q	10/21/2015	10/29/2015	11/02/2015	11/13/2015
0.615Q	01/21/2016	01/28/2016	02/01/2016	02/12/2016
0.615Q	04/21/2016	04/28/2016	05/02/2016	05/13/2016

Indicated Div: $2.46

Valuation Analysis | **Institutional Holding**

Forecast EPS	$1.76	No of Institutions
	(05/20/2016)	643
Market Cap	$9.1 Billion	Shares
Book Value	$286.9 Million	169,222,544
Price/Book	31.67	% Held
Price/Sales	1.18	80.44

TRADING VOLUME (thousand shares)

Business Summary: Equipment & Services (MIC: 9.1.3 SIC: 4923 NAIC: 221210)

Oneok is an energy company. Co.'s segments comprised of: Natural Gas Gathering and Processing, provides exploration and production companies with gathering and processing services that allow them to move their raw (unprocessed) natural gas to market; Natural Gas Liquids (NGL), owns and operates facilities that gather, fractionate, treat and distribute NGLs and store NGL products, primarily in Oklahoma, Kansas, Texas, New Mexico and the Rocky Mountain region where it provides nondiscretionary services to producers of NGLs; and Natural Gas Pipelines, which operates interstate and intrastate natural gas transmission pipelines and natural gas storage facilities.

Recent Developments: For the quarter ended Mar 31 2016, income from continuing operations increased 83.6% to US$175.9 million from US$95.8 million in the year-earlier quarter. Net income increased 82.8% to US$175.0 million from US$95.7 million in the year-earlier quarter. Revenues were US$1.77 billion, down 1.7% from US$1.81 billion the year before. Operating income was US$311.4 million versus US$196.5 million in the prior-year quarter, an increase of 58.5%. Direct operating expenses declined 8.8% to US$1.45 billion from US$1.58 billion in the comparable period the year before. Indirect operating expenses decreased 28.5% to US$17.7 million from US$24.7 million in the equivalent prior-year period.

Prospects: Our evaluation of Oneok Inc. as of June 19, 2016 is the result of our systematic analysis on three basic characteristics: earnings strength, relative valuation, and recent stock price movement. The company has managed to produce a neutral trend in earnings per share over the past 5 quarters. However, while recent estimates for the company have been lowered by analysts, OKE has posted results that fell short of analysts expectations. Based on operating earnings yield, the company is about fairly valued when compared to all of the companies in our coverage universe. Share price changes over the past year indicates that OKE will perform very poorly over the near term.

Financial Data

(US$ in Thousands)	3 Mos	12/31/2015	12/31/2014	12/31/2013	12/31/2012	12/31/2011	12/31/2010	12/31/2009
Earnings Per Share	1.27	1.16	1.49	1.27	1.71	1.68	1.55	1.44
Cash Flow Per Share	5.68	4.79	6.14	6.28	4.79	6.50	3.92	6.89
Tang Book Value Per Share	N.M.	N.M.	N.M.	5.59	5.53	5.93	6.67	5.56
Dividends Per Share	2.440	2.430	2.125	1.480	1.270	1.080	0.910	0.820
Dividend Payout %	192.13	209.48	142.62	116.54	74.27	64.29	58.71	57.14
Income Statement								
Total Revenue	1,774,459	7,763,206	12,195,091	14,602,717	12,632,559	14,805,794	13,030,051	11,111,651
EBITDA	405,788	1,167,983	1,441,071	1,348,409	1,459,579	1,465,610	1,252,840	1,215,616
Depn & Amortn	94,478	354,620	306,038	384,377	335,852	312,288	307,317	288,991
Income Before Taxes	193,063	396,576	778,870	629,826	821,422	856,316	653,284	625,803
Income Taxes	50,066	136,600	151,158	163,382	215,195	226,048	213,834	207,321
Net Income	83,446	244,977	314,107	266,533	360,619	360,594	334,632	305,451
Average Shares	211,071	210,541	210,427	209,695	210,710	214,498	215,570	212,640
Balance Sheet								
Current Assets	991,021	975,210	1,307,244	2,370,802	2,764,660	2,318,812	2,379,045	2,588,464
Total Assets	15,501,149	15,446,111	15,304,560	17,707,558	15,855,275	13,696,635	12,499,175	12,827,683
Current Liabilities	1,764,460	1,638,266	2,392,345	2,696,407	2,812,994	3,246,175	3,151,112	3,338,912
Long-Term Obligations	8,320,451	8,323,582	7,192,929	7,754,975	6,515,372	4,529,551	3,686,542	4,334,204
Total Liabilities	15,214,261	15,110,313	14,712,445	15,369,707	13,725,666	11,458,062	10,050,552	10,620,489
Stockholders' Equity	286,888	335,798	592,115	2,337,851	2,129,609	2,238,573	2,448,623	2,207,194
Shares Outstanding	210,098	209,731	208,322	206,618	204,935	206,509	213,631	211,813
Statistical Record								
Return on Assets %	1.72	1.59	1.90	1.59	2.43	2.75	2.64	2.35
Return on Equity %	65.51	52.80	21.44	11.93	16.47	15.39	14.37	14.22
EBITDA Margin %	22.87	15.05	11.82	9.23	11.55	9.90	9.62	10.94
Net Margin %	4.70	3.16	2.58	1.83	2.85	2.44	2.57	2.75
Asset Turnover	0.50	0.50	0.74	0.87	0.85	1.13	1.03	0.86
Current Ratio	0.56	0.60	0.55	0.88	0.98	0.71	0.75	0.78
Debt to Equity	29.00	24.79	12.15	3.32	3.06	2.02	1.51	1.96
Price Range	51.07-18.93	51.07-18.93	70.98-44.30	62.18-40.00	49.39-39.49	43.35-27.69	27.84-20.31	22.29-9.10
P/E Ratio	40.21-14.91	44.03-16.32	47.64-29.73	48.96-31.50	28.88-23.09	25.80-16.48	17.96-13.10	15.48-6.32
Average Yield %	7.18	6.22	3.44	2.96	2.92	3.11	3.43	5.20

Address: 100 West Fifth Street, Tulsa, OK 74103	**Web Site:** www.oneok.com	**Auditors:** PricewaterhouseCoopers LLP
Telephone: 918-588-7000	**Officers:** Terry K. Spencer - President, Chief Executive Officer Robert F. Martinovich - Executive Vice President, Executive Vice President (frmr), Senior Vice President, Chief Financial Officer, Treasurer	**Investor Contact:** 918-588-7163
Fax: 918-588-7273		**Transfer Agents:** Wells Fargo Shareowner Services, St Paul, MN

ORACLE CORP

Exchange	Symbol	Price	52Wk Range	Yield	P/E
NYS	ORCL	$40.20 (5/31/2016)	44.91-33.94	1.49	19.71

*7 Year Price Score 100.31 *NYSE Composite Index=100 *12 Month Price Score 102.78

Interim Earnings (Per Share)

Qtr.	Aug	Nov	Feb	May
2012-13	0.41	0.53	0.52	0.80
2013-14	0.47	0.56	0.56	0.80
2014-15	0.48	0.56	0.56	0.62
2015-16	0.40	0.52	0.50	...

Interim Dividends (Per Share)

Amt	Decl	Ex	Rec	Pay
0.15Q	09/15/2015	10/09/2015	10/14/2015	10/28/2015
0.15Q	12/15/2015	01/04/2016	01/06/2016	01/27/2016
0.15Q	03/14/2016	04/12/2016	04/14/2016	04/28/2016
0.15Q	06/16/2016	07/01/2016	07/06/2016	07/27/2016

Indicated Div: $0.60

Valuation Analysis

		Institutional Holding	
Forecast EPS	$2.77	No of Institutions	
	(05/20/2016)	2068	
Market Cap	$167.1 Billion	Shares	
Book Value	$45.9 Billion	2,787,384,832	
Price/Book	3.64	% Held	
Price/Sales	4.50	57.87	

TRADING VOLUME (thousand shares)

Business Summary: Internet & Software (MIC: 6.3.2 SIC: 7372 NAIC: 511210)

Oracle develops, manufactures, markets, sells and supports database and middleware software, application software, cloud infrastructure, hardware systems and related services that are engineered to work together in cloud-based and on-premises information technology environments. Co. is organized into three businesses: software and cloud, which is comprised of its new software licenses and cloud software subscriptions, cloud infrastructure-as-a-service, and software license updates and product support; hardware systems, which consist of its hardware systems products and hardware systems support; and services, which provides consulting services, managed cloud services, and education services.

Recent Developments: For the quarter ended Feb 29 2016, net income decreased 14.1% to US$2.14 billion from US$2.50 billion in the year-earlier quarter. Revenues were US$9.01 billion, down 3.4% from US$9.33 billion the year before. Operating income was US$3.03 billion versus US$3.38 billion in the prior-year quarter, a decrease of 10.5%. Direct operating expenses declined 9.3% to US$1.46 billion from US$1.61 billion in the comparable period the year before. Indirect operating expenses increased 4.4% to US$4.53 billion from US$4.34 billion in the equivalent prior-year period.

Prospects: Our evaluation of Oracle Corp. as of June 19, 2016 is the result of our systematic analysis on three basic characteristics: earnings strength, relative valuation, and recent stock price movement. The company has enjoyed a very positive trend in earnings per share over the past 5 quarters and while recent estimates for the company have remained steady, ORCL has posted results that fell short of analysts expectations. Based on operating earnings yield, the company is undervalued when compared to all of the companies in our coverage universe. Share price changes over the past year indicates that ORCL will perform in line with the market over the near term.

Financial Data

(US$ in Thousands)	9 Mos	6 Mos	3 Mos	05/31/2015	05/31/2014	05/31/2013	05/31/2012	05/31/2011
Earnings Per Share	2.04	2.10	2.14	2.21	2.38	2.26	1.96	1.67
Cash Flow Per Share	3.37	3.04	3.12	3.26	3.30	2.98	2.73	2.22
Tang Book Value Per Share	1.52	1.46	1.64	1.88	2.48	2.30	2.18	2.04
Dividends Per Share	0.600	0.570	0.540	0.510	0.480	0.300	0.240	0.210
Dividend Payout %	29.41	27.14	25.23	23.08	20.17	13.27	12.24	12.57
Income Statement								
Total Revenue	26,453,000	17,441,000	8,448,000	38,226,000	38,275,000	37,180,000	37,121,000	35,622,000
EBITDA	9,731,000	6,341,000	3,011,000	16,602,000	17,361,000	17,501,000	16,532,000	14,949,000
Depn & Amortn	1,926,000	1,304,000	671,000	2,861,000	2,908,000	2,931,000	2,916,000	2,796,000
Income Before Taxes	7,710,000	4,978,000	2,310,000	12,947,000	13,802,000	14,010,000	13,081,000	11,508,000
Income Taxes	1,623,000	1,033,000	563,000	2,896,000	2,749,000	2,973,000	2,981,000	2,864,000
Net Income	6,087,000	3,945,000	1,747,000	9,938,000	10,955,000	10,925,000	9,981,000	8,547,000
Average Shares	4,256,000	4,315,999	4,411,999	4,502,999	4,603,999	4,843,999	5,094,999	5,127,999
Balance Sheet								
Current Assets	57,069,000	58,618,000	62,122,000	63,183,000	48,138,000	41,692,000	40,023,000	39,174,000
Total Assets	104,894,000	106,483,000	109,706,000	110,903,000	90,344,000	81,812,000	78,327,000	73,535,000
Current Liabilities	11,825,000	13,754,000	15,391,000	15,291,000	14,389,000	12,872,000	15,388,000	14,192,000
Long-Term Obligations	40,106,000	39,940,000	40,050,000	39,959,000	22,667,000	18,494,000	13,524,000	14,772,000
Total Liabilities	59,024,000	60,559,000	62,609,000	62,240,000	43,466,000	37,164,000	34,639,000	33,759,000
Stockholders' Equity	45,870,000	45,924,000	47,097,000	48,663,000	46,878,000	44,648,000	43,688,000	39,776,000
Shares Outstanding	4,156,000	4,208,000	4,282,000	4,342,999	4,463,999	4,645,999	4,904,999	5,067,999
Statistical Record								
Return on Assets %	8.68	8.98	9.07	9.88	12.73	13.64	13.11	12.65
Return on Equity %	18.82	19.68	20.12	20.80	23.94	24.74	23.85	24.22
EBITDA Margin %	36.79	36.36	35.64	43.43	45.36	47.07	44.54	41.97
Net Margin %	23.01	22.62	20.68	26.00	28.62	29.38	26.89	23.99
Asset Turnover	0.36	0.37	0.36	0.38	0.44	0.46	0.49	0.53
Current Ratio	4.83	4.26	4.04	4.13	3.35	3.24	2.60	2.76
Debt to Equity	0.87	0.87	0.85	0.82	0.48	0.41	0.31	0.37
Price Range	44.91-33.94	46.23-35.44	46.23-35.45	46.23-37.56	42.20-29.96	36.34-26.00	34.22-24.78	36.37-21.46
P/E Ratio	22.01-16.64	22.01-16.88	21.60-16.57	20.92-17.00	17.73-12.59	16.08-11.50	17.46-12.64	21.78-12.85
Average Yield %	1.52	1.38	1.29	1.22	1.34	0.93	0.81	0.73

Address: 500 Oracle Parkway, Redwood City, CA 94065
Telephone: 650-506-7000

Web Site: www.oracle.com
Officers: Lawrence J. Ellison - Executive Chairman, Chief Technology Officer, Chairman, Chief Executive Officer Jeffrey O. Henley - Vice-Chairman, Chairman

Auditors: Ernst & Young LLP
Investor Contact: 650-506-4073
Transfer Agents: American Stock Transfer & Trust Company, LLC, Brooklyn, NY

ORBITAL ATK INC

Exchange	Symbol	Price	52Wk Range	Yield	P/E
NYS	OA	$87.03 (5/31/2016)	94.55-68.04	1.38	20.43

*7 Year Price Score 150.31 *NYSE Composite Index=100 ***12 Month Price Score 104.98**

Interim Earnings (Per Share)

Qtr.	Jun	Sep	Dec	Mar
2014-15	2.59	2.97	1.43	(0.51)

Qtr.	Mar	June	Sep	Dec
2015	...	0.89	1.27	0.91
2016	1.19	...	...	...

Interim Dividends (Per Share)

Amt	Decl	Ex	Rec	Pay
0.26Q	08/05/2015	08/31/2015	09/02/2015	09/24/2015
0.26Q	11/02/2015	11/16/2015	11/18/2015	12/10/2015
0.30Q	02/04/2016	03/03/2016	03/07/2016	03/24/2016
0.30Q	05/04/2016	06/06/2016	06/08/2016	06/23/2016

Indicated Div: $1.20

Valuation Analysis

		Institutional Holding	
Forecast EPS	$5.54	No of Institutions	
	(05/24/2016)	516	
Market Cap	$5.1 Billion	Shares	
Book Value	$2.0 Billion	56,450,088	
Price/Book	2.58	% Held	
Price/Sales	N/A	86.39	

TRADING VOLUME (thousand shares)

Business Summary: Defense (MIC: 7.1.2 SIC: 3761 NAIC: 336415)

Orbital ATK is an aerospace and defense systems company and supplier of related products. Co.'s products include launch vehicles and related propulsion systems; satellites and associated components and services; composite aerospace structures; tactical missiles, subsystems and defense electronics; and precision weapons, armament systems and ammunition. Co. has three segments: Flight Systems Group, which develops rockets; Defense Systems Group, which develops and produces small-, medium-, and large-caliber ammunition, precision weapons and munitions, gun systems, and propellant and energetic materials; and Space Systems Group, which develops and produces small- and medium-class satellites.

Recent Developments: For the quarter ended Apr 3 2016, income from continuing operations amounted to US$69.8 million compared with a loss of US$40.7 million in the year-earlier quarter. Net income totaled US$69.8 million versus a net loss of US$23.9 million in the year-earlier quarter. Revenues were US$1.06 billion, up 9.8% from US$969.5 million the year before. Operating income was US$115.9 million versus an operating loss of US$1.1 million in the prior-year quarter. Direct operating expenses rose 11.3% to US$842.7 million from US$757.0 million in the comparable period the year before.

Prospects: Our evaluation of Orbital ATK Inc. as of June 26, 2016 is the result of our systematic analysis on three basic characteristics: earnings strength, relative valuation, and recent stock price movement. The company has enjoyed a very positive trend in earnings per share over the past 5 quarters and while recent estimates for the company have been mixed, OA has posted better than expected results. Based on operating earnings yield, the company is undervalued when compared to all of the companies in our coverage universe. Share price changes over the past year indicates that OA will perform very well over the near term.

Financial Data

(US$ in Thousands)	3 Mos	12/31/2015	03/31/2015	03/31/2014	03/31/2013	03/31/2012	03/31/2011	03/31/2010
Earnings Per Share	4.26	3.04	5.60	10.42	8.34	7.93	9.32	8.33
Cash Flow Per Share	...	2.92	8.78	12.25	8.43	11.29	12.65	5.90
Tang Book Value Per Share	2.45	N.M.	N.M.	N.M.	3.96	N.M.	N.M.	N.M.
Dividends Per Share	1.080	1.100	1.280	1.100	0.920	0.800	0.200	...
Dividend Payout %	25.35	36.18	22.86	10.56	11.03	10.09	2.15	...
Income Statement								
Total Revenue	1,064,954	3,399,089	3,173,967	4,775,128	4,362,145	4,613,399	4,842,264	4,807,666
EBITDA	116,547	446,265	290,354	708,082	563,932	604,471	636,912	612,167
Depn & Amortn	644	123,878	85,027	117,776	106,062	108,885	111,186	99,830
Income Before Taxes	95,212	265,224	116,651	510,514	392,484	406,966	438,674	435,417
Income Taxes	25,367	83,659	39,117	169,428	120,243	143,762	124,963	156,473
Net Income	69,836	182,430	202,484	340,915	271,805	262,612	313,175	278,714
Average Shares	58,881	59,915	36,140	32,723	32,608	33,112	33,615	33,462
Balance Sheet								
Current Assets	2,408,136	2,240,442	2,388,906	2,461,598	2,218,732	2,009,695	2,059,233	1,718,978
Total Assets	5,469,043	5,353,556	5,504,402	5,771,146	4,383,010	4,541,746	4,443,845	3,869,624
Current Liabilities	954,198	966,979	1,096,784	1,130,150	906,855	919,780	1,063,486	787,815
Long-Term Obligations	1,551,481	1,450,000	1,528,504	1,843,750	1,023,877	1,272,002	1,289,709	1,379,804
Total Liabilities	3,489,594	3,416,416	3,727,404	3,859,571	2,880,841	3,314,951	3,287,087	3,071,030
Stockholders' Equity	1,979,449	1,937,140	1,776,998	1,911,575	1,502,169	1,226,795	1,156,758	798,594
Shares Outstanding	58,607	58,729	59,427	31,842	32,318	33,142	33,519	33,047
Statistical Record								
Return on Assets %	...	1.87	3.59	6.71	6.09	5.83	7.53	7.47
Return on Equity %	...	5.41	10.98	19.97	19.92	21.98	32.03	39.43
EBITDA Margin %	10.94	13.13	9.15	14.83	12.93	13.10	13.15	12.73
Net Margin %	6.56	5.37	6.38	7.14	6.23	5.69	6.47	5.80
Asset Turnover	...	0.35	0.56	0.94	0.98	1.02	1.16	1.29
Current Ratio	2.52	2.32	2.18	2.18	2.45	2.18	1.94	2.18
Debt to Equity	0.78	0.75	0.86	0.96	0.68	1.04	1.11	1.73
Price Range	94.55-68.04	90.98-68.04	79.78-47.42	66.96-32.49	33.75-20.50	35.40-23.35	38.86-28.11	42.25-31.21
P/E Ratio	22.19-15.97	29.93-22.38	14.25-8.47	6.43-3.12	4.05-2.46	4.46-2.95	4.17-3.02	5.07-3.75
Average Yield %	1.36	1.41	2.09	2.27	3.53	2.76	0.59	...

Address: 45101 Warp Drive, Dulles, VA 20166
Telephone: 703-406-5000

Web Site: www.orbitalatk.com
Officers: Ronald R. Fogleman - Chairman David W. Thompson - President, Chief Executive Officer

Auditors: PricewaterhouseCoopers LLP
Investor Contact: 952-351-3056
Transfer Agents: Computershare, Providence, R.I.

OSHKOSH CORP

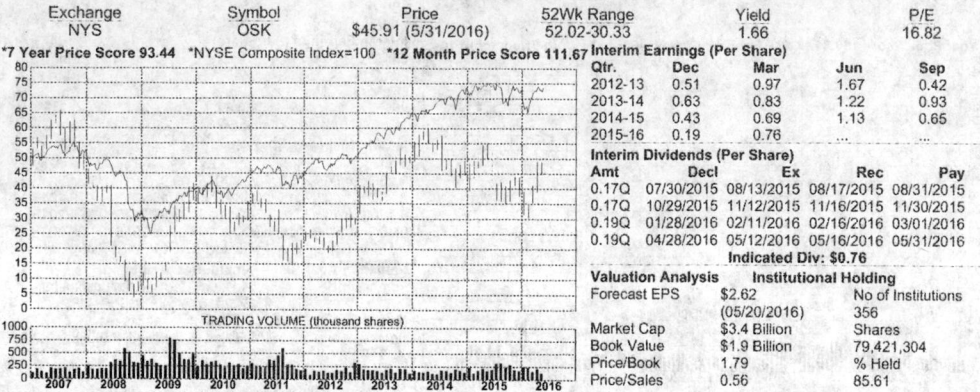

Exchange	Symbol	Price	52Wk Range	Yield	P/E
NYS	OSK	$45.91 (5/31/2016)	52.02-30.33	1.66	16.82

*7 Year Price Score 93.44 *NYSE Composite Index=100 *12 Month Price Score 111.67

Interim Earnings (Per Share)

Qtr.	Dec	Mar	Jun	Sep
2012-13	0.51	0.97	1.67	0.42
2013-14	0.63	0.83	1.22	0.93
2014-15	0.43	0.69	1.13	0.65
2015-16	0.19	0.76	...	...

Interim Dividends (Per Share)

Amt	Decl	Ex	Rec	Pay
0.17Q	07/30/2015	08/13/2015	08/17/2015	08/31/2015
0.17Q	10/29/2015	11/12/2015	11/16/2015	11/30/2015
0.19Q	01/28/2016	02/11/2016	02/16/2016	03/01/2016
0.19Q	04/28/2016	05/12/2016	05/16/2016	05/31/2016

Indicated Div: $0.76

Valuation Analysis

		Institutional Holding	
Forecast EPS	$2.62 (05/20/2016)	No of Institutions	356
Market Cap	$3.4 Billion	Shares	79,421,304
Book Value	$1.9 Billion	% Held	85.61
Price/Book	1.79		
Price/Sales	0.56		

Business Summary: Autos- Manufacturing (MIC: 1.8.1 SIC: 3711 NAIC: 336120)

Oshkosh is a designer, manufacturer and marketer of a range of vehicles and vehicle bodies. Co. operates four segments: access equipment, which includes aerial work platforms and telehandlers and Jerr-Dan-branded tow trucks and roll-back vehicle carriers; defense, which manufactures tactical wheeled vehicles and supply parts and services; fire and emergency, which manufactures firefighting vehicles and equipment, aircraft rescue and firefighting vehicles, snow removal vehicles, simulators and other emergency vehicles; and commercial, which manufactures rear- and front-discharge concrete mixers, refuse collection vehicles, portable and stationary concrete batch plants and vehicle components.

Recent Developments: For the quarter ended Mar 31 2016, net income increased 2.7% to US$56.1 million from US$54.6 million in the year-earlier quarter. Revenues were US$1.52 billion, down 1.9% from US$1.55 billion the year before. Operating income was US$91.4 million versus US$109.7 million in the prior-year quarter, a decrease of 16.7%. Direct operating expenses declined 1.0% to US$1.27 billion from US$1.28 billion in the comparable period the year before. Indirect operating expenses increased 1.1% to US$167.9 million from US$166.1 million in the equivalent prior-year period.

Prospects: Our evaluation of Oshkosh Corp. as of June 19, 2016 is the result of our systematic analysis on three basic characteristics: earnings strength, relative valuation, and recent stock price movement. The company has enjoyed a very positive trend in earnings per share over the past 5 quarters and while recent estimates for the company have been raised by analysts, OSK has posted better than expected results. Based on operating earnings yield, the company is undervalued when compared to all of the companies in our coverage universe. Share price changes over the past year indicates that OSK will perform poorly over the near term.

Financial Data

(US$ in Thousands)	6 Mos	3 Mos	09/30/2015	09/30/2014	09/30/2013	09/30/2012	09/30/2011	09/30/2010
Earnings Per Share	2.73	2.66	2.90	3.61	3.55	2.51	2.99	8.69
Cash Flow Per Share	3.39	2.79	1.06	2.03	4.99	2.93	4.27	6.89
Tang Book Value Per Share	3.94	2.96	4.02	3.78	4.07	0.48	N.M.	N.M.
Dividends Per Share	0.720	0.700	0.680	0.600	...	...	...	...
Dividend Payout %	26.37	26.32	23.45	16.62	...	...	...	...
Income Statement								
Total Revenue	2,776,300	1,252,000	6,098,100	6,808,200	7,665,100	8,180,900	7,584,700	9,842,400
EBITDA	182,900	60,600	511,800	621,900	621,500	484,100	641,800	1,539,400
Depn & Amortn	62,200	30,300	118,100	120,600	121,900	123,300	139,300	144,300
Income Before Taxes	91,500	16,200	326,100	431,900	445,000	286,700	416,500	1,211,500
Income Taxes	22,000	1,700	99,200	125,000	131,700	57,400	143,600	414,300
Net Income	70,700	14,600	229,500	309,300	318,000	230,800	273,400	790,000
Average Shares	73,861	74,853	78,981	85,457	88,953	91,893	91,573	90,954
Balance Sheet								
Current Assets	2,590,200	2,248,600	2,429,300	2,384,300	2,553,400	2,694,500	2,454,600	2,215,900
Total Assets	4,751,200	4,409,900	4,613,000	4,586,700	4,765,700	4,947,800	4,826,900	4,708,600
Current Liabilities	1,644,500	1,364,900	1,458,100	1,311,600	1,380,700	1,704,500	1,691,800	1,812,000
Long-Term Obligations	845,000	850,000	855,000	875,000	890,000	955,000	1,020,000	1,086,400
Total Liabilities	2,876,800	2,603,500	2,701,900	2,601,700	2,657,900	3,094,300	3,230,400	3,382,000
Stockholders' Equity	1,874,400	1,806,400	1,911,100	1,985,000	2,107,800	1,853,500	1,596,500	1,326,600
Shares Outstanding	73,150	73,097	75,454	79,845	86,534	91,557	91,323	90,662
Statistical Record								
Return on Assets %	4.53	4.77	4.99	6.61	6.55	4.71	5.73	16.67
Return on Equity %	11.18	11.29	11.78	15.11	16.06	13.34	18.71	85.84
EBITDA Margin %	6.59	4.84	8.39	9.13	8.11	5.92	8.46	15.64
Net Margin %	2.55	1.17	3.76	4.54	4.15	2.82	3.60	8.03
Asset Turnover	1.28	1.37	1.33	1.46	1.58	1.67	1.59	2.08
Current Ratio	1.58	1.65	1.67	1.82	1.85	1.58	1.45	1.22
Debt to Equity	0.45	0.47	0.45	0.44	0.42	0.52	0.64	0.82
Price Range	54.90-30.33	54.90-35.23	54.90-35.23	60.03-44.15	49.12-26.85	29.76-14.51	39.27-15.74	43.84-24.88
P/E Ratio	20.11-11.11	20.64-13.24	18.93-12.15	16.63-12.23	13.84-7.56	11.86-5.78	13.13-5.26	5.04-2.86
Average Yield %	1.74	1.60	1.51	1.15	...	...	...	...

Address: P.O. Box 2566, Oshkosh, WI 54903-2566
Telephone: 920-235-9151

Web Site: www.oshkoshcorporation.com
Officers: Richard M. Donnelly - Chairman Wilson R. Jones - President, Chief Executive Officer, Chief Operating Officer, Executive Vice President, Division Officer

Auditors: Deloitte & Touche LLP
Investor Contact: 920-966-5939
Transfer Agents: Computershare Investor Services, LLC, Providence, RI

OUTFRONT MEDIA INC

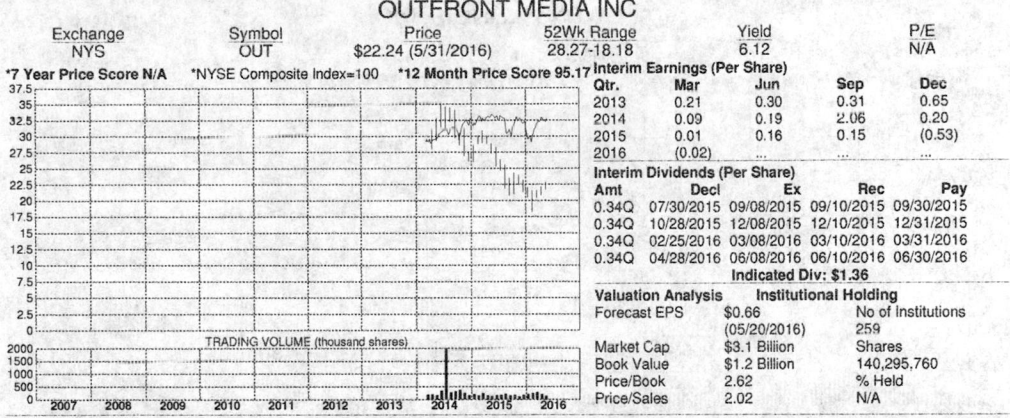

Exchange	Symbol	Price	52Wk Range	Yield	P/E
NYS	OUT	$22.24 (5/31/2016)	28.27-18.18	6.12	N/A

*7 Year Price Score N/A *NYSE Composite Index=100 *12 Month Price Score 95.17

Interim Earnings (Per Share)

Qtr.	Mar	Jun	Sep	Dec
2013	0.21	0.30	0.31	0.65
2014	0.09	0.19	2.06	0.20
2015	0.01	0.16	0.15	(0.53)
2016	(0.02)	...	...	...

Interim Dividends (Per Share)

Amt	Decl	Ex	Rec	Pay
0.34Q	07/30/2015	09/08/2015	09/10/2015	09/30/2015
0.34Q	10/28/2015	12/08/2015	12/10/2015	12/31/2015
0.34Q	02/25/2016	03/08/2016	03/10/2016	03/31/2016
0.34Q	04/28/2016	06/08/2016	06/10/2016	06/30/2016

Indicated Div: $1.36

Valuation Analysis

Forecast EPS	$0.66 (05/20/2016)
Market Cap	$3.1 Billion
Book Value	$1.2 Billion
Price/Book	2.62
Price/Sales	2.02

Institutional Holding

No of Institutions	259
Shares	140,295,760
% Held	N/A

Business Summary: REITs (MIC: 5.3.1 SIC: 6798 NAIC: 525930)

OUTFRONT Media is a real estate investment trust that provides advertising space on out-of-home advertising structures and sites across the U. S., Canada and Latin America. Co.'s portfolio includes billboard displays, which are predominantly located in densely populated main metropolitan areas and along high-traffic expressways and main commuting routes. Co. also has a number of exclusive multi-year contracts to operate advertising displays in municipal transit systems. As of Dec 31 2014, Co. had displays in 25 markets in the U.S. and over 180 markets across the U.S., Canada and Latin America. Co. manages its business through two segments: U.S. and International.

Recent Developments: For the quarter ended Mar 31 2016, net loss amounted to US$2.3 million versus net income of US$1.1 million in the year-earlier quarter. Revenues were US$348.4 million, up 1.3% from US$343.9 million the year before.

Prospects: Our evaluation of OUTFRONT Media Inc. as of June 19, 2016 is the result of our systematic analysis on three basic characteristics: earnings strength, relative valuation, and recent stock price movement. The company has enjoyed a very positive trend in earnings per share over the past 5 quarters and while recent estimates for the company have remained steady, OUT has posted results that fell short of analysts expectations. Based on operating earnings yield, the company is overvalued when compared to all of the companies in our coverage universe. Share price changes over the past year indicates that OUT will perform poorly over the near term.

Financial Data
(US$ in Thousands)

	3 Mos	12/31/2015	12/31/2014	12/31/2013	12/31/2012	12/31/2011
Earnings Per Share	(0.24)	(0.21)	2.67	1.48	1.17	1.10
Cash Flow Per Share	2.33	2.13	2.30	2.87	3.20	3.53
Tang Book Value Per Share	N.M.	N.M.	N.M.	5.41	5.64	...
Dividends Per Share	1.360	1.420	5.670	...	...	...
Dividend Payout %	...	...	212.36	...	...	...
Income Statement						
Total Revenue	348,400	1,513,800	1,353,800	1,294,000	1,284,600	1,277,100
EBITDA	55,100	113,786,000	290,000	342,100	306,100	302,200
Depn & Amortn	31,100	113,700,000	107,200	104,500	105,900	109,000
Income Before Taxes	(4,600)	(28,800)	98,000	237,600	200,200	193,200
Income Taxes	(1,300)	5,400	(206,000)	96,600	89,000	87,800
Net Income	(2,300)	(29,400)	306,900	143,500	113,400	107,100
Average Shares	137,600	137,300	114,800	97,000	97,000	97,000
Balance Sheet						
Current Assets	360,500	416,600	355,300	317,200	315,000	...
Total Assets	3,799,300	3,845,200	4,023,600	3,355,500	3,464,900	...
Current Liabilities	292,100	265,600	255,200	212,200	205,600	...
Long-Term Obligations	2,222,900	2,251,700	2,198,300	...	...	...
Total Liabilities	2,629,100	2,632,600	2,578,100	601,100	621,000	...
Stockholders' Equity	1,170,200	1,212,600	1,445,500	2,754,400	2,843,900	...
Shares Outstanding	137,900	137,600	136,600	97,000	97,000	97,000
Statistical Record						
Return on Assets %	N.M.	N.M.	8.32	4.21	...	...
Return on Equity %	N.M.	N.M.	14.61	5.13	...	...
EBITDA Margin %	15.82	7,516.58	21.42	26.44	23.83	23.66
Net Margin %	N.M.	N.M.	22.67	11.09	8.83	8.39
Asset Turnover	0.39	0.38	0.37	0.38	...	...
Current Ratio	1.23	1.57	1.39	1.49	1.53	...
Debt to Equity	1.90	1.86	1.52	...	...	...
Price Range	29.96-18.18	30.82-20.71	35.15-26.03	...	...	...
P/E Ratio	...	...	13.16-9.75	...	...	...
Average Yield %	5.70	5.50	18.34	...	...	...

Address: 405 Lexington Avenue, 17th Floor, New York, NY 10174 **Telephone:** 212-297-6400	**Web Site:** www.cbsoutdoor.com **Officers:** Jeremy J. Male - Chairman, Chief Executive Officer Donald R. Shassian - Executive Vice President, Chief Financial Officer	**Auditors:** PricewaterhouseCoopers LLP **Transfer Agents:** Wells Fargo Bank, National Association

OWENS-ILLINOIS, INC.

Exchange	Symbol	Price	52Wk Range	Yield	P/E
NYS	OI	$18.90 (5/31/2016)	24.66-12.06	N/A	N/A

*7 Year Price Score 62.07 ***NYSE Composite Index=100** ***12 Month Price Score 92.93**

Interim Earnings (Per Share)

Qtr.	Mar	Jun	Sep	Dec
2013	0.42	0.79	0.78	(0.88)
2014	0.61	0.68	0.37	(1.21)
2015	0.44	0.25	0.10	(1.26)
2016	0.41	...	...	...

Interim Dividends (Per Share)

No Dividends Paid

Valuation Analysis **Institutional Holding**

Forecast EPS	$2.31	No of Institutions
	(05/20/2016)	481
Market Cap	$3.1 Billion	Shares
Book Value	$416.0 Million	174,114,080
Price/Book	7.36	% Held
Price/Sales	0.48	94.66

Business Summary: Containers & Packaging (MIC: 8.1.3 SIC: 3221 NAIC: 327213)

Owens-Illinois is a manufacturer of glass containers. As of Dec 31 2015, Co. had glass container operations located in 23 countries. Co. produces glass containers for alcoholic beverages, including beer, flavored malt beverages, spirits and wine. Co. also produces glass packaging for a variety of food items, soft drinks, teas, juices and pharmaceuticals. Co. manufactures glass containers in a range of sizes, shapes and colors. Co. has four reportable segments based on its geographic locations: Europe, North America, South America and Asia Pacific.

Recent Developments: For the quarter ended Mar 31 2016, income from continuing operations decreased 1.3% to US$74.0 million from US$75.0 million in the year-earlier quarter. Net income decreased 2.7% to US$73.0 million from US$75.0 million in the year-earlier quarter. Revenues were US$1.59 billion, up 11.8% from US$1.42 billion the year before. Direct operating expenses rose 10.1% to US$1.27 billion from US$1.15 billion in the comparable period the year before. Indirect operating expenses increased 14.6% to US$196.0 million from US$171.0 million in the equivalent prior-year period.

Prospects: Our evaluation of Owens-Illinois Inc. as of June 19, 2016 is the result of our systematic analysis on three basic characteristics: earnings strength, relative valuation, and recent stock price movement. The company has enjoyed a very positive trend in earnings per share over the past 5 quarters. However, while recent estimates for the company have been mixed, OI has posted better than expected results. Based on operating earnings yield, the company is undervalued when compared to all of the companies in our coverage universe. Share price changes over the past year indicates that OI will perform poorly over the near term.

Financial Data

(US$ in Thousands)	3 Mos	12/31/2015	12/31/2014	12/31/2013	12/31/2012	12/31/2011	12/31/2010	12/31/2009
Earnings Per Share	(0.50)	(0.47)	0.45	1.11	1.11	(3.11)	(0.28)	0.95
Cash Flow Per Share	3.62	3.77	4.10	4.15	3.49	3.07	3.60	4.77
Income Statement								
Total Revenue	1,588,000	6,156,000	6,784,000	6,967,000	7,000,000	7,358,000	6,633,000	7,066,500
EBITDA	278,000	573,000	719,000	847,000	881,000	236,000	970,000	840,600
Depn & Amortn	125,000	323,000	335,000	350,000	378,000	405,000	369,000	374,800
Income Before Taxes	87,000	(1,000)	154,000	268,000	264,000	(472,000)	365,000	272,700
Income Taxes	27,000	106,000	92,000	120,000	108,000	85,000	129,000	127,500
Net Income	67,000	(74,000)	75,000	184,000	184,000	(510,000)	(47,000)	161,800
Average Shares	161,793	161,169	166,047	165,828	165,768	163,691	167,078	170,539
Balance Sheet								
Current Assets	2,476,000	2,334,000	2,371,000	2,550,000	2,648,000	2,694,000	2,738,000	2,796,700
Total Assets	9,688,000	9,421,000	7,858,000	8,419,000	8,598,000	8,926,000	9,754,000	8,727,400
Current Liabilities	1,886,000	2,122,000	2,328,000	2,254,000	2,162,000	2,245,000	2,079,000	2,034,300
Long-Term Obligations	5,662,000	5,345,000	2,972,000	3,245,000	3,454,000	3,627,000	3,924,000	3,257,500
Total Liabilities	9,272,000	8,955,000	6,700,000	6,963,000	7,717,000	8,087,000	7,939,000	7,189,200
Stockholders' Equity	416,000	466,000	1,158,000	1,456,000	881,000	839,000	1,815,000	1,538,200
Shares Outstanding	161,918	160,961	164,197	164,714	163,963	164,374	163,715	168,600
Statistical Record								
Return on Assets %	N.M.	N.M.	0.92	2.16	2.09	N.M.	N.M.	1.94
Return on Equity %	N.M.	N.M.	5.74	15.75	21.34	N.M.	N.M.	12.55
EBITDA Margin %	17.51	9.31	10.60	12.16	12.59	3.21	14.62	11.90
Net Margin %	4.22	N.M.	1.11	2.64	2.63	N.M.	N.M.	2.29
Asset Turnover	0.74	0.71	0.83	0.82	0.80	0.79	0.72	0.85
Current Ratio	1.31	1.10	1.02	1.13	1.22	1.20	1.32	1.37
Debt to Equity	13.61	11.47	2.57	2.23	3.92	4.32	2.16	2.12
Price Range	25.98-12.06	26.99-16.94	35.78-23.53	35.78-21.27	24.67-17.07	33.01-14.04	37.63-25.06	38.86-9.73
P/E Ratio	...	...	79.51-52.29	32.23-19.16	22.23-15.38	...	...	40.91-10.24

Address: One Michael Owens Way, Perrysburg, OH 43551 Telephone: 567-336-5000	Web Site: www.o-i.com Officers: Albert P. L. Stroucken - Executive Chairman, President, Chief Executive Officer Andres Alberto Lopez - Chief Executive Officer, Chief Operating Officer, Division Officer	Auditors: Ernst & Young LLP Investor Contact: 567-336-2400 Transfer Agents: Computershare Trust Company, N.A., Providence, RI

OWENS CORNING

Exchange	Symbol	Price	52Wk Range	Yield	P/E
NYS	OC	$51.07 (5/31/2016)	52.20-39.58	1.41	16.32

*7 Year Price Score 110.77 *NYSE Composite Index=100 *12 Month Price Score 107.54

Interim Earnings (Per Share)

Qtr.	Mar	Jun	Sep	Dec
2013	0.18	0.41	0.43	0.69
2014	1.01	0.18	0.44	0.28
2015	0.15	0.77	0.95	0.92
2016	0.49	...	...	...

Interim Dividends (Per Share)

Amt	Decl	Ex	Rec	Pay
0.17Q	09/17/2015	10/15/2015	10/19/2015	11/03/2015
0.17Q	12/04/2015	12/30/2015	01/04/2016	01/19/2016
0.18Q	02/04/2016	03/09/2016	03/11/2016	04/04/2016
0.18Q	06/16/2016	07/14/2016	07/18/2016	08/02/2016

Indicated Div: $0.72

Valuation Analysis

		Institutional Holding	
Forecast EPS	$3.05	No of Institutions	
	(05/20/2016)	388	
Market Cap	$5.9 Billion	Shares	
Book Value	$3.8 Billion	119,613,768	
Price/Book	1.56	% Held	
Price/Sales	1.10	89.43	

Business Summary: Construction Materials (MIC: 8.5.1 SIC: 3292 NAIC: 327910)

Owens Corning is a producer of glass fiber reinforcements and other materials for composites and of residential and commercial building materials. Co.'s products range from glass fiber used to reinforce composite materials for transportation, electronics, marine, infrastructure, wind-energy and other markets. Co. operates within three reporting segments, Composites, Insulation and Roofing. Co.'s Composites segment includes Co.'s Reinforcements and Downstream businesses. Co.'s insulating products include thermal and acoustical batts, loosefill insulation, foam sheathing and accessories. Co.'s primary products in the Roofing segment are laminate and strip asphalt roofing shingles.

Recent Developments: For the quarter ended Mar 31 2016, net income increased 210.5% to US$59.0 million from US$19.0 million in the year-earlier quarter. Revenues were US$1.23 billion, up 2.3% from US$1.20 billion the year before. Operating income was US$116.0 million versus US$58.0 million in the prior-year quarter, an increase of 100.0%. Direct operating expenses declined 3.5% to US$959.0 million from US$994.0 million in the comparable period the year before. Indirect operating expenses increased 3.3% to US$156.0 million from US$151.0 million in the equivalent prior-year period.

Prospects: Our evaluation of Owens Corning as of June 19, 2016 is the result of our systematic analysis on three basic characteristics: earnings strength, relative valuation, and recent stock price movement. The company has generated a negative trend in earnings per share over the past 5 quarters. However, while recent estimates for the company have been lowered by analysts, OC has posted better than expected results. Based on operating earnings yield, the company is undervalued when compared to all of the companies in our coverage universe. Share price changes over the past year indicates that OC will perform very well over the near term.

Financial Data

(US$ in Millions)	3 Mos	12/31/2015	12/31/2014	12/31/2013	12/31/2012	12/31/2011	12/31/2010	12/31/2009
Earnings Per Share	3.13	2.79	1.91	1.71	(0.16)	2.23	7.37	0.50
Cash Flow Per Share	8.26	6.33	3.75	3.54	2.76	2.36	3.89	4.33
Tang Book Value Per Share	14.05	13.57	12.79	13.47	11.41	12.27	11.85	4.12
Dividends Per Share	0.690	0.680	0.640	...	...	...	...	...
Dividend Payout %	22.04	24.37	33.51	...	...	...	...	...
Income Statement								
Total Revenue	1,231	5,350	5,276	5,295	5,172	5,335	4,997	4,803
EBITDA	192	831	629	695	402	757	505	496
Depn & Amortn	76	278	283	310	328	296	299	304
Income Before Taxes	93	453	232	273	(40)	353	96	81
Income Taxes	34	120	5	68	(28)	74	(840)	14
Net Income	57	330	226	204	(19)	276	933	64
Average Shares	116	118	118	119	119	123	126	127
Balance Sheet								
Current Assets	1,610	1,538	1,807	1,848	1,612	1,636	1,408	1,854
Total Assets	7,455	7,380	7,555	7,647	7,568	7,527	7,158	7,167
Current Liabilities	1,059	1,117	983	992	906	908	955	943
Long-Term Obligations	1,785	1,702	1,991	2,024	2,076	1,930	1,629	2,177
Total Liabilities	3,668	3,641	3,863	3,854	4,030	3,826	3,510	4,347
Stockholders' Equity	3,787	3,739	3,692	3,793	3,538	3,701	3,648	2,820
Shares Outstanding	115	115	117	117	118	120	124	127
Statistical Record								
Return on Assets %	4.87	4.42	2.97	2.68	N.M.	3.76	13.03	0.89
Return on Equity %	9.93	8.88	6.04	5.57	N.M.	7.51	28.85	2.31
EBITDA Margin %	15.60	15.53	11.92	13.13	7.77	14.19	10.11	10.33
Net Margin %	4.63	6.17	4.28	3.85	N.M.	5.17	18.67	1.33
Asset Turnover	0.71	0.72	0.69	0.70	0.68	0.73	0.70	0.67
Current Ratio	1.52	1.38	1.84	1.86	1.78	1.80	1.47	1.97
Debt to Equity	0.47	0.46	0.54	0.53	0.59	0.52	0.45	0.77
Price Range	48.08-38.31	48.08-35.04	46.05-29.00	44.95-35.62	37.05-26.13	38.51-20.55	36.18-22.98	26.59-5.33
P/E Ratio	15.36-12.24	17.23-12.56	24.11-15.18	26.29-20.83	...	17.27-9.22	4.91-3.12	53.18-10.66
Average Yield %	1.57	1.59	1.69	...	...	...	...	...

Address: One Owens Corning Parkway, Toledo, OH 43659
Telephone: 419-248-8000

Web Site: www.owenscorning.com
Officers: Michael H. Thaman - Chairman, President, Chief Executive Officer Ava Harter - Senior Vice President, General Counsel, Secretary

Auditors: PricewaterhouseCoopers LLP
Investor Contact: 419-248-5748
Transfer Agents: Wells Fargo Shareowner Services, Mendota Heights, MN

OWENS & MINOR, INC.

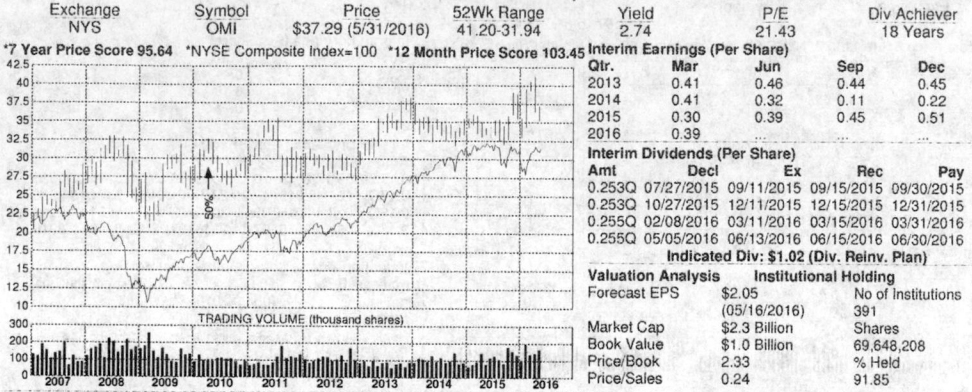

Exchange	Symbol	Price	52Wk Range	Yield	P/E	Div Achiever
NYS	OMI	$37.29 (5/31/2016)	41.20-31.94	2.74	21.43	18 Years

*7 Year Price Score 95.64   *NYSE Composite Index=100   *12 Month Price Score 103.45

Interim Earnings (Per Share)

Qtr.	Mar	Jun	Sep	Dec
2013	0.41	0.46	0.44	0.45
2014	0.41	0.32	0.11	0.22
2015	0.30	0.39	0.45	0.51
2016	0.39			

Interim Dividends (Per Share)

Amt	Decl	Ex	Rec	Pay
0.253Q	07/27/2015	09/11/2015	09/15/2015	09/30/2015
0.253Q	10/27/2015	12/11/2015	12/15/2015	12/31/2015
0.255Q	02/08/2016	03/11/2016	03/15/2016	03/31/2016
0.255Q	05/05/2016	06/13/2016	06/15/2016	06/30/2016

Indicated Div: $1.02 (Div. Reinv. Plan)

Valuation Analysis   Institutional Holding

Forecast EPS	$2.05	No of Institutions
	(05/16/2016)	391
Market Cap	$2.3 Billion	Shares
Book Value	$1.0 Billion	69,648,208
Price/Book	2.33	% Held
Price/Sales	0.24	91.85

Business Summary: Pharmaceuticals (MIC: 4.1.1 SIC: 5047 NAIC: 423450)

Owens & Minor is a healthcare services company. Co.'s business is organized into two segments: Domestic, which provides a portfolio of products and services to healthcare providers and manufacturers in the U.S., and its portfolio of medical and surgical supplies includes branded products purchased from manufacturers and its own proprietary private-label products; and International, which provides contract logistics services to the pharmaceutical, biotechnology and medical device industries, providing a range of supply chain logistics services to manufacturers, and custom procedure trays to manufacturers and healthcare provider customers throughout Europe.

Recent Developments: For the quarter ended Mar 31 2016, net income increased 27.4% to US$24.1 million from US$18.9 million in the year-earlier quarter. Revenues were US$2.46 billion, up 2.7% from US$2.39 billion the year before. Operating income was US$45.0 million versus US$41.0 million in the prior-year quarter, an increase of 9.7%. Direct operating expenses rose 3.1% to US$2.16 billion from US$2.09 billion in the comparable period the year before. Indirect operating expenses decreased 1.9% to US$251.7 million from US$256.6 million in the equivalent prior-year period.

Prospects: Our evaluation of Owens & Minor Inc. as of June 19, 2016 is the result of our systematic analysis on three basic characteristics: earnings strength, relative valuation, and recent stock price movement. The company has managed to produce a neutral trend in earnings per share over the past 5 quarters and while recent estimates for the company have remained steady, OMI has posted better than expected results. Based on operating earnings yield, the company is undervalued when compared to all of the companies in our coverage universe. Share price changes over the past year indicates that OMI will perform very well over the near term.

Financial Data

(US$ in Thousands)	3 Mos	12/31/2015	12/31/2014	12/31/2013	12/31/2012	12/31/2011	12/31/2010	12/31/2009
Earnings Per Share	1.74	1.65	1.06	1.76	1.72	1.81	1.75	1.67
Cash Flow Per Share	2.36	4.34	(0.06)	2.24	3.47	1.09	3.92	2.68
Tang Book Value Per Share	7.83	7.61	7.28	11.22	10.36	10.20	9.23	7.86
Dividends Per Share	1.013	1.010	1.000	0.960	0.880	0.800	0.708	0.613
Dividend Payout %	58.19	61.21	94.34	54.55	51.16	44.20	40.44	36.80
Income Statement								
Total Revenue	2,455,793	9,772,946	9,440,182	9,071,532	8,908,145	8,627,912	8,123,608	8,037,624
EBITDA	59,188	236,659	180,146	231,183	222,853	224,715	213,936	216,875
Depn & Amortn	14,218	36,300	35,500	33,100	26,100	21,200	18,000	15,600
Income Before Taxes	38,180	173,210	126,483	184,985	183,356	189,833	181,613	188,247
Income Taxes	14,045	69,801	59,980	74,103	74,353	74,635	71,034	71,388
Net Income	24,135	103,409	66,503	110,882	109,003	115,198	110,579	104,658
Average Shares	61,696	62,117	62,226	62,661	62,844	62,924	62,563	62,083
Balance Sheet								
Current Assets	2,001,485	1,974,700	1,870,706	1,725,932	1,628,894	1,525,825	1,403,789	1,342,067
Total Assets	2,796,841	2,777,840	2,735,406	2,324,042	2,207,701	1,946,815	1,822,039	1,747,088
Current Liabilities	1,066,938	1,063,589	1,004,555	989,179	924,287	732,365	694,481	700,116
Long-Term Obligations	567,711	572,559	608,551	213,815	215,383	212,681	209,096	208,418
Total Liabilities	1,791,920	1,785,250	1,744,568	1,300,129	1,235,175	1,028,728	964,521	977,909
Stockholders' Equity	1,004,921	992,590	990,838	1,023,913	972,526	918,087	857,518	769,179
Shares Outstanding	62,802	62,803	63,070	63,096	63,271	63,449	63,433	62,869
Statistical Record								
Return on Assets %	3.95	3.75	2.63	4.89	5.23	6.11	6.20	5.94
Return on Equity %	11.01	10.43	6.60	11.11	11.50	12.98	13.60	14.35
EBITDA Margin %	2.41	2.42	1.91	2.55	2.50	2.60	2.63	2.70
Net Margin %	0.98	1.06	0.70	1.22	1.22	1.34	1.36	1.30
Asset Turnover	3.58	3.55	3.73	4.00	4.28	4.58	4.55	4.56
Current Ratio	1.88	1.86	1.86	1.74	1.76	2.08	2.02	1.92
Debt to Equity	0.56	0.58	0.61	0.21	0.22	0.23	0.24	0.27
Price Range	40.51-31.94	39.02-31.94	37.49-31.72	38.23-28.51	31.28-27.01	35.48-26.67	32.60-26.02	31.85-20.52
P/E Ratio	23.28-18.36	23.65-19.36	35.37-29.92	21.72-16.20	18.19-15.70	19.60-14.73	18.63-14.87	19.07-12.29
Average Yield %	2.87		2.91	2.91	2.83	3.02	2.58	2.45	2.31

Address: 9120 Lockwood Boulevard, Mechanicsville, VA 23116	Web Site: www.owens-minor.com	Auditors: KPMG LLP
Telephone: 804-723-7000	Officers: Craig R. Smith - Chairman, President, Chief Executive Officer Paul Cody Phipps - President, Chief Executive Officer	Investor Contact: 804-723-7555
Fax: 804-723-7100		Transfer Agents: Computershare Shareowner Services LLC, Providence, RI

PACKAGING CORP OF AMERICA

Exchange	Symbol	Price	52Wk Range	Yield	P/E
NYS	PKG	$68.23 (5/31/2016)	73.37-45.15	3.22	14.70

*7 Year Price Score 121.32 *NYSE Composite Index=100 *12 Month Price Score 102.03

Interim Earnings (Per Share)

Qtr.	Mar	Jun	Sep	Dec
2013	0.62	0.66	0.86	2.32
2014	0.92	1.01	1.06	1.00
2015	0.92	1.16	1.31	1.08
2016	1.09	...	...	...

Interim Dividends (Per Share)

Amt	Decl	Ex	Rec	Pay
0.55Q	08/31/2015	09/11/2015	09/15/2015	10/15/2015
0.55Q	12/15/2015	12/23/2015	12/28/2015	01/15/2016
0.55Q	02/25/2016	03/11/2016	03/15/2016	04/15/2016
0.55Q	05/18/2016	06/13/2016	06/15/2016	07/15/2016

Indicated Div: $2.20

Valuation Analysis / Institutional Holding

Forecast EPS	$4.64	No of Institutions
(05/20/2016)		529
Market Cap	$6.4 Billion	Shares
Book Value	$1.6 Billion	105,291,960
Price/Book	4.04	% Held
Price/Sales	1.12	87.82

Business Summary: Containers & Packaging (MIC: 8.1.3 SIC: 2652 NAIC: 322213)

Packaging Corporation of America is a producer of containerboard, corrugated packaging products and uncoated freesheet. Co. has three reportable segments: Packaging, which produces corrugated packaging products, including shipping containers used to transport manufactured goods, multi-color boxes and displays, as well as produces packaging for meat, fresh fruit and vegetables, processed food, beverages, and other industrial and consumer products; Paper, which manufactures and sells white papers, including both commodity and specialty papers, as well as produces market pulp; and Corporate and Other, which includes corporate support staff services.

Recent Developments: For the quarter ended Mar 31 2016, net income increased 14.2% to US$103.7 million from US$90.8 million in the year-earlier quarter. Revenues were US$1.40 billion, down 1.7% from US$1.43 billion the year before. Operating income was US$180.8 million versus US$157.1 million in the prior-year quarter, an increase of 15.1%. Direct operating expenses declined 4.0% to US$1.10 billion from US$1.15 billion in the comparable period the year before. Indirect operating expenses decreased 1.8% to US$117.8 million from US$119.9 million in the equivalent prior-year period.

Prospects: Our evaluation of Packaging Corp. of America as of June 19, 2016 is the result of our systematic analysis on three basic characteristics: earnings strength, relative valuation, and recent stock price movement. The company has produced a positive trend in earnings per share over the past 5 quarters and while recent estimates for the company have been mixed, PKG has posted better than expected results. Based on operating earnings yield, the company is undervalued when compared to all of the companies in our coverage universe. Share price changes over the past year indicates that PKG will perform in line with the market over the near term.

Financial Data

(US$ in Thousands)	3 Mos	12/31/2015	12/31/2014	12/31/2013	12/31/2012	12/31/2011	12/31/2010	12/31/2009
Earnings Per Share	4.64	4.47	3.99	4.47	1.68	1.57	2.00	2.60
Cash Flow Per Share	8.98	7.89	7.59	6.30	4.18	3.48	3.44	3.01
Tang Book Value Per Share	8.31	8.51	6.92	4.85	8.80	8.60	9.38	8.23
Dividends Per Share	2.200	2.200	1.600	1.513	1.000	0.800	0.600	0.600
Dividend Payout %	47.41	49.22	40.10	33.84	59.52	50.96	30.00	23.08
Income Statement								
Total Revenue	1,401,000	5,741,700	5,852,600	3,665,308	2,843,877	2,620,111	2,435,606	2,147,589
EBITDA	263,400	1,073,000	1,050,900	664,807	609,459	434,249	339,382	500,654
Depn & Amortn	82,600	323,000	348,200	191,200	166,000	161,500	154,000	148,200
Income Before Taxes	159,200	664,500	614,300	415,332	380,559	243,504	153,104	316,971
Income Taxes	55,500	227,700	221,700	(20,951)	216,739	85,477	(52,331)	51,076
Net Income	103,700	436,800	392,600	436,283	163,820	158,027	205,435	265,895
Average Shares	94,200	96,700	97,100	97,547	97,497	100,376	102,608	102,358
Balance Sheet								
Current Assets	1,528,900	1,554,500	1,578,600	1,487,204	937,033	812,063	798,041	885,214
Total Assets	5,227,300	5,284,600	5,348,500	5,199,974	2,453,768	2,412,499	2,224,274	2,152,840
Current Liabilities	545,300	561,900	611,000	660,539	259,846	376,500	405,558	370,957
Long-Term Obligations	2,310,600	2,324,300	2,371,700	2,532,719	803,534	814,562	570,931	571,252
Total Liabilities	3,636,500	3,651,300	3,827,100	3,886,959	1,484,307	1,483,589	1,215,273	1,253,995
Stockholders' Equity	1,590,800	1,633,300	1,521,400	1,313,015	969,461	928,910	1,009,001	898,845
Shares Outstanding	94,100	96,129	98,368	98,172	98,142	98,322	102,308	103,018
Statistical Record								
Return on Assets %	8.47	8.22	7.44	11.40	6.71	6.82	9.39	12.99
Return on Equity %	28.58	27.69	27.70	38.23	17.21	16.31	21.54	33.60
EBITDA Margin %	18.80	18.69	17.96	18.14	21.43	16.57	13.93	23.31
Net Margin %	7.40	7.61	6.71	11.90	5.76	6.03	8.43	12.38
Asset Turnover	1.08	1.08	1.11	0.96	1.17	1.13	1.11	1.05
Current Ratio	2.80	2.77	2.58	2.25	3.61	2.16	1.97	2.39
Debt to Equity	1.45	1.42	1.56	1.93	0.83	0.88	0.57	0.64
Price Range	78.75-45.15	84.24-59.34	79.69-58.61	64.27-38.43	38.47-25.00	30.27-21.28	26.90-20.58	23.80-9.82
P/E Ratio	16.97-9.73	18.85-13.28	19.97-14.69	14.38-8.60	22.90-14.88	19.28-13.55	13.45-10.29	9.15-3.78
Average Yield %	3.42	3.12	2.32	2.32	2.97	3.22	2.98	3.50

Address: 1955 West Field Court, Lake Forest, IL 60045	Web Site: www.packagingcorp.com	Auditors: KPMG LLP
Telephone: 847-482-3000	Officers: Mark W. Kowlzan - Chairman, Chief Executive Officer, Senior Vice President Robert P. Mundy - Chief Financial Officer, Senior Vice President, Principal Accounting Officer, Principal Financial Officer	Investor Contact: 877-454-2509 / Transfer Agents: Computershare Trust Company N.A., Providence, RI

547

PALO ALTO NETWORKS, INC

Exchange	Symbol	Price	52Wk Range	Yield	P/E
NYS	PANW	$130.46 (5/31/2016)	197.09-115.69	N/A	N/A

*7 Year Price Score N/A   *NYSE Composite Index=100   *12 Month Price Score 87.80

Interim Earnings (Per Share)

Qtr.	Oct	Jan	Apr	Jul
2012-13	(0.05)	(0.04)	(0.10)	(0.23)
2013-14	(0.11)	(0.55)	(1.96)	(0.39)
2014-15	(0.38)	(0.53)	(0.56)	(0.55)
2015-16	(0.45)	(0.72)	(0.80)	...

Interim Dividends (Per Share)

No Dividends Paid

Valuation Analysis   **Institutional Holding**

Forecast EPS	$1.66	No of Institutions
	(05/20/2016)	672
Market Cap	$11.7 Billion	Shares
Book Value	$731.2 Million	89,370,544
Price/Book	15.99	% Held
Price/Sales	9.27	87.28

Business Summary: IT Services (MIC: 6.3.1 SIC: 3577 NAIC: 423430)

Palo Alto Networks provides a security platform that allows enterprises, service providers, and government entities to secure their organizations by safely enabling the applications running on their networks and by preventing breaches that stem from cyber attacks. Co.'s security platform consists of three primary elements: Firewall, which provides application, user, and content visibility and control as well as protection against network-based cyber threats integrated within the firewall; Endpoint Protection, which prevents cyber attacks that aim to exploit software vulnerabilities; and Threat Intelligence Cloud, which provides central intelligence capabilities.

Recent Developments: For the quarter ended Apr 30 2016, net loss amounted to US$70.2 million versus a net loss of US$45.9 million in the year-earlier quarter. Revenues were US$345.8 million, up 47.7% from US$234.2 million the year before. Operating loss was US$58.6 million versus a loss of US$36.7 million in the prior-year quarter. Direct operating expenses rose 47.4% to US$94.9 million from US$64.4 million in the comparable period the year before. Indirect operating expenses increased 49.9% to US$309.5 million from US$206.5 million in the equivalent prior-year period.

Prospects: Our evaluation of Palo Alto Networks, Inc as of June 19, 2016 is the result of our systematic analysis on three basic characteristics: earnings strength, relative valuation, and recent stock price movement. The company has generated a negative trend in earnings per share over the past 5 quarters and while recent estimates for the company have been mixed, PANW has posted better than expected results. Based on operating earnings yield, the company is overvalued when compared to all of the companies in our coverage universe. Share price changes over the past year indicates that PANW will perform well over the near term.

Financial Data

(US$ in Thousands)	9 Mos	6 Mos	3 Mos	07/31/2015	07/31/2014	07/31/2013	07/31/2012	07/31/2011
Earnings Per Share	(2.52)	(2.28)	(2.09)	(2.02)	(3.05)	(0.43)	...	(0.88)
Cash Flow Per Share	6.63	5.76	4.96	4.29	1.19	1.67	3.94	2.26
Tang Book Value Per Share	5.82	5.18	4.80	4.24	3.34	3.80	3.38	...
Income Statement								
Total Revenue	977,700	631,900	297,200	928,052	598,179	396,107	255,138	118,597
EBITDA	(119,200)	(68,300)	(22,100)	(105,052)	(203,346)	(9,229)	8,838	(9,888)
Depn & Amortn	19,800	13,100	6,500	28,200	16,931	9,911	6,057	2,167
Income Before Taxes	(156,400)	(93,000)	(34,400)	(155,577)	(222,160)	(18,656)	2,799	(12,052)
Income Taxes	15,000	8,200	4,300	9,405	4,292	10,590	2,062	476
Net Income	(171,400)	(101,200)	(38,700)	(164,982)	(226,452)	(29,246)	737	(12,528)
Average Shares	87,800	86,600	85,100	81,619	74,291	68,682	19,569	14,201
Balance Sheet								
Current Assets	1,446,200	1,307,100	1,039,900	1,074,030	958,326	529,699	381,657	76,840
Total Assets	2,507,000	2,316,600	2,094,400	1,965,178	1,478,466	585,606	407,804	91,172
Current Liabilities	1,239,000	1,186,400	1,078,200	1,032,227	348,171	206,102	122,006	67,101
Long-Term Obligations	...	...	...	...	466,875	...	...	...
Total Liabilities	1,775,800	1,646,300	1,467,900	1,389,363	1,009,883	313,186	178,733	98,135
Stockholders' Equity	731,200	670,300	626,500	575,815	468,583	272,420	229,071	(6,963)
Shares Outstanding	89,600	88,400	85,900	84,788	79,519	71,612	67,852	19,751
Statistical Record								
Return on Assets %	N.M.	N.M.	N.M.	N.M.	N.M.	N.M.	0.29	N.M.
Return on Equity %	N.M.	N.M.	N.M.	N.M.	N.M.	N.M.	0.66	...
EBITDA Margin %	N.M.	N.M.	N.M.	N.M.	N.M.	N.M.	3.46	N.M.
Net Margin %	N.M.	N.M.	N.M.	N.M.	N.M.	N.M.	0.29	N.M.
Asset Turnover	0.59	0.58	0.57	0.54	0.58	0.80	1.02	1.83
Current Ratio	1.17	1.10	0.96	1.04	2.75	2.57	3.13	1.15
Debt to Equity	...	...	...	...	1.00	...	...	...
Price Range	197.09-115.69	197.09-123.53	197.09-102.52	197.09-78.67	84.21-40.99	71.75-39.56	59.88-51.51	...

Address: 4401 Great America Parkway, Santa Clara, CA 95054 Telephone: 408-753-4000	Web Site: www.paloaltonetworks.com Officers: Mark D. McLaughlin - Chairman, President, Chief Executive Officer Lawrence J. Link - Senior Vice President, Vice President	Auditors: Ernst & Young LLP Investor Contact: 408-753-3872 Transfer Agents: Computershare, Canton, MA

PANDORA MEDIA INC

Exchange	Symbol	Price	52Wk Range	Yield	P/E
NYS	P	$11.79 (5/31/2016)	21.98-7.88	N/A	N/A

*7 Year Price Score N/A   *NYSE Composite Index=100   *12 Month Price Score 70.17

Interim Earnings (Per Share)

Qtr.	Mar	Jun	Sep	Dec
2014	(0.14)	(0.06)	(0.01)	0.06
2015	(0.23)	(0.08)	(0.40)	(0.08)
2016	(0.51)	...	...	...

Interim Dividends (Per Share)

No Dividends Paid

Valuation Analysis   Institutional Holding

Forecast EPS	$-0.43	No of Institutions
	(05/20/2016)	306
Market Cap	$2.7 Billion	Shares
Book Value	$670.4 Million	246,241,888
Price/Book	4.02	% Held
Price/Sales	2.19	101.53

Business Summary: Internet & Software (MIC: 6.3.2 SIC: 4832 NAIC: 515112)

Pandora Media provides an internet radio service which enables the listener to listen to radio on a range of smartphones, tablets, as well as internet-connected devices. Co. provides local and national advertisers capabilities to deliver targeted messages to its listeners using a combination of audio, display and video advertisements. Co. provides its Pandora service through two models: Free Service, which is Co.'s advertising-based and allows listeners access to its music and comedy catalogs and personalized playlist generating system across its delivery platforms; and Pandora One, which is a paid subscription service without any advertising and enables listeners to have more daily skips.

Recent Developments: For the quarter ended Mar 31 2016, net loss amounted to US$115.1 million versus a net loss of US$48.3 million in the year-earlier quarter. Revenues were US$297.3 million, up 28.8% from US$230.8 million the year before. Operating loss was US$109.4 million versus a loss of US$48.4 million in the prior-year quarter. Direct operating expenses rose 45.4% to US$206.9 million from US$142.3 million in the comparable period the year before. Indirect operating expenses increased 45.9% to US$199.8 million from US$136.9 million in the equivalent prior-year period.

Prospects: Our evaluation of Pandora Media Inc as of June 19, 2016 is the result of our systematic analysis on three basic characteristics: earnings strength, relative valuation, and recent stock price movement. The company has suffered a very negative trend in earnings per share over the past 5 quarters. Because the company lacks sufficient analyst estimate data, we place greater weight on the historical EPS trend as the measure of earnings strength. Based on operating earnings yield, the company is overvalued when compared to all of the companies in our coverage universe. Share price changes over the past year indicates that P will perform very poorly over the near term.

Financial Data
(US$ in Thousands)

	3 Mos	12/31/2015	12/31/2014	12/31/2013	01/31/2013	01/31/2012	01/31/2011	01/31/2010
Earnings Per Share	(1.07)	(0.79)	(0.15)	(0.15)	(0.23)	(0.19)	(1.03)	(3.84)
Cash Flow Per Share	(0.36)	(0.20)	0.10	(0.01)	(0.00)	0.06	0.30	(4.24)
Tang Book Value Per Share	1.14	1.46	2.76	2.56	0.57	0.64	3.01	2.40
Income Statement								
Total Revenue	297,305	1,164,043	920,802	600,233	427,145	274,340	137,764	55,189
EBITDA	(103,932)	(148,611)	(13,322)	(16,365)	(30,603)	(10,975)	551	(14,817)
Depn & Amortn	4,574	22,600	16,500	10,100	7,100	4,500	1,600	1,100
Income Before Taxes	(114,681)	(171,211)	(29,822)	(26,923)	(38,143)	(16,032)	(1,630)	(16,753)
Income Taxes	421	(1,550)	584	94	5	75	134	...
Net Income	(115,102)	(169,661)	(30,406)	(27,017)	(38,148)	(16,107)	(1,764)	(16,753)
Average Shares	226,659	213,790	205,273	180,968	168,294	105,955	10,761	6,482
Balance Sheet								
Current Assets	635,201	683,506	588,414	518,783	198,614	160,125	88,776	37,677
Total Assets	1,192,341	1,240,657	749,290	673,335	218,832	178,015	99,209	40,277
Current Liabilities	251,412	231,831	149,160	156,006	115,970	70,907	52,061	18,748
Long-Term Obligations	239,011	234,577	...	...	...	...	837	4,095
Total Liabilities	521,944	497,270	165,933	165,104	119,843	73,475	55,557	23,242
Stockholders' Equity	670,397	743,387	583,357	508,231	98,989	104,540	43,652	17,035
Shares Outstanding	228,750	224,970	209,071	195,395	172,506	163,569	14,510	7,102
Statistical Record								
EBITDA Margin %	N.M.	N.M.	N.M.	N.M.	N.M.	N.M.	0.40	N.M.
Asset Turnover	1.27	1.17	1.29	0.74	2.15	...	1.98	...
Current Ratio	2.53	2.95	3.94	3.33	1.71	2.26	1.71	2.01
Debt to Equity	0.36	0.32	...	...	...	...	0.02	0.24
Price Range	21.98-7.88	21.98-11.51	39.43-16.90	31.56-11.36	14.66-7.18	20.04-9.79	...	...

Address: 2101 Webster Street, Suite 1650, Oakland, CA 94612 **Telephone:** 510-451-4100 **Fax:** 510 451 4286	**Web Site:** www.pandora.com **Officers:** James M. P. Feuille - Chairman Michael S. Herring - President, Chief Financial Officer	**Auditors:** Ernst & Young LLP **Investor Contact:** 510-842-6960 **Transfer Agents:** Computershare Trust Company, N.A.

PBF ENERGY INC

Exchange	Symbol	Price	52Wk Range	Yield	P/E
NYS	PBF	$26.37 (5/31/2016)	41.48-25.96	4.55	75.34

*7 Year Price Score N/A *NYSE Composite Index=100 *12 Month Price Score 96.72

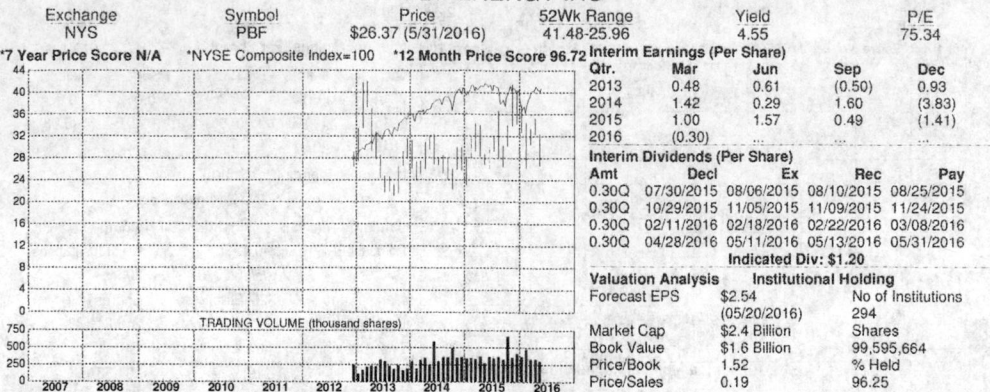

Interim Earnings (Per Share)

Qtr.	Mar	Jun	Sep	Dec
2013	0.48	0.61	(0.50)	0.93
2014	1.42	0.29	1.60	(3.83)
2015	1.00	1.57	0.49	(1.41)
2016	(0.30)			

Interim Dividends (Per Share)

Amt	Decl	Ex	Rec	Pay
0.30Q	07/30/2015	08/06/2015	08/10/2015	08/25/2015
0.30Q	10/29/2015	11/05/2015	11/09/2015	11/24/2015
0.30Q	02/11/2016	02/18/2016	02/22/2016	03/08/2016
0.30Q	04/28/2016	05/11/2016	05/13/2016	05/31/2016

Indicated Div: $1.20

Valuation Analysis

		Institutional Holding	
Forecast EPS	$2.54	No of Institutions	294
	(05/20/2016)		
Market Cap	$2.4 Billion	Shares	99,595,664
Book Value	$1.6 Billion	% Held	96.25
Price/Book	1.52		
Price/Sales	0.19		

Business Summary: Refining & Marketing (MIC: 9.1.2 SIC: 2911 NAIC: 324110)

PBF Energy is a holding company. Through its subsidiaries, Co. is engaged as an independent petroleum refiner and supplier of unbranded transportation fuels, heating oil, petrochemical feedstocks, lubricants and other petroleum products in the U.S. Co. operates in two business segments: refining, which Co. produces a variety of products at each of its refineries such as gasoline, ultra-low-sulfur diesel, heating oil, jet fuel, lubricants, petrochemicals and asphalt; and logistics, which through its PBF Logistics LP subsidiary, Co. owns or leases, operates, develops and acquires crude oil and refined petroleum products terminals, pipelines, storage facilities and similar logistics assets.

Recent Developments: For the quarter ended Mar 31 2016, net loss amounted to US$23.3 million versus net income of US$103.1 million in the year-earlier quarter. Revenues were US$2.80 billion, down 6.5% from US$3.00 billion the year before. Operating loss was US$5.4 million versus an income of US$172.4 million in the prior-year quarter. Direct operating expenses declined 3.6% to US$2.41 billion from US$2.50 billion in the comparable period the year before. Indirect operating expenses increased 22.8% to US$393.5 million from US$320.5 million in the equivalent prior-year period.

Prospects: Our evaluation of PBF Energy Inc as of June 19, 2016 is the result of our systematic analysis on three basic characteristics: earnings strength, relative valuation, and recent stock price movement. The company has suffered a very negative trend in earnings per share over the past 5 quarters. However, while recent estimates for the company have been lowered by analysts, PBF has posted results that fell short of analysts expectations. Based on operating earnings yield, the company is undervalued when compared to all of the companies in our coverage universe. Share price changes over the past year indicates that PBF will perform very well over the near term.

Financial Data

(US$ in Thousands)	3 Mos	12/31/2015	12/31/2014	12/31/2013	12/31/2012
Earnings Per Share	0.35	1.65	(0.51)	1.20	0.08
Cash Flow Per Share	4.16	6.36	6.13	8.97	34.47
Tang Book Value Per Share	17.35	16.84	14.86	16.47	17.76
Dividends Per Share	1.200	1.200	1.200	1.200	...
Dividend Payout %	342.86	72.73	...	100.00	...
Income Statement					
Total Revenue	2,800,185	13,123,929	19,828,155	19,151,455	20,138,687
EBITDA	50,286	483,226	269,542	403,963	978,888
Depn & Amortn	58,595	94,781	114,919	79,413	64,947
Income Before Taxes	(45,836)	282,258	55,859	230,766	805,312
Income Taxes	(22,500)	86,725	(22,412)	16,681	1,275
Net Income	(29,388)	146,401	(38,237)	39,540	1,956
Average Shares	97,809	94,138	74,464	33,061	97,230
Balance Sheet					
Current Assets	3,021,357	3,022,011	2,346,671	2,200,506	2,307,904
Total Assets	6,183,659	6,105,124	5,196,288	4,413,808	4,253,702
Current Liabilities	1,623,003	1,495,506	1,542,822	1,644,510	1,603,074
Long-Term Obligations	1,845,902	1,840,355	1,260,349	735,547	729,980
Total Liabilities	4,591,263	4,457,827	3,978,075	3,759,678	3,833,948
Stockholders' Equity	1,592,396	1,647,297	1,218,213	654,130	419,754
Shares Outstanding	91,754	97,781	81,981	39,665	23,571
Statistical Record					
Return on Assets %	0.52	2.59	N.M.	0.91	...
Return on Equity %	2.04	10.22	N.M.	7.36	...
EBITDA Margin %	1.80	3.68	1.36	2.11	4.86
Net Margin %	N.M.	1.12	N.M.	0.21	0.01
Asset Turnover	2.28	2.32	4.13	4.42	...
Current Ratio	1.86	2.02	1.52	1.34	1.44
Debt to Equity	1.16	1.12	1.03	1.12	1.74
Price Range	41.48-25.96	41.48-22.95	32.24-22.12	41.98-20.98	29.05-26.25
P/E Ratio	118.51-74.17	25.14-13.91	...	34.98-17.48	363.13-328.13
Average Yield %	3.82	3.91	4.42	4.18	...

Address: One Sylvan Way, Second Floor, Parsippany, NJ 07054 **Telephone:** 973-455-7500	**Web Site:** www.pbfenergy.com **Officers:** Thomas J. Nimbley - Chairman, Chief Executive Officer Matthew C. Lucey - President, Executive Vice President, Senior Vice President, Chief Financial Officer, Vice President	**Auditors:** Deloitte & Touche LLP **Investor Contact:** 973-455-7578 **Transfer Agents:** American Stock Transfer & Trust Company, Brooklyn, NY

PARKER HANNIFIN CORP.

Exchange	Symbol	Price	52Wk Range	Yield	P/E	Div Achiever
NYS	PH	$114.84 (5/31/2016)	121.25-86.51	2.19	21.27	59 Years

*7 Year Price Score 98.76 *NYSE Composite Index=100 *12 Month Price Score 105.16

Interim Earnings (Per Share)

Qtr.	Sep	Dec	Mar	Jun
2012-13	1.57	1.19	1.68	1.80
2013-14	1.61	1.66	1.60	1.99
2014-15	1.85	1.80	2.02	1.29
2015-16	1.41	1.33	1.37	...

Interim Dividends (Per Share)

Amt	Decl	Ex	Rec	Pay
0.63Q	08/13/2015	08/26/2015	08/28/2015	09/11/2015
0.63Q	10/28/2015	11/06/2015	11/10/2015	12/04/2015
0.63Q	01/21/2016	02/08/2016	02/10/2016	03/04/2016
0.63Q	04/22/2016	05/06/2016	05/10/2016	06/03/2016

Indicated Div: $2.52 (Div. Reinv. Plan)

Valuation Analysis		Institutional Holding	
Forecast EPS	$6.30	No of Institutions	
	(05/20/2016)		781
Market Cap	$15.5 Billion	Shares	
Book Value	$5.0 Billion		125,234,752
Price/Book	3.08	% Held	
Price/Sales	1.34		76.69

TRADING VOLUME (thousand shares)

Business Summary: Industrial Machinery & Equipment (MIC: 7.2.1 SIC: 3492 NAIC: 332912)

Parker Hannifin is a manufacturer of motion and control technologies and systems, providing engineered solutions for a wide variety of mobile, industrial and aerospace markets. Co. has two reporting segments: Diversified Industrial and Aerospace Systems. Co.'s Diversified Industrial segment consist of a range of motion-control and fluid systems and components, which are categorized into the following groups: Automation, Engineered Materials, Filtration, Fluid Connectors, Hydraulics, and Instrumentation. The principal products of Co.'s Aerospace Systems Segment include flight control, hydraulic, fuel, fluid conveyance, and engine systems and components.

Recent Developments: For the quarter ended Mar 31 2016, net income decreased 34.4% to US$187.1 million from US$285.5 million in the year-earlier quarter. Revenues were US$2.83 billion, down 10.6% from US$3.16 billion the year before. Direct operating expenses declined 6.9% to US$2.21 billion from US$2.37 billion in the comparable period the year before. Indirect operating expenses decreased 9.8% to US$335.9 million from US$372.3 million in the equivalent prior-year period.

Prospects: Our evaluation of Parker Hannifin Corp. as of June 19, 2016 is the result of our systematic analysis on three basic characteristics: earnings strength, relative valuation, and recent stock price movement. The company has produced a positive trend in earnings per share over the past 5 quarters and while recent estimates for the company have been raised by analysts, PH has posted better than expected results. Based on operating earnings yield, the company is undervalued when compared to all of the companies in our coverage universe. Share price changes over the past year indicates that PH will perform well over the near term.

Financial Data

(US$ in Thousands)	9 Mos	6 Mos	3 Mos	06/30/2015	06/30/2014	06/30/2013	06/30/2012	06/30/2011
Earnings Per Share	5.40	6.05	6.52	6.97	6.87	6.26	7.45	6.37
Cash Flow Per Share	8.84	8.20	7.64	9.11	9.31	7.98	10.09	7.24
Tang Book Value Per Share	8.27	6.74	6.62	8.29	15.44	8.20	5.85	7.72
Dividends Per Share	2.520	2.520	2.520	2.370	1.860	1.700	1.540	1.250
Dividend Payout %	46.67	41.65	38.65	34.00	27.07	27.16	20.67	19.62
Income Statement								
Total Revenue	8,403,603	5,574,938	2,869,348	12,711,744	13,215,971	13,015,704	13,145,942	12,345,870
EBITDA	1,114,101	731,679	389,631	1,753,422	1,854,251	1,616,275	1,879,996	1,742,663
Depn & Amortn	231,777	156,093	78,222	202,776	214,965	213,722	210,508	229,238
Income Before Taxes	778,522	505,529	275,649	1,432,240	1,556,720	1,311,001	1,576,698	1,413,721
Income Taxes	213,217	127,366	80,623	419,687	515,302	362,217	421,206	356,571
Net Income	565,044	377,960	194,978	1,012,553	1,041,418	948,784	1,155,492	1,057,150
Average Shares	136,552	137,065	138,574	145,112	151,444	151,588	154,664	164,798
Balance Sheet								
Current Assets	5,456,839	5,151,011	5,327,902	5,583,092	6,071,580	5,531,186	4,498,114	4,305,256
Total Assets	12,069,401	11,754,091	12,001,554	12,295,037	13,274,362	12,540,898	11,170,282	10,886,805
Current Liabilities	2,500,619	2,368,099	2,550,041	2,350,130	3,252,796	3,520,203	2,486,013	2,391,043
Long-Term Obligations	2,675,000	2,724,860	2,725,409	2,723,960	1,508,142	1,495,960	1,503,946	1,691,086
Total Liabilities	7,045,789	6,954,685	7,150,036	7,190,750	6,614,934	6,802,472	6,273,767	5,502,951
Stockholders' Equity	5,023,612	4,799,406	4,851,518	5,104,287	6,659,428	5,738,426	4,896,515	5,383,854
Shares Outstanding	134,681	135,102	135,980	138,558	148,902	149,288	149,630	155,090
Statistical Record								
Return on Assets %	6.10	6.93	7.49	7.92	8.07	8.00	10.45	10.17
Return on Equity %	14.64	15.97	16.22	17.21	16.80	17.84	22.42	21.68
EBITDA Margin %	13.26	13.12	13.58	13.79	14.03	12.42	14.30	14.12
Net Margin %	6.72	6.78	6.80	7.97	7.88	7.29	8.79	8.56
Asset Turnover	0.95	0.98	0.99	0.99	1.02	1.10	1.19	1.19
Current Ratio	2.18	2.18	2.09	2.38	1.87	1.57	1.81	1.80
Debt to Equity	0.53	0.57	0.56	0.53	0.23	0.26	0.31	0.31
Price Range	125.15-86.51	129.16-93.62	132.78-94.87	132.78-102.96	129.52-95.32	100.96-71.84	91.58-60.81	98.49-54.80
P/E Ratio	23.18-16.02	21.35-15.47	20.37-14.55	19.05-14.77	18.85-13.87	16.13-11.48	12.29-8.16	15.46-8.60
Average Yield %	2.34	2.23	2.13	1.96	1.61	1.95	1.94	1.56

Address: 6035 Parkland Boulevard, Cleveland, OH 44124-4141	Web Site: www.parker.com	Auditors: Deloitte & Touche LLP
Telephone: 216-896-3000	Officers: Lee C. Banks - President, Chief Operating Officer, Executive Vice President, Operating Officer Thomas L. Williams - Chief Executive Officer, Executive Vice President, Operating Officer	Investor Contact: 216-896-2240 Transfer Agents: Wells Fargo Bank, N.A., St. Paul, MN

PENNEY (J.C.) CO.,INC. (HOLDING CO.)

Exchange	Symbol	Price	52Wk Range	Yield	P/E
NYS	JCP	$7.79 (5/31/2016)	11.86-6.31	N/A	N/A

*7 Year Price Score 37.01   *NYSE Composite Index=100   *12 Month Price Score 103.66

Interim Earnings (Per Share)

Qtr.	Apr	Jul	Oct	Jan
2013-14	(1.58)	(2.66)	(1.94)	0.60
2014-15	(1.15)	(0.56)	(0.62)	(0.20)
2015-16	(0.55)	(0.45)	(0.45)	(0.23)
2016-17	(0.22)	...	...	...

Interim Dividends (Per Share)

No Dividends Paid

Valuation Analysis / Institutional Holding

Forecast EPS	$0.03	No of Institutions
	(05/20/2016)	564
Market Cap	$2.4 Billion	Shares
Book Value	$1.3 Billion	289,388,480
Price/Book	1.92	% Held
Price/Sales	0.19	73.51

Business Summary: Retail - General Merchandise/Department Stores (MIC: 2.1.1 SIC: 5311 NAIC: 452111)

J.C. Penney Company is a holding company whose principal operating subsidiary is J. C. Penney Corporation, Inc. Co.'s business consists of selling merchandise and services to consumers through its department stores and its website at jcpenney.com. Co. sells family apparel and footwear, accessories, fine and fashion jewelry, beauty products through Sephora inside JCPenney and home furnishings. In addition, Co.'s department stores provide its customers with services such as styling salon, optical, portrait photography and custom decorating. As of Jan 30 2016, Co. operated 1,021 department stores in 49 states and Puerto Rico.

Recent Developments: For the quarter ended Apr 30 2016, net loss amounted to US$68.0 million versus a net loss of US$150.0 million in the year-earlier quarter. Revenues were US$2.81 billion, down 1.6% from US$2.86 billion the year before. Operating income was US$22.0 million versus a loss of US$46.0 million in the prior-year quarter. Direct operating expenses declined 1.3% to US$1.79 billion from US$1.82 billion in the comparable period the year before. Indirect operating expenses decreased 8.4% to US$996.0 million from US$1.09 billion in the equivalent prior-year period.

Prospects: Our evaluation of Penney (J.C.) Co.,Inc. as of June 19, 2016 is the result of our systematic analysis on three basic characteristics: earnings strength, relative valuation, and recent stock price movement. The company has suffered a very negative trend in earnings per share over the past 5 quarters. However, while recent estimates for the company have been lowered by analysts, JCP has posted better than expected results. Based on operating earnings yield, the company is overvalued when compared to all of the companies in our coverage universe. Share price changes over the past year indicates that JCP will perform in line with the market over the near term.

Financial Data
(US$ in Thousands)

	3 Mos	01/30/2016	01/31/2015	02/01/2014	02/02/2013	01/28/2012	01/29/2011	01/30/2010
Earnings Per Share	(1.35)	(1.68)	(2.53)	(5.57)	(4.49)	(0.70)	1.63	1.08
Cash Flow Per Share	0.89	1.44	0.79	(7.30)	(0.04)	3.78	2.52	6.81
Tang Book Value Per Share	4.07	2.64	4.64	8.38	11.78	15.96	22.05	19.49
Dividends Per Share	...	...	...	...	0.200	0.800	0.800	0.800
Dividend Payout %	...	...	...	...	...	...	49.08	74.07
Income Statement								
Total Revenue	2,811,000	12,625,000	12,257,000	11,859,000	12,985,000	17,260,000	17,759,000	17,556,000
EBITDA	180,000	517,000	289,000	(933,000)	(767,000)	516,000	1,323,000	1,158,000
Depn & Amortn	154,000	616,000	631,000	601,000	543,000	518,000	511,000	495,000
Income Before Taxes	(69,000)	(504,000)	(748,000)	(1,886,000)	(1,536,000)	(229,000)	581,000	403,000
Income Taxes	(1,000)	9,000	23,000	(498,000)	(551,000)	(77,000)	203,000	154,000
Net Income	(68,000)	(513,000)	(771,000)	(1,388,000)	(985,000)	(152,000)	389,000	251,000
Average Shares	307,200	305,900	305,200	249,300	219,200	217,400	238,000	233,000
Balance Sheet								
Current Assets	3,798,000	4,018,000	4,331,000	4,833,000	3,683,000	5,081,000	6,370,000	6,652,000
Total Assets	9,126,000	9,442,000	10,404,000	11,801,000	9,781,000	11,424,000	13,042,000	12,581,000
Current Liabilities	2,458,000	2,412,000	2,241,000	2,846,000	2,583,000	2,756,000	2,647,000	3,249,000
Long-Term Obligations	4,395,000	4,678,000	5,360,000	4,901,000	2,956,000	2,871,000	3,099,000	2,999,000
Total Liabilities	7,876,000	8,133,000	8,490,000	8,714,000	6,610,000	7,414,000	7,582,000	7,803,000
Stockholders' Equity	1,250,000	1,309,000	1,914,000	3,087,000	3,171,000	4,010,000	5,460,000	4,778,000
Shares Outstanding	307,300	306,100	304,900	304,600	219,300	215,900	237,000	236,000
Statistical Record								
Return on Assets %	N.M.	N.M.	N.M.	N.M.	N.M.	N.M.	3.04	2.05
Return on Equity %	N.M.	N.M.	N.M.	N.M.	N.M.	N.M.	7.62	5.64
EBITDA Margin %	6.40	4.10	2.36	N.M.	N.M.	2.99	7.45	6.60
Net Margin %	N.M.	N.M.	N.M.	N.M.	N.M.	N.M.	2.19	1.43
Asset Turnover	1.30	1.28	1.11	1.10	1.20	1.41	1.39	1.43
Current Ratio	1.55	1.67	1.93	1.70	1.43	1.84	2.41	2.05
Debt to Equity	3.52	3.57	2.80	1.59	0.93	0.72	0.57	0.63
Price Range	11.86-6.31	9.98-6.31	11.20-5.08	22.47-5.77	41.93-16.28	41.42-23.81	34.47-19.50	36.81-14.18
P/E Ratio	...	...	...	...	...	...	21.15-11.96	34.08-13.13
Average Yield %	...	...	...	...	0.76	2.43	2.84	2.94

Address: 6501 Legacy Drive, Plano, TX 75024-3698	Web Site: www.jcpenney.com	Auditors: KPMG LLP
Telephone: 972-431-1000	Officers: Therace M. Risch - Executive Vice President, Chief Information Officer Myron E. Ullman - Chairman, Chief Executive Officer	Investor Contact: 972-431-5500 Transfer Agents: ComputerShare Investor Services, Providence, RI

PENTAIR PLC

Exchange	Symbol	Price	52Wk Range	Yield	P/E
NYS	PNR	$60.24 (5/31/2016)	68.75-42.88	2.26	N/A

*7 Year Price Score 96.16   ***NYSE Composite Index=100**   ***12 Month Price Score 102.68**

Interim Earnings (Per Share)

Qtr.	Mar	Jun	Sep	Dec
2013	0.25	0.75	0.85	0.78
2014	0.59	0.82	(0.95)	0.63
2015	0.62	0.81	0.63	(2.48)
2016	0.59	...	...	...

Interim Dividends (Per Share)

Amt	Decl	Ex	Rec	Pay
0.32Q	09/21/2015	10/21/2015	10/23/2015	11/06/2015
0.33Q	12/08/2015	01/27/2016	01/29/2016	02/12/2016
0.33Q	02/23/2016	04/20/2016	04/22/2016	05/06/2016
0.34Q	05/10/2016	07/20/2016	07/22/2016	08/05/2016

Indicated Div: $1.36

Valuation Analysis		Institutional Holding	
Forecast EPS	N/A	No of Institutions	625
Market Cap	$10.9 Billion	Shares	159,298,688
Book Value	$4.1 Billion	% Held	
Price/Book	2.67	N/A	
Price/Sales	1.66		

Business Summary: Industrial Machinery & Equipment (MIC: 7.2.1 SIC: 3559 NAIC: 333298)

Pentair is an industrial manufacturing company. Co. has four segments: Valves & Controls, which designs, manufactures, markets and services valves, fittings, automation and controls and actuators; Flow & Filtration Solutions, which designs, manufactures, markets and services solutions for the filtration, separation, flow and fluid management; Water Quality Systems, which designs, manufactures, markets and services water system products and solutions for filtration and fluid management; and Technical Solutions, which designs, manufactures, markets and services products that guard and protect sensitive electronics and electronic equipment, and heat management solutions.

Recent Developments: For the quarter ended Mar 31 2016, income from continuing operations decreased 9.1% to US$107.4 million from US$118.2 million in the year-earlier quarter. Net income decreased 5.7% to US$107.4 million from US$113.9 million in the year-earlier quarter. Revenues were US$1.58 billion, up 6.8% from US$1.48 billion the year before. Operating income was US$170.6 million versus US$171.2 million in the prior-year quarter, a decrease of 0.4%. Direct operating expenses rose 7.8% to US$1.04 billion from US$964.8 million in the comparable period the year before. Indirect operating expenses increased 7.6% to US$364.8 million from US$339.0 million in the equivalent prior-year period.

Prospects: Our evaluation of Pentair PLC as of July 19, 2015 is the result of our systematic analysis on three basic characteristics: earnings strength, relative valuation, and recent stock price movement. The company has generated a negative trend in earnings per share over the past 5 quarters. However, while recent estimates for the company have been lowered by analysts, PNR has posted results that fell short of analysts expectations. Based on operating earnings yield, the company is undervalued when compared to all of the companies in our coverage universe. Share price changes over the past year indicates that PNR will perform very poorly over the near term.

Financial Data

(US$ in Thousands)	3 Mos	12/31/2015	12/31/2014	12/31/2013	12/31/2012	12/31/2011	12/31/2010	12/31/2009
Earnings Per Share	(0.45)	(0.42)	1.11	2.62	(0.84)	0.34	1.99	1.17
Cash Flow Per Share	4.75	4.10	5.29	4.55	0.53	3.26	2.76	2.65
Dividends Per Share	1.290	1.280	1.100	0.960	0.880	0.800	0.760	0.720
Dividend Payout %	...	...	99.10	36.64		285.29	38.19	61.54
Income Statement								
Total Revenue	1,575,500	6,449,000	7,039,000	7,479,700	4,416,146	3,456,686	3,030,773	2,692,468
EBITDA	241,700	313,500	990,400	942,600	(30,651)	234,752	392,150	279,967
Depn & Amortn	71,100	139,500	138,700	148,900	87,835	66,235	57,995	64,823
Income Before Taxes	134,200	71,300	783,100	724,600	(186,121)	109,682	298,039	174,026
Income Taxes	27,700	139,100	177,300	183,800	(79,353)	73,059	97,200	56,428
Net Income	107,400	(76,400)	214,900	536,800	(107,186)	34,222	197,828	115,493
Average Shares	182,400	182,600	193,700	204,600	127,368	99,753	99,294	98,522
Balance Sheet								
Current Assets	3,005,900	2,780,600	2,894,100	3,232,100	3,260,368	1,237,835	1,069,297	946,298
Total Assets	12,030,200	11,857,000	10,655,200	11,743,300	11,795,311	4,586,313	3,973,533	3,911,334
Current Liabilities	1,467,600	1,486,500	1,639,500	1,610,200	1,537,921	641,841	546,796	446,279
Long-Term Obligations	4,837,100	4,709,300	2,997,400	2,552,600	2,454,278	1,304,225	702,521	803,351
Total Liabilities	7,946,000	7,848,200	5,991,400	5,648,000	5,428,451	2,652,984	1,880,380	1,899,246
Stockholders' Equity	4,084,200	4,008,800	4,663,800	6,095,300	6,366,860	1,933,329	2,093,153	2,012,088
Shares Outstanding	180,700	180,500	182,500	228,600	206,137	98,622	98,409	98,655
Statistical Record								
Return on Assets %	N.M.	N.M.	1.92	4.56	N.M.	0.80	5.02	2.90
Return on Equity %	N.M.	N.M.	3.99	8.61	N.M.	1.70	9.64	5.91
EBITDA Margin %	15.34	4.86	14.07	12.60	N.M.	6.79	12.94	10.40
Net Margin %	6.82	N.M.	3.05	7.18	N.M.	0.99	6.53	4.29
Asset Turnover	0.58	0.57	0.63	0.64	0.54	0.81	0.77	0.68
Current Ratio	2.05	1.87	1.77	2.01	2.12	1.93	1.96	2.12
Debt to Equity	1.18	1.17	0.64	0.42	0.39	0.67	0.34	0.40
Price Range	68.75-42.88	68.75-48.21	82.81-59.84	77.67-49.15	49.25-34.12	42.25-30.08	38.98-29.96	33.63-17.60
P/E Ratio	...	...	74.60-53.91	29.65-18.76	...	124.26-88.47	19.59-15.06	28.74-15.04
Average Yield %	2.30	2.13	1.54	1.51	2.09	2.21	2.26	2.68

Address: P.O. Box 471, Sharp Street, Walkden, Manchester, 55416-1259 **Telephone:** 161-703-1885	**Web Site:** www.pentair.com **Officers:** Randall J. Hogan - Chairman, President (frmr), Chief Executive Officer, Executive Vice President (frmr), Chief Operating Officer (frmr), Division Officer John L. Stauch - Executive Vice President, Chief Financial Officer	**Auditors:** Deloitte & Touche LLP **Investor Contact:** 763-656-5575 **Transfer Agents:** Wells Fargo

PEPSICO INC

Exchange	Symbol	Price	52Wk Range	Yield	P/E	Div Achiever
NYS	PEP	$101.17 (5/31/2016)	106.57-89.64	2.98	28.91	44 Years

*7 Year Price Score 108.74 *NYSE Composite Index=100 *12 Month Price Score 103.86

Interim Earnings (Per Share)

Qtr.	Mar	Jun	Aug	Dec
2013	0.69	1.28	1.23	1.12
2014	0.79	1.29	1.32	0.87
2015	0.81	1.33	0.36	1.17
2016	0.64	...	...	...

Interim Dividends (Per Share)

Amt	Decl	Ex	Rec	Pay
0.703Q	07/16/2015	09/02/2015	09/04/2015	09/30/2015
0.703Q	11/19/2015	12/02/2015	12/04/2015	01/07/2016
0.703Q	02/04/2016	03/02/2016	03/04/2016	03/31/2016
0.752Q	05/03/2016	06/01/2016	06/03/2016	06/30/2016

Indicated Div: $3.01 (Div. Reinv. Plan)

Valuation Analysis — **Institutional Holding**

Forecast EPS	$4.72 (05/20/2016)	No of Institutions 2476
Market Cap	$146.3 Billion	Shares
Book Value	$11.1 Billion	1,215,152,768
Price/Book	13.17	% Held
Price/Sales	2.33	66.68

Business Summary: Beverages (MIC: 1.2.2 SIC: 2086 NAIC: 312111)

PepsiCo is a food and beverage company. Through its operations, authorized bottlers, contract manufacturers and other third parties, Co. makes, markets, sells and distributes a range of beverages, foods and snacks. Co. has six reportable segments: Frito-Lay North America; Quaker Foods North America; North America Beverages; Latin America, which includes all of Co.'s beverage, food and snack businesses in Latin America; Europe Sub-Saharan Africa, which includes all of Co.'s beverage, food and snack businesses in Europe and Sub-Saharan Africa; and Asia, Middle East and North Africa, which includes all of Co.'s beverage, food and snack businesses in Asia, Middle East and North Africa.

Recent Developments:
For the quarter ended Mar 19 2016, net income decreased 23.2% to US$945.0 million from US$1.23 billion in the year-earlier quarter. Revenues were US$11.86 billion, down 2.9% from US$12.22 billion the year before. Operating income was US$1.62 billion versus US$1.80 billion in the prior-year quarter, a decrease of 9.9%. Direct operating expenses declined 6.4% to US$5.15 billion from US$5.50 billion in the comparable period the year before. Indirect operating expenses increased 3.6% to US$5.09 billion from US$4.92 billion in the equivalent prior-year period.

Prospects:
Our evaluation of PepsiCo Inc. as of June 19, 2016 is the result of our systematic analysis on three basic characteristics: earnings strength, relative valuation, and recent stock price movement. The company has managed to produce a neutral trend in earnings per share over the past 5 quarters and while recent estimates for the company have remained steady, PEP has posted better than expected results. Based on operating earnings yield, the company is about fairly valued when compared to all of the companies in our coverage universe. Share price changes over the past year indicates that PEP will perform well over the near term.

Financial Data
(US$ in Thousands)	3 Mos	12/26/2015	12/27/2014	12/28/2013	12/29/2012	12/31/2011	12/25/2010	12/26/2009
Earnings Per Share	3.50	3.67	4.27	4.32	3.92	4.03	3.91	3.77
Cash Flow Per Share	7.22	7.22	6.98	6.30	5.46	5.58	5.33	4.37
Tang Book Value Per Share	N.M.	N.M.	N.M.	N.M.	N.M.	N.M.	N.M.	4.86
Dividends Per Share	2.810	2.763	2.533	2.240	2.127	2.025	1.890	1.775
Dividend Payout %	80.29	75.27	59.31	51.85	54.27	50.25	48.34	47.08
Income Statement								
Total Revenue	11,862,000	63,056,000	66,683,000	66,415,000	65,492,000	66,504,000	57,838,000	43,232,000
EBITDA	1,633,000	10,676,000	12,114,000	12,287,000	11,720,000	12,242,000	10,573,000	9,607,000
Depn & Amortn	14,000	2,323,000	2,533,000	2,582,000	2,608,000	2,609,000	2,241,000	1,563,000
Income Before Taxes	1,387,000	7,442,000	8,757,000	8,891,000	8,304,000	8,834,000	7,497,000	7,714,000
Income Taxes	442,000	1,941,000	2,199,000	2,104,000	2,090,000	2,372,000	1,894,000	2,100,000
Net Income	931,000	5,452,000	6,513,000	6,740,000	6,178,000	6,443,000	6,320,000	5,946,000
Average Shares	1,459,000	1,485,000	1,527,000	1,560,000	1,575,000	1,597,000	1,614,000	1,577,000
Balance Sheet								
Current Assets	23,966,000	23,031,000	20,663,000	22,203,000	18,720,000	17,441,000	17,569,000	12,571,000
Total Assets	70,019,000	69,667,000	70,509,000	77,478,000	74,638,000	72,882,000	68,153,000	39,848,000
Current Liabilities	16,842,000	17,578,000	18,092,000	17,839,000	17,089,000	18,154,000	15,892,000	8,756,000
Long-Term Obligations	31,068,000	29,213,000	23,821,000	24,333,000	23,544,000	20,568,000	19,999,000	7,400,000
Total Liabilities	58,908,000	57,744,000	53,071,000	53,199,000	52,344,000	52,294,000	46,989,000	23,044,000
Stockholders' Equity	11,111,000	11,923,000	17,438,000	24,279,000	22,294,000	20,588,000	21,164,000	16,804,000
Shares Outstanding	1,446,000	1,448,000	1,488,000	1,529,000	1,544,000	1,564,000	1,581,000	1,565,000
Statistical Record								
Return on Assets %	7.39	7.80	8.83	8.89	8.40	8.99	11.74	15.72
Return on Equity %	38.27	37.24	31.31	29.02	28.89	30.36	33.38	41.25
EBITDA Margin %	13.77	16.93	18.17	18.50	17.90	18.41	18.28	22.22
Net Margin %	7.85	8.65	9.77	10.15	9.43	9.69	10.93	13.75
Asset Turnover	0.90	0.90	0.90	0.88	0.89	0.93	1.07	1.14
Current Ratio	1.42	1.31	1.14	1.24	1.10	0.96	1.11	1.44
Debt to Equity	2.80	2.45	1.37	1.00	1.06	1.00	0.94	0.44
Price Range	103.08-89.64	103.08-89.64	100.39-77.10	86.80-68.43	73.58-62.28	71.78-59.99	68.11-58.96	64.23-45.81
P/E Ratio	29.45-25.61	28.09-24.43	23.51-18.06	20.09-15.84	18.77-15.89	17.81-14.89	17.42-15.08	17.04-12.15
Average Yield %	2.89	2.86	2.86	2.79	3.11	3.11	2.94	3.21

Address: 700 Anderson Hill Road, Purchase, NY 10577 Telephone: 914-253-2000	Web Site: www.pepsico.com Officers: Indra K. Nooyi - Chairman, President, Chief Executive Officer Ramon Laguarta - Region Officer	Auditors: KPMG LLP Investor Contact: 914-253-3055 Transfer Agents: Computershare, Providence, RI

PERKINELMER, INC.

Exchange	Symbol	Price	52Wk Range	Yield	P/E
NYS	PKI	$54.75 (5/31/2016)	55.56-41.45	0.51	28.22

*7 Year Price Score 127.60 ***NYSE Composite Index=100** ***12 Month Price Score 101.69**

Interim Earnings (Per Share)

Qtr.	Mar	Jun	Sep	Dec
2013	0.28	0.25	0.36	0.59
2014	0.30	0.44	0.37	0.27
2015	0.36	0.43	0.48	0.60
2016	0.43	...	...	...

Interim Dividends (Per Share)

Amt	Decl	Ex	Rec	Pay
0.07Q	07/22/2015	10/14/2015	10/16/2015	11/10/2015
0.07Q	10/29/2015	01/13/2016	01/15/2016	02/10/2016
0.07Q	01/28/2016	04/13/2016	04/15/2016	05/10/2016
0.07Q	04/25/2016	07/13/2016	07/15/2016	08/10/2016

Indicated Div: $0.28

Valuation Analysis — **Institutional Holding**

Forecast EPS	$2.80	No of Institutions
	(05/20/2016)	477
Market Cap	$6.0 Billion	Shares
Book Value	$2.0 Billion	124,975,608
Price/Book	2.91	% Held
Price/Sales	2.62	93.02

Business Summary: Biotechnology (MIC: 4.1.2 SIC: 3826 NAIC: 334516)

PerkinElmer is a provider of products, services, and solutions to the diagnostics, research, environmental, industrial and laboratory services markets. Co. operates its business in two segments: The Human Health segment, engaged in developing diagnostics, tools, and applications to detect diseases and to help in the discovery and development of therapies and within this segment, Co. serves both the diagnostics and research markets; and Co.'s Environmental Health segment provides products, services and solutions to facilitate the creation of food and consumer products, which serves the environmental, industrial and laboratory services markets.

Recent Developments: For the quarter ended Apr 3 2016, income from continuing operations increased 17.8% to US$47.5 million from US$40.3 million in the year-earlier quarter. Net income increased 17.7% to US$47.5 million from US$40.3 million in the year-earlier quarter. Revenues were US$538.7 million, up 2.2% from US$526.9 million the year before. Operating income was US$68.8 million versus US$57.4 million in the prior-year quarter, an increase of 19.8%. Direct operating expenses declined 1.0% to US$288.6 million from US$291.5 million in the comparable period the year before. Indirect operating expenses increased 1.9% to US$181.3 million from US$178.0 million in the equivalent prior-year period.

Prospects: Our evaluation of PerkinElmer Inc. as of June 19, 2016 is the result of our systematic analysis on three basic characteristics: earnings strength, relative valuation, and recent stock price movement. The company has produced a positive trend in earnings per share over the past 5 quarters and while recent estimates for the company have been mixed, PKI has posted better than expected results. Based on operating earnings yield, the company is about fairly valued when compared to all of the companies in our coverage universe. Share price changes over the past year indicates that PKI will perform well over the near term.

Financial Data

(US$ in Thousands)	3 Mos	01/03/2016	12/28/2014	12/29/2013	12/30/2012	01/01/2012	01/02/2011	01/03/2010
Earnings Per Share	1.94	1.87	1.39	1.47	0.61	0.07	3.25	0.73
Cash Flow Per Share	2.55	2.51	2.51	1.42	1.34	2.00	1.41	1.26
Dividends Per Share	0.280	0.280	0.280	0.280	0.280	0.280	0.280	0.280
Dividend Payout %	14.43	14.97	20.14	19.05	45.90	400.00	8.62	38.36
Income Statement								
Total Revenue	538,684	2,262,359	2,237,219	2,166,232	2,115,205	1,921,287	1,704,346	1,812,202
EBITDA	69,254	314,739	238,506	240,706	131,227	118,153	205,443	181,398
Depn & Amortn	487	33,400	33,300	38,100	35,600	30,900	28,400	34,600
Income Before Taxes	57,681	244,015	169,603	153,332	50,587	64,354	161,984	130,677
Income Taxes	10,176	31,327	8,437	(14,592)	(17,854)	63,182	26,062	37,933
Net Income	47,466	212,425	157,778	167,212	69,940	7,655	383,919	85,599
Average Shares	111,195	113,315	113,739	113,503	114,860	113,864	117,982	116,590
Balance Sheet								
Current Assets	1,049,820	1,033,161	1,068,551	1,044,838	971,754	862,218	1,085,039	883,790
Total Assets	4,210,721	4,166,295	4,134,075	3,946,712	3,901,762	3,834,198	3,209,373	3,064,242
Current Liabilities	554,547	561,485	597,310	602,796	581,100	600,066	515,202	496,070
Long-Term Obligations	1,119,830	1,011,762	1,051,892	932,104	938,824	944,908	424,000	558,197
Total Liabilities	2,161,241	2,055,854	2,091,973	1,952,225	1,961,950	1,991,982	1,283,555	1,435,285
Stockholders' Equity	2,049,480	2,110,441	2,042,102	1,994,487	1,939,812	1,842,216	1,925,818	1,628,957
Shares Outstanding	109,015	112,034	112,481	112,626	115,036	113,157	115,715	117,023
Statistical Record								
Return on Assets %	5.33	5.04	3.92	4.27	1.81	0.22	12.27	2.81
Return on Equity %	10.69	10.07	7.84	8.52	3.71	0.41	21.66	5.27
EBITDA Margin %	12.86	13.91	10.66	11.11	6.20	6.15	12.05	10.01
Net Margin %	8.81	9.39	7.05	7.72	3.31	0.40	22.53	4.72
Asset Turnover	0.55	0.54	0.56	0.55	0.55	0.55	0.54	0.59
Current Ratio	1.89	1.84	1.79	1.73	1.67	1.44	2.11	1.78
Debt to Equity	0.55	0.48	0.52	0.47	0.48	0.51	0.22	0.34
Price Range	54.36-41.45	54.36-42.66	48.25-39.83	41.18-30.35	32.29-20.37	28.46-17.47	26.14-18.89	20.99-11.00
P/E Ratio	28.02-21.37	29.07-22.81	34.71-28.65	28.01-20.65	52.93-33.39	406.57-249.57	8.04-5.81	28.75-15.07
Average Yield %	0.56	0.56	0.63	0.79	1.02	1.18	1.24	1.67

Address: 940 Winter Street, Waltham, MA 02451	Web Site: www.perkinelmer.com	Auditors: Deloitte & Touche LLP
Telephone: 781-663-6900	Officers: Robert F. Friel - Chairman, President, Chief Executive Officer Frank Anders Wilson - Chief Financial Officer, Senior Vice President, Chief Accounting Officer	Investor Contact: 781-663-6900
Fax: 781-663-6052		Transfer Agents: Computershare, Inc., Providence, RI

PENSKE AUTOMOTIVE GROUP INC

Exchange	Symbol	Price	52Wk Range	Yield	P/E
NYS	PAG	$39.52 (5/31/2016)	54.21-29.96	2.73	10.71

*7 Year Price Score 122.06 *NYSE Composite Index=100 *12 Month Price Score 83.57

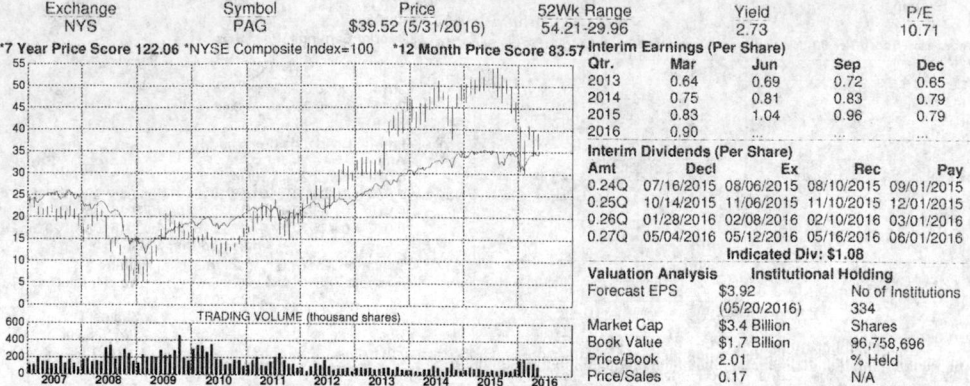

Interim Earnings (Per Share)

Qtr.	Mar	Jun	Sep	Dec
2013	0.64	0.69	0.72	0.65
2014	0.75	0.81	0.83	0.79
2015	0.83	1.04	0.96	0.79
2016	0.90			

Interim Dividends (Per Share)

Amt	Decl	Ex	Rec	Pay
0.24Q	07/16/2015	08/06/2015	08/10/2015	09/01/2015
0.25Q	10/14/2015	11/06/2015	11/10/2015	12/01/2015
0.26Q	01/28/2016	02/08/2016	02/10/2016	03/01/2016
0.27Q	05/04/2016	05/12/2016	05/16/2016	06/01/2016

Indicated Div: $1.08

Valuation Analysis   Institutional Holding

Forecast EPS	$3.92 (05/20/2016)	No of Institutions	334
Market Cap	$3.4 Billion	Shares	96,758,696
Book Value	$1.7 Billion	% Held	
Price/Book	2.01	N/A	
Price/Sales	0.17		

Business Summary: Retail - Automotive (MIC: 2.1.4 SIC: 5511 NAIC: 441110)

Penske Automotive Group is a holding company. Through its subsidiaries, Co. operates automotive and commercial truck dealerships in the U.S. and Western Europe, and distributes commercial vehicles, diesel engines, gas engines, power systems and related parts and services in Australia and New Zealand. Co. has three segments: Retail Automotive, consisting of retail automotive dealership operations; Retail Commercial Truck, consisting of its U.S. retail commercial truck dealership operations; and Other, consisting of its commercial vehicle and power systems distribution operations and other investments in non-automotive operations. At Dec 31 2015, Co. operated 355 automotive retail franchises.

Recent Developments: For the quarter ended Mar 31 2016, income from continuing operations increased 4.4% to US$80.2 million from US$76.8 million in the year-earlier quarter. Net income increased 5.7% to US$80.2 million from US$75.9 million in the year-earlier quarter. Revenues were US$4.82 billion, up 7.6% from US$4.48 billion the year before. Operating income was US$144.1 million versus US$135.5 million in the prior-year quarter, an increase of 6.3%. Direct operating expenses rose 8.1% to US$4.10 billion from US$3.79 billion in the comparable period the year before. Indirect operating expenses increased 4.6% to US$579.7 million from US$554.4 million in the equivalent prior-year period.

Prospects: Our evaluation of Penske Automotive Group Inc. as of June 19, 2016 is the result of our systematic analysis on three basic characteristics: earnings strength, relative valuation, and recent stock price movement. The company has managed to produce a neutral trend in earnings per share over the past 5 quarters. However, while recent estimates for the company have been lowered by analysts, PAG has posted better than expected results. Based on operating earnings yield, the company is undervalued when compared to all of the companies in our coverage universe. Share price changes over the past year indicates that PAG will perform in line with the market over the near term.

Financial Data

(US$ in Thousands)	3 Mos	12/31/2015	12/31/2014	12/31/2013	12/31/2012	12/31/2011	12/31/2010	12/31/2009
Earnings Per Share	3.69	3.63	3.17	2.70	2.05	1.94	1.18	0.83
Cash Flow Per Share	3.18	4.36	4.06	3.49	3.62	1.35	2.17	3.31
Tang Book Value Per Share	N.M.	0.66	0.00	0.61	0.51	N.M.	0.25	N.M.
Dividends Per Share	0.980	0.940	0.780	0.620	0.460	0.240	...	...
Dividend Payout %	26.56	25.90	24.61	22.96	22.44	12.37	...	...
Income Statement								
Total Revenue	4,824,600	19,284,900	17,177,200	14,705,400	13,163,517	11,556,232	10,713,585	9,523,105
EBITDA	164,900	644,500	590,100	497,900	401,100	347,093	291,368	286,803
Depn & Amortn	20,800	78,000	70,000	61,700	53,995	48,903	48,884	67,277
Income Before Taxes	114,100	452,600	421,200	344,700	261,416	222,937	149,599	115,620
Income Taxes	39,400	158,000	153,200	124,300	94,330	71,933	57,912	45,386
Net Income	79,300	326,100	286,700	244,200	185,540	176,881	108,281	76,461
Average Shares	88,292	89,759	90,354	90,330	90,342	91,274	92,091	91,653
Balance Sheet								
Current Assets	4,505,900	4,408,100	3,867,700	3,346,600	2,773,083	2,192,600	2,008,443	1,743,464
Total Assets	8,172,900	8,022,700	7,228,200	6,415,500	5,378,990	4,502,299	4,069,832	3,796,007
Current Liabilities	4,438,900	4,286,900	3,630,300	3,331,800	2,693,556	2,149,672	1,958,792	1,629,817
Long-Term Obligations	1,330,100	1,255,100	1,316,000	1,033,230	918,024	846,777	769,285	933,966
Total Liabilities	6,491,300	6,232,500	5,575,400	4,911,100	4,074,775	3,366,314	3,028,282	2,853,546
Stockholders' Equity	1,681,600	1,790,200	1,652,800	1,504,400	1,304,215	1,135,985	1,041,550	942,461
Shares Outstanding	85,314	89,524	90,244	90,243	90,294	90,277	92,099	91,617
Statistical Record								
Return on Assets %	4.29	4.28	4.20	4.14	3.75	4.13	2.75	1.97
Return on Equity %	19.86	18.94	18.16	17.39	15.17	16.25	10.92	8.86
EBITDA Margin %	3.42	3.34	3.44	3.39	3.05	3.00	2.72	3.01
Net Margin %	1.64	1.69	1.67	1.66	1.41	1.53	1.01	0.80
Asset Turnover	2.55	2.53	2.52	2.49	2.66	2.70	2.72	2.45
Current Ratio	1.02	1.03	1.07	1.00	1.03	1.02	1.03	1.07
Debt to Equity	0.79	0.70	0.80	0.69	0.70	0.75	0.74	0.99
Price Range	54.21-29.96	54.21-41.79	51.16-37.51	47.42-28.40	32.11-18.58	23.96-15.06	17.42-10.94	21.20-4.84
P/E Ratio	14.69-8.12	14.93-11.51	16.14-11.83	17.56-10.52	15.66-9.06	12.35-7.76	14.76-9.27	25.54-5.83
Average Yield %	2.11	1.89	1.72	1.72	1.77	1.23	...	...

Address: 2555 Telegraph Road, Bloomfield Hills, MI 48302-0954
Telephone: 248-648-2500
Fax: 248-648-2525

Web Site: www.penskeautomotive.com
Officers: Roger S. Penske - Chairman, Chief Executive Officer Bud Denke - Executive Vice President

Auditors: Deloitte & Touche LLP
Investor Contact: 866-715-5289
Transfer Agents: ComputerShare Investor Services, Providence, RI

PFIZER INC

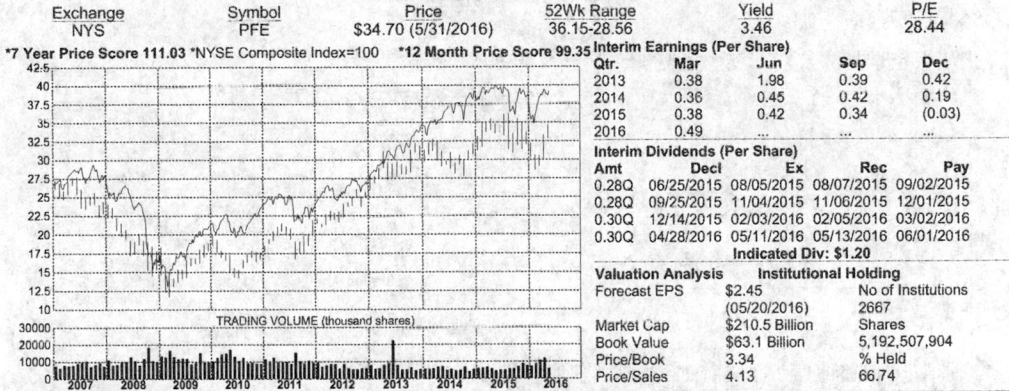

Exchange	Symbol	Price	52Wk Range	Yield	P/E
NYS	PFE	$34.70 (5/31/2016)	36.15-28.56	3.46	28.44

*7 Year Price Score 111.03 *NYSE Composite Index=100 ***12 Month Price Score 99.35**

Interim Earnings (Per Share)

Qtr.	Mar	Jun	Sep	Dec
2013	0.38	1.98	0.39	0.42
2014	0.36	0.45	0.42	0.19
2015	0.38	0.42	0.34	(0.03)
2016	0.49	...	...	...

Interim Dividends (Per Share)

Amt	Decl	Ex	Rec	Pay
0.28Q	06/25/2015	08/05/2015	08/07/2015	09/02/2015
0.28Q	09/25/2015	11/04/2015	11/06/2015	12/01/2015
0.30Q	12/14/2015	02/03/2016	02/05/2016	03/02/2016
0.30Q	04/28/2016	05/11/2016	05/13/2016	06/01/2016

Indicated Div: $1.20

Valuation Analysis

		Institutional Holding	
Forecast EPS	$2.45	No of Institutions	
	(05/20/2016)	2667	
Market Cap	$210.5 Billion	Shares	
Book Value	$63.1 Billion	5,192,507,904	
Price/Book	3.34	% Held	
Price/Sales	4.13	66.74	

Business Summary: Pharmaceuticals (MIC: 4.1.1 SIC: 2834 NAIC: 325412)

Pfizer is a research-based biopharmaceutical company involved in the discovery, development and manufacture of healthcare products. Co.'s businesses include: Global Innovative Pharmaceutical business, which comprises medicines within several therapeutic areas including inflammation, cardiovascular/metabolic, neuroscience and pain, rare diseases and women's/men's health; Global Vaccines, Oncology and Consumer Healthcare business, which focuses on the development and commercialization of vaccines and products for oncology and consumer healthcare; and Global Established Pharmaceutical business, which includes brands that have lost market exclusivity and also generic pharmaceuticals.

Recent Developments: For the quarter ended Apr 3 2016, income from continuing operations increased 27.4% to US$3.03 billion from US$2.38 billion in the year-earlier quarter. Net income increased 27.1% to US$3.03 billion from US$2.38 billion in the year-earlier quarter. Revenues were US$13.01 billion, up 19.7% from US$10.86 billion the year before. Direct operating expenses rose 55.1% to US$2.85 billion from US$1.84 billion in the comparable period the year before. Indirect operating expenses increased 11.0% to US$6.59 billion from US$5.94 billion in the equivalent prior-year period.

Prospects: Our evaluation of Pfizer Inc. as of June 19, 2016 is the result of our systematic analysis on three basic characteristics: earnings strength, relative valuation, and recent stock price movement. The company has produced a positive trend in earnings per share over the past 5 quarters and while recent estimates for the company have been mixed, PFE has posted better than expected results. Based on operating earnings yield, the company is undervalued when compared to all of the companies in our coverage universe. Share price changes over the past year indicates that PFE will perform poorly over the near term.

Financial Data

(US$ in Thousands)	3 Mos	12/31/2015	12/31/2014	12/31/2013	12/31/2012	12/31/2011	12/31/2010	12/31/2009
Earnings Per Share	1.22	1.11	1.42	3.19	1.94	1.27	1.02	1.23
Cash Flow Per Share	2.52	2.35	2.66	2.61	2.29	2.59	1.43	2.37
Dividends Per Share	1.140	1.120	1.040	0.960	0.880	0.800	0.720	0.800
Dividend Payout %	93.44	100.90	73.24	30.09	45.36	62.99	70.59	65.04
Income Statement								
Total Revenue	13,005,000	48,851,000	49,605,000	51,584,000	58,986,000	67,425,000	67,809,000	50,009,000
EBITDA	4,760,000	13,421,000	17,214,000	21,326,000	18,396,000	19,570,000	16,223,000	13,709,000
Depn & Amortn	1,006,000	3,728,000	4,039,000	4,599,000	5,175,000	5,585,000	5,404,000	2,877,000
Income Before Taxes	3,561,000	8,965,000	12,240,000	15,716,000	12,080,000	12,762,000	9,422,000	10,345,000
Income Taxes	535,000	1,990,000	3,120,000	4,306,000	2,562,000	4,023,000	1,124,000	2,197,000
Net Income	3,016,000	6,960,000	9,135,000	22,003,000	14,570,000	10,009,000	8,257,000	8,635,000
Average Shares	6,213,999	6,256,999	6,423,999	6,895,001	7,508,001	7,870,001	8,074,001	7,045,001
Balance Sheet								
Current Assets	41,298,000	43,804,000	57,702,000	56,244,000	61,415,000	57,728,000	60,468,000	61,670,000
Total Assets	162,929,000	167,460,000	169,274,000	172,101,000	185,798,000	188,002,000	195,014,000	212,949,000
Current Liabilities	28,735,000	29,399,000	21,631,000	23,366,000	28,619,000	28,069,000	28,609,000	37,225,000
Long-Term Obligations	27,824,000	28,818,000	31,541,000	30,462,000	31,036,000	34,931,000	38,410,000	43,193,000
Total Liabilities	99,861,000	102,741,000	97,973,000	95,794,000	104,538,000	105,812,000	107,201,000	122,935,000
Stockholders' Equity	63,068,000	64,720,000	71,301,000	76,307,000	81,260,000	82,190,000	87,813,000	90,014,000
Shares Outstanding	6,064,849	6,174,999	6,290,999	6,398,999	7,276,001	7,575,001	8,012,001	8,070,001
Statistical Record								
Return on Assets %	4.70	4.13	5.35	12.30	7.77	5.23	4.05	5.33
Return on Equity %	11.66	10.23	12.38	27.93	17.78	11.78	9.29	11.70
EBITDA Margin %	36.60	27.47	34.70	41.34	31.19	29.02	23.92	27.41
Net Margin %	23.19	14.25	18.42	42.65	24.70	14.84	12.18	17.27
Asset Turnover	0.32	0.29	0.29	0.29	0.31	0.35	0.33	0.31
Current Ratio	1.44	1.49	2.67	2.41	2.15	2.06	2.11	1.66
Debt to Equity	0.44	0.45	0.44	0.40	0.38	0.43	0.44	0.48
Price Range	36.15-28.56	36.15-30.82	32.75-27.70	32.20-25.08	26.04-20.95	21.83-16.66	20.00-14.14	18.85-11.66
P/E Ratio	29.63-23.41	32.57-27.77	23.06-19.51	10.09-7.86	13.42-10.80	17.19-13.12	19.61-13.86	15.33-9.48
Average Yield %	3.47	3.32	3.43	3.31	3.79	4.10	4.29	5.08

Address: 235 East 42nd Street, New York, NY 10017-5755
Telephone: 212-733-2323

Web Site: www.pfizer.com
Officers: Ian C. Read - Chairman, President, Chief Executive Officer Frank A. D'Amelio - Executive Vice President, Chief Financial Officer, Senior Vice President

Auditors: KPMG LLP
Transfer Agents: Computershare Trust Company, N.A., Canton, MA

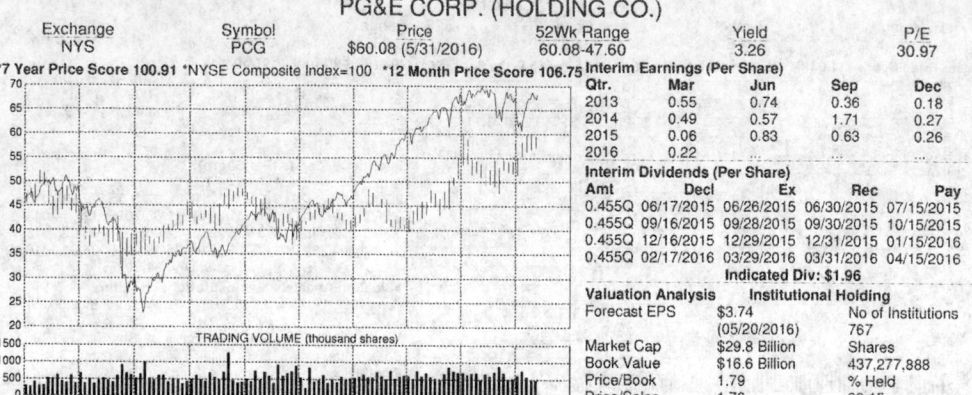

PG&E CORP. (HOLDING CO.)

Exchange	Symbol	Price	52Wk Range	Yield	P/E
NYS	PCG	$60.08 (5/31/2016)	60.08-47.60	3.26	30.97

*7 Year Price Score 100.91 *NYSE Composite Index=100 *12 Month Price Score 106.75

Interim Earnings (Per Share)

Qtr.	Mar	Jun	Sep	Dec
2013	0.55	0.74	0.36	0.18
2014	0.49	0.57	1.71	0.27
2015	0.06	0.83	0.63	0.26
2016	0.22			

Interim Dividends (Per Share)

Amt	Decl	Ex	Rec	Pay
0.455Q	06/17/2015	06/26/2015	06/30/2015	07/15/2015
0.455Q	09/16/2015	09/28/2015	09/30/2015	10/15/2015
0.455Q	12/16/2015	12/29/2015	12/31/2015	01/15/2016
0.455Q	02/17/2016	03/29/2016	03/31/2016	04/15/2016

Indicated Div: $1.96

Valuation Analysis

		Institutional Holding	
Forecast EPS	$3.74	No of Institutions	767
	(05/20/2016)		
Market Cap	$29.8 Billion	Shares	437,277,888
Book Value	$16.6 Billion	% Held	83.15
Price/Book	1.79		
Price/Sales	1.76		

TRADING VOLUME (thousand shares)

Business Summary: Electric Utilities (MIC: 3.1.1 SIC: 4931 NAIC: 221122)

PG&E is a holding company. Through its subsidiary, Pacific Gas and Electric Company (Utility), Co. engages in electricity and natural gas distribution operations, electricity generation, and natural gas transportation and storage services. The Utility owns generation facilities located in California, and owns and operates natural gas transmission, storage, and distribution system in northern and central California. At Dec 31 2015, the Utility owned approximately 18,400 circuit miles of interconnected transmission lines operating at voltages ranging from 60 kV to 500 kV. The Utility's electricity distribution network consists of approximately 142,000 circuit miles of distribution lines.

Recent Developments: For the quarter ended Mar 31 2016, net income increased 223.5% to US$110.0 million from US$34.0 million in the year-earlier quarter. Revenues were US$3.97 billion, up 1.9% from US$3.90 billion the year before. Operating income was US$95.0 million versus US$71.0 million in the prior-year quarter, an increase of 33.8%. Direct operating expenses declined 0.5% to US$3.18 billion from US$3.20 billion in the comparable period the year before. Indirect operating expenses increased 10.5% to US$697.0 million from US$631.0 million in the equivalent prior-year period.

Prospects: Our evaluation of PG&E Corp. as of June 19, 2016 is the result of our systematic analysis on three basic characteristics: earnings strength, relative valuation, and recent stock price movement. The company has enjoyed a very positive trend in earnings per share over the past 5 quarters. However, while recent estimates for the company have been mixed, PCG has posted better than expected results. Based on operating earnings yield, the company is about fairly valued when compared to all of the companies in our coverage universe. Share price changes over the past year indicates that PCG will perform in line with the market over the near term.

Financial Data

(US$ in Thousands)	3 Mos	12/31/2015	12/31/2014	12/31/2013	12/31/2012	12/31/2011	12/31/2010	12/31/2009
Earnings Per Share	1.94	1.79	3.06	1.83	1.92	2.10	2.82	3.20
Cash Flow Per Share	7.56	7.75	7.86	7.72	11.48	9.32	8.39	8.26
Tang Book Value Per Share	33.52	33.69	33.09	31.41	30.35	29.35	28.55	27.83
Dividends Per Share	1.820	1.820	1.820	1.820	1.820	1.820	1.820	1.680
Dividend Payout %	93.81	101.68	59.48	99.45	94.79	86.67	64.54	52.50
Income Statement								
Total Revenue	3,974,000	16,833,000	17,090,000	15,598,000	15,040,000	14,956,000	13,841,000	13,399,000
EBITDA	819,000	4,237,000	4,953,000	3,879,000	4,035,000	4,206,000	4,486,000	4,313,000
Depn & Amortn	697,000	2,612,000	2,433,000	2,077,000	2,272,000	2,215,000	2,151,000	1,947,000
Income Before Taxes	(77,000)	861,000	1,795,000	1,096,000	1,067,000	1,298,000	1,660,000	1,694,000
Income Taxes	(187,000)	(27,000)	345,000	268,000	237,000	440,000	547,000	460,000
Net Income	110,000	888,000	1,450,000	828,000	830,000	858,000	1,113,000	1,234,000
Average Shares	495,000	487,000	470,000	445,000	425,000	402,000	392,000	386,000
Balance Sheet								
Current Assets	5,634,000	5,822,000	6,389,000	5,977,000	5,121,000	6,480,000	5,542,000	5,657,000
Total Assets	64,650,000	63,339,000	60,127,000	55,605,000	52,449,000	49,750,000	46,025,000	42,945,000
Current Liabilities	5,974,000	6,363,000	5,920,000	7,493,000	6,256,000	7,749,000	7,185,000	6,813,000
Long-Term Obligations	16,522,000	16,030,000	15,050,000	12,717,000	12,517,000	11,766,000	11,329,000	11,208,000
Total Liabilities	48,038,000	46,763,000	44,379,000	41,263,000	39,375,000	37,649,000	34,743,000	32,612,000
Stockholders' Equity	16,612,000	16,576,000	15,748,000	14,342,000	13,074,000	12,101,000	11,282,000	10,333,000
Shares Outstanding	495,606	492,025	475,913	456,670	430,718	412,257	395,227	371,272
Statistical Record								
Return on Assets %	1.54	1.44	2.51	1.53	1.62	1.79	2.50	2.94
Return on Equity %	5.97	5.49	9.64	6.04	6.58	7.34	10.30	12.36
EBITDA Margin %	20.61	25.17	28.98	24.87	26.83	28.12	32.41	32.19
Net Margin %	2.77	5.28	8.48	5.31	5.52	5.74	8.04	9.21
Asset Turnover	0.27	0.27	0.30	0.29	0.29	0.31	0.31	0.32
Current Ratio	0.94	0.91	1.08	0.80	0.82	0.84	0.77	0.83
Debt to Equity	0.99	0.97	0.96	0.89	0.96	0.97	1.00	1.08
Price Range	59.72-47.60	60.15-47.60	54.98-39.60	48.44-40.07	46.51-39.71	47.84-36.86	48.58-40.00	45.60-34.82
P/E Ratio	30.78-24.54	33.60-26.59	17.97-12.94	26.47-21.90	24.22-20.68	22.78-17.55	17.23-14.18	14.25-10.88
Average Yield %	3.44	3.44	3.97	4.21	4.23	4.23	4.09	4.26

Address: 77 Beale Street, P.O. Box 770000, San Francisco, CA 94177
Telephone: 415-973-1000
Fax: 415-267-7265

Web Site: www.pgecorp.com
Officers: Anthony F. Earley - Chairman, President, Chief Executive Officer, holding/Parent Company Officer Edward D. Halpin - Senior Vice President, Chief Nuclear Officer

Auditors: Deloitte & Touche LLP
Investor Contact: 415-972-7080
Transfer Agents: American Stock Transfer and Trust Company, LLC, Brooklyn, NY

PHILIP MORRIS INTERNATIONAL INC

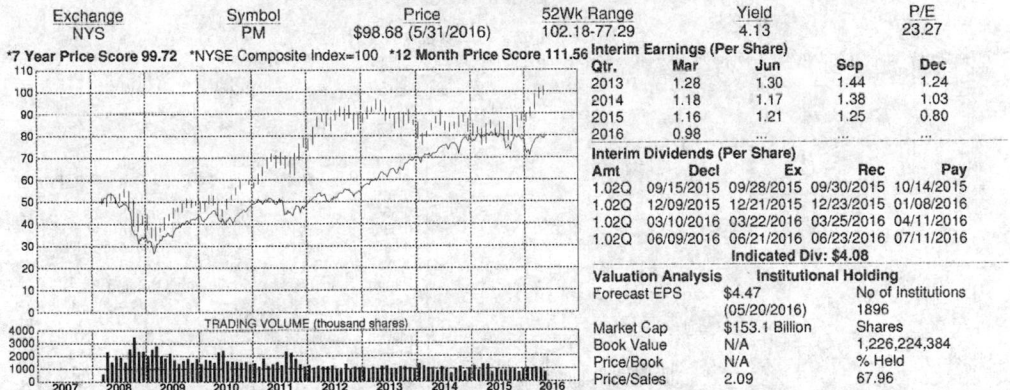

Exchange	Symbol	Price	52Wk Range	Yield	P/E
NYS	PM	$98.68 (5/31/2016)	102.18-77.29	4.13	23.27

*7 Year Price Score 99.72 *NYSE Composite Index=100 *12 Month Price Score 111.56

Interim Earnings (Per Share)

Qtr.	Mar	Jun	Sep	Dec
2013	1.28	1.30	1.44	1.24
2014	1.18	1.17	1.38	1.03
2015	1.16	1.21	1.25	0.80
2016	0.98	...	...	...

Interim Dividends (Per Share)

Amt	Decl	Ex	Rec	Pay
1.02Q	09/15/2015	09/28/2015	09/30/2015	10/14/2015
1.02Q	12/09/2015	12/21/2015	12/23/2015	01/08/2016
1.02Q	03/10/2016	03/22/2016	03/25/2016	04/11/2016
1.02Q	06/09/2016	06/21/2016	06/23/2016	07/11/2016

Indicated Div: $4.08

Valuation Analysis

Forecast EPS	$4.47
	(05/20/2016)
Market Cap	$153.1 Billion
Book Value	N/A
Price/Book	N/A
Price/Sales	2.09

Institutional Holding

No of Institutions	1896
Shares	1,226,224,384
% Held	67.96

Business Summary: Tobacco Products (MIC: 1.3.1 SIC: 2111 NAIC: 312221)

Philip Morris International is a holding company. Through its subsidiaries and affiliates, Co. is engaged in the manufacture and sale of cigarettes and other tobacco products in markets outside of the U.S. Co.'s portfolio of international and local brands include Marlboro, in category by Merit, Parliament, and Virginia Slims. Co.'s mid-price brands are L&M and Philip Morris. Other international brands include Bond Street, Chesterfield, Next and Red & White. Co. also owns a number of local cigarette brands, such as Dji Sam Soe, Sampoerna and U Mild in Indonesia; Champion, Fortune and Hope in the Philippines; Morven Gold in Pakistan; and Belmont, Canadian Classics and Number 7 in Canada.

Recent Developments: For the quarter ended Mar 31 2016, net income decreased 12.5% to US$1.61 billion from US$1.83 billion in the year-earlier quarter. Revenues were US$16.79 billion, down 3.3% from US$17.35 billion the year before. Operating income was US$2.47 billion versus US$2.87 billion in the prior-year quarter, a decrease of 13.9%. Direct operating expenses declined 1.3% to US$12.80 billion from US$12.97 billion in the comparable period the year before. Indirect operating expenses decreased 0.1% to US$1.51 billion from US$1.52 billion in the equivalent prior-year period.

Prospects: Our evaluation of Philip Morris International Inc. as of June 19, 2016 is the result of our systematic analysis on three basic characteristics: earnings strength, relative valuation, and recent stock price movement. The company has produced a positive trend in earnings per share over the past 5 quarters. However, while recent estimates for the company have been mixed, PM has posted results that fell short of analysts expectations. Based on operating earnings yield, the company is about fairly valued when compared to all of the companies in our coverage universe. Share price changes over the past year indicates that PM will perform very well over the near term.

Financial Data

(US$ in Thousands)	3 Mos	12/31/2015	12/31/2014	12/31/2013	12/31/2012	12/31/2011	12/31/2010	12/31/2009
Earnings Per Share	4.24	4.42	4.76	5.26	5.17	4.85	3.92	3.24
Cash Flow Per Share	5.61	5.08	4.94	6.25	5.55	5.98	5.13	4.06
Dividends Per Share	4.060	4.040	3.880	3.580	3.240	2.820	2.440	2.240
Dividend Payout %	95.75	91.40	81.51	68.06	62.67	58.14	62.24	69.14
Income Statement								
Total Revenue	16,788,000	73,908,000	80,106,000	80,029,000	77,393,000	76,346,000	67,713,000	62,080,000
EBITDA	2,491,000	11,377,000	12,591,000	14,397,000	14,744,000	14,325,000	12,132,000	10,893,000
Depn & Amortn	18,000	754,000	889,000	882,000	898,000	993,000	932,000	853,000
Income Before Taxes	2,226,000	9,615,000	10,650,000	12,542,000	12,987,000	12,532,000	10,324,000	9,243,000
Income Taxes	630,000	2,688,000	3,097,000	3,670,000	3,833,000	3,653,000	2,826,000	2,691,000
Net Income	1,530,000	6,873,000	7,493,000	8,576,000	8,800,000	8,591,000	7,259,000	6,342,000
Average Shares	1,550,000	1,549,000	1,566,000	1,622,000	1,692,000	1,762,000	1,842,000	1,950,000
Balance Sheet								
Current Assets	15,928,000	15,804,000	15,484,000	16,852,000	16,590,000	14,859,000	13,756,000	14,682,000
Total Assets	34,621,000	33,956,000	35,187,000	38,168,000	37,670,000	35,488,000	35,050,000	34,552,000
Current Liabilities	14,091,000	15,386,000	15,112,000	17,066,000	17,016,000	14,794,000	12,804,000	11,178,000
Long-Term Obligations	26,683,000	25,250,000	26,929,000	24,023,000	17,639,000	14,828,000	13,370,000	13,672,000
Total Liabilities	47,374,000	47,200,000	47,816,000	45,934,000	41,146,000	35,259,000	31,544,000	28,836,000
Stockholders' Equity	(12,753,000)	(13,244,000)	(12,629,000)	(7,766,000)	(3,476,000)	229,000	3,506,000	5,716,000
Shares Outstanding	1,551,257	1,549,344	1,546,899	1,589,002	1,653,612	1,725,908	1,801,783	1,887,164
Statistical Record								
Return on Assets %	19.47	19.88	20.43	22.62	23.99	24.36	20.86	18.78
Return on Equity %	...	...	...	...	...	460.03	157.43	95.97
EBITDA Margin %	14.84	15.39	15.72	17.99	19.05	18.76	17.92	17.55
Net Margin %	9.11	9.30	9.35	10.72	11.37	11.25	10.72	10.22
Asset Turnover	2.16	2.14	2.18	2.11	2.11	2.16	1.95	1.84
Current Ratio	1.13	1.03	1.02	0.99	0.97	1.00	1.07	1.31
Debt to Equity	...	...	...	...	...	64.75	3.81	2.39
Price Range	98.90-75.33	90.15-75.33	91.34-75.39	96.44-82.95	93.74-73.26	79.10-56.02	60.82-43.17	51.55-32.34
P/E Ratio	23.33-17.77	20.40-17.04	19.19-15.84	18.33-15.77	18.13-14.17	16.31-11.55	15.52-11.01	15.91-9.98
Average Yield %	4.74	4.86	4.60	4.01	3.74	4.21	4.70	5.14

Address: 120 Park Avenue, New York, NY 10017
Telephone: 917-663-2000
Fax: 917-663-5372

Web Site: www.pmi.com
Officers: Louis C. Camilleri - Chairman, Chief Executive Officer Charles R. Wall - Vice-Chairman

Auditors: PricewaterhouseCoopers SA
Investor Contact: 191 766-32233
Transfer Agents: ComputerShare LLC, Providence, RI

PHILLIPS 66

Exchange	Symbol	Price	52Wk Range	Yield	P/E
NYS	PSX	$80.36 (5/31/2016)	93.68-70.55	3.14	12.05

*7 Year Price Score N/A ***NYSE Composite Index=100** ***12 Month Price Score 99.80**

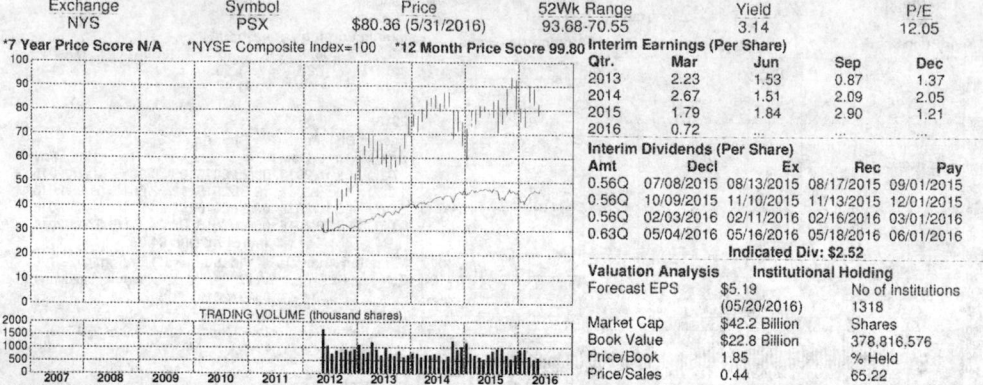

Interim Earnings (Per Share)

Qtr.	Mar	Jun	Sep	Dec
2013	2.23	1.53	0.87	1.37
2014	2.67	1.51	2.09	2.05
2015	1.79	1.84	2.90	1.21
2016	0.72			

Interim Dividends (Per Share)

Amt	Decl	Ex	Rec	Pay
0.56Q	07/08/2015	08/13/2015	08/17/2015	09/01/2015
0.56Q	10/09/2015	11/10/2015	11/13/2015	12/01/2015
0.56Q	02/03/2016	02/11/2016	02/16/2016	03/01/2016
0.63Q	05/04/2016	05/16/2016	05/18/2016	06/01/2016

Indicated Div: $2.52

Valuation Analysis   Institutional Holding

Forecast EPS	$5.19 (05/20/2016)	No of Institutions	1318
Market Cap	$42.2 Billion	Shares	378,816,576
Book Value	$22.8 Billion	% Held	65.22
Price/Book	1.85		
Price/Sales	0.44		

TRADING VOLUME (thousand shares)

Business Summary: Refining & Marketing (MIC: 9.1.2 SIC: 2911 NAIC: 324110)

Phillips 66 is an energy manufacturing and logistics company with midstream, chemicals, refining, and marketing and specialties businesses. Co.'s operating segments include: Midstream, which gathers, processes, transports and markets natural gas; and transports, fractionates and markets natural gas liquids; Chemicals, which manufactures and markets petrochemicals and plastics on a worldwide basis; Refining, which buys, sells and refines crude oil and other feedstocks at 14 refineries in the U.S. and Europe; and Marketing and Specialties, which purchases for resale and markets refined petroleum products (such as gasolines, distillates and aviation fuels), mainly in the U.S. and Europe.

Recent Developments: For the quarter ended Mar 31 2016, net income decreased 60.1% to US$398.0 million from US$997.0 million in the year-earlier quarter. Revenues were US$17.76 billion, down 24.2% from US$23.43 billion the year before. Direct operating expenses declined 27.2% to US$12.95 billion from US$17.79 billion in the comparable period the year before. Indirect operating expenses decreased 0.9% to US$4.21 billion from US$4.25 billion in the equivalent prior-year period.

Prospects: Our evaluation of Phillips 66 Inc. as of June 19, 2016 is the result of our systematic analysis on three basic characteristics: earnings strength, relative valuation, and recent stock price movement. The company has suffered a very negative trend in earnings per share over the past 5 quarters. However, while recent estimates for the company have been lowered by analysts, PSX has posted results that fell short of analysts expectations. Based on operating earnings yield, the company is undervalued when compared to all of the companies in our coverage universe. Share price changes over the past year indicates that PSX will perform very well over the near term.

Financial Data
(US$ in Millions)

	3 Mos	12/31/2015	12/31/2014	12/31/2013	12/31/2012	12/31/2011	12/31/2010	12/31/2009
Earnings Per Share	6.67	7.73	8.33	6.02	6.48	...	...	...
Cash Flow Per Share	8.69	10.53	6.24	9.83	6.81	...	...	...
Tang Book Value Per Share	35.41	35.74	31.88	30.76	26.79	...	...	...
Dividends Per Share	2.240	2.180	1.890	1.327	0.450	...	...	...
Dividend Payout %	33.58	28.20	22.69	22.05	6.94	...	...	...
Income Statement								
Total Revenue	17,760	100,949	164,093	174,809	182,922	200,614	148,656	113,951
EBITDA	962	7,432	7,007	6,748	7,790	7,549	2,200	1,727
Depn & Amortn	280	1,078	995	947	913	908	880	879
Income Before Taxes	596	6,044	5,745	5,526	6,631	6,624	1,319	847
Income Taxes	198	1,764	1,654	1,844	2,500	1,844	579	368
Net Income	385	4,227	4,762	3,726	4,124	4,775	735	476
Average Shares	534	546	571	618	636	...	...	...
Balance Sheet								
Current Assets	11,216	12,256	16,696	19,237	17,962	13,948	14,704	...
Total Assets	48,246	48,580	48,741	49,798	48,073	43,211	44,955	...
Current Liabilities	7,419	7,531	11,094	12,931	12,442	12,384	12,503	...
Long-Term Obligations	8,803	8,843	7,842	6,131	6,961	361	388	...
Total Liabilities	25,458	25,480	27,151	27,848	27,298	19,947	18,954	...
Stockholders' Equity	22,788	23,100	21,590	21,950	20,775	23,264	26,001	...
Shares Outstanding	525	529	546	590	623	...	...	...
Statistical Record								
Return on Assets %	7.45	8.69	9.67	7.61	9.01	10.83	...	...
Return on Equity %	16.27	18.92	21.87	17.44	18.68	19.38	...	...
EBITDA Margin %	5.42	7.36	4.27	3.86	4.26	3.76	1.48	1.52
Net Margin %	2.17	4.19	2.90	2.13	2.25	2.38	0.49	0.42
Asset Turnover	1.96	2.07	3.33	3.57	4.00	4.55	...	...
Current Ratio	1.51	1.63	1.50	1.49	1.44	1.13	1.18	...
Debt to Equity	0.39	0.38	0.36	0.28	0.34	0.02	0.01	...
Price Range	93.68-70.55	93.68-59.09	87.51-65.09	77.13-50.58	53.58-29.35	...	...	...
P/E Ratio	14.04-10.58	12.12-7.64	10.51-7.81	12.81-8.40	8.27-4.53	...	...	...
Average Yield %	2.74	2.74	2.40	2.14	1.09	...	...	...

Address: 3010 Briarpark Drive, Houston, TX 77042 **Telephone:** 281-293-6600	**Web Site:** www.Phillips66.com **Officers:** Greg C. Garland - Chairman, President, Chief Executive Officer Tim G. Taylor - President, Executive Vice President	**Auditors:** Ernst & Young LLP **Investor Contact:** 800-624-6440 **Transfer Agents:** Computershare, Canton, MA

PIEDMONT NATURAL GAS CO INC

Exchange	Symbol	Price	52Wk Range	Yield	P/E	Div Achiever
NYS	PNY	$60.06 (5/31/2016)	60.06-35.28	2.26	35.33	36 Years

*7 Year Price Score 127.39 *NYSE Composite Index=100* ***12 Month Price Score 115.98**

Interim Earnings (Per Share)

Qtr.	Jan	Apr	Jul	Oct
2012-13	1.18	0.74	(0.03)	(0.09)
2013-14	1.26	0.80	(0.09)	(0.12)
2014-15	1.18	0.84	(0.10)	(0.18)
2015-16	1.20	0.78	...	...

Interim Dividends (Per Share)

Amt	Decl	Ex	Rec	Pay
0.33Q	09/02/2015	09/22/2015	09/24/2015	10/15/2015
0.33Q	12/11/2015	12/22/2015	12/24/2015	01/15/2016
0.34Q	03/09/2016	03/22/2016	03/25/2016	04/15/2016
0.34Q	06/07/2016	06/22/2016	06/24/2016	07/15/2016

Indicated Div: $1.36 (Div. Reinv. Plan)

Valuation Analysis | **Institutional Holding**

Forecast EPS	$1.92	No of Institutions
	(05/20/2016)	382
Market Cap	$4.9 Billion	Shares
Book Value	$1.6 Billion	57,963,268
Price/Book	3.14	% Held
Price/Sales	4.24	53.61

Business Summary: Gas Utilities (MIC: 3.3.1 SIC: 4924 NAIC: 221210)

Piedmont Natural Gas Company is an energy services company whose principal business is the distribution of natural gas to residential, commercial, industrial and power generation customers in portions of North Carolina, South Carolina and Tennessee. Co. has three reportable business segments: regulated utility, which includes the operations of merchandising and its related service work and home service agreements; regulated non-utility activities, which consists of Co.'s equity method investments in joint venture regulated energy-related businesses; and unregulated non-utility activities, which consists of Co.'s equity method investment in an unregulated energy-related joint venture.

Recent Developments: For the quarter ended Apr 30 2016, net income decreased 4.5% to US$63.4 million from US$66.4 million in the year-earlier quarter. Revenues were US$350.2 million, down 17.6% from US$424.9 million the year before. Operating income was US$71.8 million versus US$75.1 million in the prior-year quarter, a decrease of 4.4%. Direct operating expenses declined 36.9% to US$125.8 million from US$199.3 million in the comparable period the year before. Indirect operating expenses increased 1.3% to US$152.5 million from US$150.5 million in the equivalent prior-year period.

Prospects: Our evaluation of Piedmont Natural Gas Co. Inc. as of June 19, 2016 is the result of our systematic analysis on three basic characteristics: earnings strength, relative valuation, and recent stock price movement. The company has managed to produce a neutral trend in earnings per share over the past 5 quarters. However, while recent estimates for the company have been lowered by analysts, PNY has posted results that fell short of analysts expectations. Based on operating earnings yield, the company is about fairly valued when compared to all of the companies in our coverage universe. Share price changes over the past year indicates that PNY will perform very well over the near term.

Financial Data

(US$ in Thousands)	6 Mos	3 Mos	10/31/2015	10/31/2014	10/31/2013	10/31/2012	10/31/2011	10/31/2010
Earnings Per Share	1.70	1.76	1.73	1.84	1.78	1.66	1.57	1.96
Cash Flow Per Share	3.24	4.27	4.71	5.53	4.18	4.22	4.32	4.99
Tang Book Value Per Share	18.50	18.00	17.03	16.04	14.98	13.54	13.11	12.67
Dividends Per Share	1.330	1.320	1.310	1.270	1.230	1.190	1.150	1.110
Dividend Payout %	78.24	75.00	75.72	69.02	69.10	71.69	73.25	56.63
Income Statement								
Total Revenue	811,523	461,337	1,371,718	1,469,988	1,278,229	1,122,780	1,433,905	1,552,295
EBITDA	342,028	204,629	390,107	379,548	331,452	297,449	308,648	347,181
Depn & Amortn	67,730	33,686	128,704	118,996	112,207	103,192	102,829	98,484
Income Before Taxes	240,646	153,875	192,772	205,866	194,307	174,160	161,827	204,976
Income Taxes	103,211	65,287	90,222	94,818	85,946	78,217	72,286	91,876
Net Income	161,222	97,790	137,011	143,801	134,417	119,847	113,568	141,954
Average Shares	81,388	81,266	79,231	78,193	75,333	72,278	72,266	72,525
Balance Sheet								
Current Assets	278,965	421,921	255,937	347,950	348,056	305,642	286,021	327,840
Total Assets	5,464,260	5,506,380	5,110,750	4,784,253	4,368,609	3,769,939	3,242,541	3,053,275
Current Liabilities	652,891	797,091	635,596	621,986	716,650	592,551	534,132	498,560
Long-Term Obligations	1,524,113	1,523,896	1,523,677	1,424,430	1,174,857	975,000	675,000	671,922
Total Liabilities	3,912,968	3,997,972	3,684,438	3,475,651	3,180,013	2,742,935	2,245,618	2,088,334
Stockholders' Equity	1,551,292	1,508,408	1,426,312	1,308,602	1,188,596	1,027,004	996,923	964,941
Shares Outstanding	81,196	81,072	80,883	78,531	76,099	72,250	72,318	72,282
Statistical Record								
Return on Assets %	2.69	2.69	2.77	3.14	3.30	3.41	3.61	4.60
Return on Equity %	9.31	9.80	10.02	11.52	12.13	11.81	11.58	15.00
EBITDA Margin %	42.15	44.36	28.44	25.82	25.93	26.49	21.52	22.37
Net Margin %	19.87	21.20	9.99	9.78	10.52	10.67	7.92	9.14
Asset Turnover	0.22	0.23	0.28	0.32	0.31	0.32	0.46	0.50
Current Ratio	0.43	0.53	0.40	0.56	0.49	0.52	0.54	0.66
Debt to Equity	0.98	1.01	1.07	1.09	0.99	0.95	0.68	0.70
Price Range	60.00-35.28	59.24-35.19	57.82-35.19	38.01-32.03	35.20-28.77	34.43-29.21	33.29-25.99	29.70-22.74
P/E Ratio	35.29-20.75	33.66-19.99	33.42-20.34	20.66-17.41	19.78-16.16	20.74-17.60	21.20-16.55	15.15-11.60
Average Yield %	2.75	3.07	3.42	3.65	3.74	3.74	3.88	4.18

Address: 4720 Piedmont Row Drive, Charlotte, NC 28210 **Telephone:** 704-364-3120	**Web Site:** www.piedmontng.com **Officers:** Thomas E. Skains - Chairman, President, Chief Executive Officer Karl W. Newlin - Senior Vice President, Chief Financial Officer	**Auditors:** Deloitte & Touche LLP **Investor Contact:** 704-731-4952 **Transfer Agents:** Wells Fargo Shareowner Services, St. Paul, MN

PIEDMONT OFFICE REALTY TRUST INC

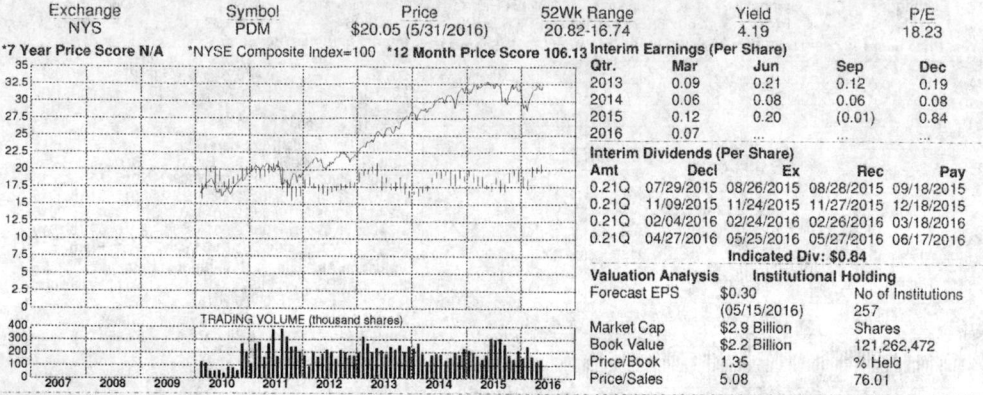

Exchange	Symbol	Price	52Wk Range	Yield	P/E
NYS	PDM	$20.05 (5/31/2016)	20.82-16.74	4.19	18.23

*7 Year Price Score N/A ***NYSE Composite Index=100** ***12 Month Price Score 106.13**

Interim Earnings (Per Share)

Qtr.	Mar	Jun	Sep	Dec
2013	0.09	0.21	0.12	0.19
2014	0.06	0.08	0.06	0.08
2015	0.12	0.20	(0.01)	0.84
2016	0.07	...	...	...

Interim Dividends (Per Share)

Amt	Decl	Ex	Rec	Pay
0.21Q	07/29/2015	08/26/2015	08/28/2015	09/18/2015
0.21Q	11/09/2015	11/24/2015	11/27/2015	12/18/2015
0.21Q	02/04/2016	02/24/2016	02/26/2016	03/18/2016
0.21Q	04/27/2016	05/25/2016	05/27/2016	06/17/2016

Indicated Div: $0.84

Valuation Analysis   **Institutional Holding**

Forecast EPS	$0.30	No of Institutions	257
	(05/15/2016)		
Market Cap	$2.9 Billion	Shares	121,262,472
Book Value	$2.2 Billion	% Held	
Price/Book	1.35	% Held	76.01
Price/Sales	5.08		

Business Summary: REITs (MIC: 5.3.1 SIC: 6798 NAIC: 525930)

Piedmont Office Realty Trust is a self-managed real estate investment trust engaged in the acquisition, development, management, and ownership of commercial real estate properties. Co. conducts business primarily through Piedmont Operating Partnership, L.P., performing the management of its buildings through two subsidiaries, Piedmont Government Services, LLC and Piedmont Office Management, LLC. As of Dec 31 2014, Co. owned interests in 74 office properties, one redevelopment asset, and one office building through an unconsolidated joint venture. Co.'s primary markets are Atlanta, Boston, Chicago, Dallas, Houston, Los Angeles, Minneapolis, New York, and Washington, D.C.

Recent Developments: For the quarter ended Mar 31 2016, net income decreased 46.1% to US$10.4 million from US$19.2 million in the year-earlier quarter. Revenues were US$138.0 million, down 7.8% from US$149.8 million the year before.

Prospects: Our evaluation of Piedmont Office Realty Trust Inc. as of June 19, 2016 is the result of our systematic analysis on three basic characteristics: earnings strength, relative valuation, and recent stock price movement. The company has generated a negative trend in earnings per share over the past 5 quarters. However, while recent estimates for the company have been lowered by analysts, PDM has posted results that fell short of analysts expectations. Based on operating earnings yield, the company is overvalued when compared to all of the companies in our coverage universe. Share price changes over the past year indicates that PDM will perform well over the near term.

Financial Data
(US$ in Thousands)

	3 Mos	12/31/2015	12/31/2014	12/31/2013	12/31/2012	12/31/2011	12/31/2010	12/31/2009
Earnings Per Share	1.10	1.15	0.28	0.60	0.55	1.30	0.70	0.47
Cash Flow Per Share	1.54	1.44	1.40	1.30	1.31	1.56	1.61	1.78
Tang Book Value Per Share	13.64	13.27	13.35	14.00	14.35	14.55	14.56	15.10
Dividends Per Share	0.840	0.840	0.810	0.800	0.800	1.260	1.260	1.260
Dividend Payout %	76.36	73.04	289.29	133.33	145.45	96.92	180.00	268.09
Income Statement								
Total Revenue	138,012	584,769	566,252	554,505	536,382	541,642	588,838	604,884
EBITDA	76,558	212,633	253,554	274,667	240,757	260,673	297,354	254,440
Depn & Amortn	49,892	134,503	138,679	123,566	113,649	109,730	104,490	106,073
Income Before Taxes	10,281	4,132	40,429	75,166	62,918	87,900	123,592	75,074
Net Income	10,372	172,990	43,348	98,728	93,204	225,041	120,379	74,700
Average Shares	145,791	150,880	154,585	165,137	170,441	172,980	170,967	158,580
Balance Sheet								
Current Assets	4,732	31,780	40,017	38,118	160,294	269,213	190,724	138,446
Total Assets	4,355,017	4,434,535	4,795,501	4,666,088	4,254,875	4,447,834	4,373,480	4,395,345
Current Liabilities	103,894	128,465	133,988	128,818	127,263	122,986	112,648	97,747
Long-Term Obligations	2,002,918	2,029,510	2,277,589	2,002,205	1,416,525	1,472,525	1,402,525	1,516,525
Total Liabilities	2,196,383	2,239,116	2,485,095	2,206,538	1,615,989	1,676,015	1,606,258	1,719,015
Stockholders' Equity	2,158,634	2,195,419	2,310,406	2,459,550	2,638,886	2,771,819	2,767,222	2,676,330
Shares Outstanding	145,093	145,511	154,324	157,460	167,556	172,629	172,658	158,916
Statistical Record								
Return on Assets %	3.58	3.75	0.92	2.21	2.14	5.10	2.75	1.67
Return on Equity %	7.39	7.68	1.82	3.87	3.44	8.13	4.42	2.72
EBITDA Margin %	55.47	36.36	44.78	49.53	44.89	48.13	50.50	42.06
Net Margin %	7.52	29.58	7.66	17.80	17.38	41.55	20.44	12.35
Asset Turnover	0.12	0.13	0.12	0.12	0.12	0.12	0.13	0.14
Current Ratio	0.05	0.25	0.30	0.30	1.26	2.19	1.69	1.42
Debt to Equity	0.93	0.92	0.99	0.81	0.54	0.53	0.51	0.57
Price Range	20.42-16.74	20.01-16.74	20.00-16.09	20.94-15.96	18.91-16.19	21.25-15.42	20.36-15.60	...
P/E Ratio	18.56-15.22	17.40-14.56	71.43-57.46	34.90-26.60	34.38-29.44	16.35-11.86	29.09-22.29	...
Average Yield %	4.58	4.56	4.43	4.33	4.60	6.70	6.73	...

Address: 11695 Johns Creek Parkway Ste. 350, Johns Creek, GA 30097 **Telephone:** 770-418-8800	**Web Site:** www.piedmontreit.com **Officers:** Michael R. Buchanan - Chairman Donald A. Miller - President, Chief Executive Officer	**Auditors:** Ernst & Young LLP **Transfer Agents:** Computershare Inc.

PINNACLE FOODS INC.

Exchange	Symbol	Price	52Wk Range	Yield	P/E
NYS	PF	$42.13 (5/31/2016)	47.41-39.89	2.42	25.38

*7 Year Price Score N/A   ***NYSE Composite Index=100**   ***12 Month Price Score 98.18**

TRADING VOLUME (thousand shares)

Interim Earnings (Per Share)

Qtr.	Mar	Jun	Sep	Dec
2013	0.29	(0.28)	0.35	0.50
2014	0.35	0.30	1.16	0.31
2015	0.35	0.37	0.41	0.67
2016	0.21	...	...	...

Interim Dividends (Per Share)

Amt	Decl	Ex	Rec	Pay
0.255Q	09/16/2015	09/24/2015	09/28/2015	10/09/2015
0.255Q	12/09/2015	12/17/2015	12/21/2015	01/08/2016
0.255Q	02/11/2016	02/19/2016	02/23/2016	04/08/2016
0.255Q	05/26/2016	06/03/2016	06/07/2016	07/08/2016

Indicated Div: $1.02

Valuation Analysis		Institutional Holding	
Forecast EPS	$2.11	No of Institutions	
	(05/20/2016)	319	
Market Cap	$4.9 Billion	Shares	
Book Value	$1.8 Billion	112,915,296	
Price/Book	2.72	% Held	
Price/Sales	1.79	92.83	

Business Summary: Food (MIC: 1.2.1 SIC: 2099 NAIC: 311999)

Pinnacle Foods is a holding company. Co. manufactures and markets food products. Co. has three segments: Birds Eye Frozen, which manages its Leadership Brands in the U.S. retail frozen vegetables (Birds Eye), frozen bagged meals (Birds Eye Voila!), and frozen seafood (Van de Kamp's and Mrs. Paul's) categories, among others; Duncan Hines Grocery, which manages its Leadership Brands in the baking mixes and frostings (Duncan Hines), pickles (Vlasic), salad dressings (Wish-Bone and Western) and syrups (Mrs. Butterworth's and Log Cabin) categories, among others; and Specialty Foods, which consists of snacks (Tim's Cascade and Snyder of Berlin) and its foodservice and private label businesses.

Recent Developments: For the quarter ended Mar 27 2016, net income decreased 40.2% to US$24.8 million from US$41.5 million in the year-earlier quarter. Revenues were US$754.3 million, up 13.4% from US$665.3 million the year before. Operating income was US$80.3 million versus US$88.5 million in the prior-year quarter, a decrease of 9.3%. Direct operating expenses rose 12.6% to US$555.7 million from US$493.6 million in the comparable period the year before. Indirect operating expenses increased 42.1% to US$118.3 million from US$83.2 million in the equivalent prior-year period.

Prospects: Our evaluation of Pinnacle Foods Inc. as of June 19, 2016 is the result of our systematic analysis on three basic characteristics: earnings strength, relative valuation, and recent stock price movement. The company has generated a negative trend in earnings per share over the past 5 quarters and while recent estimates for the company have remained steady, PF has posted results that fell short of analysts expectations. Based on operating earnings yield, the company is about fairly valued when compared to all of the companies in our coverage universe. Share price changes over the past year indicates that PF will perform well over the near term.

Financial Data
(US$ in Thousands)

	3 Mos	12/27/2015	12/28/2014	12/29/2013	12/30/2012	12/25/2011	12/26/2010
Earnings Per Share	1.66	1.81	2.13	0.82	0.61	(0.58)	0.30
Cash Flow Per Share	3.26	3.22	4.77	2.46	2.46	2.52	3.76
Dividends Per Share	1.000	0.980	0.890	0.570	...	...	...
Dividend Payout %	60.24	54.14	41.78	69.51	...	...	...
Income Statement							
Total Revenue	754,255	2,655,792	2,591,183	2,463,802	2,478,485	2,469,562	2,436,703
EBITDA	103,397	500,808	578,981	355,387	365,889	255,565	326,031
Depn & Amortn	23,116	76,106	66,710	62,350	82,295	72,299	60,879
Income Before Taxes	48,718	336,387	416,218	160,824	85,220	(24,811)	29,436
Income Taxes	23,881	123,879	167,800	71,475	32,701	22,103	7,399
Net Income	24,836	212,508	248,418	89,349	52,519	(46,914)	22,037
Average Shares	117,613	117,323	116,885	108,618	86,494	81,315	73,638
Balance Sheet							
Current Assets	929,941	857,634	715,709	792,309	705,277	725,482	...
Total Assets	6,516,680	5,340,083	5,200,945	5,081,191	4,399,988	4,451,621	...
Current Liabilities	485,315	405,647	383,436	331,304	333,724	334,148	...
Long-Term Obligations	3,133,226	2,272,932	2,285,984	2,476,167	2,576,386	2,738,650	...
Total Liabilities	4,712,089	3,534,554	3,486,956	3,483,150	3,511,262	3,606,269	...
Stockholders' Equity	1,804,591	1,805,529	1,713,989	1,598,041	888,726	845,352	...
Shares Outstanding	116,617	116,619	116,293	117,231	81,210	81,272	81,356
Statistical Record							
Return on Assets %	3.35	4.04	4.85	1.89	1.17	...	...
Return on Equity %	11.11	12.11	15.04	7.21	5.96	...	...
EBITDA Margin %	13.71	18.86	22.34	14.42	14.76	10.35	13.38
Net Margin %	3.29	8.00	9.59	3.63	2.12	N.M.	0.90
Asset Turnover	0.47	0.51	0.51	0.52	0.55	...	...
Current Ratio	1.92	2.11	1.87	2.39	2.11	2.17	...
Debt to Equity	1.74	1.26	1.33	1.55	2.90	3.24	...
Price Range	47.41-39.79	47.41-34.77	35.60-26.51	28.56-22.21	...	...	...
P/E Ratio	28.56-23.97	26.19-19.21	16.71-12.45	34.83-27.09	...	...	...
Average Yield %	2.31	2.35	2.86	2.21	...	...	...

Address: 399 Jefferson Road, Parsippany, NJ 07054 **Telephone:** 973 541-6620	**Web Site:** www.pinnaclefoods.com **Officers:** Mark A. Clouse - Chief Executive Officer Craig D. Steeneck - Chief Financial Officer, Interim Chief Executive Officer, Executive Vice President	**Auditors:** Deloitte & Touche LLP **Transfer Agents:** Computershare Trust Company, N.A.

PINNACLE WEST CAPITAL CORP

Exchange	Symbol	Price	52Wk Range	Yield	P/E
NYS	PNW	$73.59 (5/31/2016)	75.49-56.31	3.40	19.31

*7 Year Price Score 109.55 *NYSE Composite Index=100 ***12 Month Price Score 110.34**

Interim Earnings (Per Share)

Qtr.	Mar	Jun	Sep	Dec
2013	0.22	1.18	2.04	0.22
2014	0.14	1.19	2.20	0.05
2015	0.14	1.10	2.30	0.37
2016	0.04	...	...	...

Interim Dividends (Per Share)

Amt	Decl	Ex	Rec	Pay
0.595Q	06/17/2015	07/30/2015	08/03/2015	09/01/2015
0.625Q	10/21/2015	10/29/2015	11/02/2015	12/01/2015
0.625Q	12/16/2015	01/28/2016	02/01/2016	03/01/2016
0.625Q	04/21/2016	04/28/2016	05/02/2016	06/01/2016

Indicated Div: $2.50 (Div. Reinv. Plan)

Valuation Analysis / **Institutional Holding**

Forecast EPS	$4.00 (05/20/2016)	No of Institutions	596
Market Cap	$8.2 Billion	Shares	95,885,064
Book Value	$4.6 Billion	% Held	80.10
Price/Book	1.78		
Price/Sales	2.34		

Business Summary: Electric Utilities (MIC: 3.1.1 SIC: 4911 NAIC: 221122)

Pinnacle West Capital is a holding company. Through its main subsidiary, Arizona Public Service Company (APS), Co. is an electric utility that provides either retail or wholesale electric service to most of the state of Arizona, with the major exceptions of about one-half of the Phoenix metropolitan area, the Tucson metropolitan area and Mohave County in northwestern Arizona. Co.'s business segment is its regulated electricity segment, which consists of regulated retail and wholesale electricity businesses and related activities, and includes electricity generation, transmission and distribution. At Dec 31 2015, APS provided electric service to approximately 1.2 million customers.

Recent Developments: For the quarter ended Mar 31 2016, net income decreased 55.0% to US$9.3 million from US$20.7 million in the year-earlier quarter. Revenues were US$677.2 million, up 0.9% from US$671.2 million the year before. Operating income was US$50.2 million versus US$67.7 million in the prior-year quarter, a decrease of 25.9%. Direct operating expenses rose 6.0% to US$464.5 million from US$438.2 million in the comparable period the year before. Indirect operating expenses decreased 1.7% to US$162.5 million from US$165.4 million in the equivalent prior-year period.

Prospects: Our evaluation of Pinnacle West Capital Corp. as of June 19, 2016 is the result of our systematic analysis on three basic characteristics: earnings strength, relative valuation, and recent stock price movement. The company has generated a negative trend in earnings per share over the past 5 quarters and while recent estimates for the company have remained steady, PNW has posted results that fell short of analysts expectations. Based on operating earnings yield, the company is about fairly valued when compared to all of the companies in our coverage universe. Share price changes over the past year indicates that PNW will perform very well over the near term.

Financial Data

(US$ in Thousands)	3 Mos	12/31/2015	12/31/2014	12/31/2013	12/31/2012	12/31/2011	12/31/2010	12/31/2009
Earnings Per Share	3.81	3.92	3.58	3.66	3.45	3.09	3.27	0.67
Cash Flow Per Share	9.83	9.86	9.94	10.49	10.66	10.32	7.04	10.19
Tang Book Value Per Share	41.39	41.30	39.50	38.07	36.20	34.98	33.86	32.69
Dividends Per Share	2.440	2.410	2.297	2.203	2.120	2.100	2.100	2.100
Dividend Payout %	64.04	61.48	64.18	60.18	61.45	67.96	64.22	313.43
Income Statement								
Total Revenue	677,167	3,495,443	3,491,632	3,454,628	3,301,804	3,241,379	3,263,645	3,297,101
EBITDA	59,028	1,309,409	1,335,338	1,353,886	1,196,826	1,075,945	1,067,559	346,151
Depn & Amortn	2,388	573,281	537,244	523,512	364,546	338,627	350,326	35,000
Income Before Taxes	11,240	593,131	644,401	670,557	656,310	539,238	514,919	104,696
Income Taxes	1,914	136,941	220,705	230,591	237,317	183,604	164,321	37,827
Net Income	4,453	437,257	397,595	406,074	381,542	339,473	350,053	68,330
Average Shares	111,847	111,552	111,178	110,806	110,527	109,864	107,138	101,264
Balance Sheet								
Current Assets	826,025	890,516	973,435	1,043,609	1,005,726	956,470	931,930	928,737
Total Assets	15,185,101	15,028,258	14,313,532	13,508,686	13,379,615	13,111,018	12,362,703	11,808,155
Current Liabilities	1,585,902	1,442,317	1,559,143	1,618,644	1,083,542	1,342,705	1,310,736	1,083,160
Long-Term Obligations	3,463,032	3,462,391	3,031,215	2,796,465	3,199,088	3,019,054	3,045,794	3,370,524
Total Liabilities	10,585,102	10,444,341	9,946,039	9,314,216	9,406,809	9,289,168	8,679,376	8,492,046
Stockholders' Equity	4,599,999	4,583,917	4,367,493	4,194,470	3,972,806	3,821,850	3,683,327	3,316,109
Shares Outstanding	111,139	110,980	110,571	110,181	109,742	109,245	108,769	101,434
Statistical Record								
Return on Assets %	2.87	2.98	2.86	3.02	2.87	2.67	2.90	0.58
Return on Equity %	9.46	9.77	9.29	9.94	9.76	9.05	10.00	2.02
EBITDA Margin %	8.72	37.46	38.24	39.19	36.25	33.19	32.71	10.50
Net Margin %	0.66	12.51	11.39	11.75	11.56	10.47	10.73	2.07
Asset Turnover	0.24	0.24	0.25	0.26	0.25	0.25	0.27	0.28
Current Ratio	0.52	0.62	0.62	0.64	0.93	0.71	0.71	0.86
Debt to Equity	0.75	0.76	0.69	0.67	0.81	0.79	0.83	1.02
Price Range	75.07-56.31	72.47-56.31	70.63-51.28	61.48-50.98	54.32-46.06	48.71-37.98	42.37-34.50	37.73-23.00
P/E Ratio	19.70-14.78	18.49-14.36	19.73-14.32	16.80-13.93	15.74-13.35	15.76-12.29	12.96-10.55	56.31-34.33
Average Yield %	3.85	3.83	4.05	3.94	4.21	4.81	5.43	6.76

Address: 400 North Fifth Street, P.O. Box 53999, Phoenix, AZ 85072-3999
Telephone: 602-250-1000
Fax: 602-379-2625

Web Site: www.pinnaclewest.com
Officers: Donald E. Brandt - Chairman, President, Chief Executive Officer James R. Hatfield - Executive Vice President, Senior Vice President, Chief Financial Officer, Treasurer

Auditors: Deloitte & Touche LLP
Investor Contact: 602-250-5668
Transfer Agents: Computershare, Providence, RI

PIONEER NATURAL RESOURCES CO

Exchange	Symbol	Price	52Wk Range	Yield	P/E
NYS	PXD	$160.32 (5/31/2016)	168.72-107.24	0.05	N/A

*7 Year Price Score 97.67 *NYSE Composite Index=100 *12 Month Price Score 116.54

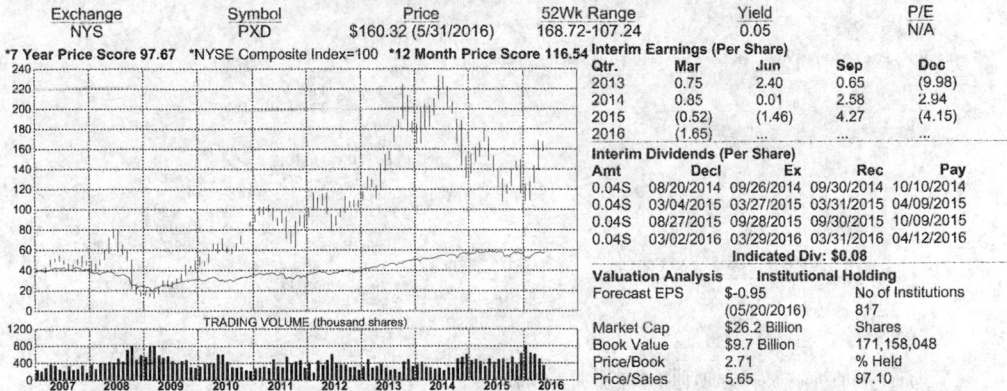

Interim Earnings (Per Share)

Qtr.	Mar	Jun	Sep	Dec
2013	0.75	2.40	0.65	(9.98)
2014	0.85	0.01	2.58	2.94
2015	(0.52)	(1.46)	4.27	(4.15)
2016	(1.65)	...	...	...

Interim Dividends (Per Share)

Amt	Decl	Ex	Rec	Pay
0.04S	08/20/2014	09/26/2014	09/30/2014	10/10/2014
0.04S	03/04/2015	03/27/2015	03/31/2015	04/09/2015
0.04S	08/27/2015	09/28/2015	09/30/2015	10/09/2015
0.04S	03/02/2016	03/29/2016	03/31/2016	04/12/2016

Indicated Div: $0.08

Valuation Analysis

	Institutional Holding	
Forecast EPS	$-0.95	No of Institutions
	(05/20/2016)	817
Market Cap	$26.2 Billion	Shares
Book Value	$9.7 Billion	171,158,048
Price/Book	2.71	% Held
Price/Sales	5.65	97.10

Business Summary: Production & Extraction (MIC: 9.1.1 SIC: 1311 NAIC: 211111)

Pioneer Natural Resources is a holding company. Through its subsidiaries, Co. is engaged as an oil and gas exploration and production company. Co. explores for, develops and produces oil and gas reserves, and sells oil, natural gas liquid and gas units. Co. has field operations in the Permian Basin in West Texas, the Eagle Ford Shale play in South Texas, the Raton field in southeastern Colorado and the West Panhandle field in the Texas Panhandle. As of Dec 31 2015, Co. had proved reserves of 664.4 million barrels of oil equivalent.

Recent Developments: For the quarter ended Mar 31 2016, loss from continuing operations was US$267.0 million compared with a loss of US$74.0 million in the year-earlier quarter. Net loss amounted to US$267.0 million versus a net loss of US$78.0 million in the year-earlier quarter. Revenues were US$685.0 million, down 21.2% from US$869.0 million the year before. Direct operating expenses rose 22.6% to US$781.0 million from US$637.0 million in the comparable period the year before. Indirect operating expenses decreased 9.0% from US$312.0 million from US$343.0 million in the equivalent prior-year period.

Prospects: Our evaluation of Pioneer Natural Resources Co as of June 19, 2016 is the result of our systematic analysis on three basic characteristics: earnings strength, relative valuation, and recent stock price movement. The company has enjoyed a very positive trend in earnings per share over the past 5 quarters. Because the company lacks sufficient analyst estimate data, we place greater weight on the historical EPS trend as the measure of earnings strength. Based on operating earnings yield, the company is overvalued when compared to all of the companies in our coverage universe. Share price changes over the past year indicates that PXD will perform very well over the near term.

Financial Data

(US$ in Thousands)	3 Mos	12/31/2015	12/31/2014	12/31/2013	12/31/2012	12/31/2011	12/31/2010	12/31/2009
Earnings Per Share	(2.99)	(1.83)	6.38	(6.16)	1.50	6.88	5.08	(0.46)
Cash Flow Per Share	7.75	8.38	16.43	15.76	14.90	13.09	11.17	4.76
Tang Book Value Per Share	57.57	54.20	55.77	44.36	43.70	42.60	33.15	28.21
Dividends Per Share	0.080	0.080	0.080	0.080	0.080	0.080	0.080	0.080
Dividend Payout %	...	...	1.25	...	5.33	1.16	1.57	...
Income Statement								
Total Revenue	685,000	4,825,000	5,055,000	3,719,510	3,228,308	2,786,585	2,471,590	1,711,516
EBITDA	(332,000)	1,386,000	3,132,000	801,293	1,502,725	1,589,626	1,608,335	632,570
Depn & Amortn	21,000	1,475,000	1,131,000	978,076	830,689	603,896	523,808	541,293
Income Before Taxes	(408,000)	(276,000)	1,817,000	(360,533)	467,814	804,070	901,443	(82,084)
Income Taxes	(141,000)	(10,000)	776,000	(10,589)	280,141	345,308	384,458	50,263
Net Income	(267,000)	(273,000)	930,000	(838,414)	192,285	834,489	605,208	(52,106)
Average Shares	162,000	149,000	144,000	136,130	126,320	119,215	116,330	114,176
Balance Sheet								
Current Assets	4,081,000	3,194,000	2,359,000	1,728,434	1,050,355	1,479,297	1,197,183	616,118
Total Assets	16,171,000	15,154,000	14,926,000	12,292,788	13,069,030	11,524,161	9,679,102	8,867,265
Current Liabilities	1,783,000	1,462,000	1,580,000	1,250,106	1,034,790	1,011,798	769,220	571,191
Long-Term Obligations	2,724,000	3,207,000	2,665,000	2,653,059	3,721,193	2,528,905	2,601,670	2,761,011
Total Liabilities	6,483,000	6,786,000	6,345,000	5,691,204	7,379,676	6,035,367	5,558,519	5,331,077
Stockholders' Equity	9,688,000	8,368,000	8,581,000	6,601,584	5,689,354	5,488,794	4,120,583	3,536,188
Shares Outstanding	163,556	149,379	149,000	142,627	123,355	121,856	115,308	114,375
Statistical Record								
Return on Assets %	N.M.	N.M.	6.83	N.M.	1.56	7.87	6.53	N.M.
Return on Equity %	N.M.	N.M.	12.25	N.M.	3.43	17.37	15.81	N.M.
EBITDA Margin %	N.M.	28.73	61.96	21.54	46.55	57.05	65.07	36.96
Net Margin %	N.M.	N.M.	18.40	N.M.	5.96	29.95	24.49	N.M.
Asset Turnover	0.30	0.32	0.37	0.29	0.26	0.26	0.27	0.19
Current Ratio	2.29	2.18	1.49	1.38	1.02	1.46	1.56	1.08
Debt to Equity	0.28	0.38	0.31	0.40	0.65	0.46	0.63	0.78
Price Range	180.23-107.24	180.23-107.24	233.07-130.60	224.95-106.59	116.24-78.78	104.66-61.82	87.53-43.62	49.55-12.10
P/E Ratio	...	...	36.53-20.47	...	77.49-52.52	15.21-8.99	17.23-8.59	...
Average Yield %	0.06	0.06	0.04	0.05	0.06	0.08	0.13	0.28

Address: 5205 N. O'Connor Blvd., Suite 200, Irving, TX 75039	**Web Site:** www.pxd.com	**Auditors:** Ernst & Young LLP
Telephone: 972-444-9001	**Officers:** Scott D. Sheffield - Chairman, Chief Executive Officer Timothy L. Dove - President, Chief Executive Officer, Chief Operating Officer	**Investor Contact:** 972-444-9001
Fax: 972-969 3587		**Transfer Agents:** Continental Stock Transfer & Trust Company, New York, NY

PITNEY BOWES INC

Exchange	Symbol	Price	52Wk Range	Yield	P/E
NYS	PBI	$18.63 (5/31/2016)	22.19-16.46	4.03	9.65

*7 Year Price Score 82.95 *NYSE Composite Index=100 *12 Month Price Score 99.39

Interim Earnings (Per Share)

Qtr.	Mar	Jun	Sep	Dec
2013	0.33	(0.05)	(0.03)	0.44
2014	0.22	0.46	0.65	0.31
2015	0.40	0.75	0.44	0.44
2016	0.30			

Interim Dividends (Per Share)

Amt	Decl	Ex	Rec	Pay
0.188Q	08/06/2015	08/19/2015	08/21/2015	09/11/2015
0.188Q	11/06/2015	11/18/2015	11/20/2015	12/11/2015
0.188Q	02/09/2016	02/17/2016	02/19/2016	03/12/2016
0.188Q	05/09/2016	05/25/2016	05/29/2016	06/13/2016

Indicated Div: $0.75 (Div. Reinv. Plan)

Valuation Analysis / Institutional Holding

Forecast EPS	$1.80 (05/15/2016)	No of Institutions 558
Market Cap	$3.6 Billion	Shares
Book Value	$123.3 Million	201,525,504
Price/Book	29.05	% Held
Price/Sales	1.01	84.88

TRADING VOLUME (thousand shares)

Business Summary: Office Equipment & Furniture (MIC: 7.5.1 SIC: 7372 NAIC: 511210)

Pitney Bowes is a technology company. Co. provides customer information management, location intelligence and customer engagement products and solutions. Co.'s business is organized around three sets of solutions: Small and Medium Business Solutions, Enterprise Business Solutions and Digital Commerce Solutions. The Small and Medium Business Solutions group includes the North America Mailing and International Mailing operations. The Enterprise Business Solutions group includes the Production Mail and Presort Services operations. The Digital Commerce Solutions group includes the sale and support services of non-equipment-based mailing.

Recent Developments: For the quarter ended Mar 31 2016, income from continuing operations decreased 26.3% to US$62.6 million from US$85.0 million in the year-earlier quarter. Net income decreased 26.5% to US$62.6 million from US$85.2 million in the year-earlier quarter. Revenues were US$844.6 million, down 5.2% from US$890.7 million the year before. Direct operating expenses declined 6.5% to US$365.2 million from US$390.5 million in the comparable period the year before. Indirect operating expenses increased 4.1% to US$379.7 million from US$364.6 million in the equivalent prior-year period.

Prospects: Our evaluation of Pitney Bowes Inc. as of June 19, 2016 is the result of our systematic analysis on three basic characteristics: earnings strength, relative valuation, and recent stock price movement. The company has produced a positive trend in earnings per share over the past 5 quarters and while recent estimates for the company have remained steady, PBI has posted results that fell short of analysts expectations. Based on operating earnings yield, the company is undervalued when compared to all of the companies in our coverage universe. Share price changes over the past year indicates that PBI will perform well over the near term.

Financial Data

(US$ in Thousands)	3 Mos	12/31/2015	12/31/2014	12/31/2013	12/31/2012	12/31/2011	12/31/2010	12/31/2009
Earnings Per Share	1.93	2.03	1.64	0.70	2.21	3.05	1.41	2.04
Cash Flow Per Share	2.44	2.58	3.25	3.10	3.29	4.56	4.62	3.99
Dividends Per Share	0.750	0.750	0.750	0.938	1.500	1.480	1.460	1.440
Dividend Payout %	38.86	36.95	45.73	133.93	67.87	48.52	103.55	70.59
Income Statement								
Total Revenue	844,589	3,578,060	3,821,504	3,869,401	4,904,015	5,277,974	5,425,254	5,569,171
EBITDA	163,265	906,199	765,646	751,541	1,003,999	825,547	978,801	1,166,882
Depn & Amortn	44,300	136,000	165,000	158,000	211,000	214,000	242,900	269,800
Income Before Taxes	99,664	610,825	431,196	403,177	604,613	414,281	534,577	693,176
Income Taxes	37,024	189,778	112,815	83,069	150,305	44,585	205,770	240,154
Net Income	58,046	407,943	333,755	142,835	445,163	617,480	292,379	423,445
Average Shares	193,181	200,945	203,961	202,957	201,366	202,766	206,753	207,322
Balance Sheet								
Current Assets	2,214,184	2,319,808	2,760,120	2,838,212	3,212,127	3,259,858	3,008,241	2,971,236
Total Assets	6,005,822	6,141,462	6,485,693	6,772,708	7,859,891	8,147,104	8,444,023	8,533,911
Current Liabilities	1,965,101	2,279,051	2,360,623	2,227,755	2,877,037	3,091,862	2,553,579	2,566,447
Long-Term Obligations	2,775,213	2,507,912	2,927,127	3,346,295	3,642,375	3,683,909	4,239,248	4,213,640
Total Liabilities	5,882,554	5,962,740	6,408,434	6,584,305	7,749,260	8,186,090	8,540,604	8,520,248
Stockholders' Equity	123,268	178,721	77,259	188,403	110,631	(38,986)	(96,581)	13,663
Shares Outstanding	192,240	195,521	201,027	202,082	200,884	199,751	203,431	207,197
Statistical Record								
Return on Assets %	6.36	6.46	5.03	1.95	5.55	7.44	3.44	4.90
Return on Equity %	432.51	318.73	251.26	95.53	1,239.30	...	...	423.55
EBITDA Margin %	19.33	25.33	20.04	19.42	20.47	15.64	18.04	20.95
Net Margin %	6.87	11.40	8.73	3.69	9.08	11.70	5.39	7.60
Asset Turnover	0.58	0.57	0.58	0.53	0.61	0.64	0.64	0.64
Current Ratio	1.13	1.02	1.17	1.27	1.12	1.05	1.18	1.16
Debt to Equity	22.51	14.03	37.89	17.76	32.92	...	...	308.40
Price Range	23.62-16.46	24.42-18.82	28.18-21.13	24.09-10.64	19.54-10.41	26.18-17.35	25.88-19.24	27.11-17.77
P/E Ratio	12.24-8.53	12.03-9.27	17.18-12.88	34.41-15.20	8.84-4.71	8.58-5.69	18.35-13.65	13.29-8.71
Average Yield %	3.62	3.45	2.93	5.67	10.01	6.71	6.44	6.25

Address: 3001 Summer Street, Stamford, CT 06926 Telephone: 203-356-5000 Fax: 203-351-7336	Web Site: www.pb.com Officers: Marc B. Lautenbach - President, Chief Executive Officer Michael Monahan - Executive Vice President, Chief Financial Officer, Chief Operating Officer	Auditors: PricewaterhouseCoopers LLP Investor Contact: 203-351-6349 Transfer Agents: Computershare Trust Company, N.A., Providence, RI

PLAINS ALL AMERICAN PIPELINE, L.P.

Exchange	Symbol	Price	52Wk Range	Yield	P/E	Div Achiever
NYS	PAA	$23.13 (5/31/2016)	47.80-15.44	12.11	47.20	16 Years

*7 Year Price Score 62.31 *NYSE Composite Index=100 *12 Month Price Score 78.05

Interim Earnings (Per Share)
Qtr.	Mar	Jun	Sep	Dec
2013	1.27	0.57	0.38	0.58
2014	0.73	0.45	0.52	0.68
2015	0.35	(0.06)	0.24	0.24
2016	0.07	...	...	...

Interim Dividends (Per Share)
Amt	Decl	Ex	Rec	Pay
0.695Q	07/07/2015	07/29/2015	07/31/2015	08/14/2015
0.70Q	10/07/2015	10/28/2015	10/30/2015	11/13/2015
0.70Q	01/12/2016	01/27/2016	01/29/2016	02/12/2016
0.70Q	04/07/2016	04/27/2016	04/29/2016	05/13/2016

Indicated Div: $2.80

Valuation Analysis / Institutional Holding
Forecast EPS	$1.22
	(05/20/2016)
Market Cap	$9.2 Billion
Book Value	N/A
Price/Book	N/A
Price/Sales	0.43

No of Institutions	571
Shares	286,554,432
% Held	64.08

Business Summary: Equipment & Services (MIC: 9.1.3 SIC: 4612 NAIC: 486110)

Plains All American Pipeline is a holding company. Co. owns and operates midstream energy infrastructure and provides logistics services for crude oil, natural gas liquids (NGL), natural gas and refined products. Co. has three operating segments: transportation, which transports crude oil and NGL on pipelines, gathering systems, trucks and barges; facilities, which provide storage, terminalling and throughput services for crude oil, refined products, NGL and natural gas, as well as NGL fractionation and isomerization services and natural gas and condensate processing services; and supply and logistics, which consists of the sale of gathered and bulk-purchased crude oil, and sales of NGL.

Recent Developments: For the quarter ended Mar 31 2016, net income decreased 28.5% to US$203.0 million from US$284.0 million in the year-earlier quarter. Revenues were US$4.11 billion, down 30.8% from US$5.94 billion the year before. Operating income was US$282.0 million versus US$372.0 million in the prior-year quarter, a decrease of 24.2%. Direct operating expenses declined 33.6% to US$3.35 billion from US$5.04 billion in the comparable period the year before. Indirect operating expenses decreased 8.9% to US$481.0 million from US$528.0 million in the equivalent prior-year period.

Prospects: Our evaluation of Plains All American Pipeline, L.P. as of June 19, 2016 is the result of our systematic analysis on three basic characteristics: earnings strength, relative valuation, and recent stock price movement. The company has enjoyed a very positive trend in earnings per share over the past 5 quarters. However, while recent estimates for the company have been lowered by analysts, PAA has posted better than expected results. Based on operating earnings yield, the company is about fairly valued when compared to all of the companies in our coverage universe. Share price changes over the past year indicates that PAA will perform very poorly over the near term.

Financial Data
(US$ in Thousands)

	3 Mos	12/31/2015	12/31/2014	12/31/2013	12/31/2012	12/31/2011	12/31/2010	12/31/2009
Earnings Per Share	0.49	0.77	2.38	2.80	2.40	2.44	1.20	1.66
Cash Flow Per Share	3.13	3.41	5.46	5.73	3.80	7.94	0.95	1.40
Dividends Per Share	2.780	2.755	2.550	2.325	2.110	1.952	1.877	1.811
Dividend Payout %	567.35	357.79	107.14	83.04	87.92	80.02	156.46	109.11
Income Statement								
Total Revenue	4,111,000	23,152,000	43,464,000	42,249,000	37,797,000	34,275,000	25,893,000	18,520,000
EBITDA	401,000	1,635,000	2,108,000	1,988,000	1,653,000	1,475,000	993,000	995,000
Depn & Amortn	114,000	380,000	319,000	259,000	222,000	196,000	235,000	216,000
Income Before Taxes	175,000	823,000	1,449,000	1,426,000	1,143,000	1,026,000	510,000	571,000
Income Taxes	19,000	100,000	171,000	99,000	54,000	45,000	(1,000)	6,000
Net Income	202,000	903,000	1,384,000	1,361,000	1,094,000	966,000	505,000	579,000
Average Shares	399,000	396,000	369,000	343,000	328,000	300,000	276,000	262,000
Balance Sheet								
Current Assets	2,780,000	2,969,000	4,179,000	4,964,000	5,147,000	4,351,000	4,381,000	3,658,000
Total Assets	22,297,000	22,288,000	22,256,000	20,360,000	19,235,000	15,381,000	13,703,000	12,358,000
Current Liabilities	3,063,000	3,407,000	4,755,000	5,411,000	5,183,000	4,511,000	4,215,000	3,782,000
Long-Term Obligations	9,153,000	10,375,000	8,762,000	6,715,000	6,320,000	4,520,000	4,631,000	4,142,000
Total Liabilities	12,984,000	14,407,000	14,123,000	12,716,000	12,598,000	9,931,000	9,361,000	8,262,000
Shares Outstanding	397,730	397,727	375,107	359,133	335,283	310,753	282,398	272,271
Statistical Record								
Return on Assets %	3.73	4.05	6.50	6.87	6.30	6.64	3.88	5.17
EBITDA Margin %	9.75	7.06	4.85	4.71	4.37	4.30	3.84	5.37
Net Margin %	4.91	3.90	3.18	3.22	2.89	2.82	1.95	3.13
Asset Turnover	0.97	1.04	2.04	2.13	2.18	2.36	1.99	1.65
Current Ratio	0.91	0.87	0.88	0.92	0.99	0.96	1.04	0.97
Price Range	51.64-15.44	52.59-18.72	60.76-45.38	59.49-45.24	46.76-36.40	36.73-28.52	32.41-25.84	26.52-17.34
P/E Ratio	105.39-31.51	68.30-24.31	25.53-19.07	21.25-16.16	19.48-15.17	15.05-11.69	27.00-21.53	15.97-10.45
Average Yield %	8.36	6.86	4.61	4.35	5.04	6.18	6.34	8.21

Address: 333 Clay Street, Suite 1600, Houston, TX 77002
Telephone: 713-646-4100

Web Site: www.plainsallamerican.com
Officers: Greg L. Armstrong - Chairman, Chief Executive Officer George N. Polydoros - Vice President

Auditors: PricewaterhouseCoopers LLP
Investor Contact: 713-646-4222
Transfer Agents: American Stock Transfer & Trust Company, Brooklyn, NY

PLANTRONICS, INC.

Exchange	Symbol	Price	52Wk Range	Yield	P/E
NYS	PLT	$44.52 (5/31/2016)	58.09-32.55	1.35	22.71

*7 Year Price Score 104.14 *NYSE Composite Index=100 *12 Month Price Score 82.46

Interim Earnings (Per Share)

Qtr.	Jun	Sep	Dec	Mar
2011-12	0.56	0.60	0.71	0.55
2012-13	0.55	0.61	0.66	0.67
2013-14	0.62	0.53	0.80	0.65
2014-15	0.68	0.65	0.71	0.60
2015-16	0.55	0.52	0.49	0.40

Interim Dividends (Per Share)

Amt	Decl	Ex	Rec	Pay
0.15Q	07/27/2015	08/18/2015	08/20/2015	09/10/2015
0.15Q	11/05/2015	11/18/2015	11/20/2015	12/10/2015
0.15Q	02/01/2016	02/17/2016	02/19/2016	03/10/2016
0.15Q	05/03/2016	05/18/2016	05/20/2016	06/10/2016

Indicated Div: $0.60

Valuation Analysis

Forecast EPS	$3.09
	(05/10/2016)
Market Cap	$1.5 Billion
Book Value	$312.4 Million
Price/Book	4.75
Price/Sales	1.73

Institutional Holding

No of Institutions	300
Shares	37,915,784
% Held	93.61

Business Summary: Manufacturing (MIC: 6.1.1 SIC: 3661 NAIC: 334210)

Plantronics designs, manufactures, and markets lightweight communications headsets, telephone headset systems, other communication endpoints, and accessories for the business and consumer markets. Co. also manufactures and markets specialty telephone products, such as telephones for the hearing impaired, and related products. Co.'s product categories are Enterprise, which includes headsets optimized for Unified Communications, other corded and cordless communication headsets, audio processors, and telephone systems; and Consumer, which includes Bluetooth® and corded products for mobile phone applications, personal computer and gaming headsets, and products for hearing impaired individuals.

Recent Developments: For the year ended Mar 31 2016, net income decreased 39.1% to US$68.4 million from US$112.3 million in the prior year. Revenues were US$856.9 million, down 0.9% from US$865.0 million the year before. Operating income was US$108.0 million versus US$149.1 million in the prior year, a decrease of 27.5%. Direct operating expenses rose 4.7% to US$422.2 million from US$403.4 million in the comparable period the year before. Indirect operating expenses increased 4.5% to US$326.6 million from US$312.5 million in the equivalent prior-year period.

Prospects: Our evaluation of Plantronics Inc. as of June 19, 2016 is the result of our systematic analysis on three basic characteristics: earnings strength, relative valuation, and recent stock price movement. The company has managed to produce a neutral trend in earnings per share over the past 5 quarters and while recent estimates for the company have remained steady, PLT has posted better than expected results. Based on operating earnings yield, the company is undervalued when compared to all of the companies in our coverage universe. Share price changes over the past year indicates that PLT will perform very poorly over the near term.

Financial Data
(US$ in Thousands)

	03/31/2016	03/31/2015	03/31/2014	03/31/2013	03/31/2012	03/31/2011	03/31/2010	03/31/2009
Earnings Per Share	1.96	2.63	2.59	2.49	2.41	2.21	1.16	(1.34)
Cash Flow Per Share	4.29	3.70	3.33	3.01	3.18	3.32	2.96	2.04
Tang Book Value Per Share	8.90	17.10	16.00	14.56	12.06	12.83	11.33	9.92
Dividends Per Share	0.600	0.600	0.400	0.400	0.200	0.200	0.200	0.200
Dividend Payout %	30.61	22.81	15.44	16.06	8.30	9.05	17.24	...
Income Statement								
Total Revenue	856,907	865,010	818,607	762,226	713,368	683,602	613,837	765,619
EBITDA	127,225	167,585	155,624	153,897	154,653	157,012	115,835	(55,372)
Depn & Amortn	19,900	18,500	15,500	15,800	13,300	16,300	18,200	25,800
Income Before Taxes	82,176	145,251	141,139	138,425	142,602	140,656	100,740	(84,716)
Income Taxes	13,784	32,950	28,722	32,023	33,566	31,413	24,287	(19,817)
Net Income	68,392	112,301	112,417	106,402	109,036	109,243	57,378	(64,899)
Average Shares	34,938	42,643	43,364	42,738	45,265	49,344	49,331	48,589
Balance Sheet								
Current Assets	596,995	602,654	556,287	566,490	524,174	617,720	569,592	463,555
Total Assets	933,437	876,042	811,815	764,605	672,470	744,647	655,351	633,120
Current Liabilities	109,167	94,822	97,607	103,486	86,193	93,602	69,616	85,970
Long-Term Obligations	489,609	34,500	...	...	37,000	...	...	...
Total Liabilities	621,038	148,645	113,151	118,158	145,226	109,795	84,017	107,753
Stockholders' Equity	312,399	727,397	698,664	646,447	527,244	634,852	571,334	525,367
Shares Outstanding	33,319	41,601	42,649	43,283	42,512	48,315	48,870	48,892
Statistical Record								
Return on Assets %	7.54	13.31	14.26	14.81	15.35	15.61	8.91	N.M.
Return on Equity %	13.12	15.75	16.71	18.13	18.71	18.11	10.46	N.M.
EBITDA Margin %	14.85	19.37	19.01	20.19	21.68	22.97	18.87	N.M.
Net Margin %	7.98	12.98	13.73	13.96	15.28	15.98	9.35	N.M.
Asset Turnover	0.94	1.02	1.04	1.06	1.00	0.98	0.95	1.11
Current Ratio	5.47	6.36	5.70	5.47	6.08	6.60	8.18	5.39
Debt to Equity	1.57	0.05	...	...	0.07	...	...	...
Price Range	58.09-32.55	55.45-41.57	49.56-41.41	45.61-28.95	40.26-27.45	38.20-26.79	32.13-11.91	26.06-7.84
P/E Ratio	29.64-16.61	21.08-15.81	19.14-15.99	18.32-11.63	16.71-11.39	17.29-12.12	27.70-10.27	...
Average Yield %	1.19	1.24	0.89	1.12	0.58	0.60	0.86	1.13

Address: 345 Encinal Street, Santa Cruz, CA 95060 **Telephone:** 831-426-5858 **Fax:** 831-426-6098	**Web Site:** www.plantronics.com **Officers:** Marvin Tseu - Chairman S. Kenneth Kannappan - President, Chief Executive Officer	**Auditors:** PricewaterhouseCoopers LLP **Investor Contact:** 831-426-5858 **Transfer Agents:** Computershare Trust Company, N.A., Providence, RI

PLATFORM SPECIALTY PRODUCTS CORP

Exchange	Symbol	Price	52Wk Range	Yield	P/E
NYS	PAH	$9.49 (5/31/2016)	28.35-5.55	N/A	N/A

*7 Year Price Score N/A   *NYSE Composite Index=100   *12 Month Price Score 67.25

TRADING VOLUME (thousand shares)

Interim Earnings (Per Share)

Qtr.	Mar	Jun	Sep	Dec
2014	(0.07)	0.00	0.08	(1.59)
2015	(0.14)	(0.06)	(0.58)	(0.71)
2016	(0.59)	...	...	...

Interim Dividends (Per Share)

No Dividends Paid

Valuation Analysis   **Institutional Holding**

Forecast EPS	$0.66	No of Institutions
	(05/20/2016)	199
Market Cap	$2.2 Billion	Shares
Book Value	$2.9 Billion	214,295,952
Price/Book	0.75	% Held
Price/Sales	0.77	97.77

Business Summary: Specialty Chemicals (MIC: 8.3.2 SIC: 5169 NAIC: 325998)

Platform Specialty Products is a producer of chemical products and provider of technical services. Co. has three operating segments: performance materials, which manufactures and markets chemistry solutions that are used in the electronics, automotive, oil and gas production and drilling industries; graphic solutions, which primarily produces and markets photopolymers through a line of flexographic plates that are used in the commercial packaging and printing industries; and agrosolutions, which focuses on products that address a need for higher crop yield and quality, as well as protection from weeds (herbicides), insects (insecticides) and diseases (fungicides).

Recent Developments: For the quarter ended Mar 31 2016, net loss amounted to US$134.4 million versus a net loss of US$26.3 million in the year-earlier quarter. Revenues were US$823.8 million, up 54.0% from US$534.8 million the year before. Operating income was US$52.1 million versus US$2.2 million in the prior-year quarter, an increase of. Direct operating expenses rose 42.8% to US$467.8 million from US$327.7 million in the comparable period the year before. Indirect operating expenses increased 48.3% to US$303.9 million from US$204.9 million in the equivalent prior-year period.

Prospects: Our evaluation of Platform Specialty Products as of June 19, 2016 is the result of our systematic analysis on three basic characteristics: earnings strength, relative valuation, and recent stock price movement. The company has suffered a very negative trend in earnings per share over the past 5 quarters and while recent estimates for the company have remained steady, PAH has posted better than expected results. Based on operating earnings yield, the company is overvalued when compared to all of the companies in our coverage universe. Share price changes over the past year indicates that PAH will perform poorly over the near term.

Financial Data
(US$ in Thousands)

	3 Mos	12/31/2015	12/31/2014	12/31/2013
Earnings Per Share	(1.94)	(1.52)	(1.94)	(2.10)
Cash Flow Per Share	0.79	1.58	0.73	0.08
Income Statement				
Total Revenue	823,800	2,542,300	843,200	118,239
EBITDA	(4,000)	33,500	26,300	(192,172)
Depn & Amortn	18,200	48,900	19,300	3,900
Income Before Taxes	(116,000)	(229,300)	(30,900)	(201,444)
Income Taxes	18,400	75,100	(6,700)	(5,819)
Net Income	(134,800)	(308,600)	(29,900)	(194,222)
Average Shares	229,500	203,200	135,300	92,563
Balance Sheet				
Current Assets	2,296,100	2,270,500	1,578,400	383,239
Total Assets	10,592,700	10,190,200	4,557,600	2,241,888
Current Liabilities	1,175,600	1,062,400	242,600	119,420
Long-Term Obligations	5,218,400	5,173,600	1,400,800	744,291
Total Liabilities	7,678,000	7,440,400	2,098,000	1,188,321
Stockholders' Equity	2,914,700	2,749,800	2,459,600	1,053,567
Shares Outstanding	229,523	229,464	182,066	103,571
Statistical Record				
EBITDA Margin %	N.M.	1.32	3.12	N.M.
Asset Turnover	0.30	0.34	0.25	...
Current Ratio	1.95	2.14	6.51	3.21
Debt to Equity	1.79	1.88	0.57	0.71
Price Range	28.35-5.55	28.35-10.12	28.70-13.83	...

Address: 1450 Centrepark Boulevard, Suite 210, West Palm Beach, FL 33401 **Telephone:** 561-207-9600	**Web Site:** www.platformspecialtyproducts.com **Officers:** Martin E. Franklin - Chairman Rakesh Sachdev - Chief Executive Officer	**Auditors:** PricewaterhouseCoopers LLP

PNC FINANCIAL SERVICES GROUP (THE)

Exchange	Symbol	Price	52Wk Range	Yield	P/E
NYS	PNC	$89.74 (5/31/2016)	99.86-78.17	2.27	12.24

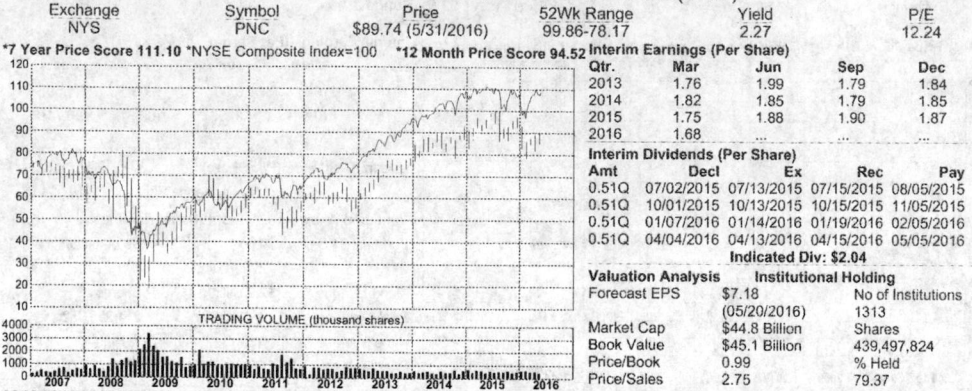

*7 Year Price Score 111.10 *NYSE Composite Index=100   *12 Month Price Score 94.52

Interim Earnings (Per Share)

Qtr.	Mar	Jun	Sep	Dec
2013	1.76	1.99	1.79	1.84
2014	1.82	1.85	1.79	1.85
2015	1.75	1.88	1.90	1.87
2016	1.68	...	...	...

Interim Dividends (Per Share)

Amt	Decl	Ex	Rec	Pay
0.51Q	07/02/2015	07/13/2015	07/15/2015	08/05/2015
0.51Q	10/01/2015	10/13/2015	10/15/2015	11/05/2015
0.51Q	01/07/2016	01/14/2016	01/19/2016	02/05/2016
0.51Q	04/04/2016	04/13/2016	04/15/2016	05/05/2016

Indicated Div: $2.04

Valuation Analysis / Institutional Holding

Forecast EPS	$7.18	No of Institutions
	(05/20/2016)	1313
Market Cap	$44.8 Billion	Shares
Book Value	$45.1 Billion	439,497,824
Price/Book	0.99	% Held
Price/Sales	2.75	79.37

Business Summary: Banking (MIC: 5.1.1 SIC: 6021 NAIC: 522110)

The PNC Financial Services Group is a bank holding company. Co. has businesses engaged in retail banking, corporate and institutional banking, asset management, and residential mortgage banking, providing its products and services nationally, as well as other products and services in its primary geographic markets located in Pennsylvania, Ohio, New Jersey, Michigan, Illinois, Maryland, Indiana, Florida, North Carolina, Kentucky, Washington, D.C., Delaware, Virginia, Alabama, Georgia, Missouri, Wisconsin and South Carolina. Co. also provides certain products and services internationally. At Dec 31 2015, Co. had total assets of $358.49 billion and total deposits of $249.00 billion.

Recent Developments: For the quarter ended Mar 31 2016, net income decreased 6.1% to US$943.0 million from US$1.00 billion in the year-earlier quarter. Net interest income increased 1.3% to US$2.10 billion from US$2.07 billion in the year-earlier quarter. Provision for loan losses was US$152.0 million versus US$54.0 million in the prior-year quarter, an increase of 181.5%. Non-interest income fell 5.5% to US$1.57 billion from US$1.66 billion, while non-interest expense declined 2.9% to US$2.28 billion.

Prospects: Our evaluation of PNC Financial Services Group as of June 19, 2016 is the result of our systematic analysis on three basic characteristics: earnings strength, relative valuation, and recent stock price movement. The company has managed to produce a neutral trend in earnings per share over the past 5 quarters. However, while recent estimates for the company have been mixed, PNC has posted results that fell short of analysts expectations. Based on operating earnings yield, the company is undervalued when compared to all of the companies in our coverage universe. Share price changes over the past year indicates that PNC will perform well over the near term.

Financial Data
(US$ in Thousands)

	3 Mos	12/31/2015	12/31/2014	12/31/2013	12/31/2012	12/31/2011	12/31/2010	12/31/2009
Earnings Per Share	7.33	7.39	7.30	7.39	5.30	5.64	5.74	4.36
Cash Flow Per Share	11.04	10.69	10.50	10.52	12.94	11.52	9.31	12.67
Tang Book Value Per Share	61.92	59.89	56.71	50.99	46.48	42.26	35.82	19.61
Dividends Per Share	2.040	2.010	1.880	1.720	1.550	1.150	0.400	0.960
Dividend Payout %	27.83	27.20	25.75	23.27	29.25	20.39	6.97	22.02
Income Statement								
Interest Income	2,407,000	9,323,000	9,431,000	10,007,000	10,734,000	10,194,000	11,150,000	12,086,000
Interest Expense	309,000	1,045,000	906,000	860,000	1,094,000	1,494,000	1,920,000	3,003,000
Net Interest Income	2,098,000	8,278,000	8,525,000	9,147,000	9,640,000	8,700,000	9,230,000	9,083,000
Provision for Losses	152,000	255,000	273,000	643,000	987,000	1,152,000	2,502,000	3,930,000
Non-Interest Income	1,567,000	6,947,000	6,850,000	6,865,000	5,872,000	5,626,000	5,946,000	7,145,000
Non-Interest Expense	2,281,000	9,463,000	9,488,000	9,801,000	10,582,000	9,105,000	8,613,000	9,073,000
Income Before Taxes	1,232,000	5,507,000	5,614,000	5,568,000	3,943,000	4,069,000	4,061,000	3,225,000
Income Taxes	289,000	1,364,000	1,407,000	1,341,000	942,000	998,000	1,037,000	867,000
Net Income	943,000	4,143,000	4,207,000	4,227,000	3,001,000	3,071,000	3,397,000	2,403,000
Average Shares	507,000	521,000	537,000	532,000	529,000	526,000	520,000	455,000
Balance Sheet								
Net Loans & Leases	206,315,000	205,509,000	203,748,000	194,259,000	185,513,000	157,603,000	149,200,000	155,010,000
Total Assets	360,985,000	358,493,000	345,072,000	320,296,000	305,107,000	271,205,000	264,284,000	269,863,000
Total Deposits	250,359,000	249,002,000	232,234,000	220,931,000	213,142,000	187,966,000	183,390,000	186,922,000
Total Liabilities	315,855,000	313,783,000	300,521,000	277,888,000	266,104,000	237,152,000	234,042,000	239,921,000
Stockholders' Equity	45,130,000	44,710,000	44,551,000	42,408,000	39,003,000	34,053,000	30,242,000	29,942,000
Shares Outstanding	499,000	504,000	523,000	533,000	528,000	527,000	526,000	462,000
Statistical Record								
Return on Assets %	1.15	1.18	1.26	1.35	1.04	1.15	1.27	0.86
Return on Equity %	9.06	9.28	9.68	10.38	8.19	9.55	11.29	8.68
Net Interest Margin %	87.16	88.79	90.39	91.41	89.81	85.34	82.78	75.15
Efficiency Ratio %	57.40	58.16	58.28	58.09	63.72	57.55	50.38	47.18
Loans to Deposits	0.82	0.83	0.88	0.88	0.87	0.84	0.81	0.83
Price Range	99.86-78.17	99.86-82.42	92.93-76.60	78.20-58.31	67.33-53.69	64.94-42.98	69.64-50.36	57.01-18.51
P/E Ratio	13.62-10.66	13.51-11.15	12.73-10.49	10.58-7.89	12.70-10.13	11.51-7.62	12.13-8.77	13.08-4.25
Average Yield %	2.29	2.21	2.22	2.52	2.56	2.13	0.69	2.32

Address: The Tower at PNC Plaza, 300 Fifth Avenue, Pittsburgh, PA 15222-2401
Telephone: 412-762-2000
Fax: 412-762-5798

Web Site: www.pnc.com
Officers: William S. Demchak - Chairman, President, Chief Executive Officer Joseph C. Guyaux - Senior Vice Chairman, Chief Risk Officer

Auditors: PricewaterhouseCoopers LLP
Investor Contact: 412-762-8257
Transfer Agents: Computershare Trust Company, N. A., Canton, MA

PNM RESOURCES INC

Exchange	Symbol	Price	52Wk Range	Yield	P/E
NYS	PNM	$32.84 (5/31/2016)	33.86-24.60	2.68	218.93

*7 Year Price Score 120.25 *NYSE Composite Index=100 *12 Month Price Score 109.25

Interim Earnings (Per Share)

Qtr.	Mar	Jun	Sep	Dec
2013	0.13	0.34	0.68	0.10
2014	0.16	0.36	0.69	0.24
2015	0.18	0.40	0.76	(1.14)
2016	0.13	...	...	...

Interim Dividends (Per Share)

Amt	Decl	Ex	Rec	Pay
0.20Q	07/14/2015	07/30/2015	08/03/2015	08/14/2015
0.20Q	09/15/2015	10/29/2015	11/02/2015	11/13/2015
0.22Q	12/10/2015	01/21/2016	01/25/2016	02/12/2016
0.22Q	02/25/2016	04/06/2016	04/08/2016	05/13/2016

Indicated Div: $0.88

Valuation Analysis		Institutional Holding	
Forecast EPS	$1.60	No of Institutions	
	(05/20/2016)	323	
Market Cap	$2.6 Billion	Shares	
Book Value	$1.7 Billion	87,003,744	
Price/Book	1.58	% Held	
Price/Sales	1.85	87.21	

Business Summary: Electric Utilities (MIC: 3.1.1 SIC: 4911 NAIC: 221121)

PNM Resources is a holding company with two regulated utilities serving residential, commercial, and industrial customers and end-users of electricity in New Mexico and Texas. Co.'s primary subsidiaries are Public Service Company of New Mexico (PNM) and Texas-New Mexico Power Company (TNMP). PNM is an electric utility that provides electric generation, transmission, and distribution service to its rate-regulated customers in New Mexico. PNM also provides electricity to firm requirements wholesale customers in New Mexico and Arizona. TNMP is a regulated utility operating in Texas. As of Dec 31 2015, PNM had 516,658 customers, while TNMP had 243,461 customers.

Recent Developments: For the quarter ended Mar 31 2016, net income decreased 21.8% to US$14.0 million from US$17.9 million in the year-earlier quarter. Revenues were US$311.0 million, down 6.6% from US$332.9 million the year before. Operating income was US$41.5 million versus US$49.6 million in the prior-year quarter, a decrease of 16.3%. Direct operating expenses declined 12.9% to US$152.4 million from US$175.0 million in the comparable period the year before. Indirect operating expenses increased 8.1% to US$117.0 million from US$108.3 million in the equivalent prior-year period.

Prospects: Our evaluation of PNM Resources Inc. as of June 19, 2016 is the result of our systematic analysis on three basic characteristics: earnings strength, relative valuation, and recent stock price movement. The company has generated a negative trend in earnings per share over the past 5 quarters. However, while recent estimates for the company have been lowered by analysts, PNM has posted results that fell short of analysts expectations. Based on operating earnings yield, the company is about fairly valued when compared to all of the companies in our coverage universe. Share price changes over the past year indicates that PNM will perform very well over the near term.

Financial Data

(US$ in Thousands)	3 Mos	12/31/2015	12/31/2014	12/31/2013	12/31/2012	12/31/2011	12/31/2010	12/31/2009
Earnings Per Share	0.15	0.20	1.45	1.25	1.31	1.96	(0.49)	1.36
Cash Flow Per Share	5.15	4.85	5.20	4.85	3.52	3.28	3.14	0.96
Tang Book Value Per Share	17.24	17.43	18.26	17.66	16.84	16.41	13.85	15.15
Dividends Per Share	0.820	0.800	0.740	0.640	0.560	0.500	0.500	0.500
Dividend Payout %	546.67	400.00	51.03	51.20	42.75	25.51	...	36.76
Income Statement								
Total Revenue	310,961	1,439,082	1,435,853	1,387,923	1,342,403	1,700,619	1,673,517	1,647,744
EBITDA	107,554	377,376	521,658	453,355	489,307	617,169	244,388	366,008
Depn & Amortn	58,563	222,861	209,867	166,881	206,499	195,366	186,067	147,296
Income Before Taxes	21,122	46,153	200,647	175,069	175,035	312,469	(48,156)	124,896
Income Taxes	7,157	15,075	69,738	59,513	54,910	121,535	(32,255)	28,818
Net Income	13,965	31,078	130,909	115,556	120,125	190,934	(31,124)	136,734
Average Shares	80,164	80,139	80,279	79,845	80,417	89,757	91,557	91,671
Balance Sheet								
Current Assets	356,961	385,570	432,817	401,539	442,191	462,819	543,880	578,205
Total Assets	6,273,812	6,009,328	5,829,325	5,500,210	5,372,583	5,204,613	5,225,083	5,359,921
Current Liabilities	771,565	641,120	704,282	492,671	434,103	373,268	520,124	563,273
Long-Term Obligations	2,108,395	1,966,969	1,642,024	1,670,420	1,669,760	1,671,626	1,563,595	1,565,206
Total Liabilities	4,621,921	4,342,986	4,096,250	3,815,112	3,752,867	3,619,099	3,576,812	3,598,675
Stockholders' Equity	1,651,891	1,666,342	1,733,075	1,685,098	1,619,716	1,585,514	1,648,271	1,761,246
Shares Outstanding	79,653	79,653	79,653	79,653	79,653	79,653	86,673	86,673
Statistical Record								
Return on Assets %	0.45	0.53	2.31	2.13	2.27	3.66	N.M.	2.38
Return on Equity %	1.61	1.83	7.66	6.99	7.48	11.81	N.M.	7.77
EBITDA Margin %	34.59	26.22	36.33	32.66	36.45	36.29	14.60	22.21
Net Margin %	4.49	2.16	9.12	8.33	8.95	11.23	N.M.	8.30
Asset Turnover	0.23	0.24	0.25	0.26	0.25	0.33	0.32	0.29
Current Ratio	0.46	0.60	0.61	0.82	1.02	1.24	1.05	1.03
Debt to Equity	1.28	1.18	0.95	0.99	1.03	1.05	0.95	0.89
Price Range	33.86-24.60	31.17-24.60	31.39-23.53	24.29-20.28	22.32-17.52	19.11-12.98	13.93-10.94	12.88-6.20
P/E Ratio	225.73-164.00	155.85-123.00	21.65-16.23	19.43-16.22	17.04-13.37	9.75-6.62	...	9.47-4.56
Average Yield %	2.89	2.89	2.74	2.82	2.85	3.19	4.10	4.77

Address: 414 Silver Ave. S.W., Albuquerque, NM 87102-3289 Telephone: 505-241-2700	Web Site: www.pnmresources.com Officers: Patricia K. Vincent-Collawn - Chairman, President, Chief Executive Officer Charles N. Eldred - Executive Vice President, Chief Financial Officer	Auditors: KPMG LLP Investor Contact: 505-241-2211 Transfer Agents: Computershare, Providence, RI

POLARIS INDUSTRIES INC.

Exchange	Symbol	Price	52Wk Range	Yield	P/E	Div Achiever
NYS	PII	$85.02 (5/31/2016)	155.34-69.61	2.59	13.80	20 Years

*7 Year Price Score 112.16 *NYSE Composite Index=100   ***12 Month Price Score 84.30**

Interim Earnings (Per Share)

Qtr.	Mar	Jun	Sep	Dec
2013	1.07	1.13	1.59	1.56
2014	1.19	1.42	2.06	1.97
2015	1.30	1.49	2.30	1.66
2016	0.71	...	...	...

Interim Dividends (Per Share)

Amt	Decl	Ex	Rec	Pay
0.53Q	07/22/2015	08/28/2015	09/01/2015	09/15/2015
0.53Q	10/23/2015	11/27/2015	12/01/2015	12/15/2015
0.55Q	01/28/2016	02/26/2016	03/01/2016	03/15/2016
0.55Q	04/28/2016	05/27/2016	06/01/2016	06/15/2016

Indicated Div: $2.20 (Div. Reinv. Plan)

Valuation Analysis **Institutional Holding**

Forecast EPS	$6.42 (05/20/2016)	No of Institutions	659
Market Cap	$5.5 Billion	Shares	
Book Value	$943.1 Million		59,425,764
Price/Book	5.83	% Held	
Price/Sales	1.18		81.89

Business Summary: Autos- Manufacturing (MIC: 1.8.1 SIC: 3799 NAIC: 336999)

Polaris Industries designs, engineers and manufactures Off-Road Vehicles (ORV), including All-Terrain Vehicles (ATV) and side-by-side vehicles for recreational and utility use, Snowmobiles, Motorcycles and Global Adjacent Markets vehicles, together with the related parts, garments and accessories. These products are sold through dealers and distributors principally located in the U.S., Canada, Western Europe, Australia and Mexico. Co.'s family of ORVs includes utility and recreational Sportsman ATVs, sport-styled Scrambler® ATVs, utility and recreational RANGER side-by-side vehicles, and recreational RZR side-by-side vehicles.

Recent Developments: For the quarter ended Mar 31 2016, net income decreased 47.1% to US$46.9 million from US$88.6 million in the year-earlier quarter. Revenues were US$983.0 million, down 4.9% from US$1.03 billion the year before. Operating income was US$77.1 million versus US$150.3 million in the prior-year quarter, a decrease of 48.7%. Direct operating expenses declined 0.6% to US$735.4 million from US$739.6 million in the comparable period the year before. Indirect operating expenses increased 18.8% to US$170.4 million from US$143.4 million in the equivalent prior-year period.

Prospects: Our evaluation of Polaris Industries Inc. as of June 19, 2016 is the result of our systematic analysis on three basic characteristics: earnings strength, relative valuation, and recent stock price movement. The company has generated a negative trend in earnings per share over the past 5 quarters. However, while recent estimates for the company have been lowered by analysts, PII has posted results that fall short of analysts expectations. Based on operating earnings yield, the company is undervalued when compared to all of the companies in our coverage universe. Share price changes over the past year indicates that PII will perform poorly over the near term.

Financial Data

(US$ in Thousands)	3 Mos	12/31/2015	12/31/2014	12/31/2013	12/31/2012	12/31/2011	12/31/2010	12/31/2009
Earnings Per Share	6.16	6.75	6.65	5.35	4.40	3.20	2.14	1.52
Cash Flow Per Share	8.84	6.67	8.00	7.18	6.03	4.40	4.45	2.98
Tang Book Value Per Share	10.28	11.56	9.82	4.79	8.50	6.17	4.96	2.74
Dividends Per Share	2.140	2.120	1.920	1.680	1.480	0.900	0.800	0.780
Dividend Payout %	34.74	31.41	28.87	31.40	33.64	28.13	37.38	51.15
Income Statement								
Total Revenue	982,996	4,719,290	4,479,648	3,777,068	3,209,782	2,656,949	1,991,139	1,565,887
EBITDA	114,957	856,133	842,187	675,153	556,534	417,003	287,740	219,878
Depn & Amortn	37,894	152,138	127,507	92,100	70,580	66,390	66,519	64,593
Income Before Taxes	74,198	692,539	703,441	576,843	480,022	346,626	218,541	151,174
Income Taxes	25,251	230,376	245,288	193,360	167,533	119,051	71,403	50,157
Net Income	46,889	455,361	454,029	377,292	312,310	227,575	147,138	101,017
Average Shares	65,892	67,484	68,229	70,546	71,005	71,057	68,764	66,148
Balance Sheet								
Current Assets	1,076,670	1,154,725	1,096,555	865,698	1,017,841	878,676	808,145	491,500
Total Assets	2,379,773	2,387,462	2,074,935	1,685,488	1,486,492	1,228,024	1,061,647	763,653
Current Liabilities	794,253	826,783	850,810	748,070	631,029	615,531	584,210	343,074
Long-Term Obligations	527,509	458,220	223,620	284,342	104,292	104,600	100,000	200,000
Total Liabilities	1,436,716	1,396,340	1,200,140	1,141,462	795,962	727,968	690,656	559,112
Stockholders' Equity	943,057	991,122	874,795	544,026	690,530	500,056	370,991	204,541
Shares Outstanding	64,620	65,309	66,307	65,623	68,647	68,430	68,468	65,296
Statistical Record								
Return on Assets %	18.55	20.41	24.15	23.79	22.95	19.88	16.12	13.34
Return on Equity %	45.46	48.81	64.00	61.12	52.32	52.25	51.13	59.15
EBITDA Margin %	11.69	18.14	18.80	17.88	17.34	15.69	14.45	14.04
Net Margin %	4.77	9.65	10.14	9.99	9.73	8.57	7.39	6.45
Asset Turnover	2.09	2.12	2.38	2.38	2.36	2.32	2.18	2.07
Current Ratio	1.36	1.40	1.29	1.16	1.61	1.43	1.38	1.43
Debt to Equity	0.56	0.46	0.26	0.52	0.15	0.21	0.27	0.98
Price Range	155.34-69.61	157.62-83.30	158.43-119.98	145.78-83.24	88.35-54.67	65.53-35.75	40.35-21.29	24.37-7.29
P/E Ratio	25.22-11.30	23.35-12.34	23.82-18.04	27.25-15.56	20.08-12.43	20.48-11.17	18.86-9.95	16.03-4.80
Average Yield %	1.81	1.59	1.22	1.37	1.96	1.78	2.70	4.67

Address: 2100 Highway 55, Medina, MN 55340 Telephone: 763-542-0500	Web Site: www.polaris.com Officers: Scott W. Wine - Chairman, Chief Executive Officer Kenneth J. Pucel - Executive Vice President	Auditors: Ernst & Young LLP Investor Contact: 763-513-3477 Transfer Agents: Wells Fargo Shareowner Services, Mendota Heights, MN

POLYONE CORP.

Exchange	Symbol	Price	52Wk Range	Yield	P/E
NYS	POL	$37.47 (5/31/2016)	40.20-24.30	1.28	21.41

*7 Year Price Score 126.06 *NYSE Composite Index=100 *12 Month Price Score 106.06

Interim Earnings (Per Share)

Qtr.	Mar	Jun	Sep	Dec
2013	0.16	1.83	0.24	0.26
2014	0.31	0.34	0.35	(0.14)
2015	0.34	0.74	0.50	0.05
2016	0.46	...	...	...

Interim Dividends (Per Share)

Amt	Decl	Ex	Rec	Pay
0.10Q	07/16/2015	09/10/2015	09/14/2015	10/07/2015
0.12Q	10/08/2015	12/16/2015	12/18/2015	01/07/2016
0.12Q	02/10/2016	03/11/2016	03/15/2016	04/06/2016
0.12Q	05/12/2016	06/15/2016	06/17/2016	07/08/2016

Indicated Div: $0.48

Valuation Analysis | **Institutional Holding**

Forecast EPS	$2.20	No of Institutions
	(05/15/2016)	299
Market Cap	$3.1 Billion	Shares
Book Value	$692.6 Million	87,583,528
Price/Book	4.55	% Held
Price/Sales	0.94	85.10

Business Summary: Plastics (MIC: 8.4.2 SIC: 2821 NAIC: 325211)

PolyOne operates in five segments: Color, Additives and Inks, which provides color and additive concentrates in solid and liquid form, dispersions, as well as specialty inks, plastisols, and vinyl slush molding solutions; Specialty Engineered Materials, which provides polymer formulations, services and solutions; Designed Structures and Solutions, which provides solutions in engineered polymer structures, rigid barrier packaging and specialty cast acrylics; Performance Products and Solutions, which provides products and services for vinyl molding and extrusion processors; as well as PolyOne Distribution, which distributes engineering and commodity grade resins.

Recent Developments: For the quarter ended Mar 31 2016, net income increased 29.1% to US$39.0 million from US$30.2 million in the year-earlier quarter. Revenues were US$847.0 million, down 3.0% from US$873.1 million the year before. Operating income was US$71.3 million versus US$70.1 million in the prior-year quarter, an increase of 1.7%. Direct operating expenses declined 5.9% to US$661.5 million from US$703.3 million in the comparable period the year before. Indirect operating expenses increased 14.5% to US$114.2 million from US$99.7 million in the equivalent prior-year period.

Prospects: Our evaluation of PolyOne Corp. as of June 19, 2016 is the result of our systematic analysis on three basic characteristics: earnings strength, relative valuation, and recent stock price movement. The company has produced a positive trend in earnings per share over the past 5 quarters and while recent estimates for the company have remained steady, POL has posted better than expected results. Based on operating earnings yield, the company is undervalued when compared to all of the companies in our coverage universe. Share price changes over the past year indicates that POL will perform poorly over the near term.

Financial Data
(US$ in Thousands)

	3 Mos	12/31/2015	12/31/2014	12/31/2013	12/31/2012	12/31/2011	12/31/2010	12/31/2009
Earnings Per Share	1.75	1.63	0.85	2.53	0.80	1.83	1.69	0.73
Cash Flow Per Share	3.02	2.59	2.26	1.14	1.20	0.79	1.51	2.49
Tang Book Value Per Share	N.M.	N.M.	N.M.	0.55	N.M.	N.M.	3.03	1.06
Dividends Per Share	0.440	0.420	0.340	0.260	0.200	0.160	...	...
Dividend Payout %	25.14	25.77	40.00	10.28	25.00	8.74	...	...
Income Statement								
Total Revenue	847,000	3,377,600	3,835,500	3,771,200	2,992,600	2,863,500	2,621,900	2,060,700
EBITDA	93,300	316,200	255,300	278,600	197,000	134,100	152,000	115,100
Depn & Amortn	21,700	84,400	104,700	91,000	56,600	53,700	51,500	61,500
Income Before Taxes	57,000	167,700	88,400	124,100	89,600	46,700	69,000	19,300
Income Taxes	18,000	23,000	11,200	58,100	41,200	26,100	(51,600)	(13,300)
Net Income	39,100	144,600	79,200	243,800	71,800	172,600	162,600	67,800
Average Shares	85,500	88,700	93,500	96,500	89,800	94,300	96,000	93,400
Balance Sheet								
Current Assets	948,900	960,800	1,042,700	1,253,600	866,900	843,500	939,000	694,700
Total Assets	2,624,400	2,595,100	2,711,200	2,944,100	2,128,000	2,080,500	1,671,900	1,391,900
Current Liabilities	518,400	498,100	601,200	608,900	459,800	442,400	434,800	375,700
Long-Term Obligations	1,174,300	1,128,000	962,000	976,200	703,100	704,000	432,900	389,200
Total Liabilities	1,931,800	1,890,900	1,934,900	1,967,300	1,498,900	1,492,200	1,155,900	1,058,300
Stockholders' Equity	692,600	704,200	776,300	976,800	629,100	588,300	516,000	333,600
Shares Outstanding	84,043	85,300	89,300	95,100	89,500	88,800	93,903	92,486
Statistical Record								
Return on Assets %	5.78	5.45	2.80	9.61	3.40	9.20	10.61	5.08
Return on Equity %	21.16	19.53	9.04	30.36	11.76	31.26	38.28	26.61
EBITDA Margin %	11.02	9.36	6.66	7.39	6.58	4.68	5.80	5.59
Net Margin %	4.62	4.28	2.06	6.46	2.40	6.03	6.20	3.29
Asset Turnover	1.26	1.27	1.36	1.49	1.42	1.53	1.71	1.54
Current Ratio	1.83	1.93	1.73	2.06	1.89	1.91	2.16	1.85
Debt to Equity	1.70	1.60	1.24	1.00	1.12	1.20	0.84	1.17
Price Range	40.89-24.30	40.89-29.27	43.14-32.19	35.44-20.42	20.74-11.77	16.34-9.63	13.60-7.05	7.67-1.34
P/E Ratio	23.37-13.89	25.09-17.96	50.75-37.87	14.01-8.07	25.92-14.71	8.93-5.26	8.05-4.17	10.51-1.84
Average Yield %	1.31	1.17	0.90	0.97	1.30	1.22	...	...

Address: 33587 Walker Road, Avon Lake, OH 44012	**Web Site:** www.polyone.com	**Auditors:** Ernst & Young LLP
Telephone: 440-930-1000	**Officers:** Robert M. Patterson - Chairman, President, Chief Executive Officer, Senior Vice President, Chief Financial Officer, Chief Operating Officer Bradley C. Richardson - Executive Vice President, Chief Financial Officer	**Investor Contact:** 440-930-1226 **Transfer Agents:** Wells Fargo Shareowner Services, Mendota Heights, MN

POST HOLDINGS INC

Exchange	Symbol	Price	52Wk Range	Yield	P/E
NYS	POST	$76.01 (5/31/2016)	76.92-43.52	N/A	N/A

*7 Year Price Score N/A ***NYSE Composite Index=100** ***12 Month Price Score 113.77**

Interim Earnings (Per Share)

Qtr.	Dec	Mar	Jun	Sep
2012-13	0.23	0.13	0.03	(0.10)
2013-14	(0.15)	(0.67)	(0.92)	(7.19)
2014-15	(2.04)	0.45	0.33	(1.31)
2015-16	0.15	0.02	...	

Interim Dividends (Per Share)

No Dividends Paid

Valuation Analysis / Institutional Holding

Valuation Analysis		Institutional Holding	
Forecast EPS	$2.26	No of Institutions	
	(05/20/2016)	330	
Market Cap	$4.9 Billion	Shares	
Book Value	$3.0 Billion	70,640,920	
Price/Book	1.63	% Held	
Price/Sales	0.97	98.59	

TRADING VOLUME (thousand shares)

Business Summary: Food (MIC: 1.2.1 SIC: 2041 NAIC: 311211)

Post Holdings is a consumer packaged goods holding company. Co. operates in four segments: Post Consumer Brands, which includes the Post branded cereal operations and the business of MOM Brands Company; Michael Foods Group, which produces egg products, refrigerated potato products and cheese and other dairy case products as well as pasta; Active Nutrition, which includes its protein shakes, bars and powders and nutritional supplement businesses, as well as its PowerBar brand; and Private Brands, which produces private label peanut and other nut butters, and dried fruits and snacking nuts, and provides peanut blanching, granulation and roasting services for the commercial peanut industry.

Recent Developments: For the quarter ended Mar 31 2016, net income decreased 83.9% to US$4.9 million from US$30.5 million in the year-earlier quarter. Revenues were US$1.27 billion, up 20.7% from US$1.05 billion the year before. Operating income was US$162.5 million versus US$49.7 million in the prior-year quarter, an increase of 227.0%. Direct operating expenses rose 10.9% to US$861.8 million from US$777.2 million in the comparable period the year before. Indirect operating expenses increased 9.3% to US$246.8 million from US$225.8 million in the equivalent prior-year period.

Prospects: Our evaluation of Post Holdings Inc. as of June 19, 2016 is the result of our systematic analysis on three basic characteristics: earnings strength, relative valuation, and recent stock price movement. The company has suffered a very negative trend in earnings per share over the past 5 quarters. However, while recent estimates for the company have been mixed, POST has posted better than expected results. Based on operating earnings yield, the company is overvalued when compared to all of the companies in our coverage universe. Share price changes over the past year indicates that POST will perform very well over the near term.

Financial Data
(US$ in Thousands)

	6 Mos	3 Mos	09/30/2015	09/30/2014	09/30/2013	09/30/2012	09/30/2011	09/30/2010
Earnings Per Share	(0.81)	(0.38)	(2.33)	(9.03)	0.30	1.45	...	...
Cash Flow Per Share	7.09	7.17	7.96	4.61	3.65	4.20	...	...
Income Statement								
Total Revenue	2,519,900	1,248,800	4,648,200	2,411,100	1,034,100	958,900	968,200	996,700
EBITDA	190,900	118,100	393,000	(87,400)	184,600	203,900	(261,600)	246,200
Depn & Amortn	2,300	1,100	272,800	155,800	76,800	63,200	58,700	55,400
Income Before Taxes	33,600	39,200	(167,300)	(426,900)	22,300	80,400	(371,800)	139,300
Income Taxes	3,200	13,700	(52,000)	(83,700)	7,100	30,500	(6,300)	49,500
Net Income	30,400	25,500	(115,300)	(343,200)	15,200	49,900	(361,300)	92,000
Average Shares	70,500	68,800	56,700	39,700	33,000	34,500	...	...
Balance Sheet								
Current Assets	1,809,900	1,716,600	1,781,700	1,219,000	668,100	209,700	135,300	147,000
Total Assets	9,204,500	9,163,400	9,220,400	7,731,100	3,473,800	2,732,300	2,786,200	3,348,000
Current Liabilities	556,600	564,400	611,000	519,900	146,000	126,400	134,300	74,200
Long-Term Obligations	4,498,200	4,506,200	4,511,400	3,830,500	1,408,600	930,300	716,500	716,500
Total Liabilities	6,197,800	6,183,800	6,244,400	5,447,900	1,975,200	1,500,800	1,288,500	1,286,300
Stockholders' Equity	3,006,700	2,979,600	2,976,000	2,283,200	1,498,600	1,231,500	1,497,700	2,061,700
Shares Outstanding	64,310	64,095	60,300	43,000	30,900	30,900	...	...
Statistical Record								
Return on Assets %	N.M.	0.09	N.M.	N.M.	0.49	...	N.M.	...
Return on Equity %	N.M.	0.29	N.M.	N.M.	1.11	...	N.M.	...
EBITDA Margin %	7.58	9.46	8.45	N.M.	17.85	21.26	N.M.	24.70
Net Margin %	1.21	2.04	N.M.	N.M.	1.47	5.20	N.M.	9.23
Asset Turnover	0.59	0.57	0.55	0.43	0.33	...	0.32	...
Current Ratio	3.25	3.04	2.92	2.34	4.58	1.66	1.01	1.98
Debt to Equity	1.50	1.51	1.52	1.68	0.94	0.76	0.48	0.35
Price Range	72.20-42.45	70.99-39.41	69.73-31.67	60.18-33.18	49.14-30.05	33.98-28.00	...	...
P/E Ratio	...	...	...	...	163.80-100.17	23.43-19.31	...	...

Address: 2503 S. Hanley Road, St. Louis, MO 63144 Telephone: 314-644-7600	Web Site: www.postholdings.com Officers: Robert V. Vitale - President, Chief Executive Officer, Chief Financial Officer James E. Dwyer - Executive Vice President, Division Officer	Auditors: PricewaterhouseCoopers LLP Investor Contact: 314-644-7600 Transfer Agents: Computershare Trust Company, N.A., Providence, RI

PPG INDUSTRIES INC

Exchange	Symbol	Price	52Wk Range	Yield	P/E	Div Achiever
NYS	PPG	$107.68 (5/31/2016)	118.29-84.51	1.49	20.43	44 Years

*7 Year Price Score 129.67 *NYSE Composite Index=100 *12 Month Price Score 106.57

Interim Earnings (Per Share)

Qtr.	Mar	Jun	Sep	Dec
2013	...	1.18	0.78	0.94
2014	4.49	1.38	1.33	0.31
2015	1.17	1.23	1.59	1.16
2016	1.29	...	...	...

Interim Dividends (Per Share)

Amt	Decl	Ex	Rec	Pay
0.36Q	07/16/2015	08/06/2015	08/10/2015	09/11/2015
0.36Q	10/15/2015	11/06/2015	11/10/2015	12/11/2015
0.36Q	01/21/2016	02/17/2016	02/19/2016	03/11/2016
0.40Q	04/21/2016	05/06/2016	05/10/2016	06/10/2016

Indicated Div: $1.60 (Div. Reinv. Plan)

Valuation Analysis — **Institutional Holding**

Forecast EPS	$6.30	No of Institutions
	(05/20/2016)	1055
Market Cap	$28.6 Billion	Shares
Book Value	$5.2 Billion	220,214,624
Price/Book	5.55	% Held
Price/Sales	1.87	70.73

Business Summary: Specialty Chemicals (MIC: 8.3.2 SIC: 2851 NAIC: 325510)

PPG Industries is engaged in the manufacturing and distribution of a range of coatings, optical and specialty materials and glass products. Co. is comprised of three reportable business segments: Performance Coatings, which is comprised of the refinish, aerospace, architectural coatings - Americas and Asia Pacific, architectural coatings - EMEA, and protective and marine coatings operating segments; Industrial Coatings, which is comprised of the automotive original equipment manufacturer coatings, industrial coatings, packaging coatings, and the specialty coatings and materials operating segments; and Glass, which is comprised of the flat glass and fiber glass businesses.

Recent Developments: For the quarter ended Mar 31 2016, income from continuing operations increased 8.6% to US$354.0 million from US$326.0 million in the year-earlier quarter. Net income increased 8.3% to US$354.0 million from US$327.0 million in the year-earlier quarter. Revenues were US$3.67 billion, up 0.3% from US$3.66 billion the year before. Direct operating expenses declined 2.5% to US$2.01 billion from US$2.07 billion in the comparable period the year before. Indirect operating expenses increased 1.8% to US$1.19 billion from US$1.17 billion in the equivalent prior-year period.

Prospects: Our evaluation of PPG Industries Inc. as of June 19, 2016 is the result of our systematic analysis on three basic characteristics: earnings strength, relative valuation, and recent stock price movement. The company has managed to produce a neutral trend in earnings per share over the past 5 quarters and while recent estimates for the company have remained steady, PPG has posted better than expected results. Based on operating earnings yield, the company is undervalued when compared to all of the companies in our coverage universe. Share price changes over the past year indicates that PPG will perform in line with the market over the near term.

Financial Data

(US$ in Thousands)	3 Mos	12/31/2015	12/31/2014	12/31/2013	12/31/2009	12/31/2008	12/31/2007	12/31/2006
Earnings Per Share	5.27	5.14	7.51	11.14	1.01	1.63	2.52	2.13
Cash Flow Per Share	8.69	6.77	5.52	6.24	4.08	4.11	3.03	3.41
Tang Book Value Per Share	N.M.	N.M.	N.M.	2.11	N.M.	N.M.	6.30	3.82
Dividends Per Share	1.440	1.415	1.310	1.210	1.065	1.045	1.020	0.955
Dividend Payout %	27.32	27.53	17.43	10.87	104.93	64.31	40.56	44.73
Income Statement								
Total Revenue	3,672,000	15,330,000	15,360,000	15,108,000	12,239,000	15,849,000	11,206,000	11,037,000
EBITDA	586,000	2,320,000	1,802,000	2,006,000	1,141,000	1,561,000	1,608,000	1,432,000
Depn & Amortn	91,000	363,000	350,000	356,000	354,000	428,000	322,000	337,000
Income Before Taxes	471,000	1,871,000	1,315,000	1,497,000	622,000	905,000	1,213,000	1,026,000
Income Taxes	117,000	456,000	259,000	333,000	191,000	284,000	355,000	278,000
Net Income	347,000	1,406,000	2,102,000	3,231,000	336,000	538,000	834,000	711,000
Average Shares	269,400	273,600	279,600	290,220	331,000	330,800	331,800	333,000
Balance Sheet								
Current Assets	6,718,000	6,554,000	6,850,000	7,214,000	5,981,000	6,348,000	7,136,000	4,592,000
Total Assets	17,315,000	17,076,000	17,583,000	15,863,000	14,240,000	14,698,000	12,629,000	10,021,000
Current Liabilities	4,556,000	4,656,000	4,876,000	4,135,000	3,577,000	4,210,000	4,661,000	2,787,000
Long-Term Obligations	4,226,000	4,042,000	3,544,000	3,372,000	3,074,000	3,009,000	1,201,000	1,155,000
Total Liabilities	12,154,000	12,093,000	12,403,000	10,931,000	10,487,000	11,365,000	8,478,000	6,787,000
Stockholders' Equity	5,161,000	4,983,000	5,180,000	4,932,000	3,753,000	3,333,000	4,151,000	3,234,000
Shares Outstanding	266,063	266,876	271,964	277,292	331,335	328,397	327,601	328,163
Statistical Record								
Return on Assets %	8.25	8.11	12.57	20.36	2.32	3.93	7.36	7.60
Return on Equity %	27.95	27.67	41.57	71.84	9.48	14.34	22.59	22.62
EBITDA Margin %	15.96	15.13	11.73	13.28	9.32	9.85	14.35	12.97
Net Margin %	9.45	9.17	13.68	21.39	2.75	3.39	7.44	6.44
Asset Turnover	0.88	0.88	0.92	0.95	0.85	1.16	0.99	1.18
Current Ratio	1.47	1.41	1.40	1.74	1.67	1.51	1.53	1.65
Debt to Equity	0.82	0.81	0.68	0.68	0.82	0.90	0.29	0.36
Price Range	118.29-84.51	118.85-84.51	116.23-88.30	94.83-28.84	31.04-14.24	35.12-18.49	41.10-32.15	34.64-28.46
P/E Ratio	22.45-16.04	23.12-16.44	15.48-11.76	8.51-2.59	30.73-14.10	21.54-11.34	16.31-12.76	16.26-13.36
Average Yield %	1.39	1.31	1.31	2.32	4.39	3.59	2.82	2.98

Address: One PPG Place, Pittsburgh, PA 15272	**Web Site:** www.ppg.com	**Auditors:** PricewaterhouseCoopers LLP
Telephone: 412-434-3131	**Officers:** Charles E. Bunch - Chairman, President, Chief Executive Officer, Executive Vice President, Chief Operating Officer, Senior Vice President Michael H. McGarry - President, Executive Vice President, Senior Vice President, Chief Operating Officer, Chief Executive Officer	**Investor Contact:** 412-434-3740 **Transfer Agents:** Computershare, Providence, R.I.

PPL CORP

Exchange	Symbol	Price	52Wk Range	Yield	P/E	Div Achiever
NYS	PPL	$38.54 (5/31/2016)	38.91-29.41	3.94	51.39	16 Years

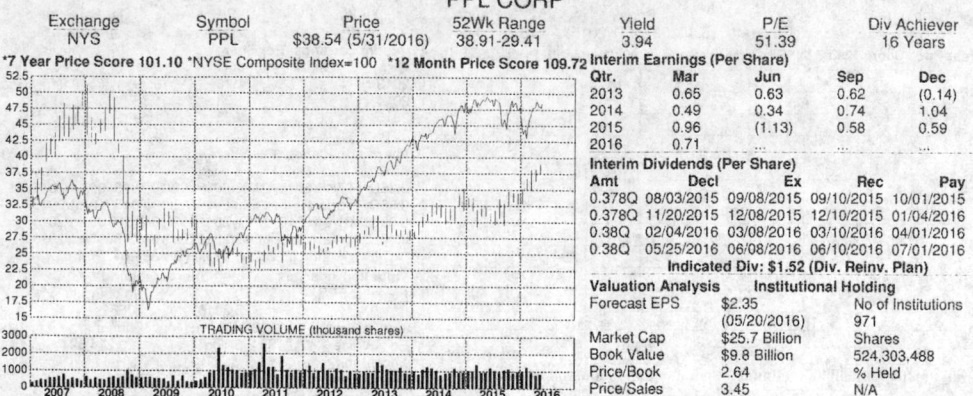

*7 Year Price Score 101.10 *NYSE Composite Index=100 *12 Month Price Score 109.72

Interim Earnings (Per Share)

Qtr.	Mar	Jun	Sep	Dec
2013	0.65	0.63	0.62	(0.14)
2014	0.49	0.34	0.74	1.04
2015	0.96	(1.13)	0.58	0.59
2016	0.71			

Interim Dividends (Per Share)

Amt	Decl	Ex	Rec	Pay
0.378Q	08/03/2015	09/08/2015	09/10/2015	10/01/2015
0.378Q	11/20/2015	12/08/2015	12/10/2015	01/04/2016
0.38Q	02/04/2016	03/08/2016	03/10/2016	04/01/2016
0.38Q	05/25/2016	06/08/2016	06/10/2016	07/01/2016

Indicated Div: $1.52 (Div. Reinv. Plan)

Valuation Analysis | **Institutional Holding**

Forecast EPS	$2.35	No of Institutions
	(05/20/2016)	971
Market Cap	$25.7 Billion	Shares
Book Value	$9.8 Billion	524,303,488
Price/Book	2.64	% Held
Price/Sales	3.45	N/A

Business Summary: Electric Utilities (MIC: 3.1.1 SIC: 4911 NAIC: 221122)

PPL is an energy and utility holding company. Through its subsidiaries, Co. delivers electricity to customers in the U.K., Pennsylvania, Kentucky, Virginia and Tennessee; delivers natural gas to customers in Kentucky; and generates electricity from power plants in the Kentucky. As of Dec 31 2015, Co.'s subsidiary, Louisville Gas and Electric Company, provided electric service to about 403,000 customers and natural gas service to 322,000 customers; Kentucky Utilities Company provided electric services to about 518,000 customers. KU also sells wholesale electricity in Kuntucky to 11 municipalities in Kentucky under load following contracts.

Recent Developments: For the quarter ended Mar 31 2016, income from continuing operations decreased 12.9% to US$481.0 million from US$552.0 million in the year-earlier quarter. Net income decreased 25.7% to US$481.0 million from US$647.0 million in the year-earlier quarter. Revenues were US$2.01 billion, down 9.8% from US$2.23 billion the year before. Operating income was US$823.0 million versus US$890.0 million in the prior-year quarter, a decrease of 7.5%. Direct operating expenses declined 15.2% to US$880.0 million from US$1.04 billion in the comparable period the year before. Indirect operating expenses increased 2.0% to US$308.0 million from US$302.0 million in the equivalent prior-year period.

Prospects: Our evaluation of PPL Corp. as of June 19, 2016 is the result of our systematic analysis on three basic characteristics: earnings strength, relative valuation, and recent stock price movement. The company has generated a negative trend in earnings per share over the past 5 quarters and while recent estimates for the company have remained steady, PPL has posted results that fell short of analysts expectations. Based on operating earnings yield, the company is undervalued when compared to all of the companies in our coverage universe. Share price changes over the past year indicates that PPL will perform very well over the near term.

Financial Data
(US$ in Thousands)

	3 Mos	12/31/2015	12/31/2014	12/31/2013	12/31/2012	12/31/2011	12/31/2010	12/31/2009
Earnings Per Share	0.75	1.01	2.61	1.76	2.60	2.70	2.17	1.08
Cash Flow Per Share	3.70	3.90	5.21	4.69	4.75	4.55	4.71	4.92
Tang Book Value Per Share	8.62	8.44	13.06	11.57	9.27	9.77	11.34	10.80
Dividends Per Share	1.508	1.500	1.490	1.470	1.440	1.400	1.400	1.380
Dividend Payout %	201.00	148.51	57.09	83.52	55.38	51.85	64.52	127.78
Income Statement								
Total Revenue	2,011,000	7,669,000	11,499,000	11,860,000	12,286,000	12,737,000	8,521,000	7,556,000
EBITDA	962,000	3,822,000	4,620,000	3,473,000	4,146,000	4,053,000	2,391,000	1,449,000
Depn & Amortn	78,000	883,000	1,237,000	1,161,000	1,100,000	961,000	567,000	471,000
Income Before Taxes	660,000	2,072,000	2,364,000	1,309,000	2,090,000	2,201,000	1,239,000	596,000
Income Taxes	179,000	469,000	781,000	180,000	545,000	691,000	263,000	130,000
Net Income	481,000	682,000	1,737,000	1,130,000	1,526,000	1,495,000	938,000	407,000
Average Shares	678,817	672,586	665,973	663,073	581,626	550,952	431,569	376,406
Balance Sheet								
Current Assets	2,713,000	2,646,000	6,159,000	5,153,000	5,068,000	6,426,000	6,188,000	4,752,000
Total Assets	38,709,000	39,301,000	48,864,000	46,259,000	43,634,000	42,648,000	32,837,000	22,165,000
Current Liabilities	4,066,000	3,876,000	7,443,000	4,912,000	5,625,000	5,255,000	5,214,000	4,182,000
Long-Term Obligations	18,074,000	18,563,000	18,856,000	20,592,000	18,725,000	17,993,000	12,161,000	7,143,000
Total Liabilities	28,947,000	29,382,000	35,236,000	33,793,000	33,154,000	31,820,000	24,627,000	16,669,000
Stockholders' Equity	9,762,000	9,919,000	13,628,000	12,466,000	10,480,000	10,828,000	8,210,000	5,496,000
Shares Outstanding	667,713	673,857	665,849	630,321	581,944	578,405	483,391	377,183
Statistical Record								
Return on Assets %	1.18	1.55	3.65	2.51	3.53	3.96	3.41	1.87
Return on Equity %	4.34	5.79	13.31	9.85	14.28	15.71	13.69	7.49
EBITDA Margin %	47.84	49.84	40.18	29.28	33.75	31.82	28.06	19.18
Net Margin %	23.92	8.89	15.11	9.53	12.42	11.74	11.01	5.39
Asset Turnover	0.17	0.17	0.24	0.26	0.28	0.34	0.31	0.35
Current Ratio	0.67	0.68	0.83	1.05	0.90	1.22	1.19	1.14
Debt to Equity	1.85	1.87	1.38	1.65	1.79	1.66	1.48	1.30
Price Range	38.07-29.41	34.75-29.14	35.21-27.46	30.97-26.40	27.98-24.84	28.06-22.60	30.26-22.49	31.87-22.70
P/E Ratio	50.76-39.21	34.41-28.85	13.49-10.52	17.60-15.00	10.76-9.55	10.39-8.37	13.94-10.37	29.51-21.02
Average Yield %	4.58	4.68	4.80	5.19	5.47	5.50	5.54	4.85

Address: Two North Ninth Street, Allentown, PA 18101-1179 **Telephone:** 610-774-5151	**Web Site:** www.pplweb.com **Officers:** William H. Spence - Chairman, President, Chief Executive Officer, Chief Operating Officer Paul A. Farr - Executive Vice President, Chief Financial Officer, Associate/Affiliate Company Officer	**Auditors:** Ernst & Young LLP **Transfer Agents:** Wells Fargo Bank, N.A., Shareowner Services, Mendota Heights, MN

PRAXAIR, INC.

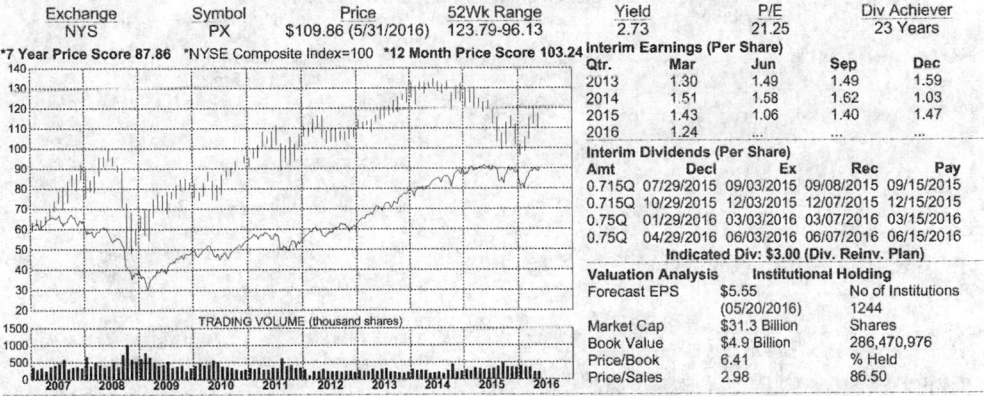

Exchange	Symbol	Price	52Wk Range	Yield	P/E	Div Achiever
NYS	PX	$109.86 (5/31/2016)	123.79-96.13	2.73	21.25	23 Years

*7 Year Price Score 87.86 *NYSE Composite Index=100 *12 Month Price Score 103.24

Interim Earnings (Per Share)

Qtr.	Mar	Jun	Sep	Dec
2013	1.30	1.49	1.49	1.59
2014	1.51	1.58	1.62	1.03
2015	1.43	1.06	1.40	1.47
2016	1.24	...	...	...

Interim Dividends (Per Share)

Amt	Decl	Ex	Rec	Pay
0.715Q	07/29/2015	09/03/2015	09/08/2015	09/15/2015
0.715Q	10/29/2015	12/03/2015	12/07/2015	12/15/2015
0.75Q	01/29/2016	03/03/2016	03/07/2016	03/15/2016
0.75Q	04/29/2016	06/03/2016	06/07/2016	06/15/2016

Indicated Div: $3.00 (Div. Reinv. Plan)

Valuation Analysis / **Institutional Holding**

Forecast EPS	$5.55	No of Institutions
	(05/20/2016)	1244
Market Cap	$31.3 Billion	Shares
Book Value	$4.9 Billion	286,470,976
Price/Book	6.41	% Held
Price/Sales	2.98	86.50

Business Summary: Specialty Chemicals (MIC: 8.3.2 SIC: 2819 NAIC: 325188)

Praxair is an industrial gases supplier in North and South America, Europe and Asia. Co.'s primary products in its industrial gases business are atmospheric gases (oxygen, nitrogen, argon, rare gases) and process gases (carbon dioxide, helium, hydrogen, electronic gases, specialty gases, acetylene). Co. also designs, engineers, and builds equipment that produces industrial gases primarily for internal use. Co.'s surface technologies segment supplies wear-resistant and high-temperature corrosion-resistant metallic and ceramic coatings and powders. Co.'s subsidiary, Praxair Surface Technologies, supplies coatings that protect metal parts from wear, corrosion and high heat.

Recent Developments: For the quarter ended Mar 31 2016, net income decreased 14.5% to US$366.0 million from US$428.0 million in the year-earlier quarter. Revenues were US$2.51 billion, down 9.0% from US$2.76 billion the year before. Operating income was US$554.0 million versus US$623.0 million in the prior-year quarter, a decrease of 11.1%. Direct operating expenses declined 9.7% to US$1.38 billion from US$1.53 billion in the comparable period the year before. Indirect operating expenses decreased 5.0% to US$574.0 million from US$604.0 million in the equivalent prior-year period.

Prospects: Our evaluation of Praxair Inc. as of June 19, 2016 is the result of our systematic analysis on three basic characteristics: earnings strength, relative valuation, and recent stock price movement. The company has managed to produce a neutral trend in earnings per share over the past 5 quarters and while recent estimates for the company have been mixed, PX has posted better than expected results. Based on operating earnings yield, the company is about fairly valued when compared to all of the companies in our coverage universe. Share price changes over the past year indicates that PX will perform well over the near term.

Financial Data
(US$ in Thousands)

	3 Mos	12/31/2015	12/31/2014	12/31/2013	12/31/2012	12/31/2011	12/31/2010	12/31/2009
Earnings Per Share	5.17	5.35	5.73	5.87	5.61	5.45	3.84	4.01
Cash Flow Per Share	9.53	9.34	9.81	9.87	9.20	8.12	6.21	7.05
Tang Book Value Per Share	4.35	2.93	6.56	9.58	11.42	9.88	11.82	10.12
Dividends Per Share	2.895	2.860	2.600	2.400	2.200	2.000	1.800	1.600
Dividend Payout %	56.00	53.46	45.38	40.89	39.22	36.70	46.88	39.90
Income Statement								
Total Revenue	2,509,000	10,776,000	12,273,000	11,925,000	11,224,000	11,252,000	10,116,000	8,956,000
EBITDA	826,000	3,427,000	3,778,000	3,734,000	3,438,000	3,471,000	3,007,000	2,421,000
Depn & Amortn	272,000	1,106,000	1,170,000	1,109,000	1,001,000	1,003,000	925,000	846,000
Income Before Taxes	489,000	2,160,000	2,395,000	2,447,000	2,296,000	2,323,000	1,964,000	1,442,000
Income Taxes	133,000	612,000	691,000	649,000	586,000	641,000	768,000	169,000
Net Income	356,000	1,547,000	1,694,000	1,755,000	1,692,000	1,672,000	1,195,000	1,254,000
Average Shares	286,665	289,055	295,608	298,965	301,845	306,722	311,395	312,382
Balance Sheet								
Current Assets	2,870,000	2,626,000	2,839,000	2,916,000	2,792,000	2,607,000	2,378,000	2,223,000
Total Assets	19,025,000	18,319,000	19,802,000	20,255,000	18,090,000	16,356,000	15,274,000	14,317,000
Current Liabilities	1,799,000	1,893,000	2,490,000	2,664,000	2,479,000	2,535,000	2,110,000	1,813,000
Long-Term Obligations	9,222,000	8,975,000	8,669,000	8,026,000	6,685,000	5,838,000	5,155,000	4,757,000
Total Liabilities	14,137,000	13,930,000	14,179,000	13,646,000	12,026,000	10,868,000	9,482,000	9,002,000
Stockholders' Equity	4,888,000	4,389,000	5,623,000	6,609,000	6,064,000	5,488,000	5,792,000	5,315,000
Shares Outstanding	285,264	284,879	289,261	294,133	296,229	298,530	303,996	306,477
Statistical Record								
Return on Assets %	7.80	8.12	8.46	9.15	9.80	10.57	8.08	9.16
Return on Equity %	30.02	30.90	27.70	27.70	29.21	29.65	21.52	26.90
EBITDA Margin %	32.92	31.80	30.78	31.31	30.63	30.85	29.73	27.03
Net Margin %	14.19	14.36	13.80	14.72	15.07	14.86	11.81	14.00
Asset Turnover	0.55	0.57	0.61	0.62	0.65	0.71	0.68	0.65
Current Ratio	1.60	1.39	1.14	1.09	1.13	1.03	1.13	1.23
Debt to Equity	1.89	2.04	1.54	1.21	1.10	1.06	0.89	0.90
Price Range	124.69-96.13	130.28-99.17	134.67-118.81	130.30-107.69	116.47-102.09	111.30-88.93	95.97-74.01	84.89-53.93
P/E Ratio	24.12-18.59	24.35-18.54	23.50-20.73	22.15-18.35	20.76-18.20	20.42-16.32	24.99-19.27	21.17-13.45
Average Yield %	2.60	2.45	2.01	2.04	2.03	2.00	2.13	2.19

Address: 39 Old Ridgebury Road, Danbury, CT 06810-5113 **Telephone:** 203-837-2000	**Web Site:** www.praxair.com **Officers:** Stephen F. Angel - Chairman, Chief Executive Officer Scott E. Telesz - Executive Vice President, Senior Vice President	**Auditors:** PricewaterhouseCoopersLLP **Investor Contact:** 203-837-2210 **Transfer Agents:** Registrar and Transfer Company, Cranford, NJ

PRESTIGE BRANDS HOLDINGS INC

Exchange	Symbol	Price	52Wk Range	Yield	P/E
NYS	PBH	$54.04 (5/31/2016)	57.60-43.62	N/A	28.74

*7 Year Price Score 176.61 *NYSE Composite Index=100 *12 Month Price Score 110.73

Interim Earnings (Per Share)

Qtr.	Jun	Sep	Dec	Mar
2011-12	0.29	0.26	0.19	0.00
2012-13	0.29	0.38	0.24	0.37
2013-14	0.40	0.63	0.06	0.31
2014-15	0.32	0.31	0.40	0.45
2015-16	0.49	0.60	0.53	0.26

Interim Dividends (Per Share)

No Dividends Paid

Valuation Analysis

		Institutional Holding	
Forecast EPS	$2.34	No of Institutions	
	(05/16/2016)	326	
Market Cap	$2.9 Billion	Shares	
Book Value	$744.3 Million	58,448,128	
Price/Book	3.83	% Held	
Price/Sales	3.54	105.06	

Business Summary: Pharmaceuticals (MIC: 4.1.1 SIC: 2834 NAIC: 325412)

Prestige Brands Holdings is a holding company. Through its subsidiaries, Co. markets, sells and distributes over-the-counter (OTC) healthcare and household cleaning brands to mass merchandisers, drug stores, supermarkets, convenience and dollar stores in North America (the U.S. and Canada) and in Australia and certain other international markets. Co.'s portfolio of OTC Healthcare products includes: DenTek oral care products, Monistat women's health products, Nix lice treatment, Chloraseptic sore throat treatments, Clear Eyes eye care products, Gaviscon antacid, and Dermoplast first-aid products. Co.'s portfolio of Household Cleaning brands includes Chore Boy, Comet and Spic and Span.

Recent Developments: For the year ended Mar 31 2016, net income increased 27.7% to US$99.9 million from US$78.3 million in the prior year. Revenues were US$806.2 million, up 12.8% from US$714.6 million the year before. Operating income was US$260.3 million versus US$207.6 million in the prior year, an increase of 25.4%. Direct operating expenses rose 9.9% to US$339.0 million from US$308.4 million in the comparable period the year before. Indirect operating expenses increased 4.1% to US$206.9 million from US$198.7 million in the equivalent prior-year period.

Prospects: Our evaluation of Prestige Brands Holdings Inc. as of June 19, 2016 is the result of our systematic analysis on three basic characteristics: earnings strength, relative valuation, and recent stock price movement. The company has generated a negative trend in earnings per share over the past 5 quarters. However, while recent estimates for the company has been lowered by analysts, PBH has posted better than expected results. Based on operating earnings yield, the company is about fairly valued when compared to all of the companies in our coverage universe. Share price changes over the past year indicates that PBH will perform very well over the near term.

Financial Data

(US$ in Thousands)

	03/31/2016	03/31/2015	03/31/2014	03/31/2013	03/31/2012	03/31/2011	03/31/2010	03/31/2009
Earnings Per Share	1.88	1.49	1.39	1.27	0.73	0.58	0.64	(3.74)
Cash Flow Per Share	3.30	3.00	2.16	2.72	1.34	1.73	1.19	1.34
Income Statement								
Total Revenue	806,247	714,623	601,881	623,597	441,085	336,510	302,023	312,715
EBITDA	247,545	212,492	173,530	192,041	103,177	87,698	89,422	(154,074)
Depn & Amortn	5,200	3,800	3,200	1,600	700	11,853	13,376	13,452
Income Before Taxes	157,185	127,458	101,748	106,034	61,157	48,528	53,111	(195,962)
Income Taxes	57,278	49,198	29,133	40,529	23,945	19,349	21,849	(9,186)
Net Income	99,907	78,260	72,615	65,505	37,212	29,220	32,115	(186,776)
Average Shares	53,143	52,670	52,349	51,440	50,748	50,338	50,084	49,935
Balance Sheet								
Current Assets	249,013	201,707	177,185	164,173	147,035	107,582	112,150	103,563
Total Assets	2,948,791	2,669,405	1,795,663	1,739,799	1,758,276	1,056,918	791,412	801,381
Current Liabilities	106,684	99,037	84,358	96,668	63,923	54,208	55,652	34,226
Long-Term Obligations	1,625,309	1,588,711	934,414	970,900	1,123,908	486,945	294,557	374,787
Total Liabilities	2,204,455	2,041,781	1,232,303	1,261,856	1,355,548	695,086	462,353	506,996
Stockholders' Equity	744,336	627,624	563,360	477,943	402,728	361,832	329,059	294,385
Shares Outstanding	52,760	52,296	51,815	51,130	50,285	50,116	50,030	49,936
Statistical Record								
Return on Assets %	3.55	3.51	4.11	3.75	2.64	3.16	4.03	N.M.
Return on Equity %	14.52	13.14	13.95	14.88	9.71	8.46	10.30	N.M.
EBITDA Margin %	30.70	29.73	28.83	30.80	23.39	26.06	29.61	N.M.
Net Margin %	12.39	10.95	12.06	10.50	8.44	8.68	10.63	N.M.
Asset Turnover	0.29	0.32	0.34	0.36	0.31	0.36	0.38	0.34
Current Ratio	2.33	2.04	2.10	1.70	2.30	1.98	2.02	3.03
Debt to Equity	2.18	2.53	1.66	2.03	2.79	1.35	0.90	1.27
Price Range	54.19-39.25	42.89-26.38	36.14-25.70	25.78-13.24	17.73-8.33	12.59-7.08	9.06-5.18	11.93-4.08
P/E Ratio	28.82-20.88	28.79-17.70	26.00-18.49	20.30-10.43	24.29-11.41	21.71-12.21	14.16-8.09	...

Address: 660 White Plains Road, Tarrytown, NY 10591 Telephone: 914-524-6800	Web Site: www.prestigebrands.com Officers: Ronald M. Lombardi - Chief Financial Officer, President, Chief Executive Officer Timothy J. Connors - Executive Vice President, Chief Marketing Officer	Auditors: PricewaterhouseCoopers LLP Investor Contact: 914-524-6819 Transfer Agents: Computershare Ltd., Canton, MA

PRIMERICA INC

Exchange	Symbol	Price	52Wk Range	Yield	P/E
NYS	PRI	$56.11 (5/31/2016)	56.11-39.93	1.21	14.73

*7 Year Price Score N/A   *NYSE Composite Index=100   *12 Month Price Score 106.79

Interim Earnings (Per Share)

Qtr.	Mar	Jun	Sep	Dec
2013	0.65	0.74	0.78	0.67
2014	0.81	0.89	0.75	0.85
2015	0.82	0.94	0.98	0.97
2016	0.92	...	...	...

Interim Dividends (Per Share)

Amt	Decl	Ex	Rec	Pay
0.16Q	08/07/2015	08/18/2015	08/20/2015	09/16/2015
0.16Q	11/09/2015	11/18/2015	11/20/2015	12/16/2015
0.17Q	02/08/2016	02/17/2016	02/19/2016	03/16/2016
0.17Q	05/09/2016	05/18/2016	05/20/2016	06/16/2016

Indicated Div: $0.68

Valuation Analysis   **Institutional Holding**

Forecast EPS	$4.22 (05/20/2016)	No of Institutions	249
Market Cap	$2.7 Billion	Shares	53,783,668
Book Value	$1.2 Billion	% Held	88.44
Price/Book	2.26		
Price/Sales	1.86		

Business Summary: Life & Health (MIC: 5.2.2 SIC: 6311 NAIC: 524113)

Primerica is a holding company. Through its subsidiaries, Co. distributes financial products in the U.S. and Canada. Co. has three operating segments: Term Life Insurance, which provides term life insurance to clients in the U.S., its territories, the District of Columbia and Canada; Investment and Savings Products, which includes mutual funds and annuities, segregated funds, and an individual annuity savings product that it underwrites in Canada; and Corporate and Other Distributed Products, which provides other products, including prepaid legal services, auto and homeowners' insurance referrals, credit information services, long-term care insurance, and debt resolution referrals.

Recent Developments: For the quarter ended Mar 31 2016, net income increased 4.1% to US$45.2 million from US$43.4 million in the year earlier quarter. Revenues were US$363.0 million, up 5.3% from US$344.8 million the year before. Net premiums earned were US$201.8 million versus US$179.9 million in the prior-year quarter, an increase of 12.2%. Net investment income was unchanged at US$21.2 million versus a year ago.

Prospects: Our evaluation of Primerica Inc as of June 19, 2016 is the result of our systematic analysis on three basic characteristics: earnings strength, relative valuation, and recent stock price movement. The company has managed to produce a neutral trend in earnings per share over the past 5 quarters. However, while recent estimates for the company have been mixed, PRI has posted better than expected results. Based on operating earnings yield, the company is undervalued when compared to all of the companies in our coverage universe. Share price changes over the past year indicates that PRI will perform poorly over the near term.

Financial Data
(US$ in Thousands)

	3 Mos	12/31/2015	12/31/2014	12/31/2013	12/31/2012	12/31/2011	12/31/2010	12/31/2009
Earnings Per Share	3.81	3.70	3.29	2.83	2.71	2.36	3.40	...
Cash Flow Per Share	4.69	5.09	4.36	3.37	1.96	1.22	0.57	...
Tang Book Value Per Share	23.58	22.52	22.68	21.03	21.39	20.82	18.62	...
Dividends Per Share	0.650	0.640	0.480	0.440	0.240	0.100	0.020	...
Dividend Payout %	17.06	17.30	14.59	15.55	8.86	4.24	0.59	...
Income Statement								
Total Revenue	362,962	1,405,314	1,340,030	1,267,448	1,190,715	1,103,093	1,361,863	2,220,401
Income Before Taxes	70,212	290,981	275,722	251,198	266,888	275,844	399,143	759,955
Income Taxes	25,036	101,110	95,888	88,473	93,082	97,568	141,365	265,366
Net Income	45,176	189,871	181,412	162,725	173,806	178,276	257,778	494,589
Average Shares	48,574	50,913	54,598	56,625	62,401	73,107	72,882	...
Balance Sheet								
Total Assets	11,012,788	10,612,119	10,738,114	10,329,950	10,337,877	9,998,544	9,884,306	13,227,781
Total Liabilities	9,840,030	9,466,347	9,492,988	9,107,923	9,062,461	8,575,903	8,452,814	8,284,008
Stockholders' Equity	1,172,758	1,145,772	1,245,126	1,222,027	1,275,416	1,422,641	1,431,492	4,943,773
Shares Outstanding	47,295	48,297	52,169	54,834	56,374	64,883	72,843	...
Statistical Record								
Return on Assets %	1.76	1.78	1.72	1.57	1.70	1.79	2.23	4.06
Return on Equity %	15.89	15.88	14.71	13.03	12.85	12.49	8.09	10.92
Net Margin %	12.45	13.51	13.54	12.84	14.60	16.16	18.93	22.27
Asset Turnover	0.13	0.13	0.13	0.12	0.12	0.11	0.12	0.18
Price Range	52.67-39.93	55.09-41.01	55.60-39.51	43.97-30.01	30.26-23.34	25.98-19.28	25.48-19.65	...
P/E Ratio	13.82-10.48	14.89-11.08	16.90-12.01	15.54-10.60	11.17-8.61	11.01-8.17	7.49-5.78	...
Average Yield %	1.42	1.34	1.01	1.18	0.89	0.44	0.09	...

Address: 1 Primerica Parkway, Duluth, GA 30099
Telephone: 770-381-1000

Web Site: www.primerica.com
Officers: Peter W. Schneider - President, Executive Vice President, Chief Administrative Officer, Corporate Secretary, General Counsel Glenn J. Williams - President, Chief Executive Officer

Auditors: KPMG LLP
Investor Contact: 866-694-0420
Transfer Agents: American Stock Transfer & Trust Company, Brooklyn, NY

PRINCIPAL FINANCIAL GROUP, INC.

Exchange	Symbol	Price	52Wk Range	Yield	P/E
NYS	PFG	$44.56 (5/31/2016)	57.98-34.34	3.50	11.34

*7 Year Price Score 109.62 *NYSE Composite Index=100   *12 Month Price Score 90.30

TRADING VOLUME (thousand shares)

Interim Earnings (Per Share)

Qtr.	Mar	Jun	Sep	Dec
2013	0.61	0.75	0.82	0.78
2014	0.95	1.03	0.77	0.90
2015	1.39	0.81	1.01	0.86
2016	1.25			

Interim Dividends (Per Share)

Amt	Decl	Ex	Rec	Pay
0.38Q	07/23/2015	09/02/2015	09/04/2015	09/25/2015
0.38Q	10/22/2015	12/03/2015	12/07/2015	12/28/2015
0.38Q	02/01/2016	03/03/2016	03/07/2016	03/25/2016
0.39Q	04/28/2016	06/02/2016	06/06/2016	06/24/2016

Indicated Div: $1.56

Valuation Analysis | Institutional Holding

Forecast EPS	$4.25	No of Institutions
	(05/20/2016)	632
Market Cap	$12.9 Billion	Shares
Book Value	$10.3 Billion	210,566,240
Price/Book	1.26	% Held
Price/Sales	1.05	67.10

Business Summary: Life & Health (MIC: 5.2.2 SIC: 6321 NAIC: 524114)

Principal Financial Group is an insurance holding company, engaged in investment management. Co. provides businesses, individuals and institutional clients a range of financial products and services, including retirement, asset management and insurance through its financial services companies. Co. provides long-term investment strategies to institutional, retirement, high net worth and retail clients by offering a range of capabilities including equity, fixed income, real estate and other alternative investments, as well as fund offerings. Co.'s segments include: Retirement and Income Solutions; Principal Global Investors; Principal International; and U.S. Insurance Solutions.

Recent Developments: For the quarter ended Mar 31 2016, net income decreased 14.0% to US$369.2 million from US$429.1 million in the year-earlier quarter. Revenues were US$3.04 billion, up 14.3% from US$2.66 billion the year before. Net premiums earned were US$1.28 billion versus US$916.4 million in the prior-year quarter, an increase of 39.9%. Net investment income rose 5.2% to US$761.7 million from US$723.9 million a year ago.

Prospects: Our evaluation of Principal Financial Group Inc. as of June 19, 2016 is the result of our systematic analysis on three basic characteristics: earnings strength, relative valuation, and recent stock price movement. The company has managed to produce a neutral trend in earnings per share over the past 5 quarters and while recent estimates for the company have been mixed, PFG has posted results that fell short of analysts expectations. Based on operating earnings yield, the company is undervalued when compared to all of the companies in our coverage universe. Share price changes over the past year indicates that PFG will perform poorly over the near term.

Financial Data

(US$ in Thousands)	3 Mos	12/31/2015	12/31/2014	12/31/2013	12/31/2012	12/31/2011	12/31/2010	12/31/2009
Earnings Per Share	3.93	4.06	3.65	2.95	2.57	2.15	2.06	1.97
Cash Flow Per Share	15.92	14.87	10.53	7.54	10.33	8.63	8.72	7.54
Tang Book Value Per Share	27.18	23.83	26.72	24.14	28.19	27.45	26.68	20.86
Dividends Per Share	1.520	1.500	1.280	0.980	0.780	0.700	0.550	0.500
Dividend Payout %	38.68	36.95	35.07	33.22	30.35	32.56	26.70	25.38
Income Statement								
Premium Income	1,282,400	5,310,300	3,722,900	3,154,100	3,219,400	2,891,000	3,555,500	3,750,600
Total Revenue	3,036,600	11,964,400	10,477,600	9,289,500	9,215,100	8,709,600	9,158,600	8,849,100
Benefits & Claims	1,658,500	6,697,700	5,231,000	4,683,600	5,123,900	4,454,100	5,338,400	5,334,500
Income Before Taxes	439,800	1,430,800	1,494,900	1,124,000	959,400	987,600	841,300	745,800
Income Taxes	70,600	177,600	318,500	187,900	134,700	236,400	124,100	100,100
Net Income	368,000	1,234,000	1,144,100	912,700	805,900	715,000	699,300	622,700
Average Shares	294,300	298,000	298,700	298,200	300,400	317,600	323,000	298,900
Balance Sheet								
Total Assets	217,570,000	218,685,900	219,087,000	208,191,400	161,926,500	148,298,000	145,631,100	137,759,400
Total Liabilities	207,267,500	209,374,300	208,903,000	198,507,200	152,173,300	138,661,000	135,903,300	129,865,900
Stockholders' Equity	10,302,500	9,311,600	10,184,000	9,684,200	9,753,200	9,637,000	9,727,800	7,893,500
Shares Outstanding	290,400	291,400	293,900	295,200	293,800	301,100	320,400	319,000
Statistical Record								
Return on Assets %	0.54	0.56	0.54	0.49	0.52	0.49	0.49	0.47
Return on Equity %	11.35	12.66	11.52	9.39	8.29	7.38	7.94	12.01
Loss Ratio %	129.33	126.13	140.51	148.49	159.16	154.07	150.14	142.23
Net Margin %	12.12	10.31	10.92	9.83	8.75	8.21	7.64	7.04
Price Range	57.98-34.34	57.98-43.82	54.62-41.71	50.63-28.52	29.93-23.23	34.69-21.22	33.32-21.45	30.83-5.88
P/E Ratio	14.75-8.74	14.28-10.79	14.96-11.43	17.16-9.67	11.65-9.04	16.13-9.87	16.17-10.41	15.65-2.98
Average Yield %	3.18	2.96	2.60	2.49	2.90	2.47	2.07	2.45

Address: 711 High Street, Des Moines, IA 50392 **Telephone:** 515-247-5111	**Web Site:** www.principal.com **Officers:** Daniel J. Houston - Chairman, President, Chief Executive Officer, Chief Operating Officer, Division Officer Karen E. Shaff - Executive Vice President, General Counsel, Second Vice Chairman	**Auditors:** Ernst & Young LLP **Investor Contact:** 515-235-9500 **Transfer Agents:** ComputerShare Investor Services, Providence, RI

PROASSURANCE CORP

Exchange	Symbol	Price	52Wk Range	Yield	P/E
NYS	PRA	$52.49 (5/31/2016)	53.42-44.76	2.36	29.16

*7 Year Price Score 104.05 *NYSE Composite Index=100 ***12 Month Price Score 99.57**

TRADING VOLUME (thousand shares)

Interim Earnings (Per Share)

Qtr.	Mar	Jun	Sep	Dec
2013	1.82	0.81	1.02	1.15
2014	0.76	0.84	0.59	1.11
2015	0.67	0.60	0.19	0.65
2016	0.36	...	...	...

Interim Dividends (Per Share)

Amt	Decl	Ex	Rec	Pay
0.31Q	12/02/2015	12/22/2015	12/24/2015	01/08/2016
1.00Sp	12/02/2015	12/22/2015	12/24/2015	01/08/2016
0.31Q	03/02/2016	03/28/2016	03/30/2016	04/12/2016
0.31Q	05/25/2016	06/22/2016	06/24/2016	07/08/2016

Indicated Div: $1.24

Valuation Analysis		Institutional Holding	
Forecast EPS	$2.30	No of Institutions	
	(05/13/2016)	296	
Market Cap	$2.8 Billion	Shares	
Book Value	$2.0 Billion	44,485,564	
Price/Book	1.41	% Held	
Price/Sales	3.69	72.78	

Business Summary: General Insurance (MIC: 5.2.1 SIC: 6331 NAIC: 524126)

ProAssurance is a holding company for property and casualty insurance companies. Co. operates in four segments: Specialty Property and Casualty, which includes its professional liability business and its medical technology and life sciences business; Workers' Compensation, which includes its workers' compensation business which it provides for employers, groups and associations; Lloyd's Syndicate, which includes operating results from its participation in Lloyd's Syndicate 1729; and Corporate, which includes its investing operations managed at the corporate level.

Recent Developments: For the quarter ended Mar 31 2016, net income decreased 48.9% to US$19.3 million from US$37.8 million in the year-earlier quarter. Revenues were US$193.4 million, down 7.0% from US$207.8 million the year before. Net premiums earned were US$177.6 million versus US$171.9 million in the prior-year quarter, an increase of 3.3%. Net investment income fell 6.8% to US$25.4 million from US$27.3 million a year ago.

Prospects: Our evaluation of ProAssurance Corp. as of June 19, 2016 is the result of our systematic analysis on three basic characteristics: earnings strength, relative valuation, and recent stock price movement. The company has managed to produce a neutral trend in earnings per share over the past 5 quarters and while recent estimates for the company have remained steady, PRA has posted results that fell short of analysts expectations. Based on operating earnings yield, the company is about fairly valued when compared to all of the companies in our coverage universe. Share price changes over the past year indicates that PRA will perform in line with the market over the near term.

Financial Data
(US$ in Thousands)

	3 Mos	12/31/2015	12/31/2014	12/31/2013	12/31/2012	12/31/2011	12/31/2010	12/31/2009
Earnings Per Share	1.80	2.11	3.30	4.80	4.46	4.66	3.60	3.35
Cash Flow Per Share	2.49	2.04	1.62	0.63	1.48	2.61	2.19	1.15
Tang Book Value Per Share	31.64	31.17	32.66	35.64	33.34	31.93	26.80	24.25
Dividends Per Share	2.240	2.240	3.860	1.050	3.125	0.250	...	...
Dividend Payout %	124.44	106.16	116.97	21.88	70.07	5.37	...	...
Income Statement								
Premium Income	177,579	694,149	699,731	527,919	550,664	565,415	519,107	497,543
Total Revenue	193,387	772,079	852,326	740,178	715,854	716,784	692,065	672,683
Benefits & Claims	128,186	456,862	379,232	243,015	161,726	151,270	252,615	265,983
Income Before Taxes	20,681	128,855	262,005	397,159	395,966	414,598	332,677	318,762
Income Taxes	1,364	12,658	65,440	99,636	120,496	127,502	101,079	96,736
Net Income	19,317	116,197	196,565	297,523	275,470	287,096	231,598	222,026
Average Shares	53,346	55,017	59,525	62,020	61,833	61,684	64,352	66,300
Balance Sheet								
Total Assets	4,894,499	4,908,163	5,169,160	5,150,891	4,876,578	4,998,878	4,875,056	4,647,414
Total Liabilities	2,909,985	2,949,809	3,011,216	2,756,477	2,605,998	2,834,425	3,019,193	2,942,819
Stockholders' Equity	1,984,514	1,958,354	2,157,944	2,394,414	2,270,580	2,164,453	1,855,863	1,704,595
Shares Outstanding	53,201	53,100	56,533	61,196	61,623	61,107	61,506	64,823
Statistical Record								
Return on Assets %	1.95	2.31	3.81	5.93	5.56	5.82	4.86	4.97
Return on Equity %	4.75	5.65	8.64	12.76	12.39	14.28	13.01	14.20
Loss Ratio %	72.19	65.82	54.20	46.03	29.37	26.75	48.66	53.46
Net Margin %	9.99	15.05	23.06	40.20	38.48	40.05	33.46	33.01
Price Range	53.42-43.73	53.42-43.73	48.48-42.90	55.28-42.19	46.48-39.35	40.60-28.98	31.16-24.59	27.48-20.33
P/E Ratio	29.68-24.29	25.32-20.73	14.69-13.00	11.52-8.79	10.42-8.82	8.71-6.22	8.65-6.83	8.20-6.07
Average Yield %	4.60	4.69	8.52	2.18	7.12	0.72	...	...

Address: 100 Brookwood Place, Birmingham, AL 35209
Telephone: 205-877-4400
Fax: 205-802-4799

Web Site: www.proassurance.com
Officers: W. Stancil Starnes - Chairman, Chief Executive Officer Victor T. Adamo - President

Auditors: Ernst & Young, LLP
Investor Contact: 205 877-4461
Transfer Agents: Mellon Investor Services, LLC, Ridgefield Park, NJ

PROCTER & GAMBLE CO.

Exchange	Symbol	Price	52Wk Range	Yield	P/E	Div Achiever
NYS	PG	$81.04 (5/31/2016)	83.81-68.06	3.27	25.48	62 Years

*7 Year Price Score 93.42 *NYSE Composite Index=100 *12 Month Price Score 103.25

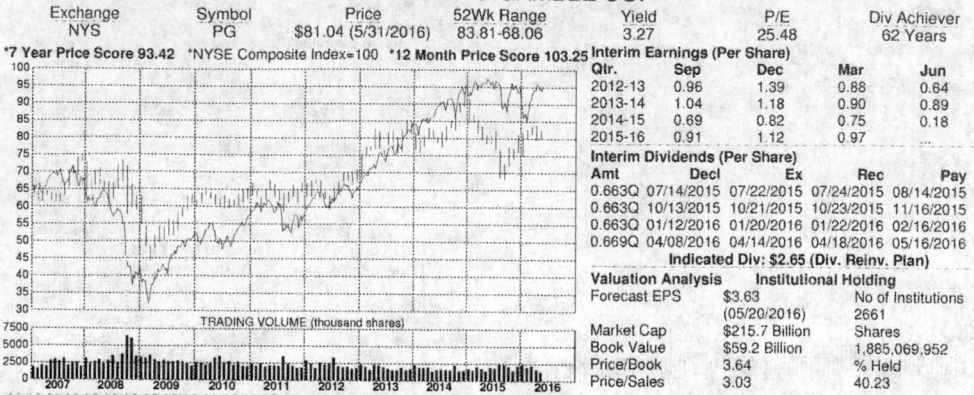

Interim Earnings (Per Share)

Qtr.	Sep	Dec	Mar	Jun
2012-13	0.96	1.39	0.88	0.64
2013-14	1.04	1.18	0.90	0.89
2014-15	0.69	0.82	0.75	0.18
2015-16	0.91	1.12	0.97	

Interim Dividends (Per Share)

Amt	Decl	Ex	Rec	Pay
0.663Q	07/14/2015	07/22/2015	07/24/2015	08/14/2015
0.663Q	10/13/2015	10/21/2015	10/23/2015	11/16/2015
0.663Q	01/12/2016	01/20/2016	01/22/2016	02/16/2016
0.669Q	04/08/2016	04/14/2016	04/18/2016	05/16/2016

Indicated Div: $2.65 (Div. Reinv. Plan)

Valuation Analysis

		Institutional Holding	
Forecast EPS	$3.63	No of Institutions	2661
	(05/20/2016)		
Market Cap	$215.7 Billion	Shares	
Book Value	$59.2 Billion		1,885,069,952
Price/Book	3.64	% Held	
Price/Sales	3.03		40.23

Business Summary: Household & Personal Products (MIC: 1.7.1 SIC: 2841 NAIC: 325611)

The Procter & Gamble provides consumer packaged goods. Co. sells its products through mass merchandisers, grocery stores, membership club stores, drug stores, department stores, salons, distributors, e-commerce, high-frequency stores and pharmacies. Co.'s segments include: Beauty, Hair and Personal Care, which include Skin and Personal Care, Cosmetics, Hair Care and Color, Prestige, and Salon Professional; Grooming, which include Shave Care, and Electronic Hair Removal; Health Care, which include Personal Health and Oral Care; Fabric Care and Home Care, which include Fabric Care, Home Care; and Baby, Feminine and Family Care, which include Baby Care, and Feminine and Family Care.

Recent Developments: For the quarter ended Mar 31 2016, income from continuing operations decreased 2.7% to US$2.34 billion from US$2.40 billion in the year-earlier quarter. Net income increased 27.2% to US$2.78 billion from US$2.19 billion in the year-earlier quarter. Revenues were US$15.76 billion, down 6.9% from US$16.93 billion the year before. Operating income was US$3.32 billion versus US$3.03 billion in the prior-year quarter, an increase of 9.7%. Direct operating expenses declined 11.3% to US$7.92 billion from US$8.93 billion in the comparable period the year before. Indirect operating expenses decreased 9.2% to US$4.52 billion from US$4.98 billion in the equivalent prior-year period.

Prospects: Our evaluation of Procter & Gamble Co. as of June 19, 2016 is the result of our systematic analysis on three basic characteristics: earnings strength, relative valuation, and recent stock price movement. The company has generated a negative trend in earnings per share over the past 5 quarters and while recent estimates for the company have remained steady, PG has posted better than expected results. Based on operating earnings yield, the company is about fairly valued when compared to all of the companies in our coverage universe. Share price changes over the past year indicates that PG will perform well over the near term.

Financial Data

(US$ in Millions)	9 Mos	6 Mos	3 Mos	06/30/2015	06/30/2014	06/30/2013	06/30/2012	06/30/2011
Earnings Per Share	3.18	2.96	2.66	2.44	4.01	3.86	3.66	3.93
Cash Flow Per Share	5.68	5.72	5.34	5.39	5.13	5.42	4.82	4.72
Dividends Per Share	2.652	2.632	2.613	2.594	2.448	2.288	2.137	1.970
Dividend Payout %	83.38	88.93	98.23	106.30	61.05	59.26	58.39	50.14
Income Statement								
Total Revenue	49,197	33,442	16,527	76,279	83,062	84,167	83,680	82,559
EBITDA	13,216	9,092	4,481	15,455	18,635	18,405	16,758	18,858
Depn & Amortn	2,239	1,454	731	3,134	3,141	2,982	3,204	2,838
Income Before Taxes	10,683	7,457	3,654	11,846	14,885	14,843	12,785	15,189
Income Taxes	2,664	1,775	877	2,916	3,178	3,441	3,468	3,392
Net Income	8,557	5,807	2,601	7,036	11,643	11,312	10,756	11,797
Average Shares	2,836	2,865	2,868	2,884	2,905	2,931	2,942	3,002
Balance Sheet								
Current Assets	34,317	36,347	35,620	29,646	31,617	23,990	21,910	21,970
Total Assets	127,508	129,143	129,265	129,495	144,266	139,263	132,244	138,354
Current Liabilities	31,357	32,053	31,567	29,790	33,726	30,037	24,907	27,293
Long-Term Obligations	19,134	17,595	17,394	18,329	19,811	19,111	21,080	22,033
Total Liabilities	68,321	67,515	66,978	67,076	75,052	71,199	68,805	70,714
Stockholders' Equity	59,187	61,628	62,287	62,419	69,214	68,064	63,439	67,640
Shares Outstanding	2,662	2,705	2,721	2,715	2,711	2,743	2,749	2,766
Statistical Record								
Return on Assets %	7.03	6.39	5.72	5.14	8.21	8.33	7.93	8.85
Return on Equity %	14.89	13.49	11.92	10.69	16.96	17.20	16.37	18.32
EBITDA Margin %	26.86	27.19	27.11	20.26	22.44	21.87	20.03	22.84
Net Margin %	17.39	17.36	15.74	9.22	14.02	13.44	12.85	14.29
Asset Turnover	0.55	0.56	0.58	0.56	0.59	0.62	0.62	0.62
Current Ratio	1.09	1.13	1.13	1.00	0.94	0.80	0.88	0.80
Debt to Equity	0.32	0.29	0.28	0.29	0.29	0.28	0.33	0.33
Price Range	83.60-68.06	91.62-68.06	93.46-68.06	93.46-77.32	85.41-75.59	82.54-61.19	67.90-58.51	67.46-59.34
P/E Ratio	26.29-21.40	30.95-22.99	35.14-25.59	38.30-31.69	21.30-18.85	21.38-15.85	18.55-15.99	17.17-15.10
Average Yield %	3.40	3.31	3.17	3.09	3.06	3.34	3.13	3.13

Address: One Procter & Gamble Plaza, Cincinnati, OH 45202
Telephone: 513-983-1100

Web Site: www.pg.com
Officers: David S. Taylor - Chairman, President, Chief Executive Officer, Division Officer Werner Geissler - Vice-Chairman, Advisor, Division Officer

Auditors: Deloitte & Touche LLP
Investor Contact: 800-742-6253
Transfer Agents: Computershare, Canton, MA

PROGRESSIVE CORP. (OH)

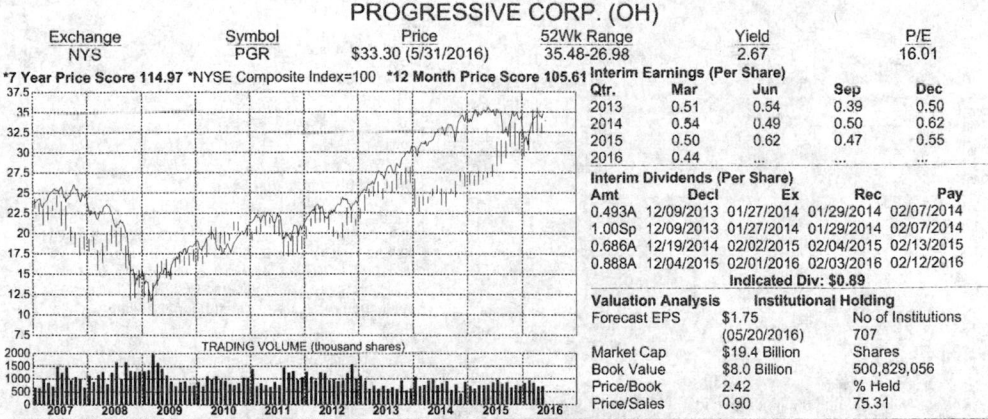

Exchange	Symbol	Price	52Wk Range	Yield	P/E
NYS	PGR	$33.30 (5/31/2016)	35.48-26.98	2.67	16.01

*7 Year Price Score 114.97 *NYSE Composite Index=100 *12 Month Price Score 105.61

Interim Earnings (Per Share)

Qtr.	Mar	Jun	Sep	Dec
2013	0.51	0.54	0.39	0.50
2014	0.54	0.49	0.50	0.62
2015	0.50	0.62	0.47	0.55
2016	0.44	...	...	...

Interim Dividends (Per Share)

Amt	Decl	Ex	Rec	Pay
0.493A	12/09/2013	01/27/2014	01/29/2014	02/07/2014
1.00Sp	12/09/2013	01/27/2014	01/29/2014	02/07/2014
0.686A	12/19/2014	02/02/2015	02/04/2015	02/13/2015
0.888A	12/04/2015	02/01/2016	02/03/2016	02/12/2016

Indicated Div: $0.89

Valuation Analysis

Forecast EPS	$1.75 (05/20/2016)	No of Institutions	707
Market Cap	$19.4 Billion	Shares	500,829,056
Book Value	$8.0 Billion	% Held	75.31
Price/Book	2.42		
Price/Sales	0.90		

Institutional Holding

Business Summary: General Insurance (MIC: 5.2.1 SIC: 6331 NAIC: 524126)

Progressive is an insurance holding company. Through its insurance subsidiaries and mutual insurance company affiliate, Co. provides personal and commercial automobile and property insurance, other property-casualty insurance and related services. Co.'s Personal Lines segment writes insurance for personal autos and recreational and other vehicles, while its commercial lines business writes liability, physical damage, and other auto-related insurance for automobiles and trucks owned and/or operated mainly by businesses. Co.'s service businesses primarily include: Commercial Auto Insurance Procedures/Plans and its commission-based service businesses.

Recent Developments: For the quarter ended Mar 31 2016, net income decreased 12.5% to US$258.7 million from US$295.6 million in the year-earlier quarter. Revenues were US$5.56 billion, up 13.5% from US$4.90 billion the year before. Net premiums earned were US$5.32 billion versus US$4.67 billion in the prior-year quarter, an increase of 14.0%. Net investment income rose 13.0% to US$118.8 million from US$105.1 million a year ago.

Prospects: Our evaluation of Progressive Corp. as of June 19, 2016 is the result of our systematic analysis on three basic characteristics: earnings strength, relative valuation, and recent stock price movement. The company has generated a negative trend in earnings per share over the past 5 quarters. However, while recent estimates for the company have been lowered by analysts, PGR has posted results that fell short of analysts expectations. Based on operating earnings yield, the company is undervalued when compared to all of the companies in our coverage universe. Share price changes over the past year indicates that PGR will perform very well over the near term.

Financial Data
(US$ in Thousands)

	3 Mos	12/31/2015	12/31/2014	12/31/2013	12/31/2012	12/31/2011	12/31/2010	12/31/2009
Earnings Per Share	2.08	2.15	2.15	1.93	1.48	1.59	1.61	1.57
Cash Flow Per Share	4.02	3.92	2.92	3.17	2.80	2.37	2.55	2.23
Tang Book Value Per Share	12.18	11.67	11.79	10.39	9.94	9.47	9.13	8.55
Dividends Per Share	0.888	0.686	1.493	0.284	1.407	0.399	1.161	0.161
Dividend Payout %	42.70	31.92	69.44	14.74	95.08	25.08	72.13	10.27
Income Statement								
Premium Income	5,317,400	19,899,100	18,398,500	17,103,400	16,018,000	14,902,800	14,314,800	14,012,800
Total Revenue	5,557,500	20,853,800	19,391,400	18,170,900	17,083,900	15,508,100	14,963,300	14,563,600
Benefits & Claims	3,913,400	14,342,000	13,306,200	12,472,400	11,948,000	10,634,800	10,131,300	9,904,900
Income Before Taxes	387,400	1,911,600	1,907,400	1,720,000	1,317,700	1,487,000	1,565,200	1,556,900
Income Taxes	128,700	611,100	626,400	554,600	415,400	471,500	496,900	499,400
Net Income	258,200	1,267,600	1,281,000	1,165,400	902,300	1,015,500	1,068,300	1,057,500
Average Shares	585,500	589,200	594,800	603,600	607,800	636,900	663,300	672,200
Balance Sheet								
Total Assets	30,721,600	29,819,300	25,787,600	24,408,200	22,694,700	21,844,800	21,150,300	20,049,300
Total Liabilities	22,694,300	22,065,000	18,859,000	18,218,700	16,687,700	16,038,100	15,101,400	14,300,700
Stockholders' Equity	8,027,300	7,754,300	6,928,600	6,189,500	6,007,000	5,806,700	6,048,900	5,748,600
Shares Outstanding	583,000	583,600	587,800	595,800	604,600	613,000	662,400	672,600
Statistical Record								
Return on Assets %	4.27	4.56	5.10	4.95	4.04	4.72	5.19	5.52
Return on Equity %	16.16	17.27	19.53	19.11	15.23	17.13	18.11	21.23
Loss Ratio %	73.60	72.07	72.32	72.92	74.59	71.36	70.78	70.68
Net Margin %	4.65	6.08	6.61	6.41	5.28	6.55	7.14	7.26
Price Range	35.17-26.55	33.64-25.85	27.35-22.59	28.14-21.10	23.30-19.24	21.94-17.09	21.97-16.21	18.05-9.89
P/E Ratio	16.91-12.76	15.65-12.02	12.72-10.51	14.58-10.93	15.74-13.00	13.80-10.75	13.65-10.07	11.50-6.30
Average Yield %	2.93	2.37	5.96	1.12	6.64	2.02	5.95	1.05

Address: 6300 Wilson Mills Road, Mayfield Village, OH 44143 **Telephone:** 440-461-5000 **Fax:** 440-446-7168	**Web Site:** www.progressive.com **Officers:** Susan Patricia Griffith - President, Chief Executive Officer, Personal Lines Chief Operating Officer, Division Officer Glenn M. Renwick Chairman, President, Chief Executive Officer	**Auditors:** PricewaterhouseCoopers LLP **Investor Contact:** 440-395-2222 **Transfer Agents:** American Stock Transfer & Trust Company, Brookly, NY

PROLOGIS INC

Exchange	Symbol	Price	52Wk Range	Yield	P/E
NYS	PLD	$47.53 (5/31/2016)	48.09-35.57	3.53	34.44

*7 Year Price Score 100.91 *NYSE Composite Index=100 *12 Month Price Score 110.33

Interim Earnings (Per Share)

Qtr.	Mar	Jun	Sep	Dec
2013	0.57	0.00	(0.02)	0.11
2014	0.01	0.13	0.23	0.81
2015	0.65	0.27	0.49	0.23
2016	0.39	...	...	...

Interim Dividends (Per Share)

Amt	Decl	Ex	Rec	Pay
0.40Q	07/21/2015	09/16/2015	09/18/2015	09/30/2015
0.40Q	12/04/2015	12/11/2015	12/15/2015	12/31/2015
0.42Q	02/26/2016	03/16/2016	03/18/2016	03/31/2016
0.42Q	05/04/2016	06/09/2016	06/13/2016	06/30/2016

Indicated Div: $1.68

Valuation Analysis

		Institutional Holding	
Forecast EPS	$1.08	No of Institutions	
	(05/20/2016)	60	
Market Cap	$25.0 Billion	Shares	
Book Value	$14.6 Billion		10,207,956
Price/Book	1.71	% Held	
Price/Sales	10.66	N/A	

Business Summary: REITs (MIC: 5.3.1 SIC: 6798 NAIC: 525930)

Prologis is a real estate investment trust. Through its approximate 97.12% common general partnership interest in Prologis, L.P., Co. is engaged in the ownership, acquisition, development and operation of industrial properties in global and regional markets throughout the Americas, Europe and Asia. Co. has investments in entities through a variety of ventures. Co. co-invests with partners and investors in entities that own multiple properties and provide asset and property management services to these entities. Co. refers to these entities as co-investment ventures. Co.'s business comprises two operating segments: Real Estate Operations and Strategic Capital.

Recent Developments: For the quarter ended Mar 31 2016, net income decreased 36.6% to US$222.8 million from US$351.3 million in the year-earlier quarter. Revenues were US$606.3 million, up 31.0% from US$462.8 million the year before. Revenues from property income rose 32.3% to US$554.1 million from US$418.8 million in the corresponding quarter a year earlier.

Prospects: Our evaluation of Prologis Inc. as of June 19, 2016 is the result of our systematic analysis on three basic characteristics: earnings strength, relative valuation, and recent stock price movement. The company has produced a positive trend in earnings per share over the past 5 quarters. Because the company lacks sufficient analyst estimate data, we place greater weight on the historical EPS trend as the measure of earnings strength. Based on operating earnings yield, the company is overvalued when compared to all of the companies in our coverage universe. Share price changes over the past year indicates that PLD will perform well over the near term.

Financial Data

(US$ in Thousands)	3 Mos	12/31/2015	12/31/2014	12/31/2013	12/31/2012	12/31/2011	12/31/2010	12/31/2009
Earnings Per Share	1.38	1.64	1.24	0.64	(0.18)	(0.51)	0.06	(0.37)
Cash Flow Per Share	2.19	1.85	1.41	1.00	1.01	0.56	1.56	1.80
Tang Book Value Per Share	27.72	27.82	27.28	27.29	27.04	28.52	18.36	18.20
Dividends Per Share	1.580	1.520	1.320	1.120	1.120	1.120	1.120	1.120
Dividend Payout %	114.49	92.68	106.45	175.00	...	...	1,866.67	...
Income Statement								
Total Revenue	606,300	2,197,074	1,760,787	1,750,486	2,005,961	1,533,291	633,500	633,842
EBITDA	247,657	1,853,116	1,548,602	1,265,568	1,151,775	801,552	349,717	201,721
Depn & Amortn	(10,595)	787,894	686,145	674,147	788,467	647,440	227,399	214,278
Income Before Taxes	180,031	789,343	579,340	239,042	(121,298)	(302,618)	(8,020)	(134,016)
Income Taxes	15,537	23,090	(25,656)	106,733	3,580	1,776	...	...
Net Income	209,730	869,439	636,183	342,921	(39,720)	(153,414)	27,119	(43,001)
Average Shares	543,562	533,944	506,391	491,546	459,895	370,534	161,988	134,321
Balance Sheet								
Current Assets	369,737	454,456	548,355	758,629	448,820	396,063	396,150	362,035
Total Assets	31,375,748	31,394,767	25,818,223	24,572,307	27,310,145	27,723,912	7,372,895	6,841,958
Current Liabilities	698,678	994,282	895,883	1,074,229	611,770	639,490	339,474	338,042
Long-Term Obligations	11,687,171	11,626,831	9,380,199	9,011,216	11,790,794	11,382,408	3,331,299	3,212,596
Total Liabilities	16,743,087	16,726,832	11,842,714	10,861,149	14,241,128	14,062,273	4,052,172	3,901,942
Stockholders' Equity	14,632,661	14,667,935	13,975,509	13,711,158	13,069,017	13,661,639	3,320,723	2,940,016
Shares Outstanding	525,132	524,512	509,498	498,799	461,770	458,597	168,736	149,258
Statistical Record								
Return on Assets %	2.58	3.04	2.53	1.32	N.M.	N.M.	0.38	N.M.
Return on Equity %	5.01	6.07	4.60	2.56	N.M.	N.M.	0.87	N.M.
EBITDA Margin %	40.85	84.34	87.95	72.30	57.42	52.28	55.20	31.83
Net Margin %	34.59	39.57	36.13	19.59	N.M.	N.M.	4.28	N.M.
Asset Turnover	0.08	0.08	0.07	0.07	0.07	0.09	0.09	0.09
Current Ratio	0.53	0.46	0.61	0.71	0.73	0.62	1.17	1.07
Debt to Equity	0.80	0.79	0.67	0.66	0.90	0.83	1.00	1.09
Price Range	44.37-35.57	47.13-36.45	43.64-36.51	44.77-34.78	36.91-28.50	37.26-22.63	31.82-22.14	26.91-9.72
P/E Ratio	32.15-25.78	28.74-22.23	35.19-29.44	69.95-54.34	...	...	530.33-369.00	...
Average Yield %	3.90	3.67	3.26	2.87	3.33	3.55	4.23	5.67

Address: Pier 1, Bay 1, San Francisco, CA 94111	Web Site: www.prologis.com	Auditors: KPMG LLP
Telephone: 415-394-9000	**Officers:** Hamid R. Moghadam - Chairman, Chief Executive Officer, Co-Chief Executive Officer	**Investor Contact:** 415-733-9565
Fax: 415-394-9001	Deborah K. Briones - Senior Vice President, Associate General Counsel	**Transfer Agents:** Computershare Investor Services, Canton, MA

PROSPERITY BANCSHARES INC.

Exchange	Symbol	Price	52Wk Range	Yield	P/E	Div Achiever
NYS	PB	$53.85 (5/31/2016)	59.23-33.73	2.23	13.40	16 Years

*7 Year Price Score 91.34   *NYSE Composite Index=100   *12 Month Price Score 99.05

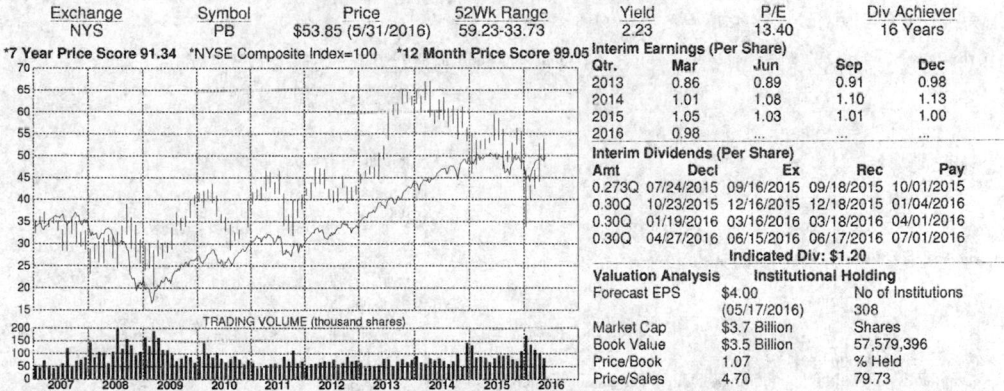

Interim Earnings (Per Share)

Qtr.	Mar	Jun	Sep	Dec
2013	0.86	0.89	0.91	0.98
2014	1.01	1.08	1.10	1.13
2015	1.05	1.03	1.01	1.00
2016	0.98	...	...	...

Interim Dividends (Per Share)

Amt	Decl	Ex	Rec	Pay
0.273Q	07/24/2015	09/16/2015	09/18/2015	10/01/2015
0.30Q	10/23/2015	12/16/2015	12/18/2015	01/04/2016
0.30Q	01/19/2016	03/16/2016	03/18/2016	04/01/2016
0.30Q	04/27/2016	06/15/2016	06/17/2016	07/01/2016

Indicated Div: $1.20

Valuation Analysis   Institutional Holding

Forecast EPS	$4.00
	(05/17/2016)
Market Cap	$3.7 Billion
Book Value	$3.5 Billion
Price/Book	1.07
Price/Sales	4.70

No of Institutions	308
Shares	57,579,396
% Held	79.73

Business Summary: Banking (MIC: 5.1.1 SIC: 6022 NAIC: 522110)

Prosperity Bancshares is a financial holding company. Through its subsidiary, Prosperity Bank®, Co. provides financial products and services to small and medium-sized businesses and consumers. Co. is a real estate lender with commercial real estate and one-four family residential loans. Co. also provides commercial loans, loans for automobiles and other consumer durables, home equity loans, debit and credit cards, internet banking and other cash management services, mobile banking, trust and wealth management, retail brokerage services, mortgage banking services and automated telephone banking. As of Dec 31 2015, Co. had total assets of $22.04 billion and total deposits of $17.68 billion.

Recent Developments: For the quarter ended Mar 31 2016, net income decreased 6.4% to US$69.0 million from US$73.6 million in the year-earlier quarter. Net interest income increased 2.1% to US$166.3 million from US$162.9 million in the year-earlier quarter. Provision for loan losses was US$14.0 million versus US$1.3 million in the prior-year quarter, an increase of. Non-interest income rose 8.3% to US$30.8 million from US$28.4 million, while non-interest expense advanced 1.3% to US$80.5 million.

Prospects: Our evaluation of Prosperity Bancshares Inc. as of June 19, 2016 is the result of our systematic analysis on three basic characteristics: earnings strength, relative valuation, and recent stock price movement. The company has enjoyed a very positive trend in earnings per share over the past 5 quarters. However, while recent estimates for the company have been lowered by analysts, PB has posted better than expected results. Based on operating earnings yield, the company is undervalued when compared to all of the companies in our coverage universe. Share price changes over the past year indicates that PB will perform poorly over the near term.

Financial Data
(US$ in Thousands)

	3 Mos	12/31/2015	12/31/2014	12/31/2013	12/31/2012	12/31/2011	12/31/2010	12/31/2009
Earnings Per Share	4.02	4.09	4.32	3.65	3.23	3.01	2.73	2.41
Cash Flow Per Share	5.06	4.44	5.06	5.09	4.04	4.65	3.81	1.59
Tang Book Value Per Share	22.27	22.06	18.80	16.25	14.99	13.25	10.70	9.43
Dividends Per Share	1.145	1.117	0.993	0.885	0.800	0.720	0.640	0.568
Dividend Payout %	28.48	27.32	22.97	24.25	24.77	23.92	23.44	23.55
Income Statement								
Interest Income	177,191	669,701	714,795	539,297	419,842	371,908	384,537	409,614
Interest Expense	10,934	39,191	43,641	40,471	39,136	45,240	66,389	102,513
Net Interest Income	166,257	630,510	671,154	498,826	380,706	326,668	318,148	307,101
Provision for Losses	14,000	7,560	18,275	17,240	6,100	5,200	13,585	28,775
Non-Interest Income	30,793	120,781	122,872	95,427	75,535	56,043	53,833	60,097
Non-Interest Expense	80,528	313,536	330,002	247,196	198,457	163,745	166,594	169,700
Income Before Taxes	102,522	430,195	445,749	329,817	251,684	213,766	191,802	168,723
Income Taxes	33,571	143,549	148,308	108,419	83,783	72,017	64,094	56,844
Net Income	68,951	286,646	297,441	221,398	167,901	141,749	127,708	111,879
Average Shares	70,181	70,049	68,911	60,578	51,941	47,017	46,832	46,354
Balance Sheet								
Net Loans & Leases	9,570,694	9,357,205	9,163,421	7,707,939	5,127,376	3,714,312	3,433,439	3,324,840
Total Assets	21,978,345	22,037,216	21,507,733	18,642,028	14,583,573	9,822,671	9,476,572	8,850,400
Total Deposits	17,872,766	17,681,119	17,693,158	15,291,271	11,641,844	8,060,254	7,454,920	7,258,550
Total Liabilities	18,479,285	18,574,306	18,262,907	15,855,210	12,494,184	8,255,406	8,024,233	7,499,155
Stockholders' Equity	3,499,060	3,462,910	3,244,826	2,786,818	2,089,389	1,567,265	1,452,339	1,351,245
Shares Outstanding	69,543	70,021	69,779	66,048	56,447	46,910	46,684	46,540
Statistical Record								
Return on Assets %	1.29	1.32	1.48	1.33	1.37	1.47	1.39	1.25
Return on Equity %	8.29	8.55	9.86	9.08	9.16	9.39	9.11	8.59
Net Interest Margin %	93.83	94.15	93.89	92.50	90.68	87.84	82.74	74.97
Efficiency Ratio %	38.72	39.66	39.40	38.95	40.06	38.26	38.00	36.13
Loans to Deposits	0.54	0.53	0.52	0.50	0.44	0.46	0.46	0.46
Price Range	59.23-33.73	59.23-45.79	67.00-53.21	65.07-42.00	47.31-39.10	46.50-31.67	43.53-28.49	40.98-20.33
P/E Ratio	14.73-8.39	14.48-11.20	15.51-12.32	17.83-11.51	14.65-12.11	15.45-10.52	15.95-10.44	17.00-8.44
Average Yield %	2.28	2.13	1.65	1.63	1.89	1.79	1.76	1.80

Address: Prosperity Bank Plaza, 4295 San Felipe, Houston, TX 77027 **Telephone:** 713-693-9300	**Web Site:** www.prosperitybankusa.com **Officers:** David Zalman - Chairman, President, Chief Executive Officer H. E. Timanus - Vice-Chairman	**Auditors:** Deloitte & Touche LLP **Investor Contact:** 713-693-9300 **Transfer Agents:** Computershare Investor Services, Golden, Co

PRUDENTIAL FINANCIAL, INC.

Exchange	Symbol	Price	52Wk Range	Yield	P/E
NYS	PRU	$79.25 (5/31/2016)	91.68-58.00	3.53	7.39

*7 Year Price Score 101.60 *NYSE Composite Index=100 ***12 Month Price Score 95.34**

Interim Earnings (Per Share)

Qtr.	Mar	Jun	Sep	Dec
2013	(1.55)	(1.13)	2.07	(0.98)
2014	2.59	2.22	0.99	(2.57)
2015	4.37	3.03	3.16	1.61
2016	2.93	...	...	...

Interim Dividends (Per Share)

Amt	Decl	Ex	Rec	Pay
0.58Q	08/11/2015	08/21/2015	08/25/2015	09/17/2015
0.70Q	11/10/2015	11/20/2015	11/24/2015	12/17/2015
0.70Q	02/09/2016	02/19/2016	02/23/2016	03/17/2016
0.70Q	05/10/2016	05/20/2016	05/24/2016	06/16/2016

Indicated Div: $2.80

Valuation Analysis

		Institutional Holding	
Forecast EPS	$9.60	No of Institutions	
	(05/20/2016)	1096	
Market Cap	$35.1 Billion	Shares	
Book Value	$49.2 Billion	313,076,320	
Price/Book	0.71	% Held	
Price/Sales	0.63	61.25	

Business Summary: Life & Health (MIC: 5.2.2 SIC: 6311 NAIC: 524113)

Prudential Financial is a holding company. Through its subsidiaries and affiliates, Co. provides financial products and services, including life insurance, annuities, retirement-related services, mutual funds and investment management. The U.S. Retirement Solutions and Investment Management division consists of Co.'s Individual Annuities, Retirement and Asset Management segments. The U.S. Individual Life and Group Insurance division consists of Co.'s Individual Life and Group Insurance segments. The International Insurance division consists of Co.'s International Insurance segment. As of Dec 31 2015, Co. had approx. $1.18 trillion of assets under management.

Recent Developments: For the quarter ended Mar 31 2016, income from continuing operations decreased 33.1% to US$1.37 billion from US$2.05 billion in the year-earlier quarter. Net income decreased 33.1% to US$1.37 billion from US$2.05 billion in the year-earlier quarter. Revenues were US$14.33 billion, down 7.9% from US$15.55 billion the year before. Net premiums earned were US$6.30 billion versus US$6.65 billion in the prior-year quarter, a decrease of 5.3%. Net investment income fell 2.6% to US$3.67 billion from US$3.77 billion a year ago.

Prospects: Our evaluation of Prudential Financial Inc. as of June 19, 2016 is the result of our systematic analysis on three basic characteristics: earnings strength, relative valuation, and recent stock price movement. The company has generated a negative trend in earnings per share over the past 5 quarters. However, while recent estimates for the company have been mixed, PRU has posted results that fell short of analysts expectations. Based on operating earnings yield, the company is undervalued when compared to all of the companies in our coverage universe. Share price changes over the past year indicates that PRU will perform well over the near term.

Financial Data
(US$ in Millions)

	3 Mos	12/31/2015	12/31/2014	12/31/2013	12/31/2012	12/31/2011	12/31/2010	12/31/2009
Earnings Per Share	10.73	12.17	3.23	(1.55)	0.94	7.22	5.75	7.63
Cash Flow Per Share	32.92	30.76	42.30	18.24	44.78	25.77	14.01	13.14
Tang Book Value Per Share	111.12	93.69	91.84	76.19	82.95	79.19	66.73	54.29
Dividends Per Share	2.560	2.440	2.170	1.730	1.600	1.450	1.150	0.700
Dividend Payout %	23.86	20.05	67.18	...	170.21	20.08	20.00	9.17
Income Statement								
Premium Income	6,297	28,521	29,293	26,237	65,354	24,338	18,260	16,545
Total Revenue	14,329	57,119	54,105	41,461	84,815	49,045	38,414	32,688
Benefits & Claims	7,031	30,627	31,587	26,733	65,131	23,614	18,285	16,346
Income Before Taxes	1,732	7,769	1,759	(1,684)	676	5,117	4,422	1,569
Income Taxes	368	2,072	349	(1,058)	204	1,599	1,310	21
Net Income	1,336	5,642	1,381	(667)	469	3,666	3,195	3,124
Average Shares	453	460	467	463	468	488	475	448
Balance Sheet								
Total Assets	772,995	757,388	766,655	731,781	709,298	624,521	539,854	480,203
Total Liabilities	723,753	715,498	724,885	696,503	670,723	587,298	507,439	455,008
Stockholders' Equity	49,242	41,890	41,770	35,278	38,575	37,223	32,415	25,195
Shares Outstanding	443	447	454	463	465	470	485	464
Statistical Record								
Return on Assets %	0.64	0.74	0.18	N.M.	0.07	0.63	0.63	0.68
Return on Equity %	10.48	13.49	3.58	N.M.	1.23	10.53	11.09	16.18
Loss Ratio %	111.66	107.38	107.83	101.89	99.66	97.03	100.14	98.80
Net Margin %	9.32	9.88	2.55	(1.61)	0.55	7.47	8.32	9.56
Price Range	91.68-58.00	91.68-74.22	93.16-77.61	92.43-53.33	64.65-44.74	67.32-43.91	65.82-47.02	54.63-11.29
P/E Ratio	8.54-5.41	7.53-6.10	28.84-24.03	...	68.78-47.60	9.32-6.08	11.45-8.18	7.16-1.48
Average Yield %	3.18	2.93	2.51	2.41	2.93	2.55	2.06	1.84

Address: 751 Broad Street, Newark, NJ 07102	**Web Site:** www.investor.prudential.com	**Auditors:** PricewaterhouseCoopers LLP
Telephone: 973-802-6000	**Officers:** John R. Strangfeld - Chairman, President, Chief Executive Officer, Division Officer Mark B. Grier - Vice-Chairman, Division Officer	**Transfer Agents:** Computershare Trust Company, N.A., Providence, RI

PUBLIC SERVICE ENTERPRISE GROUP INC

Exchange	Symbol	Price	52Wk Range	Yield	P/E
NYS	PEG	$44.75 (5/31/2016)	47.32-37.02	3.66	14.53

*7 Year Price Score 102.62 *NYSE Composite Index=100 *12 Month Price Score 107.58

Interim Earnings (Per Share)

Qtr.	Mar	Jun	Sep	Dec
2013	0.63	0.66	0.77	0.39
2014	0.76	0.42	0.88	0.94
2015	1.15	0.68	0.87	0.60
2016	0.93	...	...	...

Interim Dividends (Per Share)

Amt	Decl	Ex	Rec	Pay
0.39Q	07/21/2015	09/04/2015	09/09/2015	09/30/2015
0.39Q	11/19/2015	12/07/2015	12/09/2015	12/31/2015
0.41Q	02/16/2016	03/08/2016	03/10/2016	03/31/2016
0.41Q	04/19/2016	06/07/2016	06/09/2016	06/30/2016

Indicated Div: $1.64

Valuation Analysis | **Institutional Holding**

Forecast EPS	$2.87	No of Institutions
	(05/20/2016)	944
Market Cap	$22.6 Billion	Shares
Book Value	$13.3 Billion	366,913,344
Price/Book	1.70	% Held
Price/Sales	2.28	64.78

Business Summary: Electric Utilities (MIC: 3.1.1 SIC: 4931 NAIC: 221119)

Public Service Enterprise Group is a holding company. Through its subsidiaries, Co. is engaged in the energy industry. Co.'s Public Service Electric and Gas Company (PSE&G) subsidiary is engaged in the transmission of electricity and distribution of electricity and natural gas in certain areas of New Jersey, while its PSEG Power LLC subsidiary is a wholesale energy supply company. As of Dec 31 2015, Co.'s PSE&G subsidiary provided distribution service to 2.2 million electric customers and 1.8 million gas customers across New Jersey. Co.'s other subsidiaries include, among others, PSEG Energy Holdings L.L.C., which primarily has investments in leveraged leases.

Recent Developments: For the quarter ended Mar 31 2016, net income decreased 19.6% to US$471.0 million from US$586.0 million in the year-earlier quarter. Revenues were US$2.62 billion, down 16.6% from US$3.14 billion the year before. Operating income was US$827.0 million versus US$1.05 billion in the prior-year quarter, a decrease of 21.1%. Direct operating expenses declined 10.9% to US$1.57 billion from US$1.76 billion in the comparable period the year before. Indirect operating expenses decreased 32.1% to US$224.0 million from US$330.0 million in the equivalent prior-year period.

Prospects: Our evaluation of Public Service Enterprise Group Inc. as of June 19, 2016 is the result of our systematic analysis on three basic characteristics: earnings strength, relative valuation, and recent stock price movement. The company has generated a negative trend in earnings per share over the past 5 quarters. However, while recent estimates for the company have been mixed, PEG has posted better than expected results. Based on operating earnings yield, the company is undervalued when compared to all of the companies in our coverage universe. Share price changes over the past year indicates that PEG will perform very well over the near term.

Financial Data

(US$ in Thousands)	3 Mos	12/31/2015	12/31/2014	12/31/2013	12/31/2012	12/31/2011	12/31/2010	12/31/2009
Earnings Per Share	3.08	3.30	2.99	2.45	2.51	2.96	3.08	3.14
Cash Flow Per Share	6.84	7.76	6.25	6.24	5.49	7.03	4.28	3.67
Tang Book Value Per Share	26.12	25.63	23.89	22.85	21.21	20.01	18.74	17.25
Dividends Per Share	1.580	1.560	1.480	1.440	1.420	1.370	1.370	1.330
Dividend Payout %	51.30	47.27	49.50	58.78	56.57	46.28	44.48	42.36
Income Statement								
Total Revenue	2,616,000	10,415,000	10,886,000	9,968,000	9,781,000	11,079,000	11,793,000	12,406,000
EBITDA	860,000	4,114,000	3,816,000	3,449,000	3,264,000	3,635,000	3,880,000	3,909,000
Depn & Amortn	58,000	1,214,000	1,227,000	1,178,000	1,054,000	976,000	955,000	838,000
Income Before Taxes	752,000	2,668,000	2,443,000	2,044,000	1,999,000	2,380,000	2,612,000	2,597,000
Income Taxes	283,000	1,001,000	938,000	812,000	736,000	977,000	1,059,000	1,044,000
Net Income	471,000	1,679,000	1,518,000	1,243,000	1,275,000	1,503,000	1,564,000	1,592,000
Average Shares	508,000	508,000	508,000	507,525	507,086	506,982	507,045	507,064
Balance Sheet								
Current Assets	3,263,000	3,494,000	4,119,000	3,614,000	3,869,000	3,911,000	5,051,000	3,646,000
Total Assets	38,126,000	37,535,000	35,333,000	32,522,000	31,725,000	29,821,000	29,909,000	28,730,000
Current Liabilities	2,942,000	3,575,000	3,478,000	3,063,000	3,777,000	2,957,000	3,485,000	3,214,000
Long-Term Obligations	9,676,000	8,834,000	8,261,000	7,862,000	6,687,000	7,461,000	7,819,000	7,645,000
Total Liabilities	24,808,000	24,469,000	23,148,000	20,914,000	20,945,000	19,551,000	20,276,000	19,862,000
Stockholders' Equity	13,318,000	13,066,000	12,185,000	11,608,000	10,780,000	10,270,000	9,633,000	8,868,000
Shares Outstanding	505,000	505,282	505,836	505,857	505,892	505,945	505,974	505,989
Statistical Record								
Return on Assets %	4.23	4.61	4.47	3.87	4.13	5.03	5.33	5.51
Return on Equity %	12.09	13.30	12.76	11.10	12.08	15.10	16.91	19.04
EBITDA Margin %	32.87	39.50	35.05	34.60	33.37	32.81	32.90	31.51
Net Margin %	18.00	16.12	13.94	12.47	13.04	13.57	13.26	12.83
Asset Turnover	0.27	0.29	0.32	0.31	0.32	0.37	0.40	0.43
Current Ratio	1.11	0.98	1.18	1.18	1.02	1.32	1.45	1.13
Debt to Equity	0.73	0.68	0.68	0.68	0.62	0.73	0.81	0.86
Price Range	47.14-37.02	44.30-37.02	43.53-31.33	36.61-29.78	34.00-29.09	34.81-28.84	34.78-29.11	33.86-24.02
P/E Ratio	15.31-12.02	13.42-11.22	14.56-10.48	14.94-12.16	13.55-11.59	11.76-9.74	11.29-9.45	10.78-7.65
Average Yield %	3.83	3.80	3.93	4.36	4.54	4.24	4.31	4.30

Address: 80 Park Plaza, P.O. Box 1171, Newark, NJ 07101-1171 **Telephone:** 973-430-7000	**Web Site:** www.pseg.com **Officers:** Ralph Izzo - Chairman, President, Chief Executive Officer Daniel J. Cregg - Executive Vice President, Chief Financial Officer	**Auditors:** Deloitte and Touche LLP **Investor Contact:** 973-430-6565 **Transfer Agents:** Wells Fargo Bank, N.A., Mendota Heights, MN

PULTEGROUP INC

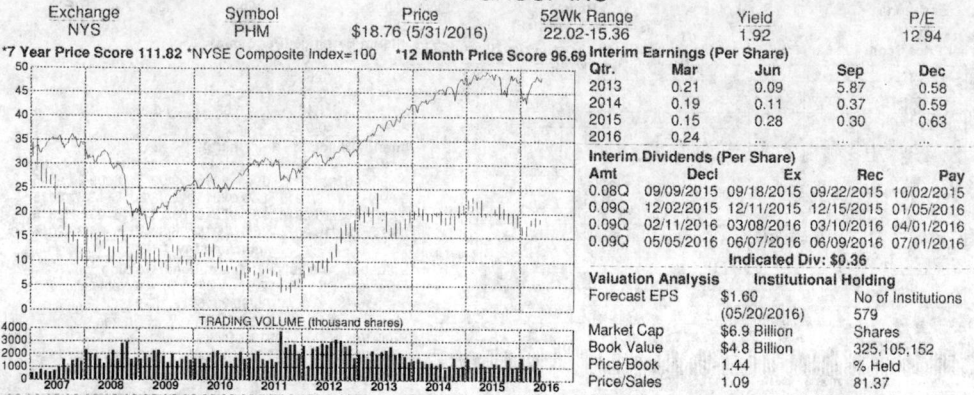

Exchange	Symbol	Price	52Wk Range	Yield	P/E
NYS	PHM	$18.76 (5/31/2016)	22.02-15.36	1.92	12.94

*7 Year Price Score 111.82 *NYSE Composite Index=100 *12 Month Price Score 96.69

Interim Earnings (Per Share)

Qtr.	Mar	Jun	Sep	Dec
2013	0.21	0.09	5.87	0.58
2014	0.19	0.11	0.37	0.59
2015	0.15	0.28	0.30	0.63
2016	0.24			

Interim Dividends (Per Share)

Amt	Decl	Ex	Rec	Pay
0.08Q	09/09/2015	09/18/2015	09/22/2015	10/02/2015
0.09Q	12/02/2015	12/11/2015	12/15/2015	01/05/2016
0.09Q	02/11/2016	03/08/2016	03/10/2016	04/01/2016
0.09Q	05/05/2016	06/07/2016	06/09/2016	07/01/2016

Indicated Div: $0.36

Valuation Analysis — **Institutional Holding**

Forecast EPS	$1.60	No of Institutions	
	(05/20/2016)	579	
Market Cap	$6.9 Billion	Shares	
Book Value	$4.8 Billion	325,105,152	
Price/Book	1.44	% Held	
Price/Sales	1.09	81.37	

Business Summary: Builders (MIC: 2.2.5 SIC: 1531 NAIC: 236117)

PulteGroup is engaged in the homebuilding business, which includes the acquisition and development of land primarily for residential purposes within the U.S. and the construction of housing on such land. Through its brands, which include Pulte Homes, Del Webb, and Centex, Co. offers home designs that include single-family detached, townhouses, condominiums, and duplexes at different prices and with varying levels of options and amenities to its customer groups: first-time, move-up, and active adult. Co. conducts its operations in 50 markets located throughout 26 states. Co.'s Homebuilding operations' reportable segments include: Northeast, Southeast, Florida, Midwest, Texas, and West.

Recent Developments: For the quarter ended Mar 31 2016, net income increased 51.5% to US$83.3 million from US$55.0 million in the year-earlier quarter. Revenues were US$1.43 billion, up 26.4% from US$1.13 billion the year before. Direct operating expenses rose 27.4% to US$1.12 billion from US$877.1 million in the comparable period the year before. Indirect operating expenses increased 22.7% to US$196.9 million from US$160.4 million in the equivalent prior-year period.

Prospects: Our evaluation of Pultegroup Inc. as of June 19, 2016 is the result of our systematic analysis on three basic characteristics: earnings strength, relative valuation, and recent stock price movement. The company has enjoyed a very positive trend in earnings per share over the past 5 quarters. However, while recent estimates for the company have been mixed, PHM has posted better than expected results. Based on operating earnings yield, the company is undervalued when compared to all of the companies in our coverage universe. Share price changes over the past year indicates that PHM will perform in line with the market over the near term.

Financial Data

(US$ in Thousands)	3 Mos	12/31/2015	12/31/2014	12/31/2013	12/31/2012	12/31/2011	12/31/2010	12/31/2009
Earnings Per Share	1.45	1.36	1.26	6.72	0.54	(0.55)	(2.90)	(3.94)
Cash Flow Per Share	(1.11)	(0.98)	0.83	2.30	1.99	0.05	1.53	2.46
Tang Book Value Per Share	12.62	13.32	12.67	11.84	5.28	4.64	4.50	5.54
Dividends Per Share	0.340	0.330	0.230	0.150	...	...	...	...
Dividend Payout %	23.45	24.26	18.25	2.23	...	...	...	...
Income Statement								
Total Revenue	1,432,578	5,981,964	5,822,363	5,679,595	4,819,998	4,136,690	4,569,290	4,084,389
EBITDA	120,744	852,549	717,400	541,509	192,301	(298,338)	(1,211,759)	(1,892,172)
Depn & Amortn	3,450	46,200	39,833	18,500	16,900	19,000	32,500	40,200
Income Before Taxes	118,043	808,668	681,350	526,692	179,495	(313,596)	(1,237,457)	(1,925,467)
Income Taxes	34,913	321,933	215,420	(2,092,294)	(22,591)	(99,912)	(137,817)	(792,552)
Net Income	83,300	494,090	474,338	2,620,116	206,145	(210,388)	(1,096,729)	(1,182,567)
Average Shares	350,477	359,793	374,102	386,866	384,564	379,877	378,585	300,179
Balance Sheet								
Current Assets	7,220,594	6,332,065	5,854,026	5,752,801	5,844,850	6,008,765	6,480,182	8,018,931
Total Assets	9,843,480	8,967,160	8,569,410	8,734,143	6,734,409	6,885,620	7,699,376	10,051,222
Current Liabilities	589,084	652,636	547,715	629,884	571,133	552,688	694,839	895,721
Long-Term Obligations	3,185,977	2,387,982	1,981,057	2,163,832	2,648,408	3,088,344	3,391,668	4,281,532
Total Liabilities	5,069,953	4,207,835	3,764,456	4,085,191	4,544,793	4,947,005	5,564,209	6,856,782
Stockholders' Equity	4,773,527	4,759,325	4,804,954	4,648,952	2,189,616	1,938,615	2,135,167	3,194,440
Shares Outstanding	365,427	349,148	369,458	381,299	386,608	382,607	382,027	380,690
Statistical Record								
Return on Assets %	5.72	5.63	5.48	33.88	3.02	N.M.	N.M.	N.M.
Return on Equity %	10.98	10.33	10.03	76.63	9.96	N.M.	N.M.	N.M.
EBITDA Margin %	8.43	14.25	12.32	9.53	3.99	N.M.	N.M.	N.M.
Net Margin %	5.81	8.26	8.15	46.13	4.28	N.M.	N.M.	N.M.
Asset Turnover	0.69	0.68	0.67	0.73	0.71	0.57	0.51	0.46
Current Ratio	12.26	9.70	10.69	9.13	10.23	10.87	9.33	8.95
Debt to Equity	0.67	0.50	0.41	0.47	1.21	1.59	1.59	1.34
Price Range	22.78-15.36	23.24-17.18	21.72-16.66	24.25-15.11	18.61-6.52	8.69-3.54	13.39-6.20	13.32-7.90
P/E Ratio	15.71-10.59	17.09-12.63	17.24-13.22	3.61-2.25	34.46-12.07	...	...	...
Average Yield %	1.78	1.63	1.18	0.80	...	...	...	...

Address: 3350 Peachtree Road NE, Suite 150, Atlanta, GA 30326 **Telephone:** 404-978-6400	**Web Site:** www.pultegroupinc.com **Officers:** Richard J. Dugas - Chairman, President, Chief Executive Officer Ryan R. Marshall - President, Region Officer	**Auditors:** Ernst & Young LLP **Investor Contact:** 248-433-4502 **Transfer Agents:** Computershare Trust Company N.A., Providence, RI

PVH CORP

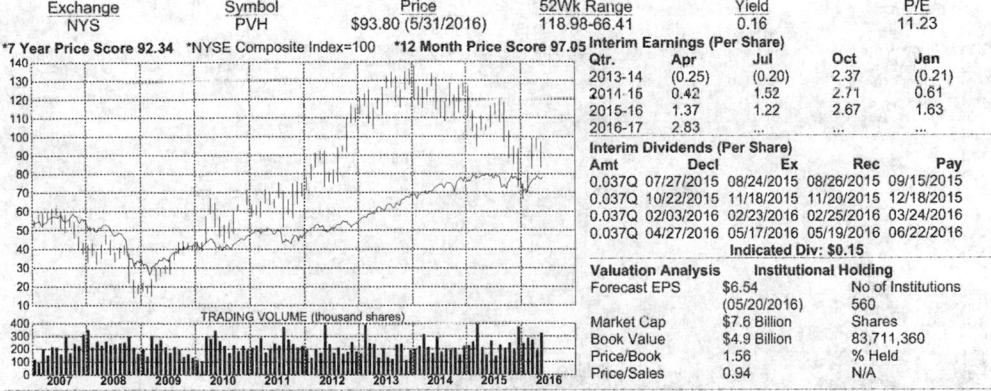

Exchange	Symbol	Price	52Wk Range	Yield	P/E
NYS	PVH	$93.80 (5/31/2016)	118.98-66.41	0.16	11.23

*7 Year Price Score 92.34 ***NYSE Composite Index=100** ***12 Month Price Score 97.05**

Interim Earnings (Per Share)

Qtr.	Apr	Jul	Oct	Jan
2013-14	(0.25)	(0.20)	2.37	(0.21)
2014-15	0.42	1.52	2.71	0.61
2015-16	1.37	1.22	2.67	1.63
2016-17	2.83	...	...	...

Interim Dividends (Per Share)

Amt	Decl	Ex	Rec	Pay
0.037Q	07/27/2015	08/24/2015	08/26/2015	09/15/2015
0.037Q	10/22/2015	11/18/2015	11/20/2015	12/18/2015
0.037Q	02/03/2016	02/23/2016	02/25/2016	03/24/2016
0.037Q	04/27/2016	05/17/2016	05/19/2016	06/22/2016

Indicated Div: $0.15

Valuation Analysis

		Institutional Holding	
Forecast EPS	$6.54	No of Institutions	
	(05/20/2016)	560	
Market Cap	$7.6 Billion	Shares	
Book Value	$4.9 Billion	83,711,360	
Price/Book	1.56	% Held	
Price/Sales	0.94	N/A	

Business Summary: Apparel, Footwear & Accessories (MIC: 1.4.2 SIC: 2321 NAIC: 315211)

PVH is an apparel company that designs and markets branded dress shirts, neckwear, sportswear, jeanswear, intimate apparel, swim products, handbags, footwear and other related products, and licenses its owned brands over a range of products. Co.'s brand portfolio includes Calvin Klein and Tommy Hilfiger, Van Heusen, IZOD, ARROW, Warner's, Olga and Eagle, which are owned, and Speedo, Geoffrey Beene, Kenneth Cole New York, Kenneth Cole Reaction, Sean John, MICHAEL Michael Kors, Michael Kors Collection and Chaps, which are licensed, and various other licensed and private label brands. Co. aggregates its segments into three main businesses: Calvin Klein, Tommy Hilfiger and Heritage Brands.

Recent Developments: For the quarter ended May 1 2016, net income increased 103.0% to US$231.6 million from US$114.1 million in the year-earlier quarter. Revenues were US$1.92 billion, up 2.0% from US$1.88 billion the year before. Direct operating expenses rose 1.9% to US$910.9 million from US$893.7 million in the comparable period the year before. Indirect operating expenses decreased 12.6% to US$712.1 million from US$814.9 million in the equivalent prior-year period.

Prospects: Our evaluation of PVH Corp. as of June 19, 2016 is the result of our systematic analysis on three basic characteristics: earnings strength, relative valuation, and recent stock price movement. The company has managed to produce a neutral trend in earnings per share over the past 5 quarters and while recent estimates for the company have been raised by analysts, PVH has posted better than expected results. Based on operating earnings yield, the company is undervalued when compared to all of the companies in our coverage universe. Share price changes over the past year indicates that PVH will perform very poorly over the near term.

Financial Data

(US$ in Thousands)	3 Mos	01/31/2016	02/01/2015	02/02/2014	02/03/2013	01/29/2012	01/30/2011	01/31/2010
Earnings Per Share	8.35	6.89	5.27	1.74	5.87	4.36	0.80	3.08
Cash Flow Per Share	11.67	10.95	9.60	5.09	7.96	7.33	5.63	4.16
Tang Book Value Per Share	N.M.	N.M.	N.M.	N.M.	N.M.	N.M.	N.M.	0.20
Dividends Per Share	0.150	0.150	0.150	0.150	0.150	0.150	0.150	0.150
Dividend Payout %	1.80	2.18	2.85	8.62	2.56	3.44	18.75	4.87
Income Statement								
Total Revenue	1,917,800	8,020,300	8,241,200	8,186,351	6,042,999	5,890,624	4,636,848	2,398,731
EBITDA	365,400	954,700	713,800	695,081	777,339	670,781	302,012	284,772
Depn & Amortn	70,600	210,800	193,800	189,675	122,424	112,495	98,617	40,960
Income Before Taxes	265,800	630,900	381,500	320,710	537,665	430,198	76,573	211,583
Income Taxes	34,000	75,100	(47,500)	185,284	109,272	113,684	22,768	49,673
Net Income	231,600	572,400	439,000	143,537	433,840	317,881	53,805	161,910
Average Shares	81,900	83,100	83,300	82,618	73,876	72,923	67,378	52,506
Balance Sheet								
Current Assets	2,528,200	2,812,600	2,901,200	2,998,592	2,437,006	1,739,235	1,810,563	994,883
Total Assets	10,885,100	10,696,400	10,931,800	11,575,578	7,781,549	6,752,361	6,735,334	2,339,679
Current Liabilities	1,394,900	1,527,200	1,428,600	1,552,397	1,162,447	1,043,871	908,162	362,881
Long-Term Obligations	2,991,600	3,054,300	3,438,700	3,878,221	2,211,642	1,832,925	2,364,002	399,584
Total Liabilities	6,022,800	6,144,100	6,567,500	7,240,399	4,528,980	4,036,912	4,292,777	1,171,126
Stockholders' Equity	4,862,300	4,552,300	4,364,300	4,335,179	3,252,569	2,715,449	2,442,557	1,168,553
Shares Outstanding	80,985	81,487	82,512	82,166	72,910	68,048	67,065	51,902
Statistical Record								
Return on Assets %	6.37	5.31	3.91	1.49	5.87	4.73	1.19	7.15
Return on Equity %	14.83	12.87	10.12	3.79	14.30	12.36	2.99	14.98
EBITDA Margin %	19.05	11.90	8.66	8.49	12.86	11.39	6.51	11.87
Net Margin %	12.08	7.14	5.33	1.75	7.18	5.40	1.16	6.75
Asset Turnover	0.74	0.74	0.73	0.85	0.82	0.88	1.02	1.06
Current Ratio	1.81	1.84	2.03	1.93	2.10	1.67	1.99	2.74
Debt to Equity	0.62	0.67	0.79	0.89	0.68	0.67	0.97	0.34
Price Range	118.98-66.41	118.98-66.41	133.66-107.87	137.62-103.85	120.86-72.70	77.94-51.47	71.23-38.60	44.15-14.50
P/E Ratio	14.25-7.95	17.27-9.64	25.36-20.47	79.09-59.68	20.59-12.39	17.88-11.81	89.04-48.25	14.33-4.71
Average Yield %	0.16	0.15	0.12	0.12	0.16	0.23	0.27	0.45

Address: 200 Madison Avenue, New York, NY 10016 Telephone: 212-381-3500	Web Site: www.pvh.com Officers: Emanuel Chirico - Chairman, Chief Executive Officer Fred Gehring - Vice-Chairman, Division Officer	Auditors: Ernst & Young LLP Transfer Agents: Wells Fargo Bank, N.A., St. Paul, MN

QEP RESOURCES INC

Exchange	Symbol	Price	52Wk Range	Yield	P/E
NYS	QEP	$18.63 (5/31/2016)	19.13-9.29	N/A	N/A

*7 Year Price Score N/A   ***NYSE Composite Index=100**   ***12 Month Price Score 115.25**

Interim Earnings (Per Share)

Qtr.	Mar	Jun	Sep	Dec
2013	(0.02)	0.99	0.21	(0.29)
2014	0.22	(0.51)	0.94	3.70
2015	(0.32)	(0.43)	0.12	(0.22)
2016	(4.55)	...	...	...

Interim Dividends (Per Share)

Amt	Decl	Ex	Rec	Pay
0.02Q	02/13/2015	02/20/2015	02/24/2015	03/06/2015
0.02Q	05/11/2015	05/21/2015	05/26/2015	06/05/2015
0.02Q	07/27/2015	08/14/2015	08/18/2015	09/04/2015
0.02Q	10/26/2015	11/13/2015	11/17/2015	12/07/2015

Valuation Analysis   **Institutional Holding**

Forecast EPS	$-1.54	No of Institutions
	(05/20/2016)	403
Market Cap	$4.0 Billion	Shares
Book Value	$3.5 Billion	197,781,280
Price/Book	1.17	% Held
Price/Sales	2.26	85.87

Business Summary: Production & Extraction (MIC: 9.1.1 SIC: 1311 NAIC: 211111)

QEP Resources is a holding company. Co.'s businesses are conducted through its two subsidiaries: QEP Energy Company (QEP Energy), which is engaged in oil and gas exploration and production; and QEP Marketing Company, which is engaged in oil and gas marketing, operation of a gas gathering system and an underground gas storage facility. Co.'s operations are focused in two geographic regions: the Northern Region and the Southern Region of the U.S. As of Dec 31 2015, QEP Energy had total proved reserves of 3,620.20 billion cubic feet of natural gas equivalents, consisting of 2,108.90 billion cubic feet of gas, 193.1 million barrels of oil and 58.8 million barrels of natural gas liquids.

Recent Developments: For the quarter ended Mar 31 2016, net loss amounted to US$863.8 million versus a net loss of US$55.6 million in the year-earlier quarter. Revenues were US$261.3 million, down 44.2% from US$468.1 million the year before. Operating loss was US$1.38 billion versus a loss of US$128.6 million in the prior-year quarter. Direct operating expenses declined 56.8% to US$91.8 million from US$212.7 million in the comparable period the year before. Indirect operating expenses increased 303.3% to US$1.55 billion from US$384.0 million in the equivalent prior-year period.

Prospects: Our evaluation of QEP Resources Inc. as of June 19, 2016 is the result of our systematic analysis on three basic characteristics: earnings strength, relative valuation, and recent stock price movement. The company has suffered a very negative trend in earnings per share over the past 5 quarters. Because the company lacks sufficient analyst estimate data, we place greater weight on the historical EPS trend as the measure of earnings strength. Based on operating earnings yield, the company is overvalued when compared to all of the companies in our coverage universe. Share price changes over the past year indicates that QEP will perform poorly over the near term.

Financial Data

(US$ in Thousands)	3 Mos	12/31/2015	12/31/2014	12/31/2013	12/31/2012	12/31/2011	12/31/2010	12/31/2009
Earnings Per Share	(5.08)	(0.85)	4.36	0.89	0.72	1.50	1.84	...
Cash Flow Per Share	4.41	2.73	8.58	6.65	7.27	7.32	5.69	...
Tang Book Value Per Share	15.95	22.33	23.23	18.87	17.97	18.34	16.77	...
Dividends Per Share	0.060	0.080	0.080	0.080	0.080	0.080	0.040	...
Dividend Payout %	...	...	1.83	8.99	11.11	5.33	2.17	...
Income Statement								
Total Revenue	261,300	2,018,600	3,414,300	2,935,800	2,349,800	3,159,200	2,246,400	2,198,500
EBITDA	(1,326,700)	786,900	561,600	1,471,700	1,225,000	1,280,200	1,180,800	1,142,700
Depn & Amortn	1,600	887,300	1,047,300	1,022,400	910,200	769,500	645,800	619,500
Income Before Taxes	(1,362,700)	(243,000)	(642,000)	291,200	198,500	424,800	452,900	459,900
Income Taxes	(498,900)	(93,600)	(232,500)	119,800	66,500	154,400	167,000	163,800
Net Income	(863,800)	(149,400)	784,400	159,400	128,300	267,200	326,200	293,500
Average Shares	189,700	176,600	179,800	179,500	178,700	178,400	177,300	...
Balance Sheet								
Current Assets	1,065,200	931,800	2,001,500	519,000	649,700	818,600	654,200	543,200
Total Assets	7,282,600	8,425,500	9,286,800	9,376,800	9,108,500	7,442,700	6,785,300	6,419,400
Current Liabilities	456,600	641,600	1,344,800	641,500	761,900	637,800	624,300	613,600
Long-Term Obligations	2,016,200	2,042,000	2,218,100	2,997,500	3,206,900	1,679,400	1,472,300	1,348,700
Total Liabilities	3,824,900	4,477,600	5,211,500	6,000,200	5,842,500	4,141,200	3,775,000	3,665,600
Stockholders' Equity	3,457,700	3,947,900	4,075,300	3,376,600	3,266,000	3,301,500	3,010,300	2,753,800
Shares Outstanding	216,800	176,800	175,400	178,900	178,400	176,800	175,900	...
Statistical Record								
Return on Assets %	N.M.	N.M.	8.41	1.72	1.55	3.76	4.94	4.64
Return on Equity %	N.M.	N.M.	21.05	4.80	3.90	8.47	11.32	10.67
EBITDA Margin %	N.M.	38.98	16.45	50.13	52.13	40.52	52.56	51.98
Net Margin %	N.M.	N.M.	22.97	5.43	5.46	8.46	14.52	13.35
Asset Turnover	0.23	0.23	0.37	0.32	0.28	0.44	0.34	0.35
Current Ratio	2.33	1.45	1.49	0.81	0.85	1.28	1.05	0.89
Debt to Equity	0.58	0.52	0.54	0.89	0.98	0.51	0.49	0.49
Price Range	23.76-9.29	23.76-11.31	35.57-18.64	33.48-26.86	34.90-24.52	45.15-24.82	38.12-28.18	...
P/E Ratio	...	...	8.16-4.28	37.62-30.18	48.47-34.06	30.10-16.55	20.72-15.32	...
Average Yield %	0.40	0.46	0.27	0.27	0.27	0.27	0.22	...

Address: 1050 17th Street, Suite 800, Denver, CO 80265 **Telephone:** 303-672-6900	**Web Site:** www.qepres.com **Officers:** Charles B. Stanley - Chairman, President, Chief Executive Officer Richard J. Doleshek - Executive Vice President, Chief Financial Officer, Chief Accounting Officer, Treasurer	**Auditors:** PricewaterhouseCoopers LLP **Investor Contact:** 303-405-6665 **Transfer Agents:** Wells Fargo Shareowner Services, Saint Paul, MN

QUANTA SERVICES, INC.

Exchange	Symbol	Price	52Wk Range	Yield	P/E
NYS	PWR	$24.03 (5/31/2016)	30.41-17.29	N/A	15.40

*7 Year Price Score 79.71   *NYSE Composite Index=100   *12 Month Price Score 99.02

TRADING VOLUME (thousand shares)

Interim Earnings (Per Share)

Qtr.	Mar	Jun	Sep	Dec
2013	0.34	0.33	0.43	0.77
2014	0.25	0.37	0.43	0.30
2015	0.25	0.22	1.15	0.06
2016	0.13	...	...	...

Interim Dividends (Per Share)

No Dividends Paid

Valuation Analysis

		Institutional Holding	
Forecast EPS	$1.68	No of Institutions	
	(05/20/2016)	572	
Market Cap	$3.7 Billion	Shares	
Book Value	$3.2 Billion	178,554,400	
Price/Book	1.16	% Held	
Price/Sales	0.50	93.90	

Business Summary: Construction Services (MIC: 7.5.4 SIC: 1731 NAIC: 238210)

Quanta Services provides contracting services, including infrastructure solutions to the electric power and oil and gas industries in the U.S., Canada and Australia and other international markets. Co.'s services include the design, installation, upgrade, repair and maintenance of infrastructure within the industries that it serves, such as electric power transmission and distribution networks, substation facilities, renewable energy facilities, pipeline transmission and distribution systems and facilities, and infrastructure services for the offshore and inland water energy markets. Co. has two segments: Electric Power Infrastructure Services and Oil and Gas Infrastructure Services.

Recent Developments: For the quarter ended Mar 31 2016, income from continuing operations decreased 60.2% to US$20.9 million from US$52.4 million in the year-earlier quarter. Net income decreased 64.2% to US$20.9 million from US$58.2 million in the year-earlier quarter. Revenues were US$1.71 billion, down 7.9% from US$1.86 billion the year before. Operating income was US$37.3 million versus US$84.2 million in the prior-year quarter, a decrease of 55.7%. Direct operating expenses declined 7.0% to US$1.51 billion from US$1.62 billion in the comparable period the year before. Indirect operating expenses increased 8.0% to US$166.0 million from US$153.8 million in the equivalent prior-year period.

Prospects: Our evaluation of Quanta Services Inc. as of June 19, 2016 is the result of our systematic analysis on three basic characteristics: earnings strength, relative valuation, and recent stock price movement. The company has enjoyed a very positive trend in earnings per share over the past 5 quarters and while recent estimates for the company have been raised by analysts, PWR has posted results that fell short of analysts expectations. Based on operating earnings yield, the company is about fairly valued when compared to all of the companies in our coverage universe. Share price changes over the past year indicates that PWR will perform poorly over the near term.

Financial Data

(US$ in Thousands)	3 Mos	12/31/2015	12/31/2014	12/31/2013	12/31/2012	12/31/2011	12/31/2010	12/31/2009
Earnings Per Share	1.56	1.59	1.35	1.87	1.44	0.62	0.72	0.81
Cash Flow Per Share	3.92	3.17	1.41	2.08	0.78	1.03	1.14	1.88
Tang Book Value Per Share	8.88	8.31	10.65	10.38	9.59	7.49	7.47	7.02
Income Statement								
Total Revenue	1,713,737	7,572,436	7,851,250	6,522,842	5,920,269	4,623,829	3,931,218	3,318,126
EBITDA	86,380	433,320	668,480	687,408	622,762	363,178	395,819	368,395
Depn & Amortn	49,005	197,648	194,007	161,615	157,991	146,053	146,068	125,852
Income Before Taxes	34,302	229,141	473,449	526,505	462,496	216,370	246,255	233,730
Income Taxes	13,443	97,472	157,408	217,940	158,859	71,954	90,698	70,195
Net Income	20,859	310,907	296,714	401,921	306,629	132,515	153,176	162,162
Average Shares	162,806	195,120	219,690	214,978	212,835	213,168	211,796	201,311
Balance Sheet								
Current Assets	2,248,374	2,277,519	2,553,976	2,313,318	2,201,727	1,765,154	1,596,364	1,582,792
Total Assets	5,295,519	5,213,543	6,312,024	5,793,245	5,140,757	4,699,114	4,341,212	4,116,954
Current Liabilities	1,235,911	1,203,744	1,137,325	1,043,520	881,179	781,076	500,395	495,688
Long-Term Obligations	404,058	475,364	72,489	...	...	...	...	126,608
Total Liabilities	2,124,974	2,128,049	1,797,551	1,559,057	1,374,209	1,317,162	975,657	1,007,771
Stockholders' Equity	3,170,545	3,085,494	4,514,473	4,234,188	3,766,548	3,381,952	3,365,555	3,109,183
Shares Outstanding	153,563	159,783	218,145	216,442	213,179	210,112	215,479	210,040
Statistical Record								
Return on Assets %	4.98	5.40	4.90	7.35	6.22	2.93	3.62	4.23
Return on Equity %	7.62	8.18	6.78	10.05	8.56	3.93	4.73	5.62
EBITDA Margin %	5.04	5.72	8.51	10.54	10.52	7.85	10.07	11.10
Net Margin %	1.22	4.11	3.78	6.16	5.18	2.87	3.90	4.89
Asset Turnover	1.30	1.31	1.30	1.19	1.20	1.02	0.93	0.87
Current Ratio	1.82	1.89	2.25	2.22	2.50	2.26	3.19	3.19
Debt to Equity	0.13	0.15	0.02	...	...	...	...	0.04
Price Range	30.41-17.29	30.41-18.74	37.20-25.53	31.56-25.74	27.60-20.34	24.03-15.46	23.03-17.05	25.41-15.91
P/E Ratio	19.49-11.08	19.13-11.79	27.56-18.91	16.88-13.76	19.17-14.13	38.76-24.94	31.99-23.68	31.37-19.64

Address: 2800 Post Oak Boulevard, Suite 2600, Houston, TX 77056 **Telephone:** 713-629-7600	**Web Site:** www.quantaservices.com **Officers:** Dale L. Querrey - Division Officer Earl C. Austin - President, Chief Executive Officer, Chief Operating Officer, Division Officer	**Auditors:** PricewaterhouseCoopers LLP **Investor Contact:** 713-341-7260 **Transfer Agents:** American Stock Transfer & Trust Company, New York, NY

QUEST DIAGNOSTICS, INC.

Exchange	Symbol	Price	52Wk Range	Yield	P/E
NYS	DGX	$77.17 (5/31/2016)	77.62-60.51	2.07	14.98

*7 Year Price Score 99.29 *NYSE Composite Index=100 *12 Month Price Score 106.63

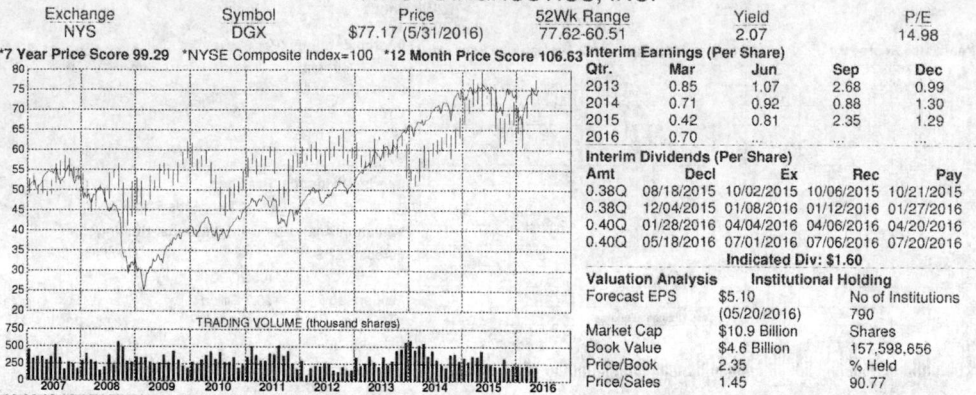

Interim Earnings (Per Share)

Qtr.	Mar	Jun	Sep	Dec
2013	0.85	1.07	2.68	0.99
2014	0.71	0.92	0.88	1.30
2015	0.42	0.81	2.35	1.29
2016	0.70			

Interim Dividends (Per Share)

Amt	Decl	Ex	Rec	Pay
0.38Q	08/18/2015	10/02/2015	10/06/2015	10/21/2015
0.38Q	12/04/2015	01/08/2016	01/12/2016	01/27/2016
0.40Q	01/28/2016	04/04/2016	04/06/2016	04/20/2016
0.40Q	05/18/2016	07/01/2016	07/06/2016	07/20/2016

Indicated Div: $1.60

Valuation Analysis

Forecast EPS	$5.10 (05/20/2016)
Market Cap	$10.9 Billion
Book Value	$4.6 Billion
Price/Book	2.35
Price/Sales	1.45

Institutional Holding

No of Institutions	790
Shares	157,598,656
% Held	90.77

Business Summary: Diagnostic & Health Related Services (MIC: 4.2.2 SIC: 8071 NAIC: 621511)

Quest Diagnostics is a provider of diagnostic information services. Co. is made up of two businesses: Diagnostic Information Services and Diagnostic Solutions. Co.'s Diagnostic Information Services business develops and delivers diagnostic testing information and services. Co.'s Diagnostics Information Services business is a provider of diagnostic information services, which includes providing clinical testing services such as routine testing, gene-based and esoteric testing, and anatomic pathology services, as well as related services and insights. In its Diagnostic Solutions group, Co. provides a variety of solutions for insurers and healthcare providers.

Recent Developments: For the quarter ended Mar 31 2016, net income increased 62.9% to US$114.0 million from US$70.0 million in the year-earlier quarter. Revenues were US$1.86 billion, up 1.3% from US$1.84 billion the year before. Operating income was US$257.0 million versus US$228.0 million in the prior-year quarter, an increase of 12.7%. Direct operating expenses declined 1.6% to US$1.14 billion from US$1.16 billion in the comparable period the year before. Indirect operating expenses increased 3.1% to US$462.0 million from US$448.0 million in the equivalent prior-year period.

Prospects: Our evaluation of Quest Diagnostics Inc. as of June 19, 2016 is the result of our systematic analysis on three basic characteristics: earnings strength, relative valuation, and recent stock price movement. The company has produced a positive trend in earnings per share over the past 5 quarters and while recent estimates for the company have been raised by analysts, DGX has posted better than expected results. Based on operating earnings yield, the company is undervalued when compared to all of the companies in our coverage universe. Share price changes over the past year indicates that DGX will perform well over the near term.

Financial Data

(US$ in Thousands)	3 Mos	12/31/2015	12/31/2014	12/31/2013	12/31/2012	12/31/2011	12/31/2010	12/31/2009
Earnings Per Share	5.15	4.87	3.81	5.54	3.46	2.92	4.05	3.87
Cash Flow Per Share	6.30	5.63	6.47	4.29	7.47	5.64	6.36	5.36
Dividends Per Share	1.520	1.470	1.290	1.200	0.680	0.400	0.400	0.400
Dividend Payout %	29.51	30.18	33.86	21.66	19.65	13.70	9.88	10.34
Income Statement								
Total Revenue	1,863,000	7,493,000	7,435,000	7,146,000	7,382,562	7,510,490	7,368,925	7,455,243
EBITDA	227,000	1,337,000	1,081,000	1,562,000	1,488,506	1,278,963	1,554,830	1,595,480
Depn & Amortn	19,000	81,000	94,000	79,000	281,047	281,102	253,964	256,687
Income Before Taxes	172,000	1,103,000	823,000	1,324,000	1,042,770	827,278	1,154,778	1,194,725
Income Taxes	68,000	373,000	262,000	500,000	401,897	349,000	425,531	460,474
Net Income	102,000	709,000	556,000	849,000	555,721	470,567	720,894	729,111
Average Shares	144,000	145,000	145,000	153,000	160,065	160,172	177,320	187,798
Balance Sheet								
Current Assets	1,493,000	1,501,000	1,603,000	1,383,000	1,560,997	1,401,260	1,605,417	1,679,425
Total Assets	10,097,000	9,962,000	9,877,000	8,948,000	9,283,863	9,313,379	8,527,630	8,563,643
Current Liabilities	1,090,000	1,173,000	1,709,000	1,132,000	1,047,603	1,561,159	1,214,268	1,059,212
Long-Term Obligations	3,740,000	3,492,000	3,244,000	3,120,000	3,354,173	3,370,522	2,641,160	2,936,792
Total Liabilities	5,461,000	5,278,000	5,576,000	5,000,000	5,120,816	5,620,507	4,494,150	4,574,004
Stockholders' Equity	4,636,000	4,684,000	4,301,000	3,948,000	4,163,047	3,692,872	4,033,480	3,989,639
Shares Outstanding	141,000	143,000	144,000	144,000	158,331	157,420	170,717	183,293
Statistical Record								
Return on Assets %	7.24	7.15	5.91	9.31	5.96	5.28	8.44	8.59
Return on Equity %	16.89	15.78	13.48	20.93	14.11	12.18	17.97	19.20
EBITDA Margin %	12.18	17.84	14.54	21.86	20.16	17.03	21.10	21.40
Net Margin %	5.48	9.46	7.48	11.88	7.53	6.27	9.78	9.78
Asset Turnover	0.73	0.76	0.79	0.78	0.79	0.84	0.86	0.88
Current Ratio	1.37	1.28	0.94	1.22	1.49	0.90	1.32	1.59
Debt to Equity	0.81	0.75	0.75	0.79	0.81	0.91	0.65	0.74
Price Range	79.60-60.51	79.60-60.51	68.10-50.80	63.70-52.79	64.68-54.62	60.83-46.02	61.61-43.50	62.07-43.46
P/E Ratio	15.46-11.75	16.34-12.43	17.87-13.33	11.50-9.53	18.69-15.79	20.83-15.76	15.21-10.74	16.04-11.23
Average Yield %	2.19	2.08	2.18	2.03	1.15		0.73	0.76	0.75

Address: 3 Giralda Farms, Madison, NJ 07940
Telephone: 973-520-2700

Web Site: www.QuestDiagnostics.com
Officers: Stephen H. Rusckowski - President, Chief Executive Officer Mark J. Guinan - Senior Vice President, Chief Financial Officer

Auditors: PricewaterhouseCoopers LLP
Investor Contact: 973-520-2900
Transfer Agents: Computershare, Providence, RI

QUESTAR CORP

Exchange	Symbol	Price	52Wk Range	Yield	P/E	Div Achiever
NYS	STR	$25.21 (5/31/2016)	25.28-18.38	3.49	21.92	36 Years

*7 Year Price Score 93.39 *NYSE Composite Index=100 *12 Month Price Score 113.96

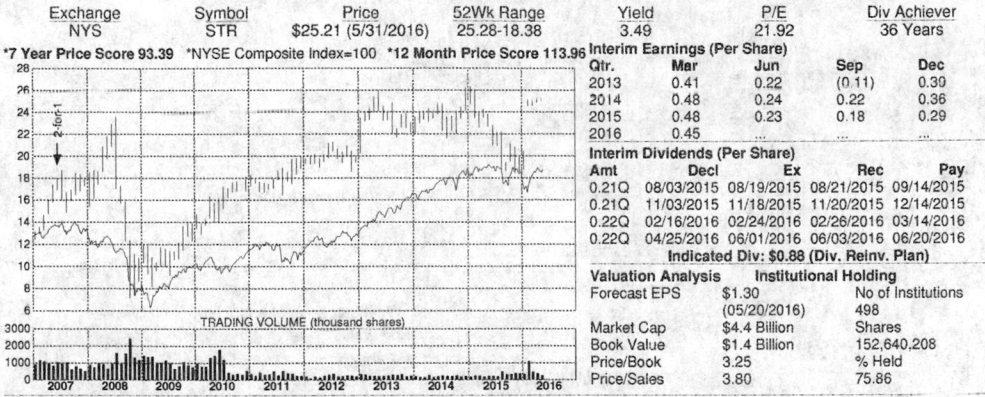

Interim Earnings (Per Share)

Qtr.	Mar	Jun	Sep	Dec
2013	0.41	0.22	(0.11)	0.39
2014	0.48	0.24	0.22	0.36
2015	0.48	0.23	0.18	0.29
2016	0.45	...	...	...

Interim Dividends (Per Share)

Amt	Decl	Ex	Rec	Pay
0.21Q	08/03/2015	08/19/2015	08/21/2015	09/14/2015
0.21Q	11/03/2015	11/18/2015	11/20/2015	12/14/2015
0.22Q	02/16/2016	02/24/2016	02/26/2016	03/14/2016
0.22Q	04/25/2016	06/01/2016	06/03/2016	06/20/2016

Indicated Div: $0.88 (Div. Reinv. Plan)

Valuation Analysis | **Institutional Holding**

Forecast EPS $1.30	No of Institutions
(05/20/2016)	498
Market Cap $4.4 Billion	Shares
Book Value $1.4 Billion	152,640,208
Price/Book 3.25	% Held
Price/Sales 3.80	75.86

TRADING VOLUME (thousand shares)

Business Summary: Gas Utilities (MIC: 3.3.1 SIC: 4923 NAIC: 221210)

Questar is a natural gas holding company with three principal complementary lines of business operated through its subsidiaries: Questar Gas Company, which distributes natural gas as a public utilityin Utah, southwestern Wyoming and a small portion of southeastern Idaho; Wexpro Company, which develops, produces and delivers natural gas from cost-of-service reserves for gas utility affiliate Questar Gas under the terms of the agreements with the states of Utah and Wyoming; and Questar Pipeline Company, which provides natural gas transportation and underground-storage services in Utah, Wyoming and Colorado, as well as gas-processing services and wellhead automation and measurement services.

Recent Developments: For the quarter ended Mar 31 2016, net income decreased 7.2% to US$78.5 million from US$84.6 million in the year-earlier quarter. Revenues were US$456.3 million, up 6.5% from US$428.6 million the year before. Operating income was US$135.7 million versus US$147.0 million in the prior-year quarter, a decrease of 7.7%. Direct operating expenses rose 13.5% to US$208.9 million from US$184.1 million in the comparable period the year before. Indirect operating expenses increased 14.6% to US$111.7 million from US$97.5 million in the equivalent prior-year period.

Prospects: Our evaluation of Questar Corp. as of June 19, 2016 is the result of our systematic analysis on three basic characteristics: earnings strength, relative valuation, and recent stock price movement. The company has managed to produce a neutral trend in earnings per share over the past 5 quarters. However, while recent estimates for the company have been mixed, STR has posted results that fell short of analysts expectations. Based on operating earnings yield, the company is undervalued when compared to all of the companies in our coverage universe. Share price changes over the past year indicates that STR will perform very well over the near term.

Financial Data

(US$ in Thousands)	3 Mos	12/31/2015	12/31/2014	12/31/2013	12/31/2012	12/31/2011	12/31/2010	12/31/2009
Earnings Per Share	1.15	1.18	1.29	0.92	1.19	1.16	1.91	2.23
Cash Flow Per Share	2.96	2.34	2.52	2.86	2.64	2.76	2.00	9.06
Tang Book Value Per Share	7.76	7.46	7.05	6.79	5.86	5.75	5.81	19.66
Dividends Per Share	0.850	0.840	0.750	0.710	0.665	0.620	0.540	0.505
Dividend Payout %	73.91	71.19	58.14	77.17	55.88	53.45	28.27	22.65
Income Statement								
Total Revenue	456,300	1,134,900	1,189,300	1,220,000	1,098,900	1,194,400	1,123,600	3,038,000
EBITDA	194,100	597,900	639,800	507,600	564,900	536,300	505,100	1,438,700
Depn & Amortn	58,400	223,500	234,400	201,800	189,200	169,400	161,800	714,600
Income Before Taxes	120,900	315,600	348,900	258,800	324,800	320,500	297,900	611,400
Income Taxes	43,400	110,600	125,900	101,300	116,500	116,400	109,400	222,000
Net Income	78,500	208,700	226,500	161,200	212,000	207,900	339,200	393,300
Average Shares	176,100	176,300	176,100	176,000	177,500	178,800	178,000	176,300
Balance Sheet								
Current Assets	234,600	440,100	414,500	351,900	345,700	335,400	399,600	831,100
Total Assets	4,179,200	4,377,800	4,249,700	4,054,300	3,757,100	3,532,800	3,373,600	8,897,700
Current Liabilities	700,500	940,200	621,400	555,800	546,700	568,800	655,100	948,100
Long-Term Obligations	992,700	1,004,100	1,257,500	1,285,500	1,138,200	993,000	898,500	2,179,900
Total Liabilities	2,818,500	3,062,700	3,003,500	2,855,500	2,721,500	2,499,300	2,337,500	5,395,500
Stockholders' Equity	1,360,700	1,315,100	1,246,200	1,198,800	1,035,600	1,033,500	1,036,100	3,502,200
Shares Outstanding	175,397	175,000	175,400	175,100	175,000	177,900	176,500	174,600
Statistical Record								
Return on Assets %	4.89	4.84	5.46	4.13	5.80	6.02	5.53	4.49
Return on Equity %	15.24	16.30	18.53	14.43	20.44	20.09	14.95	11.37
EBITDA Margin %	42.54	52.68	53.80	41.61	51.41	44.90	44.95	47.36
Net Margin %	17.20	18.39	19.04	13.21	19.29	17.41	30.19	12.95
Asset Turnover	0.28	0.26	0.29	0.31	0.30	0.35	0.18	0.35
Current Ratio	0.33	0.47	0.67	0.63	0.63	0.59	0.61	0.88
Debt to Equity	0.73	0.76	1.01	1.07	1.10	0.96	0.87	0.62
Price Range	25.00-18.38	26.29-18.38	26.18-21.59	25.89-19.76	21.24-18.50	20.02-16.41	18.08-12.83	13.87-8.14
P/E Ratio	21.74-15.98	22.28-15.58	20.29-16.74	28.14-21.48	17.85-15.55	17.26-14.15	9.47-6.72	6.22-3.65
Average Yield %	3.96	3.86	3.19	3.04	3.35	3.44	3.43	4.51

Address: 333 South State Street, P.O. Box 45433, Salt Lake City, UT 84145-0433
Telephone: 801-324-5900

Web Site: www.questar.com
Officers: Ronald W. Jibson - President, Chief Executive Officer Kevin W. Hadlock - Executive Vice President, Chief Financial Officer

Auditors: Ernst & Young LLP
Investor Contact: 801-324-5218
Transfer Agents: Wells Fargo Bank, N A Shareowner Services, Mendota Heights, MN

QUINTILES TRANSNATIONAL HOLDINGS INC

Exchange	Symbol	Price	52Wk Range	Yield	P/E
NYS	Q	$67.89 (5/31/2016)	79.10-55.91	N/A	20.70

*7 Year Price Score N/A ***NYSE Composite Index=100** ***12 Month Price Score 97.96**

Interim Earnings (Per Share)

Qtr.	Mar	Jun	Sep	Dec
2013	0.41	0.30	0.50	0.55
2014	0.68	0.64	0.71	0.69
2015	0.68	0.67	0.89	0.84
2016	0.88	...	...	...

Interim Dividends (Per Share)

No Dividends Paid

Valuation Analysis | Institutional Holding

Forecast EPS	$3.79	No of Institutions
	(05/20/2016)	N/A
Market Cap	$8.1 Billion	Shares
Book Value	N/A	N/A
Price/Book	N/A	% Held
Price/Sales	1.38	N/A

TRADING VOLUME (thousand shares)

Business Summary: Biotechnology (MIC: 4.1.2 SIC: 8731 NAIC: 541710)

Quintiles Transnational Holdings is a provider of pharmaceutical development services and commercial outsourcing services. Co. also provides a number of services designed to address the outcomes and analytical needs of the healthcare industry. Co. has two reportable segments: Product Development, which primarily serves biopharmaceutical customers engaged in research and development, provides clinical research and clinical trial services; and Integrated Healthcare Services, which provides commercialization services to biopharmaceutical customers and research, analytics, late phase research, and other services to both biopharmaceutical customers and the healthcare market.

Recent Developments: For the quarter ended Mar 31 2016, net income increased 26.1% to US$109.0 million from US$86.4 million in the year-earlier quarter. Revenues were US$1.49 billion, up 10.6% from US$1.35 billion the year before. Operating income was US$178.8 million versus US$143.2 million in the prior-year quarter, an increase of 24.8%. Direct operating expenses rose 10.5% to US$1.08 billion from US$979.4 million in the comparable period the year before. Indirect operating expenses increased 1.7% to US$228.7 million from US$224.9 million in the equivalent prior-year period.

Prospects: Our evaluation of Quintiles Transnational Holdings Inc. as of June 19, 2016 is the result of our systematic analysis on three basic characteristics: earnings strength, relative valuation, and recent stock price movement. The company has managed to produce a neutral trend in earnings per share over the past 5 quarters. However, while recent estimates for the company have been mixed, Q has posted better than expected results. Based on operating earnings yield, the company is undervalued when compared to all of the companies in our coverage universe. Share price changes over the past year indicates that Q will perform well over the near term.

Financial Data
(US$ in Thousands)

	3 Mos	12/31/2015	12/31/2014	12/31/2013	12/31/2012	12/31/2011	12/31/2010
Earnings Per Share	3.28	3.08	2.72	1.77	1.51	2.05	1.36
Cash Flow Per Share	5.46	3.87	3.37	3.20	2.89	1.38	3.25
Income Statement							
Total Revenue	1,490,085	5,737,619	5,459,998	5,099,545	4,865,513	4,327,748	3,924,020
EBITDA	179,076	781,263	727,069	572,016	506,257	411,821	482,141
Depn & Amortn	4,786	144,793	127,701	129,329	107,525	122,020	102,783
Income Before Taxes	148,961	538,995	502,189	323,116	267,428	184,675	241,727
Income Taxes	42,577	158,989	150,056	95,965	93,364	15,105	77,582
Net Income	106,668	387,205	356,383	226,591	177,546	241,772	160,596
Average Shares	121,438	125,630	131,083	127,862	117,796	117,936	118,000
Balance Sheet							
Current Assets	2,437,156	2,411,985	2,146,083	1,945,688	1,509,994	1,365,478	...
Total Assets	3,982,939	3,926,316	3,305,832	3,066,797	2,499,153	2,322,917	...
Current Liabilities	1,578,138	1,594,176	1,471,900	1,482,247	1,317,964	1,192,133	...
Long-Term Obligations	2,408,555	2,419,293	2,292,491	2,035,586	2,366,268	1,951,708	...
Total Liabilities	4,417,749	4,490,533	4,009,893	3,734,210	3,858,676	3,293,301	...
Stockholders' Equity	(434,810)	(564,217)	(704,061)	(667,413)	(1,359,523)	(970,384)	...
Shares Outstanding	119,629	119,377	124,129	129,652	115,764	115,966	116,399
Statistical Record							
Return on Assets %	11.29	10.71	11.18	8.14	7.34	...	...
EBITDA Margin %	12.02	13.62	13.32	11.22	10.41	9.52	12.29
Net Margin %	7.16	6.75	6.53	4.44	3.65	5.59	4.09
Asset Turnover	1.63	1.59	1.71	1.83	2.01	...	...
Current Ratio	1.54	1.51	1.46	1.31	1.15	1.15	...
Price Range	79.10-55.91	79.10-57.07	60.66-45.80	46.48-41.58	...	...	...
P/E Ratio	24.12-17.05	25.68-18.53	22.30-16.84	26.26-23.49	...	...	...

Address: 4820 Emperor Blvd., Durham, NC 27703 **Telephone:** 919-998-2000	**Web Site:** www.quintiles.com **Officers:** Jack M. Greenberg - Chairman Thomas H. Pike - Vice-Chairman, Chief Executive Officer	**Auditors:** PricewaterhouseCoopers LLP **Transfer Agents:** American Stock Transfer & Trust Company, LLC, Brooklyn, NY

RACKSPACE HOSTING INC

Exchange	Symbol	Price	52Wk Range	Yield	P/E
NYS	RAX	$25.00 (5/31/2016)	40.24-16.76	N/A	23.36

*7 Year Price Score 62.67 *NYSE Composite Index=100 *12 Month Price Score 85.63

Interim Earnings (Per Share)

Qtr.	Mar	Jun	Sep	Dec
2013	0.19	0.16	0.11	0.15
2014	0.18	0.16	0.18	0.26
2015	0.20	0.20	0.26	0.24
2016	0.37	...	...	...

Interim Dividends (Per Share)

No Dividends Paid

Valuation Analysis

		Institutional Holding	
Forecast EPS	$1.08	No of Institutions	
	(05/20/2016)	373	
Market Cap	$3.2 Billion	Shares	
Book Value	$975.9 Million	111,124,432	
Price/Book	3.28	% Held	
Price/Sales	1.57	81.83	

TRADING VOLUME (thousand shares)

Business Summary: Internet & Software (MIC: 6.3.2 SIC: 7371 NAIC: 541511)

Rackspace Hosting is engaged in the managed cloud segment of the business information technology market. Co. provides solutions across two primary form factors, which represent configurations of hardware and software components: dedicated cloud and private clouds, and managed public clouds. Public cloud refers to multi-tenant pools of computing resources delivered on-demand over the Internet, dedicated cloud refers to computing resources accessed by a specific customer, while private clouds refers to a pool of computing resources that is available for a specific customer workload. In addition, hybrid cloud enables customers to use the benefits of both dedicated cloud and public cloud.

Recent Developments: For the quarter ended Mar 31 2016, net income increased 77.5% to US$48.8 million from US$27.5 million in the year-earlier quarter. Revenues were US$518.1 million, up 7.9% from US$480.2 million the year before. Operating income was US$81.2 million versus US$42.9 million in the prior-year quarter, an increase of 89.3%. Direct operating expenses rose 10.8% to US$180.4 million from US$162.8 million in the comparable period the year before. Indirect operating expenses decreased 6.6% to US$256.5 million from US$274.5 million in the equivalent prior-year period.

Prospects: Our evaluation of Rackspace Hosting Inc. as of June 19, 2016 is the result of our systematic analysis on three basic characteristics: earnings strength, relative valuation, and recent stock price movement. The company has managed to produce a neutral trend in earnings per share over the past 5 quarters and while recent estimates for the company have remained steady, RAX has posted better than expected results. Based on operating earnings yield, the company is about fairly valued when compared to all of the companies in our coverage universe. Share price changes over the past year indicates that RAX will perform poorly over the near term.

Financial Data

(US$ in Thousands)	3 Mos	12/31/2015	12/31/2014	12/31/2013	12/31/2012	12/31/2011	12/31/2010	12/31/2009
Earnings Per Share	1.07	0.90	0.77	0.61	0.75	0.55	0.35	0.24
Cash Flow Per Share	4.56	4.20	3.82	3.20	2.95	2.64	1.95	1.63
Tang Book Value Per Share	6.94	6.77	6.93	6.73	5.45	3.89	2.93	2.56
Income Statement								
Total Revenue	518,100	2,001,300	1,794,357	1,534,786	1,309,239	1,025,064	780,555	628,987
EBITDA	185,200	596,500	525,729	436,336	413,641	313,271	229,502	174,041
Depn & Amortn	104,000	390,400	362,200	303,200	240,900	189,800	149,900	118,800
Income Before Taxes	71,800	193,600	159,604	130,759	168,007	116,429	71,411	46,546
Income Taxes	23,000	67,400	49,051	44,022	62,589	40,018	25,053	16,328
Net Income	48,800	126,200	110,553	86,737	105,418	76,411	46,358	30,218
Average Shares	131,000	141,000	144,498	143,011	141,265	138,064	133,429	127,420
Balance Sheet								
Current Assets	765,300	718,400	421,743	438,968	425,245	263,365	185,445	191,669
Total Assets	2,025,400	2,014,200	1,624,284	1,491,797	1,295,551	1,026,482	761,577	668,645
Current Liabilities	241,400	236,900	276,718	258,508	255,439	237,749	189,142	158,194
Long-Term Obligations	654,500	656,900	118,937	25,172	62,326	72,216	70,052	116,078
Total Liabilities	1,049,500	1,037,700	550,490	436,385	451,904	427,059	322,714	319,218
Stockholders' Equity	975,900	976,500	1,073,794	1,055,412	843,647	599,423	438,863	349,427
Shares Outstanding	128,100	130,900	140,945	141,123	137,797	131,912	126,950	123,773
Statistical Record								
Return on Assets %	7.89	6.94	7.10	6.22	9.05	8.55	6.48	4.46
Return on Equity %	13.77	12.31	10.38	9.13	14.57	14.72	11.76	9.76
EBITDA Margin %	35.75	29.81	29.30	28.43	31.59	30.56	29.40	27.67
Net Margin %	9.42	6.31	6.16	5.65	8.05	7.45	5.94	4.80
Asset Turnover	1.10	1.10	1.15	1.10	1.12	1.15	1.09	0.93
Current Ratio	3.17	3.03	1.52	1.70	1.66	1.11	0.98	1.21
Debt to Equity	0.67	0.67	0.11	0.02	0.07	0.12	0.16	0.33
Price Range	55.39-16.76	55.39-24.03	48.24-26.28	79.24-33.19	74.27-41.22	46.19-29.78	31.74-15.51	23.06-4.38
P/E Ratio	51.77-15.66	61.54-26.70	62.65-34.13	129.90-54.41	99.03-54.96	83.98-54.15	90.69-44.31	96.08-18.25

Address: 1 Fanatical Place, City of Windcrest, San Antonio, TX 78218 **Telephone:** 210-312-4000	**Web Site:** www.rackspace.com **Officers:** William Taylor Rhodes - President, Chief Executive Officer, Chief Customer Officer, Division Officer Scott Crenshaw - Senior Vice President	**Auditors:** KPMG LLP **Investor Contact:** 210-312-7291 **Transfer Agents:** American Stock & Transfer & Trust Company, Brooklyn, NY

RALPH LAUREN CORP

Exchange	Symbol	Price	52Wk Range	Yield	P/E
NYS	RL	$94.33 (5/31/2016)	140.24-83.18	2.12	20.42

*7 Year Price Score 72.07   ***NYSE Composite Index=100**   ***12 Month Price Score 81.52**

Interim Earnings (Per Share)

Qtr.	Jun	Sep	Dec	Mar
2011-12	1.90	2.46	1.78	0.99
2012-13	2.03	2.29	2.31	1.37
2013-14	1.94	2.23	2.57	1.69
2014-15	1.80	2.25	2.41	1.42
2015-16	0.73	1.86	1.54	0.51

Interim Dividends (Per Share)

Amt	Decl	Ex	Rec	Pay
0.50Q	06/11/2015	06/24/2015	06/26/2015	07/10/2015
0.50Q	09/14/2015	09/23/2015	09/25/2015	10/09/2015
0.50Q	12/11/2015	12/22/2015	12/24/2015	01/08/2016
0.50Q	03/11/2016	03/30/2016	04/01/2016	04/15/2016

Indicated Div: $2.00

Valuation Analysis

		Institutional Holding	
Forecast EPS	$5.40 (05/20/2016)	No of Institutions	582
Market Cap	$7.8 Billion	Shares	65,222,568
Book Value	$3.7 Billion	% Held	
Price/Book	2.09	N/A	
Price/Sales	1.06		

Business Summary: Apparel, Footwear & Accessories (MIC: 1.4.2 SIC: 2329 NAIC: 315211)

Ralph Lauren designs, markets, and distributes lifestyle products, including apparel, accessories, home furnishings, and other licensed product categories. Co.'s brand names include Ralph Lauren, Ralph Lauren Collection, Ralph Lauren Purple Label, Polo Ralph Lauren, Double RL, Lauren Ralph Lauren, Polo Ralph Lauren Children, Denim & Supply Ralph Lauren, Chaps, Club Monaco, and American Living. At Apr 2 2016, Co. sold directly to customers via its 493 retail stores, 583 concession-based shop-within-shops, and through its various e-commerce sites; and its international licensing partners operated 93 Ralph Lauren stores, 42 Ralph Lauren concession shops, and 133 Club Monaco stores and shops.

Recent Developments: For the year ended Apr 2 2016, net income decreased 43.6% to US$396.0 million from US$702.0 million in the prior year. Revenues were US$7.41 billion, down 2.8% from US$7.62 billion the year before. Operating income was US$582.0 million versus US$1.04 billion in the prior year, a decrease of 43.8%. Direct operating expenses declined 0.7% to US$3.22 billion from US$3.24 billion in the comparable period the year before. Indirect operating expenses increased 7.8% to US$3.61 billion from US$3.34 billion in the equivalent prior-year period.

Prospects: Our evaluation of Ralph Lauren Corp. as of June 19, 2016 is the result of our systematic analysis on three basic characteristics: earnings strength, relative valuation, and recent stock price movement. The company has generated a negative trend in earnings per share over the past 5 quarters. However, while recent estimates for the company have been lowered by analysts, RL has posted better than expected results. Based on operating earnings yield, the company is undervalued when compared to all of the companies in our coverage universe. Share price changes over the past year indicates that RL will perform very poorly over the near term.

Financial Data

(US$ in Thousands)	04/02/2016	03/28/2015	03/29/2014	03/30/2013	03/31/2012	04/02/2011	04/03/2010	03/28/2009
Earnings Per Share	4.62	7.88	8.43	8.00	7.13	5.75	4.73	4.01
Cash Flow Per Share	11.63	10.16	10.03	11.19	9.58	7.19	9.02	7.83
Tang Book Value Per Share	31.15	31.53	31.24	27.38	24.70	20.11	17.99	14.31
Dividends Per Share	2.000	1.850	1.700	1.600	0.800	0.500	0.300	0.200
Dividend Payout %	43.29	23.48	20.17	20.00	11.22	8.70	6.34	4.99
Income Statement								
Total Revenue	7,405,000	7,620,000	7,450,000	6,944,800	6,859,500	5,660,300	4,978,900	5,018,900
EBITDA	602,000	1,034,000	1,157,000	1,142,000	1,066,800	869,100	726,400	617,300
Depn & Amortn	24,000	25,000	35,000	26,800	28,900	25,400	21,700	20,200
Income Before Taxes	563,000	998,000	1,105,000	1,098,800	1,024,400	833,100	694,900	592,500
Income Taxes	156,000	285,000	320,000	339,300	334,100	257,800	209,800	181,500
Net Income	396,000	702,000	776,000	750,000	681,000	567,600	479,500	406,000
Average Shares	85,900	89,100	92,000	93,700	95,500	98,700	101,300	101,300
Balance Sheet								
Current Assets	3,053,000	3,324,000	3,329,000	2,962,800	2,899,900	2,478,000	2,275,800	2,056,700
Total Assets	6,213,000	6,106,000	6,090,000	5,418,200	5,416,400	4,981,100	4,648,900	4,356,500
Current Liabilities	1,198,000	1,186,000	970,000	1,121,300	946,200	832,000	747,300	674,100
Long-Term Obligations	863,000	536,000	555,000	38,400	312,700	332,300	320,300	483,000
Total Liabilities	2,469,000	2,215,000	2,056,000	1,633,600	1,763,900	1,676,400	1,532,300	1,621,400
Stockholders' Equity	3,744,000	3,891,000	4,034,000	3,784,600	3,652,500	3,304,700	3,116,600	2,735,100
Shares Outstanding	82,900	86,300	88,700	90,900	92,700	94,500	98,200	99,200
Statistical Record								
Return on Assets %	6.33	11.54	13.52	13.88	13.14	11.82	10.48	9.34
Return on Equity %	10.21	17.76	19.90	20.22	19.63	17.73	16.12	15.89
EBITDA Margin %	8.13	13.57	15.53	16.44	15.55	15.35	14.59	12.30
Net Margin %	5.35	9.21	10.42	10.80	9.93	10.03	9.63	8.09
Asset Turnover	1.18	1.25	1.30	1.29	1.32	1.18	1.09	1.15
Current Ratio	2.55	2.80	3.43	2.64	3.06	2.98	3.05	3.05
Debt to Equity	0.23	0.14	0.14	0.01	0.09	0.10	0.10	0.18
Price Range	140.26-83.18	186.73-127.66	189.56-148.71	178.06-136.60	179.87-114.16	127.98-71.93	86.53-42.25	76.53-31.94
P/E Ratio	30.36-18.00	23.70-16.20	22.49-17.64	22.26-17.07	25.23-16.01	22.26-12.51	18.29-8.93	19.08-7.97
Average Yield %	1.70	1.15	1.00	1.01	0.56	0.52	0.43	0.37

Address: 650 Madison Avenue, New York, NY 10022 **Telephone:** 212-318-7000	**Web Site:** www.RalphLauren.com **Officers:** Ralph Lauren - Executive Chairman, Chairman, Chief Executive Officer, Chief Creative Officer Stefan Larsson - President, Chief Executive Officer	**Auditors:** Ernst & Young LLP **Transfer Agents:** The Bank of New York Mellon, Jersey City, NJ

RANGE RESOURCES CORP

Exchange	Symbol	Price	52Wk Range	Yield	P/E
NYS	RRC	$42.59 (5/31/2016)	55.58-20.45	0.19	N/A

*7 Year Price Score 51.27   *NYSE Composite Index=100   *12 Month Price Score 111.63

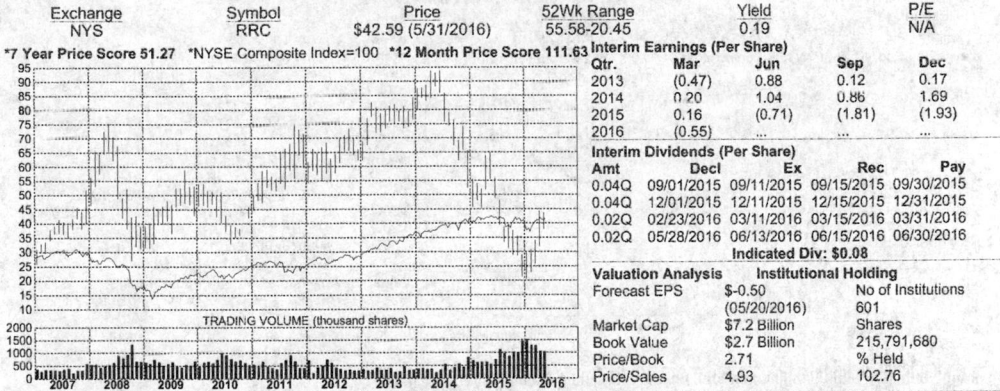

Interim Earnings (Per Share)

Qtr.	Mar	Jun	Sep	Dec
2013	(0.47)	0.88	0.12	0.17
2014	0.20	1.04	0.86	1.69
2015	0.16	(0.71)	(1.81)	(1.93)
2016	(0.55)	...	...	...

Interim Dividends (Per Share)

Amt	Decl	Ex	Rec	Pay
0.04Q	09/01/2015	09/11/2015	09/15/2015	09/30/2015
0.04Q	12/01/2015	12/11/2015	12/15/2015	12/31/2015
0.02Q	02/23/2016	03/11/2016	03/15/2016	03/31/2016
0.02Q	05/28/2016	06/13/2016	06/15/2016	06/30/2016

Indicated Div: $0.08

Valuation Analysis   Institutional Holding

Forecast EPS	$-0.50	No of Institutions
	(05/20/2016)	601
Market Cap	$7.2 Billion	Shares
Book Value	$2.7 Billion	215,791,680
Price/Book	2.71	% Held
Price/Sales	4.93	102.76

Business Summary: Production & Extraction (MIC: 9.1.1 SIC: 1311 NAIC: 211111)

Range Resources is an independent natural gas, natural gas liquids and oil company, engaged in the exploration, development and acquisition of natural gas and oil properties. Co.'s properties in the Appalachian Region are located in the Appalachian Basin in the northeastern U.S., principally in Pennsylvania. Co.'s reserves are primarily in the Marcellus Shale formation as well as the Utica/Point Pleasant, Medina and Upper Devonian formations. Co.'s other operations include drilling, production and field operations in the Texas Panhandle, as well as in the Anadarko Basin of western Oklahoma, the Nemaha Uplift of Northern Oklahoma and Kansas, the Permian Basin of West Texas and Mississippi.

Recent Developments: For the quarter ended Mar 31 2016, net loss amounted to US$91.7 million versus net income of US$27.7 million in the year-earlier quarter. Revenues were US$331.4 million, down 28.4% from US$462.8 million the year before. Direct operating expenses rose 18.0% to US$149.3 million from US$126.6 million in the comparable period the year before. Indirect operating expenses increased 11.1% to US$317.8 million from US$286.2 million in the equivalent prior-year period.

Prospects: Our evaluation of Range Resources Corp. as of June 19, 2016 is the result of our systematic analysis on three basic characteristics: earnings strength, relative valuation, and recent stock price movement. The company has suffered a very negative trend in earnings per share over the past 5 quarters. Because the company lacks sufficient analyst estimate data, we place greater weight on the historical EPS trend as the measure of earnings strength. Based on operating earnings yield, the company is overvalued when compared to all of the companies in our coverage universe. Share price changes over the past year indicates that RRC will perform very poorly over the near term.

Financial Data

(US$ in Thousands)	3 Mos	12/31/2015	12/31/2014	12/31/2013	12/31/2012	12/31/2011	12/31/2010	12/31/2009
Earnings Per Share	(5.00)	(4.29)	3.79	0.70	0.08	0.36	(1.53)	(0.35)
Cash Flow Per Share	3.36	4.11	5.83	4.63	4.05	4.00	3.27	3.83
Tang Book Value Per Share	15.74	16.30	20.50	14.78	14.51	14.85	13.91	15.04
Dividends Per Share	0.140	0.160	0.160	0.160	0.160	0.160	0.160	0.160
Dividend Payout %	...	...	4.22	22.86	200.00	44.44	...	...
Income Statement								
Total Revenue	331,413	1,598,068	2,711,695	1,862,719	1,457,704	1,218,656	1,038,975	907,341
EBITDA	(96,302)	(874,023)	1,212,762	339,336	207,054	219,515	(218,551)	90,335
Depn & Amortn	1,707	11,900	12,900	13,200	13,200	16,200	16,200	31,700
Income Before Taxes	(135,748)	(1,052,362)	1,030,885	149,579	25,056	78,263	(365,943)	(58,732)
Income Taxes	(44,038)	(338,677)	396,503	33,857	12,054	35,557	(126,687)	(4,862)
Net Income	(91,710)	(713,685)	634,382	115,722	13,002	58,026	(239,256)	(53,870)
Average Shares	166,803	166,389	164,403	161,407	160,307	159,441	156,874	154,514
Balance Sheet								
Current Assets	391,726	439,074	570,292	248,301	327,614	315,263	261,714	175,280
Total Assets	6,705,150	6,900,031	8,746,780	7,299,086	6,728,735	5,845,470	5,498,586	5,395,881
Current Liabilities	338,234	351,720	755,264	495,561	455,143	511,932	430,562	314,104
Long-Term Obligations	2,589,065	2,651,303	3,073,000	3,140,516	2,878,185	1,974,967	1,960,536	1,707,833
Total Liabilities	4,033,806	4,140,373	5,289,351	4,884,634	4,371,343	3,453,050	3,274,825	3,017,292
Stockholders' Equity	2,671,344	2,759,658	3,457,429	2,414,452	2,357,392	2,392,420	2,223,761	2,378,589
Shares Outstanding	169,696	169,316	168,628	163,342	162,514	161,131	159,909	158,118
Statistical Record								
Return on Assets %	N.M.	N.M.	7.91	1.65	0.21	1.02	N.M.	N.M.
Return on Equity %	N.M.	N.M.	21.61	4.85	0.55	2.51	N.M.	N.M.
EBITDA Margin %	N.M.	N.M.	44.72	18.22	14.20	18.01	N.M.	9.96
Net Margin %	N.M.	N.M.	23.39	6.21	0.89	4.76	N.M.	N.M.
Asset Turnover	0.19	0.20	0.34	0.27	0.23	0.21	0.19	0.17
Current Ratio	1.16	1.25	0.76	0.50	0.72	0.62	0.61	0.56
Debt to Equity	0.97	0.96	0.89	1.30	1.22	0.83	0.88	0.72
Price Range	64.75-20.45	64.75-21.17	93.70-52.28	84.31-62.05	73.28-54.02	74.40-44.74	53.93-32.80	58.74-31.18
P/E Ratio	...	...	24.72-13.79	120.44-88.64	916.00-675.25	206.67-124.28	...	...
Average Yield %	0.36	0.37	0.20	0.21	0.21	0.25	0.37	0.36

Address: 100 Throckmorton Street, Suite 1200, Fort Worth, TX 76102
Telephone: 817-870-2601

Web Site: www.rangeresources.com
Officers: Jeffrey L. Ventura - Chairman, President, Chief Executive Officer, Chief Operating Officer Roger S. Manny - Executive Vice President, Chief Financial Officer

Auditors: Ernst & Young LLP
Investor Contact: 817-870-2601
Transfer Agents: Computershare Investor Services, LLC, Cleveland, OH

RAYMOND JAMES FINANCIAL, INC.

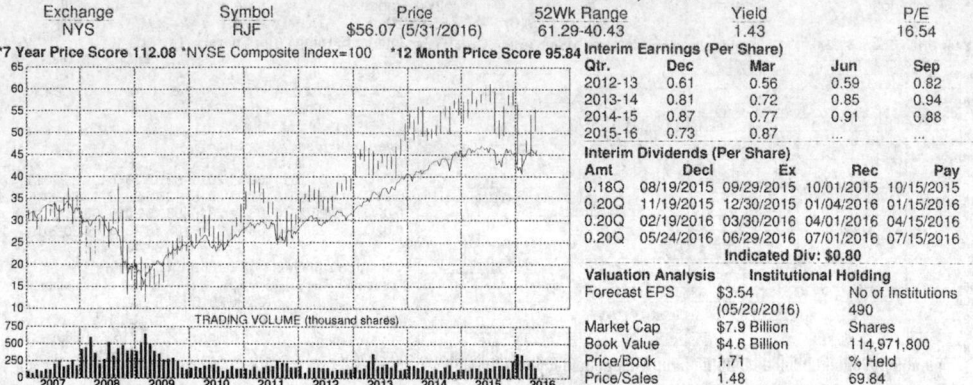

Exchange	Symbol	Price	52Wk Range	Yield	P/E
NYS	RJF	$56.07 (5/31/2016)	61.29-40.43	1.43	16.54

*7 Year Price Score 112.08 *NYSE Composite Index=100 *12 Month Price Score 95.84

Interim Earnings (Per Share)

Qtr.	Dec	Mar	Jun	Sep
2012-13	0.61	0.56	0.59	0.82
2013-14	0.81	0.72	0.85	0.94
2014-15	0.87	0.77	0.91	0.88
2015-16	0.73	0.87	...	...

Interim Dividends (Per Share)

Amt	Decl	Ex	Rec	Pay
0.18Q	08/19/2015	09/29/2015	10/01/2015	10/15/2015
0.20Q	11/19/2015	12/30/2015	01/04/2016	01/15/2016
0.20Q	02/19/2016	03/30/2016	04/01/2016	04/15/2016
0.20Q	05/24/2016	06/29/2016	07/01/2016	07/15/2016

Indicated Div: $0.80

Valuation Analysis | **Institutional Holding**

Forecast EPS	$3.54	No of Institutions
	(05/20/2016)	490
Market Cap	$7.9 Billion	Shares
Book Value	$4.6 Billion	114,971,800
Price/Book	1.71	% Held
Price/Sales	1.48	69.84

Business Summary: Finance Intermediaries & Services (MIC: 5.5.1 SIC: 6211 NAIC: 523110)

Raymond James Financial is a financial holding company. Through its broker-dealer subsidiaries, Co. is engaged in various financial services businesses, including the underwriting, distribution, trading and brokerage of equity and debt securities and the sale of mutual funds and other investment products. In addition, other subsidiaries of Co. provide investment management services for retail and institutional clients, corporate and retail banking, and trust services. Co. operates through four operating segments and its Other segment. The four operating segments include Private Client Group, Capital Markets, Asset Management, and Raymond James Bank, N.A.

Recent Developments: For the quarter ended Mar 31 2016, net income increased 8.4% to US$117.9 million from US$108.8 million in the year-earlier quarter. Revenues were US$1.34 billion, up 2.2% from US$1.31 billion the year before. Direct operating expenses rose 9.6% to US$29.4 million from US$26.8 million in the comparable period the year before. Indirect operating expenses increased 1.0% to US$1.12 billion from US$1.11 billion in the equivalent prior-year period.

Prospects: Our evaluation of Raymond James Financial Inc. as of June 19, 2016 is the result of our systematic analysis on three basic characteristics: earnings strength, relative valuation, and recent stock price movement. The company has produced a positive trend in earnings per share over the past 5 quarters and while recent estimates for the company have been mixed, RJF has posted better than expected results. Based on operating earnings yield, the company is undervalued when compared to all of the companies in our coverage universe. Share price changes over the past year indicates that RJF will perform poorly over the near term.

Financial Data

(US$ in Thousands)	6 Mos	3 Mos	09/30/2015	09/30/2014	09/30/2013	09/30/2012	09/30/2011	09/30/2010
Earnings Per Share	3.39	3.29	3.43	3.32	2.58	2.20	2.19	1.83
Cash Flow Per Share	3.19	6.20	6.31	3.63	4.79	2.98	12.73	(8.56)
Tang Book Value Per Share	30.18	29.73	29.00	26.82	23.66	21.11	19.90	17.96
Dividends Per Share	0.760	0.740	0.720	0.640	0.560	0.520	0.520	0.440
Dividend Payout %	22.42	22.49	20.99	19.28	21.71	23.64	23.74	24.04
Income Statement								
Total Revenue	2,642,444	1,301,526	5,308,164	4,965,460	4,595,798	3,897,900	3,399,886	2,979,516
EBITDA	348,527	164,762	802,483	757,307	579,638	483,904	478,081	380,702
Depn & Amortn	(3,852)	2,587	25,771	41,359	(14,272)	15,983	27,336	24,558
Income Before Taxes	352,379	162,175	776,712	715,948	593,910	467,921	450,745	356,144
Income Taxes	352,379	62,000	296,034	267,797	197,033	175,656	182,894	133,625
Net Income	232,176	106,329	502,140	480,248	367,154	295,869	278,353	228,283
Average Shares	144,012	146,141	145,939	143,589	140,541	131,791	122,836	119,592
Balance Sheet								
Current Assets	9,973,512	9,776,066	9,427,793	8,496,359	10,560,162	8,694,956	8,961,474	9,243,879
Total Assets	27,753,211	26,907,327	26,479,684	23,325,652	23,186,122	21,160,265	18,006,995	17,883,081
Current Liabilities	21,275,244	20,428,776	19,930,688	17,157,683	17,930,339	16,069,177	14,383,200	12,408,785
Long-Term Obligations	1,204,565	1,205,323	1,762,898	1,734,713	1,257,446	1,410,806	711,950	2,877,428
Total Liabilities	23,117,921	22,260,513	21,957,653	19,184,416	19,523,198	17,891,325	15,419,376	15,580,265
Stockholders' Equity	4,635,290	4,646,814	4,522,031	4,141,236	3,662,924	3,268,940	2,587,619	2,302,816
Shares Outstanding	141,102	143,720	142,918	141,203	139,557	137,736	126,407	124,701
Statistical Record								
Return on Assets %	1.88	1.88	2.02	2.07	1.66	1.51	1.55	1.26
Return on Equity %	10.98	10.81	11.59	12.31	10.59	10.08	11.38	10.53
EBITDA Margin %	13.19	12.66	15.12	15.25	12.61	12.41	14.06	12.78
Net Margin %	8.79	8.17	9.46	9.67	7.99	7.59	8.19	7.66
Asset Turnover	0.20	0.21	0.21	0.21	0.21	0.20	0.19	0.17
Current Ratio	0.47	0.48	0.47	0.50	0.59	0.54	0.62	0.74
Debt to Equity	0.26	0.26	0.39	0.42	0.34	0.43	0.28	1.25
Price Range	61.29-40.43	61.29-48.56	61.29-48.56	56.07-40.04	48.12-36.54	38.59-24.11	39.46-24.42	31.12-22.11
P/E Ratio	18.08-11.93	18.63-14.76	17.87-14.16	16.89-12.06	18.65-14.16	17.54-10.96	18.02-11.15	17.01-12.08
Average Yield %	1.41	1.31	1.28	1.27	1.33	1.56	1.60	1.69

Address: 880 Carillon Parkway, St. Petersburg, FL 33716 **Telephone:** 727-567-1000	**Web Site:** www.raymondjames.com **Officers:** Thomas A. James - Chairman Francis S. Godbold - Vice-Chairman	**Auditors:** KPMG LLP **Investor Contact:** 727-567-5133 **Transfer Agents:** Computershare Inc., College Station, TX

RAYONIER INC.

Exchange	Symbol	Price	52Wk Range	Yield	P/E
NYS	RYN	$25.93 (5/31/2016)	26.35-18.63	3.86	72.03

*7 Year Price Score 67.16 ***NYSE Composite Index=100** ***12 Month Price Score 105.51**

TRADING VOLUME (thousand shares)

Interim Earnings (Per Share)

Qtr.	Mar	Jun	Sep	Dec
2013	1.13	0.67	0.44	0.63
2014	0.34	0.14	0.25	0.07
2015	0.14	(0.01)	0.16	0.09
2016	0.12	...	...	...

Interim Dividends (Per Share)

Amt	Decl	Ex	Rec	Pay
0.25Q	07/20/2015	09/14/2015	09/16/2015	09/30/2015
0.25Q	10/19/2015	12/15/2015	12/17/2015	12/31/2015
0.25Q	02/29/2016	03/15/2016	03/17/2016	03/31/2016
0.25Q	05/24/2016	06/14/2016	06/16/2016	06/30/2016

Indicated Div: $1.00

Valuation Analysis		Institutional Holding	
Forecast EPS	$0.33	No of Institutions	
	(05/07/2016)	436	
Market Cap	$3.2 Billion	Shares	
Book Value	$1.3 Billion	123,203,368	
Price/Book	2.53	% Held	
Price/Sales	5.90	79.07	

Business Summary: REITs (MIC: 5.3.1 SIC: 6798 NAIC: 525930)

Rayonier is a timberland real estate investment trust. Co. has five business segments: Southern Timber, Pacific Northwest Timber and New Zealand Timber, which reflect activities related to the harvesting of timber and other activities, such as recreational leases; Real Estate, which reflects land sales, which are reported in five categories: improved development, unimproved development, rural, non-strategic / timberlands, and large dispositions; and Trading, which reflects the log trading activities that support Co.'s New Zealand operations. At Dec 31 2015, Co. owned, leased or managed about 2.7 million acres of timberlands located in the U.S. South, U.S. Pacific Northwest and New Zealand.

Recent Developments: For the quarter ended Mar 31 2016, net income decreased 17.2% to US$15.1 million from US$18.2 million in the year-earlier quarter. Revenues were US$134.8 million, down 3.9% from US$140.3 million the year before.

Prospects: Our evaluation of Rayonier Inc. as of June 19, 2016 is the result of our systematic analysis on three basic characteristics: earnings strength, relative valuation, and recent stock price movement. The company has enjoyed a very positive trend in earnings per share over the past 5 quarters and while recent estimates for the company have remained steady, RYN has posted better than expected results. Based on operating earnings yield, the company is overvalued when compared to all of the companies in our coverage universe. Share price changes over the past year indicates that RYN will perform in line with the market over the near term.

Financial Data
(US$ in Thousands)

	3 Mos	12/31/2015	12/31/2014	12/31/2013	12/31/2012	12/31/2011	12/31/2010	12/31/2009
Earnings Per Share	0.36	0.37	0.76	2.86	2.17	2.20	1.79	2.61
Cash Flow Per Share	1.26	1.41	2.50	4.34	3.62	3.55	4.12	2.59
Tang Book Value Per Share	10.24	10.49	11.74	13.16	11.66	10.84	10.34	9.61
Dividends Per Share	1.000	1.000	2.030	1.860	1.680	1.232	0.816	0.800
Dividend Payout %	277.78	270.27	267.11	65.03	77.42	56.00	45.67	30.69
Income Statement								
Total Revenue	134,843	544,874	603,521	1,707,822	1,571,000	1,488,642	1,315,233	1,168,567
EBITDA	23,614	195,499	264,622	636,770	585,435	508,963	432,484	577,222
Depn & Amortn	617	117,715	166,333	214,518	174,534	156,765	151,566	164,888
Income Before Taxes	14,277	43,082	44,842	380,864	366,526	302,274	231,770	361,703
Income Taxes	(781)	(859)	(9,601)	49,661	88,391	30,357	15,217	46,336
Net Income	14,472	46,165	99,337	371,896	278,685	276,005	217,586	312,541
Average Shares	122,644	125,900	131,038	130,105	128,702	125,394	121,868	120,030
Balance Sheet								
Current Assets	135,211	105,685	214,363	519,094	566,274	344,502	609,186	509,696
Total Assets	2,332,137	2,319,263	2,453,115	3,685,501	3,122,951	2,569,348	2,363,653	2,252,931
Current Liabilities	68,308	59,457	202,002	276,112	307,823	178,251	244,948	175,111
Long-Term Obligations	857,429	833,879	621,849	1,461,724	1,120,052	819,229	675,103	694,999
Total Liabilities	1,075,693	1,031,179	964,645	2,024,331	1,684,947	1,246,275	1,112,071	1,106,725
Stockholders' Equity	1,256,444	1,288,084	1,488,470	1,661,170	1,438,004	1,323,073	1,251,582	1,146,206
Shares Outstanding	122,742	122,770	126,773	126,257	123,332	122,035	121,023	119,312
Statistical Record								
Return on Assets %	1.81	1.93	3.24	10.92	9.76	11.19	9.43	14.39
Return on Equity %	3.15	3.33	6.31	24.00	20.13	21.44	18.15	30.20
EBITDA Margin %	17.51	35.88	43.85	37.29	37.27	34.19	32.88	49.40
Net Margin %	10.73	8.47	16.46	21.78	17.74	18.54	16.54	26.75
Asset Turnover	0.23	0.23	0.20	0.50	0.55	0.60	0.57	0.54
Current Ratio	1.98	1.78	1.06	1.88	1.84	1.93	2.49	2.91
Debt to Equity	0.68	0.65	0.42	0.88	0.78	0.62	0.54	0.61
Price Range	26.96-18.63	29.87-21.97	36.35-25.91	45.01-30.74	38.68-31.06	33.71-26.13	27.07-19.96	21.91-11.45
P/E Ratio	74.89-51.75	80.73-59.38	47.83-34.09	15.74-10.75	17.83-14.31	15.32-11.88	15.12-11.15	8.40-4.39
Average Yield %	4.23	3.97	6.20	4.60	4.83	4.02	3.47	4.38

Address: 225 Water Street, Suite 1400, Jacksonville, FL 32202 Telephone: 904-357-9100	Web Site: www.rayonier.com Officers: Richard D. Kincaid - Chairman David L. Nunes - President, Chief Executive Officer, Chief Operating Officer	Auditors: Ernst & Young LLP Investor Contact: 904-357-9177 Transfer Agents: Computershare, Providence, R.I.

RAYTHEON CO.

*7 Year Price Score 137.39 *NYSE Composite Index=100   ***12 Month Price Score 108.24**

Interim Earnings (Per Share)

Qtr.	Mar	Jun	Sep	Dec
2013	1.49	1.50	1.51	1.66
2014	1.89	1.76	1.65	1.88
2015	1.79	1.65	1.47	1.89
2016	1.43			

Interim Dividends (Per Share)

Amt	Decl	Ex	Rec	Pay
0.67Q	07/23/2015	10/05/2015	10/07/2015	11/12/2015
0.67Q	11/18/2015	01/04/2016	01/06/2016	02/04/2016
0.733Q	03/23/2016	04/04/2016	04/06/2016	05/12/2016
0.733Q	05/26/2016	07/01/2016	07/06/2016	08/04/2016

Indicated Div: $2.93 (Div. Reinv. Plan)

Valuation Analysis   **Institutional Holding**

Forecast EPS	$7.14	No of Institutions
	(05/20/2016)	1293
Market Cap	$38.5 Billion	Shares
Book Value	$10.1 Billion	272,571,488
Price/Book	3.80	% Held
Price/Sales	1.62	77.29

Business Summary: Defense (MIC: 7.1.2 SIC: 3812 NAIC: 334511)

Raytheon, together with its subsidiaries, is a technology company, engaged in defense and other government markets. Co. develops products, services and solutions in its core markets: sensing; effects; command, control, communications, computers, cyber and intelligence (C5Iâ,,¢); mission support; and cybersecurity. Co. serves both domestic and international customers, primarily as a prime contractor or subcontractor on a range portfolio of defense and related programs for government customers. As of Dec 31 2015, Co. had five business segments: Integrated Defense Systems; Intelligence, Information and Services; Missile Systems; Space and Airborne Systems; and Forcepoint.

Recent Developments: For the quarter ended Apr 3 2016, income from continuing operations decreased 27.1% to US$404.0 million from US$554.0 million in the year-earlier quarter. Net income decreased 26.9% to US$405.0 million from US$554.0 million in the year-earlier quarter. Revenues were US$5.76 billion, up 9.0% from US$5.29 billion the year before. Operating income was US$612.0 million versus US$840.0 million in the prior-year quarter, a decrease of 27.1%. Direct operating expenses rose 14.8% to US$4.40 billion from US$3.83 billion in the comparable period the year before. Indirect operating expenses increased 22.1% to US$751.0 million from US$615.0 million in the equivalent prior-year period.

Prospects: Our evaluation of Raytheon Co. as of June 19, 2016 is the result of our systematic analysis on three basic characteristics: earnings strength, relative valuation, and recent stock price movement. The company has enjoyed a very positive trend in earnings per share over the past 5 quarters and while recent estimates for the company have been mixed, RTN has posted better than expected results. Based on operating earnings yield, the company is about fairly valued when compared to all of the companies in our coverage universe. Share price changes over the past year indicates that RTN will perform very well over the near term.

Financial Data

(US$ in Thousands)	3 Mos	12/31/2015	12/31/2014	12/31/2013	12/31/2012	12/31/2011	12/31/2010	12/31/2009
Earnings Per Share	6.44	6.80	7.18	6.16	5.65	5.28	4.88	4.89
Cash Flow Per Share	8.79	7.74	7.00	7.35	5.86	5.99	5.21	6.98
Dividends Per Share	2.743	2.680	2.420	2.200	2.000	1.720	1.500	1.240
Dividend Payout %	31.21	38.46	33.70	35.71	35.40	32.58	30.74	25.36
Income Statement								
Total Revenue	5,763,000	23,247,000	22,826,000	23,706,000	24,414,000	24,857,000	25,183,000	24,881,000
EBITDA	738,000	3,316,000	3,487,000	3,258,000	3,289,000	3,159,000	2,846,000	3,338,000
Depn & Amortn	124,000	307,000	301,000	303,000	318,000	314,000	304,000	299,000
Income Before Taxes	560,000	2,787,000	2,983,000	2,757,000	2,779,000	2,690,000	2,432,000	2,930,000
Income Taxes	156,000	733,000	790,000	808,000	878,000	793,000	589,000	953,000
Net Income	429,000	2,074,000	2,244,000	1,996,000	1,888,000	1,866,000	1,840,000	1,935,000
Average Shares	299,600	305,200	312,600	324,200	334,200	353,600	377,000	395,700
Balance Sheet								
Current Assets	9,359,000	9,812,000	10,292,000	9,816,000	9,246,000	9,309,000	8,822,000	7,868,000
Total Assets	28,829,000	29,281,000	27,900,000	25,967,000	26,686,000	25,854,000	24,422,000	23,607,000
Current Liabilities	5,749,000	6,126,000	5,930,000	5,810,000	5,902,000	6,130,000	5,960,000	5,523,000
Long-Term Obligations	5,332,000	5,330,000	5,330,000	4,734,000	4,731,000	4,605,000	3,610,000	2,329,000
Total Liabilities	18,705,000	19,153,000	18,375,000	14,932,000	18,660,000	17,673,000	14,668,000	13,780,000
Stockholders' Equity	10,124,000	10,128,000	9,525,000	11,035,000	8,026,000	8,181,000	9,754,000	9,827,000
Shares Outstanding	297,000	299,000	307,000	315,000	328,000	339,000	359,000	378,000
Statistical Record								
Return on Assets %	6.89	7.25	8.33	7.58	7.17	7.42	7.66	8.25
Return on Equity %	19.69	21.11	21.83	20.94	23.23	20.81	18.79	20.46
EBITDA Margin %	12.81	14.26	15.28	13.74	13.47	12.71	11.30	13.42
Net Margin %	7.44	8.92	9.83	8.42	7.73	7.51	7.31	7.78
Asset Turnover	0.84	0.81	0.85	0.90	0.93	0.99	1.05	1.06
Current Ratio	1.63	1.60	1.74	1.69	1.57	1.52	1.48	1.42
Debt to Equity	0.53	0.53	0.56	0.43	0.59	0.56	0.37	0.24
Price Range	128.24-95.57	127.95-95.57	110.47-88.13	91.04-52.67	59.28-47.99	52.51-38.83	60.01-43.21	53.44-33.57
P/E Ratio	19.91-14.84	18.82-14.05	15.39-12.27	14.78-8.55	10.49-8.49	9.95-7.35	12.30-8.85	10.93-6.87
Average Yield %	1.78	2.39	2.57	3.17	3.70	3.77	2.91	2.69

REALOGY HOLDINGS CORP

Exchange	Symbol	Price	52Wk Range	Yield	P/E
NYS	RLGY	$32.80 (5/31/2016)	49.53-28.11	N/A	27.80

*7 Year Price Score N/A   *NYSE Composite Index=100   *12 Month Price Score 88.70

TRADING VOLUME (thousand shares)

Interim Earnings (Per Share)

Qtr.	Mar	Jun	Sep	Dec
2013	(0.52)	0.57	0.74	2.18
2014	(0.32)	0.46	0.68	0.14
2015	(0.22)	0.66	0.75	0.06
2016	(0.29)	...	...	...

Interim Dividends (Per Share)

No Dividends Paid

Valuation Analysis   Institutional Holding

Forecast EPS	$1.81	No of Institutions
	(05/24/2016)	344
Market Cap	$4.8 Billion	Shares
Book Value	$2.4 Billion	148,485,696
Price/Book	2.04	% Held
Price/Sales	0.83	79.28

Business Summary: Property, Real Estate & Development (MIC: 5.3.2 SIC: 6531 NAIC: 531210)

Realogy Holdings is a holding company. Through its subsidiaries, Co. is a provider of residential real estate services. Co. has four segments: real estate franchise services, which include brokerage brands including Century 21® and Coldwell Banker®; company owned real estate brokerage services, which operates real estate brokerage business under the Coldwell Banker®, Corcoran Group®, Sotheby's International Realty®, ZipRealty® and Citi Habitats brand names; relocation services, which provides clients employee relocation services such as homesale assistance; and title and settlement services, provides title, settlement and vendor management services.

Recent Developments: For the quarter ended Mar 31 2016, net loss amounted to US$42.0 million versus a net loss of US$32.0 million in the year-earlier quarter. Revenues were US$1.13 billion, up 6.8% from US$1.06 billion the year before.

Prospects: Our evaluation of Realogy Holdings Corp as of June 26, 2016 is the result of our systematic analysis on three basic characteristics: earnings strength, relative valuation, and recent stock price movement. The company has produced a positive trend in earnings per share over the past 5 quarters. However, while recent estimates for the company have been lowered by analysts, RLGY has posted results that fell short of analysts expectations. Based on operating earnings yield, the company is undervalued when compared to all of the companies in our coverage universe. Share price changes over the past year indicates that RLGY will perform well over the near term.

Financial Data
(US$ in Millions)

	3 Mos	12/31/2015	12/31/2014	12/31/2013	12/31/2012	12/31/2011	12/31/2010	12/31/2009
Earnings Per Share	1.18	1.24	0.97	2.99	(14.41)	(55.00)	(12.25)	(32.75)
Cash Flow Per Share	3.82	3.71	2.90	3.38	(2.72)	(23.95)	(14.72)	42.58
Income Statement								
Total Revenue	1,134	5,706	5,328	5,289	4,672	4,093	4,090	3,932
EBITDA	11	597	566	523	30	307	696	348
Depn & Amortn	4	84	74	67	65	74	86	99
Income Before Taxes	(66)	282	225	175	(563)	(433)	6	(334)
Income Taxes	(24)	110	87	(242)	39	32	133	(50)
Net Income	(42)	184	143	438	(543)	(441)	(99)	(262)
Average Shares	146	148	147	146	37	8	8	8
Balance Sheet								
Current Assets	844	961	1,026	917	978	806	898	874
Total Assets	7,400	7,531	7,538	7,326	7,445	7,810	8,029	8,041
Current Liabilities	1,306	1,605	878	911	1,015	1,436	1,357	1,440
Long-Term Obligations	3,203	2,962	3,891	3,886	4,256	6,825	6,698	6,674
Total Liabilities	5,050	5,113	5,359	5,316	5,929	9,320	9,103	9,024
Stockholders' Equity	2,350	2,418	2,179	2,010	1,516	(1,510)	(1,074)	(983)
Shares Outstanding	145	146	146	146	145	8	8	8
Statistical Record								
Return on Assets %	2.35	2.44	1.92	5.93	N.M.	N.M.	N.M.	...
Return on Equity %	7.72	8.01	6.83	24.84	N.M.	...	...	...
EBITDA Margin %	0.97	10.46	10.62	9.89	0.64	7.50	17.02	8.85
Net Margin %	N.M.	3.22	2.68	8.28	N.M.	N.M.	N.M.	N.M.
Asset Turnover	0.78	0.76	0.72	0.72	0.61	0.52	0.51	...
Current Ratio	0.65	0.60	1.17	1.01	0.96	0.56	0.66	0.61
Debt to Equity	1.36	1.22	1.79	1.93	2.81	...	...	...
Price Range	49.53-28.11	49.53-36.48	49.98-33.86	54.85-40.67	42.03-33.50	...	...	...
P/E Ratio	41.97-23.82	39.94-29.42	51.53-34.91	18.34-13.60	...	...	...	...

Address: 175 Park Avenue, Madison, NJ 07940 **Telephone:** 973-407-2000	**Web Site:** www.realogy.com **Officers:** Richard A. Smith - Chairman, President, Chief Executive Officer Anthony E. Hull Executive Vice President, Chief Financial Officer, Treasurer	**Auditors:** PricewaterhouseCoopers LLP **Investor Contact:** 973-407-4669 **Transfer Agents:** Computershare Trust Company, N.A.

REALTY INCOME CORP

Exchange	Symbol	Price	52Wk Range	Yield	P/E	Div Achiever
NYS	O	$60.09 (5/31/2016)	64.22-43.38	3.98	56.16	21 Years

*7 Year Price Score 111.88 *NYSE Composite Index=100 *12 Month Price Score 116.37

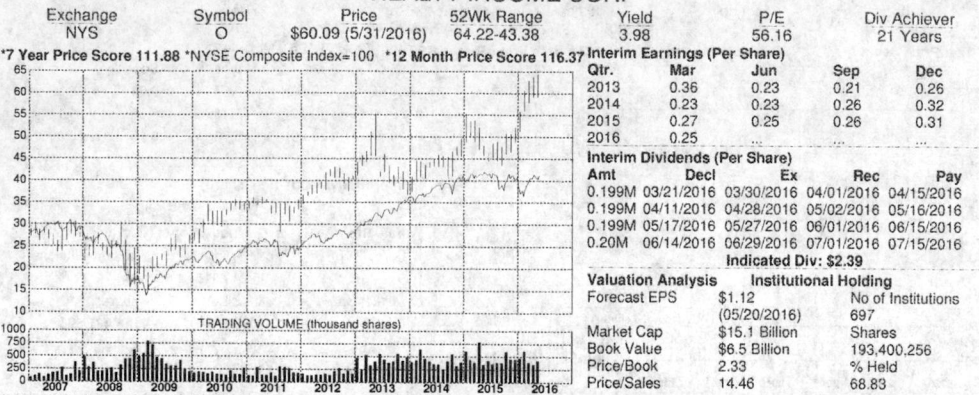

Interim Earnings (Per Share)

Qtr.	Mar	Jun	Sep	Dec
2013	0.36	0.23	0.21	0.26
2014	0.23	0.23	0.26	0.32
2015	0.27	0.25	0.26	0.31
2016	0.25	...	...	...

Interim Dividends (Per Share)

Amt	Decl	Ex	Rec	Pay
0.199M	03/21/2016	03/30/2016	04/01/2016	04/15/2016
0.199M	04/11/2016	04/28/2016	05/02/2016	05/16/2016
0.199M	05/17/2016	05/27/2016	06/01/2016	06/15/2016
0.20M	06/14/2016	06/29/2016	07/01/2016	07/15/2016

Indicated Div: $2.39

Valuation Analysis — **Institutional Holding**

Forecast EPS	$1.12	No of Institutions
	(05/20/2016)	697
Market Cap	$15.1 Billion	Shares
Book Value	$6.5 Billion	193,400,256
Price/Book	2.33	% Held
Price/Sales	14.46	68.83

Business Summary: REITs (MIC: 5.3.1 SIC: 6798 NAIC: 525930)

Realty Income is a real estate investment trust that invests in commercial real estate. Co. primary business objective is generating monthly cash dividends from a consistent level of cash flow from operations. Co. focuses on in-house acquisition, portfolio management, asset management, credit research, real estate research, legal, finance and accounting, information technology, and capital markets. Co. also engages on portfolio management, asset management and the acquisition of additional properties. At December 31, 2015, Co, owned a portfolio of 4,538 properties, located in 49 states and Puerto Rico, with over 76.0 million sq. ft. of leasable space.

Recent Developments: For the quarter ended Mar 31 2016, net income increased 4.3% to US$70.5 million from US$67.6 million in the year-earlier quarter. Revenues were US$267.1 million, up 8.2% from US$246.9 million the year before. Revenues from property income rose 8.5% to US$265.9 million from US$245.1 million in the corresponding quarter a year earlier.

Prospects: Our evaluation of Realty Income Corp. as of June 19, 2016 is the result of our systematic analysis on three basic characteristics: earnings strength, relative valuation, and recent stock price movement. The company has managed to produce a neutral trend in earnings per share over the past 5 quarters. Because the company lacks sufficient analyst estimate data, we place greater weight on the historical EPS trend as the measure of earnings strength. Based on operating earnings yield, the company is overvalued when compared to all of the companies in our coverage universe. Share price changes over the past year indicates that O will perform very well over the near term.

Financial Data

(US$ in Thousands)	3 Mos	12/31/2015	12/31/2014	12/31/2013	12/31/2012	12/31/2011	12/31/2010	12/31/2009
Earnings Per Share	1.07	1.09	1.04	1.06	0.86	1.05	1.01	1.03
Cash Flow Per Share	2.84	2.94	2.87	2.71	2.45	2.37	2.30	2.19
Tang Book Value Per Share	21.69	21.89	20.27	21.37	17.95	16.80	15.50	14.10
Dividends Per Share	2.308	2.279	2.193	2.178	1.778	1.738	1.723	1.708
Dividend Payout %	215.65	209.08	210.85	205.46	206.73	165.51	170.58	165.81
Income Statement								
Total Revenue	267,116	1,023,285	933,505	778,375	475,510	421,059	345,009	327,581
EBITDA	74,188	706,023	651,204	506,425	304,904	280,572	223,095	218,242
Depn & Amortn	3,704	421,168	382,064	327,245	158,933	129,435	101,679	96,109
Income Before Taxes	70,484	284,855	269,140	179,180	145,971	151,137	121,416	122,133
Net Income	70,243	283,766	270,635	245,564	159,152	157,032	130,784	131,127
Average Shares	250,698	236,208	218,767	191,781	132,884	126,189	105,942	103,581
Balance Sheet								
Current Assets	107,689	121,972	68,238	49,580	26,907	19,540	28,908	20,422
Total Assets	12,037,103	11,865,870	11,012,622	9,924,441	5,443,363	4,419,389	3,535,590	2,914,787
Current Liabilities	138,811	220,135	213,357	181,243	120,230	102,931	85,173	70,046
Long-Term Obligations	5,109,882	4,841,486	4,930,947	4,166,840	2,883,868	2,055,181	1,600,000	1,354,600
Total Liabilities	5,558,104	5,334,274	5,399,221	4,538,994	3,030,569	2,164,535	1,688,625	1,426,778
Stockholders' Equity	6,478,999	6,531,596	5,613,401	5,385,447	2,412,794	2,254,854	1,846,965	1,488,009
Shares Outstanding	251,081	250,416	224,881	207,485	133,452	133,223	118,058	104,286
Statistical Record								
Return on Assets %	2.48	2.48	2.59	3.20	3.22	3.95	4.06	4.44
Return on Equity %	4.73	4.67	4.92	6.30	6.80	7.66	7.84	8.62
EBITDA Margin %	27.77	69.00	69.76	65.06	64.12	66.63	64.66	66.62
Net Margin %	26.30	27.73	28.99	31.55	33.47	37.29	37.91	40.03
Asset Turnover	0.09	0.09	0.09	0.10	0.10	0.11	0.11	0.11
Current Ratio	0.78	0.55	0.32	0.27	0.22	0.19	0.34	0.29
Debt to Equity	0.79	0.74	0.88	0.77	1.20	0.91	0.87	0.91
Price Range	62.87-43.38	55.14-43.38	49.57-37.33	55.09-36.68	42.96-34.52	36.07-28.04	35.65-25.52	27.54-15.03
P/E Ratio	58.76-40.54	50.59-39.80	47.66-35.89	51.97-34.60	49.95-40.14	34.35-26.70	35.30-25.27	26.74-14.59
Average Yield %	4.61	4.68	5.05	5.03	4.51	5.12	5.44	7.63

Address: 11995 El Camino Real, San Diego, CA 92130 **Telephone:** 858-284-5000	**Web Site:** www.realtyincome.com **Officers:** Thomas A. Lewis - Vice-Chairman, Chief Executive Officer Sumit Roy - President, Chief Operating Officer, Chief Investment Officer, Executive Vice President	**Auditors:** KPMG LLP **Investor Contact:** 760-741-2111 **Transfer Agents:** Wells Fargo Shareowner Services, St. Paul, MN

RED HAT INC

Exchange	Symbol	Price	52Wk Range	Yield	P/E
NYS	RHT	$77.46 (5/31/2016)	83.65-60.93	N/A	72.39

*7 Year Price Score 125.41 *NYSE Composite Index=100   *12 Month Price Score 98.15

Interim Earnings (Per Share)

Qtr.	May	Aug	Nov	Feb
2011-12	0.17	0.20	0.19	0.19
2012-13	0.19	0.18	0.18	0.22
2013-14	0.21	0.21	0.27	0.24
2014-15	0.20	0.25	0.26	0.25
2015-16	0.26	0.28	0.25	0.29

Interim Dividends (Per Share)

No Dividends Paid

Valuation Analysis		Institutional Holding	
Forecast EPS	$2.24	No of Institutions	
	(05/20/2016)	650	
Market Cap	$14.0 Billion	Shares	
Book Value	$1.3 Billion	190,185,424	
Price/Book	10.52	% Held	
Price/Sales	6.84	92.49	

Business Summary: Internet & Software (MIC: 6.3.2 SIC: 7371 NAIC: 511210)

Red Hat is a provider of open source software solutions, using a community-powered approach to develop and provide operating system, virtualization, management, middleware, cloud, mobile and storage technologies. Co.'s software offerings include: Red Hat Enterprise Linux, an operating system built with open source software components; as well as Red Hat JBoss Middleware family of offerings for developing, deploying and managing applications, integrating applications, data and devices, and automating business processes across physical, virtual, cloud and mobile environments. Co. also provides other technologies, such as a realtime operating system, and user authentication.

Recent Developments: For the year ended Feb 29 2016, net income increased 10.6% to US$199.4 million from US$180.2 million in the prior year. Revenues were US$2.05 billion, up 14.7% from US$1.79 billion the year before. Operating income was US$288.0 million versus US$250.0 million in the prior year, an increase of 15.2%. Direct operating expenses rose 13.3% to US$309.6 million from US$273.2 million in the comparable period the year before. Indirect operating expenses increased 14.9% to US$1.45 billion from US$1.27 billion in the equivalent prior-year period.

Prospects: Our evaluation of Red Hat Inc. as of June 19, 2016 is the result of our systematic analysis on three basic characteristics: earnings strength, relative valuation, and recent stock price movement. The company has managed to produce a neutral trend in earnings per share over the past 5 quarters and while recent estimates for the company have remained steady, RHT has posted better than expected results. Based on operating earnings yield, the company is overvalued when compared to all of the companies in our coverage universe. Share price changes over the past year indicates that RHT will perform poorly over the near term.

Financial Data
(US$ in Thousands)

	02/29/2016	02/28/2015	02/28/2014	02/28/2013	02/29/2012	02/28/2011	02/28/2010	02/28/2009
Earnings Per Share	1.07	0.95	0.93	0.77	0.75	0.55	0.45	0.39
Cash Flow Per Share	3.91	3.34	2.85	2.41	2.02	1.53	1.36	1.24
Tang Book Value Per Share	0.89	1.24	3.85	3.56	3.67	3.71	3.01	2.87
Income Statement								
Total Revenue	2,052,230	1,789,489	1,534,615	1,328,817	1,133,103	909,277	748,236	652,572
EBITDA	335,222	304,557	278,072	240,325	231,214	175,987	137,485	149,230
Depn & Amortn	48,900	48,001	45,169	38,818	31,623	29,036	26,200	22,900
Income Before Taxes	274,865	255,498	239,548	209,752	208,009	153,694	121,502	121,532
Income Taxes	75,500	75,297	61,256	59,548	61,383	46,416	34,249	42,811
Net Income	199,365	180,201	178,292	150,204	146,626	107,278	87,253	78,721
Average Shares	186,119	189,246	192,036	195,804	196,451	196,353	193,546	211,344
Balance Sheet								
Current Assets	1,872,433	1,970,239	1,571,182	1,368,749	1,221,355	1,184,558	1,003,119	890,832
Total Assets	4,155,099	3,802,985	3,106,619	2,813,660	2,491,099	2,199,322	1,870,872	1,753,636
Current Liabilities	1,559,177	1,334,692	1,148,086	985,712	826,305	679,801	566,267	446,649
Long-Term Obligations	723,942	715,402	...	...	...	...	...	...
Total Liabilities	2,820,667	2,514,647	1,555,454	1,293,499	1,092,282	908,623	759,820	647,583
Stockholders' Equity	1,334,432	1,288,338	1,551,165	1,520,161	1,398,817	1,290,699	1,111,052	1,106,053
Shares Outstanding	181,185	183,551	189,712	193,021	192,654	193,046	187,351	189,998
Statistical Record								
Return on Assets %	5.00	5.22	6.02	5.66	6.24	5.27	4.81	4.11
Return on Equity %	15.16	12.69	11.61	10.29	10.87	8.93	7.87	7.65
EBITDA Margin %	16.33	17.02	18.12	18.09	20.41	19.35	18.37	22.87
Net Margin %	9.71	10.07	11.62	11.30	12.94	11.80	11.66	12.06
Asset Turnover	0.51	0.52	0.52	0.50	0.48	0.45	0.41	0.34
Current Ratio	1.20	1.48	1.37	1.39	1.48	1.74	1.77	1.99
Debt to Equity	0.54	0.56	...	...	...	...	...	...
Price Range	83.65-60.93	71.09-48.19	59.93-42.35	61.95-47.41	52.72-31.87	48.45-27.49	31.43-13.20	24.36-7.89
P/E Ratio	78.18-56.94	74.83-50.73	64.44-45.54	80.45-61.57	70.29-42.49	88.09-49.98	69.84-29.33	62.46-20.23

Address: 100 East Davie Street, Raleigh, NC 27601	Web Site: www.redhat.com	Auditors: PricewaterhouseCoopers LLP
Telephone: 919-754-3700	Officers: Henry Hugh Shelton - Chairman James M. Whitehurst - President, Chief Executive Officer	Investor Contact: 919-754-3700 Transfer Agents: Computershare, Providence, RI

REGAL BELOIT CORP

Exchange	Symbol	Price	52Wk Range	Yield	P/E	Div Achiever
NYS	RBC	$57.13 (5/31/2016)	77.70-49.38	1.68	17.31	11 Years

*7 Year Price Score 82.66 ***NYSE Composite Index=100** ***12 Month Price Score 98.44**

Interim Earnings (Per Share)

Qtr.	Mar	Jun	Sep	Dec
2013	1.09	1.13	1.16	(0.74)
2014	0.96	1.24	1.05	(2.56)
2015	0.81	1.39	1.41	(0.43)
2016	0.93	...	...	...

Interim Dividends (Per Share)

Amt	Decl	Ex	Rec	Pay
0.23Q	07/23/2015	09/30/2015	10/02/2015	10/16/2015
0.23Q	10/30/2015	12/29/2015	12/31/2015	01/15/2016
0.23Q	01/25/2016	03/30/2016	04/01/2016	04/15/2016
0.24Q	04/25/2016	06/29/2016	07/01/2016	07/15/2016

Indicated Div: $0.96

Valuation Analysis | **Institutional Holding**

Forecast EPS	$4.59	No of Institutions
	(05/20/2016)	341
Market Cap	$2.6 Billion	Shares
Book Value	$2.0 Billion	47,063,504
Price/Book	1.28	% Held
Price/Sales	0.75	94.42

Business Summary: Electrical Equipment (MIC: 7.3.1 SIC: 3621 NAIC: 335312)

Regal Beloit is a manufacturer of electric motors, electrical motion controls, power generation and power transmission products. Co.'s segments are: Commercial and Industrial Systems, which designs, manufactures and sells fractional AC and DC motors and controls for commercial and industrial applications, among others; Climate Solutions, which designs, manufactures and sells fractional motors, electronic variable speed controls and blowers, among others; and Power Transmission Solutions, which manufactures, sells and services belt and chain drives, helical and worm gearing, mounted and unmounted bearings, couplings, modular plastic belts, conveying chains and components, among others.

Recent Developments: For the quarter ended Apr 2 2016, net income increased 12.7% to US$42.7 million from US$37.9 million in the year-earlier quarter. Revenues were US$818.2 million, down 10.3% from US$911.7 million the year before. Operating income was US$69.3 million versus US$63.6 million in the prior-year quarter, an increase of 9.0%. Direct operating expenses declined 13.0% to US$600.8 million from US$690.8 million in the comparable period the year before. Indirect operating expenses decreased 5.8% to US$148.1 million from US$157.3 million in the equivalent prior-year period.

Prospects: Our evaluation of Regal Beloit Corp. as of June 19, 2016 is the result of our systematic analysis on three basic characteristics: earnings strength, relative valuation, and recent stock price movement. The company has generated a negative trend in earnings per share over the past 5 quarters and while recent estimates for the company have remained steady, RBC has posted results that fell short of analysts expectations. Based on operating earnings yield, the company is undervalued when compared to all of the companies in our coverage universe. Share price changes over the past year indicates that RBC will perform poorly over the near term.

Financial Data

(US$ in Thousands)	3 Mos	01/02/2016	01/03/2015	12/28/2013	12/29/2012	12/31/2011	01/01/2011	01/02/2010
Earnings Per Share	3.30	3.18	0.69	2.64	4.64	3.79	3.84	2.63
Cash Flow Per Share	9.44	8.55	6.52	6.80	8.44	6.70	4.60	8.98
Tang Book Value Per Share	N.M.	N.M.	16.29	16.19	11.34	2.45	10.65	10.36
Dividends Per Share	0.920	0.910	0.860	0.790	0.750	0.710	0.670	0.640
Dividend Payout %	27.88	28.62	124.64	29.92	16.16	18.73	17.45	24.33
Income Statement								
Total Revenue	818,200	3,509,700	3,257,100	3,095,700	3,166,900	2,808,332	2,237,978	1,826,277
EBITDA	109,400	348,300	213,500	292,400	394,800	320,740	290,653	209,250
Depn & Amortn	40,100	95,500	92,000	84,400	82,000	65,027	52,918	49,730
Income Before Taxes	55,400	196,900	90,300	170,500	269,900	226,337	220,729	137,955
Income Taxes	12,700	48,400	54,200	44,500	69,600	68,317	66,045	39,276
Net Income	41,600	143,300	31,000	120,000	195,600	152,290	149,379	95,048
Average Shares	45,000	45,100	45,300	45,400	42,100	40,144	38,921	36,131
Balance Sheet								
Current Assets	1,649,500	1,635,200	1,652,000	1,725,900	1,539,900	1,291,121	1,088,051	979,376
Total Assets	4,600,200	4,591,700	3,407,600	3,643,500	3,569,100	3,266,515	2,449,136	2,112,237
Current Liabilities	581,900	612,800	561,300	700,900	533,900	524,496	399,342	309,066
Long-Term Obligations	1,699,300	1,715,600	625,400	609,000	754,700	909,159	428,256	468,045
Total Liabilities	2,601,300	2,654,400	1,473,200	1,587,300	1,615,700	1,730,584	1,087,176	944,413
Stockholders' Equity	1,998,900	1,937,300	1,934,400	2,056,200	1,953,400	1,535,931	1,361,960	1,167,824
Shares Outstanding	44,700	44,700	44,700	45,100	44,900	41,579	38,615	37,399
Statistical Record								
Return on Assets %	3.10	3.59	0.87	3.34	5.74	5.34	6.57	4.52
Return on Equity %	7.53	7.42	1.53	6.00	11.24	10.54	11.84	9.38
EBITDA Margin %	13.37	9.92	6.55	9.45	12.47	11.42	12.99	11.46
Net Margin %	5.08	4.08	0.95	3.88	6.18	5.42	6.67	5.20
Asset Turnover	0.71	0.88	0.91	0.86	0.93	0.99	0.98	0.87
Current Ratio	2.83	2.67	2.94	2.46	2.88	2.46	2.72	3.17
Debt to Equity	0.85	0.89	0.32	0.30	0.39	0.59	0.31	0.40
Price Range	80.95-49.38	80.95-55.46	80.02-63.13	84.67-62.35	75.00-52.05	76.04-42.97	69.54-47.40	53.76-25.81
P/E Ratio	24.53-14.96	25.46-17.44	115.97-91.49	32.07-23.62	16.16-11.22	20.06-11.34	18.11-12.34	20.44-9.81
Average Yield %	1.41	1.30	1.18	1.11	1.15	1.14	1.14	1.54

Address: 200 State Street, Beloit, WI 53511
Telephone: 608-364-8800

Web Site: www.regal-beloit.com
Officers: Henry W. Knueppel - Executive Chairman
Mark J. Gliebe - Chief Executive Officer

Auditors: Deloitte & Touche LLP
Investor Contact: 608-364-8800
Transfer Agents: ComputerShare Investor Services, Providence, RI

REGAL ENTERTAINMENT GROUP

Exchange	Symbol	Price	52Wk Range	Yield	P/E
NYS	RGC	$21.03 (5/31/2016)	21.74-16.68	4.18	19.29

*7 Year Price Score 100.69 *NYSE Composite Index=100 *12 Month Price Score 106.15

Interim Earnings (Per Share)

Qtr.	Mar	Jun	Sep	Dec
2013	0.14	0.23	0.48	0.15
2014	(0.01)	0.22	0.17	0.30
2015	0.15	0.34	0.14	0.35
2016	0.26	...	...	...

Interim Dividends (Per Share)

Amt	Decl	Ex	Rec	Pay
0.22Q	07/30/2015	09/02/2015	09/04/2015	09/15/2015
0.22Q	10/27/2015	12/02/2015	12/04/2015	12/15/2015
0.22Q	02/09/2016	03/02/2016	03/04/2016	03/15/2016
0.22Q	04/28/2016	06/02/2016	06/06/2016	06/16/2016

Indicated Div: $0.88

Valuation Analysis		Institutional Holding	
Forecast EPS	$1.08	No of Institutions	
	(05/20/2016)	345	
Market Cap	$3.3 Billion	Shares	
Book Value	N/A	96,671,304	
Price/Book	N/A	% Held	
Price/Sales	1.02	52.18	

Business Summary: Entertainment (MIC: 2.3.2 SIC: 7832 NAIC: 512131)

Regal Entertainment Group is a holding company. Through its subsidiaries, Co. operates theatre circuits, consisting of 7,367 screens in 574 theatres in 42 states along with Guam, Saipan, American Samoa and the District of Columbia as of Jan 1 2015. Co. develops, acquires and operates multi-screen theatres mainly in mid-sized metropolitan markets and suburban growth areas of metropolitan markets throughout the U.S. Some of Co.'s theatres provide amenities such as wall-to-wall and floor-to-ceiling screens, and Sony Digital Cinemaâ,¢ 4K projection systems. Co. operates its theatre circuit using its Regal Cinemas, United Artists, Edwards, Great Escape Theatres and Hollywood Theaters brands.

Recent Developments: For the quarter ended Mar 31 2016, net income increased 77.0% to US$40.7 million from US$23.0 million in the year-earlier quarter. Revenues were US$787.1 million, up 13.9% from US$691.3 million the year before. Operating income was US$80.6 million versus US$50.4 million in the prior-year quarter, an increase of 59.9%. Direct operating expenses rose 17.7% to US$306.3 million from US$260.3 million in the comparable period the year before. Indirect operating expenses increased 5.1% to US$400.2 million from US$380.6 million in the equivalent prior-year period.

Prospects: Our evaluation of Regal Entertainment Group as of June 19, 2016 is the result of our systematic analysis on three basic characteristics: earnings strength, relative valuation, and recent stock price movement. The company has managed to produce a neutral trend in earnings per share over the past 5 quarters. However, while recent estimates for the company have been lowered by analysts, RGC has posted better than expected results. Based on operating earnings yield, the company is undervalued when compared to all of the companies in our coverage universe. Share price changes over the past year indicates that RGC will perform well over the near term.

Financial Data

(US$ in Thousands)	3 Mos	12/31/2015	01/01/2015	12/26/2013	12/27/2012	12/29/2011	12/30/2010	12/31/2009
Earnings Per Share	1.09	0.98	0.68	1.01	0.93	0.26	0.50	0.62
Cash Flow Per Share	3.29	2.80	2.21	2.25	2.25	2.31	1.70	2.69
Dividends Per Share	0.880	0.880	1.880	0.840	1.840	0.840	2.120	0.720
Dividend Payout %	80.73	89.80	276.47	83.17	197.85	323.08	424.00	116.13
Income Statement								
Total Revenue	787,100	3,127,300	2,990,100	3,038,100	2,824,200	2,681,700	2,807,900	2,893,900
EBITDA	104,200	573,700	485,000	572,900	522,300	371,300	459,500	485,000
Depn & Amortn	1,300	221,800	212,000	204,500	186,200	201,700	226,200	215,400
Income Before Taxes	70,400	222,300	146,500	227,100	201,100	19,900	85,200	118,600
Income Taxes	29,700	100,100	73,400	107,100	91,200	17,700	48,700	61,900
Net Income	40,700	153,400	105,600	157,700	144,800	40,300	77,600	95,500
Average Shares	156,773	156,511	156,310	155,723	154,990	154,556	154,517	154,092
Balance Sheet								
Current Assets	425,700	438,200	341,400	465,100	257,800	403,500	346,500	428,900
Total Assets	2,591,300	2,632,300	2,539,500	2,704,700	2,209,500	2,341,300	2,492,600	2,637,700
Current Liabilities	509,100	551,300	477,000	506,400	387,500	400,700	469,000	396,500
Long-Term Obligations	2,288,600	2,315,000	2,333,600	2,280,900	1,973,200	1,995,700	1,977,200	1,980,000
Total Liabilities	3,465,000	3,510,100	3,434,300	3,418,100	2,906,300	2,912,200	2,982,900	2,883,800
Stockholders' Equity	(873,700)	(877,800)	(894,800)	(713,400)	(696,800)	(570,900)	(490,300)	(246,100)
Shares Outstanding	156,794	156,454	156,173	155,829	155,452	154,573	154,303	154,001
Statistical Record								
Return on Assets %	6.74	5.95	3.96	6.44	6.38	1.67	3.03	3.66
EBITDA Margin %	13.24	18.34	16.22	18.86	18.49	13.85	16.36	16.76
Net Margin %	5.17	4.91	3.53	5.19	5.13	1.50	2.76	3.30
Asset Turnover	1.27	1.21	1.12	1.24	1.24	1.11	1.10	1.11
Current Ratio	0.84	0.79	0.72	0.92	0.67	1.01	0.74	1.08
Price Range	23.60-16.68	24.28-17.69	23.09-18.20	19.72-13.73	15.84-11.58	14.94-11.23	18.28-11.74	14.69-9.29
P/E Ratio	21.65-15.30	24.78-18.05	33.96-26.76	19.52-13.59	17.03-12.45	57.46-43.19	36.56-23.48	23.69-14.98
Average Yield %	4.46	4.30	9.36	4.74	13.27	6.42	14.62	5.80

Address: 7132 Regal Lane, Knoxville, TN 37918
Telephone: 865-922-1123

Web Site: www.regmovies.com
Officers: Amy E. Miles - Chairperson, Chief Executive Officer Gregory W, Dunn - President, Chief Operating Officer

Auditors: KPMG LLP
Investor Contact: 866-734-2534
Transfer Agents: Wells Fargo Bank Minnesota, St. Paul, MN

REGENCY CENTERS CORP.

Exchange	Symbol	Price	52Wk Range	Yield	P/E
NYS	REG	$76.60 (5/31/2016)	79.35-57.09	2.61	48.48

*7 Year Price Score 116.90 *NYSE Composite Index=100   *12 Month Price Score 110.41

Interim Earnings (Per Share)

Qtr.	Mar	Jun	Sep	Dec
2013	0.17	0.35	0.38	0.50
2014	0.21	0.28	0.52	0.80
2015	0.27	0.34	0.57	0.18
2016	0.49	...	...	...

Interim Dividends (Per Share)

Amt	Decl	Ex	Rec	Pay
0.485Q	08/03/2015	08/17/2015	08/19/2015	09/02/2015
0.485Q	10/28/2015	11/16/2015	11/18/2015	12/02/2015
0.50Q	02/08/2016	02/18/2016	02/22/2016	03/03/2016
0.50Q	04/28/2016	05/16/2016	05/18/2016	06/01/2016

Indicated Div: $2.00

Valuation Analysis

		Institutional Holding	
Forecast EPS	$1.35	No of Institutions	
	(05/20/2016)	378	
Market Cap	$7.4 Billion	Shares	
Book Value	$2.0 Billion	126,223,136	
Price/Book	3.64	% Held	
Price/Sales	12.86	103.63	

Business Summary: REITs (MIC: 5.3.1 SIC: 6798 NAIC: 525930)

Regency Centers is a real estate investment trust and the general partner of the Regency Centers, L.P. Operating Partnership). Co. engages in the ownership, management, leasing, acquisition, and development of retail shopping centers through the Operating Partnership. As of Dec 31 2015, Co. directly owned 200 retail shopping centers and held partial interests in an additional 118 retail shopping centers, the majority of which are grocery-anchored community and neighborhood centers. Co.'s centers are located in the top markets of 27 states and the District of Columbia.

Recent Developments: For the quarter ended Mar 31 2016, income from continuing operations increased 34.8% to US$40.7 million from US$30.2 million in the year-earlier quarter. Net income increased 72.9% to US$53.6 million from US$31.0 million in the year-earlier quarter. Revenues were US$149.6 million, up 6.6% from US$140.4 million the year before. Revenues from property income rose 6.1% to US$109.4 million from US$103.1 million in the corresponding quarter a year earlier.

Prospects: Our evaluation of Regency Centers Corp. as of June 19, 2016 is the result of our systematic analysis on three basic characteristics: earnings strength, relative valuation, and recent stock price movement. The company has enjoyed a very positive trend in earnings per share over the past 5 quarters. Because the company lacks sufficient analyst estimate data, we place greater weight on the historical EPS trend as the measure of earnings strength. Based on operating earnings yield, the company is overvalued when compared to all of the companies in our coverage universe. Share price changes over the past year indicates that REG will perform very well over the near term.

Financial Data

(US$ in Thousands)	3 Mos	12/31/2015	12/31/2014	12/31/2013	12/31/2012	12/31/2011	12/31/2010	12/31/2009
Earnings Per Share	1.58	1.36	1.80	1.40	(0.08)	0.35	(0.10)	(0.74)
Cash Flow Per Share	2.97	2.92	3.01	2.74	2.86	2.48	1.73	2.52
Tang Book Value Per Share	16.55	16.77	16.32	16.02	15.14	16.81	17.20	19.50
Dividends Per Share	1.955	1.940	1.880	1.850	1.850	1.850	1.850	2.112
Dividend Payout %	123.73	142.65	104.44	132.14	...	528.57	...	...
Income Statement								
Total Revenue	149,628	569,763	537,898	489,007	496,920	500,417	486,806	489,232
EBITDA	53,933	351,959	366,206	305,850	241,606	307,803	278,043	218,907
Depn & Amortn	2,002	154,908	155,211	144,305	139,555	145,152	131,305	121,934
Income Before Taxes	27,789	94,429	101,504	52,579	(10,078)	39,006	21,451	(12,266)
Income Taxes	...	...	(996)	...	13,224	...	...	...
Net Income	53,143	150,056	187,390	149,804	25,867	51,370	12,014	(36,704)
Average Shares	97,891	94,856	92,404	91,409	89,669	88,249	82,948	76,896
Balance Sheet								
Current Assets	132,286	175,880	248,822	205,776	152,592	160,814	140,232	217,393
Total Assets	4,147,373	4,191,074	4,197,170	3,913,516	3,853,458	3,987,071	3,973,648	3,973,806
Current Liabilities	185,949	193,942	207,188	170,956	145,331	122,278	111,837	109,773
Long-Term Obligations	1,835,300	1,872,478	2,021,357	1,854,697	1,941,891	1,982,440	2,094,469	1,886,380
Total Liabilities	2,100,702	2,136,965	2,290,578	2,070,162	2,122,693	2,178,716	2,272,213	2,098,639
Stockholders' Equity	2,046,671	2,054,109	1,906,592	1,843,354	1,730,765	1,808,355	1,701,435	1,875,167
Shares Outstanding	97,227	96,794	93,682	91,960	90,059	89,583	81,886	81,539
Statistical Record								
Return on Assets %	4.18	3.58	4.62	3.86	0.66	1.29	0.30	N.M.
Return on Equity %	8.82	7.58	9.99	8.38	1.46	2.93	0.67	N.M.
EBITDA Margin %	36.04	61.77	68.08	62.55	48.62	61.51	57.12	44.75
Net Margin %	35.52	26.34	34.84	30.63	5.21	10.27	2.47	N.M.
Asset Turnover	0.14	0.14	0.13	0.13	0.13	0.13	0.12	0.12
Current Ratio	0.71	0.91	1.20	1.20	1.05	1.32	1.25	1.98
Debt to Equity	0.90	0.91	1.06	1.01	1.12	1.10	1.23	1.01
Price Range	77.12-57.09	69.90-57.09	64.96-45.97	59.20-45.88	50.52-36.69	47.32-33.37	44.80-32.25	46.70-22.02
P/E Ratio	48.81-36.13	51.40-41.98	36.09-25.54	42.29-32.77	...	135.20-95.34	...	...
Average Yield %	2.97	2.99	3.44	3.63	4.04	4.49	4.84	6.27

Address: One Independent Drive, Suite 114, Jacksonville, FL 32202 **Telephone:** 904-598-7000	**Web Site:** www.regencycenters.com **Officers:** Martin E. Stein - Chairman, Chief Executive Officer Lisa Palmer - President, Chief Financial Officer, Executive Vice President, Senior Vice President	**Auditors:** KPMG LLP **Investor Contact:** 904-598-7000 **Transfer Agents:** Broadridge Corporate Issuer Solutions, Inc. Philadelphia, PA

REGIONS FINANCIAL CORP

Exchange	Symbol	Price	52Wk Range	Yield	P/E
NYS	RF	$9.83 (5/31/2016)	10.80-7.08	2.64	12.44

*7 Year Price Score 100.90 *NYSE Composite Index=100 *12 Month Price Score 96.46

TRADING VOLUME (thousand shares)

Interim Earnings (Per Share)

Qtr.	Mar	Jun	Sep	Dec
2013	0.23	0.18	0.20	0.15
2014	0.22	0.21	0.22	0.15
2015	0.16	0.20	0.18	0.21
2016	0.20	...	...	...

Interim Dividends (Per Share)

Amt	Decl	Ex	Rec	Pay
0.06Q	07/16/2015	09/09/2015	09/11/2015	10/01/2015
0.06Q	10/14/2015	12/09/2015	12/11/2015	01/04/2016
0.06Q	02/11/2016	03/09/2016	03/11/2016	04/01/2016
0.065Q	04/21/2016	06/08/2016	06/10/2016	07/01/2016

Indicated Div: $0.26

Valuation Analysis

Forecast EPS	$0.84
	(05/20/2016)
Market Cap	$12.5 Billion
Book Value	$17.2 Billion
Price/Book	0.73
Price/Sales	2.17

Institutional Holding

No of Institutions	832
Shares	1,033,007,360
% Held	70.94

Business Summary: Banking (MIC: 5.1.1 SIC: 6021 NAIC: 522110)

Regions Financial is a financial holding company. Co. provides commercial, retail and mortgage banking services, and other financial services in the fields of asset management, wealth management, securities brokerage, insurance brokerage, trust services, merger and acquisition advisory services, and other financing. Co. has three reportable segments: Corporate Bank, Consumer Bank, and Wealth Management. Co. provides its services in Alabama, Arkansas, Florida, Georgia, Illinois, Indiana, Iowa, Kentucky, Louisiana, Mississippi, Missouri, North Carolina, South Carolina, Tennessee, Texas and Virginia. At Dec 31 2015, Co. had total assets of $126.05 billion and total deposits of $98.43 billion.

Recent Developments: For the quarter ended Mar 31 2016, net income increased 16.7% to US$273.0 million from US$234.0 million in the year-earlier quarter. Net interest income increased 9.1% to US$889.0 million from US$815.0 million in the year-earlier quarter. Provision for loan losses was US$113.0 million versus US$49.0 million in the prior-year quarter, an increase of 130.6%. Non-interest income rose 7.7% to US$506.0 million from US$470.0 million, while non-interest expense declined 1.0% to US$896.0 million.

Prospects: Our evaluation of Regions Financial Corp. as of June 19, 2016 is the result of our systematic analysis on three basic characteristics: earnings strength, relative valuation, and recent stock price movement. The company has enjoyed a very positive trend in earnings per share over the past 5 quarters and while recent estimates for the company have been mixed, RF has posted better than expected results. Based on operating earnings yield, the company is undervalued when compared to all of the companies in our coverage universe. Share price changes over the past year indicates that RF will perform in line with the market over the near term.

Financial Data

(US$ in Thousands)	3 Mos	12/31/2015	12/31/2014	12/31/2013	12/31/2012	12/31/2011	12/31/2010	12/31/2009
Earnings Per Share	0.79	0.75	0.80	0.77	0.71	(0.34)	(0.62)	(1.27)
Cash Flow Per Share	1.61	1.19	1.52	2.72	1.76	3.78	3.44	2.02
Tang Book Value Per Share	8.65	8.20	7.94	7.19	6.84	6.06	5.68	6.68
Dividends Per Share	0.240	0.230	0.180	0.100	0.040	0.040	0.040	0.130
Dividend Payout %	30.38	30.67	22.50	12.99	5.63	...	...	...
Income Statement								
Interest Income	963,000	3,603,000	3,588,000	3,646,000	3,903,000	4,252,000	4,689,000	5,332,000
Interest Expense	74,000	268,000	309,000	384,000	603,000	842,000	1,257,000	1,997,000
Net Interest Income	889,000	3,335,000	3,279,000	3,262,000	3,300,000	3,410,000	3,432,000	3,335,000
Provision for Losses	113,000	241,000	69,000	138,000	213,000	1,530,000	2,863,000	3,541,000
Non-Interest Income	506,000	2,071,000	1,821,000	2,019,000	2,100,000	2,143,000	3,531,000	3,755,000
Non-Interest Expense	896,000	3,635,000	3,432,000	3,556,000	3,526,000	3,862,000	4,985,000	4,751,000
Income Before Taxes	386,000	1,530,000	1,599,000	1,587,000	1,661,000	161,000	(885,000)	(1,202,000)
Income Taxes	113,000	455,000	457,000	452,000	482,000	(28,000)	(346,000)	(171,000)
Net Income	273,000	1,062,000	1,155,000	1,122,000	1,120,000	(215,000)	(539,000)	(1,031,000)
Average Shares	1,291,000	1,334,000	1,345,000	1,410,000	1,387,000	1,258,000	1,227,000	989,000
Balance Sheet								
Net Loans & Leases	80,806,000	80,504,000	76,745,000	74,323,000	73,459,000	76,042,000	81,164,000	89,071,000
Total Assets	125,539,000	126,050,000	119,679,000	117,396,000	121,347,000	127,050,000	132,351,000	142,318,000
Total Deposits	98,154,000	98,430,000	94,200,000	92,453,000	95,474,000	95,627,000	94,614,000	98,680,000
Total Liabilities	108,328,000	109,206,000	102,690,000	101,628,000	105,848,000	110,551,000	115,617,000	124,437,000
Stockholders' Equity	17,211,000	16,844,000	16,989,000	15,768,000	15,499,000	16,499,000	16,734,000	17,881,000
Shares Outstanding	1,274,813	1,297,330	1,353,941	1,377,720	1,413,339	1,258,816	1,256,236	1,192,609
Statistical Record								
Return on Assets %	0.89	0.86	0.97	0.94	0.90	N.M.	N.M.	N.M.
Return on Equity %	6.43	6.28	7.05	7.18	6.98	N.M.	N.M.	N.M.
Net Interest Margin %	92.32	92.56	91.39	89.47	84.55	80.20	73.19	62.55
Efficiency Ratio %	60.99	64.06	63.45	62.77	58.74	60.39	60.64	52.28
Loans to Deposits	0.82	0.82	0.81	0.80	0.77	0.80	0.86	0.90
Price Range	10.80-7.08	10.80-8.70	11.30-9.06	10.42-7.13	7.65-4.34	8.02-3.02	8.95-5.21	8.83-2.50
P/E Ratio	13.67-8.96	14.40-11.60	14.13-11.33	13.53-9.26	10.77-6.11	...	...	...
Average Yield %	2.55	2.36	1.75	1.11	0.62	0.70	0.57	2.64

Address: 1900 Fifth Avenue North, Birmingham, AL 35203	**Web Site:** www.regions.com	**Auditors:** Ernst & Young LLP
Telephone: 205-581-7890	**Officers:** O.B. Grayson Hall - Chairman, President, Chief Executive Officer, Chief Operating Officer, Head C. Matthew Lusco - Senior Executive Vice President, Chief Risk Officer	**Investor Contact:** 205-801-0265 **Transfer Agents:** Computershare Trust Company, N.A., Providence, RI

REINSURANCE GROUP OF AMERICA, INC.

	Exchange	Symbol	Price	52Wk Range	Yield	P/E
	NYS	RGA	$99.14 (5/31/2016)	99.14-78.61	1.49	14.56

*7 Year Price Score 119.23 *NYSE Composite Index=100 ***12 Month Price Score 103.48**

TRADING VOLUME (thousand shares)

Interim Earnings (Per Share)

Qtr.	Mar	Jun	Sep	Dec
2013	2.49	(0.69)	1.93	2.02
2014	1.92	2.84	2.28	2.75
2015	1.81	1.94	1.25	2.45
2016	1.17			

Interim Dividends (Per Share)

Amt	Decl	Ex	Rec	Pay
0.37Q	07/23/2015	08/03/2015	08/05/2015	08/26/2015
0.37Q	10/29/2015	11/06/2015	11/10/2015	12/01/2015
0.37Q	01/28/2016	02/05/2016	02/09/2016	03/01/2016
0.37Q	04/28/2016	05/06/2016	05/10/2016	05/31/2016

Indicated Div: $1.48

Valuation Analysis

		Institutional Holding	
Forecast EPS	$9.00 (05/23/2016)	No of Institutions	30
Market Cap	$6.4 Billion	Shares	784,655
Book Value	$6.7 Billion	% Held	N/A
Price/Book	0.95		
Price/Sales	0.61		

Business Summary: Life & Health (MIC: 5.2.2 SIC: 6311 NAIC: 524130)

Reinsurance Group of America is an insurance holding company. Through its subsidiaries, Co. is engaged in providing traditional reinsurance, which includes individual and group life and health, disability, and critical illness reinsurance. Co. also provides non-traditional reinsurance, which includes longevity reinsurance, asset-intensive products, primarily annuities, and financial reinsurance. Co. has geographic-based and business-based operational segments: U.S. and Latin America; Canada; Europe, Middle East and Africa; Asia Pacific; and Corporate and Other.

Recent Developments: For the quarter ended Mar 31 2016, net income decreased 38.9% to US$76.5 million from US$125.1 million in the year-earlier quarter. Revenues were US$2.51 billion, down 0.3% from US$2.52 billion the year before. Net premiums earned were US$2.16 billion versus US$2.02 billion in the prior-year quarter, an increase of 6.6%. Net investment income fell 2.3% to US$417.3 million from US$426.9 million a year ago.

Prospects: Our evaluation of Reinsurance Group of America Inc. as of June 19, 2016 is the result of our systematic analysis on three basic characteristics: earnings strength, relative valuation, and recent stock price movement. The company has enjoyed a very positive trend in earnings per share over the past 5 quarters. However, while recent estimates for the company have been mixed, RGA has posted results that fell short of analysts expectations. Based on operating earnings yield, the company is undervalued when compared to all of the companies in our coverage universe. Share price changes over the past year indicates that RGA will perform well over the near term.

Financial Data

(US$ in Thousands)	3 Mos	12/31/2015	12/31/2014	12/31/2013	12/31/2012	12/31/2011	12/31/2010	12/31/2009
Earnings Per Share	6.81	7.46	9.78	5.78	8.52	8.09	7.69	5.55
Cash Flow Per Share	33.16	31.38	33.74	24.02	26.70	17.80	25.19	18.74
Tang Book Value Per Share	104.88	94.09	102.13	83.87	93.47	83.65	68.71	52.99
Dividends Per Share	1.440	1.400	1.260	1.080	0.840	0.600	0.480	0.360
Dividend Payout %	21.15	18.77	12.88	18.69	9.86	7.42	6.24	6.49
Income Statement								
Premium Income	2,157,005	8,570,741	8,669,854	8,254,027	7,906,596	7,335,687	6,659,680	5,725,161
Total Revenue	2,512,568	10,418,178	10,904,194	10,318,353	9,840,911	8,829,538	8,261,730	7,066,822
Benefits & Claims	...	7,489,382	7,406,641	7,304,332	6,665,999	6,224,800	5,547,155	4,819,426
Income Before Taxes	107,580	744,795	1,008,533	635,254	919,223	834,380	863,817	592,345
Income Taxes	31,108	242,629	324,486	216,417	287,330	234,760	289,415	185,259
Net Income	76,472	502,166	684,047	418,837	631,893	599,620	574,402	407,086
Average Shares	65,217	67,292	69,962	72,461	74,153	74,108	74,694	73,327
Balance Sheet								
Total Assets	52,186,624	50,383,152	44,679,611	39,674,473	40,360,438	32,104,032	29,081,908	25,249,501
Total Liabilities	45,467,755	44,247,771	37,656,159	33,738,946	33,450,251	25,966,927	24,041,341	21,381,574
Stockholders' Equity	6,718,869	6,135,381	7,023,452	5,935,527	6,910,187	6,137,105	5,040,567	3,867,927
Shares Outstanding	64,065	65,204	68,772	70,768	73,927	73,367	73,363	72,989
Statistical Record								
Return on Assets %	0.94	1.06	1.62	1.05	1.74	1.96	2.11	1.74
Return on Equity %	6.54	7.63	10.56	6.52	9.66	10.73	12.90	12.56
Loss Ratio %	...	87.38	85.43	88.49	84.31	84.86	83.29	84.18
Net Margin %	3.04	4.82	6.27	4.06	6.42	6.79	6.95	5.76
Price Range	98.57-78.61	98.57-82.81	89.22-71.51	77.41-53.52	60.01-48.64	63.79-44.99	55.96-43.53	48.61-21.59
P/E Ratio	14.47-11.54	13.21-11.10	9.12-7.31	13.39-9.26	7.04-5.71	7.89-5.56	7.28-5.66	8.76-3.89
Average Yield %	1.57	1.53	1.58	1.65	1.53	1.06	0.98	0.93

Address: 16600 Swingley Ridge Road, Chesterfield, MO 63017 **Telephone:** 636-736-7000	**Web Site:** www.rgare.com **Officers:** A. Greig Woodring - President, Chief Executive Officer Anna Manning - President, Senior Executive Vice President	**Auditors:** Deloitte & Touche LLP **Investor Contact:** 636-300-8828 **Transfer Agents:** Mellon Investor Services, L.L.C.

RELIANCE STEEL & ALUMINUM CO.

Exchange	Symbol	Price	52Wk Range	Yield	P/E
NYS	RS	$74.35 (5/31/2016)	74.57-51.75	2.15	18.09

*7 Year Price Score 93.25   *NYSE Composite Index=100   *12 Month Price Score 115.66

Interim Earnings (Per Share)

Qtr.	Mar	Jun	Sep	Dec
2013	1.09	1.06	1.22	0.79
2014	1.11	1.22	1.21	1.18
2015	1.30	1.20	0.69	0.95
2016	1.27	...	...	...

Interim Dividends (Per Share)

Amt	Decl	Ex	Rec	Pay
0.40Q	07/23/2015	08/12/2015	08/14/2015	09/11/2015
0.40Q	10/20/2015	11/18/2015	11/20/2015	12/18/2015
0.40Q	02/18/2016	03/09/2016	03/11/2016	03/31/2016
0.40Q	04/19/2016	05/25/2016	05/27/2016	06/17/2016

Indicated Div: $1.60

Valuation Analysis   Institutional Holding

Forecast EPS	$4.64	No of Institutions
	(05/20/2016)	439
Market Cap	$5.4 Billion	Shares
Book Value	$4.0 Billion	63,041,880
Price/Book	1.34	% Held
Price/Sales	0.60	82.00

Business Summary: Non-Precious Metals (MIC: 8.2.2 SIC: 5051 NAIC: 423510)

Reliance Steel & Aluminum is a metals service center company. Through this network, Co. provides metals processing services and distribute a line of metal products, including alloy, aluminum, brass, copper, carbon steel, stainless steel, titanium and specialty steel products.

Recent Developments: For the quarter ended Mar 31 2016, net income decreased 9.1% to US$93.5 million from US$102.9 million in the year-earlier quarter. Revenues were US$2.16 billion, down 17.3% from US$2.61 billion the year before. Operating income was US$129.8 million versus US$169.3 million in the prior-year quarter, a decrease of 23.3%. Direct operating expenses declined 21.5% to US$1.53 billion from US$1.94 billion in the comparable period the year before. Indirect operating expenses increased 1.1% to US$506.9 million from US$501.4 million in the equivalent prior-year period.

Prospects: Our evaluation of Reliance Steel & Aluminum Co. as of June 19, 2016 is the result of our systematic analysis on three basic characteristics: earnings strength, relative valuation, and recent stock price movement. The company has produced a positive trend in earnings per share over the past 5 quarters and while recent estimates for the company have been raised by analysts, RS has posted better than expected results. Based on operating earnings yield, the company is undervalued when compared to all of the companies in our coverage universe. Share price changes over the past year indicates that RS will perform well over the near term.

Financial Data
(US$ in Thousands)

	3 Mos	12/31/2015	12/31/2014	12/31/2013	12/31/2012	12/31/2011	12/31/2010	12/31/2009
Earnings Per Share	4.11	4.16	4.73	4.14	5.33	4.58	2.61	2.01
Cash Flow Per Share	14.03	13.83	4.58	8.24	7.98	3.14	2.88	12.84
Tang Book Value Per Share	13.60	14.83	14.49	12.51	17.19	13.38	12.84	10.83
Dividends Per Share	1.600	1.600	1.400	1.260	0.800	0.480	0.400	0.400
Dividend Payout %	38.93	38.46	29.60	30.43	15.01	10.48	15.33	19.90
Income Statement								
Total Revenue	2,162,700	9,350,500	10,451,600	9,223,800	8,442,300	8,134,700	6,312,795	5,318,132
EBITDA	187,000	817,900	890,900	792,700	859,900	741,700	508,660	376,107
Depn & Amortn	56,100	218,500	213,800	192,400	151,500	133,100	120,603	118,884
Income Before Taxes	109,200	458,700	544,100	476,000	607,200	509,400	295,704	194,098
Income Taxes	15,700	142,500	170,000	153,600	201,100	162,400	98,579	46,317
Net Income	92,200	311,500	371,500	321,600	403,500	343,800	194,353	148,158
Average Shares	72,708	74,902	78,615	77,646	75,694	75,041	74,472	73,701
Balance Sheet								
Current Assets	2,739,900	2,554,200	3,121,100	2,738,900	2,277,400	2,274,700	1,700,897	1,390,904
Total Assets	7,519,500	7,121,600	7,836,600	7,341,000	5,857,700	5,605,900	4,668,893	4,306,777
Current Liabilities	1,071,400	989,700	662,800	573,400	578,200	576,400	508,595	417,569
Long-Term Obligations	1,640,300	1,427,500	2,222,300	2,072,500	1,123,800	1,319,000	855,085	852,557
Total Liabilities	3,507,500	3,207,500	3,737,600	3,466,400	2,299,300	2,462,000	1,845,161	1,700,345
Stockholders' Equity	4,012,000	3,914,100	4,099,000	3,874,600	3,558,400	3,143,900	2,823,732	2,606,432
Shares Outstanding	72,222	71,739	77,337	77,492	76,042	75,007	74,639	73,750
Statistical Record								
Return on Assets %	3.93	4.16	4.90	4.87	7.02	6.69	4.33	3.12
Return on Equity %	7.57	7.77	9.32	8.65	12.01	11.52	7.16	5.88
EBITDA Margin %	8.65	8.75	8.52	8.59	10.19	9.12	8.06	7.07
Net Margin %	4.26	3.33	3.55	3.49	4.78	4.23	3.08	2.79
Asset Turnover	1.16	1.25	1.38	1.40	1.47	1.58	1.41	1.12
Current Ratio	2.56	2.58	4.71	4.78	3.94	3.95	3.34	3.33
Debt to Equity	0.41	0.36	0.54	0.53	0.32	0.42	0.30	0.33
Price Range	70.26-51.75	66.33-52.37	76.12-57.14	75.84-62.10	62.10-44.98	60.05-32.04	54.96-35.35	45.42-18.72
P/E Ratio	17.09-12.59	15.94-12.59	16.09-12.08	18.32-15.00	11.65-8.44	13.11-7.00	21.06-13.54	22.60-9.31
Average Yield %	2.66	2.71	2.02	1.82	1.50	1.00	0.90	1.15

Address: 350 South Grand Avenue, Suite 5100, Los Angeles, CA 90071	**Web Site:** www.rsac.com	**Auditors:** KPMG LLP
Telephone: 213-687 7700	**Officers:** David H. Hannah - Chairman, Chief Executive Officer Gregg J. Mollins - President, Chief Executive Officer, Chief Operating Officer	**Investor Contact:** 213-576-2428
		Transfer Agents: American Stock Transfer & Trust Company, Brooklyn, NY

RENAISSANCERE HOLDINGS LTD.

Exchange	Symbol	Price	52Wk Range	Yield	P/E
NYS	RNR	$115.51 (5/31/2016)	120.53-99.35	1.07	13.93

*7 Year Price Score 114.69 *NYSE Composite Index=100 *12 Month Price Score 103.05

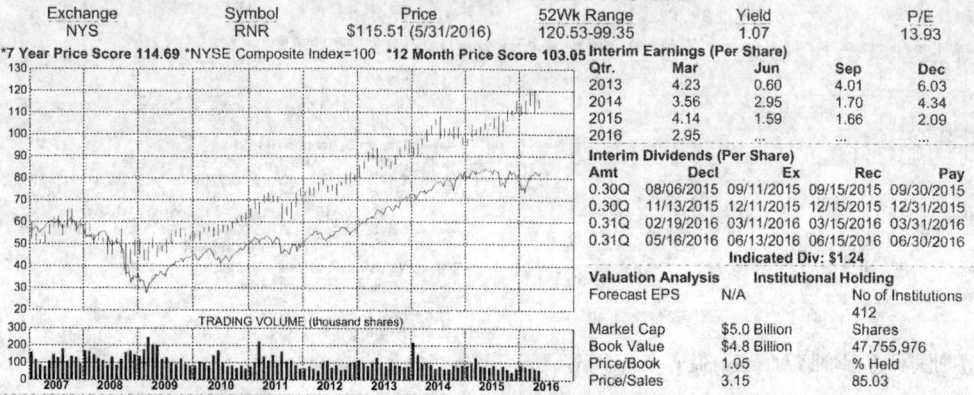

Interim Earnings (Per Share)

Qtr.	Mar	Jun	Sep	Dec
2013	4.23	0.60	4.01	6.03
2014	3.56	2.95	1.70	4.34
2015	4.14	1.59	1.66	2.09
2016	2.95	...		

Interim Dividends (Per Share)

Amt	Decl	Ex	Rec	Pay
0.30Q	08/06/2015	09/11/2015	09/15/2015	09/30/2015
0.30Q	11/13/2015	12/11/2015	12/15/2015	12/31/2015
0.31Q	02/19/2016	03/11/2016	03/15/2016	03/31/2016
0.31Q	05/16/2016	06/13/2016	06/15/2016	06/30/2016

Indicated Div: $1.24

Valuation Analysis

		Institutional Holding	
Forecast EPS	N/A	No of Institutions	412
Market Cap	$5.0 Billion	Shares	
Book Value	$4.8 Billion		47,755,976
Price/Book	1.05	% Held	
Price/Sales	3.15		85.03

Business Summary: General Insurance (MIC: 5.2.1 SIC: 6331 NAIC: 524126)

RenaissanceRe Holdings is a holding company. Co. is a global provider of reinsurance and insurance coverages and related services. Co.'s business consists of three reportable segments: Catastrophe Reinsurance, which includes catastrophe reinsurance and certain property catastrophe joint ventures managed by Co.'s ventures unit; Specialty Reinsurance, which includes specialty reinsurance and certain specialty joint ventures managed by Co.'s ventures unit; and Lloyd's, which includes reinsurance and insurance business written through Co.'s Lloyd's syndicate, RenaissanceRe Syndicate 1458. In addition, Co.'s Other category includes the remnants of its Bermuda-based insurance operations.

Recent Developments: For the quarter ended Mar 31 2016, net income decreased 16.4% to US$178.2 million from US$213.1 million in the year-earlier quarter. Revenues were US$448.1 million, up 17.3% from US$381.9 million the year before. Net premiums earned were US$353.6 million versus US$296.8 million in the prior-year quarter, an increase of 19.2%. Net investment income fell 27.3% to US$28.9 million from US$39.7 million a year ago.

Prospects: Our evaluation of RenaissanceRe Holdings Ltd. as of July 19, 2015 is the result of our systematic analysis on three basic characteristics: earnings strength, relative valuation, and recent stock price movement. The company has enjoyed a very positive trend in earnings per share over the past 5 quarters. However, while recent estimates for the company have been mixed, RNR has posted better than expected results. Based on operating earnings yield, the company is undervalued when compared to all of the companies in our coverage universe. Share price changes over the past year indicates that RNR will perform poorly over the near term.

Financial Data

(US$ in Thousands)	3 Mos	12/31/2015	12/31/2014	12/31/2013	12/31/2012	12/31/2011	12/31/2010	12/31/2009
Earnings Per Share	8.29	9.28	12.60	14.87	11.23	(1.84)	12.31	13.40
Cash Flow Per Share	12.30	9.61	16.76	18.36	14.63	3.27	8.97	9.69
Tang Book Value Per Share	95.11	93.06	89.95	80.10	67.95	59.10	62.31	50.43
Dividends Per Share	1.210	1.200	1.160	1.120	1.080	1.040	1.000	0.960
Dividend Payout %	14.60	12.93	9.21	7.53	9.62	...	8.12	7.16
Income Statement								
Premium Income	353,606	1,400,551	1,062,416	1,114,626	1,069,355	951,049	864,921	1,273,816
Total Revenue	448,120	1,515,102	1,260,077	1,380,482	1,405,934	1,095,036	1,224,671	1,667,852
Income Before Taxes	180,925	496,376	686,864	841,038	748,091	(74,817)	792,358	1,061,753
Income Taxes	2,744	(45,866)	608	1,692	1,429	(315)	(6,124)	9,094
Net Income	133,590	431,192	532,718	690,624	600,909	(57,235)	744,731	881,158
Average Shares	42,912	43,526	39,968	44,128	49,603	50,747	55,641	61,210
Balance Sheet								
Total Assets	12,153,913	11,560,871	8,203,550	8,179,131	7,928,628	7,744,912	8,138,278	7,801,041
Total Liabilities	7,393,320	6,828,687	4,337,835	4,274,747	4,425,563	4,139,719	4,201,953	3,960,255
Stockholders' Equity	4,760,593	4,732,184	3,865,715	3,904,384	3,503,065	3,605,193	3,936,325	3,840,786
Shares Outstanding	43,095	43,701	38,441	43,646	45,542	51,542	54,109	61,744
Statistical Record								
Return on Assets %	3.34	4.36	6.50	8.58	7.65	N.M.	9.34	11.16
Return on Equity %	8.20	10.03	13.71	18.65	16.86	N.M.	19.15	25.64
Net Margin %	29.81	28.46	42.28	50.03	42.74	(5.23)	60.81	52.83
Price Range	119.99-99.35	115.47-94.50	108.42-89.80	97.34-80.20	82.76-71.69	75.05-60.13	64.23-51.41	56.80-41.99
P/E Ratio	14.47-11.98	12.44-10.18	8.60-7.13	6.55-5.39	7.37-6.38	...	5.22-4.18	4.24-3.13
Average Yield %	1.12	1.15	1.11	1.16	1.26	1.42	1.53	1.74	1.92

Address: Renaissance House, 12 Crow Lane, Pembroke, HM 19
Telephone: 441-295-4513

Web Site: www.renre.com
Officers: Kevin J. O'Donnell - President, Chief Executive Officer, Executive Vice President, Global Chief Underwriting Officer Jeffrey D. Kelly - Executive Vice President, Chief Financial Officer, Chief Operating Officer

Auditors: Ernst & Young Ltd.
Investor Contact: 441-295-4513
Transfer Agents: Computershare Shareowner Services LLC, Jersey City, NJ

REPUBLIC SERVICES INC

Exchange	Symbol	Price	52Wk Range	Yield	P/E	Div Achiever
NYS	RSG	$48.28 (5/31/2016)	48.84-39.04	2.49	23.10	12 Years

*7 Year Price Score 112.26 *NYSE Composite Index=100 *12 Month Price Score 107.24

Interim Earnings (Per Share)

Qtr.	Mar	Jun	Sep	Dec
2013	0.34	0.15	0.47	0.65
2014	0.37	0.50	0.52	0.14
2015	0.49	0.54	0.61	0.49
2016	0.45	...	...	...

Interim Dividends (Per Share)

Amt	Decl	Ex	Rec	Pay
0.30Q	07/23/2015	09/29/2015	10/01/2015	10/15/2015
0.30Q	10/29/2015	12/30/2015	01/04/2016	01/15/2016
0.30Q	02/11/2016	03/30/2016	04/01/2016	04/15/2016
0.30Q	04/28/2016	06/29/2016	07/01/2016	07/15/2016

Indicated Div: $1.20

Valuation Analysis

		Institutional Holding	
Forecast EPS	$2.15 (05/17/2016)	No of Institutions	731
Market Cap	$16.6 Billion	Shares	295,228,864
Book Value	$7.8 Billion	% Held	61.04
Price/Book	2.14		
Price/Sales	1.81		

Business Summary: Sanitation Services (MIC: 7.5.3 SIC: 4953 NAIC: 562219)

Republic Services is a provider of non-hazardous solid waste collection, transfer, disposal, recycling, and energy services. As of Dec 31 2015, Co. operated in 41 states and Puerto Rico through 340 collection operations, 201 transfer stations, 193 active landfills, 67 recycling centers, eight treatment, recovery and disposal facilities, and 12 salt water disposal wells. As of the same date, Co. also operated 69 landfill gas and renewable energy projects and had post-closure responsibility for 126 closed landfills. Co. provides residential, small-container commercial, and large-container industrial solid waste collection services.

Recent Developments: For the quarter ended Mar 31 2016, net income decreased 9.0% to US$156.9 million from US$172.5 million in the year-earlier quarter. Revenues were US$2.25 billion, up 3.7% from US$2.17 billion the year before. Operating income was US$345.5 million versus US$372.8 million in the prior-year quarter, a decrease of 7.3%. Direct operating expenses rose 5.9% to US$1.38 billion from US$1.30 billion in the comparable period the year before. Indirect operating expenses increased 6.0% to US$521.7 million from US$492.3 million in the equivalent prior-year period.

Prospects: Our evaluation of Republic Services Inc. as of June 19, 2016 is the result of our systematic analysis on three basic characteristics: earnings strength, relative valuation, and recent stock price movement. The company has produced a positive trend in earnings per share over the past 5 quarters and while recent estimates for the company have been mixed, RSG has posted better than expected results. Based on operating earnings yield, the company is about fairly valued when compared to all of the companies in our coverage universe. Share price changes over the past year indicates that RSG will perform well over the near term.

Financial Data
(US$ in Thousands)

	3 Mos	12/31/2015	12/31/2014	12/31/2013	12/31/2012	12/31/2011	12/31/2010	12/31/2009
Earnings Per Share	2.09	2.13	1.53	1.62	1.55	1.56	1.32	1.30
Cash Flow Per Share	4.68	4.80	4.29	4.28	4.11	4.70	3.74	3.68
Dividends Per Share	1.180	1.160	1.080	0.990	0.910	0.840	0.780	0.760
Dividend Payout %	56.46	54.46	70.59	61.11	58.71	53.85	59.09	58.46
Income Statement								
Total Revenue	2,248,600	9,115,000	8,788,300	8,417,200	8,118,300	8,192,900	8,106,600	8,199,100
EBITDA	570,100	2,458,700	2,071,900	2,017,200	2,138,300	2,189,800	2,217,400	2,328,600
Depn & Amortn	225,300	898,700	838,500	806,700	926,900	843,600	833,700	869,700
Income Before Taxes	252,600	1,195,900	885,300	851,200	823,900	906,300	877,000	865,000
Income Taxes	95,700	445,500	337,400	262,100	251,800	317,400	369,500	368,500
Net Income	156,700	749,900	547,600	588,900	571,800	589,200	506,500	495,000
Average Shares	346,500	351,400	358,100	363,400	368,020	377,600	385,100	381,000
Balance Sheet								
Current Assets	1,183,300	1,230,300	1,391,000	1,421,900	1,231,300	1,265,700	1,246,100	1,264,900
Total Assets	20,539,200	20,577,200	20,094,000	19,949,200	19,616,900	19,551,500	19,461,900	19,540,300
Current Liabilities	1,810,300	1,834,800	1,826,000	1,717,100	1,695,000	1,897,500	2,676,500	2,548,700
Long-Term Obligations	7,554,900	7,568,700	7,050,800	7,002,400	7,051,100	6,887,000	5,865,100	6,419,600
Total Liabilities	12,776,000	12,803,100	12,348,700	12,045,700	11,913,600	11,870,200	11,615,400	11,975,800
Stockholders' Equity	7,763,200	7,774,100	7,745,300	7,903,500	7,703,300	7,681,300	7,846,500	7,564,500
Shares Outstanding	344,500	345,600	352,700	360,400	361,100	369,900	383,700	380,800
Statistical Record								
Return on Assets %	3.57	3.69	2.74	2.98	2.91	3.02	2.60	2.51
Return on Equity %	9.46	9.66	7.00	7.55	7.41	7.59	6.57	6.67
EBITDA Margin %	25.35	26.97	23.58	23.97	26.34	26.73	27.35	28.40
Net Margin %	6.97	8.23	6.23	7.00	7.04	7.19	6.25	6.04
Asset Turnover	0.45	0.45	0.44	0.43	0.41	0.42	0.42	0.42
Current Ratio	0.65	0.67	0.76	0.83	0.73	0.67	0.47	0.50
Debt to Equity	0.97	0.97	0.91	0.89	0.92	0.90	0.75	0.85
Price Range	48.72-39.04	45.25-39.04	40.89-31.53	35.44-29.33	31.14-25.39	32.94-24.76	32.65-25.62	29.57-15.85
P/E Ratio	23.31-18.68	21.24-18.33	26.73-20.61	21.88-18.10	20.09-16.38	21.12-15.87	24.73-19.41	22.75-12.19
Average Yield %	2.77	2.80	2.95	2.98	3.23	2.86	2.63	3.13

Address: 18500 North Allied Way, Phoenix, AZ 85054 **Telephone:** 480-627-2700	**Web Site:** www.republicservices.com **Officers:** James E. O'Connor - Chairman, Chief Executive Officer Harris W. Hudson - Vice-Chairman	**Auditors:** Ernst & Young LLP **Transfer Agents:** Wachovia Corp., Charlotte, NC

RESMED INC.

Exchange	Symbol	Price	52Wk Range	Yield	P/E
NYS	RMD	$59.06 (5/31/2016)	61.16-49.43	2.03	24.11

*7 Year Price Score 116.09 *NYSE Composite Index=100 ***12 Month Price Score 101.82**

Interim Earnings (Per Share)

Qtr.	Sep	Dec	Mar	Jun
2012-13	0.49	0.53	0.58	0.50
2013-14	0.56	0.60	0.63	0.61
2014-15	0.58	0.64	0.64	0.61
2015-16	0.57	0.64	0.63	

Interim Dividends (Per Share)

Amt	Decl	Ex	Rec	Pay
0.30Q	07/30/2015	08/18/2015	08/20/2015	09/17/2015
0.30Q	10/22/2015	11/17/2015	11/19/2015	12/17/2015
0.30Q	01/21/2016	02/09/2016	02/11/2016	03/17/2016
0.30Q	04/26/2016	05/17/2016	05/19/2016	06/16/2016

Indicated Div: $1.20

Valuation Analysis | **Institutional Holding**

Forecast EPS	$2.67	No of Institutions
	(05/20/2016)	502
Market Cap	$8.3 Billion	Shares
Book Value	$1.7 Billion	90,912,528
Price/Book	4.95	% Held
Price/Sales	4.68	52.19

TRADING VOLUME (thousand shares)

Business Summary: Medical Instruments & Equipment (MIC: 4.3.1 SIC: 3841 NAIC: 339112)

ResMed is a holding company. Through its operating subsidiaries, Co. is engaged in the development, manufacturing, distribution and marketing of medical products for the diagnosis, treatment and management of respiratory disorders, focusing on sleep-disordered breathing (SDB). SDB includes obstructive sleep apnea (OSA), and other respiratory disorders that occur during sleep. Co.'s noninvasive treatment for OSA, nasal Continuous Positive Airway Pressure, deliver pressurized air, typically through a nasal mask, to prevent collapse of the upper airway during sleep. Co.'s portfolio of products includes airflow generators, diagnostic products, mask systems, headgear and other accessories.

Recent Developments:
For the quarter ended Mar 31 2016, net income decreased 2.8% to US$88.5 million from US$91.0 million in the year-earlier quarter. Revenues were US$453.9 million, up 7.4% from US$422.5 million the year before. Operating income was US$104.3 million versus US$105.9 million in the prior-year quarter, a decrease of 1.5%. Direct operating expenses rose 13.4% to US$194.0 million from US$171.1 million in the comparable period the year before. Indirect operating expenses increased 6.9% to US$155.6 million from US$145.6 million in the equivalent prior-year period.

Prospects:
Our evaluation of ResMed Inc. as of June 19, 2016 is the result of our systematic analysis on three basic characteristics: earnings strength, relative valuation, and recent stock price movement. The company has enjoyed a very positive trend in earnings per share over the past 5 years and while recent estimates for the company have remained steady, RMD has posted results that fell short of analysts expectations. Based on operating earnings yield, the company is about fairly valued when compared to all of the companies in our coverage universe. Share price changes over the past year indicates that RMD will perform in line with the market over the near term.

Financial Data

(US$ in Thousands)	9 Mos	6 Mos	3 Mos	06/30/2015	06/30/2014	06/30/2013	06/30/2012	06/30/2011
Earnings Per Share	2.45	2.46	2.46	2.47	2.39	2.10	1.71	1.44
Cash Flow Per Share	3.51	3.29	2.98	2.73	2.77	2.82	2.62	1.86
Tang Book Value Per Share	7.84	7.56	8.28	9.08	10.15	9.06	9.13	9.54
Dividends Per Share	1.180	1.160	1.140	1.120	1.000	0.680	...	...
Dividend Payout %	48.16	47.15	46.34	45.34	41.84	32.38	...	...
Income Statement								
Total Revenue	1,320,066	866,187	411,647	1,678,912	1,554,973	1,514,457	1,368,515	1,243,148
EBITDA	325,400	213,977	98,329	424,154	415,704	362,775	316,839	287,810
Depn & Amortn	11,294	6,736	2,307	8,668	9,733	10,142	13,974	10,146
Income Before Taxes	322,134	213,139	99,444	435,916	431,078	385,119	331,945	303,707
Income Taxes	62,757	42,220	19,041	83,030	85,805	77,986	77,095	76,721
Net Income	259,377	170,919	80,403	352,886	345,273	307,133	254,850	226,986
Average Shares	141,040	141,148	141,946	142,687	144,359	146,410	149,316	157,195
Balance Sheet								
Current Assets	1,400,094	1,350,841	1,532,800	1,444,182	1,556,209	1,448,849	1,361,151	1,292,452
Total Assets	2,444,610	2,239,011	2,254,679	2,184,260	2,360,962	2,210,721	2,137,869	2,068,922
Current Liabilities	286,508	265,570	257,307	267,259	269,558	574,049	252,852	208,840
Long-Term Obligations	435,609	400,591	500,587	300,594	300,770	769	250,783	100,000
Total Liabilities	771,199	714,740	793,866	596,953	602,714	600,205	530,242	338,185
Stockholders' Equity	1,673,411	1,524,271	1,460,813	1,587,307	1,758,248	1,610,516	1,607,627	1,730,737
Shares Outstanding	140,367	139,994	139,539	140,474	140,304	142,013	142,021	151,668
Statistical Record								
Return on Assets %	14.69	15.30	15.34	15.53	15.10	14.13	12.08	12.29
Return on Equity %	21.61	22.45	22.48	21.10	20.50	19.09	15.23	15.04
EBITDA Margin %	24.65	24.70	23.89	25.26	26.73	23.95	23.15	23.15
Net Margin %	19.65	19.73	19.53	21.02	22.20	20.28	18.62	18.26
Asset Turnover	0.75	0.76	0.75	0.74	0.68	0.70	0.65	0.67
Current Ratio	4.89	5.09	5.96	5.40	5.77	2.52	5.38	6.19
Debt to Equity	0.26	0.26	0.34	0.19	0.17	N.M.	0.16	0.06
Price Range	74.82-49.43	74.82-49.43	74.82-46.25	74.82-46.25	57.11-42.03	51.17-30.63	35.01-23.46	35.61-29.62
P/E Ratio	30.54-20.18	30.41-20.09	30.41-18.80	30.29-18.72	23.90-17.59	24.37-14.59	20.47-13.72	24.73-20.57
Average Yield %	2.05	1.95	1.95	1.94	2.06	1.62	...	...

Address: 9001 Spectrum Center Blvd., San Diego, CA 92123
Telephone: 858-836-5000

Web Site: www.resmed.com
Officers: Robert D. Douglas - President, Chief Operating Officer, Region Officer, Office of the Chief Executive Officer Michael Farrell - Chief Executive Officer, Region Officer

Auditors: KPMG LLP
Investor Contact: 858-836-5971
Transfer Agents: Computershare Trust Company N.A., Canton, MA

RESTORATION HARDWARE HOLDINGS, INC.

Exchange	Symbol	Price	52Wk Range	Yield	P/E
NYS	RH	$33.26 (5/31/2016)	105.64-31.01	N/A	20.04

*7 Year Price Score N/A   *NYSE Composite Index=100   *12 Month Price Score 52.58

TRADING VOLUME (thousand shares)

Interim Earnings (Per Share)

Qtr.	Apr	Jul	Oct	Jan
2013-14	0.00	(0.46)	0.23	0.67
2014-15	0.04	0.66	0.47	1.02
2015-16	0.17	0.71	0.49	0.79
2016-17	(0.33)	...	...	...

Interim Dividends (Per Share)

No Dividends Paid

Valuation Analysis   **Institutional Holding**

Forecast EPS	$1.68	No of Institutions
	(05/20/2016)	327
Market Cap	$1.4 Billion	Shares
Book Value	$879.5 Million	40,850,216
Price/Book	1.54	% Held
Price/Sales	0.63	100.26

Business Summary: Retail - Furniture & Home Furnishings (MIC: 2.1.6 SIC: 5712 NAIC: 442110)

Restoration Hardware Holdings is a holding company. Together with its subsidiaries, Co. is a home furnishings retailer that provides merchandise assortments across a range of categories including furniture, lighting, textiles, bathware, decor, outdoor and garden, tableware and children's furnishings. These products are sold through the Co.'s stores, catalogs and websites. As of Jan 31 2015, Co. operated a total of 67 retail stores and 17 outlet stores in 29 states, the District of Columbia and Canada, and had sourcing operations in Shanghai and Hong Kong.

Recent Developments: For the quarter ended Apr 30 2016, net loss amounted to US$13.5 million versus net income of US$7.2 million in the year-earlier quarter. Revenues were US$455.5 million, up 7.8% from US$422.4 million the year before. Operating loss was US$11.5 million versus an income of US$17.0 million in the prior-year quarter. Direct operating expenses rose 17.5% to US$328.0 million from US$279.0 million in the comparable period the year before. Indirect operating expenses increased 9.9% to US$139.0 million from US$126.4 million in the equivalent prior-year period.

Prospects: Our evaluation of Restoration Hardware Holdings, Inc. as of June 19, 2016 is the result of our systematic analysis on three basic characteristics: earnings strength, relative valuation, and recent stock price movement. The company has generated a negative trend in earnings per share over the past 5 quarters. However, while recent estimates for the company have been lowered by analysts, RH has posted results that fell short of analysts expectations. Based on operating earnings yield, the company is undervalued when compared to all of the companies in our coverage universe. Share price changes over the past year indicates that RH will perform very well over the near term.

Financial Data
(US$ in Thousands)	3 Mos	01/30/2016	01/31/2015	02/01/2014	02/02/2013	01/28/2012	01/29/2011
Earnings Per Share	1.66	2.16	2.20	0.45	(1.36)	43,991.00	(70,510.00)
Cash Flow Per Share	1.23	3.54	2.10	2.27	(0.40)	36,683.84	(118,100.00)
Tang Book Value Per Share	17.40	17.58	13.28	9.57	7.35	75,342.00	...
Income Statement							
Total Revenue	455,456	2,109,006	1,867,422	1,550,961	1,193,046	958,084	772,752
EBITDA	(4,418)	229,761	199,426	81,351	(44,736)	53,043	24,584
Depn & Amortn	7,057	44,200	33,700	26,500	24,300	26,200	27,800
Income Before Taxes	(22,003)	149,884	148,175	49,118	(74,812)	21,709	(6,366)
Income Taxes	(8,533)	58,781	57,173	30,923	(62,023)	1,121	685
Net Income	(13,470)	91,103	91,002	18,195	(12,789)	20,588	(7,051)
Average Shares	40,588	42,256	41,378	40,416	9,428	468.00	100.00
Balance Sheet							
Current Assets	1,244,435	1,313,677	912,244	613,815	492,758	322,878	...
Total Assets	2,051,008	2,088,472	1,525,999	1,025,103	789,613	586,810	...
Current Liabilities	406,937	452,555	344,429	317,448	219,424	161,974	...
Long-Term Obligations	762,114	747,330	476,482	159,027	113,285	142,151	...
Total Liabilities	1,171,480	1,202,312	823,083	479,831	338,002	336,347	...
Stockholders' Equity	879,528	886,160	702,916	545,272	451,611	250,463	...
Shares Outstanding	40,605	40,583	39,892	39,084	37,967	1,000.00	...
Statistical Record							
Return on Assets %	3.86	5.05	7.15	2.01	N.M.	...	...
Return on Equity %	8.82	11.50	14.62	3.66	N.M.	...	...
EBITDA Margin %	N.M.	10.89	10.68	5.25	N.M.	5.54	3.18
Net Margin %	N.M.	4.32	4.87	1.17	N.M.	2.15	N.M.
Asset Turnover	1.17	1.17	1.47	1.71	1.71	...	...
Current Ratio	3.06	2.90	2.65	1.93	2.25	1.99	...
Debt to Equity	0.87	0.84	0.68	0.29	0.25	0.57	...
Price Range	105.64-36.65	105.64-60.22	99.07-54.85	77.18-32.75	37.99-31.49	...	...
P/E Ratio	63.64-22.08	48.91-27.88	45.03-24.93	171.51-72.78		...	...

Address: 15 Koch Road, Suite K, Corte Madera, CA 94925 **Telephone:** 415-924-1005	**Web Site:** www.restorationhardware.com **Officers:** Gary G. Friedman - Chairman, Co-Chief Executive Officer, Chief Executive Officer, Co-Chief Executive Officer, Creator and Curator Karen Boone - Co-President, Chief Financial Officer, Chief Administrative Officer	**Auditors:** PricewaterhouseCoopers LLP **Investor Contact:** 415-945-3500 **Transfer Agents:** ComputerShare Investor Services, Providence, RI

RETAIL PROPERTIES OF AMERICA, INC

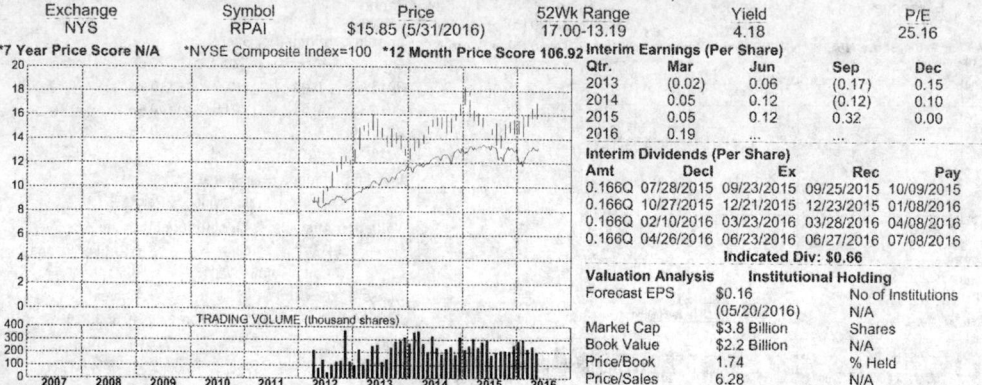

Exchange	Symbol	Price	52Wk Range	Yield	P/E
NYS	RPAI	$15.85 (5/31/2016)	17.00-13.19	4.18	25.16

*7 Year Price Score N/A *NYSE Composite Index=100 *12 Month Price Score 106.92

Interim Earnings (Per Share)

Qtr.	Mar	Jun	Sep	Dec
2013	(0.02)	0.06	(0.17)	0.15
2014	0.05	0.12	(0.12)	0.10
2015	0.05	0.12	0.32	0.00
2016	0.19	...	...	...

Interim Dividends (Per Share)

Amt	Decl	Ex	Rec	Pay
0.166Q	07/28/2015	09/23/2015	09/25/2015	10/09/2015
0.166Q	10/27/2015	12/21/2015	12/23/2015	01/08/2016
0.166Q	02/10/2016	03/23/2016	03/28/2016	04/08/2016
0.166Q	04/26/2016	06/23/2016	06/27/2016	07/08/2016

Indicated Div: $0.66

Valuation Analysis

		Institutional Holding	
Forecast EPS	$0.16 (05/20/2016)	No of Institutions	N/A
Market Cap	$3.8 Billion	Shares	N/A
Book Value	$2.2 Billion	% Held	N/A
Price/Book	1.74		
Price/Sales	6.28		N/A

TRADING VOLUME (thousand shares)

Business Summary: REITs (MIC: 5.3.1 SIC: 6798 NAIC: 525930)

Retail Properties of America is a real estate investment trust. Co. is an owner and operator of shopping centers in the in the U.S. As of Dec 31 2014, Co.'s owned 208 retail operating properties representing 30,523,000 square feet of gross leasable area. Co.'s retail operating portfolio includes power centers, neighborhood and community centers, and lifestyle centers and primarily multi-tenant retail mixed-use properties, as well as single-user retail properties. In addition to its operating portfolio, as of Dec 31 2014, Co. held interests in three retail development properties, one of which is under active development and held in a consolidated joint venture.

Recent Developments: For the quarter ended Mar 31 2016, income from continuing operations increased 202.1% to US$25.7 million from US$8.5 million in the year-earlier quarter. Net income increased 262.7% to US$47.4 million from US$13.1 million in the year-earlier quarter. Revenues were US$148.6 million, down 3.0% from US$153.2 million the year before.

Prospects: Our evaluation of Retail Properties of America as of June 19, 2016 is the result of our systematic analysis on three basic characteristics: earnings strength, relative valuation, and recent stock price movement. The company has suffered a very negative trend in earnings per share over the past 5 quarters and while recent estimates for the company have been mixed, RPAI has posted better than expected results. Based on operating earnings yield, the company is about fairly valued when compared to all of the companies in our coverage universe. Share price changes over the past year indicates that RPAI will perform well over the near term.

Financial Data
(US$ in Thousands)

	3 Mos	12/31/2015	12/31/2014	12/31/2013	12/31/2012	12/31/2011	12/31/2010	12/31/2009
Earnings Per Share	0.63	0.49	0.14	0.02	...	(0.38)	(0.50)	(0.58)
Cash Flow Per Share	1.05	1.12	1.08	1.02	0.76	0.91	0.95	1.30
Tang Book Value Per Share	8.50	8.50	8.72	9.22	9.75	10.13	10.81	...
Dividends Per Share	0.662	0.662	0.662	0.662	0.662	0.630	0.490	0.390
Dividend Payout %	105.16	135.20	473.21	3,312.50	...	...	...	...
Income Statement								
Total Revenue	148,639	603,960	600,614	551,223	567,023	605,683	632,429	648,598
EBITDA	109,870	373,360	357,412	345,909	401,037	379,897	412,413	402,953
Depn & Amortn	57,419	230,590	220,892	240,713	229,800	244,854	259,790	272,396
Income Before Taxes	25,687	3,832	2,685	(41,609)	(7,928)	(96,694)	(103,845)	(96,231)
Net Income	47,426	125,096	43,300	13,626	(447)	(72,609)	(95,843)	(112,335)
Average Shares	236,680	236,382	236,187	234,134	220,464	192,456	193,497	192,124
Balance Sheet								
Current Assets	174,362	134,228	198,305	139,008	223,500	230,931	243,128	...
Total Assets	4,687,810	4,621,251	4,803,860	4,877,576	5,237,427	5,941,894	6,386,836	...
Current Liabilities	90,681	109,097	100,316	93,595	112,183	114,460	111,421	...
Long-Term Obligations	2,248,860	2,166,238	2,334,465	2,299,633	2,592,089	3,481,218	3,757,237	...
Total Liabilities	2,526,392	2,465,914	2,615,979	2,570,236	2,863,168	3,806,870	4,091,934	...
Stockholders' Equity	2,161,418	2,155,337	2,187,881	2,307,340	2,374,259	2,135,024	2,294,902	...
Shares Outstanding	237,347	237,267	236,602	236,302	230,643	193,529	190,938	192,697
Statistical Record								
Return on Assets %	3.29	2.65	0.89	0.27	N.M.	N.M.	...	...
Return on Equity %	7.38	5.76	1.93	0.58	N.M.	N.M.	...	...
EBITDA Margin %	73.92	61.82	59.51	62.75	70.73	62.72	65.21	62.13
Net Margin %	31.91	20.71	7.21	2.47	N.M.	N.M.	N.M.	N.M.
Asset Turnover	0.12	0.13	0.12	0.11	0.10	0.10	...	...
Current Ratio	1.92	1.23	1.98	1.49	1.99	2.02	2.18	...
Debt to Equity	1.04	1.01	1.07	1.00	1.09	1.63	1.64	...
Price Range	16.12-13.19	18.21-13.19	16.87-12.30	16.03-11.94	12.56-8.64	...	...	...
P/E Ratio	25.59-20.94	37.16-26.92	120.50-87.86	801.50-597.00	...	...	...	...
Average Yield %	4.46	4.34	4.48	4.70	6.26	...	...	...

Address: 2021 Spring Road, Suite 200, Oak Brook, IL 60523 **Telephone:** 630-634-4200	**Web Site:** www.rpai.com **Officers:** Gerald M. Gorski - Chairman Steven P. Grimes - President, Chief Executive Officer	**Auditors:** Deloitte & Touche LLP **Transfer Agents:** Registrar & Transfer Company, Cranford, NJ

REYNOLDS AMERICAN INC

Exchange	Symbol	Price	52Wk Range	Yield	P/E	Div Achiever
NYS	RAI	$49.70 (5/31/2016)	51.89-35.53	3.38	10.44	11 Years

*7 Year Price Score 156.89 *NYSE Composite Index=100 *12 Month Price Score 108.11

Interim Earnings (Per Share)

Qtr.	Mar	Jun	Sep	Dec
2013	0.46	0.42	0.42	0.27
2014	0.34	0.46	0.44	0.14
2015	0.36	1.69	0.46	0.12
2016	2.49	...	...	...

Interim Dividends (Per Share)

Amt	Decl	Ex	Rec	Pay
0.36Q	07/28/2015	09/08/2015	09/10/2015	10/01/2015
0.36Q	12/02/2015	12/10/2015	12/14/2015	01/04/2016
0.42Q	02/11/2016	03/08/2016	03/10/2016	04/01/2016
0.42Q	05/05/2016	06/08/2016	06/10/2016	07/01/2016

Indicated Div: $1.68 (Div. Reinv. Plan)

Valuation Analysis

Forecast EPS	$2.35
	(05/20/2016)
Market Cap	$70.9 Billion
Book Value	$21.2 Billion
Price/Book	3.35
Price/Sales	6.15

Institutional Holding

No of Institutions	1033
Shares	707,117,952
% Held	45.41

Business Summary: Tobacco Products (MIC: 1.3.1 SIC: 2111 NAIC: 312221)

Reynolds American is a holding company whose operating subsidiaries include a tobacco company, R. J. Reynolds Tobacco Company; the manufacturer of a cigarette brand, Santa Fe Natural Tobacco Company, Inc.; a smokeless tobacco products manufacturer, American Snuff Company, LLC; R.J. Reynolds Vapor Company, a manufacturer and marketer of digital vapor cigarettes; Niconovum USA, Inc. and Niconovum AB, marketers of nicotine replacement therapy products. Co.'s operating segments are: RJR Tobacco, which includes several cigarettes brands such as CAMEL and PALL MALL; American Snuff, which brands include GRIZZLY and KODIAK; and Santa Fe, which brand includes NATURAL AMERICAN SPIRIT.

Recent Developments: For the quarter ended Mar 31 2016, net income increased 816.5% to US$3.57 billion from US$389.0 million in the year-earlier quarter. Revenues were US$2.92 billion, up 41.8% from US$2.06 billion the year before. Operating income was US$6.14 billion versus US$693.0 million in the prior-year quarter, an increase of 786.3%. Direct operating expenses rose 37.1% to US$1.17 billion from US$850.0 million in the comparable period the year before. Indirect operating income amounted to US$4.39 billion compared with an expense of US$514.0 million in the equivalent prior-year period.

Prospects: Our evaluation of Reynolds American Inc. as of June 19, 2016 is the result of our systematic analysis on three basic characteristics: earnings strength, relative valuation, and recent stock price movement. The company has produced a positive trend in earnings per share over the past 5 quarters. However, while recent estimates for the company have been lowered by analysts, RAI has posted results that fell short of analysts expectations. Based on operating earnings yield, the company is about fairly valued when compared to all of the companies in our coverage universe. Share price changes over the past year indicates that RAI will perform very well over the near term.

Financial Data
(US$ in Thousands)

	3 Mos	12/31/2015	12/31/2014	12/31/2013	12/31/2012	12/31/2011	12/31/2010	12/31/2009
Earnings Per Share	4.76	2.57	1.38	1.57	1.12	1.20	0.95	0.82
Cash Flow Per Share	0.17	0.16	1.52	1.20	1.38	1.22	1.08	1.25
Dividends Per Share	1.475	1.390	1.340	1.240	1.165	1.075	0.920	0.863
Dividend Payout %	30.99	54.09	97.45	78.98	104.02	89.58	96.34	104.55
Income Statement								
Total Revenue	2,917,000	10,675,000	8,471,000	8,236,000	8,304,000	8,541,000	8,551,000	8,419,000
EBITDA	5,920,000	7,052,000	2,640,000	3,012,000	2,311,000	2,534,000	2,563,000	1,910,000
Depn & Amortn	30,000	104,000	95,000	17,000	131,000	138,000	151,000	144,000
Income Before Taxes	5,719,000	6,384,000	2,262,000	2,741,000	1,953,000	2,186,000	2,192,000	1,534,000
Income Taxes	2,154,000	3,131,000	817,000	1,023,000	681,000	780,000	863,000	572,000
Net Income	3,565,000	3,253,000	1,470,000	1,718,000	1,272,000	1,406,000	1,113,000	962,000
Average Shares	1,431,069	1,267,715	1,069,940	1,093,898	1,135,746	1,170,766	1,169,708	1,167,304
Balance Sheet								
Current Assets	7,529,000	6,187,000	3,323,000	3,655,000	4,812,000	4,307,000	4,802,000	5,495,000
Total Assets	54,408,000	53,224,000	15,196,000	15,402,000	16,557,000	16,254,000	17,078,000	18,009,000
Current Liabilities	7,604,000	5,291,000	3,544,000	3,076,000	3,769,000	4,276,000	4,372,000	4,340,000
Long-Term Obligations	13,213,000	16,941,000	4,633,000	5,099,000	5,035,000	3,206,000	3,701,000	4,136,000
Total Liabilities	33,245,000	34,972,000	10,674,000	10,235,000	11,300,000	10,003,000	10,568,000	11,511,000
Stockholders' Equity	21,163,000	18,252,000	4,522,000	5,167,000	5,257,000	6,251,000	6,510,000	6,498,000
Shares Outstanding	1,427,341	1,427,341	1,062,567	1,076,106	1,105,881	1,152,270	1,166,087	1,165,696
Statistical Record								
Return on Assets %	18.30	9.51	9.61	10.75	7.73	8.44	6.34	5.32
Return on Equity %	50.07	28.57	30.34	32.96	22.05	22.04	17.11	15.11
EBITDA Margin %	202.95	66.06	31.17	36.57	27.83	29.67	29.97	22.69
Net Margin %	122.21	30.47	17.35	20.86	15.32	16.46	13.02	11.43
Asset Turnover	0.33	0.31	0.55	0.52	0.50	0.51	0.49	0.47
Current Ratio	0.99	1.17	0.94	1.19	1.28	1.01	1.10	1.27
Debt to Equity	0.62	0.93	1.02	0.99	0.96	0.51	0.57	0.64
Price Range	51.89-34.45	49.49-31.60	33.47-23.48	26.40-20.72	23.34-19.61	20.93-15.90	16.70-12.65	13.48-8.04
P/E Ratio	10.90-7.24	19.26-12.30	24.25-17.01	16.82-13.19	20.84-17.51	17.44-13.25	17.58-13.32	16.45-9.80
Average Yield %	3.39	3.47	4.67	5.19	5.46	5.85	6.49	8.10

Address: 401 North Main Street, Winston-Salem, NC 27101 **Telephone:** 336-741-2000 **Fax:** 336-728-8888	**Web Site:** www.reynoldsamerican.com **Officers:** Susan M. Cameron - President, Chief Executive Officer, President (frmr), Chief Executive Officer (frm) Lisa J. Caldwell - Executive Vice President, Chief Human Resources Officer	**Auditors:** KPMG LLP **Investor Contact:** 336-741-5165 **Transfer Agents:** Computershare, Providence, RI

RITE AID CORP.

Exchange	Symbol	Price	52Wk Range	Yield	P/E
NYS	RAD	$7.70 (5/31/2016)	9.32-6.05	N/A	48.13

*7 Year Price Score 187.11 *NYSE Composite Index=100   *12 Month Price Score 98.76

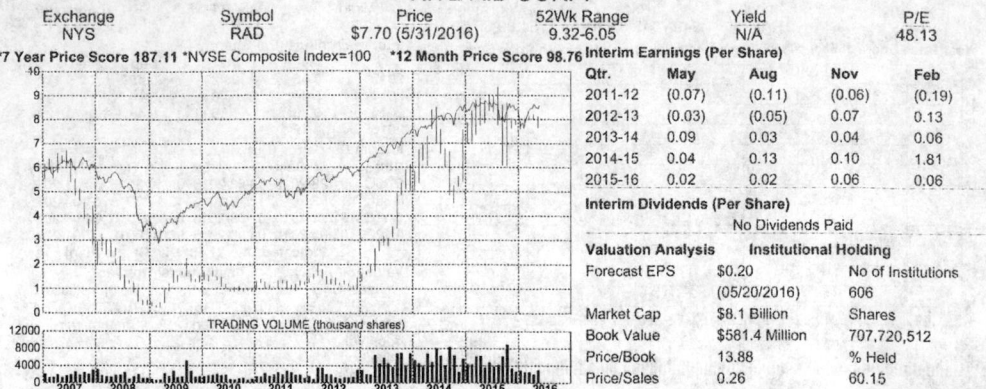

Interim Earnings (Per Share)

Qtr.	May	Aug	Nov	Feb
2011-12	(0.07)	(0.11)	(0.06)	(0.19)
2012-13	(0.03)	(0.05)	0.07	0.13
2013-14	0.09	0.03	0.04	0.06
2014-15	0.04	0.13	0.10	1.81
2015-16	0.02	0.02	0.06	0.06

Interim Dividends (Per Share)

No Dividends Paid

Valuation Analysis		Institutional Holding	
Forecast EPS	$0.20	No of Institutions	
	(05/20/2016)	606	
Market Cap	$8.1 Billion	Shares	
Book Value	$581.4 Million	707,720,512	
Price/Book	13.88	% Held	
Price/Sales	0.26	60.15	

Business Summary: Retail - Food & Beverage, Drug & Tobacco (MIC: 2.1.2 SIC: 5912 NAIC: 446110)

Rite Aid operates a pharmacy retail healthcare company. Co. operates through its two reportable segments: the Retail Pharmacy segment and the Pharmacy Services segment. The Retail Pharmacy segment's drugstores' primary business is the sale of brand and generic prescription drugs. The Retail Pharmacy segment also sells a full selection of health and beauty aids and personal care products, seasonal merchandise and a large private brand product line. Co.'s pharmacy services segment, operates, among others, pharmacy benefit management business; mail-order and specialty pharmacy services through Orchard Pharmaceutical Services and a national Medicare Part D prescription drug plan.

Recent Developments: For the year ended Feb 27 2016, net income decreased 92.2% to US$165.5 million from US$2.11 billion in the prior year. Revenues were US$30.74 billion, up 15.9% from US$26.53 billion the year before. Direct operating expenses rose 20.9% to US$22.91 billion from US$18.95 billion in the comparable period the year before. Indirect operating expenses increased 5.6% to US$7.55 billion from US$7.15 billion in the equivalent prior-year period.

Prospects: Our evaluation of Rite Aid Corp. as of June 19, 2016 is the result of our systematic analysis on three basic characteristics: earnings strength, relative valuation, and recent stock price movement. The company has enjoyed a very positive trend in earnings per share over the past 5 quarters. However, while recent estimates for the company have been mixed, RAD has posted results that fell short of analysts expectations. Based on operating earnings yield, the company is overvalued when compared to all of the companies in our coverage universe. Share price changes over the past year indicates that RAD will perform well over the near term.

Financial Data

(US$ in Thousands)	02/27/2016	02/28/2015	03/01/2014	03/02/2013	03/03/2012	02/26/2011	02/27/2010	02/28/2009
Earnings Per Share	0.16	2.08	0.23	0.12	(0.43)	(0.64)	(0.59)	(3.49)
Cash Flow Per Share	0.98	0.67	0.76	0.92	0.30	0.45	(0.37)	0.43
Income Statement								
Total Revenue	30,736,657	26,528,377	25,526,413	25,392,263	26,121,222	25,214,907	25,669,117	26,289,268
EBITDA	1,050,374	1,122,955	959,412	809,300	433,790	333,926	385,127	(1,721,496)
Depn & Amortn	322,396	298,523	284,603	286,374	296,792	331,927	349,282	383,671
Income Before Taxes	278,404	426,820	250,218	7,505	(392,257)	(545,582)	(479,918)	(2,582,794)
Income Taxes	112,939	(1,682,353)	804	(110,600)	(23,686)	9,842	26,758	329,257
Net Income	165,465	2,109,173	249,414	118,105	(368,571)	(555,424)	(506,676)	(2,915,420)
Average Shares	1,042,362	1,017,861	979,092	907,259	885,819	882,947	880,843	840,812
Balance Sheet								
Current Assets	4,550,727	4,221,758	4,285,125	4,409,047	4,504,586	4,411,365	4,508,668	4,364,932
Total Assets	11,277,010	8,863,252	6,944,871	7,078,719	7,364,291	7,555,850	8,049,911	8,326,540
Current Liabilities	2,996,895	2,485,000	2,507,452	2,578,270	2,570,319	2,420,323	2,175,692	2,302,427
Long-Term Obligations	6,967,288	5,544,567	5,707,969	5,996,220	6,248,780	6,156,820	6,319,397	5,971,026
Total Liabilities	10,695,582	8,806,196	9,058,573	9,538,153	9,951,047	9,767,217	9,723,462	9,526,192
Stockholders' Equity	581,428	57,056	(2,113,702)	(2,459,434)	(2,586,756)	(2,211,367)	(1,673,551)	(1,199,652)
Shares Outstanding	1,047,754	988,558	971,331	904,268	898,687	890,297	887,636	886,113
Statistical Record								
Return on Assets %	1.65	26.76	3.57	1.64	N.M.	N.M.	N.M.	N.M.
Return on Equity %	51.97	...	...	...	...	...	...	N.M.
EBITDA Margin %	3.42	4.23	3.76	3.19	1.66	1.32	1.50	N.M.
Net Margin %	0.54	7.95	0.98	0.47	N.M.	N.M.	N.M.	N.M.
Asset Turnover	3.06	3.37	3.65	3.53	3.44	3.24	3.14	2.66
Current Ratio	1.52	1.70	1.71	1.71	1.75	1.82	2.07	1.90
Debt to Equity	11.98	97.18	...	...	...	...	...	...
Price Range	9.32-6.05	8.50-4.51	6.74-1.65	2.05-0.97	1.67-0.91	1.74-0.87	2.24-0.21	2.99-0.20
P/E Ratio	58.25-37.81	4.09-2.17	29.30-7.17	17.08-8.07	...	...	...	...

Address: 30 Hunter Lane, Camp Hill, PA 17011	Web Site: www.riteaid.com	Auditors: Deloitte & Touche LLP
Telephone: 717-761-2633	**Officers:** John T. Standley - Chairman, President, Chief Executive Officer, Chief Operating Officer	**Investor Contact:** 717-214-8867
Fax: 717-975-5905	Kenneth A. Martindale - President, Senior Executive Vice President, Chief Operating Officer, Chief Merchandising Officer, Chief Marketing Officer, Chief Logistics Officer	**Transfer Agents:** American Stock Transfer & Trust Company, Brooklyn, NY

RLI CORP.

Exchange	Symbol	Price	52Wk Range	Yield	P/E	Div Achiever
NYS	RLI	$66.11 (5/31/2016)	68.05-48.71	1.21	21.12	39 Years

*7 Year Price Score 130.20 *NYSE Composite Index=100 *12 Month Price Score 107.89

Interim Earnings (Per Share)

Qtr.	Mar	Jun	Sep	Dec
2013	0.57	0.69	0.86	0.77
2014	0.60	0.82	0.76	0.85
2015	0.70	0.84	0.81	0.77
2016	0.71	...	...	...

Interim Dividends (Per Share)

Amt	Decl	Ex	Rec	Pay
0.19Q	11/12/2015	11/25/2015	11/30/2015	12/22/2015
2.00Sp	11/12/2015	11/25/2015	11/30/2015	12/22/2015
0.19Q	02/04/2016	02/25/2016	02/29/2016	03/18/2016
0.20Q	05/05/2016	05/26/2016	05/31/2016	06/20/2016

Indicated Div: $0.80 (Div. Reinv. Plan)

Valuation Analysis		Institutional Holding	
Forecast EPS	$2.30	No of Institutions	
	(05/15/2016)	258	
Market Cap	$2.9 Billion	Shares	
Book Value	$872.2 Million	39,591,688	
Price/Book	3.31	% Held	
Price/Sales	3.61	78.10	

Business Summary: General Insurance (MIC: 5.2.1 SIC: 6331 NAIC: 524126)

RLI is an insurance holding company. Through its subsidiaries, Co. is engaged in underwriting selected property and casualty insurance. Co. has three segments: casualty, which includes commerical and personal umbrella, general liability, professional services, commercial transportation, P&C package business, executive products, medical professional liability, and other casualty; property, which includes commercial property, marine, specialty personal, property reinsurance, and crop reinsurance; and surety; which includes miscellaneous surety coverage, commercial surety bonds, bonds for small-to-medium sized contractors, and energy surety coverages.

Recent Developments: For the quarter ended Mar 31 2016, net income increased 2.6% to US$31.4 million from US$30.6 million in the year-earlier quarter. Revenues were US$201.7 million, up 3.0% from US$195.8 million the year before. Net premiums earned were US$176.9 million versus US$169.0 million in the prior-year quarter, an increase of 4.7%. Net investment income fell 0.9% to US$13.4 million from US$13.5 million a year ago.

Prospects: Our evaluation of RLI Corp. as of June 19, 2016 is the result of our systematic analysis on three basic characteristics: earnings strength, relative valuation, and recent stock price movement. The company has generated a negative trend in earnings per share over the past 5 quarters and while recent estimates for the company have remained steady, RLI has posted better than expected results. Based on operating earnings yield, the company is about fairly valued when compared to all of the companies in our coverage universe. Share price changes over the past year indicates that RLI will perform very well over the near term.

Financial Data

(US$ in Thousands)	3 Mos	12/31/2015	12/31/2014	12/31/2013	12/31/2012	12/31/2011	12/31/2010	12/31/2009
Earnings Per Share	3.13	3.12	3.09	2.90	2.40	3.04	3.00	2.16
Cash Flow Per Share	3.45	3.52	2.86	3.16	0.85	2.80	2.38	2.96
Tang Book Value Per Share	18.32	17.27	17.92	17.54	16.94	17.92	18.25	18.95
Dividends Per Share	2.760	2.750	3.710	2.170	3.130	3.095	4.075	0.540
Dividend Payout %	88.18	88.14	120.06	74.83	130.69	101.64	135.83	25.00
Income Statement								
Premium Income	176,918	700,161	687,375	630,802	576,571	538,452	493,382	491,961
Total Revenue	201,688	794,634	775,165	705,601	660,774	619,169	583,424	546,552
Benefits & Claims	81,171	299,045	296,609	259,801	271,645	200,084	201,332	203,388
Income Before Taxes	41,842	185,768	177,149	164,751	133,879	183,232	171,389	127,385
Income Taxes	14,200	59,138	54,042	49,411	39,386	59,138	51,058	38,592
Net Income	31,393	137,544	135,445	126,255	103,346	130,591	127,432	93,845
Average Shares	44,361	44,131	43,819	43,514	43,160	42,868	42,482	43,462
Balance Sheet								
Total Assets	2,759,854	2,736,579	2,775,542	2,740,310	2,644,632	2,695,170	2,514,592	2,538,653
Total Liabilities	1,887,660	1,913,110	1,930,480	1,911,344	1,848,269	1,876,318	1,723,216	1,706,403
Stockholders' Equity	872,194	823,469	845,062	828,966	796,363	818,852	791,376	832,250
Shares Outstanding	43,671	43,544	43,102	42,982	42,525	42,324	41,929	42,529
Statistical Record								
Return on Assets %	4.99	4.99	4.91	4.69	3.86	5.01	5.04	3.79
Return on Equity %	15.95	16.49	16.18	15.54	12.76	16.22	15.70	12.18
Loss Ratio %	45.88	42.71	43.15	41.19	47.11	37.16	40.81	41.34
Net Margin %	15.57	17.31	17.47	17.89	15.64	21.09	21.84	17.17
Price Range	68.05-48.55	63.02-46.91	50.54-40.31	51.77-32.33	37.22-31.05	37.08-25.49	30.55-24.95	30.59-21.57
P/E Ratio	21.74-15.51	20.20-15.04	16.36-13.05	17.85-11.15	15.51-12.94	12.20-8.38	10.18-8.32	14.16-9.98
Average Yield %	4.87	5.14	8.25	5.42	9.18	10.04	14.72	2.12

Address: 9025 North Lindbergh Drive, Peoria, IL 61615
Telephone: 309-692-1000
Fax: 309 692 1068

Web Site: www.rlicorp.com
Officers: Gerald D. Stephens - Chairman Jonathan E. Michael - President, Chief Executive Officer

Auditors: KPMG LLP
Investor Contact: 309 693-5880
Transfer Agents: Wells Fargo Shareholder Services, St. Paul, MN

ROBERT HALF INTERNATIONAL INC.

Exchange	Symbol	Price	52Wk Range	Yield	P/E	Div Achiever
NYS	RHI	$41.59 (5/31/2016)	57.91-36.65	2.12	15.12	11 Years

*7 Year Price Score 113.75 *NYSE Composite Index=100 *12 Month Price Score 84.60

Interim Earnings (Per Share)

Qtr.	Mar	Jun	Sep	Dec
2013	0.40	0.46	0.48	0.48
2014	0.45	0.55	0.63	0.63
2015	0.58	0.67	0.73	0.71
2016	0.64			

Interim Dividends (Per Share)

Amt	Decl	Ex	Rec	Pay
0.20Q	07/30/2015	08/21/2015	08/25/2015	09/15/2015
0.20Q	10/29/2015	11/23/2015	11/25/2015	12/15/2015
0.22Q	02/11/2016	02/23/2016	02/25/2016	03/15/2016
0.22Q	05/04/2016	05/23/2016	05/25/2016	06/15/2016

Indicated Div: $0.88

Valuation Analysis

		Institutional Holding	
Forecast EPS	$2.96	No of Institutions	
	(05/17/2016)	611	
Market Cap	$5.5 Billion	Shares	
Book Value	$1.0 Billion	132,861,536	
Price/Book	5.23	% Held	
Price/Sales	1.05	84.58	

Business Summary: Business Services (MIC: 7.5.2 SIC: 7363 NAIC: 561320)

Robert Half International provides staffing and risk consulting services. Co.'s Accountemps, Robert Half Finance & Accounting, and Robert Half Management Resources divisions provide temporary, full-time, and project personnel in the fields of accounting and finance. Co.'s OfficeTeam division provides temporary administrative support personnel. Co.'s Robert Half Technology division provides information technology personnel. Co.'s Robert Half Legal division provides temporary, project, and full-time staffing of attorneys and support personnel within law firms and corporate legal departments. The Creative Group provides project staffing in the interactive media, design, and marketing fields.

Recent Developments: For the quarter ended Mar 31 2016, net income increased 7.1% to US$83.4 million from US$77.9 million in the year-earlier quarter. Revenues were US$1.30 billion, up 8.1% from US$1.21 billion the year before. Direct operating expenses rose 8.3% to US$770.7 million from US$711.5 million in the comparable period the year before. Indirect operating expenses increased 8.8% to US$398.2 million from US$365.9 million in the equivalent prior-year period.

Prospects: Our evaluation of Robert Half International Inc. as of June 19, 2016 is the result of our systematic analysis on three basic characteristics: earnings strength, relative valuation, and recent stock price movement. The company has managed to produce a neutral trend in earnings per share over the past 5 quarters and while recent estimates for the company have been mixed, RHI has posted results that fell short of analysts expectations. Based on operating earnings yield, the company is undervalued when compared to all of the companies in our coverage universe. Share price changes over the past year indicates that RHI will perform in line with the market over the near term.

Financial Data

(US$ in Thousands)	3 Mos	12/31/2015	12/31/2014	12/31/2013	12/31/2012	12/31/2011	12/31/2010	12/31/2009
Earnings Per Share	2.75	2.69	2.26	1.83	1.50	1.04	0.44	0.24
Cash Flow Per Share	3.34	3.33	2.54	2.27	2.09	1.82	1.23	1.65
Tang Book Value Per Share	6.33	6.03	5.77	5.22	4.58	4.30	4.41	4.78
Dividends Per Share	0.820	0.800	0.720	0.640	0.600	0.560	0.520	0.480
Dividend Payout %	29.82	29.74	31.86	34.97	40.00	53.85	118.18	200.00
Income Statement								
Total Revenue	1,302,625	5,094,933	4,695,014	4,245,895	4,111,213	3,776,976	3,175,093	3,036,547
EBITDA	149,021	633,945	546,306	445,349	391,772	300,680	170,547	130,586
Depn & Amortn	15,411	53,465	49,681	48,772	48,724	51,415	55,958	65,266
Income Before Taxes	133,791	581,030	497,349	397,579	344,245	250,216	115,168	66,763
Income Taxes	50,375	223,234	191,421	145,384	134,303	100,294	49,099	29,500
Net Income	83,416	357,796	305,928	252,195	209,942	149,922	66,069	37,263
Average Shares	130,137	132,930	135,541	137,589	139,409	141,790	144,028	146,611
Balance Sheet								
Current Assets	1,380,201	1,343,681	1,323,283	1,172,528	1,064,685	1,006,678	971,860	922,634
Total Assets	1,744,864	1,702,960	1,647,267	1,490,271	1,381,271	1,311,836	1,273,984	1,283,535
Current Liabilities	655,317	655,549	623,362	535,853	501,637	473,001	408,460	366,968
Long-Term Obligations	966	1,007	1,159	1,300	1,428	1,545	1,656	1,779
Total Liabilities	699,911	699,179	667,409	570,628	539,260	511,331	439,613	383,725
Stockholders' Equity	1,044,953	1,003,781	979,858	919,643	842,011	800,505	834,371	899,810
Shares Outstanding	131,318	131,156	135,134	137,466	139,438	142,085	146,182	148,645
Statistical Record								
Return on Assets %	21.48	21.36	19.50	17.57	15.55	11.60	5.17	2.76
Return on Equity %	35.80	36.07	32.21	28.63	25.49	18.34	7.62	3.96
EBITDA Margin %	11.44	12.44	11.64	10.49	9.53	7.96	5.37	4.30
Net Margin %	6.40	7.02	6.52	5.94	5.11	3.97	2.08	1.23
Asset Turnover	3.07	3.04	2.99	2.96	3.04	2.92	2.48	2.25
Current Ratio	2.11	2.05	2.12	2.19	2.12	2.13	2.38	2.51
Price Range	60.52-36.65	63.00-44.95	58.99-39.17	42.10-31.33	31.82-25.24	33.85-20.06	32.16-21.57	27.77-14.41
P/E Ratio	22.01-13.33	23.42-16.71	26.10-17.33	23.01-17.12	21.21-16.83	32.55-19.29	73.09-49.02	115.71-60.04
Average Yield %	1.61	1.45	1.52	1.76	2.12	2.04	1.92	2.14

Address: 2884 Sand Hill Road, Menlo Park, CA 94025 **Telephone:** 650-234-6000	**Web Site:** www.rhi.com **Officers:** Harold M. Messmer - Chairman, President, Chief Executive Officer M. Keith Waddell - Vice-Chairman, President, Chief Financial Officer, Treasurer	**Auditors:** PricewaterhouseCoopers LLP **Transfer Agents:** Computershare Trust Company, N.A., Canton, MA

ROCKWELL COLLINS, INC.

Exchange	Symbol	Price	52Wk Range	Yield	P/E
NYS	COL	$88.40 (5/31/2016)	95.86-78.30	1.49	17.61

*7 Year Price Score 111.75 *NYSE Composite Index=100 *12 Month Price Score 101.80

Interim Earnings (Per Share)

Qtr.	Dec	Mar	Jun	Sep
2012-13	0.94	1.17	1.20	1.28
2013-14	0.96	1.08	1.15	1.23
2014-15	1.24	1.17	1.33	1.38
2015-16	1.02	1.29	...	...

Interim Dividends (Per Share)

Amt	Decl	Ex	Rec	Pay
0.33Q	08/03/2015	08/13/2015	08/17/2015	09/08/2015
0.33Q	11/02/2015	11/12/2015	11/16/2015	12/07/2015
0.33Q	02/01/2016	02/11/2016	02/16/2016	03/07/2016
0.33Q	04/21/2016	05/12/2016	05/16/2016	06/06/2016

Indicated Div: $1.32

Valuation Analysis

		Institutional Holding	
Forecast EPS	$5.50	No of Institutions	
	(05/20/2016)	700	
Market Cap	$11.5 Billion	Shares	
Book Value	$2.0 Billion	117,552,448	
Price/Book	5.81	% Held	
Price/Sales	2.24	71.56	

TRADING VOLUME (thousand shares)

Business Summary: Aerospace (MIC: 7.1.1 SIC: 3728 NAIC: 336413)

Rockwell Collins designs, produces and supports communications and aviation systems for commercial and military customers. Co. serves a worldwide customer base through three business segments: Commercial Systems, which supplies aviation electronics systems, products and services; Government Systems, which provides a range of electronic products, systems and services to customers including the U.S. Department of Defense, other ministries of defense, other government agencies and defense contractors; and Information Management Services, which provides communications services, systems integration and security solutions across the aviation, airport, rail, transit and nuclear security markets.

Recent Developments: For the quarter ended Mar 31 2016, income from continuing operations increased 5.5% to US$172.0 million from US$163.0 million in the year-earlier quarter. Net income increased 8.9% to US$171.0 million from US$157.0 million in the year-earlier quarter. Revenues were US$1.31 billion, down 2.2% from US$1.34 billion the year before. Direct operating expenses declined 3.2% to US$907.0 million from US$937.0 million in the comparable period the year before. Indirect operating expenses increased 3.7% to US$169.0 million from US$163.0 million in the equivalent prior-year period.

Prospects: Our evaluation of Rockwell Collins Inc. as of June 19, 2016 is the result of our systematic analysis on three basic characteristics: earnings strength, relative valuation, and recent stock price movement. The company has produced a positive trend in earnings per share over the past 5 quarters. However, while recent estimates for the company have been mixed, COL has posted better than expected results. Based on operating earnings yield, the company is undervalued when compared to all of the companies in our coverage universe. Share price changes over the past year indicates that COL will perform very well over the near term.

Financial Data

(US$ in Millions)	6 Mos	3 Mos	09/30/2015	09/30/2014	09/30/2013	09/30/2012	09/30/2011	09/30/2010
Earnings Per Share	5.02	4.90	5.13	4.42	4.58	4.15	4.06	3.52
Cash Flow Per Share	5.06	5.46	5.66	4.89	4.52	3.67	4.26	4.53
Tang Book Value Per Share	N.M.	N.M.	N.M.	N.M.	4.08	1.32	2.84	2.61
Dividends Per Share	1.320	1.290	1.260	1.200	1.200	1.080	0.960	0.960
Dividend Payout %	26.29	26.33	24.56	27.15	26.20	26.02	23.65	27.27
Income Statement								
Total Revenue	2,480	1,169	5,244	4,979	4,610	4,726	4,806	4,665
EBITDA	549	230	1,172	1,075	1,061	1,044	997	957
Depn & Amortn	125	58	152	141	180	174	141	149
Income Before Taxes	392	157	959	875	855	846	842	792
Income Taxes	87	24	268	264	236	248	240	241
Net Income	306	135	686	604	632	609	634	561
Average Shares	132	132	133	136	138	146	156	159
Balance Sheet								
Current Assets	3,490	3,446	3,233	3,204	3,094	2,787	2,889	2,689
Total Assets	7,541	7,471	7,389	7,063	5,400	5,314	5,389	5,064
Current Liabilities	2,573	2,575	2,144	2,198	1,981	1,440	1,495	1,452
Long-Term Obligations	1,383	1,370	1,680	1,663	563	779	528	525
Total Liabilities	5,558	5,572	5,514	5,179	3,782	4,055	3,866	3,582
Stockholders' Equity	1,983	1,899	1,875	1,884	1,618	1,259	1,523	1,482
Shares Outstanding	130	131	131	134	135	142	153	156
Statistical Record								
Return on Assets %	9.08	8.95	9.49	9.69	11.80	11.35	12.13	11.56
Return on Equity %	33.99	34.76	36.50	34.49	43.93	43.66	42.20	40.45
EBITDA Margin %	22.14	19.67	22.35	21.59	23.02	22.09	20.74	20.51
Net Margin %	12.34	11.55	13.08	12.13	13.71	12.89	13.19	12.03
Asset Turnover	0.70	0.71	0.73	0.80	0.86	0.88	0.92	0.96
Current Ratio	1.36	1.34	1.51	1.46	1.56	1.94	1.93	1.85
Debt to Equity	0.70	0.72	0.90	0.88	0.35	0.62	0.35	0.35
Price Range	99.00-78.30	99.00-79.25	99.00-73.48	83.47-65.90	74.69-52.59	59.96-46.92	67.20-44.89	67.84-48.15
P/E Ratio	19.72-15.60	20.20-16.17	19.30-14.32	18.88-14.91	16.31-11.48	14.45-11.31	16.55-11.06	19.27-13.68
Average Yield %	1.48	1.43	1.43	1.57	1.91	2.01	1.62	1.69

Address: 400 Collins Road N.E., Cedar Rapids, IA 52498 **Telephone:** 319-295-1000	**Web Site:** www.rockwellcollins.com **Officers:** Donald R. Beall - Chairman Emeritus Robert K. Ortberg - President, Chief Executive Officer, Executive Vice President, Division Officer	**Auditors:** Deloitte LLP **Investor Contact:** 319-295 7575 **Transfer Agents:** Wells Fargo Shareowner Services, St. Paul, MN

ROCKWELL AUTOMATION, INC.

Exchange	Symbol	Price	52Wk Range	Yield	P/E
NYS	ROK	$116.05 (5/31/2016)	126.89-89.71	2.50	20.40

*7 Year Price Score 108.45 *NYSE Composite Index=100 *12 Month Price Score 103.05

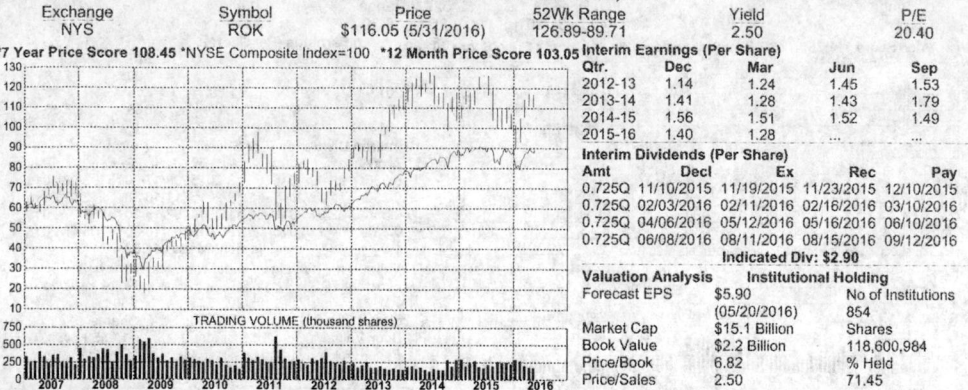

Interim Earnings (Per Share)

Qtr.	Dec	Mar	Jun	Sep
2012-13	1.14	1.24	1.45	1.53
2013-14	1.41	1.28	1.43	1.79
2014-15	1.56	1.51	1.52	1.49
2015-16	1.40	1.28	...	...

Interim Dividends (Per Share)

Amt	Decl	Ex	Rec	Pay
0.725Q	11/10/2015	11/19/2015	11/23/2015	12/10/2015
0.725Q	02/03/2016	02/11/2016	02/16/2016	03/10/2016
0.725Q	04/06/2016	05/12/2016	05/16/2016	06/10/2016
0.725Q	06/08/2016	08/11/2016	08/15/2016	09/12/2016

Indicated Div: $2.90

Valuation Analysis / **Institutional Holding**

Forecast EPS	$5.90
(05/20/2016)	No of Institutions 854
Market Cap	$15.1 Billion
Book Value	$2.2 Billion
Price/Book	6.82
Price/Sales	2.50

Shares 118,600,984
% Held 71.45

TRADING VOLUME (thousand shares)

Business Summary: Electrical Equipment (MIC: 7.3.1 SIC: 3829 NAIC: 334519)

Rockwell Automation is a provider of industrial automation power, control and information solutions. Co. has two operating segments: Architecture & Software and Control Products & Solutions. The Architecture & Software segment contains all of the hardware, software and communication components of Co.'s integrated control and information architecture capable of controlling the customer's industrial processes and connecting with their manufacturing enterprise. The Control Products & Solutions segment combines a portfolio of motor control and industrial control products, application knowledge and project management capabilities.

Recent Developments: For the quarter ended Mar 31 2016, net income decreased 18.4% to US$168.0 million from US$206.0 million in the year-earlier quarter. Revenues were US$1.44 billion, down 7.1% from US$1.55 billion the year before. Direct operating expenses declined 3.6% to US$846.2 million from US$877.6 million in the comparable period the year before. Indirect operating expenses decreased 4.9% to US$377.1 million from US$396.7 million in the equivalent prior-year period.

Prospects: Our evaluation of Rockwell Automation Inc. as of June 19, 2016 is the result of our systematic analysis on three basic characteristics: earnings strength, relative valuation, and recent stock price movement. The company has produced a positive trend in earnings per share over the past 5 quarters and while recent estimates for the company have remained steady, ROK has posted better than expected results. Based on operating earnings yield, the company is about fairly valued when compared to all of the companies in our coverage universe. Share price changes over the past year indicates that ROK will perform in line with the market over the near term.

Financial Data

(US$ in Thousands)	6 Mos	3 Mos	09/30/2015	09/30/2014	09/30/2013	09/30/2012	09/30/2011	09/30/2010
Earnings Per Share	5.69	5.92	6.09	5.91	5.36	5.13	4.80	3.22
Cash Flow Per Share	7.92	8.38	8.83	7.49	7.29	5.07	4.51	3.48
Tang Book Value Per Share	7.48	7.58	7.54	9.96	9.72	4.96	4.07	2.33
Dividends Per Share	2.750	2.675	2.600	2.320	1.980	1.745	1.475	1.220
Dividend Payout %	48.33	45.19	42.69	39.26	36.94	34.02	30.73	37.89
Income Statement								
Total Revenue	2,866,900	1,426,600	6,307,900	6,623,500	6,351,900	6,259,400	6,000,400	4,857,000
EBITDA	575,300	295,600	1,343,000	1,336,500	1,177,200	1,156,800	1,052,400	727,000
Depn & Amortn	86,400	41,300	162,500	152,500	145,200	138,600	131,300	127,300
Income Before Taxes	453,900	236,900	1,127,500	1,134,200	980,900	965,900	867,600	544,200
Income Taxes	100,400	51,400	299,900	307,400	224,600	228,900	170,500	103,800
Net Income	353,500	185,500	827,600	826,800	756,300	737,000	697,800	464,300
Average Shares	131,300	132,600	135,700	139,700	140,900	143,400	145,200	144,000
Balance Sheet								
Current Assets	4,063,000	3,957,200	4,048,000	3,934,200	3,679,900	3,387,500	3,075,100	2,586,600
Total Assets	6,539,600	6,419,700	6,404,700	6,229,500	5,844,600	5,636,500	5,284,900	4,748,300
Current Liabilities	1,504,900	1,383,400	1,327,700	1,692,100	1,544,700	1,531,600	1,329,900	1,222,300
Long-Term Obligations	1,513,200	1,492,900	1,500,900	905,600	905,100	905,000	905,000	904,900
Total Liabilities	4,324,000	4,183,200	4,147,900	3,571,400	3,259,100	3,784,800	3,536,900	3,287,900
Stockholders' Equity	2,215,600	2,236,500	2,256,800	2,658,100	2,585,500	1,851,700	1,748,000	1,460,400
Shares Outstanding	130,263	131,400	132,400	136,700	138,900	139,800	141,900	141,700
Statistical Record								
Return on Assets %	11.87	12.66	13.10	13.70	13.17	13.46	13.91	10.26
Return on Equity %	31.82	33.25	33.68	31.54	34.09	40.84	43.50	33.44
EBITDA Margin %	20.07	20.72	21.29	20.18	18.53	18.48	17.54	14.97
Net Margin %	12.33	13.00	13.12	12.48	11.91	11.77	11.63	9.56
Asset Turnover	0.94	0.98	1.00	1.10	1.11	1.14	1.20	1.07
Current Ratio	2.70	2.86	3.05	2.33	2.38	2.21	2.31	2.12
Debt to Equity	0.68	0.67	0.67	0.34	0.35	0.49	0.52	0.62
Price Range	126.89-89.71	126.89-99.62	126.89-98.60	127.83-104.39	109.13-68.73	84.55-54.55	97.84-51.54	62.83-40.28
P/E Ratio	22.30-15.77	21.43-16.83	20.84-16.19	21.63-17.66	20.36-12.82	16.48-10.63	20.38-10.74	19.51-12.51
Average Yield %	2.50	2.37	2.28	1.97	2.27	2.34	1.95	2.36

Address: 1201 South Second Street, Milwaukee, WI 53204
Telephone: 414-382-2000

Web Site: www.rockwellautomation.com
Officers: Keith D. Nosbusch - Chairman, President, Chief Executive Officer Kenneth M. Champa - Division Officer

Auditors: Deloitte & Touche LLP
Investor Contact: 414-382-8510
Transfer Agents: Wells Fargo Shareowner Services, St. Paul, MN

ROLLINS, INC.

Exchange	Symbol	Price	52Wk Range	Yield	P/E	Div Achiever
NYS	ROL	$28.42 (5/31/2016)	30.35-24.08	1.41	39.47	13 Years

*7 Year Price Score 138.72 *NYSE Composite Index=100 *12 Month Price Score 99.35

Interim Earnings (Per Share)

Qtr.	Mar	Jun	Sep	Dec
2013	0.11	0.17	0.17	0.13
2014	0.12	0.19	0.19	0.13
2015	0.14	0.21	0.21	0.15
2016	0.15	...	...	...

Interim Dividends (Per Share)

Amt	Decl	Ex	Rec	Pay
0.08Q	10/27/2015	11/06/2015	11/10/2015	12/10/2015
0.10Q	10/27/2015	11/06/2015	11/10/2015	12/10/2015
0.10Q	01/26/2016	02/08/2016	02/10/2016	03/10/2016
0.10Q	04/26/2016	05/06/2016	05/10/2016	06/10/2016

Indicated Div: $0.40

Valuation Analysis

Forecast EPS	$0.77
	(05/08/2016)
Market Cap	$6.2 Billion
Book Value	$541.6 Million
Price/Book	11.48
Price/Sales	4.12

Institutional Holding

No of Institutions	316
Shares	86,064,064
% Held	33.07

Business Summary: Business Services (MIC: 7.5.2 SIC: 7342 NAIC: 561710)

Rollins is a service company providing pest and termite control services via its subsidiaries in North America and Australia with international franchises in Central America, the Caribbean, the Middle East, Asia, the Mediterranean, Europe, Africa, and Mexico. Co.'s subsidiary, Orkin, LLC, provides pest control services and protection against termite damage, rodents and insects to homes and businesses. Co.'s other subsidiaries include Orkin Canada, which is a pest control provider in Canada; Western Pest Services, which is primarily a commercial pest control service company; and The Industrial Fumigant Company, which is a provider of pest management and sanitation services and products.

Recent Developments: For the quarter ended Mar 31 2016, net income increased 5.4% to US$31.9 million from US$30.3 million in the year-earlier quarter. Revenues were US$352.7 million, up 6.6% from US$330.9 million the year before. Direct operating expenses rose 5.8% to US$177.8 million from US$168.0 million in the comparable period the year before. Indirect operating expenses increased 6.5% to US$123.8 million from US$116.3 million in the equivalent prior-year period.

Prospects: Our evaluation of Rollins Inc. as of June 19, 2016 is the result of our systematic analysis on three basic characteristics: earnings strength, relative valuation, and recent stock price movement. The company has managed to produce a neutral trend in earnings per share over the past 5 quarters and while recent estimates for the company have remained steady, ROL has posted better than expected results. Based on operating earnings yield, the company is overvalued when compared to all of the companies in our coverage universe. Share price changes over the past year indicates that ROL will perform well over the near term.

Financial Data
(US$ in Thousands)

	3 Mos	12/31/2015	12/31/2014	12/31/2013	12/31/2012	12/31/2011	12/31/2010	12/31/2009
Earnings Per Share	0.72	0.70	0.63	0.56	0.51	0.46	0.41	0.37
Cash Flow Per Share	0.89	0.90	0.89	0.74	0.64	0.70	0.56	0.50
Tang Book Value Per Share	0.60	0.62	0.34	0.45	0.00	N.M.	N.M.	N.M.
Dividends Per Share	0.440	0.420	0.347	0.300	0.293	0.187	0.160	0.124
Dividend Payout %	61.11	60.00	55.32	53.57	57.89	40.58	39.34	33.34
Income Statement								
Total Revenue	352,736	1,485,305	1,411,566	1,337,374	1,270,909	1,205,064	1,136,890	1,073,958
EBITDA	62,768	262,418	235,857	205,636	191,868	176,716	159,957	143,129
Depn & Amortn	11,640	19,400	16,627	14,415	15,212	15,112	15,975	15,874
Income Before Taxes	51,178	243,178	219,484	191,606	176,642	161,096	143,545	126,291
Income Taxes	19,250	91,029	81,820	68,276	65,310	60,385	53,543	42,307
Net Income	31,928	152,149	137,664	123,330	111,332	100,711	90,002	83,984
Average Shares	218,686	218,583	218,694	219,121	219,459	220,419	222,346	224,435
Balance Sheet								
Current Assets	270,121	313,879	283,958	274,442	205,992	175,822	151,021	120,530
Total Assets	873,015	852,431	808,162	739,217	692,506	645,650	619,014	566,496
Current Liabilities	262,868	252,986	252,679	235,792	228,416	225,851	240,441	232,733
Total Liabilities	331,456	328,402	345,486	300,962	337,550	321,653	321,044	301,930
Stockholders' Equity	541,559	524,029	462,676	438,255	354,956	323,997	297,970	264,566
Shares Outstanding	218,698	218,753	218,482	218,796	219,022	219,376	220,772	222,534
Statistical Record								
Return on Assets %	18.37	18.32	17.79	17.23	16.59	15.93	15.18	14.75
Return on Equity %	30.50	30.84	30.56	31.10	32.71	32.38	32.00	34.07
EBITDA Margin %	17.79	17.67	16.71	15.38	15.10	14.66	14.07	13.33
Net Margin %	9.05	10.24	9.75	9.22	8.76	8.36	7.92	7.82
Asset Turnover	1.80	1.79	1.82	1.87	1.89	1.91	1.92	1.89
Current Ratio	1.03	1.24	1.12	1.16	0.90	0.78	0.61	0.52
Price Range	30.35-24.08	30.35-21.27	22.53-18.10	20.26-14.69	16.19-12.97	15.61-11.15	13.39-8.17	8.74-6.36
P/E Ratio	42.15-33.44	43.36-30.39	35.76-28.73	36.18-26.24	31.75-25.44	33.94-24.23	32.65-19.92	23.62-17.18
Average Yield %	1.64	1.62	1.72	1.75	1.99	1.40	1.59	1.59

Address: 2170 Piedmont Road, N.E., Atlanta, GA 30324 **Telephone:** 404-888 2000	**Web Site:** www.rollins.com **Officers:** R. Randall Rollins - Chairman Gary W. Rollins - Vice-Chairman, President, Chief Executive Officer, Chief Operating Officer	**Auditors:** Grant Thornton LLP **Investor Contact:** 404-888-2000 **Transfer Agents:** American Stock Transfer and Trust, Brooklyn, NY

ROPER TECHNOLOGIES INC

Exchange	Symbol	Price	52Wk Range	Yield	P/E	Div Achiever
NYS	ROP	$171.08 (5/31/2016)	194.83-152.93	0.70	25.16	23 Years

*7 Year Price Score 132.80   *NYSE Composite Index=100   *12 Month Price Score 101.24

Interim Earnings (Per Share)

Qtr.	Mar	Jun	Sep	Dec
2013	1.25	1.11	1.36	1.65
2014	1.46	1.56	1.54	1.84
2015	1.54	1.69	1.58	2.05
2016	1.48	...	...	...

Interim Dividends (Per Share)

Amt	Decl	Ex	Rec	Pay
0.25Q	09/09/2015	10/07/2015	10/09/2015	10/23/2015
0.30Q	12/17/2015	01/06/2016	01/08/2016	01/22/2016
0.30Q	03/15/2016	04/06/2016	04/08/2016	04/22/2016
0.30Q	06/14/2016	07/06/2016	07/08/2016	07/22/2016

Indicated Div: $1.20

Valuation Analysis   **Institutional Holding**

Forecast EPS	$6.95 (05/20/2016)	No of Institutions	723
Market Cap	$17.3 Billion	Shares	112,133,280
Book Value	$5.4 Billion	% Held	93.88
Price/Book	3.18		
Price/Sales	4.78		

TRADING VOLUME (thousand shares)

Business Summary: Electrical Equipment (MIC: 7.3.1 SIC: 3823 NAIC: 334513)

Roper Technologies designs and develops software (both license and software-as-a-service) and engineered products and solutions. Co. operates in four segments: Medical and Scientific Imaging, which includes products and software in medical applications; Radio Frequency (R) Technology, which provides RF identification communication technology and software solutions; Industrial Technology, which includes fluid handling pumps, materials analysis equipment, and water meter and automatic meter reading products and systems; and Energy Systems and Controls, which includes control systems, industrial valves and controls, fluid properties testing equipment, and sensors, controls and valves.

Recent Developments: For the quarter ended Mar 31 2016, net income decreased 2.8% to US$151.4 million from US$155.8 million in the year-earlier quarter. Revenues were US$902.4 million, up 4.3% from US$865.3 million the year before. Operating income was US$245.0 million versus US$246.9 million in the prior-year quarter, a decrease of 0.8%. Direct operating expenses declined 1.2% to US$342.9 million from US$347.1 million in the comparable period the year before. Indirect operating expenses increased 15.9% to US$314.5 million from US$271.3 million in the equivalent prior-year period.

Prospects: Our evaluation of Roper Technologies Inc. as of June 19, 2016 is the result of our systematic analysis on three basic characteristics: earnings strength, relative valuation, and recent stock price movement. The company has managed to produce a neutral trend in earnings per share over the past 5 quarters and while recent estimates for the company have remained steady, ROP has posted better than expected results. Based on operating earnings yield, the company is about fairly valued when compared to all of the companies in our coverage universe. Share price changes over the past year indicates that ROP will perform very well over the near term.

Financial Data
(US$ in Thousands)

	3 Mos	12/31/2015	12/31/2014	12/31/2013	12/31/2012	12/31/2011	12/31/2010	12/31/2009
Earnings Per Share	6.80	6.85	6.40	5.37	4.86	4.34	3.34	2.58
Cash Flow Per Share	8.66	9.23	8.41	8.10	6.92	6.27	5.30	4.05
Dividends Per Share	1.050	1.000	0.800	0.495	0.715	0.440	0.380	0.330
Dividend Payout %	15.44	14.60	12.50	9.22	14.71	10.14	11.38	12.79
Income Statement								
Total Revenue	902,423	3,582,395	3,549,494	3,238,128	2,993,489	2,797,089	2,386,112	2,049,668
EBITDA	295,770	1,290,831	1,197,377	1,031,359	908,954	808,778	637,948	501,760
Depn & Amortn	50,908	204,261	197,284	189,190	154,748	140,143	123,021	103,448
Income Before Taxes	217,449	1,002,345	921,456	754,130	686,681	604,987	448,394	339,768
Income Taxes	66,033	306,278	275,423	215,837	203,321	177,740	125,814	100,287
Net Income	151,416	696,067	646,033	538,293	483,360	427,247	322,580	239,481
Average Shares	102,318	101,597	100,884	100,209	99,558	98,386	96,653	92,820
Balance Sheet								
Current Assets	1,432,332	1,618,047	1,512,105	1,373,337	1,245,542	1,115,473	998,091	870,745
Total Assets	10,224,408	10,168,365	8,412,934	8,184,981	7,071,104	5,319,417	5,069,524	4,327,736
Current Liabilities	779,488	720,128	627,947	643,091	1,086,210	554,196	539,645	478,011
Long-Term Obligations	3,105,340	3,264,417	2,203,031	2,453,836	1,503,107	1,015,110	1,247,703	1,040,962
Total Liabilities	4,783,173	4,869,418	3,657,574	3,971,931	3,383,378	2,124,321	2,318,617	1,906,246
Stockholders' Equity	5,441,235	5,298,947	4,755,360	4,213,050	3,687,726	3,195,096	2,750,907	2,421,490
Shares Outstanding	101,200	100,870	100,126	99,312	98,604	96,678	95,088	93,618
Statistical Record								
Return on Assets %	7.21	7.49	7.78	7.06	7.78	8.23	6.87	5.77
Return on Equity %	13.50	13.85	14.41	13.63	14.01	14.37	12.47	10.82
EBITDA Margin %	32.78	36.03	33.73	31.85	30.36	28.91	26.74	24.48
Net Margin %	16.78	19.43	18.20	16.62	16.15	15.27	13.52	11.68
Asset Turnover	0.38	0.39	0.43	0.42	0.48	0.54	0.51	0.49
Current Ratio	1.84	2.25	2.41	2.14	1.15	2.01	1.85	1.82
Debt to Equity	0.57	0.62	0.46	0.58	0.41	0.32	0.45	0.43
Price Range	194.83-152.93	194.83-145.75	160.48-128.99	138.68-111.48	113.14-88.02	88.45-65.91	78.43-50.08	55.04-36.96
P/E Ratio	28.65-22.49	28.44-21.28	25.07-20.15	25.82-20.76	23.28-18.11	20.38-15.19	23.48-14.99	21.33-14.33
Average Yield %	0.61	0.58	0.56	0.39	0.70	0.55	0.62	0.71

Address: 6901 Professional Parkway East, Suite 200, Sarasota, FL 34240
Telephone: 941-556-2601

Web Site: www.roperind.com
Officers: Brian D. Jellison - Chairman, President, Chief Executive Officer John M. Humphrey - Executive Vice President, Vice President, Chief Financial Officer

Auditors: PricewaterhouseCoopers LLP
Transfer Agents: American Stock Transfer & Trust Company, New York, NY

ROWAN COMPANIES PLC

Exchange	Symbol	Price	52Wk Range	Yield	P/E
NYS	RDC	$16.93 (5/31/2016)	22.21-11.23	N/A	22.88

*7 Year Price Score 51.28 *NYSE Composite Index=100 *12 Month Price Score 98.88

TRADING VOLUME (thousand shares)

Interim Earnings (Per Share)

Qtr.	Mar	Jun	Sep	Dec
2013	0.55	0.67	0.42	0.40
2014	0.48	0.26	0.96	(2.63)
2015	0.99	0.68	(1.92)	1.00
2016	0.98	...	...	...

Interim Dividends (Per Share)

Amt	Decl	Ex	Rec	Pay
0.10Q	01/29/2015	02/05/2015	02/09/2015	03/03/2015
0.10Q	05/01/2015	05/08/2015	05/12/2015	05/26/2015
0.10Q	07/31/2015	08/07/2015	08/11/2015	08/25/2015
0.10Q	10/29/2015	11/05/2015	11/09/2015	11/23/2015

Valuation Analysis / Institutional Holding

Forecast EPS	$2.58 (05/20/2016)	No of Institutions	409
Market Cap	$2.1 Billion	Shares	153,998,640
Book Value	$4.9 Billion	% Held	N/A
Price/Book	0.43		
Price/Sales	1.01		

Business Summary: Equipment & Services (MIC: 9.1.3 SIC: 1381 NAIC: 213111)

Rowan Companies is a provider of offshore contract drilling services to the international oil and gas industry. As of Dec 31 2015, Co.'s fleet consisted of 31 mobile offshore drilling units, including 27 self-elevating jack-up rigs and four ultra-deepwater drillships. Co.'s fleet operates worldwide, including the U.S. Gulf of Mexico, the U.K. and Norwegian sectors of the North Sea, the Middle East and Trinidad. Co.'s jack-up rigs are capable of drilling wells to maximum depths ranging from 25,000 feet to 40,000 feet and in maximum water depths ranging from 300 feet to 550 feet, depending on rig size and location.

Recent Developments: For the quarter ended Mar 31 2016, net income decreased 0.7% to US$122.8 million from US$123.7 million in the year-earlier quarter. Revenues were US$500.2 million, down 8.6% from US$547.0 million the year before. Operating income was US$167.4 million versus US$174.5 million in the prior-year quarter, a decrease of 4.1%. Direct operating expenses declined 19.9% to US$204.8 million from US$255.7 million in the comparable period the year before. Indirect operating expenses increased 9.6% to US$128.0 million from US$116.8 million in the equivalent prior-year period.

Prospects: Our evaluation of Rowan Cos. Plc as of June 19, 2016 is the result of our systematic analysis on three basic characteristics: earnings strength, relative valuation, and recent stock price movement. The company has generated a negative trend in earnings per share over the past 5 quarters. However, while recent estimates for the company have been lowered by analysts, RDC has posted better than expected results. Based on operating earnings yield, the company is undervalued when compared to all of the companies in our coverage universe. Share price changes over the past year indicates that RDC will perform poorly over the near term.

Financial Data
(US$ in Thousands)

	3 Mos	12/31/2015	12/31/2014	12/31/2013	12/31/2012	12/31/2011	12/31/2010	12/31/2009
Earnings Per Share	0.74	0.75	(0.93)	2.03	1.46	5.83	2.36	3.24
Cash Flow Per Share	7.30	8.01	3.41	5.05	3.19	0.76	4.34	4.79
Tang Book Value Per Share	39.12	38.24	37.65	39.39	36.48	35.01	29.71	27.32
Dividends Per Share	0.300	0.400	0.300	...	...	...	...	...
Dividend Payout %	40.54	53.33	...	...	...	...	...	...
Income Statement								
Total Revenue	500,180	2,137,018	1,824,383	1,579,284	1,392,607	939,229	1,819,207	1,770,180
EBITDA	264,241	694,633	155,107	600,463	481,342	354,293	588,951	679,324
Depn & Amortn	98,852	392,735	322,641	271,008	247,900	204,872	186,563	171,445
Income Before Taxes	126,909	157,710	(269,607)	261,239	183,470	130,080	379,017	501,091
Income Taxes	4,110	64,399	(150,732)	8,663	(19,829)	(5,659)	99,022	133,587
Net Income	122,799	93,311	(114,852)	252,576	180,602	736,841	279,995	367,504
Average Shares	125,802	125,203	124,067	124,468	123,872	126,393	118,818	113,584
Balance Sheet								
Current Assets	1,041,844	921,275	941,096	1,528,878	1,552,550	821,715	1,324,769	1,549,797
Total Assets	8,392,127	8,347,267	8,411,192	7,975,761	7,699,487	6,597,845	6,217,457	5,210,694
Current Liabilities	299,257	328,671	333,221	354,584	294,094	348,371	529,230	568,272
Long-Term Obligations	2,655,043	2,692,419	2,807,324	2,008,700	2,009,598	1,089,335	1,133,745	787,490
Total Liabilities	3,492,094	3,574,808	3,719,793	3,082,000	3,167,763	2,271,858	2,465,147	2,100,324
Stockholders' Equity	4,900,033	4,772,459	4,691,399	4,893,761	4,531,724	4,325,987	3,752,310	3,110,370
Shares Outstanding	125,245	124,817	124,593	124,235	124,211	123,581	126,294	113,833
Statistical Record								
Return on Assets %	1.09	1.11	N.M.	3.22	2.52	11.50	4.90	7.53
Return on Equity %	1.90	1.97	N.M.	5.36	4.07	18.24	8.16	12.74
EBITDA Margin %	52.83	32.50	8.50	38.02	34.56	37.72	32.37	38.38
Net Margin %	24.55	4.37	N.M.	15.99	12.97	78.45	15.39	20.76
Asset Turnover	0.25	0.26	0.22	0.20	0.19	0.15	0.32	0.36
Current Ratio	3.48	2.80	2.82	4.31	5.28	2.36	2.50	2.73
Debt to Equity	0.54	0.56	0.60	0.41	0.44	0.25	0.30	0.25
Price Range	23.93-11.23	24.88-15.15	35.36-19.81	38.30-30.50	38.78-28.99	44.19-29.12	34.91-21.48	27.31-10.33
P/E Ratio	32.34-15.18	33.17-20.20	...	18.87-15.02	26.56-19.86	7.58-4.99	14.79-9.10	8.43-3.19
Average Yield %	1.67	2.02	1.03	...	...	...	...	...

Address: 2800 Post Oak Boulevard, Suite 5450, Houston, TX 77056-6189 Telephone: 713-621-7800 Fax: 713-960-7660	Web Site: www.rowancompanies.com Officers: Thomas Peter Burke - President, Chief Executive Officer, Chief Operating Officer Stephen M. Butz - Executive Vice President, Chief Financial Officer, Treasurer	Auditors: Deloitte & Touche LLP Investor Contact: 713-960-7517 Transfer Agents: Computershare Trust Company, N.A., Providence

ROYAL CARIBBEAN CRUISES LTD

Exchange	Symbol	Price	52Wk Range	Yield	P/E
NYS	RCL	$77.39 (5/31/2016)	102.73-66.29	1.94	23.67

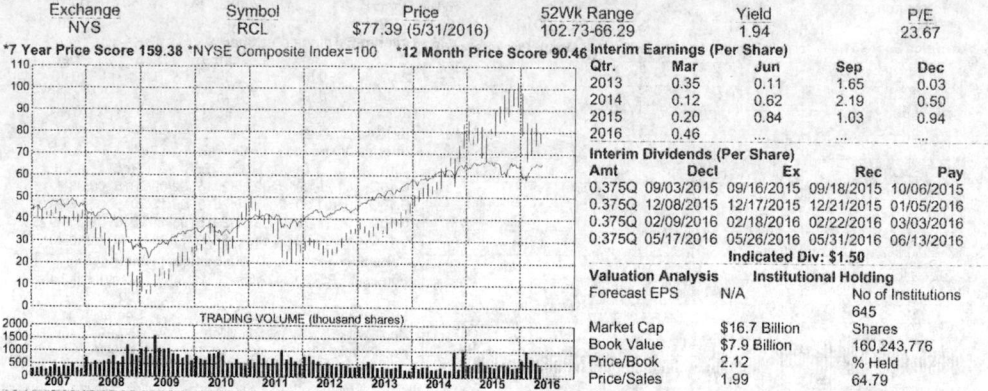

*7 Year Price Score 159.38 *NYSE Composite Index=100   *12 Month Price Score 90.46

Interim Earnings (Per Share)

Qtr.	Mar	Jun	Sep	Dec
2013	0.35	0.11	1.65	0.03
2014	0.12	0.62	2.19	0.50
2015	0.20	0.84	1.03	0.94
2016	0.46			

Interim Dividends (Per Share)

Amt	Decl	Ex	Rec	Pay
0.375Q	09/03/2015	09/16/2015	09/18/2015	10/06/2015
0.375Q	12/08/2015	12/17/2015	12/21/2015	01/05/2016
0.375Q	02/09/2016	02/18/2016	02/22/2016	03/03/2016
0.375Q	05/17/2016	05/26/2016	05/31/2016	06/13/2016

Indicated Div: $1.50

Valuation Analysis

		Institutional Holding	
Forecast EPS	N/A	No of Institutions	645
Market Cap	$16.7 Billion	Shares	160,243,776
Book Value	$7.9 Billion	% Held	64.79
Price/Book	2.12		
Price/Sales	1.99		

Business Summary: Hotels, Restaurants & Travel (MIC: 2.2.1 SIC: 4489 NAIC: 487210)

Royal Caribbean Cruises is a cruise company. Co. owns Royal Caribbean International, Celebrity Cruises, Pullmantur, Azamara Club Cruises and CDF Croisieres de France and interest in TUI Cruises. These six brands operated a combined 44 ships with an aggregate capacity of approximately 110,900 berths as of Dec 31 2015. Co.'s cruise brands provide a range of onboard services, amenities and activities, including gaming, the sale of alcoholic and other beverages, internet and other telecommunication services, gift shop items, shore excursions, photography, spa/salon and fitness services, art auctions, catalogue gifts for guests and a range of specialty restaurants and dining options.

Recent Developments: For the quarter ended Mar 31 2016, net income increased 119.2% to US$99.1 million from US$45.2 million in the year-earlier quarter. Revenues were US$1.92 billion, up 5.6% from US$1.82 billion the year before. Operating income was US$163.1 million versus US$105.7 million in the prior-year quarter, an increase of 54.4%. Direct operating expenses rose 1.6% to US$1.24 billion from US$1.22 billion in the comparable period the year before. Indirect operating expenses increased 5.3% to US$513.1 million from US$487.3 million in the equivalent prior-year period.

Prospects: Our evaluation of Royal Caribbean Cruises Ltd. as of Aug. 2, 2015 is the result of our systematic analysis on three basic characteristics: earnings strength, relative valuation, and recent stock price movement. The company has generated a negative trend in earnings per share over the past 5 quarters and while recent estimates for the company have been mixed, RCL has posted better than expected results. Based on operating earnings yield, the company is about fairly valued when compared to all of the companies in our coverage universe. Share price changes over the past year indicates that RCL will perform very poorly over the near term.

Financial Data
(US$ in Thousands)

	3 Mos	12/31/2015	12/31/2014	12/31/2013	12/31/2012	12/31/2011	12/31/2010	12/31/2009
Earnings Per Share	3.27	3.02	3.43	2.14	0.08	2.77	2.51	0.75
Cash Flow Per Share	9.21	8.87	7.87	6.43	6.32	6.71	7.73	3.95
Tang Book Value Per Share	35.21	35.67	35.86	37.96	36.00	35.30	33.27	31.35
Dividends Per Share	1.425	1.350	1.100	0.740	0.440	0.200	...	...
Dividend Payout %	43.58	44.70	32.07	34.58	550.00	7.22	...	...
Income Statement								
Total Revenue	1,917,795	8,299,074	8,073,855	7,959,894	7,688,024	7,537,263	6,752,504	5,889,826
EBITDA	372,630	1,758,491	1,784,546	1,546,927	1,083,234	1,666,945	1,521,333	1,023,631
Depn & Amortn	210,764	827,008	772,445	754,711	730,493	702,426	643,716	568,214
Income Before Taxes	99,140	665,783	764,146	473,692	18,287	607,421	547,467	162,421
Net Income	99,140	665,783	764,146	473,692	18,287	607,421	547,467	162,421
Average Shares	217,869	220,689	223,044	220,941	219,457	219,229	217,711	215,295
Balance Sheet								
Current Assets	892,286	837,022	801,083	956,374	888,060	969,288	1,015,071	1,026,391
Total Assets	20,963,413	20,921,855	20,713,190	20,072,947	19,827,930	19,804,405	19,694,904	18,233,494
Current Liabilities	4,397,944	4,292,827	3,849,247	4,267,010	4,066,151	3,067,642	3,444,498	2,749,030
Long-Term Obligations	7,806,690	7,767,378	7,644,318	6,511,426	6,970,464	7,856,962	7,951,187	7,663,555
Total Liabilities	13,075,644	12,858,816	12,428,831	11,264,682	11,519,181	11,396,582	11,752,402	10,733,777
Stockholders' Equity	7,887,769	8,063,039	8,284,359	8,808,265	8,308,749	8,407,823	7,942,502	7,499,717
Shares Outstanding	215,846	217,993	219,297	220,473	218,771	217,057	215,903	213,949
Statistical Record								
Return on Assets %	3.44	3.20	3.75	2.37	0.09	3.08	2.89	0.94
Return on Equity %	9.07	8.15	8.94	5.53	0.22	7.43	7.09	2.27
EBITDA Margin %	19.43	21.19	22.10	19.43	14.09	22.12	22.53	17.38
Net Margin %	5.17	8.02	9.46	5.95	0.24	8.06	8.11	2.76
Asset Turnover	0.40	0.40	0.40	0.40	0.39	0.38	0.36	0.34
Current Ratio	0.20	0.19	0.21	0.22	0.22	0.32	0.29	0.37
Debt to Equity	0.99	0.96	0.92	0.74	0.84	0.93	1.00	1.02
Price Range	102.73-66.29	102.73-66.69	83.56-46.06	47.44-31.82	35.53-22.46	49.96-20.01	47.00-22.77	26.89-5.50
P/E Ratio	31.42-20.27	34.02-22.08	24.36-13.43	22.17-14.87	444.13-280.75	18.04-7.22	18.73-9.07	35.85-7.33
Average Yield %	1.69	1.59	1.86	1.98	1.54	0.58	...	...

Address: 1050 Caribbean Way, Miami, FL 33132 Telephone: 305-539-6000	Web Site: www.royalcaribbean.com Officers: Richard D. Fain - Chairman, Chief Executive Officer Adam M. Goldstein - President, Chief Operating Officer, Division Officer	Auditors: PricewaterhouseCoopers LLP Investor Contact: 305-982-2625 Transfer Agents: American Stock Transfer and Trust Company, Brooklyn, NY

RPC, INC.

Exchange	Symbol	Price	52Wk Range	Yield	P/E
NYS	RES	$14.75 (5/31/2016)	15.35-8.54	N/A	N/A

*7 Year Price Score 84.17 ***NYSE Composite Index=100** ***12 Month Price Score 112.20**

Interim Earnings (Per Share)

Qtr.	Mar	Jun	Sep	Dec
2013	0.16	0.19	0.25	0 17
2014	0.18	0.29	0.30	0.37
2015	0.04	(0.16)	(0.16)	(0.18)
2016	(0.15)	...	...	...

Interim Dividends (Per Share)

Amt	Decl	Ex	Rec	Pay
0.105Q	07/23/2014	08/06/2014	08/08/2014	09/10/2014
0.105Q	10/29/2014	11/06/2014	11/10/2014	12/10/2014
0.105Q	01/28/2015	02/06/2015	02/10/2015	03/10/2015
0.05Q	04/29/2015	05/07/2015	05/11/2015	06/10/2015

Valuation Analysis   Institutional Holding

Forecast EPS	$-0.78	No of Institutions
	(05/20/2016)	258
Market Cap	$3.2 Billion	Shares
Book Value	$919.8 Million	80,249,216
Price/Book	3.49	% Held
Price/Sales	3.07	21.16

Business Summary: Equipment & Services (MIC: 9.1.3 SIC: 1389 NAIC: 213112)

RPC is a holding company for several oilfield services companies. Co. provides a range of oilfield services and equipment to independent and major oil and gas companies engaged in the exploration, production and development of oil and gas properties throughout the U.S., including the southwest, mid-continent, Gulf of Mexico, Rocky Mountain and Appalachian regions, and in selected international markets. The services and equipment provided include, among others, pressure pumping services, downhole tool services, coiled tubing services, snubbing services (hydraulic workover services), nitrogen services, the rental of drill pipe and other oilfield equipment, and well control.

Recent Developments: For the quarter ended Mar 31 2016, net loss amounted to US$32.5 million versus net income of US$7.5 million in the year-earlier quarter. Revenues were US$189.1 million, down 53.5% from US$406.3 million the year before. Operating loss was US$75.1 million versus an income of US$6.4 million in the prior-year quarter. Direct operating expenses declined 44.9% to US$161.3 million from US$292.4 million in the comparable period the year before. Indirect operating expenses decreased 4.2% to US$102.9 million from US$107.5 million in the equivalent prior-year period.

Prospects: Our evaluation of RPC Inc. as of June 19, 2016 is the result of our systematic analysis on three basic characteristics: earnings strength, relative valuation, and recent stock price movement. The company has enjoyed a very positive trend in earnings per share over the past 5 quarters. Because the company lacks sufficient analyst estimate data, we place greater weight on the historical EPS trend as the measure of earnings strength. Based on operating earnings yield, the company is overvalued when compared to all of the companies in our coverage universe. Share price changes over the past year indicates that RES will perform poorly over the near term.

Financial Data

(US$ in Thousands)	3 Mos	12/31/2015	12/31/2014	12/31/2013	12/31/2012	12/31/2011	12/31/2010	12/31/2009
Earnings Per Share	(0.65)	(0.47)	1.14	0.77	1.27	1.35	0.67	(0.11)
Cash Flow Per Share	1.53	2.22	1.50	1.70	2.59	1.77	0.78	0.78
Tang Book Value Per Share	4.08	4.24	4.83	4.28	3.98	3.34	2.32	1.74
Dividends Per Share	0.050	0.155	0.420	0.400	0.520	0.213	0.093	0.098
Dividend Payout %	...	...	36.84	51.95	40.94	15.84	14.00	...
Income Statement								
Total Revenue	189,095	1,263,840	2,337,413	1,861,489	1,945,023	1,809,807	1,096,384	587,863
EBITDA	(13,327)	123,308	634,198	493,073	659,465	662,150	373,548	99,130
Depn & Amortn	61,418	274,400	233,400	215,400	214,900	179,900	133,400	130,600
Income Before Taxes	(75,047)	(153,041)	399,386	276,270	442,619	478,815	237,532	(33,499)
Income Taxes	(42,536)	(53,480)	154,193	109,375	168,183	182,434	90,790	(10,754)
Net Income	(32,511)	(99,561)	245,193	166,895	274,436	296,381	146,742	(22,745)
Average Shares	214,111	213,632	215,889	216,733	216,796	220,249	219,805	216,686
Balance Sheet								
Current Assets	463,462	492,208	851,628	604,925	567,827	626,555	398,678	219,454
Total Assets	1,155,196	1,237,094	1,759,358	1,383,860	1,367,163	1,338,211	887,871	649,043
Current Liabilities	81,901	107,464	239,012	168,052	164,511	179,466	117,504	67,773
Long-Term Obligations	...	...	224,500	53,300	107,000	203,300	121,250	90,300
Total Liabilities	235,373	284,813	680,976	415,158	467,931	575,619	348,976	239,320
Stockholders' Equity	919,823	952,281	1,078,382	968,702	899,232	762,592	538,895	409,723
Shares Outstanding	217,607	216,991	216,539	218,985	220,144	221,187	222,263	221,320
Statistical Record								
Return on Assets %	N.M.	N.M.	15.60	12.13	20.23	26.63	19.10	N.M.
Return on Equity %	N.M.	N.M.	23.96	17.87	32.94	45.54	30.94	N.M.
EBITDA Margin %	N.M.	9.76	27.13	26.49	33.91	36.59	34.07	16.86
Net Margin %	N.M.	N.M.	10.49	8.97	14.11	16.38	13.38	N.M.
Asset Turnover	0.77	0.84	1.49	1.35	1.43	1.63	1.43	0.82
Current Ratio	5.66	4.58	3.56	3.60	3.45	3.49	3.39	3.24
Debt to Equity	...	...	0.21	0.06	0.12	0.27	0.22	0.22
Price Range	16.27-8.54	16.27-8.54	24.91-11.86	18.56-12.24	14.45-8.96	18.03-10.08	14.41-4.62	5.22-2.35
P/E Ratio	...	21.85-10.40	24.10-15.90	11.38-7.06	13.36-7.47	21.51-6.90	...	
Average Yield %	0.39	1.22	2.15	2.62	4.56	1.51	1.23	2.46

Address: 2801 Buford Highway, Suite 520, Atlanta, GA 30329
Telephone: 404-321-2140

Web Site: www.rpc.net
Officers: R. Randall Rollins - Chairman Richard A. Hubbell - President, Chief Executive Officer

Auditors: Grant Thornton LLP
Investor Contact: 404-321-2172
Transfer Agents: American Stock Transfer & Trust Company, Brooklyn, NY

RPM INTERNATIONAL INC (DE)

Exchange	Symbol	Price	52Wk Range	Yield	P/E	Div Achiever
NYS	RPM	$50.19 (5/31/2016)	51.45-37.38	2.19	20.57	42 Years

*7 Year Price Score 121.78 *NYSE Composite Index=100 *12 Month Price Score 108.44

Interim Earnings (Per Share)

Qtr.	Aug	Nov	Feb	May
2012-13	0.26	0.31	(0.33)	0.49
2013-14	0.77	0.48	0.12	0.81
2014-15	0.73	0.52	(0.44)	0.94
2015-16	0.74	0.62	0.14	

Interim Dividends (Per Share)

Amt	Decl	Ex	Rec	Pay
0.26Q	07/02/2015	07/09/2015	07/13/2015	07/31/2015
0.275Q	10/08/2015	10/15/2015	10/19/2015	10/30/2015
0.275Q	01/05/2016	01/13/2016	01/15/2016	01/29/2016
0.275Q	04/08/2016	04/14/2016	04/18/2016	04/29/2016

Indicated Div: $1.10 (Div. Reinv. Plan)

Valuation Analysis

		Institutional Holding	
Forecast EPS	$2.50	No of Institutions	
	(05/20/2016)	525	
Market Cap	$6.7 Billion	Shares	
Book Value	$1.2 Billion	107,823,888	
Price/Book	5.39	% Held	
Price/Sales	1.40	71.01	

Business Summary: Specialty Chemicals (MIC: 8.3.2 SIC: 2851 NAIC: 325510)

RPM International, through its subsidiaries, manufactures, markets and sells chemical product lines including paints, protective coatings, roofing systems, sealants and adhesives, focusing on the maintenance and improvement needs of both the industrial and consumer markets. Co.'sfamily of products includes those marketed under brand names such as API, Carboline, CAVE, DAP, Day-Glo, Dri-Eaz, Dryvit, Euclid, EUCO, Fibergrate, Flecto, Flowcrete, Grupo PV, Hummervoll, illbruck, Mohawk, Rust-Oleum, Stonhard, TCI, Toxement, Tremco, Tuf-Strand, Universal Sealants, Viapol, Watco and Zinsser. As of May 31 2015, Co.'s subsidiaries marketed products in approximately 170 countries and territories.

Recent Developments: For the quarter ended Feb 29 2016, net income amounted to US$19.3 million versus a net loss of US$79.0 million in the year-earlier quarter. Revenues were US$988.6 million, up 4.5% from US$946.4 million the year before. Direct operating expenses rose 1.6% to US$575.6 million from US$566.6 million in the comparable period the year before. Indirect operating expenses increased 7.1% to US$370.9 million from US$346.2 million in the equivalent prior-year period.

Prospects: Our evaluation of RPM Inc. as of June 19, 2016 is the result of our systematic analysis on three basic characteristics: earnings strength, relative valuation, and recent stock price movement. The company has managed to produce a neutral trend in earnings per share over the past 5 quarters and while recent estimates for the company have remained steady, RPM has posted results that fell short of analysts expectations. Based on operating earnings yield, the company is about fairly valued when compared to all of the companies in our coverage universe. Share price changes over the past year indicates that RPM will perform in line with the market over the near term.

Financial Data
(US$ in Thousands)

	9 Mos	6 Mos	3 Mos	05/31/2015	05/31/2014	05/31/2013	05/31/2012	05/31/2011
Earnings Per Share	2.44	1.86	1.76	1.78	2.18	0.74	1.65	1.45
Cash Flow Per Share	4.11	3.42	3.55	2.54	2.15	2.86	2.30	1.87
Tang Book Value Per Share	N.M.	N.M.	N.M.	N.M.	N.M.	N.M.	N.M.	0.91
Dividends Per Share	1.070	1.055	1.040	1.020	0.945	0.890	0.855	0.835
Dividend Payout %	43.85	56.72	59.09	57.30	43.35	120.27	51.82	57.59
Income Statement								
Total Revenue	3,387,065	2,398,510	1,242,526	4,594,550	4,376,353	4,078,655	3,777,416	3,381,841
EBITDA	429,379	359,520	190,685	625,629	582,966	378,009	460,563	427,807
Depn & Amortn	83,131	55,653	27,867	95,088	86,743	83,415	73,339	72,385
Income Before Taxes	282,772	261,511	141,722	451,230	421,599	221,562	320,210	295,053
Income Taxes	80,564	77,951	41,839	224,925	118,503	67,040	94,526	91,885
Net Income	201,830	183,248	99,815	239,484	291,660	98,603	215,936	189,058
Average Shares	129,068	136,734	137,307	134,893	132,288	128,956	128,717	128,066
Balance Sheet								
Current Assets	1,930,308	2,011,415	2,125,507	2,099,846	2,062,295	1,886,272	1,811,337	1,867,970
Total Assets	4,448,089	4,518,232	4,661,407	4,694,240	4,378,365	4,115,526	3,560,020	3,515,029
Current Liabilities	782,403	738,668	812,816	903,236	937,086	928,030	759,792	735,289
Long-Term Obligations	1,749,823	1,673,471	1,730,613	1,654,037	1,345,965	1,369,176	1,112,952	1,106,304
Total Liabilities	3,210,057	3,227,971	3,367,005	3,402,848	2,995,521	2,914,668	2,376,364	2,251,865
Stockholders' Equity	1,238,032	1,290,261	1,294,402	1,291,392	1,382,844	1,200,858	1,183,656	1,263,164
Shares Outstanding	132,846	133,318	133,146	133,203	133,273	132,596	131,555	130,580
Statistical Record								
Return on Assets %	7.31	5.83	5.33	5.28	6.87	2.57	6.09	5.80
Return on Equity %	26.71	18.94	17.59	17.91	22.58	8.27	17.60	16.14
EBITDA Margin %	12.68	14.99	15.35	13.62	13.32	9.27	12.19	12.65
Net Margin %	5.96	7.64	8.03	5.21	6.66	2.42	5.72	5.59
Asset Turnover	1.06	1.08	1.03	1.01	1.03	1.06	1.06	1.04
Current Ratio	2.47	2.72	2.61	2.32	2.20	2.03	2.38	2.54
Debt to Equity	1.41	1.30	1.34	1.28	0.97	1.14	0.94	0.88
Price Range	51.21-37.38	51.82-41.43	51.82-40.22	51.82-40.22	44.14-31.20	34.03-25.07	26.93-17.40	25.22-16.37
P/E Ratio	20.99-15.32	27.86-22.27	29.44-22.85	29.11-22.60	20.25-14.31	45.99-33.88	16.32-10.55	17.39-11.29
Average Yield %	2.34	2.22	2.12	2.18	2.46	3.06	3.72	3.98

Address: P.O. Box 777, 2628 Pearl Road, Medina, OH 44258 Telephone: 330-273-5090 Fax: 330-225-8743	Web Site: www.rpminc.com Officers: Frank C. Sullivan - Chairman, Chief Executive Officer Ronald A. Rice - President, Chief Operating Officer	Auditors: Deloitte & Touche LLP Investor Contact: 800-776-4488 Transfer Agents: Wells Fargo Shareowner Services, St. Paul, MN

RYDER SYSTEM, INC.

Exchange	Symbol	Price	52Wk Range	Yield	P/E	Div Achiever
NYS	R	$69.62 (5/31/2016)	95.00-47.79	2.36	12.11	11 Years

*7 Year Price Score 102.15 *NYSE Composite Index=100 *12 Month Price Score 93.39

Interim Earnings (Per Share)

Qtr.	Mar	Jun	Sep	Dec
2013	0.77	1.19	1.35	1.22
2014	0.90	1.41	1.57	0.22
2015	0.99	1.59	1.69	1.43
2016	1.04	...	...	...

Interim Dividends (Per Share)

Amt	Decl	Ex	Rec	Pay
0.41Q	07/10/2015	08/20/2015	08/24/2015	09/18/2015
0.41Q	10/02/2015	11/19/2015	11/23/2015	12/18/2015
0.41Q	02/10/2016	02/18/2016	02/22/2016	03/18/2016
0.41Q	05/06/2016	05/19/2016	05/23/2016	06/17/2016

Indicated Div: $1.64 (Div. Reinv. Plan)

Valuation Analysis

		Institutional Holding	
Forecast EPS	$6.15		No of Institutions
	(05/16/2016)		505
Market Cap	$3.7 Billion		Shares
Book Value	$2.0 Billion		61,772,900
Price/Book	1.83		% Held
Price/Sales	0.56		88.27

TRADING VOLUME (thousand shares)

Business Summary: Trucking (MIC: 7.4.1 SIC: 7513 NAIC: 532120)

Ryder System is engaged in transportation and supply chain management solutions. Co. operates in three business segments: Fleet Management Solutions, which provides service leasing, commercial rental, contract maintenance, and contract-related maintenance of trucks, tractors and trailers to customers principally in the U.S., Canada and the U.K.; Dedicated Transportation Solutions, which provides vehicles and drivers as part of a dedicated transportation solution in the U.S.; and Supply Chain Solutions, which provides supply chain solutions including distribution and transportation services in North America and Asia.

Recent Developments: For the quarter ended Mar 31 2016, income from continuing operations increased 5.4% to US$56.2 million from US$53.3 million in the year-earlier quarter. Net income increased 5.7% to US$55.8 million from US$52.8 million in the year-earlier quarter. Revenues were US$1.63 billion, up 4.0% from US$1.57 billion the year before. Direct operating expenses rose 3.7% to US$1.28 billion from US$1.24 billion in the comparable period the year before. Indirect operating expenses increased 4.8% to US$257.9 million from US$245.9 million in the equivalent prior-year period.

Prospects: Our evaluation of Ryder System Inc. as of June 19, 2016 is the result of our systematic analysis on three basic characteristics: earnings strength, relative valuation, and recent stock price movement. The company has managed to produce a neutral trend in earnings per share over the past 5 quarters. However, while recent estimates for the company have been mixed, R has posted better than expected results. Based on operating earnings yield, the company is undervalued when compared to all of the companies in our coverage universe. Share price changes over the past year indicates that R will perform poorly over the near term.

Financial Data

(US$ in Thousands)	3 Mos	12/31/2015	12/31/2014	12/31/2013	12/31/2012	12/31/2011	12/31/2010	12/31/2009
Earnings Per Share	5.75	5.71	4.11	4.53	4.09	3.28	2.25	1.11
Cash Flow Per Share	28.81	27.30	26.08	23.70	22.42	20.63	19.88	17.90
Tang Book Value Per Share	29.84	28.84	25.64	27.01	19.52	16.74	19.08	21.93
Dividends Per Share	1.600	1.560	1.420	1.300	1.200	1.120	1.040	0.960
Dividend Payout %	27.83	27.32	34.55	28.70	29.34	34.15	46.22	86.49
Income Statement								
Total Revenue	1,629,672	6,571,893	6,638,774	6,419,285	6,256,967	6,050,534	5,136,435	4,887,254
EBITDA	426,825	703,649	1,520,883	1,463,232	1,383,351	1,284,813	1,150,140	1,169,327
Depn & Amortn	300,228	84,000	1,040,259	957,141	939,677	872,262	833,841	881,216
Income Before Taxes	88,708	469,215	338,549	368,895	303,117	279,387	186,305	143,769
Income Taxes	32,523	163,226	118,090	125,699	102,218	108,019	61,697	53,652
Net Income	55,794	304,768	218,575	237,792	209,979	169,777	118,170	61,945
Average Shares	53,363	53,260	53,036	52,071	50,740	50,878	51,884	55,094
Balance Sheet								
Current Assets	1,094,546	1,098,302	1,076,197	1,062,493	1,040,237	1,088,173	1,023,301	880,373
Total Assets	11,054,530	10,967,809	9,675,986	9,103,782	8,318,979	7,617,835	6,652,374	6,259,830
Current Liabilities	1,593,540	1,680,255	1,093,591	1,231,139	1,272,665	1,173,823	1,131,519	850,274
Long-Term Obligations	4,987,217	4,883,326	4,500,275	3,929,987	3,452,821	3,107,779	2,326,878	2,265,074
Total Liabilities	9,009,212	8,980,698	7,856,512	7,207,068	6,851,492	6,299,682	5,248,061	4,832,835
Stockholders' Equity	2,045,318	1,987,111	1,819,474	1,896,714	1,467,487	1,318,153	1,404,313	1,426,995
Shares Outstanding	53,703	53,490	53,039	53,335	51,371	51,143	51,174	53,419
Statistical Record								
Return on Assets %	2.94	2.95	2.33	2.73	2.63	2.38	1.83	0.96
Return on Equity %	15.96	16.01	11.76	14.14	15.03	12.47	8.35	4.47
EBITDA Margin %	26.19	10.71	22.91	22.79	22.11	21.23	22.39	23.93
Net Margin %	3.42	4.64	3.29	3.70	3.36	2.81	2.30	1.27
Asset Turnover	0.63	0.64	0.71	0.74	0.78	0.85	0.80	0.75
Current Ratio	0.69	0.65	0.98	0.86	0.82	0.93	0.90	1.04
Debt to Equity	2.44	2.46	2.47	2.07	2.35	2.36	1.66	1.59
Price Range	99.58-47.79	99.58-54.03	95.52-68.76	73.78-49.93	57.18-33.40	59.35-35.45	52.64-32.55	46.25-19.27
P/E Ratio	17.32-8.31	17.44-9.46	23.24-16.73	16.29-11.02	13.98-8.17	18.09-10.81	23.40-14.47	41.67-17.36
Average Yield %	2.11	1.85	1.69	2.14	2.63	2.25	2.47	2.83

Address: 11690 N.W. 105th Street, Miami, FL 33178 **Telephone:** 305-500-3726	**Web Site:** www.ryder.com **Officers:** Robert E. Sanchez - Chairman, President, Chief Executive Officer, Chief Operating Officer, Division Officer Art A. Garcia - Executive Vice President, Chief Financial Officer	**Auditors:** PricewaterhouseCoopers LLP **Investor Contact:** 305-500-4053 **Transfer Agents:** Wells Fargo Bank, N.A., St. Paul, MN

S&P GLOBAL INC

Exchange	Symbol	Price	52Wk Range	Yield	P/E	Div Achiever
NYS	SPGI	$111.81 (5/31/2016)	111.81-80.77	1.29	26.56	42 Years

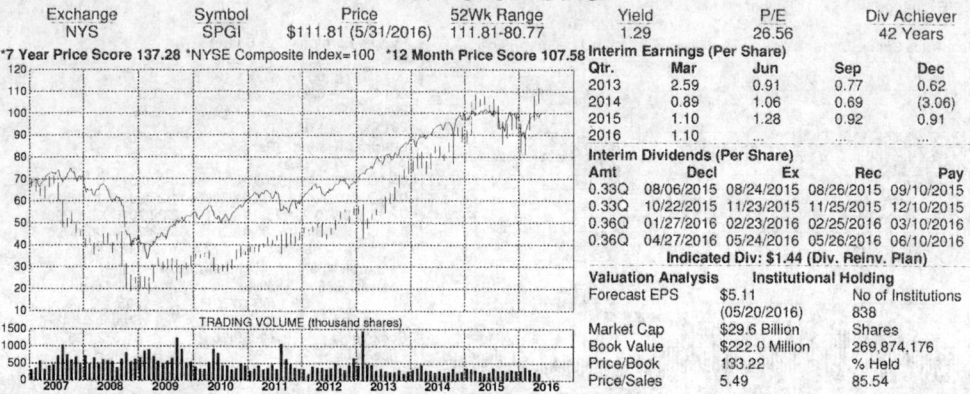

*7 Year Price Score 137.28 ***NYSE Composite Index=100** ***12 Month Price Score 107.58**

Interim Earnings (Per Share)

Qtr.	Mar	Jun	Sep	Dec
2013	2.59	0.91	0.77	0.62
2014	0.89	1.06	0.69	(3.06)
2015	1.10	1.28	0.92	0.91
2016	1.10	...	...	...

Interim Dividends (Per Share)

Amt	Decl	Ex	Rec	Pay
0.33Q	08/06/2015	08/24/2015	08/26/2015	09/10/2015
0.33Q	10/22/2015	11/23/2015	11/25/2015	12/10/2015
0.36Q	01/27/2016	02/23/2016	02/25/2016	03/10/2016
0.36Q	04/27/2016	05/24/2016	05/26/2016	06/10/2016

Indicated Div: $1.44 (Div. Reinv. Plan)

Valuation Analysis — **Institutional Holding**

Forecast EPS	$5.11	No of Institutions
	(05/20/2016)	838
Market Cap	$29.6 Billion	Shares
Book Value	$222.0 Million	269,874,176
Price/Book	133.22	% Held
Price/Sales	5.49	85.54

Business Summary: Credit & Lending (MIC: 5.4.1 SIC: 7323 NAIC: 561450)

S&P Global is a benchmarks and ratings, analytics, data and research provider serving the global capital, commodities and commercial markets. Co.'s operations consist of four segments: Standard & Poor's Ratings, which is a provider of credit ratings, research and analytics; S&P Capital IQ and SNL, which is a provider of financial research and analytical tools for capital market participants; S&P Dow Jones Indices, which is an index provider that maintains a variety of indices; and Commodities & Commercial, which focuses in commercial and commodities markets that deliver their customers access to information, data, analytic services and pricing benchmarks.

Recent Developments: For the quarter ended Mar 31 2016, net income decreased 1.8% to US$323.0 million from US$329.0 million in the year-earlier quarter. Revenues were US$1.34 billion, up 5.3% from US$1.27 billion the year before. Operating income was US$512.0 million versus US$501.0 million in the prior-year quarter, an increase of 2.2%. Direct operating expenses rose 11.5% to US$457.0 million from US$410.0 million in the comparable period the year before. Indirect operating expenses increased 2.8% to US$372.0 million from US$362.0 million in the equivalent prior-year period.

Prospects: Our evaluation of S&P Global Inc. as of June 19, 2016 is the result of our systematic analysis on three basic characteristics: earnings strength, relative valuation, and recent stock price movement. The company has managed to produce a neutral trend in earnings per share over the past 5 quarters and while recent estimates for the company have been mixed, SPGI has posted better than expected results. Based on operating earnings yield, the company is about fairly valued when compared to all of the companies in our coverage universe. Share price changes over the past year indicates that SPGI will perform in line with the market over the near term.

Financial Data

(US$ in Thousands)	3 Mos	12/31/2015	12/31/2014	12/31/2013	12/31/2012	12/31/2011	12/31/2010	12/31/2009
Earnings Per Share	4.21	4.21	(0.42)	4.91	1.53	3.00	2.65	2.33
Cash Flow Per Share	6.33	0.72	4.45	2.97	2.67	4.51	4.71	4.23
Dividends Per Share	1.350	1.320	1.200	1.120	1.020	1.000	0.940	0.900
Dividend Payout %	32.07	31.35	...	22.81	66.67	33.33	35.47	38.63
Income Statement								
Total Revenue	1,341,000	5,313,000	5,051,000	4,875,000	4,450,000	6,246,000	6,168,331	5,951,782
EBITDA	554,000	2,074,000	247,000	1,542,000	1,352,000	1,609,000	1,592,146	1,421,220
Depn & Amortn	42,000	157,000	134,000	137,000	141,000	187,000	171,087	165,484
Income Before Taxes	472,000	1,815,000	54,000	1,346,000	1,130,000	1,347,000	1,339,416	1,178,869
Income Taxes	149,000	547,000	245,000	443,000	404,000	489,000	487,547	429,108
Net Income	294,000	1,156,000	(115,000)	1,376,000	437,000	911,000	828,063	730,502
Average Shares	267,200	274,600	271,500	279,800	284,600	304,000	312,220	313,296
Balance Sheet								
Current Assets	3,448,000	3,296,000	3,966,000	2,936,000	3,899,000	2,679,000	3,294,611	2,936,396
Total Assets	8,261,000	8,183,000	6,771,000	6,061,000	7,052,000	6,427,000	7,046,561	6,475,250
Current Liabilities	2,982,000	2,908,000	3,967,000	2,372,000	3,667,000	3,130,000	2,680,874	2,451,954
Long-Term Obligations	3,469,000	3,468,000	799,000	799,000	799,000	798,000	1,197,965	1,197,791
Total Liabilities	8,039,000	7,989,000	6,283,000	4,760,000	6,285,000	4,919,000	4,836,265	4,627,963
Stockholders' Equity	222,000	194,000	488,000	1,301,000	767,000	1,508,000	2,210,296	1,847,287
Shares Outstanding	264,500	265,200	272,000	271,000	279,000	276,000	307,621	315,340
Statistical Record								
Return on Assets %	16.72	15.46	N.M.	20.99	6.47	13.52	12.25	11.64
Return on Equity %	301.18	339.00	N.M.	133.08	38.31	49.00	40.82	46.68
EBITDA Margin %	41.31	39.04	4.89	31.63	30.38	25.76	25.81	23.88
Net Margin %	21.92	21.76	N.M.	28.23	9.82	14.59	13.42	12.27
Asset Turnover	0.79	0.71	0.79	0.74	0.66	0.93	0.91	0.95
Current Ratio	1.16	1.13	1.00	1.24	1.06	0.86	1.23	1.20
Debt to Equity	15.63	17.88	1.64	0.61	1.04	0.53	0.54	0.65
Price Range	107.57-80.77	108.59-85.40	93.71-71.98	78.20-42.67	56.65-42.40	45.57-35.35	39.31-27.02	34.82-17.39
P/E Ratio	25.55-19.19	25.79-20.29	...	15.93-8.69	37.03-27.71	15.19-11.78	14.83-10.20	14.94-7.46
Average Yield %	1.39	1.33	1.47	1.89	2.08	2.45	2.86	3.22

Address: 55 Water Street, New York, NY 10041
Telephone: 212-438-1000

Web Site: www.spglobal.com
Officers: Douglas L. Peterson - President, Chief Executive Officer, Division Officer D. Edward Smyth - Executive Vice President, Executive Advisor

Auditors: Ernst & Young LLP
Investor Contact: 866-436-8502
Transfer Agents: ComputerShare, College Station, TX

ST JUDE MEDICAL INC

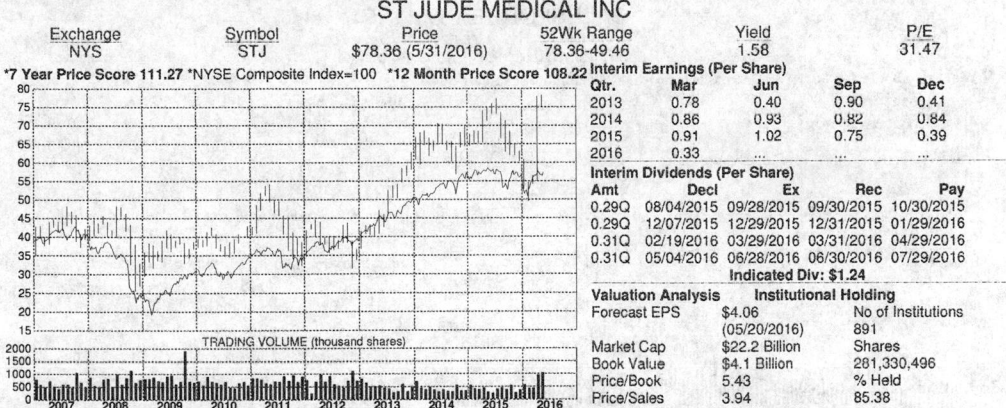

Exchange	Symbol	Price	52Wk Range	Yield	P/E
NYS	STJ	$78.36 (5/31/2016)	78.36-49.46	1.58	31.47

*7 Year Price Score 111.27 *NYSE Composite Index=100 *12 Month Price Score 108.22

Interim Earnings (Per Share)

Qtr.	Mar	Jun	Sep	Dec
2013	0.78	0.40	0.90	0.41
2014	0.86	0.93	0.82	0.84
2015	0.91	1.02	0.75	0.39
2016	0.33	...	...	...

Interim Dividends (Per Share)

Amt	Decl	Ex	Rec	Pay
0.29Q	08/04/2015	09/28/2015	09/30/2015	10/30/2015
0.29Q	12/07/2015	12/29/2015	12/31/2015	01/29/2016
0.31Q	02/19/2016	03/29/2016	03/31/2016	04/29/2016
0.31Q	05/04/2016	06/28/2016	06/30/2016	07/29/2016

Indicated Div: $1.24

Valuation Analysis

		Institutional Holding	
Forecast EPS	$4.06		No of Institutions
	(05/20/2016)		891
Market Cap	$22.2 Billion		Shares
Book Value	$4.1 Billion		281,330,496
Price/Book	5.43		% Held
Price/Sales	3.94		85.38

TRADING VOLUME (thousand shares)

Business Summary: Medical Instruments & Equipment (MIC: 4.3.1 SIC: 3845 NAIC: 334510)

St. Jude Medical, together with its subsidiaries, develops, manufactures and distributes cardiovascular medical devices for the cardiac rhythm management, cardiovascular and atrial fibrillation therapy areas, and interventional pain therapy and neurostimulation devices for the management of chronic pain and movement disorders. Co.'s seven principal product categories are as follows: tachycardia implantable cardioverter defibrillator systems, atrial fibrillation products, pacemaker systems, vascular products, structural heart products, neuromodulation products, and thoratec products. The principal geographic markets for Co.'s products are the U.S., Europe and Japan.

Recent Developments: For the quarter ended Apr 2 2016, net income decreased 62.9% to US$95.0 million from US$256.0 million in the year-earlier quarter. Revenues were US$1.45 billion, up 7.7% from US$1.35 billion the year before. Operating income was US$228.0 million versus US$325.0 million in the prior-year quarter, a decrease of 29.8%. Direct operating expenses rose 23.3% to US$487.0 million from US$395.0 million in the comparable period the year before. Indirect operating expenses increased 17.3% to US$733.0 million from US$625.0 million in the equivalent prior-year period.

Prospects: Our evaluation of St. Jude Medical Inc. as of June 19, 2016 is the result of our systematic analysis on three basic characteristics: earnings strength, relative valuation, and recent stock price movement. The company has managed to produce a neutral trend in earnings per share over the past 5 quarters and while recent estimates for the company have remained steady, STJ has posted better than expected results. Based on operating earnings yield, the company is about fairly valued when compared to all of the companies in our coverage universe. Share price changes over the past year indicates that STJ will perform poorly over the near term.

Financial Data

(US$ in Thousands)	3 Mos	01/02/2016	01/03/2015	12/28/2013	12/29/2012	12/31/2011	01/01/2011	01/02/2010
Earnings Per Share	2.49	3.07	3.46	2.49	2.39	2.52	2.75	2.26
Cash Flow Per Share	3.37	3.69	4.50	3.36	4.27	3.98	3.89	2.56
Tang Book Value Per Share	N.M.	N.M.	N.M.	N.M.	1.11	2.08	1.30	2.65
Dividends Per Share	1.180	1.160	1.080	1.000	0.920	0.840	...	...
Dividend Payout %	47.39	37.79	31.21	40.16	38.49	33.33	...	...
Income Statement								
Total Revenue	1,448,000	5,541,000	5,622,000	5,501,000	5,503,000	5,611,696	5,164,771	4,681,273
EBITDA	278,000	1,362,000	1,458,000	1,078,000	1,269,000	1,287,082	1,528,173	1,314,774
Depn & Amortn	103,000	334,000	310,000	218,000	196,000	202,600	254,074	213,835
Income Before Taxes	136,000	928,000	1,068,000	784,000	1,005,000	1,019,071	1,208,803	1,057,393
Income Taxes	41,000	62,000	113,000	92,000	253,000	193,278	301,367	280,167
Net Income	95,000	880,000	1,002,000	723,000	752,000	825,793	907,436	777,226
Average Shares	286,400	286,300	289,700	290,600	314,800	327,094	330,488	344,359
Balance Sheet								
Current Assets	2,803,000	3,265,000	3,914,000	3,910,000	3,551,000	3,390,566	2,912,148	2,560,206
Total Assets	12,552,000	13,064,000	10,207,000	10,248,000	9,271,000	9,005,193	8,566,448	6,425,811
Current Liabilities	1,630,000	2,473,000	2,666,000	1,380,000	1,775,000	1,061,725	1,017,250	1,067,313
Long-Term Obligations	5,591,000	5,229,000	2,273,000	3,518,000	2,550,000	2,713,275	2,431,966	1,587,615
Total Liabilities	8,453,000	9,022,000	6,008,000	6,017,000	5,177,000	4,530,577	4,194,777	3,102,260
Stockholders' Equity	4,099,000	4,042,000	4,199,000	4,231,000	4,094,000	4,474,616	4,371,671	3,323,551
Shares Outstanding	283,873	283,450	286,659	289,117	295,648	319,615	329,018	324,537
Statistical Record								
Return on Assets %	6.49	7.58	9.64	7.43	8.25	9.42	12.14	12.83
Return on Equity %	17.96	21.42	23.39	17.42	17.60	18.72	23.65	23.76
EBITDA Margin %	19.20	24.58	25.93	19.60	23.06	22.94	29.59	28.09
Net Margin %	6.56	15.88	17.82	13.14	13.67	14.72	17.57	16.60
Asset Turnover	0.51	0.48	0.54	0.57	0.60	0.64	0.69	0.77
Current Ratio	1.72	1.32	1.47	2.83	2.00	3.19	2.86	2.40
Debt to Equity	1.36	1.29	0.54	0.83	0.62	0.61	0.56	0.48
Price Range	77.17-49.46	77.17-60.25	70.46-56.74	62.74-36.14	44.54-31.37	54.04-32.16	42.85-34.57	41.77-29.44
P/E Ratio	30.99-19.86	25.14-19.63	20.36-16.40	25.20-14.51	18.64-13.13	21.44-12.76	15.58-12.57	18.48-13.03
Average Yield %	1.81	1.70	1.66	2.07	2.37	1.89	...	...

Address: One St. Jude Medical Drive, St. Paul, MN 55117 **Telephone:** 651-756-2000 **Fax:** 651-756-3301	**Web Site:** www.sjm.com **Officers:** Daniel J. Starks - Chairman, President, Chief Executive Officer Michael T. Rousseau - Chief Operating Officer, Division Officer, President, Chief Executive Officer	**Auditors:** Ernst & Young LLP **Investor Contact:** 651-756-4347 **Transfer Agents:** Wells Fargo Shareowner Services, Mendota Heights, MN

SALESFORCE.COM INC

*7 Year Price Score 143.35 *NYSE Composite Index=100 *12 Month Price Score 104.43

TRADING VOLUME (thousand shares)

Interim Earnings (Per Share)

Qtr.	Apr	Jul	Oct	Jan
2013-14	(0.12)	0.12	(0.21)	(0.20)
2014-15	(0.16)	(0.10)	(0.06)	(0.10)
2015-16	0.01	0.00	(0.04)	(0.04)
2016-17	0.06	...	...	...

Interim Dividends (Per Share)

No Dividends Paid

Valuation Analysis   Institutional Holding

Forecast EPS	$0.95	No of Institutions
	(05/20/2016)	1007
Market Cap	$56.7 Billion	Shares
Book Value	$5.6 Billion	610,803,200
Price/Book	10.16	% Held
Price/Sales	8.02	97.95

Business Summary: Internet & Software (MIC: 6.3.2 SIC: 7372 NAIC: 511210)

Salesforce.Com is a provider of enterprise cloud computing solutions. Co.'s service offerings include: Sales Cloud, which enables companies to store data, monitor leads and progress, forecast opportunities, gain insights through relationship intelligence and collaborate around sale on desktop and mobile devices; Service Cloud, which enables companies to deliver more personalized customer service and support; Marketing Cloud, which enables companies to plan and personalize one-to-one customer interactions; and Analytics Cloud, which is an app for business intelligence and it enables companies to deploy sales, service, marketing and custom analytics apps using any data source.

Recent Developments: For the quarter ended Apr 30 2016, net income increased 847.2% to US$38.8 million from US$4.1 million in the year-earlier quarter. Revenues were US$1.92 billion, up 26.8% from US$1.51 billion the year before. Operating income was US$52.0 million versus US$31.1 million in the prior-year quarter, an increase of 67.1%. Direct operating expenses rose 30.2% to US$497.0 million from US$381.8 million in the comparable period the year before. Indirect operating expenses increased 24.5% to US$1.37 billion from US$1.10 billion in the equivalent prior-year period.

Prospects: Our evaluation of Salesforce.com Inc. as of June 19, 2016 is the result of our systematic analysis on three basic characteristics: earnings strength, relative valuation, and recent stock price movement. The company has generated a negative trend in earnings per share over the past 5 quarters and while recent estimates for the company have been raised by analysts, CRM has posted better than expected results. Based on operating earnings yield, the company is overvalued when compared to all of the companies in our coverage universe. Share price changes over the past year indicates that CRM will perform in line with the market over the near term.

Financial Data

(US$ in Thousands)	3 Mos	01/31/2016	01/31/2015	01/31/2014	01/31/2013	01/31/2012	01/31/2011	01/31/2010
Earnings Per Share	(0.02)	(0.07)	(0.42)	(0.39)	(0.48)	(0.02)	0.12	0.16
Cash Flow Per Share	2.85	2.44	1.88	1.46	1.30	1.09	0.88	0.54
Tang Book Value Per Share	1.14	0.74	N.M.	N.M.	0.98	1.15	1.34	1.87
Income Statement								
Total Revenue	1,916,603	6,667,216	5,373,586	4,071,003	3,050,195	2,266,539	1,657,139	1,305,583
EBITDA	222,692	438,764	106,752	(94,824)	4,254	69,328	183,707	186,181
Depn & Amortn	171,299	302,000	246,600	185,900	101,100	85,600	54,500	41,800
Income Before Taxes	37,155	64,279	(213,085)	(357,935)	(127,794)	(33,317)	104,298	142,381
Income Taxes	(1,604)	111,705	49,603	(125,760)	142,651	(21,745)	34,601	57,689
Net Income	38,759	(47,426)	(262,688)	(232,175)	(270,445)	(11,572)	64,474	80,719
Average Shares	686,799	661,647	624,148	597,613	564,896	541,208	546,392	512,456
Balance Sheet								
Current Assets	3,774,672	4,347,327	3,550,072	2,680,252	2,015,880	1,672,222	1,074,924	1,706,159
Total Assets	12,817,270	12,770,772	10,692,982	9,152,930	5,528,956	4,164,154	3,091,165	2,460,201
Current Liabilities	5,085,103	5,617,005	4,390,103	3,980,188	2,917,624	2,323,471	1,276,466	908,130
Long-Term Obligations	1,293,170	1,293,947	1,370,692	1,301,930	...	...	472,538	450,198
Total Liabilities	7,233,006	7,767,903	6,717,799	6,087,715	3,157,711	2,498,053	1,814,674	1,416,399
Stockholders' Equity	5,584,264	5,002,869	3,975,183	3,065,215	2,371,245	1,666,101	1,276,491	1,043,802
Shares Outstanding	677,500	670,929	650,596	610,143	585,626	548,146	531,684	508,609
Statistical Record								
Return on Assets %	N.M.	N.M.	N.M.	N.M.	N.M.	N.M.	2.32	4.10
Return on Equity %	N.M.	N.M.	N.M.	N.M.	N.M.	N.M.	5.56	9.41
EBITDA Margin %	11.62	6.58	1.99	N.M.	0.14	3.06	11.09	14.26
Net Margin %	2.02	N.M.	N.M.	N.M.	N.M.	N.M.	3.89	6.18
Asset Turnover	0.61	0.57	0.54	0.55	0.63	0.62	0.60	0.66
Current Ratio	0.74	0.77	0.81	0.67	0.69	0.72	0.84	1.88
Debt to Equity	0.23	0.26	0.34	0.42	...	...	0.37	0.43
Price Range	82.14-54.05	82.14-57.28	66.22-49.13	61.14-36.75	44.52-29.20	39.83-24.37	37.65-15.52	18.70-6.44
P/E Ratio	...	...	...	...	...	...	313.71-129.33	116.91-40.27

SALLY BEAUTY HOLDINGS INC

Exchange	Symbol	Price	52Wk Range	Yield	P/E
NYS	SBH	$28.72 (5/31/2016)	32.75-22.13	N/A	19.94

*7 Year Price Score 110.02 *NYSE Composite Index=100 *12 Month Price Score 107.35

Interim Earnings (Per Share)

Qtr.	Dec	Mar	Jun	Sep
2012-13	0.32	0.36	0.42	0.38
2013-14	0.35	0.35	0.42	0.40
2014-15	0.35	0.39	0.39	0.36
2015-16	0.28	0.41	...	...

Interim Dividends (Per Share)

No Dividends Paid

Valuation Analysis   **Institutional Holding**

Forecast EPS	$1.74	No of Institutions
	(05/20/2016)	319
Market Cap	$4.2 Billion	Shares
Book Value	N/A	159,316,128
Price/Book	N/A	% Held
Price/Sales	1.07	90.39

Business Summary: Retail - Specialty (MIC: 2.1.3 SIC: 5999 NAIC: 446120)

Sally Beauty Holdings is a holding company. Co. is an international retailer and distributor of beauty supplies with operations primarily in North America, South America and Europe. Co. has two segments: Sally Beauty Supply, a retailer of beauty supplies providing beauty supplies to both retail consumers and salons primarily in North America, Puerto Rico, South America and Europe ; and Beauty Systems Group (BSG), a beauty supply distributor providing supplies directly to salons. As of Sep 30 2015, Sally Beauty Supply operated 3,655 Co.-operated retail stores; and BSG had 1,137 Co.-operated stores in the U.S., and in Canada, Mexico and certain European countries.

Recent Developments: For the quarter ended Mar 31 2016, net income decreased 2.2% to US$60.2 million from US$61.5 million in the year-earlier quarter. Revenues were US$980.1 million, up 4.5% from US$937.8 million the year before. Operating income was US$122.5 million versus US$129.0 million in the prior-year quarter, a decrease of 5.1%. Direct operating expenses rose 4.7% to US$492.6 million from US$470.3 million in the comparable period the year before. Indirect operating expenses increased 7.9% to US$365.0 million from US$338.4 million in the equivalent prior-year period.

Prospects: Our evaluation of Sally Beauty Holdings Inc. as of June 19, 2016 is the result of our systematic analysis on three basic characteristics: earnings strength, relative valuation, and recent stock price movement. The company has produced a positive trend in earnings per share over the past 5 quarters. However, while recent estimates for the company have been mixed, SBH has posted results that fell short of analysts expectations. Based on operating earnings yield, the company is undervalued when compared to all of the companies in our coverage universe. Share price changes over the past year indicates that SBH will perform well over the near term.

Financial Data

(US$ in Thousands)	6 Mos	3 Mos	09/30/2015	09/30/2014	09/30/2013	09/30/2012	09/30/2011	09/30/2010
Earnings Per Share	1.44	1.42	1.49	1.51	1.48	1.24	1.14	0.78
Cash Flow Per Share	2.31	2.07	1.92	1.98	1.81	1.62	1.59	1.19
Income Statement								
Total Revenue	1,978,099	998,032	3,834,343	3,753,498	3,622,216	3,523,644	3,269,131	2,916,090
EBITDA	255,072	131,842	570,426	572,096	579,762	550,355	495,769	383,330
Depn & Amortn	1,679	907	75,100	65,100	59,400	51,000	47,300	42,400
Income Before Taxes	162,479	66,992	378,484	390,679	412,667	360,943	335,939	227,948
Income Taxes	60,077	24,749	143,397	144,686	151,516	127,879	122,214	84,120
Net Income	102,402	42,243	235,087	245,993	261,151	233,064	213,725	143,828
Average Shares	148,360	152,426	158,226	163,419	176,159	188,610	188,093	184,088
Balance Sheet								
Current Assets	1,144,393	1,129,982	1,187,102	1,104,149	1,015,817	1,163,907	879,148	794,775
Total Assets	2,069,350	2,043,126	2,094,351	2,029,973	1,950,086	2,065,800	1,728,600	1,589,412
Current Liabilities	501,009	455,037	491,699	463,537	542,653	477,388	460,006	407,652
Long-Term Obligations	1,782,530	1,782,105	1,786,839	1,810,667	1,612,685	1,615,322	1,410,111	1,559,591
Total Liabilities	2,410,782	2,364,792	2,392,172	2,377,026	2,253,565	2,180,885	1,947,582	2,049,738
Stockholders' Equity	(341,432)	(321,666)	(297,821)	(347,053)	(303,479)	(115,085)	(218,982)	(460,326)
Shares Outstanding	145,854	149,155	151,452	154,668	164,425	180,241	184,057	182,230
Statistical Record								
Return on Assets %	10.52	10.74	11.40	12.36	13.01	12.25	12.88	9.34
EBITDA Margin %	12.89	13.21	14.88	15.24	16.01	15.62	15.17	13.15
Net Margin %	5.18	4.23	6.13	6.55	7.21	6.61	6.54	4.93
Asset Turnover	1.86	1.87	1.86	1.89	1.80	1.85	1.97	1.89
Current Ratio	2.28	2.48	2.41	2.38	1.87	2.44	1.91	1.95
Price Range	34.41-22.13	34.88-22.13	34.88-23.44	30.67-24.14	31.57-22.76	28.07-16.28	18.47-11.01	11.70-6.75
P/E Ratio	23.90-15.37	24.56-15.58	23.41-15.73	20.31-15.99	21.33-15.38	22.64-13.13	16.20-9.66	15.00-8.65

Address: 3001 Colorado Boulevard, Denton, TX 76210 **Telephone:** 940-898-7500	**Web Site:** www.sallybeautyholdings.com **Officers:** Gary G. Winterhalter - Chairman, President, Chief Executive Officer Christian A. Brickman - President, Chief Executive Officer, Chief Operating Officer	**Auditors:** KPMG LLP **Investor Contact:** 940-297-3877 **Transfer Agents:** Computershare Trust Company N.A., Providence, RI

SCANA CORP

Exchange	Symbol	Price	52Wk Range	Yield	P/E	Div Achiever
NYS	SCG	$69.91 (5/31/2016)	71.10-50.00	3.29	19.15	15 Years

*7 Year Price Score 108.57 *NYSE Composite Index=100 *12 Month Price Score 113.40

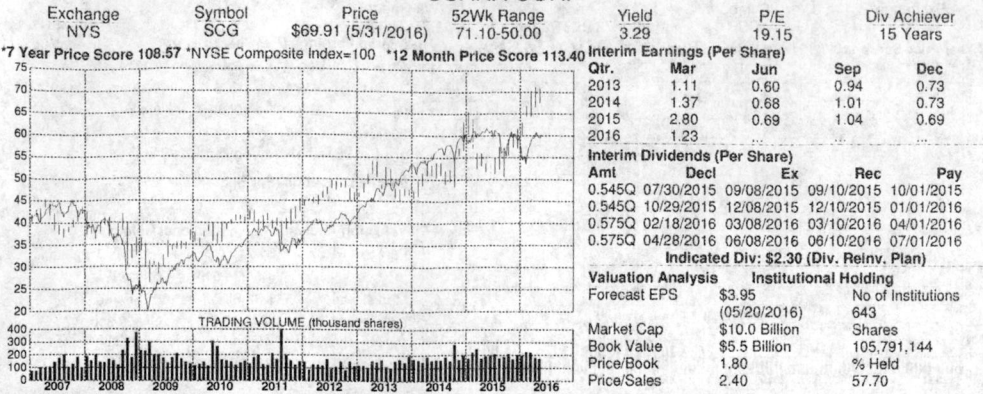

Interim Earnings (Per Share)

Qtr.	Mar	Jun	Sep	Dec
2013	1.11	0.60	0.94	0.73
2014	1.37	0.68	1.01	0.73
2015	2.80	0.69	1.04	0.69
2016	1.23	...	...	...

Interim Dividends (Per Share)

Amt	Decl	Ex	Rec	Pay
0.545Q	07/30/2015	09/08/2015	09/10/2015	10/01/2015
0.545Q	10/29/2015	12/08/2015	12/10/2015	01/01/2016
0.575Q	02/18/2016	03/08/2016	03/10/2016	04/01/2016
0.575Q	04/28/2016	06/08/2016	06/10/2016	07/01/2016

Indicated Div: $2.30 (Div. Reinv. Plan)

Valuation Analysis | **Institutional Holding**

Forecast EPS	$3.95	No of Institutions
	(05/20/2016)	643
Market Cap	$10.0 Billion	Shares
Book Value	$5.5 Billion	105,791,144
Price/Book	1.80	% Held
Price/Sales	2.40	57.70

Business Summary: Electric Utilities (MIC: 3.1.1 SIC: 4931 NAIC: 221122)

SCANA is a holding company. Through its wholly-owned regulated subsidiaries, Co. is primarily engaged in the generation, transmission, distribution and sale of electricity in South Carolina and in the purchase, transmission and sale of natural gas in North Carolina and South Carolina. Through a wholly-owned nonregulated subsidiary, Co. markets natural gas to retail customers in Georgia and to wholesale customers in the southeast. A service company subsidiary of Co. provides primarily administrative and management services to Co. and its subsidiaries. As of Dec 31 2015, Co. distributed electricity to approx. 698,000 customers and sold and transported natural gas to approx. 347,000 customers.

Recent Developments: For the quarter ended Mar 31 2016, net income decreased 56.0% to US$176.0 million from US$400.0 million in the year-earlier quarter. Revenues were US$1.17 billion, down 15.6% from US$1.39 billion the year before. Operating income was US$331.0 million versus US$586.0 million in the prior-year quarter, a decrease of 43.5%. Direct operating expenses declined 22.2% to US$687.0 million from US$883.0 million in the comparable period the year before. Indirect operating expenses amounted to US$154.0 million compared with an income of US$80.0 million in the equivalent prior-year period.

Prospects: Our evaluation of SCANA Corp. as of June 19, 2016 is the result of our systematic analysis on three basic characteristics: earnings strength, relative valuation, and recent stock price movement. The company has managed to produce a neutral trend in earnings per share over the past 5 quarters. However, while recent estimates for the company have been mixed, SCG has posted results that fell short of analysts expectations. Based on operating earnings yield, the company is undervalued when compared to all of the companies in our coverage universe. Share price changes over the past year indicates that SCG will perform very well over the near term.

Financial Data
(US$ in Thousands)

	3 Mos	12/31/2015	12/31/2014	12/31/2013	12/31/2012	12/31/2011	12/31/2010	12/31/2009
Earnings Per Share	3.65	5.22	3.79	3.39	3.15	2.97	2.98	2.85
Cash Flow Per Share	6.47	7.41	5.14	7.57	6.38	6.30	6.45	5.56
Tang Book Value Per Share	38.76	36.62	33.48	31.45	29.73	28.15	27.34	25.84
Dividends Per Share	2.210	2.180	2.100	2.030	1.980	1.940	1.900	1.880
Dividend Payout %	60.55	41.76	55.41	59.88	62.86	65.32	63.76	65.96
Income Statement								
Total Revenue	1,172,000	4,380,000	4,951,000	4,495,000	4,176,000	4,409,000	4,601,000	4,237,000
EBITDA	352,000	1,868,000	1,546,000	1,441,000	1,309,000	1,233,000	1,177,000	1,102,000
Depn & Amortn	14,000	414,000	448,000	450,000	412,000	394,000	377,000	347,000
Income Before Taxes	255,000	1,136,000	786,000	694,000	602,000	555,000	534,000	522,000
Income Taxes	79,000	390,000	248,000	223,000	182,000	168,000	159,000	167,000
Net Income	176,000	746,000	538,000	471,000	420,000	387,000	376,000	357,000
Average Shares	142,900	142,900	141,900	139,100	133,300	130,200	126,300	122,100
Balance Sheet								
Current Assets	1,217,000	1,378,000	2,145,000	1,421,000	1,527,000	1,491,000	1,631,000	1,521,000
Total Assets	17,368,000	17,146,000	16,852,000	15,164,000	14,616,000	13,534,000	12,968,000	12,094,000
Current Liabilities	2,031,000	1,952,000	2,533,000	1,442,000	1,811,000	1,642,000	1,867,000	1,256,000
Long-Term Obligations	5,879,000	5,882,000	5,531,000	5,395,000	4,949,000	4,622,000	4,152,000	4,483,000
Total Liabilities	11,829,000	11,703,000	11,865,000	10,500,000	10,462,000	9,645,000	9,266,000	8,686,000
Stockholders' Equity	5,539,000	5,443,000	4,987,000	4,664,000	4,154,000	3,889,000	3,702,000	3,408,000
Shares Outstanding	142,916	142,900	142,700	141,000	132,000	130,000	127,000	123,000
Statistical Record								
Return on Assets %	3.09	4.39	3.36	3.16	2.98	2.92	3.00	3.03
Return on Equity %	9.61	14.30	11.15	10.68	10.42	10.20	10.58	10.87
EBITDA Margin %	30.03	42.65	31.23	32.06	31.35	27.97	25.58	26.01
Net Margin %	15.02	17.03	10.87	10.48	10.06	8.78	8.17	8.43
Asset Turnover	0.25	0.26	0.31	0.30	0.30	0.33	0.37	0.36
Current Ratio	0.60	0.71	0.85	0.99	0.84	0.91	0.87	1.21
Debt to Equity	1.06	1.08	1.11	1.16	1.19	1.19	1.12	1.32
Price Range	70.15-50.00	65.36-50.00	63.18-45.67	54.20-44.86	49.65-43.71	45.34-35.12	41.69-34.55	38.44-26.37
P/E Ratio	19.22-13.70	12.52-9.58	16.67-12.05	15.99-13.23	15.76-13.88	15.27-11.82	13.99-11.59	13.49-9.25
Average Yield %	3.85	3.90	4.06	4.16	4.24	4.78	4.93	5.67

Address: 100 SCANA Parkway, Cayce, SC 29033 Telephone: 803-217-9000	Web Site: www.scana.com Officers: Kevin B. Marsh - Chairman, President, Chief Executive Officer, Chief Operating Officer W. Keller Kissam - Senior Vice President	Auditors: Deloitte & Touche LLP Investor Contact: 803-217-7512 Transfer Agents: SCANA Corporation, Columbia, SC

SCHLUMBERGER LTD.

Exchange	Symbol	Price	52Wk Range	Yield	P/E
NYS	SLB	$76.30 (5/31/2016)	91.63-61.06	2.62	60.08

*7 Year Price Score 83.65 *NYSE Composite Index=100 *12 Month Price Score 99.07

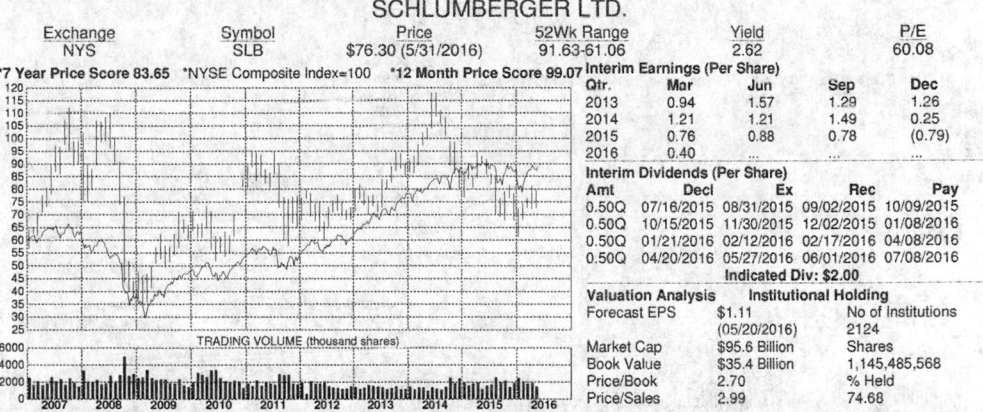

Interim Earnings (Per Share)

Qtr.	Mar	Jun	Sep	Dec
2013	0.94	1.57	1.29	1.26
2014	1.21	1.21	1.49	0.25
2015	0.76	0.88	0.78	(0.79)
2016	0.40	...	...	...

Interim Dividends (Per Share)

Amt	Decl	Ex	Rec	Pay
0.50Q	07/16/2015	08/31/2015	09/02/2015	10/09/2015
0.50Q	10/15/2015	11/30/2015	12/02/2015	01/08/2016
0.50Q	01/21/2016	02/12/2016	02/17/2016	04/08/2016
0.50Q	04/20/2016	05/27/2016	06/01/2016	07/08/2016

Indicated Div: $2.00

Valuation Analysis

		Institutional Holding	
Forecast EPS	$1.11	No of Institutions	
	(05/20/2016)	2124	
Market Cap	$95.6 Billion	Shares	
Book Value	$35.4 Billion	1,145,485,568	
Price/Book	2.70	% Held	
Price/Sales	2.99	74.68	

TRADING VOLUME (thousand shares)

Business Summary: Equipment & Services (MIC: 9.1.3 SIC: 1389 NAIC: 213112)

Schlumberger and its subsidiaries are engaged as a supplier of technology, project management and information services to customers in the international oil and gas exploration and production industry. Co. provides a range of products and services from exploration through production. Co. manages its business through three Groups: Reservoir Characterization, which consists of the technologies involved in finding and defining hydrocarbon resources; Drilling, which consists of the principal technologies involved in the drilling and positioning of oil and gas wells; and Production, which consists of the principal technologies involved in the lifetime production of oil and gas reservoirs.

Recent Developments: For the quarter ended Mar 31 2016, net income decreased 47.1% to US$523.0 million from US$988.0 million in the year-earlier quarter. Revenues were US$6.57 billion, down 36.2% from US$10.30 billion the year before. Direct operating expenses declined 32.6% to US$5.46 billion from US$8.10 billion in the comparable period the year before. Indirect operating expenses decreased 46.7% to US$483.0 million from US$907.0 million in the equivalent prior-year period.

Prospects: Our evaluation of Schlumberger Ltd. as of June 19, 2016 is the result of our systematic analysis on three basic characteristics: earnings strength, relative valuation, and recent stock price movement. The company has produced a positive trend in earnings per share over the past 5 quarters. However, while recent estimates for the company have been lowered by analysts, SLB has posted better than expected results. Based on operating earnings yield, the company is overvalued when compared to all of the companies in our coverage universe. Share price changes over the past year indicates that SLB will perform poorly over the near term.

Financial Data

(US$ in Thousands)	3 Mos	12/31/2015	12/31/2014	12/31/2013	12/31/2012	12/31/2011	12/31/2010	12/31/2009
Earnings Per Share	1.27	1.63	4.16	5.05	4.10	3.67	3.38	2.59
Cash Flow Per Share	6.57	6.95	8.64	7.40	5.11	4.57	4.40	4.43
Tang Book Value Per Share	12.10	12.30	13.89	15.34	11.57	9.17	8.90	10.90
Dividends Per Share	2.000	2.000	1.600	1.250	1.100	1.000	0.840	0.840
Dividend Payout %	157.48	122.70	38.46	24.75	26.83	27.25	24.85	32.43
Income Statement								
Total Revenue	6,565,000	35,711,000	48,871,000	46,459,000	42,321,000	39,669,000	28,931,000	22,975,000
EBITDA	1,437,000	6,427,000	11,208,000	12,182,000	10,431,000	9,336,000	7,763,000	6,631,000
Depn & Amortn	682,000	3,200,000	3,200,000	3,100,000	2,900,000	2,700,000	2,400,000	2,476,000
Income Before Taxes	622,000	2,881,000	7,639,000	8,691,000	7,191,000	6,338,000	5,156,000	3,934,000
Income Taxes	99,000	746,000	1,928,000	1,848,000	1,723,000	1,545,000	890,000	770,000
Net Income	501,000	2,072,000	5,438,000	6,732,000	5,490,000	4,997,000	4,267,000	3,134,000
Average Shares	1,259,000	1,275,000	1,308,000	1,333,000	1,339,000	1,361,000	1,263,000	1,214,000
Balance Sheet								
Current Assets	27,700,000	26,912,000	24,694,000	26,225,000	24,156,000	20,539,000	18,098,000	13,650,000
Total Assets	69,141,000	68,005,000	66,904,000	67,100,000	61,547,000	55,201,000	51,767,000	33,465,000
Current Liabilities	12,880,000	14,121,000	14,176,000	13,525,000	12,368,000	10,538,000	10,865,000	7,259,000
Long-Term Obligations	17,233,000	14,442,000	10,565,000	10,393,000	9,509,000	8,556,000	5,517,000	4,355,000
Total Liabilities	33,782,000	32,372,000	29,054,000	27,631,000	26,796,000	23,938,000	20,541,000	14,345,000
Stockholders' Equity	35,359,000	35,633,000	37,850,000	39,469,000	34,751,000	31,263,000	31,226,000	19,120,000
Shares Outstanding	1,252,334	1,256,367	1,275,312	1,307,330	1,328,255	1,333,775	1,361,171	1,194,812
Statistical Record								
Return on Assets %	2.38	3.07	8.12	10.47	9.38	9.34	10.01	9.58
Return on Equity %	4.38	5.64	14.07	18.14	16.59	15.99	16.95	17.42
EBITDA Margin %	21.89	18.00	22.93	26.22	24.65	23.53	26.83	28.86
Net Margin %	7.63	5.80	11.13	14.49	12.97	12.60	14.75	13.64
Asset Turnover	0.48	0.53	0.73	0.72	0.72	0.74	0.68	0.70
Current Ratio	2.15	1.91	1.74	1.94	1.95	1.95	1.67	1.88
Debt to Equity	0.49	0.41	0.28	0.26	0.27	0.27	0.18	0.23
Price Range	94.61-61.06	94.61-67.34	117.95-79.90	94.46-69.30	79.85-59.67	95.04-57.72	83.63-51.75	70.76-35.19
P/E Ratio	74.50-48.08	58.04-41.31	28.35-19.21	18.70-13.72	19.48-14.55	25.90-15.73	24.74-15.31	27.32-13.59
Average Yield %	2.54	2.44	1.62	1.55	1.55	1.24	1.29	1.57

Address: 42 Rue Saint-Dominique, Paris, 75007 **Telephone:** 713-513-2000	**Web Site:** www.slb.com **Officers:** Paal Kibsgaard - Chief Executive Officer Simon Ayat - Executive Vice President, Chief Financial Officer	**Auditors:** PricewaterhouseCoopers LLP **Investor Contact:** 713-375-3535 **Transfer Agents:** Computershare Trust Company, N.A., Providence, RI

SCHWAB (CHARLES) CORP.

Exchange	Symbol	Price	52Wk Range	Yield	P/E
NYS	SCHW	$30.58 (5/31/2016)	35.42-22.22	0.92	27.55

*7 Year Price Score 123.06 *NYSE Composite Index=100 *12 Month Price Score 94.34

TRADING VOLUME (thousand shares)

Interim Earnings (Per Share)

Qtr.	Mar	Jun	Sep	Dec
2013	0.15	0.18	0.22	0.23
2014	0.24	0.23	0.24	0.25
2015	0.22	0.25	0.28	0.29
2016	0.29	...	...	...

Interim Dividends (Per Share)

Amt	Decl	Ex	Rec	Pay
0.06Q	07/23/2015	08/05/2015	08/07/2015	08/21/2015
0.06Q	10/22/2015	11/04/2015	11/06/2015	11/20/2015
0.06Q	01/28/2016	02/10/2016	02/12/2016	02/26/2016
0.07Q	04/21/2016	05/11/2016	05/13/2016	05/27/2016

Indicated Div: $0.28

Valuation Analysis / Institutional Holding

Forecast EPS	$1.25	No of Institutions
	(05/20/2016)	1029
Market Cap	$40.4 Billion	Shares
Book Value	$14.5 Billion	1,119,202,560
Price/Book	2.78	% Held
Price/Sales	6.11	76.65

Business Summary: Finance Intermediaries & Services (MIC: 5.5.1 SIC: 6211 NAIC: 523120)

Charles Schwab is a savings and loan holding company. Co. is engaged, through its subsidiaries, in wealth management, securities brokerage, banking, money management and financial advisory services. Co. provides financial services to individuals and institutional clients in two segments: Investor Services and Advisor Services. The Investor Services segment provides retail brokerage and banking services, retirement plan services, and other corporate brokerage services. The Advisor Services segment provides custodial, trading, and support services to independent investment advisors, and retirement business services to independent retirement plan advisors and independent recordkeepers.

Recent Developments: For the quarter ended Mar 31 2016, net income increased 36.4% to US$412.0 million from US$302.0 million in the year-earlier quarter. Revenues were US$1.76 billion, up 15.6% from US$1.53 billion the year before. Indirect operating expenses increased 6.4% to US$1.11 billion from US$1.04 billion in the equivalent prior-year period.

Prospects: Our evaluation of Schwab (Charles) Corp. as of June 19, 2016 is the result of our systematic analysis on three basic characteristics: earnings strength, relative valuation, and recent stock price movement. The company has enjoyed a very positive trend in earnings per share over the past 5 quarters and while recent estimates for the company have been mixed, SCHW has posted results that fell short of analysts expectations. Based on operating earnings yield, the company is about fairly valued when compared to all of the companies in our coverage universe. Share price changes over the past year indicates that SCHW will perform in line with the market over the near term.

Financial Data
(US$ in Thousands)

	3 Mos	12/31/2015	12/31/2014	12/31/2013	12/31/2012	12/31/2011	12/31/2010	12/31/2009
Earnings Per Share	1.11	1.03	0.95	0.78	0.69	0.70	0.38	0.68
Cash Flow Per Share	1.65	0.95	1.80	1.29	0.99	2.01	(0.01)	1.24
Tang Book Value Per Share	8.27	7.98	7.23	6.18	5.62	4.90	4.61	3.91
Dividends Per Share	0.240	0.240	0.240	0.240	0.240	0.240	0.240	0.240
Dividend Payout %	21.62	23.30	25.26	30.77	34.78	34.29	63.16	35.29
Income Statement								
Total Revenue	1,764,000	6,380,000	6,058,000	5,435,000	4,883,000	4,691,000	4,248,000	4,193,000
EBITDA	701,000	2,503,000	2,314,000	1,907,000	1,646,000	1,683,000	925,000	1,435,000
Depn & Amortn	46,000	224,000	199,000	202,000	196,000	291,000	146,000	159,000
Income Before Taxes	655,000	2,279,000	2,115,000	1,705,000	1,450,000	1,392,000	779,000	1,276,000
Income Taxes	243,000	832,000	794,000	634,000	522,000	528,000	325,000	489,000
Net Income	412,000	1,447,000	1,321,000	1,071,000	928,000	864,000	454,000	787,000
Average Shares	1,330,000	1,327,000	1,315,000	1,293,000	1,275,000	1,229,000	1,194,000	1,160,000
Balance Sheet								
Current Assets	27,523,000	50,004,000	48,798,000	46,258,000	55,559,000	46,608,000	39,667,000	36,717,000
Total Assets	190,998,000	183,718,000	154,642,000	143,642,000	133,637,000	108,553,000	92,568,000	75,431,000
Current Liabilities	171,619,000	165,275,000	139,124,000	129,772,000	120,775,000	97,441,000	82,840,000	67,439,000
Long-Term Obligations	2,877,000	2,890,000	1,899,000	1,903,000	1,632,000	2,001,000	2,006,000	1,512,000
Total Liabilities	176,485,000	170,316,000	142,839,000	133,261,000	124,048,000	100,839,000	86,342,000	70,358,000
Stockholders' Equity	14,513,000	13,402,000	11,803,000	10,381,000	9,589,000	7,714,000	6,226,000	5,073,000
Shares Outstanding	1,321,461	1,320,337	1,310,722	1,296,886	1,277,529	1,271,164	1,202,382	1,162,107
Statistical Record								
Return on Assets %	0.89	0.86	0.89	0.77	0.76	0.86	0.54	1.24
Return on Equity %	11.68	11.48	11.91	10.73	10.70	12.40	8.04	17.23
EBITDA Margin %	39.74	39.23	38.20	35.09	33.71	35.88	21.77	34.22
Net Margin %	23.36	22.68	21.81	19.71	19.00	18.42	10.69	18.77
Asset Turnover	0.04	0.04	0.04	0.04	0.04	0.05	0.05	0.07
Current Ratio	0.16	0.30	0.35	0.36	0.46	0.48	0.48	0.54
Debt to Equity	0.20	0.22	0.16	0.18	0.17	0.26	0.32	0.30
Price Range	35.42-22.22	35.42-25.96	30.78-23.65	26.00-14.36	15.38-11.61	19.45-10.75	19.88-12.76	19.49-11.34
P/E Ratio	31.91-20.02	34.39-25.20	32.40-24.89	33.33-18.41	22.29-16.83	27.79-15.36	52.32-33.58	28.66-16.68
Average Yield %	0.79	0.77	0.84	1.19	1.81	1.58	1.46	1.42

Address: 211 Main Street, San Francisco, CA 94105 **Telephone:** 415-667-7000 **Fax:** 415-627-8894	**Web Site:** www.aboutschwab.com **Officers:** Charles R. Schwab - Chairman Walter W. Bettinger - President, Chief Executive Officer	**Auditors:** Deloitte & Touche LLP **Investor Contact:** 415-667-1841 **Transfer Agents:** Wells Fargo Bank, N.A., St. Paul, MN

SCOTTS MIRACLE-GRO CO (THE)

Exchange	Symbol	Price	52Wk Range	Yield	P/E
NYS	SMG	$69.50 (5/31/2016)	74.48-59.10	2.71	18.19

*7 Year Price Score 106.77 *NYSE Composite Index=100 *12 Month Price Score 106.29

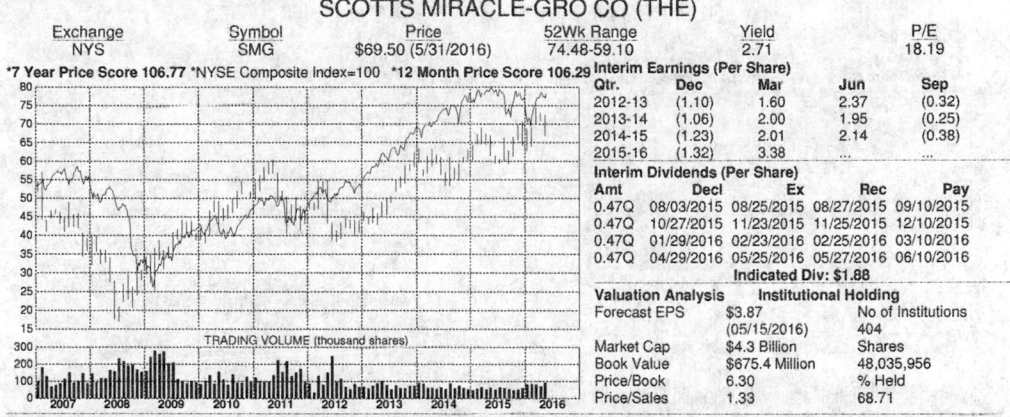

Interim Earnings (Per Share)

Qtr.	Dec	Mar	Jun	Sep
2012-13	(1.10)	1.60	2.37	(0.32)
2013-14	(1.06)	2.00	1.95	(0.25)
2014-15	(1.23)	2.01	2.14	(0.38)
2015-16	(1.32)	3.38	...	...

Interim Dividends (Per Share)

Amt	Decl	Ex	Rec	Pay
0.47Q	08/03/2015	08/25/2015	08/27/2015	09/10/2015
0.47Q	10/27/2015	11/23/2015	11/25/2015	12/10/2015
0.47Q	01/29/2016	02/23/2016	02/25/2016	03/10/2016
0.47Q	04/29/2016	05/25/2016	05/27/2016	06/10/2016

Indicated Div: $1.88

Valuation Analysis

Forecast EPS $3.87 (05/15/2016)
Market Cap $4.3 Billion
Book Value $675.4 Million
Price/Book 6.30
Price/Sales 1.33

Institutional Holding

No of Institutions 404
Shares 48,035,956
% Held 68.71

Business Summary: Agricultural Chemicals (MIC: 8.3.3 SIC: 2879 NAIC: 325320)

Scotts Miracle Gro manufactures and markets consumer lawn and garden products. Co. has two segments: Global Consumer, which manufactures, markets and sells dry, granular slow-release lawn fertilizers, combination lawn fertilizer and control products, grass seed, spreaders, water-soluble, liquid and continuous release garden and indoor plant foods, plant care products, potting, garden and lawn soils, mulches and other growing media products, pesticide and rodenticide products; and Scotts LawnService®, which provides residential and commercial lawn fertilization, disease and insect control and other services such as core aeration, tree and shrub fertilization and pest control services.

Recent Developments: For the quarter ended Apr 2 2016, income from continuing operations increased 62.9% to US$225.8 million from US$138.6 million in the year-earlier quarter. Net income increased 68.8% to US$209.8 million from US$124.3 million in the year-earlier quarter. Revenues were US$1.25 billion, up 16.2% from US$1.07 billion the year before. Operating income was US$369.2 million versus US$231.6 million in the prior-year quarter, an increase of 59.4%. Direct operating expenses rose 11.8% to US$723.6 million from US$647.0 million in the comparable period the year before. Indirect operating expenses decreased 21.1% to US$152.4 million from US$193.2 million in the equivalent prior-year period.

Prospects: Our evaluation of Scotts Co. as of June 19, 2016 is the result of our systematic analysis on three basic characteristics: earnings strength, relative valuation, and recent stock price movement. The company has generated a negative trend in earnings per share over the past 5 quarters and while recent estimates for the company have been raised by analysts, SMG has posted better than expected results. Based on operating earnings yield, the company is undervalued when compared to all of the companies in our coverage universe. Share price changes over the past year indicates that SMG will perform very well over the near term.

Financial Data

(US$ in Thousands)	6 Mos	3 Mos	09/30/2015	09/30/2014	09/30/2013	09/30/2012	09/30/2011	09/30/2010
Earnings Per Share	3.82	2.45	2.57	2.65	2.57	1.71	2.54	3.02
Cash Flow Per Share	4.36	2.85	4.04	3.91	5.54	2.51	1.89	4.46
Tang Book Value Per Share	N.M.	N.M.	N.M.	N.M.	1.79	N.M.	N.M.	0.95
Dividends Per Share	1.860	1.840	1.820	3.763	1.413	1.225	1.050	0.625
Dividend Payout %	48.69	75.10	70.82	141.98	54.96	71.64	41.34	20.70
Income Statement								
Total Revenue	1,439,700	245,700	3,016,500	2,841,300	2,816,500	2,826,100	2,835,700	3,139,900
EBITDA	299,500	(90,900)	378,200	378,500	387,500	314,200	316,100	453,800
Depn & Amortn	36,800	18,100	83,600	74,600	74,300	70,600	70,300	69,200
Income Before Taxes	227,300	(125,300)	244,100	256,600	254,000	181,800	194,800	337,800
Income Taxes	80,700	(44,500)	85,400	91,200	92,800	68,600	72,900	125,400
Net Income	129,000	(80,800)	159,800	166,500	161,100	106,500	167,900	204,100
Average Shares	62,200	61,500	62,200	62,700	62,600	62,100	66,200	67,600
Balance Sheet								
Current Assets	2,208,800	1,148,000	948,600	935,000	881,000	1,000,000	992,500	1,037,600
Total Assets	3,685,600	2,727,400	2,527,200	2,058,300	1,937,200	2,074,400	2,052,200	2,164,000
Current Liabilities	985,900	445,600	613,100	544,700	509,800	433,600	468,600	723,900
Long-Term Obligations	1,764,800	1,503,600	1,028,500	692,400	478,100	781,100	791,800	436,700
Total Liabilities	3,010,200	2,213,600	1,906,500	1,504,600	1,226,700	1,472,500	1,492,400	1,399,500
Stockholders' Equity	675,400	513,800	620,700	553,700	710,500	601,900	559,800	764,500
Shares Outstanding	61,200	61,500	61,400	60,700	62,000	61,300	60,800	65,000
Statistical Record								
Return on Assets %	7.14	6.15	6.97	8.33	8.03	5.15	7.96	9.31
Return on Equity %	38.83	31.98	27.21	26.34	24.55	18.29	25.36	30.26
EBITDA Margin %	20.80	N.M.	12.54	13.32	13.76	11.12	11.15	14.45
Net Margin %	8.96	N.M.	5.30	5.86	5.72	3.77	5.92	6.50
Asset Turnover	0.95	1.22	1.32	1.42	1.40	1.37	1.35	1.43
Current Ratio	2.24	2.58	1.55	1.72	1.73	2.31	2.12	1.43
Debt to Equity	2.61	2.93	1.66	1.25	0.67	1.30	1.41	0.57
Price Range	74.48-59.10	70.46-59.10	68.99-54.71	63.30-53.09	55.66-39.77	55.00-38.17	60.27-40.41	51.87-37.84
P/E Ratio	19.50-15.47	28.76-24.12	26.84-21.29	23.89-20.03	21.66-15.47	32.16-22.32	23.73-15.91	17.18-12.53
Average Yield %	2.87	2.87	2.92	6.44	3.03	2.70	2.01	1.42

Address: 14111 Scottslawn Road, Marysville, OH 43041
Telephone: 937-644-0011
Fax: 937-644-7614

Web Site: www.scotts.com
Officers: James Hagedorn - Chairman, Chief Executive Officer Michael C. Lukemire - President, Chief Operating Officer, Region Officer

Auditors: Deloitte & Touche LLP
Investor Contact: 937-644-0011
Transfer Agents: Wells Fargo Shareowner Services

SCRIPPS NETWORKS INTERACTIVE INC

Exchange	Symbol	Price	52Wk Range	Yield	P/E
NMS	SNI	$65.19 (3/14/2016)	68.73-48.14	1.53	10.94

*7 Year Price Score N/A   *NYSE Composite Index=100   *12 Month Price Score N/A

Interim Earnings (Per Share)

Qtr.	Mar	Jun	Sep	Dec
2013	0.72	1.08	0.87	0.73
2014	0.87	1.07	0.93	0.95
2015	0.94	1.49	0.96	1.27
2016	2.24			

Interim Dividends (Per Share)

Amt	Decl	Ex	Rec	Pay
0.23Q	08/17/2015	08/27/2015	08/31/2015	09/10/2015
0.23Q	11/12/2015	11/25/2015	11/30/2015	12/10/2015
0.25Q	02/18/2016	02/25/2016	02/29/2016	03/10/2016
0.25Q	05/11/2016	05/26/2016	05/31/2016	06/10/2016

Indicated Div: $1.00

Valuation Analysis   **Institutional Holding**

Forecast EPS	$5.17	No of Institutions
	(05/20/2016)	574
Market Cap	$8.4 Billion	Shares
Book Value	$1.8 Billion	104,711,584
Price/Book	4.56	% Held
Price/Sales	2.65	55.50

TRADING VOLUME (thousand shares)

Business Summary: Radio & Television (MIC: 2.3.1 SIC: 4841 NAIC: 515210)

Scripps Networks Interactive is a developer of lifestyle-oriented content for linear and interactive video platforms. Co. has two segments. The U.S. Networks segment includes Co.'s six domestic television networks: HGTV, Food Network, Travel Channel, DIY Network, Cooking Channel and Great American Country. Additionally, U.S. Networks includes websites associated with the aforementioned television brands and other internet and mobile businesses serving home, food, travel and other lifestyle-related categories. The International Networks segment includes the lifestyle-oriented networks available in the U.K., other European markets, the Middle East and Africa, Asia Pacific and Latin America.

Recent Developments: For the quarter ended Mar 31 2016, net income increased 104.7% to US$339.9 million from US$166.1 million in the year-earlier quarter. Revenues were US$816.9 million, up 24.1% from US$658.3 million the year before. Operating income was US$290.0 million versus US$225.8 million in the prior-year quarter, an increase of 28.4%. Direct operating expenses rose 40.4% to US$279.7 million from US$199.1 million in the comparable period the year before. Indirect operating expenses increased 6.0% to US$247.2 million from US$233.3 million in the equivalent prior-year period.

Prospects: Our evaluation of Scripps Networks Interactive Inc. as of June 19, 2016 is the result of our systematic analysis on three basic characteristics: earnings strength, relative valuation, and recent stock price movement. The company has produced a positive trend in earnings per share over the past 5 quarters and while recent estimates for the company have been raised by analysts, SNI has posted better than expected results. Based on operating earnings yield, the company is undervalued when compared to all of the companies in our coverage universe. Share price changes over the past year indicates that SNI will perform well over the near term.

Financial Data

(US$ in Thousands)	3 Mos	12/31/2015	12/31/2014	12/31/2013	12/31/2012	12/31/2011	12/31/2010	12/31/2009
Earnings Per Share	5.96	4.66	3.83	3.40	4.44	2.49	2.45	1.81
Cash Flow Per Share	6.67	6.28	5.50	5.95	4.03	4.43	2.92	3.17
Tang Book Value Per Share	N.M.	N.M.	1.62	5.95	3.97	3.90	2.84	0.19
Dividends Per Share	0.940	0.920	0.800	0.600	0.480	0.375	0.300	0.300
Dividend Payout %	15.77	19.74	20.89	17.65	10.81	15.06	12.24	16.57
Income Statement								
Total Revenue	816,878	3,018,227	2,665,456	2,530,809	2,307,182	2,072,048	2,067,162	1,541,248
EBITDA	566,405	1,286,591	1,123,489	1,077,297	1,035,304	959,490	869,920	585,911
Depn & Amortn	267,542	137,596	128,582	117,580	107,591	90,080	124,975	81,470
Income Before Taxes	265,118	1,040,948	942,220	911,007	876,899	833,289	709,778	501,631
Income Taxes	159,047	343,391	301,043	307,623	88,107	246,452	220,924	161,474
Net Income	290,897	606,828	545,275	505,070	681,478	411,558	410,972	299,326
Average Shares	129,790	130,255	142,193	148,502	153,327	165,572	168,009	165,381
Balance Sheet								
Current Assets	1,653,775	1,727,881	2,138,161	1,861,310	1,484,276	1,715,968	1,446,246	982,269
Total Assets	6,638,324	6,672,314	4,667,632	4,438,447	4,138,798	3,961,670	3,388,432	2,963,062
Current Liabilities	1,051,874	974,649	1,157,954	278,699	252,629	232,899	209,442	210,708
Long-Term Obligations	3,200,794	3,511,098	1,494,411	1,384,488	1,384,216	1,383,945	884,395	884,239
Total Liabilities	4,792,861	5,148,383	3,285,185	2,339,444	2,317,874	2,282,944	1,612,259	1,579,346
Stockholders' Equity	1,845,463	1,523,931	1,382,447	2,099,003	1,820,924	1,678,726	1,776,173	1,383,716
Shares Outstanding	128,951	128,689	132,107	146,208	148,887	157,145	167,647	165,781
Statistical Record								
Return on Assets %	14.64	10.70	11.98	11.78	16.78	11.20	12.94	12.64
Return on Equity %	51.21	41.76	31.32	25.77	38.84	23.82	26.01	23.71
EBITDA Margin %	69.34	42.63	42.15	42.57	44.87	46.31	42.08	38.02
Net Margin %	35.61	20.11	20.46	19.96	29.54	19.86	19.88	19.42
Asset Turnover	0.60	0.53	0.59	0.59	0.57	0.56	0.65	0.65
Current Ratio	1.57	1.77	1.85	6.68	5.88	7.37	6.91	4.66
Debt to Equity	1.73	2.30	1.08	0.66	0.76	0.82	0.50	0.64
Price Range	71.89-48.14	75.94-48.14	86.41-71.61	86.41-57.78	63.72-42.53	53.36-36.15	53.33-38.62	42.21-18.51
P/E Ratio	12.06-8.08	16.30-10.33	22.56-18.70	25.41-16.99	14.35-9.58	21.43-14.52	21.77-15.76	23.32-10.23
Average Yield %	1.56	1.45	1.24	1.03	0.85	0.88	0.62	0.98

Address: 9721 Sherrill Boulevard, Knoxville, TN 37932 Telephone: 865-694-2700	Web Site: www.scrippsnetworksinteractive.com Officers: Kenneth W. Lowe - Chairman, President, Chief Executive Officer Burton F. Jablin - Chief Operating Officer	Auditors: Deloitte & Touche LLP Investor Contact: 865-560-5007 Transfer Agents: BNY Mellon Shareowner Services, Pittsburgh, PA

SEALED AIR CORP

Exchange	Symbol	Price	52Wk Range	Yield	P/E
NYS	SEE	$46.44 (5/31/2016)	55.40-38.36	1.38	28.67

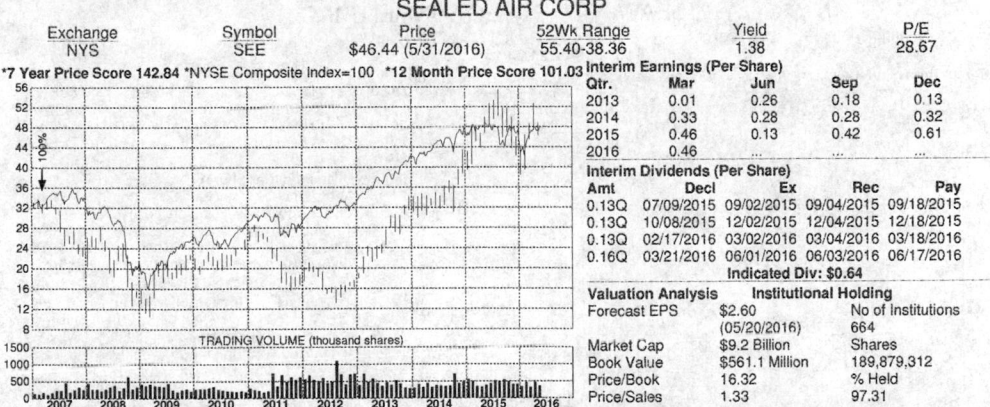

*7 Year Price Score 142.84 *NYSE Composite Index=100 *12 Month Price Score 101.03

Interim Earnings (Per Share)

Qtr.	Mar	Jun	Sep	Dec
2013	0.01	0.26	0.18	0.13
2014	0.33	0.28	0.28	0.32
2015	0.46	0.13	0.42	0.61
2016	0.46	...	...	...

Interim Dividends (Per Share)

Amt	Decl	Ex	Rec	Pay
0.13Q	07/09/2015	09/02/2015	09/04/2015	09/18/2015
0.13Q	10/08/2015	12/02/2015	12/04/2015	12/18/2015
0.13Q	02/17/2016	03/02/2016	03/04/2016	03/18/2016
0.16Q	03/21/2016	06/01/2016	06/03/2016	06/17/2016

Indicated Div: $0.64

Valuation Analysis / **Institutional Holding**

Forecast EPS	$2.60	No of Institutions
	(05/20/2016)	664
Market Cap	$9.2 Billion	Shares
Book Value	$561.1 Million	189,879,312
Price/Book	16.32	% Held
Price/Sales	1.33	97.31

Business Summary: Containers & Packaging (MIC: 8.1.3 SIC: 2671 NAIC: 322221)

Sealed Air is engaged in food safety and security, facility hygiene and product protection. Co. serves a range of end markets including food and beverage processing, food service, retail, healthcare and industrial, and commercial and consumer applications. Co. has three reportable segments: Food Care; which provides processors, retailers and food service operators a range of system solutions; Diversey Care; which provides Diversey®-branded system solutions for facility hygiene, food safety and security, and infection control; and Product Care, which provides customers a range of Product Care solutions. Co.'s other category include its Medical Applications and New Ventures businesses.

Recent Developments: For the quarter ended Mar 31 2016, net income decreased 5.5% to US$91.9 million from US$97.2 million in the year-earlier quarter. Revenues were US$1.59 billion, down 8.9% from US$1.75 billion the year before. Operating income was US$171.6 million versus US$183.6 million in the prior-year quarter, a decrease of 6.5%. Direct operating expenses declined 8.7% to US$1.00 billion from US$1.10 billion in the comparable period the year before. Indirect operating expenses decreased 10.4% to US$417.7 million from US$466.0 million in the equivalent prior-year period.

Prospects: Our evaluation of Sealed Air Corp. as of June 19, 2016 is the result of our systematic analysis on three basic characteristics: earnings strength, relative valuation, and recent stock price movement. The company has generated a negative trend in earnings per share over the past 5 quarters and while recent estimates for the company have remained steady, SEE has posted better than expected results. Based on operating earnings yield, the company is undervalued when compared to all of the companies in our coverage universe. Share price changes over the past year indicates that SEE will perform well over the near term.

Financial Data

(US$ in Thousands)	3 Mos	12/31/2015	12/31/2014	12/31/2013	12/31/2012	12/31/2011	12/31/2010	12/31/2009
Earnings Per Share	1.62	1.62	1.20	0.58	(7.31)	0.80	1.44	1.35
Cash Flow Per Share	3.34	4.75	(0.96)	3.21	2.09	2.35	3.05	3.51
Tang Book Value Per Share	N.M.	N.M.	N.M.	N.M.	N.M.	N.M.	2.88	1.58
Dividends Per Share	0.520	0.520	0.520	0.520	0.520	0.520	0.500	0.480
Dividend Payout %	32.10	32.10	43.33	89.66	...	65.00	34.72	35.56
Income Statement								
Total Revenue	1,590,600	7,031,500	7,750,500	7,690,800	7,648,100	5,640,900	4,490,100	4,242,800
EBITDA	212,500	853,400	806,100	810,200	(1,197,900)	610,500	638,100	618,700
Depn & Amortn	49,100	213,300	266,700	283,400	304,000	189,500	143,500	142,800
Income Before Taxes	112,300	425,900	267,200	176,800	(1,874,600)	212,900	341,100	328,100
Income Taxes	20,400	90,500	9,100	84,000	(261,900)	67,000	87,500	85,600
Net Income	91,900	335,400	258,100	124,200	(1,410,300)	149,100	255,900	244,300
Average Shares	197,000	206,700	213,900	213,500	192,800	185,400	176,700	182,600
Balance Sheet								
Current Assets	2,319,100	2,215,600	2,691,600	3,417,700	3,222,400	3,262,600	2,040,000	2,073,400
Total Assets	7,539,300	7,426,000	8,041,700	9,134,200	9,437,200	11,496,700	5,399,400	5,420,100
Current Liabilities	1,899,900	1,807,100	1,730,900	2,700,800	2,333,600	2,383,500	1,447,700	1,433,800
Long-Term Obligations	4,280,000	4,302,700	4,282,500	4,116,400	4,540,800	5,010,900	1,399,200	1,626,300
Total Liabilities	6,978,200	6,898,900	6,878,900	7,745,100	7,993,400	8,539,200	2,994,800	3,220,500
Stockholders' Equity	561,100	527,100	1,162,800	1,389,100	1,443,800	2,957,500	2,404,600	2,199,600
Shares Outstanding	197,157	196,013	210,531	196,198	194,557	192,062	159,305	158,938
Statistical Record								
Return on Assets %	4.29	4.34	3.01	1.34	N.M.	1.76	4.73	4.70
Return on Equity %	38.59	39.69	20.23	8.77	N.M.	5.56	11.12	11.85
EBITDA Margin %	13.36	12.14	10.40	10.53	N.M.	10.82	14.21	14.58
Net Margin %	5.78	4.77	3.33	1.61	N.M.	2.64	5.70	5.76
Asset Turnover	0.89	0.91	0.90	0.83	0.73	0.67	0.83	0.82
Current Ratio	1.22	1.23	1.56	1.27	1.38	1.37	1.41	1.45
Debt to Equity	7.63	8.16	3.68	2.96	3.15	1.69	0.58	0.74
Price Range	55.40-38.36	55.40-39.42	43.47-29.86	34.13-17.51	21.04-13.11	28.52-15.61	25.59-18.84	22.65-10.43
P/E Ratio	34.20-23.68	34.20-24.33	36.23-24.88	58.84-30.19	...	35.65-19.51	17.77-13.08	16.78-7.73
Average Yield %	1.10	1.09	1.51	2.03	3.06	2.34	2.29	2.66

Address: 8215 Forest Point Boulevard, Charlotte, NC 28273
Telephone: 201-791-7600
Fax: 201-703-4205

Web Site: www.sealedair.com
Officers: William J. Marino - Chairman Jerome A. Peribere - President, Chief Operating Officer

Auditors: Ernst & Young LLP
Investor Contact: 201-791-7600
Transfer Agents: ComputerShare Investor Services, Providence, RI

SEAWORLD ENTERTAINMENT INC.

Exchange	Symbol	Price	52Wk Range	Yield	P/E
NYS	SEAS	$17.46 (5/31/2016)	21.65-16.96	4.81	218.25

*7 Year Price Score N/A   *NYSE Composite Index=100   *12 Month Price Score 103.05

Interim Earnings (Per Share)

Qtr.	Mar	Jun	Sep	Dec
2013	(0.49)	(0.18)	1.33	(0.16)
2014	(0.56)	0.43	1.00	(0.29)
2015	(0.51)	0.07	1.14	(0.13)
2016	(1.00)			

Interim Dividends (Per Share)

Amt	Decl	Ex	Rec	Pay
0.21Q	09/16/2015	09/25/2015	09/29/2015	10/06/2015
0.21Q	01/05/2016	01/13/2016	01/15/2016	01/22/2016
0.21Q	02/22/2016	03/10/2016	03/14/2016	04/01/2016
0.21Q	06/08/2016	06/16/2016	06/20/2016	07/01/2016

Indicated Div: $0.84

Valuation Analysis

		Institutional Holding	
Forecast EPS	$0.71	No of Institutions	
	(05/20/2016)	199	
Market Cap	$1.5 Billion	Shares	
Book Value	$401.1 Million	74,316,416	
Price/Book	3.65	% Held	
Price/Sales	1.06	89.33	

Business Summary: Sporting & Recreational (MIC: 2.2.4 SIC: 7996 NAIC: 713110)

SeaWorld Entertainment is a holding company. Through its wholly-owned subsidiary, SeaWorld Parks & Entertainment, Inc. Co., owns and operates 11 theme parks within the U.S. Co. operates SeaWorld theme parks in Orlando, FL; San Antonio, TX; and San Diego, CA, and Busch Gardens theme parks in Tampa, FL, and Williamsburg, VA. Co. operates water park attractions in Orlando, FL (Aquatica); San Diego, CA (Aquatica), Tampa, FL (Adventure Island), and Williamsburg, VA (Water Country USA). Co. also operates a reservations-only attraction providing interaction with marine animals (Discovery Cove) and a seasonal park in Langhorne, PA (Sesame Place).

Recent Developments: For the quarter ended Mar 31 2016, net loss amounted to US$84.0 million versus a net loss of US$43.6 million in the year-earlier quarter. Revenues were US$220.2 million, up 2.6% from US$214.6 million the year before. Operating loss was US$119.6 million versus a loss of US$50.2 million in the prior-year quarter. Direct operating expenses rose 6.9% to US$17.0 million from US$15.9 million in the comparable period the year before. Indirect operating expenses increased 29.7% to US$322.8 million from US$248.9 million in the equivalent prior-year period.

Prospects: Our evaluation of SeaWorld Entertainment Inc. as of June 19, 2016 is the result of our systematic analysis on three basic characteristics: earnings strength, relative valuation, and recent stock price movement. The company has suffered a very negative trend in earnings per share over the past 5 quarters and while recent estimates for the company have been raised by analysts, SEAS has posted better than expected results. Based on operating earnings yield, the company is overvalued when compared to all of the companies in our coverage universe. Share price changes over the past year indicates that SEAS will perform very well over the near term.

Financial Data
(US$ in Thousands)

	3 Mos	12/31/2015	12/31/2014	12/31/2013	12/31/2012	12/31/2011	12/31/2010
Earnings Per Share	0.08	0.57	0.57	0.57	0.93	0.23	(0.56)
Cash Flow Per Share	3.35	3.33	3.00	3.31	3.67	3.30	2.50
Tang Book Value Per Share	N.M.	N.M.	0.64	1.44	N.M.	4.09	...
Dividends Per Share	0.840	0.840	0.620	0.600	...	...	...
Dividend Payout %	1,050.00	147.37	108.77	105.26	...	...	...
Income Statement							
Total Revenue	220,241	1,371,004	1,377,812	1,460,250	1,423,752	1,330,774	1,196,103
EBITDA	(118,090)	313,102	329,334	328,718	390,052	351,938	262,478
Depn & Amortn	1,335	174,700	169,000	159,700	161,700	209,300	202,800
Income Before Taxes	(134,006)	72,831	78,791	75,482	116,926	32,541	(74,705)
Income Taxes	(49,957)	23,698	28,872	25,004	39,482	13,428	(29,241)
Net Income	(84,049)	49,133	49,919	50,478	77,444	19,113	(45,464)
Average Shares	83,824	85,981	87,480	88,152	83,552	82,024	80,800
Balance Sheet							
Current Assets	143,587	109,057	142,204	243,059	158,633	166,855	...
Total Assets	2,416,825	2,391,134	2,442,474	2,582,273	2,521,052	2,547,095	...
Current Liabilities	393,286	229,314	221,085	252,694	246,281	280,236	...
Long-Term Obligations	1,546,016	1,548,893	1,589,403	1,627,183	1,802,644	1,365,387	...
Total Liabilities	2,015,773	1,887,014	1,862,939	1,928,141	2,071,204	1,674,628	...
Stockholders' Equity	401,052	504,120	579,535	654,132	449,848	872,467	...
Shares Outstanding	83,855	83,800	86,085	88,400	82,737	82,418	80,800
Statistical Record							
Return on Assets %	0.36	2.03	1.99	1.98	3.05	...	...
Return on Equity %	1.93	9.07	8.09	9.14	11.68	...	...
EBITDA Margin %	N.M.	22.84	23.90	22.51	27.40	26.45	21.94
Net Margin %	N.M.	3.58	3.62	3.46	5.44	1.44	N.M.
Asset Turnover	0.57	0.57	0.55	0.57	0.56	...	...
Current Ratio	0.37	0.48	0.64	0.96	0.64	0.60	...
Debt to Equity	3.85	3.07	2.74	2.49	4.01	1.56	...
Price Range	21.82-16.96	21.82-16.45	35.11-15.43	38.92-27.66	...	...	...
P/E Ratio	272.75-212.00	38.28-28.86	61.60-27.07	68.28-48.53	...	...	...
Average Yield %	4.42	4.44	2.40	1.81	...	...	...

Address: 9205 South Park Center Loop, Suite 400, Orlando, FL 32819 **Telephone:** 407-226-5011	**Web Site:** www.seaworldentertainment.com **Officers:** David F. D'Alessandro - Chairman, Interim Chief Executive Officer Joel K. Manby - President, Chief Executive Officer	**Auditors:** Deloitte & Touche LLP **Transfer Agents:** Computershare Trust Company, N.A.

SEMPRA ENERGY

Exchange	Symbol	Price	52Wk Range	Yield	P/E
NYS	SRE	$107.12 (5/31/2016)	107.59-87.00	2.82	21.91

*7 Year Price Score 112.70 *NYSE Composite Index=100 *12 Month Price Score 103.43

TRADING VOLUME (thousand shares)

Interim Earnings (Per Share)

Qtr.	Mar	Jun	Sep	Dec
2013	0.72	0.98	1.19	1.12
2014	0.99	1.08	1.39	1.18
2015	1.74	1.17	0.99	1.46
2016	1.27	...	...	...

Interim Dividends (Per Share)

Amt	Decl	Ex	Rec	Pay
0.70Q	09/10/2015	09/23/2015	09/25/2015	10/15/2015
0.70Q	12/15/2015	12/23/2015	12/28/2015	01/15/2016
0.755Q	02/19/2016	03/22/2016	03/25/2016	04/15/2016
0.755Q	06/14/2016	06/28/2016	06/30/2016	07/15/2016

Indicated Div: $3.02

Valuation Analysis	Institutional Holding	
Forecast EPS $4.81	No of Institutions	
(05/20/2016)	820	
Market Cap $26.7 Billion	Shares	
Book Value $11.9 Billion	227,167,504	
Price/Book 2.23	% Held	
Price/Sales 2.62	82.99	

Business Summary: Electric Utilities (MIC: 3.1.1 SIC: 4932 NAIC: 221210)

Sempra Energy is an energy-services holding company whose operating units invest in, develop and operate energy infrastructure, and provide gas and electricity services to their customers in North and South America. Co.'s principal operating units are: San Diego Gas & Electric Company and Southern California Gas Company, which are separate, reportable segments; Sempra International, which includes its Sempra South American Utilities and Sempra Mexico reportable segments; and Sempra U.S. Gas & Power, which includes its Sempra Renewables and Sempra Natural Gas reportable segments.

Recent Developments: For the quarter ended Mar 31 2016, net income decreased 27.9% to US$330.0 million from US$458.0 million in the year-earlier quarter. Revenues were US$2.62 billion, down 2.2% from US$2.68 billion the year before. Direct operating expenses was unchanged at US$1.62 billion versus the comparable period the year before. Indirect operating expenses increased 12.9% to US$439.0 million from US$389.0 million in the equivalent prior-year period.

Prospects: Our evaluation of Sempra Energy as of June 19, 2016 is the result of our systematic analysis on three basic characteristics: earnings strength, relative valuation, and recent stock price movement. The company has managed to produce a neutral trend in earnings per share over the past 5 quarters and while recent estimates for the company have been raised by analysts, SRE has posted results that fell short of analysts expectations. Based on operating earnings yield, the company is about fairly valued when compared to all of the companies in our coverage universe. Share price changes over the past year indicates that SRE will perform in line with the market over the near term.

Financial Data

(US$ in Thousands)	3 Mos	12/31/2015	12/31/2014	12/31/2013	12/31/2012	12/31/2011	12/31/2010	12/31/2009
Earnings Per Share	4.89	5.37	4.63	4.01	3.48	5.62	2.98	4.52
Cash Flow Per Share	10.76	11.70	8.79	7.32	8.34	7.79	8.80	7.71
Tang Book Value Per Share	42.95	42.63	40.51	39.10	36.04	34.82	35.30	34.41
Dividends Per Share	2.855	2.800	2.640	2.520	2.400	1.920	1.560	1.560
Dividend Payout %	58.38	52.14	57.02	62.84	68.97	34.16	52.35	34.51
Income Statement								
Total Revenue	2,622,000	10,231,000	11,035,000	10,557,000	9,647,000	10,036,000	9,003,000	8,106,000
EBITDA	913,000	3,379,000	3,125,000	3,046,000	2,820,000	2,850,000	2,364,000	2,094,000
Depn & Amortn	328,000	1,250,000	1,156,000	1,113,000	1,090,000	978,000	867,000	775,000
Income Before Taxes	477,000	1,600,000	1,443,000	1,399,000	1,262,000	1,435,000	1,078,000	977,000
Income Taxes	142,000	341,000	300,000	366,000	59,000	366,000	102,000	422,000
Net Income	330,000	1,448,000	1,262,000	1,088,000	920,000	1,407,000	733,000	1,122,000
Average Shares	251,412	250,923	250,655	249,332	246,693	241,523	247,942	247,384
Balance Sheet								
Current Assets	2,883,000	2,891,000	4,184,000	3,997,000	3,695,000	2,332,000	3,353,000	2,295,000
Total Assets	41,835,000	41,150,000	39,732,000	37,244,000	36,499,000	33,356,000	30,283,000	28,512,000
Current Liabilities	5,132,000	4,612,000	5,069,000	4,369,000	4,258,000	4,163,000	3,786,000	3,888,000
Long-Term Obligations	12,975,000	13,134,000	12,167,000	11,253,000	11,621,000	10,078,000	8,980,000	7,460,000
Total Liabilities	29,889,000	29,341,000	28,406,000	26,236,000	26,217,000	23,518,000	21,256,000	19,505,000
Stockholders' Equity	11,946,000	11,809,000	11,326,000	11,008,000	10,282,000	9,838,000	9,027,000	9,007,000
Shares Outstanding	249,000	248,298	246,330	244,461	242,368	239,934	240,447	246,507
Statistical Record								
Return on Assets %	3.24	3.58	3.28	2.95	2.63	4.42	2.49	4.09
Return on Equity %	11.26	12.52	11.30	10.22	9.12	14.92	8.13	13.22
EBITDA Margin %	34.82	33.03	28.32	28.85	29.23	28.40	26.26	25.83
Net Margin %	12.59	14.15	11.44	10.31	9.54	14.02	8.14	13.84
Asset Turnover	0.25	0.25	0.29	0.29	0.28	0.32	0.31	0.30
Current Ratio	0.56	0.63	0.83	0.91	0.87	0.56	0.89	0.59
Debt to Equity	1.09	1.11	1.07	1.02	1.13	1.02	0.99	0.83
Price Range	110.47-87.00	115.08-90.09	115.85-88.44	92.10-70.84	72.74-54.83	55.50-45.59	55.98-44.51	56.88-36.72
P/E Ratio	22.59-17.79	21.43-16.78	25.02-19.10	22.97-17.67	20.90-15.76	9.88-8.11	18.79-14.94	12.58-8.12
Average Yield %	2.86	2.71	2.61	3.04	3.71	3.65	3.08	3.23

Address: 488 8th Avenue, San Diego, CA 92101 Telephone: 619-696-2000	Web Site: www.sempra.com Officers: Debra L. Reed - Chairman, Chief Executive Officer, Executive Vice President Mark A. Snell - President, Executive Vice President, Chief Financial Officer, Division Officer	Auditors: Deloitte & Touche LLP Transfer Agents: American Stock Transfer & Trust Company, LLC, Brooklyn, NY

SENIOR HOUSING PROPERTIES TRUST

Exchange	Symbol	Price	52Wk Range	Yield	P/E
NYS	SNH	$18.68 (5/31/2016)	19.95-13.62	8.35	38.92

*7 Year Price Score 64.93   *NYSE Composite Index=100   *12 Month Price Score 109.48

Interim Earnings (Per Share)

Qtr.	Mar	Jun	Sep	Dec
2013	0.19	0.03	0.20	0.39
2014	0.21	0.19	0.18	0.23
2015	0.18	0.15	0.16	0.04
2016	0.13			

Interim Dividends (Per Share)

Amt	Decl	Ex	Rec	Pay
0.39Q	10/13/2015	10/21/2015	10/23/2015	11/19/2015
0.00Q	11/16/2015	12/15/2015	11/27/2015	12/14/2015
0.39Q	01/11/2016	01/20/2016	01/22/2016	02/23/2016
0.39Q	04/13/2016	04/21/2016	04/25/2016	05/19/2016

Indicated Div: $1.56 (Div. Reinv. Plan)

Valuation Analysis

		Institutional Holding	
Forecast EPS	$0.65	No of Institutions	454
	(05/20/2016)		
Market Cap	$4.4 Billion	Shares	185,629,712
Book Value	$3.3 Billion	% Held	85.62
Price/Book	1.34		
Price/Sales	4.31		

Business Summary: REITs (MIC: 5.3.1 SIC: 6798 NAIC: 525930)

Senior Housing Properties Trust is a real estate investment trust that acquires and invests in independent living communities, assisted living communities, nursing homes, medical related businesses, clinics and biotech laboratory tenants, and wellness centers. Co.'s day to day operations are conducted by its manager, The RMR Group LLC. As of Dec 31 2015, Co. owned 427 properties located in 43 states and Washington, D.C. Co.'s portfolio included: 296 senior living communities with 34,699 living units / beds; 121 properties (145 buildings) leased to medical providers, medical related businesses, clinics and biotech laboratory tenants; and 10 wellness centers.

Recent Developments: For the quarter ended Mar 31 2016, income from continuing operations decreased 21.9% to US$31.3 million from US$40.0 million in the year-earlier quarter. Net income decreased 21.4% to US$31.3 million from US$39.8 million in the year-earlier quarter. Revenues were US$258.4 million, up 13.0% from US$228.6 million the year before. Revenues from property income rose 10.7% to US$161.4 million from US$145.8 million in the corresponding quarter a year earlier.

Prospects: Our evaluation of Senior Housing Properties Trust as of June 19, 2016 is the result of our systematic analysis on three basic characteristics: earnings strength, relative valuation, and recent stock price movement. The company has managed to produce a neutral trend in earnings per share over the past 5 quarters. However, while recent estimates for the company have been lowered by analysts, SNH has posted results that fell short of analysts expectations. Based on operating earnings yield, the company is about fairly valued when compared to all of the companies in our coverage universe. Share price changes over the past year indicates that SNH will perform poorly over the near term.

Financial Data

(US$ in Thousands)	3 Mos	12/31/2015	12/31/2014	12/31/2013	12/31/2012	12/31/2011	12/31/2010	12/31/2009
Earnings Per Share	0.48	0.53	0.80	0.81	0.80	1.01	0.91	0.90
Cash Flow Per Share	1.79	1.74	1.76	1.64	1.67	1.71	1.68	1.72
Tang Book Value Per Share	13.99	14.15	14.48	14.76	14.99	15.20	15.00	14.92
Dividends Per Share	1.560	1.560	1.560	1.560	1.530	1.490	1.450	1.420
Dividend Payout %	325.00	294.34	195.00	192.59	191.25	147.52	159.34	157.78
Income Statement								
Total Revenue	258,375	998,773	844,887	761,438	644,842	450,017	339,009	297,780
EBITDA	135,913	533,759	476,768	417,538	393,522	361,668	286,050	244,305
Depn & Amortn	65,408	257,783	185,391	153,825	141,456	113,265	90,409	78,583
Income Before Taxes	31,289	125,474	156,688	146,605	135,943	151,592	116,786	109,318
Income Taxes	94	574	576	600	375	312	300	...
Net Income	31,272	123,968	158,637	151,164	135,884	151,419	116,485	109,715
Average Shares	237,329	232,963	198,894	187,251	169,176	149,577	128,092	121,863
Balance Sheet								
Current Assets	46,052	43,811	38,138	51,747	51,814	30,688	15,860	14,716
Total Assets	7,154,151	7,183,978	5,968,269	4,764,666	4,748,002	4,383,048	3,392,656	2,987,926
Current Liabilities	33,628	31,982	31,721	27,715	27,284	25,834	17,294	16,228
Long-Term Obligations	3,497,521	3,503,025	2,800,704	1,892,764	2,006,530	1,827,385	1,204,890	1,042,219
Total Liabilities	3,831,407	3,824,218	3,015,862	1,987,677	2,101,434	1,910,442	1,264,679	1,087,276
Stockholders' Equity	3,322,744	3,359,760	2,952,407	2,776,989	2,646,568	2,472,606	2,127,977	1,900,650
Shares Outstanding	237,471	237,471	203,910	188,167	176,553	162,646	141,854	127,377
Statistical Record								
Return on Assets %	1.69	1.89	2.96	3.18	2.97	3.89	3.65	4.00
Return on Equity %	3.35	3.93	5.54	5.57	5.29	6.58	5.78	6.04
EBITDA Margin %	52.60	53.44	56.43	54.84	61.03	80.37	84.38	82.04
Net Margin %	12.10	12.41	18.78	19.85	21.07	33.65	34.36	36.84
Asset Turnover	0.15	0.15	0.16	0.16	0.14	0.12	0.11	0.11
Current Ratio	1.37	1.37	1.20	1.87	1.90	1.19	0.92	0.91
Debt to Equity	1.05	1.04	0.95	0.68	0.76	0.74	0.57	0.55
Price Range	22.14-13.62	23.42-13.74	24.27-20.72	29.39-21.64	23.47-19.75	24.31-18.91	24.95-19.29	22.37-11.28
P/E Ratio	46.12-28.38	44.18-25.92	30.33-25.90	36.28-26.72	29.34-24.69	24.07-18.72	27.42-21.20	24.85-12.54
Average Yield %	9.32	8.50	8.25	6.95	6.30	7.00	6.63	6.60	8.20

Address: Two Newton Place, 255 Washington Street, Suite 300, Newton, MA 02458-1634 Telephone: 617-796-8350 Fax: 617-796-8349	Web Site: www.snhreit.com Officers: David J. Hegarty - President, Chief Operating Officer Richard W. Siedel - Chief Financial Officer, Treasurer	Auditors: Ernst & Young LLP Transfer Agents: Wells Fargo Bank, National Association, Mendota Heights, MN

SENSIENT TECHNOLOGIES CORP.

Exchange	Symbol	Price	52Wk Range	Yield	P/E	Div Achiever
NYS	SXT	$68.22 (5/31/2016)	70.25-53.92	1.58	29.03	10 Years

*7 Year Price Score 125.04 *NYSE Composite Index=100 *12 Month Price Score 102.74

Interim Earnings (Per Share)

Qtr.	Mar	Jun	Sep	Dec
2013	0.43	0.65	0.63	0.56
2014	(0.04)	0.59	0.44	0.53
2015	0.64	0.63	0.60	0.43
2016	0.69	...	...	...

Interim Dividends (Per Share)

Amt	Decl	Ex	Rec	Pay
0.27Q	07/23/2015	08/05/2015	08/07/2015	09/01/2015
0.27Q	10/21/2015	11/04/2015	11/06/2015	12/01/2015
0.27Q	01/22/2016	02/04/2016	02/08/2016	03/01/2016
0.27Q	04/22/2016	05/04/2016	05/06/2016	06/01/2016

Indicated Div: $1.08

Valuation Analysis — **Institutional Holding**

Forecast EPS	$3.20 (05/15/2016)	No of Institutions 320
Market Cap	$3.1 Billion	Shares
Book Value	$867.5 Million	51,064,588
Price/Book	3.53	% Held
Price/Sales	2.23	83.74

Business Summary: Specialty Chemicals (MIC: 8.3.2 SIC: 2816 NAIC: 325131)

Sensient Technologies is a manufacturer and marketer of colors, flavors and fragrances. Co.'s principal products include: flavors, flavor enhancers, ingredients and bionutrients; fragrances, aroma chemicals and essential oils; natural ingredients, including dehydrated vegetables and other food ingredients; natural and synthetic food and beverage colors; cosmetic colors and ingredients and pharmaceutical excipients and ingredients; and technical colors, inks and colors, and dyes and pigments. Co.'s three segments are the Flavors & Fragrances Group and the Color Group, which are managed on a product-and-services basis, and the Asia Pacific Group, which is managed on a geographic basis.

Recent Developments: For the quarter ended Mar 31 2016, income from continuing operations increased 1.5% to US$31.2 million from US$30.7 million in the year-earlier quarter. Net income increased 2.1% to US$31.2 million from US$30.5 million in the year-earlier quarter. Revenues were US$342.5 million, down 1.1% from US$346.2 million the year before. Operating income was US$47.5 million versus US$46.4 million in the prior-year quarter, an increase of 2.3%. Direct operating expenses declined 0.9% to US$226.6 million from US$228.8 million in the comparable period the year before. Indirect operating expenses decreased 3.8% to US$68.3 million from US$71.0 million in the equivalent prior-year period.

Prospects: Our evaluation of Sensient Technologies Corp. as of June 19, 2016 is the result of our systematic analysis on three basic characteristics: earnings strength, relative valuation, and recent stock price movement. The company has managed to produce a neutral trend in earnings per share over the past 5 quarters. However, while recent estimates for the company have been mixed, SXT has posted results that were in line with analysts expectations. Based on operating earnings yield, the company is about fairly valued when compared to all of the companies in our coverage universe. Share price changes over the past year indicates that SXT will perform poorly over the near term.

Financial Data

(US$ in Thousands)	3 Mos	12/31/2015	12/31/2014	12/31/2013	12/31/2012	12/31/2011	12/31/2010	12/31/2009
Earnings Per Share	2.35	2.31	1.51	2.27	2.49	2.41	2.17	1.78
Cash Flow Per Share	3.21	2.79	3.90	3.09	2.80	2.87	3.17	2.86
Tang Book Value Per Share	10.09	9.74	12.95	15.54	13.91	11.86	10.59	9.00
Dividends Per Share	1 060	1.040	0.980	0.910	0.870	0.840	0.790	0.760
Dividend Payout %	45.11	45.02	64.90	40.09	34.94	34.85	36.41	42.70
Income Statement								
Total Revenue	342,468	1,375,964	1,447,821	1,467,550	1,459,050	1,430,789	1,328,180	1,201,412
EBITDA	59,131	213,035	180,890	223,078	238,200	235,594	216,686	189,146
Depn & Amortn	11,612	46,694	50,225	50,716	46,992	44,771	42,109	42,183
Income Before Taxes	42,719	149,396	114,598	156,215	174,307	171,384	154,193	123,175
Income Taxes	11,526	42,149	32,827	42,920	50,399	50,900	47,049	36,614
Net Income	31,171	106,785	73,646	113,295	123,908	120,484	107,144	86,561
Average Shares	44,981	46,204	48,819	49,934	49,822	49,937	49,424	48,641
Balance Sheet								
Current Assets	753,863	753,343	759,389	789,825	751,354	706,870	672,305	658,109
Total Assets	1,742,977	1,711,437	1,765,206	1,870,734	1,776,643	1,654,164	1,599,268	1,591,691
Current Liabilities	213,832	212,922	224,905	222,893	204,236	207,275	205,063	216,145
Long-Term Obligations	629,891	613,877	451,011	348,124	333,979	312,422	324,360	388,852
Total Liabilities	875,510	866,310	718,271	628,050	622,745	604,954	615,483	682,996
Stockholders' Equity	867,467	845,127	1,046,935	1,242,684	1,153,898	1,049,210	983,785	908,695
Shares Outstanding	44,826	44,780	47,424	49,849	49,690	49,916	49,609	48,772
Statistical Record								
Return on Assets %	6.28	6.14	4.05	6.21	7.20	7.41	6.72	5.55
Return on Equity %	11.86	11.29	6.43	9.45	11.22	11.85	11.32	10.02
EBITDA Margin %	17.27	15.48	12.49	15.20	16.33	16.47	16.31	15.74
Net Margin %	9.10	7.76	5.09	7.72	8.49	8.42	8.07	7.20
Asset Turnover	0.80	0.79	0.80	0.80	0.85	0.88	0.83	0.77
Current Ratio	3.53	3.54	3.38	3.54	3.68	3.41	3.28	3.04
Debt to Equity	0.73	0.73	0.43	0.28	0.29	0.30	0.33	0.43
Price Range	70.25-53.92	70.25-57.39	62.98-46.74	53.32-35.56	40.92-33.81	39.45-30.92	37.47-24.98	29.07-18.60
P/E Ratio	29.89-22.94	30.41-24.84	41.71-30.95	23.49-15.67	16.43-13.58	16.37-12.83	17.27-11.51	16.33-10.45
Average Yield %	1.65	1.60	1.80	2.13	2.37	2.36	2.66	3.10

Address: 777 East Wisconsin Avenue, Milwaukee, WI 53202-5304 **Telephone:** 414-271-6755 **Fax:** 414-347-4795	**Web Site:** www.sensient.com **Officers:** Paul Manning - President, Chief Executive Officer, Division Officer Stephen J. Rolfs - Vice President, Senior Vice President, Chief Financial Officer	**Auditors:** Ernst & Young LLP **Investor Contact:** 414-347-3779 **Transfer Agents:** Wells Fargo Bank Minnesota, N.A., St. Paul, MN

SERVICE CORP. INTERNATIONAL

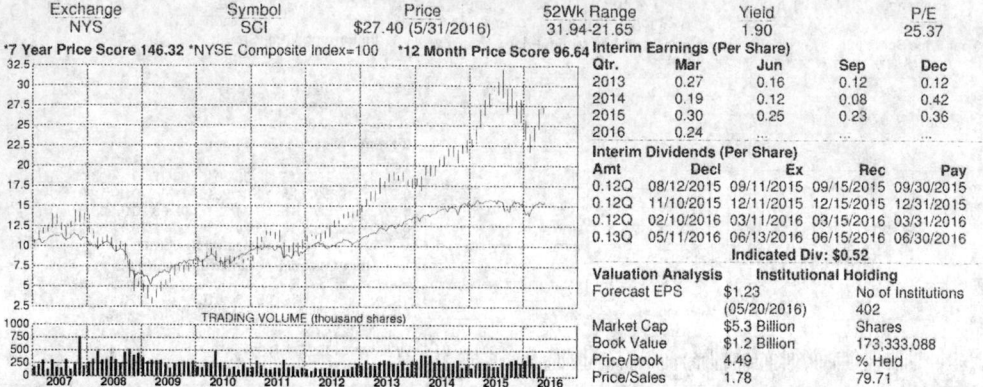

Exchange	Symbol	Price	52Wk Range	Yield	P/E
NYS	SCI	$27.40 (5/31/2016)	31.94-21.65	1.90	25.37

*7 Year Price Score 146.32 *NYSE Composite Index=100   *12 Month Price Score 96.64

Interim Earnings (Per Share)

Qtr.	Mar	Jun	Sep	Dec
2013	0.27	0.16	0.12	0.12
2014	0.19	0.12	0.08	0.42
2015	0.30	0.25	0.23	0.36
2016	0.24	...	...	...

Interim Dividends (Per Share)

Amt	Decl	Ex	Rec	Pay
0.12Q	08/12/2015	09/11/2015	09/15/2015	09/30/2015
0.12Q	11/10/2015	12/11/2015	12/15/2015	12/31/2015
0.12Q	02/10/2016	03/11/2016	03/15/2016	03/31/2016
0.13Q	05/11/2016	06/13/2016	06/15/2016	06/30/2016

Indicated Div: $0.52

Valuation Analysis

Forecast EPS	$1.23
	(05/20/2016)
Market Cap	$5.3 Billion
Book Value	$1.2 Billion
Price/Book	4.49
Price/Sales	1.78

Institutional Holding

No of Institutions	402
Shares	173,333,088
% Held	79.71

Business Summary: Miscellaneous Consumer Services (MIC: 2.2.3 SIC: 7261 NAIC: 812210)

Service Corporation International provides deathcare products and services. Co.'s funeral service and cemetery operations consist of funeral service locations, cemeteries, funeral service/cemetery combination locations, crematoria, and related businesses. Co.'s funeral service locations provide services relating to funerals and cremations, including the use of funeral facilities and motor vehicles, arranging and directing services, removal, preparation, embalming, cremations, memorialization, and catering. Co.'s cemeteries provide cemetery property interment rights, including developed lots, lawn crypts, mausoleum spaces, niches, and other cremation memorialization and interment options.

Recent Developments: For the quarter ended Mar 31 2016, net income decreased 22.8% to US$47.5 million from US$61.5 million in the year-earlier quarter. Revenues were US$749.3 million, up 0.2% from US$748.1 million the year before. Operating income was US$123.6 million versus US$141.1 million in the prior-year quarter, a decrease of 12.4%. Direct operating expenses rose 3.0% to US$587.8 million from US$570.7 million in the comparable period the year before. Indirect operating expenses increased 4.2% to US$37.9 million from US$36.3 million in the equivalent prior-year period.

Prospects: Our evaluation of Service Corp. International as of June 19, 2016 is the result of our systematic analysis on three basic characteristics: earnings strength, relative valuation, and recent stock price movement. The company has managed to produce a neutral trend in earnings per share over the past 5 quarters and while recent estimates for the company have remained steady, SCI has posted better than expected results. Based on operating earnings yield, the company is about fairly valued when compared to all of the companies in our coverage universe. Share price changes over the past year indicates that SCI will perform in line with the market over the near term.

Financial Data

(US$ in Thousands)	3 Mos	12/31/2015	12/31/2014	12/31/2013	12/31/2012	12/31/2011	12/31/2010	12/31/2009
Earnings Per Share	1.08	1.14	0.81	0.67	0.70	0.61	0.50	0.49
Cash Flow Per Share	2.40	2.36	1.51	1.82	1.71	1.66	1.42	1.48
Tang Book Value Per Share	N.M.	N.M.	N.M.	N.M.	N.M.	N.M.	N.M.	0.46
Dividends Per Share	0.460	0.440	0.340	0.270	0.280	0.190	0.160	0.160
Dividend Payout %	42.59	38.60	41.98	40.30	40.00	31.15	32.00	32.65
Income Statement								
Total Revenue	749,271	2,986,380	2,994,012	2,556,382	2,410,481	2,316,040	2,190,552	2,053,520
EBITDA	127,607	606,869	671,628	453,386	450,118	300,357	297,461	265,644
Depn & Amortn	22,881	172,915	167,186	138,198	137,660	25,591	25,197	21,698
Income Before Taxes	79,767	370,351	402,600	245,719	245,683	225,636	219,459	199,368
Income Taxes	32,313	135,027	225,980	96,615	91,548	79,404	92,458	76,275
Net Income	47,445	233,772	172,469	143,848	152,546	144,903	126,417	123,098
Average Shares	198,030	204,450	214,200	216,014	219,066	236,669	250,602	252,484
Balance Sheet								
Current Assets	352,881	308,409	396,856	393,747	286,199	328,093	381,918	377,461
Total Assets	11,756,131	11,718,888	11,923,644	12,906,070	9,683,568	9,327,812	9,190,540	8,890,981
Current Liabilities	517,811	519,396	552,008	642,584	412,104	385,608	366,627	365,515
Long-Term Obligations	3,076,342	3,071,738	2,963,794	3,155,548	1,916,621	1,861,116	1,832,380	1,840,532
Total Liabilities	10,570,765	10,534,196	10,554,918	11,491,840	8,340,541	7,935,718	7,711,084	7,408,205
Stockholders' Equity	1,185,366	1,184,692	1,368,726	1,414,230	1,343,027	1,392,094	1,479,456	1,482,776
Shares Outstanding	194,147	195,772	204,866	212,316	211,046	222,955	241,035	254,017
Statistical Record								
Return on Assets %	1.85	1.98	1.39	1.27	1.60	1.56	1.40	1.45
Return on Equity %	17.46	18.31	12.39	10.43	11.12	10.09	8.54	8.87
EBITDA Margin %	17.03	20.32	22.43	17.74	18.67	12.97	13.58	12.94
Net Margin %	6.33	7.83	5.76	5.63	6.33	6.26	5.77	5.99
Asset Turnover	0.25	0.25	0.24	0.23	0.25	0.25	0.24	0.24
Current Ratio	0.68	0.59	0.72	0.61	0.69	0.85	1.04	1.03
Debt to Equity	2.60	2.59	2.17	2.23	1.43	1.34	1.24	1.24
Price Range	31.94-21.65	31.94-22.29	23.22-16.82	19.24-13.81	14.54-10.55	12.01-8.12	9.62-7.15	8.25-2.74
P/E Ratio	29.57-20.05	28.02-19.55	28.67-20.77	28.72-20.61	20.77-15.07	19.69-13.31	19.24-14.30	16.84-5.59
Average Yield %	1.69	1.61	1.67	1.56	2.26	1.83	1.92	2.04

Address: 1929 Allen Parkway, Houston, TX 77019 **Telephone:** 713-522-5141	**Web Site:** www.sci-corp.com **Officers:** Thomas L. Ryan - Chairman, President, Chief Executive Officer Michael R. Webb - President, Executive Vice President, Chief Operating Officer	**Auditors:** PricewaterhouseCoopers LLP **Transfer Agents:** Computershare Shareowner Services, Providence, RI

SERVICENOW INC

Exchange	Symbol	Price	52Wk Range	Yield	P/E
NYS	NOW	$71.63 (5/31/2016)	89.99-47.14	N/A	N/A

*7 Year Price Score N/A *NYSE Composite Index=100 *12 Month Price Score 93.33

Interim Earnings (Per Share)

Qtr.	Mar	Jun	Sep	Dec
2013	(0.10)	(0.16)	(0.11)	(0.17)
2014	(0.30)	(0.35)	(0.28)	(0.30)
2015	(0.38)	(0.40)	(0.26)	(0.23)
2016	(2.06)	...	...	...

Interim Dividends (Per Share)

No Dividends Paid

Valuation Analysis | **Institutional Holding**

Forecast EPS	$0.62	No of Institutions
	(05/20/2016)	425
Market Cap	$11.7 Billion	Shares
Book Value	$302.4 Million	164,969,104
Price/Book	38.58	% Held
Price/Sales	10.61	92.96

Business Summary: IT Services (MIC: 6.3.1 SIC: 7372 NAIC: 511210)

ServiceNow is a provider of cloud-based solutions that define, structure, manage and automate services across the global enterprise. Co. provides business management and information technology (IT) operations management solutions that facilitate the delivery of services across the enterprise. Co.'s software applications are delivered via the Internet, or cloud, through a consumer-like interface. Co. markets its services to enterprises in a variety of industries, including financial services, consumer products, IT services, health care and technology. Co. also provides a portfolio of services to customers through its services personnel and a network of partners.

Recent Developments: For the quarter ended Mar 31 2016, net loss amounted to US$333.3 million versus a net loss of US$58.1 million in the year-earlier quarter. Revenues were US$305.9 million, up 44.3% from US$212.0 million the year before. Operating loss was US$324.2 million versus a loss of US$54.2 million in the prior-year quarter. Direct operating expenses rose 22.6% to US$94.3 million from US$76.9 million in the comparable period the year before. Indirect operating expenses increased 183.0% to US$535.8 million from US$189.3 million in the equivalent prior-year period.

Prospects: Our evaluation of ServiceNow Inc as of June 19, 2016 is the result of our systematic analysis on three basic characteristics: earnings strength, relative valuation, and recent stock price movement. The company has managed to produce a neutral trend in earnings per share over the past 5 quarters and while recent estimates for the company have remained steady, NOW has posted better than expected results. Based on operating earnings yield, the company is overvalued when compared to all of the companies in our coverage universe. Share price changes over the past year indicates that NOW will perform poorly over the near term.

Financial Data
(US$ in Thousands)

	3 Mos	12/31/2015	12/31/2014	12/31/2013	12/31/2012	12/31/2011	06/30/2011	12/31/2010
Earnings Per Share	(2.95)	(1.27)	(1.23)	(0.54)	(0.51)	(0.33)	0.08	0.04
Cash Flow Per Share	2.01	2.02	0.96	0.60	0.66	0.63	4.16	0.42
Tang Book Value Per Share	1.22	2.91	2.13	2.71	1.93	0.48	0.46	...
Income Statement								
Total Revenue	305,879	1,005,480	682,563	424,650	243,712	73,375	92,641	37,944
EBITDA	(283,253)	(106,065)	(109,735)	(43,667)	(24,084)	(2,163)	12,060	5,667
Depn & Amortn	42,232	60,300	42,100	22,600	13,500	2,000	1,500	500
Income Before Taxes	(331,559)	(193,012)	(175,540)	(71,197)	(35,980)	(5,609)	11,166	5,456
Income Taxes	1,773	5,414	3,847	2,511	1,368	1,075	1,336	653
Net Income	(333,332)	(198,426)	(179,387)	(73,708)	(37,348)	(6,684)	9,830	4,803
Average Shares	162,067	155,706	145,355	135,415	73,908	21,104	28,095	27,622
Balance Sheet								
Current Assets	1,193,258	1,085,635	906,986	797,749	422,089	130,507	96,893	...
Total Assets	1,874,043	1,807,052	1,425,079	1,168,476	478,114	156,323	108,746	...
Current Liabilities	1,048,283	731,636	506,997	328,088	211,627	126,561	87,986	...
Long-Term Obligations	482,643	474,534	443,764	414,777	...	...	...	...
Total Liabilities	1,571,687	1,240,238	996,404	774,217	234,709	145,577	99,267	...
Stockholders' Equity	302,356	566,814	428,675	394,259	243,405	10,746	9,479	...
Shares Outstanding	162,848	160,785	149,509	140,354	126,367	22,229	20,772	...
Statistical Record								
EBITDA Margin %	N.M.	N.M.	N.M.	N.M.	N.M.	N.M.	13.02	14.94
Net Margin %	N.M.	N.M.	N.M.	N.M.	N.M.	N.M.	10.61	12.66
Asset Turnover	0.65	0.62	0.53	0.52	0.77	...	...	...
Current Ratio	1.14	1.48	1.79	2.43	1.99	1.03	1.10	...
Debt to Equity	1.60	0.84	1.04	1.05	...	...	...	...
Price Range	89.99-47.14	89.99-63.63	70.81-46.42	58.37-26.07	40.37-23.74	...	...	...

Address: 2225 Lawson Lane, Santa Clara, CA 95054	Web Site: www.servicenow.com	Auditors: PricewaterhouseCoopers LLP
Telephone: 408-501-8550	Officers: Paul V. Barber - Chairman Frank Slootman - President, Chief Executive Officer	Investor Contact: 408-961-2349 Transfer Agents: Computershare Trust Company, N.A

SHERWIN-WILLIAMS CO (THE)

Exchange	Symbol	Price	52Wk Range	Yield	P/E	Div Achiever
NYS	SHW	$291.09 (5/31/2016)	300.12-218.94	1.15	25.62	36 Years

*7 Year Price Score 147.61 *NYSE Composite Index=100 *12 Month Price Score 107.92

TRADING VOLUME (thousand shares)

Interim Earnings (Per Share)

Qtr.	Mar	Jun	Sep	Dec
2013	1.11	2.46	2.55	1.15
2014	1.14	2.94	3.35	1.39
2015	1.38	3.70	3.97	2.12
2016	1.57	...	...	...

Interim Dividends (Per Share)

Amt	Decl	Ex	Rec	Pay
0.67Q	07/15/2015	08/12/2015	08/14/2015	09/04/2015
0.67Q	10/21/2015	11/10/2015	11/13/2015	12/04/2015
0.84Q	02/17/2016	02/25/2016	02/29/2016	03/11/2016
0.84Q	04/20/2016	05/18/2016	05/20/2016	06/03/2016

Indicated Div: $3.36 (Div. Reinv. Plan)

Valuation Analysis | Institutional Holding

Forecast EPS	$12.67 (05/20/2016)	No of Institutions	927
Market Cap	$26.9 Billion	Shares	90,958,944
Book Value	$1.0 Billion	% Held	71.24
Price/Book	26.90		
Price/Sales	2.35		

Business Summary: Specialty Chemicals (MIC: 8.3.2 SIC: 5231 NAIC: 444120)

Sherwin-Williams is engaged in the development, manufacture, distribution and sale of paint, coatings and related products to industrial, commercial and retail customers primarily in North and South America with additional operations in the Caribbean region, Europe and Asia. Co. has four reportable operating segments: Paint Stores Group, Consumer Group, Global Finishes Group and Latin America Coatings Group. As of Dec 31 2015, there were 4,003 Co.-operated specialty paint stores in the Paint Stores Group; 300 Co.-operated branches in the Global Finishes Group; and 276 Co.-operated stores in the Latin America Coatings Group.

Recent Developments: For the quarter ended Mar 31 2016, net income increased 12.0% to US$147.1 million from US$131.4 million in the year-earlier quarter. Revenues were US$2.57 billion, up 5.1% from US$2.45 billion the year before. Direct operating expenses declined 0.4% to US$1.31 billion from US$1.32 billion in the comparable period the year before. Indirect operating expenses increased 10.0% to US$1.02 billion from US$927.5 million in the equivalent prior-year period.

Prospects: Our evaluation of Sherwin-Williams Co. as of June 19, 2016 is the result of our systematic analysis on three basic characteristics: earnings strength, relative valuation, and recent stock price movement. The company has managed to produce a neutral trend in earnings per share over the past 5 quarters and while recent estimates for the company have been mixed, SHW has posted better than expected results. Based on operating earnings yield, the company is about fairly valued when compared to all of the companies in our coverage universe. Share price changes over the past year indicates that SHW will perform well over the near term.

Financial Data

(US$ in Thousands)	3 Mos	12/31/2015	12/31/2014	12/31/2013	12/31/2012	12/31/2011	12/31/2010	12/31/2009
Earnings Per Share	11.36	11.16	8.78	7.26	6.02	4.14	4.21	3.78
Cash Flow Per Share	15.55	15.70	11.24	10.74	8.71	7.11	6.60	7.57
Tang Book Value Per Share	N.M.	N.M.	N.M.	2.42	1.81	N.M.	N.M.	N.M.
Dividends Per Share	2.850	2.680	2.200	2.000	1.560	1.460	1.440	1.420
Dividend Payout %	25.09	24.01	25.06	27.55	25.91	35.27	34.20	37.57
Income Statement								
Total Revenue	2,574,024	11,339,304	11,129,533	10,185,532	9,534,462	8,765,699	7,776,424	7,094,249
EBITDA	296,943	1,807,920	1,518,381	1,333,224	1,126,386	961,238	920,761	831,354
Depn & Amortn	55,333	198,562	198,945	187,794	179,202	180,904	175,311	170,904
Income Before Taxes	216,365	1,548,966	1,258,226	1,085,958	907,309	741,548	677,784	622,817
Income Taxes	69,237	495,117	392,339	333,397	276,275	299,688	215,299	186,969
Net Income	147,128	1,053,849	865,887	752,561	631,034	441,860	462,485	435,848
Average Shares	93,548	94,024	98,075	103,048	103,930	105,671	108,785	113,514
Balance Sheet								
Current Assets	2,888,625	2,658,874	2,566,780	3,158,717	3,149,238	2,261,593	2,213,722	1,770,019
Total Assets	6,038,309	5,791,855	5,706,052	6,382,507	6,234,737	5,229,252	5,169,235	4,323,855
Current Liabilities	2,262,561	2,141,859	2,680,666	2,528,557	1,876,436	2,162,661	2,063,940	1,393,668
Long-Term Obligations	1,908,774	1,920,196	1,122,715	1,122,373	1,632,165	639,231	648,326	782,670
Total Liabilities	5,037,486	4,923,945	4,709,582	4,607,972	4,442,933	3,712,333	3,559,795	2,832,905
Stockholders' Equity	1,000,823	867,910	996,470	1,774,535	1,791,804	1,516,919	1,609,440	1,490,950
Shares Outstanding	92,495	92,246	94,704	100,129	103,270	103,854	107,020	109,436
Statistical Record								
Return on Assets %	17.98	18.33	14.33	11.93	10.98	8.50	9.74	9.97
Return on Equity %	145.52	113.05	62.50	42.20	38.04	28.27	29.83	28.15
EBITDA Margin %	11.54	15.94	13.64	13.09	11.81	10.97	11.84	11.72
Net Margin %	5.72	9.29	7.78	7.39	6.62	5.04	5.95	6.14
Asset Turnover	1.93	1.97	1.84	1.61	1.66	1.69	1.64	1.62
Current Ratio	1.28	1.24	0.96	1.25	1.68	1.05	1.07	1.27
Debt to Equity	1.91	2.21	1.13	0.63	0.91	0.42	0.40	0.52
Price Range	292.44-218.94	292.44-218.94	264.93-175.60	195.07-153.82	158.59-91.00	90.08-69.57	84.50-58.00	63.75-42.98
P/E Ratio	25.74-19.27	26.20-19.62	30.17-20.00	26.87-21.19	26.34-15.12	21.76-16.80	20.07-13.78	16.87-11.37
Average Yield %	1.07	0.99	1.04	1.13	1.20	1.78	2.01	2.54

Address: 101 West Prospect Avenue, Cleveland, OH 44115-1075	Web Site: www.sherwin.com	Auditors: Ernst & Young LLP
Telephone: 216-566-2000	Officers: Christopher M. Connor - Executive Chairman, Chairman, Chief Executive Officer Thomas P. Gilligan - Senior Vice President	Investor Contact: 216-566-2244
Fax: 216-566-3310		Transfer Agents: Wells Fargo Shareowner Services, St. Paul, MN

SIGNET JEWELERS LTD

Exchange	Symbol	Price	52Wk Range	Yield	P/E
NYS	SIG	$98.97 (5/31/2016)	150.94-94.71	1.05	15.81

*7 Year Price Score 152.06 ***NYSE Composite Index=100** ***12 Month Price Score 87.15**

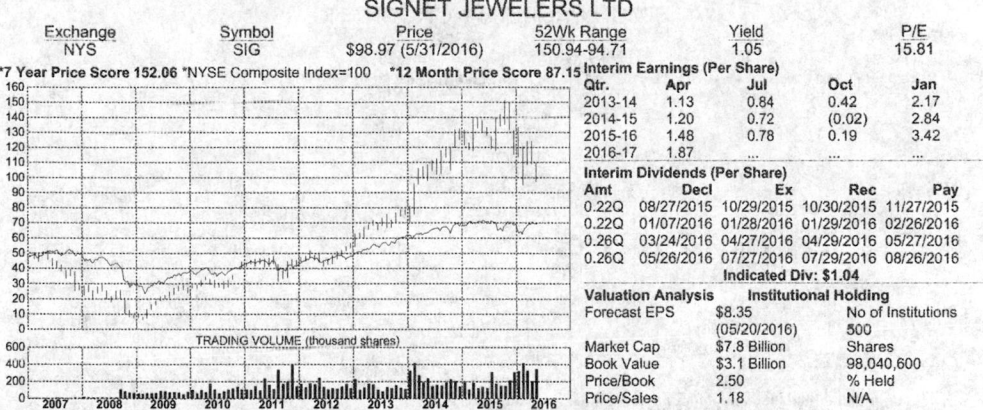

Interim Earnings (Per Share)

Qtr.	Apr	Jul	Oct	Jan
2013-14	1.13	0.84	0.42	2.17
2014-15	1.20	0.72	(0.02)	2.84
2015-16	1.48	0.78	0.19	3.42
2016-17	1.87	...	...	...

Interim Dividends (Per Share)

Amt	Decl	Ex	Rec	Pay
0.22Q	08/27/2015	10/29/2015	10/30/2015	11/27/2015
0.22Q	01/07/2016	01/28/2016	01/29/2016	02/26/2016
0.26Q	03/24/2016	04/27/2016	04/29/2016	05/27/2016
0.26Q	05/26/2016	07/27/2016	07/27/2016	08/26/2016

Indicated Div: $1.04

Valuation Analysis

		Institutional Holding	
Forecast EPS	$8.35	No of Institutions	
	(05/20/2016)	500	
Market Cap	$7.8 Billion	Shares	
Book Value	$3.1 Billion	98,040,600	
Price/Book	2.50	% Held	
Price/Sales	1.18	N/A	

Business Summary: Retail - Specialty (MIC: 2.1.3 SIC: 5944 NAIC: 448310)

Signet Jewelers is a holding company. Through its subsidiaries, Co. is a retail jeweler. Co. manages its business by store brand grouping. The Sterling Jewelers division operated 1,540 stores in all 50 U.S. states at Jan 30 2016 in malls and off-mall locations. The Zale division consists of two segments: Zale Jewelry, which operated 977 jewelry stores, is located in shopping malls in North America; and Piercing Pagoda, which operated 605 mall-based kiosks at Jan 30 2016, is located in shopping malls in the U.S. and Puerto Rico. The U.K. Jewelry division operated 503 stores at Jan 30 2016 in shopping malls and off-mall locations (i.e. high street) primarily as H.Samuel and Ernest Jones.

Recent Developments: For the quarter ended Apr 30 2016, net income increased 23.6% to US$146.8 million from US$118.8 million in the year-earlier quarter. Revenues were US$1.58 billion, up 3.2% from US$1.53 billion the year before. Operating income was US$212.0 million versus US$176.2 million in the prior-year quarter, an increase of 20.3%. Direct operating expenses rose 1.4% to US$978.5 million from US$964.7 million in the comparable period the year before. Indirect operating expenses decreased 0.3% to US$388.4 million from US$389.7 million in the equivalent prior-year period.

Prospects: Our evaluation of Signet Jewelers Limited as of June 19, 2016 is the result of our systematic analysis on three basic characteristics: earnings strength, relative valuation, and recent stock price movement. The company has managed to produce a neutral trend in earnings per share over the past 5 quarters. However, while recent estimates for the company have been lowered by analysts, SIG has posted better than expected results. Based on operating earnings yield, the company is undervalued when compared to all of the companies in our coverage universe. Share price changes over the past year indicates that SIG will perform very well over the near term.

Financial Data

(US$ in Thousands)	3 Mos	01/30/2016	01/31/2015	02/01/2014	02/02/2013	01/28/2012	01/29/2011	01/30/2010
Earnings Per Share	6.26	5.87	4.75	4.56	4.35	3.73	2.32	1.91
Cash Flow Per Share	6.24	5.59	3.55	2.94	3.74	3.78	3.79	6.06
Tang Book Value Per Share	27.40	26.67	22.97	31.62	28.32	26.32	22.18	20.74
Dividends Per Share	0.920	0.880	0.720	0.600	0.480	0.200	...	...
Dividend Payout %	14.70	14.99	15.16	13.16	11.03	5.36	...	...
Income Statement								
Total Revenue	1,578,900	6,550,200	5,736,300	4,209,200	3,983,400	3,749,200	3,437,400	3,290,700
EBITDA	208,000	865,100	716,700	680,700	659,900	599,800	470,300	384,700
Depn & Amortn	(4,000)	161,400	140,100	110,200	99,400	92,400	97,800	108,900
Income Before Taxes	200,200	657,800	540,600	566,500	556,900	502,100	300,400	241,800
Income Taxes	53,400	189,900	159,300	198,500	197,000	177,700	100,000	77,700
Net Income	146,800	467,900	381,300	368,000	359,900	324,400	200,400	164,100
Average Shares	78,700	79,700	80,200	80,700	82,800	87,000	86,400	85,700
Balance Sheet								
Current Assets	4,541,200	4,589,900	4,407,300	3,257,600	3,032,900	3,016,300	2,542,300	2,435,800
Total Assets	6,427,700	6,474,400	6,327,600	4,029,200	3,715,800	3,611,400	3,089,800	2,924,200
Current Liabilities	1,055,800	1,152,900	1,338,300	900,700	868,700	867,200	711,000	621,300
Long-Term Obligations	1,311,500	1,328,700	1,363,800	...	...	...	...	280,000
Total Liabilities	3,329,500	3,413,700	3,517,200	1,466,100	1,385,900	1,332,300	1,150,800	1,126,600
Stockholders' Equity	3,098,200	3,060,700	2,810,400	2,563,100	2,329,900	2,279,100	1,939,000	1,797,600
Shares Outstanding	78,400	79,400	80,300	80,200	81,400	86,600	86,200	85,500
Statistical Record								
Return on Assets %	7.83	7.33	7.38	9.53	9.66	9.71	6.68	5.60
Return on Equity %	16.56	15.98	14.23	15.08	15.36	15.42	10.76	9.66
EBITDA Margin %	13.17	13.21	12.49	16.17	16.57	16.00	13.68	11.69
Net Margin %	9.30	7.14	6.65	8.74	9.03	8.65	5.83	4.99
Asset Turnover	1.04	1.03	1.11	1.09	1.07	1.12	1.15	1.12
Current Ratio	4.30	3.98	3.29	3.62	3.49	3.48	3.58	3.92
Debt to Equity	0.42	0.43	0.49	...	...	...	...	0.16
Price Range	150.94-94.71	150.94-113.39	132.12-75.28	80.86-59.64	63.43-41.27	48.01-31.26	44.30-26.44	28.97-6.06
P/E Ratio	24.11-15.13	25.71-19.32	27.81-15.85	17.73-13.08	14.58-9.49	12.87-8.38	19.09-11.40	15.17-3.17
Average Yield %	0.73	0.68	0.65	0.85	0.98	0.47	...	...

Address: Clarendon House, 2 Church Street, Hamilton, HM11
Telephone: 441-296-5872

Web Site: www.signetjewelers.com
Officers: Mark S. Light - President, Chief Executive Officer, Chief Operating Officer Michele Santana - Chief Financial Officer

Auditors: KPMG LLP
Investor Contact: 440-207-3179700
Transfer Agents: Capita Registrars, Kent, United Kingdom

SIMON PROPERTY GROUP, INC.

Exchange	Symbol	Price	52Wk Range	Yield	P/E
NYS	SPG	$197.64 (5/31/2016)	213.92-171.00	3.21	31.52

*7 Year Price Score 120.04 *NYSE Composite Index=100 *12 Month Price Score 105.66

Interim Earnings (Per Share)

Qtr.	Mar	Jun	Sep	Dec
2013	0.91	1.10	1.00	1.23
2014	1.10	1.31	0.81	1.30
2015	1.16	1.52	1.36	1.84
2016	1.55	...	...	...

Interim Dividends (Per Share)

Amt	Decl	Ex	Rec	Pay
1.55Q	07/24/2015	08/13/2015	08/17/2015	08/31/2015
1.60Q	10/27/2015	11/12/2015	11/16/2015	11/30/2015
1.60Q	01/29/2016	02/10/2016	02/12/2016	02/29/2016
1.60Q	04/26/2016	05/13/2016	05/17/2016	05/31/2016

Indicated Div: $6.35

Valuation Analysis | **Institutional Holding**

Forecast EPS	$6.26	No of Institutions
	(05/20/2016)	941
Market Cap	$62.2 Billion	Shares
Book Value	$4.7 Billion	371,410,272
Price/Book	13.11	% Held
Price/Sales	11.55	94.95

Business Summary: REITs (MIC: 5.3.1 SIC: 6798 NAIC: 525930)

Simon Property Group is a self-administered and self-managed real estate investment trust. Co. owns, develops and manages retail real estate properties, which consist primarily of malls, Premium Outlets®, and The Mills®. As of Dec 31 2015, Co. owned or held an interest in 209 properties in the U.S., which consisted of 108 malls, 71 Premium Outlets, 14 Mills, four lifestyle centers, and 12 other retail properties in 37 states and Puerto Rico. Internationally, as of Dec 31 2015, Co. had ownership interests in nine Premium Outlets in Japan, three Premium Outlets in South Korea, two Premium Outlets in Canada, one Premium Outlet in Mexico, and one Premium Outlet in Malaysia.

Recent Developments: For the quarter ended Mar 31 2016, net income decreased 10.8% to US$563.8 million from US$632.4 million in the year-earlier quarter. Revenues were US$1.34 billion, up 9.9% from US$1.22 billion the year before. Revenues from property income rose 7.6% to US$1.22 billion from US$1.13 billion in the corresponding quarter a year earlier.

Prospects: Our evaluation of Simon Property Group Inc. as of June 19, 2016 is the result of our systematic analysis on three basic characteristics: earnings strength, relative valuation, and recent stock price movement. The company has managed to produce a neutral trend in earnings per share over the past 5 quarters. Because the company lacks sufficient analyst estimate data, we place greater weight on the historical EPS trend as the measure of earnings strength. Based on operating earnings yield, the company is about fairly valued when compared to all of the companies in our coverage universe. Share price changes over the past year indicates that SPG will perform well over the near term.

Financial Data

(US$ in Thousands)	3 Mos	12/31/2015	12/31/2014	12/31/2013	12/31/2012	12/31/2011	12/31/2010	12/31/2009
Earnings Per Share	6.27	5.88	4.52	4.24	4.72	3.48	2.10	1.05
Cash Flow Per Share	9.92	9.75	8.79	8.71	8.27	6.83	6.03	6.44
Tang Book Value Per Share	14.94	13.50	15.33	17.98	17.87	15.57	16.00	17.11
Dividends Per Share	6.250	6.050	5.150	4.650	4.100	3.500	2.600	2.700
Dividend Payout %	99.68	102.89	113.94	109.67	86.86	100.57	123.81	257.14
Income Statement								
Total Revenue	1,336,715	5,266,103	4,870,818	5,170,138	4,880,084	4,306,432	3,957,630	3,775,216
EBITDA	987,514	4,017,480	3,673,776	3,816,420	4,016,054	3,260,626	2,720,711	2,348,597
Depn & Amortn	317,799	1,239,214	1,285,784	1,332,950	1,301,304	1,112,438	1,016,027	1,009,490
Income Before Taxes	450,525	1,854,569	1,395,391	1,346,331	1,587,725	1,164,662	677,593	347,042
Net Income	563,839	2,139,375	1,651,526	1,551,590	1,719,632	1,245,900	753,514	387,262
Average Shares	309,416	310,102	310,731	310,255	303,138	293,573	291,350	268,472
Balance Sheet								
Current Assets	1,378,331	1,325,739	1,192,479	2,298,345	1,705,819	1,285,381	1,223,454	4,360,447
Total Assets	31,398,498	30,650,673	29,532,330	33,324,574	32,586,606	26,216,925	24,857,429	25,948,266
Current Liabilities	1,167,101	2,692,345	2,426,844	2,465,704	2,098,916	1,787,281	1,479,593	1,445,284
Long-Term Obligations	22,975,821	22,502,173	20,852,993	23,588,531	23,113,007	18,446,440	17,473,760	18,630,302
Total Liabilities	26,652,384	26,153,672	24,413,616	27,284,683	26,497,997	21,299,314	19,941,180	20,959,756
Stockholders' Equity	4,746,114	4,497,001	5,118,714	6,039,891	6,088,609	4,917,611	4,916,249	4,988,510
Shares Outstanding	314,815	309,420	310,787	310,608	309,903	293,856	292,961	285,748
Statistical Record								
Return on Assets %	7.39	7.11	5.25	4.71	5.83	4.88	2.97	1.56
Return on Equity %	46.92	44.50	29.60	25.59	31.16	25.34	15.22	9.65
EBITDA Margin %	73.88	76.29	75.42	73.82	82.29	75.72	68.75	62.21
Net Margin %	42.18	40.63	33.91	30.01	35.24	28.93	19.04	10.26
Asset Turnover	0.17	0.18	0.15	0.16	0.17	0.17	0.16	0.15
Current Ratio	1.18	0.49	0.49	0.93	0.81	0.72	0.83	3.02
Debt to Equity	4.84	5.00	4.07	3.91	3.80	3.75	3.55	3.73
Price Range	207.69-171.00	206.19-171.00	187.46-141.62	169.56-134.02	153.76-119.15	123.17-89.65	99.90-65.30	78.08-24.62
P/E Ratio	33.12-27.27	35.07-29.08	41.47-31.33	39.99-31.61	32.58-25.24	35.39-25.76	47.57-31.09	74.36-23.45
Average Yield %	3.32	3.21	3.13	3.13	3.10	2.92	3.27	5.18

Address: 225 West Washington Street, Indianapolis, IN 46204 Telephone: 317-636-1600 Fax: 317-685-7336	Web Site: www.simon.com Officers: David Simon - Chairman, Chief Executive Officer Herbert Simon - Chairman Emeritus, Chairman	Auditors: Ernst & Young LLP Investor Contact: 800-461-3439 Transfer Agents: Computershare, Pittsburgh, PA

SIX FLAGS ENTERTAINMENT CORP

Exchange	Symbol	Price	52Wk Range	Yield	P/E
NYS	SIX	$57.69 (5/31/2016)	61.33-42.34	4.02	32.05

*7 Year Price Score N/A   ***NYSE Composite Index=100**   ***12 Month Price Score 114.63**

Interim Earnings (Per Share)

Qtr.	Mar	Jun	Sep	Dec
2013	(0.61)	0.47	1.22	0.14
2014	(0.64)	0.67	1.08	(0.36)
2015	(0.75)	0.67	1.64	0.02
2016	(0.51)	...	...	...

Interim Dividends (Per Share)

Amt	Decl	Ex	Rec	Pay
0.52Q	08/20/2015	09/01/2015	09/03/2015	09/14/2015
0.58Q	11/03/2015	11/30/2015	12/02/2015	12/14/2015
0.58Q	02/04/2016	02/11/2016	02/16/2016	03/07/2016
0.58Q	05/05/2016	05/24/2016	05/26/2016	06/13/2016

Indicated Div: $2.32

Valuation Analysis / Institutional Holding

Valuation Analysis		Institutional Holding	
Forecast EPS	$1.93	No of Institutions	
	(05/15/2016)	353	
Market Cap	$5.4 Billion	Shares	
Book Value	N/A	99,473,784	
Price/Book	N/A	% Held	
Price/Sales	4.16	N/A	

Business Summary: Sporting & Recreational (MIC: 2.2.4 SIC: 7996 NAIC: 713110)

Six Flags Entertainment owns and operates theme, water and zoological parks. Of the 18 parks Co. owned or operated as of Dec 31 2014, 16 were located in the U.S., one was in Mexico City, Mexico and one was in Montreal, Canada. Co.'s parks provide a selection of rides, water attractions, themed areas, concerts and shows, restaurants, game venues and retail outlets. Co. uses Warner Bros. and DC Comics and the Hanna-Barbera and Cartoon Network characters to market its parks. Co.'s licenses include the right to sell merchandise featuring the characters at the parks, and to use the characters in its advertising, as walk-around characters and in theming for rides, attractions and retail outlets.

Recent Developments: For the quarter ended Mar 31 2016, net loss amounted to US$46.9 million versus a net loss of US$70.3 million in the year-earlier quarter. Revenues were US$115.4 million, up 35.5% from US$85.2 million the year before. Direct operating expenses rose 15.1% to US$104.2 million from US$90.5 million in the comparable period the year before. Indirect operating expenses decreased 24.7% to US$61.8 million from US$82.0 million in the equivalent prior-year period.

Prospects: Our evaluation of Six Flags Entertainment Corp. as of June 19, 2016 is the result of our systematic analysis on three basic characteristics: earnings strength, relative valuation, and recent stock price movement. The company has generated a negative trend in earnings per share over the past 5 quarters. However, while recent estimates for the company have been mixed, SIX has posted better than expected results. Based on operating earnings yield, the company is about fairly valued when compared to all of the companies in our coverage universe. Share price changes over the past year indicates that SIX will perform very well over the near term.

Financial Data

(US$ in Thousands)	3 Mos	12/31/2015	12/31/2014	12/31/2013	12/31/2012	12/31/2011	12/31/2010	04/30/2010
Earnings Per Share	1.80	1.58	0.77	1.18	3.19	(0.20)	0.45	2.80
Cash Flow Per Share	5.12	5.06	4.15	3.80	3.44	2.50	2.47	(3.22)
Dividends Per Share	2.200	2.140	1.930	1.820	1.350	0.090	0.015	...
Dividend Payout %	122.22	135.44	250.65	154.24	42.32	...	3.31	...
Income Statement								
Total Revenue	115,419	1,263,938	1,175,793	1,109,930	1,070,332	1,013,174	847,812	128,077
EBITDA	(24,776)	443,915	338,049	391,752	392,855	223,159	258,112	770,751
Depn & Amortn	26,561	104,788	105,449	113,682	132,397	150,952	106,315	45,373
Income Before Taxes	(70,795)	263,224	160,011	203,925	213,834	6,990	97,955	651,244
Income Taxes	(23,860)	70,369	46,522	47,601	(172,228)	(8,065)	11,177	112,648
Net Income	(46,935)	154,690	76,022	118,552	354,009	(22,660)	50,053	548,873
Average Shares	92,359	97,981	98,139	100,371	110,936	110,150	110,600	196,108
Balance Sheet								
Current Assets	171,917	227,977	300,924	353,858	763,474	309,529	266,913	...
Total Assets	2,393,355	2,428,440	2,534,919	2,607,814	3,056,391	2,648,178	2,733,253	...
Current Liabilities	362,875	272,058	231,671	216,810	181,863	221,749	205,249	...
Long-Term Obligations	1,497,005	1,498,022	1,389,215	1,394,334	1,398,966	921,940	938,195	...
Total Liabilities	2,466,541	2,404,224	2,311,024	2,234,477	2,164,172	1,884,700	1,869,545	...
Stockholders' Equity	(73,186)	24,216	223,895	373,337	892,219	763,478	863,708	...
Shares Outstanding	93,250	91,550	92,937	94,857	107,637	109,283	111,456	109,555
Statistical Record								
Return on Assets %	7.31	6.23	2.96	4.19	12.38	N.M.	1.77	...
Return on Equity %	692.90	124.69	25.46	18.74	42.65	N.M.	35.81	...
EBITDA Margin %	N.M.	35.12	28.75	35.30	36.70	22.03	30.44	601.79
Net Margin %	N.M.	12.24	6.47	10.68	33.07	N.M.	5.90	428.55
Asset Turnover	0.53	0.51	0.46	0.39	0.37	0.38	0.30	...
Current Ratio	0.47	0.84	1.30	1.63	4.20	1.40	1.30	...
Debt to Equity	...	61.86	6.20	3.73	1.57	1.21	1.09	...
Price Range	56.06-42.34	54.96-42.34	43.24-33.15	39.98-30.55	32.42-20.43	20.69-12.90	14.16-8.00	...
P/E Ratio	31.14-23.52	34.78-26.80	56.16-43.05	33.88-25.89	10.16-6.40	...	31.47-17.77	...
Average Yield %	4.48	4.49	4.94	5.14	5.15	0.53	0.14	...

Address: 924 Avenue J East, Grand Prairie, TX 75050	Web Site: www.sixflags.com	Auditors: KPMG LLP
Telephone: 972-595-5000	Officers: James W.P. Reid-Anderson - Executive Chairman, Chairman, President, Chief Executive Officer John M. Duffey - President, Chief Executive Officer, Chief Financial Officer	Investor Contact: 972-595-5083 Transfer Agents: Computershare

SJW CORP.

Exchange	Symbol	Price	52Wk Range	Yield	P/E	Div Achiever
NYS	SJW	$34.49 (5/31/2016)	37.83-27.64	2.35	19.49	48 Years

*7 Year Price Score 102.62 *NYSE Composite Index=100 *12 Month Price Score 107.98

Interim Earnings (Per Share)

Qtr.	Mar	Jun	Sep	Dec
2013	0.07	0.37	0.44	0.23
2014	0.04	0.34	1.88	0.28
2015	0.23	0.36	0.46	0.79
2016	0.16			

Interim Dividends (Per Share)

Amt	Decl	Ex	Rec	Pay
0.195Q	07/29/2015	08/06/2015	08/10/2015	09/01/2015
0.195Q	10/29/2015	11/05/2015	11/09/2015	12/01/2015
0.203Q	01/27/2016	02/04/2016	02/08/2016	03/01/2016
0.203Q	04/27/2016	05/05/2016	05/09/2016	06/01/2016

Indicated Div: $0.81

Valuation Analysis   **Institutional Holding**

Forecast EPS	$1.57	No of Institutions
	(05/15/2016)	171
Market Cap	$704.5 Million	Shares
Book Value	$384.2 Million	9,723,731
Price/Book	1.83	% Held
Price/Sales	2.32	53.11

Business Summary: Water Utilities (MIC: 3.2.1 SIC: 4941 NAIC: 221310)

SJW is a holding company with four subsidiaries: San Jose Water Company, a public utility providing water service to approximately 1,000,000 people in the metropolitan San Jose, CA area; SJWTX, Inc., which is doing business as Canyon Lake Water Service Company, a public utility providing water service to approximately 36,000 people in western Comal County and southern Blanco County; SJW Land Company, which owns undeveloped land in the states of California and Tennessee, owns and operates commercial buildings in the states of California, Arizona and Tennessee; and Texas Water Alliance Limited, which is undertaking activities to develop a water supply project in Texas.

Recent Developments: For the quarter ended Mar 31 2016, net income decreased 28.1% to US$3.4 million from US$4.7 million in the year-earlier quarter. Revenues were US$61.1 million, down 1.6% from US$62.1 million the year before. Operating income was US$10.6 million versus US$12.8 million in the prior-year quarter, a decrease of 17.4%. Indirect operating expenses increased 2.5% to US$50.5 million from US$49.3 million in the equivalent prior-year period.

Prospects: Our evaluation of SJW Corp. as of June 19, 2016 is the result of our systematic analysis on three basic characteristics: earnings strength, relative valuation, and recent stock price movement. The company has suffered a very negative trend in earnings per share over the past 5 quarters and while recent estimates for the company have remained steady, SJW has posted results that fell short of analysts expectations. Based on operating earnings yield, the company is about fairly valued when compared to all of the companies in our coverage universe. Share price changes over the past year indicates that SJW will perform in line with the market over the near term.

Financial Data

(US$ in Thousands)	3 Mos	12/31/2015	12/31/2014	12/31/2013	12/31/2012	12/31/2011	12/31/2010	12/31/2009
Earnings Per Share	1.77	1.85	2.54	1.12	1.18	1.11	1.30	0.81
Cash Flow Per Share	5.01	4.78	3.26	3.21	3.98	3.46	2.01	2.95
Tang Book Value Per Share	18.81	18.83	17.75	15.92	14.71	14.20	13.75	13.66
Dividends Per Share	0.787	0.780	0.750	0.730	0.710	0.690	0.680	0.660
Dividend Payout %	44.49	42.16	29.53	65.18	60.17	62.16	52.31	81.48
Income Statement								
Total Revenue	61,112	305,082	319,668	276,869	261,547	238,955	215,638	216,097
EBITDA	22,118	121,573	132,989	89,057	89,050	84,260	85,160	65,076
Depn & Amortn	11,183	38,233	35,424	32,616	31,005	29,141	26,331	23,655
Income Before Taxes	5,500	61,154	76,777	36,519	37,860	35,444	41,146	25,451
Income Taxes	2,122	23,272	24,971	14,135	15,542	14,566	16,740	10,280
Net Income	3,378	37,882	51,806	22,384	22,318	20,878	24,406	15,171
Average Shares	20,560	20,515	20,416	19,971	18,839	18,794	18,742	18,680
Balance Sheet								
Current Assets	62,626	73,376	68,093	39,652	42,911	68,915	38,027	28,010
Total Assets	1,355,576	1,340,963	1,269,304	1,109,986	1,087,499	1,038,810	935,362	878,474
Current Liabilities	97,815	79,623	44,694	59,195	49,107	28,288	29,155	31,958
Long-Term Obligations	365,823	380,825	384,365	334,997	335,598	343,848	295,704	246,879
Total Liabilities	971,377	957,180	909,149	788,811	812,895	774,806	680,330	625,718
Stockholders' Equity	384,199	383,783	360,155	321,175	274,604	264,004	255,032	252,756
Shares Outstanding	20,425	20,381	20,286	20,169	18,670	18,592	18,551	18,499
Statistical Record								
Return on Assets %	2.78	2.90	4.35	2.04	2.09	2.12	2.69	1.75
Return on Equity %	9.81	10.18	15.21	7.51	8.26	8.04	9.61	5.98
EBITDA Margin %	36.19	39.85	41.60	32.17	34.05	35.26	39.49	30.11
Net Margin %	5.53	12.42	16.21	8.08	8.53	8.74	11.32	7.02
Asset Turnover	0.23	0.23	0.27	0.25	0.25	0.24	0.24	0.25
Current Ratio	0.64	0.92	1.52	0.67	0.87	2.44	1.30	0.88
Debt to Equity	0.95	0.99	1.07	1.04	1.22	1.30	1.16	0.98
Price Range	37.50-27.64	35.60-27.64	32.87-25.64	30.03-24.58	26.62-22.69	26.47-21.10	28.23-21.76	29.94-18.72
P/E Ratio	21.19-15.62	19.24-14.94	12.94-10.09	26.81-21.95	22.56-19.23	23.85-19.01	21.72-16.74	36.96-23.11
Average Yield %	2.54	2.53	2.65	2.69	2.96	2.94	2.78	2.83

Address: 110 West Taylor Street, San Jose, CA 95110	**Web Site:** www.sjwcorp.com	**Auditors:** KPMG LLP
Telephone: 408-279-7800	**Officers:** W. Richard Roth - President, Chief Executive Officer James P. Lynch - Chief Financial Officer, Treasurer	**Investor Contact:** 800-250-5147
		Transfer Agents: American Stock Transfer & Trust Company, LLC, Brooklyn, NY

SKECHERS U S A, INC.

Exchange	Symbol	Price	52Wk Range	Yield	P/E
NYS	SKX	$31.17 (5/31/2016)	53.43-25.32	N/A	17.61

*7 Year Price Score 224.01 *NYSE Composite Index=100 *12 Month Price Score 85.88

Interim Earnings (Per Share)

Qtr.	Mar	Jun	Sep	Dec
2013	0.04	0.05	0.18	0.09
2014	0.20	0.23	0.33	0.14
2015	0.37	0.52	0.43	0.19
2016	0.63	...	...	...

Interim Dividends (Per Share)

Amt	Decl	Ex	Rec	Pay
200%	08/21/2015	10/16/2015	10/02/2015	10/15/2015

Valuation Analysis Institutional Holding

Forecast EPS	$2.11	No of Institutions
	(05/20/2016)	450
Market Cap	$4.8 Billion	Shares
Book Value	$1.4 Billion	111,922,240
Price/Book	3.34	% Held
Price/Sales	1.42	85.94

Business Summary: Apparel, Footwear & Accessories (MIC: 1.4.2 SIC: 3149 NAIC: 316219)

Skechers U.S.A. designs and markets Skechers-branded lifestyle footwear for men, women and children, and performance footwear for men and women under the Skechers GO brand name. Co.'s brands are sold through department and specialty stores, athletic and independent retailers, boutiques and internet retailers. In addition to wholesale distribution, Co.'s footwear is available at its e-commerce website and its own retail stores. As of Feb 15 2016, Co. owned and operated 119 concept stores, 155 factory outlet stores and 117 warehouse outlet stores in the U.S., and 82 concept stores, 41 factory outlet stores, and five warehouse outlet stores internationally.

Recent Developments: For the quarter ended Mar 31 2016, net income increased 77.8% to US$109.6 million from US$61.7 million in the year-earlier quarter. Revenues were US$981.4 million, up 27.5% from US$769.9 million the year before. Operating income was US$138.6 million versus US$88.2 million in the prior-year quarter, an increase of 57.1%. Direct operating expenses rose 25.5% to US$546.6 million from US$435.5 million in the comparable period the year before. Indirect operating expenses increased 20.3% to US$296.2 million from US$246.2 million in the equivalent prior-year period.

Prospects: Our evaluation of Skechers U.S.A Inc. as of June 19, 2016 is the result of our systematic analysis on three basic characteristics: earnings strength, relative valuation, and recent stock price movement. The company has generated a negative trend in earnings per share over the past 5 quarters. However, while recent estimates for the company have been lowered by analysts, SKX has posted better than expected results. Based on operating earnings yield, the company is undervalued when compared to all of the companies in our coverage universe. Share price changes over the past year indicates that SKX will perform well over the near term.

Financial Data
(US$ in Thousands)

	3 Mos	12/31/2015	12/31/2014	12/31/2013	12/31/2012	12/31/2011	12/31/2010	12/31/2009
Earnings Per Share	1.77	1.50	0.91	0.36	0.06	(0.46)	0.93	0.39
Cash Flow Per Share	1.62	1.52	1.08	0.66	(0.02)	1.13	(0.33)	0.83
Tang Book Value Per Share	9.34	8.64	7.05	6.12	5.78	5.74	6.23	5.27
Income Statement								
Total Revenue	981,419	3,159,068	2,386,668	1,854,095	1,567,425	1,613,574	2,011,436	1,438,095
EBITDA	143,950	344,030	252,466	137,761	66,880	(88,693)	200,023	73,785
Depn & Amortn	2,621	527	49,457	44,497	43,642	36,352	3,200	1,700
Income Before Taxes	140,207	333,497	191,380	82,215	10,473	(131,047)	196,603	71,110
Income Taxes	30,568	72,450	39,184	21,347	(39)	(63,467)	60,198	20,228
Net Income	97,612	231,912	138,811	54,788	9,512	(67,484)	136,148	54,699
Average Shares	154,818	154,200	153,078	151,689	149,826	145,473	147,150	141,315
Balance Sheet								
Current Assets	1,553,759	1,570,467	1,285,014	1,014,928	940,312	887,351	973,364	789,009
Total Assets	2,068,410	2,047,408	1,674,918	1,408,570	1,340,220	1,281,888	1,304,794	995,552
Current Liabilities	481,905	577,013	505,737	310,422	292,541	308,466	307,310	230,541
Long-Term Obligations	68,498	68,942	15,081	116,488	128,517	76,531	51,650	15,641
Total Liabilities	629,654	719,852	599,669	478,248	464,251	429,327	396,591	249,630
Stockholders' Equity	1,438,756	1,327,556	1,075,249	930,322	875,969	852,561	908,203	745,922
Shares Outstanding	154,001	153,602	152,271	151,674	150,885	147,768	144,615	139,767
Statistical Record								
Return on Assets %	14.46	12.46	9.00	3.99	0.72	N.M.	11.84	5.84
Return on Equity %	21.26	19.30	13.84	6.07	1.10	N.M.	16.46	7.73
EBITDA Margin %	14.67	10.89	10.58	7.43	4.27	N.M.	9.94	5.13
Net Margin %	9.95	7.34	5.82	2.95	0.61	N.M.	6.77	3.80
Asset Turnover	1.78	1.70	1.55	1.35	1.19	1.25	1.75	1.54
Current Ratio	3.22	2.72	2.54	3.27	3.21	2.88	3.17	3.42
Debt to Equity	0.05	0.05	0.01	0.13	0.15	0.09	0.06	0.02
Price Range	53.43-23.46	53.43-18.42	21.36-8.97	11.46-5.80	7.42-3.82	7.82-3.96	14.62-6.41	9.83-1.76
P/E Ratio	30.19-13.26	35.62-12.28	23.48-9.85	31.82-16.11	123.61-63.67	...	15.72-6.90	25.21-4.50

Address: 228 Manhattan Beach Blvd., Manhattan Beach, CA 90266	**Web Site:** www.skechers.com	**Auditors:** BDO USA, LLP
Telephone: 310-318-3100	**Officers:** Robert Greenberg - Chairman, Chief Executive Officer Michael Greenberg - President	**Investor Contact:** 310-829-5400
		Transfer Agents: American Stock Transfer & Trust Company, Brooklyn, NY

SL GREEN REALTY CORP

Exchange	Symbol	Price	52Wk Range	Yield	P/E
NYS	SLG	$101.36 (5/31/2016)	121.80-80.54	2.84	40.54

*7 Year Price Score 108.94 *NYSE Composite Index=100 *12 Month Price Score 94.37

TRADING VOLUME (thousand shares)

Interim Earnings (Per Share)

Qtr.	Mar	Jun	Sep	Dec
2013	0.21	0.09	0.40	0.40
2014	1.53	2.46	0.68	0.54
2015	0.44	(0.39)	1.64	1.02
2016	0.23	...	...	...

Interim Dividends (Per Share)

Amt	Decl	Ex	Rec	Pay
0.60Q	09/17/2015	09/28/2015	09/30/2015	10/15/2015
0.72Q	12/02/2015	12/30/2015	01/04/2016	01/15/2016
0.72Q	03/18/2016	03/29/2016	03/31/2016	04/15/2016
0.72Q	06/15/2016	06/28/2016	06/30/2016	07/15/2016

Indicated Div: $2.88

Valuation Analysis / Institutional Holding

Forecast EPS	$1.13	No of Institutions
	(05/20/2016)	491
Market Cap	$10.0 Billion	Shares
Book Value	$7.6 Billion	132,445,600
Price/Book	1.33	% Held
Price/Sales	5.83	103.97

Business Summary: REITs (MIC: 5.3.1 SIC: 6798 NAIC: 525930)

SL Green Realty is a self-managed real estate investment trust with in-house capabilities in property management, acquisitions and dispositions, financing, development and redevelopment, construction and leasing. As of Dec 31 2015, Co. owned interests in properties in the New York Metropolitan area, primarily in midtown Manhattan. Co.'s investments in the New York Metropolitan area also include investments in Brooklyn, Long Island, Westchester County, Connecticut and New Jersey, which are known as the Suburban properties. Co. operates two reportable segments: real estate and debt and preferred equity investments.

Recent Developments: For the quarter ended Mar 31 2016, net income decreased 41.6% to US$32.5 million from US$55.6 million in the year-earlier quarter. Revenues were US$455.4 million, up 14.9% from US$396.3 million the year before. Revenues from property income rose 13.6% to US$391.2 million from US$344.3 million in the corresponding quarter a year earlier.

Prospects: Our evaluation of SL Green Realty Corp. as of June 19, 2016 is the result of our systematic analysis on three basic characteristics: earnings strength, relative valuation, and recent stock price movement. The company has produced a positive trend in earnings per share over the past 5 quarters. Because the company lacks sufficient analyst estimate data, we place greater weight on the historical EPS trend as the measure of earnings strength. Based on operating earnings yield, the company is overvalued when compared to all of the companies in our coverage universe. Share price changes over the past year indicates that SLG will perform in line with the market over the near term.

Financial Data

(US$ in Thousands)	3 Mos	12/31/2015	12/31/2014	12/31/2013	12/31/2012	12/31/2011	12/31/2010	12/31/2009
Earnings Per Share	2.50	2.70	5.20	1.10	1.74	7.33	3.45	0.54
Cash Flow Per Share	5.28	5.30	5.12	4.19	3.95	3.74	4.11	3.95
Tang Book Value Per Share	74.22	73.50	69.73	66.88	66.49	65.37	57.58	53.41
Dividends Per Share	2.640	2.520	2.100	1.490	1.080	0.550	0.400	0.675
Dividend Payout %	105.60	93.33	40.38	135.45	62.07	7.50	11.59	125.00
Income Statement								
Total Revenue	455,444	1,662,829	1,519,978	1,469,077	1,400,255	1,263,428	1,101,246	1,010,659
EBITDA	294,404	1,100,856	798,798	763,121	712,915	663,901	552,579	456,963
Depn & Amortn	187,240	523,800	338,800	309,400	306,800	254,500	209,700	210,400
Income Before Taxes	12,492	253,186	142,598	123,506	75,546	123,484	109,232	10,263
Net Income	26,959	284,084	518,056	135,371	196,405	647,410	300,575	57,544
Average Shares	104,259	103,734	99,696	95,266	92,873	86,244	79,761	72,044
Balance Sheet								
Current Assets	1,038,981	1,107,032	914,062	836,223	744,306	568,181	739,221	695,029
Total Assets	19,585,968	19,857,941	17,096,587	14,959,001	14,387,754	13,483,852	11,300,294	10,487,577
Current Liabilities	1,016,948	554,909	441,887	374,074	317,459	343,328	224,410	212,577
Long-Term Obligations	8,550,081	10,447,108	8,199,609	6,967,579	6,557,938	6,052,509	5,268,057	4,909,571
Total Liabilities	12,012,931	12,287,960	10,088,098	8,384,046	7,918,402	7,506,305	6,421,210	6,099,139
Stockholders' Equity	7,573,037	7,569,981	7,008,489	6,574,955	6,469,352	5,977,547	4,879,084	4,388,438
Shares Outstanding	99,041	99,975	97,325	94,993	91,249	85,782	78,306	77,514
Statistical Record								
Return on Assets %	1.44	1.54	3.23	0.92	1.41	5.22	2.76	0.54
Return on Equity %	3.56	3.90	7.63	2.08	3.15	11.93	6.49	1.39
EBITDA Margin %	64.64	66.20	52.55	51.95	50.91	52.55	50.18	45.21
Net Margin %	5.92	17.08	34.08	9.21	14.03	51.24	27.29	5.69
Asset Turnover	0.09	0.09	0.09	0.10	0.10	0.10	0.10	0.09
Current Ratio	1.02	1.99	2.07	2.24	2.34	1.65	3.29	3.27
Debt to Equity	1.13	1.38	1.17	1.06	1.01	1.01	1.08	1.12
Price Range	131.64-80.54	134.00-100.95	123.10-90.96	98.15-76.65	85.14-68.16	90.01-55.14	70.27-44.18	52.74-8.69
P/E Ratio	52.66-32.22	49.63-37.39	23.67-17.49	89.23-69.68	48.93-39.17	12.28-7.52	20.37-12.81	97.67-16.09
Average Yield %	2.38	2.12	1.97	1.69	1.40	0.75	0.67	2.42

Address: 420 Lexington Avenue, New York, NY 10170	**Web Site:** www.slgreen.com	**Auditors:** Ernst & Young LLP
Telephone: 212-594-2700	**Officers:** Stephen L. Green - Chairman Andrew Mathias - President, Chief Investment Officer, Principal Operating Officer	**Transfer Agents:** Computershare Shareowner Services, Providence, RI

SM ENERGY CO.

Exchange	Symbol	Price	52Wk Range	Yield	P/E
NYS	SM	$31.52 (5/31/2016)	52.80-7.60	0.32	N/A

*7 Year Price Score 45.42   *NYSE Composite Index=100   *12 Month Price Score 94.60

Interim Earnings (Per Share)

Qtr.	Mar	Jun	Sep	Dec
2013	0.25	1.13	1.04	0.10
2014	0.96	0.88	3.05	4.89
2015	(0.79)	(0.85)	0.05	(5.02)
2016	(5.10)	...	...	...

Interim Dividends (Per Share)

Amt	Decl	Ex	Rec	Pay
0.05S	09/30/2014	10/22/2014	10/24/2014	11/05/2014
0.05S	03/27/2015	04/22/2015	04/24/2015	05/06/2015
0.05S	09/30/2015	10/21/2015	10/23/2015	11/04/2015
0.05S	03/30/2016	04/20/2016	04/22/2016	05/04/2016

Indicated Div: $0.10

TRADING VOLUME (thousand shares)

Valuation Analysis / Institutional Holding

Valuation Analysis		Institutional Holding	
Forecast EPS	$-3.31 (05/20/2016)	No of Institutions	380
Market Cap	$2.1 Billion	Shares	89,141,648
Book Value	$1.5 Billion	% Held	N/A
Price/Book	1.42		
Price/Sales	1.61		

Business Summary: Production & Extraction (MIC: 9.1.1 SIC: 1311 NAIC: 211111)

SM Energy is an independent energy company engaged in the acquisition, exploration, development, and production of crude oil and condensate, natural gas, and natural gas liquids in onshore North America. Co.'s operations are concentrated in three onshore operating areas in the U.S.: the South Texas & Gulf Coast Region; the Rocky Mountain Region; and the Permian Region. As of Dec 31 2015, Co. had total proved reserves of 471.3 million barrels of oil equivalent, consisting of 145.3 million barrels of oil, 1,264.00 billion cubic feet of natural gas, and 115.4 million barrels of natural gas liquids.

Recent Developments: For the quarter ended Mar 31 2016, net loss amounted to US$347.2 million versus a net loss of US$53.1 million in the year-earlier quarter. Revenues were US$143.1 million, down 60.9% from US$365.9 million the year before. Operating loss was US$526.7 million versus a loss of US$54.4 million in the prior-year quarter. Direct operating expenses declined 13.3% to US$358.8 million from US$413.6 million in the comparable period the year before. Indirect operating expenses increased to US$311.1 million from US$6.8 million in the equivalent prior-year period.

Prospects: Our evaluation of SM Energy Co. as of June 19, 2016 is the result of our systematic analysis on three basic characteristics: earnings strength, relative valuation, and recent stock price movement. The company has enjoyed a very positive trend in earnings per share over the past 5 quarters. Because the company lacks sufficient analyst estimate data, we place greater weight on the historical EPS trend as the measure of earnings strength. Based on operating earnings yield, the company is overvalued when compared to all of the companies in our coverage universe. Share price changes over the past year indicates that SM will perform very poorly over the near term.

Financial Data

(US$ in Thousands)	3 Mos	12/31/2015	12/31/2014	12/31/2013	12/31/2012	12/31/2011	12/31/2010	12/31/2009
Earnings Per Share	(10.92)	(6.61)	9.79	2.51	(0.83)	3.19	3.04	(1.59)
Cash Flow Per Share	11.94	14.45	21.67	20.09	14.12	11.93	7.89	6.98
Tang Book Value Per Share	22.16	27.21	33.89	23.96	21.37	22.84	19.25	15.51
Dividends Per Share	0.100	0.100	0.100	0.100	0.100	0.100	0.100	0.100
Dividend Payout %	...	...	1.02	3.98	...	3.13	3.29	...
Income Statement								
Total Revenue	143,076	1,556,965	2,522,307	2,293,374	1,505,102	1,603,318	1,092,834	832,201
EBITDA	(511,917)	334,007	1,936,931	1,196,517	714,629	913,786	688,376	185,579
Depn & Amortn	(920)	928,719	773,678	828,262	734,646	529,402	349,605	316,414
Income Before Taxes	(542,085)	(722,861)	1,064,699	278,611	(83,517)	339,001	314,896	(159,464)
Income Taxes	(194,875)	(275,151)	398,648	107,676	(29,268)	123,585	118,059	(60,094)
Net Income	(347,210)	(447,710)	666,051	170,935	(54,249)	215,416	196,837	(99,370)
Average Shares	68,077	67,723	68,044	67,998	65,138	67,564	64,689	62,457
Balance Sheet								
Current Assets	405,638	518,989	745,043	647,501	340,564	463,204	274,645	209,046
Total Assets	5,207,056	5,621,643	6,516,700	4,705,165	4,199,529	3,798,980	2,744,321	2,360,936
Current Liabilities	303,157	302,525	784,660	639,131	541,546	505,805	502,053	296,671
Long-Term Obligations	2,564,472	2,517,970	2,366,000	1,600,000	1,440,000	985,069	323,673	454,902
Total Liabilities	3,698,640	3,769,242	4,230,045	3,098,344	2,785,063	2,336,040	1,525,795	1,387,366
Stockholders' Equity	1,508,416	1,852,401	2,286,655	1,606,821	1,414,466	1,462,940	1,218,526	973,570
Shares Outstanding	68,077	68,075	67,463	67,056	66,195	64,064	63,310	62,772
Statistical Record								
Return on Assets %	N.M.	N.M.	11.87	3.84	N.M.	6.58	7.71	N.M.
Return on Equity %	N.M.	N.M.	34.21	11.32	N.M.	16.07	17.96	N.M.
EBITDA Margin %	N.M.	21.45	76.79	52.17	47.48	56.99	62.99	22.30
Net Margin %	N.M.	N.M.	26.41	7.45	N.M.	13.44	18.01	N.M.
Asset Turnover	0.23	0.26	0.45	0.52	0.38	0.49	0.43	0.33
Current Ratio	1.34	1.72	0.95	1.01	0.63	0.92	0.55	0.70
Debt to Equity	1.70	1.36	1.03	1.00	1.02	0.67	0.27	0.47
Price Range	59.01-7.60	59.01-18.22	89.58-30.17	91.98-52.21	83.35-41.80	86.85-56.04	58.93-31.64	37.22-11.58
P/E Ratio	...	...	9.15-3.08	36.65-20.80	...	27.23-17.57	19.38-10.41	...
Average Yield %	0.30	0.25	0.14	0.15	0.17	0.14	0.24	0.41

Address: 1775 Sherman Street, Suite 1200, Denver, CO 80203
Telephone: 303-861-8140
Fax: 303-861-0934

Web Site: www.sm-energy.com
Officers: William D. Sullivan - Chairman Javan D. Ottoson - President, Chief Executive Officer, Executive Vice President, Chief Operating Officer

Auditors: Ernst & Young LLP
Investor Contact: 303-861-8140
Transfer Agents: Computershare Trust Company NA, Golden, Co

SMITH (A.O.) CORP

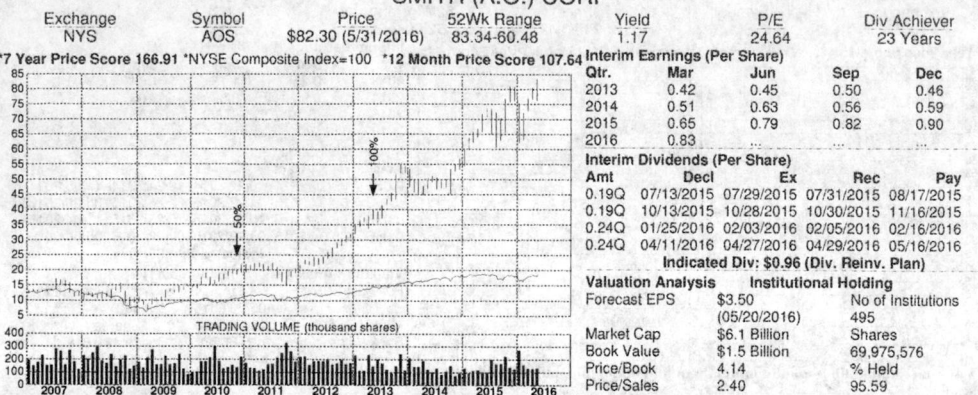

Exchange	Symbol	Price	52Wk Range	Yield	P/E	Div Achiever
NYS	AOS	$82.30 (5/31/2016)	83.34-60.48	1.17	24.64	23 Years

*7 Year Price Score 166.91 *NYSE Composite Index=100 *12 Month Price Score 107.64

Interim Earnings (Per Share)

Qtr.	Mar	Jun	Sep	Dec
2013	0.42	0.45	0.50	0.46
2014	0.51	0.63	0.56	0.59
2015	0.65	0.79	0.82	0.90
2016	0.83	...	...	...

Interim Dividends (Per Share)

Amt	Decl	Ex	Rec	Pay
0.19Q	07/13/2015	07/29/2015	07/31/2015	08/17/2015
0.19Q	10/13/2015	10/28/2015	10/30/2015	11/16/2015
0.24Q	01/25/2016	02/03/2016	02/05/2016	02/16/2016
0.24Q	04/11/2016	04/27/2016	04/29/2016	05/16/2016

Indicated Div: $0.96 (Div. Reinv. Plan)

Valuation Analysis / **Institutional Holding**

Forecast EPS	$3.50 (05/20/2016)
No of Institutions	495
Market Cap	$6.1 Billion
Book Value	$1.5 Billion
Shares	69,975,576
Price/Book	4.14
% Held	95.59
Price/Sales	2.40

TRADING VOLUME (thousand shares)

Business Summary: Household Appliances, Electronics & Goods (MIC: 1.5.1 SIC: 3639 NAIC: 335228)

A.O. Smith is a manufacturer and marketer of residential and commercial gas, gas tankless and electric water heaters. Co. is comprised of two reporting segments: North America and Rest of World. Co.'s Rest of World segment is primarily comprised of China, Europe and India. Co.'s North America segment manufactures and markets specialty commercial water heating equipment, condensing and non-condensing boilers and water systems tanks. The Rest of World segment manufactures and markets water treatment products, primarily for Asia. In addition, Co. markets in-home air purification products in China.

Recent Developments: For the quarter ended Mar 31 2016, net income increased 25.9% to US$73.5 million from US$58.4 million in the year-earlier quarter. Revenues were US$636.9 million, up 3.0% from US$618.5 million the year before. Direct operating expenses declined 3.9% to US$374.2 million from US$389.3 million in the comparable period the year before. Indirect operating expenses increased 8.7% to US$159.1 million from US$146.4 million in the equivalent prior-year period.

Prospects: Our evaluation of Smith (A.O.) Corp. as of June 19, 2016 is the result of our systematic analysis on three basic characteristics: earnings strength, relative valuation, and recent stock price movement. The company has generated a negative trend in earnings per share over the past 5 quarters and while recent estimates for the company have remained steady, AOS has posted better than expected results. Based on operating earnings yield, the company is about fairly valued when compared to all of the companies in our coverage universe. Share price changes over the past year indicates that AOS will perform in line with the market over the near term.

Financial Data
(US$ in Thousands)

	3 Mos	12/31/2015	12/31/2014	12/31/2013	12/31/2012	12/31/2011	12/31/2010	12/31/2009
Earnings Per Share	3.34	3.16	2.28	1.83	1.71	3.29	1.21	1.13
Cash Flow Per Share	4.26	3.88	2.92	3.04	1.55	0.64	1.36	3.74
Tang Book Value Per Share	10.30	8.30	7.20	6.25	4.54	3.27	4.92	0.92
Dividends Per Share	0.810	0.760	0.600	0.460	0.360	0.300	0.270	0.257
Dividend Payout %	24.25	24.05	26.32	25.14	21.11	9.13	22.31	22.71
Income Statement								
Total Revenue	636,900	2,536,500	2,356,000	2,153,800	1,939,300	1,710,500	1,489,300	1,991,500
EBITDA	121,500	472,900	352,200	301,800	297,600	217,800	122,100	198,900
Depn & Amortn	16,200	63,000	59,800	59,700	54,600	47,000	40,800	67,500
Income Before Taxes	103,600	402,500	286,700	236,400	233,800	161,500	74,400	119,600
Income Taxes	30,100	119,600	78,900	66,700	71,200	50,300	17,300	29,600
Net Income	73,500	282,900	207,800	169,700	158,700	305,700	111,700	81,300
Average Shares	88,905	89,504	90,986	92,787	93,108	93,149	92,325	71,863
Balance Sheet								
Current Assets	1,425,900	1,455,300	1,319,000	1,205,600	1,107,200	1,208,700	896,000	740,000
Total Assets	2,650,600	2,646,500	2,515,300	2,391,500	2,265,200	2,349,000	2,112,000	1,901,300
Current Liabilities	602,000	653,200	605,200	590,900	499,000	519,900	536,800	491,300
Long-Term Obligations	274,100	236,100	210,100	177,700	225,100	443,000	242,400	232,100
Total Liabilities	1,172,100	1,204,200	1,134,000	1,062,800	1,071,100	1,263,200	1,230,600	1,130,600
Stockholders' Equity	1,478,500	1,442,300	1,381,300	1,328,700	1,194,100	1,085,800	881,400	770,700
Shares Outstanding	74,428	87,948	89,399	91,239	92,426	91,653	91,666	91,040
Statistical Record								
Return on Assets %	11.43	10.96	8.47	7.29	6.86	13.71	5.57	4.30
Return on Equity %	20.67	20.04	15.34	13.45	13.88	31.08	13.52	11.52
EBITDA Margin %	19.08	18.64	14.95	14.01	15.35	12.73	8.20	9.99
Net Margin %	11.54	11.15	8.82	7.88	8.18	17.87	7.50	4.08
Asset Turnover	0.98	0.98	0.96	0.93	0.84	0.77	0.74	1.05
Current Ratio	2.37	2.23	2.18	2.04	2.22	2.32	1.67	1.51
Debt to Equity	0.19	0.16	0.15	0.13	0.19	0.41	0.28	0.30
Price Range	80.86-60.48	80.86-54.23	56.79-44.68	54.88-31.54	31.79-20.52	22.32-15.22	21.54-13.82	14.98-7.10
P/E Ratio	24.21-18.11	25.59-17.16	24.91-19.60	29.99-17.23	18.59-12.00	6.79-4.62	17.80-11.42	13.26-6.28
Average Yield %	1.15	1.11	1.21	1.11	1.42	1.52	1.56	2.24

Address: 11270 West Park Place, Milwaukee, WI 53224-9508
Telephone: 414-359-4000
Fax: 414-359-4115

Web Site: www.aosmith.com
Officers: Kevin J. Wheeler - Senior Vice President, region Officer Ajita G. Rajendra - Chairman, President, Chief Executive Officer, Chief Operating Officer, Executive Vice President, Senior Vice President, Division Officer

Auditors: Ernst & Young LLP
Investor Contact: 414-359-4130
Transfer Agents: Wells Fargo Shareowner Services, N.A., St. Paul, MN

SOTHEBY'S

Exchange	Symbol	Price	52Wk Range	Yield	P/E
NYS	BID	$29.90 (5/31/2016)	46.93-19.13	N/A	230.00

*7 Year Price Score 75.75   *NYSE Composite Index=100   *12 Month Price Score 86.79

Interim Earnings (Per Share)

Qtr.	Mar	Jun	Sep	Dec
2013	(0.33)	1.33	(0.44)	1.31
2014	(0.09)	1.11	(0.40)	1.07
2015	0.07	0.96	(0.26)	(0.16)
2016	(0.41)	...	...	...

Interim Dividends (Per Share)

Amt	Decl	Ex	Rec	Pay
0.10Q	02/26/2015	03/05/2015	03/09/2015	03/16/2015
0.10Q	05/07/2015	05/28/2015	06/01/2015	06/15/2015
0.10Q	08/06/2015	08/28/2015	09/01/2015	09/15/2015
0.10Q	11/06/2015	11/27/2015	12/01/2015	12/15/2015

Valuation Analysis / Institutional Holding

Forecast EPS	$1.65
	(05/20/2016)
Market Cap	$1.8 Billion
Book Value	$618.8 Million
Price/Book	2.88
Price/Sales	1.95

No of Institutions	339
Shares	74,150,432
% Held	104.01

TRADING VOLUME (thousand shares)

Business Summary: Miscellaneous Consumer Services (MIC: 2.2.3 SIC: 7389 NAIC: 453920)

Sotheby's is a global art business whose operations are organized under two segments: Agency and Finance. The Agency segment matches buyers and sellers of authenticated fine art, decorative art, jewelry, wine and collectibles (collectively, art or works of art or artwork or property) through the auction or private sale process. Agency segment activities also include the sale of artworks that are principally acquired incidental to the auction process and the activities of RM Sotheby's, an equity investee that operates as an auction house for investment-quality automobiles. The Finance segment provides art-related financing activities by making loans that are secured by works of art.

Recent Developments: For the quarter ended Mar 31 2016, net loss amounted to US$25.9 million versus net income of US$5.1 million in the year-earlier quarter. Revenues were US$106.5 million, down 31.6% from US$155.7 million the year before. Operating loss was US$32.0 million versus an income of US$18.4 million in the prior-year quarter. Direct operating expenses declined 8.4% to US$24.7 million from US$26.9 million in the comparable period the year before. Indirect operating expenses increased 3.2% to US$113.8 million from US$110.3 million in the equivalent prior-year period.

Prospects: Our evaluation of Sotheby's Holdings Inc. as of June 19, 2016 is the result of our systematic analysis on three basic characteristics: earnings strength, relative valuation, and recent stock price movement. The company has suffered a very negative trend in earnings per share over the past 5 quarters and while recent estimates for the company have remained steady, BID has posted results that fell short of analysts expectations. Based on operating earnings yield, the company is undervalued when compared to all of the companies in our coverage universe. Share price changes over the past year indicates that BID will perform very poorly over the near term.

Financial Data
(US$ in Thousands)

	3 Mos	12/31/2015	12/31/2014	12/31/2013	12/31/2012	12/31/2011	12/31/2010	12/31/2009
Earnings Per Share	0.13	0.63	1.68	1.88	1.57	2.46	2.34	(0.10)
Cash Flow Per Share	2.05	2.28	0.64	3.47	(0.96)	5.99	5.15	2.43
Tang Book Value Per Share	9.35	12.05	12.51	16.27	14.43	13.19	11.24	8.35
Dividends Per Share	0.300	0.400	4.740	0.200	0.520	0.230	0.200	0.300
Dividend Payout %	230.77	63.49	282.14	10.64	33.12	9.35	8.55	...
Income Statement								
Total Revenue	106,531	961,494	938,053	853,678	768,492	831,836	774,309	484,958
EBITDA	(31,561)	219,768	246,927	245,004	220,215	286,085	286,259	75,546
Depn & Amortn	381	19,500	20,600	19,400	17,900	17,200	15,600	19,800
Income Before Taxes	(39,092)	169,299	193,021	185,693	159,436	231,389	225,579	15,395
Income Taxes	(12,786)	131,145	75,761	55,702	51,395	60,032	65,273	22,162
Net Income	(25,884)	43,727	117,795	130,006	108,292	171,416	160,950	(6,528)
Average Shares	63,022	68,121	69,606	69,175	68,527	68,850	67,322	65,208
Balance Sheet								
Current Assets	1,267,515	2,109,739	2,039,522	1,972,273	1,671,123	1,693,296	1,450,404	968,367
Total Assets	2,413,997	3,274,129	3,134,820	2,893,546	2,575,095	2,399,414	2,178,628	1,586,123
Current Liabilities	554,086	1,197,583	1,429,207	1,142,489	964,879	964,312	877,384	442,475
Long-Term Obligations	1,124,409	1,156,267	745,000	515,148	515,197	464,552	472,862	512,939
Total Liabilities	1,795,182	2,467,702	2,257,123	1,754,228	1,582,269	1,495,747	1,407,120	1,009,138
Stockholders' Equity	618,815	806,427	877,697	1,139,318	992,826	903,667	771,508	576,985
Shares Outstanding	59,552	65,791	68,991	69,131	67,779	67,407	67,320	67,157
Statistical Record								
Return on Assets %	0.51	1.36	3.91	4.75	4.34	7.49	8.55	N.M.
Return on Equity %	1.71	5.19	11.68	12.19	11.39	20.47	23.87	N.M.
EBITDA Margin %	N.M.	22.86	26.32	28.70	28.66	34.39	36.97	15.58
Net Margin %	N.M.	4.55	12.56	15.23	14.09	20.61	20.79	N.M.
Asset Turnover	0.37	0.30	0.31	0.31	0.31	0.36	0.41	0.30
Current Ratio	2.29	1.76	1.43	1.73	1.73	1.76	1.65	2.19
Debt to Equity	1.82	1.43	0.85	0.45	0.52	0.51	0.61	0.89
Price Range	46.93-19.13	46.93-25.76	53.51-35.30	53.20-33.03	40.51-27.74	54.41-25.84	46.80-22.11	24.40-6.35
P/E Ratio	361.00-147.15	74.49-40.89	31.85-21.01	28.30-17.57	25.80-17.67	22.12-10.50	20.00-9.45	...
Average Yield %	0.87	1.03	11.32	0.47	1.56	0.58	0.62	2.20

Address: 1334 York Avenue, New York, NY 10021 **Telephone:** 212-606-7000	**Web Site:** www.sothebys.com **Officers:** Domenico De Sole - Chairman The Duke of Devonshire - Deputy Chairman	**Auditors:** Deloitte & Touche LLP **Investor Contact:** 800-700-6321 **Transfer Agents:** BNY Mellon Shareowner Services, Pittsburg, PA

SMUCKER (J.M.) CO.

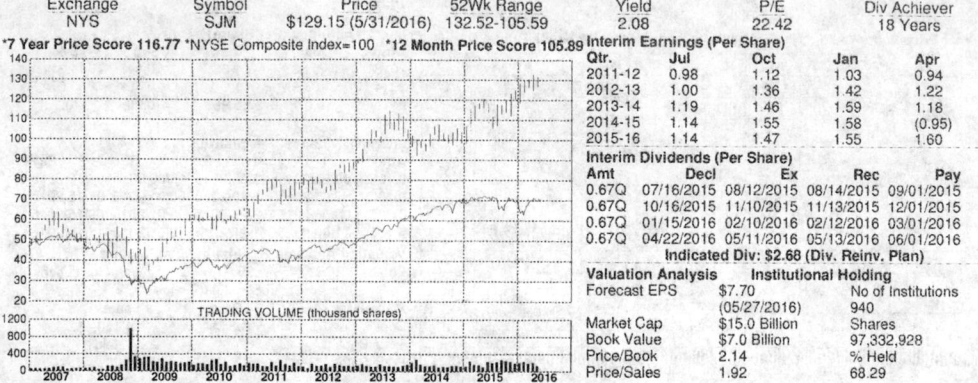

Exchange	Symbol	Price	52Wk Range	Yield	P/E	Div Achiever
NYS	SJM	$129.15 (5/31/2016)	132.52-105.59	2.08	22.42	18 Years

*7 Year Price Score 116.77 *NYSE Composite Index=100 *12 Month Price Score 105.89

Interim Earnings (Per Share)

Qtr.	Jul	Oct	Jan	Apr
2011-12	0.98	1.12	1 03	0.94
2012-13	1.00	1.36	1.42	1.22
2013-14	1.19	1.46	1.59	1.18
2014-15	1.14	1.55	1.58	(0.95)
2015-16	1.14	1.47	1.55	1.60

Interim Dividends (Per Share)

Amt	Decl	Ex	Rec	Pay
0.67Q	07/16/2015	08/12/2015	08/14/2015	09/01/2015
0.67Q	10/16/2015	11/10/2015	11/13/2015	12/01/2015
0.67Q	01/15/2016	02/10/2016	02/12/2016	03/01/2016
0.67Q	04/22/2016	05/11/2016	05/13/2016	06/01/2016

Indicated Div: $2.68 (Div. Reinv. Plan)

Valuation Analysis

		Institutional Holding	
Forecast EPS	$7.70	No of Institutions	
	(05/27/2016)	940	
Market Cap	$15.0 Billion	Shares	
Book Value	$7.0 Billion	97,332,928	
Price/Book	2.14	% Held	
Price/Sales	1.92	68.29	

Business Summary: Food (MIC: 1.2.1 SIC: 2033 NAIC: 311421)

Smucker (J.M.) manufactures and markets food and beverage products. Co.'s principal products are coffee, pet food, pet snacks, peanut butter, fruit spreads, shortening and oils, baking mixes and ready-to-spread frostings, frozen sandwiches, flour and baking ingredients, juices and beverages, and portion control products. Co. has three segments: U.S. Retail Coffee, U.S. Retail Consumer Foods, and U.S. Retail Pet Foods. The U.S. Retail Coffee segment primarily includes the domestic sales of Folgers, Dunkin' Donuts®, and Cafe Bustelo® branded coffee; and the U.S. Retail Consumer Foods segment primarily includes domestic sales of Jif®, Smucker's®, Crisco®, and Pillsbury® branded products.

Recent Developments: For the year ended Apr 30 2016, net income increased 99.7% to US$688.7 million from US$344.9 million in the prior year. Revenues were US$7.81 billion, up 37.2% from US$5.69 billion the year before. Operating income was US$1.15 billion versus US$772.0 million in the prior year, an increase of 48.4%. Direct operating expenses rose 30.1% to US$4.84 billion from US$3.72 billion in the comparable period the year before. Indirect operating expenses increased 52.3% to US$1.82 billion from US$1.20 billion in the equivalent prior-year period.

Prospects: Our evaluation of Smucker (J.M.) Co. as of June 26, 2016 is the result of our systematic analysis on three basic characteristics: earnings strength, relative valuation, and recent stock price movement. The company has produced a positive trend in earnings per share over the past 5 quarters and while recent estimates for the company have been raised by analysts, SJM has posted better than expected results. Based on operating earnings yield, the company is about fairly valued when compared to all of the companies in our coverage universe. Share price changes over the past year indicates that SJM will perform poorly over the near term.

Financial Data

(US$ in Thousands)	04/30/2016	04/30/2015	04/30/2014	04/30/2013	04/30/2012	04/30/2011	04/30/2010	04/30/2009
Earnings Per Share	5.76	3.33	5.42	5.00	4.06	4.05	4.15	3.12
Cash Flow Per Share	12.23	7.12	8.27	7.93	6.50	3.35	6.00	5.24
Dividends Per Share	2.650	2.500	2.260	2.040	1.880	1.640	1.400	6.280
Dividend Payout %	46.01	75.08	41.70	40.80	46.31	40.49	33.73	201.28
Income Statement								
Total Revenue	7,811,200	5,692,700	5,610,600	5,897,700	5,525,782	4,825,743	4,605,289	3,757,933
EBITDA	1,370,700	760,400	1,086,600	1,064,800	939,886	950,041	901,372	531,000
Depn & Amortn	221,700	157,500	157,500	154,100	158,936	165,795	108,225	79,450
Income Before Taxes	977,900	523,000	849,700	817,300	701,158	717,164	730,753	396,065
Income Taxes	289,200	178,100	284,500	273,100	241,414	237,682	236,615	130,112
Net Income	688,700	344,900	565,200	544,200	459,744	479,482	494,138	265,953
Average Shares	118,959	103,043	103,518	107,904	112,262	117,119	119,081	85,285
Balance Sheet								
Current Assets	1,573,400	2,052,300	1,539,100	1,595,200	1,643,465	1,636,999	1,223,630	1,398,891
Total Assets	15,984,100	16,882,600	9,072,100	9,031,800	9,115,226	8,324,585	7,974,853	8,192,161
Current Liabilities	1,213,000	1,022,600	891,000	596,800	616,972	482,676	478,897	1,061,236
Long-Term Obligations	5,146,000	5,944,900	1,879,800	1,967,800	2,020,543	1,304,039	900,000	910,000
Total Liabilities	8,975,600	9,795,700	4,042,500	3,883,000	3,951,840	3,032,222	2,648,533	3,252,230
Stockholders' Equity	7,008,500	7,086,900	5,029,600	5,148,800	5,163,386	5,292,363	5,326,320	4,939,931
Shares Outstanding	116,306	119,577	101,697	106,486	110,284	114,172	119,119	118,422
Statistical Record								
Return on Assets %	4.18	2.66	6.24	6.00	5.26	5.88	6.11	4.70
Return on Equity %	9.75	5.69	11.11	10.55	8.77	9.03	9.63	7.89
EBITDA Margin %	17.55	13.36	19.37	18.05	17.01	19.69	19.57	14.13
Net Margin %	8.82	6.06	10.07	9.23	8.32	9.94	10.73	7.08
Asset Turnover	0.47	0.44	0.62	0.65	0.63	0.59	0.57	0.66
Current Ratio	1.30	2.01	1.73	2.67	2.66	3.39	2.56	1.32
Debt to Equity	0.73	0.84	0.37	0.38	0.39	0.25	0.17	0.18
Price Range	132.52-105.59	118.20-96.45	114.36-91.81	105.00-73.65	81.44-67.68	75.07-54.75	63.26-39.40	56.36-34.22
P/E Ratio	23.01-18.33	35.50-28.96	21.10-16.94	21.00-14.73	20.06-16.67	18.54-13.52	15.24-9.49	18.06-10.97
Average Yield %	2.23	2.38	2.19	2.38	2.46	2.59	2.58	13.91

Address: One Strawberry Lane, Orrville, OH 44667-0280 Telephone: 330-682-3000	Web Site: www.jmsmucker.com Officers: Richard K. Smucker - Executive Chairman, Executive Chairman (frmr), President, Chief Executive Officer, Co-Chief Executive Officer Mark R. Belgya - Vice-Chairman, Senior Vice President, Chief Financial Officer	Auditors: Ernst & Young LLP Investor Contact: 330-684-3838 Transfer Agents: ComputerShare, College Station, TX

SNAP-ON, INC.

Exchange	Symbol	Price	52Wk Range	Yield	P/E
NYS	SNA	$161.82 (5/31/2016)	174.09-135.41	1.51	19.29

*7 Year Price Score 153.98 *NYSE Composite Index=100 *12 Month Price Score 98.77

Interim Earnings (Per Share)

Qtr.	Mar	Jun	Sep	Dec
2013	1.40	1.50	1.43	1.60
2014	1.62	1.80	1.76	1.96
2015	1.87	2.03	1.98	2.22
2016	2.16	...	...	...

Interim Dividends (Per Share)

Amt	Decl	Ex	Rec	Pay
0.53Q	08/06/2015	08/21/2015	08/25/2015	09/10/2015
0.61Q	11/09/2015	11/20/2015	11/24/2015	12/10/2015
0.61Q	02/11/2016	02/23/2016	02/25/2016	03/10/2016
0.61Q	04/28/2016	05/18/2016	05/20/2016	06/10/2016

Indicated Div: $2.44

Valuation Analysis / **Institutional Holding**

Forecast EPS	$9.01
	(05/20/2016)
Market Cap	$9.4 Billion
Book Value	$2.5 Billion
Price/Book	3.74
Price/Sales	2.61

No of Institutions	703
Shares	57,951,384
% Held	83.96

Business Summary: Industrial Machinery & Equipment (MIC: 7.2.1 SIC: 3429 NAIC: 332510)

Snap-on is a manufacturer and marketer of tools, equipment, diagnostics, repair information and systems solutions. Products and services include hand and power tools, tool storage, diagnostic software, information and management systems, shop equipment and solutions for vehicle dealerships and repair centers, as well as for the aviation and aerospace, agriculture, construction, government and military, mining, natural resources, power generation and technical education industries. Co. also provides financing programs to facilitate the sales of its products. Co.'s segments are: Commercial & Industrial Group; Snap-on Tools Group; Repair Systems & Information Group; and Financial Services.

Recent Developments: For the quarter ended Apr 2 2016, net income increased 16.0% to US$131.3 million from US$113.2 million in the year-earlier quarter. Revenues were US$900.5 million, up 1.7% from US$885.2 million the year before. Operating income was US$202.4 million versus US$178.2 million in the prior-year quarter, an increase of 13.6%. Direct operating expenses rose 0.8% to US$438.2 million from US$434.8 million in the comparable period the year before. Indirect operating expenses decreased 4.5% to US$259.9 million from US$272.2 million in the equivalent prior-year period.

Prospects: Our evaluation of Snap-On Inc. as of June 19, 2016 is the result of our systematic analysis on three basic characteristics: earnings strength, relative valuation, and recent stock price movement. The company has managed to produce a neutral trend in earnings per share over the past 5 quarters and while recent estimates for the company have remained steady, SNA has posted better than expected results. Based on operating earnings yield, the company is undervalued when compared to all of the companies in our coverage universe. Share price changes over the past year indicates that SNA will perform very well over the near term.

Financial Data

(US$ in Thousands)	3 Mos	01/02/2016	01/03/2015	12/28/2013	12/29/2012	12/31/2011	01/01/2011	01/02/2010
Earnings Per Share	8.39	8.10	7.14	5.93	5.20	4.71	3.19	2.32
Cash Flow Per Share	9.64	8.57	6.74	6.76	5.67	2.21	2.43	6.03
Tang Book Value Per Share	26.27	24.58	20.54	18.65	13.86	9.39	6.83	4.67
Dividends Per Share	2.280	2.200	1.850	1.580	1.400	1.300	1.220	1.200
Dividend Payout %	27.18	27.16	25.91	26.64	26.92	27.60	38.24	51.72
Income Statement								
Total Revenue	900,500	3,593,100	3,492,600	3,237,500	3,099,200	2,996,500	2,681,500	2,420,800
EBITDA	222,600	844,400	762,800	658,500	592,100	547,300	403,600	325,900
Depn & Amortn	21,000	82,500	79,500	76,700	76,700	74,600	72,700	74,600
Income Before Taxes	188,600	710,500	630,900	526,200	460,200	412,900	277,400	205,300
Income Taxes	57,600	221,200	199,500	166,700	148,200	133,700	87,600	62,700
Net Income	128,300	478,700	421,900	350,300	306,100	276,300	186,500	134,200
Average Shares	59,500	59,100	59,100	59,100	58,900	58,700	58,400	57,900
Balance Sheet								
Current Assets	1,841,500	1,898,700	1,858,600	1,796,200	1,669,000	1,530,700	1,765,500	1,676,100
Total Assets	4,436,400	4,486,900	4,310,100	4,110,000	3,902,300	3,672,900	3,729,400	3,447,400
Current Liabilities	837,200	670,500	718,700	715,400	589,200	583,800	881,100	739,900
Long-Term Obligations	714,600	861,700	862,700	858,900	970,400	967,900	954,800	902,100
Total Liabilities	1,919,300	2,074,200	2,102,300	1,996,800	2,100,200	2,142,000	2,340,900	2,157,400
Stockholders' Equity	2,517,100	2,412,700	2,207,800	2,113,200	1,802,100	1,530,900	1,388,500	1,290,000
Shares Outstanding	58,138	58,086	58,113	58,115	58,254	58,224	58,181	57,745
Statistical Record								
Return on Assets %	11.42	10.91	9.86	8.77	8.10	7.49	5.21	4.37
Return on Equity %	21.18	20.78	19.21	17.94	18.42	18.98	13.96	10.87
EBITDA Margin %	24.72	23.50	21.84	20.34	19.10	18.26	15.05	13.46
Net Margin %	14.25	13.32	12.08	10.82	9.88	9.22	6.96	5.54
Asset Turnover	0.83	0.82	0.82	0.81	0.82	0.81	0.75	0.79
Current Ratio	2.20	2.83	2.59	2.51	2.83	2.62	2.00	2.27
Debt to Equity	0.28	0.36	0.39	0.41	0.54	0.63	0.69	0.70
Price Range	174.09-135.41	174.09-131.45	139.35-97.23	108.88-77.06	80.03-51.12	64.09-42.45	57.39-39.88	43.57-20.66
P/E Ratio	20.75-16.14	21.49-16.23	19.52-13.62	18.36-12.99	15.39-9.83	13.61-9.01	17.99-12.50	18.78-8.91
Average Yield %	1.44	1.41	1.55	1.72	2.11	2.35	2.65	3.62

Address: 2801 80th Street, Kenosha, WI 53143	**Web Site:** www.snapon.com	**Auditors:** Deloitte & Touche LLP
Telephone: 262-656-5200	**Officers:** Jack D. Michaels - Chairman Nicholas T. Pinchuk - Chairman, President, Chief Executive Officer	**Investor Contact:** 262-656 6121
Fax: 262-656-5577		**Transfer Agents:** Computershare Trust Company, N.A., Providence, RI

SONIC AUTOMOTIVE, INC.

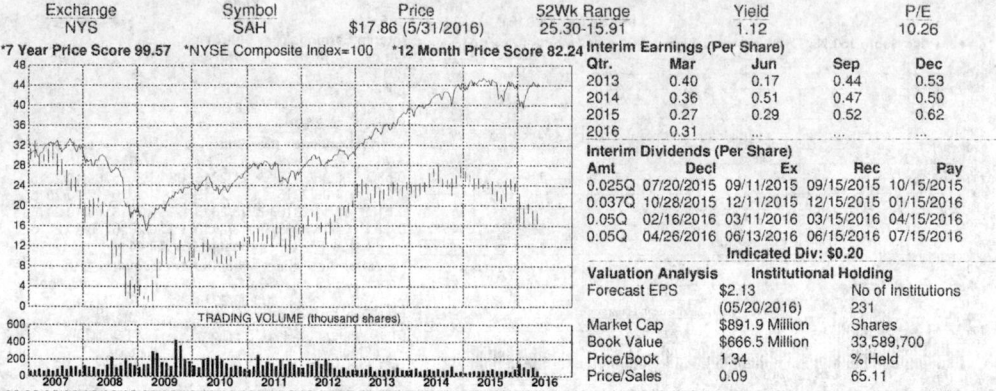

Exchange	Symbol	Price	52Wk Range	Yield	P/E
NYS	SAH	$17.86 (5/31/2016)	25.30-15.91	1.12	10.26

*7 Year Price Score 99.57 *NYSE Composite Index=100 *12 Month Price Score 82.24

Interim Earnings (Per Share)

Qtr.	Mar	Jun	Sep	Dec
2013	0.40	0.17	0.44	0.53
2014	0.36	0.51	0.47	0.50
2015	0.27	0.29	0.52	0.62
2016	0.31	...	...	...

Interim Dividends (Per Share)

Amt	Decl	Ex	Rec	Pay
0.025Q	07/20/2015	09/11/2015	09/15/2015	10/15/2015
0.037Q	10/28/2015	12/11/2015	12/15/2015	01/15/2016
0.05Q	02/16/2016	03/11/2016	03/15/2016	04/15/2016
0.05Q	04/26/2016	06/13/2016	06/15/2016	07/15/2016

Indicated Div: $0.20

Valuation Analysis

		Institutional Holding	
Forecast EPS	$2.13	No of Institutions	
	(05/20/2016)	231	
Market Cap	$891.9 Million	Shares	
Book Value	$666.5 Million	33,589,700	
Price/Book	1.34	% Held	
Price/Sales	0.09	65.11	

Business Summary: Retail - Automotive (MIC: 2.1.4 SIC: 5511 NAIC: 441110)

Sonic Automotive is an automotive retailer. As of Dec 31 2015, Co. operated 114 franchises in 13 states (representing 25 different brands of cars and light trucks) and 18 collision repair centers. As of Dec 31 2015, Co. operated 96 franchised dealership stores and three EchoPark® stores. Co. has two segments: Franchised Dealerships, which comprises retail automotive franchises that sell new vehicles and buy and sell used vehicles, replacement parts and vehicle repair and maintenance services, and finance and insurance products; and EchoPark®, which comprises stand-alone retail locations that provide customers an opportunity to search, buy, service, finance and sell pre-owned vehicles.

Recent Developments: For the quarter ended Mar 31 2016, income from continuing operations increased 0.5% to US$14.5 million from US$14.4 million in the year-earlier quarter. Net income increased 4.7% to US$14.6 million from US$14.0 million in the year-earlier quarter. Revenues were US$2.23 billion, down 0.0% from US$2.24 billion the year before. Operating income was US$42.3 million versus US$41.5 million in the prior-year quarter, an increase of 1.9%. Direct operating expenses declined 0.6% to US$1.89 billion from US$1.90 billion in the comparable period the year before. Indirect operating expenses increased 3.2% to US$302.8 million from US$293.5 million in the equivalent prior-year period.

Prospects: Our evaluation of Sonic Automotive Inc. as of June 19, 2016 is the result of our systematic analysis on three basic characteristics: earnings strength, relative valuation, and recent stock price movement. The company has managed to produce a neutral trend in earnings per share over the past 5 quarters and while recent estimates for the company have remained steady, SAH has posted results that fell short of analysts expectations. Based on operating earnings yield, the company is undervalued when compared to all of the companies in our coverage universe. Share price changes over the past year indicates that SAH will perform poorly over the near term.

Financial Data

(US$ in Thousands)	3 Mos	12/31/2015	12/31/2014	12/31/2013	12/31/2012	12/31/2011	12/31/2010	12/31/2009
Earnings Per Share	1.74	1.70	1.84	1.53	1.53	1.29	1.49	0.62
Cash Flow Per Share	2.75	1.38	3.09	2.41	(1.25)	2.93	4.88	9.21
Tang Book Value Per Share	2.29	3.54	2.10	0.94	0.03	N.M.	N.M.	N.M.
Dividends Per Share	0.138	0.113	0.100	0.100	0.100	0.100	0.025	...
Dividend Payout %	7.90	6.62	5.43	6.54	6.54	7.75	1.68	...
Income Statement								
Total Revenue	2,234,626	9,624,299	9,197,099	8,843,168	8,365,468	7,871,274	6,880,844	6,131,709
EBITDA	43,266	289,522	295,331	264,744	279,127	269,462	223,226	198,262
Depn & Amortn	857	72,130	61,621	58,284	58,350	55,628	48,129	64,448
Income Before Taxes	23,634	145,156	161,727	129,021	141,233	126,029	78,421	22,359
Income Taxes	9,170	57,065	63,168	44,343	49,972	48,382	(17,504)	(33,251)
Net Income	14,624	86,311	97,217	81,618	89,101	76,254	89,929	31,548
Average Shares	47,122	50,883	52,563	52,941	60,406	65,464	65,794	55,832
Balance Sheet								
Current Assets	1,931,458	2,083,112	1,768,959	1,732,185	1,611,033	1,180,729	1,190,350	1,085,383
Total Assets	3,431,371	3,562,381	3,183,135	3,051,170	2,776,722	2,339,629	2,250,764	2,068,855
Current Liabilities	1,804,153	1,914,621	1,647,006	1,594,536	1,524,155	1,156,675	1,105,587	1,006,901
Long-Term Obligations	817,065	781,145	742,610	730,157	610,798	536,011	546,401	552,150
Total Liabilities	2,764,914	2,833,333	2,516,417	2,437,531	2,250,177	1,816,887	1,786,069	1,700,103
Stockholders' Equity	666,457	729,048	666,718	613,639	526,545	522,742	464,695	368,752
Shares Outstanding	49,940	49,940	50,919	52,713	53,239	52,629	52,787	52,128
Statistical Record								
Return on Assets %	2.65	2.56	3.12	2.80	3.47	3.32	4.16	1.41
Return on Equity %	12.99	12.37	15.19	14.32	16.94	15.44	21.58	11.30
EBITDA Margin %	1.94	3.01	3.21	2.99	3.34	3.42	3.24	3.23
Net Margin %	0.65	0.90	1.06	0.92	1.07	0.97	1.31	0.51
Asset Turnover	2.94	2.85	2.95	3.03	3.26	3.43	3.19	2.74
Current Ratio	1.07	1.09	1.07	1.09	1.06	1.02	1.08	1.08
Debt to Equity	1.23	1.07	1.11	1.19	1.16	1.03	1.18	1.50
Price Range	25.37-15.91	27.04-20.35	27.81-21.33	25.15-20.11	20.89-12.16	16.21-10.47	13.64-8.39	14.77-0.95
P/E Ratio	14.58-9.14	15.91-11.97	15.11-11.59	16.44-13.14	13.65-7.95	12.57-8.12	9.15-5.63	23.82-1.53
Average Yield %	0.62	0.47	0.41	0.44	0.58	0.73	0.24	...

Address: 4401 Colwick Road, Charlotte, NC 28211 **Telephone:** 704-566-2400 **Fax:** 704-536-5116	**Web Site:** www.sonicautomotive.com **Officers:** O. Bruton Smith - Executive Chairman, Chairman, Chief Executive Officer David Bruton Smith - Vice-Chairman, Executive Vice President	**Auditors:** KPMG LLP **Investor Contact:** 888-766-4218 **Transfer Agents:** American Stock Transfer & Trust Company, New York, NY

SONOCO PRODUCTS CO.

Exchange	Symbol	Price	52Wk Range	Yield	P/E	Div Achiever
NYS	SON	$47.67 (5/31/2016)	49.09-37.01	3.10	21.77	32 Years

*7 Year Price Score 101.21 *NYSE Composite Index=100 *12 Month Price Score 109.70

TRADING VOLUME (thousand shares)

Interim Earnings (Per Share)

Qtr.	Mar	Jun	Sep	Dec
2013	0.47	0.54	0.59	0.53
2014	0.50	0.59	0.69	0.53
2015	0.86	0.63	0.43	0.54
2016	0.59	...	...	...

Interim Dividends (Per Share)

Amt	Decl	Ex	Rec	Pay
0.35Q	07/15/2015	08/12/2015	08/14/2015	09/10/2015
0.35Q	10/19/2015	11/10/2015	11/13/2015	12/10/2015
0.35Q	02/10/2016	02/22/2016	02/24/2016	03/10/2016
0.37Q	04/20/2016	05/11/2016	05/13/2016	06/10/2016

Indicated Div: $1.48 (Div. Reinv. Plan)

Valuation Analysis

		Institutional Holding	
Forecast EPS	$2.70	No of Institutions	
	(05/20/2016)	469	
Market Cap	$4.8 Billion	Shares	
Book Value	$1.6 Billion	81,192,864	
Price/Book	3.07	% Held	
Price/Sales	0.96	65.60	

Business Summary: Containers & Packaging (MIC: 8.1.3 SIC: 2671 NAIC: 322221)

Sonoco Products manufactures industrial and consumer packaging products and provides packaging services. Co. has four segments: Consumer Packaging, which includes round composite cans, shaped rigid paperboard containers, fiber caulk/adhesive tubes, aluminum; Display and Packaging, which includes point-of-purchase displays, custom packaging and retail packaging; Paper and Industrial Converted Products, which includes recycled paperboard, chipboard, tubeboard, lightweight corestock, boxboard, linerboard, corrugating medium, and paperboard tubes and cores; and Protective Solutions, which provides custom-engineered, paperboard-based and expanded foam protective packaging and components.

Recent Developments: For the quarter ended Apr 3 2016, net income decreased 29.8% to US$60.2 million from US$85.7 million in the year-earlier quarter. Revenues were US$1.23 billion, up 1.7% from US$1.21 billion the year before. Operating income was US$101.8 million versus US$124.1 million in the prior-year quarter, a decrease of 17.9%. Direct operating expenses declined 0.5% to US$981.0 million from US$985.7 million in the comparable period the year before. Indirect operating expenses increased 48.9% to US$143.4 million from US$96.3 million in the equivalent prior-year period.

Prospects: Our evaluation of Sonoco Products Co. as of June 19, 2016 is the result of our systematic analysis on three basic characteristics: earnings strength, relative valuation, and recent stock price movement. The company has produced a positive trend in earnings per share over the past 5 quarters. However, while recent estimates for the company have been mixed, SON has posted better than expected results. Based on operating earnings yield, the company is undervalued when compared to all of the companies in our coverage universe. Share price changes over the past year indicates that SON will perform well over the near term.

Financial Data

(US$ in Thousands)	3 Mos	12/31/2015	12/31/2014	12/31/2013	12/31/2012	12/31/2011	12/31/2010	12/31/2009
Earnings Per Share	2.19	2.44	2.32	2.12	1.91	2.13	1.96	1.50
Cash Flow Per Share	4.54	4.46	4.09	5.25	3.96	2.43	3.69	3.88
Tang Book Value Per Share	1.68	1.26	0.43	3.60	1.01	0.08	5.19	4.37
Dividends Per Share	1.400	1.370	1.270	1.230	1.190	1.150	1.110	1.080
Dividend Payout %	63.93	56.15	54.74	58.02	62.30	53.99	56.63	72.00
Income Statement								
Total Revenue	1,226,276	4,964,369	5,014,534	4,848,092	4,786,129	4,498,932	4,124,121	3,597,331
EBITDA	155,404	562,432	561,422	530,695	518,964	485,678	446,089	413,966
Depn & Amortn	53,572	179,888	169,911	169,400	171,905	163,198	156,529	161,180
Income Before Taxes	88,045	327,946	339,120	304,569	287,074	284,406	254,454	214,221
Income Taxes	29,194	87,738	108,922	96,203	103,759	78,423	64,485	66,818
Net Income	59,914	250,136	239,165	219,113	196,010	217,517	201,053	151,482
Average Shares	102,329	102,392	103,172	103,248	102,573	102,173	102,543	101,029
Balance Sheet								
Current Assets	1,320,485	1,307,378	1,390,283	1,378,474	1,499,896	1,312,791	1,157,516	996,573
Total Assets	4,048,005	4,020,269	4,209,996	3,979,291	4,176,065	3,986,170	3,281,014	3,062,580
Current Liabilities	916,268	922,516	905,445	867,225	1,044,235	836,483	780,649	805,639
Long-Term Obligations	1,015,804	1,021,854	1,200,885	946,257	1,099,454	1,232,966	603,941	462,743
Total Liabilities	2,484,295	2,507,340	2,702,873	2,268,554	2,687,079	2,574,375	1,789,223	1,696,199
Stockholders' Equity	1,563,710	1,512,929	1,507,123	1,710,737	1,488,986	1,411,795	1,491,791	1,366,381
Shares Outstanding	100,752	100,944	100,603	102,147	100,847	100,211	100,510	100,149
Statistical Record								
Return on Assets %	5.47	6.08	5.84	5.37	4.79	5.99	6.34	4.93
Return on Equity %	14.61	16.57	14.86	13.70	13.48	14.98	14.07	11.98
EBITDA Margin %	12.67	11.33	11.20	10.95	10.84	10.80	10.82	11.51
Net Margin %	4.89	5.04	4.77	4.52	4.10	4.83	4.88	4.21
Asset Turnover	1.22	1.21	1.22	1.19	1.17	1.24	1.30	1.17
Current Ratio	1.44	1.42	1.54	1.59	1.44	1.57	1.48	1.24
Debt to Equity	0.65	0.68	0.80	0.55	0.74	0.87	0.40	0.34
Price Range	48.89-37.01	47.44-37.26	44.50-37.55	41.72-29.73	34.49-29.20	36.80-27.34	34.83-26.95	30.31-16.95
P/E Ratio	22.32-16.90	19.44-15.27	19.18-16.19	19.68-14.02	18.06-15.29	17.28-12.84	17.77-13.75	20.21-11.30
Average Yield %	3.30	3.18	3.06	3.39	3.81	3.46	3.48	4.33

Address: 1 N. Second St., Hartsville, SC 29550	Web Site: www.sonoco.com	Auditors: PricewaterhouseCoopers, LLP
Telephone: 843-383-7000	Officers: Harris E. DeLoach - Chairman, Chief Executive Officer Mancil Jack Sanders - President, Chief Operating Officer, Chief Executive Officer	Investor Contact: 843-339-6018
Fax: 843-383-7008		Transfer Agents: Continental Stock Transfer & Trust Company, New York, NY

SOUTH JERSEY INDUSTRIES, INC.

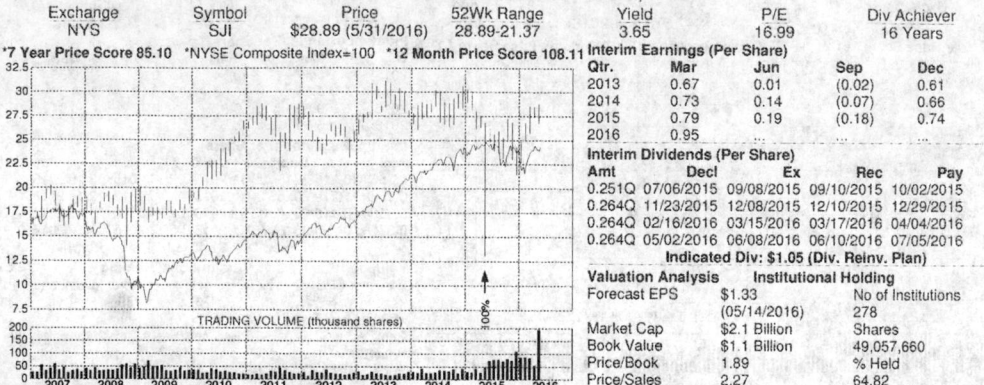

Exchange	Symbol	Price	52Wk Range	Yield	P/E	Div Achiever
NYS	SJI	$28.89 (5/31/2016)	28.89-21.37	3.65	16.99	16 Years

*7 Year Price Score 85.10 *NYSE Composite Index=100 *12 Month Price Score 108.11

Interim Earnings (Per Share)

Qtr.	Mar	Jun	Sep	Dec
2013	0.67	0.01	(0.02)	0.61
2014	0.73	0.14	(0.07)	0.66
2015	0.79	0.19	(0.18)	0.74
2016	0.95			

Interim Dividends (Per Share)

Amt	Decl	Ex	Rec	Pay
0.251Q	07/06/2015	09/08/2015	09/10/2015	10/02/2015
0.264Q	11/23/2015	12/08/2015	12/10/2015	12/29/2015
0.264Q	02/16/2016	03/15/2016	03/17/2016	04/04/2016
0.264Q	05/02/2016	06/08/2016	06/10/2016	07/05/2016

Indicated Div: $1.05 (Div. Reinv. Plan)

Valuation Analysis / **Institutional Holding**

Forecast EPS	$1.33	No of Institutions	278
	(05/14/2016)		
Market Cap	$2.1 Billion	Shares	
Book Value	$1.1 Billion		49,057,660
Price/Book	1.89	% Held	
Price/Sales	2.27		64.82

Business Summary: Gas Utilities (MIC: 3.3.1 SIC: 4924 NAIC: 221210)

South Jersey Industries is a holding company. Co. operates via its subsidiaries: South Jersey Gas Co., which is a regulated natural gas utility; South Jersey Energy Co., which acquires and markets natural gas and electricity to retail end users; South Jersey Resources Group, LLC, which markets natural gas storage assets; South Jersey Exploration, LLC, which owns oil, gas and mineral rights in the Marcellus Shale region of Pennsylvania; Marina Energy, LLC, which develops and operates energy-related projects; South Jersey Energy Service Plus, LLC, which services residential and small commercial HVAC systems; and SJI Midstream, LLC, which invests in infrastructure and other midstream projects.

Recent Developments:
For the quarter ended Mar 31 2016, income from continuing operations increased 26.6% to US$68.2 million from US$53.9 million in the year-earlier quarter. Net income increased 27.0% to US$68.1 million from US$53.6 million in the year-earlier quarter. Revenues were US$333.0 million, down 13.0% from US$383.0 million the year before. Operating income was US$114.3 million versus US$76.4 million in the prior-year quarter, an increase of 49.6%. Direct operating expenses declined 31.8% to US$196.2 million from US$287.6 million in the comparable period the year before. Indirect operating expenses increased 19.0% to US$22.6 million from US$19.0 million in the equivalent prior-year period.

Prospects:
Our evaluation of South Jersey Industries Inc. as of June 19, 2016 is the result of our systematic analysis on three basic characteristics: earnings strength, relative valuation, and recent stock price movement. The company has managed to produce a neutral trend in earnings per share over the past 5 quarters. However, while recent estimates for the company have been lowered by analysts, SJI has posted results that were in line with analysts expectations. Based on operating earnings yield, the company is about fairly valued when compared to all of the companies in our coverage universe. Share price changes over the past year indicates that SJI will perform in line with the market over the ne

Financial Data
(US$ in Thousands)	3 Mos	12/31/2015	12/31/2014	12/31/2013	12/31/2012	12/31/2011	12/31/2010	12/31/2009
Earnings Per Share	1.70	1.53	1.46	1.27	1.49	1.49	1.11	0.97
Cash Flow Per Share	3.51	2.72	2.43	2.49	1.91	3.19	2.66	2.94
Tang Book Value Per Share	14.89	14.19	13.65	12.64	11.63	10.33	9.54	9.12
Dividends Per Share	1.030	1.018	0.960	0.900	0.825	0.749	0.677	0.611
Dividend Payout %	60.59	66.50	65.75	70.59	55.56	50.42	61.04	63.02
Income Statement								
Total Revenue	333,035	959,568	886,996	731,421	706,280	828,560	925,067	845,444
EBITDA	137,157	238,855	202,426	130,252	162,338	172,998	155,061	143,801
Depn & Amortn	20,701	72,451	63,004	49,637	41,336	35,749	34,018	31,280
Income Before Taxes	107,296	134,782	109,862	61,790	102,016	113,171	99,147	93,529
Income Taxes	39,267	1,360	4,449	(19,014)	11,479	22,502	28,811	34,302
Net Income	68,069	105,107	97,046	81,593	91,608	89,291	66,652	58,105
Average Shares	71,416	68,931	66,428	64,092	61,648	60,172	59,948	59,786
Balance Sheet								
Current Assets	396,110	431,274	566,697	482,898	394,837	340,609	423,837	368,355
Total Assets	3,493,984	3,480,900	3,349,425	2,924,855	2,631,440	2,247,510	2,076,615	1,782,008
Current Liabilities	698,003	832,476	850,185	764,973	651,844	587,971	640,524	478,784
Long-Term Obligations	1,046,968	1,006,394	859,491	680,400	601,400	424,213	340,000	312,793
Total Liabilities	2,400,542	2,443,361	2,416,993	2,097,855	1,895,226	1,623,396	1,506,518	1,238,407
Stockholders' Equity	1,093,442	1,037,539	932,432	827,000	736,214	624,114	570,097	543,601
Shares Outstanding	71,425	70,965	68,334	65,430	63,306	60,424	59,745	59,592
Statistical Record								
Return on Assets %	3.48	3.08	3.09	2.94	3.74	4.13	3.45	3.25
Return on Equity %	11.58	10.67	11.03	10.44	13.43	14.95	11.97	10.98
EBITDA Margin %	41.18	24.89	22.82	17.81	22.98	20.88	16.76	17.01
Net Margin %	20.44	10.95	10.94	11.16	12.97	10.78	7.21	6.87
Asset Turnover	0.26	0.28	0.28	0.26	0.29	0.38	0.48	0.47
Current Ratio	0.57	0.52	0.67	0.63	0.61	0.58	0.66	0.77
Debt to Equity	0.96	0.97	0.92	0.82	0.82	0.68	0.60	0.58
Price Range	28.52-12.96	30.30-12.96	30.61-26.00	31.13-25.16	28.47-23.18	28.75-21.72	27.00-18.77	19.97-16.33
P/E Ratio	16.78-7.62	19.80-8.47	20.97-17.81	24.51-19.81	19.10-15.55	19.29-14.58	24.33-16.91	20.59-16.84
Average Yield %	4.10	3.94	3.41	3.41	3.15	3.23	2.81	2.99	3.43

Address: 1 South Jersey Plaza, Folsom, NJ 08037	Web Site: www.sjiindustries.com	Auditors: BDO USA, LLP
Telephone: 609-561-9000	Officers: Edward J. Graham - Chairman, President, Chief Executive Officer Walter M. Higgins - Chairman	Investor Contact: 609-561-9000Ext.42
		Transfer Agents: Computershare, Canton, MA

SOUTHERN COMPANY (THE)

Exchange	Symbol	Price	52Wk Range	Yield	P/E	Div Achiever
NYS	SO	$49.44 (5/31/2016)	51.73-41.61	4.53	19.31	14 Years

*7 Year Price Score 94.46 *NYSE Composite Index=100 *12 Month Price Score 106.63

Interim Earnings (Per Share)

Qtr.	Mar	Jun	Sep	Dec
2013	0.09	0.34	0.97	0.47
2014	0.39	0.68	0.80	0.31
2015	0.56	0.69	1.05	0.29
2016	0.53	...	...	...

Interim Dividends (Per Share)

Amt	Decl	Ex	Rec	Pay
0.542Q	07/20/2015	08/13/2015	08/17/2015	09/05/2015
0.542Q	10/19/2015	11/12/2015	11/16/2015	12/04/2015
0.542Q	01/14/2016	02/11/2016	02/16/2016	03/07/2016
0.56Q	04/18/2016	05/12/2016	05/16/2016	06/06/2016

Indicated Div: $2.24 (Div. Reinv. Plan)

Valuation Analysis / **Institutional Holding**

Forecast EPS	$2.85 (05/20/2016)
No of Institutions	1447
Market Cap	$45.4 Billion
Book Value	$21.5 Billion
Shares	507,112,832
Price/Book	2.11
% Held	51.82
Price/Sales	2.63

Business Summary: Electric Utilities (MIC: 3.1.1 SIC: 4911 NAIC: 221119)

Southern is a holding company. Through its subsidiaries, Alabama Power Company, Georgia Power Company, Gulf Power Company and Mississippi Power Company, each of which is an operating public utility company, Co. supplies electric service in the states of Alabama, Georgia, Florida, and Mississippi. In addition, Co. owns all of the common stock of Southern Power Company, which is also an operating public utility company that constructs, acquires, owns, and manages generation assets, including renewable energy projects, and sells electricity at market-based rates in the wholesale market.

Recent Developments: For the quarter ended Mar 31 2016, net income decreased 5.3% to US$497.0 million from US$525.0 million in the year-earlier quarter. Revenues were US$3.97 billion, down 5.2% from US$4.18 billion the year before. Operating income was US$933.0 million versus US$957.0 million in the prior-year quarter, a decrease of 2.5%. Direct operating expenses declined 11.9% to US$2.18 billion from US$2.48 billion in the comparable period the year before. Indirect operating expenses increased 13.6% to US$850.0 million from US$748.0 million in the equivalent prior-year period.

Prospects: Our evaluation of Southern Company as of June 19, 2016 is the result of our systematic analysis on three basic characteristics: earnings strength, relative valuation, and recent stock price movement. The company has managed to produce a neutral trend in earnings per share over the past 5 quarters and while recent estimates for the company have remained steady, SO has posted better than expected results. Based on operating earnings yield, the company is undervalued when compared to all of the companies in our coverage universe. Share price changes over the past year indicates that SO will perform well over the near term.

Financial Data

(US$ in Thousands)	3 Mos	12/31/2015	12/31/2014	12/31/2013	12/31/2012	12/31/2011	12/31/2010	12/31/2009
Earnings Per Share	2.56	2.59	2.18	1.87	2.67	2.55	2.36	2.06
Cash Flow Per Share	6.80	6.89	6.48	6.95	5.61	6.89	4.80	4.10
Tang Book Value Per Share	23.43	22.76	22.43	21.85	21.52	20.75	19.65	18.61
Dividends Per Share	2.170	2.152	2.083	2.013	1.942	1.873	1.803	1.732
Dividend Payout %	84.77	83.11	95.53	107.62	72.75	73.43	76.38	84.10
Income Statement								
Total Revenue	3,965,000	17,489,000	18,467,000	17,087,000	16,537,000	17,657,000	17,456,000	15,743,000
EBITDA	1,604,000	6,841,000	6,117,000	5,662,000	6,713,000	6,392,000	5,768,000	5,275,000
Depn & Amortn	639,000	2,395,000	2,293,000	2,298,000	2,145,000	2,048,000	1,831,000	1,788,000
Income Before Taxes	719,000	3,629,000	3,008,000	2,559,000	3,749,000	3,487,000	3,066,000	2,605,000
Income Taxes	222,000	1,194,000	977,000	849,000	1,334,000	1,219,000	1,026,000	896,000
Net Income	497,000	2,435,000	2,031,000	1,710,000	2,415,000	2,268,000	2,040,000	1,708,000
Average Shares	922,000	914,000	901,000	881,000	879,000	864,000	837,000	796,000
Balance Sheet								
Current Assets	5,461,000	6,526,000	6,370,000	5,599,000	6,162,000	6,272,000	5,883,000	5,873,000
Total Assets	78,735,000	78,318,000	70,923,000	64,546,000	63,149,000	59,267,000	55,032,000	52,046,000
Current Liabilities	7,856,000	9,129,000	8,967,000	5,536,000	7,014,000	6,577,000	6,472,000	5,584,000
Long-Term Obligations	26,091,000	24,688,000	20,841,000	21,344,000	19,274,000	18,647,000	18,154,000	18,131,000
Total Liabilities	57,211,000	56,956,000	49,583,000	44,407,000	43,770,000	40,607,000	37,748,000	36,086,000
Stockholders' Equity	21,524,000	21,362,000	21,340,000	20,139,000	19,379,000	18,660,000	17,284,000	15,960,000
Shares Outstanding	918,600	911,721	907,777	887,086	867,768	865,125	843,500	819,500
Statistical Record								
Return on Assets %	3.20	3.26	3.00	2.68	3.93	3.97	3.81	3.40
Return on Equity %	11.28	11.40	9.79	8.65	12.66	12.62	12.27	11.27
EBITDA Margin %	40.45	39.12	33.12	33.14	40.59	36.20	33.04	33.51
Net Margin %	12.53	13.92	11.00	10.01	14.60	12.84	11.69	10.85
Asset Turnover	0.23	0.23	0.27	0.27	0.27	0.31	0.33	0.31
Current Ratio	0.70	0.71	0.71	1.01	0.88	0.95	0.91	1.05
Debt to Equity	1.21	1.16	0.98	1.06	0.99	1.00	1.05	1.14
Price Range	51.73-41.61	52.79-41.61	50.88-40.40	48.65-40.12	48.42-42.03	46.59-36.80	38.47-31.13	37.47-26.81
P/E Ratio	20.21-16.25	20.38-16.07	23.34-18.53	26.02-21.45	18.13-15.74	18.27-14.43	16.30-13.19	18.19-13.01
Average Yield %	4.79	4.78	4.70	4.61	4.28	4.64	5.13	5.52

Address: 30 Ivan Allen Jr. Boulevard, N.W., Atlanta, GA 30308 Telephone: 404-506-5000 Fax: 404-506-0455	Web Site: www.southerncompany.com Officers: Thomas A. Fanning - Chairman, President, Chief Executive Officer, Executive Vice President, Chief Operating Officer Art P. Beattie - Executive Vice President, Chief Financial Officer	Auditors: Deloitte & Touche LLP Transfer Agents: ComputerShare, College Station, TX

SOUTHERN COPPER CORP

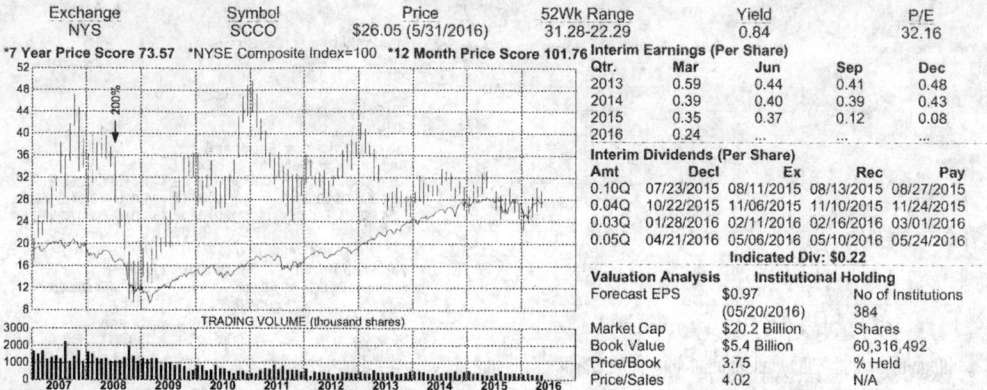

Exchange	Symbol	Price	52Wk Range	Yield	P/E
NYS	SCCO	$26.05 (5/31/2016)	31.28-22.29	0.84	32.16

*7 Year Price Score 73.57   *NYSE Composite Index=100   *12 Month Price Score 101.76

Interim Earnings (Per Share)

Qtr.	Mar	Jun	Sep	Dec
2013	0.59	0.44	0.41	0.48
2014	0.39	0.40	0.39	0.43
2015	0.35	0.37	0.12	0.08
2016	0.24	...	...	...

Interim Dividends (Per Share)

Amt	Decl	Ex	Rec	Pay
0.10Q	07/23/2015	08/11/2015	08/13/2015	08/27/2015
0.04Q	10/22/2015	11/06/2015	11/10/2015	11/24/2015
0.03Q	01/28/2016	02/11/2016	02/16/2016	03/01/2016
0.05Q	04/21/2016	05/06/2016	05/10/2016	05/24/2016

Indicated Div: $0.22

Valuation Analysis

		Institutional Holding	
Forecast EPS	$0.97	No of Institutions	
	(05/20/2016)	384	
Market Cap	$20.2 Billion	Shares	
Book Value	$5.4 Billion	60,316,492	
Price/Book	3.75	% Held	
Price/Sales	4.02	N/A	

Business Summary: Non-Precious Metals (MIC: 8.2.2 SIC: 1021 NAIC: 212234)

Southern Copper produces copper, molybdenum, zinc and silver. All of Co.'s mining, smelting and refining facilities are located in Peru and Mexico and Co. conducts exploration activities in those countries and in Argentina, Chile and Ecuador. Co.'s Peruvian copper operations involve mining, milling and flotation of copper ore to produce copper concentrates and molybdenum concentrates; the smelting of copper concentrates to produce anode copper; and the refining of anode copper to produce copper cathodes. Co. also produces molybdenum concentrate. Co.'s subsidiary, Minera Mexico S.A. de C.V., is engaged in the mining and processing of copper, molybdenum, zinc, silver, gold and lead.

Recent Developments: For the quarter ended Mar 31 2016, net income decreased 34.5% to US$185.7 million from US$283.7 million in the year-earlier quarter. Revenues were US$1.25 billion, down 2.3% from US$1.27 billion the year before. Operating income was US$346.2 million versus US$436.9 million in the prior-year quarter, a decrease of 20.8%. Direct operating expenses rose 6.9% to US$726.8 million from US$679.8 million in the comparable period the year before. Indirect operating expenses increased 8.9% to US$172.1 million from US$158.0 million in the equivalent prior-year period.

Prospects: Our evaluation of Southern Copper Corp. as of June 19, 2016 is the result of our systematic analysis on three basic characteristics: earnings strength, relative valuation, and recent stock price movement. The company has enjoyed a very positive trend in earnings per share over the past 5 quarters. However, while recent estimates for the company have been mixed, SCCO has posted better than expected results. Based on operating earnings yield, the company is overvalued when compared to all of the companies in our coverage universe. Share price changes over the past year indicates that SCCO will perform well over the near term.

Financial Data

(US$ in Thousands)	3 Mos	12/31/2015	12/31/2014	12/31/2013	12/31/2012	12/31/2011	12/31/2010	12/31/2009
Earnings Per Share	0.81	0.93	1.61	1.92	2.28	2.76	1.83	1.09
Cash Flow Per Share	0.93	1.11	1.64	2.20	2.36	2.45	2.26	1.13
Tang Book Value Per Share	6.74	6.60	7.06	6.13	5.26	4.64	4.44	4.43
Dividends Per Share	0.270	0.340	0.460	0.680	3.710	2.460	1.680	0.442
Dividend Payout %	33.33	36.56	28.57	35.42	162.72	89.13	91.80	40.55
Income Statement								
Total Revenue	1,245,100	5,045,900	5,787,694	5,952,943	6,669,266	6,818,721	5,149,500	3,734,280
EBITDA	481,000	1,892,700	2,634,999	2,942,818	3,164,216	3,907,380	2,863,067	1,766,661
Depn & Amortn	135,300	503,600	443,000	393,600	33,500	286,000	279,600	271,200
Income Before Taxes	272,900	1,189,200	2,068,706	2,372,598	2,973,542	3,448,688	2,430,780	1,404,434
Income Taxes	92,300	464,900	754,629	769,300	1,080,872	1,104,335	868,071	469,861
Net Income	185,100	736,400	1,332,973	1,618,517	1,934,632	2,336,424	1,554,051	929,381
Average Shares	773,900	794,700	828,199	842,668	848,346	845,901	850,000	850,697
Balance Sheet								
Current Assets	2,459,000	2,484,200	2,489,789	3,416,050	4,287,959	3,101,503	3,702,957	1,778,129
Total Assets	12,807,700	12,593,200	11,551,910	11,210,422	10,383,749	8,062,701	8,128,019	6,062,572
Current Liabilities	982,700	920,200	1,150,905	783,584	857,135	992,877	1,139,018	602,425
Long-Term Obligations	5,952,100	5,951,500	4,006,000	4,204,900	4,203,900	2,735,700	2,750,400	1,270,300
Total Liabilities	7,436,400	7,330,300	5,747,450	5,676,760	5,618,609	4,047,397	4,237,571	2,186,944
Stockholders' Equity	5,371,300	5,262,900	5,804,460	5,533,662	4,765,140	4,015,304	3,890,448	3,875,628
Shares Outstanding	773,707	773,707	806,690	884,596	884,596	840,980	850,000	850,000
Statistical Record								
Return on Assets %	5.31	6.10	11.71	14.99	20.92	28.86	21.90	15.72
Return on Equity %	11.61	13.31	23.51	31.43	43.95	59.11	40.02	25.61
EBITDA Margin %	38.63	37.51	45.53	49.43	47.44	57.30	55.60	47.31
Net Margin %	14.87	14.59	23.03	27.19	29.01	34.26	30.18	24.89
Asset Turnover	0.42	0.42	0.51	0.55	0.72	0.84	0.73	0.63
Current Ratio	2.50	2.70	2.16	4.36	5.00	3.12	3.25	2.95
Debt to Equity	1.11	1.13	0.69	0.76	0.88	0.68	0.71	0.33
Price Range	33.14-22.29	33.14-24.40	33.54-26.08	41.96-24.78	38.94-28.16	49.59-23.99	48.84-26.19	36.40-12.74
P/E Ratio	40.91-27.52	35.63-26.24	20.83-16.20	21.85-12.91	17.08-12.35	17.97-8.69	26.69-14.31	33.39-11.69
Average Yield %	0.97	1.09	1.53	2.17	11.20	7.04	4.93	1.84

Address: 1440 East Missouri Avenue, Suite 160, Phoenix, AZ 85014 **Telephone:** 602-264-1375 **Fax:** 602-264-1397	**Web Site:** www.southerncoppercorp.com **Officers:** German Larrea Mota Velasco - Chairman Oscar Gonzalez Rocha - President, Chief Executive Officer	**Auditors:** Deloitte Touche Tohmatsu Limited **Investor Contact:** 602-264-1375 **Transfer Agents:** Computershare, Jersey City, NJ	

SOUTHWEST AIRLINES CO

Exchange	Symbol	Price	52Wk Range	Yield	P/E
NYS	LUV	$42.48 (5/31/2016)	49.58-32.36	0.94	12.53

*7 Year Price Score 176.87 *NYSE Composite Index=100 *12 Month Price Score 106.59

Interim Earnings (Per Share)

Qtr.	Mar	Jun	Sep	Dec
2013	0.08	0.31	0.37	0.30
2014	0.22	0.67	0.48	0.28
2015	0.66	0.90	0.88	0.82
2016	0.79	...	...	...

Interim Dividends (Per Share)

Amt	Decl	Ex	Rec	Pay
0.075Q	07/30/2015	08/18/2015	08/20/2015	09/10/2015
0.075Q	11/20/2015	12/08/2015	12/10/2015	01/07/2016
0.075Q	01/28/2016	03/01/2016	03/03/2016	03/24/2016
0.10Q	05/18/2016	06/06/2016	06/08/2016	06/29/2016

Indicated Div: $0.40

Valuation Analysis

Forecast EPS	$4.15
	(05/20/2016)
Market Cap	$28.4 Billion
Book Value	$7.5 Billion
Price/Book	3.79
Price/Sales	1.40

Institutional Holding

No of Institutions	1058
Shares	564,436,800
% Held	74.24

Business Summary: Airlines/Air Freight (MIC: 7.4.4 SIC: 4512 NAIC: 481111)

Southwest Airlines operates Southwest Airlines (Southwest), a passenger airline that provides scheduled air transportation in the U.S. and near-international markets. During the year ended Dec 31 2015, Co. served 97 destinations in 40 states, the District of Columbia, the Commonwealth of Puerto Rico, and seven near-international countries including Mexico, Jamaica, The Bahamas, Aruba, Dominican Republic, Costa Rica, and Belize. Co. has added its first three destinations in Central America and also commenced Southwest service to a fourth destination in Mexico (Puerto Vallarta). As of Dec 31 2015, Southwest operated a total of 704 Boeing 737 aircraft.

Recent Developments: For the quarter ended Mar 31 2016, net income increased 12.8% to US$511.0 million from US$453.0 million in the year-earlier quarter. Revenues were US$4.83 billion, up 9.3% from US$4.41 billion the year before. Operating income was US$944.0 million versus US$780.0 million in the prior-year quarter, an increase of 21.0%. Direct operating expenses rose 1.7% to US$1.48 billion from US$1.45 billion in the comparable period the year before. Indirect operating expenses increased 10.3% to US$2.41 billion from US$2.18 billion in the equivalent prior-year period.

Prospects: Our evaluation of Southwest Airlines Co as of June 19, 2016 is the result of our systematic analysis on three basic characteristics: earnings strength, relative valuation, and recent stock price movement. The company has managed to produce a neutral trend in earnings per share over the past 5 quarters. However, while recent estimates for the company have been lowered by analysts, LUV has posted better than expected results. Based on operating earnings yield, the company is undervalued when compared to all of the companies in our coverage universe. Share price changes over the past year indicates that LUV will perform very well over the near term.

Financial Data

(US$ in Thousands)	3 Mos	12/31/2015	12/31/2014	12/31/2013	12/31/2012	12/31/2011	12/31/2010	12/31/2009
Earnings Per Share	3.39	3.27	1.64	1.05	0.56	0.23	0.61	0.13
Cash Flow Per Share	5.31	4.90	4.22	3.49	2.74	1.79	2.09	1.33
Tang Book Value Per Share	9.07	9.15	8.06	8.85	8.06	7.45	8.34	7.36
Dividends Per Share	0.300	0.285	0.220	0.130	0.035	0.018	0.018	0.018
Dividend Payout %	8.85	8.72	13.41	12.38	6.16	7.83	2.95	13.85
Income Statement								
Total Revenue	4,826,000	19,820,000	18,605,000	17,699,000	17,088,000	15,658,000	12,104,000	10,350,000
EBITDA	1,120,000	4,575,000	2,854,000	2,177,000	1,636,000	1,197,000	1,496,000	920,000
Depn & Amortn	290,000	1,015,000	938,000	867,000	832,000	702,000	614,000	604,000
Income Before Taxes	816,000	3,479,000	1,816,000	1,209,000	685,000	323,000	745,000	164,000
Income Taxes	305,000	1,298,000	680,000	455,000	264,000	145,000	286,000	65,000
Net Income	511,000	2,181,000	1,136,000	754,000	421,000	178,000	459,000	99,000
Average Shares	648,000	669,000	696,000	718,000	757,000	775,000	747,000	741,000
Balance Sheet								
Current Assets	4,574,000	4,024,000	4,404,000	4,456,000	4,227,000	4,345,000	4,279,000	3,358,000
Total Assets	22,241,000	21,312,000	20,200,000	19,345,000	18,596,000	18,068,000	15,463,000	14,269,000
Current Liabilities	8,253,000	7,406,000	5,923,000	5,676,000	4,650,000	4,533,000	3,305,000	2,676,000
Long-Term Obligations	2,355,000	2,541,000	2,434,000	2,191,000	2,883,000	3,107,000	2,875,000	3,325,000
Total Liabilities	14,745,000	13,954,000	13,425,000	12,009,000	11,604,000	11,191,000	9,226,000	8,803,000
Stockholders' Equity	7,496,000	7,358,000	6,775,000	7,336,000	6,992,000	6,877,000	6,237,000	5,466,000
Shares Outstanding	668,686	647,601	675,594	700,474	730,319	772,560	747,434	742,790
Statistical Record								
Return on Assets %	10.32	10.51	5.75	3.97	2.29	1.06	3.09	0.69
Return on Equity %	31.10	30.86	16.10	10.52	6.05	2.71	7.84	1.90
EBITDA Margin %	23.21	23.08	15.34	12.30	9.57	7.64	12.36	8.89
Net Margin %	10.59	11.00	6.11	4.26	2.46	1.14	3.79	0.96
Asset Turnover	0.93	0.95	0.94	0.93	0.93	0.93	0.81	0.72
Current Ratio	0.55	0.54	0.74	0.79	0.91	0.96	1.29	1.25
Debt to Equity	0.31	0.35	0.36	0.30	0.41	0.45	0.46	0.61
Price Range	49.58-32.36	49.58-32.36	42.32-18.84	18.95-10.24	10.56-7.88	13.32-7.35	14.26-10.63	11.61-5.01
P/E Ratio	14.63-9.55	15.16-9.90	25.80-11.49	18.05-9.75	18.86-14.07	57.91-31.96	23.38-17.43	89.31-38.54
Average Yield %	0.75	0.70	0.76	0.92	0.39	0.17	0.14	0.23

Address: P.O. Box 36611, Dallas, TX 75235-1611	Web Site: www.southwest.com	Auditors: Ernst & Young LLP
Telephone: 214-792-4000	**Officers:** Gary C. Kelly - Chairman, President, Chief Executive Officer Ron Ricks - Vice-Chairman, Executive Vice President, Chief Regulatory Officer, Executive Vice President (frmr), Corporate Secretary	**Investor Contact:** 214-792-4415
Fax: 214-792-5015		**Transfer Agents:** Wells Fargo Shareowner Services, Mendota Heights, MN

SOUTHWESTERN ENERGY COMPANY

Exchange	Symbol	Price	52Wk Range	Yield	P/E
NYS	SWN	$13.67 (5/31/2016)	25.47-5.15	N/A	N/A

*7 Year Price Score 31.66   *NYSE Composite Index=100   *12 Month Price Score 91.50

Interim Earnings (Per Share)

Qtr.	Mar	Jun	Sep	Dec
2013	0.36	0.70	0.53	0.41
2014	0.55	0.59	0.60	0.88
2015	0.12	(2.13)	(4.62)	(5.60)
2016	(3.03)	...	...	...

Interim Dividends (Per Share)

No Dividends Paid

Valuation Analysis

Forecast EPS	$-0.22	Institutional Holding	
	(05/20/2016)	No of Institutions	659
Market Cap	$5.3 Billion	Shares	
Book Value	$1.1 Billion	492,012,960	
Price/Book	4.64	% Held	
Price/Sales	1.92	102.45	

Business Summary: Production & Extraction (MIC: 9.1.1 SIC: 1311 NAIC: 211111)

Southwestern Energy is an independent natural gas and oil company. Co.'s primary business is the exploration for and production of natural gas and oil, with its operations principally focused within the U.S. on development of unconventional natural gas reservoirs located in Pennsylvania, West Virginia and Arkansas. Through its affiliated midstream subsidiaries, Co. is engaged in natural gas gathering activities in Arkansas and Louisiana. As of Dec 31 2015, Co.'s estimated proved natural gas and oil reserves were 6.20 trillion cubic ft. equivalent, comprising of 7.77 trillion cubic ft. equivalent of proved developed reserves and 443.00 billion cubic ft. equivalent of undeveloped reserves.

Recent Developments: For the quarter ended Mar 31 2016, net loss amounted to US$1.13 billion versus net income of US$78.0 million in the year-earlier quarter. Revenues were US$579.0 million, down 37.9% from US$933.0 million the year before. Operating loss was US$1.10 billion versus an income of US$165.0 million in the prior-year quarter. Direct operating expenses declined 11.7% to US$196.0 million from US$222.0 million in the comparable period the year before. Indirect operating expenses increased 171.6% to US$1.48 billion from US$546.0 million in the equivalent prior-year period.

Prospects: Our evaluation of Southwestern Energy Company as of June 19, 2016 is the result of our systematic analysis on three basic characteristics: earnings strength, relative valuation, and recent stock price movement. The company has enjoyed a very positive trend in earnings per share over the past 5 quarters. Because the company lacks sufficient analyst estimate data, we place greater weight on the historical EPS trend as the measure of earnings strength. Based on operating earnings yield, the company is overvalued when compared to all of the companies in our coverage universe. Share price changes over the past year indicates that SWN will perform very poorly over the near term.

Financial Data
(US$ in Thousands)

	3 Mos	12/31/2015	12/31/2014	12/31/2013	12/31/2012	12/31/2011	12/31/2010	12/31/2009
Earnings Per Share	(15.38)	(12.25)	2.62	2.00	(2.03)	1.82	1.73	(0.10)
Cash Flow Per Share	2.95	4.15	6.64	5.45	4.73	5.01	4.75	3.96
Tang Book Value Per Share	2.95	5.85	13.15	10.26	8.65	11.37	8.53	6.74
Income Statement								
Total Revenue	579,000	3,133,000	4,038,000	3,371,145	2,715,043	2,952,906	2,610,663	2,145,779
EBITDA	(1,115,000)	(5,360,000)	2,460,000	2,022,524	(299,836)	1,783,031	1,613,598	461,774
Depn & Amortn	2,000	1,145,000	952,000	790,553	814,710	707,966	591,943	495,291
Income Before Taxes	(1,131,000)	(6,561,000)	1,449,000	1,190,377	(1,150,203)	1,050,990	995,492	(52,155)
Income Taxes	1,000	(2,005,000)	525,000	486,874	(443,139)	413,221	391,659	(16,363)
Net Income	(1,132,000)	(4,556,000)	924,000	703,503	(707,064)	637,769	604,118	(35,650)
Average Shares	382,870	380,521	352,410	350,465	348,610	349,921	349,310	343,420
Balance Sheet								
Current Assets	1,884,000	393,000	1,115,000	644,175	808,912	978,278	580,893	564,501
Total Assets	8,518,000	8,110,000	14,925,000	8,047,726	6,737,527	7,902,897	6,017,463	4,770,250
Current Liabilities	478,000	707,000	5,428,000	688,011	767,771	884,913	693,983	536,416
Long-Term Obligations	6,442,000	4,728,000	2,466,000	1,950,096	1,668,273	1,342,100	1,093,000	997,500
Total Liabilities	7,370,000	5,828,000	10,263,000	4,425,696	3,701,655	3,933,593	3,052,587	2,439,025
Stockholders' Equity	1,148,000	2,282,000	4,662,000	3,622,030	3,035,872	3,969,304	2,964,876	2,331,225
Shares Outstanding	389,642	390,091	354,477	352,928	351,035	348,959	347,577	345,877
Statistical Record								
Return on Assets %	N.M.	N.M.	8.04	9.52	N.M.	9.16	11.20	N.M.
Return on Equity %	N.M.	N.M.	22.31	21.13	N.M.	18.39	22.81	N.M.
EBITDA Margin %	N.M.	N.M.	60.92	60.00	N.M.	60.38	61.81	21.52
Net Margin %	N.M.	N.M.	22.88	20.87	N.M.	21.60	23.14	N.M.
Asset Turnover	0.23	0.27	0.35	0.46	0.37	0.42	0.48	0.45
Current Ratio	3.94	0.56	0.21	0.94	1.05	1.11	0.84	1.05
Debt to Equity	5.61	2.07	0.53	0.54	0.55	0.34	0.37	0.43
Price Range	29.25-5.15	29.25-5.15	48.93-27.24	40.18-32.09	36.60-25.82	49.00-31.94	51.65-31.44	50.62-25.99
P/E Ratio	...	...	18.68-10.40	20.09-16.05	...	26.92-17.55	29.86-18.17	...

Address: 10000 Energy Drive, Spring, TX 77389 **Telephone:** 832-796-1000	**Web Site:** www.swn.com **Officers:** William J. Way - President, Executive Vice President, Chief Operating Officer Robert Craig Owen - Senior Vice President, Chief Financial Officer, Chief Accounting Officer, Controller	**Auditors:** PricewaterhouseCoopers LLP **Investor Contact:** 281-.61-8.4847 **Transfer Agents:** Computershare Trust Company, N.A, Providence, RI

SPECTRA ENERGY CORP

Exchange	Symbol	Price	52Wk Range	Yield	P/E
NYS	SE	$31.86 (5/31/2016)	34.92-21.97	5.08	127.44

*7 Year Price Score 84.14 *NYSE Composite Index=100 *12 Month Price Score 105.24

Interim Earnings (Per Share)

Qtr.	Mar	Jun	Sep	Dec
2013	0.51	0.30	0.39	0.35
2014	0.62	0.22	0.30	0.47
2015	0.40	0.03	0.26	(0.39)
2016	0.35	...	...	...

Interim Dividends (Per Share)

Amt	Decl	Ex	Rec	Pay
0.37Q	07/07/2015	08/10/2015	08/12/2015	09/09/2015
0.37Q	10/08/2015	11/10/2015	11/13/2015	12/08/2015
0.405Q	01/05/2016	02/10/2016	02/12/2016	03/08/2016
0.405Q	04/26/2016	05/11/2016	05/13/2016	06/07/2016

Indicated Div: $1.62

Valuation Analysis

		Institutional Holding	
Forecast EPS	$1.17 (05/27/2016)	No of Institutions	1063
Market Cap	$21.8 Billion	Shares	532,856,640
Book Value	$7.5 Billion	% Held	73.29
Price/Book	2.90		
Price/Sales	4.36		

Business Summary: Equipment & Services (MIC: 9.1.3 SIC: 4923 NAIC: 486210)

Spectra Energy owns and operates natural gas-related energy assets. Co. manages its business in four reportable segments: Spectra Energy Partners, which provides transportation and storage of natural gas in the northeastern and southeastern U.S. and a crude oil pipeline system; Distribution, which provides retail natural gas distribution service in Ontario, Canada; Western Canada Transmission & Processing, which natural gas transmission and gas gathering and processing services, and natural gas liquids extraction, fractionation, transportation, storage and marketing; and Field Services, which gathers, processes, treats, compresses, transports, stores and sells natural gas.

Recent Developments: For the quarter ended Mar 31 2016, net income decreased 4.6% to US$310.0 million from US$325.0 million in the year-earlier quarter. Revenues were US$1.38 billion, down 14.7% from US$1.62 billion the year before. Operating income was US$494.0 million versus US$541.0 million in the prior-year quarter, a decrease of 8.7%. Direct operating expenses declined 42.1% to US$250.0 million from US$432.0 million in the comparable period the year before. Indirect operating expenses decreased 1.5% to US$640.0 million from US$650.0 million in the equivalent prior-year period.

Prospects: Our evaluation of Spectra Energy Corp. as of June 26, 2016 is the result of our systematic analysis on three basic characteristics: earnings strength, relative valuation, and recent stock price movement. The company has produced a positive trend in earnings per share over the past 5 quarters. However, while recent estimates for the company have been mixed, SE has posted results that fell short of analysts expectations. Based on operating earnings yield, the company is about fairly valued when compared to all of the companies in our coverage universe. Share price changes over the past year indicates that SE will perform poorly over the near term.

Financial Data

(US$ in Millions)	3 Mos	12/31/2015	12/31/2014	12/31/2013	12/31/2012	12/31/2011	12/31/2010	12/31/2009
Earnings Per Share	0.25	0.29	1.61	1.55	1.44	1.81	1.61	1.32
Cash Flow Per Share	3.02	3.35	3.31	3.03	2.96	3.36	2.17	2.74
Tang Book Value Per Share	4.81	3.54	5.14	5.50	6.68	5.60	5.40	4.91
Dividends Per Share	1.515	1.480	1.375	1.220	1.145	1.060	1.000	1.000
Dividend Payout %	606.00	510.34	85.40	78.71	79.51	58.56	62.11	75.76
Income Statement								
Total Revenue	1,384	5,234	5,903	5,518	5,075	5,351	4,945	4,552
EBITDA	722	1,626	2,853	2,627	2,485	2,529	2,356	2,096
Depn & Amortn	196	79	870	837	827	709	650	584
Income Before Taxes	375	911	1,304	1,133	1,033	1,195	1,076	902
Income Taxes	98	161	382	419	370	487	383	353
Net Income	234	196	1,082	1,038	940	1,184	1,049	848
Average Shares	675	672	672	671	656	653	650	643
Balance Sheet								
Current Assets	1,475	1,648	2,332	2,081	1,663	1,764	1,638	1,429
Total Assets	34,091	32,923	34,040	33,533	30,587	28,138	26,686	24,079
Current Liabilities	3,163	3,392	3,809	4,039	3,791	3,101	2,523	2,495
Long-Term Obligations	13,190	12,892	12,769	12,488	10,653	10,146	10,169	8,947
Total Liabilities	26,589	26,397	25,880	25,039	21,615	20,073	18,877	16,954
Stockholders' Equity	7,502	6,526	8,160	8,494	8,972	8,065	7,809	7,125
Shares Outstanding	684	671	671	670	668	651	649	647
Statistical Record								
Return on Assets %	0.49	0.59	3.20	3.24	3.19	4.32	4.13	3.69
Return on Equity %	2.11	2.67	12.99	11.89	11.00	14.92	14.05	13.39
EBITDA Margin %	52.17	31.07	48.33	47.61	48.97	47.26	47.64	46.05
Net Margin %	16.91	3.74	18.33	18.81	18.52	22.13	21.21	18.63
Asset Turnover	0.15	0.16	0.17	0.17	0.17	0.20	0.19	0.20
Current Ratio	0.47	0.49	0.61	0.52	0.44	0.57	0.65	0.57
Debt to Equity	1.76	1.98	1.56	1.47	1.19	1.26	1.30	1.26
Price Range	38.28-21.97	38.28-21.97	43.00-33.09	36.75-27.00	32.15-26.74	30.98-23.14	25.26-19.20	20.65-11.50
P/E Ratio	153.12-87.88	132.00-75.76	26.71-20.55	23.71-17.42	22.33-18.57	17.12-12.78	15.69-11.93	15.64-8.71
Average Yield %	5.07	4.69	3.54	3.78	3.88	3.88	4.50	5.88

Address: 5400 Westheimer Court, Houston, TX 77056
Telephone: 713-627-5400

Web Site: www.spectraenergy.com
Officers: Gregory L. Ebel - President, Chief Executive Officer Patricia M. Rice - Vice President, Secretary

Auditors: Deloitte & Touche LLP
Transfer Agents: Broadridge Corporate Issuer Solutions, Inc.

SPECTRUM BRANDS HOLDINGS INC

Exchange	Symbol	Price	52Wk Range	Yield	P/E
NYS	SPB	$116.57 (5/31/2016)	118.15-89.52	1.30	31.59

*7 Year Price Score N/A   ***NYSE Composite Index=100**   ***12 Month Price Score 111.50**

TRADING VOLUME (thousand shares)

Interim Earnings (Per Share)

Qtr.	Dec	Mar	Jun	Sep
2012-13	(0.26)	(0.79)	0.69	(0.70)
2013-14	1.04	0.64	1.47	0.88
2014-15	0.94	0.52	0.79	0.40
2015-16	1.24	1.26	...	...

Interim Dividends (Per Share)

Amt	Decl	Ex	Rec	Pay
0.33Q	07/28/2015	08/14/2015	08/18/2015	09/15/2015
0.33Q	11/17/2015	11/27/2015	12/01/2015	12/17/2015
0.38Q	01/28/2016	02/11/2016	02/16/2016	03/08/2016
0.38Q	04/26/2016	05/13/2016	05/17/2016	06/14/2016

Indicated Div: $1.52

Valuation Analysis   **Institutional Holding**

Forecast EPS	$5.10	No of Institutions
	(05/20/2016)	N/A
Market Cap	$6.9 Billion	Shares
Book Value	$1.7 Billion	N/A
Price/Book	4.17	% Held
Price/Sales	1.39	N/A

Business Summary: Household & Personal Products (MIC: 1.7.1 SIC: 3691 NAIC: 335911)

Spectrum Brands Holdings is a branded consumer products company. Co. manufactures, markets and/or distributes its products in approximately 160 countries in the North America, Europe, Middle East & Africa, Latin America and Asia-Pacific regions via trade channels, including retailers, wholesalers and distributors, original equipment manufacturers, construction companies and hearing aid personnel. Co. has five segments: Global Batteries & Appliances, Global Pet Supplies, Home and Garden, Hardware & Home Improvement and Global Auto Care. Co.'s product categories are consumer batteries, small appliances, personal care, hardware and home improvement, pet supplies, home and garden and auto care.

Recent Developments: For the quarter ended Apr 3 2016, net income increased 169.9% to US$75.3 million from US$27.9 million in the year-earlier quarter. Revenues were US$1.21 billion, up 13.4% from US$1.07 billion the year before. Operating income was US$148.5 million versus US$88.4 million in the prior-year quarter, an increase of 68.0%. Direct operating expenses rose 7.9% to US$746.8 million from US$692.3 million in the comparable period the year before. Indirect operating expenses increased 9.8% to US$314.3 million from US$286.3 million in the equivalent prior-year period.

Prospects: Our evaluation of Spectrum Brands Holdings Inc. as of June 19, 2016 is the result of our systematic analysis on three basic characteristics: earnings strength, relative valuation, and recent stock price movement. The company has enjoyed a very positive trend in earnings per share over the past 5 quarters and while recent estimates for the company have remained steady, SPB has posted better than expected results. Based on operating earnings yield, the company is about fairly valued when compared to all of the companies in our coverage universe. Share price changes over the past year indicates that SPB will perform well over the near term.

Financial Data

(US$ in Thousands)	6 Mos	3 Mos	09/30/2015	09/30/2014	09/30/2013	09/30/2012	09/30/2011	09/30/2010
Earnings Per Share	3.69	2.95	2.66	4.02	(1.06)	0.91	(1.47)	(5.28)
Cash Flow Per Share	8.08	6.21	7.99	8.22	4.93	4.92	4.45	1.59
Dividends Per Share	1.370	1.320	1.290	1.150	0.750	1.000	...	...
Dividend Payout %	37.13	44.75	48.50	28.61	...	109.89	...	...
Income Statement								
Total Revenue	2,428,400	1,218,800	4,690,400	4,429,109	4,085,581	3,252,435	3,186,916	2,567,011
EBITDA	413,800	197,800	635,200	633,277	487,564	405,484	330,213	253,574
Depn & Amortn	127,100	58,800	170,000	157,630	139,893	104,616	104,760	100,742
Income Before Taxes	170,800	80,600	193,300	273,529	(27,954)	108,957	17,124	(124,183)
Income Taxes	21,800	6,900	43,900	59,023	27,359	60,385	92,295	63,189
Net Income	148,800	73,600	148,900	214,092	(55,246)	48,572	(75,171)	(190,107)
Average Shares	59,500	59,200	55,900	53,261	52,034	53,309	51,092	36,000
Balance Sheet								
Current Assets	1,779,300	1,709,000	1,732,200	1,434,626	1,482,905	1,061,427	1,048,289	1,199,712
Total Assets	7,263,000	7,165,600	7,298,000	5,513,029	5,626,673	3,751,649	3,626,706	3,873,604
Current Liabilities	820,800	792,200	1,031,500	915,704	952,370	610,631	606,912	662,772
Long-Term Obligations	4,069,100	4,093,200	3,937,200	2,894,137	3,115,942	1,652,886	1,535,522	1,723,057
Total Liabilities	5,603,400	5,594,600	5,734,900	4,469,627	4,729,652	2,762,554	2,608,209	2,827,225
Stockholders' Equity	1,659,600	1,571,000	1,563,100	1,043,402	897,021	989,095	1,018,497	1,046,379
Shares Outstanding	59,402	59,385	59,400	52,713	52,210	51,483	52,226	51,020
Statistical Record								
Return on Assets %	3.38	2.66	2.32	3.84	N.M.	1.31	N.M.	N.M.
Return on Equity %	16.37	13.18	11.43	22.07	N.M.	4.83	N.M.	N.M.
EBITDA Margin %	17.04	16.23	13.54	14.30	11.93	12.47	10.36	9.88
Net Margin %	6.13	6.04	3.17	4.83	N.M.	1.49	N.M.	N.M.
Asset Turnover	0.77	0.74	0.73	0.80	0.87	0.88	0.85	0.74
Current Ratio	2.17	2.16	1.68	1.57	1.56	1.74	1.73	1.81
Debt to Equity	2.45	2.61	2.52	2.77	3.47	1.67	1.51	1.65
Price Range	109.50-86.90	105.95-86.90	105.95-83.68	90.53-62.76	67.64-40.24	42.12-22.17	36.00-20.70	29.51-23.21
P/E Ratio	29.67-23.55	35.92-29.46	39.83-31.46	22.52-15.61	...	46.29-24.36	...	...
Average Yield %	1.41	1.38	1.41	1.51	1.38	3.14	...	...

Address: 3001 Deming Way, Middleton, WI 53562 **Telephone:** 608-275-3340	**Web Site:** www.spectrumbrands.com **Officers:** David M. Maura - Chairman Omar M. Asali - Vice-Chairman	**Auditors:** KPMG LLP **Investor Contact:** 608-275-3340 **Transfer Agents:** Computershare Shareowner Services, Jersey City, NJ

SPIRIT AEROSYSTEMS HOLDINGS INC

Exchange	Symbol	Price	52Wk Range	Yield	P/E
NYS	SPR	$46.78 (5/31/2016)	57.16-40.50	N/A	8.27

*7 Year Price Score 148.00 *NYSE Composite Index=100 *12 Month Price Score 92.80

Interim Earnings (Per Share)

Qtr.	Mar	Jun	Sep	Dec
2013	0.57	(1.47)	0.65	(4.16)
2014	1.07	1.01	1.20	(0.74)
2015	1.30	1.11	2.24	1.02
2016	1.29	...	...	...

Interim Dividends (Per Share)

No Dividends Paid

Valuation Analysis — **Institutional Holding**

Forecast EPS	$4.50	No of Institutions
	(05/20/2016)	438
Market Cap	$6.2 Billion	Shares
Book Value	$2.1 Billion	144,311,936
Price/Book	2.92	% Held
Price/Sales	0.94	96.64

Business Summary: Aerospace (MIC: 7,1,1 SIC: 3728 NAIC: 336413)

Spirit AeroSystems Holdings provides manufacturing and design expertise in a range of products and services for aircraft original equipment manufacturers. Co. has three segments: Fuselage Systems, which includes forward, mid and rear fuselage sections and systems; Propulsion Systems, which includes struts/pylons, nacelles (including thrust reversers) and related engine structural components; and Wing Systems, which includes wings and wing components such as flight control surfaces, and other miscellaneous structural parts. In addition to providing aerostructures for commercial aircraft, Co. designs, engineers and manufactures structural components for military aircraft such as Rotorcraft.

Recent Developments: For the quarter ended Mar 31 2016, net income decreased 5.7% to US$171.6 million from US$181.9 million in the year-earlier quarter. Revenues were US$1.68 billion, down 3.5% from US$1.74 billion the year before. Operating income was US$266.5 million versus US$235.3 million in the prior-year quarter, an increase of 13.3%. Direct operating expenses declined 6.2% to US$1.36 billion from US$1.45 billion in the comparable period the year before. Indirect operating expenses decreased 4.3% to US$56.1 million from US$58.6 million in the equivalent prior-year period.

Prospects: Our evaluation of Spirit AeroSystems Holdings Inc. as of June 19, 2016 is the result of our systematic analysis on three basic characteristics: earnings strength, relative valuation, and recent stock price movement. The company has managed to produce a neutral trend in earnings per share over the past 5 quarters and while recent estimates for the company have been raised by analysts, SPR has posted better than expected results. Based on operating earnings yield, the company is undervalued when compared to all of the companies in our coverage universe. Share price changes over the past year indicates that SPR will perform well over the near term.

Financial Data

(US$ in Thousands)	3 Mos	12/31/2015	12/31/2014	12/31/2013	12/31/2012	12/31/2011	12/31/2010	12/31/2009
Earnings Per Share	5.66	5.66	2.53	(4.40)	0.24	1.35	1.55	1.37
Cash Flow Per Share	7.29	9.32	2.58	1.84	3.86	(0.34)	0.91	(0.10)
Tang Book Value Per Share	15.83	15.59	11.45	10.17	13.80	13.63	12.59	11.00
Income Statement								
Total Revenue	1,681,600	6,643,900	6,799,200	5,961,000	5,397,700	4,863,800	4,172,400	4,078,500
EBITDA	269,100	875,600	368,200	(341,400)	112,700	486,700	471,900	432,400
Depn & Amortn	5,600	16,900	18,300	19,600	18,600	129,200	115,300	123,000
Income Before Taxes	252,900	808,100	262,400	(430,800)	11,440	280,300	297,800	272,800
Income Taxes	81,900	20,600	(95,900)	191,100	(24,100)	86,900	78,200	80,900
Net Income	171,600	788,700	358,800	(621,400)	34,800	192,400	218,900	191,700
Average Shares	132,700	139,400	141,600	141,300	142,700	142,300	141,000	139,800
Balance Sheet								
Current Assets	3,341,600	3,299,100	3,052,100	2,944,200	3,355,400	3,155,800	3,294,700	2,852,900
Total Assets	5,786,900	5,777,500	5,162,700	5,107,200	5,415,300	5,042,400	5,102,000	4,473,800
Current Liabilities	1,538,500	1,459,000	1,258,800	1,335,600	1,067,000	913,500	1,164,800	982,200
Long-Term Obligations	1,083,400	1,097,600	1,144,100	1,150,500	1,165,900	1,152,000	1,187,300	591,100
Total Liabilities	3,666,700	3,658,000	3,541,200	3,626,700	3,418,900	3,078,200	3,291,600	2,900,500
Stockholders' Equity	2,120,200	2,119,500	1,621,500	1,480,500	1,996,400	1,964,200	1,810,400	1,573,300
Shares Outstanding	132,475	135,617	141,089	144,798	143,697	142,865	142,098	140,734
Statistical Record								
Return on Assets %	14.08	14.42	6.99	N.M.	0.66	3.79	4.57	4.66
Return on Equity %	39.77	42.17	23.13	N.M.	1.75	10.19	12.94	13.36
EBITDA Margin %	16.00	13.18	5.42	N.M.	2.09	10.01	11.31	10.60
Net Margin %	10.20	11.87	5.28	N.M.	0.64	3.96	5.25	4.70
Asset Turnover	1.19	1.21	1.32	1.13	1.03	0.96	0.87	0.99
Current Ratio	2.17	2.26	2.42	2.20	3.14	3.45	2.83	2.90
Debt to Equity	0.51	0.52	0.71	0.78	0.58	0.59	0.66	0.38
Price Range	57.16-40.50	57.16-41.89	45.32-26.51	34.18-15.94	25.85-14.04	26.16-14.40	23.88-16.50	20.42-8.22
P/E Ratio	10.10-7.16	10.10-7.40	17.91-10.48	...	107.71-58.50	19.38-10.67	15.41-10.65	14.91-6.00

Address: 3801 South Oliver, Wichita, KS 67210	Web Site: www.spiritaero.com	Auditors: Ernst & Young LLP
Telephone: 316-526-9000	Officers: Robert D. Johnson - Chairman Thomas C. Gentile - President, Chief Executive Officer, Executive Vice President, Chief Operating Officer	Investor Contact: 316-523-7040 Transfer Agents: Computershare, Pittsburgh, PA

665

SPIRE INC

Exchange	Symbol	Price	52Wk Range	Yield	P/E	Div Achiever
NYS	SR	$63.58 (5/31/2016)	68.50-50.14	3.08	19.38	12 Years

*7 Year Price Score 115.45 *NYSE Composite Index=100 *12 Month Price Score 108.78

Interim Earnings (Per Share)

Qtr.	Dec	Mar	Jun	Sep
2012-13	1.14	1.34	0.25	(0.60)
2013-14	1.09	1.59	0.33	(0.62)
2014-15	1.09	2.18	0.32	(0.43)
2015-16	1.08	2.31	...	...

Interim Dividends (Per Share)

Amt	Decl	Ex	Rec	Pay
0.46Q	07/30/2015	09/09/2015	09/11/2015	10/02/2015
0.49Q	11/24/2015	12/09/2015	12/11/2015	01/05/2016
0.49Q	01/28/2016	03/09/2016	03/11/2016	04/04/2016
0.49Q	04/28/2016	06/08/2016	06/10/2016	07/05/2016

Indicated Div: $1.96

Valuation Analysis   **Institutional Holding**

Forecast EPS	$3.40	No of Institutions
	(05/20/2016)	294
Market Cap	$2.8 Billion	Shares
Book Value	$1.7 Billion	35,199,232
Price/Book	1.64	% Held
Price/Sales	1.86	104.15

Business Summary: Gas Utilities (MIC: 3.3.1 SIC: 4924 NAIC: 221210)

Spire is a public utility holding company. Co. has two business segments: Gas Utility and Gas Marketing. The Gas Utility segment includes the regulated operations of Laclede Gas Company, which is a natural gas distribution utility in Missouri; and Alabama Gas Corporation, which is a public utility in central and north Alabama. The Gas Marketing segment includes Laclede Energy Resources, Inc., which is engaged in the marketing of natural gas and related activities on a non-regulated basis. Co. is also engaged in compression of natural gas, oil production, real estate development, risk management, and financial investments in other enterprises, among other activities.

Recent Developments: For the quarter ended Mar 31 2016, net income increased 6.8% to US$100.8 million from US$94.4 million in the year-earlier quarter. Revenues were US$609.3 million, down 30.6% from US$877.4 million the year before. Operating income was US$167.7 million versus US$157.7 million in the prior-year quarter, an increase of 6.3%. Direct operating expenses declined 40.1% to US$397.7 million from US$664.0 million in the comparable period the year before. Indirect operating expenses decreased 21.2% to US$43.9 million from US$55.7 million in the equivalent prior-year period.

Prospects: Our evaluation of Spire Inc. as of June 19, 2016 is the result of our systematic analysis on three basic characteristics: earnings strength, relative valuation, and recent stock price movement. The company has enjoyed a very positive trend in earnings per share over the past 5 quarters and while recent estimates for the company have been mixed, SR has posted better than expected results. Based on operating earnings yield, the company is about fairly valued when compared to all of the companies in our coverage universe. Share price changes over the past year indicates that SR will perform well over the near term.

Financial Data

(US$ in Thousands)	6 Mos	3 Mos	09/30/2015	09/30/2014	09/30/2013	09/30/2012	09/30/2011	09/30/2010
Earnings Per Share	3.28	3.15	3.16	2.35	2.02	2.79	2.86	2.43
Cash Flow Per Share	6.59	9.03	7.46	3.42	6.33	5.74	7.57	4.86
Tang Book Value Per Share	16.93	15.08	14.48	13.21	24.44	26.69	25.56	24.02
Dividends Per Share	1.900	1.870	1.840	1.760	1.700	1.660	1.620	1.580
Dividend Payout %	57.93	59.37	58.23	74.89	84.16	59.50	56.64	65.02
Income Statement								
Total Revenue	1,008,700	399,400	1,976,400	1,627,200	1,017,019	1,125,475	1,603,307	1,735,029
EBITDA	324,500	122,100	404,300	246,400	147,133	153,904	157,052	144,151
Depn & Amortn	67,600	33,700	130,800	83,300	49,283	41,339	39,764	37,908
Income Before Taxes	218,600	69,400	198,900	116,900	70,336	88,929	93,007	81,134
Income Taxes	70,900	22,500	62,000	32,300	17,578	26,289	29,182	27,094
Net Income	147,700	46,900	136,900	84,600	52,758	62,640	63,825	54,040
Average Shares	43,500	43,400	43,300	35,900	25,952	22,340	22,171	22,039
Balance Sheet								
Current Assets	503,800	636,000	530,100	604,900	475,880	343,016	369,134	414,195
Total Assets	5,319,800	5,411,400	5,290,200	5,074,000	3,125,386	1,880,262	1,783,082	1,840,196
Current Liabilities	618,800	847,500	853,800	782,800	353,178	252,124	231,934	333,924
Long-Term Obligations	1,851,600	1,851,500	1,771,500	1,851,000	912,712	339,416	364,357	364,298
Total Liabilities	3,638,400	3,811,100	3,716,600	3,565,600	2,079,104	1,278,651	1,209,751	1,304,619
Stockholders' Equity	1,681,400	1,600,300	1,573,600	1,508,400	1,046,282	601,611	573,331	535,577
Shares Outstanding	43,445	43,400	43,335	43,183	32,696	22,539	22,430	22,292
Statistical Record								
Return on Assets %	2.73	2.56	2.64	2.06	2.11	3.41	3.52	3.00
Return on Equity %	8.69	8.72	8.88	6.62	6.40	10.63	11.51	10.27
EBITDA Margin %	32.17	30.57	20.46	15.14	14.47	13.67	9.80	8.31
Net Margin %	14.64	11.74	6.93	5.20	5.19	5.57	3.98	3.11
Asset Turnover	0.28	0.33	0.38	0.40	0.41	0.61	0.89	0.96
Current Ratio	0.81	0.75	0.62	0.77	1.35	1.36	1.59	1.24
Debt to Equity	1.10	1.16	1.13	1.23	0.87	0.56	0.64	0.68
Price Range	68.50-50.14	60.52-49.62	56.02-46.15	49.56-44.24	48.16-37.70	43.27-37.37	39.74-33.52	35.90-30.34
P/E Ratio	20.88-15.29	19.21-15.75	17.73-14.60	21.09-18.83	23.84-18.66	15.51-13.39	13.90-11.72	14.77-12.49
Average Yield %	3.36	3.47	3.54	3.78	3.96	4.12	4.35	4.74

Address: 700 Market Street, St. Louis, MO 63101
Telephone: 314-342-0500

Web Site: www.spireenergy.com
Officers: William E. Nasser - Chairman Suzanne Sitherwood - President, Chief Executive Officer

Auditors: Deloitte & Touche LLP
Investor Contact: 314-342-0878
Transfer Agents: Computershare Trust Company, N.A., Providence, RI

SPX CORP.

Exchange	Symbol	Price	52Wk Range	Yield	P/E
NYS	SPXC	$16.57 (5/31/2016)	18.94-7.79	9.05	N/A

*7 Year Price Score 63.95 ***NYSE Composite Index=100** ***12 Month Price Score 117.75**

Interim Earnings (Per Share)

Qtr.	Mar	Jun	Sep	Dec
2013	0.05	0.84	1.40	2.32
2014	7.06	1.17	1.50	(0.64)
2015	(0.18)	0.95	(2.58)	(0.23)
2016	0.31	...	...	...

Interim Dividends (Per Share)

Amt	Decl	Ex	Rec	Pay
0.375Q	11/20/2014	12/11/2014	12/15/2014	01/05/2015
0.375Q	02/27/2015	03/12/2015	03/16/2015	04/01/2015
0.375Q	05/28/2015	06/12/2015	06/16/2015	07/01/2015
0.00Q	09/08/2015	09/28/2015	09/16/2015	09/26/2015

Indicated Div: $1.50

Valuation Analysis / Institutional Holding

Forecast EPS	$1.14	No of Institutions
	(05/20/2016)	318
Market Cap	$688.7 Million	Shares
Book Value	$322.8 Million	39,512,324
Price/Book	2.13	% Held
Price/Sales	0.29	77.42

Business Summary: Industrial Machinery & Equipment (MIC: 7.2.1 SIC: 3429 NAIC: 332510)

SPX is a supplier of infrastructure equipment with platforms in heating, ventilation and air conditioning (HVAC) and detection and measurement markets and a presence in power and energy markets. HVAC solutions provided by Co.'s businesses include package cooling towers, residential and commercial boilers, comfort heating, and ventilation products. Co.'s detection and measurement product lines encompass underground pipe and cable locators and inspection equipment, fare collection systems, communication technologies, and specialty lighting. Within its power platform, Co. is a manufacturer of power transformers, as well as equipment for nearly every type of power plant.

Recent Developments: For the quarter ended Apr 2 2016, income from continuing operations was US$14.7 million compared with a loss of US$41.0 million in the year-earlier quarter. Net income amounted to US$13.6 million versus a net loss of US$10.0 million in the year-earlier quarter. Revenues were US$389.3 million, up 3.5% from US$376.3 million the year before. Operating income was US$20.3 million versus a loss of US$44.6 million in the prior-year quarter. Direct operating expenses declined 0.8% to US$299.5 million from US$301.8 million in the comparable period the year before. Indirect operating expenses decreased 41.6% to US$69.5 million from US$119.1 million in the equivalent prior-year period.

Prospects: Our evaluation of SPX Corp. as of June 19, 2016 is the result of our systematic analysis on three basic characteristics: earnings strength, relative valuation, and recent stock price movement. The company has managed to produce a neutral trend in earnings per share over the past 5 quarters. However, while recent estimates for the company have been mixed, SPXC has posted better than expected results. Based on operating earnings yield, the company is undervalued when compared to all of the companies in our coverage universe. Share price changes over the past year indicates that SPXC will perform in line with the market over the near term.

Financial Data

(US$ in Thousands)	3 Mos	12/31/2015	12/31/2014	12/31/2013	12/31/2012	12/31/2011	12/31/2010	12/31/2009
Earnings Per Share	(1.55)	(2.03)	9.25	4.57	5.18	3.54	4.08	0.64
Cash Flow Per Share	0.20	(0.95)	1.80	2.32	1.39	6.39	5.10	9.54
Dividends Per Share	0.375	0.750	1.500	1.000	1.000	1.000	1.000	1.000
Dividend Payout %	...	...	16.22	21.88	19.31	28.25	24.51	156.25
Income Statement								
Total Revenue	389,300	1,719,300	4,721,100	4,717,200	5,100,200	5,461,900	4,886,800	4,850,800
EBITDA	22,000	(144,500)	763,200	433,100	134,100	390,000	395,400	241,800
Depn & Amortn	900	39,200	109,200	114,800	111,100	107,400	99,100	91,200
Income Before Taxes	17,800	(204,400)	592,800	213,900	(85,100)	191,300	214,500	66,000
Income Taxes	3,500	(11,800)	214,100	54,800	31,900	34,400	53,100	47,200
Net Income	13,000	(82,700)	397,900	210,200	259,200	180,600	205,600	31,700
Average Shares	41,553	40,733	43,031	46,006	50,031	50,946	50,347	49,797
Balance Sheet								
Current Assets	665,700	782,300	2,215,100	2,772,900	3,115,000	2,895,300	2,428,500	2,312,500
Total Assets	2,052,200	2,181,300	5,902,200	6,856,200	7,130,100	7,391,800	5,993,300	5,724,400
Current Liabilities	569,200	654,800	1,609,900	2,174,400	1,736,600	1,947,800	1,722,300	1,639,300
Long-Term Obligations	337,600	342,600	1,157,800	1,090,000	1,649,900	1,925,600	1,110,500	1,128,600
Total Liabilities	1,729,400	1,835,900	4,084,300	4,698,200	4,861,400	5,164,500	3,895,600	3,833,600
Stockholders' Equity	322,800	345,400	1,817,900	2,158,000	2,268,700	2,227,300	2,097,700	1,890,800
Shares Outstanding	41,564	41,415	40,858	45,281	48,303	51,073	50,294	49,367
Statistical Record								
Return on Assets %	N.M.	N.M.	6.24	3.01	3.56	2.70	3.51	0.54
Return on Equity %	N.M.	N.M.	20.02	9.50	11.50	8.35	10.31	1.62
EBITDA Margin %	5.65	N.M.	16.17	9.18	2.63	7.14	8.09	4.98
Net Margin %	3.34	N.M.	8.43	4.46	5.08	3.31	4.21	0.65
Asset Turnover	0.60	0.43	0.74	0.67	0.70	0.82	0.83	0.82
Current Ratio	1.17	1.19	1.38	1.28	1.79	1.49	1.41	1.41
Debt to Equity	1.05	0.99	0.64	0.51	0.73	0.86	0.53	0.60
Price Range	21.81-7.79	22.77-8.34	28.01-19.59	25.08-17.19	19.75-14.81	21.77-10.58	18.09-12.93	16.30-9.76
P/E Ratio	...	...	3.03-2.12	5.49-3.76	3.81-2.86	6.15-2.99	4.43-3.17	25.47-15.25
Average Yield %	2.66	4.48	6.01	4.95	5.79	5.72	6.39	7.76

Address: 13320-A Ballantyne Corporate Place, Charlotte, NC 28277	**Web Site:** www.spx.com	**Auditors:** Deloitte & Touche LLP
Telephone: 980-474-3700	**Officers:** Patrick J. O'Leary - Chairman, Executive Vice President, Chief Financial Officer, Treasurer	**Investor Contact:** 704-752-4486
Fax: 704-752-4505	Eugene (Gene) Joseph Lowe President, Chief Executive Officer, Division Officer	**Transfer Agents:** Computershare, Providence, RI

STANLEY BLACK & DECKER INC

Exchange	Symbol	Price	52Wk Range	Yield	P/E	Div Achiever
NYS	SWK	$113.18 (5/31/2016)	114.47-90.14	1.94	18.71	48 Years

*7 Year Price Score 116.01 *NYSE Composite Index=100 *12 Month Price Score 105.76

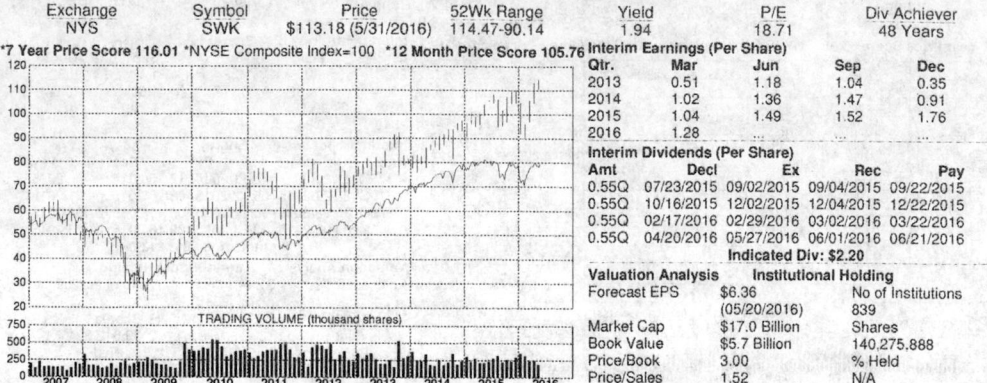

Interim Earnings (Per Share)

Qtr.	Mar	Jun	Sep	Dec
2013	0.51	1.18	1.04	0.35
2014	1.02	1.36	1.47	0.91
2015	1.04	1.49	1.52	1.76
2016	1.28			

Interim Dividends (Per Share)

Amt	Decl	Ex	Rec	Pay
0.55Q	07/23/2015	09/02/2015	09/04/2015	09/22/2015
0.55Q	10/16/2015	12/02/2015	12/04/2015	12/22/2015
0.55Q	02/17/2016	02/29/2016	03/02/2016	03/22/2016
0.55Q	04/20/2016	05/27/2016	06/01/2016	06/21/2016

Indicated Div: $2.20

Valuation Analysis / **Institutional Holding**

Forecast EPS	$6.36 (05/20/2016)	No of Institutions	839
Market Cap	$17.0 Billion	Shares	
Book Value	$5.7 Billion		140,275,888
Price/Book	3.00	% Held	
Price/Sales	1.52		N/A

Business Summary: Industrial Machinery & Equipment (MIC: 7.2.1 SIC: 3423 NAIC: 332212)

Stanley Black & Decker is a provider of hand tools, power tools and related accessories, mechanical access solutions (i.e. automatic doors and commercial locking systems), electronic security and monitoring systems, healthcare solutions, engineered fastening systems and products and services for various industrial applications. Co.'s operations are classified into three reportable segments: Tools & Storage, which is comprised of the Power Tools and Hand Tools & Storage businesses; Security, which is comprised of the Convergent Security Solutions and Mechanical Access Solutions businesses; as well as Industrial, which is comprised of the Engineered Fastening and Infrastructure businesses.

Recent Developments: For the quarter ended Apr 2 2016, income from continuing operations increased 13.5% to US$189.4 million from US$166.8 million in the year-earlier quarter. Net income increased 16.7% to US$189.4 million from US$162.3 million in the year-earlier quarter. Revenues were US$2.67 billion, up 1.6% from US$2.63 billion the year before. Direct operating expenses rose 2.3% to US$1.69 billion from US$1.66 billion in the comparable period the year before. Indirect operating expenses decreased 3.8% to US$723.5 million from US$752.3 million in the equivalent prior-year period.

Prospects: Our evaluation of Stanley Black & Decker, Inc. as of June 19, 2016 is the result of our systematic analysis on three basic characteristics: earnings strength, relative valuation, and recent stock price movement. The company has managed to produce a neutral trend in earnings per share over the past 5 quarters and while recent estimates for the company have been mixed, SWK has posted better than expected results. Based on operating earnings yield, the company is undervalued when compared to all of the companies in our coverage universe. Share price changes over the past year indicates that SWK will perform well over the near term.

Financial Data
(US$ in Thousands)

	3 Mos	01/02/2016	01/03/2015	12/28/2013	12/29/2012	12/31/2011	01/01/2011	01/02/2010
Earnings Per Share	6.05	5.79	4.76	3.09	5.30	3.97	1.32	2.79
Cash Flow Per Share	8.82	8.00	8.17	5.61	5.94	6.04	5.04	6.78
Dividends Per Share	2.170	2.140	2.040	1.980	1.800	1.640	1.340	1.300
Dividend Payout %	35.87	36.96	42.86	64.08	33.96	41.31	101.52	46.59
Income Statement								
Total Revenue	2,672,100	11,171,800	11,338,600	11,001,200	10,190,500	10,376,400	8,409,600	3,737,100
EBITDA	331,500	1,730,000	1,698,200	1,175,500	1,107,000	1,303,200	744,500	534,900
Depn & Amortn	35,900	414,000	449,800	441,300	445,300	410,100	406,800	191,000
Income Before Taxes	254,100	1,150,800	1,084,800	586,600	527,600	779,800	237,100	283,300
Income Taxes	65,500	248,600	227,100	69,300	78,900	88,600	38,900	54,500
Net Income	189,400	883,700	760,900	490,300	883,800	674,600	198,200	224,300
Average Shares	147,619	152,706	159,737	158,776	166,701	170,105	150,167	80,396
Balance Sheet								
Current Assets	4,016,800	3,662,100	3,948,800	3,968,700	4,098,300	4,322,700	4,815,600	1,411,900
Total Assets	15,607,400	15,172,300	15,849,100	16,535,100	15,844,000	15,949,000	15,139,400	4,769,100
Current Liabilities	3,696,600	2,802,600	2,832,000	3,221,000	3,073,400	3,268,500	2,742,200	1,192,000
Long-Term Obligations	3,817,200	3,836,600	3,839,800	3,799,400	3,526,500	2,925,800	3,018,100	1,084,700
Total Liabilities	9,938,800	9,360,700	9,420,000	9,735,900	9,176,900	8,945,400	8,122,400	2,783,000
Stockholders' Equity	5,668,600	5,811,600	6,429,100	6,799,200	6,667,100	7,003,600	7,017,000	1,986,100
Shares Outstanding	150,116	153,944	157,125	155,479	159,952	169,045	166,347	80,478
Statistical Record								
Return on Assets %	5.77	5.71	4.62	3.04	5.57	4.35	2.00	4.66
Return on Equity %	16.14	14.48	11.32	7.30	12.97	9.65	4.42	12.24
EBITDA Margin %	12.41	15.49	14.98	10.69	10.86	12.56	8.85	14.31
Net Margin %	7.09	7.91	6.71	4.46	8.67	6.50	2.36	6.00
Asset Turnover	0.71	0.72	0.69	0.68	0.64	0.67	0.85	0.78
Current Ratio	1.09	1.31	1.39	1.23	1.33	1.32	1.76	1.18
Debt to Equity	0.67	0.66	0.60	0.56	0.53	0.42	0.43	0.55
Price Range	110.17-90.14	110.17-90.51	97.36-75.64	92.36-73.97	81.34-59.25	77.29-47.83	67.29-49.58	53.13-22.75
P/E Ratio	18.21-14.90	19.03-15.63	20.45-15.89	29.89-23.94	15.35-11.18	19.47-12.05	50.98-37.56	19.04-8.15
Average Yield %	2.13	2.11	2.35	2.45	2.55	2.43	2.30	3.38

Address: 1000 Stanley Drive, New Britain, CT 06053 **Telephone:** 860-225-5111 **Fax:** 860-827-3895	**Web Site:** www.stanleyblackanddecker.com **Officers:** John F. Lundgren - Chairman, President, Chief Executive Officer James M. Loree - President, Executive Vice President, Chief Operating Officer	**Auditors:** Ernst & Young LLP **Transfer Agents:** Computershare Investor Services, Canton, MA

STARWOOD HOTELS & RESORTS WORLDWIDE INC

Exchange	Symbol	Price	52Wk Range	Yield	P/E
NYS	HOT	$73.43 (5/31/2016)	85.62-59.15	2.04	25.95

*7 Year Price Score 103.96 *NYSE Composite Index=100 *12 Month Price Score 105.13

TRADING VOLUME (thousand shares)

Interim Earnings (Per Share)

Qtr.	Mar	Jun	Sep	Dec
2013	1.09	0.71	0.81	0.67
2014	0.72	0.80	0.59	1.29
2015	0.58	0.79	0.53	0.98
2016	0.53	...	...	...

Interim Dividends (Per Share)

Amt	Decl	Ex	Rec	Pay
0.375Q	11/05/2015	12/07/2015	12/09/2015	12/23/2015
0.375Q	02/25/2016	03/10/2016	03/14/2016	03/28/2016
0.00Q	03/22/2016	05/13/2016	03/28/2016	05/12/2016
0.375Q	05/06/2016	05/18/2016	05/20/2016	06/03/2016

Indicated Div: $1.50

Valuation Analysis / Institutional Holding

Forecast EPS	$3.02	No of Institutions
(05/20/2016)		717
Market Cap	$12.4 Billion	Shares
Book Value	$1.3 Billion	181,914,544
Price/Book	9.26	% Held
Price/Sales	2.16	N/A

Business Summary: Hotels, Restaurants & Travel (MIC: 2.2.1 SIC; 7011 NAIC: 721110)

Starwood Hotels & Resorts Worldwide Is a hotel and leisure company. Co.'s hotel business is focused on the global operation of hotels and resorts primarily in the luxury and upper upscale segments of the lodging industry. The vacation ownership and residential business acquires, develops and operates vacation ownership resorts, markets and sells vacation ownership interests and residential units, and provides financing to customers who purchase such interests. As of Dec 31 2015, Co.'s hotel business included 1,282 owned, managed or franchised hotels, while its vacation ownership and residential business included 15 stand-alone vacation ownership resorts and residential properties.

Recent Developments: For the quarter ended Mar 31 2016, income from continuing operations decreased 9.1% to US$90.0 million from US$99.0 million in the year-earlier quarter. Net income decreased 9.1% to US$90.0 million from US$99.0 million in the year-earlier quarter. Revenues were US$1.40 billion, down 0.8% from US$1.42 billion the year before. Operating income was US$152.0 million versus US$153.0 million in the prior-year quarter, a decrease of 0.7%. Direct operating expenses declined 1.3% to US$1.06 billion from US$1.07 billion in the comparable period the year before. Indirect operating expenses increased 2.1% to US$195.0 million from US$191.0 million in the equivalent prior-year period.

Prospects: Our evaluation of Starwood Hotels & Resorts Worldwide Inc. as of June 19, 2016 is the result of our systematic analysis on three basic characteristics: earnings strength, relative valuation, and recent stock price movement. The company has managed to produce a neutral trend in earnings per share over the past 5 quarters. Because the company lacks sufficient analyst estimate data, we place greater weight on the historical EPS trend as the measure of earnings strength. Based on operating earnings yield, the company is about fairly valued when compared to all of the companies in our coverage universe. Share price changes over the past year indicates that HOT will perform well over the near ter

Financial Data

(US$ in Thousands)	3 Mos	12/31/2015	12/31/2014	12/31/2013	12/31/2012	12/31/2011	12/31/2010	12/31/2009
Earnings Per Share	2.83	2.88	3.40	3.28	2.86	2.51	2.51	0.41
Cash Flow Per Share	5.29	5.27	5.37	6.03	6.12	3.39	4.17	3.17
Tang Book Value Per Share	N.M.	N.M.	N.M.	6.92	5.76	4.58	2.09	N.M.
Dividends Per Share	1.500	1.500	4.000	1.350	1.250	0.500	0.300	0.200
Dividend Payout %	53.00	52.08	117.65	41.16	43.71	19.92	11.95	48.78
Income Statement								
Total Revenue	1,404,000	5,763,000	5,983,000	6,115,000	6,321,000	5,624,000	5,071,000	4,712,000
EBITDA	195,000	990,000	1,103,000	1,141,000	989,000	865,000	813,000	209,000
Depn & Amortn	41,000	251,000	254,000	239,000	226,000	235,000	252,000	274,000
Income Before Taxes	131,000	628,000	755,000	802,000	593,000	414,000	325,000	(292,000)
Income Taxes	53,000	180,000	139,000	263,000	148,000	(75,000)	27,000	(293,000)
Net Income	90,000	489,000	633,000	635,000	562,000	489,000	477,000	73,000
Average Shares	168,000	170,000	186,000	193,000	197,000	195,000	190,000	180,000
Balance Sheet								
Current Assets	2,480,000	2,295,000	2,321,000	1,996,000	1,919,000	2,534,000	2,306,000	1,491,000
Total Assets	8,444,000	8,268,000	8,659,000	8,762,000	8,861,000	9,560,000	9,776,000	8,761,000
Current Liabilities	2,230,000	2,236,000	2,450,000	1,924,000	2,029,000	1,992,000	2,161,000	2,027,000
Long-Term Obligations	2,429,000	2,278,000	2,574,000	1,523,000	1,656,000	2,596,000	3,215,000	2,955,000
Total Liabilities	7,100,000	6,972,000	7,134,000	5,402,000	5,724,000	6,606,000	7,305,000	6,937,000
Stockholders' Equity	1,344,000	1,296,000	1,525,000	3,360,000	3,137,000	2,954,000	2,471,000	1,824,000
Shares Outstanding	169,537	168,754	172,694	191,897	193,121	195,913	192,970	186,785
Statistical Record								
Return on Assets %	5.79	5.78	7.27	7.21	6.09	5.06	5.15	0.79
Return on Equity %	35.78	34.67	25.92	19.55	18.40	18.03	22.21	4.24
EBITDA Margin %	13.89	17.18	18.44	18.66	15.65	15.38	16.03	4.44
Net Margin %	6.41	8.49	10.58	10.38	8.89	8.69	9.41	1.55
Asset Turnover	0.69	0.68	0.69	0.69	0.68	0.58	0.55	0.51
Current Ratio	1.11	1.03	0.95	1.04	0.95	1.27	1.07	0.74
Debt to Equity	1.81	1.76	1.69	0.45	0.53	0.88	1.30	1.62
Price Range	87.53-59.15	87.53-64.53	84.65-70.87	79.45-57.36	60.70-48.46	65.09-36.90	62.41-33.32	37.31-9.52
P/E Ratio	30.93-20.90	30.39-22.41	24.90-20.84	24.22-17.49	21.22-16.94	25.93-14.70	24.86-13.27	91.00-23.22
Average Yield %	2.00	1.94	5.04	2.03	2.29	0.94	0.62	0.83

Address: One StarPoint, Stamford, CT 06902	**Web Site:** www.starwoodhotels.com	**Auditors:** Ernst & Young LLP
Telephone: 203-964-6000	**Officers:** Thomas B. Mangas - Chief Executive Officer, Chief Financial Officer, Executive Vice President Alan M. Schnaid - Chief Financial Officer, Senior Vice President, Principal Accounting Officer, Interim Chief Financial Officer, Corporate Controller	**Investor Contact:** 203-351-3500 **Transfer Agents:** American Stock Transfer & Trust Company, LLC, Brooklyn, N Y

STATE STREET CORP.

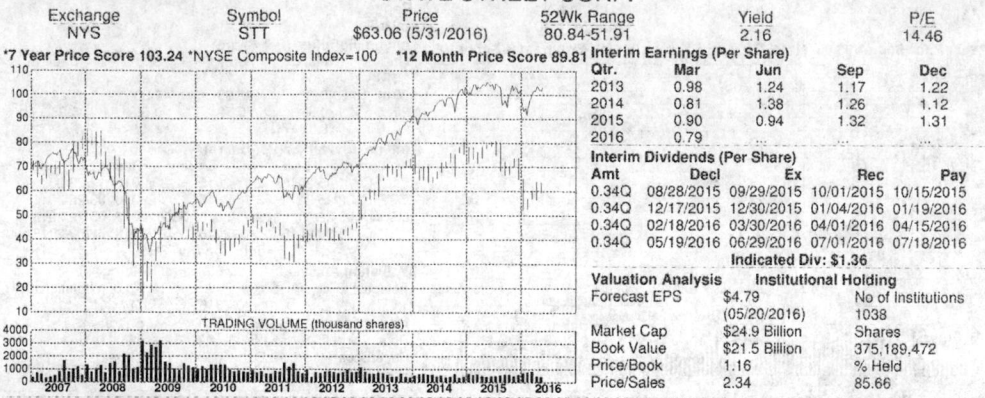

Exchange	Symbol	Price	52Wk Range	Yield	P/E
NYS	STT	$63.06 (5/31/2016)	80.84-51.91	2.16	14.46

*7 Year Price Score 103.24 *NYSE Composite Index=100 *12 Month Price Score 89.81

Interim Earnings (Per Share)

Qtr.	Mar	Jun	Sep	Dec
2013	0.98	1.24	1.17	1.22
2014	0.81	1.38	1.26	1.12
2015	0.90	0.94	1.32	1.31
2016	0.79	...		

Interim Dividends (Per Share)

Amt	Decl	Ex	Rec	Pay
0.34Q	08/28/2015	09/29/2015	10/01/2015	10/15/2015
0.34Q	12/17/2015	12/30/2015	01/04/2016	01/19/2016
0.34Q	02/18/2016	03/30/2016	04/01/2016	04/15/2016
0.34Q	05/19/2016	06/29/2016	07/01/2016	07/18/2016

Indicated Div: $1.36

Valuation Analysis | **Institutional Holding**

Forecast EPS	$4.79 (05/20/2016)	No of Institutions	1038
Market Cap	$24.9 Billion	Shares	375,189,472
Book Value	$21.5 Billion	% Held	85.66
Price/Book	1.16		
Price/Sales	2.34		

Business Summary: Banking (MIC: 5.1.1 SIC: 6022 NAIC: 522110)

State Street is a financial holding company. Through its subsidiaries, Co. provides financial products and services to institutional investors. Co. has two lines of business: Investment Servicing, which provides, among others, custody, product- and participant-level accounting, daily pricing and administration, master trust and master custody, record-keeping, cash management, foreign exchange, brokerage and other trading services; and Investment Management, which provides investment management, investment research and investment advisory services to corporations, public funds and other investors. At Dec 31 2015, Co. had total assets of $245.19 billion and total deposits of $191.63 billion.

Recent Developments: For the quarter ended Mar 31 2016, net income decreased 9.1% to US$368.0 million from US$405.0 million in the year-earlier quarter. Net interest income decreased 6.2% to US$512.0 million from US$546.0 million in the year-earlier quarter. Provision for loan losses was unchanged at US$4.0 million versus the prior-year quarter. Non-interest income fell 4.0% to US$1.97 billion from US$2.05 billion, while non-interest expense declined 2.2% to US$2.05 billion.

Prospects: Our evaluation of State Street Corp. as of June 19, 2016 is the result of our systematic analysis on three basic characteristics: earnings strength, relative valuation, and recent stock price movement. The company has managed to produce a neutral trend in earnings per share over the past 5 quarters and while recent estimates for the company have been mixed, STT has posted better than expected results. Based on operating earnings yield, the company is undervalued when compared to all of the companies in our coverage universe. Share price changes over the past year indicates that STT will perform in line with the market over the near term.

Financial Data
(US$ in Thousands)

	3 Mos	12/31/2015	12/31/2014	12/31/2013	12/31/2012	12/31/2011	12/31/2010	12/31/2009
Earnings Per Share	4.36	4.47	4.57	4.62	4.20	3.79	3.09	(4.31)
Cash Flow Per Share	2.63	(3.44)	(1.32)	(4.42)	3.84	6.85	1.66	(9.07)
Tang Book Value Per Share	28.59	27.43	28.09	26.47	25.87	22.14	19.13	16.43
Dividends Per Share	1.360	1.320	1.160	1.040	0.960	0.720	0.040	0.040
Dividend Payout %	31.19	29.53	25.38	22.51	22.86	19.00	1.29	...
Income Statement								
Interest Income	629,000	2,488,000	2,652,000	2,714,000	3,014,000	2,946,000	3,462,000	3,286,000
Interest Expense	117,000	400,000	392,000	411,000	476,000	613,000	763,000	722,000
Net Interest Income	512,000	2,088,000	2,260,000	2,303,000	2,538,000	2,333,000	2,699,000	2,564,000
Provision for Losses	4,000	12,000	10,000	6,000	(3,000)	...	25,000	149,000
Non-Interest Income	1,972,000	8,272,000	8,035,000	7,581,000	7,111,000	7,261,000	6,254,000	6,076,000
Non-Interest Expense	2,050,000	8,050,000	7,827,000	7,192,000	6,886,000	7,058,000	6,842,000	5,966,000
Income Before Taxes	430,000	2,298,000	2,458,000	2,686,000	2,766,000	2,536,000	2,086,000	2,525,000
Income Taxes	62,000	318,000	421,000	550,000	705,000	616,000	530,000	722,000
Net Income	368,000	1,980,000	2,037,000	2,136,000	2,061,000	1,920,000	1,556,000	(1,881,000)
Average Shares	403,615	413,638	432,007	455,155	481,129	496,072	497,924	474,003
Balance Sheet								
Net Loans & Leases	19,140,000	18,753,000	18,161,000	13,458,000	12,285,000	10,031,000	11,857,000	10,729,000
Total Assets	243,685,000	245,192,000	274,119,000	243,291,000	222,582,000	216,827,000	160,505,000	157,946,000
Total Deposits	185,516,000	191,627,000	209,040,000	182,268,000	164,181,000	157,287,000	98,345,000	90,062,000
Total Liabilities	222,189,000	224,089,000	252,646,000	222,913,000	201,713,000	197,429,000	142,718,000	143,455,000
Stockholders' Equity	21,496,000	21,103,000	21,473,000	20,378,000	20,869,000	19,398,000	17,787,000	14,491,000
Shares Outstanding	395,563	399,651	415,195	434,128	458,662	487,423	501,644	494,933
Statistical Record								
Return on Assets %	0.74	0.76	0.79	0.92	0.94	1.02	0.98	N.M.
Return on Equity %	9.16	9.30	9.73	10.36	10.21	10.33	9.64	N.M.
Net Interest Margin %	81.40	83.92	85.22	84.86	84.21	79.19	77.96	78.03
Efficiency Ratio %	78.82	74.81	73.24	69.86	68.01	69.15	70.42	63.73
Loans to Deposits	0.10	0.10	0.09	0.07	0.07	0.06	0.12	0.12
Price Range	80.84-51.91	80.84-64.73	80.33-63.19	73.39-47.01	47.01-38.78	50.06-30.38	48.07-32.81	55.17-14.89
P/E Ratio	18.54-11.91	18.09-14.48	17.58-13.83	15.89-10.18	11.19-9.23	13.21-8.02	15.56-10.62	...
Average Yield %	1.95	1.78	1.65	1.62	2.22	1.73	0.10	0.10

Address: One Lincoln Street, Boston, MA 02111	Web Site: www.statestreet.com	Auditors: Ernst & Young LLP
Telephone: 617-786-3000	Officers: Joseph L. Hooley - Chairman, President, Chief Executive Officer, Chief Operating Officer James S. Phalen - Vice-Chairman, Executive Vice President	Investor Contact: 617-664-3477 Transfer Agents: American Stock Transfer & Trust Company, LLC, Brooklyn, NY

STEPAN CO.

Exchange	Symbol	Price	52Wk Range	Yield	P/E	Div Achiever
NYS	SCL	$57.69 (5/31/2016)	62.47-40.58	1.32	16.02	48 Years

*7 Year Price Score 97.06   *NYSE Composite Index=100   ***12 Month Price Score 114.84**

Interim Earnings (Per Share)

Qtr.	Mar	Jun	Sep	Dec
2013	0.83	0.99	0.89	0.47
2014	0.57	1.06	0.59	0.27
2015	0.93	0.74	1.09	0.56
2016	1.21	...	...	...

Interim Dividends (Per Share)

Amt	Decl	Ex	Rec	Pay
0.18Q	07/22/2015	08/27/2015	08/31/2015	09/15/2015
0.19Q	10/20/2015	11/25/2015	11/30/2015	12/15/2015
0.19Q	02/23/2016	03/02/2016	03/04/2016	03/15/2016
0.19Q	04/25/2016	05/26/2016	05/31/2016	06/15/2016

Indicated Div: $0.76

Valuation Analysis

Forecast EPS	$3.96
	(05/15/2016)
Market Cap	$1.3 Billion
Book Value	$594.8 Million
Price/Book	2.16
Price/Sales	0.73

Institutional Holding

No of Institutions	215
Shares	14,029,729
% Held	56.84

TRADING VOLUME (thousand shares)

Business Summary: Specialty Chemicals (MIC: 8.3.2 SIC: 2843 NAIC: 325613)

Stepan is engaged in the production of specialty and intermediate chemicals, which are sold to other manufacturers for use in a variety of end products. Co. has three reportable segments: surfactants, polymers and specialty products. Surfactants are used in a variety of consumer and industrial cleaning compounds as well as in agricultural products, lubricating ingredients, oil field chemicals and other applications. Polymers are used primarily in plastics, building materials, refrigeration systems and coatings, adhesives, sealants and elastomers applications. Specialty products are used in food, flavoring, nutritional supplement and pharmaceutical applications.

Recent Developments: For the quarter ended Mar 31 2016, net income increased 29.9% to US$27.7 million from US$21.3 million in the year-earlier quarter. Revenues were US$445.9 million, down 3.2% from US$460.5 million the year before. Operating income was US$44.6 million versus US$35.2 million in the prior-year quarter, an increase of 26.8%. Direct operating expenses declined 8.2% to US$352.4 million from US$384.0 million in the comparable period the year before. Indirect operating expenses increased 18.5% to US$48.9 million from US$41.3 million in the equivalent prior-year period.

Prospects: Our evaluation of Stepan Co. as of June 19, 2016 is the result of our systematic analysis on three basic characteristics: earnings strength, relative valuation, and recent stock price movement. The company has managed to produce a neutral trend in earnings per share over the past 5 quarters and while recent estimates for the company have remained steady, SCL has posted better than expected results. Based on operating earnings yield, the company is undervalued when compared to all of the companies in our coverage universe. Share price changes over the past year indicates that SCL will perform in line with the market over the near term.

Financial Data

(US$ in Thousands)	3 Mos	12/31/2015	12/31/2014	12/31/2013	12/31/2012	12/31/2011	12/31/2010	12/31/2009
Earnings Per Share	3.60	3.32	2.49	3.18	3.49	6.42	5.90	5.84
Cash Flow Per Share	6.48	8.06	3.60	6.64	5.11	7.47	6.51	16.86
Tang Book Value Per Share	25.40	23.69	22.61	23.15	21.01	36.12	32.11	26.76
Dividends Per Share	0.740	0.730	0.690	0.650	0.580	0.530	0.490	0.450
Dividend Payout %	20.56	21.99	27.71	20.44	16.62	8.26	8.31	7.71
Income Statement								
Total Revenue	445,897	1,776,167	1,927,213	1,880,786	1,803,737	1,843,092	1,431,122	1,276,382
EBITDA	62,152	191,359	155,788	167,724	181,339	164,704	149,834	144,282
Depn & Amortn	18,070	66,985	63,804	56,400	51,294	47,099	40,351	37,171
Income Before Taxes	40,468	109,841	80,543	100,966	120,446	108,510	103,142	100,840
Income Taxes	12,811	26,819	18,454	23,293	36,035	32,292	35,888	34,028
Net Income	27,654	75,968	57,101	72,828	79,396	71,976	65,427	63,049
Average Shares	22,882	22,858	22,917	22,924	22,730	11,220	11,090	10,796
Balance Sheet								
Current Assets	639,126	619,573	575,556	608,550	523,078	479,742	427,826	349,592
Total Assets	1,259,957	1,239,661	1,162,014	1,167,202	985,478	901,118	811,431	634,203
Current Liabilities	221,349	243,244	249,513	268,993	247,167	233,226	205,627	163,295
Long-Term Obligations	312,573	313,817	246,897	235,246	149,564	164,967	159,963	93,911
Total Liabilities	665,128	682,677	626,468	614,916	506,493	499,907	461,940	344,918
Stockholders' Equity	594,829	556,984	535,546	552,286	478,985	401,211	349,491	289,285
Shares Outstanding	22,289	22,280	22,255	22,332	21,965	10,246	10,105	9,948
Statistical Record								
Return on Assets %	6.81	6.33	4.90	6.77	8.39	8.41	9.05	10.12
Return on Equity %	14.65	13.91	10.50	14.12	17.99	19.18	20.49	25.35
EBITDA Margin %	13.94	10.77	8.08	8.92	10.05	8.94	10.47	11.30
Net Margin %	6.20	4.28	2.96	3.87	4.40	3.91	4.57	4.94
Asset Turnover	1.46	1.48	1.65	1.75	1.91	2.15	1.98	2.05
Current Ratio	2.89	2.55	2.31	2.26	2.12	2.06	2.08	2.14
Debt to Equity	0.53	0.56	0.46	0.43	0.31	0.41	0.46	0.32
Price Range	56.05-40.58	55.18-37.74	66.47-37.02	66.85-52.58	55.54-39.17	41.59-31.55	39.63-23.58	33.73-11.55
P/E Ratio	15.57-11.27	16.62-11.37	26.69-14.87	21.02-16.53	15.91-11.22	6.48-4.91	6.72-4.00	5.78-1.98
Average Yield %	1.53	1.57	1.31	1.10	1.26	1.46	1.52	1.93

Address: Edens & Winnetka Road, Northfield, IL 60093 **Telephone:** 847-446-7500	**Web Site:** www.stepan.com **Officers:** F. Quinn Stepan - Chairman Arthur W. Mergner - Vice President, Division Officer	**Auditors:** Deloitte & Touche LLP **Investor Contact:** 847-446-7500 **Transfer Agents:** Computershare Investor Services, LLC, Chicago, IL

STERIS PLC

Exchange	Symbol	Price	52Wk Range	Yield	P/E
NYS	STE	$69.43 (5/31/2016)	77.73-61.96	1.44	44.51

*7 Year Price Score 134.46 *NYSE Composite Index=100 *12 Month Price Score 101.14

Interim Earnings (Per Share)

Qtr.	Jun	Sep	Dec	Mar
2011-12	0.48	0.50	0.58	0.76
2012-13	0.52	0.69	0.82	0.70
2013-14	0.54	0.50	0.48	0.65
2014-15	0.41	0.52	0.63	0.69
2015-16	0.40	0.14	0.26	0.76

Interim Dividends (Per Share)

Amt	Decl	Ex	Rec	Pay
0.25Q	02/09/2016	02/26/2016	03/01/2016	03/29/2016
0.25Q	05/18/2016	06/06/2016	06/08/2016	06/29/2016

Indicated Div: $1.00

Valuation Analysis / **Institutional Holding**

Forecast EPS	$3.94 (05/03/2016)	No of Institutions	N/A
Market Cap	$6.0 Billion	Shares	N/A
Book Value	$3.0 Billion	% Held	N/A
Price/Book	1.97		
Price/Sales	2.66		

Business Summary: Medical Instruments & Equipment (MIC: 4.3.1 SIC: 3842 NAIC: 339113)

STERIS is a provider of infection prevention and other procedural products and services. Co. has four segments: Healthcare Products, which provide infection prevention and procedural solutions, including capital equipment and related maintenance and installation services, as well as consumables; Healthcare Specialty Services, which provide a range of services including hospital sterilization services, instrument and scope repairs, and linen management; Life Sciences, which provide capital equipment and consumable products, and equipment maintenance and specialty services; and Applied Sterilization Technologies, which provide contract sterilization and laboratory services.

Recent Developments: For the year ended Mar 31 2016, net income decreased 17.4% to US$111.6 million in the prior year. Revenues were US$2.24 billion, up 21.0% from US$1.85 billion the year before. Operating income was US$212.9 million versus US$227.2 million in the prior year, a decrease of 6.3%. Direct operating expenses rose 24.8% to US$1.34 billion from US$1.08 billion in the comparable period the year before. Indirect operating expenses increased 24.8% to US$682.6 million from US$547.1 million in the equivalent prior-year period.

Prospects: Our evaluation of Steris PLC as of June 19, 2016 is the result of our systematic analysis on three basic characteristics: earnings strength, relative valuation, and recent stock price movement. The company has managed to produce a neutral trend in earnings per share over the past 5 quarters. However, while recent estimates for the company have been mixed, STE has posted results that fell short of analysts expectations. Based on operating earnings yield, the company is undervalued when compared to all of the companies in our coverage universe. Share price changes over the past year indicates that STE will perform very well over the near term.

Financial Data

(US$ in Thousands)	03/31/2016	03/31/2015	03/31/2014	03/31/2013	03/31/2012	03/31/2011	03/31/2010	03/31/2009
Earnings Per Share	1.56	2.25	2.17	2.72	2.31	0.85	2.16	1.86
Cash Flow Per Share	3.59	4.14	3.56	3.91	2.55	1.99	3.82	2.85
Tang Book Value Per Share	N.M.	3.54	4.93	4.09	8.38	7.93	7.57	7.06
Dividends Per Share	0.250	0.900	0.820	0.740	0.660	0.560	2.440	0.300
Dividend Payout %	16.03	40.00	37.79	27.21	28.57	65.88	112.96	16.13
Income Statement								
Total Revenue	2,238,764	1,850,263	1,622,252	1,501,902	1,406,810	1,207,448	1,257,733	1,298,525
EBITDA	306,885	288,692	263,844	297,914	275,296	132,984	252,989	226,705
Depn & Amortn	93,958	61,481	57,037	55,085	52,980	47,772	49,277	51,260
Income Before Taxes	171,884	208,820	188,376	227,098	211,108	73,819	191,816	166,485
Income Taxes	60,299	73,756	58,934	67,121	74,993	22,554	63,349	55,800
Net Income	110,763	135,064	129,442	159,977	136,115	51,265	128,467	110,685
Average Shares	71,184	60,045	59,745	58,844	58,963	60,148	59,423	59,544
Balance Sheet								
Current Assets	972,525	720,432	674,745	613,940	651,883	705,806	576,457	553,130
Total Assets	5,346,416	2,099,466	1,887,162	1,761,109	1,405,696	1,426,685	1,238,402	1,216,939
Current Liabilities	400,606	283,331	254,506	218,837	278,395	344,746	197,129	202,026
Long-Term Obligations	1,567,796	623,250	493,480	492,290	210,000	210,000	210,000	210,000
Total Liabilities	2,323,382	1,027,834	848,457	816,167	584,295	639,116	484,688	499,203
Stockholders' Equity	3,023,034	1,071,632	1,038,705	944,942	821,401	787,569	753,714	717,736
Shares Outstanding	85,920	59,675	58,968	58,759	57,733	59,122	59,227	58,452
Statistical Record								
Return on Assets %	2.97	6.78	7.10	10.10	9.59	3.85	10.46	9.01
Return on Equity %	5.40	12.80	13.05	18.11	16.87	6.65	17.46	15.55
EBITDA Margin %	13.71	15.60	16.26	19.84	19.57	11.01	20.11	17.46
Net Margin %	4.95	7.30	7.98	10.65	9.68	4.25	10.21	8.52
Asset Turnover	0.60	0.93	0.89	0.95	0.99	0.91	1.02	1.06
Current Ratio	2.43	2.54	2.65	2.81	2.34	2.05	2.92	2.74
Debt to Equity	0.52	0.58	0.48	0.52	0.26	0.27	0.28	0.29
Price Range	77.73-61.96	70.38-47.64	49.76-39.02	41.61-29.01	36.72-27.38	37.83-28.35	35.25-22.58	38.38-19.25
P/E Ratio	49.83-39.72	31.28-21.17	22.93-17.98	15.30-10.67	15.90-11.85	44.51-33.35	16.32-10.45	20.63-10.35
Average Yield %	0.37	1.54	1.83	2.17	2.08	1.67	8.53	1.02

Address: Chancery House,, 190 Waterside Road,, Hamilton Industrial Park, Leicester, 44060-1834 **Telephone:** 116-276-8636	**Web Site:** www.steris.com **Officers:** John P. Wareham - Chairman Walter M. Rosebrough - President, Chief Executive Officer	**Auditors:** Ernst & Young LLP **Investor Contact:** 440-392-7245 **Transfer Agents:** Computershare, Providence, RI

STONEMOR PARTNERS L P

Exchange	Symbol	Price	52Wk Range	Yield	P/E	Div Achiever
NYS	STON	$23.60 (5/31/2016)	31.49-23.08	11.19	N/A	10 Years

*7 Year Price Score 94.07   *NYSE Composite Index=100   *12 Month Price Score 87.01

Interim Earnings (Per Share)

Qtr.	Mar	Jun	Sep	Dec
2013	(0.11)	(0.54)	(0.07)	(0.16)
2014	0.02	0.00	(0.11)	(0.29)
2015	(0.30)	(0.16)	(0.11)	(0.23)
2016	(0.23)	...	...	...

Interim Dividends (Per Share)

Amt	Decl	Ex	Rec	Pay
0.65Q	07/24/2015	07/31/2015	08/04/2015	08/14/2015
0.66Q	10/27/2015	11/04/2015	11/06/2015	11/13/2015
0.66Q	01/26/2016	02/03/2016	02/05/2016	02/12/2016
0.66Q	04/26/2016	05/04/2016	05/06/2016	05/13/2016

Indicated Div: $2.64

Valuation Analysis

	Institutional Holding	
Forecast EPS	$-0.36	No of Institutions
	(05/20/2016)	124
Market Cap	$827.8 Million	Shares
Book Value	N/A	5,614,995
Price/Book	N/A	% Held
Price/Sales	2.65	19.65

TRADING VOLUME (thousand shares)

Business Summary: Miscellaneous Consumer Services (MIC: 2.2.3 SIC: 7261 NAIC: 812210)

StoneMor Partners is a provider of funeral and cemetery products and services in the death care industry. Co.'s cemetery products and services include: interment rights, which consist of burial lots, lawn crypts, mausoleum crypts, cremation niches, and perpetual care rights; merchandise, which consists of burial vaults, caskets, grave markers and grave marker bases, and memorials; and services, which consist of installation of burial vaults, installation of caskets, installation of other cemetery merchandise, and other service items. As of Dec 31 2014, Co. operated 303 cemeterics in 27 states and Puerto Rico, and also owned and operated 98 funeral homes in 19 states and Puerto Rico.

Recent Developments: For the quarter ended Mar 31 2016, net loss amounted to US$7.7 million versus a net loss of US$8.9 million in the year-earlier quarter. Revenues were US$74.6 million, up 10.6% from US$67.4 million the year before. Operating loss was US$727,000 versus a loss of US$3.4 million in the prior-year quarter. Direct operating expenses rose 7.5% to US$38.2 million from US$35.5 million in the comparable period the year before. Indirect operating expenses increased 5.3% to US$37.2 million from US$35.3 million in the equivalent prior-year period.

Prospects: Our evaluation of Stonemor Partners L.P. as of June 19, 2016 is the result of our systematic analysis on three basic characteristics: earnings strength, relative valuation, and recent stock price movement. The company has produced a positive trend in earnings per share over the past 5 quarters. Because the company lacks sufficient analyst estimate data, we place greater weight on the historical EPS trend as the measure of earnings strength. Based on operating earnings yield, the company is overvalued when compared to all of the companies in our coverage universe. Share price changes over the past year indicates that STON will perform poorly over the near term.

Financial Data
(US$ in Thousands)

	3 Mos	12/31/2015	12/31/2014	12/31/2013	12/31/2012	12/31/2011	12/31/2010	12/31/2009
Earnings Per Share	(0.73)	(0.79)	(0.40)	(0.89)	(0.15)	(0.50)	(0.10)	(0.09)
Cash Flow Per Share	0.11	0.13	0.73	1.67	1.64	0.29	0.22	1.12
Dividends Per Share	2.610	2.580	2.430	2.385	2.345	2.330	2.230	2.220
Income Statement								
Total Revenue	74,582	305,640	288,085	246,641	242,606	228,388	197,292	181,203
EBITDA	600,791	10,049	23,650	7,234	22,900	11,364	20,944	15,778
Depn & Amortn	602,400	10,600	8,900	7,500	7,200	5,900	5,800	4,400
Income Before Taxes	(7,399)	(23,136)	(6,860)	(21,336)	(4,803)	(13,734)	(6,829)	(3,031)
Income Taxes	260	1,108	3,913	(2,304)	(1,790)	(4,019)	(5,383)	(1,954)
Net Income	(7,659)	(24,244)	(10,773)	(19,032)	(3,013)	(9,715)	(1,446)	(1,077)
Average Shares	32,539	30,472	26,582	20,954	19,445	18,947	14,133	12,034
Balance Sheet								
Current Assets	109,761	107,798	101,878	93,579	81,091	81,497	65,047	58,625
Total Assets	1,708,488	1,686,125	1,699,464	1,473,329	1,343,725	1,249,125	1,147,119	858,889
Current Liabilities	41,694	35,818	38,852	41,697	32,981	29,547	26,864	28,781
Long-Term Obligations	318,136	316,399	285,378	289,016	252,774	193,835	219,008	182,821
Total Liabilities	1,534,855	1,502,447	1,490,702	1,365,809	1,208,543	1,068,846	1,018,927	743,641
Shares Outstanding	35,077	32,109	29,204	23,690	19,732	19,368	19,337	13,357
Statistical Record								
EBITDA Margin %	805.54	3.29	8.21	2.93	9.44	4.98	10.62	8.71
Asset Turnover	0.18	0.18	0.18	0.18	0.19	0.19	0.20	0.23
Current Ratio	2.63	3.01	2.62	2.24	2.46	2.76	2.42	2.04
Price Range	31.49-23.08	31.49-23.55	26.87-23.39	27.67-20.83	28.05-20.44	33.20-23.45	30.47-18.25	19.95-10.00
Average Yield %	9.23	9.02	9.67	9.49	9.67	8.41	9.75	14.50

Address: 311 Veterans Highway, Suite B, Levittown, PA 19056
Telephone: 215-826-2800

Web Site: www.stonemor.com
Officers: Lawrence Miller - Chairman, President, Chief Executive Officer David L. Meyers - Chief Operating Officer

Auditors: Deloitte & Touche LLP
Investor Contact: 215-826-2945
Transfer Agents: American Stock Transfer & Trust Company, New York, NY

STRYKER CORP.

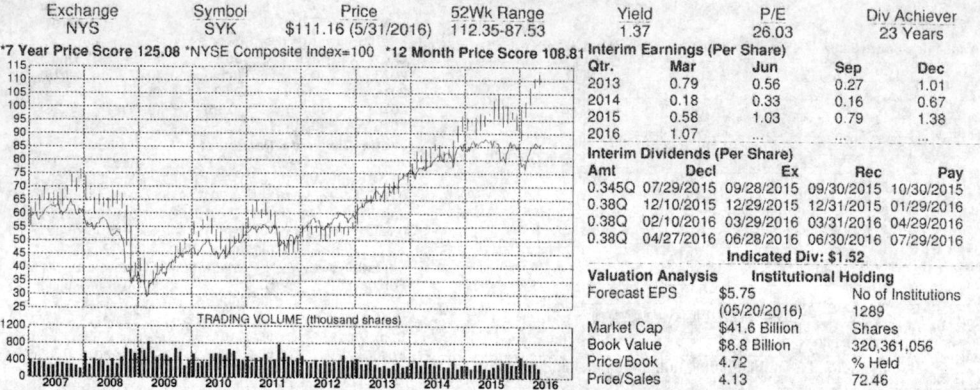

Exchange	Symbol	Price	52Wk Range	Yield	P/E	Div Achiever
NYS	SYK	$111.16 (5/31/2016)	112.35-87.53	1.37	26.03	23 Years

*7 Year Price Score 125.08 *NYSE Composite Index=100 *12 Month Price Score 108.81

Interim Earnings (Per Share)

Qtr.	Mar	Jun	Sep	Dec
2013	0.79	0.56	0.27	1.01
2014	0.18	0.33	0.16	0.67
2015	0.58	1.03	0.79	1.38
2016	1.07	...	...	...

Interim Dividends (Per Share)

Amt	Decl	Ex	Rec	Pay
0.345Q	07/29/2015	09/28/2015	09/30/2015	10/30/2015
0.38Q	12/10/2015	12/29/2015	12/31/2015	01/29/2016
0.38Q	02/10/2016	03/29/2016	03/31/2016	04/29/2016
0.38Q	04/27/2016	06/28/2016	06/30/2016	07/29/2016

Indicated Div: $1.52

Valuation Analysis | **Institutional Holding**

Forecast EPS	$5.75 (05/20/2016)	No of Institutions	1289
Market Cap	$41.6 Billion	Shares	320,361,056
Book Value	$8.8 Billion	% Held	72.46
Price/Book	4.72		
Price/Sales	4.13		

Business Summary: Medical Instruments & Equipment (MIC: 4.3.1 SIC: 3841 NAIC: 339112)

Stryker is a medical technology company. Co. segregates its operations into three reportable business segments: Orthopaedics, which provides products that consist primarily of implants used in hip and knee joint replacements and trauma and extremities surgeries; MedSurg, which provides products that include surgical equipment and surgical navigation systems, endoscopic and communications systems, patient handling and emergency medical equipment, and reprocessed and remanufactured medical devices as well as other medical device products used in a variety of medical fields; and Neurotechnology and Spine, which provides products that include both neurosurgical and neurovascular devices.

Recent Developments: For the quarter ended Mar 31 2016, net income increased 79.5% to US$402.0 million from US$224.0 million in the year-earlier quarter. Revenues were US$2.50 billion, up 4.9% from US$2.38 billion the year before. Operating income was US$519.0 million versus US$406.0 million in the prior-year quarter, an increase of 27.8%. Direct operating expenses declined 3.0% to US$801.0 million from US$826.0 million in the comparable period the year before. Indirect operating expenses increased 2.4% to US$1.18 billion from US$1.15 billion in the equivalent prior-year period.

Prospects: Our evaluation of Stryker Corp. as of June 19, 2016 is the result of our systematic analysis on three basic characteristics: earnings strength, relative valuation, and recent stock price movement. The company has managed to produce a neutral trend in earnings per share over the past 5 quarters and while recent estimates for the company have remained steady, SYK has posted better than expected results. Based on operating earnings yield, the company is about fairly valued when compared to all of the companies in our coverage universe. Share price changes over the past year indicates that SYK will perform well over the near term.

Financial Data

(US$ in Thousands)	3 Mos	12/31/2015	12/31/2014	12/31/2013	12/31/2012	12/31/2011	12/31/2010	12/31/2009
Earnings Per Share	4.27	3.78	1.34	2.63	3.39	3.45	3.19	2.77
Cash Flow Per Share	1.93	2.39	4.71	4.98	4.34	3.71	3.90	3.68
Tang Book Value Per Share	7.66	6.92	6.33	8.50	13.24	10.94	13.80	12.58
Dividends Per Share	1.450	1.415	1.260	1.100	0.902	0.752	0.630	0.250
Dividend Payout %	33.96	37.43	94.03	41.83	26.62	21.81	19.75	9.03
Income Statement								
Total Revenue	2,495,000	9,946,000	9,675,000	9,021,000	8,657,000	8,307,000	7,320,000	6,723,100
EBITDA	583,000	2,132,000	1,538,000	1,519,000	1,982,000	1,968,000	1,952,400	1,824,600
Depn & Amortn	102,000	397,000	378,000	307,000	277,000	282,000	222,800	200,700
Income Before Taxes	481,000	1,735,000	1,160,000	1,212,000	1,705,000	1,686,000	1,729,600	1,623,900
Income Taxes	79,000	296,000	645,000	206,000	407,000	341,000	456,200	516,500
Net Income	402,000	1,439,000	515,000	1,006,000	1,298,000	1,345,000	1,273,400	1,107,400
Average Shares	377,400	380,900	382,800	382,100	383,000	389,500	399,500	399,400
Balance Sheet								
Current Assets	11,325,000	7,944,000	9,673,000	8,335,000	8,148,000	7,211,000	7,631,400	5,851,200
Total Assets	19,668,000	16,247,000	17,713,000	15,743,000	13,206,000	12,405,000	10,895,100	9,071,300
Current Liabilities	3,186,000	3,503,000	4,464,000	2,657,000	1,876,000	1,828,000	1,605,000	1,441,000
Long-Term Obligations	6,706,000	3,253,000	3,246,000	2,739,000	1,746,000	1,751,000	996,500	...
Total Liabilities	10,860,000	7,736,000	9,118,000	6,696,000	4,609,000	4,722,000	3,721,500	2,476,200
Stockholders' Equity	8,808,000	8,511,000	8,595,000	9,047,000	8,597,000	7,683,000	7,173,600	6,595,100
Shares Outstanding	374,000	373,000	378,000	378,000	380,000	381,000	391,100	397,900
Statistical Record								
Return on Assets %	8.92	8.47	3.08	6.95	10.11	11.55	12.76	13.28
Return on Equity %	18.88	16.82	5.84	11.40	15.90	18.11	18.50	18.45
EBITDA Margin %	23.37	21.44	15.90	16.84	22.89	23.69	26.67	27.14
Net Margin %	16.11	14.47	5.32	11.15	14.99	16.19	17.40	16.47
Asset Turnover	0.56	0.59	0.58	0.62	0.67	0.71	0.73	0.81
Current Ratio	3.55	2.27	2.17	3.14	4.34	3.94	4.75	4.06
Debt to Equity	0.76	0.38	0.38	0.30	0.20	0.23	0.14	...
Price Range	107.29-87.53	104.53-90.07	96.61-74.63	75.39-54.82	56.57-49.84	65.07-43.80	58.89-42.88	52.20-31.19
P/E Ratio	25.13-20.50	27.65-23.83	72.10-55.69	28.67-20.84	16.69-14.70	18.86-12.70	18.46-13.44	18.84-11.26
Average Yield %	1.49	1.48	1.52	1.62	1.68	1.37	1.21	0.60

Address: 2825 Airview Boulevard, Kalamazoo, MI 49002
Telephone: 269-385-2600
Fax: 269-385-1062

Web Site: www.stryker.com
Officers: John W. Brown - Chairman Kevin A. Lobo - President, Chief Executive Officer, Division Officer

Auditors: Ernst & Young LLP
Investor Contact: 269-385-2600
Transfer Agents: American Stock Transfer & Trust Company, LLC, New York, NY

SUNOCO LOGISTICS PARTNERS L.P.

Exchange	Symbol	Price	52Wk Range	Yield	P/E	Div Achiever
NYS	SXL	$27.45 (5/31/2016)	39.75-16.49	7.13	39.21	13 Years

*7 Year Price Score 97.08   *NYSE Composite Index=100   *12 Month Price Score 93.55

Interim Earnings (Per Share)

Qtr.	Mar	Jun	Sep	Dec
2013	0.55	0.54	0.23	0.32
2014	0.33	0.53	0.50	(0.85)
2015	(0.10)	0.83	(0.07)	(0.24)
2016	0.18	...	...	...

Interim Dividends (Per Share)

Amt	Decl	Ex	Rec	Pay
0.438Q	07/23/2015	08/06/2015	08/10/2015	08/14/2015
0.458Q	10/20/2015	11/05/2015	11/09/2015	11/13/2015
0.479Q	01/28/2016	02/04/2016	02/08/2016	02/12/2016
0.489Q	04/28/2016	05/05/2016	05/09/2016	05/13/2016

Indicated Div: $1.96

Valuation Analysis

Forecast EPS	$0.92 (05/20/2016)
Market Cap	$7.7 Billion
Book Value	N/A
Price/Book	N/A
Price/Sales	0.80

Institutional Holding

No of Institutions	346
Shares	181,344,416
% Held	49.34

Business Summary: Equipment & Services (MIC: 9.1.3 SIC: 4612 NAIC: 486110)

Sunoco Logistics Partners is engaged in the transport, terminalling and storage of crude oil, refined petroleum products, and natural gas liquids. Co.'s segments are as follows: Crude Oil Pipelines, which transports crude oil principally in Oklahoma and Texas; Crude Oil Acquisition and Marketing, which gathers, purchases, markets and sells crude oil principally in the mid-continent U.S.; Terminal Facilities, which consists of refined products terminals providing storage, terminalling, blending and other ancillary services; and Refined Products Pipelines, which consists of refined products pipelines and joint venture interests in four refined products pipelines in certain areas of the U.S.

Recent Developments: For the quarter ended Mar 31 2016, net income increased 294.6% to US$146.0 million from US$37.0 million in the year-earlier quarter. Revenues were US$1.78 billion, down 30.9% from US$2.57 billion the year before. Operating income was US$183.0 million versus US$66.0 million in the prior-year quarter, an increase of 177.3%. Direct operating expenses declined 39.1% to US$1.44 billion from US$2.36 billion in the comparable period the year before. Indirect operating expenses increased 6.8% to US$158.0 million from US$148.0 million in the equivalent prior-year period.

Prospects: Our evaluation of Sunoco Logistics Partners L.P. as of June 19, 2016 is the result of our systematic analysis on three basic characteristics: earnings strength, relative valuation, and recent stock price movement. The company has suffered a very negative trend in earnings per share over the past 5 quarters. However, while recent estimates for the company have been mixed, SXL has posted better than expected results. Based on operating earnings yield, the company is about fairly valued when compared to all of the companies in our coverage universe. Share price changes over the past year indicates that SXL will perform in line with the market over the near term.

Financial Data
(US$ in Thousands)

	3 Mos	12/31/2015	12/31/2014	12/31/2013	12/31/2012	10/04/2012	12/31/2011	12/31/2010
Earnings Per Share	0.70	0.42	0.51	1.63	0.55	1.57	1.27	1.56
Cash Flow Per Share	2.81	2.38	2.66	3.61	1.35	2.61	2.12	1.79
Dividends Per Share	1.794	1.715	1.426	1.174	0.917	0.865	0.805	0.752
Dividend Payout %	256.29	408.33	279.66	72.23	166.82	55.12	63.39	48.34
Income Statement								
Total Revenue	1,777,000	10,486,000	18,088,000	16,639,000	3,194,000	9,950,000	10,918,000	7,838,000
EBITDA	187,000	921,000	676,000	824,000	221,000	556,000	524,000	495,000
Depn & Amortn	(3,000)	369,000	284,000	243,000	57,000	78,000	88,000	66,000
Income Before Taxes	151,000	418,000	325,000	504,000	150,000	413,000	347,000	356,000
Income Taxes	5,000	21,000	25,000	30,000	8,000	24,000	25,000	8,000
Net Income	145,000	393,000	291,000	463,000	139,000	381,000	313,000	346,000
Average Shares	283,100	251,700	214,100	208,600	208,200	207,800	203,600	191,400
Balance Sheet								
Current Assets	1,930,000	1,848,000	2,349,000	3,073,000	2,390,000	...	2,506,000	1,799,000
Total Assets	16,054,000	15,489,000	13,644,000	11,897,000	10,361,000	...	5,477,000	4,188,000
Current Liabilities	1,611,000	1,663,000	2,311,000	2,736,000	2,131,000	...	2,535,000	1,711,000
Long-Term Obligations	5,968,000	5,591,000	4,260,000	2,503,000	1,732,000	...	1,448,000	1,229,000
Total Liabilities	8,298,000	7,682,000	6,966,000	5,693,000	4,289,000	...	4,381,000	3,223,000
Stockholders' Equity	...	286,000	...	...	...	...	...	...
Shares Outstanding	280,900	278,266	226,072	207,699	207,546	...	206,651	198,600
Statistical Record								
Return on Assets %	3.36	2.70	2.28	4.16	1.75	...	6.48	9.50
EBITDA Margin %	10.52	8.78	3.74	4.95	6.92	5.59	4.80	6.32
Net Margin %	8.16	3.75	1.61	2.78	4.35	3.83	2.87	4.41
Asset Turnover	0.65	0.72	1.42	1.50	0.40	...	2.26	2.15
Current Ratio	1.20	1.11	1.02	1.12	1.12	...	0.99	1.05
Debt to Equity	...	19.55	...	...	...	...	...	...
Price Range	44.66-16.49	46.00-22.07	51.13-36.60	37.74-24.86	25.95-22.53	25.02-16.32	19.88-12.62	13.93-10.33
P/E Ratio	63.80-23.56	109.52-52.55	100.25-71.76	23.15-15.25	47.18-40.96	15.94-10.39	15.65-9.94	8.93-6.62
Average Yield %	5.72	4.75	3.19	3.67	3.71	4.39	5.40	6.17

Address: 3807 West Chester Pike, Newtown Square, PA 19073 **Telephone:** 866-248-4344	**Web Site:** www.sunocologistics.com **Officers:** Marshall S. McCrea - Chairman Michael J. Hennigan - President, Chief Executive Officer, Chief Operating Officer	**Auditors:** Grant Thornton LLP **Transfer Agents:** American Stock Transfer & Trust Compan, New York, NY

SUNTRUST BANKS, INC.

Exchange	Symbol	Price	52Wk Range	Yield	P/E
NYS	STI	$43.82 (5/31/2016)	45.35-31.36	2.19	12.04

*7 Year Price Score 112.40 *NYSE Composite Index=100 *12 Month Price Score 99.68

Interim Earnings (Per Share)
Qtr.	Mar	Jun	Sep	Dec
2013	0.63	0.68	0.33	0.77
2014	0.73	0.72	1.06	0.72
2015	0.78	0.89	1.00	0.91
2016	0.84			

Interim Dividends (Per Share)
Amt	Decl	Ex	Rec	Pay
0.24Q	08/11/2015	08/27/2015	08/31/2015	09/15/2015
0.24Q	11/10/2015	11/25/2015	11/30/2015	12/15/2015
0.24Q	02/09/2016	02/24/2016	02/26/2016	03/15/2016
0.24Q	04/26/2016	05/26/2016	05/31/2016	06/15/2016

Indicated Div: $0.96 (Div. Reinv. Plan)

Valuation Analysis / Institutional Holding
Forecast EPS	$3.50	No of Institutions
	(05/20/2016)	945
Market Cap	$22.1 Billion	Shares
Book Value	$24.1 Billion	476,529,600
Price/Book	0.92	% Held
Price/Sales	2.56	79.86

Business Summary: Banking (MIC: 5.1.1 SIC: 6021 NAIC: 522110)

SunTrust Banks is a financial services holding company. Through its subsidiary, SunTrust Bank (the Bank), Co. provides a line of financial services for consumers, businesses, corporations, and institutions. In addition to deposit, credit, mortgage banking, and trust and investment services provided by the Bank, other subsidiaries of Co. provide asset and wealth management, securities brokerage, and capital market services. Co. operates three business segments: Consumer Banking and Private Wealth Management, Wholesale Banking, and Mortgage Banking. As of Dec 31 2015, Co. had total assets of $190.82 billion and total deposits of $149.83 billion.

Recent Developments: For the quarter ended Mar 31 2016, net income increased 4.2% to US$449.0 million from US$431.0 million in the year-earlier quarter. Net interest income increased 12.5% to US$1.28 billion from US$1.14 billion in the year-earlier quarter. Provision for loan losses was US$101.0 million versus US$55.0 million in the prior-year quarter, an increase of 83.6%. Non-interest income fell 4.4% to US$781.0 million from US$817.0 million, while non-interest expense advanced 3.0% to US$1.32 billion.

Prospects: Our evaluation of SunTrust Banks Inc. as of June 19, 2016 is the result of our systematic analysis on three basic characteristics: earnings strength, relative valuation, and recent stock price movement. The company has managed to produce a neutral trend in earnings per share over the past 5 quarters and while recent estimates for the company have been mixed, STI has posted better than expected results. Based on operating earnings yield, the company is undervalued when compared to all of the companies in our coverage universe. Share price changes over the past year indicates that STI will perform in line with the market over the near term.

Financial Data
(US$ in Thousands)	3 Mos	12/31/2015	12/31/2014	12/31/2013	12/31/2012	12/31/2011	12/31/2010	12/31/2009
Earnings Per Share	3.64	3.58	3.23	2.41	3.59	0.94	(0.18)	(3.98)
Cash Flow Per Share	6.84	6.79	(2.24)	7.88	3.75	8.83	8.52	6.99
Tang Book Value Per Share	30.26	28.60	27.12	24.24	24.00	23.15	20.57	19.20
Dividends Per Share	0.960	0.920	0.700	0.350	0.200	0.120	0.040	0.220
Dividend Payout %	26.37	25.70	21.67	14.52	5.57	12.77	...	...
Income Statement								
Interest Income	1,411,000	5,265,000	5,384,000	5,388,000	5,867,000	6,181,000	6,343,000	6,709,747
Interest Expense	129,000	501,000	544,000	535,000	765,000	1,116,000	1,489,000	2,244,057
Net Interest Income	1,282,000	4,764,000	4,840,000	4,853,000	5,102,000	5,065,000	4,854,000	4,465,690
Provision for Losses	101,000	165,000	342,000	553,000	1,395,000	1,513,000	2,651,000	4,063,914
Non-Interest Income	781,000	3,268,000	3,323,000	3,214,000	5,373,000	3,421,000	3,729,000	3,710,278
Non-Interest Expense	1,318,000	5,160,000	5,543,000	5,880,000	6,307,000	6,237,000	5,841,000	6,523,052
Income Before Taxes	644,000	2,707,000	2,278,000	1,634,000	2,757,000	739,000	21,000	(2,450,354)
Income Taxes	195,000	764,000	493,000	273,000	773,000	79,000	(185,000)	(898,783)
Net Income	447,000	1,933,000	1,774,000	1,344,000	1,958,000	647,000	189,000	(1,563,683)
Average Shares	509,931	520,586	533,391	539,093	538,061	527,618	499,000	435,328
Balance Sheet								
Net Loans & Leases	139,887,000	136,528,000	134,407,000	127,532,000	122,695,000	122,391,000	116,502,000	115,224,667
Total Assets	194,158,000	190,817,000	190,328,000	175,335,000	173,442,000	176,859,000	172,874,000	174,164,735
Total Deposits	152,161,000	149,830,000	140,567,000	129,759,000	132,316,000	127,922,000	123,044,000	121,863,566
Total Liabilities	170,105,000	167,380,000	167,323,000	153,913,000	152,457,000	156,793,000	149,744,000	151,633,880
Stockholders' Equity	24,053,000	23,437,000	23,005,000	21,422,000	20,985,000	20,066,000	23,130,000	22,530,855
Shares Outstanding	505,443	508,712	524,540	536,097	538,959	536,967	500,436	499,156
Statistical Record								
Return on Assets %	1.02	1.01	0.97	0.77	1.11	0.37	0.11	N.M.
Return on Equity %	8.25	8.32	7.99	6.34	9.51	3.00	0.83	N.M.
Net Interest Margin %	90.86	90.48	89.90	90.07	86.96	81.94	76.53	66.56
Efficiency Ratio %	60.13	60.47	63.66	68.36	56.11	64.96	57.99	62.60
Loans to Deposits	0.92	0.91	0.96	0.98	0.93	0.96	0.95	0.95
Price Range	45.35-31.36	45.35-36.71	42.69-34.73	36.81-27.12	30.31-18.52	32.59-15.80	31.85-20.29	29.92-6.70
P/E Ratio	12.46-8.62	12.67-10.25	13.22-10.75	15.27-11.25	8.44-5.16	34.67-16.81	...	...
Average Yield %	2.36	2.20	1.81	1.10	0.81	0.50	0.16	1.24

Address: 303 Peachtree Street, N.E., Atlanta, GA 30308 **Telephone:** 800-786-8787	**Web Site:** www.suntrust.com **Officers:** William H. Rogers - Chairman, President, Chief Executive Officer Frances L. Breeden - Executive Vice President, Director	**Auditors:** Ernst & Young LLP **Investor Contact:** 877-930-8971 **Transfer Agents:** Computershare, Providence, RI

SUPERIOR ENERGY SERVICES, INC.

Exchange	Symbol	Price	52Wk Range	Yield	P/E
NYS	SPN	$17.24 (5/31/2016)	23.51-8.59	N/A	N/A

*7 Year Price Score 50.88 *NYSE Composite Index=100 *12 Month Price Score 103.13

Interim Earnings (Per Share)
Qtr.	Mar	Jun	Sep	Dec
2013	0.40	0.43	0.43	(1.96)
2014	0.23	0.47	0.51	0.44
2015	(0.07)	(5.22)	(5.45)	(1.57)
2016	(0.57)	...	...	...

Interim Dividends (Per Share)
Amt	Decl	Ex	Rec	Pay
0.08Q	04/15/2015	04/28/2015	04/30/2015	05/20/2015
0.08Q	07/15/2015	07/28/2015	07/30/2015	08/20/2015
0.08Q	10/15/2015	10/28/2015	10/30/2015	11/20/2015
0.08Q	01/15/2016	01/28/2016	02/01/2016	02/23/2016

Valuation Analysis / Institutional Holding
Forecast EPS	$-2.15	No of Institutions	
	(05/20/2016)	441	
Market Cap	$2.6 Billion	Shares	
Book Value	$2.1 Billion	165,355,936	
Price/Book	1.24	% Held	
Price/Sales	1.15	88.82	

Business Summary: Equipment & Services (MIC: 9.1.3 SIC: 1389 NAIC: 213112)

Superior Energy Services provide a range of services and products to the energy industry related to the exploration, development and production of oil and natural gas. Co. reports its operating results in four business segments: Drilling Products and Services, which includes downhole drilling tools and surface rentals; Onshore Completion and Workover Services, which include pressure pumping, fluid handling and workover and maintenance services; Production Services, which include intervention services; and Technical Solutions, which include pressure control services, completion tools and services and end-of-life services.

Recent Developments: For the quarter ended Mar 31 2016, loss from continuing operations was US$84.5 million compared with a loss of US$1.5 million in the year-earlier quarter. Net loss amounted to US$86.8 million versus a net loss of US$11.1 million in the year-earlier quarter. Revenues were US$413.1 million, down 55.0% from US$917.2 million the year before. Operating loss was US$112.0 million versus an income of US$21.8 million in the prior-year quarter. Direct operating expenses declined 51.0% to US$285.3 million from US$582.2 million in the comparable period the year before. Indirect operating expenses decreased 23.4% to US$239.8 million from US$313.2 million in the equivalent prior-year period.

Prospects: Our evaluation of Superior Energy Services Inc. as of June 19, 2016 is the result of our systematic analysis on three basic characteristics: earnings strength, relative valuation, and recent stock price movement. The company has enjoyed a very positive trend in earnings per share over the past 5 quarters. Because the company lacks sufficient analyst estimate data, we place greater weight on the historical EPS trend as the measure of earnings strength. Based on operating earnings yield, the company is overvalued when compared to all of the companies in our coverage universe. Share price changes over the past year indicates that SPN will perform very poorly over the near term.

Financial Data
(US$ in Thousands)	3 Mos	12/31/2015	12/31/2014	12/31/2013	12/31/2012	12/31/2011	12/31/2010	12/31/2009
Earnings Per Share	(12.81)	(12.33)	1.65	(0.70)	2.42	1.76	1.03	(1.31)
Cash Flow Per Share	3.02	4.20	6.66	5.61	6.91	6.19	5.79	3.53
Tang Book Value Per Share	6.39	7.10	10.76	10.51	10.76	10.85	8.77	8.85
Dividends Per Share	0.320	0.320	0.320	0.080	...	...	...	...
Dividend Payout %	...	...	19.39	...	...	...	...	...
Income Statement								
Total Revenue	413,133	2,774,565	4,556,622	4,611,824	4,568,068	2,070,166	1,681,616	1,449,300
EBITDA	32,394	(1,378,365)	1,159,523	625,391	1,185,081	497,523	376,791	115,501
Depn & Amortn	136,672	584,100	620,600	593,000	480,000	224,600	207,700	202,800
Income Before Taxes	(128,084)	(2,059,783)	442,189	(71,585)	590,569	205,306	116,857	(137,279)
Income Taxes	(43,548)	(252,020)	161,399	39,833	225,020	79,146	43,285	(57,556)
Net Income	(86,803)	(1,854,718)	257,817	(111,418)	365,935	142,554	81,817	(102,323)
Average Shares	151,324	150,461	156,726	159,206	151,106	81,095	79,734	78,171
Balance Sheet								
Current Assets	1,186,587	1,295,125	1,728,811	1,476,429	1,460,357	883,222	764,052	863,563
Total Assets	4,746,098	4,914,244	7,377,389	7,411,307	7,802,886	4,048,145	2,907,533	2,516,665
Current Liabilities	421,297	448,576	712,047	639,400	772,065	393,533	505,887	228,379
Long-Term Obligations	1,608,575	1,588,263	1,627,842	1,646,535	1,814,500	1,685,087	681,635	848,665
Total Liabilities	2,639,076	2,703,432	3,297,651	3,279,863	3,571,807	2,594,546	1,626,982	1,338,620
Stockholders' Equity	2,107,022	2,210,812	4,079,738	4,131,444	4,231,079	1,453,599	1,280,551	1,178,045
Shares Outstanding	151,412	150,861	149,708	159,158	157,933	80,425	78,951	78,559
Statistical Record								
Return on Assets %	N.M.	N.M.	3.49	N.M.	6.16	4.10	3.02	N.M.
Return on Equity %	N.M.	N.M.	6.28	N.M.	12.84	10.43	6.66	N.M.
EBITDA Margin %	7.84	N.M.	25.45	13.56	25.94	24.03	22.41	7.97
Net Margin %	N.M.	N.M.	5.66	N.M.	8.01	6.89	4.87	N.M.
Asset Turnover	0.38	0.45	0.62	0.61	0.77	0.60	0.62	0.58
Current Ratio	2.82	2.89	2.43	2.31	1.89	2.24	1.51	3.78
Debt to Equity	0.76	0.72	0.40	0.40	0.43	1.16	0.53	0.72
Price Range	26.28-8.59	26.28-12.59	36.69-17.19	28.86-20.72	30.87-17.89	41.89-23.52	35.19-18.54	25.78-11.52
P/E Ratio	...	...	22.24-10.42	...	12.76-7.39	23.80-13.36	34.17-18.00	...
Average Yield %	1.95	1.70	1.08	0.31	...	...	...	...

Address: 1001 Louisiana Street, Suite 2900, Houston, TX 77002 **Telephone:** 713-654-2200	**Web Site:** www.superiorenergy.com **Officers:** Terence E. Hall - Chairman, President, Chief Executive Officer David D. Dunlap - President, Chief Executive Officer	**Auditors:** KPMG LLP **Investor Contact:** 281-999-0047 **Transfer Agents:** Jones, Walker, LLP

SUPERVALU INC.

Exchange	Symbol	Price	52Wk Range	Yield	P/E
NYS	SVU	$4.63 (5/31/2016)	9.36-4.08	N/A	7.02

*7 Year Price Score 67.30   *NYSE Composite Index=100   *12 Month Price Score 76.07

TRADING VOLUME (thousand shares)

Interim Earnings (Per Share)

Qtr.	Jun	Aug	Nov	Feb
2012-13	0.19	(0.52)	0.08	(6.65)
2013-14	0.34	0.15	0.12	0.09
2014-15	0.17	0.11	0.30	0.15
2015-16	0.23	0.11	0.13	0.19

Interim Dividends (Per Share)

Dividend Payment Suspended

Valuation Analysis / Institutional Holding

Forecast EPS	$0.72	No of Institutions	
	(05/20/2016)	431	
Market Cap	$1.2 Billion	Shares	
Book Value	N/A	256,536,288	
Price/Book	N/A	% Held	
Price/Sales	0.07	70.59	

Business Summary: Retail - Food & Beverage, Drug & Tobacco (MIC: 2.1.2 SIC: 5411 NAIC: 445110)

Supervalu operates primarily in the U.S. grocery channel. Co.'s business is classified by management into three reportable segments: Wholesale, which provides independent retail customers a variety of food and non-food products, including national and regional brands, and Co.'s own lines of private label products; Save-A-Lot, which is a discount grocery retailer; and Retail, which at Feb 27 2016, conducted its operations through a total of 200 stores primarily organized under five regionally-based retail banners of Cub Foods, Shoppers Food & Pharmacy, Shop 'n Save, Farm Fresh and Hornbacher's, plus two Rainbow and two County Market stores.

Recent Developments: For the year ended Feb 27 2016, income from continuing operations increased 40.2% to US$178.0 million from US$127.0 million a year earlier. Net income decreased 6.5% to US$186.0 million from US$199.0 million in the prior year. Revenues were US$17.53 billion, down 2.2% from US$17.92 billion the year before. Operating income was US$454.0 million versus US$424.0 million in the prior year, an increase of 7.1%. Direct operating expenses declined 2.5% to US$14.95 billion from US$15.33 billion in the comparable period the year before. Indirect operating expenses decreased 1.6% to US$2.13 billion from US$2.16 billion in the equivalent prior-year period.

Prospects: Our evaluation of SUPERVALU Inc. as of June 19, 2016 is the result of our systematic analysis on three basic characteristics: earnings strength, relative valuation, and recent stock price movement. The company has managed to produce a neutral trend in earnings per share over the past 5 quarters and while recent estimates for the company have remained steady, SVU has posted better than expected results. Based on operating earnings yield, the company is undervalued when compared to all of the companies in our coverage universe. Share price changes over the past year indicates that SVU will perform poorly over the near term.

Financial Data

(US$ in Thousands)	02/27/2016	02/28/2015	02/22/2014	02/23/2013	02/25/2012	02/26/2011	02/27/2010	02/28/2009
Earnings Per Share	0.66	0.73	0.70	(6.91)	(4.91)	(7.13)	1.85	(13.51)
Cash Flow Per Share	1.62	1.54	0.07	4.25	4.99	5.50	6.97	7.15
Dividends Per Share	...	...	...	0.175	0.263	0.350	0.610	0.688
Dividend Payout %	...	...	...	...	...	...	32.97	...
Income Statement								
Total Revenue	17,529,000	17,820,000	17,155,000	17,097,000	36,100,000	37,534,000	40,597,000	44,564,000
EBITDA	702,000	682,000	693,000	176,000	271,000	(151,000)	2,053,000	(1,212,000)
Depn & Amortn	248,000	258,000	275,000	333,000	790,000	825,000	852,000	945,000
Income Before Taxes	258,000	181,000	11,000	(426,000)	(1,028,000)	(1,523,000)	632,000	(2,779,000)
Income Taxes	85,000	58,000	5,000	(163,000)	12,000	(13,000)	239,000	76,000
Net Income	178,000	192,000	182,000	(1,466,000)	(1,040,000)	(1,510,000)	393,000	(2,855,000)
Average Shares	268,000	264,000	258,000	212,000	212,000	212,000	213,000	211,000
Balance Sheet								
Current Assets	1,635,000	1,700,000	1,543,000	2,970,000	3,225,000	3,420,000	3,711,000	4,105,000
Total Assets	4,370,000	4,485,000	4,374,000	11,034,000	12,053,000	13,758,000	16,436,000	17,604,000
Current Liabilities	1,572,000	1,533,000	1,491,000	4,350,000	3,590,000	3,786,000	4,167,000	4,472,000
Long-Term Obligations	2,400,000	2,693,000	2,732,000	5,630,000	11,736,000	12,696,000	14,044,000	15,936,000
Total Liabilities	4,811,000	5,131,000	5,112,000	15,264,000	17,900,000	18,766,000	20,571,000	22,991,000
Stockholders' Equity	(441,000)	(646,000)	(738,000)	(1,415,000)	21,000	1,340,000	2,887,000	2,581,000
Shares Outstanding	265,000	260,000	256,000	213,000	212,000	212,000	212,000	212,000
Statistical Record								
Return on Assets %	4.03	4.26	2.37	N.M.	N.M.	N.M.	2.32	N.M.
Return on Equity %	...	...	...	...	N.M.	N.M.	14.41	N.M.
EBITDA Margin %	4.00	3.83	4.04	1.03	0.75	N.M.	5.06	N.M.
Net Margin %	1.02	1.08	1.06	N.M.	N.M.	N.M.	0.97	N.M.
Asset Turnover	3.97	3.96	2.23	1.49	2.80	2.49	2.39	2.27
Current Ratio	1.04	1.11	1.03	0.68	0.90	0.90	0.89	0.92
Debt to Equity	...	...	...	...	558.86	9.47	4.86	6.17
Price Range	11.90-4.08	10.43-6.12	8.40-3.76	6.62-1.73	11.38-6.40	17.47-7.23	17.67-12.35	35.62-9.02
P/E Ratio	18.03-6.18	14.29-8.38	12.00-5.37	...	...	...	9.55-6.68	...
Average Yield %	...	...	...	4.62	3.16	3.03	4.09	2.92

Address: 11840 Valley View Road, Eden Prairie, MN 55344 Telephone: 952-828-4000	Web Site: www.supervalu.com Officers: Mark Gross - President, Chief Executive Officer Bruce H. Besanko - Executive Vice President, Chief Financial Officer, Chief Operating Officer	Auditors: KPMG LLP Investor Contact: 952-828-4000 Transfer Agents: Wells Fargo Shareowner Services, St. Paul, MN

SYNCHRONY FINANCIAL

Exchange	Symbol	Price	52Wk Range	Yield	P/E
NYS	SYF	$31.20 (5/31/2016)	35.99-24.48	N/A	11.60

*7 Year Price Score N/A *NYSE Composite Index=100 *12 Month Price Score 95.55

Interim Earnings (Per Share)

Qtr.	Mar	Jun	Sep	Dec
2014	0.79	0.67	0.70	0.64
2015	0.66	0.65	0.69	0.65
2016	0.70	...	...	...

Interim Dividends (Per Share)

No Dividends Paid

Valuation Analysis **Institutional Holding**

Forecast EPS	$2.65	No of Institutions
	(05/20/2016)	677
Market Cap	$26.0 Billion	Shares
Book Value	$13.2 Billion	743,103,744
Price/Book	1.97	% Held
Price/Sales	1.86	94.86

TRADING VOLUME (thousand shares)

Business Summary: Banking (MIC: 5.1.1 SIC: 6141 NAIC: 522291)

Synchrony Financial is a savings and loan holding company and a consumer financial services company. Co. provides credit products through programs it has established with a group of national and regional retailers, local merchants, manufacturers, buying groups, industry associations and healthcare service providers. Co. provides its credit products primarily through its wholly-owned subsidiary, Synchrony Bank (the Bank). Through the Bank, Co. provides deposit products insured by the Federal Deposit Insurance Corporation, including certificates of deposit, individual retirement accounts, money market accounts and savings accounts. At Dec 31 2015, Co. had total assets of $84.14 billion.

Recent Developments: For the quarter ended Mar 31 2016, net income increased 5.4% to US$582.0 million from US$552.0 million in the year-earlier quarter. Net interest income increased 11.6% to US$3.21 billion from US$2.88 billion in the year-earlier quarter. Provision for loan losses was US$903.0 million versus US$687.0 million in the prior-year quarter, an increase of 31.4%. Non-interest income fell 8.9% to US$92.0 million from US$101.0 million, while non-interest expense advanced 4.6% to US$1.47 billion.

Prospects: Our evaluation of Synchrony Financial as of June 19, 2016 is the result of our systematic analysis on three basic characteristics: earnings strength, relative valuation, and recent stock price movement. The company has managed to produce a neutral trend in earnings per share over the past 5 quarters. However, while recent estimates for the company have been lowered by analysts, SYF has posted better than expected results. Based on operating earnings yield, the company is undervalued when compared to all of the companies in our coverage universe. Share price changes over the past year indicates that SYF will perform very well over the near term.

Financial Data
(US$ in Millions)

	3 Mos	12/31/2015	12/31/2014	12/31/2013	12/31/2012	12/31/2011
Earnings Per Share	2.69	2.65	2.78	...	...	...
Cash Flow Per Share	7.22	7.42	7.05	...	...	...
Tang Book Value Per Share	13.86	13.14	10.81	...	...	...
Income Statement						
Total Revenue	3,612	13,620	12,727	11,813	10,793	9,638
Income Before Taxes	928	3,531	3,386	3,142	3,376	3,010
Income Taxes	346	1,317	1,277	1,163	1,257	1,120
Net Income	582	2,214	2,109	1,979	2,119	1,890
Average Shares	836	835	757	...	...	...
Balance Sheet						
Total Assets	81,656	84,135	75,707	59,085	53,462	...
Total Liabilities	68,452	71,531	65,229	53,125	48,880	...
Stockholders' Equity	13,204	12,604	10,478	5,960	4,582	...
Shares Outstanding	833	833	833	...	...	...
Statistical Record						
Return on Assets %	2.91	2.77	3.13	3.52	...	...
Return on Equity %	18.51	19.18	25.66	37.55	...	...
Net Margin %	16.11	16.26	16.57	16.75	19.63	19.61
Asset Turnover	0.18	0.17	0.19	0.21	...	...
Price Range	35.99-24.48	35.99-28.52	30.50-22.93	...	...	...
P/E Ratio	13.38-9.10	13.58-10.76	10.97-8.25	...	...	...

Address: 777 Long Ridge Road, Stamford, CT 06902 **Telephone:** 203-585-2400	**Web Site:** www.synchronyfinancial.com **Officers:** Margaret M. Keane - President, Chief Executive Officer Brian D. Doubles - Executive Vice President, Chief Financial Officer, Treasurer	**Auditors:** KPMG LLP **Transfer Agents:** Computershare Trust Company, N.A.

SYNNEX CORP

Exchange	Symbol	Price	52Wk Range	Yield	P/E
NYS	SNX	$91.10 (5/31/2016)	101.83-71.26	0.88	17.39

*7 Year Price Score 149.81 *NYSE Composite Index=100 *12 Month Price Score 99.60

Interim Earnings (Per Share)

Qtr.	Feb	May	Aug	Nov
2012-13	0.88	0.81	0.19	1.09
2013-14	1.01	1.01	1.15	1.41
2014-15	1.16	1.30	1.21	1.56
2015-16	1.17			

Interim Dividends (Per Share)

Amt	Decl	Ex	Rec	Pay
0.125Q	06/25/2015	07/15/2015	07/17/2015	07/31/2015
0.20Q	09/28/2015	10/14/2015	10/16/2015	10/30/2015
0.20Q	01/07/2016	01/14/2016	01/19/2016	01/29/2016
0.20Q	03/28/2016	04/13/2016	04/15/2016	04/29/2016

Indicated Div: $0.80

Valuation Analysis

Forecast EPS	$6.04
	(05/20/2016)
Market Cap	$3.6 Billion
Book Value	$1.8 Billion
Price/Book	1.96
Price/Sales	0.27

Institutional Holding

No of Institutions	286
Shares	32,884,918
% Held	81.97

Business Summary: IT Services (MIC: 6.3.1 SIC: 5045 NAIC: 334119)

Synnex is a business process services company, providing services to resellers, retailers and original equipment manufacturers, financial and insurance institutions and several other industry verticals. Co. has two segments: Technology Solutions, which distributes peripherals, information technology systems including data center server and storage solutions, system components, software, consumer electronics, and complementary products, and provides systems design and integration solutions; and Concentrix, which provides solutions and services focused on customer engagement strategy, process optimization, technology innovation, front and back-office automation and business transformation.

Recent Developments: For the quarter ended Feb 29 2016, net income increased 0.7% to US$46.6 million from US$46.3 million in the year-earlier quarter. Revenues were US$3.13 billion, down 2.4% from US$3.20 billion the year before. Operating income was US$75.6 million versus US$78.9 million in the prior-year quarter, a decrease of 4.2%. Direct operating expenses declined 2.5% to US$2.84 billion from US$2.91 billion in the comparable period the year before. Indirect operating expenses decreased 0.3% to US$208.6 million from US$209.3 million in the equivalent prior-year period.

Prospects: Our evaluation of Synnex Corp. as of June 19, 2016 is the result of our systematic analysis on three basic characteristics: earnings strength, relative valuation, and recent stock price movement. The company has generated a negative trend in earnings per share over the past 5 quarters and while recent estimates for the company have been mixed, SNX has posted better than expected results. Based on operating earnings yield, the company is undervalued when compared to all of the companies in our coverage universe. Share price changes over the past year indicates that SNX will perform poorly over the near term.

Financial Data
(US$ in Thousands)

	3 Mos	11/30/2015	11/30/2014	11/30/2013	11/30/2012	11/30/2011	11/30/2010	11/30/2009
Earnings Per Share	5.24	5.24	4.57	3.06	3.99	4.08	3.58	2.70
Cash Flow Per Share	14.77	16.48	(6.10)	0.97	6.62	6.12	(1.90)	8.01
Tang Book Value Per Share	35.04	34.04	28.51	32.22	30.06	25.87	23.19	20.62
Dividends Per Share	0.650	0.575	0.125	...	...	...	...	...
Dividend Payout %	12.40	10.97	2.74	...	...	...	...	...
Income Statement								
Total Revenue	3,125,622	13,338,397	13,839,590	10,845,164	10,285,507	10,409,840	8,614,141	7,719,197
EBITDA	105,838	457,001	401,168	279,629	284,113	279,896	216,985	172,311
Depn & Amortn	26,178	103,510	91,699	24,462	24,630	24,673	16,285	19,626
Income Before Taxes	73,444	327,195	284,282	238,052	236,553	229,718	183,586	138,702
Income Taxes	26,807	118,588	104,132	85,730	84,050	79,165	66,910	50,656
Net Income	46,562	208,525	180,034	152,237	151,376	150,331	127,948	92,088
Average Shares	39,462	39,352	38,845	37,800	37,908	36,833	35,757	34,013
Balance Sheet								
Current Assets	3,388,365	3,649,781	3,899,989	2,931,733	2,580,461	2,438,415	2,209,193	1,840,559
Total Assets	4,183,700	4,444,147	4,713,042	3,325,889	2,963,262	2,833,295	2,499,861	2,100,288
Current Liabilities	1,630,423	1,918,157	2,721,729	1,789,378	1,494,707	1,372,253	1,314,008	1,077,876
Long-Term Obligations	635,250	638,798	264,246	65,405	81,152	223,822	140,333	153,160
Total Liabilities	2,362,905	2,644,766	3,059,484	1,914,667	1,644,239	1,674,916	1,507,191	1,281,918
Stockholders' Equity	1,820,795	1,799,381	1,653,558	1,411,222	1,319,023	1,158,379	992,670	818,370
Shares Outstanding	39,238	39,189	38,924	37,210	36,628	36,164	35,570	33,602
Statistical Record								
Return on Assets %	5.04	4.55	4.48	4.84	5.21	5.64	5.56	4.46
Return on Equity %	11.91	12.08	11.75	11.15	12.19	13.98	14.13	12.29
EBITDA Margin %	3.39	3.43	2.90	2.58	2.76	2.69	2.52	2.23
Net Margin %	1.49	1.56	1.30	1.40	1.47	1.44	1.49	1.19
Asset Turnover	3.20	2.91	3.44	3.45	3.54	3.90	3.75	3.74
Current Ratio	2.08	1.90	1.43	1.64	1.73	1.78	1.68	1.71
Debt to Equity	0.35	0.36	0.16	0.05	0.06	0.19	0.14	0.19
Price Range	96.10-71.23	96.10-68.43	76.94-52.36	66.42-32.60	43.89-28.42	36.60-23.20	32.09-23.06	32.14-8.86
P/E Ratio	18.34-13.59	18.34-13.06	16.84-11.46	21.71-10.65	11.00-7.12	8.97-5.69	8.96-6.44	11.90-3.28
Average Yield %	0.78	0.72	0.19	...	...	...	...	...

Address: 44201 Nobel Drive, Fremont, CA 94538 Telephone: 510-656-3333	Web Site: www.synnex.com Officers: Dwight A. Steffensen - Chairman Kevin M. Murai - President, Chief Executive Officer, Co-Chief Executive Officer	Auditors: KPMG LLP Transfer Agents: Computershare Trust Company, Providence, RI

SYNOVUS FINANCIAL CORP.

Exchange	Symbol	Price	52Wk Range	Yield	P/E
NYS	SNV	$32.17 (5/31/2016)	33.56-25.95	1.49	19.74

*7 Year Price Score 124.10 *NYSE Composite Index=100 ***12 Month Price Score 98.67**

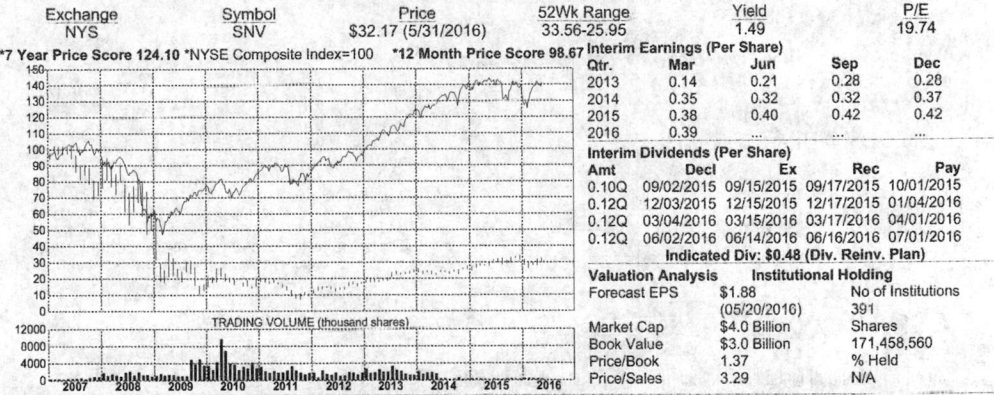

Interim Earnings (Per Share)

Qtr.	Mar	Jun	Sep	Dec
2013	0.14	0.21	0.28	0.28
2014	0.35	0.32	0.32	0.37
2015	0.38	0.40	0.42	0.42
2016	0.39	...	...	...

Interim Dividends (Per Share)

Amt	Decl	Ex	Rec	Pay
0.10Q	09/02/2015	09/15/2015	09/17/2015	10/01/2015
0.12Q	12/03/2015	12/15/2015	12/17/2015	01/04/2016
0.12Q	03/04/2016	03/15/2016	03/17/2016	04/01/2016
0.12Q	06/02/2016	06/14/2016	06/16/2016	07/01/2016

Indicated Div: $0.48 (Div. Reinv. Plan)

Valuation Analysis		Institutional Holding	
Forecast EPS	$1.88	No of Institutions	
	(05/20/2016)	391	
Market Cap	$4.0 Billion	Shares	
Book Value	$3.0 Billion	171,458,560	
Price/Book	1.37	% Held	
Price/Sales	3.29	N/A	

Business Summary: Banking (MIC: 5.1.1 SIC: 6021 NAIC: 522110)

Synovus Financial is a financial services company and a bank holding company. Through its subsidiary bank, Synovus Bank, Co. provides financial services, including commercial and retail banking, financial management, insurance, and mortgage services to its customers in Georgia, Florida, South Carolina, Alabama, and Tennessee. In addition to its banking operations, Co., through other non-bank subsidiaries, also provides various other financial services such as portfolio management and investment banking, trust, asset management and financial planning services, as well as mortgage services. As of Dec 31 2015, Co. had total assets of $28.79 billion and total deposits of $23.24 billion.

Recent Developments: For the quarter ended Mar 31 2016, net income decreased 2.7% to US$52.5 million from US$54.0 million in the year-earlier quarter. Net interest income increased 7.3% to US$218.2 million from US$203.3 million in the year-earlier quarter. Provision for loan losses was US$9.4 million versus US$4.4 million in the prior-year quarter, an increase of 113.3%. Non-interest income fell 4.1% to US$63.1 million from US$65.9 million, while non-interest expense advanced 5.2% to US$188.2 million.

Prospects: Our evaluation of Synovus Financial Corp. as of June 19, 2016 is the result of our systematic analysis on three basic characteristics: earnings strength, relative valuation, and recent stock price movement. The company has produced a positive trend in earnings per share over the past 5 quarters and while recent estimates for the company have remained steady, SNV has posted results that fell short of analysts expectations. Based on operating earnings yield, the company is undervalued when compared to all of the companies in our coverage universe. Share price changes over the past year indicates that SNV will perform well over the near term.

Financial Data

(US$ in Thousands)	3 Mos	12/31/2015	12/31/2014	12/31/2013	12/31/2012	12/31/2011	12/31/2010	12/31/2009
Earnings Per Share	1.63	1.62	1.33	0.91	5.95	(1.05)	(8.68)	(27.93)
Cash Flow Per Share	3.92	3.38	2.79	4.74	4.19	5.76	9.43	8.13
Tang Book Value Per Share	22.27	22.00	21.24	20.12	22.98	16.47	18.04	26.89
Dividends Per Share	0.440	0.420	0.240	0.280	0.280	...	0.280	0.280
Dividend Payout %	26.99	25.93	18.05	30.77	4.71	...	...	...
Income Statement								
Interest Income	249,323	945,962	928,692	929,014	1,004,140	1,141,756	1,320,581	1,509,189
Interest Expense	31,130	118,644	109,408	118,822	150,023	217,602	334,248	498,879
Net Interest Income	218,193	827,318	819,284	810,192	854,117	924,154	986,333	1,010,310
Provision for Losses	9,377	19,010	33,831	69,598	320,369	418,795	1,131,274	1,805,599
Non-Interest Income	63,147	267,920	260,537	253,242	309,285	341,213	309,389	408,967
Non-Interest Expense	188,233	717,655	743,431	741,208	811,556	906,104	1,013,618	1,219,586
Income Before Taxes	83,730	358,573	302,559	252,628	31,477	(59,532)	(849,170)	(1,605,908)
Income Taxes	31,199	132,491	107,310	93,245	(798,732)	1,312	(15,151)	(171,777)
Net Income	52,531	226,082	195,249	159,383	830,209	(60,624)	(790,678)	(1,431,705)
Average Shares	127,857	133,201	139,154	134,225	130,014	112,181	97,883	53,277
Balance Sheet								
Net Loans & Leases	22,503,687	22,177,069	20,839,988	19,760,923	19,178,975	19,573,475	21,009,581	24,476,159
Total Assets	29,171,257	28,792,653	27,051,231	26,201,604	26,760,012	27,162,845	30,093,148	32,831,418
Total Deposits	23,449,928	23,242,661	21,531,700	20,876,790	21,057,044	22,411,752	24,500,304	27,433,533
Total Liabilities	26,217,989	25,792,457	24,009,961	23,252,619	23,190,581	24,335,393	27,095,230	29,980,377
Stockholders' Equity	2,953,268	3,000,196	3,041,270	2,948,985	3,569,431	2,827,452	2,997,918	2,851,041
Shares Outstanding	125,849	129,547	136,122	138,907	112,368	112,185	112,180	69,975
Statistical Record								
Return on Assets %	0.79	0.81	0.73	0.60	3.07	N.M.	N.M.	N.M.
Return on Equity %	7.51	7.48	6.52	4.89	25.89	N.M.	N.M.	N.M.
Net Interest Margin %	87.51	87.46	88.22	87.21	85.06	80.94	74.69	66.94
Efficiency Ratio %	60.24	59.12	62.51	62.69	61.79	61.10	62.19	63.58
Loans to Deposits	0.96	0.95	0.97	0.95	0.91	0.87	0.86	0.89
Price Range	33.56-25.95	33.56-24.49	27.51-21.84	25.20-17.08	17.85-10.71	20.34-6.86	26.74-13.79	58.10-10.43
P/E Ratio	20.59-15.92	20.72-15.12	20.68-16.42	27.69-18.77	3.00-1.80	...	...	...
Average Yield %	1.46	1.42	0.99	1.33	1.92	...	1.50	1.18

Address: 1111 Bay Avenue, Suite 500, Columbus, GA 31901	Web Site: www.synovus.com	Auditors: KPMG LLP
Telephone: 706-649-2311	Officers: Kessel D. Stelling - Chairman, President, Chief Executive Officer Allan E. Kamensky - Executive Vice President, General Counsel, Corporate Secretary	Investor Contact: 706-649-3555
		Transfer Agents: American Stock Transfer & Trust Company, LLC., Brooklyn, NY

SYSCO CORP.

Exchange	Symbol	Price	52Wk Range	Yield	P/E	Div Achiever
NYS	SYY	$48.11 (5/31/2016)	50.22-35.68	2.58	34.61	39 Years

*7 Year Price Score 107.43 *NYSE Composite Index=100 *12 Month Price Score 113.55

TRADING VOLUME (thousand shares)

Interim Earnings (Per Share)

Qtr.	Sep	Dec	Mar	Jun
2012-13	0.49	0.38	0.34	0.47
2013-14	0.48	0.36	0.31	0.43
2014-15	0.47	0.27	0.30	0.12
2015-16	0.41	0.48	0.38	...

Interim Dividends (Per Share)

Amt	Decl	Ex	Rec	Pay
0.30Q	08/21/2015	09/30/2015	10/02/2015	10/23/2015
0.31Q	11/18/2015	01/06/2016	01/08/2016	01/22/2016
0.31Q	02/19/2016	03/30/2016	04/01/2016	04/22/2016
0.31Q	05/20/2016	06/29/2016	07/01/2016	07/22/2016

Indicated Div: $1.24 (Div. Reinv. Plan)

Valuation Analysis

		Institutional Holding	
Forecast EPS	$2.04	No of Institutions	1351
	(05/20/2016)		
Market Cap	$27.2 Billion	Shares	549,839,808
Book Value	$4.0 Billion	% Held	79.32
Price/Book	6.85		
Price/Sales	0.55		

Business Summary: Retail - Food & Beverage, Drug & Tobacco (MIC: 2.1.2 SIC: 5141 NAIC: 424410)

Sysco, acting through its subsidiaries and divisions, is a distributor of food and related products primarily to the foodservice or food-away-from-home industry. Co.'s segments include Broadline and SYGMA. The Broadline segment has operating companies distributing a line of food products and a variety of non-food products to their customers. The SYGMA segment has operating companies distributing a line of food products and a variety of non-food products to chain restaurant customer locations. Co.'s other segments include its produce companies, custom-cut meat companies, lodging industry products companies and a company that distributes imported products.

Recent Developments: For the quarter ended Mar 26 2016, net income increased 22.7% to US$217.1 million from US$177.0 million in the year-earlier quarter. Revenues were US$12.00 billion, up 2.2% from US$11.75 billion the year before. Operating income was US$377.6 million versus US$327.3 million in the prior-year quarter, an increase of 15.4%. Direct operating expenses rose 1.8% to US$9.86 billion from US$9.69 billion in the comparable period the year before. Indirect operating expenses increased 2.0% to US$1.77 billion from US$1.73 billion in the equivalent prior-year period.

Prospects: Our evaluation of Sysco Corp. as of June 19, 2016 is the result of our systematic analysis on three basic characteristics: earnings strength, relative valuation, and recent stock price movement. The company has produced a positive trend in earnings per share over the past 5 quarters and while recent estimates for the company have remained steady, SYY has posted better than expected results. Based on operating earnings yield, the company is about fairly valued when compared to all of the companies in our coverage universe. Share price changes over the past year indicates that SYY will perform very well over the near term.

Financial Data

(US$ in Thousands)	9 Mos	6 Mos	3 Mos	06/27/2015	06/28/2014	06/29/2013	06/30/2012	07/02/2011
Earnings Per Share	1.39	1.31	1.10	1.15	1.58	1.67	1.90	1.96
Cash Flow Per Share	2.97	2.77	2.06	2.63	2.55	2.57	2.40	1.87
Tang Book Value Per Share	3.00	3.18	5.29	5.29	5.36	5.29	4.96	5.01
Dividends Per Share	1.210	1.200	1.190	1.180	1.140	1.100	1.079	1.030
Dividend Payout %	87.05	91.60	108.18	102.61	72.15	65.87	56.32	52.55
Income Statement								
Total Revenue	36,719,028	24,716,237	12,562,611	48,680,752	46,516,712	44,411,233	42,380,939	39,323,489
EBITDA	1,369,719	962,698	514,875	1,758,754	2,093,165	2,149,450	2,282,298	2,319,721
Depn & Amortn	36,088	13,637	6,161	495,800	493,800	473,500	384,900	374,000
Income Before Taxes	1,101,790	774,919	381,807	1,008,147	1,475,624	1,547,455	1,784,002	1,827,454
Income Taxes	367,835	258,100	137,387	321,374	544,091	555,028	662,417	675,424
Net Income	733,955	516,819	244,420	686,773	931,533	992,427	1,121,585	1,152,030
Average Shares	570,814	571,452	600,789	596,849	590,216	592,675	588,991	588,691
Balance Sheet								
Current Assets	6,960,033	6,779,026	7,027,960	11,494,304	6,681,972	6,207,427	6,084,808	5,732,882
Total Assets	13,351,094	13,089,468	13,371,551	17,989,281	13,167,950	12,663,947	12,094,972	11,385,555
Current Liabilities	4,112,072	3,872,214	3,970,816	9,399,615	4,367,630	3,749,282	3,423,579	3,575,075
Long-Term Obligations	4,274,884	4,265,857	3,004,618	2,271,825	2,384,167	2,639,986	2,763,688	2,279,517
Total Liabilities	9,381,663	9,148,041	8,065,866	12,729,057	7,901,255	7,472,137	7,409,932	6,680,313
Stockholders' Equity	3,969,431	3,941,427	5,305,685	5,260,224	5,266,695	5,191,810	4,685,040	4,705,242
Shares Outstanding	564,951	566,622	596,122	594,317	586,124	586,106	585,946	591,577
Statistical Record								
Return on Assets %	5.15	4.94	4.83	4.42	7.23	8.04	9.58	10.65
Return on Equity %	17.39	16.52	12.28	13.08	17.86	20.15	23.95	27.08
EBITDA Margin %	3.73	3.90	4.10	3.61	4.50	4.84	5.39	5.90
Net Margin %	2.00	2.09	1.95	1.41	2.00	2.23	2.65	2.93
Asset Turnover	3.14	3.15	3.62	3.13	3.61	3.60	3.62	3.63
Current Ratio	1.69	1.75	1.77	1.22	1.53	1.66	1.78	1.60
Debt to Equity	1.08	1.08	0.57	0.43	0.45	0.51	0.59	0.48
Price Range	46.63-35.68	41.79-35.68	41.38-35.68	41.25-35.54	37.85-31.16	35.24-28.31	31.55-25.47	32.65-27.29
P/E Ratio	33.55-25.67	31.90-27.24	37.62-32.44	35.87-30.90	23.96-19.72	21.10-16.95	16.61-13.41	16.66-13.92
Average Yield %	3.04	3.08	3.10	3.09	3.26	3.44	3.75	3.50

Address: 1390 Enclave Parkway, Houston, TX 77077-2099	Web Site: www.sysco.com	Auditors: Ernst & Young LLP
Telephone: 281-584-1390	Officers: Thomas L. Bene - President, Chief Operating Officer, Division Officer, Executive Vice President, Chief Commercial Officer William J. DeLaney - President, Chief Executive Officer	Investor Contact: 281-584-1308
Fax: 281-584-2880		Transfer Agents: American Stock Transfer & Trust Company, New York, NY

TABLEAU SOFTWARE, INC.

Exchange	Symbol	Price	52Wk Range	Yield	P/E
NYS	DATA	$51.44 (5/31/2016)	128.74-37.22	N/A	N/A

*7 Year Price Score N/A   *NYSE Composite Index=100   *12 Month Price Score 58.56

Interim Earnings (Per Share)

Qtr.	Mar	Jun	Sep	Dec
2013	(0.12)	(0.05)	0.03	0.21
2014	(0.09)	(0.07)	(0.07)	0.27
2015	(0.14)	(0.27)	(0.19)	(0.58)
2016	(0.62)	...	...	...

Interim Dividends (Per Share)

No Dividends Paid

Valuation Analysis

		Institutional Holding	
Forecast EPS	$0.56	No of Institutions	
	(05/20/2016)	378	
Market Cap	$3.8 Billion	Shares	
Book Value	$735.2 Million	52,293,976	
Price/Book	5.21	% Held	
Price/Sales	5.51	73.84	

TRADING VOLUME (thousand shares)

Chart years: 2007 2008 2009 2010 2011 2012 2013 2014 2015 2016

Business Summary: Internet & Software (MIC: 6.3.2 SIC: 7372 NAIC: 511210)

Tableau Software provides software products that enable a population of business users to engage with their data, ask questions, and mitigate challenges. As of Dec 31 2014, Co. provided four products: Tableau Desktop, an analytics product for anyone with data; Tableau Server, a business platform for organizations; Tableau Online, a cloud-based hosted version of Tableau Server; and Tableau Public, a cloud-based platform for analyzing and sharing public data. Co's products are built on a foundation of proprietary technologies, such as VizQL, its Live Query Engine and In-Memory Data Engine, which work together to develop its Hybrid Data Architecture.

Recent Developments: For the quarter ended Mar 31 2016, net loss amounted to US$45.6 million versus a net loss of US$10.0 million in the year-earlier quarter. Revenues were US$171.7 million, up 31.9% from US$130.1 million the year before. Operating loss was US$46.4 million versus a loss of US$13.8 million in the prior-year quarter. Direct operating expenses rose 45.9% to US$22.5 million from US$15.4 million in the comparable period the year before. Indirect operating expenses increased 52.2% to US$195.6 million from US$128.5 million in the equivalent prior-year period.

Prospects: Our evaluation of Tableau Software, Inc. as of June 19, 2016 is the result of our systematic analysis on three basic characteristics: earnings strength, relative valuation, and recent stock price movement. The company has managed to produce a neutral trend in earnings per share over the past 5 quarters and while recent estimates for the company have been raised by analysts, DATA has posted better than expected results. Based on operating earnings yield, the company is overvalued when compared to all of the companies in our coverage universe. Share price changes over the past year indicates that DATA will perform very poorly over the near term.

Financial Data

(US$ in Thousands)	3 Mos	12/31/2015	12/31/2014	12/31/2013	12/31/2012	12/31/2011	12/31/2010
Earnings Per Share	(1.66)	(1.17)	0.04	0.12	...	0.04	0.03
Cash Flow Per Share	1.89	1.91	1.32	0.75	0.42	0.39	0.32
Tang Book Value Per Share	9.67	10.03	9.62	3.93	0.87	0.60	...
Income Statement							
Total Revenue	171,698	653,587	412,616	232,440	127,733	62,360	34,161
EBITDA	(37,114)	(27,107)	20,682	9,765	8,004	6,002	3,840
Depn & Amortn	7,607	23,700	13,500	6,900	3,800	2,100	1,000
Income Before Taxes	(44,721)	(50,807)	7,182	2,865	4,204	3,902	2,840
Income Taxes	857	32,893	1,309	(4,211)	2,777	523	102
Net Income	(45,578)	(83,700)	5,873	7,076	1,427	3,379	2,738
Average Shares	73,816	71,701	74,319	59,092	39,652	39,431	37,833
Balance Sheet							
Current Assets	936,459	944,739	810,261	332,181	76,161	45,440	...
Total Assets	1,044,657	1,030,711	865,662	354,927	86,992	51,277	...
Current Liabilities	282,001	272,601	180,274	104,289	51,930	28,259	...
Total Liabilities	309,465	296,766	193,656	110,267	57,018	31,523	...
Stockholders' Equity	735,192	733,945	672,006	244,660	29,974	19,754	...
Shares Outstanding	74,394	73,204	69,868	62,198	34,317	33,084	32,979
Statistical Record							
Return on Assets %	N.M.	N.M.	0.96	3.20	2.06	...	...
Return on Equity %	N.M.	N.M.	1.28	5.15	5.72	...	...
EBITDA Margin %	N.M.	N.M.	5.01	4.20	6.27	9.62	11.24
Net Margin %	N.M.	N.M.	1.42	3.04	1.12	5.42	8.01
Asset Turnover	0.72	0.69	0.68	1.05	1.84	...	...
Current Ratio	3.32	3.47	4.49	3.19	1.47	1.61	...
Price Range	128.74-37.22	128.74-77.58	100.28-54.13	74.75-48.53	...	...	...
P/E Ratio	...	...	2,507..-1,353.25	622.92-404.42	...	...	...

Address: 837 North 34th Street, Suite 200, Seattle, WA 98103
Telephone: 206-633-3400

Web Site: www.tableausoftware.com
Officers: Christian Chabot - Chairman, Chief Executive Officer, Co-Founder Kelly Wright - Executive Vice President

Auditors: PricewaterhouseCoopers LLP
Transfer Agents: American Stock Transfer & Trust Company

TAHOE RESOURCES INC.

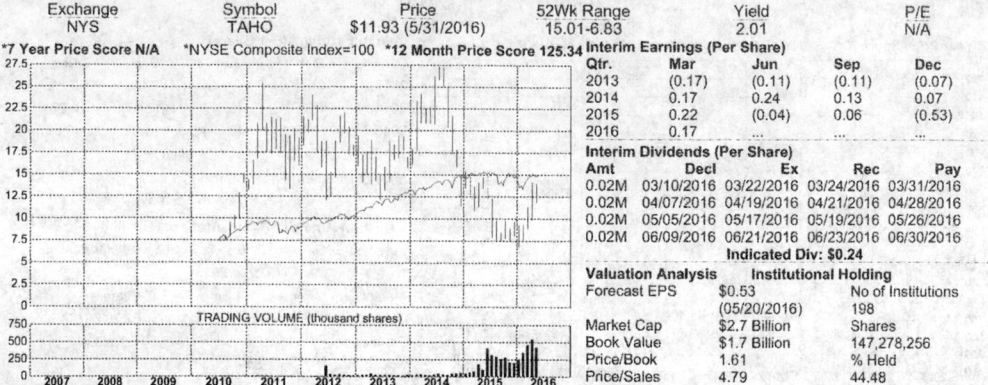

Exchange	Symbol	Price	52Wk Range	Yield	P/E
NYS	TAHO	$11.93 (5/31/2016)	15.01-6.83	2.01	N/A

*7 Year Price Score N/A   *NYSE Composite Index=100   *12 Month Price Score 125.34

Interim Earnings (Per Share)

Qtr.	Mar	Jun	Sep	Dec
2013	(0.17)	(0.11)	(0.11)	(0.07)
2014	0.17	0.24	0.13	0.07
2015	0.22	(0.04)	0.06	(0.53)
2016	0.17	...	...	...

Interim Dividends (Per Share)

Amt	Decl	Ex	Rec	Pay
0.02M	03/10/2016	03/22/2016	03/24/2016	03/31/2016
0.02M	04/07/2016	04/19/2016	04/21/2016	04/28/2016
0.02M	05/05/2016	05/17/2016	05/19/2016	05/26/2016
0.02M	06/09/2016	06/21/2016	06/23/2016	06/30/2016

Indicated Div: $0.24

Valuation Analysis

		Institutional Holding	
Forecast EPS	$0.53	No of Institutions	
	(05/20/2016)	198	
Market Cap	$2.7 Billion	Shares	
Book Value	$1.7 Billion	147,278,256	
Price/Book	1.61	% Held	
Price/Sales	4.79	44.48	

TRADING VOLUME (thousand shares)

Business Summary: Precious Metals (MIC: 8.2.1 SIC: 1044 NAIC: 212222)

Tahoe Resources is engaged in the acquisition, exploration and development of mineral properties in the Americas for the mining of precious metals. All mineral properties, land, plant and equipment are situated in Guatemala.

Recent Developments: For the quarter ended Mar 31 2016, net income increased 18.6% to US$37.8 million from US$31.9 million in the year-earlier quarter. Revenues were US$132.1 million, up 54.9% from US$85.3 million the year before. Operating income was US$46.4 million versus US$38.7 million in the prior-year quarter, an increase of 19.8%. Direct operating expenses rose 92.5% to US$77.5 million from US$40.3 million in the comparable period the year before. Indirect operating expenses increased 30.5% to US$8.3 million from US$6.3 million in the equivalent prior-year period.

Prospects: Our evaluation of Tahoe Resources Inc. as of June 19, 2016 is the result of our systematic analysis on three basic characteristics: earnings strength, relative valuation, and recent stock price movement. The company has managed to produce a neutral trend in earnings per share over the past 5 quarters and while recent estimates for the company have been raised by analysts, TAHO has posted better than expected results. Based on operating earnings yield, the company is about fairly valued when compared to all of the companies in our coverage universe. Share price changes over the past year indicates that TAHO will perform poorly over the near term.

Financial Data
(US$ in Thousands)

	3 Mos	12/31/2015	12/31/2014	12/31/2013	12/31/2012	12/31/2011	12/31/2010
Earnings Per Share	(0.34)	(0.35)	0.61	(0.45)	(0.65)	(0.48)	(0.12)
Cash Flow Per Share	...	0.80	0.81	(0.45)	(0.61)	(0.35)	(0.15)
Tang Book Value Per Share	7.18	7.06	5.95	5.30	5.71	6.36	6.78
Dividends Per Share	...	0.240	0.020	...	...	...	...
Dividend Payout %	0.240	...	3.28	...	...	...	...
Income Statement							
Total Revenue	132,133	519,721	350,265	...	...	...	...
EBITDA	67,623	...	...	...	...	...	...
Depn & Amortn	18,114	(84,945)	(47,088)	(13,029)	(6,869)	(1,200)	...
Income Before Taxes	47,636	...	...	...	...	...	...
Income Taxes	9,828	(16,321)	24,900	1,621	(310)	406	197
Net Income	37,808	(71,911)	90,790	(65,597)	(93,453)	(69,166)	(8,010)
Average Shares	227,898	207,810	147,992	145,842	144,634	142,798	67,801
Balance Sheet							
Current Assets	203,618	228,201	134,584	35,811	166,270	350,113	436,663
Total Assets	2,005,860	2,002,461	975,628	883,333	852,943	922,005	958,120
Current Liabilities	119,814	150,880	91,875	104,965	16,925	9,811	2,792
Long-Term Obligations	6,300	7,711	...	...	...	...	...
Total Liabilities	314,493	338,430	97,568	109,179	21,646	10,351	3,061
Stockholders' Equity	1,691,367	1,664,031	878,060	774,154	831,297	911,654	955,059
Shares Outstanding	227,660	227,401	147,644	146,094	145,565	143,427	140,874
Statistical Record							
Return on Assets %	N.M.	N.M.	9.77	N.M.	N.M.	N.M.	...
Return on Equity %	N.M.	N.M.	10.99	N.M.	N.M.	N.M.	...
EBITDA Margin %	51.18	...	...	...	...	...	...
Net Margin %	28.61	N.M.	25.92	...	...	...	...
Asset Turnover	0.38	0.35	0.38	...	...	...	...
Current Ratio	1.70	1.51	1.46	0.34	9.82	35.69	156.40
Price Range	15.01-6.83	15.34-7.47	27.31-11.43	19.45-12.05	24.00-12.02	25.35-13.15	15.05-7.30
P/E Ratio	...	...	44.77-18.74	...	...	...	...
Average Yield %	2.20	2.18	0.09	...	...	...	...

Address: 5310 Kietzke Lane, Suite 200, Reno, NV 89511	Web Site: www.tahoeresourcesinc.com	Auditors: Deloitte LLP
Telephone: 775-448-5800	Officers: C. Kevin McArthur - President, Chief Executive Officer Ronald W. Clayton - Vice President, Chief Operating Officer	Investor Contact: 775-448-5807
Fax: 775-398-7020		Transfer Agents: Computershare Investor Services Inc., Vancouver, British Columbia, Canada

TANGER FACTORY OUTLET CENTERS, INC.

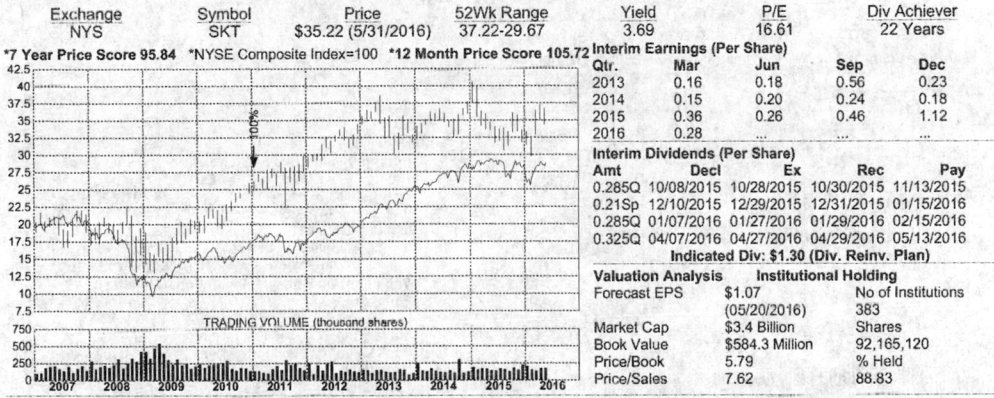

Exchange	Symbol	Price	52Wk Range	Yield	P/E	Div Achiever
NYS	SKT	$35.22 (5/31/2016)	37.22-29.67	3.69	16.61	22 Years

*7 Year Price Score 95.84 ***NYSE Composite Index=100** ***12 Month Price Score 105.72**

Interim Earnings (Per Share)

Qtr.	Mar	Jun	Sep	Dec
2013	0.16	0.18	0.56	0.23
2014	0.15	0.20	0.24	0.18
2015	0.36	0.26	0.46	1.12
2016	0.28	...	...	...

Interim Dividends (Per Share)

Amt	Decl	Ex	Rec	Pay
0.285Q	10/08/2015	10/28/2015	10/30/2015	11/13/2015
0.21Sp	12/10/2015	12/29/2015	12/31/2015	01/15/2016
0.285Q	01/07/2016	01/27/2016	01/29/2016	02/15/2016
0.325Q	04/07/2016	04/27/2016	04/29/2016	05/13/2016

Indicated Div: $1.30 (Div. Reinv. Plan)

Valuation Analysis

Valuation Analysis		Institutional Holding	
Forecast EPS	$1.07	No of Institutions	
	(05/20/2016)	383	
Market Cap	$3.4 Billion	Shares	
Book Value	$584.3 Million	92,165,120	
Price/Book	5.79	% Held	
Price/Sales	7.62	88.83	

TRADING VOLUME (thousand shares)

Business Summary: REITs (MIC: 5.3.1 SIC: 6798 NAIC: 525930)

Tanger Factory Outlet Centers, along with its subsidiaries owns and operates outlet centers in the U.S. and Canada. Co. is a self-administered and self-managed real estate investment trust, which, through its controlling interest in Tanger Properties Limited Partnership and subsidiaries, focuses on developing, acquiring, owning, operating and managing outlet shopping centers. As of Dec 31 2015, Co.'s consolidated portfolio consisted of 34 outlet centers. Co. also had partial ownership interests in nine unconsolidated outlet centers, including four outlet centers in Canada. Each of Co.'s outlet centers, except one joint venture property, carries the Tanger brand name.

Recent Developments: For the quarter ended Mar 31 2016, net income decreased 21.4% to US$28.6 million from US$36.4 million in the year-earlier quarter. Revenues were US$110.8 million, up 4.6% from US$105.9 million the year before. Revenues from property income rose 4.4% to US$109.1 million from US$104.5 million in the corresponding quarter a year earlier.

Prospects: Our evaluation of Tanger Factory Outlet Centers Inc. as of June 19, 2016 is the result of our systematic analysis on three basic characteristics: earnings strength, relative valuation, and recent stock price movement. The company has produced a positive trend in earnings per share over the past 5 quarters. Because the company lacks sufficient analyst estimate data, we place greater weight on the historical EPS trend as the measure of earnings strength. Based on operating earnings yield, the company is overvalued when compared to all of the companies in our coverage universe. Share price changes over the past year indicates that SKT will perform in line with the market over the near term.

Financial Data

(US$ in Thousands)	3 Mos	12/31/2015	12/31/2014	12/31/2013	12/31/2012	12/31/2011	12/31/2010	12/31/2009
Earnings Per Share	2.12	2.20	0.77	1.13	0.57	0.52	0.32	0.72
Cash Flow Per Share	2.32	2.33	2.01	2.01	1.80	1.64	1.48	1.77
Tang Book Value Per Share	6.08	3.81	2.96	2.78	3.85	5.31	3.61	3.81
Dividends Per Share	1.350	1.305	0.945	0.885	0.830	0.794	0.772	0.764
Dividend Payout %	63.68	59.32	122.73	78.32	145.61	152.64	241.41	106.08
Income Statement								
Total Revenue	110,805	439,369	418,558	385,009	356,997	315,223	276,303	271,685
EBITDA	42,369	350,808	206,336	228,597	183,285	164,136	137,426	171,590
Depn & Amortn	2,367	85,900	80,100	74,700	73,700	66,200	64,500	64,900
Income Before Taxes	25,118	210,684	69,099	102,281	59,771	52,554	38,806	69,007
Net Income	27,150	211,200	74,011	107,557	53,228	44,641	34,249	58,019
Average Shares	95,003	94,759	93,839	94,247	92,661	84,129	80,390	72,024
Balance Sheet								
Current Assets	18,877	142,864	62,880	15,241	10,335	7,894	6,481	3,267
Total Assets	2,190,606	2,326,707	2,097,660	2,006,456	1,672,425	1,621,815	1,216,934	1,178,861
Current Liabilities	67,608	125,784	97,946	87,850	48,233	51,413	63,425	46,110
Long-Term Obligations	1,475,668	1,563,806	1,443,194	1,328,049	1,093,537	1,025,542	714,616	584,611
Total Liabilities	1,606,334	1,751,570	1,600,841	1,484,197	1,189,816	1,161,253	850,005	716,190
Stockholders' Equity	584,272	575,137	496,819	-522,259	482,609	460,562	366,929	462,671
Shares Outstanding	96,126	95,880	95,509	94,505	94,061	86,727	80,996	80,554
Statistical Record								
Return on Assets %	9.44	9.55	3.61	5.85	3.22	3.15	2.86	5.04
Return on Equity %	37.61	39.40	14.53	21.41	11.26	10.79	8.26	16.80
EBITDA Margin %	38.24	79.84	49.30	59.37	51.34	52.07	49.74	63.16
Net Margin %	24.50	48.07	17.68	27.94	14.91	14.16	12.40	21.36
Asset Turnover	0.21	0.20	0.20	0.21	0.22	0.22	0.23	0.24
Current Ratio	0.28	1.14	0.64	0.17	0.21	0.15	0.10	0.07
Debt to Equity	2.53	2.72	2.90	2.54	2.27	2.23	1.95	1.26
Price Range	36.39-29.67	40.55-30.58	37.65-32.02	38.57-30.14	34.43-28.10	29.82-22.39	25.85-18.68	20.68-12.96
P/E Ratio	17.17-14.00	18.43-13.90	48.90-41.58	34.13-26.67	60.40-49.30	57.35-43.06	80.78-58.36	28.72-18.00
Average Yield %	4.05	3.79	2.70	2.58	2.63	2.96	3.49	4.46

Address: 3200 Northline Avenue, Suite 360, Greensboro, NC 27408	**Web Site:** www.tangeroutlet.com	**Auditors:** Deloitte & Touche LLP
Telephone: 336-292-3010	**Officers:** Steven B. Tanger - President, Chief Executive Officer James F. Williams - Chief Financial Officer, Senior Vice President, Chief Accounting Officer, Controller, Associate/Affiliate Company Officer	**Investor Contact:** 336-834-6892
Fax: 336-297-0931		**Transfer Agents:** Computershare Trust Company, NA, Providence, RI

TARGET CORP

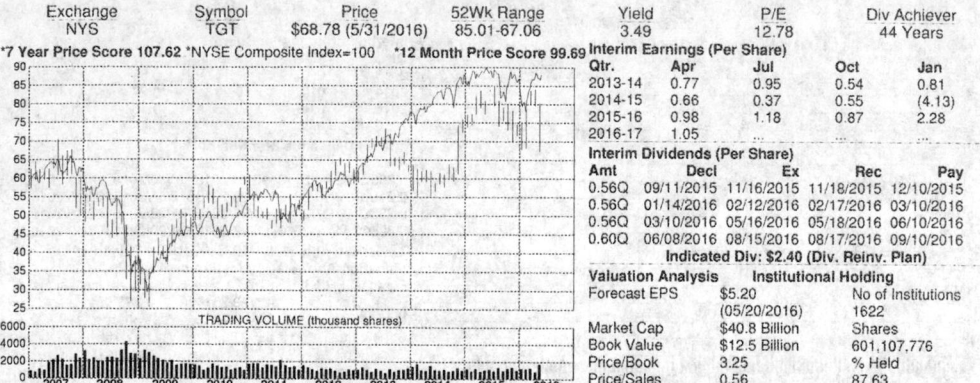

Exchange	Symbol	Price	52Wk Range	Yield	P/E	Div Achiever
NYS	TGT	$68.78 (5/31/2016)	85.01-67.06	3.49	12.78	44 Years

*7 Year Price Score 107.62 *NYSE Composite Index=100 *12 Month Price Score 99.69

Interim Earnings (Per Share)

Qtr.	Apr	Jul	Oct	Jan
2013-14	0.77	0.95	0.54	0.81
2014-15	0.66	0.37	0.55	(4.13)
2015-16	0.98	1.18	0.87	2.28
2016-17	1.05	...	...	...

Interim Dividends (Per Share)

Amt	Decl	Ex	Rec	Pay
0.56Q	09/11/2015	11/16/2015	11/18/2015	12/10/2015
0.56Q	01/14/2016	02/12/2016	02/17/2016	03/10/2016
0.56Q	03/10/2016	05/16/2016	05/18/2016	06/10/2016
0.60Q	06/08/2016	08/15/2016	08/17/2016	09/10/2016

Indicated Div: $2.40 (Div. Reinv. Plan)

Valuation Analysis   **Institutional Holding**

Forecast EPS	$5.20	No of Institutions
	(05/20/2016)	1622
Market Cap	$40.8 Billion	Shares
Book Value	$12.5 Billion	601,107,776
Price/Book	3.25	% Held
Price/Sales	0.56	87.63

Business Summary: Retail - General Merchandise/Department Stores (MIC: 2.1.1 SIC: 5331 NAIC: 452990)

Target sells a range of general merchandise and food. The majority of Co.'s general merchandise stores sell an edited food assortment, including perishables, dry grocery, dairy, and frozen items. Co.'s digital channels include a range of general merchandise, including items found in Co.'s stores, along with a complementary assortment such as additional sizes and colors sold only online. Co. also sells merchandise through periodic design and partnerships and provide in-store amenities such as Target Cafe and Target Photo, and leased or licensed departments such as Target Optical, Portrait Studio, Starbucks, and other food service offerings. At Jan. 31, 2016, Co. had 1,792 stores in the U.S.

Recent Developments: For the quarter ended Apr 30 2016, income from continuing operations decreased 5.7% to US$614.0 million from US$651.0 million in the year-earlier quarter. Net income decreased 0.5% to US$632.0 million from US$635.0 million in the year-earlier quarter. Revenues were US$16.20 billion, down 5.4% from US$17.12 billion the year before. Operating income was US$1.31 billion versus US$1.15 billion in the prior-year quarter, an increase of 13.7%. Direct operating expenses declined 6.1% to US$11.19 billion from US$11.91 billion in the comparable period the year before. Indirect operating expenses decreased 8.8% to US$3.70 billion from US$4.05 billion in the equivalent prior-year period.

Prospects: Our evaluation of Target Corp. as of June 19, 2016 is the result of our systematic analysis on three basic characteristics: earnings strength, relative valuation, and recent stock price movement. The company has managed to produce a neutral trend in earnings per share over the past 5 quarters. However, while recent estimates for the company have been lowered by analysts, TGT has posted better than expected results. Based on operating earnings yield, the company is undervalued when compared to all of the companies in our coverage universe. Share price changes over the past year indicates that TGT will perform very well over the near term.

Financial Data

(US$ in Millions)	3 Mos	01/30/2016	01/31/2015	02/01/2014	02/02/2013	01/28/2012	01/29/2011	01/30/2010
Earnings Per Share	5.38	5.31	(2.56)	3.07	4.52	4.28	4.00	3.30
Cash Flow Per Share	7.59	9.34	7.01	10.29	7.98	8.02	7.30	7.84
Tang Book Value Per Share	21.13	21.06	21.39	25.08	25.31	23.28	21.68	20.29
Dividends Per Share	2.200	2.160	1.900	1.580	1.320	1.100	0.840	0.660
Dividend Payout %	40.89	40.68	...	51.47	29.20	25.70	21.00	20.00
Income Statement								
Total Revenue	16,196	73,785	72,618	72,596	73,301	69,865	67,390	65,357
EBITDA	1,858	7,721	6,643	6,427	7,491	7,429	7,312	6,672
Depn & Amortn	546	2,191	2,108	2,198	2,120	2,107	2,060	1,999
Income Before Taxes	897	4,923	3,653	3,103	4,609	4,456	4,495	3,872
Income Taxes	283	1,602	1,204	1,132	1,610	1,527	1,575	1,384
Net Income	632	3,363	(1,636)	1,971	2,999	2,929	2,920	2,488
Average Shares	603	632	640	641	663	683	729	754
Balance Sheet								
Current Assets	13,948	14,130	14,087	11,573	16,388	16,449	17,213	18,424
Total Assets	39,908	40,262	41,404	44,553	48,163	46,630	43,705	44,533
Current Liabilities	12,019	12,622	11,736	12,777	14,031	14,287	10,070	11,327
Long-Term Obligations	12,596	11,945	12,705	12,622	14,654	13,697	15,607	15,118
Total Liabilities	27,363	27,305	27,407	28,322	31,605	30,809	28,218	29,186
Stockholders' Equity	12,545	12,957	13,997	16,231	16,558	15,821	15,487	15,347
Shares Outstanding	593	602	640	632	645	669	704	744
Statistical Record								
Return on Assets %	8.36	8.26	N.M.	4.26	6.23	6.50	6.64	5.63
Return on Equity %	25.15	25.02	N.M.	12.06	18.22	18.76	18.99	17.17
EBITDA Margin %	11.47	10.46	9.15	8.85	10.22	10.63	10.85	10.21
Net Margin %	3.90	4.56	N.M.	2.72	4.09	4.19	4.33	3.81
Asset Turnover	1.81	1.81	1.69	1.57	1.52	1.55	1.53	1.48
Current Ratio	1.16	1.12	1.20	0.91	1.17	1.15	1.71	1.63
Debt to Equity	1.00	0.92	0.91	0.78	0.89	0.87	1.01	0.99
Price Range	85.01-67.59	85.01-67.59	77.13-55.07	73.32-56.64	65.44-50.33	55.56-46.33	60.77-48.64	52.02-25.37
P/E Ratio	15.80-12.56	16.01-12.73	...	23.88-18.45	14.48-11.13	12.98-10.82	15.19-12.16	15.76-7.69
Average Yield %	2.83	2.77	3.03	2.38	2.21	2.17	1.56	1.56

Address: 1000 Nicollet Mall, Minneapolis, MN 55403 **Telephone:** 612-304-6073	**Web Site:** www.target.com **Officers:** Brian C. Cornell - Chairman, Chief Executive Officer Casey L. Carl - Executive Vice President, Chief Strategy Officer, Chief Innovation Officer	**Auditors:** Ernst & Young LLP **Investor Contact:** 800-775-3110 **Transfer Agents:** Mellon Investor Services, South Hackensack, N.J.

TARGA RESOURCES CORP

Exchange	Symbol	Price	52Wk Range	Yield	P/E
NYS	TRGP	$42.83 (5/31/2016)	93.78-15.43	8.50	46.05

*7 Year Price Score N/A ***NYSE Composite Index=100** ***12 Month Price Score 75.05**

TRADING VOLUME (thousand shares)

Interim Earnings (Per Share)

Qtr.	Mar	Jun	Sep	Dec
2013	0.32	0.36	0.39	0.49
2014	0.47	0.63	0.73	0.61
2015	0.07	0.27	0.23	0.49
2016	(0.06)	...	...	...

Interim Dividends (Per Share)

Amt	Decl	Ex	Rec	Pay
0.875Q	07/21/2015	07/30/2015	08/03/2015	08/17/2015
0.91Q	10/20/2015	10/29/2015	11/02/2015	11/16/2015
0.91Q	01/19/2016	01/29/2016	02/02/2016	02/09/2016
0.91Q	04/20/2016	04/29/2016	05/03/2016	05/16/2016

Indicated Div: $3.64

Valuation Analysis

		Institutional Holding	
Forecast EPS	$-0.07	No of Institutions	
	(05/20/2016)	399	
Market Cap	$6.9 Billion	Shares	
Book Value	$5.5 Billion	131,987,416	
Price/Book	1.25	% Held	
Price/Sales	1.07	85.38	

Business Summary: Equipment & Services (MIC: 9.1.3 SIC: 4922 NAIC: 486210)

Targa Resources has general and limited partner interests in Targa Resources Partners LP (the Partnership). The Partnership is engaged in the business of gathering, compressing, treating, processing and selling natural gas and storing, fractionating, treating, transporting, terminaling and selling natural gas liquids (NGLs) and NGL products, and gathering, storing and terminaling crude oil, and refined petroleum products. The Partnership has two primary divisions: Gathering and Processing, consisting of two segments, Field Gathering and Processing, and Coastal Gathering and Processing; and Logistics and Marketing, consisting of two segments, Logistics Assets, and Marketing and Distribution.

Recent Developments:
For the quarter ended Mar 31 2016, net loss amounted to US$700,000 versus net income of US$35.7 million in the year-earlier quarter. Revenues were US$1.44 billion, down 14.1% from US$1.68 billion the year before. Operating income was US$35.5 million versus US$138.2 million in the prior-year quarter, a decrease of 74.3%. Direct operating expenses declined 17.1% to US$1.14 billion from US$1.38 billion in the comparable period the year before. Indirect operating expenses increased 63.0% to US$263.8 million from US$161.8 million in the equivalent prior-year period.

Prospects:
Our evaluation of Targa Resources Corp. as of June 19, 2016 is the result of our systematic analysis on three basic characteristics: earnings strength, relative valuation, and recent stock price movement. The company has suffered a very negative trend in earnings per share over the past 5 quarters. Because the company lacks sufficient analyst estimate data, we place greater weight on the historical EPS trend as the measure of earnings strength. Based on operating earnings yield, the company is about fairly valued when compared to all of the companies in our coverage universe. Share price changes over the past year indicates that TRGP will perform very poorly over the near term.

Financial Data
(US$ in Thousands)	3 Mos	12/31/2015	12/31/2014	12/31/2013	12/31/2012	12/31/2011	12/31/2010	12/31/2009
Earnings Per Share	0.93	1.09	2.43	1.55	0.91	0.74	(30.94)	...
Cash Flow Per Share	9.23	19.34	18.14	9.20	10.42	9.25	32.08	87.39
Tang Book Value Per Share	20.85	N.M.	N.M.	N.M.	N.M.	3.73	3.41	100.43
Dividends Per Share	3.525	3.390	2.678	2.055	1.518	0.932	...	...
Dividend Payout %	379.03	311.01	110.19	132.58	166.76	125.89	...	...
Income Statement								
Total Revenue	1,442,400	6,658,600	8,616,500	6,556,000	5,885,700	6,994,500	5,469,200	4,536,000
EBITDA	64,300	663,000	982,900	656,600	530,900	538,900	375,400	406,600
Depn & Amortn	4,200	540,400	362,800	287,800	215,800	194,000	184,100	179,700
Income Before Taxes	7,200	(109,300)	473,000	234,700	194,300	233,200	80,400	94,800
Income Taxes	3,100	39,600	68,000	48,200	36,900	26,600	22,500	20,700
Net Income	(2,700)	(151,400)	423,000	65,100	38,100	30,700	(15,000)	29,300
Average Shares	106,600	53,600	42,100	42,100	41,800	41,400	6,500	3,842
Balance Sheet								
Current Assets	715,900	920,000	882,600	897,200	733,300	866,500	750,500	745,000
Total Assets	12,949,200	13,253,700	6,453,500	6,048,600	5,105,000	3,831,000	3,393,800	3,367,500
Current Liabilities	693,000	881,600	827,100	770,400	686,600	741,100	624,200	553,800
Long-Term Obligations	4,921,200	5,761,500	2,885,400	2,989,300	2,475,300	1,567,000	1,534,700	1,593,500
Total Liabilities	7,442,500	11,792,300	6,283,700	5,899,800	4,960,900	3,672,900	3,249,500	2,971,700
Stockholders' Equity	5,506,700	1,461,400	169,800	148,800	144,100	158,100	144,300	395,800
Shares Outstanding	160,580	56,020	42,143	42,162	42,294	42,398	42,292	3,940
Statistical Record								
Return on Assets %	N.M.	N.M.	6.77	1.17	0.85	0.85	N.M.	0.84
Return on Equity %	N.M.	N.M.	265.54	44.45	25.15	20.30	N.M.	7.14
EBITDA Margin %	4.46	9.96	11.41	10.02	9.02	7.70	6.86	8.96
Net Margin %	N.M.	N.M.	4.91	0.99	0.65	0.44	N.M.	0.65
Asset Turnover	0.48	0.68	1.38	1.18	1.31	1.94	1.62	1.29
Current Ratio	1.03	1.04	1.07	1.16	1.07	1.17	1.20	1.35
Debt to Equity	0.89	3.94	16.99	20.09	17.18	9.91	10.64	4.03
Price Range	107.22-15.43	107.22-25.74	150.62-85.34	88.46-52.84	52.84-39.62	41.05-26.68	27.53-24.70	...
P/E Ratio	115.29-16.59	98.37-23.61	61.98-35.12	57.07-34.09	58.07-43.54	55.47-36.05	...	...
Average Yield %	5.86	4.40	2.32	2.98	3.30	2.85	...	...

Address: 1000 Louisiana St., Suite 4300, Houston, TX 77002
Telephone: 713-584 1000
Fax: 713 584-1100

Web Site: www.targaresources.com
Officers: James W. Whalen - Executive Chairman, Advisor Joe Bob Perkins - President, Chief Executive Officer

Auditors: PricewaterhouseCoopers LLP
Investor Contact: 713-584-1000
Transfer Agents: Computershare Trust Company, N.A.

TAUBMAN CENTERS, INC.

Exchange	Symbol	Price	52Wk Range	Yield	P/E
NYS	TCO	$68.57 (5/31/2016)	78.75-66.67	3.47	40.34

*7 Year Price Score 97.18   *NYSE Composite Index=100   *12 Month Price Score 96.38

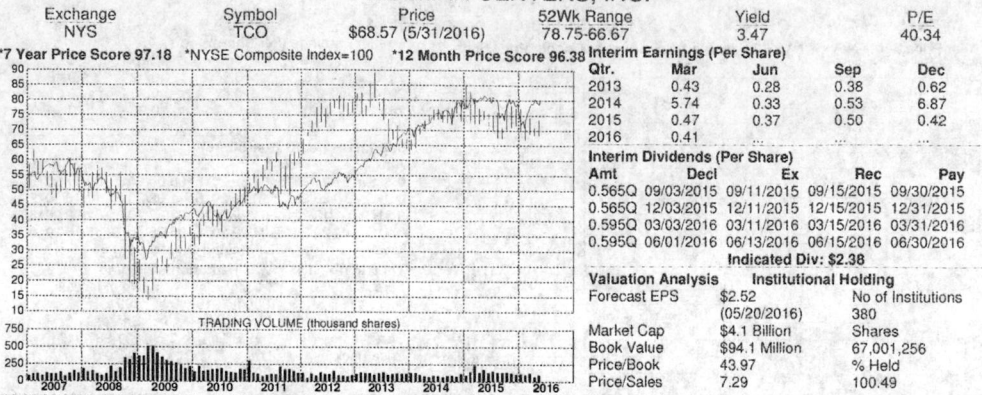

Interim Earnings (Per Share)

Qtr.	Mar	Jun	Sep	Dec
2013	0.43	0.28	0.38	0.62
2014	5.74	0.33	0.53	6.87
2015	0.47	0.37	0.50	0.42
2016	0.41			

Interim Dividends (Per Share)

Amt	Decl	Ex	Rec	Pay
0.565Q	09/03/2015	09/11/2015	09/15/2015	09/30/2015
0.565Q	12/03/2015	12/11/2015	12/15/2015	12/31/2015
0.595Q	03/03/2016	03/11/2016	03/15/2016	03/31/2016
0.595Q	06/01/2016	06/13/2016	06/15/2016	06/30/2016

Indicated Div: $2.38

Valuation Analysis

		Institutional Holding	
Forecast EPS	$2.52 (05/20/2016)	No of Institutions	380
Market Cap	$4.1 Billion	Shares	67,001,256
Book Value	$94.1 Million	% Held	100.49
Price/Book	43.97		
Price/Sales	7.29		

Business Summary: REITs (MIC: 5.3.1 SIC: 6798 NAIC: 525930)

Taubman Centers is a self-administered and self-managed real estate investment trust. The Taubman Realty Group Limited Partnership is a majority-owned partnership subsidiary of Co. that owns direct or indirect interests in all of Co.'s real estate properties. Co. owns, leases, acquires, disposes of, develops, expands, and manages regional shopping centers and interests therein. As of Dec 31 2015, Co. owned interests in 19 operating centers, which are located in metropolitan areas, including Denver, Detroit, Los Angeles, Miami, Nashville, New York City, Orlando, Salt Lake City, San Francisco, San Juan, Sarasota, St. Louis, Tampa, and Washington, D.C.

Recent Developments: For the quarter ended Mar 31 2016, net income decreased 13.1% to US$44.3 million from US$51.0 million in the year-earlier quarter. Revenues were US$139.5 million, up 8.1% from US$129.0 million the year before. Revenues from property income rose 9.4% to US$84.7 million from US$77.5 million in the corresponding quarter a year earlier.

Prospects: Our evaluation of Taubman Centers Inc. as of June 19, 2016 is the result of our systematic analysis on three basic characteristics: earnings strength, relative valuation, and recent stock price movement. The company has managed to produce a neutral trend in earnings per share over the past 5 quarters. Because the company lacks sufficient analyst estimate data, we place greater weight on the historical EPS trend as the measure of earnings strength. Based on operating earnings yield, the company is overvalued when compared to all of the companies in our coverage universe. Share price changes over the past year indicates that TCO will perform in line with the market over the near term.

Financial Data

(US$ in Thousands)	3 Mos	12/31/2015	12/31/2014	12/31/2013	12/31/2012	12/31/2011	12/31/2010	12/31/2009
Earnings Per Share	1.70	1.76	13.47	1.71	1.37	3.03	0.86	(1.31)
Cash Flow Per Share	5.30	5.01	5.75	5.84	5.40	4.75	4.85	4.44
Tang Book Value Per Share	1.56	1.87	5.03	...	...	...	...	...
Dividends Per Share	2.290	2.260	6.910	2.000	1.850	1.763	1.866	1.660
Dividend Payout %	134.71	128.41	51.30	116.96	135.04	58.17	216.97	...
Income Statement								
Total Revenue	139,455	557,172	679,129	767,154	747,974	644,918	654,558	666,104
EBITDA	75,027	299,983	312,736	412,835	391,803	345,422	355,257	196,378
Depn & Amortn	29,746	98,800	110,100	142,500	134,900	127,200	144,900	139,700
Income Before Taxes	26,153	138,142	111,833	140,312	114,287	95,945	57,649	(88,992)
Income Taxes	302	2,248	2,267	3,409	4,964	610	734	1,657
Net Income	30,909	134,127	893,013	132,590	106,174	192,871	63,868	(53,512)
Average Shares	60,791	62,161	64,921	64,575	61,376	58,529	55,702	53,239
Balance Sheet								
Current Assets	231,056	270,107	364,002	121,036	109,237	380,759	70,611	65,701
Total Assets	3,729,381	3,563,380	3,214,901	3,506,222	3,268,495	3,336,792	2,546,873	2,606,853
Current Liabilities	777,763	798,611	769,453	663,829	661,391	447,403	418,224	390,581
Long-Term Obligations	2,843,155	2,643,958	2,025,505	3,058,053	2,952,030	3,145,602	2,656,560	2,691,019
Total Liabilities	3,635,284	3,450,573	2,896,538	3,626,349	3,524,113	3,552,916	2,910,634	2,935,410
Stockholders' Equity	94,097	112,807	318,363	(120,127)	(255,618)	(216,124)	(363,761)	(328,557)
Shares Outstanding	60,342	60,233	63,324	63,101	63,310	58,022	54,696	54,321
Statistical Record								
Return on Assets %	3.75	3.96	26.57	3.91	3.21	6.56	2.48	N.M.
Return on Equity %	75.54	62.22	900.96	...	...	...	...	...
EBITDA Margin %	53.80	53.84	46.05	53.81	52.38	53.56	54.27	29.48
Net Margin %	22.16	24.07	131.49	17.28	14.19	29.91	9.76	N.M.
Asset Turnover	0.16	0.16	0.20	0.23	0.23	0.22	0.25	0.23
Current Ratio	0.30	0.34	0.47	0.18	0.17	0.85	0.17	0.17
Debt to Equity	30.22	23.44	6.36	...	...	...	...	...
Price Range	78.75-66.67	84.70-67.14	80.06-63.34	88.95-63.65	81.34-62.03	62.71-48.27	50.76-31.66	37.66-13.56
P/E Ratio	46.32-39.22	48.13-38.15	5.94-4.70	52.02-37.22	59.37-45.28	20.70-15.93	59.02-36.81	...
Average Yield %	3.15	3.03	9.43	2.68	2.46	3.13	4.43	6.22

Address: 200 East Long Lake Road, Suite 300, Bloomfield Hills, MI 48304-2324 **Telephone:** 248-258-6800	**Web Site:** www.taubman.com **Officers:** Robert S. Taubman - Chairman, President, Chief Executive Officer William S. Taubman - Chief Operating Officer	**Auditors:** KPMG LLP **Investor Contact:** 248-258-7367 **Transfer Agents:** Computershare, Providence, R.I.

TAYLOR MORRISON HOME CORP

Exchange	Symbol	Price	52Wk Range	Yield	P/E
NYS	TMHC	$14.90 (5/31/2016)	21.33-11.30	N/A	11.73

*7 Year Price Score N/A *NYSE Composite Index=100 *12 Month Price Score 85.10

Interim Earnings (Per Share)

Qtr.	Mar	Jun	Sep	Dec
2013	0.00	0.16	0.43	0.78
2014	0.33	0.45	0.54	0.84
2015	0.79	0.15	0.37	0.54
2016	0.21	...	...	...

Interim Dividends (Per Share)

No Dividends Paid

Valuation Analysis | **Institutional Holding**

Forecast EPS	$1.63	No of Institutions
	(05/20/2016)	136
Market Cap	$1.8 Billion	Shares
Book Value	$522.3 Million	29,864,574
Price/Book	3.45	% Held
Price/Sales	0.58	27.26

TRADING VOLUME (thousand shares)

2007 2008 2009 2010 2011 2012 2013 2014 2015 2016

Business Summary: Builders (MIC: 2.2.5 SIC: 1531 NAIC: 238990)

Taylor Morrison Home is a holding company. Co. provides a variety of homes across a range of price points. Co.'s primary focus is on move-up buyers where Co. designs, builds and sells single-family detached and attached homes. Co. operates under the Taylor Morrison and Darling Homes brand names in the U.S. Co. also provides financial services to customers through its wholly owned mortgage subsidiary, Taylor Morrison Home Funding, LLC. Co.'s business has 10 homebuilding operating divisions, and a mortgage division, which are managed as three reportable segments: East; West; Mortgage Operations.

Recent Developments: For the quarter ended Mar 31 2016, income from continuing operations decreased 35.0% to US$26.1 million from US$40.2 million in the year-earlier quarter. Net income decreased 73.0% to US$26.1 million from US$96.8 million in the year-earlier quarter. Revenues were US$645.3 million, up 26.7% from US$509.4 million the year before. Direct operating expenses rose 27.0% to US$526.7 million from US$414.8 million in the comparable period the year before. Indirect operating expenses increased 35.7% to US$77.3 million from US$56.9 million in the equivalent prior-year period.

Prospects: Our evaluation of Taylor Morrison Home Corp as of June 19, 2016 is the result of our systematic analysis on three basic characteristics: earnings strength, relative valuation, and recent stock price movement. The company has managed to produce a neutral trend in earnings per share over the past 5 quarters. However, while recent estimates for the company have been mixed, TMHC has posted results that fell short of analysts expectations. Based on operating earnings yield, the company is undervalued when compared to all of the companies in our coverage universe. Share price changes over the past year indicates that TMHC will perform very poorly over the near term.

Financial Data
(US$ in Thousands)

	3 Mos	12/31/2015	12/31/2014	12/31/2013	12/31/2012
Earnings Per Share	1.27	1.85	2.17	1.38	...
Cash Flow Per Share	(3.42)	(7.95)	(4.06)	(4.63)	...
Tang Book Value Per Share	3.74	3.77	3.68	3.10	1.00
Income Statement					
Total Revenue	645,329	2,976,820	2,708,432	2,323,237	...
EBITDA	39,200	262,336	300,749	62,197	...
Depn & Amortn	1,078	3,300	3,000	2,300	...
Income Before Taxes	38,209	259,228	296,589	60,373	...
Income Taxes	12,887	90,001	76,395	3,068	...
Net Income	6,813	61,049	71,469	45,420	...
Average Shares	121,267	122,384	122,313	122,319	...
Balance Sheet					
Current Assets	3,439,202	248,197	511,941	599,321	107
Total Assets	4,249,992	4,137,290	4,133,113	3,438,558	107
Current Liabilities	406,221	473,424	443,583	478,575	106
Long-Term Obligations	1,787,298	1,691,189	1,743,804	1,415,082	...
Total Liabilities	3,727,654	3,617,372	3,654,716	3,022,741	106
Stockholders' Equity	522,338	519,918	478,397	415,817	1,000.00
Shares Outstanding	120,993	121,332	122,287	122,308	1,000.00
Statistical Record					
Return on Assets %	1.03	1.48	1.89	...	...
Return on Equity %	8.21	12.23	15.98	...	...
EBITDA Margin %	6.07	8.81	11.10	2.68	...
Net Margin %	1.06	2.05	2.64	1.96	...
Asset Turnover	0.77	0.72	0.72	...	...
Current Ratio	8.47	0.52	1.15	1.25	1.01
Debt to Equity	3.42	3.25	3.65	3.40	...
Price Range	21.33-11.30	21.33-15.43	26.09-15.13	26.89-19.96	...
P/E Ratio	16.80-8.90	11.53-8.34	12.02-6.97	19.49-14.46	...

Address: 4900 N. Scottsdale Road, Suite 2000, Scottsdale, AZ 85251 Telephone: 480-840-8100	Web Site: www.taylormorrison.com Officers: Timothy R. Eller - Chairman Sheryl D. Palmer - President, Chief Executive Officer	Auditors: Deloitte & Touche LLP Transfer Agents: Computershare Trust Company, N.A.

TC PIPELINES, LP

Exchange	Symbol	Price	52Wk Range	Yield	P/E	Div Achiever
NYS	TCP	$55.23 (5/31/2016)	64.19-35.44	6.45	276.15	16 Years

*7 Year Price Score 90.06   *NYSE Composite Index=100   *12 Month Price Score 102.89

Interim Earnings (Per Share)

Qtr.	Mar	Jun	Sep	Dec
2013	0.52	0.40	0.58	0.19
2014	0.90	0.58	0.48	0.71
2015	0.88	0.66	0.70	0.00
2016	1.10			

Interim Dividends (Per Share)

Amt	Decl	Ex	Rec	Pay
0.89Q	07/23/2015	07/31/2015	08/04/2015	08/14/2015
0.89Q	10/22/2015	10/30/2015	11/03/2015	11/13/2015
0.89Q	01/21/2016	01/29/2016	02/02/2016	02/12/2016
0.89Q	04/21/2016	04/28/2016	05/02/2016	05/13/2016

Indicated Div: $3.56

Valuation Analysis

		Institutional Holding	
Forecast EPS	$3.12 (05/20/2016)	No of Institutions	213
Market Cap	$3.7 Billion	Shares	41,429,664
Book Value	N/A	% Held	56.39
Price/Book	N/A		
Price/Sales	8.16		

Business Summary: Equipment & Services (MIC: 9.1.3 SIC: 4922 NAIC: 486210)

TC PipeLines and its subsidiaries are engaged in acquiring, owning and participating in the management of energy infrastructure businesses in North America. Co. is managed by TC PipeLines GP, Inc., (its General Partner), which is an indirect, wholly-owned subsidiary of TransCanada Corporation (TransCanada). Co. has equity ownership interests in natural gas interstate pipeline systems. As of Dec 31 2014, these systems transported about 8.90 billion cubic feet per day of natural gas from producing regions and import facilities to market hubs and consuming markets mainly in the Western and Midwestern U.S. All of Co.'s pipeline systems are operated by subsidiaries of TransCanada.

Recent Developments: For the quarter ended Mar 31 2016, net income increased 14.1% to US$73.0 million from US$64.0 million in the year-earlier quarter. Revenues were US$128.0 million, up 8.5% from US$118.0 million the year before. Indirect operating expenses increased 1.9% to US$55.0 million from US$54.0 million in the equivalent prior-year period.

Prospects: Our evaluation of TC PipeLines L.P. as of June 19, 2016 is the result of our systematic analysis on three basic characteristics: earnings strength, relative valuation, and recent stock price movement. The company has generated a negative trend in earnings per share over the past 5 quarters. However, while recent estimates for the company have been mixed, TCP has posted better than expected results. Based on operating earnings yield, the company is undervalued when compared to all of the companies in our coverage universe. Share price changes over the past year indicates that TCP will perform well over the near term.

Financial Data
(US$ in Thousands)

	3 Mos	12/31/2015	12/31/2014	12/31/2013	12/31/2012	12/31/2011	12/31/2010	12/31/2009
Earnings Per Share	0.20	(0.03)	2.67	2.13	2.51	3.02	2.91	2.34
Cash Flow Per Share	4.64	...	4.91	4.62	2.85	3.31	3.38	3.19
Dividends Per Share	3.510	3.460	3.300	3.180	3.100	3.040	2.940	2.870
Dividend Payout %	1,755.00	...	123.60	149.30	123.51	100.66	101.03	122.65
Income Statement								
Total Revenue	128,000	...	424,000	408,000	194,000	223,900	195,100	167,300
EBITDA	95,000	158,000	337,000	319,000	170,000	185,000	160,700	134,600
Depn & Amortn	22,000	85,000	86,000	86,000	11,000	15,200	15,000	14,700
Income Before Taxes	73,000	20,000	204,000	191,000	137,000	157,400	137,100	106,100
Net Income	73,000	13,000	172,000	155,000	137,000	157,400	137,100	106,100
Average Shares	64,700	...	62,700	58,900	53,500	51,100	46,200	38,700
Balance Sheet								
Current Assets	97,000	...	68,000	69,000	12,000	38,300	12,300	11,700
Total Assets	3,238,000	...	3,349,000	3,443,000	1,998,000	2,082,000	1,650,500	1,675,100
Current Liabilities	55,000	59,000	291,000	55,000	11,000	9,200	506,600	72,100
Long-Term Obligations	2,059,000	1,896,000	1,446,000	1,575,000	685,000	739,400	30,100	487,900
Total Liabilities	2,142,000	1,982,000	1,997,000	2,094,000	697,000	749,000	538,000	571,600
Shares Outstanding	66,600	66,217	63,561	62,327	53,472	53,472	46,227	46,227
Statistical Record								
Return on Assets %	0.84	...	5.06	5.70	6.70	8.43	8.25	6.79
EBITDA Margin %	74.22	35.83	79.48	78.19	87.63	82.63	82.37	80.45
Net Margin %	57.03	...	40.57	37.99	70.62	70.30	70.27	63.42
Asset Turnover	0.13	0.14	0.12	0.15	0.09	0.12	0.12	0.11
Current Ratio	1.76	...	0.23	1.25	1.09	4.16	0.02	0.16
Price Range	69.14-35.44	72.53-41.48	76.59-45.52	52.18-40.36	47.58-38.50	54.45-40.17	52.00-34.40	41.10-23.25
P/E Ratio	345.70-177.20	...	28.69-17.05	24.50-18.95	18.96-15.34	18.03-13.30	17.87-11.82	17.56-9.94
Average Yield %	6.58	5.94	5.92	6.75	7.05	6.36	7.05	8.61

Address: 700 Louisiana Street, Suite 700, Houston, TX 77002-2761 **Telephone:** 877-290-2772	**Web Site:** www.tcpipelineslp.com **Officers:** Janine Watson - Associate/Affiliate Company Officer Nancy Priemer - Associate/Affiliate Company Officer	**Auditors:** KPMG LLP (USA) **Investor Contact:** 877-.29-0.2772 **Transfer Agents:** Computershare

TCF FINANCIAL CORP

Exchange	Symbol	Price	52Wk Range	Yield	P/E
NYS	TCB	$14.37 (5/31/2016)	17.16-10.47	2.09	12.72

*7 Year Price Score 86.36   *NYSE Composite Index=100   *12 Month Price Score 91.26

Interim Earnings (Per Share)

Qtr.	Mar	Jun	Sep	Dec
2013	0.16	0.21	0.23	0.22
2014	0.24	0.29	0.29	0.11
2015	0.21	0.29	0.29	0.29
2016	0.26	...	...	...

Interim Dividends (Per Share)

Amt	Decl	Ex	Rec	Pay
0.05Q	07/20/2015	08/12/2015	08/14/2015	09/01/2015
0.075Q	10/19/2015	11/10/2015	11/13/2015	12/01/2015
0.075Q	01/22/2016	02/10/2016	02/12/2016	03/01/2016
0.075Q	04/20/2016	05/11/2016	05/13/2016	06/01/2016

Indicated Div: $0.30 (Div. Reinv. Plan)

Valuation Analysis

Forecast EPS	$1.15	No of Institutions
	(05/15/2016)	351
Market Cap	$2.5 Billion	Shares
Book Value	$2.3 Billion	152,207,504
Price/Book	1.05	% Held
Price/Sales	1.80	82.49

Institutional Holding

Business Summary: Banking (MIC: 5.1.1 SIC: 6021 NAIC: 522110)

TCF Financial is a bank holding company. Through its subsidiary, Co. provides retail banking and commercial banking products. Co.'s segments are: Lending, which includes consumer real estate, commercial real estate and business lending, leasing and equipment finance, inventory finance and auto finance; funding, which includes branch banking and treasury services; and support services, which includes corporate functions that provide data processing, bank operations and other professional services to the operating segments. At Dec 31 2015, Co. had total assets of $20.69 billion and total deposits of $16.72 billion.

Recent Developments: For the quarter ended Mar 31 2016, net income increased 20.7% to US$48.0 million from US$39.8 million in the year-earlier quarter. Net interest income increased 4.0% to US$211.7 million from US$203.4 million in the year-earlier quarter. Provision for loan losses was US$18.8 million versus US$12.8 million in the prior-year quarter, an increase of 47.3%. Non-interest income rose 11.9% to US$112.6 million from US$100.6 million, while non-interest expense advanced 0.7% to US$228.3 million.

Prospects: Our evaluation of TCF Financial Corp. as of June 19, 2016 is the result of our systematic analysis on three basic characteristics: earnings strength, relative valuation, and recent stock price movement. The company has generated a negative trend in earnings per share over the past 5 quarters and while recent estimates for the company have remained steady, TCB has posted better than expected results. Based on operating earnings yield, the company is undervalued when compared to all of the companies in our coverage universe. Share price changes over the past year indicates that TCB will perform poorly over the near term.

Financial Data

(US$ in Thousands)	3 Mos	12/31/2015	12/31/2014	12/31/2013	12/31/2012	12/31/2011	12/31/2010	12/31/2009
Earnings Per Share	1.13	1.07	0.94	0.82	(1.37)	0.71	1.05	0.54
Cash Flow Per Share	3.38	2.19	1.91	2.55	3.12	3.22	3.72	2.87
Tang Book Value Per Share	10.87	10.61	9.75	8.87	8.41	10.24	9.23	7.92
Dividends Per Share	0.250	0.225	0.200	0.200	0.200	0.200	0.200	0.400
Dividend Payout %	22.12	21.03	21.28	24.39	...	28.17	19.05	74.07
Income Statement								
Interest Income	232,342	891,930	874,229	864,540	884,623	937,951	969,877	958,181
Interest Expense	20,684	71,542	58,600	61,916	104,604	238,263	270,675	325,175
Net Interest Income	211,658	820,388	815,629	802,624	780,019	699,688	699,202	633,006
Provision for Losses	18,842	52,944	95,737	118,368	247,443	200,843	236,437	258,536
Non-Interest Income	112,602	441,998	433,267	404,058	490,423	444,434	537,985	525,855
Non-Interest Expense	228,334	894,747	871,777	845,269	1,362,554	764,451	763,124	767,784
Income Before Taxes	77,084	314,695	281,382	243,045	(339,555)	178,828	237,626	132,541
Income Taxes	26,803	108,872	99,766	84,345	(132,858)	64,441	87,765	45,854
Net Income	48,046	197,123	174,187	151,668	(212,884)	109,394	146,564	87,097
Average Shares	167,435	166,241	164,084	161,926	159,268	154,509	138,812	126,593
Balance Sheet								
Net Loans & Leases	17,904,518	17,437,570	16,369,743	15,674,477	15,168,885	13,908,904	14,522,485	14,346,273
Total Assets	21,321,102	20,691,704	19,394,611	18,379,840	18,225,917	18,979,388	18,465,025	17,885,175
Total Deposits	17,312,369	16,719,989	15,449,882	14,432,776	14,050,786	12,202,004	11,585,115	11,568,319
Total Liabilities	18,978,189	18,400,788	17,272,962	16,426,872	16,362,544	17,111,255	16,993,362	16,709,813
Stockholders' Equity	2,342,913	2,290,916	2,121,649	1,952,968	1,863,373	1,868,133	1,471,663	1,175,362
Shares Outstanding	170,604	169,844	167,461	165,122	163,386	160,323	142,913	129,202
Statistical Record								
Return on Assets %	0.99	0.98	0.92	0.83	N.M.	0.58	0.81	0.50
Return on Equity %	9.12	8.93	8.55	7.95	N.M.	6.55	11.07	6.53
Net Interest Margin %	91.10	91.98	93.30	92.84	88.18	74.60	72.09	66.06
Efficiency Ratio %	66.19	67.08	66.68	66.63	99.09	55.30	50.61	51.74
Loans to Deposits	1.03	1.04	1.06	1.09	1.08	1.14	1.25	1.24
Price Range	17.16-10.47	17.16-13.95	17.19-14.26	16.45-12.15	12.44-9.85	16.99-8.79	18.87-13.07	16.51-9.00
P/E Ratio	15.19-9.27	16.04-13.04	18.29-15.17	20.06-14.82	...	23.93-12.38	17.97-12.45	30.57-16.67
Average Yield %	1.69	1.44	1.26	1.37	1.77	1.54	1.30	3.02

Address: 200 Lake Street East, Wayzata, MN 55391-1693 **Telephone:** 952-745-2760	**Web Site:** www.tcfbank.com **Officers:** William A. Cooper - Chairman, Chief Executive Officer Craig R. Dahl - Vice-Chairman, President, Executive Vice President, Chief Executive Officer	**Auditors:** KPMG LLP **Investor Contact:** 952-745-2756 **Transfer Agents:** Computershare Trust Company, N.A., Providence, RI

TE CONNECTIVITY LTD

Exchange	Symbol	Price	52Wk Range	Yield	P/E
NYS	TEL	$60.00 (5/31/2016)	69.67-52.27	2.47	11.45

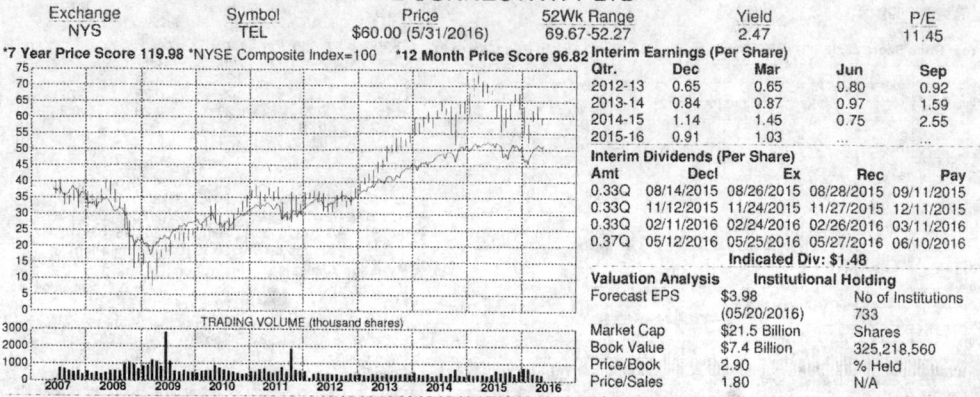

*7 Year Price Score 119.98 *NYSE Composite Index=100   *12 Month Price Score 96.82

Interim Earnings (Per Share)

Qtr.	Dec	Mar	Jun	Sep
2012-13	0.65	0.65	0.80	0.92
2013-14	0.84	0.87	0.97	1.59
2014-15	1.14	1.45	0.75	2.55
2015-16	0.91	1.03		

Interim Dividends (Per Share)

Amt	Decl	Ex	Rec	Pay
0.33Q	08/14/2015	08/26/2015	08/28/2015	09/11/2015
0.33Q	11/12/2015	11/24/2015	11/27/2015	12/11/2015
0.33Q	02/11/2016	02/24/2016	02/26/2016	03/11/2016
0.37Q	05/12/2016	05/25/2016	05/27/2016	06/10/2016

Indicated Div: $1.48

Valuation Analysis

		Institutional Holding	
Forecast EPS	$3.98	No of Institutions	
	(05/20/2016)	733	
Market Cap	$21.5 Billion	Shares	
Book Value	$7.4 Billion	325,218,560	
Price/Book	2.90	% Held	
Price/Sales	1.80	N/A	

TRADING VOLUME (thousand shares)

Business Summary: Electrical Equipment (MIC: 7.3.1 SIC: 5065 NAIC: 334111)

TE Connectivity designs and manufactures connectivity and sensors solutions. Co. operates through three reportable segments: Transportation Solutions, which provides terminals and connector systems and components, sensors, relays, application tooling, and wire and heat shrink tubing products; Industrial Solutions, which is a supplier of products that connect and distribute power, data, and signals and is used in the industrial equipment (aerospace, defense, oil, and gas), and energy markets; and Communications Solutions, which is a supplier of electronic components for the data and devices and appliances markets.

Recent Developments: For the quarter ended Mar 25 2016, income from continuing operations increased 23.1% to US$389.0 million from US$316.0 million in the year-earlier quarter. Net income decreased 36.6% to US$380.0 million from US$599.0 million in the year-earlier quarter. Revenues were US$2.95 billion, down 4.2% from US$3.08 billion the year before. Operating income was US$535.0 million versus US$448.0 million in the prior-year quarter, an increase of 19.4%. Direct operating expenses declined 2.0% to US$1.99 billion from US$2.03 billion in the comparable period the year before. Indirect operating expenses decreased 29.2% to US$427.0 million from US$603.0 million in the equivalent prior-year period.

Prospects: Our evaluation of TE Connectivity Ltd. as of June 19, 2016 is the result of our systematic analysis on three basic characteristics: earnings strength, relative valuation, and recent stock price movement. The company has produced a positive trend in earnings per share over the past 5 quarters and while recent estimates for the company have remained steady, TEL has posted better than expected results. Based on operating earnings yield, the company is undervalued when compared to all of the companies in our coverage universe. Share price changes over the past year indicates that TEL will perform in line with the market over the near term.

Financial Data

(US$ in Millions)	6 Mos	3 Mos	09/25/2015	09/26/2014	09/27/2013	09/28/2012	09/30/2011	09/24/2010
Earnings Per Share	5.24	5.66	5.89	4.27	3.02	2.59	2.81	2.41
Cash Flow Per Share	4.78	5.15	4.74	5.09	4.91	4.58	4.00	3.72
Tang Book Value Per Share	3.63	6.54	8.14	7.56	6.83	5.47	7.63	7.77
Dividends Per Share	1.320	1.280	1.240	1.080	0.920	0.780	0.680	0.640
Dividend Payout %	25.19	22.61	21.05	25.29	30.46	30.12	24.20	26.56
Income Statement								
Total Revenue	5,785	2,833	12,233	13,912	13,280	13,282	14,312	12,070
EBITDA	1,243	552	2,157	2,610	1,869	2,070	2,274	2,182
Depn & Amortn	290	146	463	502	496	502	506	489
Income Before Taxes	901	382	1,575	1,996	1,248	1,415	1,629	1,558
Income Taxes	188	58	337	207	(29)	249	376	493
Net Income	733	353	2,420	1,781	1,276	1,112	1,245	1,103
Average Shares	368	390	411	417	423	430	443	457
Balance Sheet								
Current Assets	5,414	6,505	7,887	7,544	6,309	6,503	6,632	6,731
Total Assets	17,841	19,223	20,608	20,152	18,461	19,306	17,723	16,992
Current Liabilities	3,097	3,266	3,577	3,954	3,924	4,004	3,401	3,460
Long-Term Obligations	3,732	3,370	3,403	3,281	2,303	2,696	2,668	2,307
Total Liabilities	10,435	10,646	11,023	11,145	10,081	11,335	10,249	9,944
Stockholders' Equity	7,406	8,577	9,585	9,007	8,380	7,971	7,474	7,048
Shares Outstanding	357	375	393	407	411	422	423	443
Statistical Record								
Return on Assets %	10.93	11.69	11.91	9.25	6.78	6.02	7.06	6.66
Return on Equity %	25.40	25.94	26.10	20.54	15.65	14.44	16.87	15.73
EBITDA Margin %	21.49	19.48	17.63	18.76	14.07	15.59	15.89	18.08
Net Margin %	12.67	12.46	19.78	12.80	9.61	8.37	8.70	9.14
Asset Turnover	0.62	0.61	0.60	0.72	0.71	0.72	0.81	0.73
Current Ratio	1.75	1.99	2.20	1.91	1.61	1.62	1.95	1.95
Debt to Equity	0.50	0.39	0.36	0.36	0.27	0.34	0.36	0.33
Price Range	71.73-52.27	73.42-55.53	73.42-51.47	64.97-49.91	53.54-32.03	37.30-27.25	38.51-27.86	32.85-21.12
P/E Ratio	13.69-9.98	12.97-9.81	12.47-8.74	15.22-11.69	17.73-10.61	14.40-10.52	13.70-9.91	13.63-8.76
Average Yield %	2.08	1.95	1.92	1.86	2.18	2.31	2.01	2.46

Address: Rheinstrasse 20, Schaffhausen, CH-8200
Telephone: 526-336-661

Web Site: www.te.com
Officers: Thomas J. Lynch - Chairman, Chief Executive Officer, Division Officer Terrence R. Curtin - President, Executive Vice President, Vice President, Chief Financial Officer, Corporate Controller, Division Officer

Auditors: Deloitte & Touche LLP
Investor Contact: 610-893-9551
Transfer Agents: Computershare Shareowner Services LLC, Jersey City, NJ

TECO ENERGY INC.

Exchange	Symbol	Price	52Wk Range	Yield	P/E
NYS	TE	$27.54 (5/31/2016)	27.78-17.66	3.34	34.42

*7 Year Price Score 116.00 *NYSE Composite Index=100 *12 Month Price Score 108.89

Interim Earnings (Per Share)

Qtr.	Mar	Jun	Sep	Dec
2013	0.19	0.24	0.29	0.20
2014	0.23	0.27	0.04	0.04
2015	0.25	0.05	0.23	0.21
2016	0.31	...	...	...

Interim Dividends (Per Share)

Amt	Decl	Ex	Rec	Pay
0.225Q	07/29/2015	08/12/2015	08/14/2015	08/28/2015
0.225Q	11/04/2015	11/10/2015	11/13/2015	11/30/2015
0.23Q	02/03/2016	02/10/2016	02/12/2016	02/29/2016
0.23Q	05/04/2016	05/12/2016	05/16/2016	05/27/2016

Indicated Div: $0.92

Valuation Analysis

Institutional Holding	
Forecast EPS	$1.18
	(05/20/2016)
Market Cap	$6.5 Billion
Book Value	$2.6 Billion
Price/Book	2.51
Price/Sales	2.39

No of Institutions 550
Shares 186,995,728
% Held 67.36

Business Summary: Electric Utilities (MIC: 3.1.1 SIC: 4911 NAIC: 221122)

TECO Energy is a holding company for regulated utilities and other businesses. Co. holds the common stock of Tampa Electric Company (TEC) and, through its subsidiaries, New Mexico Gas Intermediate, Inc., owns New Mexico Gas Company, Inc. (NMGC). TEC has two business segments: Tampa Electric, which is engaged in the generation, purchase, transmission, distribution and sale of electric energy; and Peoples Gas System, which is engaged in the purchase, distribution and sale of natural gas for residential, commercial, industrial and electric power generation customers. NMGC is engaged in the purchase, distribution and sale of natural gas for residential, commercial and industrial customers.

Recent Developments: For the quarter ended Mar 31 2016, income from continuing operations increased 15.5% to US$73.7 million from US$63.8 million in the year-earlier quarter. Net income increased 27.2% to US$73.8 million from US$58.0 million in the year-earlier quarter. Revenues were US$659.5 million, down 4.8% from US$693.0 million the year before. Operating income was US$148.1 million versus US$146.2 million in the prior-year quarter, an increase of 1.3%. Direct operating expenses declined 10.0% to US$368.7 million from US$409.5 million in the comparable period the year before. Indirect operating expenses increased 3.9% to US$142.7 million from US$137.3 million in the equivalent prior-year period.

Prospects: Our evaluation of TECO Energy Inc. as of June 19, 2016 is the result of our systematic analysis on three basic characteristics: earnings strength, relative valuation, and recent stock price movement. The company has produced a positive trend in earnings per share over the past 5 quarters and while recent estimates for the company have remained steady, TE has posted better than expected results. Based on operating earnings yield, the company is about fairly valued when compared to all of the companies in our coverage universe. Share price changes over the past year indicates that TE will perform very well over the near term.

Financial Data

(US$ in Thousands)	3 Mos	12/31/2015	12/31/2014	12/31/2013	12/31/2012	12/31/2011	12/31/2010	12/31/2009
Earnings Per Share	0.80	0.74	0.58	0.92	0.99	1.27	1.11	1.00
Cash Flow Per Share	2.97	2.62	2.98	3.06	3.52	3.53	3.13	3.42
Tang Book Value Per Share	9.23	9.14	9.22	10.74	10.58	10.25	9.84	9.47
Dividends Per Share	0.905	0.900	0.880	0.880	0.880	0.850	0.815	0.800
Dividend Payout %	113.13	121.62	151.72	95.65	88.89	66.93	73.42	80.00
Income Statement								
Total Revenue	659,500	2,743,500	2,566,400	2,851,300	2,996,600	3,343,400	3,487,900	3,310,500
EBITDA	245,100	922,000	823,900	790,100	876,600	938,500	927,600	768,000
Depn & Amortn	89,800	339,100	307,500	316,500	309,300	306,600	297,100	275,200
Income Before Taxes	109,400	396,500	345,300	306,700	383,800	426,800	399,200	265,800
Income Taxes	35,700	155,300	138,900	108,900	137,800	153,900	170,000	98,600
Net Income	73,800	173,500	130,400	197,700	212,700	272,600	239,000	213,900
Average Shares	235,200	234,500	223,700	215,500	215,000	215,100	214,800	213,100
Balance Sheet								
Current Assets	547,200	570,300	755,600	857,700	856,800	797,900	757,600	651,600
Total Assets	8,981,100	8,961,100	8,726,200	7,448,000	7,356,500	7,322,200	7,194,600	7,219,500
Current Liabilities	1,200,600	1,198,700	1,097,900	765,400	602,200	1,019,700	752,300	771,300
Long-Term Obligations	3,489,700	3,516,900	3,354,000	2,837,800	2,972,700	2,687,300	3,148,100	3,201,600
Total Liabilities	6,398,800	6,402,100	6,151,500	5,114,300	5,064,700	5,055,600	5,024,900	5,134,100
Stockholders' Equity	2,582,300	2,559,000	2,574,700	2,333,700	2,291,800	2,266,600	2,169,700	2,085,400
Shares Outstanding	235,500	235,300	234,900	217,300	216,600	215,800	214,900	213,900
Statistical Record								
Return on Assets %	2.13	1.96	1.61	2.67	2.89	3.76	3.32	2.98
Return on Equity %	7.32	6.76	5.31	8.55	9.31	12.29	11.23	10.45
EBITDA Margin %	37.16	33.61	32.10	27.71	29.25	28.07	26.59	23.20
Net Margin %	11.19	6.32	5.08	6.93	7.10	8.15	6.85	6.46
Asset Turnover	0.31	0.31	0.32	0.39	0.41	0.46	0.48	0.46
Current Ratio	0.46	0.48	0.69	1.12	1.42	0.78	1.01	0.84
Debt to Equity	1.35	1.37	1.30	1.22	1.30	1.19	1.45	1.54
Price Range	27.55-17.66	27.22-17.66	21.20-16.18	19.13-16.29	19.17-16.21	19.60-16.12	17.90-14.69	16.61-8.60
P/E Ratio	34.44-22.07	36.78-23.86	36.55-27.90	20.79-17.71	19.36-16.37	15.43-12.69	16.13-13.23	16.61-8.60
Average Yield %	3.81	4.09	4.93	5.07	4.98	4.64	4.95	6.34

Address: TECO Plaza, 702 N. Franklin Street, Tampa, FL 33602	Web Site: www.tecoenergy.com	Auditors: PricewaterhouseCoopers LLP
Telephone: 813-228-1111	Officers: John B. Ramil - President, Chief Executive Officer Chalres A. Attal - Senior Vice President, Chief Legal Officer, General Counsel	Investor Contact: 800-810-2032
Fax: 813-228-1670		Transfer Agents: Wells Fargo Shareowner Services, St Paul, MN

TEEKAY CORP

Exchange	Symbol	Price	52Wk Range	Yield	P/E
NYS	TK	$10.52 (5/31/2016)	48.27-4.92	2.09	N/A

*7 Year Price Score 57.47   *NYSE Composite Index=100   *12 Month Price Score 42.22

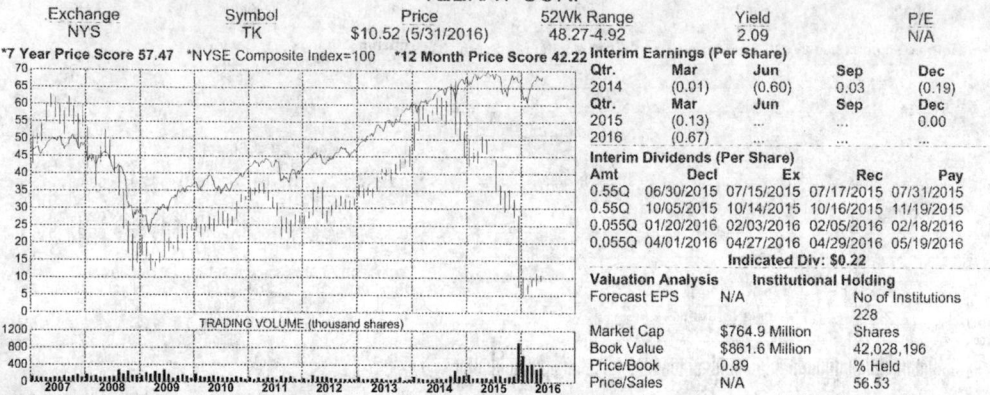

Interim Earnings (Per Share)

Qtr.	Mar	Jun	Sep	Dec
2014	(0.01)	(0.60)	0.03	(0.19)

Qtr.	Mar	Jun	Sep	Dec
2015	(0.13)	...	...	0.00
2016	(0.67)	...		

Interim Dividends (Per Share)

Amt	Decl	Ex	Rec	Pay
0.55Q	06/30/2015	07/15/2015	07/17/2015	07/31/2015
0.55Q	10/05/2015	10/14/2015	10/16/2015	11/19/2015
0.055Q	01/20/2016	02/03/2016	02/05/2016	02/18/2016
0.055Q	04/01/2016	04/27/2016	04/29/2016	05/19/2016

Indicated Div: $0.22

Valuation Analysis

		Institutional Holding	
Forecast EPS	N/A	No of Institutions	228
Market Cap	$764.9 Million	Shares	42,028,196
Book Value	$861.6 Million	% Held	56.53
Price/Book	0.89		
Price/Sales	N/A		

Business Summary: Equipment & Services (MIC: 9.1.3 SIC: 4412 NAIC: 483111)

Teekay is a provider of international crude oil and gas marine transportation services. Co. also provides offshore oil production, storage and offloading services. Co.'s shuttle tanker and FSO and FPSO segment includes its shuttle tanker operations, floating storage and off-take (FSO) units, and its floating production, storage and offloading (FPSO) units, which primarily operate under long-term fixed-rate contracts. Co.'s liquefied gas segment includes its liquefied natural gas and liquefied petroleum gas carriers that are subject to long-term, fixed-rate time-charter contracts. Co.'s conventional tanker segment, consisting of the spot tanker sub-segment and fixed-rate tanker sub-segment.

Recent Developments: For the quarter ended Mar 31 2016, net loss amounted to US$39.2 million versus net income of US$43.9 million in the year-earlier quarter. Revenues were US$641.1 million, up 17.4% from US$545.9 million the year before. Operating income was US$135.3 million versus US$137.4 million in the prior-year quarter, a decrease of 1.5%. Direct operating expenses rose 23.1% to US$31.6 million from US$25.7 million in the comparable period the year before. Indirect operating expenses increased 23.9% to US$474.2 million from US$382.8 million in the equivalent prior-year period.

Prospects: Our evaluation of Teekay Corp. as of Apr. 17, 2016 is the result of our systematic analysis on three basic characteristics: earnings strength, relative valuation, and recent stock price movement. The company has suffered a very negative trend in earnings per share over the past 5 quarters and while recent estimates for the company have remained steady, TK has posted better than expected results. Based on operating earnings yield, the company is undervalued when compared to all of the companies in our coverage universe. Share price changes over the past year indicates that TK will perform very poorly over the near term.

Financial Data
(US$ in Thousands)

	3 Mos	12/31/2015	12/31/2014	12/31/2013	12/31/2012	12/31/2011	12/31/2010	12/31/2009
Earnings Per Share	...	1.13	(0.76)	(1.63)	(2.31)	(5.25)	(3.67)	1.76
Cash Flow Per Share	...	10.60	6.19	4.15	4.16	1.53	5.65	5.08
Tang Book Value Per Share	...	8.78	11.52	12.12	14.67	16.39	22.49	25.08
Dividends Per Share	1.471	1.732	1.265	1.265	1.265	1.265	1.265	1.265
Dividend Payout %	...	153.32	...	...	...	...	...	71.88
Income Statement								
Total Revenue	641,108	2,450,382	1,993,920	1,830,085	1,956,235	1,953,782	2,068,878	2,172,049
EBITDA	160,421	1,001,718	589,728	442,888	139,688	162,576	353,841	663,072
Depn & Amortn	144,157	479,415	381,965	369,386	382,965	382,172	392,451	361,199
Income Before Taxes	(54,617)	285,822	6,061	(98,186)	(404,733)	(347,122)	(161,718)	180,424
Income Taxes	...	(16,767)	10,173	2,872	(14,406)	4,290	(6,340)	22,889
Net Income	(48,784)	82,151	(54,757)	(114,738)	(160,180)	(368,916)	(267,287)	128,412
Average Shares	72,742	73,190	72,066	70,457	69,263	70,234	72,862	73,058
Balance Sheet								
Current Assets	1,211,916	1,319,644	1,335,252	1,674,590	1,555,425	1,212,756	1,262,090	864,378
Total Assets	12,903,234	13,061,248	11,864,212	11,555,701	11,002,025	11,131,396	9,911,098	9,510,916
Current Liabilities	1,650,740	1,886,788	1,365,976	1,945,514	1,522,901	1,130,930	1,153,638	845,863
Long-Term Obligations	6,230,242	6,332,563	6,141,492	5,679,706	5,329,605	5,642,841	4,626,308	4,931,216
Total Liabilities	12,041,609	12,142,223	10,765,884	10,423,913	9,686,636	9,701,700	7,932,651	7,270,826
Stockholders' Equity	861,625	919,025	1,098,328	1,131,788	1,315,389	1,429,696	1,978,447	2,240,090
Shares Outstanding	...	72,711	72,500	70,729	69,704	68,732	72,012	72,694
Statistical Record								
Return on Assets %	...	0.66	N.M.	N.M.	N.M.	N.M.	N.M.	1.30
Return on Equity %	...	8.14	N.M.	N.M.	N.M.	N.M.	N.M.	5.96
EBITDA Margin %	25.02	40.88	29.58	24.20	7.14	8.32	17.10	30.53
Net Margin %	N.M.	3.35	N.M.	N.M.	N.M.	N.M.	N.M.	5.91
Asset Turnover	...	0.20	0.17	0.16	0.18	0.19	0.21	0.22
Current Ratio	0.73	0.70	0.98	0.86	1.02	1.07	1.09	1.02
Debt to Equity	7.23	6.89	5.59	5.02	4.05	3.95	2.34	2.20
Price Range	50.88-4.92	50.89-7.27	67.12-44.66	48.01-32.10	36.12-25.30	37.18-21.43	33.81-21.40	25.24-11.84
P/E Ratio	...	45.04-6.43	...	...	...	...	...	14.34-6.73
Average Yield %	5.00	4.51	2.25	3.25	4.14	4.21	4.68	6.64

Address: 4th floor, Belvedere Building, 69 Pitts Bay Road, Hamilton, HM 08
Telephone: 604-683-3529

Web Site: www.teekay.com
Officers: Peter Evensen - President, Chief Executive Officer Arthur Bensler - Executive Vice President, General Counsel, Secretary

Auditors: KPMG LLP
Investor Contact: 604-844-6654
Transfer Agents: ComputerShare Investor Services, Providence, RI

TELEFLEX INCORPORATED

Exchange	Symbol	Price	52Wk Range	Yield	P/E
NYS	TFX	$161.10 (5/31/2016)	162.61-123.24	0.84	30.28

*7 Year Price Score 141.64 *NYSE Composite Index=100 ***12 Month Price Score 113.31**

TRADING VOLUME (thousand shares)

Interim Earnings (Per Share)

Qtr.	Mar	Jun	Sep	Dec
2013	0.63	0.98	1.08	0.77
2014	0.76	1.02	1.18	1.08
2015	0.81	0.93	1.25	2.10
2016	1.04	...	...	...

Interim Dividends (Per Share)

Amt	Decl	Ex	Rec	Pay
0.34Q	07/30/2015	08/12/2015	08/14/2015	09/14/2015
0.34Q	10/29/2015	11/10/2015	11/13/2015	12/14/2015
0.34Q	02/25/2016	03/02/2016	03/04/2016	03/15/2016
0.34Q	05/02/2016	05/12/2016	05/16/2016	06/15/2016

Indicated Div: $1.36 (Div. Reinv. Plan)

Valuation Analysis | **Institutional Holding**

Forecast EPS $7.23 (05/15/2016)	No of Institutions 456
Market Cap $7.0 Billion	Shares 46,559,768
Book Value $2.1 Billion	% Held 96.68
Price/Book 3.39	
Price/Sales 3.89	

Business Summary: Medical Instruments & Equipment (MIC: 4 3.1 SIC: 3841 NAIC: 339112)

Teleflex is a provider of medical technology products. Co. designs, develops, manufactures and supplies single-use medical devices used by hospitals and healthcare providers for diagnostic and therapeutic procedures in care and surgical applications. Co. has six segments: Vascular North America; Anesthesia North America; Surgical North America; Europe, the Middle East and Africa; Asia; and OEM. All of Co.'s segments, other than the OEM segment, design, manufacture and distribute medical devices used in critical care, surgical applications and cardiac care. Co.'s OEM segment designs, manufactures and supplies devices and instruments for other medical device manufacturers.

Recent Developments: For the quarter ended Mar 27 2016, income from continuing operations increased 30.3% to US$51.2 million from US$39.3 million in the year-earlier quarter. Net income increased 31.9% to US$50.9 million from US$38.6 million in the year-earlier quarter. Revenues were US$424.9 million, down 1.1% from US$429.4 million the year before. Operating income was US$67.5 million versus US$65.6 million in the prior-year quarter, an increase of 2.9%. Direct operating expenses declined 3.4% to US$199.7 million from US$206.8 million in the comparable period the year before. Indirect operating expenses increased 0.4% to US$157.7 million from US$157.0 million in the equivalent prior-year period.

Prospects: Our evaluation of Teleflex Inc. as of June 19, 2016 is the result of our systematic analysis on three basic characteristics: earnings strength, relative valuation, and recent stock price movement. The company has generated a negative trend in earnings per share over the past 5 quarters and while recent estimates for the company have been mixed, TFX has posted better than expected results. Based on operating earnings yield, the company is about fairly valued when compared to all of the companies in our coverage universe. Share price changes over the past year indicates that TFX will perform in line with the market over the near term.

Financial Data

(US$ in Thousands)	3 Mos	12/31/2015	12/31/2014	12/31/2013	12/31/2012	12/31/2011	12/31/2010	12/31/2009
Earnings Per Share	5.32	5.10	4.04	3.45	(4.65)	7.92	4.99	7.59
Cash Flow Per Share	7.87	7.30	7.02	5.59	4.73	2.55	5.18	4.78
Tang Book Value Per Share	N.M.	N.M.	N.M.	N.M.	N.M.	N.M.	N.M.	3.04
Dividends Per Share	1.360	1.360	1.360	1.360	1.360	1.360	1.360	1.360
Dividend Payout %	25.56	26.67	33.66	39.42	...	17.17	27.25	17.92
Income Statement								
Total Revenue	424,893	1,809,690	1,839,832	1,696,271	1,551,009	1,528,911	1,801,705	1,890,062
EBITDA	99,833	413,830	395,995	324,987	(16,907)	303,377	319,152	370,825
Depn & Amortn	32,336	108,393	111,133	92,976	80,468	85,617	92,189	101,057
Income Before Taxes	53,793	244,646	220,110	175,730	(165,369)	148,703	147,793	182,846
Income Taxes	2,613	7,838	28,650	23,547	16,413	27,000	21,887	39,904
Net Income	50,689	244,863	187,679	150,881	(190,057)	323,329	201,094	302,994
Average Shares	48,782	48,058	46,470	43,693	40,859	40,801	40,280	39,936
Balance Sheet								
Current Assets	1,085,009	1,006,431	1,053,209	1,200,554	1,069,079	1,280,256	921,233	1,003,934
Total Assets	3,943,466	3,878,516	3,977,255	4,209,007	3,739,497	3,924,103	3,643,155	3,839,005
Current Liabilities	674,675	666,712	634,899	635,120	274,405	271,007	420,763	337,107
Long-Term Obligations	641,973	646,000	700,000	930,000	965,280	954,809	813,409	1,192,491
Total Liabilities	1,871,370	1,869,244	2,065,946	2,295,480	1,960,547	1,943,515	1,859,779	2,258,764
Stockholders' Equity	2,072,096	2,009,272	1,911,309	1,913,527	1,778,950	1,980,588	1,783,376	1,580,241
Shares Outstanding	43,579	41,609	41,439	41,179	40,972	40,740	39,995	39,755
Statistical Record								
Return on Assets %	6.54	6.23	4.59	3.80	N.M.	8.55	5.38	7.80
Return on Equity %	13.09	12.49	9.81	8.17	N.M.	17.18	11.96	21.44
EBITDA Margin %	23.50	22.87	21.52	19.16	N.M.	19.84	17.71	19.62
Net Margin %	11.93	13.53	10.20	8.89	N.M.	21.15	11.16	16.03
Asset Turnover	0.46	0.46	0.45	0.43	0.40	0.40	0.48	0.49
Current Ratio	1.61	1.51	1.66	1.89	3.90	4.72	2.19	2.98
Debt to Equity	0.31	0.32	0.37	0.49	0.54	0.48	0.46	0.75
Price Range	154.74-119.49	140.26-109.41	119.15-90.94	98.82-71.31	71.38-57.73	63.81-49.51	66.02-48.06	54.95-38.15
P/E Ratio	29.09-22.46	27.50-21.45	29.49-22.51	28.64-20.67	...	8.06-6.25	13.23-9.63	7.24-5.03
Average Yield %	1.03	1.07	1.28	1.66	2.13	2.42	2.39	2.88

Address: 550 East Swedesford Road, Suite 400, Wayne, PA 19087 Telephone: 610-225-6800	Web Site: www.teleflex.com Officers: Benson F. Smith - Chairman, President, Chief Executive Officer Liam Kelly - President, Executive Vice President, Chief Operating Officer, Division Officer	Auditors: PricewaterhouseCoopers LLP Investor Contact: 610-948-2836 Transfer Agents: American Stock Transfer & Trust Company, New York, NY

TELEPHONE & DATA SYSTEMS, INC.

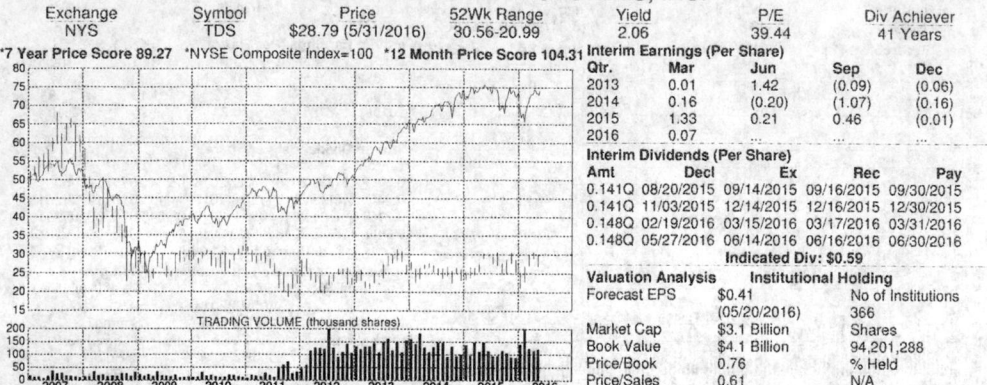

Exchange	Symbol	Price	52Wk Range	Yield	P/E	Div Achiever
NYS	TDS	$28.79 (5/31/2016)	30.56-20.99	2.06	39.44	41 Years

*7 Year Price Score 89.27   *NYSE Composite Index=100   *12 Month Price Score 104.31

Interim Earnings (Per Share)

Qtr.	Mar	Jun	Sep	Dec
2013	0.01	1.42	(0.09)	(0.06)
2014	0.16	(0.20)	(1.07)	(0.16)
2015	1.33	0.21	0.46	(0.01)
2016	0.07	...	...	...

Interim Dividends (Per Share)

Amt	Decl	Ex	Rec	Pay
0.141Q	08/20/2015	09/14/2015	09/16/2015	09/30/2015
0.141Q	11/03/2015	12/14/2015	12/16/2015	12/30/2015
0.148Q	02/19/2016	03/15/2016	03/17/2016	03/31/2016
0.148Q	05/27/2016	06/14/2016	06/16/2016	06/30/2016

Indicated Div: $0.59

Valuation Analysis   **Institutional Holding**

Forecast EPS	$0.41 (05/20/2016)	No of Institutions	366
Market Cap	$3.1 Billion	Shares	
Book Value	$4.1 Billion		94,201,288
Price/Book	0.76	% Held	
Price/Sales	0.61	N/A	

Business Summary: Services (MIC: 6.1.2 SIC: 4813 NAIC: 517110)

Telephone and Data Systems is a telecommunications company. Co. provided services to approximately 4.9 million wireless customers and 1.2 million wireline and cable connections at Dec 31 2015. Co. conducts its wireless operations through its majority-owned subsidiary, United States Cellular Corporation. Co. provides broadband, video, voice and hosted and managed services, through its subsidiary, TDS Telecommunications Corporation. Co. has four business segments comprised of: U.S. Cellular, which provides a range of wireless devices such as handsets, modems, mobile hotspots, home phones and tablets; and TDS Telecom's Wireline, Cable, and Hosted and Managed Services operations.

Recent Developments: For the quarter ended Mar 31 2016, net income decreased 94.3% to US$10.0 million from US$175.8 million in the year-earlier quarter. Revenues were US$1.24 billion, down 0.7% from US$1.25 billion the year before. Operating income was US$15.0 million versus US$282.6 million in the prior-year quarter, a decrease of 94.7%. Direct operating expenses rose 2.4% to US$579.0 million from US$565.6 million in the comparable period the year before. Indirect operating expenses increased 60.9% to US$649.0 million from US$403.3 million in the equivalent prior-year period.

Prospects: Our evaluation of Telephone and Data Systems Inc. as of June 19, 2016 is the result of our systematic analysis on three basic characteristics: earnings strength, relative valuation, and recent stock price movement. The company has suffered a very negative trend in earnings per share over the past 5 quarters and while recent estimates for the company have remained steady, TDS has posted results that fell short of analysts expectations. Based on operating earnings yield, the company is overvalued when compared to all of the companies in our coverage universe. Share price changes over the past year indicates that TDS will perform well over the near term.

Financial Data

(US$ in Thousands)	3 Mos	12/31/2015	12/31/2014	12/31/2013	12/31/2012	12/31/2011	12/31/2010	12/31/2009
Earnings Per Share	0.73	1.98	(1.26)	1.29	0.75	1.83	1.36	1.77
Cash Flow Per Share	6.24	7.27	3.64	4.56	10.14	11.57	10.67	10.08
Tang Book Value Per Share	11.52	11.25	12.91	15.29	15.52	14.95	15.35	15.10
Dividends Per Share	0.571	0.564	0.536	0.510	0.490	0.470	0.450	0.430
Dividend Payout %	78.22	28.48	...	39.53	65.33	25.68	33.09	24.29
Income Statement								
Total Revenue	1,243,000	5,176,241	5,009,438	4,901,236	5,345,277	5,180,471	4,986,829	5,020,674
EBITDA	227,000	1,207,962	607,851	1,234,269	966,165	1,131,863	1,022,703	1,133,906
Depn & Amortn	212,000	810,500	797,600	984,400	785,300	741,600	734,800	724,100
Income Before Taxes	(12,000)	294,526	(284,189)	160,150	103,368	281,207	183,191	296,370
Income Taxes	13,000	171,992	(4,932)	126,043	73,582	113,503	92,283	133,376
Net Income	8,000	219,037	(136,355)	141,927	81,861	200,566	143,856	193,902
Average Shares	110,000	109,910	108,485	109,132	108,937	109,100	105,506	109,577
Balance Sheet								
Current Assets	2,173,000	2,158,343	1,766,955	2,087,337	1,763,437	1,705,680	1,596,076	1,644,142
Total Assets	9,383,000	9,422,462	8,906,939	8,904,147	8,623,900	8,201,005	7,762,519	7,608,784
Current Liabilities	890,000	944,384	1,063,256	1,191,756	924,608	874,133	810,633	780,296
Long-Term Obligations	2,437,000	2,439,827	1,993,586	1,720,074	1,721,571	1,529,857	1,499,862	1,492,908
Total Liabilities	5,256,000	5,296,088	4,979,837	4,785,486	4,611,539	4,238,014	3,947,767	3,830,647
Stockholders' Equity	4,127,000	4,126,374	3,927,102	4,118,661	4,012,361	3,962,991	3,814,752	3,778,137
Shares Outstanding	109,041	108,966	107,899	108,757	108,031	108,456	103,936	106,022
Statistical Record								
Return on Assets %	0.88	2.39	N.M.	1.62	0.97	2.51	1.87	2.54
Return on Equity %	1.98	5.44	N.M.	3.49	2.05	5.16	3.79	5.14
EBITDA Margin %	18.26	23.34	12.13	25.18	18.08	21.85	20.51	22.58
Net Margin %	0.64	4.23	N.M.	2.90	1.53	3.87	2.88	3.86
Asset Turnover	0.56	0.56	0.56	0.56	0.63	0.65	0.65	0.66
Current Ratio	2.44	2.29	1.66	1.75	1.91	1.95	1.97	2.11
Debt to Equity	0.59	0.59	0.51	0.42	0.43	0.39	0.39	0.40
Price Range	30.56-20.99	30.56-23.25	27.84-22.23	31.38-20.71	28.61-19.42	31.86-18.42	32.04-25.28	30.86-22.19
P/E Ratio	41.86-28.75	15.43-11.74	...	24.33-16.05	38.15-25.89	17.41-10.07	23.56-18.59	17.44-12.54
Average Yield %	2.09	2.07	2.07	2.10	2.00	2.08	1.81	1.58

Address: 30 North LaSalle Street, Suite 4000, Chicago, IL 60602 **Telephone:** 312-630-1900 **Fax:** 312-630-1908	**Web Site:** www.teldta.com **Officers:** LeRoy T. Carlson - President, Chief Executive Officer Kenneth R. Meyers - Chief Financial Officer, Executive Vice President	**Auditors:** PricewaterhouseCoopers LLP **Investor Contact:** 312-592-5341 **Transfer Agents:** Computershare Trust Company, N.A., College Station, TX

TEMPUR SEALY INTERNATIONAL, INC.

Exchange	Symbol	Price	52Wk Range	Yield	P/E
NYS	TPX	$58.22 (5/31/2016)	81.89-52.51	N/A	40.71

*7 Year Price Score 121.74 ***NYSE Composite Index=100** ***12 Month Price Score 86.51**

Price chart and Trading Volume (thousand shares), 2007–2016

Interim Earnings (Per Share)

Qtr.	Mar	Jun	Sep	Dec
2013	0.20	(0.03)	0.65	0.45
2014	0.44	(0.04)	0.60	0.75
2015	0.38	0.34	0.64	(0.19)
2016	0.64	...	...	...

Interim Dividends (Per Share)

No Dividends Paid

Valuation Analysis | Institutional Holding

Valuation Analysis		Institutional Holding	
Forecast EPS	$3.90	No of Institutions	
	(05/15/2016)	381	
Market Cap	$3.5 Billion	Shares	
Book Value	$252.4 Million	77,640,384	
Price/Book	14.05	% Held	
Price/Sales	1.13	95.73	

Business Summary: Furniture (MIC: 1.6.2 SIC: 2515 NAIC: 337910)

Tempur Sealy International is a developer, manufacturer, marketer, and distributor of bedding products. Co.'s brand portfolio includes TEMPUR®, Tempur-Pedic®, Sealy®, Sealy Posturepedic®, and Stearns & Foster®. Co.'s bedding product category includes mattresses, foundations and adjustable foundations. Co.'s other products include pillows, mattress covers, sheets, cushions and various other comfort products. Co. sells its products through two distribution channels: Retail, which includes furniture and bedding retailers, department stores, specialty retailers and warehouse clubs; and Other, which includes third party distributors; hospitality and healthcare customers.

Recent Developments:
For the quarter ended Mar 31 2016, net income increased 56.0% to US$39.0 million from US$25.0 million in the year-earlier quarter. Revenues were US$721.0 million, down 2.5% from US$739.5 million the year before. Operating income was US$76.7 million versus US$54.4 million in the prior-year quarter, an increase of 41.0%. Direct operating expenses declined 6.7% to US$430.0 million from US$460.8 million in the comparable period the year before. Indirect operating expenses decreased 4.5% to US$214.3 million from US$224.3 million in the equivalent prior-year period.

Prospects:
Our evaluation of Tempur-Sealy International Inc. as of June 19, 2016 is the result of our systematic analysis on three basic characteristics: earnings strength, relative valuation, and recent stock price movement. The company has managed to produce a neutral trend in earnings per share over the past 5 quarters and while recent estimates for the company have been raised by analysts, TPX has posted better than expected results. Based on operating earnings yield, the company is undervalued when compared to all of the companies in our coverage universe. Share price changes over the past year indicates that TPX will perform in line with the market over the near term.

Financial Data

(US$ in Thousands)	3 Mos	12/31/2015	12/31/2014	12/31/2013	12/31/2012	12/31/2011	12/31/2010	12/31/2009
Earnings Per Share	1.43	1.17	1.75	1.28	1.70	3.18	2.16	1.12
Cash Flow Per Share	3.58	3.80	3.70	1.63	3.08	3.71	2.62	1.80
Income Statement								
Total Revenue	721,000	3,151,200	2,989,800	2,464,300	1,402,900	1,417,938	1,105,421	831,156
EBITDA	82,800	337,800	316,200	293,800	278,900	369,258	273,365	174,396
Depn & Amortn	7,900	53,500	57,700	59,400	30,900	28,919	27,999	29,010
Income Before Taxes	53,500	188,200	166,600	123,600	229,200	328,391	230,865	128,037
Income Taxes	17,300	125,400	64,900	49,100	122,400	108,783	73,720	43,044
Net Income	39,600	73,500	108,900	78,600	106,800	219,608	157,145	84,993
Average Shares	62,600	62,600	62,100	61,600	62,900	69,149	72,792	76,048
Balance Sheet								
Current Assets	708,900	809,100	766,400	727,500	821,100	379,470	271,480	208,983
Total Assets	2,576,800	2,655,500	2,662,600	2,729,900	1,313,000	828,640	716,003	643,379
Current Liabilities	655,100	713,000	538,300	441,500	212,100	183,179	146,234	136,525
Long-Term Obligations	1,293,700	1,273,300	1,535,900	1,796,900	1,025,000	585,000	407,000	297,470
Total Liabilities	2,324,400	2,365,300	2,459,900	2,611,300	1,290,700	797,849	589,970	471,086
Stockholders' Equity	252,400	290,200	202,700	118,600	22,300	30,791	126,033	172,293
Shares Outstanding	60,921	62,400	60,900	60,600	59,700	63,770	68,484	75,112
Statistical Record								
Return on Assets %	3.43	2.76	4.04	3.89	9.95	28.43	23.12	13.18
Return on Equity %	40.14	29.82	67.79	111.57	401.23	280.07	105.35	69.46
EBITDA Margin %	11.48	10.72	10.58	11.92	19.88	26.04	24.73	20.98
Net Margin %	5.49	2.33	3.64	3.19	7.61	15.49	14.22	10.23
Asset Turnover	1.20	1.19	1.11	1.22	1.31	1.84	1.63	1.29
Current Ratio	1.08	1.13	1.42	1.65	3.87	2.07	1.86	1.53
Debt to Equity	5.13	4.39	7.58	15.15	45.96	19.00	3.23	1.73
Price Range	81.89-52.51	81.89-49.17	61.34-45.64	54.19-31.49	87.26-21.02	72.24-39.40	40.62-23.63	24.28-3.93
P/E Ratio	57.27-36.72	69.99-42.03	35.05-26.08	42.34-24.60	51.33-12.36	22.72-12.39	18.81-10.94	21.68-3.51

Address: 1000 Tempur Way, Lexington, KY 40511 **Telephone:** 800-878-8889	**Web Site:** www.tempursealy.com **Officers:** Scott L. Thompson - Chairman, President, Chief Executive Officer Robert B. Trussell - Vice-Chairman	**Auditors:** Ernst & Young LLP **Investor Contact:** 800-805-3635 **Transfer Agents:** American Stock Transfer & Trust Company, LLC

TENET HEALTHCARE CORP.

Exchange	Symbol	Price	52Wk Range	Yield	P/E
NYS	THC	$28.94 (5/31/2016)	60.78-22.63	N/A	N/A

*7 Year Price Score 97.59 *NYSE Composite Index=100 *12 Month Price Score 80.63

Interim Earnings (Per Share)

Qtr.	Mar	Jun	Sep	Dec
2013	(0.85)	(0.49)	0.27	(0.25)
2014	(0.33)	(0.27)	0.09	0.62
2015	0.47	(0.61)	(0.29)	(0.98)
2016	(0.60)	...	...	...

Interim Dividends (Per Share)

Amt	Decl	Ex	Rec	Pay
1-for-4	...	10/10/2012	...	...

Valuation Analysis   Institutional Holding

Forecast EPS	$1.89	No of Institutions
	(05/20/2016)	444
Market Cap	$2.9 Billion	Shares
Book Value	$625.0 Million	173,036,512
Price/Book	4.60	% Held
Price/Sales	0.15	N/A

Business Summary: Hospitals & Health Care Facilities (MIC: 4.2.1 SIC: 8062 NAIC: 622110)

Tenet Healthcare is a healthcare services company whose subsidiaries and affiliates as of Dec 31 2015 operated 86 hospitals, 20 short-stay surgical hospitals, over 475 outpatient centers, nine facilities in the U.K. and six health plans through its subsidiaries, partnerships and joint ventures, and Co.'s Conifer Holdings, Inc. (Conifer) subsidiary, which provides healthcare business process services. Co.'s business lines are classified into three reportable business segments: Hospital Operations and other, Ambulatory Care and Conifer.

Recent Developments: For the quarter ended Mar 31 2016, income from continuing operations decreased 49.3% to US$38.0 million from US$75.0 million in the year-earlier quarter. Net income decreased 55.3% to US$34.0 million from US$76.0 million in the year-earlier quarter. Revenues were US$5.07 billion, up 14.5% from US$4.43 billion the year before. Operating income was US$347.0 million versus US$290.0 million in the prior-year quarter, an increase of 19.7%. Indirect operating expenses increased 14.1% to US$4.72 billion from US$4.14 billion in the equivalent prior-year period.

Prospects: Our evaluation of Tenet Healthcare Corp. as of June 19, 2016 is the result of our systematic analysis on three basic characteristics: earnings strength, relative valuation, and recent stock price movement. The company has produced a positive trend in earnings per share over the past 5 quarters and while recent estimates for the company have been raised by analysts, THC has posted better than expected results. Based on operating earnings yield, the company is about fairly valued when compared to all of the companies in our coverage universe. Share price changes over the past year indicates that THC will perform poorly over the near term.

Financial Data
(US$ in Millions)

	3 Mos	12/31/2015	12/31/2014	12/31/2013	12/31/2012	12/31/2011	12/31/2010	12/31/2009
Earnings Per Share	(2.48)	(1.41)	0.12	(1.32)	1.30	0.48	8.16	1.48
Cash Flow Per Share	12.45	10.35	7.02	5.79	5.68	4.24	3.90	3.54
Tang Book Value Per Share	N.M.	N.M.	N.M.	N.M.	N.M.	N.M.	2.78	N.M.
Income Statement								
Total Revenue	5,068	18,634	16,615	11,102	9,119	8,854	9,205	9,014
EBITDA	358	1,894	1,778	880	1,198	979	1,007	1,036
Depn & Amortn	10	838	877	564	452	443	425	386
Income Before Taxes	105	144	147	(158)	334	161	158	205
Income Taxes	67	68	49	(65)	125	61	(977)	(23)
Net Income	34	78	76	(104)	133	94	1,152	197
Average Shares	98	99	100	101	108	121	140	126
Balance Sheet								
Current Assets	5,129	5,171	4,717	3,710	2,681	2,357	2,311	2,472
Total Assets	23,766	23,682	18,141	16,130	9,044	8,462	8,500	7,953
Current Liabilities	4,268	4,308	3,577	2,928	1,763	1,815	1,725	1,783
Long-Term Obligations	14,350	14,383	11,695	10,690	5,158	4,294	3,997	4,272
Total Liabilities	23,141	22,991	17,490	15,375	7,901	7,039	6,734	7,307
Stockholders' Equity	625	691	651	755	1,143	1,423	1,766	646
Shares Outstanding	99	98	98	96	104	103	121	120
Statistical Record								
Return on Assets %	N.M.	0.37	0.44	N.M.	1.52	1.11	14.00	2.44
Return on Equity %	N.M.	11.62	10.81	N.M.	10.34	5.90	95.52	52.60
EBITDA Margin %	7.06	10.16	10.70	7.93	13.14	11.06	10.94	11.49
Net Margin %	0.67	0.42	0.46	N.M.	1.46	1.06	12.51	2.19
Asset Turnover	0.91	0.89	0.97	0.88	1.04	1.04	1.12	1.12
Current Ratio	1.20	1.20	1.32	1.27	1.52	1.30	1.34	1.39
Debt to Equity	22.96	20.81	17.96	14.16	4.51	3.02	2.26	6.61
Price Range	60.78-22.63	60.78-27.23	63.27-38.75	49.25-32.47	33.50-17.56	30.52-14.36	27.32-15.68	24.96-3.60
P/E Ratio	...	...	527.25-322.92	...	25.77-13.51	63.58-29.92	3.35-1.92	16.86-2.43

Address: 1445 Ross Avenue, Suite 1400, Dallas, TX 75202 Telephone: 469-893-2200	Web Site: www.tenethealth.com Officers: Edward A. Kangas - Chairman Keith B. Pitts - Vice-Chairman	Auditors: Deloitte & Touche LLP Transfer Agents: Computershare

TENNANT CO.

Exchange	Symbol	Price	52Wk Range	Yield	P/E	Div Achiever
NYS	TNC	$53.70 (5/31/2016)	66.70-46.54	1.49	31.22	43 Years

*7 Year Price Score 101.45 *NYSE Composite Index=100 *12 Month Price Score 92.75

Interim Earnings (Per Share)

Qtr.	Mar	Jun	Sep	Dec
2013	0.27	0.76	0.56	0.55
2014	0.31	0.83	0.63	0.93
2015	0.27	0.79	(0.05)	0.73
2016	0.25	...	...	...

Interim Dividends (Per Share)

Amt	Decl	Ex	Rec	Pay
0.20Q	08/19/2015	08/27/2015	08/31/2015	09/15/2015
0.20Q	11/09/2015	11/25/2015	11/30/2015	12/15/2015
0.20Q	02/17/2016	02/25/2016	02/29/2016	03/15/2016
0.20Q	04/27/2016	05/26/2016	05/31/2016	06/15/2016

Indicated Div: $0.80 (Div. Reinv. Plan)

Valuation Analysis — **Institutional Holding**

Forecast EPS	$2.39
(04/09/2016)	No of Institutions 191
Market Cap	$948.5 Million — Shares
Book Value	$251.7 Million — 16,189,487
Price/Book	3.77 — % Held
Price/Sales	1.18 — 85.56

Business Summary: Industrial Machinery & Equipment (MIC: 7.2.1 SIC: 3589 NAIC: 333319)

Tennant is engaged in designing, manufacturing and marketing solutions. Co. provides products and solutions consisting of mechanized cleaning equipment, detergent-free and other sustainable cleaning technologies, aftermarket parts and consumables, equipment maintenance and repair service, specialty surface coatings, and business solutions such as financing, rental and leasing programs, and machine-to-machine asset management solutions. Co. markets and sells the following brands: Tennant®, Nobles®, Green Machinesâ,,¢, Alfa Uma Empresa Tennantâ,,¢, IRIS® and Orbio®. Co.'s Orbio Technologies Group markets and sells Orbio-branded products and solutions.

Recent Developments: For the quarter ended Mar 31 2016, net income decreased 11.7% to US$4.4 million from US$5.0 million in the year-earlier quarter. Revenues were US$179.9 million, down 3.2% from US$185.7 million the year before. Operating income was US$7.1 million versus US$8.3 million in the prior-year quarter, a decrease of 14.0%. Direct operating expenses declined 4.9% to US$102.4 million from US$107.7 million in the comparable period the year before. Indirect operating expenses increased 0.8% to US$70.4 million from US$69.8 million in the equivalent prior-year period.

Prospects: Our evaluation of Tennant Co. as of June 19, 2016 is the result of our systematic analysis on three basic characteristics: earnings strength, relative valuation, and recent stock price movement. The company has generated a negative trend in earnings per share over the past 5 quarters and while recent estimates for the company have remained steady, TNC has posted better than expected results. Based on operating earnings yield, the company is about fairly valued when compared to all of the companies in our coverage universe. Share price changes over the past year indicates that TNC will perform poorly over the near term.

Financial Data

(US$ in Thousands)	3 Mos	12/31/2015	12/31/2014	12/31/2013	12/31/2012	12/31/2011	12/31/2010	12/31/2009
Earnings Per Share	1.72	1.74	2.70	2.14	2.18	1.69	1.80	(1.42)
Cash Flow Per Share	2.33	2.51	3.26	3.27	2.56	3.02	2.26	4.06
Tang Book Value Per Share	13.11	13.09	13.40	12.22	10.50	9.39	8.95	7.19
Dividends Per Share	0.800	0.800	0.780	0.720	0.690	0.680	0.590	0.530
Dividend Payout %	46.51	45.98	28.89	33.64	31.65	40.24	32.78	...
Income Statement								
Total Revenue	179,864	811,799	821,983	752,011	738,980	753,998	667,667	595,875
EBITDA	11,156	68,115	88,652	78,935	79,410	68,304	54,239	(2,251)
Depn & Amortn	4,368	16,550	17,694	17,686	18,072	18,088	18,026	19,632
Income Before Taxes	6,527	50,424	69,538	59,878	59,890	48,730	34,727	(24,320)
Income Taxes	2,088	18,336	18,887	19,647	18,306	16,017	(76)	1,921
Net Income	4,439	32,088	50,651	40,231	41,584	32,713	34,803	(26,241)
Average Shares	17,977	18,493	18,740	18,833	19,102	19,360	19,332	18,507
Balance Sheet								
Current Assets	259,446	293,644	347,089	315,296	273,446	272,096	248,269	215,912
Total Assets	412,700	432,295	486,932	456,306	420,760	424,262	403,668	377,726
Current Liabilities	115,770	133,216	145,630	131,526	121,694	123,992	116,144	116,152
Long-Term Obligations	19,189	21,194	24,571	28,000	30,281	32,289	27,674	30,192
Total Liabilities	160,968	180,088	206,281	192,460	185,706	203,410	187,535	193,447
Stockholders' Equity	251,732	252,207	280,651	263,846	235,054	220,852	216,133	184,279
Shares Outstanding	17,662	17,744	18,415	18,491	18,464	18,834	19,038	18,750
Statistical Record								
Return on Assets %	7.27	6.98	10.74	9.17	9.82	7.90	8.91	N.M.
Return on Equity %	12.02	12.04	18.60	16.13	18.19	14.97	17.38	N.M.
EBITDA Margin %	6.20	8.39	10.79	10.50	10.75	9.06	8.12	N.M.
Net Margin %	2.47	3.95	6.16	5.35	5.63	4.34	5.21	N.M.
Asset Turnover	1.86	1.77	1.74	1.71	1.74	1.82	1.71	1.43
Current Ratio	2.24	2.20	2.38	2.40	2.25	2.19	2.14	1.86
Debt to Equity	0.08	0.08	0.09	0.11	0.13	0.15	0.13	0.16
Price Range	68.12-46.54	72.17-54.49	76.52-58.21	68.70-43.95	48.45-35.30	44.25-32.92	38.82-21.84	31.92-7.74
P/E Ratio	39.60-27.06	41.48-31.32	28.34-21.56	32.10-20.54	22.22-16.19	26.18-19.48	21.57-12.13	...
Average Yield %	1.36	1.28	1.15	1.35	1.67	1.73	1.86	2.61

Address: 701 North Lilac Drive, P.O. Box 1452, Minneapolis, MN 55440
Telephone: 763-540-1200

Web Site: www.tennantco.com
Officers: H. Chris Killingstad - President, Chief Executive Officer Heidi M. Wilson - Senior Vice President, General Counsel, Secretary

Auditors: KPMG LLP
Investor Contact: 763-540-1204
Transfer Agents: Wells Fargo Bank, N.A., St. Paul, MN

TENNECO INC

Exchange	Symbol	Price	52Wk Range	Yield	P/E
NYS	TEN	$53.72 (5/31/2016)	61.53-35.59	N/A	12.49

*7 Year Price Score 105.75 *NYSE Composite Index=100 *12 Month Price Score 103.91

TRADING VOLUME (thousand shares)

Interim Earnings (Per Share)

Qtr.	Mar	Jun	Sep	Dec
2013	0.88	1.02	0.19	0.88
2014	0.75	1.32	1.27	0.33
2015	0.80	1.26	0.88	1.17
2016	0.99			

Interim Dividends (Per Share)

No Dividends Paid

Valuation Analysis   **Institutional Holding**

Forecast EPS	$5.64	No of Institutions	
	(05/20/2016)	367	
Market Cap	$3.1 Billion	Shares	
Book Value	$505.0 Million	57,544,952	
Price/Book	6.09	% Held	
Price/Sales	0.37	87.12	

Business Summary: Auto Parts (MIC: 1.8.2 SIC: 3714 NAIC: 336330)

Tenneco designs, manufactures and sells clean air and ride performance systems and products for light vehicle, commercial truck, off-highway and other applications. Co. serves both original equipment manufacturers and replacement markets through brands such as Monroe® and Clevite® Elastomers. As a parts supplier, Co. produces individual component parts for vehicles as well as groups of components that are combined as modules or systems within vehicles. Co. has six operating segments: North America Clean Air; North America Ride Performance; Europe, South America and India Clean Air; Europe, South America and India Ride Performance; Asia Pacific Clean Air and Asia Pacific Ride Performance.

Recent Developments: For the quarter ended Mar 31 2016, net income increased 14.3% to US$72.0 million from US$63.0 million in the year-earlier quarter. Revenues were US$2.14 billion, up 5.6% from US$2.02 billion the year before. Direct operating expenses rose 5.0% to US$1.77 billion from US$1.69 billion in the comparable period the year before. Indirect operating expenses increased 11.1% to US$240.0 million from US$216.0 million in the equivalent prior-year period.

Prospects: Our evaluation of Tenneco Automotive Inc. as of June 19, 2016 is the result of our systematic analysis on three basic characteristics: earnings strength, relative valuation, and recent stock price movement. The company has produced a positive trend in earnings per share over the past 5 quarters and while recent estimates for the company have been raised by analysts, TEN has posted better than expected results. Based on operating earnings yield, the company is undervalued when compared to all of the companies in our coverage universe. Share price changes over the past year indicates that TEN will perform in line with the market over the near term.

Financial Data
(US$ in Thousands)

	3 Mos	12/31/2015	12/31/2014	12/31/2013	12/31/2012	12/31/2011	12/31/2010	12/31/2009
Earnings Per Share	4.30	4.11	3.66	2.97	4.50	2.55	0.63	(1.50)
Cash Flow Per Share	9.42	8.66	5.61	8.32	6.07	4.09	4.12	4.96
Tang Book Value Per Share	7.42	6.09	6.63	5.49	2.30	...	...	...
Income Statement								
Total Revenue	2,136,000	8,209,000	8,420,000	7,964,000	7,363,000	7,205,000	5,937,000	4,649,000
EBITDA	178,000	722,000	700,000	629,000	633,000	586,000	497,000	313,000
Depn & Amortn	54,000	203,000	208,000	205,000	205,000	207,000	216,000	221,000
Income Before Taxes	106,000	452,000	401,000	344,000	323,000	271,000	132,000	(41,000)
Income Taxes	34,000	149,000	131,000	122,000	19,000	88,000	69,000	13,000
Net Income	57,000	247,000	226,000	183,000	275,000	157,000	39,000	(73,000)
Average Shares	57,445	60,193	61,782	61,594	61,083	61,520	60,998	48,572
Balance Sheet								
Current Assets	2,662,000	2,311,000	2,426,000	2,290,000	2,124,000	1,979,000	1,790,000	1,393,000
Total Assets	4,348,000	3,967,000	4,010,000	3,830,000	3,608,000	3,337,000	3,167,000	2,841,000
Current Liabilities	1,921,000	1,794,000	1,799,000	1,838,000	1,649,000	1,570,000	1,468,000	1,201,000
Long-Term Obligations	1,311,000	1,124,000	1,069,000	1,019,000	1,067,000	1,158,000	1,160,000	1,145,000
Total Liabilities	3,843,000	3,534,000	3,513,000	3,397,000	3,362,000	3,337,000	3,171,000	2,862,000
Stockholders' Equity	505,000	433,000	497,000	433,000	246,000	...	(4,000)	(21,000)
Shares Outstanding	57,287	57,593	61,209	60,870	60,494	60,406	60,247	59,495
Statistical Record								
Return on Assets %	6.01	6.19	5.77	4.92	7.90	4.83	1.30	N.M.
Return on Equity %	52.09	53.12	48.60	53.90	222.97	...	...	...
EBITDA Margin %	8.33	8.80	8.31	7.90	8.60	8.13	8.37	6.73
Net Margin %	2.67	3.01	2.68	2.30	3.73	2.18	0.66	N.M.
Asset Turnover	1.96	2.06	2.15	2.14	2.11	2.22	1.98	1.64
Current Ratio	1.39	1.29	1.35	1.25	1.29	1.26	1.22	1.16
Debt to Equity	2.60	2.60	2.15	2.35	4.34	...	...	...
Price Range	61.53-35.59	61.53-42.24	68.60-47.93	57.53-34.57	39.76-24.72	46.58-23.90	43.03-17.68	19.30-0.70
P/E Ratio	14.31-8.28	14.97-10.28	18.74-13.10	19.37-11.64	8.84-5.49	18.27-9.37	68.30-28.06	...

Address: 500 North Field Drive, Lake Forest, IL 60045
Telephone: 847-482-5000

Web Site: www.tenneco.com
Officers: Gregg M. Sherrill - Chairman, Chief Executive Officer Kenneth R. Trammell - Executive Vice President, Chief Financial Officer

Auditors: PricewaterhouseCoopers LLP
Investor Contact: 847-482-5162
Transfer Agents: Wells Fargo Bank, N.A. Shareowner Services, Mendota Heights, MN

TERADATA CORP (DE)

Exchange	Symbol	Price	52Wk Range	Yield	P/E
NYS	TDC	$28.34 (5/31/2016)	40.00-22.60	N/A	N/A

*7 Year Price Score 55.35   *NYSE Composite Index=100   *12 Month Price Score 88.44

Interim Earnings (Per Share)

Qtr.	Mar	Jun	Sep	Dec
2013	0.35	0.65	0.59	0.68
2014	0.37	0.60	0.60	0.76
2015	0.15	(1.87)	0.55	(0.37)
2016	(0.36)	...	...	...

Interim Dividends (Per Share)

No Dividends Paid

Valuation Analysis		Institutional Holding	
Forecast EPS	$2.40	No of Institutions	
	(05/20/2016)	555	
Market Cap	$3.7 Billion	Shares	
Book Value	$794.0 Million	136,659,840	
Price/Book	4.62	% Held	
Price/Sales	1.47	94.89	

Business Summary: IT Services (MIC: 6.3.1 SIC: 7372 NAIC: 511210)

Teradata is a provider of analytic data solutions and related services. Co.'s analytic data solutions comprise software, hardware, and related business consulting and support services for analytics across a company's analytical ecosystem, which includes components such as data warehousing, big data, discovery tools, integration tools, and business intelligence tools as well as the services to architect, manage, and integrate this ecosystem. Co. helps customers access and manage data and extract business value and insight from their data. Co. also provides marketing and analytic applications that are designed to utilize data to help customers discover and exploit new insights.

Recent Developments: For the quarter ended Mar 31 2016, net loss amounted to US$46.0 million versus net income of US$22.0 million in the year-earlier quarter. Revenues were US$545.0 million, down 6.4% from US$582.0 million the year before. Operating loss was US$42.0 million versus an income of US$30.0 million in the prior-year quarter. Direct operating expenses declined 9.5% to US$276.0 million from US$305.0 million in the comparable period the year before. Indirect operating expenses increased 25.9% to US$311.0 million from US$247.0 million in the equivalent prior-year period.

Prospects: Our evaluation of Teradata Corp. as of June 19, 2016 is the result of our systematic analysis on three basic characteristics: earnings strength, relative valuation, and recent stock price movement. The company has produced a positive trend in earnings per share over the past 5 quarters. However, while recent estimates for the company have been lowered by analysts, TDC has posted better than expected results. Based on operating earnings yield, the company is undervalued when compared to all of the companies in our coverage universe. Share price changes over the past year indicates that TDC will perform poorly over the near term.

Financial Data

(US$ in Millions)	3 Mos	12/31/2015	12/31/2014	12/31/2013	12/31/2012	12/31/2011	12/31/2010	12/31/2009
Earnings Per Share	(2.05)	(1.53)	2.33	2.27	2.44	2.05	1.77	1.46
Cash Flow Per Share	3.32	2.87	4.38	3.12	3.41	3.05	2.47	2.65
Tang Book Value Per Share	1.57	1.97	2.87	3.56	2.95	2.68	5.57	4.14
Income Statement								
Total Revenue	545	2,530	2,732	2,692	2,665	2,362	1,936	1,709
EBITDA	(8)	(6)	616	612	667	514	474	393
Depn & Amortn	34	129	122	104	89	33	60	59
Income Before Taxes	(45)	(144)	494	508	578	481	414	334
Income Taxes	1	70	127	131	159	128	113	80
Net Income	(46)	(214)	367	377	419	353	301	254
Average Shares	129	139	157	166	171	171	170	173
Balance Sheet								
Current Assets	1,677	1,734	1,572	1,563	1,534	1,412	1,406	1,152
Total Assets	2,464	2,530	3,132	3,096	3,066	2,616	1,883	1,569
Current Liabilities	968	953	995	776	806	695	569	543
Long-Term Obligations	560	570	195	248	274	290	...	...
Total Liabilities	1,670	1,681	1,425	1,239	1,287	1,122	694	659
Stockholders' Equity	794	849	1,707	1,857	1,779	1,494	1,189	910
Shares Outstanding	129	130	147	159	165	167	168	168
Statistical Record								
Return on Assets %	N.M.	N.M.	11.79	12.24	14.71	15.69	17.44	16.94
Return on Equity %	N.M.	N.M.	20.59	20.74	25.53	26.31	28.68	30.11
EBITDA Margin %	N.M.	N.M.	22.55	22.73	25.03	21.76	24.48	23.00
Net Margin %	N.M.	N.M.	13.43	14.00	15.72	14.94	15.55	14.86
Asset Turnover	0.90	0.89	0.88	0.87	0.94	1.05	1.12	1.14
Current Ratio	1.73	1.82	1.58	2.01	1.90	2.03	2.47	2.12
Debt to Equity	0.71	0.67	0.11	0.13	0.15	0.19	...	...
Price Range	45.89-22.60	46.98-25.58	49.19-39.54	69.34-39.52	80.62-47.37	62.33-41.16	43.50-27.66	32.08-13.02
P/E Ratio	...	...	21.11-16.97	30.55-17.41	33.04-19.41	30.40-20.08	24.58-15.63	21.97-8.92

Address: 10000 Innovation Drive, Dayton, OH 45342
Telephone: 866-548-8348

Web Site: www.teradata.com
Officers: James M. Ringler - Chairman Victor L. Lund - President, Chief Executive Officer

Auditors: PricewaterhouseCoopers LLP
Investor Contact: 937-242-4878
Transfer Agents: Computershare Shareowner Services

TERADYNE, INC.

Exchange	Symbol	Price	52Wk Range	Yield	P/E
NYS	TER	$19.81 (5/31/2016)	21.75-16.78	1.21	18.51

*7 Year Price Score 106.43 *NYSE Composite Index=100   *12 Month Price Score 99.99

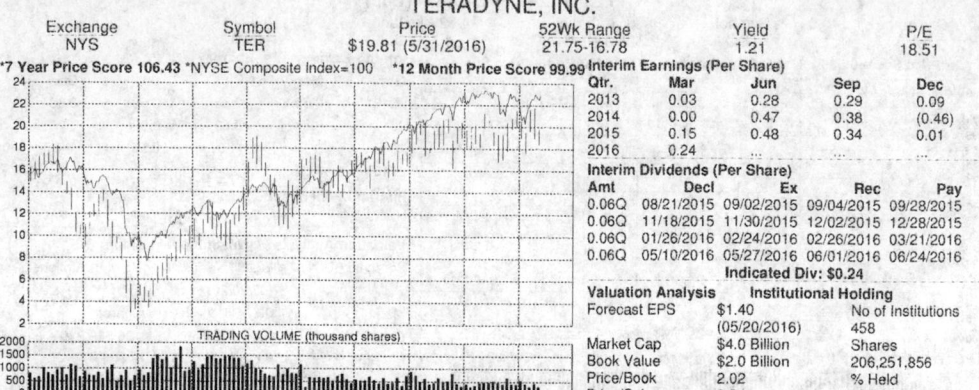

Interim Earnings (Per Share)

Qtr.	Mar	Jun	Sep	Dec
2013	0.03	0.28	0.29	0.09
2014	0.00	0.47	0.38	(0.46)
2015	0.15	0.48	0.34	0.01
2016	0.24	...	...	...

Interim Dividends (Per Share)

Amt	Decl	Ex	Rec	Pay
0.06Q	08/21/2015	09/02/2015	09/04/2015	09/28/2015
0.06Q	11/18/2015	11/30/2015	12/02/2015	12/28/2015
0.06Q	01/26/2016	02/24/2016	02/26/2016	03/21/2016
0.06Q	05/10/2016	05/27/2016	06/01/2016	06/24/2016

Indicated Div: $0.24

Valuation Analysis

		Institutional Holding	
Forecast EPS	$1.40	No of Institutions	
	(05/20/2016)	458	
Market Cap	$4.0 Billion	Shares	
Book Value	$2.0 Billion	206,251,856	
Price/Book	2.02	% Held	
Price/Sales	2.34	96.78	

Business Summary: Semiconductors (MIC: 6.2.4 SIC: 3825 NAIC: 334515)

Teradyne is a global supplier of automation equipment for test and industrial applications. Co. designs, develops, manufactures and sells automatic test systems used to test semiconductors, wireless products, data storage and electronics systems in the consumer electronics, wireless, automotive, industrial, computing, communications, and aerospace and defense industries. Co.'s automatic test equipment and industrial automation products and services include: semiconductor test systems; defense/aerospace test instrumentation and systems, storage test systems, and circuit-board test and inspection systems; wireless test systems; and industrial automation products.

Recent Developments: For the quarter ended Apr 3 2016, net income increased 52.5% to US$50.0 million from US$32.8 million in the year-earlier quarter. Revenues were US$431.0 million, up 25.9% from US$342.4 million the year before. Operating income was US$56.1 million versus US$35.1 million in the prior-year quarter, an increase of 59.8%. Direct operating expenses rose 33.8% to US$200.7 million from US$150.0 million in the comparable period the year before. Indirect operating expenses increased 10.8% to US$174.2 million from US$157.3 million in the equivalent prior-year period.

Prospects: Our evaluation of Teradyne Inc. as of June 19, 2016 is the result of our systematic analysis on three basic characteristics: earnings strength, relative valuation, and recent stock price movement. The company has generated a negative trend in earnings per share over the past 5 quarters. However, while recent estimates for the company have been mixed, TER has posted better than expected results. Based on operating earnings yield, the company is undervalued when compared to all of the companies in our coverage universe. Share price changes over the past year indicates that TER will perform in line with the market over the near term.

Financial Data

(US$ in Thousands)	3 Mos	12/31/2015	12/31/2014	12/31/2013	12/31/2012	12/31/2011	12/31/2010	12/31/2009
Earnings Per Share	1.07	0.97	0.37	0.70	0.94	1.65	1.73	(0.77)
Cash Flow Per Share	1.97	1.95	2.43	1.40	2.16	1.48	3.15	0.70
Tang Book Value Per Share	6.27	6.08	7.46	7.15	5.91	4.14	5.49	2.93
Dividends Per Share	0.240	0.240	0.180	...	...	...	...	...
Dividend Payout %	22.43	24.74	48.65	...	...	...	...	...
Income Statement								
Total Revenue	430,994	1,639,578	1,647,824	1,427,933	1,656,750	1,429,061	1,608,650	819,407
EBITDA	92,922	385,017	240,251	320,359	415,868	327,254	496,265	(30,027)
Depn & Amortn	36,662	137,231	144,200	129,700	128,500	91,540	82,797	92,394
Income Before Taxes	57,192	253,124	95,376	201,922	265,976	218,637	394,512	(142,637)
Income Taxes	7,206	46,647	14,104	36,975	48,927	(129,256)	14,782	(8,800)
Net Income	49,986	206,477	81,272	164,947	217,049	373,809	379,730	(133,837)
Average Shares	205,732	213,321	222,550	235,599	230,246	226,820	226,807	173,604
Balance Sheet								
Current Assets	1,242,722	1,259,968	1,243,846	1,440,277	1,236,061	1,099,887	1,176,618	762,292
Total Assets	2,548,974	2,548,674	2,538,520	2,629,824	2,429,345	2,188,639	1,810,355	1,235,337
Current Liabilities	344,522	372,857	292,406	475,632	297,828	373,684	363,704	283,357
Long-Term Obligations	...	...	...	...	171,059	159,956	150,182	141,100
Total Liabilities	553,073	582,888	459,540	644,730	650,990	683,579	688,167	570,758
Stockholders' Equity	1,995,901	1,965,786	2,078,980	1,985,094	1,778,355	1,505,060	1,122,188	664,579
Shares Outstanding	203,707	203,641	216,613	191,731	187,908	183,587	182,035	174,908
Statistical Record								
Return on Assets %	8.84	8.12	3.14	6.52	9.37	18.70	24.94	N.M.
Return on Equity %	11.04	10.21	4.00	8.77	13.18	28.46	42.50	N.M.
EBITDA Margin %	21.56	23.48	14.58	22.44	25.10	22.90	30.85	N.M.
Net Margin %	11.60	12.59	4.93	11.55	13.10	26.16	23.61	N.M.
Asset Turnover	0.68	0.64	0.64	0.56	0.72	0.71	1.06	0.66
Current Ratio	3.61	3.38	4.25	3.03	4.15	2.94	3.24	2.69
Debt to Equity	...	...	...	...	...	0.10	0.11	0.13
Price Range	21.75-16.78	21.48-16.78	20.72-16.16	18.56-14.30	17.39-13.05	19.07-10.55	14.39-8.98	10.80-3.44
P/E Ratio	20.33-15.68	22.14-17.30	56.00-43.68	26.51-20.43	18.50-13.88	11.56-6.39	8.32-5.19	...
Average Yield %	1.23	1.24	0.94	...	...	...	...	...

Address: 600 Riverpark Drive, North Reading, MA 01864 **Telephone:** 978-370-2700	**Web Site:** www.teradyne.com **Officers:** Mark E. Jagiela - President, Chief Executive Officer, Vice President, Division Officer Gregory R. Beecher - Vice President, Chief Financial Officer, Treasurer	**Auditors:** PricewaterhouseCoopers LLP **Investor Contact:** 978-370-2425 **Transfer Agents:** Broadridge Corporate Issue Services, Brentwood, NY

TEREX CORP.

Exchange	Symbol	Price	52Wk Range	Yield	P/E
NYS	TEX	$21.18 (5/31/2016)	26.78-14.46	1.32	31.15

*7 Year Price Score 71.67   ***NYSE Composite Index=100**   ***12 Month Price Score 106.84**

Interim Earnings (Per Share)

Qtr.	Mar	Jun	Sep	Dec
2013	0.21	0.18	0.81	0.73
2014	0.30	1.21	0.56	0.72
2015	0.01	0.78	0.40	0.15
2016	(0.65)	...	...	...

Interim Dividends (Per Share)

Amt	Decl	Ex	Rec	Pay
0.06Q	07/17/2015	08/06/2015	08/10/2015	09/18/2015
0.06Q	10/19/2015	11/06/2015	11/10/2015	12/18/2015
0.07Q	02/16/2016	03/08/2016	03/10/2016	03/18/2016
0.07Q	05/13/2016	06/08/2016	06/10/2016	06/20/2016

Indicated Div: $0.28

Valuation Analysis   **Institutional Holding**

Forecast EPS	$1.36	No of Institutions 438
	(05/20/2016)	
Market Cap	$2.3 Billion	Shares 97,741,840
Book Value	$1.9 Billion	% Held 83.73
Price/Book	1.24	
Price/Sales	0.35	

Business Summary: Industrial Machinery & Equipment (MIC: 7.2.1 SIC: 3537 NAIC: 333924)

Terex is a lifting and material handling solutions company. Co. has five business segments: Aerial Work Platforms, which provides aerial work platform equipment, telehandlers, and light towers; Cranes, which provides mobile telescopic cranes, tower cranes, lattice boom crawler cranes, lattice boom truck cranes, utility equipment and truck-mounted cranes (boom trucks), and related components and replacement parts; Material Handling & Port Solutions, which provides industrial cranes, as well as a portfolio of port and rail equipment; Materials Processing, which provides materials processing equipment; and Construction, which provides compact construction equipment and specialty equipment.

Recent Developments: For the quarter ended Mar 31 2016, net loss amounted to US$71.0 million versus net income of US$1.6 million in the year-earlier quarter. Revenues were US$1.43 billion, down 4.6% from US$1.50 billion the year before. Operating loss was US$41.7 million versus an income of US$44.2 million in the prior-year quarter. Direct operating expenses declined 1.3% to US$1.20 billion from US$1.22 billion in the comparable period the year before. Indirect operating expenses increased 14.1% to US$265.2 million from US$232.4 million in the equivalent prior-year period.

Prospects: Our evaluation of Terex Corp. as of June 19, 2016 is the result of our systematic analysis on three basic characteristics: earnings strength, relative valuation, and recent stock price movement. The company has suffered a very negative trend in earnings per share over the past 5 quarters. However, while recent estimates for the company have been mixed, TEX has posted results that fell short of analysts expectations. Based on operating earnings yield, the company is undervalued when compared to all of the companies in our coverage universe. Share price changes over the past year indicates that TEX will perform very well over the near term.

Financial Data

(US$ in Thousands)	3 Mos	12/31/2015	12/31/2014	12/31/2013	12/31/2012	12/31/2011	12/31/2010	12/31/2009
Earnings Per Share	0.68	1.33	2.79	1.93	0.93	0.41	3.30	(3.88)
Cash Flow Per Share	1.79	1.98	3.74	1.70	2.64	0.17	(5.61)	(0.67)
Tang Book Value Per Share	4.95	5.61	5.21	4.55	2.62	1.18	14.71	10.62
Dividends Per Share	0.250	0.240	0.200	0.050	...	...	...	...
Dividend Payout %	36.76	18.05	7.17	2.59	...	...	...	...
Income Statement								
Total Revenue	1,426,900	6,543,100	7,308,900	7,084,000	7,348,400	6,504,600	4,418,200	4,043,100
EBITDA	(15,600)	430,600	527,500	523,600	421,400	302,700	(16,200)	(388,600)
Depn & Amortn	29,900	98,400	110,400	104,400	100,400	89,500	78,600	73,600
Income Before Taxes	(69,400)	226,600	297,200	291,300	155,600	84,500	(238,300)	(581,700)
Income Taxes	5,000	81,000	37,700	87,400	54,200	50,400	(26,800)	(132,100)
Net Income	(70,800)	145,900	319,000	226,000	105,800	45,200	358,500	(398,400)
Average Shares	108,800	109,600	114,200	117,000	113,900	110,700	108,700	102,600
Balance Sheet								
Current Assets	3,160,200	3,144,200	3,356,200	3,639,400	3,797,400	4,013,500	3,968,900	3,914,600
Total Assets	5,737,500	5,637,100	5,928,000	6,536,700	6,746,200	7,050,700	5,516,400	5,713,800
Current Liabilities	1,634,600	1,458,600	1,643,100	1,724,700	1,708,800	1,891,700	1,674,200	1,554,700
Long-Term Obligations	1,668,900	1,751,000	1,636,300	1,889,900	2,014,900	2,223,400	1,339,500	1,892,700
Total Liabilities	3,882,400	3,759,700	3,922,100	4,346,600	4,738,500	5,144,300	3,433,200	4,063,600
Stockholders' Equity	1,855,100	1,877,400	2,005,900	2,190,100	2,007,700	1,906,400	2,083,200	1,650,200
Shares Outstanding	108,500	107,700	105,400	109,900	109,900	108,800	108,100	107,300
Statistical Record								
Return on Assets %	1.29	2.52	5.12	3.40	1.53	0.72	6.38	N.M.
Return on Equity %	4.11	7.51	15.20	10.77	5.39	2.27	19.21	N.M.
EBITDA Margin %	N.M.	6.58	7.22	7.39	5.73	4.65	N.M.	N.M.
Net Margin %	N.M.	2.23	4.36	3.19	1.44	0.69	8.11	N.M.
Asset Turnover	1.13	1.13	1.17	1.07	1.06	1.04	0.79	0.72
Current Ratio	1.93	2.16	2.04	2.11	2.22	2.12	2.37	2.52
Debt to Equity	0.90	0.93	0.82	0.86	1.00	1.17	0.64	1.15
Price Range	28.85-14.46	28.85-16.83	44.74-25.66	41.99-26.01	28.11-14.11	38.30-9.61	31.04-17.30	24.11-7.57
P/E Ratio	42.43-21.26	21.69-12.65	16.04-9.20	21.76-13.48	30.23-15.17	93.41-23.44	9.41-5.24	...
Average Yield %	1.12	1.03	0.54	0.15	...	...	...	...

Address: 200 Nyala Farm Road, Westport, CT 06880	Web Site: www.terex.com	Auditors: PricewaterhouseCoopers LLP
Telephone: 203-222-7170	Officers: John L. Garrison - President, Chief Executive Officer Eric I. Cohen - Senior Vice President, Secretary, General Counsel	Investor Contact: 203-222-5943
Fax: 203-222-7976		Transfer Agents: American Stock Transfer & Trust Company, New York, NY

TEGNA INC

Exchange	Symbol	Price	52Wk Range	Yield	P/E
NYS	TGNA	$22.96 (5/31/2016)	32.97-21.37	2.44	12.15

*7 Year Price Score 127.63 *NYSE Composite Index=100   *12 Month Price Score 89.95

Interim Earnings (Per Share)

Qtr.	Mar	Jun	Sep	Dec
2013	0.44	0.48	0.34	0.39
2014	0.25	0.90	0.51	2.92
2015	0.49	0.50	0.38	0.63
2016	0.38			

Interim Dividends (Per Share)

Amt	Decl	Ex	Rec	Pay
0.14Q	07/29/2015	09/02/2015	09/04/2015	10/01/2015
0.14Q	10/27/2015	12/02/2015	12/04/2015	01/04/2016
0.14Q	02/23/2016	03/02/2016	03/04/2016	04/01/2016
0.14Q	05/05/2016	06/01/2016	06/03/2016	07/01/2016

Indicated Div: $0.56 (Div. Reinv. Plan)

Valuation Analysis | **Institutional Holding**
Forecast EPS $2.32 | No of Institutions
(05/16/2016) | 663
Market Cap $5.0 Billion | Shares
Book Value $2.2 Billion | 216,928,288
Price/Book 2.32 | % Held
Price/Sales 1.33 | 89.70

Business Summary: Radio & Television (MIC: 2.3.1 SIC: 2711 NAIC: 511110)

Tegna is involved in media and digital businesses. Co. operates two reportable segments: TEGNA Media, which provides core advertising, political advertising, retransmission, and digital; and TEGNA Digital, which is comprised of four business units including; Cars.com, which provides online subscription advertising products targeting car dealerships and national advertisers; CareerBuilder, which provides a range of solutions that help match the right candidate to the right opportunity; G/O Digital, which connect with media consumers through digital marketing; and Cofactor, which enables brands and retailers to engage shoppers with personalized ad content on any device or channel.

Recent Developments: For the quarter ended Mar 31 2016, income from continuing operations increased 23.1% to US$103.4 million from US$84.0 million in the year-earlier quarter. Net income decreased 24.7% to US$95.9 million from US$127.5 million in the year-earlier quarter. Revenues were US$781.7 million, up 6.9% from US$731.5 million the year before. Operating income was US$201.9 million versus US$182.5 million in the prior-year quarter, an increase of 10.7%. Direct operating expenses rose 9.6% to US$248.3 million from US$226.6 million in the comparable period the year before. Indirect operating expenses increased 2.8% to US$331.6 million from US$322.4 million in the equivalent prior-year period.

Prospects: Our evaluation of Tegna Inc. as of June 19, 2016 is the result of our systematic analysis on three basic characteristics: earnings strength, relative valuation, and recent stock price movement. The company has produced a positive trend in earnings per share over the past 5 quarters. However, while recent estimates for the company have been mixed, TGNA has posted better than expected results. Based on operating earnings yield, the company is undervalued when compared to all of the companies in our coverage universe. Share price changes over the past year indicates that TGNA will perform in line with the market over the near term.

Financial Data
(US$ in Thousands)

	3 Mos	12/31/2015	12/28/2014	12/29/2013	12/30/2012	12/25/2011	12/26/2010	12/27/2009
Earnings Per Share	1.89	2.00	4.58	1.66	1.79	1.89	2.43	1.51
Cash Flow Per Share	2.71	2.71	3.64	2.24	3.20	3.41	3.25	3.72
Dividends Per Share	0.620	0.680	0.800	0.800	0.800	0.240	0.160	0.160
Dividend Payout %	32.80	34.00	17.47	48.19	44.69	12.70	6.58	10.60
Income Statement								
Total Revenue	781,732	3,050,945	6,008,174	5,161,362	5,353,197	5,239,989	5,438,678	5,612,993
EBITDA	254,821	1,163,873	1,727,709	880,925	992,528	1,015,243	1,214,490	990,791
Depn & Amortn	50,523	262,244	265,724	189,572	194,039	197,373	214,684	242,809
Income Before Taxes	142,585	628,000	1,188,741	515,289	648,020	644,730	826,820	572,234
Income Taxes	42,108	202,314	225,600	113,200	195,400	152,800	244,013	193,800
Net Income	85,444	459,522	1,062,171	388,680	424,280	458,748	588,201	355,270
Average Shares	223,254	229,721	231,907	234,189	236,690	242,768	241,605	236,027
Balance Sheet								
Current Assets	748,054	805,159	1,480,465	1,923,485	1,072,720	1,075,545	1,139,134	1,049,042
Total Assets	8,469,173	8,537,758	11,205,455	9,240,706	6,379,886	6,616,450	6,816,844	7,148,432
Current Liabilities	579,022	606,783	1,127,936	1,007,192	934,516	901,937	893,186	900,103
Long-Term Obligations	4,196,722	4,200,816	4,488,028	3,707,010	1,432,100	1,760,363	2,352,242	3,061,951
Total Liabilities	6,311,592	6,345,787	7,950,541	6,547,608	4,029,272	4,288,559	4,653,090	5,544,507
Stockholders' Equity	2,157,581	2,191,971	3,254,914	2,693,098	2,350,614	2,327,891	2,163,754	1,603,925
Shares Outstanding	217,587	219,754	226,739	227,568	230,042	237,036	239,509	237,156
Statistical Record								
Return on Assets %	4.44	4.62	10.42	4.99	6.42	6.85	8.45	4.77
Return on Equity %	15.85	16.74	35.81	15.45	17.84	20.48	31.31	26.79
EBITDA Margin %	32.60	38.15	28.76	17.07	18.54	19.37	22.33	17.65
Net Margin %	10.93	15.06	17.68	7.53	7.93	8.75	10.82	6.33
Asset Turnover	0.39	0.31	0.59	0.66	0.81	0.78	0.78	0.75
Current Ratio	1.29	1.33	1.31	1.91	1.15	1.19	1.28	1.17
Debt to Equity	1.95	1.92	1.38	1.38	0.61	0.76	1.09	1.91
Price Range	32.97-21.37	32.97-21.85	27.63-20.75	23.43-14.40	15.17-9.86	13.74-6.84	14.93-9.40	12.50-1.56
P/E Ratio	17.44-11.31	16.48-10.93	6.03-4.53	14.12-8.67	8.47-5.51	7.27-3.62	6.14-3.87	8.28-1.03
Average Yield %	2.35	2.51	3.34	4.25	6.49	2.25	1.36	2.86

Address: 7950 Jones Branch Drive, McLean, VA 22107-0150 **Telephone:** 703-854-7000	**Web Site:** www.gannett.com **Officers:** John Jeffry Louis - Chairman Maryam Banikarim - Senior Vice President, Chief Marketing Officer	**Auditors:** Ernst & Young LLP **Investor Contact:** 703-854-6917 **Transfer Agents:** Wells Fargo Bank, N.A., St Paul, MN

TESORO CORPORATION

Exchange	Symbol	Price	52Wk Range	Yield	P/E
NYS	TSO	$78.08 (5/31/2016)	118.24-68.64	2.56	6.60

*7 Year Price Score 176.51 ***NYSE Composite Index=100** ***12 Month Price Score 85.15**

Interim Earnings (Per Share)

Qtr.	Mar	Jun	Sep	Dec
2013	0.67	1.64	0.72	(0.03)
2014	0.58	1.70	3.05	1.14
2015	1.15	4.59	6.13	0.54
2016	0.57	...	...	...

Interim Dividends (Per Share)

Amt	Decl	Ex	Rec	Pay
0.50Q	08/05/2015	08/26/2015	08/28/2015	09/14/2015
0.50Q	10/27/2015	11/25/2015	11/30/2015	12/15/2015
0.50Q	01/29/2016	02/25/2016	02/29/2016	03/15/2016
0.50Q	05/03/2016	05/26/2016	05/31/2016	06/15/2016

Indicated Div: $2.00

Valuation Analysis		Institutional Holding	
Forecast EPS	$6.91	No of Institutions	
	(05/20/2016)	750	
Market Cap	$9.4 Billion	Shares	
Book Value	$5.2 Billion	126,748,264	
Price/Book	1.79	% Held	
Price/Sales	0.34	90.23	

Business Summary: Refining & Marketing (MIC: 9.1.2 SIC: 2911 NAIC: 324110)

Tesoro is a petroleum refining and marketing company. Co.'s subsidiaries operate through three business segments: refining, which owns and operates six refineries in the western U.S., refines crude oil and other feedstocks into transportation fuels, such as gasoline and gasoline blendstocks, jet fuel and diesel fuel, as well as other products, including heavy fuel oils, liquefied petroleum gas and petroleum coke for sale in bulk markets; logistics, which is comprised of Tesoro Logistics LP's assets and operations; and marketing, which sells transportation fuels in 16 states through a network of retail stations under the ARCO®, Shell®, Exxon®, Mobil®, USA Gasolineâ,,¢ and Tesoro® brands.

Recent Developments: For the quarter ended Mar 31 2016, income from continuing operations decreased 47.9% to US$98.0 million from US$188.0 million in the year-earlier quarter. Net income decreased 42.0% to US$109.0 million from US$188.0 million in the year-earlier quarter. Revenues were US$5.10 billion, down 21.1% from US$6.46 billion the year before. Operating income was US$179.0 million versus US$340.0 million in the prior-year quarter, a decrease of 47.4%. Direct operating expenses declined 23.9% to US$4.01 billion from US$5.27 billion in the comparable period the year before. Indirect operating expenses increased 6.5% to US$914.0 million from US$858.0 million in the equivalent prior-year period.

Prospects: Our evaluation of Tesoro Petroleum Corp. as of June 19, 2016 is the result of our systematic analysis on three basic characteristics: earnings strength, relative valuation, and recent stock price movement. The company has suffered a very negative trend in earnings per share over the past 5 quarters. However, while recent estimates for the company have been lowered by analysts, TSO has posted better than expected results. Based on operating earnings yield, the company is undervalued when compared to all of the companies in our coverage universe. Share price changes over the past year indicates that TSO will perform very well over the near term.

Financial Data

(US$ in Thousands)	3 Mos	12/31/2015	12/31/2014	12/31/2013	12/31/2012	12/31/2011	12/31/2010	12/31/2009
Earnings Per Share	11.83	12.36	6.44	3.00	5.25	3.81	(0.21)	(1.01)
Cash Flow Per Share	20.59	17.30	10.61	6.36	11.34	4.87	2.74	4.80
Tang Book Value Per Share	33.00	31.94	24.30	30.33	28.96	24.33	20.48	19.84
Dividends Per Share	1.925	1.850	1.100	0.900	0.270	...	...	0.350
Dividend Payout %	16.27	14.97	17.08	30.00	5.14	...	...	...
Income Statement								
Total Revenue	5,101,000	28,711,000	40,633,000	37,601,000	32,974,000	30,303,000	20,583,000	16,872,000
EBITDA	398,000	3,331,000	2,052,000	1,140,000	1,671,000	1,342,000	395,000	377,000
Depn & Amortn	212,000	491,000	363,000	322,000	295,000	262,000	266,000	439,000
Income Before Taxes	126,000	2,623,000	1,454,000	669,000	1,212,000	905,000	(25,000)	(188,000)
Income Taxes	30,000	936,000	547,000	246,000	442,000	342,000	4,000	(48,000)
Net Income	69,000	1,540,000	843,000	412,000	743,000	546,000	(29,000)	(140,000)
Average Shares	121,200	124,600	130,800	137,300	141,500	143,300	140,600	138,200
Balance Sheet								
Current Assets	3,503,000	4,307,000	5,074,000	5,326,000	4,636,000	4,151,000	2,928,000	2,223,000
Total Assets	16,011,000	16,332,000	16,584,000	13,389,000	10,702,000	9,892,000	8,732,000	8,070,000
Current Liabilities	2,268,000	2,530,000	3,466,000	3,408,000	2,881,000	3,249,000	2,496,000	1,889,000
Long-Term Obligations	4,046,000	4,067,000	4,254,000	2,823,000	1,587,000	1,283,000	1,843,000	1,837,000
Total Liabilities	10,789,000	11,119,000	12,130,000	9,087,000	6,451,000	6,224,000	5,517,000	4,983,000
Stockholders' Equity	5,222,000	5,213,000	4,454,000	4,302,000	4,251,000	3,668,000	3,215,000	3,087,000
Shares Outstanding	119,926	119,393	124,960	131,804	138,162	139,964	143,180	140,427
Statistical Record								
Return on Assets %	9.07	9.36	5.63	3.42	7.20	5.86	N.M.	N.M.
Return on Equity %	29.99	31.86	19.26	9.63	18.71	15.87	N.M.	N.M.
EBITDA Margin %	7.80	11.60	5.05	3.03	5.07	4.43	1.92	2.23
Net Margin %	1.35	5.36	2.07	1.10	2.25	1.80	N.M.	N.M.
Asset Turnover	1.69	1.74	2.71	3.12	3.19	3.25	2.45	2.18
Current Ratio	1.54	1.70	1.46	1.56	1.61	1.28	1.17	1.18
Debt to Equity	0.77	0.78	0.96	0.66	0.37	0.35	0.57	0.60
Price Range	118.24-68.64	118.24-66.67	78.55-47.47	64.90-40.22	44.73-21.55	29.18-17.98	18.68-10.54	19.11-10.89
P/E Ratio	9.99-5.80	9.57-5.39	12.20-7.37	21.63-13.41	8.52-4.10	7.66-4.72	...	...
Average Yield %	2.04	1.97	1.84	1.72	0.86	...	...	2.43

Address: 19100 Ridgewood Pkwy, San Antonio, TX 78259-1828	Web Site: www.tsocorp.com	Auditors: Ernst & Young LLP
Telephone: 210-626-6000	Officers: Gregory J. Goff - Chairman, President, Chief Executive Officer Steven M. Sterin - Executive Vice President, Chief Financial Officer	Transfer Agents: American Stock Transfer & Trust Company, New York, NY

TEXTRON INC

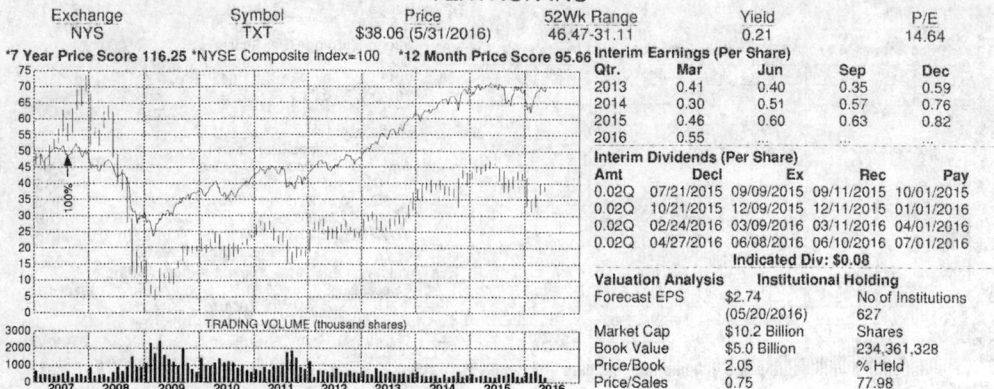

Exchange	Symbol	Price	52Wk Range	Yield	P/E
NYS	TXT	$38.06 (5/31/2016)	46.47-31.11	0.21	14.64

*7 Year Price Score 116.25 *NYSE Composite Index=100 ***12 Month Price Score 95.66**

Interim Earnings (Per Share)

Qtr.	Mar	Jun	Sep	Dec
2013	0.41	0.40	0.35	0.59
2014	0.30	0.51	0.57	0.76
2015	0.46	0.60	0.63	0.82
2016	0.55	...	...	...

Interim Dividends (Per Share)

Amt	Decl	Ex	Rec	Pay
0.02Q	07/21/2015	09/09/2015	09/11/2015	10/01/2015
0.02Q	10/21/2015	12/09/2015	12/11/2015	01/01/2016
0.02Q	02/24/2016	03/09/2016	03/11/2016	04/01/2016
0.02Q	04/27/2016	06/08/2016	06/10/2016	07/01/2016

Indicated Div: $0.08

Valuation Analysis

		Institutional Holding	
Forecast EPS	$2.74	No of Institutions	627
	(05/20/2016)		
Market Cap	$10.2 Billion	Shares	234,361,328
Book Value	$5.0 Billion	% Held	77.98
Price/Book	2.05		
Price/Sales	0.75		

TRADING VOLUME (thousand shares)

Business Summary: Aerospace (MIC: 7.1.1 SIC: 3721 NAIC: 336411)

Textron has five operating segments: Textron Aviation, which manufactures, sells and services Beechcraft and Cessna aircraft, and services the Hawker brand of business jets; Bell, which supplies military and commercial helicopters, tiltrotor aircraft, and related spare parts and services; Textron Systems, which includes unmanned aircraft systems, marine and land systems, weapons and sensors, simulation, training and other defense and aviation mission support products and services; Industrial, which provides fuel systems and functional components, specialized vehicles and equipment, and tools and test equipment; as well as Finance, which is a commercial finance business.

Recent Developments: For the quarter ended Apr 2 2016, income from continuing operations increased 18.0% to US$151.0 million from US$128.0 million in the year-earlier quarter. Net income increased 17.2% to US$150.0 million from US$128.0 million in the year-earlier quarter. Revenues were US$3.20 billion, up 4.2% from US$3.07 billion the year before. Direct operating expenses rose 5.0% to US$2.64 billion from US$2.51 billion in the comparable period the year before. Indirect operating expenses decreased 7.6% to US$351.0 million from US$380.0 million in the equivalent prior-year period.

Prospects: Our evaluation of Textron Inc. as of June 19, 2016 is the result of our systematic analysis on three basic characteristics: earnings strength, relative valuation, and recent stock price movement. The company has produced a positive trend in earnings per share over the past 5 quarters and while recent estimates for the company have remained steady, TXT has posted better than expected results. Based on operating earnings yield, the company is undervalued when compared to all of the companies in our coverage universe. Share price changes over the past year indicates that TXT will perform poorly over the near term.

Financial Data

(US$ in Millions)	3 Mos	01/02/2016	01/03/2015	12/28/2013	12/29/2012	12/31/2011	01/01/2011	01/02/2010
Earnings Per Share	2.60	2.50	2.13	1.75	2.00	0.79	0.28	(0.12)
Cash Flow Per Share	3.54	3.95	4.25	2.91	3.32	3.84	3.60	3.87
Tang Book Value Per Share	10.70	10.72	8.12	9.39	4.95	3.98	4.86	4.42
Dividends Per Share	0.080	0.080	0.080	0.080	0.080	0.080	0.080	0.080
Dividend Payout %	3.08	3.20	3.76	4.57	4.00	10.13	28.57	...
Income Statement								
Total Revenue	3,201	13,423	13,878	12,104	12,237	11,275	10,525	10,500
EBITDA	367	1,523	1,423	1,182	1,368	900	664	471
Depn & Amortn	109	383	379	335	315	317	308	317
Income Before Taxes	215	971	853	674	841	337	86	(149)
Income Taxes	64	273	248	176	260	95	(6)	(76)
Net Income	150	697	600	498	589	242	86	(31)
Average Shares	273	278	281	284	294	307	302	262
Balance Sheet								
Current Assets	6,737	6,478	6,273	5,572	5,389	5,263	5,047	5,933
Total Assets	15,099	14,708	14,605	12,944	13,033	13,615	15,282	18,940
Current Liabilities	3,877	3,792	3,638	3,003	3,512	2,931	2,657	2,868
Long-Term Obligations	3,688	3,348	3,866	3,179	3,453	4,780	6,269	9,117
Total Liabilities	10,110	9,744	10,333	8,560	10,042	10,870	12,310	16,114
Stockholders' Equity	4,989	4,964	4,272	4,384	2,991	2,745	2,972	2,826
Shares Outstanding	268	274	276	282	271	278	275	272
Statistical Record								
Return on Assets %	4.82	4.77	4.29	3.84	4.43	1.68	0.50	N.M.
Return on Equity %	15.33	15.13	13.64	13.54	20.59	8.49	2.97	N.M.
EBITDA Margin %	11.47	11.35	10.25	9.77	11.18	7.98	6.31	4.49
Net Margin %	4.69	5.19	4.32	4.11	4.81	2.15	0.82	N.M.
Asset Turnover	0.91	0.92	0.99	0.93	0.92	0.78	0.62	0.54
Current Ratio	1.74	1.71	1.72	1.86	1.53	1.80	1.90	2.07
Debt to Equity	0.74	0.67	0.90	0.73	1.15	1.74	2.11	3.23
Price Range	46.86-31.11	46.86-37.00	44.23-32.28	37.29-24.79	28.89-18.64	28.50-14.88	24.55-16.07	20.73-3.75
P/E Ratio	18.02-11.97	18.74-14.80	20.77-15.15	21.31-14.17	14.45-9.32	36.08-18.84	87.68-57.39	...
Average Yield %	0.20	0.19	0.21	0.28	0.32	0.36	0.39	0.60

Address: 40 Westminster Street, Providence, RI 02903 **Telephone:** 401-421-2800	**Web Site:** www.textron.com **Officers:** Scott C. Donnelly - Chairman, President, Chief Executive Officer Frank T. Connor - Executive Vice President, Chief Financial Officer	**Auditors:** Ernst & Young LLP **Investor Contact:** 401-457-2288 **Transfer Agents:** American Stock Transfer & Trust Cmpany, LLC, Brooklyn, NY

706

THE GAP, INC.

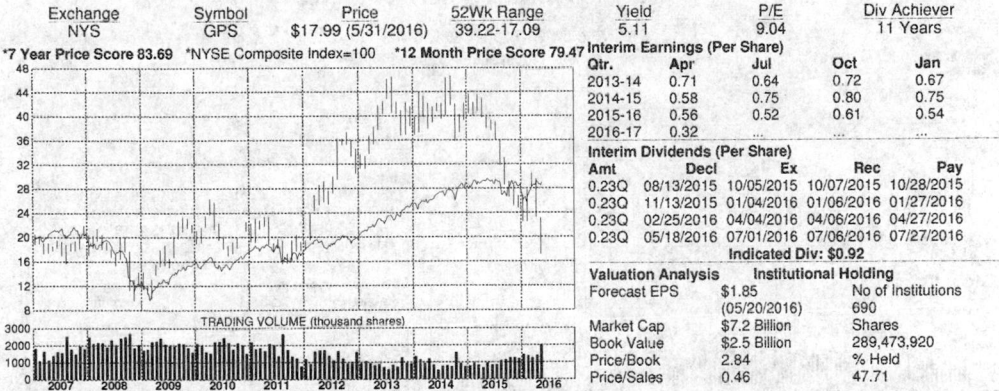

Exchange	Symbol	Price	52Wk Range	Yield	P/E	Div Achiever
NYS	GPS	$17.99 (5/31/2016)	39.22-17.09	5.11	9.04	11 Years

*7 Year Price Score 83.69 *NYSE Composite Index=100 *12 Month Price Score 79.47

Interim Earnings (Per Share)

Qtr.	Apr	Jul	Oct	Jan
2013-14	0.71	0.64	0.72	0.67
2014-15	0.58	0.75	0.80	0.75
2015-16	0.56	0.52	0.61	0.54
2016-17	0.32			

Interim Dividends (Per Share)

Amt	Decl	Ex	Rec	Pay
0.23Q	08/13/2015	10/05/2015	10/07/2015	10/28/2015
0.23Q	11/13/2015	01/04/2016	01/06/2016	01/27/2016
0.23Q	02/25/2016	04/04/2016	04/06/2016	04/27/2016
0.23Q	05/18/2016	07/01/2016	07/06/2016	07/27/2016

Indicated Div: $0.92

Valuation Analysis | **Institutional Holding**

Forecast EPS	$1.85	No of Institutions
	(05/20/2016)	690
Market Cap	$7.2 Billion	Shares
Book Value	$2.5 Billion	289,473,920
Price/Book	2.84	% Held
Price/Sales	0.46	47.71

TRADING VOLUME (thousand shares)

Business Summary: Retail - Apparel and Accessories (MIC: 2.1.5 SIC: 5651 NAIC: 448140)

The Gap is a retailer providing apparel, accessories, and personal care products for men, women, and children under the Gap, Banana Republic, Old Navy, Athleta, and Intermix brands. Co. has stores in the U.S., Canada, the U.K., France, Ireland, Japan, Italy, China, Hong Kong, Taiwan, and Mexico, and has franchise agreements with unaffiliated franchisees to operate Gap, Banana Republic, and Old Navy stores throughout Asia, Australia, Europe, Latin America, the Middle East, and Africa. Under these agreements, third parties operate, or will operate, stores that sell apparel and related products under Co.'s brand names. At Jan. 30, 2016, Co. had 3,721 Co.-operated and franchise store locations.

Recent Developments: For the quarter ended Apr 30 2016, net income decreased 46.9% to US$127.0 million from US$239.0 million in the year-earlier quarter. Revenues were US$3.44 billion, down 6.0% from US$3.66 billion the year before. Operating income was US$222.0 million versus US$386.0 million in the prior-year quarter, a decrease of 42.5%. Direct operating expenses declined 2.0% to US$2.23 billion from US$2.28 billion in the comparable period the year before. Indirect operating expenses decreased 0.9% to US$987.0 million from US$996.0 million in the equivalent prior-year period.

Prospects: Our evaluation of The Gap Inc. as of June 19, 2016 is the result of our systematic analysis on three basic characteristics: earnings strength, relative valuation, and recent stock price movement. The company has managed to produce a neutral trend in earnings per share over the past 5 quarters. However, while recent estimates for the company have been lowered by analysts, GPS has posted better than expected results. Based on operating earnings yield, the company is undervalued when compared to all of the companies in our coverage universe. Share price changes over the past year indicates that GPS will perform very poorly over the near term.

Financial Data
(US$ in Thousands)	3 Mos	01/30/2016	01/31/2015	02/01/2014	02/02/2013	01/28/2012	01/29/2011	01/30/2010
Earnings Per Share	1.99	2.23	2.87	2.74	2.33	1.56	1.88	1.58
Cash Flow Per Share	3.90	3.89	4.91	3.71	3.95	2.58	2.75	2.79
Tang Book Value Per Share	6.34	5.73	6.44	6.17	5.57	5.32	6.64	6.96
Dividends Per Share	0.920	0.920	0.880	0.700	0.500	0.450	0.400	0.340
Dividend Payout %	46.23	41.26	30.66	25.55	21.46	28.85	21.28	21.52
Income Statement								
Total Revenue	3,438,000	15,797,000	16,435,000	16,148,000	15,651,000	14,549,000	14,664,000	14,197,000
EBITDA	206,000	2,112,000	2,643,000	2,679,000	2,497,000	2,026,000	2,611,000	2,464,000
Depn & Amortn	(16,000)	588,000	560,000	530,000	555,000	588,000	643,000	649,000
Income Before Taxes	204,000	1,471,000	2,013,000	2,093,000	1,861,000	1,369,000	1,982,000	1,816,000
Income Taxes	77,000	551,000	751,000	813,000	726,000	536,000	778,000	714,000
Net Income	127,000	920,000	1,262,000	1,280,000	1,135,000	833,000	1,204,000	1,102,000
Average Shares	399,000	413,000	440,000	467,000	488,000	533,000	641,000	699,000
Balance Sheet								
Current Assets	3,945,000	3,985,000	4,317,000	4,430,000	4,132,000	4,309,000	3,926,000	4,664,000
Total Assets	7,507,000	7,473,000	7,690,000	7,849,000	7,470,000	7,422,000	7,065,000	7,985,000
Current Liabilities	2,555,000	2,535,000	2,234,000	2,445,000	2,344,000	2,128,000	2,095,000	2,131,000
Long-Term Obligations	1,318,000	1,310,000	1,332,000	1,369,000	1,246,000	1,606,000	...	...
Total Liabilities	4,985,000	4,928,000	4,707,000	4,787,000	4,576,000	4,667,000	2,985,000	3,094,000
Stockholders' Equity	2,522,000	2,545,000	2,983,000	3,062,000	2,894,000	2,755,000	4,080,000	4,891,000
Shares Outstanding	398,000	397,000	421,000	446,000	463,000	485,000	588,000	676,000
Statistical Record								
Return on Assets %	10.77	12.17	16.29	16.76	15.00	11.53	16.04	14.21
Return on Equity %	29.92	33.38	41.87	43.10	39.53	24.44	26.92	23.82
EBITDA Margin %	5.99	13.37	16.08	16.59	15.95	13.93	17.81	17.36
Net Margin %	3.69	5.82	7.68	7.93	7.25	5.73	8.21	7.76
Asset Turnover	2.08	2.09	2.12	2.11	2.07	2.01	1.95	1.83
Current Ratio	1.54	1.57	1.93	1.81	1.76	2.02	1.87	2.19
Debt to Equity	0.52	0.51	0.45	0.45	0.43	0.58	...	...
Price Range	40.16-22.43	43.45-22.45	46.59-35.74	46.48-31.22	37.27-18.83	23.29-15.52	26.21-16.86	23.21-9.85
P/E Ratio	20.18-11.27	19.48-10.07	16.23-12.45	16.96-11.39	16.00-8.08	14.93-9.95	13.94-8.97	14.69-6.23
Average Yield %	3.02	2.70	2.15	1.78	1.64	2.33	1.94	1.92

Address: Two Folsom Street, San Francisco, CA 94105
Telephone: 415-427-0100

Web Site: www.gapinc.com
Officers: Arthur L. Peck - Executive Vice President, Division Officer, Region Officer, Division Officer, Chief Executive Officer, President Michelle A. Banks - Executive Vice President, Chief Compliance Officer, Corporate Secretary, General Counsel

Auditors: Deloitte & Touche LLP
Investor Contact: 415-427-0100
Transfer Agents: Wells Fargo Bank, N.A., Mendota Heights, MN

THERMO FISHER SCIENTIFIC INC

Exchange	Symbol	Price	52Wk Range	Yield	P/E
NYS	TMO	$151.77 (5/31/2016)	152.13-118.13	0.40	30.60

*7 Year Price Score 137.81 *NYSE Composite Index=100 *12 Month Price Score 107.82

Interim Earnings (Per Share)

Qtr.	Mar	Jun	Sep	Dec
2013	0.93	0.76	0.86	0.92
2014	1.36	0.69	1.17	1.49
2015	0.96	1.27	1.18	1.50
2016	1.01	...	...	...

Interim Dividends (Per Share)

Amt	Decl	Ex	Rec	Pay
0.15Q	07/10/2015	09/11/2015	09/15/2015	10/15/2015
0.15Q	11/12/2015	12/11/2015	12/15/2015	01/15/2016
0.15Q	02/25/2016	03/11/2016	03/15/2016	04/15/2016
0.15Q	05/18/2016	06/13/2016	06/15/2016	07/15/2016

Indicated Div: $0.60

Valuation Analysis / **Institutional Holding**

Forecast EPS	$8.13	No of Institutions
	(05/20/2016)	1370
Market Cap	$59.7 Billion	Shares
Book Value	$20.9 Billion	410,946,496
Price/Book	2.85	% Held
Price/Sales	3.44	99.66

Business Summary: Biotechnology (MIC: 4.1.2 SIC: 3829 NAIC: 334519)

Thermo Fisher Scientific is a provider of analytical instruments, equipment, reagents and consumables, software and services for research, manufacturing, analysis, discovery and diagnostics. Markets served include pharmaceutical and biotech, academic and government, industrial and applied, as well as healthcare and diagnostics. Co. serves its customers through its five brands: Thermo Scientific, Applied Biosystems, Invitrogen, Fisher Scientific and Unity Lab Services. Co. has four business segments: Life Sciences Solutions, Analytical Instruments, Specialty Diagnostics and Laboratory Products and Services.

Recent Developments: For the quarter ended Apr 2 2016, income from continuing operations increased 4.5% to US$402.3 million from US$385.1 million in the year-earlier quarter. Net income increased 4.4% to US$402.2 million from US$385.1 million in the year-earlier quarter. Revenues were US$4.29 billion, up 9.6% from US$3.92 billion the year before. Operating income was US$517.9 million versus US$487.3 million in the prior-year quarter, an increase of 6.3%. Direct operating expenses rose 11.5% to US$2.34 billion from US$2.10 billion in the comparable period the year before. Indirect operating expenses increased 7.8% to US$1.44 billion from US$1.34 billion in the equivalent prior-year period.

Prospects: Our evaluation of Thermo Fisher Scientific Inc. as of June 19, 2016 is the result of our systematic analysis on three basic characteristics: earnings strength, relative valuation, and recent stock price movement. The company has produced a positive trend in earnings per share over the past 5 quarters and while recent estimates for the company have remained steady, TMO has posted better than expected results. Based on operating earnings yield, the company is undervalued when compared to all of the companies in our coverage universe. Share price changes over the past year indicates that TMO will perform very well over the near term.

Financial Data

(US$ in Thousands)	3 Mos	12/31/2015	12/31/2014	12/31/2013	12/31/2012	12/31/2011	12/31/2010	12/31/2009
Earnings Per Share	4.96	4.92	4.71	3.48	3.21	3.46	2.53	2.01
Cash Flow Per Share	7.65	7.07	6.58	5.58	5.59	4.44	3.71	4.02
Tang Book Value Per Share	N.M.	N.M.	N.M.	N.M.	N.M.	N.M.	0.13	0.27
Dividends Per Share	0.600	0.600	0.600	0.600	0.540	...	...	...
Dividend Payout %	12.10	12.20	12.74	17.24	16.82	...	...	...
Income Statement								
Total Revenue	4,294,800	16,965,400	16,889,600	13,090,300	12,509,900	11,725,900	10,788,700	10,109,700
EBITDA	934,500	4,008,900	4,204,200	2,553,500	2,469,500	2,138,500	1,435,100	1,219,400
Depn & Amortn	416,100	1,688,200	1,684,800	999,900	983,700	863,500	198,300	190,300
Income Before Taxes	423,000	1,936,400	2,087,200	1,319,500	1,269,400	1,126,600	1,164,600	927,100
Income Taxes	20,700	(43,900)	191,700	40,400	11,000	107,000	131,500	75,800
Net Income	402,200	1,975,400	1,894,400	1,273,300	1,177,900	1,329,900	1,035,600	850,300
Average Shares	398,700	401,900	402,300	365,800	366,600	384,800	409,400	422,800
Balance Sheet								
Current Assets	6,539,000	5,741,200	6,539,800	9,880,700	4,834,800	4,821,900	4,135,000	4,530,900
Total Assets	42,952,700	40,889,000	42,852,100	31,863,400	27,444,600	26,833,700	21,349,400	21,625,000
Current Liabilities	6,322,800	4,147,300	5,349,800	3,126,000	2,093,300	3,113,100	1,709,800	1,639,300
Long-Term Obligations	11,653,000	11,473,900	12,351,600	9,499,600	7,031,200	5,755,200	2,031,300	2,064,000
Total Liabilities	22,028,300	19,538,800	22,304,000	15,007,300	11,979,900	11,795,600	5,988,400	6,194,100
Stockholders' Equity	20,924,400	21,350,200	20,548,100	16,856,100	15,464,700	15,038,100	15,361,000	15,430,900
Shares Outstanding	393,512	399,630	400,469	361,961	357,443	371,383	391,369	409,310
Statistical Record								
Return on Assets %	4.70	4.72	5.07	4.29	4.33	5.52	4.82	3.98
Return on Equity %	9.76	9.43	10.13	7.88	7.70	8.75	6.73	5.60
EBITDA Margin %	21.76	23.63	24.89	19.51	19.74	18.24	13.30	12.06
Net Margin %	9.36	11.64	11.22	9.73	9.42	11.34	9.60	8.41
Asset Turnover	0.41	0.41	0.45	0.44	0.46	0.49	0.50	0.47
Current Ratio	1.03	1.38	1.22	3.16	2.31	1.55	2.42	2.76
Debt to Equity	0.56	0.54	0.60	0.56	0.45	0.38	0.13	0.13
Price Range	143.03-118.13	143.03-118.13	129.29-109.63	111.35-63.78	65.28-45.95	65.57-43.54	55.94-42.12	49.03-32.39
P/E Ratio	28.84-23.82	29.07-24.01	27.45-23.28	32.00-18.33	20.34-14.31	18.95-12.58	22.11-16.65	24.39-16.11
Average Yield %	0.45	0.46	0.50	0.69	0.96	...	...	...

Address: 81 Wyman Street, Waltham, MA 02451 **Telephone:** 781-622-1000 **Fax:** 781-933-4476	**Web Site:** www.thermofisher.com **Officers:** Jim P. Manzi - Chairman, Chairman (frmr) Marc N. Casper - President, Chief Executive Officer, Executive Vice President (frmr), Senior Vice President, Chief Operating Officer	**Auditors:** PricewaterhouseCoopers LLP **Investor Contact:** 781-622-1111 **Transfer Agents:** American Stock Transfer & Trust Company, LLC, Brooklyn, NY

THOMSON REUTERS CORP

Exchange	Symbol	Price	52Wk Range	Yield	P/E	Div Achiever
NYS	TRI	$42.05 (5/31/2016)	42.28-34.62	3.23	26.96	22 Years

*7 Year Price Score 95.91 *NYSE Composite Index=100 *12 Month Price Score 103.45

Price chart and Trading Volume (thousand shares), 2007–2016

Interim Earnings (Per Share)

Qtr.	Mar	Jun	Sep	Dec
2013	(0.04)	0.30	0.33	(0.42)
2014	0.34	0.31	0.28	1.42
2015	0.38	0.33	0.36	0.53
2016	0.34	...	...	...

Interim Dividends (Per Share)

Amt	Decl	Ex	Rec	Pay
0.335Q	07/29/2015	08/18/2015	08/20/2015	09/15/2015
0.335Q	10/22/2015	11/17/2015	11/19/2015	12/15/2015
0.34Q	02/10/2016	02/19/2016	02/23/2016	03/15/2016
0.34Q	04/26/2016	05/17/2016	05/19/2016	06/15/2016

Indicated Div: $1.36 (Div. Reinv. Plan)

Valuation Analysis		Institutional Holding	
Forecast EPS	$2.05	No of Institutions	
	(05/17/2016)	403	
Market Cap	$31.6 Billion	Shares	
Book Value	$12.3 Billion	248,668,256	
Price/Book	2.56	% Held	
Price/Sales	2.65	29.34	

Business Summary: Publishing (MIC: 2.3.3 SIC: 2721 NAIC: 511120)

Thomson Reuters provides information to businesses and professionals. Co.'s business units are: Financial and Risk, a provider of critical news, information and analytics, and regulatory and operational risk management solutions; Legal, a provider of online and print information, decision support tools, software and services; Tax and Accounting, a provider of tax compliance and accounting information, software and services; and Intellectual Property and Science (IP&S), a provider of IP&S information, decision support tools and services. Co. also operates Reuters, a provider of multimedia news and information services to newspapers, television and cable networks, radio stations and websites.

Recent Developments: For the quarter ended Mar 31 2016, net income decreased 15.0% to US$272.0 million from US$320.0 million in the year-earlier quarter. Revenues were US$2.79 billion, down 1.0% from US$2.82 billion the year before. Operating income was US$310.0 million versus US$362.0 million in the prior-year quarter, a decrease of 14.4%. Indirect operating expenses increased 1.6% to US$2.49 billion from US$2.45 billion in the equivalent prior-year period.

Prospects: Our evaluation of Thomson Reuters Corp as of June 19, 2016 is the result of our systematic analysis on three basic characteristics: earnings strength, relative valuation, and recent stock price movement. The company has generated a negative trend in earnings per share over the past 5 quarters and while recent estimates for the company have remained steady, TRI has posted better than expected results. Based on operating earnings yield, the company is about fairly valued when compared to all of the companies in our coverage universe. Share price changes over the past year indicates that TRI will perform well over the near term.

Financial Data

(US$ in Thousands)	3 Mos	12/31/2015	12/31/2014	12/31/2013	12/31/2012	12/31/2011	12/31/2010	12/31/2009
Earnings Per Share	1.56	1.60	2.35	0.16	2.49	(1.67)	1.08	1.01
Cash Flow Per Share	...	3.63	2.93	2.54	3.26	3.12	3.19	3.21
Dividends Per Share	1.345	1.340	1.320	1.300	1.280	1.240	1.160	1.960
Dividend Payout %	86.22	83.75	56.17	812.50	51.41	...	107.41	194.06
Income Statement								
Total Revenue	2,793,000	12,209,000	12,607,000	12,702,000	13,278,000	13,807,000	13,070,000	12,997,000
Depn & Amortn	378,000	986,000	1,028,000	998,000	890,000	833,000	660,000	538,000
Income Taxes	(26,000)	56,000	62,000	848,000	157,000	293,000	139,000	(299,000)
Net Income	262,000	1,255,000	1,909,000	137,000	2,070,000	(1,390,000)	909,000	844,000
Average Shares	762,216	784,138	810,930	830,984	828,185	833,459	836,447	832,942
Balance Sheet								
Current Assets	4,841,000	3,540,000	3,646,000	3,900,000	4,151,000	3,914,000	3,659,000	3,663,000
Total Assets	29,048,000	29,095,000	30,597,000	32,439,000	32,572,000	32,476,000	35,531,000	34,573,000
Current Liabilities	6,221,000	5,390,000	4,597,000	4,761,000	4,995,000	4,604,000	5,011,000	4,712,000
Long-Term Obligations	6,379,000	6,829,000	7,576,000	7,470,000	6,223,000	7,160,000	6,873,000	6,821,000
Total Liabilities	16,702,000	16,482,000	16,419,000	16,403,000	15,427,000	16,071,000	16,209,000	15,306,000
Stockholders' Equity	12,346,000	12,613,000	14,178,000	16,036,000	17,145,000	16,405,000	19,322,000	19,267,000
Shares Outstanding	752,425	764,594	796,016	820,155	826,902	827,867	833,396	829,758
Statistical Record								
Return on Assets %	4.12	4.20	6.06	0.42	6.35	N.M.	2.59	2.44
Return on Equity %	9.41	9.37	12.64	0.83	12.31	N.M.	4.71	4.48
Net Margin %	9.38	10.28	15.14	1.08	15.59	N.M.	6.95	6.49
Asset Turnover	0.41	0.41	0.40	0.39	0.41	0.41	0.37	0.38
Current Ratio	0.78	0.66	0.79	0.82	0.83	0.85	0.73	0.78
Debt to Equity	0.52	0.54	0.53	0.47	0.36	0.44	0.36	0.35
Price Range	42.32-34.62	42.32-36.97	41.22-33.43	38.52-29.06	30.47-26.97	41.95-25.36	38.89-31.74	35.33-22.26
P/E Ratio	27.13-22.19	26.45-23.11	17.54-14.23	240.75-181.63	12.24-10.83	...	36.01-29.39	34.98-22.04
Average Yield %	3.50	3.38	3.54	3.85	4.49	3.60	3.19	6.61

Address: 3 Times Square, New York, NY 10036 Telephone: 646-223-4000 Fax: 416-360-8812	Web Site: www.thomsonreuters.com Officers: David Thomson - Chairman Andrew Rashbass - President, Editor-in Chief	Auditors: PricewaterhouseCoopers LLP Transfer Agents: Computershare Trust Company N.A., Jersey City, New Jersey, United States

THOR INDUSTRIES, INC.

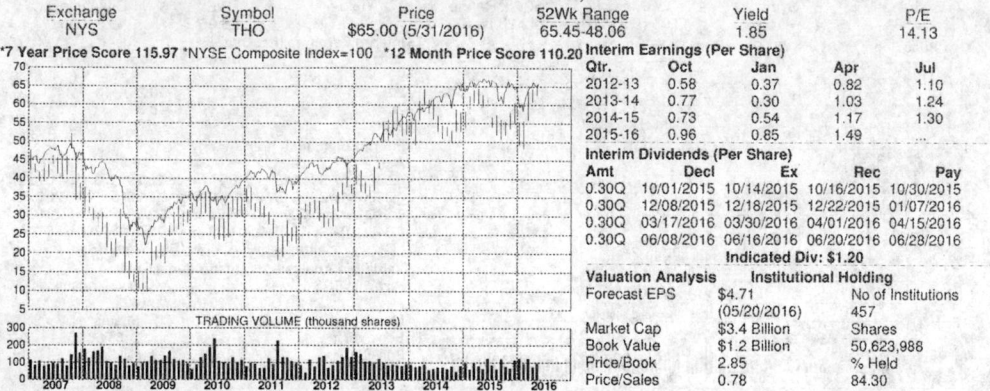

Exchange	Symbol	Price	52Wk Range	Yield	P/E
NYS	THO	$65.00 (5/31/2016)	65.45-48.06	1.85	14.13

*7 Year Price Score 115.97 *NYSE Composite Index=100 *12 Month Price Score 110.20

Interim Earnings (Per Share)

Qtr.	Oct	Jan	Apr	Jul
2012-13	0.58	0.37	0.82	1.10
2013-14	0.77	0.30	1.03	1.24
2014-15	0.73	0.54	1.17	1.30
2015-16	0.96	0.85	1.49	...

Interim Dividends (Per Share)

Amt	Decl	Ex	Rec	Pay
0.30Q	10/01/2015	10/14/2015	10/16/2015	10/30/2015
0.30Q	12/08/2015	12/18/2015	12/22/2015	01/07/2016
0.30Q	03/17/2016	03/30/2016	04/01/2016	04/15/2016
0.30Q	06/08/2016	06/16/2016	06/20/2016	06/28/2016

Indicated Div: $1.20

Valuation Analysis

		Institutional Holding	
Forecast EPS	$4.71	No of Institutions	457
	(05/20/2016)		
Market Cap	$3.4 Billion	Shares	50,623,988
Book Value	$1.2 Billion	% Held	84.30
Price/Book	2.85		
Price/Sales	0.78		

Business Summary: Autos- Manufacturing (MIC: 1.8.1 SIC: 3716 NAIC: 336213)

Thor Industries manufacture a variety of recreational vehicles in the U.S. and sell those vehicles primarily throughout the U.S. and Canada, as well as related parts and accessories. The principal types of towable recreational vehicles that Co. produces include conventional travel trailers and fifth wheels. In addition, Co. also produces truck and folding campers and equestrian and other specialty towable recreational vehicles, as well as Class A, Class C and Class B motorhomes. As of July 31 2015, Co. had two reportable segments: towable recreational vehicles and motorized recreational vehicles.

Recent Developments: For the quarter ended Apr 30 2016, income from continuing operations increased 24.6% to US$79.2 million from US$63.6 million in the year-earlier quarter. Net income increased 25.0% to US$78.6 million from US$62.8 million in the year-earlier quarter. Revenues were US$1.28 billion, up 9.4% from US$1.17 billion the year before. Direct operating expenses rose 7.4% to US$1.08 billion from US$1.01 billion in the comparable period the year before. Indirect operating expenses increased 18.8% to US$86.6 million from US$72.9 million in the equivalent prior-year period.

Prospects: Our evaluation of Thor Industries Inc. as of June 19, 2016 is the result of our systematic analysis on three basic characteristics: earnings strength, relative valuation, and recent stock price movement. The company has generated a negative trend in earnings per share over the past 5 quarters and while recent estimates for the company have been raised by analysts, THO has posted better than expected results. Based on operating earnings yield, the company is undervalued when compared to all of the companies in our coverage universe. Share price changes over the past year indicates that THO will perform well over the near term.

Financial Data

(US$ in Thousands)	9 Mos	6 Mos	3 Mos	07/31/2015	07/31/2014	07/31/2013	07/31/2012	07/31/2011
Earnings Per Share	4.60	4.28	3.97	3.74	3.35	2.88	2.26	1.92
Cash Flow Per Share	5.74	4.70	4.14	4.66	2.80	2.74	2.20	2.08
Tang Book Value Per Share	14.12	12.78	11.90	11.14	11.28	10.47	9.29	8.36
Dividends Per Share	1.170	1.140	1.110	1.080	1.920	2.220	0.600	0.400
Dividend Payout %	25.43	26.64	27.96	28.88	57.31	77.08	26.55	20.83
Income Statement								
Total Revenue	3,289,476	2,005,422	1,030,351	4,006,819	3,525,456	3,241,795	3,084,660	2,755,508
EBITDA	295,010	166,518	89,160	310,160	277,086	244,337	202,464	172,938
Depn & Amortn	35,113	22,840	11,433	18,377	25,834	24,987	24,978	24,009
Income Before Taxes	259,862	143,579	77,691	292,895	252,819	221,972	180,691	152,627
Income Taxes	84,686	47,596	26,955	90,886	77,303	70,296	58,952	46,354
Net Income	173,747	95,165	50,497	199,385	179,002	152,862	121,739	106,273
Average Shares	52,601	52,561	52,545	53,275	53,361	53,115	53,899	55,373
Balance Sheet								
Current Assets	974,392	868,105	841,915	775,841	844,049	830,704	684,886	623,767
Total Assets	1,697,880	1,586,363	1,572,383	1,503,248	1,408,718	1,328,268	1,243,054	1,198,070
Current Liabilities	441,595	397,203	410,415	378,335	370,715	361,672	311,090	278,598
Total Liabilities	501,689	454,969	472,009	438,061	431,021	435,654	392,227	361,796
Stockholders' Equity	1,196,191	1,131,394	1,100,374	1,065,187	977,697	892,614	850,827	836,274
Shares Outstanding	52,482	52,482	52,482	52,394	53,329	53,186	52,920	55,840
Statistical Record								
Return on Assets %	14.94	14.92	14.15	13.69	13.08	11.89	9.95	9.83
Return on Equity %	21.43	21.11	20.06	19.52	19.14	17.54	14.39	14.23
EBITDA Margin %	8.97	8.30	8.65	7.74	7.86	7.54	6.56	6.28
Net Margin %	5.28	4.75	4.90	4.98	5.08	4.72	3.95	3.86
Asset Turnover	2.68	2.79	2.76	2.75	2.58	2.52	2.52	2.55
Current Ratio	2.21	2.19	2.05	2.05	2.28	2.30	2.20	2.24
Price Range	64.31-48.06	64.38-49.25	64.38-50.68	64.38-50.03	64.16-49.03	55.27-27.22	34.47-18.00	37.71-23.24
P/E Ratio	13.98-10.45	15.04-11.51	16.22-12.77	17.21-13.38	19.15-14.64	19.19-9.45	15.25-7.96	19.64-12.10
Average Yield %	2.07	1.99	1.93	1.90	3.42	5.63	2.21	1.29

Address: 601 East Beardsley Ave., Elkhart, IN 46514-3305 **Telephone:** 574-970-7460	**Web Site:** www.thorindustries.com **Officers:** Peter B. Orthwein - Chairman, President, Chief Executive Officer Robert W. Martin - President, Chief Executive Officer, Chief Operating Officer, Division Officer	**Auditors:** Deloitte & Touche LLP **Transfer Agents:** Computershare Investor Services

3M CO

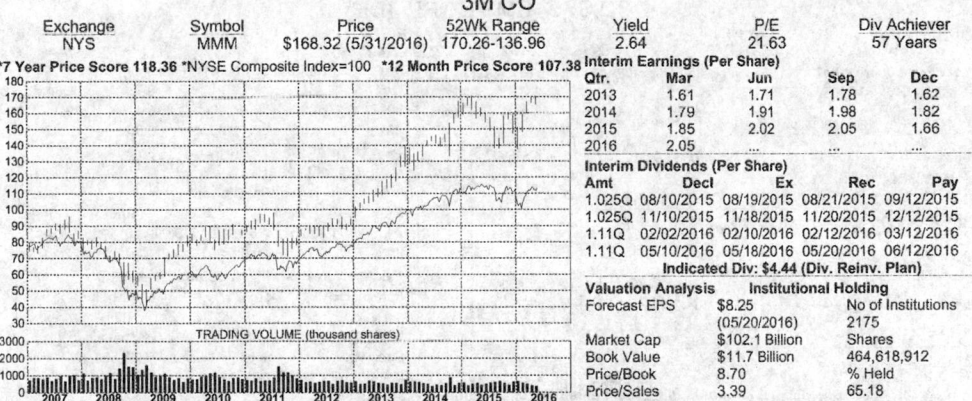

Exchange	Symbol	Price	52Wk Range	Yield	P/E	Div Achiever
NYS	MMM	$168.32 (5/31/2016)	170.26-136.96	2.64	21.63	57 Years

*7 Year Price Score 118.36 ***NYSE Composite Index=100** ***12 Month Price Score 107.38**

Interim Earnings (Per Share)

Qtr.	Mar	Jun	Sep	Dec
2013	1.61	1.71	1.78	1.62
2014	1.79	1.91	1.98	1.82
2015	1.85	2.02	2.05	1.66
2016	2.05	...	...	...

Interim Dividends (Per Share)

Amt	Decl	Ex	Rec	Pay
1.025Q	08/10/2015	08/19/2015	08/21/2015	09/12/2015
1.025Q	11/10/2015	11/18/2015	11/20/2015	12/12/2015
1.11Q	02/02/2016	02/10/2016	02/12/2016	03/12/2016
1.11Q	05/10/2016	05/18/2016	05/20/2016	06/12/2016

Indicated Div: $4.44 (Div. Reinv. Plan)

Valuation Analysis		Institutional Holding	
Forecast EPS	$8.25	No of Institutions	
	(05/20/2016)		2175
Market Cap	$102.1 Billion	Shares	
Book Value	$11.7 Billion		464,618,912
Price/Book	8.70	% Held	
Price/Sales	3.39		65.18

Business Summary: Medical Instruments & Equipment (MIC: 4.3.1 SIC: 3841 NAIC: 339112)

3M is a technology company. Co.'s segments are: Industrial, providing tapes, a range of coated, non-woven and bonded abrasives, and adhesives, among others; Safety and Graphics, providing personal protection products; and traffic safety and security products, among others; Electronics and Energy, providing LCD computer monitors, LCD televisions, and automotive displays, among others; Health Care, providing medical and surgical supplies, skin health and infection prevention products, and food safety products, among others; and Consumer, providing office supply products, stationery products, and home care products, among others.

Recent Developments: For the quarter ended Mar 31 2016, net income increased 6.4% to US$1.28 billion from US$1.20 billion in the year-earlier quarter. Revenues were US$7.41 billion, down 2.2% from US$7.58 billion the year before. Operating income was US$1.79 billion versus US$1.73 billion in the prior-year quarter, an increase of 3.4%. Direct operating expenses declined 3.7% to US$3.68 billion from US$3.82 billion in the comparable period the year before. Indirect operating expenses decreased 4.1% to US$1.94 billion from US$2.03 billion in the equivalent prior-year period.

Prospects: Our evaluation of 3M Co as of June 19, 2016 is the result of our systematic analysis on three basic characteristics: earnings strength, relative valuation, and recent stock price movement. The company has produced a positive trend in earnings per share over the past 5 quarters. However, while recent estimates for the company have been mixed, MMM has posted better than expected results. Based on operating earnings yield, the company is about fairly valued when compared to all of the companies in our coverage universe. Share price changes over the past year indicates that MMM will perform well over the near term.

Financial Data

(US$ in Millions)	3 Mos	12/31/2015	12/31/2014	12/31/2013	12/31/2012	12/31/2011	12/31/2010	12/31/2009
Earnings Per Share	7.78	7.58	7.49	6.72	6.32	5.96	5.63	4.52
Cash Flow Per Share	10.87	10.26	10.21	8.53	7.62	7.46	7.25	7.05
Tang Book Value Per Share	N.M.	N.M.	7.28	12.77	12.03	9.29	9.86	7.87
Dividends Per Share	4.185	4.100	3.420	2.540	2.360	2.200	2.100	2.040
Dividend Payout %	53.79	54.09	45.66	37.80	37.34	36.91	37.30	45.13
Income Statement								
Total Revenue	7,409	30,274	31,821	30,871	29,904	29,611	26,662	23,123
EBITDA	2,144	8,381	8,543	8,037	7,771	7,414	7,038	5,971
Depn & Amortn	356	1,435	1,408	1,371	1,288	1,236	1,120	1,157
Income Before Taxes	1,746	6,823	7,026	6,562	6,351	6,031	5,755	4,632
Income Taxes	468	1,982	2,028	1,841	1,840	1,674	1,592	1,388
Net Income	1,275	4,833	4,956	4,659	4,444	4,283	4,085	3,193
Average Shares	621	637	662	693	703	719	725	706
Balance Sheet								
Current Assets	10,874	10,986	11,765	12,733	13,630	12,240	12,215	10,795
Total Assets	32,982	32,718	31,269	33,550	33,876	31,616	30,156	27,250
Current Liabilities	7,178	7,118	5,998	7,498	6,200	5,441	6,089	4,897
Long-Term Obligations	8,927	8,799	6,790	4,384	4,987	4,563	4,277	5,204
Total Liabilities	21,249	21,010	18,160	16,048	16,301	16,196	14,493	14,486
Stockholders' Equity	11,733	11,708	13,109	17,502	17,575	15,420	15,663	12,764
Shares Outstanding	606	609	635	663	687	694	711	710
Statistical Record								
Return on Assets %	15.43	15.11	15.29	13.82	13.53	13.87	14.23	12.10
Return on Equity %	38.28	38.95	32.38	26.56	26.86	27.56	28.74	28.20
EBITDA Margin %	28.94	27.68	26.85	26.03	25.99	25.04	26.40	25.82
Net Margin %	17.21	15.96	15.57	15.09	14.86	14.46	15.32	13.81
Asset Turnover	0.95	0.95	0.98	0.92	0.91	0.96	0.93	0.88
Current Ratio	1.51	1.54	1.96	1.70	2.20	2.25	2.01	2.20
Debt to Equity	0.76	0.75	0.52	0.25	0.28	0.30	0.27	0.41
Price Range	167.07-136.96	170.50-137.58	167.27-123.90	140.25-92.85	95.37-82.51	97.97-70.93	90.90-74.74	84.13-41.83
P/E Ratio	21.47-17.60	22.49-18.15	22.33-16.54	20.87-13.82	15.09-13.06	16.44-11.90	16.15-13.28	18.61-9.25
Average Yield %	2.72	2.62	2.40	2.23	2.65	2.54	2.51	3.19

Address: 3M Center, St. Paul, MN 55144	Web Site: www.3M.com	Auditors: PricewaterhouseCoopers LLP
Telephone: 651-733-1110	Officers: Inge G. Thulin - Chairman, President, Chief Executive Officer, Executive Vice President, Chief Operating Officer Hak Cheol Shin - Executive Vice President, Executive Vice President (frmr)	Investor Contact: 651-737-8503
Fax: 651-733-9973		Transfer Agents: Wells Fargo Shareowner Services, St. Paul, MN

3D SYSTEMS CORP. (DE)

Exchange	Symbol	Price	52Wk Range	Yield	P/E
NYS	DDD	$13.39 (5/31/2016)	21.98-6.42	N/A	N/A

*7 Year Price Score 45.42 ***NYSE Composite Index=100** ***12 Month Price Score 119.00**

TRADING VOLUME (thousand shares)

Interim Earnings (Per Share)

Qtr.	Mar	Jun	Sep	Dec
2013	0.06	0.10	0.17	0.11
2014	0.05	0.02	0.03	0.02
2015	(0.12)	(0.12)	(0.29)	(5.32)
2016	(0.16)	...	...	...

Interim Dividends (Per Share)

Amt	Decl	Ex	Rec	Pay
2-for-1	04/28/2011	05/19/2011	05/09/2011	05/18/2011
3-for-2	02/06/2013	02/25/2013	02/15/2013	02/22/2013

Valuation Analysis

		Institutional Holding	
Forecast EPS	$0.33	No of Institutions	
	(05/20/2016)	339	
Market Cap	$1.5 Billion	Shares	
Book Value	$665.7 Million	56,534,164	
Price/Book	2.25	% Held	
Price/Sales	2.28	55.07	

Business Summary: Computer Hardware & Equipment (MIC: 6.2.1 SIC: 7372 NAIC: 511210)

3D Systems is a holding company. Through its subsidiaries, Co. provides 3D products and services, including 3D printers, print materials, on-demand parts services and digital design and manufacturing tools. Co. provides a range of 3D printers, which includes: Stereolithography, Selective Laser Sintering, Direct Metal Printing, MultiJet Printing, ColorJet Printing and PlasticJet Printing; print materials, which includes plastic, nylon, metal, composite, elastomeric, wax and Class IV bio-compatible materials; software; haptic devices; scanners and virtual surgical simulators.

Recent Developments: For the quarter ended Mar 31 2016, net loss amounted to US$17.8 million versus a net loss of US$13.1 million in the year-earlier quarter. Revenues were US$152.6 million, down 5.1% from US$160.7 million the year before. Operating loss was US$16.8 million versus a loss of US$17.5 million in the prior-year quarter. Direct operating expenses declined 8.2% to US$75.0 million from US$81.7 million in the comparable period the year before. Indirect operating expenses decreased 2.3% to US$94.3 million from US$96.5 million in the equivalent prior-year period.

Prospects: Our evaluation of 3D Systems Corp. as of June 19, 2016 is the result of our systematic analysis on three basic characteristics: earnings strength, relative valuation, and recent stock price movement. The company has produced a positive trend in earnings per share over the past 5 quarters. However, while recent estimates for the company have been mixed, DDD has posted results that were in line with analysts expectations. Based on operating earnings yield, the company is overvalued when compared to all of the companies in our coverage universe. Share price changes over the past year indicates that DDD will perform poorly over the near term.

Financial Data
(US$ in Thousands)

	3 Mos	12/31/2015	12/31/2014	12/31/2013	12/31/2012	12/31/2011	12/31/2010	12/31/2009
Earnings Per Share	(5.89)	(5.85)	0.11	0.45	0.47	0.47	0.28	0.02
Cash Flow Per Share	0.14	(0.03)	0.47	0.26	0.65	0.37	0.46	0.11
Tang Book Value Per Share	2.88	2.77	4.05	4.08	1.47	1.23	0.80	0.77
Income Statement								
Total Revenue	152,555	666,163	653,652	513,400	353,633	230,423	159,868	112,835
EBITDA	(10,759)	(620,945)	41,042	90,607	69,012	41,169	27,038	7,955
Depn & Amortn	6,000	20,979	14,727	9,746	8,441	6,267	6,118	4,882
Income Before Taxes	(16,633)	(654,953)	17,387	64,006	43,279	32,446	19,739	1,913
Income Taxes	1,179	8,972	5,441	19,887	4,338	(2,974)	173	774
Net Income	(17,788)	(655,492)	11,637	44,107	38,941	35,420	19,566	1,066
Average Shares	112,197	111,969	108,023	98,393	81,723	76,084	70,392	67,815
Balance Sheet								
Current Assets	432,515	432,467	580,690	526,855	287,438	261,380	100,140	70,153
Total Assets	896,714	893,275	1,525,970	1,097,856	677,442	462,974	208,800	150,403
Current Liabilities	147,985	145,471	148,491	110,456	75,153	59,023	57,665	33,435
Long-Term Obligations	8,090	8,187	8,905	18,693	87,974	138,716	8,055	8,254
Total Liabilities	231,045	237,366	233,052	165,210	197,109	208,186	75,681	45,706
Stockholders' Equity	665,669	655,909	1,292,918	932,646	480,333	254,788	133,119	104,697
Shares Outstanding	111,981	112,223	111,524	103,218	89,250	75,976	70,020	68,100
Statistical Record								
Return on Assets %	N.M.	N.M.	0.89	4.97	6.81	10.55	10.89	0.70
Return on Equity %	N.M.	N.M.	1.05	6.24	10.57	18.26	16.45	1.03
EBITDA Margin %	N.M.	N.M.	6.28	17.65	19.52	17.87	16.91	7.05
Net Margin %	N.M.	N.M.	1.78	8.59	11.01	15.37	12.24	0.94
Asset Turnover	0.55	0.55	0.50	0.58	0.62	0.69	0.89	0.74
Current Ratio	2.92	2.97	3.91	4.77	3.82	4.43	1.74	2.10
Debt to Equity	0.01	0.01	0.01	0.02	0.18	0.54	0.06	0.08
Price Range	32.50-6.42	32.87-8.52	96.42-28.38	92.93-29.16	35.57-10.24	19.25-9.00	11.30-3.50	3.90-1.30
P/E Ratio	...	...	876.55-258.00	206.51-64.80	75.67-21.79	40.96-19.15	40.36-12.50	195.17-64.83

Address: 333 Three D Systems Circle, Rock Hill, SC 29730 **Telephone:** 803-326-3900	**Web Site:** www.3DSystems.com **Officers:** G. Walter Loewenbaum - Chairman Vyomesh I. Joshi - President, Chief Executive Officer	**Auditors:** BDO USA, LLP **Investor Contact:** 803-326-4010 **Transfer Agents:** U.S. Stock Transfer Corporation

TIDEWATER INC.

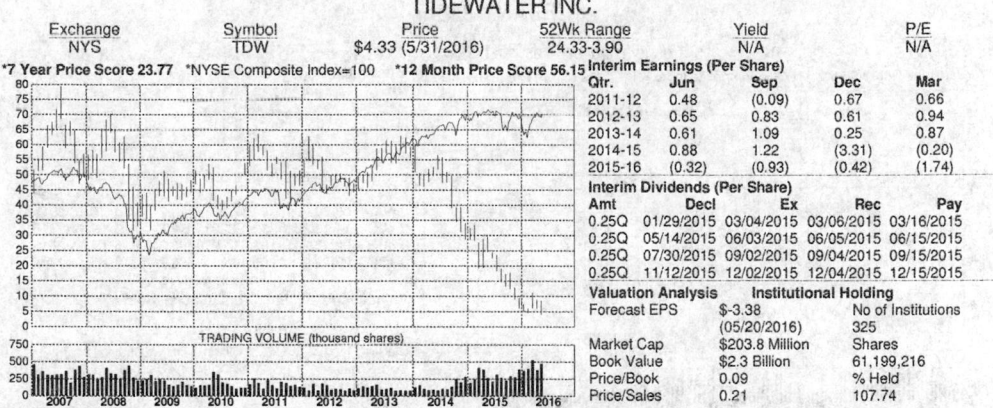

Exchange	Symbol	Price	52Wk Range	Yield	P/E
NYS	TDW	$4.33 (5/31/2016)	24.33-3.90	N/A	N/A

*7 Year Price Score 23.77   *NYSE Composite Index=100   *12 Month Price Score 56.15

Interim Earnings (Per Share)

Qtr.	Jun	Sep	Dec	Mar
2011-12	0.48	(0.09)	0.67	0.66
2012-13	0.65	0.83	0.61	0.94
2013-14	0.61	1.09	0.25	0.87
2014-15	0.88	1.22	(3.31)	(0.20)
2015-16	(0.32)	(0.93)	(0.42)	(1.74)

Interim Dividends (Per Share)

Amt	Decl	Ex	Rec	Pay
0.25Q	01/29/2015	03/04/2015	03/06/2015	03/16/2015
0.25Q	05/14/2015	06/03/2015	06/05/2015	06/15/2015
0.25Q	07/30/2015	09/02/2015	09/04/2015	09/15/2015
0.25Q	11/12/2015	12/02/2015	12/04/2015	12/15/2015

Valuation Analysis | **Institutional Holding**

Forecast EPS	$-3.38	No of Institutions	
	(05/20/2016)	325	
Market Cap	$203.8 Million	Shares	
Book Value	$2.3 Billion	61,199,216	
Price/Book	0.09	% Held	
Price/Sales	0.21	107.74	

Business Summary: Equipment & Services (MIC: 9.1.3 SIC: 4424 NAIC: 213112)

Tidewater provides offshore service vessels and marine support services to the global offshore energy industry through the operation of a fleet of marine service vessels. Co.'s vessels and associated vessel services provide support of all phases of offshore exploration, field development and production. These services include towing of, and anchor handling for, mobile offshore drilling units; transporting supplies and personnel necessary to sustain drilling, workover and production activities; offshore construction, remotely operated vehicle operations, and seismic and subsea support; and a variety of services such as pipe and cable laying.

Recent Developments: For the year ended Mar 31 2016, net loss amounted to US$160.4 million versus a net loss of US$65.3 million in the prior year. Revenues were US$979.1 million, down 34.5% from US$1.50 billion the year before. Operating loss was US$69.5 million versus a loss of US$37.2 million in the prior year. Direct operating expenses declined 32.6% to US$579.9 million from US$860.9 million in the comparable period the year before. Indirect operating expenses decreased 30.2% to US$468.6 million from US$671.8 million in the equivalent prior-year period.

Prospects: Our evaluation of Tidewater Inc. as of June 19, 2016 is the result of our systematic analysis on three basic characteristics: earnings strength, relative valuation, and recent stock price movement. The company has enjoyed a very positive trend in earnings per share over the past 5 years. Because the company lacks sufficient analyst estimate data, we place greater weight on the historical EPS trend as the measure of earnings strength. Based on operating earnings yield, the company is overvalued when compared to all of the companies in our coverage universe. Share price changes over the past year indicates that TDW will perform very well over the near term.

Financial Data

(US$ in Thousands)	03/31/2016	03/31/2015	03/31/2014	03/31/2013	03/31/2012	03/31/2011	03/31/2010	03/31/2009
Earnings Per Share	(3.41)	(1.34)	2.82	3.03	1.70	2.05	5.02	7.89
Cash Flow Per Share	5.38	7.37	2.12	4.32	4.34	5.16	6.38	10.25
Tang Book Value Per Share	48.86	52.62	48.17	45.75	43.48	42.12	41.20	37.06
Dividends Per Share	0.750	1.000	1.000	1.000	1.000	1.000	1.000	1.000
Dividend Payout %	...	...	35.46	33.00	58.82	48.78	19.92	12.67
Income Statement								
Total Revenue	979,062	1,495,517	1,435,103	1,244,165	1,067,007	1,055,388	1,168,634	1,390,835
EBITDA	107,382	146,701	366,418	356,542	255,219	282,214	374,624	594,395
Depn & Amortn	182,309	175,204	167,480	147,299	138,356	140,600	130,200	126,231
Income Before Taxes	(125,976)	(76,605)	157,247	182,974	97,995	135,910	249,627	474,537
Income Taxes	20,819	(1,077)	32,793	44,413	23,625	42,479	8,258	84,617
Net Income	(160,183)	(65,190)	140,255	150,750	87,411	105,616	259,476	406,898
Average Shares	46,981	48,658	49,680	49,734	51,429	51,487	51,689	51,546
Balance Sheet								
Current Assets	1,323,314	868,815	820,209	508,090	694,100	579,147	585,627	634,451
Total Assets	4,990,547	4,756,162	4,885,829	4,168,055	4,061,618	3,748,116	3,293,357	3,073,804
Current Liabilities	2,459,128	482,234	401,681	266,629	238,929	183,589	204,712	203,350
Long-Term Obligations	...	1,524,295	1,505,358	1,000,000	950,000	700,000	275,000	300,000
Total Liabilities	2,691,027	2,281,674	2,206,445	1,606,299	1,535,261	1,234,172	829,327	829,126
Stockholders' Equity	2,299,520	2,474,488	2,679,384	2,561,756	2,526,357	2,513,944	2,464,030	2,244,678
Shares Outstanding	47,067	47,029	49,730	49,485	51,250	51,876	51,830	51,696
Statistical Record								
Return on Assets %	N.M.	N.M.	3.10	3.66	2.23	3.00	8.15	13.97
Return on Equity %	N.M.	N.M.	5.35	5.93	3.46	4.24	11.02	19.49
EBITDA Margin %	10.97	9.81	25.53	28.66	23.92	26.74	32.06	42.74
Net Margin %	N.M.	N.M.	9.77	12.12	8.19	10.01	22.20	29.26
Asset Turnover	0.20	0.31	0.32	0.30	0.27	0.30	0.37	0.48
Current Ratio	0.54	1.80	2.04	1.91	2.91	3.15	2.86	3.12
Debt to Equity	...	0.62	0.56	0.39	0.38	0.28	0.11	0.13
Price Range	29.48-4.43	56.40-19.14	62.76-45.97	55.93-42.98	62.72-40.53	63.50-38.33	51.37-37.13	70.18-31.44
P/E Ratio	...	...	22.26-16.30	18.46-14.18	36.89-23.84	30.98-18.70	10.23-7.40	8.89-3.98
Average Yield %	4.96	2.45	1.80	2.09	1.91	2.07	2.20	2.01

Address: 601 Poydras St., Suite 1500, New Orleans, LA 70130 Telephone: 504-568-1010	Web Site: www.tdw.com Officers: Richard A. Pattarozzi - Chairperson Jeffrey M. Platt - President, Chief Executive Officer, Executive Vice President, Chief Operating Officer	Auditors: Deloitte & Touche LLP Investor Contact: 713-470-5300 Transfer Agents: ComputerShare Investor Services, Providence, RI

TIFFANY & CO.

*7 Year Price Score 95.61   *NYSE Composite Index=100   *12 Month Price Score 88.83

Interim Earnings (Per Share)

Qtr.	Apr	Jul	Oct	Jan
2013-14	0.65	0.83	0.73	(0.80)
2014-15	0.97	0.96	0.29	1.51
2015-16	0.81	0.81	0.70	1.27
2016-17	0.69			

Interim Dividends (Per Share)

Amt	Decl	Ex	Rec	Pay
0.40Q	08/20/2015	09/17/2015	09/21/2015	10/13/2015
0.40Q	11/19/2015	12/17/2015	12/21/2015	01/11/2016
0.40Q	02/18/2016	03/17/2016	03/21/2016	04/11/2016
0.45Q	05/26/2016	06/16/2016	06/20/2016	07/11/2016

Indicated Div: $1.80

Valuation Analysis   **Institutional Holding**

Forecast EPS	$3.64	No of Institutions
	(05/20/2016)	713
Market Cap	$7.8 Billion	Shares
Book Value	$2.9 Billion	126,121,160
Price/Book	2.65	% Held
Price/Sales	1.94	83.39

Business Summary: Retail - Specialty (MIC: 2.1.3 SIC: 5944 NAIC: 448310)

Tiffany & Co. is a holding company. Through its subsidiary, Tiffany and Company, Co. is engaged as a jeweler and retailer whose principal merchandise offering is jewelry. Co. also sells timepieces, leather goods, sterling silverware, china, crystal, stationery, fragrances and accessories. Through its subsidiaries, Co. designs and manufactures products and operates TIFFANY & CO. retail stores worldwide, and also sells its products through Internet, catalog, business-to-business and wholesale operations. Co. has five reportable segments: Americas, Asia-Pacific, Japan, Europe, and Other. As of Jan 31 2016, Co. operated a total of 307 TIFFANY & CO. stores.

Recent Developments: For the quarter ended Apr 30 2016, net income decreased 16.6% to US$87.5 million from US$104.9 million in the year-earlier quarter. Revenues were US$891.3 million, down 7.4% from US$962.4 million the year before. Operating income was US$134.6 million versus US$170.0 million in the prior-year quarter, a decrease of 20.8%. Direct operating expenses declined 12.1% to US$345.7 million from US$393.4 million in the comparable period the year before. Indirect operating expenses increased 3.0% to US$411.0 million from US$399.0 million in the equivalent prior-year period.

Prospects: Our evaluation of Tiffany & Co. as of June 19, 2016 is the result of our systematic analysis on three basic characteristics: earnings strength, relative valuation, and recent stock price movement. The company has managed to produce a neutral trend in earnings per share over the past 5 quarters. However, while recent estimates for the company have been lowered by analysts, TIF has posted better than expected results. Based on operating earnings yield, the company is undervalued when compared to all of the companies in our coverage universe. Share price changes over the past year indicates that TIF will perform well over the near term.

Financial Data

(US$ in Thousands)	3 Mos	01/31/2016	01/31/2015	01/31/2014	01/31/2013	01/31/2012	01/31/2011	01/31/2010
Earnings Per Share	3.47	3.59	3.73	1.41	3.25	3.40	2.87	2.11
Cash Flow Per Share	5.94	6.33	4.76	1.21	2.58	1.65	2.36	5.53
Tang Book Value Per Share	23.36	22.96	21.92	21.20	20.47	18.54	17.15	14.91
Dividends Per Share	1.600	1.580	1.480	1.340	1.250	1.120	0.950	0.680
Dividend Payout %	46.11	44.01	39.68	95.04	38.46	32.94	33.10	32.23
Income Statement								
Total Revenue	891,300	4,104,900	4,249,913	4,031,130	3,794,249	3,642,937	3,085,290	2,709,704
EBITDA	132,500	955,200	983,201	488,972	861,663	862,634	751,172	582,720
Depn & Amortn	(2,100)	196,300	182,761	171,452	159,018	149,109	149,403	137,705
Income Before Taxes	123,100	709,900	737,537	254,866	643,576	664,951	547,434	389,974
Income Taxes	35,600	246,000	253,358	73,497	227,419	225,761	179,031	124,298
Net Income	87,500	463,900	484,179	181,369	416,157	439,190	368,403	264,823
Average Shares	126,500	129,100	129,918	128,867	127,934	129,083	128,406	125,383
Balance Sheet								
Current Assets	3,522,200	3,508,400	3,611,387	3,228,388	3,151,589	2,889,675	2,684,545	2,445,666
Total Assets	5,148,200	5,129,700	5,180,603	4,752,351	4,630,850	4,158,992	3,735,669	3,488,360
Current Liabilities	717,800	729,900	658,033	696,740	586,592	626,677	479,913	600,273
Long-Term Obligations	790,000	798,100	882,535	751,154	765,238	538,352	588,494	519,592
Total Liabilities	2,205,300	2,218,300	2,345,544	2,031,914	2,032,118	1,810,087	1,558,194	1,605,121
Stockholders' Equity	2,942,900	2,911,400	2,835,059	2,720,437	2,598,732	2,348,905	2,177,475	1,883,239
Shares Outstanding	126,000	126,800	129,326	128,312	126,934	126,676	126,969	126,326
Statistical Record								
Return on Assets %	8.67	9.00	9.75	3.87	9.44	11.13	10.20	8.04
Return on Equity %	15.37	16.15	17.43	6.82	16.78	19.41	18.14	15.26
EBITDA Margin %	14.87	23.27	23.13	12.13	22.71	23.68	24.35	21.50
Net Margin %	9.82	11.30	11.39	4.50	10.97	12.06	11.94	9.77
Asset Turnover	0.78	0.80	0.86	0.86	0.86	0.92	0.85	0.82
Current Ratio	4.91	4.81	5.49	4.63	5.37	4.61	5.59	4.07
Debt to Equity	0.27	0.27	0.31	0.28	0.29	0.23	0.27	0.28
Price Range	95.70-60.75	95.70-60.93	108.67-80.88	92.78-62.17	73.27-50.29	83.82-56.27	65.44-36.29	46.89-16.94
P/E Ratio	27.58-17.51	26.66-16.97	29.13-21.68	65.80-44.09	22.54-15.47	24.65-16.55	22.80-12.64	22.22-8.03
Average Yield %	2.01	1.88	1.54	1.73	2.04	1.63	1.96	2.12

TIME INC

Exchange	Symbol	Price	52Wk Range	Yield	P/E
NYS	TIME	$15.87 (5/31/2016)	24.05-12.40	4.79	N/A

*7 Year Price Score N/A ***NYSE Composite Index=100** ***12 Month Price Score 83.39**

Interim Earnings (Per Share)

Qtr.	Mar	Jun	Sep	Dec
2013	(0.07)	0.69	0.62	0.61
2014	(0.67)	(0.30)	0.44	1.33
2015	(0.08)	0.22	(8.30)	(0.15)
2016	(0.10)	...	...	...

Interim Dividends (Per Share)

Amt	Decl	Ex	Rec	Pay
0.19Q	08/04/2015	08/27/2015	08/31/2015	09/15/2015
0.19Q	11/05/2015	11/25/2015	11/30/2015	12/15/2015
0.19Q	02/11/2016	02/25/2016	02/29/2016	03/15/2016
0.19Q	05/05/2016	05/26/2016	05/31/2016	06/15/2016

Indicated Div: $0.76

Valuation Analysis

		Institutional Holding	
Forecast EPS	$1.44	No of Institutions	
	(05/20/2016)	379	
Market Cap	$1.6 Billion	Shares	
Book Value	$1.7 Billion	97,039,312	
Price/Book	0.95	% Held	
Price/Sales	0.52	95.58	

TRADING VOLUME (thousand shares)

Business Summary: Publishing (MIC: 2,3,3 SIC: 2721 NAIC: 511120)

Time together with its subsidiaries is engaged as a media company. Co.'s brands include People, Sports Illustrated, InStyle, Time, Real Simple, Southern Living, Entertainment Weekly, Travel + Leisure, Cooking Light, Fortune and Food & Wine, as well as other titles in the U.K. such as Decanter, Horse & Hound and Wallpaper*. Co. also provides content marketing, targeted local print and digital advertising programs, branded book publishing, and marketing and support services, including subscription sales services for magazines and other products, retail distribution and marketing services and customer service and fulfillment services.

Recent Developments: For the quarter ended Mar 31 2016, net loss amounted to US$10.0 million versus a net loss of US$9.0 million in the year-earlier quarter. Revenues were US$690.0 million, up 1.5% from US$680.0 million the year before. Operating loss was US$3.0 million versus an income of US$5.0 million in the prior-year quarter. Direct operating expenses rose 8.4% to US$297.0 million from US$274.0 million in the comparable period the year before. Indirect operating expenses decreased 1.2% to US$396.0 million from US$401.0 million in the equivalent prior-year period.

Prospects: Our evaluation of Time Inc. as of June 19, 2016 is the result of our systematic analysis on three basic characteristics: earnings strength, relative valuation, and recent stock price movement. The company has managed to produce a neutral trend in earnings per share over the past 5 quarters. However, while recent estimates for the company have been mixed, TIME has posted better than expected results. Based on operating earnings yield, the company is undervalued when compared to all of the companies in our coverage universe. Share price changes over the past year indicates that TIME will perform very poorly over the near term.

Financial Data

(US$ in Millions)	3 Mos	12/31/2015	12/31/2014	12/31/2013	12/31/2012
Earnings Per Share	(8.33)	(8.32)	0.80	1.85	2.41
Cash Flow Per Share	1.19	1.45	2.58	3.84	4.23
Dividends Per Share	0.760	0.760	0.190	...	...
Dividend Payout %	...	...	23.75	...	...
Income Statement					
Total Revenue	690	3,103	3,281	3,354	3,436
EBITDA	(4)	(653)	353	456	544
Depn & Amortn	...	172	179	127	127
Income Before Taxes	(21)	(902)	123	326	414
Income Taxes	(11)	(21)	36	125	151
Net Income	(10)	(881)	87	201	263
Average Shares	102	105	109	108	108
Balance Sheet					
Current Assets	1,087	1,417	1,256	763	...
Total Assets	4,587	4,884	5,900	5,674	...
Current Liabilities	963	1,126	1,086	983	...
Long-Term Obligations	1,251	1,286	1,368	38	...
Total Liabilities	2,867	3,075	3,029	1,632	...
Stockholders' Equity	1,720	1,809	2,871	4,042	...
Shares Outstanding	102	106	109	...	...
Statistical Record					
Return on Assets %	N.M.	N.M.	1.50	...	...
Return on Equity %	N.M.	N.M.	2.52	...	...
EBITDA Margin %	N.M.	N.M.	10.76	13.60	15.83
Net Margin %	N.M.	N.M.	2.65	5.99	7.65
Asset Turnover	0.60	0.58	0.57	...	...
Current Ratio	1.13	1.26	1.16	0.78	...
Debt to Equity	0.73	0.71	0.48	0.01	...
Price Range	24.05-12.40	25.60-14.96	25.62-19.41	...	...
P/E Ratio	...	...	32.02-24.26	...	...
Average Yield %	4.01	3.58	0.81	...	...

Address: 225 Liberty Street, New York, NY 10281
Telephone: 212-522-1212

Web Site: www.timeinc.com
Officers: Joseph A. Ripp - Chairman, Chief Executive Officer Jeffrey John Bairstow - Executive Vice President, Chief Financial Officer

Auditors: Ernst & Young LLP

715

TIME WARNER INC

Exchange	Symbol	Price	52Wk Range	Yield	P/E
NYS	TWX	$75.66 (5/31/2016)	91.01-60.07	2.13	15.16

*7 Year Price Score 124.99 *NYSE Composite Index=100 *12 Month Price Score 99.07

Interim Earnings (Per Share)

Qtr.	Mar	Jun	Sep	Dec
2013	0.75	0.81	1.26	1.07
2014	1.42	0.95	1.11	0.85
2015	1.15	1.16	1.26	1.06
2016	1.51	...	...	...

Interim Dividends (Per Share)

Amt	Decl	Ex	Rec	Pay
0.35Q	08/05/2015	08/27/2015	08/31/2015	09/15/2015
0.35Q	10/29/2015	11/25/2015	11/30/2015	12/15/2015
0.403Q	02/10/2016	02/25/2016	02/29/2016	03/15/2016
0.403Q	04/28/2016	05/26/2016	05/31/2016	06/15/2016

Indicated Div: $1.61

Valuation Analysis	Institutional Holding	
Forecast EPS	$5.39	No of Institutions
	(05/20/2016)	1384
Market Cap	$59.7 Billion	Shares
Book Value	$23.8 Billion	866,132,096
Price/Book	2.50	% Held
Price/Sales	2.11	N/A

TRADING VOLUME (thousand shares)

Business Summary: Entertainment (MIC: 2.3.2 SIC: 7812 NAIC: 512110)

Time Warner is a media and entertainment company. Co. has three reportable segments: Turner, consisting principally of cable networks and digital media properties; Home Box Office, consisting principally of premium pay television services domestically and premium pay and basic tier television services internationally; and Warner Bros., consisting principally of television, feature film, home video and videogame production and distribution. Co. also holds interests in companies that operate broadcast networks, including Central European Media Enterprises Ltd., as well as The CW broadcast network, a 50-50 joint venture between Co.'s Warner Bros segment and CBS Corporation.

Recent Developments: For the quarter ended Mar 31 2016, income from continuing operations increased 25.8% to US$1.17 billion from US$933.0 million in the year-earlier quarter. Net income increased 25.2% to US$1.21 billion from US$970.0 million in the year-earlier quarter. Revenues were US$7.31 billion, up 2.5% from US$7.13 billion the year before. Operating income was US$2.00 billion versus US$1.79 billion in the prior-year quarter, an increase of 11.8%. Direct operating expenses declined 2.0% to US$4.01 billion from US$4.09 billion in the comparable period the year before. Indirect operating expenses increased 4.3% to US$1.31 billion from US$1.25 billion in the equivalent prior-year period.

Prospects: Our evaluation of Time Warner Inc. as of June 19, 2016 is the result of our systematic analysis on three basic characteristics: earnings strength, relative valuation, and recent stock price movement. The company has generated a negative trend in earnings per share over the past 5 quarters. However, while recent estimates for the company have been mixed, TWX has posted better than expected results. Based on operating earnings yield, the company is undervalued when compared to all of the companies in our coverage universe. Share price changes over the past year indicates that TWX will perform in line with the market over the near term.

Financial Data

(US$ in Thousands)	3 Mos	12/31/2015	12/31/2014	12/31/2013	12/31/2012	12/31/2011	12/31/2010	12/31/2009
Earnings Per Share	4.99	4.62	4.34	3.92	3.09	2.71	2.25	2.07
Cash Flow Per Share	4.55	4.73	4.26	4.04	3.60	3.30	2.94	2.86
Dividends Per Share	1.452	1.400	1.270	1.150	1.040	0.940	0.850	0.563
Dividend Payout %	29.11	30.30	29.26	29.34	33.66	34.69	37.78	27.17
Income Statement								
Total Revenue	7,308,000	28,118,000	27,359,000	29,795,000	28,729,000	28,974,000	26,888,000	25,785,000
EBITDA	4,102,000	6,921,000	6,203,000	6,896,000	6,089,000	5,885,000	5,355,000	4,820,000
Depn & Amortn	2,112,000	189,000	202,000	251,000	248,000	269,000	264,000	319,000
Income Before Taxes	1,706,000	5,569,000	4,832,000	5,455,000	4,588,000	4,406,000	3,913,000	3,346,000
Income Taxes	498,000	1,651,000	785,000	1,749,000	1,526,000	1,484,000	1,348,000	1,194,000
Net Income	1,214,000	3,833,000	3,827,000	3,691,000	3,019,000	2,886,000	2,578,000	2,468,000
Average Shares	802,300	829,500	882,600	942,600	976,300	1,064,500	1,145,300	1,195,100
Balance Sheet								
Current Assets	11,792,000	12,513,000	13,180,000	12,844,000	13,288,000	13,432,000	13,138,000	13,007,000
Total Assets	63,254,000	63,848,000	63,259,000	67,994,000	68,304,000	67,801,000	66,524,000	65,730,000
Current Liabilities	7,194,000	8,002,000	9,204,000	8,383,000	9,829,000	8,922,000	8,643,000	8,765,000
Long-Term Obligations	23,622,000	23,594,000	21,376,000	20,099,000	19,122,000	19,501,000	16,523,000	15,357,000
Total Liabilities	39,411,000	40,229,000	38,783,000	38,090,000	38,427,000	37,844,000	33,584,000	32,347,000
Stockholders' Equity	23,843,000	23,619,000	24,476,000	29,904,000	29,877,000	29,957,000	32,940,000	33,383,000
Shares Outstanding	789,000	795,000	832,000	895,000	932,000	974,000	1,099,000	1,157,000
Statistical Record								
Return on Assets %	6.50	6.03	5.83	5.42	4.42	4.30	3.90	2.75
Return on Equity %	16.97	15.94	14.08	12.35	10.06	9.18	7.77	6.52
EBITDA Margin %	56.13	24.61	22.67	23.14	21.19	20.31	19.92	18.69
Net Margin %	16.61	13.63	13.99	12.39	10.51	9.96	9.59	9.57
Asset Turnover	0.45	0.44	0.42	0.44	0.42	0.43	0.41	0.29
Current Ratio	1.64	1.56	1.43	1.53	1.35	1.51	1.52	1.48
Debt to Equity	0.99	1.00	0.87	0.67	0.64	0.65	0.50	0.46
Price Range	91.01-60.07	91.01-63.41	87.36-58.98	67.41-45.86	46.27-32.37	36.62-26.59	32.48-25.70	29.32-13.97
P/E Ratio	18.24-12.04	19.70-13.73	20.13-13.59	17.20-11.70	14.97-10.47	13.51-9.81	14.44-11.42	14.16-6.75
Average Yield %	1.92	1.77	1.74	1.98	2.70	2.86	2.88	2.46

Address: One Time Warner Center, New York, NY 10019-8016 **Telephone:** 212-484-8000 **Fax:** 212-489-6183	**Web Site:** www.timewarner.com **Officers:** Jeffrey L. Bewkes - Chairman, Chief Executive Officer Howard M. Averill - Executive Vice President, Chief Financial Officer	**Auditors:** Ernst & Young LLP **Investor Contact:** 212-484-8920 **Transfer Agents:** Computershare Trust Company, N.A., Providence, RI

TIMKEN CO. (THE)

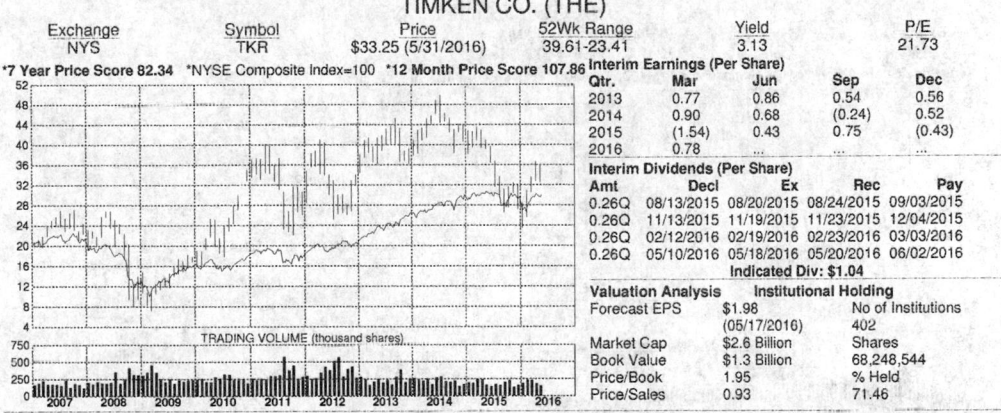

Exchange	Symbol	Price	52Wk Range	Yield	P/E
NYS	TKR	$33.25 (5/31/2016)	39.61-23.41	3.13	21.73

*7 Year Price Score 82.34   *NYSE Composite Index=100   *12 Month Price Score 107.86

Interim Earnings (Per Share)

Qtr.	Mar	Jun	Sep	Dec
2013	0.77	0.86	0.54	0.56
2014	0.90	0.68	(0.24)	0.52
2015	(1.54)	0.43	0.75	(0.43)
2016	0.78	...	...	...

Interim Dividends (Per Share)

Amt	Decl	Ex	Rec	Pay
0.26Q	08/13/2015	08/20/2015	08/24/2015	09/03/2015
0.26Q	11/13/2015	11/19/2015	11/23/2015	12/04/2015
0.26Q	02/12/2016	02/19/2016	02/23/2016	03/03/2016
0.26Q	05/10/2016	05/18/2016	05/20/2016	06/02/2016

Indicated Div: $1.04

Valuation Analysis   Institutional Holding

Forecast EPS	$1.98	No of Institutions
	(05/17/2016)	402
Market Cap	$2.6 Billion	Shares
Book Value	$1.3 Billion	68,248,544
Price/Book	1.95	% Held
Price/Sales	0.93	71.46

Business Summary: Industrial Machinery & Equipment (MIC: 7.2 1 SIC: 3562 NAIC: 332991)

Timken engineers, manufactures and markets bearings, transmissions, gearboxes, belts, chain and related products and provides a range of power system rebuild and repair services. Co.'s product and services portfolio features various brands, including Timken, Fafnir, Philadelphia Gear, Carlisle, Drives and Interlube. Co.'s segments include: Mobile Industries, which provides a portfolio of bearings, seals, lubrication devices and systems, as well as power transmission components, engineered chain, augers, belts and related products and maintenance services; and Process Industries, which supplies industrial bearings and assemblies, and power transmission components such as gears and gearboxes.

Recent Developments: For the quarter ended Mar 31 2016, net income amounted to US$62.9 million versus a net loss of US$134.8 million in the year-earlier quarter. Revenues were US$684.0 million, down 5.3% from US$722.5 million the year before. Operating income was US$50.9 million versus a loss of US$147.4 million in the prior-year quarter. Direct operating expenses declined 3.3% to US$503.1 million from US$520.0 million in the comparable period the year before. Indirect operating expenses decreased 62.8% to US$130.0 million from US$349.9 million in the equivalent prior-year period.

Prospects: Our evaluation of Timken Co. as of June 19, 2016 is the result of our systematic analysis on three basic characteristics: earnings strength, relative valuation, and recent stock price movement. The company has enjoyed a very positive trend in earnings per share over the past 5 quarters and while recent estimates for the company have been raised by analysts, TKR has posted better than expected results. Based on operating earnings yield, the company is undervalued when compared to all of the companies in our coverage universe. Share price changes over the past year indicates that TKR will perform in line with the market over the near term.

Financial Data

(US$ in Thousands)	3 Mos	12/31/2015	12/31/2014	12/31/2013	12/31/2012	12/31/2011	12/31/2010	12/31/2009
Earnings Per Share	1.53	(0.84)	1.87	2.74	5.07	4.59	2.81	(1.39)
Cash Flow Per Share	5.08	4.43	3.40	4.53	6.46	2.17	3.24	6.11
Tang Book Value Per Share	9.54	9.04	12.16	22.11	17.40	14.94	16.07	12.64
Dividends Per Share	1.040	1.030	1.000	0.920	0.920	0.780	0.530	0.450
Dividend Payout %	67.97	...	53.48	33.58	18.15	16.99	18.86	...
Income Statement								
Total Revenue	684,000	2,872,300	3,076,200	4,341,200	4,987,000	5,170,200	4,055,500	3,141,627
EBITDA	122,100	(64,300)	343,800	615,500	973,200	906,500	619,600	134,460
Depn & Amortn	23,500	94,600	115,500	175,900	179,000	178,500	179,600	188,711
Income Before Taxes	90,500	(189,600)	204,000	417,100	766,000	696,800	405,500	(94,230)
Income Taxes	27,600	(121,600)	54,700	154,100	270,100	240,200	136,000	(28,193)
Net Income	63,000	(70,800)	170,800	262,700	495,500	454,300	274,800	(133,961)
Average Shares	80,437	84,631	91,224	95,823	97,602	98,655	97,516	96,135
Balance Sheet								
Current Assets	1,274,900	1,206,400	1,481,900	1,937,500	2,174,100	2,292,300	2,399,200	2,022,560
Total Assets	2,850,100	2,785,300	3,001,400	4,477,900	4,244,700	4,352,100	4,180,400	4,006,893
Current Liabilities	442,600	505,300	533,800	980,100	667,900	844,600	719,900	540,433
Long-Term Obligations	673,400	580,600	522,100	206,600	455,100	478,800	481,700	469,287
Total Liabilities	1,500,400	1,460,800	1,425,200	1,841,300	2,012,500	2,323,800	2,255,400	2,429,309
Stockholders' Equity	1,349,700	1,324,500	1,576,200	2,636,600	2,232,200	2,028,300	1,925,000	1,577,584
Shares Outstanding	79,222	80,263	88,591	93,122	95,898	97,666	97,803	96,854
Statistical Record								
Return on Assets %	4.49	N.M.	4.57	6.02	11.50	10.65	6.71	N.M.
Return on Equity %	9.26	N.M.	8.11	10.79	23.20	22.98	15.69	N.M.
EBITDA Margin %	17.85	N.M.	11.18	14.18	19.51	17.53	15.28	4.28
Net Margin %	9.21	N.M.	5.55	6.05	9.94	8.79	6.78	N.M.
Asset Turnover	1.00	0.99	0.82	1.00	1.16	1.21	0.99	0.74
Current Ratio	2.88	2.39	2.78	1.98	3.26	2.71	3.33	3.74
Debt to Equity	0.50	0.44	0.33	0.08	0.20	0.24	0.25	0.30
Price Range	42.88-23.41	43.50-26.46	49.73-37.75	45.26-33.98	41.01-25.02	40.06-21.95	34.94-15.92	18.20-7.13
P/E Ratio	28.03-15.30	...	26.59-20.19	16.52-12.40	8.09-4.93	8.73-4.78	12.43-5.67	...
Average Yield %	3.17	2.88	2.30	2.31	2.85	2.44	2.23	3.31

Address: 4500 Mount Pleasant Street N.W., North Canton, OH 44720-5450	**Web Site:** www.timken.com	**Auditors:** Ernst & Young LLP
Telephone: 234-262-3000	**Officers:** Richard G. Kyle - President, Group President, Chief Executive Officer, Chief Operating Officer Christpher A. Coughlin - Group President, Executive Vice President, Division Officer	**Investor Contact:** 330-471-7446 **Transfer Agents:** Wells Fargo Shareowner Services, Saint Paul, MN

TJX COMPANIES, INC.

Exchange	Symbol	Price	52Wk Range	Yield	P/E	Div Achiever
NYS	TJX	$76.12 (5/31/2016)	78.78-64.21	1.37	22.39	19 Years

*7 Year Price Score 137.74 *NYSE Composite Index=100 *12 Month Price Score 104.89

TRADING VOLUME (thousand shares)

Interim Earnings (Per Share)

Qtr.	Apr	Jul	Oct	Jan
2013-14	0.62	0.66	0.86	0.80
2014-15	0.64	0.73	0.85	0.93
2015-16	0.69	0.80	0.86	0.98
2016-17	0.76	...	...	...

Interim Dividends (Per Share)

Amt	Decl	Ex	Rec	Pay
0.21Q	09/18/2015	11/09/2015	11/12/2015	12/03/2015
0.21Q	12/09/2015	02/09/2016	02/11/2016	03/03/2016
0.26Q	03/29/2016	05/10/2016	05/12/2016	06/02/2016
0.26Q	06/08/2016	08/09/2016	08/11/2016	09/01/2016

Indicated Div: $1.04

Valuation Analysis

		Institutional Holding	
Forecast EPS	$3.46	No of Institutions	1351
	(05/20/2016)		
Market Cap	$50.3 Billion	Shares	654,215,360
Book Value	$4.5 Billion	% Held	85.35
Price/Book	11.10		
Price/Sales	1.59		

Business Summary: Retail - Apparel and Accessories (MIC: 2.1.5 SIC: 5651 NAIC: 448140)

TJX Companies is an apparel and home fashions retailer. Co. operates its business in four main segments. In the U.S., Co.'s two segments are comprised of Marmaxx (T.J. Maxx, Marshalls and tjmaxx.com) and HomeGoods. The TJX Canada segment operates Winners, HomeSense and Marshalls in Canada, and the TJX International segment operates T.K. Maxx, HomeSense and tkmaxx.com in Europe and Trade Secret in Australia. All of Co.'s stores, with the exception of HomeGoods and HomeSense, sell family apparel and home fashions. HomeGoods and HomeSense provide home fashions. As of Jan 30 2016, Co. operated a total of 2,689 stores in the U.S.; 387 stores in Canada; and 530 stores in Europe and Australia.

Recent Developments: For the quarter ended Apr 30 2016, net income increased 7.1% to US$508.3 million from US$474.6 million in the year-earlier quarter. Revenues were US$7.54 billion, up 9.9% from US$6.87 billion the year before. Direct operating expenses rose 9.2% to US$5.37 billion from US$4.92 billion in the comparable period the year before. Indirect operating expenses increased 14.2% to US$1.34 billion from US$1.17 billion in the equivalent prior-year period.

Prospects: Our evaluation of TJX Companies Inc. as of June 19, 2016 is the result of our systematic analysis on three basic characteristics: earnings strength, relative valuation, and recent stock price movement. The company has managed to produce a neutral trend in earnings per share over the past 5 quarters and while recent estimates for the company have been raised by analysts, TJX has posted better than expected results. Based on operating earnings yield, the company is about fairly valued when compared to all of the companies in our coverage universe. Share price changes over the past year indicates that TJX will perform very well over the near term.

Financial Data
(US$ in Thousands)

	3 Mos	01/30/2016	01/31/2015	02/01/2014	02/02/2013	01/28/2012	01/29/2011	01/30/2010
Earnings Per Share	3.40	3.33	3.15	2.94	2.55	1.93	1.65	1.42
Cash Flow Per Share	4.40	4.37	4.35	3.64	4.08	2.52	2.48	2.73
Tang Book Value Per Share	6.34	5.97	5.78	5.56	4.63	4.06	3.75	3.31
Dividends Per Share	0.840	0.805	0.670	0.550	0.440	0.360	0.285	0.235
Dividend Payout %	24.71	24.17	21.27	18.71	17.25	18.65	17.27	16.55
Income Statement								
Total Revenue	7,542,356	30,944,938	29,078,407	27,422,696	25,878,372	23,191,455	21,942,193	20,288,444
EBITDA	992,177	4,321,396	4,178,646	3,899,393	3,108,226	2,449,262	2,205,429	1,993,271
Depn & Amortn	157,014	616,696	588,975	548,823	1,700	2,200	2,200	2,200
Income Before Taxes	824,969	3,658,300	3,549,884	3,319,489	3,077,351	2,411,414	2,164,092	1,951,562
Income Taxes	316,623	1,380,642	1,334,756	1,182,093	1,170,664	915,324	824,562	737,990
Net Income	508,346	2,277,658	2,215,128	2,137,396	1,906,687	1,496,090	1,343,141	1,213,572
Average Shares	670,388	683,251	703,545	726,376	747,555	773,772	812,826	855,238
Balance Sheet								
Current Assets	6,877,701	6,772,560	6,715,061	6,067,998	5,711,543	5,132,632	5,099,527	4,803,856
Total Assets	11,704,722	11,499,482	11,128,381	10,201,022	9,511,855	8,281,605	7,971,763	7,463,977
Current Liabilities	4,296,735	4,402,230	3,929,634	3,517,843	3,760,596	3,063,423	3,133,121	2,894,986
Long-Term Obligations	1,615,477	1,709,268	1,684,597	1,274,216	774,552	784,623	787,517	790,169
Total Liabilities	7,169,753	7,192,407	6,864,151	5,971,129	5,845,918	5,072,315	4,871,864	4,574,701
Stockholders' Equity	4,534,969	4,307,075	4,264,230	4,229,893	3,665,937	3,209,290	3,099,899	2,889,276
Shares Outstanding	661,083	663,495	684,733	705,016	723,902	746,702	779,314	818,772
Statistical Record								
Return on Assets %	20.04	20.19	20.83	21.74	21.08	18.46	17.45	17.84
Return on Equity %	52.38	53.29	52.30	54.29	54.57	47.56	44.98	48.45
EBITDA Margin %	13.15	13.96	14.37	14.22	12.01	10.56	10.05	9.82
Net Margin %	6.74	7.36	7.62	7.79	7.37	6.45	6.12	5.98
Asset Turnover	2.74	2.74	2.73	2.79	2.86	2.86	2.85	2.98
Current Ratio	1.60	1.54	1.71	1.72	1.52	1.68	1.63	1.66
Debt to Equity	0.36	0.40	0.40	0.30	0.21	0.24	0.25	0.27
Price Range	78.78-64.21	76.78-64.21	68.60-52.23	64.05-43.58	46.64-33.73	33.98-23.57	24.31-18.76	20.11-9.71
P/E Ratio	23.17-18.89	23.06-19.28	21.78-16.58	21.79-14.82	18.29-13.23	17.61-12.21	14.73-11.37	14.16-6.84
Average Yield %	1.18	1.16	1.12	1.03	1.04	1.30	1.30	1.44

Address: 770 Cochituate Road, Framingham, MA 01701 Telephone: 508-390-1000 Fax: 508-390-2091	Web Site: www.tjx.com Officers: Carol Meyrowitz - Chairwoman, Chief Executive Officer Ernie L. Herrman - President, Chief Executive Officer	Auditors: PricewaterhouseCoopers LLP Investor Contact: 508-390-2323 Transfer Agents: Computershare, Providence, RI

TOLL BROTHERS INC.

Exchange	Symbol	Price	52Wk Range	Yield	P/E
NYS	TOL	$29.15 (5/31/2016)	41.88-24.10	N/A	14.15

*7 Year Price Score 101.80 *NYSE Composite Index=100 *12 Month Price Score 84.18

TRADING VOLUME (thousand shares)

Interim Earnings (Per Share)

Qtr.	Jan	Apr	Jul	Oct
2012-13	0.03	0.14	0.26	0.54
2013-14	0.25	0.35	0.53	0.71
2014-15	0.44	0.37	0.36	0.79
2015-16	0.40	0.51	...	...

Interim Dividends (Per Share)

No Dividends Paid

Valuation Analysis　**Institutional Holding**

Forecast EPS	$2.60	No of Institutions
	(05/20/2016)	557
Market Cap	$4.9 Billion	Shares
Book Value	$4.2 Billion	151,125,488
Price/Book	1.17	% Held
Price/Sales	1.08	82.81

Business Summary: Builders (MIC: 2.2.5 SIC: 1531 NAIC: 236117)

Toll Brothers designs, builds, markets and arranges financing for detached and attached homes in residential communities. Co. also builds and sells homes in urban infill markets through Toll Brothers City Living®. Co. operates its own land development, architectural, engineering, mortgage, title, landscaping, security monitoring, lumber distribution, house component assembly, and manufacturing operations. In certain markets, Co. develops land for sale to other builders, often through joint venture structures with other builders or with financial partners. Co. also develops, owns, and operates golf courses and country clubs, which are associated with several of Co.'s planned communities.

Recent Developments: For the quarter ended Apr 30 2016, net income increased 31.1% to US$89.1 million from US$67.9 million in the year-earlier quarter. Revenues were US$1.12 billion, up 30.8% from US$852.6 million the year before. Operating income was US$116.6 million versus US$66.4 million in the prior-year quarter, an increase of 75.7%. Direct operating expenses rose 28.3% to US$870.6 million from US$678.5 million in the comparable period the year before. Indirect operating expenses increased 19.2% to US$128.3 million from US$107.7 million in the equivalent prior-year period.

Prospects: Our evaluation of Toll Brothers Inc. as of June 19, 2016 is the result of our systematic analysis on three basic characteristics: earnings strength, relative valuation, and recent stock price movement. The company has enjoyed a very positive trend in earnings per share over the past 5 quarters. However, while recent estimates for the company have been mixed, TOL has posted better than expected results. Based on operating earnings yield, the company is undervalued when compared to all of the companies in our coverage universe. Share price changes over the past year indicates that TOL will perform poorly over the near term.

Financial Data

(US$ in Thousands)	6 Mos	3 Mos	10/31/2015	10/31/2014	10/31/2013	10/31/2012	10/31/2011	10/31/2010
Earnings Per Share	2.06	1.92	1.97	1.84	0.97	2.86	0.24	(0.02)
Cash Flow Per Share	0.49	0.40	0.34	1.76	(3.36)	(1.01)	0.32	(0.88)
Tang Book Value Per Share	24.81	24.33	24.15	22.02	19.68	18.51	15.61	15.36
Income Statement								
Total Revenue	2,044,123	928,566	4,171,248	3,911,602	2,674,299	1,882,781	1,475,881	1,494,771
EBITDA	249,551	113,308	528,204	420,248	226,277	86,015	(26,929)	(132,692)
Depn & Amortn	11,029	5,533	15,700	22,999	25,210	22,586	23,142	20,044
Income Before Taxes	239,458	108,179	514,443	463,441	253,305	89,350	(28,172)	(140,657)
Income Taxes	94,980	43,637	172,395	164,550	97,091	(374,204)	(69,161)	(113,813)
Net Income	162,234	73,180	363,167	340,032	170,606	487,146	39,795	(3,374)
Average Shares	176,414	182,391	184,703	185,875	177,963	170,154	168,381	165,666
Balance Sheet								
Current Assets	7,737,426	7,545,644	8,141,760	7,357,425	5,793,960	5,384,411	4,576,395	4,681,148
Total Assets	8,964,225	8,763,437	9,206,515	8,416,902	6,827,459	6,181,044	5,055,246	5,171,555
Current Liabilities	2,007,216	1,852,676	1,188,196	1,156,619	984,631	800,229	807,758	901,574
Long-Term Obligations	2,792,061	2,754,796	3,790,240	3,399,586	2,503,664	2,252,944	1,654,937	1,710,968
Total Liabilities	4,805,086	4,613,288	4,983,958	4,562,526	3,494,472	3,059,344	2,468,893	2,616,102
Stockholders' Equity	4,159,139	4,150,149	4,222,557	3,854,376	3,332,987	3,121,700	2,586,353	2,555,453
Shares Outstanding	167,623	170,551	174,847	175,046	169,353	168,637	165,729	166,408
Statistical Record								
Return on Assets %	4.29	4.13	4.12	4.46	2.62	8.65	0.78	N.M.
Return on Equity %	9.17	8.76	8.99	9.46	5.29	17.02	1.55	N.M.
EBITDA Margin %	12.21	12.20	12.66	10.74	8.46	4.57	N.M.	N.M.
Net Margin %	7.94	7.88	8.71	8.69	6.38	25.87	2.70	N.M.
Asset Turnover	0.51	0.49	0.47	0.51	0.41	0.33	0.29	0.28
Current Ratio	3.85	4.07	6.85	6.36	5.88	6.73	5.67	5.19
Debt to Equity	0.67	0.66	0.90	0.88	0.75	0.72	0.64	0.67
Price Range	41.88-24.10	41.88-26.79	41.88-30.92	39.55-29.18	37.98-29.73	36.43-17.05	21.90-13.75	23.15-16.02
P/E Ratio	20.33-11.70	21.81-13.95	21.26-15.70	21.49-15.86	39.15-30.65	12.74-5.96	91.25-57.29	...

Address: 250 Gibraltar Road, Horsham, PA 19044	Web Site: www.tollbrothers.com	Auditors: Ernst & Young LLP
Telephone: 215-938-8000	Officers: Robert I. Toll - Executive Chairman Richard T. Hartman - President, Chief Operating Officer	Investor Contact: 215-938-8312
Fax: 215-938-8023		Transfer Agents: American Stock Transfer and Trust Company, New York, NY

TOOTSIE ROLL INDUSTRIES INC

Exchange	Symbol	Price	52Wk Range	Yield	P/E	Div Achiever
NYS	TR	$35.79 (5/31/2016)	36.21-29.49	1.01	33.45	52 Years

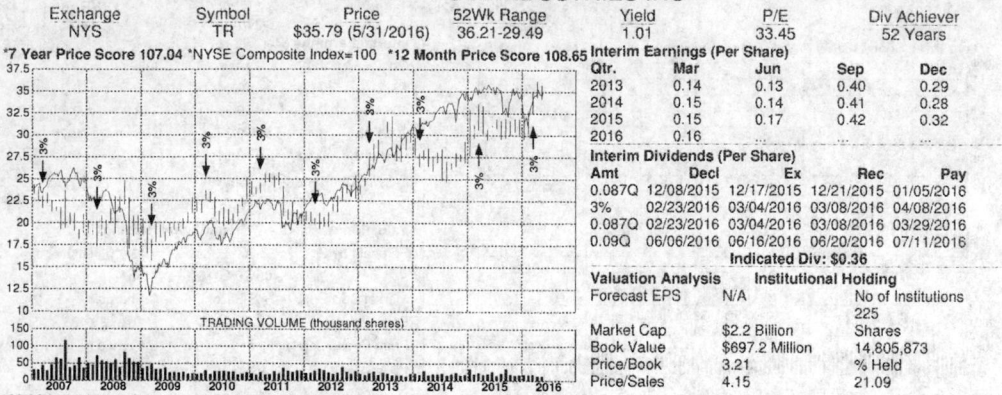

*7 Year Price Score 107.04 *NYSE Composite Index=100 *12 Month Price Score 108.65

Interim Earnings (Per Share)

Qtr.	Mar	Jun	Sep	Dec
2013	0.14	0.13	0.40	0.29
2014	0.15	0.14	0.41	0.28
2015	0.15	0.17	0.42	0.32
2016	0.16			

Interim Dividends (Per Share)

Amt	Decl	Ex	Rec	Pay
0.087Q	12/08/2015	12/17/2015	12/21/2015	01/05/2016
3%	02/23/2016	03/04/2016	03/08/2016	04/08/2016
0.087Q	02/23/2016	03/04/2016	03/08/2016	03/29/2016
0.09Q	06/06/2016	06/16/2016	06/20/2016	07/11/2016

Indicated Div: $0.36

Valuation Analysis

Forecast EPS	N/A	**Institutional Holding**
		No of Institutions 225
Market Cap	$2.2 Billion	Shares
Book Value	$697.2 Million	14,805,873
Price/Book	3.21	% Held
Price/Sales	4.15	21.09

Business Summary: Food (MIC: 1.2.1 SIC: 2064 NAIC: 311340)

Tootsie Roll Industries and its consolidated subsidiaries are engaged in the manufacture and sale of confectionary products. This is the only industry segment in which Co. operates and is its only line of business. The majority of Co.'s products are sold under the registered trademarks TOOTSIE ROLL, TOOTSIE POPS, CHILD'S PLAY, CARAMEL APPLE POPS, CHARMS, BLOW-POP, CHARMS MINI POPS, CELLA'S, DOTS, JUNIOR MINTS, CHARLESTON CHEW, SUGAR DADDY, SUGAR BABIES, ANDES, FLUFFY STUFF, DUBBLE BUBBLE, RAZZLES, CRY BABY, NIK-L-NIP, and TUTSI POP (Mexico). Co.'s principal markets are in the U.S., Canada and Mexico.

Recent Developments: For the quarter ended Mar 31 2016, net income increased 8.3% to US$9.9 million from US$9.1 million in the year-earlier quarter. Revenues were US$104.4 million, down 1.8% from US$106.3 million the year before. Operating income was US$14.2 million versus US$13.0 million in the prior-year quarter, an increase of 9.7%. Direct operating expenses declined 1.9% to US$66.1 million from US$67.4 million in the comparable period the year before. Indirect operating expenses decreased 7.4% to US$24.1 million from US$26.0 million in the equivalent prior-year period.

Prospects: Our evaluation of Tootsie Roll Industries Inc. as of June 19, 2016 is the result of our systematic analysis on three basic characteristics: earnings strength, relative valuation, and recent stock price movement. The company has managed to produce a neutral trend in earnings per share over the past 5 quarters. Because the company lacks sufficient analyst estimate data, we place greater weight on the historical EPS trend as the measure of earnings strength. Based on operating earnings yield, the company is about fairly valued when compared to all of the companies in our coverage universe. Share price changes over the past year indicates that TR will perform in line with the market over the ne

Financial Data

(US$ in Thousands)	3 Mos	12/31/2015	12/31/2014	12/31/2013	12/31/2012	12/31/2011	12/31/2010	12/31/2009
Earnings Per Share	1.07	1.05	0.99	0.96	0.79	0.68	0.81	0.80
Cash Flow Per Share	1.58	1.44	1.38	1.74	1.54	0.77	1.25	1.12
Tang Book Value Per Share	7.19	7.18	6.94	6.88	6.13	6.46	6.43	6.08
Dividends Per Share	0.350	0.338	0.299	0.291	0.726	0.274	0.266	0.258
Dividend Payout %	32.59	32.19	30.26	30.24	91.87	40.58	32.81	32.47
Income Statement								
Total Revenue	104,395	540,112	543,525	543,383	549,870	532,505	521,448	499,331
EBITDA	14,929	111,621	110,569	104,155	93,707	79,175	91,631	85,478
Depn & Amortn	748	20,388	20,758	20,050	19,925	19,229	18,279	17,862
Income Before Taxes	14,181	92,578	91,294	85,458	75,014	60,912	74,089	68,812
Income Taxes	4,325	26,451	28,434	23,634	22,160	16,974	20,375	10,704
Net Income	9,896	66,089	63,298	60,849	52,004	43,938	53,714	53,475
Average Shares	62,499	63,284	64,250	63,265	66,114	65,157	66,075	66,952
Balance Sheet								
Current Assets	255,274	293,806	264,621	240,111	197,241	212,201	237,591	211,878
Total Assets	896,449	908,983	910,386	888,409	846,737	857,856	860,383	838,247
Current Liabilities	59,770	72,062	64,459	60,121	60,765	58,355	58,505	56,066
Long-Term Obligations	7,864	7,883	8,194	7,500	7,500	7,500	7,500	7,500
Total Liabilities	199,285	210,800	219,577	208,104	196,922	191,921	191,429	185,762
Stockholders' Equity	697,164	698,183	690,809	680,305	649,815	665,935	668,954	652,485
Shares Outstanding	62,445	62,669	63,753	62,795	65,507	64,641	65,445	66,453
Statistical Record								
Return on Assets %	7.40	7.27	7.04	7.01	6.08	5.11	6.32	6.48
Return on Equity %	9.65	9.52	9.23	9.15	7.88	6.58	8.13	8.31
EBITDA Margin %	14.30	20.67	20.34	19.17	17.04	14.87	17.57	17.12
Net Margin %	9.48	12.24	11.65	11.20	9.46	8.25	10.30	10.71
Asset Turnover	0.60	0.59	0.60	0.63	0.64	0.62	0.61	0.61
Current Ratio	4.27	4.08	4.11	3.99	3.25	3.64	4.06	3.78
Debt to Equity	0.01	0.01	0.01	0.01	0.01	0.01	0.01	0.01
Price Range	34.98-29.46	33.53-27.56	29.78-24.65	32.14-23.03	25.41-19.28	25.71-19.71	24.99-19.55	22.82-15.61
P/E Ratio	32.69-27.53	31.94-26.25	30.08-24.90	33.48-23.99	32.17-24.41	37.80-28.99	30.85-24.13	28.52-19.51
Average Yield %	1.12	1.09	1.10	1.03	3.35	1.19	1.22	1.34

Address: 7401 South Cicero Avenue, Chicago, IL 60629	**Web Site:** www.tootsie.com	**Auditors:** PricewaterhouseCoopers LLP
Telephone: 773-838-3400	**Officers:** Ellen R. Gordon - Chairwoman, President, Chief Operating Officer G. Howard Ember - Vice President, Chief Financial Officer	**Transfer Agents:** American Stock Transfer & Trust Company, Brooklyn, NY
Fax: 773-838-3534		

TORCHMARK CORP.

Exchange	Symbol	Price	52Wk Range	Yield	P/E	Div Achiever
NYS	TMK	$61.63 (5/31/2016)	63.12-48.58	0.91	14.57	10 Years

*7 Year Price Score 126.00 *NYSE Composite Index=100 *12 Month Price Score 99.59

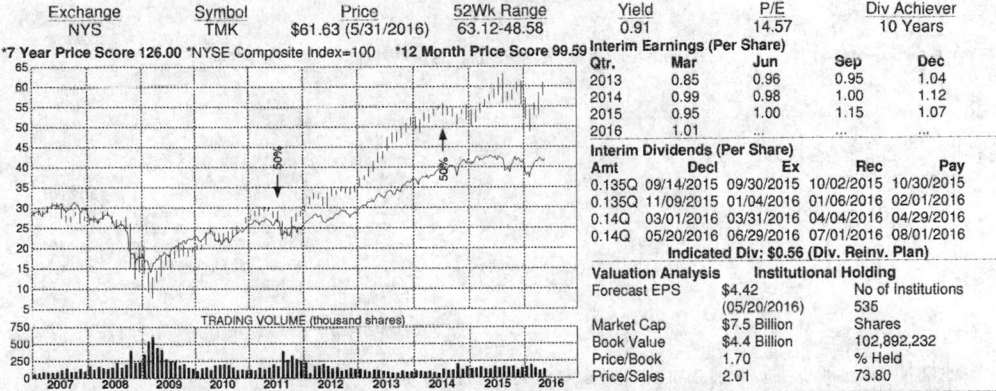

Interim Earnings (Per Share)

Qtr.	Mar	Jun	Sep	Dec
2013	0.85	0.96	0.95	1.04
2014	0.99	0.98	1.00	1.12
2015	0.95	1.00	1.15	1.07
2016	1.01	...	...	...

Interim Dividends (Per Share)

Amt	Decl	Ex	Rec	Pay
0.135Q	09/14/2015	09/30/2015	10/02/2015	10/30/2015
0.135Q	11/09/2015	01/04/2016	01/06/2016	02/01/2016
0.14Q	03/01/2016	03/31/2016	04/04/2016	04/29/2016
0.14Q	05/20/2016	06/29/2016	07/01/2016	08/01/2016

Indicated Div: $0.56 (Div. Reinv. Plan)

Valuation Analysis — **Institutional Holding**

Forecast EPS	$4.42
(05/20/2016)	No of Institutions 535
Market Cap	$7.5 Billion
Book Value	$4.4 Billion Shares 102,892,232
Price/Book	1.70
Price/Sales	2.01 % Held 73.80

TRADING VOLUME (thousand shares)

Business Summary: Life & Health (MIC: 5.2.2 SIC: 6311 NAIC: 524113)

Torchmark is an insurance holding company for a group of insurance companies which market primarily individual life, and supplemental health insurance to middle income households. Co.'s segment comprised of Insurance, which consist of life, health, and annuities; and Investments, which consist of investment-grade securities. Life insurance products include traditional and interest-sensitive whole life insurance as well as term life insurance. Health insurance products are generally guaranteed-renewable and include Medicare Supplement, critical illness, accident, long-term care, and limited-benefit supplemental hospital and surgical coverages. Annuities include fixed-benefit contracts.

Recent Developments: For the quarter ended Mar 31 2016, income from continuing operations increased 2.1% to US$133.6 million from US$130.8 million in the year-earlier quarter. Net income increased 2.0% to US$124.0 million from US$121.6 million in the year-earlier quarter. Revenues were US$977.6 million, up 4.6% from US$934.4 million the year before. Net premiums earned were US$779.9 million versus US$742.1 million in the prior-year quarter, an increase of 5.1%. Net investment income rose 2.8% to US$197.1 million from US$191.6 million a year ago.

Prospects: Our evaluation of Torchmark Corp. as of June 19, 2016 is the result of our systematic analysis on three basic characteristics: earnings strength, relative valuation, and recent stock price movement. The company has managed to produce a neutral trend in earnings per share over the past 5 quarters and while recent estimates for the company have remained steady, TMK has posted better than expected results. Based on operating earnings yield, the company is undervalued when compared to all of the companies in our coverage universe. Share price changes over the past year indicates that TMK will perform in line with the market over the near term.

Financial Data

(US$ in Thousands)	3 Mos	12/31/2015	12/31/2014	12/31/2013	12/31/2012	12/31/2011	12/31/2010	12/31/2009
Earnings Per Share	4.23	4.16	4.09	3.79	3.61	3.15	2.80	2.17
Cash Flow Per Share	9.70	8.95	6.61	8.13	6.49	5.29	5.62	5.22
Tang Book Value Per Share	32.62	29.53	33.27	24.84	27.73	25.40	20.30	15.96
Dividends Per Share	0.545	0.405	0.507	0.553	0.380	0.296	0.271	0.187
Dividend Payout %	12.88	9.74	12.39	14.61	10.54	9.39	9.68	8.61
Income Statement								
Premium Income	779,860	2,998,720	3,209,420	3,052,274	2,856,462	2,656,318	2,651,758	2,687,199
Total Revenue	977,627	3,766,065	3,964,296	3,771,938	3,589,516	3,377,401	3,367,632	3,222,397
Benefits & Claims	524,973	2,016,212	2,219,200	2,088,846	1,955,682	1,793,276	1,793,044	1,812,800
Income Before Taxes	195,448	766,187	778,468	763,126	765,993	755,666	778,567	605,193
Income Taxes	61,874	249,894	235,529	234,654	236,669	237,326	256,274	200,240
Net Income	124,033	527,100	542,939	528,472	529,324	517,885	517,064	404,953
Average Shares	123,312	126,757	132,640	139,563	146,847	164,723	184,685	186,825
Balance Sheet								
Total Assets	20,621,021	19,853,213	20,214,730	18,191,744	18,776,910	17,156,391	16,159,762	16,023,759
Total Liabilities	16,229,278	15,797,661	15,517,264	14,415,402	14,415,124	12,927,483	12,143,521	12,624,868
Stockholders' Equity	4,391,743	4,055,552	4,697,466	3,776,342	4,361,786	4,228,908	4,016,241	3,398,891
Shares Outstanding	121,093	122,369	127,930	134,252	141,353	150,869	178,296	186,391
Statistical Record								
Return on Assets %	2.56	2.63	2.83	2.86	2.94	3.11	3.21	2.74
Return on Equity %	11.42	12.04	12.81	12.99	12.29	12.56	13.95	14.41
Loss Ratio %	67.32	67.24	69.15	68.44	68.47	67.51	67.62	67.46
Net Margin %	12.69	14.00	13.70	14.01	14.75	15.33	15.35	12.57
Price Range	63.12-48.58	63.12-50.07	55.68-48.37	52.35-34.45	35.31-28.91	30.16-22.12	27.55-19.53	20.79-7.58
P/E Ratio	14.92-11.48	15.17-12.04	13.61-11.83	13.81-9.09	9.78-8.01	9.57-7.02	9.84-6.98	9.58-3.49
Average Yield %	0.95	0.71	0.96	1.25	1.15	1.16	1.16	1.13

Address: 3700 South Stonebridge Drive, McKinney, TX 75070 **Telephone:** 972-569-4000	**Web Site:** www.torchmarkcorp.com **Officers:** Gary L. Coleman - Co-Chairman, Co-Chief Executive Officer, Executive Vice President, Chief Financial Officer Larry M. Hutchison - Co-Chairman, Co-Chief Executive Officer, Executive Vice President, General Counsel	**Auditors:** Deloitte & Touche LLP **Investor Contact:** 972-569-3627 **Transfer Agents:** Wells Fargo Shareowner Services, St. Paul, MN

TORO CO. (THE)

Exchange	Symbol	Price	52Wk Range	Yield	P/E	Div Achiever
NYS	TTC	$89.31 (5/31/2016)	89.71-65.50	1.34	22.61	12 Years

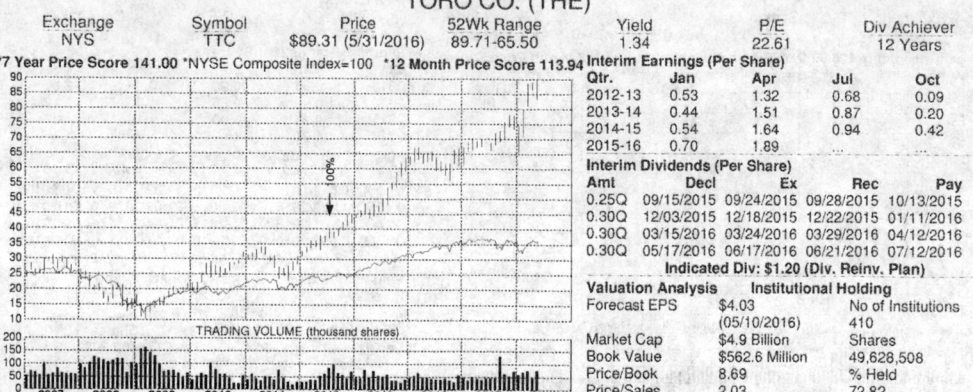

*7 Year Price Score 141.00 *NYSE Composite Index=100 *12 Month Price Score 113.94

Interim Earnings (Per Share)

Qtr.	Jan	Apr	Jul	Oct
2012-13	0.53	1.32	0.68	0.09
2013-14	0.44	1.51	0.87	0.20
2014-15	0.54	1.64	0.94	0.42
2015-16	0.70	1.89	...	...

Interim Dividends (Per Share)

Amt	Decl	Ex	Rec	Pay
0.25Q	09/15/2015	09/24/2015	09/28/2015	10/13/2015
0.30Q	12/03/2015	12/18/2015	12/22/2015	01/11/2016
0.30Q	03/15/2016	03/24/2016	03/29/2016	04/12/2016
0.30Q	05/17/2016	06/17/2016	06/21/2016	07/12/2016

Indicated Div: $1.20 (Div. Reinv. Plan)

Valuation Analysis — **Institutional Holding**

Forecast EPS	$4.03	No of Institutions
	(05/10/2016)	410
Market Cap	$4.9 Billion	Shares
Book Value	$562.6 Million	49,628,508
Price/Book	8.69	% Held
Price/Sales	2.03	72.82

TRADING VOLUME (thousand shares)

Business Summary: Industrial Machinery & Equipment (MIC: 7.2.1 SIC: 3524 NAIC: 333112)

Toro designs, manufactures, and markets turf maintenance equipment and services, turf irrigation systems, landscaping equipment and lighting, agricultural micro-irrigation systems, rental and construction equipment, and residential yard and snow removal products. Co. has three segments: Professional, which designs turf, landscape, construction, and agricultural products; Residential, which includes walk power mower products, riding products, home solutions products, and snow thrower products; and Distribution, which comprises Co.-owned domestic distributorships.

Recent Developments: For the quarter ended Apr 29 2016, net income increased 12.7% to US$105.7 million from US$93.8 million in the year-earlier quarter. Revenues were US$836.4 million, up 1.2% from US$826.2 million the year before. Operating income was US$155.1 million versus US$138.5 million in the prior-year quarter, an increase of 12.0%. Direct operating expenses declined 2.0% to US$533.3 million from US$544.3 million in the comparable period the year before. Indirect operating expenses increased 3.2% to US$148.1 million from US$143.5 million in the equivalent prior-year period.

Prospects: Our evaluation of Toro Co. as of June 19, 2016 is the result of our systematic analysis on three basic characteristics: earnings strength, relative valuation, and recent stock price movement. The company has managed to produce a neutral trend in earnings per share over the past 5 quarters and while recent estimates for the company have been mixed, TTC has posted better than expected results. Based on operating earnings yield, the company is about fairly valued when compared to all of the companies in our coverage universe. Share price changes over the past year indicates that TTC will perform very well over the near term.

Financial Data
(US$ in Thousands)

	6 Mos	3 Mos	10/31/2015	10/31/2014	10/31/2013	10/31/2012	10/31/2011	10/31/2010
Earnings Per Share	3.95	3.70	3.55	3.02	2.62	2.14	1.85	1.40
Cash Flow Per Share	5.08	4.75	4.26	3.24	3.83	3.12	1.82	2.93
Tang Book Value Per Share	4.63	2.73	2.70	5.26	4.20	3.23	2.35	2.65
Dividends Per Share	1.100	1.050	1.000	0.800	0.560	0.440	0.400	0.360
Dividend Payout %	27.85	28.38	28.17	26.49	21.37	20.56	21.62	25.81
Income Statement								
Total Revenue	1,322,839	486,398	2,390,875	2,172,691	2,041,431	1,958,690	1,883,953	1,690,378
EBITDA	248,840	74,092	351,263	311,280	283,586	253,226	228,581	196,834
Depn & Amortn	31,526	15,741	50,322	47,136	48,207	46,840	43,539	42,108
Income Before Taxes	207,939	53,697	282,678	249,183	219,616	190,266	169,144	138,669
Income Taxes	62,997	14,436	89,440	82,575	71,868	66,721	57,168	48,031
Net Income	144,942	39,261	201,591	173,870	154,845	129,541	117,658	93,237
Average Shares	55,986	56,163	56,757	57,628	59,105	60,618	63,594	66,874
Balance Sheet								
Current Assets	950,107	805,089	710,679	824,036	653,267	612,134	532,882	584,973
Total Assets	1,542,741	1,393,834	1,303,658	1,192,415	1,002,748	935,199	870,663	885,622
Current Liabilities	600,601	550,414	443,734	400,420	388,845	378,122	359,080	368,283
Long-Term Obligations	337,909	341,127	354,818	347,316	223,544	223,482	225,178	223,578
Total Liabilities	980,133	933,905	841,493	783,688	644,010	622,797	603,896	609,812
Stockholders' Equity	562,608	459,929	462,165	408,727	358,738	312,402	266,767	275,810
Shares Outstanding	54,759	54,482	54,650	55,678	56,788	58,266	59,206	62,789
Statistical Record								
Return on Assets %	14.68	15.46	16.15	15.84	15.98	14.31	13.40	10.61
Return on Equity %	43.26	48.05	46.30	45.31	46.14	44.61	43.37	31.55
EBITDA Margin %	18.81	15.23	14.69	14.33	13.89	12.93	12.13	11.64
Net Margin %	10.96	8.07	8.43	8.00	7.59	6.61	6.25	5.52
Asset Turnover	1.60	1.77	1.92	1.98	2.11	2.16	2.15	1.92
Current Ratio	1.58	1.46	1.60	2.06	1.68	1.62	1.48	1.59
Debt to Equity	0.60	0.74	0.77	0.85	0.62	0.72	0.84	0.81
Price Range	88.94-65.50	78.11-64.91	75.78-60.81	66.93-56.15	58.95-40.79	42.22-26.00	33.95-22.82	29.14-18.50
P/E Ratio	22.52-16.58	21.11-17.54	21.35-17.13	22.16-18.59	22.50-15.57	19.73-12.15	18.35-12.33	20.81-13.22
Average Yield %	1.49	1.49	1.48	1.29	1.18	1.22	1.25	1.47

Address: 8111 Lyndale Avenue South, Bloomington, MN 55420 Telephone: 952-888-8801	Web Site: www.thetorocompany.com Officers: Michael J. Hoffman - Chairman, President, Chief Executive Officer Richard M. Olson - President, Chief Operating Officer, Vice President	Auditors: KPMG LLP Transfer Agents: Wells Fargo Shareowner Services, St. Paul, MN

TOTAL SYSTEM SERVICES, INC.

Exchange	Symbol	Price	52Wk Range	Yield	P/E
NYS	TSS	$53.70 (5/31/2016)	56.37-37.96	0.74	26.32

*7 Year Price Score 152.22 *NYSE Composite Index=100 *12 Month Price Score 107.64

Interim Earnings (Per Share)

Qtr.	Mar	Jun	Sep	Dec
2013	0.30	0.31	0.34	0.35
2014	0.26	0.58	0.45	0.43
2015	0.42	0.45	0.65	0.45
2016	0.49	...	...	...

Interim Dividends (Per Share)

Amt	Decl	Ex	Rec	Pay
0.10Q	09/01/2015	09/15/2015	09/17/2015	10/01/2015
0.10Q	12/02/2015	12/15/2015	12/17/2015	01/04/2016
0.10Q	03/08/2016	03/22/2016	03/24/2016	04/01/2016
0.10Q	06/07/2016	06/21/2016	06/23/2016	07/01/2016

Indicated Div: $0.40

Valuation Analysis / **Institutional Holding**

Forecast EPS	$2.83 (05/20/2016)	No of Institutions 599
Market Cap	$9.9 Billlion	Shares 149,153,344
Book Value	$1.9 Billion	% Held 71.90
Price/Book	5.13	
Price/Sales	3.45	

Business Summary: Business Services (MIC: 7.5.2 SIC: 7389 NAIC: 561499)

Total System Services is a payment solutions provider that provides services to financial and nonfinancial institutions. Co.'s operating segments include: North America Services, which provides issuer account solutions for financial institutions and other organizations; International Services, which provides issuer card solutions to financial institutions and other organizations; Merchant Services, which provides merchant services and related services; and NetSpend, which is a program manager for FDIC-insured depository institutions that issue general purpose reloadable cards and payroll cards and provide alternative financial services to underbanked and other consumers.

Recent Developments: For the quarter ended Mar 31 2016, net income increased 17.1% to US$92.4 million from US$78.9 million in the year-earlier quarter. Revenues were US$739.4 million, up 11.7% from US$662.2 million the year before. Operating income was US$151.7 million versus US$122.5 million in the prior-year quarter, an increase of 23.8%. Direct operating expenses rose 6.9% to US$480.6 million from US$449.7 million in the comparable period the year before. Indirect operating expenses increased 19.1% to US$107.1 million from US$90.0 million in the equivalent prior-year period.

Prospects: Our evaluation of Total System Services Inc. as of June 19, 2016 is the result of our systematic analysis on three basic characteristics: earnings strength, relative valuation, and recent stock price movement. The company has enjoyed a very positive trend in earnings per share over the past 5 quarters and while recent estimates for the company have been raised by analysts, TSS has posted better than expected results. Based on operating earnings yield, the company is about fairly valued when compared to all of the companies in our coverage universe. Share price changes over the past year indicates that TSS will perform very well over the near term.

Financial Data
(US$ in Thousands)

	3 Mos	12/31/2015	12/31/2014	12/31/2013	12/31/2012	12/31/2011	12/31/2010	12/31/2009
Earnings Per Share	2.04	1.97	1.72	1.29	1.29	1.15	0.99	1.09
Cash Flow Per Share	3.23	3.29	3.04	2.42	2.43	2.28	1.99	2.16
Tang Book Value Per Share	N.M.	N.M.	N.M.	N.M.	2.08	2.57	2.18	3.39
Dividends Per Share	0.400	0.400	0.400	0.400	0.400	0.310	0.280	0.280
Dividend Payout %	19.61	20.30	23.26	31.01	31.01	26.96	28.28	25.69
Income Statement								
Total Revenue	739,378	2,779,541	2,446,877	2,132,353	1,870,972	1,808,966	1,717,577	1,688,062
EBITDA	162,031	757,390	643,147	568,764	525,762	485,876	471,077	495,217
Depn & Amortn	10,488	260,502	250,218	212,845	170,908	169,325	163,265	156,625
Income Before Taxes	129,247	496,888	392,929	355,919	354,854	316,551	307,812	338,592
Income Taxes	43,429	151,364	129,761	112,369	115,102	102,597	106,088	121,238
Net Income	90,628	364,044	322,872	244,750	244,280	220,559	193,947	215,213
Average Shares	182,807	183,622	185,756	188,793	188,665	191,239	195,378	195,623
Balance Sheet								
Current Assets	2,426,434	882,902	690,553	653,933	574,726	650,181	721,813	810,896
Total Assets	5,423,933	3,908,300	3,733,581	3,686,568	2,023,838	1,858,392	1,952,261	1,710,954
Current Liabilities	283,697	339,218	296,513	297,215	230,519	380,576	227,270	220,779
Long-Term Obligations	2,887,247	1,383,634	1,405,106	1,435,751	192,014	63,593	225,276	205,123
Total Liabilities	3,502,392	2,065,282	2,040,819	2,105,491	598,628	557,103	711,137	535,153
Stockholders' Equity	1,921,541	1,843,018	1,692,762	1,581,077	1,425,210	1,301,289	1,241,124	1,175,801
Shares Outstanding	183,436	182,781	184,939	187,717	187,031	189,031	194,528	197,180
Statistical Record								
Return on Assets %	8.19	9.53	8.70	8.57	12.55	11.58	10.59	13.20
Return on Equity %	20.77	20.59	19.72	16.28	17.87	17.35	16.05	19.87
EBITDA Margin %	21.91	27.25	26.28	26.67	28.10	26.86	27.43	29.34
Net Margin %	12.26	13.10	13.20	11.48	13.06	12.19	11.29	12.75
Asset Turnover	0.62	0.73	0.66	0.75	0.96	0.95	0.94	1.04
Current Ratio	8.55	2.60	2.33	2.20	2.49	1.71	3.18	3.67
Debt to Equity	1.50	0.75	0.83	0.91	0.13	0.05	0.18	0.17
Price Range	56.37-37.89	56.37-33.27	34.41-28.70	33.30-21.42	24.39-19.40	20.42-15.38	17.27-13.60	17.59-11.40
P/E Ratio	27.63-18.57	28.61-16.89	20.01-16.69	25.81-16.60	18.91-15.04	17.76-13.37	17.44-13.74	16.14-10.46
Average Yield %	0.88	0.91	1.28	1.51	1.76	1.70	1.85	1.91

Address: One TSYS Way, P.O. Box 1755, Columbus, GA 31902 Telephone: 706-644-6081 Fax: 706-649-2456	Web Site: www.tsys.com Officers: M. Troy Woods - Chairman, President, Chief Executive Officer, Chief Operating Officer Pamela A. Joseph - President, Chief Operating Officer	Auditors: KPMG LLP Investor Contact: 706-644-6081 Transfer Agents: American Stock Transfer & Trust Company, LLC, Brookly, NY

TRANSOCEAN LTD.

Exchange	Symbol	Price	52Wk Range	Yield	P/E
NYS	RIG	$9.79 (5/31/2016)	19.28-8.20	6.13	2.35

*7 Year Price Score 22.88   ***NYSE Composite Index=100**   ***12 Month Price Score 76.66**

TRADING VOLUME (thousand shares)

Interim Earnings (Per Share)

Qtr.	Mar	Jun	Sep	Dec
2013	0.88	0.84	1.50	0.64
2014	1.25	1.61	(6.12)	(2.05)
2015	(1.33)	0.93	0.88	1.67
2016	0.68	...	...	...

Interim Dividends (Per Share)

Amt	Decl	Ex	Rec	Pay
0.75Q	11/04/2014	11/12/2014	11/14/2014	12/17/2014
0.75Q	02/06/2015	02/18/2015	02/20/2015	03/18/2015
0.15Q	05/15/2015	05/27/2015	05/29/2015	06/17/2015
0.15Q	08/14/2015	08/21/2015	08/25/2015	09/23/2015

Indicated Div: $0.60

Valuation Analysis   **Institutional Holding**

Forecast EPS	N/A	No of Institutions
		602
Market Cap	$3.6 Billion	Shares
Book Value	$14.8 Billion	307,362,240
Price/Book	0.24	% Held
Price/Sales	0.53	75.77

Business Summary: Equipment & Services (MIC: 9.1.3 SIC: 1389 NAIC: 213112)

Transocean is a provider of offshore contract drilling services for oil and gas wells. Co. focuses on deepwater and harsh environment drilling services. Co. contracts its drilling rigs, related equipment and work crews primarily on a dayrate basis to drill oil and gas wells. At Dec 31 2015, Co. owned or had partial ownership interests in and operated 60 mobile offshore drilling units, including 27 ultra-deepwater floaters, seven harsh environment floaters, five deepwater floaters, 11 midwater floaters and 10 high-specification jackups. At Dec 31 2015, Co. also had seven ultra-deepwater drillships and five high-specification jackups under construction or under contract to be constructed.

Recent Developments: For the quarter ended Mar 31 2016, income from continuing operations was US$256.0 million compared with a loss of US$467.0 million in the year-earlier quarter. Net income amounted to US$255.0 million versus a net loss of US$469.0 million in the year-earlier quarter. Revenues were US$1.34 billion, down 34.4% from US$2.04 billion the year before. Operating income was US$414.0 million versus a loss of US$321.0 million in the prior-year quarter. Direct operating expenses declined 38.7% to US$665.0 million from US$1.08 billion in the comparable period the year before. Indirect operating expenses decreased 79.5% to US$262.0 million from US$1.28 billion in the equivalent prior-year period.

Prospects: Our evaluation of Transocean Ltd. as of Aug. 2, 2015 is the result of our systematic analysis on three basic characteristics: earnings strength, relative valuation, and recent stock price movement. The company has suffered a very negative trend in earnings per share over the past 5 quarters. Because the company lacks sufficient analyst estimate data, we place greater weight on the historical EPS trend as the measure of earnings strength. Based on operating earnings yield, the company is undervalued when compared to all of the companies in our coverage universe. Share price changes over the past year indicates that RIG will perform in line with the market over the near term.

Financial Data

(US$ in Millions)	3 Mos	12/31/2015	12/31/2014	12/31/2013	12/31/2012	12/31/2011	12/31/2010	12/31/2009
Earnings Per Share	4.16	2.16	(5.29)	3.87	(0.62)	(17.79)	2.99	9.84
Cash Flow Per Share	9.75	9.49	6.13	5.33	7.59	5.54	12.33	17.49
Tang Book Value Per Share	40.42	39.83	37.74	37.99	35.49	35.72	41.53	38.66
Dividends Per Share	0.300	1.050	2.810	1.680	0.790	2.370	...	...
Dividend Payout %	7.21	48.61	...	43.41	...	...	...	...
Income Statement								
Total Revenue	1,341	7,386	9,174	9,484	9,196	9,142	9,576	11,556
EBITDA	630	2,388	(232)	3,290	1,491	(4,902)	1,745	4,122
Depn & Amortn	217	948	1,124	1,094	(42)	(45)	(98)	(281)
Income Before Taxes	330	1,030	(1,800)	1,664	866	(5,434)	1,299	3,924
Income Taxes	74	206	146	258	50	395	311	754
Net Income	249	791	(1,913)	1,407	(219)	(5,725)	961	3,181
Average Shares	364	363	362	360	356	322	320	321
Balance Sheet								
Current Assets	4,700	4,785	6,001	6,772	8,647	7,609	6,195	4,476
Total Assets	26,245	26,329	28,413	32,546	34,255	35,088	36,811	36,436
Current Liabilities	2,588	2,669	3,770	3,554	5,463	5,358	3,836	3,618
Long-Term Obligations	7,253	7,397	9,059	10,379	11,092	11,497	9,209	9,849
Total Liabilities	11,487	11,831	14,742	15,855	18,510	19,387	15,428	15,884
Stockholders' Equity	14,758	14,498	13,671	16,691	15,745	15,701	21,383	20,552
Shares Outstanding	365	364	362	360	359	349	319	321
Statistical Record								
Return on Assets %	5.71	2.89	N.M.	4.21	N.M.	N.M.	2.62	8.88
Return on Equity %	10.89	5.62	N.M.	8.68	N.M.	N.M.	4.58	17.16
EBITDA Margin %	46.98	32.33	N.M.	34.69	16.21	N.M.	18.22	35.67
Net Margin %	18.57	10.71	N.M.	14.84	N.M.	N.M.	10.04	27.53
Asset Turnover	0.25	0.27	0.30	0.28	0.26	0.25	0.26	0.32
Current Ratio	1.82	1.79	1.59	1.91	1.58	1.42	1.61	1.24
Debt to Equity	0.49	0.51	0.66	0.62	0.70	0.73	0.43	0.48
Price Range	21.39-8.20	21.39-11.60	49.42-16.25	59.30-44.38	58.70-38.97	85.47-38.39	93.02-42.58	92.75-46.39
P/E Ratio	5.14-1.97	9.90-5.37	...	15.32-11.47	...	...	31.11-14.24	9.43-4.71
Average Yield %	2.13	6.72	7.50	3.34	1.68	3.76	...	...

Address: 10 Chemin de Blandonnet, Vernier, 1214 **Telephone:** 229-309-000	**Web Site:** www.deepwater.com **Officers:** Ian C. Strachan - Chairman Jeremy D. Thigpen - President, Chief Executive Officer	**Auditors:** Ernst & Young LLP **Investor Contact:** 713-232-7551 **Transfer Agents:** Computershare Shareowner Services LLC, Pittsburgh, PA

TRAVELERS COMPANIES INC (THE)

Exchange	Symbol	Price	52Wk Range	Yield	P/E	Div Achiever
NYS	TRV	$114.14 (5/31/2016)	117.56-96.14	2.35	10.73	10 Years

*7 Year Price Score 121.71 *NYSE Composite Index=100 *12 Month Price Score 103.56

TRADING VOLUME (thousand shares)

Interim Earnings (Per Share)

Qtr.	Mar	Jun	Sep	Dec
2013	2.33	2.41	2.30	2.69
2014	2.95	1.95	2.69	3.10
2015	2.55	2.53	2.97	2.84
2016	2.30	...	...	...

Interim Dividends (Per Share)

Amt	Decl	Ex	Rec	Pay
0.61Q	07/21/2015	09/08/2015	09/10/2015	09/30/2015
0.61Q	10/20/2015	12/08/2015	12/10/2015	12/31/2015
0.61Q	01/21/2016	03/08/2016	03/10/2016	03/31/2016
0.67Q	04/21/2016	06/08/2016	06/10/2016	06/30/2016

Indicated Div: $2.68 (Div. Reinv. Plan)

Valuation Analysis / Institutional Holding

Valuation Analysis		Institutional Holding	
Forecast EPS	$9.50	No of Institutions	
	(05/20/2016)	1300	
Market Cap	$33.4 Billion	Shares	
Book Value	$24.2 Billion	306,187,680	
Price/Book	1.38	% Held	
Price/Sales	1.24	N/A	

Business Summary: General Insurance (MIC: 5.2.1 SIC: 6331 NAIC: 524126)

Travelers Companies is a holding company. Through its subsidiaries, Co. provides a range of commercial and personal property and casualty insurance products and services. Co.'s segments include: The Business and International Insurance, which provides a range of property and casualty insurance and insurance related services to its clients; The Bond & Specialty Insurance, which provides surety, crime, management and professional liability coverages and related risk management services to a range of primarily domestic customers; and Personal Insurance, which writes a range of property and casualty insurance covering individuals' personal risks.

Recent Developments: For the quarter ended Mar 31 2016, net income decreased 17.0% to US$691.0 million from US$833.0 million in the year-earlier quarter. Revenues were US$6.69 billion, up 0.9% from US$6.63 billion the year before. Net premiums earned were US$5.98 billion versus US$5.89 billion in the prior-year quarter, an increase of 1.6%. Net investment income fell 8.1% to US$544.0 million from US$592.0 million a year ago.

Prospects: Our evaluation of The Travelers Companies Inc. as of June 19, 2016 is the result of our systematic analysis on three basic characteristics: earnings strength, relative valuation, and recent stock price movement. The company has generated a negative trend in earnings per share over the past 5 quarters. However, while recent estimates for the company have been mixed, TRV has posted results that fell short of analysts expectations. Based on operating earnings yield, the company is undervalued when compared to all of the companies in our coverage universe. Share price changes over the past year indicates that TRV will perform very well over the near term.

Financial Data
(US$ in Thousands)

	3 Mos	12/31/2015	12/31/2014	12/31/2013	12/31/2012	12/31/2011	12/31/2010	12/31/2009
Earnings Per Share	10.64	10.88	10.70	9.74	6.30	3.36	6.62	6.33
Cash Flow Per Share	13.89	11.06	10.90	10.31	8.34	5.22	6.41	7.51
Tang Book Value Per Share	69.44	66.73	64.93	58.87	57.39	52.65	49.56	44.94
Dividends Per Share	2.440	2.380	2.150	1.960	1.790	1.590	1.410	1.230
Dividend Payout %	22.93	21.88	20.09	20.12	28.41	47.32	21.30	19.43
Income Statement								
Premium Income	5,981,000	23,874,000	23,713,000	22,637,000	22,357,000	22,090,000	21,432,000	21,418,000
Total Revenue	6,686,000	26,800,000	27,162,000	26,191,000	25,740,000	25,446,000	25,112,000	24,680,000
Benefits & Claims	3,712,000	13,723,000	13,870,000	13,307,000	14,676,000	16,276,000	13,210,000	12,408,000
Income Before Taxes	917,000	4,740,000	5,089,000	4,945,000	3,166,000	1,352,000	4,306,000	4,711,000
Income Taxes	226,000	1,301,000	1,397,000	1,272,000	693,000	(74,000)	1,090,000	1,089,000
Net Income	691,000	3,439,000	3,692,000	3,673,000	2,473,000	1,426,000	3,216,000	3,622,000
Average Shares	297,900	313,900	342,500	374,300	389,800	420,500	482,500	568,600
Balance Sheet								
Total Assets	101,680,000	100,184,000	103,078,000	103,812,000	104,938,000	104,602,000	105,181,000	109,560,000
Total Liabilities	77,514,000	76,586,000	78,242,000	79,016,000	79,533,000	80,125,000	79,706,000	82,145,000
Stockholders' Equity	24,166,000	23,598,000	24,836,000	24,796,000	25,405,000	24,477,000	25,475,000	27,415,000
Shares Outstanding	292,400	295,900	322,200	353,500	377,400	392,800	434,600	520,300
Statistical Record								
Return on Assets %	3.23	3.38	3.57	3.52	2.35	1.36	3.00	3.30
Return on Equity %	13.45	14.20	14.88	14.63	9.89	5.71	12.16	13.74
Loss Ratio %	62.06	57.48	58.49	58.78	65.64	73.68	61.64	57.93
Net Margin %	10.34	12.83	13.59	14.02	9.61	5.60	12.81	14.68
Price Range	117.43-96.14	115.83-96.14	106.95-80.26	90.99-71.82	74.33-56.87	64.05-46.80	57.44-47.94	54.31-33.52
P/E Ratio	11.04-9.04	10.65-8.84	10.00-7.50	9.34-7.37	11.80-9.03	19.06-13.93	8.68-7.24	8.58-5.30
Average Yield %	2.30	2.25	2.33	2.35	2.78	2.81	2.72	2.78

Address: 485 Lexington Avenue, New York, NY 10017 **Telephone:** 917-778-6000	**Web Site:** www.travelers.com **Officers:** Jay Steven Fishman - Executive Chairman designate, Chairman, Chief Executive Officer, President William H. Heyman - Vice-Chairman, Chief Investment Officer	**Auditors:** KPMG LLP **Investor Contact:** 917-778-9844 **Transfer Agents:** Wells Fargo Bank, N.A. Shareowner Services, St. Paul, MN

TRAVELCENTERS OF AMERICA LLC

Exchange	Symbol	Price	52Wk Range	Yield	P/E
NYS	TA	$7.07 (5/31/2016)	16.70-6.47	N/A	117.83

*7 Year Price Score 121.59 *NYSE Composite Index=100   *12 Month Price Score 67.11

Interim Earnings (Per Share)

Qtr.	Mar	Jun	Sep	Dec
2013	(0.41)	0.54	0.53	0.40
2014	0.01	0.36	0.34	0.91
2015	0.41	0.10	0.26	(0.04)
2016	(0.26)	...	...	...

Interim Dividends (Per Share)

No Dividends Paid

Valuation Analysis		Institutional Holding	
Forecast EPS	$0.35	No of Institutions	
	(05/20/2016)	172	
Market Cap	$274.3 Million	Shares	
Book Value	$540.7 Million	21,512,234	
Price/Book	0.51	% Held	
Price/Sales	0.05	71.29	

Business Summary: Retail - Automotive (MIC: 2.1.4 SIC: 5541 NAIC: 447110)

TravelCenters of America is engaged in operating and franchising travel center and gasoline station/convenience store locations. Co.'s customers include trucking fleets and their drivers, independent truck drivers and motorists. Co. provides a range of products and services, including diesel fuel and gasoline, truck repair and maintenance services, restaurants, more than 35 different brands of quick service restaurants, travel/convenience stores and various driver amenities. As of Dec 31 2014, Co.'s business included 250 travel centers located in 43 states in the U.S., primarily along the U.S. interstate highway system, and the province of Ontario, Canada.

Recent Developments: For the quarter ended Mar 31 2016, net loss amounted to US$9.9 million versus net income of US$15.7 million in the year-earlier quarter. Revenues were US$1.16 billion, down 17.3% from US$1.41 billion the year before. Operating loss was US$8.8 million versus an income of US$32.2 million in the prior-year quarter. Direct operating expenses declined 22.9% to US$824.2 million from US$1.07 billion in the comparable period the year before. Indirect operating expenses increased 14.0% to US$349.1 million from US$306.3 million in the equivalent prior-year period.

Prospects: Our evaluation of TravelCenters of America LLC as of June 19, 2016 is the result of our systematic analysis on three basic characteristics: earnings strength, relative valuation, and recent stock price movement. The company has suffered a very negative trend in earnings per share over the past 5 quarters. However, while recent estimates for the company have been lowered by analysts, TA has posted results that fell short of analysts expectations. Based on operating earnings yield, the company is about fairly valued when compared to all of the companies in our coverage universe. Share price changes over the past year indicates that TA will perform very poorly over the near term.

Financial Data
(US$ in Thousands)

	3 Mos	12/31/2015	12/31/2014	12/31/2013	12/31/2012	12/31/2011	12/31/2010	12/31/2009
Earnings Per Share	0.06	0.72	1.62	1.06	1.12	0.98	(3.78)	(5.38)
Cash Flow Per Share	2.48	3.75	4.49	2.55	3.05	1.25	1.63	3.16
Tang Book Value Per Share	11.08	11.42	12.10	10.77	11.29	10.31	12.52	16.55
Income Statement								
Total Revenue	1,164,450	5,850,633	7,778,633	7,944,731	7,995,724	7,888,857	5,962,481	4,699,820
EBITDA	10,778	132,789	176,360	76,123	87,573	74,298	(2,175)	(39,678)
Depn & Amortn	20,525	70,042	63,880	57,456	46,888	42,344	39,362	37,278
Income Before Taxes	(16,568)	40,202	95,768	2,331	31,812	23,784	(64,907)	(89,359)
Income Taxes	(5,677)	16,539	38,023	(26,618)	1,491	1,379	1,421	901
Net Income	(9,944)	27,719	60,969	31,623	32,198	23,574	(65,571)	(89,874)
Average Shares	36,891	36,485	35,856	28,081	27,193	24,104	17,362	16,694
Balance Sheet								
Current Assets	465,576	495,340	562,532	470,394	393,488	484,250	402,176	410,598
Total Assets	1,637,970	1,635,094	1,425,174	1,257,282	1,018,281	1,016,531	894,089	885,360
Current Liabilities	330,908	295,622	267,138	303,613	283,127	287,748	237,009	219,685
Long-Term Obligations	698,696	715,498	562,934	453,926	351,135	364,369	98,464	101,248
Total Liabilities	1,097,300	1,085,775	906,564	803,405	664,847	697,930	642,784	570,607
Stockholders' Equity	540,670	549,319	518,610	453,877	353,434	318,601	251,305	314,753
Shares Outstanding	38,799	38,808	38,336	37,625	29,536	28,775	18,016	17,269
Statistical Record								
Return on Assets %	0.13	1.81	4.55	2.78	3.16	2.47	N.M.	N.M.
Return on Equity %	0.38	5.19	12.54	7.83	9.56	8.27	N.M.	N.M.
EBITDA Margin %	0.93	2.27	2.27	0.96	1.10	0.94	N.M.	N.M.
Net Margin %	N.M.	0.47	0.78	0.40	0.40	0.30	N.M.	N.M.
Asset Turnover	3.58	3.82	5.80	6.98	7.84	8.26	6.70	5.30
Current Ratio	1.41	1.68	2.11	1.55	1.39	1.68	1.70	1.87
Debt to Equity	1.29	1.30	1.09	1.00	0.99	1.14	0.39	0.32
Price Range	17.80-6.61	17.80-9.10	12.62-7.26	12.25-4.70	6.78-4.19	12.36-3.01	5.79-2.09	8.05-1.72
P/E Ratio	296.67-110.17	24.72-12.64	7.79-4.48	11.56-4.43	6.05-3.74	12.61-3.07	...	...

Address: 24601 Center Ridge Road, Suite 200, Westlake, OH 44145-5639
Telephone: 440-808-9100

Web site: www.tatravelcenters.com
Officers: Thomas M. O'Brien - President, Chief Executive Officer, Managing Director Andrew J. Rebholz - Executive Vice President, Chief Financial Officer, Treasurer

Auditors: RSM US LLP
Investor Contact: 617-796-8251
Transfer Agents: Wells Fargo Shareowner Services, St. Paul, MN

TREEHOUSE FOODS INC

Exchange	Symbol	Price	52Wk Range	Yield	P/E
NYS	THS	$94.70 (5/31/2016)	94.89-67.32	N/A	43.84

*7 Year Price Score 112.00 *NYSE Composite Index=100 *12 Month Price Score 107.46

Interim Earnings (Per Share)

Qtr.	Mar	Jun	Sep	Dec
2013	0.62	0.50	0.61	0.61
2014	0.38	0.57	0.47	0.80
2015	0.41	0.72	0.65	0.85
2016	(0.06)	...	...	...

Interim Dividends (Per Share)

No Dividends Paid

Valuation Analysis   **Institutional Holding**

Forecast EPS	$3.07	No of Institutions
	(05/20/2016)	381
Market Cap	$5.3 Billion	Shares
Book Value	$2.7 Billion	66,547,232
Price/Book	1.97	% Held
Price/Sales	1.45	99.61

Business Summary: Food (MIC: 1.2.1 SIC: 2033 NAIC: 311421)

TreeHouse Foods is a food manufacturer servicing primarily the retail grocery and foodservice distribution channels. Co. has three business segments: North American Retail Grocery, which sells branded and private label products including non-dairy powdered creamers; condensed and ready to serve soups, broths and gravies to customers in the U.S. and Canada; Food Away From Home, which sells non-dairy powdered creamers; sweeteners; pickles and related products; Mexican sauces; refrigerated dressings; aseptic products and hot cereals to foodservice customers; as well as Industrial and Export, which includes Co.'s co-pack business and non-dairy powdered creamer sales to industrial customers.

Recent Developments: For the quarter ended Mar 31 2016, net loss amounted to US$3.3 million versus net income of US$17.9 million in the year-earlier quarter. Revenues were US$1.27 billion, up 62.2% from US$783.1 million the year before. Operating income was US$18.9 million versus US$46.7 million in the prior-year quarter, a decrease of 59.5%. Direct operating expenses rose 65.8% to US$1.05 billion from US$630.7 million in the comparable period the year before. Indirect operating expenses increased 94.5% to US$205.6 million from US$105.7 million in the equivalent prior-year period.

Prospects: Our evaluation of TreeHouse Foods Inc. as of June 19, 2016 is the result of our systematic analysis on three basic characteristics: earnings strength, relative valuation, and recent stock price movement. The company has generated a negative trend in earnings per share over the past 5 quarters and while recent estimates for the company have remained steady, THS has posted better than expected results. Based on operating earnings yield, the company is about fairly valued when compared to all of the companies in our coverage universe. Share price changes over the past year indicates that THS will perform well over the near term.

Financial Data

(US$ in Thousands)	3 Mos	12/31/2015	12/31/2014	12/31/2013	12/31/2012	12/31/2011	12/31/2010	12/31/2009
Earnings Per Share	2.16	2.63	2.23	2.33	2.38	2.56	2.51	2.48
Cash Flow Per Share	5.97	6.63	5.39	5.95	5.64	4.36	6.97	3.28
Tang Book Value Per Share	N.M.	N.M.	N.M.	N.M.	N.M.	N.M.	N.M.	5.66
Income Statement								
Total Revenue	1,270,173	3,206,405	2,946,102	2,293,927	2,182,125	2,049,985	1,817,024	1,511,653
EBITDA	77,505	275,271	240,916	245,329	239,875	241,437	225,491	174,421
Depn & Amortn	59,436	61,500	63,300	73,300	64,700	48,616	43,400	33,962
Income Before Taxes	(4,780)	171,264	136,570	124,910	124,209	139,798	136,400	122,074
Income Taxes	(1,434)	56,354	46,690	37,922	35,846	45,391	45,481	40,760
Net Income	(3,346)	114,910	89,880	86,988	88,363	94,407	90,919	81,314
Average Shares	52,708	43,709	40,238	37,396	37,118	36,950	36,172	32,798
Balance Sheet								
Current Assets	1,461,629	847,203	949,436	649,689	588,411	468,394	440,803	370,652
Total Assets	6,864,247	3,702,796	3,903,004	2,721,054	2,525,873	2,404,529	2,391,248	1,384,428
Current Liabilities	562,593	275,473	311,233	240,364	187,030	171,479	203,360	149,725
Long-Term Obligations	2,942,336	1,221,741	1,445,488	938,945	898,100	902,929	976,452	401,640
Total Liabilities	4,144,910	1,847,937	2,143,747	1,447,936	1,346,618	1,331,012	1,413,282	628,199
Stockholders' Equity	2,719,337	1,854,859	1,759,257	1,273,118	1,179,255	1,073,517	977,966	756,229
Shares Outstanding	56,433	43,126	42,663	36,493	36,196	35,921	35,439	31,998
Statistical Record								
Return on Assets %	1.75	3.02	2.71	3.32	3.57	3.94	4.82	5.94
Return on Equity %	4.18	6.36	5.93	7.09	7.82	9.20	10.49	11.82
EBITDA Margin %	6.10	8.59	8.18	10.69	10.99	11.78	12.41	11.54
Net Margin %	N.M.	3.58	3.05	3.79	4.05	4.61	5.00	5.38
Asset Turnover	0.69	0.84	0.89	0.87	0.88	0.85	0.96	1.10
Current Ratio	2.60	3.08	3.05	2.70	3.15	2.73	2.17	2.48
Debt to Equity	1.08	0.66	0.82	0.74	0.76	0.84	1.00	0.53
Price Range	88.11-67.32	92.90-69.44	87.95-63.59	75.19-52.13	65.52-48.42	66.45-47.85	52.85-37.37	40.15-24.88
P/E Ratio	40.79-31.17	35.32-26.40	39.44-28.52	32.27-22.37	27.53-20.34	25.96-18.69	21.06-14.89	16.19-10.03

Address: 2021 Spring Road, Suite 600, Oak Brook, IL 60523

Telephone: 708-483-1300

Web Site: www.treehousefoods.com

Officers: Sam K. Reed - Chairman, Chief Executive Officer David B. Vermylen - President, Chief Operating Officer

Auditors: Deloitte & Touche LLP

Transfer Agents: BNY Mellon Shareowner Services, South Hackensack, NJ

TRI POINTE GROUP INC

Exchange	Symbol	Price	52Wk Range	Yield	P/E
NYS	TPH	$11.66 (5/31/2016)	16.05-9.05	N/A	8.57

*7 Year Price Score N/A   *NYSE Composite Index=100   *12 Month Price Score 89.55

Interim Earnings (Per Share)

Qtr.	Mar	Jun	Sep	Dec
2013	0.01	0.07	0.15	0.27
2014	0.14	0.19	0.07	0.27
2015	0.09	0.34	0.31	0.53
2016	0.18			

Interim Dividends (Per Share)

No Dividends Paid

Valuation Analysis

		Institutional Holding	
Forecast EPS	$1.22	No of Institutions	
	(05/20/2016)	262	
Market Cap	$1.9 Billion	Shares	
Book Value	$1.7 Billion	164,637,808	
Price/Book	1.11	% Held	
Price/Sales	0.77	100.17	

Business Summary: Builders (MIC: 2.2.5 SIC: 1531 NAIC: 236117)

TRI Pointe Group is engaged in the design, construction and sale of single-family detached and attached homes. As of Dec 31 2015, Co. had a portfolio of six homebuilding brands operating in 10 markets across eight states: Maracay Homes in Arizona; Pardee Homes in California and Nevada; Quadrant Homes in Washington; Trendmaker Homes in Texas; TRI Pointe Homes in California and Colorado; and Winchester Homes in Maryland and Virginia. As of the same date, Co.'s operations consisted of 104 active selling communities and 27,602 lots owned or controlled. Co.'s operations are organized in two principal businesses: homebuilding and financial services.

Recent Developments: For the quarter ended Mar 31 2016, net income increased 87.7% to US$28.7 million from US$15.3 million in the year-earlier quarter. Revenues were US$424.1 million, up 12.4% from US$377.3 million the year before. Direct operating expenses rose 7.6% to US$325.8 million from US$302.8 million in the comparable period the year before. Indirect operating expenses increased 6.2% to US$54.9 million from US$51.7 million in the equivalent prior-year period.

Prospects: Our evaluation of Tri Pointe Group Inc as of June 19, 2016 is the result of our systematic analysis on three basic characteristics: earnings strength, relative valuation, and recent stock price movement. The company has suffered a very negative trend in earnings per share over the past 5 quarters and while recent estimates for the company have remained steady, TPH has posted better than expected results. Based on operating earnings yield, the company is undervalued when compared to all of the companies in our coverage universe. Share price changes over the past year indicates that TPH will perform very poorly over the near term.

Financial Data
(US$ in Thousands)

	3 Mos	12/31/2015	12/31/2014	12/31/2013	12/31/2012	12/31/2011	12/31/2010
Earnings Per Share	1.36	1.27	0.58	0.50	...	...	...
Cash Flow Per Share	(0.00)	0.19	(0.78)	(7.16)	...	...	...
Tang Book Value Per Share	9.46	9.29	8.00	10.20	4.72	...	...
Income Statement							
Total Revenue	424,138	2,400,149	1,703,616	257,955	78,550	19,329	18,987
EBITDA	46,104	336,778	148,301	28,990	2,937	(3,835)	(633)
Depn & Amortn	2,605	20,209	20,049	3,237	431	758	1,542
Income Before Taxes	43,499	316,569	128,252	25,753	2,506	(4,593)	(2,175)
Income Taxes	15,490	112,079	43,767	10,379	...	...	...
Net Income	28,550	205,461	84,197	15,374	2,506	(4,593)	(2,175)
Average Shares	162,192	162,319	145,531	30,797	...	...	...
Balance Sheet							
Current Assets	3,008,770	2,908,125	2,628,751	497,211	214,455	92,258	27,958
Total Assets	3,234,077	3,138,071	2,913,524	506,035	217,516	93,776	30,096
Current Liabilities	139,915	125,409	135,272	45,617	10,995	4,412	1,776
Long-Term Obligations	1,246,641	1,172,947	1,171,691	138,112	57,368	6,873	3,462
Total Liabilities	1,539,320	1,473,388	1,459,344	183,729	68,363	11,285	5,238
Stockholders' Equity	1,694,757	1,664,683	1,454,180	322,306	149,153	82,491	24,858
Shares Outstanding	162,007	161,813	161,355	31,597	31,597	...	...
Statistical Record							
Return on Assets %	6.99	6.79	4.92	4.25	1.61	N.M.	...
Return on Equity %	13.70	13.18	9.48	6.52	2.16	N.M.	...
EBITDA Margin %	10.87	14.03	8.71	11.24	3.74	N.M.	N.M.
Net Margin %	6.73	8.56	4.94	5.96	3.19	N.M.	N.M.
Asset Turnover	0.79	0.79	1.00	0.71	0.50	0.31	...
Current Ratio	21.50	23.19	19.43	10.90	19.50	20.91	15.74
Debt to Equity	0.74	0.70	0.81	0.43	0.38	0.08	0.14
Price Range	16.05-9.05	16.05-12.50	19.93-12.73	20.51-13.66	...	...	...
P/E Ratio	11.80-6.65	12.64-9.84	34.36-21.95	41.02-27.32	...	...	...

Address: 19540 Jamboree Road, Suite 300, Irvine, CA 92612 Telephone: 949-438-1400	Web Site: www.TRIPointeGroup.com Officers: Barry S. Sternlicht - Chairman Thomas J. Mitchell - President, Chief Operating Officer, Secretary	Auditors: Ernst & Young LLP Investor Contact: 949-478-8696 Transfer Agents: American Stock Transfer & Trust Company, LLC

TRINITY INDUSTRIES, INC.

Exchange	Symbol	Price	52Wk Range	Yield	P/E
NYS	TRN	$18.06 (5/31/2016)	30.70-15.64	2.44	3.94

*7 Year Price Score 99.06 ***NYSE Composite Index=100** ***12 Month Price Score 78.02**

TRADING VOLUME (thousand shares)

Interim Earnings (Per Share)

Qtr.	Mar	Jun	Sep	Dec
2013	0.50	0.53	0.63	0.72
2014	1.43	1.01	0.90	0.86
2015	1.13	1.33	1.31	1.30
2016	0.64	...	...	...

Interim Dividends (Per Share)

Amt	Decl	Ex	Rec	Pay
0.11Q	09/09/2015	10/13/2015	10/15/2015	10/30/2015
0.11Q	12/10/2015	01/13/2016	01/15/2016	01/29/2016
0.11Q	03/10/2016	04/13/2016	04/15/2016	04/29/2016
0.11Q	05/02/2016	07/13/2016	07/15/2016	07/29/2016

Indicated Div: $0.44

Valuation Analysis		Institutional Holding	
Forecast EPS	$2.10	No of Institutions	
	(05/20/2016)	534	
Market Cap	$2.7 Billion	Shares	
Book Value	$3.7 Billion	116,838,568	
Price/Book	0.73	% Held	
Price/Sales	0.46	82.14	

Business Summary: Industrial Machinery & Equipment (MIC: 7.2.1 SIC: 3743 NAIC: 336510)

Trinity Industries is an industrial company that owns a range of businesses providing products and services to the energy, transportation, chemical, and construction sectors. Co. manufactures and sells a range of products and services including: railcars and railcar parts; parts and steel components; the leasing, management, and maintenance of railcars; highway products; aggregates; inland barges; structural wind towers; steel utility structures; storage and distribution containers; and trench shields and shoring products. Co. has five business groups: Rail Group; Railcar Leasing and Management Services Group; Construction Products Group; Energy Equipment Group; and Inland Barge Group.

Recent Developments: For the quarter ended Mar 31 2016, net income decreased 46.0% to US$102.1 million from US$189.0 million in the year-earlier quarter. Revenues were US$1.19 billion, down 27.0% from US$1.63 billion the year before. Operating income was US$203.4 million versus US$333.1 million in the prior-year quarter, a decrease of 38.9%. Direct operating expenses declined 26.5% to US$889.9 million from US$1.21 billion in the comparable period the year before. Indirect operating expenses increased 14.7% to US$94.6 million from US$82.5 million in the equivalent prior-year period.

Prospects: Our evaluation of Trinity Industries Inc. as of June 19, 2016 is the result of our systematic analysis on three basic characteristics: earnings strength, relative valuation, and recent stock price movement. The company has suffered a very negative trend in earnings per share over the past 5 quarters and while recent estimates for the company have been mixed, TRN has posted results that fell short of analysts expectations. Based on operating earnings yield, the company is undervalued when compared to all of the companies in our coverage universe. Share price changes over the past year indicates that TRN will perform very poorly over the near term.

Financial Data

(US$ in Thousands)	3 Mos	12/31/2015	12/31/2014	12/31/2013	12/31/2012	12/31/2011	12/31/2010	12/31/2009
Earnings Per Share	4.58	5.08	4.19	2.38	1.60	0.89	0.42	(0.91)
Cash Flow Per Share	7.53	6.26	5.43	4.33	3.40	0.67	1.07	4.32
Tang Book Value Per Share	19.63	18.97	14.28	13.72	11.46	10.21	9.82	10.26
Dividends Per Share	0.430	0.420	0.350	0.250	0.200	0.170	0.160	0.160
Dividend Payout %	9.39	8.27	8.35	10.53	12.54	19.21	37.65	...
Income Statement								
Total Revenue	1,187,900	6,392,700	6,170,000	4,365,300	3,811,900	3,075,100	2,189,100	2,575,200
EBITDA	273,500	1,586,800	1,385,600	904,700	772,800	614,200	486,800	135,400
Depn & Amortn	69,400	142,300	130,000	129,000	193,700	192,900	189,600	160,800
Income Before Taxes	159,500	1,252,000	1,064,100	590,500	385,900	237,500	116,500	(146,900)
Income Taxes	57,400	426,000	354,800	204,400	134,000	91,800	40,900	(9,400)
Net Income	97,200	796,500	678,200	375,500	255,200	142,200	67,400	(137,700)
Average Shares	148,300	152,200	156,700	153,000	155,000	155,600	154,000	152,800
Balance Sheet								
Current Assets	2,168,600	2,278,800	2,495,200	1,765,600	1,630,700	1,286,900	1,082,700	1,084,300
Total Assets	8,909,700	8,885,900	8,733,800	7,313,400	6,669,900	6,121,000	5,760,000	4,656,400
Current Liabilities	676,100	746,400	1,005,000	783,700	771,300	628,700	508,400	451,300
Long-Term Obligations	3,171,000	3,195,400	3,553,000	2,989,800	3,055,000	2,974,900	2,907,700	1,845,100
Total Liabilities	5,197,100	5,232,000	5,737,900	4,911,300	4,616,900	4,257,200	3,995,200	2,850,100
Stockholders' Equity	3,712,600	3,653,900	2,995,900	2,402,100	2,053,000	1,863,800	1,764,800	1,806,300
Shares Outstanding	150,700	152,900	155,600	154,800	158,200	160,400	159,600	158,400
Statistical Record								
Return on Assets %	8.09	9.04	8.45	5.37	3.98	2.39	1.29	N.M.
Return on Equity %	20.79	23.96	25.13	16.86	13.00	7.84	3.77	N.M.
EBITDA Margin %	23.02	24.82	22.46	20.72	20.27	19.97	22.24	5.26
Net Margin %	8.18	12.46	10.99	8.60	6.69	4.62	3.08	N.M.
Asset Turnover	0.68	0.73	0.77	0.62	0.59	0.52	0.42	0.54
Current Ratio	3.21	3.05	2.48	2.25	2.11	2.05	2.13	2.40
Debt to Equity	0.85	0.87	1.19	1.24	1.49	1.60	1.65	1.02
Price Range	36.80-15.64	36.80-22.37	50.30-26.57	28.32-17.65	18.02-10.93	18.88-9.97	13.34-7.61	9.72-3.23
P/E Ratio	8.03-3.41	7.24-4.40	12.00-6.34	11.90-7.41	11.27-6.83	21.21-11.20	31.76-18.12	...
Average Yield %	1.67	1.48	0.93	1.16	1.33	1.34	1.54	2.18

Address: 2525 N. Stemmons Freeway, Dallas, TX 75207-2401	Web Site: www.trin.net	Auditors: Ernst & Young LLP
Telephone: 214-631-4420	Officers: Timothy R. Wallace - Chairman, President, Chief Executive Officer William A. McWhirter - Senior Vice President, Chief Financial Officer, Group President	Investor Contact: 214-589-8909
Fax: 214-589-8501		Transfer Agents: American Stock Transfer & Trust Company

TRIUMPH GROUP INC.

Exchange	Symbol	Price	52Wk Range	Yield	P/E
NYS	TGI	$37.73 (5/31/2016)	68.78-23.53	0.42	N/A

*7 Year Price Score 68.72 *NYSE Composite Index=100 *12 Month Price Score 81.78

TRADING VOLUME (thousand shares)

Interim Earnings (Per Share)

Qtr.	Jun	Sep	Dec	Mar
2011-12	0.98	1.13	1.27	2.03
2012-13	1.46	1.53	1.43	1.24
2013-14	1.50	0.94	0.67	0.80
2014-15	2.46	1.32	(0.79)	1.64
2015-16	1.27	1.25	(1.80)	(22.01)

Interim Dividends (Per Share)

Amt	Decl	Ex	Rec	Pay
0.04Q	07/17/2015	08/28/2015	09/01/2015	09/15/2015
0.04Q	11/13/2015	11/27/2015	12/01/2015	12/15/2015
0.04Q	02/05/2016	02/26/2016	03/01/2016	03/15/2016
0.04Q	05/02/2016	05/26/2016	05/31/2016	06/15/2016

Indicated Div: $0.16

Valuation Analysis

		Institutional Holding	
Forecast EPS	$5.86	No of Institutions	
	(05/20/2016)	346	
Market Cap	$1.9 Billion	Shares	
Book Value	$934.9 Million	66,208,944	
Price/Book	1.99	% Held	
Price/Sales	0.48	88.63	

Business Summary: Aerospace (MIC: 7.1.1 SIC: 3724 NAIC: 336412)

Triumph Group designs, engineers, manufactures, repairs, overhauls and distributes aerostructures, aircraft components, accessories, subassemblies and systems. Co. realigns its segments into four units: Integrated Systems, which designs, develops and supports proprietary components, subsystems, systems, and produces complex assemblies; Aerospace Structures, which supplies commercial, business, regional and military manufacturers with metallic and composite structures; Precision Components, which produces close-tolerance parts, including aluminum, hard metal and composite structure capabilities; and Product Support, which provides solutions for commercial, regional and military aircraft.

Recent Developments: For the year ended Mar 31 2016, net loss amounted to US$1.05 billion versus net income of US$238.7 million in the prior year. Revenues were US$3.89 billion, unchanged from the year before. Operating loss was US$1.09 billion versus an income of US$434.7 million in the prior year. Direct operating expenses rose 14.5% to US$3.60 billion from US$3.14 billion in the comparable period the year before. Indirect operating expenses increased 341.4% to US$1.38 billion from US$312.6 million in the equivalent prior-year period.

Prospects: Our evaluation of Triumph Group Inc. as of June 19, 2016 is the result of our systematic analysis on three basic characteristics: earnings strength, relative valuation, and recent stock price movement. The company has generated a negative trend in earnings per share over the past 5 quarters. However, while recent estimates for the company have been mixed, TGI has posted results that fell short of analysts expectations. Based on operating earnings yield, the company is undervalued when compared to all of the companies in our coverage universe. Share price changes over the past year indicates that TGI will perform very poorly over the near term.

Financial Data

(US$ in Thousands)	03/31/2016	03/31/2015	03/31/2014	03/31/2013	03/31/2012	03/31/2011	03/31/2010	03/31/2009
Earnings Per Share	(21.29)	4.68	3.91	5.67	5.41	3.15	2.04	2.81
Cash Flow Per Share	1.70	9.20	2.61	6.46	4.65	3.16	5.15	4.12
Tang Book Value Per Share	N.M.	N.M.	N.M.	N.M.	N.M.	N.M.	8.36	6.38
Dividends Per Share	0.160	0.160	0.160	0.160	0.140	0.080	0.080	0.080
Dividend Payout %	...	3.42	4.09	2.82	2.59	2.54	3.93	2.85
Income Statement								
Total Revenue	3,886,072	3,888,722	3,763,254	3,702,702	3,407,929	2,905,348	1,294,780	1,240,378
EBITDA	(968,909)	543,020	517,557	625,061	600,526	382,927	195,035	191,330
Depn & Amortn	122,197	108,347	117,553	93,848	85,811	68,891	39,715	36,836
Income Before Taxes	(1,159,147)	349,294	312,233	463,057	437,577	234,477	126,455	143,398
Income Taxes	(111,187)	110,597	105,977	165,710	155,955	82,066	41,167	45,586
Net Income	(1,047,960)	238,697	206,256	297,347	280,857	149,899	67,762	93,067
Average Shares	49,218	51,005	52,787	52,446	51,873	47,488	33,332	33,168
Balance Sheet								
Current Assets	1,742,641	2,044,614	1,782,343	1,626,336	1,418,383	1,239,855	784,733	678,818
Total Assets	4,835,093	6,069,443	5,553,283	5,183,505	4,554,757	4,470,237	1,712,677	1,592,907
Current Liabilities	1,135,874	897,443	640,199	736,423	719,981	962,546	296,953	306,659
Long-Term Obligations	1,374,879	1,337,141	1,500,808	1,195,933	1,016,625	1,011,752	413,851	386,219
Total Liabilities	3,900,149	3,933,659	3,269,372	3,138,347	2,761,388	2,835,514	851,991	813,257
Stockholders' Equity	934,944	2,135,784	2,283,911	2,045,158	1,793,369	1,634,723	860,686	779,650
Shares Outstanding	49,328	49,273	52,159	50,123	49,531	48,513	33,346	33,179
Statistical Record								
Return on Assets %	N.M.	4.11	3.84	6.11	6.21	4.85	4.10	6.19
Return on Equity %	N.M.	10.80	9.53	15.49	16.34	12.01	8.26	12.64
EBITDA Margin %	N.M.	13.96	13.75	16.88	17.62	13.18	15.06	15.43
Net Margin %	N.M.	6.14	5.48	8.03	8.24	5.16	5.23	7.50
Asset Turnover	0.71	0.67	0.70	0.76	0.75	0.94	0.78	0.82
Current Ratio	1.53	2.28	2.78	2.21	1.97	1.29	2.64	2.21
Debt to Equity	1.47	0.63	0.66	0.58	0.57	0.62	0.48	0.50
Price Range	69.50-23.53	71.62-53.96	85.00-61.52	79.30-54.37	65.54-40.41	48.29-30.75	35.48-17.95	36.49-14.07
P/E Ratio	...	15.30-11.53	21.74-15.73	13.99-9.59	12.11-7.47	15.33-9.76	17.39-8.80	12.99-5.01
Average Yield %	0.34	0.25	0.22	0.25	0.27	0.20	0.34	0.34

Address: 899 Cassatt Road, Suite 210, Berwyn, PA 19312
Telephone: 610-251-1000

Web Site: www.triumphgroup.com
Officers: Daniel J. Crowley - President, Chief Executive Officer Jeffry D. Frisby - President, Chief Executive Officer, Chief Operating Officer

Auditors: Ernst & Young LLP
Investor Contact: 610-251-1000
Transfer Agents: Computershare, Inc., Canton, MA

TRANSDIGM GROUP INC

Exchange	Symbol	Price	52Wk Range	Yield	P/E
NYS	TDG	$263.54 (5/31/2016)	263.54-187.29	N/A	30.33

*7 Year Price Score 144.08 *NYSE Composite Index=100 *12 Month Price Score 102.95

TRADING VOLUME (thousand shares)

Interim Earnings (Per Share)

Qtr.	Dec	Mar	Jun	Sep
2012-13	0.66	1.25	0.71	(0.23)
2013-14	1.44	1.49	(1.66)	1.90
2014-15	1.63	1.96	1.75	2.50
2015-16	1.97	2.47	...	...

Interim Dividends (Per Share)

Amt	Decl	Ex	Rec	Pay
12.85U	10/15/2012	10/23/2012	10/25/2012	11/05/2012
22.00U	07/03/2013	07/11/2013	07/15/2013	07/25/2013
25.00U	06/04/2014	06/12/2014	06/16/2014	06/26/2014

Valuation Analysis / Institutional Holding

Forecast EPS	$11.23	No of Institutions	479
(05/20/2016)			
Market Cap	$14.0 Billion	Shares	61,544,784
Book Value	N/A	% Held	98.96
Price/Book	N/A		
Price/Sales	4.65		

Business Summary: Aerospace (MIC: 7.1.1 SIC: 3728 NAIC: 336412)

TransDigm Group is a holding company. Through its subsidiaries, Co. is a designer, producer and supplier of engineered aircraft components for use on commercial and military aircraft. Co.'s products include mechanical/electro-mechanical actuators and controls, ignition systems and engine technology, pumps and valves, power conditioning devices, electric motors and generators, NiCad batteries and chargers, engineered latching and locking devices, rods and locking devices, engineered connectors and elastomers, cockpit security components and systems, cockpit displays, aircraft audio systems, lavatory components, seatbelts and safety restraints, engineered interior surfaces and others.

Recent Developments: For the quarter ended Apr 2 2016, net income increased 25.0% to US$138.6 million from US$110.9 million in the year-earlier quarter. Revenues were US$796.8 million, up 28.7% from US$619.0 million the year before. Operating income was US$312.1 million versus US$256.6 million in the prior-year quarter, an increase of 21.6%. Direct operating expenses rose 33.8% to US$371.1 million from US$277.4 million in the comparable period the year before. Indirect operating expenses increased 33.5% to US$113.6 million from US$85.1 million in the equivalent prior-year period.

Prospects: Our evaluation of Transdigm Group Inc. as of June 19, 2016 is the result of our systematic analysis on three basic characteristics: earnings strength, relative valuation, and recent stock price movement. The company has managed to produce a neutral trend in earnings per share over the past 5 quarters. However, while recent estimates for the company have been mixed, TDG has posted better than expected results. Based on operating earnings yield, the company is about fairly valued when compared to all of the companies in our coverage universe. Share price changes over the past year indicates that TDG will perform in line with the market over the near term.

Financial Data
(US$ in Thousands)

	6 Mos	3 Mos	09/30/2015	09/30/2014	09/30/2013	09/30/2012	09/30/2011	09/30/2010
Earnings Per Share	8.69	8.18	7.84	3.16	2.39	5.97	3.17	2.52
Cash Flow Per Share	10.82	8.73	9.20	9.50	8.54	7.66	4.89	3.73
Dividends Per Share	...	...	...	25.000	34.850	...	...	7.650
Dividend Payout %	...	...	...	791.14	1,458.16	...	...	303.57
Income Statement								
Total Revenue	1,498,496	701,695	2,707,115	2,372,906	1,924,400	1,700,208	1,206,021	827,654
EBITDA	651,318	306,074	1,149,272	892,583	792,689	768,002	475,141	393,234
Depn & Amortn	63,201	30,033	93,663	96,385	73,515	68,227	60,460	30,165
Income Before Taxes	364,846	164,058	636,824	448,510	448,489	487,869	229,425	250,835
Income Taxes	111,317	49,157	189,612	141,600	145,700	162,900	77,200	87,390
Net Income	253,529	114,901	447,212	306,910	302,789	324,969	172,134	163,445
Average Shares	56,134	56,805	56,606	56,993	55,080	53,882	53,333	52,923
Balance Sheet								
Current Assets	1,758,000	1,860,775	1,831,962	1,689,576	1,320,495	1,050,531	870,292	583,508
Total Assets	8,359,474	8,329,978	8,427,050	6,756,848	6,148,879	5,459,617	4,513,636	2,677,818
Current Liabilities	675,996	656,442	658,215	585,907	322,500	233,915	206,859	113,012
Long-Term Obligations	8,091,934	8,099,159	8,183,502	7,233,836	5,700,193	3,598,625	3,122,875	1,771,646
Total Liabilities	9,321,292	9,294,248	9,465,356	8,312,947	6,485,260	4,240,783	3,702,687	2,084,839
Stockholders' Equity	(961,818)	(964,270)	(1,038,306)	(1,556,099)	(336,381)	1,218,834	810,949	592,979
Shares Outstanding	52,966	53,584	53,684	52,417	52,667	51,651	50,335	49,434
Statistical Record								
Return on Assets %	6.34	6.12	5.89	4.76	5.22	6.50	4.79	6.37
Return on Equity %	...	...	...	...	68.62	31.93	24.52	23.15
EBITDA Margin %	43.46	43.62	42.45	37.62	41.19	45.17	39.40	47.51
Net Margin %	16.92	16.37	16.52	12.93	15.73	19.11	14.27	19.75
Asset Turnover	0.38	0.37	0.36	0.37	0.33	0.34	0.34	0.32
Current Ratio	2.60	2.83	2.78	2.88	4.09	4.49	4.21	5.16
Debt to Equity	...	...	...	...	...	2.95	3.85	2.99
Price Range	244.35-187.29	244.35-196.45	244.35-171.82	197.00-137.86	162.48-125.52	145.61-77.38	93.94-61.00	63.56-39.18
P/E Ratio	28.12-21.55	29.87-24.02	31.17-21.92	62.34-43.63	67.98-52.52	24.39-12.96	29.63-19.24	25.22-15.55
Average Yield %	...	...	...	14.67	24.38	...	...	14.92

Address: 1301 East 9th Street, Suite 3000, Cleveland, OH 44114	**Web Site:** www.transdigm.com	**Auditors:** Ernst & Young LLP
Telephone: 216-706-2960	**Officers:** W. Nicholas Howley - Chairman, Chief Executive Officer Gregory Rufus - Senior Executive Vice President, Executive Vice President, Chief Financial Officer, Secretary	**Investor Contact:** 216-706-2945 **Transfer Agents:** Computershare, Providence, RI

TUPPERWARE BRANDS CORP

Exchange	Symbol	Price	52Wk Range	Yield	P/E
NYS	TUP	$56.58 (5/31/2016)	67.48-43.97	4.81	14.29

*7 Year Price Score 77.95 ***NYSE Composite Index=100** ***12 Month Price Score 102.14**

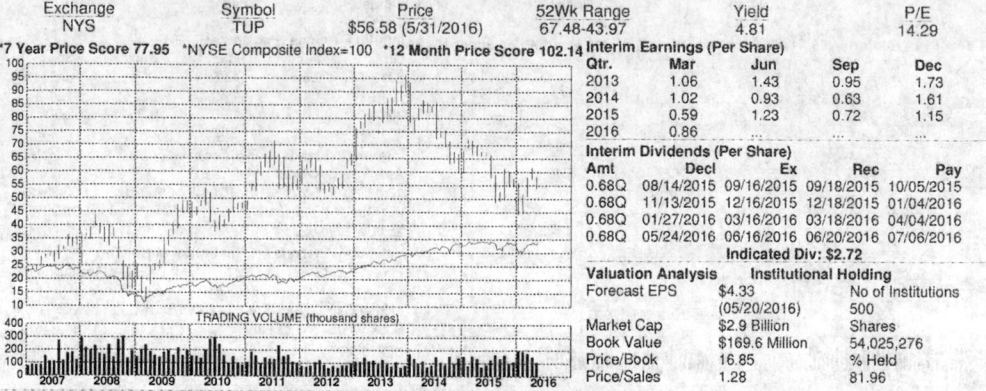

Interim Earnings (Per Share)

Qtr.	Mar	Jun	Sep	Dec
2013	1.06	1.43	0.95	1.73
2014	1.02	0.93	0.63	1.61
2015	0.59	1.23	0.72	1.15
2016	0.86	...	...	...

Interim Dividends (Per Share)

Amt	Decl	Ex	Rec	Pay
0.68Q	08/14/2015	09/16/2015	09/18/2015	10/05/2015
0.68Q	11/13/2015	12/16/2015	12/18/2015	01/04/2016
0.68Q	01/27/2016	03/16/2016	03/18/2016	04/04/2016
0.68Q	05/24/2016	06/16/2016	06/20/2016	07/06/2016

Indicated Div: $2.72

Valuation Analysis

		Institutional Holding	
Forecast EPS	$4.33	No of Institutions	
	(05/20/2016)	500	
Market Cap	$2.9 Billion	Shares	
Book Value	$169.6 Million	54,025,276	
Price/Book	16.85	% Held	
Price/Sales	1.28	81.96	

Business Summary: Plastics (MIC: 8.4.2 SIC: 3089 NAIC: 326199)

Tupperware Brands is engaged in the manufacture and sale of Tupperware® products and cosmetics and personal care products under a range of trade names, including Avroy Shlain®, BeautiControl®, Fuller®, NaturCare®, Nutrimetics® and Nuvo®. Each business manufactures and/or markets a line of products. Co. operates in three geographic regions: Europe (Europe, Africa and the Middle East), Asia Pacific and the Americas. The Tupperware product line consists of preparation, storage, and serving solutions for the kitchen and home. Co. also manufactures and distributes skin and hair care products, cosmetics, bath and body care, toiletries, fragrances, jewelry and nutritional products.

Recent Developments: For the quarter ended Mar 26 2016, net income increased 47.1% to US$43.4 million from US$29.5 million in the year-earlier quarter. Revenues were US$525.7 million, down 9.6% from US$581.8 million the year before. Operating income was US$70.0 million versus US$61.2 million in the prior-year quarter, an increase of 14.4%. Direct operating expenses declined 13.4% to US$166.0 million from US$191.6 million in the comparable period the year before. Indirect operating expenses decreased 11.9% to US$289.7 million from US$329.0 million in the equivalent prior-year period.

Prospects: Our evaluation of Tupperware Corp. as of June 19, 2016 is the result of our systematic analysis on three basic characteristics: earnings strength, relative valuation, and recent stock price movement. The company has produced a positive trend in earnings per share over the past 5 quarters. However, while recent estimates for the company have been lowered by analysts, TUP has posted better than expected results. Based on operating earnings yield, the company is undervalued when compared to all of the companies in our coverage universe. Share price changes over the past year indicates that TUP will perform poorly over the near term.

Financial Data
(US$ in Thousands)

	3 Mos	12/26/2015	12/27/2014	12/28/2013	12/29/2012	12/31/2011	12/25/2010	12/26/2009
Earnings Per Share	3.96	3.69	4.20	5.17	3.42	3.55	3.53	2.75
Cash Flow Per Share	4.56	4.54	5.65	6.25	5.42	4.50	4.80	4.03
Tang Book Value Per Share	N.M.	N.M.	N.M.	N.M.	2.64	1.68	5.19	2.93
Dividends Per Share	2.720	2.720	2.720	2.480	1.440	1.200	1.050	0.910
Dividend Payout %	68.69	73.71	64.76	47.97	42.11	33.80	29.75	33.09
Income Statement								
Total Revenue	525,700	2,283,800	2,606,100	2,671,600	2,583,800	2,585,000	2,300,400	2,127,500
EBITDA	69,700	357,300	393,400	448,000	352,800	388,000	372,300	312,400
Depn & Amortn	100	52,200	51,700	50,000	47,600	46,900	45,800	46,600
Income Before Taxes	58,200	259,900	298,200	360,400	272,800	295,300	299,700	237,100
Income Taxes	14,800	74,100	83,800	86,200	79,800	77,000	74,100	62,000
Net Income	43,400	185,800	214,400	274,200	193,000	218,300	225,600	175,100
Average Shares	50,600	50,400	51,000	53,100	56,400	61,400	63,800	63,400
Balance Sheet								
Current Assets	622,900	550,500	753,600	779,000	766,500	769,400	849,200	696,800
Total Assets	1,657,300	1,598,200	1,783,100	1,843,900	1,821,800	1,844,200	2,015,800	1,795,300
Current Liabilities	676,700	614,000	747,400	737,500	694,500	675,400	500,400	460,500
Long-Term Obligations	608,100	608,200	615,200	619,900	414,400	415,200	426,800	426,200
Total Liabilities	1,487,700	1,437,200	1,597,300	1,591,000	1,342,700	1,343,400	1,226,000	1,157,600
Stockholders' Equity	169,600	161,000	185,800	252,900	479,100	500,800	789,800	637,700
Shares Outstanding	50,501	50,436	49,682	50,324	54,059	56,507	62,706	63,054
Statistical Record								
Return on Assets %	11.78	11.02	11.85	15.00	10.56	11.13	11.87	9.73
Return on Equity %	119.30	107.45	98.01	75.12	39.50	33.28	31.69	31.59
EBITDA Margin %	13.26	15.64	15.10	16.77	13.65	15.01	16.18	14.68
Net Margin %	8.26	8.14	8.23	10.26	7.47	8.44	9.81	8.23
Asset Turnover	1.31	1.35	1.44	1.46	1.41	1.32	1.21	1.18
Current Ratio	0.92	0.90	1.01	1.06	1.10	1.14	1.70	1.51
Debt to Equity	3.59	3.78	3.31	2.45	0.86	0.83	0.54	0.67
Price Range	70.37-43.97	72.68-48.42	95.54-59.64	96.00-64.00	66.56-51.16	71.45-45.63	53.92-37.45	49.15-11.40
P/E Ratio	17.77-11.10	19.70-13.12	22.75-14.20	18.57-12.38	19.46-14.96	20.13-12.85	15.27-10.61	17.87-4.15
Average Yield %	4.69	4.40	3.53	3.01	2.47	2.05	2.34	3.00

Address: 14901 South Orange Blossom Trail, Orlando, FL 32837 **Telephone:** 407-826-5050	**Web Site:** www.tupperwarebrands.com **Officers:** E. V. Goings - Chairman, Chief Executive Officer Simon C. Hemus - President, Chief Operating Officer	**Auditors:** PricewaterhouseCoopers LLP **Investor Contact:** 407-826-4475 **Transfer Agents:** Wells Fargo Bank, N.A., South St. Paul, MN

TWITTER INC

Exchange	Symbol	Price	52Wk Range	Yield	P/E
NYS	TWTR	$15.22 (5/31/2016)	37.00-14.01	N/A	N/A

*7 Year Price Score N/A   *NYSE Composite Index=100   *12 Month Price Score 63.66

Interim Earnings (Per Share)

Qtr.	Mar	Jun	Sep	Dec
2013	(0.21)	(0.32)	(0.48)	(5.80)
2014	(0.23)	(0.24)	(0.29)	(0.20)
2015	(0.25)	(0.21)	(0.20)	(0.13)
2016	(0.12)	...	...	...

Interim Dividends (Per Share)

No Dividends Paid

Valuation Analysis		Institutional Holding	
Forecast EPS	$0.53	No of Institutions	
	(05/20/2016)	604	
Market Cap	$10.7 Billion	Shares	
Book Value	$4.5 Billion	308,963,072	
Price/Book	2.38	% Held	
Price/Sales	4.48	86.84	

Business Summary: Internet & Software (MIC: 6.3.2 SIC: 7371 NAIC: 541511)

Twitter provides products and services for users, advertisers, developers and platform and data partners. Co.'s products and services for users include Twitter, a platform for public self-expression and conversation and Vine, where users create and distribute their videos to their followers on Vine, with the option of tweeting them to their Twitter followers. Co.'s products and services for advertisers include Promoted Tweets, Promoted Accounts, and Promoted Trends. Co.'s products for platform partners and developers include a set of tools, public application program interfaces and embeddable widgets. Co.'s products for data partners include subscription access to its public data feed.

Recent Developments: For the quarter ended Mar 31 2016, net loss amounted to US$79.7 million versus a net loss of US$162.4 million in the year-earlier quarter. Revenues were US$594.5 million, up 36.4% from US$435.9 million the year before. Operating loss was US$59.1 million versus a loss of US$146.6 million in the prior-year quarter. Direct operating expenses rose 38.3% to US$198.4 million from US$143.5 million in the comparable period the year before. Indirect operating expenses increased 3.7% to US$455.2 million from US$439.1 million in the equivalent prior-year period.

Prospects: Our evaluation of Twitter Inc as of June 19, 2016 is the result of our systematic analysis on three basic characteristics: earnings strength, relative valuation, and recent stock price movement. The company has enjoyed a very positive trend in earnings per share over the past 5 quarters and while recent estimates for the company have remained steady, TWTR has posted better than expected results. Based on operating earnings yield, the company is overvalued when compared to all of the companies in our coverage universe. Share price changes over the past year indicates that TWTR will perform very poorly over the near term.

Financial Data
(US$ in Thousands)

	3 Mos	12/31/2015	12/31/2014	12/31/2013	12/31/2012	12/31/2011	12/31/2010
Earnings Per Share	(0.66)	(0.79)	(0.96)	(6.82)	(0.68)	(1.60)	(0.89)
Cash Flow Per Share	0.66	0.58	0.14	0.01	(0.24)	(0.69)	(0.64)
Tang Book Value Per Share	4.61	4.47	4.51	4.40	4.39	4.96	...
Income Statement							
Total Revenue	594,521	2,218,032	1,403,002	1,329,780	316,933	106,313	28,278
EBITDA	(34,440)	(177,927)	(372,766)	(1,091,056)	(22,884)	(109,441)	(64,696)
Depn & Amortn	18,370	257,200	171,600	188,800	53,800	19,500	2,900
Income Before Taxes	(77,703)	(533,305)	(578,351)	(1,294,292)	(79,170)	(129,746)	(67,541)
Income Taxes	2,028	(12,274)	(531)	(3,646)	229	(1,444)	(217)
Net Income	(79,731)	(521,031)	(577,820)	(1,290,646)	(79,399)	(128,302)	(67,324)
Average Shares	691,564	662,424	604,990	379,020	117,401	102,544	75,992
Balance Sheet							
Current Assets	4,388,909	4,381,792	4,255,853	5,149,358	554,466	596,068	...
Total Assets	6,476,168	6,442,439	5,583,082	6,732,480	831,568	720,675	...
Current Liabilities	422,765	506,039	393,794	450,860	109,879	47,744	...
Long-Term Obligations	1,520,991	1,514,790	1,494,970	221,040	65,732	21,104	...
Total Liabilities	1,998,682	2,074,392	1,956,679	832,468	207,204	87,391	...
Stockholders' Equity	4,477,486	4,368,047	3,626,403	5,900,012	624,364	633,284	...
Shares Outstanding	700,203	694,132	642,385	1,139,844	125,597	118,967	96,463
Statistical Record							
Asset Turnover	0.39	0.37	0.23	0.35	0.41	...	...
Current Ratio	10.38	8.66	10.81	11.42	5.05	12.48	...
Debt to Equity	0.34	0.35	0.41	0.04	0.11	0.03	...
Price Range	52.87-14.31	52.87-22.14	69.00-30.50	73.31-39.06	...	...	...

Address: 1355 Market Street, Suite 900, San Francisco, CA 94103
Telephone: 415-222-9670

Web Site: www.twitter.com
Officers: Omid R. Kordestani - Executive Chairman Jack Dorsey - Chairman, Chief Executive Officer, Interim Chief Executive Officer

Auditors: PricewaterhouseCoopers LLP
Transfer Agents: Computershare Trust Company, N.A., Canton, MA

TYLER TECHNOLOGIES, INC.

Exchange	Symbol	Price	52Wk Range	Yield	P/E
NYS	TYL	$153.29 (5/31/2016)	180.61-119.36	N/A	89.12

*7 Year Price Score 192.24 *NYSE Composite Index=100 *12 Month Price Score 96.00

Interim Earnings (Per Share)

Qtr.	Mar	Jun	Sep	Dec
2013	0.25	0.26	0.32	0.30
2014	0.33	0.42	0.48	0.43
2015	0.48	0.52	0.55	0.21
2016	0.44	...	...	...

Interim Dividends (Per Share)

No Dividends Paid

Valuation Analysis		Institutional Holding	
Forecast EPS	$3.41	No of Institutions	
	(05/20/2016)	361	
Market Cap	$5.5 Billion	Shares	
Book Value	$792.0 Million	37,783,856	
Price/Book	6.99	% Held	
Price/Sales	8.71	93.27	

Business Summary: Internet & Software (MIC: 6.3.2 SIC: 7372 NAIC: 511210)

Tyler Technologies provides integrated information management solutions and services for the public sector, with a focus on local governments. Co. has two segments. The Enterprise Software Solutions segment provides municipal and county governments and schools with software systems and services to meet their information technology and automation needs for functions such as financial management and courts and justice processes. The Appraisal and Tax Software Solutions and Services segment provides systems and software that automate the appraisal and assessment of real and personal property as well as property appraisal outsourcing services for local governments and taxing authorities.

Recent Developments: For the quarter ended Mar 31 2016, net income decreased 1.1% to US$17.1 million from US$17.3 million in the year-earlier quarter. Revenues were US$179.3 million, up 32.8% from US$135.0 million the year before. Operating income was US$28.0 million versus US$27.2 million in the prior-year quarter, an increase of 3.2%. Direct operating expenses rose 36.7% to US$97.2 million from US$71.1 million in the comparable period the year before. Indirect operating expenses increased 47.3% to US$54.1 million from US$36.7 million in the equivalent prior-year period.

Prospects: Our evaluation of Tyler Technologies Inc. as of June 19, 2016 is the result of our systematic analysis on three basic characteristics: earnings strength, relative valuation, and recent stock price movement. The company has generated a negative trend in earnings per share over the past 5 quarters. However, while recent estimates for the company have been mixed, TYL has posted results that were in line with analysts expectations. Based on operating earnings yield, the company is overvalued when compared to all of the companies in our coverage universe. Share price changes over the past year indicates that TYL will perform in line with the market over the near term.

Financial Data
(US$ in Thousands)

	3 Mos	12/31/2015	12/31/2014	12/31/2013	12/31/2012	12/31/2011	12/31/2010	12/31/2009
Earnings Per Share	1.72	1.77	1.66	1.13	1.00	0.83	0.71	0.74
Cash Flow Per Share	3.59	2.61	3.74	2.07	1.93	1.80	1.04	1.22
Tang Book Value Per Share	N.M.	N.M.	5.32	2.63	N.M.	N.M.	N.M.	0.35
Income Statement								
Total Revenue	179,293	591,022	493,101	416,643	363,304	309,391	288,628	290,286
EBITDA	30,936	123,429	106,913	76,736	63,747	52,744	48,224	51,743
Depn & Amortn	3,362	15,005	12,446	10,917	9,879	8,631	8,325	7,105
Income Before Taxes	27,574	108,424	94,467	65,819	53,868	44,113	39,899	44,638
Income Taxes	10,495	43,555	35,527	26,718	20,874	16,556	14,845	17,628
Net Income	17,079	64,869	58,940	39,101	32,994	27,557	25,054	27,010
Average Shares	38,557	36,552	35,401	34,590	32,916	33,154	35,528	36,624
Balance Sheet								
Current Assets	225,536	268,215	346,710	217,235	122,757	107,092	98,449	109,687
Total Assets	1,318,009	1,356,570	573,982	444,488	338,315	295,391	264,032	270,670
Current Liabilities	289,684	337,572	232,839	192,110	169,795	151,640	124,649	129,253
Long-Term Obligations	140,000	66,000	...	...	18,000	60,700	26,500	...
Total Liabilities	526,020	497,713	237,009	198,169	193,016	217,281	157,060	136,312
Stockholders' Equity	791,989	858,857	336,973	246,319	145,299	78,110	106,972	134,358
Shares Outstanding	36,104	36,774	33,469	32,838	31,331	29,971	32,293	35,120
Statistical Record								
Return on Assets %	6.86	6.72	11.57	9.99	...	9.85	9.37	10.34
Return on Equity %	11.17	10.85	20.21	19.97	...	29.78	20.76	21.73
EBITDA Margin %	17.25	20.88	21.68	18.42	17.55	17.05	16.71	17.82
Net Margin %	9.53	10.98	11.95	9.38	9.08	8.91	8.68	9.30
Asset Turnover	0.67	0.61	0.97	1.06	...	1.11	1.08	1.11
Current Ratio	0.78	0.79	1.49	1.13	0.72	0.71	0.79	0.85
Debt to Equity	0.18	0.08	...	...	0.12	0.78	0.25	...
Price Range	180.61-119.36	180.61-104.17	114.09-76.00	104.62-48.44	49.00-30.34	32.65-20.28	22.02-15.09	20.88-11.51
P/E Ratio	105.01-69.40	102.04-58.85	68.73-45.78	92.58-42.87	49.00-30.34	39.34-24.43	31.01-21.25	28.22-15.55

Address: 5101 Tennyson Parkway, Plano, TX 75024 Telephone: 972-713-3700	Web Site: www.tylertech.com Officers: John M. Yeaman - Chairman John S. Marr - President, Chief Executive Officer	Auditors: Ernst & Young LLP Investor Contact: 972-713-3720 Transfer Agents: American Stock Transfer & Company, New York, NY

TYSON FOODS, INC.

Exchange	Symbol	Price	52Wk Range	Yield	P/E
NYS	TSN	$63.78 (5/31/2016)	69.27-39.75	0.94	17.19

*7 Year Price Score 159.28 *NYSE Composite Index=100 *12 Month Price Score 125.44

Interim Earnings (Per Share)

Qtr.	Dec	Mar	Jun	Sep
2012-13	0.48	0.26	0.68	0.70
2013-14	0.72	0.60	0.73	0.32
2014-15	0.74	0.75	0.83	0.63
2015-16	1.15	1.10	...	...

Interim Dividends (Per Share)

Amt	Decl	Ex	Rec	Pay
0.15Q	08/04/2015	11/27/2015	12/01/2015	12/15/2015
0.15Q	11/19/2015	02/26/2016	03/01/2016	03/15/2016
0.15Q	02/04/2016	05/27/2016	06/01/2016	06/15/2016
0.15Q	05/05/2016	08/30/2016	09/01/2016	09/15/2016

Indicated Div: $0.60

Valuation Analysis | **Institutional Holding**

Forecast EPS	$4.31	No of Institutions
	(05/17/2016)	819
Market Cap	$23.6 Billion	Shares
Book Value	$9.8 Billion	303,272,512
Price/Book	2.41	% Held
Price/Sales	0.61	82.55

Business Summary: Food (MIC: 1.2.1 SIC: 2015 NAIC: 311615)

Tyson Foods is engaged as a producer of chicken, beef and pork as well as prepared foods. Co. has four segments: chicken, which includes raising and processing live chickens into fresh and frozen chicken products, as well as logistics operations; beef, which includes processing live fed cattle and fabricating dressed beef carcasses into primal and sub-primal meat cuts and case-ready products; pork, which includes processing live market hogs and fabricating pork carcasses into primal and sub-primal cuts and case-ready products; and prepared foods, which includes manufacturing and marketing frozen and refrigerated food products and logistics operations.

Recent Developments: For the quarter ended Apr 2 2016, net income increased 39.5% to US$434.0 million from US$311.0 million in the year-earlier quarter. Revenues were US$9.17 billion, down 8.1% from US$9.98 billion the year before. Operating income was US$704.0 million versus US$547.0 million in the prior-year quarter, an increase of 28.7%. Direct operating expenses declined 11.2% to US$7.99 billion from US$8.99 billion in the comparable period the year before. Indirect operating expenses increased 8.4% to US$479.0 million from US$442.0 million in the equivalent prior-year period.

Prospects: Our evaluation of Tyson Foods Inc. as of June 19, 2016 is the result of our systematic analysis on three basic characteristics: earnings strength, relative valuation, and recent stock price movement. The company has produced a positive trend in earnings per share over the past 5 quarters and while recent estimates for the company have been raised by analysts, TSN has posted better than expected results. Based on operating earnings yield, the company is undervalued when compared to all of the companies in our coverage universe. Share price changes over the past year indicates that TSN will perform very well over the near term.

Financial Data

(US$ in Thousands)	6 Mos	3 Mos	10/03/2015	09/27/2014	09/28/2013	09/29/2012	10/01/2011	10/02/2010
Earnings Per Share	3.71	3.36	2.95	2.37	2.12	1.58	1.97	2.06
Cash Flow Per Share	7.39	7.22	6.24	3.34	3.74	3.28	2.81	3.85
Tang Book Value Per Share	N.M.	N.M.	N.M.	N.M.	12.10	11.12	9.77	8.24
Dividends Per Share	0.500	0.450	0.400	0.300	0.300	0.160	0.160	0.160
Dividend Payout %	13.48	13.39	13.56	12.66	14.15	10.13	8.12	7.77
Income Statement								
Total Revenue	18,322,000	9,152,000	41,373,000	37,580,000	34,374,000	33,278,000	32,266,000	28,430,000
EBITDA	1,832,000	949,000	2,814,000	1,871,000	1,869,000	1,714,000	1,738,000	1,952,000
Depn & Amortn	348,000	172,000	609,000	494,000	474,000	443,000	433,000	416,000
Income Before Taxes	1,356,000	712,000	1,921,000	1,252,000	1,257,000	927,000	1,074,000	1,203,000
Income Taxes	461,000	251,000	697,000	396,000	409,000	351,000	341,000	438,000
Net Income	893,000	461,000	1,220,000	864,000	778,000	583,000	750,000	780,000
Average Shares	393,000	400,000	413,000	364,000	367,000	370,000	380,000	379,000
Balance Sheet								
Current Assets	4,927,000	5,677,000	5,381,000	6,221,000	5,604,000	5,403,000	4,780,000	4,618,000
Total Assets	22,511,000	23,290,000	23,004,000	23,956,000	12,177,000	11,896,000	11,071,000	10,752,000
Current Liabilities	2,610,000	3,668,000	3,535,000	3,797,000	3,010,000	2,830,000	2,374,000	2,545,000
Long-Term Obligations	6,270,000	5,988,000	6,010,000	7,535,000	1,895,000	1,917,000	2,112,000	2,135,000
Total Liabilities	12,720,000	13,528,000	13,313,000	15,066,000	5,976,000	5,884,000	5,414,000	5,586,000
Stockholders' Equity	9,791,000	9,762,000	9,691,000	8,890,000	6,201,000	6,012,000	5,657,000	5,166,000
Shares Outstanding	370,000	363,000	369,000	376,000	344,000	359,000	370,000	377,000
Statistical Record								
Return on Assets %	6.49	5.83	5.11	4.80	6.48	5.09	6.89	7.33
Return on Equity %	15.61	14.53	12.92	11.48	12.78	10.02	13.90	16.44
EBITDA Margin %	10.00	10.37	6.80	4.98	5.44	5.15	5.39	6.87
Net Margin %	4.87	5.04	2.95	2.30	2.26	1.75	2.32	2.74
Asset Turnover	1.69	1.69	1.73	2.09	2.86	2.91	2.97	2.67
Current Ratio	1.89	1.55	1.52	1.64	1.86	1.91	2.01	1.81
Debt to Equity	0.64	0.61	0.62	0.85	0.31	0.32	0.37	0.41
Price Range	68.09-38.11	53.95-37.42	45.01-37.12	44.01-27.56	31.83-16.02	20.91-14.17	19.92-14.84	20.40-12.02
P/E Ratio	18.35-10.27	16.06-11.14	15.26-12.58	18.57-11.63	15.01-7.56	13.23-8.97	10.11-7.53	9.90-5.83
Average Yield %	1.04	1.05	0.97	0.82	1.27	0.87	0.91	1.00

Address: 2200 West Don Tyson Parkway, Springdale, AR 72762-6999
Telephone: 479-290-4000
Fax: 479-290-7984

Web Site: www.tyson.com
Officers: John Tyson - Chairman Tom Hayes - President

Auditors: PricewaterhouseCoopers LLP
Investor Contact: 479-290-4235
Transfer Agents: Computershare, Inc., Providence , RI

UDR INC

Exchange	Symbol	Price	52Wk Range	Yield	P/E
NYS	UDR	$36.03 (5/31/2016)	38.56-31.14	3.28	34.31

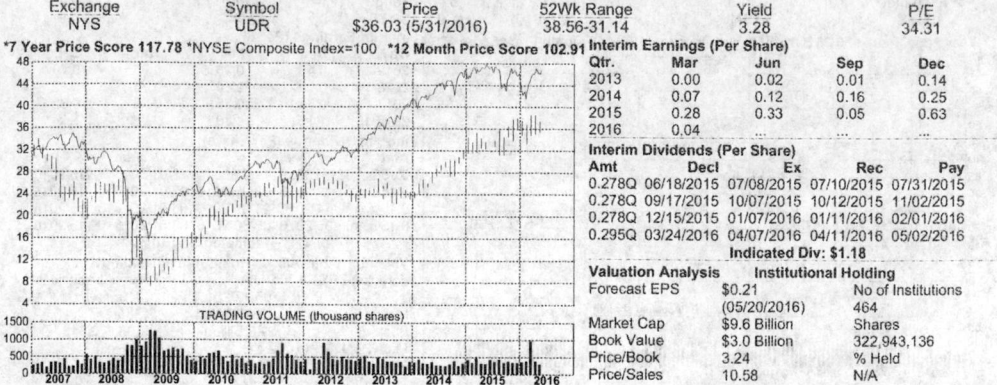

*7 Year Price Score 117.78 *NYSE Composite Index=100 *12 Month Price Score 102.91

Interim Earnings (Per Share)

Qtr.	Mar	Jun	Sep	Dec
2013	0.00	0.02	0.01	0.14
2014	0.07	0.12	0.16	0.25
2015	0.28	0.33	0.05	0.63
2016	0.04	...	...	...

Interim Dividends (Per Share)

Amt	Decl	Ex	Rec	Pay
0.278Q	06/18/2015	07/08/2015	07/10/2015	07/31/2015
0.278Q	09/17/2015	10/07/2015	10/12/2015	11/02/2015
0.278Q	12/15/2015	01/07/2016	01/11/2016	02/01/2016
0.295Q	03/24/2016	04/07/2016	04/11/2016	05/02/2016

Indicated Div: $1.18

Valuation Analysis | **Institutional Holding**

Forecast EPS	$0.21 (05/20/2016)	No of Institutions	464
Market Cap	$9.6 Billion	Shares	322,943,136
Book Value	$3.0 Billion	% Held	N/A
Price/Book	3.24		
Price/Sales	10.58		

TRADING VOLUME (thousand shares)

Business Summary: REITs (MIC: 5.3.1 SIC: 6798 NAIC: 525930)

UDR is a real estate investment trust that owns, operates, acquires, renovates, develops, redevelops, and manages multifamily apartment communities generally located in markets located throughout the U.S. Co. reports in two segments: Same-Store Communities and Non-Mature Communities/Other. As of Dec 31 2015, Co.'s consolidated real estate portfolio included 133 communities located in 18 markets, with a total of 40,728 completed apartment homes, which are held through its subsidiaries. In addition, Co. has an ownership interest in 28 communities containing 6,696 apartment homes through unconsolidated joint ventures or partnerships.

Recent Developments: For the quarter ended Mar 31 2016, income from continuing operations decreased 88.8% to US$8.5 million from US$76.4 million in the year-earlier quarter. Net income decreased 84.8% to US$11.6 million from US$76.4 million in the year-earlier quarter. Revenues were US$234.8 million, up 6.9% from US$219.8 million the year before. Revenues from property income rose 12.0% to US$232.0 million from US$207.0 million in the corresponding quarter a year earlier.

Prospects: Our evaluation of UDR Inc. as of June 19, 2016 is the result of our systematic analysis on three basic characteristics: earnings strength, relative valuation, and recent stock price movement. The company has enjoyed a very positive trend in earnings per share over the past 5 quarters. Because the company lacks sufficient analyst estimate data, we place greater weight on the historical EPS trend as the measure of earnings strength. Based on operating earnings yield, the company is overvalued when compared to all of the companies in our coverage universe. Share price changes over the past year indicates that UDR will perform very well over the near term.

Financial Data

(US$ in Thousands)	3 Mos	12/31/2015	12/31/2014	12/31/2013	12/31/2012	12/31/2011	12/31/2010	12/31/2009
Earnings Per Share	1.05	1.29	0.59	0.16	0.85	0.05	(0.68)	(0.64)
Cash Flow Per Share	1.71	1.67	1.56	1.36	1.32	1.21	1.29	1.54
Tang Book Value Per Share	10.95	14.51	11.65	11.90	12.67	11.03	8.73	8.76
Dividends Per Share	1.110	1.093	1.015	0.925	0.875	0.770	0.725	0.665
Dividend Payout %	105.71	84.69	172.03	578.13	102.94	1,540.00	...	...
Income Statement								
Total Revenue	234,815	894,638	818,046	758,926	729,363	708,685	646,596	617,173
EBITDA	42,004	558,885	490,693	465,151	472,016	440,799	374,670	373,674
Depn & Amortn	3,879	399,294	363,929	348,231	367,404	393,862	332,187	303,393
Income Before Taxes	7,452	39,267	8,168	(4,544)	(34,457)	(104,207)	(103,579)	(71,099)
Income Taxes	(403)	(3,886)	(15,098)	(7,299)	...	...	...	...
Net Income	10,393	340,383	154,334	44,812	212,177	20,023	(102,899)	(87,532)
Average Shares	264,285	263,752	253,445	249,969	238,851	201,294	165,857	149,090
Balance Sheet								
Current Assets	24,698	27,540	37,564	53,045	35,676	37,137	28,799	52,514
Total Assets	7,601,568	7,663,844	6,846,534	6,807,722	6,888,509	6,721,354	5,529,540	5,132,617
Current Liabilities	245,370	246,002	244,999	253,918	261,926	247,725	232,949	208,288
Long-Term Obligations	3,411,825	3,570,795	3,583,105	3,523,703	3,409,333	3,918,370	3,567,504	3,426,589
Total Liabilities	4,628,701	3,817,653	3,828,957	3,778,477	3,672,175	4,170,829	3,804,140	3,638,418
Stockholders' Equity	2,972,867	3,846,191	3,017,577	3,029,245	3,216,334	2,550,525	1,725,400	1,494,199
Shares Outstanding	267,137	261,844	255,114	250,749	250,139	219,650	182,496	155,465
Statistical Record								
Return on Assets %	3.83	4.69	2.26	0.65	3.11	0.33	N.M.	N.M.
Return on Equity %	9.58	9.92	5.10	1.43	7.34	0.94	N.M.	N.M.
EBITDA Margin %	17.89	62.47	59.98	61.29	64.72	62.20	57.94	60.55
Net Margin %	4.43	38.05	18.87	5.90	29.09	2.83	N.M.	N.M.
Asset Turnover	0.13	0.12	0.12	0.11	0.11	0.12	0.12	0.12
Current Ratio	0.10	0.11	0.15	0.21	0.14	0.15	0.12	0.25
Debt to Equity	1.15	0.93	1.19	1.16	1.06	1.54	2.07	2.29
Price Range	38.53-31.14	37.89-30.82	31.74-23.27	26.82-22.24	27.06-22.51	27.14-20.77	24.05-14.70	16.98-7.10
P/E Ratio	36.70-29.66	29.37-23.89	53.80-39.44	167.63-139.00	31.84-26.48	542.80-415.40	...	...
Average Yield %	3.22	3.24	3.66	3.80	3.47	3.17	3.65	5.58

Address: 1745 Shea Center Drive, Suite 200, Highlands Ranch, CO 80129 **Telephone:** 720-283-6120	**Web Site:** www.udrt.com **Officers:** Robert C. Larson - Chairman James D. Klingbeil - Vice-Chairman	**Auditors:** Ernst & Young LLP **Investor Contact:** 720-348-7762 **Transfer Agents:** Wells Fargo Shareowner Services, Saint Paul, MN

UGI CORP.

Exchange	Symbol	Price	52Wk Range	Yield	P/E	Div Achiever
NYS	UGI	$42.92 (5/31/2016)	43.43-31.67	2.21	21.68	28 Years

*7 Year Price Score 121.61 *NYSE Composite Index=100 *12 Month Price Score 111.89

Interim Earnings (Per Share)

Qtr.	Dec	Mar	Jun	Sep
2012-13	0.60	0.99	0.09	(0.07)
2013-14	0.70	1.23	0.12	(0.12)
2014-15	0.19	1.40	0.05	(0.05)
2015-16	0.65	1.33	...	...

Interim Dividends (Per Share)

Amt	Decl	Ex	Rec	Pay
0.228Q	07/28/2015	09/11/2015	09/15/2015	10/01/2015
0.228Q	11/20/2015	12/15/2015	12/15/2015	01/01/2016
0.228Q	01/28/2016	03/11/2016	03/15/2016	04/01/2016
0.237Q	04/28/2016	06/13/2016	06/15/2016	07/01/2016

Indicated Div: $0.95 (Div. Reinv. Plan)

Valuation Analysis | **Institutional Holding**

Forecast EPS	$1.97
	(05/20/2016)
No of Institutions	531
Market Cap	$7.4 Billion
Shares	
Book Value	$2.9 Billion
148,863,520	
Price/Book	2.52
% Held	
Price/Sales	1.28
76.10	

Business Summary: Gas Utilities (MIC: 3.3.1 SIC: 4932 NAIC: 221210)

UGI is a holding company. Through its subsidiaries, Co. provides energy products and related services. Co. is a distributor of propane and butane (which are liquefied petroleum gases); a provider of natural gas and electric service through regulated local distribution utilities; a generator of electricity; a marketer of energy commodities; an owner and manager of midstream assets; and a provider of heating, ventilation, air conditioning, refrigeration, and electrical contracting services. Co.'s subsidiaries and affiliates operate in six segments: AmeriGas Propane, UGI International - UGI France, UGI International - Flaga and Other, Energy Services, Electric Generation, and Gas Utility.

Recent Developments: For the quarter ended Mar 31 2016, net income decreased 15.4% to US$408.0 million from US$482.2 million in the year-earlier quarter. Revenues were US$1.97 billion, down 19.7% from US$2.46 billion the year before. Operating income was US$615.4 million versus US$702.1 million in the prior-year quarter, a decrease of 12.3%. Direct operating expenses declined 35.5% to US$776.9 million from US$1.21 billion in the comparable period the year before. Indirect operating expenses increased 5.8% to US$579.8 million from US$548.1 million in the equivalent prior-year period.

Prospects: Our evaluation of UGI Corp. as of June 19, 2016 is the result of our systematic analysis on three basic characteristics: earnings strength, relative valuation, and recent stock price movement. The company has managed to produce a neutral trend in earnings per share over the past 5 quarters. However, while recent estimates for the company have been lowered by analysts, UGI has posted results that fell short of analysts expectations. Based on operating earnings yield, the company is about fairly valued when compared to all of the companies in our coverage universe. Share price changes over the past year indicates that UGI will perform well over the near term.

Financial Data
(US$ in Thousands)

	6 Mos	3 Mos	09/30/2015	09/30/2014	09/30/2013	09/30/2012	09/30/2011	09/30/2010
Earnings Per Share	1.98	2.05	1.60	1.92	1.61	1.17	1.37	1.57
Cash Flow Per Share	6.51	7.36	6.72	5.82	4.69	4.18	3.31	3.64
Tang Book Value Per Share	N.M.	N.M.	N.M.	N.M.	N.M.	N.M.	1.60	0.67
Dividends Per Share	0.910	0.900	0.890	0.791	0.737	0.707	0.680	0.600
Dividend Payout %	45.96	43.90	55.63	41.19	45.85	60.23	49.52	38.14
Income Statement								
Total Revenue	3,578,700	1,606,600	6,691,100	8,277,300	7,194,700	6,519,200	6,091,300	5,591,400
EBITDA	1,098,200	395,000	1,148,500	1,307,700	1,130,300	769,800	776,800	843,900
Depn & Amortn	169,100	85,700	313,200	305,700	301,400	264,200	201,200	187,600
Income Before Taxes	813,900	251,400	594,200	767,900	590,800	286,500	439,900	525,400
Income Taxes	237,900	83,400	179,000	235,200	162,800	99,600	130,800	167,600
Net Income	347,800	114,600	281,000	337,200	278,100	199,400	232,900	261,000
Average Shares	174,845	175,218	175,667	175,231	173,281	170,148	169,416	165,766
Balance Sheet								
Current Assets	1,707,000	1,674,000	1,459,800	1,663,000	1,627,300	1,504,500	1,306,100	1,220,100
Total Assets	10,955,400	10,780,400	10,546,600	10,093,000	10,008,800	9,709,700	6,663,300	6,374,300
Current Liabilities	1,466,700	1,911,700	1,678,900	1,430,900	1,424,900	1,487,000	1,077,900	1,674,700
Long-Term Obligations	3,630,500	3,422,400	3,441,800	3,433,600	3,542,200	3,347,600	2,110,300	1,432,200
Total Liabilities	8,015,200	8,061,000	7,854,600	7,433,900	7,516,300	7,476,600	4,685,600	4,549,800
Stockholders' Equity	2,940,200	2,719,400	2,692,000	2,659,100	2,492,500	2,233,100	1,977,700	1,824,500
Shares Outstanding	172,680	173,825	172,388	172,273	171,643	168,930	167,754	165,560
Statistical Record								
Return on Assets %	3.29	3.41	2.72	3.35	2.82	2.43	3.57	4.20
Return on Equity %	12.13	13.47	10.50	13.09	11.77	9.45	12.25	15.28
EBITDA Margin %	30.69	24.59	17.16	15.80	15.71	11.81	12.75	15.09
Net Margin %	9.72	7.13	4.20	4.07	3.87	3.06	3.82	4.67
Asset Turnover	0.55	0.59	0.65	0.82	0.73	0.79	0.93	0.90
Current Ratio	1.16	0.88	0.87	1.16	1.14	1.01	1.21	0.73
Debt to Equity	1.23	1.26	1.28	1.29	1.42	1.50	1.07	0.78
Price Range	40.58-31.67	38.57-31.67	39.60-31.78	36.33-25.50	28.69-20.33	21.17-16.59	22.20-17.29	19.19-15.57
P/E Ratio	20.49-15.99	18.81-15.45	24.75-19.86	18.92-13.28	17.82-12.63	18.09-14.18	16.20-12.62	12.23-9.92
Average Yield %	2.58	2.57	2.50	2.61	2.99	3.68	3.30	3.48

Address: 460 North Gulph Road, King of Prussia, PA 19406
Telephone: 610-337-1000

Web Site: www.ugicorp.com
Officers: Marvin O. Schlanger - Chairman John L. Walsh - President, Chief Executive Officer, Chief Operating Officer

Auditors: Ernst & Young LLP
Investor Contact: 610-337-1000
Transfer Agents: ComputerShare Investor Services, Providence, RI

UNDER ARMOUR INC

Exchange	Symbol	Price	52Wk Range	Yield	P/E
NYS	UA	$37.73 (5/31/2016)	53.78-34.67	N/A	69.87

*7 Year Price Score 194.07 *NYSE Composite Index=100 *12 Month Price Score 93.02

TRADING VOLUME (thousand shares)

Interim Earnings (Per Share)

Qtr.	Mar	Jun	Sep	Dec
2013	0.02	0.04	0.17	0.15
2014	0.03	0.04	0.20	0.20
2015	0.03	0.04	0.23	0.23
2016	0.04	...	...	...

Interim Dividends (Per Share)

Amt	Decl	Ex	Rec	Pay
100%	06/11/2012	07/10/2012	06/25/2012	07/09/2012
100%	03/17/2014	04/15/2014	03/28/2014	04/14/2014
0.00U	03/16/2016	04/08/2016	03/28/2016	04/07/2016

Valuation Analysis   Institutional Holding

Forecast EPS	$0.58	No of Institutions
	(05/20/2016)	787
Market Cap	$16.4 Billion	Shares
Book Value	$1.7 Billion	158,245,872
Price/Book	9.43	% Held
Price/Sales	3.90	79.40

Business Summary: Apparel, Footwear & Accessories (MIC: 1.4.2 SIC: 5136 NAIC: 448110)

Under Armour is engaged in the development, marketing and distribution of apparel, footwear and accessories for men, women and youth. Co.'s apparel is provided in a range of styles and fits. Co. markets its apparel for consumers to choose HEATGEAR® when it is hot, COLDGEAR® when it is cold and ALLSEASONGEAR® between the extremes. Co.'s footwear offerings include football, baseball, lacrosse, softball and soccer cleats, slides and performance training, running, basketball and outdoor footwear. Co.'s accessories primarily include the sale of headwear, bags and gloves. Co. also has agreements with its licensees to develop Under Armour apparel and accessories.

Recent Developments: For the quarter ended Mar 31 2016, net income increased 63.5% to US$19.2 million from US$11.7 million in the year-earlier quarter. Revenues were US$1.05 billion, up 30.2% from US$804.9 million the year before. Operating income was US$34.9 million versus US$27.7 million in the prior-year quarter, an increase of 26.1%. Direct operating expenses rose 32.7% to US$567.1 million from US$427.3 million in the comparable period the year before. Indirect operating expenses increased 27.4% to US$445.8 million from US$350.0 million in the equivalent prior-year period.

Prospects: Our evaluation of Under Armour Inc. as of June 19, 2016 is the result of our systematic analysis on three basic characteristics: earnings strength, relative valuation, and recent stock price movement. The company has generated a negative trend in earnings per share over the past 5 quarters. However, while recent estimates for the company have been lowered by analysts, UA has posted better than expected results. Based on operating earnings yield, the company is overvalued when compared to all of the companies in our coverage universe. Share price changes over the past year indicates that UA will perform well over the near term.

Financial Data
(US$ in Thousands)

	3 Mos	12/31/2015	12/31/2014	12/31/2013	12/31/2012	12/31/2011	12/31/2010	12/31/2009
Earnings Per Share	0.54	0.53	0.47	0.38	0.30	0.23	0.17	0.12
Cash Flow Per Share	(0.08)	(0.10)	0.51	0.28	0.48	0.04	0.12	0.30
Tang Book Value Per Share	2.48	2.33	2.81	2.14	1.94	1.52	1.20	0.98
Income Statement								
Total Revenue	1,047,702	3,963,313	3,084,370	2,332,051	1,834,921	1,472,684	1,063,927	856,411
EBITDA	69,606	488,413	411,145	312,226	248,422	193,403	139,877	110,062
Depn & Amortn	32,021	87,100	63,600	48,300	39,800	32,700	28,700	25,300
Income Before Taxes	33,053	386,685	342,210	260,993	203,439	156,862	108,919	82,418
Income Taxes	13,873	154,112	134,168	98,663	74,661	59,943	40,442	35,633
Net Income	19,180	232,573	208,042	162,330	128,778	96,919	68,477	46,785
Average Shares	443,260	441,736	438,760	431,916	425,520	420,208	410,256	405,200
Balance Sheet								
Current Assets	1,768,783	1,498,763	1,549,399	1,128,811	903,598	689,663	555,850	448,000
Total Assets	3,218,124	2,868,900	2,095,083	1,577,741	1,157,083	919,210	675,378	545,588
Current Liabilities	605,900	478,810	421,627	426,630	252,228	183,607	149,147	120,162
Long-Term Obligations	767,525	627,000	255,250	47,951	52,757	70,842	9,077	10,948
Total Liabilities	1,476,807	1,200,678	744,783	524,387	340,161	282,778	178,412	145,591
Stockholders' Equity	1,741,317	1,668,222	1,350,300	1,053,354	816,922	636,432	496,966	399,997
Shares Outstanding	435,182	432,192	427,791	423,257	419,044	413,969	409,282	401,981
Statistical Record								
Return on Assets %	8.33	9.37	11.33	11.87	12.37	12.16	11.22	9.06
Return on Equity %	15.36	15.41	17.31	17.36	17.67	17.10	15.27	12.80
EBITDA Margin %	6.64	12.32	13.33	13.39	13.54	13.13	13.15	12.85
Net Margin %	1.83	5.87	6.75	6.96	7.02	6.58	6.44	5.46
Asset Turnover	1.46	1.60	1.68	1.71	1.76	1.85	1.74	1.66
Current Ratio	2.92	3.13	3.67	2.65	3.58	3.76	3.73	3.73
Debt to Equity	0.44	0.38	0.19	0.05	0.06	0.11	0.02	0.03
Price Range	53.78-34.67	53.78-33.17	37.55-21.18	22.55-11.85	15.51-9.32	11.11-6.82	7.75-3.09	4.27-1.59
P/E Ratio	99.58-64.20	101.46-62.59	79.89-45.06	59.34-31.17	51.68-31.07	48.29-29.64	45.59-18.19	35.61-13.27

Address: 1020 Hull Street, Baltimore, MD 21230 **Telephone:** 410-454-6428	**Web Site:** www.underarmour.com **Officers:** Kevin A. Plank - Chairman, President, Chief Executive Officer William J. Kraus - Senior Vice President	**Auditors:** PricewaterhouseCoopers LLP **Transfer Agents:** American Stock Transfer & Trust Company, New York, NY

UNION PACIFIC CORP

Exchange	Symbol	Price	52Wk Range	Yield	P/E
NYS	UNP	$84.19 (5/31/2016)	102.31-68.79	2.61	15.74

*7 Year Price Score 108.78 *NYSE Composite Index=100 *12 Month Price Score 97.03

Interim Earnings (Per Share)

Qtr.	Mar	Jun	Sep	Dec
2013	1.01	1.19	1.24	1.27
2014	1.19	1.43	1.53	1.61
2015	1.30	1.38	1.50	1.31
2016	1.16	...	...	...

Interim Dividends (Per Share)

Amt	Decl	Ex	Rec	Pay
0.55Q	07/30/2015	08/27/2015	08/31/2015	09/30/2015
0.55Q	11/19/2015	11/25/2015	11/30/2015	12/30/2015
0.55Q	02/04/2016	02/25/2016	02/29/2016	03/31/2016
0.55Q	05/12/2016	05/26/2016	05/31/2016	06/30/2016

Indicated Div: $2.20

Valuation Analysis

Forecast EPS	$5.15 (05/20/2016)
Market Cap	$70.8 Billion
Book Value	$20.5 Billion
Price/Book	3.46
Price/Sales	3.37

Institutional Holding

No of Institutions	1806
Shares	725,439,936
% Held	79.90

TRADING VOLUME (thousand shares)

Business Summary: Rail (MIC: 7.4.3 SIC: 4011 NAIC: 482111)

Union Pacific, through its operating subsidiary, Union Pacific Railroad Company, is a Class I railroad operating in the U.S. As of Dec 31 2015, Co.'s network included 32,084 route miles, linking Pacific Coast and Gulf Coast ports with the Midwest and eastern U.S. gateways and providing several corridors to key Mexican gateways. Co. serves the Western two-thirds of the country and maintains coordinated schedules with other rail carriers to move freight to and from the Atlantic Coast, the Pacific Coast, the Southeast, the Southwest, Canada, and Mexico. Co.'s freight traffic consists of bulk, manifest, and premium business.

Recent Developments: For the quarter ended Mar 31 2016, net income decreased 14.9% to US$979.0 million from US$1.15 billion in the year-earlier quarter. Revenues were US$4.83 billion, down 14.0% from US$5.61 billion the year before. Operating income was US$1.69 billion versus US$1.98 billion in the prior-year quarter, a decrease of 14.7%. Direct operating expenses declined 16.4% to US$1.68 billion from US$2.01 billion in the comparable period the year before. Indirect operating expenses decreased 10.2% to US$1.46 billion from US$1.63 billion in the equivalent prior-year period.

Prospects: Our evaluation of Union Pacific Corp. as of June 19, 2016 is the result of our systematic analysis on three basic characteristics: earnings strength, relative valuation, and recent stock price movement. The company has managed to produce a neutral trend in earnings per share over the past 5 quarters. However, while recent estimates for the company have been lowered by analysts, UNP has posted better than expected results. Based on operating earnings yield, the company is undervalued when compared to all of the companies in our coverage universe. Share price changes over the past year indicates that UNP will perform poorly over the near term.

Financial Data

(US$ in Thousands)	3 Mos	12/31/2015	12/31/2014	12/31/2013	12/31/2012	12/31/2011	12/31/2010	12/31/2009
Earnings Per Share	5.35	5.49	5.75	4.71	4.13	3.36	2.77	1.88
Cash Flow Per Share	8.83	8.48	8.23	7.36	6.49	6.05	4.12	3.21
Tang Book Value Per Share	24.35	24.38	23.99	23.27	21.17	19.35	18.07	16.77
Dividends Per Share	2.200	2.200	1.910	1.480	1.245	0.965	0.655	0.540
Dividend Payout %	41.12	40.07	33.22	31.42	30.11	28.72	23.69	28.80
Income Statement								
Total Revenue	4,829,000	21,813,000	23,988,000	21,963,000	20,926,000	19,557,000	16,965,000	14,143,000
EBITDA	2,233,000	10,285,000	10,804,000	9,347,000	8,610,000	7,450,000	6,518,000	5,026,000
Depn & Amortn	502,000	2,012,000	1,904,000	1,777,000	1,760,000	1,617,000	1,487,000	1,444,000
Income Before Taxes	1,566,000	7,656,000	8,343,000	7,048,000	6,318,000	5,264,000	4,433,000	2,987,000
Income Taxes	587,000	2,884,000	3,163,000	2,660,000	2,375,000	1,972,000	1,653,000	1,089,000
Net Income	979,000	4,772,000	5,180,000	4,388,000	3,943,000	3,292,000	2,780,000	1,898,000
Average Shares	846,700	869,400	901,100	931,600	953,000	979,600	1,005,800	1,011,600
Balance Sheet								
Current Assets	5,083,000	4,130,000	4,679,000	3,990,000	3,614,000	3,727,000	3,432,000	3,680,000
Total Assets	55,772,000	54,600,000	52,716,000	49,731,000	47,153,000	45,096,000	43,088,000	42,410,000
Current Liabilities	3,287,000	3,206,000	3,765,000	3,791,000	3,119,000	3,317,000	2,952,000	2,682,000
Long-Term Obligations	14,791,000	13,607,000	11,018,000	8,872,000	8,801,000	8,697,000	9,003,000	9,636,000
Total Liabilities	35,297,000	33,898,000	31,527,000	28,506,000	27,276,000	26,518,000	25,325,000	25,469,000
Stockholders' Equity	20,475,000	20,702,000	21,189,000	21,225,000	19,877,000	18,578,000	17,763,000	16,941,000
Shares Outstanding	840,938	849,211	883,366	912,001	938,930	959,859	983,131	1,010,079
Statistical Record								
Return on Assets %	8.45	8.89	10.11	9.06	8.53	7.47	6.50	4.62
Return on Equity %	22.15	22.78	24.43	21.35	20.45	18.12	16.02	11.72
EBITDA Margin %	46.24	47.15	45.04	42.56	41.14	38.09	38.42	35.54
Net Margin %	20.27	21.88	21.59	19.98	18.84	16.83	16.39	13.42
Asset Turnover	0.39	0.41	0.47	0.45	0.45	0.44	0.40	0.34
Current Ratio	1.55	1.29	1.24	1.05	1.16	1.12	1.16	1.37
Debt to Equity	0.72	0.66	0.52	0.42	0.44	0.47	0.51	0.57
Price Range	111.42-68.79	123.83-75.43	123.31-82.58	84.00-62.86	64.22-52.49	53.38-39.91	47.27-30.25	33.12-16.81
P/E Ratio	20.83-12.86	22.56-13.74	21.45-14.36	17.83-13.35	15.55-12.71	15.89-11.88	17.07-10.92	17.61-8.94
Average Yield %	2.45	2.21	1.89	1.96	2.13	1.99	1.71	2.03

Address: 1400 Douglas Street, Omaha, NE 68179 **Telephone:** 402-544-5000	**Web Site:** www.up.com **Officers:** Lance M. Fritz - Chairman, President, Chief Executive Officer Eric L. Butler - Executive Vice President	**Auditors:** Deloitte & Touche LLP **Investor Contact:** 187-754-77261 **Transfer Agents:** Computershare Investor Services, LLC, Providence, RI

UNIT CORP.

Exchange	Symbol	Price	52Wk Range	Yield	P/E
NYS	UNT	$13.97 (5/31/2016)	32.56-4.41	N/A	N/A

*7 Year Price Score 30.18 *NYSE Composite Index=100 *12 Month Price Score 77.30

TRADING VOLUME (thousand shares)

Interim Earnings (Per Share)

Qtr.	Mar	Jun	Sep	Dec
2013	0.83	1.22	0.70	1.05
2014	1.17	1.11	1.37	(0.87)
2015	(5.07)	(5.58)	(4.18)	(6.29)
2016	(0.83)	...	...	...

Interim Dividends (Per Share)

No Dividends Paid

Valuation Analysis | Institutional Holding

Forecast EPS	$-0.95	No of Institutions
	(05/20/2016)	267
Market Cap	$718.6 Million	Shares
Book Value	$1.3 Billion	53,838,708
Price/Book	0.56	% Held
Price/Sales	0.98	94.13

Business Summary: Production & Extraction (MIC: 9.1.1 SIC: 1311 NAIC: 213111)

Unit is an oil and natural gas contract drilling company. In addition to its drilling operations, Co. has operations in the exploration and production and mid-stream areas. Co. operates three segments: Oil and Natural Gas, which explores, develops, acquires, and produces oil and natural gas properties for its own account; Contract Drilling, which contracts to drill onshore oil and natural gas wells for others and for its own account; and Mid-Stream, which buys, sells, gathers, processes, and treats natural gas. As of Dec 31 2015, Co. had total proved reserves of 16.7 million barrels of oil, 37.7 million barrels of natural gas liquid, and 484.87 billion cubic feet of natural gas.

Recent Developments: For the quarter ended Mar 31 2016, net loss amounted to US$41.1 million versus a net loss of US$248.4 million in the year-earlier quarter. Revenues were US$136.2 million, down 46.6% from US$255.1 million the year before. Operating loss was US$58.2 million versus a loss of US$398.3 million in the prior-year quarter. Direct operating expenses declined 71.2% to US$185.8 million from US$644.6 million in the comparable period the year before. Indirect operating expenses decreased 3.4% to US$8.5 million from US$8.8 million in the equivalent prior-year period.

Prospects: Our evaluation of Unit Corp. as of June 19, 2016 is the result of our systematic analysis on three basic characteristics: earnings strength, relative valuation, and recent stock price movement. The company has enjoyed a very positive trend in earnings per share over the past 5 quarters. Because the company lacks sufficient analyst estimate data, we place greater weight on the historical EPS trend as the measure of earnings strength. Based on operating earnings yield, the company is overvalued when compared to all of the companies in our coverage universe. Share price changes over the past year indicates that UNT will perform very poorly over the near term.

Financial Data

(US$ in Thousands)	3 Mos	12/31/2015	12/31/2014	12/31/2013	12/31/2012	12/31/2011	12/31/2010	12/31/2009
Earnings Per Share	(16.88)	(21.12)	2.78	3.80	0.48	4.08	3.09	(1.18)
Cash Flow Per Share	7.16	9.10	14.59	13.99	14.38	12.77	8.25	10.44
Tang Book Value Per Share	23.68	24.81	45.76	42.98	39.33	39.09	34.33	31.50
Income Statement								
Total Revenue	136,184	854,231	1,572,944	1,351,850	1,315,123	1,208,371	881,845	709,898
EBITDA	(35,055)	(1,576,211)	399,998	387,678	134,546	402,836	307,191	(41,861)
Depn & Amortn	12,195	56,135	159,688	71,194	81,007	79,667	69,970	45,326
Income Before Taxes	(56,867)	(1,664,309)	222,939	301,469	39,402	319,002	237,221	(87,726)
Income Taxes	(15,718)	(626,948)	86,663	116,723	16,226	123,135	90,737	(32,226)
Net Income	(41,149)	(1,037,361)	136,276	184,746	23,176	195,867	146,484	(55,500)
Average Shares	49,880	49,110	49,083	48,572	48,154	47,951	47,454	46,990
Balance Sheet								
Current Assets	124,092	140,258	252,491	212,031	195,644	228,465	188,180	128,095
Total Assets	2,681,088	2,808,509	4,473,728	4,022,390	3,761,120	3,256,720	2,669,240	2,228,399
Current Liabilities	139,411	150,891	304,171	243,573	207,139	212,750	147,128	105,147
Long-Term Obligations	920,314	950,128	838,039	645,696	716,359	300,000	163,000	30,000
Total Liabilities	1,400,048	1,494,929	2,141,334	1,848,998	1,786,819	1,309,703	958,623	662,589
Stockholders' Equity	1,281,040	1,313,580	2,332,394	2,173,392	1,974,301	1,947,017	1,710,617	1,565,810
Shares Outstanding	51,440	50,413	49,593	49,107	48,581	48,151	47,910	47,530
Statistical Record								
Return on Assets %	N.M.	N.M.	3.21	4.75	0.66	6.61	5.98	N.M.
Return on Equity %	N.M.	N.M.	6.05	8.91	1.18	10.71	8.94	N.M.
EBITDA Margin %	N.M.	N.M.	25.43	28.68	10.23	33.34	34.84	N.M.
Net Margin %	N.M.	N.M.	8.66	13.67	1.76	16.21	16.61	N.M.
Asset Turnover	0.22	0.23	0.37	0.35	0.37	0.41	0.36	0.30
Current Ratio	0.89	0.93	0.83	0.87	0.94	1.07	1.28	1.22
Debt to Equity	0.72	0.72	0.36	0.30	0.36	0.15	0.10	0.02
Price Range	35.82-4.41	35.82-10.96	69.94-29.98	51.99-41.13	50.56-32.81	63.43-34.88	49.91-33.82	46.94-17.83
P/E Ratio	...	...	25.16-10.78	13.68-10.82	105.33-68.35	15.55-8.55	16.15-10.94	

Address: 7130 South Lewis, Suite 1000, Tulsa, OK 74136 Telephone: 918-493-7700	Web Site: www.unitcorp.com Officers: John G. Nikkel - Chairman Larry D. Pinkston - President, Chief Executive Officer, Chief Operating Officer	Auditors: PricewaterhouseCoopers LLP Investor Contact: 918-493-7700 Transfer Agents: American Stock Transfer & Trust Co., New York, NY

UNITED CONTINENTAL HOLDINGS INC

Exchange	Symbol	Price	52Wk Range	Yield	P/E
NYS	UAL	$45.09 (5/31/2016)	61.56-43.78	N/A	2.35

*7 Year Price Score 142.45 *NYSE Composite Index=100 *12 Month Price Score 88.64

Interim Earnings (Per Share)

Qtr.	Mar	Jun	Sep	Dec
2013	(1.26)	1.21	0.98	0.38
2014	(1.66)	2.01	2.37	0.09
2015	1.32	3.14	12.82	2.32
2016	0.88	...	...	...

Interim Dividends (Per Share)

No Dividends Paid

Valuation Analysis | **Institutional Holding**

Forecast EPS	$7.95	No of Institutions
	(05/20/2016)	735
Market Cap	$15.3 Billion	Shares
Book Value	$7.8 Billion	351,982,176
Price/Book	1.95	% Held
Price/Sales	0.41	N/A

TRADING VOLUME (thousand shares)

Business Summary: Airlines/Air Freight (MIC: 7.4.4 SIC: 4512 NAIC: 481111)

United Continental Holdings is a holding company and its principal, wholly-owned subsidiary is United Airlines, Inc. (United). Co. is engaged in the transportation of people and cargo through its mainline and its regional operations. As of Dec 31 2015, Co., through United and its regional carriers, operated an average of nearly 5,000 flights a day to 342 airports across six continents from its hubs. Co. also has contractual relationships with various regional carriers to provide regional jet and turboprop service branded as United Express. Including aircraft operating by United's regional carriers, United operated 1,236 aircraft as of Dec 31 2015.

Recent Developments: For the quarter ended Mar 31 2016, net income decreased 38.4% to US$313.0 million from US$508.0 million in the year-earlier quarter. Revenues were US$8.20 billion, down 4.8% from US$8.61 billion the year before. Operating income was US$649.0 million versus US$741.0 million in the prior-year quarter, a decrease of 12.4%. Direct operating expenses declined 20.4% to US$2.85 billion from US$3.58 billion in the comparable period the year before. Indirect operating expenses increased 9.5% to US$4.70 billion from US$4.29 billion in the equivalent prior-year period.

Prospects: Our evaluation of United Continental Holdings Inc. as of June 19, 2016 is the result of our systematic analysis on three basic characteristics: earnings strength, relative valuation, and recent stock price movement. The company has generated a negative trend in earnings per share over the past 5 quarters. However, while recent estimates for the company have been lowered by analysts, UAL has posted better than expected results. Based on operating earnings yield, the company is undervalued when compared to all of the companies in our coverage universe. Share price changes over the past year indicates that UAL will perform very well over the near term.

Financial Data
(US$ in Thousands)

	3 Mos	12/31/2015	12/31/2014	12/31/2013	12/31/2012	12/31/2011	12/31/2010	12/31/2009
Earnings Per Share	19.16	19.47	2.93	1.53	(2.18)	2.26	1.08	(4.32)
Cash Flow Per Share	15.16	15.94	7.10	4.15	2.82	7.32	9.21	6.41
Tang Book Value Per Share	N.M.	0.84	N.M.	N.M.	N.M.	N.M.	N.M.	...
Income Statement								
Total Revenue	8,195,000	37,864,000	38,901,000	38,279,000	37,152,000	37,110,000	23,229,000	16,335,000
EBITDA	1,110,000	4,907,000	1,870,000	1,324,000	132,000	1,875,000	2,133,000	875,000
Depn & Amortn	479,000	93,000	81,000	72,000	81,000	133,000	1,115,000	999,000
Income Before Taxes	494,000	4,219,000	1,128,000	539,000	(724,000)	845,000	250,000	(672,000)
Income Taxes	181,000	(3,121,000)	(4,000)	(32,000)	(1,000)	5,000	...	(17,000)
Net Income	313,000	7,340,000	1,132,000	571,000	(723,000)	840,000	253,000	(651,000)
Average Shares	355,000	377,000	390,000	390,000	331,000	383,000	253,000	150,700
Balance Sheet								
Current Assets	7,224,000	7,828,000	8,138,000	8,702,000	10,049,000	10,997,000	12,045,000	5,105,000
Total Assets	40,373,000	40,861,000	37,353,000	36,812,000	37,628,000	37,988,000	39,598,000	18,684,000
Current Liabilities	13,380,000	12,414,000	12,508,000	12,107,000	12,818,000	11,394,000	12,645,000	6,473,000
Long-Term Obligations	10,197,000	10,440,000	10,692,000	10,924,000	11,232,000	11,424,000	12,470,000	7,572,000
Total Liabilities	32,533,000	31,895,000	34,957,000	33,828,000	37,147,000	36,182,000	37,871,000	21,495,000
Stockholders' Equity	7,840,000	8,966,000	2,396,000	2,984,000	481,000	1,806,000	1,727,000	(2,811,000)
Shares Outstanding	339,304	364,609	374,525	362,283	332,472	330,906	327,922	167,610
Statistical Record								
Return on Assets %	17.98	18.77	3.05	1.53	N.M.	2.17	0.87	N.M.
Return on Equity %	131.73	129.20	42.08	32.96	N.M.	47.55	...	N.M.
EBITDA Margin %	13.54	12.96	4.81	3.46	0.36	5.05	9.18	5.36
Net Margin %	3.82	19.39	2.91	1.49	N.M.	2.26	1.09	N.M.
Asset Turnover	0.94	0.97	1.05	1.03	0.98	0.96	0.80	0.86
Current Ratio	0.54	0.63	0.65	0.72	0.78	0.97	0.95	0.79
Debt to Equity	1.30	1.16	4.46	3.66	23.35	6.33	7.22	...
Price Range	67.25-45.12	73.62-50.78	66.89-37.73	39.83-23.38	25.17-17.48	27.48-15.53	29.53-12.23	13.09-3.17
P/E Ratio	3.51-2.35	3.78-2.61	22.83-12.88	26.03-15.28	...	12.16-6.87	27.34-11.32	...

Address: 233 South Wacker Drive, Chicago, IL 60606
Telephone: 872-825-4000

Web Site: www.unitedcontinentalholdings.com
Officers: James E. Compton - Vice-Chairman, Executive Vice President, Chief Revenue Officer
Oscar Munoz - President, President (frmr-frmr), Chief Executive Officer, Chief Executive Officer (trmr)

Auditors: Ernst & Young LLP
Investor Contact: 312-997-8610
Transfer Agents: ComputerShare Investor Services, Chicago, IL

UNITED PARCEL SERVICE INC

Exchange	Symbol	Price	52Wk Range	Yield	P/E
NYS	UPS	$103.09 (5/31/2016)	106.84-88.70	3.03	18.78

*7 Year Price Score 104.14 *NYSE Composite Index=100 *12 Month Price Score 102.78

Interim Earnings (Per Share)

Qtr.	Mar	Jun	Sep	Dec
2013	1.08	1.13	1.16	1.24
2014	0.98	0.49	1.32	0.50
2015	1.12	1.35	1.39	1.48
2016	1.27	...	...	...

Interim Dividends (Per Share)

Amt	Decl	Ex	Rec	Pay
0.73Q	08/06/2015	08/13/2015	08/17/2015	09/01/2015
0.73Q	11/05/2015	11/12/2015	11/16/2015	12/02/2015
0.78Q	02/10/2016	02/18/2016	02/22/2016	03/09/2016
0.78Q	05/05/2016	05/12/2016	05/16/2016	06/01/2016

Indicated Div: $3.12

Valuation Analysis — **Institutional Holding**

Forecast EPS	$5.80 (05/20/2016)	No of Institutions	1634
Market Cap	$91.1 Billion	Shares	553,337,600
Book Value	$2.5 Billion	% Held	52.11
Price/Book	37.09		
Price/Sales	1.55		

TRADING VOLUME (thousand shares)

Business Summary: Airlines/Air Freight (MIC: 7.4.4 SIC: 4215 NAIC: 492110)

United Parcel Service focuses its operations in the field of transportation services, primarily domestic and international letter and package delivery. Co. reports its operations in three segments: U.S. Domestic Package operations, which provides a range of U.S. domestic guaranteed ground and air package transportation services; International Package operations, which includes the small package operations in Europe, Asia, Canada and Latin America, the Indian sub-continent, Middle East and Africa; and Supply Chain & Freight operations, which consists of Co.'s forwarding and logistics services, its UPS Freight business, and its financial offerings through its UPS Capital.

Recent Developments: For the quarter ended Mar 31 2016, net income increased 10.2% to US$1.13 billion from US$1.03 billion in the year-earlier quarter. Revenues were US$14.42 billion, up 3.2% from US$13.98 billion the year before. Operating income was US$1.82 billion versus US$1.67 billion in the prior-year quarter, an increase of 9.0%. Direct operating expenses declined 0.3% to US$2.84 billion from US$2.85 billion in the comparable period the year before. Indirect operating expenses increased 3.2% to US$9.76 billion from US$9.46 billion in the equivalent prior-year period.

Prospects: Our evaluation of United Parcel Service Inc. as of June 19, 2016 is the result of our systematic analysis on three basic characteristics: earnings strength, relative valuation, and recent stock price movement. The company has managed to produce a neutral trend in earnings per share over the past 5 quarters. However, while recent estimates for the company have been mixed, UPS has posted better than expected results. Based on operating earnings yield, the company is undervalued when compared to all of the companies in our coverage universe. Share price changes over the past year indicates that UPS will perform in line with the market over the near term.

Financial Data

(US$ in Millions)	3 Mos	12/31/2015	12/31/2014	12/31/2013	12/31/2012	12/31/2011	12/31/2010	12/31/2009
Earnings Per Share	5.49	5.35	3.28	4.61	0.83	3.84	3.48	2.14
Cash Flow Per Share	8.27	8.25	6.25	7.77	7.50	7.21	3.86	5.30
Tang Book Value Per Share	N.M.	N.M.	N.M.	3.80	1.97	4.52	5.35	4.97
Dividends Per Share	2.970	2.920	2.680	2.480	2.280	2.080	1.880	1.800
Dividend Payout %	54.10	54.58	81.71	53.80	274.70	54.17	54.02	84.11
Income Statement								
Total Revenue	14,418	58,363	58,232	55,438	54,127	53,105	49,545	45,297
EBITDA	2,392	9,767	6,913	8,921	3,225	7,906	7,669	5,558
Depn & Amortn	552	2,084	1,923	1,867	1,858	1,782	1,792	1,747
Income Before Taxes	1,747	7,342	4,637	6,674	974	5,776	5,523	3,366
Income Taxes	616	2,498	1,605	2,302	167	1,972	2,035	1,214
Net Income	1,131	4,844	3,032	4,372	807	3,804	3,488	2,152
Average Shares	894	906	924	948	969	991	1,003	1,004
Balance Sheet								
Current Assets	13,912	13,208	11,808	13,387	15,591	12,284	11,569	9,275
Total Assets	39,168	38,311	35,471	36,212	38,863	34,701	33,597	31,883
Current Liabilities	11,098	10,696	8,639	7,131	8,390	6,514	5,902	6,239
Long-Term Obligations	11,569	11,316	9,864	10,824	11,089	11,095	10,491	8,668
Total Liabilities	36,711	35,841	33,330	29,738	34,210	27,666	25,618	24,253
Stockholders' Equity	2,457	2,470	2,141	6,474	4,653	7,035	7,979	7,630
Shares Outstanding	884	886	905	923	953	963	991	994
Statistical Record								
Return on Assets %	12.94	13.13	8.46	11.65	2.19	11.14	10.65	6.75
Return on Equity %	230.94	210.11	70.39	78.58	13.77	50.67	44.69	29.87
EBITDA Margin %	16.59	16.73	11.87	16.09	5.96	14.89	15.48	12.27
Net Margin %	7.84	8.30	5.21	7.89	1.49	7.16	7.04	4.75
Asset Turnover	1.54	1.58	1.62	1.48	1.47	1.56	1.51	1.42
Current Ratio	1.25	1.23	1.37	1.88	1.86	1.89	1.96	1.49
Debt to Equity	4.71	4.58	4.61	1.67	2.38	1.58	1.31	1.14
Price Range	106.80-88.70	114.25-94.46	112.45-93.62	105.08-73.73	81.11-70.02	76.47-61.70	73.76-56.15	59.29-38.30
P/E Ratio	19.45-16.16	21.36-17.66	34.28-28.54	22.79-15.99	97.72-84.36	19.91-16.07	21.20-16.14	27.71-17.90
Average Yield %	2.99	2.90	2.66	2.80	3.01	2.94	2.91	3.45

Address: 55 Glenlake Parkway, N.E.
Atlanta, GA 30328
Telephone: 404-828-6000

Web Site: www.ups.com
Officers: David P. Abney - Chairman, Chief Executive Officer, Senior Vice President, Chief Executive Officer, Senior Vice President, Chief Operating Officer, Chief Operating Officer D. Scott Davis - Chairman, Chief Executive Officer

Auditors: Deloitte & Touche LLP
Investor Contact: 404-828-6059
Transfer Agents: Computershare Shareowner Services, Pittsburgh, PA

UNITED RENTALS, INC.

Exchange	Symbol	Price	52Wk Range	Yield	P/E
NYS	URI	$69.67 (5/31/2016)	92.58-43.34	N/A	11.73

*7 Year Price Score 116.37 ***NYSE Composite Index=100** ***12 Month Price Score 94.28**

TRADING VOLUME (thousand shares)

Interim Earnings (Per Share)

Qtr.	Mar	Jun	Sep	Dec
2013	0.19	0.78	1.53	1.31
2014	0.56	0.90	1.84	1.86
2015	1.16	0.88	2.25	1.80
2016	1.01	...	...	...

Interim Dividends (Per Share)

No Dividends Paid

Valuation Analysis / Institutional Holding

Valuation Analysis		Institutional Holding	
Forecast EPS	$7.75	No of Institutions	
	(05/20/2016)	714	
Market Cap	$6.2 Billion	Shares	
Book Value	$1.5 Billion	105,468,200	
Price/Book	4.15	% Held	
Price/Sales	1.07	97.42	

Business Summary: Construction Services (MIC: 7.5.4 SIC: 7359 NAIC: 532412)

United Rentals is an equipment rental company. Co. provides equipment for rent to construction and industrial companies, manufacturers, utilities, municipalities, homeowners, government entities and other customers. Co. has two reportable segments: general rentals and trench, power and pump. The general rentals segment includes the rental of construction, aerial, industrial and homeowner equipment and related services and activities. The trench, power and pump segment is comprised of: the Trench Safety region, the Power and HVAC region, and the Pump Solutions region, which rents pumps primarily used by energy and petrochemical customers.

Recent Developments: For the quarter ended Mar 31 2016, net income decreased 20.0% to US$92.0 million from US$115.0 million in the year-earlier quarter. Revenues were US$1.31 billion, down 0.4% from US$1.32 billion the year before. Operating income was US$254.0 million versus US$300.0 million in the prior-year quarter, a decrease of 15.3%. Direct operating expenses rose 2.4% to US$810.0 million from US$791.0 million in the comparable period the year before. Indirect operating expenses increased 9.8% to US$246.0 million from US$224.0 million in the equivalent prior-year period.

Prospects: Our evaluation of United Rentals Inc. as of June 19, 2016 is the result of our systematic analysis on three basic characteristics: earnings strength, relative valuation, and recent stock price movement. The company has generated a negative trend in earnings per share over the past 5 quarters and while recent estimates for the company have been raised by analysts, URI has posted better than expected results. Based on operating earnings yield, the company is undervalued when compared to all of the companies in our coverage universe. Share price changes over the past year indicates that URI will perform poorly over the near term.

Financial Data
(US$ in Thousands)

	3 Mos	12/31/2015	12/31/2014	12/31/2013	12/31/2012	12/31/2011	12/31/2010	12/31/2009
Earnings Per Share	5.94	6.07	5.15	3.64	0.79	1.38	(0.44)	(1.02)
Cash Flow Per Share	21.26	20.96	18.47	16.60	8.67	9.78	7.48	7.29
Income Statement								
Total Revenue	1,310,000	5,817,000	5,685,000	4,955,000	4,117,000	2,611,000	2,237,000	2,358,000
EBITDA	499,000	2,506,000	2,326,000	1,935,000	1,303,000	822,000	589,000	532,000
Depn & Amortn	245,000	976,000	921,000	852,000	699,000	423,000	389,000	417,000
Income Before Taxes	147,000	963,000	850,000	605,000	88,000	164,000	(63,000)	(107,000)
Income Taxes	55,000	378,000	310,000	218,000	13,000	63,000	(41,000)	(47,000)
Net Income	92,000	585,000	540,000	387,000	75,000	101,000	(26,000)	(62,000)
Average Shares	90,943	96,379	104,956	106,291	94,848	73,349	60,455	60,100
Balance Sheet								
Current Assets	1,182,000	1,294,000	1,546,000	1,362,000	1,343,000	723,000	725,000	705,000
Total Assets	11,784,000	12,083,000	12,467,000	11,231,000	11,026,000	4,143,000	3,693,000	3,859,000
Current Liabilities	1,229,000	1,233,000	1,478,000	1,286,000	1,351,000	864,000	569,000	461,000
Long-Term Obligations	7,203,000	7,555,000	7,434,000	6,569,000	6,734,000	2,647,000	2,700,000	2,950,000
Total Liabilities	10,283,000	10,607,000	10,669,000	9,383,000	9,452,000	4,040,000	3,713,000	3,878,000
Stockholders' Equity	1,501,000	1,476,000	1,798,000	1,848,000	1,574,000	103,000	(20,000)	(19,000)
Shares Outstanding	89,376	91,776	97,877	93,288	92,984	62,877	60,621	60,163
Statistical Record								
Return on Assets %	4.67	4.77	4.56	3.48	0.99	2.58	N.M.	N.M.
Return on Equity %	37.52	35.74	29.62	22.62	8.92	243.37	...	...
EBITDA Margin %	38.09	43.08	40.91	39.05	31.65	31.48	26.33	22.56
Net Margin %	7.02	10.06	9.50	7.81	1.82	3.87	N.M.	N.M.
Asset Turnover	0.48	0.47	0.48	0.45	0.54	0.67	0.59	0.59
Current Ratio	0.96	1.05	1.05	1.06	0.99	0.84	1.27	1.53
Debt to Equity	4.80	5.12	4.13	3.55	4.28	25.70	...	...
Price Range	105.13-43.34	105.13-59.48	119.02-74.46	77.95-45.52	46.82-27.23	34.09-13.11	23.51-7.02	11.03-3.03
P/E Ratio	17.70-7.30	17.32-9.80	23.11-14.46	21.41-12.51	59.27-34.47	24.70-9.50	...	...

Address: 100 First Stamford Place, Suite 700, Stamford, CT 06902
Telephone: 203-622-3131

Web Site: www.unitedrentals.com
Officers: Jenne K. Britell - Chairman Michael J. Kneeland - President, Chief Executive Officer

Auditors: Ernst & Young LLP
Investor Contact: 203-618-7318
Transfer Agents: American Stock Transfer & Trust Company, New York, NY

UNITED STATES STEEL CORP.

Exchange	Symbol	Price	52Wk Range	Yield	P/E
NYS	X	$14.47 (5/31/2016)	25.78-6.67	1.38	N/A

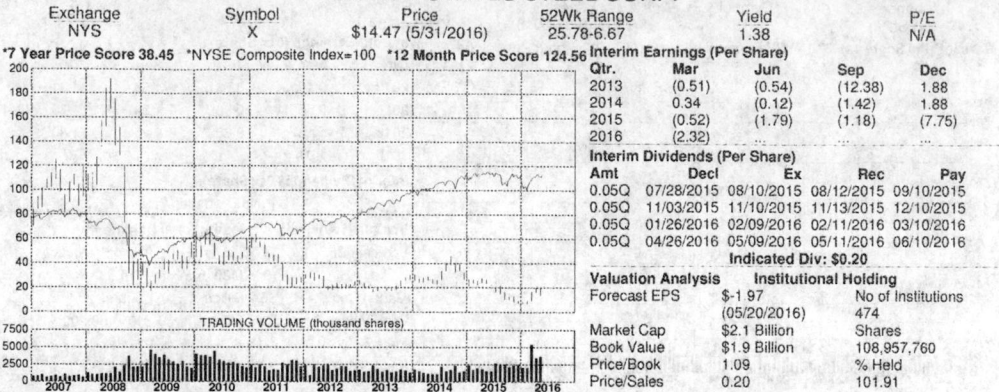

*7 Year Price Score 38.45 *NYSE Composite Index=100 *12 Month Price Score 124.56

Interim Earnings (Per Share)

Qtr.	Mar	Jun	Sep	Dec
2013	(0.51)	(0.54)	(12.38)	1.88
2014	0.34	(0.12)	(1.42)	1.88
2015	(0.52)	(1.79)	(1.18)	(7.75)
2016	(2.32)	...	...	...

Interim Dividends (Per Share)

Amt	Decl	Ex	Rec	Pay
0.05Q	07/28/2015	08/10/2015	08/12/2015	09/10/2015
0.05Q	11/03/2015	11/10/2015	11/13/2015	12/10/2015
0.05Q	01/26/2016	02/09/2016	02/11/2016	03/10/2016
0.05Q	04/26/2016	05/09/2016	05/11/2016	06/10/2016

Indicated Div: $0.20

Valuation Analysis — **Institutional Holding**

Forecast EPS	$-1.97	No of Institutions
	(05/20/2016)	474
Market Cap	$2.1 Billion	Shares
Book Value	$1.9 Billion	108,957,760
Price/Book	1.09	% Held
Price/Sales	0.20	101.91

Business Summary: Non-Precious Metals (MIC: 8.2.2 SIC: 3312 NAIC: 331111)

United States Steel is a steel producer of flat-rolled and tubular products. Co. has three operating segments: Flat-rolled Products, which includes the production of slabs, rounds, strip mill plates, sheets and tin mill products, as well as iron ore and coke production; U.S. Steel Europe, which produces and sells slabs, sheet, strip mill plate, tin mill products and spiral welded pipe, as well as heating radiators and refractory ceramic materials; and Tubular Products, which produces and sells seamless and electric resistance welded steel casing and tubing, standard and line pipe and mechanical tubing. Co.'s other business activities consist of railroad services and real estate operations.

Recent Developments: For the quarter ended Mar 31 2016, net loss amounted to US$340.0 million versus a net loss of US$75.0 million in the year-earlier quarter. Revenues were US$2.34 billion, down 28.5% from US$3.27 billion the year before. Operating loss was US$261.0 million versus a loss of US$187.0 million in the prior-year quarter. Direct operating expenses declined 20.5% to US$2.44 billion from US$3.07 billion in the comparable period the year before. Indirect operating expenses decreased 57.8% to US$166.0 million from US$393.0 million in the equivalent prior-year period.

Prospects: Our evaluation of United States Steel Corp. as of June 19, 2016 is the result of our systematic analysis on three basic characteristics: earnings strength, relative valuation, and recent stock price movement. The company has enjoyed a very positive trend in earnings per share over the past 5 quarters. Because the company lacks sufficient analyst estimate data, we place greater weight on the historical EPS trend as the measure of earnings strength. Based on operating earnings yield, the company is overvalued when compared to all of the companies in our coverage universe. Share price changes over the past year indicates that X will perform very poorly over the near term.

Financial Data
(US$ in Millions)

	3 Mos	12/31/2015	12/31/2014	12/31/2013	12/31/2012	12/31/2011	12/31/2010	12/31/2009
Earnings Per Share	(13.04)	(11.24)	0.69	(11.56)	(0.86)	(0.37)	(3.36)	(10.42)
Cash Flow Per Share	2.30	2.46	10.28	2.86	7.85	1.17	(2.64)	(0.45)
Tang Book Value Per Share	11.93	15.31	24.68	21.24	9.72	10.10	12.64	18.63
Dividends Per Share	0.200	0.200	0.200	0.200	0.200	0.200	0.200	0.450
Dividend Payout %	...	...	28.99	...	...	...	...	...
Income Statement								
Total Revenue	2,341	11,574	17,507	17,424	19,328	19,884	17,374	11,048
EBITDA	(177)	(739)	877	(1,325)	730	807	441	(1,006)
Depn & Amortn	129	547	627	684	661	681	658	661
Income Before Taxes	(371)	(1,497)	28	(2,272)	(138)	(58)	(405)	(1,816)
Income Taxes	14	183	68	(560)	131	80	97	(439)
Net Income	(340)	(1,642)	102	(1,672)	(124)	(53)	(482)	(1,401)
Average Shares	146	146	152	144	144	143	143	134
Balance Sheet								
Current Assets	3,683	3,917	6,431	6,078	5,374	5,774	5,304	5,015
Total Assets	8,936	9,190	12,314	13,143	15,217	16,073	15,350	15,422
Current Liabilities	2,193	2,148	3,569	3,245	2,990	3,649	3,147	2,474
Long-Term Obligations	3,076	3,116	3,120	3,616	3,936	3,828	3,517	3,345
Total Liabilities	6,994	6,754	8,515	9,795	11,740	12,573	11,499	10,746
Stockholders' Equity	1,942	2,436	3,799	3,348	3,477	3,500	3,851	4,676
Shares Outstanding	146	146	145	144	144	144	143	143
Statistical Record								
Return on Assets %	N.M.	N.M.	0.80	N.M.	N.M.	N.M.	N.M.	N.M.
Return on Equity %	N.M.	N.M.	2.85	N.M.	N.M.	N.M.	N.M.	N.M.
EBITDA Margin %	N.M.	N.M.	5.01	N.M.	3.78	4.06	2.54	N.M.
Net Margin %	N.M.	N.M.	0.58	N.M.	N.M.	N.M.	N.M.	N.M.
Asset Turnover	1.04	1.08	1.38	1.23	1.23	1.27	1.13	0.70
Current Ratio	1.68	1.82	1.80	1.87	1.80	1.58	1.69	2.03
Debt to Equity	1.58	1.28	0.82	1.08	1.13	1.09	0.91	0.72
Price Range	27.33-6.67	27.33-7.09	46.00-22.73	30.09-16.18	32.25-17.89	63.64-20.19	69.71-37.66	56.86-16.88
P/E Ratio	...	...	66.67-32.94	...	...	...	...	...
Average Yield %	1.31	1.07	0.66	0.95	0.85	0.50	0.40	1.25

Address: 600 Grant Street, Pittsburgh, PA 15219-2800 **Telephone:** 412-433-1121 **Fax:** 412-433-4818	**Web Site:** www.ussteel.com **Officers:** Mario Longhi - President, Chief Executive Officer, Executive Vice President, Chief Operating Officer David B. Burritt - Executive Vice President, Chief Financial Officer	**Auditors:** PricewaterhouseCoopers LLP **Investor Contact:** 412-433-1121 **Transfer Agents:** Wells Fargo Bank Shareowner Services, St. Paul, MN

UNITEDHEALTH GROUP INC

Exchange	Symbol	Price	52Wk Range	Yield	P/E
NYS	UNH	$133.67 (5/31/2016)	134.24-109.23	1.87	21.49

*7 Year Price Score 154.17 *NYSE Composite Index=100 *12 Month Price Score 107.30

TRADING VOLUME (thousand shares)

Interim Earnings (Per Share)

Qtr.	Mar	Jun	Sep	Dec
2013	1.16	1.40	1.53	1.41
2014	1.10	1.42	1.63	1.55
2015	1.46	1.64	1.65	1.26
2016	1.67	...	...	...

Interim Dividends (Per Share)

Amt	Decl	Ex	Rec	Pay
0.50Q	08/12/2015	09/09/2015	09/11/2015	09/22/2015
0.50Q	11/06/2015	12/02/2015	12/04/2015	12/15/2015
0.50Q	02/10/2016	03/09/2016	03/11/2016	03/22/2016
0.625Q	06/08/2016	06/15/2016	06/17/2016	06/28/2016

Indicated Div: $2.50

Valuation Analysis

		Institutional Holding	
Forecast EPS	$7.88	No of Institutions	
	(05/20/2016)	1652	
Market Cap	$127.5 Billion	Shares	
Book Value	$35.2 Billion	953,499,712	
Price/Book	3.63	% Held	
Price/Sales	0.77	84.89	

Business Summary: Life & Health (MIC: 5.2.2 SIC: 6324 NAIC: 524114)

UnitedHealth Group is a health and well-being company. Co. provides a range of products and services through two busienss platforms: UnitedHealthcare, which provides health care coverage and benefits services; and Optum, which provides information and technology-enabled health services. As of Dec. 31, 2015, Co. had four reportable segments across its two business platforms, UnitedHealthcare and Optum: UnitedHealthcare, which includes UnitedHealthcare Employer & Individual, UnitedHealthcare Medicare & Retirement, UnitedHealthcare Community & State and UnitedHealthcare Global; OptumHealth; OptumInsight; and OptumRx.

Recent Developments: For the quarter ended Mar 31 2016, net income increased 15.1% to US$1.63 billion from US$1.41 billion in the year-earlier quarter. Revenues were US$44.53 billion, up 24.5% from US$35.76 billion the year before. Net premiums earned were US$34.81 billion versus US$31.67 billion in the prior-year quarter, an increase of 9.9%.

Prospects: Our evaluation of UnitedHealth Group Inc. as of June 19, 2016 is the result of our systematic analysis on three basic characteristics: earnings strength, relative valuation, and recent stock price movement. The company has produced a positive trend in earnings per share over the past 5 quarters and while recent estimates for the company have been raised by analysts, UNH has posted better than expected results. Based on operating earnings yield, the company is about fairly valued when compared to all of the companies in our coverage universe. Share price changes over the past year indicates that UNH will perform in line with the market over the near term.

Financial Data
(US$ in Thousands)

	3 Mos	12/31/2015	12/31/2014	12/31/2013	12/31/2012	12/31/2011	12/31/2010	12/31/2009
Earnings Per Share	6.22	6.01	5.70	5.50	5.28	4.73	4.10	3.24
Cash Flow Per Share	10.27	10.22	8.28	6.95	6.95	6.51	5.60	4.82
Tang Book Value Per Share	N.M.	N.M.	N.M.	N.M.	N.M.	1.46	0.16	0.43
Dividends Per Share	2.000	1.875	1.405	1.053	0.800	0.613	0.405	0.030
Dividend Payout %	32.15	31.20	24.65	19.14	15.15	12.95	9.88	0.93
Income Statement								
Total Revenue	44,527,000	157,107,000	130,474,000	122,489,000	110,618,000	101,862,000	94,155,000	87,138,000
Income Before Taxes	2,701,000	10,231,000	9,656,000	8,915,000	8,622,000	7,959,000	7,383,000	5,808,000
Income Taxes	1,074,000	4,363,000	4,037,000	3,242,000	3,096,000	2,817,000	2,749,000	1,986,000
Net Income	1,611,000	5,813,000	5,619,000	5,625,000	5,526,000	5,142,000	4,634,000	3,822,000
Average Shares	967,000	967,000	986,000	1,023,000	1,046,000	1,087,000	1,131,000	1,179,000
Balance Sheet								
Total Assets	117,855,000	111,383,000	86,382,000	81,882,000	80,885,000	67,889,000	63,063,000	59,045,000
Total Liabilities	82,686,000	77,553,000	53,928,000	49,733,000	49,707,000	39,597,000	37,238,000	35,439,000
Stockholders' Equity	35,169,000	33,830,000	32,454,000	32,149,000	31,178,000	28,292,000	25,825,000	23,606,000
Shares Outstanding	954,000	953,000	954,000	988,000	1,019,000	1,039,000	1,086,000	1,147,000
Statistical Record								
Return on Assets %	5.79	5.88	6.68	6.91	7.41	7.85	7.59	6.66
Return on Equity %	17.93	17.54	17.40	17.76	18.53	19.00	18.75	17.22
Net Margin %	3.62	3.70	4.31	4.59	5.00	5.05	4.92	4.39
Price Range	129.83-109.23	125.86-98.92	103.04-69.74	75.30-51.40	60.26-50.35	53.13-36.11	38.05-27.85	32.32-16.35
P/E Ratio	20.87-17.56	20.94-16.46	18.08-12.24	13.69-9.35	11.41-9.54	11.23-7.63	9.28-6.79	9.98-5.05
Average Yield %	1.69	1.61	1.68	1.61	1.45	1.32	1.23	0.11

Address: UnitedHealth Group Center, 9900 Bren Road East, Minnetonka, MN 55343
Telephone: 952-936-1300

Web Site: www.unitedhealthgroup.com
Officers: Larry C. Renfro - Vice-Chairman, Executive Vice President, Division Officer David S. Wichmann - President, Chief Financial Officer, Executive Vice President, Division Officer

Auditors: Deloitte & Touche LLP
Investor Contact: 800-328-5979
Transfer Agents: Wells Fargo Shareowner Services, St. Paul, MN

UNITED STATES CELLULAR CORP

Exchange	Symbol	Price	52Wk Range	Yield	P/E
NYS	USM	$37.78 (5/31/2016)	45.87-34.42	N/A	35.64

*7 Year Price Score 82.29 *NYSE Composite Index=100 *12 Month Price Score 105.98

Interim Earnings (Per Share)

Qtr.	Mar	Jun	Sep	Dec
2013	0.06	1.69	(0.12)	0.01
2014	0.23	(0.22)	(0.26)	(0.26)
2015	1.89	0.23	0.75	(0.02)
2016	0.10	...	...	...

Interim Dividends (Per Share)

Amt	Decl	Ex	Rec	Pay
5.75U	05/17/2013	06/07/2013	06/11/2013	06/25/2013

Valuation Analysis   Institutional Holding

Forecast EPS	$0.48	No of Institutions
	(05/20/2016)	169
Market Cap	$3.2 Billion	Shares
Book Value	$3.6 Billion	12,656,595
Price/Book	0.89	% Held
Price/Sales	0.80	15.32

Business Summary: Services (MIC: 6.1.2 SIC: 4812 NAIC: 517212)

United States Cellular provides wireless telecommunications services. Co.'s postpaid customers are able to choose from a range of national plans with voice, messaging and data usage options and pricing. Co. also provides prepaid service plans, which include voice, messaging and data options in a variety of ways, for a fee. In addition, Co. provides a range of wireless devices such as handsets, modems, mobile hotspots, home phone and tablets for use by its customers. Co. also sells a range of accessories, such as carrying cases, hands-free devices, batteries, battery chargers, memory cards and other items. At Dec 31 2014, Co.'s consolidated operating markets covered customers in 23 states.

Recent Developments: For the quarter ended Mar 31 2016, net income decreased 94.5% to US$9.0 million from US$165.0 million in the year-earlier quarter. Revenues were US$958.0 million, down 0.7% from US$965.0 million the year before. Operating loss was US$1.0 million versus an income of US$250.0 million in the prior-year quarter. Direct operating expenses rose 2.6% to US$440.0 million from US$429.0 million in the comparable period the year before. Indirect operating expenses increased 81.5% to US$519.0 million from US$286.0 million in the equivalent prior-year period.

Prospects: Our evaluation of United States Cellular Corp. as of June 5, 2016 is the result of our systematic analysis on three basic characteristics: earnings strength, relative valuation, and recent stock price movement. The company has suffered a very negative trend in earnings per share over the past 5 quarters. However, while recent estimates for the company have been lowered by analysts, USM has posted results that fell short of analysts expectations. Based on operating earnings yield, the company is overvalued when compared to all of the companies in our coverage universe. Share price changes over the past year indicates that USM will perform very well over the near term.

Financial Data

(US$ in Thousands)	3 Mos	12/31/2015	12/31/2014	12/31/2013	12/31/2012	12/31/2011	12/31/2010	12/31/2009
Earnings Per Share	1.06	2.84	(0.51)	1.65	1.31	2.05	1.53	2.48
Cash Flow Per Share	5.51	6.59	2.05	3.46	10.60	11.64	10.15	10.14
Tang Book Value Per Share	16.54	16.08	17.70	19.03	22.04	19.56	17.92	16.99
Dividends Per Share	...	...	...	5.750	...	...	...	...
Dividend Payout %	...	...	...	348.48	...	...	...	...
Income Statement								
Total Revenue	958,000	3,996,853	3,892,747	3,918,836	4,452,084	4,343,346	4,177,681	4,214,611
EBITDA	153,000	908,908	449,970	956,809	751,138	856,575	757,046	882,749
Depn & Amortn	153,000	595,500	593,200	791,100	597,700	565,100	561,600	554,900
Income Before Taxes	(15,000)	263,546	(188,468)	125,707	114,689	229,256	137,699	255,079
Income Taxes	11,000	156,334	(11,782)	113,134	63,977	114,078	79,609	114,103
Net Income	9,000	241,347	(42,812)	140,038	111,006	175,041	132,324	216,008
Average Shares	85,000	84,891	84,213	84,730	85,067	85,335	86,518	87,168
Balance Sheet								
Current Assets	1,708,000	1,671,642	1,279,175	1,401,191	1,196,476	1,292,843	1,109,624	1,005,588
Total Assets	7,057,000	7,059,978	6,487,268	6,445,708	6,587,450	6,327,976	5,933,610	5,745,217
Current Liabilities	723,000	747,938	856,894	1,006,173	754,999	722,280	665,995	644,565
Long-Term Obligations	1,626,000	1,628,507	1,151,819	878,032	878,858	880,320	867,941	867,522
Total Liabilities	3,483,000	3,499,465	3,185,277	3,054,502	2,853,595	2,708,015	2,453,027	2,340,921
Stockholders' Equity	3,574,000	3,560,513	3,301,991	3,391,206	3,733,855	3,619,961	3,480,583	3,404,296
Shares Outstanding	84,395	84,359	84,080	84,205	84,168	84,557	85,547	86,540
Statistical Record								
Return on Assets %	1.32	3.56	N.M.	2.15	1.71	2.86	2.27	3.82
Return on Equity %	2.57	7.03	N.M.	3.93	3.01	4.93	3.84	6.53
EBITDA Margin %	15.97	22.74	11.56	24.42	16.87	19.72	18.12	20.94
Net Margin %	0.94	6.04	N.M.	3.57	2.49	4.03	3.17	5.13
Asset Turnover	0.58	0.59	0.60	0.60	0.69	0.71	0.72	0.75
Current Ratio	2.36	2.24	1.49	1.39	1.58	1.79	1.67	1.56
Debt to Equity	0.45	0.46	0.35	0.26	0.24	0.24	0.25	0.25
Price Range	45.69-34.42	43.36-34.42	44.45-31.93	48.80-32.62	47.61-33.76	51.99-36.07	50.05-34.75	47.08-30.34
P/E Ratio	43.10-32.47	15.27-12.12	...	29.58-19.77	36.34-25.77	25.36-17.60	32.71-22.71	18.98-12.23
Average Yield %	...	...	...	14.35	...	...	...	...

Address: 8410 West Bryn Mawr, Chicago, IL 60631 **Telephone:** 773-399-8900	**Web Site:** www.uscellular.com **Officers:** LeRoy T. Carlson - Chairman Kenneth R. Meyers - President, Chief Executive Officer, Vice President, Assistant Treasurer	**Auditors:** PricewaterhouseCoopers LLP **Investor Contact:** 312-592-5379 **Transfer Agents:** Computershare Trust Company, N.A., TX

U.S. BANCORP (DE)

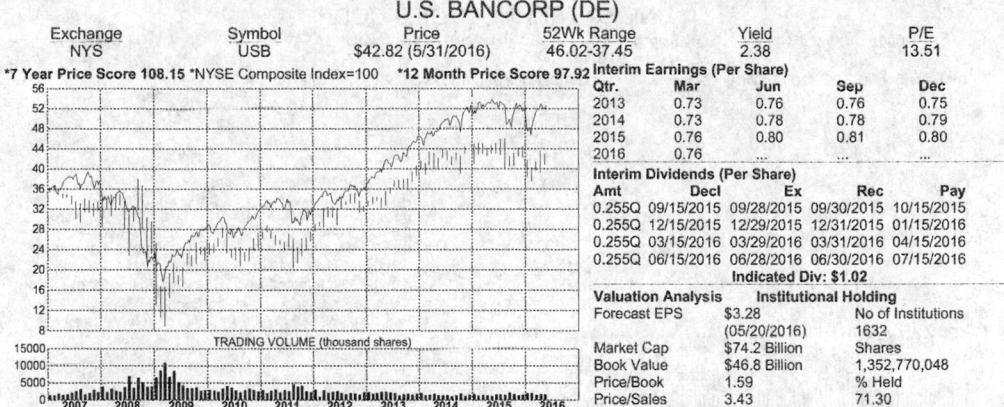

Exchange	Symbol	Price	52Wk Range	Yield	P/E
NYS	USB	$42.82 (5/31/2016)	46.02-37.45	2.38	13.51

*7 Year Price Score 108.15 *NYSE Composite Index=100 ***12 Month Price Score 97.92**

Interim Earnings (Per Share)

Qtr.	Mar	Jun	Sep	Dec
2013	0.73	0.76	0.76	0.75
2014	0.73	0.78	0.78	0.79
2015	0.76	0.80	0.81	0.80
2016	0.76	...	...	...

Interim Dividends (Per Share)

Amt	Decl	Ex	Rec	Pay
0.255Q	09/15/2015	09/28/2015	09/30/2015	10/15/2015
0.255Q	12/15/2015	12/29/2015	12/31/2015	01/15/2016
0.255Q	03/15/2016	03/29/2016	03/31/2016	04/15/2016
0.255Q	06/15/2016	06/28/2016	06/30/2016	07/15/2016

Indicated Div: $1.02

Valuation Analysis

		Institutional Holding	
Forecast EPS	$3.28	No of Institutions	
	(05/20/2016)		1632
Market Cap	$74.2 Billion	Shares	
Book Value	$46.8 Billion		1,352,770,048
Price/Book	1.59	% Held	
Price/Sales	3.43		71.30

Business Summary: Banking (MIC: 5.1.1 SIC: 6021 NAIC: 522110)

U.S. Bancorp is a financial services holding company. Through its subsidiaries, Co. provides a range of financial services, including lending and depository services, cash management, capital markets, and trust and investment management services. Co. also engages in credit card services, merchant and automatic teller machine processing, mortgage banking, insurance, brokerage and leasing. Lending services include credit products as well as credit card services, lease financing, and other products. Depository services include checking accounts, savings accounts and time certificate contracts. At Dec 31 2015, Co. had total assets of $421.85 billion and deposits of $300.40 billion.

Recent Developments: For the quarter ended Mar 31 2016, net income decreased 3.0% to US$1.40 billion from US$1.44 billion in the year-earlier quarter. Net interest income increased 5.1% to US$2.84 billion from US$2.70 billion in the year-earlier quarter. Provision for loan losses was US$330.0 million versus US$264.0 million in the prior-year quarter, an increase of 25.0%. Non-interest income was unchanged at US$2.15 billion, while non-interest expense advanced 3.2% to US$2.75 billion.

Prospects: Our evaluation of U.S. Bancorp as of June 19, 2016 is the result of our systematic analysis on three basic characteristics: earnings strength, relative valuation, and recent stock price movement. The company has managed to produce a neutral trend in earnings per share over the past 5 quarters. However, while recent estimates for the company have been mixed, USB has posted better than expected results. Based on operating earnings yield, the company is undervalued when compared to all of the companies in our coverage universe. Share price changes over the past year indicates that USB will perform in line with the market over the near term.

Financial Data

(US$ in Thousands)	3 Mos	12/31/2015	12/31/2014	12/31/2013	12/31/2012	12/31/2011	12/31/2010	12/31/2009
Earnings Per Share	3.17	3.16	3.08	3.00	2.84	2.46	1.73	0.97
Cash Flow Per Share	4.77	4.98	2.96	6.22	4.21	5.13	2.74	4.11
Tang Book Value Per Share	16.65	16.00	14.66	12.95	11.97	10.32	8.03	6.30
Dividends Per Share	1.020	1.010	0.965	0.885	0.780	0.500	0.200	0.200
Dividend Payout %	32.18	31.96	31.33	29.50	27.46	20.33	11.56	20.62
Income Statement								
Interest Income	3,221,000	12,402,000	12,228,000	12,285,000	12,883,000	12,639,000	12,158,000	11,538,000
Interest Expense	386,000	1,401,000	1,453,000	1,681,000	2,138,000	2,516,000	2,579,000	3,020,000
Net Interest Income	2,835,000	11,001,000	10,775,000	10,604,000	10,745,000	10,123,000	9,579,000	8,518,000
Provision for Losses	330,000	1,132,000	1,229,000	1,340,000	1,882,000	2,343,000	4,356,000	5,557,000
Non-Interest Income	2,149,000	9,092,000	9,164,000	8,774,000	9,319,000	8,760,000	8,360,000	7,952,000
Non-Interest Expense	2,749,000	10,931,000	10,715,000	10,274,000	10,456,000	9,911,000	9,383,000	8,281,000
Income Before Taxes	1,905,000	8,030,000	7,995,000	7,764,000	7,726,000	6,629,000	4,200,000	2,632,000
Income Taxes	504,000	2,097,000	2,087,000	2,032,000	2,236,000	1,841,000	935,000	395,000
Net Income	1,386,000	5,879,000	5,851,000	5,836,000	5,647,000	4,872,000	3,317,000	2,205,000
Average Shares	1,743,000	1,772,000	1,813,000	1,849,000	1,896,000	1,923,000	1,921,000	1,859,000
Balance Sheet								
Net Loans & Leases	264,674,000	260,170,000	248,604,000	234,253,000	226,881,000	212,238,000	200,122,000	195,101,000
Total Assets	428,638,000	421,853,000	402,529,000	364,021,000	353,855,000	340,122,000	307,786,000	281,176,000
Total Deposits	306,348,000	300,400,000	282,733,000	262,123,000	249,183,000	230,885,000	204,252,000	183,242,000
Total Liabilities	381,883,000	375,722,000	359,050,000	322,908,000	314,857,000	306,144,000	278,267,000	255,213,000
Stockholders' Equity	46,755,000	46,131,000	43,479,000	41,113,000	38,998,000	33,978,000	29,519,000	25,963,000
Shares Outstanding	1,732,006	1,745,190	1,785,866	1,824,748	1,869,431	1,909,821	1,920,903	1,912,938
Statistical Record								
Return on Assets %	1.39	1.43	1.53	1.63	1.62	1.50	1.13	0.81
Return on Equity %	12.82	13.12	13.83	14.57	15.43	15.35	11.96	8.44
Net Interest Margin %	88.02	88.70	88.12	86.32	83.40	80.09	78.79	73.83
Efficiency Ratio %	51.19	50.86	50.09	48.79	47.09	46.32	45.73	42.49
Loans to Deposits	0.86	0.87	0.88	0.89	0.91	0.92	0.98	1.06
Price Range	46.02-37.45	46.02-39.76	45.91-38.78	40.60-31.94	35.19-27.57	28.70-20.31	28.26-20.71	25.35-8.82
P/E Ratio	14.52-11.81	14.56-12.58	14.91-12.59	13.53-10.65	12.39-9.71	11.67-8.26	16.34-11.97	26.13-9.09
Average Yield %	2.40	2.33	2.30	2.47	2.45	1.97	0.82	1.03

Address: 800 Nicollet Mall, Minneapolis, MN 55402 **Telephone:** 651-466-3000	**Web Site:** www.usbank.com **Officers:** Richard K. Davis - Chairman, President, Chief Executive Officer, Chief Operating Officer Andrew Cecere - Vice-Chairman, President, Chief Operating Officer, Chief Financial Officer	**Auditors:** Ernst & Young LLP **Investor Contact:** 612-303-0778 **Transfer Agents:** Computershare, Providence, R.I.

UNITED TECHNOLOGIES CORP

Exchange	Symbol	Price	52Wk Range	Yield	P/E	Div Achiever
NYS	UTX	$100.58 (5/31/2016)	118.51-84.66	2.62	11.89	22 Years

*7 Year Price Score 93.99   *NYSE Composite Index=100   *12 Month Price Score 102.98

Interim Earnings (Per Share)

Qtr.	Mar	Jun	Sep	Dec
2013	1.39	1.71	1.57	1.59
2014	1.32	1.84	2.04	1.62
2015	1.58	1.73	1.54	3.76
2016	1.43			

Interim Dividends (Per Share)

Amt	Decl	Ex	Rec	Pay
0.64Q	10/14/2015	11/10/2015	11/13/2015	12/10/2015
0.64Q	02/08/2016	02/17/2016	02/19/2016	03/10/2016
0.66Q	04/25/2016	05/18/2016	05/20/2016	06/10/2016
0.66Q	06/08/2016	08/17/2016	08/19/2016	09/10/2016

Indicated Div: $2.64 (Div. Reinv. Plan)

Valuation Analysis

		Institutional Holding	
Forecast EPS	$6.55 (05/20/2016)	No of Institutions	1999
Market Cap	$84.2 Billion	Shares	802,763,456
Book Value	$28.4 Billion	% Held	
Price/Book	2.97		79.65
Price/Sales	1.46		

Business Summary: Aerospace (MIC: 7.1.1 SIC: 3724 NAIC: 336412)

United Technologies provides technology products and services to the building systems and aerospace industries. Co. operates in the following segments: Otis, UTC Climate, Controls & Security, Pratt & Whitney, and UTC Aerospace Systems. Co.'s principal products and services include elevators, escalators, heating, ventilating, air conditioning and refrigeration systems, aircraft engines for the commercial, military, business jet and general aviation markets, aerospace products and aftermarket service solutions for aircraft manufacturers, airlines, regional, business and general aviation markets, military, space and undersea operations.

Recent Developments: For the quarter ended Mar 31 2016, revenues were US$13.36 billion, up 0.3% from US$13.32 billion the year before. Operating income was US$1.95 billion versus US$2.18 billion in the prior-year quarter, a decrease of 10.9%. Direct operating expenses rose 1.6% to US$9.65 billion from US$9.51 billion in the comparable period the year before. Indirect operating expenses increased 7.7% to US$1.76 billion from US$1.63 billion in the equivalent prior-year period.

Prospects: Our evaluation of United Technologies Corp. as of June 19, 2016 is the result of our systematic analysis on three basic characteristics: earnings strength, relative valuation, and recent stock price movement. The company has enjoyed a very positive trend in earnings per share over the past 5 quarters. However, while recent estimates for the company have been mixed, UTX has posted better than expected results. Based on operating earnings yield, the company is undervalued when compared to all of the companies in our coverage universe. Share price changes over the past year indicates that UTX will perform in line with the market over the near term.

Financial Data
(US$ in Millions)

	3 Mos	12/31/2015	12/31/2014	12/31/2013	12/31/2012	12/31/2011	12/31/2010	12/31/2009
Earnings Per Share	8.46	8.61	6.82	6.25	5.66	5.49	4.74	4.12
Cash Flow Per Share	7.49	7.68	8.17	8.33	7.36	7.39	6.51	5.83
Tang Book Value Per Share	N.M.	N.M.	N.M.	N.M.	N.M.	0.02	N.M.	0.25
Dividends Per Share	2.560	2.560	2.360	2.195	2.030	1.865	1.700	1.540
Dividend Payout %	30.26	29.73	34.60	35.12	35.87	33.97	35.86	37.38
Income Statement								
Total Revenue	13,357	56,098	65,100	62,626	57,708	58,190	54,326	52,920
EBITDA	2,411	8,359	10,891	10,259	8,604	8,989	8,086	7,317
Depn & Amortn	466	1,068	1,122	1,050	920	890	900	852
Income Before Taxes	1,722	6,467	8,887	8,312	6,911	7,605	6,538	5,760
Income Taxes	461	2,111	2,264	2,238	1,711	2,231	1,827	1,581
Net Income	1,191	7,608	6,220	5,721	5,130	4,979	4,373	3,829
Average Shares	831	883	911	915	906	906	922	928
Balance Sheet								
Current Assets	27,527	26,706	29,758	29,442	29,610	25,758	23,510	23,194
Total Assets	88,571	87,484	91,289	90,594	89,409	61,452	58,493	55,762
Current Liabilities	20,523	22,618	22,895	22,800	23,786	18,616	17,732	17,913
Long-Term Obligations	21,688	19,320	17,872	19,741	21,597	9,501	10,010	8,257
Total Liabilities	60,218	60,126	60,076	58,728	63,495	39,572	37,108	35,696
Stockholders' Equity	28,353	27,358	31,213	31,866	25,914	21,880	21,385	20,066
Shares Outstanding	836	838	909	915	918	907	921	936
Statistical Record								
Return on Assets %	8.32	8.51	6.84	6.36	6.78	8.30	7.65	6.82
Return on Equity %	26.25	25.98	19.72	19.80	21.41	23.02	21.10	21.28
EBITDA Margin %	18.05	14.90	16.73	16.38	14.91	15.45	14.88	13.83
Net Margin %	8.92	13.56	9.55	9.14	8.89	8.56	8.05	7.24
Asset Turnover	0.64	0.63	0.72	0.70	0.76	0.97	0.95	0.94
Current Ratio	1.34	1.18	1.30	1.29	1.24	1.38	1.33	1.29
Debt to Equity	0.76	0.71	0.57	0.62	0.83	0.43	0.47	0.41
Price Range	119.14-84.66	124.11-86.82	120.09-99.17	113.80-82.01	86.89-70.88	91.39-67.44	79.52-63.22	70.49-37.56
P/E Ratio	14.08-10.01	14.41-10.08	17.61-14.54	18.21-13.12	15.35-12.52	16.65-12.28	16.78-13.34	17.11-9.12
Average Yield %	2.54	2.39	2.11	2.22	2.59	2.33	2.38	2.79

Address: 10 Farm Springs Road, Farmington, CT 06032
Telephone: 860-728-7000
Fax: 860-728-7028

Web Site: www.utc.com
Officers: Gregory J. Hayes - President, Chief Executive Officer, Senior Vice President, Chief Financial Officer Elizabeth B. Amato - Senior Vice President

Auditors: PricewaterhouseCoopers LLP
Transfer Agents: Computershare Trust Company, N. A., Canton, MA

UNIVERSAL CORP.

Exchange	Symbol	Price	52Wk Range	Yield	P/E	Div Achiever
NYS	UVV	$54.70 (5/31/2016)	58.41-46.98	3.88	13.95	45 Years

*7 Year Price Score 96.62   *NYSE Composite Index=100   *12 Month Price Score 100.42

Interim Earnings (Per Share)

Qtr.	Jun	Sep	Dec	Mar
2011-12	0.52	(0.51)	2.06	0.91
2012-13	0.81	1.68	1.26	0.91
2013-14	2.05	0.90	1.36	0.94
2014-15	(0.13)	0.48	1.87	1.63
2015-16	(0.43)	0.81	1.60	1.74

Interim Dividends (Per Share)

Amt	Decl	Ex	Rec	Pay
0.52Q	08/04/2015	10/08/2015	10/13/2015	11/09/2015
0.53Q	11/05/2015	01/07/2016	01/11/2016	02/08/2016
0.53Q	02/03/2016	04/07/2016	04/11/2016	05/09/2016
0.53Q	05/24/2016	07/07/2016	07/11/2016	08/08/2016

Indicated Div: $2.12 (Div. Reinv. Plan)

Valuation Analysis

		Institutional Holding	
Forecast EPS	N/A	No of Institutions	279
Market Cap	$1.2 Billion	Shares	27,266,684
Book Value	$1.4 Billion	% Held	93.71
Price/Book	0.88		
Price/Sales	0.59		

Business Summary: Tobacco Products (MIC: 1.3.1 SIC: 5159 NAIC: 424590)

Universal is a holding company. Through its subsidiaries, Co.'s primary business is procuring, financing, processing, packing, storing, and shipping leaf tobacco. Co.'s North America, South America, Africa, Europe, and Asia segments are primarily involved in flue-cured and burley leaf tobacco operations for supply to cigarette manufacturers. Co.'s Dark Air-Cured group supplies dark air-cured tobacco principally to manufacturers of cigars, pipe tobacco, and smokeless tobacco products, and Co.'s Oriental business supplies oriental tobacco to cigarette manufacturers. Co.'s Special Services group provides laboratory services.

Recent Developments: For the year ended Mar 31 2016, net income decreased 1.9% to US$118.1 million from US$120.5 million in the prior year. Revenues were US$2.12 billion, down 6.7% from US$2.27 billion the year before. Operating income was US$181.6 million versus US$167.9 million in the prior year, an increase of 8.2%. Direct operating expenses declined 8.0% to US$1.71 billion from US$1.86 billion in the comparable period the year before. Indirect operating expenses decreased 6.9% to US$225.7 million from US$242.4 million in the equivalent prior-year period.

Prospects: Our evaluation of Universal Corp. as of June 19, 2016 is the result of our systematic analysis on three basic characteristics: earnings strength, relative valuation, and recent stock price movement. The company has produced a positive trend in earnings per share over the past 5 quarters. Because the company lacks sufficient analyst estimate data, we place greater weight on the historical EPS trend as the measure of earnings strength. Based on operating earnings yield, the company is undervalued when compared to all of the companies in our coverage universe. Share price changes over the past year indicates that UVV will perform well over the near term.

Financial Data

(US$ in Thousands)	03/31/2016	03/31/2015	03/31/2014	03/31/2013	03/31/2012	03/31/2011	03/31/2010	03/31/2009
Earnings Per Share	3.92	4.06	5.25	4.66	3.25	5.42	5.68	4.57
Cash Flow Per Share	8.07	9.83	(0.15)	10.04	8.58	2.27	6.56	3.87
Tang Book Value Per Share	48.58	46.56	45.91	40.55	37.46	37.57	33.05	28.42
Dividends Per Share	2.090	2.050	2.010	1.970	1.930	1.890	1.850	1.810
Dividend Payout %	53.32	50.49	38.29	42.27	59.38	34.87	32.57	39.61
Income Statement								
Total Revenue	2,120,373	2,271,801	2,542,115	2,461,699	2,446,877	2,571,527	2,491,738	2,554,659
EBITDA	218,401	203,268	283,408	266,417	222,462	298,254	298,497	250,693
Depn & Amortn	36,754	35,394	37,257	43,408	42,158	43,654	41,288	40,761
Income Before Taxes	167,156	151,330	226,793	201,650	158,783	234,265	234,252	176,606
Income Taxes	54,430	38,006	75,535	66,366	61,159	78,349	86,283	64,588
Net Income	109,016	114,608	149,009	132,750	92,057	156,565	168,397	131,739
Average Shares	27,825	28,221	28,392	28,478	28,339	28,888	29,662	25,570
Balance Sheet								
Current Assets	1,638,546	1,634,610	1,673,247	1,745,973	1,690,629	1,578,234	1,693,076	1,503,919
Total Assets	2,232,797	2,198,473	2,270,907	2,306,155	2,266,919	2,227,867	2,371,040	2,138,176
Current Liabilities	246,270	270,913	454,776	622,597	392,708	512,351	614,999	549,875
Long-Term Obligations	370,000	370,000	240,000	181,250	392,500	320,193	414,764	331,808
Total Liabilities	818,575	835,748	892,677	1,047,584	1,083,468	1,042,261	1,248,470	1,108,703
Stockholders' Equity	1,414,222	1,362,725	1,378,230	1,258,571	1,183,451	1,185,606	1,122,570	1,029,473
Shares Outstanding	22,717	22,593	23,216	23,343	23,257	23,240	24,325	24,999
Statistical Record								
Return on Assets %	4.91	5.13	6.51	5.81	4.08	6.81	7.47	6.17
Return on Equity %	7.83	8.36	11.30	10.87	7.75	13.57	15.65	12.28
EBITDA Margin %	10.30	8.95	11.15	10.82	9.09	11.60	11.98	9.81
Net Margin %	5.14	5.04	5.86	5.39	3.76	6.09	6.76	5.16
Asset Turnover	0.95	1.02	1.11	1.08	1.09	1.12	1.11	1.20
Current Ratio	6.65	6.03	3.68	2.80	4.31	3.08	2.75	2.74
Debt to Equity	0.26	0.27	0.17	0.14	0.33	0.27	0.37	0.32
Price Range	58.41-46.80	56.82-38.53	63.36-48.43	58.36-44.03	48.11-35.11	55.92-35.44	55.19-29.27	65.53-25.82
P/E Ratio	14.90-11.94	14.00-9.49	12.07-9.22	12.52-9.45	14.80-10.80	10.32-6.54	9.72-5.15	14.34-5.65
Average Yield %	3.94	4.26	3.65	3.99	4.61	4.48	4.43	4.11

Address: 9201 Forest Hill Avenue, Richmond, VA 23235	**Web Site:** www.universalcorp.com	**Auditors:** Ernst & Young LLP
Telephone: 804-359-9311	**Officers:** George C. Freeman - Chairman, President, Chief Executive Officer Airton L. Hentschke - Senior Vice President, Chief Operating Officer	**Investor Contact:** 804-359-9311
		Transfer Agents: Wells Fargo Bank, N.A., St. Paul, MN

UNIVERSAL HEALTH REALTY INCOME TRUST

Exchange	Symbol	Price	52Wk Range	Yield	P/E	Div Achiever
NYS	UHT	$53.50 (5/31/2016)	57.85-43.54	4.86	29.23	28 Years

*7 Year Price Score 101.21 *NYSE Composite Index=100   ***12 Month Price Score 107.44**

Interim Earnings (Per Share)

Qtr.	Mar	Jun	Sep	Dec
2013	0.27	0.23	0.26	0.28
2014	0.29	0.26	2.18	1.25
2015	0.28	0.90	0.27	0.33
2016	0.33	...	...	...

Interim Dividends (Per Share)

Amt	Decl	Ex	Rec	Pay
0.64Q	09/09/2015	09/17/2015	09/21/2015	09/30/2015
0.645Q	12/10/2015	12/17/2015	12/21/2015	12/31/2015
0.645Q	03/03/2016	03/14/2016	03/16/2016	03/31/2016
0.65Q	06/09/2016	06/16/2016	06/20/2016	06/30/2016

Indicated Div: $2.60 (Div. Reinv. Plan)

Valuation Analysis | **Institutional Holding**

Forecast EPS	N/A	No of Institutions
		185
Market Cap	$713.0 Million	Shares
Book Value	$191.1 Million	7,466,253
Price/Book	3.73	% Held
Price/Sales	11.15	50.93

Business Summary: REITs (MIC: 5.3.1 SIC: 6798 NAIC: 525930)

Universal Health Realty Income Trust is real estate investment trust. Co. invests in health care and human service related facilities including acute care hospitals, rehabilitation hospitals, sub-acute facilities, surgery centers, free-standing emergency departments, childcare centers and medical office buildings. As of Feb 29 2016, Co. had 62 real estate investments or commitments located in the U.S. consisting of: six hospital facilities including three acute care, one rehabilitation and two sub-acute,; three free-standing emergency departments; 49 medical office buildings, including five owned by unconsolidated limited liability companies; and; four preschool and childcare centers.

Recent Developments: For the quarter ended Mar 31 2016, net income increased 19.8% to US$4.4 million from US$3.7 million in the year-earlier quarter. Revenues were US$16.2 million, unchanged from the year before.

Prospects: Our evaluation of Universal Health Realty Income Trust as of June 19, 2016 is the result of our systematic analysis on three basic characteristics: earnings strength, relative valuation, and recent stock price movement. The company has managed to produce a neutral trend in earnings per share over the past 5 quarters. Because the company lacks sufficient analyst estimate data, we place greater weight on the historical EPS trend as the measure of earnings strength. Based on operating earnings yield, the company is overvalued when compared to all of the companies in our coverage universe. Share price changes over the past year indicates that UHT will perform well over the near term.

Financial Data
(US$ in Thousands)

	3 Mos	12/31/2015	12/31/2014	12/31/2013	12/31/2012	12/31/2011	12/31/2010	12/31/2009
Earnings Per Share	1.83	1.78	3.99	1.04	1.54	5.83	1.33	1.56
Cash Flow Per Share	2.93	2.87	2.54	2.47	2.42	1.69	1.88	2.10
Tang Book Value Per Share	12.85	13.15	13.64	11.26	11.93	12.69	11.49	11.66
Dividends Per Share	2.570	2.560	2.520	2.495	2.460	2.425	2.415	2.380
Dividend Payout %	140.44	143.82	63.16	239.90	159.74	41.60	181.58	152.56
Income Statement								
Total Revenue	16,226	63,950	59,786	54,280	53,950	29,494	28,878	31,914
EBITDA	5,485	51,352	78,162	36,956	44,439	80,444	21,587	24,331
Depn & Amortn	(56)	21,973	20,663	18,410	19,559	7,306	6,286	6,399
Income Before Taxes	3,369	21,155	49,123	11,074	17,112	70,736	13,362	15,484
Net Income	4,428	23,691	51,551	13,169	19,477	73,794	16,310	18,576
Average Shares	13,314	13,301	12,934	12,701	12,669	12,649	12,262	11,897
Balance Sheet								
Current Assets	11,235	10,302	10,166	8,700	7,872	15,687	3,863	6,057
Total Assets	471,107	458,901	428,866	373,145	383,038	370,929	216,135	228,825
Current Liabilities	160,188	504	545	491	539	473	113	142
Long-Term Obligations	109,332	252,704	213,155	199,987	197,936	174,836	67,563	84,267
Total Liabilities	280,045	263,859	224,285	207,515	205,367	182,068	70,722	87,863
Stockholders' Equity	191,062	195,042	204,581	165,630	177,671	188,861	145,413	140,962
Shares Outstanding	13,328	13,327	13,301	12,858	12,688	12,666	12,653	12,089
Statistical Record								
Return on Assets %	5.35	5.34	12.86	3.48	5.15	25.14	7.33	8.26
Return on Equity %	12.49	11.86	27.85	7.67	10.60	44.15	11.39	13.00
EBITDA Margin %	33.80	80.30	130.74	68.08	82.37	272.75	74.75	76.24
Net Margin %	27.29	37.05	86.23	24.26	36.10	250.20	56.48	58.21
Asset Turnover	0.14	0.14	0.15	0.14	0.14	0.10	0.13	0.14
Current Ratio	0.07	20.44	18.65	17.72	14.60	33.16	34.19	42.65
Debt to Equity	0.57	1.30	1.04	1.21	1.11	0.93	0.46	0.60
Price Range	56.80-43.54	56.87-43.54	49.13-40.06	58.85-38.52	50.61-37.77	43.38-32.21	38.40-30.79	35.28-25.11
P/E Ratio	31.04-23.79	31.95-24.46	12.31-10.04	56.59-37.04	32.86-24.53	7.44-5.52	28.87-23.15	22.62-16.10
Average Yield %	5.17	5.13	5.75	5.22	5.76	6.33	7.08	7.51

Address: Universal Corporate Center, 367 South Gulph Road, P.O. Box 61558, King of Prussia, PA 19406-0958
Telephone: 610-265-0688
Fax: 610-768-3336

Web Site: www.uhrit.com
Officers: Alan B. Miller - Chairman, President, Chief Executive Officer Charles F. Boyle - Vice President, Chief Financial Officer

Auditors: KPMG LLP
Transfer Agents: Computershare, Providence, RI

UNIVERSAL HEALTH SERVICES, INC.

Exchange	Symbol	Price	52Wk Range	Yield	P/E
NYS	UHS	$134.86 (5/31/2016)	146.24-101.65	0.30	19.40

*7 Year Price Score 157.73 *NYSE Composite Index=100 ***12 Month Price Score 102.83**

Interim Earnings (Per Share)

Qtr.	Mar	Jun	Sep	Dec
2013	1.21	1.53	1.15	1.25
2014	1.38	1.51	0.82	1.71
2015	1.73	1.80	1.48	1.74
2016	1.93	...	...	...

Interim Dividends (Per Share)

Amt	Decl	Ex	Rec	Pay
0.10Q	07/15/2015	08/28/2015	09/01/2015	09/15/2015
0.10Q	11/18/2015	11/27/2015	12/01/2015	12/15/2015
0.10Q	01/20/2016	02/26/2016	03/01/2016	03/15/2016
0.10Q	05/19/2016	06/01/2016	06/01/2016	06/15/2016

Indicated Div: $0.40

Valuation Analysis — **Institutional Holding**

Forecast EPS	$7.54	No of Institutions
	(05/20/2016)	628
Market Cap	$13.1 Billion	Shares
Book Value	$4.3 Billion	101,754,744
Price/Book	3.05	% Held
Price/Sales	1.41	84.72

Business Summary: Hospitals & Health Care Facilities (MIC: 4.2.1 SIC: 8062 NAIC: 622110)

Universal Health Services owns and operates, through its subsidiaries, acute care hospitals, behavioral health centers, surgical hospitals, ambulatory surgery centers and radiation oncology centers. Services provided by Co.'s hospitals include general and specialty surgery, internal medicine, obstetrics, emergency room care, radiology, oncology, diagnostic care, coronary care, pediatric services, pharmacy services and/or behavioral health services. As of Feb 25 2016, Co. owned and/or operated 24 acute care hospitals, three free-standing emergency departments and 229 behavioral health care facilities located in 37 states, Washington, D.C., the U.K., Puerto Rico and the U.S. Virgin Islands.

Recent Developments: For the quarter ended Mar 31 2016, net income increased 11.0% to US$215.7 million from US$194.3 million in the year-earlier quarter. Revenues were US$2.45 billion, up 10.1% from US$2.23 billion the year before. Operating income was US$356.3 million versus US$327.1 million in the prior-year quarter, an increase of 8.9%. Indirect operating expenses increased 10.3% to US$2.09 billion from US$1.90 billion in the equivalent prior-year period.

Prospects: Our evaluation of Universal Health Services Inc. as of June 19, 2016 is the result of our systematic analysis on three basic characteristics: earnings strength, relative valuation, and recent stock price movement. The company has managed to produce a neutral trend in earnings per share over the past 5 quarters and while recent estimates for the company have been mixed, UHS has posted better than expected results. Based on operating earnings yield, the company is undervalued when compared to all of the companies in our coverage universe. Share price changes over the past year indicates that UHS will perform in line with the market over the near term.

Financial Data
(US$ in Thousands)

	3 Mos	12/31/2015	12/31/2014	12/31/2013	12/31/2012	12/31/2011	12/31/2010	12/31/2009
Earnings Per Share	6.95	6.76	5.42	5.14	4.53	4.04	2.34	2.64
Cash Flow Per Share	12.44	10.33	10.48	9.02	8.40	7.39	5.18	5.45
Tang Book Value Per Share	7.15	6.65	4.51	2.04	N.M.	N.M	N.M.	10.51
Dividends Per Share	0.400	0.400	0.300	0.200	0.600	0.200	0.200	0.170
Dividend Payout %	5.76	5.92	5.54	3.89	13.25	4.95	8.55	6.44
Income Statement								
Total Revenue	2,449,798	9,043,451	8,065,326	7,283,822	6,961,400	7,500,198	5,568,185	5,202,379
EBITDA	460,373	1,596,895	1,377,805	1,301,063	1,213,081	1,165,628	708,497	705,132
Depn & Amortn	104,049	337,500	314,500	285,600	270,500	268,500	202,800	184,600
Income Before Taxes	326,724	1,145,901	929,667	869,332	763,663	696,336	428,097	474,722
Income Taxes	111,005	395,203	324,671	315,309	274,616	247,466	152,302	170,475
Net Income	190,759	680,528	545,343	510,733	443,446	398,167	230,183	260,373
Average Shares	98,895	100,694	100,544	99,361	97,711	98,537	97,973	98,275
Balance Sheet								
Current Assets	1,635,438	1,718,304	1,615,138	1,432,329	1,407,496	1,364,905	1,331,116	796,197
Total Assets	9,565,009	9,634,113	8,974,443	8,311,723	8,200,843	7,665,245	7,527,936	3,964,463
Current Liabilities	1,685,440	1,100,406	1,182,827	1,059,888	894,058	836,933	826,299	582,817
Long-Term Obligations	2,792,144	3,387,303	3,210,215	3,209,762	3,727,431	3,651,428	3,912,102	956,429
Total Liabilities	5,275,791	5,384,466	5,238,497	5,061,744	5,487,498	5,368,893	5,549,164	2,213,392
Stockholders' Equity	4,289,218	4,249,647	3,735,946	3,249,979	2,713,345	2,296,352	1,978,772	1,751,071
Shares Outstanding	97,046	98,296	98,716	98,311	97,591	96,609	97,450	96,914
Statistical Record								
Return on Assets %	7.47	7.31	6.31	6.19	5.57	5.24	4.01	6.76
Return on Equity %	17.01	17.04	15.61	17.13	17.66	18.63	12.34	15.80
EBITDA Margin %	18.79	17.66	17.08	17.86	17.43	15.54	12.72	13.55
Net Margin %	7.79	7.53	6.76	7.01	6.37	5.31	4.13	5.00
Asset Turnover	0.99	0.97	0.93	0.88	0.88	0.99	0.97	1.35
Current Ratio	0.97	1.56	1.37	1.35	1.57	1.63	1.61	1.37
Debt to Equity	0.65	0.80	0.86	0.99	1.37	1.59	1.98	0.55
Price Range	146.24-101.65	146.24-102.53	114.84-74.35	83.12-48.35	49.46-36.82	56.41-31.91	43.74-28.75	33.17-15.39
P/E Ratio	21.04-14.63	21.63-15.17	21.19-13.72	16.17-9.41	10.92-8.13	13.96-7.90	18.69-12.29	12.57-5.83
Average Yield %	0.32	0.32	0.32	0.29	1.43	0.45	0.54	0.67

Address: Universal Corporate Center, 367 South Gulph Road, King of Prussia, PA 19406
Telephone: 610-768-3300

Web Site: www.uhsinc.com
Officers: Alan B. Miller - Chairman, Chief Executive Officer, Division Officer Marc D. Miller - President

Auditors: PricewaterhouseCoopers LLP
Investor Contact: 610-768-3300
Transfer Agents: Computershare, Canton, MA

751

UNUM GROUP

Exchange	Symbol	Price	52Wk Range	Yield	P/E
NYS	UNM	$36.92 (5/31/2016)	37.61-24.07	2.00	10.43

*7 Year Price Score 104.65 *NYSE Composite Index=100 *12 Month Price Score 100.48

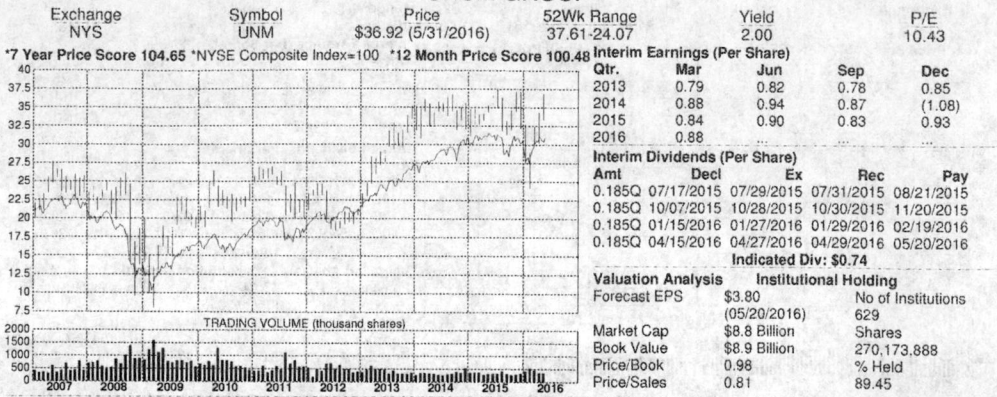

Interim Earnings (Per Share)

Qtr.	Mar	Jun	Sep	Dec
2013	0.79	0.82	0.78	0.85
2014	0.88	0.94	0.87	(1.08)
2015	0.84	0.90	0.83	0.93
2016	0.88	...	...	...

Interim Dividends (Per Share)

Amt	Decl	Ex	Rec	Pay
0.185Q	07/17/2015	07/29/2015	07/31/2015	08/21/2015
0.185Q	10/07/2015	10/28/2015	10/30/2015	11/20/2015
0.185Q	01/15/2016	01/27/2016	01/29/2016	02/19/2016
0.185Q	04/15/2016	04/27/2016	04/29/2016	05/20/2016

Indicated Div: $0.74

Valuation Analysis

Forecast EPS	$3.80
	(05/20/2016)
Market Cap	$8.8 Billion
Book Value	$8.9 Billion
Price/Book	0.98
Price/Sales	0.81

Institutional Holding

No of Institutions	629
Shares	270,173,888
% Held	89.45

Business Summary: Life & Health (MIC: 5.2.2 SIC: 6321 NAIC: 524114)

Unum Group is an insurance holding company. Through its subsidiaries, Co. provides disability insurance products and other insurance products. Co.'s three main segments are: Unum U.S., which includes group disability insurance, group life and accidental death and dismemberment products, and supplemental and voluntary lines of business; Unum U.K., which includes group disability, group life, and supplemental lines of business; and Colonial Life, which includes insurance for accident, sickness, and disability products, life products, and cancer and critical illness products. Other segment includes the Closed Block, which consists of individual disability, group and individual long-term care.

Recent Developments: For the quarter ended Mar 31 2016, net income decreased 1.1% to US$210.6 million from US$212.9 million in the year-earlier quarter. Revenues were US$2.73 billion, up 2.9% from US$2.65 billion the year before. Net premiums earned were US$2.09 billion versus US$2.01 billion in the prior-year quarter, an increase of 4.0%. Net investment income rose 0.7% to US$606.4 million from US$602.0 million a year ago.

Prospects: Our evaluation of UNUM Group as of June 19, 2016 is the result of our systematic analysis on three basic characteristics: earnings strength, relative valuation, and recent stock price movement. The company has managed to produce a neutral trend in earnings per share over the past 5 quarters and while recent estimates for the company have remained steady, UNM has posted better than expected results. Based on operating earnings yield, the company is undervalued when compared to all of the companies in our coverage universe. Share price changes over the past year indicates that UNM will perform in line with the market over the near term.

Financial Data

(US$ in Thousands)	3 Mos	12/31/2015	12/31/2014	12/31/2013	12/31/2012	12/31/2011	12/31/2010	12/31/2009
Earnings Per Share	3.54	3.50	1.61	3.23	3.17	0.78	2.71	2.57
Cash Flow Per Share	4.95	5.23	4.79	3.90	4.89	3.95	3.67	3.73
Tang Book Value Per Share	36.56	35.00	33.11	32.53	31.13	28.61	27.62	25.01
Dividends Per Share	0.720	0.700	0.620	0.550	0.470	0.395	0.350	0.315
Dividend Payout %	20.34	20.00	38.51	17.03	14.83	50.64	12.92	12.26
Income Statement								
Premium Income	2,087,500	8,082,400	7,797,200	7,624,700	7,716,100	7,514,200	7,431,400	7,475,500
Total Revenue	2,725,400	10,731,300	10,509,700	10,353,800	10,515,400	10,278,000	10,193,200	10,091,000
Income Before Taxes	304,200	1,238,300	527,200	1,205,200	1,249,500	257,200	1,331,300	1,292,300
Income Taxes	93,600	371,200	113,800	347,100	355,100	21,800	445,200	439,700
Net Income	210,600	867,100	413,400	858,100	894,400	235,400	886,100	852,600
Average Shares	239,930	247,854	256,652	265,949	281,756	303,571	327,221	332,136
Balance Sheet								
Total Assets	61,967,900	60,589,700	62,497,100	59,403,600	62,236,100	60,179,000	57,307,700	54,477,000
Total Liabilities	53,047,600	51,925,800	53,944,700	50,744,500	53,623,500	51,602,000	48,363,300	45,976,900
Stockholders' Equity	8,920,300	8,663,900	8,552,400	8,659,100	8,612,600	8,577,000	8,944,400	8,500,100
Shares Outstanding	237,733	240,917	252,309	260,017	270,205	292,715	316,573	331,809
Statistical Record								
Return on Assets %	1.38	1.41	0.68	1.41	1.46	0.40	1.59	1.64
Return on Equity %	9.82	10.07	4.80	9.94	10.38	2.69	10.16	11.45
Net Margin %	7.73	8.08	3.93	8.29	8.51	2.29	8.69	8.45
Price Range	37.61-24.07	37.61-31.05	36.81-30.71	35.16-20.82	24.68-18.36	26.90-19.91	26.41-18.73	22.89-7.99
P/E Ratio	10.62-6.80	10.75-8.87	22.86-19.07	10.89-6.45	7.79-5.79	34.49-25.53	9.75-6.91	8.91-3.11
Average Yield %	2.16	2.04	1.81	1.90	2.24	1.63	1.56	1.81

Address: 1 Fountain Square, Chattanooga, TN 37402 **Telephone:** 423-294-1011	**Web Site:** www.unum.com **Officers:** Kevin P. McCarthy - Executive Vice President, Chief Operating Officer, Region Officer Richard P. McKenney - Executive Vice President, Chief Financial Officer, President, Chief Executive Officer	**Auditors:** Ernst & Young LLP **Transfer Agents:** Computershare Trust Company, N.A., Providence, RI

URBAN EDGE PROPERTIES

Exchange	Symbol	Price	52Wk Range	Yield	P/E
NYS	UE	$26.85 (5/31/2016)	27.80-20.12	2.98	38.91

*7 Year Price Score N/A   *NYSE Composite Index=100   *12 Month Price Score 110.34

Interim Earnings (Per Share)

Qtr.	Mar	Jun	Sep	Dec
2014	0.18	0.18	0.14	0.00
2015	(0.12)	0.16	0.19	0.15
2016	0.19	...	...	...

Interim Dividends (Per Share)

Amt	Decl	Ex	Rec	Pay
0.20Q	08/17/2015	09/11/2015	09/15/2015	09/30/2015
0.20Q	11/03/2015	12/11/2015	12/15/2015	12/31/2015
0.20Q	02/18/2016	03/11/2016	03/15/2016	03/31/2016
0.20Q	05/16/2016	06/13/2016	06/15/2016	06/30/2016

Indicated Div: $0.80 (Div. Reinv. Plan)

Valuation Analysis   Institutional Holding

Forecast EPS	$0.75	No of Institutions
	(05/15/2016)	231
Market Cap	$2.7 Billion	Shares
Book Value	$437.6 Million	90,832,864
Price/Book	6.10	% Held
Price/Sales	8.28	N/A

Business Summary: REITs (MIC: 5.3.1 SIC: 6798 NAIC: 525930)

Urban Edge Properties is a real estate investment trust focused on managing, developing, redeveloping, and acquiring retail real estate in urban communities, primarily in the New York metropolitan region. Urban Edge Properties LP is a Delaware limited partnership formed to serve as Co.'s majority-owned partnership subsidiary and to own, through affiliates, all of Co.'s real estate properties and other assets. As of Dec 31 2015, Co. owned 80 shopping centers, three malls and a warehouse park adjacent to one of its centers totaling 14.8 million square feet.

Recent Developments: For the quarter ended Mar 31 2016, net income amounted to US$19.8 million versus a net loss of US$12.0 million in the year-earlier quarter. Revenues were US$83.1 million, down 0.9% from US$83.8 million the year before. Revenues from property income rose 2.3% to US$58.9 million from US$57.6 million in the corresponding quarter a year earlier.

Prospects: Our evaluation of Urban Edge Properties as of June 19, 2016 is the result of our systematic analysis on three basic characteristics: earnings strength, relative valuation, and recent stock price movement. The company has produced a positive trend in earnings per share over the past 5 quarters. Because the company lacks sufficient analyst estimate data, we place greater weight on the historical EPS trend as the measure of earnings strength. Based on operating earnings yield, the company is overvalued when compared to all of the companies in our coverage universe. Share price changes over the past year indicates that UE will perform well over the near term.

Financial Data

(US$ in Thousands)	3 Mos	12/31/2015	12/31/2014	12/31/2013	12/31/2012
Earnings Per Share	0.69	0.39	...	...	...
Cash Flow Per Share	1.41	1.39	...	...	...
Tang Book Value Per Share	4.07	4.07	2.13	...	...
Dividends Per Share	0.800	0.800	...	...	...
Dividend Payout %	115.94	205.13	...	...	...
Income Statement					
Total Revenue	83,068	322,945	315,676	362,995	304,233
EBITDA	32,170	151,206	168,991	214,979	168,488
Depn & Amortn	(1,216)	53,130	46,551	47,766	43,522
Income Before Taxes	20,124	42,642	67,515	111,435	71,214
Income Taxes	336	1,294	1,721	2,100	1,364
Net Income	18,638	38,785	65,772	109,314	69,837
Average Shares	99,363	99,278	...	...	...
Balance Sheet					
Current Assets	276,510	285,688	123,447	120,767	...
Total Assets	1,907,994	1,918,931	1,741,529	1,749,965	...
Current Liabilities	39,508	45,331	26,924	30,538	...
Long-Term Obligations	1,230,349	1,233,983	1,288,535	1,200,762	...
Total Liabilities	1,470,411	1,481,011	1,483,007	1,408,700	...
Stockholders' Equity	437,583	437,920	258,522	341,265	...
Shares Outstanding	99,381	99,290	104,964	...	...
Statistical Record					
Return on Assets %	3.58	...	3.77	...	...
Return on Equity %	17.76	...	21.93	...	...
EBITDA Margin %	38.73	46.82	53.53	59.22	55.38
Net Margin %	22.44	12.01	20.84	30.11	22.96
Asset Turnover	0.17	...	0.18	...	...
Current Ratio	7.00	6.30	4.59	3.95	...
Debt to Equity	2.81	2.82	4.98	3.52	...
Price Range	25.99-20.12	25.00-20.12	...	...	...
P/E Ratio	37.67-29.16	64.10-51.59	...	...	...
Average Yield %	3.51	3.52	...	...	...

Address: 888 Seventh Avenue, New York, NY 10019
Telephone: 212-956-2556

Web Site: www.uedge.com
Officers: Jeffrey S. Olson - Chairman, President, Chief Executive Officer Mark Langer - Executive President, Chief Financial Officer

Auditors: Deloitte & Touche LLP

URSTADT BIDDLE PROPERTIES INC

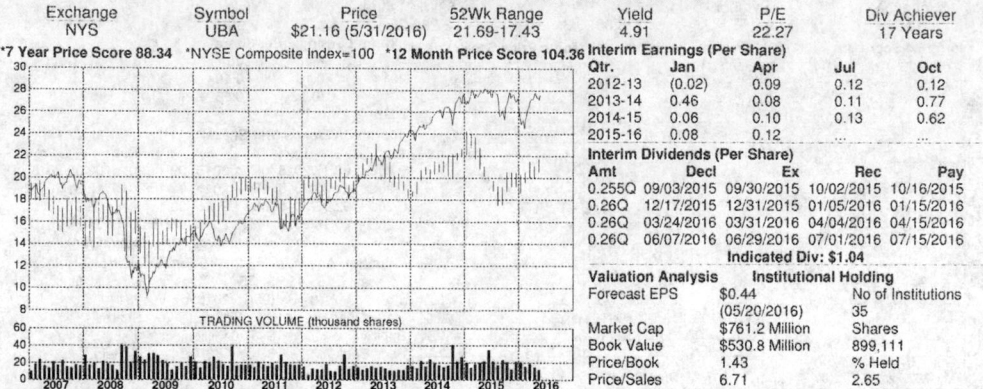

Exchange	Symbol	Price	52Wk Range	Yield	P/E	Div Achiever
NYS	UBA	$21.16 (5/31/2016)	21.69-17.43	4.91	22.27	17 Years

*7 Year Price Score 88.34   *NYSE Composite Index=100   *12 Month Price Score 104.36

Interim Earnings (Per Share)

Qtr.	Jan	Apr	Jul	Oct
2012-13	(0.02)	0.09	0.12	0.12
2013-14	0.46	0.08	0.11	0.77
2014-15	0.06	0.10	0.13	0.62
2015-16	0.08	0.12	...	...

Interim Dividends (Per Share)

Amt	Decl	Ex	Rec	Pay
0.255Q	09/03/2015	09/30/2015	10/02/2015	10/16/2015
0.26Q	12/17/2015	12/31/2015	01/05/2016	01/15/2016
0.26Q	03/24/2016	03/31/2016	04/04/2016	04/15/2016
0.26Q	06/07/2016	06/29/2016	07/01/2016	07/15/2016

Indicated Div: $1.04

Valuation Analysis

		Institutional Holding	
Forecast EPS	$0.44	No of Institutions	
	(05/20/2016)	35	
Market Cap	$761.2 Million	Shares	
Book Value	$530.8 Million	899,111	
Price/Book	1.43	% Held	
Price/Sales	6.71	2.65	

Business Summary: REITs (MIC: 5.3.1 SIC: 6798 NAIC: 525930)

Urstadt Biddle Properties is a real estate investment trust engaged in the acquisition, ownership and management of commercial real estate. Co.'s sole business is the ownership of real estate investments, which consist principally of investments in income-producing properties, with primary emphasis on properties in the metropolitan New York tri-state area outside of the City of New York. At Oct. 31, 2015, Co. owned or had equity interests in 74 properties comprised of neighborhood and community shopping centers, office buildings, single tenant retail or restaurant properties and office/retail mixed use properties located in four states throughout the U.S.

Recent Developments: For the quarter ended Apr 30 2016, net income increased 14.4% to US$8.6 million from US$7.5 million in the year-earlier quarter. Revenues were US$29.2 million, down 2.9% from US$30.1 million the year before. Revenues from property income fell 4.7% to US$28.3 million from US$29.7 million in the corresponding quarter a year earlier.

Prospects: Our evaluation of Urstadt Biddle Properties Inc. as of June 19, 2016 is the result of our systematic analysis on three basic characteristics: earnings strength, relative valuation, and recent stock price movement. The company has generated a negative trend in earnings per share over the past 5 quarters. Because the company lacks sufficient analyst estimate data, we place greater weight on the historical EPS trend as the measure of earnings strength. Based on operating earnings yield, the company is overvalued when compared to all of the companies in our coverage universe. Share price changes over the past year indicates that UBA will perform poorly over the near term.

Financial Data

(US$ in Thousands)	6 Mos	3 Mos	10/31/2015	10/31/2014	10/31/2013	10/31/2012	10/31/2011	10/31/2010
Earnings Per Share	0.95	0.93	0.90	1.42	0.31	0.41	0.60	0.52
Cash Flow Per Share	1.59	1.53	1.49	1.64	1.66	1.86	1.68	1.78
Tang Book Value Per Share	9.08	9.17	9.42	8.40	7.84	9.09	11.41	11.69
Dividends Per Share	1.030	1.025	1.020	1.010	1.000	0.990	0.980	0.970
Dividend Payout %	108.42	110.22	113.33	71.13	322.58	241.46	163.33	186.54
Income Statement								
Total Revenue	56,617	27,451	115,312	102,328	94,245	91,295	91,011	85,149
EBITDA	32,074	15,197	63,576	80,837	53,352	53,875	53,862	49,896
Depn & Amortn	11,347	5,688	22,435	19,249	17,816	16,721	15,292	15,066
Income Before Taxes	14,308	6,289	27,894	51,487	27,787	28,898	31,556	27,641
Net Income	14,786	6,447	49,264	65,151	29,795	28,260	31,643	27,542
Average Shares	35,180	34,910	35,060	31,963	31,740	29,168	28,665	26,118
Balance Sheet								
Current Assets	28,100	28,333	31,167	95,513	25,515	164,614	29,043	37,972
Total Assets	862,243	862,783	861,075	819,005	650,026	724,243	576,264	557,053
Current Liabilities	40,359	36,422	3,438	1,622	1,450	1,632	893	1,397
Long-Term Obligations	257,506	259,000	283,207	245,697	175,496	154,836	159,985	129,802
Total Liabilities	331,394	328,404	320,297	343,962	204,112	239,725	177,843	153,399
Stockholders' Equity	530,849	534,379	540,778	475,043	445,914	484,518	398,421	403,654
Shares Outstanding	35,972	35,969	35,721	32,805	32,565	32,315	29,563	29,281
Statistical Record								
Return on Assets %	5.85	5.70	5.86	8.87	4.34	4.33	5.58	5.19
Return on Equity %	9.58	9.33	9.70	14.15	6.40	6.38	7.89	7.12
EBITDA Margin %	56.65	55.36	55.13	79.00	56.61	59.01	59.18	58.60
Net Margin %	26.12	23.49	42.72	63.67	31.61	30.95	34.77	32.35
Asset Turnover	0.13	0.13	0.14	0.14	0.14	0.14	0.16	0.16
Current Ratio	0.70	0.78	9.07	58.89	17.60	100.87	32.52	27.18
Debt to Equity	0.49	0.48	0.52	0.52	0.39	0.32	0.40	0.32
Price Range	21.46-17.43	24.01-17.43	24.22-17.43	22.08-18.15	23.05-18.12	20.78-15.61	20.05-15.31	19.55-13.72
P/E Ratio	22.59-18.35	25.82-18.74	26.91-19.37	15.55-12.77	74.35-58.45	50.68-38.07	33.42-25.52	37.60-26.38
Average Yield %	5.24	5.09	4.89	5.02	4.88	5.25	5.35	5.84

| **Address:** 321 Railroad Avenue, Greenwich, CT 06830
Telephone: 203-863-8200 | **Web Site:** www.ubproperties.com
Officers: Charles J. Urstadt - Chairman, Chief Executive Officer Robert R. Douglass - Vice-Chairman | **Auditors:** PKF O‚ÄôConnor Davies, LLP
Investor Contact: 203-863-8200
Transfer Agents: BNY Mellon Shareowner Services, Jersey City, N |

USG CORP

Exchange	Symbol	Price	52Wk Range	Yield	P/E
NYS	USG	$28.86 (5/31/2016)	32.73-16.48	N/A	4.10

*7 Year Price Score 103.26 *NYSE Composite Index=100 *12 Month Price Score 105.42

Interim Earnings (Per Share)

Qtr.	Mar	Jun	Sep	Dec
2013	0.02	0.22	0.21	(0.04)
2014	0.32	0.38	(0.09)	(0.37)
2015	0.16	0.54	0.52	5.52
2016	0.46	...	...	...

Interim Dividends (Per Share)

No Dividends Paid

Valuation Analysis   **Institutional Holding**

Forecast EPS	$1.75	No of Institutions
	(05/20/2016)	356
Market Cap	$4.2 Billion	Shares
Book Value	$1.5 Billion	126,989,544
Price/Book	2.77	% Held
Price/Sales	1.10	81.21

Business Summary: Construction Materials (MIC: 8.5.1 SIC: 3275 NAIC: 327420)

USG is a manufacturer and distributor of building materials. Co. operates four segments: Gypsum, which manufactures and markets gypsum and related products in the U.S., Canada, Mexico and Latin America; Ceilings, which manufactures and markets interior systems products in the U.S., Canada, Mexico, and Latin America; Distribution, which consists of L&W Supply Corporation, a distributor of gypsum wallboard and other building materials in the U.S.; as well as USG Boral Building Products, which manufactures and distributes products for wall, ceiling, floor lining and exterior systems that utilize gypsum wallboard, mineral fiber ceiling tiles, steel grid and joint compound.

Recent Developments: For the quarter ended Mar 31 2016, net income increased 179.2% to US$67.0 million from US$24.0 million in the year-earlier quarter. Revenues were US$970.0 million, up 6.7% from US$909.0 million the year before. Operating income was US$127.0 million versus US$76.0 million in the prior-year quarter, an increase of 67.1%. Direct operating expenses rose 2.5% to US$775.0 million from US$756.0 million in the comparable period the year before. Indirect operating expenses decreased 11.7% to US$68.0 million from US$77.0 million in the equivalent prior-year period.

Prospects: Our evaluation of USG Corp. as of June 19, 2016 is the result of our systematic analysis on three basic characteristics: earnings strength, relative valuation, and recent stock price movement. The company has generated a negative trend in earnings per share over the past 5 quarters. However, while recent estimates for the company have been mixed, USG has posted better than expected results. Based on operating earnings yield, the company is undervalued when compared to all of the companies in our coverage universe. Share price changes over the past year indicates that USG will perform well over the near term.

Financial Data
(US$ in Thousands)

	3 Mos	12/31/2015	12/31/2014	12/31/2013	12/31/2012	12/31/2011	12/31/2010	12/31/2009
Earnings Per Share	7.04	6.73	0.25	0.42	(1.19)	(3.76)	(4.03)	(7.93)
Cash Flow Per Share	2.35	2.28	1.22	0.70	0.64	(1.87)	(0.94)	1.40
Tang Book Value Per Share	10.41	9.86	2.81	4.65	0.06	1.48	6.02	9.37
Income Statement								
Total Revenue	970,000	3,776,000	3,724,000	3,570,000	3,224,000	3,024,000	2,939,000	3,235,000
EBITDA	164,000	492,000	323,000	394,000	168,000	(51,000)	(83,000)	27,000
Depn & Amortn	36,000	130,000	134,000	135,000	136,000	144,000	178,000	203,000
Income Before Taxes	90,000	201,000	11,000	59,000	(170,000)	(400,000)	(439,000)	(337,000)
Income Taxes	30,000	(729,000)	7,000	11,000	12,000	(10,000)	(34,000)	450,000
Net Income	67,000	991,000	37,000	47,000	(126,000)	(390,000)	(405,000)	(787,000)
Average Shares	146,986	147,246	144,296	111,434	106,382	103,902	100,472	99,238
Balance Sheet								
Current Assets	1,370,000	1,400,000	1,152,000	1,700,000	1,327,000	1,226,000	1,437,000	1,431,000
Total Assets	4,662,000	4,736,000	3,994,000	4,121,000	3,723,000	3,719,000	4,087,000	4,097,000
Current Liabilities	909,000	991,000	563,000	568,000	551,000	525,000	529,000	492,000
Long-Term Obligations	1,676,000	1,675,000	2,205,000	2,292,000	2,305,000	2,297,000	2,301,000	1,955,000
Total Liabilities	3,144,000	3,300,000	3,587,000	3,483,000	3,717,000	3,563,000	3,468,000	3,167,000
Stockholders' Equity	1,518,000	1,436,000	407,000	638,000	6,000	156,000	619,000	930,000
Shares Outstanding	145,853	145,667	144,768	137,314	107,850	105,329	102,876	99,300
Statistical Record								
Return on Assets %	24.14	22.70	0.91	1.20	N.M.	N.M.	N.M.	N.M.
Return on Equity %	107.71	107.54	7.08	14.60	N.M.	N.M.	N.M.	N.M.
EBITDA Margin %	16.91	13.03	8.67	11.04	5.21	N.M.	N.M.	0.83
Net Margin %	6.91	26.24	0.99	1.32	N.M.	N.M.	N.M.	N.M.
Asset Turnover	0.90	0.87	0.92	0.91	0.86	0.77	0.72	0.73
Current Ratio	1.51	1.41	2.05	2.99	2.41	2.34	2.72	2.91
Debt to Equity	1.10	1.17	5.42	3.59	384.17	14.72	3.72	2.10
Price Range	32.73-16.48	32.73-22.91	35.85-24.55	30.44-22.19	28.43-10.56	19.40-6.13	24.97-11.48	19.64-4.21
P/E Ratio	4.65-2.34	4.86-3.40	143.40-98.20	72.48-52.83	...	...	...	...

Address: 550 West Adams Street, Chicago, IL 60661-3676 **Telephone:** 312-436-4000	**Web Site:** www.usg.com **Officers:** James S. Metcalf - Chairman, President, Chief Executive Officer Matthew F. Hilzinger - Executive Vice President, Principal Accounting Officer, Chief Financial Officer	**Auditors:** Deloitte & Touche LLP **Investor Contact:** 312-436-6098 **Transfer Agents:** Computershare Trust Company, Providence, RI

VALERO ENERGY CORP.

Exchange	Symbol	Price	52Wk Range	Yield	P/E
NYS	VLO	$54.70 (5/31/2016)	73.03-54.09	4.39	7.61

*7 Year Price Score 151.26 *NYSE Composite Index=100 *12 Month Price Score 91.51

Interim Earnings (Per Share)

Qtr.	Mar	Jun	Sep	Dec
2013	1.18	0.85	0.57	2.36
2014	1.54	1.10	2.00	2.21
2015	1.87	2.66	2.79	0.69
2016	1.05	...	...	...

Interim Dividends (Per Share)

Amt	Decl	Ex	Rec	Pay
0.40Q	07/13/2015	07/31/2015	08/04/2015	09/02/2015
0.50Q	10/28/2015	11/19/2015	11/23/2015	12/17/2015
0.60Q	01/21/2016	02/05/2016	02/09/2016	03/03/2016
0.60Q	05/12/2016	05/23/2016	05/25/2016	06/21/2016

Indicated Div: $2.40

Valuation Analysis | **Institutional Holding**

Forecast EPS	$5.44 (05/20/2016)	No of Institutions	1243
Market Cap	$25.7 Billion	Shares	440,677,504
Book Value	$20.7 Billion	% Held	78.43
Price/Book	1.24		
Price/Sales	0.31		

Business Summary: Refining & Marketing (MIC: 9.1.2 SIC: 2911 NAIC: 324110)

Valero Energy is a petroleum refining and marketing company. Co. markets branded and unbranded refined products on a wholesale basis in the U.S., Canada, the Caribbean, the U.K., and Ireland through a bulk and rack marketing network and through outlets that carry the Valero®, Diamond Shamrock®, Shamrock®, Ultramar®, Beacon®, and Texaco® brand names. Co. has two reportable segments: refining and ethanol. Co.'s refining segment includes refining and marketing operations in the U.S., Canada, the U.K., Aruba, and Ireland. Co.'s ethanol segment includes ethanol and marketing operations in the U.S.

Recent Developments: For the quarter ended Mar 31 2016, net income decreased 47.0% to US$513.0 million from US$968.0 million in the year-earlier quarter. Revenues were US$15.71 billion, down 26.3% from US$21.33 billion the year before. Operating income was US$829.0 million versus US$1.50 billion in the prior-year quarter, a decrease of 44.5%. Direct operating expenses declined 26.0% to US$14.24 billion from US$19.25 billion in the comparable period the year before. Indirect operating expenses increased 9.0% to US$641.0 million from US$588.0 million in the equivalent prior-year period.

Prospects: Our evaluation of Valero Energy Corp. as of June 19, 2016 is the result of our systematic analysis on three basic characteristics: earnings strength, relative valuation, and recent stock price movement. The company has suffered a very negative trend in earnings per share over the past 5 quarters. However, while recent estimates for the company have been lowered by analysts, VLO has posted results that fell short of analysts expectations. Based on operating earnings yield, the company is undervalued when compared to all of the companies in our coverage universe. Share price changes over the past year indicates that VLO will perform very well over the near term.

Financial Data

(US$ in Thousands)	3 Mos	12/31/2015	12/31/2014	12/31/2013	12/31/2012	12/31/2011	12/31/2010	12/31/2009
Earnings Per Share	7.19	7.99	6.85	4.97	3.75	3.68	0.57	(3.67)
Cash Flow Per Share	10.27	11.29	8.06	10.27	9.56	7.17	5.41	3.37
Tang Book Value Per Share	43.97	43.39	40.20	36.04	32.28	29.09	26.04	25.67
Dividends Per Share	1.900	1.700	1.050	0.850	0.650	0.300	0.200	0.600
Dividend Payout %	26.43	21.28	15.33	17.10	17.33	8.15	35.09	...
Income Statement								
Total Revenue	15,714,000	87,804,000	130,844,000	138,074,000	139,250,000	125,987,000	82,233,000	68,144,000
EBITDA	1,323,000	7,704,000	7,149,000	5,547,000	5,119,000	4,823,000	2,967,000	932,000
Depn & Amortn	485,000	1,300,000	1,200,000	1,200,000	1,100,000	1,100,000	985,000	973,000
Income Before Taxes	730,000	5,971,000	5,552,000	3,982,000	3,706,000	3,322,000	1,498,000	(449,000)
Income Taxes	217,000	1,870,000	1,777,000	1,254,000	1,626,000	1,226,000	575,000	(97,000)
Net Income	495,000	3,990,000	3,630,000	2,720,000	2,083,000	2,090,000	324,000	(1,982,000)
Average Shares	471,000	500,000	530,000	548,000	556,000	569,000	568,000	541,000
Balance Sheet								
Current Assets	14,861,000	14,972,000	16,614,000	19,277,000	16,460,000	15,972,000	13,518,000	10,923,000
Total Assets	44,259,000	44,343,000	45,550,000	47,260,000	44,477,000	42,783,000	37,621,000	35,629,000
Current Liabilities	6,775,000	7,360,000	9,980,000	13,123,000	11,929,000	12,708,000	8,784,000	7,798,000
Long-Term Obligations	7,207,000	7,250,000	5,780,000	6,261,000	6,463,000	6,732,000	7,515,000	7,195,000
Total Liabilities	23,603,000	23,816,000	24,873,000	27,800,000	26,445,000	26,360,000	22,596,000	20,904,000
Stockholders' Equity	20,656,000	20,527,000	20,677,000	19,460,000	18,032,000	16,423,000	15,025,000	14,725,000
Shares Outstanding	469,789	473,039	514,298	535,569	552,095	556,812	568,388	564,702
Statistical Record								
Return on Assets %	7.82	8.88	7.82	5.93	4.76	5.20	0.88	N.M.
Return on Equity %	17.00	19.37	18.09	14.51	12.06	13.29	2.18	N.M.
EBITDA Margin %	8.42	8.77	5.46	4.02	3.68	3.83	3.61	1.37
Net Margin %	3.15	4.54	2.77	1.97	1.50	1.66	0.39	N.M.
Asset Turnover	1.83	1.95	2.82	3.01	3.18	3.13	2.25	1.95
Current Ratio	2.19	2.03	1.66	1.47	1.38	1.26	1.54	1.40
Debt to Equity	0.35	0.35	0.28	0.32	0.36	0.41	0.50	0.49
Price Range	73.03-54.82	73.03-44.07	58.51-43.76	50.40-31.17	31.41-17.91	28.07-15.68	21.33-14.30	23.61-14.22
P/E Ratio	10.16-7.62	9.14-5.52	8.54-6.39	10.14-6.27	8.37-4.78	7.63-4.26	37.42-25.08	...
Average Yield %	2.99	2.76	2.05	2.20	2.65	1.34	1.17	3.42

Address: One Valero Way, San Antonio, TX 78249
Telephone: 210-345-2000
Fax: 210-246-2646

Web Site: www.valero.com
Officers: Joseph W. Gorder - Chairman, President, Chief Executive Officer, Executive Vice President, Chief Operating Officer, Chief Commercial Officer Michael S. Ciskowski - Executive Vice President, Chief Financial Officer

Auditors: KPMG LLP
Investor Contact: 800-531-7911
Transfer Agents: ComputerShare Investor Services, Providence, RI

VALLEY NATIONAL BANCORP

Exchange	Symbol	Price	52Wk Range	Yield	P/E
NYS	VLY	$9.53 (5/31/2016)	11.14-8.31	4.62	21.66

*7 Year Price Score 77.66   ***NYSE Composite Index=100**   ***12 Month Price Score 95.73**

Interim Earnings (Per Share)

Qtr.	Mar	Jun	Sep	Dec
2013	0.16	0.17	0.14	0.20
2014	0.17	0.15	0.14	0.11
2015	0.13	0.14	0.15	0.01
2016	0.14	...	...	...

Interim Dividends (Per Share)

Amt	Decl	Ex	Rec	Pay
0.11Q	08/19/2015	09/11/2015	09/15/2015	10/01/2015
0.11Q	11/24/2015	12/11/2015	12/15/2015	01/04/2016
0.11Q	02/23/2016	03/11/2016	03/15/2016	04/01/2016
0.11Q	05/26/2016	06/13/2016	06/15/2016	07/01/2016

Indicated Div: $0.44 (Div. Reinv. Plan)

Valuation Analysis

Forecast EPS	$0.65 (05/15/2016)	**Institutional Holding**
		No of Institutions 304
Market Cap	$2.4 Billion	**Shares**
Book Value	$2.2 Billion	138,601,520
Price/Book	1.09	**% Held**
Price/Sales	3.00	58.25

Business Summary: Banking (MIC: 5.1.1 SIC: 6021 NAIC: 522110)

Valley National Bancorp is a bank holding company. Co. operates through its principal subsidiary, Valley National Bank (the Bank), which provides a range of commercial, retail, insurance and wealth management financial services products. The Bank provides a variety of banking services including automated teller machines, telephone and internet banking, remote deposit capture, overdraft facilities, drive-in and night deposit services, and safe deposit facilities. The Bank also provides certain international banking services to customers. At Dec 31 2015, Co. had total assets of $21.60 billion and total deposits of $16.30 billion.

Recent Developments: For the quarter ended Mar 31 2016, net income increased 19.3% to US$36.2 million from US$30.3 million in the year-earlier quarter. Net interest income increased 12.2% to US$148.2 million from US$132.1 million in the year-earlier quarter. Non-interest income rose 15.0% to US$21.4 million from US$18.6 million, while non-interest expense advanced 9.3% to US$118.2 million.

Prospects: Our evaluation of Valley National Bancorp as of June 19, 2016 is the result of our systematic analysis on three basic characteristics: earnings strength, relative valuation, and recent stock price movement. The company has generated a negative trend in earnings per share over the past 5 quarters and while recent estimates for the company have remained steady, VLY has posted results that fell short of analysts expectations. Based on operating earnings yield, the company is undervalued when compared to all of the companies in our coverage universe. Share price changes over the past year indicates that VLY will perform well over the near term.

Financial Data

(US$ in Thousands)	3 Mos	12/31/2015	12/31/2014	12/31/2013	12/31/2012	12/31/2011	12/31/2010	12/31/2009
Earnings Per Share	0.44	0.42	0.56	0.66	0.73	0.75	0.73	0.58
Cash Flow Per Share	0.61	0.66	0.89	1.43	1.63	1.07	1.57	0.63
Tang Book Value Per Share	5.40	5.36	5.38	5.39	5.26	5.19	5.35	5.26
Dividends Per Share	0.440	0.440	0.440	0.598	0.652	0.656	0.654	0.657
Dividend Payout %	100.00	104.76	78.57	90.53	89.29	87.20	89.01	113.50
Income Statement								
Interest Income	185,597	707,023	636,603	616,097	671,193	673,824	676,812	712,184
Interest Expense	37,444	156,754	161,846	168,377	181,312	199,013	214,060	262,870
Net Interest Income	148,153	550,269	474,757	447,720	489,881	474,811	462,752	449,314
Provision for Losses	800	8,101	1,884	16,095	25,552	53,335	49,456	47,992
Non-Interest Income	21,448	83,802	77,616	128,653	120,946	112,297	91,327	72,251
Non-Interest Expense	118,225	499,075	403,255	381,338	374,900	336,588	317,682	306,028
Income Before Taxes	50,576	126,895	147,234	178,940	210,375	197,185	186,941	167,545
Income Taxes	14,389	23,938	31,062	46,979	66,748	63,532	55,771	51,484
Net Income	36,187	102,957	116,172	131,961	143,627	133,653	131,170	116,061
Average Shares	254,347	234,437	205,716	199,309	197,354	178,426	177,577	167,223
Balance Sheet								
Net Loans & Leases	16,045,919	15,953,311	13,395,855	11,464,483	11,012,829	9,691,008	9,300,049	9,293,573
Total Assets	21,727,523	21,612,616	18,793,855	16,156,541	16,012,646	14,244,507	14,143,826	14,284,153
Total Deposits	16,408,426	16,253,551	14,034,116	11,319,262	11,264,018	9,673,102	9,363,614	9,547,285
Total Liabilities	19,507,921	19,405,525	16,930,838	14,615,501	14,510,269	12,978,259	12,848,621	13,031,299
Stockholders' Equity	2,219,602	2,207,091	1,863,017	1,541,040	1,502,377	1,266,248	1,295,205	1,252,854
Shares Outstanding	254,285	253,787	232,110	199,593	198,438	178,683	178,010	177,102
Statistical Record								
Return on Assets %	0.53	0.51	0.66	0.82	0.95	0.94	0.92	0.80
Return on Equity %	5.32	5.06	6.83	8.67	10.35	10.44	10.30	8.87
Net Interest Margin %	79.83	77.83	74.58	72.67	72.99	70.47	68.37	63.09
Efficiency Ratio %	57.10	63.11	56.46	51.20	47.33	42.82	41.36	39.01
Loans to Deposits	0.98	0.98	0.95	1.01	0.98	1.00	0.99	0.97
Price Range	11.14-8.31	11.14-9.05	10.80-9.21	10.65-8.85	12.59-8.72	13.52-9.42	14.47-11.27	16.66-7.24
P/E Ratio	25.32-18.89	26.52-21.55	19.29-16.45	16.14-13.41	17.25-11.95	18.03-12.56	19.82-15.43	28.72-12.48
Average Yield %	4.50	4.46	4.44	6.05	6.07	5.50	5.19	6.06

Address: 1455 Valley Road, Wayne, NJ 07470	**Web Site:** www.valleynationalbank.com	**Auditors:** KPMG LLP
Telephone: 973-305-8800	**Officers:** Gerald H. Lipkin - Chairman, President, Chief Executive Officer Rudy E. Schupp - Senior Executive Vice President, Division Officer	**Investor Contact:** 973-305-8800
		Transfer Agents: American Stock & Transfer & Trust Company, Brooklyn, NY

VALMONT INDUSTRIES INC

Exchange	Symbol	Price	52Wk Range	Yield	P/E	Div Achiever
NYS	VMI	$138.32 (5/31/2016)	143.76-93.99	1.08	73.97	14 Years

*7 Year Price Score 85.86   *NYSE Composite Index=100   *12 Month Price Score 115.49

TRADING VOLUME (thousand shares)

Interim Earnings (Per Share)

Qtr.	Mar	Jun	Sep	Dec
2013	2.89	3.33	2.10	2.04
2014	2.08	2.38	0.92	1.66
2015	1.28	1.19	0.52	(1.29)
2016	1.45	...	...	...

Interim Dividends (Per Share)

Amt	Decl	Ex	Rec	Pay
0.375Q	09/08/2015	09/23/2015	09/25/2015	10/15/2015
0.375Q	12/07/2015	12/23/2015	12/28/2015	01/15/2016
0.375Q	03/07/2016	03/23/2016	03/28/2016	04/15/2016
0.375Q	06/06/2016	06/22/2016	06/24/2016	07/15/2016

Indicated Div: $1.50 (Div. Reinv. Plan)

Valuation Analysis   **Institutional Holding**

Forecast EPS	$6.42	No of Institutions
	(05/15/2016)	327
Market Cap	$3.9 Billion	Shares
Book Value	$931.1 Million	24,593,008
Price/Book	4.14	% Held
Price/Sales	1.52	86.21

Business Summary: Construction Services (MIC: 7.5.4 SIC: 3499 NAIC: 332323)

Valmont Industries is a producer of fabricated metal products. Co. is a producer of steel, aluminum and composite pole, tower and other structures in its Engineered Support Structures segment, steel and concrete pole structures in its Utilities Support Structures segment and is a producer of mechanized irrigation systems in its Irrigation segment. Co. also provides metal coating services, including galvanizing, painting and anodizing in its Coatings segment. Customers and end-users of Co.'s products include state and federal governments, contractors, utility and telecommunications companies, manufacturers of commercial lighting fixtures and farms as well as the general manufacturing sector.

Recent Developments: For the quarter ended Mar 28 2016, net income increased 8.5% to US$34.2 million from US$31.5 million in the year-earlier quarter. Revenues were US$596.6 million, down 11.0% from US$670.4 million the year before. Operating income was US$62.4 million versus US$57.7 million in the prior-year quarter, an increase of 8.1%. Direct operating expenses declined 13.7% to US$435.6 million from US$504.9 million in the comparable period the year before. Indirect operating expenses decreased 8.5% to US$98.6 million from US$107.8 million in the equivalent prior-year period.

Prospects: Our evaluation of Valmont Industries Inc. as of June 19, 2016 is the result of our systematic analysis on three basic characteristics: earnings strength, relative valuation, and recent stock price movement. The company has enjoyed a very positive trend in earnings per share over the past 5 quarters and while recent estimates for the company have remained steady, VMI has posted better than expected results. Based on operating earnings yield, the company is about fairly valued when compared to all of the companies in our coverage universe. Share price changes over the past year indicates that VMI will perform well over the near term.

Financial Data

(US$ in Thousands)	3 Mos	12/26/2015	12/27/2014	12/28/2013	12/29/2012	12/31/2011	12/25/2010	12/26/2009
Earnings Per Share	1.87	1.71	7.09	10.35	8.75	8.60	3.57	5.73
Cash Flow Per Share	13.10	11.72	6.79	14.92	7.47	5.59	5.85	13.51
Tang Book Value Per Share	15.49	18.00	25.37	37.33	31.75	25.08	15.75	19.45
Dividends Per Share	1.500	1.500	1.375	0.975	0.855	0.705	0.480	0.580
Dividend Payout %	80.21	87.72	19.39	9.42	9.77	8.20	13.45	10.12
Income Statement								
Total Revenue	596,605	2,618,924	3,123,143	3,304,211	3,029,541	2,661,480	1,975,505	1,786,601
EBITDA	81,285	225,476	404,255	552,878	452,861	335,227	238,752	285,082
Depn & Amortn	20,598	91,144	89,328	77,436	70,218	74,560	59,663	44,748
Income Before Taxes	50,444	93,007	284,183	449,417	359,290	233,757	152,982	226,084
Income Taxes	16,273	47,427	94,894	157,781	126,502	4,590	55,008	72,894
Net Income	32,969	40,117	183,976	278,489	234,072	228,308	94,379	150,562
Average Shares	22,816	23,405	25,719	26,899	26,764	26,550	26,422	26,289
Balance Sheet								
Current Assets	1,252,838	1,226,852	1,392,941	1,597,840	1,425,940	1,252,943	1,094,226	715,422
Total Assets	2,399,862	2,399,428	2,729,668	2,776,494	2,568,551	2,306,076	2,090,743	1,302,169
Current Liabilities	364,577	366,554	397,214	436,580	412,433	408,070	346,914	256,817
Long-Term Obligations	756,878	763,964	766,654	470,907	472,593	474,415	468,596	160,251
Total Liabilities	1,468,808	1,480,987	1,527,835	1,254,469	1,218,639	1,159,114	1,174,851	515,908
Stockholders' Equity	931,054	918,441	1,201,833	1,522,025	1,349,912	1,146,962	915,892	786,261
Shares Outstanding	27,900	22,857	24,229	26,824	26,674	26,481	26,374	26,297
Statistical Record								
Return on Assets %	1.70	1.57	6.70	10.45	9.63	10.22	5.58	11.49
Return on Equity %	4.17	3.79	13.55	19.45	18.80	21.78	11.12	21.41
EBITDA Margin %	13.62	8.61	12.94	16.73	14.95	12.60	12.09	15.96
Net Margin %	5.53	1.53	5.89	8.43	7.73	8.58	4.78	8.43
Asset Turnover	1.02	1.02	1.14	1.24	1.25	1.19	1.17	1.36
Current Ratio	3.44	3.35	3.51	3.66	3.46	3.07	3.15	2.79
Debt to Equity	0.81	0.83	0.64	0.31	0.35	0.41	0.51	0.20
Price Range	128.26-93.99	130.26-93.99	161.61-123.75	164.50-132.08	141.13-92.07	110.26-74.27	87.74-67.03	88.50-38.45
P/E Ratio	68.59-50.26	76.18-54.96	22.72-17.45	15.89-12.76	16.13-10.52	12.82-8.64	24.58-18.78	15.45-6.71
Average Yield %	1.33	1.29	0.95	0.67	0.70	0.76	0.62	0.85

Address: One Valmont Plaza, Omaha, NE 68154-5215 **Telephone:** 402-963-1000 **Fax:** 402-963-1198	**Web Site:** www.valmont.com **Officers:** Mogens C. Bay - Chairman, Chief Executive Officer Barry Ruffalo - Executive Vice President	**Auditors:** Deloitte & Touche LLP **Investor Contact:** 402-963-1000 **Transfer Agents:** Wells Fargo Shareowner Services, Mendota Heights, MN

VALSPAR CORP

Exchange	Symbol	Price	52Wk Range	Yield	P/E	Div Achiever
NYS	VAL	$108.32 (5/31/2016)	108.32-70.82	1.22	26.04	37 Years

*7 Year Price Score 128.60 *NYSE Composite Index=100 *12 Month Price Score 124.09

Interim Earnings (Per Share)

Qtr.	Jan	Apr	Jul	Oct
2012-13	0.60	0.84	1.04	0.72
2013-14	0.61	0.99	1.14	1.27
2014-15	1.24	1.09	1.25	1.27
2015-16	0.65	0.99	...	...

Interim Dividends (Per Share)

Amt	Decl	Ex	Rec	Pay
0.30Q	08/20/2015	08/28/2015	09/01/2015	09/15/2015
0.33Q	11/24/2015	12/03/2015	12/07/2015	12/16/2015
0.33Q	02/24/2016	03/03/2016	03/07/2016	03/18/2016
0.33Q	05/19/2016	05/27/2016	06/01/2016	06/15/2016

Indicated Div: $1.32

Valuation Analysis

Forecast EPS	$4.85
	(05/17/2016)
Market Cap	$8.6 Billion
Book Value	$968.2 Million
Price/Book	8.87
Price/Sales	2.02

Institutional Holding

No of Institutions	461
Shares	71,350,592
% Held	70.25

Business Summary: Specialty Chemicals (MIC: 8.3.2 SIC: 2851 NAIC: 325510)

Valspar develops, manufactures and distributes a range of coatings, paints and related products. Co. has two reportable segments: Coatings, which provides coatings for metal, wood and plastic, as well as interior and exterior of metal packaging containers, principally metal food containers and beverage cans; and Paints, which provides consumer paints including interior and exterior decorative paints, stains, primers, varnishes and specialty decorative products, such as enamels, aerosols and faux finishes, as well as automotive paint refinish product. Co. also manufactures and sells resins and colorants, as well as furniture protection plans and furniture care and repair products.

Recent Developments: For the quarter ended Apr 29 2016, net income decreased 11.4% to US$80.0 million from US$90.3 million in the year-earlier quarter. Revenues were US$1.06 billion, down 2.1% from US$1.08 billion the year before. Direct operating expenses declined 4.5% to US$655.4 million from US$686.1 million in the comparable period the year before. Indirect operating expenses increased 14.0% to US$270.5 million from US$237.3 million in the equivalent prior-year period.

Prospects: Our evaluation of Valspar Corp. as of June 19, 2016 is the result of our systematic analysis on three basic characteristics: earnings strength, relative valuation, and recent stock price movement. The company has enjoyed a very positive trend in earnings per share over the past 5 quarters. However, while recent estimates for the company have been lowered by analysts, VAL has posted results that fell short of analysts expectations. Based on operating earnings yield, the company is about fairly valued when compared to all of the companies in our coverage universe. Share price changes over the past year indicates that VAL will perform well over the near term.

Financial Data
(US$ in Thousands)

	6 Mos	3 Mos	10/30/2015	10/31/2014	10/25/2013	10/26/2012	10/28/2011	10/29/2010
Earnings Per Share	4.16	4.26	4.85	4.01	3.20	3.10	(1.47)	2.20
Cash Flow Per Share	5.55	5.42	4.78	4.08	4.55	3.83	3.10	2.71
Dividends Per Share	1.260	1.230	1.200	1.040	0.920	0.800	0.720	0.640
Dividend Payout %	30.29	28.87	24.74	25.94	28.75	25.81	...	29.09
Income Statement								
Total Revenue	1,942,553	885,756	4,392,622	4,522,424	4,103,776	4,020,851	3,952,954	3,226,687
EBITDA	270,950	116,114	728,112	649,849	569,675	571,979	48,466	451,503
Depn & Amortn	47,683	23,021	82,963	92,637	81,122	87,151	90,109	74,039
Income Before Taxes	178,063	70,678	563,801	491,882	423,795	417,224	(103,154)	319,197
Income Taxes	45,605	18,247	164,295	146,481	134,540	124,727	35,447	97,141
Net Income	132,458	52,431	399,506	345,401	289,255	292,497	(138,601)	222,056
Average Shares	80,878	80,612	82,446	86,046	90,526	94,380	94,309	100,866
Balance Sheet								
Current Assets	1,620,326	1,501,722	1,631,230	1,577,257	1,580,290	1,449,177	1,325,137	1,284,922
Total Assets	4,346,471	4,175,241	4,318,575	4,033,951	4,025,509	3,626,836	3,500,151	3,867,936
Current Liabilities	1,281,727	1,225,322	1,366,739	1,704,421	1,480,573	1,026,772	1,259,933	884,851
Long-Term Obligations	1,707,042	1,708,431	1,706,933	950,035	1,037,392	1,012,578	679,805	943,216
Total Liabilities	3,378,258	3,320,515	3,463,566	3,022,860	2,902,959	2,403,313	2,287,601	2,237,571
Stockholders' Equity	968,213	854,726	855,009	1,011,091	1,122,550	1,223,523	1,212,550	1,630,365
Shares Outstanding	79,258	79,011	78,983	82,213	85,793	90,165	93,554	98,027
Statistical Record								
Return on Assets %	8.11	8.51	9.59	8.43	7.58	8.23	N.M.	6.04
Return on Equity %	36.71	38.29	42.93	31.85	24.73	24.08	N.M.	14.21
EBITDA Margin %	13.95	13.11	16.58	14.37	13.88	14.23	1.23	13.99
Net Margin %	6.82	5.92	9.09	7.64	7.05	7.27	N.M.	6.88
Asset Turnover	1.02	1.04	1.05	1.10	1.08	1.13	1.08	0.88
Current Ratio	1.26	1.23	1.19	0.93	1.07	1.41	1.05	1.45
Debt to Equity	1.76	2.00	2.00	0.94	0.92	0.83	0.56	0.58
Price Range	107.16-70.82	88.16-70.82	88.16-70.82	82.16-68.10	73.81-54.96	59.75-33.72	40.18-27.59	32.91-25.25
P/E Ratio	25.76-17.02	20.69-16.62	18.18-14.60	20.49-16.98	23.07-17.18	19.27-10.88	...	14.96-11.48
Average Yield %	1.51	1.51	1.45	1.40	1.42	1.68	2.05	2.16

Address: 1101 South 3rd Street, Minneapolis, MN 55415
Telephone: 612-851-7000

Web Site: www.valsparglobal.com
Officers: Gary E. Hendrickson - Chairman, President, Chief Executive Officer James L. Muehlbauer - Executive Vice President, Chief Financial Officer, Chief Administrative Officer

Auditors: Ernst & Young LLP
Investor Contact: 612-851-7358
Transfer Agents: Computershare

VANTIV INC

| Exchange NYS | Symbol VNTV | Price $53.77 (5/31/2016) | 52Wk Range 56.49-37.76 | Yield N/A | P/E 50.25 |

*7 Year Price Score N/A ***NYSE Composite Index=100** ***12 Month Price Score 112.82**

Interim Earnings (Per Share)

Qtr.	Mar	Jun	Sep	Dec
2013	0.18	0.20	0.24	0.25
2014	0.18	(0.01)	0.20	0.35
2015	0.13	0.24	0.27	0.31
2016	0.25			

Interim Dividends (Per Share)

No Dividends Paid

Valuation Analysis   **Institutional Holding**

Forecast EPS	$2.64 (05/20/2016)	No of Institutions 445
Market Cap	$10.3 Billion	Shares
Book Value	$998.5 Million	157,773,824
Price/Book	10.31	% Held
Price/Sales	3.14	79.25

Business Summary: Business Services (MIC: 7.5.2 SIC: 7389 NAIC: 561499)

Vantiv is a holding company. Through its subsidiaries, Co. provides electronic payment processing services to merchants and financial institutions. Co. operates two segments: Merchant Services, which provides merchant acquiring and payment processing services to national merchants, regional and small-to-mid sized businesses; and Financial Institution Services, which provides card issuer processing, payment network processing, fraud protection, card production, prepaid program management, automated teller machine driving and network gateway and switching services that utilize Co.'s proprietary Jeanie debit payment network to a set of financial institutions.

Recent Developments: For the quarter ended Mar 31 2016, net income increased 94.3% to US$52.4 million from US$27.0 million in the year-earlier quarter. Revenues were US$818.6 million, up 16.0% from US$705.6 million the year before. Operating income was US$109.7 million versus US$74.0 million in the prior-year quarter, an increase of 48.1%. Direct operating expenses rose 17.0% to US$387.4 million from US$331.1 million in the comparable period the year before. Indirect operating expenses increased 7.0% to US$321.6 million from US$300.4 million in the equivalent prior-year period.

Prospects: Our evaluation of Vantiv Inc as of June 19, 2016 is the result of our systematic analysis on three basic characteristics: earnings strength, relative valuation, and recent stock price movement. The company has generated a negative trend in earnings per share over the past 5 quarters and while recent estimates for the company have remained steady, VNTV has posted better than expected results. Based on operating earnings yield, the company is overvalued when compared to all of the companies in our coverage universe. Share price changes over the past year indicates that VNTV will perform very well over the near term.

Financial Data

(US$ in Thousands)	3 Mos	12/31/2015	12/31/2014	12/31/2013	12/31/2012	12/31/2011	12/31/2010	12/31/2009
Earnings Per Share	1.07	0.95	0.75	0.87	0.47	0.40	0.25	(0.02)
Cash Flow Per Share	4.41	5.23	4.18	3.46	2.51	2.61	2.19	0.35
Income Statement								
Total Revenue	818,623	3,159,938	2,577,203	2,108,077	1,863,239	1,622,421	1,162,132	506,002
EBITDA	112,771	479,742	384,868	389,602	252,883	260,354	182,481	77,273
Depn & Amortn	8,768	76,600	70,000	56,800	40,700	31,700	12,500	4,000
Income Before Taxes	76,274	297,406	235,167	291,900	157,611	117,119	53,961	14,396
Income Taxes	23,826	88,177	66,177	83,760	46,853	32,309	(956)	(191)
Net Income	39,738	147,946	125,292	133,572	57,610	36,240	21,993	(2,141)
Average Shares	196,777	200,934	199,170	206,027	122,747	89,514	89,515	89,515
Balance Sheet								
Current Assets	1,038,700	1,117,499	1,214,736	807,913	921,077	819,997	630,950	...
Total Assets	6,355,739	6,465,426	6,336,083	4,189,553	3,979,529	3,489,710	3,370,517	...
Current Liabilities	1,204,615	1,295,379	963,333	685,313	869,468	440,720	424,827	...
Long-Term Obligations	2,935,778	2,965,439	3,292,016	1,730,794	1,171,880	1,750,820	1,740,527	...
Total Liabilities	5,357,234	5,512,638	5,433,070	3,421,622	3,161,603	2,866,012	2,775,060	...
Stockholders' Equity	998,505	952,788	903,013	767,931	817,926	623,698	595,457	...
Shares Outstanding	191,378	190,531	188,497	190,581	211,484	89,514	89,515	...
Statistical Record								
Return on Assets %	2.71	2.31	2.38	3.27	1.54	1.06	...	...
Return on Equity %	17.49	15.94	15.00	16.85	7.97	5.95	...	...
EBITDA Margin %	13.78	15.18	14.93	18.48	13.57	16.05	15.70	15.27
Net Margin %	4.85	4.68	4.86	6.34	3.09	2.23	1.89	N.M.
Asset Turnover	0.53	0.49	0.49	0.52	0.50	0.47	...	...
Current Ratio	0.86	0.86	1.26	1.18	1.06	1.86	1.49	...
Debt to Equity	2.94	3.11	3.65	2.25	1.43	2.81	2.92	...
Price Range	53.88-37.57	52.84-33.25	34.82-28.79	32.61-19.97	24.03-19.50	...	...	...
P/E Ratio	50.36-35.11	55.62-35.00	46.43-38.39	37.48-22.95	51.13-41.49	...	...	...

Address: 8500 Governor's Hill Drive, Symmes Township, OH 45249
Telephone: 513-900-5250

Web Site: www.vantiv.com
Officers: Jeffrey E. Stiefler - Chairman Charles D. Drucker - President, Chief Executive Officer

Auditors: Deloitte & Touche LLP
Investor Contact: 513-.90-0.4811
Transfer Agents: American Stock Transfer & Trust Company, LLC

VARIAN MEDICAL SYSTEMS, INC.

Exchange	Symbol	Price	52Wk Range	Yield	P/E
NYS	VAR	$82.79 (5/31/2016)	90.39-71.44	N/A	20.49

*7 Year Price Score 99.77 ***NYSE Composite Index=100** ***12 Month Price Score 101.68**

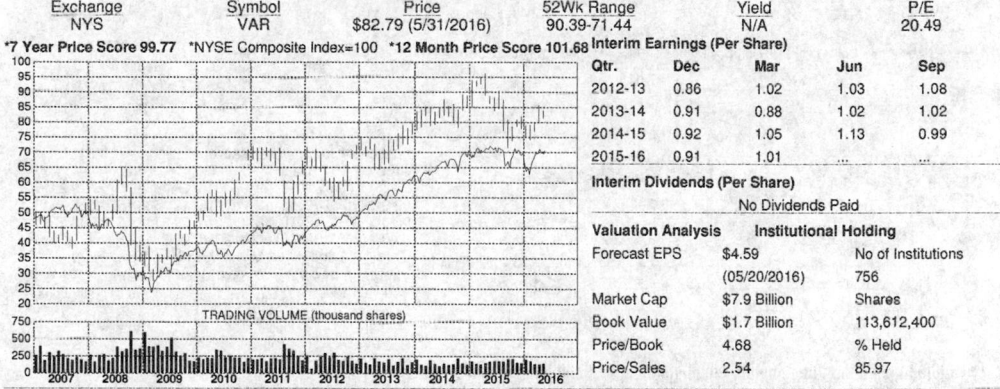

Interim Earnings (Per Share)

Qtr.	Dec	Mar	Jun	Sep
2012-13	0.86	1.02	1.03	1.08
2013-14	0.91	0.88	1.02	1.02
2014-15	0.92	1.05	1.13	0.99
2015-16	0.91	1.01	...	...

Interim Dividends (Per Share)

No Dividends Paid

Valuation Analysis   **Institutional Holding**

Forecast EPS	$4.59	No of Institutions
	(05/20/2016)	756
Market Cap	$7.9 Billion	Shares
Book Value	$1.7 Billion	113,612,400
Price/Book	4.68	% Held
Price/Sales	2.54	85.97

TRADING VOLUME (thousand shares)

Business Summary: Medical Instruments & Equipment (MIC: 4.3.1 SIC: 3845 NAIC: 334510)

Varian Medical Systems is a manufacturer of medical devices and software for treating cancer and other medical conditions with radiotherapy, radiosurgery, proton therapy and brachytherapy. Co.'s operations are grouped into two reportable operating segments: Oncology Systems, which designs, manufactures, sells and services hardware and software products for treating cancer with radiotherapy, and other treatments; and Imaging Components, which designs, manufactures, sells and services X-ray imaging components for use in a range of applications. Co.'s Ginzton Technology Center and Varian Particle Therapy business are reflected in the Other category.

Recent Developments: For the quarter ended Apr 1 2016, net income decreased 8.5% to US$97.0 million from US$106.0 million in the year-earlier quarter. Revenues were US$758.8 million, down 0.1% from US$759.4 million the year before. Operating income was US$134.0 million versus US$146.0 million in the prior-year quarter, a decrease of 8.3%. Direct operating expenses rose 1.1% to US$441.5 million from US$436.9 million in the comparable period the year before. Indirect operating expenses increased 3.8% to US$183.2 million from US$176.5 million in the equivalent prior-year period.

Prospects: Our evaluation of Varian Medical Systems Inc. as of June 19, 2016 is the result of our systematic analysis on three basic characteristics: earnings strength, relative valuation, and recent stock price movement. The company has enjoyed a very positive trend in earnings per share over the past 5 quarters and while recent estimates for the company have been mixed, VAR has posted better than expected results. Based on operating earnings yield, the company is undervalued when compared to all of the companies in our coverage universe. Share price changes over the past year indicates that VAR will perform well over the near term.

Financial Data

(US$ in Thousands)	6 Mos	3 Mos	10/02/2015	09/26/2014	09/27/2013	09/28/2012	09/30/2011	10/01/2010
Earnings Per Share	4.04	4.08	4.09	3.83	3.98	3.76	3.36	2.91
Cash Flow Per Share	4.67	4.82	4.63	4.33	4.21	4.44	4.06	3.79
Tang Book Value Per Share	14.71	14.02	13.82	13.22	13.98	11.77	9.18	9.04
Income Statement								
Total Revenue	1,515,900	757,133	3,099,111	3,049,800	2,942,897	2,807,015	2,596,666	2,356,585
EBITDA	288,561	135,120	617,487	633,612	671,749	655,056	641,042	582,495
Depn & Amortn	37,928	18,470	68,520	62,457	62,859	60,982	52,591	48,293
Income Before Taxes	253,338	118,369	554,662	574,510	612,083	595,924	588,710	532,925
Income Taxes	67,313	29,327	142,644	170,807	173,835	168,875	180,084	165,444
Net Income	185,998	89,027	411,485	403,703	438,248	427,049	398,933	360,422
Average Shares	96,179	97,843	100,552	105,271	110,053	113,473	118,735	124,025
Balance Sheet								
Current Assets	2,773,217	2,640,216	2,525,045	2,494,165	2,704,783	2,170,515	1,854,617	1,681,344
Total Assets	3,866,258	3,726,662	3,600,748	3,357,290	3,468,474	2,878,726	2,498,761	2,323,952
Current Liabilities	1,694,140	1,589,055	1,382,904	1,201,654	1,160,579	1,236,531	1,125,912	903,541
Long-Term Obligations	312,500	345,000	337,500	387,500	450,000	6,250	6,250	17,869
Total Liabilities	2,176,487	2,098,858	1,889,148	1,740,870	1,754,627	1,368,950	1,254,870	1,048,585
Stockholders' Equity	1,689,771	1,627,804	1,711,600	1,616,420	1,713,847	1,509,776	1,243,891	1,275,367
Shares Outstanding	95,550	95,999	98,070	100,942	106,491	109,407	112,344	118,007
Statistical Record								
Return on Assets %	10.87	11.43	11.64	11.86	13.85	15.93	16.59	15.60
Return on Equity %	23.67	25.11	24.33	24.31	27.26	31.10	31.76	27.94
EBITDA Margin %	19.04	17.85	19.92	20.78	22.83	23.34	24.69	24.72
Net Margin %	12.27	11.76	13.28	13.24	14.89	15.21	15.36	15.29
Asset Turnover	0.85	0.88	0.88	0.90	0.93	1.05	1.08	1.02
Current Ratio	1.64	1.66	1.83	2.08	2.33	1.76	1.65	1.86
Debt to Equity	0.18	0.21	0.20	0.24	0.26	N.M.	0.01	0.01
Price Range	96.14-71.44	96.14-71.44	96.14-71.44	87.52-72.50	76.27-57.08	71.70-50.10	71.96-49.63	60.80-39.14
P/E Ratio	23.80-17.68	23.56-17.51	23.51-17.47	22.85-18.93	19.16-14.34	19.07-13.32	21.42-14.77	20.89-13.45

Address: 3100 Hansen Way, Palo Alto, CA 94304-1038	**Web Site:** www.varian.com	**Auditors:** PricewaterhouseCoopers LLP
Telephone: 650-493-4000	**Officers:** R. Andrew Eckert - Chairman Timothy E. Guertin - Vice-Chairman, President, Chief Executive Officer	**Investor Contact:** 650-424-5782
		Transfer Agents: Computershare Trust Company, N.A., Providence, RI

VECTOR GROUP LTD

Exchange	Symbol	Price	52Wk Range	Yield	P/E	Div Achiever
NYS	VGR	$21.47 (5/31/2016)	25.43-20.81	7.45	45.68	17 Years

*7 Year Price Score 121.83 *NYSE Composite Index=100   *12 Month Price Score 93.00

Interim Earnings (Per Share)

Qtr.	Mar	Jun	Sep	Dec
2013	(0.02)	0.13	(0.36)	0.62
2014	0.03	0.07	0.13	0.10
2015	0.17	0.14	0.10	0.07
2016	0.16	...	...	...

Interim Dividends (Per Share)

Amt	Decl	Ex	Rec	Pay
5%	09/02/2015	09/14/2015	09/16/2015	09/29/2015
0.40Q	12/01/2015	12/11/2015	12/15/2015	12/29/2015
0.40Q	03/02/2016	03/17/2016	03/21/2016	03/30/2016
0.40Q	06/01/2016	06/20/2016	06/22/2016	06/29/2016

Indicated Div: $1.60 (Div. Reinv. Plan)

Valuation Analysis / Institutional Holding

Forecast EPS	$0.76	No of Institutions
	(04/18/2016)	279
Market Cap	$2.7 Billion	Shares
Book Value	N/A	63,569,268
Price/Book	N/A	% Held
Price/Sales	1.58	49.66

Business Summary: Tobacco Products (MIC: 1.3.1 SIC: 2111 NAIC: 312221)

Vector Group is a holding company. Co. is principally engaged in the manufacture and sale of cigarettes in the U.S. through its Liggett Group LLC and Vector Tobacco Inc. subsidiaries; the sale of electronic cigarettes (e-cigarettes) in the U.S. through its Zoom E-Cigs LLC subsidiary; and the real estate business through its New Valley LLC subsidiary, which is seeking to acquire additional operating companies and real estate properties. Co. has three segments: Tobacco; E-Cigarettes, which includes the operations of Co.'s e-cigarette business; as well as Real Estate, which includes Co.'s investments in consolidated and non-consolidated real estate businesses.

Recent Developments: For the quarter ended Mar 31 2016, net income decreased 0.4% to US$21.4 million from US$21.5 million in the year-earlier quarter. Revenues were US$380.8 million, up 5.6% from US$360.8 million the year before. Operating income was US$62.2 million versus US$43.7 million in the prior-year quarter, an increase of 42.2%. Direct operating expenses declined 2.3% to US$236.4 million from US$242.0 million in the comparable period the year before. Indirect operating expenses increased 9.6% to US$82.2 million from US$75.0 million in the equivalent prior-year period.

Prospects: Our evaluation of Vector Group Ltd. as of June 19, 2016 is the result of our systematic analysis on three basic characteristics: earnings strength, relative valuation, and recent stock price movement. The company has generated a negative trend in earnings per share over the past 5 quarters and while recent estimates for the company have been mixed, VGR has posted results that were in line with analysts expectations. Based on operating earnings yield, the company is about fairly valued when compared to all of the companies in our coverage universe. Share price changes over the past year indicates that VGR will perform in line with the market over the near term.

Financial Data
(US$ in Thousands)

	3 Mos	12/31/2015	12/31/2014	12/31/2013	12/31/2012	12/31/2011	12/31/2010	12/31/2009
Earnings Per Share	0.47	0.49	0.33	0.37	0.30	0.77	0.56	0.25
Cash Flow Per Share	1.12	1.23	0.99	0.52	0.86	0.38	0.71	0.06
Dividends Per Share	1.562	1.543	1.469	1.399	1.333	1.269	1.209	1.151
Dividend Payout %	330.28	314.87	440.86	376.29	440.88	165.92	217.31	453.81
Income Statement								
Total Revenue	380,800	1,657,197	1,591,315	1,056,200	1,084,546	1,133,380	1,063,289	801,494
EBITDA	67,330	242,461	255,976	181,706	145,924	215,363	156,493	91,720
Depn & Amortn	...	20,423	17,843	11,063	10,608	10,607	10,790	10,398
Income Before Taxes	37,934	108,385	77,142	38,496	25,214	104,050	61,607	13,324
Income Taxes	14,363	41,233	33,251	24,795	23,095	48,137	31,486	3,731
Net Income	19,338	59,198	36,978	38,944	30,622	75,020	54,084	24,806
Average Shares	118,253	117,792	108,142	101,147	98,042	95,875	95,330	93,243
Balance Sheet								
Current Assets	526,645	583,739	857,846	588,311	639,056	509,741	526,763	389,208
Total Assets	1,228,789	1,310,756	1,573,392	1,260,159	1,086,731	927,768	949,595	735,542
Current Liabilities	191,317	216,292	270,095	405,005	195,159	315,198	226,872	149,008
Long-Term Obligations	864,554	886,249	860,711	540,766	586,946	493,356	506,052	334,920
Total Liabilities	1,462,860	1,516,803	1,630,419	1,355,195	1,165,983	1,016,798	995,829	740,224
Stockholders' Equity	(234,071)	(206,047)	(57,027)	(95,036)	(79,252)	(89,030)	(46,234)	(4,682)
Shares Outstanding	123,792	123,792	120,226	107,475	104,068	96,562	95,643	95,498
Statistical Record								
Return on Assets %	4.14	4.11	2.61	3.32	3.03	7.99	6.42	3.41
Return on Equity %	...	...	...	...	...	...	...	171.53
EBITDA Margin %	17.68	14.63	16.09	17.20	13.45	19.00	14.72	11.44
Net Margin %	5.08	3.57	2.32	3.69	2.82	6.62	5.09	3.09
Asset Turnover	1.21	1.15	1.12	0.90	1.07	1.21	1.26	1.10
Current Ratio	2.75	2.70	3.18	1.45	3.27	1.62	2.32	2.61
Price Range	25.43-20.73	25.43-20.00	21.67-14.66	15.12-12.85	15.25-12.56	15.09-12.44	15.51-10.21	11.87-8.01
P/E Ratio	54.11-44.11	51.90-40.82	65.66-44.42	40.87-34.72	50.84-41.87	19.60-16.16	27.70-18.23	47.47-32.04
Average Yield %	6.85	6.88	7.68	9.89	9.42	9.05	9.39	11.10

Address: 4400 Biscayne Boulevard, Miami, FL 33137 **Telephone:** 305-579-8000	**Web Site:** www.vectorgroupltd.com **Officers:** Bennett S. LeBow - Chairman Howard M. Lorber - President, Chief Executive Officer	**Auditors:** Deloitte & Touche LLP **Investor Contact:** 212-687-8080 **Transfer Agents:** American Stock Transfer & Trust Company, LLC, Brooklyn, NY

Exchange	Symbol	Price	52Wk Range	Yield	P/E	Div Achiever
NYS	VVC	$49.68 (5/31/2016)	50.93-38.39	3.22	21.79	40 Years

*7 Year Price Score 112.63 *NYSE Composite Index=100 *12 Month Price Score 111.22

Interim Earnings (Per Share)

Qtr.	Mar	Jun	Sep	Dec
2013	0.61	(0.07)	0.52	0.61
2014	0.62	0.14	0.57	0.68
2015	0.69	0.43	0.48	0.79
2016	0.58	...	...	...

Interim Dividends (Per Share)

Amt	Decl	Ex	Rec	Pay
0.38Q	05/04/2015	05/13/2015	05/15/2015	06/01/2015
0.38Q	08/05/2015	08/13/2015	08/17/2015	09/01/2015
0.40Q	11/05/2015	11/12/2015	11/16/2015	12/01/2015
0.40Q	02/03/2016	02/11/2016	02/16/2016	03/01/2016

Indicated Div: $1.60 (Div. Reinv. Plan)

Valuation Analysis / **Institutional Holding**

Forecast EPS	$2.45
	(05/20/2016)
Market Cap	$4.1 Billion
Book Value	$1.7 Billion
Price/Book	2.42
Price/Sales	1.78

No of Institutions 419
Shares 60,652,176
% Held 58.41

Business Summary: Electric Utilities (MIC: 3.1.1 SIC: 4932 NAIC: 221210)

Vectren is an energy holding company. Co.'s subsidiary, Vectren Utility Holdings, Inc., served as the intermediate holding company for three public utilities that provides natural gas distribution and transportation services and electric transmission and distribution services. At Dec 31 2014, Co. supplied natural gas service to approximately 1.0 million Indiana and Ohio customers and electric service to approximately 144,000 Indiana customers, including residential, commercial, and industrial and other customers. Co., through Vectren Enterprises, Inc. subsidiary, is involved in nonutility activities in two primary business areas: infrastructure services and energy services.

Recent Developments: For the quarter ended Mar 31 2016, net income decreased 15.3% to US$48.3 million from US$57.0 million in the year-earlier quarter. Revenues were US$584.8 million, down 17.2% from US$706.2 million the year before. Operating income was US$92.2 million versus US$106.1 million in the prior-year quarter, a decrease of 13.1%. Direct operating expenses declined 26.3% to US$211.1 million from US$286.4 million in the comparable period the year before. Indirect operating expenses decreased 10.3% to US$281.5 million from US$313.7 million in the equivalent prior-year period.

Prospects: Our evaluation of Vectren Corp. as of June 19, 2016 is the result of our systematic analysis on three basic characteristics: earnings strength, relative valuation, and recent stock price movement. The company has managed to produce a neutral trend in earnings per share over the past 5 quarters. However, while recent estimates for the company have been mixed, VVC has posted results that fell short of analysts expectations. Based on operating earnings yield, the company is about fairly valued when compared to all of the companies in our coverage universe. Share price changes over the past year indicates that VVC will perform very well over the near term.

Financial Data

(US$ in Thousands)	3 Mos	12/31/2015	12/31/2014	12/31/2013	12/31/2012	12/31/2011	12/31/2010	12/31/2009
Earnings Per Share	2.28	2.39	2.02	1.66	1.94	1.73	1.64	1.64
Cash Flow Per Share	6.13	6.11	5.92	7.13	4.71	5.10	4.74	5.57
Tang Book Value Per Share	16.99	16.79	15.94	15.68	15.37	14.69	14.65	14.24
Dividends Per Share	1.560	1.540	1.460	1.425	1.405	1.385	1.365	1.345
Dividend Payout %	68.42	64.44	72.28	85.84	72.42	80.06	83.23	82.01
Income Statement								
Total Revenue	584,800	2,434,700	2,611,700	2,491,200	2,232,800	2,325,200	2,129,500	2,088,900
EBITDA	161,800	616,400	595,100	621,600	607,900	604,800	545,500	497,000
Depn & Amortn	63,900	256,300	273,400	277,800	254,600	244,300	229,100	211,900
Income Before Taxes	75,800	293,600	247,500	263,400	264,800	260,000	217,000	193,800
Income Taxes	27,300	95,700	81,100	67,100	82,500	86,400	74,700	64,100
Net Income	48,300	197,300	166,900	136,600	159,000	141,600	133,700	133,100
Average Shares	82,800	82,700	82,500	82,400	82,100	81,800	81,300	81,000
Balance Sheet								
Current Assets	521,700	659,400	686,400	630,400	678,400	610,000	645,200	581,900
Total Assets	5,323,200	5,409,900	5,162,300	5,102,600	5,089,100	4,878,900	4,764,200	4,671,800
Current Liabilities	409,100	527,800	762,700	510,500	794,300	693,500	820,700	747,700
Long-Term Obligations	1,713,200	1,722,800	1,407,300	1,777,100	1,553,400	1,559,600	1,435,200	1,540,500
Total Liabilities	3,622,800	3,726,100	3,555,700	3,548,300	3,563,000	3,413,400	3,325,300	3,274,600
Stockholders' Equity	1,700,400	1,683,800	1,606,600	1,554,300	1,526,100	1,465,500	1,438,900	1,397,200
Shares Outstanding	82,800	82,800	82,600	82,400	82,200	81,900	81,700	81,100
Statistical Record								
Return on Assets %	3.64	3.73	3.25	2.68	3.18	2.94	2.83	2.86
Return on Equity %	11.31	11.99	10.56	8.87	10.60	9.75	9.43	9.68
EBITDA Margin %	27.67	25.32	22.79	24.95	27.23	26.01	25.62	23.79
Net Margin %	8.26	8.10	6.39	5.48	7.12	6.09	6.28	6.37
Asset Turnover	0.45	0.46	0.51	0.49	0.45	0.48	0.45	0.45
Current Ratio	1.28	1.25	0.90	1.23	0.85	0.88	0.79	0.78
Debt to Equity	1.01	1.02	0.88	1.14	1.02	1.06	1.00	1.10
Price Range	50.93-38.39	49.31-38.39	48.12-34.89	37.56-29.40	30.27-27.62	30.54-23.90	27.74-22.41	26.72-18.27
P/E Ratio	22.34-16.84	20.63-16.06	23.82-17.27	22.63-17.71	15.60-14.24	17.65-13.82	16.91-13.66	16.29-11.14
Average Yield %	3.65	3.59	3.63	4.17	4.83	5.06	5.52	5.83

Address: One Vectren Square, Evansville, IN 47708 **Telephone:** 812-491-4000 **Fax:** 812-491-4149	**Web Site:** www.vectren.com **Officers:** Carl L. Chapman - President, Chief Executive Officer Eric J. (Rick) Schach - Chief Operating Officer, Executive Vice President, Division Officer	**Auditors:** Deloitte & Touche, LLP **Investor Contact:** 812-491-4080 **Transfer Agents:** Wells Fargo Shareowner Services, St. Paul, MN

VENTAS, INC.

Exchange	Symbol	Price	52Wk Range	Yield	P/E
NYS	VTR	$66.33 (5/31/2016)	67.23-48.43	4.40	49.87

*7 Year Price Score 94.26   ***NYSE Composite Index=100**   ***12 Month Price Score 110.04**

TRADING VOLUME (thousand shares)

Interim Earnings (Per Share)

Qtr.	Mar	Jun	Sep	Dec
2013	0.38	0.39	0.40	0.37
2014	0.41	0.47	0.37	0.36
2015	0.37	0.45	0.07	0.37
2016	0.44	...	...	...

Interim Dividends (Per Share)

Amt	Decl	Ex	Rec	Pay
0.73Q	09/03/2015	09/11/2015	09/15/2015	09/30/2015
0.73Q	12/11/2015	12/17/2015	12/21/2015	12/30/2015
0.73Q	02/12/2016	03/03/2016	03/07/2016	03/31/2016
0.73Q	05/10/2016	06/02/2016	06/06/2016	06/30/2016

Indicated Div: $2.92

Valuation Analysis

		Institutional Holding	
Forecast EPS	$1.51	No of Institutions	
	(05/20/2016)	775	
Market Cap	$22.4 Billion	Shares	
Book Value	$9.6 Billion	362,557,312	
Price/Book	2.33	% Held	
Price/Sales	6.56	101.82	

Business Summary: REITs (MIC: 5.3.1 SIC: 6798 NAIC: 525930)

Ventas is a real estate investment trust. Co. primarily invests in seniors housing and healthcare properties through acquisitions and leases its properties to unaffiliated tenants or operates them through independent third-party managers. Through its Lillibridge Healthcare Services, Inc. subsidiary and its ownership interests in PMB Real Estate Services LLC, Co. provides medical office building management, leasing, marketing, facility development and advisory services to hospitals and health systems. Co. also makes secured and non-mortgage loans and other investments relating to seniors housing and healthcare operators or properties. As of Dec 31 2015, Co. owned about 1,300 properties.

Recent Developments: For the quarter ended Mar 31 2016, income from continuing operations increased 27.8% to US$123.3 million from US$96.5 million in the year-earlier quarter. Net income increased 23.4% to US$149.0 million from US$120.8 million in the year-earlier quarter. Revenues were US$852.3 million, up 5.8% from US$805.6 million the year before. Revenues from property income rose 6.0% to US$829.8 million from US$783.1 million in the corresponding quarter a year earlier.

Prospects: Our evaluation of Ventas Inc. as of June 19, 2016 is the result of our systematic analysis on three basic characteristics: earnings strength, relative valuation, and recent stock price movement. The company has managed to produce a neutral trend in earnings per share over the past 5 quarters and while recent estimates for the company have remained steady, VTR has posted better than expected results. Based on operating earnings yield, the company is overvalued when compared to all of the companies in our coverage universe. Share price changes over the past year indicates that VTR will perform well over the near term.

Financial Data

(US$ in Thousands)	3 Mos	12/31/2015	12/31/2014	12/31/2013	12/31/2012	12/31/2011	12/31/2010	12/31/2009
Earnings Per Share	1.33	1.25	1.60	1.54	1.23	1.58	1.56	1.74
Cash Flow Per Share	3.94	4.21	4.27	4.08	3.39	3.38	2.86	2.77
Tang Book Value Per Share	25.36	26.02	28.08	28.91	29.73	30.87	15.18	15.74
Dividends Per Share	2.980	3.040	2.965	2.735	2.480	2.300	2.140	2.050
Dividend Payout %	224.06	243.20	185.31	177.60	201.63	145.57	137.18	117.82
Income Statement								
Total Revenue	852,289	3,286,398	3,075,746	2,810,053	2,485,299	1,764,991	1,016,867	936,094
EBITDA	215,798	1,673,771	1,634,643	1,550,817	1,281,227	1,001,682	614,934	575,333
Depn & Amortn	(2,591)	954,982	809,284	737,343	707,714	434,382	208,274	200,938
Income Before Taxes	115,116	351,675	448,517	478,990	280,112	330,493	227,797	195,892
Income Taxes	(8,421)	(39,284)	(8,732)	(11,828)	(6,282)	(31,137)	5,201	(1,719)
Net Income	148,980	419,222	477,186	454,889	361,775	363,261	249,729	269,360
Average Shares	339,202	334,007	296,677	295,110	294,488	230,790	157,657	152,758
Balance Sheet								
Current Assets	51,701	53,023	55,348	94,816	67,908	45,807	21,812	107,397
Total Assets	22,261,292	22,261,918	21,226,171	19,731,494	18,980,000	17,271,910	5,758,021	5,616,245
Current Liabilities	1,138,669	1,232,966	1,411,666	1,306,031	1,302,436	1,384,013	467,772	457,769
Long-Term Obligations	11,247,730	11,206,996	10,888,092	9,364,992	8,413,646	6,429,116	2,900,044	2,670,101
Total Liabilities	12,647,097	12,501,062	12,373,971	10,750,553	9,786,317	7,894,116	3,371,295	3,150,734
Stockholders' Equity	9,614,195	9,760,856	8,852,200	8,980,941	9,193,683	9,377,794	2,386,726	2,465,511
Shares Outstanding	337,485	334,342	298,471	294,189	291,866	288,809	157,265	156,612
Statistical Record								
Return on Assets %	1.91	1.93	2.33	2.35	1.99	3.15	4.39	4.73
Return on Equity %	4.33	4.50	5.35	5.01	3.89	6.18	10.29	11.68
EBITDA Margin %	25.32	50.93	53.15	55.19	51.55	56.75	60.47	61.46
Net Margin %	17.48	12.76	15.51	16.19	14.56	20.58	24.56	28.77
Asset Turnover	0.15	0.15	0.15	0.15	0.14	0.15	0.18	0.16
Current Ratio	0.05	0.04	0.04	0.07	0.05	0.03	0.05	0.23
Debt to Equity	1.17	1.15	1.23	1.04	0.92	0.69	1.22	1.08
Price Range	67.35-48.43	70.89-49.68	65.19-49.73	72.63-48.39	58.97-47.01	50.09-38.50	48.54-35.86	39.16-17.80
P/E Ratio	50.64-36.41	56.71-39.74	40.75-31.08	47.16-31.43	47.94-38.22	31.70-24.37	31.12-22.99	22.50-10.23
Average Yield %	5.24	5.14	5.23	4.64	4.65	4.96	5.01	7.11

Address: 353 N. Clark Street, Suite 3300, Chicago, Il. 60654 **Telephone:** 877-483-6827	**Web Site:** www.ventasreit.com **Officers:** Debra A. Cafaro - Chairman, Chief Executive Officer Robert F. Probst - Executive Vice President, Chief Financial Officer, Acting Chief Accounting Officer	**Auditors:** KPMG LLP **Investor Contact:** 312-660-3848 **Transfer Agents:** Wells Fargo Shareowner Services, St. Paul, MN

VERIFONE SYSTEMS INC.

Exchange	Symbol	Price	52Wk Range	Yield	P/E
NYS	PAY	$26.40 (5/31/2016)	38.93-20.65	N/A	41.25

*7 Year Price Score 81.14 *NYSE Composite Index=100 *12 Month Price Score 95.56

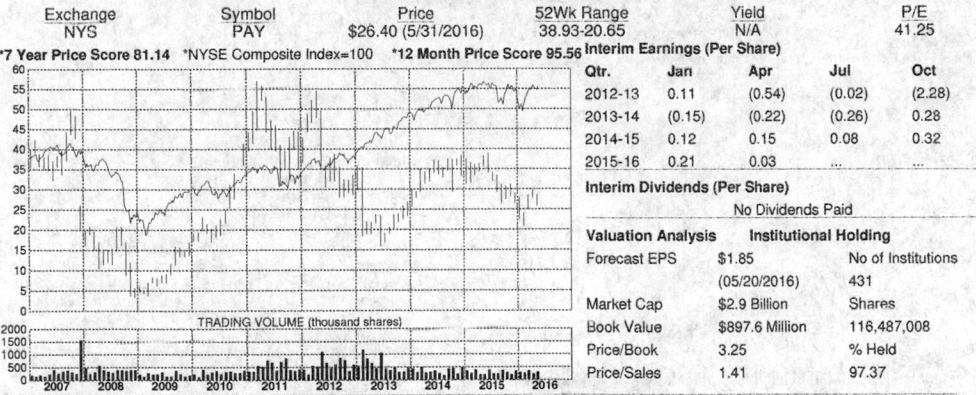

Interim Earnings (Per Share)

Qtr.	Jan	Apr	Jul	Oct
2012-13	0.11	(0.54)	(0.02)	(2.28)
2013-14	(0.15)	(0.22)	(0.26)	0.28
2014-15	0.12	0.15	0.08	0.32
2015-16	0.21	0.03	...	...

Interim Dividends (Per Share)

No Dividends Paid

Valuation Analysis

Forecast EPS	$1.85
	(05/20/2016)
Market Cap	$2.9 Billion
Book Value	$897.6 Million
Price/Book	3.25
Price/Sales	1.41

Institutional Holding

No of Institutions	431
Shares	116,487,008
% Held	97.37

Business Summary: Internet & Software (MIC: 6.3.2 SIC: 3578 NAIC: 333313)

VeriFone Systems is a holding company. Through its subsidiaries, Co. designs, manufactures, markets and supplies payment solutions and complementary services that enable secure electronic payment transactions and value-added services at the point of sale. Co. provides: System Solutions, which include Countertop and PIN pads, Multimedia, Portable and Mobile, Petroleum, Unattended and Self-Service, and Network Access Solutions; and Services, which include Payment-as-a-Service, Managed Services and Terminal Management Solutions, Payment-Enabled Media, In-Taxi Payment Solutions, Security Solutions, Server-based Payment Processing Software and Middleware, and Support Services.

Recent Developments: For the quarter ended Apr 30 2016, net income decreased 81.1% to US$3.3 million from US$17.7 million in the year-earlier quarter. Revenues were US$526.3 million, up 7.4% from US$490.1 million the year before. Operating income was US$19.8 million versus US$29.7 million in the prior-year quarter, a decrease of 33.4%. Direct operating expenses rose 10.4% to US$315.9 million from US$286.2 million in the comparable period the year before. Indirect operating expenses increased 9.4% to US$190.6 million from US$174.2 million in the equivalent prior-year period.

Prospects: Our evaluation of Verifone Systems Inc. as of June 19, 2016 is the result of our systematic analysis on three basic characteristics: earnings strength, relative valuation, and recent stock price movement. The company has generated a negative trend in earnings per share over the past 5 quarters. However, while recent estimates for the company have been lowered by analysts, PAY has posted results that fell short of analysts expectations. Based on operating earnings yield, the company is undervalued when compared to all of the companies in our coverage universe. Share price changes over the past year indicates that PAY will perform very well over the near term.

Financial Data
(US$ in Thousands)

	6 Mos	3 Mos	10/31/2015	10/31/2014	10/31/2013	10/31/2012	10/31/2011	10/31/2010
Earnings Per Share	0.64	0.76	0.68	(0.34)	(2.73)	0.59	2.92	1.13
Cash Flow Per Share	2.41	2.44	2.19	1.78	2.18	2.03	1.89	1.83
Tang Book Value Per Share	N.M.	N.M.	N.M.	N.M.	N.M.	N.M.	3.49	N.M.
Income Statement								
Total Revenue	1,039,817	513,539	2,000,457	1,868,874	1,702,221	1,865,971	1,303,866	1,001,537
EBITDA	90,606	53,662	245,595	159,868	88,346	256,479	149,176	134,035
Depn & Amortn	41,600	19,626	141,192	157,280	150,960	129,695	31,829	28,724
Income Before Taxes	32,159	25,732	72,948	(39,884)	(106,958)	68,353	90,992	78,245
Income Taxes	5,086	1,999	(7,409)	(3,442)	188,043	2,050	(191,412)	(20,582)
Net Income	26,400	23,501	79,097	(38,130)	(296,055)	65,033	282,404	98,827
Average Shares	111,314	112,351	115,934	111,586	108,609	110,315	96,616	87,785
Balance Sheet								
Current Assets	840,614	797,309	782,264	785,572	824,992	1,135,443	1,160,448	761,091
Total Assets	2,708,386	2,541,182	2,473,062	2,702,243	2,993,720	3,490,607	2,313,561	1,075,326
Current Liabilities	614,212	546,827	541,241	492,414	587,664	570,390	703,280	259,806
Long-Term Obligations	899,456	883,214	760,241	851,040	943,325	1,252,701	211,756	468,231
Total Liabilities	1,810,737	1,719,512	1,573,558	1,668,453	1,879,114	2,182,812	1,119,368	869,301
Stockholders' Equity	897,649	821,670	899,504	1,033,790	1,114,606	1,307,795	1,194,193	206,025
Shares Outstanding	110,525	110,164	112,684	113,314	110,160	107,930	105,697	86,832
Statistical Record								
Return on Assets %	2.84	3.52	3.06	N.M.	N.M.	2.23	16.67	9.91
Return on Equity %	8.12	10.16	8.18	N.M.	N.M.	5.18	40.34	83.02
EBITDA Margin %	8.71	10.45	12.28	8.55	5.19	13.75	11.44	13.38
Net Margin %	2.54	4.58	3.95	N.M.	N.M.	3.49	21.66	9.87
Asset Turnover	0.79	0.80	0.77	0.66	0.53	0.64	0.77	1.00
Current Ratio	1.37	1.46	1.45	1.60	1.40	1.99	1.65	2.93
Debt to Equity	1.00	1.07	0.85	0.82	0.85	0.96	0.18	2.27
Price Range	38.93-20.65	38.93-22.32	38.93-26.20	37.53-22.41	35.94-15.75	54.45-27.85	56.84-31.12	33.83-13.26
P/E Ratio	60.83-32.27	51.22-29.37	57.25-38.53	...	...	92.29-47.20	19.47-10.66	29.94-11.73

Address: 88 West Plumeria Drive, San Jose, CA 95134	**Web Site:** www.verifone.com	**Auditors:** Ernst & Young LLP
	Officers: Alex W. Hart - Chairman Paul Galant	**Transfer Agents:** Computershare,
Telephone: 408-232-7800	Chief Executive Officer	Canton, MA

VERIZON COMMUNICATIONS INC

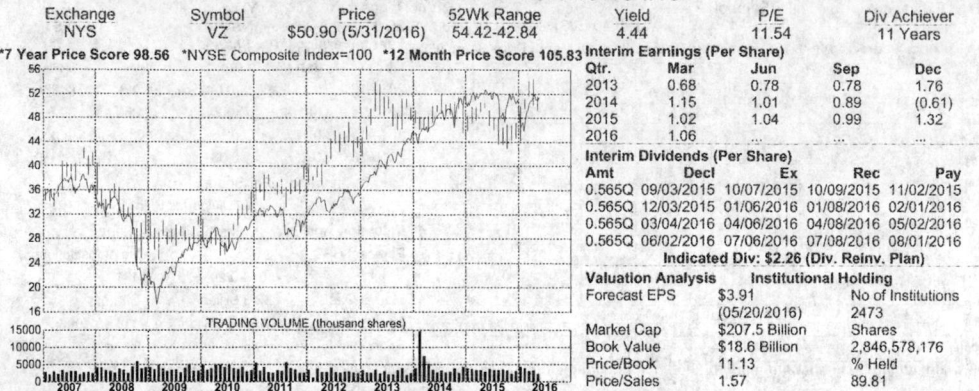

Exchange	Symbol	Price	52Wk Range	Yield	P/E	Div Achiever
NYS	VZ	$50.90 (5/31/2016)	54.42-42.84	4.44	11.54	11 Years

*7 Year Price Score 98.56   *NYSE Composite Index=100   *12 Month Price Score 105.83

Interim Earnings (Per Share)

Qtr.	Mar	Jun	Sep	Dec
2013	0.68	0.78	0.78	1.76
2014	1.15	1.01	0.89	(0.61)
2015	1.02	1.04	0.99	1.32
2016	1.06	...	...	...

Interim Dividends (Per Share)

Amt	Decl	Ex	Rec	Pay
0.565Q	09/03/2015	10/07/2015	10/09/2015	11/02/2015
0.565Q	12/03/2015	01/06/2016	01/08/2016	02/01/2016
0.565Q	03/04/2016	04/06/2016	04/08/2016	05/02/2016
0.565Q	06/02/2016	07/06/2016	07/08/2016	08/01/2016

Indicated Div: $2.26 (Div. Reinv. Plan)

Valuation Analysis   **Institutional Holding**

Forecast EPS	$3.91	No of Institutions
	(05/20/2016)	2473
Market Cap	$207.5 Billion	Shares
Book Value	$18.6 Billion	2,846,578,176
Price/Book	11.13	% Held
Price/Sales	1.57	89.81

TRADING VOLUME (thousand shares)

Business Summary: Services (MIC: 6.1.2 SIC: 4813 NAIC: 517110)

Verizon Communications is a holding company. Through its subsidiaries, Co. provides communications, information and entertainment products and services to consumers, businesses and governmental agencies. Co. has two reportable segments: Wireless, which includes wireless voice and data services and equipment sales, which are provided to consumer, business and government customers across the U.S; and Wireline, which includes voice, data and video communications products and services including broadband video and data, corporate networking solutions, data center and cloud services, security and managed network services and local and long distance voice services.

Recent Developments: For the quarter ended Mar 31 2016, net income increased 2.1% to US$4.43 billion from US$4.34 billion in the year-earlier quarter. Revenues were US$32.17 billion, up 0.6% from US$31.98 billion the year before. Operating income was US$7.94 billion versus US$7.96 billion in the prior-year quarter, a decrease of 0.2%. Direct operating expenses rose 4.3% to US$12.61 billion from US$12.10 billion in the comparable period the year before. Indirect operating expenses decreased 2.6% to US$11.62 billion from US$11.93 billion in the equivalent prior-year period.

Prospects: Our evaluation of Verizon Communications Inc. as of June 19, 2016 is the result of our systematic analysis on three basic characteristics: earnings strength, relative valuation, and recent stock price movement. The company has generated a negative trend in earnings per share over the past 5 quarters. However, while recent estimates for the company have been lowered by analysts, VZ has posted better than expected results. Based on operating earnings yield, the company is undervalued when compared to all of the companies in our coverage universe. Share price changes over the past year indicates that VZ will perform well over the near term.

Financial Data

(US$ in Thousands)	3 Mos	12/31/2015	12/31/2014	12/31/2013	12/31/2012	12/31/2011	12/31/2010	12/31/2009
Earnings Per Share	4.41	4.37	2.42	4.00	0.31	0.85	0.90	1.29
Cash Flow Per Share	8.87	9.53	7.71	13.54	11.01	10.51	11.79	11.11
Dividends Per Share	2.230	2.215	2.140	2.075	2.015	1.962	1.913	1.855
Dividend Payout %	50.57	50.69	88.43	51.88	650.00	230.88	212.50	143.80
Income Statement								
Total Revenue	32,171,000	131,620,000	127,079,000	120,550,000	115,846,000	110,875,000	106,565,000	107,808,000
EBITDA	11,976,000	47,454,000	33,263,000	46,757,000	27,007,000	27,789,000	29,200,000	28,604,000
Depn & Amortn	4,017,000	14,323,000	14,966,000	15,019,000	14,920,000	14,991,000	14,593,000	14,562,000
Income Before Taxes	6,786,000	28,326,000	13,490,000	29,135,000	9,573,000	10,039,000	12,176,000	11,015,000
Income Taxes	2,336,000	9,865,000	3,314,000	5,730,000	(660,000)	285,000	2,467,000	1,210,000
Net Income	4,310,000	17,879,000	9,625,000	11,497,000	875,000	2,404,000	2,549,000	3,651,000
Average Shares	4,085,000	4,093,000	3,981,000	2,874,000	2,862,000	2,839,000	2,833,000	2,841,000
Balance Sheet								
Current Assets	23,615,000	22,280,000	29,623,000	70,994,000	21,235,000	30,939,000	22,348,000	22,608,000
Total Assets	244,587,000	244,640,000	232,708,000	274,098,000	225,222,000	230,461,000	220,005,000	227,251,000
Current Liabilities	33,312,000	35,052,000	28,064,000	27,050,000	26,956,000	30,761,000	30,597,000	29,136,000
Long-Term Obligations	103,615,000	103,705,000	110,536,000	89,658,000	47,618,000	50,303,000	45,252,000	55,051,000
Total Liabilities	225,946,000	228,212,000	220,410,000	235,262,000	192,065,000	194,491,000	181,436,000	185,645,000
Stockholders' Equity	18,641,000	16,428,000	12,298,000	38,836,000	33,157,000	35,970,000	38,569,000	41,606,000
Shares Outstanding	4,076,288	4,073,175	4,154,964	2,862,000	2,858,569	2,834,016	2,827,023	2,835,668
Statistical Record								
Return on Assets %	7.48	7.49	3.80	4.61	0.38	1.07	1.14	1.70
Return on Equity %	128.45	124.48	37.65	31.94	2.52	6.45	6.36	8.76
EBITDA Margin %	37.23	36.05	26.18	38.79	23.31	25.06	27.40	26.53
Net Margin %	13.40	13.58	7.57	9.54	0.76	2.17	2.39	3.39
Asset Turnover	0.55	0.55	0.50	0.48	0.51	0.49	0.48	0.50
Current Ratio	0.71	0.64	1.06	2.62	0.79	1.01	0.73	0.78
Debt to Equity	5.56	6.31	8.99	2.31	1.44	1.40	1.17	1.32
Price Range	54.08-42.84	50.55-42.84	51.97-45.42	53.91-41.51	47.26-36.80	40.12-33.12	35.78-25.16	32.36-24.46
P/E Ratio	12.26-9.71	11.57-9.80	21.48-18.77	13.48-10.38	152.45-118.71	47.20-38.96	39.76-27.95	25.09-18.96
Average Yield %	4.69	4.70	4.40	4.27	4.78	5.36	6.50	6.52

Address: 1095 Avenue of the Americas, New York, NY 10036 **Telephone:** 212-395-1000	**Web Site:** www.verizon.com **Officers:** Lowell C. McAdam - Chairman, President, Chief Executive Officer, Chief Operating Officer, Division Officer Francis J. Shammo - Executive Vice President, Chief Financial Officer, Division Officer	**Auditors:** Ernst & Young LLP **Transfer Agents:** EquiServe Trust Company, N.A., Providence, RI

VF CORP.

Exchange	Symbol	Price	52Wk Range	Yield	P/E	Div Achiever
NYS	VFC	$62.32 (5/31/2016)	77.09-54.00	2.37	22.26	43 Years

*7 Year Price Score 131.12 *NYSE Composite Index=100   ***12 Month Price Score 94.00**

Interim Earnings (Per Share)

Qtr.	Mar	Jun	Sep	Dec
2013	0.60	0.31	0.97	0.82
2014	0.67	0.36	1.08	0.28
2015	0.67	0.40	1.07	0.72
2016	0.61	...	...	...

Interim Dividends (Per Share)

Amt	Decl	Ex	Rec	Pay
0.32Q	07/21/2015	09/03/2015	09/08/2015	09/18/2015
0.37Q	10/20/2015	12/04/2015	12/08/2015	12/18/2015
0.37Q	02/19/2016	03/04/2016	03/08/2016	03/18/2016
0.37Q	04/29/2016	06/08/2016	06/10/2016	06/20/2016

Indicated Div: $1.48 (Div. Reinv. Plan)

Valuation Analysis / Institutional Holding

Valuation Analysis		Institutional Holding	
Forecast EPS	$3.24 (05/20/2016)	No of Institutions	1059
Market Cap	$26.0 Billion	Shares	441,184,896
Book Value	$4.9 Billion	% Held	101.26
Price/Book	5.31		
Price/Sales	2.10		

TRADING VOLUME (thousand shares)

Business Summary: Apparel, Footwear & Accessories (MIC: 1 4 2 SIC: 2320 NAIC: 315228)

VF is an apparel and footwear company. Co. designs, produces, procures, markets and distributes a variety of products, including jeanswear, outerwear, footwear, backpacks, luggage, sportswear, and occupational and performance apparel, for consumers of all ages. Products are marketed under Co.-owned brand names, primarily The North Face®, Vans®, Timberland®, Wrangler®, Lee®, Nautica®, Majestic® and Kipling®. Co.'s products are marketed to consumers shopping in specialty stores, department stores, national chains, mass merchants and Co.'s own direct-to-consumer operations. Co.'s groupings of businesses are Outdoor & Action Sports, Jeanswear, Imagewear, Sportswear and Contemporary Brands.

Recent Developments: For the quarter ended Apr 2 2016, net income decreased 9.9% to US$260.3 million from US$288.7 million in the year-earlier quarter. Revenues were US$2.84 billion, unchanged from the year before. Operating income was US$336.3 million versus US$397.8 million in the prior-year quarter, a decrease of 15.5%. Direct operating expenses rose 1.8% to US$1.47 billion from US$1.45 billion in the comparable period the year before. Indirect operating expenses increased 3.8% to US$1.03 billion from US$992.9 million in the equivalent prior-year period.

Prospects: Our evaluation of VF Corp. as of June 19, 2016 is the result of our systematic analysis on three basic characteristics: earnings strength, relative valuation, and recent stock price movement. The company has managed to produce a neutral trend in earnings per share over the past 5 quarters and while recent estimates for the company have remained steady, VFC has posted better than expected results. Based on operating earnings yield, the company is about fairly valued when compared to all of the companies in our coverage universe. Share price changes over the past year indicates that VFC will perform in line with the market over the near term.

Financial Data

(US$ in Thousands)	3 Mos	01/02/2016	01/03/2015	12/28/2013	12/29/2012	12/31/2011	12/31/2010	01/02/2010
Earnings Per Share	2.80	2.85	2.38	2.71	2.42	2.00	1.29	1.03
Cash Flow Per Share	3.39	2.70	3.86	3.44	2.91	2.47	2.31	2.21
Tang Book Value Per Share	2.20	3.06	2.78	2.21	0.29	N.M.	2.69	1.97
Dividends Per Share	1.380	1.330	1.107	0.915	0.757	0.652	0.608	0.593
Dividend Payout %	49.29	46.67	46.53	33.76	31.24	32.71	46.91	57.38
Income Statement								
Total Revenue	2,839,300	12,376,744	12,282,161	11,419,648	10,879,855	9,459,232	7,702,589	7,220,286
EBITDA	405,572	1,934,726	1,646,684	1,846,719	1,709,025	1,406,454	981,824	892,052
Depn & Amortn	68,030	272,075	214,504	203,597	196,898	168,911	156,210	153,707
Income Before Taxes	317,387	1,580,389	1,352,366	1,562,490	1,421,875	1,164,743	750,212	654,673
Income Taxes	57,118	348,796	304,861	352,371	335,737	274,350	176,700	196,215
Net Income	260,269	1,231,593	1,047,505	1,210,119	1,085,999	888,089	571,362	461,271
Average Shares	429,133	432,079	440,153	446,809	447,616	445,152	441,312	446,420
Balance Sheet								
Current Assets	3,972,874	4,163,136	4,185,854	3,882,982	3,449,583	3,187,944	2,826,060	2,629,356
Total Assets	9,832,263	9,639,542	9,980,140	10,315,443	9,633,021	9,313,126	6,457,556	6,470,657
Current Liabilities	2,529,467	1,941,713	1,620,241	1,568,001	1,732,212	1,666,032	1,109,475	1,092,583
Long-Term Obligations	1,401,233	1,401,820	1,423,581	1,426,829	1,429,166	1,831,781	935,882	938,494
Total Liabilities	4,938,317	4,254,704	4,349,258	4,238,405	4,507,396	4,787,135	2,596,337	2,655,506
Stockholders' Equity	4,893,946	5,384,838	5,630,882	6,077,038	5,125,625	4,525,991	3,861,219	3,815,151
Shares Outstanding	417,005	426,614	432,859	440,310	440,818	442,227	431,752	441,140
Statistical Record								
Return on Assets %	12.30	12.59	10.16	12.17	11.50	11.26	8.89	7.17
Return on Equity %	24.56	22.42	17.60	21.66	22.57	21.18	14.97	12.55
EBITDA Margin %	14.28	15.63	13.41	16.17	15.71	14.87	12.75	12.35
Net Margin %	9.17	9.95	8.53	10.60	9.98	9.39	7.42	6.39
Asset Turnover	1.27	1.27	1.19	1.15	1.15	1.20	1.20	1.12
Current Ratio	1.57	2.14	2.58	2.48	1.99	1.91	2.55	2.41
Debt to Equity	0.29	0.26	0.25	0.23	0.28	0.40	0.24	0.25
Price Range	77.09-54.00	77.61-61.81	75.46-55.99	62.08-36.44	42.22-32.42	35.26-20.34	22.33-17.48	19.62-11.91
P/E Ratio	27.53-19.29	27.23-21.69	31.71-23.53	22.91-13.44	17.44-13.40	17.63-10.17	17.31-13.55	19.05-11.57
Average Yield %	2.02	1.87	1.73	1.94	2.05	2.38	3.06	3.73

Address: 105 Corporate Center Boulevard, Greensboro, NC 27408 Telephone: 336-424-6000	Web Site: www.vfc.com Officers: Eric C. Wiseman - Chairman, President, Chief Executive Officer Steven E. Rendle - Vice President, Division Officer, President, Chief Operating Officer	Auditors: PricewaterhouseCoopers LLP Transfer Agents: Computershare Trust Company, N.A, Providence, RI

VISA INC

Exchange	Symbol	Price	52Wk Range	Yield	P/E
NYS	V	$78.94 (5/31/2016)	81.45-66.72	0.71	27.99

*7 Year Price Score 155.01 *NYSE Composite Index=100 *12 Month Price Score 105.37

Interim Earnings (Per Share)

Qtr.	Dec	Mar	Jun	Sep
2012-13	0.48	0.48	0.47	0.46
2013-14	0.55	0.63	0.54	0.43
2014-15	0.63	0.63	0.69	0.62
2015-16	0.80	0.71	...	...

Interim Dividends (Per Share)

Amt	Decl	Ex	Rec	Pay
0.12Q	07/22/2015	08/12/2015	08/14/2015	09/01/2015
0.14Q	10/21/2015	11/10/2015	11/13/2015	12/01/2015
0.14Q	02/05/2016	02/17/2016	02/19/2016	03/01/2016
0.14Q	04/20/2016	05/11/2016	05/13/2016	06/07/2016

Indicated Div: $0.56

Valuation Analysis

		Institutional Holding	
Forecast EPS	$2.76	No of Institutions	
	(05/20/2016)	1871	
Market Cap	$171.2 Billion	Shares	
Book Value	$29.1 Billion	1,823,274,368	
Price/Book	5.88	% Held	
Price/Sales	11.99	58.13	

TRADING VOLUME (thousand shares)

Business Summary: Business Services (MIC: 7.5.2 SIC: 7389 NAIC: 561499)

Visa is a payments technology company that connects consumers, businesses, financial institutions and governments to electronic payments. Co. operates a processing network, VisaNet, which facilitates authorization, clearing and settlement of payment transactions. It also provides fraud protection for account holders and payment for merchants. Co. provides a variety of payment solutions that support payment products that issuers can provide to their account holders: pay now with debit; pay ahead with prepaid; or pay later with credit products. Co. also provides a range of digital, eCommerce, person-to-person payments and mobile products and services.

Recent Developments: For the quarter ended Mar 31 2016, net income increased 10.1% to US$1.71 billion from US$1.55 billion in the year-earlier quarter. Revenues were US$3.63 billion, up 6.4% from US$3.41 billion the year before. Operating income was US$2.43 billion versus US$2.28 billion in the prior-year quarter, an increase of 6.7%. Indirect operating expenses increased 5.7% to US$1.19 billion from US$1.13 billion in the equivalent prior-year period.

Prospects: Our evaluation of Visa Inc. as of June 19, 2016 is the result of our systematic analysis on three basic characteristics: earnings strength, relative valuation, and recent stock price movement. The company has generated a negative trend in earnings per share over the past 5 quarters and while recent estimates for the company have been mixed, V has posted better than expected results. Based on operating earnings yield, the company is about fairly valued when compared to all of the companies in our coverage universe. Share price changes over the past year indicates that V will perform well over the near term.

Financial Data
(US$ in Thousands)

	6 Mos	3 Mos	09/30/2015	09/30/2014	09/30/2013	09/30/2012	09/30/2011	09/30/2010
Earnings Per Share	2.82	2.74	2.58	2.15	1.90	0.79	1.29	1.00
Cash Flow Per Share	3.49	3.51	2.96	2.34	0.95	1.54	1.17	0.80
Tang Book Value Per Share	2.75	2.88	3.00	1.39	1.23	1.40	1.03	0.62
Dividends Per Share	0.520	0.500	0.480	0.400	0.330	0.220	0.150	0.125
Dividend Payout %	18.44	18.25	18.60	18.56	17.39	27.85	11.63	12.47
Income Statement								
Total Revenue	7,191,000	3,565,000	13,880,000	12,702,000	11,778,000	10,421,000	9,188,000	8,065,000
EBITDA	6,818,000	3,456,000	9,426,000	8,093,000	7,585,000	2,426,000	5,897,000	4,956,000
Depn & Amortn	1,577,000	788,000	431,000	369,000	328,000	265,000	225,000	265,000
Income Before Taxes	5,080,000	2,639,000	8,995,000	7,724,000	7,257,000	2,207,000	5,656,000	4,645,000
Income Taxes	1,432,000	698,000	2,667,000	2,286,000	2,277,000	65,000	2,010,000	1,674,000
Net Income	3,648,000	1,941,000	6,328,000	5,438,000	4,980,000	2,144,000	3,650,000	2,966,000
Average Shares	2,401,000	2,430,000	2,457,000	2,524,000	2,624,000	2,712,000	2,828,000	2,956,000
Balance Sheet								
Current Assets	24,303,000	25,473,000	10,892,000	9,562,000	7,822,000	11,786,000	9,190,000	8,734,000
Total Assets	54,326,000	54,977,000	40,236,000	38,569,000	35,956,000	40,013,000	34,760,000	33,408,000
Current Liabilities	5,125,000	5,357,000	5,374,000	6,006,000	4,335,000	7,954,000	3,451,000	3,498,000
Long-Term Obligations	15,876,000	15,877,000	...	...	...	...	...	32,000
Total Liabilities	25,195,000	25,501,000	10,394,000	11,156,000	9,086,000	12,383,000	8,323,000	8,397,000
Stockholders' Equity	29,131,000	29,476,000	29,842,000	27,413,000	26,870,000	27,630,000	26,437,000	25,011,000
Shares Outstanding	2,169,000	2,190,000	2,215,000	3,048,000	3,120,000	3,244,000	3,248,000	3,340,000
Statistical Record								
Return on Assets %	14.72	14.28	16.06	14.59	13.11	5.72	10.71	9.03
Return on Equity %	23.91	23.34	22.10	20.04	18.28	7.91	14.19	12.31
EBITDA Margin %	94.81	96.94	67.91	63.71	64.40	23.28	64.18	61.45
Net Margin %	50.73	54.45	45.59	42.81	42.28	20.57	39.73	36.78
Asset Turnover	0.31	0.30	0.35	0.34	0.31	0.28	0.27	0.25
Current Ratio	4.74	4.76	2.03	1.59	1.80	1.48	2.66	2.50
Debt to Equity	0.54	0.54	...	...	...	...	...	N.M.
Price Range	80.46-64.52	80.46-61.59	76.38-50.06	58.25-45.63	49.71-34.00	33.75-21.07	23.21-16.73	24.15-16.37
P/E Ratio	28.53-22.88	29.36-22.48	29.60-19.40	27.09-21.22	26.16-17.89	42.72-26.66	17.99-12.97	24.15-16.37
Average Yield %	0.72	0.71	0.72	0.76	0.79	0.78	0.77	0.62

Address: P.O. Box 8999, San Francisco, CA 94128-8999 Telephone: 650-432-3200	Web Site: www.corporate.visa.com Officers: Joseph W. Saunders - Chairman, Chief Executive Officer Ryan McInerney - President	Auditors: KPMG LLP Investor Contact: 650-432-7644 Transfer Agents: Wells Fargo Shareowner Services, St. Paul, MN

VISHAY INTERTECHNOLOGY, INC.

Exchange	Symbol	Price	52Wk Range	Yield	P/E
NYS	VSH	$12.96 (5/31/2016)	13.06-9.30	1.93	N/A

*7 Year Price Score 82.63   *NYSE Composite Index=100   *12 Month Price Score 106.21

Interim Earnings (Per Share)

Qtr.	Mar	Jun	Sep	Dec
2013	0.19	0.21	0.22	0.20
2014	0.17	0.23	0.57	0.20
2015	0.20	0.17	(0.19)	(0.92)
2016	0.19	...	...	...

Interim Dividends (Per Share)

Amt	Decl	Ex	Rec	Pay
0.06Q	08/11/2015	08/31/2015	09/02/2015	09/24/2015
0.06Q	11/10/2015	12/01/2015	12/03/2015	12/22/2015
0.063Q	02/16/2016	03/09/2016	03/11/2016	03/29/2016
0.063Q	05/24/2016	06/13/2016	06/15/2016	06/29/2016

Indicated Div: $0.25

Valuation Analysis

		Institutional Holding	
Forecast EPS	$0.86	No of Institutions	
	(05/20/2016)	351	
Market Cap	$1.9 Billion	Shares	
Book Value	$1.7 Billion	169,030,352	
Price/Book	1.14	% Held	
Price/Sales	0.84	100.48	

TRADING VOLUME (thousand shares)

Business Summary: Electrical Equipment (MIC: 7,3,1 SIC: 3679 NAIC: 334419)

Vishay Intertechnology is a manufacturer and supplier of discrete semiconductors and passive components. Semiconductors include MOSFETs, diodes, and optoelectronic components. Passive components include resistive products, capacitors, and inductors. Co.'s semiconductor components are used for various functions, including power control, power conversion, power management, signal switching, signal routing, signal blocking, signal amplification, and circuit isolation. Co.'s passive components are used to restrict current flow, suppress voltage increases, store and discharge energy, control alternating current and voltage, filter out unwanted electrical signals, and perform other functions.

Recent Developments: For the quarter ended Apr 2 2016, net income decreased 9.0% to US$28.2 million from US$30.9 million in the year-earlier quarter. Revenues were US$570.6 million, down 3.8% from US$593.4 million the year before. Operating income was US$40.5 million versus US$47.6 million in the prior-year quarter, a decrease of 14.7%. Direct operating expenses declined 3.4% to US$433.3 million from US$448.4 million in the comparable period the year before. Indirect operating expenses decreased 0.7% to US$96.8 million from US$97.5 million in the equivalent prior-year period.

Prospects: Our evaluation of Vishay Intertechnology Inc. as of June 19, 2016 is the result of our systematic analysis on three basic characteristics: earnings strength, relative valuation, and recent stock price movement. The company has enjoyed a very positive trend in earnings per share over the past 5 quarters and while recent estimates for the company have remained steady, VSH has posted better than expected results. Based on operating earnings yield, the company is undervalued when compared to all of the companies in our coverage universe. Share price changes over the past year indicates that VSH will perform poorly over the near term.

Financial Data

(US$ in Thousands)	3 Mos	12/31/2015	12/31/2014	12/31/2013	12/31/2012	12/31/2011	12/31/2010	12/31/2009
Earnings Per Share	(0.75)	(0.73)	0.77	0.81	0.79	1.42	1.89	(0.31)
Cash Flow Per Share	1.71	1.66	2.01	2.02	1.92	2.35	2.97	1.56
Tang Book Value Per Share	9.71	9.36	10.13	11.54	10.15	9.48	8.35	7.30
Dividends Per Share	0.242	0.240	0.240	...	...	...	...	...
Dividend Payout %	...	...	31.17	...	...	...	...	...
Income Statement								
Total Revenue	570,606	2,300,488	2,493,282	2,370,979	2,230,097	2,594,029	2,725,092	2,042,033
EBITDA	83,822	250,368	347,465	350,033	338,816	505,029	583,405	172,698
Depn & Amortn	40,017	154,340	160,804	155,064	153,801	165,022	169,724	206,009
Income Before Taxes	38,472	74,740	167,143	176,405	170,037	331,116	405,533	(39,715)
Income Taxes	10,320	182,473	49,300	52,636	46,506	91,119	45,240	16,800
Net Income	28,014	(108,514)	117,629	122,980	122,738	238,821	359,106	(57,188)
Average Shares	150,628	147,700	153,716	151,417	155,844	168,514	190,227	186,605
Balance Sheet								
Current Assets	1,888,618	1,887,492	1,926,450	1,980,680	1,791,263	1,830,676	1,794,504	1,407,543
Total Assets	3,146,624	3,152,986	3,298,773	3,237,139	3,016,277	2,993,730	2,966,093	2,719,546
Current Liabilities	438,027	457,724	456,739	449,065	412,170	439,788	527,161	407,501
Long-Term Obligations	400,124	436,738	454,922	364,911	392,931	399,054	431,682	320,052
Total Liabilities	1,469,600	1,530,510	1,473,407	1,364,383	1,392,949	1,390,724	1,474,362	1,203,100
Stockholders' Equity	1,677,024	1,622,476	1,825,366	1,872,756	1,623,328	1,603,006	1,491,731	1,516,446
Shares Outstanding	147,693	147,590	147,453	147,331	143,272	157,188	164,964	186,636
Statistical Record								
Return on Assets %	N.M.	N.M.	3.60	3.93	4.07	8.01	12.63	N.M.
Return on Equity %	N.M.	N.M.	6.36	7.04	7.59	15.43	23.88	N.M.
EBITDA Margin %	14.69	10.88	13.94	14.76	15.19	19.47	21.41	8.46
Net Margin %	4.91	N.M.	4.72	5.19	5.50	9.21	13.18	N.M.
Asset Turnover	0.72	0.71	0.76	0.76	0.74	0.87	0.96	0.74
Current Ratio	4.31	4.12	4.22	4.41	4.35	4.16	3.40	3.45
Debt to Equity	0.24	0.27	0.25	0.19	0.24	0.25	0.29	0.21
Price Range	13.92-9.30	14.59-9.30	16.17-12.68	15.32-10.28	12.74-8.18	19.08-8.09	15.31-6.59	7.72-1.97
P/E Ratio	...	...	21.00-16.47	18.91-12.69	16.13-10.35	13.44-5.70	8.10-3.49	...
Average Yield %	2.10	1.98	1.66	...	...	...	...	...

Address: 63 Lancaster Avenue,	Web Site: www.vishay.com	Auditors: Ernst & Young LLP
Malvern, PA 19355-2143	Officers: Marc Zandman - Executive Chairman, Chief	Investor Contact: 610-644-1300
Telephone: 610-644-1300	Business Development Officer Gerald Paul - President,	Transfer Agents: American Stock
	Chief Executive Officer, Chief Technical Officer	Transfer & Trust Company, New York, NY

VISTA OUTDOOR INC

Exchange	Symbol	Price	52Wk Range	Yield	P/E
NYS	VSTO	$50.18 (5/31/2016)	52.87-41.78	N/A	21.35

*7 Year Price Score N/A   *NYSE Composite Index=100   *12 Month Price Score 105.14

TRADING VOLUME (thousand shares)

Interim Earnings (Per Share)

Qtr.	Jun	Sep	Dec	Mar
2014-15	0.64	0.53	(0.17)	0.25
2015-16	0.53	0.52	0.70	0.60

Interim Dividends (Per Share)

No Dividends Paid

Valuation Analysis   Institutional Holding

Forecast EPS	$2.80	No of Institutions
	(05/17/2016)	275
Market Cap	$3.1 Billion	Shares
Book Value	$1.7 Billion	54,184,712
Price/Book	1.84	% Held
Price/Sales	1.34	N/A

Business Summary: Sporting & Recreational (MIC: 2.2.4 SIC: 3949 NAIC: 339920)

Vista Outdoor is a designer, manufacturer and marketer of consumer products in the outdoor sports and recreation markets. Co. has two operating segments: Shooting Sports, which designs, develops, produces, and sources ammunition and firearms for the hunting and sport shooting markets, as well as ammunition for local law enforcement, the U.S. government and international markets; and Outdoor Products, which includes hunting arrows, game calls, hunting blinds, game cameras, waterfowl decoys, eyewear, helmets, laser rangefinders, hydration packs, water bottles, binoculars, riflescopes, telescopes, reloading equipment, clay targets, holsters, duty gear, and stand up paddle boards.

Recent Developments: For the year ended Mar 31 2016, net income increased 84.9% to US$147.0 million from US$79.5 million in the prior year. Revenues were US$2.27 billion, up 9.0% from US$2.08 billion the year before. Operating income was US$262.8 million versus US$184.2 million in the prior year, an increase of 42.7%. Direct operating expenses rose 6.2% to US$1.65 billion from US$1.55 billion in the comparable period the year before. Indirect operating expenses increased 3.5% to US$356.7 million from US$344.8 million in the equivalent prior-year period.

Prospects: Our evaluation of Vista Outdoor Inc. as of June 19, 2016 is the result of our systematic analysis on three basic characteristics: earnings strength, relative valuation, and recent stock price movement. The company has produced a positive trend in earnings per share over the past 5 quarters. However, while recent estimates for the company have been mixed, VSTO has posted better than expected results. Based on operating earnings yield, the company is undervalued when compared to all of the companies in our coverage universe. Share price changes over the past year indicates that VSTO will perform very well over the near term.

Financial Data

(US$ in Thousands)	03/31/2016	03/31/2015	03/31/2014	03/31/2013	03/31/2012
Earnings Per Share	2.35	1.25	...	...	...
Cash Flow Per Share	3.17	2.43	...	...	...
Tang Book Value Per Share	N.M.	5.47	...	...	...
Income Statement					
Total Revenue	2,270,734	2,083,414	1,873,919	1,196,031	1,042,914
EBITDA	335,372	250,705	278,709	126,583	54,794
Depn & Amortn	72,614	66,551	44,902	25,128	24,490
Income Before Taxes	238,407	154,046	218,338	101,462	30,307
Income Taxes	91,370	74,518	85,081	36,770	19,647
Net Income	147,037	79,528	133,257	64,692	10,660
Average Shares	62,568	63,857	...	...	...
Balance Sheet					
Current Assets	1,049,664	1,065,061	849,674	415,529	...
Total Assets	2,942,634	2,573,124	2,457,658	797,812	...
Current Liabilities	368,901	307,912	332,627	214,577	...
Long-Term Obligations	652,787	332,500	1,014,911	...	...
Total Liabilities	1,282,467	924,360	1,586,927	265,912	...
Stockholders' Equity	1,660,167	1,648,764	870,731	531,900	...
Shares Outstanding	60,825	63,873	...	...	...
Statistical Record					
Return on Assets %	5.32	...	8.19	...	...
Return on Equity %	8.86	...	19.00	...	...
EBITDA Margin %	14.77	12.03	14.87	10.58	5.25
Net Margin %	6.48	3.82	7.11	5.41	1.02
Asset Turnover	0.82	...	1.15	...	...
Current Ratio	2.85	3.46	2.55	1.94	...
Debt to Equity	0.39	0.20	1.17	...	...
Price Range	52.87-41.78	45.64-34.03	...	...	...
P/E Ratio	22.50-17.78	36.51-27.22	...	...	...

Address: 262 N University Avenue, Farmington, UT 84025
Telephone: 801-447-3000

Web Site: www.vistaoutdoor.com
Officers: Mark W. DeYoung - Chairman, Chief Executive Officer Stephen M. Nolan - Senior Vice President, Chief Financial Officer

Auditors: Deloitte & Touche LLP
Transfer Agents: Computershare Trust Company, N.A.

VISTEON CORP.

Exchange	Symbol	Price	52Wk Range	Yield	P/E
NYS	VC	$74.98 (5/31/2016)	120.72-60.45	N/A	1.46

*7 Year Price Score N/A   *NYSE Composite Index=100   *12 Month Price Score 80.72

TRADING VOLUME (thousand shares)

Interim Earnings (Per Share)

Qtr.	Mar	Jun	Sep	Dec
2013	1.33	1.29	0.85	10.06
2014	0.38	(3.35)	(0.46)	(2.94)
2015	1.10	49.73	0.12	1.08
2016	0.49	...	...	...

Interim Dividends (Per Share)

Amt	Decl	Ex	Rec	Pay
43.40U	12/10/2015	01/25/2016	01/15/2016	01/22/2016

Valuation Analysis   **Institutional Holding**

Forecast EPS	$3.57	No of Institutions
	(05/20/2016)	399
Market Cap	$2.5 Billion	Shares
Book Value	$586.0 Million	47,574,020
Price/Book	4.35	% Held
Price/Sales	0.79	N/A

Business Summary: Auto Parts (MIC: 1.8.2 SIC: 3714 NAIC: 336399)

Visteon is an automotive supplier that designs, engineers and manufactures products for original equipment vehicle manufacturer. Co.'s operations are organized by product lines including: Electronics, which provides vehicle cockpit electronics products to customers, including audio systems, information displays, instrument clusters, head up displays, infotainment systems, and telematics solutions; and Other, which includes entities located in Europe previously associated with the Interiors business as well as includes entities in South America and South Africa previously associated with the Climate business.

Recent Developments: For the quarter ended Mar 31 2016, income from continuing operations increased 50.0% to US$36.0 million from US$24.0 million in the year-earlier quarter. Net income decreased 67.1% to US$23.0 million from US$70.0 million in the year-earlier quarter. Revenues were US$802.0 million, down 1.7% from US$816.0 million the year before. Direct operating expenses declined 3.3% to US$681.0 million from US$704.0 million in the comparable period the year before. Indirect operating expenses increased 8.2% to US$66.0 million from US$61.0 million in the equivalent prior-year period.

Prospects: Our evaluation of Visteon Corp. as of June 19, 2016 is the result of our systematic analysis on three basic characteristics: earnings strength, relative valuation, and recent stock price movement. The company has generated a negative trend in earnings per share over the past 5 quarters and while recent estimates for the company have remained steady, VC has posted better than expected results. Based on operating earnings yield, the company is about fairly valued when compared to all of the companies in our coverage universe. Share price changes over the past year indicates that VC will perform very well over the near term.

Financial Data

(US$ in Millions)	3 Mos	12/31/2015	12/31/2014	12/31/2013	12/31/2012	12/31/2011	12/31/2010	10/01/2010
Earnings Per Share	51.42	52.63	(6.25)	13.50	1.88	1.54	1.66	7.21
Cash Flow Per Share	2.81	7.99	6.20	6.24	4.51	3.42	3.07	0.20
Tang Book Value Per Share	13.44	23.10	10.41	30.69	20.25	18.35	16.94	...
Dividends Per Share	43.400	...	...	...	...	...	...	...
Dividend Payout %	84.40	...	...	...	...	...	...	...
Income Statement								
Total Revenue	802	3,245	7,509	7,439	6,857	8,047	1,887	5,579
EBITDA	68	146	492	925	325	419	157	1,407
Depn & Amortn	17	70	218	217	225	277	64	225
Income Before Taxes	49	62	246	669	65	113	83	1,022
Income Taxes	13	27	124	107	121	127	19	131
Net Income	19	2,284	(295)	690	100	80	86	940
Average Shares	38	43	47	51	53	52	51	130
Balance Sheet								
Current Assets	1,732	4,053	3,134	3,753	2,663	2,498	2,702	...
Total Assets	2,368	4,682	5,323	6,027	5,156	4,973	5,208	...
Current Liabilities	928	2,772	1,832	1,802	1,552	1,557	1,842	...
Long-Term Obligations	346	347	839	624	473	512	483	...
Total Liabilities	1,782	3,625	4,458	4,107	3,771	3,666	3,948	...
Stockholders' Equity	586	1,057	865	1,920	1,385	1,307	1,260	...
Shares Outstanding	34	40	44	48	52	52	51	...
Statistical Record								
Return on Assets %	58.47	45.66	N.M.	12.34	1.97	1.57	1.68	...
Return on Equity %	306.74	237.67	N.M.	41.75	7.41	6.23	35.25	...
EBITDA Margin %	8.48	4.50	6.55	12.43	4.74	5.21	8.32	25.22
Net Margin %	2.37	70.39	N.M.	9.28	1.46	0.99	4.56	16.85
Asset Turnover	0.84	0.65	1.32	1.33	1.35	1.58	0.37	...
Current Ratio	1.87	1.46	1.71	2.08	1.72	1.60	1.47	...
Debt to Equity	0.59	0.33	0.97	0.33	0.34	0.39	0.38	...
Price Range	120.72-60.45	120.72-95.47	108.29-78.74	81.89-53.37	55.93-28.42	75.75-40.68	74.25-57.00	...
P/E Ratio	2.35-1.18	2.29-1.81	...	6.07-3.95	29.75-15.12	49.19-26.42	44.73-34.34	...
Average Yield %	43.53	...	...	...	...	...	...	...

Address: One Village Center Drive, Van Buren Township, MI 48111 **Telephone:** 734-710-5800	**Web Site:** www.visteon.com **Officers:** Sachin S. Lawande - President, Chief Executive Officer Robert C. Pallash - Senior Vice President, Division Officer	**Auditors:** Ernst & Young LLP **Investor Contact:** 734-710-5800 **Transfer Agents:** Computershare Shareholders Services, Providence, RI

VMWARE INC

*7 Year Price Score 71.37 *NYSE Composite Index=100 *12 Month Price Score 84.79

Interim Earnings (Per Share)

Qtr.	Mar	Jun	Sep	Dec
2013	0.40	0.57	0.60	0.77
2014	0.46	0.38	0.45	0.75
2015	0.45	0.40	0.60	0.88
2016	0.38	...	...	...

Interim Dividends (Per Share)

No Dividends Paid

Valuation Analysis

		Institutional Holding	
Forecast EPS	$4.16	No of Institutions	
	(05/17/2016)	522	
Market Cap	$25.7 Billion	Shares	
Book Value	$8.3 Billion	95,798,816	
Price/Book	3.11	% Held	
Price/Sales	3.86	19.08	

Business Summary: Internet & Software (MIC: 6.3.2 SIC: 7372 NAIC: 511210)

VMware is engaged in virtualization infrastructure solutions utilized by organizations to help them transform the way they build, deliver and consume information technology resources. Co.'s virtualization infrastructure solutions, which include a suite of products and services designed to deliver a software-defined data center, run on industry-standard desktop computers and servers and support a range of operating system and application environments, as well as networking and storage infrastructures. Co. develops and markets its product and service offerings within three main product groups: Software-Defined Data Center, Hybrid Cloud Computing, and End-User Computing.

Recent Developments: For the quarter ended Mar 31 2016, net income decreased 17.9% to US$161.0 million from US$196.0 million in the year-earlier quarter. Revenues were US$1.59 billion, up 5.2% from US$1.51 billion the year before. Operating income was US$192.0 million versus US$218.0 million in the prior-year quarter, a decrease of 11.9%. Direct operating expenses rose 3.3% to US$251.0 million from US$243.0 million in the comparable period the year before. Indirect operating expenses increased 9.1% to US$1.15 billion from US$1.05 billion in the equivalent prior-year period.

Prospects: Our evaluation of VMware Inc. as of June 19, 2016 is the result of our systematic analysis on three basic characteristics: earnings strength, relative valuation, and recent stock price movement. The company has managed to produce a neutral trend in earnings per share over the past 5 quarters. However, while recent estimates for the company have been lowered by analysts, VMW has posted better than expected results. Based on operating earnings yield, the company is undervalued when compared to all of the companies in our coverage universe. Share price changes over the past year indicates that VMW will perform very poorly over the near term.

Financial Data

(US$ in Thousands)	3 Mos	12/31/2015	12/31/2014	12/31/2013	12/31/2012	12/31/2011	12/31/2010	12/31/2009
Earnings Per Share	2.26	2.34	2.04	2.34	1.72	1.68	0.84	0.49
Cash Flow Per Share	4.57	4.48	5.07	5.91	4.44	4.81	2.87	2.50
Tang Book Value Per Share	8.71	7.84	6.68	7.39	5.04	6.15	4.87	3.81
Income Statement								
Total Revenue	1,589,000	6,571,000	6,035,000	5,207,000	4,605,047	3,767,096	2,857,343	2,023,937
EBITDA	295,000	1,429,000	1,262,000	1,292,000	1,028,668	924,619	534,644	332,707
Depn & Amortn	88,000	190,000	190,000	141,000	130,900	126,300	114,200	102,300
Income Before Taxes	200,000	1,213,000	1,048,000	1,147,000	893,114	794,413	416,375	223,449
Income Taxes	39,000	216,000	162,000	133,000	147,412	70,477	58,936	26,351
Net Income	161,000	997,000	886,000	1,014,000	745,702	723,936	357,439	197,098
Average Shares	424,180	426,547	434,513	433,415	433,974	431,750	423,446	399,776
Balance Sheet								
Current Assets	9,494,000	9,360,000	9,130,000	7,681,000	6,120,039	5,677,772	4,297,655	3,182,480
Total Assets	15,836,000	15,746,000	15,216,000	12,327,000	10,596,392	8,680,808	6,797,319	5,066,984
Current Liabilities	3,909,000	4,129,000	3,996,000	3,293,000	2,960,234	2,401,506	1,789,152	1,294,042
Long-Term Obligations	1,500,000	1,500,000	1,500,000	450,000	450,000	450,000	450,000	450,000
Total Liabilities	7,567,000	7,827,000	7,635,000	5,511,000	4,856,411	3,910,526	2,988,876	2,324,033
Stockholders' Equity	8,269,000	7,919,000	7,581,000	6,816,000	5,739,981	4,770,282	3,808,443	2,742,951
Shares Outstanding	424,086	421,947	429,359	430,349	428,688	423,610	416,701	402,785
Statistical Record								
Return on Assets %	6.29	6.44	6.43	8.85	7.72	9.35	6.03	4.43
Return on Equity %	12.23	12.86	12.31	16.15	14.15	16.88	10.91	8.19
EBITDA Margin %	18.57	21.75	20.91	24.81	22.34	24.54	18.71	16.44
Net Margin %	10.13	15.17	14.68	19.47	16.19	19.22	12.51	9.74
Asset Turnover	0.43	0.42	0.44	0.45	0.48	0.49	0.48	0.45
Current Ratio	2.43	2.27	2.28	2.33	2.07	2.36	2.40	2.46
Debt to Equity	0.18	0.19	0.20	0.07	0.08	0.09	0.12	0.16
Price Range	91.14-43.84	91.14-55.42	111.80-76.43	99.00-65.53	114.62-80.29	107.75-74.81	91.02-41.58	45.57-19.89
P/E Ratio	40.33-19.40	38.95-23.68	54.80-37.47	42.31-28.00	66.64-46.68	64.14-44.53	108.36-49.50	93.00-40.59

VORNADO REALTY TRUST

Exchange	Symbol	Price	52Wk Range	Yield	P/E
NYS	VNO	$95.52 (5/31/2016)	103.41-80.15	2.64	37.75

*7 Year Price Score 99.75 ***NYSE Composite Index=100** ***12 Month Price Score 100.08**

Interim Earnings (Per Share)

Qtr.	Mar	Jun	Sep	Dec
2013	1.24	0.78	0.44	(0.37)
2014	0.33	0.41	0.69	2.72
2015	0.45	0.87	1.05	1.22
2016	(0.61)	...	...	...

Interim Dividends (Per Share)

Amt	Decl	Ex	Rec	Pay
0.63Q	07/30/2015	08/07/2015	08/11/2015	08/21/2015
0.63Q	10/29/2015	11/06/2015	11/10/2015	11/23/2015
0.63Q	01/20/2016	01/28/2016	02/01/2016	02/16/2016
0.63Q	04/27/2016	05/06/2016	05/10/2016	05/20/2016

Indicated Div: $2.52

Valuation Analysis | **Institutional Holding**

Forecast EPS	$0.79	No of Institutions	
	(05/20/2016)		607
Market Cap	$18.0 Billion	Shares	
Book Value	$6.5 Billion		211,373,472
Price/Book	2.76	% Held	
Price/Sales	7.19		89.73

Business Summary: REITs (MIC: 5.3.1 SIC: 6798 NAIC: 525930)

Vornado Realty Trust is a real estate investment trust. Co. conducts its business through, and substantially all of its interests in properties are held by, Vornado Realty L.P. Co. owns and operates office and retail properties in New York and Washington, DC/ Northern Virginia area. As of Dec 31 2015, Co. owned all or portions of, among others: office space, retail space, units in residential properties and Hotel Pennsylvania in New York, a 32.4% interest in Alexander's, Inc. that owned seven properties in New York, office space and residential properties in Washington DC, theMart in Chicago, and a 70.0% controlling interest in an office complex in San Francisco.

Recent Developments: For the quarter ended Mar 31 2016, loss from continuing operations was US$92.3 million compared with income of US$109.1 million in the year-earlier quarter. Net loss amounted to US$91.6 million versus net income of US$125.2 million in the year-earlier quarter. Revenues were US$613.0 million, up 1.0% from US$606.8 million the year before. Revenues from property income rose 2.1% to US$579.1 million from US$567.2 million in the corresponding quarter a year earlier.

Prospects: Our evaluation of Vornado Realty Trust as of June 19, 2016 is the result of our systematic analysis on three basic characteristics: earnings strength, relative valuation, and recent stock price movement. The company has generated a negative trend in earnings per share over the past 5 quarters. Because the company lacks sufficient analyst estimate data, we place greater weight on the historical EPS trend as the measure of earnings strength. Based on operating earnings yield, the company is overvalued when compared to all of the companies in our coverage universe. Share price changes over the past year indicates that VNO will perform in line with the market over the near term.

Financial Data

(US$ in Thousands)	3 Mos	12/31/2015	12/31/2014	12/31/2013	12/31/2012	12/31/2011	12/31/2010	12/31/2009
Earnings Per Share	2.53	3.59	4.15	2.09	2.94	3.23	3.24	0.28
Cash Flow Per Share	4.00	3.57	6.05	5.57	4.43	3.81	4.23	3.69
Tang Book Value Per Share	26.64	27.54	27.63	27.58	28.06	29.65	28.23	27.46
Dividends Per Share	2.520	2.520	2.920	2.920	3.760	2.760	2.600	3.200
Dividend Payout %	99.60	70.19	70.36	139.71	127.89	85.45	80.25	1,142.86
Income Statement								
Total Revenue	613,037	2,502,267	2,635,940	2,760,909	2,766,457	2,915,665	2,779,727	2,742,578
EBITDA	(15,796)	1,499,334	1,377,389	1,324,381	900,561	1,486,619	1,663,495	1,262,077
Depn & Amortn	(17,507)	487,154	536,622	509,122	503,529	517,946	490,110	486,572
Income Before Taxes	(96,537)	661,022	400,282	369,708	(70,331)	476,098	657,128	24,892
Income Taxes	2,831	(84,695)	11,002	(6,406)	8,132	24,827	22,476	20,737
Net Income	(93,799)	760,434	864,852	475,971	617,260	662,302	647,883	106,169
Average Shares	188,658	189,564	188,690	187,709	186,530	186,021	184,159	173,503
Balance Sheet								
Current Assets	1,880,058	2,192,565	1,715,456	1,153,509	1,737,481	1,617,740	1,814,873	1,407,406
Total Assets	20,873,374	21,143,293	21,248,320	20,097,224	21,965,975	20,446,487	20,517,471	20,185,472
Current Liabilities	447,700	443,955	499,702	422,276	484,746	423,512	438,479	475,242
Long-Term Obligations	11,059,832	11,091,010	10,898,859	9,978,718	11,296,190	10,562,002	10,893,639	10,939,615
Total Liabilities	14,348,450	14,445,698	14,502,894	13,331,992	15,115,040	13,618,171	14,201,761	13,942,703
Stockholders' Equity	6,524,924	6,697,595	6,745,426	6,765,232	6,850,935	6,828,316	6,315,710	6,242,769
Shares Outstanding	188,771	188,576	187,887	187,284	186,734	185,080	183,661	181,214
Statistical Record								
Return on Assets %	2.80	3.59	4.18	2.26	2.90	3.23	3.18	0.51
Return on Equity %	8.78	11.31	12.80	6.99	9.00	10.08	10.32	1.78
EBITDA Margin %	N.M.	59.92	52.25	47.97	32.55	50.99	59.84	46.02
Net Margin %	N.M.	30.39	32.81	17.24	22.31	22.72	23.31	3.87
Asset Turnover	0.13	0.12	0.13	0.13	0.13	0.14	0.14	0.13
Current Ratio	4.20	4.94	3.43	2.73	3.58	3.82	4.14	2.96
Debt to Equity	1.70	1.66	1.62	1.48	1.65	1.55	1.72	1.75
Price Range	112.62-80.15	114.75-84.80	108.02-80.28	82.52-69.50	79.77-66.33	89.30-63.37	82.49-56.60	65.66-26.22
P/E Ratio	44.51-31.68	31.96-23.62	26.03-19.35	39.48-33.25	27.13-22.56	27.65-19.62	25.46-17.47	234.52-93.64
Average Yield %	2.63	2.49	3.12	3.78	5.09	3.56	3.65	6.74

Address: 888 Seventh Avenue, New York, NY 10019	**Web Site:** www.vno.com	**Auditors:** Deloitte & Touche LLP
Telephone: 212-894-7000	**Officers:** Steven Roth - Chairman, Chief Executive Officer Joseph Macnow - Executive Vice President, Chief Administrative Officer, Chief Financial Officer	**Investor Contact:** 201-587-1000 **Transfer Agents:** American Stock Transfer & Trust Co., New York, NY

VOYA FINANCIAL INC

Exchange	Symbol	Price	52Wk Range	Yield	P/E
NYS	VOYA	$32.86 (5/31/2016)	48.14-25.98	0.12	17.20

*7 Year Price Score N/A *NYSE Composite Index=100 *12 Month Price Score 82.38

Interim Earnings (Per Share)

Qtr.	Mar	Jun	Sep	Dec
2013	(0.92)	(0.33)	1.32	2.17
2014	0.98	0.96	1.58	5.47
2015	0.77	1.24	0.18	(0.43)
2016	0.92	...		

Interim Dividends (Per Share)

Amt	Decl	Ex	Rec	Pay
0.01Q	07/30/2015	08/27/2015	08/31/2015	09/30/2015
0.01Q	10/30/2015	11/24/2015	11/27/2015	12/30/2015
0.01Q	02/04/2016	02/24/2016	02/26/2016	03/30/2016
0.01Q	04/27/2016	05/26/2016	05/31/2016	06/29/2016

Indicated Div: $0.04

Valuation Analysis / Institutional Holding

Forecast EPS	$3.10	No of Institutions
	(05/20/2016)	425
Market Cap	$6.7 Billion	Shares
Book Value	$14.5 Billion	200,130,368
Price/Book	0.46	% Held
Price/Sales	0.57	N/A

Business Summary: Life & Health (MIC: 5.2.2 SIC: 6311 NAIC: 524210)

Voya Financial is a holding company. Co. provides a range of retirement services, annuities, investment management services, mutual funds, life insurance, group insurance and supplemental health products, guaranteed investment contracts and funding agreements. Co. provides these products and services in three ongoing businesses (Retirement Solutions, Investment Management and Insurance Solutions) and reports results through five segments, including Retirement, Annuities, Investment Management, Individual Life and Employee Benefits. Co. also has a Closed Block segment, which includes its run-off and legacy business lines. At Dec 31 2014, Co. had $136.30 billion of assets under management.

Recent Developments: For the quarter ended Mar 31 2016, net income decreased 10.8% to US$192.3 million from US$215.7 million in the year-earlier quarter. Revenues were US$3.01 billion, up 15.5% from US$2.60 billion the year before. Net premiums earned were US$966.8 million versus US$608.8 million in the prior-year quarter, an increase of 58.8%. Net investment income fell 4.7% to US$1.09 billion from US$1.15 billion a year ago.

Prospects: Our evaluation of Voya Financial Inc. as of June 19, 2016 is the result of our systematic analysis on three basic characteristics: earnings strength, relative valuation, and recent stock price movement. The company has produced a positive trend in earnings per share over the past 5 quarters and while recent estimates for the company have been raised by analysts, VOYA has posted results that fell short of analysts expectations. Based on operating earnings yield, the company is undervalued when compared to all of the companies in our coverage universe. Share price changes over the past year indicates that VOYA will perform in line with the market over the near term.

Financial Data
(US$ in Thousands)

	3 Mos	12/31/2015	12/31/2014	12/31/2013	12/31/2012	12/31/2011	12/31/2010
Earnings Per Share	1.91	1.80	9.02	2.38	2.06	(0.38)	(0.53)
Cash Flow Per Share	13.75	14.40	14.34	13.02	...	...	...
Tang Book Value Per Share	69.70	63.06	65.42	49.48	58.81	52.05	...
Dividends Per Share	0.040	0.040	0.040	0.020	...	...	...
Dividend Payout %	2.09	2.22	0.44	0.84	...	...	...
Income Statement							
Total Revenue	3,009,300	11,341,200	11,070,900	8,758,500	9,615,300	9,718,800	9,274,200
EBITDA	412,500	1,077,300	1,211,000	1,157,200	903,000	521,700	454,300
Depn & Amortn	102,500	24,100	26,600	33,700	36,900	36,200	34,200
Income Before Taxes	241,300	584,500	785,200	758,100	606,000	277,800	37,800
Income Taxes	49,000	45,900	(1,752,200)	(32,500)	(5,200)	175,000	171,000
Net Income	191,600	408,300	2,299,700	600,500	473,000	(88,100)	(122,900)
Average Shares	209,100	227,400	255,100	251,800	...	...	...
Balance Sheet							
Current Assets	15,414,500	14,537,900	13,506,800	11,306,100	15,821,300	13,036,000	...
Total Assets	214,007,700	218,249,600	226,951,400	221,023,200	216,394,200	203,572,800	...
Current Liabilities	3,339,000	2,257,400	2,689,400	1,995,000	3,822,700	4,144,000	...
Long-Term Obligations	3,455,900	3,485,900	3,515,700	3,514,700	3,171,100	1,343,100	...
Total Liabilities	199,546,400	204,813,800	210,843,500	207,751,000	202,519,300	191,218,900	...
Stockholders' Equity	14,461,300	13,435,800	16,107,900	13,272,200	13,874,900	12,353,900	...
Shares Outstanding	203,958	209,095	241,875	261,675	230,000	230,000	230,000
Statistical Record							
Return on Assets %	0.19	0.18	1.03	0.27	0.22	...	...
Return on Equity %	2.68	2.76	15.65	4.42	3.60	...	...
EBITDA Margin %	13.71	9.50	10.94	13.21	9.39	5.37	4.90
Net Margin %	6.37	3.60	20.77	6.86	4.92	N.M.	N.M.
Asset Turnover	0.05	0.05	0.05	0.04	0.05	...	...
Current Ratio	4.62	6.44	5.02	5.67	4.14	3.15	...
Debt to Equity	0.24	0.26	0.22	0.26	0.23	0.11	...
Price Range	48.14-25.98	48.14-36.04	43.07-33.11	35.89-20.67	...	...	...
P/E Ratio	25.20-13.60	26.74-20.02	4.77-3.67	15.08-8.68	...	...	...
Average Yield %	0.10	0.09	0.09	0.11	0.07	...	...

Address: 230 Park Avenue, New York, NY 10169 **Telephone:** 212-309-8200	**Web Site:** www.ing.us **Officers:** Rodney O. Martin - Chairman, Chief Executive Officer Alain M. Karaoglan - Executive Vice President, Chief Operating Officer	**Auditors:** Ernst & Young LLP **Transfer Agents:** Computershare Trust Company, N.A, Canton, MA

VULCAN MATERIALS CO (HOLDING COMPANY)

Exchange	Symbol	Price	52Wk Range	Yield	P/E
NYS	VMC	$116.75 (5/31/2016)	120.07-81.60	0.69	56.40

*7 Year Price Score 144.37 *NYSE Composite Index=100 ***12 Month Price Score 113.78**

TRADING VOLUME (thousand shares)

Interim Earnings (Per Share)

Qtr.	Mar	Jun	Sep	Dec
2013	(0.42)	0.22	0.31	0.07
2014	0.41	0.35	0.50	0.28
2015	(0.30)	0.36	0.91	0.66
2016	0.14	...	...	...

Interim Dividends (Per Share)

Amt	Decl	Ex	Rec	Pay
0.10Q	07/10/2015	08/21/2015	08/25/2015	09/10/2015
0.10Q	10/09/2015	11/20/2015	11/24/2015	12/10/2015
0.20Q	02/12/2016	02/22/2016	02/24/2016	03/10/2016
0.20Q	05/13/2016	05/24/2016	05/26/2016	06/10/2016

Indicated Div: $0.80 (Div. Reinv. Plan)

Valuation Analysis | **Institutional Holding**

Forecast EPS	$3.46	No of Institutions
(05/17/2016)		674
Market Cap	$15.6 Billion	Shares
Book Value	$4.4 Billion	147,529,312
Price/Book	3.52	% Held
Price/Sales	4.39	90.01

Business Summary: Mining (MIC: 8.2.4 SIC: 1429 NAIC: 212319)

Vulcan Materials is a producer of construction aggregates (primarily crushed stone, sand and gravel) and a producer of asphalt mix and ready-mixed concrete. Co. has four operating segments organized around its principal product lines: Aggregates, which produces and sells aggregates (crushed stone, sand and gravel, sand, and other aggregates) and related products and services (transportation and other); Asphalt Mix, which produces and sells asphalt mix in four states; Concrete, which produces and sells ready-mixed concrete in six states, Washington D.C. and the Bahamas; and Calcium, which consists of a Florida facility that mines, produces and sells calcium products.

Recent Developments: For the quarter ended Mar 31 2016, income from continuing operations was US$20.7 million compared with a loss of US$36.7 million in the year-earlier quarter. Net income amounted to US$18.9 million versus a net loss of US$39.7 million in the year-earlier quarter. Revenues were US$754.7 million, up 19.6% from US$631.3 million the year before. Operating income was US$64.9 million versus US$10.8 million in the prior-year quarter, an increase of 503.4%. Direct operating expenses rose 6.6% to US$590.0 million from US$553.4 million in the comparable period the year before. Indirect operating expenses increased 48.7% to US$99.8 million from US$67.1 million in the equivalent prior-year period.

Prospects: Our evaluation of Vulcan Materials Co. as of June 19, 2016 is the result of our systematic analysis on three basic characteristics: earnings strength, relative valuation, and recent stock price movement. The company has managed to produce a neutral trend in earnings per share over the past 5 quarters. However, while recent estimates for the company have been lowered by analysts, VMC has posted better than expected results. Based on operating earnings yield, the company is overvalued when compared to all of the companies in our coverage universe. Share price changes over the past year indicates that VMC will perform very well over the near term.

Financial Data

(US$ in Thousands)	3 Mos	12/31/2015	12/31/2014	12/31/2013	12/31/2012	12/31/2011	12/31/2010	12/31/2009
Earnings Per Share	2.07	1.64	1.54	0.19	(0.41)	(0.55)	(0.75)	0.25
Cash Flow Per Share	3.94	3.78	1.98	2.74	1.83	1.31	1.58	3.81
Tang Book Value Per Share	4.30	4.45	2.45	1.22	N.M.	0.06	1.37	2.19
Dividends Per Share	0.500	0.400	0.220	0.040	0.040	0.760	1.000	1.480
Dividend Payout %	24.15	24.39	14.29	21.05	...	...	...	592.00
Income Statement								
Total Revenue	754,728	3,422,181	2,994,169	2,770,709	2,567,310	2,564,550	2,558,862	2,690,490
EBITDA	133,633	776,966	780,856	469,122	392,654	391,518	337,994	515,289
Depn & Amortn	69,406	228,866	239,611	271,180	301,146	328,072	349,460	361,530
Income Before Taxes	30,495	327,857	298,838	(3,703)	(120,418)	(153,738)	(192,206)	(19,221)
Income Taxes	9,764	94,943	91,692	(24,459)	(66,492)	(78,483)	(89,663)	(37,869)
Net Income	18,924	221,177	204,923	24,382	(52,593)	(70,778)	(96,490)	30,314
Average Shares	135,452	135,093	132,991	131,467	129,745	129,381	128,050	119,430
Balance Sheet								
Current Assets	1,007,503	1,084,591	920,469	951,496	984,972	863,100	772,106	743,289
Total Assets	8,247,025	8,301,632	8,061,902	8,259,143	8,126,599	8,229,314	8,337,891	8,532,950
Current Liabilities	356,485	353,479	451,878	299,135	436,411	406,253	565,672	856,695
Long-Term Obligations	1,981,425	1,980,334	1,855,447	2,522,243	2,526,401	2,680,677	2,427,516	2,116,120
Total Liabilities	3,825,972	3,847,444	3,885,203	4,321,037	4,365,537	4,437,697	4,372,911	4,480,928
Stockholders' Equity	4,421,053	4,454,188	4,176,699	3,938,106	3,761,062	3,791,617	3,964,980	4,052,022
Shares Outstanding	133,348	133,172	131,907	130,200	129,721	129,245	128,570	125,912
Statistical Record								
Return on Assets %	3.37	2.70	2.51	0.30	N.M.	N.M.	N.M.	0.35
Return on Equity %	6.52	5.13	5.05	0.63	N.M.	N.M.	N.M.	0.80
EBITDA Margin %	17.71	22.70	26.08	16.93	15.29	15.27	13.21	19.15
Net Margin %	2.51	6.46	6.84	0.88	N.M.	N.M.	N.M.	1.13
Asset Turnover	0.43	0.42	0.37	0.34	0.31	0.31	0.30	0.31
Current Ratio	2.83	3.07	2.04	3.18	2.26	2.12	1.36	0.87
Debt to Equity	0.45	0.44	0.44	0.64	0.67	0.71	0.61	0.52
Price Range	105.93-80.91	105.70-64.98	69.01-55.28	59.49-45.59	53.25-32.57	46.98-26.19	58.89-35.70	69.95-34.55
P/E Ratio	51.17-39.09	64.45-39.62	44.81-35.90	313.11-239.95	...	...	...	279.80-138.20
Average Yield %	0.54	0.45	0.35	0.08	0.09	2.02	2.24	3.07

Address: 1200 Urban Center Drive, Birmingham, AL 35242 **Telephone:** 205-298-3000 **Fax:** 205-298-2963	**Web Site:** www.vulcanmaterials.com **Officers:** J. Thomas Hill - Chairman, President, Chief Executive Officer, Executive Vice President, Chief Operating Officer John R. McPherson - Executive Vice President, Senior Vice President, Chief Financial Officer, Chief Strategy Officer	**Auditors:** Deloitte & Touche LLP **Investor Contact:** 205-298-3220 **Transfer Agents:** Computershare Shareowner Services LLC, Providence, RI

WABTEC CORP

Exchange	Symbol	Price	52Wk Range	Yield	P/E
NYS	WAB	$77.38 (5/31/2016)	102.39-60.58	0.52	18.74

*7 Year Price Score 136.81 *NYSE Composite Index=100 *12 Month Price Score 96.51

Interim Earnings (Per Share)

Qtr.	Mar	Jun	Sep	Dec
2013	0.72	0.77	0.76	0.76
2014	0.83	0.91	0.93	0.95
2015	0.99	1.04	1.02	1.05
2016	1.02	...	...	...

Interim Dividends (Per Share)

Amt	Decl	Ex	Rec	Pay
0.08Q	10/27/2015	11/12/2015	11/16/2015	11/30/2015
0.08Q	01/26/2016	02/10/2016	02/12/2016	02/26/2016
0.08Q	04/19/2016	05/11/2016	05/13/2016	05/27/2016
0.10Q	05/11/2016	08/11/2016	08/15/2016	08/29/2016

Indicated Div: $0.40

Valuation Analysis

		Institutional Holding	
Forecast EPS	$4.35	No of Institutions	577
	(05/17/2016)		
Market Cap	$7.0 Billion	Shares	103,686,216
Book Value	$1.7 Billion	% Held	90.67
Price/Book	4.16		
Price/Sales	2.14		

TRADING VOLUME (thousand shares)

Business Summary: Construction Services (MIC: 7.5.4 SIC: 3743 NAIC: 336510)

Westinghouse Air Brake Technologies is a provider of technology-based equipment and services for the rail industry. Co. has two segments, the Freight Segment, which manufactures and services components for new and existing locomotive and freight cars, supplies railway electronics, positive train control equipment, signal design and engineering services, builds switcher locomotives, rebuilds freight locomotives and provides heat exchangers and cooling systems for rail and other industrial markets; and the Transit Segment, which manufactures and services components for passenger transit vehicles, typically subway cars and buses, builds new commuter locomotives and refurbishes subway cars.

Recent Developments: For the quarter ended Mar 31 2016, net income decreased 2.1% to US$94.2 million from US$96.2 million in the year-earlier quarter. Revenues were US$772.0 million, down 5.7% from US$818.6 million the year before. Operating income was US$142.2 million versus US$148.4 million in the prior-year quarter, a decrease of 4.2%. Direct operating expenses declined 8.2% to US$516.9 million from US$563.2 million in the comparable period the year before. Indirect operating expenses increased 5.7% to US$113.0 million from US$106.9 million in the equivalent prior-year period.

Prospects: Our evaluation of Wabtec Corp. as of June 19, 2016 is the result of our systematic analysis on three basic characteristics: earnings strength, relative valuation, and recent stock price movement. The company has managed to produce a neutral trend in earnings per share over the past 5 quarters and while recent estimates for the company have remained steady, WAB has posted better than expected results. Based on operating earnings yield, the company is undervalued when compared to all of the companies in our coverage universe. Share price changes over the past year indicates that WAB will perform well over the near term.

Financial Data

(US$ in Thousands)	3 Mos	12/31/2015	12/31/2014	12/31/2013	12/31/2012	12/31/2011	12/31/2010	12/31/2009
Earnings Per Share	4.13	4.10	3.62	3.01	2.60	1.75	1.28	1.20
Cash Flow Per Share	5.26	4.67	4.93	2.47	2.48	2.60	1.85	1.69
Tang Book Value Per Share	4.13	4.36	5.42	4.31	3.17	2.09	1.43	1.11
Dividends Per Share	0.300	0.280	0.200	0.130	0.080	0.040	0.020	0.020
Dividend Payout %	7.26	6.83	5.52	4.32	3.08	2.28	1.56	1.67
Income Statement								
Total Revenue	772,031	3,307,998	3,044,454	2,566,392	2,391,122	1,967,637	1,507,012	1,401,616
EBITDA	158,567	645,356	564,229	469,928	420,509	300,221	231,150	205,733
Depn & Amortn	16,232	43,100	38,800	33,500	28,900	29,900	28,400	25,700
Income Before Taxes	137,464	585,368	507,855	421,087	377,358	255,314	186,827	163,359
Income Taxes	43,301	186,740	156,175	128,852	125,626	85,165	63,728	48,304
Net Income	94,163	398,628	351,680	292,235	251,732	170,149	123,099	115,055
Average Shares	92,149	97,006	96,885	96,832	96,742	96,658	96,010	95,954
Balance Sheet								
Current Assets	1,686,565	1,612,448	1,637,864	1,333,047	1,092,938	1,055,782	801,953	689,509
Total Assets	3,380,785	3,300,335	3,303,841	2,821,997	2,351,542	2,158,953	1,803,081	1,585,835
Current Liabilities	657,668	664,776	738,802	579,400	553,059	541,385	348,374	305,348
Long-Term Obligations	801,883	695,294	520,403	450,288	317,853	395,805	382,007	359,039
Total Liabilities	1,704,224	1,600,728	1,496,599	1,236,738	1,074,712	1,113,764	903,310	808,928
Stockholders' Equity	1,676,561	1,699,607	1,807,242	1,585,259	1,276,830	1,045,189	899,771	776,907
Shares Outstanding	90,104	91,836	96,274	95,909	95,407	95,892	95,908	95,377
Statistical Record								
Return on Assets %	12.11	12.07	11.48	11.30	11.13	8.59	7.26	7.44
Return on Equity %	22.71	22.73	20.73	20.42	21.62	17.50	14.68	16.18
EBITDA Margin %	20.54	19.51	18.53	18.31	17.59	15.26	15.34	14.68
Net Margin %	12.20	12.05	11.55	11.39	10.53	8.65	8.17	8.21
Asset Turnover	1.00	1.00	0.99	0.99	1.06	0.99	0.89	0.91
Current Ratio	2.56	2.43	2.22	2.30	1.98	1.95	2.30	2.26
Debt to Equity	0.48	0.41	0.29	0.28	0.25	0.38	0.42	0.46
Price Range	102.39-60.58	102.39-68.89	91.24-70.82	74.27-43.77	44.34-34.40	35.78-25.07	26.62-18.45	21.20-11.68
P/E Ratio	24.79-14.67	24.97-16.80	25.20-19.56	24.67-14.54	17.06-13.23	20.45-14.33	20.80-14.41	17.67-9.73
Average Yield %	0.35	0.31	0.25	0.23	0.21	0.13	0.09	0.11

Address: 1001 Air Brake Avenue, Wilmerding, PA 15148 **Telephone:** 412-825-1000 **Fax:** 412-825-1019	**Web Site:** www.wabtec.com **Officers:** Albert J. Neupaver - Executive Chairman, Chairman, President, Chief Executive Officer Emilio A. Fernandez - Vice-Chairman	**Auditors:** Ernst & Young LLP **Transfer Agents:** Wells Fargo Shareowner Services, St Paul, MN

WADDELL & REED FINANCIAL, INC.

Exchange	Symbol	Price	52Wk Range	Yield	P/E
NYS	WDR	$21.37 (5/31/2016)	49.85-18.87	8.61	8.25

*7 Year Price Score 71.88   *NYSE Composite Index=100   *12 Month Price Score 63.88

Interim Earnings (Per Share)
Qtr.	Mar	Jun	Sep	Dec
2013	0.63	0.61	0.80	0.93
2014	0.88	0.98	0.89	0.97
2015	0.80	0.80	0.58	0.76
2016	0.45	...	...	...

Interim Dividends (Per Share)
Amt	Decl	Ex	Rec	Pay
0.43Q	09/21/2015	10/07/2015	10/12/2015	11/02/2015
0.46Q	10/28/2015	01/07/2016	01/11/2016	02/01/2016
0.46Q	03/28/2016	04/14/2016	04/18/2016	05/02/2016
0.46Q	06/20/2016	07/07/2016	07/11/2016	08/01/2016

Indicated Div: $1.84

Valuation Analysis / Institutional Holding
Forecast EPS	$2.04	No of Institutions
	(05/20/2016)	413
Market Cap	$1.7 Billion	Shares
Book Value	$835.2 Million	81,537,072
Price/Book	2.09	% Held
Price/Sales	1.20	81.09

Business Summary: Finance Intermediaries & Services (MIC: 5.5.1 SIC: 6211 NAIC: 523120)

Waddell & Reed Financial is a holding company. Co. provides investment management, investment advisory, investment product underwriting and distribution, and shareholder services administration to mutual fund families, its Ivy Global Investors sub-funds (the IGI Funds) and institutional and separately managed accounts. In addition to performing investment management services for the mutual fund families, Co. acts as an investment adviser for the IGI Funds, institutional and other private investors and Co. provides subadvisory services to other investment companies. As of Dec 31 2015, Co. had $104.40 billion in assets under management.

Recent Developments: For the quarter ended Mar 31 2016, net income decreased 44.2% to US$37.5 million from US$67.1 million in the year-earlier quarter. Revenues were US$323.8 million, down 16.0% from US$385.5 million the year before. Operating income was US$71.4 million versus US$104.4 million in the prior-year quarter, a decrease of 31.6%. Direct operating expenses declined 11.0% to US$173.8 million from US$195.4 million in the comparable period the year before. Indirect operating expenses decreased 8.2% to US$78.5 million from US$85.6 million in the equivalent prior-year period.

Prospects: Our evaluation of Waddell & Reed Financial Inc. as of June 19, 2016 is the result of our systematic analysis on three basic characteristics: earnings strength, relative valuation, and recent stock price movement. The company has generated a negative trend in earnings per share over the past 5 quarters. However, while recent estimates for the company have been lowered by analysts, WDR has posted results that fell short of analysts expectations. Based on operating earnings yield, the company is undervalued when compared to all of the companies in our coverage universe. Share price changes over the past year indicates that WDR will perform in line with the market over the near term.

Financial Data
(US$ in Thousands)	3 Mos	12/31/2015	12/31/2014	12/31/2013	12/31/2012	12/31/2011	12/31/2010	12/31/2009
Earnings Per Share	2.59	2.94	3.71	2.96	1.76	2.05	1.83	1.23
Cash Flow Per Share	1.17	2.80	4.08	3.35	2.72	3.30	1.64	1.82
Tang Book Value Per Share	8.28	8.31	7.51	6.16	4.06	3.53	2.75	1.72
Dividends Per Share	1.750	1.720	1.360	1.120	1.750	0.850	0.770	0.760
Dividend Payout %	67.57	58.50	36.66	37.84	99.43	41.46	42.08	61.79
Income Statement								
Total Revenue	323,816	1,516,631	1,597,759	1,370,354	1,173,805	1,195,177	1,044,885	839,089
EBITDA	73,212	426,608	515,805	417,275	325,514	309,341	273,207	188,551
Depn & Amortn	11,997	16,000	14,600	12,800	13,200	15,200	14,000	13,700
Income Before Taxes	58,447	399,540	490,163	393,231	301,003	282,728	246,484	162,156
Income Taxes	20,978	154,004	176,832	140,233	108,475	107,269	89,525	56,651
Net Income	36,968	245,536	313,331	252,998	150,952	175,459	156,959	105,505
Average Shares	82,104	83,499	84,485	85,589	85,728	85,793	85,647	85,544
Balance Sheet								
Current Assets	1,114,827	1,217,745	1,172,633	1,006,325	804,893	699,611	605,050	618,716
Total Assets	1,444,713	1,555,719	1,511,866	1,336,965	1,152,843	1,082,196	976,931	983,382
Current Liabilities	351,901	443,213	462,966	419,729	365,333	288,898	281,942	360,757
Long-Term Obligations	189,475	190,000	190,000	190,000	190,000	190,000	189,999	199,984
Total Liabilities	609,513	709,264	725,782	649,623	642,603	558,553	519,770	614,327
Stockholders' Equity	835,200	846,455	786,084	687,342	510,240	523,643	457,161	369,055
Shares Outstanding	81,758	82,850	83,654	85,236	85,679	85,564	85,751	85,807
Statistical Record								
Return on Assets %	14.74	16.01	22.00	20.32	13.47	17.04	16.01	12.00
Return on Equity %	25.89	30.08	42.53	42.25	29.12	35.78	37.99	30.62
EBITDA Margin %	22.61	28.13	32.28	30.45	27.73	25.88	26.15	22.47
Net Margin %	11.42	16.19	19.61	18.46	12.86	14.68	15.02	12.57
Asset Turnover	1.00	0.99	1.12	1.10	1.05	1.16	1.07	0.95
Current Ratio	3.17	2.75	2.53	2.40	2.20	2.42	2.15	1.72
Debt to Equity	0.23	0.22	0.24	0.28	0.37	0.36	0.42	0.54
Price Range	50.93-20.77	51.39-28.30	75.96-43.85	65.47-34.82	35.49-25.00	42.16-23.39	39.05-21.83	31.00-11.84
P/E Ratio	19.66-8.02	17.48-9.63	20.47-11.82	22.12-11.76	20.16-14.20	20.57-11.41	21.34-11.93	25.20-9.63
Average Yield %	4.69	4.00	2.30	2.29	5.68	2.52	2.57	3.19

Address: 6300 Lamar Avenue, Overland Park, KS 66202 **Telephone:** 913-236-2000	**Web Site:** www.waddell.com **Officers:** Henry J. Herrmann - Chairman, Chief Executive Officer Alan W. Kosloff - Chairman	**Auditors:** KPMG LLP **Investor Contact:** 913-236-1880 **Transfer Agents:** Computershare Trust Company, N.A., Providence, RI

WAL-MART STORES, INC.

Exchange	Symbol	Price	52Wk Range	Yield	P/E	Div Achiever
NYS	WMT	$70.78 (5/31/2016)	74.89-56.42	2.83	15.62	40 Years

*7 Year Price Score 86.32 *NYSE Composite Index=100 *12 Month Price Score 101.30

TRADING VOLUME (thousand shares)

Interim Earnings (Per Share)

Qtr.	Apr	Jul	Oct	Jan
2013-14	1.14	1.24	1.14	1.36
2014-15	1.11	1.26	1.15	1.54
2015-16	1.03	1.08	1.03	1.44
2016-17	0.98	...	...	...

Interim Dividends (Per Share)

Amt	Decl	Ex	Rec	Pay
0.50Q	02/18/2016	12/07/2016	12/09/2016	01/03/2017
0.50Q	02/18/2016	03/09/2016	03/11/2016	04/04/2016
0.50Q	02/18/2016	05/11/2016	05/13/2016	06/06/2016
0.50Q	02/18/2016	08/10/2016	08/12/2016	09/06/2016

Indicated Div: $2.00 (Div. Reinv. Plan)

Valuation Analysis		Institutional Holding	
Forecast EPS	$4.29	No of Institutions	
	(05/20/2016)	2093	
Market Cap	$221.2 Billion	Shares	
Book Value	$75.2 Billion	1,164,080,768	
Price/Book	2.94	% Held	
Price/Sales	0.46	30.24	

Business Summary: Retail - General Merchandise/Department Stores (MIC: 2.1.1 SIC: 5331 NAIC: 452990)

Wal-Mart Stores operates retail and other stores in various formats. Co.'s operations comprise of three business segments: Walmart U.S., which is a merchandiser of consumer products, operating under the Walmart or Wal-Mart brands, as well as walmart.com., and operating retail stores in all 50 states, Washington D.C. and Puerto Rico.; Walmart International, which consists of operations in 27 countries outside of the U.S. and includes numerous formats divided into three categories: retail, wholesale and other; and Sam's Club, which operates membership-only warehouse clubs, as well as samsclub.com, in the U.S., and its members include both business owners and individual consumers.

Recent Developments: For the quarter ended Apr 30 2016, net income decreased 2.0% to US$3.22 billion from US$3.28 billion in the year-earlier quarter. Revenues were US$115.90 billion, up 0.9% from US$114.83 billion the year before. Operating income was US$5.28 billion versus US$5.68 billion in the prior-year quarter, a decrease of 7.1%. Direct operating expenses rose 0.1% to US$86.54 billion from US$86.48 billion in the comparable period the year before. Indirect operating expenses increased 6.3% to US$24.09 billion from US$22.66 billion in the equivalent prior-year period.

Prospects: Our evaluation of Wal-Mart Stores Inc. as of June 19, 2016 is the result of our systematic analysis on three basic characteristics: earnings strength, relative valuation, and recent stock price movement. The company has enjoyed a very positive trend in earnings per share over the past 5 quarters and while recent estimates for the company have been raised by analysts, WMT has posted better than expected results. Based on operating earnings yield, the company is undervalued when compared to all of the companies in our coverage universe. Share price changes over the past year indicates that WMT will perform poorly over the near term.

Financial Data

(US$ in Thousands)	3 Mos	01/31/2016	01/31/2015	01/31/2014	01/31/2013	01/31/2012	01/31/2011	01/31/2010
Earnings Per Share	4.53	4.57	5.05	4.88	5.02	4.52	4.47	3.70
Cash Flow Per Share	9.27	8.54	8.84	7.11	7.56	7.01	6.47	6.79
Tang Book Value Per Share	18.70	20.19	19.61	17.55	16.85	14.82	14.73	14.43
Dividends Per Share	1.970	1.960	1.920	1.880	1.590	1.460	1.210	1.090
Dividend Payout %	43.49	42.89	38.02	38.52	31.67	32.30	27.07	29.46
Income Statement								
Total Revenue	115,904,000	482,130,000	485,651,000	476,294,000	469,162,000	446,950,000	421,849,000	408,214,000
EBITDA	7,663,000	33,505,000	36,247,000	35,672,000	36,201,000	34,658,000	33,142,000	31,150,000
Depn & Amortn	2,388,000	9,400,000	9,100,000	8,800,000	8,400,000	8,100,000	7,600,000	7,200,000
Income Before Taxes	4,714,000	21,638,000	24,799,000	24,656,000	25,737,000	24,398,000	23,538,000	22,066,000
Income Taxes	1,498,000	6,558,000	7,985,000	8,105,000	7,981,000	7,944,000	7,579,000	7,139,000
Net Income	3,079,000	14,694,000	16,363,000	16,022,000	16,999,000	15,699,000	16,389,000	14,335,000
Average Shares	3,154,000	3,217,000	3,243,000	3,283,000	3,389,000	3,474,000	3,670,000	3,877,000
Balance Sheet								
Current Assets	59,097,000	60,239,000	63,278,000	61,185,000	59,940,000	54,975,000	51,893,000	48,331,000
Total Assets	198,705,000	199,581,000	203,706,000	204,751,000	203,105,000	193,406,000	180,663,000	170,706,000
Current Liabilities	70,282,000	64,619,000	65,272,000	69,345,000	71,818,000	62,300,000	58,484,000	55,561,000
Long-Term Obligations	43,393,000	44,030,000	43,692,000	44,559,000	41,417,000	47,079,000	43,842,000	36,401,000
Total Liabilities	123,522,000	119,035,000	122,312,000	128,496,000	126,762,000	122,091,000	112,121,000	99,957,000
Stockholders' Equity	75,183,000	80,546,000	81,394,000	76,255,000	76,343,000	71,315,000	68,542,000	70,749,000
Shares Outstanding	3,125,000	3,162,000	3,228,000	3,233,000	3,314,000	3,418,000	3,516,000	3,786,000
Statistical Record								
Return on Assets %	7.23	7.29	8.01	7.86	8.55	8.39	9.33	8.58
Return on Equity %	19.02	18.15	20.76	21.00	22.96	22.45	23.53	21.08
EBITDA Margin %	6.61	6.95	7.46	7.49	7.72	7.75	7.86	7.63
Net Margin %	2.66	3.05	3.37	3.36	3.62	3.51	3.89	3.51
Asset Turnover	2.42	2.39	2.38	2.34	2.36	2.39	2.40	2.44
Current Ratio	0.84	0.93	0.97	0.88	0.83	0.88	0.89	0.87
Debt to Equity	0.58	0.55	0.54	0.58	0.54	0.66	0.64	0.51
Price Range	79.92-56.42	87.33-56.42	90.47-72.66	81.21-68.76	77.15-57.36	61.47-48.41	57.57-48.00	55.01-46.42
P/E Ratio	17.64-12.45	19.11-12.35	17.91-14.39	16.64-14.09	15.37-11.43	13.60-10.71	12.88-10.74	14.87-12.55
Average Yield %	2.94	2.78	2.46	2.48	2.33	2.67	2.28	2.15

Address: 702 S.W. 8th Street, Bentonville, AR 72716 Telephone: 479-273-4000	Web Site: www.walmart.com Officers: S. Robson Walton - Chairman Eduardo Castro-Wright - Vice-Chairman, Division Officer	Auditors: Ernst & Young LLP Investor Contact: 479-273-8446 Transfer Agents: Computershare Trust Company, N.A., Providence, RI

WASTE MANAGEMENT, INC. (DE)

Exchange	Symbol	Price	52Wk Range	Yield	P/E	Div Achiever
NYS	WM	$60.95 (5/31/2016)	61.78-46.35	2.69	24.19	12 Years

*7 Year Price Score 113.38 *NYSE Composite Index=100 *12 Month Price Score 109.85

TRADING VOLUME (thousand shares)

Interim Earnings (Per Share)

Qtr.	Mar	Jun	Sep	Dec
2013	0.36	0.52	0.62	(1.29)
2014	0.49	0.45	0.58	1.27
2015	(0.28)	0.60	0.74	0.60
2016	0.58	...	...	...

Interim Dividends (Per Share)

Amt	Decl	Ex	Rec	Pay
0.385Q	08/20/2015	09/10/2015	09/14/2015	09/24/2015
0.385Q	11/09/2015	12/02/2015	12/04/2015	12/18/2015
0.41Q	02/26/2016	03/03/2016	03/07/2016	03/18/2016
0.41Q	05/11/2016	06/01/2016	06/03/2016	06/17/2016

Indicated Div: $1.64 (Div. Reinv. Plan)

Valuation Analysis / Institutional Holding

Forecast EPS	$2.80	No of Institutions
	(05/20/2016)	1123
Market Cap	$27.1 Billion	Shares
Book Value	$5.3 Billion	393,186,112
Price/Book	5.12	% Held
Price/Sales	2.07	77.20

Business Summary: Sanitation Services (MIC: 7.5.3 SIC: 4953 NAIC: 562211)

Waste Management is a holding company. Through its subsidiaries, Co. is a provider of waste management environmental services. Co. partners with its residential, commercial, industrial and municipal customers and the communities it serves to manage and reduce waste at each stage from collection to disposal, while recovering resources and creating renewable energy. Co.'s Solid Waste business provides collection, transfer, recycling and resource recovery, and disposal services. Through its subsidiaries, Co. is also a developer, operator and owner of landfill gas-to-energy facilities. At Dec 31 2015, Co. owned or operated 244 solid waste landfills and five hazardous waste landfills.

Recent Developments: For the quarter ended Mar 31 2016, net income amounted to US$256.0 million versus a net loss of US$131.0 million in the year-earlier quarter. Revenues were US$3.18 billion, up 4.5% from US$3.04 billion the year before. Operating income was US$508.0 million versus US$440.0 million in the prior-year quarter, an increase of 15.5%. Direct operating expenses rose 2.4% to US$1.99 billion from US$1.95 billion in the comparable period the year before. Indirect operating expenses increased 3.2% to US$675.0 million from US$654.0 million in the equivalent prior-year period.

Prospects: Our evaluation of Waste Management Inc. as of June 19, 2016 is the result of our systematic analysis on three basic characteristics: earnings strength, relative valuation, and recent stock price movement. The company has managed to produce a neutral trend in earnings per share over the past 5 quarters and while recent estimates for the company have been raised by analysts, WM has posted better than expected results. Based on operating earnings yield, the company is about fairly valued when compared to all of the companies in our coverage universe. Share price changes over the past year indicates that WM will perform very well over the near term.

Financial Data

(US$ in Thousands)	3 Mos	12/31/2015	12/31/2014	12/31/2013	12/31/2012	12/31/2011	12/31/2010	12/31/2009
Earnings Per Share	2.52	1.65	2.79	0.21	1.76	2.04	1.98	2.01
Cash Flow Per Share	6.06	5.52	5.04	5.25	4.94	5.26	4.74	4.81
Tang Book Value Per Share	N.M.	N.M.	N.M.	N.M.	N.M.	N.M.	0.50	0.85
Dividends Per Share	1.565	1.540	1.500	1.460	1.420	1.360	1.260	1.160
Dividend Payout %	62.10	93.33	53.76	695.24	80.68	66.67	63.64	57.71
Income Statement								
Total Revenue	3,176,000	12,961,000	13,996,000	13,983,000	13,649,000	13,378,000	12,515,000	11,791,000
EBITDA	810,000	2,652,000	3,484,000	2,258,000	3,061,000	3,202,000	3,274,000	3,025,000
Depn & Amortn	312,000	1,169,000	1,214,000	1,253,000	1,228,000	1,178,000	1,153,000	1,137,000
Income Before Taxes	403,000	1,098,000	1,804,000	528,000	1,349,000	1,551,000	1,652,000	1,475,000
Income Taxes	140,000	308,000	413,000	364,000	443,000	511,000	629,000	413,000
Net Income	258,000	753,000	1,298,000	98,000	817,000	961,000	953,000	994,000
Average Shares	448,600	455,900	465,600	469,800	464,400	471,400	482,200	493,600
Balance Sheet								
Current Assets	2,302,000	2,345,000	3,641,000	2,499,000	2,423,000	2,379,000	2,482,000	3,010,000
Total Assets	20,781,000	20,419,000	21,412,000	22,603,000	23,097,000	22,569,000	21,476,000	21,154,000
Current Liabilities	2,560,000	2,510,000	3,485,000	3,014,000	3,036,000	3,068,000	2,485,000	2,901,000
Long-Term Obligations	9,072,000	8,728,000	8,345,000	9,500,000	9,173,000	9,125,000	8,674,000	8,124,000
Total Liabilities	15,491,000	15,074,000	15,546,000	16,896,000	16,743,000	16,499,000	15,216,000	14,869,000
Stockholders' Equity	5,290,000	5,345,000	5,866,000	5,707,000	6,354,000	6,070,000	6,260,000	6,285,000
Shares Outstanding	444,723	447,177	458,537	464,320	464,220	460,532	475,046	486,120
Statistical Record								
Return on Assets %	5.50	3.60	5.90	0.43	3.57	4.36	4.47	4.80
Return on Equity %	21.03	13.43	22.43	1.63	13.12	15.59	15.19	16.31
EBITDA Margin %	25.50	20.46	24.89	16.15	22.43	23.93	26.16	25.66
Net Margin %	8.12	5.81	9.27	0.70	5.99	7.18	7.61	8.43
Asset Turnover	0.63	0.62	0.64	0.61	0.60	0.61	0.59	0.57
Current Ratio	0.90	0.93	1.04	0.83	0.80	0.78	1.00	1.04
Debt to Equity	1.71	1.63	1.42	1.66	1.44	1.50	1.39	1.29
Price Range	59.71-46.35	55.18-46.35	51.58-40.41	46.10-33.74	36.08-30.96	39.61-28.17	36.99-31.29	34.10-22.23
P/E Ratio	23.69-18.39	33.44-28.09	18.49-14.48	219.52-160.67	20.50-17.59	19.42-13.81	18.68-15.80	16.97-11.06
Average Yield %	3.00	2.98	3.33	3.60	4.22	3.89	3.69	3.96

Address: 1001 Fannin Street, Suite 4000, Houston, TX 77002	**Web Site:** www.wm.com	**Auditors:** Ernst & Young LLP
Telephone: 713-512-6200	**Officers:** David P. Steiner - President, Chief Executive Officer James C. Fish - Executive Vice President, Chief Financial Officer	**Investor Contact:** 713-265-1656
Fax: 713-512-6299		**Transfer Agents:** Computershare, Canton, MA

WATERS CORP.

Exchange	Symbol	Price	52Wk Range	Yield	P/E
NYS	WAT	$137.55 (5/31/2016)	138.31-113.62	N/A	24.35

*7 Year Price Score 117.57 *NYSE Composite Index=100 *12 Month Price Score 103.80

Interim Earnings (Per Share)

Qtr.	Mar	Jun	Sep	Dec
2013	1.39	1.03	1.14	1.64
2014	0.82	1.13	1.34	1.78
2015	1.15	1.27	1.40	1.83
2016	1.15	...	...	...

Interim Dividends (Per Share)

No Dividends Paid

Valuation Analysis		Institutional Holding	
Forecast EPS	$6.35	No of Institutions	
	(05/20/2016)	658	
Market Cap	$11.1 Billion	Shares	
Book Value	$2.1 Billion	86,775,896	
Price/Book	5.30	% Held	
Price/Sales	5.41	88.97	

Business Summary: Biotechnology (MIC: 4.1.2 SIC: 3826 NAIC: 334516)

Waters is a holding company. Co. is an analytical instrument manufacturer that primarily designs, manufactures, sells and services, through its Waters Division, high performance liquid chromatography, ultra performance liquid chromatography and mass spectrometry technology systems and support products, including chromatography columns, other consumable products and post-warranty service plans. Through its TA Division, Co. primarily designs, manufactures, sells and services thermal analysis, rheometry and calorimetry instruments. Co. is also a developer and supplier of software-based products that are typically purchased by customers as part of the instrument system.

Recent Developments: For the quarter ended Apr 2 2016, net income decreased 2.1% to US$94.1 million from US$96.1 million in the year-earlier quarter. Revenues were US$475.2 million, up 3.2% from US$460.4 million the year before. Operating income was US$112.7 million versus US$120.0 million in the prior-year quarter, a decrease of 6.1%. Direct operating expenses rose 6.3% to US$201.2 million from US$189.2 million in the comparable period the year before. Indirect operating expenses increased 6.8% to US$161.4 million from US$151.2 million in the equivalent prior-year period.

Prospects: Our evaluation of Waters Corp. as of June 19, 2016 is the result of our systematic analysis on three basic characteristics: earnings strength, relative valuation, and recent stock price movement. The company has produced a positive trend in earnings per share over the past 5 quarters and while recent estimates for the company have remained steady, WAT has posted better than expected results. Based on operating earnings yield, the company is about fairly valued when compared to all of the companies in our coverage universe. Share price changes over the past year indicates that WAT will perform well over the near term.

Financial Data

(US$ in Thousands)	3 Mos	12/31/2015	12/31/2014	12/31/2013	12/31/2012	12/31/2011	12/31/2010	12/31/2009
Earnings Per Share	5.65	5.65	5.07	5.20	5.19	4.69	4.06	3.34
Cash Flow Per Share	6.96	6.80	6.07	5.68	5.10	5.48	4.96	4.37
Tang Book Value Per Share	18.80	18.21	15.72	13.84	10.77	8.29	6.49	3.97
Income Statement								
Total Revenue	475,246	2,042,332	1,989,344	1,904,218	1,843,641	1,851,184	1,643,371	1,498,700
EBITDA	136,093	657,438	612,139	595,463	580,321	594,987	512,490	451,874
Depn & Amortn	23,431	89,987	94,231	79,695	68,831	66,387	62,558	57,272
Income Before Taxes	106,630	541,919	490,740	490,105	487,625	509,252	437,863	386,652
Income Taxes	12,578	72,866	59,120	40,102	26,182	76,284	56,100	63,339
Net Income	94,052	469,053	431,620	450,003	461,443	432,968	381,763	323,313
Average Shares	81,974	83,087	85,151	86,546	88,979	92,325	94,057	96,862
Balance Sheet								
Current Assets	3,310,619	3,213,533	2,853,736	2,556,255	2,257,726	1,942,104	1,586,641	1,172,376
Total Assets	4,368,395	4,268,677	3,877,934	3,582,629	3,168,150	2,723,234	2,327,670	1,907,931
Current Liabilities	524,030	564,076	581,595	487,532	504,242	601,863	385,850	394,568
Long-Term Obligations	1,593,301	1,493,027	1,240,000	1,190,000	1,045,000	700,000	700,000	500,000
Total Liabilities	2,266,709	2,209,826	1,983,268	1,819,456	1,700,793	1,496,656	1,258,873	1,058,982
Stockholders' Equity	2,101,686	2,058,851	1,894,666	1,763,173	1,467,357	1,226,578	1,068,797	848,949
Shares Outstanding	80,919	81,472	83,147	84,819	86,390	88,996	91,848	94,118
Statistical Record								
Return on Assets %	11.33	11.52	11.57	13.33	15.62	17.14	18.03	18.31
Return on Equity %	23.56	23.73	23.60	27.86	34.16	37.73	39.81	42.82
EBITDA Margin %	28.64	32.19	30.77	31.27	31.48	32.14	31.19	30.15
Net Margin %	19.79	22.97	21.70	23.63	25.03	23.39	23.23	21.57
Asset Turnover	0.50	0.50	0.53	0.56	0.62	0.73	0.78	0.85
Current Ratio	6.32	5.70	4.91	5.24	4.48	3.23	4.11	2.97
Debt to Equity	0.76	0.73	0.65	0.67	0.71	0.57	0.65	0.59
Price Range	136.50-113.62	136.50-112.53	116.98-95.08	107.73-86.22	94.03-73.71	99.56-71.61	80.47-56.18	62.58-30.75
P/E Ratio	24.16-20.11	24.16-19.92	23.07-18.75	20.72-16.58	18.12-14.20	21.23-15.27	19.82-13.84	18.74-9.21

Address: 34 Maple Street, Milford, MA 01757
Telephone: 508-478-2000
Fax: 508-872-1990

Web Site: www.waters.com
Officers: Douglas A. Berthiaume - Chairman, President, President (frmr), Chief Executive Officer Christopher J. O'Connell - President, Chief Executive Officer

Auditors: PricewaterhouseCoopers LLP
Investor Contact: 508-482-2349
Transfer Agents: Computershare, Providence, RI

WATSCO INC.

Exchange	Symbol	Price	52Wk Range	Yield	P/E
NYS	WSO	$134.23 (5/31/2016)	136.99-108.09	2.53	27.17

*7 Year Price Score 128.52 ***NYSE Composite Index=100** ***12 Month Price Score 105.57**

Interim Earnings (Per Share)

Qtr.	Mar	Jun	Sep	Dec
2013	0.39	1.48	1.32	0.50
2014	0.48	1.60	1.56	0.68
2015	0.65	1.85	1.64	0.74
2016	0.71	...	...	...

Interim Dividends (Per Share)

Amt	Decl	Ex	Rec	Pay
0.70Q	07/01/2015	07/13/2015	07/15/2015	07/31/2015
0.70Q	10/01/2015	10/13/2015	10/15/2015	10/30/2015
0.85Q	01/04/2016	01/13/2016	01/15/2016	01/29/2016
0.85Q	04/01/2016	04/13/2016	04/15/2016	04/29/2016

Indicated Div: $3.40

Valuation Analysis

Forecast EPS	$5.50 (05/17/2016)
Market Cap	$4.1 Billion
Book Value	$968.1 Million
Price/Book	4.21
Price/Sales	0.98

Institutional Holding

No of Institutions	342
Shares	26,222,014
% Held	85.98

Business Summary: Industrial Machinery & Equipment (MIC: 7.2.1 SIC: 5075 NAIC: 423730)

Watsco is a distributor of air conditioning, heating and refrigeration equipment and related parts and supplies. The products Co. distributes consist of: equipment, including residential ducted and ductless air conditioners, gas, electric and oil furnaces, commercial air conditioning and heating equipment and systems, and other equipment; parts, including replacement compressors, evaporator coils, motors and other component parts; and supplies, including thermostats, insulation material, refrigerants, ductwork, grills, registers, sheet metal, tools, copper tubing, concrete pads, tape, adhesives and other ancillary supplies.

Recent Developments: For the quarter ended Mar 31 2016, net income increased 9.2% to US$34.2 million from US$31.3 million in the year-earlier quarter. Revenues were US$851.4 million, up 5.2% from US$809.0 million the year before. Operating income was US$50.7 million versus US$47.0 million in the prior-year quarter, an increase of 7.8%. Direct operating expenses rose 5.7% to US$639.0 million from US$604.7 million in the comparable period the year before. Indirect operating expenses increased 2.9% to US$161.8 million from US$157.2 million in the equivalent prior-year period.

Prospects: Our evaluation of Watsco Inc. as of June 19, 2016 is the result of our systematic analysis on three basic characteristics: earnings strength, relative valuation, and recent stock price movement. The company has produced a positive trend in earnings per share over the past 5 quarters and while recent estimates for the company have remained steady, WSO has posted results that fell short of analysts expectations. Based on operating earnings yield, the company is about fairly valued when compared to all of the companies in our coverage universe. Share price changes over the past year indicates that WSO will perform well over the near term.

Financial Data

(US$ in Thousands)	3 Mos	12/31/2015	12/31/2014	12/31/2013	12/31/2012	12/31/2011	12/31/2010	12/31/2009
Earnings Per Share	4.94	4.90	4.32	3.68	2.70	2.74	2.49	1.40
Cash Flow Per Share	8.61	6.83	4.49	4.67	5.46	2.00	5.02	3.10
Tang Book Value Per Share	13.86	11.85	8.86	7.02	3.81	12.36	12.45	11.71
Dividends Per Share	2.950	2.800	2.000	1.150	7.480	2.230	2.040	1.890
Dividend Payout %	59.72	57.14	46.30	31.25	277.04	81.39	81.93	135.00
Income Statement								
Total Revenue	851,424	4,113,239	3,944,540	3,743,330	3,431,712	2,977,759	2,844,595	2,001,815
EBITDA	55,625	350,550	317,905	282,886	235,894	208,414	176,343	89,593
Depn & Amortn	4,957	13,802	12,158	11,677	10,986	9,364	10,771	8,533
Income Before Taxes	49,682	331,201	300,541	265,379	220,243	194,592	162,082	78,329
Income Taxes	15,508	104,677	91,839	77,660	62,642	56,850	50,360	26,756
Net Income	25,537	172,929	151,387	127,723	103,334	90,450	80,760	43,314
Average Shares	32,537	32,480	32,358	32,258	31,744	30,753	30,578	28,521
Balance Sheet								
Current Assets	1,261,925	1,181,265	1,157,335	1,021,102	1,015,451	828,177	838,004	755,298
Total Assets	1,876,890	1,788,442	1,791,067	1,669,531	1,682,055	1,268,148	1,237,227	1,160,613
Current Liabilities	347,251	270,301	287,022	243,506	282,358	223,039	266,005	223,926
Long-Term Obligations	238,366	245,814	303,885	230,557	316,196	...	10,016	13,429
Total Liabilities	908,822	831,132	907,107	829,135	933,841	465,358	472,766	422,587
Stockholders' Equity	968,068	957,310	883,960	840,396	748,214	802,790	764,461	738,026
Shares Outstanding	30,342	35,311	35,006	34,727	34,521	33,005	32,449	32,138
Statistical Record								
Return on Assets %	9.31	9.66	8.75	7.62	6.99	7.22	6.74	4.62
Return on Equity %	18.99	18.78	17.56	16.08	13.29	11.54	10.75	6.62
EBITDA Margin %	6.53	8.52	8.06	7.56	6.87	7.00	6.20	4.48
Net Margin %	3.00	4.20	3.84	3.41	3.01	3.04	2.84	2.16
Asset Turnover	2.21	2.30	2.28	2.23	2.32	2.38	2.37	2.13
Current Ratio	3.63	4.37	4.03	4.19	3.60	3.71	3.15	3.37
Debt to Equity	0.25	0.26	0.34	0.27	0.42	...	0.01	0.02
Price Range	134.84-108.09	131.89-104.92	108.20-85.53	97.47-74.13	80.12-66.22	72.76-51.10	64.55-47.86	56.82-30.97
P/E Ratio	27.30-21.88	26.92-21.41	25.05-19.80	26.49-20.14	29.67-24.53	26.55-18.65	25.92-19.22	40.59-22.12
Average Yield %	2.39	2.30	2.05	1.32	10.29	3.54	3.60	4.10

Address: 2665 South Bayshore Drive, Suite 901, Miami, FL 33133	Web Site: www.watsco.com	Auditors: KPMG LLP
Telephone: 305-714-4100	Officers: Albert H. Nahmad - Chairman, President, Chief Executive Officer Aaron J. Nahmad - Vice President, President	Investor Contact: 305-714-4100
		Transfer Agents: American Stock Transter & Trust Company, New York, NY

WEBSTER FINANCIAL CORP (WATERBURY, CONN)

Exchange	Symbol	Price	52Wk Range	Yield	P/E
NYS	WBS	$39.16 (5/31/2016)	40.96-30.35	2.55	18.21

*7 Year Price Score 126.70 *NYSE Composite Index=100 *12 Month Price Score 98.54

Interim Earnings (Per Share)

Qtr.	Mar	Jun	Sep	Dec
2013	0.44	0.48	0.49	0.45
2014	0.53	0.50	0.53	0.53
2015	0.52	0.55	0.54	0.55
2016	0.51	...	...	...

Interim Dividends (Per Share)

Amt	Decl	Ex	Rec	Pay
0.23Q	07/27/2015	08/06/2015	08/10/2015	08/24/2015
0.23Q	10/27/2015	11/06/2015	11/10/2015	11/24/2015
0.23Q	01/26/2016	02/05/2016	02/09/2016	02/23/2016
0.25Q	04/25/2016	05/05/2016	05/09/2016	05/23/2016

Indicated Div: $1.00 (Div. Reinv. Plan)

Valuation Analysis / Institutional Holding

Forecast EPS	$2.16 (05/20/2016)	No of Institutions 336
Market Cap	$3.6 Billion	Shares 88,586,536
Book Value	$2.4 Billion	% Held 89.71
Price/Book	1.47	
Price/Sales	3.49	

Business Summary: Banking (MIC: 5.1.1 SIC: 6021 NAIC: 522110)

Webster Financial is a bank holding company and financial holding company. Co., through Webster Bank, N.A. and non-banking financial services subsidiaries, provides financial services to individuals, families and businesses pimarily from New York to Massachusetts. Co. provides business and consumer banking, mortgage lending, financial planning, trust, and investment services through banking offices, ATMs, telephone banking, mobile banking and its internet website www.websterbank.com or or www.wbst.com. Co. has four segments: Commercial Banking, Community Banking, HSA Bank and Private Banking. At Dec 31 2015, Co. had total assets of $24.68 billion and total deposits of $17.95 billion.

Recent Developments: For the quarter ended Mar 31 2016, net income decreased 2.2% to US$48.6 million from US$49.7 million in the year-earlier quarter. Net interest income increased 10.3% to US$176.2 million from US$159.8 million in the year-earlier quarter. Provision for loan losses was US$15.6 million versus US$9.8 million in the prior-year quarter, an increase of 60.0%. Non-interest income rose 10.6% to US$64.0 million from US$57.9 million, while non-interest expense advanced 13.2% to US$151.7 million.

Prospects: Our evaluation of Webster Financial Corp. (CT) as of June 19, 2016 is the result of our systematic analysis on three basic characteristics: earnings strength, relative valuation, and recent stock price movement. The company has managed to produce a neutral trend in earnings per share over the past 5 quarters. However, while recent estimates for the company have been lowered by analysts, WBS has posted results that fell short of analysts expectations. Based on operating earnings yield, the company is undervalued when compared to all of the companies in our coverage universe. Share price changes over the past year indicates that WBS will perform in line with the market over the near term.

Financial Data

(US$ in Thousands)	3 Mos	12/31/2015	12/31/2014	12/31/2013	12/31/2012	12/31/2011	12/31/2010	12/31/2009
Earnings Per Share	2.15	2.15	2.08	1.86	1.86	1.61	0.60	(2.14)
Cash Flow Per Share	2.86	3.38	3.03	5.37	2.94	3.06	4.31	1.87
Tang Book Value Per Share	19.03	18.73	18.13	16.92	16.50	14.58	13.74	12.45
Dividends Per Share	0.920	0.890	0.750	0.550	0.350	0.160	0.040	0.040
Dividend Payout %	42.79	41.40	36.06	29.57	18.82	9.94	6.67	...
Income Statement								
Interest Income	202,335	760,040	718,941	687,640	693,502	699,723	706,186	745,342
Interest Expense	26,183	95,415	90,500	90,912	114,594	135,955	171,376	250,704
Net Interest Income	176,152	664,625	628,441	596,728	578,908	563,768	534,810	494,638
Provision for Losses	15,600	49,300	37,250	33,500	21,500	22,500	115,000	303,000
Non-Interest Income	64,024	239,545	202,108	191,050	192,758	177,042	206,856	187,108
Non-Interest Expense	151,742	554,554	502,138	498,059	501,804	510,976	538,974	507,394
Income Before Taxes	72,834	300,316	291,161	256,219	248,362	207,334	87,692	(128,648)
Income Taxes	24,217	93,976	91,409	76,670	74,665	57,951	13,468	(52,736)
Net Income	48,617	206,340	199,752	179,549	173,697	151,379	74,315	(75,632)
Average Shares	91,809	91,533	90,620	90,261	91,649	91,688	82,172	63,916
Balance Sheet								
Net Loans & Leases	15,714,579	15,533,836	13,808,713	12,568,005	11,959,200	11,049,308	10,755,198	10,708,053
Total Assets	24,935,509	24,677,820	22,533,010	20,852,999	20,146,765	18,714,340	18,038,068	17,739,197
Total Deposits	18,724,523	17,952,778	15,651,605	14,854,420	14,530,835	13,656,025	13,608,785	13,632,127
Total Liabilities	22,497,542	22,262,249	20,210,329	18,643,811	18,053,235	16,868,566	16,264,646	15,790,804
Stockholders' Equity	2,437,967	2,415,571	2,322,681	2,209,188	2,093,530	1,845,774	1,773,422	1,948,393
Shares Outstanding	91,379	91,561	90,381	89,959	84,963	87,215	86,858	77,896
Statistical Record								
Return on Assets %	0.85	0.87	0.92	0.88	0.89	0.82	0.42	N.M.
Return on Equity %	8.56	8.71	8.82	8.35	8.79	8.37	3.99	N.M.
Net Interest Margin %	87.06	87.45	87.41	86.78	83.48	80.57	75.73	66.36
Efficiency Ratio %	56.97	55.48	54.52	56.68	56.62	58.28	59.03	54.42
Loans to Deposits	0.84	0.87	0.88	0.85	0.82	0.81	0.79	0.79
Price Range	40.96-30.35	40.96-29.11	33.05-27.65	31.18-20.55	24.65-19.10	23.65-14.60	21.67-11.87	14.12-2.97
P/E Ratio	19.05-14.12	19.05-13.54	15.89-13.29	16.76-11.05	13.25-10.27	14.69-9.07	36.12-19.78	...
Average Yield %	2.50	2.43	2.46	2.17	1.62	0.80	0.23	0.44

Address: 145 Bank Street, Waterbury, CT 06702	**Web Site:** www.websterbank.com	**Auditors:** Ernst & Young LLP
Telephone: 203-578-2202	**Officers:** James C. Smith - Chairman, President, Chief Executive Officer Joseph J. Savage - Executive Vice-Chairman, President, Executive Vice President	**Investor Contact:** 203-578-2202 **Transfer Agents:** Computershare, Pittsburgh, PA

WEC ENERGY GROUP INC

Exchange	Symbol	Price	52Wk Range	Yield	P/E	Div Achiever
NYS	WEC	$60.14 (5/31/2016)	60.18-44.97	3.29	23.31	12 Years

*7 Year Price Score 99.83 *NYSE Composite Index=100 *12 Month Price Score 109.88

Interim Earnings (Per Share)

Qtr.	Mar	Jun	Sep	Dec
2013	0.76	0.52	0.60	0.63
2014	0.91	0.58	0.56	0.54
2015	0.86	0.35	0.58	0.56
2016	1.09	...	...	...

Interim Dividends (Per Share)

Amt	Decl	Ex	Rec	Pay
0.234Q	06/12/2015	08/12/2015	08/14/2015	09/01/2015
0.458Q	10/15/2015	11/10/2015	11/13/2015	12/01/2015
0.495Q	12/03/2015	02/10/2016	02/12/2016	03/01/2016
0.495Q	04/21/2016	05/11/2016	05/13/2016	06/01/2016

Indicated Div: $1.98 (Div. Reinv. Plan)

Valuation Analysis / **Institutional Holding**

Forecast EPS	$2.93 (05/17/2016)
No of Institutions	829
Market Cap	$19.0 Billion
Shares	234,167,296
Book Value	$8.8 Billion
% Held	75.35
Price/Book	2.15
Price/Sales	2.82

Business Summary: Electric Utilities (MIC: 3.1.1 SIC: 4931 NAIC: 221121)

WEC Energy Group is a holding company. Co. has six segments: Wisconsin, which includes the electric and natural gas utility and non-utility operations, including electric and natural gas operations in Michigan; Illinois, which includes the natural gas utility and non-utility operations; other states, which includes the natural gas utility and non-utility operations; electric transmission, which includes Co.'s approximate 60.0% ownership interest in American Transmission Company LLC, an electric transmission company; We Power, which includes Co.'s nonregulated entity that owns and leases generating facilities to its subsidiary, Wisconsin Electric Power Company; and corporate and other.

Recent Developments: For the quarter ended Mar 31 2016, net income increased 76.7% to US$346.5 million from US$196.1 million in the year-earlier quarter. Revenues were US$2.19 billion, up 58.1% from US$1.39 billion the year before. Operating income was US$589.3 million versus US$358.8 million in the prior-year quarter, an increase of 64.2%. Direct operating expenses rose 53.2% to US$1.37 billion from US$894.6 million in the comparable period the year before. Indirect operating expenses increased 74.8% to US$235.1 million from US$134.5 million in the equivalent prior-year period.

Prospects: Our evaluation of WEC Energy Group Inc. as of June 19, 2016 is the result of our systematic analysis on three basic characteristics: earnings strength, relative valuation, and recent stock price movement. The company has enjoyed a very positive trend in earnings per share over the past 5 quarters. However, while recent estimates for the company have been mixed, WEC has posted better than expected results. Based on operating earnings yield, the company is about fairly valued when compared to all of the companies in our coverage universe. Share price changes over the past year indicates that WEC will perform well over the near term.

Financial Data
(US$ in Thousands)

	3 Mos	12/31/2015	12/31/2014	12/31/2013	12/31/2012	12/31/2011	12/31/2010	12/31/2009
Earnings Per Share	2.58	2.34	2.59	2.51	2.35	2.24	1.93	1.62
Cash Flow Per Share	5.26	4.77	5.31	5.41	5.09	4.27	3.47	2.69
Tang Book Value Per Share	18.44	17.84	17.64	16.78	16.12	15.28	14.37	13.37
Dividends Per Share	1.815	1.743	1.560	1.445	1.200	1.040	0.800	0.675
Dividend Payout %	70.36	74.48	60.23	57.57	51.06	46.43	41.45	41.67
Income Statement								
Total Revenue	2,194,800	5,926,100	4,997,100	4,519,000	4,246,400	4,486,400	4,202,500	4,127,900
EBITDA	813,900	1,892,900	1,544,900	1,499,100	1,406,800	1,286,400	969,600	810,800
Depn & Amortn	191,900	583,500	419,400	400,200	371,700	336,400	119,000	118,700
Income Before Taxes	521,100	978,000	884,000	846,800	786,900	714,200	644,200	535,400
Income Taxes	213,100	433,800	361,700	337,900	306,300	263,900	249,900	217,300
Net Income	346,500	640,300	588,300	577,400	546,300	526,200	456,500	382,400
Average Shares	317,100	272,700	227,500	229,700	232,800	235,400	236,800	235,800
Balance Sheet								
Current Assets	1,896,400	2,206,800	1,535,400	1,551,100	1,313,900	1,426,200	1,331,100	1,461,700
Total Assets	29,104,600	29,355,200	15,163,400	14,769,400	14,285,000	13,862,100	13,059,800	12,697,900
Current Liabilities	2,229,800	2,709,000	1,668,700	1,496,400	1,443,300	1,364,500	1,721,100	1,881,900
Long-Term Obligations	8,955,800	9,124,100	4,186,400	4,363,200	4,453,800	4,614,300	3,932,000	3,875,800
Total Liabilities	20,286,300	20,670,000	10,713,300	10,506,000	10,119,500	9,868,400	9,227,300	9,100,600
Stockholders' Equity	8,818,300	8,685,200	4,450,100	4,263,400	4,165,500	3,993,700	3,832,500	3,597,300
Shares Outstanding	315,647	315,683	225,517	225,962	229,039	230,486	233,771	233,816
Statistical Record								
Return on Assets %	3.58	2.88	3.93	3.97	3.87	3.91	3.54	3.02
Return on Equity %	11.87	9.75	13.50	13.70	13.35	13.45	12.29	10.98
EBITDA Margin %	37.08	31.94	30.92	33.17	33.13	28.67	23.07	19.64
Net Margin %	15.79	10.80	11.77	12.78	12.87	11.73	10.86	9.26
Asset Turnover	0.30	0.27	0.33	0.31	0.30	0.33	0.33	0.33
Current Ratio	0.85	0.81	0.92	1.04	0.91	1.05	0.77	0.78
Debt to Equity	1.02	1.05	0.94	1.02	1.07	1.16	1.03	1.08
Price Range	60.07-44.97	57.47-44.97	55.23-40.31	44.94-36.85	41.28-33.92	61.02-27.94	60.49-47.66	50.42-36.55
P/E Ratio	23.28-17.43	24.56-19.22	21.32-15.56	17.90-14.68	17.57-14.43	27.24-12.47	31.34-24.69	31.12-22.56
Average Yield %	3.57	3.49	3.41	3.49	3.23	2.90	1.49	1.58

Address: 231 West Michigan Street, P.O. Box 1331, Milwaukee, WI 53201 Telephone: 414-221-2345 Fax: 414-221-2172	Web Site: www.wisconsinenergy.com Officers: Gale E. Klappa - Chairman, President, Chief Executive Officer Allen L. Leverett - President, Chief Executive Officer, Chief Operating Officer, Chief Financial Officer, Executive Vice President	Auditors: Deloitte & Touche LLP Transfer Agents: Computershare Shareowner Services LLC, Providence, RI

WEINGARTEN REALTY INVESTORS

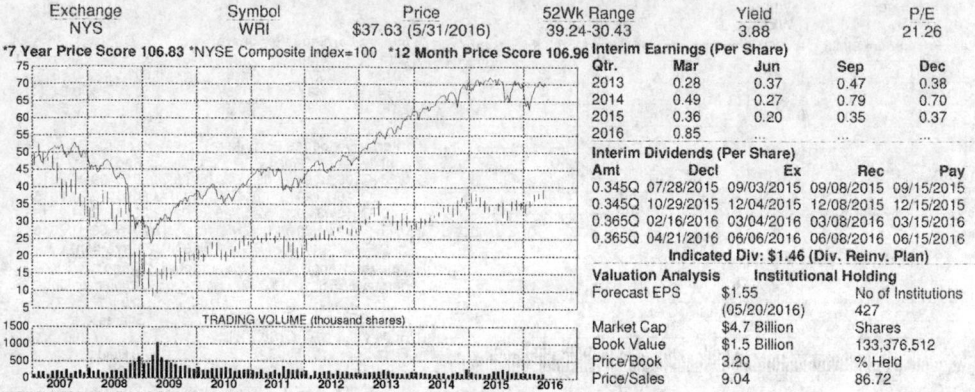

Exchange	Symbol	Price	52Wk Range	Yield	P/E
NYS	WRI	$37.63 (5/31/2016)	39.24-30.43	3.88	21.26

*7 Year Price Score 106.83 *NYSE Composite Index=100 *12 Month Price Score 106.96

Interim Earnings (Per Share)

Qtr.	Mar	Jun	Sep	Dec
2013	0.28	0.37	0.47	0.38
2014	0.49	0.27	0.79	0.70
2015	0.36	0.20	0.35	0.37
2016	0.85			

Interim Dividends (Per Share)

Amt	Decl	Ex	Rec	Pay
0.345Q	07/28/2015	09/03/2015	09/08/2015	09/15/2015
0.345Q	10/29/2015	12/04/2015	12/08/2015	12/15/2015
0.365Q	02/16/2016	03/04/2016	03/08/2016	03/15/2016
0.365Q	04/21/2016	06/06/2016	06/08/2016	06/15/2016

Indicated Div: $1.46 (Div. Reinv. Plan)

Valuation Analysis | **Institutional Holding**

Forecast EPS	$1.55 (05/20/2016)	No of Institutions	427
Market Cap	$4.7 Billion	Shares	133,376,512
Book Value	$1.5 Billion	% Held	86.72
Price/Book	3.20		
Price/Sales	9.04		

TRADING VOLUME (thousand shares)

Business Summary: REITs (MIC: 5.3.1 SIC: 6798 NAIC: 525930)

Weingarten Realty Investors is a real estate investment trust in the business of owning, managing and developing retail shopping centers. Co.'s primary business is leasing space to tenants in the shopping centers it owns or leases. Co. also provides property management services for which it charges fees to either joint ventures where it is partners or other outside owners. At Dec 31 2015, Co. owned or operated under long-term leases, either directly or through its interest in real estate joint ventures or partnerships, a total of 232 properties, which are located in 18 states. At the same time, Co. also owned interests in 30 parcels of land held for development.

Recent Developments: For the quarter ended Mar 31 2016, income from continuing operations increased 137.9% to US$63.5 million from US$26.7 million in the year-earlier quarter. Net income increased 120.8% to US$108.7 million from US$49.2 million in the year-earlier quarter. Revenues were US$132.4 million, up 5.4% from US$125.6 million the year before. Revenues from property income rose 4.8% to US$128.5 million from US$122.7 million in the corresponding quarter a year earlier.

Prospects: Our evaluation of Weingarten Realty Investors as of June 19, 2016 is the result of our systematic analysis on three basic characteristics: earnings strength, relative valuation, and recent stock price movement. The company has managed to produce a neutral trend in earnings per share over the past 5 quarters. Because the company lacks sufficient analyst estimate data, we place greater weight on the historical EPS trend as the measure of earnings strength. Based on operating earnings yield, the company is overvalued when compared to all of the companies in our coverage universe. Share price changes over the past year indicates that WRI will perform well over the near term.

Financial Data

(US$ in Thousands)	3 Mos	12/31/2015	12/31/2014	12/31/2013	12/31/2012	12/31/2011	12/31/2010	12/31/2009
Earnings Per Share	1.77	1.29	2.25	1.50	0.90	(0.17)	0.09	1.23
Cash Flow Per Share	1.92	1.99	1.98	1.93	1.88	1.78	1.79	2.23
Tang Book Value Per Share	11.75	11.21	12.13	11.30	12.98	13.70	14.94	15.83
Dividends Per Share	1.400	1.380	1.550	1.220	1.160	1.100	1.040	1.275
Dividend Payout %	79.10	106.98	68.89	81.33	128.89	...	1,155.56	103.66
Income Statement								
Total Revenue	132,417	512,844	514,406	497,725	503,538	541,561	554,667	572,108
EBITDA	86,695	334,163	338,013	347,217	330,839	300,921	330,572	391,626
Depn & Amortn	699	148,590	154,257	150,147	147,251	162,505	156,124	157,971
Income Before Taxes	65,316	102,353	92,787	107,311	73,824	1,721	35,479	91,875
Income Taxes	5,899	52	(1,261)	7,051	79	395	240	6,338
Net Income	107,074	174,352	288,008	220,262	146,640	15,621	46,206	171,102
Average Shares	126,271	124,329	124,370	122,460	121,705	120,331	120,780	110,178
Balance Sheet								
Current Assets	101,294	106,950	100,970	173,927	99,144	100,172	119,718	249,956
Total Assets	4,033,840	3,901,945	3,814,094	4,223,929	4,184,784	4,588,226	4,807,855	4,890,385
Current Liabilities	88,738	112,205	112,479	108,535	119,699	124,888	126,767	137,727
Long-Term Obligations	2,189,324	2,113,277	1,938,188	2,299,844	2,204,030	2,531,837	2,589,448	2,531,847
Total Liabilities	2,566,252	2,512,483	2,328,908	2,845,754	2,607,654	2,932,846	3,007,866	2,989,095
Stockholders' Equity	1,467,588	1,389,462	1,485,186	1,378,175	1,577,130	1,655,380	1,799,989	1,901,290
Shares Outstanding	124,871	123,951	122,489	121,949	121,505	120,844	120,492	120,098
Statistical Record								
Return on Assets %	5.94	4.52	7.17	5.24	3.33	0.33	0.95	3.42
Return on Equity %	15.64	12.13	20.12	14.91	9.05	0.90	2.50	10.28
EBITDA Margin %	65.47	65.16	65.71	69.76	65.70	55.57	59.60	68.45
Net Margin %	80.86	34.00	55.99	44.25	29.12	2.88	8.33	29.91
Asset Turnover	0.13	0.13	0.13	0.12	0.11	0.12	0.11	0.11
Current Ratio	1.14	0.95	0.90	1.60	0.83	0.80	0.94	1.81
Debt to Equity	1.49	1.52	1.31	1.67	1.40	1.53	1.44	1.33
Price Range	37.84-30.43	38.41-30.43	36.96-27.42	35.84-26.77	28.85-21.56	26.80-19.35	25.92-18.16	22.29-8.41
P/E Ratio	21.38-17.19	29.78-23.59	16.43-12.19	23.89-17.85	32.06-23.96	...288.00-201.78		18.12-6.84
Average Yield %	4.09	3.99	4.80	4.00	4.41	4.63	4.79	7.80

Address: 2600 Citadel Plaza Drive, P.O. Box 924133, Houston, TX 77292-4133 **Telephone:** 713-866-6000	**Web Site:** www.weingarten.com **Officers:** Stanford Alexander - Chairman Andrew M. Alexander - President, Chief Executive Officer	**Auditors:** Doloitte & Touche LLP **Investor Contact:** 713-866-6000 **Transfer Agents:** Computershare Trust Company, National Association, Canton, MA

WELLCARE HEALTH PLANS INC

Exchange	Symbol	Price	52Wk Range	Yield	P/E
NYS	WCG	$101.42 (5/31/2016)	101.42-70.06	N/A	32.61

*7 Year Price Score 130.37 *NYSE Composite Index=100 ***12 Month Price Score 107.99**

TRADING VOLUME (thousand shares)

Interim Earnings (Per Share)

Qtr.	Mar	Jun	Sep	Dec
2013	0.49	1.07	1.45	0.97
2014	1.00	(0.17)	0.44	0.17
2015	0.39	1.17	0.82	0.29
2016	0.83	...	...	...

Interim Dividends (Per Share)

No Dividends Paid

Valuation Analysis | **Institutional Holding**

Forecast EPS	$4.63	No of Institutions
	(05/17/2016)	358
Market Cap	$4.5 Billion	Shares
Book Value	$1.8 Billion	52,961,332
Price/Book	2.54	% Held
Price/Sales	0.32	98.63

Business Summary: Hospitals & Health Care Facilities (MIC: 4.2 1 SIC: 6324 NAIC: 524114)

WellCare Health Plans is a managed care company with a focus on government-sponsored managed care services. Co. manages its business in three reportable segments: Medicaid Health Plans, which includes plans for beneficiaries of Temporary Assistance for Needy Families, and other state-based programs that are not part of the Medicaid program; Medicare Health Plans, which provides eligible persons age 65 and over and some disabled persons with a variety of hospital, medical and prescription drug benefits; and Medicare Prescription Drug Plans (PDPs), which provides stand-alone Medicare Part D coverage to Medicare-eligible beneficiaries in its Medicare PDPs segment.

Recent Developments: For the quarter ended Mar 31 2016, net income increased 112.0% to US$37.1 million from US$17.5 million in the year-earlier quarter. Revenues were US$3.54 billion, up 2.0% from US$3.47 billion the year before. Net premiums earned were US$3.54 billion versus US$3.47 billion in the prior-year quarter, an increase of 2.0%.

Prospects: Our evaluation of WellCare Health Plans Inc. as of June 19, 2016 is the result of our systematic analysis on three basic characteristics: earnings strength, relative valuation, and recent stock price movement. The company has managed to produce a neutral trend in earnings per share over the past 5 quarters and while recent estimates for the company have been mixed, WCG has posted better than expected results. Based on operating earnings yield, the company is about fairly valued when compared to all of the companies in our coverage universe. Share price changes over the past year indicates that WCG will perform poorly over the near term.

Financial Data
(US$ in Thousands)

	3 Mos	12/31/2015	12/31/2014	12/31/2013	12/31/2012	12/31/2011	12/31/2010	12/31/2009
Earnings Per Share	3.11	2.67	1.44	3.98	4.22	6.10	(1.26)	0.95
Cash Flow Per Share	15.86	16.17	6.82	4.11	(0.71)	3.78	5.27	1.38
Tang Book Value Per Share	32.23	31.40	28.05	27.75	24.21	23.24	16.68	17.87
Income Statement								
Total Revenue	3,540,500	13,890,200	12,959,900	9,527,900	7,409,032	6,106,868	5,440,225	6,878,164
EBITDA	125,500	452,300	264,000	326,900	329,804	449,906	(50,207)	121,235
Depn & Amortn	20,800	62,000	46,800	36,700	29,243	24,922	22,413	21,804
Income Before Taxes	88,900	336,100	177,800	278,300	296,439	418,474	(72,849)	93,020
Income Taxes	51,800	217,500	114,100	103,000	111,711	154,228	(19,449)	53,149
Net Income	37,100	118,600	63,700	175,300	184,728	264,246	(53,400)	39,871
Average Shares	44,493	44,391	44,163	44,000	43,826	43,328	42,365	42,150
Balance Sheet								
Current Assets	4,410,500	4,268,500	3,526,300	2,692,700	2,100,710	2,119,894	1,815,171	1,717,465
Total Assets	5,319,800	5,193,600	4,495,000	3,450,700	2,675,516	2,488,111	2,247,293	2,118,447
Current Liabilities	2,361,900	2,441,600	1,935,700	1,237,100	1,113,426	1,123,140	1,185,701	1,180,070
Long-Term Obligations	1,097,100	912,100	900,000	600,000	120,000	135,000	...	...
Total Liabilities	3,552,700	3,465,300	2,899,100	1,932,800	1,352,352	1,371,265	1,415,247	1,237,547
Stockholders' Equity	1,767,100	1,728,300	1,595,900	1,517,900	1,323,164	1,116,846	832,046	880,900
Shares Outstanding	44,251	44,113	43,914	43,766	43,212	42,848	42,541	42,361
Statistical Record								
Return on Assets %	2.77	2.45	1.60	5.72	7.14	11.16	N.M.	1.85
Return on Equity %	8.17	7.14	4.09	12.34	15.10	27.12	N.M.	4.73
EBITDA Margin %	3.54	3.26	2.04	3.43	4.45	7.37	N.M.	1.76
Net Margin %	1.05	0.85	0.49	1.84	2.49	4.33	N.M.	0.58
Asset Turnover	2.79	2.87	3.26	3.11	2.86	2.58	2.49	3.18
Current Ratio	1.87	1.75	1.82	2.18	1.89	1.89	1.53	1.46
Debt to Equity	0.62	0.53	0.56	0.40	0.09	0.12	...	...
Price Range	98.51-70.06	98.51-72.85	84.25-56.64	74.76-45.78	74.24-45.90	58.45-29.90	37.18-22.92	38.63-6.23
P/E Ratio	31.68-22.53	36.90-27.28	58.51-39.33	18.78-11.50	17.59-10.88	9.58-4.90	...	40.66-6.56

Address: 8725 Henderson Road, Renaissance One, Tampa, FL 33634	**Web Site:** www.wellcare.com	**Auditors:** Deloitte & Touche, LLP
Telephone: 813-290-6200	**Officers:** Christian P. Michalik - Chairman Kenneth A. Burdick - President, Chief Executive Officer, Chief Operating Officer, Division Officer	**Investor Contact:** 813-206-3916
		Transfer Agents: Computershare Trust Company, N.A., Providence, RI

WELLS FARGO & CO.

Exchange	Symbol	Price	52Wk Range	Yield	P/E
NYS	WFC	$50.72 (5/31/2016)	58.52-45.16	3.00	12.46

*7 Year Price Score 115.93 *NYSE Composite Index=100 *12 Month Price Score 92.58

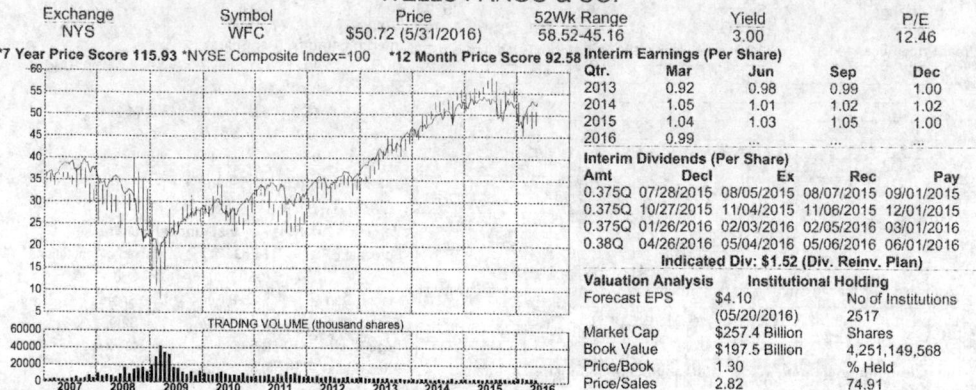

Interim Earnings (Per Share)

Qtr.	Mar	Jun	Sep	Dec
2013	0.92	0.98	0.99	1.00
2014	1.05	1.01	1.02	1.02
2015	1.04	1.03	1.05	1.00
2016	0.99	...	...	...

Interim Dividends (Per Share)

Amt	Decl	Ex	Rec	Pay
0.375Q	07/28/2015	08/05/2015	08/07/2015	09/01/2015
0.375Q	10/27/2015	11/04/2015	11/06/2015	12/01/2015
0.375Q	01/26/2016	02/03/2016	02/05/2016	03/01/2016
0.38Q	04/26/2016	05/04/2016	05/06/2016	06/01/2016

Indicated Div: $1.52 (Div. Reinv. Plan)

Valuation Analysis / Institutional Holding

Forecast EPS	$4.10 (05/20/2016)	No of Institutions	2517
Market Cap	$257.4 Billion	Shares	4,251,149,568
Book Value	$197.5 Billion	% Held	74.91
Price/Book	1.30		
Price/Sales	2.82		

Business Summary: Banking (MIC: 5.1.1 SIC: 6021 NAIC: 522110)

Wells Fargo is a financial holding company and a bank holding company.Co. has three operating segments: Community Banking; Wholesale Banking; and Wealth, Brokerage and Retirement. The Community Banking segment provides a line of financial products and services to consumers and businesses. The Wholesale Banking segment provides financial solutions to businesses across the U.S. and to financial institutions globally. The Wealth, Brokerage and Retirement segment provides a range of personalized wealth management, investment and retirement products and services to clients across U.S. based businesses. At Dec 31 2015, Co. had total assets of $1.79 trillion and total deposits of $1.22 trillion.

Recent Developments: For the quarter ended Mar 31 2016, net income decreased 6.3% to US$5.51 billion from US$5.88 billion in the year-earlier quarter. Net interest income increased 6.2% to US$11.67 billion from US$10.99 billion in the year-earlier quarter. Provision for loan losses was US$1.09 billion versus US$608.0 million in the prior-year quarter, an increase of 78.6%. Non-interest income rose 2.3% to US$10.53 billion from US$10.29 billion, while non-interest expense advanced 4.2% to US$13.03 billion.

Prospects: Our evaluation of Wells Fargo & Co. as of June 19, 2016 is the result of our systematic analysis on three basic characteristics: earnings strength, relative valuation, and recent stock price movement. The company has managed to produce a neutral trend in earnings per share over the past 5 quarters. However, while recent estimates for the company have been lowered by analysts, WFC has posted better than expected results. Based on operating earnings yield, the company is undervalued when compared to all of the companies in our coverage universe. Share price changes over the past year indicates that WFC will perform well over the near term.

Financial Data
(US$ in Thousands)

	3 Mos	12/31/2015	12/31/2014	12/31/2013	12/31/2012	12/31/2011	12/31/2010	12/31/2009
Earnings Per Share	4.07	4.12	4.10	3.89	3.36	2.82	2.21	1.75
Cash Flow Per Share	3.46	2.88	3.35	10.90	11.04	2.59	3.59	6.30
Tang Book Value Per Share	25.60	25.21	23.42	20.10	18.81	15.34	12.60	9.35
Dividends Per Share	1.500	1.475	1.350	1.150	0.880	0.480	0.200	0.490
Dividend Payout %	36.86	35.80	32.93	29.56	26.19	17.02	9.05	28.00
Income Statement								
Interest Income	12,972,000	49,277,000	47,552,000	47,089,000	48,391,000	49,412,000	52,796,000	56,274,000
Interest Expense	1,305,000	3,976,000	4,025,000	4,289,000	5,161,000	6,649,000	8,039,000	9,950,000
Net Interest Income	11,667,000	45,301,000	43,527,000	42,800,000	43,230,000	42,763,000	44,757,000	46,324,000
Provision for Losses	1,086,000	2,442,000	1,395,000	2,309,000	7,217,000	7,899,000	15,753,000	21,668,000
Non-Interest Income	10,528,000	40,756,000	40,820,000	40,980,000	42,856,000	38,185,000	40,453,000	42,362,000
Non-Interest Expense	13,028,000	49,974,000	49,037,000	48,842,000	50,398,000	49,393,000	50,456,000	49,020,000
Income Before Taxes	8,081,000	33,641,000	33,915,000	32,629,000	28,471,000	23,656,000	19,001,000	17,998,000
Income Taxes	2,567,000	10,365,000	10,307,000	10,405,000	9,103,000	7,445,000	6,338,000	5,331,000
Net Income	5,462,000	22,894,000	23,057,000	21,878,000	18,897,000	15,869,000	12,362,000	12,275,000
Average Shares	5,139,399	5,209,799	5,324,399	5,371,199	5,351,499	5,323,399	5,263,099	4,562,699
Balance Sheet								
Net Loans & Leases	935,917,000	905,293,000	850,954,000	811,430,000	782,624,000	751,597,000	735,535,000	763,987,000
Total Assets	1,849,182,000	1,787,632,000	1,687,155,000	1,527,015,000	1,422,968,000	1,313,867,000	1,258,128,000	1,243,646,000
Total Deposits	1,241,490,000	1,223,312,000	1,168,310,000	1,079,177,000	1,002,835,000	920,070,000	847,942,000	824,018,000
Total Liabilities	1,651,686,000	1,594,634,000	1,502,761,000	1,356,873,000	1,265,414,000	1,173,626,000	1,131,720,000	1,131,860,000
Stockholders' Equity	197,496,000	192,998,000	184,394,000	170,142,000	157,554,000	140,241,000	126,408,000	111,786,000
Shares Outstanding	5,075,902	5,092,128	5,170,348	5,257,162	5,266,313	5,262,611	5,262,282	5,178,624
Statistical Record								
Return on Assets %	1.26	1.32	1.43	1.48	1.38	1.23	0.99	0.96
Return on Equity %	11.68	12.13	13.01	13.35	12.66	11.90	10.38	11.64
Net Interest Margin %	89.94	91.93	91.54	90.89	89.33	86.54	84.77	82.32
Efficiency Ratio %	55.44	55.51	55.49	55.46	55.23	56.39	54.11	49.70
Loans to Deposits	0.75	0.74	0.73	0.75	0.78	0.82	0.87	0.93
Price Range	58.52-45.16	58.52-50.02	55.71-44.23	45.54-34.18	36.13-28.43	34.10-22.88	33.88-23.25	31.38-8.12
P/E Ratio	14.38-11.10	14.20-12.14	13.59-10.79	11.71-8.79	10.75-8.46	12.09-8.11	15.33-10.52	17.93-4.64
Average Yield %	2.80	2.69	2.68	2.86	2.68	1.71	0.71	2.09

Address: 420 Montgomery Street, San Francisco, CA 94163 Telephone: 866-878-5865	Web Site: www.wellsfargo.com Officers: John G. Stumpf - Chairman, President, Chief Executive Officer John R. Shrewsberry - Senior Executive Vice President, Chief Financial Officer	Auditors: KPMG LLP Investor Contact: 415-371-2921 Transfer Agents: Wells Fargo Shareowners Services, St. Paul, MN

WELLTOWER INC

Exchange	Symbol	Price	52Wk Range	Yield	P/E	Div Achiever
NYS	HCN	$68.91 (5/31/2016)	74.70-53.68	4.99	31.32	12 Years

*7 Year Price Score 98.09   ***NYSE Composite Index=100**   ***12 Month Price Score 104.75**

Interim Earnings (Per Share)

Qtr.	Mar	Jun	Sep	Dec
2013	0.21	(0.03)	0.07	0.04
2014	0.17	0.24	0.44	0.59
2015	0.56	0.89	0.52	0.37
2016	0.42	...	...	...

Interim Dividends (Per Share)

Amt	Decl	Ex	Rec	Pay
0.825Q	07/30/2015	08/07/2015	08/11/2015	08/20/2015
0.825Q	10/29/2015	11/06/2015	11/10/2015	11/20/2015
0.86Q	01/28/2016	02/05/2016	02/09/2016	02/22/2016
0.86Q	04/28/2016	05/06/2016	05/10/2016	05/20/2016

Indicated Div: $3.44 (Div. Reinv. Plan)

Valuation Analysis	Institutional Holding
Forecast EPS	$1.96	No of Institutions
(05/20/2016)	842
Market Cap	$24.6 Billion	Shares
Book Value	$14.5 Billion	364,039,808
Price/Book	1.69	% Held
Price/Sales	6.13	101.75

TRADING VOLUME (thousand shares)

Business Summary: REITs (MIC: 5.3.1 SIC: 6798 NAIC: 525930)

Welltower is a real estate investment trust that invests in seniors housing and health care real estate. Co.'s segments include: triple-net, which include independent living facilities and independent supportive living facilities (Canada), continuing care retirement communities, assisted living facilities, care homes with and without nursing (U.K), Alzheimer's/dementia care facilities, long-term/post-acute care facilities and hospitals; seniors housing operating, which include independent living and supportive living facilities, assisted living facilities, care homes and Alzheimer's/dementia care facilities; and outpatient medical, which include outpatient medical buildings.

Recent Developments: For the quarter ended Mar 31 2016, income from continuing operations increased 8.5% to US$165.5 million from US$152.6 million in the year-earlier quarter. Net income decreased 21.0% to US$165.5 million from US$209.4 million in the year-earlier quarter. Revenues were US$1.05 billion, up 17.1% from US$894.2 million the year before. Revenues from property income rose 9.5% to US$415.7 million from US$379.6 million in the corresponding quarter a year earlier.

Prospects: Our evaluation of Welltower Inc. as of June 19, 2016 is the result of our systematic analysis on three basic characteristics: earnings strength, relative valuation, and recent stock price movement. The company has generated a negative trend in earnings per share over the past 5 quarters. Because the company lacks sufficient analyst estimate data, we place greater weight on the historical EPS trend as the measure of earnings strength. Based on operating earnings yield, the company is overvalued when compared to all of the companies in our coverage universe. Share price changes over the past year indicates that HCN will perform in line with the market over the near term.

Financial Data

(US$ in Thousands)	3 Mos	12/31/2015	12/31/2014	12/31/2013	12/31/2012	12/31/2011	12/31/2010	12/31/2009
Earnings Per Share	2.20	2.34	1.45	0.28	0.98	0.90	0.83	1.49
Cash Flow Per Share	4.28	3.94	3.72	3.57	3.64	3.39	2.86	3.34
Tang Book Value Per Share	37.69	38.10	36.80	35.67	35.35	31.44	28.96	28.43
Dividends Per Share	3.335	3.300	3.180	3.060	2.960	2.835	2.740	2.720
Dividend Payout %	151.59	141.03	219.31	1,092.86	302.04	315.00	330.12	182.55
Income Statement								
Total Revenue	1,047,050	3,859,826	3,343,546	2,880,608	1,822,099	1,421,162	680,530	568,973
EBITDA	168,917	1,471,366	1,236,053	984,762	734,588	594,378	294,899	340,360
Depn & Amortn	1,348	835,249	851,840	882,517	548,935	437,949	216,856	178,622
Income Before Taxes	167,569	636,117	384,213	102,245	185,653	156,429	78,043	161,738
Income Taxes	(1,725)	6,451	(1,267)	7,491	7,612	1,388	364	168
Net Income	165,474	888,549	512,300	138,280	294,840	212,716	128,884	192,927
Average Shares	356,051	349,424	307,747	278,761	225,953	174,401	128,208	114,612
Balance Sheet								
Current Assets	418,125	818,252	553,423	231,601	1,141,421	233,102	210,639	58,713
Total Assets	29,088,293	29,023,845	25,014,296	23,083,957	19,549,109	14,924,606	9,451,734	6,367,186
Long-Term Obligations	13,063,198	12,967,686	10,828,013	10,652,014	8,531,899	7,240,752	4,469,736	2,414,022
Total Liabilities	14,568,699	14,433,285	11,839,143	11,669,374	9,254,308	7,799,842	4,848,883	2,570,147
Stockholders' Equity	14,519,594	14,590,560	13,175,153	11,414,583	10,294,801	7,124,764	4,602,851	3,797,039
Shares Outstanding	356,772	354,777	328,790	289,563	260,373	192,275	147,097	123,385
Statistical Record								
Return on Assets %	3.03	3.29	2.13	0.65	1.71	1.75	1.63	3.07
Return on Equity %	5.81	6.40	4.17	1.27	3.38	3.63	3.07	5.51
EBITDA Margin %	16.13	38.12	36.97	34.19	40.32	41.82	43.33	59.82
Net Margin %	15.80	23.02	15.32	4.80	16.18	14.97	18.94	33.91
Asset Turnover	0.14	0.14	0.14	0.14	0.11	0.12	0.09	0.09
Debt to Equity	0.90	0.89	0.82	0.93	0.83	1.02	0.97	0.64
Price Range	79.44-53.68	84.31-58.21	77.98-53.05	78.98-52.58	62.24-52.40	54.98-41.11	51.71-40.00	46.19-27.27
P/E Ratio	36.11-24.40	36.03-24.88	53.78-36.59	282.07-187.79	63.51-53.47	61.09-45.68	62.30-48.19	31.00-18.30
Average Yield %	4.97	4.68	4.97	4.75	5.16	5.62	6.08	7.12

Address: 4500 Dorr Street, Toledo, OH 43615	Web Site: www.welltower.com/#investors/governance	Auditors: Ernst & Young LLP
Telephone: 419-247-2800	Officers: Thomas J. DeRosa - Chief Executive Officer Scott M. Brinker - Executive Vice President, Chief Investment Officer, Executive Vice President (firm), Senior Vice President, Vice President	Transfer Agents: Computershare, Providence, RI

WESCO INTERNATIONAL, INC.

Exchange	Symbol	Price	52Wk Range	Yield	P/E
NYS	WCC	$58.33 (5/31/2016)	74.19-36.05	N/A	14.33

*7 Year Price Score 76.93 *NYSE Composite Index=100 *12 Month Price Score 106.43

TRADING VOLUME (thousand shares)

Interim Earnings (Per Share)

Qtr.	Mar	Jun	Sep	Dec
2013	1.60	1.25	1.32	1.08
2014	0.97	1.29	1.52	1.40
2015	0.90	1.00	1.28	1.02
2016	0.77			

Interim Dividends (Per Share)

No Dividends Paid

Valuation Analysis   **Institutional Holding**

Forecast EPS	$4.00	No of Institutions
	(05/16/2016)	320
Market Cap	$2.5 Billion	Shares
Book Value	$1.9 Billion	57,468,712
Price/Book	1.30	% Held
Price/Sales	0.33	103.48

Business Summary: Electrical Equipment (MIC: 7.3.1 SIC: 5063 NAIC: 444190)

WESCO International is a provider of electrical, industrial, and communications maintenance, repair and operating and original equipment manufacturers products, construction materials, and supply chain management and logistics services. Co.'s main product categories include general electrical and industrial supplies, wire, cable and conduit, data and broadband communications, power distribution equipment, lighting and lighting control systems, control and automation. Co. also provides a portfolio of services, including supply chain management, logistics and transportation, procurement, warehousing and inventory management, as well as kitting, assembly of products and system installation.

Recent Developments: For the quarter ended Mar 31 2016, net income decreased 26.2% to US$34.5 million from US$46.8 million in the year-earlier quarter. Revenues were US$1.78 billion, down 2.2% from US$1.82 billion the year before. Operating income was US$69.5 million versus US$87.2 million in the prior-year quarter, a decrease of 20.3%. Direct operating expenses declined 1.9% to US$1.42 billion from US$1.45 billion in the comparable period the year before. Indirect operating expenses increased 1.8% to US$285.7 million from US$280.5 million in the equivalent prior-year period.

Prospects: Our evaluation of Wesco International Inc. as of June 19, 2016 is the result of our systematic analysis on three basic characteristics: earnings strength, relative valuation, and recent stock price movement. The company has enjoyed a very positive trend in earnings per share over the past 5 quarters. However, while recent estimates for the company have been mixed, WCC has posted better than expected results. Based on operating earnings yield, the company is undervalued when compared to all of the companies in our coverage universe. Share price changes over the past year indicates that WCC will perform poorly over the near term.

Financial Data

(US$ in Thousands)	3 Mos	12/31/2015	12/31/2014	12/31/2013	12/31/2012	12/31/2011	12/31/2010	12/31/2009
Earnings Per Share	4.07	4.18	5.18	5.25	3.95	3.96	2.50	2.46
Cash Flow Per Share	6.43	6.52	5.65	7.14	6.58	3.88	2.99	6.90
Tang Book Value Per Share	N.M.	N.M.	N.M.	N.M.	N.M.	4.17	0.06	1.22
Income Statement								
Total Revenue	1,775,961	7,518,487	7,889,626	7,513,342	6,579,301	6,125,718	5,063,862	4,623,954
EBITDA	85,882	391,542	484,717	483,658	343,801	345,479	226,904	204,605
Depn & Amortn	16,374	17,800	18,500	18,200	14,400	12,500	11,700	13,700
Income Before Taxes	50,679	303,910	384,153	379,851	281,639	279,376	157,641	137,151
Income Taxes	16,145	95,537	108,716	103,333	79,880	83,136	42,164	32,063
Net Income	36,053	210,687	275,906	276,430	201,777	196,251	115,477	105,088
Average Shares	46,813	50,373	53,258	52,650	51,133	49,623	46,112	42,671
Balance Sheet								
Current Assets	2,274,442	2,257,534	2,350,338	2,198,541	2,101,837	1,737,420	1,513,686	1,331,004
Total Assets	4,690,828	4,587,425	4,754,437	4,617,108	4,629,629	3,078,452	2,826,774	2,494,193
Current Liabilities	983,302	947,801	1,063,872	1,044,589	1,007,995	845,846	708,233	680,834
Long-Term Obligations	1,391,227	1,456,761	1,366,430	1,447,634	1,695,413	642,922	725,893	597,869
Total Liabilities	2,793,024	2,810,753	2,825,785	2,852,299	3,075,832	1,732,454	1,678,180	1,497,904
Stockholders' Equity	1,897,804	1,776,672	1,928,652	1,764,809	1,553,797	1,345,998	1,148,594	996,289
Shares Outstanding	42,233	42,173	44,489	44,267	44,061	43,424	43,009	42,416
Statistical Record								
Return on Assets %	4.29	4.51	5.89	5.98	5.22	6.65	4.34	4.03
Return on Equity %	10.69	11.37	14.94	16.66	13.88	15.73	10.77	12.16
EBITDA Margin %	4.84	5.21	6.14	6.44	5.23	5.64	4.48	4.42
Net Margin %	2.03	2.80	3.50	3.68	3.07	3.20	2.28	2.27
Asset Turnover	1.61	1.61	1.68	1.63	1.70	2.07	1.90	1.77
Current Ratio	2.31	2.38	2.21	2.10	2.09	2.05	2.14	1.95
Debt to Equity	0.73	0.82	0.71	0.82	1.09	0.48	0.63	0.60
Price Range	74.19-36.05	76.21-40.04	93.81-71.18	91.12-65.46	67.60-52.31	63.79-32.09	53.21-27.01	30.14-13.42
P/E Ratio	18.23-8.86	18.23-9.58	18.11-13.74	17.36-12.47	17.11-13.24	16.11-8.10	21.28-10.80	12.25-5.46

<table>
<tr><td>Address: 225 West Station Square Drive, Suite 700, Pittsburgh, PA 15219
Telephone: 412-454-2200</td><td>Web Site: www.wesco.com
Officers: John J. Engel - Chairman, President, Chief Executive Officer Timothy A. Hibbard - Interim Chief Financial Officer, Corporate Controller</td><td>Auditors: PricewaterhouseCoopers LLP
Transfer Agents: Computershare, Providence, RI</td></tr>
</table>

WEST PHARMACEUTICAL SERVICES, INC.

Exchange	Symbol	Price	52Wk Range	Yield	P/E	Div Achiever
NYS	WST	$75.08 (5/31/2016)	75.08-53.70	0.64	65.29	23 Years

*7 Year Price Score 152.11 *NYSE Composite Index=100 *12 Month Price Score 115.12

Interim Earnings (Per Share)

Qtr.	Mar	Jun	Sep	Dec
2013	0.45	0.43	0.37	0.32
2014	0.38	0.52	0.43	0.43
2015	0.45	0.38	0.02	0.45
2016	0.30	...	...	...

Interim Dividends (Per Share)

Amt	Decl	Ex	Rec	Pay
0.11Q	07/01/2015	07/20/2015	07/22/2015	08/05/2015
0.12Q	07/14/2015	10/19/2015	10/21/2015	11/04/2015
0.12Q	12/17/2015	01/15/2016	01/20/2016	02/03/2016
0.12Q	03/04/2016	04/18/2016	04/20/2016	05/04/2016

Indicated Div: $0.48 (Div. Reinv. Plan)

Valuation Analysis

		Institutional Holding	
Forecast EPS	$2.19	No of Institutions	
	(04/18/2016)	335	
Market Cap	$5.5 Billion	Shares	
Book Value	$1.1 Billion	75,889,840	
Price/Book	5.11	% Held	
Price/Sales	3.85	93.22	

Business Summary: Rubber Products (MIC: 8.4.1 SIC: 3069 NAIC: 326299)

West Pharmaceutical Services is a manufacturer of components and systems for the packaging and delivery of injectable drugs as well as delivery system components. Co. has two segments: Pharmaceutical Packaging Systems, which develops, manufactures and sells primary packaging components and systems for injectable drug delivery, including stoppers and seals for vials, closures and other components used in syringe, intravenous and blood collection systems, and prefillable syringe components; and Pharmaceutical Delivery Systems, which develops, manufactures and sells safety and administration systems, multi-component systems for drug administration, and contract-manufacturing solutions.

Recent Developments: For the quarter ended Mar 31 2016, net income decreased 32.8% to US$22.1 million from US$32.9 million in the year-earlier quarter. Revenues were US$362.1 million, up 7.8% from US$335.9 million the year before. Operating income was US$30.0 million versus US$47.8 million in the prior-year quarter, a decrease of 37.2%. Direct operating expenses rose 5.6% to US$238.8 million from US$226.2 million in the comparable period the year before. Indirect operating expenses increased 50.7% to US$93.3 million from US$61.9 million in the equivalent prior-year period.

Prospects: Our evaluation of West Pharmaceutical Services Inc. as of June 19, 2016 is the result of our systematic analysis on three basic characteristics: earnings strength, relative valuation, and recent stock price movement. The company has enjoyed a very positive trend in earnings per share over the past 5 quarters and while recent estimates for the company have remained steady, WST has posted better than expected results. Based on operating earnings yield, the company is overvalued when compared to all of the companies in our coverage universe. Share price changes over the past year indicates that WST will perform well over the near term.

Financial Data

(US$ in Thousands)	3 Mos	12/31/2015	12/31/2014	12/31/2013	12/31/2012	12/31/2011	12/31/2010	12/31/2009
Earnings Per Share	1.15	1.30	1.75	1.57	1.15	1.08	0.94	1.06
Cash Flow Per Share	3.00	2.95	2.58	3.17	2.75	1.94	2.08	2.10
Tang Book Value Per Share	12.90	12.20	11.31	10.60	8.25	7.29	6.88	6.20
Dividends Per Share	0.460	0.450	0.410	0.385	0.365	0.345	0.325	0.305
Dividend Payout %	40.00	34.62	23.43	24.52	31.74	31.94	34.39	28.77
Income Statement								
Total Revenue	362,100	1,399,800	1,421,400	1,368,400	1,266,400	1,192,300	1,104,700	1,055,700
EBITDA	52,300	214,700	266,800	243,200	196,300	180,700	159,500	161,400
Depn & Amortn	22,300	86,100	84,800	81,000	72,800	71,100	68,800	63,900
Income Before Taxes	27,800	116,100	169,000	147,100	108,600	92,700	74,500	83,100
Income Taxes	6,900	26,300	47,200	40,200	32,700	23,500	13,600	13,500
Net Income	22,100	95,600	127,100	112,300	80,700	75,500	65,300	72,600
Average Shares	74,100	73,800	72,800	71,400	71,800	74,000	73,400	72,600
Balance Sheet								
Current Assets	630,700	673,700	659,300	650,700	557,300	472,000	436,600	397,200
Total Assets	1,668,200	1,695,100	1,670,900	1,671,600	1,564,000	1,399,100	1,294,300	1,271,000
Current Liabilities	241,100	314,300	252,500	236,900	261,800	243,200	169,700	171,100
Long-Term Obligations	229,500	228,900	309,500	371,300	378,800	299,300	358,100	379,100
Total Liabilities	594,200	671,200	714,000	765,200	835,100	744,200	668,600	691,900
Stockholders' Equity	1,074,000	1,023,900	956,900	906,400	728,900	654,900	625,700	579,100
Shares Outstanding	73,077	72,300	71,300	70,200	68,600	67,400	66,600	66,000
Statistical Record								
Return on Assets %	5.20	5.68	7.61	6.94	5.43	5.61	5.09	5.95
Return on Equity %	8.42	9.65	13.64	13.73	11.63	11.79	10.84	13.62
EBITDA Margin %	14.44	15.34	18.77	17.77	15.50	15.16	14.44	15.29
Net Margin %	6.10	6.83	8.94	8.21	6.37	6.33	5.91	6.88
Asset Turnover	0.87	0.83	0.85	0.85	0.85	0.89	0.86	0.87
Current Ratio	2.62	2.14	2.61	2.75	2.13	1.94	2.57	2.32
Debt to Equity	0.21	0.22	0.32	0.41	0.52	0.46	0.57	0.65
Price Range	69.32-53.09	64.13-49.19	55.08-39.26	50.08-27.38	27.86-18.90	23.72-17.82	22.29-16.52	20.76-14.06
P/E Ratio	60.28-46.17	49.33-37.84	31.47-22.43	31.90-17.44	24.23-16.43	21.96-16.50	23.71-17.57	19.58-13.26
Average Yield %	0.78	0.79	0.90	1.04	1.54	1.67	1.71	1.69

Address: 530 Herman O. West Drive, Exton, PA 19341 0645 Telephone: 610-594-2900	Web Site: www.westpharma.com Officers: Eric M. Green - President, Chief Executive Officer William J. Federici - Vice President, Chief Financial Officer	Auditors: PricewaterhouseCoopers LLP Investor Contact: 610-594-3345 Transfer Agents: Broadridge Corporate Issuer Solutions, Philadelphia, PA

WESTAR ENERGY INC

Exchange	Symbol	Price	52Wk Range	Yield	P/E	Div Achiever
NYS	WR	$56.33 (5/31/2016)	56.33-34.11	2.70	26.08	12 Years

*7 Year Price Score 116.35 *NYSE Composite Index=100 *12 Month Price Score 122.16

Interim Earnings (Per Share)

Qtr.	Mar	Jun	Sep	Dec
2013	0.40	0.52	1.04	0.31
2014	0.52	0.40	1.10	0.31
2015	0.38	0.46	0.97	0.27
2016	0.46	...	...	...

Interim Dividends (Per Share)

Amt	Decl	Ex	Rec	Pay
0.36Q	08/26/2015	09/04/2015	09/09/2015	10/01/2015
0.36Q	11/25/2015	12/07/2015	12/09/2015	01/04/2016
0.38Q	02/24/2016	03/07/2016	03/09/2016	04/01/2016
0.38Q	05/18/2016	06/07/2016	06/09/2016	07/01/2016

Indicated Div: $1.52 (Div. Reinv. Plan)

Valuation Analysis — **Institutional Holding**

Forecast EPS	$2.44 (05/20/2016)	No of Institutions 495
Market Cap	$8.0 Billion	Shares 118,988,408
Book Value	$3.7 Billion	
Price/Book	2.17	% Held
Price/Sales	3.27	74.86

Business Summary: Electric Utilities (MIC: 3.1.1 SIC: 4931 NAIC: 221210)

Westar Energy is an electric utility. As of Dec 31 2015, Co. provided electric generation, transmission and distribution services to approximately 700,000 customers in Kansas. Co. provides these services in central and northeastern Kansas, including the cities of Topeka, Lawrence, Manhattan, Salina and Hutchinson. Kansas Gas and Electric Company, Co.'s wholly owned subsidiary, provides these services in south-central and southeastern Kansas, including the city of Wichita. Co. also supplies electric energy at wholesale to municipalities and electric cooperatives in Kansas, and has contracts for the sale or purchase of wholesale electricity with other utilities.

Recent Developments: For the quarter ended Mar 31 2016, net income increased 29.2% to US$68.7 million from US$53.2 million in the year-earlier quarter. Revenues were US$569.5 million, down 3.6% from US$590.8 million the year before. Operating income was US$141.8 million versus US$125.6 million in the prior-year quarter, an increase of 12.9%. Direct operating expenses declined 19.8% to US$238.6 million from US$297.4 million in the comparable period the year before. Indirect operating expenses increased 12.6% to US$189.1 million from US$167.9 million in the equivalent prior-year period.

Prospects: Our evaluation of Westar Energy Inc. as of June 19, 2016 is the result of our systematic analysis on three basic characteristics: earnings strength, relative valuation, and recent stock price movement. The company has enjoyed a very positive trend in earnings per share over the past 5 quarters. However, while recent estimates for the company have been mixed, WR has posted better than expected results. Based on operating earnings yield, the company is about fairly valued when compared to all of the companies in our coverage universe. Share price changes over the past year indicates that WR will perform very well over the near term.

Financial Data
(US$ in Thousands)

	3 Mos	12/31/2015	12/31/2014	12/31/2013	12/31/2012	12/31/2011	12/31/2010	12/31/2009
Earnings Per Share	2.16	2.09	2.35	2.27	2.15	1.93	1.80	1.58
Cash Flow Per Share	5.22	5.18	6.34	5.51	4.72	3.96	5.44	4.37
Tang Book Value Per Share	25.92	25.87	25.02	23.88	22.89	22.03	21.28	20.62
Dividends Per Share	1.460	1.440	1.400	1.360	1.320	1.280	1.240	1.200
Dividend Payout %	67.59	68.90	59.57	59.91	61.40	66.32	68.89	75.95
Income Statement								
Total Revenue	569,450	2,459,164	2,601,703	2,370,654	2,261,470	2,170,991	2,056,171	1,858,231
EBITDA	159,977	918,498	920,513	856,651	832,735	774,584	717,797	586,140
Depn & Amortn	12,216	287,900	263,800	249,900	247,800	262,600	249,200	228,600
Income Before Taxes	107,330	453,796	473,595	424,584	408,598	339,524	293,656	200,180
Income Taxes	38,622	152,000	151,270	123,721	126,136	103,344	85,032	58,850
Net Income	65,585	291,929	313,259	292,520	275,146	230,239	203,896	175,075
Average Shares	142,311	139,278	132,824	128,298	126,898	118,290	112,014	109,648
Balance Sheet								
Current Assets	675,579	717,141	700,922	706,798	643,075	633,585	601,609	629,482
Total Assets	10,805,597	10,705,666	10,347,001	9,597,111	9,265,231	8,682,851	8,079,638	7,525,483
Current Liabilities	1,073,933	836,935	849,631	955,399	846,141	827,287	782,846	682,478
Long-Term Obligations	3,150,478	3,302,047	3,382,104	3,163,760	3,042,014	2,740,392	2,776,547	2,600,034
Total Liabilities	7,134,207	7,048,945	7,052,145	6,534,337	6,369,091	5,892,204	5,671,870	5,255,255
Stockholders' Equity	3,671,390	3,656,721	3,294,856	3,062,774	2,896,140	2,790,647	2,407,768	2,270,228
Shares Outstanding	141,628	141,353	131,687	128,254	126,503	125,698	112,128	109,072
Statistical Record								
Return on Assets %	2.89	2.77	3.14	3.10	3.06	2.75	2.61	2.34
Return on Equity %	8.78	8.40	9.85	9.82	9.65	8.86	8.72	7.81
EBITDA Margin %	28.09	37.35	35.38	36.14	36.82	35.68	34.91	31.54
Net Margin %	11.52	11.87	12.04	12.34	12.17	10.61	9.92	9.42
Asset Turnover	0.23	0.23	0.26	0.25	0.25	0.26	0.26	0.25
Current Ratio	0.63	0.86	0.82	0.74	0.76	0.77	0.77	0.92
Debt to Equity	0.86	0.90	1.03	1.03	1.05	0.98	1.15	1.15
Price Range	49.91-34.11	43.96-34.11	42.93-31.77	34.96-28.62	30.97-26.90	28.96-22.76	25.55-20.80	22.18-14.95
P/E Ratio	23.11-15.79	21.03-16.32	18.27-13.52	15.40-12.61	14.40-12.51	15.01-11.79	14.19-11.56	14.04-9.46
Average Yield %	3.68	3.73	3.89	4.28	4.58	4.85	5.32	6.26

Address: 818 South Kansas Avenue, Topeka, KS 66612
Telephone: 785-575-6300

Web Site: www.WestarEnergy.com
Officers: Charles Q. Chandler - Chairman Mark A. Ruelle - President, Chief Executive Officer, Chief Financial Officer

Auditors: Deloitte & Touche LLP
Investor Contact: 785-575-8227
Transfer Agents: Continental Stock Transfer & Trust Company, New York, NY

WABCO HOLDINGS INC

Exchange	Symbol	Price	52Wk Range	Yield	P/E
NYS	WBC	$107.90 (5/31/2016)	127.14-84.83	N/A	33.20

*7 Year Price Score 130.04 *NYSE Composite Index=100   *12 Month Price Score 98.68

Stock price chart 2007–2016 and Trading Volume (thousand shares)

Interim Earnings (Per Share)

Qtr.	Mar	Jun	Sep	Dec
2013	1.15	1.31	1.26	6.59
2014	1.12	1.23	1.37	1.10
2015	1.22	1.12	0.67	1.70
2016	(0.24)	...	...	...

Interim Dividends (Per Share)

No Dividends Paid

Valuation Analysis   Institutional Holding

Forecast EPS	$5.60	No of Institutions
	(05/20/2016)	409
Market Cap	$6.1 Billion	Shares
Book Value	$743.2 Million	59,810,760
Price/Book	8.17	% Held
Price/Sales	2.28	90.21

Business Summary: Construction Services (MIC: 7.5.4 SIC: 3711 NAIC: 336111)

WABCO is a provider of electronic, mechanical, electro-mechanical and aerodynamic products for manufacturers of commercial trucks, buses and trailers, as well as passenger cars. Co.'s key products are pneumatic anti-lock braking systems, electronic braking systems, electronic stability control, brake controls, automated manual transmission systems, air disc brakes, and a variety of mechanical products. Co. supplies commercial vehicle aftermarket distributors and service partners as well as fleet operators with replacement parts, fleet management solutions, diagnostic tools, training and other services. Co. also provides remanufacturing services globally.

Recent Developments: For the quarter ended Mar 31 2016, net loss amounted to US$9.8 million versus net income of US$74.8 million in the year-earlier quarter. Revenues were US$688.7 million, up 5.6% from US$652.2 million the year before. Operating income was US$87.0 million versus US$85.5 million in the prior-year quarter, an increase of 1.8%. Direct operating expenses rose 8.3% to US$475.2 million from US$438.6 million in the comparable period the year before. Indirect operating expenses decreased 1.2% to US$126.5 million from US$128.1 million in the equivalent prior-year period.

Prospects: Our evaluation of WABCO Holdings Inc. as of June 19, 2016 is the result of our systematic analysis on three basic characteristics: earnings strength, relative valuation, and recent stock price movement. The company has produced a positive trend in earnings per share over the past 5 quarters. However, while recent estimates for the company have been mixed, WBC has posted better than expected results. Based on operating earnings yield, the company is undervalued when compared to all of the companies in our coverage universe. Share price changes over the past year indicates that WBC will perform in line with the market over the near term.

Financial Data
(US$ in Thousands)

	3 Mos	12/31/2015	12/31/2014	12/31/2013	12/31/2012	12/31/2011	12/31/2010	12/31/2009
Earnings Per Share	3.25	4.72	4.81	10.31	4.62	5.19	(3.50)	0.29
Cash Flow Per Share	7.12	6.84	5.25	10.66	5.59	4.98	(2.94)	2.29
Tang Book Value Per Share	4.55	6.10	5.86	11.85	4.23	2.90	N.M.	3.07
Dividends Per Share	...	...	...	...	...	...	...	0.070
Dividend Payout %	...	...	...	...	...	...	...	24.14
Income Statement								
Total Revenue	688,700	2,627,500	2,851,000	2,720,500	2,477,400	2,794,100	2,175,700	1,491,500
EBITDA	113,300	369,200	434,400	703,500	396,400	468,300	(101,700)	99,200
Depn & Amortn	26,200	96,700	101,600	85,200	76,900	78,200	83,300	89,600
Income Before Taxes	84,100	265,400	333,000	623,200	318,000	388,400	(187,200)	10,100
Income Taxes	101,100	11,500	55,600	(21,000)	23,600	36,700	36,900	(10,700)
Net Income	(13,400)	275,200	291,500	653,200	302,000	357,000	(226,100)	18,800
Average Shares	56,485	58,274	60,546	63,382	65,323	68,829	64,562	65,030
Balance Sheet								
Current Assets	1,544,600	1,386,400	1,182,500	1,234,600	792,600	750,700	657,700	815,700
Total Assets	2,742,600	2,589,500	2,432,700	2,392,800	1,747,000	1,623,200	1,524,900	1,715,600
Current Liabilities	504,700	464,800	417,700	485,400	445,700	451,600	500,500	355,200
Long-Term Obligations	630,700	498,700	307,100	47,000	...	52,000	96,800	154,400
Total Liabilities	1,999,400	1,803,200	1,591,100	1,240,000	1,070,600	1,036,000	1,112,600	1,075,500
Stockholders' Equity	743,200	786,700	841,600	1,152,800	676,400	587,200	412,300	640,100
Shares Outstanding	56,249	56,759	58,425	61,359	62,747	64,765	66,458	64,077
Statistical Record								
Return on Assets %	7.41	10.96	12.08	31.56	17.87	22.68	N.M.	1.08
Return on Equity %	24.89	33.80	29.23	71.42	47.67	71.44	N.M.	3.03
EBITDA Margin %	16.45	14.05	15.24	25.86	16.00	16.76	N.M.	6.65
Net Margin %	N.M.	10.47	10.22	24.01	12.19	12.78	N.M.	1.26
Asset Turnover	1.04	1.05	1.18	1.31	1.47	1.78	1.34	0.85
Current Ratio	3.06	2.98	2.83	2.54	1.78	1.66	1.31	2.30
Debt to Equity	0.85	0.63	0.36	0.04	...	0.09	0.23	0.24
Price Range	133.21-84.83	133.21-94.54	110.68-84.36	93.41-62.66	65.19-44.66	74.30-35.47	60.93-25.06	25.94-8.18
P/E Ratio	40.99-26.10	28.22-20.03	23.01-17.54	9.06-6.08	14.11-9.67	14.32-6.83	...	89.45-28.21
Average Yield %	...	...	...	...	...	...	...	0.38

Address: Chaussée de la Hulpe 166, Brussels, 48309-3511	**Web Site:** www.wabco-auto.com	**Auditors:** Ernst & Young Belgium
Telephone: 266-398-00	**Officers:** Jacques R. Esculier - Chairman, Chief Executive Officer Leon Liu - Executive Vice	**Investor Contact:** 732-369-7477
Fax: 267-543-42	President, Region Officer, Division Officer	

WESTERN REFINING INC

Exchange	Symbol	Price	52Wk Range	Yield	P/E
NYS	WNR	$21.24 (5/31/2016)	50.24-20.78	7.16	6.07

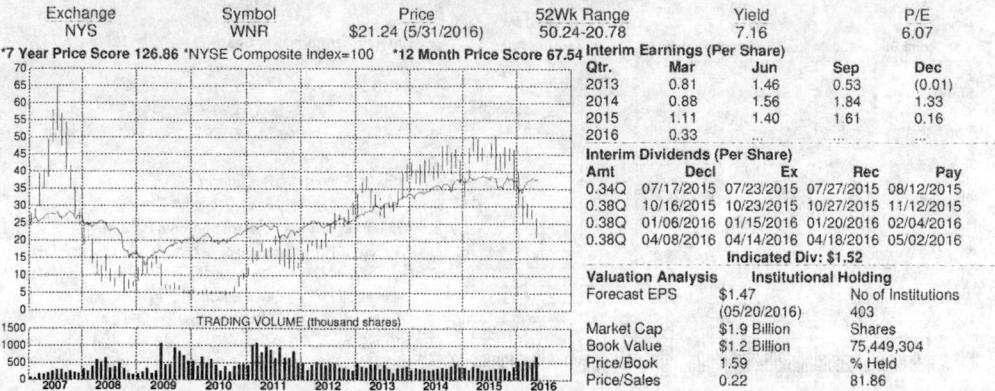

*7 Year Price Score 126.86 *NYSE Composite Index=100 *12 Month Price Score 67.54

Interim Earnings (Per Share)

Qtr.	Mar	Jun	Sep	Dec
2013	0.81	1.46	0.53	(0.01)
2014	0.88	1.56	1.84	1.33
2015	1.11	1.40	1.61	0.16
2016	0.33	...	...	...

Interim Dividends (Per Share)

Amt	Decl	Ex	Rec	Pay
0.34Q	07/17/2015	07/23/2015	07/27/2015	08/12/2015
0.38Q	10/16/2015	10/23/2015	10/27/2015	11/12/2015
0.38Q	01/06/2016	01/15/2016	01/20/2016	02/04/2016
0.38Q	04/08/2016	04/14/2016	04/18/2016	05/02/2016

Indicated Div: $1.52

Valuation Analysis   **Institutional Holding**

Forecast EPS	$1.47 (05/20/2016)	No of Institutions 403
Market Cap	$1.9 Billion	Shares 75,449,304
Book Value	$1.2 Billion	% Held 81.86
Price/Book	1.59	
Price/Sales	0.22	

Business Summary: Refining & Marketing (MIC: 9.1.2 SIC: 2911 NAIC: 324110)

Western Refining is a holding company. Through its subsidiaries, Co. is a crude oil refiner and marketer of refined products. Co. has four business segments: refining, which operates refineries that makes various grades of gasoline, diesel fuel, jet fuel and other products from crude oil, other feedstocks and blending components; Northern Tier Energy LP, which process a range of light, heavy, sweet and sour crudes into refined products; Western Refining Logistics, LP, which owns and operates terminal, storage, transportation and wholesale assets; and retail, which operates retail stores and unmanned commercial fueling locations that sell various grades of gasoline and diesel fuel.

Recent Developments: For the quarter ended Mar 31 2016, net income decreased 77.4% to US$39.6 million from US$175.0 million in the year-earlier quarter. Revenues were US$1.46 billion, down 37.2% from US$2.32 billion the year before. Operating income was US$78.6 million versus US$256.0 million in the prior-year quarter, a decrease of 69.3%. Direct operating expenses declined 35.0% to US$1.27 billion from US$1.96 billion in the comparable period the year before. Indirect operating expenses decreased 0.2% to US$105.9 million from US$106.1 million in the equivalent prior-year period.

Prospects: Our evaluation of Western Refining Inc. as of June 19, 2016 is the result of our systematic analysis on three basic characteristics: earnings strength, relative valuation, and recent stock price movement. The company has generated a negative trend in earnings per share over the past 5 quarters. However, while recent estimates for the company have been lowered by analysts, WNR has posted results that fell short of analysts expectations. Based on operating earnings yield, the company is undervalued when compared to all of the companies in our coverage universe. Share price changes over the past year indicates that WNR will perform very well over the near term.

Financial Data

(US$ in Thousands)	3 Mos	12/31/2015	12/31/2014	12/31/2013	12/31/2012	12/31/2011	12/31/2010	12/31/2009
Earnings Per Share	3.50	4.28	5.61	2.79	3.71	1.34	(0.19)	(4.43)
Cash Flow Per Share	8.03	8.88	8.13	5.36	10.24	5.71	1.52	1.78
Tang Book Value Per Share	N.M.	N.M.	N.M.	N.M.	9.98	8.68	6.97	7.12
Dividends Per Share	1.440	1.360	3.080	0.640	2.740	...	...	...
Dividend Payout %	41.14	31.78	54.90	22.94	73.85	...	...	...
Income Statement								
Total Revenue	1,455,504	9,787,036	15,153,573	10,086,070	9,503,134	9,071,037	7,965,053	6,807,368
EBITDA	137,959	1,144,486	1,285,650	642,014	795,200	476,845	243,321	(125,561)
Depn & Amortn	53,228	201,200	187,100	114,700	90,600	131,300	130,600	137,700
Income Before Taxes	58,214	838,386	1,002,676	453,479	617,087	202,528	(43,126)	(391,204)
Income Taxes	18,629	223,955	292,604	153,925	218,202	69,861	(26,077)	(40,583)
Net Income	30,538	406,756	559,926	275,994	398,885	132,667	(17,049)	(350,621)
Average Shares	92,144	94,899	101,190	104,904	111,822	109,792	88,204	79,163
Balance Sheet								
Current Assets	1,853,333	1,922,218	1,768,463	1,847,736	1,292,403	1,210,655	825,703	944,158
Total Assets	5,753,762	5,833,393	5,682,558	5,512,965	2,480,407	2,570,344	2,628,146	2,824,654
Current Liabilities	786,682	807,852	1,013,701	1,399,061	733,190	665,674	552,953	632,904
Long-Term Obligations	1,652,592	1,644,894	1,515,037	1,172,965	499,657	800,395	1,006,531	1,053,664
Total Liabilities	4,534,528	4,534,096	4,562,850	4,618,913	1,571,337	1,750,516	1,952,553	2,136,202
Stockholders' Equity	1,219,234	1,299,297	1,119,708	894,052	909,070	819,828	675,593	688,452
Shares Outstanding	91,276	93,684	96,200	79,725	86,938	89,303	88,327	87,990
Statistical Record								
Return on Assets %	5.77	7.06	10.00	6.91	15.75	5.10	N.M.	N.M.
Return on Equity %	27.69	33.63	55.61	30.61	46.02	17.74	N.M.	N.M.
EBITDA Margin %	9.48	11.69	8.48	6.37	8.37	5.26	3.05	N.M.
Net Margin %	2.10	4.16	3.70	2.74	4.20	1.46	N.M.	N.M.
Asset Turnover	1.55	1.70	2.71	2.52	3.75	3.49	2.92	2.31
Current Ratio	2.36	2.38	1.74	1.32	1.76	1.82	1.49	1.49
Debt to Equity	1.36	1.27	1.35	1.31	0.55	0.98	1.49	1.53
Price Range	50.24-24.81	50.24-32.51	47.72-36.16	42.41-26.51	31.04-13.98	21.44-10.23	10.62-4.11	15.43-4.49
P/E Ratio	14.35-7.09	11.74-7.60	8.51-6.45	15.20-9.50	8.37-3.77	16.00-7.63	...	...
Average Yield %	3.54	3.13	7.50	1.97	12.15	...	...	...

Address: 123 W. Mills Ave., Suite 200, El Paso, TX 79901 Telephone: 915-534-1400	Web Site: www.wnr.com Officers: Paul L. Foster - Executive Chairman Jeff A. Stevens - President, Chief Executive Officer	Auditors: Deloitte & Touche LLP Investor Contact: 602-286-1530 Transfer Agents: American Stock Transfer & Trust Company, New York, NY

WESTERN UNION CO

Exchange	Symbol	Price	52Wk Range	Yield	P/E
NYS	WU	$19.45 (5/31/2016)	22.23-16.44	3.29	12.16

*7 Year Price Score 91.68 ***NYSE Composite Index=100** ***12 Month Price Score 102.34**

TRADING VOLUME (thousand shares)

Interim Earnings (Per Share)

Qtr.	Mar	Jun	Sep	Dec
2013	0.37	0.36	0.39	0.32
2014	0.37	0.36	0.44	0.42
2015	0.39	0.36	0.45	0.42
2016	0.37	...	...	...

Interim Dividends (Per Share)

Amt	Decl	Ex	Rec	Pay
0.155Q	07/16/2015	09/14/2015	09/16/2015	09/30/2015
0.155Q	11/24/2015	12/15/2015	12/17/2015	12/31/2015
0.16Q	02/09/2016	03/15/2016	03/17/2016	03/31/2016
0.16Q	05/12/2016	06/14/2016	06/16/2016	06/30/2016

Indicated Div: $0.64

Valuation Analysis / Institutional Holding

Forecast EPS	$1.63 (05/20/2016)	No of Institutions 827
Market Cap	$9.6 Billion	Shares
Book Value	$1.2 Billion	579,118,784
Price/Book	7.72	% Held
Price/Sales	1.75	86.39

Business Summary: Business Services (MIC: 7.5.2 SIC: 7389 NAIC: 522320)

Western Union is a holding company. Through its subsidiaries, Co. is engaged in money movement and payment services. Co. has three segments: consumer-to-consumer, which facilitates money transfers between two consumers, primarily through a network of third-party agents; consumer-to-business, which facilitates bill payments from consumers to businesses and other organizations, including utilities, auto finance companies, mortgage servicers, government agencies and other businesses; and business solutions, which facilitates payment and foreign exchange solutions, primarily cross-border, cross-currency transactions, for small and medium size enterprises and other organizations and individuals.

Recent Developments: For the quarter ended Mar 31 2016, net income decreased 8.9% to US$185.7 million from US$203.9 million in the year-earlier quarter. Revenues were US$1.30 billion, down 1.8% from US$1.32 billion the year before. Operating income was US$258.6 million versus US$272.3 million in the prior-year quarter, a decrease of 5.0%. Direct operating expenses rose 1.0% to US$779.4 million from US$771.8 million in the comparable period the year before. Indirect operating expenses decreased 6.2% to US$259.7 million from US$276.8 million in the equivalent prior-year period.

Prospects: Our evaluation of Western Union Co as of June 19, 2016 is the result of our systematic analysis on three basic characteristics: earnings strength, relative valuation, and recent stock price movement. The company has managed to produce a neutral trend in earnings per share over the past 5 quarters and while recent estimates for the company have remained steady, WU has posted results that fell short of analysts expectations. Based on operating earnings yield, the company is undervalued when compared to all of the companies in our coverage universe. Share price changes over the past year indicates that WU will perform in line with the market over the near term.

Financial Data
(US$ in Thousands)

	3 Mos	12/31/2015	12/31/2014	12/31/2013	12/31/2012	12/31/2011	12/31/2010	12/31/2009
Earnings Per Share	1.60	1.62	1.59	1.43	1.69	1.84	1.36	1.21
Cash Flow Per Share	2.14	2.09	1.96	1.96	1.95	1.86	1.49	1.74
Dividends Per Share	0.625	0.620	0.500	0.500	0.425	0.310	0.250	0.060
Dividend Payout %	39.06	38.27	31.45	34.97	25.15	16.85	18.38	4.96
Income Statement								
Total Revenue	1,297,700	5,483,700	5,607,200	5,542,000	5,664,800	5,491,400	5,192,700	5,083,600
EBITDA	322,700	1,166,500	1,199,900	1,177,300	1,404,600	1,512,300	1,373,800	1,335,900
Depn & Amortn	65,000	67,700	66,600	64,200	61,700	61,000	61,500	55,900
Income Before Taxes	217,500	941,800	968,200	926,900	1,168,800	1,274,600	1,145,200	1,131,500
Income Taxes	31,800	104,000	115,800	128,500	142,900	109,200	235,300	282,700
Net Income	185,700	837,800	852,400	798,400	1,025,900	1,165,400	909,900	848,800
Average Shares	503,200	516,700	536,800	559,700	607,400	634,200	668,900	701,000
Balance Sheet								
Current Assets	1,160,000	1,399,300	1,846,200	2,157,000	1,849,000	1,443,800	2,245,400	1,774,400
Total Assets	9,418,300	9,458,900	9,890,400	10,121,300	9,465,700	9,069,900	7,929,200	7,353,400
Current Liabilities	801,200	1,090,700	1,071,700	1,200,100	1,157,100	1,557,700	1,900,500	1,334,500
Long-Term Obligations	3,225,700	3,225,600	3,720,400	4,213,000	4,029,200	3,286,200	2,593,600	3,048,500
Total Liabilities	8,179,300	8,054,000	8,590,000	9,016,600	8,525,100	8,175,100	7,346,500	6,999,900
Stockholders' Equity	1,239,000	1,404,900	1,300,400	1,104,700	940,600	894,800	582,700	353,500
Shares Outstanding	491,700	502,400	521,500	548,800	572,100	619,400	654,000	686,500
Statistical Record								
Return on Assets %	8.29	8.66	8.52	8.15	11.04	13.71	11.91	13.13
Return on Equity %	63.32	61.94	70.88	78.07	111.48	157.75	194.38	491.49
EBITDA Margin %	24.87	21.27	21.40	21.24	24.80	27.54	26.46	26.28
Net Margin %	14.31	15.28	15.20	14.41	18.11	21.22	17.52	16.70
Asset Turnover	0.55	0.57	0.56	0.57	0.61	0.65	0.68	0.79
Current Ratio	1.45	1.28	1.72	1.80	1.60	0.93	1.18	1.33
Debt to Equity	2.60	2.30	2.86	3.81	4.28	3.67	4.45	8.62
Price Range	22.56-16.44	22.56-16.96	18.58-15.15	19.37-13.36	19.73-11.95	21.99-14.89	20.13-14.90	20.56-10.43
P/E Ratio	14.10-10.28	13.93-10.47	11.69-9.53	13.55-9.34	11.67-7.07	11.95-8.09	14.80-10.96	16.99-8.62
Average Yield %	3.24	3.19	2.98	3.05	2.52	1.64	1.46	0.36

Address: 12500 East Belford Avenue, Englewood, CO 80112 **Telephone:** 866-405-5012	**Web Site:** www.westernunion.com **Officers:** Odilon Almeida - Region Officer Hikmet Ersek - President, Chief Executive Officer	**Auditors:** Ernst & Young LLP **Transfer Agents:** Wells Fargo Bank, National Association, South St. Paul, MN

WESTLAKE CHEMICAL CORP

Exchange	Symbol	Price	52Wk Range	Yield	P/E	Div Achiever
NYS	WLK	$44.13 (5/31/2016)	72.94-41.01	1.65	9.37	11 Years

*7 Year Price Score 114.96 *NYSE Composite Index=100 *12 Month Price Score 86.09

Interim Earnings (Per Share)

Qtr.	Mar	Jun	Sep	Dec
2013	0.92	1.09	1.27	1.27
2014	1.18	1.26	1.25	1.38
2015	1.10	1.54	1.39	0.84
2016	0.94	...	...	...

Interim Dividends (Per Share)

Amt	Decl	Ex	Rec	Pay
0.181Q	08/24/2015	09/02/2015	09/04/2015	09/22/2015
0.181Q	11/23/2015	12/02/2015	12/04/2015	12/18/2015
0.181Q	02/18/2016	02/25/2016	02/29/2016	03/14/2016
0.181Q	05/10/2016	05/19/2016	05/23/2016	06/07/2016

Indicated Div: $0.73

Valuation Analysis   Institutional Holding

Forecast EPS	$3.90	No of Institutions
	(05/17/2016)	363
Market Cap	$5.7 Billion	Shares
Book Value	$3.4 Billion	40,580,268
Price/Book	1.69	% Held
Price/Sales	1.33	57.56

Business Summary: Specialty Chemicals (MIC: 8.3.2 SIC: 2869 NAIC: 325211)

Westlake Chemical operates a manufacturer and marketer of basic chemicals, vinyls, polymers and building products. Co. operates in two principal operating segments: Olefins and Vinyls. The Olefins segment manufactures and markets polyethylene, styrene monomer and various ethylene co-products. The Vinyls segment manufactures and markets polyvinyl chloride (PVC), vinyl chloride monomer, ethylene dichloride, chlorine, caustic soda and ethylene. Co. also manufactures and sells products fabricated from PVC that it produces, including pipe, fittings, profiles, foundation building products, fence and deck components, window and door components and film and sheet products.

Recent Developments: For the quarter ended Mar 31 2016, net income decreased 14.3% to US$128.9 million from US$150.4 million in the year-earlier quarter. Revenues were US$975.2 million, down 11.6% from US$1.10 billion the year before. Operating income was US$202.3 million versus US$229.3 million in the prior-year quarter, a decrease of 11.8%. Direct operating expenses declined 12.1% to US$719.6 million from US$819.0 million in the comparable period the year before. Indirect operating expenses decreased 3.5% to US$53.3 million from US$55.3 million in the equivalent prior-year period.

Prospects: Our evaluation of Westlake Chemical Corp. as of June 19, 2016 is the result of our systematic analysis on three basic characteristics: earnings strength, relative valuation, and recent stock price movement. The company has generated a negative trend in earnings per share over the past 5 quarters. However, while recent estimates for the company have been mixed, WLK has posted better than expected results. Based on operating earnings yield, the company is undervalued when compared to all of the companies in our coverage universe. Share price changes over the past year indicates that WLK will perform in line with the market over the near term.

Financial Data

(US$ in Thousands)	3 Mos	12/31/2015	12/31/2014	12/31/2013	12/31/2012	12/31/2011	12/31/2010	12/31/2009
Earnings Per Share	4.71	4.86	5.07	4.54	2.88	1.94	1.67	0.40
Cash Flow Per Share	7.81	8.18	7.76	5.65	4.69	2.75	2.14	1.79
Tang Book Value Per Share	24.51	23.44	20.27	16.95	13.63	12.83	10.96	9.31
Dividends Per Share	0.710	0.693	0.582	0.412	2.136	0.137	0.121	0.110
Dividend Payout %	15.06	14.26	11.48	9.08	74.30	7.09	7.25	27.50
Income Statement								
Total Revenue	975,187	4,463,336	4,415,350	3,759,484	3,571,041	3,619,848	3,171,787	2,325,723
EBITDA	261,182	1,195,092	1,286,092	1,081,476	743,688	556,937	484,857	208,843
Depn & Amortn	56,261	209,271	174,173	129,222	120,924	110,268	105,744	100,333
Income Before Taxes	198,236	957,199	1,078,035	937,258	583,725	398,542	340,748	74,935
Income Taxes	69,300	298,396	398,902	331,747	199,614	142,466	121,567	25,758
Net Income	123,128	646,010	678,523	610,425	385,555	258,966	221,393	52,995
Average Shares	130,600	132,301	133,643	133,779	133,282	132,600	132,685	132,025
Balance Sheet								
Current Assets	2,191,734	2,175,189	2,011,287	1,649,082	1,751,413	1,756,156	1,475,960	988,378
Total Assets	5,724,401	5,575,252	5,213,990	4,060,909	3,412,196	3,266,821	2,954,144	2,446,356
Current Liabilities	506,161	522,642	537,180	404,858	398,510	364,595	323,578	286,566
Long-Term Obligations	758,300	764,115	763,997	763,879	763,761	764,563	764,482	515,400
Total Liabilities	2,317,875	2,309,374	2,302,479	1,642,306	1,539,940	1,510,509	1,449,074	1,161,374
Stockholders' Equity	3,406,526	3,265,878	2,911,511	2,418,603	1,872,256	1,756,312	1,505,070	1,284,982
Shares Outstanding	130,291	130,218	132,891	133,327	133,805	133,064	132,512	131,959
Statistical Record								
Return on Assets %	11.42	11.98	14.63	16.34	11.51	8.33	8.20	2.24
Return on Equity %	19.50	20.92	25.46	28.45	21.19	15.88	15.87	4.20
EBITDA Margin %	26.78	26.78	29.13	28.77	20.83	15.39	15.29	8.98
Net Margin %	12.63	14.47	15.37	16.24	10.80	7.15	6.98	2.28
Asset Turnover	0.80	0.83	0.95	1.01	1.07	1.16	1.17	0.98
Current Ratio	4.33	4.16	3.74	4.07	4.39	4.82	4.56	3.45
Debt to Equity	0.22	0.23	0.26	0.32	0.41	0.44	0.51	0.40
Price Range	78.59-41.01	78.59-49.82	97.96-53.67	61.03-39.31	40.05-20.43	33.09-16.16	21.80-8.78	14.09-5.20
P/E Ratio	16.69-8.71	16.17-10.25	19.32-10.59	13.44-8.66	13.90-7.09	17.06-8.33	13.05-5.26	35.23-13.00
Average Yield %	1.21	1.10	0.78	0.84	6.67	0.59	0.89	1.05

Address: 2801 Post Oak Boulevard, Suite 600, Houston, TX 77056 Telephone: 713-960-9111	Web Site: www.westlake.com Officers: James Chao - Chairman Albert Chao - President, Chief Executive Officer	Auditors: PricewaterhouseCoopers LLP Transfer Agents: American Stock Transfer & Trust Company, New York, NY

WESTWOOD HOLDINGS GROUP, INC.

Exchange	Symbol	Price	52Wk Range	Yield	P/E	Div Achiever
NYS	WHG	$57.32 (5/31/2016)	62.30-42.20	3.98	18.55	13 Years

*7 Year Price Score 103.06 *NYSE Composite Index=100 *12 Month Price Score 103.91

TRADING VOLUME (thousand shares)

Interim Earnings (Per Share)

Qtr.	Mar	Jun	Sep	Dec
2013	0.38	0.65	0.57	0.75
2014	0.75	1.14	0.92	0.72
2015	0.71	1.23	0.87	0.55
2016	0.44	...	...	...

Interim Dividends (Per Share)

Amt	Decl	Ex	Rec	Pay
0.50Q	07/29/2015	09/09/2015	09/11/2015	10/01/2015
0.57Q	10/28/2015	12/11/2015	12/15/2015	01/04/2016
0.57Q	02/03/2016	03/09/2016	03/11/2016	04/01/2016
0.57Q	04/27/2016	06/08/2016	06/10/2016	07/01/2016

Indicated Div: $2.28

Valuation Analysis

		Institutional Holding	
Forecast EPS	N/A	No of Institutions	107
Market Cap	$502.1 Million	Shares	5,753,174
Book Value	$129.0 Million	% Held	63.26
Price/Book	3.89		
Price/Sales	3.85		

Business Summary: Wealth Management (MIC: 5.5.2 SIC: 6282 NAIC: 523930)

Westwood Holdings Group is a holding company. Through Its subsidiaries, Co. manages investment assets and provides services for its clients. Westwood Management Corp. provides investment advisory services to corporate retirement plans, public retirement plans, endowments and foundations, mutual funds, individuals and clients of Westwood Trust. Westwood Trust provides institutions and individuals with trust and custodial services and participation in its sponsored common trust funds. Westwood International Advisors Inc. provides investment advisory services to corporate retirement plans, public retirement plans, endowments and foundations, mutual funds and other pooled investment vehicles.

Recent Developments: For the quarter ended Mar 31 2016, net income decreased 37.2% to US$3.5 million from US$5.6 million in the year-earlier quarter. Revenues were US$29.1 million, down 1.6% from US$29.6 million the year before. Indirect operating expenses increased 10.6% to US$23.5 million from US$21.2 million in the equivalent prior-year period.

Prospects: Our evaluation of Westwood Holdings Group Inc. as of June 19, 2016, is the result of our systematic analysis on three basic characteristics: earnings strength, relative valuation, and recent stock price movement. The company has generated a negative trend in earnings per share over the past 5 quarters. Because the company lacks sufficient analyst estimate data, we place greater weight on the historical EPS trend as the measure of earnings strength. Based on operating earnings yield, the company is undervalued when compared to all of the companies in our coverage universe. Share price changes over the past year indicates that WHG will perform well over the near term.

Financial Data

(US$ in Thousands)	3 Mos	12/31/2015	12/31/2014	12/31/2013	12/31/2012	12/31/2011	12/31/2010	12/31/2009
Earnings Per Share	3.09	3.33	3.45	2.34	1.65	2.04	1.58	1.18
Cash Flow Per Share	7.46	7.12	3.53	2.96	1.92	2.66	2.77	1.67
Tang Book Value Per Share	9.02	9.67	11.47	9.00	7.61	7.12	5.79	5.91
Dividends Per Share	2.140	2.070	1.820	1.640	1.510	1.420	1.650	1.230
Dividend Payout %	69.26	62.16	52.75	70.09	91.52	69.61	104.43	104.24
Income Statement								
Total Revenue	29,129	130,936	113,241	91,825	77,495	68,909	55,313	42,553
EBITDA	6,394	44,816	42,974	29,038	20,847	23,871	18,150	12,572
Depn & Amortn	748	2,596	938	769	821	762	429	254
Income Before Taxes	5,646	42,220	42,036	28,269	20,026	23,109	17,721	12,318
Income Taxes	2,124	15,115	14,787	10,378	7,936	8,423	6,441	4,423
Net Income	3,522	27,105	27,249	17,891	12,090	14,686	11,280	7,895
Average Shares	8,047	8,149	7,906	7,643	7,338	7,208	6,795	6,664
Balance Sheet								
Current Assets	99,239	117,604	118,764	96,189	77,370	72,482	55,882	54,343
Total Assets	164,452	181,336	139,874	116,020	96,615	90,597	72,628	59,886
Current Liabilities	32,722	44,853	27,204	24,853	18,826	17,523	11,744	11,361
Total Liabilities	35,441	47,369	29,867	27,387	20,064	19,840	11,951	12,668
Stockholders' Equity	129,011	133,967	110,007	88,633	76,551	70,757	60,677	47,218
Shares Outstanding	8,759	8,630	8,308	8,176	8,031	7,707	7,645	7,151
Statistical Record								
Return on Assets %	17.18	16.88	21.30	16.83	12.88	17.99	17.02	14.26
Return on Equity %	21.03	22.22	27.44	21.66	16.37	22.35	20.91	18.36
EBITDA Margin %	21.95	34.23	37.95	31.62	26.90	34.64	32.81	29.54
Net Margin %	12.09	20.70	24.06	19.48	15.60	21.31	20.39	18.55
Asset Turnover	0.90	0.82	0.89	0.86	0.83	0.84	0.83	0.77
Current Ratio	3.03	2.62	4.37	3.87	4.11	4.14	4.76	4.78
Price Range	64.07-42.20	64.07-50.37	67.84-51.72	61.91-39.97	40.92-34.15	40.91-31.11	40.62-28.98	44.19-24.90
P/E Ratio	20.73-13.66	19.24-15.13	19.66-14.99	26.46-17.08	24.80-20.70	20.05-15.25	25.71-18.34	37.45-21.10
Average Yield %	3.83	3.55	3.09	3.47	3.98	3.87	4.52	3.31

Address: 200 Crescent Court, Suite 1200, Dallas, TX 75201 Telephone: 214-756-6900	Web Site: www.westwoodgroup.com Officers: Susan M. Byrne - Chairman, Chief Investment Officer Brian O. Casey - President, Chief Executive Officer, Secretary	Auditors: Grant Thornton LLP Investor Contact: 214-756-6900 Transfer Agents: American Stock Transfer & Trust Company, Brooklyn, NY

WEX INC

Exchange	Symbol	Price	52Wk Range	Yield	P/E
NYS	WEX	$92.26 (5/31/2016)	117.37-58.09	N/A	34.95

*7 Year Price Score 111.19 *NYSE Composite Index=100 *12 Month Price Score 98.36

Interim Earnings (Per Share)

Qtr.	Mar	Jun	Sep	Dec
2013	0.73	1.08	1.12	0.89
2014	0.93	1.11	1.91	1.22
2015	0.57	0.68	0.83	0.54
2016	0.59	...	...	...

Interim Dividends (Per Share)

No Dividends Paid

Valuation Analysis		Institutional Holding	
Forecast EPS	$4.25	No of Institutions	
	(05/20/2016)	290	
Market Cap	$3.6 Billion	Shares	
Book Value	$1.1 Billion	44,193,932	
Price/Book	3.20	% Held	
Price/Sales	4.16	N/A	

Business Summary: Miscellaneous Consumer Services (MIC: 2.2.3 SIC: 7389 NAIC: 561499)

Wex is a provider of corporate card payment solutions. Co. operates in three business segments: Fleet Solutions, provides fleet vehicle payment processing services which include: customer service, account activation and account retention; authorization and billing inquiries and account maintenance; fleet services; credit and collections services; and merchant services; Travel and Corporate Solutions consist of virtual and prepaid products that provide corporate purchasing and payment capabilities; and Health and Employee Benefit Solutions include its healthcare payment products and SaaS platforms which provides payment in a healthcare market as well as employee benefit products in Brazil.

Recent Developments: For the quarter ended Mar 31 2016, net income increased 15.9% to US$23.2 million from US$20.0 million in the year-earlier quarter. Revenues were US$205.9 million, up 1.8% from US$202.3 million the year before. Operating income was US$41.1 million versus US$48.2 million in the prior-year quarter, a decrease of 14.7%. Direct operating expenses declined 18.4% to US$905,000 from US$1.1 million in the comparable period the year before. Indirect operating expenses increased 7.2% to US$163.9 million from US$152.9 million in the equivalent prior-year period.

Prospects: Our evaluation of Wex Inc. as of June 19, 2016 is the result of our systematic analysis on three basic characteristics: earnings strength, relative valuation, and recent stock price movement. The company has produced a positive trend in earnings per share over the past 5 quarters and while recent estimates for the company have remained steady, WEX has posted better than expected results. Based on operating earnings yield, the company is about fairly valued when compared to all of the companies in our coverage universe. Share price changes over the past year indicates that WEX will perform poorly over the near term.

Financial Data
(US$ in Thousands)

	3 Mos	12/31/2015	12/31/2014	12/31/2013	12/31/2012	12/31/2011	12/31/2010	12/31/2009
Earnings Per Share	2.64	2.62	5.18	3.82	2.48	3.43	2.25	3.55
Cash Flow Per Share	9.29	11.48	7.62	1.02	1.84	1.32	(0.27)	(0.87)
Tang Book Value Per Share	N.M.	N.M.	N.M.	N.M.	N.M.	1.29	N.M.	2.39
Income Statement								
Total Revenue	205,928	854,637	817,647	717,463	623,151	553,076	390,406	318,224
EBITDA	60,826	273,613	378,456	300,895	260,025	259,427	181,956	261,077
Depn & Amortn	23,036	83,077	70,380	58,208	48,852	45,369	31,504	22,559
Income Before Taxes	36,404	184,908	301,639	238,400	206,183	208,605	145,082	225,244
Income Taxes	13,183	75,296	101,621	90,102	109,474	74,983	57,453	85,585
Net Income	23,086	111,317	202,211	149,208	96,922	133,622	87,629	139,659
Average Shares	38,850	38,843	39,000	39,103	39,092	38,998	39,052	39,364
Balance Sheet								
Current Assets	2,194,762	1,881,325	2,198,131	2,073,547	1,753,476	1,357,871	1,178,527	889,608
Total Assets	4,143,777	3,857,946	4,118,347	3,433,043	3,106,684	2,278,060	2,097,951	1,499,662
Current Liabilities	1,658,854	1,408,241	1,542,736	1,710,209	1,537,266	1,164,518	1,013,910	810,778
Long-Term Obligations	1,191,566	1,201,819	1,354,539	685,000	621,000	295,300	407,300	128,000
Total Liabilities	3,025,482	2,774,702	3,058,022	2,530,265	2,288,753	1,568,745	1,538,944	1,058,346
Stockholders' Equity	1,118,295	1,083,244	1,060,325	902,778	817,931	709,315	559,007	441,316
Shares Outstanding	38,746	38,746	38,897	38,987	38,908	38,765	38,437	38,196
Statistical Record								
Return on Assets %	2.67	2.79	5.36	4.56	3.59	6.11	4.87	8.98
Return on Equity %	10.40	10.39	20.60	17.34	12.66	21.07	17.52	37.95
EBITDA Margin %	29.54	32.02	46.29	41.94	41.73	46.91	46.61	82.04
Net Margin %	11.21	13.03	24.73	20.80	15.55	24.16	22.45	43.89
Asset Turnover	0.20	0.21	0.22	0.22	0.23	0.25	0.22	0.20
Current Ratio	1.32	1.34	1.42	1.21	1.14	1.17	1.16	1.10
Debt to Equity	1.07	1.11	1.28	0.76	0.76	0.42	0.73	0.29
Price Range	118.50-58.09	118.50-84.66	118.43-79.93	100.38-67.91	75.37-53.29	57.05-36.36	46.39-27.98	32.60-11.20
P/E Ratio	44.89-22.00	45.23-32.31	22.86-15.43	26.28-17.78	30.39-21.49	16.63-10.60	20.62-12.44	9.18-3.15

Address: 97 Darling Avenue, South Portland, ME 04106 Telephone: 207-773-8171	Web Site: www.wrightexpress.com Officers: Melissa D. Smith - President, Chief Executive Officer, Region Officer Kenneth W. Janosick - Senior Vice President, General Manager	Auditors: Deloitte & Touche LLP Investor Contact: 866-230-1633 Transfer Agents: American Stock Transfer & Trust Company, Brooklyn, NY

WEYERHAEUSER CO

Exchange	Symbol	Price	52Wk Range	Yield	P/E
NYS	WY	$31.50 (5/31/2016)	32.96-22.22	3.94	37.50

*7 Year Price Score 87.49 ***NYSE Composite Index=100** ***12 Month Price Score 105.52**

Interim Earnings (Per Share)

Qtr.	Mar	Jun	Sep	Dec
2013	0.26	0.35	0.27	0.07
2014	0.31	0.47	2.15	0.35
2015	0.17	0.26	0.35	0.12
2016	0.11	...	...	...

Interim Dividends (Per Share)

Amt	Decl	Ex	Rec	Pay
0.31Q	08/27/2015	09/09/2015	09/11/2015	09/25/2015
0.31Q	10/14/2015	10/28/2015	10/30/2015	11/20/2015
0.31Q	02/10/2016	03/04/2016	03/08/2016	03/18/2016
0.31Q	05/20/2016	06/08/2016	06/10/2016	06/24/2016

Indicated Div: $1.24

Valuation Analysis

Forecast EPS	$0.95
	(05/20/2016)
Market Cap	$23.9 Billion
Book Value	$10.3 Billion
Price/Book	2.33
Price/Sales	3.32

Institutional Holding

No of Institutions	1060
Shares	637,174,720
% Held	73.84

Business Summary: REITs (MIC: 5.3.1 SIC: 6798 NAIC: 525930)

Weyerhaeuser is a private owner of timberland. As of Dec. 31, 2015, Co. owned or controlled nearly 7.0 million acres of timberlands, primarily in the U.S., and managed additional timberlands under licenses in Canada. Co. is also a manufacturer of wood and specialty cellulose fibers products. Co. is a real estate investment trust. Co. has three segments: Timberlands, which include logs, timber, minerals, oil and gas and international wood products; Wood Products, which include softwood lumber, engineered lumber, structural panels and building materials distribution; and Cellulose Fibers, which include pulp, liquid packaging board and an equity interest in a newsprint joint venture.

Recent Developments: For the quarter ended Mar 31 2016, net income decreased 19.8% to US$81.0 million from US$101.0 million in the year-earlier quarter. Revenues were US$1.84 billion, up 6.3% from US$1.73 billion the year before.

Prospects: Our evaluation of Weyerhaeuser Co. as of June 19, 2016 is the result of our systematic analysis on three basic characteristics: earnings strength, relative valuation, and recent stock price movement. The company has produced a positive trend in earnings per share over the past 5 quarters. However, while recent estimates for the company have been mixed, WY has posted better than expected results. Based on operating earnings yield, the company is about fairly valued when compared to all of the companies in our coverage universe. Share price changes over the past year indicates that WY will perform very well over the near term.

Financial Data

(US$ in Thousands)	3 Mos	12/31/2015	12/31/2014	12/31/2013	12/31/2012	12/31/2011	12/31/2010	12/31/2009
Earnings Per Share	0.84	0.89	3.18	0.95	0.71	0.61	3.99	(2.58)
Cash Flow Per Share	1.64	2.06	1.95	1.77	1.07	0.54	2.33	(0.77)
Tang Book Value Per Share	13.47	9.43	10.01	11.55	7.43	7.87	8.53	18.94
Dividends Per Share	1.220	1.200	1.020	0.810	0.620	0.600	26.663	0.600
Dividend Payout %	145.24	134.83	32.08	85.26	87.32	98.36	668.26	...
Income Statement								
Total Revenue	1,835,000	7,082,000	7,403,000	8,529,000	7,059,000	6,216,000	6,552,000	5,528,000
EBITDA	328,000	1,233,000	1,820,000	1,219,000	1,191,000	1,074,000	968,000	88,000
Depn & Amortn	142,000	314,000	500,000	472,000	456,000	480,000	503,000	508,000
Income Before Taxes	98,000	608,000	1,013,000	434,000	439,000	257,000	96,000	(854,000)
Income Taxes	20,000	(3,000)	185,000	(129,000)	55,000	(62,000)	(1,187,000)	(274,000)
Net Income	81,000	506,000	1,826,000	563,000	385,000	331,000	1,281,000	(545,000)
Average Shares	634,872	519,618	560,899	571,239	542,310	539,879	321,096	211,342
Balance Sheet								
Current Assets	1,830,000	2,174,000	3,033,000	2,326,000	2,140,000	2,068,000	2,590,000	3,674,000
Total Assets	21,779,000	12,486,000	13,457,000	14,498,000	12,592,000	12,598,000	13,429,000	15,250,000
Current Liabilities	984,000	875,000	918,000	1,128,000	1,230,000	941,000	1,074,000	955,000
Long-Term Obligations	9,149,000	5,402,000	5,402,000	5,407,000	3,951,000	4,466,000	5,060,000	5,683,000
Total Liabilities	11,498,000	7,617,000	8,153,000	7,703,000	8,522,000	8,335,000	8,817,000	11,206,000
Stockholders' Equity	10,281,000	4,869,000	5,304,000	6,795,000	4,070,000	4,263,000	4,612,000	4,044,000
Shares Outstanding	759,044	510,483	524,474	583,548	542,392	536,425	535,975	211,358
Statistical Record								
Return on Assets %	2.79	3.90	13.06	4.16	3.05	2.54	8.93	N.M.
Return on Equity %	6.35	9.95	30.18	10.36	9.22	7.46	29.60	N.M.
EBITDA Margin %	17.87	17.41	24.58	14.29	16.87	17.28	14.77	1.59
Net Margin %	4.41	7.14	24.67	6.60	5.45	5.32	19.55	N.M.
Asset Turnover	0.41	0.55	0.53	0.63	0.56	0.48	0.46	0.35
Current Ratio	1.86	2.48	3.30	2.06	1.74	2.20	2.41	3.85
Debt to Equity	0.89	1.11	1.02	0.80	0.97	1.05	1.10	1.41
Price Range	33.15-22.22	36.69-26.87	36.64-27.72	32.60-26.65	28.52-18.69	25.20-15.25	53.30-15.23	44.15-19.36
P/E Ratio	39.46-26.45	41.22-30.19	11.52-8.72	34.32-28.05	40.17-26.32	41.31-25.00	13.36-3.82	...
Average Yield %	4.11	3.79	3.20	2.73	2.68	2.98	86.30	1.78

Address: 33663 Weyerhaeuser Way South, Federal Way, WA 98063-9777 **Telephone:** 253-924-2345	**Web Site:** www.weyerhaeuser.com **Officers:** Charles R. Williamson - Chairman Daniel S. Fulton Vice-Chairman, President, Chief Executive Officer	**Auditors:** KPMG LLP **Investor Contact:** 253-924-2058 **Transfer Agents:** Computershare Investor Services, Canton, MA

WGL HOLDINGS INC

Exchange	Symbol	Price	52Wk Range	Yield	P/E	Div Achiever
NYS	WGL	$65.23 (5/31/2016)	73.33-52.24	2.99	20.51	39 Years

*7 Year Price Score 121.70 *NYSE Composite Index=100 *12 Month Price Score 108.56

Interim Earnings (Per Share)

Qtr.	Dec	Mar	Jun	Sep
2012-13	1.01	1.73	(0.19)	(1.00)
2013-14	0.36	1.18	(0.23)	0.74
2014-15	1.28	1.63	(0.32)	0.03
2015-16	1.36	2.11		

Interim Dividends (Per Share)

Amt	Decl	Ex	Rec	Pay
0.463Q	09/22/2015	10/07/2015	10/10/2015	11/01/2015
0.463Q	12/16/2015	01/06/2016	01/10/2016	02/01/2016
0.487Q	02/03/2016	04/06/2016	04/10/2016	05/01/2016
0.487Q	05/11/2016	07/06/2016	07/10/2016	08/01/2016

Indicated Div: $1.95 (Div. Reinv. Plan)

Valuation Analysis / **Institutional Holding**

Forecast EPS	$3.10	No of Institutions
	(05/20/2016)	383
Market Cap	$3.3 Billion	Shares
Book Value	$1.4 Billion	42,446,704
Price/Book	2.31	% Held
Price/Sales	1.39	60.03

Business Summary: Gas Utilities (MIC: 3.3.1 SIC: 4924 NAIC: 221210)

WGL Holdings is a holding company. Through its subsidiaries, Co. sells and delivers natural gas and provides energy-related products and services. Co.'s segments include: Regulated Utility, which is a regulated public utility that sells and delivers natural gas to retail customers and owns full and partial interests in underground natural gas storage facilities; Retail Energy-Marketing, which sells natural gas and/or electricity to residential, commercial and industrial customers; Commercial Energy Systems, which focuses on clean and energy efficient solutions; and Midstream Energy Services, which engages in investing in and optimizing natural gas pipelines and storage facilities.

Recent Developments: For the quarter ended Mar 31 2016, net income increased 30.4% to US$106.6 million from US$81.8 million in the year-earlier quarter. Revenues were US$835.7 million, down 16.6% from US$1.00 billion the year before. Operating income was US$174.4 million versus US$142.9 million in the prior-year quarter, an increase of 22.1%. Direct operating expenses declined 23.9% to US$609.9 million from US$801.1 million in the comparable period the year before. Indirect operating expenses decreased 11.0% to US$51.4 million from US$57.8 million in the equivalent prior-year period.

Prospects: Our evaluation of WGL Holdings Inc. as of June 19, 2016 is the result of our systematic analysis on three basic characteristics: earnings strength, relative valuation, and recent stock price movement. The company has generated a negative trend in earnings per share over the past 5 quarters and while recent estimates for the company have remained steady, WGL has posted results that fell short of analysts expectations. Based on operating earnings yield, the company is about fairly valued when compared to all of the companies in our coverage universe. Share price changes over the past year indicates that WGL will perform very well over the near term.

Financial Data

(US$ in Thousands)	6 Mos	3 Mos	09/30/2015	09/30/2014	09/30/2013	09/30/2012	09/30/2011	09/30/2010
Earnings Per Share	3.18	2.70	2.62	2.05	1.55	2.71	2.28	2.16
Cash Flow Per Share	6.70	8.72	10.12	7.38	6.15	4.21	5.78	5.76
Tang Book Value Per Share	28.27	26.43	25.00	24.61	24.62	24.60	23.41	22.63
Dividends Per Share	1.850	1.827	1.805	1.720	1.640	1.575	1.530	1.490
Dividend Payout %	58.18	67.69	68.89	83.90	105.81	58.12	67.11	68.98
Income Statement								
Total Revenue	1,449,073	613,384	2,659,830	2,780,947	2,466,138	2,425,310	2,751,501	2,708,876
EBITDA	295,019	118,813	385,810	311,326	273,097	369,166	347,449	323,292
Depn & Amortn	1,325	325	124,384	112,268	104,731	98,251	101,383	98,464
Income Before Taxes	267,935	105,728	210,915	161,320	132,355	234,487	205,520	184,761
Income Taxes	98,847	38,490	83,804	57,254	52,292	93,349	87,150	73,556
Net Income	175,119	68,501	132,579	107,260	81,573	141,138	118,370	111,205
Average Shares	50,282	50,030	50,060	51,770	51,808	51,589	51,295	50,765
Balance Sheet								
Current Assets	924,208	917,996	781,383	835,515	820,011	832,761	724,733	717,265
Total Assets	5,659,565	5,500,255	5,294,201	4,856,499	4,260,060	4,110,947	3,809,034	3,643,894
Current Liabilities	985,902	1,180,949	982,914	1,020,285	950,077	757,015	576,740	544,051
Long-Term Obligations	1,194,251	945,582	944,201	679,228	524,067	589,202	587,213	592,875
Total Liabilities	4,236,278	4,182,980	4,022,781	3,581,750	2,957,342	2,813,218	2,578,146	2,462,326
Stockholders' Equity	1,423,287	1,317,275	1,271,420	1,274,749	1,302,718	1,297,729	1,230,888	1,181,568
Shares Outstanding	50,338	49,847	49,728	50,656	51,774	51,611	51,365	50,974
Statistical Record								
Return on Assets %	2.99	2.57	2.61	2.35	1.95	3.55	3.18	3.18
Return on Equity %	11.74	10.58	10.41	8.32	6.27	11.13	9.81	9.64
EBITDA Margin %	20.36	19.37	14.51	11.19	11.07	15.22	12.63	11.93
Net Margin %	12.08	11.17	4.98	3.86	3.31	5.82	4.30	4.11
Asset Turnover	0.44	0.47	0.52	0.61	0.59	0.61	0.74	0.77
Current Ratio	0.94	0.78	0.79	0.82	0.86	1.10	1.26	1.32
Debt to Equity	0.84	0.72	0.74	0.53	0.40	0.45	0.48	0.50
Price Range	73.33-52.24	65.12-51.28	58.57-42.12	45.40-35.88	46.80-36.85	44.70-37.34	41.60-35.06	37.78-31.27
P/E Ratio	23.06-16.43	24.12-18.99	22.35-16.08	22.15-17.50	30.19-23.77	16.49-13.78	18.25-15.38	17.49-14.48
Average Yield %	3.10	3.22	3.37	4.24	3.89	3.85	4.01	4.35

Address: 101 Constitution Ave., N.W., Washington, DC 20080 **Telephone:** 703-750-2000	**Web Site:** www.wglholdings.com **Officers:** Terry D. McCallister - Chairman, Chief Executive Officer Adrian P. Chapman - President, Chief Operating Officer	**Auditors:** Deloitte & Touche LLP **Investor Contact:** 202-624-6129 **Transfer Agents:** Computershare, Pittsburgh, PA

WHIRLPOOL CORP

Exchange	Symbol	Price	52Wk Range	Yield	P/E
NYS	WHR	$174.62 (5/31/2016)	190.15-127.21	2.29	18.64

*7 Year Price Score 122.73 *NYSE Composite Index=100 *12 Month Price Score 107.42

TRADING VOLUME (thousand shares)

Interim Earnings (Per Share)

Qtr.	Mar	Jun	Sep	Dec
2013	3.12	2.44	2.42	2.27
2014	2.02	2.25	2.88	1.01
2015	2.38	2.21	2.95	2.29
2016	1.92	...	...	...

Interim Dividends (Per Share)

Amt	Decl	Ex	Rec	Pay
0.90Q	08/18/2015	08/26/2015	08/28/2015	09/15/2015
0.90Q	10/21/2015	11/18/2015	11/20/2015	12/15/2015
0.90Q	02/16/2016	02/24/2016	02/26/2016	03/15/2016
1.00Q	04/18/2016	05/18/2016	05/20/2016	06/15/2016

Indicated Div: $4.00

Valuation Analysis

		Institutional Holding	
Forecast EPS	$14.70	No of Institutions	
	(05/17/2016)	770	
Market Cap	$13.3 Billion	Shares	
Book Value	$4.8 Billion	82,703,392	
Price/Book	2.79	% Held	
Price/Sales	0.64	90.45	

Business Summary: Household Appliances, Electronics & Goods (MIC: 1.5.1 SIC: 3630 NAIC: 335228)

Whirlpool is a manufacturer and marketer of home appliances and related products. Co.'s main products are laundry appliances, refrigerators and freezers, cooking appliances, dishwashers, mixers and other small domestic appliances. Co. also produces hermetic compressors for refrigeration systems. Co. markets products under brand names such as Whirlpool, KitchenAid, Maytag, Consul, Brastemp, Amana, Bauknecht, Jenn-Air and Indesit. Co. has four geographic segments, which consist of North America, EMEA (Europe, Middle East and Africa), Latin America and Asia.

Recent Developments: For the quarter ended Mar 31 2016, net income decreased 21.2% to US$156.0 million from US$198.0 million in the year-earlier quarter. Revenues were US$4.62 billion, down 4.7% from US$4.85 billion the year before. Operating income was US$283.0 million versus US$303.0 million in the prior-year quarter, a decrease of 6.6%. Direct operating expenses declined 5.0% to US$3.80 billion from US$3.99 billion in the comparable period the year before. Indirect operating expenses decreased 2.2% to US$538.0 million from US$550.0 million in the equivalent prior-year period.

Prospects: Our evaluation of Whirlpool Corp. as of June 19, 2016 is the result of our systematic analysis on three basic characteristics: earnings strength, relative valuation, and recent stock price movement. The company has produced a positive trend in earnings per share over the past 5 quarters and while recent estimates for the company have been raised by analysts, WHR has posted results that fell short of analysts expectations. Based on operating earnings yield, the company is undervalued when compared to all of the companies in our coverage universe. Share price changes over the past year indicates that WHR will perform in line with the market over the near term.

Financial Data

(US$ in Thousands)	3 Mos	12/31/2015	12/31/2014	12/31/2013	12/31/2012	12/31/2011	12/31/2010	12/31/2009
Earnings Per Share	9.37	9.83	8.17	10.24	5.06	4.99	7.97	4.34
Cash Flow Per Share	14.66	15.57	18.89	15.91	8.89	6.90	14.15	20.78
Tang Book Value Per Share	N.M.	N.M.	N.M.	19.35	10.34	9.12	9.29	1.85
Dividends Per Share	3.600	3.450	2.875	2.375	2.000	1.930	1.720	1.720
Dividend Payout %	38.42	35.10	35.19	23.19	39.53	38.68	21.58	39.63
Income Statement								
Total Revenue	4,616,000	20,891,000	19,872,000	18,769,000	18,143,000	18,666,000	18,366,000	17,099,000
EBITDA	469,000	1,953,000	1,748,000	1,789,000	1,420,000	1,350,000	1,563,000	1,213,000
Depn & Amortn	186,000	668,000	560,000	540,000	551,000	558,000	555,000	525,000
Income Before Taxes	215,000	1,031,000	881,000	917,000	558,000	(28,000)	586,000	294,000
Income Taxes	59,000	209,000	189,000	68,000	133,000	(436,000)	(64,000)	(61,000)
Net Income	150,000	783,000	650,000	827,000	401,000	390,000	619,000	328,000
Average Shares	78,100	79,700	79,600	80,800	79,300	78,100	77,600	75,600
Balance Sheet								
Current Assets	7,894,000	7,325,000	8,098,000	7,022,000	6,827,000	6,422,000	7,315,000	7,025,000
Total Assets	19,672,000	19,010,000	20,002,000	15,544,000	15,396,000	15,181,000	15,584,000	15,094,000
Current Liabilities	8,687,000	7,744,000	8,403,000	6,794,000	6,510,000	6,297,000	6,149,000	5,941,000
Long-Term Obligations	3,251,000	3,470,000	3,544,000	1,846,000	1,944,000	2,129,000	2,195,000	2,502,000
Total Liabilities	14,914,000	14,267,000	15,117,000	10,620,000	11,136,000	11,000,000	11,358,000	11,430,000
Stockholders' Equity	4,758,000	4,743,000	4,885,000	4,924,000	4,260,000	4,181,000	4,226,000	3,664,000
Shares Outstanding	76,000	77,221	77,956	77,417	78,407	76,451	76,000	75,000
Statistical Record								
Return on Assets %	3.82	4.01	3.66	5.35	2.62	2.54	4.04	2.29
Return on Equity %	15.48	16.27	13.25	18.01	9.48	9.28	15.69	9.84
EBITDA Margin %	10.16	9.35	8.80	9.53	7.83	7.23	8.51	7.09
Net Margin %	3.25	3.75	3.27	4.41	2.21	2.09	3.37	1.92
Asset Turnover	1.06	1.07	1.12	1.21	1.18	1.21	1.20	1.19
Current Ratio	0.91	0.95	0.96	1.03	1.05	1.02	1.19	1.18
Debt to Equity	0.68	0.73	0.73	0.37	0.46	0.51	0.52	0.68
Price Range	202.06-127.21	215.00-142.27	193.74-126.69	157.80-101.75	102.73-48.51	91.28-45.37	112.42-71.62	83.65-19.39
P/E Ratio	21.56-13.58	21.87-14.47	23.71-15.51	15.41-9.94	20.30-9.59	18.29-9.09	14.11-8.99	19.27-4.47
Average Yield %	2.17	1.93	1.88	1.86	2.69	2.75	1.99	3.30

Address: 2000 North M-63, Benton Harbor, MI 49022-2692 Telephone: 269-923-5000	Web Site: www.whirlpoolcorp.com Officers: Jeff M. Fettig - Chairman, Chief Executive Officer Marc R. Bitzer - Vice-Chairman, President, Chief Operating Officer, Region Officer	Auditors: Ernst & Young LLP Investor Contact: 269-923-2641 Transfer Agents: Computershare Trust Company, N.A., Providence, RI

WHITE MOUNTAINS INSURANCE GROUP, LTD.

*7 Year Price Score 124.16 *NYSE Composite Index=100 *12 Month Price Score 107.43

Interim Earnings (Per Share)

Qtr.	Mar	Jun	Sep	Dec
2013	19.17	4.26	9.26	19.06
2014	15.48	15.53	8.45	11.71
2015	14.09	0.72	(10.01)	45.63
2016	2.34	...	...	...

Interim Dividends (Per Share)

Amt	Decl	Ex	Rec	Pay
1.00A	02/28/2013	03/14/2013	03/18/2013	03/27/2013
1.00A	02/27/2014	03/13/2014	03/17/2014	03/26/2014
1.00A	02/26/2015	03/12/2015	03/16/2015	03/25/2015
1.00A	02/26/2016	03/17/2016	03/21/2016	03/30/2016

Indicated Div: $1.00

Valuation Analysis | **Institutional Holding**

Forecast EPS	$5.00 (05/08/2016)	No of Institutions	271
Market Cap	$4.4 Billion	Shares	5,398,219
Book Value	$3.8 Billion	% Held	
Price/Book	1.15		81.04
Price/Sales	2.15		

Business Summary: General Insurance (MIC: 5.2.1 SIC: 6331 NAIC: 524126)

White Mountains Insurance Group is an insurance holding company. Co. has four reportable segments: OneBeacon, which owns a family of property and casualty insurance companies; Sirius Group, which provides insurance and reinsurance products for property, accident and health, aviation and space, trade credit, marine, agriculture and certain other exposures; HG Global/BAM, which consists of investment in HG Global Ltd. and Build America Mutual Assurance Company; and Other Operations, which includes, Co. and its intermediate holding companies, its investment management subsidiary, and its variable annuity reinsurance business, as well as various other investments and entities.

Recent Developments: For the quarter ended Mar 31 2016, income from continuing operations was US$20.2 million compared with a loss of US$4.1 million in the year-earlier quarter. Net income decreased 74.9% to US$19.3 million from US$77.0 million in the year-earlier quarter. Revenues were US$427.1 million, up 9.0% from US$391.8 million the year before. Net premiums earned were US$282.1 million versus US$289.3 million in the prior-year quarter, a decrease of 2.5%. Net investment income rose 42.1% to US$17.9 million from US$12.6 million a year ago.

Prospects: Our evaluation of White Mountains Insurance Group Ltd. as of June 19, 2016 is the result of our systematic analysis on three basic characteristics: earnings strength, relative valuation, and recent stock price movement. The company has suffered a very negative trend in earnings per share over the past 5 quarters and while recent estimates for the company have remained steady, WTM has posted results that fell short of analysts expectations. Based on operating earnings yield, the company is overvalued when compared to all of the companies in our coverage universe. Share price changes over the past year indicates that WTM will perform very well over the near term.

Financial Data
(US$ in Thousands)

	3 Mos	12/31/2015	12/31/2014	12/31/2013	12/31/2012	12/31/2011	12/31/2010	12/31/2009
Earnings Per Share	38.68	50.60	51.21	51.89	30.50	97.44	10.12	53.10
Cash Flow Per Share	25.70	30.23	19.71	(16.53)	(33.57)	(14.66)	6.63	(5.33)
Tang Book Value Per Share	630.49	629.03	606.43	632.29	593.20	539.43	445.76	412.79
Dividends Per Share	1.000	1.000	1.000	1.000	1.000	1.000	1.000	1.000
Dividend Payout %	2.59	1.98	1.95	1.93	3.28	1.03	9.88	1.88
Income Statement								
Premium Income	282,100	1,188,200	2,058,900	1,987,300	2,063,600	1,927,800	3,162,400	3,600,400
Total Revenue	427,100	1,808,600	2,510,200	2,317,400	2,435,700	2,178,100	3,571,100	4,448,100
Benefits & Claims	161,100	708,900	1,169,300	1,040,500	1,193,900	1,206,900	2,068,000	2,119,100
Income Before Taxes	11,500	154,900	301,700	344,900	262,800	61,600	150,500	764,000
Income Taxes	(8,700)	(700)	53,300	76,600	(15,700)	(122,700)	20,900	208,800
Net Income	13,000	297,600	312,700	321,800	207,400	767,900	86,500	470,000
Average Shares	5,486	5,811	6,026	6,109	6,708	7,811	8,549	8,764
Balance Sheet								
Total Assets	10,391,800	10,284,500	10,456,900	12,144,300	12,895,400	14,064,000	14,534,100	15,443,200
Total Liabilities	6,605,900	6,371,300	6,460,300	8,238,800	9,163,600	9,976,300	10,881,100	11,785,800
Stockholders' Equity	3,785,900	3,913,200	3,996,600	3,905,500	3,731,800	4,087,700	3,653,000	3,657,400
Shares Outstanding	5,415	5,623	5,986	6,176	6,290	7,577	8,194	8,860
Statistical Record								
Return on Assets %	2.17	2.87	2.77	2.57	1.53	5.37	0.58	3.00
Return on Equity %	5.80	7.52	7.91	8.43	5.29	19.84	2.37	14.34
Loss Ratio %	57.11	59.66	56.79	52.36	57.86	62.61	65.39	58.86
Net Margin %	3.04	16.45	12.46	13.89	8.52	35.26	2.42	10.57
Price Range	808.00-636.06	808.00-618.00	674.71-559.26	610.50-515.00	547.67-439.94	453.46-335.60	362.90-297.22	338.08-150.00
P/E Ratio	20.89-16.44	15.97-12.21	13.18-10.92	11.77-9.92	17.96-14.42	4.65-3.44	35.86-29.37	6.37-2.82
Average Yield %	0.14	0.14	0.16	0.17	0.20	0.25	0.30	0.39

Address: 14 Wesley Street, 5th Floor, Hamilton, HM 11 **Telephone:** 603-640-2200	**Web Site:** www.whitemountains.com **Officers:** Raymond Barrette - Chairman, Chief Executive Officer David T. Foy - Executive Vice President, Chief Financial Officer	**Auditors:** PricewaterhouseCoopers LLP **Investor Contact:** 203-458-5850 **Transfer Agents:** Computershare Trust Company, N.A., Providence, RI, United States

WHITEWAVE FOODS CO.

Exchange	Symbol	Price	52Wk Range	Yield	P/E
NYS	WWAV	$44.65 (5/31/2016)	52.16-33.59	N/A	44.65

*7 Year Price Score N/A   *NYSE Composite Index=100   *12 Month Price Score 97.02

Interim Earnings (Per Share)

Qtr.	Mar	Jun	Sep	Dec
2013	0.14	0.18	0.14	0.11
2014	0.18	0.19	0.23	0.17
2015	0.19	0.21	0.28	0.27
2016	0.24	...	...	...

Interim Dividends (Per Share)

No Dividends Paid

Valuation Analysis   Institutional Holding

Forecast EPS	$1.40	No of Institutions
	(05/17/2016)	516
Market Cap	$7.9 Billion	Shares
Book Value	$1.3 Billion	152,591,360
Price/Book	6.03	% Held
Price/Sales	1.98	83.27

Business Summary: Food (MIC: 1.2.1 SIC: 5451 NAIC: 445299)

Whitewave Foods is a consumer packaged food and beverage company. Co. manufactures, markets, distributes, and sells plant-based foods and beverages, coffee creamers and beverages, dairy products and organic produce throughout North America and Europe. Co.'s brands distributed in North America include Silk®, So Delicious® and Vegaâ,,¢ plant-based foods and beverages, International Delight® and LAND O LAKES® coffee creamers and beverages, Horizon Organic® and Wallaby Organic® dairy products and Earthbound Farm® organic salads, fruits and vegetables. Co.'s plant-based foods and beverages brands in Europe include Alpro® and Provamel®.

Recent Developments: For the quarter ended Mar 31 2016, net income increased 27.7% to US$42.6 million from US$33.3 million in the year-earlier quarter. Revenues were US$1.04 billion, up 14.1% from US$911.1 million the year before. Operating income was US$83.8 million versus US$70.1 million in the prior-year quarter, an increase of 19.6%. Direct operating expenses rose 13.8% to US$685.9 million from US$602.6 million in the comparable period the year before. Indirect operating expenses increased 13.2% to US$269.9 million from US$238.5 million in the equivalent prior-year period.

Prospects: Our evaluation of The Whitewave Foods Co. as of June 19, 2016 is the result of our systematic analysis on three basic characteristics: earnings strength, relative valuation, and recent stock price movement. The company has managed to produce a neutral trend in earnings per share over the past 5 quarters and while recent estimates for the company have remained steady, WWAV has posted better than expected results. Based on operating earnings yield, the company is overvalued when compared to all of the companies in our coverage universe. Share price changes over the past year indicates that WWAV will perform poorly over the near term.

Financial Data
(US$ in Thousands)

	3 Mos	12/31/2015	12/31/2014	12/31/2013	12/31/2012	12/31/2011	12/31/2010
Earnings Per Share	1.00	0.94	0.79	0.57	0.74	0.72	0.53
Cash Flow Per Share	1.69	1.80	1.64	1.07	1.53	1.60	1.21
Tang Book Value Per Share	N.M.	N.M.	0.05	1.09	0.11	...	...
Income Statement							
Total Revenue	1,039,695	3,866,295	3,436,605	2,542,063	2,289,438	2,025,751	1,821,313
EBITDA	82,506	430,663	361,220	240,261	251,096	240,972	188,298
Depn & Amortn	1,108	104,800	99,800	79,000	71,800	65,400	63,200
Income Before Taxes	67,718	267,736	224,448	143,234	169,372	166,423	114,515
Income Taxes	22,908	87,908	78,279	44,193	56,858	52,089	33,159
Net Income	42,600	168,393	140,185	99,041	113,694	107,395	79,098
Average Shares	180,284	180,084	177,949	174,581	153,770	150,000	150,000
Balance Sheet							
Current Assets	643,040	606,677	539,187	456,221	382,821	373,769	...
Total Assets	4,305,733	4,228,869	3,372,841	2,283,184	2,168,011	2,108,685	...
Current Liabilities	564,099	604,205	491,418	386,400	322,542	237,250	...
Long-Term Obligations	2,089,244	2,078,940	1,495,822	647,650	765,550	456,171	...
Total Liabilities	2,997,134	3,017,961	2,296,354	1,321,745	1,383,055	972,766	...
Stockholders' Equity	1,308,599	1,210,908	1,076,487	961,439	784,956	1,135,919	...
Shares Outstanding	176,858	176,246	174,388	173,452	173,000	...	...
Statistical Record							
Return on Assets %	4.63	4.43	4.96	4.45	5.30	...	...
Return on Equity %	14.88	14.72	13.76	11.34	11.81	...	...
EBITDA Margin %	7.94	11.14	10.51	9.45	10.97	11.90	10.34
Net Margin %	4.10	4.36	4.08	3.90	4.97	5.30	4.34
Asset Turnover	1.04	1.02	1.22	1.14	1.07	...	...
Current Ratio	1.14	1.00	1.10	1.18	1.19	1.58	...
Debt to Equity	1.60	1.72	1.39	0.67	0.98	0.40	...
Price Range	52.16-33.59	52.16-32.64	37.46-22.57	23.45-14.85	16.75-14.31	...	...
P/E Ratio	52.16-33.59	55.49-34.72	47.42-28.57	41.14-26.05	22.64-19.34	...	...

Address: 1225 Seventeenth Street, Suite 1000, Denver, CO 80202 **Telephone:** 303-635-4500	**Web Site:** www.whitewave.com **Officers:** Gregg L. Engles - Chairman, Chief Executive Officer, Holding/Parent Company Officer Gregory S. Christenson - Executive Vice President, Chief Financial Officer	**Auditors:** Deloitte & Touche LLP **Investor Contact:** 303-635-4747 **Transfer Agents:** Computershare, Providence, RI

WHITING PETROLEUM CORP

Exchange	Symbol	Price	52Wk Range	Yield	P/E
NYS	WLL	$12.35 (5/31/2016)	35.97-3.53	N/A	N/A

*7 Year Price Score 29.22 *NYSE Composite Index=100 *12 Month Price Score 68.87

TRADING VOLUME (thousand shares)

Interim Earnings (Per Share)

Qtr.	Mar	Jun	Sep	Dec
2013	0.72	1.14	1.71	(0.50)
2014	0.91	1.26	1.32	(2.95)
2015	(0.63)	(0.73)	(9.14)	(0.34)
2016	(0.84)	...	...	...

Interim Dividends (Per Share)

Amt	Decl	Ex	Rec	Pay
100%	...	02/23/2011	02/07/2011	02/22/2011

Valuation Analysis

		Institutional Holding	
Forecast EPS	$-2.23 (05/20/2016)	No of Institutions	522
Market Cap	$2.5 Billion	Shares	
Book Value	$4.6 Billion		192,873,824
Price/Book	0.55	% Held	
Price/Sales	1.39		85.29

Business Summary: Production & Extraction (MIC: 9.1.1 SIC: 1311 NAIC: 211111)

Whiting Petroleum is an independent oil and gas company that explores for, develops, acquires and produces crude oil, natural gas liquids and natural gas primarily in the Rocky Mountains and Permian Basin regions of the U.S. Co. sells its oil and gas production to end users, marketers and other purchasers that have access to nearby pipeline facilities. In areas with no access to pipelines, oil is trucked to terminals, refineries or storage facilities. As of Dec 31 2014, Co. had estimated total proved reserves of 780.3 million barrels of oil equivalent, consisting of 643.6 million barrels of oil, 54.7 million barrels of natural gas liquids and 492.02 billion cubic feet of natural gas.

Recent Developments: For the quarter ended Mar 31 2016, net loss amounted to US$171.8 million versus a net loss of US$106.1 million in the year-earlier quarter. Revenues were US$292.0 million, down 44.8% from US$529.2 million the year before. Indirect operating expenses decreased 23.3% to US$528.9 million from US$689.2 million in the equivalent prior-year period.

Prospects: Our evaluation of Whiting Petroleum Corp. as of June 19, 2016 is the result of our systematic analysis on three basic characteristics: earnings strength, relative valuation, and recent stock price movement. The company has enjoyed a very positive trend in earnings per share over the past 5 quarters. Because the company lacks sufficient analyst estimate data, we place greater weight on the historical EPS trend as the measure of earnings strength. Based on operating earnings yield, the company is overvalued when compared to all of the companies in our coverage universe. Share price changes over the past year indicates that WLL will perform very poorly over the near term.

Financial Data

(US$ in Thousands)	3 Mos	12/31/2015	12/31/2014	12/31/2013	12/31/2012	12/31/2011	12/31/2010	12/31/2009
Earnings Per Share	(11.05)	(11.35)	0.53	3.06	3.48	4.14	2.55	(1.18)
Cash Flow Per Share	4.38	5.38	14.86	14.75	11.88	10.16	9.38	4.35
Tang Book Value Per Share	22.43	23.27	28.88	32.27	29.29	25.74	21.62	22.32
Income Statement								
Total Revenue	292,007	2,050,798	3,085,097	2,828,385	2,173,452	1,899,622	1,516,099	979,360
EBITDA	(135,395)	(2,649,706)	320,051	689,507	740,893	845,523	602,812	(95,080)
Depn & Amortn	19,622	9,664	5,494	4,700	3,672	2,688	2,291	3,147
Income Before Taxes	(236,924)	(2,993,495)	143,915	571,871	662,011	780,319	541,443	(162,835)
Income Taxes	(65,166)	(774,227)	79,170	205,868	247,912	288,691	204,790	(55,953)
Net Income	(171,748)	(2,219,182)	64,807	366,055	414,189	491,687	336,653	(106,882)
Average Shares	204,367	195,472	122,519	119,588	119,028	118,668	107,846	100,088
Balance Sheet								
Current Assets	419,506	535,190	842,999	1,069,618	384,412	298,703	233,543	176,025
Total Assets	11,181,237	11,389,085	14,019,504	8,833,470	7,272,419	6,045,609	4,648,777	4,029,542
Current Liabilities	491,182	599,813	1,208,516	777,685	636,979	567,034	459,205	282,732
Long-Term Obligations	5,334,595	5,197,704	5,628,782	2,653,834	1,800,000	1,380,000	800,000	779,585
Total Liabilities	6,596,511	6,638,481	8,324,530	5,004,903	3,827,431	3,024,752	2,117,462	1,759,457
Stockholders' Equity	4,584,726	4,750,604	5,694,974	3,828,567	3,444,988	3,020,857	2,531,315	2,270,085
Shares Outstanding	204,385	204,147	166,889	118,657	117,631	117,380	117,098	101,690
Statistical Record								
Return on Assets %	N.M.	N.M.	0.57	4.55	6.20	9.20	7.76	N.M.
Return on Equity %	N.M.	N.M.	1.36	10.07	12.78	17.71	14.02	N.M.
EBITDA Margin %	N.M.	N.M.	10.37	24.38	34.09	44.51	39.76	N.M.
Net Margin %	N.M.	N.M.	2.10	12.94	19.06	25.88	22.21	N.M.
Asset Turnover	0.14	0.16	0.27	0.35	0.33	0.36	0.35	0.24
Current Ratio	0.85	0.89	0.70	1.38	0.60	0.53	0.51	0.62
Debt to Equity	1.16	1.09	0.99	0.69	0.52	0.46	0.32	0.34
Price Range	37.95-3.53	40.95-8.31	92.66-25.04	69.75-42.48	62.47-36.41	74.50-30.66	59.10-32.70	37.34-9.87
P/E Ratio	...	...	174.83-47.25	22.79-13.88	17.95-10.46	18.00-7.41	23.18-12.82	...

Address: 1700 Broadway, Suite 2300, Denver, CO 80290-2300 **Telephone:** 303-837-1661	**Web Site:** www.whiting.com **Officers:** James J. Volker - Chairman, President, Chief Executive Officer Peter W. Hagist - Senior Vice President	**Auditors:** Deloitte & Touche LLP **Investor Contact:** 303-390-4051

WILEY (JOHN) & SONS INC.

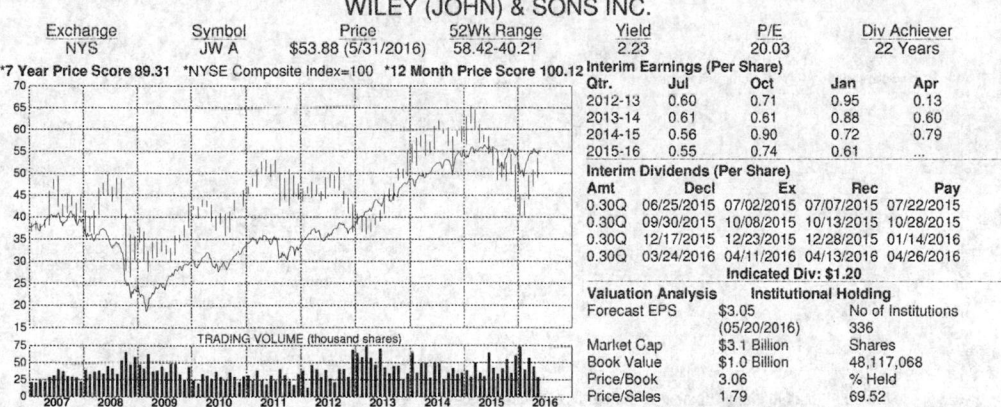

Exchange	Symbol	Price	52Wk Range	Yield	P/E	Div Achiever
NYS	JW A	$53.88 (5/31/2016)	58.42-40.21	2.23	20.03	22 Years

*7 Year Price Score 89.31 *NYSE Composite Index=100 *12 Month Price Score 100.12

Interim Earnings (Per Share)

Qtr.	Jul	Oct	Jan	Apr
2012-13	0.60	0.71	0.95	0.13
2013-14	0.61	0.61	0.88	0.60
2014-15	0.56	0.90	0.72	0.79
2015-16	0.55	0.74	0.61	...

Interim Dividends (Per Share)

Amt	Decl	Ex	Rec	Pay
0.30Q	06/25/2015	07/02/2015	07/07/2015	07/22/2015
0.30Q	09/30/2015	10/08/2015	10/13/2015	10/28/2015
0.30Q	12/17/2015	12/23/2015	12/28/2015	01/14/2016
0.30Q	03/24/2016	04/11/2016	04/13/2016	04/26/2016

Indicated Div: $1.20

Valuation Analysis		Institutional Holding	
Forecast EPS	$3.05	No of Institutions	
	(05/20/2016)	336	
Market Cap	$3.1 Billion	Shares	
Book Value	$1.0 Billion	48,117,068	
Price/Book	3.06	% Held	
Price/Sales	1.79	69.52	

TRADING VOLUME (thousand shares)

Business Summary: Publishing (MIC: 2.3.3 SIC: 2731 NAIC: 511130)

John Wiley & Sons provides knowledge and knowledge-enabled services. Co. has three operating segments: research, professional development, and education. Through the research segment, Co. provides digital and print scientific, technical, medical and scholarly journals, reference works, books, database services and advertising. The professional development segment provides digital and print books, online learning, assessment and training services, and test prep and certification. In education, Co. provides print and digital content, and education solutions including online program management services for higher education institutions and course management tools for instructors and students.

Recent Developments: For the quarter ended Jan 31 2016, net income decreased 16.5% to US$35.5 million from US$42.5 million in the year-earlier quarter. Revenues were US$436.4 million, down 6.3% from US$465.9 million the year before. Operating income was US$39.6 million versus US$54.0 million in the prior-year quarter, a decrease of 26.7%. Direct operating expenses declined 3.2% to US$120.2 million from US$124.2 million in the comparable period the year before. Indirect operating expenses decreased 3.8% to US$276.5 million from US$287.6 million in the equivalent prior-year period.

Prospects: Our evaluation of Wiley (John) & Sons Inc. as of June 19, 2016 is the result of our systematic analysis on three basic characteristics: earnings strength, relative valuation, and recent stock price movement. The company has generated a negative trend in earnings per share over the past 5 quarters. However, while recent estimates for the company have been lowered by analysts, JW.A has posted better than expected results. Based on operating earnings yield, the company is undervalued when compared to all of the companies in our coverage universe. Share price changes over the past year indicates that JW.A will perform in line with the market over the near term.

Financial Data

(US$ in Thousands)	9 Mos	6 Mos	3 Mos	04/30/2015	04/30/2014	04/30/2013	04/30/2012	04/30/2011
Earnings Per Share	2.69	2.80	2.96	2.97	2.70	2.39	3.47	2.80
Cash Flow Per Share	5.51	5.55	5.68	6.05	5.94	5.67	6.29	6.24
Dividends Per Share	1.190	1.180	1.170	1.160	1.000	0.960	0.800	0.640
Dividend Payout %	44.24	42.14	39.53	39.06	37.04	40.17	23.05	22.86
Income Statement								
Total Revenue	1,292,736	856,343	422,981	1,822,440	1,775,195	1,760,778	1,782,742	1,742,551
EBITDA	264,300	182,991	83,390	352,767	309,665	295,385	365,305	327,045
Depn & Amortn	118,118	77,859	38,561	113,286	103,000	97,999	87,147	81,085
Income Before Taxes	135,789	98,543	41,920	225,461	195,534	186,922	272,095	231,060
Income Taxes	24,214	22,486	9,463	48,593	35,024	42,697	59,349	59,171
Net Income	111,575	76,057	32,457	176,868	160,510	144,225	212,746	171,889
Average Shares	58,204	58,790	59,366	59,594	59,514	60,224	61,272	61,359
Balance Sheet								
Current Assets	896,941	618,787	706,939	740,919	789,662	634,971	574,600	527,490
Total Assets	3,114,408	2,882,827	2,981,600	3,004,243	3,077,365	2,806,375	2,532,946	2,430,141
Current Liabilities	826,936	593,399	659,834	803,683	729,587	667,169	640,930	756,365
Long-Term Obligations	814,728	739,051	750,473	650,090	700,100	673,000	475,000	330,500
Total Liabilities	2,098,325	1,815,154	1,900,936	1,949,203	1,895,117	1,818,019	1,515,378	1,452,252
Stockholders' Equity	1,016,083	1,067,673	1,080,664	1,055,040	1,182,248	988,356	1,017,568	977,889
Shares Outstanding	57,725	58,066	58,551	58,838	59,052	58,670	59,515	60,709
Statistical Record								
Return on Assets %	5.28	5.71	5.81	5.82	5.46	5.40	8.55	7.24
Return on Equity %	15.08	14.84	15.35	15.81	14.79	14.38	21.26	20.22
EBITDA Margin %	20.45	21.37	19.71	19.36	17.44	16.78	20.49	18.77
Net Margin %	8.63	8.88	7.67	9.71	9.04	8.19	11.93	9.86
Asset Turnover	0.58	0.61	0.60	0.60	0.60	0.66	0.72	0.73
Current Ratio	1.08	1.04	1.07	0.92	1.08	0.95	0.90	0.70
Debt to Equity	0.80	0.69	0.69	0.62	0.59	0.68	0.47	0.34
Price Range	65.21-40.29	65.21-48.16	65.21-51.45	65.21-51.45	58.83-38.15	51.32-36.09	53.00-42.35	52.64-35.59
P/E Ratio	24.24-14.98	23.29-17.20	22.03-17.38	21.96-17.32	21.79-14.13	21.47-15.10	15.27-12.20	18.80-12.71
Average Yield %	2.21	2.08	2.00	1.97	2.04	2.23	1.68	1.48

Address: 111 River Street, Hoboken, NJ 07030
Telephone: 201-748-6000

Web Site: www.wiley.com
Officers: Mathew S. Kissner - Chairman Mark J. Allin - President, Chief Executive Officer, Executive Vice President, Chief Operating Officer, Senior Vice President

Auditors: KPMG LLP
Investor Contact: 201-748-6874
Transfer Agents: Registrar and Transfer Company, Cranford, NJ

WILLIAMS COS INC (THE)

Exchange	Symbol	Price	52Wk Range	Yield	P/E	Div Achiever
NYS	WMB	$22.16 (5/31/2016)	60.86-11.16	11.55	N/A	12 Years

*7 Year Price Score 90.68   *NYSE Composite Index=100   *12 Month Price Score 56.47

Stock price chart 2007–2016 with TRADING VOLUME (thousand shares)

Interim Earnings (Per Share)

Qtr.	Mar	Jun	Sep	Dec
2013	0.23	0.21	0.20	(0.03)
2014	0.20	0.15	2.22	0.24
2015	0.09	0.15	(0.05)	(0.95)
2016	(0.09)	...		

Interim Dividends (Per Share)

Amt	Decl	Ex	Rec	Pay
0.64Q	09/11/2015	09/22/2015	09/24/2015	09/30/2015
0.64Q	11/19/2015	12/09/2015	12/11/2015	12/28/2015
0.64Q	03/03/2016	03/10/2016	03/14/2016	03/28/2016
0.64Q	06/08/2016	06/16/2016	06/20/2016	06/27/2016

Indicated Div: $2.56 (Div. Reinv. Plan)

Valuation Analysis

		Institutional Holding	
Forecast EPS	$0.71	No of Institutions	1005
	(05/20/2016)		
Market Cap	$16.6 Billion	Shares	690,963,072
Book Value	$5.7 Billion	% Held	98.22
Price/Book	2.92		
Price/Sales	2.28		

Business Summary: Equipment & Services (MIC: 9.1.3 SIC: 4922 NAIC: 486210)

Williams Companies is an energy infrastructure company focused on connecting North America's hydrocarbon resource plays to markets for natural gas, natural gas liquids, and olefins. Co.'s operations are located principally in the U.S., but span from the deepwater Gulf of Mexico to the Canadian oil sands. As of Dec 31 2015, Co.'s interstate gas pipelines, midstream, and olefins production interests were mainly held through its investments in Williams Partners L.P. Substantially all Co.'s operations are conducted through its subsidiaries. Co.'s business segments include Williams Partners, and Williams NGL & Petchem Services, and other, which include its Canadian construction services company.

Recent Developments: For the quarter ended Mar 31 2016, net loss was unchanged at US$13.0 million versus US$13.0 million the year-earlier quarter. Revenues were US$1.66 billion, down 3.3% from US$1.72 billion the year before. Operating income was US$262.0 million versus US$227.0 million in the prior-year quarter, an increase of 15.4%. Direct operating expenses declined 16.5% to US$709.0 million from US$849.0 million in the comparable period the year before. Indirect operating expenses increased 7.7% to US$689.0 million from US$640.0 million in the equivalent prior-year period.

Prospects: Our evaluation of Williams Cos Inc. as of June 19, 2016 is the result of our systematic analysis on three basic characteristics: earnings strength, relative valuation, and recent stock price movement. The company has generated a negative trend in earnings per share over the past 5 quarters and while recent estimates for the company have been raised by analysts, WMB has posted results that fell short of analysts expectations. Based on operating earnings yield, the company is about fairly valued when compared to all of the companies in our coverage universe. Share price changes over the past year indicates that WMB will perform very poorly over the near term.

Financial Data

(US$ in Thousands)	3 Mos	12/31/2015	12/31/2014	12/31/2013	12/31/2012	12/31/2011	12/31/2010	12/31/2009
Earnings Per Share	(0.94)	(0.76)	2.92	0.62	1.37	0.63	(1.88)	0.49
Cash Flow Per Share	3.72	3.57	2.94	3.25	2.95	5.84	4.54	4.42
Tang Book Value Per Share	N.M.	N.M.	N.M.	3.77	3.52	3.03	12.44	12.75
Dividends Per Share	2.510	2.450	1.958	1.438	1.196	0.775	0.485	0.440
Dividend Payout %	...	...	67.04	231.85	87.32	123.02	...	89.80
Income Statement								
Total Revenue	1,660,000	7,360,000	7,637,000	6,860,000	7,486,000	7,930,000	9,616,000	8,255,000
EBITDA	204,000	378,000	2,610,000	2,208,000	2,399,000	2,271,000	969,000	2,885,000
Depn & Amortn	21,000	1,382,000	967,000	752,000	712,000	658,000	1,500,000	1,500,000
Income Before Taxes	(108,000)	(2,048,000)	896,000	946,000	1,178,000	1,047,000	(1,109,000)	807,000
Income Taxes	2,000	(399,000)	1,249,000	401,000	360,000	124,000	(30,000)	359,000
Net Income	(65,000)	(571,000)	2,114,000	430,000	859,000	376,000	(1,097,000)	285,000
Average Shares	750,332	749,271	723,641	687,185	625,486	598,175	584,552	589,385
Balance Sheet								
Current Assets	1,261,000	1,527,000	1,890,000	1,683,000	1,924,000	1,894,000	2,530,000	3,793,000
Total Assets	48,807,000	49,020,000	50,563,000	27,142,000	24,327,000	16,502,000	24,972,000	25,280,000
Current Liabilities	2,789,000	2,497,000	2,567,000	1,983,000	1,549,000	1,675,000	2,574,000	2,477,000
Long-Term Obligations	23,701,000	23,812,000	20,888,000	11,353,000	10,735,000	8,369,000	8,600,000	8,259,000
Total Liabilities	43,116,000	42,872,000	41,786,000	22,278,000	19,575,000	14,709,000	17,684,000	16,833,000
Stockholders' Equity	5,691,000	6,148,000	8,777,000	4,864,000	4,752,000	1,793,000	7,288,000	8,447,000
Shares Outstanding	750,000	749,000	747,000	683,000	681,000	591,000	585,000	583,000
Statistical Record								
Return on Assets %	N.M.	N.M.	5.44	1.67	4.20	1.81	N.M.	1.11
Return on Equity %	N.M.	N.M.	30.99	8.94	26.18	8.28	N.M.	3.38
EBITDA Margin %	12.29	5.14	34.18	32.19	32.05	28.64	10.08	34.95
Net Margin %	N.M.	N.M.	27.68	6.27	11.47	4.74	N.M.	3.45
Asset Turnover	0.15	0.15	0.20	0.27	0.37	0.38	0.38	0.32
Current Ratio	0.45	0.61	0.74	0.85	1.24	1.13	0.98	1.53
Debt to Equity	4.16	3.87	2.38	2.33	2.26	4.67	1.18	0.98
Price Range	60.86-11.16	60.86-21.54	59.44-38.03	38.57-31.65	36.77-26.82	27.09-19.07	20.21-14.43	17.45-8.03
P/E Ratio	...	...	20.36-13.02	62.21-51.05	26.84-19.58	42.99-30.27	...	35.61-16.38
Average Yield %	6.50	5.37	4.00	4.05	3.79	3.26	2.79	3.33

Address: One Williams Center, Tulsa, OK 74172	Web Site: www.williams.com	Auditors: Ernst & Young LLP
Telephone: 918-573-2000	Officers: Alan S. Armstrong - President, Chief Executive Officer Donald R. Chappel - Senior Vice President, Chief Financial Officer	Transfer Agents: Computershare Trust Company, N.A., College Station, TX

WILLIAMS SONOMA INC

Exchange	Symbol	Price	52Wk Range	Yield	P/E
NYS	WSM	$53.04 (5/31/2016)	88.67-48.02	2.79	15.88

*7 Year Price Score 120.13 *NYSE Composite Index=100   ***12 Month Price Score 82.41**

Interim Earnings (Per Share)

Qtr.	Apr	Jul	Oct	Jan
2013-14	0.40	0.49	0.58	1.36
2014-15	0.48	0.53	0.68	1.55
2015-16	0.48	0.58	0.77	1.55
2016-17	0.44	...	...	...

Interim Dividends (Per Share)

Amt	Decl	Ex	Rec	Pay
0.35Q	09/18/2015	10/23/2015	10/27/2015	11/25/2015
0.35Q	12/18/2015	01/22/2016	01/26/2016	02/24/2016
0.37Q	03/16/2016	04/27/2016	04/29/2016	05/27/2016
0.37Q	06/17/2016	07/20/2016	07/22/2016	08/26/2016

Indicated Div: $1.48

Valuation Analysis   **Institutional Holding**

Forecast EPS	$3.59	No of Institutions	
	(05/20/2016)	518	
Market Cap	$4.7 Billion	Shares	
Book Value	$1.2 Billion	96,070,000	
Price/Book	4.08	% Held	
Price/Sales	0.94	81.18	

Business Summary: Retail - Furniture & Home Furnishings (MIC: 2.1.6 SIC: 5712 NAIC: 442110)

Williams-Sonoma is a retailer of products for the home. As of Jan 31 2016, the e-commerce channel had the following merchandising concepts: Williams-Sonoma, Pottery Barn, Pottery Barn Kids, West Elm, PBteen, Williams-Sonoma Home, Rejuvenation and Mark and Graham, which sell its products through its e-commerce websites and direct-mail catalogs. As of Jan 31 2016, Co. operated 618 stores comprising 571 stores in 43 states, Washington, D.C., and Puerto Rico, 27 stores in Canada, 19 stores in Australia and one store in the U.K. Co. also operates 48 franchised stores and/or e-commerce websites in a number of countries in the Middle East, the Philippines and Mexico.

Recent Developments: For the quarter ended May 1 2016, net income decreased 11.6% to US$39.6 million from US$44.8 million in the year-earlier quarter. Revenues were US$1.10 billion, up 6.5% from US$1.03 billion the year before. Operating income was US$63.5 million versus US$71.9 million in the prior-year quarter, a decrease of 11.7%. Direct operating expenses rose 8.2% to US$705.3 million from US$651.8 million in the comparable period the year before. Indirect operating expenses increased 7.2% to US$329.0 million from US$306.9 million in the equivalent prior-year period.

Prospects: Our evaluation of Williams-Sonoma Inc. as of June 19, 2016 is the result of our systematic analysis on three basic characteristics: earnings strength, relative valuation, and recent stock price movement. The company has managed to produce a neutral trend in earnings per share over the past 5 quarters and while recent estimates for the company have been raised by analysts, WSM has posted better than expected results. Based on operating earnings yield, the company is undervalued when compared to all of the companies in our coverage universe. Share price changes over the past year indicates that WSM will perform poorly over the near term.

Financial Data

(US$ in Thousands)	3 Mos	01/31/2016	02/01/2015	02/02/2014	02/03/2013	01/29/2012	01/30/2011	01/31/2010
Earnings Per Share	3.34	3.37	3.24	2.82	2.54	2.22	1.83	0.72
Cash Flow Per Share	6.03	6.01	4.94	4.71	3.61	2.80	3.34	4.65
Tang Book Value Per Share	13.01	13.38	13.33	13.35	13.39	12.50	12.00	11.33
Dividends Per Share	1.420	1.400	1.320	1.240	0.880	0.730	0.580	0.480
Dividend Payout %	42.51	41.54	40.74	43.97	34.65	32.88	31.69	66.67
Income Statement								
Total Revenue	1,097,817	4,976,090	4,698,719	4,387,889	4,042,870	3,720,895	3,504,158	3,102,704
EBITDA	57,538	631,673	640,119	576,511	516,922	484,738	430,929	236,439
Depn & Amortn	(5,987)	143,039	137,854	124,413	107,759	103,006	107,515	114,997
Income Before Taxes	63,593	488,007	502,203	452,682	409,956	381,830	323,060	120,289
Income Taxes	23,996	177,939	193,349	173,780	153,226	144,899	122,833	42,847
Net Income	39,597	310,068	308,854	278,902	256,730	236,931	200,227	77,442
Average Shares	90,514	92,102	95,200	98,765	101,051	106,582	109,522	107,373
Balance Sheet								
Current Assets	1,212,662	1,336,100	1,391,923	1,419,103	1,316,772	1,276,366	1,347,594	1,180,193
Total Assets	2,290,368	2,417,427	2,330,277	2,336,734	2,187,679	2,060,838	2,131,762	2,079,169
Current Liabilities	871,756	996,427	875,948	861,096	657,127	571,799	611,716	563,482
Long-Term Obligations	...	...	...	1,968	3,753	5,478	7,130	8,672
Total Liabilities	1,127,512	1,219,201	1,105,571	1,080,732	878,541	805,576	872,899	867,574
Stockholders' Equity	1,162,856	1,198,226	1,224,706	1,256,002	1,309,138	1,255,262	1,258,863	1,211,595
Shares Outstanding	89,350	89,563	91,891	94,049	97,734	100,451	104,888	106,962
Statistical Record								
Return on Assets %	13.43	13.10	13.27	12.36	11.89	11.33	9.54	3.87
Return on Equity %	25.95	25.66	24.97	21.81	19.70	18.90	16.25	6.58
EBITDA Margin %	5.24	12.69	13.62	13.14	12.79	13.03	12.30	7.62
Net Margin %	3.61	6.23	6.57	6.36	6.35	6.37	5.71	2.50
Asset Turnover	2.22	2.10	2.02	1.94	1.87	1.78	1.67	1.55
Current Ratio	1.39	1.34	1.59	1.65	2.00	2.23	2.20	2.09
Debt to Equity	...	...	...	N.M.	N.M.	N.M.	0.01	0.01
Price Range	88.67-48.99	88.67-48.99	80.94-52.85	61.33-43.96	47.93-33.06	45.24-28.81	36.09-18.93	23.23-7.55
P/E Ratio	26.55-14.67	26.31-14.54	24.98-16.31	21.75-15.59	18.87-13.02	20.38-12.98	19.72-10.34	32.26-10.49
Average Yield %	2.05	1.87	1.96	2.28	2.19	1.98	2.00	3.09

Address: 3250 Van Ness Avenue, San Francisco, CA 94109
Telephone: 415-421-7900
Fax: 415-434-0881

Web Site: www.williams-sonomainc.com
Officers: Adrian D.P. Bellamy - Chairman Laura J. Alber - President, Chief Executive Officer

Auditors: Deloitte & Touche LLP
Transfer Agents: Wilson Sonsini Goodrich & Rosati Professional Corporation, Palo Alto, CA

WORKDAY INC

Exchange	Symbol	Price	52Wk Range	Yield	P/E
NYS	WDAY	$75.84 (5/31/2016)	84.80-48.90	N/A	N/A

*7 Year Price Score N/A   ***NYSE Composite Index=100**   ***12 Month Price Score 99.75**

Interim Earnings (Per Share)

Qtr.	Apr	Jul	Oct	Jan
2013-14	(0.20)	(0.21)	(0.27)	(0.33)
2014-15	(0.32)	(0.38)	(0.33)	(0.32)
2015-16	(0.33)	(0.37)	(0.41)	(0.43)
2016-17	(0.41)			

Interim Dividends (Per Share)

No Dividends Paid

Valuation Analysis		Institutional Holding	
Forecast EPS	$0.03	No of Institutions	
	(05/20/2016)	365	
Market Cap	$14.9 Billion	Shares	
Book Value	$1.1 Billion	140,491,488	
Price/Book	13.24	% Held	
Price/Sales	11.89	56.91	

Business Summary: IT Services (MIC: 6.3.1 SIC: 7374 NAIC: 518210)

Workday is a provider of enterprise cloud applications for finance and human resources. Co.'s applications include: Workday Financial Management, a unified application built on a single core with a range of financial capabilities, analytics and metrics, and auditable process management built to help manage financial processes for organizations; Workday Human Capital Management, which allows an organization to staff, pay, organize, and develop its global workforce; and Workday Insight Applications, which is a suite of applications that utilize data science and machine learning methodologies to help customers make financial and workforce decisions.

Recent Developments: For the quarter ended Apr 30 2016, net loss amounted to US$80.6 million versus a net loss of US$61.6 million in the year-earlier quarter. Revenues were US$345.4 million, up 37.6% from US$251.0 million the year before. Operating loss was US$73.6 million versus a loss of US$53.4 million in the prior-year quarter. Direct operating expenses rose 39.4% to US$108.6 million from US$77.9 million in the comparable period the year before. Indirect operating expenses increased 37.1% to US$310.5 million from US$226.4 million in the equivalent prior-year period.

Prospects: Our evaluation of Workday Inc as of June 19, 2016 is the result of our systematic analysis on three basic characteristics: earnings strength, relative valuation, and recent stock price movement. The company has produced a positive trend in earnings per share over the past 5 quarters and while recent estimates for the company have been raised by analysts, WDAY has posted better than expected results. Based on operating earnings yield, the company is overvalued when compared to all of the companies in our coverage universe. Share price changes over the past year indicates that WDAY will perform poorly over the near term.

Financial Data
(US$ in Thousands)

	3 Mos	01/31/2016	01/31/2015	01/31/2014	01/31/2013	01/31/2012	01/31/2011	12/31/2010
Earnings Per Share	(1.62)	(1.53)	(1.35)	(1.01)	(1.62)	(2.71)	(0.20)	(2.22)
Cash Flow Per Share	1.68	1.36	0.56	0.27	0.15	(0.47)	(0.46)	(0.60)
Tang Book Value Per Share	5.38	5.49	5.77	6.40	3.51	...	...	...
Income Statement								
Total Revenue	345,430	1,162,346	787,860	468,938	273,657	134,427	7,282	68,055
EBITDA	(39,198)	(190,824)	(171,872)	(123,905)	(102,363)	(69,654)	(4,903)	(51,085)
Depn & Amortn	34,472	71,000	46,000	29,300	15,900	8,900	500	4,900
Income Before Taxes	(79,487)	(288,901)	(245,972)	(170,831)	(119,066)	(79,462)	(5,440)	(56,118)
Income Taxes	1,135	1,017	2,010	1,678	124	167	10	97
Net Income	(80,622)	(289,918)	(247,982)	(172,509)	(119,190)	(79,629)	(5,450)	(56,215)
Average Shares	194,529	190,016	183,702	171,297	74,011	29,478	27,642	25,367
Balance Sheet								
Current Assets	2,372,131	2,362,308	2,109,039	2,023,658	884,302	183,172	...	67,275
Total Assets	2,776,153	2,730,094	2,358,633	2,176,265	959,080	232,638	...	100,605
Current Liabilities	970,252	922,679	641,265	421,890	254,774	145,238	...	71,340
Long-Term Obligations	514,075	507,476	490,501	472,001	12,972	8,641	...	2,495
Total Liabilities	1,647,997	1,593,937	1,232,658	989,048	366,797	237,293	...	122,689
Stockholders' Equity	1,128,156	1,136,157	1,125,975	1,187,217	592,283	(4,655)	...	(22,084)
Shares Outstanding	197,000	194,479	188,416	183,406	166,424	35,924	28,065	27,555
Statistical Record								
Asset Turnover	0.49	0.46	0.35	0.30	0.46	...	...	...
Current Ratio	2.44	2.56	3.29	4.80	3.47	1.26	...	0.94
Debt to Equity	0.46	0.45	0.44	0.40	0.02	...	...	...
Price Range	92.49-48.90	93.94-62.03	115.47-67.06	94.00-50.44	56.50-46.99	...	...	...

Address: 6230 Stoneridge Mall Road, Pleasanton, CA 94588 **Telephone:** 925-951-9000	**Web Site:** www.workday.com **Officers:** David A. Duffield - Chairman, Co-Chief Executive Officer Michael A. Stankey - Vice-Chairman, President, Chief Operating Officer	**Auditors:** Ernst & Young LLP **Investor Contact:** 925-951-9005 **Transfer Agents:** American Stock Transfer & Trust Co., New York, NY

WORLD FUEL SERVICES CORP.

Exchange	Symbol	Price	52Wk Range	Yield	P/E
NYS	INT	$45.97 (5/31/2016)	50.79-34.44	0.52	17.55

*7 Year Price Score 96.18   ***NYSE Composite Index=100**   ***12 Month Price Score 108.05**

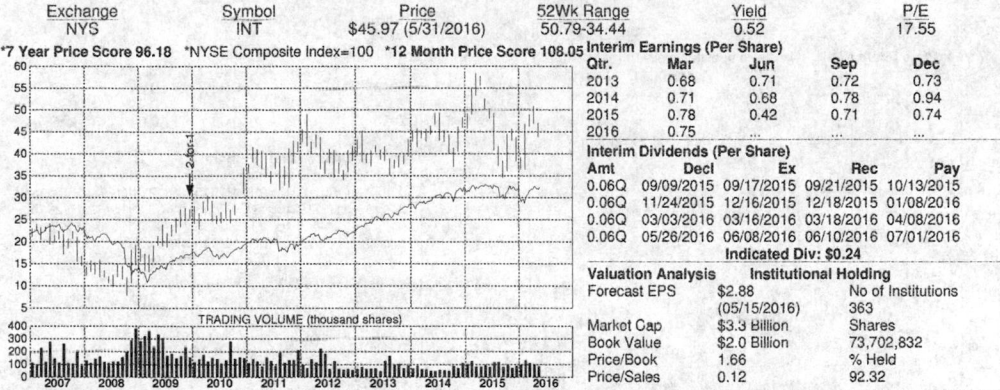

Interim Earnings (Per Share)

Qtr.	Mar	Jun	Sep	Dec
2013	0.68	0.71	0.72	0.73
2014	0.71	0.68	0.78	0.94
2015	0.78	0.42	0.71	0.74
2016	0.75	...	...	...

Interim Dividends (Per Share)

Amt	Decl	Ex	Rec	Pay
0.06Q	09/09/2015	09/17/2015	09/21/2015	10/13/2015
0.06Q	11/24/2015	12/16/2015	12/18/2015	01/08/2016
0.06Q	03/03/2016	03/16/2016	03/18/2016	04/08/2016
0.06Q	05/26/2016	06/08/2016	06/10/2016	07/01/2016

Indicated Div: $0.24

Valuation Analysis

		Institutional Holding	
Forecast EPS	$2.88	No of Institutions	
	(05/15/2016)	363	
Market Cap	$3.3 Billion	Shares	
Book Value	$2.0 Billion	73,702,832	
Price/Book	1.66	% Held	
Price/Sales	0.12	92.32	

Business Summary: Equipment & Services (MIC: 9.1.3 SIC: 5172 NAIC: 424720)

World Fuel Services is a fuel logistics, transaction management and payment processing company, which provides energy management solutions to the aviation, marine and land transportation industries. Co. primarily contracts with third parties for the delivery and storage of fuel products, however, Co. also operates storage facilities and transportation assets. Co. operates in three reportable segments: aviation, which provides fuel and related products and services; marine, which include fuel, lubricants and related products and services to a base of customers; and land, which provides fuel, crude oil, lubricants, natural gas and related products and services to customers.

Recent Developments: For the quarter ended Mar 31 2016, net income decreased 4.2% to US$52.3 million from US$54.6 million in the year-earlier quarter. Revenues were US$5.19 billion, down 29.3% from US$7.34 billion the year before. Operating income was US$63.3 million versus US$71.5 million in the prior-year quarter, a decrease of 11.5%. Direct operating expenses declined 30.3% to US$4.97 billion from US$7.13 billion in the comparable period the year before. Indirect operating expenses increased 11.5% to US$160.5 million from US$143.9 million in the equivalent prior-year period.

Prospects: Our evaluation of World Fuel Services Corp. as of June 19, 2016 is the result of our systematic analysis on three basic characteristics: earnings strength, relative valuation, and recent stock price movement. The company has enjoyed a very positive trend in earnings per share over the past 5 quarters and while recent estimates for the company have remained steady, INT has posted results that were in line with analysts expectations. Based on operating earnings yield, the company is undervalued when compared to all of the companies in our coverage universe. Share price changes over the past year indicates that INT will perform well over the near term.

Financial Data

(US$ in Thousands)	3 Mos	12/31/2015	12/31/2014	12/31/2013	12/31/2012	12/31/2011	12/31/2010	12/31/2009
Earnings Per Share	2.62	2.64	3.11	2.83	2.64	2.71	2.31	1.96
Cash Flow Per Share	6.89	6.37	2.00	3.71	2.04	(2.02)	(0.57)	1.32
Tang Book Value Per Share	18.07	12.41	11.83	12.24	12.12	12.35	10.37	8.53
Dividends Per Share	0.240	0.240	0.150	0.150	0.150	0.150	0.150	0.150
Dividend Payout %	9.16	9.09	4.82	5.30	5.68	5.54	6.49	7.65
Income Statement								
Total Revenue	5,192,600	30,379,700	43,386,389	41,561,947	38,945,338	34,622,854	19,131,147	11,295,177
EBITDA	83,100	284,300	325,088	285,952	277,292	269,528	201,381	170,528
Depn & Amortn	18,400	35,100	30,300	22,000	18,600	15,500	19,106	16,956
Income Before Taxes	57,100	219,300	269,551	246,665	239,595	238,203	177,530	149,909
Income Taxes	4,800	36,300	51,144	39,505	38,244	39,001	31,027	32,346
Net Income	52,400	186,900	221,747	203,075	189,345	194,029	146,865	117,139
Average Shares	70,000	70,700	71,323	71,800	71,817	71,510	63,441	59,901
Balance Sheet								
Current Assets	3,110,600	3,254,600	3,674,843	3,815,501	3,281,377	3,122,227	2,067,867	1,463,978
Total Assets	4,419,700	4,549,400	4,879,980	4,739,277	4,107,751	3,697,246	2,566,450	1,741,228
Current Liabilities	1,555,000	1,762,800	2,241,354	2,514,515	2,149,298	2,026,142	1,358,484	947,742
Long-Term Obligations	776,500	746,700	671,954	449,064	354,253	269,348	24,566	9,925
Total Liabilities	2,457,700	2,638,000	3,024,622	3,065,379	2,590,577	2,364,285	1,439,242	1,008,207
Stockholders' Equity	1,962,000	1,911,400	1,855,358	1,673,898	1,517,174	1,332,961	1,127,208	733,021
Shares Outstanding	70,900	70,788	72,082	71,883	72,147	71,154	69,602	59,385
Statistical Record								
Return on Assets %	3.99	3.96	4.61	4.59	4.84	6.20	6.82	7.45
Return on Equity %	9.58	9.92	12.57	12.73	13.25	15.77	15.79	17.47
EBITDA Margin %	1.60	0.94	0.75	0.69	0.71	0.78	1.05	1.51
Net Margin %	1.01	0.62	0.51	0.49	0.49	0.56	0.77	1.04
Asset Turnover	6.13	6.44	9.02	9.40	9.95	11.06	8.88	7.18
Current Ratio	2.00	1.85	1.64	1.52	1.53	1.54	1.52	1.54
Debt to Equity	0.40	0.39	0.36	0.27	0.23	0.20	0.02	0.01
Price Range	57.72-34.44	58.28-34.44	49.24-36.87	45.11-35.00	48.94-34.00	42.87-31.65	36.70-22.68	27.58-13.07
P/E Ratio	22.03-13.15	22.08-13.05	15.83-11.86	15.94-12.37	18.54-12.88	15.82-11.68	15.89-9.82	14.07-6.67
Average Yield %	0.54	0.51	0.34	0.38	0.38	0.40	0.55	0.72

Address: 9800 N.W. 41st Street, Miami, FL 33178	**Web Site:** www.wfscorp.com	**Auditors:** PricewaterhouseCoopers LLP
Telephone: 305-428-8000	**Officers:** Michael J. Kasbar - Chairman, President, Chief Operating Officer, Chief Executive Officer Ira M. Birns - Executive Vice President, Chief Financial Officer, Acting Principal Accounting Officer	**Investor Contact:** 305-428-8000
Fax: 305-392-5621		**Transfer Agents:** Wells Fargo Shareowner Services, St. Paul, MN

WP GLIMCHER INC

Exchange	Symbol	Price	52Wk Range	Yield	P/E
NYS	WPG	$10.22 (5/31/2016)	14.31-7.41	9.78	N/A

*7 Year Price Score N/A *NYSE Composite Index=100 *12 Month Price Score 90.53

TRADING VOLUME (thousand shares)

Interim Earnings (Per Share)

Qtr.	Mar	Jun	Sep	Dec
2013	0.30	0.22	0.21	0.27
2014	0.22	0.45	0.21	0.22
2015	(0.07)	0.02	0.02	(0.53)
2016	0.05	...	...	...

Interim Dividends (Per Share)

Amt	Decl	Ex	Rec	Pay
0.25Q	08/03/2015	08/31/2015	09/02/2015	09/15/2015
0.25Q	11/02/2015	11/30/2015	12/02/2015	12/15/2015
0.25Q	02/25/2016	03/03/2016	03/07/2016	03/15/2016
0.25Q	05/17/2016	06/01/2016	06/03/2016	06/15/2016

Indicated Div: $1.00

Valuation Analysis

		Institutional Holding	
Forecast EPS	$0.33	No of Institutions	
	(05/17/2016)	322	
Market Cap	$1.9 Billion	Shares	
Book Value	$1.2 Billion	170,197,088	
Price/Book	1.62	% Held	
Price/Sales	2.12	N/A	

Business Summary: REITs (MIC: 5.3.1 SIC: 6798 NAIC: 525930)

WP Glimcher operates as a self-administered and self-managed real estate investment trust. Washington Prime Group, L.P. is Co.'s majority-owned partnership subsidiary that owns, through its affiliates, all of Co.'s real estate properties and other assets. Co. owns, develops and manages retail real estate properties. As of Dec 31 2015, Co. had interests in 121 shopping centers in the U.S., consisting of community centers and malls.

Recent Developments: For the quarter ended Mar 31 2016, income from continuing operations was US$15.9 million compared with a loss of US$9.6 million in the year-earlier quarter. Net income amounted to US$13.7 million versus a net loss of US$9.6 million in the year-earlier quarter. Revenues were US$210.0 million, down 11.6% from US$237.7 million the year before. Revenues from property income fell 12.4% to US$204.5 million from US$233.4 million in the corresponding quarter a year earlier.

Prospects: Our evaluation of WP Glimcher Inc. as of June 19, 2016 is the result of our systematic analysis on three basic characteristics: earnings strength, relative valuation, and recent stock price movement. The company has enjoyed a very positive trend in earnings per share over the past 5 quarters. However, while recent estimates for the company have been mixed, WPG has posted results that fell short of analysts' expectations. Based on operating earnings yield, the company is about fairly valued when compared to all of the companies in our coverage universe. Share price changes over the past year indicates that WPG will perform very poorly over the near term.

Financial Data
(US$ in Thousands)

	3 Mos	12/31/2015	12/31/2014	12/31/2013	12/31/2012
Earnings Per Share	(0.44)	(0.55)	1.10	1.00	0.84
Cash Flow Per Share	1.72	1.69	1.79	2.17	2.26
Tang Book Value Per Share	5.20	5.47	5.09	...	...
Dividends Per Share	1.000	1.000	0.500	...	...
Dividend Payout %	...	...	45.45	...	...
Income Statement					
Total Revenue	210,031	921,656	661,126	626,289	623,927
EBITDA	124,776	366,949	485,868	425,443	403,921
Depn & Amortn	70,377	329,895	198,934	184,467	189,715
Income Before Taxes	17,051	(102,875)	204,482	185,918	155,362
Net Income	12,022	(85,297)	170,029	155,481	129,731
Average Shares	220,269	218,408	187,490	186,738	186,738
Balance Sheet					
Current Assets	178,948	207,856	178,384	86,978	...
Total Assets	5,364,794	5,479,484	3,528,003	3,002,658	...
Current Liabilities	379,349	383,995	209,312	192,324	...
Long-Term Obligations	3,630,073	3,668,476	2,348,864	918,614	...
Total Liabilities	4,198,898	4,263,490	2,738,952	1,437,489	...
Stockholders' Equity	1,165,896	1,215,994	789,051	1,565,169	...
Shares Outstanding	185,309	185,304	155,162	...	...
Statistical Record					
Return on Assets %	N.M.	N.M.	5.21	...	...
Return on Equity %	N.M.	N.M.	14.44	...	...
EBITDA Margin %	59.41	39.81	73.49	67.93	64.74
Net Margin %	5.72	N.M.	25.72	24.83	20.79
Asset Turnover	0.14	0.20	0.20	...	...
Current Ratio	0.47	0.54	0.85	0.45	...
Debt to Equity	3.11	3.02	2.98	0.59	...
Price Range	16.63-7.41	18.18-9.91	20.60-16.20	...	...
P/E Ratio	...	...	18.73-14.73	...	...
Average Yield %	8.33	7.15	2.75	...	...

Address: 180 East Broad Street, Columbus, OH 43215
Telephone: 614-621-9000

Web Site: www.wpglimcher.com
Officers: Michael P. Glimcher - Vice-Chairman, Chief Executive Officer Keric M. Knerr - Executive Vice President, Chief Operating Officer

Auditors: Ernst & Young LLP

WORTHINGTON INDUSTRIES, INC.

Exchange	Symbol	Price	52Wk Range	Yield	P/E
NYS	WOR	$37.36 (5/31/2016)	38.26-21.88	2.03	21.60

*7 Year Price Score 102.05 *NYSE Composite Index=100 *12 Month Price Score 119.72

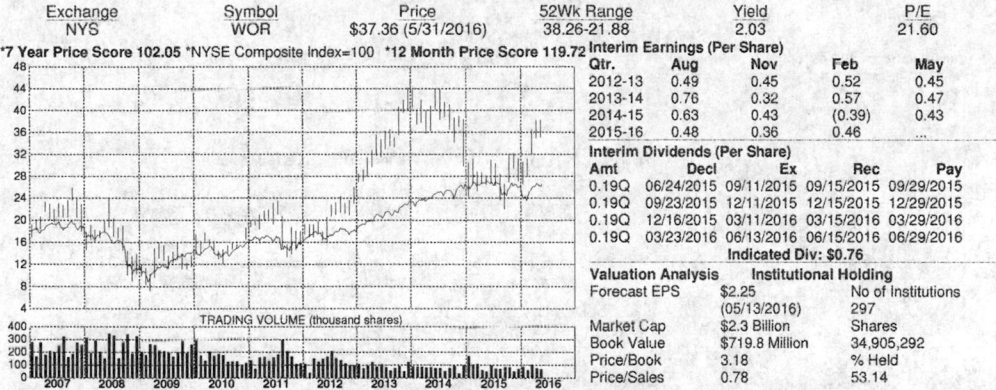

Interim Earnings (Per Share)

Qtr.	Aug	Nov	Feb	May
2012-13	0.49	0.45	0.52	0.45
2013-14	0.76	0.32	0.57	0.47
2014-15	0.63	0.43	(0.39)	0.43
2015-16	0.48	0.36	0.46	...

Interim Dividends (Per Share)

Amt	Decl	Ex	Rec	Pay
0.19Q	06/24/2015	09/11/2015	09/15/2015	09/29/2015
0.19Q	09/23/2015	12/11/2015	12/15/2015	12/29/2015
0.19Q	12/16/2015	03/11/2016	03/15/2016	03/29/2016
0.19Q	03/23/2016	06/13/2016	06/15/2016	06/29/2016

Indicated Div: $0.76

Valuation Analysis

		Institutional Holding	
Forecast EPS	$2.25	No of Institutions	297
	(05/13/2016)		
Market Cap	$2.3 Billion	Shares	34,905,292
Book Value	$719.8 Million	% Held	53.14
Price/Book	3.18		
Price/Sales	0.78		

Business Summary: Non-Precious Metals (MIC: 8.2.2 SIC: 3312 NAIC: 331111)

Worthington Industries is a metals manufacturing company, focused on steel processing and manufactured metal products. Co. operates three segments: Steel Processing, which buys coils of steel from steel mills and mini-mills and processes them to customer specifications; Pressure Cylinders, which manufactures and sells filled and unfilled pressure cylinders, tanks, hand torches, and oil and gas equipment with accessories and related products for end-use market applications; and Engineered Cabs, which designs and manufactures open and enclosed cabs and operator stations and custom fabrications for mobile equipment, and provides complementary products such as machined structural components.

Recent Developments: For the quarter ended Feb 29 2016, net income amounted to US$33.9 million versus a net loss of US$23.2 million in the year-earlier quarter. Revenues were US$647.1 million, down 19.6% from US$804.8 million the year before. Operating income was US$25.1 million versus a loss of US$52.1 million in the prior-year quarter. Direct operating expenses declined 22.0% to US$551.2 million from US$706.3 million in the comparable period the year before. Indirect operating expenses decreased 52.9% to US$70.9 million from US$150.5 million in the equivalent prior-year period.

Prospects: Our evaluation of Worthington Industries Inc. as of June 19, 2016 is the result of our systematic analysis on three basic characteristics: earnings strength, relative valuation, and recent stock price movement. The company has enjoyed a very positive trend in earnings per share over the past 5 quarters and while recent estimates for the company have been mixed, WOR has posted results that fell short of analysts expectations. Based on operating earnings yield, the company is undervalued when compared to all of the companies in our coverage universe. Share price changes over the past year indicates that WOR will perform well over the near term.

Financial Data

(US$ in Thousands)	9 Mos	6 Mos	3 Mos	05/31/2015	05/31/2014	05/31/2013	05/31/2012	05/31/2011
Earnings Per Share	1.73	0.88	0.95	1.12	2.11	1.91	1.65	1.53
Cash Flow Per Share	5.97	5.52	4.64	3.23	3.32	3.94	2.49	0.96
Tang Book Value Per Share	6.22	6.18	6.24	6.10	6.73	6.74	6.48	8.04
Dividends Per Share	0.740	0.730	0.720	0.690	0.450	0.640	0.460	0.400
Dividend Payout %	42.77	82.95	75.79	61.61	21.33	33.51	27.88	26.14
Income Statement								
Total Revenue	2,105,043	1,457,963	758,147	3,384,234	3,126,426	2,612,244	2,534,701	2,442,624
EBITDA	134,511	85,373	51,858	126,018	215,060	186,596	154,573	182,718
Depn & Amortn	62,748	41,987	21,440	64,666	62,344	56,002	50,644	57,765
Income Before Taxes	48,224	27,733	22,564	25,552	126,045	106,676	84,432	106,197
Income Taxes	35,121	23,508	14,708	25,772	57,349	64,465	51,904	58,496
Net Income	84,227	54,651	31,410	76,785	151,300	136,442	115,595	115,066
Average Shares	63,727	64,527	65,729	68,483	71,664	71,314	70,252	75,409
Balance Sheet								
Current Assets	847,658	871,896	934,836	992,193	1,198,922	866,883	914,239	891,635
Total Assets	1,959,928	1,961,005	2,045,910	2,085,142	2,296,381	1,950,857	1,877,797	1,667,249
Current Liabilities	427,648	451,770	495,439	524,392	589,663	448,914	658,263	525,002
Long-Term Obligations	579,515	579,016	580,901	579,352	554,790	406,236	257,462	250,254
Total Liabilities	1,240,152	1,247,999	1,296,026	1,336,030	1,445,569	1,120,035	1,180,623	977,339
Stockholders' Equity	719,776	713,006	749,884	749,112	850,812	830,822	697,174	689,910
Shares Outstanding	61,285	62,101	63,343	64,141	67,408	69,752	67,906	71,683
Statistical Record								
Return on Assets %	5.41	2.71	2.91	3.50	7.12	7.13	6.50	7.22
Return on Equity %	15.28	7.29	7.93	9.60	17.99	17.86	16.62	16.42
EBITDA Margin %	6.39	5.86	6.84	3.72	6.88	7.14	6.10	7.48
Net Margin %	4.00	3.75	4.14	2.27	4.84	5.22	4.56	4.71
Asset Turnover	1.41	1.46	1.49	1.54	1.47	1.36	1.43	1.53
Current Ratio	1.98	1.93	1.89	1.89	2.03	1.93	1.39	1.70
Debt to Equity	0.81	0.81	0.77	0.77	0.65	0.49	0.37	0.36
Price Range	32.14-21.88	38.36-21.88	40.99-23.52	43.85-24.18	44.05-31.35	35.59-15.88	23.45-13.21	21.83-12.05
P/E Ratio	18.58-12.65	43.59-24.86	43.15-24.76	39.15-21.59	20.88-14.86	18.63-8.31	14.21-8.01	14.27-7.88
Average Yield %	2.64	2.57	2.34	2.02	1.19	2.54	2.59	2.34

Address: 200 Old Wilson Bridge Road, Columbus, OH 43085	**Web Site:** www.worthingtonindustries.com	**Auditors:** KPMG LLP
Telephone: 614-438-3210	**Officers:** John P. McConnell - Chairman, Chief Executive Officer Mark A. Russell - President, Chief Operating Officer	**Investor Contact:** 614-438-3077
Fax: 614-438-3256		**Transfer Agents:** Wells Fargo Shareowner Services, Saint Paul, MN

W.P. CAREY INC

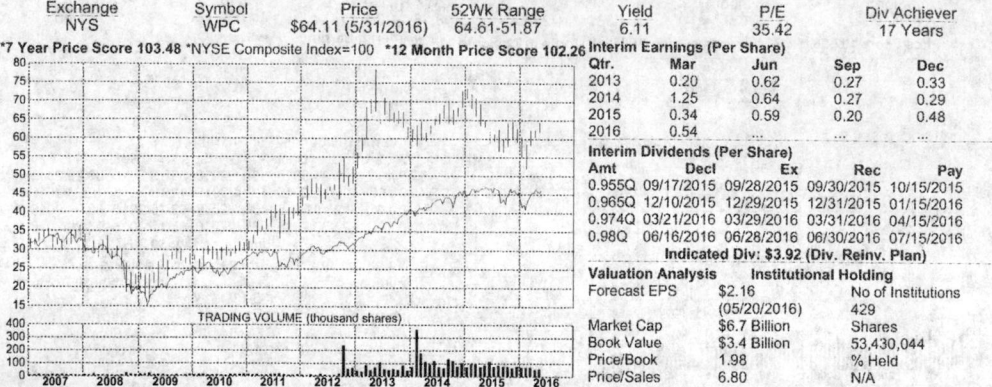

Exchange	Symbol	Price	52Wk Range	Yield	P/E	Div Achiever
NYS	WPC	$64.11 (5/31/2016)	64.61-51.87	6.11	35.42	17 Years

*7 Year Price Score 103.48 *NYSE Composite Index=100 *12 Month Price Score 102.26

Interim Earnings (Per Share)

Qtr.	Mar	Jun	Sep	Dec
2013	0.20	0.62	0.27	0.33
2014	1.25	0.64	0.27	0.29
2015	0.34	0.59	0.20	0.48
2016	0.54	...	...	...

Interim Dividends (Per Share)

Amt	Decl	Ex	Rec	Pay
0.955Q	09/17/2015	09/28/2015	09/30/2015	10/15/2015
0.965Q	12/10/2015	12/29/2015	12/31/2015	01/15/2016
0.974Q	03/21/2016	03/29/2016	03/31/2016	04/15/2016
0.98Q	06/16/2016	06/28/2016	06/30/2016	07/15/2016

Indicated Div: $3.92 (Div. Reinv. Plan)

Valuation Analysis

		Institutional Holding	
Forecast EPS	$2.16	No of Institutions	
	(05/20/2016)	429	
Market Cap	$6.7 Billion	Shares	
Book Value	$3.4 Billion	53,430,044	
Price/Book	1.98	% Held	
Price/Sales	6.80	N/A	

Business Summary: REITs (MIC: 5.3.1 SIC: 6798 NAIC: 525930)

W. P. Carey owns and manages commercial real estate, primarily net leased to companies on a long-term basis. Co.'s owned real estate portfolio is comprised primarily of single-tenant, office, industrial, warehouse/distribution, and retail facilities. In addition to managing its owned real estate portfolio, Co. acts as the advisor to publicly-owned, non-traded REITs for which it raises equity capital through public offerings of their shares, invests those funds and manages their assets. Co.'s business operates in two segments: real estate ownership and investment management. At Dec 31 2014, Co.'s portfolio had 783 net-leased properties, two self-storage properties, and two hotels.

Recent Developments: For the quarter ended Mar 31 2016, income from continuing operations increased 61.0% to US$60.2 million from US$37.4 million in the year-earlier quarter. Net income increased 57.8% to US$60.9 million from US$38.6 million in the year-earlier quarter. Revenues were US$270.2 million, up 22.6% from US$220.4 million the year before. Revenues from property income rose 25.3% to US$221.0 million from US$176.4 million in the corresponding quarter a year earlier.

Prospects: Our evaluation of W.P.Carey Inc. as of June 19, 2016 is the result of our systematic analysis on three basic characteristics: earnings strength, relative valuation, and recent stock price movement. The company has managed to produce a neutral trend in earnings per share over the past 5 quarters. Because the company lacks sufficient analyst estimate data, we place greater weight on the historical EPS trend as the measure of earnings strength. Based on operating earnings yield, the company is about fairly valued when compared to all of the companies in our coverage universe. Share price changes over the past year indicates that WPC will perform in line with the market over the near term.

Financial Data

(US$ in Thousands)	3 Mos	12/31/2015	12/31/2014	12/31/2013	12/31/2012	12/31/2011	12/31/2010	12/31/2009
Earnings Per Share	1.81	1.61	2.39	1.41	1.28	3.42	1.86	1.74
Cash Flow Per Share	4.94	4.52	4.04	3.03	1.70	2.01	2.19	1.91
Tang Book Value Per Share	13.36	13.09	14.82	12.38	14.03	14.01	13.62	13.79
Dividends Per Share	3.848	3.826	3.685	3.500	2.442	2.190	2.030	2.000
Dividend Payout %	212.59	237.65	154.18	248.23	190.78	64.04	109.14	114.94
Income Statement								
Total Revenue	270,240	938,383	906,193	489,851	373,995	336,409	273,910	235,876
EBITDA	57,802	663,573	655,391	297,355	121,448	170,632	113,818	107,754
Depn & Amortn	(36,309)	303,906	292,606	152,213	48,509	23,325	24,443	24,476
Income Before Taxes	45,716	165,341	184,663	42,506	23,762	127,388	74,409	69,803
Income Taxes	525	37,621	17,609	1,252	6,783	37,228	25,822	22,793
Net Income	57,439	172,258	239,826	98,876	62,132	139,079	73,972	69,023
Average Shares	106,405	106,507	99,827	69,708	48,078	40,098	40,007	39,712
Balance Sheet								
Current Assets	328,612	219,445	233,160	149,553	159,906	67,666	103,486	54,448
Total Assets	8,703,251	8,754,673	8,637,328	4,678,950	4,609,042	1,462,623	1,172,326	1,093,336
Current Liabilities	518,197	445,089	393,924	273,171	335,791	149,152	102,324	126,906
Long-Term Obligations	4,563,664	4,492,793	4,088,546	2,067,410	1,968,397	589,369	396,982	326,330
Total Liabilities	5,305,247	5,327,430	4,886,439	2,774,535	2,581,896	780,042	547,313	467,703
Stockholders' Equity	3,398,004	3,427,243	3,750,889	1,904,415	2,027,146	682,581	625,013	625,633
Shares Outstanding	104,866	104,448	104,040	68,266	68,485	39,729	39,454	39,204
Statistical Record								
Return on Assets %	2.22	1.98	3.60	2.13	2.04	10.56	6.53	6.26
Return on Equity %	5.55	4.80	8.48	5.03	4.57	21.27	11.83	10.84
EBITDA Margin %	21.39	70.71	72.32	60.70	32.47	50.72	41.55	45.68
Net Margin %	21.25	18.36	26.47	20.18	16.61	41.34	27.01	29.26
Asset Turnover	0.11	0.11	0.14	0.11	0.12	0.26	0.24	0.21
Current Ratio	0.63	0.49	0.59	0.55	0.48	0.45	1.01	0.43
Debt to Equity	1.34	1.31	1.09	1.09	0.97	0.86	0.64	0.52
Price Range	69.33-51.87	73.58-56.23	72.84-57.87	78.58-51.89	54.70-41.65	44.34-29.85	31.96-25.00	30.27-17.00
P/E Ratio	38.30-28.66	45.70-34.93	30.48-24.21	55.73-36.80	42.73-32.54	12.96-8.73	17.18-13.44	17.40-9.77
Average Yield %	6.34	6.02	5.71	5.39	5.07	5.91	7.02	7.91

Address: 50 Rockefeller Plaza, New York, NY 10020 **Telephone:** 212-492-1100	**Web Site:** www.wpcarey.com **Officers:** Polk Carey - Chairman Mark J. DeCesaris - Chief Executive Officer, Chief Financial Officer, Acting Chief Financial Officer, Chief Administrative Officer, Managing Director	**Auditors:** PricewaterhouseCoopers LLP **Investor Contact:** 212-492-8920 **Transfer Agents:** Computershare Shareowner Services, LLC, Pittsburgh, PA

WPX ENERGY, INC.

Exchange	Symbol	Price	52Wk Range	Yield	P/E
NYS	WPX	$10.29 (5/31/2016)	13.40-3.56	N/A	N/A

*7 Year Price Score N/A *NYSE Composite Index=100 *12 Month Price Score 111.49

Interim Earnings (Per Share)

Qtr.	Mar	Jun	Sep	Dec
2013	(0.58)	0.09	(0.57)	(4.85)
2014	0.09	(0.66)	0.30	1.07
2015	0.32	(0.14)	(0.93)	(6.53)
2016	(0.06)	...	...	...

Interim Dividends (Per Share)

No Dividends Paid

Valuation Analysis — **Institutional Holding**

Forecast EPS	$-0.68	No of Institutions
	(05/20/2016)	409
Market Cap	$2.8 Billion	Shares
Book Value	$3.5 Billion	271,035,232
Price/Book	0.81	% Held
Price/Sales	1.86	93.73

TRADING VOLUME (thousand shares)

Business Summary: Production & Extraction (MIC: 9.1.1 SIC: 1311 NAIC: 211111)

WPX Energy is an independent oil and natural gas exploration and production company engaged in the exploitation and development of properties. Co. is focused on exploiting, developing and growing its oil positions in the Williston Basin in North Dakota and the Permian and San Juan Basins in the southwestern U. S. Co.'s activity in the Delaware Basin is primarily focused on the Bone Spring interval (which includes the Avalon sand and shales, and the Bone Springs sands, shales and carbonates), the shallower Delaware sand interval, and the Wolfcamp Shale formation. Co.'s proved reserves at Dec 31 2015 were 583.0 million barrels of oil equivalents.

Recent Developments: For the quarter ended Mar 31 2016, income from continuing operations decreased 100.0% to nil from US$52.0 million in the year-earlier quarter. Net loss amounted to US$12.0 million versus net income of US$68.0 million in the year-earlier quarter. Revenues were US$216.0 million, down 48.6% from US$420.0 million the year before. Operating income was US$90.0 million versus US$113.0 million in the prior-year quarter, a decrease of 20.4%. Indirect operating expenses decreased 59.0% to US$126.0 million from US$307.0 million in the equivalent prior-year period.

Prospects: Our evaluation of WPX Energy Inc. as of June 19, 2016 is the result of our systematic analysis on three basic characteristics: earnings strength, relative valuation, and recent stock price movement. The company has managed to produce a neutral trend in earnings per share over the past 5 quarters. Because the company lacks sufficient analyst estimate data, we place greater weight on the historical EPS trend as the measure of earnings strength. Based on operating earnings yield, the company is overvalued when compared to all of the companies in our coverage universe. Share price changes over the past year indicates that WPX will perform very poorly over the near term.

Financial Data
(US$ in Millions)

	3 Mos	12/31/2015	12/31/2014	12/31/2013	12/31/2012	12/31/2011	12/31/2010	12/31/2009
Earnings Per Share	(7.66)	(7.42)	0.80	(5.91)	(1.12)	(1.53)	(6.55)	0.68
Cash Flow Per Share	2.29	3.46	5.28	3.17	3.98	6.12	5.36	5.97
Tang Book Value Per Share	11.48	11.60	21.20	20.44	26.43	28.82	...	...
Income Statement								
Total Revenue	216	1,888	3,493	2,761	3,189	3,988	4,034	3,681
EBITDA	99	(1,392)	1,226	(794)	721	623	(454)	1,201
Depn & Amortn	7	975	899	972	1,001	956	882	894
Income Before Taxes	35	(2,554)	204	(1,869)	(374)	(441)	(1,444)	225
Income Taxes	35	(915)	75	(655)	(111)	(145)	(149)	96
Net Income	(12)	(1,727)	164	(1,185)	(223)	(302)	(1,291)	134
Average Shares	276	234	206	200	198	197	197	197
Balance Sheet								
Current Assets	1,563	850	1,869	922	772	1,674	958	...
Total Assets	8,140	8,350	8,798	8,429	9,456	10,432	9,846	...
Current Liabilities	1,029	690	1,209	1,007	726	1,156	3,167	...
Long-Term Obligations	2,746	3,189	2,280	1,916	1,508	1,503	...	...
Total Liabilities	4,625	4,815	4,479	4,320	4,188	4,754	5,434	...
Stockholders' Equity	3,515	3,535	4,319	4,109	5,268	5,678	4,412	...
Shares Outstanding	276	275	203	201	199	197	...	...
Statistical Record								
Return on Assets %	N.M.	N.M.	1.90	N.M.	N.M.	N.M.	...	...
Return on Equity %	N.M.	N.M.	3.89	N.M.	N.M.	N.M.	...	...
EBITDA Margin %	45.83	N.M.	35.10	N.M.	22.61	15.62	N.M.	32.63
Net Margin %	N.M.	N.M.	4.70	N.M.	N.M.	N.M.	N.M.	3.64
Asset Turnover	0.19	0.22	0.41	0.31	0.32	0.39	...	...
Current Ratio	1.52	1.23	1.55	0.92	1.06	1.45	0.30	...
Debt to Equity	0.78	0.90	0.53	0.47	0.29	0.26	...	...
Price Range	14.55-3.56	14.55-5.16	26.62-10.27	23.45-14.19	19.67-13.37	...	...	...
P/E Ratio	...	...	33.27-12.84	...	...	...	...	...

Address: 3500 One Williams Center, Tulsa, OK 74172-0172	**Web Site:** www.wpxenergy.com	**Auditors:** Ernst &Young LLP
Telephone: 855-979 2012	**Officers:** William G. Lowrie - Chairman Richard E. Muncrief - President, Chief Executive Officer	**Investor Contact:** 539-573-9360
		Transfer Agents: Computershare Trust Company, N.A., Canton, MA

WYNDHAM WORLDWIDE CORP

Exchange	Symbol	Price	52Wk Range	Yield	P/E
NYS	WYN	$67.39 (5/31/2016)	87.29-61.63	2.97	13.51

*7 Year Price Score 123.45 *NYSE Composite Index=100 *12 Month Price Score 93.76

Interim Earnings (Per Share)

Qtr.	Mar	Jun	Sep	Dec
2013	0.19	0.98	1.40	0.66
2014	0.69	1.20	1.64	0.67
2015	1.00	1.33	1.61	1.21
2016	0.84	...	...	...

Interim Dividends (Per Share)

Amt	Decl	Ex	Rec	Pay
0.42Q	08/13/2015	08/26/2015	08/28/2015	09/14/2015
0.42Q	11/12/2015	11/25/2015	11/30/2015	12/15/2015
0.50Q	02/25/2016	03/09/2016	03/11/2016	03/24/2016
0.50Q	05/10/2016	05/25/2016	05/27/2016	06/10/2016

Indicated Div: $2.00

Valuation Analysis

		Institutional Holding	
Forecast EPS	$5.69	No of Institutions	
	(05/17/2016)	652	
Market Cap	$7.5 Billion	Shares	
Book Value	$837.0 Million	121,088,392	
Price/Book	9.01	% Held	
Price/Sales	1.35	86.89	

Business Summary: Hotels, Restaurants & Travel (MIC: 2.2.1 SIC: 7011 NAIC: 721110)

Wyndham Worldwide is a hospitality company. Co. has three segments: hotel group, which franchises in the upscale, upper midscale, midscale, economy and extended stay segments with a concentration in economy brands, and provides property management services; destination network, which provides vacation accommodations; and vacation ownership, which develops and markets Vacation Ownership Interests (VOIs) to individual consumers, provides consumer financing in connection with the sale of VOIs and provides property management services at resorts. Co.'s brands include Wyndham Hotels and Resorts, Ramada, Days Inn, Super 8, Howard Johnson, Wingate by Wyndham, and Dolce Hotels and Resorts.

Recent Developments: For the quarter ended Mar 31 2016, net income decreased 21.3% to US$96.0 million from US$122.0 million in the year-earlier quarter. Revenues were US$1.30 billion, up 3.2% from US$1.26 billion the year before. Operating income was US$195.0 million versus US$216.0 million in the prior-year quarter, a decrease of 9.7%. Direct operating expenses rose 8.6% to US$668.0 million from US$615.0 million in the comparable period the year before. Indirect operating expenses increased 2.1% to US$440.0 million from US$431.0 million in the equivalent prior-year period.

Prospects: Our evaluation of Wyndham Worldwide Corp. as of June 19, 2016 is the result of our systematic analysis on three basic characteristics: earnings strength, relative valuation, and recent stock price movement. The company has generated a negative trend in earnings per share over the past 5 quarters. However, while recent estimates for the company have been mixed, WYN has posted better than expected results. Based on operating earnings yield, the company is undervalued when compared to all of the companies in our coverage universe. Share price changes over the past year indicates that WYN will perform in line with the market over the near term.

Financial Data
(US$ in Millions)

	3 Mos	12/31/2015	12/31/2014	12/31/2013	12/31/2012	12/31/2011	12/31/2010	12/31/2009
Earnings Per Share	4.99	5.14	4.18	3.21	2.75	2.51	2.05	1.61
Cash Flow Per Share	8.84	8.40	7.87	7.58	7.00	6.19	3.57	3.85
Tang Book Value Per Share	N.M.	N.M.	N.M.	N.M.	N.M.	N.M.	1.53	1.41
Dividends Per Share	1.760	1.680	1.400	1.160	0.920	0.600	0.480	0.160
Dividend Payout %	35.27	32.68	33.49	36.14	33.45	23.90	23.41	9.94
Income Statement								
Total Revenue	1,303	5,536	5,281	5,009	4,534	4,254	3,851	3,750
EBITDA	256	1,229	1,144	985	783	924	870	750
Depn & Amortn	62	197	196	180	31	146	145	150
Income Before Taxes	163	916	845	683	628	650	563	493
Income Taxes	67	304	316	250	229	233	184	200
Net Income	96	612	529	432	400	417	379	293
Average Shares	114	119	127	135	145	166	185	182
Balance Sheet								
Current Assets	2,349	1,869	1,867	1,940	1,866	1,730	1,752	1,740
Total Assets	10,165	9,716	9,679	9,741	9,463	9,023	9,416	9,352
Current Liabilities	2,256	1,957	1,859	1,790	1,931	1,563	1,575	1,885
Long-Term Obligations	5,180	4,955	4,792	4,608	4,018	3,773	3,510	3,138
Total Liabilities	9,328	8,766	8,424	8,118	7,533	6,791	6,499	6,664
Stockholders' Equity	837	950	1,255	1,623	1,930	2,232	2,917	2,688
Shares Outstanding	111	113	121	128	137	147	173	178
Statistical Record								
Return on Assets %	5.84	6.31	5.45	4.50	4.32	4.52	4.04	3.10
Return on Equity %	61.07	55.51	36.76	24.32	19.17	16.20	13.52	11.65
EBITDA Margin %	19.65	22.20	21.66	19.66	17.27	21.72	22.59	20.00
Net Margin %	7.37	11.05	10.02	8.62	8.82	9.80	9.84	7.81
Asset Turnover	0.56	0.57	0.54	0.52	0.49	0.46	0.41	0.40
Current Ratio	1.04	0.96	1.00	1.08	0.97	1.11	1.11	0.92
Debt to Equity	6.19	5.22	3.82	2.84	2.08	1.69	1.20	1.17
Price Range	91.59-61.63	94.11-70.18	86.77-68.62	73.69-53.21	55.04-36.87	38.09-25.38	31.08-20.12	21.20-2.92
P/E Ratio	18.35-12.35	18.31-13.65	20.76-16.42	22.96-16.58	20.01-13.41	15.18-10.11	15.16-9.81	13.17-1.81
Average Yield %	2.25	2.03	1.84	1.87	1.87	1.87	1.89	1.30

Address: 22 Sylvan Way, Parsippany, NJ 07054	Web Site: www.wyndhamworldwide.com	Auditors: Deloitte & Touche LLP
Telephone: 973-753-6000	Officers: Stephen P. Holmes - Chairman, Chief Executive Officer Thomas F. Anderson - Executive Vice President, Chief Real Estate Development Officer	Investor Contact: 973-753-5500
Fax: 973-496-8906		Transfer Agents: Wells Fargo Shareowner Services, St. Paul, MN

XCEL ENERGY, INC.

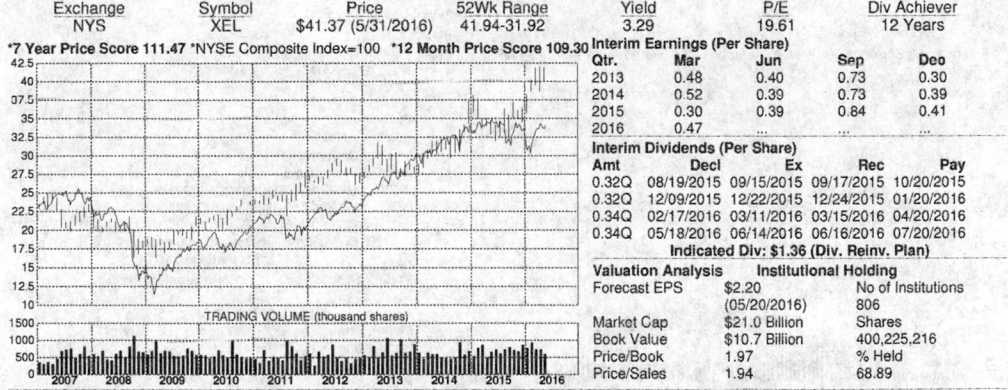

*7 Year Price Score 111.47 *NYSE Composite Index=100 *12 Month Price Score 109.30

Interim Earnings (Per Share)

Qtr.	Mar	Jun	Sep	Deo
2013	0.48	0.40	0.73	0.30
2014	0.52	0.39	0.73	0.39
2015	0.30	0.39	0.84	0.41
2016	0.47	...	...	...

Interim Dividends (Per Share)

Amt	Decl	Ex	Rec	Pay
0.32Q	08/19/2015	09/15/2015	09/17/2015	10/20/2015
0.32Q	12/09/2015	12/22/2015	12/24/2015	01/20/2016
0.34Q	02/17/2016	03/11/2016	03/15/2016	04/20/2016
0.34Q	05/18/2016	06/14/2016	06/16/2016	07/20/2016

Indicated Div: $1.36 (Div. Reinv. Plan)

Valuation Analysis / **Institutional Holding**

Forecast EPS	$2.20	No of Institutions
	(05/20/2016)	806
Market Cap	$21.0 Billion	Shares
Book Value	$10.7 Billion	400,225,216
Price/Book	1.97	% Held
Price/Sales	1.94	68.89

Business Summary: Electric Utilities (MIC: 3.1.1 SIC: 4931 NAIC: 221121)

Xcel Energy is a holding company. Co. has four wholly owned utility subsidiaries that serves electric and natural gas customers in eight states. Co.'s regulated electric utility segment generates, transmits and distributes electricity in Minnesota, Wisconsin, Michigan, North Dakota, South Dakota, Colorado, Texas and New Mexico. This segment also includes sales for resale and provides wholesale transmission service to various entities in the U.S. Regulated electric utility also includes commodity and trading operations. Co.'s regulated natural gas utility segment transports, stores and distributes natural gas primarily in portions of Minnesota, Wisconsin, North Dakota, Michigan and Colorado.

Recent Developments: For the quarter ended Mar 31 2016, net income increased 58.7% to US$241.3 million from US$152.1 million in the year-earlier quarter. Revenues were US$2.77 billion, down 6.4% from US$2.96 billion the year before. Operating income was US$489.9 million versus US$350.8 million in the prior-year quarter, an increase of 39.6%. Direct operating expenses declined 12.8% to US$1.76 billion from US$2.02 billion in the comparable period the year before. Indirect operating expenses decreased 11.8% to US$522.8 million from US$593.0 million in the equivalent prior-year period.

Prospects: Our evaluation of Xcel Energy Inc. as of June 19, 2016 is the result of our systematic analysis on three basic characteristics: earnings strength, relative valuation, and recent stock price movement. The company has generated a negative trend in earnings per share over the past 5 quarters and while recent estimates for the company have remained steady, XEL has posted better than expected results. Based on operating earnings yield, the company is about fairly valued when compared to all of the companies in our coverage universe. Share price changes over the past year indicates that XEL will perform very well over the near term.

Financial Data
(US$ in Thousands)

	3 Mos	12/31/2015	12/31/2014	12/31/2013	12/31/2012	12/31/2011	12/31/2010	12/31/2009
Earnings Per Share	2.11	1.94	2.03	1.91	1.85	1.72	1.62	1.48
Cash Flow Per Share	5.56	5.96	5.26	5.21	4.10	4.96	4.10	4.20
Tang Book Value Per Share	21.01	20.89	20.20	19.21	18.19	17.44	16.76	15.92
Dividends Per Share	1.300	1.280	1.200	1.110	1.070	1.033	1.002	0.973
Dividend Payout %	61.61	65.98	59.11	58.12	57.84	60.03	61.88	65.71
Income Statement								
Total Revenue	2,772,273	11,024,486	11,686,135	10,914,922	10,128,223	10,654,770	10,310,947	9,644,303
EBITDA	528,768	3,305,449	3,187,370	3,030,577	2,928,372	2,844,818	2,689,143	2,477,794
Depn & Amortn	25,605	1,249,338	1,151,547	1,100,710	1,047,001	1,013,377	992,902	938,693
Income Before Taxes	356,780	1,492,814	1,514,970	1,402,190	1,325,431	1,279,163	1,158,643	1,032,174
Income Taxes	128,650	542,719	523,815	483,976	450,203	468,316	436,635	371,314
Net Income	241,312	984,485	1,021,306	948,234	905,229	841,172	755,834	680,887
Average Shares	509,150	508,168	504,117	496,532	488,434	485,615	463,391	457,139
Balance Sheet								
Current Assets	2,732,617	2,910,445	3,364,380	3,218,040	2,625,139	2,982,564	2,732,643	2,763,411
Total Assets	39,069,844	39,053,535	36,957,884	33,907,490	31,140,686	29,497,267	27,387,690	25,488,428
Current Liabilities	3,188,568	4,058,297	4,064,583	3,654,498	2,937,073	3,588,639	2,536,533	3,015,257
Long-Term Obligations	13,148,395	12,490,719	11,499,634	10,910,754	10,143,905	8,848,513	9,263,144	7,888,628
Total Liabilities	28,398,210	28,452,615	26,743,402	24,341,540	22,266,609	21,015,069	19,199,191	18,100,203
Stockholders' Equity	10,671,634	10,600,920	10,214,482	9,565,950	8,874,077	8,482,198	8,188,499	7,388,225
Shares Outstanding	507,952	507,535	505,733	497,971	487,959	486,493	482,333	457,509
Statistical Record								
Return on Assets %	2.83	2.59	2.88	2.92	2.98	2.96	2.86	2.70
Return on Equity %	10.28	9.46	10.33	10.28	10.40	10.09	9.70	9.42
EBITDA Margin %	19.07	29.98	27.27	27.77	28.91	26.70	26.08	25.69
Net Margin %	8.70	8.93	8.74	8.69	8.94	7.89	7.33	7.06
Asset Turnover	0.29	0.29	0.33	0.34	0.33	0.37	0.39	0.38
Current Ratio	0.86	0.72	0.83	0.88	0.89	0.83	1.08	0.92
Debt to Equity	1.23	1.18	1.13	1.14	1.14	1.04	1.13	1.07
Price Range	41.82-31.92	38.11-31.92	37.25-27.35	31.79-26.71	29.58-26.00	27.71-21.82	24.33-20.04	21.77-16.19
P/E Ratio	19.82-15.13	19.64-16.45	18.35-13.47	16.64-13.98	15.99-14.05	16.11-12.69	15.02-12.37	14.71-10.94
Average Yield %	3.66	3.68	3.84	3.87	3.90	4.22	4.55	5.15

Address: 414 Nicollet Mall,	Web Site: www.xcelenergy.com	Auditors: Deloitte & Touche LLP
Minneapolis, MN 55401	Officers: Benjamin G.S. Fowke - Chairman,	Transfer Agents: Wells Fargo
Telephone: 612-330-5500	President, Chief Executive Officer Teresa S. Madden -	Shareowner Services, Mendota Heights,
	Executive Vice President, Chief Financial Officer,	MN
	Senior Vice President, Principal Financial Officer,	
	Vice President, Controller	

XEROX CORP

Exchange	Symbol	Price	52Wk Range	Yield	P/E
NYS	XRX	$9.97 (5/31/2016)	11.53-8.69	3.11	39.88

*7 Year Price Score 88.38 *NYSE Composite Index=100 *12 Month Price Score 96.84

Interim Earnings (Per Share)

Qtr.	Mar	Jun	Sep	Dec
2013	0.23	0.21	0.22	0.24
2014	0.23	0.22	0.22	0.14
2015	0.19	0.01	(0.04)	0.25
2016	0.03	...	...	...

Interim Dividends (Per Share)

Amt	Decl	Ex	Rec	Pay
0.07Q	07/22/2015	09/28/2015	09/30/2015	10/30/2015
0.07Q	10/20/2015	12/29/2015	12/31/2015	01/29/2016
0.077Q	01/29/2016	03/29/2016	03/31/2016	04/29/2016
0.077Q	05/20/2016	06/28/2016	06/30/2016	07/29/2016

Indicated Div: $0.31

Valuation Analysis   **Institutional Holding**

Forecast EPS	$1.10	No of Institutions
	(05/20/2016)	755
Market Cap	$10.1 Billion	Shares
Book Value	$9.5 Billion	1,018,316,032
Price/Book	1.07	% Held
Price/Sales	0.57	77.43

TRADING VOLUME (thousand shares)

Business Summary: Peripherals (MIC: 6.2.2 SIC: 3577 NAIC: 333315)

Xerox is a provider of business process and document management solutions. Co. also provides document technology, services, software and Xerox supplies for graphic communication and office printing environments. Co. organizes its business around two main reportable segments: Services and Document Technology. Co.'s Services segment is comprised of business process outsourcing and document outsourcing services. Co.'s Document Technology segment is comprised of its document technology and related supplies, technical service and equipment financing (excluding contracts related to document outsourcing) and its product groups within this segment include Entry, Mid-Range and High-End products.

Recent Developments: For the quarter ended Mar 31 2016, income from continuing operations decreased 81.6% to US$36.0 million from US$196.0 million in the year-earlier quarter. Net income decreased 84.3% to US$36.0 million from US$230.0 million in the year-earlier quarter. Revenues were US$4.28 billion, down 4.2% from US$4.47 billion the year before. Direct operating expenses declined 2.4% to US$2.97 billion from US$3.04 billion in the comparable period the year before. Indirect operating expenses increased 8.4% to US$1.33 billion from US$1.23 billion in the equivalent prior-year period.

Prospects: Our evaluation of Xerox Corp. as of June 19, 2016 is the result of our systematic analysis on three basic characteristics: earnings strength, relative valuation, and recent stock price movement. The company has enjoyed a very positive trend in earnings per share over the past 5 years and while recent estimates for the company have remained steady, XRX has posted results that fell short of analysts expectations. Based on operating earnings yield, the company is undervalued when compared to all of the companies in our coverage universe. Share price changes over the past year indicates that XRX will perform in line with the market over the near term.

Financial Data

(US$ in Thousands)	3 Mos	12/31/2015	12/31/2014	12/31/2013	12/31/2012	12/31/2011	12/31/2010	12/31/2009
Earnings Per Share	0.25	0.42	0.81	0.91	0.88	0.90	0.43	0.55
Cash Flow Per Share	1.45	1.51	1.79	1.94	1.98	1.41	2.06	2.54
Tang Book Value Per Share	N.M.	N.M.	N.M.	N.M.	N.M.	N.M.	N.M.	3.08
Dividends Per Share	0.287	0.280	0.250	0.230	0.170	0.170	0.170	0.170
Dividend Payout %	115.00	66.67	30.86	25.27	19.32	18.89	39.53	30.91
Income Statement								
Total Revenue	4,281,000	18,045,000	19,540,000	21,435,000	22,390,000	22,626,000	21,633,000	15,179,000
EBITDA	159,000	1,344,000	2,212,000	2,470,000	2,822,000	2,828,000	2,396,000	1,773,000
Depn & Amortn	89,000	587,000	639,000	763,000	1,059,000	806,000	1,008,000	640,000
Income Before Taxes	(16,000)	412,000	1,206,000	1,312,000	1,348,000	1,565,000	815,000	627,000
Income Taxes	(15,000)	(23,000)	259,000	276,000	277,000	386,000	256,000	152,000
Net Income	34,000	474,000	969,000	1,159,000	1,195,000	1,295,000	606,000	485,000
Average Shares	1,013,033	1,076,224	1,198,563	1,273,527	1,329,184	1,443,774	1,350,728	879,520
Balance Sheet								
Current Assets	6,808,000	6,685,000	8,874,000	8,511,000	8,273,000	7,912,000	8,639,000	9,731,000
Total Assets	24,857,000	24,817,000	27,658,000	29,036,000	30,015,000	30,116,000	30,600,000	24,032,000
Current Liabilities	6,146,000	5,254,000	6,076,000	5,686,000	5,910,000	6,381,000	6,417,000	4,461,000
Long-Term Obligations	5,359,000	6,382,000	6,358,000	6,904,000	7,447,000	7,088,000	7,237,000	8,276,000
Total Liabilities	15,382,000	15,394,000	16,675,000	16,387,000	18,145,000	17,891,000	18,245,000	16,982,000
Stockholders' Equity	9,475,000	9,423,000	10,983,000	12,649,000	11,870,000	12,225,000	12,355,000	7,050,000
Shares Outstanding	1,013,002	1,012,836	1,116,745	1,188,320	1,223,772	1,337,341	1,397,578	869,381
Statistical Record								
Return on Assets %	1.10	1.81	3.42	3.93	3.96	4.27	2.22	2.09
Return on Equity %	2.83	4.65	8.20	9.45	9.89	10.54	6.25	7.30
EBITDA Margin %	3.71	7.45	11.32	11.52	12.60	12.50	11.08	11.68
Net Margin %	0.79	2.63	4.96	5.41	5.34	5.72	2.80	3.20
Asset Turnover	0.69	0.69	0.69	0.73	0.74	0.75	0.79	0.65
Current Ratio	1.11	1.27	1.46	1.50	1.40	1.24	1.35	2.18
Debt to Equity	0.57	0.68	0.58	0.55	0.63	0.58	0.59	1.17
Price Range	13.26-8.69	14.00-9.29	14.32-10.30	12.23-6.82	8.76-6.23	11.71-6.72	12.01-7.91	9.57-4.17
P/E Ratio	53.04-34.76	33.33-22.12	17.68-12.72	13.44-7.49	9.95-7.08	13.01-7.47	27.93-18.40	17.40-7.58
Average Yield %	2.72	2.45	2.01	2.43	2.27	1.81	1.71	2.37

Address: P.O. Box 4505, 45 Glover Avenue, Norwalk, CT 06856-4505 **Telephone:** 203-968-3000	**Web Site:** www.xerox.com **Officers:** Ursula M. Burns - Chairman, President, Chief Executive Officer Lynn R. Blodgett - Executive Vice President, Division Officer	**Auditors:** PricewaterhouseCoopers LLP **Transfer Agents:** Computershare Trust Company, N.A., Providence, RI

XL GROUP PLC

*7 Year Price Score 117.65 ***NYSE Composite Index=100** ***12 Month Price Score 91.97**

TRADING VOLUME (thousand shares)

Interim Earnings (Per Share)

Qtr.	Mar	Jun	Sep	Dec
2013	1.17	0.93	0.47	1.06
2014	0.91	(1.03)	0.27	0.51
2015	0.14	3.11	0.09	0.75
2016	0.07	...	...	...

Interim Dividends (Per Share)

Amt	Decl	Ex	Rec	Pay
0.20Q	08/06/2015	09/11/2015	09/15/2015	09/30/2015
0.20Q	10/30/2015	12/11/2015	12/15/2015	12/31/2015
0.20Q	02/19/2016	03/11/2016	03/15/2016	03/31/2016
0.20Q	05/13/2016	06/13/2016	06/15/2016	06/30/2016

Indicated Div: $0.80

Valuation Analysis **Institutional Holding**

Forecast EPS	$2.23	No of Institutions	
	(05/20/2016)	521	
Market Cap	$0.8 Billion	Shares	
Book Value	$11.7 Billion	305,763,904	
Price/Book	0.84	% Held	
Price/Sales	0.95	N/A	

Business Summary: General Insurance (MIC: 5.2.1 SIC: 6331 NAIC: 524126)

XL Group is a holding company. Through its subsidiaries, Co. is an insurance and reinsurance company providing property, casualty and specialty products to industrial, commercial and professional firms, insurance companies and other enterprises. Co. is organized into two operating segments: insurance, which include four business groups: Global Casualty, Global Energy, Property and Construction, Global Professional Lines, and Global Specialty Lines, as well as four regions: Americas; Europe, Middle East & Africa; U.K. & Ireland; and Asia Pacific; and reinsurance which include five geographical regions: Bermuda; North America; London; EMEA; and Latin America, Asia Pacific & Credit.

Recent Developments: For the quarter ended Mar 31 2016, net income increased 12.7% to US$83.0 million from US$73.7 million in the year-earlier quarter. Revenues were US$2.42 billion, up 69.9% from US$1.42 billion the year before. Net premiums earned were US$2.35 billion versus US$1.33 billion in the prior-year quarter, an increase of 76.5%. Net investment income fell 1.3% to US$205.9 million from US$208.5 million a year ago.

Prospects: Our evaluation of XL Group plc as of June 19, 2016 is the result of our systematic analysis on three basic characteristics: earnings strength, relative valuation, and recent stock price movement. The company has enjoyed a very positive trend in earnings per share over the past 5 quarters. However, while recent estimates for the company have been lowered by analysts, XL has posted results that fell short of analysts expectations. Based on operating earnings yield, the company is undervalued when compared to all of the companies in our coverage universe. Share price changes over the past year indicates that XL will perform very well over the near term.

Financial Data

(US$ in Thousands)	3 Mos	12/31/2015	12/31/2014	12/31/2013	12/31/2012	12/31/2011	12/31/2010	12/31/2009
Earnings Per Share	4.02	4.15	0.69	3.63	2.10	(1.52)	1.73	0.61
Cash Flow Per Share	1.40	2.15	3.61	2.71	3.43	1.05	1.77	(0.13)
Tang Book Value Per Share	33.03	32.12	37.56	34.45	33.82	28.57	31.11	25.63
Dividends Per Share	0.760	0.720	0.640	0.560	0.440	0.440	0.400	0.400
Dividend Payout %	18.91	17.35	92.75	15.43	20.95	...	23.12	65.57
Income Statement								
Premium Income	2,354,610	8,226,425	5,895,070	6,309,521	6,090,441	5,690,130	5,414,061	5,706,840
Total Revenue	2,417,227	9,308,926	6,602,267	7,541,234	7,230,480	6,696,803	6,398,582	6,193,647
Benefits & Claims	1,382,485	4,766,200	3,258,393	3,731,464	3,765,482	4,078,391	3,211,800	3,168,837
Income Before Taxes	92,673	909,031	258,517	1,094,348	708,606	(420,962)	684,746	134,714
Income Taxes	22,295	(19,161)	96,897	77,505	34,028	59,707	162,737	120,307
Net Income	21,885	1,207,152	188,340	1,059,916	651,134	(403,883)	643,377	74,991
Average Shares	296,666	290,999	271,527	292,069	310,282	312,896	337,709	340,966
Balance Sheet								
Total Assets	60,645,692	58,682,938	45,046,819	45,652,887	45,387,779	44,626,077	45,023,351	45,579,675
Total Liabilities	48,956,948	47,005,859	35,013,067	35,655,254	34,877,707	35,201,139	34,340,698	35,966,890
Stockholders' Equity	11,688,744	11,677,079	10,033,752	9,997,633	10,510,072	9,424,938	10,682,653	9,612,785
Shares Outstanding	286,273	294,745	255,182	278,253	298,681	315,645	316,396	342,118
Statistical Record								
Return on Assets %	2.24	2.33	0.42	2.33	1.44	N.M.	1.42	0.16
Return on Equity %	10.88	11.12	1.88	10.34	6.51	N.M.	6.34	0.92
Loss Ratio %	58.71	57.94	55.27	59.14	61.83	71.67	59.32	55.53
Net Margin %	0.91	12.97	2.85	14.05	9.01	(6.03)	10.05	1.21
Price Range	40.41-33.20	40.41-34.37	36.30-27.96	33.03-25.06	25.76-19.06	25.19-18.17	22.22-15.97	18.95-2.67
P/E Ratio	10.05-8.26	9.74-8.28	52.61-40.52	9.10-6.90	12.27-9.08	...	12.84-9.23	31.07-4.38
Average Yield %	2.04	1.93	1.98	1.84	1.99	2.04	2.09	3.46

Address: XL House, 8 St. Stephen's Green, Dublin, 2
Telephone: 140-055-00

Web Site: www.xlgroup.com
Officers: Stephen Catlin - Executive Deputy Chairman Michael S. McGavick - Chief Executive Officer

Auditors: PricewaterhouseCoopers LLP
Investor Contact: 203-964-3470

XYLEM INC.

Exchange	Symbol	Price	52Wk Range	Yield	P/E
NYS	XYL	$44.66 (5/31/2016)	44.74-30.46	1.32	23.63

*7 Year Price Score N/A   *NYSE Composite Index=100   *12 Month Price Score 114.29

Interim Earnings (Per Share)

Qtr.	Mar	Jun	Sep	Dec
2013	0.22	0.25	0.39	0.36
2014	0.27	0.47	0.58	0.52
2015	0.35	0.41	0.48	0.63
2016	0.37	...	...	...

Interim Dividends (Per Share)

Amt	Decl	Ex	Rec	Pay
0.141Q	08/19/2015	08/31/2015	09/02/2015	09/23/2015
0.141Q	10/14/2015	11/02/2015	11/04/2015	12/02/2015
0.155Q	02/04/2016	02/16/2016	02/18/2016	03/16/2016
0.155Q	05/12/2016	05/23/2016	05/25/2016	06/22/2016

Indicated Div: $0.59

Valuation Analysis

		Institutional Holding	
Forecast EPS	$2.05	No of Institutions	
	(05/17/2016)	572	
Market Cap	$8.0 Billion	Shares	
Book Value	$2.2 Billion	161,991,744	
Price/Book	3.70	% Held	
Price/Sales	2.18	85.39	

Business Summary: Industrial Machinery & Equipment (MIC: 7.2.1 SIC: 3561 NAIC: 333911)

Xylem is an equipment and service provider for water and wastewater applications with a portfolio of products and services addressing the cycle of water, from collection, distribution and use to the return of water to the environment. Co. operates in two segments: Water Infrastructure, which focuses on the transportation, treatment and testing of water, providing a range of products including water and wastewater pumps, treatment and testing equipment, and controls and systems; and Applied Water, which focuses on the residential, commercial, industrial and agricultural markets. The Applied Water segment's products include pumps, valves, heat exchangers, controls and dispensing equipment.

Recent Developments: For the quarter ended Mar 31 2016, net income increased 3.1% to US$66.0 million from US$64.0 million in the year-earlier quarter. Revenues were US$847.0 million, up 1.2% from US$837.0 million the year before. Operating income was US$79.0 million versus US$83.0 million in the prior-year quarter, a decrease of 4.8%. Direct operating expenses declined 0.8% to US$518.0 million from US$522.0 million in the comparable period the year before. Indirect operating expenses increased 7.8% to US$250.0 million from US$232.0 million in the equivalent prior-year period.

Prospects: Our evaluation of Xylem Inc. as of June 19, 2016 is the result of our systematic analysis on three basic characteristics: earnings strength, relative valuation, and recent stock price movement. The company has enjoyed a very positive trend in earnings per share over the past 5 quarters and while recent estimates for the company have remained steady, XYL has posted better than expected results. Based on operating earnings yield, the company is about fairly valued when compared to all of the companies in our coverage universe. Share price changes over the past year indicates that XYL will perform well over the near term.

Financial Data
(US$ in Millions)

	3 Mos	12/31/2015	12/31/2014	12/31/2013	12/31/2012	12/31/2011	12/31/2010	12/31/2009
Earnings Per Share	1.89	1.87	1.83	1.22	1.59	1.50	...	...
Cash Flow Per Share	2.61	2.56	2.27	1.75	2.13	2.43	...	...
Tang Book Value Per Share	0.35	0.36	0.33	0.19	N.M.	N.M.	...	...
Dividends Per Share	0.577	0.563	0.512	0.466	0.405	0.101	...	...
Dividend Payout %	30.54	30.12	27.98	38.16	25.46	6.75	...	...
Income Statement								
Total Revenue	847	3,653	3,916	3,837	3,791	3,803	3,202	2,849
EBITDA	111	544	568	449	533	490	480	347
Depn & Amortn	32	88	95	99	94	93	92	70
Income Before Taxes	65	403	421	298	388	383	388	277
Income Taxes	(1)	63	84	70	91	104	59	14
Net Income	66	340	337	228	297	279	329	263
Average Shares	179	181	184	186	186	185	...	...
Balance Sheet								
Current Assets	2,575	2,005	2,102	2,009	1,874	1,642	1,336	1,088
Total Assets	5,304	4,657	4,864	4,896	4,679	4,393	3,735	2,535
Current Liabilities	1,432	823	908	853	781	817	649	571
Long-Term Obligations	1,153	1,196	1,199	1,199	1,199	1,201	...	...
Total Liabilities	3,145	2,573	2,737	2,655	2,605	2,566	1,016	848
Stockholders' Equity	2,159	2,084	2,127	2,241	2,074	1,827	2,719	1,687
Shares Outstanding	178	178	182	184	185	184	...	...
Statistical Record								
Return on Assets %	6.89	7.14	6.91	4.76	6.53	...	10.49	...
Return on Equity %	16.49	16.15	15.43	10.57	15.19	...	14.93	...
EBITDA Margin %	13.11	14.89	14.50	11.70	14.06	12.88	14.99	12.18
Net Margin %	7.79	9.31	8.61	5.94	7.83	7.34	10.27	9.23
Asset Turnover	0.74	0.77	0.80	0.80	0.83	...	1.02	...
Current Ratio	1.80	2.44	2.31	2.36	2.40	2.01	2.06	1.91
Debt to Equity	0.53	0.57	0.56	0.54	0.58	0.66	...	...
Price Range	41.04-30.46	38.08-30.46	39.78-31.91	34.77-24.19	28.73-23.16	27.31-23.06	...	...
P/E Ratio	21.71-16.12	20.36-16.29	21.74-17.44	28.50-19.83	18.07-14.57	18.21-15.37	...	...
Average Yield %	1.62	1.59	1.39	1.63	1.58	0.41	...	...

Address: 1 International Drive, Rye Brook, NY 10573 **Telephone:** 914-323-5700 **Fax:** 914-323-5800	**Web Site:** www.xyleminc.com **Officers:** Markos I. Tambakeras - Chairman Patrick K. Decker - President, Chief Executive Officer	**Auditors:** Deloitte & Touche LLP **Investor Contact:** 914-323-5930 **Transfer Agents:** Wells Fargo Shareowner Services, St. Paul, MN

YELP INC

Exchange	Symbol	Price	52Wk Range	Yield	P/E
NYS	YELP	$26.19 (5/31/2016)	48.58-15.23	N/A	N/A

*7 Year Price Score N/A   ***NYSE Composite Index=100**   ***12 Month Price Score 83.94**

Interim Earnings (Per Share)

Qtr.	Mar	Jun	Sep	Dec
2013	(0.08)	(0.01)	(0.04)	(0.03)
2014	(0.04)	0.04	0.05	0.43
2015	(0.02)	(0.02)	(0.11)	(0.30)
2016	(0.20)	...	...	...

Interim Dividends (Per Share)

No Dividends Paid

Valuation Analysis		Institutional Holding	
Forecast EPS	$-0.27	No of Institutions	
	(05/20/2016)	246	
Market Cap	$2.0 Billion	Shares	
Book Value	$700.7 Million	63,196,124	
Price/Book	2.86	% Held	
Price/Sales	3.39	89.90	

Business Summary: Internet & Software (MIC: 6.3.2 SIC: 7299 NAIC: 519190)

Yelp is a local business review site. Co.'s core business are the communities of contributors that contribute the content on Co.'s online platform. These contributors provide information about businesses in the form of reviews and ratings, tips, photos and videos. Co.'s platform covers business categories that include restaurants, shopping, beauty and fitness, arts, entertainment and events, home and local services, health, nightlife, travel and hotel, and auto. Co.'s products include: local advertising, which provides free and paid business listing products to businesses; brand advertising, which provides advertising solutions; and other services.

Recent Developments: For the quarter ended Mar 31 2016, net loss amounted to US$15.5 million versus a net loss of US$1.3 million in the year-earlier quarter. Revenues were US$158.6 million, up 33.8% from US$118.5 million the year before. Operating loss was US$14.3 million versus a loss of US$4.2 million in the prior-year quarter. Direct operating expenses rose 73.3% to US$15.1 million from US$8.7 million in the comparable period the year before. Indirect operating expenses increased 38.4% to US$157.8 million from US$114.1 million in the equivalent prior-year period.

Prospects: Our evaluation of Yelp Inc as of June 19, 2016 is the result of our systematic analysis on three basic characteristics: earnings strength, relative valuation, and recent stock price movement. The company has produced a positive trend in earnings per share over the past 5 quarters. Because the company lacks sufficient analyst estimate data, we place greater weight on the historical EPS trend as the measure of earnings strength. Based on operating earnings yield, the company is overvalued when compared to all of the companies in our coverage universe. Share price changes over the past year indicates that YELP will perform very poorly over the near term.

Financial Data
(US$ in Thousands)

	3 Mos	12/31/2015	12/31/2014	12/31/2013	12/31/2012	12/31/2011	12/31/2010	12/31/2009
Earnings Per Share	(0.63)	(0.44)	0.48	(0.15)	(0.35)	(1.10)	(0.71)	(0.19)
Cash Flow Per Share	0.73	0.77	0.81	0.33	(0.00)	0.02	(0.57)	(0.05)
Tang Book Value Per Share	6.40	6.35	7.06	5.95	1.75	1.83	2.31	...
Income Statement								
Total Revenue	158,613	549,711	377,536	232,988	137,567	83,285	47,731	25,808
EBITDA	(7,450)	1,440	24,853	(1,392)	(13,142)	(12,379)	(7,221)	(1,120)
Depn & Amortn	6,876	23,000	14,300	7,900	5,900	4,200	2,300	1,200
Income Before Taxes	(14,015)	(20,938)	11,280	(9,230)	(18,991)	(16,566)	(9,491)	(2,300)
Income Taxes	1,437	11,962	(25,193)	838	122	102	75	8
Net Income	(15,452)	(32,900)	36,473	(10,068)	(19,113)	(16,668)	(9,566)	(2,308)
Average Shares	75,884	74,683	76,712	65,665	54,149	15,291	13,774	12,344
Balance Sheet								
Current Assets	447,340	443,282	420,758	416,833	111,774	31,726	35,395	...
Total Assets	772,967	755,427	629,650	515,977	187,696	43,821	41,015	...
Current Liabilities	58,941	49,777	33,973	24,989	21,507	12,730	6,654	...
Total Liabilities	72,273	61,807	41,500	29,494	22,034	12,733	6,658	...
Stockholders' Equity	700,694	693,620	588,150	486,483	165,662	31,088	34,357	...
Shares Outstanding	76,424	75,982	72,920	70,874	63,505	16,956	14,848	13,559
Statistical Record								
Return on Assets %	N.M.	N.M.	6.37	N.M.	N.M.	N.M.	...	...
Return on Equity %	N.M.	N.M.	6.79	N.M.	N.M.	N.M.	...	...
EBITDA Margin %	N.M.	0.26	6.58	N.M.	N.M.	N.M.	N.M.	N.M.
Net Margin %	N.M.	N.M.	9.66	N.M.	N.M.	N.M.	N.M.	N.M.
Asset Turnover	0.79	0.79	0.66	0.66	1.19	1.96	...	...
Current Ratio	7.59	8.91	12.39	16.68	5.20	2.49	5.32	...
Price Range	51.28-15.23	57.47-20.87	98.04-50.04	74.89-18.85	28.89-15.22	...	...	...
P/E Ratio	...	...	204.25-104.25	...	...	...	...	...

Address: 140 New Montgomery Street, 9th Floor, San Francisco, CA 94105 **Telephone:** 415-908-3801	**Web Site:** www.yelp.com **Officers:** Jeremy Stoppelman - Chief Executive Officer Joseph R. Nachman - Senior Vice President, Chief Revenue Officer	**Auditors:** Deloitte & Touche LLP **Transfer Agents:** Computershare Trust Company, N.A

YUM! BRANDS, INC.

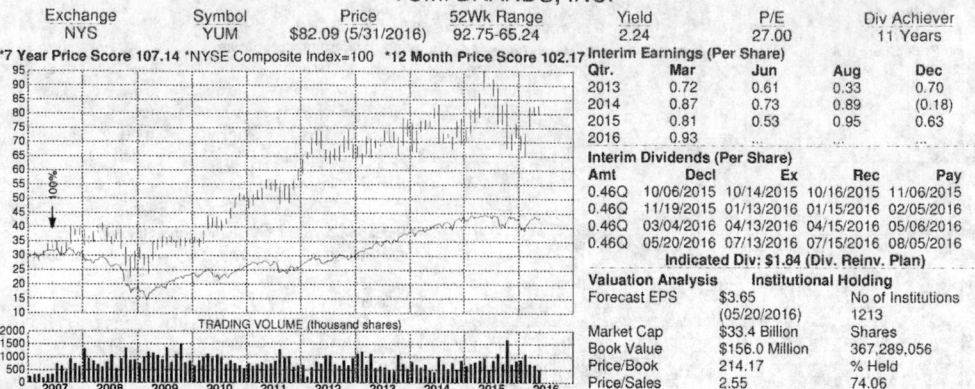

Exchange	Symbol	Price	52Wk Range	Yield	P/E	Div Achiever
NYS	YUM	$82.09 (5/31/2016)	92.75-65.24	2.24	27.00	11 Years

*7 Year Price Score 107.14 *NYSE Composite Index=100 *12 Month Price Score 102.17

Interim Earnings (Per Share)

Qtr.	Mar	Jun	Aug	Dec
2013	0.72	0.61	0.33	0.70
2014	0.87	0.73	0.89	(0.18)
2015	0.81	0.53	0.95	0.63
2016	0.93			

Interim Dividends (Per Share)

Amt	Decl	Ex	Rec	Pay
0.46Q	10/06/2015	10/14/2015	10/16/2015	11/06/2015
0.46Q	11/19/2015	01/13/2016	01/15/2016	02/05/2016
0.46Q	03/04/2016	04/13/2016	04/15/2016	05/06/2016
0.46Q	05/20/2016	07/13/2016	07/15/2016	08/05/2016

Indicated Div: $1.84 (Div. Reinv. Plan)

Valuation Analysis

		Institutional Holding	
Forecast EPS	$3.65	No of Institutions	
	(05/20/2016)	1213	
Market Cap	$33.4 Billion	Shares	
Book Value	$156.0 Million	367,289,056	
Price/Book	214.17	% Held	
Price/Sales	2.55	74.06	

Business Summary: Hotels, Restaurants & Travel (MIC: 2.2.1 SIC: 5812 NAIC: 722211)

Yum! Brands, through its three concepts of KFC, Pizza Hut and Taco Bell, develops, operates, franchises and licenses a system of restaurants which prepare, package and sell a menu of food items. Co. operates in five segments: China Division, including operations in mainland China; India Division, including operations in India, Bangladesh, Nepal and Sri Lanka; The KFC Division, including operations of the KFC concept outside of China and India Divisions; The Pizza Hut Division, including operations of the Pizza Hut concept outside of China and India Divisions; and The Taco Bell Division. As of Dec 26 2015, Co. had over 42,000 restaurants in more than 130 countries and territories.

Recent Developments: For the quarter ended Mar 19 2016, net income increased 9.4% to US$395.0 million from US$361.0 million in the year-earlier quarter. Revenues were US$2.62 billion, unchanged from the year before. Operating income was US$564.0 million versus US$506.0 million in the prior-year quarter, an increase of 11.5%. Direct operating expenses declined 3.6% to US$1.73 billion from US$1.80 billion in the comparable period the year before. Indirect operating expenses increased 1.3% to US$323.0 million from US$319.0 million in the equivalent prior-year period.

Prospects: Our evaluation of Yum! Brands Inc. as of June 19, 2016 is the result of our systematic analysis on three basic characteristics: earnings strength, relative valuation, and recent stock price movement. The company has managed to produce a neutral trend in earnings per share over the past 5 quarters. However, while recent estimates for the company have been mixed, YUM has posted better than expected results. Based on operating earnings yield, the company is about fairly valued when compared to all of the companies in our coverage universe. Share price changes over the past year indicates that YUM will perform in line with the market over the near term.

Financial Data

(US$ in Millions)	3 Mos	12/26/2015	12/27/2014	12/28/2013	12/29/2012	12/31/2011	12/25/2010	12/26/2009
Earnings Per Share	3.04	2.92	2.32	2.36	3.38	2.74	2.38	2.22
Cash Flow Per Share	5.49	4.92	4.63	4.75	4.99	4.55	4.16	2.99
Tang Book Value Per Share	N.M.	N.M.	1.22	1.44	0.95	1.83	0.94	N.M.
Dividends Per Share	1.740	1.690	1.520	1.375	1.190	1.035	0.880	0.780
Dividend Payout %	57.24	57.88	65.52	58.26	35.21	37.77	36.97	35.14
Income Statement								
Total Revenue	2,619	13,105	13,279	13,084	13,633	12,626	11,343	10,836
EBITDA	684	2,592	2,229	2,458	2,876	2,367	2,292	2,107
Depn & Amortn	136	712	702	686	629	599	565	553
Income Before Taxes	511	1,746	1,397	1,525	2,098	1,612	1,552	1,360
Income Taxes	132	489	406	487	537	324	416	313
Net Income	391	1,293	1,051	1,091	1,597	1,319	1,158	1,071
Average Shares	422	443	453	461	473	481	486	483
Balance Sheet								
Current Assets	1,963	1,688	1,646	1,691	1,909	2,321	2,313	1,208
Total Assets	8,221	8,075	8,345	8,695	9,011	8,834	8,316	7,148
Current Liabilities	4,648	3,088	2,411	2,265	2,188	2,450	2,448	1,653
Long-Term Obligations	2,510	3,054	3,077	2,918	2,932	2,997	2,915	3,207
Total Liabilities	8,065	7,164	6,798	6,529	6,857	7,011	6,740	6,123
Stockholders' Equity	156	911	1,547	2,166	2,154	1,823	1,576	1,025
Shares Outstanding	407	420	434	443	451	460	469	469
Statistical Record								
Return on Assets %	16.00	15.79	12.37	12.36	17.95	15.13	15.02	15.71
Return on Equity %	141.92	105.50	56.77	50.65	80.53	76.36	89.29	234.23
EBITDA Margin %	26.12	19.78	16.79	18.79	21.10	18.75	20.21	19.44
Net Margin %	14.93	9.87	7.91	8.34	11.71	10.45	10.21	9.88
Asset Turnover	1.59	1.60	1.56	1.48	1.53	1.45	1.47	1.59
Current Ratio	0.42	0.55	0.68	0.75	0.87	0.95	0.94	0.73
Debt to Equity	16.09	3.35	1.99	1.35	1.36	1.64	1.85	3.13
Price Range	94.88-65.24	94.88-67.12	83.29-66.16	78.30-62.08	74.47-58.57	59.58-46.40	51.90-32.72	36.64-23.47
P/E Ratio	31.21-21.46	32.49-22.99	35.90-28.52	33.18-26.31	22.03-17.33	21.74-16.93	21.81-13.75	16.50-10.57
Average Yield %	2.19	2.11	2.05	1.97	1.77	2.04	2.09	2.38

Address: 1441 Gardiner Lane, Louisville, KY 40213 Telephone: 502-874-8300	Web Site: www.yum.com Officers: David C. Novak - Executive Chairman, Chairman, President, Chief Executive Officer Greg Creed - Chief Executive Officer, Division Officer	Auditors: KPMG LLP Investor Contact: 502-874-8006 Transfer Agents: American Stock Transfer & Trust Company, New York, NY

ZIMMER BIOMET HOLDINGS INC

Exchange	Symbol	Price	52Wk Range	Yield	P/E
NYS	ZBH	$122.11 (5/31/2016)	123.07-91.68	0.79	321.34

*7 Year Price Score 115.65 *NYSE Composite Index=100 ***12 Month Price Score 108.82**

TRADING VOLUME (thousand shares)

Interim Earnings (Per Share)

Qtr.	Mar	Jun	Sep	Dec
2013	1.28	0.89	0.90	1.36
2014	1.29	1.03	0.96	0.90
2015	1.02	(0.91)	0.11	0.66
2016	0.52	...	...	...

Interim Dividends (Per Share)

Amt	Decl	Ex	Rec	Pay
0.22Q	08/24/2015	09/28/2015	09/30/2015	10/30/2015
0.22Q	12/14/2015	12/29/2015	12/31/2015	01/29/2016
0.24Q	02/24/2016	03/29/2016	03/31/2016	04/29/2016
0.24Q	05/23/2016	06/22/2016	06/24/2016	07/29/2016

Indicated Div: $0.96

Valuation Analysis

		Institutional Holding	
Forecast EPS	$7.96	No of Institutions	
	(05/20/2016)	1096	
Market Cap	$24.3 Billion	Shares	
Book Value	$9.7 Billion	214,432,752	
Price/Book	2.52	% Held	
Price/Sales	3.59	84.28	

Business Summary: Medical Instruments & Equipment (MIC: 4.3.1 SIC: 3842 NAIC: 339113)

Zimmer Biomet Holdings is engaged in musculoskeletal healthcare. Co. designs, manufactures and markets orthopaedic reconstructive products; sports medicine, biologics, extremities and trauma products; spine, bone healing, craniomaxillofacial and thoracic products; dental implants; and related surgical products. Co. manages its operations through three operating segments are the Americas; Europe, the Middle East and Africa; and Asia Pacific. Co.'s four product category operating segments: Americas Spine; Bone Healing; Craniomaxillofacial and Thoracic; and Dental.

Recent Developments: For the quarter ended Mar 31 2016, net income decreased 38.2% to US$105.8 million from US$171.1 million in the year-earlier quarter. Revenues were US$1.90 billion, up 67.8% from US$1.13 billion the year before. Operating income was US$245.5 million versus US$269.9 million in the prior-year quarter, a decrease of 9.0%. Direct operating expenses rose 123.0% to US$635.2 million from US$284.9 million in the comparable period the year before. Indirect operating expenses increased 76.6% to US$1.02 billion from US$579.6 million in the equivalent prior-year period.

Prospects: Our evaluation of Zimmer Biomet Holdings Inc. as of June 19, 2016 is the result of our systematic analysis on three basic characteristics: earnings strength, relative valuation, and recent stock price movement. The company has produced a positive trend in earnings per share over the past 5 quarters and while recent estimates for the company have been mixed, ZBH has posted better than expected results. Based on operating earnings yield, the company is undervalued when compared to all of the companies in our coverage universe. Share price changes over the past year indicates that ZBH will perform well over the near term.

Financial Data

(US$ in Thousands)	3 Mos	12/31/2015	12/31/2014	12/31/2013	12/31/2012	12/31/2011	12/31/2010	12/31/2009
Earnings Per Share	0.38	0.77	4.19	4.43	4.29	4.03	2.97	3.32
Cash Flow Per Share	4.95	4.36	6.23	5.68	6.57	6.27	5.97	5.20
Tang Book Value Per Share	N.M.	N.M.	20.05	17.54	14.85	11.70	12.08	9.78
Dividends Per Share	0.900	0.880	0.880	0.800	0.720	...	...	...
Dividend Payout %	236.84	114.29	21.00	18.06	16.78	...	...	...
Income Statement								
Total Revenue	1,904,000	5,997,800	4,673,300	4,623,400	4,471,700	4,451,800	4,220,200	4,095,400
EBITDA	368,300	1,142,800	1,263,700	1,298,200	1,313,400	1,290,200	1,164,600	1,263,000
Depn & Amortn	126,600	712,400	268,600	262,600	266,000	266,100	247,900	244,220
Income Before Taxes	154,800	153,200	943,900	981,100	990,100	978,900	860,200	998,200
Income Taxes	49,000	7,000	224,900	221,900	237,200	218,900	263,300	280,800
Net Income	105,900	147,000	720,100	761,000	755,000	760,800	596,900	717,400
Average Shares	202,000	189,800	171,700	171,800	176,000	188,700	201,100	215,800
Balance Sheet								
Current Assets	5,082,000	5,862,900	4,289,000	4,197,700	3,708,700	3,276,600	3,009,700	2,738,000
Total Assets	26,297,300	27,219,500	9,634,700	9,580,600	9,012,400	8,515,300	7,999,900	7,785,500
Current Liabilities	1,514,600	1,617,900	1,038,000	1,031,600	866,000	867,100	702,500	690,700
Long-Term Obligations	11,117,400	11,556,300	1,425,500	1,672,300	1,720,800	1,576,000	1,142,100	1,127,600
Total Liabilities	16,637,600	17,331,600	3,113,900	3,283,300	3,151,500	3,008,100	2,228,600	2,146,800
Stockholders' Equity	9,659,700	9,887,900	6,520,800	6,297,300	5,860,900	5,507,200	5,771,300	5,638,700
Shares Outstanding	199,100	202,700	169,700	169,800	171,600	178,000	195,600	204,200
Statistical Record								
Return on Assets %	0.45	0.80	7.50	8.19	8.59	9.21	7.56	9.55
Return on Equity %	1.20	1.79	11.24	12.52	13.25	13.49	10.46	12.71
EBITDA Margin %	19.34	19.05	27.04	28.08	29.37	28.98	27.60	30.84
Net Margin %	5.56	2.45	15.41	16.46	16.88	17.09	14.14	17.52
Asset Turnover	0.31	0.33	0.49	0.50	0.51	0.54	0.53	0.55
Current Ratio	3.36	3.62	4.13	4.07	4.28	3.78	4.28	3.96
Debt to Equity	1.15	1.17	0.22	0.27	0.29	0.29	0.20	0.20
Price Range	118.76-91.68	121.76-92.41	115.05-90.87	93.43-66.66	68.80-53.21	69.69-47.42	63.71-46.97	60.34-32.13
P/E Ratio	312.53-241.26	158.13-120.01	27.46-21.69	21.09-15.05	16.04-12.40	17.29-11.77	21.45-15.81	18.17-9.68
Average Yield %	0.86	0.81	0.87	1.00	1.15	...	...	...

Address: 345 East Main Street, Warsaw, IN 46580 **Telephone:** 574-267-6131	**Web Site:** www.zimmer.com **Officers:** David C. Dvorak - President, Chief Executive Officer Daniel P. Florin - Senior Vice President, Chief Financial Officer	**Auditors:** PricewaterhouseCoopers LLP **Investor Contact:** 574-267-6131 **Transfer Agents:** American Stock Transfer & Trust Company LLC

ZOETIS INC

Exchange	Symbol	Price	52Wk Range	Yield	P/E
NYS	ZTS	$47.42 (5/31/2016)	55.38-39.33	0.80	61.58

*7 Year Price Score N/A *NYSE Composite Index=100 *12 Month Price Score 102.06

Interim Earnings (Per Share)

Qtr.	Mar	Jun	Sep	Dec
2013	0.28	0.26	0.26	0.21
2014	0.31	0.27	0.33	0.25
2015	0.33	(0.07)	0.38	0.05
2016	0.41	...	...	...

Interim Dividends (Per Share)

Amt	Decl	Ex	Rec	Pay
0.083Q	10/01/2015	11/03/2015	11/05/2015	12/01/2015
0.095Q	12/16/2015	01/19/2016	01/21/2016	03/01/2016
0.095Q	02/19/2016	04/05/2016	04/07/2016	06/01/2016
0.095Q	05/12/2016	06/28/2016	06/30/2016	08/30/2016

Indicated Div: $0.38

Valuation Analysis

		Institutional Holding	
Forecast EPS	$1.87	No of Institutions	
	(05/20/2016)	735	
Market Cap	$23.5 Billion	Shares	479,555,328
Book Value	$1.2 Billion	% Held	91.78
Price/Book	20.21		
Price/Sales	4.88		

TRADING VOLUME (thousand shares)

Business Summary: Pharmaceuticals (MIC: 4.1.1 SIC: 2834 NAIC: 325412)

Zoetis engages in the discovery, development, manufacture and commercialization of animal health medicines and vaccines, with a focus on both livestock and companion animals. Co. organizes and operates its business in two segments: the U.S. and International. Co.'s main product categories are anti-infectives, vaccines, parasiticides, medicated feed additives, and other pharmaceutical products such as pain and sedation, oncology, antiemetic, allergy and dermatology, and reproductive products. Co.'s other product categories include nutritionals and agribusiness, as well as products and services in complementary areas, including biodevices, diagnostics and genetics.

Recent Developments: For the quarter ended Apr 3 2016, net income increased 23.6% to US$204.0 million from US$165.0 million in the year-earlier quarter. Revenues were US$1.16 billion, up 5.4% from US$1.10 billion the year before. Direct operating expenses declined 1.3% to US$389.0 million from US$394.0 million in the comparable period the year before. Indirect operating expenses decreased 4.9% to US$428.0 million from US$450.0 million in the equivalent prior-year period.

Prospects: Our evaluation of Zoetis Inc as of June 19, 2016 is the result of our systematic analysis on three basic characteristics: earnings strength, relative valuation, and recent stock price movement. The company has generated a negative trend in earnings per share over the past 5 quarters and while recent estimates for the company have been mixed, ZTS has posted better than expected results. Based on operating earnings yield, the company is about fairly valued when compared to all of the companies in our coverage universe. Share price changes over the past year indicates that ZTS will perform in line with the market over the near term.

Financial Data

(US$ in Millions)	3 Mos	12/31/2015	12/31/2014	12/31/2013	12/31/2012	12/31/2011	12/31/2010	12/31/2009
Earnings Per Share	0.77	0.68	1.16	1.01	0.87	...	...	...
Cash Flow Per Share	1.32	1.33	1.25	1.36	0.91	...	...	...
Tang Book Value Per Share	N.M.	N.M.	N.M.	N.M.	4.35	...	...	...
Dividends Per Share	0.344	0.332	0.288	0.195		...	...	...
Dividend Payout %	44.68	48.82	24.83	19.31	...	...	...	...
Income Statement								
Total Revenue	1,162	4,765	4,785	4,561	4,336	4,233	3,582	2,760
EBITDA	396	865	1,138	1,009	938	499	273	(89)
Depn & Amortn	21	196	201	206	197	69	58	33
Income Before Taxes	332	545	820	690	710	394	178	(148)
Income Taxes	128	206	233	187	274	146	67	(47)
Net Income	204	339	583	504	436	245	110	(100)
Average Shares	499	502	502	500	500	...	...	...
Balance Sheet								
Current Assets	3,307	3,830	3,465	3,357	2,864	2,311	2,116	...
Total Assets	7,453	7,913	6,607	6,558	6,262	5,711	5,284	...
Current Liabilities	1,163	1,781	1,086	1,415	1,123	843	808	...
Long-Term Obligations	4,464	4,463	3,643	3,642	509	575	673	...
Total Liabilities	6,288	6,845	5,296	5,618	2,236	1,991	1,940	...
Stockholders' Equity	1,165	1,068	1,311	940	4,026	3,720	3,344	...
Shares Outstanding	496	497	501	500	500	...	...	...
Statistical Record								
Return on Assets %	5.45	4.67	8.86	7.86	...	4.46	...	...
Return on Equity %	30.95	28.50	51.80	20.30	...	6.94	...	...
EBITDA Margin %	34.08	18.15	23.78	22.12	21.63	11.79	7.62	N.M.
Net Margin %	17.56	7.11	12.18	11.05	10.06	5.79	3.07	N.M.
Asset Turnover	0.70	0.66	0.73	0.71	...	0.77	...	...
Current Ratio	2.84	2.15	3.19	2.37	2.55	2.74	2.62	...
Debt to Equity	3.83	4.18	2.78	3.87	0.13	0.15	0.20	...
Price Range	55.38-39.33	55.38-39.65	44.93-28.40	34.64-29.15	...	...	...	...
P/E Ratio	71.92-51.08	81.44-58.31	38.73-24.48	34.30-28.86	...	...	...	...
Average Yield %	0.76	0.72	0.85	0.61	...	...	...	...

Address: 100 Campus Drive, Florham Park, NJ 07932
Telephone: 973-822-7000

Web Site: www.zoetis.com
Officers: Frank A. D'Amelio - Chairman Kristin C. Peck - Group President, Executive Vice President

Auditors: KPMG LLP
Transfer Agents: Computershare Trust Company, N.A., College Station, TX

CONDENSED

STATISTICAL

TABULATION

The tab section consists of statistical highlights for all U.S. companies listed on the New York Stock Exchange.

Statistics for companies whose fiscal year ends prior to June 30 are listed under the prior calendar year. Statistics for companies whose fiscal year ends June 30 or after are listed under the current calendar year. Dividends and price ranges are on a calendar year basis.

Because of editorial constraints a column for fourth quarter results was not included. At fiscal year-end, full fiscal year per share earnings are listed and quarterly figures are eliminated. Quarterly per share earnings are inserted as the company reports in the current fiscal year.

NOTE: Figures listed under "Earnings Per Share" for investment companies are net asset value per share.

For abbreviations, see the blue section of the Handbook.

SYMBOL	COMPANY	NATURE OF BUSINESS	FISCAL YEAR-END	TOTAL REV. $MILL	NET INCOME $MILL	TOTAL ASSETS $MILL	NET STK EQUITY $MILL	NO OF INST	INST. HOLDINGS (SHARES)
DDD	3D Systems Corp. (DE)	Computer Hardware & Equipment	12/31/15	666.2	-655.5	893.3	655.9	339	56534163
MMM	3M Co	Medical Instruments & Equipment	12/31/15	30274.0	4833.0	32718.0	11708.0	2175	464618926
WBAI	500.com Ltd.	Sporting & Recreational	12/31/15	99.6	-323.9	2084.5	1767.9	49	8798271
WUBA	58.com Inc	IT Services	12/31/15	714.8	-263.0	4067.2	2829.8	185	55993199
ATEN	A10 Networks Inc	Manufacturing	12/31/15	199.0	-40.0	192.6	80.1	118	30560033
AAC	AAC Holdings Inc	Diagnostic & Health Related Service	12/31/15	212.3	11.2	316.0	141.7	7	251904
AIR	AAR Corp	Aerospace	5/31/15	1594.3	10.2	1515.0	845.1	220	34363714
AAN	Aaron's Inc	Retail - Furniture & Home Furnishing	12/31/15	3179.8	135.7	2658.9	1366.6	300	72023673
ABB	ABB Ltd	Electrical Equipment	12/31/15	35481.0	1933.0	41356.0	14481.0	439	116190870
ABT	Abbott Laboratories	Pharmaceuticals	12/31/15	20405.0	4423.0	41247.0	21211.0	2056	1190967254
ABBV	AbbVie Inc.	Biotechnology	12/31/15	22859.0	5144.0	53050.0	3945.0	1856	1165989952
ANF	Abercrombie & Fitch Co.	Retail - Apparel and Accessories	1/30/16	3518.7	35.6	2433.0	1291.1	428	84567695
GCH	Aberdeen Greater China Fund Inc	Holding and other Investment Office	12/31/15	3.5	1.6	95.8	91.2	39	4679305
JEQ	Aberdeen Japan Equity Fund Inc	Holding and other Investment Office	10/31/15	1.8	0.7	118.9	118.7	43	8507619
SGF	Aberdeen Singapore Fund Inc	Holding and other Investment Office	10/31/15	3.4	2.0	84.0	83.6	33	3873977
ABM	ABM Industries, Inc.	Sanitation Services	10/31/15	4897.8	76.3	2149.8	1007.5	274	54062587
AKR	Acadia Realty Trust	REITs	12/31/15	217.3	65.7	3032.3	1100.5	220	76756492
ACN	Accenture plc	IT Services	8/31/15	32914.4	3053.6	18266.1	6133.7	-	-
ACCO	Acco Brands Corp	Office Equipment & Furniture	12/31/15	1510.4	85.9	1953.4	581.2	286	108968326
ACW	Accuride Corp	Auto Parts	12/31/15	685.6	-8.1	606.7	57.0	128	32186515
ATV	Acorn International Inc	Retail - Specialty	12/31/14	94.8	-44.3	125.7	91.2	9	317818
ATU	Actuant Corp.	Industrial Machinery & Equipment	8/31/15	1249.3	19.9	1636.9	673.0	261	67220932
AYI	Acuity Brands Inc (Holding Compan	Electrical Equipment	8/31/15	2706.7	222.1	2429.6	1360.0	572	48169966
ADX	Adams Diversified Equity Fund Inc	Holding and other Investment Office	12/31/15	26.7	12.1	1475.7	1472.1	124	25096318
PEO	Adams Natural Resources Fund Inc	Holding and other Investment Office	12/31/15	19.0	10.3	596.2	582.7	94	6300005
AGRO	Adecoagro SA	Agricultural Crop Production	12/31/15	725.9	17.1	1370.7	535.4	127	75205772
ADPT	Adeptus Health Inc	Hospitals & Health Care Facilities	12/31/15	364.7	13.2	525.3	92.0	178	18023536
AAP	Advance Auto Parts Inc	Retail - Automotive	1/2/16	9737.0	473.4	8134.6	2460.6	678	83836188
WMS	Advanced Drainage Systems Inc	Plastics	3/31/15	1180.1	8.6	1041.7	298.2	112	44861199
ASX	Advanced Semiconductor Engineeri	Semiconductors	12/31/15	283302.5	20013.5	365268.2	154713.8	167	119378724
AAV	Advantage Oil & Gas Ltd	Production & Extraction	12/31/15	126.5	21.4	1517.4	1121.9	-	-
LCM	Advent / Claymore Enhanced Growt	Holding and other Investment Office	10/31/15	5.9	2.8	190.6	136.8	46	5696977
AVK	Advent Claymore Convertible Secur	Holding and other Investment Office	10/31/15	26.2	15.4	678.0	403.6	85	9003511
AGC	Advent Claymore Convertible Secur	Holding and other Investment Office	10/31/15	15.9	7.9	430.5	246.1	63	13890760
ACM	AECOM	Construction Services	9/30/15	17989.9	-154.8	14014.3	3407.7	359	133203398
ANW	Aegean Marine Petroleum Network	Equipment & Services	12/31/15	4231.7	35.9	1456.7	621.5	137	31659527
AEG	AEGON N.V.	Life & Health	12/31/15	29060.0	711.0	417175.0	27488.0	262	194475556
AER	Aercap Holdings NV	Aerospace	12/31/15	5287.6	1178.7	43914.5	8349.0	373	174533398
HIVE	Aerohive Networks Inc	Internet & Software	12/31/15	151.7	-46.2	140.9	34.2	69	21422087
AJRD	Aerojet Rocketdyne Holdings Inc	Defense	11/30/15	1708.3	-16.2	2034.9	-145.5	227	76496578
AES	AES Corp.	Electric Utilities	12/31/15	14963.0	306.0	36850.0	3687.0	611	700441968
AET	Aetna Inc.	Life & Health	12/31/15	60336.5	2390.2	53424.1	16114.3	1122	384480856
AMG	Affiliated Managers Group Inc.	Wealth Management	12/31/15	2484.5	516.0	7784.8	2837.1	661	64229802
AFL	AFLAC Inc.	Life & Health	12/31/15	20872.0	2533.0	118296.0	17708.0	1188	309988743
MITT	AG Mortgage Investment Trust Inc	REITs	12/31/15	141.3	13.8	3164.1	666.9	137	18710383
AGCO	AGCO Corp.	Industrial Machinery & Equipment	12/31/15	7467.3	264.0	6501.3	2838.3	525	89088747
A	Agilent Technologies, Inc.	Medical Instruments & Equipment	10/31/15	4038.0	401.0	7479.0	4167.0	818	324995038
ATG PR	AGL Capital Trust II	Gas Utilities		-	-	-	-	-	-
GAS	AGL Resources Inc.	Gas Utilities	12/31/15	3941.0	353.0	14754.0	3929.0	623	89540291
AEM	Agnico Eagle Mines Ltd	Precious Metals	12/31/15	1985.4	24.6	6683.2	4141.0	400	148740759
ADC	Agree Realty Corp.	REITs	12/31/15	70.0	39.0	792.5	451.1	225	16187917
GRO	Agria Corp	Agricultural Crop Production	6/30/15	944.7	-0.5	498.9	56.6	16	7681206
AGU	Agrium, Inc.	Agricultural Chemicals	12/31/15	14795.0	988.0	16377.0	6003.0	463	107766836
AHC	AH Belo Corp	Publishing	12/31/15	272.1	-17.8	221.5	117.8	92	14962271
AL	Air Lease Corp	Miscellaneous Transportation Servic	12/31/15	1222.8	253.4	12355.1	3019.9	282	95814804
APD	Air Products & Chemicals, Inc.	Specialty Chemicals	9/30/15	9894.9	1277.9	17438.1	7249.0	1139	231194828
AYR	Aircastle Ltd.	Aerospace	12/31/15	819.2	121.7	6570.0	1779.5	198	54956957
AKS	AK Steel Holding Corp.	Non-Precious Metals	12/31/15	6692.9	-509.0	4084.4	-977.6	303	104700449
ALP PRO	Alabama Power Co.	Electric Utilities	12/31/15	5768.0	811.0	21721.0	6273.0	-	-
ALG	Alamo Group, Inc.	Construction Services	12/31/15	879.6	43.2	603.5	360.5	152	10627359
AGI	Alamos Gold Inc (New)	Precious Metals	12/31/14	169.9	-2.1	879.5	783.3	153	175636661
ALK	Alaska Air Group, Inc.	Airlines/Air Freight	12/31/15	5598.0	848.0	6533.0	2411.0	594	116530830
AIN	Albany International Corp	Industrial Machinery & Equipment	12/31/15	709.9	57.3	1009.6	498.9	211	30475448
ALB	Albemarle Corp.	Specialty Chemicals	12/31/15	3651.3	334.9	9615.0	3254.4	479	114505150
AA	Alcoa, Inc.	Non-Precious Metals	12/31/15	22534.0	-322.0	36528.0	12046.0	987	1008072065
ALR	Alere Inc.	Medical Instruments & Equipment	12/31/14	2586.7	9.9	6718.0	1958.0	359	89056913
ALEX	Alexander & Baldwin Inc.	Property, Real Estate & Developmen	12/31/15	570.5	29.6	2243.5	1235.2	-	-
ALX	Alexander's, Inc.	REITs	12/31/15	207.9	76.9	1447.8	352.9	136	1997123
ARE	Alexandria Real Estate Equities, Inc	REITs	12/31/15	843.5	144.2	8911.1	3975.1	410	78383062
BABA	Alibaba Group Holding Ltd	Internet & Software	3/31/16	101143.0	71460.0	364450.0	217337.0	857	645578768
Y	Alleghany Corp.	General Insurance	12/31/15	4999.5	560.3	22846.3	7554.7	428	16865138
ATI	Allegheny Technologies, Inc	Non-Precious Metals	12/31/15	3719.6	-377.9	5751.7	2082.8	403	106710287
ALLE	Allegion Plc	Services	12/31/15	2068.1	153.9	2285.3	25.6	439	86548916
AGN	Allergan PLC	Pharmaceuticals	12/31/15	15071.0	3915.2	135840.7	76591.4	1259	346698075
ALE	Allete Inc.	Electric Utilities	12/31/15	1486.4	141.1	4907.1	1820.2	319	40069619
AKP	Alliance California Municipal Income	Holding and other Investment Office	10/31/15	8.2	6.4	209.9	159.5	25	1359630
ADS	Alliance Data Systems Corp.	Business Services	12/31/15	6439.7	605.4	22421.8	2010.0	713	66266913
AOI	Alliance One International Inc	Tobacco Products	3/31/15	2065.8	-15.4	1664.6	233.0	109	17443653
AWF	AllianceBernstein Global High Inco	Holding and other Investment Office	3/31/15	99.1	86.3	1429.6	1208.0	133	17237310
AB	AllianceBernstein Holding LP	Wealth Management	12/31/15	212.5	188.2	1590.0		265	40139539

T2

1st	2nd	3rd	2015	2014	2013	P/E	RATIO	Div 2015	Div 2014	Div 2013	AV. YLD %	AMOUNT	PAYABLE	PR High	PR Low
-0.16	-	-	-5.85	0.11	0.45	-		-	-	-	-	-	-	22.0	6.4
2.05	-	-	7.58	7.49	6.72	22.5	18.1	4.10	3.42	2.54	2.6	1.110Y	61/28/99	170.3	137.0
-	-	-	0.84	0.44	0.41			-	-	-	-	-		30.0	13.5
-	-	-	-1.07	0.13	0.13			-	-	-	-	-		81.8	40.6
-0.15	-	-	-0.64	-0.74	-3.14			-	-	-	-	-		8.1	4.9
0.03	-	-	0.48	0.41	0.12	93.2	32.4	-	-	-	-	-		44.8	15.5
-	-	0.14	0.24	1.83	1.38	135.8	77.9	0.30	0.30	0.30	1.2	0.0750Y	5/10/16	32.6	18.7
0.68	-	-	1.86	1.08	1.58	21.8	10.9	-	0.09	0.07	-	0.0250Y	61/28/99	40.5	20.3
-	-	0.36	0.87	1.13	1.21	26.6	18.5	0.75	0.77	0.70	3.9	-		23.1	16.1
0.21	-	-	2.92	1.49	1.62	17.5	12.4	0.96	0.88	0.56	2.2	0.260Y	61/28/99	51.2	36.3
0.83	-	-	3.13	1.10	2.56	22.8	15.4	2.02	1.66	1.60	3.3	0.570Y	61/28/99	71.2	48.3
-0.59	-	-	0.71	0.69	2.85	45.7	23.2	0.80	0.80	0.70	3.3	0.20Y	61/28/99	32.5	16.4
-	-	-	0.18	0.08	-0.04	60.2	0.0	0.51	0.23	1.34	5.8	0.0785B	1/12/16	10.8	0.0
-	-	-	0.05	0.04	0.07	166.4	129.4	0.07	0.15	0.06	0.9	0.0272B	1/12/16	8.3	6.5
-	-	-	0.26	0.29	0.39	44.2	0.0	1.05	0.89	1.26	11.4	0.260	1/12/16	11.5	0.0
-	0.08	-	1.33	1.32	1.30	25.7	20.0	0.64	0.62	0.60	2.1	0.1650Y	61/28/99	34.2	26.6
0.40	-	-	0.94	1.18	0.72	38.0	30.3	1.22	1.23	0.86	3.8	0.250Z	7/15/16	35.7	28.5
-	-	1.41	4.76	4.52	4.93			2.04	1.86	1.62	-	1.10	61/28/99		
0.04	-	-	0.78	0.79	0.67	12.7	7.2	-	-	-	-	-		9.9	5.7
-0.10	-	-	-0.16	-0.05	-0.81			-	-	-	-	-		4.6	0.8
-	-	-0.13	-	0.54	-0.47			-	-	-	-	-		19.2	0.0
-	-2.70	-	0.32	2.26	0.40	85.3	54.9	0.04	0.04	0.04	0.2	0.040Y	10/15/15	27.3	17.6
-	1.49	-	5.09	4.05	2.95	51.0	33.4	0.52	0.52	0.52	0.2	0.130Y	61/28/99	259.5	169.9
-	-	-	0.13	0.20	0.20	110.4	85.1	0.93	1.18	0.84	7.2	0.050	6/1/16	14.4	11.1
-	-	-	0.37	0.50	0.44	65.2	40.5	1.38	1.89	1.88	7.2	0.10	6/1/16	24.1	15.0
-	-	-0.05	0.14	0.02	-0.21	94.5	54.2	-	-	-	-	-		13.2	7.6
0.32	-	-	1.09	-0.34		110.9	35.4	-	-	-	-	-		120.9	38.5
2.14	-	-	6.40	6.71	5.32	31.3	21.6	0.24	0.24	0.24	0.1	0.060Y	61/28/99	200.4	138.4
-	-	0.13	-0.06	-0.07	0.41			0.08	1.68	0.10	0.3	0.060Y	6/30/16	33.0	18.3
-	-	0.57	2.51	2.79	1.99	2.8	0.0	7.18	4.53	3.61	129.7	-		7.0	0.0
-	-	0.04	0.12	0.09	-0.02	68.0	0.0	-	-	-	-	-		8.2	0.0
-	-	-	0.21	0.21	0.23	45.6	33.9	0.84	0.84	0.84	10.0	0.210	5/31/16	9.6	7.1
-	-	-	0.65	0.71	0.74	26.6	17.2	1.13	1.13	1.13	8.0	0.09390	6/30/16	17.3	11.2
-	-	-	-	0.24	0.27			-	0.56	0.56	-	0.0470	6/30/16	7.0	4.5
-	0.27	-	-1.04	2.33	2.35			-	-	-	-	-		35.4	23.1
-	-	-	0.73	0.37	0.58			0.08	0.05	0.04	-	0.020	6/21/16		
-	-	0.08	0.27	0.29	0.36	29.3	17.3	0.24	0.22	0.22	3.9	0.25560Z	9/15/16	7.9	4.7
-	-	0.73	5.72	4.54	2.54			-	-	-	-	-			
-0.25	-	-	-0.98	-0.85	-4.84			-	-	-	-	-		8.0	4.3
0.08	-	-	-0.27	-0.92	2.11			-	-	-	-	0.030Y	5/28/04	24.3	14.0
0.19	-	-	0.44	1.06	0.15	31.7	19.4	0.40	0.20	0.16	3.6	0.110Y	61/28/99	13.9	8.5
2.06	-	-	6.78	-	5.33	19.6	13.9	1.00	-	0.80	0.9	0.250Y	61/28/99	132.6	94.3
1.92	-	-	9.28	8.01	6.55	24.6	12.7	-	-	-	-	0.39040Z	5/16/16	227.9	117.8
1.74	-	-	5.85	6.50	6.76	11.9	9.4	1.58	1.50	1.42	2.5	0.410Y	61/28/99	69.8	55.2
-0.21	-	-	0.01	3.37	-1.61	1910.0	1078.0	2.27	2.40	2.80	15.3	0.4750Z	7/29/16	19.1	10.8
0.09	-	-	3.06	4.36	6.01	18.9	14.3	0.48	0.44	0.40	1.0	0.130Y	61/28/99	57.9	43.8
-	0.28	-	1.20	1.49	2.10	38.2	27.8	0.40	0.53	0.46	1.0	0.1150Y	61/28/00	45.9	33.4
1.51	-	-	2.94	4.04	2.64	22.6	15.8	2.04	1.96	1.88	3.4	0.530Y	61/28/99	66.4	46.6
-	-	0.01	0.11	0.39	-2.35	566.7	0.0	0.32	0.32	0.88	0.9	0.080	6/15/16	62.3	0.0
0.36	-	-	2.16	1.24	1.50	20.1	12.9	1.85	1.74	1.64	5.5	0.480Z	7/15/16	43.4	27.8
-	-	-	-	0.05	-7.67			-	-	-	-	-		1.8	0.9
0.02	-	-	6.98	4.97	7.20	19.9	0.0	3.40	3.03	2.50	3.2	0.8750	7/21/16	138.8	0.0
-0.03	-	-	-0.84	4.13	0.71			0.32	4.07	0.28	6.1	0.080Y	9/2/16	6.4	4.3
0.85	-	-	2.34	2.38	1.80	16.4	9.7	0.17	0.13	0.11	0.5	0.050Y	61/28/99	38.5	22.7
-	-2.17	-	5.88	4.61	4.68	25.4	19.8	3.20	3.02	2.77	2.3	0.860Y	61/28/99	149.2	116.3
0.46	-	-	1.50	1.25	0.40			0.90	0.82	0.69	-	0.240Y	6/15/16		
-0.08	-	-	-2.86	-0.65	-0.34			-	-	-	-	0.050Y	61/28/99	5.6	1.8
-	-	-	-	-	-			1.61	1.61	1.61	6.4	0.40630Y	7/1/16	30.9	0.0
0.75	-	-	3.76	3.42	2.96	16.4	11.8	0.32	0.28	0.28	0.6	0.090Y	4/29/16	61.6	44.3
-	-	-0.13	-	-0.02	0.30			-	-	-	-	0.010	4/29/16	9.6	0.0
1.46	-	-	6.56	4.42	3.58	13.2	9.2	0.80	0.50	0.20	1.1	0.2750	61/28/99	86.3	60.6
0.42	-	-	1.79	1.30	0.55	23.1	15.7	0.67	0.63	0.59	1.9	0.170Y	7/8/16	41.3	28.2
2.02	-	-	3.00	1.69	4.90	26.7	13.9	1.16	1.10	0.96	2.1	0.3050Y	61/28/99	80.1	41.8
0.00	-	-	-0.31	0.21	-2.14			0.12	0.12	0.12	1.3	0.93750Y	61/28/99	12.6	6.7
-	-	-	-	-0.14	-1.13			-	-	-	-	3.0Y	7/15/16	55.4	35.5
-0.15	-	-	0.54	1.25	0.82	76.3	54.3	0.21	0.17	0.04	0.6	0.060Y	61/28/99	41.2	29.3
4.31	-	-	15.04	13.29	11.14	28.6	0.0	14.00	13.00	11.00	3.6	4.0Z	5/20/16	430.0	0.0
-0.05	-	-	1.63	1.01	1.60	60.3	44.0	3.05	2.88	2.61	3.4	0.80Z	61/28/99	98.3	71.7
11.92	-	-	9.70	10.00	3.57	9.4	5.9	-	-	-	-	-		90.8	57.4
9.96	-	-	35.13	41.40	37.44	15.5	12.8	-	-	-	-	3.80360Y	6/15/09	544.8	450.9
-0.94	-	-	-3.53	-0.03	1.44			0.62	0.72	0.72	3.7	0.080Y	61/28/99	33.3	7.6
0.60	-	-	1.59	1.80	0.32			0.40	0.32	-	-	0.120	6/30/16		
0.47	-	-	10.01	-7.42	-5.27			-	-	-	-	13.750	61/28/99		
0.93	-	-	2.92	2.90	2.63	19.9	15.6	2.02	1.96	1.90	3.9	0.520Y	6/1/16	58.1	45.7
-	-	-	0.75	0.77	0.74	20.2	17.6	0.75	0.75	0.77	5.3	0.0517M	7/15/16	15.2	13.2
2.36	-	-	8.85	7.87	7.42	34.5	20.0	-	-	-	-	-		305.5	177.1
-	-	1.30	-1.70	-9.90	2.50			-	-	-	-	0.030Y	9/23/05	26.4	8.7
-	-	-	1.00	1.14	1.21	12.4	10.1	1.44	1.58	1.44	12.8	0.0810	7/15/16	12.4	10.1
0.56	-	-	1.80	1.86	1.71	16.8	8.9	1.93	1.80	1.59	7.8	0.40	5/19/16	31.8	16.8

SYMBOL	COMPANY	NATURE OF BUSINESS	FISCAL YEAR-END	TOTAL REV. $MILL	NET INCOME $MILL	TOTAL ASSETS $MILL	NET STK EQUITY $MILL	NO OF INST	INST. HOLDINGS (SHARES)
AFB	AllianceBernstein National Municipa	Holding and other Investment Office	10/31/15	28.3	23.4	712.2	519.7	67	4393296
LNT	Alliant Energy Corp	Electric Utilities	12/31/15	3253.6	388.4	12495.2	3724.1	550	82752746
NCV	AllianzGI Convertible & Income Fun	Holding and other Investment Office	2/28/15	85.8	76.2	1114.1	1097.0	101	20413910
NCZ	AllianzGI Convertible & Income Fun	Holding and other Investment Office	2/28/15	65.8	58.7	846.2	833.3	85	15157035
ACV	AllianzGI Diversified Income & Conv	Holding and other Investment Office	4/13/15	-	-	0.1			
NIE	AllianzGI Equity & Convertible Inco	Holding and other Investment Office	1/31/15	21.8	14.7	620.7	613.1	73	7075304
NFJ	AllianzGI NFJ Dividend Interest & P	Holding and other Investment Office	1/31/15	54.7	38.1	1621.4	1606.7	131	22146485
AWH	Allied World Assurance Company H	General Insurance	12/31/15	2546.4	83.9	13511.9	3532.5	306	82650097
ALSN	Allison Transmission Holdings Inc	Construction Services	12/31/15	1985.8	182.3	4408.4	1188.6	304	247717255
ALL	Allstate Corp.	General Insurance	12/31/15	35653.0	2171.0	104656.0	20025.0	1160	350592127
ALLY	Ally Financial Inc	Credit & Lending	12/31/15	9487.0	1289.0	158581.0	13439.0	3	107200
ALJ	Alon USA Energy Inc	Refining & Marketing	12/31/15	4338.2	52.8	2176.1	639.1	210	46052544
ALDW	Alon USA Partners LP	Refining & Marketing	12/31/15	2157.2	156.9	748.6		58	3975231
AGD	Alpine Global Dynamic Dividend Fu	Holding and other Investment Office	10/31/15	11.8	10.1	138.2	135.4	47	3913900
AWP	Alpine Global Premier Properties Fu	Holding and other Investment Office	10/31/14	27.8	18.9	708.5	672.1	112	30320268
AOD	Alpine Total Dynamic Dividend Fun	Holding and other Investment Office	10/31/14	82.2	69.9	1095.6	1077.1	113	40636198
RESI	Altisource Residential Corp	REITs	12/31/15	248.1	-46.0	2457.9	1152.4	135	49831057
MO	Altria Group Inc	Tobacco Products	12/31/15	25434.0	5241.0	32535.0	2880.0	1945	1442590023
ACH	Aluminum Corp of China Ltd.	Non-Precious Metals	12/31/15	123445.9	206.3	189269.3	38840.1	69	2642958
AMBR	Amber Road Inc	Internet & Software	12/31/15	67.1	-28.1	114.7	44.5	68	14049635
ABEV	Ambev SA	Beverages	12/31/15	46720.2	12423.8	90176.3	48331.9		
AMC	AMC Entertainment Holdings Inc.	Entertainment	12/31/15	2946.9	103.9	5110.1	1540.1	149	21368871
AMFW	AMEC Foster Wheeler PLC	Equipment & Services	12/31/15	5455.0	-256.0	5572.0	1599.0	84	10566525
AEE	Ameren Corp	Electric Utilities	12/31/15	6098.0	630.0	23640.0	6946.0	666	191316728
AMRC	Ameresco Inc.	Construction Services	12/31/15	630.8	30.4	728.7	289.5	99	13629593
AMX	America Movil, S.A.B. de C.V.	Services	12/31/15	894216.6	35054.8	1296486.8	112278.0	458	261087366
AAT	American Assets Trust Inc	Property, Real Estate & Developmen	12/31/15	275.6	53.9	1978.4	799.6	205	51533891
AXL	American Axle & Manufacturing Hol	Auto Parts	12/31/15	3903.1	235.6	3202.7	301.5	317	79044862
ACC	American Campus Communities Inc	REITs	12/31/15	753.4	116.0	6025.9	2770.2	403	142444552
AEO	American Eagle Outfitters, Inc.	Retail - Apparel and Accessories	1/30/16	3521.8	218.1	1612.2	1051.4	547	221033657
AEP	American Electric Power Company,	Electric Utilities	12/31/15	16453.2	2047.1	61683.1	17891.7	1109	384335197
AEL	American Equity Investment Life Ho	Life & Health	12/31/15	1518.9	219.8	49041.2	1944.5	318	89180264
AXP	American Express Co.	Credit & Lending	12/31/15	34441.0	5163.0	161184.0	20673.0	1800	892601234
AFG	American Financial Group Inc	General Insurance	12/31/15	6145.0	352.0	49859.0	4592.0	422	64209585
AMH	American Homes 4 Rent	REITs	12/31/15	630.6	-47.9	6807.8	3259.3		
AIG	American International Group Inc	General Insurance	12/31/15	58327.0	2196.0	496943.0	89658.0	1421	1114214668
AMID	American Midstream Partners LP	Equipment & Services	12/31/15	236.4	-127.5	891.3	169.7	58	14797526
ARL	American Realty Investors, Inc.	Property, Real Estate & Developmen	12/31/15	104.2	-2.0	1117.4	123.0	19	71223
ARA	American Renal Associates Holding	Diagnostic & Health Related Service	12/31/15	653.0	18.8	939.5	-128.7		
AWR	American States Water Co	Water Utilities	12/31/15	458.6	60.5	1348.6	465.9	286	24632713
AMT	American Tower Corp (New)	REITs	12/31/15	4771.5	685.1	26904.3	6651.7	1048	456415663
AVD	American Vanguard Corp.	Agricultural Chemicals	12/31/15	289.4	6.6	443.5	268.4	172	25393080
AWK	American Water Works Co, Inc.	Water Utilities	12/31/15	3159.0	476.0	17241.0	5049.0	703	172625950
APU	AmeriGas Partners, L.P.	Gas Utilities	9/30/15	2885.3	211.2	4141.7		297	27446022
AMP	Ameriprise Financial Inc	Wealth Management	12/31/15	12170.0	1562.0	145342.0	7217.0	897	166305271
ABC	AmerisourceBergen Corp.	Pharmaceuticals	9/30/15	135961.8	-134.9	27736.2	633.5	957	210632875
AME	AMETEK, Inc.	Electrical Equipment	12/31/15	3974.3	590.9	6664.5	3254.6	615	229519244
ANFI	Amira Nature Foods Ltd	Food	3/31/15	700.2	42.1	497.1	193.4	51	5448090
AHS	AMN Healthcare Services, Inc.	Diagnostic & Health Related Service	12/31/15	1463.1	81.9	880.4	347.9	341	57695222
AP	Ampco-Pittsburgh Corp.	Non-Precious Metals	12/31/15	238.5	1.4	506.2	211.4	82	6202203
APH	Amphenol Corp.	Electrical Equipment	12/31/15	5568.7	763.5	7458.4	3238.5	689	329710022
BETR	Amplify Snack Brands Inc	Food	12/31/15	183.9	9.9	360.8	15.4	109	64770474
AXR	AMREP Corp.	Business Services	4/30/15	49.8	11.3	138.7	93.3	37	1834084
APC	Anadarko Petroleum Corp	Production & Extraction	12/31/15	8698.0	-6692.0	46414.0	12819.0	1225	552077394
AU	AngloGold Ashanti Ltd	Precious Metals	12/31/15	4015.0	-85.0	7204.0	2430.0	261	214030951
BUD	Anheuser-Busch Inbev SA	Beverages	12/31/15	43604.0	8273.0	134635.0	42137.0	608	94601179
AXE	Anixter International Inc	Electrical Equipment	1/1/16	6190.5	127.6	4142.0	1179.4	267	35560979
NLY	Annaly Capital Management Inc	REITs	12/31/15	1135.6	466.6	75190.9	11896.0	728	587398902
AM	Antero Midstream Partners LP	Equipment & Services	12/31/15	387.3	117.6	1980.0		100	68458137
AR	Antero Resources Corp	Production & Extraction	12/31/15	3954.9	941.4	14155.2	5934.4	288	438618051
ANTM	Anthem Inc	Hospitals & Health Care Facilities	12/31/15	79156.5	2560.0	61717.8	23044.1	837	223709588
ANH	Anworth Mortgage Asset Corp.	REITs	12/31/15	72.5	14.7	6636.3	702.2	212	62289829
AON	Aon Plc	Brokers & Intermediaries	12/31/15	11682.0	1385.0	27164.0	6106.0	710	250098124
APA	Apache Corp.	Production & Extraction	12/31/15	6366.0	-23528.0	18842.0	2566.0	1139	423797836
AIV	Apartment Investment & Manageme	REITs	12/31/15	981.3	248.7	6144.2	1622.4	437	190615374
ARI	Apollo Commercial Real Estate Fina	REITs	12/31/15	192.2	103.3	2719.9	1375.4	210	43697570
APO	Apollo Global Management LLC	Finance Intermediaries & Services	12/31/15	1041.7	134.5	4559.8	649.5	187	121839774
AMTG	Apollo Residential Mortgage, Inc.	REITs	12/31/15	160.1	-11.6	3663.0	694.9	151	22994329
AFT	Apollo Senior Floating Rate Fund In	Holding and other Investment Office	12/31/14	27.5	18.4	469.1	285.0	56	5344350
AIF	Apollo Tactical Income Fund Inc	Holding and other Investment Office	12/31/14	29.8	21.6	425.4	263.4	40	5462609
APLE	Apple Hospitality REIT Inc	REITs	12/31/15	898.3	117.3	3722.8	2647.1	147	70097961
AIT	Applied Industrial Technologies, Inc.	Industrial Machinery & Equipment	6/30/15	2751.6	115.5	1435.0	741.3	249	40393027
ATR	AptarGroup Inc.	Plastics	12/31/15	2317.1	199.3	2438.7	1149.4	426	74086648
WTR	Aqua America Inc	Water Utilities	12/31/15	814.2	201.8	5741.0	1725.9	521	93571655
ARMK	Aramark	Hotels, Restaurants & Travel	10/2/15	14329.1	235.9	10224.0	1883.4	351	229725384
ABR	Arbor Realty Trust Inc	REITs	12/31/15	142.6	53.4	1827.4	565.1	102	22552873
ARC	ARC Document Solutions, Inc.	Office Equipment & Furniture	12/31/15	428.7	97.0	476.1	202.1	146	35259280
ARCX	ARC Logistics Partners LP	Equipment & Services	12/31/15	81.8	10.7	648.5		29	10109183
MT	ArcelorMittal SA	Non-Precious Metals	12/31/15	63578.0	-7946.0	76846.0	25272.0	38	1295104
ADM	Archer Daniels Midland Co.	Food	12/31/15	67702.0	1849.0	40157.0	17899.0	992	557304699

T4

| EARNINGS PER SHARE | | | | | | P/E RATIO | | DIVIDENDS PER SHARE | | | AV. YLD | DIV. DECLARED | | PRICE RANGE 2015 | |
| QUARTERLY | | | ANNUAL | | | | | | | | % | | | | |
1st	2nd	3rd	2015	2014	2013			2015	2014	2013		AMOUNT	PAYABLE		
-	-	-	0.81	0.85	0.82	18.5	16.1	0.82	0.87	0.89	6.0	0.0552M	7/15/16	15.0	13.0
0.42	-	-	1.68	1.73	1.62	22.3	16.2	2.20	2.04	1.80	6.9	0.29380Y	61/28/99	37.5	27.3
-	-	-	0.87	1.02	1.02	10.2	5.2	1.08	1.08	1.08	17.4	0.0650	7/1/16	8.9	4.5
-	-	-	0.80	0.95	0.93	9.9	5.0	1.02	1.02	1.02	18.3	0.05750	7/1/16	7.9	4.0
-	-	-	-	-	-	-	-	-	-	-	-	0.1670	7/1/16	25.0	14.8
-	-	-	0.53	0.56	0.39	38.4	29.9	1.32	1.36	1.12	7.3	0.380	6/24/16	20.3	15.9
-	-	-	0.41	0.49	0.53	39.3	25.8	1.80	1.80	1.80	13.9	0.30	6/24/16	16.1	10.6
0.81	-	-	0.89	4.92	3.98	-	-	1.00	0.84	0.63	-	0.260	61/28/99	-	-
0.28	-	-	1.03	1.25	0.88	29.8	21.0	0.60	0.51	0.42	2.2	0.150Y	61/28/99	30.7	21.6
0.57	-	-	5.05	6.27	4.81	13.7	11.3	1.20	1.12	1.00	1.9	0.39060Y	61/28/99	69.4	57.0
0.49	-	-	-2.66	1.83	-1.64	-	-	-	-	-	-	0.53130Y	5/16/16	23.7	15.3
-0.51	-	-	0.75	0.55	0.33	30.5	9.9	0.55	0.53	0.38	3.7	0.150Y	6/6/16	22.9	7.4
-0.14	-	-	2.51	2.71	2.18	10.5	3.6	3.43	2.02	2.76	17.8	0.080	2/29/16	26.3	9.2
-	-	-	0.80	0.70	0.78	13.0	9.3	0.77	0.64	-	8.6	0.0650	7/29/16	10.4	7.5
-	-	-	-	0.22	0.34	-	-	-	0.60	0.60	-	0.050	7/29/16	6.9	4.7
-	-	-	-	0.64	0.68	-	-	-	0.56	-	-	0.05750	7/29/16	9.1	6.6
-0.82	-	-	-0.81	3.34	1.61	-	-	1.83	2.03	0.35	13.6	0.150Z	7/15/16	18.4	8.7
0.62	-	-	2.67	2.56	2.26	24.4	17.8	2.17	2.00	1.84	3.8	0.5650Y	61/28/99	65.0	47.5
-	-	-	0.01	-1.20	0.07	1501.0	695.0	-	-	-	-	-	-	15.0	7.0
-0.22	-	-	-1.07	-1.46	-5.11	-	-	-	-	-	-	-	-	7.7	3.5
-	-	-	0.78	0.76	0.74	8.0	5.0	0.62	0.72	-	12.1	-	-	6.3	3.9
0.29	-	-	1.06	0.66	4.76	31.0	18.9	0.80	0.60	-	3.0	0.20	6/20/16	32.9	20.1
-	-	-	0.77	0.27	0.60	18.4	6.2	0.28	0.42	0.37	3.1	-	-	14.2	4.8
0.43	-	-	2.59	2.40	1.18	19.6	14.5	1.66	1.61	1.60	3.8	0.4250Y	61/28/99	50.8	37.5
0.02	-	-	0.06	0.22	0.05	131.8	65.5	-	-	-	-	-	-	7.9	3.9
-	-	0.23	0.52	0.67	1.02	41.5	23.4	11.13	4.78	4.45	68.1	-	-	21.6	12.2
0.17	-	-	0.86	0.51	0.38	50.6	40.2	0.95	0.89	0.85	2.4	0.250Z	6/24/16	34.5	34.6
0.78	-	-	3.02	1.85	1.23	8.4	3.9	-	-	-	-	0.020Y	12/29/08	25.3	11.8
0.36	-	-	1.02	0.58	0.98	47.1	31.6	1.58	1.50	1.42	3.9	0.420Z	61/28/99	48.0	32.3
0.22	-	-	0.42	0.43	1.16	43.7	31.2	0.50	0.38	2.05	3.1	0.1250Y	61/28/99	18.4	13.1
1.02	-	-	4.17	3.34	3.04	16.1	12.6	2.15	2.03	1.95	3.7	0.560Y	61/28/99	67.0	52.5
-0.55	-	-	2.72	1.58	3.38	10.9	4.7	0.22	0.20	0.18	1.0	0.220Y	61/28/99	29.5	12.8
1.45	-	-	5.05	5.56	4.88	16.1	10.1	1.10	0.98	0.86	1.6	0.290Y	61/28/99	81.4	51.1
1.14	-	-	3.94	-	5.16	19.1	16.1	2.03	-	1.80	2.9	0.280Y	61/28/99	75.2	63.5
-0.02	-	-	-0.40	-0.34	-0.36	-	-	0.20	0.20	0.05	1.2	0.34380Z	61/28/99	18.6	13.2
-0.16	-	-	1.65	5.20	6.13	39.1	30.4	0.81	0.50	0.20	1.4	0.220Y	61/28/99	64.5	50.2
-0.33	-	-	-6.00	-8.58	-7.00	-	-	1.89	1.85	1.75	18.3	0.41250	5/13/16	18.8	4.0
-0.24	-	-	-0.21	2.28	3.37	-	-	-	-	-	-	-	-	7.5	0.0
0.16	-	-	0.83	0.73	-0.94	34.2	31.9	-	-	-	-	-	-	28.4	26.5
0.28	-	-	1.60	1.57	1.61	29.5	22.5	0.87	0.83	0.76	2.2	0.2240Y	61/28/99	47.2	36.0
0.58	-	-	1.41	2.00	1.38	76.0	59.3	1.81	1.40	1.10	1.9	0.530Z	61/28/99	107.2	83.7
0.10	-	-	0.23	0.17	1.19	73.7	43.8	0.02	0.17	0.22	0.1	0.010Y	7/12/16	17.0	10.1
0.46	-	-	2.64	2.35	2.06	28.5	18.4	1.33	1.21	0.84	2.2	0.3750Y	61/28/99	75.2	48.6
-	1.74	-	1.91	2.82	2.14	25.8	16.9	3.60	3.44	3.28	8.5	0.940	5/18/16	49.3	32.2
2.09	-	-	8.48	8.30	6.44	15.3	9.0	2.59	2.26	2.01	2.4	0.750Y	61/28/99	129.9	76.3
-	2.68	-	-0.62	1.17	1.84	-	-	1.16	0.94	0.84	1.2	0.340Y	61/28/99	115.0	73.7
0.57	-	-	2.45	2.37	2.10	23.5	18.3	0.36	0.33	0.24	0.7	0.090Y	61/28/99	57.5	44.8
-	0.18	-	1.46	1.04	0.63	-	-	-	-	-	-	-	-	-	-
0.53	-	-	1.68	0.69	0.09	22.9	13.0	-	-	-	-	-	-	38.5	21.9
-0.26	-	-	0.13	-0.11	1.20	146.8	71.5	0.72	0.72	0.72	5.6	0.090Y	4/29/16	19.1	9.3
0.50	-	-	2.41	2.21	1.96	24.5	18.8	0.53	0.45	0.30	1.0	0.140Y	61/28/99	59.0	45.4
0.11	-	-	0.13	0.06	1895.01	125.8	72.5	-	-	-	-	-	-	16.4	9.4
-	-	-0.07	1.43	-0.42	-0.47	3.7	0.0	-	-	-	-	1.7	8/24/07	5.3	0.0
-2.03	-	-	-13.18	-3.47	1.58	-	-	1.08	0.99	0.54	1.8	0.050Y	61/28/99	84.8	30.5
-	-	-0.09	-0.20	-0.14	-6.31	-	-	-	-	-	-	-	-	16.4	5.7
-	-	0.84	4.96	5.54	8.72	26.6	20.9	3.95	3.24	3.03	3.3	-	-	131.8	103.9
0.68	-	-	3.81	5.84	6.04	18.4	10.0	-	-	5.00	-	5.7	61/28/99	70.1	38.3
-0.96	-	-	0.42	-0.96	3.74	26.5	20.7	1.97	1.97	1.97	19.8	0.30Z	61/28/99	11.1	8.7
0.23	-	-	0.76	0.05	-	38.6	22.3	0.67	-	-	2.9	0.2350	5/25/16	29.3	16.9
-0.02	-	-	3.43	2.57	-0.07	11.7	5.6	-	-	-	-	-	-	40.1	19.1
2.63	-	-	0.30	8.99	8.20	18.2	12.5	2.50	1.75	1.50	1.8	0.650Y	61/28/99	171.0	117.2
-0.22	-	-	0.08	0.18	0.49	66.6	48.6	0.60	0.56	0.50	12.5	0.150Z	7/29/16	5.3	3.9
1.15	-	-	4.88	4.66	3.53	-	-	1.15	0.93	0.68	-	0.330	5/16/16	-	-
-1.29	-	-	-61.20	-14.06	5.50	-	-	1.00	0.95	0.77	2.1	0.250Y	61/28/99	59.6	34.4
0.15	-	-	1.52	2.06	1.40	28.4	22.9	1.18	1.04	0.96	3.0	0.330Z	61/28/99	43.1	34.9
0.18	-	-	1.54	1.72	1.26	11.7	9.8	1.78	1.60	1.60	10.8	0.53910Z	7/15/16	17.9	15.1
-0.19	-	-	0.61	0.62	4.03	37.5	20.7	1.96	3.11	3.95	11.1	0.250	5/31/16	22.9	12.6
-0.52	-	-	-0.81	2.55	-2.02	-	-	1.92	1.71	2.20	14.5	0.50Z	7/29/16	16.0	9.7
-	-	-	-	1.18	1.34	-	-	-	1.23	1.26	-	0.090	7/29/16	18.2	13.8
-	-	-	-	1.50	1.03	-	-	-	1.66	0.97	-	0.1170	7/29/16	16.5	12.6
0.20	-	-	0.65	0.04	1.26	31.8	25.2	0.80	-	-	4.2	0.10Z	7/18/16	20.7	16.4
-	-	-1.14	2.80	2.67	2.78	16.5	13.1	1.04	0.96	0.88	2.5	0.280Y	8/31/16	46.1	36.7
0.67	-	-	3.09	2.85	2.52	25.9	19.9	1.14	1.09	1.00	1.6	0.30Y	61/28/99	80.0	61.4
0.29	-	-	1.14	1.31	1.25	28.9	21.5	0.69	0.63	0.62	2.4	0.1780Y	61/28/99	32.9	24.5
-	0.27	-	0.96	0.63	0.33	35.8	30.0	0.34	0.23	-	1.1	0.0950Y	61/28/99	34.3	28.8
0.02	-	-	0.90	1.70	0.39	8.1	6.7	0.58	0.52	0.50	8.7	0.46090Z	8/15/16	7.3	6.0
0.05	-	-	2.04	0.15	-0.33	3.8	1.7	-	-	-	-	-	-	7.8	3.4
0.15	-	-	0.39	0.05	0.10	48.6	24.2	1.69	1.40	-	12.0	0.440	5/13/16	19.0	9.4
-	-	-0.12	-4.43	-1.00	-1.46	-	-	0.17	0.17	0.17	2.8	0.3750Z	1/15/16	11.4	3.0
0.39	-	-	2.98	3.43	2.02	17.8	10.2	1.12	0.06	0.76	2.7	0.30Y	61/28/99	53.0	30.5

SYMBOL	COMPANY	NATURE OF BUSINESS	FISCAL YEAR-END	TOTAL REV. $MILL	NET INCOME $MILL	TOTAL ASSETS $MILL	NET STK EQUITY $MILL	NO OF INST	INST. HOLDINGS (SHARES)
AROC	Archrock Inc	Equipment & Services	12/31/15	998.1	-105.8	2706.8	733.9	241	66486838
AROC	Archrock Inc	Equipment & Services	12/31/15	998.1	-105.8	2706.8	733.9	241	66486838
ARCO	Arcos Dorados Holdings Inc	Hotels, Restaurants & Travel	12/31/15	3052.7	-51.6	1407.0	286.3	107	81738081
ASC	Ardmore Shipping Corp	Shipping	12/31/15	157.9	32.0	778.2	347.6	117	19288091
ACRE	Ares Commercial Real Estate Corp	REITs	12/31/15	121.8	43.3	1379.0	409.5	121	19147208
ARDC	Ares Dynamic Credit Allocation Fun	Finance Intermediaries & Services	10/31/14	30.0	21.4	478.0	321.4	56	7752451
ARES PR	Ares Management LP	Venture Capital	12/31/15	814.4	19.4	4321.4	23.5	40	9311034
AGX	Argan Inc	Construction Services	1/31/16	413.3	36.3	410.9	218.5	175	11529805
ANET	Arista Networks Inc	Computer Hardware & Equipment	12/31/15	837.6	121.1	1159.9	788.2	231	34162145
AI	Arlington Asset Investment Corp	Credit & Lending	12/31/15	2.2	-69.4	4204.8	484.0	149	24663102
AHH	Armada Hoffler Properties Inc	Property, Real Estate & Developmen	12/31/15	252.4	19.6	689.5	49.5	147	21742728
ARR	ARMOUR Residential REIT Inc.	REITs	12/31/15	5.7	-31.2	13055.3	1225.2	139	20452695
AFI	Armstrong Flooring Inc	Plastics	12/31/15	1188.7	48.9	863.4	617.9		
AFI	Armstrong Flooring Inc	Plastics	12/31/15	1188.7	48.9	863.4	617.9		
AWI	Armstrong World Industries Inc	Metal Products	12/31/15	2420.0	94.2	2691.9	768.8	246	62010249
ARW	Arrow Electronics, Inc.	Electrical Equipment	12/31/15	23282.0	497.7	13021.9	4142.4	505	108102276
APAM	Artisan Partners Asset Management	Wealth Management	12/31/15	805.5	81.8	946.5	130.0	193	40699919
ASA	ASA Gold and Precious Metals Ltd	Holding and other Investment Office	11/30/14	2.2	-1.5	223.3	221.8	67	7515171
ABG	Asbury Automotive Group, Inc	Retail - Automotive	12/31/15	6588.3	169.2	2305.9	314.5	286	27025310
AHP	Ashford Hospitality Prime Inc	REITs	12/31/15	349.5	-6.7	1352.8	401.1	147	23889818
AHT	Ashford Hospitality Trust Inc	REITs	12/31/15	1337.0	270.9	4965.1	811.1	236	88937121
ASH	Ashland Inc	Specialty Chemicals	9/30/15	5387.0	309.0	10064.0	3037.0	520	59996542
APB	Asia Pacific Fund, Inc. (The)	Holding and other Investment Office	3/31/15	5.0	2.4	138.8	135.2	46	7148590
GRR	Asia Tigers Fund, Inc. (The)	Holding and other Investment Office	10/31/15	1.2	0.3	40.2	39.9	29	1493340
ASPN	Aspen Aerogels Inc	Paper & Forest Products	12/31/15	122.5	-6.4	140.1	122.5	60	18012975
AHL	Aspen Insurance Holdings Ltd	General Insurance	12/31/15	2753.4	323.1	11048.8	3418.6	330	61243047
ASB	Associated Banc-Corp	Banking	12/31/15	1082.1	188.3	27715.0	2937.2	301	120909592
AC	Associated Capital Group Inc	Brokers & Intermediaries	12/31/15	22.8	-0.1	836.7	754.9	74	2362193
AIZ	Assurant Inc	Life & Health	12/31/15	10325.5	141.6	30043.1	4524.0	511	71834546
AGO	Assured Guaranty Ltd	General Insurance	12/31/15	2207.0	1056.0	14544.0	6063.0	361	150219052
AF	Astoria Financial Corp.	Credit & Lending	12/31/15	528.0	88.1	15076.2	1663.4	251	85803389
AZN	AstraZeneca Plc	Pharmaceuticals	12/31/15	24708.0	2825.0	60124.0	18490.0	530	270648484
T	AT&T Inc	Services	12/31/15	146801.0	13345.0	402672.0	122671.0	2552	3703483933
ATTO	Atento SA	Services	12/31/15	1965.6	49.1	1378.4	397.8	36	70110435
ATKR	Atkore International Group Inc	Electrical Equipment	9/25/15	1729.2	-5.0	1113.8	156.3		
ARP	Atlas Resource Partners, L.P.	Production & Extraction	12/31/15	740.0	-808.8	1731.0		84	27936324
ATO	Atmos Energy Corp.	Gas Utilities	9/30/15	4142.1	315.1	9092.9	3194.8	503	83546390
ATW	Atwood Oceanics, Inc.	Equipment & Services	9/30/15	1395.9	432.6	4809.0	2947.2	376	78507527
AUO	AU Optronics Corp.	Electrical Equipment	12/31/15	360346.5	7242.2	399237.1	158012.5	149	80381352
ATHM	Autohome Inc	IT Services	12/31/15	3464.0	990.6	7530.1	4851.0	137	36972482
ALV	Autoliv Inc.	Auto Parts	12/31/15	9169.6	456.8	7525.5	3455.6	369	38416149
AN	AutoNation, Inc.	Retail - Automotive	12/31/15	20862.0	442.6	9558.3	2349.3	525	88980049
AZO	AutoZone, Inc.	Retail - Automotive	8/29/15	10187.3	1160.2	8102.3	-1701.4	807	37224000
AVB	AvalonBay Communities, Inc.	REITs	12/31/15	1856.0	741.7	16931.3	9840.5	643	151626864
AGR	Avangrid Inc	Electric Utilities	12/31/14	4594.0	424.0	24252.0	12440.0	200	40831081
ACP	Avenue Income Credit Strategies F	Finance Intermediaries & Services	10/31/14	27.6	20.5	348.3	235.8	47	5222927
AVY	Avery Dennison Corp.	Containers & Packaging	1/2/16	5966.9	274.3	4133.7	965.7	671	101634444
AVG	AVG Technologies N.V.	IT Services	12/31/15	428.3	48.9	681.6	90.6	171	44296022
AVH	Avianca Holdings SA	Airlines/Air Freight	12/31/15	4361.3	-155.4	6361.9	1354.0	54	8202642
AVA	Avista Corp.	Electric Utilities	12/31/15	1484.8	123.2	4906.6	1528.6	321	46763175
AV	Aviva Plc	General Insurance	12/31/15	23728.0	918.0	387874.0	17087.0	7	158507
AVT	Avnet Inc	Electrical Equipment	6/27/15	27924.7	571.9	10800.0	4685.0	565	150785483
AVP	Avon Products, Inc.	Household & Personal Products	12/31/15	6160.5	-1148.9	3879.5	-1070.3	503	423354969
AVX	AVX Corp.	Electrical Equipment	3/31/15	1195.5	101.5	2409.8	2177.1	194	47999101
AXTA	Axalta Coating Systems Ltd	Miscellaneous Transportation Servic	12/31/15	4113.3	93.7	5854.2	1073.7	282	236446486
AXLL	Axiall Corp	Specialty Chemicals	12/31/15	3361.1	-816.4	4539.4	1578.3	270	72114708
AXS	AXIS Capital Holdings Ltd	General Insurance	12/31/15	4130.3	641.6	19981.9	5866.9	381	88371634
AXON	Axovant Sciences Ltd	Pharmaceuticals	3/31/16	-	-133.1	282.5	266.7	82	25307942
AZZ	AZZ Inc	Business Services	2/29/16	903.2	76.8	983.4	481.2	231	22464714
BGS	B&G Foods Inc	Food	1/2/16	966.4	69.1	2571.7	457.7	331	57301435
BW	Babcock & Wilcox Enterprises Inc	Industrial Machinery & Equipment	12/31/15	1757.3	19.1	1663.0	747.7	185	50060659
MCI	Babson Capital Corporate Investors	Holding and other Investment Office	12/31/15	26.8	20.4	315.7	275.9	54	2290376
BGH	Babson Capital Global Short Durati	Finance Intermediaries & Services	12/31/14	53.6	42.5	613.2	441.2		
MPV	Babson Capital Participating Investo	Holding and other Investment Office	12/31/15	12.5	9.8	154.7	135.3	31	1785529
BMI	Badger Meter, Inc.	Electronic Instruments & Related Pro	12/31/15	377.7	25.9	355.5	232.3	188	13533366
BHI	Baker Hughes Inc.	Equipment & Services	12/31/15	15742.0	-1967.0	24080.0	16298.0	948	402970381
BLL	Ball Corp	Metal Products	12/31/15	7997.0	280.9	9777.0	1251.3	614	134862887
BANC	Banc of California Inc	Banking	12/31/15	486.6	62.1	8235.6	652.4	194	38668360
BBVA	Banco Bilbao Vizcaya Argentaria S	Banking	12/31/15	37360.0	2642.0	750078.0	47290.0	286	114909324
BBD	Banco Bradesco S.A.	Banking	12/31/15	139483.7	18132.9	1026703.5	90789.4	281	587667864
BCH	Banco de Chile	Banking	12/31/15	2228770.0	609903.0	31057596.0	3175322.0	91	2755542
BLX	Banco Latinoamericano de Comerci	Banking	12/31/15	248.7	104.0	8286.2	971.9	51	9325336
BMA	Banco Macro S.A.	Banking	12/31/15	26633.7	5008.4	104952.0	15876.1	130	10512675
BSBR	Banco Santander Brasil SA	Banking	12/31/15	72814.9	9783.7	605394.5	79400.2	98	62372001
BSAC	Banco Santander Chile	Banking	12/31/15	2244137.0	448466.0	34637660.0	2772374.0	172	82581123
SAN	Banco Santander SA	Banking	12/31/15	76745.0	5966.0	1340260.0	88040.0	367	111146707
CIB	BanColombia, S.A.	Banking	12/31/15	5644477.0	2518890.0	92972867.0	19279449.0	172	49871132
BXS	BancorpSouth Inc.	Banking	12/31/15	742.3	127.5	13798.7	1655.4	233	66104337
BAC	Bank of America Corp.	Banking	12/31/15	93056.0	15888.0	2144316.0	256205.0	2201	6728425178
BOH	Bank of Hawaii Corp	Banking	12/31/15	618.3	160.7	15455.0	1116.3	360	40563134

T6

| EARNINGS PER SHARE | | | | | | P/E RATIO | | DIVIDENDS PER SHARE | | | AV. YLD % | DIV. DECLARED | | PRICE RANGE 2015 | |
| QUARTERLY | | | ANNUAL | | | | | | | | | | | | |
1st	2nd	3rd	2015	2014	2013			2015	2014	2013		AMOUNT	PAYABLE		
-	-	-0.09	-1.55	1.40	1.86	-		0.60	0.60	-	6.3	0.0950Y	5/18/16	14.1 -	0.0
-	-	-0.09	-1.55	1.40	1.86	-		0.60	0.60	-	5.5	0.0950Y	5/18/16	21.0 -	3.7
-	-	-	-0.25	-0.52	0.26	-		-	0.24	0.24		0.05950	1/2/15	-	
-	-	-	1.23	0.07	0.31	-		0.61	0.40	0.07	-	0.160	5/31/16	-	
0.18	-	-	1.20	0.85	0.72	10.9 -	7.5	1.00	1.00	1.00	8.6	0.260Z	7/15/16	13.1 -	9.0
-	-	-	1.24	1.09		-		-	1.40	1.17	-	0.110	6/30/16	16.1 -	12.0
-0.04	-	-	0.23	0.43	-	-		-	-	-	-	0.150	6/7/16	-	
0.81	-	-	2.05	2.78	1.65	20.2 -	14.0	0.70	0.75	0.60	2.0	0.70Y	11/5/15	41.4 -	28.7
0.48	-	-	1.67	1.29	0.72	52.5 -	31.7	-	-	-	-	-	-	87.7 -	53.0
-1.38	-	-	-3.02	0.29	3.06	-		3.00	3.50	3.50	20.2	0.6250Y	7/29/16	21.1 -	10.2
0.57	-	-	0.75	0.37	0.39	16.4 -	12.7	0.68	0.64	0.40	6.4	0.180	7/7/16	12.3 -	9.5
-7.73	-	-	-1.09	-4.32	-4.40	-		1.65	4.80	6.48	7.8	0.220Z	5/27/16	24.1 -	17.5
														13.7 -	12.0
														17.6 -	12.0
-0.18	-	-	1.68	1.14	1.60	30.9 -	18.7	-	-	-	-	8.557	61/28/99	52.0 -	31.5
1.14	-	-	5.20	4.98	3.85	12.6 -	9.0	-	-	-	-	0.025	61/28/99	65.3 -	46.7
0.35	-	-	1.86	-0.37	-2.04	25.8 -	13.0	3.35	3.83	0.86	9.1	0.60	5/31/16	47.9 -	24.2
-	-	-	-0.08	0.02		-		-	0.04	0.18	-	0.020	5/27/16	-	
1.27	-	-	6.41	3.71	3.51	14.9 -	7.0	-	-	-	-	0.2250Y	61/28/99	95.5 -	45.1
-0.04	-	-	-0.34	0.07	-0.73	-		0.35	0.20	0.05	2.7	0.3438GZ	7/15/16	15.9 -	9.7
-0.20	-	-	2.35	-0.75	-1.00	3.8 -	1.9	0.48	0.48	0.48	7.2	0.56250Z	7/15/16	8.9 -	4.6
-	1.38	-	4.48	3.00	8.57	28.6 -	19.9	1.46	1.36	1.13	1.3	0.390Y	61/28/99	128.3 -	89.3
-	-	-	0.23	-0.02	-0.03	56.5 -	0.0	-	-	-	-	0.510	1/8/16	13.0 -	0.0
-	-	-	0.08	0.05	0.07	144.4 -	0.0	0.47	0.29	2.66	5.3	0.0326B	1/12/16	11.6 -	0.0
-0.08	-	-	-0.28	-5.37	404.12	-		-	-	-	-	-	-	8.9 -	3.5
1.68	-	-	4.54	4.82	4.14	-		0.83	0.78	0.71	-	0.37190	61/28/99	-	
0.27	-	-	1.19	1.16	1.10	17.5 -	13.0	0.41	0.37	0.33	2.2	0.38280Y	61/28/99	20.8 -	15.5
0.06	-	-	0.00			-		-	-	-	-	0.1GY	6/28/16	35.2 -	0.0
3.34	-	-	2.05	6.44	6.30	43.3 -	32.0	1.37	1.06	0.96	1.8	0.50Y	61/28/99	88.7 -	65.5
0.43	-	-	7.08	6.26	4.30	4.2 -	3.1	0.48	0.44	0.40	1.9	0.130	61/28/99	29.5 -	22.0
0.16	-	-	0.79	0.88	0.60	22.7 -	16.3	0.16	0.16	0.16	1.0	0.40630Z	7/15/16	17.9 -	12.9
-	-	0.99	2.23	0.98	2.04	15.6 -	12.5	1.38	1.40	1.40	4.4	-	-	34.8 -	27.9
0.61	-	-	2.37	1.19	3.39	16.7 -	13.4	1.88	1.84	1.80	5.3	0.480Y	61/28/99	39.5 -	31.8
-	-	-	0.66	-0.61	-2.02	-		-	-	-	-	-	-	-	
-	-	-	-0.08	-2.02		-		-	-	-	-	-	-	-	
0.09	-	-	-8.63	-8.42	-2.03	-		1.38	2.53	2.09	57.8	0.01250	4/14/16	7.7 -	0.3
-	1.38	-	3.09	2.96	2.64	24.3 -	16.6	1.56	1.48	1.40	2.5	0.420Y	61/28/99	75.0 -	51.3
-	1.89	-	6.65	5.24	5.32	4.7 -	0.8	1.00	-	-	6.8	0.0750Y	61/28/99	31.3 -	5.3
-	-	-	0.70	1.69	0.40	7.6 -	3.4	3.19	1.26	-	102.4	-	-	5.3 -	2.4
-	-	-	8.57	6.64	4.37	6.0 -	2.8	-	-	-	-	-	-	51.5 -	22.5
1.51	-	-	5.17	5.06	5.07	24.9 -	18.7	2.22	2.12	2.00	1.9	0.500Y	61/28/99	128.9 -	96.6
0.89	-	-	3.89	3.52	3.04	17.0 -	10.7	-	-	-	-	-	-	66.2 -	41.5
-	-	10.77	36.03	31.57	27.79	22.4 -	18.4	-	-	-	-	-	-	805.4 -	663.2
1.73	-	-	5.51	5.21	2.78	34.7 -	28.9	5.00	4.64	4.28	2.9	1.350Y	01/28/99	191.0 -	159.1
0.69	-	-	-	1.70	-0.30	-		-	-	-	-	0.4320	7/1/16	42.0 -	33.3
-	-	-	-	1.57	1.56	-		-	1.61	1.44	-	0.120	6/30/16	15.2 -	9.5
0.98	-	-	2.95	2.60	2.16	26.0 -	18.8	1.46	1.34	1.14	2.3	0.410Y	61/28/99	76.7 -	55.6
-	-	0.09	0.89	1.02	1.16	32.3 -	18.5	-	-	-	-	-	-	28.8 -	16.5
-	-	-	-0.14	0.13	0.27	-		0.52	0.29	-	8.9	-	-	11.0 -	3.5
0.89	-	-	1.97	3.10	1.85	21.1 -	15.2	1.32	1.27	1.22	3.7	0.34250Y	61/28/99	41.6 -	29.9
-	-	-	0.22	0.50	0.65	76.4 -	52.9	0.37	0.29	0.29	2.6	0.51560Z	6/1/16	16.8 -	11.6
-	-	0.94	4.12	3.89	3.21	11.4 -	9.2	0.64	0.60	-	1.5	0.170	61/28/99	47.0 -	37.8
-0.38	-	-	-2.60	-0.88	-0.13	-		0.24	0.24	0.24	5.5	0.060Y	61/28/99	7.0 -	2.4
-	-	0.03	1.34	0.75	-0.38	10.6 -	8.0	0.40	0.36	0.30	3.1	0.1050Y	61/28/99	14.3 -	10.7
0.12	-	-	0.39	0.12	-0.97	93.3 -	54.0	-	-	-	-	-	-	36.4 -	21.1
-0.76	-	-	-11.59	0.65	2.44	-		0.64	0.64	0.48	2.8	0.160Y	7/8/16	39.9 -	9.2
0.41	-	-	6.04	7.29	5.93	-		1.22	1.10	1.02	-	0.34380	9/1/16	-	
-	-	-0.64	-1.32	-		-		-	-	-	-	-	-	29.9 -	9.5
-	-	0.91	2.52	2.32	2.37	23.8 -	18.8	0.58	0.56	0.53	1.1	0.150Y	5/6/16	59.9 -	47.3
0.56	-	-	1.22	0.76	0.98	36.0 -	23.3	1.38	1.36	1.23	4.0	0.420Y	8/1/16	44.0 -	28.4
0.20	-	-	0.36			65.7 -	44.7	-	-	-	-	-	-	23.7 -	16.1
-	-	-	1.04	1.23	1.18	17.3 -	15.0	1.20	1.20	1.20	7.2	0.30	5/13/16	18.0 -	15.7
-	-	-	2.12	2.05		-		-	2.60	2.32	-	0.15341	9/1/16	20.5 -	14.8
-	-	-	0.95	1.04	1.00	15.4 -	13.0	1.08	1.08	1.08	8.0	0.270	5/13/16	14.6 -	12.3
0.55	-	-	1.80	2.06	1.70	41.7 -	29.6	0.78	0.74	0.70	1.3	0.20Y	61/28/99	75.0 -	53.2
-2.22	-	-	-4.49	3.92	2.47	-		0.68	0.64	0.60	1.3	0.170Y	61/28/99	65.2 -	38.9
-0.90	-	-	1.99	3.30	2.73	38.1 -	30.4	0.52	0.52	0.52	0.8	0.130Y	61/28/99	75.8 -	60.5
0.36	-	-	1.34	0.91	-0.14	15.5 -	8.8	0.48	0.48	0.48	3.3	0.6128GHY	6/15/16	20.8 -	11.8
-	-	0.03	0.39	0.44		27.3 -	15.3	0.28	0.40	0.42	3.5	-	-	10.7 -	6.0
-	-	-	3.12	2.64	2.13	2.7 -	1.2	1.10	0.87	0.59	18.2	-	-	8.5 -	3.7
-	-	-	6.34	6.29	5.79	10.5 -	8.9	1661.46	1555.68	1564.52	2659.1	-	-	66.4 -	56.3
-	-	0.59	2.66	2.75	2.20	12.5 -	7.7	1.16	1.78	1.20	4.5	0.3850	5/11/16	33.2 -	20.4
-	-	-	-	-		-		-	-	-	-	-	-	73.0 -	37.1
-	-	176.00	1.24	0.71	0.01	4.5 -	2.4	0.96	2.05	0.28	22.5	-	-	5.8 -	3.0
-	-	0.54	2.38	3.02	2.35	8.9 -	6.7	555.94	423.12	385.03	2949.6	-	-	21.2 -	16.0
-	-	0.11	0.40	0.48	0.40	19.0 -	9.3	0.40	0.60	0.60	7.4	-	-	7.6 -	3.7
-	-	-	2680.00	2591.00		0.0 -	0.0	3333.93	3088.70	-	9838.5	-	-	43.9 -	24.0
0.24	-	-	1.33	1.21	0.99	20.2 -	14.3	0.35	0.25	0.12	1.5	0.10Y	61/28/99	26.9 -	19.0
0.21	-	-	1.31	0.36	0.90	14.1 -	8.5	0.20	0.12	0.04	1.3	1.750Y	61/28/99	18.4 -	11.2
1.16	-	-	3.70	3.69	3.38	19.4 -	14.9	1.80	1.00	1.80	2.8	0.480Y	61/28/99	71.8 -	55.3

SYMBOL	COMPANY	NATURE OF BUSINESS	FISCAL YEAR-END	TOTAL REV. $MILL	NET INCOME $MILL	TOTAL ASSETS $MILL	NET STK EQUITY $MILL	NO OF INST	INST. HOLDINGS (SHARES)
BMO	Bank of Montreal	Banking	10/31/15	23784.0	4370.0	641881.0	39422.0	474	325298993
BK	Bank of New York Mellon Corp	Banking	12/31/15	15494.0	3158.0	393780.0	38037.0	1208	953949361
BNS	Bank of Nova Scotia Halifax	Banking	10/31/15	31244.0	6897.0	856497.0	52019.0	414	668310149
RATE	Bankrate Inc (DE)	Internet & Software	12/31/15	370.5	-13.3	1132.8	761.2		
BKU	BankUnited Inc.	Banking	12/31/15	983.0	251.7	23883.5	2243.9	297	119595997
BCS	Barclays PLC	Banking	12/31/15	31803.0	-49.0	1120012.0	59810.0	340	130282783
BCR	Bard (CR) Inc	Medical Instruments & Equipment	12/31/15	3416.0	135.4	4942.9	1455.3	869	79713656
BNED	Barnes & Noble Education Inc	Educational Services	5/2/15	1773.0	19.1	1129.9	790.1	170	31393830
BKS	Barnes & Noble Inc	Retail - Specialty	4/30/16	4163.8	-24.4	2012.8	603.5	282	61248216
B	Barnes Group Inc.	Industrial Machinery & Equipment	12/31/15	1194.0	121.4	2061.9	1127.8	275	52000909
CUDA	Barracuda Networks Inc	IT Services	2/29/16	320.2	-4.4	419.8	-32.1	144	26044684
BBG	Barrett (Bill) Corp.	Production & Extraction	12/31/15	207.9	-487.8	1515.2	549.4	227	62151392
ABX	Barrick Gold Corp.	Precious Metals	12/31/15	9029.0	-2838.0	26308.0	7178.0	681	758770714
BAS	Basic Energy Services Inc	Equipment & Services	12/31/15	805.6	-241.7	1161.4	106.3	186	34081438
BAX	Baxter International Inc.	Medical Instruments & Equipment	12/31/15	9968.0	968.0	20975.0	8846.0	1346	550421936
BTE	Baytex Energy Corp	Production & Extraction	12/31/15	888.4	-1133.7	5488.5	2414.5		
BBT	BB&T Corp.	Banking	12/31/15	10346.0	2123.0	209947.0	27306.0	1039	526730942
BFR	BBVA Banco Frances S.A. (Argenti	Banking	12/31/15	23271.8	3784.5	110736.2	13716.4	72	11210776
BBX	BBX Capital Corp	Finance Intermediaries & Services	12/31/15	131.5	21.8	393.5	334.8	63	5569879
BCE	BCE Inc	Services	12/31/15	21514.0	2526.0	47993.0	17023.0	589	474324949
BZH	Beazer Homes USA, Inc.	Builders	9/30/15	1627.4	344.1	2421.2	630.4	206	39293054
BDX	Becton, Dickinson and Co.	Medical Instruments & Equipment	9/30/15	10282.0	695.0	26820.0	7164.0	1305	209204890
BDC	Belden Inc	Electrical Equipment	12/31/15	2309.2	66.2	3315.8	824.1	286	52929318
BXE	Bellatrix Exploration Ltd	Production & Extraction	12/31/14	468.6	163.1	2213.5	1248.3	85	68394064
T 28A	BellSouth Telecommunications, Inc.	Services	12/31/99	17478.0	2770.0	25295.0	8805.0		
BEL	Belmond Ltd	Hotels, Restaurants & Travel	12/31/15	571.7	16.3	1509.5	658.1	202	88375880
BMS	Bemis Co Inc	Containers & Packaging	12/31/15	4071.4	239.3	3489.8	1207.4	511	94427936
BHE	Benchmark Electronics, Inc.	Electrical Equipment	12/31/15	2540.9	95.4	1893.9	1321.9	269	54768718
WRB	Berkley (WR) Corp	General Insurance	12/31/15	7206.5	504.1	21731.0	4600.2	495	111624258
BRK B	Berkshire Hathaway Inc	General Insurance	12/31/15	210821.0	24083.0	552257.0	255550.0	2223	886035294
BHLB	Berkshire Hills Bancorp, Inc.	Banking	12/31/15	301.3	49.5	7831.9	887.2	193	23612790
BERY	Berry Plastics Group Inc	Plastics	9/26/15	4881.0	86.0	5028.0	-68.0	307	125425522
BBY	Best Buy Inc	Retail - Appliances and Electronics	1/30/16	39528.0	897.0	13519.0	4378.0	750	299658128
BHP	BHP Billiton Ltd.	Non-Precious Metals	6/30/15	44636.0	1910.0	124580.0	64768.0	521	61480228
BBL	BHP Billiton Plc	Non-Precious Metals	6/30/15	44636.0	1910.0	124580.0	64768.0	191	35500983
BIG	Big Lots, Inc.	Retail - General Merchandise/Depart	1/30/16	5190.6	142.9	1640.4	720.5	413	64444248
BH	Biglari Holdings Inc.	Retail - Food & Beverage, Drug & To	12/31/15	861.5	-15.8	1003.9	451.4	149	3195404
BIO	Bio-Rad Laboratories, Inc.	Biotechnology	12/31/15	2019.4	113.1	3711.5	2490.5	320	19664596
BIOA	BioAmber Inc	Specialty Chemicals	12/31/15	2.2	-37.2	143.1	46.4	41	12187380
BITA	Bitauto Holdings Ltd	Internet & Software	12/31/15	4011.6	-424.4	13089.5	8492.0	103	15955415
BKH	Black Hills Corporation	Electric Utilities	12/31/15	1304.6	-32.1	4655.5	1465.9	324	50382990
BKFS	Black Knight Financial Services Inc	IT Services	12/31/15	930.7	20.0	3703.7	818.7	107	61872883
BSM	Black Stone Minerals LP	Production & Extraction	12/31/15	392.9	-101.3	1061.4	79.2	60	16890515
BJZ	BlackRock California Municipal 2018	Holding and other Investment Office	12/31/15	2.9	2.3	97.5	97.4	25	863586
BFZ	BlackRock California Municipal Inco	Holding and other Investment Office	7/31/15	34.4	26.5	840.5	505.0	38	2496315
BHK	BlackRock Core Bond Trust	Holding and other Investment Office	8/31/15	48.9	42.1	1090.3	770.8	97	20529429
HYT	BlackRock Corporate High Yield Fu	Holding and other Investment Office	8/31/15	132.7	110.7	2170.9	1527.3	150	39154286
BTZ	BlackRock Credit Allocation Income	Holding and other Investment Office	10/31/14	125.3	107.0	2463.8	1660.4	143	49383584
DSU	BlackRock Debt Strategies Fund Inc	Holding and other Investment Office	2/28/15	64.5	54.4	1148.2	801.9	143	82991123
BHL	Blackrock Defined Opportunity Cred	Holding and other Investment Office	8/31/14	9.5	7.0	189.6	130.4	27	2423248
BGR	Blackrock Energy & Resources Trus	Holding and other Investment Office	12/31/15	15.6	8.7	422.1	419.0	101	5746297
CII	BlackRock Enhanced Capital & Inco	Holding and other Investment Office	12/31/15	11.4	4.9	672.6	666.5	81	7682947
BDJ	BlackRock Enhanced Equity Divide	Holding and other Investment Office	12/31/15	45.5	31.2	1660.8	1643.5	160	50674038
EGF	BlackRock Enhanced Government	Holding and other Investment Office	12/31/15	4.5	3.3	144.8	103.1	29	5489266
FRA	BlackRock Floating Rate Income Str	Holding and other Investment Office	12/31/15	39.1	30.3	785.3	555.1	107	13891832
BGT	BlackRock Floating Rate Income Tr	Holding and other Investment Office	10/31/15	23.7	18.4	453.0	335.4	82	6508513
BFO	BlackRock Florida Municipal 2020 T	Holding and other Investment Office	7/31/15	2.9	2.3	85.8	85.5	18	704710
BOE	BlackRock Global Opportunities Eq	Holding and other Investment Office	12/31/15	18.7	7.6	1000.8	990.3	97	23232900
BME	BlackRock Health Sciences Trust	Holding and other Investment Office	12/31/15	3.2	-0.4	301.0	297.5	39	2144393
BKT	BlackRock Income Trust Inc. (The)	Holding and other Investment Office	8/31/15	25.0	20.5	725.3	452.6	84	39381659
BGY	BlackRock International Growth & In	Holding and other Investment Office	12/31/14	1.3	-0.2	852.4	836.6	96	34278912
BKN	BlackRock Investment Quality Muni	Holding and other Investment Office	4/30/15	19.5	15.4	436.6	276.3	57	1465386
BLW	Blackrock Limited Duration Income	Holding and other Investment Office	8/31/15	50.5	43.1	903.6	630.4	91	13873193
BTA	BlackRock Long-Term Municipal Ad	Holding and other Investment Office	4/30/15	11.7	9.2	253.8	167.9	45	3578475
BIT	Blackrock Multi-Sector Income Trust	Holding and other Investment Office	10/31/14	78.2	62.7	1495.4	763.4	71	15063466
MUI	BlackRock Muni Intermediate Durati	Holding and other Investment Office	4/30/15	38.8	29.5	950.9	607.4	80	6655398
MNE	BlackRock Muni New York Intermed	Holding and other Investment Office	7/31/15	4.0	2.9	101.1	64.7	23	599112
MUA	BlackRock MuniAssets Fund, Inc.	Holding and other Investment Office	4/30/15	30.4	26.3	569.1	505.3	61	2063078
BPK	Blackrock Municipal 2018 Term Tru	Holding and other Investment Office	12/31/15	7.7	6.5	248.9	244.0	47	1420028
BKK	BlackRock Municipal 2020 Term Tr	Holding and other Investment Office	4/30/15	14.8	12.4	387.6	329.8	52	2565774
BTT	BlackRock Municipal 2030 Target T	Holding and other Investment Office	7/31/15	94.3	77.2	2544.3	1602.4	67	11755396
BBK	Blackrock Municipal Bond Trust	Holding and other Investment Office	8/31/15	12.5	9.5	277.3	173.4	43	916627
BAF	BlackRock Municipal Income Invest	Holding and other Investment Office	8/31/15	9.3	7.2	214.8	138.2	31	1416838
BBF	BlackRock Municipal Income Invest	Holding and other Investment Office	7/31/15	7.6	5.8	166.1	101.5	27	544509
BYM	BlackRock Municipal Income Qualit	Holding and other Investment Office	8/31/15	28.3	22.2	644.1	401.5	67	2599730
BFK	BlackRock Municipal Income Trust	Holding and other Investment Office	4/30/15	49.9	39.3	1064.9	667.1	72	5188574
MEN	BlackRock MuniEnhanced Fund Inc	Holding and other Investment Office	4/30/15	26.2	21.0	589.8	362.7	50	3496510
MUC	BlackRock MuniHoldings California	Holding and other Investment Office	7/31/15	41.4	31.9	1066.2	646.9	52	4490046
MUH	BlackRock MuniHoldings Fund II Inc	Holding and other Investment Office	4/30/15	13.2	10.5	282.9	183.2	40	998956
MHD	BlackRock MuniHoldings Fund Inc	Holding and other Investment Office	4/30/15	18.3	14.5	390.7	248.6	35	1090000

T8

EARNINGS PER SHARE QUARTERLY 1st	2nd	3rd	ANNUAL 2015	2014	2013	P/E RATIO		DIVIDENDS PER SHARE 2015	2014	2013	AV. YLD %	DIV. DECLARED AMOUNT	PAYABLE	PRICE RANGE 2015	
-	-	1.67	6.57	6.41	6.26	12.8 -	0.0	3.24	3.08	2.94	4.9	14.625G	8/25/16	84.3 -	0.0
0.73	-	-	2.71	2.15	1.74	16.7 -	12.1	0.68	0.66	0.58	1.7	0.3250Y	61/28/99	45.3 -	32.7
1.43	-	-	5.67	5.66	5.15	11.8 -	0.0	2.72	2.56	2.39	5.2	0.5086GH	7/27/16	66.7 -	0.0
0.00	-	-	-0.13	0.05	-0.10									15.2 -	7.3
0.51	-	-	2.35	1.95	2.01	16.7 -	12.7	0.63	1.05	0.63	1.8	0.210Y	61/28/99	39.3 -	29.9
-	-	-	-0.02	-0.01	0.04			0.25	0.25	0.26	1.9			18.0 -	8.2
1.54	-	-	1.77	3.76	8.39	125.4 -	95.1	0.92	0.86	0.82	0.5	0.260Y	61/28/99	221.9 -	168.3
-	-	-0.07	0.33	0.88	0.78	46.3 -	26.0	-	-	-	-			15.3 -	8.6
-	-	1.04	0.21	-1.12	-3.02	89.4 -	34.9					0.150	61/28/99	18.8 -	7.3
0.53	-	-	2.19	2.12	4.92	19.0 -	13.9	0.48	0.45	0.42	1.3	0.130Y	6/10/16	41.6 -	30.5
-	-	-0.03	-1.30	-0.10	-0.29									42.7 -	10.1
-0.96	-	-	-10.10	0.31	-4.06									9.4 -	2.5
-	-	-0.12	-2.44	-2.50	-10.14			0.14	0.20	0.50	1.2	0.020	6/15/16	25.0 -	0.0
-2.00	-	-	-5.97	-0.20	-0.89									8.9 -	1.6
6.12	-	-	1.76	4.56	3.66	26.4 -	18.3	1.27	2.05	1.92	3.3	0.130Y	61/28/99	46.4 -	32.3
-	-	-2.49	-5.72	-0.89	1.32			0.80	2.64	2.64	12.2	0.10	9/15/15	21.9 -	0.0
0.67	-	-	2.56	2.75	2.19	16.3 -	11.8	1.05	0.95	1.12	2.9	0.3203GHY	61/28/99	41.6 -	30.3
-	-	-	-	-	-									24.8 -	14.6
-0.02	-	-	1.30	0.28	2.94	14.2 -	9.1							18.4 -	11.8
0.82	-	-	2.98	2.97	2.54	20.4 -	0.0	2.00	2.47	2.33	5.3	0.05630	7/12/16	60.9 -	0.0
-	-0.04	-	10.83	1.08	-1.37	1.9 -	0.6					0.46880Z	7/15/15	21.1 -	6.3
-	1.56	-	3.35	5.99	6.49	50.3 -	38.9	2.40	2.18	1.98	1.6	0.660Y	61/28/99	168.6 -	130.4
0.39	-	-	1.54	1.69	2.31	56.1 -	24.1	0.20	0.20	0.20	0.3	0.050Y	61/28/99	86.3 -	37.1
-	-	-0.26	-	0.88	0.62									3.7 -	0.0
-0.02	-	-	0.16	-0.02	-0.31							0.0250	11/4/08		
0.59	-	-	2.44	1.89	2.04	22.2 -	16.1	1.12	1.08	1.04	2.4	0.290Y	61/28/99	54.1 -	39.2
0.22	-	-	1.83	1.52	2.03	12.9 -	10.3							23.6 -	18.8
0.93	-	-	3.87	4.86	3.55	15.1 -	12.4	0.47	1.43	0.39	0.9	0.130Y	61/28/99	58.4 -	48.0
3401.00	-	-	14656.00	2092.00	1850.00	0.0 -	0.0							147.6 -	124.1
0.52	-	-	1.73	1.36	1.65	17.6 -	14.5	0.76	0.72	0.72	2.7	0.20Y	5/26/16	30.4 -	25.0
-	0.47	-	0.70	0.51	0.48	56.1 -	40.6							39.3 -	28.4
0.70	-	-	3.49	1.53	-1.30	11.2 -	7.4	0.72	0.68	0.66	2.2	0.280Y	61/28/99	39.0 -	25.9
-	-	-	0.36	2.59	2.04	125.1 -	53.8	2.48	2.36	2.28	8.0			45.0 -	19.4
-	-	-	0.36	2.59	2.04	119.8 -	47.4	2.48	2.36	2.28	8.6			43.1 -	17.1
0.79	-	-	2.06	2.16	2.93	25.4 -	17.4	0.51	-	-	1.2	0.210Y	61/28/99	52.3 -	35.9
41.16	-	-	-10.18	48.45	97.90									448.0 -	323.7
0.42	-	-	3.85	3.05	2.69	39.5 -	32.2							161.9 -	123.9
-0.39	-	-	1.52	-2.32	-2.13									8.8 -	2.9
-	-	-	-7.30	10.88	5.74									63.5 -	16.4
0.77	-	-	-0.71	2.89	2.59			1.62	1.56	1.52	3.4	0.420Y	61/28/99	61.7 -	37.3
0.17	-	-	0.29	-	-	125.0 -	89.7							36.3 -	26.0
0.09	-	-	-0.56	0.07	0.07			0.42	-	-	2.8	0.26250	5/26/16	18.2 -	10.8
-	-	-	0.36	0.40	0.61	42.3 -	0.0	0.38	0.54	0.63	2.6	0.0277M	7/1/16	15.2 -	0.0
-	-	-	0.83	0.87	0.89	20.3 -	17.4	0.87	0.93	0.93	5.6	0.0672M	7/1/16	16.8 -	14.4
-	-	-	0.86	0.87	0.89	15.8 -	14.4	1.08	0.91	0.94	8.3	0.0710	6/30/16	13.6 -	12.4
-	-	-	0.87	0.98	1.00	13.0 -	10.6	0.97	1.04	1.02	9.6	0.070	6/30/16	11.3 -	9.2
-	-	-	-	0.99	0.97				0.97	0.98		0.0760	6/30/16	13.2 -	11.7
-	-	-	0.29	0.30	0.33	12.9 -	10.8	0.29	0.34	0.33	8.4	0.020	6/30/16	3.7 -	3.1
-	-	-	-	0.77	0.87				0.83	0.84		0.0510	6/30/16	13.5 -	12.6
-	-	-	0.29	0.25	0.12	68.3 -	35.9	1.50	2.76	1.62	10.5	0.07760	6/30/16	19.8 -	10.4
-	-	-	0.11	0.40	0.31	140.4 -	106.1	1.20	1.20	1.20	8.6	0.10	6/30/16	15.4 -	11.7
-	-	-	0.17	0.04	0.18	48.2 -	38.8	0.56	0.56	0.56	7.4	0.04670	6/30/16	8.2 -	6.6
-	-	-	0.41	0.49	0.47	33.8 -	32.5	0.62	0.66	0.76	4.6	0.0490	6/30/16	13.9 -	13.3
-	-	-	0.81	0.87	0.99	17.1 -	14.8	0.81	0.89	1.03	6.2	0.0610	6/30/16	13.8 -	12.0
-	-	-	0.78	0.99	0.94	17.3 -	15.0	0.81	0.84	1.04	6.4	0.05830	6/30/16	13.5 -	11.7
-	-	-	0.42	0.47	0.68	36.4 -	0.0	0.44	0.61	0.76	3.0	0.031M	7/29/16	15.3 -	0.0
-	-	-	0.11	0.00	0.12	128.0 -	95.7	1.16	1.24	1.25	9.3	0.0970	6/30/16	14.1 -	10.5
-	-	-	-0.06	-0.01	0.12			6.70	4.20	2.39	16.8	0.20	6/30/16	47.5 -	31.6
-	-	-	0.32	0.35	0.32	20.8 -	19.6	0.40	0.43	0.48	6.2	0.02650	6/30/16	6.7 -	6.3
-	-	-	-	0.00	0.13			-	0.66	0.67		0.0490	6/30/16	7.6 -	5.3
-	-	-	0.90	0.94	0.94	19.3 -	16.1	0.95	0.96	0.98	6.1	0.072M	7/1/16	17.3 -	14.5
-	-	-	1.16	1.26	1.30	13.9 -	11.5	1.29	1.22	1.39	8.8	0.0870	6/30/16	16.2 -	13.3
-	-	-	0.69	0.71	0.74	18.1 -	15.5	0.72	0.74	0.76	6.3	0.0545GH	7/1/16	12.5 -	10.7
-	-	-	-	1.62	1.02			-	1.40	0.82	-	0.11670	6/30/16	17.2 -	14.8
-	-	-	0.77	0.80	0.82	19.8 -	17.6	0.82	0.91	1.00	5.8	0.0555M	7/1/16	15.3 -	13.5
-	-	-	0.68	0.69	0.72	23.1 -	0.0	0.69	0.73	0.75	4.8	0.0498M	7/1/16	15.7 -	0.0
-	-	-	0.73	0.77	0.77	20.8 -	18.3	0.76	0.75	0.78	5.4	0.0575M	7/1/16	15.2 -	13.4
-	-	-	0.41	0.61	0.72	38.6 -	37.0	0.60	0.68	0.77	3.9	0.0278M	7/1/16	15.8 -	15.2
-	-	-	0.90	0.74	0.90	18.0 -	0.0	0.67	0.81	0.91	4.2	0.0448M	7/1/16	16.2 -	0.0
-	-	-	1.09	1.12	0.80	21.8 -	17.9	0.96	1.11	0.98	4.5	0.08M	7/1/16	23.7 -	19.6
-	-	-	0.90	0.97	0.96	19.6 -	16.5	0.98	1.05	1.11	6.1	0.075M	7/1/16	17.6 -	14.9
-	-	-	0.83	0.83	0.81	19.3 -	16.6	0.82	0.82	0.83	5.6	0.0685M	7/1/16	16.1 -	13.7
-	-	-	0.87	0.87	0.85	18.5 -	15.2	0.87	0.87	0.87	6.1	0.0724M	7/1/16	16.1 -	13.2
-	-	-	0.84	0.86	0.91	18.9 -	15.9	0.86	0.92	0.94	6.0	0.066M	7/1/16	15.8 -	13.4
-	-	-	0.80	0.93	0.93	18.0 -	15.1	0.91	0.91	0.96	6.3	0.0711M	7/1/16	15.8 -	13.3
-	-	-	0.71	0.73	0.71	17.9 -	15.4	0.73	0.72	0.70	6.2	0.0565M	7/1/16	12.7 -	10.9
-	-	-	0.78	0.82	0.86	20.9 -	17.8	0.82	0.86	0.93	5.5	0.0615M	7/1/16	16.3 -	13.9
-	-	-	0.93	0.95	0.98	18.2 -	15.3	0.97	1.09	1.20	6.3	0.0745M	7/1/16	16.0 -	14.2
-	-	-	1.03	1.04	1.07	18.1 -	15.3	1.06	1.10	1.31	6.2	0.081M	7/1/16	18.7 -	15.8

SYMBOL	COMPANY	NATURE OF BUSINESS	FISCAL YEAR-END	TOTAL REV. $MILL	NET INCOME $MILL	TOTAL ASSETS $MILL	NET STK EQUITY $MILL	NO OF INST	INST. HOLDINGS (SHARES)
MFL	BlackRock MuniHoldings Investmen	Holding and other Investment Office	8/31/15	42.3	33.5	938.1	573.9	64	6103331
MUJ	BlackRock MuniHoldings New Jerse	Holding and other Investment Office	7/31/15	26.1	20.1	764.0	470.9	43	2196784
MHN	BlackRock MuniHoldings New York	Holding and other Investment Office	8/31/15	32.0	24.9	762.3	461.2	42	2073373
MUE	BlackRock MuniHoldings Quality Fu	Holding and other Investment Office	7/31/15	22.8	17.9	510.7	325.9	64	3505881
MUS	BlackRock MuniHoldings Quality Fu	Holding and other Investment Office	4/30/15	13.4	10.5	299.6	189.6	44	2988577
MVT	BlackRock MuniVest Fund II Inc	Holding and other Investment Office	4/30/15	25.8	20.7	544.9	336.3	42	1068007
MYC	BlackRock MuniYield California Fun	Holding and other Investment Office	7/31/15	23.5	18.7	578.8	348.8	35	2291588
MCA	BlackRock MuniYield California Qua	Holding and other Investment Office	7/31/15	35.9	28.5	907.3	554.1	39	4359960
MYD	BlackRock MuniYield Fund Inc	Holding and other Investment Office	4/30/15	52.1	42.4	1132.8	713.2	64	4589125
MYF	BlackRock MuniYield Investment Fu	Holding and other Investment Office	7/31/15	16.1	13.0	349.3	212.7	36	1782582
MFT	BlackRock MuniYield Investment Q	Holding and other Investment Office	7/31/15	9.1	7.1	203.5	126.7	38	1157217
MIY	BlackRock MuniYield Michigan Qual	Holding and other Investment Office	7/31/15	19.3	15.1	455.0	282.5	45	2350178
MYN	BlackRock MuniYield New York Qu	Holding and other Investment Office	7/31/15	37.7	29.5	913.5	560.4	46	2094289
MYJ	BlackRock MuniYield NJ Fund Inc	Holding and other Investment Office	7/31/15	16.4	12.9	371.8	228.6	25	947642
MPA	BlackRock MuniYield Pennsylvania	Holding and other Investment Office	7/31/15	12.5	9.7	323.0	210.5	40	1258126
MQT	BlackRock MuniYield Quality Fund I	Holding and other Investment Office	4/30/15	22.9	18.1	518.1	319.8	52	2362338
MYI	BlackRock MuniYield Quality Fund I	Holding and other Investment Office	7/31/15	73.3	59.1	1617.6	1003.6	82	9040543
MQY	BlackRock MuniYield Quality Fund I	Holding and other Investment Office	4/30/15	35.4	28.1	792.7	494.5	57	4271119
BNJ	Blackrock New Jersey Municipal Inc	Holding and other Investment Office	7/31/15	8.8	6.6	196.4	119.2	26	506995
BLH	Blackrock New York Municipal 2018	Holding and other Investment Office	12/31/15	1.3	0.9	54.9	54.8	11	176885
BQH	Blackrock New York Municipal Bond	Holding and other Investment Office	8/31/15	3.0	2.1	72.1	44.1	16	144134
BSE	BlackRock New York Municipal Inco	Holding and other Investment Office	8/31/15	6.2	4.6	155.8	96.6	29	687196
BNY	Blackrock New York Municipal Inco	Holding and other Investment Office	7/31/15	13.6	10.2	321.7	193.3	23	829392
BCX	Blackrock Resources & Commoditie	Holding and other Investment Office	12/31/14	4.2	2.8	1168.8	1156.5	103	34237263
BST	BlackRock Science & Technology T	Holding and other Investment Office	12/31/14	0.5	-0.2	443.2	437.4	37	6200963
BSD	Blackrock Strategic Municipal Trust	Holding and other Investment Office	4/30/15	7.9	6.1	170.8	107.8	31	1238755
BBN	BlackRock Taxable Municipal Bond	Holding and other Investment Office	7/31/15	109.1	93.3	2011.6	1283.7	101	8835238
BUI	Blackrock Utility & Infrastructure Tru	Holding and other Investment Office	12/31/14	2.5	1.8	386.2	379.8	45	2626531
BLK	BlackRock, Inc.	Finance Intermediaries & Services	12/31/15	11401.0	3345.0	225261.0	28503.0	1119	157735580
BGX	Blackstone / GSO Long-Short Credi	Holding and other Investment Office	12/31/14	16.4	11.9	315.3	226.3	50	6292617
BSL	Blackstone / GSO Senior Floating R	Holding and other Investment Office	12/31/14	22.8	14.1	441.7	275.2	48	6103774
BGB	Blackstone / GSO Strategic Credit F	Holding and other Investment Office	12/31/14	71.8	52.1	1255.3	803.0	74	20128911
BX	Blackstone Group LP (The)	Wealth Management	12/31/15	4646.6	709.8	22526.1		671	301375824
BXMT	Blackstone Mortgage Trust Inc	REITs	12/31/15	410.6	196.8	9376.6	2492.6	252	75596162
HRB	Block (H & R), Inc.	Miscellaneous Consumer Services	4/30/16	3038.2	374.3	2857.8	23.1	672	238439173
BCRH	Blue Capital Reinsurance Holdings	General Insurance	12/31/15	38.1	20.7	217.6	187.6	49	5966655
BXC	BlueLinx Holdings Inc	Construction Services	1/2/16	1916.6	-11.6	513.1	-45.9	47	74411216
BWP	Boardwalk Pipeline Partners LP	Equipment & Services	12/31/15	1249.2	222.0	8300.3		232	235008618
BA	Boeing Co. (The)	Aerospace	12/31/15	96114.0	5176.0	94408.0	6335.0	1862	556782675
BCC	Boise Cascade Co. (DE)	Construction Materials	12/31/15	3633.4	52.2	1248.6	534.7	210	38214181
BCEI	Bonanza Creek Energy, Inc.	Production & Extraction	12/31/15	292.7	-745.5	1273.4	209.4	189	49863689
BOOT	Boot Barn Holdings Inc	Retail - Apparel and Accessories	3/26/16	569.0	9.9	539.3	161.5	88	27576909
BAH	Booz Allen Hamilton Holding Corp.	Business Services	3/31/16	5405.7	294.1	3010.2	408.5	269	226380524
BWA	BorgWarner Inc	Auto Parts	12/31/15	8023.2	609.7	8841.5	3553.7	656	220899513
SAM	Boston Beer Co Inc (The)	Beverages	12/26/15	959.9	98.4	645.4	461.2	289	10886599
BXP	Boston Properties, Inc.	REITs	12/31/15	2490.8	583.1	18379.5	5709.4	660	170972949
BSX	Boston Scientific Corp.	Medical Instruments & Equipment	12/31/15	7477.0	-239.0	18133.0	6320.0	747	1347941560
BIF	Boulder Growth & Income Fund Inc	Holding and other Investment Office	11/30/15	17.0	3.8	1104.8	1053.4	91	28120836
BOX	Box Inc	Internet & Software	1/31/16	302.7	-202.9	497.5	137.9	109	23777242
BYD	Boyd Gaming Corp.	Hotels, Restaurants & Travel	12/31/15	2199.4	47.2	4350.9	508.0	314	93630389
BP	BP p.l.c.	Production & Extraction	12/31/15	225316.0	-6482.0	261832.0	97216.0	1220	379163290
BPT	BP Prudhoe Bay Royalty Trust	Oil Royalty Traders	12/31/15	126.8	125.5	1.0	0.8	155	1630135
BRC	Brady Corp	Printing	7/31/15	1171.7	3.0	1062.9	587.7	229	44152929
BDN	Brandywine Realty Trust	REITs	12/31/15	602.6	-30.4	4554.5	1933.9	322	217113607
LND	Brasilagro Cia Brasileira De Proprie	Agricultural Crop Production	6/30/15	374.6	180.8	1017.8	752.1		
BAK	Braskem S A	Refining & Marketing	12/31/15	47283.0	3140.3	59961.3	2022.6	96	14295261
BRFS	BRF S.A.	Food	12/31/15	32196.6	3111.2	40388.0	13516.9	204	64267545
BPI	Bridgepoint Education, Inc.	Educational Services	12/31/15	561.7	-70.5	506.8	303.6	96	71425092
BGG	Briggs & Stratton Corp.	Industrial Machinery & Equipment	6/28/15	1894.8	45.7	1459.0	574.3	300	45323680
BFAM	Bright Horizons Family Solutions, In	Services	12/31/15	1458.4	93.9	2150.5	727.6		
EAT	Brinker International, Inc.	Hotels, Restaurants & Travel	6/24/15	3002.3	196.7	1435.9	-78.5	458	72344192
BCO	Brinks Co (The)	Business Services	12/31/15	3061.4	-11.9	1946.7	317.9	289	53423660
BMY	Bristol-Myers Squibb Co.	Pharmaceuticals	12/31/15	16560.0	1565.0	31748.0	14266.0	2036	1396721121
BRS	Bristow Group Inc	Miscellaneous Transportation Servic	3/31/16	1715.5	-72.4	3271.9	1499.2	240	44241456
BRX	Brixmor Property Group Inc	REITs	12/31/15	1266.0	193.7	9498.0	2869.8	278	317830064
BR	Broadridge Financial Solutions Inc	Finance Intermediaries & Services	6/30/15	2694.2	287.1	2368.1	927.8	626	122023391
BKD	Brookdale Senior Living Inc	Hospitals & Health Care Facilities	12/31/15	4960.6	-458.2	10048.6	2458.9	341	199099465
BAM	Brookfield Asset Management Inc	Property, Real Estate & Developmen	12/31/15	19913.0	2341.0	139514.0	25307.0	477	565972922
BBU	Brookfield Business Partners LP	Business Services	12/31/15	6753.0	208.0	7635.0	1787.0		
BBU	Brookfield Business Partners LP	Business Services	12/31/15	6753.0	208.0	7635.0	1787.0		
BOXC	Brookfield Canada Office Properties	REITs	12/31/15	516.9	98.6	6356.5	923.8	34	15265931
DTLA PR	Brookfield DTLA Fund Office Trust I	REITs	12/31/15	299.1	-22.0	2798.0	365.6	1	10000
INF	Brookfield Global Listed Infrastructu	Holding and other Investment Office	12/31/14	9.3	4.0	327.9	237.4	56	4740897
HHY	Brookfield High Income Fund Inc	Holding and other Investment Office	9/30/15	24.0	19.4	296.1	211.0	64	3523364
BIP	Brookfield Infrastructure Partners L.	Electric Utilities	12/31/15	1855.0	232.0	17735.0	4050.0	234	83612257
BOI	Brookfield Mortgage Opportunity Inc	Holding and other Investment Office	6/30/15	42.2	32.3	576.8	412.6		
BPY	Brookfield Property Partners LP	Property, Real Estate & Developmen	12/31/15	4853.0	3766.0	71866.0	7431.0	133	150207513
BEP	Brookfield Renewable Partners LP	Electric Utilities	12/31/15	1750.0	2.0	19507.0	2827.0		
HTR	Brookfield Total Return Fund Inc	Holding and other Investment Office	9/30/15	33.5	27.8	488.6	353.1	63	2713880
BRO	Brown & Brown, Inc.	Brokers & Intermediaries	12/31/15	1660.5	243.3	5012.7	2149.8	340	122393073

T10

EARNINGS PER SHARE QUARTERLY			EARNINGS PER SHARE ANNUAL			P/E RATIO		DIVIDENDS PER SHARE			AV. YLD %	DIV. DECLARED AMOUNT	PAYABLE	PRICE RANGE 2015	
1st	2nd	3rd	2015	2014	2013			2015	2014	2013					
-	-	-	0.89	0.89	0.87	17.6 -	14.9	0.86	0.86	0.90	5.9	0.0715M	7/1/16	15.6 -	13.3
-	-	-	0.84	0.86	0.86	19.1 -	15.7	0.89	0.89	0.89	6.3	0.0675M	7/1/16	16.1 -	13.2
-	-	-	0.00	0.83	0.87	19.6 -	16.7	0.82	0.87	0.92	5.7	0.058M	7/1/16	15.7 -	13.4
-	-	-	0.80	0.82	0.81	18.4 -	15.9	0.83	0.85	0.85	6.1	0.064M	7/1/16	14.7 -	12.7
-	-	-	0.80	0.82	0.83	18.4 -	15.8	0.81	0.82	0.89	6.0	0.0675M	7/1/16	14.7 -	12.6
-	-	-	0.99	1.03	1.06	17.9 -	14.8	1.04	1.08	1.10	6.5	0.079M	7/1/16	17.7 -	14.6
-	-	-	0.87	0.91	0.91	19.9 -	17.2	0.90	0.95	0.95	5.6	0.07M	7/1/16	17.3 -	15.0
-	-	-	0.83	0.87	0.88	20.0 -	17.2	0.88	0.91	0.91	5.7	0.065M	7/1/16	16.6 -	14.3
-	-	-	0.91	0.94	0.95	17.6 -	15.1	0.95	0.99	1.02	6.4	0.072M	7/1/16	16.0 -	13.8
-	-	-	0.95	0.96	0.94	17.3 -	15.0	0.97	0.95	0.95	6.3	0.078M	7/1/16	16.4 -	14.3
-	-	-	0.84	0.85	0.84	18.0 -	15.4	0.85	0.85	0.85	6.1	0.071M	7/1/16	15.1 -	12.9
-	-	-	0.83	0.86	0.90	18.4 -	15.7	0.86	0.90	0.92	6.2	0.064M	7/1/16	15.3 -	13.0
-	-	-	0.75	0.78	0.83	19.5 -	17.1	0.77	0.83	0.85	5.7	0.054M	7/1/16	14.6 -	12.9
-	-	-	0.90	0.90	0.89	18.8 -	15.8	0.90	0.93	0.96	5.8	0.075M	7/1/16	16.9 -	14.3
-	-	-	0.81	0.87	0.90	19.4 -	16.5	0.88	0.89	0.89	6.1	0.0623M	7/1/16	15.7 -	13.3
-	-	-	0.91	0.83	0.82	16.1 -	13.6	0.85	0.84	0.83	6.4	0.062M	7/1/16	14.7 -	12.4
-	-	-	0.87	0.89	0.89	17.9 -	15.7	0.89	0.87	0.87	6.1	0.068M	7/1/16	15.6 -	13.7
-	-	-	0.92	0.95	-	18.3 -	15.9	0.96	0.98	0.96	6.1	0.0725M	7/1/16	16.8 -	14.6
-	-	-	0.86	0.88	0.88	19.3 -	16.3	0.85	0.90	0.94	5.6	0.0696M	7/1/16	16.6 -	14.0
-	-	-	0.25	0.35	0.44	60.4 -	0.0	0.33	0.37	0.57	2.3	0.0177M	7/1/16	15.1 -	0.0
-	-	-	0.74	0.79	0.84	21.4 -	0.0	0.79	0.80	1.05	5.5	0.059M	7/1/16	15.8 -	0.0
-	-	-	0.70	0.72	0.78	21.1 -	18.3	0.73	0.77	0.83	5.4	0.052M	7/1/16	14.8 -	12.8
-	-	-	0.79	0.81	0.87	20.8 -	17.5	0.83	0.83	0.87	5.5	0.06M	7/1/16	16.4 -	13.8
-	-	-	-	0.04	0.25	-		-	0.93	1.16	-	0.04460	6/30/16	9.8 -	5.8
-	-	-	-	-0.01	-	-		-	0.10		-	0.10	6/30/16	18.5 -	14.1
-	-	-	1.04	0.86	0.85	15.2 -	12.5	0.88	0.89	0.89	6.3	0.065M	7/1/16	15.8 -	13.0
-	-	-	1.63	1.59	1.58	14.7 -	12.1	1.58	1.58	1.58	7.4	0.13180	6/30/16	23.9 -	19.8
-	-	-	-	0.11	0.57	-		-	1.45	1.45	-	0.1210	6/30/16	19.7 -	15.0
3.92	-	-	19.79	19.25	16.87	18.6 -	14.6	8.72	7.72	6.72	2.6	2.290Y	61/28/99	367.5 -	289.7
-	-	-	-	0.94	1.13	-		-	1.20	1.35	-	0.0980	9/30/16	16.2 -	12.3
-	-	-	-	0.92	1.17	-		-	1.21	1.21	-	0.0970	9/30/16	17.8 -	13.4
-	-	-	-	1.17	1.21	-		-	1.28	1.40	-	0.1050	9/30/16	16.4 -	12.2
0.23	-	-	1.04	2.58	1.98	41.1 -	22.1	2.90	1.92	1.18	9.2	0.280Z	5/9/16	42.7 -	23.0
0.61	-	-	2.41	1.86	8.10	12.6 -	9.4	2.28	1.98	0.72	8.3	0.620Z	7/15/16	30.4 -	22.7
-	-	-0.35	1.71	1.72	1.58	21.9 -	11.4	0.80	0.80	0.80	2.5	0.220Y	61/28/99	37.4 -	19.5
0.57	-	-	2.36	1.72	-0.31	8.2 -	6.8	1.56	0.90	-	8.9	0.30	7/15/16	19.3 -	16.1
-0.70	-	-	-1.30	-1.60	-5.10	-		-			-	0.1250Y	12/28/07	11.3 -	3.4
0.40	-	-	0.87	0.94	0.96	20.3 -	11.0	0.40	0.40	2.13	3.0	0.10	5/19/16	17.7 -	9.6
1.83	-	-	7.44	7.38	5.96	20.1 -	14.6	3.64	2.92	1.94	2.7	1.090Y	61/28/99	149.4 -	108.4
0.13	-	-	1.33	2.03	2.91	29.5 -	10.4	-			-			39.2 -	13.9
-0.90	-	-	-15.57	0.49	1.71	-		-			-			21.0 -	1.1
-	0.37	-	0.54	0.28	0.03	62.9 -	10.2	-			-			34.0 -	5.5
-	0.71	-	1.52	1.54	1.45	20.5 -	16.3	1.46	2.40	8.36	5.2	0.150Y	61/28/99	31.1 -	24.8
0.13	-	-	2.70	2.86	2.70	22.8 -	10.5	0.52	0.51	0.25	1.2	0.130Y	61/28/99	61.6 -	28.2
0.53	-	-	7.25	6.69	5.18	36.0 -	20.2	-			-			261.3 -	146.4
1.18	-	-	3.73	2.83	4.86	35.7 -	29.0	3.85	7.10	4.85	3.1	0.32810Z	61/28/99	133.1 -	108.2
0.15	-	-	-0.18	-0.09	-0.09	-		-			-			22.7 -	15.8
-	-	-	0.03	0.03	0.06	292.3 -	222.7	0.33	0.44	0.35	4.2	0.0330	7/29/16	8.8 -	6.7
-0.31	-	-	-11.48	-14.89	-14.68	-		-			-			19.4 -	9.1
0.29	-	-	0.42	-0.48	-0.83	50.8 -	34.8	-			-	0.150Y	6/2/08	21.4 -	14.6
-	-	0.07	-0.35	0.20	1.23	-		2.38	2.34	2.19	7.1	-		41.9 -	27.6
-	-	-	5.86	10.60	9.04	11.6 -	2.1	5.86	10.60	9.04	16.8	0.0720	4/20/16	67.9 -	12.3
-	-	0.42	0.06	-0.89	-3.02	534.3 -	325.3	0.80	0.78	0.76	3.3	0.20250Y	61/28/99	32.1 -	19.5
0.25	-	-	-0.21	0.00	0.23	-		0.60	0.60	0.60	4.5	0.43130Z	61/28/99	15.8 -	11.3
-	-	-	3.10	-0.23	0.49	1.2 -	0.0	-	0.09	-	-	-		3.7 -	0.0
-	-	-	3.95	1.09	0.64	3.9 -	1.6	1.11	1.12	-	10.1	-		15.4 -	6.4
-	-	0.33	3.72	2.56	1.22	6.0 -	3.0	1.25	0.61	0.50	7.7	-		22.2 -	11.2
-0.22	-	-	-1.54	0.21	0.74	-		-			-			10.6 -	6.3
-	-	0.61	1.00	0.59	-0.73	24.0 -	15.8	0.50	0.48	0.48	2.5	0.1350Y	6/30/16	24.0 -	15.8
0.40	-	-	1.50	1.07	0.20	46.8 -	37.2	-			-			70.2 -	55.9
-	-	1.00	3.05	2.26	2.20	19.6 -	14.2	1.12	0.96	0.80	2.2	0.320Y	61/28/99	59.9 -	43.4
-0.06	-	-	-0.24	-1.71	1.16	-		0.40	0.40	0.40	1.3	0.10Y	6/1/16	35.2 -	26.0
0.71	-	-	0.93	1.20	1.54	78.3 -	61.6	1.49	1.45	1.76	2.3	0.380Y	61/28/99	72.8 -	57.3
-	-	0.09	2.37	5.09	3.57	25.5 -	4.8	1.28	1.00	0.80	4.3	0.070Y	6/29/16	60.5 -	11.5
0.20	-	-	0.65	0.36	-0.50	41.2 -	32.5	0.90	0.73	-	3.7	0.24502	61/28/99	26.8 -	21.1
-	-	0.52	2.32	2.12	1.69	28.2 -	21.4	1.08	0.84	0.72	1.9	0.30Y	61/28/99	65.4 -	49.6
-0.26	-	-	-2.48	-1.01	-0.03	-		-			-	0.250Y	61/28/99	37.8 -	11.8
-	-	0.27	2.26	3.11	2.08	15.9 -	11.8	0.47	0.45	0.39	1.5	0.05631	7/12/16	36.0 -	26.7
-	-	-	-	-	-	-		-			-			0.0 -	0.0
-	-	-	-	-	-	-		-			-			32.5 -	32.5
-	-	0.54	3.76	1.24	-	7.8 -	0.0	1.24	1.22	1.17	5.8	0.10920	8/15/16	29.4 -	0.0
-	-	-	-	-	-	-		2.25			10.8	2.25GJ	1/4/16	24.4 -	0.0
-	-	-	0.38	0.69		-		-	2.06	2.35	-	0.11670	6/23/16	17.9 -	8.8
-	-	-	0.76	0.21	0.92	11.5 -	8.0	0.93	0.92	0.91	12.8	0.060	6/23/16	8.8 -	6.1
-	-	-	1.04	0.67	-0.43	-		2.12	1.92	1.72	-	0.34380	6/30/16	-	
-	-	-	1.42	1.32	0.17	11.4 -	9.8	1.53	1.53	0.25	10.3	0.12710	6/23/16	16.2 -	14.0
-	-	-	3.60	5.31	1.41	-		1.06	1.00	0.63	-	0.280	6/30/16	-	
-	0.03	-	0.01	0.42	0.52	-		-			-	0.2639GH	8/2/16	-	
-	-	-	1.99	1.85	2.08	12.3 -	10.3	2.28	2.28	2.28	10.1	0.190	6/23/16	24.5 -	20.5
0.44	-	-	1.70	1.41	1.48	21.2 -	17.0	0.45	0.41	0.37	1.4	0.12250Y	61/28/99	36.1 -	28.9

SYMBOL	COMPANY	NATURE OF BUSINESS	FISCAL YEAR-END	TOTAL REV. $MILL	NET INCOME $MILL	TOTAL ASSETS $MILL	NET STK EQUITY $MILL	NO OF INST	INST. HOLDINGS (SHARES)
BF B	Brown-Forman Corp.	Beverages	4/30/16	3089.0	1067.0	4183.0	1562.0	156	42442192
BRT	BRT Realty Trust	REITs	9/30/15	-	-2.4	835.9	122.7	45	3882988
BC	Brunswick Corp.	Leisure Equipment	12/31/15	4105.7	241.4	3152.5	1281.3	454	98980991
BT	BT Group Plc	Services	3/31/16	19042.0	2588.0	42592.0	10380.0	230	24511478
BPL	Buckeye Partners, L.P.	Equipment & Services	12/31/15	3453.4	437.2	8369.3		478	100822319
BKE	Buckle, Inc. (The)	Retail - Apparel and Accessories	1/30/16	1119.6	147.3	572.8	412.6	249	34280919
BBW	Build-A-Bear Workshop Inc	Retail - Specialty	1/2/16	377.7	27.3	213.3	99.4	162	15041639
BG	Bunge Ltd.	Food	12/31/15	43455.0	791.0	17922.0	6441.0	569	122526047
BURL	Burlington Stores Inc	Retail - General Merchandise/Depart	1/30/16	5129.8	150.5	2580.1	-99.0	293	81695421
BWXT	BWX Technologies inc	Industrial Machinery & Equipment	12/31/15	1415.5	131.5	1382.1	265.7	321	102227663
BWXT	BWX Technologies inc	Industrial Machinery & Equipment	12/31/15	1415.5	131.5	1382.1	265.7	321	102227663
CJES	C&J Energy Services Ltd	Equipment & Services	12/31/15	1748.9	-872.5	2232.9	632.6		
BNK	C1 Financial Inc	Banking	12/31/15	87.5	14.3	1725.5	201.0	73	4372198
CAB	Cabelas Inc	Retail - Specialty	1/2/16	3997.7	189.3	8472.5	1828.6	370	60454239
CABO	Cable One Inc	Radio & Television	12/31/15	807.3	89.0	1408.6	435.3	235	4147375
CBT	Cabot Corp.	Specialty Chemicals	9/30/15	2871.0	-334.0	3075.0	1234 0	377	60005942
COG	Cabot Oil & Gas Corp.	Production & Extraction	12/31/15	1357.1	-113.9	5261.9	2009.2	617	475470170
CACI	CACI International Inc.	IT Services	6/30/15	3313.5	126.2	3257.1	1480.1	323	26980084
CAE	CAE Inc.	Aerospace	3/31/16	2512.6	229.7	4996.7	1888.7	161	167666953
CAI	CAI International Inc	Shipping	12/31/15	249.7	26.8	1986.5	460 3	114	12727438
CAA	CalAtlantic Group Inc	Builders	12/31/15	3540.1	213.5	8345.5	3861.4	426	137050205
CAL	Caleres Inc	Retail - Apparel and Accessories	1/30/16	2577.4	81.5	1303.3	601.5	265	45729570
CCC	Calgon Carbon Corp.	Specialty Chemicals	12/31/15	535.0	43.5	656.5	394.0	237	52487389
CRC	California Resources Corp	Production & Extraction	12/31/15	2403.0	-3554.0	7053.0	-916.0	589	243254297
CWT	California Water Service Group (DE	Water Utilities	12/31/15	588.4	45.0	2246.1	642.2	253	35696174
CALX	Calix Inc	Manufacturing	12/31/15	407.5	-26.3	323.9	235.8	130	33571054
ELY	Callaway Golf Co (DE)	Leisure Equipment	12/31/15	843.8	14.6	631.2	412.9	275	84296009
CPE	Callon Petroleum Co. (DE)	Production & Extraction	12/31/15	137.5	-240.1	788.6	362.8	225	106151983
CPN	Calpine Corp	Electric Utilities	12/31/15	6472.0	235.0	18833.0	3109.0	450	333933488
CBM	Cambrex Corp	Pharmaceuticals	12/31/15	433.3	57.2	505.5	310.8	308	37256986
CPT	Camden Property Trust	REITs	12/31/15	900.3	258.3	6037.6	2816.6	473	94697876
CCJ	Cameco Corp.	Mining	12/31/15	2754.4	65.3	8794.6	5547.0	378	264669995
CPB	Campbell Soup Co.	Food	8/2/15	8082.0	691.0	8089.0	1380.0	835	168573650
CM	Canadian Imperial Bank of Commer	Banking	10/31/15	17424.0	3576.0	463309.0	21360.0	317	227951533
CNI	Canadian National Railway Co.	Rail	12/31/15	12611.0	3538.0	36402.0	14950.0	694	512699940
CNQ	Canadian Natural Resources Ltd.	Production & Extraction	12/31/15	12363.0	-637.0	59275.0	27381.0	488	804128845
CP	Canadian Pacific Railway Ltd	Rail	12/31/15	6712.0	1352.0	19637 0	4796.0	482	132701674
CAJ	Canon, Inc.	Leisure Equipment	12/31/15	3800271.0	220209.0	4427773.0	2966415.0	243	20665796
CMN	Cantel Medical Corp	Medical Instruments & Equipment	7/31/15	565.0	48.0	584.0	406.6	268	36180620
COF	Capital One Financial Corp	Credit & Lending	12/31/15	25038.0	4050.0	334048.0	47284.0	1120	497403263
CSU	Capital Senior Living Corp	Hospitals & Health Care Facilities	12/31/15	412.2	-14.3	1019.0	135.7	147	33893034
CMO	Capstead Mortgage Corp.	REITs	12/31/15	-	108.3	14446.4	1298.3	271	68635491
CRR	Carbo Ceramics Inc.	Equipment & Services	12/31/15	279.6	-109.5	836.4	642 3	225	28007333
CAH	Cardinal Health, Inc.	Pharmaceuticals	6/30/15	102531.0	1215.0	30142.0	6256.0	1052	311892103
CCP	Care Capital Properties Inc	REITs	12/31/15	327.9	143.2	2955.0	1214.4	348	76667131
CRCM	Care.com Inc	Services	12/26/15	138.7	-35.0	142.5	88.3	76	23857069
CSL	Carlisle Companies Inc.	Rubber Products	12/31/15	3543.2	319.7	3954.1	2347.4	427	61416330
KMX	Carmax Inc.	Retail - Automotive	2/29/16	15149.7	623.4	14481.6	2904.8	587	253724754
CCL	Carnival Corp	Hotels, Restaurants & Travel	11/30/15	15714.0	1757.0	39237.0	23771.0	894	485970778
CUK	Carnival Plc	Hotels, Restaurants & Travel	11/30/15	15714.0	1757.0	39237.0	23771.0	139	6625510
CRS	Carpenter Technology Corp.	Non-Precious Metals	6/30/15	2226.7	58.7	2905.9	1325.9	303	47019898
CSV	Carriage Services, Inc.	Miscellaneous Consumer Services	12/31/15	242.5	20.9	837.4	157.6	142	13560800
CRI	Carter's Inc	Apparel, Footwear & Accessories	1/2/16	3013.9	237.8	2009.1	875.1	471	53144590
CSH	Cash America International Inc	Credit & Lending	12/31/15	1029.5	27.6	1379.0	998.2	263	29514196
CAS	Castle (A.M.) & Co.	Non-Precious Metals	12/31/15	770.8	-209.8	497.7	47.0	82	19202640
CSLT	Castlight Health Inc	Internet & Software	12/31/15	75.3	-79.9	173.3	118.4	110	52521844
CTLT	Catalent Inc	Pharmaceuticals	6/30/15	1830.8	212.2	3145.4	634.0	208	125967157
CTT	Catchmark Timber Trust Inc	REITs	12/31/15	69.1	-8.4	599.1	411.0	125	29303209
CAT	Caterpillar Inc.	Construction Services	12/31/15	47011.0	2102.0	78497.0	14809.0	1552	479145791
CATO	Cato Corp.	Retail - Apparel and Accessories	1/30/16	1011.1	66.8	642 3	412.7	207	23745077
CBZ	CBIZ Inc	Business Services	12/31/15	750.4	34.1	998.2	427.9	188	51345309
CBL	CBL & Associates Properties Inc	REITs	12/31/15	1055.0	103.4	6480.0	1285.0	327	172798873
IGR	CBRE Clarion Global Real Estate In	Holding and other Investment Office	12/31/15	44.9	31.5	1256.0	1053.9	138	34891801
CBG	CBRE Group Inc	Property, Real Estate & Developmen	12/31/15	10855.8	547.1	110179	2712.7	665	366548951
CBS	CBS Corp	Radio & Television	12/31/15	13886.0	1413.0	23765.0	5563.0	968	415748031
CDI	CDI Corp.	Business Services	12/31/15	985.5	-37.0	339.1	221 2	124	9435355
CEB	CEB Inc	Business Services	12/31/15	928.4	92.5	1338.6	43.7	313	34873273
FUN	Cedar Fair L.P	Sporting & Recreational	12/31/15	1235.8	112.2	1994.9		228	36904628
CDR	Cedar Realty Trust, Inc.	REITs	12/31/15	149.2	22.1	1321.6	596.0	205	83685519
CGI	Celadon Group, Inc.	Trucking	6/30/15	900.8	37.2	1175.7	366 3	166	28665498
CE	Celanese Corp (DE)	Specialty Chemicals	12/31/15	5674.0	304.0	8586.0	2378.0	516	160455244
CLS	Celestica, Inc.	Electrical Equipment	12/31/15	5639.2	66.9	2612.0	1091.0	169	95964881
CEL	Cellcom Israel Ltd	Services	12/31/15	4180.0	95.0	6278.0	1169.0	64	10727272
CPAC	Cementos Pacasmayo S.A.A. (Peru	Construction Materials	12/31/15	1231.0	215.5	3413.8	1943.1	20	4449940
CX	Cemex S.A.B. de C.V.	Construction Materials	12/31/15	225742.0	1201.0	542264.0	143479.0	358	433461885
CNCO	Cencosud SA	Retail - General Merchandise/Depart	12/31/15	10991337.7	231940.9	10110725.0	3971745.8	48	3033306
CVE	Cenovus Energy Inc.	Production & Extraction	12/31/15	13064.0	618.0	25791.0	12391.0	351	574768314
CNC	Centene Corp	Hospitals & Health Care Facilities	12/31/15	22760.0	355.0	7339.0	2157.0	669	169530353
CEN	Center Coast MLP & Infrastructure	Finance Intermediaries & Services	11/30/14	1.2	-3.5	485.2	297.9	25	3837593
CNP	CenterPoint Energy, Inc	Electric Utilities	12/31/15	7386.0	-692.0	21334.0	3461.0	641	325819645

EARNINGS PER SHARE						P/E RATIO		DIVIDENDS PER SHARE			AV. YLD	DIV. DECLARED		PRICE RANGE
QUARTERLY			ANNUAL								%			2015
1st	2nd	3rd	2015	2014	2013			2015	2014	2013		AMOUNT	PAYABLE	
-	-	0.94	3.21	3.06	2.75	34.5 -	28.2	1.21	1.09	4.98	1.2	0.340Y	61/28/99	110.8 - 90.6
-	1.76	-	-0.17	-0.66	0.35	-						1.157Y	10/00/09	7.2 - 0.0
0.70	-	-	2.56	2.50	8.20	21.7 -	14.8	0.53	0.45	0.10	1.1	0.150Y	61/28/99	55.5 - 38.0
-	-	-	0.26	0.25	0.26	144.2 -	119.8	0.18	0.48	0.42	0.5	-		37.5 - 31.1
1.01	-	-	3.40	2.28	1.49	23.2 -	14.8	4.63	4.42	4.22	6.9	1.20	61/28/99	79.0 - 50.4
0.48	-	-	3.38	3.39	3.44	14.0 -	6.8	3.66	2.02	5.30	10.5	0.250Y	7/27/16	47.2 - 23.1
0.22	-	-	1.59	0.81	-0.13	13.3 -	6.8					-		21.1 - 10.9
1.54	-	-	5.07	3.17	1.55			1.44	1.28	1.14		1.21880Z	61/28/99	
0.52	-	-	0.87	-0.39	-2.92	70.1 -	46.8					-		61.0 - 40.7
0.46	-	-	1.22	0.27	3.07	0.0 -	0.0	0.32	0.40	0.34	1.$	0.090Y	61/28/99	0.0 - 0.0
0.46	-	-	1.22	0.27	3.07	28.8 -	18.7	0.32	0.40	0.34	1.1	0.090Y	61/28/99	35.2 - 22.8
-3.65	-	-	-8.48	1.22	1.20							-		15.1 - 0.3
0.29	-	-	0.89	0.48	1.05	27.9 -	20.1					-		24.8 - 17.9
0.33	-	-	2.67	2.81	3.13	20.1 -	12.5					-		53.6 - 33.4
4.65	-	-	15.14	7309.00	4511.00	32.8 -	0.0	1.50			0.4	1.50Y	61/28/99	498.5 - 0.0
-	0.76	-	-5.27	3.03	2.36			0.88	0.84	0.80	2.2	0.30Y	61/28/99	50.2 - 30.9
-0.12	-	-	-0.28	0.25	0.66			0.08	0.08	0.06	0.3	0.020Y	61/28/99	34.2 - 15.0
-	-	1.38	5.17	5.38	6.35	21.3 -	14.2					-		110.3 - 73.6
-	-	0.21	0.76	0.73	0.54	21.7 -	0.0	0.27	0.22	0.19	2.1	0.0750	6/30/16	16.5 - 0.0
0.36	-	-	1.28	2.85	2.82	17.4 -	3.8					-		22.0 - 4.9
0.52	-	-	2.26	2.70	2.35	20.8 -	12.3	0.04			0.1	0.040Y	61/28/99	46.5 - 27.9
0.41	-	-	1.89	0.88	0.64	17.8 -	11.4	0.28	0.28	0.28	1.0	0.070Y	7/1/16	33.6 - 21.5
0.11	-	-	0.82	0.92	0.84	25.9 -	16.3	0.20			1.2	0.050Y	6/15/16	21.3 - 13.4
-1.30	-	-	-92.70	-37.50				0.30			1.0	0.010Y	10/15/15	81.8 - 3.0
-0.02	-	-	0.94	1.19	1.02	31.0 -	20.9	0.67	0.65	0.04	2.8	0.1/250Y	61/28/99	29.1 - 19.7
-0.22	-	-	-0.51	-0.41	-0.35							-		9.0 - 5.7
0.40	-	-	0.17	0.20	-0.31	60.4 -	47.4	0.04	0.04	0.04	0.4	0.010Y	6/15/16	10.3 - 8.1
-0.51	-	-	-3.77	0.65	-0.01							1.250Y	6/30/16	11.7 - 5.2
-0.56	-	-	0.64	2.31	0.03	31.5 -	18.4					-		20.1 - 11.8
0.44	-	-	1.76	1.81	0.84	30.6 -	17.7					14.7	5/3/07	53.8 - 31.1
0.46	-	-	2.76	3.27	3.78	31.4 -	25.2	2.80	2.64	2.52	3.6	0.750Z	61/28/99	86.8 - 69.5
-	-	-0.01	0.16	0.47	0.81	120.5 -	0.0	0.40	0.40	0.40	2.7	0.10	7/15/16	19.3 - 0.0
-	-	0.59	2.21	2.59	1.44	30.1 -	20.9	1.25	1.25	1.16	2.3	0.3120Y	61/28/99	66.5 - 46.1
2.43	-	-	8.87	7.86	8.23	11.7 -	0.0	4.30	3.94	3.80	5.2	0.2250	7/28/16	103.4 - 0.0
1.00	-	-	4.39	3.85	3.09	19.0 -	0.0	1.25	1.00	0.86	1.9	0.3750	6/30/16	83.5 - 0.0
-0.10	-	-	-0.58	3.58	2.08			0.92	0.90	0.57	3.0	0.230	7/1/16	38.5 - 0.0
3.51	-	-	8.40	8.46	4.96	25.1 -	0.0	1.40	1.40	1.40	0.9	0.50	7/25/16	210.6 - 0.0
42.11	-	-	201.65	229.03	200.78	0.2 -	0.1	75.43	215.45	139.96	249.5	-		34.6 - 26.8
-	-	0.34	1.15	1.04	0.95	62.8 -	40.3	0.10	0.09	0.07	0.2	0.060Y	7/29/16	72.2 - 46.4
1.84	-	-	7.07	7.59	6.96	13.0 -	8.3	1.50	1.20	0.95	2.0	0.38750Y	61/28/99	91.7 - 58.7
0.21	-	-	-0.50	-0.83	-0.58							-		26.3 - 14.7
0.25	-	-	0.97	1.33	0.93	12.3 -	8.1	1.14	1.36	1.24	11.3	0.46880Z	7/15/16	11.9 - 7.9
-1.07	-	-	-4.76	2.41	3.67			0.63	1.28	1.14	2.8	0.10Y	61/28/99	46.0 - 10.6
-	-	1.17	3.62	3.38	0.97	25.1 -	21.0	1.41	1.25	1.09	1.7	0.44890Y	61/28/99	90.8 - 76.2
0.36	-	-	1.71		-	20.8 -	0.0	1.14			4.0	0.570Z	61/28/99	35.6 - 0.0
0.20	-	-	-1.09	-2.77	-9.45							-		8.9 - 5.0
1.05	-	-	4.82	3.82	3.22	21.7 -	16.1	1.10	0.94	0.84	1.2	0.30Y	61/28/99	104.6 - 77.8
-	-	0.63	2.73	2.16	1.87	27.0 -	15.4					-		73.7 - 42.1
0.18	-	-	2.26	1.59	1.39	24.4 -	18.5	1.10	1.00	1.50	2.2	0.350Y	61/28/99	55.1 - 41.9
0.18	-	-	2.26	1.59	1.39	25.5 -	19.4	1.10	1.00	1.50	2.1	-		57.5 - 43.9
-	-	-0.51	1.11	2.47	2.73	38.6 -	22.7	0.72	0.72	0.72	2.1	0.180Y	61/28/99	42.9 - 25.2
0.27	-	-	1.12	0.85	1.00	22.8 -	17.9	0.10	0.10	0.10	0.4	0.0250Y	6/1/16	25.6 - 20.1
1.04	-	-	4.50	3.62	2.75	24.2 -	18.7	0.88	0.76	0.48	0.9	0.330Y	61/28/99	109.0 - 84.1
0.42	-	-	1.01	3.36	4.66	40.3 -	23.8	0.20	0.14	0.14	0.6	0.080Y	5/25/16	40.7 - 24.0
-1.56	-	-	-8.91	-5.77	-1.46							0.060Y	4/2/09	6.5 - 1.4
-0.22	-	-	-0.85	-1.16	-6.28							-		10.3 - 2.6
-	-	0.08	1.75	0.21	-0.62	19.5 -	11.9					-		34.2 - 20.9
-0.02	-	-	-0.21	0.02	-1.03			0.50	0.47		4.6	0.1350Z	6/16/16	12.0 - 9.7
0.46	-	-	3.50	5.88	5.75	25.3 -	16.5	2.94	2.60	1.72	4.0	0.770Y	61/28/99	88.5 - 57.9
1.29	-	-	2.15	1.86	2.11	18.8 -	15.3	1.20	0.20	2.98	3.2	0.330Y	6/20/16	40.5 - 32.8
0.41	-	-	0.65	0.58	1.75	17.4 -	13.9					-		11.3 - 9.1
0.17	-	-	0.34	1.02	0.24	52.3 -	27.6	1.06	1.00	0.94	7.9	0.41410Z	61/28/99	17.8 - 9.4
-	-	-	0.27	0.30	0.33	31.4 -	24.3	0.57	0.54	0.54	7.4	0.050	6/30/16	8.5 - 6.6
0.24	-	-	1.63	1.45	0.95	23.7 -	14.3					-		38.6 - 23.3
1.02	-	-	2.89	5.27	3.01	21.5 -	13.4	0.60	0.54	0.48	1.2	0.150Y	61/28/99	62.2 - 38.7
-0.24	-	-	-1.88	0.16	0.65			0.52	0.52	0.39	6.4	0.130Y	12/2/15	13.7 - 4.4
0.14	-	-	2.75	1.50	0.94	32.8 -	18.1	1.50	1.05	0.90	2.2	0.41250Y	61/28/99	90.2 - 49.7
-0.87	-	-	1.99	1.86	1.94	30.2 -	25.0	3.08	2.85	2.58	5.5	0.8250	6/15/16	60.0 - 49.8
-0.03	-	-	0.09	0.18	-0.03	81.8 -	65.6	0.20	0.20	0.67	2.9	0.45310Z	5/20/16	7.4 - 5.9
-	-	0.19	1.52	1.29	1.17	15.3 -	4.5	0.08	0.08	0.08	0.6	0.020Y	7/22/16	23.2 - 6.8
1.73	-	-	2.00	4.00	6.91	36.9 -	27.2	1.15	0.93	0.53	1.7	0.360Y	61/28/99	73.7 - 54.5
-	0.08	-	0.42	0.60	0.64	41.7 -	0.0					-		17.5 - 0.0
-	-	1.85	0.95	3.48	2.86					0.85		0.850	12/12/13	
-	-	-	0.38	0.33	0.27	24.9 -	0.0	1.27	0.90		17.8	-		9.5 - 0.0
-	-	-	0.03	-0.17	-0.28	309.9 -	127.2					-		9.3 - 3.8
-	-	-	81.00	58.30	89.80	0.1 -	0.1	58.32	37.67	114.50	869.4	-		8.7 - 5.2
-	-	2.16	0.75	0.98	0.87	29.6 -	0.0	0.85	1.06	0.97	5.3	0.050	6/30/16	22.2 - 0.0
-0.14	-	-	2.88	2.25	1.47	28.3 -	18.3					-		81.5 - 52.7
-	-	-	-	-0.24	-				1.46	0.10		0.10420	8/29/16	15.9 - 6.5
0.36	-	-	-1.61	1.42	0.72			0.99	0.95	0.83	5.2	0.35750Y	61/28/99	22.5 - 16.1

SYMBOL	COMPANY	NATURE OF BUSINESS	FISCAL YEAR-END	TOTAL REV. $MILL	NET INCOME $MILL	TOTAL ASSETS $MILL	NET STK EQUITY $MILL	NO OF INST	INST. HOLDINGS (SHARES)
CEE	Central Europe, Russia and Turkey	Holding and other Investment Office	10/31/15	6.5	3.7	178.0	174.7	38	4682460
CPF	Central Pacific Financial Corp	Banking	12/31/15	195.0	45.9	5131.3	494.6	190	40684814
CCS	Century Communities, Inc	Construction Services	12/31/15	734.5	39.9	917.7	409.5	98	13192487
CTL	CenturyLink, Inc.	Services	12/31/15	17900.0	878.0	47604.0	14060.0	916	434947598
CVO	Cenveo Inc	Printing	1/2/16	1741.8	-30.9	1079.9	-669.8	110	35554658
CF	CF Industries Holdings Inc	Agricultural Chemicals	12/31/15	4308.3	699.9	12738.9	4035.2	724	234615844
CGG	CGG	Equipment & Services	12/31/15	2102.3	-1450.2	5513.0	1312.2	45	769694
GIB	CGI Group, Inc.	IT Services	9/30/15	10287.1	977.6	11787.3	6082.2	268	215077268
ECOM	ChannelAdvisor Corp	IT Services	12/31/15	100.6	-21.0	131.0	83.9	114	21603179
CRL	Charles River Laboratories Internati	Biotechnology	12/26/15	1363.3	149.3	2068.5	733.1	389	56712730
CLDT	Chatham Lodging Trust	REITs	12/31/15	276.9	33.0	1339.9	692.9	162	36425874
CMCM	Cheetah Mobile Inc	Services	12/31/15	3684.4	176.6	4942.6	2911.9	76	16089688
CHGG	Chegg Inc	Educational Services	12/31/15	301.4	-59.2	291.4	231.1	120	62064746
CHE	Chemed Corp	Diagnostic & Health Related Service	12/31/15	1543.4	110.3	852.3	513.3	315	19604084
CC	Chemours Co (The)	Specialty Chemicals	12/31/15	5717.0	-90.0	6298.0	126.0	485	121882394
CHMT	Chemtura Corp	Specialty Chemicals	12/31/15	1745.0	136.0	2366.0	1001.0	302	77176899
CHMI	Cherry Hill Mortgage Investment Co	REITs	12/31/15	19.6	13.4	636.3	151.3	42	3829493
CHK	Chesapeake Energy Corp.	Production & Extraction	12/31/15	12764.0	-14685.0	17357.0	2138.0	779	565060011
CHKR	Chesapeake Granite Wash Trust	Production & Extraction	12/31/15	36.4	53.3	63.4	63.2	-	
CHSP	Chesapeake Lodging Trust	REITs	12/31/15	582.6	67.5	2094.3	1209.6	214	61311910
CPK	Chesapeake Utilities Corp.	Gas Utilities	12/31/15	459.2	41.1	1068.6	358.1	203	8959876
CVX	Chevron Corporation	Refining & Marketing	12/31/15	138477.0	4587.0	266103.0	152716.0	2503	1401759704
CBI	Chicago Bridge & Iron Co., N.V. (Ne	Construction Services	12/31/15	12929.5	-504.4	9202.4	2014.0	622	85073835
CHS	Chico's FAS Inc	Retail - Apparel and Accessories	1/30/16	2642.3	1.9	1166.1	639.8	387	139221412
CIM	Chimera Investment Corp	REITs	12/31/15	603.1	250.3	15344.6	2946.2	317	193437331
CO	China Cord Blood Corp	Diagnostic & Health Related Service	3/31/15	635.1	107.3	4119.5	1537.8	-	
STV	China Digital TV Holding Co Ltd	Radio & Television	12/31/15	52.9	1.5	130.8	101.5	36	16274079
DL	China Distance Education Holdings	Educational Services	9/30/15	108.2	24.6	174.1	90.8	-	
CEA	China Eastern Airlines Corp., Ltd.	Airlines/Air Freight	12/31/15	93969.0	4537.0	197992.0	37411.0	36	1336711
CHN	China Fund, Inc. (The)	Holding and other Investment Office	10/31/15	8.6	4.0	336.0	312.2	66	9305404
CGA	China Green Agriculture Inc	Agricultural Chemicals	6/30/15	263.4	31.4	429.6	372.9	38	1529395
LFC	China Life Insurance Co Ltd	Life & Health	12/31/15	509423.0	34699.0	2448315.0	322492.0	174	16992822
CHL	China Mobile Limited	Services	12/31/14	641448.0	109279.0	1296449.0	856576.0	467	83938112
NPD	China Nepstar Chain Drugstore Ltd	Retail - Food & Beverage, Drug & To	12/31/15	3232.4	39.8	1621.8	871.4	31	3849955
BORN	China New Borun Corp	Beverages	12/31/15	2652.0	128.9	3091.0	1805.1	18	841075
COE	China Online Education Group	Educational Services	12/31/15	154.7	-327.1	291.6	-86.3	-	
SNP	China Petroleum & Chemical Corp	Production & Extraction	12/31/15	2018883.0	32438.0	1443129.0	674029.0	194	7935350
ZNH	China Southern Airlines Co Ltd	Airlines/Air Freight	12/31/15	111652.0	3736.0	185989.0	39045.0	58	1308881
CHA	China Telecom Corp Ltd	Services	12/31/15	331202.0	20054.0	629561.0	303784.0	76	4530991
CHU	China Unicom (Hong Kong) Ltd	Services	12/31/15	277049.0	10562.0	610346.0	231216.0	140	30023657
XNY	China Xiniya Fashion Ltd.	Apparel, Footwear & Accessories	12/31/15	472.2	-600.3	934.7	731.8	3	2632876
CYD	China Yuchai International Ltd.	Auto Parts	12/31/15	13733.4	341.1	18815.6	7239.6	80	9439344
ZX	China Zenix Auto International Ltd.	Auto Parts	12/31/15	2445.8	-28.6	3835.3	2563.5	10	9735452
CMG	Chipotle Mexican Grill Inc	Hotels, Restaurants & Travel	12/31/15	4501.2	475.6	2725.1	2128.0	748	32776537
CHH	Choice Hotels International, Inc.	Hotels, Restaurants & Travel	12/31/15	859.9	128.0	717.0	-395.9	181	29439948
CBK	Christopher & Banks Corp	Retail - Apparel and Accessories	1/30/16	383.8	-49.1	150.9	88.4	139	25355298
CB	Chubb Ltd	General Insurance	12/31/15	18987.0	2834.0	102366.0	29135.0	1148	408445080
CHT	Chunghwa Telecom Co Ltd	Services	12/31/14	226609.0	36970.0	446498.0	360788.0	176	44941113
CHD	Church & Dwight Co., Inc.	Household & Personal Products	12/31/15	3394.8	410.4	4256.9	2023.2	821	124886670
CBR	CIBER, Inc.	IT Services	12/31/15	787.0	3.3	502.3	319.3	171	66687145
CIEN	Ciena Corp	IT Services	10/31/15	2445.7	11.7	2695.1	620.9	453	149908747
CI	Cigna Corp	Life & Health	12/31/15	37876.0	2094.0	57088.0	12035.0	982	250656683
XEC	Cimarex Energy Co	Production & Extraction	12/31/15	1452.6	-2408.9	5243.3	2797.7	606	106580172
CBB	Cincinnati Bell Inc	Services	12/31/15	1167.8	353.7	1454.4	-298.2	250	187385444
CNK	Cinemark Holdings Inc	Entertainment	12/31/15	2852.6	216.9	4126.5	1099.7	392	110218362
CINR	Ciner Resources LP	Mining	12/31/15	486.4	51.5	423.2		41	2033333
CIR	Circor International Inc	Industrial Machinery & Equipment	12/31/15	656.3	9.9	669.9	400.8	168	17334273
CIT	CIT Group, Inc.	Banking	12/31/15	3884.9	1056.6	67498.8	10978.1	538	226213425
C	Citigroup Inc	Banking	12/31/15	88275.0	17242.0	1731210.0	221867.0	1893	2538979135
CFG	Citizens Financial Group Inc (New)	Banking	12/31/15	5276.0	840.0	138208.0	19646.0	499	503395181
CIA	Citizens, Inc. (Austin, TX)	Life & Health	12/31/15	236.3	-3.6	1484.0	242.5	79	9379364
CIO	City Office REIT Inc	REITs	12/31/15	55.1	-6.6	443.6	65.8	88	8096794
CVEO	Civeo Corp (Canada)	Business Services	12/31/15	518.0	-131.8	1071.2	563.2	156	79220901
CIVI	Civitas Solutions Inc	Hospitals & Health Care Facilities	9/30/15	1366.9	3.1	1063.2	121.3	96	34198111
CLC	Clarcor Inc.	Industrial Machinery & Equipment	11/28/15	1481.0	134.7	1818.5	1109.6	337	55418147
CLH	Clean Harbors, Inc	Sanitation Services	12/31/15	3275.1	44.1	3431.4	1096.3	333	61891405
CCO	Clear Channel Outdoor Holdings Inc	Advertising	12/31/15	2806.2	-96.1	6357.2	-757.4	146	35238073
CBA	ClearBridge American Energy MLP	Finance Intermediaries & Services	11/30/14	2.7	-16.8	1531.0	1095.5	-	
CEM	ClearBridge Energy MLP Fund Inc	Holding and other Investment Office	11/30/14	10.3	-20.5	3226.3	2032.6	100	16671222
EMO	ClearBridge Energy MLP Opportunit	Holding and other Investment Office	11/30/14	3.0	-9.1	1257.1	797.8	42	7454455
CTR	ClearBridge Energy MLP Total Retu	Holding and other Investment Office	11/30/14	6.4	-9.3	1410.1	935.4	52	7177741
CLW	Clearwater Paper Corp	Paper & Forest Products	12/31/15	1752.4	56.0	1527.4	474.9	202	15203243
CLF	Cliffs Natural Resources, Inc.	Non-Precious Metals	12/31/15	2013.3	-749.3	2135.5	-1981.4	374	108096605
CLX	Clorox Co (The)	Household & Personal Products	6/30/15	5655.0	580.0	4164.0	118.0	1126	111276643
CLD	Cloud Peak Energy Inc	Mining	12/31/15	1124.1	-204.9	1802.2	887.9	195	58313872
MYCC	ClubCorp Holdings Inc	Sporting & Recreational	12/29/15	1052.9	-9.5	2170.9	168.4	173	65692122
CMS	CMS Energy Corp	Electric Utilities	12/31/15	6456.0	525.0	20340.0	3938.0	629	279913095
CNA	CNA Financial Corp.	General Insurance	12/31/15	9101.0	479.0	55047.0	11756.0	227	272283489
CNHI	CNH Industrial N.V	Industrial Machinery & Equipment	12/31/15	25912.0	253.0	46746.0	4802.0	136	300323876
CNO	CNO Financial Group Inc	Life & Health	12/31/15	3811.9	270.7	31125.1	4138.5	310	222713406

EARNINGS PER SHARE QUARTERLY			EARNINGS PER SHARE ANNUAL			P/E RATIO		DIVIDENDS PER SHARE			AV. YLD %	DIV. DECLARED AMOUNT	DIV. DECLARED PAYABLE	PRICE RANGE 2015	
1st	2nd	3rd	2015	2014	2013			2015	2014	2013					
-	-	-	0.43	0.43	0.68	51.4 -	0.0	0.97	2.49	1.09	5.3	0.48640	1/28/16	22.1 -	0.0
0.35	-	-	1.40	1.07	4.07	17.5 -	13.3	0.82	0.36	0.16	3.8	0.140Y	6/15/16	24.5 -	18.6
0.38	-	-	1.88	1.03	0.95	12.4 -	7.2	-	-	-	-	-	-	23.4 -	13.5
0.44	-	-	1.58	1.36	-0.40	20.9 -	14.1	2.16	2.16	2.16	7.6	0.540Y	61/28/99	33.0 -	22.2
0.15	-	-	-0.45	-1.25	-1.07	-		-	-	-	-	-	-	2.6 -	0.4
0.11	-	-	2.96	5.42	4.95	23.3 -	9.3	1.20	1.00	0.44	2.7	0.30Y	61/28/99	68.9 -	27.6
-	-	0.01	-7.45	-6.52	-3.95	-		-	-	-	-	1.2961E	12/27/05	7.1 -	0.6
0.75	-	-	3.04	2.69	1.44	20.8 -	0.0	-	-	-	-	-	-	63.3 -	0.0
-0.18	-	-	-0.84	-1.40	-1.51	-		-	-	-	-	-	-	14.6 -	8.7
0.78	-	-	3.13	2.66	2.12	27.5 -	19.7	-	-	-	-	-	-	86.0 -	61.6
0.08	-	-	0.86	2.30	0.13	33.4 -	19.7	1.20	0.93	0.84	5.3	0.110Z	7/29/16	28.7 -	16.9
-	-	-	0.12	0.05	0.05	291.3 -	81.9	-	-	-	-	-	-	35.0 -	9.8
-0.18	-	-	-0.68	-0.78	-7.58	-		-	-	-	-	-	-	8.7 -	3.5
1.45	-	-	6.33	5.57	4.16	25.1 -	19.7	0.92	0.84	0.76	0.7	0.240Y	6/15/16	158.7 -	124.6
0.28	-	-	-0.50	-	-	-		0.58	-	-	7.3	0.030	6/15/16	20.9 -	3.1
-1.46	-	-	1.98	8.34	-1.81	16.2 -	12.3	-	-	-	-	0.050Y	9/2/08	32.1 -	24.3
-0.94	-	-	1.76	0.31	12.50	9.9 -	7.2	1.98	2.03	0.45	13.2	0.490Y	7/26/16	17.5 -	12.7
-1.44	-	-	-22.43	1.87	0.73	-		0.17	0.35	0.35	2.6	14.3750Y	61/28/99	14.1 -	1.6
0.16	-	-	-	-	-	-		1.52	2.40	2.72	34.9	0.04030	5/31/16	7.9 -	1.8
0.13	-	-	0.99	1.00	0.75	32.8 -	22.7	1.50	1.20	1.00	5.5	0.484407	7/15/16	32.5 -	22.5
1.33	-	-	2.72	2.47	2.26	24.4 -	17.1	1.13	1.07	1.01	2.0	0.3050Y	61/28/99	66.4 -	46.6
-0.39	-	-	2.45	10.14	11.09	42.4 -	28.6	4.28	4.21	3.90	4.7	1.070Y	61/28/99	103.8 -	70.0
1.01	-	-	-4.72	4.98	4.23	-		0.28	0.28	0.20	0.7	0.070Y	61/28/99	56.7 -	31.5
0.23	-	-	0.42	0.41	1.08	40.9 -	23.1	0.30	0.24	0.21	2.2	0.080Y	61/28/99	17.2 -	9.7
0.44	-	-	1.25	2.85	1.75	12.1 -	9.1	1.44	1.80	2.80	10.4	0.0960Z	61/28/99	15.1 -	11.4
-	0.33	-	1.36	1.60	1.49	-		-	-	-	-	-	-	-	
-	-	0.08	0.02	0.34	0.41	249.0 -	60.5	-	0.48	-	-	0.217	0/0/00	5.0 -	1.2
-	-	0.02	0.17	0.17	0.10	110.0 -	48.5	-	0.58	0.48	-	0.97	1/13/16	18.7 -	8.3
-	-	-	0.35	0.27	0.20	141.4 -	60.6	-	-	-	-	-	-	49.5 -	21.2
-	-	-	0.26	0.33	0.41	84.1 -	49.4	3.77	3.31	3.25	23.3	0.4363B	1/6/16	21.9 -	12.9
-	-	0.22	0.93	0.81	1.61	2.5 -	1.2	0.10	-	-	6.1	0.1GY	1/31/15	2.4 -	1.1
-	-	-	1.22	1.14	0.88	19.7 -	8.5	2.00	1.33	0.58	12.6	-	-	24.1 -	10.3
-	-	-	5.35	5.98	-	-		-	11.33	12.35	-	-	-	67.3 -	50.7
-	-	-0.02	0.20	-0.07	0.06	14.8 -	9.5	-	-	1.82	-	-	-	3.0 -	1.9
-	-	0.42	5.01	3.08	3.09	0.4 -	0.2	-	-	-	-	-	-	1.8 -	1.0
-2.06	-	-	-5.57	-1.71	-0.24	-		-	-	-	-	-	-	-	
-	-	-	0.27	0.40	0.53	327.4 -	184.5	17.88	21.48	20.02	26.6	-	-	88.4 -	49.8
-	-	-	0.38	0.18	0.20	166.6 -	66.9	1.70	1.68	2.12	4.5	-	-	63.3 -	25.4
-	-	-	-	-	-	-		6.84	6.89	6.05	13.3	-	-	67.6 -	43.0
-	-	-	0.44	0.49	0.43	39.2 -	23.6	1.83	1.46	1.07	14.3	-	-	17.3 -	10.4
-	-	-	-2.64	-0.75	0.43	-		-	-	-	-	-	-	2.4 -	0.0
-	-	-	8.81	10.36	18.79	-		6.82	7.48	5.53	-	0.850	6/29/16	-	
-	-	0.29	-0.14	0.38	1.13	-		-	-	-	-	-	-	1.3 -	0.0
-0.88	-	-	15.10	14.13	10.47	50.2 -	26.8	-	-	-	-	-	-	757.8 -	404.3
0.35	-	-	2.22	2.10	1.91	25.7 -	18.9	0.79	0.75	0.74	1.6	0.2050Y	61/28/99	57.1 -	41.9
0.00	-	-	1.28	0.23	-0.45	4.4 -	0.8	-	-	-	-	0.060Y	10/20/11	5.7 -	1.0
0.97	-	-	8.62	8.42	10.92	14.8 -	11.6	2.66	3.21	1.51	2.4	0.690	61/28/99	127.2 -	99.7
-	-	1.37	-	4.76	5.34	-		-	39.84	43.26	-	-	-	34.6 -	29.2
0.86	-	-	3.07	3.01	2.79	32.3 -	25.5	1.34	1.24	1.12	1.5	0.3550Y	61/28/99	99.1 -	78.2
-1.21	-	-	0.04	-0.25	-0.19	94.8 -	24.5	-	-	-	-	-	-	3.8 -	1.0
-	0.10	-	0.10	-0.38	-0.83	260.3 -	157.3	-	-	-	-	-	-	26.0 -	15.7
2.00	-	-	8.04	7.83	5.18	21.1 -	15.5	0.04	0.04	0.04	0.0	0.040Y	61/28/99	169.8 -	124.8
-2.00	-	-	-25.92	5.78	6.47	-		0.64	0.62	0.54	0.6	0.080Y	61/28/99	123.0 -	75.6
0.02	-	-	1.63	0.31	-0.32	2.5 -	1.8	-	-	-	-	0.84380Y	7/1/16	4.1 -	2.9
0.50	-	-	1.87	1.66	1.28	22.5 -	14.5	1.00	1.00	0.92	2.8	0.270Y	61/28/99	42.1 -	27.1
1.02	-	-	2.58	2.23	0.65	11.5 -	7.6	2.17	2.10	0.57	9.1	0.5640	5/13/16	29.6 -	19.6
0.23	-	-	0.58	2.84	2.67	105.8 -	56.8	0.15	0.15	0.15	0.3	0.03750Y	6/10/16	61.4 -	32.9
0.73	-	-	5.67	5.96	3.35	8.6 -	4.5	0.60	0.50	0.10	1.5	0.150Y	5/27/16	48.5 -	25.6
1.10	-	-	5.40	2.20	4.35	11.2 -	6.5	0.16	0.04	0.04	0.3	0.53130Y	61/28/99	60.3 -	35.0
0.41	-	-	1.55	1.55	-6.12	18.3 -	11.7	0.40	0.10	2.12	1.7	0.120Y	5/18/16	28.3 -	18.1
-0.06	-	-	-0.07	-0.13	0.10	-		-	-	-	-	0.05640	3/20/79	10.1 -	5.8
-0.56	-	-	-0.53	-0.59	-	-		0.70	0.65	-	6.0	0.2350Z	7/21/16	13.1 -	10.4
-0.25	-	-	-1.24	-1.77	1.70	-		-	0.26	-	-	-	-	3.9 -	0.8
-	0.20	-	0.08	-0.89	-0.72	374.3 -	192.4	-	-	-	-	-	-	29.9 -	15.4
-	1.09	-	2.67	2.83	2.34	23.8 -	16.6	0.82	0.71	0.57	1.5	0.220Y	61/28/99	63.5 -	44.3
-0.36	-	-	0.76	-0.47	1.57	74.4 -	51.8	-	-	-	-	-	-	56.5 -	39.4
0.39	-	-	-0.27	-0.03	-0.14	-		-	0.49	0.56	-	1.49377Y	61/28/99	11.6 -	3.4
-	-	-	-	-0.29	-0.09	-		-	1.21	0.60	-	0.20	5/27/16	15.6 -	4.8
-	-	-	-	-0.30	-0.27	-		-	1.63	1.56	-	0.3550	5/27/16	25.3 -	9.5
-	-	-	-	-0.29	-0.31	-		-	1.40	1.37	-	0.320	5/27/16	21.2 -	6.9
-	-	-	-	-0.24	-0.31	-		-	1.33	1.32	-	0.290	5/27/16	20.0 -	6.8
1.05	-	-	2.97	-0.11	4.80	21.1 -	11.8	-	-	-	-	-	-	62.6 -	35.1
0.62	-	-	-5.13	-47.52	2.37	-		-	0.60	0.60	-	0.150Y	61/28/99	5.5 -	1.3
-	-	1.23	4.37	4.23	4.30	30.4 -	23.8	2.96	2.84	2.56	2.4	0.80Y	61/28/99	132.9 -	104.0
-0.59	-	-	-3.36	1.29	0.85	-		-	-	-	-	-	-	5.6 -	1.2
-0.13	-	-	-0.15	0.21	-0.75	-		0.52	0.49	0.12	2.9	0.130Y	7/15/16	24.7 -	9.8
0.59	-	-	1.89	1.74	1.66	22.6 -	16.6	1.16	1.08	1.02	3.2	0.310Y	61/28/99	42.7 -	31.4
0.25	-	-	1.77	2.55	3.47	22.8 -	15.9	3.00	2.00	0.80	8.6	0.250Y	61/28/99	40.4 -	28.2
-	-	-	0.19	0.52	0.54	-		0.21	0.28	0.29	-	0.130	5/3/16	-	
0.26	-	-	1.39	0.24	2.06	14.9 -	10.9	0.27	0.24	0.11	1.6	0.000Y	6/24/16	20.8 -	15.1

SYMBOL	COMPANY	NATURE OF BUSINESS	FISCAL YEAR-END	TOTAL REV. $MILL	NET INCOME $MILL	TOTAL ASSETS $MILL	NET STK EQUITY $MILL	NO OF INST	INST. HOLDINGS (SHARES)
CEO	Cnooc Ltd.	Production & Extraction	12/31/14	274634.0	60199.0	662859.0	379610.0	258	9313453
CNXC	CNX Coal Resources LP	Mining	12/31/15	261.6	50.7	422.1	182.4	27	7441735
COH	Coach, Inc.	Apparel, Footwear & Accessories	6/27/15	4191.6	402.4	4666.9	2489.9	916	280524877
CIE	Cobalt International Energy Inc.	Production & Extraction	12/31/15	-694.4	4094.1	1446.1		260	519851871
KO	Coca-Cola Co (The)	Beverages	12/31/15	44294.0	7351.0	90093.0	25554.0	2295	3059275088
CCE	Coca-Cola European Partners plc	Manufacturing	12/31/15	2919.8	191.1	2641.0	2109.8		
KOF	Coca-Cola FEMSA SAB de CV	Beverages	12/31/15	152360.0	10235.0	210249.0	104749.0	149	16298797
CDE	Coeur Mining, Inc.	Precious Metals	12/31/15	646.1	-367.2	1332.5	421.5	263	102212273
FOF	Cohen & Steers Closed-End Opport	Holding and other Investment Office	12/31/14	22.7	18.9	393.4	392.4	53	5723984
INB	Cohen & Steers Global Income Buil	Holding and other Investment Office	12/31/14	9.9	5.0	346.5	269.6	52	2957619
CNS	Cohen & Steers Inc	Wealth Management	12/31/15	328.7	64.6	305.3	231.8	172	21623556
UTF	Cohen & Steers Infrastructure Fund,	Holding and other Investment Office	12/31/15	102.3	57.7	2752.4	1895.5	156	27946594
LDP	Cohen & Steers Limited Duration Pr	Holding and other Investment Office	12/31/14	63.0	51.1	1066.1	740.9	62	6239839
MIE	Cohen & Steers MLP Income & Ene	Finance Intermediaries & Services	11/30/15	17.0	1.7	574.6	348.6	39	6409315
RQI	Cohen & Steers Quality Income Re	Holding and other Investment Office	12/31/15	58.8	32.0	1935.3	1469.1	138	21885369
RNP	Cohen & Steers Reit & Preferred In	Holding and other Investment Office	12/31/15	60.4	43.2	1382.5	1029.0	110	10792484
PSF	Cohen & Steers Select Preferred & I	Holding and other Investment Office	12/31/15	30.0	24.8	462.2	325.6	45	1262253
RFI	Cohen & Steers Total Return Realty	Holding and other Investment Office	12/31/15	10.6	7.4	356.2	355.5	66	2924170
CFX	Colfax Corp	Industrial Machinery & Equipment	12/31/15	3967.1	167.7	6732.9	3070.0		
CL	Colgate-Palmolive Co.	Household & Personal Products	12/31/15	16034.0	1384.0	11958.0	-299.0	1715	726320782
CLNY	Colony Capital Inc	REITs	12/31/15	842.0	150.0	10039.3	2846.9	267	110425736
SFR	Colony Starwood Homes	REITs	12/31/15	271.8	-44.4	3007.7	1008.9	185	38594395
CPGX	Columbia Pipeline Group Inc	Equipment & Services	12/31/15	1334.9	307.1	10056.2	4056.6	457	327627143
CPPL	Columbia Pipeline Partners LP	Production & Extraction	12/31/15	1331.8	530.2	9162.0	1258.5	110	51942044
CXP	Columbia Property Trust Inc	REITs	12/31/15	566.1	44.6	4678.1	2614.2	253	73147700
STK	Columbia Seligman Premium Techn	Holding and other Investment Office	12/31/14	2.0	-1.1	272.6	271.3	34	1927302
CCZ	Comcast Holdings Corp	Radio & Television	12/31/04	8586.0	986.0	41942.0	19912.0	3	297000
CMA	Comerica, Inc.	Banking	12/31/15	2834.0	521.0	71877.0	7560.0	589	173864641
FIX	Comfort Systems USA Inc	Construction Services	12/31/15	1580.5	49.4	691.6	346.7	270	40730927
CMC	Commercial Metals Co.	Non-Precious Metals	8/31/15	5988.6	141.6	3372.3	1319.2	362	112059109
CBU	Community Bank System, Inc.	Banking	12/31/15	382.9	91.2	8552.7	1140.6	204	31184907
CYH	Community Health Systems, Inc.	Hospitals & Health Care Facilities	12/31/15	19437.0	158.0	26861.0	4019.0	434	123012769
CHCT	Community Healthcare Trust Inc	REITs	12/31/15	8.6	-1.5	142.8	122.3	63	5812597
CBD	Companhia Brasileira de Distribuica	Retail - General Merchandise/Depart	12/31/14	65525.0	1270.0	45500.0	10580.0		
SBS	Companhia de Saneamento Basico	Water Utilities	12/31/15	11711.6	536.3	33706.6	13716.6	234	124513766
CIG	Companhia Energetica de Minas G	Electric Utilities	12/31/14	19540.0	3137.0	35000.0	11281.0	220	177552043
ELP	Companhia Paranaense De Energia	Electric Utilities	12/31/13	9180.2	1072.6	23111.4	12651.3	132	33408022
SID	Companhia Siderurgica Nacional	Non-Precious Metals	12/31/13	17312.4	509.0	50402.5	8096.6		
CCU	Compania Cervecerias Unidas S.A.	Beverages	12/31/15	1498371.7	120808.1	1823356.6	1057816.4	135	29066820
BVN	Compania de Minas Buenaventura	Precious Metals	12/31/15	951.9	-317.2	4547.2	3161.1	214	133835982
CODI	Compass Diversified Holdings	Auto Parts	12/31/15	805.4	161.8	1425.6	826.1	138	24353842
CMP	Compass Minerals International Inc	Mining	12/31/15	1098.7	159.2	1628.9	639.7	360	43877489
CSC	Computer Sciences Corp	IT Services	4/1/16	7106.0	251.0	7736.0	2025.0	511	148418206
CRK	Comstock Resources, Inc.	Production & Extraction	12/31/15	252.4	-1047.1	1195.8	-171.3	168	31718118
CAG	ConAgra Foods, Inc.	Food	5/31/15	15832.4	-252.6	17542.2	4526.0	931	386446819
CXO	Concho Resources Inc	Production & Extraction	12/31/15	1803.6	65.9	12641.9	6942.6	554	140551630
CCM	Concord Medical Services Holdings	Diagnostic & Health Related Service	12/31/15	616.5	-79.3	3601.4	1391.5	33	27005723
CNNX	CONE Midstream Partners LP	Gas Utilities	12/31/15	203.4	71.2	924.4		69	13365186
COP	ConocoPhillips	Production & Extraction	12/31/15	30935.0	-4428.0	97484.0	39762.0	1981	909579698
CNX	CONSOL Energy Inc	Mining	12/31/15	3114.4	-374.9	10929.9	4702.0	460	281212371
ED	Consolidated Edison Inc	Electric Utilities	12/31/15	12554.0	1193.0	45642.0	13052.0	993	178255584
STZ	Constellation Brands Inc	Beverages	2/29/16	6548.4	1054.9	16965.0	6559.6	906	183602843
CSTM	Constellium N.V.	Non-Precious Metals	12/31/15	5153.0	-554.0	3628.0	-551.0		
CMS PRB	Consumers Energy Co	Electric Utilities	12/31/15	6165.0	594.0	18658.0	5546.0		
TCS	Container Store Group, Inc	Retail - Furniture & Home Furnishing	2/27/16	794.6	5.1	763.8	207.1	108	40991779
CBPX	Continental Building Products Inc	Construction Materials	12/31/15	421.7	16.7	643.0	300.8	165	44412596
CLR	Continental Resources Inc.	Production & Extraction	12/31/15	2680.2	-353.7	14919.8	4668.9	470	93557442
VLRS	Controladora Vuela Compania De A	Airlines/Air Freight	12/31/15	18179.7	2463.9	15261.0	6824.8		
CVG	Convergys Corp	Miscellaneous Consumer Services	12/31/15	2950.6	169.0	2358.1	1276.2	362	106198081
COO	Cooper Companies, Inc. (The)	Medical Instruments & Equipment	10/31/15	1797.1	203.5	4460.6	2667.5	501	58475904
CTB	Cooper Tire & Rubber Co.	Auto Parts	12/31/15	2972.9	212.8	2436.2	979.2	352	65375243
CPS	Cooper-Standard Holdings, Inc.	Auto Parts	12/31/15	3342.8	111.9	2304.3	603.4	175	16950899
CPA	Copa Holdings S.A.	Airlines/Air Freight	12/31/15	2250.1	-225.0	3715.5	1587.4	291	35815573
CLB	Core Laboratories N.V. (Netherland	Equipment & Services	12/31/15	797.5	114.8	625.3	-29.1	494	48967686
CLGX	CoreLogic Inc.	Business Services	12/31/15	1528.1	127.8	3701.0	1049.5	355	87230762
CORR	CorEnergy Infrastructure Trust Inc	REITs	12/31/15		12.3	678.5	418.0	112	9175845
COR	CoreSite Realty Corp.	REITs	12/31/15	333.3	34.7	1162.5	416.1	268	31280907
GLW	Corning Inc	Electrical Equipment	12/31/15	9111.0	1339.0	28547.0	18788.0	1254	941245246
OFC	Corporate Office Properties Trust	REITs	12/31/15	625.5	178.3	3909.3	1544.5	334	101210149
CXW	Corrections Corporation of America	REITs	12/31/15	1793.1	221.9	3356.0	1462.7	384	126767462
CZZ	Cosan Ltd	Refining & Marketing	12/31/15	12458.3	459.8	52307.7	6017.0	156	93843962
CMRE	Costamare Inc.	Shipping	12/31/15	490.4	143.8	2638.6	963.5	97	10840585
COTV	Cotiviti Holdings Inc	Business Services	12/31/15	541.3	13.9	2147.0	787.6		
COT	Cott Corp.	Beverages	1/2/16	2944.0	-3.4	2887.3	639.3	181	98955634
COTY	Coty, Inc.	Household & Personal Products	6/30/15	4395.2	232.5	6018.9	969.8	206	57771255
CUZ	Cousins Properties Inc	REITs	12/31/15	381.6	125.5	2597.8	1683.4	291	225660437
CVA	Covanta Holding Corp	Electric Utilities	12/31/15	1645.0	68.0	4259.0	638.0	327	116865362
CPL	CPFL Energia SA	Electric Utilities	12/31/15	20205.9	864.9	40532.5	7674.2	128	13763540
CR	Crane Co.	Industrial Machinery & Equipment	12/31/15	2740.5	230.0	3341.6	1139.4	350	45758757
CRD B	Crawford & Co.	Brokers & Intermediaries	12/31/15	1241.5	-45.5	783.4	113.7	44	11044367

1st	2nd	3rd	2015	2014	2013	P/E High	P/E Low	Div 2015	Div 2014	Div 2013	AV. YLD %	AMOUNT	PAYABLE	Price High	Price Low
			1.35	1.26					41.02	40.50				193.0 -	0.0
0.11			0.99			16.1 -	6.2	0.48			4.6	0.51250	5/12/16	15.9 -	6.1
		0.40	1.45	2.79	3.61	29.0 -	18.9	1.35	1.35	1.24	4.0	0.33750Y	61/28/99	42.0 -	27.4
-0.11			-1.70	-1.25	-1.45									10.7 -	2.1
0.34			1.67	1.60	1.90	28.1 -	22.7	1.32	1.22	1.12	3.1	0.350Y	61/28/99	46.9 -	38.0
			0.13	0.12	0.07	298.5 -	298.5							38.8 -	38.8
								30.79	28.84	28.86	40.8			87.3 -	64.5
-0.14			-2.83	-11.28	-6.65									8.5 -	1.7
				0.69	0.64				1.04	1.04		0.260	6/30/16	13.1 -	9.5
				0.22	0.21				1.12	1.12		0.230	6/30/16	11.7 -	7.9
0.39			1.41	1.65	1.51	29.8 -	18.8	1.50	1.88	1.80	4.6	0.260Y	6/23/16	42.0 -	26.5
			0.68	0.72	0.61	33.3 -	23.7	1.60	1.48	1.44	8.2	0.40	6/23/16	22.6 -	16.1
				1.77	1.79				2.17	1.90		0.1560	6/30/16	24.0 -	21.2
			0.06	-0.01	-0.03	320.3 -	92.2	1.32	1.26	0.63	11.4	0.230	6/30/16	19.2 -	5.5
			0.29	0.31	0.25	44.3 -	35.4	0.96	0.76	0.72	8.3	0.240	6/30/16	12.9 -	10.3
			0.91	0.96	0.83	21.5 -	17.9	1.40	1.29	1.20	8.2	0.370	6/30/16	19.6 -	16.3
				2.07	2.05				2.56	2.28		0.1720	6/30/16	26.5 -	23.1
			0.28	0.28	0.28	47.9 -	39.3	1.30	1.30	1.15	10.5	0.240	6/30/16	13.4 -	11.0
0.18			1.34	3.02	1.56	38.2 -	14.4							51.2 -	19.3
0.59			1.52	2.36	2.38	47.8 -	39.7	1.50	1.42	1.33	2.2	0.390Y	61/28/99	72.7 -	00.4
0.16			0.96	1.01	1.20	26.7 -	15.8	1.15	1.44	1.40	5.8	0.4GZ	7/15/16	25.6 -	15.2
-0.43			-1.17	-1.12		3424.00		0.66	0.28		2.8	0.220Z	7/15/16	27.3 -	20.2
0.18			0.81			39.0 -	19.6	0.25			1.1	0.13880	8/19/16	31.6 -	15.9
0.25			0.74			36.9 -	15.2	0.43			2.5	0.18750	5/20/16	27.3 -	11.3
0.05			0.36	0.74	0.12	72.7 -	55.0	1.20	1.20	0.30	5.2	0.30Y	61/28/99	26.2 -	19.8
			-0.07	-0.07					1.85	1.85		0.46250	5/24/16	19.6 -	14.7
												0.39460Z	4/15/16	57.0 -	0.0
0.34			2.84	3.16	2.85	18.5 -	10.9	0.83	0.79	0.68	1.9	0.220Y	61/28/99	52.6 -	31.0
0.26			1.30	0.61	0.73	25.9 -	17.4	0.25	0.23	0.21	0.9	0.070Y	5/24/16	33.7 -	22.7
	0.09		1.20	0.97	0.66	15.3 -	10.8	0.48	0.48	0.48	3.1	0.120Y	61/28/99	18.3 -	12.9
0.55			2.19	2.22	1.94	19.7 -	15.6	1.22	1.16	1.10	3.2	0.310Y	61/28/99	43.1 -	34.2
0.10			1.37	0.82	1.51	38.5 -	8.7					0.25G7	61/28/99	52.7 -	12.0
0.02			-0.31					0.52			2.8	0.380	6/3/16	19.9 -	15.9
				4.51	3.75				0.92	0.92				27.3 -	8.0
			0.78	1.32	2.81	10.1 -	4.6	0.27	0.63	1.74	5.1			7.8 -	3.6
		0.82		2.49	2.47				3.01	1.18				4.6 -	1.0
					3.74					1.98				11.5 -	4.3
					0.35					1.04				3.8 -	0.7
		65.02	326.95	287.52	370.81	0.1 -	0.1	198.49	242.47	327.26	908.3			25.2 -	18.8
		0.26	-1.25	-0.30	-0.40				0.03	0.30		0.02250	4/21/97	11.2 -	3.4
-0.31			2.61	5.38	1.05	6.6 -	5.4	1.44	1.44	1.44	9.0	0.360	4/28/16	17.2 -	14.0
1.46			4.69	6.44	3.88	18.8 -	14.2	2.64	2.40	2.18	3.4	0.6950Y	61/28/99	88.1 -	66.6
		0.30	-0.05	4.47	6.18			0.92	0.80	0.80	2.6	0.140Y	61/28/99	50.6 -	27.1
-1.14			22.71	-1.24	0.85				0.50	0.38		0.1250	12/15/14	4 0 -	0.6
		0.46	-0.60	0.70	1.85			1.00	1.00	0.99	2.4	0.250Y	61/28/99	46.4 -	37.4
-7.95			0.54	4.88	2.39	232.7 -	134.3							125.7 -	72.5
		0.20	-0.58	0.92	0.64			6.35	9.79		123.2			8.0 -	3.6
0.42			1.20			16.9 -	6.5	0.88			7.0	0.2450	5/13/16	20.2 -	7 8
1.18			-3.58	5.51	7.38			2.94	2.04	2.70	6.1	0.250Y	61/28/99	64.1 -	31.9
-0.43			-1.64	0.70	2.87			0.14	0.25	0.38	1.1	0.010Y	61/28/99	28.4 -	5.0
1.05			4.05	3.71	3.61	19.0 -	14.1	2.60	2.52	2 46	3.9	0.670Y	61/28/99	77.0 -	57.2
		1.33	4.17	9.83	2.04	39.2 -	27.7					0.360	61/28/99	163.5 -	115.5
		0.43	-5.27	0.48	0.99										
								4.50	4.50	4.50	6.5	1.1250Y	7/1/16	105.0 -	0.0
		-0.04	0.47	-2.87	-30.78	39.8 -	8.4							18.7 -	3.9
0.30			0.39	0.37	0.07	61.4 -	35.7							24.0 -	13.9
-0.54			-0.96	2.64	2.06									47.6 -	16.0
			2.44	0.60	0.31	8.8 -	4.8							21.5 -	11.7
0.43			1.61	1.13	0.56	17.5 -	13.1	0.31	0.27	0.24	1.2	0.090Y	61/28/99	28.2 -	21.2
	1.52		4.14	5.51	5.96	44.6 -	29.2	0.06	0.06	0.06	0.0	0.030Y	61/28/99	184.8 -	121.0
1.05			3.69	3.42	1.73	11 6 -	8.4	0.42	0.42	0.42	1.1	0.1050Y	6/30/16	42.8 -	30.9
1.64			6.08	2.39	2.24	14.1 -	9.0							86.0 -	55.0
		2.84	-5.13	8.15	9.63			3.36	3.84	1.46	5.6	0.510	6/15/16	88.7 -	40.4
0.35			2.68	5.77	5.28			2.20	2.00	1.28		0.550	5/24/16		
0.31			1.41	0.79	1.11	29.9 -	22.8							42.2 -	32.2
0.20			0.79	1.05	0.95	43.7 -	14.6	2 75	2.57	1.88	12.1	0.750	5/31/16	34.5 -	11.5
0.37			1.03	0.66	0.49	75.8 -	43.7	1.79	1.47	1.16	3.1	0.45310Z	7/15/16	78.1 -	45.0
-0.36			1.00	1.73	1.34	21.2 -	16.0	0.48	0.40	0.39	2.6	0.1350Y	61/28/99	21.2 -	16.0
0.03			1.74	0.25	0.83	15.6 -	11.5	1.10	1.10	1.10	4.7	0.46090Z	61/28/99	27.1 -	20.0
0.39			1.88	1.66	2.70	18.9 -	13.1	2.16	2.04	8.60	7.1	0.540Z	61/28/99	35.5 -	24.6
	1.26		1.68	0.58	0.33			0.35	0.70	0.72		0.09090	6/2/16		
			1.68	1.38	1.36			1.15	1.11	1.08		0.54690	4/15/16		
0.10			0.18	-0.40		101.4 -	95.1							18.3 -	17.1
-0.03			-0.03	0.10	0.18			0.24	0.23	0.23	1.8	0.060	6/15/16	19.2 -	0.0
		-0.08	0.64	-0.26	0.42	51.1 -	34.0	0.20	0.20	0.15	0.7	0.250	61/28/99	32.7 -	21.8
0.11			0.58	0.22	0.76	18.8 -	13.8	0.32	0.30	0.18	3.3	0.082Z	5/27/16	10.9 -	8.0
-0.29			0.51	-0.01	-0.05	44.3 -	24.7	1.00	0.86	0.66	5.8	0.250Y	61/28/99	22.6 -	12.6
			0.83	0.92	0.90	14.9 -	7.9		1.88	1.68				12.4 -	6.6
0.93			3.89	3.23	3.73	15.8 -	11.1	1.32	1.26	1.16	2.5	0 330Y	61/20/99	81.6 -	43.1
0.16			-0.79	0.57	0.03			0.20	0.18	0.14	3.2	0.050Y	6/9/16	9.0 -	4.0

SYMBOL	COMPANY	NATURE OF BUSINESS	FISCAL YEAR-END	TOTAL REV. $MILL	NET INCOME $MILL	TOTAL ASSETS $MILL	NET STK EQUITY $MILL	NO OF INST	INST. HOLDINGS (SHARES)
BAP	CrediCorp Ltd	Banking	12/31/15	16022.9	3092.3	155480.2	16128.0	326	53762159
CS	Credit Suisse Group	Banking	12/31/15	23797.0	-2944.0	820805.0	44382.0	246	49219917
CPG	Crescent Point Energy Corp	Production & Extraction	12/31/15	3242.9	-870.2	17616.0	10125.0	191	191335987
CEQP	Crestwood Equity Partners LP	Equipment & Services	12/31/15	2632.8	-1666.9	5803.7	-	170	53032691
CRH	CRH Plc	Construction Materials	12/31/15	23635.0	724.0	32007.0	13015.0	156	24179430
CRT	Cross Timbers Royalty Trust	Oil Royalty Traders	12/31/15	8.9	8.1	11.5	10.5	55	662296
CAPL	CrossAmerica Partners LP	Equipment & Services	12/31/15	2214.8	11.4	853.1	0.0	65	12107145
CCI	Crown Castle International Corp (N	REITs	12/31/15	3663.9	1521.0	22036.2	7089.2	758	343534959
CCK	Crown Holdings Inc	Metal Products	12/31/15	8762.0	393.0	10020.0	144.0	506	139374452
CRY	CryoLife, Inc.	Medical Instruments & Equipment	12/31/15	145.9	4.0	181.2	155.3	157	20441317
CSRA	CSRA Inc	Computer Hardware & Equipment	4/1/16	4250.4	87.1	4846.3	64.5	360	142182000
CSS	CSS Industries, Inc.	Printing	3/31/16	317.0	17.2	309.9	271.5	115	7824777
CST	CST Brands Inc	Retail - Food & Beverage, Drug & To	12/31/15	11444.0	149.0	3840.0	910.0	353	68512156
CTS	CTS Corp	Electrical Equipment	12/31/15	382.3	7.0	484.1	281.7	155	32555292
CUBE	CubeSmart	REITs	12/31/15	444.5	77.7	3114.8	1643.3	316	223414819
CUB	Cubic Corp	Electronic Instruments & Related Pro	9/30/15	1431.0	22.9	1300.3	756.3	217	27179107
CFR	Cullen/Frost Bankers, Inc.	Banking	12/31/15	1078.2	279.3	28567.1	2890.3	424	63942279
CFI	Culp Inc.	Textiles	5/3/15	310.2	15.1	171.4	119.4	125	10664450
CMI	Cummins, Inc.	Auto Parts	12/31/15	19110.0	1399.0	15134.0	7406.0	1100	169972301
CW	Curtiss-Wright Corp.	Industrial Machinery & Equipment	12/31/15	2205.7	145.5	3029.4	1255.4	284	41948568
SRF	Cushing Energy Income Fund	Holding and other Investment Office	11/30/14	1.3	-0.2	209.2	150.7	22	153007
SRV	Cushing MLP Total Return Fund	Holding and other Investment Office	11/30/14	6.7	-7.7	326.0	199.8	41	1716057
SZC	Cushing Renaissance Fund	Holding and other Investment Office	11/30/15	6.2	3.5	126.2	118.6	36	1415673
CUBI	Customers Bancorp Inc	Banking	12/31/15	277.6	58.6	8401.3	553.9	166	21919463
CSI	Cutwater Select Income Fund	Holding and other Investment Office	3/31/15	12.2	10.5	232.7	230.5	50	2496951
CVT	Cvent, Inc	IT Services	12/31/15	187.7	-18.8	301.6	174.3	154	29824674
CVI	CVR Energy Inc	Refining & Marketing	12/31/15	5432.5	169.6	3305.8	984.1	220	91105691
UAN	CVR Partners LP	Agricultural Crop Production	12/31/15	289.2	62.0	536.5	-	90	4376642
CVRR	CVR Refining LP	Refining & Marketing	12/31/15	5161.9	291.2	2195.2	-	123	18299033
CVS	CVS Health Corporation	Retail - Food & Beverage, Drug & To	12/31/15	153290.0	5237.0	93657.0	37196.0	2075	1042203034
CELP	Cypress Energy Partners LP	Equipment & Services	12/31/15	371.2	4.1	192.7	-	21	515758
CYS	CYS Investments, Inc.	REITs	12/31/15	331.2	-4.8	14330.7	1694.6	227	101644214
DAN	Dana Holding Corp	Auto Parts	12/31/15	6060.0	159.0	4326.0	728.0	340	162804256
DHR	Danaher Corp	Industrial Machinery & Equipment	12/31/15	20563.1	3357.4	48222.2	23690.3	1415	581837208
DAC	Danaos Corp	Shipping	12/31/15	567.9	117.0	3697.1	841.9	46	5082256
DQ	DAQO New Energy Corp	Semiconductors	12/31/15	182.0	13.0	660.9	240.4	37	3192204
DRI	Darden Restaurants, Inc.	Hotels, Restaurants & Travel	5/31/15	6764.0	709.5	5994.7	2333.5	797	136720137
DAR	Darling Ingredients Inc	Food	1/2/16	3397.4	78.5	4789.6	1870.7	367	177911469
DVA	DaVita HealthCare Partners Inc	Diagnostic & Health Related Service	12/31/15	13781.8	269.7	18514.9	4870.8	678	186439636
DPM	DCP Midstream Partners LP	Equipment & Services	12/31/15	1898.0	228.0	5477.0	-	182	82469943
DCT	DCT Industrial Trust Inc	REITs	12/31/15	354.7	94.0	3632.4	1752.0	265	105649789
DDR	DDR Corp.	REITs	12/31/15	1028.1	-72.2	9097.1	3455.2	347	402074405
DF	Dean Foods Co.	Food	12/31/15	8121.7	-8.5	2528.0	545.5	405	132332062
DECK	Deckers Outdoor Corp.	Apparel, Footwear & Accessories	3/31/16	1875.2	122.3	1278.1	967.5	386	36767231
DE	Deere & Co.	Industrial Machinery & Equipment	10/31/15	28862.8	1940.0	57947.6	6743.4	1301	262691397
DEX	Delaware Enhanced Global Dividen	Holding and other Investment Office	11/30/14	13.4	9.3	313.3	209.3	56	5033900
DDF	Delaware Investments Dividend & I	Holding and other Investment Office	11/30/15	5.4	3.8	126.2	86.9	44	1526241
DKL	Delek Logistics Partners LP	Equipment & Services	12/31/15	589.6	66.8	375.3	-	57	8078248
DK	Delek US Holdings Inc	Refining & Marketing	12/31/15	5762.0	19.4	3324.9	1153.3	244	53658384
DEG	Delhaize Group SA	Retail - Food & Beverage, Drug & To	12/31/15	24395.0	366.0	13032.0	6168.0	124	10220276
DLPH	Delphi Automotive Plc	Auto Parts	12/31/15	15165.0	1450.0	11973.0	2250.0	605	265205152
DAL	Delta Air Lines, Inc. (DE)	Airlines/Air Freight	12/31/15	40704.0	4526.0	53134.0	10850.0	1088	755213168
DEL	Deltic Timber Corp.	Paper & Forest Products	12/31/15	193.9	2.7	539.2	254.0	146	10736860
DLX	Deluxe Corp.	Printing	12/31/15	1772.8	218.6	1844.4	745.1	432	49462210
DMD	Demand Media Inc	Internet & Software	12/31/15	126.0	-43.5	101.5	79.1	-	-
DWRE	Demandware Inc	Internet & Software	12/31/15	237.3	-36.6	377.4	287.5	169	40124960
DNR	Denbury Resources, Inc. (DE)	Production & Extraction	12/31/15	1257.6	-4385.4	5919.8	1248.9	415	352340201
DB	Deutsche Bank AG	Banking	12/31/15	43610.0	-6794.0	1629130.0	67354.0	259	315905567
LBF	Deutsche Global High Income Fund	Holding and other Investment Office	10/31/15	4.6	3.2	79.4	55.4	38	3244774
DHG	Deutsche High Income Opportunitie	Holding and other Investment Office	9/30/14	22.2	17.0	369.1	249.9	56	9123819
KHI	Deutsche High Income Trust	Holding and other Investment Office	11/30/15	12.0	9.6	193.9	137.7	44	4582523
KMM	Deutsche Multi-Market Income Trus	Holding and other Investment Office	11/30/15	15.8	12.5	309.8	202.3	54	6021853
KTF	Deutsche Municipal Income Trust	Holding and other Investment Office	11/30/15	39.7	32.1	839.0	528.2	65	4224108
KST	Deutsche Strategic Income Trust	Holding and other Investment Office	11/30/15	4.1	3.1	81.1	54.6	37	1428135
KSM	Deutsche Strategic Municipal Incom	Holding and other Investment Office	11/30/15	11.7	9.2	223.2	144.0	24	210803
DVN	Devon Energy Corp.	Production & Extraction	12/31/15	13145.0	-14454.0	29532.0	7049.0	1149	452284740
DV	DeVry Education Group Inc	Educational Services	6/30/15	1909.9	139.9	2074.2	1584.8	283	70144052
DHX	DHI Group Inc	Internet & Software	12/31/15	259.8	-11.0	370.5	138.6	203	49903207
DHT	DHT Holdings, Inc.	Equipment & Services	12/31/15	365.1	105.3	1423.8	737.9	215	71159819
DEO	Diageo Plc	Beverages	6/30/15	10813.0	2381.0	25804.0	7771.0	836	94154693
DO	Diamond Offshore Drilling, Inc.	Equipment & Services	12/31/15	2419.4	-274.3	7164.9	4112.8	478	147045198
DRII	Diamond Resorts International Inc	Hotels, Restaurants & Travel	12/31/15	954.0	149.5	1993.0	271.0	210	63976584
DRH	DiamondRock Hospitality Co.	REITs	12/31/15	931.0	85.6	3320.5	1824.6	302	272780131
DSX	Diana Shipping Inc	Shipping	12/31/15	157.7	-64.7	1837.0	1218.4	119	43218158
DKS	Dick's Sporting Goods, Inc	Retail - Specialty	1/30/16	7271.0	330.4	3559.3	1789.2	569	91356904
DBD	Diebold, Inc.	Computer Hardware & Equipment	12/31/15	2419.3	73.7	2249.3	412.4	354	81104120
DLR	Digital Realty Trust, Inc.	REITs	12/31/15	1763.3	296.7	11451.3	4500.1	621	171989134
DGI	DigitalGlobe Inc	Services	12/31/15	702.4	23.3	2925.1	1248.1	217	66609132
DDS	Dillard's Inc.	Retail - General Merchandise/Depart	1/30/16	6754.5	269.4	3865.6	1795.3	320	38068462
DIN	DineEquity Inc	Retail - Food & Beverage, Drug & To	12/31/15	681.1	104.9	2331.8	267.2	239	20567805

T18

EARNINGS PER SHARE QUARTERLY			ANNUAL			P/E RATIO		DIVIDENDS PER SHARE			AV. YLD	DIV. DECLARED		PRICE RANGE 2015	
1st	2nd	3rd	2015	2014	2013			2015	2014	2013	%	AMOUNT	PAYABLE		
-	-	-	38.84	29.27	7.12	3.8 -	2.2	6.83	5.30	2.60	5.7	2.3160	5/13/16	146.9 -	87.1
-	-	0.26	-1.73	1.07	1.22			1.17	0.70	0.10	5.5	-	-	29.7 -	12.7
-	-	-0.40	-1.82	1.21	0.37			2.11	2.76	2.76	13.0	0.030	7/15/16	28.4 -	0.0
-1.47	-	-	-54.00	3.00	0.60							0.60	5/13/16	51.3 -	8.1
-	-	-	0.89	0.79	-0.41	34.8 -	26.7	0.63	0.62	0.63	2.2	-		30.9 -	23.7
0.36	-	-	1.35	2.66	2.31	14.0 -	8.9	1.35	2.66	2.31	8.8	0.06090	7/15/16	18.9 -	12.0
0.03	-	-	0.35	-0.32	1.18	97.9 -	53.7	2.23	2.08	1.73	9.1	0.59750	5/31/16	34.3 -	18.8
0.11	-	-	4.42	1.04	0.26	20.7 -	17.3	3.35	0.82		4.0	0.8850Y	61/28/99	91.3 -	76.6
0.57	-	-	2.82	2.79	2.30	20.0 -	15.7							56.5 -	44.2
0.08	-	-	0.14	0.25	0.57	91.2 -	64.1	0.12	0.12	0.11	1.1	0.030Y	12/18/15	12.8 -	9.0
-	-	0.29										0.10Y	7/11/16	33.0 -	22.3
-	-	1.06	1.80	1.99	1.59	17.3 -	13.6	0.63	0.60	0.60	2.3	0.20Y	6/15/16	31.1 -	24.5
0.24	-	-	1.95	2.63	1.84	21.2 -	16.4	0.25	0.25	0.13	0.7	0.06250Y	61/28/99	41.3 -	32.0
0.24	-	-	0.21	0.78	-0.12	96.0 -	63.0	0.16	0.16	0.14	0.9	0.040Y	7/29/16	20.2 -	13.2
0.08	-	-	0.42	0.14	0.26	79.3 -	54.1	0.69	0.55	0.46	2.4	0.48440Z	7/15/16	33.3 -	22.7
-	0.38	-	0.85	2.59	0.74	58.7 -	30.2	0.27	0.24	0.24	0.6	0.1350Y	3/21/16	49.9 -	30.8
1.07	-	-	4.28	4.29	3.80	18.7 -	9.9	2.10	2.03	1.98	3.3	0.33590Y	61/28/99	80.1 -	42.5
-	-	0.39	1.21	1.41	1.47	28.0 -	19.1	0.62	0.18	0.62	2.2	0.217	7/15/16	33.9 -	23.1
1.87	-	-	7.84	9.02	7.91	17.6 -	10.7	3.51	2.81	2.25	3.2	0.9750Y	61/28/99	137.8 -	83.5
0.73	-	-	3.05	2.31	2.88	27.5 -	20.3	0.52	0.52	0.39	0.7	0.130Y	01/28/99	83.8 -	62.0
-	-	-	-0.25	0.00								0.0570	6/30/16	25.5 -	5.8
-	-	-	-5.60	-4.80								0.090	6/30/16	20.2 -	7.5
-	-	-	0.58	0.53	0.72	36.5 -	19.4	1.64	1.64	1.48	10.5	0.410	6/17/16	21.2 -	11.2
0.57	-	-	1.96	1.55	1.30	15.8 -	11.1					0.2105GHY	6/15/16	31.0 -	21.8
-	-	-	0.98	1.05	1.06	19.8 -	18.4	1.06	1.06	1.08	5.6	0.2250	8/23/16	19.4 -	18.0
-0.03	-	-	-0.45	0.04	-0.13									36.9 -	19.0
-0.19	-	-	1.95	2.00	4.27	24.5 -	10.0	2.00	5.00	14.25	5.7	0.50Y	5/16/16	47.8 -	19.5
0.25	-	-	0.85	1.04	1.62	16.7 -	5.7	1.25	1.41	1.75	13.6	0.270	5/16/16	14.2 -	4.9
-0.46	-	-	1.97	2.43	3.47	11.4 -	5.1	3.12	2.93	3.23	18.4	1.010	11/16/15	22.5 -	10.1
1.04	-	-	4.63	3.96	3.74	24.5 -	19.4	1.40	1.10	0.90	1.4	0.4250Y	61/28/99	113.5 -	89.7
0.00	-	-	0.35	-1.72		49.5 -	16.6	1.63	1.10		15.3	0.40640	5/13/16	17.3 -	5.8
0.37	-	-	-0.17	2.50	-2.90			1.10	1.24	1.32	14.2	0.46880Z	7/15/16	8.9 -	6.3
0.30	-	-	0.99	1.84	-0.09	22.4 -	11.1	0.23	0.20	0.20	1.5	0.060Y	61/28/99	22.1 -	11.0
1.09	-	-	4.74	3.63	3.80	21.1 -	17.4	0.54	0.40	0.10	0.6	0.160Y	61/28/99	100.0 -	82.4
-	-	0.08	1.07	-0.04	0.34							0.4650	11/19/08		
-	-	-	0.05	0.08	-0.41	539.0 -	231.6					-		26.9 -	11.6
-	-	0.82	5.47	2.15	3.13	12.4 -	9.9	2.20	2.20	2.00	3.5	0.50Y	61/28/99	67.8 -	53.9
0.01	-	-	0.48	0.39	0.91	33.3 -	16.5					-		16.0 -	7.9
0.47	-	-	1.25	3.33	2.95	67.2 -	49.8					-		84.0 -	62.2
0.36	-	-	0.91	2.84	1.34	41.8 -	17.1	3.12	3.00	2.02	11.5	0.780	5/13/16	38.0 -	15.6
0.41	-	-	1.05	0.58	0.20	41.1 -	29.8	1.13	0.28	1.12	3.1	0.290Z	7/13/16	43.1 -	31.3
0.11	-	-	-0.27	0.25	-0.14			0.69	0.62	0.54	4.2	0.190Z	61/28/99	18.4 -	14.8
0.43	-	-	-0.09	-0.22	8.58			0.28	0.28		1.6	0.090Y	61/28/99	21.0 -	15.8
-	-	4.78	4.66	-0.08	4.18	16.3 -	9.1					-		76.1 -	42.3
-	1.56	-	5.77	8.63	9.09	16.9 -	12.4	2.40	2.22	1.99	2.9	0.60Y	61/28/99	97.3 -	71.8
-	-	-	0.59	0.58					0.90	0.90		0.0750	6/24/16	11.5 -	8.0
-	-	-	0.44	0.44	0.44	23.7 -	17.3	0.63	0.63	0.63	7.0	0.05250	6/24/16	10.4 -	7.6
0.54	-	-	2.52	2.85	1.93	18.9 -	9.0	2.16	1.00	1.41	6.4	0.610	5/13/16	47.6 -	22.7
-0.47	-	-	0.32	3.35	1.96	125.0 -	40.2	0.70	1.00	0.95	2.8	0.150Y	6/14/16	40.0 -	12.9
-	-	-0.85	3.54	0.87	1.76	7.5 -	5.6	0.29	0.28	0.26	1.2	-		26.7 -	19.8
1.53	-	-	5.06	4.48	3.89			1.00	1.00	0.60		0.290	61/28/99		
1.21	-	-	5.63	0.78	12.29	9.3 -	7.1	0.45	0.30	0.12	1.0	0.1350Y	61/28/99	52.3 -	40.0
0.03	-	-	0.21	1.55	2.05	330.8 -	244.5	0.40	0.40	0.40	0.6	0.10Y	9/15/16	69.5 -	51.4
1.18	-	-	4.36	3.96	3.65	15.0 -	11.7	1.20	1.15	1.00	2.0	0.30Y	61/28/99	65.4 -	51.0
-0.59	-	-	-2.18	-14.26	-1.15							-		6.7 -	4.1
-0.32	-	-	-1.02	-0.78	-0.68							-		75.6 -	28.1
-0.53	-	-	-12.57	1.81	1.11			0.19	0.25		5.6	0.06250	61/28/99	7.3 -	1.0
1.03	-	-	-5.06	1.31	0.65			0.75	0.75	0.75		-			
-	-	-	0.50	0.54	0.55	16.7 -	14.0	0.55	0.54	0.55	7.0	0.0480	6/30/16	8.4 -	7.0
-	-	-		1.08	1.14				1.05	1.19		0.06250	6/30/16	14.8 -	12.1
-	-	-	0.62	0.67	0.69	14.2 -	12.0	0.66	0.72	0.75	8.0	0.0460	6/30/16	8.8 -	7.4
-	-	-	0.54	0.64	0.70	15.7 -	13.3	0.60	0.68	0.88	7.8	0.04250	6/30/16	8.5 -	7.2
-	-	-	0.82	0.83	0.85	17.4 -	15.3	0.86	0.85	0.85	6.4	0.07M	6/30/16	14.3 -	12.6
-	-	-	0.69	0.83		16.9 -	14.5	0.95	0.96	1.10	8.8	0.0550	6/30/16	11.7 -	10.0
-	-	-	0.83	0.87	0.87	17.0 -	14.9	0.91	0.93	0.92	6.9	0.0650	6/30/16	14.1 -	12.4
-6.44	-	-	-35.55	3.91	-0.06			0.96	0.94	0.86	2.5	0.060Y	61/28/99	64.8 -	18.6
-	-	0.81	2.14	2.07	1.65	15.9 -	7.5	0.36	0.34	0.34	1.5	0.180Y	61/28/99	34.0 -	16.0
0.02	-	-	-0.21	0.51	0.27							-		10.0 -	6.1
-	-	-0.26	1.04	0.18	-0.24			0.53	0.08	0.08		0.250	5/25/16		
-	-	-	0.95	0.89	0.99	128.4 -	106.9	2.09	2.00	1.81	1.9	-		122.0 -	101.5
0.64	-	-	-2.00	2.81	3.95			0.50	3.50	3.50	2.3	0.1250Y	61/28/99	31.4 -	15.6
0.48	-	-	1.98	0.77	-0.04	17.5 -	8.5					-		34.6 -	16.8
0.08	-	-	0.43	0.83	0.25	32.1 -	18.1	0.50	0.41	0.34	4.6	0.1250Z	7/12/16	13.8 -	7.8
-	-	-0.04	-0.89	-0.19	-0.26							0.55470	7/15/16		
0.50	-	-	2.84	2.69	2.31	19.1 -	12.1	0.50	0.50	2.50	1.1	0.15130Y	61/28/99	54.2 -	34.2
2.56	-	-	1.12	1.76	-2.85	33.8 -	20.5	1.15	1.15	1.15	3.8	0.28750Y	61/28/99	37.8 -	23.0
0.27	-	-	1.56	0.99	2.12	62.4 -	39.4	3.40	3.32	3.12	4.5	0.39690Z	61/28/99	97.3 -	61.5
0.11	-	-	0.26	0.18	-1.00	116.7 -	48.1					-		30.0 -	12.5
2.17	-	-	7.79	7.10	6.87	15.0 -	7.1	0.24	0.22	5.20	0.3	0.070Y	61/28/99	117.2 -	55.5
1.37	-	-	5.52	1.00	0.70	19.0 -	14.4	3.54	3.13	3.00	3.0	0.920Y	7/8/16	104.9 -	79.5

SYMBOL	COMPANY	NATURE OF BUSINESS	FISCAL YEAR-END	TOTAL REV. $MILL	NET INCOME $MILL	TOTAL ASSETS $MILL	NET STK EQUITY $MILL	NO OF INST	INST. HOLDINGS (SHARES)
DPLO	Diplomat Pharmacy Inc	Diagnostic & Health Related Service	12/31/15	3366.6	25.8	1005.9	512.0	189	48796892
DFS	Discover Financial Services	Credit & Lending	12/31/15	10002.0	2297.0	86936.0	11275.0	969	397841333
DIS	Disney (Walt) Co (The)	Entertainment	10/3/15	52465.0	8382.0	88182.0	44525.0	2344	1191815739
DRA	Diversified Real Asset Income Fund	Holding and other Investment Office	5/31/15	31.3	26.5	588.8	409.6	74	6955378
DNI	Dividend & Income Fund	Holding and other Investment Office	12/31/15	5.1	2.8	146.8	138.4	44	2854893
DNP	DNP Select Income Fund Inc	Holding and other Investment Office	10/31/15	123.2	80.2	3458.0	2440.2	204	14430656
DLB	Dolby Laboratories Inc	Manufacturing	9/25/15	970.6	181.4	2133.3	1807.1	317	54355248
DG	Dollar General Corp	Retail - General Merchandise/Depart	1/29/16	20368.6	1165.1	11257.9	5377.9	773	272303710
DDC	Dominion Diamond Corp	Precious Metals	1/31/16	720.6	-34.0	2164.8	1280.5	163	37254453
DM	Dominion Midstream Partners LP	Gas Utilities	12/31/15	369.6	196.5	4125.2	-	89	18676542
D	Dominion Resources Inc	Electric Utilities	12/31/15	11683.0	1899.0	58797.0	12664.0	1303	436348452
DPZ	Dominos Pizza Inc.	Hotels, Restaurants & Travel	1/3/16	2216.5	192.8	799.8	-1800.3	399	52495626
UFS	Domtar Corp	Paper & Forest Products	12/31/15	5264.0	142.0	5663.0	2652.0	-	
DCI	Donaldson Co. Inc.	Industrial Machinery & Equipment	7/31/15	2371.2	208.1	1809.5	774.8	417	128120030
LPG	Dorian LPG Ltd.	Shipping	3/31/15	289.2	129.7	1865.9	985.6	97	28547939
DSL	DoubleLine Income Solutions Fund	Holding and other Investment Office	9/30/14	230.7	180.1	3430.6	2348.6	135	44398354
DBL	Doubleline Opportunistic Credit Fun	Holding and other Investment Office	9/30/14	32.8	27.1	437.4	345.7	76	3903406
PLOW	Douglas Dynamics, Inc.	Industrial Machinery & Equipment	12/31/15	400.4	44.2	505.5	200.5	173	19339040
DEI	Douglas Emmett Inc	REITs	12/31/15	635.8	58.4	6066.2	1926.2	317	170668533
DOV	Dover Corp	Industrial Machinery & Equipment	12/31/15	6956.3	869.8	8619.8	3644.6	819	161049012
DDE	Dover Downs Gaming & Entertainm	Hotels, Restaurants & Travel	12/31/15	182.9	1.9	174.0	115.0	52	5904234
DVD	Dover Motorsports, Inc.	Sporting & Recreational	12/31/15	46.5	5.3	82.4	52.0	50	11227618
DOW	Dow Chemical Co.	Plastics	12/31/15	48778.0	7685.0	68026.0	25374.0	1543	855534858
DOW	Dow Chemical Co.	Plastics	12/31/15	48778.0	7685.0	68026.0	25374.0	1543	855534858
DPS	Dr Pepper Snapple Group Inc	Beverages	12/31/15	6282.0	764.0	8869.0	2183.0	789	192417818
RDY	Dr. Reddy's Laboratories Ltd.	Pharmaceuticals	3/31/15	2901721.0	442731.0	3542366.0	111302.0	227	30150418
DRD	DRDGold Ltd	Precious Metals	6/30/15	2105.3	67.8	2503.0	1529.9	48	3966878
DW	Drew Industries, Inc.	Auto Parts	12/31/15	1403.1	74.3	622.9	438.6	218	24949540
DHF	Dreyfus High Yield Strategies Fund	Holding and other Investment Office	3/31/15	28.1	23.1	407.9	279.3	72	8571778
DMB	Dreyfus Municipal Bond Infrastructu	Holding and other Investment Office	2/28/15	17.5	13.4	369.5	329.6	33	3143771
DSM	Dreyfus Strategic Municipal Bond F	Holding and other Investment Office	11/30/15	30.1	25.6	614.5	514.4	76	4905213
LEO	Dreyfus Strategic Municipals, Inc.	Holding and other Investment Office	9/30/15	40.1	33.9	830.6	683.6	79	4325652
DRQ	Dril-Quip Inc	Equipment & Services	12/31/15	844.3	192.0	1428.3	1324.5	362	45127188
DST	DST Systems Inc. (DE)	IT Services	12/31/15	2825.1	358.2	2813.2	1046.0	450	33352517
DSW	DSW Inc	Retail - Apparel and Accessories	1/30/16	2620.2	136.0	1369.1	904.9	322	76830708
DTE	DTE Energy Co	Electric Utilities	12/31/15	10337.0	727.0	28737.0	8772.0	687	134036150
DTF	DTF Tax-Free Income, Inc.	Holding and other Investment Office	10/31/15	8.5	5.9	204.0	139.0	38	1005614
DD	Du Pont (E.I.) de Nemours & Co	Diversified Chemicals	12/31/15	25130.0	1953.0	41166.0	9993.0	1675	721502081
DCO	Ducommun Inc.	Aerospace	12/31/15	666.0	-73.3	561.4	187.3	123	9635043
DPG	Duff & Phelps Global Utility Income	Holding and other Investment Office	10/31/14	48.5	35.0	1185.2	924.1	70	7764321
DSE	Duff & Phelps Select Energy MLP F	Holding and other Investment Office	11/30/14	1.7	-2.3	651.0	448.6	-	
DUC	Duff & Phelps Utility & Corporate Bo	Holding and other Investment Office	10/31/14	15.7	11.3	408.2	282.9	56	9471083
DUK	Duke Energy Corp	Electric Utilities	12/31/15	23459.0	2816.0	121156.0	39727.0	1504	489475985
DRE	Duke Realty Corp	REITs	12/31/15	949.4	621.9	6917.1	3181.9	478	345162568
DNB	Dun & Bradstreet Corp (DE)	Business Services	12/31/15	1637.1	168.8	2273.6	-1116.8	498	40868301
DFT	DuPont Fabros Technology Inc	REITs	12/31/15	452.4	1.9	2815.5	1435.6	300	78762762
DY	Dycom Industries, Inc.	Construction Services	7/25/15	2022.3	84.3	1358.9	507.2	375	40233182
DLNG	Dynagas LNG Partners LP	Equipment & Services	12/31/15	145.2	60.0	1108.1	-	49	11171254
DYN	Dynegy Inc (New) (DE)	Electric Utilities	12/31/15	3870.0	50.0	11539.0	2921.0	263	130576768
DX	Dynex Capital, Inc.	REITs	12/31/15	100.2	16.5	3670.0	492.0	142	25214986
DANG	E-Commerce China Dangdang Inc	Internet & Software	12/31/15	9312.0	91.5	4621.0	866.2	-	
EJ	E-House (China) Holdings, Ltd	Property, Real Estate & Developmen	12/31/15	1023.7	-39.9	1784.5	907.7	111	43610977
EGIF	Eagle Growth & Income Opportuniti	Holding and other Investment Office	5/19/15			0.4		14	1880200
EXP	Eagle Materials Inc	Construction Materials	3/31/16	1143.5	152.6	1883.6	1040.5	360	50770615
ECC	Eagle Point Credit Company Inc	Holding and other Investment Office	12/31/14	5.7	4.3	-		15	10666559
DEA	Easterly Government Properties Inc	REITs	12/31/15	71.4	-1.7	912.0	377.3	95	12175563
EGP	EastGroup Properties, Inc.	REITs	12/31/15	235.0	48.4	1666.2	554.9	289	34047924
EMN	Eastman Chemical Co.	Plastics	12/31/15	9648.0	848.0	15611.0	3941.0	778	140253606
KODK	Eastman Kodak Co.	Leisure Equipment	12/31/15	1798.0	-80.0	2138.0	78.0	189	52615968
ETN	Eaton Corp plc	Electrical Equipment	12/31/15	20855.0	1979.0	31031.0	15186.0	954	338290450
EV	Eaton Vance Corp	Wealth Management	10/31/15	1403.6	230.3	2116.5	620.2	444	96012128
EOI	Eaton Vance Enhanced Equity Inco	Holding and other Investment Office	9/30/15	15.5	9.1	526.9	525.0	76	7008626
EOS	Eaton Vance Enhanced Equity Inco	Holding and other Investment Office	12/31/15	13.9	6.2	689.9	686.6	90	8468521
EFF	Eaton Vance Floating Rate Income	Finance Intermediaries & Services	5/31/15	11.9	8.5	236.9	139.9	35	2088316
EFT	Eaton Vance Floating Rate Income	Holding and other Investment Office	5/31/15	48.8	35.2	1017.4	623.4	116	15233761
ETX	Eaton Vance Municipal Income 202	Holding and other Investment Office	1/31/15	13.1	10.0	361.8	223.7	39	3245643
EVN	Eaton Vance Municipal Income Trus	Holding and other Investment Office	11/30/15	26.5	21.0	586.7	429.5	42	1825590
EOT	Eaton Vance National Municipal Op	Holding and other Investment Office	3/31/15	19.5	16.6	399.8	350.6	49	2633775
ETJ	Eaton Vance Risk-Managed Diversif	Holding and other Investment Office	12/31/14	13.1	4.2	774.0	769.2	104	22951913
EFR	Eaton Vance Senior Floating Rate T	Holding and other Investment Office	12/31/15	44.7	34.7	881.6	659.9	105	9122550
EVF	Eaton Vance Senior Income Trust	Holding and other Investment Office	6/30/15	21.3	15.2	448.1	376.0	78	16990063
EVG	Eaton Vance Short Duration Diversif	Holding and other Investment Office	10/31/14	20.0	14.2	407.5	275.7	71	12108619
EVT	Eaton Vance Tax Advantaged Divid	Holding and other Investment Office	8/31/15	81.2	58.8	2034.0	1545.3	120	16370945
ETW	Eaton Vance Tax Managed Global	Holding and other Investment Office	10/31/14	33.7	19.5	1242.9	1230.4	139	23078584
ETG	Eaton Vance Tax-Advantage Global	Holding and other Investment Office	10/31/15	108.4	88.7	1788.4	1338.5	98	13488167
EXD	Eaton Vance Tax-Advantaged Bond	Holding and other Investment Office	12/31/14	3.2	0.9	156.4	147.6	35	2842989
ETO	Eaton Vance Tax-Advantaged Glob	Holding and other Investment Office	12/31/15	20.0	14.5	473.9	349.3	45	2007304
ETB	Eaton Vance Tax-Managed Buy-Wri	Holding and other Investment Office	12/31/15	9.3	4.9	387.0	382.9	65	3761630
ETV	Eaton Vance Tax-Managed Buy-Wri	Holding and other Investment Office	12/31/15	17.2	6.9	938.9	929.4	120	12932557
ETY	Eaton Vance Tax-Managed Diversifi	Holding and other Investment Office	10/31/14	68.1	48.4	1870.9	1844.4	132	37564725

1st	2nd	3rd	2015	2014	2013	P/E hi	P/E lo	2015	2014	2013	AV. YLD %	AMOUNT	PAYABLE	hi	lo
0.23	-	-	0.41	0.11	-0.79	125.1	59.5	-	-	-	-	-	-	51.3	24.4
1.35	-	-	5.13	4.90	4.96	11.6	8.4	1.08	0.92	0.60	2.0	0.40630Y	61/28/99	59.7	43.3
-	1.30	-	4.90	4.26	3.38	24.8	18.1	1.81	0.86	0.75	1.7	0.710Y	61/28/99	121.7	88.8
-	-	-	1.14	-	-	15.8	11.8	1.04	-	-	6.4	0.110	7/1/16	18.0	13.5
-	-	-	0.31	0.34	0.40	48.8	30.6	1.63	1.63	1.63	13.8	0.250	6/30/16	15.1	9.5
-	-	-	0.29	0.35	0.27	37.1	30.0	0.78	0.78	0.78	8.0	0.0650	10/11/16	10.8	8.7
-	0.66	-	1.75	1.99	1.84	27.4	17.4	0.40	-	4.00	1.1	0.120Y	61/28/99	47.9	30.5
1.03	-	-	3.49	3.17	2.85	25.8	17.2	-	-	-	-	0.250Y	61/28/99	89.9	60.0
-	-	0.05	0.77	5.59	0.41	31.2	0.0	-	-	-	-	0.20	6/2/16	24.1	0.0
0.58	-	-	2.08	0.15	-	20.2	12.0	0.70	-	-	2.2	0.22450	5/13/16	42.0	25.1
0.88	-	-	3.20	2.24	2.93	23.8	20.3	2.59	2.40	2.25	3.7	0.70Y	61/28/99	76.2	64.9
0.89	-	-	3.47	2.86	2.48	40.3	29.3	1.24	1.00	0.80	1.1	0.380Y	61/28/99	140.0	101.6
0.06	-	-	2.24	6.64	1.36	24.9	0.0	1.60	1.40	1.05	3.6	0.4150	61/28/99	55.9	0.0
-	-	0.41	1.49	1.76	1.64	24.4	17.6	0.67	0.57	0.41	2.2	0.1750Y	61/28/99	36.4	26.2
-	-	0.97	0.45	0.09	-	-	-	-	-	-	-	-	-	-	-
-	-	-	1.76	0.56	-	-	-	-	1.80	0.60	-	0.150	6/30/16	20.6	15.0
-	-	-	1.83	1.63	-	-	-	-	2.00	2.48	-	0.1670	6/30/16	26.8	22.8
0.23	-	-	1.94	1.77	0.51	12.1	9.0	0.89	0.87	0.83	4.2	0.2350Y	61/28/99	23.6	17.4
0.10	-	-	0.39	0.30	0.31	87.3	64.0	0.85	0.81	0.74	2.9	0.220Z	61/28/99	34.0	24.9
0.64	-	-	5.46	4.59	5.78	13.9	9.6	1.64	1.55	1.45	2.6	0.420Y	61/28/99	75.8	52.6
-0.01	-	-	0.06	-0.02	-	19.3	13.8	-	-	-	-	0.020Y	12/10/12	1.2	0.8
-0.06	-	-	0.14	0.09	0.05	17.7	0.0	0.05	0.05	0.05	2.3	0.050Y	12/10/15	2.5	0.0
0.15	-	-	6.15	2.87	3.68	7.9	0.0	1.72	1.53	1.28	4.3	0.460Y	61/28/99	48.5	0.0
0.15	-	-	6.15	2.87	3.68	9.3	6.4	1.72	1.53	1.28	3.5	0.460Y	61/28/99	57.0	39.4
0.96	-	-	3.97	3.56	3.05	24.1	18.3	1.92	1.64	1.52	2.2	0.530Y	61/28/99	95.6	72.8
-	-	-	-2588.37	2194.24	1709.08	0.0	0.0	16.62	13.48	13.01	31.6	-	-	67.8	41.2
-0.03	-	-	0.17	-0.12	0.16	35.0	6.5	0.16	1.13	1.78	6.5	-	-	6.0	1.1
1.45	-	-	3.02	2.56	2.11	25.6	17.4	2.00	-	2.00	3.3	0.30Y	6/17/16	77.4	52.4
-	-	-	0.32	0.36	0.38	11.3	8.5	0.36	0.40	0.44	11.4	0.02650	7/27/16	3.6	2.7
-	-	-	0.73	0.60	-	18.9	15.8	0.75	0.50	-	6.1	0.0625M	7/1/16	13.8	11.5
-	-	-	0.52	0.52	0.53	17.1	14.6	0.50	0.57	0.57	6.2	0.0415M	6/30/16	8.9	7.6
-	-	-	0.55	0.55	0.54	16.7	14.2	0.53	0.59	0.59	6.3	0.043M	6/30/16	9.2	7.8
0.97	-	-	4.98	5.19	4.16	15.9	10.0	-	-	-	-	-	-	79.1	49.9
1.70	-	-	9.83	14.66	8.00	13.6	9.7	1.20	1.20	1.20	1.1	0.330Y	61/28/99	134.2	95.6
0.36	-	-	1.69	1.65	1.62	21.2	11.4	0.75	0.38	1.44	2.8	0.20Y	61/28/99	35.8	19.2
1.37	-	-	4.05	5.10	3.76	22.6	18.2	2.84	2.69	2.59	3.5	0.770Y	61/28/99	91.3	73.8
-	-	-	0.69	0.73	0.84	24.1	20.8	0.84	0.85	0.85	5.5	0.07M	9/30/16	16.6	14.3
1.39	-	-	2.16	3.92	5.18	34.5	21.9	1.72	1.84	1.78	2.8	0.380Y	61/28/99	74.5	47.3
1.21	-	-	-6.63	1.79	0.86	-	-	-	-	-	-	0.0750Y	3/4/11	26.6	12.9
-	-	-	0.92	0.82	-	-	-	-	1.40	1.40	-	0.350	9/30/16	19.5	11.9
-	-	-	-0.09	-	-	-	-	-	0.32	-	-	0.220	5/19/16	14.0	3.3
-	-	-	0.41	0.35	0.45	23.8	22.2	0.60	0.82	0.84	6.4	0.050	9/30/16	9.0	9.1
1.01	-	-	4.05	2.66	3.76	20.0	16.3	3.24	3.15	3.09	4.4	0.8250Y	61/28/99	81.1	65.8
0.12	-	-	1.77	0.60	0.47	13.4	9.9	0.69	0.68	0.68	3.4	0.180Z	61/28/99	23.7	17.6
0.82	-	-	4.64	7.99	6.54	28.2	18.9	1.85	1.76	1.60	1.7	0.48250Y	61/28/99	130.6	87.9
0.36	-	-	-0.40	1.18	0.32	-	-	1.73	1.47	0.95	5.2	0.4095GHZ	8/15/16	43.2	25.1
-	-	1.00	2.41	1.15	1.04	36.9	20.2	-	-	-	-	0.0228G	7/15/81	88.9	48.6
-	-	-	1.60	1.58	2.95	-	-	1.69	1.29	-	-	0.56250	5/12/16	-	-
-0.13	-	-	0.22	2.65	-3.56	154.5	33.8	-	-	-	-	1.34380Y	8/1/16	34.0	7.4
-0.81	-	-	0.14	0.34	1.10	56.6	39.3	0.96	1.00	1.12	14.2	0.47660Z	7/15/16	7.9	5.5
-	-	-0.07	0.22	0.21	-0.36	52.2	24.3	-	-	-	-	-	-	11.5	5.3
-	-	0.14	-0.28	0.26	0.38	-	-	0.14	0.37	0.14	2.3	-	-	7.1	5.0
-	-	-	-	-	-	-	-	-	-	-	-	0.10	6/30/16	22.4	13.4
-	-	0.92	3.71	2.49	1.22	22.8	12.6	0.40	0.40	0.40	0.6	0.10Y	61/28/99	84.5	46.9
-	-	-	-	0.32	-	-	-	-	0.55	-	-	0.43750Y	9/30/16	20.8	0.0
0.03	-	-	-0.08	-	-	-	-	0.54	-	-	3.2	0.230Y	6/23/16	19.0	15.3
0.67	-	-	1.49	1.52	1.08	43.1	33.6	2.34	2.22	2.14	4.1	0.60Z	6/30/16	64.2	50.1
1.69	-	-	5.66	4.97	7.44	14.8	10.3	1.66	1.45	1.25	2.3	0.460Y	61/28/99	83.8	58.4
-0.43	-	-	-1.91	-2.95	-1.94	-	-	-	-	-	-	0.250Y	12/12/08	19.9	8.1
0.88	-	-	4.23	3.76	3.90	17.2	11.2	2.20	1.96	1.68	3.8	0.570	61/28/99	72.9	47.3
-	0.48	-	1.92	2.44	1.53	21.5	14.2	1.01	0.91	1.82	2.9	0.2650Y	61/28/99	41.4	27.2
-	-	-	0.23	0.08	0.12	59.6	49.1	1.04	1.04	1.04	8.2	0.08640	6/30/16	13.7	11.3
-	-	-	0.13	-	0.05	111.1	86.1	1.05	1.05	1.05	8.0	0.08750	6/30/16	14.4	11.2
-	-	-	1.11	0.99	-	15.3	11.6	1.42	0.97	-	9.6	0.0850	6/30/16	17.0	12.9
-	-	-	0.88	0.89	-	16.5	13.3	0.89	0.97	1.04	6.8	0.0750	6/30/16	14.5	11.7
-	-	-	0.92	0.72	-	22.3	18.2	0.85	0.57	-	4.6	0.0708M	6/30/16	20.5	16.7
-	-	-	0.89	0.89	0.89	16.3	13.7	0.89	0.90	0.93	6.6	0.0625M	6/20/16	14.5	12.2
-	-	-	1.09	1.10	-	20.9	18.3	1.03	1.03	1.08	4.8	0.0858M	6/30/16	22.8	20.0
-	-	-	-	0.07	0.09	-	-	-	1.12	1.12	-	0.0930	6/30/16	11.2	9.1
-	-	-	0.94	0.93	1.01	15.4	12.2	0.94	0.99	1.04	7.3	0.0780	6/30/16	14.5	11.4
-	-	-	0.40	0.41	0.47	16.3	13.0	0.40	0.44	0.48	6.8	0.0340	6/20/16	6.5	5.2
-	-	-	0.78	0.80	0.82	18.6	16.2	1.08	1.08	1.08	8.0	0.090	6/30/16	14.5	12.6
-	-	-	0.81	1.43	1.39	25.5	20.7	1.45	1.32	1.29	7.5	0.1450	6/30/16	20.6	16.8
-	-	-	0.18	0.23	0.17	67.8	51.6	1.17	1.17	1.17	10.6	0.09730	6/30/16	12.2	9.3
-	-	-	1.16	1.30	1.24	15.5	11.1	1.23	1.23	1.23	8.0	0.10250	6/30/16	18.0	12.9
-	-	-	-	0.09	0.07	-	-	-	1.40	1.70	-	0.290	6/30/16	13.0	11.8
-	-	-	1.00	1.55	1.61	24.8	18.1	3.13	2.35	1.65	14.3	0.180	6/30/16	24.8	18.1
-	-	-	0.20	0.17	0.18	84.5	69.2	1.30	1.30	1.30	8.2	0.1080	6/30/16	16.9	13.8
-	-	-	0.11	0.11	0.13	140.7	119.8	1.33	1.33	1.33	9.0	0.11080	6/30/16	15.5	13.2
-	-	-	-	0.32	0.20	-	-	-	1.01	1.10	-	0.08430	6/30/16	11.8	9.7

SYMBOL	COMPANY	NATURE OF BUSINESS	FISCAL YEAR-END	TOTAL REV. $MILL	NET INCOME $MILL	TOTAL ASSETS $MILL	NET STK EQUITY $MILL	NO OF INST	INST. HOLDINGS (SHARES)
EXG	Eaton Vance Tax-Managed Global	Holding and other Investment Office	10/31/14	164.1	129.0	3231.6	3198.3	184	54490730
ECT	ECA Marcellus Trust I	Oil Royalty Traders	12/31/15	6.2	5.0	62.7	61.5	40	981575
ECR	Eclipse Resources Corp	Production & Extraction	12/31/15	255.3	-971.4	1266.4	620.6	94	50643564
ECL	Ecolab, Inc.	Specialty Chemicals	12/31/15	13545.1	1002.1	18641.7	6909.9	1100	262049299
EC	Ecopetrol SA	Refining & Marketing	12/31/15	52347271.0	-71933859.0	23588190.0	41225908.0	164	41883659
EPC	Edgewell Personal Care Co	Household & Personal Products	9/30/15	2421.2	-275.3	4991.7	1864.1	541	58253494
EPC	Edgewell Personal Care Co	Household & Personal Products	9/30/15	2421.2	-275.3	4991.7	1864.1	541	58253494
EIX	Edison International	Electric Utilities	12/31/15	11524.0	1020.0	50310.0	11368.0	767	286858034
EDR	Education Realty Trust Inc	REITs	12/31/15	255.2	19.9	2001.8	1236.7	264	88620449
EW	Edwards Lifesciences Corp	Medical Instruments & Equipment	12/31/15	2493.7	494.9	4059.3	2503.1	820	193709553
EHIC	eHi Car Services Ltd	Miscellaneous Consumer Services	12/31/15	1450.6	696.3	7800.9	3948.1	44	29778173
EE	El Paso Electric Company	Electric Utilities	12/31/15	849.9	81.9	3233.9	1016.5	230	44569216
EGO	Eldorado Gold Corp	Precious Metals	12/31/15	863.3	-1540.9	5464.3	3751.7	254	412571935
ELLI	Ellie Mae Inc	Internet & Software	12/31/15	253.9	22.3	364.9	290.9	256	31004108
EFC	Ellington Financial LLC	Property, Real Estate & Developmen	12/31/15	104.6	66.2	2991.6	732.0		
EARN	Ellington Residential Mortgaging Re	REITs	12/31/15	40.8	0.0	1556.7	144.9	47	5382232
AKO B	Embotelladora Andina S.A.	Beverages	12/31/15	1877394.3	87863.5	2209361.0	830473.8	21	1154432
ERJ	Embraer SA	Aerospace	12/31/15	5928.1	69.2	11669.5	3741.8	263	104198211
EMC	EMC Corp. (MA)	Computer Hardware & Equipment	12/31/15	24704.0	1990.0	46612.0	21140.0	1676	1803362107
EME	EMCOR Group, Inc.	Construction Services	12/31/15	6718.7	172.3	3546.5	1476.7	359	71020036
EMES	Emerge Energy Services LP	Equipment & Services	12/31/15	711.6	-9.4	420.0		60	10420341
EBS	Emergent BioSolutions Inc	Biotechnology	12/31/15	522.8	62.9	1043.6	660.0	264	36196245
EMG	Emergent Capital Inc	Finance Intermediaries & Services	12/31/15	46.9	-31.0	509.9	220.4	55	16421332
EMR	Emerson Electric Co.	Electrical Equipment	9/30/15	22304.0	2710.0	22088.0	8081.0	1731	543647886
EDE	Empire District Electric Co.	Electric Utilities	12/31/15	605.6	56.6	2455.3	802.7	232	29520438
ESRT	Empire State Realty Trust Inc	REITs	12/31/15	657.6	79.9	3300.6	524.7	213	128277092
EIG	Employers Holdings Inc	General Insurance	12/31/15	752.1	94.4	3755.8	760.8	213	29404635
EDN	Empresa Distribuidora y Comerciali	Electric Utilities	12/31/15	3802.2	1142.4	12980.9	1525.1	31	3080685
EOCC	Empresa Nacional de Electricidad S	Electric Utilities	12/31/15	1543810.3	392868.1	7278770.3	2648189.9	128	8802654
ICA	Empresas ICA S.A. de C.V.	Construction Services	12/31/15	33124.1	-20422.7	108294.9	-3061.1	40	5054846
ENBL	Enable Midstream Partners L.P.	Equipment & Services	12/31/15	2418.0	-752.0	11238.0		85	69015893
EEQ	Enbridge Energy Management LLC	Equipment & Services	12/31/15	-379.7	-512.4	133.3	133.3	192	59794123
EEP	Enbridge Energy Partners, L. P.	Equipment & Services	12/31/15	5146.1	454.3	18815.8		402	154315036
ENB	Enbridge Inc	Equipment & Services	12/31/15	33794.0	251.0	84664.0	18898.0	429	674130854
ECA	EnCana Corp	Production & Extraction	12/31/15	4422.0	-5165.0	15644.0	6167.0	517	582466980
EXK	Endeavour Silver Corp	Precious Metals	12/31/15	183.6	-149.9	114.2	50.9	80	23715468
EOCA	Endesa Americas SA	Electric Utilities							
EOCA	Endesa Americas SA	Electric Utilities							
GI	EndoChoice Holdings Inc	Medical Instruments & Equipment	12/31/15	72.3	-59.4	164.3	99.3	58	10793003
ENH	Endurance Specialty Holdings Ltd	General Insurance	12/31/15	2097.5	344.1	13241.5	4856.3	372	66056148
NDRO	Enduro Royalty Trust	Oil Royalty Traders	12/31/15	14.5	13.8	121.0	121.0	37	38893829
EGN	Energen Corp.	Production & Extraction	12/31/15	878.6	-945.7	4613.7	2895.9	439	102303301
ENR	Energizer Holdings Inc (New)	Household & Personal Products	9/30/15	1631.6	-4.0	1629.6	-60.1	329	56471384
TXU 19	Energy Future Holdings Corp	Electric Utilities	12/31/15	5370.0	-5342.0	23330.0	-25061.0	68	17905858
ETC WI	Energy Transfer Corp LP	Gas Utilities							
ETE	Energy Transfer Equity LP	Equipment & Services	12/31/15	42126.0	1189.0	71189.0	33.0	500	499802161
ETP	Energy Transfer Partners LP	Equipment & Services	12/31/15	34292.0	1364.0	65173.0	33.0	676	327819529
ERF	Enerplus Corp	Production & Extraction	12/31/15	1027.1	-1523.4	2581.2	897.8		
ENIA	Enersis Americas SA	Electric Utilities	12/31/15	5301439.6	661586.9	15449154.4	6026149.3	200	86757284
ENIC	Enersis Chile SA	Electric Utilities	12/31/15	2399029.1	251838.4	5325468.9	2592681.5		
ENIC	Enersis Chile SA	Electric Utilities	12/31/15	2399029.1	251838.4	5325468.9	2592681.5		
ENS	Enersys	Electrical Equipment	3/31/16	2316.2	136.2	2214.5	1013.1	308	46167645
EGL	Engility Holdings Inc (New)	Services	12/31/15	2085.6	-235.4	2275.0	693.8	186	35718691
E	ENI S.p.A.	Production & Extraction	12/31/15	68945.0	-8783.0	134792.0	51753.0	206	26731201
ENLC	EnLink Midstream LLC	Equipment & Services	12/31/15	4452.1	-355.2	9565.1	2285.7	161	41720441
ENLK	EnLink Midstream Partners LP	Refining & Marketing	12/31/15	4452.1	-1377.8	8115.8		188	127114789
EBF	Ennis Inc	Printing	2/29/16	569.0	35.7	392.2	298.5	205	26326224
ENVA	Enova International Inc	Credit & Lending	12/31/15	652.6	44.0	880.9	206.0	132	21169016
NPO	EnPro Industries Inc	Industrial Machinery & Equipment	12/31/15	1204.4	-20.9	1503.5	459.8	234	23557096
ESV	Ensco plc	Equipment & Services	12/31/15	4063.4	-1594.8	13637.0	6512.9	607	241399050
ETM	Entercom Communications Corp	Radio & Television	12/31/15	411.4	29.2	1022.1	389.1	134	23011891
EAA	Entergy Arkansas, Inc.	Electric Utilities	12/31/15	2253.6	74.3	8747.8	2008.0		
ETR	Entergy Corp	Electric Utilities	12/31/15	11513.3	-156.7	44647.7	9575.0	756	157901102
ELJ	Entergy Louisiana LLC (New)	Electric Utilities	12/31/15	4417.1	446.6	16387.4	4737.3	1	66887
EMZ	Entergy Mississippi Inc	Electric Utilities	12/31/15	1397.0	92.7	3477.4	1062.4	2	800
ENO	Entergy New Orleans Inc.	Electric Utilities	12/31/15	671.4	44.9	1215.1	369.8		
EZT	Entergy Texas Inc	Electric Utilities	12/31/15	1707.2	69.6	3898.6	961.5		
EPD	Enterprise Products Partners L.P.	Equipment & Services	12/31/15	27027.9	2558.4	48952.0		1049	772764032
EVC	Entravision Communications Corp.	Radio & Television	12/31/15	254.1	25.6	528.2	167.3	191	60441550
ENV	Envestnet Inc	Internet & Software	12/31/15	420.9	4.4	885.6	440.4	177	44383391
EVHC	Envision Healthcare Holdings Inc	Hospitals & Health Care Facilities	12/31/15	5447.9	144.9	6388.2	1966.5	291	204636411
EVA	Enviva Partners LP	Miscellaneous	12/31/15	457.4	23.2	574.5		53	22691663
ENZ	Enzo Biochem, Inc.	Biotechnology	7/31/15	97.6	-2.3	68.4	42.6	136	23800286
EOG	EOG Resources, Inc.	Production & Extraction	12/31/15	8757.4	-4524.5	26975.2	12943.0	1210	534612475
EPE	EP Energy Corp.	Production & Extraction	12/31/15	1908.0	-3748.0	5833.0	619.0	154	192565815
EPAM	Epam Systems, Inc.	Internet & Software	12/31/15	914.1	84.5	778.5	613.2	263	46939132
EPR	EPR Properties	REITs	12/31/15	421.0	194.5	4217.3	2073.9	377	71352988
EQT	EQT Corp.	Production & Extraction	12/31/15	2339.8	85.2	13976.2	5077.8	660	151142530
EQGP	EQT GP Holdings LP	Production & Extraction	12/31/15	614.1	145.9	2634.3		78	28315308
EQM	EQT Midstream Partners LP	Equipment & Services	12/31/15	614.1	393.4	2633.8		208	60715918

| EARNINGS PER SHARE | | | | | | P/E RATIO | | DIVIDENDS PER SHARE | | | AV. YLD | DIV. DECLARED | | PRICE RANGE | |
| QUARTERLY | | | ANNUAL | | | | | | | | % | | | 2015 | |
1st	2nd	3rd	2015	2014	2013			2015	2014	2013		AMOUNT	PAYABLE		
-	-	-	-	0.43	0.18	-		-	0.98	1.06	-	0.08130	6/30/16	10.1 -	7.5
0.03	-	-	0.28	1.00	1.67	12.0 -	3.5	0.40	1.18	1.99	21.6	0.0250	5/31/16	3.4 -	1.0
-0.18	-	-	-4.46	-1.27	-	-		-	-	-	-			6.5 -	0.7
0.77	-	-	3.32	3.93	3.16	36.8 -	30.2	1.34	1.16	0.96	1.2	0.350Y	61/28/99	122.1 -	100.1
-	-	-	--175.00	122.70	-	-		2639.93	5129.26	-	34278.1			17.9 -	0.0
-	1.10	-	-4.44	5.69	6.47	-		-	-	-	-			35.0 -	33.0
-	1.10	-	-4.44	5.69	6.47	-		-	-	-	-			105.7 -	69.8
0.82	-	-	3.10	4.89	2.78	23.5 -	17.9	1.73	1.48	1.37	2.8	0.480Y	61/28/99	72.8 -	55.6
0.26	-	-	0.40	1.09	0.12	107.3 -	70.2	1.46	1.38	1.26	4.1	0.370Z	5/13/16	42.9 -	28.1
0.66	-	-	2.25	3.74	1.72	48.4 -	29.2	-	-	-	-			108.9 -	65.6
-	-	-	5.42	-17.91	-60.98	3.4 -	1.6	-	-	-	-			18.2 -	8.5
-0.14	-	-	2.03	2.27	2.20	22.9 -	16.7	1.17	1.11	1.04	3.0	0.310Y	6/30/16	46.5 -	34.0
-	-	-0.13	-2.15	0.14	-0.91	-		0.02	0.02	0.12	0.5	0.010	8/26/15	6.5 -	0.0
0.08	-	-	0.72	0.50	0.44	127.5 -	82.2	-	-	-	-			91.8 -	59.2
0.36	-	-	1.98	2.10	2.11	9.9 -	7.8	2.45	3.08	3.83	13.8	0.50	6/15/16	19.6 -	15.5
-0.03	-	-	-	1.77	-0.29	-		2.00	2.20	1.14	15.6	0.40Z	7/27/16	15.8 -	10.1
-	-	15.50	88.40	52.19	89.53	0.3 -	0.2	293.99	282.39	386.45	1543.7			24.0 -	14.6
-	-	0.07	0.09	0.45	0.47	355.4 -	231.3	0.16	0.48	0.40	0.6			32.0 -	20.8
0.14	-	-	1.01	1.32	1.33	28.1 -	22.4	0.46	0.55	0.20	1.8	0.1150	61/28/99	28.4 -	22.7
0.56	-	-	2.72	2.52	1.82	19.0 -	15.6	0.32	0.32	0.18	0.7	0.080Y	61/28/99	51.7 -	42.5
-	-	-0.49	-0.39	3.70	0.92	-		3.08	4.68	1.23	26.7	0.670	8/13/15	40.2 -	2.3
0.10	-	-	1.41	0.88	0.85	31.1 -	20.0	-	-	-	-			43.9 -	28.3
-0.27	-	-	-1.25	-0.26	3.08	-		-	-	-	-			6.1 -	3.6
-	0.57	-	3.99	3.03	2.76	15.1 -	10.6	1.88	1.72	1.64	3.8	0.4750Y	61/28/99	60.3 -	42.3
0.32	-	-	1.29	1.55	1.48	26.3 -	16.1	1.04	1.02	1.00	3.9	0.260Y	6/15/16	33.9 -	20.8
0.00	-	-	0.29	0.27	0.79	67.8 -	50.6	0.34	0.34	0.08	1.9	0.1050Z	6/30/16	19.7 -	14.7
0.64	-	-	2.90	3.14	2.00	10.4 -	7.2	0.24	0.24	0.24	0.9	0.090Y	5/25/16	30.2 -	21.0
-	-	-0.62	1.27	-0.87	0.89	15.6 -	9.4	-	-	-	-			19.8 -	11.9
-	-	-	47.90	33.65	43.15	0.6 -	0.5	465.40	526.42	339.28	1749.1			30.3 -	23.0
-	-	-	-33.28	-4.97	0.69	-		-	-	-	-			3.4 -	0.4
0.19	-	-	-1.78	1.29	0.74	-		1.26	0.55	-	11.0	0.3180	5/13/16	17.0 -	5.5
-1.56	-	-	-7.26	0.41	-0.33	-		-	-	-	-			35.9 -	14.7
0.07	-	-	-0.25	0.67	-0.39	-		2.31	2.20	2.17	9.5	0.5830	5/13/16	37.2 -	14.7
1.38	-	-	-0.04	1.37	0.55	-		1.86	1.40	1.26	4.1	0.2750	6/1/16	60.6 -	0.0
-	-	-1.47	-6.28	4.58	0.32	-		0.28	0.28	0.67	3.5	0.0150	6/30/16	15.6 -	0.0
-	-	-0.14	-1.47	-0.74	-0.90	-		-	-	-	-			5.2 -	0.0
-	-	-	-	-	-	-		-	-	-	-			0.0 -	0.0
-	-	-	-	-	-	-		-	-	-	-			14.1 -	0.0
-0.68	-	-	-2.82	-	-	-		-	-	-	-			19.3 -	3.8
1.58	-	-	5.73	7.06	6.37	-		1.40	1.36	1.28	-	0.39690	61/28/99		
0.08	-	-	-	-	-	-		0.38	0.80	1.46	12.3	0.01340Z	7/15/16	4.6 -	1.8
-2.34	-	-	-12.43	7.75	2.82	-		0.08	0.47	0.58	0.2	0.020Y	61/28/99	75.5 -	22.9
-	0.26	-	-0.06	-	-	-		0.25	-	-	0.6	0.250	61/28/99	47.3 -	30.2
-	-	-	-	-	-	-		-	-	-	-				
0.30	-	-	1.11	0.57	0.17	31.7 -	3.6	1.02	0.75	0.65	5.5	0.2850	61/28/99	35.2 -	4.0
-0.15	-	-	-0.10	1.77	-0.18	-		4.10	3.79	3.59	10.4	1.0550	5/16/16	56.2 -	19.8
-	-	-1.42	-7.39	1.44	0.24	-		0.64	1.17	1.08	10.8	0.010Y	7/15/16	12.1 -	0.0
-	-	-	13.48	11.65	14.56	0.7 -	0.4	6.21	6.71	5.45	84.8			9.0 -	5.7
-	-	-	-	-	-	-		-	-	-	-			6.7 -	6.3
-	-	-	-	-	-	-		-	-	-	-			6.4 -	5.3
-	0.06	-	3.77	3.02	3.42	19.3 -	11.5	0.70	0.50	-	1.2	0.1750	6/24/16	72.8 -	43.4
-0.09	-	-	-7.02	1.97	2.81	-		-	-	-	-			35.6 -	11.6
-	-	1.10	-2.44	0.06	1.42	-		1.35	1.69	1.75	4.3			38.1 -	25.0
-2.56	-	-	-2.17	0.55	-	-		0.98	0.63	-	5.3	0.2550	5/13/16	33.6 -	7.1
-1.74	-	-	-4.66	0.59	-1.71	-		1.53	1.46	1.33	9.7	0.390	5/12/16	25.1 -	7.7
-	-	0.41	-1.72	0.50	0.95	-		0.70	0.53	0.88	3.8	1.57Y	8/8/16	21.5 -	15.5
0.30	-	-	1.33	3.38	2.36	15.0 -	3.7	-	3.71	2.27	-			19.9 -	5.0
-2.15	-	-	-0.93	0.85	1.17	-		0.80	-	-	1.6	0.210	6/15/16	60.7 -	38.3
0.74	-	-	-6.88	-16.88	6.07	-		0.60	3.00	2.25	-	0.010	61/28/99		
0.10	-	-	0.73	0.69	0.68	17.4 -	12.5	-	-	-	-	0.0750Y	6/15/16	12.7 -	9.1
-	-	-	-	-	-	-		1.44	1.44	1.44	5.7	0.40310Y	7/1/16	25.9 -	24.9
1.28	-	-	-0.99	5.22	3.99	-		3.34	3.32	3.32	4.7	0.850Y	61/28/99	80.0 -	61.5
-	-	-	-	-	-	-		-	-	-	-	0.3750Z	9/15/16	26.1 -	24.2
-	-	-	-	-	-	-		1.50	1.50	1.50	5.9	0.38750Z	7/15/16	26.9 -	0.0
-	-	-	-	-	-	-		-	-	-	-	1.390Y	7/1/16	26.5 -	25.3
-	-	-	-	-	-	-		1.41	0.76	-	5.4	0.35160Z	9/1/16	27.3 -	0.0
0.32	-	-	1.26	1.47	1.41	25.5 -	15.7	1.51	1.43	1.35	5.8	0.3950	61/28/99	32.2 -	19.8
0.02	-	-	0.28	0.30	1.50	33.1 -	23.0	0.11	0.10	0.13	1.4	0.03130Y	6/30/16	9.3 -	6.4
-0.26	-	-	0.12	0.38	0.10	384.3 -	163.7	-	-	-	-			46.1 -	19.6
0.14	-	-	0.76	0.66	0.04	59.6 -	25.0	-	-	-	-			45.3 -	19.0
0.58	-	-	1.58	-	-	15.2 -	7.6	0.70	-	-	4.0	0.510	5/27/16	24.0 -	12.0
-	-	-0.05	-0.05	-0.23	-0.46	-		-	-	-	-			6.3 -	2.5
-0.86	-	-	-8.29	5.32	4.02	-		0.67	0.51	0.37	0.9	0.16750Y	61/28/99	90.7 -	60.2
0.38	-	-	-15.37	3.02	2.16	-		-	-	-	-			13.7 -	1.6
0.45	-	-	1.62	1.40	1.28	50.9 -	35.2	-	-	-	-			82.5 -	57.0
0.77	-	-	2.93	2.86	3.24	24.5 -	16.9	3.63	3.42	3.16	6.2	0.41410Z	61/28/99	71.8 -	49.6
0.04	-	-	0.56	2.54	2.57	153.7 -	85.3	0.12	0.12	0.12	0.2	0.030Y	61/28/99	86.1 -	47.8
0.19	-	-	0.39	-	-	88.9 -	46.3	0.15	-	-	0.6	0.1340	5/23/16	34.7 -	18.0
1.39	-	-	4.70	3.52	2.46	18.1 -	12.6	2.50	2.02	1.55	3.4	0.7450	5/13/16	84.9 -	59.0

SYMBOL	COMPANY	NATURE OF BUSINESS	FISCAL YEAR-END	TOTAL REV. $MILL	NET INCOME $MILL	TOTAL ASSETS $MILL	NET STK EQUITY $MILL	NO OF INST	INST. HOLDINGS (SHARES)
EFX	Equifax Inc	Business Services	12/31/15	2663.6	429.1	4509.0	2310.9	731	142055735
EQC	Equity Commonwealth	REITs	12/31/15	714.9	99.9	5244.4	3368.5	337	131934980
ELS	Equity Lifestyle Properties Inc	REITs	12/31/15	821.7	150.5	3420.1	925.1	322	81807968
EQY	Equity One, Inc.	REITs	12/31/15	360.2	65.5	3375.9	1564.0	281	96978056
EQR	Equity Residential	REITs	12/31/15	2745.0	908.0	23157.3	10470.4	719	424239643
EQS	Equus Total Return, Inc.	Holding and other Investment Office	12/31/15	0.4	-2.4	52.5	37.3	18	1092446
ERA	ERA Group Inc	Equipment & Services	12/31/15	281.8	8.7	1007.1	471.3	127	18850303
EROS	Eros International Plc	Entertainment	3/31/15	284.2	40.3	1149.5	697.3	103	16029723
ESE	ESCO Technologies, Inc.	Industrial Machinery & Equipment	9/30/15	537.3	42.5	864.2	584.2	215	26336553
ESNT	Essent Group Ltd	General Insurance	12/31/15	353.3	157.3	1469.1	1119.2	172	71534091
ESS	Essex Property Trust Inc	REITs	12/31/15	1194.4	232.1	12005.1	6237.7	538	74133100
ESL	Esterline Technologies Corp	Electronic Instruments & Related Pro	10/2/15	1774.4	59.6	3007.0	1537.5	299	30732233
ETH	Ethan Allen Interiors, Inc.	Furniture	6/30/15	754.6	37.1	607.3	370.3	232	30186996
EURN	Euronav NV	Shipping	12/31/15	846.5	350.3	3040.7	1905.7	122	53089221
EEA	European Equity Fund Inc (The)	Holding and other Investment Office	12/31/15	2.1	0.8	78.3	77.5	38	3883611
EVER	EverBank Financial Corp	Credit & Lending	12/31/15	1094.6	130.5	26601.0	1868.3	182	109371040
EVR	Evercore Partners Inc	Finance Intermediaries & Services	12/31/15	1223.3	42.9	1479.2	504.6	292	36998725
RE	Everest Re Group Ltd	General Insurance	12/31/15	5837.9	977.9	21426.2	7608.6	530	44054615
EVRI	Everi Holdings Inc	Credit & Lending	12/31/15	827.0	-105.0	1574.1	137.4	172	65192207
ES	Eversource Energy	Electric Utilities	12/31/15	7954.8	886.0	30580.3	10352.2	131	24724103
EVTC	Evertec, Inc.	Business Services	12/31/15	373.5	85.4	870.1	98.2	144	61722525
EVDY	Everyday Health, Inc.	Internet & Software	12/31/15	232.0	-11.6	369.6	180.3	107	22279673
EVGN	Evogene Ltd	Agricultural Chemicals	12/31/15	11.1	-17.2	112.6	103.8	23	7387543
EVH	Evolent Health Inc	Business Services	12/31/15	96.9	332.5	1015.5	649.3	80	16415438
EXAM	ExamWorks Group Inc	Diagnostic & Health Related Service	12/31/15	819.6	5.6	1051.7	360.0	193	44053064
EXAR	Exar Corp.	Semiconductors	3/27/16	149.4	-16.0	255.4	214.5	166	41611891
XCO	Exco Resources Inc.	Production & Extraction	12/31/15	328.3	-1192.4	954.1	-662.3	211	206116405
EXC	Exelon Corp	Electric Utilities	12/31/15	29447.0	2250.0	95384.0	25986.0	1112	753670608
EXPR	Express, Inc.	Retail - Apparel and Accessories	1/30/16	2350.1	116.5	1178.6	618.0	314	88445439
STAY	Extended Stay America Inc	Hotels, Restaurants & Travel	12/31/15	1284.8	283.0	4528.9	879.7	155	211931732
EXTN	Exterran Corp	Business Services	12/31/15	1869.9	46.2	1842.4	909.9	143	28175703
EXR	Extra Space Storage Inc	REITs	12/31/15	782.3	209.5	6071.4	2089.1	494	144640280
XOM	Exxon Mobil Corp.	Production & Extraction	12/31/15	268882.0	16150.0	336758.0	170811.0	2839	2599308589
FNB	F.N.B. Corp.	Banking	12/31/15	709.2	159.6	17557.7	2096.2	333	152789326
FN	Fabrinet	Manufacturing	6/26/15	773.6	43.6	672.5	478.9	211	37274508
FDS	FactSet Research Systems Inc.	Business Services	8/31/15	1006.8	241.1	736.7	531.6	490	46213174
FICO	Fair Isaac Corp	Internet & Software	9/30/15	838.8	86.5	1230.2	437.0	313	36369228
FMSA	Fairmount Santrol Holdings Inc	Equipment & Services	12/31/15	828.7	-92.1	1369.0	-61.2	109	88681517
FPI	Farmland Partners Inc	REITs	12/31/15	13.8	1.2	345.0	108.4	58	3257608
FFG	FBL Financial Group, Inc.	Life & Health	12/31/15	722.8	113.5	9132.0	1134.4	148	7642917
FCB	FCB Financial Holdings Inc	Banking	12/31/15	223.7	53.4	7331.5	876.1	169	36991006
AGM	Federal Agricultural Mortgage Corp	Credit & Lending	12/31/15	285.0	68.7	15540.4	553.5	127	7735635
FRT	Federal Realty Investment Trust (M	REITs	12/31/15	744.0	210.2	4911.7	1663.7	493	75912151
FSS	Federal Signal Corp.	Industrial Machinery & Equipment	12/31/15	768.0	63.5	666.5	405.6	247	58440888
FII	Federated Investors Inc (PA)	Wealth Management	12/31/15	926.6	169.8	1187.2	647.8	425	100937013
FPT	Federated Premier Intermediate Mu	Holding and other Investment Office	11/30/15	6.5	5.0	162.5	115.6	29	1911713
FMN	Federated Premier Municipal Incom	Holding and other Investment Office	11/30/15	6.8	5.4	148.7	112.6	18	379627
FDX	FedEx Corp	Airlines/Air Freight	5/31/15	47453.0	1050.0	37069.0	14993.0	1408	230811151
FCH	FelCor Lodging Trust Inc	REITs	12/31/15	886.3	-8.9	1884.0	260.2	238	131233843
RACE	Ferrari NV (New)	Autos- Manufacturing	12/31/15	2854.4	287.8	3875.4	-25.1	184	50985650
FGP	Ferrellgas Partners LP	Gas Utilities	7/31/15	2024.4	29.6	2464.1	-	156	9715240
FOE	Ferro Corp	Specialty Chemicals	12/31/15	1075.3	64.1	1225.4	316.5	236	79418073
FCAU	Fiat Chrysler Automobiles NV	Autos- Manufacturing	12/31/15	110595.0	334.0	105040.0	16092.0	226	332964752
FBR	Fibria Celulose SA	Paper & Forest Products	12/31/15	10080.7	342.2	29434.0	12752.4	166	52343361
FGL	Fidelity & Guaranty Life	Life & Health	9/30/15	961.0	118.0	24925.0	1502.0	114	10446399
FNF	Fidelity National Financial Inc	General Insurance	12/31/15	9132.0	527.0	13931.0	5754.0	520	262570810
FIS	Fidelity National Information Service	Business Services	12/31/15	6595.2	631.5	26268.8	9321.0	774	313677518
FMO	Fiduciary / Claymore MLP Opportun	Holding and other Investment Office	11/30/15	9.2	-3.6	894.8	528.4	95	7001659
FAC	First Acceptance Corp	General Insurance	12/31/15	331.9	-1.9	402.1	103.7	42	8499519
FAF	First American Financial Corp	General Insurance	12/31/15	5175.5	288.1	8254.4	2758.5	304	100395803
FBP	First Bancorp	Banking	12/31/15	686.9	21.3	12573.0	1694.1	215	195078827
FCF	First Commonwealth Financial Corp	Banking	12/31/15	265.4	50.1	6566.9	719.5	182	60358099
FDC	First Data Corp (New)	IT Services	12/31/15	11451.0	-1481.0	34362.0	668.0	266	271390182
FHN	First Horizon National Corp	Banking	12/31/15	1253.7	85.9	26195.1	2344.2	370	201920121
FR	First Industrial Realty Trust Inc	REITs	12/31/15	365.8	73.8	2718.1	1073.1	317	139014082
AG	First Majestic Silver Corp	Precious Metals	12/31/15	219.4	-108.4	789.7	544.7	133	58445698
FMD	First Marblehead Corp	Credit & Lending	6/30/15	46.2	-47.8	240.8	102.2	81	8078692
FPO	First Potomac Realty Trust	REITs	12/31/15	172.8	-33.0	1450.4	624.5	203	58347876
FRC	First Republic Bank (San Francisco,	Banking	12/31/15	1989.1	522.1	58981.3	5705.7	506	164070441
FEO	First Trust / Aberdeen Emerging Op	Holding and other Investment Office	12/31/14	6.0	4.1	105.6	99.1	34	2925731
FAM	First Trust / Aberdeen Global Oppor	Holding and other Investment Office	12/31/15	19.0	14.3	288.4	201.3	65	7550527
FAV	First Trust Dividend & Income Fund	Holding and other Investment Office	11/30/14	4.2	2.6	116.1	84.2	38	3117508
FDEU	First Trust Dynamic Europe Equity I	Holding and other Investment Office	8/20/15	-	-	0.1	0.1	26	2576458
FIF	First Trust Energy Infrastructure Fu	Holding and other Investment Office	11/30/14	11.7	3.8	625.1	455.8	49	4631054
FFA	First Trust Enhanced Equity Income	Holding and other Investment Office	12/31/15	7.7	4.2	307.5	299.4	63	7292487
FSD	First Trust High Income Long / Shor	Holding and other Investment Office	10/31/14	59.5	47.0	871.9	702.0	80	13860168
FPF	First Trust Intermediate Duration Pr	Finance Intermediaries & Services	10/31/14	136.8	112.1	2159.6	1482.5	69	10308545
FEI	First Trust MLP & Energy Income F	Finance Intermediaries & Services	10/31/14	15.4	-1.5	1586.3	1057.3	59	10394009
FMY	First Trust Mortgage Income Fund	Holding and other Investment Office	10/31/14	5.4	4.3	75.2	67.6	30	3037804
FPL	First Trust New Opportunities MLP	Finance Intermediaries & Services	10/31/14	4.6	-0.4	681.5	484.7	40	4211685

T24

EARNINGS PER SHARE QUARTERLY			ANNUAL			P/E RATIO		DIVIDENDS PER SHARE			AV. YLD %	DIV. DECLARED		PRICE RANGE 2015	
1st	2nd	3rd	2015	2014	2013			2015	2014	2013		AMOUNT	PAYABLE		
0.85	-	-	3.55	2.97	2.84	35.6 -	26.1	1.16	1.00	0.88	1.1	0.330Y	61/28/99	126.3 -	92.7
0.31	-	-	0.56	-0.19	-1.97	53.0 -	45.1	-	0.25	1.00	-	0.35940Z	8/1/16	29.7 -	25.3
0.60	-	-	1.54	1.41	1.28	49.0 -	33.9	1.50	1.30	1.00	2.4	0.42190Z	61/28/99	75.5 -	52.2
0.15	-	-	0.51	0.39	0.65	59.2 -	44.5	0.88	0.88	0.88	3.3	0.220Z	61/28/99	30.2 -	22.7
9.76	-	-	2.36	1.73	5.16	34.7 -	28.3	2.21	2.00	1.85	3.0	0.50380Z	61/28/99	82.0 -	66.8
-0.06	-	-	-0.19	-0.20	-0.30	-	-	-	-	-	-	0.1580	9/29/08	2.0 -	0.0
-0.19	-	-	0.42	0.84	0.88	50.5 -	17.9	-	-	-	-	-	-	21.2 -	7.5
-	-	-	0.72	0.65	0.23	-	-	-	-	-	-	-	-	-	-
-	0.33	-	1.62	0.02	-0.96	24.9 -	19.9	0.32	0.40	0.32	0.9	0.080Y	7/19/16	40.3 -	32.3
0.52	-	-	1.72	1.03	0.70	17.1 -	9.7	-	-	-	-	-	-	29.5 -	16.6
1.19	-	-	3.49	2.06	4.04	70.0 -	55.1	5.76	5.11	4.84	2.6	1.60Z	61/28/99	244.3 -	192.3
-	0.50	-	1.91	3.16	5.19	56.9 -	27.1	-	-	-	-	0.09	61/28/99	108.7 -	51.8
-	-	0.36	1.27	1.47	1.11	27.1 -	18.4	0.46	0.39	0.77	1.6	0.170Y	7/25/16	34.4 -	23.4
-	-	-	2.22	-0.39	-1.79	-	-	0.87	-	-	-	-	-	-	-
-	-	-	0.09	0.09	0.10	98.0 -	0.0	0.17	0.11	-	2.1	0.02030	7/18/16	8.8 -	0.0
0.20	-	-	0.95	1.10	1.02	22.2 -	13.2	0.20	0.14	0.10	1.2	0.42190Y	7/5/16	21.1 -	12.6
0.12	-	-	0.98	2.08	1.38	60.4 -	43.4	1.15	1.03	0.91	2.2	0.310Y	6/10/16	59.1 -	42.5
4.00	-	-	22.10	25.91	25.44	9.0 -	7.6	4.00	3.20	2.19	2.2	1.150	61/28/99	199.3 -	167.7
-0.20	-	-	-1.59	0.18	0.36	-	-	-	-	-	-	-	-	8.5 -	1.1
0.45	-	-	2.76	2.58	2.49	21.3 -	16.5	1.67	1.57	1.47	3.2	0.4450Y	61/28/99	58.8 -	45.4
0.26	-	-	1.11	0.86	-0.31	20.8 -	10.3	0.40	0.40	0.20	2.4	0.10Y	6/10/16	23.1 -	11.4
-0.49	-	-	-0.36	0.17	-3.57	-	-	-	-	-	-	-	-	14.0 -	4.0
-	-	-	-0.68	-0.58	-0.45	-	-	-	-	-	-	-	-	-	-
-2.91	-	-	6.93	-53.83	3.96	3.2 -	1.2	-	-	-	-	-	-	22.5 -	8.5
0.08	-	-	0.13	0.25	-0.29	324.8 -	174.5	-	-	-	-	-	-	42.2 -	22.7
-	-	-0.15	-0.05	0.12	0.06	-	-	-	-	-	-	-	-	10.9 -	5.0
-0.47	-	-	-4.36	0.45	0.10	-	-	-	0.15	0.20	-	0.050Y	9/30/14	1.8 -	0.5
0.19	-	-	2.54	1.88	2.00	14.1 -	10.0	1.24	1.24	1.46	4.0	0.3180Y	61/28/99	35.9 -	25.5
0.16	-	-	0.81	1.37	1.60	26.4 -	17.8	-	-	-	-	0.567	12/23/10	21.4 -	14.4
0.08	-	-	0.55	0.19	0.19	36.3 -	19.9	0.91	0.53	-	5.5	0.190	5/24/16	19.9 -	10.9
-	-	-	1.35	-	-	13.5 -	0.0	-	-	-	-	-	-	18.2 -	0.0
0.66	-	-	1.56	1.53	1.53	60.3 -	41.7	2.24	1.81	1.45	2.8	0.780Z	61/28/99	94.0 -	65.0
0.43	-	-	3.85	7.60	7.37	23.4 -	17.8	2.88	2.70	2.46	3.6	0.750Y	61/28/99	90.3 -	68.7
0.12	-	-	0.86	0.80	0.80	17.0 -	13.0	0.48	0.48	0.48	3.6	0.120Y	6/15/16	14.6 -	11.2
-	-	0.56	1.21	2.58	1.98	29.8 -	14.8	-	-	-	-	-	-	36.0 -	17.9
-	1.63	-	5.71	4.92	4.45	30.8 -	23.9	1.66	1.48	1.32	1.0	0.50Y	61/28/99	176.0 -	136.4
-	0.72	-	2.65	2.72	2.48	42.1 -	30.4	0.08	0.08	0.08	0.1	0.020Y	61/28/99	111.6 -	80.7
-0.07	-	-	-0.57	1.03	0.63	-	-	-	-	-	-	-	-	9.1 -	1.2
-0.15	-	-	0.08	-0.15	-	154.6 -	123.1	0.50	0.33	-	4.6	0.12750Y	7/15/16	12.4 -	9.8
1.04	-	-	4.53	4.39	4.21	15.3 -	12.2	3.60	1.40	2.52	6.0	0.420Y	6/30/16	69.4 -	55.3
0.52	-	-	1.23	0.58	0.40	31.7 -	23.3	-	-	-	-	-	-	39.0 -	28.7
0.94	-	-	4.19	3.37	6.41	10.4 -	5.3	0.64	0.56	0.48	2.1	0.3750Y	7/17/16	43.5 -	22.4
1.10	-	-	3.03	2.41	2.46	52.6 -	41.2	3.62	3.30	3.02	2.5	0.940Z	61/28/99	159.5 -	125.0
0.22	-	-	1.00	1.00	2.53	17.1 -	11.4	0.25	0.09	-	1.7	0.070Y	6/7/16	17.1 -	11.4
0.44	-	-	1.62	1.42	1.55	21.8 -	14.4	1.00	1.00	0.98	3.3	0.250Y	61/28/99	35.3 -	23.3
-	-	-	0.72	0.67	0.71	20.4 -	17.0	0.67	0.71	0.73	5.0	0.054M	7/1/16	14.7 -	12.2
-	-	-	0.87	0.89	0.91	18.7 -	15.9	0.88	0.90	0.91	5.9	0.07M	7/1/16	16.3 -	13.8
-	-	1.84	3.65	6.75	4.91	50.7 -	33.7	0.80	0.60	0.56	0.5	0.40Y	61/28/99	185.0 -	123.2
-0.08	-	-	-0.33	0.43	-0.81	-	-	0.16	0.08	-	2.0	0.48/50Z	4/29/16	11.0 -	5.8
-	-	-	1.52	1.38	1.27	-	-	-	-	-	-	0.46G	5/30/16	-	-
-	-	0.19	0.35	0.41	0.71	69.4 -	41.0	2.00	2.00	2.00	10.3	0.51250	6/14/16	24.3 -	14.4
-0.12	-	-	0.72	0.99	0.82	23.7 -	12.0	-	-	-	-	0.010Y	3/10/09	17.1 -	8.6
-	-	-	0.22	0.46	0.74	-	-	-	-	-	-	0.01090	1/7/16	-	-
-	-	-	0.62	0.28	-1.28	23.8 -	12.8	3.93	-	-	32.8	-	-	14.8 -	7.9
-	0.16	-	2.02	2.90	7.40	13.8 -	10.9	0.26	0.20	-	1.0	0.0650Y	5/30/16	27.8 -	22.1
0.26	-	-	1.89	0.75	1.71	21.2 -	15.7	0.80	0.37	0.66	2.3	0.180Y	61/28/99	40.0 -	29.6
0.17	-	-	2.19	2.35	1.68	34.0 -	25.6	1.04	0.96	0.88	1.6	0.260Y	61/28/99	74.4 -	56.0
-	-	-	-0.11	-0.26	-0.38	-	-	1.71	1.68	1.63	11.1	0.43080	5/31/16	24.9 -	8.4
-0.13	-	-	-0.05	0.68	0.22	-	-	-	-	-	-	0.0067	6/28/02	3.3 -	1.3
0.47	-	-	2.62	2.15	1.71	16.2 -	12.4	1.00	0.84	0.48	2.7	0.260Y	61/28/99	42.4 -	32.4
0.11	-	-	0.10	1.87	-0.80	65.3 -	20.8	-	-	-	-	1.050	6/30/09	6.5 -	2.1
0.14	-	-	0.56	0.48	0.43	17.6 -	14.1	0.28	0.28	0.23	3.1	0.070Y	5/20/16	9.9 -	7.9
-0.06	-	-	-7.70	-	-	-	-	-	-	-	-	-	-	17.8 -	8.7
0.20	-	-	0.34	0.91	0.10	47.6 -	34.2	0.24	0.20	0.20	1.7	0.38750Y	61/28/99	16.2 -	11.6
0.14	-	-	0.67	0.42	0.24	37.2 -	27.9	0.51	0.41	0.34	2.4	0.190Z	7/18/16	24.9 -	18.7
-	-	-0.01	-0.84	-0.52	-0.33	-	-	-	-	-	-	-	-	15.6 -	0.0
-	-	-0.46	4.16	-3.33	-4.70	-	-	-	-	-	-	1.20Y	12/21/07	6.5 -	3.1
-0.07	-	-	-0.79	0.07	-0.03	-	-	0.60	0.60	0.60	5.9	0.48440Z	5/16/16	12.0 -	8.1
0.88	-	-	3.18	3.07	3.10	22.8 -	17.8	0.59	0.54	0.36	0.9	0.160Y	61/28/99	72.5 -	56.6
-	-	-	-	0.77	0.79	-	-	-	1.40	1.40	-	0.350	6/30/16	16.5 -	11.8
-	-	-	0.82	1.03	1.07	14.0 -	11.7	1.14	1.38	1.56	11.0	0.0750	7/15/16	11.5 -	9.6
-	-	-	-	0.32	0.20	-	-	-	0.66	0.63	-	0.170	4/29/16	8.9 -	7.3
-	-	-	-	-	-	-	-	-	-	-	-	0.1210	7/15/16	20.5 -	14.1
-	-	-	0.22	0.22	-	-	-	-	2.75	4.13	-	0.110	7/15/16	22.1 -	10.9
-	-	0.20	0.24	0.21	-	75.9 -	57.4	0.94	0.92	0.90	7.1	0.240	6/30/16	15.2 -	11.5
-	-	-	1.31	1.35	-	-	-	-	1.31	1.40	-	0.080	7/15/16	16.3 -	13.0
-	-	-	1.85	0.70	-	-	-	-	1.91	0.46	-	0.16250	7/15/16	23.2 -	20.2
-	-	-	-0.03	-0.05	-	-	-	-	1.33	0.98	-	0.11830	7/15/16	20.6 -	8.8
-	-	-	1.02	1.02	1.25	14.5 -	0.0	1.02	1.02	1.25	7.2	0.0750	7/15/16	14.0 -	0.0
-	-	-	-	-0.02	-	-	-	-	0.50	-	-	0.1050	7/15/10	16.8 -	7.7

SYMBOL	COMPANY	NATURE OF BUSINESS	FISCAL YEAR-END	TOTAL REV. $MILL	NET INCOME $MILL	TOTAL ASSETS $MILL	NET STK EQUITY $MILL	NO OF INST	INST. HOLDINGS (SHARES)
FCT	First Trust Senior Floating Rate Inco	Holding and other Investment Office	5/31/15	30.0	23.3	573.6	392.7	79	10911799
FGB	First Trust Specialty Finance and Fi	Holding and other Investment Office	11/30/14	11.3	9.3	138.3	110.4	29	1273803
FHY	First Trust Strategic High Income Fu	Holding and other Investment Office	10/31/14	15.1	11.7	199.9	140.7	55	2481871
FE	FirstEnergy Corp	Electric Utilities	12/31/15	15026.0	578.0	52187.0	12421.0	745	343587799
FIT	Fitbit Inc	Computer Hardware & Equipment	12/31/15	1858.0	175.7	1519.1	981.5	289	72710342
OAKS	Five Oaks Investment Corp	REITs	12/31/15	100.7	0.5	2498.4	177.5	40	2802521
FBC	Flagstar Bancorp, Inc.	Credit & Lending	12/31/15	825.0	158.0	13715.0	1529.0	192	58779586
DFP	Flaherty & Crumrine Dynamic Prefe	Finance Intermediaries & Services	11/30/14	41.4	33.7	711.6	475.2	44	3524514
PFD	Flaherty & Crumrine Preferred Inco	Holding and other Investment Office	11/30/15	15.0	12.2	226.3	148.6	30	528907
PFO	Flaherty & Crumrine Preferred Inco	Holding and other Investment Office	11/30/15	13.7	11.1	210.7	138.4	41	1168174
FFC	Flaherty & Crumrine Preferred Secu	Holding and other Investment Office	11/30/15	82.1	70.2	1267.3	831.7	104	7247439
FLC	Flaherty & Crumrine Total Return F	Holding and other Investment Office	11/30/15	20.0	16.3	306.8	201.6	44	1879850
FLT	FleetCor Technologies Inc	Business Services	12/31/15	1702.9	362.4	7891.9	2830.0	416	88797530
FLTX	Fleetmatics Group Plc	IT Services	12/31/15	284.8	38.8	402.4	302.2	234	42134733
FTK	Flotek Industries Inc	Specialty Chemicals	12/31/15	334.4	-13.5	403.1	293.7	209	53059525
FLO	Flowers Foods, Inc.	Food	1/2/16	3778.5	189.2	2885.2	1243.1	398	139583916
FLS	Flowserve Corp	Industrial Machinery & Equipment	12/31/15	4561.0	267.7	5103.8	1666.5	606	141151283
FLR	Fluor Corp.	Construction Services	12/31/15	18114.0	412.5	7631.5	2997.3	777	130798891
FLY	Fly Leasing Ltd	Airlines/Air Freight	12/31/14	426.7	56.1	4224.7	758.9	122	22970298
FMC	FMC Corp.	Agricultural Chemicals	12/31/15	3276.5	489.0	6325.9	1865.7	533	131550515
FTI	FMC Technologies Inc	Equipment & Services	12/31/15	6362.7	393.1	6437.9	2511.8	599	214202407
FMX	Fomento Economico Mexicano, S.A	Beverages	12/31/15	311589.0	17683.0	409332.0	181524.0	348	105802707
FL	Foot Locker, Inc.	Retail - Apparel and Accessories	1/30/16	7412.0	541.0	3775.0	2553.0	753	164352768
F	Ford Motor Co. (DE)	Autos- Manufacturing	12/31/15	149558.0	7373.0	224925.0	28642.0	1479	2642330240
F 12A	Ford Motor Credit Company LLC	Credit & Lending	12/31/15	3641.0	1363.0	137448.0	11713.0	1	2
FELP	Foresight Energy LP	Mining	12/31/15	984.9	-39.5	1837.0		35	12662804
FCE A	Forest City Realty Trust Inc	REITs	12/31/15	978.2	496.0	9993.0	3518.3	255	223934636
FOR	Forestar Group Inc	Property, Real Estate & Developmen	12/31/15	262.4	-213.0	980.5	501.6	172	36978487
FTV WI	Fortive Corp	Industrial Machinery & Equipment							
FIG	Fortress Investment Group LLC	Wealth Management	12/31/15	1213.9	78.5	2275.3	570.7	180	119314546
FTAI	Fortress Transportation & Infrastruct	Industrial Machinery & Equipment	12/31/15	136.6	-11.8	1649.6	1166.3	57	23512034
FSM	Fortuna Silver Mines Inc	Precious Metals	12/31/15	154.7	-10.6	379.7	264.2		
FBHS	Fortune Brands Home & Security, In	Household Appliances, Electronics &	12/31/15	4579.4	315.0	4878.6	2450.9	507	148596365
FET	Forum Energy Technologies Inc	Equipment & Services	12/31/15	1073.7	-119.4	1886.0	1257.0	186	95065009
FCPT	Four Corners Property Trust Inc	REITs	12/31/15	33.5	5.7	929.4	441.6	301	52656578
FNV	Franco-Nevada Corp	Precious Metals	12/31/15	443.6	24.6	3674.3	3163.0		
FI	Frank's International NV	Equipment & Services	12/31/15	974.6	79.1	1726.8	1212.0	171	38433617
FC	Franklin Covey Co	Business Services	8/31/15	209.9	11.1	200.6	125.5	92	8868859
FSB	Franklin Financial Network Inc	Banking	12/31/15	81.6	16.1	2167.8	188.8	91	4189949
BEN	Franklin Resources, Inc.	Wealth Management	9/30/15	7948.7	2035.3	16335.7	11841.0	816	318657922
FT	Franklin Universal Trust	Holding and other Investment Office	8/31/15	15.1	11.2	240.0	178.7	54	6639435
FCX	Freeport-McMoRan Inc	Non-Precious Metals	12/31/15	15877.0	-12089.0	46577.0	7828.0	1134	952140774
FMS	Fresenius Medical Care AG & Co K	Diagnostic & Health Related Service	12/31/15	16737.6	1029.4	25533.5	9887.1	237	15855019
FDP	Fresh Del Monte Produce Inc.	Food	1/1/16	4056.5	62.4	2596.1	1708.0	201	34042797
FRO	Frontline Ltd	Equipment & Services	12/31/15	567.9	154.6	2886.7	1446.3	187	14114965
FSIC	FS Investment Corp	Finance Intermediaries & Services	12/31/15	474.8	265.1	4149.7	2208.9	175	78972376
FCN	FTI Consulting Inc.	Business Services	12/31/15	1779.1	66.1	2229.0	1147.6	264	48817185
FUL	Fuller (H.B.) Company	Specialty Chemicals	11/28/15	2083.7	86.7	2042.3	872.9	265	57160219
FF	FutureFuel Corp	Specialty Chemicals	12/31/15	299.6	46.4	489.1	394.3	145	17924700
FXCM	FXCM Inc	Finance Intermediaries & Services	12/31/15	402.3	-553.9	1230.5	-263.1	48	2632663
GCV	Gabelli Convertible and Income Sec	Holding and other Investment Office	12/31/15	2.3	1.0	100.8	98.7	31	2452049
GDV	Gabelli Dividend & Income Trust	Holding and other Investment Office	12/31/15	50.6	30.1	2203.1	2198.2		
GAB	Gabelli Equity Trust Inc.	Holding and other Investment Office	12/31/15	30.5	12.9	1607.2	1582.8	115	27062999
GGZ	Gabelli Global Small & Mid Cap Val	Holding and other Investment Office	12/31/14	0.2	-0.6	100.2	97.9	52	1866760
GRX	Gabelli Healthcare & WellnessRx Tr	Holding and other Investment Office	12/31/14	2.7	-0.5	301.1	299.6	62	5303338
GGT	Gabelli Multimedia Trust Inc.	Holding and other Investment Office	12/31/15	3.7	0.8	243.9	238.0	55	3895459
GUT	Gabelli Utility Trust	Holding and other Investment Office	12/31/15	8.8	5.7	273.6	270.5	54	2088566
GFA	Gafisa S.A.	Builders	12/31/15	2294.3	74.4	6760.3	3095.5		
GCAP	GAIN Capital Holdings Inc	Finance Intermediaries & Services	12/31/15	435.3	10.3	1424.8	306.1	111	25708540
AJG	Gallagher (Arthur J.) & Co.	Brokers & Intermediaries	12/31/15	5392.4	356.8	10913.8	3638.3	611	158977309
GBL	GAMCO Investors Inc	Finance Intermediaries & Services	12/31/15	381.0	83.4	104.0	-276.3	110	7564139
GNT	GAMCO Natural Resources, Gold &	Holding and other Investment Office	12/31/14	3.3	0.5	191.2	184.1	48	4960672
GME	GameStop Corp	Retail - Appliances and Electronics	1/30/16	9363.8	402.8	4334.9	2081.0	664	140582953
GCI	Gannett Co Inc (New)	Publishing	12/27/15	2885.0	146.1	2427.8	1058.6	302	107564802
GCI	Gannett Co Inc (New)	Publishing	12/27/15	2885.0	146.1	2427.8	1058.6	302	107564802
IT	Gartner Inc	IT Services	12/31/15	2163.1	175.6	2174.7	-132.4	435	126459023
GLOG	GasLog Ltd	Equipment & Services	12/31/15	415.1	10.8	4039.6	1001.7		
GLOP	GasLog Partners LP	Shipping	12/31/15	199.7	72.0	1347.2	578.2	59	9711633
GMT	GATX Corp	Services	12/31/15	1449.9	205.3	6894.2	1280.2	335	55223972
GZT	Gazit-Globe Ltd	Property, Real Estate & Developmen	12/31/15	7303.0	620.0	84236.0	7512.0	31	19473740
GCP	GCP Applied Technologies Inc	Specialty Chemicals	12/31/15	1418.6	40.1	833.1	470.6	155	57430439
GCP	GCP Applied Technologies Inc	Specialty Chemicals	12/31/15	1418.6	40.1	833.1	470.6	155	57430439
GDL	GDL Fund	Holding and other Investment Office	12/31/14	4.3	-3.5	428.5	244.9	63	9933483
GEGI 26	GE Global Insurance Holdings Corp	Brokers & Intermediaries	12/31/03	11621.0	656.0	52542.0	7943.0		
GNK	Genco Shipping & Trading Ltd	Shipping	12/31/15	154.0	-194.9	1724.1	1106.0	77	46856593
GNRT	Gener8 Maritime Inc	Equipment & Services	12/31/15	429.9	129.6	2389.7	1347.8	101	61751315
GNRC	Generac Holdings Inc	Electrical Equipment	12/31/15	1317.3	77.7	1792.8	465.9	262	72163642
GAM	General American Investors Co., In	Holding and other Investment Office	12/31/15	27.5	13.7	1277.8	1258.1	98	10281470
BGC	General Cable Corp. (DE)	Electrical Equipment	12/31/15	4225.1	-135.8	2466.7	228.0	276	54788008
GD	General Dynamics Corp.	Aerospace	12/31/15	31469.0	2965.0	31997.0	10738.0	1237	293849266

T26

EARNINGS PER SHARE						P/E RATIO		DIVIDENDS PER SHARE			AV. YLD	DIV. DECLARED		PRICE RANGE	
QUARTERLY			ANNUAL											2015	
1st	2nd	3rd	2015	2014	2013			2015	2014	2013	%	AMOUNT	PAYABLE		
-	-	-	0.87	0.84	1.01	15.7 -	13.5	0.84	0.94	1.03	6.6	0.070	7/15/16	13.7 -	11.7
-	-	-	-	0.65	0.62	-		-	0.69	0.67	-	0.1750	5/31/16	7.2 -	4.7
-	-	-	-	1.38	1.48	-		-	1.44	1.45	-	0.10	7/15/16	13.8 -	9.9
0.77	-	-	1.37	0.71	0.94	26.5 -	21.3	1.44	1.44	2.20	4.4	0.360Y	61/28/99	36.3 -	29.1
0.05	-	-	0.75	0.63	-1.32	68.9 -	16.2	-	-	-	-	-	-	51.6 -	12.2
-1.22	-	-	-0.21	0.03	0.52	-		1.35	1.50	1.30	21.3	0.18230	9/27/16	10.1 -	4.0
0.54	-	-	2.24	-1.72	4.37	11.1 -	7.8	-	-	-	-	0.50Y	12/31/07	24.9 -	17.5
-	-	-	-	1.76	0.72	-		-	1.97	0.78	-	0.160	6/30/16	24.2 -	21.4
-	-	-	1.10	1.12	1.13	14.1 -	11.1	1.08	1.16	1.20	8.0	0.090	6/30/16	15.5 -	12.2
-	-	-	0.90	0.92	0.93	13.7 -	11.0	0.88	0.95	0.99	8.0	0.0730	6/30/16	12.3 -	9.9
-	-	-	1.61	1.64	1.68	13.1 -	10.9	1.63	1.68	1.75	8.3	0.1360	6/30/16	21.2 -	17.6
-	-	-	1.65	1.67	1.68	13.1 -	10.9	1.63	1.72	1.72	8.3	0.1360	6/30/16	21.6 -	18.0
1.17	-	-	3.85	4.24	3.36	42.6 -	29.5	-	-	-	-	-	-	163.9 -	113.4
0.14	-	-	0.99	0.71	0.82	62.4 -	35.6	-	-	-	-	-	-	61.8 -	35.2
-0.55	-	-	-0.25	0.97	0.67	-		-	-	-	-	-	-	21.0 -	5.5
0.28	-	-	0.89	0.82	1.09	30.4 -	17.7	0.57	0.48	0.44	2.7	0.160Y	61/28/99	27.1 -	15.7
0.29	-	-	2.00	3.76	3.41	27.8 -	17.7	0.72	0.64	0.56	1.6	0.190Y	61/28/99	55.6 -	35.4
0.74	-	-	2.81	3.20	4.06	20.3 -	14.6	0.84	0.84	0.64	1.7	0.210Y	61/28/99	57.1 -	40.9
-	-	0.00	-	1.32	1.50	-		-	1.00	0.88	-	-	-	16.2 -	10.8
0.36	-	-	3.66	2.29	2.16	15.7 -	9.0	0.66	0.60	0.54	1.6	0.1650Y	61/28/99	57.5 -	32.0
0.09	-	-	1.70	2.95	2.10	25.4 -	13.4	-	-	-	-	-	-	43.3 -	22.8
-	-	-	0.88	0.83	0.79	115.9 -	93.1	21.99	-	39.81	24.0	-	-	102.0 -	81.9
1.39	-	-	3.56	2.85	2.58	21.3 -	15.2	0.88	0.80	0.72	1.3	0.2750Y	61/28/99	75.8 -	54.1
0.61	-	-	1.84	0.80	1.76	8.5 -	6.1	0.60	0.50	0.40	4.3	0.150Y	61/28/99	15.7 -	11.2
-0.32	-	-	-0.25	0.54	-	-		1.28	0.38	-	24.3	0.170	11/25/15	14.9 -	1.1
0.92	-	-	1.97	-0.04	-0.03	12.1 -	8.5	-	-	-	-	0.060Y	6/24/16	23.8 -	16.7
-0.13	-	-	-6.22	0.38	0.80	-		-	-	-	-	-	-	14.6 -	8.4
-0.04	-	-	0.28	0.43	0.79	28.4 -	14.0	0.62	0.50	0.24	11.1	0.117	5/20/16	8.0 -	3.9
-0.08	-	-	-0.18	-	-	-		0.48	-	-	3.8	0.330	5/31/16	19.0 -	8.7
-	-	0.02	-0.08	0.12	-0.15	-		-	-	-	-	-	-	8.6 -	0.0
0.35	-	-	1.93	0.95	1.34	30.7 -	22.9	0.56	0.48	0.30	1.1	0.160Y	61/28/99	59.2 -	44.1
-0.25	-	-	-1.33	1.83	1.37	-		-	-	-	-	-	-	22.0 -	8.5
1.57	-	-	0.91	-	-	26.6 -	16.0	-	-	-	-	0.24250Z	7/15/16	24.2 -	14.5
0.18	-	-	0.16	0.70	0.08	566.2 -	0.0	0.83	0.78	0.72	1.4	0.220	6/30/16	90.6 -	0.0
-	-	-	0.50	1.03	1.85	41.2 -	25.0	0.60	0.45	0.07	3.7	0.150	61/28/99	20.6 -	12.5
-	-0.03	-	0.66	1.07	0.80	31.3 -	21.3	-	-	-	-	-	-	20.7 -	14.1
0.56	-	-	1.54	1.27	1.10	21.3 -	14.1	-	-	-	-	-	-	32.8 -	21.8
-	0.61	-	3.29	3.79	3.37	15.6 -	9.6	1.10	0.48	1.39	2.7	0.180Y	61/28/99	51.4 -	31.4
-	-	-	0.45	0.47	0.43	15.5 -	11.8	0.47	0.47	0.46	7.7	0.03950	7/15/16	7.0 -	5.3
-3.35	-	-	-11.31	-1.26	2.64	-		0.26	1.25	2.25	2.4	0.050	61/28/99	20.6 -	3.7
-	-	0.90	3.38	3.46	3.65	13.5 -	11.1	0.30	0.37	0.33	0.7	-	-	45.7 -	37.5
1.57	-	-	1.17	2.53	-0.61	45.2 -	31.5	0.50	0.50	0.50	1.2	0.1250	6/3/16	52.9 -	36.9
-	-	-2.30	1.29	-8.15	-11.80	-		0.25	-	-	-	0.40	6/20/16	-	
0.21	-	-	1.10	0.97	0.30	9.6 -	7.0	0.89	1.08	-	9.4	0.22280	7/5/16	10.5 -	7.7
0.73	-	-	1.58	1.44	-0.27	28.9 -	19.2	-	-	-	-	-	-	45.7 -	30.4
0.37	-	-	1.69	0.97	1.89	27.0 -	19.4	0.51	0.46	0.39	1.3	0.140Y	61/28/99	45.7 -	32.7
0.24	-	-	1.06	1.22	1.71	14.9 -	8.8	0.24	0.48	0.69	2.0	0.060Y	12/15/16	15.8 -	9.3
8.88	-	-	-108.89	3.90	4.40	-		-	2.40	2.40	-	0.60Y	12/31/14	19.8 -	5.3
-	-	-	0.07	0.07	0.09	86.9 -	56.9	0.48	0.51	0.48	9.7	0.3750	6/27/16	6.1 -	4.0
-	-	-	0.30	0.41	0.36	71.5 -	51.1	1.24	1.18	1.03	6.6	0.3750	6/27/16	21.4 -	15.3
-	-	-	0.06	0.07	0.06	109.3 -	75.0	0.64	0.64	0.62	11.5	0.3255GH	6/27/16	6.6 -	4.5
-	-	-	-	-0.07	-	-		-	-	-	-	0.1779GH	6/27/16	10.9 -	9.2
-	-	-	-	0.01	0.04	-		-	0.62	0.91	-	0.36720	6/27/16	11.6 -	9.0
-	-	-	0.03	0.05	0.06	317.7 -	205.7	0.94	1.05	0.92	12.0	0.3750	6/27/16	9.5 -	6.2
-	-	-	0.13	0.13	0.14	54.7 -	42.6	-	-	-	-	0.35160	6/27/16	7.1 -	5.5
-	-	0.04	0.20	-0.11	2.02	8.4 -	4.6	-	0.10	0.51	-	-	-	1.7 -	0.9
0.17	-	-	0.22	0.71	0.79	47.2 -	28.2	0.20	0.20	0.20	2.6	0.050Y	6/20/16	10.4 -	6.2
0.26	-	-	2.06	1.97	2.06	23.9 -	17.6	1.48	1.44	1.40	3.4	0.380Y	61/28/99	49.3 -	36.2
0.88	-	-	3.24	4.28	4.54	12.6 -	8.3	0.28	0.50	0.72	0.8	0.020Y	6/28/16	40.9 -	26.8
-	-	-	-	0.02	0.06	-		-	1.08	1.50	-	0.070	9/23/16	8.2 -	4.7
0.63	-	-	3.47	2.99	-2.13	13.7 -	7.2	1.32	1.10	0.80	3.6	0.370Y	61/28/99	47.4 -	25.1
0.26	-	-	1.25	-	-	11.9 -	11.2	0.32	-	-	2.2	0.160Y	61/28/99	14.9 -	13.9
0.26	-	-	1.25	-	-	14.2 -	9.0	0.32	-	-	2.1	0.160Y	61/28/99	17.8 -	11.3
0.48	-	-	2.06	2.03	1.93	49.7 -	38.8	-	-	-	-	-	-	102.3 -	79.9
-	-	-	0.04	0.54	0.91	-		0.56	0.50	0.45	-	0.54690	7/1/16	-	
-	-	-	2.38	0.75	728.28	-		1.78	0.58	-	-	0.4780Y	5/13/16	-	
1.66	-	-	4.69	4.48	3.59	12.3 -	7.5	1.52	1.32	1.24	3.3	0.40Y	61/28/99	57.5 -	35.1
-	-	1.89	3.45	0.39	5.64	4.5 -	0.0	1.84	1.35	1.72	29.9	0.350	6/16/16	15.6 -	0.0
0.24	-	-	0.57	-	-	35.1 -	0.0	-	-	-	-	-	-	20.0 -	0.0
0.24	-	-	0.57	-	-	42.6 -	27.2	-	-	-	-	-	-	24.3 -	15.5
-	-	-	-	-0.26	-0.33	-		-	0.80	1.28	-	0.3750	6/27/16	10.4 -	9.5
-0.75	-	-	-2.96	-3.38	-3.42	-		-	-	-	-	1.0Y	11/28/08	-	
0.74	-	-	2.06	-1.54	-8.64	-		-	-	-	-	0.010Y	11/26/10	-	
0.15	-	-	1.12	2.49	2.51	37.2 -	24.0	-	-	5.00	-	5.7Y	6/21/13	41.7 -	26.9
-	-	-	0.48	0.32	0.17	74.5 -	56.0	1.15	3.50	2.10	3.6	0.37190Y	6/24/16	35.8 -	26.9
-0.10	-	-	-2.49	-12.86	-0.37	-		0.54	0.72	0.72	3.8	0.180Y	61/28/99	21.1 -	6.6
2.30	-	-	9.08	7.42	6.67	16.9 -	13.7	2.69	2.42	1.68	1.9	0.760Y	01/28/99	153.3 -	124.2

T27

SYMBOL	COMPANY	NATURE OF BUSINESS	FISCAL YEAR-END	TOTAL REV. $MILL	NET INCOME $MILL	TOTAL ASSETS $MILL	NET STK EQUITY $MILL	NO OF INST	INST. HOLDINGS (SHARES)
GEK	General Electric Capital Corp.	Credit & Lending	12/31/14		7234.0	500216.0	87499.0		
GE	General Electric Co	Electrical Equipment	12/31/15	117386.0	-6126.0	492692.0	98274.0	2799	5992432203
GE	General Electric Co	Electrical Equipment	12/31/15	117386.0	-6126.0	492692.0	98274.0	2799	5992432203
GGP	General Growth Properties Inc	REITs	12/31/15	2403.9	1374.6	24073.6	8270.0		
GIS	General Mills, Inc.	Food	5/31/15	17630.3	1221.3	21964.5	4996.7	1513	477512479
GM	General Motors Co	Autos- Manufacturing	12/31/15	152356.0	9687.0	194520.0	39871.0	1138	1185356542
GM 26	General Motors Financial Co Inc	Credit & Lending	12/31/14		537.0	47724.0	7392.0	52	9475070
GSI	General Steel Holdings Inc	Non-Precious Metals	12/31/14	2289.4	-48.7	2565.2	-345.0	29	384482
GCO	Genesco Inc	Retail - Apparel and Accessories	1/30/16	3022.2	94.6	1541.5	955.2	265	23391708
GWR	Genesee & Wyoming Inc.	Rail	12/31/15	2000.4	225.0	6795.6	2519.5	379	62094714
GEL	Genesis Energy L.P.	Equipment & Services	12/31/15	2246.5	422.5	5459.6		223	88816354
GEN	Genesis Healthcare Inc	Hospitals & Health Care Facilities	12/31/15	5619.2	-526.8	6091.5	-436.3	28	1463447
GNE	Genie Energy Ltd.	Electric Utilities	12/31/15	210.1	-7.5	155.8	123.4	65	4713770
G	Genpact Ltd	Business Services	12/31/15	2461.0	239.8	2793.5	1304.4	280	189366782
GPC	Genuine Parts Co.	Auto Parts	12/31/15	15280.0	705.7	8144.8	3146.6	893	130603441
GNW	Genworth Financial, Inc. (Holding C	Life & Health	12/31/15	8548.0	-615.0	106431.0	12824.0	499	413711639
GEO	Geo Group Inc (The) (New)	REITs	12/31/15	1843.3	139.4	3503.3	1006.7	320	72626237
GPRK	GeoPark Ltd	Production & Extraction	12/31/15	209.7	-234.0	703.8	146.7		
GPE PRA	Georgia Power Co.	Electric Utilities	12/31/15	8326.0	1277.0	32865.0	10985.0		
GGB	Gerdau S.A.	Non-Precious Metals	12/31/15	43581.2	-4551.4	70094.7	31685.8	184	209495088
GTY	Getty Realty Corp.	REITs	12/31/15	110.7	37.4	899.1	406.6	171	19305260
GIMO	Gigamon Inc	IT Services	12/26/15	222.0	6.2	279.9	155.4	220	28046575
GIL	Gildan Activewear Inc	Apparel, Footwear & Accessories	1/3/16	2959.2	304.9	2834.3	2188.4	275	186523891
GKOS	Glaukos Corp	Medical Instruments & Equipment	12/31/15	71.7	-37.2		95.2	81	20550182
GSK	GlaxoSmithKline Plc	Pharmaceuticals	12/31/15	23923.0	8422.0	53446.0	5114.0	1000	267780323
BRSS	Global Brass & Copper Holdings Inc	Metal Products	12/31/15	1506.2	35.6	557.2	56.4	157	20623829
GRME	Global Medical REIT Inc	Services	12/31/15	2.1	-1.6	65.3	-0.1		
GNL	Global Net Lease Inc	REITs	12/31/15	205.3	-2.1	2548.0	1205.4	127	56728094
GLP	Global Partners LP	Equipment & Services	12/31/15	10314.9	43.6	2663.7		95	15950623
GPN	Global Payments, Inc.	Business Services	5/31/15	2773.7	278.0	5793.5	758.0	556	135462358
GSL	Global Ship Lease, Inc	Shipping	12/31/15	164.9	-28.9	904.9	396.8		
GLOB	Globant SA	IT Services	12/31/15	253.8	31.7	222.9	160.1	109	16584989
GMED	Globus Medical Inc	Medical Instruments & Equipment	12/31/15	544.8	112.8	834.1	715.3		
GMS	GMS Inc	Construction Materials	4/30/15	1570.1	-13.8	1154.6	297.5		
GNC	GNC Holdings Inc	Retail - Food & Beverage, Drug & To	12/31/15	2639.2	219.3	2552.0	468.6	299	71505448
GDDY	GoDaddy Inc	Internet & Software	12/31/15	1607.3	-75.6	3498.8	425.8	170	68157378
GOL	Gol Linhas Aereas Inteligentes SA	Airlines/Air Freight	12/31/15	9778.0	-4460.9	10368.4	-4546.5	83	10367591
GFI	Gold Fields Ltd.	Precious Metals	12/31/15	2545.4	-345.0	5513.8	2554.9	244	382961243
GG	Goldcorp Inc	Precious Metals	12/31/15	4375.0	-4158.0	21428.0	12848.0	562	554998275
GSBD	Goldman Sachs BDC Inc	Finance Intermediaries & Services	12/31/15	118.4	74.6	1132.8	688.6	56	10744233
GS	Goldman Sachs Group, Inc.	Finance Intermediaries & Services	12/31/15	39208.0	6083.0	861395.0	86728.0	1519	346847610
GER	Goldman Sachs MLP Energy Renai	Finance Intermediaries & Services	11/30/14	17.0	4.1	1821.5	1242.6		
GMZ	Goldman Sachs MLP Income Oppor	Finance Intermediaries & Services	11/30/14	15.4	0.0	1177.5	846.8	54	6861560
GPX	GP Strategies Corp.	Business Services	12/31/15	490.3	18.8	302.3	158.3	110	15922882
GRA	Grace (WR) & Co	Specialty Chemicals	12/31/15	3051.5	144.2	3676.0	207.8	377	64234200
GGG	Graco Inc	Industrial Machinery & Equipment	12/25/15	1286.5	345.7	1391.4	635.6	442	60384627
GHM	Graham Corp.	Industrial Machinery & Equipment	3/31/16	90.0	6.1	143.1	109.4	117	9059934
GHC	Graham Holdings Co.	Educational Services	12/31/15	2586.1	-100.7	4353.0	2490.7	333	4557944
GWW	Grainger (W.W.) Inc.	Electrical Equipment	12/31/15	9973.4	769.0	5857.8	2266.6	828	61815746
GPT	Gramercy Property Trust	REITs	12/31/15	237.3	-47.9	5840.9	2911.3	292	331080560
GRAM	Grana y Montero S.A.A. (Peru)	Construction Services	12/31/15	7832.4	88.2	8991.8	2654.6	33	15891438
GVA	Granite Construction Inc.	Construction Services	12/31/15	2371.0	60.5	1627.9	839.2	270	42068167
GRP U	Granite Real Estate Investment Tru	REITs	12/31/15	216.3	193.3	2731.8	1849.0		
GPK	Graphic Packaging Holding Co	Containers & Packaging	12/31/15	4160.2	230.1	4256.1	1101.7	338	447348017
GTN	Gray Television Inc	Radio & Television	12/31/15	597.4	39.3	2143.2	429.3	229	61149592
AJX	Great Ajax Corp	REITs	12/31/15	37.5	24.8	615.4	227.8	57	10087591
GXP	Great Plains Energy Inc	Electric Utilities	12/31/15	2502.2	213.0	10738.6	3695.5	421	135127355
GWB	Great Western Bancorp Inc	Banking	9/30/15	397.3	109.1	9798.7	1459.3	210	58393694
GB	Greatbatch Inc	Medical Instruments & Equipment	1/1/16	800.4	-7.6	2982.1	850.6	277	33227195
GDOT	Green Dot Corp	Credit & Lending	12/31/15	694.7	38.4	1691.4	663.3	214	42660662
GBX	Greenbrier Companies Inc (The)	Construction Services	8/31/15	2605.3	192.8	1790.5	732.8	309	28190987
GHL	Greenhill & Co Inc	Finance Intermediaries & Services	12/31/15	261.6	25.6	423.8	283.4	250	35017618
GEF	Greif Inc	Containers & Packaging	10/31/15	3616.7	71.9	3315.7	1015.6	258	26974998
GFF	Griffon Corp.	Metal Products	9/30/15	2016.0	34.3	1731.4	430.5	172	36846322
GPI	Group 1 Automotive, Inc.	Retail - Automotive	12/31/15	10632.5	94.0	4414.9	918.3	294	29077142
GRUB	GrubHub Inc	Internet & Software	12/31/15	361.8	38.1	1060.2	877.6	189	97083497
PAC	Grupo Aeroportuario del Pacifico, S.	Airlines/Air Freight	12/31/15	8106.9	2726.0	31473.4	21274.0	127	6717434
ASR	Grupo Aeroportuario del Sureste SA	Airlines/Air Freight	12/31/15	8994.6	2913.7	26125.9	20408.1	126	10003428
AVAL	Grupo Aval Acciones Y Valores SA	Banking	12/31/15	4075598.0	2041364.0	216679264.0	14567621.0	50	76659211
BSMX	Grupo Financiero Santander Mexico	Banking	12/31/15	85.0	14.0	1176.0	109.6		
SUPV	Grupo Supervielle SA	Banking	12/31/15		674.1	33045.8	2373.7		
TV	Grupo Televisa, S.A.	Radio & Television	12/31/15	88051.8	10899.1	281473.8	87382.9	326	326815384
GTT	GTT Communications, Inc	Internet & Software	12/31/15	369.3	19.3	596.5	110.5	121	22078061
GSH	Guangshen Railway Co., Ltd.	Rail	12/31/15	15725.3	1070.8	31943.3	27462.5	44	1143489
GES	GUESS ?, Inc.	Retail - Apparel and Accessories	1/30/16	2204.3	81.9	1538.7	1018.5	306	73233172
GBAB	Guggenheim Build America Bonds	Holding and other Investment Office	5/31/15	31.2	25.7	533.5	406.7	41	3963289
GGM	Guggenheim Credit Allocation Fund	Holding and other Investment Office	5/31/15	16.1	12.9	230.8	154.8	22	702466
GPM	Guggenheim Enhanced Equity Inco	Holding and other Investment Office	12/31/15	4.4	1.2	241.8	159.7	54	5465277
GGE	Guggenheim Enhanced Equity Strat	Holding and other Investment Office	10/31/15	2.5	0.6	138.7	91.8	51	1521842
GEQ	Guggenheim Equal Weight Enhanc	Holding and other Investment Office	12/31/14	4.2	1.1	233.8	182.9	34	1559264

EARNINGS PER SHARE QUARTERLY			ANNUAL			P/E RATIO		DIVIDENDS PER SHARE			AV. YLD	DIV. DECLARED		PRICE RANGE 2015	
1st	2nd	3rd	2015	2014	2013			2015	2014	2013	%	AMOUNT	PAYABLE		
-	-	-	-	-	-	-	-	-	1.22	1.24	-	0.29380Z	8/16/16	26.3 -	24.3
-0.01	-	-	-0.61	1.50	1.27	-	-	0.92	0.89	0 79	6.8	0.230Y	01/20/99	30.7 -	0.0
-0.01	-	-	-0.61	1.50	1.27	-	-	0.92	0.89	0.79	3.2	0.230Y	61/28/99	31.9 -	23.3
0.20	-	-	1.43	0.69	0.31	21.1 -	17.0	0.71	0.63	0.51	2.6	0.39840Z	61/28/99	30.2 -	24.4
-	-	0.59	1.97	2.83	2.79	33.2 -	27.5	1.67	1.55	1.32	2.9	0.460Y	61/28/99	65.4 -	54.1
1.24	-	-	5.91	1.65	2.38	6.2 -	4.6	1.38	1.20	-	4.3	0.380Y	61/28/99	36.5 -	26.9
-	-	-4.39	-	-4.30	-3.00	-	-	-	-	-	-	-	-	4.1 -	0.7
0.50	-	-	4.12	3.92	4.60	17.5 -	12.7	-	-	-	-	0.3750Y	4/30/13	72.3 -	52.1
0.47	-	-	3.89	4.58	4.79	21.8 -	11.5	-	-	-	-	1.250	10/1/15	84.8 -	44.5
0.32	-	-	4.09	1.18	1.03	12.2 -	5.0	2.47	2.23	2.02	6.7	0.67250	61/28/99	49.8 -	20.4
-0.48	-	-	-4.97	-0.02	-0.28	-	-	-	-	-	-	-	-	7.7 -	1.4
0.26	-	-	-0.40	-1.31	-0.36	-	-	0.12	0.06	-	1.2	0.060	5/20/16	13.5 -	6.4
0.27	-	-	1.09	0.85	0.97	26.0 -	19.5	-	-	-	-	2.24G7	61/28/99	28.4 -	21.2
1.05	-	-	4.63	4.61	4.40	21.6 -	16.7	2.46	2.30	2.15	2.8	0.65750Y	61/28/99	99.8 -	77.4
0.11	-	-	-1.24	-2.51	1.12	-	-	-	-	-	-	-	-	8.1 -	1.6
0.44	-	-	1.88	1.98	1.61	20.5 -	13.9	2.51	0.62	-	7.9	0.650Z	5/12/16	38.5 -	26.1
-	-	-	-4.05	0.13	0.47	-	-	-	-	-	-	-	-	-	-
-	-	-	-	-	-	-	-	6.50	6.50	6.50	24.2	1.6250Y	7/1/16	31.4 -	0.0
-	-	-	-	-	-	-	-	0.17	0.21	0.16	10 4	-	-	2.9 -	0.8
-	-	0.35	-2.69	0.82	0.93	-	-	-	-	-	-	-	-	-	-
0.23	-	-	1.11	0.69	2.08	18.8 -	13.7	1.15	0.96	0.85	6 6	0.250Z	7/7/16	20.9 -	15.3
0.08	-	-	0.17	-1.27	-0.39	204.6 -	112.4	-	-	-	-	-	-	34.8 -	19.1
-	-	0.41	1.25	1.46	1.30	36.5 -	0.0	0.26	0.22	0.18	0.8	0.0780	6/13/16	45.7 -	0.0
0.03	-	-	-2.13	-5.29	-6.21	-	-	-	-	-	-	-	-	32.9 -	14.8
-	-	0.11	1 72	0.57	1.11	26.2 -	21.8	1.55	1.60	1.55	3.8	-	-	45.1 -	37.6
0.57	-	-	1.66	1.49	0.49	16.8 -	9.7	0.15	0.15	0.04	0.7	0.03750	5/26/16	27.8 -	16.0
-3.11	-	-	-6.44	-1.64	-4.00	-	-	1.02	0.09	-	1632.0	0.08520Z	4/29/16	0.1 -	0.0
0.04	-	-	-0.01	-0.43	-1.28	-	-	0.37	0.71	0.71	4.4	0.05920Y	9/15/16	9.3 -	6.5
-0.21	-	-	1.11	3.95	1.42	37.5 -	11.1	2.73	2.53	2.34	11.5	0.46250	61/28/99	41.6 -	12.3
-	-	0.53	2.06	1.69	1.38	37.7 -	24.8	0.04	0.04	0.04	0.1	0.010Y	61/28/99	77.7 -	51.1
-	-	0.15	-0.67	0.10	0.68	-	-	0.20	-	-	-	0.54690	7/1/16	-	-
0.11	-	-	0.90	0.79	0.48	44.6 -	25.7	-	-	-	-	-	-	40.1 -	23.1
0.29	-	-	1.17	0.97	0.73	24.1 -	17.7	-	-	-	-	-	-	28.2 -	20.7
-	-	-	-0.43	-0.59	-	-	-	-	-	-	-	-	-	22.8 -	21.9
0.69	-	-	2.60	2.81	2.72	19.6 -	9.1	0.72	0.64	0.60	2.0	0.20Y	61/28/99	50.9 -	23.6
-0.15	-	-	-0.81	-1.11	-1.58	-	-	-	-	-	-	-	-	34.2 -	23.6
-	-	-	-0.42	-0.13	-2.88	-	-	-	-	-	-	-	-	25.4 -	2.5
-	-	-	-0.45	-0.04	-0.33	-	-	0.02	0.03	0.07	0.6	-	-	4.7 -	2.1
-	-	-0.23	-5.03	-2.66	-3.34	-	-	0.45	0.60	0.60	2.7	0.020	3/28/16	25.3 -	0.0
0.58	-	-	2.14	1.77	0.67	11.8 -	8.1	1.00	1.69	0.50	8.8	0.450	7/15/16	25.2 -	17.4
2.68	-	-	12.14	17.07	15.46	18 0 -	11.6	2.55	2.25	2.05	1.4	0.40630Z	8/1/16	218.4 -	140.7
-	-	-	-	0.05	-	-	-	-	0.32	-	-	0.160	5/27/16	14.7 -	3.4
-	-	-	-	-	-	-	-	-	1.29	-	-	0.210	5/27/16	17.7 -	5.2
0.23	-	-	1.09	1.43	1.23	32.2 -	20.0	-	-	-	-	0.025	2/1/89	35.1 -	21.8
-0.04	-	-	1.99	3.63	3.30	42.2 -	31.7	-	-	-	-	0.170Y	61/28/99	83.9 -	63.1
0.70	-	-	5.86	3.65	3.36	14.7 -	10.8	1.20	1.10	1.00	1.6	0.330Y	61/28/99	86.0 -	63.6
-	-	0.13	1.45	1.00	1.11	15.0 -	10.3	0.20	0.13	0.11	1.1	0.090Y	6/23/16	21.8 -	14.9
6.59	-	-	-17 87	195.03	32.05	-	-	9.10	10.20	-	1.6	1.210Y	61/28/99	718.7 -	428.1
2.98	-	-	11.56	11.45	11.13	21.2 -	15.8	4.59	4.17	3.59	2.1	1.220Y	61/28/99	245.4 -	182.8
-0.01	-	-	-0.30	0.08	0.34	-	-	0.51	0.50	0.40	6.7	0.110Z	7/15/16	9.1 -	6.5
-	-	-	0.13	0.45	0.53	58 8 -	16.9	0.76	0.81	-	16.4	-	-	7.6 -	2.2
-0.28	-	-	1.52	0.64	-0.94	31.5 -	19.2	0.52	0.52	0.52	1.4	0.130Y	61/28/99	47.9 -	29.1
-	-	-	-	-	3.09	-	-	2.30	2.21	2.11	6.8	0.2030	7/15/16	44.4 -	0.0
0.18	-	-	0.70	0.27	0.42	21.7 -	15.3	0.20	-	-	1.5	0.050Y	7/5/16	15.2 -	10.7
0.12	-	-	0.57	0.82	0.32	31.3 -	17.7	-	-	-	-	0.030Y	10/15/08	17.9 -	10.1
0.50	-	-	1.68	0.40	-	8.6 -	5.5	0.64	-	-	5.1	0.250Y	5/20/16	14.4 -	9.2
0.17	-	-	1.37	1.57	1.62	23.9 -	17.6	1.00	0.94	0.88	3.6	1.050Y	61/28/99	32.7 -	24.2
-	0.55	-	1.90	1.81	484.29	17.9 -	12.1	0.36	1.76	208.32	1.3	0.140	5/24/16	34.0 -	22.9
-0.41	-	-	-0.29	2.14	1.43	-	-	-	-	-	-	-	-	39.3 -	19.3
0.63	-	-	0.72	0.90	0.76	32.6 -	20.5	-	-	-	-	-	-	23.5 -	14.8
-	1.41	-	5.93	3.44	-0.41	10.4 -	3.5	0.60	0.15	-	1.7	0.20Y	5/11/16	61.4 -	21.0
0.14	-	-	0.82	1.43	1.55	51.3 -	23.0	1.80	1.80	1.80	6.3	0.450Y	6/22/16	42.1 -	18.9
-	0.53	-	1.23	1.56	2.52	31.9 -	19.5	1.68	1.68	1.68	5.2	0.630Y	61/28/99	39.2 -	24.0
-	0.14	-	0.73	0.00	0.07	26.1 -	18.8	0.16	0.12	0.10	1.0	0.050Y	6/23/16	19.0 -	13.8
1.47	-	-	3.90	3.60	4.32	24.9 -	12.8	0.83	0.70	0.65	1.1	0.230Y	61/28/99	97.0 -	49.8
0.12	-	-	0.44	0.30	0.12	92.7 -	41.7	-	-	-	-	-	-	40.8 -	18.3
-	-	-	5.98	4.27	4.24	17.1 -	11.5	56.10	58.57	22.59	66.1	-	-	102.5 -	68.5
-	-	1.70	9.71	7.61	7.66	17.1 -	12.5	50.05	-	82.72	34.1	-	-	165.8 -	121.4
-	-	-	-	-	-	-	-	2019.35	354.76	-	26191.7	-	-	9.9 -	5.6
-	-	-	2.06	1.96	3.93	4.8 -	3.3	4.45	2.39	14.97	52.2	-	-	9.8 -	6.9
-	-	-	-	-	-	-	-	-	-	-	-	-	-	11.5 -	11.2
-	-	-	3.52	1.74	2.50	11.3 -	6.7	1.58	-	3.19	5.4	-	-	39.7 -	23.5
0.02	-	-	0.54	-0.85	-0.95	48.2 -	23.5	-	-	-	-	-	-	26.1 -	12.7
-	-	-	0.15	0.09	0.18	224.5 -	126.7	2.16	3.52	3.44	9.1	-	-	33.7 -	19.0
-0.30	-	-	1.11	1.80	2.05	21.0 -	14.1	0.90	0.80	2.00	4.5	0.2250Y	61/28/99	23.3 -	15.6
-	-	-	1.48	1.63	1.65	16 6 -	13.7	1.66	1.66	1.80	7.5	0.13820	6/30/16	24.6 -	20.3
-	-	-	1.95	1.64	-	11.9 -	9.0	2.16	1.46	-	10.7	0.18130	6/30/16	23.3 -	17.5
-	-	-	0.06	-0.06	-0.05	146.2 -	106.0	0.96	0.96	0.96	12.7	0.240	6/30/16	8.8 -	6.4
-	-	-	0.12	-0.26	-0.15	146.9 -	110.1	1.94	1 94	1 77	12.4	0.4050	5/31/16	17.6 -	13.2
-	-	-	-	0.12	0.07	-	-	-	1.75	1.76	-	0.43750	4/29/16	20.2 -	13.8

SYMBOL	COMPANY	NATURE OF BUSINESS	FISCAL YEAR-END	TOTAL REV. $MILL	NET INCOME $MILL	TOTAL ASSETS $MILL	NET STK EQUITY $MILL	NO OF INST	INST. HOLDINGS (SHARES)
GOF	Guggenheim Strategic Opportunitie	Holding and other Investment Office	5/31/15	28.1	21.1	522.4	343.0	52	5071047
GWRE	Guidewire Software Inc	Internet & Software	7/31/15	380.5	9.9	799.9	689.4	244	77560090
GLF	GulfMark Offshore, Inc.	Equipment & Services	12/31/15	274.8	-215.2	1370.3	698.3	174	27337052
HAE	Haemonetics Corp.	Medical Instruments & Equipment	4/2/16	908.8	-55.6	1319.1	721.6	249	58094618
HK	Halcon Resources Corp	Production & Extraction	12/31/15	550.3	-1922.6	3458.7	52.4	162	49546479
HAL	Halliburton Company	Equipment & Services	12/31/15	23633.0	-671.0	36942.0	15462.0	1338	782868126
HYH	Halyard Health Inc	Medical Instruments & Equipment	12/31/15	1574.4	-426.3	2000.2	1055.3	389	38443568
HPS	Hancock John Preferred Income Fd	Holding and other Investment Office	7/31/15	55.6	45.5	912.8	601.1	58	4430887
HPF	Hancock John Preferred Income Fu	Holding and other Investment Office	7/31/15	42.5	34.8	698.1	458.7	65	1629311
HTD	Hancock John Tax-Advantaged Divi	Holding and other Investment Office	10/31/15	64.4	50.4	1268.8	835.7	85	7127375
HBI	HanesBrands Inc	Apparel, Footwear & Accessories	1/2/16	5731.5	428.9	5619.0	1275.9	706	338245700
HASI	Hannon Armstrong Sustainable Infr	REITs	12/31/15	32.3	8.0	1469.6	428.2	147	27928254
THG	Hanover Insurance Group Inc	General Insurance	12/31/15	5034.0	331.5	13790.9	2844.4	381	44929217
HOG	Harley-Davidson Inc	Autos- Manufacturing	12/31/15	5995.4	752.2	9991.2	1839.7	785	191154963
HAR	Harman International Industries, Inc	Household Appliances, Electronics &	6/30/15	6155.3	342.7	5929.8	2374.6	616	77362890
HMY	Harmony Gold Mining Co. Ltd.	Precious Metals	6/30/15	1348.0	-374.0	2972.0	2200.0	124	169940312
HRS	Harris Corp.	Defense	7/3/15	5083.0	334.0	13129.0	3397.0	807	145904594
HSC	Harsco Corp.	Industrial Machinery & Equipment	12/31/15	1723.1	6.2	2071.3	271.6	323	69299759
HHS	Harte-Hanks Inc	Advertising	12/31/15	495.3	-170.9	414.6	140.3	177	36933822
HIG	Hartford Financial Services Group I	General Insurance	12/31/15	18377.0	1682.0	228348.0	17642.0	938	432511306
HNR	Harvest Natural Resources Inc	Production & Extraction	12/31/15	-	-98.6	47.8	36.8	96	12594366
HTS	Hatteras Financial Corp	REITs	12/31/15	313.0	51.6	16137.5	2143.4	257	82104204
HVT	Haverty Furniture Cos., Inc.	Retail - Furniture & Home Furnishing	12/31/15	805.2	27.8	471.3	301.7	152	17836562
HE	Hawaiian Electric Industries Inc	Electric Utilities	12/31/15	2603.0	161.8	11790.2	1961.9	314	50635303
HCA	HCA Holdings Inc	Hospitals & Health Care Facilities	12/31/15	39678.0	2129.0	32744.0	-7599.0	753	313804354
HCI	HCI Group Inc	General Insurance	12/31/15	286.0	65.9	637.0	237.7	148	8247635
HCP	HCP, Inc.	REITs	12/31/15	2544.3	-559.2	21449.8	9343.6	890	465498360
HDB	HDFC Bank Ltd	Banking		-		-		361	158438137
HW	Headwaters Inc	Refining & Marketing	9/30/15	895.3	130.8	979.0	237.9	303	74066768
HR	Healthcare Realty Trust, Inc.	REITs	12/31/15	388.5	69.4	2816.7	1242.7	303	111279617
HTA	Healthcare Trust Of America Inc	REITs	12/31/15	403.8	32.9	3172.3	1379.4	270	134881095
HLS	HealthSouth Corp	Hospitals & Health Care Facilities	12/31/15	3115.7	183.1	4606.1	611.4	339	104558194
HL	Hecla Mining Co	Precious Metals	12/31/15	443.6	-87.0	2221.9	1338.9	263	217247096
HEI A	Heico Corp.	Aerospace	10/31/15	1188.6	133.4	1736.4	809.9	251	21507185
HLX	Helix Energy Solutions Group Inc	Equipment & Services	12/31/15	695.8	-377.0	2412.0	1279.0	298	99751191
HP	Helmerich & Payne, Inc.	Production & Extraction	9/30/15	3165.4	422.2	7152.0	4897.5	730	136276709
HLF	Herbalife Ltd.	Household & Personal Products	12/31/15	4469.0	339.1	2477.9	-53.5	343	104108716
HTGC	Hercules Capital Inc	Holding and other Investment Office	12/31/15	140.3	73.5	1334.8	717.1	197	33682875
HRTG	Heritage Insurance Holdings Inc	General Insurance	12/31/15	394.8	92.5	837.4	356.6	140	16480428
HT	Hersha Hospitality Trust	REITs	12/31/15	470.4	42.2	1969.8	678.0	224	64956422
HSY	Hershey Company (The)	Food	12/31/15	7386.6	513.0	5344.4	998.0	936	133571065
HTZ	Hertz Global Holdings Inc	Miscellaneous Transportation Servic	12/31/15	10535.0	273.0	23358.0	2019.0	509	555236567
HES	Hess Corp	Production & Extraction	12/31/15	6561.0	-3056.0	34195.0	19386.0	838	286106396
HPE	Hewlett Packard Enterprise Co	IT Services	10/31/15	52107.0	2461.0	81270.0	33535.0	820	1335419232
HXL	Hexcel Corp.	Plastics	12/31/15	1861.2	237.2	2187.4	1179.6	416	109117384
HF	HFF Inc	Credit & Lending	12/31/15	502.0	84.0	742.5	214.5	218	36592697
HGG	hhgregg Inc	Retail - Appliances and Electronics	3/31/16	1960.0	-54.9	385.4	121.4	78	19148048
HCLP	Hi-Crush Partners LP	Mining	12/31/15	339.6	28.3	419.6	-	84	8356192
ONE	Higher One Holdings Inc.	Business Services	12/31/15	158.0	10.9	193.0	108.7	101	25522087
HIW	Highwoods Properties, Inc.	REITs	12/31/15	604.7	101.3	4493.4	1601.3	330	110080436
HIL	Hill International Inc	Business Services	12/31/15	720.6	6.9	442.6	114.0	89	29044532
HRC	Hill-Rom Holdings, Inc.	Medical Instruments & Equipment	9/30/15	1988.2	47.7	4457.6	1146.9	27	4651596
HI	Hillenbrand Inc	Industrial Machinery & Equipment	9/30/15	1596.8	111.4	1808.1	594.1	246	51952134
HTH	Hilltop Holdings, Inc.	Banking	12/31/15	1697.5	211.0	11867.0	1737.0	211	57850912
HLT	Hilton Worldwide Holdings Inc	Hotels, Restaurants & Travel	12/31/15	11272.0	1404.0	25716.0	5985.0	428	934635922
HNI	HNI Corp	Office Equipment & Furniture	1/2/16	2304.4	105.4	1263.9	477.0	228	41908640
HMLP	Hoegh LNG Partners LP	Shipping	12/31/15	57.5	41.3	763.7	249.8	32	9467070
HEP	Holly Energy Partners LP	Equipment & Services	12/31/15	358.9	148.3	1534.5	-	135	28623421
HFC	HollyFrontier Corp.	Refining & Marketing	12/31/15	13237.9	740.1	8388.3	5253.4	592	159212327
HD	Home Depot Inc	Retail - Hardware & Home Improvem	1/31/16	88519.0	7009.0	42549.0	6316.0	2227	1080127128
HMC	Honda Motor Co., Ltd.(Honda Giken	Autos- Manufacturing	3/31/15	13328099.0	509435.0	18425837.0	7108627.0	327	61163947
HON	Honeywell International Inc	Auto Parts	12/31/15	38581.0	4768.0	49316.0	18573.0	1739	667302155
HMN	Horace Mann Educators Corp	General Insurance	12/31/15	1080.4	93.5	10059.3	1264.7	238	44878275
HZN	Horizon Global Corp	Auto Parts	12/31/15	575.5	8.3	331.6	2.0	106	17341925
HRL	Hormel Foods Corp.	Food	10/25/15	9263.9	686.1	6139.8	3998.2	660	187118628
HOS	Hornbeck Offshore Services Inc	Equipment & Services	12/31/15	476.1	66.8	2984.4	1446.2	222	42844429
DHI	Horton (D.R.) Inc.	Builders	9/30/15	10824.0	750.7	11151.0	5894.3	723	341810375
HST	Host Hotels & Resorts Inc	REITs	12/31/15	5387.0	558.0	11784.0	7064.0	636	896551130
HLI	Houlihan Lokey Inc	Wealth Management	3/31/16	693.8	69.7	1070.9	651.2	85	13794280
HOV	Hovnanian Enterprises, Inc.	Builders	10/31/15	2148.5	-16.1	2603.3	-128.1	186	50437347
HHC	Howard Hughes Corp	Property, Real Estate & Developmen	12/31/15	797.1	126.7	5721.6	2360.1	278	35855731
HPQ	HP Inc	Computer Hardware & Equipment	10/31/15	103355.0	4554.0	106882.0	27768.0	1356	1582915013
HPQ	HP Inc	Computer Hardware & Equipment	10/31/15	103355.0	4554.0	106882.0	27768.0	1356	1582915013
HRG	HRG Group Inc	Household & Personal Products	9/30/15	5815.9	-556.8	32334.1	586.7	161	208062604
HSFC PRB	HSBC Finance Corp	Credit & Lending	12/31/15	1689.0	-431.0	24145.0	6635.0	-	
HSBC	HSBC Holdings Plc	Banking	12/31/15	91617.0	13522.0	2409656.0	188460.0	508	107886908
HUSI PRG	HSBC USA, Inc.	Banking	12/31/15	5173.0	330.0	188278.0	20525.0	5	158072
HNP	Huaneng Power International, Inc.	Electric Utilities	12/31/15	128904.9	13651.9	308866.4	84141.9	125	3606281
HUBB	Hubbell Inc.	Electrical Equipment	12/31/15	3390.4	277.3	3208.7	1740.6	324	49352318
HUBS	HubSpot Inc	Internet & Software	12/31/15	181.9	-46.1	220.4	121.7	156	30721941

T30

1st	2nd	3rd	2015	2014	2013	P/E	RATIO	2015	2014	2013	AV. YLD %	AMOUNT	PAYABLE	2015	
-	-	-	1.28	1.44	1.68	16.6	11.8	2.19	2.19	1.95	12.3	0.18210	6/30/16	21.2	15.1
-	-	-0.01	0.14	0.21	0.25	442.1	307.5	-	-	-	-	-	-	61.9	43.0
-3.66	-	-	-8.70	2.39	2.70	-	-	-	1.00	1.00	-	0.250Y	12/29/14	13.2	2.6
-	-	-1.17	0.32	0.67	0.74	135.8	81.7	-	-	-	-	-	-	43.4	26.1
-4.72	-	-	-18.66	2.95	-16.25	-	-	-	-	-	-	14.3750	12/1/15	6.6	0.2
-2.81	-	-	-0.79	4.11	2.36	-	-	0.72	0.63	0.53	1.9	0.180Y	61/28/99	46.2	28.5
0.30	-	-	-9.15	0.58	-	-	-	-	-	-	-	-	-	43.1	23.3
-	-	-	1.44	1.46	1.49	13.5	11.1	1.47	1.47	1.47	8.3	0.12220	6/30/16	19.4	16.1
-	-	-	1.64	1.64	1.71	13.6	11.1	1.68	1.68	1.68	8.4	0.140	6/30/16	22.2	18.3
-	-	-	1.38	1.54	1.30	18.1	13.7	1.45	1.35	1.18	6.9	0.1210	6/30/16	25.0	18.9
0.21	-	-	1.06	1.32	1.08	32.5	22.5	0.40	0.30	0.15	1.3	0.110Y	61/28/99	34.5	23.8
0.07	-	-	0.21	0.43	-0.68	101.5	77.9	1.08	0.92	0.42	5.8	0.30Z	7/14/16	21.3	16.4
1.80	-	-	7.40	6.28	5.59	12.3	9.6	1.69	1.52	1.36	2.1	0.460Y	61/28/99	91.2	71.3
1.36	-	-	3.69	3.88	3.28	16.4	10.2	1.24	1.10	0.84	2.5	0.350Y	61/28/99	60.4	37.5
-	-	1.22	4.84	3.36	2.04	26.2	13.9	1.32	1.20	0.60	1.4	0.350Y	61/28/99	126.9	67.5
0.03	-	-	-0.86	-0.27	-0.53	-	-	-	-	0.10	-	-	-	4.2	0.5
-	-	1.34	3.11	4.95	1.01	28.8	22.6	1.88	1.68	1.48	2.4	0.50Y	61/28/99	89.5	70.3
-0.14	-	-	0.08	-0.31	-2.82	222.0	45.9	0.82	0.82	0.82	8.6	0.05120Y	2/16/16	17.8	3.7
-0.09	-	-	-2.77	0.38	0.21	-	-	0.34	0.34	0.26	9.2	0.0850Y	3/15/16	6.5	1.0
0.79	-	-	3.96	1.73	0.34	12.5	9.5	0.78	0.66	0.50	1.8	0.210Y	61/28/99	40.6	07.0
-0.27	-	-	-2.18	-4.60	-2.25	-	-	-	-	-	-	-	-	2.1	0.3
-0.81	-	-	0.31	0.36	-1.59	58.2	36.0	1.90	2.00	2.45	12.6	0.47660Z	7/15/16	18.0	11.2
0.41	-	-	1.22	0.37	1.41	20.0	14.5	0.36	1.32	0.24	1.7	0.10Y	6/9/16	24.4	17.7
0.30	-	-	1.50	1.64	1.62	22.7	18.2	1.24	1.24	1.24	4.1	0.310Y	61/28/99	34.0	27.2
1.69	-	-	4.99	4.16	3.37	19.0	12.6	-	-	-	-	2.7Y	61/28/99	94.8	62.8
0.60	-	-	5.90	5.36	5.63	7.8	4.8	1.20	1.10	0.95	3.2	0.50Z	8/1/16	45.9	28.5
0.25	-	-	-1.21	2.00	2.13	-	-	2.26	2.18	2.10	6.3	0.5750Z	61/28/99	40.7	26.1
-	8.20	-	-	-	-	-	-	19.33	14.97	12.19	32.3	-	-	65.0	51.8
-	0.03	-	1.73	0.20	0.10	12.4	8.2	-	-	-	-	-	-	21.4	14.2
0.09	-	-	0.70	0.33	0.08	45.4	31.6	1.20	1.20	1.20	4.5	0.30Z	5/31/16	31.8	22.1
0.08	-	-	0.26	0.37	0.20	118.3	87.3	1.17	0.29	-	4.4	0.2950Z	61/28/99	30.8	22.7
0.61	-	-	1.91	2.29	2.58	25.0	16.2	0.88	0.78	0.36	2.3	0.230Y	7/15/16	47.7	30.9
-	-	-	-0.23	0.05	-0.08	-	-	0.01	0.01	0.02	0.4	0.8750Y	7/1/16	4.6	1.5
-	0.57	-	1.97	1.80	1.53	28.2	20.5	0.14	0.47	1.82	0.3	0.080Y	7/19/16	55.5	40.5
-0.26	-	-	-3.58	1.85	1.04	-	-	-	-	-	-	-	-	16.2	2.6
-	0.19	-	3.87	6.46	6.79	19.4	11.1	2.75	2.44	0.87	4.8	0.70Y	61/28/99	75.1	42.9
1.13	-	-	3.97	3.40	4.91	-	-	-	0.30	1.20	-	0.30	61/28/99	-	-
0.28	-	-	1.04	1.13	1.22	12.4	9.6	1.24	1.24	1.11	10.8	0.43750Z	7/30/16	12.9	10.0
0.24	-	-	3.05	1.82	2.36	8.9	4.2	0.05	-	-	0.3	0.060Y	7/1/16	27.1	12.9
-0.26	-	-	0.56	1.04	0.64	50.5	29.5	0.84	1.04	0.96	3.7	0.280Z	7/15/16	28.3	16.5
1.06	-	-	2.32	3.77	3.61	41.8	35.9	2.24	2.04	1.81	2.5	0.530Y	61/28/99	97.1	83.3
-0.12	-	-	0.60	-0.18	0.76	35.3	11.8	-	-	-	-	-	-	21.2	7.1
-1.72	-	-	-10.78	7.53	14.82	-	-	1.00	1.00	0.70	1.8	0.250Y	61/28/99	70.2	34.4
-	0.18	-	1.34	-	-	13.8	9.0	-	-	-	-	0.0550Y	61/28/99	18.5	12.1
0.59	-	-	2.44	2.12	1.04	22.3	15.7	0.40	-	-	0.9	0.110Y	61/28/99	54.5	38.4
0.36	-	-	2.18	1.61	1.36	21.0	9.9	1.80	1.83	-	5.4	1.87Y	2/19/16	45.8	21.7
-	-	-0.97	-4.72	0.01	0.74	-	-	-	-	-	-	-	-	6.4	1.5
-1.39	-	-	0.73	3.00	2.08	44.4	5.0	1.83	2.23	1.92	16.9	0.4750	8/14/15	32.4	3.7
0.08	-	-	0.23	0.31	0.20	16.7	8.2	-	-	-	-	-	-	4.3	1.9
4.49	-	-	1.00	1.19	1.44	48.9	36.8	1.70	1.70	1.70	4.0	21.56250Z	61/28/99	48.9	36.8
0.03	-	-	0.14	-0.25	0.04	39.1	20.4	-	-	-	-	-	-	5.5	2.9
-	0.33	-	0.82	1.04	1.74	70.5	52.8	0.63	0.59	0.53	1.2	0.170Y	61/28/99	57.8	43.3
-	0.41	-	1.74	1.72	1.01	18.4	14.2	0.80	0.79	0.78	2.8	0.20250Y	6/30/16	31.9	24.6
0.28	-	-	2.09	1.17	1.40	11.7	6.8	-	-	-	-	0.51560Y	7/30/10	24.5	14.3
0.31	-	-	1.42	0.68	0.45	20.7	12.1	0.14	-	-	0.6	0.070Y	61/28/99	29.4	17.2
0.26	-	-	2.32	1.35	1.39	22.9	13.3	1.04	0.99	0.96	2.4	0.2750Y	61/28/99	53.2	30.9
-	-	-	1.56	0.50	-	-	-	1.35	0.18	-	-	0.41250	5/13/16	-	-
0.52	-	-	1.60	1.20	0.88	23.0	14.1	2.17	2.04	1.93	6.9	0.5750	5/13/16	36.8	22.5
0.12	-	-	3.90	1.42	3.64	13.8	6.8	1.31	3.26	3.20	3.2	0.330Y	61/28/99	53.8	26.6
1.44	-	-	4.71	3.76	3.00	29.2	23.3	1.88	1.56	1.16	1.5	0.690Y	61/28/99	137.5	109.6
-	70.88	-	282.66	318.54	203.71	0.1	0.1	88.63	79.67	71.92	292.3	-	-	35.6	24.9
1.53	-	-	6.04	5.33	4.92	19.2	15.2	2.15	1.87	1.68	2.1	0.5950Y	61/28/99	115.8	91.6
0.61	-	-	2.20	2.47	2.66	17.2	12.5	1.00	0.92	0.78	3.0	0.2650Y	6/30/16	37.7	27.6
0.12	-	-	0.46	-	-	35.3	0.0	-	-	-	-	-	-	16.3	0.0
-	0.40	-	1.27	1.12	0.97	35.0	22.1	0.50	0.40	0.34	1.4	0.1450Y	61/28/99	44.5	26.0
-0.21	-	-	1.84	2.41	3.05	12.1	3.2	-	-	-	-	-	-	22.2	5.8
-	0.52	-	2.03	1.50	1.33	16.3	11.4	0.25	0.14	0.19	0.9	0.080Y	61/28/99	33.0	23.2
0.24	-	-	0.74	0.96	0.42	28.8	17.3	0.80	0.75	0.46	4.7	0.20Z	61/28/99	21.3	12.8
-	-	0.35	135.88	104.31	-	0.2	0.2	-	-	-	-	0.170Y	6/15/16	26.2	20.9
-	-0.06	-	-0.11	1.87	0.22	-	-	-	-	-	-	0.47660Z	10/15/07	3.2	1.3
2.69	-	-	1.60	-0.60	-1.87	92.5	50.8	-	-	-	-	-	-	148.0	81.3
-	0.36	-	2.48	2.62	2.62	5.0	4.7	0.67	0.61	0.55	5.6	0.1240Y	61/28/99	12.4	11.7
-	0.36	-	2.48	2.62	2.62	6.2	3.6	0.67	0.61	0.55	5.4	0.1240Y	61/28/99	15.4	9.0
-	-0.18	-	-2.81	-0.51	-0.67	-	-	-	-	-	-	-	-	14.5	10.3
-	-	-	-	-	-	-	-	1.59	1.59	1.59	6.3	0.39750Y	6/15/16	25.9	24.0
-	-	-	0.64	0.69	0.84	74.8	45.7	2.50	2.45	2.40	6.6	0.50780	7/15/16	47.9	29.3
-	-	-	-	-	-	-	-	1.63	1.63	1.63	7.0	0.40630Y	4/1/16	25.3	20.1
-	-	-	0.94	0.76	0.74	59.4	27.6	13.65	13.71	7.27	34.4	-	-	55.8	25.9
1.08	-	-	4.77	5.48	5.47	22.9	18.1	-	-	-	-	0.630Y	61/20/99	109.2	86.3
-0.29	-	-	-1.39	-1.40	-2.24	-	-	-	-	1.85	-	-	-	59.5	27.5

SYMBOL	COMPANY	NATURE OF BUSINESS	FISCAL YEAR-END	TOTAL REV. $MILL	NET INCOME $MILL	TOTAL ASSETS $MILL	NET STK EQUITY $MILL	NO OF INST	INST. HOLDINGS (SHARES)
HBM	HudBay Minerals Inc	Precious Metals	12/31/15	886.1	-331.4	4479.6	1787.3	106	170167683
HPP	Hudson Pacific Properties Inc	REITs	12/31/15	520.9	-16.1	6254.0	1676.0	201	95900904
HGT	Hugoton Royalty Trust (TX)	Oil Royalty Traders	12/31/15	8.2	7.8	88.2	86.9	122	5256092
HUM	Humana Inc	Life & Health	12/31/15	54289.0	1276.0	24705.0	10346.0	791	160487098
HII	Huntington Ingalls Industries, Inc.	Defense	12/31/15	7020.0	404.0	6024.0	1490.0	437	43041596
HUN	Huntsman Corp	Specialty Chemicals	12/31/15	10299.0	93.0	9820.0	1442.0	419	189424237
H	Hyatt Hotels Corp	Hotels, Restaurants & Travel	12/31/15	4328.0	124.0	7596.0	3991.0	203	25995458
HY	Hyster-Yale Materials Handling, Inc.	Autos- Manufacturing	12/31/15	2578.1	74.7	1095.9	460.8	153	9352250
IAG	IAMGold Corp	Precious Metals	12/31/15	917.0	-755.3	3251.4	1895.8	205	236202584
IBN	ICICI Bank Ltd (India)	Banking	3/31/15	902162.3	122468.7	8260791.7	847045.4	419	652651766
IDA	Idacorp Inc	Electric Utilities	12/31/15	1270.3	194.7	6023.3	2057.9	328	46552065
IEX	IDEX Corporation	Industrial Machinery & Equipment	12/31/15	2020.7	282.8	2805.4	1443.3	398	81631290
IDT	IDT Corp	Services	7/31/15	1596.8	84.5	485.7	133.8	130	13265163
IHS	IHS Inc	Business Services	11/30/15	2184.3	240.2	5601.1	2200.9	394	77737616
ITW	Illinois Tool Works, Inc.	Industrial Machinery & Equipment	12/31/15	13405.0	1899.0	15729.0	5224.0	1311	356302903
IMN	Imation Corp.	Electrical Equipment	12/31/15	529.2	-194.0	168.4	24.4	146	36954212
IMAX	IMAX Corp.	Entertainment	12/31/15	373.8	64.6	931.0	623.9	265	64088964
IMPV	Imperva Inc.	Internet & Software	12/31/15	234.3	-48.9	397.7	240.2	238	29731346
IMPR	Imprivata Inc	Computer Hardware & Equipment	12/31/15	119.1	-23.1	120.8	48.6	62	14348347
IMS	IMS Health Holdings Inc	Internet & Software	12/31/15	2921.0	417.0	7459.0	1572.0	273	300506772
ICD	Independence Contract Drilling Inc	Business Services	12/31/15	88.4	-7.9	314.8	232.7	58	14460631
IHC	Independence Holding Co.	Life & Health	12/31/15	532.9	29.9	1198.0	323.4	71	4755176
IFN	India Fund, Inc. (The)	Holding and other Investment Office	12/31/15	11.9	0.4	807.7	759.1	127	9753406
IBA	Industrias Bachoco S.A.B. de C.V.	Food	12/31/15	46229.0	3812.8	40446.6	27728.9	-	-
BLOX	Infoblox Inc	Internet & Software	7/31/15	306.1	-27.1	459.3	275.2	195	54188588
INFY	Infosys Ltd.	IT Services	3/31/15	9501.0	2052.0	11378.0	9324.0	377	410786428
HIFR	InfraREIT Inc	REITs	12/31/15	151.2	13.3	1663.7	678.1	132	33826825
ING	ING Groep N.V.	Banking	12/31/15	51660.0	4926.0	837855.0	44972.0	308	76740467
IR	Ingersoll-Rand Plc	Industrial Machinery & Equipment	12/31/15	13300.7	664.6	16738.8	5816.7	-	-
NGVT	Ingevity Corp	Specialty Chemicals	12/31/15	968.0	80.0	782.0	517.0	-	-
NGVT	Ingevity Corp	Specialty Chemicals	12/31/15	968.0	80.0	782.0	517.0	-	-
IM	Ingram Micro Inc.	Computer Hardware & Equipment	12/31/15	43025.9	215.1	12307.3	3967.8	489	165511131
INGR	Ingredion Inc	Food	12/31/15	5621.0	402.0	5074.0	2144.0	572	76946291
IPHI	Inphi Corp	Semiconductors	12/31/15	246.6	-13.6	505.0	290.7	232	37140729
NSP	Insperity Inc	Business Services	12/31/15	2603.6	39.4	784.9	172.5	256	19678069
IBP	Installed Building Products Inc	Construction Services	12/31/15	662.7	26.5	374.1	114.5	137	20326465
INST	Instructure Inc	IT Services	12/31/15	73.2	-53.0	121.1	45.6	59	8151079
I	Intelsat SA	Services	12/31/15	2352.5	-3923.4	12253.6	-4649.6	-	-
ICE	Intercontinental Exchange Inc.	Finance Intermediaries & Services	12/31/15	3338.0	1274.0	77987.0	14808.0	-	-
IHG	InterContinental Hotels Group Plc	Hotels, Restaurants & Travel	12/31/15	1803.0	1222.0	3769.0	309.0	139	16179811
IBM	International Business Machines Co	IT Services	12/31/15	81741.0	13190.0	110495.0	14262.0	2400	718716420
IFF	International Flavors & Fragrances I	Specialty Chemicals	12/31/15	3023.2	419.2	3721.5	1590.3	606	85444844
IGT	International Game Technology PL	Miscellaneous	12/31/15	4689.1	-75.6	15114.7	3017.6	-	-
IP	International Paper Co	Containers & Packaging	12/31/15	22365.0	938.0	30587.0	3884.0	983	406224324
IOC	InterOil Corp.	Production & Extraction	12/31/15	23.1	-242.0	1191.4	799.7	155	27797517
IPG	Interpublic Group of Companies Inc.	Advertising	12/31/15	7613.8	454.6	12585.1	1965.5	631	436238477
IPL PRD	Interstate Power & Light Co	Electric Utilities	12/31/15	1774.5	196.2	6709.1	2195.3	-	-
INXN	InterXion Holding NV	IT Services	12/31/15	386.6	48.6	1252.1	507.4	197	59132588
IL	IntraLinks Holdings Inc	IT Services	12/31/15	276.2	-30.4	461.7	282.2	141	56417441
SNOW	Intrawest Resorts Holdings Inc	Sporting & Recreational	6/30/15	587.6	-6.9	1095.0	276.2	105	37826210
IPI	Intrepid Potash Inc	Agricultural Chemicals	12/31/15	287.2	-524.8	640.5	426.5	193	39439200
XON	Intrexon Corp	Biotechnology	12/31/15	173.6	-84.5	982.0	694.1	-	-
IVC	Invacare Corp	Medical Instruments & Equipment	12/31/15	1142.3	-26.2	838.1	462.8	206	37218563
INVN	InvenSense, Inc.	Semiconductors	4/3/16	418.4	-21.2	622.5	378.7	-	-
VBF	Invesco Bond Fund	Holding and other Investment Office	2/28/15	10.9	9.6	241.9	233.1	46	3949613
VCV	Invesco California Value Municipal I	Holding and other Investment Office	2/28/15	44.7	37.8	1032.1	662.1	49	3843244
VTA	Invesco Dynamic Credit Opportuniti	Holding and other Investment Office	2/28/15	93.3	67.9	1641.3	983.8	117	27060819
VLT	Invesco High Income Trust II	Holding and other Investment Office	2/28/15	11.7	9.6	193.7	138.9	45	2312774
IVZ	Invesco Ltd	Wealth Management	12/31/15	5122.9	968.1	25073.2	7885.3	697	377521074
IVR	Invesco Mortgage Capital Inc.	REITs	12/31/15	437.6	104.0	16772.7	2241.0	224	74957052
OIA	Invesco Municipal Income Opportun	Holding and other Investment Office	2/28/15	22.0	19.3	417.6	359.6	65	4073024
VMO	Invesco Municipal Opportunity Trust	Holding and other Investment Office	2/28/15	71.0	56.2	1613.2	960.2	95	7382686
VKQ	Invesco Municipal Trust	Holding and other Investment Office	2/29/16	58.0	46.0	1273.6	780.5	84	9109038
VPV	Invesco Pennsylvania Value Munici	Holding and other Investment Office	2/28/15	24.1	18.6	553.2	348.1	47	2911655
IQI	Invesco Quality Municipal Income T	Holding and other Investment Office	2/29/12	23.1	19.8	524.2	443.1	-	-
VVR	Invesco Senior Income Trust	Holding and other Investment Office	2/28/15	78.3	57.9	1403.4	908.7	144	65267673
VGM	Invesco Trust for Investment Grade	Holding and other Investment Office	2/28/15	59.6	46.8	1339.9	798.9	100	6621263
VTN	Invesco Trust For Investment Grade	Holding and other Investment Office	2/28/15	20.5	16.6	472.0	296.3	37	1211279
IIM	Invesco Value Municipal Income Tr	Holding and other Investment Office	2/28/15	47.5	40.6	1192.8	779.3	-	-
ITG	Investment Technology Group Inc.	Finance Intermediaries & Services	12/31/15	634.8	91.6	1709.0	454.8	226	37572959
IRET	Investors Real Estate Trust	REITs	4/30/15	283.2	24.1	1997.8	652.1	201	59290816
NVTA	Invitae Corp	Diagnostic & Health Related Service	12/31/15	8.4	-89.8	156.7	138.4	53	21465260
IO	ION Geophysical Corp	Equipment & Services	12/31/15	221.5	-25.1	438.4	112.0	150	13674153
IRM	Iron Mountain Inc (New)	Business Services	12/31/15	3008.0	123.2	6350.6	508.8	478	211644205
IRS	IRSA Inversiones y Representacion	Property, Real Estate & Developmen	6/30/15	3402.6	-41.2	9629.4	1881.7	68	13179073
ICL	Israel Chemicals Ltd	Agricultural Chemicals	12/31/15	5405.0	509.0	9077.0	3028.0	88	93395288
STAR	iStar Inc	REITs	12/31/15	514.6	-2.4	5622.9	1059.1	230	77830987
ITCB	Itau CorpBanca	Banking	12/31/15	1542586.0	216321.0	20805351.0	1220552.0	51	1840523
ITUB	Itau Unibanco Holding S.A.	Banking	12/31/15	188934.0	25740.0	1276415.0	112252.0	368	718391785
ITC	ITC Holdings Corp	Electric Utilities	12/31/15	1044.8	242.4	7582.1	1709.1	508	139268978

T32

1st	2nd	3rd	2015	2014	2013	P/E	RATIO	2015	2014	2013	AV. YLD %	AMOUNT	PAYABLE	2015	
-	-	-0.05	-1.41	0.34	-0.59	-		0.02	0.02	0.11	0.4	0.010	3/31/16	11.9 -	0.0
0.02	-	-	-0.19	0.15	-0.27	-		0.57	0.50	0.50	2.0	0.20Z	6/30/16	31.7 -	23.0
0.00	-	-	0.19	1.10	0.86	21.4 -	5.2	0.19	1.10	0.86	8.2	0.00710Z	1/15/16	4.1 -	1.0
1.56	-	-	8.44	7.36	7.73	25.5 -	18.6	1.15	1.11	1.07	0.6	0.290Y	61/28/99	214.9 -	157.0
2.87	-	-	8.36	6.86	5.18	18.7 -	12.4	1.70	1.00	0.50	1.4	0.50Y	61/28/99	156.2 -	104.0
0.24	-	-	0.38	1.31	0.53	61.8 -	20.8	0.50	0.50	0.50	3.5	0.1250Y	61/28/99	23.5 -	7.9
0.25	-	-	0.86	2.23	1.30	69.5 -	41.6	-	-	-	-			59.8 -	35.8
0.61	-	-	4.57	6.58	6.54	15.8 -	10.2	1.13	1.08	1.00	1.9	0.2950Y	6/15/16	72.4 -	46.6
-	-	-0.21	-1.93	-0.55	-2.21	-		-	-	-	-	0.1250	7/12/13	5.2 -	0.0
-	4.07	-	20.94	19.03	16.57	0.5 -	0.2	9.15	7.50	6.46	113.5			10.6 -	5.2
0.51	-	-	3.87	3.85	3.64	19.3 -	14.4	1.92	1.76	1.57	2.9	0.510Y	61/28/99	74.8 -	55.8
0.89	-	-	3.62	3.45	3.09	23.3 -	18.9	1.24	1.07	0.89	1.6	0.340Y	61/28/99	84.3 -	68.3
-	-	0.19	3.63	0.82	0.52	5.4 -	3.0	2.03	0.59	0.75	13.9	0.190Y	6/17/16	19.6 -	10.9
0.66	-	-	3.47	2.81	1.95	38.6 -	27.1	-	-	-	-			133.8 -	94.0
1.29	-	-	5.13	7.28	3.74	20.7 -	15.6	2.07	1.81	1.60	2.2	0.550Y	61/28/99	106.0 -	80.1
-2.46	-	-	-4.84	-2.80	-1.10	-		-	-	-	-	0.080Y	12/29/08	4.7 -	0.6
0.14	-	-	0.78	0.56	0.64	55.4 -	33.3	-	-	-	-			43.2 -	26.0
-0.75	-	-	-1.64	-2.28	-1.04	-		-	-	-	-			77.4 -	33.3
-0.27	-	-	-0.94	-1.37	-3.12	-		-	-	-	-			21.5 -	9.4
0.13	-	-	1.23	-0.59	0.29	27.0 -	18.3	-	-	-	-			33.1 -	22.5
-0.02	-	-	-0.33	-1.85	-0.10	-		-	-	-	-			9.1 -	3.4
-	-	0.85	1.71	0.92	0.77	9.7 -	6.8	0.08	0.07	0.04	0.6	0.0450Y	7/20/16	16.7 -	11.6
-	-	-	0.01	0.08	0.10	2839.0 -	1965.0	1.82	1.86	0.95	7.6	1.3621C	1/12/16	28.4 -	19.6
-	-	0.59	6.36	6.55	3.40	10.0 -	6.5	17.75	-	18.66	33.7			63.5 -	41.2
-	-	-0.10	-0.48	-0.45	-0.09	-		-	-	-	-			27.9 -	14.1
-	0.17	-	0.88	0.77	0.76	22.7 -	17.5	1.20	0.79	0.85	6.9			20.0 -	15.4
0.14	-	-	0.31	-86.35	1.07	109.5 -	48.7	0.81	-	-	3.5	0.250Z	7/21/16	33.9 -	15.1
-	-	-	1.27	0.06	1.06	13.6 -	8.3	0.31	0.12	0.00	2.2	0.38280Z	7/15/16	17.3 -	10.6
0.58	-	-	2.48	3.40	2.07	-		1.16	1.00	0.84	-	0.320	61/28/99	28.2 -	23.5
0.19	-	-	-	-	-	-		-	-	-	-			28.2 -	23.5
0.19	-	-	-	-	-	-		-	-	-	-			29.1 -	23.5
0.01	-	-	1.37	1.67	1.99	26.7 -	17.6	0.20	-	-	0.7	0.10Y	61/28/99	36.5 -	24.1
1.73	-	-	5.51	4.74	5.05	21.8 -	14.4	1.74	1.68	1.56	1.8	0.450Y	61/28/99	120.3 -	79.3
0.01	-	-	-0.35	-0.69	-0.45	-		-	-	-	-			34.7 -	20.9
1.53	-	-	1.58	1.05	1.25	45.6 -	26.9	0.85	2.74	0.68	1.7	0.250Y	6/21/16	72.0 -	42.5
0.19	-	-	0.85	-0.20	-0.01	39.3 -	21.9	-	-	-	-			33.4 -	18.6
-0.50	-	-	-6.07	-7.50	-6.26	-		-	-	-	-			22.6 -	13.8
-	-	-	-36.68	1.99	-2.70	-		-	-	-	-	0.71880	5/2/16	11.0 -	1.5
3.08	-	-	11.39	8.55	3.21	23.8 -	19.5	2.90	2.60	0.65	1.2	0.850Y	61/28/99	271.1 -	221.9
-	-	-	5.13	1.56	1.51	10.1 -	7.2	0.78	0.25	-	1.7			51.8 -	37.2
2.09	-	-	13.42	11.90	14.94	12.9 -	8.8	5.00	4.25	3.70	3.4	1.40Y	61/28/99	173.2 -	117.8
1.47	-	-	5.16	5.06	4.29	25.1 -	19.5	2.06	1.72	1.46	1.8	0.560Y	61/28/99	129.3 -	100.5
-	-	-	-0.39	0.49	1.16	-		0.40	-	-	2.4	0.20	6/23/16	19.8 -	12.7
0.81	-	-	2.23	1.29	3.11	23.2 -	14.6	1.64	1.45	1.25	3.9	0.440Y	61/28/99	51.8 -	32.6
-	-2.09	-	-4.89	5.82	0.83	-		-	-	-	-			61.0 -	22.4
0.01	-	-	1.09	1.12	0.61	21.9 -	16.8	0.48	0.38	0.30	2.2	0.150Y	61/28/99	23.9 -	18.3
-	-	-	-	-	-	-		1.27	1.27	0.94	5.0	0.31870Y	6/15/16	27.3 -	24.8
-	-	-0.24	0.69	0.50	0.10	-		-	-	-	-			12.7 -	6.5
-0.08	-	-	-0.53	-0.47	-0.28	-		-	-	-	-			12.7 -	7.0
-	-	4.08	-0.15	-4.37	-7.07	-		-	-	-	-				
-0.24	-	-	-6.94	0.13	0.30	-		-	-	-	-	0.75G7	12/27/12	12.2 -	0.7
-0.55	-	-	-0.76	-0.83	-1.40	-		-	-	-	-			68.7 -	21.4
-0.27	-	-	-0.81	-1.75	1.03	-		0.05	0.05	0.06	0.3	0.01140Y	7/13/16	23.5 -	10.2
-	-	0.02	-0.01	0.07	0.59	-		-	-	-	-			16.3 -	5.5
-	-	-	0.85	0.86	0.86	22.1 -	19.9	1.38	1.18	1.51	7.7	0.0690	6/30/16	18.8 -	16.9
-	-	-	0.79	0.80	0.80	18.1 -	15.5	-	-	-	-	0.063M	6/30/16	14.3 -	12.2
-	-	-	0.92	0.84	0.91	13.2 -	10.5	0.90	0.90	0.90	8.3	0.0750	6/30/16	12.2 -	9.7
-	-	-	1.18	1.28	1.35	12.7 -	10.0	1.29	1.37	1.39	9.6	0.09750	6/30/16	15.0 -	11.9
0.38	-	-	2.26	2.27	2.10	17.6 -	11.2	1.06	0.97	0.85	3.2	0.280	61/28/99	39.9 -	25.4
-1.39	-	-	0.67	-1.76	0.99	23.8 -	14.6	1.70	1.95	2.30	13.0	0.48440Z	9/27/16	16.0 -	9.8
-	-	-	0.40	0.42	0.41	19.9 -	16.5	0.40	0.42	0.42	5.6	0.0328M	6/30/16	8.0 -	6.6
-	-	-	0.83	0.83	0.83	17.4 -	14.4	0.79	0.84	1.01	6.0	0.0733M	6/30/16	14.5 -	12.0
-	-	-	0.80	0.80	0.81	17.1 -	14.8	0.81	0.83	0.95	6.4	0.068M	6/30/16	13.7 -	11.9
-	-	-	0.78	0.81	0.82	18.3 -	15.4	-	-	-	-	0.0662M	6/30/16	14.3 -	12.0
-	-	-	-	-	-	-		-	-	-	-	0.0635M	6/30/16	13.6 -	11.6
-	-	-	0.32	0.31	0.34	14.8 -	11.5	-	-	-	-	0.02450	6/30/16	4.7 -	3.7
-	-	-	0.86	0.86	0.86	17.0 -	14.6	0.89	0.92	1.04	6.7	0.073M	6/30/16	14.6 -	12.5
-	-	-	0.85	0.89	0.89	18.8 -	15.6	0.86	1.01	1.01	6.0	0.0708M	6/30/16	16.0 -	13.2
-	-	-	0.86	0.86	0.85	20.3 -	16.4	0.90	0.90	0.90	5.6	0.07M	6/30/16	17.4 -	14.1
-0.08	-	-	2.63	1.40	0.82	10.6 -	4.8	0.21	-	-	1.1	0.070	6/14/16	27.8 -	12.7
-	-	0.30	0.11	-0.23	0.17	76.3 -	54.3	0.52	0.52	0.52	7.4	0.49690Z	6/30/16	8.4 -	6.0
-0.80	-	-	-3.18	-56.14	-36.13	-		-	-	-	-			15.5 -	6.0
-3.30	-	-	-2.29	-11.70	-23.85	-		-	-	-	-			22.9 -	2.7
0.30	-	-	0.58	1.66	0.51	65.8 -	42.3	1.91	5.37	1.08	6.2	0.4850Y	61/28/99	38.1 -	24.6
0.06	-	-	-0.07	-1.37	0.41	-		0.63	2.83	4.54	4.3			19.2 -	8.6
-	-	0.31	0.40	0.36	0.64	-		0.05	0.59	0.51	-				
-0.27	-	-	-0.62	-0.40	-1.83	-		-	-	-	-	0.56250Z	6/15/16	14.8 -	7.6
-	-	0.08	0.64	0.69	0.48	28.8 -	17.0	1224.66	295.28	288.24	9023.1			18.4 -	10.9
-	-	0.86	4.28	3.92	3.30	2.4 -	1.3	1.21	0.73	0.68	15.4			10.3 -	5.5
0.42	-	-	1.56	1.54	1.47	28.6 -	20.1	0.70	0.61	0.54	1.9	0.19750Y	61/20/99	44.8 -	31.3

SYMBOL	COMPANY	NATURE OF BUSINESS	FISCAL YEAR-END	TOTAL REV. $MILL	NET INCOME $MILL	TOTAL ASSETS $MILL	NET STK EQUITY $MILL	NO OF INST	INST. HOLDINGS (SHARES)
ESI	ITT Educational Services, Inc.	Educational Services	12/31/15	849.8	23.3	664.0	161.1	173	26913266
ITT	ITT Inc	Industrial Machinery & Equipment	12/31/15	2485.6	351.8	3723.6	1362.1	525	101913205
IVH	Ivy High Income Opportunities Fund	Finance Intermediaries & Services	9/30/14	34.1	27.6	466.4	320.5	53	3853084
JAX	J Alexander's Holdings Inc	Hotels, Restaurants & Travel	1/3/16	217.9	5.4	156.2	97.6	128	10053665
JBL	Jabil Circuit, Inc.	Electrical Equipment	8/31/15	17899.2	284.0	9603.2	2314.9	501	201291177
JEC	Jacobs Engineering Group, Inc.	Construction Services	10/2/15	12114.8	303.0	7785.9	4291.7	669	127802579
JHX	James Hardie Industries Plc	Construction Materials	3/31/16	1728.2	244.4	2040.4	-225.2	60	4164545
JNS	Janus Capital Group Inc	Wealth Management	12/31/15	1076.2	155.8	2871.5	1582.7	353	194574289
JOF	Japan Smaller Capitalization Fund I	Holding and other Investment Office	2/28/15	5.1	1.8	311.7	311.1	66	20866837
JCAP	Jernigan Capital Inc	REITs		1.7	-2.9	105.4	101.3	40	2420553
JKS	JinkoSolar Holding Co., Ltd.	Semiconductors	12/31/15	16076.5	683.8	27144.5	4321.9	99	6136253
JMP	JMP Group LLC	Finance Intermediaries & Services	12/31/15	172.1	-0.2	1277.5	125.1	49	4312619
JBT	John Bean Technologies Corp	Industrial Machinery & Equipment	12/31/15	1107.3	55.9	876.1	129.7	245	28599356
DECR 19	John Deere Capital Corp.	Credit & Lending	10/31/15	1951.7	498.2	34652.8	3749.4		
BTO	John Hancock Financial Opportuniti	Holding and other Investment Office	12/31/15	3.3	1.8	596.4	486.1	75	3911467
HEQ	John Hancock Hedged Equity & Inc	Holding and other Investment Office	12/31/14	9.3	6.3	249.1	248.5	37	2587705
JHS	John Hancock Income Securities Tr	Holding and other Investment Office	10/31/15	12.2	9.5	269.3	176.4	32	3525407
HTY	John Hancock Investment Trust	Holding and other Investment Office	8/31/92	3.9	2.6	119.5	119.5		
JHI	John Hancock Investors Trust	Holding and other Investment Office	10/31/15	14.8	12.4	244.1	151.3	49	1026410
HPI	John Hancock Preferred Income Fu	Holding and other Investment Office	7/31/15	52.2	42.8	859.5	565.1	70	2739312
PDT	John Hancock Premium Dividend F	Holding and other Investment Office	10/31/15	61.6	47.7	1118.0	732.6	90	6090386
JNJ	Johnson & Johnson	Pharmaceuticals	1/3/16	70074.0	15409.0	133411.0	71150.0	2936	2175478276
JCI	Johnson Controls Inc	Auto Parts	9/30/15	37179.0	1563.0	29673.0	10376.0	1147	521964657
JONE	Jones Energy Inc	Production & Extraction	12/31/15	197.4	-2.4	1945.4	400.0	90	42341799
JLL	Jones Lang LaSalle Inc	Property, Real Estate & Developmen	12/31/15	5965.7	438.7	6205.2	2688.8	527	44288759
JOY	Joy Global Inc	Industrial Machinery & Equipment	10/30/15	3172.1	-1178.0	3712.4	1420.0	490	116529700
JPEP	JP Energy Partners LP	Equipment & Services	12/31/15	680.6	-58.7	735.3		39	11455420
JPM	JPMorgan Chase & Co	Banking	12/31/15	101006.0	24442.0	2351698.0	247573.0	2637	3094806046
JFC	JPMorgan China Region Fund Inc	Holding and other Investment Office	12/31/15	3.3	0.7	134.3	113.2	31	5120712
JMEI	Jumei International Holding Ltd	Retail - Apparel and Accessories	12/31/15	7343.0	122.9	4991.7	3630.4	96	51303678
JNPR	Juniper Networks Inc	Peripherals	12/31/15	4857.8	633.7	8619.2	4574.4	695	392154889
JP	Jupai Holdings Ltd	Wealth Management	12/31/15	94.4	24.3	241.7	167.4	6	20507
JE	Just Energy Group Inc.	Electric Utilities	3/31/16	4105.9	64.6	1247.4	-651.1		
LRN	K12 Inc	Educational Services	6/30/15	948.3	11.0	708.6	536.9	170	32509589
KAI	Kadant Inc	Industrial Machinery & Equipment	1/2/16	390.1	34.4	415.5	266.6	185	12763627
KAMN	Kaman Corp.	Industrial Machinery & Equipment	12/31/15	1775.1	60.4	1441.2	543.1	233	28152947
KSU	Kansas City Southern	Rail	12/31/15	2418.8	483.5	8341.0	3914.3	668	120625294
KS	KapStone Paper & Packaging Corp	Paper & Forest Products	12/31/15	2789.3	106.4	3222.1	845.3	281	86326591
KAR	KAR Auction Services Inc.	Retail - Automotive	12/31/15	2639.6	214.6	5791.8	1386.1		
KATE	Kate Spade & Co	Apparel, Footwear & Accessories	1/2/16	1242.7	17.1	980.4	245.2	360	142194273
KED	Kayne Anderson Energy Developm	Holding and other Investment Office	11/30/14	9.5	-1.6	551.3	348.5	60	3393151
KYE	Kayne Anderson Energy Total Retur	Holding and other Investment Office	11/30/15	44.9	10.9	833.3	477.3	86	6907309
KMF	Kayne Anderson Midstream / Energ	Holding and other Investment Office	11/30/14	32.1	-0.2	1246.3	854.3	56	5163132
KYN	Kayne Anderson MLP Investment C	Holding and other Investment Office	11/30/15	72.5	-58.5	4108.3	2141.6	240	34189620
KB	KB Financial Group, Inc.	Banking	12/31/15	13909742.0	1698318.0	29065467.0	28680621.0	145	29996138
KBH	KB HOME	Builders	11/30/15	3032.0	84.6	5015.4	1690.8	342	87607525
KBR	KBR Inc	Construction Services	12/31/15	5096.0	203.0	3412.0	1065.0	376	154416993
KCG	KCG Holdings Inc	Finance Intermediaries & Services	12/31/15	1599.1	249.1	6051.2	1444.1		
K	Kellogg Co	Food	1/2/16	13525.0	614.0	15265.0	2128.0	990	415320543
KEM	KEMET Corp.	Electrical Equipment	3/31/16	734.8	-53.6	702.5	112.5	110	30128917
KMPR	Kemper Corp. (DE)	General Insurance	12/31/15	2340.8	85.7	8036.1	1992.4	226	30504025
KMT	Kennametal Inc.	Industrial Machinery & Equipment	6/30/15	2647.2	-373.9	2849.5	1345.8	365	81617295
KW	Kennedy-Wilson Holdings Inc	Property, Real Estate & Developmen	12/31/15	603.7	59.0	7640.1	1133.8	4	2975087
KEN	Kenon Holdings Ltd	Energy	12/31/15	1289.1	73.0	4482.8	1061.2	14	447375
KEG	Key Energy Services, Inc.	Equipment & Services	12/31/15	792.3	-917.7	1327.8	140.3	166	101779506
KEY	KeyCorp	Banking	12/31/15	4502.0	916.0	95133.0	10746.0	831	746229302
KEYS	Keysight Technologies Inc	Industrial Machinery & Equipment	10/31/15	2856.0	513.0	3508.0	1302.0	379	145804998
KRC	Kilroy Realty Corp	REITs	12/31/15	581.3	234.1	5939.5	3171.0	349	119763069
KMB	Kimberly-Clark Corp.	Household & Personal Products	12/31/15	18591.0	1013.0	14842.0	-110.0	1691	307206771
KIM	Kimco Realty Corp.	REITs	12/31/15	1166.8	894.1	11344.2	5046.3	580	420304162
KMI	Kinder Morgan Inc.	Equipment & Services	12/31/15	14403.0	253.0	84104.0	35119.0	1249	1404334502
KND	Kindred Healthcare Inc	Hospitals & Health Care Facilities	12/31/15	7054.9	-93.4	6518.9	1499.9	274	86539234
KFS	Kingsway Financial Services Inc.	General Insurance	12/31/15	160.0	1.3	241.0	48.3	24	7981919
KGC	Kinross Gold Corp.	Precious Metals	12/31/15	3052.2	-984.5	7735.4	3889.3	338	835726279
KEX	Kirby Corp.	Shipping	12/31/15	2147.5	226.7	4156.3	2268.8	387	63413228
KRG	Kite Realty Group Trust	REITs	12/31/15	347.0	27.1	3766.0	1726.0	274	84973622
KKR	KKR & Co LP (DE)	Finance Intermediaries & Services	12/31/15	1043.8	488.5	71057.8		399	298316369
KIO	KKR Income Opportunities Fund	Finance Intermediaries & Services	10/31/14	29.3	22.5	434.1	289.5	41	3337048
KMG	KMG Chemicals, Inc.	Specialty Chemicals	7/31/15	320.5	12.1	242.4	123.4	96	9190450
KNX	Knight Transportation Inc.	Trucking	12/31/15	1183.0	116.7	1120.2	738.4	246	83207951
KNL	Knoll Inc	Office Equipment & Furniture	12/31/15	1104.4	66.0	856.1	255.3	221	52663459
KNOP	KNOT Offshore Partners LP	Shipping	12/31/15	155.0	40.4	1223.9	520.8	45	13558029
KN	Knowles Corp	Electronic Instruments & Related Pro	12/31/15	1084.6	-233.8	1697.7	1006.8	312	104847365
KSS	Kohl's Corp.	Retail - General Merchandise/Depart	1/30/16	19204.0	673.0	13606.0	5491.0	889	212672832
PHG	Koninklijke Philips NV	Household Appliances, Electronics &	12/31/15	24244.0	645.0	30976.0	11662.0	316	62040203
KOP	Koppers Holdings Inc	Paper & Forest Products	12/31/15	1626.9	-72.0	1125.4	-18.5	213	21487253
KEP	Korea Electric Power Corp	Electric Utilities	12/31/15	58957722.0	13289127.0	175257359.0	66634467.0	197	105994990
KEF	Korea Equity Fund, Inc.	Holding and other Investment Office	10/31/15	1.0	-0.2	85.4	84.6	29	7433328
KF	Korea Fund, Inc. (The)	Holding and other Investment Office	6/30/15	3.7	-0.2	368.4	329.5	50	5188019
KFY	Korn/Ferry International (DE)	Business Services	4/30/15	1066.1	88.4	1317.8	815.2	306	53597720

T34

| EARNINGS PER SHARE | | | | | | P/E RATIO | | DIVIDENDS PER SHARE | | | AV. YLD | DIV. DECLARED | | PRICE RANGE | |
| QUARTERLY | | | ANNUAL | | | | | | | | | | | 2015 | |
1st	2nd	3rd	2015	2014	2013	2015		2015	2014	2013	%	AMOUNT	PAYABLE		
0.17	-	-	0.97	1.23	-1.15	5.8 -	2.1	-	-	-	-	-	-	5.7 -	2.0
0.41	-	-	3.88	1.99	5.29	11.2 -	7.7	0.47	0.44	0.40	1.3	0.124GY	7/1/16	43.4 -	29.9
-	-	-	1.67	0.45				-	1.85	0.25	-	0.1250	6/30/16	16.1 -	10.7
0.15	-	-	0.36			32.3 -	24.9							11.6 -	9.0
-	0.41	-	1.45	1.19	1.79	17.9 -	11.6	0.32	0.32	0.32	1.5	0.080Y	61/28/99	25.9 -	16.9
-	0.54	-	2.40	2.48	3.23	21.1 -	14.6	-	-	-	-	0.00710	61/28/99	50.7 -	35.1
-	0.12	-	0.65	0.22	0.10	23.7 -	15.8	0.88	0.45	0.43	6.8			15.4 -	10.3
0.19	-	-	0.80	0.81	0.62	23.4 -	14.3	0.35	0.31	0.21	2.4	0.110Y	61/28/99	18.8 -	11.5
-	-	-	0.06	0.05	0.07	182.2 -	142.2	0.13	0.20	0.08	1.3	0.1429B	12/28/15	10.9 -	8.5
0.18	-	-	-0.69					1.05	-	-	6.4	0.350Z	7/15/16	21.2 -	10.2
-	-	1.10	5.35	3.86	1.96	6.0 -	2.9							31.9 -	15.7
-	-	-0.14	-0.01	0.57	0.16			0.49	0.23	0.14	8.0	0.030	7/15/16	8.1 -	5.0
0.17	-	-	1.88	1.03	1.11	32.5 -	17.1	0.37	0.36	0.34	0.8	0.10Y	6/9/16	61.1 -	32.1
-	-	-	0.10	0.35	0.29	293.1 -	199.9					0.37010	6/30/16	29.3 -	20.0
-	-	-		0.46	0.14			-	1.50	1.35	-	0.3760	6/30/16	16.7 -	12.8
-	-	-	0.81	0.86	0.91	17.8 -	16.1	0.90	0.95	1.03	6.5	0.22090	6/30/16	14.4 -	13.0
-	-	-										0.320	6/30/16	11.5 -	9.0
-	-	-	1.41	1.58	1.61	12.4 -	9.5	1.49	1.64	1.71	9.9	0.34110	6/30/16	17.5 -	13.4
-	-	-	1.65	1.67	1.74	13.6 -	11.3	1.68	1.68	1.68	8.3	0.140	6/30/16	22.4 -	18.6
-	-	-	0.97	0.98	0.96	16.7 -	12.9	1.09	1.31	0.91	7.9	0.09750	7/29/16	16.2 -	12.5
1.54	-	-	5.48	5.70	4.81	20.9 -	16.6	2.95	2.76	2.59	2.9	0.80Y	61/28/99	114.7 -	90.7
-	-0.82	-	2.36	1.80	1.71	22.7 -	14.5	1.04	0.88	0.76	2.5	0.290Y	61/28/99	53.6 -	34.2
0.62	-	-	-0.09	3.26	-0.17			-	-	-	-			9.9 -	1.3
0.56	-	-	9.65	8.52	5.98	18.6 -	10.2	0.56	0.48	0.44	0.4	0.310Y	61/28/99	179.3 -	98.6
-	-0.10	-	-12.08	3.28	4.99			0.80	0.75	0.70	4.2	0.010Y	61/28/99	40.2 -	8.8
-0.09	-	-	-1.60	-0.51	-1.67			1.28	-	-	16.9	0.3250	5/13/16	14.8 -	2.1
1.35	-	-	6.00	5.29	4.35	11.7 -	8.8	1.68	1.56	1.36	2.7	0.480Y	61/28/99	70.1 -	53.1
-	-	-	0.10	0.14	0.10	205.0 -	0.0	0.97	0.13	0.13	6.5	0.2707B	1/8/16	20.5 -	0.0
-	-	-	0.82	0.45	0.19	30.5 -	5.8							25.0 -	4.8
0.23	-	-	1.59	-0.73	0.86	20.3 -	13.6	0.40	0.20	-	1.5	0.10	61/28/99	32.2 -	21.6
0.04	-	-	0.16	0.06	0.09	69.3 -	0.0							11.1 -	0.0
-0.26	-	-	-3.07	0.94	3.27			0.58	0.84	1.24	8.2	0.1250	6/30/16	10.1 -	0.0
-	-	0.37	0.29	0.50	0.72	51.3 -	25.2							14.9 -	7.3
0.62	-	-	3.10	2.56	2.07	16.1 -	11.2	0.66	0.57	0.38	1.5	0.190Y	8/11/16	49.8 -	34.6
0.35	-	-	2.17	2.08	2.10	20.2 -	16.5	0.72	0.64	0.64	1.8	0.180Y	7/7/16	43.9 -	35.7
0.99	-	-	4.40	4.55	3.18	23.0 -	14.6	1.32	1.12	0.86	1.5	0.250Y	61/28/99	101.1 -	64.3
0.17	-	-	1.09	1.76	1.32	24.8 -	8.3	0.40	0.10	-	2.1	0.10Y	7/13/16	27.0 -	9.1
0.44	-	-	1.51	1.19	0.48	27.3 -	21.2	1.08	1.02	0.82	2.9	0.290Y	61/28/99	41.2 -	32.0
0.09	-	-	0.13	1.25	0.59	201.8 -	119.2	-	-	-	-	0.06630Y	61/20/99	28.2 -	15.5
-	-	-	-0.15	-0.14				-	2.04	1.76	-	0.480	7/15/16	28.1 -	10.2
-	-	-	0.30	0.14	-0.28	79.2 -	16.9	1.94	1.93	1.92	15.5	0.250	7/15/16	23.8 -	5.1
-	-	-	-0.01	-0.06				-	1.91	1.81	-	0.350	7/15/16	32.7 -	7.0
-	-	-	-0.53	-0.76	-0.73			2.63	2.52	2.29	12.4	0.09580	8/1/16	34.3 -	11.0
-	-1100.00	4376.00	3611.00	3240.00		0.0 -	0.0	765.23	500.96	588.61	2613.1			36.0 -	23.2
0.14	-	-	0.85	9.25	0.46	20.4 -	11.3	0.10	0.10	0.10	0.7	0.0250Y	61/28/99	17.3 -	9.6
0.30	-	-	1.40	-8.66	1.54	14.7 -	8.4	0.32	0.32	0.32	1.9	0.080Y	61/28/99	20.6 -	11.8
0.41	-	-	2.42	0.52	1.75	5.8 -	4.1							14.1 -	9.9
0.49	-	-	1.72	1.75	4.94	45.4 -	35.6	1.90	1.90	1.80	2.8	0.50Y	61/28/99	78.1 -	61.3
-	-	-0.19	-0.31	-1.52	-1.83									3.2 -	1.3
-0.04	-	-	1.65	2.12	3.80	25.1 -	14.4	0.96	0.96	0.96	2.8	0.240Y	61/28/00	41.4 -	20.8
-	-	0.20	-4.71	1.99	2.52			0.72	0.72	0.64	2.8	0.20Y	61/28/99	36.4 -	15.9
-0.07	-	-	0.66	0.14	-0.21	39.8 -	24.0	0.48	0.36	0.28	2.1	0.140Z	7/7/16	26.3 -	15.8
-	-	-	1.36	8.76	-11.72			-	-	-	-				
-0.51	-	-	-5.86	-1.16	-0.14									2.3 -	0.2
0.22	-	-	1.05	0.99	0.97	14.9 -	9.5	0.29	0.25	0.22	2.2	1.93750Y	61/28/99	15.7 -	10.0
-	0.51	-	3.00	2.35		11.2 -	7.1							33.7 -	21.2
1.84	-	-	2.42	1.95	0.36	30.4 -	19.6	1.40	1.40	1.40	2.2	0.39840Z	61/28/99	73.5 -	47.4
1.50	-	-	2.77	4.04	5.53	49.9 -	37.3	3.52	3.36	3.24	2.9	0.920Y	61/28/99	138.1 -	103.3
0.31	-	-	2.00	0.89	0.43	14.9 -	11.1	0.97	0.92	0.85	3.7	0.35160Z	61/28/99	29.7 -	22.3
0.12	-	-	0.10	0.80	1.15	412.9 -	120.1	1.93	1.70	1.56	7.8	0.1250Y	61/28/99	41.3 -	12.0
0.15	-	-	-1.11	-1.36	-3.23			0.48	0.48	0.24	3.2	18.750	61/28/99	22.9 -	8.3
-	-0.05	-	0.04	-0.75	-2.56	190.5 -	0.0	-	-	-	-	0.080	6/30/09	7.6 -	0.0
-	-0.05	-	-0.86	-1.02	-3.28			-	-	0.08	-	0.080	3/28/13	7.2 -	0.0
0.71	-	-	4.11	4.93	4.44	19.6 -	11.1	-	-	-	-	0.05	61/28/99	80.4 -	45.8
0.02	-	-	0.18	-0.24	-0.48	157.4 -	127.4	1.08	0.26	0.96	4.1	0.28750Z	7/14/16	28.3 -	22.9
-0.73	-	-	1.01	1.16	2.30	24.4 -	11.0	1.58	2.03	1.62	9.2	0.4125GH	6/15/16	24.6 -	11.1
-	-	-	1.48	0.27				-	1.66	0.13	-	0.1250	7/29/16	16.3 -	12.3
-	0.53	-	1.03	-0.09	0.81	30.6 -	18.5	0.12	0.12	0.12	0.5	0.030Y	6/30/16	31.5 -	19.0
0.28	-	-	1.42	1.25	0.86	20.9 -	14.8	0.24	0.30	0.24	0.9	0.060Y	6/24/16	29.6 -	21.0
0.36	-	-	1.36	0.97	0.49	19.0 -	12.4	0.51	0.48	0.48	2.3	0.150Y	6/30/16	25.9 -	16.9
-	-	-	1.50	1.37	1.06			2.03	1.79	0.75	-	0.520	5/16/16		
-0.33	-	-	-2.69	-1.02	1.24									22.0 -	10.0
0.09	-	-	4.24	4.05	4.17	15.5 -	8.2	1.56	1.40	1.28	3.1	0.50Y	61/28/99	65.7 -	34.6
-	-	0.31	0.70	0.45	1.27	40.8 -	33.1	0.80	0.80	-	3.0			28.6 -	23.2
-0.06	-	-	-3.51	-1.58	1.94			0.00	1.00	1.00	0.0	0.250Y	1/5/15	27.1 -	14.3
-	-	-1518.00	20701.00	4290.00	96.00	0.0 -	0.0	248.49	44.48	-	1114.2	0.08821	4/20/97	26.9 -	19.3
-	-	-	-0.03	-0.07	-0.08			0.09	1.25	1.05	1.2	0.1124B	12/28/15	8.0 -	0.0
-	-	-	-0.02	-0.14	-0.13			-	-	-	-	4.35C	1/15/15	41.9 -	28.9
-	-	-0.30	1.76	1.48	0.70	21.8 -	14.5	-	-	-	-	0.10	7/15/16	38.3 -	25.6

SYMBOL	COMPANY	NATURE OF BUSINESS	FISCAL YEAR-END	TOTAL REV. $MILL	NET INCOME $MILL	TOTAL ASSETS $MILL	NET STK EQUITY $MILL	NO OF INST	INST. HOLDINGS (SHARES)
KOS	Kosmos Energy Ltd	Production & Extraction	12/31/15	471.6	-69.8	3203.0	1325.5	135	462798343
KRA	Kraton Performance Polymers Inc	Plastics	12/31/15	1034.6	-10.5	1092.7	358.7	195	31105752
KKD	Krispy Kreme Doughnuts Inc	Hotels, Restaurants & Travel	1/31/16	518.7	32.4	342.9	256.1	226	54083267
KR	Kroger Co (The)	Retail - Food & Beverage, Drug & To	1/30/16	109830.0	2039.0	33897.0	6820.0	1099	862304497
KRO	Kronos Worldwide Inc	Specialty Chemicals	12/31/15	1348.8	-173.6	1242.7	461.9	134	17566526
KT	KT Corp (Korea)	Services	12/31/15	22281221.0	552964.0	29341185.0	10845069.0	176	115124781
KYO	Kyocera Corp	Electrical Equipment	3/31/15	1526536.0	115875.0	3021184.0	2215319.0	101	1804078
LB	L Brands, Inc	Retail - Apparel and Accessories	1/30/16	12154.0	1253.0	8493.0	-259.0	751	245569127
LLL	L-3 Communications Holdings, Inc.	Aerospace	12/31/15	10466.0	-240.0	12085.0	4355.0		
LQ	La Quinta Holdings Inc	Hotels, Restaurants & Travel	12/31/15	1030.0	26.4	2985.8	743.6	174	132714169
LZB	La-Z-Boy Inc.	Furniture	4/30/16	1525.4	79.3	800.0	547.1	248	46378078
LH	Laboratory Corporation of America	Diagnostic & Health Related Service	12/31/15	8680.1	436.9	14221.7	4944.4	895	113256915
LADR	Ladder Capital Corp	REITs	12/31/15	442.8	146.1	5895.2	828.2	85	40178673
LDR	Landauer, Inc.	Diagnostic & Health Related Service	9/30/15	151.3	14.5	208.7	11.2	172	9453381
LKB 04	Landesbank Baden-Wurttemberg	Banking	12/31/14	18197.0	434.0	266230.0	13189.0		
LCI	Lannett Co., Inc.	Pharmaceuticals	6/30/15	406.8	149.9	508.8	463.4	278	28274733
LPI	Laredo Petroleum, Inc	Production & Extraction	12/31/15	606.6	-2209.9	1813.3	131.4	207	314208537
LVS	Las Vegas Sands Corp	Hotels, Restaurants & Travel	12/31/15	11688.5	1966.2	20987.4	6816.7	688	343321738
LHO	LaSalle Hotel Properties	REITs	12/31/15	1216.6	135.6	4074.8	2374.3	336	131922545
LFL	LATAM Airlines Group SA	Airlines/Air Freight	12/31/15	9740.0	-219.3	18101.4	2856.5	99	19845417
LDF	Latin American Discovery Fund, Inc.	Holding and other Investment Office	12/31/15	1.5	0.4	57.7	57.3	32	4034110
EL	Lauder (Estee) Cos., Inc. (The)	Household & Personal Products	6/30/15	10780.4	1088.9	8239.2	3643.2	844	226457459
LGI	Lazard Global Total Return & Incom	Holding and other Investment Office	12/31/15	6.2	3.8	163.3	146.6	38	3435387
LAZ	Lazard Ltd	Finance Intermediaries & Services	12/31/15	2404.8	986.4	4486.8	1313.5	390	110091355
LOR	Lazard World Dividend & Income Fu	Holding and other Investment Office	12/31/15	5.2	3.5	82.7	72.8	34	3126538
LEA	Lear Corp.	Auto Parts	12/31/15	18211.4	745.5	9405.8	2927.4	631	92075915
LEE	Lee Enterprises, Inc.	Publishing	9/27/15	648.5	23.3	763.5	-159.4	108	23339160
BWG	Legg Mason BW Global Income Op	Holding and other Investment Office	10/31/14	37.3	30.0	557.1	420.1	56	8176854
LM	Legg Mason, Inc.	Wealth Management	3/31/16	2660.8	-25.0	7520.4	4213.6	579	119797656
LEG	Leggett & Platt, Inc.	Furniture	12/31/15	3917.2	325.1	2967.6	1085.6	607	112890164
LEH 06	Lehman Brothers, Inc.	Finance Intermediaries & Services	11/30/02	12124.0	740.0	196219.0	3152.0		
LDOS	Leidos Holdings Inc	IT Services	1/1/16	4712.0	242.0	3377.0	1068.0	398	71882844
LEJU	Leju Holdings Ltd	Property, Real Estate & Developmen	12/31/15	575.8	35.3	626.8	424.7	52	7505013
LC	LendingClub Corp	Credit & Lending	12/31/15	979.7	-5.0	5793.6	1041.9	220	356554928
LEN	Lennar Corp.	Builders	11/30/15	9474.0	802.9	14419.5	5648.9	677	210539031
LII	Lennox International Inc	Industrial Machinery & Equipment	12/31/15	3467.4	186.6	1680.2	101.2	371	35694263
LUK	Leucadia National Corp.	Agricultural Livestock	12/31/15	10886.5	252.1	46339.8	10526.2	604	273569564
LVLT	Level 3 Communications, Inc.	Services	12/31/15	8229.0	3433.0	24145.0	10126.0	623	495182884
LXP	Lexington Realty Trust	REITs	12/31/15	430.8	111.7	3830.2	1440.0	346	188402152
LXK	Lexmark International, Inc.	Peripherals	12/31/15	3551.2	-40.4	3912.4	1118.0	383	73700994
LPL	LG Display Co Ltd	Electrical Equipment	12/31/15	28383884.0	966553.0	22577160.0	12192952.0	156	27715860
USA	Liberty All-Star Equity Fund	Holding and other Investment Office	12/31/15	19.3	7.0	1190.7	1136.6	141	64749413
ASG	Liberty All-Star Growth Fund Inc.	Holding and other Investment Office	12/31/15	1.2	-0.6	149.0	124.3	46	3943402
LPT	Liberty Property Trust	REITs	12/31/15	808.8	238.0	6557.6	2952.9	463	161523660
LOCK	Lifelock Inc	Miscellaneous Consumer Services	12/31/15	587.5	-51.0	592.8	318.1	209	88702574
LITB	Lightinthebox Holding Co., Ltd.	Retail - Apparel and Accessories	12/31/15	323.8	-39.4	55.5	-2.1	20	3028573
LLY	Lilly (Eli) & Co.	Pharmaceuticals	12/31/15	19958.7	2408.4	35568.9	14571.3	1633	936653799
LNC	Lincoln National Corp.	Life & Health	12/31/15	13572.0	1154.0	251937.0	13617.0	850	227123859
LNN	Lindsay Corp	Industrial Machinery & Equipment	8/31/15	560.2	26.3	536.5	288.6	228	15774085
LNKD	LinkedIn Corp	Internet & Software	12/31/15	2990.9	-164.8	7011.2	4468.6	661	102190927
LGF	Lions Gate Entertainment Corp.	Entertainment	3/31/16	2347.4	50.2	3855.5	850.3	322	155805625
LAD	Lithia Motors, Inc.	Retail - Automotive	12/31/15	7864.3	183.0	3227.3	828.2	345	26441063
LYV	Live Nation Entertainment, Inc.	Entertainment	12/31/15	7245.7	-32.5	6156.2	1237.0	352	136028439
LYG	Lloyds Banking Group Plc	Banking	12/31/15	30889.0	860.0	806688.0	46589.0	273	298947306
SCD	LMP Capital & Income Fund Inc	Holding and other Investment Office	11/30/15	14.6	10.4	354.1	275.4	68	6608058
LMT	Lockheed Martin Corp.	Defense	12/31/15	46132.0	3605.0	49128.0	3097.0	1445	304227486
L	Loews Corp.	General Insurance	12/31/15	13415.0	260.0	76029.0	17561.0	590	237735874
LPX	Louisiana-Pacific Corp.	Paper & Forest Products	12/31/15	1892.5	-88.1	2176.3	1017.0	295	167999662
LOW	Lowe's Companies Inc	Retail - Hardware & Home Improvem	1/29/16	59074.0	2546.0	31266.0	7654.0	1629	807029074
LXU	LSB Industries, Inc.	Specialty Chemicals	12/31/15	711.8	-34.8	1361.8	598.9	192	18510007
LTC	LTC Properties, Inc.	REITs	12/31/15	136.2	73.1	1275.4	659.2	258	33258341
LUB	Luby's, Inc.	Hotels, Restaurants & Travel	8/26/15	394.1	-2.1	264.3	174.7	84	12836958
LL	Lumber Liquidators Holdings Inc	Retail - Hardware & Home Improvem	12/31/15	978.8	-56.4	456.2	277.6	204	20928391
LXFR	Luxfer Holdings Plc	Industrial Machinery & Equipment	12/31/15	460.3	16.1	435.7	169.7	58	22365244
LXFT	Luxoft Holding, Inc.	IT Services	3/31/15	520.5	63.1	304.3	218.1	183	17711635
LUX	Luxottica Group S P.A.	Medical Instruments & Equipment	12/31/15	8836.6	804.1	9649.1	5412.5	173	7052067
LDL	Lydall, Inc.	Industrial Machinery & Equipment	12/31/15	524.5	46.3	358.3	245.2	176	15773342
WLH	Lyon (William) Homes	Builders	12/31/15	1106.6	57.3	1923.4	632.1	135	34373022
LYB	LyondellBasell Industries NV	Diversified Chemicals	12/31/15	32735.0	4476.0	22757.0	6550.0	893	308306013
MTB	M & T Bank Corp	Banking	12/31/15	5010.1	1079.7	122787.9	16173.3	736	136637055
MTB PRA	M & T Capital Trust IV	Banking						3	104665
MDC	M.D.C. Holdings, Inc.	Builders	12/31/15	1909.0	65.8	2415.9	1256.3	263	43170167
MHO	M/I Homes Inc	Builders	12/31/15	1418.4	51.8	1415.6	596.6	167	26160432
MAC	Macerich Co. (The)	REITs	12/31/15	1288.1	487.6	11258.6	4715.4	479	172083726
CLI	Mack Cali Realty Corp	REITs	12/31/15	594.9	-142.1	4063.5	1455.7	340	103929352
MGU	Macquarie Global Infrastructure Tot	Holding and other Investment Office	11/30/15	16.5	8.4	444.7	300.7	68	5595472
MIC	Macquarie Infrastructure Corp	Business Services	12/31/15	1639.3	-108.5	7378.8	3030.2	425	72915863
MFD	Macquarie/First Trust Global Infrastr	Holding and other Investment Office	11/30/14	15.1	12.3	168.0	115.4	46	1027977
M	Macy's Inc	Retail - General Merchandise/Depart	1/30/16	27079.0	1072.0	20576.0	4250.0	984	315898185
MCN	Madison Covered Call & Equity Stra	Holding and other Investment Office	12/31/15	2.6	0.7	166.0	163.4	54	8027066

EARNINGS PER SHARE QUARTERLY			EARNINGS PER SHARE ANNUAL			P/E RATIO		DIVIDENDS PER SHARE			AV. YLD %	DIV. DECLARED		PRICE RANGE 2015	
1st	2nd	3rd	2015	2014	2013			2015	2014	2013		AMOUNT	PAYABLE		
-0.15	-	-	-0.18	0.72	-0.24	-								9.0	3.5
2.84	-	-	-0.34	0.07	-0.02									27.2	13.7
0.14	-	-	0.44	0.48	0.30	49.0	29.9							21.5	13.2
-	-	0.43	1.72	1.45	1.39	24.8	19.6	0.34	0.31	0.25	0.9	0.120Y	61/28/99	42.6	33.7
-0.03	-	-	-1.50	0.86	-0.88			0.60	0.60	0.60	8.4	0.150Y	6/16/16	12.5	4.0
-	-	435.00	2258.09	4316.00	-666.00	0.0	0.0	-	400.43	988.90				14.5	11.0
-	-	72.05	315.85	241.93	181.18	0.2	0.1	79.00	110.71	60.22	166.0			54.5	38.5
0.52	-	-	3.50	3.05	2.54	28.6	17.3	2.36	1.20	5.00	2.7	0.60Y	61/28/99	100.2	60.6
2.87	-	-	-2.93	7.56	8.54			2.60	2.40	2.20	2.2	0.70Y	61/28/99	138.3	101.9
-0.31	-	-	0.20	-2.67		122.4	48.0							24.5	9.6
-	-	0.43	1.34	1.02	0.85	21.6	14.8	0.28	0.20	0.08	1.1	0.10Y	6/10/16	29.0	19.9
1.55	-	-	4.34	5.91	6.25	29.5	23.3					0.0826L	6/30/00	128.2	100.9
-0.09	-	-	1.42	0.86		13.0	6.8	2.23			16.3	0.2750Z	7/1/16	18.5	9.6
-	0.45	-	1.52	-2.65	0.49	27.4	18.0	1.38	2.20	2.20	3.9	0.2750Y	7/5/16	41.7	27.4
-	-	-0.15	4.04	1.62	0.46	15.5	4.3					0.0076	12/14/79	62.7	17.2
-0.85	-	-	-11.10	1.85	0.88									15.1	4.1
0.40	-	-	2.47	3.52	2.79	23.2	15.0	2.60	2.00	1.40	5.5	0.720Z	61/28/99	57.2	37.0
0.05	-	-	1.09	1.88	0.73	35.1	18.5	1.73	1.41	0.96	6.1	0.2188GHZ	61/28/99	38.3	20.1
-	-	-	-0.40	-0.48	-0.06					0.01				8.3	4.5
-	-	-	0.05	0.09	0.12	211.3	0.0	0.00	0.16	0.51	0.4	0.00310	7/15/16	10.6	0.0
-	-	0.71	2.82	3.06	2.58	34.4	26.9	0.92	0.78	1.08	1.1	0.30Y	61/28/99	97.1	75.7
-	-	-	0.39	0.37	0.39	41.9	27.7	1.11	1.25	1.09	8.4	0.07950	7/22/16	16.3	10.8
0.50	-	-	7.40	3.20	1.21			2.35	1.20	1.00		0.380	61/28/99		
-	-	-	0.51	0.85	0.59	24.4	14.7	0.92	1.03	0.94	9.5	0.05740	7/22/16	12.5	7.5
3.29	-	-	9.59	8.23	4.99	13.2	9.9	1.00	0.80	0.68	0.9	0.30Y	61/28/99	126.3	95.0
-	0.36	-	0.43	0.13	-1.51	7.9	2.7					0.190Y	10/1/08	3.4	1.2
-	-	-	1.43	1.43				-	1.77	1.43		0.090	8/26/16	15.5	10.3
-	-	-1.31	2.04	2.33	-2.65	26.8	12.4	0.64	0.52	0.44	1.6	0.220Y	61/28/99	54.8	25.2
0.63	-	-	2.28	0.68	1.34	22.4	16.6	1.26	1.22	1.18	2.8	0.340Y	61/28/99	51.0	37.8
0.66	-	-	3.27	1.94	6.16	18.1	11.6	1.60	0.64	1.92	3.4	0.320Y	61/28/99	59.0	38.0
-	-	-	0.26	0.50	0.35	38.8	13.0	0.18			3.1			10.1	3.4
0.01	-	-	-0.01	-0.44	0.00									19.3	3.5
0.63	-	-	3.46	2.80	2.15	16.1	10.9	0.16	0.16	0.16	0.3	0.040Y	61/28/99	55.6	37.8
0.56	-	-	4.09	4.23	3.39	34.7	26.2	1.38	1.14	0.92	1.1	0.430Y	61/28/99	142.0	107.2
-0.60	-	-	0.74	0.54	1.06	34.1	19.5	0.25	0.25	0.25	1.3	0.06250Y	61/28/99	25.2	14.4
0.34	-	-	9.58	1.21	-0.49	5.8	4.3							56.0	41.6
0.21	-	-	0.45	0.38	-0.07	21.0	14.7	0.68	0.68	0.61	8.1	0.81250Z	11/15/16	9.5	6.6
-0.63	-	-	-0.86	1.25	4.08			1.44	1.38	1.20	4.2	0.360Y	61/28/99	47.3	24.4
-	-	885.00	2701.00	2527.00	1191.00	0.0	0.0	250.23			2430.9			13.7	8.6
-	-	-	0.04	0.02	0.03	148.3	107.7	0.51	0.39	0.35	9.8	0.120	6/13/16	5.9	4.3
-	-	-	-0.03	-0.04	-0.04			0.77	0.33	0.31	16.9	0.090	6/13/16	5.3	3.5
0.39	-	-	1.60	1.47	1.60	23.4	17.1	1.90	1.90	1.90	5.8	0.4750Z	61/28/99	37.4	27.3
-0.12	-	-	-0.54	0.03	0.55									17.2	7.3
-	-	-0.02	-0.41	-0.30	-0.09									6.1	2.0
0.41	-	-	2.26	2.23	4.32	39.8	30.6	2.00	1.96	1.96	2.5	0.510Y	61/28/99	90.0	69.1
0.82	-	-	4.51	5.67	4.52	13.7	6.8	0.80	0.64	0.48	1.7	0.250Y	61/28/00	61.6	30.8
-	-0.37	-	2.22	4.00	5.47	40.4	28.9	1.09	0.92	0.47	1.6	0.200Y	61/28/99	89.7	64.1
-0.35	-	-	-1.29	-0.13	0.23									255.5	101.0
-	-	0.26	1.23	1.04	1.61	33.4	15.1	0.26	0.10		0.8	0.090Y	8/5/16	41.1	18.5
1.55	-	-	6.91	5.26	4.05	18.2	10.7	0.76	0.61	0.39	0.7	0.250Y	61/28/99	126.1	73.8
-0.29	-	-	-0.33	-0.49	-0.22									29.2	19.4
-	-	-	0.01	0.02	-0.01	555.0	332.0	0.04	0.04	0.04	0.9	0.48440	7/15/15	5.5	3.3
-	-	-	0.58	-	0.72	28.5	17.4	1.12	1.12	1.12	8.7	0.310	6/24/16	16.5	10.1
2.58	-	-	11.46	11.21	9.13	21.4	16.2	6.15	5.49	4.78	2.9	1.650Y	61/28/99	244.9	185.5
0.30	-	-	0.72	1.55	1.53	56.6	47.5	0.25	0.25	0.25	0.7	0.06250Y	61/28/99	40.7	34.2
0.07	-	-	-0.62	-0.53	1.23							0.150Y	61/28/99	18.7	13.8
0.98	-	-	2.71	2.14	1.69	29.6	23.4	0.87	0.70	0.62	1.2	0.350Y	61/28/99	80.3	63.4
-1.08	-	-	-1.67	0.83	2.33							10.0Y	4/1/10	43.8	4.3
0.53	-	-	1.94	1.99	1.63	25.0	20.0	2.07	2.04	1.91	4.8	0.180Z	6/30/16	48.5	38.9
-	-0.02	-	-0.07	-0.12	0.11							0.10	9/25/00	5.3	3.8
-1.20	-	-	-2.08	2.31	2.77									22.3	11.1
-	-	0.60	0.59	1.05	1.22	23.5	15.8	0.38	0.38	0.38	3.3			13.9	9.3
-	-	0.73	1.91	1.59	1.24				1.00	0.91					
-	-	-	1.67	1.34	1.14	44.3	31.6	1.04	0.52	0.47	1.6			74.0	52.7
0.54	-	-	2.71	1.28	1.14	14.2	9.4					0.0194	9/15/82	38.5	25.5
0.24	-	-	1.48	1.34	4.95	17.5	5.4							25.9	8.0
2.37	-	-	9.59	7.99	6.75			3.04	2.70	2.00		0.850	6/7/16		
1.73	-	-	7.18	7.42	8.20	18.6	14.0	2.80	2.80	2.80	2.4	0.70Y	61/28/99	133.2	100.8
												0.53130Z	12/16/13		
0.20	-	-	1.34	1.29	6.34	23.2	14.6	1.00	1.00		3.9	0.250Y	61/28/99	31.1	19.6
0.30	-	-	1.68	1.65	5.24	15.8	9.4					0.60940Y	6/15/16	26.6	15.7
2.76	-	-	3.08	10.45	3.00	27.9	23.5	6.63	2.51	2.36	8.4	0.680Z	61/28/99	85.9	72.5
0.69	-	-	-1.41	0.32	-0.17			0.60	0.90	1.50	2.8	0.150Z	61/28/99	26.4	17.0
-	-	-	0.67	0.90	1.59	37.9	23.8	1.44	1.40	1.28	7.0	0.370	6/30/16	25.4	16.0
0.28	-	-	-1.39	16.10	0.61			2.24	3.89	3.35	3.1	1.20Y	5/17/16	87.2	52.9
-	-	-	1.44	1.23	1.29	11.7	6.9	1.40	1.40	1.40	10.9	0.30	5/31/16	16.8	9.9
0.37	-	-	4.22	3.86	3.24	17.3	7.1	1.19	0.95	0.80	2.4	0.37750Y	61/28/99	72.8	30.1
-	-	-	0.04	-0.02	0.00	208.5	105.3	0.72	0.72	0.72	9.6	0.180	6/30/16	8.3	6.6

SYMBOL	COMPANY	NATURE OF BUSINESS	FISCAL YEAR-END	TOTAL REV. $MILL	NET INCOME $MILL	TOTAL ASSETS $MILL	NET STK EQUITY $MILL	NO OF INST	INST. HOLDINGS (SHARES)
MSG	Madison Square Garden Co (The) (	Sporting & Recreational	6/30/15	1071.6	-40.7	2148.9	1223.3	-	-
MSG	Madison Square Garden Co (The) (	Sporting & Recreational	6/30/15	1071.6	-40.7	2148.9	1223.3	-	-
MSP	Madison Strategic Sector Premium	Holding and other Investment Office	12/31/15	1.2	0.4	74.0	72.8	31	2240324
MMP	Magellan Midstream Partners LP	Equipment & Services	12/31/15	2188.5	819.1	6041.6	-	692	158172577
MGA	Magna International Inc.	Auto Parts	12/31/15	32134.0	2013.0	19706.0	8966.0	540	262136188
MX	MagnaChip Semiconductor Corp	Semiconductors	12/31/15	633.7	-84.9	477.9	-62.3	79	30698152
MAIN	Main Street Capital Corp	Holding and other Investment Office	12/31/15	164.6	107.1	1878.9	1070.9	173	23695809
MMD	MainStay DefinedTerm Municipal Hi	Holding and other Investment Office	5/31/15	40.9	32.7	810.4	524.4	-	-
MNK	Mallinckrodt plc	Pharmaceuticals	9/25/15	3346.9	324.7	16404.1	5311.2	540	107315810
MZF	Managed Duration Investment Grad	Holding and other Investment Office	7/31/15	7.4	6.0	171.9	170.6	36	2823714
MANU	Manchester United Plc	Entertainment	6/30/15	395.2	-0.9	1301.6	477.9	-	-
MTW	Manitowoc Company Inc (The)	Construction Services	12/31/15	3435.8	63.5	3448.9	819.5	350	131466604
MFS	Manitowoc Foodservice Inc	Industrial Machinery & Equipment	12/31/15	1570.1	157.1	1754.0	1208.7	179	108663455
MFS	Manitowoc Foodservice Inc	Industrial Machinery & Equipment	12/31/15	1570.1	157.1	1754.0	1208.7	179	108663455
MN	Manning & Napier Inc.	Wealth Management	12/31/15	327.8	13.2	230.8	168.8	97	11760916
MAN	ManpowerGroup	Business Services	12/31/15	19329.9	419.2	7517.5	2624.7	537	83544594
MFC	Manulife Financial Corp.	Life & Health	12/31/15	34430.0	2191.0	704643.0	41346.0	484	1085976720
MRO	Marathon Oil Corp.	Production & Extraction	12/31/15	5861.0	-2204.0	32311.0	18553.0	986	761694989
MPC	Marathon Petroleum Corp.	Refining & Marketing	12/31/15	72258.0	2852.0	43115.0	13237.0	988	410919780
MMI	Marcus & Millichap Inc	Property, Real Estate & Developmen	12/31/15	689.1	66.3	321.2	189.0	156	13129019
MCS	Marcus Corp. (The)	Hotels, Restaurants & Travel	12/31/15	324.3	23.6	807.9	363.4	165	17202919
MRIN	Marin Software Inc.	IT Services	12/31/15	108.5	-33.3	116.2	94.1	92	17551672
MHG	Marine Harvest ASA	Food	12/31/15	27880.7	1417.1	40260.1	18178.3	66	48908548
MPX	Marine Products Corp.	Leisure Equipment	12/31/15	207.1	14.3	110.7	90.2	61	7983694
HZO	MarineMax Inc	Retail - Specialty	9/30/15	751.4	48.3	467.6	283.6	182	28269972
MKL	Markel Corp (Holding Co)	General Insurance	12/31/15	5370.0	589.1	24941.3	7834.1	507	15182810
VAC	Marriott Vacations Worldwide Corp	Hotels, Restaurants & Travel	1/1/16	1830.5	122.8	2395.0	976.3	288	21268081
MMC	Marsh & McLennan Companies Inc.	Brokers & Intermediaries	12/31/15	12893.0	1599.0	18216.0	6513.0	829	513800408
MLM	Martin Marietta Materials, Inc.	Construction Materials	12/31/15	3539.6	288.8	6961.7	4057.3	572	71512441
MAS	Masco Corp.	Construction Materials	12/31/15	7142.0	355.0	5680.0	-135.0	748	358948424
DOOR	Masonite International Corp (New)	Construction Materials	1/3/16	1872.0	-47.1	1499.1	642.4	189	32665045
MTZ	MasTec Inc. (FL)	Construction Services	12/31/15	4208.3	-79.1	2940.2	939.6	274	67850889
MA	MasterCard Inc	Business Services	12/31/15	9667.0	3808.0	16269.0	6028.0	1540	872115916
MTDR	Matador Resources Co	Production & Extraction	12/31/15	316.2	-679.8	1140.9	488.0	220	80901010
MTRN	Materion Corp	Metal Products	12/31/15	1025.3	32.2	742.6	483.0	189	18750539
MATX	Matson Inc	Shipping	12/31/15	1884.9	103.0	1669.8	450.6	306	40000901
MLP	Maui Land & Pineapple Co., Inc	Property, Real Estate & Developmen	12/31/15	22.8	6.8	46.6	-10.9	38	3783588
MMS	MAXIMUS Inc.	Business Services	9/30/15	2099.8	157.8	1280.2	612.4	346	68950220
MXL	MaxLinear Inc	Semiconductors	12/31/15	300.4	-42.3	334.5	262.9	237	49709963
MBI	MBIA Inc.	General Insurance	12/31/15	853.0	180.0	14855.0	3729.0	318	149762452
MNI	McClatchy Co (The)	Publishing	12/27/15	1056.6	-300.2	1923.0	192.8	117	38564181
MKC	McCormick & Co., inc.	Food	11/30/15	4296.3	401.6	4507.8	1670.2	828	118236099
MDR	McDermott International, Inc. (Pana	Industrial Machinery & Equipment	12/31/15	3070.3	-18.0	3387.1	1486.8	390	215140018
MCD	McDonald's Corp	Hotels, Restaurants & Travel	12/31/15	25413.0	4529.3	37938.7	7087.9	2177	746253621
MUX	McEwen Mining Inc.	Precious Metals	12/31/15	73.0	-20.4	475.1	418.3	126	60141548
MCK	McKesson Corp.	Pharmaceuticals	3/31/16	190884.0	2258.0	56563.0	8924.0	1329	227516013
MDU	MDU Resources Group Inc.	Electric Utilities	12/31/15	4191.5	-657.7	6627.6	2396.5	452	133620549
MJN	Mead Johnson Nutrition Co	Food	12/31/15	4071.3	653.5	3998.1	-632.3	727	196549752
MTL	Mechel OAO	Non-Precious Metals	12/31/15	253141.0	-115163.0	342072.0	-267802.0	88	20262785
MEG	Media General Inc (New)	Radio & Television	12/31/15	1304.9	-39.5	4408.4	1448.0	234	131858988
MPW	Medical Properties Trust Inc	REITs	12/31/15	441.9	139.6	5609.4	2102.3	375	201630450
MED	Medifast Inc	Household & Personal Products	12/31/15	272.8	20.1	117.3	88.6	177	11602397
MCC	Medley Capital Corp	Holding and other Investment Office	9/30/15	149.2	72.9	1257.2	619.9	120	18404997
MDLY	Medley Management Inc	Finance Intermediaries & Services	12/31/15	67.4	3.1	121.5	-0.0	44	4459052
MD	Mednax, Inc.	Diagnostic & Health Related Service	12/31/15	2780.0	336.3	4547.2	2437.5	503	101727330
MDT	Medtronic PLC	Medical Instruments & Equipment	4/29/16	28833.0	3538.0	99782.0	52063.0	-	-
MRK	Merck & Co., Inc	Pharmaceuticals	12/31/15	39498.0	4442.0	101779.0	44676.0	2300	2182931178
MCY	Mercury General Corp.	General Insurance	12/31/15	3009.3	74.5	4628.6	1820.9	281	27460731
MDP	Meredith Corp	Publishing	6/30/15	1594.2	136.8	2843.3	951.8	311	42873233
MTH	Meritage Homes Corp	Builders	12/31/15	2579.5	128.7	2690.5	1258.9	227	40475580
MTOR	Meritor Inc	Auto Parts	9/30/15	3505.0	64.0	2195.0	-671.0	261	88999784
MTR	Mesa Royalty Trust	Oil Royalty Traders	12/31/15	2.1	1.9	4.1	3.7	22	119574
MSB	Mesabi Trust	Non-Precious Metals	1/31/15	26.1	24.8	10.1	1.6	59	1973250
MPG	Metaldyne Performance Group Inc	Auto Parts	12/31/15	3047.3	125.3	3177.2	636.1	88	64436742
MEI	Methode Electronics, Inc.	Electrical Equipment	4/30/16	809.1	84.6	655.9	470.1	274	35855171
MET	MetLife Inc	Life & Health	12/31/15	69951.0	5310.0	877933.0	68026.0	1376	910268952
MTD	Mettler-Toledo International, Inc.	Biotechnology	12/31/15	2395.4	352.8	2018.5	580.5	519	32416952
MXE	Mexico Equity & Income Fund, Inc.	Holding and other Investment Office	7/31/15	1.3	-0.6	106.7	103.1	27	4231467
MXF	Mexico Fund, Inc.	Holding and other Investment Office	10/31/15	6.8	1.5	311.8	311.2	53	2519947
MFA	MFA Financial, Inc.	REITs	12/31/15	491.4	313.2	13167.3	2967.3	343	340131815
MFCB	MFC Bancorp Ltd	Business Services	12/31/15	1579.7	-487.6	977.4	367.2	18	1360787
MCR	MFS Charter Income Trust	Holding and other Investment Office	11/30/15	30.7	26.0	585.9	484.0	90	29464269
MGF	MFS Government Markets Income	Holding and other Investment Office	11/30/15	6.9	5.5	201.5	184.8	58	20658616
CXE	MFS High Income Municipal Trust	Holding and other Investment Office	11/30/15	14.3	10.6	268.3	175.4	47	2695011
CMU	MFS High Yield Municipal Trust	Holding and other Investment Office	11/30/15	11.3	8.7	212.9	140.9	42	1361278
CIF	MFS Intermediate High Income Fun	Holding and other Investment Office	11/30/15	5.2	4.1	78.6	56.4	37	6215876
MIN	MFS Intermediate Income Trust	Holding and other Investment Office	10/31/15	17.7	13.7	599.8	594.5	104	54572708
CXH	MFS Investment Grade Municipal Tr	Holding and other Investment Office	11/30/15	8.4	6.3	179.3	123.7	36	3421492
MMT	MFS Multimarket Income Trust	Holding and other Investment Office	10/31/15	32.8	27.4	625.1	515.1	113	35487658
MFM	MFS Municipal Income Trust	Holding and other Investment Office	10/31/15	22.2	17.2	423.6	310.0	60	3661990

T38

\-\- EARNINGS PER SHARE \-\-						P/E RATIO		DIVIDENDS PER SHARE			AV. YLD %	DIV. DECLARED		PRICE RANGE 2015	
QUARTERLY			ANNUAL												
1st	2nd	3rd	2015	2014	2013			2015	2014	2013		AMOUNT	PAYABLE		
-	-	-2.47	-	-	-	-	-	-	-	-	-	-	-	180.0	0.0
-	-	-2.47	-	-	-	-	-	-	-	-	-	-	-	182.7	141.0
-	-	-	0.07	-0.01	0.01	174.5	140.9	1.04	1.04	1.04	9.4	0.260	6/30/16	12.2	9.9
0.91	-	-	3.59	3.69	2.56	22.1	15.3	2.92	2.50	2.10	4.3	0.80250	61/28/99	79.2	55.1
1.22	-	-	4.88	4.34	3.38	15.1	0.0	0.88	0.76	0.64	1.7	0.250	6/10/16	73.9	0.0
0.23	-	-	-2.47	-3.44	-1.82	-	-	-	-	-	-	-	-	9.6	3.3
0.54	-	-	2.18	2.20	2.06	15.2	12.1	2.66	2.55	2.67	8.9	0.38280Z	10/3/16	33.1	26.4
-	-	-	1.19	1.16	0.92	17.2	14.4	1.17	1.50	1.06	6.3	0.098M	6/30/16	20.5	17.2
-	1.06	-	2.75	-4.92	1.02	47.2	19.4	-	-	-	-	-	-	129.9	53.4
-	-	-	0.88	0.95	1.02	16.4	14.5	0.76	0.84	0.94	5.6	0.06160	6/30/16	14.4	12.8
-0.00	-	-	-0.55	0.15	0.90	-	-	-	-	-	-	0.0450	6/10/16	-	-
-1.49	-	-	0.46	1.05	1.05	13.2	5.7	0.08	0.08	0.08	2.1	0.080Y	61/28/99	6.0	2.6
0.13	-	-	1.15	1.17	1.07	11.6	0.0	-	-	-	-	-	-	13.4	0.0
0.13	-	-	1.15	1.17	1.07	14.3	12.0	-	-	-	-	-	-	16.5	13.8
0.16	-	-	0.90	0.67	0.19	13.7	6.3	0.72	0.72	0.64	8.2	0.160	8/1/16	12.3	5.7
0.98	-	-	5.40	5.30	3.62	17.9	13.0	1.60	0.98	0.92	1.9	0.860Y	61/28/99	96.6	70.3
-	-	0.30	1.05	1.80	1.62	22.9	0.0	0.67	0.57	0.52	3.7	0.4411GH	6/19/16	24.0	0.0
-0.56	-	-	-3.26	4.46	2.47	-	-	0.68	0.80	0.72	4.3	0.050Y	61/28/99	27.8	6.7
0.00	-	-	5.26	4.39	3.32	11.3	5.8	1.14	0.92	0.77	2.5	0.320Y	61/28/99	59.3	30.7
0.38	-	-	1.69	1.27	0.24	31.3	11.2	-	-	-	-	-	-	52.0	19.0
0.20	-	-	0.04	0.92	0.63	25.0	21.3	0.41	0.35	1.34	2.1	0.11250Y	6/15/16	21.0	17.9
-0.12	-	-	-0.91	-0.97	-1.36	-	-	-	-	-	-	-	-	7.6	2.1
4.00	-	-	3.21	2.28	6.70	5.2	3.5	5.08	8.21	-	37.8	-	-	16.7	11.1
0.10	-	-	0.39	0.24	0.20	22.3	13.4	0.20	0.16	0.15	2.9	0.060Y	6/10/16	8.7	5.2
-	0.10	-	1.92	0.46	0.63	13.5	7.2	-	-	-	-	-	-	25.9	13.9
11.15	-	-	41.74	22.27	22.48	23.5	18.5	-	-	-	-	-	-	982.8	774.2
0.82	-	-	3.82	2.33	2.18	24.1	12.2	1.05	0.25	-	1.6	0.30Y	6/9/16	91.9	46.6
0.91	-	-	2.98	2.65	2.43	22.2	17.2	1.18	1.06	0.96	2.1	0.340Y	61/28/99	66.1	51.3
0.69	-	-	4.29	2.71	2.61	45.0	27.3	1.60	1.60	1.60	1.0	0.40Y	61/28/99	193.2	117.0
0.32	-	-	1.02	2.38	0.76	32.1	22.2	0.36	0.33	0.30	1.3	0.0950Y	61/28/99	32.7	22.6
0.57	-	-	-1.56	-1.26	-0.39	-	-	-	-	-	-	-	-	71.4	45.6
-0.03	-	-	-0.98	1.35	1.66	-	-	-	-	-	-	-	-	23.5	12.8
0.86	-	-	3.35	3.10	2.56	30.3	24.1	0.64	0.44	0.21	0.7	0.190Y	61/28/99	101.5	80.7
-1.26	-	-	-8.34	1.56	0.77	-	-	-	-	-	-	-	-	28.4	12.6
0.27	-	-	1.58	2.00	0.94	24.6	13.7	0.35	0.34	0.32	1.2	0.0950Y	6/1/16	38.9	21.6
0.41	-	-	2.34	1.63	1.25	22.6	13.3	0.70	0.66	0.62	1.7	0.190Y	9/1/16	52.8	31.0
-0.07	-	-	0.36	0.94	-0.06	17.3	0.0	-	-	-	-	0.1250	3/31/00	6.2	0.0
-	0.74	-	2.35	2.11	1.67	29.7	19.5	0.18	0.18	0.18	0.3	0.0450Y	5/31/16	69.8	45.9
0.29	-	-	-0.79	-0.19	-0.37	-	-	-	-	-	-	-	-	20.7	9.2
-0.58	-	-	1.06	2.76	1.29	8.9	5.1	-	-	-	-	0.340Y	61/28/99	9.4	5.4
-1.60	-	-	-34.70	42.30	2.20	-	-	-	-	-	-	0.090Y	4/1/09	16.0	8.1
0.73	-	-	3.11	3.34	2.91	32.4	24.4	1.60	1.48	1.36	1.9	0.430Y	61/28/99	100.7	76.0
-0.01	-	-	-0.08	-0.32	-2.19	-	-	-	-	-	-	0.01670	7/1/00	5.9	2.3
1.23	-	-	4.80	4.82	5.55	27.4	19.0	3.44	3.28	3.12	3.1	0.890Y	61/28/99	131.6	91.2
0.04	-	-	-0.07	1.05	-0.50	-	-	0.01	-	-	0.7	0.005D	2/12/16	3.5	0.0
-	-	2.73	6.27	5.41	5.59	38.0	23.9	0.96	0.92	0.80	0.5	0.280Y	61/28/99	238.3	150.0
0.13	-	-	-3.20	1.55	1.47	-	-	0.73	0.71	0.69	3.9	1.2750Z	61/28/99	22.9	16.0
0.39	-	-	3.27	3.54	3.19	29.7	20.7	1.65	1.50	1.36	2.0	0.41250Y	61/28/99	97.0	67.6
-	-	-	-276.65	-318.79	-7.03	-	-	-	-	-	-	-	-	2.6	1.3
-0.20	-	-	-0.31	0.58	0.10	-	-	-	-	-	-	-	-	17.8	10.0
0.24	-	-	0.63	0.29	0.63	23.3	15.7	0.88	0.84	0.81	7.2	0.230Z	61/28/99	14.7	9.9
0.36	-	-	1.66	1.03	1.73	21.1	16.1	0.25	-	-	0.8	0.250Y	8/10/16	35.0	26.7
-	0.26	-	1.27	1.58	1.53	7.5	4.2	1.27	1.48	1.45	16.8	0.40630Z	7/30/16	9.5	5.4
-0.01	-	-	0.46	0.24	-	26.7	7.9	0.60	0.20	-	8.3	0.20Y	6/2/16	12.3	3.6
0.73	-	-	3.58	3.18	2.78	23.9	17.3	-	-	-	-	-	-	85.5	62.0
-	-	0.77	2.41	3.02	3.37	34.0	26.8	0.30	1.12	1.04	0.4	0.380	61/28/99	81.9	64.5
0.40	-	-	1.56	4.07	1.47	38.9	31.0	1.81	1.77	1.73	3.3	0.460Y	61/28/99	60.8	48.4
0.42	-	-	1.35	3.23	2.04	42.6	31.9	2.47	2.46	2.45	4.7	0.620Y	61/28/99	57.5	43.1
-	-	1.79	3.02	2.50	2.74	17.7	12.1	1.78	1.68	1.58	3.8	0.4950Y	61/28/99	53.4	36.5
0.50	-	-	3.09	3.46	3.25	15.9	8.7	-	-	-	-	-	-	49.2	26.0
-	0.35	-	0.64	2.51	-0.22	22.5	9.5	-	-	-	-	0.10Y	12/8/08	14.4	6.1
0.08	-	-	1.03	3.51	1.86	18.0	0.0	1.03	3.51	1.86	10.4	0.03580Z	7/29/16	18.5	0.0
-0.03	-	-	1.89	1.61	2.34	7.5	1.7	1.84	1.62	2.33	21.1	0.20	5/20/16	14.2	3.1
0.36	-	-	1.80	1.06	0.86	13.3	6.2	0.27	-	-	1.5	0.09250Y	6/21/16	23.9	11.2
-	-	0.45	2.57	2.51	1.08	18.9	9.3	0.36	0.30	0.28	1.2	0.090Y	7/29/16	48.6	24.0
1.98	-	-	4.57	5.42	2.91	12.6	7.7	1.48	1.33	1.01	3.1	0.40Y	61/28/99	57.7	35.2
2.40	-	-	12.48	11.44	9.96	30.1	22.2	-	-	-	-	-	-	375.3	277.6
-	-	-	-0.09	0.01	-0.09	-	-	1.62	2.13	0.19	14.3	0.56C	1/29/16	12.7	9.4
-	-	-	0.09	0.09	0.08	244.7	162.6	2.20	3.01	2.94	12.3	0.28310	7/26/16	22.0	14.6
0.20	-	-	0.80	0.81	0.78	10.0	7.2	0.80	0.80	1.64	11.4	0.20Z	61/28/99	8.0	5.8
-	0.11	-	-7.72	0.01	0.15	-	-	-	0.24	0.24	-	0.060	1/5/15	4.6	1.5
-	-	-	0.49	0.52	0.57	18.3	15.1	0.81	0.58	0.62	10.0	0.06140	6/30/16	9.0	7.4
-	-	-	0.17	0.18	0.20	32.9	30.4	0.43	0.45	0.48	8.0	0.03410	6/30/16	5.6	5.2
-	-	-	0.34	0.32	0.33	16.1	13.4	0.31	0.31	0.32	6.3	0.0245M	6/30/16	5.5	4.5
-	-	-	0.31	0.30	0.30	16.1	13.2	0.28	0.29	0.29	6.2	0.0225M	6/30/16	5.0	4.1
-	-	-	0.20	0.21	0.23	13.6	10.3	0.24	0.23	0.24	10.1	0.02140	6/30/16	2.7	2.1
-	-	-	0.12	0.15	0.18	40.1	37.2	0.45	0.48	0.51	9.8	0.03490	6/30/16	4.8	4.5
-	-	-	0.55	0.55	0.57	19.0	16.3	0.51	0.53	0.55	5.2	0.0405M	6/30/16	10.4	9.0
-	-	-	0.36	0.39	0.44	18.0	14.7	0.57	0.55	0.46	9.8	0.0440	6/30/16	6.5	5.3
-	-	-	0.42	0.41	0.43	17.9	14.9	0.39	0.41	0.44	6.8	0.0015M	6/30/16	7.5	6.3

SYMBOL	COMPANY	NATURE OF BUSINESS	FISCAL YEAR-END	TOTAL REV. $MILL	NET INCOME $MILL	TOTAL ASSETS $MILL	NET STK EQUITY $MILL	NO OF INST	INST. HOLDINGS (SHARES)
MFV	MFS Special Value Trust	Holding and other Investment Office	10/31/15	2.4	1.7	43.3	43.1	23	768896
MTG	MGIC Investment Corp. (WI)	Credit & Lending	12/31/15	1040.8	1172.0	5879.5	2236.1	395	360146484
MGP	MGM Growth Properties LLC	REITs	12/31/15		-262.0	7793.6	6059.0	-	
MGM	MGM Resorts International	Hotels, Restaurants & Travel	12/31/15	9190.1	-447.7	25215.2	5119.9	523	457591417
KORS	Michael Kors Holdings Ltd	Retail - Apparel and Accessories	4/2/16	4712.1	837.7	2566.8	1995.7	569	150049148
MAA	Mid-America Apartment Communiti	REITs	12/31/15	1042.8	332.3	6847.8	3000.3	456	76426557
MEP	Midcoast Energy Partners LP	Gas Utilities	12/31/15	2842.7	-284.5	5273.9		48	15920480
MSL	MidSouth Bancorp, Inc.	Banking	12/31/15	102.2	11.0	1927.7	213.1	57	4207584
MCRN	Milacron Holdings Corp	Industrial Machinery & Equipment	12/31/15	1179.5	-38.8	1696.3	440.9	71	108913652
MLR	Miller Industries Inc. (TN)	Auto Parts	12/31/15	541.0	16.0	270.9	173.9	107	9861683
HIE	Miller/Howard High Income Equity F	Holding and other Investment Office	11/3/14			0.1	0.1	26	1543246
MTX	Minerals Technologies, Inc.	Specialty Chemicals	12/31/15	1797.6	107.9	2980.0	910.5	294	38132070
MP PRD	Mississippi Power Co.	Electric Utilities	12/31/15	1138.0	-6.0	7840.0	2392.0	-	
MG	Mistras Group, Inc.	Business Services	5/31/15	711.3	16.1	471.7	244.8	126	20120473
MTU	Mitsubishi UFJ Financial Group Inc	Banking	3/31/15	4361475.0	1531127.0	280886326.0	14679065.0	301	187598065
MIXT	MiX Telematics Ltd.	Miscellaneous Transportation Servic	3/31/15	1389.4	149.6	2228.6	1865.4	36	2801693
MFG	Mizuho Financial Group Inc	Banking	3/31/15		803048.0	190119734.0	7930338.0	136	39600468
MBT	Mobile TeleSystems PJSC	Services	12/31/15	431232.0	49489.0	653378.0	160115.0	314	298310811
MBLY	Mobileye NV Amsterdam	Internet & Software	12/31/15	240.9	68.5	577.6	515.5	387	165319098
MODN	Model N, Inc	IT Services	9/30/15	93.8	-19.6	122.0	83.1	77	20352616
MOD	Modine Manufacturing Co	Auto Parts	3/31/16	1352.5	-1.6	920.9	376.2	185	43732844
MC	Moelis & Co	Banking	12/31/15	551.9	33.1	539.5	168.4	109	17183715
MHK	Mohawk Industries, Inc.	Construction Materials	12/31/15	8071.6	615.3	9942.4	4854.2	662	72619634
MOH	Molina Healthcare Inc	Hospitals & Health Care Facilities	12/31/15	14178.0	143.0	6576.0	1557.0	371	53065983
TAP	Molson Coors Brewing Co.	Beverages	12/31/15	3567.5	359.5	12276.3	7043.0	705	185391064
MNR	Monmouth Real Estate Investment	REITs	9/30/15	78.0	25.6	916.0	446.0	207	35666898
MORE	Monogram Residential Trust Inc	REITs	12/31/15	238.1	73.8	3283.1	1166.7	185	118002532
MON	Monsanto Co.	Agricultural Chemicals	8/31/15	15001.0	2314.0	21920.0	6990.0	1342	406199562
MWW	Monster Worldwide Inc	Business Services	12/31/15	666.9	73.6	1159.9	481.4	300	98902428
MCO	Moody's Corp.	Business Services	12/31/15	3484.5	941.3	5123.4	-565.0	737	206472853
MOG A	Moog, Inc.	Industrial Machinery & Equipment	10/3/15	2525.5	131.9	3086.5	994.5	262	31798273
MS	Morgan Stanley	Finance Intermediaries & Services	12/31/15	37897.0	6127.0	787465.0	75182.0	1196	1742195963
APF	Morgan Stanley Asia-Pacific Fund, I	Holding and other Investment Office	12/31/15	5.3	2.2	218.1	215.6	61	10066776
CAF	Morgan Stanley China A Share Fun	Holding and other Investment Office	12/31/14	15.9	6.0	797.9	759.3	84	10331853
MSD	Morgan Stanley Emerging Markets	Holding and other Investment Office	12/31/15	15.2	12.5	239.9	216.8	65	10300974
EDD	Morgan Stanley Emerging Markets	Holding and other Investment Office	10/31/14	89.0	66.0	1434.5	954.5	97	18936106
MSF	Morgan Stanley Emerging Markets	Holding and other Investment Office	12/31/15	4.2	0.7	212.4	207.2	54	8412309
ICB	Morgan Stanley Funds - Income Se	Holding and other Investment Office	9/30/15	7.3	6.0	172.6	171.2	38	4612662
IIF	Morgan Stanley India Investment Fu	Holding and other Investment Office	12/31/15	3.9	-2.4	436.0	434.6	69	6706034
ICB	Morgan Stanley Trusts	Holding and other Investment Office	10/31/02	5.5	4.8	103.9	103.8	-	
MOS	Mosaic Co (The)	Agricultural Chemicals	12/31/15	8895.3	1000.4	17412.4	9531.8	763	337517970
MSI	Motorola Solutions Inc.	Manufacturing	12/31/15	5695.0	610.0	8387.0	-106.0	801	318354917
MOV	Movado Group, Inc.	Miscellaneous Consumer Goods	1/31/16	594.9	45.1	585.2	440.6	221	19023342
MPLX	MPLX LP	Equipment & Services	12/31/15	703.0	156.0	15677.0		323	208912342
MRC	MRC Global Inc	Industrial Machinery & Equipment	12/31/15	4528.6	-331.6	2501.5	1311.3	234	101271515
MSA	MSA Safety Inc	Office Equipment & Furniture	12/31/15	1129.9	70.8	1424.8	516.5	228	26560405
MSM	MSC Industrial Direct Co., Inc.	Industrial Machinery & Equipment	8/29/15	2910.4	231.3	2101.2	1332.9	384	54831879
MSCI	MSCI Inc	Publishing	12/31/15	1075.0	223.6	3147.0	901.5	381	96854423
MSGN	MSG Network Inc	Entertainment	6/30/15	1621.6	254.7	3019.8	1723.5	477	75258135
MSGN	MSG Network Inc	Entertainment	6/30/15	1621.6	254.7	3019.8	1723.5	477	75258135
MLI	Mueller Industries Inc	Industrial Machinery & Equipment	12/26/15	2100.0	87.9	1338.8	827.3	235	59780711
MWA	Mueller Water Products Inc	Industrial Machinery & Equipment	9/30/15	1164.5	30.9	1229.8	366.3	277	143680895
MPSX	Multi Packaging Solutions Internatio	Paper & Forest Products	6/30/15	1617.6	6.5	1882.1	282.0	67	45337487
MUR	Murphy Oil Corp	Production & Extraction	12/31/15	3033.1	-2270.8	11493.8	5306.7	588	176886509
MUSA	Murphy USA Inc	Retail - General Merchandise/Depart	12/31/15	12699.4	176.3	1886.2	792.3	-	
MVO	MV Oil Trust	Production & Extraction	12/31/15	15.5	14.7	22.2	22.2	43	1034692
MVC	MVC Capital Inc	Holding and other Investment Office	10/31/15	23.7	9.3	516.8	294.1	89	14462543
MYE	Myers Industries Inc.	Plastics	12/31/15	601.5	17.8	429.9	97.7	161	28687570
NBR	Nabors Industries Ltd.	Production & Extraction	12/31/15	3791.7	-372.7	9537.8	4282.7	537	293453872
NC	NACCO Industries Inc.	Household Appliances, Electronics &	12/31/15	915.9	22.0	655.4	201.1	121	3802259
NTP	Nam Tai Property Inc	Property, Real Estate & Developmen	12/31/15	1.0	-13.2	271.5	265.6	70	8701633
NBHC	National Bank Holdings Corp	Banking	12/31/15	192.9	4.9	4683.9	617.5	130	30288440
NFG	National Fuel Gas Co. (NJ)	Gas Utilities	9/30/15	1760.9	-379.4	6702.1	2025.4	469	62957461
NGG	National Grid plc	Electric Utilities	3/31/16	15115.0	2591.0	58934.0	13555.0	460	47481320
NHI	National Health Investors, Inc.	REITs	12/31/15	229.0	150.3	2146.3	1133.3	264	27937439
NOV	National Oilwell Varco Inc	Equipment & Services	12/31/15	14757.0	-769.0	26725.0	16383.0	1042	404831548
NPK	National Presto Industries, Inc.	Defense	12/31/15	427.7	40.5	387.4	339.3	182	4307857
NNN	National Retail Properties Inc	REITs	12/31/15	482.9	197.8	5460.0	3342.1	418	153857533
NSA	National Storage Affiliates Trust	REITs	12/31/15	133.9	12.4	1101.9	236.6	119	19883605
NW PRC	National Westminster Bank Plc	Banking	12/31/15	8437.0	-1205.0	302430.0	14821.0	-	
NSM	Nationstar Mortgage Holdings Inc	Credit & Lending	12/31/15	1988.6	38.8	16654.1	1758.1	157	111201439
NGS	Natural Gas Services Group Inc	Equipment & Services	12/31/15	95.9	10.1	285.6	224.0	126	12867267
NGVC	Natural Grocers By Vitamin Cottage	Retail - Food & Beverage, Drug & To	9/30/15	624.7	16.2	233.9	115.5	96	8334464
NRP	Natural Resources Partners L.P.	Mining	12/31/15	488.8	-571.7	1684.1		125	9872824
NTZ	Natuzzi S.p.A	Furniture	12/31/15	488.5	-16.5	349.4	157.3	23	12141443
NLS	Nautilus Inc	Leisure Equipment	12/31/15	335.8	26.6	315.9	127.0	226	36406628
NCI	Navigant Consulting, Inc.	Business Services	12/31/15	919.5	60.3	1015.9	593.5	240	48529157
NVGS	Navigator Holdings Ltd.	Miscellaneous Transportation Servic	12/31/15	315.2	98.1	1570.6	910.1	-	
NNA	Navios Maritime Acquisition Corp	Equipment & Services	12/31/15	313.4	89.7	1774.1	547.4	109	35610895
NM	Navios Maritime Holdings Inc	Shipping	12/31/15	497.0	-134.1	2958.8	989.0	121	33654388

1st	2nd	3rd	2015	2014	2013	P/E RATIO		2015	2014	2013	AV. YLD %	AMOUNT	PAYABLE	PRICE RANGE 2015	
			0.25	0.28	0.33	25.9 -	19.0	0.65	0.70	0.70	12.0	0.04890	6/30/16	6.5 -	4.7
0.17			2.60	0.64	-0.16	4.5 -	2.2					0.0250Y	9/2/08	11.6 -	5.7
												0.2632GHY	7/15/16	23.0 -	21.8
0.12			-0.82	-0.31	-0.32							0.05G	61/28/99	24.1 -	16.6
		1.59	4.28	3.22	1.97										
0.58			4.41	1.97	2.25	23.5 -	16.5	3.08	2.92	2.78	3.5	0.820Z	61/28/99	103.7 -	72.8
-0.44			-3.55	1.39	0.68			1.40	1.14		15.7	0.35750	5/13/16	13.4 -	3.9
0.17			0.90	1.58	1.12	17.3 -	7.5	0.36	0.35	0.31	3.3	0.090Y	7/1/16	15.6 -	6.7
0.14			-0.65	-0.28	-0.55									21.1 -	12.0
0.30			1.41	1.31	0.82	16.7 -	12.3	0.64	0.60	0.56	3.1	0.170Y	6/20/16	23.6 -	17.3
												0.1160	6/30/16	17.7 -	8.8
0.97			3.08	2.65	2.30	23.0 -	12.0	0.20	0.20	0.20	0.4	0.050Y	61/28/99	70.9 -	37.0
								1.31	1.31	1.31	6.7	1.31250Y	7/1/16	27.9 -	0.0
		0.12	0.54	0.77	0.40	48.1 -	23.7							26.0 -	12.8
19.74			107.50	69.98	74.16	0.1 -	0.0	17.79	14.17	12.06	299.6			7.5 -	3.9
			0.19	0.20	0.19	42.8 -	17.9							8.1 -	3.4
			31.64	19.64	34.47	0.1 -	0.1	13.83	12.15	12.06	372.1			4.5 -	2.7
		9.09	24.87	26.06	40.14	0.4 -	0.2	46.79	46.99	38.45	603.5			10.3 -	5.2
-0.61			0.29	-0.15	-6.03										
	-0.33		0.76	-0.86	-0.06	16.4 -	12.4							12.4	0.4
		0.17	0.45	2.72	-0.52	25.3 -	13.4					0.10Y	12/5/08	11.4 -	6.0
0.31			1.55	-0.19		19.8 -	15.3	1.00	1.40		3.6	0.30	6/3/16	30.7 -	23.6
2.30			8.31	7.25	4.82	25.4 -	18.3							211.3 -	151.8
0.43			2.58	1.29	1.13	31.6 -	17.6							81.5 -	45.3
0.78			1.93	2.76	3.08	51.9 -	33.8	1.64	1.48	1.28	1.9	0.410Y	61/28/99	100.2 -	65.2
	0.08		0.43	0.40	0.50	28.3 -	21.2	0.60	0.60	0.60	5.8	0.49220Z	6/15/16	12.2 -	9.1
-0.05			0.44	-0.04	0.18	23.8 -	17.6	0.30	0.07	0.35	3.1	0.0750Z	7/8/16	10.4 -	7.8
	2.41		4.81	5.22	4.60	24.2 -	17.3	1.96	1.72	1.50	2.0	0.540Y	61/28/99	116.6 -	83.1
0.02			0.78	-3.29		10.4 -	3.2							8.1 -	2.5
0.93			4.63	4.61	3.60	24.4 -	16.9	1.36	1.12	0.90	1.4	0.370Y	61/28/99	112.9 -	78.5
	0.85		3.35	3.52	2.63	21.5 -	11.7					0.01480	10/5/88	72.1 -	39.1
0.55			2.90	1.60	1.36	14.0 -	7.5	0.55	0.35	0.20	1.7	0.150Y	61/28/99	40.5 -	21.7
			0.16	0.15	0.15	101.1 -	0.0	0.14	1.22	0.22	1.0	0.14410	1/15/16	16.2 -	0.0
				0.27	0.11				1.72	0.11		1.7548B	12/28/15	37.9 -	14.4
			0.57	0.53	0.56	16.8 -	13.8	0.60	0.57	0.97	6.9	0.150	7/15/16	9.6 -	7.9
				0.94	1.19				1.65	1.00		0.180	7/15/16	9.2 -	6.1
			0.05	0.07	0.09	303.6 -	227.2	0.05	0.12	0.05	0.4	0.02770	7/15/16	15.2 -	11.4
			0.67	0.64	0.75	27.4 -	24.5	0.81	0.70	0.69	4.7	0.050	6/24/16	18.4 -	16.4
			-0.16	-0.08	-0.07			0.04			0.2	0.4494C	7/15/16	29.3 -	21.5
												0.050	6/24/16	18.4 -	16.4
0.73			2.78	2.68	0.80	16.9 -	7.9	1.08	1.00	1.00	3.3	0.2750Y	61/28/99	46.9 -	22.1
0.10			3.02	5.29	4.06	25.3 -	18.8	1.43	1.30	1.14	2.1	0.410Y	61/28/99	76.3 -	56.8
0.14			2.02	1.97	2.22	15.1 -	10.2	0.40	0.26	1.45	1.5	0.130Y	6/21/16	30.5 -	20.5
-0.33			1.22	1.55	1.05	62.3 -	13.5	1.70	1.34	1.03	4.2	0.5050	5/13/16	76.0 -	16.5
-0.14			3.38	1.40	1.48									16.0 -	8.7
0.31			1.87	2.33	2.34	28.1 -	20.5	1.27	1.23	1.18	2.8	0.56250Y	61/28/99	52.6 -	38.3
	0.80		3.74	3.76	3.75	20.8 -	14.7	4.60	1.32	1.20	6.8	0.430Y	61/28/99	77.8 -	55.0
0.60			2.03	2.43	1.83	39.3 -	28.5	0.80	0.18		1.2	0.220	61/28/99	79.8 -	57.8
		0.59	3.28	1.47	1.83	6.3 -	5.7							20.7 -	18.6
		0.59	3.28	1.47	1.83	8.0 -	4.7							26.1 -	15.4
0.50			1.54	1.79	3.06	23.5 -	15.5	0.30	0.30	0.25	1.0	0.10	6/15/16	36.2 -	23.8
	0.10		0.19	0.34	0.25	58.4 -	39.3	0.07	0.07	0.07	0.8	0.030Y	5/20/16	11.1 -	7.5
		0.05	0.10	-1.17	-203.74	180.4 -	136.9							18.0 -	13.7
-1.16			-13.03	5.03	5.94			1.40	1.33	1.25	4.9	0.350Y	61/28/99	43.9 -	15.8
2.08			4.02	5.26	5.02	17.0 -	12.1							68.4 -	48.7
0.10			1.27	3.40	3.22	9.2 -	2.9	1.27	3.40	3.22	20.2	0.030Z	4/25/16	11.7 -	3.7
0.22			0.41	0.07	-0.15	25.3 -	16.6	0.54	0.54	0.54	6.5	0.45310Z	10/17/16	10.4 -	6.8
-0.11			0.57	-0.27	0.76	34.1 -	18.2	0.54	0.52	0.36	3.8	0.1350Y	7/5/16	19.4 -	10.4
-1.41			-1.29	-2.28	0.47			0.24	0.20	0.16	2.4	0.060	61/28/99	15.1 -	5.5
0.41			3.13	-5.02	5.47	19.9 -	12.9	1.04	1.02	1.00	2.0	0.26750Y	6/15/16	62.4 -	40.5
		0.40	0.32	-0.58	0.01			0.08	0.08	0.47		0.020	10/31/16		
0.01			0.14	0.22	0.14	165.5 -	133.2	0.20	0.20	0.20	1.0	0.050Y	6/15/16	23.2 -	18.6
	-1.74		-4.50	3.52	3.08			1.56	1.52	1.48	3.1	0.4050Y	61/28/99	64.3 -	37.9
			0.53	0.66	0.62	140.4 -	121.1							74.4 -	64.2
0.85			3.95	3.04	3.74	18.1 -	13.7	3.40	3.08	3.12	5.5	0.90Z	61/28/99	71.3 -	54.1
-0.32			-1.99	5.82	5.44			1.84	1.64	0.91	5.0	0.050Y	61/28/99	50.2 -	26.3
1.04			5.83	3.82	5.97	16.0 -	12.1	4.05	5.05		4.9	4.056Y	3/15/16	93.4 -	70.3
0.44			1.20	1.24	1.10	39.7 -	28.3	1.71	1.65	1.60	4.3	0.4350Z	61/28/99	47.6 -	34.0
0.07			0.17			132.4 -	68.3	0.54			3.4	0.220Z	6/30/16	22.5 -	11.6
								1.27	1.18	1.24	4.9			26.3 -	24.4
-1.28			0.37	2.45	2.40	54.0 -	23.3							20.0 -	8.6
0.20			0.79	1.11	1.15	31.2 -	20.5							24.6 -	16.2
	0.16		0.72	0.60	0.47	37.1 -	17.9							26.7 -	12.9
1.88			-45.75	9.40	15.40				14.00	22.00		0.45G	5/13/16	41.4 -	6.9
		-0.34	-0.30	-0.90	-1.25									2.4 -	0.0
0.37			0.84	0.59	1.52	27.2 -	16.8					0.10Y	9/10/07	22.8 -	14.2
0.26			1.23	-0.75	1.02	14.4 -	11.1							17.7 -	13.6
			1.76	1.52	0.89										
		-0.03	0.56	0.08	-0.57			0.20	0.20	0.20		0.050	6/22/16		
		-0.13	-1.42	-0.65	-1.09			0.18	0.24	0.24		0.000	9/25/15		

SYMBOL	COMPANY	NATURE OF BUSINESS	FISCAL YEAR-END	TOTAL REV. $MILL	NET INCOME $MILL	TOTAL ASSETS $MILL	NET STK EQUITY $MILL	NO OF INST	INST. HOLDINGS (SHARES)
NAP	Navios Maritime Midstream Partner	Shipping	12/31/15	83.4	27.1	480.6		29	3402865
NMM	Navios Maritime Partners LP	Shipping	12/31/15	223.7	41.8	1350.3		99	12631598
NAV	Navistar International Corp.	Autos- Manufacturing	10/31/15	10140.0	-184.0	6692.0	-5167.0	233	95218990
NCS	NCI Building Systems, Inc.	Metal Products	11/1/15	1563.7	17.8	1079.7	272.0	193	68988869
NCR	NCR Corp.	Computer Hardware & Equipment	12/31/15	6373.0	-178.0	7635.0	1518.0	487	127118440
NP	Neenah Paper Inc	Paper & Forest Products	12/31/15	887.7	51.1	751.4	311.6	256	19718568
NEFF	Neff Corp (New)	Industrial Machinery & Equipment	12/31/15	383.9	15.6	653.7	-94.6	61	7469653
NNI	Nelnet Inc	Credit & Lending	12/31/15	1202.2	268.0	30485.9	1884.4	176	18654685
NPTN	NeoPhotonics Corp	Semiconductors	12/31/15	339.4	3.7	341.9	211.7	157	34408479
N	Netsuite Inc	Internet & Software	12/31/15	741.1	-124.7	1141.0	306.2	253	47853569
NSR	NeuStar, Inc.	Services	12/31/15	1050.0	175.5	2202.2	723.5	359	76061336
NVRO	Nevro Corp	Medical Instruments & Equipment	12/31/15	69.6	-67.4	291.2	234.6	155	27578445
HYB	New America High Income Fund, In	Holding and other Investment Office	12/31/15	21.6	17.8	289.2	206.5	73	11750848
GF	New Germany Fund, Inc.	Holding and other Investment Office	12/31/15	5.2	2.1	284.0	257.8	57	10313111
IRL	New Ireland Fund, Inc. (The)	Holding and other Investment Office	10/31/15	2.3	1.0	84.4	82.1	36	2070004
NJR	New Jersey Resources Corp	Gas Utilities	9/30/15	2734.0	181.0	3339.0	1107.0	344	56360195
NEWM	New Media Investment Group Inc	Publishing	12/27/15	1195.8	67.6	1200.3	647.1	180	39796693
NMFC	New Mountain Finance Corp	Wealth Management	12/31/15	153.9	82.5	1602.1	836.9	130	27870006
EDU	New Oriental Education & Technolo	Educational Services	5/31/15	1246.8	193.0	1951.5	1220.3	263	127552806
NEWR	New Relic Inc	Internet & Software	3/31/16	181.3	-67.5	294.4	193.2	122	28057313
NRZ	New Residential Investment Corp	REITs	12/31/15	371.1	281.9	15192.7	2795.9	284	162356120
SNR	New Senior Investment Group Inc	REITs	12/31/15	388.5	-82.4	3017.5	767.3	170	61225550
NWY	New York & Company Inc	Retail - Apparel and Accessories	1/30/16	950.1	-10.1	283.5	93.8	106	27870345
NYCB	New York Community Bancorp Inc.	Credit & Lending	12/31/15	1902.3	-47.2	50317.8	5934.7	619	291852457
NYRT	New York REIT Inc	Property, Real Estate & Developmen	12/31/15	174.5	-39.1	2071.8	1034.7	213	127621781
NYT	New York Times Co.	Publishing	12/27/15	1579.2	63.2	2417.7	826.8	304	133161324
NCT	Newcastle Investment Corp	REITs	12/31/15	391.7	21.6	1468.0	210.4	167	55816915
NWL	Newell Brands Inc	Plastics	12/31/15	5915.7	350.0	7278.0	1822.9	730	338771155
NFX	Newfield Exploration Co	Production & Extraction	12/31/15	1557.0	-3362.0	4768.0	1379.0	576	213766507
NEU	NewMarket Corp	Specialty Chemicals	12/31/15	2140.8	238.6	1289.9	387.6	323	8543760
NEM	Newmont Mining Corp (Holding Co)	Precious Metals	12/31/15	7729.0	220.0	25182.0	11350.0	895	460794132
NR	Newpark Resources, Inc.	Equipment & Services	12/31/15	676.9	-90.8	848.9	520.3	229	90665557
NHF	NexPoint Credit Strategies Fund	Holding and other Investment Office	12/31/15	159.6	139.8	627.6	366.1	75	7271980
NXRT	NexPoint Residential Trust Inc	REITs	12/31/15	117.7	-10.8	976.3	221.5	104	8727989
NEE PRK	NextEra Energy Capital Holdings In	Electric Utilities							
NEE	NextEra Energy Inc	Electric Utilities	12/31/15	17486.0	2762.0	82479.0	22574.0	1511	368087329
NEP	NextEra Energy Partners LP	Electric Utilities	12/31/15	471.0	10.0	6092.0	0.0	140	37037213
NGL	NGL Energy Partners LP	Refining & Marketing	3/31/16	11742.1	-187.1	5560.2		124	56910936
NLSN	Nielsen Holdings PLC	Business Services	12/31/15	6172.0	570.0	15303.0	4433.0	482	341304681
NKE	NIKE Inc	Apparel, Footwear & Accessories	5/31/15	30601.0	3273.0	21600.0	12707.0	1695	1120565284
NMBL	Nimble Storage Inc	Internet & Software	1/31/16	322.2	-120.1	331.7	155.6	159	53466729
NTT	Nippon Telegraph & Telephone Cor	Services	3/31/15	1095317.0	518066.0	20702427.0	8710132.0	274	32193245
NKA	Niska Gas Storage Partners LLC	Equipment & Services	3/31/16	54.3	-101.5	991.9	80.6	53	61789378
NI	NiSource Inc. (Holding Co.)	Electric Utilities	12/31/15	4651.8	286.5	17492.5	3843.5	609	294714007
NL	NL Industries, Inc.	Electrical Equipment	12/31/15	109.0	-23.9	349.3	149.9	59	3716440
NOAH	Noah Holdings Ltd	Wealth Management	12/31/15	2119.9	535.8	4097.0	2448.9	101	24914081
NE	Noble Corp plc	Equipment & Services	12/31/15	3352.3	511.0	12892.0	6699.2		
NBL	Noble Energy, Inc.	Production & Extraction	12/31/15	3133.0	-2441.0	24196.0	10370.0	730	427384283
NOK	Nokia Corp	Manufacturing	12/31/15	12499.0	2466.0	20926.0	10503.0	546	327073402
NOK	Nokia Corp	Manufacturing	12/31/15	12499.0	2466.0	20926.0	10503.0	546	327073402
NOMD	Nomad Foods Ltd	Food	12/31/15	894.2	-337.3	4929.7	1888.1	66	137659830
NMR	Nomura Holdings Inc	Finance Intermediaries & Services	3/31/15	1003015.0	224785.0	41783236.0	2707774.0	151	42228208
OSB	Norbord Inc	Paper & Forest Products	12/31/15	1509.0	-56.0	1633.0	519.0		
NORD	Nord Anglia Education Inc	Educational Services	8/31/15	577.0	7.4	2423.3	275.4	68	30047048
NAO	Nordic American Offshore Ltd	Miscellaneous Transportation Servic	12/31/15	36.4	-10.8	337.4	280.9	72	4330854
NAT	Nordic American Tankers Ltd	Equipment & Services	12/31/15	445.7	114.6	1244.6	880.7	243	32418805
JWN	Nordstrom, Inc.	Retail - General Merchandise/Depart	1/30/16	14437.0	600.0	7698.0	871.0	835	133360608
NSC	Norfolk Southern Corp.	Rail	12/31/15	10511.0	1556.0	34260.0	12188.0	1323	232756700
NTL	Nortel Inversora S.A.	Services	12/31/15	40539.0	1891.0	38542.0	9605.0		
NOA	North American Energy Partners Inc	Equipment & Services	12/31/15	281.3	-7.5	360.7	171.6	48	19397133
NADL	North Atlantic Drilling Ltd	Production & Extraction	12/31/15	747.7	-94.8	3255.1	392.2	67	2441126
NRT	North European Oil Royalty Trust	Oil Royalty Traders	10/31/15	12.4	11.6	2.2	0.1	59	1196131
NOC	Northrop Grumman Corp	Defense	12/31/15	23526.0	1990.0	24454.0	5522.0	1057	200726097
NSAM	NorthStar Asset Management Grou	REITs	12/31/15	435.8	119.8	374.8	175.1	265	165311577
NRE	NorthStar Realty Europe Corp	REITs	12/31/15	120.5	-143.1	2683.0	787.1	225	44058338
NRF	NorthStar Realty Finance Corp	REITs	12/31/15	2036.2	-267.3	15403.0	3799.2	411	152394276
NRF	NorthStar Realty Finance Corp	REITs	12/31/15	2036.2	-267.3	15403.0	3799.2	411	152394276
NWN	Northwest Natural Gas Co.	Gas Utilities	12/31/15	723.8	53.7	3076.7	781.0	255	18423602
NWE	Northwestern Corp.	Electric Utilities	12/31/15	1214.3	151.2	5278.6	1600.2	303	53625665
NVS	Novartis AG Basel	Pharmaceuticals	12/31/15	50387.0	17783.0	131556.0	77046.0	1222	272689088
NVO	Novo-Nordisk A/S	Pharmaceuticals	12/31/15	107927.0	34860.0	91799.0	46969.0	702	210014660
DNOW	Now Inc	Equipment & Services	12/31/15	3010.0	-502.0	1832.0	1403.0	360	107145693
NQ	NQ Mobile Inc	IT Services	12/31/15	406.7	-1.3	802.1	463.7	79	9075172
NRG	NRG Energy Inc	Electric Utilities	12/31/15	14674.0	-6382.0	32882.0	3009.0	554	351436860
NYLD	NRG Yield Inc	Electrical Equipment	12/31/15	869.0	33.0	7775.0	1841.0	154	60783103
DCM	NTT DoCoMo Inc	Services	3/31/15	4383397.0	410093.0	7146340.0	5380072.0	166	24373660
NUS	NU Skin Enterprises, Inc.	Household & Personal Products	12/31/15	2247.0	133.0	1505.8	825.6	304	48168220
NUE	Nucor Corp.	Non-Precious Metals	12/31/15	16439.3	357.7	14250.4	7416.9	895	311677134
NS	NuStar Energy LP	Equipment & Services	12/31/15	2084.0	306.7	5149.3		291	44657219
NSH	NuStar GP Holdings LLC	Equipment & Services	12/31/15	79.7	72.2	360.5	287.1	117	32618764

T42

EARNINGS PER SHARE						P/E RATIO		DIVIDENDS PER SHARE			AV. YLD	DIV. DECLARED		PRICE RANGE	
QUARTERLY			ANNUAL					PER SHARE			%			2015	
1st	2nd	3rd	2015	2014	2013			2015	2014	2013		AMOUNT	PAYABLE		
-	-	-	1.33	0.13	-2.65	-		1.44			-	0.42250	5/12/16		
-	-	-	0.48	0.93	0.84	-		1.54	1.77	1.77	-	0.21250	11/13/15		
-	0.05	-	-2.25	-7.60	-11.17	-		-	-	-	-			27.1 -	6.2
-	0.03	-	0.24	0.15	-0.29	67.1 -	38.2	-	-	-				16.1 -	9.2
0.16	-	-	-1.09	1.12	2.62	-		-	-	-				34.7 -	19.1
1.11	-	-	2.98	4.03	3.12	23.3 -	18.6	1.20	1.02	0.70	1.9	0.330Y	6/2/16	69.4 -	55.5
-0.01	-	-	1.29	0.13	4.14	8.4 -	3.0	-	-	-				10.9 -	3.8
1.11	-	-	5.89	6.62	6.50	7.6 -	4.9	0.42	0.40	0.40	1.1	0.120Y	6/15/16	44.8 -	28.8
0.05	-	-	0.09	-0.61	-1.11	161.0 -	64.0	-	-	-				14.5 -	5.8
-0.37	-	-	-1.59	-1.31	-0.95	-		-	-	-				99.7 -	53.1
0.57	-	-	3.14	2.75	2.46	10.2 -	6.5	-	-	-				31.9 -	20.4
-0.33	-	-	-2.54	-6.94	-29.84	-		-	-	-				71.0 -	37.1
-	-	-	0.76	0.80	0.83	12.1 -	9.3	0.81	0.83	0.86	10.0	0.060	6/30/16	9.2 -	7.0
-	-	-	0.13	0.21	0.22	121.8 -	94.5	1.23	4.34	4.48	8.5	0.0976B	7/18/16	15.8 -	12.3
-	-	-	0.21	-0.04	0.11	72.0 -	56.4	1.13	0.37	-	8.4	0.30760	6/21/16	15.1 -	11.8
-	0.84	-	2.10	1.67	1.38	17.6 -	13.0	0.92	0.85	0.81	2.9	0.240Y	61/28/99	36.9 -	27.3
0.11	-	-	1.52	-0.10	0.24	14.8 -	9.4	1.29	0.54	-	7.7	0.330Y	5/19/16	22.5 -	14.3
0.34	-	-	0.55	1.10	-	27.4 -	20.2	1.36	1.48	1.48	10.1	0.340Y	6/30/16	15.1 -	11.1
0.81	-	-	1.23	1.37	0.87	34.9 -	15.1	-	0.35	0.30				42.9 -	18.5
-	-	-0.37	-1.98	-2.58	-1.49	-		-	-	-				39.9 -	20.8
0.48	-	-	1.32	2.53	2.06	12.9 -	7.5	1.75	0.38	0.99	13.5	0.460Z	7/29/16	17.1 -	9.9
-0.26	-	-	-1.08	-0.70	-	-		0.75	0.23	-	6.9	0.260Z	6/22/16	16.0 -	8.3
-0.09	-	-	-0.27	0.04	0.03	-		-	-	-				4.0 -	1.7
0.27	-	-	-0.11	1.09	1.08	-		1.00	1.00	1.00	6.0	0.170Y	61/28/99	19.2 -	14.4
-	-	-	-0.24	-0.56	-0.26	-		0.46	0.31	-	4.5	0.03830	7/15/16	11.8 -	9.0
-0.05	-	-	0.38	0.20	0.41	38.1 -	30.4	0.16	0.16	0.04	1.2	0.040Y	61/28/99	14.5 -	11.6
1.05	-	-	0.24	0.44	3.06	21.6 -	12.1	0.48	0.12	3.54	11.0	0.120Y	4/29/16	5.2 -	2.9
0.15	-	-	1.29	1.35	1.63	38.1 -	26.2	0.76	0.66	0.60	1.8	0.190Y	61/28/99	49.2 -	33.8
-3.52	-	-	-21.18	6.52	0.94	-		-	-	-				41.2 -	22.3
5.22	-	-	19.45	18.38	19.90	23.8 -	16.7	5.80	4.70	3.80	1.5	1.60Y	61/28/99	463.9 -	324.9
0.10	-	-	0.43	1.02	-4.94	82.7 -	36.2	0.10	0.23	1.23	0.5	0.0250Y	61/28/99	35.5 -	15.6
-0.16	-	-	-1.10	1.07	0.69	-		-	-	-				9.1 -	3.4
-	-	-	8.75	3.28	2.52	3.6 -	1.9	0.72	-	-	3.2	0.240	6/30/16	31.8 -	16.9
0.00	-	-	-0.51	-0.73	-0.01	-		0.62	-	-	4.7	0.2060Z	6/30/16	15.3 -	10.8
												0.31250Z	7/15/16		
1.37	-	-	6.06	5.60	4.47	20.0 -	15.6	3.08	2.90	2.64	2.9	0.870Y	61/28/99	121.5 -	94.6
0.14	-	-	0.46	0.16	-	103.7 -	43.3	0.91	0.19	-	3.1	0.31870	5/13/16	47.7 -	19.9
-	-	0.03	-0.29	0.51	0.96	-		2.37	2.01	1.69	13.7	0.390	5/13/16	33.6 -	5.7
0.27	-	-	1.54	1.00	1.94	-		0.28	0.95	0.72		0.310	61/28/99	-	
-	-	0.55	1.85	1.49	1.36	36.3 -	27.4	0.54	0.47	0.41	0.9	0.160Y	61/28/99	67.2 -	50.7
-0.51	-	-	-1.37	-1.61	-1.53	-		-	-	-				31.6 -	5.7
-	87.13	-	236.85	254.60	216.22	0.2 -	0.1	89.35	80.60	75.67	224.9	-		46.8 -	34.2
-	-	-0.54	-9.34	-0.25	-0.63	-		1.05	1.40	1.40	31.5	0.350	11/20/14	4.1 -	1.3
0.56	-	-	0.90	1.67	1.70	27.0 -	18.0	0.83	1.02	0.98	4.2	0.1650Y	61/28/99	24.3 -	16.2
-0.05	-	-	-0.49	0.50	-1.14	-		-	-	0.50		0.1250Y	12/24/13	7.9 -	1.9
-	-	0.12	18.31	2.57	1.84	2.0 -	1.0	-	-	-	0.12	-		35.9 -	19.1
0.42	-	-	2.06	0.03	3.05	8.4 -	3.4	1.27	1.50	0.25	10.9	0.020Y	61/28/99	17.3 -	6.9
-0.67	-	-	-6.07	3.27	2.69	-		0.72	0.68	0.55	2.1	0.10Y	61/28/99	46.6 -	25.7
-	-	-0.02	0.63	0.85	-0.17	11.5 -	0.0	0.14	0.37	-	3.5			7.2 -	0.0
-	-	-0.02	0.63	0.85	-0.17	12.0 -	8.1	0.14	0.37	-	2.1			7.6 -	5.1
-	-	-	-2.32	-	-	-		-	-	-					
-	-	12.65	60.03	55.81	28.37	0.1 -	0.1	14.94	13.60	4.05	264.1	-		7.3 -	4.0
-	-	-0.11	-0.66	0.48	2.79	-		0.55	2.18	1.72	2.8	0.10	6/21/16	28.6 -	0.0
0.02	-	-	0.07	-1.07	-1.24	-		-	-	-		0.0880	5/27/16		
-	-	-	-0.47	0.34	-0.01	-		0.94	1.35	-		0.0880	5/27/16		
0.33	-	-	1.29	-0.15	-1.64	-		1.38	0.63	0.64		0.430	5/27/16		
0.26	-	-	3.72	3.71	3.56	21.4 -	9.8	1.32	1.20	1.08	2.2	0.370Y	61/28/99	79.5 -	36.4
1.29	-	-	5.10	6.39	6.04	19.1 -	13.1	2.36	2.22	2.04	2.9	0.590Y	61/28/99	97.6 -	66.6
-	-	45.01	629.52	195.27	164.72	0.0 -	0.0	-	-	-		2.10	10/15/98	28.0 -	0.0
-	-	-0.07	-0.23	-0.03	1.89	-		0.08	0.08	-	3.4	0.020	7/8/16	3.8 -	0.0
-	-	-	-3.93	13.90	10.40	-		0.00	4.80	9.05		0.240	9/18/14		
-	0.23	-	1.26	1.96	2.25	9.8 -	4.7	1.43	2.09	2.23	15.6	0.240Z	5/25/16	12.4 -	5.9
3.03	-	-	10.39	9.75	8.35	21.0 -	15.1	3.10	2.71	2.38	1.7	0.90Y	61/28/99	218.0 -	156.7
0.09	-	-	0.60	0.10	-	36.5 -	15.5	0.40	0.10	-	2.8	0.10Y	5/20/16	21.9 -	9.3
-0.49	-	-	-2.30	-	-	-		0.15	-	-	1.4	0.150Z	5/27/16	13.9 -	8.4
-0.79	-	-	-1.87	-3.78	-2.60	-		0.75	-	3.40	3.8	0.40Z	5/20/16	20.7 -	19.0
-0.79	-	-	-1.87	-3.78	-2.60	-		0.75	-	3.40	3.6	0.40Z	5/20/16	36.6 -	8.6
1.33	-	-	1.96	2.16	2.24	29.4 -	21.5	1.86	1.85	1.83	3.8	0.46750Y	61/28/99	57.7 -	42.2
0.79	-	-	3.17	2.99	2.46	19.7 -	15.4	1.92	1.60	1.52	3.5	0.50Y	6/30/16	62.4 -	48.8
-	-	0.77	7.29	4.13	3.70	14.6 -	9.8	2.67	2.76	2.43	3.1	-		106.1 -	71.1
-	-	3.26	13.52	10.07	9.35	4.5 -	3.4	3.71	3.28	2.61	6.7	-		60.2 -	46.6
-0.59	-	-	-4.68	1.06	-	-		-	-	-				23.4 -	12.5
-	-	-0.01	-0.00	-0.19	-0.01	-		-	-	-				6.3 -	2.9
0.24	-	-	19.46	0.23	-1.22	-		0.58	0.54	0.45	3.7	0.030Y	61/28/99	25.1 -	9.0
0.05	-	-	0.40	0.59	0.57	67.8 -	27.2	0.63	1.42	0.23	4.0	0.230Y	6/15/16	27.1 -	10.9
-	38.22	-	101.55	112.07	119.52	0.3 -	0.2	60.00	60.00	58.00	284.7	-		25.9 -	16.6
0.06	-	-	2.25	3.11	5.94	22.7 -	12.5	1.40	1.38	1.20	3.6	0.3550Y	61/28/99	51.2 -	28.1
0.22	-	-	1.11	2.22	1.52	45.6 -	31.4	1.49	1.48	1.47	3.4	0.3750Y	61/28/99	50.6 -	34.9
0.57	-	-	3.30	2.10	-4.00	18.9 -	8.0	4.38	4.38	4.38	9.6	1.0950	5/13/16	62.5 -	26.5
0.09	-	-	1.68	1.44	-0.26	23.7 -	7.8	2.18	2.18	2.18	8.4	0.6450	5/17/16	39.8 -	13.2

SYMBOL	COMPANY	NATURE OF BUSINESS	FISCAL YEAR-END	TOTAL REV. $MILL	NET INCOME $MILL	TOTAL ASSETS $MILL	NET STK EQUITY $MILL	NO OF INST	INST. HOLDINGS (SHARES)
JMLP	Nuveen All Cap Energy MLP Opport	Finance Intermediaries & Services	11/30/14	0.6	-3.4	350.0	236.3	27	1458445
NEA	Nuveen AMT-Free Municipal Incom	Holding and other Investment Office	10/31/15	78.0	60.8	1746.2	1168.8	115	7775940
NUW	Nuveen AMT-Free Municipal Value	Holding and other Investment Office	10/31/14	12.5	10.8	235.0	226.9	27	797586
NAZ	Nuveen Arizona Premium Income M	Holding and other Investment Office	2/28/15	11.8	9.1	256.5	173.6	27	820573
NBB	Nuveen Build America Bond Fund	Holding and other Investment Office	3/31/15	42.6	36.2	764.9	612.1	57	7625411
NBD	Nuveen Build America Bond Opport	Holding and other Investment Office	3/31/15	11.6	9.8	193.0	172.3	-	
NKX	Nuveen California AMT-Free Munici	Holding and other Investment Office	2/28/15	50.8	39.3	1100.7	760.8	54	4298086
NAC	Nuveen California Dividend Advanta	Holding and other Investment Office	2/28/15	98.2	78.5	2516.7	1713.6	67	6020370
NCA	Nuveen California Municipal Value	Holding and other Investment Office	2/28/15	13.2	11.6	273.7	268.0	47	2609423
NXC	Nuveen California Select Tax-Free I	Holding and other Investment Office	3/31/15	4.5	4.1	101.3	97.4	22	460350
NTC	Nuveen Connecticut Premium Inco	Holding and other Investment Office	5/31/15	13.8	10.2	335.1	208.6	39	1482024
JCE	Nuveen Core Equity Alpha Fund	Holding and other investment Office	12/31/14	5.5	2.5	283.9	280.3	49	3400133
JQC	Nuveen Credit Strategies Income F	Holding and other Investment Office	7/31/15	111.5	84.7	2258.7	1344.8	170	50166976
JDD	Nuveen Diversified Dividend and In	Holding and other Investment Office	7/31/15	14.1	9.1	370.7	248.7	55	4126894
NAD	Nuveen Dividend Advantage Munici	Holding and other Investment Office	10/31/15	41.5	33.0	901.7	606.6	89	3823516
DIAX	Nuveen Dow 30SM Dynamic Overw	Holding and other Investment Office	12/31/14	4.6	2.3	618.9	607.3	66	8143770
JMF	Nuveen Energy MLP Total Return F	Holding and other Investment Office	11/30/14	3.4	-12.7	1401.3	871.9	79	9206652
NVG	Nuveen Enhanced AMT-Free Munic	Holding and other Investment Office	10/31/15	28.4	20.5	631.0	433.1	68	6476804
NZF	Nuveen Enhanced Municipal Credit	Holding and other Investment Office	10/31/14	39.0	28.6	856.1	574.7	86	10513987
NEV	Nuveen Enhanced Municipal Value	Holding and other Investment Office	10/31/14	23.7	20.3	355.4	330.9	32	2230635
JPW	Nuveen Flexible Investment Income	Holding and other Investment Office	7/31/15	6.4	5.1	101.1	68.9	22	482782
JFR	Nuveen Floating Rate Income Fund	Holding and other Investment Office	7/31/15	56.6	41.2	1139.8	662.8	109	21371236
JRO	Nuveen Floating Rate Income Oppo	Holding and other Investment Office	7/31/15	41.4	30.4	797.7	463.7	98	10981590
NKG	Nuveen Georgia Dividend Advantag	Holding and other Investment Office	5/31/15	9.5	7.1	226.6	147.4	25	687522
JGV	Nuveen Global Equity Income Fund	Holding and other Investment Office	12/31/14	5.5	2.6	231.3	230.8	52	7048705
JGH	Nuveen Global High Income Fund	Holding and other Investment Office	12/31/14	4.9	4.0	685.9	624.9	59	8512591
JHY	Nuveen High Income 2020 Target T	Finance Intermediaries & Services	5/27/15	-	-	0.5	0.1	14	1133979
NID	Nuveen Intermediate Duration Muni	Finance Intermediaries & Services	5/31/15	40.4	32.5	840.6	643.4	53	8315388
NIQ	Nuveen Intermediate Duration Quali	Holding and other Investment Office	5/31/15	9.7	7.6	238.2	179.3	29	3679830
NQM	Nuveen Investment Quality Municip	Holding and other Investment Office	10/31/15	48.1	37.8	1008.3	665.5	69	2554409
NMY	Nuveen Maryland Premium Income	Holding and other Investment Office	5/31/15	21.7	16.3	535.4	344.3	56	2547453
NMT	Nuveen Massachusetts Premium In	Holding and other Investment Office	5/31/15	8.9	6.2	212.0	137.1	28	303684
NUM	Nuveen Michigan Quality Income M	Holding and other Investment Office	2/28/15	21.7	16.6	499.5	329.2	55	1740708
NMS	Nuveen Minnesota Municipal Incom	Holding and other Investment Office	5/31/15	5.2	3.8	135.8	86.2	19	268197
JLS	Nuveen Mortgage Opportunity Term	Holding and other Investment Office	12/31/14	29.1	19.8	563.7	415.6	56	6920378
JMT	Nuveen Mortgage Opportunity Term	Holding and other Investment Office	12/31/14	9.0	5.9	170.4	123.8	26	1572324
JMM	Nuveen Multi-Market Income Fund	Holding and other Investment Office	6/30/15	5.4	4.4	114.7	79.5	32	3755049
NMI	Nuveen Municipal Income Fund, Inc	Holding and other Investment Office	10/31/15	4.9	4.2	99.0	95.1	32	475179
NMO	Nuveen Municipal Market Opportuni	Holding and other Investment Office	10/31/15	46.9	35.5	1075.4	697.8	92	9565639
NUV	Nuveen Municipal Value Fund, Inc.	Holding and other Investment Office	10/31/15	96.4	85.4	2115.0	2096.5	200	26937304
NXJ	Nuveen New Jersey Dividend Adva	Holding and other Investment Office	4/30/15	23.7	17.3	993.8	668.7	58	2649089
NRK	Nuveen New York AMT-Free Munici	Holding and other Investment Office	9/30/15	81.1	63.1	1877.0	1257.9	84	7644253
NAN	Nuveen New York Dividend Advant	Holding and other Investment Office	9/30/15	15.7	11.6	708.3	474.8	41	3230937
NNY	Nuveen New York Municipal Value	Holding and other Investment Office	9/30/15	7.0	6.1	156.0	152.1	34	1100992
NXN	Nuveen New York Select Tax-Free I	Holding and other Investment Office	3/31/15	2.4	2.2	58.6	57.0	12	232882
NNC	Nuveen North Carolina Premium Inc	Holding and other Investment Office	5/31/15	13.9	10.0	377.0	246.3	49	1693809
NUO	Nuveen Ohio Quality Income Munici	Holding and other Investment Office	2/28/15	20.7	15.7	464.8	315.1	50	2044046
NQP	Nuveen Pennsylvania Investment Q	ETFs	4/30/15	40.3	30.8	892.9	592.5	73	2816934
NPP	Nuveen Performance Plus Municipa	Holding and other Investment Office	10/31/15	67.7	51.8	1544.6	969.1	106	7386597
JPI	Nuveen Preferred & Income Term F	Holding and other Investment Office	7/31/15	54.2	44.7	803.3	566.1	52	3343084
JPC	Nuveen Preferred Income Opportun	Holding and other Investment Office	7/31/15	93.8	77.1	1437.4	1012.8	143	20729081
JPS	Nuveen Preferred Securities Incom	Holding and other Investment Office	7/31/15	102.0	82.5	1655.3	1174.3	138	17014540
NPF	Nuveen Premier Municipal Income	Holding and other Investment Office	10/31/15	20.4	15.7	449.5	298.0	60	3059596
NPM	Nuveen Premium Income Municipal	Holding and other Investment Office	10/31/15	75.2	58.6	1657.6	1087.3	108	10814259
NPI	Nuveen Premium Income Municipal	Holding and other Investment Office	10/31/15	66.8	52.2	1501.7	981.3	107	10460840
JRI	Nuveen Real Asset Income & Growt	Holding and other Investment Office	12/31/14	17.3	13.4	276.0	194.0	44	1970386
BXMX	Nuveen S&P 500 Buy-Write Income	Holding and other Investment Office	12/31/14	30.3	17.5	1400.0	1381.9	107	18587494
SPXX	Nuveen S&P 500 Dynamic Overwrit	Holding and other Investment Office	12/31/14	5.5	3.3	242.2	237.8	51	4973167
NIM	Nuveen Select Maturities Municipal	Holding and other Investment Office	3/31/15	5.0	4.2	133.4	131.8	43	1574354
NQS	Nuveen Select Quality Municipal Fu	Holding and other Investment Office	10/31/15	35.9	27.2	837.3	548.3	77	8266658
NXQ	Nuveen Select Tax Free Income Po	Holding and other Investment Office	3/31/15	11.2	10.2	261.3	259.4	58	1627524
NXP	Nuveen Select Tax-Free Income Po	Holding and other Investment Office	3/31/15	10.7	9.9	257.2	251.3	53	1708287
NXR	Nuveen Select Tax-Free Income Po	Holding and other Investment Office	3/31/15	8.6	7.8	203.8	200.2	44	1390293
NSL	Nuveen Senior Income Fund	Holding and other Investment Office	7/31/15	23.9	17.2	479.4	276.5	82	14980581
JSD	Nuveen Short Duration Credit Oppo	Holding and other Investment Office	7/31/15	15.7	12.3	285.2	188.0	37	3781549
JTD	Nuveen Tax-Advantaged Dividend	Holding and other Investment Office	12/31/14	14.4	9.5	364.3	250.7	53	3637600
JTA	Nuveen Tax-Advantaged Total Retu	Holding and other Investment Office	12/31/14	10.2	6.6	268.1	181.4	54	3530907
NTX	Nuveen Texas Quality Income Muni	Holding and other Investment Office	2/28/15	9.8	6.2	238.9	157.6	29	480118
NPV	Nuveen Virginia Premium Income M	Holding and other Investment Office	5/31/15	17.2	12.8	407.7	260.1	32	884605
NVR	NVR Inc.	Builders	12/31/15	5169.6	382.9	2515.1	1239.2	407	5096217
OAK	Oaktree Capital Group LLC	Wealth Management	12/31/15	201.9	71.3	51811.1	733.9	217	37975095
OAS	Oasis Petroleum Inc.	Production & Extraction	12/31/15	789.7	-40.2	5649.4	2319.3	294	164252471
OXY	Occidental Petroleum Corp	Production & Extraction	12/31/15	12699.0	-7829.0	43437.0	24350.0	1465	681238989
OII	Oceaneering International, Inc.	Equipment & Services	12/31/15	3062.8	231.0	3429.5	1578.7	499	106734097
OZM	Och-Ziff Capital Management Grou	Wealth Management	12/31/15	1323.0	25.7	10691.5	416.5	148	99295952
OCIP	OCI Partners LP	Specialty Chemicals	12/31/15	309.4	52.0	733.6		33	12183160
OCN	Ocwen Financial Corp.	Credit & Lending	12/31/15	-	-247.0	7404.8	851.6	251	96403276
OFG	OFG Bancorp	Banking	12/31/15	459.0	-2.5	7099.1	897.1	177	48711938
OGE	OGE Energy Corp.	Electric Utilities	12/31/15	2196.9	271.3	9597.4	3326.0	482	141550412
OIS	Oil States International, Inc.	Equipment & Services	12/31/15	1100.0	28.6	1599.1	1255.7	320	61495619

EARNINGS PER SHARE QUARTERLY 1st	2nd	3rd	ANNUAL 2015	2014	2013	P/E RATIO	DIVIDENDS PER SHARE 2015	2014	2013	AV. YLD %	DIV. DECLARED AMOUNT	PAYABLE	PRICE RANGE 2015
-	-	-	-	-0.32	-	-	-	1.00			0.2460	5/16/16	15.7 - 4.1
-	-	-	0.77	0.79	0.72	19.3 - 16.4	0.80	0.82	0.82	5.9	0.0625M	7/1/16	14.8 - 12.6
-	-	-	-	0.82	0.85	-	-	0.90	0.81	-	0.065M	7/1/16	18.6 - 16.0
-	-	-	0.79	0.55	0.75	20.8 - 18.2	0.79	0.77	0.77	5.2	0.0665M	7/1/16	16.5 - 14.4
-	-	-	1.37	1.39	1.35	16.4 - 14.0	1.39	1.40	1.31	6.8	0.1080	7/1/16	22.4 - 19.1
-	-	-	1.37	1.40	1.34	16.1 - 14.1	1.37	1.35	1.29	6.7	0.10350	7/1/16	22.1 - 19.3
-	-	-	0.85	0.84	0.77	19.4 - 16.4	0.85	0.86	0.90	5.6	0.072M	7/1/16	16.5 - 13.9
-	-	-	0.87	0.84	0.84	19.1 - 16.3	0.93	0.89	0.92	6.1	0.074M	7/1/16	16.6 - 14.2
-	-	-	0.46	0.47	0.47	24.1 - 22.0	0.47	0.47	0.47	4.4	0.039M	7/1/16	11.1 - 10.1
-	-	-	0.66	0.67	0.69	25.8 - 21.9	0.80	0.93	0.68	5.1	0.0525M	7/1/16	17.0 - 14.5
-	-	-	0.70	0.60	0.56	19.5 - 17.4	0.68	0.69	0.70	5.3	0.055M	7/1/16	13.7 - 12.2
-	-	-	-	0.16	0.13	-	-	2.51	1.45	-	0.290	7/1/16	16.9 - 12.1
-	-	-	0.62	0.60	0.42	14.4 - 11.5	0.56	0.64	0.80	7.0	0.05150	7/1/16	8.9 - 7.1
-	-	-	0.46	0.48	0.43	27.1 - 20.3	1.08	1.03	1.00	9.9	0.270	7/1/16	12.5 - 9.4
-	-	-	0.84	0.87	0.81	18.7 - 15.9	0.87	0.90	0.88	6.1	0.0695M	7/1/16	15.7 - 13.4
-	-	-	-	0.18	-	-	-	-	-	-	0.2660	7/1/16	15.3 - 0.0
-	-	-	-	-0.32	-0.29	-	-	1.28	1.26	-	0.3370	5/16/16	18.3 - 6.2
-	-	-	-	0.71	0.60	-	-	0.77	0.85	-	0.076M	7/1/16	15.8 - 13.6
-	-	-	-	0.72	0.71	-	-	0.72	0.75	-	0.076M	7/1/16	15.5 - 13.3
-	-	-	-	0.96	0.96	-	-	0.96	0.96	-	0.08M	7/1/16	16.3 - 14.3
-	-	-	1.37	1.42	0.03	12.7 - 9.8	1.96	1.51	-	12.8	0.1130	7/1/16	17.5 - 13.1
-	-	-	0.75	0.75	0.90	14.9 - 12.1	0.72	0.76	0.97	7.1	0.06150	7/1/16	11.2 - 9.1
-	-	-	0.79	-	0.95	14.4 - 11.2	0.76	0.79	1.04	7.6	0.06450	7/1/16	11.4 - 8.8
-	-	-	0.67	0.54	0.60	21.7 - 0.0	0.64	0.64	0.67	4.8	0.0535M	7/1/16	14.6 - 0.0
-	-	-	0.14	0.23	0.35	95.4 - 67.3	0.99	1.06	1.09	8.9	0.2340	7/1/16	13.4 - 9.4
-	-	-	-	0.12	-	-	-	-	-	-	0.1320	7/1/16	17.3 - 12.1
-	-	-	-	-	-	-	-	-	-	-	0.0570	7/1/16	10.5 - 9.5
-	-	-	0.69	0.69	0.26	20.1 - 17.5	0.68	0.67	0.22	5.3	0.057M	7/1/16	13.9 - 12.1
-	-	-	0.58	0.60	0.14	23.7 - 20.9	0.60	0.58	0.10	4.7	0.045M	7/1/16	13.7 - 12.2
-	-	-	0.91	0.93	0.92	18.1 - 15.9	0.98	0.97	0.97	6.4	0.0735M	7/1/16	16.5 - 14.5
-	-	-	0.68	0.60	0.58	20.3 - 17.9	0.67	0.67	0.77	5.3	0.0555M	7/1/16	13.8 - 12.2
-	-	-	0.65	0.58	0.62	23.4 - 20.0	0.68	0.68	0.76	4.9	0.059M	7/1/16	15.2 - 13.0
-	-	-	0.80	0.80	0.74	18.6 - 16.3	0.86	0.89	0.89	6.3	0.062M	7/1/16	14.9 - 13.1
-	-	-	0.74	-	-	22.3 - 0.0	0.48	-	-	3.2	0.06650	7/1/16	16.5 - 0.0
-	-	-	-	1.25	1.08	-	-	1.55	2.82	-	0.11350	7/1/16	23.1 - 22.1
-	-	-	-	1.22	1.06	-	-	1.56	3.72	-	0.11250	7/1/16	22.9 - 21.4
-	-	-	0.47	0.40	0.53	16.0 - 0.0	0.28	-	-	3.9	0.0360	7/1/16	7.5 - 0.0
-	-	-	0.51	0.50	0.54	25.4 - 20.5	0.51	0.55	0.57	4.4	0.0415M	7/1/16	12.9 - 10.5
-	-	-	0.77	0.80	0.79	19.4 - 16.7	0.79	0.80	0.79	5.8	0.061M	7/1/16	14.9 - 12.9
-	-	-	0.42	0.43	0.44	25.2 - 22.2	0.40	0.44	0.45	4.0	0.0325M	7/1/16	10.6 - 9.3
-	-	-	0.67	0.71	0.63	22.0 - 18.7	0.77	0.68	0.75	5.7	0.065M	7/1/16	14.7 - 12.6
-	-	-	0.72	0.76	0.76	19.4 - 17.3	0.73	0.82	0.76	5.6	0.0585M	7/1/16	14.0 - 12.4
-	-	-	0.71	0.67	0.70	21.5 - 18.5	0.77	0.76	0.79	5.5	0.065M	7/1/16	15.3 - 13.1
-	-	-	0.40	0.41	0.40	25.7 - 23.7	0.39	0.39	0.41	3.9	0.0325M	7/1/16	10.3 - 9.5
-	-	-	0.56	0.60	0.63	26.2 - 0.0	0.57	0.63	0.71	4.2	0.046M	7/1/16	14.7 - 0.0
-	-	-	0.61	0.54	0.56	23.4 - 20.6	0.64	0.60	0.67	4.8	0.049M	7/1/16	14.3 - 12.6
-	-	-	0.85	0.76	0.89	19.2 - 16.7	0.93	0.99	0.96	6.2	0.065M	7/1/16	16.4 - 14.2
-	-	-	0.81	0.74	0.80	18.5 - 15.9	0.84	0.85	0.91	6.1	0.084M	7/1/16	15.0 - 12.9
-	-	-	0.86	0.91	0.88	19.1 - 16.1	0.91	0.92	0.93	6.1	0.073M	7/1/16	16.4 - 13.9
-	-	-	1.96	1.98	1.89	12.2 - 11.0	1.94	2.46	1.96	8.5	0.16250	7/1/16	24.0 - 21.6
-	-	-	0.80	0.79	0.46	12.6 - 10.8	0.77	0.76	0.76	8.3	0.0670	7/1/16	10.1 - 8.6
-	-	-	0.64	0.69	0.69	14.6 - 12.9	0.73	0.66	0.66	8.1	0.0590	7/1/16	9.3 - 8.3
-	-	-	0.79	-0.85	0.82	18.9 - 16.2	0.83	0.86	0.84	6.1	0.062M	7/1/16	15.0 - 12.8
-	-	-	0.83	0.85	0.84	18.4 - 15.9	0.87	0.87	0.87	6.2	0.0665M	7/1/16	15.2 - 13.2
-	-	-	0.82	0.82	0.82	18.5 - 15.9	0.83	0.86	0.87	6.0	0.067M	7/1/16	15.2 - 13.0
-	-	-	-	1.37	1.53	-	-	2.79	3.40	-	0.110	7/1/16	19.3 - 13.0
-	-	-	0.17	0.17	0.20	79.1 - 65.8	1.00	1.00	1.08	7.9	0.2380	7/1/16	13.4 - 11.2
-	-	-	0.20	0.19	0.22	70.8 - 58.4	1.04	1.04	1.12	7.8	0.250	7/1/16	14.2 - 11.7
-	-	-	0.34	0.36	0.37	31.9 - 29.2	0.34	0.34	0.37	3.3	0.026M	7/1/16	10.8 - 9.9
-	-	-	0.77	0.82	0.77	19.8 - 17.1	0.79	0.80	0.86	5.7	0.06M	7/1/16	15.3 - 13.1
-	-	-	0.58	0.62	0.65	25.4 - 22.2	0.60	0.63	0.63	4.4	0.0445M	7/1/16	14.7 - 12.9
-	-	-	0.60	0.66	0.69	25.4 - 22.1	0.61	0.64	0.69	4.3	0.0455M	7/1/16	15.2 - 13.3
-	-	-	0.60	0.64	0.66	25.6 - 22.5	0.61	0.63	0.66	4.3	0.0455M	7/1/16	15.4 - 13.5
-	-	-	0.45	0.44	0.54	14.9 - 11.6	0.42	0.44	0.56	7.1	0.0360	7/1/16	6.7 - 5.2
-	-	-	1.22	1.29	1.61	14.2 - 11.2	1.20	1.70	1.68	7.8	0.0970	7/1/16	17.3 - 13.7
-	-	-	-	0.66	0.52	-	-	1.22	1.11	-	0.310	7/1/16	16.4 - 12.1
-	-	-	0.47	0.49	0.34	29.3 - 20.9	1.09	1.03	0.93	9.2	0.2580	7/1/16	13.8 - 9.8
-	-	-	0.62	0.66	0.68	24.7 - 21.4	0.68	0.70	0.77	4.8	0.0545M	7/1/16	15.3 - 13.3
-	-	-	0.72	0.71	0.66	20.5 - 18.4	0.75	0.73	0.77	5.4	0.0545M	7/1/16	14.7 - 13.3
15.79	-	-	89.99	63.50	54.81	20.0 - 14.9	-	-	-				1799.2 - 1340.0
0.45	-	-	1.45	2.97	6.35	38.2 - 27.8	2.10	3.15	4.71	4.3	0.550	5/13/16	55.4 - 40.3
-0.40	-	-	-0.31	5.05	2.44	-	-	-	-	-	-	-	17.5 - 4.3
0.10	-	-	-10.23	0.79	7.32	-	2.97	2.88	2.56	4.2	0.750Y	61/28/99	79.4 - 59.6
0.26	-	-	2.34	4.00	3.42	21.9 - 11.2	1.08	1.03	0.84	2.8	0.270Y	61/28/99	51.2 - 26.2
-0.38	-	-	0.14	0.80	1.62	93.7 - 23.6	0.87	1.72	1.42	11.8	0.040	11/20/15	13.1 - 3.3
-0.07	-	-	0.61	1.48	0.59	30.7 - 9.7	0.74	1.76	-	7.4	0.060	7/8/16	18.7 - 5.9
-0.90	-	-	-1.97	-3.60	2.02	-	-	-	-	-	-	-	11.8 - 1.5
0.24	-	-	-0.37	1.51	1.73	-	0.36	0.34	0.26	4.3	0.14580	9/30/16	14.3 - 4.8
0.13	-	-	1.36	1.98	1.94	23.1 - 17.5	1.02	0.93	0.83	3.7	0.2750Y	61/28/99	31.4 - 23.0
-0.26	-	-	0.56	3.31	7.53	70.1 - 39.9	-	-	-				42.0 - 22.4

SYMBOL	COMPANY	NATURE OF BUSINESS	FISCAL YEAR-END	TOTAL REV. $MILL	NET INCOME $MILL	TOTAL ASSETS $MILL	NET STK EQUITY $MILL	NO OF INST	INST. HOLDINGS (SHARES)
ODC	Oil-Dri Corp. of America	Household & Personal Products	7/31/15	261.4	11.4	190.0	110.5	87	4026452
ORI	Old Republic International Corp.	General Insurance	12/31/15	5766.1	422.1	17110.5	3880.8	497	214125100
OLN	Olin Corp.	Diversified Chemicals	12/31/15	2854.4	-1.4	9321.8	2418.8	421	162848787
OLN	Olin Corp.	Diversified Chemicals	12/31/15	2854.4	-1.4	9321.8	2418.8	421	162848787
OMAM	OM Asset Management PLC	Finance Intermediaries & Services	12/31/15	699.3	155.5	1014.1	165.9	103	38545059
OHI	Omega Healthcare Investors, Inc.	REITs	12/31/15	743.6	233.3	8019.0	3738.0	525	179085722
OME	Omega Protein Corp.	Food	12/31/15	359.3	24.0	407.2	295.2	185	19908974
OMC	Omnicom Group, Inc.	Advertising	12/31/15	15134.4	1093.9	22110.7	2452.4	905	280483991
OMN	Omnova Solutions Inc	Specialty Chemicals	11/30/15	838.0	-17.8	687.2	109.1	137	39930962
ASGN	On Assignment, Inc.	Business Services	12/31/15	2065.0	97.6	1767.3	784.8	292	51108953
ONDK	On Deck Capital Inc	Credit & Lending	12/31/15	254.8	-2.2	749.3	322.8	94	50881190
OGS	ONE Gas, Inc.	Electric Utilities	12/31/15	1547.7	119.0	4644.4	1841.6	319	38013091
OLP	One Liberty Properties, Inc.	REITs	12/31/15	65.7	20.5	650.4	260.5	140	6678423
OB	OneBeacon Insurance Group Ltd	General Insurance	12/31/15	1186.4	36.8	3604.5	1000.9	132	19478601
OMF	OneMain Holdings Inc	Credit & Lending	12/31/15	2192.0	-242.0	21056.0	2751.0	202	134916650
OKE	Oneok Inc	Equipment & Services	12/31/15	7763.2	245.0	15446.1	335.8	643	169222545
OKS	ONEOK Partners LP	Equipment & Services	12/31/15	7761.1	589.5	14927.6	-	393	112123496
OOMA	OOMA Inc	Internet & Software	1/31/16	88.8	-14.1	76.5	42.9	36	3764286
OPY	Oppenheimer Holdings Inc	Finance Intermediaries & Services	12/31/15	928.4	2.0	2693.0	518.1	87	6523769
ORCL	Oracle Corp	Internet & Software	5/31/16	37047.0	8901.0	112180.0	47289.0	2068	2787384765
ORAN	Orange	Services	12/31/15	40198.0	2652.0	91430.0	30907.0	209	34326603
OA	Orbital ATK Inc	Defense	12/31/15	3399.1	182.4	5353.6	1937.1	516	56450087
ORC	Orchid Island Capital, Inc.	REITs	12/31/15	16.2	1.1	2241.8	253.3	65	4484843
OEC	Orion Engineered Carbons SA	Specialty Chemicals	12/31/15	1111.8	42.9	970.5	49.7	81	17417415
ORN	Orion Group Holdings Inc	Construction Services	12/31/15	466.5	-8.1	465.5	227.7	123	31702460
IX	Orix Corp. (Japan)	Credit & Lending	3/31/15	2150609.0	234948.0	11443628.0	2152198.0	143	5276450
ORA	Ormat Technologies Inc	Electric Utilities	12/31/15	594.6	119.6	2293.0	990.0	198	22032216
OSK	Oshkosh Corp (New)	Autos- Manufacturing	9/30/15	6098.1	229.5	4613.0	1911.1	356	79421304
OUT	OUTFRONT Media Inc	REITs	12/31/15	1513.8	-29.4	3845.2	1212.6	259	140295758
OSG	Overseas Shipholding Group Inc (N	Equipment & Services	12/31/15	964.5	284.0	3275.0	1580.5	81	4755948
OMI	Owens & Minor, Inc.	Pharmaceuticals	12/31/15	9772.9	103.4	2777.8	992.6	391	69648212
OC	Owens Corning	Construction Materials	12/31/15	5350.0	330.0	7380.0	3739.0	388	119613767
OI	Owens-Illinois, Inc.	Containers & Packaging	12/31/15	6156.0	-74.0	9421.0	466.0	481	174114081
OXM	Oxford Industries, Inc.	Apparel, Footwear & Accessories	1/30/16	969.3	30.6	582.7	334.4	229	15813256
TLK	P.T. Telekomunikasi Indonesia (Per	Services	12/31/15	102470000.0	15451000.0	165928000.0	74934000.0	189	38212744
T 34D	Pacific Bell	Services	12/31/98	9406.0	1077.0	15093.0	3260.0		-
ROYT	Pacific Coast Oil Trust	Oil Royalty Traders	12/31/15	11.9	10.0	229.1	229.1	35	4054662
PACD	Pacific Drilling SA	Production & Extraction	12/31/15	1085.1	126.2	5832.5	2692.1	79	34602355
PKG	Packaging Corp of America	Containers & Packaging	12/31/15	5741.7	436.8	5284.6	1633.3	529	105291959
PANW	Palo Alto Networks, Inc	IT Services	7/31/15	928.1	-165.0	1965.2	575.8	672	89370543
PAM	Pampa Energia SA	Electric Utilities	12/31/15	7160.8	3065.1	29149.6	6990.6		-
P	Pandora Media Inc	Internet & Software	12/31/15	1164.0	-169.7	1240.7	743.4	306	246241893
PHX	Panhandle Oil & Gas Inc	Production & Extraction	9/30/15	70.9	9.3	238.8	127.0	96	8412148
PAR	Par Technology Corp.	Electronic Instruments & Related Pro	12/31/15	229.0	-0.9	115.3	68.1	49	3598555
PGRE	Paramount Group Inc	REITs	12/31/15	662.4	21.1	8794.1	3761.0	202	141225133
PKE	Park Electrochemical Corp.	Electrical Equipment	2/28/16	145.9	18.0	314.8	180.9	134	16994388
PKD	Parker Drilling Co	Production & Extraction	12/31/15	712.2	-95.1	1376.9	568.5	193	91818475
PH	Parker Hannifin Corp.	Industrial Machinery & Equipment	6/30/15	12711.7	1012.6	12295.0	5104.3	781	125234755
PKY	Parkway Properties Inc.	REITs	12/31/15	474.0	67.3	3619.2	1388.7	234	115517473
PE	Parsley Energy Inc	Production & Extraction	12/31/15	266.1	-50.5	2514.2	1264.5	232	128842547
PRTY	Party City Holdco Inc	Retail - General Merchandise/Depart	12/31/15	2294.5	10.5	3292.4	913.0	117	114983101
PN	Patriot National Inc	Brokers & Intermediaries	12/31/15	209.7	-5.4	308.2	86.7	57	4081389
PAYC	Paycom Software Inc	Internet & Software	12/31/15	224.7	20.9	876.8	98.3	203	42254563
PBF	PBF Energy Inc	Refining & Marketing	12/31/15	13123.9	146.4	6105.1	1647.3	294	99595667
PBFX	PBF Logistics LP	Refining & Marketing	12/31/15	142.1	75.1	422.9	-185.7	57	14912680
PCM	PCM Fund Inc	Holding and other Investment Office	6/30/15	6.4	5.1	214.2	123.2	37	2156502
PSO	Pearson Plc	Publishing	12/31/15	4468.0	823.0	11635.0	6414.0	141	35415022
PEB	Pebblebrook Hotel Trust	REITs	12/31/15	770.9	94.7	3062.9	1758.4	232	88656741
PBA	Pembina Pipeline Corp	Equipment & Services	12/31/15	4669.0	406.0	12936.0	7424.0	274	178615009
PGH	Pengrowth Energy Corp	Production & Extraction	12/31/15	1017.7	-1093.1	4550.7	1765.0	209	101957605
PWE	Penn West Petroleum Ltd	Production & Extraction	12/31/15	1265.0	-2646.0	5924.0	2935.0	245	85075149
JCP	Penney (J.C.) Co.,Inc. (Holding Co)	Retail - General Merchandise/Depart	1/30/16	12625.0	-513.0	9442.0	1309.0	564	289388483
PEI	Pennsylvania Real Estate Investme	REITs	12/31/15	425.4	-116.7	2806.5	629.3	252	77826754
PFSI	Pennymac Financial Services Inc	Credit & Lending	12/31/15	713.1	47.2	3505.3	270.8	98	23586654
PMT	Pennymac Mortgage Investment Tr	REITs	12/31/15	373.5	90.1	5826.9	1496.1		-
PAG	Penske Automotive Group Inc	Retail - Automotive	12/31/15	19284.9	326.1	8022.7	1790.2	334	96758698
PNR	Pentair PLC	Industrial Machinery & Equipment	12/31/15	6449.0	-76.4	11857.0	4008.8	625	159298691
PEN	Penumbra Inc	Medical Instruments & Equipment	12/31/15	186.1	2.4	263.8	232.5	81	10919767
PEP	PepsiCo Inc	Beverages	12/26/15	63056.0	5452.0	69667.0	11923.0	2476	1215152766
PFGC	Performance Food Group Co	Retail - Food & Beverage, Drug & To	6/27/15	15270.0	56.5	3390.9	493.0	94	79769482
PSG	Performance Sports Group Ltd	Leisure Equipment	5/31/15	654.7	3.3	844.9	311.8	141	35554960
PKI	PerkinElmer, Inc.	Biotechnology	1/3/16	2262.4	212.4	4166.3	2110.4	477	124975608
PBT	Permian Basin Royalty Trust	Oil Royalty Traders	12/31/15	17.8	16.0	2.1	0.7	102	6594130
PRGO	Perrigo Company plc	Pharmaceuticals	12/31/15	2769.5	5.6	19393.9	10036.7		-
PZE	Petrobras Argentina SA	Production & Extraction	12/31/15	21955.0	853.0	29097.0	12936.0		-
PTR	PetroChina Co Ltd	Production & Extraction	12/31/15	1725428.0	35517.0	2393844.0	1179716.0	208	5406968
PBR	Petroleo Brasileiro S.A	Production & Extraction	12/31/15	97314.0	-8450.0	230521.0	65236.0	462	383430774
PQ	PetroQuest Energy Inc	Production & Extraction	12/31/15	116.0	-294.8	379.3	-163.1	118	29976527
PFE	Pfizer Inc	Pharmaceuticals	12/31/15	48851.0	6960.0	167460.0	64720.0	2667	5192507675
PCG	PG&E Corp. (Holding Co.)	Electric Utilities	12/31/15	16833.0	888.0	63339.0	16576.0	767	437277902

EARNINGS PER SHARE						P/E RATIO		DIVIDENDS PER SHARE			AV. YLD %	DIV. DECLARED		PRICE RANGE 2015	
1st	2nd	3rd	2015	2014	2013			2015	2014	2013		AMOUNT	PAYABLE		
-	-	-0.13	1.59	1.17	2.07	24.1 -	13.9	0.80	0.76	0.72	2.6	0.1650Y	61/28/99	38.3 -	22.1
0.43	-	-	1.48	1.44	1.74	13.0 -	10.1	0.74	0.73	0.72	4.3	0.18750Y	61/28/99	19.3 -	14.9
-0.23	-	-	-0.01	1.33	2.21			0.80	0.80	0.80	5.3	0.20Y	61/28/99	18.0 -	0.0
-0.23	-	-	-0.01	1.33	2.21			0.80	0.80	0.80	4.0	0.20Y	61/28/99	29.5 -	12.8
0.26	-	-	1.29	0.43		15.2 -	8.1	0.32			2.1	0.080	6/30/16	19.6 -	10.4
0.29	-	-	1.29	1.74	1.46	28.7 -	21.3	2.18	2.02	1.86	6.4	0.580Z	61/28/99	37.0 -	27.5
0.37	-	-	1.07	0.85	1.45	23.4 -	12.3							25.0 -	13.1
0.90	-	-	4.41	4.24	3.71	19.3 -	14.7	2.00	1.90	1.60	2.7	0.550Y	61/28/99	85.3 -	64.8
-0.03	-	-	-0.39	0.25	0.42							0.050	5/31/01	8.2 -	4.7
0.32	-	-	1.84	1.42	1.55	25.9 -	16.1							47.6 -	29.7
-0.18	-	-	-0.02	-0.60	-8.64									15.2 -	4.3
1.22	-	-	2.24	2.07		27.6 -	18.5	1.20	0.84		2.4	0.350Y	61/28/99	61.8 -	41.4
0.18	-	-	1.22	1.37	1.14	20.2 -	16.1	1.58	1.50	1.42	7.2	0.410Z	7/7/16	24.7 -	19.6
0.49	-	-	0.38	0.35	1.52			0.84	0.84	0.84		0.210	6/23/16		
1.13	-	-	-1.89	4.38	-0.19									51.4 -	18.9
0.40	-	-	1.16	1.49	1.27	37.3 -	16.3	2.43	2.13	1.48	7.5	0.6150Y	61/28/99	43.3 -	18.9
0.52	-	-	0.73	2.33	2.35	54.2 -	30.4	3.16	3.01	2.87	10.0	0.790	5/13/16	39.5 -	22.2
-0.23	-	-	-2.81	-1.18	-3.54									11.2 -	5.8
-0.29	-	-	0.14	0.62	1.77	198.6 -	97.9	0.44	0.44	0.44	2.4	0.110	5/27/16	27.8 -	13.7
-	-	0.50	2.21	2.38	2.26	20.3 -	15.4	0.51	0.48	0.30	1.3	0.150Y	61/28/99	44.9 -	33.9
-	-	-	0.92	0.31	0.71	19.9 -	16.0	0.01	0.70	0.51	3.7			18.3 -	14.7
1.19	-	-	3.04	10.42	8.34	31.1 -	22.4	1.10	1.10	0.92	1.4	0.30Y	61/28/99	94.5 -	68.0
-0.21	-	-	0.05	2.48	-0.23	273.4 -	155.4	1.92	2.16	1.40	19.5	0.140Z	6/30/16	13.7 -	7.8
-	-	-	0.72	-1.11				0.51	0.67			0.18840	6/29/16		
-0.04	-	-	-0.29	0.25	0.01									8.2 -	3.3
-	00.89	-	179.21	142.77	87.37	0.5 -	0.3	114.45	62.73	45.58	161.5			81.4 -	59.0
0.59	-	-	2.43	1.18	0.91	18.0 -	13.7	0.26	0.21	0.08	0.7	0.070Y	5/24/16	43.8 -	33.3
-	0.76	-	2.90	3.61	3.55	17.9 -	10.5	0.68	0.60		1.7	0.190Y	61/28/99	52.0 -	30.3
-0.02	-	-	-0.21	2.67	1.48			1.42	5.67		6.2	0.340	61/28/99	28.3 -	18.2
0.54	-	-	-	-	-114.22							0.17970	5/13/16	19.8 -	0.0
0.39	-	-	1.65	1.06	1.76	25.0 -	19.4	1.01	1.00	0.96	2.8	0.2550Y	61/28/99	41.2 -	31.9
0.49	-	-	2.79	1.91	1.71	18.7 -	14.2	0.68	0.64		1.5	0.180	61/28/99	52.2 -	39.6
0.41	-	-	-0.47	0.45	1.11							0.59380 Y	2/15/08	24.7 -	12.1
1.21	-	-	2.78	2.75	1.89	32.5 -	20.1	0.84	0.72	0.60	1.2	0.270Y	7/29/16	90.4 -	55.9
-	-	-	157.38	147.78	145.77	0.4 -	0.2	17551.80	20492.05	16991.60	38861.0			56.9 -	34.7
0.01	-	-	0.26	1.40	1.80	15.5 -	3.0	0.26	1.40	1.66	12.4	0.00590Z	1/13/16	4.0 -	0.8
-	-	1.40	6.00	8.70	1.20										
1.09	-	-	4.47	3.99	4.47	16.4 -	10.1	2.20	1.60	1.51	3.5	0.550Y	61/28/99	73.4 -	45.1
-	-	-0.80	-2.02	-3.05	-0.43									197.1 -	115.7
-	-	-	2.28	0.51	0.22	11.5 -	5.7							26.2 -	13.0
-0.51	-	-	-0.79	-0.15	-0.15									22.0 -	7.9
-	-0.44	-	0.56	1.49	0.83	39.2 -	21.6	0.16	0.16	0.14	0.9	0.040Y	6/13/16	22.0 -	12.1
0.00	-	-	-0.06	-0.24	0.02									7.4 -	0.0
-0.03	-	-	-0.02	0.27				0.42			2.5	0.0950Z	7/15/16	18.6 -	14.4
-	-	0.20	0.96	-2.03	0.81	23.0 -	14.3	1.90	2.90	2.90	11.4	0.10Y	8/3/16	22.1 -	13.8
-0.78	-	-	-0.78	0.19	0.22							0.01	2/17/87	3.8 -	1.1
-	-	1.37	6.97	6.87	6.26	17.4 -	12.4	2.37	1.86	1.70	2.2	0.630Y	61/28/99	121.3 -	86.5
0.55	-	-	0.60	0.42	-0.45	30.9 -	20.0	0.75	0.75	0.64	4.7	0.18750Z	6/29/16	18.5 -	12.0
-0.14	-	-	-0.45	0.42										26.1 -	13.7
0.00	-	-	0.09	0.59	0.04	248.0 -	85.6							22.3 -	7.7
0.12	-	-	-0.20	0.66	-0.43									18.9 -	3.6
0.31	-	-	0.36	0.11	0.02	127.0 -	62.5							45.7 -	22.5
-0.30	-	-	1.65	-0.51	1.20	25.1 -	15.7	1.20	1.20	1.20	3.8	0.30Y	61/28/99	41.5 -	26.0
1.06	-	-	4.36	1.87		5.7 -	3.6	1.44	0.46		7.1	0.420	5/31/16	25.0 -	15.8
-	-	-	0.44	0.94	1.12	24.6 -	19.5	1.05	1.05	1.10	11.0	0.080	7/1/16	10.8 -	8.6
-	-	-	1.01	0.58	0.67	19.9 -	9.3	0.53	0.49	0.47	3.7			20.1 -	9.4
0.09	-	-	0.95	0.71	0.32	48.7 -	23.1	1.24	0.92	0.64	3.8	0.1594GHZ	7/15/16	46.2 -	22.0
-	-	0.29	1.02	1.06	1.12	41.2 -	0.0	1.80	1.72	1.65	6.0	0.160	7/15/16	42.0 -	0.0
-	-0.02	-	-2.02	-1.10	-0.61			0.19	0.48	0.48	13.2	0.010Y	12/15/15	3.4 -	0.0
-	-	-1.52	-5.27	-3.51	-1.72			0.03	0.56	0.82	2.5	0.010	10/15/15	2.6 -	0.0
-0.22	-	-	-2.53	-5.57	-4.49					0.20		0.20Y	61/28/99	11.9 -	6.3
-0.03	-	-	-1.93	-0.44	0.31			0.84	0.80	0.74	4.0	0.46090Z	6/15/16	23.8 -	16.7
0.23	-	-	2.17	1.73	0.82	9.0 -	5.0							19.5 -	10.8
0.20	-	-	1.16	2.47	2.96	16.3 -	9.7	2.16	2.99	2.28	14.2	0.470Z	7/28/16	18.9 -	11.2
0.90	-	-	3.63	3.17	2.70	14.9 -	8.3	0.94	0.78	0.62	2.1	0.270Y	61/28/99	54.2 -	30.0
0.59	-	-	-0.42	1.11	2.62			1.28	0.60			0.340	61/28/99		
0.02	-	-	0.08	-0.18	0.14	696.4 -	456.3							55.7 -	36.5
0.64	-	-	3.67	4.27	4.32	29.0 -	24.4	2.76	2.53	2.24	2.8	0.75250Y	61/28/99	106.6 -	89.6
-	-	0.09	0.64	0.18	0.10	42.9 -	30.0			2.53				27.4 -	19.2
-	-	-4.13	0.07	0.53	0.69	357.0 -	0.0							25.0 -	0.0
0.43	-	-	1.87	1.39	1.47	29.7 -	22.2	0.28	0.28	0.28	0.6	0.070Y	61/28/99	55.6 -	41.5
0.05	-	-	0.34	1.02	0.87	25.1 -	12.7	0.34	1.02	0.87	5.3	0.03450	7/15/16	8.6 -	4.3
-2.34	-	-	0.04	1.77	4.68	4926.5 -	2209.0	0.50	0.21	0.35	0.3	0.1450	6/14/16	197.1 -	88.4
-	-	0.13	0.42	0.23	0.39	17.5 -	11.4	-	-	-				7.4 -	4.8
-	-	0.03	0.19	0.59	0.71	622.9 -	284.5	14.12	29.07	25.82	18.2			118.4 -	54.0
-	-	-	-0.65	-0.56	0.85				0.41	0.21				9.7 -	2.9
-2.32	-	-	-18.44	1.56	0.56			3.44	3.44	3.44	86.2	0.85940Y	1/15/16	9.3 -	1.5
0.49	-	-	1.11	1.42	3.19	32.6 -	25.7	1.12	1.04	0.96	3.4	0.30Y	61/28/99	36.1 -	28.6
0.22	-	-	1.79	3.06	1.83	33.6 -	20.8	1.82	1.82	1.82	3.4	0.4550Y	61/28/99	60.1 -	47.6

SYMBOL	COMPANY	NATURE OF BUSINESS	FISCAL YEAR-END	TOTAL REV. $MILL	NET INCOME $MILL	TOTAL ASSETS $MILL	NET STK EQUITY $MILL	NO OF INST	INST. HOLDINGS (SHARES)
GLT	PH Glatfelter Co	Paper & Forest Products	12/31/15	1666.7	64.6	1503.6	663.2	225	43268047
PMC	PharMerica Corp	Pharmaceuticals	12/31/15	2028.5	35.1	1153.7	519.4	266	31854457
PHH	PHH Corp	Credit & Lending	12/31/15	790.0	-145.0	3652.0	1318.0	208	64903092
PM	Philip Morris International Inc	Tobacco Products	12/31/15	73908.0	6873.0	33956.0	-13244.0	1896	1226224411
PHI	Philippine Long Distance Telephone	Services	12/31/15	171103.0	22065.0	455095.0	113608.0	124	22165311
PSX	Phillips 66	Refining & Marketing	12/31/15	100949.0	4227.0	48580.0	23100.0	1318	378816568
PSXP	Phillips 66 Partners LP	Equipment & Services	12/31/15	348.1	194.2	1523.5	-1.5	142	23253934
FENG	Phoenix New Media Ltd	Radio & Television	12/31/15	1609.2	73.6	2567.2	1805.6	60	15937347
DOC	Physicians Realty Trust	REITs	12/31/15	129.4	12.7	1644.9	1021.1	-	-
PNY	Piedmont Natural Gas Co Inc	Gas Utilities	10/31/15	1371.7	137.0	5110.8	1426.3	382	57963267
PDM	Piedmont Office Realty Trust Inc	REITs	12/31/15	584.8	173.0	4434.5	2195.4	257	121262472
PIR	Pier 1 Imports Inc.	Retail - Furniture & Home Furnishing	2/27/16	1892.2	39.6	819.2	284.8	261	82800578
PCQ	Pimco California Municipal Income	Holding and other Investment Office	12/31/15	14.4	12.2	452.8	422.3	32	1348344
PCK	Pimco California Municipal Income	Holding and other Investment Office	12/31/15	14.3	12.2	478.4	448.1	34	1433116
PZC	Pimco California Municipal Income	Holding and other Investment Office	12/31/15	4.5	3.8	383.2	353.2	26	1317951
PTY	PIMCO Corporate & Income Opport	Holding and other Investment Office	7/31/15	54.0	47.7	1360.2	1244.4	119	9289870
PCN	PIMCO Corporate & Income Strateg	Holding and other Investment Office	7/31/15	32.9	28.2	760.1	739.1	-	-
PCI	PIMCO Dynamic Credit Income Fun	Holding and other Investment Office	6/30/15	144.7	104.0	5586.4	3155.7	159	44924494
PDI	PIMCO Dynamic Income Fund	Holding and other Investment Office	6/30/15	46.2	36.2	2412.4	1426.9	84	10347181
PGP	PIMCO Global StocksPLUS & Inco	Holding and other Investment Office	6/30/15	4.4	3.6	210.7	135.5	34	741249
PHK	Pimco High Income Fund	Holding and other Investment Office	7/31/15	29.7	26.3	1306.4	1217.6	106	7578882
PKO	PIMCO Income Opportunity Fund	Holding and other Investment Office	6/30/15	29.4	23.1	668.9	388.4	66	3902082
PFL	PIMCO Income Strategy Fund	Holding and other Investment Office	7/31/15	23.8	19.9	359.3	341.2	65	5938741
PFN	PIMCO Income Strategy Fund II	Holding and other Investment Office	7/31/15	48.4	41.1	742.1	699.4	112	15103321
PMF	Pimco Municipal Income Fund	Holding and other Investment Office	12/31/15	19.4	16.7	544.0	528.3	49	1661715
PML	Pimco Municipal Income Fund II	Holding and other Investment Office	12/31/15	34.0	29.0	1195.3	1127.2	91	6127267
PMX	Pimco Municipal Income Fund III	Holding and other Investment Office	12/31/15	7.7	6.6	590.7	552.8	46	2455947
PNI	Pimco New York Municipal Fund II	Holding and other Investment Office	12/31/15	5.8	4.8	214.5	205.1	23	426119
PNF	Pimco New York Municipal Income	Holding and other Investment Office	12/31/15	4.4	3.6	151.3	140.2	27	762379
PYN	Pimco New York Municipal Income	Holding and other Investment Office	12/31/15	1.0	0.8	91.6	86.2	16	240418
RCS	PIMCO Strategic Income Fund Inc	Holding and other Investment Office	6/30/15	14.3	12.6	997.9	357.7	65	3032179
PF	Pinnacle Foods Inc.	Food	12/27/15	2655.8	212.5	5340.1	1805.5	319	112915298
PNW	Pinnacle West Capital Corp	Electric Utilities	12/31/15	3495.4	437.3	15028.3	4583.9	596	95885067
PES	Pioneer Energy Services Corp	Production & Extraction	12/31/15	540.8	-155.1	829.8	342.6	185	52610999
PHD	Pioneer Floating Rate Trust	Holding and other Investment Office	11/30/15	24.5	18.8	468.0	304.4	86	10548312
PHT	Pioneer High Income Trust	Holding and other Investment Office	3/31/15	44.1	39.1	502.7	344.3	56	3410615
MAV	Pioneer Municipal High Income Adv	Holding and other Investment Office	3/31/15	26.1	22.5	450.7	450.3	48	1053512
MHI	Pioneer Municipal High Income Tru	Holding and other Investment Office	4/30/15	23.7	20.5	404.1	403.7	51	1905578
PXD	Pioneer Natural Resources Co	Production & Extraction	12/31/15	4825.0	-273.0	15154.0	8368.0	817	171158056
PJC	Piper Jaffray Companies	Finance Intermediaries & Services	12/31/15	672.9	52.1	2138.5	783.7	255	12657114
PBI	Pitney Bowes Inc	Office Equipment & Furniture	12/31/15	3578.1	407.9	6141.5	178.7	558	201525509
PBI 08	Pitney-Bowes Credit Corp	Credit & Lending	12/31/01	587.8	160.1	5721.0	1476.4	-	-
PJT	PJT Partners Inc	Finance Intermediaries & Services	12/31/15	405.9	7.6	467.3	-110.8	-	-
PAA	Plains All American Pipeline, L.P.	Equipment & Services	12/31/15	23152.0	903.0	22288.0		571	286554434
PAGP	Plains GP Holdings, L.P	Equipment & Services	12/31/15	23152.0	118.0	24142.0		299	205307682
PLNT	Planet Fitness Inc	Sporting & Recreational	12/31/15	330.5	18.5	699.2	-15.4	98	84206068
PLT	Plantronics, Inc.	Manufacturing	3/31/16	856.9	68.4	933.4	312.4	300	37915785
PAH	Platform Specialty Products Corp	Specialty Chemicals	12/31/15	2542.3	-308.6	10190.2	2749.8	199	214295054
PGEM	PLY Gem Holdings Inc	Construction Materials	12/31/15	1839.7	32.3	1285.9	-76.8	118	18553894
PNC	PNC Financial Services Group (The	Banking	12/31/15	16270.0	4143.0	358493.0	44710.0	1313	439497815
PNM	PNM Resources Inc	Electric Utilities	12/31/15	1439.1	31.1	6009.3	1666.3	323	87003741
PII	Polaris Industries Inc.	Autos- Manufacturing	12/31/15	4719.3	455.4	2387.5	991.1	659	59425763
POL	PolyOne Corp.	Plastics	12/31/15	3377.6	144.6	2595.1	704.2	299	87583527
POR	Portland General Electric Co.	Electric Utilities	12/31/15	1898.0	172.0	7221.0	2258.0	360	105467492
PKX	POSCO (South Korea)	Non-Precious Metals	12/31/15	58192344.6	180646.9	80408759.2	41235349.8	205	23265298
POST	Post Holdings Inc	Food	9/30/15	4648.2	-115.3	9220.4	2976.0	330	70640917
PPS	Post Properties Inc	REITs	12/31/15	384.0	80.6	2271.8	1248.6	321	55237301
POT	Potash Corp. of Saskatchewan Inc.	Agricultural Chemicals	12/31/15	6279.0	1270.0	17469.0	8382.0	772	539831157
PPG	PPG Industries Inc	Specialty Chemicals	12/31/15	15330.0	1406.0	17076.0	4983.0	1055	220214627
PPL	PPL Corp	Electric Utilities	12/31/15	7669.0	682.0	39301.0	9919.0	971	524303482
PX	Praxair, Inc.	Specialty Chemicals	12/31/15	10776.0	1547.0	18319.0	4389.0	1244	286470961
PDS	Precision Drilling Corp.	Production & Extraction	12/31/15	1555.6	-363.4	4878.7	2121.2	205	224250086
APTS	Preferred Apartment Communities I	REITs	12/31/15	109.3	-2.4	1295.5	523.0	101	8873476
PGND	Press Ganey Holdings Inc	Miscellaneous Consumer Services	12/31/15	318.7	-36.6	935.8	562.6	101	48369598
PBH	Prestige Brands Holdings Inc	Pharmaceuticals	3/31/16	806.2	99.9	2948.8	744.3	326	58448128
PVG	Pretium Resources Inc	Precious Metals	12/31/15		-0.5	1479.7	967.6	-	-
PRI	Primerica Inc	Life & Health	12/31/15	1405.3	189.9	10612.1	1145.8	249	53783668
PPP	Primero Mining Corp	Precious Metals	12/31/15	291.3	-106.9	925.0	648.9	111	104535573
PFG	Principal Financial Group, Inc	Life & Health	12/31/15	11964.4	1234.0	218685.9	9311.6	632	210566240
PGZ	Principal Real Estate Income Fund	Finance Intermediaries & Services	10/31/14	14.5	10.8	208.2	145.0	-	-
PRA	ProAssurance Corp	General Insurance	12/31/15	772.1	116.2	4908.2	1958.4	296	44485563
PG	Procter & Gamble Co.	Household & Personal Products	6/30/15	76279.0	7036.0	129495.0	62419.0	2661	1885069993
PGR	Progressive Corp. (OH)	General Insurance	12/31/15	20853.8	1267.6	29819.3	7754.3	707	500829061
PLD	Prologis Inc	REITs	12/31/15	2197.1	869.4	31394.8	14667.9	60	10207956
PRO	Pros Holdings Inc	Internet & Software	12/31/15	168.2	-65.8	263.7	55.4	136	28624229
PB	Prosperity Bancshares Inc.	Banking	12/31/15	790.5	286.6	22037.2	3462.9	308	57579395
PRLB	Proto Labs Inc	Manufacturing	12/31/15	264.1	46.5	361.0	327.6	256	29729318
PFS	Provident Financial Services Inc	Credit & Lending	12/31/15	347.0	83.7	8911.7	1196.1	206	42319742
PRU	Prudential Financial, Inc.	Life & Health	12/31/15	57119.0	5642.0	757388.0	41890.0	1096	313076308
GHY	Prudential Global Short Duration Hi	Finance Intermediaries & Services	7/31/15	58.7	47.1	984.3	698.6	73	12705565

T48

| EARNINGS PER SHARE | | | | | | P/E RATIO | | DIVIDENDS PER SHARE | | | AV. YLD | DIV. DECLARED | | PRICE RANGE 2015 | |
| QUARTERLY | | | ANNUAL | | | | | | | | % | | | | |
1st	2nd	3rd	2015	2014	2013			2015	2014	2013		AMOUNT	PAYABLE		
0.37	-	-	1.47	1.57	1.52	16.1 -	9.7	0.48	0.44	0.40	2.5	0.1250Y	8/1/16	23.6 -	14.3
0.13	-	-	1.14	0.22	0.63	32.2 -	17.5	-	-	-	-	-	-	36.7 -	20.0
0.56	-	-	-2.62	1.47	2.06	-	-	-	-	-	-	-	-	27.8 -	8.8
0.98	-	-	4.42	4.76	5.26	23.1 -	17.5	4.04	3.88	3.58	4.6	1.020Y	61/28/99	102.2 -	77.3
-	-	42.72	101.85	157.51	163.67	0.6 -	0.3	151.70	182.97	174.89	317.6	0.8	10/14/94	65.0 -	34.3
0.72	-	-	7.73	8.33	6.02	12.1 -	9.1	2.18	1.89	1.33	2.7	0.630Y	61/28/99	93.7 -	70.5
0.44	-	-	3.26	2.93	0.80	22.9 -	13.7	1.54	1.12	0.15	2.6	0.4810	5/12/16	74.6 -	44.6
-	-	0.13	0.13	0.43	0.45	73.2 -	25.5	-	-	-	-	-	-	9.5 -	3.3
0.04	-	-	0.15	-0.12	-0.13	130.4 -	93.7	0.90	0.90	0.18	5.4	0.2250	7/18/16	19.6 -	14.1
-	0.78	-	1.73	1.84	1.78	34.7 -	20.4	1.31	1.27	1.23	2.6	0.340Y	61/28/99	60.1 -	35.3
0.07	-	-	1.15	0.28	0.60	18.1 -	14.6	0.84	0.81	0.80	4.5	0.210	61/28/99	20.8 -	16.7
-	-	0.13	0.82	1.01	1.20	16.1 -	4.6	0.24	0.21	0.17	3.1	0.070Y	5/11/16	13.2 -	3.8
-	-	-	0.65	0.99	1.02	26.7 -	21.7	0.92	0.92	0.92	5.9	0.077M	7/1/16	17.3 -	14.1
-	-	-	0.38	0.68	0.69	28.9 -	24.6	0.65	0.73	0.75	6.5	0.0537M	7/1/16	11.0 -	9.3
-	-	-	0.17	0.69	0.79	71.9 -	60.2	0.72	0.72	0.72	6.3	0.06M	7/1/16	12.2 -	10.2
-	-	-	0.68	1.14	1.43	22.4 -	17.7	2.21	3.40	2.58	16.1	0.130	7/1/16	15.2 -	12.0
-	-	-	0.73	0.99	1.28	20.8 -	17.3	1.70	2.30	1.56	12.4	0.11250	7/1/16	15.2 -	12.7
-	-	-	0.76	1.79	1.33	27.4 -	22.0	2.47	2.47	1.93	13.4	0.16410	7/1/16	20.8 -	16.7
-	-	-	0.80	3.70	2.79	37.4 -	31.1	4.19	3.52	2.45	15.0	0.22050	7/1/16	30.0 -	24.9
-	-	-	0.34	1.39	-	62.4 -	40.1	2.20	2.20	2.20	12.4	0.18340	7/1/16	21.2 -	13.6
-	-	-	0.21	0.84	0.81	55.5 -	33.2	1.46	1.46	1.46	16.5	0.10350	7/1/16	11.7 -	7.0
-	-	-	1.54	2.71	2.87	17.1 -	12.4	3.87	2.88	2.83	17.4	0.190	7/1/16	26.3 -	19.1
-	-	-	0.79	0.79	0.92	14.3 -	11.2	1.22	1.08	1.40	12.3	0.090	7/1/16	11.3 -	8.8
-	-	-	0.70	0.72	0.92	14.8 -	11.4	1.11	0.96	1.46	12.4	0.080	7/1/16	10.3 -	8.0
-	-	-	0.65	0.94	0.95	25.9 -	21.0	0.97	0.97	0.97	8.4	0.0813M	7/1/16	16.8 -	13.7
-	-	-	0.47	0.81	0.82	29.4 -	24.4	0.78	0.78	0.78	6.3	0.065M	7/1/16	13.8 -	11.5
-	-	-	0.20	0.75	0.75	64.0 -	52.9	0.75	0.79	0.84	6.5	0.0623M	7/1/16	12.8 -	10.6
-	-	-	0.43	0.75	0.69	32.5 -	27.3	0.80	0.80	0.80	6.4	0.0663M	7/1/16	14.0 -	11.7
-	-	-	0.47	0.67	0.70	29.3 -	23.3	0.68	0.68	0.68	5.7	0.057M	7/1/16	13.8 -	10.9
-	-	-	0.14	0.56	0.62	80.6 -	0.0	0.63	0.63	0.63	6.2	0.0525M	7/1/16	11.3 -	0.0
-	-	-	0.30	0.99	1.05	31.9 -	25.9	1.02	1.11	1.25	11.6	0.080	7/1/16	9.6 -	7.8
0.21	-	-	1.81	2.13	0.82	26.2 -	22.0	0.98	0.89	0.57	2.2	0.2550Y	61/28/99	47.4 -	39.9
0.04	-	-	3.92	3.58	3.66	19.3 -	14.4	2.41	2.30	2.20	3.7	0.6250Y	61/28/99	75.5 -	56.3
-0.43	-	-	-2.41	-0.60	-0.58	-	-	-	-	-	-	-	-	7.5 -	1.1
-	-	-	0.76	0.75	1.01	15.4 -	13.4	0.69	0.80	0.90	6.2	0.060	6/30/16	11.7 -	10.2
-	-	-	1.36	1.50	1.74	9.2 -	6.3	1.61	1.65	1.65	15.7	0.0850	6/30/16	12.6 -	8.5
-	-	-	0.95	1.08	1.07	14.9 -	12.9	1.14	1.14	1.14	8.6	0.07M	6/30/16	14.1 -	12.3
-	-	-	0.91	1.05	1.14	16.1 -	13.2	1.08	1.14	1.14	8.3	0.07M	6/30/16	14.7 -	12.0
-1.65	-	-	-1.83	6.38	-6.16	-	-	0.08	0.08	0.08	0.1	0.040Y	61/28/99	168.7 -	107.2
0.16	-	-	3.34	3.87	2.70	14.8 -	9.8	-	-	-	-	-	-	49.6 -	32.6
0.30	-	-	2.03	1.64	0.70	10.9 -	8.1	0.75	0.75	0.94	3.7	0.18750Y	61/28/99	22.2 -	16.5
0.01	-	-	-0.61	-	-	-	-	-	-	-	-	0.050Y	6/22/16	29.2 -	0.0
0.07	-	-	0.77	2.38	2.80	62.1 -	20.1	2.75	2.55	2.33	9.5	0.70	61/28/99	47.8 -	15.4
0.14	-	-	0.53	0.47	0.10	53.1 -	10.0	0.88	0.67	-	6.1	0.2310	5/13/16	28.1 -	5.3
0.09	-	-	0.11	-	-	173.6 -	120.5	-	-	-	-	-	-	19.1 -	13.3
-	-	0.49	2.63	2.59	2.49	22.1 -	12.4	0.60	0.40	0.40	1.2	0.150Y	61/28/99	58.1 -	32.5
-0.59	-	-	-1.52	-1.94	-2.10	-	-	-	-	-	-	-	-	28.4 -	5.5
-0.40	-	-	0.47	-0.46	-1.32	33.2 -	19.0	-	-	-	-	-	-	15.6 -	8.9
1.68	-	-	7.39	7.30	7.39	13.5 -	10.6	-	-	-	-	24.250Y	61/28/99	99.9 -	78.2
0.13	-	-	0.20	1.45	1.25	169.3 -	123.0	0.80	0.74	0.64	2.7	0.220Y	61/28/99	33.9 -	24.6
0.71	-	-	6.75	6.65	5.35	23.0 -	10.3	2.12	1.92	1.68	1.9	0.550Y	61/28/99	155.3 -	69.6
0.46	-	-	1.63	0.85	2.53	24.7 -	14.9	0.42	0.34	0.26	1.3	0.120Y	61/28/99	40.2 -	24.3
0.68	-	-	2.04	2.18	1.35	20.4 -	16.3	1.18	1.12	1.10	3.2	0.320Y	7/15/16	41.7 -	33.2
-	-	-7190.00	1845.00	7432.00	7409.00	0.0 -	0.0	1983.43	1971.69	1971.57	4736.8	-	-	55.0 -	32.3
-	0.02	-	-2.33	-9.03	0.30	-	-	-	-	-	-	0.6250	5/16/16	76.9 -	43.5
0.36	-	-	1.41	-	1.96	44.2 -	38.0	1.72	-	1.24	3.0	1.06250Z	6/30/16	62.4 -	53.6
0.09	-	-	1.52	1.82	2.04	25.9 -	0.0	1.49	1.40	1.19	6.1	0.250	8/2/16	39.3 -	0.0
1.29	-	-	5.14	7.51	11.14	23.0 -	16.4	1.42	1.31	1.21	1.4	0.40Y	61/28/99	118.3 -	84.5
0.71	-	-	1.01	2.61	1.76	38.5 -	29.1	1.50	1.49	1.47	4.4	0.380Y	61/28/99	38.9 -	29.4
1.24	-	-	5.35	5.73	5.87	23.1 -	18.0	2.86	2.60	2.40	2.6	0.750Y	61/28/99	123.8 -	96.1
-	-0.30	-	-1.24	0.11	0.66	-	-	0.28	0.25	0.21	5.5	0.070	11/18/15	8.8 -	0.0
-0.49	-	-	-0.95	-0.31	-1.59	-	-	0.73	0.66	0.60	6.3	0.20250Z	7/15/16	14.0 -	9.8
0.15	-	-	-0.75	0.36	0.00	-	-	-	-	-	-	-	-	35.2 -	24.1
-	-	0.53	1.49	1.39	1.27	38.7 -	29.3	-	-	-	-	-	-	57.6 -	43.6
-	-0.02	-	0.00	-0.11	-0.16	-	-	-	-	-	-	-	-	11.0 -	0.0
0.92	-	-	3.70	3.29	2.83	15.2 -	10.8	0.64	0.48	0.44	1.4	0.170Y	61/28/99	56.1 -	39.9
-	-0.03	-	-0.66	-1.48	-0.04	-	-	-	-	-	-	-	-	5.4 -	0.0
1.25	-	-	4.06	3.65	2.95	14.3 -	8.5	1.50	1.28	0.98	3.2	0.390Y	61/28/99	58.0 -	34.3
-	-	-	1.57	0.33	-	-	-	-	1.67	0.41	-	0.1450	7/28/16	20.0 -	14.7
0.36	-	-	2.11	3.30	4.80	25.3 -	21.2	2.24	3.86	1.05	4.5	0.310Y	61/28/99	53.4 -	44.8
-	-	0.97	2.44	4.01	3.86	34.3 -	27.9	2.59	2.45	2.29	3.3	0.66950Y	61/28/99	83.8 -	68.1
0.44	-	-	2.15	2.15	1.93	16.5 -	12.5	0.69	1.49	0.28	2.2	0.88820Y	61/28/99	35.5 -	27.0
0.39	-	-	1.64	1.24	0.64	29.3 -	21.7	1.52	1.32	1.12	3.7	1.06750Z	61/28/99	48.1 -	35.6
-0.68	-	-	-2.23	-1.27	0.11	-	-	-	-	-	-	-	-	25.1 -	9.3
0.98	-	-	4.09	4.32	3.65	14.5 -	8.2	1.12	0.99	0.89	2.2	0.30Y	61/28/99	59.2 -	33.7
0.40	-	-	1.77	1.60	1.36	46.0 -	29.9	-	-	-	-	-	-	81.5 -	52.9
0.33	-	-	1.33	1.22	1.23	15.9 -	13.5	0.65	0.60	0.56	3.3	0.180Y	5/31/16	21.2 -	17.9
2.93	-	-	12.17	3.23	-1.55	7.5 -	4.8	2.44	2.17	1.73	3.1	0.356307	61/28/99	91.7 -	58.0
-	-	-	1.15	1.23	0.64	13.7 -	11.6	1.75	1.50	0.75	12.1	0.110	8/31/16	15.8 -	13.3

SYMBOL	COMPANY	NATURE OF BUSINESS	FISCAL YEAR-END	TOTAL REV. $MILL	NET INCOME $MILL	TOTAL ASSETS $MILL	NET STK EQUITY $MILL	NO OF INST	INST. HOLDINGS (SHARES)
PUK	Prudential Plc	Life & Health	12/31/15	41543.0	2579.0	386985.0	12955.0	233	22012075
ISD	Prudential Short Duration High Yield	Holding and other Investment Office	5/31/15	49.3	39.8	785.9	593.2	67	9350408
PSB PRT	PS Business Parks, Inc	REITs	12/31/15	373.7	130.5	2186.7	1660.5	251	22427148
PSAV	PSAV Inc	Business Services							
PEG 31	PSEG Power LLC	Electric Utilities	12/31/15	4928.0	856.0	12250.0	6002.0		
PEG	Public Service Enterprise Group Inc	Electric Utilities	12/31/15	10415.0	1679.0	37535.0	13066.0	944	366913339
PSA	Public Storage	REITs	12/31/15	2381.7	1311.2	9778.2	9170.6	790	168131961
PHM	PulteGroup Inc	Builders	12/31/15	5982.0	494.1	8967.2	4759.3	579	325105164
PBYI	Puma Biotechnology, Inc.	Biotechnology	12/31/15	-	-239.3	239.8	206.0	158	30451371
PSTG	PURE Storage Inc	Internet & Software	1/31/16	440.3	-213.8	870.8	563.4	111	81877960
PCF	Putnam High Income Securities Fun	Holding and other Investment Office	8/31/15	6.7	5.4	128.3	127.0	50	5115495
PMM	Putnam Managed Municipal Income	Holding and other Investment Office	10/31/15	28.6	24.7	570.3	553.5	90	7013830
PIM	Putnam Master Intermediate Incom	Holding and other Investment Office	9/30/15	16.9	14.0	575.0	278.1	77	25992897
PMO	Putnam Municipal Opportunities Tru	Holding and other Investment Office	4/30/15	34.5	29.5	746.7	701.0	84	7592514
PPT	Putnam Premier Income Trust	Holding and other Investment Office	7/31/15	40.3	34.0	1001.5	669.9	125	60443339
PVH	PVH Corp	Apparel, Footwear & Accessories	1/31/16	8020.3	572.4	10694.4	4552.3	560	83711361
PZN	Pzena Investment Management Inc	Wealth Management	12/31/15	116.6	7.7	114.3	18.4	84	9339908
QTWO	Q2 Holdings Inc	IT Services	12/31/15	108.9	-25.1	204.5	118.0	135	34145173
QEP	QEP Resources Inc	Production & Extraction	12/31/15	2018.6	-149.4	8425.5	3947.9	403	197781285
QIHU	Qihoo 360 Technology Co, Ltd.	Internet & Software	12/31/15	1804.6	307.0	3655.2	1191.9	269	38390314
QTS	QTS Realty Trust Inc	REITs	12/31/15	311.1	20.3	1757.5	618.0	217	51180430
QUAD	Quad/Graphics, Inc.	Printing	12/31/15	4677.7	-641.9	2847.5	423.9	153	24506597
KWR	Quaker Chemical Corp.	Specialty Chemicals	12/31/15	737.6	51.2	685.5	373.0	206	12601272
NX	Quanex Building Products Corp	Construction Materials	10/31/15	645.5	16.1	572.0	395.3	162	32212541
PWR	Quanta Services, Inc.	Construction Services	12/31/15	7572.4	310.9	5213.5	3085.5	572	178554395
QTM	Quantum Corp.	Computer Hardware & Equipment	3/31/16	476.0	-74.7	-	-126.9	179	207834618
DGX	Quest Diagnostics, Inc.	Diagnostic & Health Related Service	12/31/15	7493.0	709.0	9962.0	4684.0	790	157598654
STR	Questar Corp	Gas Utilities	12/31/15	1134.9	208.7	4377.8	1315.1	498	152640213
Q	Quintiles Transnational Holdings Inc	Biotechnology	12/31/15	5737.6	387.2	3926.3	-564.2		
QHC	Quorum Health Corp	Hospitals & Health Care Facilities	12/31/15	2187.3	1.3	2294.9	3.2		
QHC	Quorum Health Corp	Hospitals & Health Care Facilities	12/31/15	2187.3	1.3	2294.9	3.2		
QUOT	Quotient Technology Inc	Internet & Software	12/31/15	237.3	-26.7	321.1	265.5	104	63003053
CTQ	Qwest Corp	Services	12/31/15	8964.0	1074.0	21470.0	8907.0	5	145808
RAX	Rackspace Hosting Inc	Internet & Software	12/31/15	2001.3	126.2	2014.2	976.5	373	111124430
RDN	Radian Group, Inc.	Credit & Lending	12/31/15	1193.3	286.9	5642.1	2496.9	316	227060235
RAS	RAIT Financial Trust	REITs	12/31/15	324.0	63.5	4447.3	489.9	174	65017919
RL	Ralph Lauren Corp	Apparel, Footwear & Accessories	4/2/16	7405.0	396.0	6213.0	3744.0	582	65222566
RPT	Ramco-Gershenson Properties Trus	REITs	12/31/15	251.8	65.1	2128.7	884.2	206	89137270
RRC	Range Resources Corp	Production & Extraction	12/31/15	1598.1	-713.7	6900.0	2759.7	601	215791674
RJF	Raymond James Financial, Inc.	Finance Intermediaries & Services	9/30/15	5308.2	502.1	26479.7	4522.0	490	114971802
RYAM	Rayonier Advanced Materials Inc.	Plastics	12/31/15	941.4	55.3	1288.5	-17.1	239	31891157
RYN	Rayonier Inc.	REITs	12/31/15	544.9	46.2	2319.3	1288.1	436	123203366
RTN	Raytheon Co.	Defense	12/31/15	23247.0	2074.0	29281.0	10128.0	1293	272571481
RMAX	Re/Max Holdings Inc	Property, Real Estate & Developmen	12/31/15	176.9	16.7	385.3	449.7	152	18027797
RLGY	Realogy Holdings Corp	Property, Real Estate & Developmen	12/31/15	5706.0	184.0	7531.0	2418.0	344	148485693
O	Realty Income Corp	REITs	12/31/15	1023.3	283.8	11865.9	6531.6	697	193400257
RHT	Red Hat Inc	Internet & Software	2/29/16	2052.2	199.4	4155.1	1334.4	650	190185418
RLH	Red Lions Hotels Corp	Hotels, Restaurants & Travel	12/31/15	142.9	2.7	287.2	134.0	74	13319683
RWT	Redwood Trust Inc.	REITs	12/31/15	-	102.1	6231.0	1146.3	246	77923497
RBC	Regal Beloit Corp	Electrical Equipment	1/2/16	3509.7	143.3	4591.7	1937.3	341	47063504
RGC	Regal Entertainment Group	Entertainment	12/31/15	3127.3	153.4	2632.3	-877.8	345	96671303
REG	Regency Centers Corp.	REITs	12/31/15	569.8	150.1	4191.1	2054.1	378	126223132
RM	Regional Management Corp	Credit & Lending	12/31/15	217.3	23.4	629.1	205.2	93	11316221
RF	Regions Financial Corp	Banking	12/31/15	5674.0	1062.0	126050.0	16844.0	832	1033007353
RGS	Regis Corp.	Miscellaneous Consumer Services	6/30/15	1837.3	-33.8	1162.0	627.4	226	54758967
RGA	Reinsurance Group of America, Inc.	Life & Health	12/31/15	10418.2	502.2	50383.2	6135.4	30	784655
RS	Reliance Steel & Aluminum Co.	Non-Precious Metals	12/31/15	9350.5	311.5	7121.6	3914.1	439	63041880
RENX	RELX NV	Publishing	12/31/15	-	787.0	4325.0	4218.0	125	13964331
RELX	RELX PLC	Publishing	12/31/15			3169.0	3114.0	139	24535867
RNR	RenaissanceRe Holdings Ltd.	General Insurance	12/31/15	1515.1	431.2	11560.9	4732.2	412	47755977
SOL	Renesola Ltd.	Semiconductors	12/31/15	1282.0	-5.1	1346.3	111.9		
RENN	Renren Inc	Internet & Software	12/31/15	41.1	-220.1	1267.8	930.5	84	9415756
RSG	Republic Services Inc	Sanitation Services	12/31/15	9115.0	749.9	20577.2	7774.1	731	295228868
RMD	ResMed Inc.	Medical Instruments & Equipment	6/30/15	1678.9	352.9	2184.3	1587.3	502	90912530
REN	Resolute Energy Corp	Production & Extraction	12/31/15	154.6	-742.3	391.0	-203.3	59	35431297
RFP	Resolute Forest Products Inc	Paper & Forest Products	12/31/15	3645.0	-257.0	4220.0	1932.0	163	97331361
RSO	Resource Capital Corp	REITs	12/31/15	167.7	17.2	2760.4	818.9	127	18407285
QSR	Restaurant Brands International Inc	Hotels, Restaurants & Travel	12/31/15	4052.2	375.1	18411.1	4633.6	245	169154338
RH	Restoration Hardware Holdings, Inc.	Retail - Furniture & Home Furnishing	1/30/16	2109.0	91.1	2088.5	886.2	327	40850214
RPAI	Retail Properties of America, Inc	REITs	12/31/15	604.0	125.1	4621.3	2155.3		
REV	Revlon Inc	Household & Personal Products	12/31/15	1914.3	56.1	2014.3	-587.5	116	15038175
REX	REX American Resources Corp	Refining & Marketing	1/31/16	436.5	31.4	414.7	311.3	165	6882113
REXR	Rexford Industrial Realty Inc	REITs	12/31/15	93.9	1.9	1153.3	672.1	150	59882299
RXN	Rexnord Corp (New)	Industrial Machinery & Equipment	3/31/16	1923.8	67.9	3354.8	588.6	184	100857040
RAI	Reynolds American Inc	Tobacco Products	12/31/15	10675.0	3253.0	53224.0	18252.0	1033	707117933
RICE	Rice Energy Inc	Production & Extraction	12/31/15	502.1	-291.3	3970.5	1279.9	234	138308611
RMP	Rice Midstream Partners LP	Production & Extraction	12/31/15	114.5	52.5	689.8		64	39135064
RNG	RingCentral Inc	IT Services	12/31/15	296.2	-32.1	214.8	110.1	187	49527819
RIO	Rio Tinto Plc	Mining	12/31/15	34829.0	-853.0	91564.0	37349.0	408	96266125
RBA	Ritchie Bros Auctioneers Inc	Business Services	12/31/15	515.9	136.2	1120.1	678.4	254	105722691

| EARNINGS PER SHARE | | | | | | P/E RATIO | | DIVIDENDS PER SHARE | | | AV. YLD | DIV. DECLARED | | PRICE RANGE | |
| QUARTERLY | | | ANNUAL | | | | | | | | | | | 2015 | |
1st	2nd	3rd	2015	2014	2013			2015	2014	2013	%	AMOUNT	PAYABLE		
-	-	-	1.01	0.87	0.53	50.7	31.3	0.78	0.70	0.61	1.8	0.42190Z	9/23/16	51.2	31.6
-	-	-	1.20	1.22	1.24	13.2	11.6	1.59	1.60	1.56	10.6	0.110	8/31/16	15.9	13.9
0.54	-	-	2.52	4.19	1.77	10.5	9.7	2.20	4.75	1.76	8.6	0.35630Z	6/30/16	26.5	24.5
0.93	-	-	3.30	2.99	2.45	14.3	11.2	1.56	1.48	1.44	3.7	0.410Y	61/28/99	47.3	37.0
1.39	-	-	6.07	5.25	4.89	45.5	30.1	6.50	5.60	5.15	2.8	0.1602GHZ	6/30/16	276.3	183.0
0.24	-	-	1.36	1.26	6.72	16.2	11.3	0.33	0.23	0.15	1.8	0.090Y	61/28/99	22.0	15.4
-2.19	-	-	-7.45	-4.73	-1.90	-	-	-	-	-	-	-	-	170.0	21.9
-0.34	-	-	-6.56	-3.24		-	-	-	-	-	-	-	-	19.7	11.6
-	-	-	0.35	0.36	0.44	23.4	18.7	0.37	0.43	0.48	5.0	0.03090Z	8/1/16	8.2	6.5
-	-	-	0.45	0.45	0.47	17.6	15.4	0.44	0.46	0.47	6.0	0.0363MZ	8/1/16	7.9	6.9
-	-	-	0.25	0.29	0.30	19.4	16.4	0.31	0.31	0.31	6.9	0.0260Z	8/1/16	4.8	4.1
-	-	-	0.73	0.73	0.73	18.2	15.8	0.71	0.70	0.71	5.8	0.0595MZ	8/1/16	13.3	11.6
-	-	-	0.28	0.32	0.32	18.7	15.9	0.31	0.31	0.33	6.3	0.0260Z	8/1/16	5.2	4.4
2.83	-	-	5.27	1.74	5.87	22.6	12.6	0.15	0.15	0.15	0.2	0.03750Y	61/28/99	119.0	66.4
0.10	-	-	0.50	0.53	0.45	23.5	12.0	0.41	0.35	0.25	4.6	0.030Y	5/19/16	11.8	6.0
-0.25	-	-	-0.67	-0.67	-1.51	-	-	-	-	-	-	-	-	30.0	16.8
-4.55	-	-	-0.85	4.36	0.89	-	-	0.08	0.08	0.08	0.6	0.020Y	61/28/99	19.1	9.3
-	-	0.23	1.58	1.13	0.52	48.1	26.7	-	-	-	-	-	-	76.0	42.2
0.14	-	-	0.53	0.51	0.11	98.7	68.4	1.28	1.16	0.24	2.9	0.360Z	7/6/16	52.3	36.3
0.08	-	-	-13.40	0.38	0.65	-	-	1.20	1.20	1.20	9.0	0.30Y	6/17/16	20.5	7.8
0.98	-	-	3.84	4.26	4.27	24.3	18.1	1.24	1.10	0.99	1.5	0.3450Y	7/29/16	93.2	69.6
-	0.11	-	0.47	0.78	-0.32	46.6	34.3	0.16	0.16	0.16	0.8	0.040Y	6/30/16	21.9	16.1
0.13	-	-	1.59	1.35	1.87	19.1	10.9	-	-	-	-	-	-	30.4	17.3
-	-	0.00	0.06	-0.09	-0.22	33.7	6.3	-	-	-	-	-	-	2.0	0.4
0.70	-	-	4.87	3.81	5.54	15.9	12.4	1.47	1.29	1.20	2.1	0.40Y	61/28/99	77.6	60.5
0.45	-	-	1.18	1.29	0.92	21.4	15.6	0.84	0.75	0.71	3.9	0.220Y	61/28/99	25.3	18.4
0.88	-	-	3.08	2.72	1.77	25.7	18.2	-	-	-	-	-	-	79.1	55.9
-	-	-	-	-	-	-	-	-	-	-	-	-	-	17.8	0.0
-	-	-	-	-	-	-	-	-	-	-	-	-	-	13.3	9.1
-0.10	-	-	-0.32	-0.35	-0.57	-	-	-	-	-	-	-	-	13.1	5.2
-	-	-	-	-	-	-	-	1.53	1.53	0.80	6.0	0.41410Z	9/15/16	26.5	24.8
0.37	-	-	0.90	0.77	0.61	44.7	18.6	-	-	-	-	-	-	40.2	16.8
0.29	-	-	1.22	4.16	-1.18	15.5	7.7	0.01	0.01	0.01	0.1	0.00250Y	6/6/16	18.9	9.4
-0.20	-	-	0.08	-3.92	-4.54	81.9	23.8	0.72	0.69	0.50	17.4	0.44530Z	8/30/16	6.5	1.9
-	-	1.54	7.88	8.43	8.00	17.8	10.6	1.85	1.70	1.60	1.7	0.50Y	61/28/99	140.2	83.2
0.13	-	-	0.73	-0.14	0.06	25.7	20.3	0.82	0.78	0.71	4.9	0.90630Z	7/1/16	18.8	14.8
-0.55	-	-	-4.29	3.79	0.70	-	-	0.16	0.16	0.16	0.5	0.020Y	61/28/99	55.6	20.4
-	0.87	-	3.43	3.32	2.58	17.9	11.8	0.72	0.64	0.58	1.4	0.20Y	61/28/99	61.3	40.4
0.49	-	-	1.30	0.75		13.4	4.6	0.28	0.14		2.7	0.070Y	6/30/16	17.5	6.0
0.12	-	-	0.37	0.76	2.86	71.2	50.4	1.00	2.03	1.86	4.3	0.250Z	61/28/99	26.4	18.6
1.43	-	-	6.80	7.18	6.16	19.4	14.1	2.62	1.81	2.20	2.2	0.73250Y	61/28/99	132.0	95.6
0.26	-	-	1.30	1.10	0.12	33.2	23.5	2.00	0.25		5.5	0.150Y	6/2/16	43.1	30.5
-0.20	-	-	1.24	0.97	2.99	39.9	22.7	-	-	-	-	-	-	49.5	28.1
0.25	-	-	1.09	1.04	1.06	58.9	39.8	2.28	2.19	2.18	4.4	0.1380Z	61/28/99	64.2	43.4
-	-	0.25	0.95	0.93	0.77	88.1	64.1	-	-	-	-	-	-	83.7	60.9
-0.24	-	-	0.13	0.12	-0.87	71.2	42.8	-	-	-	-	-	-	9.3	5.6
0.15	-	-	1.18	1.15	1.94	14.4	7.9	1.12	1.12	1.12	8.2	0.280Z	6/30/16	17.0	9.4
0.93	-	-	3.18	0.69	2.64	24.4	15.5	0.91	0.86	0.79	1.4	0.240Y	61/28/99	77.7	49.4
0.26	-	-	0.98	0.68	1.01	22.2	17.0	0.88	1.88	0.04	4.5	0.220Y	61/28/99	21.7	16.7
0.49	-	-	1.36	1.80	1.40	58.3	42.0	1.94	1.88	1.85	2.9	0.50Z	61/28/99	79.3	57.1
0.40	-	-	1.79	1.14	2.23	11.1	6.7	-	-	-	-	-	-	19.9	11.9
0.20	-	-	0.75	0.80	0.77	14.4	9.4	0.23	0.18	0.10	2.5	0.39840Y	61/28/99	10.8	7.1
-	-	-0.04	-0.62	-2.40	0.51	-	-	-	0.12	0.24	-	0.060Y	11/19/13	18.0	10.7
1.17	-	-	7.46	9.78	5.78	13.3	10.5	1.40	1.26	1.08	1.5	0.370Y	61/28/99	99.1	78.6
1.27	-	-	4.16	4.73	4.14	17.9	12.4	1.60	1.40	1.26	2.6	0.40Y	61/28/99	74.6	51.8
-	-	-	0.45	0.48		-	-	0.83	0.88	0.78	4.3	-	-	49.6	14.9
-	-	-	0.42	0.48		-	-	0.84	0.99	0.93	3.9	-	-	67.8	15.6
2.95	-	-	9.28	12.60	14.87	-	-	1.20	1.16	1.12	-	0.310	61/28/99		
0.00	-	-	-0.02	-0.17	-1.42	-	-	-	-	-	-	-	-	1.9	0.9
-	-	-0.02	-0.22	0.06	0.06	-	-	-	-	-	-	-	-	4.3	1.8
0.45	-	-	2.13	1.53	1.62	22.9	18.3	1.16	1.08	0.99	2.7	0.30Y	61/28/99	48.8	39.0
-	-	0.63	2.47	2.39	2.10	24.8	20.0	1.12	1.00	0.68	2.0	0.30Y	61/28/99	61.2	49.4
-5.65	-	-	-49.55	-1.50	-8.35	-	-	-	-	-	-	-	-	6.7	1.8
-0.09	-	-	-2.78	-2.93	-6.75	-	-	-	-	-	-	-	-	15.4	0.0
0.31	-	-	-0.43	1.36	1.32	-	-	1.06	3.20	3.20	8.4	0.53910Z	8/1/16	17.4	9.3
0.21	-	-	0.50	-2.34	0.65	115.8	0.0	0.44	0.30	0.24	1.0	0.150Y	7/6/16	57.9	0.0
-0.33	-	-	2.20	0.45	-1.36	48.0	14.1	-	-	-	-	-	-	105.6	31.0
0.19	-	-	0.49	0.14	0.02	34.7	26.9	0.66	0.66	0.66	4.4	0.43750Z	61/28/99	17.0	13.2
0.21	-	-	1.07	0.78	-0.11	35.5	22.9	-	-	-	-	0.16740Y	10/8/13	38.0	24.5
0.43	-	-	10.76	4.29	-0.28	6.1	4.1	-	-	-	-	-	-	65.3	43.9
0.02	-	-	0.03	0.02	-0.03	666.3	423.0	0.51	0.48	0.21	3.2	0.1350	7/15/16	20.0	12.7
-	-	0.24	0.80	0.30	0.50	33.3	18.3	-	-	-	-	-	-	26.6	14.7
2.49	-	-	2.57	1.38	1.57	20.2	13.8	1.39	1.34	1.24	3.1	0.420Y	61/28/99	51.9	35.5
-0.15	-	-	-2.14	1.70		-	-	-	-	-	-	-	-	23.3	8.3
0.97	-	-	0.76	0.02		24.1	12.0	0.59	-	-	4.0	0.210	5/12/16	18.3	9.1
-0.09	-	-	-0.46	-0.72	-1.39	-	-	-	-	-	-	-	-	25.5	14.4
-	-	-	-0.47	3.51	1.97	-	-	2.21	2.02	1.76	6.6	-	-	44.7	22.7
0.27	-	-	1.27	0.85	0.88	33.9	0.0	0.60	0.54	0.51	2.0	0.180	6/14/16	43.0	0.0

SYMBOL	COMPANY	NATURE OF BUSINESS	FISCAL YEAR-END	TOTAL REV. $MILL	NET INCOME $MILL	TOTAL ASSETS $MILL	NET STK EQUITY $MILL	NO OF INST	INST. HOLDINGS (SHARES)
RAD	Rite Aid Corp.	Retail - Food & Beverage. Drug & To	2/27/16	30736.7	165.5	11277.0	581.4	606	707720481
RIV	RiverNorth Opportunities Fund Inc	Finance Intermediaries & Services	11/20/15	-	0.2	-	0.1	-	-
RLI	RLI Corp.	General Insurance	12/31/15	794.6	137.5	2736.6	823.5	258	39591686
RLJ	RLJ Lodging Trust	REITs	12/31/15	1136.3	218.2	3980.2	2182.8	228	136841977
RRTS	Roadrunner Transportation System	Miscellaneous Transportation Servic	12/31/15	1995.0	48.0	1326.1	613.3	169	43414324
RHI	Robert Half International Inc.	Business Services	12/31/15	5094.9	357.8	1703.0	1003.8	611	132861535
ROK	Rockwell Automation, Inc.	Electrical Equipment	9/30/15	6307.9	827.6	6404.7	2256.8	854	118600987
COL	Rockwell Collins, Inc.	Aerospace	9/30/15	5244.0	686.0	7389.0	1875.0	700	117552451
RCI 14A	Rogers Cable Inc.	Radio & Television	12/31/06	3201.0	177.0	5245.0	419.0	-	-
RCI	Rogers Communications Inc	Services	12/31/15	13414.0	1381.0	29175.0	5745.0	351	284194267
ROG	Rogers Corp.	Plastics	12/31/15	641.4	46.3	932.5	584.6	211	18281479
ROL	Rollins, Inc.	Business Services	12/31/15	1485.3	152.1	852.4	524.0	316	86064063
ROP	Roper Technologies Inc	Electrical Equipment	12/31/15	3582.4	696.1	10168.4	5298.9	723	112133281
RRMS	Rose Rock Midstream LP	Equipment & Services	12/31/15	844.7	49.7	1257.8	-	81	13044240
RST	Rosetta Stone, Inc.	Internet & Software	12/31/15	217.7	-46.8	228.5	22.4	85	20923613
RSE	Rouse Properties Inc	REITs	12/31/15	305.4	41.7	2529.3	519.7	176	57520754
RDC	Rowan Companies Plc	Equipment & Services	12/31/15	2137.0	93.3	8347.3	4772.5	409	153998645
RY	Royal Bank of Canada (Montreal, Q	Banking	10/31/15	43279.0	9925.0	1074208.0	62146.0	533	789614745
RY	Royal Bank of Canada (Montreal, Q	Banking	10/31/15	43279.0	9925.0	1074208.0	62146.0	533	789614745
RBS	Royal Bank of Scotland Group Plc	Banking	12/31/15	16890.0	-1891.0	815408.0	53431.0	123	16099519
RCL	Royal Caribbean Cruises Ltd	Hotels, Restaurants & Travel	12/31/15	8299.1	665.8	20921.9	8063.0	645	160243778
RDS A	Royal Dutch Shell Plc	Production & Extraction	12/31/15	272156.0	1939.0	340157.0	162876.0	932	306690345
RGT	Royce Global Value Trust Inc	ETFs	12/31/14	2.9	1.3	95.8	95.3	76	3711252
RMT	Royce Micro-Cap Trust, Inc.	Holding and other Investment Office	12/31/15	5.5	0.9	359.2	312.4	88	10679775
RVT	Royce Value Trust, Inc.	Holding and other Investment Office	12/31/15	17.3	9.2	1143.5	1072.0	171	28494356
RES	RPC, Inc.	Equipment & Services	12/31/15	1263.8	-99.6	1237.1	952.3	258	80249216
RPM	RPM International Inc (DE)	Specialty Chemicals	5/31/15	4594.6	239.5	4694.2	1291.4	525	107823891
RSPP	RSP Permian Inc	Production & Extraction	12/31/15	284.0	-18.3	2979.6	1858.6	211	89514511
RUBI	Rubicon Project Inc	Internet & Software	12/31/15	248.5	0.4	536.7	278.1	151	32888898
RT	Ruby Tuesday, Inc.	Hotels, Restaurants & Travel	6/2/15	1126.6	-3.2	929.4	465.6	196	60912981
RTEC	Rudolph Technologies, Inc.	Semiconductors	12/31/15	221.7	18.0	379.8	270.7	220	35705534
R	Ryder System, Inc.	Trucking	12/31/15	6571.9	304.8	10967.8	1987.1	505	61772901
RYI	Ryerson Holding Corp	Non-Precious Metals	12/31/15	3167.2	-0.5	1556.2	-141.5	75	10377093
RHP	Ryman Hospitality Properties Inc	REITs	12/31/15	1092.1	111.5	2331.4	379.6	310	48716276
SPGI	S&P Global Inc	Credit & Lending	12/31/15	5313.0	1156.0	8183.0	194.0	838	269874175
SBR	Sabine Royalty Trust	Oil Royalty Traders	12/31/15	48.4	46.0	6.1	5.2	84	1958130
SB	Safe Bulkers Inc	Shipping	12/31/15	127.3	-47.9	1309.6	634.1	79	13082827
SFE	Safeguard Scientifics, Inc.	Venture Capital	12/31/15	-	-59.5	257.6	195.5	148	25814065
CRM	Salesforce.Com Inc	Internet & Software	1/31/16	6667.2	-47.4	12770.8	5002.9	1007	610803185
SMM	Salient Midstream & MLP Fund	Holding and other Investment Office	11/30/14	4.9	-1.9	757.5	492.7	43	5071708
SBH	Sally Beauty Holdings Inc	Retail - Specialty	9/30/15	3834.3	235.1	2094.4	-297.8	319	159316133
SJT	San Juan Basin Royalty Trust	Oil Royalty Traders	12/31/15	19.5	17.0	10.5	8.7	132	14778725
SN	Sanchez Energy Corp.	Production & Extraction	12/31/15	475.8	-1454.6	1542.3	-456.2	171	35650412
SDT	SandRidge Mississippian Trust I	Oil Royalty Traders	12/31/15	38.0	34.8	79.8	79.8	44	558827
SDR	SandRidge Mississippian Trust II	Oil Royalty Traders	12/31/15	47.2	42.3	135.9	135.9	41	2383010
PER	SandRidge Permian Trust	Oil Royalty Traders	12/31/15	87.8	81.0	158.5	158.5	-	-
SNY	Sanofi	Pharmaceuticals	12/31/15	34861.0	4287.0	102321.0	58049.0	650	235461823
SC	Santander Consumer USA Holdings	Credit & Lending	12/31/15	6697.2	827.3	36570.4	4425.0	203	122751911
SAN PRB	Santander Finance Preferred SA Un	Finance Intermediaries & Services	12/31/14	-	0.8	2191.5	4.0	-	-
SOV PRC	Santander Holdings USA Inc.	Banking	12/31/15	10473.7	-1454.6	127633.0	17141.4	56	9131130
SAP	SAP SE	Internet & Software	12/31/15	20793.0	3056.0	41390.0	23267.0	426	50290039
SAR	Saratoga Investment Corp	Holding and other Investment Office	2/29/16	30.1	10.7	295.0	125.1	34	3343928
SSL	Sasol Ltd.	Production & Extraction	6/30/15	185266.0	29716.0	323599.0	191610.0	193	97790061
BFS	Saul Centers, Inc.	REITs	12/31/15	209.1	42.5	1304.1	303.3	164	9724824
SCG	SCANA Corp	Electric Utilities	12/31/15	4380.0	746.0	17146.0	5443.0	643	105791147
SLB	Schlumberger Ltd.	Equipment & Services	12/31/15	35711.0	2072.0	68005.0	35633.0	2124	1145485534
SCHW	Schwab (Charles) Corp.	Finance Intermediaries & Services	12/31/15	6380.0	1447.0	183718.0	13402.0	1029	1119202603
SWM	Schweitzer-Mauduit International, In	Paper & Forest Products	12/31/15	764.1	89.7	1290.0	467.9	242	28282933
SAIC	Science Applications International C	IT Services	1/29/16	4315.0	117.0	2122.0	380.0	282	29440912
SALT	Scorpio Tankers Inc.	Shipping	12/31/15	62.5	-510.8	1485.4	934.5	81	23963760
STNG	Scorpio Tankers Inc.	Shipping	12/31/15	755.7	217.7	3523.5	1413.9	226	147571554
SMG	Scotts Miracle-Gro Co (The)	Agricultural Chemicals	9/30/15	3016.5	159.8	2527.2	620.7	404	48035957
SSP	Scripps (E.W.) Co (The)	Radio & Television	12/31/15	715.7	-82.5	1680.9	901.0	227	67748723
SA	Seabridge Gold Inc	Precious Metals	12/31/15	-	-9.1	300.5	282.0	107	11956569
CKH	SEACOR Holdings Inc	Equipment & Services	12/31/15	1054.7	-68.8	3185.4	1270.8	203	20203645
SDRL	Seadrill Ltd	Production & Extraction	12/31/15	4335.0	-738.0	23470.0	9371.0	362	173932865
SDLP	Seadrill Partners LLC	Production & Extraction	12/31/15	1741.6	257.2	6841.1	-	81	7144157
SEE	Sealed Air Corp	Containers & Packaging	12/31/15	7031.5	335.4	7426.0	527.1	664	189879307
SSW	Seaspan Corp	Shipping	12/31/15	819.0	199.4	6109.2	1776.2	137	19532138
SEAS	SeaWorld Entertainment Inc.	Sporting & Recreational	12/31/15	1371.0	49.1	2391.1	504.1	199	74316414
SEM	Select Medical Holdings Corp	Hospitals & Health Care Facilities	12/31/15	3742.7	130.7	4426.7	859.3	195	107981056
SEMG	SemGroup Corp	Equipment & Services	12/31/15	1455.1	30.3	2870.7	1115.5	206	45642144
SMI	Semiconductor Manufacturing Inter	Semiconductors	12/31/15	2236.4	253.4	7115.3	3729.9	41	10418250
SRE	Sempra Energy	Electric Utilities	12/31/15	10231.0	1448.0	41150.0	11809.0	822	227167509
ST	Sensata Technologies Holding NV	Electrical Equipment	12/31/15	2975.0	347.7	6337.3	1668.6	321	162945809
SXT	Sensient Technologies Corp.	Specialty Chemicals	12/31/15	1376.0	106.8	1711.4	845.1	320	51064587
SQNS	Sequans Communications S A	Semiconductors	12/31/15	32.5	-27.4	48.9	-1.2	25	17177670
SRG	Seritage Growth Properties	REITs	12/31/15	113.6	-38.8	2833.4	886.7	120	18844050
SCI	Service Corp. International	Miscellaneous Consumer Services	12/31/15	2986.4	233.8	11718.9	1184.7	402	173333086
SERV	ServiceMaster Global Holdings, Inc	Miscellaneous Consumer Services	12/31/15	2594.0	160.0	5098.0	545.0	278	138861163

T52

| EARNINGS PER SHARE | | | | | | P/E RATIO | | DIVIDENDS PER SHARE | | | AV. YLD | DIV. DECLARED | | PRICE RANGE 2015 | |
| QUARTERLY | | | ANNUAL | | | | | | | | | | | | |
1st	2nd	3rd	2015	2014	2013			2015	2014	2013	%	AMOUNT	PAYABLE		
-	-	0.06	2.08	0.23	0.12	4.5	2.9	-	-	-	-	0.1150	61/28/99	9.3	6.0
												0.140	7/28/16	19.9	0.0
0.71	-	-	3.12	3.09	2.90	21.8	15.6	2.75	3.71	2.17	4.7	0.20Y	61/28/99	68.0	48.7
0.20	-	-	1.68	1.06	0.95	19.0	10.2	1.32	1.04	0.85	5.4	0.330Z	7/15/16	31.9	17.2
0.08	-	-	1.23	1.32	1.29	23.0	5.4	-	-	-	-			28.3	6.7
0.64	-	-	2.69	2.26	1.83	21.5	13.6	0.80	0.72	0.64	1.7	0.220Y	61/28/99	57.9	36.6
-	1.28	-	6.09	5.91	5.36	20.8	14.7	2.60	2.32	1.98	2.4	0.7250Y	61/28/99	126.9	89.7
-	1.29	-	5.13	4.42	4.58	18.7	15.3	1.26	1.20	1.20	1.4	0.330	61/28/99	95.9	78.3
0.48	-	-	2.67	2.56	3.22	20.2	0.0	1.92	1.83	1.74	4.6	0.480	7/4/16	53.9	0.0
0.82	-	-	2.48	2.83	2.13	29.5	17.2	-	-	-	-	0.0075	2/12/92	73.1	42.8
0.15	-	-	0.70	0.63	0.56	43.4	34.4	0.42	0.35	0.30	1.5	0.10Y	61/28/99	30.4	24.1
1.48	-	-	6.85	6.40	5.37	28.4	22.3	1.00	0.80	0.50	0.6	0.30Y	61/28/99	194.8	152.9
0.56	-	-	0.79	1.69	1.66	63.3	9.2	2.56	2.07	1.72	10.5	0.660	5/13/16	50.0	7.3
-0.34	-	-	-2.17	-3.47	-0.75	-	-	-	-	-	-			8.7	6.4
-0.21	-	-	0.70	-0.90	-1.11	26.0	18.7	0.71	0.64	0.46	4.2	0.180Z	1/29/16	18.6	13.1
0.98	-	-	0.75	-0.93	2.03	29.6	15.0	0.40	0.30	-	2.3	0.10	61/28/99	22.2	11.2
1.58	-	-	6.73	6.00	5.54	8.6	0.0	3.08	2.84	2.53	24.1	0.29380	8/24/16	58.1	0.0
1.58	-	-	6.73	6.00	5.54	12.0	0.0	3.08	2.84	2.53	4.7	0.29380	8/24/16	80.5	0.0
-	-	-0.07	-0.17	-0.30	-0.80	-	-	-	-	-	-	0.53130	3/31/00	11.5	5.8
0.46	-	-	3.02	0.40	2.14	-	-	1.35	1.10	0.74	-	0.3750	61/28/99		
-	-	-1.16	0.30	2.36	2.60	198.7	122.9	3.76	3.72	3.56	7.4			59.6	36.9
-	-	-	-	0.13	-	-	-	-	-	-	-	0.18	12/28/15	8.6	6.2
-	-	-	0.03	0.12	0.01	324.7	200.3	1.26	2.90	1.38	16.3	0.160	6/27/16	9.7	6.0
-	-	-	0.12	0.12	0.12	119.6	81.5	1.24	1.02	0.79	10.3	0.250	6/27/16	14.4	9.8
-0.15	-	-	-0.47	1.14	0.77	-	-	0.16	0.42	0.40	1.3	0.050Y	61/28/99	15.4	8.5
-	-	0.14	1.78	2.18	0.74	28.9	21.0	1.02	0.94	0.89	2.2	0.2750Y	61/28/99	51.5	37.4
-0.17	-	-	-0.21	0.03	-	-	-	-	-	-	-			33.5	18.3
0.05	-	-	0.01	-0.70	-1.17	2018.0	1187.0	-	-	-	-			20.2	11.9
-	-	-0.05	-0.05	-1.07	-0.65	-	-	-	-	-	-	0.250Y	8/7/07	7.4	3.8
0.44	-	-	0.56	-0.14	0.10	26.5	19.6	-	-	-	-			14.8	10.9
1.04	-	-	5.71	4.11	4.53	16.6	8.4	1.56	1.42	1.30	2.2	0.410Y	61/28/99	95.0	47.8
0.42	-	-	-0.02	-1.01	5.99	-	-	-	-	-	-			14.2	2.6
0.51	-	-	2.16	2.17	2.22	27.0	20.2	2.70	2.20	2.00	5.2	0.750	7/15/16	58.3	43.5
1.10	-	-	4.21	-0.42	4.91	26.6	19.2	1.32	1.20	1.12	1.4	0.360Y	61/28/99	111.8	80.8
0.42	-	-	3.15	4.03	4.03	12.7	7.7	3.11	4.10	3.92	9.6	0.10260Z	6/29/16	39.9	24.2
-	-	0.14	-0.74	0.06	1.05	-	-	0.04	0.22	0.21	-	0.50	5/2/16		
-0.76	-	-	-2.85	-0.25	-1.66	-	-	-	-	-	-	0.02670	12/31/79	19.8	11.8
0.06	-	-	-0.42	-0.39	-0.48	-	-	-	-	-	-			83.8	54.0
-	-	-	-	-0.19	-0.11	-	-	-	1.43	1.07	-	0.3250	5/31/16	22.2	5.7
-	0.41	-	1.49	1.51	1.48	22.0	14.9	-	-	-	-			32.8	22.1
0.04	-	-	0.36	1.28	0.78	31.1	11.2	0.36	1.28	0.78	4.9	0.00270	7/15/16	11.2	4.0
-1.20	-	-	-25.70	-1.06	0.22	-	-	-	-	-	-	0.81250Y	4/1/16	11.0	2.3
0.31	-	-	1.24	1.53	2.46	3.8	1.5	1.24	1.53	2.46	39.8	0.13840Z	5/27/16	4.7	1.9
0.18	-	-	1.14	2.01	2.30	4.0	1.2	1.14	2.02	2.31	45.0	0.1010Z	5/27/16	4.6	1.3
0.19	-	-	1.90	2.55	2.34	4.1	1.1	1.97	2.54	2.35	47.4	0.090Z	5/27/16	7.7	2.2
-	-	-	3.25	3.30	2.78	16.9	11.8	2.85	2.80	2.77	6.3			55.0	38.4
0.56	-	-	2.31	2.15	2.01	11.5	3.8	-	0.15	0.84	-	0.15G	5/30/14	26.5	8.9
-	-	-	-	-	-	-	-	-	0.77	0.76	-	0.40630	8/1/16	23.7	18.0
-	-	-	-	-	-	-	-	1.83	1.83	1.83	9.4	0.45620Y	5/16/16	26.7	0.0
-	-	0.75	2.56	2.74	2.78	31.7	24.8	-	-	-	-			81.2	63.4
-	-	0.61	1.80	1.85	1.71	9.8	7.5	1.88	1.44	4.25	11.9	0.46880Z	8/15/16	17.7	13.5
-	-	-	48.70	48.27	43.31	0.8	0.4	16.87	17.85	14.57	56.0			37.1	21.9
0.46	-	-	1.42	1.54	0.57	41.5	33.6	1.69	1.56	1.44	3.2	0.42970Z	7/15/16	58.9	47.6
1.23	-	-	5.22	3.79	3.39	13.6	9.6	2.18	2.10	2.03	3.6	0.5750Y	61/28/99	71.1	50.0
0.40	-	-	1.63	4.16	5.05	56.2	37.5	2.00	1.60	1.25	2.6	0.50	61/28/99	91.6	61.1
0.29	-	-	1.03	0.95	0.78	34.4	21.6	0.24	0.24	0.24	0.8	0.3473GHY	61/28/99	35.4	22.2
0.69	-	-	2.94	2.93	2.42	14.7	10.0	1.54	1.46	1.26	4.2	0.40Y	6/24/16	43.1	29.3
0.71	-	-	2.91	2.27	-	18.8	13.7	1.12	0.56	-	2.3	0.310	7/29/16	54.6	39.9
-	-	-	-23.86	-10.20	-1.92	-	-	-	-	-	-	0.46880Z	6/15/16		
-	-	0.00	1.20	0.30	0.11	-	-	0.50	0.39	0.13	-	0.46880Z	10/17/16		
-	3.38	-	2.57	2.65	2.57	29.0	23.0	1.82	3.76	1.41	2.8	0.470Y	61/28/99	74.5	59.1
0.06	-	-	-1.06	0.18	-0.01	-	-	1.03	-	-	5.4	0.15GY	9/10/08	24.6	14.7
-	-	-0.05	-0.18	-0.27	-0.60	-	-	-	-	-	-			19.7	0.0
-1.62	-	-	-3.94	4.71	1.82	-	-	-	-	-	-	5.7Y	12/26/12	73.0	42.4
-	-	0.60	-1.49	8.30	5.47	-	-	-	2.98	2.74	-	1.0	9/18/14	12.7	1.6
-	-	0.48	2.45	1.75	2.15	5.8	0.7	2.27	2.05	1.52	29.7	0.250	5/13/16	14.3	1.7
0.46	-	-	1.62	1.20	0.58	34.2	23.7	0.52	0.52	0.52	1.1	0.160Y	61/28/99	55.4	38.4
-	-	0.42	1.46	0.79	2.93	-	-	1.47	1.35	1.19	-	0.39840Z	8/1/16		
-1.00	-	-	0.57	0.57	0.57	38.0	29.8	0.84	0.62	0.60	4.5	0.210	61/28/99	21.6	17.0
0.42	-	-	0.99	0.91	0.82	17.1	7.6	0.10	0.40	0.30	0.8	0.10Y	3/11/15	17.0	7.5
-0.35	-	-	0.69	0.68	1.13	118.6	21.5	1.59	1.03	0.60	3.8	0.450Y	5/26/16	81.9	14.8
-	-	0.00	0.01	0.00	0.01	606.0	390.0	-	-	-	-			6.1	3.9
1.27	-	-	5.37	4.63	4.01	20.0	16.2	2.80	2.64	2.52	2.8	0.7550Y	61/28/99	107.6	87.0
0.35	-	-	2.03	1.65	1.05	27.7	14.9	-	-	-	-			56.3	30.3
0.69	-	-	2.31	1.51	2.27	30.4	23.3	1.04	0.98	0.91	1.6	0.270Y	61/28/99	70.3	53.9
-	-	-0.20	-0.46	-0.58	-0.78	-	-	-	-	-	-			3.0	1.0
-0.27	-	-	-0.71	-	-	-	-	0.50	-	-	1.2	0.250	7/14/16	56.5	33.8
0.24	-	-	1.14	0.81	0.67	28.0	19.0	0.44	0.34	0.27	1.6	0.130Y	01/28/99	31.9	21.6
0.28	-	-	1.17	-0.50	-5.49	36.1	27.8	-	-	-	-			42.2	32.5

SYMBOL	COMPANY	NATURE OF BUSINESS	FISCAL YEAR-END	TOTAL REV. $MILL	NET INCOME $MILL	TOTAL ASSETS $MILL	NET STK EQUITY $MILL	NO OF INST	INST. HOLDINGS (SHARES)
NOW	ServiceNow Inc	IT Services	12/31/15	1005.5	-198.4	1807.1	566.8	425	164969099
SHAK	Shake Shack Inc	Hotels, Restaurants & Travel	12/30/15	190.6	-8.8	379.5	100.6	152	18190363
SJR	Shaw Communications Inc	Radio & Television	8/31/15	5488.0	856.0	14564.0	5409.0	274	258588477
SHLX	Shell Midstream Partners LP	Equipment & Services	12/31/15	326.5	167.1	715.5	98.7	160	74808772
SHW	Sherwin-Williams Co (The)	Specialty Chemicals	12/31/15	11339.3	1053.8	5791.9	867.9	927	90958944
SHG	Shinhan Financial Group Co. Ltd.	Banking	12/31/15	5695849.0	2367171.0	70539622.0	30839655.0	133	10727944
SFL	Ship Finance International Ltd	Equipment & Services	12/31/15	406.7	200.8	3064.8	1241.8	236	33360630
SHOP	Shopify Inc	IT Services	12/31/15	205.2	-18.8	243.7	195.3	117	37682395
SSTK	Shutterstock Inc	Internet & Software	12/31/15	425.1	19.6	469.1	288.6	136	22631094
SBGL	Sibanye Gold Ltd	Mining	12/31/15	22717.4	716.9	28265.7	14875.0	111	82421799
SIG	Signet Jewelers Ltd	Retail - Specialty	1/30/16	6550.2	467.9	6474.4	3060.7	500	98040602
SBY	Silver Bay Realty Trust Corp	REITs	12/31/15	113.7	-10.0	1224.4	530.1	163	24021015
SSNI	Silver Spring Networks Inc	Computer Hardware & Equipment	12/31/15	489.6	80.0	457.7	-33.9	144	39045218
SLW	Silver Wheaton Corp	Precious Metals	12/31/15	648.7	-162.0	5632.2	4150.7	449	239329226
SPG	Simon Property Group, Inc.	REITs	12/31/15	5266.1	2139.4	30650.7	4497.0	941	371410269
SSD	Simpson Manufacturing Co., Inc. (D	Metal Products	12/31/15	794.1	67.9	961.3	849.8	228	48133001
SHI	Sinopec Shanghai Petrochemical C	Refining & Marketing	12/31/15	67037.2	3274.3	27820.6	19797.3	43	342188
SITE	SiteOne Landscape Supply Inc	Services	1/3/16	1451.6	26.9	668.7	304.6	-	-
SIX	Six Flags Entertainment Corp	Sporting & Recreational	12/31/15	1263.9	154.7	2428.4	24.2	353	99473784
SJW	SJW Corp.	Water Utilities	12/31/15	305.1	37.9	1341.0	383.8	171	9723731
SKM	SK Telecom Co Ltd (South Korea)	Internet & Software	12/31/15	17136734.0	1518604.0	28581387.0	15251079.0	231	97291769
SKX	Skechers U S A, Inc.	Apparel, Footwear & Accessories	12/31/15	3159.1	231.9	2047.4	1327.6	450	111922238
SLG	SL Green Realty Corp	REITs	12/31/15	1662.8	284.1	19857.9	7570.0	491	132445602
SM	SM Energy Co.	Production & Extraction	12/31/15	1557.0	-447.7	5621.6	1852.4	380	89141646
SFS	Smart & Final Stores Inc	Retail - Food & Beverage, Drug & To	1/3/16	3971.0	38.3	1821.3	566.6	110	70782881
SNN	Smith & Nephew Plc	Medical Instruments & Equipment	12/31/15	4634.0	410.0	7167.0	3966.0	239	30168111
AOS	Smith (A.O.) Corp	Household Appliances, Electronics &	12/31/15	2536.5	282.9	2646.5	1442.3	495	69975574
SJM	Smucker (J.M.) Co.	Food	4/30/16	7811.2	688.7	15984.1	7008.5	940	97332929
SNA	Snap-On, Inc.	Industrial Machinery & Equipment	1/2/16	3593.1	478.7	4486.9	2412.7	703	57951384
SNH PRZ	SNH Capital Trust I	REITs							
SQM	Sociedad Quimica y Minera de Chil	Agricultural Chemicals	12/31/15	1728.3	213.2	4643.8	2339.8	184	56786605
SAH	Sonic Automotive, Inc	Retail - Automotive	12/31/15	9624.3	86.3	3562.4	729.0	231	33589699
SON	Sonoco Products Co.	Containers & Packaging	12/31/15	4964.4	250.1	4020.3	1512.9	469	81192863
SNE	Sony Corp	Household Appliances, Electronics &	3/31/15	8215880.0	-125980.0	15834331.0	2317077.0	319	88098017
BID	Sotheby's	Miscellaneous Consumer Services	12/31/15	961.5	43.7	3274.1	806.4	339	74150431
SFUN	SouFun Holdings Ltd	Internet & Software	12/31/15	883.5	-15.1	2295.3	853.8	198	239935135
SOR	Source Capital, Inc.	Holding and other Investment Office	12/31/15	5.9	0.2	638.2	632.5	90	1097573
SJI	South Jersey Industries, Inc.	Gas Utilities	12/31/15	959.6	105.1	3480.9	1037.5	278	49057661
SXE	Southcross Energy Partners LP	Gas Utilities	12/31/15	698.5	-55.5	1319.0		-	-
SO	Southern Company (The)	Electric Utilities	12/31/15	17489.0	2435.0	78318.0	21362.0	1447	507112825
SCCO	Southern Copper Corp	Non-Precious Metals	12/31/15	5045.9	736.4	12593.2	5262.9	384	60316491
LUV	Southwest Airlines Co	Airlines/Air Freight	12/31/15	19820.0	2181.0	21312.0	7358.0	1058	564436828
SWX	Southwest Gas Corporation	Gas Utilities	12/31/15	2463.6	138.3	5358.7	1594.4	298	41104617
SWN	Southwestern Energy Company	Production & Extraction	12/31/15	3133.0	-4556.0	8110.0	2282.0	659	492012951
SSS	Sovran Self Storage Inc	REITs	12/31/15	366.6	112.5	2122.2	1202.3	369	41232865
SPA	Sparton Corp.	Electrical Equipment	6/30/15	382.1	11.0	337.6	116.9	83	8564839
SPE	Special Opportunities Fund, Inc.	Holding and other Investment Office	12/31/15	6.8	4.2	152.7	151.4	45	7528227
SE	Spectra Energy Corp	Equipment & Services	12/31/15	5234.0	196.0	32923.0	6526.0	1063	532856634
SEP	Spectra Energy Partners LP	Equipment & Services	12/31/15	2455.0	1225.0	18851.0		272	59212698
SPB	Spectrum Brands Holdings Inc	Household & Personal Products	9/30/15	4690.4	148.9	7298.0	1563.1	-	-
TRK	Speedway Motorsports, Inc.	Sporting & Recreational	12/31/15	496.5	-34.4	1539.2	784.8	119	11579325
SR	Spire Inc	Gas Utilities	9/30/15	1976.4	136.9	5290.2	1573.6	294	35199233
SPR	Spirit AeroSystems Holdings Inc	Aerospace	12/31/15	6643.9	788.7	5777.5	2119.5	438	144311935
SRC	Spirit Realty Capital, Inc (New)	REITs	12/31/15	667.3	114.7	7919.0	3489.8	-	-
SRLP	Sprague Resources LP	Equipment & Services	12/31/15	3481.9	78.3	1000.3		35	6548231
SLFC 17A	Springleaf Finance Corp	Credit & Lending	12/31/15	1240.0	9.0	12055.0	2069.0	-	-
S	Sprint Corp (New)	Services	3/31/16	32180.0	-1995.0	78975.0	19783.0	582	796474975
SPXC	SPX Corp.	Industrial Machinery & Equipment	12/31/15	1719.3	-82.7	2181.3	345.4	318	39512323
FLOW	SPX Flow Inc	Industrial Machinery & Equipment	12/31/15	2388.5	87.5	3309.4	1259.1	214	33352455
FLOW	SPX Flow Inc	Industrial Machinery & Equipment	12/31/15	2388.5	87.5	3309.4	1259.1	214	33352455
SQ	Square Inc	IT Services	12/31/15	1267.1	-179.8	894.8	508.0	136	40860314
STJ	St Jude Medical Inc	Medical Instruments & Equipment	1/2/16	5541.0	880.0	13064.0	4042.0	891	281330486
JOE	St. Joe Co. (The)	Property, Real Estate & Developmen	12/31/15	103.9	-1.7	984.8	665.3	203	76148365
STAG	STAG Industrial Inc.	REITs	12/31/15	218.6	-29.4	1906.2	820.1	222	57143580
SSI	Stage Stores Inc.	Retail - Apparel and Accessories	1/30/16	1604.4	3.8	848.1	429.8	196	31488089
SMP	Standard Motor Products, Inc.	Auto Parts	12/31/15	972.0	46.0	681.1	392.0	181	18401012
SXI	Standex International Corp	Industrial Machinery & Equipment	6/30/15	772.1	54.7	660.3	348.6	207	12970792
SWK	Stanley Black & Decker Inc	Industrial Machinery & Equipment	1/2/16	11171.8	883.7	15172.3	5811.6	839	140275893
STN	Stantec Inc	Business Services	12/31/15	2373.7	156.4	2341.9	1323.3	1	6402
SGU	Star Gas Partners L.P.	Gas Utilities	9/30/15	1674.3	37.6	707.0		66	12972505
SCX	Starrett (L.S.) Co.	Industrial Machinery & Equipment	6/30/15	241.5	5.2	212.3	114.4	56	3334619
SRT	Startek, Inc.	Business Services	12/31/15	282.1	-15.6	115.7	41.9	53	7180067
HOT	Starwood Hotels & Resorts Worldwi	Hotels, Restaurants & Travel	12/31/15	5763.0	489.0	8268.0	1296.0	717	181914537
STWD	Starwood Property Trust Inc.	REITs	12/31/15	735.9	450.7	85738.1	4140.3	404	190199862
STT	State Street Corp.	Banking	12/31/15	10760.0	1980.0	245192.0	21103.0	1038	375189479
STO	Statoil ASA	Refining & Marketing	12/31/15	482800.0	-37500.0	966700.0	354800.0	294	174951001
SPLP	Steel Partners Holdings LP	Metal Products	12/31/15	998.0	136.7	1684.8		23	4583354
SCS	Steelcase, Inc.	Office Equipment & Furniture	2/26/16	3060.0	170.3	1808.6	736.9	299	86260788
SCM	Stellus Capital Investment Corp	Finance Intermediaries & Services	12/31/15	35.2	16.5	369.3	164.7	40	3131728
SCL	Stepan Co.	Specialty Chemicals	12/31/15	1776.2	76.0	1239.7	557.0	215	14029729

T54

| EARNINGS PER SHARE | | | | | | P/E RATIO | | DIVIDENDS PER SHARE | | | AV. YLD | DIV. DECLARED | | PRICE RANGE | |
| QUARTERLY | | | ANNUAL | | | 2015 | | 2015 | 2014 | 2013 | % | | | 2015 | |
1st	2nd	3rd	2015	2014	2013							AMOUNT	PAYABLE		
-2.06			-1.27	-1.23	-0.54									90.0	47.1
0.07			-0.65	0.07	0.18									78.9	31.9
	0.32		1 79	1.84	1.63	15.7	0.0	1.14	1.06	0.99	5.1	0.28130	6/30/16	28.1	0.0
0.36			1.16	0.10		41.5	21.7	0.67			1.8	0.2350	5/12/16	48.2	25.2
1.57			11.16	8.78	7.26	26.9	19.6	2.68	2.20	2.00	1.0	0.840Y	61/28/99	300.1	218.9
		-1055.00	4789.00	4195.00	3819.00	0.0	0.0	935.99	651.73	692.10	2685.3			39.5	29.7
			1.88	1.24	0.99			1.74	1.63	1.17		0.450	6/29/16		
		-0.06	-0.30	-0.57	-0.13									40.4	19.3
0.17			0.54	0.61	0.77	117.6	48.3							63.5	26.1
			0.79	1.82	2.55	20.7	5.3	2.32	4.18	1.12	27.3			16.4	4.2
1.87			4.75	4.56	4.35	31.8	19.9	0.72	0.60	0.48	0.6	0.260	61/28/99	150.9	94.7
-0.09			-0.26	-1.49	-0.63			0.46	0.16	0.04	3.0	0.130Z	7/15/16	28.1	12.2
-0.36			1.55	-1.84	-4.54	10.4	6.3							16.1	9.7
		-0.24	-0.41	0.56	1.05			0.20	0.26	0.45	1.2	0.050	6/2/16	26.3	0.0
1.55			5.88	4.52	4.24	36.4	29.1	6.05	5.15	4.65	3.2	1.04690Z	61/28/99	213.9	171.0
0.34			1.38	1.29	1.05	28.7	22.1	0.60	0.41	0.38	1.7	0.180Y	7/28/16	39.6	30.5
			0.30	-0.06	0.19	190.7	102.2		4.43	2.71				57.2	30.7
-0.85			-1.04	-0.29	-0.73									29.3	26.7
-0.51			1.58	0.77	1.18	38.8	26.8	2.14	1.93	1.82	4.2	0.580Y	61/28/99	61.3	42.3
0.16			1.85	2.54	1.12	20.4	14.9	0.78	0.75	0.73	2.4	0.20250Y	61/28/99	37.8	27.6
		-7086.02	20988.00	15154.00	23211.00	0.0	0.0	1027.39	1041.26	1040.26	4675.7			26.0	17.9
0.63			1.50	0.91	0.36	35.6	16.9							53.4	25.3
0.23			2.70	5.20	1.10	45.1	29.8	2.52	2.10	1.49	2.4	0.40630Z	61/28/99	121.8	80.5
-5.10			-6.61	9.79	2.51			0.10	0.10	0.10	0.3	0.050Y	61/28/99	52.8	7.6
-0.03			0.50	0.52	0.14	37.4	28.7							18.7	14.3
		0.14	0.46	0.56	0.61	82.1	66.4	0.60	0.78	0.37	1.8			37.8	30.6
0.83			3.16	2.28	1.83	26.4	19.1	0.76	0.60	0.46	1.0	0.240Y	61/28/99	83.3	60.5
		1.55	3.33	5.42	5.00	39.8	31.7	2.50	2.26	2.04	2.1	0.670Y	61/28/99	132.5	105.6
2.16			8.10	7.14	5.93	21.5	16.7	2.20	1.85	1.58	1.4	0.610Y	61/28/99	174.1	135.4
		0.53	0.81	1.13	1.77	28.8	16.1	0.38	1.12	0.83	2.2			23.4	13.0
0.31			1.70	1.84	1.53	14.9	9.4	0.11	0.10	0.10	0.5	0.050Y	61/28/99	25.3	15.9
0.59			2.44	2.32	2.12	20.1	15.2	1.37	1.27	1.23	3.2	0.370Y	61/28/99	49.1	37.0
		23.09	-113.04	-124.99	40.19			12.47	24.56	24.99	48.1			31.2	20.3
-0.41			0.63	1.68	1.88	74.5	30.4	0.40	4.74	0.20	1.3	0.10Y	61/28/99	46.9	19.1
		1.22	-0.18	2.87	3.54			0.19	0.19	0.20	2.9			9.9	4.4
			0.02	0.14	0.14	3749.5	1774.5	4.00	4.20	3.00	6.4	0.410Y	6/15/16	75.0	35.5
0.95			1.53	1.46	1.27	18.9	14.0	1.02	0.96	0.90	4.0	0.26370Y	61/28/99	28.9	21.4
-0.27			-0.93	-0.93	-0.71			1.60	1.60	1.44	32.5	0.40	11/13/15	13.8	0.4
0.53			2.59	2.18	1.87	20.0	16.1	2.15	2.08	2.01	4.6	0.560Y	61/28/99	51.7	41.6
0.24			0.93	1.61	1.92	33.6	24.0	0.34	0.46	0.68	1.3	0.050	61/28/99	31.3	22.3
0.70			3.27	1.64	1.05	15.2	9.9	0.28	0.22	0.13	0.7	0.10Y	61/28/99	49.6	32.4
1.58			2.92	3.01	3.11	24.1	17.4	1.58	1.43	1.28	2.7	0.450Y	9/1/16	70.3	50.8
-3.03			-12.25	2.62	2.00							0.00750	61/28/99	25.5	5.2
0.73			3.16	2.67	2.36	37.3	27.3	3.20	2.72	2.02	3.2	0.950Z	4/26/16	118.0	86.1
		0.12	1.10	1.28	1.33	26.3	11.3					0.09070	10/5/05	29.0	12.5
			0.41	0.22	0.92	37.8	29.0	1.19	1.48	2.21	8.6	0.05B	12/31/15	15.5	11.9
0.35			0.29	1.61	1.55	120.4	75.8	1.48	1.38	1.22	5.1	0.4050Y	61/28/99	34.9	22.0
0.80			3.30	2.84	7.15	15.6	11.5	2.43	2.25	2.02	5.3	0.65130	5/27/16	51.4	37.9
	1.26		2.66	4.02	-1.06	44.4	33.7	1.29	1.15	0.75	1.3	0.380Y	61/28/99	118.2	89.5
0.02			-0.83	0.75	-0.16			0.60	0.60	0.60	3.1	0.150Y	6/6/16	23.4	16.9
	2.31		3.16	2.35	2.02	21.7	15.9	1.84	1.76	1.70	3.1	0.490Y	61/28/99	68.5	50.1
1.29			5.66	2.53	-4.40	10.1	7.2							57.2	40.5
0.06			0.26	-0.09	0.00	46.0	34.8	0.69	0.67	0.30	6.7	0.1750Z	7/15/16	12.0	9.0
1.38			3.65	5.84	-1.50	7.7	4.3	1.92	1.56	0.28	8.7	0.53250	5/13/16	28.2	15.9
		-0.21	-0.85	-0.04	-0.54									5.2	2.5
0.31			-2.03	9.25	4.57			0.75	1.50	1.00	5.6	0.3750Y	61/28/99	18.9	7.8
-0.75			2.14			0.0	0.0							0.0	0.0
-0.75			2.14			19.1	7.4							41.0	15.8
-0.29			-1.24	-1.08	-0.82									15.5	8.4
0.33			3.07	3.46	2.49	25.5	16.1	1.16	1.08	1.00	1.8	0.310Y	61/28/99	78.4	49.5
0.12			-0.02	4.40	0.05							0.160Y	9/28/07	21.4	14.4
0.12			-0.61	-0.28	-0.10			1.37	1.29	1.20	7.1	0 4965GHZ	6/30/16	21.6	15.1
-0.57			0.96	0.51	1.19	19.2	4.7	0.53	0.47	0.38	5.0	0.150Y	6/15/16	18.4	4.5
0.53			1.99	1.85	2.21	22.5	15.1	0.60	0.52	0.44	1.7	0.170Y	6/1/16	44.7	30.0
		0.91	4.27	3.35	3.51	21.5	15.6	0.46	0.38	0.31	0.6	0.140Y	5/25/16	91.7	66.4
1.28			5.79	4.76	3.09	19.8	15.6	2.14	2.04	1.98	2.1	0.550Y	61/28/99	114.5	90.1
		0.53	1.65	1.74	1.55	22.9	0.0	0.42	0.37	0.33	1.5	0.11250	7/14/16	37.8	0.0
	0.79		0.59	0.57	0.47	16.9	11.9	0.36	0.34	0.32	4.3	0.10250	5/6/16	10.0	7.0
		0.08	0.75	0.97	-0.02	23.4	11.3	0.40	0.40	0.40	3.3	0.10Z	6/29/16	17.5	8.5
			-1.01	-0.35	-0.42							0.250Y	11/27/06	6.5	0.0
0.53			2.88	3.40	3.28	29.7	20.5	1.50	4.00	1.35	2.0	0.3750Y	61/28/99	85.6	59.1
0.11			1.91	2.24	1.82	12.5	8.9	1.92	1.92	1.82	9.4	0.480Z	7/15/16	24.0	16.9
0.79			4.47	4.57	4.62	18.1	11.6	1.32	1.16	1.04	2.0	0.340Y	61/28/99	80.8	51.9
		4.47	-11.80	6.87	12.50			6.73	10.51	6.70	43.1			18.9	11.4
0.07			4.98	-0.27	0.63	3.6	0.0							18.0	0.0
		0.28	0.68	0.69	0.30	29.9	17.3	0.42	0.40	0.36	2.5	0.120Y	7/15/16	20.3	11.8
0.33			1.33	1.34	1.33	9.2	5.9	1.36	1.42	1.36	13.3	0.40630Z	8/15/16	12.2	7.0
1.21			3.32	2.40	3.18	18.8	12.2	0.73	0.69	0.65	1.4	0.190Y	61/28/99	02.5	40.6

SYMBOL	COMPANY	NATURE OF BUSINESS	FISCAL YEAR-END	TOTAL REV. $MILL	NET INCOME $MILL	TOTAL ASSETS $MILL	NET STK EQUITY $MILL	NO OF INST	INST. HOLDINGS (SHARES)
STE	Steris Plc	Medical Instruments & Equipment	3/31/16	2238.8	110.8	5346.4	3023.0		
STL	Sterling Bancorp (DE)	Banking	12/31/15	410.9	66.1	11956.0	1665.1	16	1276749
STC	Stewart Information Services Corp.	General Insurance	12/31/15	2033.9	-6.2	1321.6	629.3	211	26202095
SF	Stifel Financial Corp.	Finance Intermediaries & Services	12/31/15	2377.0	92.3	13335.9	2492.4	307	62207937
SWC	Stillwater Mining Co.	Precious Metals	12/31/15	726.3	-11.9	1282.2	909.2	261	122500061
STM	STMicroelectronics N.V.	Semiconductors	12/31/15	6897.0	104.0	8195.0	4632.0	148	21606110
SGY	Stone Energy Corp.	Production & Extraction	12/31/15	544.6	-1090.9	1410.2	-39.8	238	42742595
EDF	Stone Harbor Emerging Markets Inc	Holding and other Investment Office	11/30/14	38.8	32.3	435.7	293.0		
EDI	Stone Harbor Emerging Markets Tot	Finance Intermediaries & Services	5/31/15	22.7	18.9	252.3	160.5	37	1842171
SGM	Stonegate Mortgage Corp	Finance Intermediaries & Services	12/31/15	182.7	-22.3	1280.6	261.6	51	12533049
STON	StoneMor Partners L P	Miscellaneous Consumer Services	12/31/15	305.6	-24.2	1686.1		124	5614995
SRI	Stoneridge Inc.	Auto Parts	12/31/15	644.8	22.8	364.3	93.1	155	26091342
STOR	STORE Capital Corp	REITs	12/31/15	284.8	83.8	3911.4	2059.8	194	144163317
SYK	Stryker Corp.	Medical Instruments & Equipment	12/31/15	9946.0	1439.0	16247.0	8511.0	1289	320361042
RGR	Sturm, Ruger & Co., Inc.	Leisure Equipment	12/31/15	551.1	62.1	315.9	227.7	271	15745421
SPH	Suburban Propane Partners LP	Gas Utilities	9/26/15	1417.0	84.4	2485.7		232	22448519
SCNB	Suffolk Bancorp	Banking	12/31/15	81.4	17.7	2168.6	197.3	101	7961242
SMFG	Sumitomo Mitsui Financial Group In	Banking	3/31/15	4851736.0	753610.0	83442585.0	9022248.0		
INN	Summit Hotel Properties Inc	REITs	12/31/15	463.5	124.4	1581.0	852.7	232	84562294
SUM	Summit Materials Inc	Mining	1/2/16	1432.3	3.3	2396.2	628.3	173	52443284
SMLP	Summit Midstream Partners LP	Equipment & Services	12/31/15	371.3	-186.8	2040.5		87	29787555
SUI	Sun Communities, Inc.	REITs	12/31/15	674.7	170.5	4190.6	1538.6	295	67414199
SLF	Sun Life Financial Inc	Life & Health	12/31/15	19274.0	6655.0	246853.0	21418.0	339	296434051
SXC	SunCoke Energy Inc	Non-Precious Metals	12/31/15	1362.7	-22.0	2255.5	289.9	210	53937621
SXCP	SunCoke Energy Partners LP	Metal Products	12/31/15	838.5	86.0	1768.9			
SU	Suncor Energy Inc.	Refining & Marketing	12/31/15	29680.0	-1995.0	77527.0	39039.0	723	1098874024
SXL	Sunoco Logistics Partners L.P.	Equipment & Services	12/31/15	10486.0	393.0	15489.0	286.0	346	181344419
SUN	Sunoco LP	Equipment & Services	12/31/15	16935.3	183.6	6247.6	3074.2	138	33665887
SHO	Sunstone Hotel Investors Inc	REITs	12/31/15	1249.2	355.5	3863.3	2300.8	292	273031593
STI 15	SunTrust Bank, Middle Georgia, N.	Banking							
STI	SunTrust Banks, Inc.	Banking	12/31/15	8533.0	1933.0	190817.0	23437.0	945	476529589
SPN	Superior Energy Services, Inc.	Equipment & Services	12/31/15	2774.6	-1854.7	4914.2	2210.8	441	165355938
SUP	Superior Industries International, Inc	Auto Parts	12/27/15	727.9	23.9	539.9	413.9	191	21767380
SVU	Supervalu Inc.	Retail - Food & Beverage, Drug & To	2/27/16	17529.0	178.0	4370.0	-441.0	431	256536294
SWFT	Swift Transportation Co	Trucking	12/31/15	4229.3	197.6	2922.4	617.0	290	106667754
SWZ	Swiss Helvetia Fund, Inc. (The)	Holding and other Investment Office	12/31/15	7.2	3.0	357.0	344.1	83	16173859
SYF	Synchrony Financial	Banking	12/31/15	13620.0	2214.0	84135.0	12604.0	677	743103734
SYF	Synchrony Financial	Banking	12/31/15	13620.0	2214.0	84135.0	12604.0	677	743103734
SYT	Syngenta AG	Agricultural Chemicals	12/31/15	13411.0	1339.0	18977.0	8401.0	406	25874252
SNX	Synnex Corp	IT Services	11/30/15	13338.4	208.5	4444.1	1799.4	286	32884918
SNV	Synovus Financial Corp.	Banking	12/31/15	1213.9	226.1	28792.7	3000.2	391	171458557
SYY	Sysco Corp	Retail - Food & Beverage, Drug & To	6/27/15	48680.8	686.8	17989.3	5260.2	1351	549839791
SYX	Systemax, Inc.	Retail - Appliances and Electronics	12/31/15	1854.7	-99.8	710.1	253.9	84	10853647
DATA	Tableau Software, Inc.	Internet & Software	12/31/15	653.6	-83.7	1030.7	733.9	378	52293974
TAHO	Tahoe Resources Inc.	Precious Metals	12/31/15	519.7	-71.9	2002.5	1664.0	198	147278258
TLRD	Tailored Brands Inc	Retail - Apparel and Accessories	1/30/16	3496.3	-1026.7	2244.3	-100.1	268	53414309
TWN	Taiwan Fund, Inc. (The)	Holding and other Investment Office	8/31/15	3.5	0.6	139.1	137.6	32	7812597
TSM	Taiwan Semiconductor Manufacturi	Semiconductors	12/31/15	843512.5	302850.9	1657397.4	1194007.7	753	1121858219
XRS	TAL Education Group	Educational Services	2/29/16	619.9	102.9	1061.4	437.0	201	44130853
TAL	TAL International Group Inc	Miscellaneous Transportation Servic	12/31/15	670.2	88.2	4434.1	665.0	196	23813406
TLN	Talen Energy Corp	Electric Utilities	12/31/15	4481.0	-341.0	12826.0	4303.0	327	136151639
TEGP	Tallgrass Energy GP LP	Production & Extraction	12/31/15	536.2	32.0	3016.7	422.3	104	85727412
TEP	Tallgrass Energy Partners, LP	Gas Utilities	12/31/15	536.2	160.5	2562.1		120	33425561
SKT	Tanger Factory Outlet Centers, Inc.	REITs	12/31/15	439.4	211.2	2326.7	575.1	383	92165117
TRGP	Targa Resources Corp	Equipment & Services	12/31/15	6658.6	-151.4	13253.7	1461.4	399	131987416
TGT	Target Corp	Retail - General Merchandise/Depart	1/30/16	73785.0	3363.0	40262.0	12957.0	1622	601107761
TARO	Taro Pharmaceutical Industries Ltd.	Pharmaceuticals	3/31/15	862.9	484.3	1737.7	1411.7	190	7218264
TTM	Tata Motors Ltd	Autos- Manufacturing	3/31/15	2625265.2	128291.2	2345643.4	534941.7	326	85760505
TCO	Taubman Centers, Inc.	REITs	12/31/15	557.2	134.1	3563.4	112.8	380	67001258
TMHC	Taylor Morrison Home Corp	Builders	12/31/15	2976.8	61.0	4137.3	519.9	136	29864574
TCP	TC PipeLines, LP	Equipment & Services	12/31/15	344.0	13.0			213	41429666
TCB	TCF Financial Corp	Banking	12/31/15	1333.9	197.1	20691.7	2290.9	351	152207508
TCPI	TCP International Holdings Ltd	Electrical Equipment	12/31/14	489.5	12.4	405.6	85.7	25	1632609
TSI	TCW Strategic Income Fund Inc	Holding and other Investment Office	12/31/15	13.0	10.5	281.0	277.9	89	18593892
TEL	TE Connectivity Ltd	Electrical Equipment	9/25/15	12233.0	2420.0	20608.0	9585.0	733	325218557
TMH	Team Health Holdings Inc	Business Services	12/31/15	3597.2	82.7	4060.8	642.5	312	81546989
TISI	Team Inc	Equipment & Services	12/31/15	571.7	8.9	799.0	338.1	173	28724645
TCK	Teck Resources Ltd	Mining	12/31/15	8259.0	-2474.0	34688.0	16407.0	300	391761004
TE	TECO Energy Inc.	Electric Utilities	12/31/15	2743.5	173.5	8961.1	2559.0	550	186995732
TK	Teekay Corp	Equipment & Services	12/31/15	2450.4	82.2	13061.2	919.0	228	42028196
TGP	Teekay LNG Partners LP	Equipment & Services	12/31/15	398.0	217.5	4053.0		166	46836495
TOO	Teekay Offshore Partners LP	Equipment & Services	12/31/15	1229.4	100.1	5744.2	252.5	124	55509449
TNK	Teekay Tankers Ltd	Equipment & Services	12/31/15	514.2	179.6	2169.5	877.5	204	75470275
TGNA	Tegna Inc	Radio & Television	12/31/15	3050.9	459.5	8537.8	2192.0	663	216928290
TRC	Tejon Ranch Co	Property, Real Estate & Developmen	12/31/15	51.1	2.9	431.9	291.6	112	16679651
HQH	Tekla Healthcare Investors	Holding and other Investment Office	9/30/15	4.3	-7.9	1118.1	1104.4	105	8794471
THQ	Tekla Healthcare Opportunities Fun	Finance Intermediaries & Services	9/30/14	1.2	-0.6	928.3	848.2	52	6663515
HQL	Tekla Life Sciences Investors	Holding and other Investment Office	9/30/15	1.3	-4.7	467.9	462.8	66	3288158
THW	Tekla World Healthcare Fund	Holding and other Investment Office	5/19/15			0.2	0.1	36	2836799
TDOC	Teladoc Inc	Diagnostic & Health Related Service	12/31/15	77.4	-58.0	229.7	178.6	96	15772807

T56

| EARNINGS PER SHARE | | | | | | P/E RATIO | | DIVIDENDS PER SHARE | | | AV. YLD | DIV. DECLARED | | PRICE RANGE | |
| QUARTERLY | | | ANNUAL | | | | | | | | | | | 2015 | |
1st	2nd	3rd	2015	2014	2013			2015	2014	2013	%	AMOUNT	PAYABLE		
-	-	0.26	2.25	2.17	2.72	34.5 -	27.5	0.90	0.82	0.74	1.3	0.250	61/28/99	77.7 -	62.0
0.18	-	-	0.60	0.20	0.58	29.4 -	22.0	0.28	0.28	0.24	1.8	0.070Y	5/23/16	17.6 -	13.2
-0.40	-	-	-0.28	1.24	2.60	-	-	0.80	0.10	0.10	2.1	0.30Y	6/30/16	43.5 -	32.0
0.36	-	-	1.18	2.31	2.20	50.6 -	22.7	-	-	-	-	0.33590Z	10/17/16	59.7 -	26.7
-0.08	-	-	-0.10	0.56	-2.28	-	-	-	-	-	-	-	-	14.5 -	5.3
-	-	-0.16	0.12	0.14	-0.56	71.3 -	43.7	0.34	0.34	0.34	5.0	-	-	8.6 -	5.2
-33.90	-	-	-197.50	-36.00	23.60	-	-	-	-	-	-	-	-	144.8 -	2.9
-	-	-	-	2.05	1.67	-	-	-	2.16	2.16	-	0.180	7/28/16	16.8 -	10.0
-	-	-	1.96	1.69	0.95	7.6 -	4.8	1.81	1.81	1.00	14.8	0.15110Y	7/28/16	14.8 -	9.4
-1.45	-	-	-0.86	-1.19	1.32	-	-	-	-	-	-	-	-	10.9 -	3.7
-0.23	-	-	-0.79	-0.40	-0.89	-	-	2.58	2.43	2.38	9.4	0.660	61/28/99	31.5 -	23.1
0.26	-	-	0.81	-1.75	0.56	20.7 -	12.8	-	-	-	-	-	-	16.8 -	10.4
0.18	-	-	0.68	0.61	0.52	39.6 -	29.1	1.04	0.11	-	4.5	0.270	7/15/16	26.9 -	19.8
1.07	-	-	3.78	1.34	2.63	29.7 -	23.2	1.42	1.26	1.10	1.4	0.380Y	61/28/99	112.3 -	87.5
1.21	-	-	3.21	1.95	5.58	23.8 -	15.2	1.10	1.62	2.12	1.8	0.480Y	5/27/16	76.3 -	49.0
-	1.51	-	1.38	1.56	1.34	31.5 -	16.3	3.52	3.50	3.48	11.0	0.88750	5/10/16	43.4 -	21.1
0.41	-	-	1.49	1.31	1.10	21.0 -	15.7	0.32	0.12	-	1.2	0.10Y	5/25/16	31.2 -	23.4
-	-	-	550.85	611.14	585.94	0.0 -	0.0	-	-	-	-	-	-	9.3 -	5.1
0.51	-	-	1.24	0.05	-0.12	11.7 -	7.5	0.47	0.46	0.45	3.9	0.44530Z	5/31/16	14.5 -	9.3
0.42	-	-	0.52	-	-	52.5 -	26.6	-	-	-	-	-	-	27.3 -	13.8
-0.12	-	-	-0.00	-0.93	1.85	-	-	2.27	2.04	1.73	10.8	0.5750	5/13/16	35.0 -	12.4
0.14	-	-	2.52	0.54	0.31	29.0 -	24.4	2.60	2.60	2.52	3.9	0.40630Z	6/30/16	73.1 -	61.6
-	-	0.79	3.55	2.86	1.55	12.9 -	0.0	1.51	1.44	1.44	4.1	0.26560	6/30/16	45.8 -	0.0
-0.06	-	-	-0.34	-1.83	0.36	-	-	0.43	0.06	-	5.8	0.150	12/7/15	16.4 -	2.2
0.64	-	-	1.92	1.57	1.81	11.4 -	2.7	2.29	2.02	1.16	20.8	0.5040	6/1/16	21.9 -	5.3
0.17	-	-	-1.38	1.84	2.60	-	-	1.14	1.02	0.73	3.7	0.290	6/24/16	39.8 -	0.0
0.18	-	-	0.42	0.51	1.63	94.6 -	39.3	1.72	1.43	1.17	5.9	0.4890	61/28/99	39.8 -	16.5
0.47	-	-	1.11	0.85	1.69	42.5 -	20.9	2.68	2.05	1.80	7.4	0.81730	5/16/16	47.2 -	23.2
-0.02	-	-	1.62	0.37	0.29	9.9 -	6.3	1.41	0.51	0.10	10.3	0.2016GHZ	7/15/16	16.0 -	10.1
0.84	-	-	3.58	3.23	2.41	12.7 -	8.8	0.92	0.70	0.35	2.3	0.36720Y	61/28/99	45.4 -	31.4
-0.57	-	-	-12.33	1.65	-0.70	-	-	0.32	0.32	0.08	2.1	0.080	61/28/99	23.5 -	8.6
0.56	-	-	0.90	0.33	0.83	30.2 -	18.4	0.72	0.72	0.02	3.6	0.180Y	7/19/16	27.1 -	16.6
-	-	0.13	0.73	0.70	-6.91	12.8 -	5.6	-	-	0.17	-	0.08750Y	61/28/99	9.4 -	4.1
0.23	-	-	1.38	1.12	1.09	17.8 -	8.9	-	-	-	-	-	-	24.6 -	12.4
-	-	-	0.11	0.08	0.08	112.6 -	85.8	0.71	2.38	1.09	6.6	0.206B	8/12/16	12.4 -	9.4
0.70	-	-	2.65	2.78	-	12.6 -	11.4	-	-	-	-	-	-	33.3 -	30.3
0.70	-	-	2.65	2.78	-	13.6 -	9.2	-	-	-	-	-	-	36.0 -	24.5
-	-	-	14.52	17.60	17.78	6.4 -	4.3	2.35	2.28	2.03	3.0	-	-	36.9 -	61.9
1.17	-	-	5.24	4.57	3.06	19.4 -	13.6	0.57	0.13	-	0.7	0.20Y	61/28/99	101.8 -	71.3
0.39	-	-	1.62	1.33	0.91	20.7 -	16.0	0.42	0.24	0.28	1.4	0.120Y	61/28/99	33.6 -	26.0
-	-	0.38	1.15	1.58	1.67	43.7 -	31.0	1.18	1.14	1.10	2.8	0.310Y	61/28/99	50.2 -	35.7
-0.47	-	-	-2.69	-1.01	-1.18	-	-	-	-	-	-	0.257	12/21/12	100 -	6.7
-0.62	-	-	-1.17	-	0.12	-	-	-	-	-	-	-	-	128.7 -	37.2
0.17	-	-	-0.35	0.61	-0.45	-	-	0.24	0.02	-	2.1	0.020	61/28/99	18.5 -	0.0
0.03	-	-	-0.01	1.70	2.55	-	-	0.72	0.72	0.72	2.2	0.180Y	9/23/16	65.8 -	10.7
-	-	-	0.07	0.08	0.13	259.0 -	0.0	2.63	-	-	17.8	2.6332C	1/9/15	18.1 -	0.0
-	-	2.91	11.68	9.81	7.10	2.3 -	1.6	17.90	11.97	12.05	78.7	-	-	26.5 -	18.8
-	0.15	-	0.41	0.38	0.21	142.7 -	70.7	-	-	0.49	-	-	-	58.5 -	29.0
0.19	-	-	2.67	3.68	4.25	13.5 -	3.4	2.61	2.88	2.68	14.3	0.547	6/15/16	36.0 -	9.2
1.17	-	-	-3.10	-	-	-	-	-	-	-	-	-	-	20.1 -	5.8
0.16	-	-	0.51	1.36	0.17	65.5 -	20.3	0.22	-	-	1.0	0.210	5/13/16	33.4 -	10.4
0.35	-	-	1.91	1.36	0.17	27.0 -	13.5	2.19	1.43	0.44	5.2	0.7050	5/13/16	51.5 -	25.9
0.28	-	-	2.20	0.77	1.13	16.9 -	13.5	1.30	0.94	0.89	3.9	0.3250Z	61/28/99	37.2 -	29.7
-0.06	-	-	1.09	2.43	1.55	86.0 -	14.2	3.39	2.68	2.06	6.8	3.9583GH	61/28/99	93.8 -	15.4
1.05	-	-	-2.56	3.07	4.52	-	-	1.90	1.58	1.32	2.5	0.60Y	61/28/99	85.0 -	67.1
-	2.15	-	11.31	8.14	5.96	13.9 -	11.4	-	-	-	-	-	-	157.0 -	129.1
-	-	-	39.40	40.60	27.80	1.0 -	0.5	8.61	7.87	18.47	30.4	-	-	37.9 -	20.6
0.41	-	-	1.76	13.47	1.71	44.7 -	37.9	2.26	6.91	2.00	3.1	0.39060Z	61/28/99	78.8 -	66.7
0.21	-	-	1.85	2.17	1.38	11.5 -	6.1	-	-	-	-	-	-	21.3 -	13.7
1.10	-	-	-0.03	2.67	2.13	-	-	3.48	3.30	3.18	6.8	0.890	61/28/99	64.2 -	35.4
0.26	-	-	1.07	0.94	0.82	16.0 -	9.8	0.23	0.20	0.20	1.6	0.40310Y	61/28/99	17.2 -	10.5
-	-0.06	-	0.52	0.40	-	-	-	-	-	-	-	-	-	-	-
-	-	-	0.22	0.24	0.31	24.8 -	23.0	0.21	0.25	0.39	4.0	0.0520	7/15/16	5.5 -	5.1
-	1.03	-	5.89	4.27	3.02	11.8 -	8.9	1.24	1.08	0.92	2.0	0.370Y	61/28/99	69.7 -	52.3
0.01	-	-	1.12	1.35	1.24	60.3 -	30.0	-	-	-	-	-	-	67.6 -	33.6
-0.27	-	-	0.41	1.40	1.53	113.4 -	53.7	-	-	-	-	0.010	3/1/93	46.5 -	22.0
-	0.14	-	-4.29	0.63	1.66	-	-	0.20	0.90	0.90	2.5	0.050	6/30/16	15.4 -	0.0
0.31	-	-	0.74	0.58	0.92	37.5 -	23.9	0.90	0.88	0.88	3.6	0.230Y	61/28/99	27.8 -	17.7
-0.67	-	-	1.13	-0.76	-1.63	-	-	1.73	1.26	1.26	-	0.0550	61/28/99	-	-
-	-	-	2.21	2.30	2.48	-	-	2.80	2.77	2.70	-	0.140	5/13/16	-	-
-	-	-	0.32	-0.22	0.88	-	-	2.18	2.15	2.09	-	0.53130	5/13/16	-	-
-	-	-0.17	1.35	0.66	-0.10	-	-	0.12	0.12	0.12	-	0.090	6/3/16	-	-
0.38	-	-	2.00	4.58	1.66	16.5 -	10.7	0.68	0.80	0.80	2.7	0.140Y	61/28/99	33.0 -	21.4
0.06	-	-	0.14	0.27	0.20	199.4 -	121.7	-	-	-	-	0.0250	12/10/99	27.9 -	17.0
-	-	-	-0.22	-0.24	-0.20	-	-	2.61	2.13	1.61	8.8	0.490	6/30/16	38.9 -	21.0
-	-	-	-	-0.01	-	-	-	-	0.11	-	-	0.11250	6/30/16	20.7 -	14.0
-	-	-	-0.25	-0.23	-0.22	-	-	2.09	1.70	1.30	9.0	0.820	8/12/16	31.1 -	15.9
-	-	-	-	-	-	-	-	-	-	-	-	0.11670	6/30/16	20.0 -	12.2
-0.40	-	-	-2.91	-10.25	-8.05	-	-	-	-	-	-	-	-	34.8 -	9.5

SYMBOL	COMPANY	NATURE OF BUSINESS	FISCAL YEAR-END	TOTAL REV. $MILL	NET INCOME $MILL	TOTAL ASSETS $MILL	NET STK EQUITY $MILL	NO OF INST	INST. HOLDINGS (SHARES)
TEO	Telecom Argentina SA	Services	12/31/15	40540.0	3403.0	38465.0	17194.0	99	18470831
TI	Telecom Italia SPA	Radio & Television	12/31/15	20661.0	-72.0	71232.0	17610.0	118	17997881
TDY	Teledyne Technologies, Inc.	Electronic Instruments & Related Pro	1/3/16	2298.1	195.8	2718.5	1344.1	295	34915310
TFX	Teleflex Incorporated	Medical Instruments & Equipment	12/31/15	1809.7	244.9	3878.5	2009.3	456	46559767
VIV	Telefonica Brasil SA	Services	12/31/15	40286.8	3420.2	101685.1	68642.6	227	178718853
TEF	Telefonica SA	Services	12/31/15	47219.0	2745.0	122974.0	17891.0	316	76983263
TDS	Telephone & Data Systems, Inc.	Services	12/31/15	5176.2	219.0	9422.5	4126.4	366	94201288
TU	TELUS Corp.	Services	12/31/15	12430.0	1382.0	26406.0	7672.0	294	343285793
TDF	Templeton Dragon Fund, Inc.	Holding and other Investment Office	12/31/15	23.0	10.5	715.5	713.8	95	19542773
EMF	Templeton Emerging Markets Fund	Holding and other Investment Office	8/31/15	8.0	3.7	241.0	240.3	59	6977711
TEI	Templeton Emerging Markets Inco	Holding and other Investment Office	8/31/15	51.3	44.5	581.3	576.1	113	10105967
GIM	Templeton Global Income Fund (DE	Holding and other Investment Office	8/31/15	52.8	44.8	1031.6	989.6	172	32507916
TRF	Templeton Russia and East Europe	Holding and other Investment Office	3/31/15	3.3	2.1	56.1	56.0	13	58209
TPX	Tempur Sealy International, Inc.	Furniture	12/31/15	3151.2	73.5	2655.5	290.2	381	77640384
TS	Tenaris SA	Equipment & Services	12/31/15	7100.8	-80.2	14887.0	11713.3	227	100671899
THC	Tenet Healthcare Corp.	Hospitals & Health Care Facilities	12/31/15	18634.0	78.0	23682.0	691.0	444	173036518
TNC	Tennant Co.	Industrial Machinery & Equipment	12/31/15	811.8	32.1	432.3	252.2	191	16189487
TEN	Tenneco Inc	Auto Parts	12/31/15	8209.0	247.0	3967.0	433.0	367	57544952
TVE	Tennessee Valley Authority	Electric Utilities	9/30/15	11003.0	1111.0	48825.0	7203.0	-	-
TDC	Teradata Corp (DE)	IT Services	12/31/15	2530.0	-214.0	2530.0	849.0	555	136659848
TER	Teradyne, Inc.	Semiconductors	12/31/15	1639.6	206.5	2548.7	1965.8	458	206251857
TEX	Terex Corp.	Industrial Machinery & Equipment	12/31/15	6543.1	145.9	5637.1	1877.4	438	97741844
TX	Ternium S A	Non-Precious Metals	12/31/15	7877.4	8.1	8062.6	4033.1	132	40831214
TNH	Terra Nitrogen Co., L.P.	Agricultural Chemicals	12/31/15	581.7	306.9	443.7	-	99	1503939
TRNO	Terreno Realty Corp	REITs	12/31/15	95.9	14.6	1152.1	733.1	143	44319336
TSO	Tesoro Corporation	Refining & Marketing	12/31/15	28711.0	1540.0	16332.0	5213.0	750	126748266
TLLP	Tesoro Logistics LP	Production & Extraction	12/31/15	1112.0	272.0	4892.0	-	171	60291140
TTI	TETRA Technologies, Inc.	Equipment & Services	12/31/15	1130.1	-209.5	1656.4	241.2	224	87798131
TEVA	Teva Pharmaceutical Industries Ltd	Pharmaceuticals	12/31/15	19652.0	1588.0	54258.0	29769.0	1230	636167635
TPL	Texas Pacific Land Trust	Property, Real Estate & Developmen	12/31/15	79.4	50.0	50.4	45.7	104	5195698
TGH	Textainer Group Holdings Ltd	Shipping	12/31/15	542.2	106.9	4386.3	1202.7	137	9005033
TXT	Textron Inc	Aerospace	1/2/16	13423.0	697.0	14708.0	4964.0	627	234361330
TTF	Thai Fund, Inc. (The)	Holding and other Investment Office	12/31/15	3.2	1.9	100.2	98.6	36	8196479
GPS	The Gap, Inc.	Retail - Apparel and Accessories	1/30/16	15797.0	920.0	7473.0	2545.0	690	289473933
NWHM	The New Home Company Inc	Builders	12/31/15	430.1	21.7	351.3	220.8	66	12609177
TMO	Thermo Fisher Scientific Inc	Biotechnology	12/31/15	16965.4	1975.4	40889.0	21350.2	1370	410946495
THR	Thermon Group Holdings Inc	Electrical Equipment	3/31/16	281.9	23.0	468.7	294.4	121	33150012
TPRE	Third Point Reinsurance Ltd	General Insurance	12/31/15	574.8	-87.4	3545.1	1379.7	101	72198791
TSLF	THL Credit Senior Loan Fund	Finance Intermediaries & Services	12/31/14	12.7	9.2	193.2	139.0	27	1978838
TRI	Thomson Reuters Corp	Publishing	12/31/15	12209.0	1255.0	29095.0	12613.0	403	248668250
THO	Thor Industries, Inc.	Autos- Manufacturing	7/31/15	4006.8	199.4	1503.2	1065.2	457	50623988
TDW	Tidewater Inc.	Equipment & Services	3/31/16	979.1	-160.2	4990.5	2299.5	325	61199218
TIER	Tier REIT Inc	REITs	12/31/15	282.4	-34.2	1873.7	676.3	136	14941250
TIF	Tiffany & Co.	Retail - Specialty	1/31/16	4104.9	463.9	5129.7	2911.4	713	126121162
TLYS	Tilly's Inc	Retail - Apparel and Accessories	1/30/16	551.0	7.5	270.8	173.2	103	9782846
TSU	TIM Participacoes S.A.	Services	12/31/15	17138.9	2071.1	35403.7	16933.0	151	99801760
TIME	Time Inc	Publishing	12/31/15	3103.0	-881.0	4884.0	1809.0	379	97039315
TWX	Time Warner Inc	Entertainment	12/31/15	28118.0	3833.0	63848.0	23619.0	1384	866132061
TKR	Timken Co. (The)	Industrial Machinery & Equipment	12/31/15	2872.3	-70.8	2785.3	1324.5	402	68248545
TMST	Timkensteel Corp	Metal Products	12/31/15	1106.2	-72.4	1141.8	686.4	201	25306940
TWI	Titan International Inc	Industrial Machinery & Equipment	12/31/15	1394.8	-75.6	1275.2	422.2	218	52396063
TJX	TJX Companies, Inc.	Retail - Apparel and Accessories	1/30/16	30944.9	2277.7	11499.5	4307.1	1351	654215345
TOL	Toll Brothers Inc.	Builders	10/31/15	4171.2	363.2	9206.5	4222.6	557	151125482
TR	Tootsie Roll Industries Inc	Food	12/31/15	540.1	66.1	909.0	698.2	225	14805873
BLD	TopBuild Corp	Construction Materials	12/31/15	1616.6	79.0	1642.2	915.7	252	35691183
TMK	Torchmark Corp.	Life & Health	12/31/15	3766.1	527.1	19853.2	4055.6	535	102892230
TTC	Toro Co. (The)	Industrial Machinery & Equipment	10/31/15	2390.9	201.6	1303.7	462.2	410	49628507
TD	Toronto Dominion Bank	Banking	10/31/15	37909.0	7813.0	1104373.0	65418.0	592	1056463695
NDP	Tortoise Energy Independence Fun	Holding and other Investment Office	11/30/14	3.9	-1.8	400.1	330.5	48	2663510
TYG	Tortoise Energy Infrastructure Corp	Holding and other Investment Office	11/30/15	31.7	-29.7	2793.9	1405.7	195	19288551
NTG	Tortoise MLP Fund, Inc.	Holding and other Investment Office	11/30/14	-2.7	-25.4	2282.9	1401.9	-	-
TTP	Tortoise Pipeline & Energy Fund Inc	Holding and other Investment Office	11/30/14	8.3	0.8	443.6	351.0	50	3275211
TPZ	Tortoise Power & Energy Infrastruct	Holding and other Investment Office	11/30/14	8.7	5.6	259.4	216.0	53	2116923
TOT	Total S.A.	Production & Extraction	12/31/15	143421.0	5087.0	224484.0	92494.0	691	170170532
TSS	Total System Services, Inc.	Business Services	12/31/15	2779.5	364.0	3908.3	1843.0	599	149153336
TOWR	Tower International Inc	Auto Parts	12/31/15	1955.7	194.1	1215.5	197.5	182	18806766
TSQ	Townsquare Media Inc	Radio & Television	12/31/15	441.2	9.8	1060.7	362.8	77	12260201
TM	Toyota Motor Corp	Autos- Manufacturing	3/31/15	27234521.0	2173338.0	47729830.0	16788131.0	496	21100321
TSLX	TPG Specialty Lending Inc	Credit & Lending	12/31/15	173.4	95.3	1516.9	820.7	76	30973953
TAC	TransAlta Corp.	Electric Utilities	12/31/15	2267.0	22.0	10947.0	3361.0	136	137065238
TRP	TransCanada Corp	Equipment & Services	12/31/15	11300.0	-1146.0	64483.0	16438.0	469	443132389
TCI	Transcontinental Realty Investors, I	Property, Real Estate & Developmen	12/31/15	102.2	-7.6	1110.2	206.7	18	27530
TDG	TransDigm Group Inc	Aerospace	9/30/15	2707.1	447.2	8427.0	-1038.3	479	61544782
TLP	TransMontaigne Partners L.P.	Equipment & Services	12/31/15	152.5	41.7	656.7	-	108	9233291
RIG	Transocean Ltd.	Equipment & Services	12/31/15	7386.0	791.0	26339.0	14498.0	602	307362247
RIGP	Transocean Partners LLC	Production & Extraction	12/31/15	580.0	-71.0	2231.0	1262.0	56	11052523
TGS	Transportadora de Gas del Sur S.A.	Equipment & Services	12/31/15	4226.6	-172.1	6646.6	1695.4	-	-
TRU	TransUnion	Miscellaneous Consumer Services	12/31/15	1506.8	5.9	4446.7	1231.4	138	177703055
TRV	Travelers Companies Inc (The)	General Insurance	12/31/15	26800.0	3439.0	100184.0	23598.0	1300	306187669
TVPT	Travelport Worldwide Ltd	Hotels, Restaurants & Travel	12/31/15	2221.0	16.0	2929.0	-357.0	174	114203603

EARNINGS PER SHARE QUARTERLY			EARNINGS PER SHARE ANNUAL			P/E RATIO		DIVIDENDS PER SHARE			AV. YLD	DIV. DECLARED		PRICE RANGE 2015	
1st	2nd	3rd	2015	2014	2013	2015	2014	2015	2014	2013	%	AMOUNT	PAYABLE		
-	-	0.89	3.51	3.79	3.27	5.8 -	3.9	-	-	-	-	-	-	20.4 -	13.9
-	-	-	0.00	0.07	-0.03			-	-	0.16	-	-	-	14.0 -	9.1
1.10	-	-	5.44	5.75	4.87	20.5 -	14.1					-	-	111.5 -	76.6
1.04	-	-	5.10	4.04	3.45	31.9 -	24.2	1.36	1.36	1.36	1.0	0.340Y	61/28/99	162.6 -	123.2
-	-	-	2.15	4.12	3.10	6.7 -	3.7	3.14	2.73	4.10	28.5	-	-	14.4 -	8.0
-	-	-	0.51	0.61	1.01	30.4 -	18.9	0.89	0.73	0.35	7.3	-	-	15.5 -	9.7
0.07	-	-	1.98	-1.26	1.29	15.4 -	10.6	0.56	0.54	0.51	2.0	0.1480Z	61/28/99	30.6 -	21.0
0.64	-	-	2.29	2.31	2.01	19.7 -	0.0	1.68	1.52	1.36	4.7	0.460	7/4/16	45.0 -	0.0
-	-	-	0.30	0.49	0.53	91.1 -	49.3	4.01	4.31	1.67	20.9	1.7229C	12/31/15	27.3 -	14.8
-	-	-	0.21	0.29	0.26	72.0 -	41.2	1.18	1.69	0.46	10.3	0.9578B	12/31/15	15.1 -	8.7
-	-	-	0.93	1.02	1.07	11.9 -	9.6	1.14	1.39	1.87	11.3	0.20	7/14/16	11.1 -	8.9
-	-	-	0.33	0.35	0.38	21.9 -	17.8	0.64	0.62	1.01	9.9	0.0250Z	6/30/16	7.2 -	5.9
-	-	-	0.40	0.29	-	27.9 -	23.4	0.46	0.19	0.23	4.5	0.44250	12/16/15	11.2 -	9.4
0.64	-	-	1.17	1.75	1.28	70.0 -	44.9	-	-	-	-	0.080Y	61/28/99	81.9 -	52.5
-	-	0 25	-0.07	0.98	1.31			0.90	0.90	0.86	3.6	-	-	29.9 -	19.3
-0.60	-	-	-1.41	0.12	-1.32			-	-	-	-	0.0267F	61/28/99	60.8 -	22.6
0.25	-	-	1.74	2.70	2.14	38.3 -	26.7	0.80	0.78	0.72	1.4	0.20Y	61/28/99	66.7 -	46.5
0.99	-	-	4.11	3.66	2.97	15.0 -	8.7	-	-	-	-	0.050	61/28/99	61.5 -	35.6
-	-	-	-	-	-			0.95	0.99	1.03	3.8	0.210Z	5/2/16	25.9 -	23.8
-0.00	-	-	-1.53	2.33	2.27			-	-	-	-	-	-	40.0 -	22.6
0.24	-	-	0.97	0.37	0.70	22.4 -	17.3	0.24	0.18	-	1.2	0.060Y	61/28/99	21.8 -	16.8
-0.65	-	-	1.33	2.79	1.93	20.1 -	10.9	0.24	0.20	0.05	1.1	0.070	61/28/99	26.8 -	14.5
-	-	0.05	0.00	-0.10	0.23			0.90	0.75	0.65	5.8	-	-	20.6 -	10.6
1.44	-	-	10.06	12.07	15.77	13.0 -	9.0	9.75	10.00	14.35	8.9	1 510	5/31/16	130.5 -	90.7
0.15	-	-	0.26	0.23	0.15	92.1 -	74.6	0.66	0.57	0.51	3.0	0.48440Z	6/30/16	23.9 -	19.4
0.57	-	-	12.36	6.44	3.00	9.6 -	5.6	1.85	1.10	0.90	2.0	0.50Y	61/28/99	118.2 -	68.6
0.64	-	-	2.33	0.96	1.47	25.7 -	15.7	2.84	2.41	2.02	5.8	0.810	5/13/16	59.9 -	36.7
-1.11	-	-	-1.59	-2.16	0.00			-	-	-	-	-	-	9.3 -	4.7
-	-	0.12	1.82	3.56	1.49	39.6 -	27.6	1.16	1.15	1.09	1.9	17.50	6/15/16	72.0 -	50.3
0.90	-	-	6.10	4.14	3.16	27.9 -	17.8	0.29	0.27	0.00	0.2	0.310Y	3/16/16	170.0 -	108.7
-	-	0.71	1.87	3.32	3.21			1.65	1.88	1.85	-	0.240	5/25/16	-	-
0.55	-	-	2.50	2.13	1.75	18.6 -	12.4	0.08	0.08	0.08	0.2	0.020Y	61/28/99	46.5 -	31.1
-	-	-	0.15	0.21	0.47	57.5 -	42.5	3.06	9.16	0.92	41.4	0.12280	1/15/16	8.6 -	6.4
0.32	-	-	2.87	2.74	2.33	13.7 -	6.0	0.88	0.70	0.50	3.1	0.230Y	61/28/99	39.2 -	17.1
-0.04	-	-	1.28	0.30	0.76	13.9 -	6.0	-	-	-	-	-	-	17.8 -	7.7
1.01	-	-	4.92	4.71	3.48	30.9 -	24.0	0.60	0.60	0.60	0.4	0.150Y	61/28/99	152.1 -	118.1
-	-	0.26	1.52	0.80	0.85	16.6 -	10.0	-	-	-	-	-	-	25.3 -	15.2
-0.49	-	-	-0.84	0.47	2.54			-	-	-	-	-	-	15.3 -	10.5
-	-	-	-	1.25	-			-	1.43	0.24	-	0.1050	6/30/16	17.9 -	14.3
0.34	-	-	1.60	2.35	0.16	34.6 -	0.0	-	-	-	-	0.340	61/28/99	55.3 -	0.0
-	-	1.49	3.74	3.35	2.88	17.5 -	12.9	1.08	1.92	2.22	1.9	0.30Y	61/28/99	65.5 -	48.1
-	-	-0.42	-1.34	2.82	3.03			1.00	1.00	1.00	8.4	0.250Y	61/28/99	24.3 -	3.9
-0.27	-	-	-0.66	-0.36	0.30			0.38	-	-	2.4	0.180Z	7/8/16	18.3 -	12.8
0.69	-	-	3.73	1.41	3.25	25.7 -	16.3	1.48	1.34	1.25	1.9	0.450Y	61/28/99	95.7 -	60.8
-0.10	-	-	0.50	0.65	0.92	20.5 -	11.2	-	-	-	-	-	-	10.2 -	5.6
-	-	0.13	0.86	0.64	0.62	20.1 -	8.3	0.66	1.64	1.36	6.0	-	-	17.3 -	7.1
-0.10	-	-	-8.32	0.80	1.85			0.76	0.19	-	4.3	0.190	61/28/99	24.1 -	12.4
1.51	-	-	4.62	4.34	3.92	19.7 -	13.0	1.40	1.27	1.15	1.9	0.40250Y	61/28/99	91.0 -	60.1
0.78	-	-	-0.84	1.87	2.74			1.03	1.00	0.92	3.3	0.260Y	61/28/99	39.6 -	23.4
-0.31	-	-	-1.63	2.27	1.94			0.42	0.28	-	3.1	0.140Y	9/10/15	31.7 -	4.0
-0.27	-	-	-1.74	-1.50	0.64			0.02	0.02	0.02	0.3	0.0050Y	7/15/16	11.2 -	2.7
0.76	-	-	3.15	2.94	2.55	25.0 -	20.4	0.67	0.55	0.44	0.9	0.260Y	61/28/99	78.8 -	64.2
-	0.51	-	1.97	1.84	0.97	21.3 -	12.2	-	-	-	-	-	-	41.9 -	24.1
0.16	-	-	1.05	0.99	0.96	34.5 -	28.1	0.34	0.30	0.29	1.1	0.090Y	61/28/99	36.2 -	29.5
0.29	-	-	2.09	-	-	17.4 -	0.0	-	-	-	-	-	-	36.4 -	0.0
1.01	-	-	4.16	4.09	3.79	15.2 -	11.7	0.41	0.51	0.55	0.7	0.140Y	61/28/99	63.1 -	48.6
-	1.89	-	3.55	3.02	2.62	25.3 -	18.5	1.00	0.80	0.56	1.3	0.30Y	61/28/99	89.7 -	65.5
1.17	-	-	4.21	4.14	3.46	13.7 -	0.0	2.00	1.84	1.62	4.3	0.550	7/31/16	57.7 -	0.0
-	-	-	-	-0.12	0.01			-	1.75	1.75	-	0.43750	5/31/16	19.6 -	7.9
-	-	-	-0.62	-0.66	0.73			2.59	2.38	2.29	8.8	0.6550	5/31/16	41.9 -	19.1
-	-	-	-0.54	-0.42				-	1.69	1.67	-	0.42250	5/31/16	24.2 -	12.2
-	-	-	0.08	0.10				-	1.63	1.63	-	0.40750	5/31/16	27.5 -	9.8
-	-	-	0.81	0.76				-	1.50	1.50	-	0.1250	8/31/16	26.7 -	12.5
-	-	0.45	2.16	1.86	3.72	24.1 -	18.6	-	-	-	-	-	-	52.1 -	40.2
0.49	-	-	1.97	1.72	1.29	28.6 -	19.3	0.40	0.40	0.40	0.8	0.10Y	61/28/99	56.4 -	38.0
0.39	-	-	9.06	1.01	-0.99	3.5 -	2.2	0.10	-	-	0.4	0.10	6/10/16	31.3 -	20.0
-0.08	-	-	0.37	-1.41		37.8 -	22.1	-	-	-	-	-	-	14.0 -	8.2
-	192.51	-	687.66	574.92	303.78	0.2 -	0.1	351.14	255.11	120.20	296.7	-	-	137.4 -	98.3
0.32	-	-	1.18	1.68	1.66	15.5 -	12.8	1.56	1.53	-	9.3	0.390Y	7/29/16	18.3 -	15.2
-	-0.18	-	-0.09	0.52	-0.27			0.72	0.72	1.16	12.6	0.33120	6/30/16	10.8 -	0.0
0.36	-	-	-1.75	2.46	2.42			2.08	1.92	1.84	5.0	0.154GH	5/31/16	54.5 -	0.0
-0.43	-	-	-0.98	4.74	6.82			-	-	-	-	0.180	9/20/00	14.3 -	0.0
-	2.47	-	7.84	3.16	2.39	33.6 -	23.9	-	25.00	34.85	-	25.7Y	61/28/99	263.5 -	187.3
0.41	-	-	2.12	1.57	1.90	20.2 -	9.8	2.66	2.64	2.58	8.1	0.680	5/9/16	42.8 -	20.8
0.68	-	-	2.16	-5.29	3.87			1.05	2.81	1.68	-	0.150	61/28/99	-	-
0.45	-	-	-1.02	0.52				1.45	0.22	-	-	0.36250	5/24/16	-	-
-	-	-0.06	-0.22	0.13	0.14			-	0.85	0.64	-	-	-	7.0 -	3.8
0.07	-	-	0.04	-0.08	-0.24	827.5 -	524.5	-	-	-	-	-	-	33.1 -	21.0
2.30	-	-	10.88	10.70	9.74	10.8 -	8.8	2.38	2.15	1.96	2.2	0.670Y	61/28/99	117.6 -	96.1
0.13	-	-	0.13	0.98	-4.52	121.8 -	66.1	0.30	0.07	-	2.2	0.0750	6/16/16	15.8 -	8.6

SYMBOL	COMPANY	NATURE OF BUSINESS	FISCAL YEAR-END	TOTAL REV. $MILL	NET INCOME $MILL	TOTAL ASSETS $MILL	NET STK EQUITY $MILL	NO OF INST	INST. HOLDINGS (SHARES)
TRR	TRC Companies, Inc.	Sanitation Services	6/30/15	414.6	19.4	362.9	148.3	106	16831568
TREC	Trecora Resources	Refining & Marketing	12/31/15	242.0	18.6	258.8	142.1	75	8146740
TG	Tredegar Corp.	Plastics	12/31/15	876.1	-32.1	623.3	272.7	164	21495734
THS	TreeHouse Foods Inc	Food	12/31/15	3206.4	114.9	3702.8	1854.9	381	66547231
TRMR	Tremor Video Inc	Advertising	12/31/15	173.8	-43.2	168.1	101.4	59	19786845
TREX	Trex Co Inc	Metal Products	12/31/15	440.8	48.1	212.0	116.5	242	30647757
TPH	TRI Pointe Group Inc	Builders	12/31/15	2400.1	205.5	3138.1	1664.7	262	164637805
TY	Tri-Continental Corp.	Holding and other Investment Office	12/31/15	56.2	48.7	1426.2	1420.3	106	15985575
TCAP	Triangle Capital Corp	Holding and other Investment Office	12/31/15	121.3	71.6	1039.3	508.4	134	9039407
TRCO	Tribune Media Co.	Radio & Television	12/31/15	2010.5	-319.9	9758.5	3826.2	271	101898102
TSL	Trina Solar Ltd	Semiconductors	12/31/15	3035.5	76.5	4694.0	1050.7	172	61485937
TNET	Trinet Group Inc.	Services	12/31/15	2659.3	31.7	2098.2	8.1	162	59219060
TRN	Trinity Industries, Inc.	Industrial Machinery & Equipment	12/31/15	6392.7	796.5	8885.9	3653.9	534	116838587
TSE	Trinseo SA	Synthetic Materials	12/31/15	3971.9	133.6	2284.6	389.0	155	48267476
GTS	Triple-S Management Corp	Hospitals & Health Care Facilities	12/31/15	2902.7	52.1	2206.1	847.5	162	22784338
TPVG	TriplePoint Venture Growth BDC Co	Finance Intermediaries & Services	12/31/15	42.1	22.0	382.3	231.6	50	9547599
TGI	Triumph Group Inc.	Aerospace	3/31/15	3886.1	-1048.0	4835.1	934.9	346	66208944
TROX	Tronox Ltd	Specialty Chemicals	12/31/15	2112.0	-318.0	5072.0	998.0		
TBI	TrueBlue Inc	Business Services	12/25/15	2695.7	71.2	1266.8	535.6	250	41794046
TNP	Tsakos Energy Navigation Ltd.	Equipment & Services	12/31/15	587.7	158.2	2900.7	1403.5	138	32178161
TUMI	Tumi Holdings Inc	Apparel, Footwear & Accessories	12/31/15	547.7	63.0	611.9	480.8	220	60185770
TUP	Tupperware Brands Corp	Plastics	12/26/15	2283.8	185.8	1598.2	161.0	500	54025277
TKC	Turkcell Iletisim Hizmetleri AS	Services	12/31/15	12769.4	2067.7	26207.3	14354.8	146	56537829
TKF	Turkish Investment Fund, Inc. (The)	Holding and other Investment Office	10/31/15	1.5	0.7	47.2	47.1	37	1940748
TPB	Turning Point Brands Inc	Tobacco Products	12/31/15	197.3	9.1	248.7	-81.6		
TRQ	Turquoise Hill Resources Ltd.	Precious Metals	12/31/14	1644.1	31.8	8167.2	8237.6	212	611278799
TPC	Tutor Perini Corp	Construction Services	12/31/15	4920.5	45.3	4042.4	1420.2	25	447716
TWLO	Twilio Inc	IT Services							
TWTR	Twitter Inc	Internet & Software	12/31/15	2218.0	-521.0	6442.4	4368.0	604	308963074
TWO	Two Harbors Investment Corp	REITs	12/31/15	769.4	492.2	14575.8	3576.6	351	257654750
TYC	Tyco International PLC	Business Services	9/25/15	9902.0	551.0	12321.0	4041.0	771	463547799
TYL	Tyler Technologies, Inc.	Internet & Software	12/31/15	591.0	64.9	1356.6	858.9	361	37783857
TSN	Tyson Foods, Inc.	Food	10/3/15	41373.0	1220.0	23004.0	9691.0	819	303272503
USB	U.S. Bancorp (DE)	Banking	12/31/15	21494.0	5879.0	421853.0	46131.0	1632	1352770077
USPH	U.S. Physical Therapy, Inc.	Hospitals & Health Care Facilities	12/31/15	331.3	22.3	279.9	162.8	185	12406282
UBS	UBS Group AG	Holding and other Investment Office	12/31/15	37166.0	6203.0	942819.0	55313.0		
UCP	UCP Inc	Construction Services	12/31/15	278.8	2.4	416.2	90.2	41	7057163
UDR	UDR Inc	REITs	12/31/15	894.6	340.4	7663.8	3846.2	464	322943129
UGI	UGI Corp.	Gas Utilities	9/30/15	6691.1	281.0	10546.6	2692.0	531	148863527
UGP	Ultrapar Participacoes SA	Equipment & Services	12/31/15	75655.3	1503.5	20966.0	7945.0	128	20545857
UMH	UMH Properties Inc	REITs	12/31/15	81.5	2.1	604.0	246.2	113	11504757
UA	Under Armour Inc	Apparel, Footwear & Accessories	12/31/15	3963.3	232.6	2868.9	1668.2	787	158245870
UFI	Unifi, Inc.	Textiles	6/28/15	687.1	42.2	476.4	297.5	164	13764622
UNF	Unifirst Corp.	Business Services	8/29/15	1456.6	124.3	1533.2	1242.2	257	17521033
UN	Unilever N.V.	Household & Personal Products	12/31/15	53272.0	4909.0	52298.0	15439.0	643	149654479
UL	Unilever Plc	Household & Personal Products	12/31/15	53272.0	4909.0	52298.0	15439.0	648	139998885
UNP	Union Pacific Corp	Rail	12/31/15	21813.0	4772.0	54600.0	20702.0	1806	725439964
UIS	Unisys Corp.	IT Services	12/31/15	3015.1	-109.9	2143.2	-1389.7	243	85761777
UNT	Unit Corp.	Production & Extraction	12/31/15	854.2	-1037.4	2808.5	1313.6	267	53838707
UAL	United Continental Holdings Inc	Airlines/Air Freight	12/31/15	37864.0	7340.0	40861.0	8966.0	735	351982164
UMC	United Microelectronics Corp.	Semiconductors	12/31/15	144830.4	13254.1	335354.3	222825.6	129	170753644
UPS	United Parcel Service Inc	Airlines/Air Freight	12/31/15	58363.0	4844.0	38311.0	2470.0	1634	553337573
URI	United Rentals, Inc.	Construction Services	12/31/15	5817.0	585.0	12083.0	1476.0	714	105468200
UZC	United States Cellular Corp	Services	12/31/15	3996.9	241.3	7060.0	3560.5	169	12656595
X	United States Steel Corp.	Non-Precious Metals	12/31/15	11574.0	-1642.0	9190.0	2436.0	474	108957764
UTX	United Technologies Corp	Aerospace	12/31/15	56098.0	7608.0	87484.0	27358.0	1999	802763484
UNH	UnitedHealth Group Inc	Life & Health	12/31/15	157107.0	5813.0	111383.0	33830.0	1652	953499691
UTL	UNITIL Corp	Electric Utilities	12/31/15	426.8	26.3	1046.4	282.8	154	8428859
UNVR	Univar Inc	Construction Services	12/31/15	8981.8	16.5	5612.4	816.7	98	98189443
UAM	Universal American Corp (New)	Life & Health	12/31/15	1491.7	-164.0	1737.1	382.4	89	71276577
UVV	Universal Corp.	Tobacco Products	3/31/16	2120.4	109.0	2232.8	1414.2	279	27266683
UHT	Universal Health Realty Income Tru	REITs	12/31/15	63.9	23.7	458.9	195.0	185	7466253
UHS	Universal Health Services, Inc.	Hospitals & Health Care Facilities	12/31/15	9043.5	680.5	9634.1	4249.6	628	101754745
UVE	Universal Insurance Holdings Inc	General Insurance	12/31/15	546.5	106.5	993.5	293.1	213	26990371
UTI	Universal Technical Institute, Inc.	Educational Services	9/30/15	362.7	-9.1	274.3	113.5	122	23011971
UNM	Unum Group	Life & Health	12/31/15	10731.3	867.1	60589.7	8663.9	629	270173884
UE	Urban Edge Properties	REITs	12/31/15	322.9	38.8	1918.9	437.9	231	90832862
UBA	Urstadt Biddle Properties Inc	REITs	10/31/15	115.3	49.3	861.1	540.8	35	899111
USFD	US Foods Holding Corp	Retail - Food & Beverage, Drug & To	1/2/16	23127.5	167.5	9239.4	1911.6		
SLCA	US Silica Holdings, Inc.	Equipment & Services	12/31/15	643.0	11.9	1106.6	384.2	270	67967208
USAC	USA Compression Partners, LP	Equipment & Services	12/31/15	270.5	-154.3	1509.8		78	57212397
USNA	USANA Health Sciences Inc	Household & Personal Products	1/2/16	918.5	94.7	423.2	280.9	202	5784963
USB PRI	USB Capital X	Banking						1	15070
USDP	USD Partners LP	Rail	12/31/15	81.8	17.7	328.4		32	6313705
USG	USG Corp	Construction Materials	12/31/15	3776.0	991.0	4736.0	1436.0	356	126989543
EGY	VAALCO Energy, Inc.	Production & Extraction	12/31/15	80.4	-158.7	124.0	26.1	123	31173065
MTN	Vail Resorts Inc.	Sporting & Recreational	7/31/15	1399.9	114.8	2489.6	866.6	353	41297036
RIO 34	Vale Overseas Ltd	Finance Intermediaries & Services	12/31/05	84.1	0.0	1289.4	-0.0		
VALE	Vale SA	Non-Precious Metals	12/31/15	25609.0	-24749.0	88492.0	33589.0	456	491480755
VRX	Valeant Pharmaceuticals Internation	Pharmaceuticals	12/31/15	10446.5	-291.7	48964.5	5911.0	631	285183084

T60

EARNINGS PER SHARE						P/E RATIO		DIVIDENDS PER SHARE			AV. YLD	DIV. DECLARED		PRICE RANGE	
QUARTERLY			ANNUAL					PER SHARE						2015	
1st	2nd	3rd	2015	2014	2013	2015	2013	2015	2014	2013	%	AMOUNT	PAYABLE		
-	-	-0.46	0.63	0.40	1.23	19.3 -	9.2	-	-	-	-	-	-	12.2 -	5.8
0.29	-	-	0.74	0.63	0.79	22.0 -	12.0	-	-	-	-	-	-	16.3 -	8.8
0.22	-	-	-0.99	1.13	0.67	-	-	0.42	0.35	0.28	2.7	0.110Y	7/1/16	23.8 -	11.7
-0.06	-	-	2.63	2.23	2.33	36.1 -	25.6	-	-	-	-	-	-	94.9 -	67.3
-0.21	-	-	-0.84	-0.46	-1.02	-	-	-	-	-	-	-	-	3.2 -	1.6
0.78	-	-	1.52	1.27	1.01	34.7 -	21.2	-	-	-	-	-	-	52.8 -	32.1
0.18	-	-	1.27	0.58	0.50	12.6 -	7.1	-	-	-	-	-	-	16.1 -	9.1
-	-	-	0.81	0.73	0.69	27.1 -	21.8	0.81	0.75	0.68	4.0	0.22010	6/28/16	22.0 -	17.6
0.29	-	-	2.16	2.08	2.23	11.4 -	7.2	2.36	2.56	2.16	12.0	0.39840Z	6/15/16	24.7 -	15.6
0.12	-	-	-3.38	4.75	2.41	-	-	7.48	-	-	18.7	0.250	6/6/16	55.6 -	27.4
-	-	0.00	0.02	0.01	-0.02	652.0 -	387.5	-	-	-	-	-	-	13.0 -	7.8
0.16	-	-	0.45	0.22	0.24	66.1 -	27.3	-	-	-	-	-	-	29.7 -	12.3
0.64	-	-	5.08	4.19	2.38	6.0 -	3.1	0.42	0.35	0.25	1.8	0.110Y	61/28/99	30.7 -	15.6
1.56	-	-	2.73	-1.55	-0.60	17.4 -	8.2	-	-	-	-	0.3G	7/20/16	47.6 -	22.5
0.14	-	-	2.02	2.41	2.01	13.6 -	8.8	-	-	-	-	-	-	27.5 -	17.7
0.41	-	-	1.46	1.30	-	9.6 -	6.1	1.44	1.22	-	12.7	0.421902	7/15/16	14.1 -	8.9
-	-1.80	-	4.68	3.91	5.67	14.7 -	5.0	0.16	0.16	0.16	0.4	0.040Y	61/28/99	68.8 -	23.5
-0.78	-	-	-2.75	-3.74	-1.11	-	-	1.00	1.00	1.00	-	0.0450	5/27/16	-	-
0.17	-	-	1.71	1.59	1.11	18.3 -	10.5	-	-	-	-	-	-	31.3 -	18.0
-	-	-0.04	1.69	0.32	-0.73	-	-	0.24	0.15	0.15	-	0.080	8/10/16	-	-
0.12	-	-	0.93	0.85	0.80	29.2 -	16.6	-	-	-	-	-	-	27.1 -	15.4
0.86	-	-	3.69	4.20	5.17	18.3 -	11.9	2.72	2.72	2.48	4.8	0.680Y	61/28/99	67.5 -	44.0
-	-	0.16	0.94	0.39	0.56	12.7 -	8.4	3.73	-	-	37.8	-	-	11.9 -	7.9
-	-	-	0.15	0.02	0.20	68.3 -	0.0	0.27	3.35	0.23	3.1	0.14960	1/15/16	10.2 -	0.0
0.27	-	-	1.10	-4.07	-	10.9 -	9.2	-	-	-	-	-	-	11.9 -	10.1
-	-	0.01	-	0.02	-0.09	-	-	-	-	-	-	-	-	5.5 -	0.0
0.31	-	-	0.91	2.20	1.80	26.3 -	11.7	-	-	-	-	1.7Y	11/12/10	23.9 -	10.7
-0.12	-	-	-0.79	-0.96	-6.82	-	-	-	-	-	-	-	-	37.0 -	14.0
-0.25	-	-	1.35	0.46	1.65	7.9 -	5.2	1.04	1.04	1.17	11.9	0.230Z	7/20/16	10.7 -	7.1
-	0.34	-	1.29	3.97	1.14	33.1 -	23.1	0.59	0.68	-	1.6	0.2050	8/17/16	42.7 -	29.8
0.44	-	-	1.77	1.66	1.13	102.0 -	67.4	-	-	-	-	-	-	180.6 -	119.4
-	1.10	-	2.95	2.37	2.12	23.5 -	13.5	0.40	0.30	0.30	0.8	0.1350Y	61/28/99	69.3 -	39.8
0.76	-	-	3.16	3.08	3.00	14.6 -	11.9	1.01	0.96	0.89	2.4	25.6250Y	61/28/99	46.0 -	37.5
0.43	-	-	1.77	1.62	1.05	33.0 -	24.3	0.60	0.48	0.40	1.2	0.170Z	6/3/16	58.3 -	43.0
-	-	-	1.64	0.91	0.83	-	-	1.50	-	-	-	0.257	5/17/16	-	-
0.01	-	-	0.30	-0.63	-0.25	28.1 -	18.2	-	-	-	-	-	-	8.4 -	5.5
0.04	-	-	1.29	0.59	0.16	29.9 -	24.1	1.09	1.01	0.93	3.1	0.33220Z	61/28/99	38.6 -	31.1
-	1.33	-	1.60	1.92	1.61	27.1 -	19.8	0.89	0.79	0.74	2.5	0.23750Y	61/28/99	43.4 -	31.7
-	-	0.61	2.74	2.26	2.28	8.2 -	4.8	1.44	1.41	1.30	7.9	-	-	22.5 -	13.1
0.07	-	-	0.08	0.19	0.31	133.1 -	113.5	0.72	0.72	0.72	7.4	0.50Y	6/15/16	10.7 -	9.1
0.04	-	-	0.53	0.47	0.38	101.5 -	65.4	-	-	-	-	-	-	53.8 -	34.7
-	-	0.53	2.24	1.47	0.80	15.2 -	9.5	-	-	-	-	0.140	5/8/98	33.9 -	21.3
-	1.16	-	6.15	5.95	5.81	19.1 -	15.9	0.15	0.15	0.15	0.1	0.030Y	7/1/16	117.4 -	98.0
-	-	-	1.72	1.79	1.66	27.4 -	22.3	1.20	1.13	1.04	2.8	-	-	47.0 -	38.4
-	-	-	1.72	1.79	1.66	27.8 -	22.7	1.18	1.12	1.04	2.7	-	-	47.8 -	39.1
1.16	-	-	5.49	5.75	4.71	18.6 -	12.5	2.20	1.91	1.48	2.6	0.550Y	61/28/99	102.3 -	68.8
-0.80	-	-	-2.20	0.89	2.08	-	-	-	-	-	-	1.56250Y	12/1/13	21.1 -	7.2
-0.83	-	-	-21.12	2.78	3.80	-	-	-	-	-	-	-	-	32.6 -	4.4
0.88	-	-	19.47	2.93	1.53	3.2 -	2.2	-	-	-	-	2.15G7Y	61/28/99	61.6 -	43.8
-	-	0.26	1.02	0.89	0.96	2.2 -	1.6	1.84	2.23	1.43	97.0	-	-	2.2 -	1.5
1.27	-	-	5.35	3.28	4.61	20.0 -	16.6	2.92	2.68	2.48	2.9	0.780Y	61/28/99	106.8 -	88.7
1.01	-	-	6.07	5.15	3.64	15.3 -	7.1	-	-	-	-	-	-	92.6 -	43.3
0.10	-	-	2.84	-0.51	1.65	9.1 -	8.5	-	-	5.75	-	5.75GY	61/28/99	25.9 -	24.2
-2.32	-	-	-11.24	0.69	-11.56	-	-	0.20	0.20	0.20	1.4	0.050Y	61/28/99	25.8 -	6.7
1.43	-	-	8.61	6.82	6.25	13.8 -	9.8	2.56	2.36	2.19	2.6	0.660Y	61/28/99	118.5 -	84.7
1.67	-	-	6.01	5.70	5.50	22.3 -	18.2	1.88	1.41	1.05	1.6	0.6250Y	61/28/99	134.2 -	109.2
0.78	-	-	1.89	1.79	1.57	22.7 -	17.4	1.40	1.38	1.38	3.8	0.3550Y	5/27/16	43.0 -	32.9
0.10	-	-	0.14	-0.20	-0.83	194.6 -	79.4	-	-	-	-	-	-	27.3 -	11.1
0.00	-	-	-1.99	-0.35	-2.20	-	-	0.75	-	1.60	9.9	0.757	10/26/15	10.9 -	5.7
-	-	1.60	4.06	5.25	4.66	14.4 -	11.6	2.05	2.01	1.97	3.8	16.8750Y	61/28/99	58.4 -	47.0
0.33	-	-	1.78	3.99	1.04	32.5 -	24.5	2.56	2.52	2.50	5.1	0.650Z	61/28/99	57.9 -	43.5
1.93	-	-	6.76	5.42	5.14	21.6 -	15.0	0.40	0.30	0.20	0.3	0.10Y	61/28/99	146.2 -	101.7
0.71	-	-	2.97	2.08	1.56	12.2 -	5.5	0.63	0.55	0.49	2.7	0.140Y	7/5/16	36.3 -	16.4
-	-1.32	-	-0.38	0.08	0.15	-	-	0.32	0.40	0.40	6.6	0.020Y	3/31/16	8.8 -	2.9
0.88	-	-	3.50	1.61	3.23	10.7 -	6.9	0.70	0.62	0.55	2.1	0.1850Y	61/28/99	37.6 -	24.1
0.19	-	-	0.39	-	-	71.3 -	51.6	0.80	-	-	3.4	0.20	61/28/99	27.8 -	20.1
-	0.12	-	0.90	1.42	0.31	24.1 -	19.4	1.02	1.01	1.00	5.2	0.421902	61/28/99	21.7 -	17.4
0.07	-	-	0.98	-0.43	-0.34	25.5 -	25.4	-	-	-	-	-	-	25.0 -	24.9
-0.20	-	-	0.22	2.23	1.41	149.8 -	61.8	0.44	0.50	0.38	2.1	0.06250Y	7/6/16	33.0 -	13.6
0.24	-	-	-3.15	0.60	0.32	-	-	2.08	1.98	1.25	14.1	0.5250	5/13/16	21.8 -	7.2
1.77	-	-	7.18	5.60	5.56	24.5 -	13.2	-	-	-	-	-	-	176.1 -	94.8
0.19	-	-	0.83	-0.29	-	15.8 -	6.2	1.11	-	-	12.0	0.30750	5/13/16	13.1 -	5.1
0.46	-	-	6.73	0.25	0.42	4.9 -	2.4	-	-	-	-	0.0250	61/28/99	32.7 -	16.5
-0.14	-	-	-2.72	-1.36	0.74	-	-	-	-	-	-	0.001F	8/1/09	2.4 -	0.8
-	-	4.23	3.07	0.77	1.03	43.6 -	33.0	2.08	1.25	0.79	1.8	0.810Z	7/13/16	133.7 -	101.3
-	-	0.68	-2.35	0.13	0.11	-	-	0.25	0.67	0.72	5.7	-	-	6.9 -	2.1
-1.08	-	-	-0.85	2.63	-2.70	-	-	-	-	-	-	1.7	12/22/10	346.3 -	0.0

SYMBOL	COMPANY	NATURE OF BUSINESS	FISCAL YEAR-END	TOTAL REV. $MILL	NET INCOME $MILL	TOTAL ASSETS $MILL	NET STK EQUITY $MILL	NO OF INST	INST. HOLDINGS (SHARES)
VLO	Valero Energy Corp.	Refining & Marketing	12/31/15	87804.0	3990.0	44343.0	20527.0	1243	440677502
VLP	Valero Energy Partners LP	Equipment & Services	12/31/15	243.6	101.8	850.1		114	20576579
VHI	Valhi, Inc.	Specialty Chemicals	12/31/15	1564.9	-133.6	2537.4	268.7	76	3932077
VR	Validus Holdings Ltd	General Insurance	12/31/15	2345.3	374.9	10515.8	3639.0	321	83469054
VLY	Valley National Bancorp	Banking	12/31/15	790.8	103.0	21612.6	2207.1	304	138601515
VMI	Valmont Industries Inc	Construction Services	12/26/15	2618.9	40.1	2399.4	918.4	327	24593008
VAL	Valspar Corp	Specialty Chemicals	10/30/15	4392.6	399.5	4318.6	855.0	461	71350593
VNTV	Vantiv Inc	Business Services	12/31/15	3159.9	147.9	6465.4	952.8	445	157773818
VAR	Varian Medical Systems, Inc.	Medical Instruments & Equipment	10/2/15	3099.1	411.5	3600.7	1711.6	756	113612403
VGR	Vector Group Ltd	Tobacco Products	12/31/15	1657.2	59.2	1310.8	-206.0	279	63569268
VVC	Vectren Corp	Electric Utilities	12/31/15	2434.7	197.3	5409.9	1683.8	419	60652175
VVC 13	Vectren Utility Holdings Inc.	Electric Utilities	12/31/15	1394.5	160.9	4601.3	1535.2		
VEC	Vectrus Inc	Services	12/31/15	1180.7	31.0	484.4	89.3	177	8645485
VEDL	Vedanta Ltd	Non-Precious Metals	3/31/15	733579.0	-128350.0	2161704.0	561119.0	114	33316422
VEEV	Veeva Systems Inc	IT Services	1/31/16	409.2	54.5	705.8	505.2	219	89501678
VTR	Ventas, Inc.	REITs	12/31/15	3286.4	419.2	22261.9	9760.9	775	362557302
VER	VEREIT Inc	REITs	12/31/15	1556.0	-316.4	17405.9	8524.0	415	751204683
PAY	VeriFone Systems Inc.	Internet & Software	10/31/15	2000.5	79.1	2473.1	899.5	431	116487010
VRTV	Veritiv Corp	Industrial Machinery & Equipment	12/31/15	8717.7	26.7	2476.9	530.1	198	16012430
VZ	Verizon Communications Inc	Services	12/31/15	131620.0	17879.0	244640.0	16428.0	2473	2846578299
VET	Vermilion Energy Inc.	Production & Extraction	12/31/15	873.7	-217.3	4209.2	1858.7		
VFC	VF Corp.	Apparel, Footwear & Accessories	1/2/16	12376.7	1231.6	9639.5	5384.8	1059	441184898
VVI	Viad Corp.	Business Services	12/31/15	1089.0	26.6	692.3	322.6	204	20348933
VCO	Vina Concha y Toro S.A. (Chile)	Beverages	12/31/15	636194.1	49797.4	987471.0	452711.0	28	205551
VNCE	Vince Holding Corp	Retail - Apparel and Accessories	1/30/16	302.5	5.1	363.6	78.5	104	10837219
VMEM	Violin Memory Inc	IT Services	1/31/16	50.9	-99.1	112.8	-54.9	88	29826901
VIPS	Vipshop Holdings Ltd	Retail - Apparel and Accessories	12/31/15	40203.2	1589.7	20035.5	3539.2	321	356546318
VGI	Virtus Global Multi-Sector Income F	Holding and other Investment Office	12/31/14	18.4	13.8	286.0	204.2	40	4690427
DCA	Virtus Total Return Fund	Holding and other Investment Office	11/30/15	7.3	4.8	171.9	126.5	50	11568481
V	Visa Inc	Business Services	9/30/15	13880.0	6328.0	40236.0	29842.0	1871	1823274394
VSH	Vishay Intertechnology, Inc.	Electrical Equipment	12/31/15	2300.5	-108.5	3153.0	1622.5	351	169030347
VPG	Vishay Precision Group Inc	Electronic Instruments & Related Pro	12/31/15	232.2	-13.0	264.3	172.3	117	10743526
VSTO	Vista Outdoor Inc	Sporting & Recreational	3/31/16	2270.7	147.0	2942.6	1660.2	275	54184712
VC	Visteon Corp.	Auto Parts	12/31/15	3245.0	2284.0	4682.0	1057.0	399	47574019
VSI	Vitamin Shoppe Inc	Retail - Specialty	12/26/15	1266.5	53.2	748.7	475.3	195	30085842
VSLR	Vivint Solar Inc	Miscellaneous Consumer Goods	12/31/15	64.2	13.1	1609.1	518.9	99	97011807
VMW	VMware Inc	Internet & Software	12/31/15	6571.0	997.0	15746.0	7919.0	522	95798812
VOC	VOC Energy Trust	Oil Royalty Traders	12/31/15	8.6	8.0	93.5	93.5	39	1209286
VCRA	Vocera Communications, Inc.	Computer Hardware & Equipment	12/31/15	104.1	-17.1	162.3	104.4	134	27898309
VG	Vonage Holdings Corp	Services	12/31/15	895.1	22.7	784.6	388.7	252	175115459
VNO	Vornado Realty Trust	REITs	12/31/15	2502.3	760.4	21143.3	6697.6	607	211373472
VJET	voxeljet AG	Industrial Machinery & Equipment	12/31/15	24.1	-9.6	70.1	61.5	39	1265426
IAE	VOYA Asia Pacific Dividend Equity I	Holding and other Investment Office	2/28/15	5.9	3.4	166.7	165.8	49	5323647
IHD	VOYA Emerging Markets High Divid	Holding and other Investment Office	2/28/15	9.3	5.8	227.5	226.2	44	9465684
VOYA	Voya Financial Inc	Life & Health	12/31/15	11341.2	408.3	218249.6	13435.8	425	200130368
IGA	VOYA Global Advantage & Premiu	Holding and other Investment Office	2/28/15	5.4	3.1	242.3	237.4	42	4970089
IGD	VOYA Global Equity Dividend & Pre	Holding and other Investment Office	2/28/15	32.7	21.3	924.7	908.6	106	22782494
IDE	VOYA Infrastructure Industrials & M	Holding and other Investment Office	2/28/15	9.6	5.2	342.7	340.4	50	5825920
IID	VOYA International High Dividend E	Holding and other Investment Office	2/28/15	2.8	1.8	73.0	72.2	33	991942
PPR	VOYA Prime Rate Trust	Holding and other Investment Office	2/28/15	67.7	49.2	1266.9	876.4	137	48624506
IRR	VOYA Risk Managed Natural Reso	Holding and other Investment Office	2/28/15	5.6	2.6	213.4	212.3	62	4900891
VTTI	VTTI Energy Partners LP	Equipment & Services	12/31/15	289.7	22.5	1551.4	225.6	58	18895565
VMC	Vulcan Materials Co (Holding Comp	Mining	12/31/15	3422.2	221.2	8301.6	4454.2	674	147529307
WTI	W & T Offshore Inc	Production & Extraction	12/31/15	507.3	-1044.7	1208.0	-526.5	137	32599986
WPC	W.P. Carey Inc	REITs	12/31/15	938.4	172.3	8754.7	3427.2	429	53430043
WNC	Wabash National Corp.	Autos- Manufacturing	12/31/15	2027.5	104.3	950.1	439.8	295	80502386
WBC	WABCO Holdings Inc	Construction Services	12/31/15	2627.5	275.2	2589.9	786.7	409	59810759
WAB	Wabtec Corp	Construction Services	12/31/15	3308.0	398.6	3300.3	1699.6	577	103686215
WDR	Waddell & Reed Financial, Inc.	Finance Intermediaries & Services	12/31/15	1516.6	245.5	1555.7	846.5	413	81537070
WAGE	WageWorks Inc	Business Services	12/31/15	334.3	22.9	888.7	337.0	204	39813521
WMT	Wal-Mart Stores, Inc.	Retail - General Merchandise/Depart	1/31/16	482130.0	14694.0	199581.0	80546.0	2093	1164080749
WD	Walker & Dunlop Inc	Business Services	12/31/15	468.2	82.6	3515.0	487.9	190	25044862
WAC	Walter Investment Management Cor	Credit & Lending	12/31/15	1274.3	-263.2	18591.5	804.7	125	39974980
WRE	Washington Real Estate Investment	REITs	12/31/15	306.4	89.7	2191.2	835.6	296	63515155
WCN	Waste Connections Inc (Canada)	Sanitation Services	12/31/15	1925.6	123.9	3244.9	1128.9	206	82149785
WM	Waste Management, Inc. (DE)	Sanitation Services	12/31/15	12961.0	753.0	20419.0	5345.0	1123	393186107
WAT	Waters Corp.	Biotechnology	12/31/15	2042.3	469.1	4268.7	2058.9	658	86775896
WSO	Watsco Inc.	Industrial Machinery & Equipment	12/31/15	4113.2	172.9	1788.4	957.3	342	26222014
WTS	Watts Water Technologies Inc	Industrial Machinery & Equipment	12/31/15	1467.7	-112.9	1692.8	704.9	247	31317820
W	Wayfair Inc	Retail - Furniture & Home Furnishing	12/31/15	2249.9	-77.4	694.6	242.5	179	55246156
WCIC	WCI Communities Inc	Builders	12/31/15	563.6	35.4	861.6	472.0	144	25709753
WFT	Weatherford International Plc	Equipment & Services	12/31/15	9433.0	-1985.0	14787.0	4304.0		
WBS	Webster Financial Corp (Waterbury,	Banking	12/31/15	999.6	206.3	24677.8	2415.6	336	88586537
WEC	WEC Energy Group Inc	Electric Utilities	12/31/15	5926.1	640.3	29355.2	8685.2	829	234167293
WTW	Weight Watchers International, Inc.	Miscellaneous Consumer Services	1/2/16	1164.4	32.9	1422.1	-1290.2	254	67043955
WRI	Weingarten Realty Investors	REITs	12/31/15	512.8	174.4	3901.9	1389.5	427	133376514
WMK	Weis Markets, Inc.	Retail - Food & Beverage, Drug & To	12/26/15	2876.7	59.3	1236.0	871.7	145	9969029
WCG	WellCare Health Plans Inc	Hospitals & Health Care Facilities	12/31/15	13890.2	118.6	5193.6	1728.3	358	52961331
WFC	Wells Fargo & Co.	Banking	12/31/15	90033.0	22894.0	1787632.0	192998.0	2517	4251149679
WSF	Wells Fargo Capital IV	Banking							

T62

| EARNINGS PER SHARE QUARTERLY | | | EARNINGS PER SHARE ANNUAL | | | P/E RATIO | | DIVIDENDS PER SHARE | | | AV. YLD | DIV. DECLARED | | PRICE RANGE 2015 | |
1st	2nd	3rd	2015	2014	2013			2015	2014	2013	%	AMOUNT	PAYABLE		
1.05	-	-	7.99	6.85	4.97	9.1 -	6.8	1.70	1.05	0.85	2.7	0.60Y	61/28/99	73.0 -	54.1
0.61	-	-	4.19	2.02	0.06	12.8 -	9.2	1.14	0.71	0.04	2.4	0.340	5/10/16	53.8 -	38.4
-0.06	-	-	0.30	0.16	0.20	-		0.08	0.11	0.20	3.1	0.020Y	6/23/16	7.1 -	0.9
1.98	-	-	4.34	5.08	4.94			1.28	1.20	3.20		0.350	6/30/16		
0.14	-	-	0.42	0.56	0.66	26.5 -	19.8	0.44	0.44	0.60	4.5	0.39060Y	61/28/99	11.1 -	8.3
1.45	-	-	1.71	7.09	10.35	84.1 -	55.0	1.50	1.38	0.97	1.3	0.3750Y	61/28/99	143.8 -	94.0
-	0.99	-	4.85	4.01	3.20	22.3 -	14.6	1.20	1.04	0.92	1.4	0.330Y	61/28/99	108.3 -	70.8
0.25	-	-	0.95	0.75	0.87	59.5 -	39.7	-	-	-		-		56.5 -	37.8
-	1.01	-	4.09	3.83	3.98	22.1 -	17.5	-	-	-		0.0250	61/28/99	90.4 -	71.4
0.16	-	-	0.49	0.33	0.37	51.9 -	42.5	1.54	1.47	1.40	6.7	0.40Y	61/28/99	25.4 -	20.8
0.58	-	-	2.39	2.02	1.66	21.3 -	16.1	1.54	1.46	1.43	3.5	0.40Y	61/28/99	50.9 -	38.4
0.61	-	-	2.86	2.13	-	9.4 -	6.2	-	-	-		-		26.9 -	17.8
-	-	-	-43.29	5.22	16.03			-	-	-		-		12.3 -	3.7
0.18	-	-	0.28	0.15	0.11	117.7 -	73.6	-	-	-		-		33.0 -	20.6
0.44	-	-	1.25	1.60	1.54	53.8 -	38.7	3.04	2.96	2.73	5.3	0.730Z	61/28/99	67.2 -	48.4
-0.15	-	-	-0.43	-1.36	-2.36			0.28	1.08	0.91	3.3	0.13960Z	9/15/16	9.9 -	7.1
-	0.03	-	0.68	-0.34	-2.73	57.2 -	30.4	-	-	-		-		38.9 -	20.6
0.21	-	-	1.67	-1.62		26.1 -	16.8	-	-	-		-		43.6 -	28.0
1.06	-	-	4.37	2.42	4.00	12.5 -	9.8	2.21	2.14	2.08	4.6	0.5650Y	61/28/99	54.4 -	42.8
-	-	-0.76	-1.98	2.51	3.20			2.58	2.58	2.40	7.0	0.2150	7/15/16	55.6 -	0.0
0.61	-	-	2.85	2.38	2.71	27.0 -	18.9	1.33	1.11	0.92	2.0	0.370Y	61/28/99	77.1 -	54.0
-0.35	-	-	1.32	2.59	1.06	24.8 -	19.1	0.40	1.90	2.90	1.4	0.10Y	7/1/16	32.7 -	25.2
-	-	-	66.66	50.06	-	0.6 -	0.0	358.67	296.00	248.00	1170.0			37.5 -	0.0
-0.05	-	-	0.93	-0.98	-0.00	17.1 -	3.7	-	-	-		-		15.9 -	3.4
-0.22	-	-	-1.20	-3.88	-8.01			-	-	-		-		3.2 -	0.3
-	-	0.10	13.23	2.28	0.45	2.0 -	0.8	-	-	-		-		25.9 -	10.4
-	-	-	-	1.23	1.34			-	1.62	1.53		0.1560	9/19/16	16.8 -	12.4
-	-	-	0.18	0.32	0.20	25.9 -	17.5	0.40	0.36	0.21	10.0	0.10	7/18/16	4.7 -	3.1
-	0.71	-	2.58	2.15	1.90	31.6 -	25.9	0.48	0.40	0.33	0.6	0.140Y	61/28/99	81.5 -	66.7
0.19	-	-	-0.73	0.77	0.81	-		0.24	0.24	-	2.1	0.06250	61/28/99	13.1 -	9.3
0.04	-	-	-0.96	0.28	0.31			-	-	-		-		15.6 -	10.5
-	-	0.70	1.25	-		42.3 -	33.4	-	-	-		-		52.9 -	41.8
0.49	-	-	52.63	-6.25	13.50	2.3 -	1.1	-	-	-		43.4G7	61/28/99	120.7 -	60.5
0.59	-	-	1.82	2.00	2.18	22.1 -	14.6	-	-	-		-		40.2 -	26.5
-0.29	-	-	0.12	-0.35	0.07	132.2 -	18.5	-	-	-		-		15.9 -	2.2
0.38	-	-	2.34	2.04	2.34	38.9 -	18.7	-	-	-		-		91.1 -	43.8
0.04	-	-	0.47	1.85	1.68	13.0 -	4.3	0.47	1.85	1.68	12.7	0.050	5/13/16	6.1 -	2.0
-0.14	-	-	-0.66	-1.12	-0.43			-	-	-		-		14.9 -	10.1
0.04	-	-	0.10	0.09	0.13	69.5 -	39.0	-	-	-		-		7.0 -	3.9
-0.61	-	-	3.59	4.15	2.09	28.8 -	22.3	2.52	2.92	2.02	2.7	0.33750Z	61/28/99	103.4 -	80.2
-	-	-	2.68	1.22	1.21			-	-	-		-		7.9 -	3.7
-	-	-	0.27	0.35	0.29	44.5 -	28.3	1.28	1.35	1.50	13.7	0.2550	7/15/16	12.0 -	7.7
-	-	-	0.30	0.34	0.30	34.4 -	21.1	1.15	1.30	1.52	14.6	0.230	7/15/16	10.3 -	6.3
0.92	-	-	1.80	9.02	2.38	26.7 -	14.4	0.04	0.04	0.02	0.1	0.010Y	61/28/99	48.1 -	26.0
-	-	-	0.17	0.19	0.21	74.7 -	52.2	1.12	1.12	1.18	10.5	0.280	7/15/16	12.7 -	8.9
-	-	-	0.22	0.27	0.27	38.2 -	27.6	0.01	0.97	1.07	12.6	0.0760	7/15/16	8.4 -	6.0
-	-	-	0.26	0.48	0.28	59.1 -	40.4	1.62	1.62	1.71	12.8	0.3650	7/15/16	15.4 -	10.5
-	-	-	0.22	0.25	0.23	37.9 -	24.9	0.83	0.88	0.99	12.5	0.0690	7/15/16	8.3 -	5.5
-	-	-	0.33	0.40	0.46	16.7 -	13.9	0.35	0.41	0.42	6.9	0.02650	6/22/16	5.5 -	4.6
-	-	-	0.12	0.10	0.10	68.3 -	36.9	1.01	1.06	1.22	16.6	0.2020	7/15/16	8.2 -	4.4
-	-	-	0.55	0.23				1.11	0.16			0.31090	5/13/16		
0.14	-	-	1.64	1.54	0.19	73.2 -	49.8	0.40	0.22	0.04	0.4	0.20Y	61/28/99	120.1 -	81.6
-2.49	-	-	-13.76	-0.16	0.68			-	0.40	0.78		0.10Y	12/3/14	5.7 -	1.4
0.54	-	-	1.61	2.39	1.41	40.1 -	32.2	3.83	3.69	3.50	6.4	0.980Z	61/28/99	64.6 -	51.9
0.42	-	-	1.50	0.85	0.67	9.6 -	6.8	-	-	-		0.0450Y	10/10/08	14.4 -	10.2
-0.24	-	-	4.72	4.81	10.31	26.9 -	18.0	-	-	-		0.070Y	61/28/99	127.1 -	84.8
1.02	-	-	4.10	3.62	3.01	25.0 -	14.8	0.28	0.20	0.13	0.3	0.10Y	61/28/99	102.4 -	60.6
0.45	-	-	2.94	3.71	2.96	17.0 -	6.4	1.72	1.36	1.12	5.3	0.460Y	61/28/99	49.9 -	18.9
0.16	-	-	0.63	0.50	0.62	90.6 -	62.3	-	-	-		-		57.1 -	39.2
0.98	-	-	5.05	4.88	5.02	14.8 -	11.2	1.92	1.88	1.59	2.9	0.50Y	61/28/99	74.9 -	56.4
0.50	-	-	2.65	1.58	1.21	12.1 -	7.4	-	-	-		-		32.1 -	19.7
-4.85	-	-	-7.00	-2.93	6.63			-	-	-		0.22427Z	11/15/11	23.3 -	4.3
0.03	-	-	1.31	1.67	0.55	22.7 -	18.3	1.20	1.20	1.20	4.5	0.30Z	6/30/16	29.7 -	23.9
-	-	0.44	2.33	2.28	2.12	39.5 -	0.0	-	-	-		-		92.0 -	0.0
0.58	-	-	1.65	2.79	0.21	37.4 -	28.1	1.54	1.50	1.46	2.9	0.410Y	61/28/99	61.8 -	46.4
1.15	-	-	5.65	5.07	5.20	24.5 -	20.1	-	-	-		-		138.3 -	113.6
0.71	-	-	4.90	4.32	3.68	28.0 -	22.1	2.80	2.00	1.15	2.2	0.850Y	61/28/99	137.0 -	108.1
0.47	-	-	-3.24	1.42	1.65			0.66	0.58	0.50	1.2	0.180Y	6/16/16	59.8 -	44.9
-0.49	-	-	-0.92	-2.97	-0.99			-	-	-		-		53.6 -	28.8
0.25	-	-	1.34	0.82	5.86	20.0 -	11.7	-	-	-		-		26.8 -	15.6
-0.61	-	-	-2.55	-0.75	-0.45			-	-	-		-		14.4 -	4.9
0.51	-	-	2.15	2.08	1.86	19.1 -	14.1	0.89	0.75	0.55	2.4	0.40Y	61/28/99	41.0 -	30.4
1.09	-	-	2.34	2.59	2.51	25.7 -	19.2	1.74	1.56	1.45	3.3	0.4950Y	61/28/99	60.2 -	45.0
-0.17	-	-	0.56	1.74	3.63	47.5 -	6.7	0.00	0.00	0.53	0.0	0.1750Y	10/11/13	26.6 -	3.8
0.85	-	-	1.29	2.25	1.50	30.4 -	23.6	1.38	1.55	1.22	4.0	0.3650Z	61/28/99	39.2 -	30.4
0.75	-	-	2.21	2.05	2.67	22.9 -	17.3	1.20	1.20	1.20	2.8	0.30Y	5/16/16	50.6 -	38.2
0.83	-	-	2.67	1.44	3.98	38.0 -	26.2	-	-	-		-		101.4 -	70.1
0.99	-	-	4.12	4.10	3.89	14.2 -	11.0	1.48	1.35	1.15	2.8	0.380Y	61/28/99	58.5 -	45.2

SYMBOL	COMPANY	NATURE OF BUSINESS	FISCAL YEAR-END	TOTAL REV. $MILL	NET INCOME $MILL	TOTAL ASSETS $MILL	NET STK EQUITY $MILL	NO OF INST	INST. HOLDINGS (SHARES)
EOD	Wells Fargo Global Dividend Opport	Holding and other Investment Office	10/31/14	43.0	38.4	428.6	419.3	73	14561278
WFE PRA	Wells Fargo Real Estate Investment	REITs	12/31/15	680.8	646.0	13244.9	12412.9	-	
HCN	Welltower Inc	REITs	12/31/15	3859.8	888.5	29023.8	14590.6	842	364039793
WAIR	Wesco Aircraft Holdings Inc.	Aerospace	9/30/15	1497.6	-154.7	2021.0	817.6	169	142225761
WCC	Wesco International, Inc.	Electrical Equipment	12/31/15	7518.5	210.7	4587.4	1776.7	320	57468710
WST	West Pharmaceutical Services, Inc.	Rubber Products	12/31/15	1399.8	95.6	1695.1	1023.9	335	75889841
WR	Westar Energy Inc	Electric Utilities	12/31/15	2459.2	291.9	10705.7	3656.7	495	118988405
WAL	Western Alliance Bancorporation	Banking	12/31/15	554.9	194.2	14275.1	1591.5	313	89529620
TLI	Western Asset Corporate Loan Fun	Holding and other Investment Office	9/30/15	10.2	7.9	178.3	117.4	48	3951572
ESD	Western Asset Emerging Markets D	Holding and other Investment Office	12/31/15	39.4	32.2	606.7	504.1	93	11862371
EMD	Western Asset Emerging Markets In	Holding and other Investment Office	5/31/15	27.2	22.1	439.1	374.9	42	2066318
GDO	Western Asset Global Credit Define	Holding and other Investment Office	10/31/14	23.9	19.9	390.3	307.6	51	6261982
EHI	Western Asset Global High Income	Holding and other Investment Office	5/31/15	36.7	30.8	521.4	382.7	68	8386452
GDF	Western Asset Global Partners Inco	Holding and other Investment Office	8/31/15	15.8	13.0	216.9	156.7	57	5067267
HIX	Western Asset High Income Fund II	Holding and other Investment Office	4/30/15	79.7	68.5	1019.3	738.4	100	12545390
HIO	Western Asset High Income Opport	Holding and other Investment Office	9/30/15	39.0	34.5	485.2	457.4	105	24306066
HYI	Western Asset High Yield Defined	Holding and other Investment Office	8/31/15	33.3	29.6	388.1	386.5	-	
PAI	Western Asset Income Fund	Holding and other Investment Office	12/31/15	7.7	6.7	131.1	131.0	33	2205482
IGI	Western Asset Investment Grade D	Holding and other Investment Office	11/30/14	12.8	10.9	233.1	232.7	28	2329119
MHY	Western Asset Managed High Inco	Holding and other Investment Office	2/28/15	22.0	19.3	282.4	276.9	81	13472523
MMU	Western Asset Managed Municipals	Holding and other Investment Office	5/31/15	39.3	33.3	872.7	649.2	76	6500678
WMC	Western Asset Mortgage Capital Co	REITs	12/31/15	152.7	-9.5	3414.6	511.6	-	
DMO	Western Asset Mortgage Defined O	Holding and other Investment Office	12/31/14	25.7	19.5	407.9	257.6	32	1367894
MHF	Western Asset Municipal High Inco	Holding and other Investment Office	10/31/15	9.1	7.9	172.4	172.2	46	2456803
MNP	Western Asset Municipal Partners F	Holding and other Investment Office	11/30/15	10.2	7.8	247.6	181.7	44	1521140
MTT	Western Asset Municipal Term Trus	Holding and other Investment Office	11/30/14	14.9	13.0	276.8	276.5	33	1387081
WEA	Western Asset Premier Bond Fund	Holding and other Investment Office	12/31/15	14.3	11.8	214.2	155.7	50	2601418
GFY	Western Asset Variable Rate Strate	Holding and other Investment Office	9/30/15	6.0	4.6	131.5	117.0	36	4634790
SBW	Western Asset Worldwide Income F	Holding and other Investment Office	12/31/15	12.0	9.6	184.6	154.3	50	3512100
WIW	Western Asset/Claymore Inflation-Li	Holding and other Investment Office	12/31/15	24.3	15.5	1078.2	744.1	100	36431041
WIA	Western Asset/Claymore Inflation-Li	Holding and other Investment Office	12/31/15	6.1	1.9	521.1	363.4	62	17033834
WGP	Western Gas Equity Partners LP	Production & Extraction	12/31/15	1561.4	87.9	6709.4		122	29591404
WES	Western Gas Partners LP	Equipment & Services	12/31/15	1632.6	-73.5	6707.3		-	
WNR	Western Refining Inc	Refining & Marketing	12/31/15	9787.0	406.8	5833.4	1299.3	403	75449302
WNRL	Western Refining Logistics LP	Equipment & Services	12/31/15	2599.9	63.6	501.0	-68.4	62	13233013
WU	Western Union Co	Business Services	12/31/15	5483.7	837.8	9458.9	1404.9	827	579118753
WLK	Westlake Chemical Corp	Specialty Chemicals	12/31/15	4463.3	646.0	5575.3	3265.9	363	40580269
WLKP	Westlake Chemical Partners LP	Specialty Chemicals	12/31/15	1007.2	39.8	1290.3		58	11228685
WMLP	Westmoreland Resource Partners L	Mining	12/31/15	384.7	-33.7	425.3		14	48434
WBK	Westpac Banking Corp	Banking	9/30/15	39670.0	8012.0	812156.0	53098.0	199	17425780
WRK	WestRock Co	Containers & Packaging	9/30/15	11381.3	507.1	25356.8	11651.8	519	223885201
WRK	WestRock Co	Containers & Packaging	9/30/15	11381.3	507.1	25356.8	11651.8	519	223885201
WHG	Westwood Holdings Group, Inc.	Wealth Management	12/31/15	130.9	27.1	181.3	134.0	107	5753174
WEX	Wex Inc	Miscellaneous Consumer Services	12/31/15	854.6	111.3	3857.9	1083.2	290	44193932
WY	Weyerhaeuser Co	REITs	12/31/15	7082.0	506.0	12486.0	4869.0	1060	637174694
WGL	WGL Holdings Inc	Gas Utilities	9/30/15	2659.8	132.6	5294.2	1271.4	383	42446702
WHR	Whirlpool Corp	Household Appliances, Electronics &	12/31/15	20891.0	783.0	19010.0	4743.0	770	82703390
WTM	White Mountains Insurance Group,	General Insurance	12/31/15	1806.6	297.6	10284.5	3913.2	271	5308219
WSR	Whitestone REIT	REITs	12/31/15	93.4	6.7	783.9	243.0	114	11348617
WWAV	WhiteWave Foods Co.	Food	12/31/15	3866.3	168.4	4228.9	1210.9	516	152591366
WLL	Whiting Petroleum Corp	Production & Extraction	12/31/15	2050.8	-2219.2	11389.1	4750.6	522	192873823
JW A	Wiley (John) & Sons Inc.	Publishing	4/30/15	1822.4	176.9	3004.2	1055.0	336	48117067
WG	Willbros Group Inc (DE)	Equipment & Services	12/31/15	909.0	31.5	445.6	177.4	-	
CWEI	Williams (Clayton) Energy, Inc.	Production & Extraction	12/31/15	232.4	-98.2	1294.8	299.6	119	6008343
WMB	Williams Cos Inc (The)	Equipment & Services	12/31/15	7360.0	-571.0	49020.0	6148.0	1005	690963079
WPZ	Williams Partners LP (New)	Equipment & Services	12/31/15	7331.0	-1449.0	47870.0		19	5331382
WSM	Williams Sonoma Inc	Retail - Furniture & Home Furnishing	1/31/16	4976.1	310.1	2417.4	1198.2	518	96070004
WGO	Winnebago Industries, Inc.	Autos- Manufacturing	8/29/15	976.5	41.2	362.2	221.0	199	27499263
FUR	Winthrop Realty Trust	REITs	12/31/15			745.6	516.4	148	27646042
WIT	Wipro Ltd	IT Services	3/31/15	963552.0	173137.0	588718.0	406336.0	158	55781550
WNS	WNS (Holdings) Ltd	IT Services	3/31/16	562.2	59.9	525.5	408.2	153	47317534
WWW	Wolverine World Wide, Inc.	Apparel, Footwear & Accessories	1/2/16	2691.6	122.8	2444.6	963.7	350	100156351
WF	Woori Bank (Korea)	Banking	12/31/01	7459439.0	705352.0	77849060.0		34	1643547
WDAY	Workday Inc	IT Services	1/31/16	1162.3	-289.9	2730.1	1136.2	365	140491483
WK	Workiva Inc	Internet & Software	12/31/15	145.3	-43.4	143.9	25.7	70	8887035
INT	World Fuel Services Corp.	Equipment & Services	12/31/15	30379.7	186.9	4549.4	1911.4	363	73702835
WPT	World Point Terminals, LP	Equipment & Services	12/31/15	96.1	33.1	206.4		31	5436319
WWE	World Wrestling Entertainment Inc	Entertainment	12/31/15	658.8	24.1	409.1	209.3	208	37987140
WOR	Worthington Industries, Inc.	Non-Precious Metals	5/31/15	3384.2	76.8	2085.1	749.1	297	34905293
WPG	WP Glimcher Inc	REITs	12/31/15	921.7	-85.3	5479.5	1216.0	322	170197086
WPX	WPX Energy, Inc.	Production & Extraction	12/31/15	1888.0	-1727.0	8350.0	3535.0	409	271035223
WYN	Wyndham Worldwide Corp	Hotels, Restaurants & Travel	12/31/15	5536.0	612.0	9716.0	950.0	652	121088395
XTLY	Xactly Corp	Internet & Software	1/31/16	76.0	-24.7	86.9	10.4	59	10496170
XEL	Xcel Energy, Inc.	Electric Utilities	12/31/15	11024.5	984.5	39053.5	10600.9	806	400225231
XHR	Xenia Hotels & Resorts Inc	Hotels, Restaurants & Travel	12/31/15	976.1	88.8	3005.9	1727.4	197	59418503
XRM	Xerium Technologies Inc	Industrial Machinery & Equipment	12/31/15	477.2	-4.4	550.4	-113.1	110	12450234
XRX	Xerox Corp	Peripherals	12/31/15	18045.0	474.0	24817.0	9423.0	755	1018316007
XIN	Xinyuan Real Estate Co Ltd	Property, Real Estate & Developmen	12/31/15	1164.3	66.5	3561.4	936.0	57	26570110
XL	XL Group Plc	General Insurance	12/31/15	9308.9	1207.2	58682.9	11677.1	521	305763890
XOXO	XO Group Inc	Internet & Software	12/31/15	141.6	5.5	196.7	159.5	174	24570799

Table headers: EARNINGS PER SHARE — QUARTERLY (1st, 2nd, 3rd) / ANNUAL (2015, 2014, 2013); P/E RATIO; DIVIDENDS PER SHARE (2015, 2014, 2013); AV. YLD %; DIV. DECLARED (AMOUNT, PAYABLE); PRICE RANGE 2015.

1st	2nd	3rd	2015	2014	2013	P/E hi	P/E lo	Div 2015	Div 2014	Div 2013	AV.YLD%	AMOUNT	PAYABLE	Price hi	Price lo
-	-	-	-	0.78	0.84	-	-	-	0.72	0.84	-	0.1350	7/1/16	7.5 -	5.2
10.90	-	-	48.71	49.07	19.95	0.6 -	0.5	1.69	46.74	24.81	6.4	0.39840	6/30/16	27.6 -	24.8
0.42	-	-	2.34	1.45	0.28	31.9 -	22.9	3.30	3.18	3.06	5.0	0.860Z	61/28/99	74.7 -	53.7
-	0.24	-	-1.60	1.05	1.09	-	-	-	-	-	-	-	-	16.0 -	10.2
0.77	-	-	4.18	5.18	5.25	17.7 -	8.6	-	-	-	-	-	-	74.2 -	36.0
0.30	-	-	1.30	1.75	1.57	57.8 -	41.3	0.45	0.41	0.39	0.7	0.120Y	61/28/99	75.1 -	53.7
0.46	-	-	2.09	2.35	2.27	27.0 -	16.3	1.44	1.40	1.36	3.4	0.380Y	61/28/99	56.3 -	34.1
0.60	-	-	2.03	1.67	1.31	19.1 -	13.5	-	-	-	-	0.4557GHZ	10/1/16	38.8 -	27.4
-	-	-	0.80	0.78	0.77	14.7 -	11.1	0.87	0.87	0.87	8.6	0.07250	8/26/16	11.8 -	8.9
-	-	-	1.05	1.15	1.12	15.1 -	11.8	1.31	1.42	1.44	9.2	0.1050	7/29/16	15.9 -	12.4
-	-	-	0.77	0.78	0.82	14.6 -	11.5	0.94	1.02	1.02	9.3	0.210	6/24/16	11.2 -	8.8
-	-	-	-	1.30	1.24	-	-	-	1.39	1.42	-	0.11350	8/26/16	17.9 -	15.2
-	-	-	0.99	1.06	1.11	11.1 -	7.7	1.16	1.16	1.16	12.5	0.09630	6/24/16	11.0 -	7.7
-	-	-	0.83	0.90	0.98	11.6 -	8.6	0.87	0.96	1.11	10.6	0.07250	6/24/16	9.6 -	7.1
-	-	-	0.79	0.85	0.90	10.1 -	7.2	0.83	0.89	0.97	12.3	0.06150	8/26/16	8.0 -	5.7
-	-	-	0.41	0.43	0.45	13.0 -	10.4	0.43	0.44	0.48	9.0	0.03550	6/24/16	5.3 -	4.3
-	-	-	1.30	1.38	1.49	12.4 -	9.8	1.32	1.46	1.65	9.2	0.110	8/26/16	16.1 -	12.7
-	-	-	0.70	0.73	0.73	19.9 -	17.9	0.69	0.69	0.69	5.2	0.05750	9/30/16	13.9 -	12.6
-	-	-	-	1.02	1.03	-	-	-	1.51	1.27	-	0.10	8/26/16	22.0 -	19.4
-	-	-	0.41	0.44	0.47	12.5 -	9.9	0.42	0.45	0.49	9.2	0.03450	6/24/16	5.1 -	4.1
-	-	-	0.78	0.79	0.81	19.8 -	16.9	0.78	0.78	0.78	5.4	0.065M	8/26/16	15.4 -	13.2
-0.88	-	-	-0.25	2.67	-1.19	-	-	2.49	2.74	5.10	21.3	0.310	7/26/16	15.6 -	8.8
-	-	-	-	1.87	1.44	-	-	-	3.09	3.70	-	0.2350	8/26/16	25.1 -	22.1
-	-	-	0.36	0.36	0.38	23.4 -	19.5	0.35	0.37	0.38	4.6	0.0265M	8/26/16	8.4 -	7.0
-	-	-	0.81	0.86	0.87	21.3 -	18.1	0.87	0.85	0.92	5.5	0.0725M	8/26/16	17.3 -	14.6
-	-	-	-	1.08	1.08	-	-	-	1.01	1.01	-	0.0840	8/26/16	25.1 -	22.2
-	-	-	1.00	1.04	1.13	13.7 -	11.4	1.08	1.08	1.14	8.6	0.0850	9/30/16	13.7 -	11.4
-	-	-	0.69	0.78	0.78	24.3 -	21.3	0.88	0.87	0.87	5.6	0.07750	8/26/16	16.7 -	14.7
-	-	-	0.74	0.79	0.78	15.5 -	12.2	0.91	0.99	1.01	8.9	0.07250	7/29/16	11.4 -	9.0
-	-	-	0.25	0.38	0.16	45.7 -	40.0	0.37	0.44	0.40	3.5	0.03350	6/30/16	11.4 -	10.0
-	-	-	0.07	0.29	0.10	165.0 -	147.9	0.35	0.42	0.38	3.2	0.0320	6/30/16	11.6 -	10.4
0.32	-	-	0.39	1.02	0.71	164.8 -	50.9	1.40	1.04	0.63	3.3	0.42380	5/22/16	64.3 -	19.9
0.31	-	-	-1.95	2.12	1.83	-	-	2.95	2.55	2.20	6.0	0.8150	5/13/16	68.0 -	26.6
0.33	-	-	4.28	5.61	2.79	11.7 -	4.9	1.36	3.08	0.64	3.6	0.380Y	61/28/99	50.2 -	20.8
0.28	-	-	2.60	2.30	0.19	12.2 -	6.7	1.43	1.16	-	6.0	0.40250	5/27/16	31.8 -	17.4
0.37	-	-	1.62	1.59	1.43	13.7 -	10.1	0.62	0.50	0.50	3.3	0.160Y	61/28/99	22.2 -	16.4
0.94	-	-	4.86	5.07	4.54	15.0 -	8.4	0.69	0.58	0.41	1.3	0.18150Y	61/28/99	72.9 -	41.0
0.45	-	-	1.47	0.50	-	16.6 -	10.6	1.15	0.17	-	5.9	0.31680	5/24/16	24.5 -	15.6
-0.41	-	-	-4.62	-0.58	-10.27	-	-	0.60	-	-	10.6	0.20	5/13/16	11.3 -	0.0
-	-	-	2.49	2.39	2.15	10.5 -	0.0	1.74	1.83	1.72	7.7	-	-	26.1 -	0.0
-	0.22	-	2.93	3.29	4.98	21.6 -	0.0	0.38	0.70	0.53	0.7	0.3750	5/16/16	63.4 -	0.0
-	0.22	-	2.93	3.29	4.98	20.0 -	9.2	0.38	0.70	0.53	0.9	0.3750	5/16/16	58.6 -	27.0
0.44		-	3.33	3.45	2.34	18.7 -	12.7	2.07	1.82	1.64	3.7	0.570Y	61/28/99	62.3 -	42.2
0.59		-	2.62	5.18	3.82	44.8 -	22.2	-	-	-	-	-	-	117.4 -	58.1
0.11		-	0.89	3.18	0.95	37.0 -	25.0	1.20	1.02	0.81	4.1	0.79690Z	61/28/99	33.0 -	22.2
-	2.11	-	2.62	2.05	1.55	28.0 -	19.9	1.80	1.72	1.64	2.9	0.48750Y	61/28/99	73.3 -	52.2
1.92		-	9.83	8.17	10.24	19.3 -	12.9	3.45	2.88	2.38	2.1	1.0Y	61/28/99	190.2 -	127.2
2.34		-	50.60	51.21	51.00	10.5 -	12.8	1.00	1.00	1.00	0.1	1.0	61/28/99	834.0 -	636.1
0.18		-	0.24	0.32	0.20	59.1 -	41.1	1.14	1.14	1.04	9.3	0.09502	9/9/16	14.2 -	9.9
0.24		-	0.94	0.79	0.57	55.5 -	35.7	-	-	-	-	-	-	52.2 -	33.6
-0.84		-	-11.35	0.53	3.06	-	-	-	-	-	-	1.56250Y	6/17/13	36.0 -	3.5
-	-	0.61	2.97	2.70	2.39	19.7 -	13.5	1.16	1.00	0.96	2.3	0.310Y	61/28/99	58.4 -	40.2
-0.25	-	-	0.54	-1.62	-0.32	6.0 -	1.3	-	-	-	-	-	-	3.3 -	0.7
-2.90	-	-	-8.07	3.61	-2.04	-	-	-	-	-	-	-	-	73.0 -	7.1
-0.09	-	-	-0.76	2.92	0.62	-	-	2.45	1.96	1.44	7.4	0.640Y	61/28/99	60.9 -	11.2
-0.25	-	-	-3.27	1.01	0.95	-	-	3.40	2.20	1.83	10.6	0.850	5/13/16	56.0 -	13.3
0.44	-	-	3.24	2.82	2.54	27.4 -	14.8	1.32	1.24	0.88	2.0	0.370Y	61/28/99	88.7 -	48.0
-	0.35	-	1.52	1.64	1.13	16.1 -	10.9	0.36	-	-	1.8	0.10Y	7/27/16	24.5 -	16.5
-	-	-	-	0.16	0.51	-	-	2.25	2.58	0.65	16.5	1.25A	7/1/16	17.0 -	9.8
-	7.85	-	70.31	63.95	52.00	0.2 -	0.2	9.90	7.96	6.08	82.6	-	-	13.0 -	10.9
-	0.18	-	1.10	0.79	0.41	31.0 -	23.4	-	-	-	-	-	-	34.1 -	25.7
0.18	-	-	1.20	1.30	0.99	24.6 -	12.7	0.24	0.24	0.18	1.1	0.060Y	8/1/16	29.5 -	15.2
-	-	-	-	-	-	-	-	-	-	-	-	-	-	28.3 -	0.0
-0.41	-	-	-1.35	-1.01	-1.62	-	-	-	-	-	-	-	-	84.8 -	48.9
-0.30	-	-	-1.09	-1.28	-	-	-	-	-	-	-	-	-	18.8 -	11.0
0.75	-	-	2.64	3.11	2.83	19.2 -	13.0	0.24	0.15	0.15	0.6	0.060Y	61/28/99	50.8 -	34.4
0.27	-	-	0.95	0.98	0.42	18.5 -	12.6	1.20	1.20	0.16	8.3	0.30	5/13/16	17.6 -	11.9
0.18	-	-	0.32	-0.40	0.04	71.9 -	43.0	0.48	0.48	0.48	2.7	0.120Y	6/27/16	23.0 -	13.8
-	-	0.46	1.12	2.11	1.91	34.2 -	19.5	0.69	0.45	0.64	2.3	0.190Y	61/28/99	38.3 -	21.9
0.05	-	-	-0.55	1.10	1.00	-	-	1.00	0.50	-	9.0	0.42970Z	61/28/99	14.3 -	7.4
-0.06	-	-	-7.42	0.80	-5.91	-	-	-	-	-	-	0.78130Y	8/1/16	13.4 -	3.6
0.84	-	-	5.14	4.18	3.21	17.0 -	12.0	1.68	1.40	1.16	2.2	0.50Y	61/28/99	87.3 -	61.6
-0.15	-	-	-6.69	-5.73	-4.16	-	-	-	-	-	-	-	-	10.3 -	4.7
0.47	-	-	1.94	2.03	1.91	21.6 -	16.5	1.28	1.20	1.11	3.5	0.340Y	61/28/99	41.9 -	31.9
-0.08	-	-	0.79	-	-	30.8 -	16.1	0.84	-	-	4.8	0.2750Z	7/15/16	24.3 -	12.7
-0.09	-	-	-0.28	-0.48	0.26	-	-	-	-	-	-	0.11250Y	12/17/07	18.5 -	4.3
0.03	-	-	0.42	0.81	0.91	27.5 -	20.7	0.28	0.25	0.23	2.7	0.07750Y	61/28/99	11.5 -	8.7
-	-	0.20	0.45	0.29	0.85	12.2 -	5.4	0.19	0.19	0.19	5.3	-	-	5.5 -	2.4
0.07	-	-	4.15	0.69	3.63	9.7 -	7.8	0.72	0.64	0.56	2.0	0.20	61/28/99	40.4 -	32.3
0.12	-	-	0.21	0.02	0.23	86.3 -	65.1	-	-	-	-	-	-	18.1 -	13.7

SYMBOL	COMPANY	NATURE OF BUSINESS	FISCAL YEAR-END	TOTAL REV. $MILL	NET INCOME $MILL	TOTAL ASSETS $MILL	NET STK EQUITY $MILL	NO OF INST	INST. HOLDINGS (SHARES)
XPO	XPO Logistics, Inc.	Airlines/Air Freight	12/31/15	7623.2	-191.6	12643.2	2717.1	254	120567718
XYL	Xylem Inc.	Industrial Machinery & Equipment	12/31/15	3853.0	340.0	4657.0	2084.0	572	161991742
YDKN	Yadkin Financial Corp	Banking	12/31/15	219.1	44.6	4474.1	562.5	166	37015226
AUY	Yamana Gold Inc	Precious Metals	12/31/15	1824.9	-2114.8	9518.1	4841.3	391	494537472
YZC	Yanzhou Coal Mining Co., Ltd.	Mining	12/31/15	36404.1	164.5	142471.9	42031.6	58	4220780
YELP	Yelp Inc	Internet & Software	12/31/15	549.7	-32.9	755.4	693.6	246	63196123
YGE	Yingli Green Energy Holding Co Ltd	Semiconductors	12/31/15	9965.8	-5600.5	17640.3	-5939.7	94	6652292
YRD	Yirendai Ltd	Wealth Management	12/31/15	209.1	43.8	338.1	150.8	34	1822877
YPF	YPF SA	Refining & Marketing	12/31/15	156136.0	4579.0	363453.0	120413.0	188	103092297
YUM	Yum! Brands, Inc.	Hotels, Restaurants & Travel	12/26/15	13105.0	1293.0	8075.0	911.0	1213	367289058
YUME	YuMe Inc	Advertising	12/31/15	173.3	-16.7	149.1	102.6	50	6238104
ZFC	ZAIS Financial Corp	REITs	12/31/15	86.7	-1.4	775.1	159.2	49	3185113
ZAYO	Zayo Group Holdings Inc	Manufacturing	6/30/15	1347.1	-155.3	6094.6	1211.2	213	129966531
ZEN	Zendesk Inc	Internet & Software	12/31/15	208.8	-84.1	422.7	293.3	159	78648487
ZPIN	Zhaopin Ltd	Miscellaneous Consumer Services	6/30/15	1271.3	251.2	2248.0	1019.7	41	11790108
ZBH	Zimmer Biomet Holdings Inc	Medical Instruments & Equipment	12/31/15	5997.8	147.0	27219.5	9887.9	1096	214432754
ZOES	Zoe's Kitchen Inc	Hotels, Restaurants & Travel	12/28/15	226.6	1.1	198.0	125.0	142	22169908
ZTS	Zoetis Inc	Pharmaceuticals	12/31/15	4765.0	339.0	7913.0	1068.0	735	479555324
ZF	Zweig Fund, Inc. (The)	Holding and other Investment Office	12/31/15	6.1	2.2	311.1	296.8	64	8944806
ZTR	Zweig Total Return Fund, Inc. (The)	Holding and other Investment Office	12/31/15	11.7	7.0	442.1	431.3	79	16686419

| EARNINGS PER SHARE | | | | | | P/E RATIO | | DIVIDENDS PER SHARE | | | AV. YLD | DIV. DECLARED | | PRICE RANGE | |
| QUARTERLY | | | ANNUAL | | | | | | | | | | | 2015 | |
1st	2nd	3rd	2015	2014	2013			2015	2014	2013	%	AMOUNT	PAYABLE		
-0.21	-		-2.65	-2.00	-2.26	-		-				-		49.5 -	19.6
0.37	-	-	1.87	1.83	1.22	23.9 -	16.3	0.56	0.51	0.47	1.5	0.15490Y	61/28/99	44.7 -	30.5
0.20	-	-	1.38	0.88	1.19	19.6 -	14.2	0.20	-	-	0.9	0.10	5/19/16	27.1 -	19.6
-	-	-0.12	-2.26	-1.69	0.59			0.06	0.13	0.26	2.0	0.0050	7/14/16	6.6 -	0.0
-	-	0.37	0.03	0.16	-	317.0 -	125.3	0.16	0.16	3.08	3.0	-		9.5 -	3.8
-0.20	-	-	-0.44	0.48	-0.15			-				-		48.6 -	15.2
-	-	-2.05	-30.81	-7.49	-12.41			-				-		14.0 -	3.0
-	-	-	0.44	-0.04	-0.08	33.0 -	8.1	-				-		14.5 -	3.6
-	-	3.60	11.68	22.95	13.05	2.5 -	1.1	0.66	0.71	0.53	3.3	-		28.9 -	12.8
0.93	-	-	2.92	2.32	2.36	31.8 -	22.3	1.69	1.52	1.38	2.1	0.460Y	61/28/99	92.8 -	65.2
-0.10	-	-	-0.49	-0.27	0.02			-				-		5.6 -	2.5
-0.38	-	-	-0.16	3.08	0.92			1.60	1.60	2.12	10.7	0.40Z	7/15/16	17.5 -	12.7
-	-	-0.08	-0.66	-0.80	-0.61			-				-		29.4 -	21.9
-0.30	-	-	-0.99	-1.26	-1.04			-				-		27.3 -	14.8
-	-	-	2.23	1.97	-20.51	7.5 -	5.3	-				-		16.7 -	11.8
0.52	-	-	0.77	4.19	4.43	159.8 -	119.1	0.88	0.88	0.80	0.8	0.240Y	61/28/99	123.1 -	91.7
0.07	-	-	0.06	-0.58	-0.30	760.0 -	401.2	-				-		45.6 -	24.1
0.41	-	-	0.68	1.16	1.01	81.4 -	57.8	0.33	0.29	0.20	0.7	0.0950Y	61/28/99	55.4 -	39.3
-	-	-	0.11	0.11	0.14	138.0 -	100.6	1.22	1.03	0.88	9.2	0.3620	4/18/16	15.2 -	11.1
-	-	-	0.22	0.25	0.29	61.1 -	48.8	1.11	1.09	1.02	9.2	0.110	6/20/16	13.4 -	10.7

This Page left intentionally blank